# INTRODUCTION TO
# PSYCHOLOGY

## 6TH EDITION

# INTRODUCTION TO
# PSYCHOLOGY

## 6TH EDITION

## ROD PLOTNIK
### San Diego State University

**WADSWORTH**
™
**THOMSON LEARNING**

Australia • Canada • Mexico • Singapore • Spain • United Kingdom • United States

**WADSWORTH**

**THOMSON LEARNING**

Psychology Publisher: *Vicki Knight*
Development Editor: *Penelope Sky*
Assistant Editor: *Jennifer Wilkinson*
Editorial Assistant: *Dan Moneypenny*
Marketing Manager: *Joanne Terhaar*
Marketing Assistant: *Justine Ferguson*
Production Editor: *Kirk Bomont*
Production Service: *Nancy Shammas, New Leaf*
 *Publishing Services*
Manuscript Editor: *Carol Reitz*

Permissions Editor: *Linda Rill*
Photo Researcher: *Linda Rill*
Interior Design: *Rod Plotnik*
Concept Illustrators: *Phillip Dvorak & Bill Ogden*
Cover Design: *Vernon T. Boes*
Cover Illustration: *Tana Powell*
Indexer: *Do Mi Stauber*
Print Buyer: *Vena Dyer*
Typesetting: *LaurelTech*
Printing and Binding: *R. R. Donnelley & Sons/Willard*

*For more information about this or any other Wadsworth product, contact:*
WADSWORTH–THOMSON LEARNING
511 Forest Lodge Road
Pacific Grove, CA 93950 USA
www.wadsworth.com
1-800-423-0563 (Thomson Learning Academic Resource Center)

Printed in the United States of America

10  9  8  7  6  5  4  3  2

**Library of Congress Cataloging-in-Publication Data**
Plotnik, Rod.
      Introduction to psychology / Rod Plotnik—6th ed.
         p. cm.
      Includes bibliographical references and index.
      ISBN 0-534-57996-5
         1. Psychology.      I. Title.
   BF121 .P626  2001
   150—dc21                              2001026231

BF121 .P626

## To All Students Everywhere

While revising this text, there were times when my mood and motivation waned and I really needed a pick-me-up. Right about then, I would receive a grateful student comment that made me smile with delight and helped me go merrily on my way. I'm dedicating the 6th edition to all those students who will take the time to send me their comments (there's a form on the last page in this book). Here's a sample of some of the wonderful students' comments that made my day!

"The best textbook I've ever read! It held my interest!"

*Lindy,* International Institute of Technology

"I thought the pictures and diagrams were extremely helpful in understanding new concepts."

*Gini,* Oregon State University

"This was the first textbook in college that I actually read all of!"

*Lauren,* Dallas Baptist University

"I loved every part of this text and used it on many occasions to share interesting information with my family and friends. My sister and friend read some chapters after I showed them the book—just because it was so good. . . . I'm not selling this book to another student because I'm keeping it for myself."

*Carolyn,* York College

"I read the whole book without the teacher telling me to."

*Aubrey,* Masters Institute

"I can honestly say this was the most interesting and easy to read book I have had in my history of college. I love the way you used real-life examples."

*Carmen,* Miami-Dade Community College

"This is an excellent textbook. It doesn't seem like one, because it is so fun to read. I even read it in my spare time. . . . I love it. Well done."

*Intesar,* Trocaire College

"The stories at the beginning of each module made it really easy to apply the concepts and themes."

*Andrea,* San Diego State University

"Next week is the time to sell back books. Your book will be staying with me and added to my health/science/knowledge library!"

*Jennifer,* Santa Rosa Junior College

"I loved the pictures and the personal stories that made the topics so much more interesting. I learn from visual stimulation more than from anything else and it's amazing to realize how much I remember at the end of the module! I think this book is great!"

*Maria Luisa,* Miami-Dade Community College

"I found the book to be the most interesting book I have had in college. The photos and figures made it easy to read, and very compelling. Also, I really enjoyed the way current events were incorporated into examples. . . . Thank you so much for not making it boring!"

*Raechal,* Northwestern State University

"I really enjoyed this book. I think it was the only text I actually read because I wanted to, not because I had to."

*Jane,* Owens Community College

"The book is one of the best textbooks I have ever used for any subject."

*Steve,* Owens Community College

# Contents

Module 1    *Discovering Psychology*   2

Module 2    *Psychology & Science*   26

Module 3    *Brain's Building Blocks*   46

Module 4    *Incredible Nervous System*   66

Module 5    *Sensation*   92

Module 6    *Perception*   120

Module 7    *Consciousness, Sleep, & Dreams*   146

Module 8    *Hypnosis & Drugs*   168

Module 9    *Classical Conditioning*   194

Module 10    *Operant & Cognitive Approaches*   212

Module 11    *Types of Memory*   238

Module 12    *Remembering & Forgetting*   260

Module 13    *Intelligence*   280

Module 14    *Thought & Language*   304

Module 15    *Motivation*   328

Module 16    *Emotion*   358

Module 17    *Infancy & Childhood*   376

Module 18    *Adolescence & Adulthood*   406

Module 19    *Freudian & Humanistic Theories*   432

Module 20    *Social Cognitive & Trait Theories*   456

Module 21    *Health, Stress, & Coping*   480

Module 22    *Assessment & Anxiety Disorders*   508

Module 23    *Mood Disorder & Schizophrenia*   530

Module 24    *Therapies*   554

Module 25    *Social Psychology*   580

Appendix A:    *Statistics in Psychology*   610

Appendix B:    *Critical Thinking Study Questions with Answers*   618

## Module 1: Discovering Psychology 2

**A. Definition & Goals  4**
* Definition of Psychology  4
* Goals of Psychology  4

**B. Modern Approaches  5**
* Biological Approach  6
* Cognitive Approach  7
* Behavioral Approach  8
* Psychoanalytic Approach  9
* Humanistic Approach  10
* Cross-Cultural Approach  11

**C. Historical Approaches  12**
* Structuralism  12
* Functionalism  12
* Gestalt Approach  13
* Behaviorism  13
* Survival of Approaches  13

**D. Cultural Diversity: Early Discrimination  14**
* Women in Psychology  14
* Minorities in Psychology  14
* Righting the Wrongs  14

**Concept Review  15**

**E. Research Focus: Class Notes  16**
* Best Strategy for Taking Class Notes?  16

**F. Careers in Psychology  17**
* Psychologist versus Psychiatrist  17
* Many Career Settings  17

**G. Research Areas  18**
* Social and Personality  18
* Developmental  18
* Experimental  18
* Biological  19
* Cognitive  19
* Psychometrics  19

**H. Application: Study Skills  20**
* Improving Study Habits  20
* Setting Goals  20
* Rewarding Yourself  21
* Taking Notes  21
* Stopping Procrastination  21

**Summary Test  22**

**Critical Thinking  24**

**Links to Learning  25**

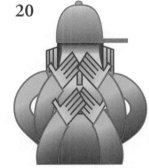

## Module 2: Psychology & Science 26

**A. Answering Questions  28**
* Survey  28
* Case Study  28
* Experiment  28

**B. Surveys  29**
* Kind of Information  29
* Disadvantages  29
* Advantages  29

**C. Case Study  30**
* Kind of Information  30
* Personal Case Study: Testimonial  30
* Error and Bias  30

**D. Cultural Diversity: Use of Placebos  31**
* Remarkable Treatments  31
* Conclusion: Testimonials and Placebos  31

**E. Correlation  32**
* Definition  32
* Correlation Coefficients  32
* Correlation versus Causation  33
* Correlation as Clues  33
* Correlation and Predictions  33

**F. Decisions about Doing Research  34**
* Choosing Research Techniques  34
* Choosing Research Settings  35

**G. Scientific Method: Experiment  36**
* Advantages of Scientific Method  36
* Conducting an Experiment: Seven Rules  36
* Conclusion  37

**Concept Review  38**

**H. Research Focus: ADHD Controversies  39**
* Controversy: Diagnosis  39
* Controversy: Treatment  39
* Controversy: Long-Term Effects  39

**I. Application: Research Concerns  40**
* Concerns about Being a Subject  40
* Code of Ethics  40
* Role of Deception  40
* Ethics of Animal Research  41

**Summary Test  42**

**Critical Thinking  44**

**Links to Learning  45**

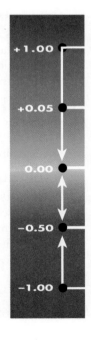

## Module 3: Brain's Building Blocks 46

A. **Overview: Human Brain** 48
  ✳ Development of the Brain 48
  ✳ Structure of the Brain 48
  ✳ Growth of New Neurons 49
  ✳ Brain versus Mind 49

B. **Neurons: Structure & Function** 50
  ✳ Three Parts of the Neuron 50
  ✳ Alzheimer's Disease and Neurons 50

C. **Neurons versus Nerves** 51
  ✳ Reattaching Arms 51
  ✳ Peripheral Nervous System 51
  ✳ Central Nervous System 51

D. **Sending Information** 52
  ✳ Sequence: Action Potential 52
  ✳ Sequence: Nerve Impulse 52

E. **Transmitters** 54
  ✳ Excitatory and Inhibitory Transmitters 54
  ✳ Neurotransmitters 54
  ✳ Alcohol 55
  ✳ New Transmitters 55

F. **Reflex Responses** 56
  ✳ Definition and Sequence 56
  ✳ Functions of a Reflex 56

**Concept Review** 57

G. **Research Focus: What Is a Phantom Limb?** 58
  ✳ Case Study 58
  ✳ Definition and Data 58
  ✳ Answers: Old and New 58

H. **Cultural Diversity: Plants & Drugs** 59
  ✳ Cocaine 59
  ✳ Curare 59
  ✳ Mescaline 59

I. **Application: Fetal Tissue Transplant** 60
  ✳ Parkinson's Disease 60
  ✳ Issues Involving Transplants 60
  ✳ Fetal Tissue Transplants 61

**Summary Test** 62

**Critical Thinking** 64

**Links to Learning** 65

## Module 4: Incredible Nervous System 66

A. **Genes & Evolution** 68
  ✳ Genetic Instructions 68
  ✳ Evolution of the Human Brain 69

B. **Studying the Living Brain** 70
  ✳ New Techniques 70
  ✳ MRI Brain Scans 70
  ✳ PET Brain Scans 71
  ✳ Picturing Thoughts 71

C. **Organization of the Brain** 72
  ✳ Divisions of the Nervous System 72
  ✳ Major Parts of the Brain 73

D. **Control Centers: Four Lobes** 74
  ✳ Overall View of the Cortex 74
  ✳ Frontal Lobe: Functions 75
  ✳ Parietal Lobe: Functions 77
  ✳ Temporal Lobe: Functions 78
  ✳ Occipital Lobe: Functions 79

E. **Limbic System: Old Brain** 80
  ✳ Structures and Functions 80
  ✳ Autonomic Nervous System 81

F. **Endocrine System** 82
  ✳ Definition 82
  ✳ Control Center 82
  ✳ Other Glands 82

**Concept Review** 83

G. **Research Focus: Sex Differences in the Brain** 84
  ✳ Science and Politics 84

H. **Cultural Diversity: Brain Size & Racial Myths** 85
  ✳ Skull Size and Intelligence 85
  ✳ Brain Size and Intelligence 85

I. **Application: Split Brain** 86
  ✳ Definition and Testing 86
  ✳ Behaviors Following Split Brain 87
  ✳ Different Functions 87
  ✳ What Am I? 87

**Summary Test** 88

**Critical Thinking** 90

**Links to Learning** 91

## Module 5: Sensation 92

**A. Eye: Vision   94**
* Stimulus: Light Waves  94
* Structure and Function  94
* Retina  96
* Visual Pathways  97
* Color Vision  98

**B. Ear: Audition   100**
* Stimulus: Sound Waves  100
* Outer, Middle, and Inner Ear  102
* Auditory Brain Areas  103
* Auditory Cues  104

**C. Vestibular System: Balance   105**
* Position and Balance  105
* Motion Sickness  105
* Meniere's Disease and Vertigo  105

**D. Chemical Senses   106**
* Taste  106
* Smell, or Olfaction  107

**E. Touch   108**
* Definition  108
* Receptors in the Skin  108
* Brain Areas  108

**Concept Review   109**

**F. Cultural Diversity: Disgust versus Delight   110**
* Sensations and Psychological Factors  110

**G. Research Focus: Mind Over Body?   111**
* Definitions and Research Methods  111
* Placebo Results  111
* Conclusion: Mind Over Body!  111

**H. Pain   112**
* Definition  112
* Gate Control Theory  112
* Endorphins  113
* Acupuncture  113

**I. Application: Artificial Senses   114**
* Artificial Visual System  114
* Kinds of Deafness  115
* Cochlear Implants  115

**Summary Test   116**

**Critical Thinking   118**

**Links to Learning   119**

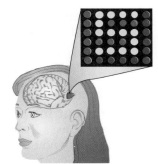

## Module 6: Perception 120

**A. Perceptual Thresholds   122**
* Becoming Aware of a Stimulus  122
* Weber's Law  123
* Just Noticeable Difference (JND) and Soft Towels  123

**B. Sensation versus Perception   124**
* Basic Differences  124
* Changing Sensations into Perceptions  125

**C. Rules of Organization   126**
* Structuralists versus Gestalt Psychologists  126
* Evidence for Rules  126
* Organizational Rules  126

**D. Perceptual Constancy   128**
* Size, Shape, Brightness, and Color Constancy  128

**E. Depth Perception   129**
* Binocular (Two Eyes) Depth Cues  129
* Monocular Depth Cues  130

**F. Illusions   132**
* Strange Perceptions  132
* Learning from Illusions  133

**Concept Review   134**

**G. Research Focus: Subliminal Perception   135**
* Can "Unsensed Messages" Change Behavior?  135

**H. Cultural Diversity: Influence on Perceptions   136**
* What Do Cultural Influences Do?  136

**I. ESP: Extrasensory Perception   138**
* Definition and Controversy  138
* Trickery and Magic  138
* ESP Experiment  139
* Status of ESP  139

**J. Application: Creating Perceptions   140**
* Creating Movement  140
* Creating Movies  140
* Creating Virtual Reality  141
* Creating First Impressions  141

**Summary Test   142**

**Critical Thinking   144**

**Links to Learning   145**

## Module 7: Consciousness, Sleep, & Dreams 146

A. **Continuum of Consciousness** 148
 ❋ Different States 148
 ❋ Several Kinds 149

B. **Rhythms of Sleeping & Waking** 150
 ❋ Biological Clocks 150
 ❋ Location of Biological Clocks 150
 ❋ Circadian Problems and Treatments 151

C. **World of Sleep** 152
 ❋ Stages of Sleep 152
 ❋ Non-REM Sleep 152
 ❋ REM Sleep 153
 ❋ Awake and Alert 153
 ❋ Sequence of Stages 154

D. **Research Focus: Circadian Preference** 155
 ❋ Are You a Morning or a Night Person? 155
 ❋ Body Temperature 155
 ❋ Behavioral Differences 155

E. **Questions about Sleep** 156
 ❋ How Much Sleep Do I Need? 156
 ❋ Why Do I Sleep? 156
 ❋ What If I Miss Sleep? 157
 ❋ What Causes Sleep? 157

**Concept Review** 158

F. **Cultural Diversity: Incidence of SAD** 159
 ❋ Problem and Treatment 159
 ❋ Occurrence of SAD 159
 ❋ Cultural Differences 159

G. **World of Dreams** 160
 ❋ Theories of Dream Interpretation 160
 ❋ Typical Dreams 161

H. **Application: Sleep Problems & Treatments** 162
 ❋ Occurrence 162
 ❋ Insomnia 162
 ❋ Nondrug Treatment 162
 ❋ Drug Treatment 162
 ❋ Sleep Apnea 163
 ❋ Narcolepsy 163
 ❋ Sleep Disturbances 163

**Summary Test** 164

**Critical Thinking** 166

**Links to Learning** 167

## Module 8: Hypnosis & Drugs 168

A. **Hypnosis** 170
 ❋ Definition 170
 ❋ Theories of Hypnosis 171
 ❋ Behaviors 172
 ❋ Medical and Therapeutic Applications 173

B. **Drugs: Overview** 174
 ❋ Reasons for Use 174
 ❋ Definition of Terms 174
 ❋ Use of Drugs 175
 ❋ Effects on Nervous System 175

C. **Stimulants** 176
 ❋ Definition 176
 ❋ Amphetamines 176
 ❋ Cocaine 177
 ❋ Caffeine 178
 ❋ Nicotine 178

D. **Opiates** 179
 ❋ Opium, Morphine, Heroin 179
 ❋ Treatment 179

E. **Hallucinogens** 180
 ❋ Definition 180
 ❋ LSD 180
 ❋ Psilocybin 180
 ❋ Mescaline 181
 ❋ Designer Drugs 181

F. **Alcohol** 182
 ❋ History and Use 182
 ❋ Definition and Effects 182
 ❋ Risk Factors 183
 ❋ Problems with Alcohol 183

**Concept Review** 184

G. **Cultural Diversity: Alcoholism Rates** 185
 ❋ Definition and Differences in Rates 185

H. **Marijuana** 186
 ❋ Use and Effects 186

I. **Research Focus: Drug Prevention** 187
 ❋ How Effective Is the Dare Program? 187

J. **Application: Treatment for Drug Abuse** 188
 ❋ Developing a Problem 188
 ❋ Substance Abuse and Treatment 188

**Summary Test** 190

**Critical Thinking** 192

**Links to Learning** 193

## Module 9: Classical Conditioning 194

**A. Three Kinds of Learning  196**
* Classical Conditioning  196
* Operant Conditioning  196
* Cognitive Learning  196

**B. Procedure: Classical Conditioning  197**
* Pavlov's Experiment  197
* Terms in Classical Conditioning  198

**C. Other Conditioning Concepts  199**
* Generalization  199
* Discrimination  199
* Extinction  199
* Spontaneous Recovery  199

**D. Adaptive Value & Uses  200**
* Taste-Aversion Learning  200
* Explanation  200
* Examples of Classical Conditioning  201
* Conditioned Emotional Response  201
* Classical Conditioning and Dyslexia  201

**E. Three Explanations  202**
* Theories of Classical Conditioning  202
* Stimulus Substitution and Contiguity Theory  202
* Cognitive Perspective  202

**Concept Review  203**

**F. Research Focus: Conditioning Little Albert  204**
* Can Emotional Responses Be Conditioned?  204

**G. Cultural Diversity: Conditioning Dental Fears  205**
* In the Dentist's Chair  205
* Cultural Practices  205
* Origins  205
* Effects of Fear  205

**H. Application: Conditioned Fear & Nausea  206**
* Examples of Classical Conditioning  206
* Systematic Desensitization  207

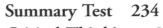

MOST STRESSFUL

8. Vomiting
7. Feeling nausea
6. Receiving injection
5. In treatment room
4. Smelling chemicals
3. In waiting room
2. Entering clinic
1. Driving to clinic

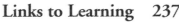

**Summary Test  208**

**Critical Thinking  210**

**Links to Learning  211**

## Module 10: Operant & Cognitive Approaches 212

**A. Operant Conditioning  214**
* Background: Thorndike and Skinner  214
* Principles and Procedures  215
* Examples of Operant Conditioning  215
* Operant versus Classical Conditioning  217

**B. Reinforcers  218**
* Consequences  218
* Reinforcement  218
* Reinforcers  219
* Punishment  219

**C. Schedules of Reinforcement  220**
* Skinner's Contributions  220
* Measuring Ongoing Behavior  220
* Schedules of Reinforcement  220
* Partial Reinforcement Schedules  221

**D. Other Conditioning Concepts  222**
* Generalization  222
* Discrimination  222
* Extinction and Spontaneous Recovery  222

**E. Cognitive Learning  223**
* Three Viewpoints of Cognitive Learning  223
* Observational Learning  224
* Bandura's Social Cognitive Theory  225
* Insight Learning  226

**Concept Review  227**

**F. Biological Factors  228**
* Definition  228
* Imprinting  228
* Prepared Learning  229

**G. Research Focus: Noncompliance  230**
* How Can Parents Deal with "NO"?  230

**H. Cultural Diversity: East Meets West  231**
* Different Cultures but Similar Learning Principles  231

**I. Application: Behavior Modification  232**
* Definition  232
* Behavior Modification and Autism  232
* Biofeedback  233
* Pros and Cons of Punishment  233

**Summary Test  234**

**Critical Thinking  236**

**Links to Learning  237**

## Module 11: Types of Memory  238

**A. Three Types of Memory  240**
* Sensory Memory  240
* Short-Term Memory  240
* Long-Term Memory  240
* Memory Processes  240

**B. Sensory Memory: Recording  241**
* Iconic Memory  241
* Echoic Memory  241
* Functions of Sensory Memory  241

**C. Short-Term Memory: Working  242**
* Definition  242
* Two Features  242
* Chunking  243
* Functions of Short-Term Memory  243

**D. Long-Term Memory: Storing  244**
* Steps in the Memory Process  244
* Features of Long-Term Memory  244
* Separate Memory Systems  245
* Declarative versus Procedural or Nondeclarative  246

**E. Research Focus: Do Emotions Affect Memories?  247**
* Hormones and Memories  247
* Memories of Emotional Events  247

**F. Encoding: Transferring  248**
* Two Kinds of Encoding  248
* Rehearsing and Encoding  249
* Levels of Processing  249

**G. Repressed Memories  250**
* Recovered Memories  250
* Definition of Repressed Memories  250
* Therapist's Role in Recovered Memories  250
* Implanting False Memories  251
* Accuracy of Recovered Memories  251

**Concept Review  252**

**H. Cultural Diversity: Oral versus Written  253**
* United States versus Africa  253
* Remembering Spoken Information  253

**I. Application: Unusual Memories  254**
* Photographic Memory  254
* Eidetic Imagery  254
* Flashbulb Memory  255

**Summary Test  256**

**Critical Thinking  258**

**Links to Learning  259**

## Module 12: Remembering & Forgetting  260

**A. Organization of Memories  262**
* Filing and Organizing 87,967 Memories  262
* Network Theory of Memory Organization  262
* Organization of Network Hierarchy  263
* Categories in the Brain  263

**B. Forgetting Curves  264**
* Early Memories  264
* Unfamiliar and Uninteresting  264
* Familiar and Interesting  264

**C. Reasons for Forgetting  265**
* Overview: Four Reasons for Forgetting  265
* Interference  266
* Retrieval Cues  267
* State-Dependent Learning  267

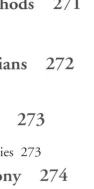

**D. Biological Bases of Memory  268**
* Location of Memories in the Brain  268
* Making a Short-Term Memory  269
* Genetically Altering Memory  269
* Making a Long-Term Memory  269

**Concept Review  270**

**E. Mnemonics: Memorization Methods  271**
* Improving Your Memory  271

**F. Cultural Diversity: Aborigines versus White Australians  272**
* Retrieval Cues  272
* Visual versus Verbal Memory  272

**G. Research Focus: False Memories  273**
* Can False Memories Be Implanted?  273
* Research Method to Create False Memories  273

**H. Application: Eyewitness Testimony  274**
* How Accurate Is an Eyewitness?  274
* Can an Eyewitness Be Misled?  274
* Can Questions Change the Answers?  275
* Is What You Say, What You Believe?  275
* Which Interview Technique Works Best?  275

**Summary Test  276**

**Critical Thinking  278**

**Links to Learning  279**

## Module 13: Intelligence  280

**A. Defining Intelligence  282**
* Problem: Definition  282
* Two-Factor Theory  282
* Multiple-Intelligence Theory  283
* Triarchic Theory  283
* Current Status  283

**B. Measuring Intelligence  284**
* Earlier Attempts to Measure Intelligence  284
* Binet's Breakthrough  285
* Formula for IQ  285
* Examples of IQ Tests  286
* Two Characteristics of Tests  287

**C. Distribution & Use of IQ Scores  288**
* Normal Distribution of IQ Scores  288
* Mental Retardation: IQ Scores  288
* Vast Majority: IQ Scores  289
* Gifted: IQ Scores  289

**D. Potential Problems of IQ Testing  290**
* Binet's Two Warnings  290
* Racial Discrimination  290
* Cultural Bias  291
* Culture-Free Tests  291
* Nonintellectual Factors  291

**E. Nature-Nurture Question  292**
* Definitions  292
* Twin Studies  292
* Adoption Studies  293
* Interaction: Nature and Nurture  293
* Racial Controversy  294

**Concept Review  295**

**F. Cultural Diversity: Races, IQs, & Immigration  296**
* Misuse of IQ Tests?  296

**G. Research Focus: New Approaches  297**
* Can Genius Be Found in the Brain?  297
* Can Spearman's *g* Be Found in the Brain?  297

**H. Application: Intervention Programs  298**
* Definition of Intervention Programs  298
* Raising IQ Scores  299
* Need for Intervention Programs  299

**Summary Test  300**

**Critical Thinking  302**

**Links to Learning  303**

## Module 14: Thought & Language  304

**A. Forming Concepts  306**
* Definition Theory  306
* Prototype Theory  306
* Early Formation of Concepts  307
* Concepts in the Brain  307
* Two Functions of Concepts  307

**B. Solving Problems  308**
* Different Ways of Thinking  308
* Three Strategies for Solving Problems  309

**C. Thinking Creatively  310**
* How Is Creativity Defined?  310
* Is IQ Related to Creativity?  311
* How Do Creative People Think and Behave?  311
* Is Creativity Related to Mental Disorders?  311

**D. Language: Basic Rules  312**
* Four Rules of Language  312
* Understanding Language  313
* Different Structure, Same Meaning  313

**E. Acquiring Language  314**
* Four Stages in Acquiring Language  314
* Going Through the Stages  315
* What Are Innate Factors?  316
* What Are Environmental Factors?  316

**Concept Review  317**

**F. Reason, Thought, & Language  318**
* Two Kinds of Reasoning  318
* Why Reasoning Fails  318
* Words and Thoughts  319

**G. Research Focus: Dyslexia  320**
* What Kind of Problem Is Dyslexia?  320

**H. Cultural Diversity: Influences on Thinking  321**
* Differences in Thinking  321
* Male–Female Differences  321

**I. Application: Do Animals Have Language?  322**
* Criteria for Language  322
* Dolphins  322
* Gorilla and Chimpanzee  323
* Bonobo Chimp: Star Pupil  323

**Summary Test  324**

**Critical Thinking  326**

**Links to Learning  327**

## Module 15: Motivation  328

**A. Theories of Motivation  330**
* Instinct Theory  330
* Drive-Reduction Theory  330
* Incentive Theory  331
* Cognitive Theory  331
* Explaining Human Motivation  331

**B. Biological & Social Needs  332**
* Biological Needs  332
* Social Needs  332
* Satisfying Needs  332
* Maslow's Hierarchy of Needs  333

**C. Hunger  334**
* Optimal Weight  334
* Overweight  334
* Three Hunger Factors  334
* Biological Hunger Factors  335
* Genetic Hunger Factors  336
* Psychosocial Hunger Factors  337

**D. Sexual Behavior  338**
* Genetic Influences on Sexual Behavior  338
* Biological Influences  339
* Psychological Influences on Sexual Behavior  340
* Male–Female Sex Differences  342
* Homosexuality  343
* Sexual Responses, Problems, and Treatments  344
* AIDS: Acquired Immune Deficiency Syndrome  345

**E. Cultural Diversity: Female Circumcision  346**
* Good Tradition or Cruel Mutilation?  346

**Concept Review  347**

**F. Achievement  348**
* Kinds of Achievement  348
* Fear of Failure  349
* Underachievement  349
* Three Components of Success  349
* Cognitive Influences  350
* Intrinsic Motivation  350

**G. Research Focus: Immigrant Students  351**
* Why Did Immigrant Children Do Well?  351

**H. Application: Eating Problems & Treatments  352**
* Dieting: Problems, Concerns, and Benefits  352
* Serious Eating Disorders  353

**Summary Test  354**

**Critical Thinking  356**

**Links to Learning  357**

## Module 16: Emotion  358

**A. Peripheral Theories  360**
* Sequence for Emotions  360
* James-Lange Theory  360
* Facial Feedback Theory  361

**B. Cognitive Appraisal Theory  362**
* Schachter-Singer Experiment  362
* Which Comes First: Feeling or Thinking?  363
* Cognitive Appraisal Theory  363
* Affective-Primacy Theory  363

**C. Universal Facial Expressions  364**
* Definition of Universal  364
* Cross-Cultural Evidence  364
* Genetic Evidence  364

**D. Functions of Emotions  365**
* Send Social Signals  365
* Adapt and Survive  365
* Arouse and Motivate  365

**E. Happiness  366**
* Kinds of Happiness  366
* Adaptation Level Theory  366
* Long-Term Happiness  366

**F. Cultural Diversity: Emotions Across Cultures  367**
* Showing Emotions  367
* Perceiving Emotions  367

**Concept Review  368**

**G. Research Focus: Emotional Intelligence  369**
* What Is Emotional Intelligence?  369

**H. Application: Lie Detection  370**
* What Is the Theory?  370
* What Is a Lie Detector Test?  370
* How Accurate Are Lie Detector Tests?  371

**Summary Test  372**

**Critical Thinking  374**

**Links to Learning  375**

## Module 17: Infancy & Childhood 376

**A. Prenatal Influences   378**
- ✳ Nature and Nurture   378
- ✳ Genetic and Environmental Factors   378
- ✳ Prenatal Period: Three Stages   379
- ✳ Drugs and Prenatal Development   381

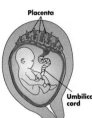

Placenta

Umbilical cord

**B. Newborns' Abilities   382**
- ✳ Genetic Developmental Program   382
- ✳ Sensory Development   382
- ✳ Motor Development   383

**C. Emotional Development   384**
- ✳ Definition and Kinds of Temperament   384
- ✳ Temperament and Emotions   384
- ✳ Attachment   385

**D. Research Focus: Temperament   386**
- ✳ Are Some Infants Born Fearful?   386

**E. Cognitive Development   388**
- ✳ Piaget's Theory   388
- ✳ Piaget's Stages of Cognitive Development   388
- ✳ Evaluation of Piaget's Theory   391

**F. Social Development   392**
- ✳ Freud's Psychosexual Stages   392
- ✳ Erikson's Psychosocial Stages   393
- ✳ Bandura's Social Cognitive Theory   394
- ✳ Resiliency   394
- ✳ Gender Differences   395
- ✳ Differences in Gender Traits   396
- ✳ Questions about Gender Differences   396
- ✳ Review: The Big Picture   397

1. Sensorimotor
2. Preoperational
3. Concrete
4. Formal

**Concept Review   398**

**G. Cultural Diversity: Gender Roles   399**
- ✳ Identifying Gender Roles   399
- ✳ Gender Roles Across Cultures   399
- ✳ Two Answers   399

**H. Application: Child Abuse   400**
- ✳ Kinds of Abuse   400
- ✳ Who Abuses Children?   401
- ✳ What Problems Do Abused Children Have?   401
- ✳ How Are Abusive Parents Helped?   401

**Summary Test   402**

**Critical Thinking   404**

**Links to Learning   405**

## Module 18: Adolescence & Adulthood 406

**A. Puberty & Sexual Behavior   408**
- ✳ Girls During Puberty   408
- ✳ Boys During Puberty   408
- ✳ Adolescents: Sexually Mature   409

**B. Cognitive & Emotional Changes   410**
- ✳ Definition   410
- ✳ Piaget's Cognitive Stages: Continued   410
- ✳ Brain Development: Reason and Emotion   411
- ✳ Kohlberg's Theory of Moral Reasoning   412
- ✳ Parenting Styles and Effects   413
- ✳ Adolescence: Big Picture   414
- ✳ Beyond Adolescence   415

**C. Personality & Social Changes   416**
- ✳ Definition   416
- ✳ Development of Self-Esteem   416
- ✳ Adulthood: Erikson's Psychosocial Stages   417
- ✳ Personality Change   417

**D. Gender Roles, Love, & Relationships   418**
- ✳ Definition: Gender Roles   418
- ✳ Expectations   419
- ✳ Kinds of Love   419
- ✳ Choosing a Partner   420
- ✳ Long-Term Relationship: Success or Failure?   420

**Concept Review   421**

**E. Research Focus: Happy Marriages   422**
- ✳ Why Do Marriages Succeed or Fail?   422

**F. Cultural Diversity: Preferences for Partners   423**
- ✳ Measuring Cultural Influences   423
- ✳ Desirable Traits   423
- ✳ Reasons for Marrying   423

**G. Physical Changes: Aging   424**
- ✳ Kinds of Aging   424
- ✳ Reasons for Aging   424
- ✳ Sexual Changes with Aging   425

**H. Application: Suicide   426**
- ✳ Teenage Suicide   426
- ✳ Problems Related to Teenage Suicide   426
- ✳ Preventing Teenage Suicide   427
- ✳ Suicide in the Elderly   427

**Summary Test   428**

**Critical Thinking   430**

**Links to Learning   431**

## Module 19: Freudian & Humanistic Theories 432

### A. Freud's Psychodynamic Theory 434
✳ Definition 434
✳ Conscious versus Unconscious Forces 434
✳ Techniques to Discover the Unconscious 435

### B. Divisions of the Mind 436
✳ Id, Ego, and Superego 436
✳ Anxiety 437
✳ Defense Mechanisms 437

### C. Developmental Stages 438
✳ Development: Dealing with Conflicts 438
✳ Fixation: Potential Personality Problems 438
✳ Five Psychosexual Stages 439

### D. Freud's Followers & Critics 440
✳ Disagreements 440
✳ Neo-Freudians 440
✳ Freudian Theory Today 441

### E. Humanistic Theories 442
✳ Three Characteristics of Humanistic Theories 442
✳ Maslow: Need Hierarchy and Self-Actualization 443
✳ Rogers: Self Theory 444
✳ Applying Humanistic Ideas 446
✳ Evaluation of Humanistic Theories 446

### Concept Review 447

### F. Cultural Diversity: Unexpected High Achievement 448
✳ Boat People: Remarkable Achievement 448
✳ Values and Motivation 448
✳ Parental Attitudes 448

### G. Research Focus: Shyness 449
✳ What Is Shyness and What Causes It? 449
✳ Psychodynamic Approach 449
✳ Social Cognitive Theory 449

### H. Application: Assessment— Projective Tests 450
✳ Definition of Projective Tests 450
✳ Examples of Projective Tests 450
✳ Two Characteristics 451
✳ Usefulness of Projective Tests 451

### Summary Test 452
### Critical Thinking 454
### Links to Learning 455

1. Oral
2. Anal
3. Phallic
4. Latency
5. Genital

## Module 20: Social Cognitive & Trait Theories 456

### A. Social Cognitive Theory 458
✳ Review and Definition 458
✳ Interaction of Three Factors 458
✳ Bandura's Social Cognitive Theory 459
✳ Evaluation of Social Cognitive Theory 461

### B. Trait Theory 462
✳ Definition 462
✳ Identifying Traits 462
✳ Finding Traits: Big Five 463
✳ Person versus Situation 464
✳ Stability versus Change 465

### C. Genetic Influences on Traits 466
✳ Behavioral Genetics 466
✳ Studying Genetic Influences 466
✳ Data from Twin Studies 467
✳ Influences on Personality 467

### D. Evaluation of Trait Theory 468
✳ How Good Is the List? 468
✳ Can Traits Predict? 468
✳ What Influences Traits? 468

### Concept Review 469

### E. Research Focus: 180-Degree Change 470
✳ How Much Can People Change in a Day? 470

### F. Cultural Diversity: Resolving Conflicts 471
✳ Interpersonal Conflicts 471
✳ Cultural Differences 471
✳ Using Different Strategies 471

### G. Four Theories of Personality 472
✳ Psychodynamic Theory 472
✳ Humanistic Theories 472
✳ Social Cognitive Theory 473
✳ Trait Theory 473

### H. Application: Assessment— Objective Tests 474
✳ Definition 474
✳ Examples of Objective Tests 474
✳ Reliability and Validity 475
✳ Usefulness 475

### Summary Test 476
### Critical Thinking 478
### Links to Learning 479

Should I take one marsh-mallow now or wait and get two?

I read my horo-scope every day, and it's always right on the mark.

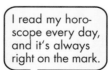

## Module 21: Health, Stress, & Coping 480

**A. Appraisal 482**
* Primary Appraisals 482
* Situations and Primary Appraisals 482
* Appraisal and Stress Level 483
* Same Situation, Different Appraisals 483
* Sequence: Appraisal to Arousal 483

**B. Physiological Responses 484**
* Fight-Flight Response 484
* Psychosomatic Symptoms 486
* Kinds of Symptoms 486
* General Adaptation Syndrome 487
* Mind-Body Connection 487
* Immune System 488

**C. Stressful Experiences 490**
* Kinds of Stressors 490
* Situational Stressors 491
* Conflict 492
* Anxiety 493

**D. Personality & Social Factors 494**
* Hardiness 494
* Locus of Control 495
* Optimism versus Pessimism 495
* Type A Behavior 496
* Social Support 497

**Concept Review 498**

**E. Kinds of Coping 499**
* Appraisal 499
* Kinds of Coping 499
* Choosing a Coping Strategy 499

**F. Research Focus: Coping with Trauma 500**
* How Do People Cope with Severe Burns? 500

**G. Cultural Diversity: Tibetan Monks 501**
* Monks' Amazing Claims 501
* Mind-Body Interaction 501

**H. Application: Stress Management Programs 502**
* Definition 502
* Changing Thoughts 502
* Changing Behaviors 503
* Changing Physiological Responses 503

**Summary Test 504**

**Critical Thinking 506**

**Links to Learning 507**

## Module 22: Assessment & Anxiety Disorders 508

**A. Three Approaches 510**
* Causes of Abnormal Behavior 510
* Definitions of Abnormal Behavior 511

**B. Assessing Mental Disorders 512**
* Definition of Assessment 512
* Three Methods of Assessment 512

**C. Diagnosing Mental Disorders 513**
* Real-Life Assessment 513
* DSM-IV-TR 513
* Nine Major Problems: Axis I 514
* Other Problems and Disorders: Axes II, III, IV, V 515
* Potential Problems with Using DSM-IV-TR 516
* Frequency of Mental Disorders 516

**D. Anxiety Disorders 517**
* Generalized Anxiety Disorder 517
* Panic Disorder 517
* Phobias 518
* Obsessive-Compulsive Disorders 519

**E. Somatoform Disorders 520**
* Definition and Examples 520
* Mass Hysteria 520

**Concept Review 521**

**F. Cultural Diversity: An Asian Disorder 522**
* Taijin Kyofusho, or TKS 522
* Social Customs 522

**G. Research Focus: School Shootings 523**
* What Drove Teens to Kill Fellow Students and Teachers? 523

**H. Application: Treating Phobias 524**
* Specific Phobia: Flying 524
* Cognitive-Behavioral Therapy 524
* Exposure Therapy 524
* Social Phobia: Public Speaking 525
* Drug Treatment of Phobias 525

**Summary Test 526**

**Critical Thinking 528**

**Links to Learning 529**

## Module 23: Mood Disorder & Schizophrenia 530

**A. Mood Disorders 532**
* Kinds of Mood Disorders 532
* Causes of Mood Disorders 533
* Treatment of Mood Disorders 534

**B. Electroconvulsive Therapy 535**
* Definition and Usage 535
* Effectiveness of ECT 535

**C. Personality Disorders 536**
* Definition 536
* Antisocial Personality Disorder 536
* Psychopaths: Causes and Treatment 537

**D. Schizophrenia 538**
* Definition and Types 538
* Symptoms 538
* Biological Causes 539
* Neurological Causes 540
* Environmental Causes 540
* Treatment 541
* Evaluation of Neuroleptic Drugs 542

**Concept Review 543**

**E. Dissociative Disorders 544**
* Definition 544
* Dissociative Amnesia 544
* Dissociative Fugue 544
* Dissociative Identity Disorder 545

**F. Cultural Diversity: Interpreting Symptoms 546**
* Spirit Possession 546
* Cultural Differences in Occurrence 546
* Cultural Differences in Gender Roles 546

**G. Research Focus: Exercise versus Drugs 547**
* Choice of Therapy for Depression 547
* Exercise Experiment: Seven Rules 547

**H. Application: Dealing with Mild Depression 548**
* Mild versus Major Depression 548
* Beck's Theory of Depression 548
* Overcoming Mild Depression 549

**Summary Test 550**

**Critical Thinking 552**

**Links to Learning 553**

## Module 24: Therapies 554

**A. Historical Background 556**
* Definition 556
* Early Treatments 556
* Reform Movement 556
* Phenothiazines and Deinstitutionalization 557
* Community Mental Health Centers 557

**B. Questions about Psychotherapy 558**
* Do I Need Professional Help? 558
* Are There Different Kinds of Therapists? 558
* Are There Different Approaches? 559
* How Effective Is Psychotherapy? 559

**C. Insight Therapies 560**
* Psychoanalysis 560
* Techniques to Reveal the Unconscious 561
* Problems During Therapy 562
* Psychoanalysis: Evaluation 563
* Client-Centered Therapy 564
* Cognitive Therapy 565

**D. Behavior Therapy 566**
* Definition 566
* Systematic Desensitization 567
* Cognitive-Behavior Therapy 568
* Kinds of Problems 568

**Concept Review 569**

**E. Review: Evaluation of Approaches 570**
* Assumptions, Methods, and Techniques 570
* Effectiveness of Psychotherapy 571
* Common Factors 571

**F. Cultural Diversity: Different Healer 572**
* Case Study: Young Woman 572
* Healer's Diagnosis and Treatment 572
* Healers versus Western Therapists 572

**G. Research Focus: EMDR—New Therapy 573**
* Does New Therapy Method Eliminate Traumatic Memories? 573

**H. Application: Cognitive-Behavior Techniques 574**
* Thought Problems 574
* Thought-Stopping Programs 574
* Thought Substitution 575
* Treatment for Insomnia 575

**Summary Test 576**

**Critical Thinking 578**

**Links to Learning 579**

## Module 25: Social Psychology 580

### A. Perceiving Others 582
* Person Perception 582
* Physical Appearance 582
* Stereotypes 583
* Schemas 584

### B. Attributions 585
* Definition 585
* Internal versus External 585
* Kelley's Model of Covariation 585
* Biases and Errors 586

### C. Research Focus: Attributions & Grades 587
* Can Changing Attributions Change Grades? 587

### D. Attitudes 588
* Definition 588
* Components of Attitudes 588
* Functions of Attitudes 589
* Attitude Change 590
* Persuasion 591

### E. Social & Group Influences 592
* Conformity 592
* Compliance 593
* Obedience 593
* Helping: Prosocial Behavior 595
* Why People Help 595
* Group Dynamics 596
* Behavior in Crowds 597
* Group Decisions 598

### Concept Review 599

### F. Aggression 600
* Definition 600
* Biological Factors 600
* Social Cognitive and Personality Factors 601
* Environmental Factors 601
* Sexual Harassment and Aggression 602

### G. Cultural Diversity: National Attitudes & Behaviors 603
* Niger: Beauty Ideal 603
* Japan: Organ Transplants 603
* Egypt: Women's Rights 603

### H. Application: Controlling Aggression 604
* Case Study 604
* Controlling Aggression in Children 604
* Controlling Anger in Adults 605
* Controlling Sexual Aggression 605

### Summary Test 606

### Critical Thinking 608

### Links to Learning 609

## Appendix A: Statistics in Psychology 610

### Descriptive Statistics 610
* Frequency Distributions 610
* Measures of Central Tendency 611
* Measures of Variability 612

**Figure A.1**
**A normal curve.**

Number of subjects

Measurements

### Inferential Statistics 613
* Chance & Reliability 614
* Tests of Statistical Significance 614
* Analysis of Variance 615
* Chi-Square 616

### Summary 617

## Appendix B: Critical Thinking Study Questions with Answers 618

### Glossary 638
### References 662
### Credits 700
### Name Index 709
### Subject Index 715

## What's Different about the 6th Edition?

One of the first things instructors notice about this textbook is that it looks different from more traditional texts. As one reviewer said, "When I first adopted the 5th edition, I wasn't sure how students would approach the text. It looks very different from other books and is very visual." This text looks different because its method of presenting information is based on several well-known principles of learning and memory.

One principle is that if information is presented in an interesting way, concepts are learned and remembered much more readily. Like previous editions, the 6th edition applies this principle by integrating the text with interesting graphics so that students have visual cues to help them learn and remember. As students often say, "I'm a visual learner so this text is perfect for me."

Another principle is that if information is organized or "chunked" into smaller units, the material will be better learned and remembered. As in previous editions, the 6th edition applies this principle by organizing information into smaller and smaller segments to help students remember the hundreds of terms and concepts. As one reviewer said, "The material is broken down into small, friendly pieces that are easy for students to understand."

Thus, this text looks different because it uses "chunking" and visual learning, which help students better learn and remember. As one reviewer said, "I was very pleased to find that students were reading the text, discussing the material and using the study guide. In fact, they sometimes asked questions about parts of the chapters not assigned."

I have received many dozens of reviewers' comments and hundreds of students' responses. They agree that the visual learning approach used in this and previous editions motivates students not only to read but also to learn the material.

## What Are the Major Changes in the 6th Edition?

During the past decade, new findings in the related areas of biology, genetics, and cognitive neuroscience have had a great impact on the field of psychology. For example, a new and interesting finding is that teenagers' brains, especially their "executive" areas (prefrontal cortex), are not fully developed. As a result, teenagers may show poor planning, bad reasoning, and muddled thinking. Because such findings help psychologists better understand and explain behavior, I have included many new and exciting discoveries not only from the field of psychology but also from the related fields of biology, genetics, and cognitive neuroscience.

I have also used feedback from readers and reviewers in revising and adding new figures and illustrations, which provide visual cues for learning. Finally, in updating the 6th edition, I have added 670 new references (65% of them from 2000 and 2001).

Here are some of the major changes in the 6th edition:

**Module 1: Discovering Psychology.** Discussion of new medical tests used to identify infants who are likely to develop autism; differences between how normal and autistic brains process human faces; how autism is diagnosed in different cultures; updated research on test anxiety; relationship between cognitive neuroscience and cognitive approach; how students respond to test anxiety in different cultures; and, in the Critical Thinking section, a new newspaper article: "Is There a New Treatment for Autism?" along with new questions and suggested answers.

**Module 2: Psychology & Science.** Discussion of new guidelines by the American Academy of Pediatrics for diagnosing ADHD; new survey data on frequency of ADHD; new behavioral/medical test with the potential to diagnose ADHD; possibility of using the effects of Ritalin on brain activity to diagnose children with ADHD; new discussion of the controversies surrounding ADHD, including diagnosis, treatment, and long-term concerns; and new examples of placebo effects that occurred while testing drugs to treat impotency and using magnets to reduce chronic pain.

**Module 3: Brain's Building Blocks.** New information on the diagnosis, causes, and treatment of Alzheimer's disease; MRIs comparing brain activity in normal and Alzheimer's brains; photos showing size decrease in Alzheimer's brains; possibility of transplanting a donor's hand; Christopher Reeve's spinal cord damage and likelihood of walking again; transplanting human fetal tissue and fetal pig brain cells to treat Parkinson's patients; and, in the Critical Thinking section, a new newspaper article, "Would You Want a Head Transplant?" along with new questions and suggested answers.

**Module 4: Incredible Nervous System.** New information on Project Genome (identifying and mapping the location of all human genes); use of brain scans (fMRI) to study such cognitive functions as identifying various objects and faces; involvement of the cerebellum in classical conditioning; involvement of motor cortex in remembering the sequence of events; importance of frontal lobe's executive function; relationship between emotions (limbic system) and executive functions (prefrontal area); why men may be better than women at remembering and following directions; increased environmental experiences may stimulate growth of new neurons in adult brains; and, in the Critical Thinking section, a new newspaper article: "Can Brain Damage Disrupt Right and Wrong?" along with new questions and suggested answers.

**Module 5: Sensation.** New information on using eye surgery (LASIK) to correct nearsighted vision (myopia); revised figure explaining the three layers of the retina; PET scan showing activity in brain's visual association areas; new figure showing why people can't always agree on how to adjust the colors on their TV sets; revised auditory figures showing amplitude, pitch, and direction of sound; new figure showing vestibular system; cultural influences on emotions, such as disgust; using double-blind research method to study placebo effects; importance of psychological, emotional, and social factors in the experience and treatment of pain; research on the mechanisms and effectiveness of acupuncture; and discussion of cochlear implants.

**Module 6: Perception.** New information comparing the accuracy of X rays with digital mammograms; revised figure explaining how sensations become perceptions; new explanation of the moon illusion;

revised explanation of the Ames' room illusion; effectiveness of subliminal stimuli on perceptions and specific behaviors; examples of how different cultures produce differences in perceiving and thinking; how not replicating findings creates a major problem in ESP research; psychic hot lines; using virtual reality technology to perform robotic surgery and treat phobias; and, in the Critical Thinking section, a new newspaper article, "What's It Like to Talk to a Clairvoyant?" along with new questions and suggested answers.

**Module 7: Consciousness, Sleep, & Dreams.** New information on the hazards of driving while talking on a cell phone; comparison of Freud's idea of the unconscious with cognitive psychology's theory of implicit (nondeclarative) memory; finding that the circadian sleep-wake clock is set for an average of 24 hours, 18 minutes, rather than 25 hours, as previously thought; how sunlight affects the suprachiasmatic nucleus; melatonin found to be no better than a placebo in reducing jet lag; REM sleep helps to store or encode previously learned information; adolescents need more sleep than previously believed; cultural differences influence occurrence of seasonal affective disorder (SAD); activity in certain brain areas explains why dreams are so strange; cause and treatment of narcolepsy; and, in the Critical Thinking section, a new newspaper article, "Want to be Treated by a Sleep-Deprived Doctor?" along with new questions and suggested answers.

**Module 8: Hypnosis & Drugs.** New information on altered states compared to the sociocognitive theory of hypnosis; reasons people use drugs; legalization and decriminalization of illegal drugs; genetic factors involved in drug use and abuse; methamphetamine becoming the most popular illegal drug in Japan; cocaine increasing heart attacks; increase in teenage smokers and the fact that 75% become adult smokers; use and dangers of ecstasy (MDMA); genetic risk factors for alcoholism; medical use of marijuana; ineffectiveness of Drug Abuse Resistance Program (DARE ); total abstinence versus learning to drink responsibly; and, in the Critical Thinking section, new questions and suggested answers for the newspaper article.

**Module 9: Classical Conditioning.** New information on the development of dental phobias in children and adults; discussion of taste-aversion learning; using classical conditioning to diagnose dyslexia; possibility of being classically conditioned in the dentist's office; explanation of systematic desensitization; and, in the Critical Thinking section, new newspaper article, "Can Your Beliefs Make You Sick?" along with new questions and suggested answers.

**Module 10: Operant & Cognitive Approaches.** New example of 3-year-old boy learning to play golf through cognitive learning; accidentally shaping superstitious behaviors; comparing operant and classical conditioning; nonpunishment treatments for self-injurious behaviors; Skinner's impact and critics' responses; parents using operant conditioning to deal with noncompliance in young children; follow-up data on the success of Dr. Lovaas's behavior modification program for treating autistic children; and, in the Critical Thinking section, a new newspaper article, "Is It OK for Parents to Spank Their Kids?" along with new questions and suggested answers.

**Module 11: Types of Memory.** New discussion of how iconic memory lets us "see" when our eyes close during blinking; involvement of prefrontal cortex in working memory; steps in the memory processes; retrieving information from long-term memory; evidence of two separate memory systems; declarative and procedural (nondeclarative) memory systems; emotional experiences increase or decrease memory for related events; accuracy of repressed and recovered memories; photographic memory; and, in the Critical Thinking section, a new newspaper article, "Preschool Teachers Accused of Child Abuse," along with new questions and suggested answers.

**Module 12: Remembering & Forgetting.** New discussion of how we file and organize memories; organization of the network hierarchy; the brain having different areas for storing different categories (faces, tools, plants, animals); earliest childhood memories; state-dependent learning; different memories located in different parts of the brain; long-term memory can be genetically altered; memory-enhancing drugs; comparison of retrieval cues used by Aborigines and White Australians; effects of own-race bias on eyewitness testimony.

**Module 13: Intelligence.** Discussion of different kinds of intelligence; Spearman's, Gardner's, and Sternberg's theories of intelligence; brain size, sex differences, and intelligence; intelligence results from nature and nurture interaction; skin color is not a scientific basis for assigning people to different races; differences in Einstein's brain; search for Spearman's *g* using PET scans; Head Start's emphasis on preparing disadvantaged children for kindergarten; and, in the Critical Thinking section, a new newspaper article, "Can a Successful Bookie Have an IQ of 55?" along with new questions and suggested answers.

**Module 14: Thought & Language.** Discussion of breakthrough in artificial intelligence; increasing connections between neurons associated with development of language; going through the language stages; language development of Genie, who was deprived of social interactions for her first 13 years; diagnosis, cause, and treatment of dyslexia; new Research Focus on how cultural factors influence what we see; dolphins' ability to use language; and, in the Critical Thinking section, new questions and suggested answers for the newspaper article.

**Module 15: Motivation.** New information on increasing percentage of overweight people and related health risks; women overestimate and men underestimate their weights; effects of sex chromosomes and sex hormones on development of brain and behavior; child's gender identity resistant to change despite sex surgery; explanations of male–female sex differences according to social role and evolutionary theories; genetic, biological, and psychological factors involved in developing a homosexual orientation; spread of AIDS worldwide and current treatment programs; using self-handicapping to protect one's self-esteem; how external rewards affect intrinsic motivation; problems with dieting and weight control; and, in the Critical Thinking section, a new newspaper article, "How Effective Is Viagra?" along with new questions and suggested answers.

**Module 16: Emotion.** New discussion of the four components of emotions; new figure that summarizes the James-Lange theory of emotions; new figure that summarizes the facial-feedback theory of emotions; new figure that summarizes the Schachter-Singer experiment on emotions; discussion of how to achieve long-term happiness; new Research Focus on measuring emotional intelligence; using lie detector tests to screen new employees; and, in the Critical Thinking section, a new newspaper article, "Why Are They Learning to Smile?" along with new questions and suggested answers for the newspaper article.

**Module 17: Infancy & Childhood.** New discussion of the interaction of genes and environment; potential problems during the fetal stage; short- and long-term effects of drugs used during pregnancy; brain areas most active during a newborn's first three months; interaction of temperament and emotions; change in temperament across time; criticism of Piaget's theory of cognitive development; fathers tend to model being assertive and dominant, while mothers model being concerned and nurturing; differences in gender roles, careers, and cognitive abilities; and, in the Critical Thinking section, new questions and suggested answers for the newspaper article.

**Module 18: Adolescence & Adulthood.** New discussion of factors influencing teenagers' decisions whether or not to become sexually active; adolescence not all storm and stress but also a time for growth; association between development of the adolescent brain and ability to think and reason; evaluation of Kohlberg's theory of moral reasoning involving recent evidence of the importance of the prefrontal cortex in executive functions; review of major physical, sexual, cognitive, and moral changes during adolescence; cognitive changes from young adulthood through old age; changes in personality and social development during adolescence; the current status, development, and function of gender roles; why couples succeed or fail in long-term relationships; doctor-assisted suicide; and, in the Critical Thinking section, a new newspaper article, "Am I Losing My Memory?" as well as new questions and suggested answers.

**Module 19: Freudian & Humanistic Theories.** New discussion of Freud's theory of dream interpretation; having a dominant or most-often-used defense mechanism; new figure showing Freud's five psychosexual stages; current status of Freud's psychoanalytic theory; advantages and disadvantages of projective tests; and, in the Critical Thinking section, new questions and suggested answers for the newspaper article.

**Module 20: Social Cognitive & Trait Theories.** New figure showing the importance of three cognitive factors on personality; how self-efficacy influences learning and motivation in students; sexual bias and discrimination against women in majority of police departments; why the Big Five traits are important; new example of person/situation interaction; how much personality traits change and how much they remain the same across the life span; validity and predictability of five factor trait theory; how researchers studied quantum personality changes; validity and reliability of objective personality tests; and, in the Critical Thinking section, new questions and suggested answers for the newspaper article.

**Module 21: Health, Stress, & Coping.** New discussion of how we make different appraisals of the same situation (waiting in line); men are more likely to respond to stress by fighting or escaping and women are more likely to respond by nurturing and seeking social support; interaction between the fight-flight response and development of psychosomatic symptoms; women report significantly more numerous and intense experiences of stressful and emotional events than men; how optimism and pessimism influence emotional feelings, levels of stress, and psychosomatic symptoms; hostility associated with heart disease in men but not in women; advantages and disadvantages of emotion-focused and problem-focused coping; Tibetan monks use meditation to control responses of the normally involuntary autonomic nervous system; and, in the Critical Thinking section, new questions and suggested answers for the newspaper article.

**Module 22: Assessment & Anxiety Disorders.** New discussion of the medical, cognitive-behavioral, and psychodynamic approaches to mental disorders; DSM-IV-TR's five axes and how they are used to diagnose mental disorders; genetic and neurological factors involved in obsessive-compulsive disorder (OCD) as well as possible treatments; occurrence and symptoms involved in mass hysteria; personality traits and risk factors of students who shoot fellow students; using virtual reality technology to treat specific phobias, such as fear of heights, flying, and spiders; and, in the Critical Thinking section, new questions and suggested answers for the newspaper article.

**Module 23: Mood Disorder & Schizophrenia.** New information on neurological factors (prefrontal cortex) involved in mood disorders; clinicians' recommendation that SSRIs (selective serotonin reuptake inhibitors) are better tolerated than older tricyclic antidepressants; high rates of relapse (70%) following treatment for depression; new belief that for many patients depression is a chronic disorder requiring long-term treatment; electroconvulsive shock therapy (ECT) as seen through the eyes of an actual patient; increased risk for developing an antisocial personality because of brain damage or maldevelopment of the prefrontal cortex; multiple genes are involved in the development of schizophrenia; differences in action, side effects, and effectiveness of typical and atypical neuroleptics for treating schizophrenia; new Research Focus showing that exercise is as effective in treating major depression as antidepressants; and, in the Critical Thinking section, new questions and suggested answers for the newspaper article.

**Module 24: Therapies.** New report that about 20–30% of Americans experience a mental disorder in the course of a year; experimental program to train clinical psychologists in prescribing drugs to treat mental disorders; reasons for the decline in popularity of psychoanalysis and current attempts to evaluate its concepts and effectiveness; effectiveness of traditional healers (Balians) in Bali, Indonesia; EMDR (eye movement desensitization and reprocessing) therapy found to be another form of exposure therapy; suppressing unwanted thoughts is difficult and often results in the opposite effect of thinking more about the unwanted thought; and, in the Critical Thinking section, a new newspaper article, "What Is Exorcism?" along with new questions and suggested answers.

**Module 25: Social Psychology.** New information on what makes faces attractive and how facial attractiveness strongly influences first impressions; use of schemas in analyzing and responding in social situations and in relationships; how group makeup and cultural factors affect conformity in Asch-type studies; genetic factors associated with regulating levels of serotonin and its involvement in aggression; social cognitive and personality factors influencing the development and performance of aggressive behaviors; cultural attitudes influence the relationship between body weight and attractiveness; successful programs for treating aggressive children; cognitive-behavioral program for reducing anger in college students; females' friendliness misperceived by sexually aggressive males; and, in the Critical Thinking section, new questions and answers for the newspaper article.

Now that you've read about all the changes in the 6th edition, we'll discuss the major features of the text.

## Module 5: Sensation

**A. Eye: Vision**     **94**
* STIMULUS: LIGHT WAVES
* STRUCTURE AND FUNCTION
* RETINA
* VISUAL PATHWAYS
* COLOR VISION

**B. Ear: Audition**     **100**
* STIMULUS: SOUND WAVES
* OUTER, MIDDLE, AND INNER EAR
* AUDITORY BRAIN AREAS
* AUDITORY CUES

**C. Vestibular System: Balance**     **105**
* POSITION AND BALANCE
* MOTION SICKNESS
* MENIERE'S DISEASE AND VERTIGO

**D. Chemical Senses**     **106**
* TASTE
* SMELL, OR OLFACTION

**E. Touch**     **108**
* DEFINITION
* RECEPTORS IN THE SKIN
* BRAIN AREAS

**Concept Review**     **109**

**F. Cultural Diversity: Disgust versus Delight**     **110**
* SENSATIONS AND PSYCHOLOGICAL FACTORS

**G. Research Focus: Mind over Body?**     **111**
* DEFINITIONS AND RESEARCH METHODS
* PLACEBO RESULTS
* CONCLUSION: MIND OVER BODY!

**H. Pain**     **112**
* DEFINITION
* GATE CONTROL THEORY
* ENDORPHINS
* ACUPUNCTURE

**I. Application: Artificial Senses**     **114**
* ARTIFICIAL VISUAL SYSTEM
* KINDS OF DEAFNESS
* COCHLEAR IMPLANTS

**Summary Test**     **116**

**Critical Thinking**     **118**
* CAN MUSIC RAISE A CHILD'S IQ?

**Links to Learning**     **119**

92

**Feature.** One of the features best-liked by both instructors and students is that the text is organized into smaller units called *modules*, which are shorter (20–30 pages) and more manageable than traditional chapters (45–50 pages). The 6th edition has 25 *modules*, which can easily be organized, omitted, or rearranged into any order. Because individual modules all have the same structure, each one can stand on its own.

**Advantage.** Instructors said that, compared to longer and more traditional chapters, they preferred the shorter *modules*, which allow greater flexibility in planning and personalizing one's course.

**Example and outline.** The sample page on your left, which is the opening page of Module 5, Sensation, shows that each *module* begins with a complete outline. In this outline, the major heads are designated by letter (A. Eye: Vision) and provide students with an overview of the entire module.

Under each major head are a number of subheads, which provide a more detailed outline of the major concepts covered in the module.

Students can use a *module's* outline to organize their lecture notes as well as to review the material.

# Visual Organization Explains Difficult Concepts

**Step-by-step approach.** One way to help students understand difficult or complex concepts is to use visual organization, which involves breaking concepts down into smaller, more manageable "chunks" of text that are integrated with related graphics. For example, the sample page at top right uses the step-by-step approach to explain the sequence for hearing (Module 5) by leading the student through a series of smaller steps.

**Side-by-side approach.** The sample page at bottom right also uses a form of visual organization, called the side-by-side approach, which places concepts—different states of consciousness—side by side for easy comparison. Student feedback indicates that visual organization—*step-by-step* and *side-by-side approach*—makes difficult concepts easier to understand.

**Definitions.** These two sample pages also show that students need never search for *definitions,* which are always **boldface and printed in blue.** Students need only look for **blue** words to easily find and review definitions.

**Integration of figures.** Finally, these two sample pages show that text and graphics are always integrated so students never have to search for an explanation or figure in some distant place. Students especially like this integration of text and graphics.

## B. Ear: Audition

### Outer, Middle, and Inner Ear

**Is that the Rolling Stones or a barking dog?**

Most of us think that we hear with our ears and that's how we tell the difference between, for example, the music of the Rolling Stones and the barking of a dog. But nothing is further from the truth. What really happens is that both music and a dog's barks produce only sound waves, which are just the stimulus for hearing (audition). Your ears receive sound waves, but it is your brain that actually does the hearing, distinguishing the difference between the Stones' song, "(I Can't Get No) Satisfaction," and a dog's barks. It's a complicated journey; the first step begins in the outer ear.

**1** *Outer Ear*
The only reason your ear has that peculiar shape and sticks out from the side of your head is to gather in sound waves. Thus, sound waves produced by the Rolling Stones are gathered by your outer ear.

The *outer ear* consists of three structures: external ear, auditory canal, and tympanic membrane.

The *external ear* is an oval-shaped structure that protrudes from the side of the head. The function of the external ear is to pick up sound waves and send them down a long, narrow tunnel called the auditory canal.

**1a** The *auditory canal* is a long tube that funnels sound waves down its length so that the waves strike a thin, taut membrane—the eardrum, or tympanic membrane.

In some cases, the auditory canal may become clogged with ear wax, which interferes with sound waves on their way to the eardrum. Ear wax should be removed by a professional so as not to damage the fragile eardrum.

**1b** The *tympanic (tim-PAN-ick) membrane* is a taut, thin structure commonly called the eardrum. Sound waves strike the tympanic membrane and cause it to vibrate. The tympanic membrane passes the vibrations on to the first of three small bones to which it is attached.

The tympanic membrane marks the boundary between the outer ear and the middle ear, described below left in #2.

**Sound waves**

**3** *Inner Ear*
The inner ear contains two main structures that are sealed in bony cavities: the

## A. Continuum of Consciousness

### Different States

**Are you conscious now?**

One curious and amazing feature of consciousness is that, at some point, the person is actually observing himself or herself (Damasio, 1999). For example, how do you know that at this very moment you are conscious?

*Consciousness* refers to different levels of awareness of one's thoughts and feelings. It may include creating images in one's mind, following one's thought processes, or having unique emotional experiences.

One way you know that you are conscious is that you are aware of your own thoughts and existence (Pinker, 2000). You may think that when awake you are conscious and when asleep you are unconscious, but there is actually a continuum of consciousness.

The *continuum of consciousness* refers to a wide range of experiences, from being acutely aware and alert to being totally unaware and unresponsive.

We'll summarize some of the experiences that make up the continuum of consciousness.

**Controlled Processes**

A big problem with people driving while using car phones is that we have the ability to focus all of our attention on only one thing, which is an example of controlled processes.

*Controlled processes* are activities that require full awareness, alertness, and concentration to reach some goal. The focused attention required in

**Automatic Processes**

Eating while reading is an automatic process.

Since this woman's atten-

**Daydreaming**

Many of us engage in a pleasurable form of consciousness that is called daydreaming.

*Daydreaming* is an activity that requires a low level of awareness, often occurs during automatic processes, and involves fantasizing or dreaming while awake.

We may begin daydreaming in a relatively conscious

**Altered States**

Over 3,000 years ago, Egyptians brewed alcohol to reach altered states of consciousness (Samuel, 1996).

*Altered states of consciousness* result from using any number of procedures—such as meditation, psychoactive drugs, hypnosis, or sleep deprivation—to produce an awareness that differs from normal consciousness.

# Concept Review Tests Knowledge of Major Concepts

## ✓ Concept Review

**1.** An emotion is defined in terms of four components: you interpret or (a)_____ some stimulus, thought, or event in terms of your well-being; you have a subjective (b)_____, such as being happy or fearful; you experience bodily responses, such as increased heart rate and breathing, which are called (c)_____ responses; and you often show (d)_____ behaviors, such as crying or smiling.

**2.** One theory says that emotions result from specific physiological changes in our bodies and that each emotion has a different physiological pattern. This theory, which says that we feel fear because we run, is called the (a)_____ theory. Two major criticisms of this theory are that researchers have not identified a different (b)_____ response pattern to match each emotion and that individuals with severed spinal cords, which prevents feedback from the body's physiological responses, still experience (c)_____.

**3.** A second theory says that feedback from the movement of facial muscles and skin is interpreted by your brain as an emotion; this theory is called the (a)_____ theory. Researchers found that emotions do occur without feedback from facial muscles and skin. However, facial feedback may initiate the occurrence of emotions and contribute to the (b)_____ of an emotion, as well as to our mood.

**4.** A third theory of emotions, which grew out of the work of Schachter and Singer, says that you interpret or appraise a situation as having a positive or negative impact on your life and this results in a subjective feeling that you call an emotion; this is called the _____ theory.

**5.** The fourth theory of emotions, which says that in some situations you feel an emotion before you have time to interpret or appraise the situation, is called the (a)_____. This theory says that, for some emotions, you (b)_____ before you think. In comparison, the cognitive appraisal theory says that you (c)_____ before you feel. This question about which comes first, feeling or thinking, is called the (d)_____.

**6.** Specific inherited facial patterns or expressions that signal specific feelings or emotional states across cultures, such as a smile signaling a happy state, are called _____. These emotions are thought to have evolved because they had important adaptive and survival functions for our ancestors.

**7.** According to one theory, we inherit the neural structure and physiology to express and experience emotions and we evolved basic emotional patterns to adapt to and solve problems important for our survival; this is called the (a)_____ theory. Facial expressions that accompany emotions communicate the state of our personal or subjective (b)_____ and provide (c)_____ signals that communicate with, and elicit responses from, those around us.

**8.** Your performance on a task depends on the amount of physiological arousal and the difficulty of the task. For many tasks, moderate arousal helps performance; for new or difficult tasks, low arousal is better; and for easy or well-learned tasks, high arousal may facilitate performance. This relationship between arousal and performance is known as the _____.

**9.** According to one theory, big events in your life, such as doing well on final exams, getting a car, obtaining a degree, or winning the lottery, do not produce long-lasting increases in happiness because in a relatively short period of time you become accustomed to your good fortune and it contributes less to your level of happiness; this theory is called the (a)_____. Long-term happiness is less dependent upon wealth and more dependent upon developing and achieving long-term (b)_____.

**10.** Specific cultural norms that regulate when, where, and how much emotion we should or should not express in different situations are called _____. These rules explain why the expression and intensity of emotions differ across cultures.

***Answers:*** *1. (a) appraise, (b) feeling, (c) physiological, (d) observable; 2. (a) James-Lange, (b) physiological, (c) emotions; 3. (a) facial feedback, (b) intensity; 4. cognitive appraisal; 5. (a) affective-primacy theory, (b) feel, (c) think, (d) primacy question; 6. universal emotions; 7. (a) psychoevolutionary, (b) feelings, (c) social; 8. Yerkes-Dodson law; 9. (a) adaptation level theory, (b) goals; 10. display rules*

368

---

**Feature.** How many times have students asked, "What should I study for the test?" One way to answer this question is to tell students to complete the two built-in quizzes that appear in each module. One quiz is the *Concept Review* (shown here) and the second is the *Summary Test* (shown on page xxix).

**Linking graphics and concepts.** The sample page on the left shows a *Concept Review* (Module 16), which has the unique feature of repeating the graphics that were first linked to the major concepts discussed in the text. This repeated use of visual cues has been shown to increase the learning or encoding of information as well to promote visual learning.

**Reading versus knowing.** One reason for including quizzes within the text is that students may think that they know the material because that have read it. However, studies show that students cannot judge how well they actually know the material unless they test their knowledge of specific information. The *Concept Review* gives students a chance to test their knowledge of major terms discussed in the text.

Student feedback on the *Concept Review* has been very positive. Students like the visual learning approach of having the graphics integrated with the concepts and find that the *Concept Review* is a great way to test their knowledge.

# Cultural Diversity Opens Students' Minds

**Feature.** One goal of an Introductory Psychology course is to challenge and broaden students' viewpoints by providing information about other cultures. Because of their limited experience of other cultures, students may be unaware that similar behaviors are viewed very differently in other cultures. For this reason, each of the 25 modules includes a *Cultural Diversity* feature.

**Example.** In the sample page on the right, the *Cultural Diversity* feature (Module 25) compares the different attitudes and behaviors regarding beauty standards, organ transplants, and women's rights in non-Western cultures.

**Topics.** Other *Cultural Diversity* topics include:

**Module 1:** Early Discrimination
**Module 2:** Use of Placebos
**Module 4:** Brain Size and Racial Myths
**Module 7:** Incidence of SAD
**Module 8:** Rates of Alcoholism
**Module 9:** Dental Fears
**Module 16:** Emotions Across Cultures
**Module 17:** Gender Roles
**Module 19:** High Achievement
**Module 20:** Resolving Conflicts
**Module 22:** An Asian Disorder
**Module 24:** Different Healer

The *Cultural Diversity* feature gives students a chance to see the world through very different eyes.

---

## G. Cultural Diversity: National Attitudes & Behaviors

### Niger: Beauty Ideal

**How do African women judge beauty?**

One reason that the concept of attitude has been so dominant in social psychology is that our attitudes push or predispose us to think and behave in certain ways. What we often don't realize is how much our culture shapes our attitudes. For example, in the United States, the current attitude, especially among the middle and upper classes, is that for a woman to be attractive, she should be slender. This thin-is-beautiful attitude can pressure women to behave in certain ways, such as to constantly worry about their weight and go on strict diets, which in some cases may result in eating disorders (Heatherton et al., 1997).

But thin is not always beautiful. For example, in Niger, Africa, a small group of young women were discussing who had the most beautiful body. They all agreed on Monique, age 15, because she was already heavy for her age and on her way to being

*The beauty ideal in Niger is to be heavy.*

very rotund. As one woman said, "I want to gain weight like Monique. I don't want to be thin" (Onishi, 2001, p. A4).

In Niger, as well as in many parts of Africa, being fat is the beauty ideal for women and beauty contests are won by the heaviest women. Before getting married, young brides-to-be are sent to so-called fattening rooms, where the goal is to eat to get fat and round so that the bride will be admired for her fullness. If a married woman is not round and fleshy, the villagers will accuse the husband of not taking care of her.

As one African doctor said, "In America, you are rich and have everything and the women want to be thin as if they had nothing. Here in Africa, we have nothing but women buy products to become fat and show they had everything" (Onishi, 2001, p. A4). This comparison of beauty attitudes between America and Africa clearly shows how cultural values not only shape attitudes but also predispose us to behave in certain ways.

A different debate over attitudes is going on in Japan.

### Japan: Organ Transplants

**How do Japanese view heart transplants?**

Miss Wakana Kume, who lives in Japan, was going to die unless she received a liver transplant. However, since 1968, it has been illegal in Japan to transplant organs from donors who are brain-dead. Like all Japanese, Miss Kume grew up with the attitude that brain-dead was not really dead, so she was very reluctant to get a transplant from a brain-dead donor. But because of the seriousness of her condition, Miss Kume flew to Australia, where she underwent a liver transplant. In a very real sense, Miss Kume engaged in counterattitudinal behavior by doing a behavior opposite of what she believed—getting a transplanted organ. Since her life-saving transplant, Miss Kume has changed her attitude toward transplant organs and now approves of them. This is a real example of changing attitudes by engaging in counterattitudinal behavior.

*There are almost no organ transplants in Japan.*

The reason there were about 24,000 organ transplants in the United States in 1997 but none in Japan is that cultures have different definitions of death. In the United States, death is defined as brain death—when a person's brain no longer shows electrical activity, even though the heart is still beating. In Japan, however, death is defined only as the moment when a person's heart stops beating, and donor organs can be removed only after the heart stops. But to be useful, donor organs must be removed when a person's heart is still beating. Currently, the Japanese are debating changing their definition of death to include brain death, which goes against a long cultural tradition. If brain death is legalized in Japan, organ transplants will be possible, provided that the Japanese change their attitudes toward death and accept organ transplants (WuDunn, 1997).

A debate over attitudes and behaviors is also going on in Egypt.

### Egypt: Women's Rights

**How do Egyptians view women?**

Since the early 1900s, Egyptian women have been fighting for their sexual, political, and legal rights in a society that is dominated by Muslim religious principles, which grant women few rights. For example, while women are supposed to wear veils to preserve their dignity, a husband may strike his wife as long as he doesn't hit her in the face and hits lightly. Many women are not given birth certificates, which means that they cannot vote, get a passport, or go to court. Although female circumcision is illegal in Egypt, virtually all women in certain areas have been circumcised (p. 346). There are no public hotlines to help battered women and no statistics on rape,

*Egyptian women are fighting for equal rights.*

although both are common in certain areas. Although Egyptian women are currently fighting for equal rights, such as not wearing veils in public (photo below), they are having limited success because these traditional attitudes are backed by powerful social forces, including political, cultural, and religious institutions (Daniszewski, 1999; Lief, 1994). In getting Egyptians to change their attitudes toward women, the persuaders will need to use some of the methods that we have discussed, such as using trustworthy and honest sources, presenting one- or two-sided arguments, and, depending on the audience, using either the central or peripheral approach.

Next, we'll examine programs psychologists have developed to change attitudes toward aggression.

**G.** *CULTURAL DIVERSITY: NATIONAL ATTITUDES & BEHAVIORS* **603**

---

## G. Research Focus: Sex Differences in the Brain?

### Science and Politics

**Is this kind of research sexist?**

Throughout history, politicians have criticized or misused research depending on what was "politically correct" (Azar, 1997). For example, in the 1920s, United States politicians misused research on IQ scores to justify passing discriminatory immigration quotas (see p. 296) (Gould, 1981). In the 1980s, many politicians were critical of homosexuality and denied federal money for AIDS research until the virus became a threat to the heterosexual population (Shilts, 1988). In the 1980s and 1990s, research on sex differences was criticized as "sexist" because it went against the "politically correct" belief that male and female brains are essentially the same (Azar, 1997).

However, using PET scans, researchers have recently reported interesting differences in the structure and function of male and female brains, which are called sex differences (Hausmann & Gunturkun, 1999).

*Sex, or gender, differences refer to structural or functional differences in cognitive, behavioral, or brain processes that arise from being a male or a female.*

Sex differences are neither good nor bad nor sexist but simply ways in which males and females differ. Here are some interesting sex differences.

### Differences in Solving Problems

The rotating figure problem is a rather difficult spatial problem, as follows. First, study the target figure on the left. Then, from the three choices at the right, identify the same figure, even though it has been rotated.

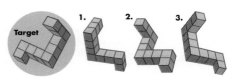

The key to solving this problem is the ability to rotate the target figure in your mind until it matches the rotation of one of the three choices. Researchers consistently report faster or more accurate performance by males than by females in solving rotating figure problems (Kimura, 1992). (Correct answer is 1.)

There are other tasks at which women perform better than men.

For example, look at the house outlined in black (figure above) and find its twin among the three choices. Women are generally faster on these kinds of tests, which measure perceptual speed. In addition, women usually score higher on tests of verbal fluency, in which you must list as many words as you can that begin with the same letter, as in the figure below (Halpern, 2000).

One explanation for these sex differences in skills is that they result from differences in

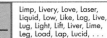

Limp, Livery, Love, Laser, Liquid, Low, Like, Lag, Live, Lug, Light, Lift, Liver, Lime, Leg, Load, Lap, Lucid, . . .

socialization and learning. Another explanation is that these sex differences have evolved from different skills needed by early humans. Males with good spatial skills had an advantage in hunting, and females with good communication skills had an advantage in child-rearing (Springer & Deutsch, 1997).

Researchers have now begun to look for sex differences in how the brain itself functions.

### Differences between Female and Male Brains

To check for sex differences between male and female brains, researchers took PET scans while subjects were solving rotating figure problems.

For male brains, PET scans taken during problem solving showed that maximum neural activity occurred in the right frontal area (upper right figure).

In contrast, PET scans of female brains taken during problem solving showed that maximum neural activity occurred in the right parietal-temporal area (lower right figure). Researchers concluded that solving rotating figure problems showed a significant sex difference in terms of which brain areas were activated and that these brain differences may be the basis for sex differences in performance (Alivisatos & Petrides, 1997).

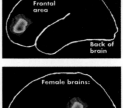

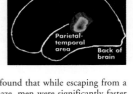

Another interesting PET study found that while escaping from a three-dimensional virtual-reality maze, men were significantly faster (average: 2 min. 22 sec) than women (average: 3 min. 16 sec). Also, men used both sides of their hippocampus, which is used to save data into permanent storage, while women used only the right hippocampus. Researchers concluded that these brain differences may explain why men are better at finding a specific place in a strange city (Gron et al., 2000).

Besides differences in cognitive tasks, researchers are also finding sex differences in emotional tasks.

Because women are consistently reported to be more sensitive, concerned, and nurturing, is it possible that women process emotional information differently than men (Halpern, 2000)? Researchers took PET scans while subjects induced emotional states (happy, sad). PET scans showed that while inducing emotional states, women used more of their limbic structures (involved in emotions) than men. Researchers speculate that these kinds of sex differences in the brain may underlie other male-female emotional behaviors (George et al., 1996).

In finding sex differences in the brain, researchers warn against using such differences as the basis for promoting discriminatory practices or furthering someone's political agenda (Azar, 1997).

 **84** **Module 4** *INCREDIBLE NERVOUS SYSTEM*

---

**Feature.** In teaching Introductory Psychology, an important but difficult goal is to explain how psychologists use a variety of research methods and techniques to answer questions. To help instructors reach this goal, each of the 25 modules includes a *Research Focus* that explains how psychologists answer questions through experiments, case studies, self-reports, and surveys.

**Example.** In the sample page on the left, the *Research Focus* (Module 4) explains how psychologists answer questions about sex differences in the brain by combining behavioral and neurological techniques and findings.

**Topics.** Other *Research Focus* topics include:

**Module 2:** ADHD Controversies

**Module 3:** Phantom Limb

**Module 5:** Pain and Placebos

**Module 7:** Circadian Preference

**Module 8:** Drug Prevention

**Module 10:** Noncompliance

**Module 12:** False Memories

**Module 16:** Emotional Intelligence

**Module 17:** Temperament

**Module 19:** Shyness

**Module 20:** 180-Degree Change

**Module 22:** School Shootings

Each of the 25 modules includes a *Research Focus,* which discusses the research methods and techniques that psychologists use to answer questions.

# Application Shows Psychology's Practical Side

**Feature.** A feature that is well-liked by students and instructors is the *Application*, which demonstrates how psychologists use basic principles to solve or treat real-life problems.

**Example.** In the sample page on the right, the *Application* (Module 16) explains how current "lie detector" machines measure only physiological arousal (increased heart rate, breathing, and finger sweating), which may result from a number of factors, including fear, nervousness, or emotional responses, such as feeling guilt after telling a lie.

**Topics.** Other *Application* topics include:

**Module 1:** Study Skills
**Module 4:** Split Brain
**Module 7:** Sleep Problems and Treatments
**Module 8:** Treatment for Drug Abuse
**Module 9:** Conditioned Fear and Nausea
**Module 10:** Behavior Modification
**Module 11:** Unusual Memories
**Module 17:** Child Abuse
**Module 18:** Suicide
**Module 20:** Assessment— Objective Tests
**Module 21:** Stress Management Program
**Module 22:** Treating Phobias
**Module 23:** Dealing with Mild Depression
**Module 25:** Controlling Aggression

The *Application* sections show the practical side of psychology—how psychological principles are applied to real-life situations.

---

## H. Application: Lie Detection

**How did a spy pass a lie detector test twice?**

From 1985 to 1994, the Russians paid or promised $4.6 million to Aldrich Ames (photo on right), who was a high-level Central Intelligence Agency official. Later, Ames pleaded guilty to espionage, which involved selling secrets to the Russians. Ames is currently serving a life sentence in prison. The Ames case brings up the issue of lie detection because he reportedly

*I lied, but I passed two lie detector tests.*

passed at least two lie detector (polygraph) tests during the time that he was selling U.S. secrets to Russia (Jackson, 1994). The publicity surrounding this case made people ask, "How could Ames be selling secrets and pass two lie detector tests?" The Ames case raises three questions: What is the theory behind lie detection? How is a lie detector test given? How accurate are lie detector tests?

### What Is the Theory?

**Does the test measure lying?**

The lie detector test is based on the four components of an emotion that we discussed earlier. The first component of an emotion is interpreting or appraising a stimulus. In this case, Ames will need to interpret questions such as "Have you ever sold secrets to Russia?" The second component of an emotion is a subjective feeling, such as whether Ames will feel any guilt or fear when he answers "Yes" or "No" to the question "Have you ever sold secrets to Russia?" The third component of an emotion is the occurrence of various physiological responses (figure below). If Mr. Ames feels guilty about selling secrets, then his guilt feeling will be accompanied by physiological arousal, which includes increases in heart rate, blood pressure, breathing, and sweating of the hands. These physiological responses occur automatically and are usually involuntary because they are controlled by the autonomic nervous system (discussed in Module 4). The fourth component of an emotion is the occurrence of some overt behavior, such as a facial expression. Mr. Ames may be able to control his facial expressions and put on a nonemotional poker face. However, neither the presence nor the absence of expressions is critical to the theory behind lie detector tests.

*Lie detector (polygraph) tests* are based on the theory that, if a person tells a lie, he or she will feel some emotion, such as guilt or fear. Feeling guilty or fearful will be accompanied by involuntary physiological responses, which are difficult to suppress or control and can be measured with a machine called a polygraph.

A polygraph (lie detector) is about the size of a laptop computer (right figure) and measures chest and abdominal muscle movement during respiration, heart rate, blood pressure, and skin conductance or galvanic skin response.

The *galvanic skin response* refers to changes in sweating of the fingers (or palms) that accompany emotional experiences and are independent of perspiration under normal temperatures (Cacioppo et al., 1993).

Chest movement during respiration
Abdominal movement during respiration
Heart rate and blood pressure
Skin conductance

For example, you may remember having sweaty or clammy palms when taking exams, giving a public talk, or meeting someone important, even though the temperature was not unduly hot.

We'll focus on the galvanic skin response because its changes are often the most obvious.

**Man hooked up to lie detector (polygraph)**

### What Is a Lie Detector Test?

**Is the suspect lying?**

Very few details have been released about how Mr. Ames, who apparently lied, passed two lie detector tests. Instead, we'll use a more detailed report of a man named Floyd, who told the truth but failed two lie detector tests.

Floyd was very surprised when two police officers came to his home. They had a warrant and arrested him for the armed robbery of a liquor store. However, the case against Floyd was weak, since none of the witnesses could positively identify him as the robber. Soon after his arrest, the prosecutor offered to drop all charges if Floyd agreed to take, and pass, a lie detector test. Floyd jumped at the chance to prove his innocence and took the test. He failed the lie detector test but insisted that he had not lied and that he be allowed to take a second one, which he also failed. Eventually Floyd was tried, found guilty, and sent to prison. He served several years behind bars before his lawyer tracked down the real robbers, which proved Floyd's innocence (*Los Angeles Times,* December 22, 1980).

Floyd was given the most commonly used procedure for lie detection in criminal investigations, which is called the Control Question Technique (Bashore & Rapp, 1993; Saxe, 1994).

The *Control Question Technique* refers to a lie detection procedure in which the examiner asks two kinds of questions: neutral

## Summary Test

### A. OVERVIEW: HUMAN BRAIN

**1.** The brain is composed of a trillion cells that can be divided into two groups. One group of cells has specialized extensions for receiving and transmitting information. These cells, which are called (a)_____, are involved in communicating with other neurons, receiving sensory information, and regulating muscles, glands, and organs. The other group of cells provide the scaffolding to guide and support neurons, insulate neurons, and release chemicals that influence neuron functions. These cells are much more numerous than neurons and are called (b)_____.

**2.** There is a major difference between the growth of neurons in the brains of humans and in the brains of birds. A mature human brain is normally not capable of developing new (a)_____, which are almost totally present at the time of birth. In contrast, a mature (b)_____ brain has the capacity to develop new neurons.

**3.** The age-old question of how the brain's membranes, fluids, and chemicals are involved in generating complex mental activities, such as thoughts, images, and feelings, is called the _____ question.

### B. NEURONS: STRUCTURE & FUNCTION

**4.** Although neurons come in wondrous shapes and sizes, they all share three structures. The structure that maintains the entire neuron in working order, manufactures chemicals, and provides fuel is called the (a)_____. The structure with many branchlike extensions that receive signals from other neurons, muscles, or organs and conduct these signals to the cell body is called a (b)_____. The single threadlike extension that leaves the cell body and carries signals to other neurons, muscles, or organs is called the (c)_____. At the very end of this structure are individual swellings called (d)_____, which contain tiny vesicles filled with (e)_____.

**5.** Surrounding most axons is a fatty material called the (a)_____. This material acts like (b)_____ and diminishes interference from electrical signals traveling in neighboring axons.

**6.** Neurons do not make physical contact with one another or with other organs. Instead, there is an infinitely small space between a neuron's end bulbs and neighboring dendrites, cell bodies, or other organs. This space is called the (a)_____. When an axon's end bulbs secrete a neurotransmitter, it flows across this

space and affects the (b)_____ on the neighboring membrane.

### C. NEURONS VERSUS NERVES

**7.** There are major differences between neurons and nerves. Cells with specialized extensions for conducting electrical signals are called (a)_____. These cells, which are located in the brain and spinal cord, make up the (b)_____ nervous system. Stringlike bundles of neurons' axons and dendrites, which are held together by connective tissue, are called (c)_____. These stringlike bundles, which are located throughout the body, make up the (d)_____ nervous system. Nerves carry information back and forth between the body and the spinal cord. If a neuron in the central nervous system is damaged, it normally does not have the capacity to (e)_____. In comparison, a nerve in the (f)_____ nervous system has the capacity to regrow or reattach if cut or damaged. The mature human brain has a limited ability to regrow (g)_____ throughout adulthood.

### D. SENDING INFORMATION

**Action Potential**

**8.** The axon membrane has (a)_____ that can be opened or closed. These gates keep some ions inside the membrane and other ions outside. If the axon is ready to conduct but not actually conducting an impulse, the axon is said to be in the (b)_____ state. In this state, most of the positively charged (c)_____ ions are on the outside of the membrane and all the negatively charged (d)_____ ions are trapped inside. In the resting state, the outside of the membrane has a (e)_____ charge compared to the (f)_____ charge on the inside. The process responsible for picking up and transporting sodium ions from the inside to the outside of the axon membrane is called the (g)_____.

**9.** If a stimulus is strong enough to excite a neuron, two things happen to its axon. First, the stimulus will eventually open the axon's (a)_____. Second, after the gates are opened, the (b)_____ pump is stopped, and all the positive (c)_____ ions rush inside because they are attracted to the negatively charged protein ions. The rush of sodium ions inside generates a tiny electrical current that is called the

---

**Problem.** How often have you heard students say, "I read the material three times but still did poorly on the test"? The problem is that students may think they know the material because they have a general idea of what they have read. However, researchers found that students are poor judges of how well they really know material unless they test themselves on specific questions.

**Feature.** The sample page on the left shows the *Summary Test* (Module 3), which gives students a chance to test their knowledge by answering specific questions. The reason the *Summary Test* (and the *Concept Review*) uses fill-in-the-blank questions instead of multiple choice is that fill-in-the-blank questions require recall, which is more difficult than recognition (multiple-choice questions). Thus, fill-in-the-blank questions are a better test of how well students know the material.

**Two tests.** Each module contains two tests. The first is the *Concept Review* (discussed on page xxiv), which occurs toward the end of each module and allows students to test their knowledge of major concepts. The second is the *Summary Test*, which occurs at the end of each module and allows students to check their knowledge of the entire module.

Students say that they like the *Summary Test* because it's a great way to review the entire module.

# Critical Thinking Challenges Students

**Feature.** Another goal of an Introductory Psychology course is to give students practice in critical thinking, which includes using concepts that they have learned to evaluate information from other sources. To accomplish this goal, we ask students to apply what they have learned by reading and evaluating an interesting and current newspaper article.

Recent research indicates that newspaper articles are a good way to create interest, nurture curiosity, and stimulate critical thinking and writing (Hollander, 2000).

**Example.** The sample page on the right shows the *Critical Thinking* feature (Module 10), which contains an interesting newspaper article that relates to one of the major topics (punishment) discussed in the module. Students are asked to think about and evaluate the article by answering five to seven questions that are placed next to it. Because many students need help in thinking about and answering questions, there are brief suggested answers at the bottom of the page to help them get on the right track. The suggested answers show students how they can use information in the module to evaluate statements in the article.

A newspaper article and its suggested answers appear at the end of each module and are great for stimulating class discussions.

## Critical Thinking

### Newspaper Article

### IS IT OK FOR PARENTS TO SPANK THEIR KIDS?

**Questions**

**1.** What is your own attitude toward spanking and how much, if at all, do these findings influence your attitude?

**2.** Which approach to answering questions did this study use and what are some of the problems with this study?

**3.** How do Dr. Trumbull's beliefs about spanking differ from those of Straus's study, which shows spanking has damaging effects?

Today, about 64% of American adults approve of spanking. The do-or-don't spanking controversy was sparked by a recent study.

Sociologist Murray Straus reported that the more a parent spanks a child for misbehaving, the worse—over time—that child behaves (*Archives of Pediatrics & Adolescent Medicine*, 1997). Straus says, "We are now able to show that when parents attempt to correct their child's behavior by spanking, it backfires . . . the more they spanked (3 or more times a week), the worse a child behaved two years and four years later" (Schulte, 1997, p. A1).

However, Straus's study has several problems. First, the mothers ranged in age from 14 to 21, not a representative sample of mothers in the United States. Second, the study looked at children ages 6 to 9 but not younger children. Third, the mothers were interviewed twice, two years apart, so there is a question about the reliability and truthfulness of their answers.

Dr. Den Trumbull, a pediatrician and critic of Straus's conclusions, says that spanking is effective and not harmful to development if limited to children between18 months and 6 years. On the other hand, spanking may be humiliating and traumatic to children in the 6 to 9 years age group and lead to problems down the line. Dr. Trumbull says that he favors spanking (one or two slaps to the buttocks) only as a last resort.

Psychologist Robert Larzelere, director of residential research at Boys Town in Nebraska, which does not allow spanking, reviewed 35 studies and could not find any convincing evidence that nonabusive spanking, as typically used by parents, had damaging effects. Larzelere concluded that whether or not parents spank is less important than how they spank. He says, "If parents use spanking as an occasional backup for say, a time-out, and as part of discipline in the context of a loving relationship, then an occasional spanking can have a beneficial role" (Rosellini, 1998, p. 58). The American Academy of Pediatrics also concluded that in certain circumstances, spanking may be an effective backup to other forms of discipline.

However, psychologist Irwin Hyman concludes, "There's enough evidence to decide we don't need spanking, even if the evidence isn't that strong." (Adapted from M. D. Lemonick, Spare the rod? Maybe, *Time*, August 25, 1997, p. 65; L. Rosellini, When to spank, *U.S. News & World Report*, April 15, 1998, pp. 52–58; B. Schulte, Spanking backfires, the latest study says, Knight-Ridder, appeared in *San Diego Union-Tribune*, August 15, 1997, p. A1).

**4.** What does Dr. Larzelere conclude is important about using spanking?

**5.** How do spanking and time-out differ?

**6.** Do you agree with Dr. Hyman that spanking should be banned?

*Try InfoTrac to search for terms:* spanking; disciplining children.

### Suggested answers to Newspaper Article questions

1. Your attitude toward spanking will be influenced by how you or your brothers and sisters were disciplined by your parents, such as how much they used spanking and any negative effects. If you disapprove of spanking, this study will confirm your belief; if you approve of spanking, this study may cause you to rethink.
2. This study used the survey approach, which is an efficient method to gather data from a large number of people, but they may misremember, forget, or give answers they think the interviewers want to hear. Problems with this study include choosing a very small sample of mothers (ages 14–21) and not including younger children (below the age of 6).
3. Dr. Trumbull believes that spanking is not harmful to younger children—18 months to 6 years—who are the group of children that Straus did not study.

4. Dr. Larzelere believes that how parents spank (doing it in the context of a loving relationship and as a backup to time-out) is MORE important than if they spank.
5. Spanking is an example of positive punishment—presenting an aversive stimulus (pain); time-out is an example of negative punishment—removing a reinforcer (attention, toys, television).
6. It is almost impossible not to have an emotional reaction when discussing spanking—I feel spanking may be OK as a last resort; I feel it's never all right to hurt a child. This means that your emotional feelings will influence how you respond to research findings. Research findings rarely answer any question absolutely but rather give you some data or facts to think about. For example, if you're against spanking, you'll agree with Dr. Hyman to ban spanking, even if the research doesn't totally support such a ban.

**236** **Module 10** *OPERANT & COGNITIVE APPROACHES*

## Links to Learning

### Web Sites

- **WADSWORTH ONLINE STUDY CENTER**
  **http://psychology.wadsworth.com**
  Quizzes, learning activities and exercises, a discussion forum, and hot links to Internet sites related to sensation, including:

- **OPERANT CONDITIONING AND BEHAVIORISM—A HISTORICAL OUTLINE**
  **http://www.biozentrum.uni-wuerzburg.de/genetics/behavior/learning/behaviorism.html**
  Here is a nice history of research on operant conditioning and behaviorism, including work by Thorndike, Watson, and Skinner.

- **POSITIVE REINFORCEMENT: A SELF-INSTRUCTIONAL EXERCISE**
  **http://server.bmod.athabascau.ca/html/prtut/reinpair.htm**
  This site offers a tutorial in positive reinforcement, and includes examples, activities, and practice exercises.

- **PARENT SOUP**
  **http://www.parentsoup.com/**
  This site is dedicated to that ongoing experiment in operant conditioning known as parenthood. There are areas for parents of children of various ages, and special features such as how to raise moral children.

### Learning Activities

- **POWERSTUDY™ CD, BY ROD PLOTNIK & TOM DOYLE**
  A 40-minute, fully narrated, self-paced, multimedia presentation that includes animations, interactive activities, videos, quizzes, pronunciation of terms, personal note-taking, and direct-to-Web connections.

- **STUDY GUIDE TO ACCOMPANY INTRODUCTION TO PSYCHOLOGY, 6TH EDITION, by Matthew Enos**
  In Module 10, read a tribute to B. F. Skinner, decide whether Bandura's classic Bobo doll experiment disproves Skinner, and come up with everyday examples of reinforcement.

- **WEBTUTOR**
  **http://webtutor.thomsonlearning.com**
  WebTUTOR Visit this site for interactive versions of the Study Guide features. Take a quiz, get your score—should you study a topic some more, or can you move on? For example, is there a difference between learning a behavior and performing it? What do you call the spanking a child gets for running into the street?

- **INFOTRAC ONLINE LIBRARY**
  **http://www.infotrac-college.com**
   Use your password and then key in search terms such as those below to find popular and scientific articles on subjects covered in Module 10. Make the library work for you!

  | Behavior modification | Biofeedback |
  | Imprinting | Ethologists |

- **PSYCHNOW!**
  CD for Macintosh and Windows includes a study guide, glossary, Web sites, and animations. For Module 10, see:
  - Classical Conditioning
  - Operant Conditioning

### Study Questions

*Use InfoTrac to search for topics mentioned in the main heads below (e.g., operant conditioning, cognitive learning, behavior modification).*

**\*A. Operant Conditioning**—How do you explain why your significant other sulks every time something is wrong even though you've told him or her that it bugs you? (**Suggested answer page 625**)

**\*B. Reinforcers**—How would you use operant conditioning to change a rude friend into a more likable and friendly person? (**Suggested answer page 625**)

**C. Schedules of Reinforcement**—Which schedules of partial reinforcement best apply to the following behaviors: eating, studying, going to the movies, dating?

**D. Other Conditioning Concepts**—The first time you visit your 2-year-old niece, she takes one look at you and starts to cry. What happened?

**E. Cognitive Learning**—Why should parents be especially concerned about what they say and do in the presence of their children?

**F. Biological Factors**—A 14-year-old boy graduated from college with outstanding grades. How could he learn so much so early?

**G. Research Focus: Noncompliance**—Why might parents yell, threaten, or spank rather than use a time-out to deal with a child's constant refusals?

**\*H. Cultural Diversity: East Meets West**—Why do the same principles of learning work in very different cultures? (**Suggested answer page 625**)

**I. Application: Behavior Modification**—How could techniques of behavior modification be used in a computer program to teach children how to do math problems?

*\*These questions are answered in Appendix B.*

*LINKS TO LEARNING* **237**

---

**Feature.** At the end of each module is the *Links to Learning* feature, which offers students the following learning opportunities:

*PowerStudy,* new to the 6th edition, is a revolutionary way of presenting information. *PowerStudy* consists of two cross-platform CDs that contain 40-to-50-minute multimedia presentations. Each presentation is fully narrated and includes animations, interactive activities, and many quizzes. *PowerStudy* covers core content for Modules 3, 4, 9, 10, 11, and 12, and selective coverage that is applicable to other modules. A more detailed description of *PowerStudy* appears on pages xxxv–xxxviii.

*Web Sites* direct students to additional information on related topics on the Internet.

*WebTutor* offers students online tutorials and quizzes.

*Study Guide,* by Matt Enos (hard copy or computer disk), offers study aids and quizzes.

*InfoTrac* gives students free access to online full-length psychological articles and journals.

*PsychNow!* is a CD that allows students to take quizzes and see animations for selected topics.

*Study Questions* ask students to apply what they have learned. Questions with an asterisk have suggested answers and possible strategies for answering study questions.

# Supplements

## PowerStudy Student CD-ROM

0-534-58013-0

Two cross-platform CD-ROMs, created by Rod Plotnik and Tom Doyle. PowerStudy includes six 40–50-minute multimedia presentations to accompany six modules in *Introduction to Psychology, 6th Edition*. These modules sometimes cause difficulty for students: Module 3: Brain's Building Blocks; Module 4: Incredible Nervous System; Module 9: Classical Conditioning; Module 10: Operant and Cognitive Approaches; Module 11: Types of Memory; and Module 12: Remembering & Forgetting. Each of the six PowerStudy modules is also relevant to other modules throughout the text.

## Instructor's Resource Guide

0-534-57998-1

Updated by Susan Barnett, Virginia Cecchini, Teddi Deka, and Patrice Moulton, the Instructor's Resource Guide includes teaching tips for new instructors; module outlines; a resource integration guide; inquiries for student learning; electronic classroom assignments; suggested videos, films, and Web sites; complete active learning exercises and handout masters; and chapter-by-chapter correlations to the active learning exercises, transparency masters, and ancillary CD-ROMs.

## Test Bank

0-534-58011-4

Greg Cutler completely revised and updated his excellent Test Bank, which includes approximately 4,000 test items! Ten test items per module are available to students as online quizzes and are clearly identified as such. Approximately 10–15 questions per module are reproduced from the Study Guide and are also clearly identified. Each test item has a main text page reference and is labeled with question type (applied, conceptual, or factual) and level of difficulty.

## Multimedia Manager for Introductory Psychology 2002

A Microsoft, PowerPoint, Link Tool (Cross-Platform CD-ROM)
0-534-58025-4

This Microsoft PowerPoint lecture tool makes it easy to assemble, edit, publish, and deliver custom lectures for your introductory psychology course, bringing together art from this CD-ROM, the Web, and your own material. The Multimedia Manager includes lecture outlines for each module, written by Shaunna Crossen; they incorporate hundreds of art pieces from the text, relevant CNN Today video clips, and animations. It also contains a very simple wizard to guide you in publishing your 2002 lectures online for student reference and distance learning.

## Transparency Acetates

0-534-57999-X

Approximately 100 4-color transparency acetates

## InfoTrac, College Edition

Available exclusively from Wadsworth/Thomson Learning. Packaged free with each new copy of Plotnik's book, this virtual library can be accessed from students' own computers. InfoTrac, College Edition is a comprehensive and powerful reference resource that includes tens of thousands of articles from major encyclopedias, reference books, magazines, pamphlets, and other sources onto a single Web site with fast and easy search tools for all your reference needs. InfoTrac, College Edition is the ideal one-stop reference source for instructors and students. Available to North American colleges and universities only.

## ExamView

0-534-58012-2 (Cross-Platform)

Create, deliver, and customize tests and study guides (both print and online) in minutes with this easy-to-use assessment and tutorial system. ExamView offers both a Quick Test Wizard and an Online Test Wizard that guide you step-by-step through the process of creating tests, and its unique WYSIWYG capability allows you to see the test you are creating on the screen exactly as it will print or display online. You can build tests of up to 250 questions, using up to 12 question types. With ExamView's complete word-processing capabilities, you can enter an unlimited number of new questions or edit existing questions. ExamView also includes an electronic test bank of text-specific questions for this edition of the text.

## The Wadsworth Psychology Resource Center Web Site

*http://psychology.wadsworth.com*

When you adopt Plotnik's text, you and your students will have access to the Wadsworth Psychology Study Center! It includes text-specific, chapter-by-chapter online quizzes; interactive Internet activities; links to psychology-related sites on the Web; hot topics; research and teaching showcase; teaching tips and ideas; and bulletin boards. Thousands of students and instructors visit this free Web site every week. Think of it as a complete resource that will engage and support your students.

## The Wadsworth Video and Film Library

Qualified adopters can choose from a variety of continually updated film and video resources. Contact your local Wadsworth/Thomson Learning representative for details.

## CNN Today Videos: Introductory Psychology

Volume I: ISBN: 0-534-36634-1
Volume II: ISBN: 0-534-50420-5
Volume III: ISBN: 0-534-50749-2
Volume IV: ISBN: 0-534-50751-4

These 1- to 4-minute video clips allow professors to integrate the news gathering and programming power of CNN into the classroom to show students the relevance of psychology to their everyday lives. Contact your local Wadsworth/Thomson Learning representative for additional details.

**Teaching Modules: The Brain Video, Second Edition**

This video offers your students extensive new footage of research into the inner workings of the human brain. Included are the latest findings on Alzheimer's disease; schizophrenia; autism; Parkinson's disease; and many other topics. Contact your local Wadsworth/Thomson Learning representative for details.

**Seeing Beyond the Obvious: Understanding Perception in Everyday and Novel Environments**

This 46-minute video, created by the NASA Ames Research Center in conjunction with the University of Virginia, provides a college-level introduction to the basic concepts of visual perception. Contact your local Wadsworth/Thomson Learning representative for details.

**Discovering Psychology Video Series**
Annenberg/CPB

The programs in the Discovering Psychology series encourage personal development while stimulating curiosity and critical thinking. Available on 26 half-hour programs, two per tape. Contact your local Wadsworth/Thomson Learning representative for details.

**Sniffy™, The Virtual Rat**

By Tom Alloway, Greg Wilson, Jeff Graham, and Lester Krames
Pro Version: ISBN: 0-534-35865-9
Lite Version: ISBN: 0-534-35869-1

The world's most famous virtual rat! Available in Lite and Pro versions, Sniffy the Virtual Rat is an enjoyable interactive software program that gives undergraduate students a virtual laboratory experience without the drawbacks of working with a live laboratory rat. Sniffy helps students explore operant and classical conditioning as they perform experiments that demonstrate most of the major conditioning phenomena. Sniffy is priced affordably for student budgets.

**Study Guide**

ISBN: 0-534-58002-5

The wonderful Study Guide, again written by Matthew Enos, includes module outlines; effective student tips; key terms; language development tools written by Robert Keser; "Big Picture" questions; and true/false, matching, and multiple-choice questions. Answers to all test items are at the end.

**Thomson Learning WebTutor™**

on WebCT and BlackBoard
WebCT: 0-534-58003-3
Packaged with the casebound text: ISBN: 0-534-68873-X
Blackboard: 0-534-58004-1
Packaged with the casebound text: ISBN: 0-534-68909-4

Take your course beyond the classroom! Now instructors who adopt Plotnik's text can offer their students an affordable, content-rich, Web-based teaching and learning tool. WebTutor is filled with pre-loaded content tied directly to the Sixth Edition and is ready to use as soon as you log on. Instructors can customize the content, from uploading images and other resources, to adding Web links, to creating your own practice materials. For students, WebTutor has real-time access to a full array of study tools, including flashcards with audio; practice quizzes; online tutorials; and Web links. Use WebTutor to provide virtual office hours; post syllabi; set up threaded discussions; track student progress with the quizzing material; and more. WebTutor provides rich communication tools, including a course calendar; asynchronous discussion; "real time" chat; a whiteboard; and an integrated e-mail system. Try WebTutor today at *http://e.thomsonlearning.com*

**Psychology: Careers for the Twenty-First Century**
0-534-34292-2

This pamphlet is produced by the American Psychological Association and is exclusive to APA and Wadsworth. It describes the field of psychology, as well as the "how to" for career preparation in the many areas of specialization.

**Cross-Cultural Perspectives In Introductory Psychology, Third Edition**
0-534-33570-6

By William F. Price, North Country Community College, and Richley H. Crapo, Utah State University. This timely revision contains 26 articles on cultural groups around the globe and is an ideal companion volume to any introductory psychology text. Where appropriate in the standard curriculum of the introductory course, the authors include a cross-cultural reading or vignette that enriches the traditional material. The book increases student understanding of the similarities and differences among the peoples of the world as they relate to psychological principles, concepts, and issues. As topics are covered in the introductory course, readings offer another dimension.

**Writing Papers In Psychology: A Student Guide, Fifth Edition**
0-534-53975-5

By Ralph L. Rosnow, Temple University, and Mimi Rosnow. For more than a decade this brief, inexpensive, and easy-to-understand manual has helped thousands of students in psychology and related fields write term papers and research reports. Now updated, this best-seller includes a wealth of new information and reflects the latest APA manual style.

**Challenging Your Preconceptions: Thinking Critically About Psychology, Second Edition**
0-534-26739-4

By Randolph A. Smith, Ouachita Baptist University. This is an ideal supplement for any introductory psychology text. The book covers critical thinking within the context of research methods and statistics; biological bases of behavior; sensation and perception; altered states of consciousness; learning; memory; testing; motivation; therapy; and abnormal and social psychology.

**Looks different.** This textbook looks different because it uses visual learning techniques, such as breaking material into smaller units and integrating text and graphics. Every definition is boldface and printed in blue so that you can identify it easily.

**Concept Review.** This is a test of how well you remember some of the key concepts. As you fill in the blanks of the Concept Review, you'll be learning important terms and concepts.

**Summary Test.** This lets you check how well you remember the material from the entire module. Taking the Summary Test is also an excellent way to review all the major terms discussed in the module.

**Critical Thinking.** At the end of each module are several Critical Thinking activities, including study questions and questions about an interesting newspaper article. There are also lists of Web sites where you can find additional information.

**Study Guide.** To give you additional help in mastering a module, the *Study Guide* contains outlines of each module, plus a variety of questions (multiple-choice, true-false, matching) that give you many chances to test your mastery of the material.

**PowerStudy.** This is an exciting new way to study the material, is explained on the following pages.

---

## D. Cultural Diversity: Use of Placebos

### Remarkable Treatments

**Can your beliefs reduce pain?**

If you happen to take a prescription drug, read its brochure, which discusses what the drug does, its side effects, and, most interesting, how its effectiveness has compared to a placebo.

A *placebo* is some intervention, such as taking a pill, receiving an injection, or undergoing an operation, that resembles medical therapy but that, in fact, has no medical effects.

A *placebo effect* is a change in the patient's illness that is attributable to an imagined treatment rather than to a medical treatment.

For example, the results of studies involving 3,000 men showed that a new drug (Uprima) allowed about 56% to have erections and engage in intercourse. However, about 35% of the men reported equally good results from taking another pill that proved to be a sugar pill or placebo (Cowley, 2000b). In these studies,

**Placebo**

Placebos are sugar pills.

none of the men who reported problems with impotency knew whether they had been given the drug or a placebo. Researchers estimate that between 35 and 75% of patients benefit from taking placebos or dummy drugs (Talbot, 2000).

Researchers have proposed that placebos work by reducing tension and distress and by creating powerful self-fulfilling prophecies so that individuals think and behave as if the drug, actually a placebo, will work (Brown, 1997). Self-fulfilling prophecies are strongest and placebos are most effective when they are administered by trusted and sincere professionals who convince their patients of the drugs' effectiveness, even though the "medications" are actually placebos (Madon et al., 1997).

Perhaps the most convincing evidence for the effectiveness of placebos comes from testimonials, which claim that taking various vitamins, animal parts, or herbs cure a wide variety of symptoms. We'll review some of the more common placebos in use worldwide.

| Rhino Horn | Bear Gallbladders | Tiger Bones | Magnets |
|---|---|---|---|

*Rhino Horn*

Millions of people in China, Thailand, South Korea, and Taiwan claim that rhino horn is an aphrodisiac, will increase their sexual desire and stamina, and is a cure for everything from headaches and nosebleeds to high fevers and typhoid. However, the basic ingredient of rhino horn is compacted hair (keratin), which has no proven medicinal powers (*Sierra,* November/ December 1989). A single rhino horn weighing about 4 to 5 pounds will bring from $25,000 to $50,000 on the black market. In the early 1900s, there were about 1 million rhinos. By 1994, poachers had reduced the total number of rhinos to about 10,000, as the desire for rhino horns continued to grow (Berger & Cunningham, 1994).

*Bear Gallbladders*

In parts of Asia, a very popular "medicine" to treat many kinds of physical problems is a tablet made from bear gallbladders. Some traders are substituting pig gallbladders for bears' and customers are none the wiser, since bear or pig gallbladders are nothing more than placebos (*Time,* November 4, 1991). The price of a single bear gallbladder has risen to an amazing $18,000, and there is now an illegal global trade in animal parts. Poachers threaten some endangered species of bears, such as the grizzly bear in the United States.

*Tiger Bones*

In the early 1900s, there were 100,000 tigers in Asia, but by 1994 there were fewer than 5,000. The chief reason for this precipitous decline is the use of tiger bones to treat ulcers, typhoid, malaria, dysentery, and burns, to increase longevity, to guard newborn babies from infection, and to cure devil possession (Friend, 1997b). In addition, wealthy Taiwanese pay $320 for a bowl of tiger penis soup that is thought to increase flagging libidos (Nagarahole, 1994). Tiger bones and tiger penises function as powerful placebos in traditional Asian medicine.

*Magnets*

Beginning in the early 1990s, athletes reported a decrease in pain after wearing small magnet pads over their painful injuries. Such testimonials resulted in millions of dollars in sales for magnet pads. Although several earlier studies supported such claims, a recent study that was better designed to eliminate error and bias found no difference in pain reduction between magnets and placebos (Christopher, 2000; Collacott et al., 2000). These researchers doubt that magnetic pads can reduce pain.

### Conclusion: Testimonials and Placebos

**Why are placebos so popular?**

Perhaps the main reason placebos are used worldwide, even to the point of destroying certain wild animals, is that the placebo's beneficial "medical" effects are supported by countless testimonials. For example, compared to the results of surveys, testimonials are much more convincing because they are based on real-life experiences of friends, peers, and parents, who are honest and believable. However, it is common for people, honest and trustworthy, to unknowingly make a mistake and conclude that a rhino horn, bear gallbladder, tiger bone, or magnet is producing a beneficial "medical" effect when the beneficial effect is actually being caused by the individual's mental thought influencing the body's functioning (H. Brody, 2000).

As you'll see next, people often make mistakes about the effect of placebos because there is often no way to figure out what causes what.

**D.** *CULTURAL DIVERSITY: USE OF PLACEBOS* **31**

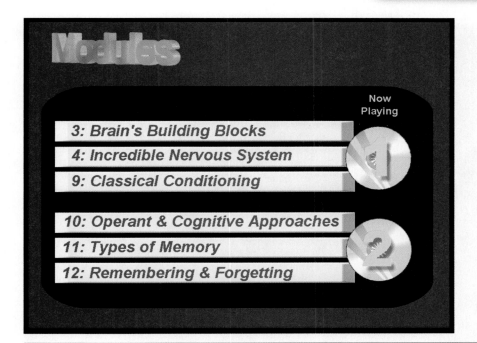

**Modules**

Now Playing

3: Brain's Building Blocks
4: Incredible Nervous System
9: Classical Conditioning

10: Operant & Cognitive Approaches
11: Types of Memory
12: Remembering & Forgetting

*PowerStudy* consists of two cross-platform CDs that contain multimedia presentations.

*PowerStudy* covers core content for Modules 3, 4, 9, 10, 11, and 12, and has selective coverage that is applicable for all other modules.

Each of the presentations is 40–50 minutes long and is fully narrated so users both see and hear explanations of the material. Each presentation includes numerous animations, interactive activities, many quizzes, and critical thinking exercises that help students understand and remember the material.

**Matching outline.** On the right is the *PowerStudy* title screen for Module 4. *PowerStudy* uses the same organization and covers the same topics as the text modules. Because of this, students can use *PowerStudy* to receive additional help on all of these topics.

**Easy navigation.** At the bottom of this screen are seven icons with their functions as well as three navigation arrows with their functions.

Thus, any module or topic is only a click away.

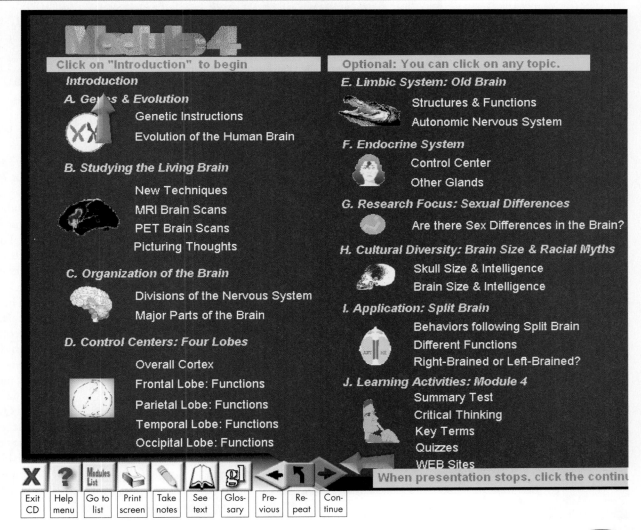

**Module 4**

Click on "Introduction" to begin | Optional: You can click on any topic.

Introduction

A. Genes & Evolution
Genetic Instructions
Evolution of the Human Brain

B. Studying the Living Brain
New Techniques
MRI Brain Scans
PET Brain Scans
Picturing Thoughts

C. Organization of the Brain
Divisions of the Nervous System
Major Parts of the Brain

D. Control Centers: Four Lobes
Overall Cortex
Frontal Lobe: Functions
Parietal Lobe: Functions
Temporal Lobe: Functions
Occipital Lobe: Functions

E. Limbic System: Old Brain
Structures & Functions
Autonomic Nervous System

F. Endocrine System
Control Center
Other Glands

G. Research Focus: Sexual Differences
Are there Sex Differences in the Brain?

H. Cultural Diversity: Brain Size & Racial Myths
Skull Size & Intelligence
Brain Size & Intelligence

I. Application: Split Brain
Behaviors following Split Brain
Different Functions
Right-Brained or Left-Brained?

J. Learning Activities: Module 4
Summary Test
Critical Thinking
Key Terms
Quizzes
WEB Sites

When presentation stops, click the continu

| X | ? | Modules List | | | | gl | ← | ↰ | → |
|---|---|---|---|---|---|---|---|---|---|
| Exit CD | Help menu | Go to list | Print screen | Take notes | See text | Glos-sary | Pre-vious | Re-peat | Con-tinue |

**On-screen menu.** Navigation is very easy in *PowerStudy* because there is always an on-screen menu. As shown here, the menu appears on the left side of the screen and lists the same major topics and subtopics as those discussed in the corresponding modules of the 6th edition. Thus, if students are confused or need further explanation of any of the topics in Modules 3, 4, 9, 10, 11, or 12 of the 6th edition, they can hear and see a multimedia presentation of that particular topic simply by going to *PowerStudy* and clicking first on the specific module and then on the particular topic.

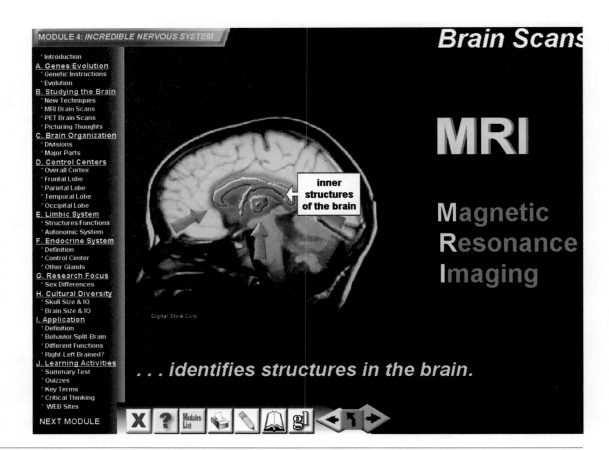

MODULE 4: *INCREDIBLE NERVOUS SYSTEM*

* Introduction
A. Genes/Evolution
* Genetic Instructions
* Evolution
B. Studying the Brain
* New Techniques
* MRI Brain Scans
* PET Brain Scans
* Picturing Thoughts
C. Brain Organization
* Divisions
* Major Parts
D. Control Centers
* Overall Cortex
* Frontal Lobe
* Parietal Lobe
* Temporal Lobe
* Occipital Lobe
E. Limbic System
* Structures/Functions
* Autonomic System
F. Endocrine System
* Definition
* Control Center
* Other Glands
G. Research Focus
* Sex Differences
H. Cultural Diversity
* Skull Size & IQ
* Brain Size & IQ
I. Application
* Definition
* Behavior/Split-Brain
* Different Functions
* Right-Left Brained?
J. Learning Activities
* Summary Test
* Quizzes
* Key Terms
* Critical Thinking
* WEB Sites

NEXT MODULE

**Brain Scans**

inner structures of the brain

Digital Stock Corp.

**MRI**

Magnetic Resonance Imaging

*. . . identifies structures in the brain.*

---

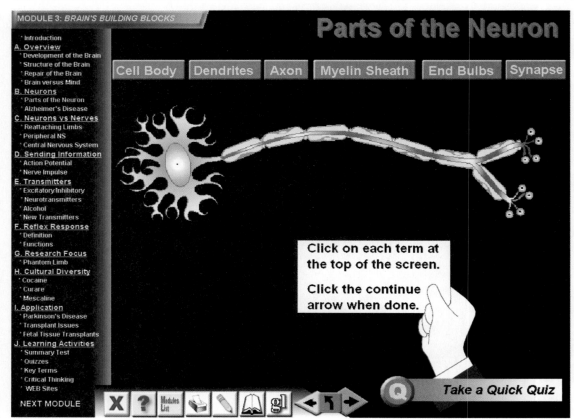

MODULE 3: *BRAIN'S BUILDING BLOCKS*

* Introduction
A. Overview
* Development of the Brain
* Structure of the Brain
* Repair of the Brain
* Brain versus Mind
B. Neurons
* Parts of the Neuron
* Alzheimer's Disease
C. Neurons vs Nerves
* Reattaching Limbs
* Peripheral NS
* Central Nervous System
D. Sending Information
* Action Potential
* Nerve Impulse
E. Transmitters
* Excitatory/Inhibitory
* Neurotransmitters
* Alcohol
* New Transmitters
F. Reflex Response
* Definition
* Functions
G. Research Focus
* Phantom Limb
H. Cultural Diversity
* Cocaine
* Curare
* Mescaline
I. Application
* Parkinson's Disease
* Transplant Issues
* Fetal Tissue Transplants
J. Learning Activities
* Summary Test
* Quizzes
* Key Terms
* Critical Thinking
* WEB Sites

NEXT MODULE

**Parts of the Neuron**

Cell Body | Dendrites | Axon | Myelin Sheath | End Bulbs | Synapse

Click on each term at the top of the screen.

Click the continue arrow when done.

**Q** Take a Quick Quiz

**Interactive activities.** There are many interactive activities throughout *PowerStudy* because they actively involve students in the learning process.

For example, the text box in the left screen asks students to click on each part of the neuron to have it identified and explained. After completing this task, they can check their understanding and memory by taking an interactive quiz.

**Quiz.** The purple bar tells the student that they can take a quiz by clicking the round button with the "Q," which stands for quiz.

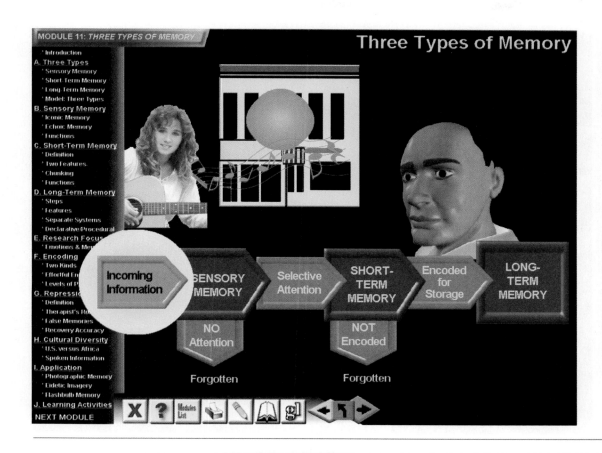

**Animations.** A real advantage of a multimedia format like *PowerStudy* is the ability to use animations to help explain difficult material.

For example, the screen at left (Module 11) shows the beginning of an animation that, step-by-step, guides students through the relatively complex memory process. In this animation, students see how information gets into sensory memory, how information may or may not reach short-term memory, why some information is forgotten, and how information may or may not be stored or encoded in long-term memory.

**Quizzes.** *PowerStudy* is loaded with a wide variety of interactive quizzes for every topic. Students can immediately check their answers.

For example, the screen on the right shows the quiz for functions of the sympathetic and parasympathetic nervous systems (CD M 4). Students are asked to click on a function listed on the right or left sides, drag it next to the correct organ, and place it under the correct nervous system. (Drag "salivation," next to mouth, under parasympathetic nervous system.) They can click on the green button to see the correct answers.

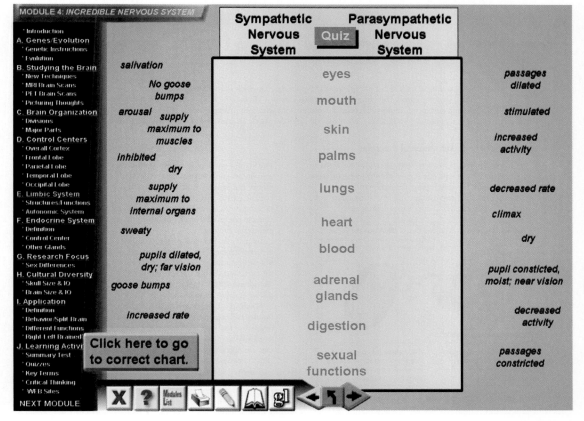

## Learning activities.

As the screen on the right shows, *PowerStudy* offers a variety of learning activities. Students can check their knowledge by taking the Summary Test, True-False Quiz, Multiple-Choice Quiz, or Matching Quiz. They will get immediate feedback on their answers.

Students can click on Web addresses and go directly to the Internet sites.

Finally, students can engage in Critical Thinking activities by answering questions about interesting newspaper articles or applying their knowledge to answer study questions.

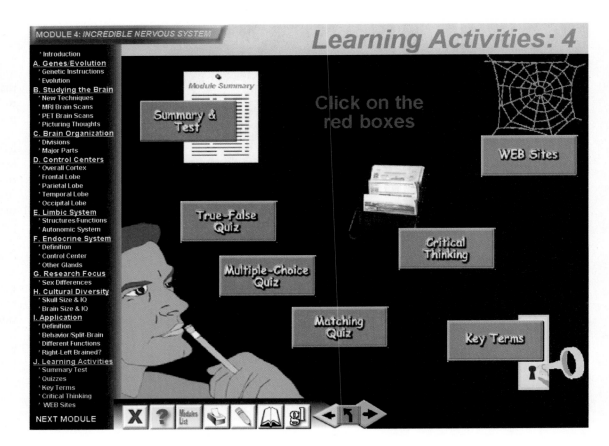

MODULE 4: INCREDIBLE NERVOUS SYSTEM

**Learning Activities: 4**

° Introduction
**A. Genes/Evolution**
° Genetic Instructions
° Evolution
**B. Studying the Brain**
° New Techniques
° MRI Brain Scans
° PET Brain Scans
° Picturing Thoughts
**C. Brain Organization**
° Divisions
° Major Parts
**D. Control Centers**
° Overall Cortex
° Frontal Lobe
° Parietal Lobe
° Temporal Lobe
° Occipital Lobe
**E. Limbic System**
° Structures/Functions
° Autonomic System
**F. Endocrine System**
° Definition
° Control Center
° Other Glands
**G. Research Focus**
° Sex Differences
**H. Cultural Diversity**
° Skull Size & IQ
° Brain Size & IQ
**I. Application**
° Definition
° Behavior/Split-Brain
° Different Functions
° Right-Left Brained?
**J. Learning Activities**
° Summary Test
° Quizzes
° Key Terms
° Critical Thinking
° WEB Sites

NEXT MODULE

Click on the red boxes

Module Summary

Summary & Test

WEB Sites

True-False Quiz

Critical Thinking

Multiple-Choice Quiz

Matching Quiz

Key Terms

---

## B. Newborns' Abilities

**Power Study ™**

**Check out CD: Module 3**
A. Overview: Human Brain
B. Neurons: Structure & Function

*Why can't a newborn walk?*

Some animals, such as baby elephants (150 pounds), can walk immediately after birth. In comparison, baby humans (7 pounds) cannot walk because neither their leg muscles nor brain areas are well enough developed. However, human infants are born with a surprising number of sensory and motor abilities, such as hearing, grasping, and sucking. How these abilities develop is explained by an inherited genetic program.

### Genetic Developmental Program

Conception results in a fertilized egg, which has a genetic program that is equivalent to 300,000 pages of typed instructions for developing the body and brain. The mother contributes 23 chromosomes and the father contributes 23, so that each child receives a unique genetic program.

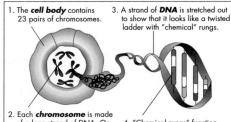

1. The *cell body* contains 23 pairs of chromosomes.

2. Each *chromosome* is made of a long strand of DNA. On the 23 pairs of chromosomes are about 30,000 *genes,* which are pieces of DNA that contain specific instructions.

3. A strand of *DNA* is stretched out to show that it looks like a twisted ladder with "chemical" rungs.

4. "Chemical rungs" function like a *chemical alphabet* that writes instructions (genes) for development of millions of parts for your brain and body.

**Brain growth.** After birth, the genetic program regulates how the brain develops, such as making thousands of connections

### Sensory Development

During the nine months of development in the womb, the genetic program is guiding the development of a number of motor and sensory functions that are important for the newborn's survival. For example, each newborn is equipped with a sucking reflex to ensure getting food and a very loud cry to demand attention. Here's a summary of a newborn's sensory and perceptual abilities.

**Faces.** At 1 month of age, an infant can distinguish his or her mother's face from that of a stranger, provided the infant also hears the mother's voice. By 3 months of age, an infant can visually distinguish his or her mother's face from a stranger's (Burnham, 1993). By 3 to 4 years of age, an infant's visual abilities are equal to those of an adult.

**Hearing.** One-month-old infants have very keen hearing and can discriminate small sound variations, such as the difference between *bah* and *pah*. By 6 months, infants have developed the ability to make all the sounds that are necessary to learn the language in which they are raised (Bower, 1994).

**Touch.** Newborns also have a well-developed sense of touch and will turn their head when lightly touched on the cheek. Touch will also elicit a

**Concepts.** On the left is page 382 from Module 17, which does not have a core *Power-Study* presentation. However, at the top of page 382, students are told to check CD: Module 3, because it contains two related presentations.

In this case, students can go to CD: Module 3, click on the menu topics, (A. Overview of Human Brain, or B. Neurons: Structure & Function) to review related concepts.

The round *Power-Study* icon in the text indicates topics that are covered in *PowerStudy*.

PS

# Acknowledgments and Thanks

In developing the 6th edition, I worked with a remarkable group of creative people, each of whom deserves special thanks.

## Publisher:

For the past 15 years my editor has been Vicki Knight, who is surely one of the best editors in publishing. She always has great advice and, best of all, understands what this book is about and how to make it happen.

## Developmental Editor:

Penelope Sky was involved in a hundred difficult tasks, each of which took great time and effort and really improved the text. Penelope found and checked out all the Web sites and developed Links for Learning.

## Editorial Associates:

Julie Dillemuth and Dan Moneypenny had the trying job of making sure that all the modules were sent to reviewers.

## Cover Designer:

As always, Vernon Boes came up with a great design for the cover, which is difficult because we all have very strong opinions.

## Concept Illustrators:

In every module you'll discover Bill Ogden and Philip Dvorak's creative drawings and figures that help make the book visually exciting.

## Photo Researcher:

Once again, Linda Rill was in charge of photo research and permissions, and there is no one as good at this as Linda.

## Manuscript Editor:

I had the best manuscript editor ever in Carol Reitz, whose editorial skills really did improve the book.

## Production:

The job of Nancy Shammas at New Leaf Publishing Services was to make sure that every page was perfect and ready for print.

Keeping track of everything at Wadsworth Publishing was Kirk Bomont, Senior Production Editor, who made sure that everything was where it should be.

## Production:

The person who made sure the individual pages were turned into a complete book is "geeze" Louise Gelinas of LaurelTech. She kept track of a record number of photos and artwork (more than 2000 pieces) and kept the pages rolling out.

Special thanks goes to Carol Perrella at LaurelTech whose knowledge of QuarkXpress is astronomical. She explained all of Quark's nuances to me.

## Marketing Communication:

When you read the great advertising copy and see the brochures, think of Margaret Parks and Tami Strang, who were able to describe the "soul" of the book.

You can also go online to the Wadsworth site and see a virtual tour of the 6th edition created by Jean Thompson and Shelley Tweddell.

## Sales:

Joanne Terhaar's job is to make sure that all the sales representatives knew what the book was about and how to describe it to potential adopters.

## Study Guide:

Matthew Enos used his friendly and helpful teaching skills to write the *Study Guide,* whose previous editions were so highly praised by students. Robert Keser did a great job on the *Study Guide's* language development section.

## Supplements:

Jennifer Wilkinson, senior assistant editor, was responsible for organizing and keeping track of all the many supplements.

A number of very talented people worked on revising the *Instructor's Resource Guide:* Teddi Deka at Missouri Western State; Patrice Moulton, Susan Barnett, and Virginia Checcini, all at Northwestern State University, Natchitoches, LA. Their creative efforts make the resource guide one of the best ever.

Once again Greg Cutler at Bay de Noc Community College, MA, used his critical thinking skills to write the *Test Bank,* which received high marks in previous editions.

Shaunna Crossen at Penn State University at Schuylkill developed the lecture outlines for the popular PowerPoint Presentation Tool, PsychLink.

## Special Colleague:

While working on the 6th edition I alternated between "It's wonderful," and "I quit." Through it all, my friend and colleague Sandy Mollenauer provided emotional support, encouragement, and understanding.

## PowerStudy:

One of the most exciting projects that I have ever been involved in was working with Professor Tom Doyle to develop a new and revolutionary multimedia presentation for students, called *PowerStudy*.

Tom is an absolute genius for figuring out how to use Director, a nightmare software, and to create the best animations and interactive activities that you'll ever see. Printed samples of Tom's wonderful work can be seen on pages xxxvi-xxxvii but his true creativity is best appreciated by viewing the two *PowerStudy* CDs.

Penelope Sky deserves a second mention because she spent many hours reviewing and identifying problems and making suggestions for *PowerStudy*.

Leslie Krongold, Technology Project Manager, helped guide us through many potential pitfalls associated with developing a multimedia project like *PowerStudy*.

## CEO:

Last, I must thank my big boss, CEO Susan Badger, who not only fully supported the non-traditional look of the 6th edition but also supported Tom and me in creating *PowerStudy*. In fact, Susan was the one who early on suggested that we use an on-screen menu, which helped make navigation through *PowerStudy* a breeze.

# Reviewers and Many Thanks

I especially want to thank the many reviewers who put in an amazing amount of time and energy to consider and comment on various aspects of this textbook.

I would like to explain why I was not able to include all your valuable suggestions.

Sometimes your suggestions were great but required inserting material for which there simply was no room.

Other times, one reviewer might suggest changing something that another reviewer really liked, so I tried to work out the best compromise.

Still other times, reviewers forcefully argued for entirely different points so that I felt like the proverbial starving donkey trying to decide which way to turn between two stacks of hay.

For all these reasons, I could not make all your suggested changes but I did give them a great deal of thought and used as many as I possibly could.

I do want each reviewer to know that his or her efforts were invaluable in the process of revising and developing a textbook. If it were within my power, I would triple your honorariums and give you each a year-long sabbatical.

**Glen Adams,** Harding University
**Nelson Adams,** Winston-Salem State University
**Marlene Adelman,** Norwalk Community Technical College
**George Bagwell,** Colorado Mountain College-
   Alpine Campus
**Roger Bailey,** Southwestern College
**Beth Barton,** Coastal Carolina Community College
**Beth Benoit,** University of Massachusetts-Lowell
**John B. Benson,** Texarcana College
**Kristen Biondolillo,** Arkansas State University
**Linda Brunton,** Columbia State Community College
**Lawrence Burns,** Grand Valley State University
**Ronald Caldwell,** Blue Mountain Community College
**James Calhoun,** University of Georgia
**Peter Caprioglio,** Middlesex Community-Technical College
**Donna M. Casperson,** Harrisburg Area
   Community College
**Hank Cetola,** Adrian College
**Larry Christensen,** Salt Lake Community College
**Saundra K. Ciccarelli,** Gulf Coast Community College
**Gerald S. Clack,** Loyola University
**J. Craig Clarke,** Salisbury State University
**Richard T. Colgan,** Bridgewater State College
**Laurie Corey,** Westchester Community College
**Sandy Deabler,** North Harris College
**Paul H. Del Nero,** Towson State University
**Jean Edwards,** Jones County Junior College
**Tami Eggleston,** McKendree College
**Nolen U. Embry,** Lexington Community College
**Charles H. Evans,** LaGrange College
**Melissa Faber,** Lima Technical College
**Mike Fass,** Miami-Dade Community College,
   North Campus

**Mary Beth Foster,** Purdue University
**Jan Francis,** Santa Rosa Junior College
**Grace Galliano,** Kennesaw State College
**John T. Garrett,** Texas State Technical College
**Philip Gray,** D'Youville College
**Charles M. Greene,** Florida Community College at
   Jacksonville
**Lynn Haller,** Morehead State University
**Sheryl Hartman,** Miami Dade Community College
**Debra Lee Hollister,** Valencia Community College
**Donna Holmes,** Becker College
**Lucinda Hutman,** Elgin Community College
**Terry Isbell,** Northwestern State University
**Eleanor Jones,** Tidewater Community College
**Stan Kary,** St. Louis Community College at Florissant
   Valley
**Paul Kasenow,** Henderson Community College
**Don Kates,** College of Dupage
**Mark Kelland,** Lansing Community College
**Richard Kirk,** Texas State Technical College
**John C. Koeppel,** University of Southern Mississippi
**Jan Kottke,** California State University-San Bernardino
**Joan Krueger,** Harold Washington College
**Doug Krull,** Northern Kentucky University
**Diane J. Krumm,** College of Lake County
**Raymond Launier,** Santa Barbara City College
**Eamonn J. Lester,** St. Philips College
**John Lindsay,** Georgia College & State University
**Alan Lipman,** Georgetown University
**Karsten Look,** Columbus State Community College
**Jerry Lundgren,** Flathead Valley Community College
**Frank MacHovec,** Rappahannock Community College
**Sandra Madison,** Delgado Community College

Mary Lee Meiners, San Diego Miramar College
Diane Mello-Goldner, Pine Manor College
Laurence Miller, Western Washington University
Alinde Moore, Ashland University
John T. Nixon, SUNY-Canton
Art Olguin, Santa Barbara City College
Carol Pandey, Pierce College
Christine Panyard, University of Detroit-Mercy
Jeff Parsons, Rockefeller University
Bob Pellegrini, San Jose State University
James Previte, Victor Valley College
Joan Rafter, Hudson Community College
Robert R. Rainey, Jr., Florida Community College
    at Jacksonville
Lillian Range, University of Southern Mississippi
S. Peter Resta, Prince George's Community College
Bret Roark, Oklahoma Baptist University
Ann E. Garrett Robinson, Gateway Community
    Technical College
Alan Schultz, Prince George's Community College
Robert Schultz, Fulton Montgomery Community
    College
Harold Siegel, Rutger's University
N. Clayton Silver, University of Nevada, Las Vegas
James Spencer, West Virginia State College
Deborah Steinberg, Jefferson Community College
Julie Stokes, California State University-Fullerton
Ted Sturman, University of Southern Maine
Clayton N. Tatro, Garden City Community College
Annette Taylor, University of San Diego
Andy Thomas, Tennessee Technical University
Larry Till, Cerritos College
Susan Troy, Northeast Iowa Community College
Jane Vecchio, Holyoke Community College
Randy Vinzant, Hinds Community College
Benjamin Wallace, Cleveland State University
James Ward, Western New England College
Mary Scott West, Virginia Intermont College
Fred W. Whitford, Montana State University
John Whittle, Northern Essex Community College
Ellen Williams, Mesa Community College
Matthew J. Zagumny, Tennessee Technological
    University

## Special help on the 6th edition

Edward Aronow, Montclair State University
Irwin Badin, Montclair State University
Susan Barnett, Northwestern State University
Angela Blankenship, Halifax Community College
Pamela Braverman Schmidt, Salem State College
Shaunna Crossen, Penn State University, Berk-Lehigh
    Valley College
Lorry J. Cology, Owens Community College
Jay Coleman, University of South Carolina, Columbia
Bradley Donohue, University of Nevada, Las Vegas
Verneda Hamm Baugh, Kean University
Sheryl M. Hartman, Ph.D., Miami Dade
    Community College
Debra Hollister, Valencia Community College
Charles Jeffreys, Seattle Central Community College
Haig Kouyoumdjian, University of Nebraska, Lincoln
Arthur D. Kemp, Ph.D., Central Missouri State
    University
Dan Klaus, Community College of Beaver City
Gail Knapp, Mott Community College
Linda V. Jones, Ph.D., Blinn College
Richard McCulloch, Kaskaskia College
Lesley Annette Miller, Triton College
Ron Payne, San Joaquin Delta College
James Previte, Victor Valley College
Vicki Ritts, St. Louis Community College, Meramac
Michael Schuller, Fresno City College
Kimberly Eretzian Smirles, Ph.D., Emmanuel
    College
Kimberly Stoker, MS, Holmes Community College
Debra Schwiesow, Creighton University
Gene Zingarelli, Santa Rosa Community College

# Module 1: Discovering Psychology

**A. Definition & Goals**     4
- DEFINITION OF PSYCHOLOGY
- GOALS OF PSYCHOLOGY

**B. Modern Approaches**     5
- BIOLOGICAL APPROACH
- COGNITIVE APPROACH
- BEHAVIORAL APPROACH
- PSYCHOANALYTIC APPROACH
- HUMANISTIC APPROACH
- CROSS-CULTURAL APPROACH

**C. Historical Approaches**     12
- STRUCTURALISM
- FUNCTIONALISM
- GESTALT APPROACH
- BEHAVIORISM
- SURVIVAL OF APPROACHES

**D. Cultural Diversity: Early Discrimination**     14
- WOMEN IN PSYCHOLOGY
- MINORITIES IN PSYCHOLOGY
- RIGHTING THE WRONGS

**Concept Review**     15

**E. Research Focus: Taking Class Notes**     16
- BEST STRATEGY FOR TAKING CLASS NOTES?

**F. Careers in Psychology**     17
- PSYCHOLOGIST VERSUS PSYCHIATRIST
- MANY CAREER SETTINGS

**G. Research Areas**     18
- SOCIAL AND PERSONALITY
- DEVELOPMENTAL
- EXPERIMENTAL
- BIOLOGICAL
- COGNITIVE
- PSYCHOMETRICS

**H. Application: Study Skills**     20
- IMPROVING STUDY HABITS
- SETTING GOALS
- REWARDING YOURSELF
- TAKING NOTES
- STOPPING PROCRASTINATION

**Summary Test**     22

**Critical Thinking**     24
- A NEW TREATMENT FOR AUTISM?

**Links to Learning**     25

## Growing Up in a Strange World

**Why does Donna flap her hands?**

When Donna was about 3 years old, she ate lettuce because she liked rabbits and they ate lettuce. She ate jelly because it looked like colored glass and she liked to look at colored glass.

She was told to make friends, but Donna had her own friends. She had a pair of green eyes named Willie, which hid under her bed, and wisps, which were tiny, transparent spots that hung in the air around her.

When people spoke, their words were strange sounds with no meaning, like mumble jumble. Donna did learn the sounds of letters and how they fit together to make words. Although she didn't learn the meanings of words, she loved their sounds when she said them out loud. As a child, she was tested for deafness because she did not use language like other children. She did not learn that words had meaning until she was a teenager.

When people talked to Donna, especially people with loud or excited voices, she heard only "blah, blah, blah." Too much excited talk or overstimulation caused Donna to stare straight ahead and appear to be frozen. Donna later called this state "involuntarily anesthetized."

Donna was in and out of many schools because she failed her exams, refused to take part in any class activities, walked out of classes she didn't like, and sometimes threw things. Because of her strange behaviors, other students called her "Zombie."

When Donna did make a friend, she tried to avoid getting a friendly hug, which made her feel as if she were burning up inside and going to faint. Eventually she learned to tolerate being hugged but never liked it (Williams, 1992).

Donna Williams has all the symptoms of autism, which is a relatively rare problem that occurs about once in 1,000 births, affects two to four times as many boys as girls, and is found in all parts of the world (Berney, 2000).

*Autism* is marked by especially abnormal or impaired development in social interactions, such as hiding to avoid people, not making eye contact, not wanting to be touched. Autism is marked by difficulties in communicating, such as grave problems in developing spoken language or in initiating conversations. Autistics are characterized by having very few activities and interests, spending long periods repeating the same behaviors (hand flapping), or following the same rituals. Signs of autism usually appear when a child is about 2 or 3 years old (American Psychiatric Association, 1994).

Some autistic children show rapid hand flapping.

Some autistic children avoid social interactions.

Among autistic individuals, about 1–2% possess a special skill at which they excel. These individuals, called savants, may create intricate drawings with no instruction, play a song on a musical instrument after hearing the song only once, do mathematical calculations as fast as a hand calculator, or solve calendar puzzles, such as figuring out the day of the week for a date ten years ago.

Donna Williams (1992) is an example of a savant who developed exceptional language skills. At age 25, in four almost-nonstop weeks, she wrote a 500-page book that described what it was like to be autistic. In this and her more recent book (D. Williams, 1994), Donna describes how common sights, sounds, and images become strangely distorted, which makes getting through an ordinary day like finding one's way out of a terribly complex maze.

As we describe Donna's experiences, you'll see how psychologists try to answer questions about complex behaviors, such as autism, as well as countless other behaviors that are discussed in the 25 modules of this text. For example, one question that psychologists have studied involves a problem that many students have—test anxiety.

## Test Anxiety

**What happens during tests?**

If you're like many other students, you probably experience some degree of test anxiety.

*Test anxiety* refers to a combination of physiological, emotional, and cognitive components that are caused by the stress of taking exams and that may interfere with one's ability to think, reason, and plan (Zeidner, 1998).

For some students, test anxiety is an unpleasant experience but doesn't necessarily interfere with exam performance. For other students, test anxiety not only is an unpleasant experience but also seriously interferes with exam performance. We'll discuss the components of test anxiety, why students differ in how much test anxiety they feel, and, probably most important, how to decrease test anxiety.

There are several ways to decrease test anxiety.

## What's Coming

In this module, we'll explore the goals of psychology, the major approaches that psychologists use to understand behavior and answer questions, the historical roots of psychology, current research areas, and possible careers in the broad field of psychology. Let's begin with how psychologists study complex problems, such as Donna's autistic behaviors.

---

### Definition of Psychology

**What do psychologists study?**

When you think of psychology, you may think of helping people with mental problems. However, psychologists study a broad range of behaviors, including Donna's autistic behaviors and students' test anxiety, as well as hundreds of other behaviors. For this reason, we need a very broad definition of psychology.

*Psychology* is the systematic, scientific study of behaviors and mental processes.

What's important about this definition is that each of its terms has a broader meaning. For example, *behaviors* refers to observable actions or responses in both humans and animals. Behaviors might include eating, speaking, laughing, running, reading, and sleeping. *Mental processes,* which are not directly observable, refer to a wide range of complex mental processes, such as thinking, imagining, studying, and dreaming. The current broad definition of psychology grew out of discussions and heated arguments among early psychologists, who defined psychology much more specifically, as we'll discuss later in this module.

Although the current definition of psychology is very broad, psychologists usually have four specific goals in mind when they study some behavior or mental process, such as Donna's autistic experiences.

---

### Goals of Psychology

**What are some of Donna's unusual behaviors?**

Donna (photo below) knows that she has some unusual behaviors. For example, she says that she doesn't like to be touched, held, or hugged, doesn't like to make eye contact when speaking to people, hates to talk to someone who has a loud voice, and really dislikes meeting strangers. If you were a psychologist studying Donna's unusual behaviors, you would have the following four goals in mind: to describe, explain, predict, and control her behavior.

**1 Describe** Donna says that, when she was a child, she wondered what people were saying to her because words were just lists of meaningless sounds. When people or things bothered her, she would endlessly tap or twirl her fingers to create movements that completely held her attention and helped her escape from a world that often made no sense.

*The first goal of psychology is to describe the different ways that organisms behave.*

As psychologists begin to describe the behaviors and mental processes of autistic children, such as difficulties in learning language, they begin to understand how autistic children behave. After describing behavior, psychologists try to explain behavior, the second goal.

**2 Explain** Donna's mother believed that autism was caused by evil spirits. Donna thinks her autism may result from metabolic imbalance.

*The second goal of psychology is to explain the causes of behavior.*

The explanation of autism has changed as psychologists learn more about this complex problem. In the 1950s, psychologists explained that children became autistic if they were reared by parents who were cold and rejecting (Blakeslee, 2000a). In the 1990s, researchers discovered that autism is caused by genetic and biological factors that result in a maldeveloped brain (Berney, 2000; Rodier, 2000). Being able to describe and explain behavior helps psychologists reach the third goal, which is to predict behavior.

Psychologists' goals are to describe, explain, predict, and control Donna's autistic behaviors.

**3 Predict** Donna says that one of her biggest problems is being so overloaded by visual sensations that she literally freezes in place. She tries to predict when she will freeze up by estimating how many new stimuli she must adjust to.

*The third goal of psychology is to predict how organisms will behave in certain situations.*

However, psychologists may have difficulty predicting how autistic children will behave in certain situations unless they have already described and explained their behaviors. For example, from the first two goals, psychologists know that autistic children are easily overwhelmed by strange stimuli and have difficulty paying attention. Based on this information, psychologists can predict that autistic children will have difficulty learning in a school environment because there is too much activity and stimuli in the classroom (Gresham et al., 1999). However, if psychologists can predict behavior, then they can often control behavior.

**4 Control** Donna knows one reason she fears meeting people is that social interactions cause a tremendous sensory overload that makes her freeze up. She controls her social fear by making a rule to meet only one person at a time.

*For some psychologists, the fourth goal of psychology is to control an organism's behavior.*

The idea of control has both positive and negative sides. The positive side is that psychologists can help people, such as Donna, learn to control undesirable behaviors (Howlin, 1997). The negative side is that people's behaviors might be controlled without their knowledge or consent. In Module 2, we'll discuss the strict guidelines that psychologists have established to prevent potential abuse of controlling behavior and to protect the rights and privacy of individuals, patients, and subjects in experiments.

Because many behaviors, such as autism, are enormously complex, psychologists use a combination of different approaches to reach the four goals of describing, explaining, predicting, and controlling behavior. To reach these goals, psychologists may use one or a combination of the following six approaches.

### More Approaches, More Answers

**How do psychologists answer questions?**

Psychologists have many questions about Donna's unusual behaviors. For example, why did Donna believe that objects were alive and made their own sounds? "My bed was my friend; my coat protected me and kept me inside; things that made noise had their own unique voices, which said vroom, ping, or whatever. I told my shoes where they were going so they would take me there" (Blakely, 1994, p. 14).

Why did Donna initially hear words as meaningless sounds that people were constantly saying to her? Why did she develop her own signaling

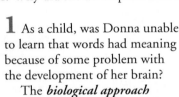

Donna would tell her shoes where she was going so they would take her there.

system, such as raising two fingers or scrunching her toes to signal that no one could reach her? Why did she freeze up when staring at soap bubbles in the sink? In trying to answer questions about Donna's strange and intriguing behaviors, psychologists would use a combination of different approaches.

*Approaches to understanding behavior* include the biological, cognitive, behavioral, psychoanalytic, humanistic, and cross-cultural. Each approach has a different focus or perspective and may use a different research method or technique.

We'll summarize these six commonly used approaches and then discuss them in more detail on the following pages.

**1** As a child, was Donna unable to learn that words had meaning because of some problem with the development of her brain?

The ***biological approach*** focuses on how our genes, hormones, and nervous system interact with our environments to influence learning, personality, memory, motivation, emotions, and coping techniques.

**2** How was Donna able to develop her own signaling system that involved gestures instead of words?

The ***cognitive approach*** examines how we process, store, and use information and how this information influences what we attend to, perceive, learn, remember, believe, and feel.

**3** Why did Donna make it a rule to avoid leaving soap bubbles in the sink?

The ***behavioral approach*** studies how organisms learn new behaviors or modify existing ones, depending on whether events in their environments reward or punish these behaviors.

**4** Why did Donna develop alternate personalities, such as Willie who had "hateful glaring eyes, a rigid corpselike stance, and clenched fists"?

The ***psychoanalytic approach*** stresses the influence of unconscious fears, desires, and motivations on thoughts, behaviors, and the development of personality traits and psychological problems later in life.

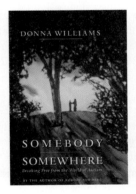

**5** How was Donna able to overcome her early language problems and write a book in four weeks?

The ***humanistic approach*** emphasizes that each individual has great freedom in directing his or her future, a large capacity for personal growth, a considerable amount of intrinsic worth, and enormous potential for self-fulfillment.

**6** Why did her mother believe that autism was caused by evil spirits? What do other peoples and cultures believe causes it?

The ***cross-cultural approach*** examines the influence of cultural and ethnic similarities and differences on psychological and social functioning of a culture's members.

By using one or more of these six different approaches, psychologists can look at autism from different viewpoints and stand a better chance of reaching psychology's four goals: to describe, explain, predict, and control behavior. We'll use the problems of autism and test anxiety to show how each approach examines these problems from a different perspective.

## Biological Approach

**Are their brains different?**

As Donna explains, autism has a huge effect on all parts of her life. "Autism makes me feel everything at once without knowing what I am feeling. Or it cuts me off from feeling anything at all" (D. Williams, 1994, p. 237). Donna's description of how autism so changes her life leads researchers to question whether her brain has not developed normally or perhaps functions differently. To answer this question, researchers use the biological approach.

The *biological approach* examines how our genes, hormones, and nervous system interact with our environments to influence learning, personality, memory, motivation, emotions, coping techniques, and other traits and abilities.

Researchers who use the biological approach are also called psychobiologists and use a number of different research methods, including taking computerized photos of living brains. For example, the top figure (based on computerized photos of living brains) shows that the normal brain uses one area (blue—fusiform gyrus) to process faces of people and a different area (red—inferior temporal gyrus) to process inanimate objects, such as a chair. In comparison, the autistic brain uses the area usually used to process inanimate objects (red—inferior temporal gyrus) to also process human faces (Schultz et al., 2000). The finding that the autistic brain uses the same area to process both objects and human faces suggests that the autistic individual may have difficulty distinguishing objects from human faces. In fact, autistic individuals have a preference for inanimate objects and show little interest in looking at human faces and are poor at recognizing and interpreting human facial expressions and emotions. This study is an example of using

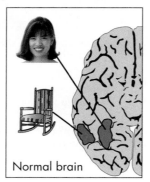

Normal brain

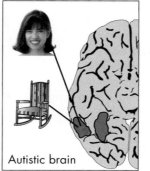

Autistic brain

the biological approach to look inside the human brain to understand why autistic individuals have little interest in human facial responses.

Psychobiologists have shown that genetic factors influence a wide range of human behaviors, which we'll discuss throughout this text. The genes (p. 68) use a chemical alphabet to write instructions for the development of the brain and body and the manufacture of chemicals that affect everything we do, such as mental health, learning, emotions, and personality traits (Plomin, 2000). For example, researchers found that autistic children share a genetic defect in regulating a chemical (serotonin) that has an important role in brain functioning (Berney, 2000). This finding is an example of using the biological approach to answer questions by looking for defects in the genes.

Finally, using the biological approach, researchers recently developed a test that identified high levels of certain proteins in the blood of infants who later developed autism (Grether, 2000). If this finding is repeated, it will be the first medical test to identify infants who are very likely to develop autism. At present, autism must be diagnosed with behavioral symptoms but not until around age 2 or 3.

Using new methods to study the structures and functions of the living brain, psychobiologists are studying one of the oldest puzzles in psychology: How do the mind, brain, and body interact? In fact, your mind, brain, and body interact each time you take an exam and experience what many students know as test anxiety.

### Biological Approach to Test Anxiety

**Why do my hands sweat?**

You've probably experienced one component of test anxiety, called the emotional component. This component includes a variety of physiological responses, such as increased heart rate, dry mouth, and sweaty palms. An interesting feature of sweaty palms, called palmar sweating, is that it is caused by stressful feelings and is not related to changes in room temperature (Kohler & Troester, 1991). In fact, palmar sweating is one of the measures used in the lie detection test, which we'll discuss in Module 16.

As you take an exam—or even think about taking one—your stressful thoughts trigger the emotional component, which can interfere with processing information and increase your chances of making mistakes (Zeidner, 1998).

Sweaty hands often indicate stress.

The figure on the right shows how easily your stressful thoughts can trigger palmar sweating, which is one measure of the emotional component of test anxiety. As subjects did mental arithmetic, which involved counting backward from 2007 in steps of 7, there was a significant increase in this palmar sweating (Kohler & Troester, 1991). If a simple task of counting backward increased palmar sweating, a sign of physiological and emotional arousal, imagine the increased arousal that occurs while taking an exam!

One way to reduce the emotional and physiological component of test anxiety is through stress-reducing activities. For example, students who completed a stress-reduction program that included relaxation exercises and soothing imagining reported less test anxiety than students who were on a waiting list for the program (Zeidner, 1998). In Module 21, we'll describe several methods of reducing stress that will be especially useful in reducing the emotional component of test anxiety.

## Cognitive Approach

**Was Donna an unusual autistic?**

Autistic individuals usually have difficulty developing language skills. For example, Donna writes, "Autism makes me hear other people's words but be unable to know what the words mean. Autism stops me from finding and using my own words when I want to. Or makes me use all the words and silly things I do not want to say" (D. Williams, 1994, p. 237). In spite of these difficulties, Donna eventually learned to both speak and write. Her success shows that, among autistic individuals, there is a wide range of cognitive abilities that can be divided into three groups (Nordin & Gillberg, 1998).

In the first group are individuals whose intellectual functioning is in the retarded range, which means their IQs are below 70, compared to the average IQ of 100. These individuals develop no language skills, are often handicapped, and need special care.

In the second group are individuals who have some amazing skills, such as performing complex mathematical calculations, memorizing vast quantities of data, and excelling at musical or artistic feats (Miller, 1999). These individuals are termed *autistic savants*, or just *savants*.

Individuals in the third group have IQs above 70 and relatively fluent speech, but they do not do well in academic subjects and have impaired social skills. These individuals, called high-functioning autistics, make up the largest group (Minshew et al., 1995).

Donna Williams is said to be a high-functioning autistic, or savant (Blakely, 1994). Although Donna did not understand words until she was an adolescent, she has learned to speak and write, has written two very creative books (Williams, 1992, 1994), and has

*I'm trying to find out why things go in one ear and out the other.*

learned French and German. To discover why autistic individuals differ in development of language and social skills, psychologists use the cognitive approach.

The *cognitive approach* focuses on how we process, store, and use information and how this information influences what we attend to, perceive, learn, remember, believe, and feel.

For example, when listening to a conversation, 95% of right-handers use primarily the left sides of their brains and very little of the right sides to process this verbal information. In contrast, researchers found that autistic individuals used primarily the right sides of their brains and very little of the left sides when listening to a conversation (Muller et al., 1999). This reversing of brain sides as well as having difficulties in processing verbal information may help explain why autistic individuals have problems acquiring cognitive, language, and communication skills.

One of the more recent approaches in studying a wide variety of cognitive processes is called cognitive neuroscience.

*Cognitive neuroscience* involves taking pictures of the structures and functions of the living brain during performance of a wide variety of mental or cognitive processes, such as thinking, planning, naming, and recognizing objects.

Throughout this text, we'll discuss how cognitive psychologists study many aspects of human behavior, such as learning and memory, personality, emotion, stress, motivation, and social behaviors. In recent years, the cognitive approach has become very popular because it has proved very useful in answering questions about human behavior (Murray, 2000; Potter, 2000).

For example, the cognitive approach has much to say about test anxiety, especially about worrying too much.

### *Cognitive Approach to Test Anxiety*

**Can you worry too much?**

Students who experience test anxiety must deal with two components. The first component, which we already described, is increased physiological arousal, which is the emotional component. Cognitive psychologists have identified a second component, the cognitive component, which is excessive worrying, usually about doing poorly on exams.

Excessive worrying about your performance can interfere with your ability to read accurately, understand what you are reading, and identify important concepts (Zeidner, 1998). For these reasons, it is easy to see how excessive worrying can impair performance on exams and result in lower grades. An interesting finding, shown in the right graph, was that female college freshmen reported significantly more

*What happens if I worry too much about exams?*

worry and anxiety than did males (Everson et al., 1994). Women may report more worry and anxiety than men because women are generally more sensitive to negative feedback, such as grades and exam scores (Zeidner, 1998).

In related studies, researchers found that the cognitive component could either help or hinder performance. Students who channeled their worry into complaining rather than studying performed poorly because their worry interfered with their reading the exam material and caused them to make more reading errors (Calvo & Carreiras, 1993). In contrast, students who channeled their worry into studying performed better and achieved higher grades because they were better prepared (Endler et al., 1994).

These studies indicate that the cognitive component of test anxiety—excessive worrying—may either help or hinder cognitive performance, depending on how students channel their worries.

**Differences in Levels of Anxiety**

| | |
|---|---|
| 7 | Men |
| 18 | Women |

# B. Modern Approaches

**Power Study**

**Check out CD: Module 10**
A. Operant Conditioning
E. Cognitive Learning

---

## Behavioral Approach

---

### No leaving soap suds in the sink!

**Why have a "no soap suds" rule?**

If Donna happened to leave soap suds in the sink, she might see a rainbow of colors reflected in the bubbles. She would become so completely absorbed in looking at the brilliant colors that she could not move; she would be in a state of temporary paralysis. Donna made her "no soap suds" rule to prevent the environment from triggering an autistic behavior—temporary paralysis. Donna and her husband, who is also autistic, have developed many rules to control some of their unwanted behaviors. Here are some of their rules: *No lining feet up with furniture; No making the fruit in the bowl symmetrical; No reading newspaper headlines in gas stations or at newsstands* (Blakely, 1994, p. 43). These rules, which help Donna and her husband avoid performing repetitive and stereotyped behaviors, illustrate the behavioral approach.

The ***behavioral approach*** analyzes how organisms learn new behaviors or modify existing ones, depending on whether events in their environments reward or punish these behaviors.

Donna and her husband's rules are examples of a basic behavioral principle: rewards or punishments can modify, change, or control behavior. Psychologists use behavioral principles to teach people to be more assertive or less depressed, to toilet train young children, and to change many other behaviors. Psychologists use behavioral principles to train animals to press levers, to use symbols to communicate, and to perform behaviors on cue in movies and television shows.

Seeing a dazzling rainbow in soap suds stopped Donna in her tracks.

Largely through the creative work and original ideas of B. F. Skinner (1989), the behavioral approach has grown into a major force in psychology. Skinner's ideas stress the study of observable behaviors, the importance of environmental reinforcers (reward and punishment), and the exclusion of mental processes. His ideas, often referred to as strict behaviorism, continue to have an impact on psychology. In Module 10, we'll explain how Skinner's ideas were integrated into a program that taught autistic children new social behaviors that enabled them to enter and do well in public grade schools.

However, some behaviorists, such as Albert Bandura (1989b), disagree with strict behaviorism and have formulated a theory that includes mental or cognitive processes in addition to observable behaviors. According to Bandura's *social learning approach,* our behaviors are influenced not only by environmental events and reinforcers but also by observation, imitation, and thought processes. In Module 10, we'll discuss how Bandura's ideas explain why some children develop a fear of bugs.

Behaviorists have developed a number of techniques for changing behaviors. As we mentioned earlier, they used relaxation exercises to reduce the emotional component of test anxiety. Next, you'll see how they have used self-management skills to reduce the cognitive component of test anxiety.

---

### Behavioral Approach to Test Anxiety

**Can I redirect my worrying?**

We discussed how excessive worrying, which is the cognitive component of test anxiety, can improve test performance if you can channel your worry into studying for exams. One method to redirect worry into studying more is to use a system of *self-management* based on a number of behavioral principles (Kennedy & Doepke, 1999).

Researchers found that the following self-management practices are related to increasing studying time and achieving better grades: (1) select a place that you use exclusively for study; (2) reward yourself for studying; (3) keep a record of your study time; (4) establish priorities among projects; (5) specify a time for each task; (6) complete one task before going on to another. Notice that each of these self-management practices derives from our basic behavioral principle: Events in your environment can modify your behaviors through rewards and punishments. As the graph on the right shows, 53% of freshmen who learned and used self-management practices survived into their sophomore year compared to the survival rate of only 7% of freshmen who did not learn self-management practices (Long et al., 1994).

I heard that self-management can help me stay in college.

In later modules, we'll give many examples of how behavioral principles can be used to modify a wide range of behaviors and thought patterns.

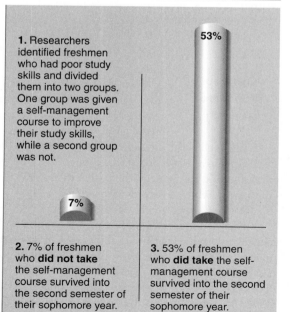

**1.** Researchers identified freshmen who had poor study skills and divided them into two groups. One group was given a self-management course to improve their study skills, while a second group was not.

**53%**

**7%**

**2.** 7% of freshmen who **did not take** the self-management course survived into the second semester of their sophomore year.

**3.** 53% of freshmen who **did take** the self-management course survived into the second semester of their sophomore year.

How was
Donna's
childhood?

When she was about 3 years old, Donna faced a number of personal problems: having an alcoholic mother who hit and verbally abused her, having a father who was often gone, and being sent to a "special needs" school. Apparently in trying to deal with these problems, Donna developed other personalities. One personality was Willie, a child with "hateful glaring eyes, a pinched-up mouth, rigid corpselike stance, and clenched fists," who stamped and spit but also did well in school. The other was Carol, a charming, cooperative little girl who could act normal and make friends (Reed & Cook, 1993). Why Donna developed other personalities to deal with difficult childhood experiences would be carefully looked at in the psychoanalytic approach (Lanyado & Horne, 1999).

The *psychoanalytic approach* is based on the belief that childhood experiences greatly influence the development of later personality traits and psychological problems. It also stresses the influence of unconscious fears, desires, and motivations on thoughts and behaviors.

In the late 1800s, Sigmund Freud, a physician, treated a number of patients with psychological problems. On the basis of insights from therapy sessions, Freud proposed a number of revolutionary ideas about the human mind and personality development. For

Donna had an alcoholic and verbally abusive mother and a mostly absent father.

example, one hallmark of Sigmund Freud's psychoanalytic approach is the idea that the first five years have a profound effect on later personality development. According to the psychoanalytic approach, Donna's first five years with a verbally abusive mother and mostly absent father would profoundly affect her later personality development.

In addition, Freud reasoned that thoughts or feelings that make us feel fearful or guilty, that threaten our self-esteem, or that come from unresolved sexual conflicts are automatically placed deep into our unconscious. In turn, these unconscious, threatening thoughts and feelings give rise to anxiety, fear, or psychological problems. Because Freud's patients could not uncover their unconscious fears, he developed several techniques, such as dream interpretation, to bring hidden fears to the surface. Freud's belief in an unconscious force that influenced human thought and behavior was another of his revolutionary ideas (Hansen, 2000).

Many of Freud's beliefs, such as the existence of unconscious feelings and fears, have survived, while other ideas, such as the all-importance of a person's first five years, have received less support. Many of Freud's terms, such as id, ego, superego, and libido, have become part of our everyday language. We'll discuss Freud's theory of personality in Module 19.

Unlike the biological, cognitive, and behavioral approaches, the psychoanalytic approach would search for hidden or unconscious forces underlying test anxiety.

### *Psychoanalytic Approach to Test Anxiety*

Is test anxiety
related to
procrastination?

We discussed two components of test anxiety—excessive worrying and increased physiological responses—that can impair a student's performance on exams. Researchers also found that students with high test anxiety are much more likely to procrastinate than students with low test anxiety (Milgram et al., 1992).

*Procrastination* refers to the tendency to always put off completing a task to the point of feeling anxious or uncomfortable about one's delay.

Researchers estimate that about 20% of adults are chronic procrastinators and from 30 to 70% of students procrastinate or deliberately delay completing assignments or studying for exams (Ferrari & Tice, 2000). Some of the more obvious reasons students give for procrastinating include being lazy or undisciplined, lacking motivation, or not knowing how to organize their time (Senécal et al., 1995).

However, the psychoanalytic approach would look beneath these obvious reasons and try to identify unconscious personality problems that may underlie procrastination. Because unconscious reasons for procrastination are difficult to uncover, psychologists studied the personality of procrastinators by giving them standard paper-and-pencil personality tests.

Based on personality tests, researchers concluded that students who are regular procrastinators may have low self-esteem, are too dependent on others, or have such a strong fear of failure that they do not start the

task (Blunt & Pychyl, 2000; Ferrari, 1994). Thus, the psychoanalytic approach would point to underlying personality problems as the probable cause of procrastination.

The psychoanalytic approach would also study how childhood experience may have led to being a procrastinator. For instance, researchers find that procrastinators tend to be raised by parents who stress overachievement, set unrealistic goals for their children, or link achievement to giving parental love and approval. A child who is raised by parents like these may feel very anxious when he or she fails at some task and will be tempted to put off such tasks in the future (Ferrari et al., 1997).

The best thing to do is to put off doing it for a few more days.

Psychologists know that ingrained personality characteristics, such as procrastination, remain relatively stable and persist across time unless a person makes a deliberate effort to change them. In Modules 21, 23, and 24, we'll discuss several effective methods that psychologists have developed to change personality characteristics.

### Humanistic Approach

**What was Donna's potential?**

Donna says that one reason she wrote her books was to escape her prison of autism. Autism has trapped her in a world where she sometimes blinks compulsively, switches lights on and off for long periods of time, rocks back and forth, freezes up, stares off into space without being able to stop herself, hates to be touched, cannot stand to enter public places, and hates to make eye contact with others (Williams, 1992).

When Donna and her husband were dating, they confided to each other that they didn't feel sexual attraction or sexual feelings like other couples. Something had been left out of their lives and made them asexual (D. Williams, 1994).

Donna's struggle to free herself from autism, develop close personal relationships, and reach her true potential characterizes the humanistic approach.

The *humanistic approach* emphasizes that each individual has great freedom in directing his or her future, a large capacity for achieving personal growth, a considerable amount of intrinsic worth, and enormous potential for self-fulfillment.

Donna echoes the humanistic approach when she writes, "Autism tried to rob me of life, of friendship, of caring, of sharing, of showing interest, of using my intelligence . . . it tries to bury me alive. . . ." The last words in her book are "I CAN

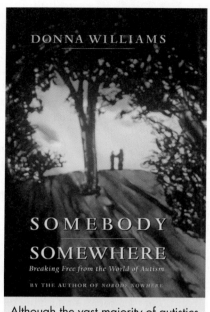

Although the vast majority of autistics have great difficulty with language, Donna had an amazing ability for written and spoken language.

FIGHT AUTISM. . . . I WILL CONTROL IT. . . . IT WILL NOT CONTROL ME" (D. Williams, 1994, p. 238).

Humanists believe that, like Donna, we may have to struggle to reach our potential, but we have control of our fate and are free to become whatever we are capable of being. The humanistic approach emphasizes the positive side of human nature, its creative tendencies, and its inclination to build caring relationships. This concept of human nature—freedom, potential, creativity—is the most distinctive feature of the humanistic approach and sets it far apart from the behavioral and psychoanalytic approaches (Hansen, 2000).

The humanistic approach officially began in the early 1960s with the publication of the *Journal of Humanistic Psychology.* One of the major figures behind establishing the journal and the humanistic approach was Abraham Maslow, who had become dissatisfied with the behavioral and psychoanalytic approaches. To paraphrase Maslow (1968), the humanistic approach was to be a new way of perceiving and thinking about the individual's capacity, freedom, and potential for growth. Many of humanism's ideas have been incorporated into approaches for counseling and psychotherapy.

Because of its free-will concept of human nature and its lack of rigorous experimental methods, many behaviorists regard the humanistic approach as more of a philosophy of life than a science of human behavior.

The humanistic approach also applies to dealing with a student's problems, such as test anxiety and procrastination.

### *Humanistic Approach to Test Anxiety*

**How can students reach their potentials?**

We've all had the experience of getting exams back and looking at the grades. Researchers wanted to know if you would give different reasons for earning high scores than for earning low scores. For example, researchers asked children to explain why they performed well or poorly on reading and math exams. Children who performed well said that their good performance resulted from their effort and ability. Children who performed poorly said it was primarily because the task was too difficult and they lacked the ability (Bell et al., 1994). Based on these findings, researchers suggested that teachers be especially encouraging and supportive to children who do poorly, so that they will not give up but rather try to develop their academic potential. This advice to teachers is a good example of applying the humanistic approach to help individuals reach their highest potential.

What are the ways that I can improve?

Psychologists have also studied students whose academic performance ranged from poor to very good in order to develop a profile of a successful student. Studies showed that successful students share a number of similar characteristics: they feel competent about meeting the demands of their classes; they believe they can handle test situations; they are very good at organizing their study time and leisure time; they prepare themselves for tests and do not procrastinate (Kleijn et al., 1994).

Based on studies of students' performances, the humanistic approach would say that just as successful students found ways to reach their academic potential, all students should search for ways to reach their own potentials. The humanistic approach emphasizes that students have the capacity to choose, that each is unique or special, and that students should have faith in their personal or subjective feelings (Hansen, 2000).

## Cross-Cultural Approach

**How is autism diagnosed in other cultures?**

Although autism is now recognized in most countries, there are differences among countries in the age at which the diagnosis is first made.

**United States.** A psychologist in the United States first described the symptoms of autism almost 60 years ago (Kanner, 1943). At that time, autism was thought to be caused by environmental factors, such as having "cold" parents. However, in the 1960s, the focus changed to searching for biological causes (Rimland, 1964). In the United States, the diagnosis of autism usually occurs very early, between 2 and 3 years of age. At this writing, there is no cure for autism but there are a variety of treatment programs, one of which is described on page 232.

**China.** The problem of autism was not recognized in China until 1987, when a published article described 15 cases of children with autistic symptoms (Tao, 1987). There are several reasons for this time lag in recognizing autism in China. First, most Chinese could not imagine that any disorder, such as autism, could occur in infancy. Second, many Chinese parents were unaware of an

infant's developmental stages, such as when an infant first develops social responses and verbal skills. Third, Chinese parents generally believed that infants would grow out of any early difficulties. Efforts are under way to alert parents and medical professionals to the importance of making an early diagnosis and beginning early treatment (Tao & Yang, 1997).

**Germany.** Similar to the United States, the recognition of autism in Germany began in the late 1940s. However, unlike the United States' policy of making an early diagnosis of autism, the diagnosis of autism in Germany is hardly ever made in 3-year-olds and generally not until children are 5 or 6 years of age. Efforts are under way to change this policy and diagnose autism and begin treatment at an earlier age (Schmidt, 1997).

These differences in diagnosing autism show the influence of cultural factors and illustrate one of the newer approaches in psychology, the cross-cultural approach (Kagitcibasi & Poortinga, 2000).

The *cross-cultural approach* studies the influence of cultural and ethnic similarities and differences on psychological and social functioning.

As you'll see next, there are also cross-cultural differences in how students respond to test anxiety.

### Cross-Cultural Approach to Test Anxiety

**How do other cultures deal with test anxiety?**

Culture plays an important role in determining the intensity and expression of anxiety. For example, the highest test anxiety scores were reported by students in Egypt, Jordan, and Hungary. The lowest test anxiety scores were reported by students in China, Italy, Japan, and the Netherlands. Test anxiety scores of students in the United States were somewhere in the middle (Zeidner, 1998).

Some cultural factors that play a role in determining levels of text anxiety include importance of academic success, career opportunities, parental expectations, perceptions of being evaluated, and students' expectations. Researchers suggest that higher test anxiety may also result from special envi-

Students' level of test anxiety depends on their cultural values.

ronmental and educational problems or increased competition because of fewer educational opportunities (Zeidner, 1998).

Researchers also discovered that how students evaluate success depends on their cultural values. For example, students in Chile admired successful students, whether or not they thought the success resulted from expending great effort or having natural ability. In contrast, students in America admired successful students much more if they thought the success resulted from expending great effort rather than having natural ability (Betancourt & Lopez, 1993). This study shows how the cross-cultural approach provides different and interesting answers to the same question (Keller & Greenfield, 2000).

### Many Approaches, Many Answers

Of the six approaches that we have discussed, the cross-cultural approach is the most recent. This approach began in the early 1970s with the publication of the *Journal of Cross-Cultural Psychology* and has since grown in popularity (Massimini & Fave, 2000). In each module, we will highlight a cross-cultural study, which will be indicated by the symbol of multicultural people shown here on the right.

The reason modern psychology uses many different approaches to study the same behavior is that the different viewpoint of each approach serves to provide

This symbol indicates a cultural diversity topic.

additional information. By combining information from the biological, cognitive, behavioral, psychoanalytic, humanistic, and cross-cultural approaches, psychologists stand a better chance of reaching their four goals of describing, explaining, predicting, and controlling behavior.

We have discussed the approaches used by modern psychologists so that you can compare them with the different approaches used by early psychologists. As you compare early and modern approaches, you can appreciate how much psychology has changed in the past 100 years.

| | |
|---|---|
| **How did psychology begin?** | Imagine living in the late 1800s and early 1900s, when the electric light, radio, and airplane were being invented and the average human life span was about 30 years. This was the time when psychology broke away from philosophy and became a separate field of study. As they developed this new area, early psychologists hotly debated its definition, approach, and goals (Benjamin, 2000). We'll highlight those early psychologists whose ideas and criticisms shaped the field. We'll begin with the person considered to be the father of psychology, Wilhelm Wundt. |

### Structuralism: Elements of the Mind

**WILHELM WUNDT**
**1832–1920**

**Who established the first lab?**

There were no bands or celebrations when Wilhelm Wundt established the first psychology laboratory in 1879, in Leipzig, Germany. In fact, his laboratory was housed in several rooms in a shabby building that contained rather simple equipment, such as platforms, various balls, telegraph keys, and metronomes. The heavily bearded Wundt, now considered the father of psychology, would ask subjects to drop balls from a platform or listen to a metronome (figure below) and report their own sensations. Wundt and his followers were analyzing their sensations, which they thought was the key to analyzing the structure of the mind (Evans, 1999). For this reason they were called structuralists and their approach was called structuralism.

*Structuralism* was the study of the most basic elements, primarily sensations and perceptions, that make up our conscious mental experiences.

Just as you might assemble hundreds of pieces of a jigsaw puzzle into a completed picture, structuralists tried to combine hundreds of sensations into a complete conscious experience. Perhaps Wundt's greatest contribution was his method of introspection.

*Introspection* was a method of exploring conscious mental processes by asking subjects to look inward and report their sensations and perceptions.

For example, after listening to a beating metronome, the subjects would be asked to report whether their sensations were pleasant, unpleasant, exciting, or relaxing. However, introspection was heavily criticized for being an unscientific method because it was solely dependent on subjects' self-reports, which could be biased, rather than on objective measurements. Although Wundt's approach was the first, it had little impact on modern psychology. The modern-day cognitive approach also studies mental processes, but with different scientific methods and much broader interests than those of Wundt.

It wasn't long before Wundt's approach was criticized for being too narrow and subjective in primarily studying sensations. These criticisms resulted in another new approach, called functionalism.

Can you describe each sensation you hear?

### Functionalism: Functions of the Mind

**WILLIAM JAMES**
**1842–1910**

**Who wrote the first textbook?**

For twelve years, William James labored over a book called *Principles of Psychology*, which was published in 1890 and included almost every topic that is now part of psychology textbooks: learning, sensation, memory, reasoning, attention, feelings, consciousness, and a revolutionary theory of emotions.

For example, why do you feel fear when running from a raging wolf? You might answer that an angry wolf (figure below) is a terrifying creature that causes fear and makes you run—fear makes you run. Not so, according to James, who reasoned that the act of running causes a specific set of physiological responses that your brain interprets as fear—running makes you afraid. According to James, emotions were caused by physiological changes; thus, running produced fear. You'll find out if James's theory of emotions was correct in Module 16.

Unlike Wundt, who saw mental activities as composed of basic elements, James viewed mental activities as having developed through ages of evolution because of their adaptive functions, such as helping humans survive. James was interested in the goals, purposes, and functions of the mind, an approach called functionalism.

*Functionalism,* which was the study of the function rather than the structure of consciousness, was interested in how our minds adapt to our changing environment.

Functionalism did not last as a unique approach, but many of James's ideas grew into current areas of study, such as emotions, attention, and memory (Hunt, 1993). In addition, James suggested ways to apply psychological principles to teaching, which had a great impact on educational psychology. For all these reasons, James is considered the father of modern psychology.

Notice that James disagreed with Wundt's structural approach and pushed psychology toward looking at how the mind functions and adapts to our ever-changing world. About the same time that James was criticizing Wundt's structuralism, another group also found reasons to disagree with Wundt; this group was the Gestalt psychologists.

Does running from an angry wolf cause fear?

## Gestalt Approach: Sensations versus Perceptions

**Who said, "Wundt is wrong"?**

When you see a road hazard sign like the one in the photo below, you think the lights forming the arrow are actually moving in one direction. This motion, however, is only an illusion; the lights are stationary and are only flashing on and off.

The illusion that flashing lights appear to move was first studied in 1912 by three psychologists; Max Wertheimer, Wolfgang Köhler, and Kurt Koffka. They reported that they had created the perception of movement by briefly flashing one light and then, a short time later, a second light. Although the two bulbs were fixed, the light actually appeared to move from one to the other. They called this the *phi phenomenon;* today it is known as *apparent motion.*

**MAX WERTHEIMER
1883–1943**

Wertheimer and his colleagues believed that the perception of apparent motion could not be explained by the structuralists, who said that the movement resulted from simply adding together the sensations from two fixed lights. Instead, Wertheimer argued that perceptual experiences, such as perceiving moving lights, resulted from analyzing a "whole pattern," or, in German, a *Gestalt.*

The *Gestalt approach* emphasized that perception is more than the sum of its parts and studied how sensations are assembled into meaningful perceptual experiences.

In our example, Gestalt psychologists would explain that your experience of perceiving moving traffic lights is much more than and very different from what is actually happening—fixed lights flashing in sequence. These kinds of findings could not be explained by the structuralists and pointed out the limitations of their approach (Murray et al., 2000).

After all these years, many principles of the Gestalt approach are still used to explain how we perceive objects. We'll discuss many of the Gestalt principles of perception in Module 6.

Why do blinking lights seem to move?

## Behaviorism: Observable Behaviors

**Who offered a guarantee?**

"Give me a dozen healthy infants, well-formed, and my own special world to bring them up in and I'll guarantee to take any one at random and train him to become any type of specialist I might select—doctor, lawyer, artist . . ." (Watson, 1924).

These words come from John B. Watson, who published a landmark paper in 1913 titled "Psychology as a Behaviorist Views It." In it, he rejected Wundt's structuralism and its study of mental elements and conscious processes. He rejected introspection as a psychological technique because its results could not be scientifically verified by other psychologists. Instead, John Watson very boldly stated that psychology should be considered an objective, experimental science, whose goal should be the analysis of observable behaviors and the prediction and control of those behaviors (Rilling, 2000). It is a small step from these ideas to Watson's famous boast, "Give me a dozen healthy infants . . . ," which illustrates the behavioral approach.

**JOHN B. WATSON
1878–1958**

The *behavioral approach* emphasized the objective, scientific analysis of observable behaviors.

Can anyone guarantee what I will become?

From the 1920s to the 1960s, behaviorism was the dominant force in American psychology. Part of this dominance was due to the work of B. F. Skinner and other behaviorists, who expanded and developed Watson's ideas into the modern-day behavioral approach, which is fully discussed in Module 10. However, beginning in the 1970s and continuing into the present, behaviorism's dominance was challenged by the cognitive approach, whose popularity throughout the 1990s surpassed behaviorism (Evans, 1999).

## Survival of Approaches

**Which approaches survived?**

The survival of each approach—structuralism, functionalism, Gestalt, and behaviorism—depended on its ability to survive its criticisms. Criticisms of Wundt's structural approach gave rise to the functional approach of James and the Gestalt approach of Wertheimer, Köhler, and Koffka. Criticisms of all three approaches—structural, functional, and Gestalt—gave rise to Watson's behavioral approach. Another approach, Sigmund Freud's psychoanalytic approach (see p. 9), which emphasized the influence of unconscious processes, disagreed with Watson's strict behavioral approach and developed largely in parallel to these other approaches. These disagreements in approaches resulted in heated debates among early psychologists, but they helped psychology develop into the scientific field it is today (Evans, 1999).

Although early American psychologists differed in their approaches, they shared one underlying theme that was a sign of their times. They discriminated against women and minorities in both academic and career settings. Such discriminatory practices were widespread, and we'll examine that issue next.

Because psychologists focus on studying and understanding human behavior, you would expect them to be among the first to recognize the mistreatment of and discrimination against other groups. However, psychologists are human and being human, they knowingly or unknowingly adopted and carried out the discriminatory practices that were operating at the time. This means that, for the first 75 of its more than 100 years of existence, the academic policies and career opportunities of American psychology were determined by White males, who both intentionally and unintentionally discriminated against women and people of color. Here are just a few examples.

## Women in Psychology

**Why couldn't she enter graduate school?**

The reason Mary Calkins (on right) could not enter graduate school was that she was a woman, and many universities (Johns Hopkins, Harvard, Columbia) would not admit women. Since Calkins was a faculty member and had established a laboratory in psychology at Wellesley College in 1891, she petitioned and was allowed to take seminars at Harvard. There, she completed all requirements for a Ph.D. and was recommended for a doctorate by her professors, but the Harvard administration declined to grant it because she was a woman (Furumoto, 1989). It was not until 1908 that a woman, Margaret Washburn, was awarded a Ph.D. in psychology.

Mary Calkins was not given a Ph.D. because she was a woman.

Even after women began obtaining doctorates, the only positions open to them were teaching jobs at women's colleges or normal schools, which trained high school teachers (Furumoto & Scarborough, 1986). During the past 25 years, women have made great progress in the field. However, even though women currently earn more Ph.D.s in psychology than men, in 1991 there were more full-time male psychologists (39,180) than women (20,100). In addition, female psychologists earn less than male psychologists, and few women are editors of psychology journals (Rabasca, 2000). Not only did women face discrimination in psychology, but so did people of color.

## Minorities in Psychology

**Why so few minority students?**

In psychology's early days, only a few northern White universities accepted Black students, while all southern White universities denied admission to Black students.

The first African American woman to receive a Ph.D. in psychology was Ruth Howard (photo below), who graduated from the University of Minnesota in 1934. She had a successful career as a clinical psychologist and school consultant.

Between 1920 and 1966, only 8 Ph.D.s in psychology were awarded to Black students, compared to 3,767 doctorates to Whites (Guthrie, 1976). In 1996, there were 168 Ph.D.s awarded to African Americans, 183 to Hispanics, 23 to Native Americans, 131 to Asians, and 2,939 to Whites (Rabasca, 2000).

During the early 1900s, few degrees were awarded to Hispanics. One early exception was

Ruth Howard was the first black woman to get a Ph.D. in 1934.

George Sanchez (photo below), who conducted pioneering work on the cultural bias of intelligence tests given to minority students. Sanchez criticized the claim that Mexican Americans were mentally inferior, saying that this claim was based solely on intelligence tests. Sanchez showed that intelligence tests contained many questions that were biased against minorities and thus resulted in their lower scores (Guthrie, 1976).

From the founding of the American Psychological Association in 1892 up until 1990, its cumulative membership was 128,000. Of those members, only 700 were African American, 700 were Latino, and 70 were Native American. This limited minority membership indicates how much further psychology must go to remedy its earlier discriminatory practices (Barinaga, 1996).

George Sanchez found that intelligence tests were culturally biased.

## Righting the Wrongs

**How much success?**

Today, people of color are still underrepresented in academic departments and in graduate programs in psychology, although their numbers and influence are increasing (Evans, 1999). For example, the American Psychological Association has recognized the need to recruit minority members and has formed a special group to carry out this goal. An increasing number of journals *(Psychology of Women Quarterly, Hispanic Journal of Behavioral Science,* and *Journal of Black Psychology)* are promoting the causes of women and minorities and are fighting discriminatory practices (DeAngelis, 1966). The American Psychological Association (APA) has an official policy supporting equal opportunities "for persons regardless of race, gender, age, religion, disability, sexual orientation and national origin" (Tomes, 2000).

In the late 1990s, several states banned affirmative action programs, which helped minority students enter college. As a result, university enrollments of Hispanic and African American students in these states have dropped significantly (Wildavsky, 1999). Colleges are searching for other ways to recruit minority students.

# Concept Review

**1.** The systematic, scientific study of behaviors and mental processes is called _____.

**2.** The four goals of psychology are to (a)_____ what organisms do, to (b)_____ the causes of behavior, to (c)_____ behavior in new situations, and to (d)_____ behavior, which has both positive and negative aspects.

**3.** The approach that focuses on how one's nervous system, hormones, and genes interact with the environment is called the _____ approach.

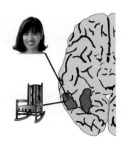

**4.** The approach that studies how people think, solve problems, and process information is called the _____ approach.

**5.** The approach that analyzes how environmental rewards and punishments shape, change, or motivate behavior is called the _____ approach.

**6.** The approach that stresses the influence of unconscious feelings, fears, or desires on the development of behavior, personality, and psychological problems is called the (a)_____ approach. This approach also emphasizes the importance of early (b)_____ experiences.

**7.** The approach that emphasizes freedom of choice, self-fulfillment, and attaining one's potential is called the (a)_____ approach. Many of this approach's concepts have been taken up and used in (b)_____.

**8.** The newest approach, which focuses on cultural and ethnic influences on behavior, is called the _____ approach.

**9.** Wundt studied the elements that made up the conscious mind and called this approach (a)_____. Subjects were asked to observe the workings of their minds, a technique that Wundt called (b)_____. Modern-day psychologists who study mental activities with more objective and scientific methods are said to use the (c)_____ approach.

**10.** William James disagreed with Wundt's structuralism and instead emphasized the functions, goals, and purposes of the mind and its adaptation to the environment; he called this approach (a)_____. James also applied the principles of psychology to teaching, so his approach had a great effect on the field of (b)_____ psychology.

**11.** Some psychologists disagreed with Wundt's approach of structuralism and instead believed that perceptions are more than the sum of many individual (a)_____. These psychologists called their approach the (b)_____ approach, which studied how sensations were assembled into meaningful (c)_____.

**12.** John Watson disagreed with Wundt's approach, which was called (a)_____, and disagreed with Wundt's technique of studying the mind, which was called (b)_____. Instead, Watson emphasized the objective, scientific analysis of observable behaviors, which was known as the (c)_____ approach. Later, this approach became a dominant force in psychology through the work of behaviorist (d)_____.

**Answers:** 1. psychology; 2. (a) describe, (b) explain, (c) predict, (d) control; 3. biological; 4. cognitive; 5. behavioral; 6. (a) psychoanalytic, (b) childhood; 7. (a) humanistic, (b) counseling or psychotherapy; 8. cross-cultural; 9. (a) structuralism, (b) introspection, (c) cognitive; 10. (a) functionalism, (b) educational; 11. (a) sensations, (b) Gestalt, (c) perceptions; 12. (a) structuralism, (b) introspection, (c) behavioral, (d) B. F. Skinner

## Best Strategy for Taking Class Notes?

**How good are your class notes?**

As you listen to lectures in class, you'll probably be taking notes. But how do you know if you're using the best system or strategy? To research some particular behavior, such as note-taking, psychologists first ask a very specific research question: Which system or strategy for taking notes results in the best performance on tests? One researcher answered this question by using a combination of behavioral and cognitive approaches (King, 1992). As we describe this interesting study, notice how it involves the four goals of psychology, beginning with the first goal, describing behavior.

How can I make my notes better?

### 1st Goal: Describe Behavior

The researcher divided college students into three different groups. Each group was given a different method or strategy for taking notes. As described below, students practiced three different strategies for taking notes: review notes, summarize notes, and answer questions about notes.

**A. Review Notes**

The strategy that most students use is to try to write down as much as possible of what the professor says. Then, before exams, students review their notes, hoping they took good class notes.

**B. Summarize Notes**

Students took notes as usual but, after the lecture, used their notes to write a summary of the lecture in their own words.

Students were shown how to identify a main topic and, in their own words, write a sentence about it. Then they identified a subtopic and wrote a sentence that related it to the main topic. When linked together, these sentences created a summary of the lecture, written in the students' own words.

**C. Answer Questions about Notes**

Students took notes as usual but, after the lecture, used their notes to ask and answer questions about the lecture material. Students were given a set of 13 general questions, such as: **What is the main idea of . . . ? How would you use . . . to . . . ? What is a new example of . . . ? What is the difference between . . . and . . . ?** Students answered each of these questions using their class notes.

After practicing one of these three note-taking strategies, students watched a videotaped lecture and used their particular strategy for taking notes.

### 2nd Goal: Explain Behavior

A week after each group had watched a videotaped lecture, they were given an exam. The graph on the right shows that the group who used the strategy of taking notes plus answering questions scored significantly higher than the other two groups. The researcher explained that students who took notes and then answered questions about their notes retained more information than students who employed the other two strategies (King, 1992).

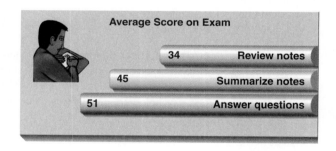

**Average Score on Exam**

| 34 | Review notes |
| 45 | Summarize notes |
| 51 | Answer questions |

### 3rd Goal: Predict Behavior

On the basis of these results, the researcher predicts that students who use the strategy that combines note-taking with answering questions are likely to retain more information and perform better on exams than students who use traditional note-taking methods, such as writing as much as they can and then reviewing their notes before exams.

### 4th Goal: Control Behavior

Students can increase their chances of getting better grades by taking the time to learn a better note-taking strategy. This new strategy involves taking notes and then answering, in their own words, a series of general questions about the lecture material. Although this new note-taking strategy takes a little time to learn, the payoff will be better performance on exams. This and other studies show how students can improve their test-taking performance by using a better strategy of taking notes (Armbruster, 2000).

### Purpose of the Research Focus

This study shows how psychologists answered a very practical and important question about how best to take lecture notes. We'll use the Research Focus to show how psychologists use different approaches and research techniques to answer a variety of interesting questions about human behavior.

Each time you see this symbol, it will indicate a Research Focus, which occurs in each module.

Although a large percentage of psychologists engage in research, you'll see next how many others work in a variety of career settings that may or may not involve research.

---

## Psychologist versus Psychiatrist

---

**What's a psychologist?**

Many students think that psychologists are primarily counselors and therapists, even though advanced degrees in psychology are awarded in a dozen different areas. Obtaining an advanced degree in psychology requires that one finish college and spend about two to three years in postgraduate study to obtain a master's degree or four to five years in postgraduate study to obtain a Ph.D. Some careers or work settings require a master's degree, while others require a Ph.D. Many students are confused about the difference between a psychologist, a clinical or counseling psychologist, and a psychiatrist.

A *psychologist* is usually someone who has completed four to five years of postgraduate education and has obtained a Ph.D., PsyD., or Ed.D. in psychology.

Some states permit individuals with master's degrees to call themselves psychologists.

It usually takes about 4–5 years after college to become a psychologist.

A *clinical psychologist* has a Ph.D., PsyD., or Ed.D., has specialized in a clinical subarea, and has spent an additional year in a supervised therapy setting to gain experience in diagnosing and treating a wide range of abnormal behaviors.

Similar to clinical psychologists are *counseling psychologists,* who provide many of the same services but usually work with different problems, such as those involving marriage, family, or career counseling. Neither clinical nor counseling psychologists assess the neurological causes of mental problems and do not yet have the authority to prescribe drugs like psychiatrists.

A *psychiatrist* is a medical doctor (M.D.) who has spent several years in clinical training, which includes diagnosing possible physical and neurological causes of abnormal behaviors and treating these behaviors, often with prescription drugs.

After becoming a psychologist, you could choose among the following career settings.

---

## Many Career Settings

---

**Are psychologists usually therapists?**

As you can see in the pie chart below, the majority (49%) of psychologists are therapists, while the rest work in four other settings. In the United States and Canada, most psychologists have a Ph.D., PsyD., or Ed.D., which require four to five years of study after college. In many other countries, most psychologists have a college degree, which requires four to five years of study after high school (Rosenzweig, 1992). Since the 1950s, there has been an increase in psychologists who provide therapy/health services and a decline in those who work in academic/research settings.

The U.S. Department of Labor predicts that employment opportunities for psychologists will grow much faster than the average for other occupations in the coming years (Chamberlin, 2000). Here's a breakdown of where psychologists in the United States currently work.

**49%** The largest percentage (49%) of psychologists work as clinical or counseling psychologists in either a *private practice* or *therapy setting,* such as a psychological or psychiatric clinic; a mental health center; a psychiatric, drug, or rehabilitation ward of a hospital; or a private office. The duties of clinical or counseling psychologists might involve doing individual or group therapy; helping patients with problems involving drugs, stress, weight, marriage, family, or career; designing programs for healthier living; or testing patients for psychological problems that developed from some neurological problem.

**28%** The second largest percentage (28%) of psychologists work in the *academic settings* of universities and colleges. Academic psychologists often engage in some combination of classroom teaching, mentoring or helping students, and doing research in their areas of interest.

**13%** The third largest percentage (13%) of psychologists work in a variety of other kinds of jobs and career settings.

**6%** The fourth largest percentage (6%) of psychologists work in *industrial settings,* such as businesses, corporations, and consulting firms. These psychologists, often called industrial/organizational psychologists, may work at selecting personnel, increasing production, or improving job satisfaction and employer–employee relations.

**4%** The smallest percentage (4%) work in *secondary schools and other settings.* For example, school psychologists conduct academic and career testing and provide counseling for a variety of psychological problems (learning disabilities, attention-deficit/hyperactivity disorder).

If you are thinking of entering the field of psychology today, you have a wide and exciting range of career choices. For those who decide to engage in research, we'll next discuss seven of the more popular research areas that psychologists choose.

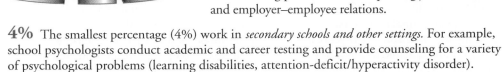

# G. Research Areas

---
**Areas of Specialization**
---

**Which area should I choose?**

As you proceed through your introductory psychology course, you'll find that the world of psychology has been divided into at least seven general areas. And, if you go on and enter graduate school in psychology, you'll be expected to specialize in one of these seven areas. Students often find it difficult to choose only one special area of psychology, since they may be interested in two or three. For example, I switched areas three times before deciding upon one of the seven. The reason graduate students are asked to choose one area is that there is such an enormous amount of information that it takes great effort to master even one area. As you read about each research area, think about which one you might prefer. (Percentages given below do not add up to 100% because some miscellaneous areas are not included.)

## Social and Personality

**How important are first impressions?**

**How does one develop certain personality traits?**

**Why do we use stereotypes?**

**What causes aggression?**

These questions come from the two different and sometimes overlapping areas of social psychology and personality psychology.

*Social psychology* involves the study of social interactions, stereotypes, prejudices, attitudes, conformity, group behaviors, and aggression.

*Personality psychology* involves the study of personality development, personality change, assessment, and abnormal behaviors.

Many social/personality psychologists work in academic settings, but some work as consultants and personnel managers in business. About 22% of psychologists choose social psychology and 5% choose personality.

## Developmental

**When does a newborn recognize his or her parents?**

**What happens to teenagers at puberty?**

**When does a child know he or she is a boy or girl?**

You would be asking these kinds of questions if you were a developmental psychologist.

*Developmental psychology* examines moral, social, emotional, and cognitive development throughout a person's entire life.

Some developmental psychologists focus on changes in infancy and childhood, while others trace changes through adolescence, adulthood, and old age. They work in academic settings and may consult on day care or programs for the aging. About 25% of psychologists choose this specialty.

## Experimental

**Why does an animal press a bar to obtain food?**

**Can learning principles be used to treat a phobia?**

**Why do we feel fear when we see a snake?**

**What is taste aversion?**

These kinds of questions interest experimental psychologists.

*Experimental psychology* includes areas of sensation, perception, learning, human performance, motivation, and emotion.

Experimental psychologists conduct much of their research under carefully controlled laboratory conditions, with both animal and human subjects. About 16% of psychologists specialize in experimental psychology. Most work in academic settings, but some also work in business, industry, and government.

## Biological

**How do brain cells change during Alzheimer's disease?**

**Do people have predispositions for mental disorders?**

**Does coffee improve your memory?**

**Do genes affect your intelligence and personality?**

Physiological psychologists or psychobiologists study the biological basis of learning and memory; the effects of brain damage; the causes of sleep and wakefulness; the basis of hunger, thirst, and sex; the effects of stress on the body; and the ways in which drugs influence behavior.

*Biological psychology* or *psychobiology* involves research on the physical and chemical changes that occur during stress, learning, and emotions, as well as how our genetic makeup, brain, and nervous system interact with our environments and influence our behaviors.

Psychobiologists work in academic settings, hospitals, and private research laboratories. About 8% of psychologists choose this area.

## Cognitive

**What was unique about Einstein's thought processes?**

**Can you learn something but not remember it?**

**Does memory get worse with age?**

**What are repressed memories?**

If these questions interest you, think about being a cognitive psychologist.

*Cognitive psychology* involves how we process, store, and retrieve information and how cognitive processes influence our behaviors.

Cognitive research includes memory, thinking, language, creativity, and decision making. Newer areas, such as artificial intelligence, combine knowledge of the brain's functions with computer programming in an attempt to duplicate human thinking and intelligence.

Earlier we discussed a relatively new area that combines cognitive and biological approaches and is called cognitive neuroscience. About 5% of psychologists select this area.

## Psychometrics

**What do college entrance tests show?**

**What career best fits my abilities?**

**How do tests assess abnormal behaviors?**

These questions introduce an area called psychometrics, which involves the construction, administration, and interpretation of psychological tests.

*Psychometrics* focuses on the measurement of people's abilities, skills, intelligence, personality, and abnormal behaviors.

To accomplish their goals, psychologists in this area focus on developing a wide range of psychological tests, which must be continually updated and checked for usefulness and cultural biases. Some of these tests are used to assess people's skills and abilities, as well as to predict their performance in certain careers and situations, such as college or business. About 5% of psychologists select this area.

---

### Making Decisions

**What should I do?**

If you decide to become a psychologist, you will need to make a series of decisions. The first is whether to obtain a master's degree or Ph.D. The next decision involves which setting to work in: choosing among private practice, clinic or hospital setting, academic research and/or teaching, industry/business, or counseling and testing in a school setting. You'll also need to specialize in one of the seven areas: social, personality, developmental, experimental, biological, cognitive, or psychometrics. After making all these decisions, you are on your way to having a very interesting and exciting career.

Next, we're going to use research findings from several research areas, including personality, experimental, and cognitive, and give you tips on how to improve your study skills.

---
### Improving Study Habits
---

**What problems do over 50% of freshmen report?**

In a survey of college freshmen, 57% reported that they had poor study habits, and 54% said that they had problems managing their time (Thombs, 1995). We'll discuss ways to deal with both of these problems, beginning with methods to improve study habits.

**Common complaint.** The most common student complaint that I hear after exams is, "I read the book and went over my notes three times and still got a C." This complaint points to the most common mistake students make in studying for exams. Because students do read the material and go over their notes several times, they may have a general feeling that they know the material. For example, you have just read about the six modern approaches, the historical approaches, and the differences between a psychologist, clinical psychologist, and psychiatrist. Having read this material, you may generally feel that you know it. However, researchers have discovered a startling fact: There is almost no relationship between how well students think they know material and how well they perform on an exam (Cull & Zechmeister, 1994; Mazzoni & Cornoldi, 1993).

*How do I know when I've studied enough to take a test?*

**Poor judges.** The reason students tend to be poor judges of what they know is that they base their judgments more on what they *generally* know rather than on what they *specifically* remember (Glenberg et al., 1987). For example, you might generally remember the six approaches. However, on an exam you will be asked for specific information, such as names and definitions. One of the best ways to judge how prepared you are for an exam is to test yourself and get feedback from answering specific questions. For instance, can you list the six approaches and define each one? Because answering specific questions is one way to judge your learning, we have built specific questions and answers into this text. You can test yourself by answering the questions in the Concept Review in each module and by answering the questions in the Summary Test at the end of each module.

**Time management.** A common problem that students have involves managing their time—specifically, underestimating how long it will take to study all the material. For example, researchers found that about 50% of college students repeatedly anticipated finishing a task earlier than they actually did (Buehler et al., 1994). Part of the problem is that students do not allow enough time for studying more difficult items. Researchers found that students who plan to set aside extra time for studying more difficult items increase their chances of remembering the material (Allgood et al., 2000). One way to achieve better time management involves setting the right kinds of goals.

> *Remember:*
> *To judge how well prepared you are for an exam, ask yourself specific questions about the material. You can do that by taking the tests built into each module—the Concept Review and the Summary Test.*

---
### Setting Goals
---

**What's the best kind of goal to set?**

Another way to better manage your study time is to set the right goals, which can vary from studying for a certain period of time to studying until you feel you are well prepared (Flippo & Caverly, 2000). Which of the following goals do you think would make your study time more efficient and improve your test performance?

**1** Set a **time goal,** such as studying 10 hours a week or more, and then keep track of your study time during the semester.

*Should my goal be to study 10 hours a week?*

**2** Set a **general goal,** such as trying to study hard and stay on schedule; then, try to reach this goal during the semester.

**3** Set a **specific performance goal,** such as answering at least 80% of the Summary Test questions correctly for each module.

To determine which of these three goals leads to more effective studying, researchers told three different groups of students to set time goals, general goals, or specific performance goals when they studied on their own. The researchers found that students who set specific performance goals did significantly better on the final exam than students who set time or general goals (Morgan, 1985). Thus, if you want to improve your study skills, you should think less about the total time you study and concentrate more on reaching a specific performance goal every week. For example, the first week your goal might be to correctly answer 80% of the Summary Test questions. Once you have reached this goal, you could aim to answer 90% of the questions correctly. Setting performance goals rather than time goals is the key to better time management (Barling et al., 1996).

As you'll see next, one way to motivate yourself to reach your performance goals is to reward yourself at the right times.

> *Remember:*
> *One way to make your study time more efficient is to set a specific performance goal and keep track of your progress.*

## Rewarding Yourself

**What if you reach a goal?**

One problem many students have is getting and staying motivated. One reliable solution is to give yourself a reward when you reach a specific goal, such as answering 80% of the questions correctly. The reward may be a special treat (such as a CD, meal, movie, or time with friends) or a positive statement (such as "I'm doing really well" or "I'm going to get a good grade on the test"). Giving yourself a reward (self-reinforcement) is an effective way to improve performance (Allgood et al., 2000).

Motivate yourself with rewards.

*Remember:*
*Immediately after you reach a specific goal, give yourself a reward, which will both maintain and improve your motivation.*

## Taking Notes

Another way to improve your performance is to take great notes. Students generally make two kinds of mistakes in taking notes. One is to try to write down everything the instructor says, which is impossible and leads to confusing notes. The other is to mechanically copy down terms or concepts that they do not understand but hope to learn by sheer memorization, which is difficult. Researchers have several suggestions for taking good notes (Armbruster, 2000):

1 Write down the information in your own words. This approach will ensure that you understand the material and will increase your chances of remembering it.

2 Use headings or an outline format. This method will help you better organize and remember the material.

3 Try to associate new lecture or text material with material that you already know. It's easier to remember new information if you can relate it to your existing knowledge. That is the reason we have paired terms in the Concept Review section with illustrations, drawings, and photos that you are familiar with from earlier in the text.

4 As we discussed in the Research Focus (p. 16), you can improve your note-taking by asking yourself questions, such as: What is the main idea of . . . ? What is an example of . . . ? How is . . . related to what we studied earlier? Writing the answers in your own words will give you a better chance of remembering the material (King, 1992).

Even though you may take great notes and set performance goals, if you procrastinate and put off getting started, as 30 to 70% of students report doing, your best-laid plans will come to nothing (Senécal et al., 1995). We already discussed some of the reasons behind procrastination (p. 9) and here we'll look at ways to overcome it.

*Remember:*
*Go through your lecture notes, ask questions, and write down answers in your own words.*

## Stopping Procrastination

**How do you get started?**

Some students find the task of reading assignments, studying for exams, or writing papers so difficult that they cannot bring themselves to start. If you have problems with procrastinating, here are three things you should do to get started (Blunt & Pychyl, 2000; Peterson, 1997):

1 *Stop thinking about the final goal*—reading 30 pages or taking two midterm exams—which may seem too overwhelming.

2 Break the final assignment down into a number of *smaller goals* that are less overwhelming and easier to accomplish. Work on the first small goal, and when you finish it, go on to the next small goal. Continue until you have completed all the small goals.

3 Write down a *realistic schedule* for reaching each of your smaller goals. This schedule should indicate the time and place for study and what you will accomplish that day. Use a variety of self-reinforcements to stay on your daily schedule and accomplish your specific goals.

Everyone procrastinates a little, but it becomes a problem if you continually put off starting important projects with deadlines, such as exams and papers (Harriott & Ferrari, 1966). Take the advice of professionals on stopping procrastination: get organized, set specific goals, and reward yourself (Zane, 1996).

Use three steps to overcome procrastination.

If you adopt these tested methods for improving your study skills, you'll greatly increase your chances of being a successful student (Flippo et al., 2000).

*Remember:*
*One of the most effective ways to start a large assignment is to break it down into a series of smaller goals and work on each goal separately.*

### Unusual Excuses for Missing Exams

✔ I missed the exam because of my uncle's funeral, and I can't take the make-up tomorrow because I just found out my aunt has a brain tumor.

✔ I can't be at the exam because my cat is having kittens and I'm her coach.

✔ I want to reschedule the final because my grandmother is a nun.

✔ I can't take the exam on Monday because my mom is getting married on Sunday and I'll be too drunk to drive back to school.

✔ I couldn't be at the exam because I had to attend the funeral of my girlfriend's dog.

✔ I can't take the test Friday because my mother is having a vasectomy. (Bernstein, 1993, p. 4)

## A. DEFINITION & GOALS

**1.** The broad definition of psychology is the systematic, scientific study of (a)_____ and (b)_____. The term in (a) refers to observable responses of animals and humans, and the term in (b) refers to processes that are not directly observable, such as thoughts, ideas, and dreams.

**2.** All psychologists agree that the first three goals of psychology are to (a)_____ what organisms do, to (b)_____ how organisms behave as they do, and to (c)_____ how they will respond in the future and in different situations. Some psychologists add a fourth goal, which is to (d)_____ behavior and thus curb or eliminate psychological and social problems.

## B. MODERN APPROACHES

**3.** Because behavior is often so complex, psychologists study it using six different approaches. The approach that focuses on how a person's genetic makeup, hormones, and nervous system interact with the environment to influence a wide range of behaviors is called the _____ approach.

**4.** The approach that studies how organisms learn new behaviors or change or modify existing ones in response to influences from the environment is called the (a)_____ approach. There are two versions of this approach. One that primarily studies observable behaviors and excludes mental events is called (b)_____ and is best expressed by the ideas of B. F. Skinner; the other, which includes observable behaviors plus cognitive processes, is called the (c)_____ approach and is expressed by the ideas of Albert Bandura and his colleagues.

**5.** An approach that examines how our unconscious fears, desires, and motivations influence behaviors, thoughts, and personality and cause psychological problems is called the _____ approach. Sigmund Freud developed this approach, as well as the technique of dream interpretation, to bring unconscious ideas to the surface.

**6.** The approach that investigates how people attend to, store, and process information and how this information affects learning, remembering, feeling, and believing is called the _____ approach.

**7.** An approach that emphasizes people's capacity for personal growth, freedom in choosing their future, and potential for self-fulfillment is called the _____ approach. One of the founders of this approach was Abraham Maslow.

**8.** The approach that studies how cultural and ethnic similarities and differences influence psychological and social functioning is called the _____ approach.

## C. HISTORICAL APPROACHES

**9.** Considered the father of psychology, Wilhelm Wundt developed an approach called (a)_____. This approach studied the elements of the conscious mind by using a self-report technique called (b)_____. Wundt's approach was the beginning of today's cognitive approach.

**10.** Disagreeing with Wundt's approach, William James said that it was important to study functions rather than elements of the mind. Accordingly, James studied the functions of consciousness as well as how mental processes continuously flow and adapt to input from the environment. This approach is called _____. James's ideas contributed to the modern area of psychology and have also influenced educational psychology.

**11.** Also disagreeing with Wundt's approach was a group of psychologists, led by Wertheimer, Köhler, and Koffka, who stated that perceptions cannot be explained by breaking them down into individual elements or sensations. Instead, they believed that perceptions are more than the sum of individual sensations, an idea called the _____ approach.

**12.** Another psychologist who disagreed with Wundt's approach was John B. Watson. He stated that psychology should use scientific principles to study only observable behaviors and not mental events, an approach called _____. Watson's approach gave rise to the modern behavioral approach.

## D. CULTURAL DIVERSITY: EARLY DISCRIMINATION

**13.** During the first 75 of its more than 100 years of existence, the field of psychology discriminated against (a)_____ and (b)_____, as indicated by the very limited number of these individuals who were granted Ph.D.s or offered positions in major universities. During the past 25 years, the

American Psychological Association, minority organizations, and most universities and colleges have been actively recruiting minorities and helping them enter the field of psychology.

## E. RESEARCH FOCUS: TAKING CLASS NOTES

**14.** Three different strategies for note-taking were studied: note-taking plus review, which means writing down almost everything the instructor says; note-taking plus questions, which means asking and answering questions about the lecture material; and note-taking plus summary, which means writing a summary of the lecture in your own words. The note-taking strategy that resulted in the highest exam grades involved (a)_____, and the note-taking strategy that resulted in the lowest exam grades involved (b)_____.

## F. CAREERS IN PSYCHOLOGY

**15.** There are five major settings in which psychologists work and establish careers. The largest percentage of psychologists work in private practice or (a)_____ settings, where they diagnose and help clients with psychological problems. The second largest group work in (b)_____ settings, doing a combination of teaching and research. The third largest group work in a (c)_____ of settings. The fourth largest group work in (d)_____ settings, where they are involved in selecting personnel, increasing job satisfaction, and improving worker–management relations. The fifth largest group work in other settings, such as (e)_____, where they do academic testing and counseling.

## G. RESEARCH AREAS

**16.** There are six common subareas in which psychologists specialize. Those who are interested in prejudice, attitudes, and group behaviors or in personality development and change specialize in (a)_____ psychology. Those interested in social, emotional, and cognitive changes across the life span specialize in (b)_____ psychology. Those interested in studying sensation, perceptions, learning,

and motivation, often under laboratory conditions, specialize in (c)_____ psychology. Those interested in the interaction among genes, the nervous system, and the environment choose (d)_____. Those interested in how people process, store, and retrieve information choose (e)_____ psychology, and those who are interested in the measurement and testing of skills, abilities, personality, and mental problems specialize in (f)_____.

## H. APPLICATION: STUDY SKILLS

**17.** A common mistake that many students make is that, when they plan their study schedules, they often _____ the time it will take to complete a task.

**18.** Another common mistake that students make is that they think they know the material after reading the text and reviewing their notes. A better way to judge how prepared you are for an exam is to ask yourself specific (a)_____ rather than to trust your judgment about what you think you know. A good way to make your study time more efficient is to set specific (b)_____

and keep track of your progress. Immediately after you reach a specific performance goal, give yourself a (c)_____, which will both maintain and improve your motivation. To improve your lecture notes, try to associate new lecture material with what you already know, and use your notes to ask and answer (d)_____ in your own words. One of the most effective ways to overcome a strong tendency to delay starting a task, known as (e)_____, is to stop thinking about the final goal. Instead, break down a large assignment into a series of smaller goals and work on each goal separately. Finally, it's best to set a realistic (f)_____ in order to accomplish each of the smaller goals.

***Answers:*** *1. (a) behaviors, (b) mental processes; 2. (a) describe, (b) explain, (c) predict, (d) control; 3. biological; 4. (a) behavioral, (b) strict behaviorism, (c) social learning; 5. psychoanalytic; 6. cognitive; 7. humanistic; 8. cross-cultural; 9. (a) structuralism, (b) introspection; 10. functionalism; 11. Gestalt; 12. behaviorism; 13. (a) women, (b) minorities; 14. (a) answering questions, (b) reviewing notes; 15. (a) therapy or clinical, (b) academic, (c) variety, (d) industrial, (e) schools; 16. (a) social and personality, (b) developmental, (c) experimental, (d) biological or physiological psychology, (e) cognitive, (f) psychometrics; 17. underestimate; 18. (a) questions, (b) performance goals, (c) reward, (d) questions, (e) procrastination, (f) schedule*

# Critical Thinking

## Questions

Test your thinking power by answering the following questions. If you need help, check the suggested answers on the right.

**1.** What kind of symptoms would doctors use to decide whether or not young Parker Beck was autistic?

**2.** What did researchers believe was the cause of autism in the past and what do they believe is the cause today?

**3.** Based on the results from only Parker and three other autistic children, why would parents want their autistic children to be treated with secretin?

## Newspaper Article

### A New Treatment for Autism?

Young Parker Beck, who was diagnosed as being autistic, had to see a doctor for his gastrointestinal problems. As part of a regular procedure for diagnosing these problems, Dr. Karoly Horvath, of the University of Maryland Medical Center, gave Parker an injection of a hormone called secretin. In the days following the injection of secretin, Victoria Beck, Parker's mother, noticed a dramatic reduction in Parker's autistic symptoms. Besides seeing an improvement in Parker's digestive problems, Victoria also noticed that Parker was sleeping through the night and even began saying words.

Encouraged by the improvements in Parker's behavior, Victoria persuaded Dr. Horvath to follow up and treat other children with secretin, which was extracted from the small intestine of pigs. Subsequently, Dr. Horvath published a report on three other autistic children who also seemed to have improved after injections of secretin.

After the popular television program "Dateline" reported on Parker's improvement, parents around the country began asking their doctors to treat their autistic children with injections of secretin.

Because of the sudden and widespread use of secretin, the National Institute of Child Health and Human Development quickly organized clinical trials to scientifically evaluate possible benefits of using secretin to reduce autistic symptoms.

One of the first such studies, by Dr. James W. Bodfish and his colleagues at the University of North Carolina, reported that injections of secretin caused some improvement in autistic children but the improvement was about the same as observed in children receiving a placebo or sugar pill. Dr. Adrian Sandler of Thoms Rehabilitation Hospital in Asheville said, "We have been unable to show any benefit from the secretin treatment." Another colleague added that, because both secretin and the placebo resulted in equal improvements, such improvement in symptoms probably resulted from the increased attention from both doctors and parents.

However, Dr. Bernard Rimland of the Autism Research Institute in San Diego downplayed the finding, saying that there were about a dozen other studies being done. Dr. Rimland remained very optimistic about the value of secretin in reducing autistic symptoms based on the observations of parents. (Adapted from Thomas H. Maugh II, *Los Angeles Times,* December 9, 1999, p. A1)

**4.** Why did the National Institute decide to evaluate the effects of secretin on autism?

**5.** Why might a secretin injection result in the same improvement as taking a placebo?

**6.** Why did Dr. Rimland downplay the negative results of the reported study?

*Try these InfoTrac search terms:* autism; secretin; clinical trials; placebo.

---

### Suggested answers to Newspaper Article questions

1. Autism is marked by especially abnormal or impaired development in social interactions, such as hiding to avoid people, not making eye contact, and not wanting to be touched, and by difficulties in communicating, such as grave problems in developing spoken language or in initiating conversations. Autistics are characterized by having very few activities and interests and spending long periods repeating the same behaviors (hand flapping).

2. In the past, researchers mistakenly believed that autism was caused by having "cold" or withdrawn parents. Today, researchers believe there are genetic and biological causes of autism.

3. At this writing, there is no medical treatment or cure for autism. Lacking medical treatment, many parents are desperate for any treatment that claims to reduce or cure autism.

4. The original finding that secretin helped autistic children was based on limited observations from only four children. The National Institute used a more reliable and scientific approach to determine if secretin really was a useful medical treatment for autism.

5. The parents' belief that their child is being treated for autism (not knowing if it's secretin or a placebo) may result in giving their child more attention, care, and support, which may itself improve an autistic child's behavior.

6. Dr. Rimland puts considerable faith in the observations of parents with autistic children. In addition, like many researchers, he isn't convinced by a single study but waits to see if other studies confirm the finding that secretin is no better than a placebo.

# Links to Learning

- WADSWORTH ONLINE PSYCHOLOGY STUDY CENTER

  **http://psychology.wadsworth.com**

  Quizzes, learning activities and exercises, a discussion forum, and hot links to Internet sites related to the history and practice of psychology, including:

- APA PSYCHNET

  **http://www.apa.org/**

  Join educators, scientists, doctors, and mental health practitioners at the richly layered Web site of the American Psychological Association. It's a very good place to start surfing!

- CYBERPSYCHLINK

  **http://cctr.umkc.edu/~dmartin/psych2.html**

  This index of psychology sites includes list servers, newsgroups, electronic journals, self-help links, software for psychologists, and information about the history and teaching of psychology.

- *POWERSTUDY™ CD BY ROD PLOTNIK & TOM DOYLE*

- *STUDY GUIDE TO ACCOMPANY INTRODUCTION TO PSYCHOLOGY, 6TH EDITION,* **by Matthew Enos**

  In Module 1 you'll be introduced to the "Effective Student Tips" that appear throughout the *Study Guide,* along with key terms, a detailed chapter outline with critical thinking questions, language enrichment tools, a special quiz for psychology majors, and a variety of helpful quizzes with their answers.

| Power Study™ |
| --- |
| **Check out CD: Module 4** |
| A. Genes & Evolution (book page 68) |
| B. Studying the Living Brain (book page 70) |
| **Check out CD: Module 10** |
| A. Operant Conditioning (book page 214) |
| E. Cognitive Learning (book page 223) |
| I. Application: Behavior Modification (book page 232) |

- *WEBTUTOR*

  WebTUTOR **http://webtutor.thomsonlearning.com**

  Visit this site for interactive versions of Study Guide features. Take a quiz, get your score—should you study a topic some more, or can you move on? For example, what is Sigmund Freud's relation to humanist psychology? Your professor's class syllabus and course calendar are also posted—you'll never have to get behind in class again!

- *INFOTRAC ONLINE LIBRARY*

   **http://www.infotrac-college.com**

  Use your password and then key in search terms such as those below to find popular and scientific articles on subjects covered in Module 1. Make the library work for you!

  | Behaviorism | Gestalt psychology | Minorities |
  | --- | --- | --- |
  | Psychiatry | Study habits | Procrastination |

- *PSYCHNOW!*

  CD for Macintosh and Windows includes a study guide, glossary, Web sites, and animations. For Module 1, see:

  Study Skills
  Critical Thinking in Psychology
  Psychology and Its History

*Use InfoTrac to search for topics mentioned in the following questions (e.g., alcoholism, psychological discrimination, stress management).*

**\*A. Definition & Goals**—How would you rank the four goals of psychology in terms of importance? (**Suggested answer page 619**)

**B. Modern Approaches**—How would psychologists use the six modern approaches to study whether alcoholism runs in families?

**C. Historical Approaches**—Do any of these historical approaches match your stereotype of what psychology is all about?

**\*D. Cultural Diversity: Early Discrimination**—Why would discriminatory practices exist in psychology, an area devoted to studying human behavior? (**Suggested answer page 619**)

**E. Research Focus: Taking Class Notes**—What could you do to improve your note-taking skills?

**F. Careers in Psychology**—If you're thinking about a career in psychology, what setting would you choose?

**G. Research Areas**—Which of the six subareas of psychology would you study to help people manage stress?

**\*H. Application: Study Skills**—What changes would you make to study most efficiently? (**Suggested answer page 619**)

\*These questions are answered in Appendix B.

**A. Answering Questions**     28
* SURVEY
* CASE STUDY
* EXPERIMENT

**B. Surveys**     29
* KIND OF INFORMATION
* DISADVANTAGES
* ADVANTAGES

**C. Case Study**     30
* KIND OF INFORMATION
* PERSONAL CASE STUDY: TESTIMONIAL
* ERROR AND BIAS

**D. Cultural Diversity: Use of Placebos**     31
* REMARKABLE TREATMENTS
* CONCLUSION: TESTIMONIALS AND PLACEBOS

**E. Correlation**     32
* DEFINITION
* CORRELATION COEFFICIENTS
* CORRELATION VERSUS CAUSATION
* CORRELATIONS AS CLUES
* CORRELATION AND PREDICTIONS

**F. Decisions about Doing Research**     34
* CHOOSING RESEARCH TECHNIQUES
* CHOOSING RESEARCH SETTINGS

**G. Scientific Method: Experiment**     36
* ADVANTAGES OF THE SCIENTIFIC METHOD
* CONDUCTING AN EXPERIMENT: SEVEN RULES
* CONCLUSION

**Concept Review**     38

**H. Research Focus: ADHD Controversies**     39
* CONTROVERSY: DIAGNOSIS
* CONTROVERSY: TREATMENT
* CONTROVERSY: LONG-TERM EFFECTS

**I. Application: Research Concerns**     40
* CONCERNS ABOUT BEING A SUBJECT
* CODE OF ETHICS
* ROLE OF DECEPTION
* ETHICS OF ANIMAL RESEARCH

**Summary Test**     42

**Critical Thinking**     44
* DOES FREQUENT SEX HELP MEN LIVE LONGER?

**Links to Learning**     45

## Several Controversies

**What is Dusty's problem?**

It was 5:00 in the morning when Dusty began throwing a fit. As if driven by an inner motor, all 50 pounds of him was flying around the room, wailing and kicking. This raging activity went on for about 30 minutes; then he headed downstairs for breakfast. While his mother was busy in the kitchen, Dusty grabbed a box of cereal and kicked it around the room, spreading cereal everywhere. When his mother told him to clean up the mess, he got the plastic dustpan but began picking it apart, piece by piece. Next he grabbed three rolls of toilet paper and unraveled them around the house. By then, it was only 7:30. Dusty had not been given his pill because he was seeing his doctor at 4:00 that day (adapted from *Time,* July 18, 1994).

Seven-year-old Dusty has been diagnosed with ADHD.

Seven-year-old Dusty has a behavioral problem that has been surrounded with controversy. Dusty was diagnosed as being hyperactive, a problem that is officially called attention-deficit/hyperactivity disorder, or ADHD (American Psychiatric Association, 1994).

*Attention-deficit/hyperactivity disorder,* or *ADHD,* is not diagnosed by any medical tests but on the basis of the occurrence of certain behavioral problems. A child must have six or more symptoms of inattention, such as making careless mistakes in schoolwork, not following instructions, and being easily distracted, and six or more symptoms of hyperactivity, such as fidgeting, leaving classroom seat, running about when should not, and talking excessively. These symptoms should have been present from an early age, persisted for at least six months, and contributed to maladaptive development.

One controversy surrounding ADHD involves diagnosis. Since ADHD is based not on medical tests but rather on the occurrence of certain behavioral problems, how can children with ADHD be distinguished from those who are naturally outgoing and rambunctious (Sciutto et al., 2000)? Because of this difficulty, the American Academy of Pediatrics issued its first guidelines for diagnosing ADHD (Tanner, 2000). These guidelines stressed that, before the diagnosis of ADHD is made, a number of the symptoms described above should be present for at least six months. The guidelines focused on children aged 6 to 12 because there isn't sufficient evidence for making the diagnosis of ADHD at earlier ages. These guidelines were issued in the hope of preventing merely rambunctious youngsters from being overmedicated while ensuring that children with ADHD get the help they need (Tanner, 2000).

To help control his ADHD, Dusty is given a drug that is a relatively powerful stimulant, called Ritalin (*WRIT-ah-lin*). Ritalin's effects are similar to those of another stimulant, amphetamine. For reasons researchers do not yet understand, stimulants, such as Ritalin and amphetamine, decrease activity in children, and Ritalin has become the most popular medical treatment of ADHD (Shute et al., 2000; Spencer et al., 2000).

Perhaps the major questions surrounding the use of Ritalin concern whether it is being overprescribed, whether it is the most effective treatment, and how long a child with ADHD should remain on the drug (Zito et al., 2000). In addition, Ritalin, especially in larger doses, does have side effects that may include loss of appetite and problems with sleeping. A related question is whether children with ADHD should be kept on a diet free of artificial dyes, sweeteners, or sugar, which some parents claim worsen the symptoms. We'll answer these questions in this module.

We're going to use Dusty's problem with ADHD to show how researchers pursue the four goals of psychology that we discussed in Module 1. In Dusty's case, the four goals are (1) to describe Dusty's symptoms, (2) to explain their causes, (3) to predict their occurrence, and (4) to control Dusty's behavior through some behavioral therapy or drug treatment.

## Rhino Horn and Magnets

**Can beliefs cure like real medicine?**

One interesting aspect of trying to control unwanted symptoms with a drug treatment is that sometimes the drug is not really a drug because it has no proven medical effects. For example, in many parts of Asia, people take powdered rhino horn because they believe that it is a medicine for treating hundreds of physical and mental problems. Similarly, in the United States, people are spending $300 million annually on wearing tiny magnets to decrease pain in joints and muscles, even though there is no reliable scientific evidence that magnets work. The use of rhino horn and tiny magnets, both questionable medical treatments, raises the interesting question of how much one's mind or one's beliefs contribute to the development or treat-

Can rhino horn cure all kinds of problems?

ment of physical symptoms. We'll discuss methods that researchers use to decide whether the effectiveness of a treatment is due to a drug's medical effect or the person's beliefs.

## What's Coming

Our main focus in this module is to explore the methods that researchers use to answer questions, such as how to treat ADHD and why placebos work. Specifically, we'll discuss the advantages and disadvantages of three major research methods—surveys, case studies, and experiments. We'll explain which research procedures can identify cause-and-effect relationships and which cannot. We begin with an overview of the three major research methods that psychologists use to answer questions.

**How do researchers study ADHD?**

As you look at the photo of Dusty on the right, you see a young boy ready to explode into an uncontrolled burst of activity, a major symptom of ADHD. However, 25 years ago, ADHD was a relatively small problem in the United States, while today it is the most commonly diagnosed behavioral problem in children. ADHD is surrounded with controversy. For example, its name has been changed from hyperactivity to minimal brain damage to attention-deficit disorder and most recently to attention-deficit/hyperactivity disorder (ADHD). The diagnosis of ADHD is not straightforward, since it is based on behavioral symptoms rather than medical tests. The proposed causes of ADHD

Researchers use three different research methods to study ADHD.

are many, including various genetic, hormonal, neurological, and dietary factors. Finally, the most popular treatment of ADHD involves giving children a stimulant drug.

In the middle of these controversies are parents like Dusty's mother, who after dealing with a hyperactive and impulsive child from an early age, have little doubt that ADHD exists and that Ritalin decreases hyperactivity and impulsivity. At the same time, critics warn that ADHD may be misdiagnosed or overdiagnosed and that while Ritalin may reduce activity it may fail to improve academic performance (Jensen, 1999).

As researchers work to resolve all the controversies surrounding ADHD, they are using three major research methods—survey, case study, and experiment.

### Survey

Suppose you wish to know how many children have ADHD, whether it occurs more in boys or girls, which treatment is the most popular, and how many children continue to have problems when they become adults. Researchers obtain this information with surveys.

A *survey* is a way to obtain information by asking many individuals—either person to person, by telephone, or by mail—to answer a fixed set of questions about particular subjects.

The disadvantage of a survey is that such information can contain errors or be biased because people may not remember accurately or answer truthfully. The advantage of a survey is that it is an efficient way to obtain much information from a large number of people.

But if researchers wanted to know more about a particular person, they would use a case study.

### Case Study

Suppose you wish to know in greater detail about how a single child, such as Dusty, developed ADHD, performs in school, makes friends, plays team sports, and deals with everyday problems. Or suppose you wish to know about how a family copes with a child who has ADHD. For example, one mother said, "Ritalin doesn't take away the problems at all. It just helps him focus on what he's doing. You can talk to him; he can get his school work done. It still takes him a long time to get things done. He's still behind, emotionally and socially" (*San Diego Tribune,* November 27, 1989). When another mother was told that sugar doesn't increase activity, she replied, "I say, they're nuts! Where were they last Christmas when my sons ate candy canes and green frosting for days and never slept!" (*Los Angeles Times,* February 9, 1994). Researchers gather in-depth data about a particular individual with a case study.

A *case study* is an in-depth analysis of the thoughts, feelings, beliefs, experiences, behaviors, or problems of a single individual.

One disadvantage of a case study is that its detailed information about a particular person, such as Dusty, may not apply to other children with ADHD.

One advantage of a case study is that its detailed information allows greater understanding of a particular person's life.

But if researchers wanted to establish whether sugar really increases activity in children with ADHD, they would use an experiment.

### Experiment

Suppose you thought that sugar or artificial dyes caused hyperactivity in your child and you wondered if this were true. For example, based on case studies and parents' reports, one researcher thought that certain artificial dyes, chemicals, and sweeteners increased the activity and impulsive behavior of children diagnosed with ADHD (Feingold, 1975). When researchers want to identify a cause-and-effect relationship, such as whether sugar increases activity, they would use an experiment.

An *experiment* is a method for identifying cause-and-effect relationships by following a set of rules and guidelines that minimize the possibility of error, bias, and chance occurrences.

A disadvantage of an experiment is that information obtained in one experimental situation or laboratory setting may not apply to other situations. An experiment's primary advantage is that it has the greatest potential for identifying cause-and-effect relationships with less error and bias than either surveys or case studies.

**Which method is best?**

Very often, researchers use all three research methods—survey, case study, and experiment—because each provides a different kind of information. Surveys provide information about fixed questions from a large number of people. Case studies give in-depth information about a single person. Experiments point to cause-and-effect relationships. We'll discuss the advantages and disadvantages of each of the three methods, beginning with surveys.

---

## Kind of Information

---

**What do surveys tell us?**

Almost every day the media report some new survey. Although surveys tell us what others believe or how they behave, survey questions can be written to bias the answers; moreover, people may not always answer truthfully (Schwartz, 1999). For example, how many people do you think always wash their hands after going to the bathroom? We'll sample some surveys and then discuss their problems.

### Do you wash your hands?

Although 94% of the people surveyed by telephone said that they always washed their hands after going to the bathroom, direct observation of 6,333 people in five major cities found that only 68% really do and that women (74%) washed their hands more often than men (61%) (Manning, 1996).

### What's your biggest worry?

A survey of 251,323 college freshmen (class of 2000) reported that 66% are worried about not having the money to finish college (Weiss, 1997). In a random sample of 1,003 adults in 50 states, 60% agreed that lying is sometimes necessary, especially to protect someone's feelings (Smiley, 2000).

### How many children are diagnosed with ADHD?

Recent surveys report that about 4–12% of United States school-age children are diagnosed with ADHD (Allen, 2000); about 30–50% of children with ADHD continue to have symptoms as adults (Schweitzer et al., 2000); the incidence of ADHD in China is about the same as in the United States, but France and England have one-tenth that of the United States, and Japan is just beginning to study ADHD (Leung et al., 1996).

These examples show that surveys provide a great deal of useful information. However, surveys have potential problems with accuracy (hand-washing survey) as well as with wording of questions and who asks the questions.

---

## Disadvantages

### How questions are worded

You may be surprised to learn that surveys may get very different results depending on how questions are worded. Here are two examples:

QUESTION: "Would you say that **industry** contributes more or less to air pollution than **traffic**?"
**Traffic** contributes more: **24%**
**Industry** contributes more: 57%

QUESTION: "Would you say that **traffic** contributes more or less to air pollution than **industry**?"
**Traffic** contributes more: **45%**
**Industry** contributes more: 32%

These two examples indicate that the way questions are phrased and the way the possible answers are ordered can greatly influence people's responses and, in this case, produce opposite results (reported in *U.S. News & World Report,* Dec. 4, 1995, p. 55).

### Who asks the questions

You may also be surprised to learn that the sex or race of the questioner can also affect how people answer the questions.

QUESTION: "The problems faced by blacks were brought on by blacks themselves."
When the interviewer was **white, 62%** of whites who were interviewed agreed.
When the interviewer was **black, 46%** of whites who were interviewed agreed.

These two examples indicate that when asked about sensitive or emotional issues, people take into account the race of the interviewer and tend to give socially acceptable rather than honest answers (*U.S. News & World Report,* Dec. 4, 1995, p. 55).

We can conclude that surveys may be biased because people may not answer questions truthfully, may give socially acceptable answers, or feel pressured to answer in certain ways. Also, surveys can be biased by how questions are worded and by interviewing a group of people who are not representative of the general population (Schwartz, 1999). Despite these potential problems, surveys do have advantages.

---

## Advantages

While guarding against error and bias, surveys can be a useful research tool to quickly and efficiently collect information on behaviors, beliefs, experiences, and attitudes from a large sample of people and can compare answers from various ethnic, age, socioeconomic, and cultural groups.

For example, surveys suggest that ADHD interferes with performance in school settings, decreases the chances of graduating from high school, and may lead to conduct disorder problems in adolescence as well as continued problems in adulthood (Biederman et al., 1996).

Because surveys indicate that children with ADHD have major problems in school settings, psychologists are developing methods for improving performance. These methods include: teaching ADHD children how to organize their work; giving them constant feedback on reaching their goals; and starting programs that train teachers and families to work together to help ADHD children control their disruptive behaviors (DuPaul & Eckert, 1997). Thus, another advantage of surveys is their ability to identify problems and evaluate treatment programs.

However, if researchers wish to focus on a particular individual rather than a group, they would use a case study.

# C. Case Study

### What's a case study?

Sometimes researchers answer questions by studying a single individual in great detail, which is called a case study.

A *case study* is an in-depth analysis of the thoughts, feelings, beliefs, or behaviors of a single person.

We'll use a different case study, this time focusing on Nick, who is now 11 years old and diagnosed as having ADHD. From the age of 3, Nick has had problems paying attention and completing tasks. Because he was so easily distracted, Nick needed to be called as many as 19 times before he answered,

couldn't seem to finish tying his shoes, couldn't pay attention in school, and alternated between bouts of frustration and being an angel. In the first grade, Nick was put on Ritalin, and it made an immediate difference. He called it a "concentrating medicine," and although he still has academic problems, he can better focus on and complete a project (Leavy, 1996). This case study tells us that Ritalin helped Nick concentrate but only partially solved his academic problems. Sometimes case studies help answer questions, but as you'll see next, case studies can also result in wrong or biased answers.

---

**Personal Case Study: Testimonial**

### Why did parents make a mistake?

Observations from case studies may be misinterpreted if the observer has preconceived notions of what to look for. For example, beginning in the mid-1970s, parents were told that food with artificial additives, dyes, and preservatives could cause hyperactivity in children (Feingold, 1975). Shortly after, parents reported that, yes indeed, artificial additives caused a sudden increase in restlessness and irritability in their hyperactive children (Feingold, 1975). The parents' reports and beliefs that additives cause hyperactivity are examples of another kind of case study, called a testimonial.

A *testimonial* is a statement in support of a particular viewpoint based on detailed observations of a person's own personal experience.

However, contrary to the parents' testimonials, researchers have generally found that amounts of artificial additives within a normal

| Average Ratings of Parents and Teachers | |
| --- | --- |
| 13.5 | Placebo |
| 13 | Aspartame |

range did not affect hyperactivity (Kinsbourne, 1994). More recently, there are testimonials from parents that children with attention deficit disorder who ate foods with an artificial sweetener, aspartame (Nutrasweet), showed noticeable increases in symptoms.

To test the accuracy of these recent testimonials, researchers asked teachers and parents to evaluate the behaviors and cognitive functions of children who were given a capsule containing either ten times their normal daily intake of aspartame or a placebo. Neither parent, child, nor teacher knew if the capsule contained aspartame or the placebo. As the figure on the left shows, there was little or no difference between the effect of aspartame (Nutrasweet) and that of the placebo on the behaviors or cognitive functions of children with attention deficit disorder (Shaywitz et al., 1994). Although testimonials from parents, friends, or peers can be very convincing, we'll point out two problems that make testimonials especially susceptible to error.

---

**Error and Bias**

### What's the problem with testimonials?

One of the major problems with testimonials is that they are based on our personal observations, which have great potential for error and bias. For example, if parents reported that sweeteners increased their son's activity, we would have to rule out personal beliefs and self-fulfilling prophecies.

**Personal beliefs.** If parents hear that artificial sweeteners may cause physical or psychological problems, they may interpret their child's problems as caused by artificial sweeteners. Because of biased perceptions, parents may overlook other potential causes, such as frustration, anger, or changes in the child's environment, and make the error of focusing only on artificial sweeteners. If we believe strongly in something, it may bias our perception and cause us to credit an unrelated treatment or event as the reason for some change.

Parents mistakenly believed that artificial sweeteners caused ADHD.

**Self-fulfilling prophecy.** If parents believe that artificial sweeteners cause problems, they may behave in ways—being more strict or less sympathetic—that cause the problems to occur. This phenomenon is called a self-fulfilling prophecy.

A *self-fulfilling prophecy* involves having a strong belief or making a statement (prophecy) about a future behavior and then acting, usually unknowingly, to fulfill or carry out the behavior.

If we strongly believe that something is going to happen, we may unknowingly behave in such a way as to make it happen (Madon et al., 1997). Self-fulfilling prophecies reinforce testimonials and thus keep our biased beliefs alive.

The main disadvantage of testimonials is their high potential for error and bias. But they have the advantage of providing detailed information that may point to potential answers or lead to future studies. We'll discuss how case studies are used in developmental research in Module 18 and clinical research in Module 21.

Next, we'll discuss how testimonials are a popular source of information, especially when we are talking about placebos.

## Remarkable Treatments

**Can your beliefs reduce pain?**

If you happen to take a prescription drug, read its brochure, which discusses what the drug does, its side effects, and, most interesting, how its effectiveness has compared to a placebo.

A *placebo* is some intervention, such as taking a pill, receiving an injection, or undergoing an operation, that resembles medical therapy but that, in fact, has no medical effects.

A *placebo effect* is a change in the patient's illness that is attributable to an imagined treatment rather than to a medical treatment.

For example, the results of studies involving 3,000 men showed that a new drug (Uprima) allowed about 56% to have erections and engage in intercourse. However, about 35% of the men reported equally good results from taking another pill that proved to be a sugar pill or placebo (Cowley, 2000b). In these studies,

### Placebo

Placebos are sugar pills.

none of the men who reported problems with impotency knew whether they had been given the drug or a placebo. Researchers estimate that between 35 and 75% of patients benefit from taking placebos or dummy drugs (Talbot, 2000).

Researchers have proposed that placebos work by reducing tension and distress and by creating powerful self-fulfilling prophecies so that individuals think and behave as if the drug, actually a placebo, will work (Brown, 1997). Self-fulfilling prophecies are strongest and placebos are most effective when they are administered by trusted and sincere professionals who convince their patients of the drugs' effectiveness, even though the "medications" are actually placebos (Madon et al., 1997).

Perhaps the most convincing evidence for the effectiveness of placebos comes from testimonials, which claim that taking various vitamins, animal parts, or herbs cure a wide variety of symptoms. We'll review some of the more common placebos in use worldwide.

### Rhino Horn

Millions of people in China, Thailand, South Korea, and Taiwan claim that rhino horn is an aphrodisiac, will increase their sexual desire and stamina, and is a cure for everything from headaches and nosebleeds to high fevers and typhoid. However, the basic ingredient of rhino horn is compacted hair (keratin), which has no proven medicinal powers (*Sierra,* November/ December 1989). A single rhino horn weighing about 4 to 5 pounds will bring from $25,000 to $50,000 on the black market. In the early 1900s, there were about 1 million rhinos. By 1994, poachers had reduced the total number of rhinos to about 10,000, as the desire for rhino horns continued to grow (Berger & Cunningham, 1994).

### Bear Gallbladders

In parts of Asia, a very popular "medicine" to treat many kinds of physical problems is a tablet made from bear gallbladders. Some traders are substituting pig gallbladders for bears' and customers are none the wiser, since bear or pig gallbladders are nothing more than placebos (*Time,* November 4, 1991). The price of a single bear gallbladder has risen to an amazing $18,000, and there is now an illegal global trade in animal parts. Poachers threaten some endangered species of bears, such as the grizzly bear in the United States.

### Tiger Bones

In the early 1900s, there were 100,000 tigers in Asia, but by 1994 there were fewer than 5,000. The chief reason for this precipitous decline is the use of tiger bones to treat ulcers, typhoid, malaria, dysentery, and burns, to increase longevity, to guard newborn babies from infection, and to cure devil possession (Friend, 1997b). In addition, wealthy Taiwanese pay $320 for a bowl of tiger penis soup that is thought to increase flagging libidos (Nagarahole, 1994). Tiger bones and tiger penises function as powerful placebos in traditional Asian medicine.

### Magnets

Beginning in the early 1990s, athletes reported a decrease in pain after wearing small magnet pads over their painful injuries. Such testimonials resulted in millions of dollars in sales for magnet pads. Although several earlier studies supported such claims, a recent study that was better designed to eliminate error and bias found no difference in pain reduction between magnets and placebos (Christopher, 2000; Collacott et al., 2000). These researchers doubt that magnetic pads can reduce pain.

## Conclusion: Testimonials and Placebos

**Why are placebos so popular?**

Perhaps the main reason placebos are used worldwide, even to the point of destroying certain wild animals, is that the placebo's beneficial "medical" effects are supported by countless testimonials. For example, compared to the results of surveys, testimonials are much more convincing because they are based on real-life experiences of friends, peers, and parents, who are honest and believable. However, it is common for people, honest and trustworthy, to unknowingly make a mistake and conclude that a rhino horn, bear gallbladder, tiger bone, or magnet is producing a beneficial "medical" effect when the beneficial effect is actually being caused by the individual's mental thought influencing the body's functioning (H. Brody, 2000).

As you'll see next, people often make mistakes about the effect of placebos because there is often no way to figure out what causes what.

# E. Correlation

## Definition

Research suggests that ADHD has a genetic basis.

**What's a correlation?**

The photo on the left shows Dusty running wild in a supermarket. Researchers would like to know if Dusty's hyperactivity has a genetic basis. One way to identify genetic factors is to study genetic twins, since they share 100% of their genes in common. Suppose you were studying the occurrence of ADHD in identical male twins and found that, about 70% of the time, if one identical twin had ADHD so did the second twin (Barkley, 1998). This strong relationship among behaviors in identical twins suggests a genetic basis for ADHD. Such a relationship is called a correlation.

A *correlation* is an association or relationship between the occurrence of two or more events.

For example, if one twin has hyperactivity, a correlation will tell us the likelihood that the other twin also has hyperactivity. The likelihood or strength of a relationship between two events is called a correlation coefficient.

A *correlation coefficient* is a number that indicates the strength of a relationship between two or more events: the closer the number is to −1.00 or +1.00, the greater is the strength of the relationship.

We'll explain correlation coefficients in more detail because they can be confusing.

## Correlation Coefficients

**What are these numbers?**

There are two major points to understand about correlations:

First, a correlation means there is an association between two or more events. For example, there is an association, or correlation, between the sex of a child and the occurrence of ADHD; two to three times more boys are diagnosed with ADHD than girls.

A second point to understand about correlations is that the strength of the relationship or association is measured by a number called a correlation coefficient. Because the correlation coefficient ranges from +1.00 to −1.00, its meaning can be confusing. In the boxes on the right, we'll describe what correlation coefficients mean, beginning at the top of the table with a +1.00.

+1.00

+0.05

0.00

−0.50

−1.00

If each of 20 identical pairs showed equal levels of hyperactivity, the correlation coefficient would be positive and perfect and would be indicated by a +1.00 correlation coefficient.

A **perfect positive correlation coefficient** of +1.00 means that an increase in one event is always matched by an equal increase in a second event.

That is, a coefficient of +1.00 means that if one twin of an identical pair has hyperactivity, the other twin always has hyperactivity.

---

If some identical pairs but not all 20 pairs were similar in hyperactivity, the result would be a positive correlation coefficient, which can range from +0.01 to +0.99.

A **positive correlation coefficient** indicates that as one event tends to increase, the second event tends to, but does not always, increase.

As the coefficient increases from +0.01 to +0.99, it indicates a strengthening of the relationship between the occurrence of two events.

---

If one twin of 20 pairs showed hyperactivity while the other twin sometimes did and sometimes did not show hyperactivity, the result would be no association, or zero correlation (0.00).

A **zero correlation** indicates that there is no relationship between the occurrence of one event and the occurrence of a second event.

---

If, in some identical pairs, one twin showed an increase while the other showed an equivalent decrease in activity, the result would be a negative correlation coefficient, which can range from −0.01 to −0.99.

A **negative correlation coefficient** indicates that as one event tends to increase, the second event tends to, but does not always, decrease.

As the coefficient increases in absolute magnitude from −0.01 to −0.99, it indicates a strengthening in the relationship of one event increasing and the other decreasing.

---

If one twin of 20 identical pairs showed hyperactivity and the second twin always showed decreased activity, the correlation coefficient would be negative and perfect and would be indicated by a −1.00 correlation coefficient.

A **perfect negative correlation coefficient** of −1.00 means that an increase in one event is always matched by an equal decrease in a second event.

That is, a coefficient of −1.00 means that if one twin of an identical pair has hyperactivity, the other twin always has decreased activity.

The media often headline interesting findings: Thin people live longer than heavier ones; overweight people earn less money than their peers; school uniforms decrease violence. Before you assume that one event causes the other, such as thinness causing one to live longer, you must check to see what researchers did. If researchers measured

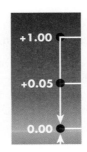

only the relationship between two events, such as thinness and length of life, then it's a correlation. In fact, all three findings reported here are correlations. The reason you should check whether some finding is a correlation is that correlations have one very important limitation: They do not identify what causes what. For example, let's look closely at the findings about school uniforms and student behavior problems.

## Correlation versus Causation

The biggest mistake people make in discussing correlations is assuming that they show cause and effect. For instance, many school districts are considering the adoption of mandatory school uniforms because wearing uniforms was related to decreased problems with students' behavior. The graph on the right shows that wearing school uniforms was related to or correlated with a large decrease in carrying weapons, fighting, assaults, and vandalism. Since an increase in wearing uniforms was associated with a drop in problems, this is a negative correlation.

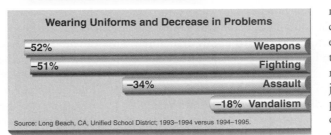

**Wearing Uniforms and Decrease in Problems**

−52% Weapons
−51% Fighting
−34% Assault
−18% Vandalism

Source: Long Beach, CA, Unified School District; 1993–1994 versus 1994–1995.

Although the correlation between wearing uniforms and decreased problems was impressive, you must keep in mind that correlations,

no matter how impressive, cannot indicate a cause-and-effect relationship. To make the point that correlations do not indicate cause and effect, just remember that over the past 26 years, there is a +0.88 correlation between which professional football team (American or National League) wins the Super Bowl and whether the stock market rises or falls. Although +0.88 is a very high positive correlation, it indicates only a relationship; winning a Super Bowl could not possibly cause a rising or falling stock market.

Although correlations do not indicate cause-and-effect relationships, they do serve two very useful purposes: Correlations help predict behavior and also point to where to look for possible causes, as has happened in the case of lung cancer.

Does wearing uniforms decrease school problems?

## Correlation as Clues

Although cigarette smoke was positively correlated with lung cancer (right graph), it was unknown whether smoking was the *cause* of cancer. Acting on the clue that some ingredient of cigarette smoke might trigger the development of lung cancer, researchers rubbed tar, an ingredient of cigarette smoke, on the skin of animals. After repeated applications over a period of time, the animals developed cancerous growths. This research proved that

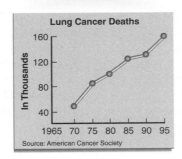

**Lung Cancer Deaths**

In Thousands
160
120
80
40

1965 70 75 80 85 90 95
Source: American Cancer Society

tar could cause cancer. More recently, researchers discovered that one particular ingredient of cigarette smoke (benzo[a]pyrene) turns off a gene that normally suppresses tumors. When that particular gene is turned off by cigarette smoke, lung cancer develops (Sozzi et al., 1996). In this case, correlations told researchers where to look for causes of lung cancer. In other cases, correlations help predict behavior.

## Correlation and Predictions

One way to predict how well students will do in academic settings is by looking at their IQ scores. For example, there is a reasonably high correlation, from +0.60 to +0.70, between IQ scores and performance in academic settings (Anastasi & Urbina, 1997). Thus, we would predict that individuals who score high on IQ scores have the skills to do well in college. However, IQ scores are only relatively good predictors for any single individual because doing well in college involves not only academic skills but

Do IQ scores predict academic success?

many other motivational, emotional, and personality factors that we'll discuss in Module 13.

So far, we have discussed the advantages and disadvantages of two major research methods—surveys and case studies—that psychologists use to answer questions. We have also explained a statistical procedure—correlation—that shows the strength of relationships and points to possible causes of behaviors. Next, we'll describe the other kinds of research decisions that psychologists make as they try to understand and explain behavior.

## Choosing Research Techniques

**What's the best technique for answering a question?**

You are constantly asking questions about human behavior, such as "Why did she say that?" or "Why did he behave that way?" Similarly, psychologists are continually asking questions, such as "What percentage of the population is gay?" or "Of what use are SAT scores?" or "How do we diagnose ADHD?"or "Does a specific gene cause obesity?" After asking one of these questions, psychologists must decide which research technique or procedure best answers it. We'll describe four different techniques for finding answers.

### Questionnaires and Interviews

**What percentage of the population is gay?** This question is often answered by doing a survey using interviews or questionnaires.

An *interview* is a technique for obtaining information by asking questions, ranging from open-ended to highly structured, about a subject's behaviors and attitudes, usually in a one-on-one situation.

A *questionnaire* is a technique for obtaining information by asking subjects to read a list of written questions and check off specific answers.

You might think this question about what percentage of the population is gay would be relatively easy to answer. But three different surveys have reported three different answers: 2.3%, 10%, and 22% (Billy et al., 1993; Janus & Janus, 1993; Kinsey et al., 1948). These different answers resulted from surveys using differently worded questions, different groups of people, and different kinds of interview techniques. As we discussed earlier, when it comes to surveys on personal issues—such as Did you vote? Do you wear seat belts? Do you go to church? or What is your sexual preference?—people may give the desirable rather than the honest answer.

### Standardized Tests

**Of what use are SAT scores?** The standardized test that you may be most familiar with is the SAT, which is given to many high school seniors to help predict how they will perform in college. Each year only 0.05% of students who take the SAT score a perfect 1600, a feat accomplished for the first time in 1997 by twins, Courtney and Chris (photo on left).

A *standardized test* is a technique to obtain information by administering a psychological test that has been standardized, which means that the test has been given to hundreds of people and shown to reliably measure thought patterns, personality traits, emotions, or behaviors.

One disadvantage of standardized tests, such as the SAT, is that they may be biased toward a certain group of people. One advantage of standardized tests is that they allow comparisons to be made across schools, states, and groups of people (Anastasi & Urbina, 1997). Another well-known standardized test is the IQ test, which we'll discuss in Module 13.

Courtney and Chris scored perfect 1600s on the SAT.

### Laboratory Experiments

**How do we diagnose ADHD?** As of this writing, the diagnosis of ADHD is based primarily on behavioral symptoms, which are less reliable than medical tests. For this reason, researchers are currently searching for more reliable tests to diagnose ADHD. To identify such tests, researchers are using laboratory experiments.

A *laboratory experiment* is a technique to gather information about the brain, genes, or behavior with the least error and bias by using a controlled environment that allows careful observation and measurement.

Can a laboratory or psychological test be used to diagnose ADHD?

For example, in the photo on the right is an 11-year-old boy who is believed to have ADHD. He is taking a laboratory test that involves pressing a key when he sees a certain star on the screen. In addition, researchers took pictures of his brain (discussed in Module 4) before and after he received Ritalin. By combining these laboratory tests, researchers believe they may be on the track of identifying a more reliable method to diagnose ADHD (Teicher, 2000).

### Animal Models

**Does a specific gene cause obesity?** Over one-third of the adult population in the United States is now overweight, which may lead to serious medical problems, such as heart disease and high blood pressure. To understand the physiological causes of obesity, researchers are using animal models (Foster et al., 1997).

An *animal model* involves examining or manipulating some behavioral, genetic, or physiological factor that closely approximates some human problem, disease, or condition.

For example, researchers have identified a gene in mice that is involved in obesity (Gura, 1997). In the photo, an obese mouse on the left without the gene is compared to a normal mouse on the right. One advantage of the animal model is that it answers questions about physiological factors that cannot be investigated in humans.

Genetically altered mice are used to study obesity.

Deciding which one or combination of these four research techniques to use depends on the kind of question being asked. As you'll see next, the kind of question also influences which research setting to use.

## Choosing Research Settings

**Which problems do children with ADHD have?**

In trying to understand the kinds of problems faced by children with ADHD, psychologists study these children in different research settings, which may include observing them in the home, in the classroom, on the playground, or at their individual work. In addition, researchers may try to find the causes of ADHD by using different research settings, which may include studying children in the laboratory, hospital, or clinic. All these research settings can be grouped under either laboratory or naturalistic environments. We'll explain each setting and compare their advantages and disadvantages, beginning with more naturalistic environments.

### Naturalistic Setting

Parents and teachers want to know if ADHD children have different problems at home (photo below) than in school. Researchers answer this question by studying ADHD children in different naturalistic settings (home versus school) (Allen, 2000).

Does this ADHD child have different problems in school than at home?

A *naturalistic setting* is a relatively normal environment in which researchers gather information by observing individuals' behaviors without attempting to change or control the situation.

For example, observations of children with ADHD in school settings indicate that they have difficulty remaining in their seats, don't pay attention to the teacher, don't complete their projects, can't sit still, get into trouble, are rude to other students, and get angry when they don't get their way. Parents report that, at home, ADHD children do not respond when called, throw tantrums when frustrated, and have periods of great activity (Hancock, 1996; Henker & Whalen, 1989). Based on these naturalistic observations, researchers and pediatricians developed a list of primary symptoms of ADHD (Tanner, 2000). Similarly, psychologists study how normal people behave in different naturalistic settings, including schools, workplaces, college dormitories, bars, sports arenas, and homeless shelters. One problem with naturalistic observations is that the psychologists' own beliefs or values may bias their observations and cause them to misperceive or misinterpret behaviors. One advantage of naturalistic observations is the opportunity to study behaviors in real-life situations and environments, which cannot or would not be duplicated in the laboratory.

**Case studies.** As we discussed earlier, a single individual may be studied in his or her natural environment, and this is called a case study. The case study approach is often used in clinical psychology to understand the development of a personality or psychological problem or, in developmental psychology, to examine a person's behavior across his or her life span.

One *disadvantage* of a case study is that the information obtained is unique to an individual and may not apply to, or help us understand, the behaviors of others. One *advantage* of a case study is that psychologists can obtain detailed descriptions and insights into aspects of an individual's complex life and behaviors that cannot be obtained in other ways.

As you can see, naturalistic settings are very useful for observing how individuals behave in relatively normal environments. However, since naturalistic settings are uncontrolled and many things happen, researchers find it difficult to identify what causes what. For this reason, researchers may have to answer some questions in a more controlled setting, such as a laboratory or clinic.

### Laboratory Setting

Is there something different about the brains of children with ADHD? Questions about the brain are usually answered under very controlled conditions, such as in a laboratory setting.

A *laboratory setting* involves studying individuals under systematic and controlled conditions, with many of the real-world influences eliminated.

For example, researchers used special techniques (MRI brain scans, p. 70) that actually took pictures of the living brains of boys with and without ADHD. Researchers focused on an area called the basal ganglia (shown below in red) because it is involved in paying attention, which is difficult for ADHD children. In boys without ADHD, Ritalin caused decreased activity in the basal ganglia. However, in boys with ADHD, Ritalin caused increased activity in the basal ganglia and increased attention (Gabrieli, 1998). Researchers believe that this is one of the first laboratory tests to clearly distinguish children with and without ADHD.

Researchers use laboratory settings to study and identify a wide range of psychological and biological factors involved in motivation, emotion, learning, memory, drug use, sleep, intelligence, and mental disorders.

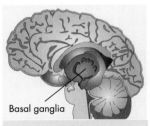

Basal ganglia

Is part of the brain (basal ganglia) involved in ADHD?

One disadvantage of laboratory settings is that they may be so controlled or artificial that their results are not always transferable to, or meaningful for, real-life situations. However, one advantage of the laboratory setting is that psychologists can carefully control and manipulate one or more treatments while reducing error or bias from other situational or environmental factors.

Psychologists may use both naturalistic and laboratory settings to obtain a broader understanding of some behavior or problem, such as ADHD (Jensen, 1999).

Researchers may combine the advantages of naturalistic and laboratory settings to identify cause-and-effect relationships. That's what happened when psychologists answered the difficult question: Does Ritalin help children with ADHD?

---
## Advantages of the Scientific Method
---

**How do researchers reduce error and bias?**

There have been many different treatments, including diets, vitamins, drugs, and behavior therapy, that claimed to help children with ADHD, such as Dusty (right photo). To discover which of these claims were valid, researchers followed a general approach called the scientific method.

The *scientific method* is an approach of gathering information and answering questions so that errors and biases are minimized.

Remember that information from surveys, case studies, and testimonials has considerable potential for error and bias. Remember too that information from correlations can suggest, but not pinpoint, cause-and-effect relationships. One way to both reduce error

It takes 7 rules to do an experiment on ADHD.

and bias and identify cause-and-effect relationships is to do an experiment.

An *experiment* is a method of identifying cause-and-effect relationships by following a set of rules and guidelines that minimize the possibility of error, bias, and chance occurrences.

An experiment, which is an example of using the scientific method, is the most powerful method for finding what causes what. We will divide an experiment into seven rules that are intended to reduce error and bias and identify the cause of an effect.

---
## Conducting an Experiment: Seven Rules
---

**Why seven rules?**

Some researchers and parents claimed that diets without sugar, artificial colors, and additives reduced ADHD symptoms, but most of these claims proved false because the rules to reduce error had not been followed (Kinsbourne, 1994). Here are seven rules that reduce error and bias and that researchers follow when conducting an experiment.

## Rule 1: Ask

Every experiment begins with one or more specific questions that are changed into specific hypotheses.

A *hypothesis* is an educated guess about some phenomenon and is stated in precise, concrete language to rule out any confusion or error in the meaning of its terms.

> **Hypothesis:**
> Ritalin will decrease negative classroom behaviors of children diagnosed with ADHD.

Researchers develop different hypotheses based on their own observations or previous research findings. Following this first rule, researchers change the general question— Does Ritalin help children with ADHD?—into a very concrete hypothesis: Ritalin will decrease the negative classroom behaviors of children with ADHD.

## Rule 2: Identify

After researchers have made their hypothesis, they identify a treatment that will be administered to the subjects. This treatment is called the independent variable.

The *independent variable* is a treatment or something that the researcher controls or manipulates.

The independent variable may be a single treatment, such as a single drug dose, or various levels of the same treatment, such as different doses of the same drug.

> **Ritalin**
>
> **Independent Variable:**
>
> Drug treatment

In our experiment, the independent variable is administering three different doses of Ritalin and a placebo.

After researchers choose the treatment, they next identify the behavior(s) of the subjects, called the dependent variable, that will be used to measure the effects of the treatment.

> **Dependent Variable:**
>
> Child's negative classroom behaviors

The *dependent variable* is one or more of the subjects' behaviors that are used to measure the potential effects of the treatment or independent variable.

The dependent variable, so called because it is dependent on the treatment, can include a wide range of behaviors, such as observable responses, self-reports of cognitive processes, or recordings of physiological responses from the body or brain. In the present experiment, the dependent variable is the teacher's rating of the child's disruptive classroom behaviors.

## Rule 3: Choose

After researchers identify the independent and dependent variables, they next choose the subjects for the experiment. Researchers want to choose subjects who are representative of the entire group or population, and they do this through a process called random selection.

*Random selection* means that each subject in a sample population has an equal chance of being selected to participate in the experiment.

> **Random Selection**

There are many ways to select randomly, such as taking every tenth child from a list of children with ADHD.

The reason researchers randomly select subjects is to avoid any potential error or bias that may come from their knowingly or unknowingly wanting to choose the "best" subjects for their experiment.

## Rule 4: Assign

After randomly choosing the subjects, researchers then randomly assign subjects to different groups, either an experimental group or a control group.

**Ritalin**

**Experimental Group**

The *experimental group* is composed of subjects who receive the treatment.

The *control group* is composed of subjects who undergo all the same procedures as the experimental subjects except that the control subjects do not receive the treatment.

**Placebo**

**Control Group**

In this study, some of the children are assigned to the experimental group and receive Ritalin; the other children are assigned to the control group and receive a similar-looking pill that is a placebo.

The reason subjects are randomly assigned to either the experimental or control group is to take into account or control for other factors or traits, such as intelligence, social class, economic level, age, personality variables, sex, and genetic differences. Randomly assigning subjects reduces the chances that these factors will bias the results.

## Rule 5: Manipulate

After assigning subjects to experimental and control groups, researchers manipulate the independent variable by administering the treatment (or one level of the treatment) to the experimental group. Researchers give the same conditions to the control group but give them a different level of the treatment, no treatment, or a placebo.

For example, in this study, researchers give the experimental group a pill containing Ritalin, while the control group receives a placebo. Drugs and placebos are given with special care in a double-blind procedure.

A *double-blind procedure* means that neither the subjects nor the researchers know which group is receiving which treatment.

A double-blind procedure is essential in drug research to control for self-fulfilling prophecies, placebo effects (see p. 31), or possible influences or biases of the experimenters.

Double-blind procedure is an important research tool.

## Rule 6: Measure

By manipulating the treatment so that the experimental group receives a different treatment than the control group, researchers are able to measure how the independent variable (treatment) affects those behaviors that have been selected as the dependent variables.

For example, the hypothesis in this study is: Ritalin will decrease negative classroom behaviors of children with ADHD. Researchers observe whether treatment (Ritalin or placebo) changes negative behaviors of ADHD children in the classroom. Negative behaviors, whose frequencies are counted for 30-minute periods, include: getting out of seat, engaging in destructive behavior, disturbing others, swearing, teasing, and not following instructions. As the graph below indicates, ADHD children given placebos show 9.8 negative behaviors per 30-minute period, compared with 4.8 for the children given Ritalin (Pelham et al., 1985). Thus, compared to placebos, Ritalin decreases negative behaviors

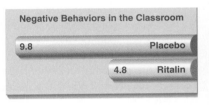

**Negative Behaviors in the Classroom**

| 9.8 | Placebo |
| 4.8 | Ritalin |

in ADHD children in the classroom. However, to be absolutely sure, researchers must analyze the results more carefully by using statistical procedures.

## Rule 7: Analyze

Although there appears to be a large decrease in negative behaviors, from 9.8 for the placebo control group to 4.8 for the Ritalin experimental group, researchers must analyze the size of these differences with statistical procedures.

*Statistical procedures* are used to determine whether differences observed in dependent variables (behaviors) are due to independent variables (treatment) or to error or chance occurrence.

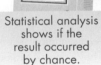

Statistical analysis shows if the result occurred by chance.

Using statistical procedures, which are described in Appendix A, researchers compared the effect of the placebo with that of Ritalin on negative behaviors. They concluded that, compared with the placebo, Ritalin significantly reduced negative behaviors. In this case, significantly means there was a 95% likelihood that it was Ritalin and not some error or chance occurrence that decreased negative behaviors (Pelham et al., 1985).

These significant findings support the hypothesis that Ritalin decreases negative classroom behaviors of children with ADHD.

---

## Conclusion

**What does an experiment tell you?**

By following these seven rules for conducting an experiment, researchers reduced the chances that error or bias would distort the major finding, which was that Ritalin reduced negative behaviors of children in the classroom. This example shows that when an experiment is run according to these seven rules, it is a much more powerful method for identifying cause-and-effect relationships than are surveys, testimonials, correlations, or case studies. Even so, researchers usually repeat experiments many times before being confident that the answers they found were correct. That's why a newly reported finding, no matter how significant, is usually regarded as questionable until other researchers have been able to repeat the experiment and replicate the finding.

After the Concept Review, we'll discuss why, after 20 years of research, there are still controversies surrounding ADHD.

# Concept Review

**1.** If psychologists obtain information through an in-depth analysis of the thoughts, beliefs, or behaviors of a single person, this method is called a (a)_____. If a method is used that minimizes error and identifies cause-and-effect relationships, it is called an (b)_____. If individuals are asked a fixed set of questions, it is called a (c)_____. If individuals make statements in support of a particular viewpoint on the basis of personal experience, it is called a (d)_____.

**2.** Some intervention that is designed to look like a medical treatment but that has no actual medical effect is called a (a)_____. A change in a patient's illness that is due to a supposed treatment and not to any medical therapy is called a (b)_____.

**3.** Psychologists describe the association, relationship, or linkage among two or more events as a (a)_____. They describe the strength of such a relationship by a number called the (b)_____, which may vary from −1.00 to +1.00. If an increase in one event is associated with an increase in a second event, this relationship is called a (c)_____ correlation. If an increase in one event is associated with a decrease in a second event, this relationship is called a (d)_____ correlation. Finding that two or more events are linked together does not prove that one event (e)_____ the other.

**4.** Psychologists use at least five common research techniques. They can ask subjects oral or written questions by using (a)_____ and (b)_____. They might ask subjects to answer questions on established tests, which are called (c)_____ tests. They might observe and measure behaviors, brains, or genes with the least error and bias by using a controlled environment, called a (d)_____. They could study some question or problem in animals by developing an (e)_____ that closely approximates the human condition.

**5.** If psychologists study individuals in their real-life environments, without trying to control the situation, they are using a (a)_____ setting. A variation of this approach is to study a single individual in great depth in his or her own environment, which is called a (b)_____. If psychologists study individuals under carefully controlled conditions, they are using a (c)_____ setting.

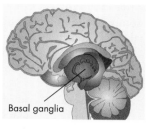

Basal ganglia

**6.** One example of searching for cause-and-effect relationships by following the rules and guidelines of the scientific method is to answer questions by conducting an _____, which has seven rules.

**7.** If you are conducting an experiment, you should follow 7 rules. Rule 1 is to *ask* specific questions in very concrete terms: these statements are called (a)_____. Rule 2 is to *identify* the treatment, which is called the (b)_____, and to choose the behaviors or responses that will be observed to judge the effectiveness of the treatment. These behaviors or responses are called the (c)_____. Rule 3 is to *choose* subjects through a process called (d)_____, which gives everyone in a sample population an equal chance of being selected. Rule 4 is to *assign* subjects to different groups by random selection. The group that will receive the treatment is called the (e)_____, and the group that undergoes everything but the treatment is called the (f)_____. Rule 5 is to *manipulate* the (g)_____ by administering it to the experimental group but not the control group. Rule 6 is to *measure* the effects of the independent variable on behaviors that have been selected as the (h)_____. Rule 7 is to *analyze* the difference between the experimental and control groups by using (i)_____.

**8.** Researchers usually repeat experiments many times to make sure that their _____ are correct.

**Answers:** 1. (a) case study, (b) experiment, (c) survey, (d) testimonial; 2. (a) placebo, (b) placebo effect; 3. (a) correlation, (b) correlation coefficient, (c) positive, (d) negative, (e) causes; 4. (a) questionnaires, (b) interviews, (c) standardized, (d) laboratory experiment, (e) animal model; 5. (a) naturalistic, (b) case study, (c) laboratory; 6. experiment; 7. (a) hypotheses, (b) independent variable, (c) dependent variable, (d) random selection, (e) experimental group, (f) control group, (g) independent variable, (h) dependent variables, (i) statistical procedures; 8. answers or results

# H. Research Focus: ADHD Controversies

**Why do controversies still remain?**

You might ask why, after 30 years of research, there are still controversies over how best to diagnose and treat ADHD. Although researchers have reached the first goal of psychology, which is to describe ADHD, they have not reached the second goal, which is to explain the causes of ADHD, which will lead to better treatment. Explaining the causes of ADHD means combining biological, psychological, and behavioral factors, which is a slow, ongoing process. We'll review the current controversies involving ADHD to show how far researchers have come and how far they have to go.

## Controversy: Diagnosis

The first controversy involves the accuracy and reliability of how ADHD is diagnosed. In the United States, about 4 to 12% of school-age children are diagnosed with ADHD (2 to 3 million children), with 4 to 5 times as many boys having ADHD as girls (Allen, 2000).

The controversy arises from the fact that the current diagnosis of ADHD is based solely on reported and observed behavioral symptoms rather than on medical or laboratory tests. Because the behavioral symptoms vary in severity (more or less) and setting (home versus school), there is the potential for misdiagnosis. For example, parents or teachers may label a child as having ADHD when the child is simply outgoing, rambunctious, or difficult to discipline (Tanner, 2000). Or, a child may feel anxious or overwhelmed by the

There are three big controversies surrounding ADHD.

demands of school and act hyperactive or distracted and be labeled as ADHD. Because of diagnostic difficulties, pediatricians and family doctors were recently given the following guidelines for diagnosing ADHD: children should be 6–12 years old, show six or more symptoms of inattention and hyperactivity, have symptoms for at least 6 months, and symptoms should occur in both home and school (Allen, 2000). The purpose of the guidelines is to prevent the merely rambunctious child from being diagnosed with ADHD and given unnecessary drugs.

The controversy regarding the diagnosis of ADHD will continue until the development of medical tests that confirm the behavioral symptoms, which are not always clear cut (Tanner, 2000).

## Controversy: Treatment

The second controversy involves how best to treat ADHD. As we discussed earlier (p. 30), researchers found that using certain diets that avoid artificial flavors or colors, preservatives, artificial sweeteners, or sugars did little to reduce or stop hyperactive behaviors (Kinsbourne, 1994).

There is a nondrug treatment program, called behavior modification (p. 232), that involves changing or modifying undesirable behaviors by using learning principles. Using behavior modification, which requires considerable efforts by the parents, has been effective in reducing ADHD symptoms (Miranda & Presentacion, 2000).

The most popular treatment for ADHD involves Ritalin (methylphenidate), whose use has risen 600% since 1993 (Thomas, 2000). A recent study found that a combination of Ritalin plus behavior modification was more effective than behavior modification alone in reducing ADHD symptoms (Jensen, 1999).

We'll review the advantages and disadvantages of using stimulant drugs, such as Ritalin, to treat ADHD.

**Use of Ritalin 1993–2000 600% Increase**

### STIMULANTS—ADVANTAGES

1. They decrease the child's activity, physical and verbal aggression, and impulsive and negative behaviors (such as teasing and swearing) and generally make the child more manageable at home and in school settings.

2. They increase the child's ability to concentrate, pay attention, and improve the amount and accuracy of schoolwork (Thomas, 2000).

### STIMULANTS—DISADVANTAGES

1. They cause side effects—most frequently, problems with eating and sleeping and dampening of emotional feelings.

2. Even during treatment, there were no significant improvements in reading skills, athletic or game skills, or social skills in grade school.

Ritalin has become so popular because it can decrease hyperactivity and at the same time increase a child's ability to pay attention, which makes the child easier to manage at home and in school (Thomas, 2000). However, there are numerous cases of children who were diagnosed with ADHD and given Ritalin but showed no improvement because they had been misdiagnosed and actually had other kinds of learning problems or disabilities (Murray, 1997). As found in a recent study, a combination of Ritalin and behavior modification was the most effective treatment (Jensen, 1999).

## Controversy: Long-Term Effects

The third controversy involves the long-term effects of ADHD. Many children diagnosed and treated for ADHD have now reached their early twenties. Researchers found that even when ADHD children are treated with Ritalin, between 30 and 70% continue to have problems as adolescents and adults. They are less likely to graduate from high school or attend college (only 1% finish college) and are at risk for showing antisocial behaviors, such as fighting, trouble with the law, or drug abuse (Wilens et al., 1997). Because ADHD is a continuing

problem, researchers encourage parents and teachers to include behavioral programs such as setting goals, establishing rules, and rewarding performance to help those with ADHD deal with adolescence and adulthood (Jensen, 1999). The controversies surrounding ADHD point out the difficulties in understanding, explaining, and treating complex human problems, such as ADHD.

The use of Ritalin to treat young children also raises questions about the rights of subjects, both human and animals, in research.

## Concerns about Being a Subject

**What's it like to be a subject?**

Each time you hear about a new research finding—such as a drug to control weight or treat depression, or the discovery of a gene related to happiness, or ways to improve memory—you rarely think about the treatment of subjects, humans and animals, used in these experiments.

For example, if you were asked to volunteer to be a subject, you would certainly be concerned about whether someone has checked to ensure that the experiment is safe, that there are safeguards to protect you from potential psychological or physical harm, and that you won't be unfairly deceived or made to feel foolish. These are all real concerns, and we'll answer each one in turn.

Additionally, a separate and controversial question concerns the use of animals in research. We'll answer this question in some detail since there are many misconceptions about the use and misuse of animals in research.

We'll begin by considering the concerns of human subjects.

## Code of Ethics

If you are a college student, there is a good possibility that you will be asked to participate in a psychology experiment. If you are considering becoming a subject, you may wonder what kinds of safeguards are used to protect subjects' rights and privacy.

The American Psychological Association has published a code of ethics and conduct for psychologists to follow when doing research, counseling, teaching, and related activities (American Psychological Association, 1992). This code of ethics spells out the responsibilities of psychologists and the rights of subjects participating in research.

Besides having to follow a code of ethics, psychologists must submit the details of their research programs, especially those with the potential for causing psychological or physical harm, to university research committees. These research committees carefully check the proposed experiments for any harmful procedures (R. Rosenthal, 1994).

*Are my rights protected?*

Experiments are not approved unless any potentially damaging effects can be eliminated or counteracted. Counteracting potentially harmful effects is usually done by thoroughly describing the experiment, a process called debriefing.

*Debriefing* includes explaining the purpose and method of the experiment, asking the subjects their feelings about being participants in the experiment, and helping the subjects deal with possible doubts or guilt that arise from their behaviors in the experiment.

During the debriefing sessions, researchers will answer any questions or discuss any problems that subjects may have. The purpose of debriefing is to make sure that subjects have been treated fairly and have no lingering psychological or physical concerns or worries that come from being a subject in an experiment (Gurman, 1994).

## Role of Deception

When recruiting subjects for their experiments, psychologists usually give the experiments titles, such as "Study of eyewitness testimony" or "Effects of alcohol on memory." The reason for using such general titles is that researchers do not want to create specific expectations that may bias how potential subjects will behave. It is well known that an experiment's results may be biased by a number of factors: by subjects' expectations of how they should behave, by their unknowingly behaving according to self-fulfilling prophecies, or by their efforts to make themselves look good or to please the experimenter.

One way that researchers control for subjects' expectations is to use bogus procedures or instructions that prevent subjects from learning the experiment's true purpose. However, before researchers can use bogus or deceptive methodology, they must satisfy

*Will they try to trick or deceive me?*

the American Psychological Association's (1992) code of ethics. For example, researchers must justify the deceptive techniques by the scientific, educational, or applied value of the study and by giving subjects a sufficient explanation of the study as soon as possible (Fisher & Fryberg, 1994).

Another way to avoid bias from subjects' expectations is to keep both the researcher and subjects in the dark about the experiment's true purpose by using a double-blind procedure. As discussed earlier (p. 37), a double-blind procedure means that neither the subjects nor the researcher is aware of the experiment's treatment or purpose.

Thus, researchers must be careful not to reveal too many details about their experiments lest they bias how potential subjects may behave.

## How many animals are used in research?

An estimated 18 to 22 million animals are used each year in biomedical research, which includes the fields of psychology, biology, medicine, and pharmaceuticals (Mukerjee, 1997). Although these numbers seem large, they are small in comparison to the 5 billion chickens eaten annually by citizens in the United States. However, it is the use of animals in research that has generated the most concern and debate.

In the field of psychology, about 85% of the nonhuman animals used by researchers are rats and mice, while 10% are cats, dogs, monkeys, and birds (Mukerjee, 1997). We'll examine the justification for using animals in research and how their rights are protected.

## Are research animals mistreated?

You may have seen a disturbing photo or heard about a laboratory animal being mistreated (Barnard & Kaufman, 1997). The fact is that, of the millions of animals used in research, only a few cases of animal mistreatment have been confirmed. That is because scientists know that proper care and treatment of their laboratory animals are vital to the success of their research. To abolish the use of all laboratory animals because of one or two isolated cases of mistreatment would be like abolishing all medical practice because of isolated cases of malpractice. Instead, researchers suggest balancing the rights of animals with the needs for advancing the medical, physiological, and psychological health of humans.

## Is the use of animals justified?

Adrian Morrison, director of the National Institute of Mental Health's Program for Animal Research Issues, recently wrote,

"Because I do experimental surgery, I go through a soul-searching every couple of months, asking myself whether I really want to continue working on cats. The answer is always yes because I know that there is no other way for medicine to progress but through animal experimentation and that basic research ultimately leads to unforeseen benefits" (Morrison, 1993).

According to Frederick King, the former chair of the American Psychological Association's Committee on Animal Research and Experimentation, animal research has resulted in major medical advances, the discovery of treatments for human diseases, and a better understanding of human disorders (King et al., 1988).

In the field of psychology, animal research and animal models have led to a better understanding of how stress affects one's psychological and physical health, mechanisms underlying learning and memory, and effects of sensory deprivation on development, to mention but a few (Mukerjee, 1997).

Researchers are currently using animals to study epilepsy, Alzheimer's disease, fetal alcohol syndrome, schizophrenia, AIDS, and transplantation of brain tissue, none of which is possible with human subjects.

## Who checks on the use of animals in research?

Numerous government and university regulations ensure the proper care and humane treatment of laboratory animals. For example, the U.S. Department of Agriculture conducts periodic inspections of all animal research facilities to ensure proper housing and to oversee experimental procedures that might cause pain or distress. Universities hire veterinarians to regularly monitor the care and treatment of laboratory animals. Finally, universities have animal subject committees with authority to decide whether sufficient justification exists for using animals in specific research projects (Mukerjee, 1997).

## How do we strike a balance?

One of the basic issues in animal research is how to strike the right balance between animal rights and research needs (Barnard & Kaufman, 1997). Based on past, present, and potential future benefits of animal research, many experts in the scientific, medical, and mental health communities believe that the conscientious and responsible use of animals in research is justified and should continue. This is especially true in light of recent rules that regulate the safe and humane treatment of animals kept in laboratories or used in research (Botting & Morrison, 1997).

If we stop animal research, who'll stop the real killers?

Without animal research, we couldn't have put an end to polio, smallpox, rubella and diphtheria. Now, some would like to put an end to animal research. Obviously, they don't have cancer, heart disease or AIDS.

Foundation for Biomedical Research

The small print in poster reads, "Without animal research, we couldn't have put an end to polio, smallpox, rubella and diphtheria. Now, some would like to put an end to animal research. Obviously, they don't have cancer, heart disease or AIDS."

# Summary Test

## A. ANSWERING QUESTIONS

**1.** Psychologists use at least three methods to answer questions or obtain information. An in-depth analysis of a single person's thoughts and behaviors is called a (a)_____. One advantage of this method is that researchers ob- 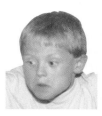 tain detailed information about a person, but one disadvantage is that such information may not apply to others. Asking a large number of individuals a fixed set of questions is called a (b)_____. Gathering information in a controlled laboratory setting is called an (c)_____.

## B. SURVEYS

 **2.** Measuring the attitudes, beliefs, and behaviors of a large sample of individuals by asking a set of ques-tions is called a _____. One advantage of this method is that psychologists can quickly and efficiently collect information about a large number of people. One disadvantage is that people may answer in a way that they think is more socially acceptable.

## C. CASE STUDY

**3.** A statement that supports a particular viewpoint and is based on a person's own experience is called a (a)_____, which has several poten-tial sources of error and bias. First, strongly held personal beliefs may bias an individual's (b)_____ of events. Second, believ-ing strongly that something will happen and then unknowingly acting in such a way as to make that something occur is a source of error called (c)_____. This source of error is one of the major reasons that people believe that their (d)_____ are true.

## D. CULTURAL DIVERSITY: USE OF PLACEBOS

 **4.** Some intervention that resembles a medical therapy but that, in fact, has no medical effects is called a (a)_____. If a per-son reports an improvement in some medical con-dition that is due to a supposed treatment rather than some medical therapy, that is called a (b)_____. One reason people around the world believe in placebos is that people give (c)_____ to their effectiveness.

## E. CORRELATION

**5.** If two or more events are associated or linked to-gether, they are said to be (a)_____. The strength of this association is indicated by a number called the (b)_____, which has a range from −1.00 to +1.00.

**6.** If there were a perfect association between two events—for example, when one increased, the other did also—this would be called a (a)_____. If an increase in one event is usually, but not always, accompanied by an increase in a second event, this would be called a (b)_____. If an increase in one event is always accompanied by a decrease in a second event, this is called a (c)_____. If an increase in one event is usually, but not always, accompanied by a decrease in a second event, this is called a (d)_____.

**7.** Although a correlation indicates that two or more events are oc-curring in some pattern, a correlation does not identify which event may (a)_____ the other(s). Although correlations do not identify cause-and-effect relationships, they do provide (b)_____ as to where to look for causes and they help to (c)_____ behavior.

## F. DECISIONS ABOUT DOING RESEARCH

**8.** Psychologists may answer some question by using one or more of five commonly used research techniques. Asking questions about people's attitudes and behaviors, usually in a one-on-one sit-uation, is using an (a)_____. Asking subjects to read a list of questions and indicate a specific answer is using a (b)_____. Asking subjects to complete established tests that measure personality, intelligence, or other behaviors is using (c)_____. If psychologists study subjects' behaviors under carefully controlled conditions that allow manipulation of the treatment, they are conducting a (d)_____. Psychologists can study a problem using ani-mals by developing an (e)_____, which closely approxi-mates the human disease or condition.

Basal ganglia

**9.** Psychologists conduct research in two common settings. If psy-chologists obtain information by observing an individual's behaviors in his or her environment, without attempts to control or manipulate the situation, they would be using a _____. The *advantage* of this method is that it gives information that would be difficult to obtain or duplicate in a laboratory. The *disadvantage* of this method is that the psychologists' own beliefs or values may bias their observations and cause them to misinterpret the behaviors under observation.

**10.** If psychologists study a single individual in considerable depth in his or her own environment, they are using a _____. The *advantage* of this method is that it results in detailed descriptions and insights into many aspects of an individual's life. The *disadvantage* is that the information obtained may be unique and not applicable to others.

**11.** If psychologists want to study individuals under controlled and systematic conditions, with many of the real-life factors removed, they do the study in a _____. The *advantage* of this setting is that it permits greater control and manipulation of many conditions while ruling out possible contaminating factors. The *disadvantage* of this setting is that it may be too artificial or controlled, so that the results may not necessarily apply to real-life situations.

## G. SCIENTIFIC METHOD: EXPERIMENT

**12.** The scientific method offers a set of rules or guidelines on how to conduct research with a minimum of error or bias. We have divided these guidelines into seven rules. **Rule 1** is to make a statement in precise, concrete terms. Such a statement is called a (a)_____, which researchers often develop based on previous observations or studies. **Rule 2** is to identify the treatment or something the experimenter manipulates, which is called the (b)_____. In addition, the experimenter selects behaviors that are to be used to measure the potential effects of the treatment. These selected behaviors are called the (c)_____, and they may include a wide range of behaviors, such as cognitive processes, observable behaviors, or measurable physiological responses. **Rule 3** is to choose subjects so that each one in a sample has an equal chance of being selected. One procedure for doing so is called (d)_____. **Rule 4** is to assign subjects randomly to one of two groups. The group that will receive the treatment is called the (e)_____, and the group that will undergo everything but the treatment is called the (f)_____. **Rule 5** is to manipulate the (g)_____ by administering it (or one level of it) to the experimental group but not to the control group. The procedure for preventing researchers or

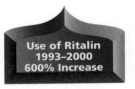

subjects from knowing who is getting the treatment is called the (h)_____. **Rule 6** is to measure the effects of the independent variable on behaviors that have been selected as the (i)_____. **Rule 7** is to analyze differences between behaviors of subjects in the experimental group and those in the control group by using various (j)_____, which determine whether differences were due to the treatment or to chance occurrences. By following these seven rules, researchers reduce the chances that (k)_____ caused their results.

## H. RESEARCH FOCUS: ADHD CONTROVERSIES

Use of Ritalin 1993–2000 600% Increase

**13.** One controversy over ADHD is that, as of this writing, the diagnosis of ADHD is based on (a)_____ observations, which are not always clear cut, rather than on more reliable (b)_____ tests. Another controversy involves how best to treat ADHD. A recent study found that the most effective treatment was a combination of (c)_____ and (d)_____ modification. However, even though Ritalin can decrease hyperactivity in children and increase their ability to pay (e)_____, Ritalin does not necessarily improve reading or social skills and does not reduce problems occurring during adolescence and adulthood.

## I. APPLICATION: RESEARCH CONCERNS

**14.** One method of counteracting potential harmful effects on experimental subjects is by thoroughly _____ them. This includes explaining the purpose and method of the experiment, asking subjects about their feelings, and helping subjects deal with possible doubts or problems arising from the experiment.

**15.** The justification for using _____ in research is that it has resulted in major medical advances, treatments for diseases, and understanding of human disorders.

***Answers:*** *1. (a) case study, (b) survey, (c) experiment; 2. survey; 3. (a) testimonial, (b) perceptions, (c) self-fulfilling prophecy, (d) testimonials; 4. (a) placebo, (b) placebo effect, (c) testimonials; 5. (a) correlated, (b) correlation coefficient; 6. (a) perfect positive correlation, (b) positive correlation, (c) perfect negative correlation, (d) negative correlation; 7. (a) cause, (b) clues, (c) predict; 8. (a) interview, (b) questionnaire, (c) standardized tests, (d) laboratory study or experiment, (e) animal model; 9. naturalistic setting; 10. case study; 11. laboratory setting; 12. (a) hypothesis, (b) independent variable, (c) dependent variables, (d) random selection, (e) experimental group, (f) control group, (g) independent variable, (h) double-blind procedure, (i) dependent variables, (j) statistical procedures, (k) error or bias; 13. (a) behavioral, (b) medical or laboratory, (c) Ritalin, (d) behavior, (e) attention; 14. debriefing; 15. animals*

# Critical Thinking

## Does Frequent Sex Help Men Live Longer?

*by Lawrence K. Altman*

### Questions

**1.** Was the original research question to study sex, or was this "sex" finding unexpected?

**2.** What are the three major methods for answering questions, and which method was used in this study?

**3.** Does the major finding indicate a cause-and-effect relationship or only a correlation?

Men who have more orgasms seem to live longer, a statistical study of Welsh villagers in *The British Medical Journal* has found. . . . "Sexual activity seems to have a protective effect on men's health," Dr. George Davey-Smith's team concluded after analyzing death rates of nearly 1,000 men from 45 to 59 in Caerphilly.

Davey-Smith's team assessed the existence of heart disease in the men when they entered the study from 1979 to 1983. After explaining the purpose of their question, they asked the men about the frequency of sexual activity. The answers were put into categories ranging from "never" to "daily." . . . The participants' names were flagged in the British national health service's central registry and the researchers were automatically notified if they died. The death rate was analyzed 10 years after the participants entered the study.

Men who said they had sex twice a week had a risk of dying half that of the less passionate participants who said they had sex once a month, Davey-Smith's team said. . . . Further studies of both sexes are needed to confirm their findings, the authors said.

Two other scientists added a few drops of cold water, cautioning that because of its design (use of surveys), the epidemiological study might not have been able to identify a number of factors that could have inadvertently influenced the findings. One possibility is that the link could be reversed—ill people may be less likely to have sex, according to the critics who commented in the same issue.

The authors said that they had tried to adjust the study's design to account for a factor that might explain the findings—that healthier, fitter men with more healthy life styles engaged in more sex. Even so, they could not explain the differences in risk. Hormonal effects on the body resulting from frequent sex could be among other possible explanations for the findings, Davey-Smith said. (*Source:* New York Times News Service, appeared in *San Diego Union-Tribune*, December 23, 1997)

**4.** Why couldn't this study show a cause-and-effect relationship between more sex and living longer?

**5.** What are the advantage and the disadvantage of this study?

*Try these InfoTrac search terms:* **sex; epidemiology; heart disease; male hormones.**

---

### Suggested answers to Newspaper Article questions

1. The original purpose of this study was to assess heart disease in men. However, in answering the original research question, researchers found another interesting link between sexual activity and length of life, which raised new questions.

2. The three major methods for answering questions are survey, case study, and experiment. In this study, researchers asked men questions about their health and sexual activity, so this study primarily used the survey method.

3. Surveys cannot show cause-and-effect relationships but only associations or correlations between events: men who had sex more often lived longer than men who had sex less often.

4. To show a cause-and-effect relationship, this study must have been designed as an experiment in which an experimental group got one treatment (more sex) while a control group got no or different treatment (less sex). For ethical reasons, such an experiment could not be conducted on humans, so it would be difficult to demonstrate this cause-and-effect relationship.

5. The advantage of this survey study is that it suggests an unexpected cause or explanation of why men live longer (having more sex). One disadvantage of this survey study is that it cannot identify cause-and-effect relationships because many other factors (hormones, different lifestyles) cannot be ruled out.

# Links to Learning

## Web Sites

- WADSWORTH ONLINE PSYCHOLOGY STUDY CENTER
  **http://psychology.wadsworth.com**
  Quizzes, learning activities and exercises, a discussion forum, and hot links to Internet sites related to psychology and science, including:

- TWENTY SCIENCE ATTITUDES
  **http://psg.com/~ted/bcskeptics/ratenq/Re3.3-Attitude.html**
  An annotated list of the 20 traits of a good psychologist.

- APA SCIENCE INFORMATION FOR STUDENTS
  **http://www.apa.org/science/infostu.html**
  This is a great site for learning what scientific opportunities are available to psychology students.

- MEGASITE RESEARCH LINKS
  **http://www.oklahoma.net/~jnichols/research.html**
  This is a great place to go to participate in psychological research online. There are links to specific studies, to lots of research opportunites, and to research databases.

## Learning Activities

- *POWERSTUDY*™ CD
  BY ROD PLOTNIK &
  TOM DOYLE

  **Power Study**™
  **Check out CD: Module 4**
  B. Studying the Living Brain
  (book page 70)

- *STUDY GUIDE TO ACCOMPANY INTRODUCTION TO PSYCHOLOGY, 6TH EDITION,* by Matthew Enos
  In Module 2 you can compare your school attendance history with the author's, consider rhinoceros horn as a metaphor for beliefs and practices, learn a light bulb joke about psychologists, and benefit from numerous study aids as well.

- *WEBTUTOR*
  Web**TUTOR**
  **http://webtutor.thomsonlearning.com**
  Visit this site for interactive versions of Study Guide features. Take a quiz, get your score—should you study a topic some more, or can you move on? For instance, can you explain why a control group is needed in a scientific experiment? Your professor's class syllabus and course calendar are also posted—you'll never have to get behind in class again!

- *INFOTRAC ONLINE LIBRARY*
  **http://www.infotrac-college.com**
  Use your password and then key in search terms such as those below to find popular and scientific articles on subjects covered in Module 2. Make the library work for you!

  Placebos                   Attention-Deficit/Hyperactivity Disorder
  Animal research        Sex and longevity

- *PSYCHNOW!*
  CD for Macintosh and Windows includes a study guide, glossary, Web sites, and animations. For Module 2, see:

  Research Methods
  Critical Thinking in Psychology

## Study Questions

*Use InfoTrac to search for topics mentioned in the following questions (e.g., caffeine, research questions, scientific method).*

**\*A. Answering Questions**—Which method would you use to find out if caffeine improves memory? (**Suggested answer page 619**)

**B. Surveys**—How believable is a recent survey that reported that people never lie to their best friends?

**C. Case Study**—Why do some people put more faith in testimonials than in proven research?

**\*D. Cultural Diversity: Use of Placebos**—Why do Americans think it strange that Asians use rhino horn as medicine? (**Suggested answer page 620**)

**E. Correlation**—How would you explain the positive correlation (0.60) researchers found between drinking coffee and being sexually active after age 60?

**\*F. Decisions about Doing Research**—Which research techniques and settings would you use to study mental problems in the homeless? (**Suggested answer page 620**)

**G. Scientific Method: Experiment**—How would you determine whether taking vitamin B reduces stress?

**H. Research Focus: ADHD Controversies**—If you had a child who might have ADHD, what would you do?

**I. Application: Research Concerns**—What concerns might a student have about volunteering to be a subject in an experiment?

\*These questions are answered in Appendix B.

# Module 3: Brain's Building Blocks

**A. Overview: Human Brain**      48
  * DEVELOPMENT OF THE BRAIN
  * STRUCTURE OF THE BRAIN
  * GROWTH OF NEW NEURONS
  * BRAIN VERSUS MIND

**B. Neurons: Structure & Function**      50
  * PARTS OF THE NEURON
  * ALZHEIMER'S DISEASE AND NEURONS

**C. Neurons versus Nerves**      51
  * REATTACHING LIMBS
  * PERIPHERAL NERVOUS SYSTEM
  * CENTRAL NERVOUS SYSTEM

**D. Sending Information**      52
  * SEQUENCE: ACTION POTENTIAL
  * SEQUENCE: NERVE IMPULSE

**E. Transmitters**      54
  * EXCITATORY AND INHIBITORY
  * NEUROTRANSMITTERS
  * ALCOHOL
  * NEW TRANSMITTERS

**F. Reflex Responses**      56
  * DEFINITION AND SEQUENCE
  * FUNCTIONS OF A REFLEX

**Concept Review**      57

**G. Research Focus:
What Is a Phantom Limb?**      58
  * CASE STUDY
  * DEFINITION AND DATA
  * ANSWERS: OLD AND NEW

**H. Cultural Diversity: Plants & Drugs**      59
  * COCAINE
  * CURARE
  * MESCALINE

**I. Application: Fetal Tissue Transplant**      60
  * PARKINSON'S DISEASE
  * ISSUES INVOLVING TRANSPLANTS
  * FETAL TISSUE TRANSPLANTS

**Summary Test**      62

**Critical Thinking**      64
  * WOULD YOU WANT A HEAD TRANSPLANT?

**Links to Learning**      65

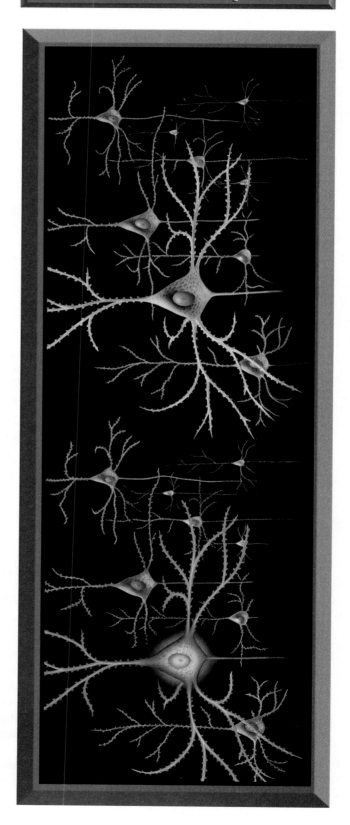

PowerStudy ™

## Losing One's Mind

**Why does 71-year-old Ina think the baby is hers?**

Her children had always called their mother, Ina, "the Rock of Gibraltar." Ina could fix the plumbing, hang wallpaper, and prepare a full dinner from scratch every night, while keeping her six children out of trouble. She could swim faster than anyone, she wanted to be a basketball player, and her late husband called her the most beautiful woman he had ever seen.

But that was before she started to forget things and repeat herself, which could just be part of getting old. But how to explain her mopping the kitchen floor at 2:00 in the morning and refusing to go to bed? Or wearing the same dirty clothes day after day, something she had never done in her entire life? Or being confused at housework? Or thinking that her granddaughter (right photo) is her own child?

Because Ina had always been so healthy, her six grown children thought she must have suffered a stroke or be depressed. When they took Ina in for a checkup, a neurologist confirmed their worst fears. Ina had Alzheimer's (*ALTS-hi-mers*) disease.

In 10% of the cases, *Alzheimer's disease* begins after age 50, but in 90% of the cases, it begins after age 65. Its initial symptoms are problems with memory, such as forgetting and repeating things, getting lost, and being mildly confused. There are also cognitive deficits, such as problems with language, difficulties in recognizing objects, and inability to plan and organize tasks. Over a period of five to ten years, these symptoms worsen and result in profound memory loss, lack of recognition of family and friends, deterioration in personality, and emotional outbursts. There is widespread damage to the brain, especially the hippocampus, which is involved in memory. At present, there is no cure for Alzheimer's, which is always fatal (American Psychiatric Association, 1994).

In the United States, Alzheimer's is the fourth leading cause of death among adults. In 2000, approximately 4 million people—or 5% of adults over age 65—had Alzheimer's disease, and the number of patients is projected to rise dramatically in the coming decades (graph on right) as people are expected to live longer (Cowley, 2000a).

Ina's condition worsened through the coming months. She had trouble completing even the simplest tasks, and the day after having a big Thanksgiving celebration with her family, she asked where she had spent the holiday. At times, she recognized her grown children; at other times, she thought they were her cousins. Ina must now be watched almost every minute so that she does not hurt herself or wander off and get lost (adapted from *Newsweek,* December 18, 1989).

She was the family's "Rock of Gibraltar" until she developed Alzheimer's.

For Ina, the worst is yet to come. Her memory will totally disintegrate, she will be completely bedridden, and she will not know who she is or recognize the family she has lovingly raised. When she dies—for Alzheimer's has, at present, no cure—Ina will have lost her memory, her wonderful personality, and all signs of humanity.

## Diagnosis and Causes

In Ina's case as well as all cases of individuals with memory and cognitive difficulties, Alzheimer's is diagnosed by identifying a combination of behavioral symptoms and by eliminating the possibility of other physical problems. At the time of this writing, the only foolproof test for Alzheimer's involves examination of the patient's brain after death (Cowley, 2000a).

Researchers now believe they are very close to figuring out the causes of Alzheimer's disease, which involve genetic, neurological, and possible environmental factors (Greengard, 2000). For example, Alzheimer's incidence is three times higher among individuals who have one parent with Alzheimer's and five times higher if both parents have the disease (Tanzi, 2000). Researchers have also identified several chemicals (proteins and peptides) that occur naturally in all brains but, for some reason, begin to multiply and are believed to cause Alzheimer's. These chemicals seem to act like glue that eventually destroy brain cells (Naslund et al., 2000). With these new leads, researchers are optimistic about finding the causes of and developing treatments for Alzheimer's (Morrison-Bogorad, 2000).

New treatments are badly needed because current drugs are only mildly effective and short acting (Cowley, 2000a).

**Dementia on the rise**
**Alzheimer's patients in the U.S.**

Millions

10.2

10

8

6

4

3.7

0

1990　　2010　　2030　　2050
**(projection)**

## What's Coming

The reason Alzheimer's disease gradually destroys a person's memory, personality, and humanity is that it progressively breaks down the building blocks that make up the brain's informational network. We'll explain the two groups of brain cells—glial cells and neurons—that make up this network. We'll discuss how the cells in one group—neurons—have a remarkable ability to transport information. You'll discover that brain cells communicate with chemicals that have the ability to start or stop the flow of information. Finally, we'll explain a remarkable new treatment of implanting neurons to treat brain diseases. We'll use the story of Ina and Alzheimer's disease to illustrate the brain's building blocks.

As Alzheimer's disease slowly destroys Ina's brain, she is also slowly losing her mind. Alzheimer's disease has progressed to the point that Ina can no longer recognize her own children or remember what she did on Thanksgiving day. We'll use Ina's brain and her current problems to answer four basic questions: Why isn't the brain a nose? What's in the brain? Can a brain grow new neurons? Can you take a picture of the mind? We'll answer each of these questions in order.

## Development of the Brain

**Why isn't the brain a nose?**

The fact that your brain does not develop into a nose is because of instructions contained in your genes.

*Genes* are chains of chemicals that are arranged like rungs on a twisting ladder (right figure). There are about 30,000 genes that contain chemical instructions that equal about 300,000 pages of written instructions. The chemical instructions in the genes program the development of millions of individual parts into a complex body and brain.

An amazing feature of the 30,000 genes is that they are contained in a fertilized egg, which is a single cell about the size of a grain of sand. We'll explain more about the genes and their chemical instructions in the next module (p. 68).

In the brain's early stages of development, it looks nothing like the final product. For example, the figure below looks more like some strange animal than what it really is, a six-week-old human embryo with a developing brain.

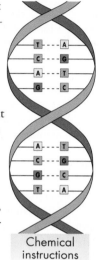

Chemical instructions

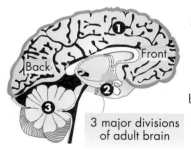

3 major divisions of 6-week-old brain

**SIX-WEEK-OLD BRAIN.** This drawing represents a greatly enlarged six-week-old human embryo. The 3 labeled areas (in 3 colors) will eventually develop into the 3 major divisions of the mature human brain that is shown below.

**MATURE BRAIN.** The 3 labeled areas represent the 3 major divisions of the mature brain that we'll discuss in the next module. The mature human brain (side view) weighs almost 3 pounds and contains about 1 trillion cells (Fischbach, 1992).

Front
Back
3 major divisions of adult brain

In the case of Ina, who developed Alzheimer's disease, researchers think that some of her genetic instructions were faulty. The faulty instructions resulted in an abnormal buildup in the brain of a gluelike substance that gradually destroys brain cells (Cowley, 2000c). Next, we'll explain the two different kinds of brain cells and which ones are destroyed by Alzheimer's disease.

## Structure of the Brain

**What's in your brain?**

Top view of human brain

On the left is a top view of a human brain. It is shaped like a small wrinkled melon, weighs about 1,350 grams (less than 3 pounds), has a pinkish-white color, and has the consistency of firm Jell-O. Your brain is fueled by sugar (glucose) and has about 1 trillion cells that can be divided into two groups—glial cells and neurons.

**GLIAL CELLS.** The most numerous brain cells, about 900 billion, are called glial (*GLEE-all*) cells.

*Glial cells* have at least three functions: they provide scaffolding to guide the growth of developing neurons and support mature neurons; they wrap themselves around neurons and form a kind of insulation to prevent interference from other electrical signals; and they release chemicals that influence a neuron's growth and function (Coyle & Schwarcz, 2000).

Glial cell

A star-shaped glial cell (astrocyte) is shown above. Glial cells grow throughout one's lifetime. If something causes the uncontrolled growth of glial cells, the result is brain cancer. Alzheimer's disease does not usually destroy glial cells, but it does destroy the second kind of brain cells, which are called neurons.

**NEURONS.** The second group of brain cells, which number about 100 billion, are called neurons (*NER-ons*); one is shown on the right.

A *neuron* is a brain cell with two specialized extensions. One extension is for receiving electrical signals, and a second, longer extension is for transmitting electrical signals.

Depending upon their size, neurons receive and transmit electrical signals at speeds of up to 200 miles per hour over distances from a fraction of an inch to over 3 feet, such as from your toe to your spinal cord.

Neurons form a vast, miniaturized informational network that allows us to receive sensory information, control muscle movement, regulate digestion, secrete hormones, and engage in complex mental processes such as thinking, imagining, dreaming, and remembering.

Neuron

Ina's brain was constructed from two kinds of building blocks—glial cells and neurons. However, it is the neurons that Alzheimer's disease gradually destroys; the result is that Ina's brain is losing its ability to transmit information, causing memory and cognitive difficulties. Why neurons do not repair or replace themselves is our next topic.

## Growth of New Neurons

**Can a brain grow new neurons?**

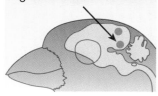

The two red dots show two areas of the mature canary's brain that increase by 50% with the growth of new neurons.

If you had a bird's brain, you could grow new neurons every spring. That's because a male canary learns to sing a breeding song in the spring, but when breeding season is over, the ability to sing the song disappears. However, come next spring, an adult canary's brain begins growing about 20,000 new neurons a day and, during this short period, relearns the breeding song. These new neurons result in a 50% or more increase in two areas of the canary's brain (left figure) that control singing (Ball & Hulse, 1998). Without a doubt, an adult canary brain can regularly grow new neurons (Hoffman, 1999).

**PRIMATE BRAINS.** Does the fact that adult canaries as well as adult mice, rats, and other animals can grow new neurons also hold true for adult human brains (Blakeslee, 2000)? Until very recently, researchers believed that the brains of adult primates, such as humans and chimpanzees, could not grow new neurons. Instead, primates were believed to have developed almost all their neurons at birth and adult brains did not grow new neurons (Rakic, 1985).

However, recent studies found that adult primate brains (humans and monkeys) did grow new neurons in certain areas of the brain (frontal and temporal cortex, hippocampus) which are involved in learning and memory (Gould et al., 1999; Kempermann & Gage, 1999). According to these findings, adult monkey and human brains are capable of growing a relatively limited number of new neurons throughout adulthood and these new neurons may play an important role in our continuing ability to learn and remember new things (Gould et al., 1999).

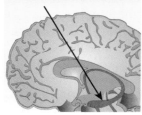

Growth of new neurons is found in this area of mature human brain (hippocampus).

**REPAIRING THE BRAIN.** Besides having a limited capacity to grow new neurons throughout adulthood, mature human brains also have a limited capacity to replace, rewire, or repair damaged neurons, such as after a stroke, gunshot wound, or blow to the head (Hoffman, 1999). For instance, after the brain is accidentally injured, healthy neurons have the ability to send out very short extensions to make some new connections with neurons whose normal connections were damaged (Barinaga, 1992a). One reason neurons have only a limited capacity to be repaired or rewired after damage is that there is a genetic program that turns off regrowth when neurons become fully grown (Schneider, 1995). This limited capacity of the adult brain to rewire itself by forming new connections helps explain why people may recover some, but rarely all, of the functions initially lost after brain damage (Hoffman, 1999).

The reason Alzheimer's disease is so destructive and eventually leads to death is that this disease destroys neurons many times faster than the brain's limited capacity for regrowth, repair, or rewiring. As Alzheimer's destroys Ina's brain, what is happening to her mind?

## Brain versus Mind

**Can you take a picture of the mind?**

As Alzheimer's destroys Ina's brain, she is also losing her mind, which raises the mind-body question.

The ***mind-body question*** asks how complex mental activities, such as feeling, thinking, and learning, can be explained by the physical, chemical, and electrical activities of the brain.

Through the centuries, philosophers and scientists have answered the mind-body question differently, some believing the mind and brain are separate things and others saying the mind and brain are one and the same (Damasio, 1999).

For example, Nobel Prize winner and geneticist Francis Crick (1994) believes the mind ***is*** the brain: "You, your joys and your sorrows, your memories and your ambition, your sense of personal identity and free will, are in fact no more than the behavior of a vast assembly of nerve cells and their associated molecules." Although some agree with Crick's answer, that the mind and brain are the same, others reply that mental activities cannot be reduced to the physical activities of the brain (Gold & Stoljar, 1999).

Another answer comes from Nobel Prize winner and neurophysiologist Roger Sperry (1993), who said that the brain is like a coin with two sides. One side consists of physical reactions, such as making chemicals that neurons use for communicating. The other side consists of all of our mental functions, such as thinking, imagining, and deciding. According to Sperry, the brain's chemicals (physical side) influence consciousness and mental activities, which, in turn, influence the production of more or different brain chemicals. There is considerable support for Sperry's idea of continuous interaction between the physical and mental sides (Pinker, 2000).

**ALZHEIMER'S.** In Ina's case, as Alzheimer's disease destroys her brain, she also loses more and more of her mental activities, such as knowing, thinking, and deciding. Researchers can now study a person's mental activities by taking pictures or brain scans of the neural activities going on inside the living brain (brain scans are discussed on pp. 70–71). For example, the top right brain scan shows a great amount of neural activity occurring inside a normal brain (red/yellow indicate most neural activity, blue/green indicate least activity). In comparison, the bottom right brain scan shows relatively little neural activity and thus relatively little mental activity occurring inside an Alzheimer's brain. These kinds of brain scans show that neural activities and mental activities are closely linked, and researchers are studying how these links occur (Gold & Stoljar, 1999).

Knowing now how important neurons are to your mental and physical functions, we next examine them in more detail.

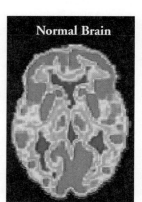

**Normal Brain**

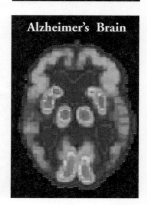

**Alzheimer's Brain**

## Parts of the Neuron

**Why could Ina think, move, and talk?**

Before Ina developed Alzheimer's disease, she was able to engage in an incredible variety of cognitive and physical behaviors. She was able to think, remember, walk, smile, and speak—all because of the activity of millions of microscopic brain cells called neurons. We'll examine the neuron, which comes in many wondrous shapes and sizes and has only three basic structures—cell body, dendrites, and axon.

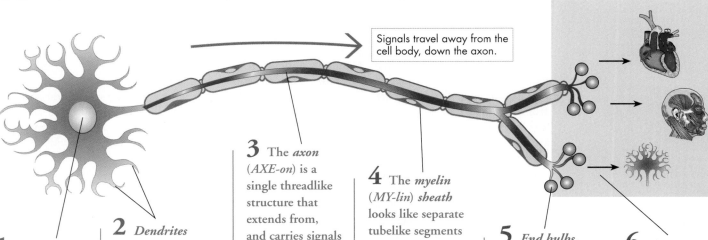

Signals travel away from the cell body, down the axon.

**1** The *cell body* (or soma) is a relatively large, egg-shaped structure that provides fuel, manufactures chemicals, and maintains the entire neuron in working order.

In the center of the cell body is a small, oval shape representing the nucleus, which contains genetic instructions (in the form of DNA) for both the manufacture of chemicals and the regulation of the neuron.

**2** *Dendrites* (*DEN-drites*) are branchlike extensions that arise from the cell body; they receive signals from other neurons, muscles, or sense organs and pass these signals to the cell body.

At the time of birth, a neuron has few dendrites. After birth, dendrites undergo dramatic growth that accounts for much of the increase in brain size. As dendrites grow, they make connections and form communication networks between neurons and other cells or organs.

**3** The *axon* (*AXE-on*) is a single threadlike structure that extends from, and carries signals away from, the cell body to neighboring neurons, organs, or muscles.

Here the axon is indicated by an orange line inside the tube composed of separate gray segments. Axons vary in length from less than a hair's breadth to as long as 3 feet (from your spinal cord to your toes). An axon conducts electrical signals to a neighboring organ (heart), a muscle, or another neuron.

**4** The *myelin* (*MY-lin*) *sheath* looks like separate tubelike segments composed of fatty material that wraps around and insulates an axon. The myelin sheath prevents interference from electrical signals generated in adjacent axons.

The axons of most large neurons, including motor neurons, have myelin sheaths. You may have heard the brain described as consisting of gray and white matter. Gray is the color of cell bodies, while white is the color of myelin sheaths.

**5** *End bulbs,* which look like tiny bubbles, are located at the extreme ends of the axon's branches. Each end bulb is like a miniature container that stores chemicals called neurotransmitters, which are used to communicate with neighboring cells.

End bulbs reach right up to, but do not physically touch, the surface of a neighboring organ (heart), muscle (head), or another cell body.

**6** The *synapse* (*SIN-apse*) is an infinitely small space (20–30 billionths of a meter) that exists between an end bulb and its adjacent body organ (heart), muscles (head), or cell body.

When stimulated by electrical signals from the axon, the end bulbs eject neurotransmitters into the synapse. The neurotransmitters cross the synapse and act like switches to turn adjacent cells on or off. We'll explain this switching process a little later.

## Alzheimer's Disease and Neurons

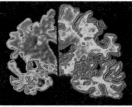

Alzheimer's brain is smaller because it has lost many neurons.

Size of normal brain with all of its neurons intact.

A major result of Alzheimer's disease is an excessive buildup of gluelike, toxic substances, which gradually destroy neurons. In Ina's case, these toxic substances will destroy more and more of her neurons, causing her brain to actually shrink, as indicated by the very deep creases in the Alzheimer's brain (left photo). Researchers are searching for ways to stop the buildup of these toxic and killer substances.

We have discussed the structure and function of neurons, but it is important not to confuse neurons (in your brain and spinal cord) with nerves (in your body).

## Reattaching Limbs

### What's unusual about John's arms?

John Thomas was 18 when a farm machine ripped off both of his arms just below his shoulders. Since he was home alone, he had to walk to the farmhouse, kick open the front door, and with a pencil clenched in his teeth, dial the phone for help. When paramedics arrived, he reminded them to get his two arms, which were still stuck in the farm equipment. John was taken to the hospital, where doctors reattached both arms (indicated by red arrows in left photo).

Three months later, John could raise his arms up in the air but could not move them below his elbows. After three years of physical therapy and 15 operations, John could raise both of his reattached arms over his head, make fists, and grip with his hands. Surgeons believe that John will recover additional movement and feelings in his arms, but that may require 2–5 years of physical therapy (*USA Today,* January 12, 1995).

**Both his arms were torn off and then reattached.**

More recently, doctors have taken a hand from a donor body and reattached the hand to the arm (stump) of a person whose own limb was severed or damaged (Horowitz, 2000). During this operation, nerves, blood vessels, and muscles from a donor's hand (right figure) are reattached to those in the patient's remaining limb. About a year after surgery, one patient with a reattached donor's hand can feel hot and cold, drive a car, lift his kids, and tie his shoe laces using his new hand, but cannot yet perform fine movements, such as picking up a dime (Horowitz, 2000). The fact that severed nerves in limbs, such as arms, hands, or legs, can be reattached but neurons in a severed spinal cord are very difficult to reattach illustrates a major difference between the peripheral and central nervous systems.

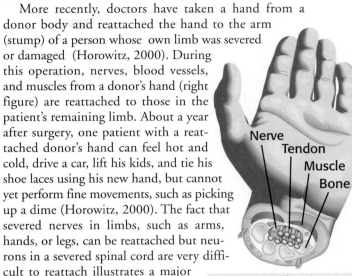

Nerve
Tendon
Muscle
Bone

**A donor's hand was attached to a different arm.**

## Peripheral Nervous System

### Why can limbs be reattached?

Severed limbs can be reattached and regain movement and sensation because their nerves are part of the peripheral nervous system.

The *peripheral nervous system* is made up of nerves, which are located throughout the body except in the brain and spinal cord.

*Nerves* are stringlike bundles of axons and dendrites that come from the spinal cord and are held together by connective tissue (shown in red in right figure). Nerves carry information from the senses, skin, muscles, and the body's organs to and from the spinal cord. Nerves in the peripheral nervous system have the ability to regrow or reattach if severed or damaged.

**Peripheral nerves can be reattached.**

The fact that nerves can regrow means that severed limbs can be reattached and limb transplants are possible. However, limb transplants are risky because a person must take drugs long-term to suppress his or her own immune system, whose normal job is to destroy "foreign" things, such as a donor's transplanted limb. By suppressing his or her own immune system, a person is at risk for getting serious infectious diseases (Gajilan & Leland, 1999).

The remarkable ability of nerves to regrow and be reattached distinguishes them from neurons.

## Central Nervous System

### Why wheelchairs?

People may find themselves in wheelchairs after damage to their spinal cords because of what neurons cannot easily do.

The *central nervous system* is made up of neurons located in the brain and spinal cord (shown in blue in left figure). The adult human brain has a limited capacity to grow new neurons and a limited ability to make new connections. Once damaged, neurons usually die and are not replaced.

Because neurons have such a limited capacity for repair or regrowth, people who have an injured or damaged brain or spinal cord experience some loss of sensation and motor movement, depending upon the severity of the damage. For example, Christopher Reeve (right photo) injured his spinal cord in the upper neck. Since his riding accident, Reeve has been confined to a wheelchair because neurons usually have a very limited capacity for regrowth or repair (Kluger, 1999).

**It is most unlikely that Reeve will ever walk.**

Currently, one of the most exciting areas of research involves techniques that stimulate the regrowth or repair of damaged neurons (Scott & Pawson, 2000). For example, axons, which carry information up and down the spinal cord, normally wither and die after injury, as happened to Reeve. However, in experiments with animals, those axons provided with tubes made from peripheral nerves to guide their growth or injected with growth-producing chemicals regrew and made new connections (Olson et al., 1997). These research findings in animals offer hope of developing similar methods to treat humans who have suffered brain or spinal cord injury (Seppa, 2000). Another approach for treating brain damage is to replace damaged neurons by transplanting fetal neurons into the damaged area. This method has great potential for treating brain diseases, such as Alzheimer's (Bjorklund, 2000). We'll discuss fetal tissue transplants in the Application section.

Now that you know the structure of the neuron, we'll explain one of its amazing functions: sending information at speeds approaching 200 miles per hour.

# D. Sending Information

## 1 Feeling a Sharp Object

When you step on a sharp object, you seem to feel the pain almost immediately because neurons send signals at speeds approaching 200 mph. To feel the pain involves the following series of electrochemical events:

A. Some stimulus, such as a tack, causes a change in physical energy. The tack produces mechanical pressure on the bottom of your foot.

B. Your skin has sensors that pick up the mechanical pressure and transform it into electrical signals. (We'll discuss various kinds of sensors in Module 5.)

C. The sensors' electrical signals are sent by the neuron's axon to various areas in the spinal cord and brain.

D. Finally, your brain interprets these electrical signals as "pain."

We're going to focus on step C and explain how axons send electrical signals by using the analogy of a battery. We'll begin by enlarging the inside of an axon.

## 2 Axon Membrane: Chemical Gates

Just as a battery has a protective covering, so too does the axon. Think of an axon as a long tube that is not only filled with fluid but also surrounded with fluid. The axon's tube is formed by a thin membrane, similar to a battery's outside covering, which keeps the fluid separate and also has special gates.

The *axon membrane* has chemical gates (shown in red) that can open to allow electrically charged particles to enter or can close to keep out electrically charged particles.

Just as a battery's power comes from its electrically charged chemicals, so does the axon's power to send information. In fact, the axon's electrically charged particles are the key to making it a living battery.

**Axon**

**Gates**

## 3 Ions: Charged Particles

The fluid inside and outside the axon contains ions.

*Ions* are chemical particles that have electrical charges. Ions follow two rules: opposite charges attract (figure below), and like charges repel.

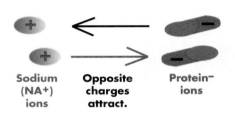

Sodium (NA+) ions — Opposite charges attract. — Protein⁻ ions

The fluid contains several different ions, such as sodium, potassium, chloride, and protein. The axon's function is often explained by discussing sodium and potassium ions. However, it is simpler and easier to focus on just sodium ions, which have positive charges and are abbreviated $Na^+$, and large protein ions, which have negative charges and are labeled protein⁻. Because they have opposite charges, $Na^+$ ions will be attracted to protein⁻ ions (figure above).

Because the axon's membrane separates the positive sodium ions from the negative protein ions, we have the makings of a living battery, as shown in section 4 on the next page.

---

## 6 Sending Information

One mistake students make is to think that the axon has ONE action potential, similar to the bang of a gunshot. However, unlike a gunshot, the axon has numerous individual action potentials that move down the axon, segment by segment; this movement is called the nerve impulse.

The *nerve impulse* refers to the series of separate action potentials that take place segment by segment as they move down the length of an axon.

Thus, instead of a single bang, a nerve impulse goes down the length of the axon very much like a lit fuse. Once lit, a fuse doesn't go off in a single bang but rather burns continuously until it reaches the end. This movement of a nerve impulse all the way down to the end of an axon is actually a natural law.

## 7 All-or-None Law

Why does a nerve impulse travel down the axon's entire length? The answer is the all-or-none law.

The *all-or-none law* says that, if an action potential starts at the beginning of an axon, the action potential will continue at the same speed, segment by segment, to the very end of the axon.

You'll see how the all-or-none law works in the next figure.

## 8 Nerve Impulse

Notice in this drawing, which continues on the next page, that the nerve impulse is made up of a sequence of six action potentials, with the first action potential occurring at the beginning of the axon.

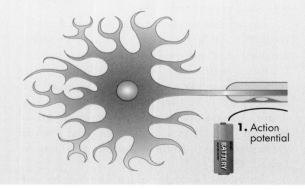

**1.** Action potential

BATTERY

---

## 4 Resting State: Charged Battery

The axon membrane separates positively charged sodium ions on the outside from negatively charged protein ions on the inside. This separation produces a miniature chemical battery that is not yet discharging and, thus, is said to be in its resting state.

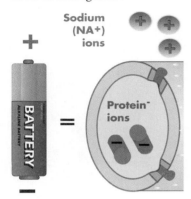

**Sodium (NA+) ions**

**Protein ions**

The *resting state* means that the axon has a charge, or potential; it resembles a battery. The charge, or potential, results from the axon membrane separating positive ions on the outside from negative ions on the inside (left figure).

The axon membrane has a charge across it during the resting state because of several factors, the primary one being the sodium pump. (To simplify our explanation of the resting state, we won't discuss other pump or transport systems.)

The *sodium pump* is a transport process that picks up any sodium ions that enter the axon's chemical gates and returns them back outside. Thus, the sodium pump is responsible for keeping the axon charged by returning and keeping sodium ions outside the axon membrane.

In the resting state, the axon is similar to a fully charged battery. Let's see what happens when the resting state is disrupted and the battery discharges.

## 5 Action Potential: Sending Information

If a stimulus, such as stepping on a tack, is large enough to excite a neuron, two things will happen to its axon. First, the stimulus will eventually open the axon's chemical gates by stopping the sodium pump. Second, when the stoppage of the sodium pump causes the gates to open, thousands of positive sodium ions will rush inside because of their attraction to the negative protein ions. The rush of sodium ions inside the axon is called the action potential.

The *action potential* is a tiny electrical current that is generated when the positive sodium ions rush inside the axon. The enormous increase of sodium ions inside the axon causes the inside of the axon to reverse its charge. The inside becomes positive, while the outside becomes negative.

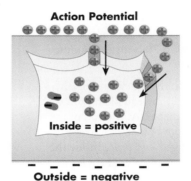

**Action Potential**

**Inside = positive**

**Outside = negative**

**5a** Just as a current flows when you connect the poles of a battery, current also flows when sodium ions rush through the opened gates of the axon membrane.

**5b** During an action potential, the inside of the axon changes to positive and the outside changes to negative. Immediately after the action potential, the sodium pump starts up and returns the axon to the resting state.

At this point, imagine that an action potential has started at the beginning of an axon. How action potentials whiz at race-car speeds down the entire length of an axon is what we'll examine next in the section below, Sequence: Nerve Impulse.

**8a** According to the all-or-none law, once a nerve impulse begins, it goes to the end of the axon. This means that when action potential 1 occurs, it will be followed in order by potentials 2, 3, 4, 5, and 6. After the occurrence of each action potential, the axon membrane at that point quickly returns to its resting state.

**8b** Notice that the *myelin sheath* has regular breaks where the axon is bare and uninsulated. It is at these bare points that the axon's gates open and the action potential takes place.

## 9 End Bulbs and Neurotransmitters

Once the nerve impulse reaches the end of the axon, the very last action potential, 6, affects the end bulbs, which are located at the very end of the axon. This last action potential triggers the end bulbs to release their neurotransmitters. Once released, neurotransmitters cross the synapse and, depending upon the kind, they will either excite or inhibit the function of neighboring organs (heart), muscles (head), or cell bodies.

As you can now see, neurotransmitters are critical for communicating with neighboring organs, muscles, and other neurons. We'll examine transmitters in more detail and show you how they excite or inhibit.

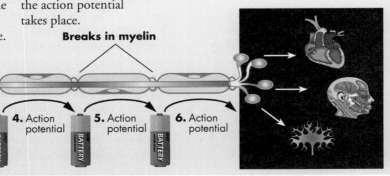

**Breaks in myelin**

**2.** Action potential  **3.** Action potential  **4.** Action potential  **5.** Action potential  **6.** Action potential

## E. Transmitters

### Excitatory and Inhibitory

**What makes your heart pound?**

There's no doubt that you have felt your heart pounding when you are afraid, stressed, or angry. One reason for your pounding heart has to do with transmitters.

A *transmitter* is a chemical messenger that transmits information between nerves and body organs, such as muscles and heart.

Everything you do, including thinking, deciding, talking, and getting angry, involves transmitters. For example, imagine seeing someone back into your brand new car and then just drive away. You would certainly become angry and your heart would pound. Let's see why getting angry can increase your heart rate from a normal 60 to 70 beats per minute to over 180.

Why does my heart rate increase when I get angry?

**1** In the figure on the left, you see the end of an axon with 3 branches. At the end of the bottom branch is a greatly enlarged *end bulb.* Inside the bulb are 4 colored circles that represent transmitters.

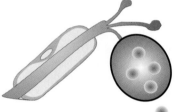

**2** When the action potential hits the *end bulb,* it causes a miniature explosion, and the transmitters are ejected outside. Once ejected, transmitters cross a tiny space, or synapse, and, in this case, reach the nearby heart muscle. Think of transmitters as chemical keys that fit into chemical locks on the surface of the heart muscle. End bulbs usually hold either excitatory or inhibitory transmitters, which have opposite effects.

**Transmitters**

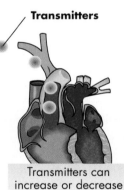

Transmitters can increase or decrease heart rate.

**3** Strong emotions cause the release of *excitatory transmitters,* which open chemical locks in the heart muscle and cause it to beat

**Excitatory**

faster (left figure). When you get very angry, excitatory transmitters may cause your heart rate to double or even triple its rate. When you start to calm down, there is a release of *inhibitory transmitters,* which block chemical locks in the heart muscle and decrease its rate (right figure). Think of transmitters acting like chemical messengers that either excite or inhibit nearby body organs (heart), neurons, or muscle fibers. One special class of transmitters that are made in the brain are called neurotransmitters.

**Inhibitory**

### Neurotransmitters

**What makes your brain work?**

Writing a paper on a computer requires your brain to use millions of neurons that communicate with one another by using chemicals called neurotransmitters. *Neurotransmitters* refer to about a dozen different chemicals that are made by neurons and then used for communication between neurons during the performance of mental or physical activities.

Since billions of neurons that are packed tightly together use different neurotransmitters for eating, sleeping, talking, thinking, and dreaming, why don't neurotransmitters get all mixed up? The answer is that neurotransmitters are similar to chemical keys that fit into only specific chemical locks.

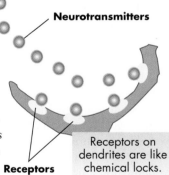
What happens in my brain when I use my computer?

**1** The figure on the left again shows the end of an axon with 3 branches. We have again enlarged one *end bulb* to show that it contains neurotransmitters (4 colored circles).

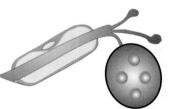

**2** The action potential causes the end bulbs to eject their neurotransmitters (colored circles), which, in turn, cross the synapse and, in this case, land on the surface of nearby dendrites. The surface of one dendrite is enlarged (right figure) to show its *receptors* (yellow ovals), which are special areas that function like chemical locks.

**Neurotransmitters**

Receptors on dendrites are like chemical locks.

**Receptors**

**3** Although there are many different neurotransmitters, each one has a unique chemical key that fits and opens only certain chemical locks, or receptors. Thus, billions of neurons use this system of chemical keys that open or close matching locks to communicate and to participate in so many different activities. Also, remember that some neurotransmitters are *excitatory*—they open receptor locks and turn on neurons—while others are *inhibitory*—they close locks and turn off neurons.

Since neurons use neurotransmitters to communicate, any drug that acts like or interferes with neurotransmitters has the potential to change how the brain functions and how we feel, think, and behave. For example, here's what alcohol does.

## Alcohol

**What does alcohol do?**

Drinking alcoholic beverages usually raises the level of alcohol in the blood, which is measured in terms of blood alcohol content (BAC). For example, at low to medium doses (0.01–0.06 BAC), alcohol causes friendliness, loss of inhibitions, decreased self-control, and impaired social judgment; after 3 or 4 drinks, the average person's BAC will range from 0.08 to 0.1, which meets the legal definition of drunkenness in most states. (Alcohol is discussed more fully in Module 8.)

*Why do I feel different after drinking?*

*Alcohol* (ethyl alcohol) is a psychoactive drug that is classified as a depressant, which means that it depresses the activity of the central nervous system.

Although alcohol has been around for 3,000 years, it is only recently that researchers have determined its effects on the brain. The effects of alcohol have proved difficult to pin down since it has so many. We'll discuss one of its major effects on the brain.

**GABA neurons.** Alcohol affects the nervous system in a number of ways, blocking some neural receptors and stimulating others. For example, some neurons are excited by a neurotransmitter called GABA (*GAH-bah*), which the brain normally manufactures. This means that GABA neurons (figure above) have chemical locks that can be opened by chemical keys in the form of the neurotransmitter GABA (Tsai et al., 1995).

**GABA keys.** Now here's the interesting part. Alcohol molecules so closely resemble those of the GABA neurotransmitter that alcohol can function like GABA keys and open GABA receptors (figure below right). Opening GABA receptors excites GABA neurons.

Although it seems backward, when GABA neurons are *excited*, they *decrease* neural activity and overall produce inhibitory effects, such as reduction in anxiety and tension, loss of inhibitions and self-control, and often an increase in friendliness. Thus, one reason alcohol is such a popular drug is that it reduces tension and anxiety (Stritzke et al., 1996).

One way that alcohol affects the brain is by imitating a naturally occurring neurotransmitter, GABA. Other drugs have different effects on the brain's neurotransmitters, several of which have been recently discovered.

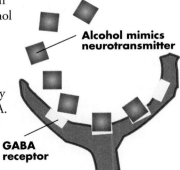

**Alcohol mimics neurotransmitter**

**GABA receptor**

## New Transmitters

**What are the latest discoveries?**

There are a number of well-known neurotransmitters, such as acetylcholine, GABA, norepinephrine, epinephrine, dopamine, and serotonin. However, researchers continue to discover new ones to add to the list of neurotransmitters.

**Endorphins.** In the 1970s, researchers discovered that the brain makes its own painkiller, very similar to morphine. They called this neurotransmitter endorphin, which is secreted to decrease the effects of pain during great bodily stress, such as an accident (Hughes et al., 1975). We'll discuss the effects of endorphins on page 113.

**Anandamide.** In the early 1990s, researchers discovered a somewhat surprising neurotransmitter, called anandamide, which is similar in chemical makeup to THC, the active ingredient in marijuana (discussed on page 186) (Fackelmann, 1993). The figure on the right shows a horizontal section of a rat brain that has been treated with a radioactive version of anandamide. The yellow areas, which were most affected by anandamide, are involved in memory, motor coordination, and emotions (Herkenham, 1996). Researchers speculate that anandamide may help humans deal with stress and pain (Fackelmann, 1993).

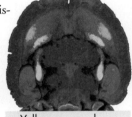

Yellow areas show where marijuana like anandamide acts.

**Nitric oxide.** In the mid-1990s, researchers discovered that a gas, nitric oxide, functions like a neurotransmitter and may be involved in regulation of emotions. For example, mice genetically altered to lack nitric oxide were six times more likely to pick a fight (right figure) compared to normal mice (Nelson et al., 1995). Based on these results, researchers think that nitric oxide may be involved in turning off aggression in mice and perhaps in humans.

**Other chemicals.** Currently, researchers have identified over a dozen chemicals that have all the characteristics of neurotransmitters and

Changing neurotransmitter levels in rats causes increased aggression.

another 40 to 50 chemicals that influence communication between neurons but do not have all the characteristics of true neurotransmitters (Klein, 2000). The important point to remember about neurotransmitters is that their system of chemical keys and locks permits very effective communication among billions of neurons, which allow us to move, sense, think, feel, and perform hundreds of other functions.

Now that you are familiar with the structure and function of the neuron and the importance of neurotransmitters, we'll use this knowledge to explain a response that many of you have experienced—what happened when you touched a hot object.

### Definition and Sequence

**Can you move without thinking?**

If you accidentally touched a hot light bulb, your hand would instantly jerk away, without any conscious thought or effort on your part. This is an example of a reflex.

A *reflex* is an unlearned, involuntary reaction to some stimulus. The neural connections or network underlying a reflex is prewired by genetic instructions.

In some cases, such as when a doctor taps your knee, the knee-jerk reflex is controlled by the spinal cord. In other cases, such as when someone shines a bright light into your eye, the pupillary reflex causes the pupil to constrict. We are all born with a number of programmed reflexes, and all reflexes share the same two or three steps, depending upon how they are wired in the nervous system.

One reason reflexes occur so quickly is that they are genetically programmed and involve relatively few neural connections, which saves time. Here's the sequence for how a reflex occurs:

**1 Sensors.** The skin of your fingers has specialized sensors, or receptors, that are sensitive to heat. When you touch a hot light bulb, these skin sensors trigger neurons that start the withdrawal reflex.

**2 Afferent neuron.** From the receptors in your skin, long dendrites carry "pain information" in the form of electrical signals to the spinal cord. These dendrites are part of sensory, or afferent, neurons (red arrows).

*Afferent* (AFF-er-ent), or *sensory, neuron*s carry information from the senses to the spinal cord.

Sensory neurons may have dendrites 2 to 3 feet long, to reach from the tips of your fingers to the spinal cord. When the pain information enters the spinal cord, it is transmitted to a second neuron.

**3 Interneuron.** Once the afferent neuron reaches the spinal cord, it transmits the pain information to a second neuron, called an interneuron.

An *interneuron* is a relatively short neuron whose primary task is making connections between other neurons.

In this example, an interneuron transmits the pain information to a third neuron, called the efferent, or motor, neuron.

**4 Efferent neuron.** Inside the spinal cord, an interneuron transfers information to a third neuron, called an efferent, or motor, neuron (blue arrows).

*Efferent* (EFF-er-ent), or *motor, neuron*s carry information away from the spinal cord to produce responses in various muscles and organs throughout the body.

From the spinal cord, an efferent (motor) neuron sends electrical signals on its 2- to 3-foot-long axon to the muscles in the hand. These electrical signals contain "movement information" and cause the hand to withdraw quickly and without any thought on your part.

In addition, an interneuron will send the pain information to other neurons that speed this information to different parts of the brain. These different parts interpret the electrical signals coming from your hand as being hot and painful. At this point your brain may direct motor neurons to move your facial and vocal muscles so that you look pained and yell "Ouch!" or something much more intense.

Afferent or sensory neuron

Efferent or motor neuron

3. Interneuron makes connections between neurons which carries message to the brain.

4. Efferent or motor neuron carries neural messages from spinal cord to hand.

2. Afferent or sensory neuron carries neural messages from hand to spinal cord.

### Functions of a Reflex

The primary reason you automatically withdraw your hand when touching a hot object, turn your head in the direction of a loud noise, or vomit after eating tainted food has to do with survival. Reflexes, which have evolved through millions of years, protect body parts from injury and harm and automatically regulate physiological responses, such as heart rate, respiration, and blood pressure. One primitive reflex that is no longer useful in our modern times is called piloerection, which causes the hair to stand up on your arms when you are cold. Piloerection helped keep heat in by fluffing hair for better insulation, but clothes now do a better job.

After the Concept Review, we'll discuss a very strange neural phenomenon that you may have heard of—phantom limb.

# Concept Review

**1.** The structure that nourishes and maintains the entire neuron is the (a)_____. Branchlike extensions that receive signals from senses and the environment are called (b)_____. A single thread-like extension that speeds signals away from the cell body toward a neighboring cell is the (c)_____. A tubelike structure that insulates the axon from interference by neighboring signals is the (d)_____. Tiny swellings at the very end of the axon are called (e)_____, which store neurotransmitters.

**2.** Chemicals that have electrical charges are called (a)_____. They obey the rule that opposite charges attract and like charges repel. Although the fluid of the axon contains a number of ions, we have focused on only two, a positively charged (b)_____ ion whose symbol is Na$^+$ and a negatively charged (c)_____ ion.

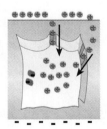

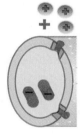

**3.** If an axon membrane has a potential similar to a charged battery, the axon is in the (a)_____. During this state, the ions outside the membrane are positively charged (b)_____ ions; the ions inside the membrane are negatively charged (c)_____ ions.

**4.** If an axon membrane is in a state similar to a discharging battery, the axon is generating an (a)_____. During this potential, the chemical gates open and positively charged (b)_____ rush inside, changing the inside of the membrane to a (c)_____ charge, while the outside of the membrane has a (d)_____ charge. As the action potential moves down the axon, it is called an (e)_____. Once it is generated, the impulse travels from the beginning to the end of the axon; this phenomenon is referred to as the (f)_____.

**5.** The end bulbs of one neuron are separated from the dendrites of a neighboring neuron by an extremely small space called the (a)_____. Into this space, end bulbs release chemicals, called (b)_____, which open/excite or block/inhibit neighboring receptors.

**6.** From end bulbs are secreted chemical keys or (a)_____ into the synapse. These chemical keys open matching locks called (b)_____, which are located on the surface of neighboring dendrites, muscles, or organs. Neurotransmitters that open a receptor's lock are called (c)_____; neurotransmitters that block a receptor's lock are called (d)_____.

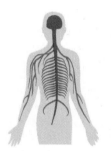

**7.** Neurons in the brain and spinal cord make up the (a)_____. If neurons are damaged, they have little ability to (b)_____ and usually die. The mature human brain has a limited ability to regrow (c)_____ throughout adulthood. Information from the body's senses, skin, organs, and muscles is carried to and from the spinal cord by nerves that make up the (d)_____. If this nervous system is damaged, (e)_____ in this system have a remarkable ability to regrow and make new connections. If your finger were accidentally cut off, it could be (f)_____ and there is a good chance that your finger would regain most of its sensory and motor functions.

**8.** If you touch a sharp object, your hand automatically withdraws because of a prewired reflex response. Neurons that carry "pain information" into the spinal cord are called (a)_____ neurons. Inside the spinal cord, there are short neurons, called (b)_____, that make connections between other neurons that carry information to the brain. Neurons that carry information away from the spinal cord to muscles or organs are called (c)_____ neurons.

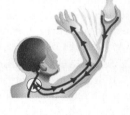

**Answers:** 1. (a) cell body or soma, (b) dendrites, (c) axon, (d) myelin sheath, (e) end bulbs; 2. (a) ions, (b) sodium, (c) protein; 3. (a) resting state, (b) sodium, (c) protein; 4. (a) action potential, (b) sodium ions, (c) positive, (d) negative, (e) impulse, or nerve impulse, (f) all-or-none law; 5. (a) synapse, (b) neurotransmitters; 6. (a) neurotransmitters, (b) receptors, (c) excitatory, (d) inhibitory; 7. (a) central nervous system, (b) regrow, repair, or reconnect, (c) neurons, (d) peripheral nervous system, (e) nerves, (f) reattached; 8. (a) sensory, or afferent, (b) interneurons, (c) motor, or efferent

# G. Research Focus: What Is a Phantom Limb?

## Case Study

**Why did Donald cut off his leg?**

Each Research Focus is about some interesting and puzzling question that researchers are trying to answer. This particular question, "How can you feel a phantom limb?" was first raised in 1866 and is closer now to being answered.

Donald Wyman was a bulldozer driver working in a remote forest when a giant oak tree accidentally fell and pinned him to the ground. All alone and with no one close enough to hear his shouts for help, Donald realized his only hope to get out from under the tree and survive was to cut off his leg, which he did with a 3-inch pocket knife.

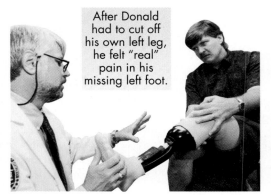

After Donald had to cut off his own left leg, he felt "real" pain in his missing left foot.

Although bleeding badly, he dragged himself to his truck and drove a mile and a half to get help. Even though his leg was recovered, it was too damaged to be reattached. Donald is now learning to walk with an artificial leg (left photo) that is fitted to the stump.

Donald's recovery is proceeding very well, but he says, "The toughest part since the accident is dealing with phantom pain. It feels like somebody's holding an electrical shock to your foot that's not there. It makes you jump around" (*USA Today*, August 31, 1993, p. 2A). Donald's case introduces you to the strange phenomenon of phantom limb.

## Definition and Data

**What is phantom limb?**

Very few symptoms have so surprised doctors as when patients reported feeling strange sensations or movements in arms or legs that had been amputated, a phenomenon called phantom limb.

*Phantom limb* refers to feeling sensations or movements coming from a limb that has been amputated. The sensations and movements are extremely vivid, as if the limb were still present.

As the figure on the right shows, the vast majority of individuals felt sensations ("pins and needles") or intense pain coming from their removed limbs. Patients insist that the phantom limb pain is real pain and not merely memories of previous pain (Hill et al., 1996).

| Patients' Reports after Removal of Limbs | |
|---|---|
| 80–100% | Report sensations |
| 70–80% | Report pain |

In other cases, amputees felt that their removed limbs were not only still present but stuck in certain positions, such as straight out from their bodies, so they felt they had to be very careful not to hit their phantom limbs when going through doorways (Katz, 1992).

From 1866 to the present, there have been at least three answers for what causes the feelings of sensations and movements coming from phantom limbs.

## Answers: Old and New

**1** **Sensations come from cut nerves in the stump.**

Early researchers thought that the phantom limb sensations come from cut nerves remaining in the stump. However, when these nerves were cut near the spinal cord, phantom limb should have been prevented; but the sensations still remained, so this early answer has been rejected (Melzack, 1997).

**2** **Sensations come from the spinal cord.**

If sensations from phantom limbs do not come from the stump, perhaps they originate in the spinal cord. However, even individuals whose spinal cords have been severed above the stump report phantom limb sensations. Since a severed spinal cord prevents sensations (electrical signals) from reaching the brain, this answer too has been rejected (Melzack, 1997).

**3** **Sensations come from a body image stored in the brain.**

Researchers now have enough data to indicate that the origin of phantom limb sensations must be the brain itself (Melzack, 1997). But having said that, researchers are puzzled about how the brain generates sensations from phantom limbs.

This newest and most creative answer to the origin of phantom limb sensations comes from researcher Ronald Melzack, who has

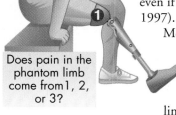

Does pain in the phantom limb come from 1, 2, or 3?

been studying this problem for about 40 years (Melzack, 1989, 1997). A simplified version of his theory is that each of us has a genetically programmed system of sensations that results in our knowing where our body parts are and in our developing an image of our body. Based on sensations from body parts, the brain pieces together a complete body image. Thus, having a body image, the brain itself can generate sensations as coming from any body part, even if that part is a phantom limb (Melzack, 1997).

Melzack admits that some of his theory must still be tested, but many researchers agree that it is so far one of the best answers to the 40-year-old question involving phantom limbs (Flor et al., 1995).

The phantom limb phenomenon points out that the brain sometimes functions in mysterious ways. Less mysterious is how certain drugs affect the functioning of the brain and the body.

# H. Cultural Diversity: Plants & Drugs

**Where did the first drugs come from?**

The very first drugs that affected neurotransmitters came from various plants, which people used long before researchers knew what those plants contained. We'll discuss three such drugs—cocaine, curare, and mescaline—which come from plants found in different parts of the world. We'll explain what these plants contain and their actions on the nervous systems.

## Cocaine: Blocking Reuptake

For almost 3,500 years, South American Indians have chewed leaves of the coca plant. Following this ancient custom, adult Indians habitually carry bags of toasted coca leaves, which contain cocaine. Throughout the day, they chew small amounts of coca leaves to relieve fatigue and feelings of hunger. Here's how cocaine affects neurotransmitters.

The drawing on the right shows a neuron's end bulb containing the neurotransmitter dopamine (*DOPE-ah-mean*). Once released, dopamine (colored blue circles) reaches the dendrite's receptors, opens their chemical locks, and activates the neuron. However, after a short period of time, the neurotransmitter is normally removed by being transported back into the end bulb through a process called reuptake.

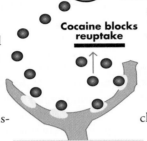

**Cocaine blocks reuptake**

Cocaine works by blocking reuptake.

*Reuptake* is a process through which some neurotransmitters, such as dopamine, are removed from the synapse by being transported back into the end bulbs.

If reuptake does not occur, the released neurotransmitter would continually affect the neuron by remaining longer in the synapse. What cocaine does is block reuptake so that dopamine remains longer in the synapse (Stahl, 2000). Because cocaine blocks reuptake, neurons are stimulated longer, resulting in the physiological arousal and feelings of euphoria that are associated with cocaine usage. Researchers now understand why South American Indians chewed coca leaves. The cocaine released from chewing coca leaves blocked the reuptake of dopamine, which in turn caused physiological arousal that relieved fatigue and feelings of hunger.

## Curare: Blocking Receptors

When hunting animals, the Indians of Peru and Ecuador coat the ends of blowdarts with the juice of a tropical vine that contains the paralyzing drug curare.

*Curare* (*cure-RAH-ree*) is a drug that enters the bloodstream, reaches the muscles, and blocks receptors on muscles. As a result, the neurotransmitter that normally activates muscles, which is called acetylcholine, is blocked, and muscles are paralyzed.

Once hit by a curare-tipped blowdart, an animal's limb muscles become paralyzed, followed by paralysis of chest muscles used to breathe.

Why did Indians coat blowdarts with curare?

Curare is an example of a drug that stops neural transmission by blocking the muscles' receptors. Today, the purified active ingredient in curare (tubocurarine chloride) is used to induce muscle paralysis in humans, such as when doctors insert a breathing tube down a patient's throat. Curare doesn't easily enter the brain because the body's blood must go through a filtering system before it can enter the brain. This filtering system, called the *blood-brain barrier,* prevents some, but not all, potentially harmful substances in the body's blood supply from reaching the brain.

## Mescaline: Mimicking a Neurotransmitter

A golf-ball-sized, gray-green plant (right photo) called peyote cactus grows in Mexico and the southwestern United States. Peyote contains mescaline.

*Mescaline* (*MESS-ka-lin*) is a drug that causes physiological arousal as well as visual hallucinations. Mescaline's chemical keys are similar to those of the neurotransmitter norepinephrine (*nor-epee-NEFF-rin*).

Because mescaline's chemical keys open the same chemical locks (receptors) as norepinephrine, mescaline produces its effects by mimicking the actions of norepinephrine.

In 1965, an estimated 250,000 members of the Native American Church in the United States and Canada won a Supreme Court case that permits them to be the only group legally authorized to use peyote in their religious services. To enhance meditation, members may eat from 4 to 12 peyote buttons, which results in visual sensations, euphoria, and sometimes nausea and vomiting.

Mescaline comes from peyote cactus.

**Conclusion.** These three plants—cocaine, curare, and mescaline—contain potent drugs that illustrate three different ways of affecting the nervous system. Researchers have discovered numerous plants, including the opium poppy, marijuana, and "magic" mushrooms, which contain drugs that in turn affect neurotransmitters (discussed in Module 8).

Neurotransmitters are the keys that turn the brain's functions on or off. For example, Alzheimer's disease interferes with neurons and neurotransmitters and turns off the brain's functions. Such is the case with another terrible disease, called Parkinson's, which we'll discuss next.

## Parkinson's Disease

**Why does Bob's arm shake?**

Part of Bob's job was to climb poles and make electrical repairs. He was good at his job until he began to notice that, for no apparent reason, his hands would shake or become rigid. The shakes and tremors in his arms grew worse until he couldn't hold his tools. When his symptoms forced him to stop working, his tremors were so bad that he was too embarrassed to eat out or be seen in public. Many days he had trouble walking because his legs would suddenly become stiff and rigid and he couldn't move. It was like being frozen in space.

Bob had all the symptoms of Parkinson's disease.

*Parkinson's disease* includes symptoms of tremors and shakes in the limbs, a slowing of voluntary movements, and feelings of depression. As the disease progresses,

patients develop a peculiar shuffling walk and may suddenly freeze in space for minutes or hours at a time. Parkinson's is caused by a destruction of neurons that produce the neurotransmitter dopamine (*DOPE-ah-mean*).

Like most Parkinson's patients, Bob was placed on a medication called L-dopa, which boosts the levels of dopamine in the brain. However, patients must take ever-increasing amounts of L-dopa, until the drug itself causes involuntary jerky movements that may be as bad as those produced by Parkinson's. Thus, L-dopa controls but does not cure the symptoms of Parkinson's, and after prolonged use, L-dopa's beneficial effects may be replaced by unwanted jerky movements.

In spite of taking L-dopa, Bob's symptoms were getting worse. He had heard about an experimental treatment in which fetal brain tissue that contained dopamine-producing neurons was transplanted into an area of the brain called the basal ganglia.

The *basal ganglia* are a group of structures located in the center of the brain and are involved in regulating movements. To function properly, neurons in the basal ganglia must have a sufficient supply of the neurotransmitter dopamine.

The reason Bob's symptoms had worsened was that neurons in his basal ganglia were running out of dopamine. After Bob reached what he called the "point of no return," he chose to have an experimental treatment, a fetal tissue transplant (*Los Angeles Times,* November 26, 1992).

In the United States, about 1.5 million adults, usually over age 50, have Parkinson's disease (Perry, 2000). Causes of Parkinson's disease include genetic and possible environmental factors (Lucking et al., 2000). To date, Parkinson's has no known cure.

## Issues Involving Transplants

**Why not just use drugs?**

**Human cells.** The majority of patients, like Bob, have found that using L-dopa for 10 years or more to treat Parkinson's disease produces unwanted side effects, such as involuntary movements, as well as the return of some of the original symptoms described above (Troster, 2000).

Because of the disappointing long-term results of using L-dopa to treat Parkinson's disease, a search has begun for alternative treatments, such as the use of fetal brain tissue transplants.

Previously, researchers had shown that when fetal rat brain tissue was transplanted into older rats, the fetal neurons lived, grew, functioned, and allowed brain-damaged older rats to relearn the solutions to mazes (Shetty & Turner, 1996). Following successful fetal transplants in rats and monkeys, researchers began to transplant human fetal brain tissue into patients who were suffering from Parkinson's disease.

The primary reason for using 6- to 8-week-old fetal tissue for transplants is that this fetal tissue has a unique ability to survive and

A neuron from an 8-week-old fetus has almost no dendritic branches but is primed for development. After being transplanted, a fetal neuron develops extensive dendritic branches.

A neuron from an adult human brain has developed elaborate dendritic branches. Thus, if a mature neuron is transplanted, it develops few, if any, new branches.

make connections in a patient's brain or body. For example, the figure on the left shows that dendrites of fetal neurons are barely developed compared to the well-developed dendrites of adult neurons. Because fetal brain tissue is primed for growth, it has a far greater chance of survival after transplantation than does tissue from mature brains (Barinaga, 2000b).

**Pig cells.** Because of ethical and legal questions surrounding the use of human fetal cells, researchers have tried using cells from fetal pig brains. Ten patients with advanced Parkinson's disease were each given transplants of 12 million fetal pig brain cells. Three years after transplant, six patients showed slight to moderate improvement (Dinsmore, 2000). However, transplanting animal cells into human brains increases the danger of also transferring animal bacteria, diseases, or viruses. So far, no animal diseases or related problems have been found in Parkinson's patients who received fetal pig transplants.

Next we'll explain how fetal brain cells are transplanted into a human brain.

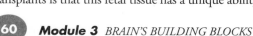

Fetal pig brain cells have been implanted into human brains.

**Procedure.** The neurosurgeon first removes nervous tissue from a 6- to 8-week-old aborted human fetus brain and then transplants the tissue into the basal ganglia of Bob's brain.

The method used to transplant fetal cells into a precise location in either animal or human brains is called the stereotaxic procedure.

The *stereotaxic procedure* (right figure) involves fixing a patient's head in a holder and drilling a small hole through the skull. The holder has a syringe that can be precisely guided into a predetermined location in the brain.

As shown on the right, Bob's head has been fixed in the stereotaxic holder. In this figure, a large part of the skull has been removed to show the brain, but in actual surgery, only a small, pencil-sized hole is drilled in the patient's skull. A long needle from the syringe (lower left in the figure) extends from the holder into the basal ganglia of his brain. The surgeon will slowly inject human fetal cells into Bob's basal ganglia.

The advantages of the stereotaxic procedure are that a thin syringe can be placed in precise locations in the brain and that it causes relatively little damage to the brain. The stereotaxic procedure can be used to either inject solutions or destroy diseased brain tissue.

**Results.** Before surgery, Bob had suffered severe tremors and rigidity. About a year after surgery, Bob and a friend drove a motor home across country. Bob said, "I was able to take care of myself for the first time in a long time—buying groceries, filling the car with gas, and driving. I tried golf and played nine holes several times." Bob says that he still has ups and downs but that his symptoms are much more controllable (*Los Angeles Times,* November 26, 1992).

To date, about 150 Parkinson's patients worldwide have been treated with fetal tissue transplants. About 30 to 60% of these patients showed substantial improvement, but none have been completely cured. Patients under 60 years old showed the most improvement, while those over 60 reported little or no improvement in symptoms (Freed, 1999).

However, a number of questions remain: Should Parkinson's patients be treated before symptoms become too severe, how much fetal tissue should be implanted, what are the best areas for implantation, and should fetal tissue from pigs' brains be used since human fetal cells are in very short supply (six human fetuses are required to supply tissue for one Parkinson's patient)? Researchers believe that answering these questions will lead to higher rates of success (Barinaga, 2000b; Dinsmore, 2000). One way to determine how well the transplanted neural tissue is functioning is by doing brain scans.

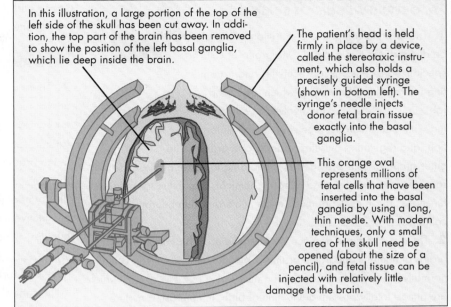

In this illustration, a large portion of the top of the left side of the skull has been cut away. In addition, the top part of the brain has been removed to show the position of the left basal ganglia, which lie deep inside the brain.

The patient's head is held firmly in place by a device, called the stereotaxic instrument, which also holds a precisely guided syringe (shown in bottom left). The syringe's needle injects donor fetal brain tissue exactly into the basal ganglia.

This orange oval represents millions of fetal cells that have been inserted into the basal ganglia by using a long, thin needle. With modern techniques, only a small area of the skull need be opened (about the size of a pencil), and fetal tissue can be injected with relatively little damage to the brain.

### Before Transplant

This brain scan shows few dopamine-producing neurons in basal ganglia, as indicated by mostly white and small yellow areas but few red areas.

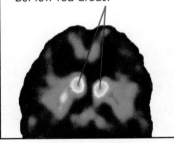

### After Transplant

This brain scan shows that 33 months after transplant there are new dopamine-producing neurons in basal ganglia, as indicated by larger yellow and red areas.

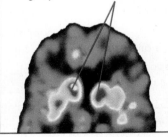

**Brain scans.** The critical question is: Once transplanted, does fetal tissue survive and produce neurotransmitter? One way to answer this question is with brain scans, which take pictures of the living brain and show the activity of neurons. For example, a brain scan before transplant (upper left) shows the low activity level of dopamine-producing neurons, as indicated by the small yellow areas and almost no red areas.

However, a brain scan 33 months after transplant (lower left) shows that the red and yellow areas have increased significantly, which indicates that transplanted neurons are actually producing dopamine. These scans offer dramatic evidence that fetal tissue does survive and produce dopamine when transplanted into other brains (Freed et al., 1992).

**Significance of fetal tissue transplant.** Since diseased or damaged neurons do not usually regrow, the use of fetal tissue transplants, with human or possibly animal donor tissue, is currently the only treatment for replacing diseased neurons.

Researchers hope that fetal tissue transplants will become a new treatment for various currently incurable brain diseases, which include about 1.5 million Parkinson's patients and, like Ina, whom we described at the beginning of this module, about 4 million Alzheimer's patients (Perry, 2000).

## A. OVERVIEW: HUMAN BRAIN

**1.** The brain is composed of a trillion cells that can be divided into two groups. One group of cells has specialized extensions for receiving and transmitting information. These cells, which are called (a)_____, are involved in communicating with other neurons, receiving sensory information, and regulating muscles, glands, and organs. The other group of cells provide the scaffolding to guide and support neurons, insulate neurons, and release chemicals that influence neuron functions. These cells are much more numerous than neurons and are called (b)_____.

**2.** There is a major difference between the growth of neurons in the brains of humans and in the brains of birds. A mature human brain is normally not capable of developing new (a)_____, which are almost totally present at the time of birth. In contrast, a mature (b)_____ brain has the capacity to develop new neurons.

**3.** The age-old question of how the brain's membranes, fluids, and chemicals are involved in generating complex mental activities, such as thoughts, images, and feelings, is called the _____ question.

## B. NEURONS: STRUCTURE & FUNCTION

**4.** Although neurons come in wondrous shapes and sizes, they all share three structures. The structure that maintains the entire neuron in working order, manufactures chemicals, and provides fuel is called the (a)_____. The structure with many branchlike extensions that receive signals from other neurons, muscles, or organs and conduct these signals to the cell body is called a (b)_____. The single threadlike extension that leaves the cell body and carries signals to other neurons, muscles, or organs is called the (c)_____. At the very end of this structure are individual swellings called (d)_____, which contain tiny vesicles filled with (e)_____.

**5.** Surrounding most axons is a fatty material called the (a)_____. This material acts like (b)_____ and diminishes interference from electrical signals traveling in neighboring axons.

**6.** Neurons do not make physical contact with one another or with other organs. Instead, there is an infinitely small space between a neuron's end bulbs and neighboring dendrites, cell bodies, or other organs. This space is called the (a)_____. When an axon's end bulbs secrete a neurotransmitter, it flows across this space and affects the (b)_____ on the neighboring membrane.

## C. NEURONS VERSUS NERVES

**7.** There are major differences between neurons and nerves. Cells with specialized extensions for conducting electrical signals are called (a)_____. These cells, which are located in the brain and spinal cord, make up the (b)_____ nervous system. Stringlike bundles of neurons' axons and dendrites, which are held together by connective tissue, are called (c)_____. These stringlike bundles, which are located throughout the body, make up the (d)_____ nervous system. Nerves carry information back and forth between the body and the spinal cord. If a neuron in the central nervous system is damaged, it normally does not have the capacity to (e)_____. In comparison, a nerve in the (f)_____ nervous system has the capacity to regrow or reattach if cut or damaged. The mature human brain has a limited ability to regrow (g)_____ throughout adulthood.

## D. SENDING INFORMATION

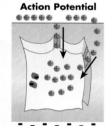

**Action Potential**

**8.** The axon membrane has (a)_____ that can be opened or closed. These gates keep some ions inside the membrane and other ions outside. If the axon is ready to conduct but not actually conducting an impulse, the axon is said to be in the (b)_____ state. In this state, most of the positively charged (c)_____ ions are on the outside of the membrane and all the negatively charged (d)_____ ions are trapped inside. In the resting state, the outside of the membrane has a (e)_____ charge compared to the (f)_____ charge on the inside. The process responsible for picking up and transporting sodium ions from the inside to the outside of the axon membrane is called the (g)_____.

**9.** If a stimulus is strong enough to excite a neuron, two things happen to its axon. First, the stimulus will eventually open the axon's (a)_____. Second, after the gates are opened, the (b)_____ pump is stopped, and all the positive (c)_____ ions rush inside because they are attracted to the negatively charged protein ions. The rush of sodium ions inside generates a tiny electrical current that is called the (d)_____. When this current is generated, the inside of the axon membrane changes to a (e)_____ charge and the outside changes to a (f)_____ charge.

**10.** Once an action potential starts in the axon, it continues, segment by segment, down the entire length of the axon, creating the (a)_____. Once an action potential is triggered in the segment at the beginning of the axon, other action potentials will be triggered in sequence down the entire length of the axon; this phenomenon is called the (b)_____.

## E. TRANSMITTERS

**11.** Once started, the action potential will reach the end bulbs at the end of the axon. The action potential excites the end bulbs and causes them to secrete (a)_____ that were stored in the end bulbs. Neurotransmitters function like chemical keys that unlock chemical locks or (b)_____, which are located on neighboring neurons, muscles, or other organs. If neurotransmitters open the receptors' locks on neighboring cells, they are said to be (c)_____. If neurotransmitters block the receptors' locks, they are said to be (d)_____. Because of these different actions, neurotransmitters can cause different and even opposite responses in neurons, muscles, or organs. There are about a dozen well-known neurotransmitters. One of the newly discovered neurotransmitters that has a chemical makeup similar to THC in marijuana is called (e)_____ and is involved in emotions and motor coordination.

## F. REFLEX RESPONSES

**12.** The movement of automatically withdrawing your hand after touching a hot object is called a (a)_____, which involves several or more neurons. Information is carried to the spinal cord by the (b)_____ neuron. Information is carried from the spinal cord to the muscle by the (c)_____ neuron. Connections between efferent (motor) and afferent (sensory) neurons are made by relatively short (d)_____, which also send signals to the brain. The functions of reflexes include protecting body parts from (e)_____ and automatically regulating the (f)_____ responses of the body.

## G. RESEARCH FOCUS: WHAT IS A PHANTOM LIMB?

**13.** The experience of sensations from a limb that has been amputated is called the (a)_____ phenomenon. About 70–80% of patients report sensations of intense pain coming from limbs that have been amputated. A recent explanation of phantom limb sensations is that they arise from the brain's genetically programmed system of sensations that allows the brain to know the locations of all the body's (b)_____.

## H. CULTURAL DIVERSITY: PLANTS & DRUGS

**14.** One of cocaine's effects on the nervous system is to block the process of (a)_____ so that the neurotransmitter remains longer in the synapse, which causes physiological arousal. A drug that blocks receptors on muscles and causes muscle paralysis is (b)_____. A drug that mimics the naturally occurring neurotransmitter norepinephrine and can produce visual hallucinations is (c)_____.

## I. APPLICATION: FETAL TISSUE TRANSPLANT

**15.** The tremors and rigidity of Parkinson's disease result when a group of structures that regulate movement, called the (a)_____, lose their supply of dopamine. In an experimental operation, fetal brain cells are transplanted into a precise location of a patient's brain by a technique called the (b)_____ procedure. By this procedure, fetal transplants have been used with slight to moderate success to treat (c)_____ disease, which destroys neurons that produce dopamine.

***Answers:*** *1. (a) neurons, (b) glial cells; 2. (a) neurons, (b) bird; 3. mind-body; 4. (a) cell body, or soma, (b) dendrite, (c) axon, (d) end bulbs, (e) neurotransmitters; 5. (a) myelin sheath, (b) insulation; 6. (a) synapse, (b) receptors; 7. (a) neurons, (b) central, (c) nerves, (d) peripheral, (e) regrow, (f) peripheral, (g) neurons; 8. (a) chemical gates, (b) resting, (c) sodium, (d) protein, (e) positive, (f) negative, (g) sodium pump; 9. (a) chemical gates, (b) sodium, (c) sodium, (d) action potential, (e) positive, (f) negative; 10. (a) nerve impulse, (b) all-or-none law; 11. (a) neurotransmitters, (b) receptors, (c) excitatory, (d) inhibitory, (e) anandamide; 12. (a) reflex, or reflex response, (b) sensory, or afferent, (c) motor, or efferent, (d) interneurons, (e) injury or harm, (f) physiological; 13. (a) phantom limb, (b) parts; 14. (a) reuptake, (b) curare, (c) mescaline; 15. (a) basal ganglia, (b) stereotaxic, (c) Parkinson's*

# Critical Thinking

## Would You Want a Head Transplant?

### Questions

**1.** From what you know about the central nervous system, what's the major problem in transplanting a head?

**2.** Why do researchers first develop new medical procedures in animals before trying them on humans?

**3.** Why do damaged neurons usually wither and die instead of regrowing?

Everyone knows the story of Dr. Frankenstein, who transplanted a brain into a dead body and brought this creature to life with a jolt from a lightning bolt. As a serious and respected researcher, Dr. Robert J. White, Harvard Medical School graduate and professor of neurosurgery at Case Western Reserve University, believes that a complete head (including brain) transplant is becoming increasingly possible.

Dr. White has been working for the past 40 years on the possibility of transplanting a head. In the 1960s, he succeeded in removing brains from monkeys and keeping the brains alive in special solutions for up to 22 hours. In the 1970s, he successfully removed the complete head from one rhesus monkey and transplanted it onto the body of another monkey. He reports that this "new" monkey with the transplanted head regained consciousness, tried to bite the researchers, moved its eyes, and lived for eight days—dying of lung failure. Although transplanting a head has a number of practical applications, it also raises ethical, religious, and moral questions.

As to practical applications, a head transplant would mean that if quadriplegics' bodies developed life-threatening problems, they could have their healthy heads (and brains) transplanted onto healthy donor bodies and thus keep on living. (Quadriplegics have damaged spinal cords that prevent all movement and sensations from the neck down and

often develop life-threatening lung problems.) Because researchers have not yet solved the problem of how to reconnect spinal cords, the quadriplegic's head could not send or receive information from the donor's body. But if you were a quadriplegic with a diseased and dying body, would you want the choice and chance of living a little longer by having your healthy head transplanted onto a donor's healthy body?

Among the ethical and moral questions are whether someone with a healthy head should be allowed to live on top of a stranger's body. Or, how would a family react to knowing that their dead son's or daughter's body is still alive? Among the religious questions are what happens to a person's mind or soul when the person's head is now transplanted onto a different body. Or, is it right to separate the head from the body for any reason?

Dr. White answers these questions by saying that defining death is a medical and not a religious issue. He believes the body is essentially an "energy pack" and concludes by saying, "If a procedure can help somebody live longer, I think most doctors and patients are willing to do what they can, particularly if the alternative is death." (Adapted from S. LaFee, At hand and ahead, *San Diego Union-Tribune,* March 8, 2000, p. E-1)

**4.** What advances have been made in getting damaged neurons to regrow?

**5.** How do many neuroscientists view the mind-brain distinction?

**6.** How does Dr. White answer questions about the mind and soul?

*Try these InfoTrac search terms:* **organ**  **transplant; neurosurgery; quadriplegia; mind-brain.**

---

*Suggested answers to Newspaper Article questions*

1. Surgeons can transplant many body organs (hearts, lungs, kidneys, even hands) because peripheral nerves regrow. However, the major problem in transplanting a complete head involves reconnecting the head's spinal cord to the spinal cord in the donor's body. That's because damaged or severed neurons that are in the central nervous system do not usually reconnect or regrow.
2. As discussed on page 41, this raises the ethical question of whether animals should be used in research. The major reason researchers first use animals to develop complicated medical procedures, such as heart or future head transplants, is to work out problems and avoid life-threatening risks to humans.
3. As discussed on page 49, damaged neurons (central nervous system) usually wither and die because of a built-in genetic program

that turns off future regrowth or repair once a neuron is fully grown.
4. As discussed on page 51, researchers are stimulating damaged neurons to regrow by providing tubes to guide regrowth and by injecting growth-producing chemicals.
5. As discussed on page 49, the age-old mind-body (brain) question has several answers. Some philosophers believe that the mind (spirit or soul) and brain are separate things. In contrast, many researchers believe that the mind and the brain are either the same thing or like two sides of a coin.
6. Dr. White seems to believe that the mind (soul, spirit) and brain are one and the same since he defines death as being a medical rather than a spiritual problem.

# Links to Learning

## Web Sites

- **WADSWORTH ONLINE STUDY CENTER**
  http://psychology.wadsworth.com
  Quizzes, learning activities and exercises, a discussion forum, and hot links to Internet sites related to the brain, including:

- **BASIC NEURAL PROCESS TUTORIALS**
  http://psych.hanover.edu/Krantz/neurotut.html
  The interactive tutorials on neural processes were designed for undergraduate students.

- **NEUROSURGERY AT NEW YORK UNIVERSITY**
  http://mcns10.med.nyu.edu
  This fascinating site contains fully illustrated examples of brain surgery, and case studies highlighting a full range of nervous system disorders.

- **ALZHEIMER WEB HOME PAGE**
  http://www.alzweb.org
  Devoted to research on Alzheimer's disease, this site is visited more than 1000 times per day. There are many links in a variety of categories, including one to the *Journal of Alzheimer's Disease.*

- **FOUNDERS OF NEUROLOGY**
  http://www.uic.edu/depts/mcne/founders
  This is a wonderful list of links from the Department of Neurology at the University of Illinois. Thumbnail descriptions and photos of 88 neurologists from A (Edward Actin) to W (Wilhelm Wundt) may inspire you to research one or more in greater depth, for a report or simply to satisfy your curiosity about this fascinating field.

## Learning Activities

- ***POWERSTUDY*™ CD, BY ROD PLOTNIK & TOM DOYLE**
  Check out Module 3, "Brain's Building Blocks," for a  40-minute, fully narrated, self-paced, interactive, multimedia presentation on the brain. Includes animations, videos, hot links to the Web, quizzes, pronunciation of terms, and personal note-taking capability.

- ***STUDY GUIDE TO ACCOMPANY INTRODUCTION TO PSYCHOLOGY, 6TH EDITION,* by Matthew Enos**
  In Module 3, "a mini-course in biology," you're encouraged to concentrate on the processes of neurology, and not get bogged down in details.

- ***WEBTUTOR***
  http://webtutor.thomsonlearning.com
  Visit this site for interactive versions of Study Guide features. Take a quiz, get your score—should you study a topic some more, or can you move on? Can you define the terms *action potential, mescaline,* and *neurotransmitters?* Your professor's class syllabus and course calendar are also posted—you'll never have to get behind in class again!

- ***INFOTRAC ONLINE LIBRARY***
  http://www.infotrac-college.com
   Use your password and then key in search terms such as those below to find popular and scientific articles on subjects covered in Module 3. Make the library work for you!

  | | | |
  |---|---|---|
  | Human brain | Neurons | Nerves |
  | Central nervous system | Reflexes | Cocaine |

- ***PSYCHNOW!***
  CD for Macintosh and Windows includes a study guide, glossary, Web sites, and animations. For Module 3, see:

  Neurons and Synaptic Transmission

## Study Questions

*Use InfoTrac to search for topics mentioned in the following questions (e.g., neurotransmitters, phantom limb, fetal tissue transplant).*

*A. **Overview: Human Brain**—Why is it really smart to drive a car only if it is equipped with driver- and passenger-side airbags? (**Suggested answer page 620**)

B. **Neurons: Structure & Function**—How would you decide if a piece of tissue came from the brain or from a muscle?

C. **Neurons versus Nerves**—Headline—"Chimp Brain Transplanted into Human Skull." Is this possible?

*D. **Sending Information**—How are the structure and function of the axon like those of a battery? (**Suggested answer page 620**)

E. **Transmitters**—What are some of the ways that nerve gas could cause death?

F. **Reflex Responses**—How might the reflexes of professional tennis players differ from those of amateurs?

G. **Research Focus: What Is a Phantom Limb?**—What problems might you have after your hand was amputated?

*H. **Cultural Diversity: Plants & Drugs**—What are the different ways that drugs can affect neurotransmitters? (**Suggested answer page 620**)

I. **Application: Fetal Tissue Transplant**—Would you recommend that a family member with Parkinson's be treated with a fetal transplant?

*These questions are answered in Appendix B.

# Module 4: Incredible Nervous System

A. Genes & Evolution    68
  * GENETIC INSTRUCTIONS
  * EVOLUTION OF THE HUMAN BRAIN

B. Studying the Living Brain    70
  * NEW TECHNIQUES
  * MRI BRAIN SCANS
  * PET BRAIN SCANS
  * PICTURING THOUGHTS

C. Organization of the Brain    72
  * DIVISIONS OF THE NERVOUS SYSTEM
  * MAJOR PARTS OF THE BRAIN

D. Control Centers: Four Lobes    74
  * OVERALL VIEW OF THE CORTEX
  * FRONTAL LOBE: FUNCTIONS
  * PARIETAL LOBE: FUNCTIONS
  * TEMPORAL LOBE: FUNCTIONS
  * OCCIPITAL LOBE: FUNCTIONS

E. Limbic System: Old Brain    80
  * STRUCTURES AND FUNCTIONS
  * AUTONOMIC NERVOUS SYSTEM

F. Endocrine System    82
  * DEFINITION
  * CONTROL CENTER
  * OTHER GLANDS

Concept Review    83

G. Research Focus: Sex Differences in the Brain?    84
  * SCIENCE AND POLITICS

H. Cultural Diversity: Brain Size & Racial Myths    85
  * SKULL SIZE AND INTELLIGENCE
  * BRAIN SIZE AND INTELLIGENCE

I. Application: Split Brain    86
  * DEFINITION AND TESTING
  * BEHAVIORS FOLLOWING SPLIT BRAIN
  * DIFFERENT FUNCTIONS
  * WHAT AM I?

Summary Test    88

Critical Thinking    90
  * CAN DAMAGED BRAIN LEARN MORALS?

Links to Learning    91

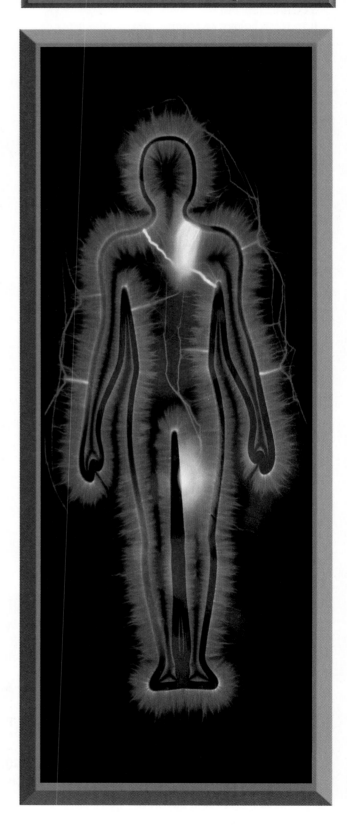

PowerStudy™

## Lucy's Brain: Earliest Ancestor

Although Lucy was fully grown, she was short and slightly built, standing a little under 4 feet tall and weighing about 55 pounds. She had an apelike head, and her face (left drawing) had a large brow above her eyes and a protruding jaw that held big, uneven front teeth. Lucy had a lot of hair, was very muscular, walked upright on slightly bent legs, and had powerful arms for climbing trees to search for fruits and nuts.

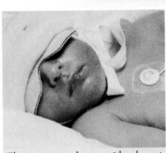

Possible human ancestor lived 3 million years ago.

Anthropologists think that Lucy did not make tools, knew nothing of fire, and conversed with hand gestures, waves, and grunts. Lucy's small skull held a brain that was only about the size of a chimpanzee's, which is about one-third the size of ours. The males of her species were about a foot taller than Lucy and at least two-thirds heavier.

Anthropologists believe that Lucy's species, formally named *Australopithecus afarensis,* lived about 3 million years ago and may be the earliest ancestor of modern humans (Johanson, 1996).

We'll use Lucy's brain as an example of how the human brain is thought to have evolved and increased in size over 3 million years.

## Baby Theresa's Brain: Fatal Flaw

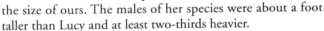

Theresa was born with almost all of her brain missing.

The press called her Baby Theresa. She was one of about 1,000 babies born each year in the United States with a disorder that is always fatal.

Baby Theresa (left photo) had almost no brain and therefore would never develop the functions we associate with being human, such as thinking, talking, reasoning, and planning. She survived for 9 days because a very primitive part of her brain was still functioning. This small, primitive brain area lies directly above the spinal cord and regulates vital reflexes, such as breathing, blood pressure, and heart rate. These vital reflexes kept her alive for a little over a week.

We'll use Baby Theresa's tragic case to illustrate some of the different structures and functions of the brain.

## Steve's Brain: Cruel Fate

When Steve walked into the hotel, he felt an incredible pain in his head. He was 28 years old, a successful journalist, and in excellent health, but something terrible was happening.

He could barely talk to the hotel clerk, who said that Steve's room wasn't ready. He slowly walked to a chair and sat down

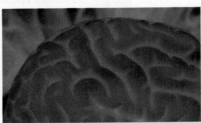

What happened to Steve's brain that prevented him from telling time?

to wait. He glanced at the clock on the wall to check the time. He could clearly see the hands of the clock, but he could not figure out the time. Like a small child, he said out loud, "The big hand is on twelve and the little hand is on eight." When he heard the words, he knew it was 8 o'clock and wondered why he could tell time by sound but not by sight (Fishman, 1988).

We'll use Steve's unsettling experience to show some of the symptoms of brain damage and how neurologists can examine the living brain.

## Scott's Brain: Wrong Instructions

"As a very young baby, Scott seemed okay," said his mother, Cindy. "He cooed and smiled at the right times. He babbled at the right times. He seemed normal" (LaFee, 1996, p. E-1). But it was his constant crying that scared her. Scott would walk outside and burst into tears, and no one could comfort him.

As Scott (right photo) got older, other problems developed. He couldn't sit up, he refused to play with other children, and often he was off in a world of his own. Finally, an examination of Scott's genetic makeup revealed that he had inherited fragile X syndrome, which is the most common genetic disorder in America (Fisch et al., 1996).

Scott has a genetic defect that affects his functioning.

We'll use Scott's problem to explain how genetic instructions are written and what happens if the instructions have errors.

## What's Coming

The brains of Lucy, Baby Theresa, Steve, and Scott raise a number of questions. Lucy's brain brings up the question of evolution, which says that modern brains have been evolving for 3 million years. Baby Theresa's brain raises the question of what it means to be human. Steve's brain brings up the questions of what happens when brains are damaged and whether doctors can look inside living brains. Finally, Scott's brain raises the questions of how brains develop and why things go wrong. We'll answer these questions as well as discuss all the major structures and functions of the human brain.

Let's begin with how genetic instructions are written.

### Genetic Instructions

**What makes brains different?**

Your brain and body developed according to complex chemical instructions that were written in a human cell no larger than a grain of sand. The reason brains and bodies have different shapes, colors, and abilities is that they develop from different instructions, which are written at the moment of fertilization.

**1 Fertilization.** Human life has its beginnings when a father's sperm, which contains 23 chromosomes, penetrates a mother's egg, which contains 23 chromosomes. The result is a fertilized cell called a zygote, which is shown in the figure below.

**2 Zygote.** A zygote (figure above), which is about the size of a grain of sand, is the largest human cell.

A *zygote* is a cell that results when an egg is fertilized. A zygote contains 46 chromosomes arranged in 23 pairs.

A zygote contains the equivalent of 300,000 pages of typewritten instructions. For simplicity, the zygote shown above has only 1 pair of chromosomes instead of the usual 23 pairs.

**3 Chromosomes.** Inside the very tiny zygote are 23 pairs of chromosomes, which contain chemical instructions for development of the brain and body.

A *chromosome* is a hairlike strand that contains tightly coiled strands of the chemical DNA, which is an abbreviation for deoxyribonucleic (*dee-ox-ee-RYE-bow-new-CLEE-ick*) acid. Each cell of the human body (except for the sperm and egg) contains 46 chromosomes arranged in 23 pairs.

For the sake of simplicity, the cell at the right contains only 4 pairs of chromosomes instead of the usual 23 pairs.

**4 Chemical alphabet.** Each chromosome is made up of long strands of DNA. A long strand of DNA resembles a ladder (left figure) that has been twisted over and over upon itself.

Each rung of the DNA ladder is made up of four chemicals. The order in which the four different chemicals combine to form rungs creates a microscopic chemical alphabet. The 23 pairs of chromosomes contain the equivalent of 300,000 pages of specific instructions for making such things as a nose, finger, brain, or toe. Thus, a chemical alphabet is used to write instructions for the development and assembly of billions of parts that make up the brain and body.

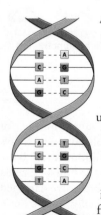

Instructions are written in a chemical alphabet.

**5 Genes and proteins.** Each chromosome has specific segments that contain particular instructions. In the chromosome on the right, each segment is represented by a green band, which is the location of a gene.

A *gene* is a specific segment on the long strand of DNA that contains instructions for making proteins. Proteins are chemical building blocks from which all the parts of the brain and body are constructed.

For example, one or more genes determine your eye color, how much your ear lobes are attached, and if you are likely to become obese (Gura, 1997). Researchers estimate that there are about 30,000 human genes located on the 23 pairs of chromosomes (Wade, 2001). When researchers discover a new gene, it means they have identified the exact location of the gene on its chromosome.

**6 Genome.** After 13 years and $250 million, researchers are completing project Genome, which is to identify all the human genes. Unlike earlier estimates of 100,000 human genes, researchers now find there are only about 30,000 human genes (Wade, 2001). By identifying all the human genes, researchers hope to create a blueprint of how humans develop, to provide clues for developing beneficial drugs, and to use gene therapy to treat genetic problems (Begley, 2000).

**7 Scott's brain: An error in instructions.** Earlier, we told you about Scott's unusual physical and behavioral problems. Scott has the most common inherited genetic disorder, called fragile X syndrome.

*Fragile X syndrome* is caused by a defect in the X chromosome. This defect (shown here as the pinched end of the X chromosome) can result in physical changes, such as a relatively large head with protruding ears, as well as mild to profound levels of mental retardation.

Fragile X syndrome, which can include changes in both physical features and brain development, illustrates what happens when there is an error in genetic instructions (Fisch et al., 1996). We'll discuss other problems caused by errors in genetic instructions, such as Down syndrome, on page 380.

In the last 10 years, researchers have shown the importance of genetic instructions in affecting the development of physical traits, personality characteristics, mental disorders, and various cognitive abilities (Cowley & Underwood, 2000; Plomin, 2000).

Scott has fragile X syndrome.

Next we'll discuss how genetic changes are thought to have affected brain development over millions of years.

# Evolution of the Human Brain

### What is evolution?

In 1859, Charles Darwin stunned much of the Western world by publishing *Origin of Species*, a revolutionary theory of how species originate, which was the basis for his now famous theory of evolution.

The *theory of evolution* says that different species arose from a common ancestor and that those species that survived were best adapted to meet the demands of their environments.

Although Darwin's theory of evolution is just that—a theory—it has received broad scientific support from both fossil records and more recent examination of genetic similarities and differences among species (Lemonick & Dorfman, 1999). The fact that many scientists hold to the theory of evolution clashes with deeply held religious beliefs that place humans on a family tree of their own. According to the theory of evolution, present-day humans descended from a creature that split off from apes millions of years ago. Supporting the theory of evolution is the finding that humans and chimpanzees share at least 98.5% of their DNA or genetic instructions (Gibbons, 1998).

We will discuss three supposed human ancestors that represent three major milestones in how the human brain is thought to have evolved and developed.

*Australopithecus afarensis*    *Homo erectus*    *Homo sapiens*

Increasing skull and brain size of proposed ancestors

---

### Perhaps the First Human Brain

Of the three skulls shown above, the smallest one (far left) is thought to have belonged to one of our earliest ancestors, who lived about 3 to 4 million years ago. This proposed ancestor has been given a common name, Lucy, and a scientific name, *Australopithecus afarensis*. Lucy's brain weighed about 500 grams, which is about the size of a chimpanzee's brain and about one-third the size of our brains. Lucy's brain size and skeleton suggest a closer resemblance to apes than to humans. She had long powerful arms and short legs and is thought to have lived mainly on leaves and fruit.

Anthropologists conclude, on the basis of Lucy's rather limited brain size, that her species did not make tools, did not have language, knew nothing of fire, and thus represents the most primitive kind of human (Gore, 1997; Lemonick & Dorfman, 1999). Lucy's line died out about a million years ago. Anthropologists believe that another line branched out from Lucy's and gave rise to our genus, which is called *Homo;* this process was accompanied eventually by a threefold increase in brain size.

### Brain Doubles in Size

The skull in the middle, which is almost twice as large as Lucy's, belongs to a species named *Homo erectus*. (*Homo* means "man" and *erectus* means "upright.") *Homo erectus,* who lived about one and a half million years ago, is thought to be part of the genus from which modern humans eventually evolved. *Homo erectus* developed a thick-boned skeleton designed for walking upright and was about as tall as modern humans. They are thought to have added meat to their diets.

With a brain size of about 1,000 grams, which was twice as large as Lucy's, *Homo erectus* had increased abilities and made a wide variety of stone tools. The finest was a tear-shaped hand ax, whose production required much more extensive work than any previous tools. There is considerable debate about whether tool-making or the development of language was the main pressure for the doubling in brain size in *Homo erectus* (Gore, 1997; Lewin, 1993). Descendants of *Homo erectus* evolved a still larger brain; these individuals were called *Homo sapiens*.

### Brain Triples in Size

The largest skull, on the far right, comes from a modern human, who is called *Homo sapiens* (*sapiens* means "wise"). Our species began about 400,000 years ago and continues to the present day. *Homo sapiens* evolved a brain that weighs about 1,350 grams, or about 3 pounds, which is the average size of our brains today and almost three times the size of Lucy's. With such a significant increase in brain size came four dramatic changes: *Homo sapiens* began growing crops instead of relying on hunting; started to live in social communities instead of roaming the country; developed language, which was a far better way to communicate compared to grunts and gestures; and painted beautiful and colorful representations of animals and humans.

Two forces are thought to be responsible for the evolution of the human brain and its tripling in size: genetic changes or mutations, which are accidental changes in genetic instructions, and natural selection, which means that only those best fitted to their environments will survive (Kurten, 1993).

Anthropologists believe that it took millions of years for our brains to evolve to their current size. Next, we'll describe how researchers study our modern brains.

**A.** *GENES & EVOLUTION*    **69**

## New Techniques

**Can we look inside the human skull?**

We have explained how genetic instructions guide the development and assembly of billions of parts that make up the human brain. We have discussed the anthropologists' belief that the human brain tripled in size through 3 million years of evolution. Now we begin exploring the structure and function of your own brain.

Looking at the skull on the right raises an interesting question: How can researchers look inside the half-inch-thick skull and study the living brain without causing any

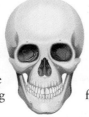

New techniques can take pictures through the skull.

damage? The answer is that during the past 10 years, researchers have developed several brain scanning techniques that can look through the thick skull and picture the brain with astonishing clarity yet cause no damage to the extremely delicate brain cells. By using these almost science-fiction techniques, researchers are mapping a variety of cognitive functions (reading, listening, doing arithmetic, searching, identifying shapes, faces, and animals) as well as sites of emotional feelings and hunger sensations (Blakeslee, 2000b; Gordon et al., 2000). We'll discuss several brain scanning techniques that take pictures through the skull.

## MRI Brain Scans

**Why would Steve have an MRI?**

At the beginning of this module, we told you about Steve, who was a successful journalist in excellent health. As he walked into his hotel, he felt a sudden searing pain in his head. As he waited for his room, he looked up at the clock and suddenly felt fear because he could clearly see the numbers and the hands but could not figure out the time.

Later, the neurologist told Steve that a blood vessel had burst and blood had flowed into the surrounding area of the brain. The neurologist could identify the exact location and extent of the damaged area by using one of the new brain scanning techniques, called an MRI (photo below).

*MRI,* or *magnetic resonance imaging,* involves passing nonharmful radio frequencies through the brain. A computer measures how these signals interact with brain cells and transforms this interaction into an incredibly detailed image of the brain (or body). MRIs are used to study the structure of the brain.

During an MRI procedure, Steve would lie with his head in the center of a giant, donut-shaped machine. Reflections from the radio waves are computer analyzed and developed into very detailed pictures of the living brain, as shown in the photo (below left).

There is also a newer and different version of the MRI, called the fMRI.

The "f" in *fMRI* (functional magnetic resonance imaging) stands for functional and measures the activity of specific neurons that are functioning during cognitive tasks, such as thinking, listening, or reading.

For example, the fMRI on the right shows that while a person was doing mathematical calculations, maximum neural activity occurred in the left frontal area of the brain (Butterworth, 1999). Notice that *fMRI* scans identify or map activities of neurons that are involved in various cognitive *functions.* In comparison, *MRI* scans show the location of *structures* inside the brain as well as identify tumors and sites of brain damage (left photo).

**fMRI: View of left side**

"three times five is fifteen"

Left frontal area

Front of brain

**Brain damage.** During Steve's MRI scan, images of his brain—slice by slice—appeared on a television screen. Suddenly, standing out from the normal grayish image of a brain slice was an unusual area that indicated dead brain cells (small red area on right of MRI scan). Because the damaged neurons were located in a brain area involved with processing visual information, Steve had experienced visual problems, such as being unable to tell the time by looking at a clock, even though he could see the hands of the clock. However, since only a small part of his visual area was affected, most other functions, such as walking, feeling, speaking, and hearing, were normal. The reason Steve could figure out the time by saying aloud where the big and little hands of the clock were located was that his hearing areas were undamaged.

**Advantage.** The advantage of the two kinds of MRI scans is that they use nonharmful radio frequencies and give very detailed views of structures and functions inside the living brain. The use of these two kinds of MRI scans has greatly increased our understanding of the brain.

We'll discuss one other brain scanning technique, called the PET scan, which, similar to the fMRI, is also used to identify cognitive functions.

**MRI Brain Scan: Side View of Head**

Skull: about 1/2 inch thick

Outer surface of brain

Brain damage

Nose

Inner structures of brain

Top of spinal cord

**Are there pictures of thinking?**

Currently, one of the most exciting advances in biological psychology, specifically the area of cognitive neuroscience (see p. 7), involves using an imaging technique that literally lights up your thoughts. This imaging technique is called the PET scan.

*PET scan*, or *positron emission tomography*, involves injecting a slightly radioactive solution into the blood and then measuring the amount of radiation absorbed by brain cells. Very active brain cells—neurons—absorb more radioactive solution than less active ones. A computer transforms the different levels of absorption into colors that indicate activity of neurons. The colors red and yellow indicate maximum activity of neurons, while blue and green indicate minimal activity.

For example, which parts of the brain are active when you "look at a word" compared to when you "speak a word"? Subjects were asked to either "look at a word" or "speak a word" while researchers took PET scans of their brains.

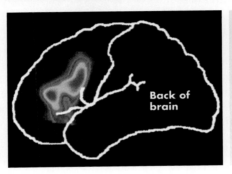

PET scan indicates that when you LOOK at a word, maximum neural activity—areas of red and yellow—occurs in the BACK of your brain.

PET scan indicates that when you SPEAK a word, maximum neural activity—areas of red and yellow—occurs in the FRONT of your brain.

**Looking at words.** PET scans in the top left figure show that when subjects were "looking at words" but not speaking them, most neural activity occurred near the back of the brain, which is involved in processing visual information.

**Speaking words.** PET scans in the bottom left figure show that when subjects were "speaking words" instead of just thinking about them, most neural activity occurred near the front-middle part of the brain, which is involved in speaking (Raichle, 1994).

**Mapping areas.** By using PET scans, researchers can map the brain's neural activity as we perform complex cognitive tasks, such as thinking and speaking. Researchers mapped activity of neurons that shows which areas are involved in something we do every day—naming animals and objects (Martin et al., 1996).

---

**Picturing Thoughts**

**Is it possible to see your thoughts?**

Using PET scans, researchers were even able to identify brain areas that are activated when we silently think very specific thoughts, such as names of tools and animals.

**Naming animals.** As shown at the top right, the thoughts of subjects as they *silently* named animals (camel) activated an area in the back of the brain, which is involved in processing visual information. Researchers think this visual area helps us distinguish sizes, shapes, and colors, such as distinguishing a camel from a horse.

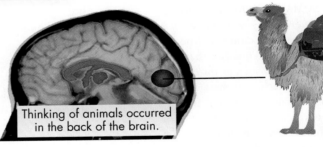

Thinking of animals occurred in the back of the brain.

**Naming tools.** As shown at the bottom right, the thoughts of subjects as they silently named tools (pliers) activated an area in the front of the brain. Researchers think this frontal area helps us think about how we use tools (Martin et al., 1996).

Researchers concluded that the brain has two separate systems: one for thoughts about naming animals, which involves distinguishing between sizes, shapes, and colors; and another for thoughts about naming tools, which involves thinking about how tools are used (Martin et al., 1996). Other researchers report that the brain is genetically wired to place things, such as tools, animals, faces, and vegetables, into different categories so that we can quickly and easily perceive and make sense of all the things in our world (Ishai, 1999; Moscovitch, 1997).

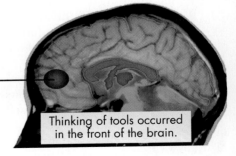

Thinking of tools occurred in the front of the brain.

As we discussed in Module 1 (p. 7), the above study is an example of a relatively new area, called *cognitive neuroscience,* which identifies differences in neural activity as the bases for cognitive functions (Gold & Stoljar, 1999). Throughout this text, we'll include many experiments that show how cognitive processes, emotions, memo-ries, and mental disorders are being studied using MRI and PET scans.

Now that you are familiar with ways to study the living brain, we can begin to examine the brain's specific structures and interesting functions.

## C. Organization of the Brain

### Divisions of the Nervous System

**How many nervous systems?**

Because you have one brain, you may think that means you have one nervous system. In fact, your brain is much more complex: It has two major nervous systems, one of which has four subdivisions. We'll explain the overall organization of the brain's several nervous systems, beginning with its two major divisions, the central and peripheral nervous systems.

### A. Major Divisions of the Nervous System

#### CENTRAL NERVOUS SYSTEM—CNS

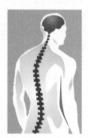

You are capable of many complex cognitive functions—such as thinking, speaking, and reading, as well as moving, feeling, seeing, and hearing—because of your central nervous system.

The *central nervous system* is made up of the brain and spinal cord. From the bottom of the brain emerges the spinal cord, which is made up of neurons and bundles of axons and dendrites that carry information back and forth between the brain and the body.

We'll discuss the major parts of the brain throughout this module.

#### PERIPHERAL NERVOUS SYSTEM—PNS

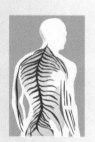

You are able to move your muscles, receive sensations from your body, and perform many other bodily responses because of the peripheral nervous system.

The *peripheral nervous system* includes all the nerves that extend from the spinal cord and carry messages to and from various muscles, glands, and sense organs located throughout the body.

The peripheral nervous system has two subdivisions, the somatic and autonomic nervous systems.

### B. Subdivisions of the PNS

#### SOMATIC NERVOUS SYSTEM

The *somatic nervous system* consists of a network of nerves that connect either to sensory receptors or to muscles that you can move voluntarily, such as muscles in your limbs, back, neck, and chest. Nerves in the somatic nervous system usually contain two kinds of fibers. Afferent, or sensory, fibers carry information from sensory receptors in the skin, muscles, and other organs to the spinal cord and brain. Efferent, or motor, fibers carry information from the brain and spinal cord to the muscles.

For example, this gymnast controls her muscles, knows where her arms and legs are located in space, and maintains her coordination and balance because the somatic nervous system sends electrical signals back and forth to her brain.

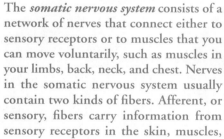

#### ANS—AUTONOMIC NERVOUS SYSTEM

The *autonomic nervous system* regulates heart rate, breathing, blood pressure, digestion, hormone secretion, and other functions. The autonomic nervous system usually functions without conscious effort, which means that only a few of its responses, such as breathing, can also be controlled voluntarily.

The autonomic nervous system also has two subdivisions, the sympathetic and parasympathetic divisions.

### C. Subdivisions of the ANS

#### SYMPATHETIC DIVISION

The *sympathetic division,* which is triggered by threatening or challenging physical or psychological stimuli, increases physiological arousal and prepares the body for action.

For example, the sight of a frightening snake would trigger the sympathetic division, which, in turn, would arouse the body for action, such as fighting or fleeing.

#### PARASYMPATHETIC DIVISION

The *parasympathetic division* returns the body to a calmer, relaxed state and is involved in digestion.

For example, when you are feeling calm and relaxed or digesting food, your parasympathetic system is activated.

Now that you know the overall organization of the nervous system, we'll focus on major parts of the brain.

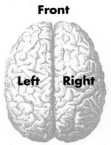

**Front**

**Left    Right**

**Back**

A human brain (right figure), which can easily be held in one hand, weighs about 1,350 grams, or 3 pounds, and has the consistency of firm Jell-O. The brain is protected by a thick skull and covered with thin, tough, plasticlike membranes. If shot in the head, a person may or may not die depending on which area was damaged. For example, damage to an area in the forebrain would result in paralysis, damage to an area in the midbrain would result in coma, but damage to an area in the hindbrain would certainly result in death.

We'll begin our exploration of the brain by looking at its three major parts—forebrain, midbrain, and hindbrain—beginning with the forebrain.

## 1 Forebrain

When you look at the brain, what you are actually seeing is almost all forebrain (figure above).

The *forebrain,* which is the largest part of the brain, has right and left sides that are called hemispheres. The hemispheres, which are connected by a wide band of fibers, are responsible for an incredible number of functions, including learning and memory, speaking and language, emotional responses, experiencing sensations, initiating voluntary movements, planning, and making decisions.

The large structure outlined in orange to the left shows only the right hemisphere of the forebrain. The forebrain's right and left hemispheres are both shown in the figure at the top right. The forebrain is very well developed in humans.

## 2 Midbrain

If a boxer is knocked unconscious, part of the reason lies in the midbrain.

The *midbrain* is involved in visual and auditory reflexes, such as automatically turning your head toward a noise. Extending down from the top of the midbrain to the spinal cord is a long column of neurons called the reticular formation. The reticular formation alerts and arouses the forebrain so that it is ready to process incoming information from the senses.

If the reticular formation were seriously damaged—by a blow to the head, for example—a person would be unconscious and might go into a coma because the forebrain could not be aroused (Steriade, 1966).

Side view of the brain's right hemisphere

## 3c Cerebellum

A person suspected of drunken driving may fail the test of rapidly touching a finger to the nose because of alcohol's effects on the cerebellum.

The *cerebellum,* which is located at the very back and underneath the brain, is involved in coordinating movements but not in initiating voluntary movements. The cerebellum is also involved in performing timed motor responses, such as those required in playing games or sports (Allen et al., 1997).

More recently, researchers reported that the cerebellum is involved in automatic or reflexive learning, such as blinking the eye to a signal, which is called classical conditioning (discussed in Module 9) (Green & Woodruff-Pak, 2000).

Because alcohol is a depressant drug and interferes with the functions of the cerebellum, an intoxicated person would experience decreased coordination and have difficulty rapidly touching a finger to the nose, which is one of the tests for being drunk.

## 3 Hindbrain

The structures and functions of the hindbrain, which are found in very primitive brains, such as the alligator's, have remained constant through millions of years of evolution. The *hindbrain* has three distinct structures: the pons, medulla, and cerebellum.

## 3a Pons

If someone has a serious sleep disorder, it may involve the pons. In Latin, *pons* means "bridge," which suggests its function.

The *pons* functions as a bridge to interconnect messages between the spinal cord and brain. The pons also makes chemicals involved in sleep (Cirelli et al., 1996).

## 3b Medulla

If someone dies of a drug overdose, the cause of death probably involved the medulla.

The *medulla,* which is located at the top of the spinal cord, includes a group of cells that control vital reflexes, such as respiration, heart rate, and blood pressure.

Large amounts of alcohol, heroin, or other depressant drugs suppress the functions of cells in the medulla and cause death by stopping breathing.

Of the brain's three parts, the forebrain is the largest, most evolved, and most responsible for an enormous range of personal, social, emotional, and cognitive behaviors. For those reasons, we'll examine the forebrain in more detail.

## Overall View of the Cortex

**How do you package 1 trillion cells?**

How would you design a brain to hold 1 trillion cells (100 billion neurons and 900 billion glial cells) and be no bigger than a small melon and weigh no more than 3 pounds? First, the cells need to be microscopic in size, which they are. But the second part of the solution might not have occurred to you: make the the brain's surface very wrinkled. And, here's why.

### WRINKLED CORTEX

In the photo below you see a computer-enhanced photo of the outside of an adult human brain, which has a very wrinkled surface that is called the cortex (in Latin, *cortex* means "cover").

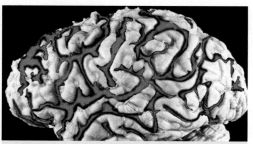

Brain's surface shows its wrinkled cortex.

The *cortex* is a thin layer of cells that essentially covers the entire surface of the forebrain. The vast majority of our neurons are located in the cortex, which folds over on itself so that it forms a large surface area.

To understand the advantage of having a wrinkled cortex, just imagine having to put a large sheet of paper about 18 inches square into a small match box that is 3 inches square. One solution is to crumple (wrinkle) the sheet of paper until it easily fits into the tiny match box. Similarly, imagine many billions of neurons laid on a sheet of paper about 18 inches square. When this large sheet of neurons is wrinkled, the cortex can fit snugly into our much smaller, rounded skulls.

Early researchers divided the wrinkled cortex into four different areas, or lobes, each of which has different functions.

### FOUR LOBES

As you look at the brain's cortex, you see a wrinkled surface of peaks and valleys with very few distinguishing features. However, the cortex's appearance is deceiving because its hundreds of different functions are organized into four separate areas called lobes.

The cortex is divided into four separate areas, or *lobes,* each with different functions: the *frontal lobe* is involved with personality, emotions, and motor behaviors; the *parietal* (*puh-RYE-it-all*) *lobe* is involved with perception and sensory experiences; the *occipital* (*ock-SIP-pih-tull*) *lobe* is involved with processing visual information; and the *temporal* (*TEM-purr-all*) *lobe* is involved with hearing and speaking.

Cortex is divided into four different areas, or lobes.

The one brain structure that most clearly distinguishes you from animals is your well-developed cortex, which allows you to read, understand, talk about, and remember the concepts in this text. To understand what life would be like without a cortex, we'll return to the case of Baby Theresa, who was born without any lobes and thus no cortex.

### BABY THERESA'S BRAIN: A FATAL DEFECT

At the beginning of this module, we told you about Baby Theresa, who was one of the 1,000 babies born each year in the United States with almost no brain. This rare condition, caused by errors in genetic instructions, is called anencephaly (Chen et al., 1996).

*Anencephaly* (*an-in-CEPH-ah-lee*) refers to the condition of being born with little or no brain. If some brain or nervous tissue is present, it is totally exposed and often damaged because the top of the skull is missing. Survival is usually limited to days; the longest has been two months.

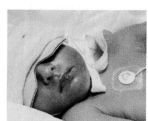

Theresa has anencephaly, meaning little or no brain.

Anencephaly is always fatal because it also includes other serious physical defects, such as damage to the heart (Stumpf et al., 1990). Baby Theresa (photo above), who survived only nine days, had almost no brain tissue and almost no skull (bandaged area above eyes). Lacking most of a brain means that she would be incapable of perceiving, thinking, speaking, planning, or making decisions.

The figure below shows that a baby born with anencephaly has no forebrain. One reason babies with anencephaly may survive for days or weeks is that they may have parts of their hindbrain. As discussed earlier, the hindbrain contains the pons (blue) and medulla (red). The medulla controls vital reflexes, such as breathing, heart rate, and blood pressure, which together can maintain life for a period of time.

This example of anencephaly shows that without the forebrain, a baby may be physiologically alive but show no signs of having a mind or possessing cognitive abilities associated with being human.

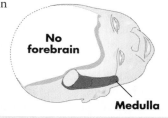

No forebrain

Medulla

Medulla kept Theresa alive.

In a real sense, it is the functions of the forebrain's four lobes that define us as human and distinguish us from all other creatures.

Because the four lobes are vital to our existence as humans, we'll discuss each lobe in turn. We'll begin with the frontal lobe and a tragic accident.

**What does the biggest lobe do?**

The frontal lobe (right figure), which is the largest and most noticeable of the brain's four lobes, has a number of important functions.

The *frontal lobe*, which is located in the front part of the brain, includes a huge area of cortex. The frontal lobe is involved in many functions: performing voluntary motor movements, interpreting and performing emotional behaviors, behaving normally in social situations, maintaining a healthy personality, paying attention to things in the environment, making decisions, and executing plans. Because the frontal lobe is involved in making decisions, planning, reasoning, and carrying out behaviors, it is said to have executive functions, much like the duties of a company's executive officer.

Our first clue about the functions of the frontal lobe came from an unusual accident in 1848, while our more recent knowledge comes from research using PET scans. Let's first go back in time and meet Phineas Gage, whose accident led to the discovery of one of the frontal lobe's important functions.

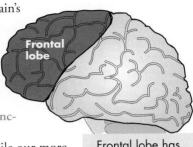

Frontal lobe has executive functions.

### A TERRIBLE ACCIDENT

The accident occurred at about half past four on the afternoon of September 13, 1848, near the small town of Cavendish, Vermont. Railroad crewmen were about to blast a rock that blocked their way. Foreman Phineas Gage filled a deep, narrow hole in the rock with powder and rammed in a long iron rod to tamp down the charge before covering it with sand. But the tamping iron rubbed against the side of the shaft, and a spark ignited the powder. The massive rod—$3\frac{1}{2}$ feet long, $1\frac{1}{4}$ inches in diameter, and weighing 13 pounds—shot from the hole under the force of the explosion. It struck Phineas just beneath his left eye and tore through his skull. It shot out the top of his head and landed some 50 yards away.

Phineas survived, but, following the accident, his personality changed: He went from being a popular, friendly foreman to acting impatient, cursing his workers, and refusing to honor his promises.

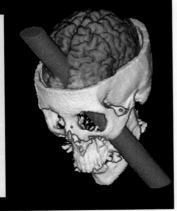

A massive rod (right diagram) weighing 13 pounds was accidentally driven through the front part of Phineas Gage's frontal lobe. The result, which was similar to having a frontal lobotomy, caused Phineas to have emotional outbursts and problems in making decisions, something he did not experience before this accident.

Researchers recently used Phineas's preserved skull to reconstruct the site and extent of his brain damage. As the figure above shows, the iron rod had passed through and extensively damaged Phineas's frontal lobe. Researchers concluded that Phineas had suffered a crude form of frontal lobotomy, which caused deficits in processing of emotion and decision making that result after damage to the frontal lobe (Damasio et al., 1994).

Beginning in the 1930s, doctors performed thousands of lobotomies to treat various mental and behavioral problems.

### FRONTAL LOBOTOMY

In 1936, Egas Moniz, a Portuguese neurologist, used an untested surgical treatment, called frontal lobotomy, to treat individuals with severe emotional problems.

A *frontal lobotomy* was a surgical procedure in which about one-third of the front part of the frontal lobe (figure below) was cut away from the rest of the brain.

Moniz first reported that frontal lobotomies did reduce emotional problems in about 35% of severely agitated human patients, although he did no controlled or follow-up studies to check long-term effects (Weinberger et al., 1995). Based on Moniz's reports of success, about 18,000 frontal lobotomies were performed in the 1940s and 1950s on emotionally disturbed patients who were primarily confined to state mental hospitals, which had no other treatments.

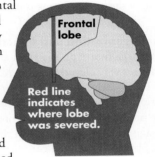

Red line indicates where lobe was severed.

### RESULTS OF LOBOTOMIES

Initially, neurologists reported good short-term effects, but better controlled, long-term studies on frontal lobotomies found mixed results: Some patients did become less violent, but others showed no improvement and some became worse (Swayze, 1995). Even those whose social-emotional behaviors improved were often left with serious problems in other areas, such as having difficulty in making and carrying out plans, adjusting to new social demands, or behaving with appropriate emotional responses in social situations (Valenstein, 1986).

Two things happened in the early 1950s that ended the use of frontal lobotomies to treat social-emotional problems. First, follow-up research indicated that lobotomies were no more successful in relieving social-emotional problems than doing nothing. Second, antipsychotic drugs were discovered and showed greater success in treating serious social-emotional problems (Swayze, 1995).

From using frontal lobotomies as treatment, researchers learned two things: (1) careful follow-up work is essential before declaring a treatment successful and (2) the frontal lobe has many different, important functions, which we'll look at next.

## Frontal Lobe: Functions

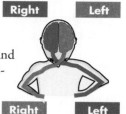

The organization of the frontal lobe is somewhat confusing because it has such a wide range of functions, from motor movements to cognitive processes. We'll first focus on motor movements, which have a very unusual feature.

**How do you move your right hand?**

In the figure on the right, notice that nerves from the right hemisphere (blue) cross over and control the movements of the left hand and left side of the body; nerves from the left hemisphere (red) cross over and control the movements of the right hand and right side of the body. The ability to move your hand or any other part of your body depends on the motor cortex in the right and left frontal lobes.

### 1 Location of Motor Cortex

To move your right hand, you will use the motor cortex in your left frontal lobe.

The *motor cortex* is a narrow strip of cortex that is located on the back edge of the frontal lobe and extends down its side. The motor cortex is involved in the initiation of all voluntary movements. The right motor cortex controls muscles on the left side of the body and vice versa.

You can move any individual part of your body at will because of how the motor cortex is organized.

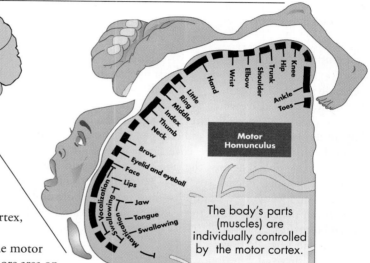

Motor Homunculus

The body's parts (muscles) are individually controlled by the motor cortex.

### 2 Organization and Function of Motor Cortex

The large figure on the right shows an enlarged part of the motor cortex, which is very cleverly organized.

**First,** notice the different sizes of the body parts drawn on top of the motor cortex. A larger body part (notice huge hand area) indicates relatively more area on the motor cortex and thus more ability to perform complex movements. A smaller body part (notice small knee area) indicates relatively less area on the motor cortex and thus less ability to perform complex movements. This unusual drawing, which uses sizes of body parts to show the ability to perform complex movements, is called the *motor homunculus* (*ho-MONK-you-luss*). Notice that the motor cortex makes up only a small part of the frontal lobe.

**Second,** notice that each body part has its own area on the motor cortex. This means that damage to one part of the motor cortex could result in paralysis of that part, yet completely spare all other parts.

In a surprising finding, researchers discovered that the motor cortex was involved in remembering the order of events across time, such as the order in which signals occurred (Georgopoulos, 1999). This means that besides triggering voluntary movements, the motor cortex is also involved in memory for the order of events across time. Next, we'll explain the frontal lobe's other functions.

### 3 Other Functions of Frontal Lobe

**Brain damage.** Much of our knowledge of other frontal lobe functions comes from individuals who had damage to that area. By studying patients like Phineas Gage, researchers found that damage to frontal lobes may result in disruption of personality as well as emotional swings. From studying patients with damage to frontal lobes, researchers found that frontal lobes are involved in paying attention, remembering things, making good decisions, and planning and organizing events (Waltz et al., 1999).

**PET scans.** Researchers have also identified many cognitive functions of the frontal lobe by taking PET scans while subjects perform various tasks. For example, subjects were shown a noun, such as *hammer,* and asked to think of an appropriate verb, such as *hit.* PET scans, such as the one shown here, indicated that maximum activity (red and yellow areas)

Frontal lobe

Maximum activity

Back of brain

occurred in the frontal lobe. This means that the frontal lobe is involved in our thinking processes (Fiez & Petersen, 1993). Other PET studies indicate that the frontal lobes are also involved in paying attention (Wheeler et al., 1997).

**Executive function.** We now know that the frontal lobes are involved in paying attention, organizing, planning, deciding, and carrying out many different kinds of tasks. For all these reasons, the frontal lobes are often said to have an executive function, that is, act similar to a successful executive of a large organization (Waltz et al., 1999).

Immediately behind the frontal lobe is the parietal lobe, which keeps track of your body's limbs.

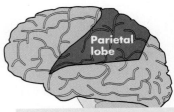

Parietal lobe processes information from body parts.

**How do you know where your feet are?**

Every second of every minute of every day, your brain must keep track of what's touching your skin, where your feet and hands are, and whether you're walking or running. All this is automatically and efficiently done by your parietal lobe (right figure).

The *parietal lobe* is located directly behind the frontal lobe. The parietal lobe's functions include processing sensory information from body parts, which includes touching, locating positions of limbs, and feeling temperature and pain, and carrying out several cognitive functions, such as attending to and perceiving objects.

For example, the ability to know what you're touching involves the parietal lobe's somatosensory cortex.

## 1 Location of Somatosensory Cortex

Knowing what you're touching or how hot to make the water for your shower involves the somatosensory cortex.

The *somatosensory cortex* is a narrow strip of cortex that is located on the front edge of the parietal lobe and extends down its side. The somatosensory cortex processes sensory information about touch, location of limbs, pain, and temperature. The right somatosensory cortex receives information from the left side of the body and vice versa.

Your lips are much more sensitive than your elbows because of the way the somatosensory cortex is organized.

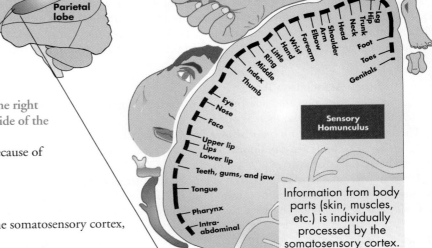

Information from body parts (skin, muscles, etc.) is individually processed by the somatosensory cortex.

## 2 Organization of Somatosensory Cortex

The large figure on the right shows an enlarged part of the somatosensory cortex, which is also cleverly organized.

First, notice the different sizes of the body parts drawn on top of the somatosensory cortex. A larger body part (notice large area for lips) indicates relatively more area on the somatosensory cortex and thus more sensitivity to external stimulation. A smaller body part (notice small nose area) indicates relatively less area on the somatosensory cortex and thus less sensitivity to external stimulation. This unusual drawing, which uses sizes of body parts to indicate amount of sensitivity to external stimulation, is called the *sensory homunculus* (*ho-MONK-you-luss*). In Latin, *homunculus* means "little man." Notice that the somatosensory cortex makes up only a small part of the parietal lobe.

Second, notice that each body part has its own area on the somatosensory cortex. This means that damage to one part of the somatosensory cortex could result in loss of feeling to one part of the body, yet completely spare all others. Next, we'll explain the parietal lobe's other functions.

## 3 Other Functions of Parietal Lobe

**Brain damage.** When you put your hand in your pocket, you can easily tell a key from a nickel from a stick of chewing gum because your parietal lobe digests information about texture, shape, and size and "tells you" what the object is. However, patients with damage to the back of their parietal lobes cannot recognize common objects by touch or feel (Bear et al., 1996). Evidence that the parietal lobes are involved in other cognitive processes comes from studies using PET scans (Banati et al., 2000).

**PET scans.** Researchers asked subjects to remember letters they saw on a screen by repeating them over and over in their minds. PET scans, such as the one shown here, indicated that

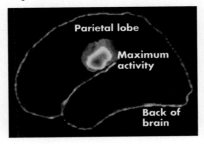

maximum activity during this task occurred in the parietal lobe. Researchers concluded that the parietal lobe is involved when we try to remember things (Paulesu et al., 1993). Other PET studies on chess players indicated that the parietal lobe was involved in perceiving and analyzing the positions of chess pieces on the board (Nichelli et al., 1994).

Thus, case studies and PET scans indicate that the parietal lobe is involved in several cognitive functions, including recognizing objects, remembering items, and perceiving and analyzing objects in space.

Immediately below the parietal lobe is the temporal lobe, which we'll examine next.

---------- **Temporal Lobe: Functions** ----------

**Did you hear your name?**

You recognize your name when you hear it spoken; because of the way sound is processed in the temporal lobe, you know it's not just some meaningless noise.

The *temporal lobe* is located directly below the parietal lobe and is involved in hearing, speaking coherently, and understanding verbal and written material.

As you'll see, the process of hearing and recognizing your name involves two steps and two different brain areas.

## 1a Primary Auditory Cortex

The first step in hearing your name occurs when sounds reach specific areas in the temporal lobe called the primary auditory (hearing) cortex—there is one in each lobe.

The *primary auditory cortex* (**shown in red**), which is located on the top edge of each temporal lobe, receives electrical signals from receptors in the ears and transforms these signals into meaningless sound sensations, such as vowels and consonants.

At this point, you would not be able to recognize your name because the primary auditory cortex only changes electrical signals from the ears into basic sensations, such as individual sounds, clicks, or noises. For these meaningless sound sensations to become recognizable words, they must be sent to another area in the temporal lobe, called the auditory association area (Feng & Ratnam, 2000).

**Temporal lobe**

Temporal lobe processes auditory (hearing) information.

## 1b Auditory Association Area

The second step in recognizing your name is when the primary auditory cortex sends its electrical signals to the auditory association area; there is one in each lobe.

The *auditory association area* (**shown in blue**), which is located directly below the primary auditory cortex, transforms basic sensory information, such as noises or sounds, into recognizable auditory information, such as words or music.

It is only after auditory information is sent by the primary auditory cortex to the auditory association area that you would recognize sounds as your name, or words, or music (Feng & Ratnam, 2000). So, it is safe to say that you hear with your brain, rather than your ears.

Besides being involved in hearing, the temporal lobe has other areas that are critical for speaking and understanding words and sentences.

## 2 Broca's Area—Frontal Lobe

Just as hearing your name is a two-step process, so is speaking a sentence. The first step is putting words together, which involves an area in the frontal lobe called Broca's (*BROKE-ahs*) area.

*Broca's area*, which is usually located in the left frontal lobe, is necessary for combining sounds into words and arranging words into meaningful sentences. Damage to this area results in *Broca's aphasia* (*ah-PHASE-zz-ah*), which means a person cannot speak in fluent sentences but can understand written and spoken words.

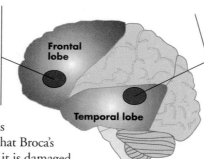

**Frontal lobe**

**Temporal lobe**

The reason that saying words and putting words into sentences come naturally to small children is that Broca's area is genetically programmed to do this task. If it is damaged, people with Broca's aphasia have difficulty putting words into sentences. For example, a patient was asked, "What have you been doing in the hospital?" The patient answered, "Yes, sure. Me go, er, uh, P.T. non o'cot, speech . . . two times . . . read . . . wr . . . ripe, er, rike, er, write . . . practice . . . get-ting better" (Gardner, 1976, p. 61). The patient was trying to say, "I go to P.T. (physical therapy) at one o'clock to practice speaking, reading, and writing, and I'm getting better."

A patient with Broca's aphasia cannot speak fluently but can still understand words and sentences because of a second area in the temporal lobe—Wernicke's area (Hotz, 2000).

## 3 Wernicke's Area—Temporal Lobe

The first step in speaking is using Broca's area to combine sounds into words and arrange words into sentences. The second step is to understand sentences, which involves Wernicke's (*VERN-ick-ees*) area.

*Wernicke's area*, which is usually located in the left temporal lobe, is necessary for speaking in coherent sentences and for understanding speech. Damage to this area results in *Wernicke's aphasia*, which is a difficulty in understanding spoken or written words and a difficulty in putting words into meaningful sentences.

For example, a patient with Wernicke's aphasia said, "You know, once in awhile I get caught up, I mention the tarripoi, a month ago, quite a little, I've done a lot well" (Gardner, 1976, p. 68). As this meaningless sentence shows, Wernicke's area is critical for combining words into meaningful sentences and being able to speak coherently (Basso, 2000).

In almost all right-handed people (96%) and the vast majority of left-handed people (70%), Broca's and Wernicke's areas are in the left hemisphere; the remaining percentages of people have these two areas in the right hemisphere (Risse et al., 1997).

Compared to many other animals, humans rely more heavily on visual information, which is processed in the occipital lobe, our next topic.

**Can you see better than dogs?**

Dogs have very poor color vision and rely much more on their sense of smell. In comparison, all primates, which include monkeys, apes, and humans, have a relatively poor sense of smell and rely much more on vision for gathering information about their environments.

If you have ever been hit on the back of the head and saw "stars," you already know that vision is located in the occipital lobe.

The *occipital lobe* is located at the very back of the brain and is involved in processing visual information, which includes seeing colors and perceiving and recognizing objects, animals, and people.

Although you see and recognize things with great ease, it is actually a complicated two-step process. Here, we'll give only an overview of that process; we'll go into more detail in Module 5.

### 1 Vision

When you look in the mirror and see your face, you don't realize that seeing your face involves two steps and two different areas in the occipital lobe (Maldonado et al., 1997). The first step in seeing your face involves the primary visual cortex.

Occipital lobe

Occipital lobe processes visual (seeing) information.

The *primary visual cortex*, which is located at the very back of the occipital lobe, receives electrical signals from receptors in the eyes and transforms these signals into meaningless basic visual sensations, such as lights, lines, shadows, colors, and textures.

Since the primary visual cortex produces only meaningless visual sensations (lights, lines, shadows), you do not yet see your face. Transforming meaningless visual sensations into a meaningful visual object occurs in the visual association area (Logothetis, 1999).

The *visual association area*, which is located next to the primary visual cortex, transforms basic sensations, such as lights, lines, colors, and textures, into complete, meaningful visual perceptions, such as persons, objects, or animals.

If there are problems in the second step, such as damage to the visual association area, the person can still see parts of objects but has difficulty combining the parts and seeing or recognizing the whole object (Bower, 1996). We'll discuss two unusual visual problems that result from damage to association areas.

### 2 Visual Agnosia

Since the visual association area is critical for recognizing faces, shapes, and objects, damage to this area results in difficulties of recognition, a condition called visual agnosia (*ag-NO-zee-ah*).

In *visual agnosia*, the individual fails to recognize some object, person, or color, yet has the ability to see and even describe pieces or parts of some visual stimulus.

Here's what happens when patients with damage to the visual association area were asked to simply copy an object.

A patient who has visual agnosia was asked to make a copy of this horse, something most everyone can do.

The patient drew each part of the horse separately and could not combine individual parts into a meaningful image.

Patients with visual agnosia can see individual parts of an object, such as a horse's leg, but, because of damage to visual association areas, have great difficulty combining parts to perceive or draw a complete and recognizable image, such as a complete horse (Maratsos & Matheny, 1994). Damage to association areas can also result in seeing only half of one's world.

### 3 Neglect Syndrome

Individuals who have damage to association areas, usually in occipital and parietal lobes, and usually in the right hemisphere, experience a very strange problem called the neglect syndrome.

The *neglect syndrome* refers to the failure of a patient to see objects or parts of the body on the side opposite the brain damage. Patients may dress only one side of their body and deny that opposite body parts are theirs ("that's not my leg").

Here's how a patient with neglect syndrome drew an object.

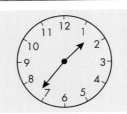 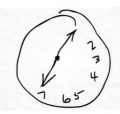

A patient with neglect syndrome caused by right-sided brain damage was asked to copy this clock.

The patient drew only the right side of the clock because he did not see or recognize things on his left side.

After a stroke or other damage, usually to the occipital and parietal association areas in the right hemisphere, patients may behave as if the left sides of objects or their own bodies no longer exist: they may not shave or dress the left sides of their bodies, which they do not recognize. Neglect syndrome shows the important function of association areas in recognizing things (Springer & Deutsch, 1997).

Now we'll journey beneath the cortex and explore a group of structures that existed in evolutionarily very old, primitive brains.

### Structures and Functions

**How are you like an alligator?**

Like alligators, humans have limbic systems.

Your cortex is involved in numerous cognitive functions, such as thinking, deciding, planning, and speaking, as well as other sensory and motor behaviors. But what triggers your wide range of emotional experiences, such as feeling happy, sad, fearful, and angry? If we peeled away the cortex, you would be looking deeper inside the brain at a number of structures that are involved in emotions and that make up the limbic system (LeDoux & Phelps, 2000).

The *limbic system* refers to a group of about half a dozen interconnected structures that make up the core of the forebrain. The limbic system's structures are involved with many motivational behaviors such as obtaining food, drink, and sex; with organizing emotional behaviors such as fear, anger, and aggression; and with the storing of memories.

The limbic system is often referred to as our primitive, or animal, brain because its same structures are found in the brains of animals that are evolutionarily very old, such as alligators. The alligator's limbic system, which essentially makes up its entire forebrain, is primarily involved in smelling out prey, defending territory, hunting, fighting, reproducing, eating, and remembering. The human limbic system, which makes up only a small part of the human forebrain, is involved in similar behaviors.

Limbic system is involved in emotional behavior.

We'll discuss some of the major structures and functions of the limbic system. The drawing below shows the right hemisphere (left hemisphere cut away). Notice that the limbic structures are surrounded by the forebrain, whose executive functions regulate the limbic system's emotional and motivational behaviors.

**1** One limbic structure that is a master control for many emotional responses is the hypothalamus (*high-po-THAL-ah-mus*).

The *hypothalamus* regulates many motivational behaviors, including eating, drinking, and sexual responses; emotional behaviors, such as arousing the body when fighting or fleeing; and the secretion of hormones, such as occurs at puberty.

In addition, the hypothalamus controls the two divisions of the autonomic nervous system discussed on the right-hand page.

The next limbic structure, the amygdala, is also involved in emotions but more so in the forming and remembering of them.

**3** This limbic structure, which is like a miniature computer that gathers and processes information from your senses, is called the thalamus (*THAL-ah-mus*).

The *thalamus* is involved in receiving sensory information, doing some initial processing, and then relaying the sensory information to areas of the cortex, including the somatosensory cortex, primary auditory cortex, and primary visual cortex.

For example, if the thalamus malfunctions and slows down the processing of auditory information, the result can be difficulty in learning to read, which is one sign of dyslexia (Begley, 1994).

Our last limbic structure, the hippocampus, is involved in saving your memories.

**2** The *amygdala* (*ah-MIG-duh-la*), which is located in the tip of the temporal lobe, is involved in forming, recognizing, and remembering emotional experiences, especially fear, as well as emotional facial expressions.

For example, researchers found that patients with amygdala damage had difficulty recognizing personal facial expressions, and animals that have had their amygdalas removed do not learn to fear dangerous situations (Anderson & Phelps, 2000). The amygdala's role is to attach emotional feelings to different events or situations, especially those involving danger, panic, fear, or anxiety (Damasio, 2000).

**4** The *hippocampus,* which is a curved structure inside the temporal lobe, is involved in saving many kinds of fleeting memories by putting them into permanent storage in various parts of the brain.

For example, humans with damage to the hippocampus have difficulty remembering new facts, places, faces, or conversations because these new events cannot be placed into permanent storage (Rolls, 2000; Squire & Zola-Morgan, 1991). Think of the hippocampus, which is involved in saving things in long-term storage (see p. 268), as functioning like the "Save" command on your computer.

Some of the basic emotional feelings triggered by the limbic system (anger, rage, fear, panic) carry the potential for self-injury or injury to others. Researchers believe that our larger and evolutionarily newer frontal lobe, which is involved in thinking, deciding, and planning, regulates the limbic system's powerful urges (LeDoux & Phelps, 2000). One particular structure in the limbic system, the hypothalamus, also has an important role in regulating the autonomic nervous system, which we'll examine next.

**Why don't you worry about breathing?**

You are unaware of what regulates your breathing, heart rate, hormone secretions, or body temperature. You're not concerned about these vital functions because they are usually controlled by a separate nervous system, called the autonomic nervous system, which, in turn, is regulated by a master control center, the hypothalamus (discussed on the previous page).

The autonomic nervous system, which regulates numerous physiological responses, has two divisions, the sympathetic and parasympathetic nervous systems. The sympathetic division is activated when you suddenly see a snake; then the parasympathetic division helps you relax (Cacioppo et al., 2000). We'll explain some of the specific and automatic functions of the sympathetic and parasympathetic divisions.

## Sympathetic Nervous System

If you were on a nature hike and suddenly saw a snake, your cortex would activate the hypothalamus, which in turn triggers the sympathetic division of the autonomic nervous system (Jansen et al., 1995).

The *sympathetic division,* which is one part of the autonomic nervous system, is triggered by threatening or challenging physical stimuli, such as a snake, or by psychological stimuli, such as the thought of having to give a public speech. Once triggered, the sympathetic division increases the body's physiological arousal.

All of the physiological responses listed in the left column under *Sympathetic,* such as increased heart rate, increased blood pressure, and dilated pupils, put your body into a state of heightened physiological arousal, which is called the fight-flight response.

The *fight-flight response*, which is a state of increased physiological arousal caused by activation of the sympathetic division, helps the body cope with and survive threatening situations.

You have no doubt experienced the fight-flight response many times, such as when you felt your heart pound and your mouth go dry. Later, we'll discuss the role of the fight-flight response in stressful situations and its role in psychosomatic diseases (pp. 484–489).

## Parasympathetic Nervous System

After you have been physiologically aroused by seeing a snake, it is usually some time before your body returns to a calmer state. The process of decreasing physiological arousal and calming down your body is triggered by the hypothalamus, which activates the parasympathetic division.

The *parasympathetic division*, which is the other part of the autonomic nervous system, decreases physiological arousal and helps return the body to a calmer, more relaxed state. It also stimulates digestion during eating.

As shown in the right column under the heading *Parasympathetic,* the parasympathetic division, once activated, decreases physiological arousal by decreasing heart rate, lowering blood pressure, and stimulating digestion. These responses result in the body returning to a more relaxed state.

In dealing with stress, we'll discuss many relaxation techniques (pp. 502–503), such as the relaxation response, various forms of meditation, and biofeedback, which help increase parasympathetic activity, decrease body arousal, and thus help you calm down after stressful experiences.

| Sympathetic | | Parasympathetic |
|---|---|---|
| Pupils dilated, dry; far vision | Eyes | Pupils constricted, moist; near vision |
| Dry | Mouth | Salivation |
| Goose bumps | Skin | No goose bumps |
| Sweaty | Palms | Dry |
| Passages dilated | Lungs | Passages constricted |
| Increased rate | Heart | Decreased rate |
| Supply maximum to muscles | Blood | Supply maximum to internal organs |
| Increased activity | Adrenal glands | Decreased activity |
| Inhibited | Digestion | Stimulated |
| Climax | Sexual functions | Arousal |

## Homeostasis

One problem that some students face is becoming too stressed or upset by life's events. Because it is potentially harmful to your body to stay stressed or aroused, the autonomic nervous system tries to keep the body's arousal at an optimum level, a state called homeostasis.

*Homeostasis* (*ho-me-oh-STAY-sis*) means that sympathetic and parasympathetic systems work together to keep the body's level of arousal in balance for optimum functioning.

Homeostasis—physiological arousal kept in balance

For instance, your body's balance, or homeostasis, may be upset by the continuous stress of final exams or a difficult relationship. Such stress usually results in continuous physiological arousal and any number of physical problems, including headaches, stomachaches, tight muscles, or fatigue. These physical symptoms, which are called psychosomatic problems, may result in real pain. We'll discuss these problems in Module 21: Health, Stress, & Coping (pp. 480–507).

Besides triggering your autonomic nervous system, the hypothalamus is also involved in regulating a complex hormonal system, which we'll examine next.

# F. Endocrine System

## Definition

**What is your chemical system?**

You have two major systems for sending signals to the body's muscles, glands, and organs. We have already discussed the nervous system, which uses neurons, nerves, and neurotransmitters to send information throughout the body. The second major system for sending information is called the endocrine system.

The *endocrine system* is made up of numerous glands that are located throughout the body. These glands secrete various chemicals, called *hormones,* which affect organs, muscles, and other glands in the body.

The location and function of some of the endocrine system's glands are shown in the figure below.

## Control Center

In many ways, the *hypothalamus,* which is located in the lower middle part of the brain, controls much of the endocrine system by regulating the pituitary gland, which is located directly below and outside the brain. The hypothalamus is often called the control center of the endocrine system.

The drawing on the left shows that the hypothalamus is connected to the pituitary gland.

## Other Glands

We'll describe some of the endocrine system's major glands as well as their dysfunctions.

The *pituitary gland,* a key component of the endocrine system, hangs directly below the hypothalamus, to which it is connected by a narrow stalk. The pituitary gland is divided into anterior (front) and posterior (back) sections.

*Posterior pituitary.* The rear portion of the pituitary regulates water and salt balance.

**Dysfunction:** Lack of hormones causes a less common form of diabetes.

*Anterior pituitary.* The front part of the pituitary regulates growth through secretion of growth hormone and produces hormones that control the adrenal cortex, pancreas, thyroid, and gonads.

**Dysfunction:** Too little growth hormone produces dwarfism; too much causes gigantism. Other problems in the pituitary cause problems in the glands it regulates.

*Pancreas.* This organ regulates the level of sugar in the bloodstream by secreting insulin.

**Dysfunction:** Lack of insulin results in the more common form of diabetes, while too much causes hypoglycemia (low blood sugar).

Endocrine system controls glands located throughout the body.

*Thyroid.* This gland, which is located in the neck, regulates metabolism through secretion of hormones.

**Dysfunction:** Hormone deficiency during development leads to stunted growth and mental retardation. Undersecretion during adulthood leads to reduction in motivation. Oversecretion results in high metabolism, weight loss, and nervousness.

*Adrenal glands.* The adrenal cortex (outside part) secretes hormones that regulate sugar and salt balances and help the body resist stress; they are also responsible for growth of pubic hair, a secondary sexual characteristic. The adrenal medulla (inside part) secretes two hormones that arouse the body to deal with stress and emergencies: epinephrine (adrenaline) and norepinephrine (noradrenaline).

**Dysfunction:** With a lack of cortical hormones, the body's responses are unable to cope with stress.

*Gonads.* In females, the ovaries produce hormones that regulate sexual development, ovulation, and growth of sex organs. In males, the testes produce hormones that regulate sexual development, production of sperm, and growth of sex organs.

**Dysfunction:** Lack of sex hormones during puberty results in lack of secondary sexual characteristics (facial and body hair, muscles in males, breasts in females).

Up to this point, we have examined many of the structures and functions that make up the incredible nervous and endocrine systems. After the Concept Review, we'll discuss a question that students often ask: Do the brains of males differ from those of females?

# Concept Review

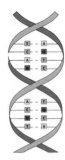

**1.** A hairlike structure that contains tightly coiled strands of the chemical DNA (deoxyribonucleic acid) is called a (a)_____. A specific segment on the strand of DNA that contains instructions for making proteins is called a (b)_____. A theory that different species arose from a common ancestor and that those species survived that were best adapted to meet the demands of their environments is called the theory of (c)_____.

**2.** There are several techniques for studying the living brain. One method for identifying structures in the brain involves measuring nonharmful radio frequencies as they pass through the brain; this is called an (a)_____ scan. Another method that is used to study functions of the brain involves measuring amounts of low-level radioactive substances absorbed by brain cells; this is called a (b)_____ scan.

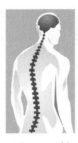

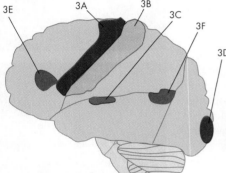

**3. The numbers/letters on the drawing match those of the questions below.**

**3A.** The cortical area that controls voluntary movements is called the (a)_____ and is located in the (b)_____ lobe.

**3B.** The cortical area that receives input from sensory receptors in the skin, muscles, and joints is called the (a)_____ and is located in the (b)_____ lobe.

**3C.** The cortical area that receives input from sensory receptors in the ears is called the (a)_____ and is located in the (b)_____ lobe.

**3D.** The cortical area that receives input from sensory receptors in the eyes is called the (a)_____ and is located in the (b)_____ lobe.

**3E.** The cortical area that is necessary to produce words and arrange them into sentences is called (a)_____ and is located in the (b)_____ lobe.

**3F.** The cortical area that is necessary for understanding spoken and written words and putting words into meaningful sentences is called (a)_____ and is located in the (b)_____ lobe.

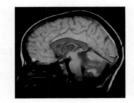

**4.** The two major divisions of the nervous system include the (a)_____ and the (b)_____. In turn, the peripheral nervous system has two parts: one part is a network of nerves that are connected either to sensory receptors or to muscles that you can move voluntarily and is called the (c)_____; another part regulates heart rate, breathing, blood pressure, digestion, secretion of hormones, and other functions and is called the (d)_____. The brain itself is divided into three major parts: (e)_____, _____, and _____.

**5.** The old brain that is involved with many motivational and emotional behaviors is called the (a)_____. One structure of the limbic system, the hypothalamus, controls the autonomic nervous system, which has two divisions. The division that responds by increasing the body's physiological arousal is called the (b)_____. This division triggers an increased state of physiological arousal so that the body can cope with threatening situations; this state is called the (c)_____. The other division of the autonomic nervous system that is primarily responsible for returning the body to a calm or relaxed state and is involved in digestion is called the (d)_____. These two divisions work together to keep the body in physiological balance so that it remains or returns to a state of optimal functioning; this state is called (e)_____.

**6.** A system made up of numerous glands that are located throughout the body and that secrete various hormones is called the (a)_____. The brain area that can be considered the master control for this system is the (b)_____. This brain area is connected to and controls one of the endocrine system's major glands that has an anterior and posterior part and is collectively called the (c)_____.

*Answers:* 1. (a) chromosome, (b) gene, (c) evolution; 2. (a) MRI, (b) PET; 3A. (a) motor cortex, (b) frontal; 3B. (a) somatosensory cortex, (b) parietal; 3C. (a) primary auditory cortex, (b) temporal; 3D. (a) primary visual cortex, (b) occipital; 3E. (a) Broca's area, (b) frontal; 3F. (a) Wernicke's area, (b) temporal; 4. (a) central nervous system, (b) peripheral nervous system, (c) somatic nervous system, (d) autonomic nervous system, (e) forebrain, midbrain, hindbrain; 5. (a) limbic system, (b) sympathetic nervous system, (c) fight-flight response, (d) parasympathetic nervous system, (e) homeostasis; 6. (a) endocrine system, (b) hypothalamus, (c) pituitary gland

## Science and Politics

**Is this kind of research sexist?**

Throughout history, politicians have criticized or misused research depending on what was "politically correct" (Azar, 1997). For example, in the 1920s, United States politicians misused research on IQ scores to justify passing discriminatory immigration quotas (see p. 296) (Gould, 1981). In the 1980s, many politicians were critical of homosexuality and denied federal money for AIDS research until the virus became a threat to the heterosexual population (Shilts, 1988). In the 1980s and 1990s, research on sex differences was criticized as "sexist" because it went against the "politically correct" belief that male and female brains are essentially the same (Azar, 1997).

However, using PET scans, researchers have recently reported interesting differences in the structure and function of male and female brains, which are called sex differences (Hausmann & Gunturkun, 1999). *Sex, or gender, differences* refer to structural or functional differences in cognitive, behavioral, or brain processes that arise from being a male or a female.

Sex differences are neither good nor bad nor sexist but simply ways in which males and females differ. Here are some interesting sex differences.

### Differences in Solving Problems

The rotating figure problem is a rather difficult spatial problem, as follows. First, study the target figure on the left. Then, from the three choices at the right, identify the same figure, even though it has been rotated.

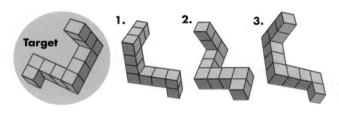

The key to solving this problem is the ability to rotate the target figure in your mind until it matches the rotation of one of the three choices. Researchers consistently report faster or more accurate performance by males than by females in solving rotating figure problems (Kimura, 1992). (Correct answer is 1.)

There are other tasks at which women perform better than men.

For example, look at the house outlined in black (figure above) and find its twin among the three choices. Women are generally faster on these kinds of tests, which measure perceptual speed. In addition, women usually score higher on tests of verbal fluency, in which you must list as many words as you can that begin with the same letter, as in the figure below (Halpern, 2000).

One explanation for these sex differences in skills is that they result from differences in

L___ Limp, Livery, Love, Laser, Liquid, Low, Like, Lag, Live, Lug, Light, Lift, Liver, Lime, Leg, Load, Lap, Lucid, . . .

socialization and learning. Another explanation is that these sex differences have evolved from different skills needed by early humans. Males with good spatial skills had an advantage in hunting, and females with good communication skills had an advantage in child-rearing (Springer & Deutsch, 1997).

Researchers have now begun to look for sex differences in how the brain itself functions.

### Differences between Female and Male Brains

To check for sex differences between male and female brains, researchers took PET scans while subjects were solving rotating figure problems.

For male brains, PET scans taken during problem solving showed that maximum neural activity occurred in the right frontal area (upper right figure).

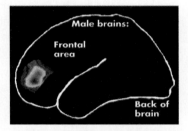

In contrast, PET scans of female brains taken during problem solving showed that maximum neural activity occurred in the right parietal-temporal area (lower right figure). Researchers concluded that solving rotating figure problems showed a significant sex difference in terms of which brain areas were activated and that these brain differences may be the basis for sex differences in performance (Alivisatos & Petrides, 1997).

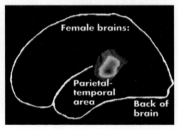

Another interesting PET study found that while escaping from a three-dimensional virtual-reality maze, men were significantly faster (average: 2 min. 22 sec) than women (average: 3 min. 16 sec). Also, men used both sides of their hippocampus, which is used to save data into permanent storage, while women used only the right hippocampus. Researchers concluded that these brain differences may explain why men are better at finding a specific place in a strange city (Gron et al., 2000).

Besides differences in cognitive tasks, researchers are also finding sex differences in emotional tasks.

Because women are consistently reported to be more sensitive, concerned, and nurturing, is it possible that women process emotional information differently than men (Halpern, 2000)? Researchers took PET scans while subjects induced emotional states (happy, sad). PET scans showed that while inducing emotional states, women used more of their limbic structures (involved in emotions) than men. Researchers speculate that these kinds of sex differences in the brain may underlie other male-female emotional behaviors (George et al., 1996).

In finding sex differences in the brain, researchers warn against using such differences as the basis for promoting discriminatory practices or furthering someone's political agenda (Azar, 1997).

## Skull Size and Intelligence

**Which race had the biggest brain?**

When he died in 1851, the *New York Times* proudly said that Samuel George Morton, scientist and physician, had one of the best reputations among scholars throughout the world. Morton had spent his lifetime collecting skulls of different races to determine which race had the biggest brain. During Morton's time, it was generally accepted that a bigger brain meant greater intelligence and innate mental ability.

**Results in 1839.** Morton estimated the size of a brain by pouring tiny lead pellets (the size of present-day BBs) into each skull and then measuring the number of pellets. Using this procedure, he arrived at the following ranking of

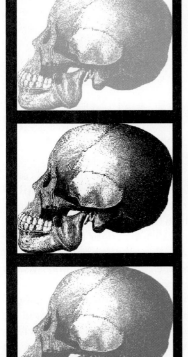

**No significant differences in brain size among races**

brain size in different races, from biggest to smallest (see skulls on left): 1, White (Caucasian); 2, yellow (Mongolian); 3, brown (American Indian); and 4, Black (Negro). Along with his racial ranking of decreasing brain size, Morton also believed there was a corresponding decrease in behavioral and cognitive skills (Morton, 1839, cited in Gould, 1981).

**Reanalyzed in 1980.** Stephen Jay Gould, a renowned evolutionary biologist, reanalyzed Morton's data on brain size and, unlike Morton's findings, found *no significant difference* in brain size among the four races. Furthermore, Gould concluded that Morton's strong biases that Caucasians should have the biggest brains had unknowingly swayed his scientific judgment to fit his racial prejudices of the 1800s (Gould, 1981).

**Major error.** Morton's major error was that he included skulls that matched his personal biased expectations and omitted skulls that did not support his racial beliefs. That is, Morton chose bigger skulls to match his bias of Whites being more intelligent and smaller skulls for other races, whom he considered to be less intelligent (Gould, 1994).

Although Morton had the reputation for being a respected scholar and although he had asked a legitimate research question—Are their differences in brain size?—he was unable to prevent his strong personal beliefs from biasing his research and finding what he strongly but mistakenly believed.

One way current researchers guard against the problem of biasing their results is by having scientists in other laboratories repeat their studies. If the original findings are repeated in other laboratories, then they can be reasonably confident that their original results are valid.

## Brain Size and Intelligence

**Is a bigger brain more intelligent?**

Currently, researchers are again studying the relationship between brain size and intelligence with MRI scans (see p. 70), which can measure more precisely the size of the human brain. In four different studies, researchers found a moderate correlation of about +0.40 between brain size and intelligence (Wickett et al., 1994). These results suggest a positive relationship between brain size and intelligence, meaning that, generally, the larger the brain the higher the IQ.

**Female brains.** If there is a positive relationship between brain size and intelligence, then women should generally be less intelligent than men because their brains, as well as their heads, are about 10% smaller than men's (Holden, 1995). Since there is no evidence that women are less intelligent than men, how do we explain this contradiction?

Women's heads and brains are about 10% smaller than men's.

Although women's brains may be smaller, perhaps their brain cells are more tightly packed together. This idea received considerable support when the brains of men and women were examined after death. Researchers reported that in some areas of women's brains there were 11–17% more neurons than in corresponding parts of men's larger brains (Witelson et al., 1995). Researchers think that women's brains are not simply scaled-down versions of men's brains but rather that neurons in women's brains are more densely packed.

**Correlations.** Since studies report a positive correlation between brain size and intelligence, we'll briefly review what *correlation* means. A correlation indicates only the existence of a relationship between two events but does not identify cause and effect. For example, being in a stimulating environment may promote brain growth and result in higher IQ scores, or being born with a larger brain may allow one to absorb more from one's environment and score higher on IQ tests.

Thus, at this point in time, a positive correlation between brain size and intelligence may be scientifically interesting but has little practical application.

Before we complete our journey through the brain, we'll take you on one last trip, perhaps the most interesting of all. We'll see what happens when the brain is literally cut in two.

**Definition and Testing**

**Why did Victoria choose a split brain?**

Since about the age of 6, Victoria had seizures (also called epileptic seizures). During the seizures, she would lose consciousness, fall to the floor, and although her muscles would jerk uncontrollably, she felt no pain and would remember nothing of the experience. She was given anticonvulsant medicine, which prevented any further seizures until she was 18.

**Split-brain operation.** When Victoria was 18, for some unknown reason, her seizures returned with greater intensity. And to her dismay, anticonvulsant medication no longer had any effect. The seizures continued for ten years. Finally, when she was 27, she decided that her best chance of reducing her frightening, uncontrollable seizures was to have an operation that had a high probability of producing serious side effects. In this operation, a neurosurgeon would sever the major connection between her right and left hemispheres, leaving her with what is called a split brain (figure below).

Having to choose between a future of uncontrollable seizures and the potential problems of having a split brain, Victoria chose the operation (Sidtis et al., 1981).

In addition to Victoria (identified as V.P. in published reports), dozens of other individuals have also chosen to have a split-brain operation when they found that medicine no longer prevented their severe, uncontrollable seizures.

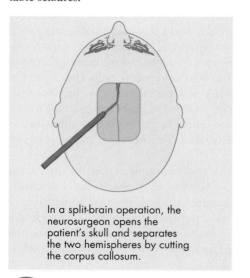

In a split-brain operation, the neurosurgeon opens the patient's skull and separates the two hemispheres by cutting the corpus callosum.

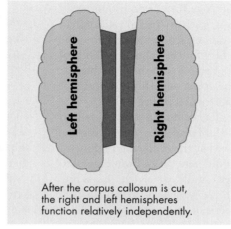

Left hemisphere　　Right hemisphere

After the corpus callosum is cut, the right and left hemispheres function relatively independently.

A *split-brain operation* involves cutting the wide band of fibers, called the corpus callosum, that connects the right and left hemispheres (figure above). The corpus callosum has 200 million nerve fibers that allow information to pass back and forth between the hemispheres.

A split-brain operation not only disrupts the major pathway between the hemispheres but, to a large extent, leaves each hemisphere functioning independently. In many split-brain patients, severing the corpus callosum prevented the spread of seizures from one hemisphere to the other and thus reduced their frequency and occurrence (Gazzaniga, 1996).

**Major breakthrough.** It was 1961 when researcher Michael S. Gazzaniga and his colleagues tested the first split-brain patient, known as W.J. in the literature. Researchers first flashed on a screen a number of colors, letters, and pictures of objects. These stimuli were flashed so that they went only to W.J.'s left hemisphere, and he had no difficulty naming them. Then researchers flashed the same stimuli so that they went only to W.J.'s right hemisphere, and W.J. seemed to see nothing, to be blind (Gazzaniga et al., 1962). Gazzaniga calls the discovery that W.J.'s right hemisphere was saying nothing "one of those unforgettable moments in life." Was it true that W.J.'s left hemisphere could talk but not his right?

**Testing a patient.** To determine what each hemisphere can and cannot do, we can watch as Gazzaniga tests Victoria after her split-brain operation.

Victoria is asked to stare at the black dot between *HE* and *ART* as the word *HEART* is displayed on a screen. Because Victoria's hemispheres are split, information from each side of the black dot will go only to the opposite hemisphere (figure below). This means that Victoria's left hemisphere will see only the word *ART* and her right hemisphere will see only the word *HE*.

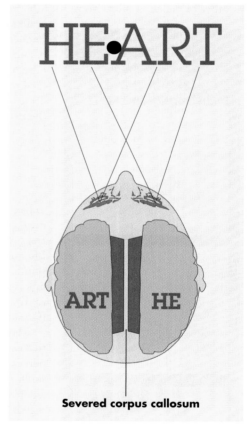

Severed corpus callosum

When asked, "What did you see?" Victoria says that she saw the word "ART," because it was projected to the left hemisphere, which has the ability to speak.

Although Victoria's right hemisphere saw the word *HE,* the right hemisphere turns out to be mute, meaning that it cannot say what it saw. However, Victoria can point with her left hand to a photo of a man (HE), indicating that the right hemisphere understood the question and saw the word *HE.* (Victoria points with her left hand because her right hemisphere controls the left side of the body.) Although the effects of having a split brain are obvious under special testing, the effects are not so apparent in everyday life.

## Behaviors Following Split Brain

**How does a split brain affect behavior?**

Initially, after her operation, Victoria reported that when she would choose clothes from her closet, her right hand would grab a blouse but then her left hand would put it back. However, examples of obvious conflicts between hemispheres are rare and disappear over the coming months.

Four months after her operation, Victoria was alert and talked easily about past and present events. She could read, write, reason, and perform everyday functions such as eating, dressing, and walking, as well as carry on normal conversations. For Victoria with her split brain, as well as for most of us with normal brains, only the left hemisphere can express itself through the spoken word (Springer & Deutsch, 1997). If the speech area is in the left hemisphere, then the right hemisphere is usually mute. (For a small percentage of left-handers, the speech area is in the right hemisphere and the left hemisphere is usually mute.) Thus, one reason a split-brain person appears normal in casual conversation is that only one hemisphere is directing speech. After testing split-brain patients, researchers discovered that each hemisphere is specialized for performing certain tasks.

## Different Functions

Before observing split-brain patients, researchers knew very little about how each hemisphere functioned. But after studying the behaviors of split-brain patients, researchers gained a whole new understanding of what task each hemisphere does best.

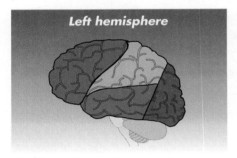

**Left hemisphere**

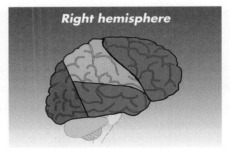

**Right hemisphere**

**Verbal.** Left hemisphere is very good at all language-related abilities: speaking, understanding language, carrying on a conversation, reading, writing, spelling.

**Mathematical.** Left hemisphere is very good at mathematical skills: adding, subtracting, multiplying, dividing, solving complex problems in calculus and physics, and so on. Generally, the right hemisphere can perform simple addition and subtraction but not more complex mathematics (Sperry, 1974).

**Analytic.** Left hemisphere appears to process information by analyzing each separate piece that makes up a whole. For example, the left hemisphere would recognize a face by analyzing piece by piece its many separate parts: nose, eyes, lips, cheeks, and so on—a relatively slow process (Levy & Trevarthen, 1976).

**Nonverbal.** Although usually mute, the right hemisphere has a childlike ability to read, write, spell, and understand speech (Gazzaniga, 1998). For example, when spoken to, the right hemisphere can understand simple sentences and read simple words.

**Spatial.** Right hemisphere is very good at solving spatial problems, such as arranging blocks to match a geometric design. Because hemispheres control opposite sides of the body, the left hand (right hemisphere) is best at arranging blocks, a spatial task.

**Holistic.** Right hemisphere appears to process information by combining parts into a meaningful whole. For this reason, the right hemisphere is better at recognizing and identifying whole faces (Levy et al., 1972). The right hemisphere is also good at making and recognizing emotional facial expressions (Springer & Deutsch, 1997).

After comparing the left and right hemispheres' functions, you can see that each hemisphere has specialized skills and is better at performing different tasks. These differences raise a popular question: Am I primarily right-brained or left-brained?

## What Am I?

**Am I "left-brained" or "right-brained"?** The popular press has exaggerated the idea that we are either "right-brained"—creative, intuitive, and artistic—or "left-brained"—reasonable, logical, and rational.

According to Jerre Levy (1985), who has devoted her career to studying how the brain's hemispheres interact, these distinctions are much too simple. She believes that we are constantly using both hemispheres, since each hemisphere is specialized for processing certain kinds of information. For example, when you read a novel, you are probably using programs in the left hemisphere that allow you to understand language in written form. But at the same time, you are using programs in the right hemisphere to keep track of the overall story, appreciate its humor and emotional content, and interpret any illustrations. Although hemispheres may sometimes work alone, they share much of their information by passing it quickly back and forth through the corpus callosum.

**How is my brain organized?** Michael Gazzaniga (1998), a cognitive neuroscientist who has studied split-brain patients for over 40 years, believes that each hemisphere of the brain has many different mental programs, such as sensing, thinking, learning, feeling, and speaking, all of which can function simultaneously. For example, when you see someone smile, your brain uses dozens of mental programs from each hemisphere to receive, interpret, and respond to this relatively simple emotional facial expression.

According to Gazzaniga, the brain and mind are built from separate units or modules that are interconnected and work together to carry out specific functions. Gazzaniga's modular model of how the brain functions is similar to your computer, which has many separate programs that allow you to perform many different tasks.

**Does the brain get better with use?** You have about 100 billion neurons, which you can think of as an extremely powerful living computer that has the ability to improve with use. For example, researchers found that adult mice given increased physical and social interactions or adult rats given increased learning experiences grew double the number of new neurons compared to animals that just lived in cages (Gould, 1999; van Praag, 1999). These results in animals suggest that the adult human brain may grow more neurons the more it is exposed to new experiences and lends support to the old saying "Use it or lose it" (Gage, 1999).

## A. GENES & EVOLUTION

**1.** A fertilized egg, which is called a (a)_____, contains 46 chromosomes arranged in 23 pairs. A hairlike structure that contains tightly coiled strands of the chemical DNA (deoxyribonucleic acid) is called a (b)_____. A specific segment on the strand of DNA that contains instructions for making proteins is called a (c)_____.

**2.** In 1859, Charles Darwin published a revolutionary theory of (a)_____, which said that different species arose from a common (b)_____ and that those species survived that were best adapted to meet the demands of their (c)_____.

## B. STUDYING THE LIVING BRAIN

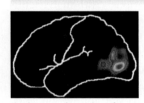

**3.** There are several recently developed techniques for studying the living brain. One technique, which measures nonharmful radio frequencies as they pass through the brain, is called an (a)_____ and is used to identify structures in the living brain. Another technique measures how much of a radioactive substance is taken up by brain cells and is called a (b)_____. This kind of scan is used to study brain function and identify the most and least active parts.

## C. ORGANIZATION OF THE BRAIN

**4.** The human nervous system is divided into two major parts. The brain and spinal cord make up the (a)_____. The network of nerves outside the brain and spinal cord makes up the (b)_____.

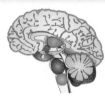

**5.** The peripheral nervous system is further divided into two parts. One part is made up of a network of nerves that either carry messages to muscles and organs throughout the body or carry input from sensory receptors to the spinal cord; this is called the (a)_____. The second part of the peripheral nervous system, which regulates heart rate, breathing, digestion, secretion of hormones, and related responses, is called the (b)_____.

**6.** The human brain is divided into three major parts. The largest part is involved in cognitive responses that we characterize as most human. This part is called the (a)_____, which is divided into right and left hemispheres. The part that is involved in controlling vital reflexes, sleeping, and coordinating body movements is called the (b)_____. The part that is involved in visual

and auditory reflexes, as well as alerting the brain to incoming sensations, is called the (c)_____.

**7.** Beginning in the midbrain and extending downward is a long column of cells called the _____ that alerts the forebrain to incoming sensory information.

**8.** The hindbrain consists of three structures. The structure that serves as a bridge to connect the brain and body and also manufactures chemicals involved in sleep is called the (a)_____. The structure that controls vital reflexes, such as heart rate, blood pressure, and respiration, is called the (b)_____. The structure that was assumed to be involved primarily in coordinating body movements but has recently been found to have a role in cognitive functions, such as short-term memory, following rules, and carrying out plans, is called the (c)_____.

## D. CONTROL CENTERS: FOUR LOBES

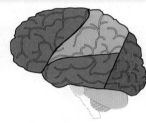

**9.** The thin outside layer of cells that has a wrinkled look and covers almost the entire forebrain is called the (a)_____. This layer of cells is divided into four separate areas or lobes: (b)_____, _____, _____, and _____.

**10.** The lobe that is involved in controlling social-emotional behaviors, maintaining a healthy personality, and making and carrying out plans is called the _____ lobe.

**11.** At the back edge of the frontal lobe is a continuous strip called the _____, which controls the movement of voluntary muscles. Body parts that have greater capacity for complicated muscle movement have more area on the motor cortex devoted to them.

**12.** Along the front edge of the parietal lobe is a continuous strip that receives sensations from the body and is called the _____. Body parts with greater sensitivity have more area on the somatosensory cortex devoted to them.

**13.** An area on the upper edge of the temporal lobe that receives signals from receptors in the ears and changes them into basic auditory sensations is called the (a)_____. For most individuals, an area in the left temporal lobe is involved in understanding and speaking coherently; it is called (b)_____ area. Damage to this area results in inability to understand spoken and written speech or to speak coherently, a problem called (c)_____. An area in the frontal lobe, called (d)_____, is necessary for producing words and arranging them into fluent sentences. If this area is damaged, the result is a speech problem called (e)_____.

**14.** An area at the very back of the occipital lobe that receives signals from receptors in the eyes and changes them into basic visual sensations is called the _____.

**15.** The vast majority of the cortex making up the four lobes is involved in adding meaning, interpretations, and associations to sensory stimuli, as well as in many cognitive functions. Together, these areas are called _____ areas.

## E. LIMBIC SYSTEM: OLD BRAIN

**16.** Inside the forebrain is a central core of interconnected structures known as the primitive, or "animal," brain or, more technically, the (a)_____. Four of the areas that make up the limbic system are the (b)_____,

_____, _____, and _____, which are all involved in motivational and emotional behaviors.

**17.** One structure of the limbic system, the hypothalamus, controls the autonomic nervous system, which has two divisions. The one that arouses the body, increases physiological responses (such as heart rate and blood pressure), and prepares the body for the fight-flight response is called the (a)_____. The division that calms down the body and aids digestion is called the (b)_____. These two divisions work together to keep the body's internal organs in a balanced physiological state, which is called (c)_____.

## F. ENDOCRINE SYSTEM

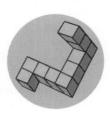

**18.** Besides the nervous system, a network of glands regulates organs through the secretion of hormones. This chemical system is called the (a)_____. A major gland that controls other glands in this system is the (b)_____ gland, which has an anterior and posterior part.

## G. RESEARCH FOCUS: SEX DIFFERENCES IN THE BRAIN?

**19.** Structural or functional differences in the brain that arise from being male or female are called _____. One example of sex differences in the brain is that males primarily use the frontal area to solve spatial problems, while females use the parietal-temporal area.

## H. CULTURAL DIVERSITY: BRAIN SIZE & RACIAL MYTHS

**20.** In the 1800s, one scientist measured skull size and concluded that a larger brain indicated more intelligence and that the races could be ranked by brain size. However, further analysis of this researcher's data indicated that there was no basis for ranking races by (a)_____. More recent experiments that precisely measured brain size with MRI scans found a modest correlation between brain size and (b)_____. However, we do not know if a stimulating environment causes the brain to grow more or if a larger brain is able to absorb more from the environment.

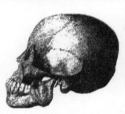

## I. APPLICATION: SPLIT BRAIN

**21.** The two hemispheres are connected by a major bundle of fibers that is called the _____. Severing this structure produces a condition called a split brain. Study of such patients reveals that each hemisphere generally processes information in a different way.

**22.** For most individuals, mental programs for language, speech, and mathematics are located in the (a)_____; mental programs for solving spatial problems and processing emotional responses are located in the (b)_____. In addition, the hemispheres process information in different ways. The left hemisphere processes information in a more piece-by-piece fashion or (c)_____ way. In comparison, the right hemisphere processes information as a meaningful whole; that is, it uses a more (d)_____ approach.

**23.** One theory of brain organization says that your brain has many separate but interconnected _____ programs that function and work together so that you can perform many cognitive skills.

*Answers:* 1. (a) zygote, (b) chromosome, (c) gene; 2. (a) evolution, (b) ancestor, (c) environment; 3. (a) MRI scan, (b) PET scan; 4. (a) central nervous system, (b) peripheral nervous system; 5. (a) somatic nervous system, (b) autonomic nervous system; 6. (a) forebrain, (b) hindbrain, (c) midbrain; 7. reticular formation; 8. (a) pons, (b) medulla, (c) cerebellum; 9. (a) cortex, (b) frontal, parietal, temporal, occipital; 10. frontal; 11. motor cortex; 12. somatosensory cortex; 13. (a) primary auditory cortex, (b) Wernicke's, (c) Wernicke's aphasia, (d) Broca's area, (e) Broca's aphasia; 14. primary visual cortex; 15. association; 16. (a) limbic system, (b) hippocampus, hypothalamus, thalamus, amygdala; 17. (a) sympathetic division, (b) parasympathetic division, (c) homeostasis; 18. (a) endocrine system, (b) pituitary; 19. sex differences; 20. (a) brain size, (b) intelligence; 21. corpus callosum; 22. (a) left hemisphere, (b) right hemisphere, (c) analytic, (d) holistic; 23. mental

# Critical Thinking

Newspaper Article

## Can Damaged Brain Learn Morals?

### Questions

**1.** In Module 1, you learned about three major research methods for answering questions about human behavior (p. 28). Which major research method is used in this study?

**2.** What are the major structures and functions of the limbic system?

**3.** What does Dr. Damasio expect will happen if the prefrontal cortex is damaged?

When Sheryl (not her real name) was 15 months old, she was run over by a car. The accident damaged an area, called the prefrontal cortex, which is located in the very front part of the frontal lobe, just above the bridge of the nose. Although Sheryl seemed to recover from the injury, by the time she was 3 years old, she didn't respond when her parents told her not to misbehave or physically punished her for doing so.

When Tom (not his real name) was 3 months old, doctors removed a tumor that had damaged his prefrontal cortex. Although Tom recovered from the surgery, by the time he was 9 years old, he showed little motivation, had few friends, and at times would explode with anger.

The effects of early damage to Tom and Sheryl's prefrontal cortexes were studied by Dr. Antonio Damasio and colleagues at the University of Iowa College of Medicine. According to Dr. Damasio, our emotional behaviors are triggered by a primitive brain, called the limbic system, whose urges and emotions are in turn dampened and controlled by the prefrontal cortex, which is involved in making plans and decisions. Dr. Damasio asked what would happen to a person's emotions and urges if one of its major controls, the prefrontal cortex, was damaged in infancy.

As a teenager, Sheryl was disruptive at home and in school, stole from her family, shoplifted, never expressed guilt

or remorse for misdeeds, blamed others for all her problems, and had no plans for her future. Although Tom managed to graduate from high school, he developed a variety of problems, including stealing, getting into fights, and being unable to hold a job.

Dr. Damasio describes Tom and Sheryl as going through life never showing guilt or remorse for bad behaviors, not learning normal social and moral rules. Dr. Damasio believes that Sheryl and Tom never learned the basic moral rules of what's right and wrong because of early brain damage to their prefrontal cortexes.

Some experts believe that Dr. Damasio's findings might be used by criminal lawyers to show that there is a biological basis for bad or antisocial behaviors. However, Dr. Damasio warns that these findings do not show a biological basis for being a psychopath since true psychopaths are very good at deciding, planning, and purposely carrying out a wide range of antisocial behaviors. In comparison, although Tom and Sheryl lacked normal rules of social and moral behavior, they sort of bumbled through life rather than purposely planning their bad behaviors. (Adapted from S. Blakeslee, Brain damage during infancy stunts moral learning, study finds, *Los Angeles Times,* October 19, 1999, p. A-1)

**4.** Do Tom and Sheryl's behaviors fit with the fact that their prefrontal cortexes were damaged?

**5.** Do you think these findings will help a lawyer get a client off for committing antisocial behaviors?

**6.** Why don't these findings provide a biological basis for psychopathic behavior?

*Use InfoTrac to search for topics:* prefrontal cortex; frontal lobe; antisocial behavior; psychopathology.

---

### *Suggested answers to Newspaper Article questions*

1. Three major research methods for answering questions are survey, case study, and experiment. In this article, researchers used the case study approach, which is an in-depth study of individual subjects, in this case, Tom and Sheryl.
2. Hypothalamus regulates many motivational behaviors; amygdala is involved in forming emotional experiences; thalamus receives and relays sensory information; and hippocampus saves certain kinds of memories in long-term storage.
3. Dr. Damasio expects damage to the prefrontal cortex, which is involved in planning and deciding, to cause major problems or deficits in social, emotional, and moral behaviors.

4. Beginning during childhood and continuing through adolescence, Sheryl and Tom show deficits in planning, deciding, and reasoning, which are functions of the prefrontal cortex, which was damaged in infancy.
5. If you were a defense lawyer, why wouldn't you use these findings, that brain damage may decrease moral behavior, to help your client go free instead of going to prison?
6. Psychopaths are individuals who commit antisocial acts but feel little or no guilt, sorrow, or remorse. Dr. Damasio adds that psychopaths purposely plan their antisocial behaviors, while Sheryl and Tom showed little evidence of such planning.

# Links to Learning

## Web Sites

- WADSWORTH ONLINE STUDY CENTER
  http://psychology.wadsworth.com
  Quizzes, learning activities and exercises, a discussion forum, and hot links to Internet sites related to the nervous system, including:

- THE WHOLE BRAIN ATLAS
  http://www.med.harvard.edu/AANLIB/home.html
  This amazing site from Harvard University features dozens of scans of the human brain in health and sickness.

- REB PAGE NEWS
  http://www.uni-hohenheim.de/~rebhan/rp.html
  This site is devoted to the brain in health and disease, and includes links to online journals and discussion groups from 1995 to the present.

- ABOUT BRAIN INJURY
  http://www.waiting.com/waitingabouttbi.html
  This site contains a wealth of information about brain injury. Topics include neuroanatomy, intercranial pressure and its consequences, coma, neurosurgery, and a glossary of terms.

## Learning Activities

- *POWERSTUDY*™ CD BY ROD PLOTNIK & TOM DOYLE

  Check out Module 4, "Incredible Nervous System," for a 50-minute, fully narrated, self-paced, interactive, multimedia presentation. Includes animations, videos, hot links to the Web, quizzes, pronunciation of terms, and personal note-taking capability.

- *STUDY GUIDE TO ACCOMPANY INTRODUCTION TO PSYCHOLOGY, 6TH EDITION,*
  by Matthew Enos
  Module 4 explores the current "Golden Age of biology." This can be tough going, but Baby Theresa, Phineas Gage, and Tarzan and Jane will help you navigate.

- *WEBTUTOR*
  http://webtutor.thomsonlearning.com
  Visit this site for interactive versions of Study Guide features. Take a quiz, get your score—should you study a topic some more, or can you move on? For example, what do we know about the relationship between brain size and intelligence? Your professor's class syllabus and course calendar are also posted—you'll never have to get behind in class again!

- *INFOTRAC ONLINE LIBRARY*
  http://www.infotrac-college.com

  Use your password and then key in search terms such as those below to find popular and scientific articles on subjects covered in Module 4. Make the library work for you!

  | | | |
  |---|---|---|
  | Genes | Brain scans | Cortex |
  | Autonomic nervous system | Endocrine system | Brain size |

- *PSYCHNOW!*
  CD for Macintosh and Windows includes a study guide, glossary, Web sites, and animations. For Module 4, see:
    - Brain and Behavior

## Study Questions

*Use InfoTrac to search for topics mentioned in the main heads below (e.g., brain evolution, split brain).*

*A. **Genes & Evolution**—If a species of humans with 5-pound brains was discovered, would their behavior differ from ours? (**Suggested answer page 621**)

*B. **Studying the Living Brain**—How would you know if a professional boxer had brain damage? (**Suggested answer page 621**)

C. **Organization of the Brain**—If you had to give up one part of your brain, which one would you sacrifice?

D. **Control Centers: Four Lobes**—Which brain functions would computers be the best and worst at imitating?

E. **Limbic System: Old Brain**—What would happen if your limbic system were replaced with one from an alligator?

F. **Endocrine System**—What is one reason for the different bodies of football players, soccer players, and jockeys?

G. **Research Focus: Sex Differences in the Brain?**—What's the danger of identifying sex differences in the brain?

*H. **Cultural Diversity: Brain Size & Racial Myths**—Why is there a continuing interest in whether a bigger brain is more intelligent? (**Suggested answer page 621**)

I. **Application: Split Brain**—If you were supposed to act like a person with a split brain, what would you do differently?

*These questions are answered in Appendix B.

# Module 5: Sensation

**A. Eye: Vision**      **94**
* STIMULUS: LIGHT WAVES
* STRUCTURE AND FUNCTION
* RETINA
* VISUAL PATHWAYS
* COLOR VISION

**B. Ear: Audition**      **100**
* STIMULUS: SOUND WAVES
* OUTER, MIDDLE, AND INNER EAR
* AUDITORY BRAIN AREAS
* AUDITORY CUES

**C. Vestibular System: Balance**      **105**
* POSITION AND BALANCE
* MOTION SICKNESS
* MENIERE'S DISEASE AND VERTIGO

**D. Chemical Senses**      **106**
* TASTE
* SMELL, OR OLFACTION

**E. Touch**      **108**
* DEFINITION
* RECEPTORS IN THE SKIN
* BRAIN AREAS

**Concept Review**      **109**

**F. Cultural Diversity:**
**Disgust versus Delight**      **110**
* SENSATIONS AND PSYCHOLOGICAL FACTORS

**G. Research Focus: Mind over Body?**      **111**
* DEFINITIONS AND RESEARCH METHODS
* PLACEBO RESULTS
* CONCLUSION: MIND OVER BODY!

**H. Pain**      **112**
* DEFINITION
* GATE CONTROL THEORY
* ENDORPHINS
* ACUPUNCTURE

**I. Application: Artificial Senses**      **114**
* ARTIFICIAL VISUAL SYSTEM
* KINDS OF DEAFNESS
* COCHLEAR IMPLANTS

**Summary Test**      **116**

**Critical Thinking**      **118**
* CAN MUSIC RAISE A CHILD'S IQ?

**Links to Learning**      **119**

### Electric Billboard in the Brain

**Can Katie see without her eyes?**

Katie was looking at an electric billboard made up of 36 dots of blue, purple, red, and yellow light. The billboard wasn't on the front of a store or sports stadium; it was in her own head.

When Katie was 22, she lost her eyesight to glaucoma and lived in total darkness for the next 20 years. At the age of 42, she volunteered to have experimental surgery in which 36 tiny gold wires were implanted into the occipital lobe in the back of her brain, which is the area that processes visual information. When researchers pushed a switch, a low-level, nonharmful electrical current passed through these gold wires and activated brain cells. When the brain cells in Katie's visual area were activated, she reported seeing flashes of colored light. By adjusting the electrical current, researchers could vary the brightness and size of the flashes from a tiny dot to the size of a nickel.

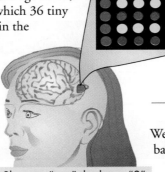

She can "see" the letter "S" when her brain is stimulated.

Because the implanted gold wires formed a rectangular grid of 36 dots (see figure above), researchers could apply current to particular wires in the grid to form patterns of flashing dots. For example, when the flashing dots formed the pattern shown in the figure, Katie reported seeing the letter "S" (adapted from *Los Angeles Times,* October 30, 1992).

Although Katie is officially blind because her eyes are not functioning, she can still "see" flashes of colored lights when the visual area of her brain is electrically stimulated. This fact raises an interesting question: How is it possible to see without using one's eyes? As we answer this question, you'll discover that the eye, ear, nose, tongue, and skin are smaller, more complicated, and better recorders than any of the newest, miniaturized, high-tech video cameras, recorders, or digital disks on the market.

### What's Coming

We'll discuss six of the major human senses—vision, hearing, balance (vestibular system), taste, olfaction (smell), and touch. We'll also explain how you see color, why some long-playing rock-and-roll musicians have become partially deaf, why you get motion sickness, and why your sense of taste decreases when you have a cold. Although your sense organs—eye, ear, tongue, nose, and skin—look so very different, they all share the following three characteristics.

### Three Characteristics of All Senses

Your eyes, ears, nose, skin, and tongue are complex, miniaturized, living sense organs that automatically gather information about your environment. Although physically very different, all senses share the following three characteristics.

**1 Transduction.** The first thing each sense organ must do is to change or transform some physical energy, such as molecules of skunk spray, into electrical signals, a process called transduction.

**Electrical signal**

*Transduction* refers to the process in which a sense organ changes, or transforms, physical energy into electrical signals that become neural impulses, which may be sent to the brain for processing.

For example, transduction occurs when a skunk's molecules enter your nose, which transforms the molecules into electrical signals, or impulses, that are interpreted by your brain as the very unpleasant odor of a skunk.

**2 Adaptation.** A short period of time after putting on glasses, jewelry, or clothes, you no longer "feel" them, a process called adaptation.

*Adaptation* refers to the decreasing response of the sense organs, the more they are exposed to a continuous level of stimulation.

For example, the continuous stimulation of glasses, jewelry, or clothes on your skin results in adaptation so that soon you no longer feel them. Some sense organs adapt very quickly, and some very slowly. However, sense organs do not adapt to intense forms of stimulation, because such stimulation may cause physical damage. Instead, intense stimulation, such as from a very hot shower, may cause pain, which warns us of possible injury.

**3 Sensations versus perceptions.** Gathering information about the world involves two steps. In the first step, electrical signals reach the brain and are changed into sensations.

*Sensations* are relatively meaningless bits of information (left figure) that result when the brain processes electrical signals that come from the sense organs.

In the second step, the brain quickly changes sensations, which you're not aware of, into perceptions.

*Perceptions* are meaningful sensory experiences (right figure) that result after the brain combines hundreds of sensations.

For example, visual sensations would resemble the top figure, showing meaningless lines, colors, and shapes. Visual perceptions would be like the bottom figure, showing a complete "sad-happy" face.

While all sensations begin with step 1, transduction, sense organs use different mechanisms to do it. We'll start with how the visual system does it.

# A. Eye: Vision

## Stimulus: Light Waves

**Why can't you see radio waves?**

Each sense organ has a different shape and structure; it can receive only a certain kind of stimulus, or physical energy. For instance, the reason you cannot see radio waves is that their waves are not the right length. Although radio waves, along with light waves from the sun, are all forms of electromagnetic energy, they vary in wavelength. For example, the figure below shows that X rays are very short and AM radio waves are very long. Notice that only a small, specific range of wavelengths that come from the sun, called the visible spectrum, is able to excite receptors in your eyes.

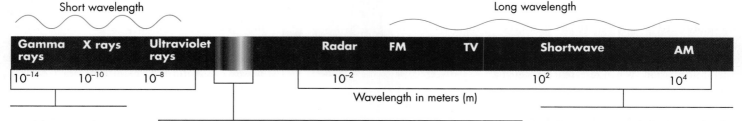

Short wavelength — Long wavelength

| Gamma rays | X rays | Ultraviolet rays | | Radar | FM | TV | Shortwave | AM |
|---|---|---|---|---|---|---|---|---|
| $10^{-14}$ | $10^{-10}$ | $10^{-8}$ | | $10^{-2}$ | | | $10^{2}$ | $10^{4}$ |

Wavelength in meters (m)

Violet Blue  Green  Yellow  Red

400    500    600    700
Wavelength in nanometers (nm)

**Invisible—too short.** On this side of the electromagnetic energy spectrum are shorter wavelengths, including gamma rays, X rays, and ultraviolet rays. These waves are invisible to the human eye because their lengths are too short to stimulate our receptors. However, some birds (such as hummingbirds) and insects can see ultraviolet rays to help them find food.

**Visible—just right.** Near the middle of the electromagnetic spectrum is a small range of waves that make up the visible spectrum.

The *visible spectrum* is one particular segment of electromagnetic energy that we can see because these waves are the right length to stimulate receptors in the eye.

The reason you can see a giraffe is that its body reflects light waves from the visible spectrum back to your eyes. One function of the eyes is to absorb light waves that are reflected back from all the objects in your environment.

**Invisible—too long.** On this side of the electromagnetic spectrum are longer wavelengths, such as radio and television waves. These waves are invisible to the human eye because their lengths are too long to stimulate the receptors in the eye. Imagine the awful distraction of seeing radio and television waves all day long!

**Stimulus.** Thus, the most effective stimulus for vision is energy (light waves) from the visible spectrum. However, for you to see anything, reflected light waves must be gathered and changed into electrical signals, and for that process—transduction—we must look inside the eye itself.

## Structure and Function

**How can you see a giraffe?**

For you to see a 16-foot-tall giraffe, your eyes perform two separate processes. First, the eyes gather and focus light waves into a precise area at the back of your eyes. Second, this area absorbs and transforms light waves into impulses, a process known as transduction. We'll follow the path of light waves from the giraffe to the back of your eyes in a series of 7 steps.

**1 Image reversed.** Notice that, at the back of the eye, the giraffe appears upside down. Even though the giraffe is focused upside down in the eye, somehow the brain turns the giraffe—and all other objects we see—right side up so that we see the world as it really is.

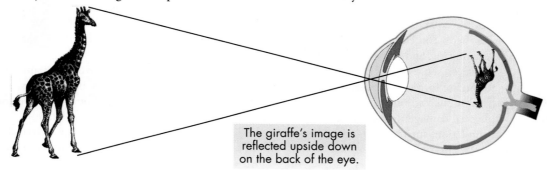

The giraffe's image is reflected upside down on the back of the eye.

**2 Light waves.** The problem with light waves is that after they strike an object, such as a giraffe, they are reflected back in a broad beam. You cannot see the giraffe unless your eyes change this broad beam of light waves into a narrow, focused one. Your eye has two structures, the cornea and the lens, that bring an image into focus, much as a camera does.

**3 Cornea.** The broad beam of light reflected from the giraffe passes first through the cornea.

The *cornea* is the rounded, transparent covering over the front of your eye. As the light waves pass through the cornea, its curved surface bends, or focuses, the waves into a narrower beam.

**4 Pupil.** After passing through the cornea, light waves next go through the pupil.

The *pupil* is a round opening at the front of your eye that allows light waves to pass into the eye's interior.

Your pupil grows larger or smaller because of a muscle called the iris.

**5 Iris.** The opening of the pupil is surrounded by the iris.

The *iris* is a circular muscle that surrounds the pupil and controls the amount of light entering the eye. In dim light, the iris relaxes, allowing more light to enter—the pupil dilates; in bright light, the iris constricts, allowing less light to enter—the pupil constricts. The iris muscle contains the pigment that gives your eye its characteristic color.

If you look in a mirror in bright light, you will see that the iris is constricted and that your pupil—the black dot in the center of your eye—is very small.

**6 Lens.** After passing through the cornea and pupil, light waves reach the lens.

The *lens* is a transparent, oval structure whose curved surface bends and focuses light waves into an even narrower beam. The lens is attached to muscles that adjust the curve of the lens, which, in turn, adjusts the focusing.

For the eye to see distant objects, light waves need less bending (focusing), so muscles automatically stretch the lens so that its surface is less curved. To see near objects, light waves need more focusing, so muscles relax and allow the surface of the lens to become very curved. Making the lens more or less curved causes light waves to be focused into a very narrow beam that must be projected precisely onto an area at the very back of the eye, called the retina.

**7 Retina.** Although light waves have been bent and focused, transduction hasn't yet occurred. That is about to change as light waves reach the retina.

The *retina,* located at the very back of the eyeball, is a thin film that contains cells that are extremely sensitive to light. These light-sensitive cells, called photoreceptors, begin the process of transduction by absorbing light waves.

On the following page, we'll describe the two kinds of photoreceptors, how they absorb light waves, and how they carry out the process of transduction. For some people, light waves cannot be focused precisely on the retina because of a problem with the shape of their eyeballs.

### Eyeball's Shape and Laser Eye Surgery

**Eyeball.** Some of us are born with perfectly shaped eyeballs, which contributes to having almost perfect vision. Others, however, are born with eyeballs that are a little too long or too short, resulting in two common visual problems: nearsightedness and farsightedness.

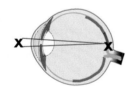

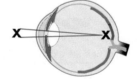

**Normal vision.** The shape of your eyeball is primarily determined by genetic instructions. If your eyeball is shaped so that objects are perfectly focused on the back of your retina (**black X**), then both the near and distant objects will appear clear and sharp and you will have very good vision (20/20).

**Nearsighted.** If you inherit an eyeball that is too long, you are likely nearsighted.

*Nearsightedness (myopia)* results when the eyeball is too long so that objects are focused at a point in front of the retina (**black X**). In this case, near objects are clear, but distant objects appear blurry.

Common treatments involve corrective lenses or eye surgery.

**Farsighted.** If you inherit an eyeball that is too short, you are likely farsighted.

*Farsightedness (presbyopia)* occurs when the eyeball is too short so that objects are focused at a point slightly behind the retina (**black X**). In this case, distant objects are clear, but near objects appear blurry.

Common treatments involve corrective lenses or eye surgery.

**Eye surgery.** Currently, a popular and successful treatment to correct nearsighted vision is called LASIK. In this procedure the surface of the eye is folded back and a laser is used to reshape the exposed cornea so that light waves are correctly bent and focused on the retina (Chang, 2000).

Next, we'll examine the retina more closely and see exactly how transduction occurs.

### Retina: Miniature Camera–Computer

**What happens to light waves?**

Some miniaturized electronic cameras can record amazingly detailed video pictures. But they are primitive compared to the retina, whose microscopic cells can transform light waves into impulses that carry detailed information to the brain about all kinds of shapes, shadows, sizes, textures, and colors. Think of the retina as a combination of a video camera and a computer whose batteries never run out as it transforms light waves into impulses—the process of transduction. And here's how transduction occurs.

**1** You already know that an object, such as a giraffe, reflects light waves that enter the eye and are bent, focused, and projected precisely on the retina, at the very back of the eyeball.

The *retina* has three layers of cells. The back layer contains two kinds of photoreceptors that begin the process of transduction, changing light waves into electrical signals. One kind of photoreceptor with a rodlike shape is called a rod and is located primarily in the periphery of the retina. The other photoreceptor with a conelike shape is called a cone and is located primarily in the center of the retina in an area called the *fovea (FOH-vee-ah).*

We have enlarged a section of retina to show that it has three layers. We'll explain the function of each layer. Start with #2, located below the figure on the far right, and move left to #5.

**Retina,** located at the back of the eye, contains photoreceptors.

**Fovea**

**Optic nerve** sends signals to the brain.

**Retina blown up to show its 3 layers.**

**Light waves** pass through spaces between cells to reach rods and cones in back layer of the retina.

**Front layer** of retina contains **nerve fibers** that carry impulses to the brain.

*Nerve fibers*

**Middle layer** of retina contains **ganglion cells,** in which impulses begin.

**Ganglion cells**

**Back layer** of retina contains photoreceptors, **rods** and **cones,** where transduction occurs.

**Cone**

**Rod**

**Rod**

**Neural impulses** move from ganglion cells to nerve fibers and then to the brain.

**Rods** and **cones** change light waves into electrical signals.

**5** *Nerve impulses* generated in ganglion cells exit the back of the eye through the *optic nerve,* which carries impulses toward the brain. The point where the optic nerve exits the eye has no receptors and is called the *blind spot.* You don't notice the blind spot because your eyes are continually moving.

What's surprising about the eye is that it does not "see" but rather is a sophisticated computer for transduction, for changing light waves into impulses. In order to "see something," impulses must reach the visual areas in the brain, our next stop.

**4** The process of *transduction* begins when chemicals in the rods and cones break down after absorbing light waves. This chemical breakdown generates a tiny electrical force that, if large enough, triggers *nerve impulses* in neighboring *ganglion cells;* now, transduction is complete.

**3** There are about 3 million cones, most located in the retina's fovea.

*Cones* are photoreceptors that contain three chemicals called opsins *(OP-sins),* which are activated in bright light and allow us to see color. Unlike rods, cones are wired individually to neighboring cells; this one-on-one system of relaying information allows us to see fine details.

Next, we finally get to transduction, which begins in the rods and cones.

**2** There are about 60 million rods, most located in the retina's periphery.

*Rods* are photoreceptors that contain a single chemical, called rhodopsin *(row-DOP-sin),* which is activated by small amounts of light. Because rods are extremely light sensitive, they allow us to see in dim light, but to see only black, white, and shades of gray.

To see color, we need the cones.

# Visual Pathways: Eye to Brain

*How do you see rock stars?*

There is a lot of truth to the old saying, "Seeing is believing," but most people don't realize that the "seeing" takes place in the brain, not in the eye. So far, we have traced the paths along which light waves enter the eye, are focused on the retina, are changed into impulses, and leave the eye on the optic nerve. Now we will follow the optic nerve as it reaches its final destination in the occipital lobe, at the back of the brain. There, the occipital lobe changes light waves into colorful rock stars.

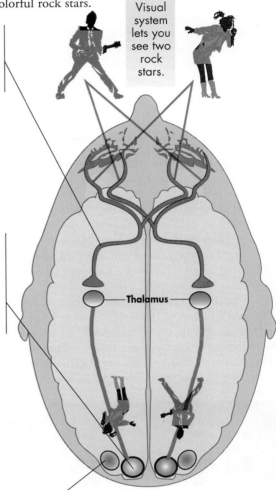

Visual system lets you see two rock stars.

Thalamus

**1 Optic nerve.** Nerve impulses flow through the optic nerve as it exits from the back of the eye. This exit point creates a blind spot that we do not normally see because our eyes are constantly moving and cover any areas that might be in the blind spot.

The optic nerves partially cross over and make a major stop in the *thalamus,* which does some initial processing. The thalamus relays the impulses to the back of the occipital lobe in the right and left hemispheres.

**2 Primary visual cortex.** At the very back of each occipital lobe lies a primary visual cortex, which transforms nerve impulses into simple visual sensations, such as texture, lines, and colors. At this point, you would report seeing only these basic sensations (left figure), not the complete figure of a rock star.

Researchers estimate that about 25% of the entire cortex is devoted to processing visual information, more area than to any other sensory input (Van Essen, 1997). The visual cortex contains many different cells that respond to many different kinds of visual stimulation.

*Meaningless stimuli*

**Specialized cells.** From the Nobel Prize–winning research of David Hubel and Torsten Wiesel (1979), we know that different cells in the *primary visual cortex* respond to specific kinds of visual stimuli. For example, some cortical cells respond to lines of a particular width, others to lines at a particular angle, and still others to lines moving in a particular direction. These specialized cortical cells transform different stimuli into simple visual sensations, such as shadows, lines, textures, or angles.

**Stimulation or blindness.** At the beginning of this module, we told you about Katie, who had 36 tiny wires implanted into her primary visual cortex. When electricity was passed through these wires to stimulate neurons, Katie reported seeing flashes of colored light. She did not see meaningful images, such as a singer, because neurons in the primary visual cortex produce only simple visual sensations.

If part of your primary visual cortex were damaged, you would have a blind spot in the visual field, similar to looking through glasses with tiny black spots painted on the lens. Damage to the entire primary visual cortex in both hemispheres would result in almost total blindness; the ability to tell night from day might remain.

However, to make sense of what you see, such as a rock star, nerve impulses must be sent from the primary visual cortex to neighboring visual association areas.

**3 Visual association areas.** The primary visual cortex sends simple visual sensations (actually, impulses) to neighboring association areas, which add meaning or *associations* (Van Essen et al., 1992). In our example, the association area receives sensations of texture, line, movement, orientation, and color and assembles them into a meaningful image of a complete rock star (left figure). There are visual association areas in each hemisphere. If part of your visual association area were damaged, you would experience *visual agnosia,* which is difficulty in assembling simple visual sensations into more complex, meaningful images (Zeki, 1993). For instance, a person with visual agnosia could see pieces of things but would have difficulty combining pieces and recognizing them as whole, meaningful objects (see p. 79).

*Meaningful rock star*

Researchers can use brain scans to show actual neural activity that is occurring in the visual association areas.

**4** This slightly modified PET scan shows that when a subject is silently looking at and reading words, maximum neural activity occurs in the primary visual cortex and nearby visual association areas (red and yellow indicate maximum neural activity; blue and green indicate least) (Posner & Raichle, 1994). These visual areas are located in the occipital lobe (back of the brain). The visual association areas are involved in many visual activities, such as reading, writing, and perceiving objects, animals, people, and colors.

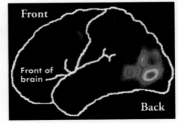

Front
Front of brain
Back

Next we'll explain how the visual system transforms light waves into all the colors of the rainbow.

## Color Vision

Debra was born with opaque films over her lenses (cataracts) that made her almost totally blind. For her first 28 years, she could tell night from day but see little else. When a newly developed operation restored much of her vision, she cried with delight as she looked around her hospital room and saw things she had only imagined. "Colors were a real surprise to me," Debra said. "They were so bright. You can't conceive what colors are until you've seen them. I couldn't imagine what a red apple looked like and now I can hold one and actually see red" (*San Diego Tribune*, April 3, 1984).

Red is actually long light waves.

Like Debra, you might assume that a red apple is really red, but you are about to discover otherwise. Objects, such as a red apple, do not have colors. Instead, objects reflect light waves whose different wavelengths are transformed by your visual system into the experience of seeing colors. So, What is red? The answer is that the color red, is actually a wavelength.

How light waves are turned into millions of colors is a wondrous and interesting process, which begins with a ray of sunlight.

### *Making Colors from Wavelengths*

1. A ray of sunlight is called white light because it contains all the light waves in the visible spectrum, which is what humans can see.

2. As white light passes through a prism, it is separated into light waves that vary in length. Nature creates prisms in the form of raindrops, which separate the passing sunlight into waves of different lengths, creating a spectrum of colors that we call a rainbow.

3. Our visual system transforms light waves of various lengths into millions of different colors. For example, in the figure below, notice that the numbers, which vary from about 400 to 700 (nanometers, or nm), indicate the length of light waves. We see shorter wavelengths as shades of

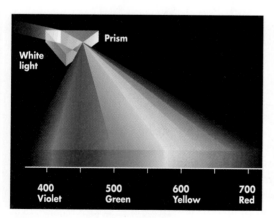

Prism
White light
400 Violet
500 Green
600 Yellow
700 Red

violet, blue, and green, and longer wavelengths as shades of yellow, orange, and red (Abramov & Gordon, 1994).

You see an apple as red because the apple reflects longer light waves, which your brain interprets as red.

Actually, how our visual system transforms light waves into color is explained by two different theories—the trichromatic and opponent-process theories—which we'll examine next.

### *Trichromatic Theory*

The explanation of how you see the many colors in the native face (left photo) began over 200 hundred years ago with the early work of an American chemist, John Young. It was his research that laid the basis for a theory of how you see colors, called the trichromatic *(TRI-crow-MAH-tic)* theory of color.

The ***trichromatic theory*** says that there are three different kinds of cones in the retina, and each cone contains one of three different light-sensitive chemicals, called opsins. Each of the three opsins is most responsive to wavelengths that correspond to each of the three primary colors, blue, green, and red. All other colors can be mixed from these three primary colors.

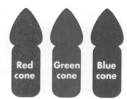

Red cone    Green cone    Blue cone

According to the recent version of the trichromatic theory, you see the red around the man's eyes because this area reflects light waves of a longer wavelength. You see the green in the feathers because they reflect light waves of medium length. You see the blue in the headband because it reflects light waves of shorter length. The different lengths of light waves are absorbed by three different cones whose chemicals (opsins) are most sensitive to one of the three primary colors—red, green, blue (right figure). Thus, wavelenghts of different lengths are changed into one of the three primary colors, which are mixed to produce all colors (Goldstein, 1999).

Until recently, color vision was believed to involve only three genes, one each to code the three primary colors of red, green, and blue. Researchers discovered that we had as many as two to nine genes (thus two to nine cones) that code the longer wavelengths involved in seeing red (Neitz & Neitz, 1995). This means that seeing a particular color, such as red, depends on how many color genes you have. For example, which bar on the TV (below) do you think is really "red"? One person may see "red" as deep scarlet and another as pale red. The color of

People do NOT all see the same color of red.

"red" that you see depends on how many genes (two to nine) that you have for seeing red (longer light waves). This means that different people may see the "same" color, red, very differently (scarlet to pale red) and explains why people may not agree about adjusting the color (red) on their television sets (Lipkin, 1995). Thus, your perception of "red" may differ from how someone else sees "red."

To understand how color coding occurs in the brain, we need to examine the second theory of color vision, the opponent-process theory.

All colors are made from mixing 3 primary colors: red, green, and blue.

## Opponent-Process Theory

If you stare at a red square for about 20 seconds and then immediately look at a white piece of paper, you'll see a green square, which is called an afterimage.

An *afterimage* is a visual sensation that continues after the original stimulus is removed.

And if you stare at a blue square, you'll see a yellow afterimage. On the basis of his work with afterimages, physiologist Ewald Hering suggested that the visual system codes color by using two complementary pairs—red-green and blue-yellow. Hering's idea became known as the opponent-process theory.

The *opponent-process theory* says that ganglion cells in the retina and cells in the thalamus of the brain respond to two pairs of colors—red-green and blue-yellow. When these cells are excited, they respond to one color of the pair; when inhibited, they respond to the complementary pair.

For example, some ganglion and thalamic cells use a *red-green* paired combination: they signal red when excited and green when inhibited.

Other ganglion and thalamic cells use a *yellow-blue* paired combination: they signal blue when excited and yellow when inhibited.

Thus, different parts of the visual system use different methods to code different colors.

## Theories Combined

Because we see colors so automatically and naturally, we don't realize it involves both the opponent-process and trichromatic theories. Here's what happens when we combine the two theories to explain color vision.

First, the trichromatic theory says that there are usually three different kinds of cones (there may be as many as nine) in the retina. Each cone absorbs light waves of different lengths, which correspond to the three primary colors of blue, green, and red. Second, when electrical signals (color information) reach the ganglion cells in the retina and neurons in the thalamus, they use the opponent-process theory, which involves a pair of colors: Activation results in one color of a pair, and inhibition results in the other color. Third, nerve impulses carry this color information to the visual cortex, where other neurons respond and give us the experience of seeing thousands of colors, which can be made by combining the three primary colors of red, green, and blue.

Although most of us have good color vision, some individuals have varying degrees of color blindness.

## Color Blindness

This is normal color vision.

The vast majority of us have normal color vision. We see the man on the left with a pinkish face, pale yellow scarf, purple hat, blue coat with orange trim, and brown pipe giving off yellow smoke, all against a two-toned orange background. However, about 1 out of 20 men in the United States see this same man in different shades of greens (photo below right) because they have inherited the most common form of color blindness.

*Color blindness* is the inability to distinguish two or more shades in the color spectrum. There are several kinds of color blindness.

*Monochromats* (MOHN-oh-crow-mats) have total color blindness; their worlds look like black-and-white movies. This kind of color blindness is rare and results from individuals having only rods or only one kind of functioning cone (instead of three).

This is red-green color blindness.

*Dichromats* (DIE-crow-mats) usually have trouble distinguishing red from green because they have just two kinds of cones. This is an inherited genetic defect, found mostly in males, that results in seeing mostly shades of green (photo right) but differs in severity (Neitz et al., 1996).

People don't always realize they have color blindness. For example, a little boy came home complaining about being chased by a green dog. The dog really looked green to the little boy; he did not know he had a form of color blindness.

People in some occupations, such as electrical technicians, are screened for color blindness because they must identify differently colored wires.

Below, you'll see two circles filled with colored dots that are part of a test for color blindness. An individual taking this test is asked to look at each circle and identify what, if any, number is formed by the colored dots.

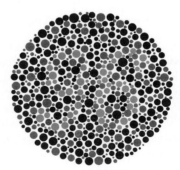

Individuals with normal vision see the number 96, while people with red-green color deficits find this number difficult or impossible to see.

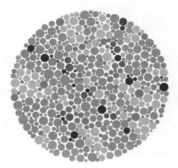

Individuals with red-green color deficits see the number 2, while those with normal vision see nothing.

From our discussion of the eye's structure and function, you can see that the eye is an engineering marvel that makes even the most sophisticated video camera seem like an expensive toy.

Next we'll examine an equally astonishing sense organ, the ear.

## Stimulus: Sound Waves

**What happens when someone yells?**

When a cheerleader gives a big yell, she is actually producing the yell by letting out air so that it is alternately compressed and expanded into traveling waves, called sound waves.

*Sound waves*, which are the stimuli for hearing (audition), resemble ripples of different sizes. Similar to ripples on a pond, sound waves travel through space with varying heights and speeds. Height, which is the distance from the bottom to the top of a sound wave, is called amplitude. Speed, which is the number of sound waves that occur within 1 second, is called frequency.

We'll demonstrate the concept of amplitude by comparing sound waves of a cheerleader's yell with a child's whisper.

### Amplitude and Loudness

**Yell.** As a cheerleader yells, she lets out an enormous amount of air that is compressed and expanded into very large traveling waves (shown below). Large sound waves are described as having high amplitude, which the brain interprets as loud sounds.

YELL! — Large amplitude means big sound waves and loud sounds.

**Whisper.** As a child whispers a secret to his friend, he lets out a small amount of air that is compressed and expanded into very small traveling waves. Small sound waves are described as having low amplitude, which the brain interprets as soft sounds.

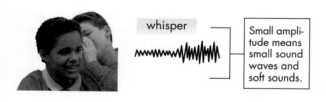

whisper — Small amplitude means small sound waves and soft sounds.

**Relationship: amplitude and loudness.** You have no difficulty distinguishing between a cheerleader's yell and a child's whisper because your auditory system automatically uses the amplitude of the sound waves to calculate loudness (Zeng & Shannon, 1994).

*Loudness* is your subjective experience of a sound's intensity. The brain calculates loudness from specific physical energy, in this case the amplitude of sound waves.

A whisper, which results in low-amplitude sound waves, is just above our threshold of hearing. The loudest yell on record, which resulted in high-amplitude sound waves, was about as loud as sound heard near speakers at a rock concert.

If the brain uses amplitude to calculate loudness, what does it use to calculate a sound's low or high pitch?

### Frequency and Pitch

**Screech or boom.** As you listen to someone playing a keyboard, you can tell the difference between high and low notes because your brain is continually discriminating between high and low sounds, which is called pitch.

Fast frequency means sound waves are close together, resulting in high sounds or pitch.

Slow frequency means sound waves are far apart, resulting in low sounds or pitch.

**High note.** Striking the top key on a keyboard produces sound waves that travel rapidly and are described as having fast frequency. The brain interprets fast frequency as high notes or high pitch.

**Low note.** Striking the bottom key on a keyboard produces sound waves that travel slowly and are described as having slow frequency. The brain interprets slow frequency as low notes or low pitch.

**Relationship: frequency and pitch.** When you hear a sound, your auditory system automatically uses frequency to calculate pitch.

*Pitch* is our subjective experience of a sound being high or low, which the brain calculates from specific physical stimuli, in this case the speed or frequency of sound waves. The frequency of sound waves is measured in cycles, which refers to how many sound waves occur within 1 second.

For example, playing the keyboard's highest key produces sound waves with a fast frequency (4,000 cycles per second), which results in high sounds or high pitch; the keyboard's lowest key produces sound waves of slower frequency (27 cycles per second), which results in low sounds or low pitch.

**Hearing range.** Humans hear sounds only within a certain range of frequencies and this range decreases with age. For example, infants have the widest range of hearing, from frequencies of 20 to 20,000 cycles per second. For college students, it is perhaps 30 to 18,000 cycles per second. With further aging, the hearing range decreases even more so that by age 70, many people have trouble hearing sounds above 6,000 cycles per second.

Next, we'll see how loud a jet plane is compared to a whisper.

**How loud is the library?**

## MEASURING SOUND WAVES

If the sign on the right were posted in the library, you might not know that it refers to loudness, which is measured in decibels (dB).

A *decibel* is a unit to measure loudness, just as an inch is a measure of length. Our threshold for hearing ranges from 0 decibels, which is absolutely no sound, to 140 decibels, which can produce pain and permanent hearing loss.

The following table contains common sounds with their decibel levels. Notice especially those sound levels that can cause permanent hearing loss.

**Please Do Not Talk Above 30 Decibels**

| Decibel (dB) level | Sounds and their decibel levels | Exposure time and permanent hearing loss |
|---|---|---|
| 140 | Jet engine, gun muzzle blast | Any exposure to sounds this loud is painful and dangerous. That's why aircraft ground personnel should wear ear protectors. |
| 120 | Rock concert near speakers, thunderclap, record-setting human yell (115 dB) | Fifteen minutes or less of exposure can produce hearing loss. Rock musicians and fans who do not use ear plugs risk hearing loss. |
| 100 | Chain saw, jackhammer, baby screaming, inside of racing car, firecracker | Exposure for 2 hours or more can cause hearing loss. Workers using loud power tools who do not use ear protectors risk hearing loss. |
| 80 | Heavy city traffic, alarm clock at 2 feet, subway, personal tape recorders | Constant exposure for 8 hours can produce hearing loss. Music lovers should know that stereo headphones can produce sounds from 80 to 115 dB. |
| 60 | Conversation, air conditioner at 20 feet, typewriter | Aging decreases hearing sensitivity, and that's why older adults may ask, "What did you say?" indicating that they may not easily hear normal conversations. |
| 30 | Whisper, quiet library, car idling in neutral (45 dB) | Today's cars are engineered for quietness. At idle, many cars are almost as quiet as a library; and at 65 mph (70 dB), they are not much louder than a conversation. |
| 0 | Threshold of hearing | If you were boating in the middle of a calm lake, you might say, "Now, this is really quiet." In comparison, most of us are accustomed to relatively noisy city environments. |

## DECIBELS AND DEAFNESS

It is now well established that continuous exposure to sounds with higher decibel levels for certain periods of time can produce permanent hearing loss. For example, rock musicians, rock fans, hunters, drivers of heavy machinery, airplane workers, and stereo headphone listeners who take no precautions against high decibel levels may suffer significant, permanent hearing losses later (Kulman, 1999).

At the end of this module (p. 115) we'll discuss different causes of deafness and treatment. Now, we'll take you inside the ear and explain how it turns sound waves into wonderful sounds.

**B.** *EAR: AUDITION* 101

## Outer, Middle, and Inner Ear

**Is that the Rolling Stones or a barking dog?**

Most of us think that we hear with our ears and that's how we tell the difference between, for example, the music of the Rolling Stones and the barking of a dog. But nothing is further from the truth. What really happens is that both music and a dog's barks produce only sound waves, which are just the stimulus for hearing (audition). Your ears receive sound waves, but it is your brain that actually does the hearing, distinguishing the difference between the Stones' song, "(I Can't Get No) Satisfaction," and a dog's barks. It's a complicated journey; the first step begins in the outer ear.

### 1 Outer Ear

The only reason your ear has that peculiar shape and sticks out from the side of your head is to gather in sound waves. Thus, sound waves produced by the Rolling Stones are gathered by your outer ear.

The *outer ear* consists of three structures: external ear, auditory canal, and tympanic membrane.

The *external ear* is an oval-shaped structure that protrudes from the side of the head. The function of the external ear is to pick up sound waves and send them down a long, narrow tunnel called the auditory canal.

**1a** The *auditory canal* is a long tube that funnels sound waves down its length so that the waves strike a thin, taut membrane—the eardrum, or tympanic membrane.

In some cases, the auditory canal may become clogged with ear wax, which interferes with sound waves on their way to the eardrum. Ear wax should be removed by a professional so as not to damage the fragile eardrum.

**1b** The *tympanic (tim-PAN-ick) membrane* is a taut, thin structure commonly called the eardrum. Sound waves strike the tympanic membrane and cause it to vibrate. The tympanic membrane passes the vibrations on to the first of three small bones to which it is attached.

The tympanic membrane marks the boundary between the outer ear and the middle ear, described below left in #2.

**Sound waves**

### 2 Middle Ear

The middle ear functions like a radio's amplifier; it picks up and increases, or amplifies, vibrations.

The *middle ear* is a bony cavity that is sealed at each end by membranes. The two membranes are connected by three small bones.

The three tiny bones are collectively called *ossicles (AW-sick-culls)* and, because of their shapes, are referred to as the hammer, anvil, and stirrup. The first ossicle—hammer—is attached to the back of the tympanic membrane. When the tympanic membrane vibrates, so does the hammer. In turn, the hammer sends the vibrations to the attached anvil, which further sends the vibrations to the attached stirrup. The stirrup makes the connection with the end membrane, the oval window. The three ossicles act like levers that greatly amplify the vibrations, which, in turn, cause the attached oval window to vibrate.

Thus, the function of the middle ear is to pick up vibrations produced by the tympanic membrane, amplify these vibrations, and pass them on to the oval window, which marks the end of the middle ear and beginning of the inner ear.

### 3 Inner Ear

The inner ear contains two main structures that are sealed in bony cavities: the cochlea, which is involved in hearing, and the vestibular system, which is involved in balance. We'll discuss the vestibular system on page 105; now, we'll focus on the cochlea.

The *cochlea* (KOCK-lee-ah), located in the inner ear, has a bony coiled exterior that resembles a snail's shell. The cochlea contains the receptors for hearing, and its function is transduction—transforming vibrations into nerve impulses that are sent to the brain for processing into auditory information.

Researchers liken the cochlea to an exquisite miniature box that is made of bone and contains precious jewels, which in this case are miniature cells that are the receptors for hearing.

On the next page, we have enlarged and opened the cochlea so you can see the auditory receptors.

## 3 Inner Ear (continued)

**3a** If you were to take two drinking straws, hold them side by side, and then wind them around your finger, you would have a huge imitation of a cochlea. The cochlea consists of two long narrow tubes (straws) separated by membranes (basilar and tectorial) but joined together and rolled up, or coiled. The beginning of the coiled compartments is sealed by a membrane, the oval window. So when the ossicles vibrate the oval window, the oval window vibrates the fluid in the cochlea's tubes, where the auditory receptors are located.

**3b** The auditory receptors, called *hair cells,* are miniature hair-shaped cells that stick up from the cochlea's bottom membrane, called the *basilar (BAZ-ih-lahr) membrane.* Vibration of fluid in the cochlear tubes causes movement of the basilar membrane, which literally bends the hair cells. The mechanical bending of the hair cells generates miniature electrical forces that, if large enough, trigger nerve impulses (transduction). Nerve impulses leave the cochlea as explained above right in #3c.

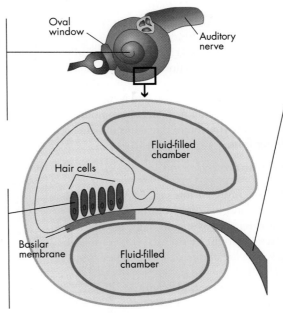

Cochlea changes vibrations into electrical signals.

Oval window

Auditory nerve

Fluid-filled chamber

Hair cells

Basilar membrane

Fluid-filled chamber

**Cross Section of Cochlea**

**3c** The *auditory nerve* is a band of fibers that carry nerve impulses (electrical signals) to the auditory cortex of the brain for processing.

Now the cochlea has completed its role of transduction—transforming vibrations into nerve impulses. However, you won't report hearing anything until the impulses reach your brain.

---

## Auditory Brain Areas

**How do we tell noise from music?**

Just as your eye does not see, your ear does not hear. Rather, sense organs, such as the ear, perform only transduction—transform physical energy into nerve impulses. You don't hear or recognize sound as noise, music, or words until nerve impulses are processed by various auditory areas in the temporal lobes of your brain.

### 4 Sensations and Perceptions

After nerve impulses reach the brain, a two-step process occurs in which nerve impulses are first transformed into meaningless bits of sounds and then into meaningful sounds. The first step occurs in the primary auditory area, explained in #4a.

**4a** The *primary auditory cortex*, which is located at the top edge of the temporal lobe, transforms nerve impulses (electrical signals) into basic auditory sensations, such as meaningless sounds and tones of various pitches and loudness.

Next, the primary auditory cortex sends impulses (sensations) to the auditory association areas, explained in #4b.

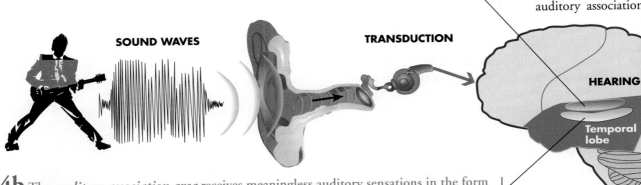

SOUND WAVES

TRANSDUCTION

HEARING

Temporal lobe

**4b** The *auditory association area* receives meaningless auditory sensations in the form of neural impulses from the neighboring primary auditory area. The auditory association areas combine meaningless auditory sensations into perceptions, which are meaningful melodies, songs, words, or sentences.

It takes only a moment from the time sound waves enter your ear until you say, "That's the Stones' song, '(I Can't Get No) Satisfaction.'" But during that amazing moment, sound waves were changed into impulses, impulses into sensations, and finally, sensations into perceptions (Feng & Ratnam, 2000).

Now we'll explain how the brain uses nerve impulses to calculate where a sound is coming from, whether it is a high or low sound, and whether it is a loud or soft sound.

### Auditory Cues

**Where's the sound coming from?**

If someone yelled, "Watch out!" you would immediately turn your head toward the source of the sound because your brain automatically calculates the source's location. The brain calculates not only the source of the voice but also whether the voice calling your name is high or low or loud or soft. Thus, sound waves contain an amazing amount of information. We'll begin with how your brain calculates the direction of where a sound is coming from.

#### Calculating Direction

You automatically turn toward the source of the yell, "Watch out!" because your brain instantly calculates the direction or source.

The brain determines the *direction of a sound* by calculating the slight difference in time (see 1 in right figure) that it takes sound waves to reach the two ears, which are about six inches apart (see 2 in right figure) (Goldstein, 1999).

If you have difficulty telling where a sound is coming from, the sound is probably arriving at both ears simultaneously. To locate the direction, you can turn your head from side to side, causing the sound to reach one ear before the other.

The brain uses other cues to calculate a sound's high or low pitch.

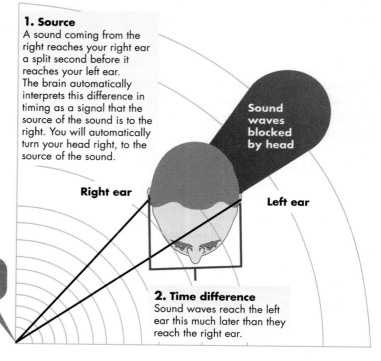

**1. Source**
A sound coming from the right reaches your right ear a split second before it reaches your left ear. The brain automatically interprets this difference in timing as a signal that the source of the sound is to the right. You will automatically turn your head right, to the source of the sound.

Sound waves blocked by head

**Right ear**

**Left ear**

**WATCH OUT!**

**2. Time difference**
Sound waves reach the left ear this much later than they reach the right ear.

#### Calculating Pitch

Imagine the low, menacing growl of a lion and then the high screech of fingernails on the chalkboard. Your subjective experience of a sound being high or low is referred to as pitch. Exactly how the cochlea codes pitch and the brain interprets the code is rather complicated. We'll focus on two better known theories of pitch, the frequency and place theories.

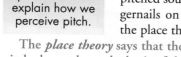

The frequency and place theories explain how we perceive pitch.

The *frequency theory*, which applies only to low-pitched sounds, says that the rate at which nerve impulses reach the brain determines how low the pitch of a sound is.

For example, the brain interprets a frequency rate of 50 impulses per second as a lower sound than one with a frequency rate of 200 impulses per second. Hearing the low-pitched roar of a lion involves the frequency theory. Hearing higher-pitched sounds, however, such as the screech of fingernails on a chalkboard, involves another theory, the place theory.

The *place theory* says that the brain determines medium- to higher-pitched sounds on the basis of the place on the basilar membrane where maximum vibration occurs.

For example, lower-pitched sounds cause maximum vibrations near the beginning of the cochlea's basilar membrane, while higher-pitched sounds cause maximum vibrations near the end of the membrane. Our auditory system combines the frequency and place theories to transform sound waves into perceptions of low- to high-pitched sounds (Goldstein, 1999).

The brain does one more thing: It calculates how loud a sound is.

#### Calculating Loudness

You can easily tell the difference between a yell and a whisper because your auditory system transforms the intensity of sound waves into the subjective experiences of a soft whisper or a loud yell. This transformation occurs inside the cochlea.

Compared to a yell, a whisper produces low-amplitude sound waves that set off the following chain of events: fewer vibrations of the tympanic membrane, less movement of fluid in the cochlea, less movement of the basilar membrane, fewer bent hair cells, less electrical force, and finally, fewer nerve impulses sent to the brain, which interprets these signals as a soft sound.

The brain calculates *loudness* primarily from the frequency or rate of how fast or how slowly nerve impulses arrive from the auditory nerve.

For example, the brain interprets a slower rate of impulses as a softer tone (whisper) and a faster rate as a louder tone (yell) (Goldstein, 1999).

Earlier, we said that there are two structures in the inner ear, the cochlea and the vestibular system. If you have ever stood on your head, you have firsthand experience with the vestibular system, our next topic.

The brain calculates loudness from frequency of nerve impulses.

### Position and Balance

**What else is in the inner ear?**

I guarantee that one question you never ask is, "Where is my head?" Even though your head is in a hundred different positions throughout the day, you rarely forget to duck it as you enter a car or forget whether you're standing on your feet or your hands. That's because the position of your head is automatically tracked by another sense, called your vestibular system.

The *vestibular system*, which is located above the cochlea in the inner ear, includes three *semicircular canals,* resembling bony arches, which are set at different angles (right figure). Each of the semicircular canals is filled with fluid that moves in response to movements of your head. In the canals are sensors (hair cells) that respond to the movement of the fluid. The functions of the vestibular system include sensing the position of the head, keeping the head upright, and maintaining balance.

The vestibular system uses information on the position of your head to indicate whether you're standing on your hands or your feet. A gymnast (left figure) relies heavily on his or her vestibular system to keep balance. Sometimes an inner ear infection affects the vestibular system and results in dizziness, nausea, and the inability to balance. And as you'll see next, the vestibular system is also involved in motion sickness.

**Semicircular canals**

Vestibular system says you're upside down.

### Motion Sickness

**Why am I getting sick?**

One of my terrible childhood memories is sitting in the back seat of a moving car and after 30 minutes of curving roads feeling a cold sweat followed by nausea, dizziness, and an extreme desire to lie down anywhere—stationary. Along with about 25% of the United States population, I experienced moderate to severe signs of motion sickness. About 55% of people experience only mild symptoms, while the remaining 20% are lucky and rarely experience any. Researchers think that motion sickness results when information provided by the vestibular system doesn't match information coming from other senses (Turner & Griffin, 1999).

*Motion sickness*, which consists of feelings of discomfort, nausea, and dizziness in a moving vehicle, is thought to develop when there is a sensory mismatch between the information from the vestibular system—that your head is physically bouncing around—and the information reported by your eyes—that objects in the distance look fairly steady.

Infants below age 2 rarely have motion sickness, but susceptibility increases from 2 to about 12. After 12, susceptibility decreases in both men and women. Researchers suspect that genetic and not personality factors determine susceptibility to motion sickness (Stern & Koch, 1996).

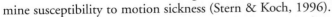

Motion sickness results from mismatch between vestibular and visual systems.

A number of drugs reduce the symptoms of motion sickness (Attias et al., 1987). As an alternative to drugs, fliers reported a significant reduction in motion sickness after completing a behavioral training program that taught them to perform relaxation responses, think positive thoughts, or use calming images at the first sign of symptoms. Of 53 fliers who had been grounded because of chronic, severe motion sickness, 49 were able to overcome their problem and start flying again after completing the behavioral program (Jones et al., 1985).

Malfunctioning of the vestibular system can cause terrible symptoms.

### Meniere's Disease and Vertigo

**Why is the room spinning?**

Imagine suddenly having ringing in your ears like Niagara Falls, walking into the bathroom to find the toilet spinning out of range, or vomiting more than 30 times a day. These are all symptoms of the dreaded Meniere's disease.

*Meniere's* (*main-YERS*) *disease* results from a malfunction of the semicircular canals of the vestibular system. The symptoms include sudden attacks of dizziness, nausea, vomiting, spinning, and head-splitting buzzing sounds.

About 7 million Americans suffer from Meniere's disease, which is thought to be caused by a viral infection of the inner ear (Milstein, 1993). Doctors no longer believe that the famous Dutch artist Vincent van Gogh suffered from Meniere's disease (Rosenfeld, 1998).

The vestibular system is also involved in vertigo.

*Vertigo,* whose symptoms are dizziness and nausea, results from malfunction of the semicircular canals of the vestibular system.

For example, a friend of mine slipped in a bathtub, fell, and struck the side of his head. He had severe vertigo for about a week, most likely because he temporarily damaged his vestibular system.

Meniere's disease and vertigo, which have no known cures, indicate what happens if the vestibular system malfunctions.

If you happen to be reading this book in a car or on a plane and feel a little queasy, relax before reading the next section, which is about tasting and smelling food.

### Taste

You rarely think about the thousands of chemicals you put into your mouth every day, but you do know when something tastes very good or very bad. You also know that if you burn your tongue on hot foods or liquids, your sense of taste can be markedly decreased.

*Taste* is called a chemical sense because the stimuli are various chemicals. On the surface of the tongue are receptors, called taste buds, for four basic tastes: sweet, salty, sour, and bitter. The function of taste buds is to perform transduction, which means transforming chemical reactions into nerve impulses.

As you imagine biting into and chewing a very bitter slice of lemon, we'll explain how your tongue tastes.

### 1 Tongue: Four Basic Taste Areas

Imagine sucking on a piece of lemon and tasting its sourness, which is one of the four basic tastes: *sweet, salty, sour, and bitter.* The right figure shows that particular areas on the tongue respond most to each of the four basic tastes. Overlapping areas result in combinations, such as sweet-salty.

The reason many of us have a sweet tooth comes from the fact that, as newborns, we inherited an innate preference for sweet and salt (J. Williams, 1994). Like most animals, humans avoid bitter-tasting substances, presumably because many poisonous substances taste bitter (Barinaga, 2000a). If you are one of those who likes sour lemonade, you know that people can learn to like bitter substances. Tasting begins with what happens in the trenches on the surface of your tongue.

### 2 Surface of the Tongue

As you chew the lemon, its chemicals, which are the *stimuli* for taste, break down into molecules. In turn, these molecules mix with saliva and run down into narrow trenches on the surface of the tongue. Once inside the trenches, the molecules stimulate the taste buds.

### 3 Taste Buds

Buried in the trenches on the surface of the tongue are many hundreds of bulblike taste buds.

*Taste buds*, which are shaped like miniature onions, are the receptors for taste. Chemicals dissolved in the saliva activate the taste buds, which produce nerve impulses that eventually reach areas in the brain's parietal lobe. The brain transforms these nerve impulses into sensations of taste.

Taste buds live in a relatively toxic environment and are continually exposed to heat, cold, spices, bacteria, and saliva. As a result, taste buds wear out and are replaced about every ten days. The human tongue can have as many as 10,000 taste buds and as few as 500; the number remains constant throughout life (Fackelmann, 1997b).

**Tongue contains taste buds that are most sensitive to four tastes.**

Bitter

**1. Tongue: Four basic taste areas**

Sour — Sour

Salty — Salty

Sweet

**2. Surface of the tongue**

**Trench contains buried taste buds.**

**3. Taste buds**

**Taste buds change dissolved chemicals into electrical signals.**

### 4 All Tongues Are Not the Same

In rare cases, individuals are born without any taste buds and cannot taste anything because they have a genetically determined disorder (Bartoshuk & Beauchamp, 1994). In contrast, about 25% of the population are supertasters, which means they may have two to three times more taste buds than normal, which results in increased sensitivity to sweet, bitter, sour, and salty. For example, supertasters taste sugar to be twice as sweet as most people and get more intense oral burning sensations from the chemical (capsaicin) in chili peppers. Supertasters find grapefruit juice too bitter and don't like broccoli because it also contains a bitter chemical (Drewnowski, 1997).

Researchers found that being a supertaster is an inherited trait and speculate that it may have had some evolutionary advantage. For example, supertasters would be better able to judge whether fruits or berries were poisonous (Bartoshuk, 1997). Today, supertasters may work for food manufacturers and rate the taste of new food products.

But for all of us, our ability to taste is greatly affected by our ability to smell.

### 5 Flavor: Taste and Smell

If taste receptors are sensitive to only four basic tastes, how can you tell the difference between two sweet tastes, such as a brownie and vanilla ice cream, or between two sour tastes, such as lemon juice and vinegar? The truth is that a considerable percentage of the sensations we attribute to taste are actually contributed by our sense of smell.

We experience *flavor* when we combine sensations of taste and smell.

You have no doubt experienced the limitations of your taste buds' abilities when you had a cold, which blocks the nasal passages and cuts out the sense of smell. Without smell, foods we usually love now taste very bland.

Since our taste of foods is greatly enhanced by the sense of smell, we'll examine olfaction next.

**How does your nose smell?**

Every year people in the United States spend about $5 billion on perfumes to make themselves smell better. You may have been impressed that your tongue has up to 10,000 taste buds, but that number pales in comparison to the nose's 6 million receptor cells (Silver, 1997). That's why the sense of smell, more properly called olfaction, is 10,000 times more sensitive than taste (Reyneri, 1984).

*Olfaction* is called a chemical sense because its stimuli are various chemicals that are carried by the air. The upper part of the nose has a small area that contains receptor cells for olfaction. The function of the olfactory receptors is transduction, to transform chemical reactions into nerve impulses.

We'll explain the steps for olfaction by having you imagine crossing paths with an angry skunk.

### 1 Stimulus

An angry skunk protects itself by spraying thousands of molecules, which are carried by the air and drawn into your nose as you breathe. The reason you can smell substances such as skunk spray is that these substances are volatile. A volatile substance is one that can release molecules into the air at room temperature. For example, volatile substances include skunk spray, perfumes, and warm brownies, but not glass or steel. We can smell only volatile substances, but first they must reach the olfactory cells in the nose.

Olfactory bulb contains olfactory cells that change dissolved molecules into electrical signals.

**Olfactory bulb**

**Olfactory cell**

**Volatile molecules entering nose**

### 2 Olfactory Cells

*Olfactory cells,* which are the receptors for smell, are located in two 1-inch-square patches of tissue in the uppermost part of the nasal passages. Olfactory cells are covered with mucus, a thick, gluey film into which volatile molecules dissolve. As molecules dissolve in the mucus, they stimulate the underlying olfactory cells, which trigger nerve impulses that travel to the brain.

As you breathe, a small percentage of the total air entering your nose reaches the uppermost surface of your nasal passages, where the olfactory receptors are located. People can lose their sense of smell in several ways. For example, a virus or inflammation can destroy olfactory receptors in their nose, or a blow to the head can damage the neural network that carries impulses to the brain (Bartoshuk & Beauchamp, 1994). Even though the olfactory cells change volatile molecules into impulses, you do not really smell anything until neural impulses reach the brain.

### 3 Sensations and Memories

Nerve impulses from the olfactory cells travel first to the olfactory bulb, which is a tiny, grape-shaped area (green structure in diagram of nose) that lies directly above the olfactory cells at the bottom of the brain. From here, impulses are relayed to the primary olfactory cortex (also called the piriform cortex) located underneath the brain. This cortex transforms nerve impulses into the olfactory sensations of a skunk's spray or a sweet perfume (Firestein et al., 1996).

Although we can identify as many as 10,000 different odors, we soon stop smelling our deodorants or perfumes because of adaptation in the olfactory cells (Kurahashi & Menini, 1997).

Smell, in terms of evolution, is a very primitive sense and has important functions.

---

### A nose worth $100,000?

Sophia Grojsman is one of only a dozen master perfumers in the United States who are responsible for creating some of the best-known perfumes (Calvin Klein, Estée Lauder). Known in the trade as a "nose," she earns over $100,000 a

year because there is no scientific/computer substitute for her nose and brain's ability to identify, remember, and mix fragrances that elicit pleasant memories and moods. One reason a computerized nose has not yet replaced a human nose is that scientists are only now beginning to understand which combinations of molecular qualities (weight, shape) and olfactory receptors determine which of 10,000 different odors humans can smell (Buck, 1999).

### 4 Functions of Olfaction

One function of smell is to intensify the taste of food. For example, you could not tell a licorice from an orange jelly bean with your nose held closed. A second is to warn us of potentially dangerous foods; the repulsive odor of spoiled or rotten food does this very effectively. A third and more recently discovered function is that smells elicit strong memories, often associated with emotional feelings; for example, the smell of pumpkin pie may remind you of a festive family gathering (Silver, 1997). For many animals, such as cats and dogs, smell also functions to locate food, mates, and territory.

Next, we examine the sense of touch and explain what happens when you pet a cat.

# E. Touch

## Definition

**What happens when fingers feel fur?**

If you were to draw your hand across the surface of a cat, you would have the sensations of touching something soft and furry. These sensations are part of the sense of touch.

The sense of *touch* includes pressure, temperature, and pain. Beneath the outer layer of skin are a half-dozen miniature sensors that are receptors for the sense of touch. The function of the touch sensors is to change mechanical pressure or changes in temperature into nerve impulses that are sent to the brain for processing.

We'll examine several miniature mechanical sensors and explain how they function.

## Receptors in the Skin

If you were to closely examine the surface of your skin, you would see a relatively smooth membrane covered in some places with hair. Some "touch" sensors are wound around hair follicles (the backs of your arms) and are slightly different from sensors in skin without hair (your palms). However, before we discuss several major touch receptors, we need to examine the different layers of the skin.

**1 Skin.** The skin, which is the body's largest organ, has three layers. The *outermost layer* of skin is a thin film of dead cells containing no receptors. Immediately below the dead layer are the first receptors, which look like groups of threadlike extensions. In the *middle and fatty layers* of skin are a variety of receptors with different shapes and functions. Some of the major sensors in the middle layer of skin are hair receptors.

**2 Hair receptors.** In the middle layer are free nerve endings that are wrapped around the base of each hair follicle; these are called *hair receptors.* Hair receptors respond or fire with a burst of activity when hairs are first bent. However, if hairs remain bent for a period of time, the receptors cease firing, an example of *sensory adaptation.* When you first put on a watch, it bends hairs, causing hair receptors to fire; your brain interprets this firing as pressure on your wrist. If you keep the watch on and it remains in place, keeping the hairs bent, the hair receptors adapt or cease firing, and you no longer feel pressure from your watch, even though it is still there. Your skin contains some receptors that adapt rapidly (hair receptors) and others that adapt slowly. Adaptation prevents your sense of touch from being overloaded.

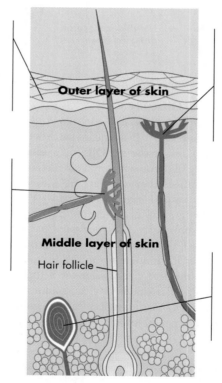

Outer layer of skin

Middle layer of skin

Hair follicle

**3 Free nerve endings.** Near the bottom of the outer layer of skin is a group of threadlike extensions; these are called *free nerve endings* because they have nothing protecting or surrounding them. One question about free nerve endings is how the same receptor can transmit information about both temperature and pain. Researchers think that different patterns of neural activity may signal different sensations—for example, slow bursts of firing for temperature and fast bursts for pain (Ferster & Spruston, 1995).

**4 Pacinian corpuscle.** In the fatty layer of skin is the largest touch sensor, called the *Pacinian corpuscle* (*pa-SIN-ee-in core-PUS-sole*). This receptor, which has distinctive layers like a slice of onion, is highly sensitive to touch, is the only receptor that responds to vibration, and adapts very quickly.

All these receptors send their electrical signals to the brain.

## Brain Areas

**Did I touch my nose or my toe?**

**PS** When pressure (touch), temperature, or pain stimulates the skin's receptors, they perform transduction and change these forms of energy into nerve impulses. The impulses go up the spinal cord and eventually reach the brain's somatosensory cortex.

The *somatosensory cortex,* which is located in the parietal lobe, transforms nerve impulses into sensations of touch, temperature, and pain. You know which part is being stimulated because, as we explained earlier (p. 77), different parts of the body are represented on different areas of the somatosensory cortex.

Somatosensory cortex

Parietal lobe

Compared with touch and temperature, the sense of pain is different because it has no specific stimulus and can be suppressed by psychological factors. We'll discuss these interesting aspects of pain, along with acupuncture, later in this module. We'll also discuss later how psychological factors can make foods that we think are truly disgusting become delicacies in other parts of the world. But first, try out your memory on the Concept Review.

# Concept Review

## EYE: Numbers on the eye match the numbers of the questions.

**1.** A transparent, curved structure at the front of the eye, called the _____, focuses or bends light waves into a more narrow beam.

**2.** A round opening at the front of the eye that allows varying amounts of light to enter the eye is called the _____.

**3.** A circular, pigmented muscle that dilates or constricts, thus increasing or decreasing the size of the pupil, is called the _____.

**4.** The function of the transparent, oval structure called the _____ is to bend light waves into a narrower beam of light and focus the beam precisely on a layer of cells in the very back of the eye.

**5.** Lining the back of the eye is a filmlike layer called the (a)_____, which contains several layers of cells. The back layer of cells has two kinds of photoreceptors, called (b)_____ and (c)_____.

**6.** This band of nerve fibers, called the (a)_____, exits from the back of the eye and carries impulses to the brain. The point at which this nerve exits is called the (b)_____ because it contains no rods or cones.

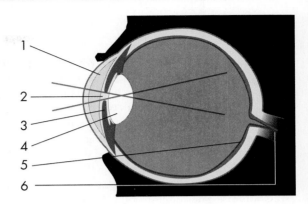

## EAR: Numbers on the ear match the numbers of the questions.

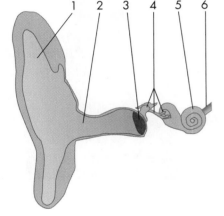

**1.** The funnel-like structure called the _____ gathers in sound waves from the environment.

**2.** The short tunnel called the _____ carries sound waves that strike a membrane.

**3.** The thin, taut membrane at the end of the auditory canal, called the _____, transforms sound waves into vibrations.

**4.** The three small bones (hammer, anvil, and stirrup) called the (a)_____ are part of the middle ear. They transform vibrations of the tympanic membrane into mechanical movements, which in turn vibrate a second membrane, called the (b)_____.

**5.** The coiled, fluid-filled structure called the (a)_____ is one part of the inner ear. It contains auditory receptors called (b)_____ that are attached to the basilar membrane.

**6.** The band of fibers called the _____ carries nerve impulses from the cochlea to the brain.

**7.** The inner ear contains a group of structures shaped like three tiny arches set at different angles. These structures signal body movement and position and are called the _____ system.

**9.** Substances give off volatile molecules that are drawn into the nose, dissolve in mucus, and activate the (a)_____. The function of these cells is to produce (b)_____ that are sent to the olfactory bulb and brain for processing.

**8.** Various areas of the tongue respond most to one of the four basic tastes, which are (a)_____, _____, _____, and _____. The receptors for taste are called (b)_____.

Hair follicle

**10.** There are several kinds of touch receptors: the (a)_____ is fast adapting; the (b)_____ is also fast adapting; the (c)_____ responds to both touch and vibration.

**Answers:** EYE: 1. cornea; 2. pupil; 3. iris; 4. lens; 5. (a) retina, (b) rods, (c) cones; 6. (a) optic nerve, (b) blind spot; EAR: 1. external ear; 2. auditory canal; 3. tympanic membrane (eardrum); 4. (a) ossicles, (b) oval window; 5. (a) cochlea, (b) hair cells; 6. auditory nerve; 7. vestibular; 8. (a) sweet, salty, sour, bitter, (b) taste buds; 9. (a) olfactory cells, (b) nerve impulses; 10. (a) free nerve ending, (b) hair receptor, (c) Pacinian corpuscle

## Sensations and Physiological Factors

**Would you eat a worm?**

We have discussed how senses transform physical energy into impulses, which eventually become sensations and then perceptions. However, your perceptions are usually influenced by psychological factors, such as learning, emotion, and motivation, so that you never perceive the world exactly like someone else. For example, when offered a fish eye to eat, many of us would react with great disgust. The facial expression to express disgust (right photo) is similar across cultures.

*Disgust* is triggered by the presence of a variety of contaminated or offensive things, including certain foods, body products, and

gore. We show disgust, which is a universally recognized facial expression, by closing the eyes, narrowing the nostrils, curling the lips downward, and sometimes sticking out the tongue.

Disgust is considered a basic emotion and is specifically related to a particular motivational system (hunger). Children begin to show the facial expression for disgust between the ages of 2 and 4, a time when they are learning which foods in their culture are judged edible and which are considered repugnant (Rozin et al., 2000).

**Cultural influence.** Your particular culture has a strong influence on which foods you learn to perceive as disgusting and which you think are delicious. We'll describe three foods that are considered delicious in some cultures and disgusting in others.

### Plump Grubs

For most U.S. citizens, eating a round, soft, white worm would be totally un-thinkable. For the Asmat of New Guinea, however, a favorite delicacy is a plump, white, 2-inch larva—the beetle grub. The natives harvest dozens of the grubs, put them on bamboo slivers, and roast them. A photographer from the United States who did a story on the Asmat tried to eat a roasted grub, but his American tastes would not let him swallow it (Kirk, 1972).

### Fish Eyes and Whale Fat

Although some Americans have developed a taste for raw fish (sushi), a common dish in Japan, most would certainly gag at the thought of eating raw fish eyes. Yet for some Inuit (Eskimo) children, raw fish eyes are like candy. Here you see a young girl using the Inuits' all-purpose knife to gouge out the eye of an already-filleted Arctic fish.

Eskimos also hunt a type of whale (the narwhal) that provides much of their protein. They consider the layer of fat under the skin (*mukluk*) a delicacy, and they eat it raw or dried.

### Milk and Blood

Several tribes in East Africa supplement their diet with fresh blood that is sometimes mixed with milk. They obtain the blood by puncturing a cow's jugular vein with a sharp arrow. A cow can be bled many times and suffer no ill effects. The blood-milk drink provides a rich source of protein and iron.

### CULTURAL INFLUENCES ON DISGUST

The reaction of U.S. college students to eating white, plump grubs (on right, actual size) or cold, glassy fish eyes or having a warm drink of blood mixed with milk is almost always disgust. Researchers believe that showing disgust originally evolved to signal rejection of potentially contaminated or dangerous foods. Today, however, because of cultural and psychological influences, we may show disgust for eating a variety of noncontaminated foods (cat, dog, or horse meat) or situations (touching a dead person) (Rozin et al., 2000). The fact that the same things are viewed as all right in one culture but as disgusting in another graphically shows how much cultural values can influence and bias perceptions.

Just as psychological factors are involved in perceiving taste, they are also involved in experiencing pain.

## Definitions and Research Methods

**Can sugar pills reduce pain?**

One of the truly amazing research findings is how sugar pills or placebos can somehow "trick" us into feeling or getting better. For example, because many of us believe that we will be helped by taking pills, about one-third of the population report feeling much better or having less pain after taking a pill, not knowing that it was only a sugar pill—a placebo.

A *placebo* is some intervention, such as taking a pill, receiving an injection, or undergoing an operation, that resembles medical therapy but that, in fact, has no medical effects.

A *placebo effect* is a change in the patient's illness (for better or worse) that is due to the patient's beliefs or expectations rather than the medical treatment.

For example, if people take a pill for headache pain and **believe** or **expect** that the pill will decrease their pain, about 30 to 60% of people will actually feel less pain after taking a placebo (Talbot, 2000).

Because the placebo effect can occur after taking any pill (injection or medical procedure), researchers needed to find a method that could separate a person's expectations and beliefs from the actual effects of a new drug or medical treatment. The method that researchers use to separate the effects of a person's expectations (placebo effect) from a pill or medical treatment is called the double-blind design.

In a ***double-blind procedure,*** neither the researchers ("blind") nor the subjects ("blind") know who is receiving what treatment. Because neither researchers nor subjects know who is receiving which treatment, the researchers' or subjects' expectations have a chance to equally affect both treatments (drug and placebo).

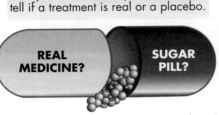

Only a double-blind procedure can tell if a treatment is real or a placebo.

REAL MEDICINE?    SUGAR PILL?

For example, in a double-blind design, headache sufferers would be told that they will be given two different kinds of pills to decrease pain. Unknown to the subjects ("blind") and the researchers ("blind"), one of the pills is a drug and one is a placebo. If subjects taking the drug report the same decrease in pain as those taking the placebo, researchers conclude that the drug is no better than a placebo. If subjects taking the drug report less pain than those taking the placebo, researchers conclude that the drug is medically useful because it is better than a placebo.

Over the past 25 years, hundreds of double-blind experiments have found that 30 to 98% of people have reported beneficial effects after taking placebos (Talbot, 2000). What follows is a sample of these findings, which demonstrate how people's expectations and beliefs can change placebos into powerful medicine.

## Placebo Results

Here are four convincing examples of pain reduction that involved placebos and double-blind procedures (J. A. Turner et al., 1994).

**98%** of patients originally reported marked or complete relief of pain from ulcers after medical treatment (gastric freezing). However, in a later double-blind procedure, this treatment was shown to be ineffective.

**85%** of patients originally reported a reduction in pain from *Herpes simplex* (cold sores and genital sores) after a drug treatment. However, in a later double-blind procedure, this drug was proved to be ineffective.

**56%** of patients reported a decrease in heart pain (angina pectoris) after being given a medical procedure that, unknown to the patient, involved only a skin incision.

**35%** (range 15–58%) of patients reported that placebos reduced pain following major and serious surgical procedures in hospitals.

## Conclusion: Mind over Body!

Based on findings like those given above, researchers have reached three conclusions (Brown, 1997; Talbot, 2000).

*First,* potentially very powerful placebo effects, such as reducing pain, getting over colds, or speeding recovery from medical procedures, have been greatly underestimated.

*Second,* both medication (pills, injections) and fake surgeries can produce significant placebo effects, such as reducing pain, in 15 to 98% of patients.

*Third,* and of great interest to psychologists, placebos indicate a powerful mind-over-body interaction. This mind-over-body interaction explains why people may really experience and report surprising health benefits from taking a wide variety of placebos on the market, such as unproven herbal remedies.

Researchers suggest that placebos may work by creating positive expectations and beliefs that reduce anxiety and stress. In turn, the reduction of anxiety results in perceiving less pain. And the reduction in stress improves functioning of the immune system so that the body can better fight off toxins and make a quicker recovery from some problem (Brown, 1997). Thus, there is no question that our minds have powerful effects on our bodies.

Next we'll examine pain in more detail and see how mental factors can affect the perception of pain.

---

### Definition

---

**What causes pain?**

All of us can relate to pain because at one time or another we have all felt various degrees of pain.

*Pain* is an unpleasant sensory and emotional experience that may result from tissue damage, one's thoughts or beliefs, or environmental stressors (job, traffic). Pain receptors in the body send nerve impulses to the somatosensory and limbic areas of the brain, where impulses are changed into pain sensations. Pain is essential for survival: it warns us to avoid or escape dangerous situations or stimuli and makes us take time to recover from injury.

This definition of pain differs from the other senses in three ways. First, pain results from many different stimuli (physical injury, loud noises, bright lights, psychological and social stressors), while each of the other senses responds primarily to a single stimulus. Second, the pain's intensity depends not only on the physical stimulus but also on a number of social and psychological factors, including attentional or emotional states. Third, the treatment of pain depends not only on treating any physical injury but also on reducing psychological and

Pain is different from all other senses.

emotional distress that may have caused or contributed to the painful sensations (Keefe & France, 1999).

In many cases, pain lasts for relatively short periods of time and is called short-acting, or acute, pain. In acute pain, such as after an injury, there is a sharp, localized pain, which is shortly replaced by a dull, more generalized pain. In other cases, when pain lasts for six months or more, it is called long-acting, or chronic, pain.

In the past, pain was usually thought of as resulting only from tissue damage. Now, researchers recognize that pain is a complex process that may or may not include tissue damage and usually involves social, psychological, and emotional factors, which can either cause, increase, or decrease painful sensations (Chapman & Nakamura, 1999; Price, 2000). For example, researchers found that painkillers may lose their effectiveness, especially in treating chronic pain. In these cases, the patients' social, emotional, and psychological factors must also be dealt with, such as patients' feelings of having little control over their lives or having little social support (Turk, 1996).

We'll examine how our perception of pain can be influenced by psychological factors.

---

### Gate Control Theory

---

**How does the mind stop pain?**

Although a headache is painful, the pain may come and go as you shift your attention or become absorbed in some project. This phenomenon is explained by the gate control theory of pain (Melzack & Wall, 1983).

The *gate control theory of pain* says that nonpainful nerve impulses (shifting attention) compete with pain impulses (headache) in trying to reach the brain. This competition creates a bottleneck, or neural gate, that limits the number of impulses that can be transmitted. Thus, shifting one's attention or rubbing an injured area may increase the passage of nonpainful impulses and thereby decrease the passage of painful impulses; as a result, the sensation of pain is dulled. The neural gate isn't a physical structure but rather refers to the competition between nonpainful and painful impulses as they try to reach the brain.

The gate control theory explains that you may not notice pain from a headache or injury while thoroughly involved in some other activity because impulses from that activity close the neural gate and block the passage of painful impulses (right figure above: NO PAIN). However, when you become less involved, there are fewer nonpainful impulses, the neural gate opens (left figure above: PAIN), and you again notice the pain as painful impulses reach the brain (Kugelmann, 1998).

An example of the gate control theory in real life is the football player who plays for hours with a broken bone

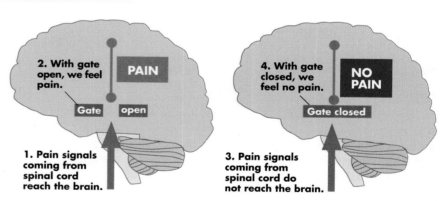

2. With gate open, we feel pain.

**PAIN**

Gate open

1. Pain signals coming from spinal cord reach the brain.

4. With gate closed, we feel no pain.

**NO PAIN**

Gate closed

3. Pain signals coming from spinal cord do not reach the brain.

but doesn't feel any pain (Warga, 1987). According to the gate control theory, a football player's intense attentional and emotional involvement in the game causes the brain to send nonpainful impulses that close neural gates in the spinal cord. The closed neural gates block pain impulses from reaching the brain and thus prevent feelings of pain. Later, when the game is over and the player's attentional and emotional states calm down, neural gates open, impulses from the broken bone reach his brain, and he feels pain.

#### PAIN: PHYSICAL AND PSYCHOLOGICAL

According to the gate control theory, your perception of pain depends not only on some stressful mental state or physical injury but also on a variety of psychological, emotional, and social factors, which can either decrease or increase your perception of pain (Chapman & Nakamura, 1999).

Besides the effects of psychological factors, our initial perception of pain from a serious injury can be reduced by our brain's ability to secrete its own pain-reducing chemicals called endorphins.

**Does the brain make its own painkillers?**

Someone who has experienced a serious injury—in football, for example—will usually report that initially the pain was bearable but with time the pain became much worse. One reason pain seems less intense immediately after injury is that the brain produces endorphins.

*Endorphins* (*en-DOOR-fins*) are chemicals produced by the brain and secreted in response to injury or severe physical or psychological stress. The pain-reducing properties of endorphins are similar to those of morphine, a powerful painkilling drug.

The brain produces endorphins in situations that evoke great fear, anxiety, stress, or bodily injury, as well as after intense aerobic activity (Tripathi et al., 1993). For example, subjects showed increased levels of endorphins after being stressed by receiving painful electric shocks or by holding their hands in ice water (Millan, 1986). Patients showed increased levels of endorphins after their teeth nerves were touched or their bandages were removed from badly burned areas of the body (Szyfelbein et al., 1985). These studies indicate that the brain produces endorphins to reduce pain during periods of intense physical stress. Endorphins and other painkillers (heroin, morphine, codeine) act mostly to stop receptors from signaling severe, persistent pain but do not stop receptors from signaling quick, sharp pain as from a pinprick (Taddese et al., 1995).

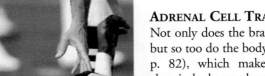

Brain releases endorphins in times of great pain, stress, or fear.

Researchers have identified the genetic code responsible for the development of the endorphin-morphine receptor in the brain. This receptor, which is activated by morphine, heroin, or endorphin, is the key to both reducing pain and causing addiction (Chen et al., 1993). Researchers hope that, as they better understand how this receptor works, they can develop drugs that reduce pain but are not addicting.

### ADRENAL CELL TRANSPLANTS

Not only does the brain make endorphins, but so too do the body's adrenal glands (see p. 82), which make an endorphin-like chemical that reduces pain. Researchers removed pain-reducing adrenal gland cells from individuals who were brain-dead and transplanted these cells into the spinal cords of patients suffering from chronic and severe cancer pain. Four of five patients who received transplanted cells reported dramatic decreases in pain (Pappas et al., 1997). Researchers were very encouraged and suggested that transplants of adrenal gland cells that make an endorphin-like chemical represent a promising approach to treating chronic pain.

Endorphins may also be involved in explaining how acupuncture reduces pain.

## Acupuncture

**Can an ancient technique reduce pain?**

Initially, scientists trained in the rigorous methods of the West (in particular, the United States) expressed great doubt about an ancient Chinese pain-reducing procedure, traced back to 2500 B.C., called acupuncture.

*Acupuncture* is a procedure in which a trained practitioner inserts thin needles into various points on the body's surface and then manually twirls or electrically stimulates the needles. After 10–20 minutes of needle stimulation, patients often report a reduction in various kinds of pain.

The mysterious part of this procedure is that the points of insertion—such as those shown in the photograph on the right—were mapped thousands of years ago and, as researchers now know, are often far removed from the sites of painful injury.

Today, modern scientists have explained some of the mystery surrounding acupuncture. First, the points of needle insertion, which seem unrelated to the points of injury, are often

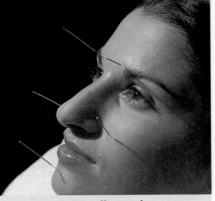

Acupuncture is effective for nausea, headaches, and some kinds of pain.

close to known pathways that conduct pain. Second, there is some evidence that stimulation of these points causes secretion of endorphins, which we know can reduce pain. For example, if patients are first given a drug (naloxone) that blocks secretion of endorphins, acupuncture does not reduce pain. Third, fMRI brain scans showed that acupuncture decreased neural activity in brain areas involved in pain sensations (Ceniceros & Brown, 1998; Hui et al., 2000).

Studies on the effectiveness of acupuncture in reducing pain of headaches and back pain indicate that 50 to 80% of patients reported short-term improvement but after six months, about 50% of the patients reported a return of their painful symptoms (Ceniceros & Brown, 1998).

There is some evidence that acupuncture decreases certain kinds of chronic pain (rotator cuff tendinitis) in athletes (Kleinhenz et al., 1999). The National Institutes of Health concluded that acupuncture is effective for nausea (from chemotherapy or morning sickness) and some kinds of pain (after dental treatment) (Holden, 1997). There is little convincing evidence that acupuncture is effective in treating either heroin, cocaine, or nicotine dependency (Ceniceros & Brown, 1998).

Next we turn to a very practical question: Can a sense be replaced if damaged? Of the five major senses—vision, audition, taste, olfaction, and touch—damage to vision and audition is especially disastrous to the quality of life. For that reason, researchers are trying to develop artificial eyes and ears.

## Artificial Visual System

**Is an artificial eye possible?**

The cause and degree of blindness depend on which part of the visual system is affected. For example, a person would be totally blind if the photoreceptors (rods and cones) in the retina were destroyed (retinitis pigmentosa, an inherited disease) or if the entire retina or optic nerve were damaged. First, we'll look at a microchip that could be implanted into the retina to replace photoreceptors damaged by disease.

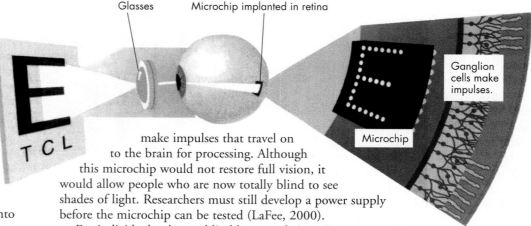

Glasses  Microchip implanted in retina

Ganglion cells make impulses.

Microchip

**1 Artificial photoreceptors.** Some individuals are blind because the front part of the eye is functioning but the photoreceptors (rods and cones) in the retina are damaged by accident or disease. For these individuals, researchers are developing a microchip the size of a match head (black square with white "E") that would be implanted in the back of the retina. This microchip would change light waves into electrical signals that would activate the middle layer of ganglion cells, which are undamaged. The ganglion cells would then make impulses that travel on to the brain for processing. Although this microchip would not restore full vision, it would allow people who are now totally blind to see shades of light. Researchers must still develop a power supply before the microchip can be tested (LaFee, 2000).

For individuals who are blind because their entire eye or optic nerve is damaged, researchers are developing a complete artificial eye that would send impulses directly to the brain.

**2 Artificial eye and brain implant.** At the beginning of this module, we told you about Katie, who was completely blind because both her eyes were damaged. In Katie's case, 36 tiny wires or electrodes were implanted directly into her visual cortex. When these electrodes were stimulated, Katie saw 36 dots of light, which is far less than needed for something as simple as avoiding objects while walking.

In another attempt to restore some vision (figure below) a blind patient was fitted with a miniature camera that sent electrical signals to 100 electrodes that were implanted directly into the visual cortex, located in the occipital lobe. When activated, the electrodes stimulated neurons in the visual cortex and produced 100 tiny spots of light. This patient could see the letter S when 26 of 100 electrodes were stimulated (LaFee, 2000). Although the 100 electrodes in this patient's visual cortex provided more visual information than did Katie's 36, neither patient was able to see the outlines of objects or walk around without using canes.

However, recently, researchers made a significant step forward in developing an artificial visual system.

Camera sent electrical signals directly to brain.

**3 Functional vision.** The major goal in developing an artificial visual system is to provide enough visual information so that a blind person can function, such as reading letters and distinguishing between and avoiding objects while walking around a room. Researchers are getting closer to reaching this goal (Ritter, 2000).

Recently, Jerry, a 62-year-old man who has been blind since the age of 36, volunteered for having electrodes implanted into his brain's visual cortex (right photo). Jerry also wears a pair of glasses that, on one side, hold a tiny camera and, on the other side, an ultrasonic range finder. The range finder analyzes echoes from high-frequency

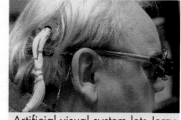

Artificial visual system lets Jerry "see" a 2-inch-high letter.

sounds (beyond our range of hearing) that provide information on location, size, and distance of objects. The tiny camera provides visual information that is like looking through a tunnel opening about 2 inches wide and 8 inches high. Both devices send electrical signals to a small computer that Jerry wears on his hip. In turn, the computer analyzes and relays electrical information to a panel of electrodes that were implanted into and stimulate the visual area in Jerry's occipital lobe (white cords going into skull).

Using this device, Jerry can recognize a 2-inch letter from 5 feet away and avoid large objects as he moves around a room. This is one of the first examples of using a camera and brain implant to provide useful vision (Dobelle, 2000). Although Jerry's artificial visual system is still relatively primitive, it is a good beginning to providing a blind person with useful and functional visual information (LaFee, 2000).

Researchers are also working on developing an artificial cochlea for the inner ear.

# Kinds of Deafness

**What causes deafness?** There are two major kinds of deafness that have different effects, causes, and treatments. The most severe kind of deafness is caused by damage to the inner ear and is called neural deafness. A less severe kind of deafness is caused by problems in the middle ear and is called conduction deafness.

### Conduction Deafness

It is not uncommon to see older people wearing hearing aids, which are often used to treat conduction deafness.

*Conduction deafness* can be caused by wax in the auditory canal, injury to the tympanic membrane, or malfunction of the ossicles. All of these conditions interfere with the transmission of vibrations from the tympanic membrane to the fluid of the cochlea.

Conduction deafness can often be treated with a hearing aid, which replaces the function of the middle ear. Hearing aids pick up sound waves, change them to vibrations, and send them through the skull to the inner ear.

### Neural Deafness

Hellen Keller, who was born deaf and blind, said, "To be deaf is a greater affliction than to be blind." Hellen Keller had neural deafness, which is not helped by hearing aids.

*Neural deafness* can be caused by damage to the auditory receptors (hair cells), which prevents the production of impulses, or by damage to the auditory nerve, which prevents nerve impulses from reaching the brain. Since neither hair cells nor auditory nerve fibers regenerate, neural deafness was generally untreatable until the development of the cochlear implant.

Currently, the only approved treatment for certain kinds of neural deafness is the cochlear implant described below.

## Cochlear Implants

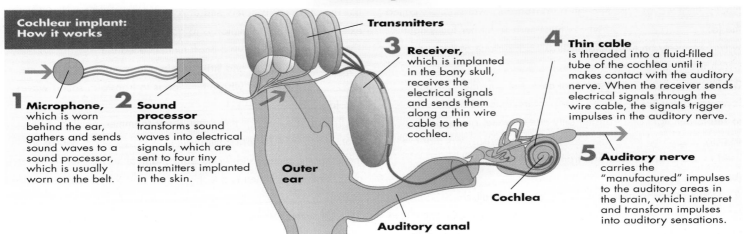

**Cochlear implant: How it works**

**1 Microphone,** which is worn behind the ear, gathers and sends sound waves to a sound processor, which is usually worn on the belt.

**2 Sound processor** transforms sound waves into electrical signals, which are sent to four tiny transmitters implanted in the skin.

**Transmitters**

**3 Receiver,** which is implanted in the bony skull, receives the electrical signals and sends them along a thin wire cable to the cochlea.

**4 Thin cable** is threaded into a fluid-filled tube of the cochlea until it makes contact with the auditory nerve. When the receiver sends electrical signals through the wire cable, the signals trigger impulses in the auditory nerve.

**5 Auditory nerve** carries the "manufactured" impulses to the auditory areas in the brain, which interpret and transform impulses into auditory sensations.

**Outer ear**

**Auditory canal**

**Cochlea**

**What can deaf people hear?** If the auditory nerve is intact, a cochlear implant (figure above) can be used to treat neural deafness caused by damaged hair cells, which affects about 90% of those with hearing impairment (Manning, 2000).

The *cochlear implant* is a miniature electronic device that is surgically implanted into the cochlea. The cochlear implant changes sound waves into electrical signals that are fed into the auditory nerve, which carries them to the brain for processing.

As you proceed step by step through the figure above, notice that the cochlear implant first changes sound waves into electrical signals (1, 2, and 3) and then sends the electrical signals into the auditory nerve (4), which sends impulses to the brain (5).

Worldwide, about 32,000 adults and children with severe neural deafness have received cochlear implants, and the demand for them grows about 25% a year (Manning, 2000). For example, the child in the photo, deaf from birth, is reacting to hearing his first sounds after receiving a cochlear implant.

Using the newest cochlear implants (costs up to $50,000), adults who had learned to speak before they became deaf were able to understand about 80% of sen-

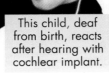

This child, deaf from birth, reacts after hearing with cochlear implant.

tences without any facial cues and from 90 to 100% of sentences when watching the speaker's face and lips (speech reading) (Svirsky et al., 2000).

The results are more complicated for very young children (up to age 2) who did not learn to speak before becoming deaf. Some clinicians believe that with cochlear implants they can easily learn sign language but may have a very difficult time learning to speak (Lane, 1997). However, long-term studies reported that young children (deaf before learning to speak) with cochlear implants were able to understand about 4% of spoken words and sentences after one year, 31% after two years, and 74% after four years (Mondain et al., 1997). But clinicians warn that very young children need intensive speech rehabilitation after cochlear implants (Sharp, 2000). Thus, cochlear implants are most effective in adults, adolescents, and children who spoke before becoming deaf; they may be somewhat less effective but still useful in young children who became deaf before learning to speak (Svirsky et al., 2000).

As we end this module, notice that we primarily discussed how senses transform energy into electrical impulses. Next, in Module 6, we'll focus on how "meaningless" sensations turn into meaningful perceptions.

## A. EYE: VISION

**1.** Waves in about the middle of the electromagnetic spectrum are visible because they can be absorbed by the human eye. These waves make up the _____ and can be absorbed by receptors at the back of the eye.

**2.** Upon entering the eye, light waves pass first through a curved, thin, transparent structure called the (a)_____, whose function is to bend or focus light waves into a narrower beam. Next, light waves pass through an opening in the eye called the (b)_____. Around this opening is a circular, pigmented muscle called the (c)_____; its function is to dilate or constrict, thus increasing or decreasing the amount of entering light. Finally, light waves pass through a transparent, oval structure called the (d)_____, whose function is to further focus light waves precisely on the photosensitive back surface of the eye, which is called the (e)_____.

**3.** The retina has several layers of cells, but only the very back layer contains photoreceptors. The photoreceptors that are used to see in dim light and transmit only black, white, and shades of gray are called (a)_____. Photoreceptors that are used to see in bright light and transmit colors are called (b)_____.

**4.** When rods absorb light waves, a chemical called (a)_____ breaks down and in turn generates tiny electrical forces that trigger (b)_____ in neighboring cells. Similarly, when cones absorb light waves, chemicals called (c)_____ break down and generate tiny electrical forces.

**5.** Nerve impulses generated in the eye travel along fibers that combine to form the (a)_____ nerve. This nerve carries nerve impulses to an area in the back of each occipital lobe called the (b)_____, which transforms impulses into simple visual (c)_____, such as lines, shadows, colors, and textures. If the primary visual cortex were totally damaged, the person would be essentially blind. Simple, meaningless sensations are transformed into complete, meaningful images when nerve impulses reach an area of the brain known as (d)_____.

**6.** We see color because our eyes absorb light waves of different (a)_____, which are transformed by the visual system into our experience of seeing colors. One theory of color applies to how the cones function; this is the (b)_____ theory. A second theory of color applies to how the ganglion and thalamic cells function; this is called the (c)_____ theory of color.

## B. EAR: AUDITION

**7.** The stimuli for hearing, or audition, are sound waves, which have several physical characteristics. The physical characteristic of amplitude or height of sound waves is transformed into the subjective experience of (a)_____, which is measured in units called (b)_____. The frequency of sound waves (cycles per second) is transformed into the subjective experience of (c)_____, which for humans ranges from about 20 to 20,000 cycles per second.

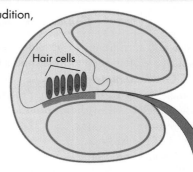

Hair cells

**8.** The outer ear is composed of a funnel-like shape, called the external ear, whose function is to gather (a)_____. These waves travel down a short tunnel called the (b)_____ and strike a thin, taut membrane called the (c)_____, whose function is to transform sound waves into (d)_____.

**9.** The middle ear has three tiny bones (hammer, anvil, and stirrup), which together are called (a)_____. Vibrations in the tympanic membrane produce mechanical movements in the ossicles, the third of which is attached to another thin membrane, called the (b)_____, which is made to vibrate.

**10.** Of several structures in the inner ear, one is a coiled, fluid-filled, tubelike apparatus called the (a)_____, which contains the auditory receptors, called (b)_____. Movement of the fluid in the tube causes movement of the basilar membrane, which in turn causes bending of the hair cells, generating a tiny (c)_____. If this is large enough, it will trigger nerve impulses, which leave the cochlea via the (d)_____ and travel to the brain.

**11.** Nerve impulses are transformed into rather simple, meaningless auditory sensations when they reach the (a)_____, which is located in the temporal lobe. These sensations are transformed into meaningful and complete melodies, songs, words, or sentences by the auditory (b)_____.

**12.** To tell the direction of a sound, the brain analyzes the differences in time and intensity between (a)_____ arriving at the left and right ears. The brain determines degrees of loudness by using the (b)_____ of the arriving impulses. The discrimination of different tones or pitches is explained by the (c)_____ and _____ theories.

## C. VESTIBULAR SYSTEM: BALANCE

**13.** Besides the cochlea, the inner ear contains three arch-shaped, fluid-filled structures called _____. The movement of fluid in these organs provides signals that the brain interprets in terms of the movement and position of the head and body. The vestibular system is also involved in motion sickness, Meniere's disease, and vertigo.

## D. CHEMICAL SENSES

**14.** Particular areas on our tongues respond most to each of the four basic tastes: (a)_____, _____, _____, and _____. The receptors for taste, which are called (b)_____, trigger nerve impulses that travel to the brain, which then transforms them into the sensations of taste.

**15.** Volatile airborne substances are drawn into the upper part of the nose, where they dissolve in a thin film of mucus. Underneath the mucus are layers of receptors for olfaction (smell), which are called (a)_____. These receptors trigger impulses that travel to an area underneath the brain called the (b)_____. This area transforms impulses into hundreds of different odors.

## E. TOUCH

**16.** The sense of touch actually provides information on three different kinds of stimuli: (a)_____, _____, and _____. The various layers of skin contain different kinds of touch receptors that have different speeds of adaptation. Receptors for the sense of touch trigger nerve impulses that travel to an area in the brain's parietal lobe, called the (b)_____. This area transforms impulses into sensations of pressure, temperature, and pain. The more sensitive the area of the body is to touch, the larger is its area on the cortex.

Hair follicle

## F. CULTURAL DIVERSITY: DISGUST VERSUS DELIGHT

**17.** A universal facial expression that indicates rejection of food is called (a)_____. Besides our innate preferences for sweet and salty foods and avoidance of bitter substances, most of our tastes are (b)_____ and particular to our culture. The fact that foods considered fine in one culture may seem disgusting to people in another culture indicates how much psychological factors influence taste.

## G. RESEARCH FOCUS: MIND OVER BODY?

**18.** In order to control for the placebo effect, researchers use an experimental design in which neither the researchers nor subjects know who is receiving what treatment. This is the _____ design, which controls for the expectations of both researchers and subjects.

## H. PAIN

**19.** After an injury, you feel two different kinds of pain sensations: at first, there is sharp, localized pain, which is followed by a duller, more generalized pain. The receptors for pain are (a)_____, which send impulses to two areas of the brain, specifically the (b)_____ and _____. If you rub an injured area or become totally absorbed in another activity, you may experience a reduction of pain, which is explained by the (c)_____. Immediately following a serious injury or great physical stress, the brain produces pain-reducing chemicals called (d)_____.

## I. APPLICATION: ARTIFICIAL SENSES

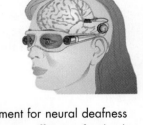

**20.** There are two basic causes of deafness. If the cause is wax in the auditory canal, injury to the tympanic membrane, or malfunction of the ossicles, it is called (a)_____ deafness. If the cause is damage to hair cells in the cochlea or to the auditory nerve, it is called (b)_____ deafness. One treatment for neural deafness is to use a (c)_____, which is more effective if individuals have learned to speak before becoming deaf.

**Answers:** *1. visible spectrum; 2. (a) cornea, (b) pupil, (c) iris, (d) lens, (e) retina; 3. (a) rods, (b) cones; 4. (a) rhodopsin, (b) impulses, (c) opsins; 5. (a) optic, (b) primary visual cortex, (c) sensations, (d) association areas; 6. (a) lengths, (b) trichromatic, (c) opponent-process; 7. (a) loudness, (b) decibels, (c) pitch; 8. (a) sound waves, (b) auditory canal, (c) eardrum or tympanic membrane, (d) vibrations; 9. (a) ossicles, (b) oval window; 10. (a) cochlea, (b) hair cells, (c) electrical force, (d) auditory nerve; 11. (a) primary auditory cortex, (b) association areas; 12. (a) sound waves, (b) rate, (c) frequency, place; 13. vestibular organs; 14. (a) bitter, sour, salty, sweet, (b) taste buds; 15. (a) olfactory cells, (b) primary olfactory cortex; 16. (a) pressure, temperature, pain, (b) somatosensory cortex; 17. (a) disgust, (b) learned; 18. double-blind; 19. (a) free nerve endings, (b) somatosensory area, limbic system, (c) gate control theory, (d) endorphins; 20. (a) conduction, (b) neural, (c) cochlear implant*

# Critical Thinking

## Newspaper Article

### Can Music Raise a Child's IQ?

**Questions**

**1.** The sales clerk supports the Mozart effect by saying that a lot of women are buying the Mozart CD. The sales clerk's statement illustrates what kind of supporting evidence? How good is this kind of evidence?

**2.** What did the original study say about playing Mozart to children or boosting general intelligence?

**3.** In what ways did the press and the public change and distort the researchers' original findings?

The young woman, who was 8 months pregnant, asked the sales clerk for the Mozart CD that was supposed to increase a baby's intelligence. The sales clerk said that the Mozart CD was a big seller and that a lot of women were playing Mozart to their unborn children to take full advantage of the Mozart effect.

The "Mozart effect," as it came to be called, began in 1993 with a short study from researchers at the University of Wisconsin–Oshkosh. The researchers played 10 minutes' worth of Mozart's Sonata for Two Pianos in D Major to college students. Then the students took a test that required them to visualize how objects changed over time, such as how a piece of paper that was folded and cut would look when it was unfolded. Subjects who had listened to Mozart showed a slight but temporary rise in scores on this test compared to subjects who sat through 10 minutes of silence. However, the researchers reported that the Mozart effect was not long lasting and had little effect on overall intelligence.

Within no time, the Mozart effect was making headlines around the country: "Mozart Can Boost Intelligence." Advertising for the Mozart CD claimed that listening to Mozart would stimulate young minds, improve intelligence, and raise IQs. Many parents believed the advertising and bought thousands of "Baby Mozart" videotapes and CDs. One mother said, "I am six months into my pregnancy and almost immediately upon playing the Mozart CD my baby started actively moving. I can really tell he enjoys it even though I can't see him yet." One governor even wanted to pass a law that would give a free Mozart CD to all pregnant women in his state so that their children would have a boost in intelligence.

However, when researchers looked closely at the Mozart effect they reported a different story. A Harvard neuropsychologist analyzed a dozen studies and reported that listening to classical music had no lasting effect on intelligence. Other researchers at Appalachian State University tried repeating the original Mozart study but were unable to find a "Mozart effect" and concluded that listening to classical music did not affect intelligence scores.

However, one nursery had positive proof of one effect. They had been playing classical music to their young children for the past 30 years. Without a doubt, listening to classical music helps kids relax and take their naps. (Adapted from J. Weiss, So-called Mozart effect may be (yawn) just a dream, *San Diego Union-Tribune*, February, 12, 2000, p. E-5)

**4.** In what ways did the new research differ from the original findings?

**5.** Is it possible that listening to melodic music, such as Mozart, could improve performance on a test?

*Use InfoTrac to search for term:* **Mozart effect.**

---

*Suggested answers to Newspaper Article questions*

1. The sales clerk's statement about other mothers buying the Mozart CD is called a testimonial, which has great potential for error and bias and thus is not very reliable evidence.
2. The original study used college students, not children, did not claim that listening to Mozart boosted general intelligence, and said the effect was not long lasting.
3. Greatly distorting the original findings, the press and general public said that the Mozart effect applied to children, that it boosted IQ scores, and that it would help unborn children.
4. A neuropsychologist reviewed all the previous studies and found that listening to classical music had no effect on intelligence. Recent attempts by researchers to repeat or replicate the original study's Mozart effect were not successful; that is, listening to classical music had no effect on test scores.
5. Just as listening to melodic classical music, such as Mozart, relaxed and helped children nap, it may have the same relaxing or calming effect on college students. Thus, feeling more relaxed or less anxious and stressed may improve performance on tests since we know that stress and anxiety may interfere with and decrease test performance.

# Links to Learning

## Web Sites

- WADSWORTH ONLINE STUDY CENTER
  **http://psychology.wadsworth.com**
  Quizzes, learning activities and exercises, a discussion forum, and hot links to Internet sites related to sensation, including:

- SEEING, HEARING, AND SMELLING THE WORLD
  **http://www.hhmi.org/senses**
  How do we see colors and movement? How do we locate a thing by its sound? Why can a smell be a sexual signal? These and many other questions about sensation are answered at this site.

- EDUCATIONAL AUDITORY RESOURCES
  **http://www.neurophys.wisc.edu/www/aud/aud_educ.html**
  Interactive tutorials, demonstrations, and research cover every aspect of the ear and hearing.

- VIRTUAL TOUR OF THE EAR
  **http://ctl.augie.edu/perry/ear/hearmech.htm**
  This comprehensive site contains information about the anatomy of the ear, speech perception, hearing disorders, and audiology.

## Learning Activities

- *POWERSTUDY*™ CD, BY ROD PLOTNIK & TOM DOYLE

  > **Power Study**™
  >
  > **Check out CD: Module 4**
  > A. Studying the Living Brain (book page 70)
  > D. Control Centers: Four Lobes (book page 74)

- *STUDY GUIDE TO ACCOMPANY INTRODUCTION TO PSYCHOLOGY, 6TH EDITION,* **by Matthew Enos**
  What is real? In Module 5 you'll study how we relate to the world through sensation, as well as receive encouragement to get up your nerve and ask your teacher when you don't understand something—this would be a good time to start!

- *WEBTUTOR*
  **http://webtutor.thomsonlearning.com**
  Visit this site for interactive versions of the Study Guide features. Take a quiz, get your score—should you study a topic some more, or can you move on? For instance, you can "see" a giraffe because it emits light waves the human eye can detect: true, or false? Your professor's class syllabus and course calendar are posted—you'll never have to get behind in class again!

- *INFOTRAC Online Library*
  **http://www.infotrac-college.com**

  Use your password and then key in search terms such as those below to find popular and scientific articles on subjects covered in Module 5. Make the library work for you!

  | | |
  |---|---|
  | Human vision | Vestibular system |
  | Ear and hearing | Cochlear implants |

- *PSYCHNOW!*
  CD for Macintosh and Windows includes a study guide, glossary, Web sites, and animations. For Module 5, see:
  - Vision and Hearing
  - Chemical and Somesthetic Senses

## Study Questions

*Use InfoTrac to search for topics mentioned in the main heads below (e.g., chemical senses, disgust, pain).*

*A. **Eye: Vision**—What kinds of problems in the visual system could result in some forms of blindness? (**Suggested answer page 621**)

*B. **Ear: Audition**—What kinds of problems in the auditory system could result in some form of deafness? (**Suggested answer page 622**)

*C. **Vestibular System: Balance**—How do placebos help about 40–60% of people who suffer from motion sickness?

D. **Chemical Senses**—How might a master chef's chemical senses differ from yours? (**Suggested answer page 622**)

E. **Touch**—What would happen if touch receptors did not show adaptation?

F. **Cultural Diversity: Disgust versus Delight**—Why do people often show disgust when offered a new but edible food?

G. **Research Focus: Mind over Body?**—Why are some drugs initially reported to be effective but later proven to be worthless?

H. **Pain**—Why can some individuals stand more pain than others?

I. **Application: Artificial Senses**—Why is it so difficult to build an artificial eye or ear that duplicates the real one?

*These questions are answered in Appendix B.

# Module 6: Perception

A. Perceptual Thresholds      122
* BECOMING AWARE OF A STIMULUS
* WEBER'S LAW
* JUST NOTICEABLE DIFFERENCE (JND)

B. Sensation versus Perception      124
* BASIC DIFFERENCES
* CHANGING SENSATIONS INTO PERCEPTIONS

C. Rules of Organization      126
* STRUCTURALISTS VERSUS GESTALT PSYCHOLOGISTS
* EVIDENCE FOR RULES
* ORGANIZATIONAL RULES

D. Perceptual Constancy      128
* SIZE, SHAPE, BRIGHTNESS, & COLOR CONSTANCY

E. Depth Perception      129
* BINOCULAR DEPTH CUES
* MONOCULAR DEPTH CUES

F. Illusions      132
* STRANGE PERCEPTIONS
* LEARNING FROM ILLUSIONS

Concept Review      134

G. Research Focus:
Subliminal Perception      135
* CAN "UNSENSED MESSAGES" CHANGE BEHAVIOR?

H. Cultural Diversity:
Influence on Perceptions      136
* WHAT DO CULTURAL INFLUENCES DO?

I. ESP: Extrasensory Perception      138
* DEFINITION AND CONTROVERSY
* TRICKERY AND MAGIC
* ESP EXPERIMENT
* STATUS OF ESP

J. Application: Creating Perceptions      140
* CREATING MOVEMENT
* CREATING MOVIES
* CREATING VIRTUAL REALITY
* CREATING FIRST IMPRESSIONS

Summary Test      142

Critical Thinking      144
* TALK TO A CLAIRVOYANT?

Links to Learning      145

### Silent Messages

**How can I be more confident?**

Although it seemed like an ordinary week, Maria and her 7-year-old daughter, Gabrielle, would be involved in three relatively normal events that could change their lives forever.

On Tuesday, Maria's new boss unfairly criticized her work and made her feel insecure and unsure of herself. During her lunch hour, she browsed through a bookstore to find something on building confidence. She was intrigued by an audiotape titled "Improve Self-Esteem." The instructions read, "The listener hears only relaxing music, but the unconscious hears and automatically processes subliminal messages that boost self-esteem. In a few short weeks, the listener is guaranteed to have more confidence and self-esteem. If you're not completely satisfied, return the tape for a full refund." Maria had heard about tapes with subliminal persuasion from a friend who claimed that she used a weight-reduction tape that helped her lose 20 pounds. When Maria asked about the effectiveness of subliminal tapes, the salesperson said that he had a friend who increased his motivation to study by listening to one of these tapes. Maria smiled and said, "Well, it's guaranteed, so what have I got to lose?" She bought the tape, put it in her purse, and as she walked out the door, she was already feeling a little more confident.

Can subliminal tapes change a person's behaviors?

### Nice Dog, Mean Dog

**What's a mean dog?**

On Saturday afternoon, Maria took her daughter, Gabrielle, to play at the local park, which had slides, swings, ropes, and even a small trampoline. As Gabrielle was walking toward the trampoline, she saw a beautiful brown dog sitting by its owner. Gabrielle loved animals, and she ran toward the dog. The dog's owner was deep in conversation and did not notice the cute little girl running toward the beautiful Doberman. As Gabrielle came closer, she thrust out her hands to pet the dog's smooth black nose. The movement of Gabrielle's hands startled the dog, who reflexively snarled and then snapped at the hands coming at its nose. Gabrielle felt the pain as the dog's teeth nipped two of her fingers, which immediately started to bleed. The owner turned to see what had happened and quickly pulled the dog away as Maria came running. Maria took Gabrielle in her arms, soothed her, and then examined the small cuts on her fingers. Gabrielle looked at her bleeding fingers and then at the big, ugly, brown dog that had bit her and said in a tearful voice, "I hate that dog. Bad dog." Seeing her daughter's reaction, Maria began to have doubts about her plans to surprise Gabrielle with a cute little puppy for her birthday.

How does a bad experience create a bad perception?

### White Spot

**Can the doctor be sure?**

On Friday, Maria had to take time from work for her annual physical exam, which included a mammogram. In the past, the doctor had simply said that the results of her mammogram were negative. This time, the doctor brought in her mammogram, which looked like an X ray. He pointed to a small white spot and said in a concerned voice, "I'm afraid that this tiny white dot may be a cancerous tumor." The doctor's words took her breath away. Finally, Maria asked in a terrified whisper, "Are you absolutely sure that spot is cancer?" The doctor paused for a minute, looked again at the mammogram, and said, "I can't be absolutely sure the spot is cancerous until we do a biopsy. All I can say is that there is a good possibility that it is." As Maria scheduled her biopsy, she would never forget seeing that white spot on the mammogram.

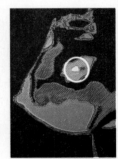

Why should two doctors read each mammogram?

### Perceiving Things

**What are the three questions?**

At first glance, these three events—buying a subliminal tape, being bitten by a dog, and seeing a spot on a mammogram—seem to have nothing in common. In fact, these events raise three basic questions about how we perceive things.

Maria's subliminal tape raises the first question: Are there things that we perceive but are not aware of, and can these things influence our behaviors (Abrams & Greenwald, 2000)?

Maria's mammogram raises the second question: How large or unusual must things be before our senses can detect them? This is a very important question since the answer may have serious health consequences (Swets et al., 2000).

Finally, Gabrielle's painful experience with a dog raises the third question: How much are the things we perceive influenced or biased by our cultural, learning, emotional, and personal experiences (NAMHC, 1996)? These three questions are the key to understanding how we perceive our world.

### What's Coming

We'll discuss what perceptual thresholds are, how sensations differ from perceptions, how sensations are combined to form perceptions, how objects can undergo great changes yet appear the same to us, how our senses are fooled by illusions, how cultural experiences change perceptions, whether there is good evidence for ESP (extrasensory perception), and whether the newest kind of perceiving, called virtual reality, can fool our senses into believing we're in a three-dimensional world.

Let's start with the first and most basic perceptual question: At what point do you become aware of seeing, hearing, smelling, tasting, or feeling some stimulus, object, or event?

## Becoming Aware of a Stimulus

**When do you know something is happening?**

Imagine suddenly becoming deaf or blind, unable to hear what people are saying or to see where you are going. Only then would you realize that your senses provide a continuous stream of information about your world. Your senses tell you that something is out there, and your perceptions tell you what that something is. However, there are some sounds and objects you may not be aware of because the level of stimulation is too low and does not exceed the threshold of a particular sense.

*Threshold* refers to a point above which a stimulus is perceived and below which it is not perceived. The threshold determines when we first become aware of a stimulus.

**IMPROVE SELF-ESTEEM**

Subliminal means that a person has less than a 50% chance of detecting the message.

For example, the reason Maria is not aware of, or does not hear, subliminal messages recorded on tape is that these messages are below her absolute threshold for hearing. To understand how the absolute threshold is determined, imagine that Maria is presented with a series of auditory messages that slowly increase in intensity. Maria is asked to press a button when she first hears a message. You may think that there will be a certain level or absolute value of intensity (loudness) at which Maria will first report hearing a tone. The idea that there is an absolute threshold was initially proposed by Gustav Fechner (1860), an important historical figure in perceptual research. However, as you'll see, Fechner had difficulty identifying the absolute threshold as he defined it.

**1** At first, ***Gustav Fechner*** (*FECK-ner*) defined the absolute threshold as the smallest amount of stimulus energy (such as sound or light) that can be observed or experienced.

According to Fechner's definition, if Maria's hearing could always be measured under exactly the same conditions, her absolute threshold would always remain the same. Although Fechner tried various methods to identify absolute thresholds, he found that an individual's threshold was not absolute and, in fact, differed depending on the subject's alertness and the test situation. Because of this variability in measurement, researchers had to redefine absolute threshold.

**2** The graph below shows how the absolute threshold was redefined.

*Absolute threshold* is the intensity level of a stimulus such that a person will have a 50% chance of detecting it.

According to this updated definition, Maria's absolute threshold is the point on the graph where she has a 50% chance of hearing the message.

Once we have determined Maria's absolute threshold for hearing messages, we can define a subliminal stimulus.

Absolute threshold: 50% chance of hearing message

Subliminal stimulus: 0–49% chance of hearing message

100% chance of hearing message

Increasing intensity

**3** The graph above shows that a subliminal stimulus can occur at any point below the absolute threshold (50% chance of hearing).

A *subliminal stimulus* has an intensity that gives a person less than a 50% chance of detecting the stimulus.

Because subliminal messages can occur in a wide range (0–49%), Maria may or may not report hearing them on the tape. For example, Maria would never report hearing messages of very low intensity (0% level) but may sometimes report hearing messages of higher intensity (49%).

We'll discuss whether subliminal messages can change behaviors or attitudes, such as increasing self-esteem, in the Research Focus (p. 135).

**4** Although the concept of an absolute threshold may seem abstract, it has very real consequences in detecting breast cancer.

Each year, doctors read about 25 million mammograms (X rays of breasts) to look for white spots that usually stand out on a black background; these white spots indicate tumors (photo right). The problem is that

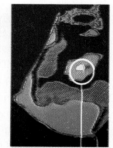

Possible cancerous breast tumor stands out as a white spot.

about 40% of women have so much connective breast tissue, which also appears white, that tiny white tumors go undetected. For this and other reasons, doctors fail to detect about 5 to 17% of tumors on mammograms (Rubin, 1999a). After lung cancer, breast cancer is the second most frequently occurring cancer in American women, with approximately 200,000 new cases each year.

**Improving accuracy.** The task is to increase the accuracy of mammograms. Researchers found that if a mammogram is read independently by two doctors, the accuracy of identifying cancerous tumors was improved by 20% (Healy, 2000). In addition, a new technique, called digital mammograms, is currently being used because it can detect tumors better than X-ray mammograms (Rubin, 1999b). Thus, mammogram testing for breast cancer is a practical example of finding ways to lower the threshold for detecting cancerous tumors and thus save patients' lives.

Besides being involved in subliminal messages and mammogram tests, the problem of determining thresholds also applies to the question of how we know a stimulus has decreased or increased in intensity. We'll discuss this next.

**Why is that music still too loud?**

Suppose people are playing music too loud and you ask them to turn down the volume. Even after they turn it down, it may still seem just as loud as before. The explanation for this phenomenon can be found in the work of another historical figure in perception, E. H. Weber (*VEY-ber*).

Weber worked on the problem of how we judge whether a stimulus, such as loud music, has increased or decreased in intensity. This problem involves measuring the difference in thresholds between two stimuli, such as very loud music and not-quite-so-loud music. To solve this problem, Weber (1834) developed the concept of a just noticeable difference.

A *just noticeable difference*, or *JND*, refers to the smallest increase or decrease in the intensity of a stimulus that a person is able to detect.

*Smallest detectable increase or decrease in intensity is a JND.*

For example, to measure a just noticeable difference in weight, Weber asked people to compare stimuli of varying intensities and indicate when they could detect a difference between them. He discovered that if he presented two stimuli with very low intensities, such as a 2-ounce weight versus a 3-ounce weight, people could easily detect the difference between them. However, if he presented stimuli with high intensities, such as a 40-pound weight versus a 41-pound weight, people could no longer detect the difference. For higher-intensity stimuli, such as heavy weights, a much larger difference in intensity was required for the difference to be noticed (Hellstrom, 2000).

Weber's observations on what it takes to detect just noticeable differences were the basis for what became known as Weber's law.

*Weber's law* states that the increase in intensity of a stimulus needed to produce a just noticeable difference grows in proportion to the intensity of the initial stimulus.

We'll use Weber's law (please read right figure) to explain how if someone is playing the stereo very loud, it must be turned down a great deal, usually more than the person prefers to turn it down, for you to detect a just noticeable decrease in volume.

### Weber's Law Explained

Weber's law explains that, at lower intensities, small changes between two stimuli can be detected as just noticeable differences (JNDs); however, at higher intensities, only larger changes between two stimuli can be detected as JNDs.

**Stimulus: Lighter ⟶ Heavier**

**1 JND.** The same height of each step illustrates your ability to detect "one sensory unit" of a *just noticeable difference* between the loudness of two sounds.

**3 Higher intensities.** The considerable width of this step indicates that, at higher sound intensities, you need a *larger difference* to detect a just noticeable difference between the loudness of two sounds. This statement follows from Weber's law, which says that a larger difference in intensity is required for you to detect a just noticeable difference when judging stimuli of higher intensity.

Besides explaining the problem with loud stereos, Weber's law has many practical applications, such as how to detect a difference in the softness of towels.

**2 Lower intensities.** The small width of this step indicates that, at lower intensities, you need only a *small difference* in order to detect a just noticeable difference between the loudness of two sounds. This statement follows from Weber's law, which says that only a small difference in intensity is required for you to detect a just noticeable difference when judging stimuli of lower intensity.

## Just Noticeable Difference (JND) and Soft Towels

**Which towel is softer?**

Every year, industry and business spend billions of dollars to make sure that consumers can detect just noticeable differences between this year's and last year's cars, shampoos, cereals, and fashions. For example, consumers spend millions of dollars each year on fabric softeners, which are added during washing and are claimed to make clothes feel softer. To test such claims, researchers asked subjects to feel towels washed with and without a fabric softener and rate the softness of the towels on a scale from 1 (hard) to 30 (very soft). Subjects gave an average softness rating of 5 to towels washed repeatedly without softener and an average rat-

ing of 18 to towels washed with softener. Researchers concluded that fabric softeners worked, since subjects could easily detect a just noticeable difference in softness (Ali & Begum, 1994). This is but one practical application of Weber's law and just noticeable difference (JND) in industry.

So far, we've focused on how you become aware of and detect stimuli and distinguish between their intensities. Next, we'll discuss one of the most interesting questions in perception: How do you change meaningless bits of sensations into meaningful and complete perceptions?

*The just noticeable difference (JND) is used in industry.*

## B. Sensation versus Perception

### Basic Differences

*How can I be successful and happy?*

Much of your success in being happy and successful depends on your ability to respond intelligently and adapt appropriately to changes in your environment (NAMHC, 1996). The first step in responding and adapting involves gathering millions of meaningless sensations and changing them into useful perceptions. Because your brain changes sensations into perceptions so quickly, automatically, and with very little awareness, you might assume that what you see (sense) is what you perceive. However, the process of changing sen-

sations into perceptions is influenced by whether you are alert, sleepy, worried, emotional, motivated, or affected by the use of a legal or illegal drug. For example, drinking alcohol causes perceptions in social situations to be less rational and more uninhibited, causing people under its influence to act aggressively, make terrible decisions, create problems, or say really dumb things (Carey & Correia, 1997; Ito et al., 1996; Stritzke et al., 1996). As you are about to discover, sensing and perceiving are as different as night and day.

For example, quickly glance at the black-and-white figure below on the left and then look away and describe what you saw.

### *Sensations*

Initially, the left figure appears to be a bunch of meaningless lines, spaces, and blobs, which, for the sake of simplicity, we'll take the liberty of calling visual sensations. In real life, we rarely if ever experience sensations because, as we'll explain on the next page, they are immediately turned into perceptions.

A *sensation* is our first awareness of some outside stimulus. An outside stimulus activates sensory receptors, which in turn produce electrical signals that are transformed by the brain into meaningless bits of information.

Sensations are MEANINGLESS bits of information.

You can approximate how visual sensations may look by placing half of a ping-pong ball over your eye. As you look through this nearly opaque ping-pong ball, you'll see shadows, textures, and dark shapes but nothing meaningful; these are similar to sensations.

Another example that illustrates the difference between sensations and perceptions is the photo below. Your first impression consists of meaningless shapes, textures, and blotches of color, which we'll again take the liberty of calling visual sensations. However, you can turn these meaningless sensations into a meaningful image—a perception—by using the following clues. This photo is an ultrasound image of a fetus in the womb. The fetus is lying on his back with his rounded tummy on the left and his large head on the right. Above his head is the right arm and hand, and you can even count the five tiny fingers. You can also see that the fetus is sucking on his thumb. Once you know what to look for, you automatically change the random blotches of colors and shapes into the perception of a fetus.

Obviously, it would be impossible to respond, adapt, and survive if you had to rely only on sensations. You can now appreciate the importance of changing sensations into perceptions.

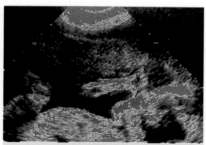

You can turn this sensation into a perception by reading the text (left).

### *Perceptions*

As you look at the right stimulus, your brain is processing many thousands of visual sensations involving lines, curves, textures, shadows, and colors. Then, instantaneously, automatically, and without awareness, your brain combines these thousands of sensations into a perception—an orange tiger's face against a green background.

A *perception* is the experience we have after our brain assembles and combines thousands of individual, meaningless sensations into a meaningful pattern or image. However, our perceptions are rarely exact replicas of the original stimuli. Rather, our perceptions are usually changed, biased, colored, or distorted by our unique set of experiences. Thus, perceptions are our personal interpretations of the real world.

Perceptions are MEANINGFUL patterns, images, or sounds.

If you now look at the black-and-white drawing on the upper left, your brain will automatically combine the formerly meaningless shapes and blobs into a tiger's face. This is an approximate example of how meaningless sensations are automatically combined to form meaningful perceptions.

One important feature of perceptions is that they are rarely exact copies of the real world. To study how experience can bias our perceptions, researchers asked 20 college students who liked rock music and 20 who disliked it to listen to a 10-second sample of rock music. Then, the subjects in each group were asked to adjust the volume of the rock-music sample to match different levels of intensity, ranging from very soft to extremely loud. Researchers reported that subjects who liked rock music consistently set the volume louder than the reference level, while subjects who disliked rock music consistently set the volume lower (Fucci et al., 1993). This study shows how our experiences can bias our perceptions, usually without our awareness.

To show that no two individuals perceive the world in exactly the same way, we'll explain how your personal experiences change, bias, and even distort your perceptions.

## Changing Sensations into Perceptions

**How does a "nice" doggie become a "bad" doggie?**

It is most unlikely that you have ever experienced a "pure" sensation because your brain automatically and instantaneously changes sensations into perceptions. Despite what you may think, perceptions do not exactly mirror events, people, situations, and objects in your environment. Rather, perceptions are interpretations, which means that your perceptions are changed or biased by your personal experiences, memories, emotions, and motivations. For

There are five steps in forming perceptions.

example, at the beginning of this module we told you how 7-year-old Gabrielle's perception of a dog was changed from "nice" to "bad" by her personal experience of being bitten. The next time Gabrielle sees a dog, she won't see just a four-legged creature with ears, nose, and tail; she will see a "bad" four-legged creature. To understand how sensations become perceptions, we have divided the perceptual process into a series of discrete steps that, in real life, are much more complex and interactive.

**1 Stimulus.** Since normally we experience only perceptions, we are not aware of many preceding steps. The first step begins with some stimulus, which is any change of energy in the environment, such as light waves, sound waves, mechanical pressure, or chemicals. The stimulus activates sense receptors in the eyes, ears, skin, nose, or mouth. In Gabrielle's case, the stimuli are light waves reflecting off the body of a large, brown dog.

A stimulus (dog) activates receptors in the senses.

**2 Transduction.** After entering Gabrielle's eyes, light waves are focused on the retina, which contains photoreceptors that are sensitive to light. The light waves are absorbed by photoreceptors, which change physical energy into electrical signals, called transduction. The electrical signals are changed into impulses that travel to the brain. Sense organs, such as the eye, do not produce sensations but simply transform energy into electrical signals.

Senses change stimulus into electrical signals.

**3 Brain: primary areas.** Impulses from sense organs first go to different primary areas of the brain. For example, impulses from the ear go to the temporal lobe, from touch to the parietal lobe, and from the eye to areas in the occipital lobe. When impulses reach primary areas in the occipital lobe, they are first changed into sensations. However, Gabrielle would not report seeing sensations.

Occipital lobe

Primary areas of brain change electrical signals into sensations.

**4 Brain: association areas.** Each sense sends its particular impulses to a different primary area of the brain where impulses are changed into sensations, which are meaningless bits of information, such as shapes, colors, and textures (top right). The "sensation" impulses are then sent to the appropriate association area in the brain. The association areas change meaningless bits into meaningful images, called perceptions, such as a dog (bottom right).

In Gabrielle's case, impulses from her eyes would be changed into visual sensations by the primary visual area and into perceptions by the visual association areas. However, Gabrielle's perception of a dog would be changed, biased, and even distorted by many psychological, emotional, and cultural factors.

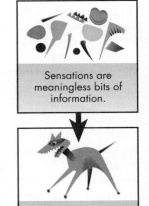

Sensations are meaningless bits of information.

Association areas change sensations into perceptions—dog.

**5 Personalized perceptions.** Each of us has a unique set of personal experiences, emotions, and memories that are automatically added to our perceptions by other areas of the brain. As a result, our perceptions are not a mirror but a changed, biased, or even distorted copy of the real world (Goldstein, 1999). For example, the visual areas of Gabrielle's brain automatically assemble many thousands of sensations into a meaningful pattern, which in this case is a dog. Now, however, Gabrielle doesn't see just an ordinary brown dog because other brain areas add her emotional experience of being bitten. Thus, Gabrielle perceives this brown, four-legged creature to be a "bad dog." For this same reason, two people can look at the same dog and have very different perceptions, such as cute dog, great dog, bad dog, smelly dog, or friendly dog. Thus, your perceptions are personalized interpretations rather than true copies of objects, animals, people, and situations in the real world.

The process of assembling and organizing sensations into perceptions was of great interest to early psychologists, who disagreed on how perceptions were formed. As you'll see next, their debate resulted in a very interesting perceptual controversy.

Perceptions do not mirror reality but rather include our biases, emotions, and memories to reflect reality.

# C. Rules of Organization

## Structuralists versus Gestalt Psychologists

**What was the great debate?**

In the early 1900s, two groups of psychologists engaged in a heated debate over how perceptions are formed. One group, called the structuralists, strongly believed that we added together thousands of sensations to form a perception. Another group, called the Gestalt psychologists, just as strongly believed that sensations were not added but rather combined according to a set of innate rules to form a perception (Murray et al., 2000). One group won the debate and you might guess which one before you read further.

### Structuralists

As you look at the scene in the middle of this page, you perceive a fountain at the bottom with shrubs and palm trees on the sides, all topped by a large dome of glass windows. Is it possible that your brain combined many thousands of individual sensations to produce this complex perception? If you answer yes, you agree with the structuralists.

The *structuralists* believed that you add together hundreds of basic elements to form complex perceptions. They also believed that you can work backward to break down perceptions into smaller and smaller units, or elements.

Structuralists spent hundreds of hours analyzing how perceptions, such as a falling ball, might be broken down into basic units or elements. They believed that once they understood the process of breaking down perceptions, they would know how basic units are recombined to form perceptions. Thus, structuralists believed that you add together basic units to form perceptions, much as you would add a column of numbers to get a total.

For example, structuralists would say that you add together hundreds of basic units, such as colors, bricks, leaves, branches, tiles, pieces of glass, and bits of steel, to form the perception of the scene above. However, the structuralists' explanation of adding bits to form a perception was hotly denied by Gestalt psychologists.

Do you add together basic elements to form perceptions or does your brain have rules for forming perceptions?

### Gestalt Psychologists

The Gestalt psychologists said that perceptions were much too complex to be formed by simply adding sensations together; instead, they believed that perceptions were formed according to a set of rules.

*Gestalt psychologists* believed that our brains followed a set of rules that specified how individual elements were to be organized into a meaningful pattern, or perception.

Unlike the structuralists, the Gestalt psychologists said that perceptions do not result from adding sensations. Rather, perceptions result from our brain's ability to organize sensations according to a set of rules, much as our brain follows a set of rules for organizing words into meaningful sentences.

So how would Gestalt psychologists explain your perception of the scene on the left? They would say that your perception was not formed by simply adding bits of tile, steel, and foliage into a whole image. Rather, your brain automatically used a set of rules to combine these elements to form a unified whole. To emphasize their point, Gestalt psychologists came up with a catchy phrase, "The whole is more than the sum of its parts," to mean that perceptions are not merely combined sensations. The Gestalt psychologists went one step further; they came up with a list of organizational rules.

## Evidence for Rules

**Who won the debate?**

Gestalt psychologists won their debate with the structuralists for two reasons. The first reason comes from our own personal perceptual experiences. For example, as you look again at the beautiful scene above, we must reveal that it is entirely fake. The scene, which looks so realistic and three-dimensional, is actually painted on a flat wall. It seems impossible that we could have such a complex, three-dimensional perceptual experience from simply combining bits and pieces of bricks, branches, leaves, and steel. This fake but truly realistic scene makes the Gestalt motto come to life: "The whole is more than the sum of its parts."

Equally convincing evidence that the whole is greater than the sum of its parts came from a remarkably detailed series of studies in which Gestalt psychologists presented stimuli to subjects and then asked them to describe what they perceived (Rock & Palmer, 1990). On the basis of subjects' reports, Gestalt psychologists discovered that forming perceptions involved more than adding and combining individual elements. They discovered that our brains actually did follow a set of rules for forming perceptions. We'll explain these rules for organizing perceptions next.

## Organizational Rules

**How many rules are there?**

It is very hard to believe that the scene on the previous page (repeated here on the right) was actually painted on a flat wall. One reason you perceive this scene as complex and 3-dimensional is that the painter followed many of the Gestalt rules of organization (Han & Humphreys, 1999).

*Rules of organization,* which were identified by Gestalt psychologists, specify how our brains combine and organize individual pieces or elements into a meaningful perception.

As you look at the scene, your brain automatically organizes many hundreds of visual stimuli, including colors, textures, shadows, bricks, steel, glass, leaves, and branches, according to one or more of the six perceptual rules of organization described below. We'll use a relatively simple figure to illustrate each rule.

### Figure-Ground

One of the most basic rules in organizing perceptions is picking out the object from its background. As you look at the figure on the left, you will automatically see a white object standing out against a red background, which illustrates the figure-ground principle.

The *figure-ground rule* states that, in organizing stimuli, we tend to automatically distinguish between a figure and a ground: The figure, with more detail, stands out against the background, which has less detail.

There is some evidence that our ability to separate figure from ground is an innate response. For example, individuals who were blind from an early age and had their sight restored as adults were able to distinguish between figure and ground with little or no training (Senden, 1960). The figure-ground rule is one of the first rules that our brain uses to organize stimuli into a perception (Peterson & Gibson, 1994). This particular image is interesting because, as you continue to stare at it, the figure and ground will suddenly reverse and you'll see profiles of two faces. However, in the real world, the images and objects we usually perceive are not reversible because they have more distinct shapes (Humphreys & Muller, 2000).

### Similarity

As you look at this figure filled with light and dark blue dots, you see a dark blue numeral 2.

The *similarity rule* states that, in organizing stimuli, we group together elements that appear similar.

The similarity rule causes us to group the dark blue dots together and prevents us from seeing the figure as a random arrangement of light and dark blue dots.

### Closure

Although the lines are incomplete, you can easily perceive this drawing as a cat or dog.

The *closure rule* states that, in organizing stimuli, we tend to fill in any missing parts of a figure and see the figure as complete.

For example, the closure rule explains why you can fill in letters missing on a sign or pieces missing in a jigsaw puzzle.

### Proximity

Notice that although there are exactly eight circles in each horizontal line, you perceive each line as formed by a different number of groups of circles.

The *proximity rule* states that, in organizing stimuli, we group together objects that are physically close to one another.

You automatically group circles that are close together and thus perceive the first line as composed of three groups (Kubovy & Wagemans, 1995).

### Simplicity

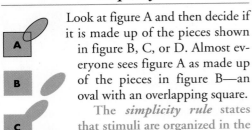

Look at figure A and then decide if it is made up of the pieces shown in figure B, C, or D. Almost everyone sees figure A as made up of the pieces in figure B—an oval with an overlapping square.

The *simplicity rule* states that stimuli are organized in the simplest way possible.

For example, almost no one sees figure A as having been formed from the complicated pieces shown in figure C or figure D. This rule says that we tend to perceive complex figures as divided into several simpler figures (Shimaya, 1997).

### Continuity

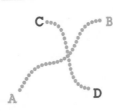

As you scan this figure, keep track of the path that your eyes follow. If you are like most people, your eyes will move from left to right in a continuous line, following the path from A to B or from C to D.

The *continuity rule* states that, in organizing stimuli, we tend to favor smooth or continuous paths when interpreting a series of points or lines.

For example, the rule of continuity predicts that you do not see a line that begins at A and then turns abruptly to C or to D.

**Conclusion.** These figures demonstrate the Gestalt rules of organizing stimuli into perceptions. Young children slowly learn these perceptual rules and are able to use them around the age of 2 (Spelke et al., 1993). As adults we often use these rules to organize thousands of stimuli into perceptions, especially stimuli in print and advertisements.

Next, we turn to another interesting perceptual question: How can objects change yet appear to remain the same?

# D. Perceptual Constancy

## Size, Shape, Brightness, and Color Constancy

**Why don't speeding cars shrink?**

Perception is full of interesting puzzles, such as how cars, people, and pets can constantly change their shapes as they move about yet we perceive them as remaining the same size and shape. For example, a car doesn't grow smaller as it speeds away, even though its shape on your retina grows smaller and smaller. A door doesn't become a trapezoid as you walk through it, even though that's what happens to its shape on your retina. These are examples of how perceptions remain constant, a phenomenon called perceptual constancy.

*Perceptual constancy* refers to our tendency to perceive sizes, shapes, brightness, and colors as remaining the same even though their physical characteristics are constantly changing.

We'll discuss four kinds of perceptual constancy—size, shape, brightness, and color.

### Size Constancy

Imagine a world in which you perceived that every car, person, or animal became smaller as it moved away. Fortunately, we are spared from coping with so much stimulus change by perceptual constancy, one type of which is size constancy.

*Size constancy* refers to our tendency to perceive objects as remaining the same size even when their images on the retina are continually growing or shrinking.

As a car drives away, it projects a smaller and smaller image on your retina (left figure). Although the retinal image grows smaller, you do not perceive the car as shrinking because of size constancy. A similar process happens as a car drives toward you.

As the same car drives closer, notice in the below figure how it projects a larger image on your retina. However, because of size constancy, you do not perceive the car as becoming larger.

Size constancy is something you have learned from experience with moving objects. You have learned that objects do not increase or decrease in size as they move about. For example, an individual who was blind since birth and had his vision restored as an adult looked out a fourth-story window and reported seeing tiny creatures moving on the sidewalk. Because he had not learned size constancy, he did not know the tiny creatures were full-size people (Gregory, 1974).

We also perceive shapes as remaining the same.

### Shape Constancy

Each time you move a book, its image on your retina changes from a rectangle to a trapezoid. But you see the book's shape as remaining the same because of shape constancy.

*Shape constancy* refers to your tendency to perceive an object as retaining its same shape even though when you view it from different angles, its shape is continually changing its image on the retina.

The figure below shows that when you look down at a rectangular book, it projects a rectangular shape on your retina.

However, if you move the book farther away, it projects trapezoidal shapes on your retina (figure below), but you still perceive the book as rectangular because of shape constancy.

Besides size and shape constancy, there is also brightness and color constancy.

### Brightness and Color Constancy

If you look into your dimly lit closet, all the brightly colored clothes will appear dull and grayish. However, because of brightness and color constancy, you still perceive brightness and colors and have no trouble selecting a red shirt.

*Brightness constancy* refers to the tendency to perceive brightness as remaining the same in changing illumination.

*Color constancy* refers to the tendency to perceive colors as remaining stable despite differences in lighting.

For example, if you looked at this young girl's sweater in bright sunlight, it would be a bright yellow.

If you looked at her same yellow sweater in dim light, you would still perceive the color as a shade of yellow, although it is duller. Because of color constancy, colors seem about the same even when lighting conditions change.

However, if the light is very dim, objects will appear mostly gray because you lose color vision in very dim light.

Perceptual constancy is important because it transforms a potentially ever-changing, chaotic world into one with stability and comforting sameness.

Our next perceptual puzzle is how our eyes can see only two-dimensional images but our brain can transform them into a three-dimensional world.

## Binocular (Two Eyes) Depth Cues

**How can you see in three dimensions?**

Normally, movies are shown in only two dimensions, height and width. But if you have ever seen a movie in 3-D (using special glasses to see three dimensions: height, width, and depth), you know the thrill of watching objects or animals come leaping off the screen so realistically that you duck or turn your head. You may not have realized that your eyes automatically give you a free, no-glasses, 3-D view of the world. And the amazing part of seeing in 3-D is that everything projected on the retina is in only two dimensions, height and width, which means that your eye and brain somehow add the third dimension—depth.

Seeing in 3-D means seeing length, width, and DEPTH.

*Depth perception* refers to the ability of your eye and brain to add a third dimension, depth, to all visual perceptions, even though images projected on the retina are in only two dimensions, height and width.

The object on the left has been given a three-dimensional look by making it seem to have depth. It is impossible for most sighted people to imagine a world without depth, since they rely on depth perception to move and locate objects in space. The cues for depth perception are divided into two major classes: binocular and monocular. *Binocular depth cues* depend on the movement of both eyes (*bi* means "two"; *ocular* means "eye").

We'll start with two binocular cues, convergence and retinal disparity.

### Convergence

When you have an eye exam, the doctor usually asks you to follow the end of her finger as she holds it a few feet away and then slowly moves it closer until it touches your nose. This is a test for convergence.

*Convergence* refers to a binocular cue for depth perception based on signals sent from muscles that turn the eyes. To focus on near or approaching objects, these muscles turn the eyes inward, toward the nose. The brain uses the signals sent by these muscles to determine the distance of the object.

The woman in the photo at the right is demonstrating the ultimate in convergence as she looks at

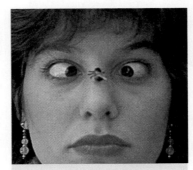

During convergence the eyes turn inward to see objects up close.

the fly on her nose. You can experience convergence by holding a finger in front of your nose and slowly bringing it closer to your nose. Your finger appears to move closer to your nose because the muscles that are turning the eyes inward produce signals corresponding to convergence. The more your eyes turn inward or converge, the nearer the object appears in space. The woman in the photo knows the fly is on her nose because of convergent clues from her turned-in eyes.

The second binocular cue comes from having an eye on each side of your face.

### Retinal Disparity

One reason it's an advantage to have an eye on each side of your face is that each eye has a slightly different view of the world, which provides another binocular cue for depth perception called retinal disparity.

*Retinal disparity* refers to a binocular depth cue that depends on the distance between the eyes. Because of their different positions, each eye receives a slightly different image. The difference between the right and left eyes' images is the retinal disparity. The brain interprets a large retinal disparity to mean a close object and a small retinal disparity to mean a distant object.

The figure at the left shows how retinal disparity occurs: The difference between the image seen by the left eye (1) and the one seen by the right eye (2) results in retinal disparity (3).

1. Left eye sees a slightly different image of the fly.

3. Brain combines the two slightly different images from left and right eyes and gives us a perception of depth.

2. Right eye sees a slightly different image of the fly.

Another example of retinal disparity occurs when viewers wear special glasses to watch a 3-D movie, which has width, height, and depth. Standard 3-D glasses have two different-colored lenses—a red lens and a green lens. The brain receives two slightly different images of a scene: The right eye sees the scene through a red lens, and the left eye sees the same scene through a green lens. The brain automatically combines the slightly different red and green images to give us the feeling of depth—for example, seeing a mad dog jump out at us from the movie screen.

Individuals who have only one eye still have depth perception because there are a number of one-eyed, or monocular, cues for depth perception, which we'll explain next.

**Monocular Depth Cues**

**Could a cyclops land an airplane?**

A mythical creature called the Cyclops had only one eye in the middle of his forehead. Although a Cyclops would lack depth perception cues associated with retinal disparity, he would have depth perception cues associated with having one eye, or being monocular (*mon* means "one").

*I could land an airplane with one eye!*

This means that a Cyclops or an individual with one good eye could land an airplane because of monocular depth cues.

*Monocular depth cues* are produced by signals from a single eye. Monocular cues most commonly arise from the way objects are arranged in the environment.

We'll show you seven of the most common monocular cues for perceiving depth.

Linear perspective makes you see the road as going on forever.

### 1 Linear Perspective

As you look down a long stretch of highway, the parallel lines formed by the sides of the road appear to come together, or converge, at a distant point. This convergence is a monocular cue for distance and is called linear perspective.

*Linear perspective* is a monocular depth cue that results as parallel lines come together, or converge, in the distance.

Relative size makes you see the larger man as closer and smaller men as farther away.

### 2 Relative Size

You expect the runners in the photo above to be the same size. However, since the runner on the right appears larger, you perceive him as closer, while the runner on the left appears smaller and, thus, farther away. The relative size of objects is a monocular cue for distance.

*Relative size* is a monocular cue for depth that results when we expect two objects to be the same size and they are not. In that case, the larger of the two objects will appear closer and the smaller will appear farther away.

Interposition makes you see the fish in front as closer and those in back as farther away.

### 3 Interposition

As you look at the school of fish in the photo above, you can easily perceive which fish are in front and which are in back, even though all the fish are about the same size. You can identify and point out which fish are closest to you and which are farthest away by using the monocular depth cue of overlap, which is called interposition.

*Interposition* is a monocular cue for depth perception that comes into play when objects overlap. The overlapping object appears closer and the object that is overlapped appears farther away.

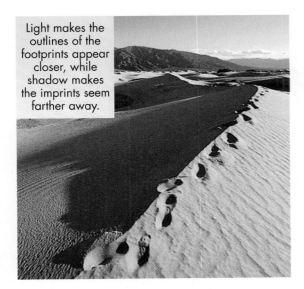

Light makes the outlines of the footprints appear closer, while shadow makes the imprints seem farther away.

## 4 Light and Shadow

Notice how the brightly lit edges of the footprints appear closer, while the shadowy imprint in the sand appears to recede. Also, the sunny side of the sand dune seems closer, while the back side in shadows appears farther away. The monocular depth cues shown here involve the interplay of light and shadows.

*Light and shadow* make up monocular cues for depth perception: Brightly lit objects appear closer, while objects in shadows appear farther away.

Texture gradient makes you see the sharply detailed, cracked mud as being closer.

## 5 Texture Gradient

You can't help but notice how the wide, detailed surface cracks in the mud seem closer, while the less detailed and narrower cracks appear farther away. These sharp changes in surface details are monocular depth cues created by texture gradients.

*Texture gradient* is a monocular depth cue in which areas with sharp, detailed texture are interpreted as being closer and those with less sharpness and poorer detail are perceived as more distant.

## 6 Atmospheric Perspective

One of the depth cues you may have overlooked is created by changes in the atmosphere. For example, both the man sitting on the chair and the edge of the cliff appear much closer than the fog-shrouded hills and landscape in the background. These monocular depth cues are created by changes in the atmosphere.

*Atmospheric perspective* is a monocular depth cue that is created by the presence of dust, smog, clouds, or water vapor. We perceive clearer objects as being nearer, and we perceive hazy or cloudy objects as being farther away.

Atmospheric perspective makes clear objects seem nearer and hazy objects as being farther away.

## 7 Motion Parallax

In this photo, you can easily tell which riders seem closer to you and which appear farther away. That's because you perceive fast-moving or blurry objects (horsemen on the right) as being closer to you and slower-moving or clearer objects (horsemen on the left) as being farther away. These monocular depth cues come from the way you perceive motion.

Motion parallax makes blurry objects appear closer and clear objects as being farther away.

*Motion parallax* is a monocular depth cue based on the speed of moving objects. We perceive objects that appear to be moving at high speed as closer to us than those moving more slowly or appearing stationary.

We have just discussed seven monocular cues involved in perceiving depth and distance accurately. Because they are monocular cues—needing only one eye—it means that people with only one eye have depth perception good enough to land a plane, drive a car, or play various sports such as baseball and tennis. If you wish to try some of these monocular cues, just hold your hand over one eye and see if you can avoid objects as you walk around a room.

We turn next to occasions where our perceptual system is fooled, and we see things that are not there. Welcome to the world of illusions.

## Strange Perceptions

**What is an illusion?**

There are two reasons why much of the time your perceptions of cars, people, food, trees, animals, furniture, and professors are reasonably accurate reflections but, because of emotional, motivational, and cultural influences, never exact copies of reality.

First, we inherit similar sensory systems whose information is processed and interpreted by similar areas of the brain (Franz et al., 2000). However, damage to sensory areas of the brain can result in very distorted perceptions, such as the neglect syndrome (p. 79), in which people do not perceive one side of their body or one side of their environment. The second reason our perceptions are reasonably accurate is that we learn from common experience about the sizes, shapes, and colors of objects. But we've already discussed how perceptions can be biased or distorted by previous emotional and learning experiences, such as perceiving dogs differently after being bitten by one. Now we come to another way that perceptions can be distorted: by changing the actual perceptual cues so you perceive something unlikely, which is called an illusion.

An *illusion* is a perceptual experience in which you perceive an image as being so strangely distorted that, in reality, it cannot and does not exist. An illusion is created by manipulating the perceptual cues so that your brain can no longer correctly interpret space, size, and depth cues.

This impossible figure seems to have two or three prongs!

For example, if you look at the right end of this tuning fork, it appears to have two prongs. But if you look at the left end, it appears to have three prongs. You're looking at a figure that most of us cannot draw because it seems impossible.

An *impossible figure* is a perceptual experience in which a drawing seems to defy basic geometric laws.

One reason the tuning fork appears impossible to figure out and is almost impossible for you to draw has to do with your previous experience with line drawings in books. Because you have seen many three-dimensional objects drawn in books, you tend to perceive the left side of the tuning fork as being three-dimensional (three forks) but you tend to perceive the right side as being two-dimensional (two forks). Later on in the Cultural Diversity feature (p. 137), you'll learn why Africans can easily draw this impossible figure while most college professors cannot (Coren & Ward, 1993).

In this example, we perceive an illusion because the tuning fork is drawn to confuse our previous experiences with two- and three-dimensional objects. One of the oldest illusions that you have often experienced is the moon illusion, which has proven very difficult to explain (L. Kaufman, 2000).

### Moon Illusion

Moon appears to be huge when it's near the horizon.

Moon appears 50% smaller when it's high in the sky.

The moon illusion has intrigued people for centuries because it is so impressive. The left photo shows that when a full moon is near the horizon, it appears (or gives the illusion of being) as much as 50% larger than when it is high in the sky (right photo). Here's the interesting part: You perceive this 50% increase in size even though the size of both moons on your retinas is exactly the same.

For the past 50 years, researchers have proposed different explanations for the moon illusion. The most current explanation is based on the theory that your brain automatically estimates how far away an object is and then interprets its size—the farther away the object is, the larger the object is perceived. For example, when look-

ing at a far-off car, your brain automatically estimates the distance as being far away and thus interprets or perceives the car as being a full-sized car and not a small toy car. Similar to you seeing a far-off car and perceiving it as being large or full-sized (not a toy), researchers found that subjects estimated the horizon moon to be much farther away and thus interpreted its size as being larger. In contrast, subjects estimated the elevated moon to be closer and thus perceived it as being smaller (L. Kaufman, 2000).

Besides naturally occurring illusions, there are others that humans have created. One of the most interesting illusions comes from looking inside the Ames room.

Adult woman appears smaller than young boy.

In the Ames room (left photo) you perceive the boy on the right to be twice as tall as the woman on the left. In fact, the boy is smaller than the woman but appears larger because of the design of the Ames room.

The *Ames room*, named after its designer, Albert Ames, shows that our perception of size can be distorted by changing depth cues.

The reason the boy appears to be twice as tall as the woman is that the room has a peculiar shape and you are looking in from a fixed peephole. To see how the Ames room changes your depth cues, look at the diagram of the Ames room in the drawing below right.

If you view the Ames room from the fixed peephole, the room appears rectangular and matches your previous

experience with rooms, which are usually rectangular. However, as the right figure shows, the Ames room is actually shaped in an odd way: the left corner is twice as far away from the peephole as the right corner. This means that the woman is actually twice as far away from you as the boy. However, the Ames room's odd shape makes you think that you are seeing the two people from the same distance, and this (illusion) makes the farther woman appear to be shorter than the boy (Goldstein, 1999).

The next two illusions either change your perceptual cues or rely too much on your previous perceptual experiences.

## Ponzo Illusion

Black bars are the samel length.

In the figure above, the top black bar appears to be much longer than the bottom black bar. However, if you measure these two bars, you will discover that they are exactly the same size. This is the *Ponzo illusion.* I clearly remember measuring the first time I saw this picture because I couldn't believe the bars were the same size. You perceive the top bar as being farther away, and you have learned from experience that if two objects appear to be the same size but one is farther away, the more distant object must be larger; thus, the top bar appears longer.

## Müller-Lyer Illusion

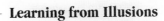

The figures at the left and right illustrate the *Müller-Lyer illusion.* Notice that the left arrow appears noticeably shorter than the right arrow. However, if you measure them, you'll prove that the arrows are of equal length.

One explanation for this illusion is that you are relying on size cues learned from your previous experience with corners of rooms. You have learned that if a corner of a room extends outward, it is closer; this experience distorts your perception so that the left arrow appears to be shorter. In contrast, you have learned that if a corner of a room recedes inward, it is farther away, and this experience makes you perceive the right arrow as longer (Goldstein, 1999). Illusions are fun, but what have we learned?

Left and right arrows are the same length.

## Learning from Illusions

Most of the time, you perceive the world with reasonable accuracy by using a set of proven perceptual cues for size, shape, and depth. However, illusions teach us that when proven perceptual cues are changed or manipulated, our reliable perceptual processes can be deceived, and we see something unreal or an illusion. Illusions also teach us that perception is a very active process, in which we continually rely on and apply previous experiences with objects when we perceive new situations. For example, you'll discover later (p. 140) how the entertainment industry changes the perceptual rule of closure to create movies, whose motion is a brilliant illusion. After the Concept Review, we'll discuss a form of perception that the United States Congress almost outlawed.

# Concept Review

**1.** This figure illustrates the concept of the _____, which is defined as the intensity level of a stimulus such that a person will have a 50% chance of detecting it.

**2.** The smallest increase or decrease in the intensity of a stimulus that a person can detect is called a (a)_____. The increase in intensity of a stimulus needed to produce a just noticeable difference grows in proportion to the intensity of the initial stimulus; this is called (b)_____ law.

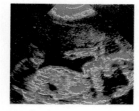

**3.** Our first awareness of sensory information, in the form of meaningless bits of information, is called a (a)_____. When many bits of sensory information have been assembled into a meaningful image, it is called a (b)_____, which can be biased or distorted by our unique set of experiences.

**4.** Early psychologists discovered a set of rules or principles that our brains use to automatically group or arrange stimuli into perceptual experiences. These early researchers, who were called _____ psychologists, disagreed with other early psychologists, who were called structuralists.

**5.** You automatically separate an image into a more dominant, detailed figure and a less detailed background according to the _____ rule.

**6.** You fill in missing parts to form a complete image as a result of the _____ rule.

**7.** You see this image as formed by an oval and an overlying square because of the _____ rule.

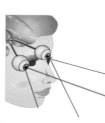

**8.** You divide each line of this figure into separate groups of objects according to the _____ rule.

**9.** In this figure, you see a blue numeral 2 instead of light and dark blue circles because of the _____ rule.

**10.** In this figure, you see a continuous line from A to B, rather than a line from A to C, following the _____ rule.

**11.** Although physical qualities of stimuli may change, you may perceive them as remaining the same because of (a)_____. For example, as a car drives away from you, its image on your retina becomes smaller but you know that the car does not shrink in size because of (b)_____ constancy. When you close a door, its shape on your retina changes from a rectangle to a trapezoid, but you perceive the door as remaining the same because of (c)_____ constancy. If you had a bright red car, it would appear red in bright light and still appear to be red in dimmer light because of (d)_____ constancy.

**12.** Cues for depth perception that depend on both eyes are called (a)_____ cues. Cues for depth perception that depend on a single eye are called (b)_____ cues. The binocular cue that occurs when your eyes move inward to track a fly landing on your nose is called (c)_____. The binocular cue that occurs when each eye receives a slightly different image is called (d)_____.

**13.** Monocular cues for depth perception include: cues from overlapping objects, called (a)_____; cues from two parallel lines converging, called (b)_____; cues from larger and smaller images, called (c)_____; cues from the presence of dust and smog, called (d)_____; and cues from nearer and farther objects moving at different speeds, called (e)_____.

**14.** If perceptual cues are so changed that our brains can no longer interpret them correctly, we perceive a distorted image of reality, called an (a)_____. Such a distorted perception illustrates that perception is an active process and that we rely on previous (b)_____ when perceiving new situations.

# G. Research Focus: Subliminal Perception

## Can "Unsensed Messages" Change Behavior?

***Why did people buy more popcorn?***

Sometimes research questions come from unusual places—in this case, a movie theatre. In the late 1950s, moviegoers were reported to have bought 50% more popcorn and 18% more Coca-Cola when the words "Eat popcorn" and "Drink Coca-Cola" were projected subliminally (1/3,000 of a second) during the regular movie (McConnell et al., 1958). The concern that advertisers might change consumers' buying habits without their knowledge prompted the United States Congress to consider banning any form of subliminal advertising. Congress did not take legislative action

because subliminal advertising proved to be ineffective (Pratkanis, 1992). However, history seems to be repeating itself as advertisers now claim that subliminal tapes can change specific behaviors (Epley et al., 1999).

### Changing Specific Behaviors

At the beginning of this module, we told you about Maria, who, like millions of other Americans, purchased an audiotape because it claimed to contain subliminal persuasion that would effortlessly change her behavior.

A *subliminal message* is a brief auditory or visual message that is presented below the absolute threshold, which means that there is less than a 50% chance that the message will be perceived.

To answer the research question, Can subliminal messages change specific behaviors? researchers conducted a well-designed experiment that used a double-blind procedure.

Labels did not match subliminal messages.

**Method.** For several weeks, subjects listened to two different tapes titled either "Improve Self-Esteem" or "Improve Memory." Then they rated any improvement in these behaviors.

**Double-blind procedure.** Researchers had to control for any possible placebo effects, such as subjects' showing improvement because they believed they were hearing powerful subliminal messages. Therefore, subjects were not told which subliminal messages the tapes contained. For example, some tapes labeled "Improve Memory" contained subliminal messages for improving memory, while others contained subliminal messages for improving self-esteem. Thus, by using a double-blind procedure, subjects never knew if the tapes' subliminal messages actually matched the tapes' labels.

But, subjects believed what the labels said.

**Results.** About 50% of the subjects reported improvements in either self-esteem or memory. However, subjects reported improvements in behavior based on what the ***tapes' labels promised*** rather than on what the subliminal messages were. For example, a subject who listened to a tape labeled "Improve Self-Esteem" reported improvements in self-esteem even though the tape contained subliminal messages for improving memory. These results suggest a self-fulfilling prophecy at work.

*Self-fulfilling prophecies* involve having strong beliefs about changing some behavior and then acting, unknowingly, to change that behavior.

Researchers concluded that subliminal messages in self-help tapes did not affect the behavior they were designed to change. Instead, any changes in behavior resulted from listeners' beliefs that the tapes would be effective (Epley et al., 1999).

Although subliminal messages are ineffective in changing specific behaviors, there is evidence that your emotional state can unknowingly or subliminally influence perception.

### Changing Perceptions

When you're in a happy mood, do you unknowingly or subliminally notice more smiley faces? This is similar to the question that researchers asked: Would subjects who were in a happy mood perceive "happy" words faster than "sad" words, and vice versa (Niedenthal & Setterlund, 1994)?

**Method.** Subjects were put into happy or sad moods by listening to music that made them feel happy or sad.

After being put into a sad or happy mood, subjects sat in front of a screen that projected strings of words, such as joy, habit, hurt, code, comedy, and weep. As each word appeared, subjects rated it as happy (joy, comedy), sad (hurt, weep), or neutral (habit, code). We have simplified the results by reporting only a sample of their data.

**Time in Milliseconds to Recognize Words**

| | |
|---|---|
| 530 | Happy words |
| 592 | Sad words |

**Results.** As shown in the graph above, researchers found that subjects in happy moods perceived happy words significantly faster than subjects in sad moods. Not shown is that subjects in sad moods also perceived sad words faster than subjects in happy moods.

Researchers concluded that being in a particular emotional state can affect our perceptions without our awareness. Researchers suggested that these findings may explain what occurs in real life: When we are in a happy state, we are more likely to notice and perceive the things that bring us joy rather than things that make us sad.

These and other studies indicate that subliminal stimuli can influence emotional and cognitive processes, including preferring shapes, liking individuals, recognizing words, and being classically conditioned to respond to sad or happy faces, all without any conscious awareness (Abrams & Greenwald, 2000; Bunce et al., 1999; Epley et al., 1999). However, there are yet no well-designed studies to show that subliminal advertising can persuade consumers to choose a specific item or brand (Channouf et al., 2000).

Not only can emotional states unknowingly affect perceptions, but next you'll see how cultural values and experiences can also unknowingly change what you perceive.

## What Do Cultural Influences Do?

If you visit ethnic sections of large U.S. cities, such as Chinatown or Little Italy, or visit foreign countries, you become aware of cultural differences and influences. For example, this photo shows two Japanese women in traditional robes and setting, which symbolize the different cultural influences of Japan compared to Western countries.

*Cultural influences* are persuasive pressures that encourage members of a particular society or ethnic group to conform to shared behaviors, values, and beliefs.

What if you were born and raised in Asia?

No one doubts that cultural influences affect the way people eat, dress, talk, and socialize. But you are less likely to notice how cultural influences also affect how you perceive things in your own environment.

For example, cultural anthropologists, who study behaviors in natural settings in other cultures, have reported intriguing examples of how cultural experiences influence perceptual processes. We'll begin with a remarkable finding of why natives were unable to perceive common objects in photos.

### Perception of Photos

Could not recognize a dog in a black/white photo

A cultural anthropologist showed African natives black-and-white photos of a cow and a dog, two animals the natives were very familiar with. But when the natives looked at the black-and-white photos, they seemed very puzzled because they did not see any animals. Their expressions suggested that the anthropologist was lying about the black-and-white photos showing a cow and dog. Next, the anthropologist showed the natives color photos of the same two animals. The natives looked at the color photos and smiled and nodded as they now recognized and pointed to the color photos of the cow and dog (Deregowski, 1980).

Because the people of this tribe had never seen black-and-white photos, they had no experience in recognizing

*The thing without color is nothing.*

*The thing with color is a dog.*

Could recognize a dog in a color photo

animals in this format. But when they were shown color photographs, which showed a world more similar to the one they experienced, they immediately recognized the cow and dog. Most likely, the natives drew on their everyday experiences with objects in full color and could recognize what they saw in the photo from what they saw in the real world. This is an example of how cultural experiences can influence perceptual skills, such as the ability to recognize familiar images presented in different photo formats.

How we describe images is another example of how culture influences what we perceive.

### Perception of Images

Please look at the photo below for a few seconds and then close your eyes and tell what you saw. Dr. Richard Nisbett (2000) and colleagues found that what you see or think about depends, to a large extent, on your culture.

For example, after looking at the underwater scene, Americans tended to begin their descriptions by focusing on the largest fish and making statements like "There was what looked like a trout swimming to the left." Americans are much more likely to zero in on the biggest fish, the brightest object, the fish moving the fastest. "That's where the money is as far as Americans are concerned" (Goode, 2000, p. D4).

Compared to Americans, Japanese subjects were much more likely to begin by setting the scene, saying, for example, "There was a lake or pond" or "The bottom was rocky" or "The water was green." On average, Japanese subjects made 70% more statements about how the background looked than Americans did

Look at the photo briefly and then close your eyes and describe it.

and twice as many statements about the relationships between the fish and the backgrounds. For instance, compared to Americans, Japanese subjects were more likely to say, "The big fish swam past the gray seaweed." This kind of statement indicates that Japanese focus much more on describing relationships between objects and their backgrounds than do Americans.

Generally, Americans tend to analyze each object separately, which is called analytical thinking—seeing a forest and focusing more on separate trees. In comparison, Easterners (Japanese, Chinese, and Koreans) tend to think more about the relationship between objects and backgrounds, which is called holistic thinking—seeing a forest and thinking about how trees combine to make up a forest. Researchers suggest that these differences in thinking and perceiving (analytical versus holistic) may come from differences in social and religious practices, languages, and even geography (Nisbett, 2000).

Cultures also influence how we see cartoons.

## Perception of Motion

For just a moment, look at the cartoon drawing of the dog (below) and notice what its tail is doing. Then look at the female figure (right) and describe what the figure is doing.

Most people in Western cultures immediately perceive what is happening: the dog is wagging its tail and the figure is spinning. Because of our Western cultural experience with cartoon drawings, we have learned to recognize that certain kinds of repeated images (the dog's tail) and certain lines and circles (the dancing figure) indicate movement. We have learned and become so accustomed to seeing these kinds of cartoon drawings indicate motion that the tail and the dancer really do seem to be in motion.

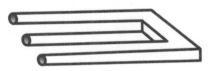

What is the dog's tail doing?

However, people from non-Western cultures, who have no experience with these cartoon drawings, do not perceive the dog's tail or the figure as moving. Non-Westerners see only an unusual dog that has three tails and a strange figure that is surrounded by circles; they do not perceive any indication of movement in these drawings (Friedman & Stevenson, 1980). This is a perfect example of how Western cultural influences shape our perceptions, often without our realizing.

If part of your cultural experience involves seeing 3-dimensional objects in books, you won't be able to draw the next figure.

What is this dancer doing?

## Perception of 3 Dimensions

Can you draw this impossible figure?

This is the same impossible figure that you saw earlier. As you look at it, it changes almost magically back and forth between a two-pronged and a three-pronged tuning fork. The illusion is that the middle fork is unreal because it seems to come out of nowhere.

When people from industrialized nations try to draw this figure from memory, they almost surely fail. What is interesting is that Africans who have no formal education do not see any illusion but perceive only a two-dimensional pattern of flat lines, which they find easy to draw from memory. In contrast, people with formal education, who have spent years looking at three-dimensional representations in books, perceive this object as having three dimensions, a pattern that is almost impossible to draw (Coren & Ward, 1993).

I can draw that strange thing.

## Perception of Beauty

Do you think this woman is attractive?

In the past, when Burmese girls were about 5 years old, they put a brass coil one-third-inch wide around their necks. As they grew older, girls added more brass coils until they had from 19 to 25 wrapped around their necks. The appearance of long necks caused by the brass coils was perceived as being very attractive by Burmese people, who live in southeast Asia. This custom eventually declined as neck coils were no longer considered beautiful, just cruel and uncomfortable. Recently, however, the custom has been revived because now tourists come and pay $12 to see and take photos of women with brass neck coils (Stevens, 1994).

This example illustrates how cultural values influence our perceptions of personal beauty.

## Perceptual Sets

Do you think this muscular body is beautiful?

From our previous cultural experiences with images and objects, we develop certain expectations about how things should be; these expectations are called perceptual sets.

*Perceptual sets* are learned expectations that are based on our personal, social, or cultural experiences. These expectations automatically add information, meaning, or feelings to our perceptions and thus change or bias our perceptions.

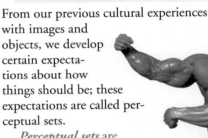

For example, as you look at this bodybuilder, you automatically add personal feelings, such as like/dislike and approve/disapprove, as well as impressions of physical characteristics: height, about 6 feet, and weight, about 225 pounds. Because of your perceptual set for bodybuilders, you expect them to be large, and so you will be surprised to learn that this bodybuilder is only 5 feet 2 inches tall and weighs 182 pounds. One function of perceptual sets is to automatically fill in information or add feelings that can greatly modify our perceptions.

These examples show that we rarely perceive the world exactly as it is. Rather, our perceptions can be changed, biased, or distorted by experiences, such as cultural influences and perceptual sets.

Next, we'll discuss a controversial kind of perception that goes by the initials ESP.

## Definition and Controversy

**What are psychic powers?**

No one doubts your ability to receive information through one or more of your major senses—seeing, hearing, tasting, smelling, and touching—because this ability has been repeatedly demonstrated and reliably measured. In comparison, most research psychologists do not believe that you can receive information outside normal sensory channels, which is called extrasensory perception, because this phenomenon has been neither repeatedly demonstrated nor reliably measured (Bem & Honorton, 1994).

*Extrasensory perception (ESP)* is a group of psychic experiences that involve perceiving or sending information (images) outside normal sensory processes or channels. ESP includes four general abilities—telepathy, precognition, clairvoyance, and psychokinesis. Telepathy is the ability to transfer one's thoughts to another or to read the thoughts of others. Precognition is the ability to foretell events. Clairvoyance is the ability to perceive events or objects that are out of sight. Psychokinesis is the ability to exert mind over matter—for example, by moving objects without touching them. Together, these psychic powers or extrasensory perceptions are called psi phenomena.

The term *psi* refers to the processing of information or transfer of energy by methods that have no known physical or biological mechanisms and that seem to stretch the laws of physics.

**Believing in ESP.** According to Gallup polls, 49% of adult Americans believe in ESP, 36% believe in communication between minds without the use of regular senses, 26% believe in psychics, and

*Psi refers to receiving information by methods that defy the laws of physics.*

25 to 50% claim to have had one or more extrasensory experiences (Gallup & Newport, 1991; Nisbet, 1998). The reason so many Americans but so few research psychologists believe in ESP is that researchers demand hard, scientific evidence rather than evidence from testimonials, which are based on personal beliefs or experiences and have a high potential for error and bias.

**Testimonials as evidence.** In discussing testimonials earlier (p. 30), we pointed out that they seem convincing because they are based on personal experiences. However, there are many examples of very convincing testimonials that, when evaluated with scientifically designed experiments, were found to be unproven. For example, researchers found that 35 to 98% of individuals who gave testimonials about becoming ill or getting well after taking a pill, dietary supplement, or herb had unknowingly taken a placebo, a medically useless treatment (Cowley, 2000b). Because many people are so convinced and so willing to provide testimonials that some treatment works (actually a placebo), scientists must seriously question any evidence arising from testimonials. Questioning testimonial evidence applies especially to ESP, which is outside normal senses, defies physical and biological explanations, and stretches the laws of physics (Kurtz, 1995; Nisbet, 1998).

Another reason researchers demand reliable and repeatable evidence to prove the existence of ESP is that some demonstrations of psi phenomena have involved trickery or questionable methodology. For example, at least one well-known researcher has used trickery and magic to duplicate many of the better-known demonstrations of ESP, such as mentally bending spoons, starting broken watches, moving objects, and reading messages in sealed envelopes. This researcher's name is the Amazing Randi.

## Trickery and Magic

**Could you spot a trick?**

According to James Randi, known as the Amazing Randi (on the left in the photo), and others acquainted with magic, much of what passes for extrasensory perception is actually done through trickery (Steiner, 1989; Ybarra, 1991). For example, to show how easily people may be fooled, Randi sent two young magicians (also in the photo) to a lab that studied psychic phenomena. Instead of admitting they were magicians, the pair claimed to have psychic powers and to perform psychic feats, such as mentally bending keys and making images on film. After 120 hours of testing, the lab's researchers, who had carefully conducted and supervised the ESP demonstrations, concluded that the two did indeed have genuine psychic abilities. The lab's researchers were not expecting trickery, had not taken steps to prevent it, and were thus totally fooled into believing they were witnessing ESP.

The Amazing Randi (left), professional magician, sent two young magicians to fool researchers into believing that they had psychic powers.

Several years ago, a 2-hour television show under the supervision of James Randi offered $100,000 to anyone who could demonstrate psychic powers. Twelve people claimed to have psychic powers, such as identifying through interviews the astrological signs under which people were born, seeing the auras of people standing behind screens, and correctly reading Zener cards (showing five symbols: square, circle, wavy lines, plus sign, and star). Of the 12 people who claimed psychic powers, none scored above chance on any of these tasks (Steiner, 1989). Although people may claim psychic powers, most cannot demonstrate such powers under controlled conditions, which eliminate trickery, magic, and educated guessing.

James Randi has repeatedly shown that people untrained in recognizing trickery cannot distinguish between psychic feats and skillful tricks. To eliminate any trickery, claims of psychic abilities must withstand the scrutiny of scientific investigation. Let's see how a controlled ESP experiment is designed and conducted.

**How do researchers study psychic abilities?**

One of the more common demonstrations of psychic ability is to use Zener cards, which show five symbols—circle, waves, square, plus sign, and star (on right). A researcher holds up the back of one card and asks the subject to guess the symbol on the front. If there were 100 trials, the subject could identify 20 symbols correctly simply by guessing (chance level). However, if a subject identifies 25 symbols correctly, which is above chance level, does that mean the subject has psychic powers? This is a simplified example of a very complicated statistical question: How can we determine whether a person has psychic powers or is just guessing correctly? Therefore, to solve one major problem in psi research—how to eliminate guesswork and trickery—researchers use a state-of-the-art method called the Ganzfeld procedure.

The *Ganzfeld procedure* is a controlled method for eliminating trickery, error, and bias while testing telepathic communication between a sender—the person who sends the message—and a receiver—the person who receives the message.

Symbols used to study ESP

In the Ganzfeld procedure, the receiver is placed in a reclining chair in an acoustically isolated room. Translucent ping-pong ball halves are taped over the eyes, and headphones are placed over the ears. The sender, who is isolated in a separate soundproof room, concentrates for about 30 minutes on a target, which is a randomly selected visual stimulus, such as a photo or art print (right figure). At the end of this period, the receiver is shown four different stimuli and asked which one most closely matches what the receiver was imagining. Because there are four stimuli, the receiver will guess the target correctly 25% of the time. Thus, if the receiver correctly identifies the target more than 25% of the time, it is above chance level and indicates something else is occurring, perhaps extrasensory perception (Bem & Honorton, 1994).

We have described the Ganzfeld procedure in detail to illustrate the precautions and scientific methodology that researchers must use to rule out the potential for trickery, error, and bias. The next question is perhaps the most interesting of all: What have researchers learned from recent Ganzfeld experiments?

Ganzfeld procedure involves mentally sending this picture to a person in another room.

**What is the scientific status of ESP?**

The history of psychic research is filled with controversy. The most recent was when one of psychology's most prestigious academic journals, *Psychological Bulletin*, published for the first time an article on ESP. Because of the controversial nature of ESP, four prominent researchers had carefully studied this article and found no methodological errors. In the article, Daryl Bem and Charles Honorton (1994), two respected researchers, reported that the Ganzfeld procedure (described above) provided evidence for mental telepathy, that is, one person mentally transferred information to a person in another room. However, their study has been criticized because the method may have been biased in favor of the subjects' success (Hyman, 1994). But the biggest question about Bem and Honorton's controversial mental telepathy results was whether their findings could be replicated by other researchers.

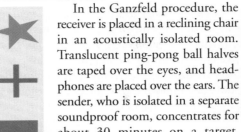

The best-known mental telepathy results (Ganzfeld studies) could not be replicated.

**Importance of replication.** Science has a powerful weapon for evaluating research findings, called *replication*, that simply says, if other scientists cannot repeat the results, the results probably occurred by chance. Recently, 2 researchers evaluated the results of 30 Ganzfeld experiments conducted by 7 independent researchers. These two researchers reported that the original Ganzfeld finding, which supported some kind of mental telepathy, could not be

replicated (Milton & Wiseman, 1999). This failure to replicate the Ganzfeld experiments, which represent the best controlled studies on ESP to date, means that there is currently little or no reliable scientific evidence to support the existence of ESP or psi phenomenon (Milton & Wiseman, 1999). One of the biggest problems with ESP is that those who claim to have it are rarely subjected to scientific study. Such is the case with so-called hotline psychics.

**Television psychics.** Started in the early 1990s was something called psychic hotlines. These hotlines involved over 2,000 self-claimed "psychics" who answered calls from people seeking answers to personal and financial questions. Psychic hotlines became very popular, taking in about $100 million a year. The problem with hotline psychics, who claimed the ability to reveal the future, was that they were often recruited through want ads and paid $15 to $20 an hour to answer questions from perfect strangers (Nisbet, 1998). There is no test or training for becoming a psychic, other than personally claiming to be one. As with other claims for ESP, there is no scientific evidence that self-proclaimed psychics are any more successful at knowing or predicting the future than would occur by chance (Sheaffer, 1997).

Ever wonder what it's like to talk to a clairvoyant or psychic? Check out the conversation on page 144.

Next we'll discuss several other forms of perceptions that fool our senses into believing that fixed things are moving.

**Can we create new perceptions?**

About 20,000 years ago, early humans *(Homo sapiens)* created some of the earliest images by using earth pigments to paint prancing horses on the sides of their caves (right photo) (Fritz, 1995). About 3,000 years ago, Egyptians created some of the most impressive images with their enormous and long-lasting pyramids. Today, computer researchers are using virtual reality techniques to develop new images and perceptions that can put you in the middle of a mind-blowing three-dimensional world. We'll begin our look at how perceptions are created with an old perceptual device that is used in modern billboards.

Painted 20,000 years ago

## Creating Movement

The father of the flashing lights used in today's billboards, movie marquees, and traffic arrows was a distinguished Gestalt psychologist named Max Wertheimer. In the early 1900s, Wertheimer spent a considerable amount of time in a darkened room, where he experimented with flashing first one light and then a second light that was positioned some distance away. He discovered that if the time between flashing one light and then the other was adjusted just right, the two flashes were actually perceived as a moving spot of light rather than as two separate flashes. He called this illusion *phi movement*.

Neon billboards use flashing lights to create the illusion of movement.

*Phi movement* refers to the illusion that lights that are actually stationary seem to be moving. This illusionary movement, which today is called apparent motion, is created by flashing closely positioned stationary lights at regular intervals.

Each time you pass a traffic arrow composed of flashing lights or perceive a moving string of lights used in an advertising sign, you are seeing a practical application of Wertheimer's phi movement. This phi movement was one of the first examples of how ordinary visual stimuli could be adjusted to create an illusion.

Another example of creating wonderful moving illusions with stationary visual stimuli came from the remarkable genius of Thomas Edison, who invented motion pictures in 1893.

## Creating Movies

Movies create the illusion of motion by showing a series of fixed images.

If you attend a track meet and watch a 100-meter race and then, minutes later, watch a videotaped replay of the same race, you perceive motion produced in two very different ways. One kind of motion is real, while the other is an illusion.

*Real motion* refers to your perception of any stimulus or object that actually moves in space.

As you watch a live 100-meter race, you are perceiving real motion. However, when you watch a replay of that same race, you are seeing apparent motion.

*Apparent motion* refers to an illusion that a stimulus or object is moving in space when, in fact, the stimulus or object is stationary. The illusion of apparent motion is created by rapidly showing a series of stationary images, each of which has a slightly different position or posture than the one before.

The principle for creating apparent motion is deceptively simple and can be easily discovered by examining the positions of the runner's body in each frame of the time-lapse photo shown above.

Beginning on the left side of the photo, notice that each frame shows only a slight change in the position of the runner's body. However, if these frames were presented rapidly—for example, at the movie standard of 24 frames per second—you would perceive the illusion of an athlete running down the track.

In a series of ingenious experiments, researchers discovered that several complex mechanisms built into our visual system detect cues that produce the illusion of motion (Ramachandran & Anstis, 1986). One such cue is the closure principle, which means that our brains fill in the motion expected to occur between images that vary only slightly in position and are presented in rapid sequence. Without apparent motion, there would be no movies, television, or flip books.

Currently, researchers have developed a procedure that creates a three-dimensional perceptual experience of walking through a house, dissecting a frog, or doing complicated human surgery. This is the brave new world of virtual reality.

## Creating Virtual Reality

**What is a surgical robot?**

The invention of the movie camera was revolutionary because it created a new perceptual experience: the illusion that still pictures moved. Currently, another perceptual revolution is under way, and it's called virtual reality.

*Virtual reality* refers to a perceptual experience of being inside an object, moving through an environment, or carrying out some action that is created or simulated by computer.

**Remote and robotic surgery.** In a medical application of virtual reality, researchers are developing programs that will allow surgeons to practice their skills with surgical simulators on virtual cadavers as well as perform remote surgery using a surgical robot. For example, the top left photo shows a surgeon inserting and maneuvering a tiny camera and surgical tools into a patient through a pencil-thin incision between the ribs (Cray, 2000). The surgeon operates by maneuvering the robotic arms (bottom left photo), which are steadier and more precise than a human's. Robotic surgery has already been used in heart bypass surgery, without opening the patient's chest (Mackenzie, 2000). Virtual reality technology will soon be used to perform a wide variety of robotic surgical procedures, such as hip replacement and operating on microscopic body tissues or difficult-to-see areas in the brain (Kockro et al., 2000; Riva, 2000).

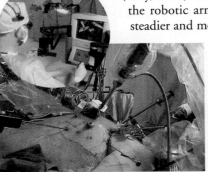

Doctors use virtual reality to guide a robot to perform operations.

**Psychotherapy.** In a psychological application of virtual reality, clients with such fears as spiders, flying, or heights are exposed to the feared stimuli in a three-dimensional environment where everything appears very real.

In this photo, a client is being treated for fear of spiders. She wears a plastic helmet that contains a computer monitor that puts her inside a virtual reality kitchen in which she sees, touches, and kills spiders. For example, Joanne Cartwright suffered a debilitating fear of spiders. "I washed my truck every night before I went to work in case there were webs," she said. "I put all my clothes in plastic bags and taped duct tape around my doors so spiders couldn't get in. I thought I was going to have a mental breakdown. I wasn't living" (Robbins, 2000, p. D6). Dr. Albert Carlin at the University of Washington gave Joanne 12 virtual reality sessions that decreased her fear, or as she said, "I'm amazed because I am doing all this stuff I could never do—camping, hunting and hiking" (Carlin, 2000). Psychotherapists report success in using virtual reality therapy to treat a wide variety of phobias (Hoffman, 2000; Robbins, 2000).

The next topic focuses on how much your first impressions of other people depend on your perceptions of their physical appearances.

Therapists use virtual reality to treat phobias (fear of spiders).

## Creating First Impressions

**Can you name these faces?**

Social psychologists have discovered that facial features have a significant effect on our first impressions and perceptions of people. For example, researchers found that we perceive an attractive person as being more interesting, sociable, intelligent, outgoing, and kind (Lemley, 2000). Similarly, first impressions are also influenced by racial stereotypes, both positive and negative, based on physical features such as skin color and hair style. Hollywood hair stylists know that the kind, amount, color, and style of actors' hair can radically change their appearance and our impressions of them. In fact, they use different hair styles to match different roles. For instance, look at the three photos on the right and try to correctly identify each of these famous personalities (answers at the end).

Besides hair color and style, skin color has a considerable impact on first perceptions and impressions. To illustrate how skin color can greatly change your perceptions of people, look at the two photos on the far right and try to correctly identify these two famous people.

Who . . .

. . am . .

. . . I?

You may have guessed correctly that the two people are the actor Arnold Schwarzenegger of the United States and Queen Elizabeth of England. The editors of *Colors, the Multicultural Magazine* published these interesting computer-colored images to ask their readers: What percentage of your understanding of someone is formed by race? After looking at Queen Elizabeth with the skin color of an Indian and at Arnold Schwarzenegger with the skin color of an African American, you can judge for yourself how much facial coloring influences your impressions and perceptions of others. We'll discuss more on how we perceive people and form impressions in Module 25.

The factors involved in forming first impressions as well as in creating moving lights, movies, and virtual reality illustrate an important, underlying principle of perception: Our perceptions, which may be changed or biased by personal experiences, are interpretations rather than exact copies of reality.

(Correct answers top to bottom: actress Marilyn Monroe, radio personality Howard Stern, actress Julia Roberts)

Who are we?

# Summary Test

## A. PERCEPTUAL THRESHOLDS

**1.** We discussed three basic questions that psychologists ask about perception. Our first question—At what point are we aware of a stimulus?— can be answered by measuring the threshold of a stimulus, which is a point above which a stimulus is perceived and below which it is not. The intensity level at which a person has a 50% chance of perceiving the stimulus is called the _____.

**2.** Our second question—At what point do we know a stimulus intensity has increased or decreased?—can be answered by measuring the smallest increase or decrease in the intensity of a stimulus that a person can detect; this is called a (a) _____. It has been found that the increase in stimulus intensity needed to produce a just noticeable difference increases in proportion to the intensity of the initial stimulus; this is called (b) _____ law.

## B. SENSATION VERSUS PERCEPTION

 **3.** Our third question—How are meaningless sensations combined into meaningful perceptions?—can be answered by analyzing our own perceptual experiences. Our first awareness of some outside stimulus is called a (a) _____. This awareness results when some change in energy activates sensory receptors, which produce signals that, in turn, are transformed by the brain into meaningless sensory experiences. When many individual sensations are assembled into a meaningful experience, image, or pattern, it is called a (b) _____. The latter is not an exact replica of the real world but rather a copy that has been changed, biased, or distorted by our unique set of (c) _____. Our brain transforms sensations into perceptions instantaneously, automatically, and without our awareness.

**4.** The (a) _____ argued that we can explain how perceptions are formed by dividing perceptions into smaller and smaller elements. They believed that we combine basic elements to form a perception. In contrast, the (b) _____ psychologists replied that the formation of perceptions cannot be understood by simply breaking perceptions down into individual components and then studying how we reassemble them. They argued that "the whole is more than the sum of its parts," by which they meant that perceptions are more than a combination of individual elements. The Gestalt psychologists believed that the brain has rules for assembling perceptions, which they called principles of (c) _____.

## C. RULES OF ORGANIZATION

**5.** Many of the rules of perceptual organization involve ways of grouping or arranging stimuli. According to one of these rules, the first thing we do is automatically separate an image into two parts: the more detailed feature of an image becomes the (a) _____ and the less detailed aspects become the (b) _____. According to the (c) _____ rule, stimuli tend to be organized in the most basic, elementary way. According to the (d _____ rule, stimuli that appear the same tend to be grouped together. According to the (e) _____ rule, stimuli that are near one another tend to be grouped together. According to the (f) _____ rule, stimuli that are arranged in a smooth line or curve tend to be perceived as forming a continuous path. According to the (g) _____ rule, we tend to fill in the missing parts of a figure and perceive it as complete.

## D. PERCEPTUAL CONSTANCY

 **6.** Although the size, shape, brightness, and color of objects are constantly changing, we tend to see them as remaining the same, a phenomenon that is called (a) _____. A person walking away does not appear to grow smaller, even though the image on the retina is decreasing in size, because of (b) _____ constancy. Even though the image of a door that is opened and closed changes on the retina from a rectangle to a trapezoid, we see it as retaining its rectangular outline because of (c) _____ constancy. Even though the color and brightness inside a car are altered when we drive from bright into dim light, we tend to see little change because of (d) _____ and _____ constancy.

## E. DEPTH PERCEPTION

**7.** The visual system transforms the two-dimensional image (height and width) of stimuli projected onto the retina into a three-dimensional experience by adding depth. Cues for depth that are dependent on both eyes are called (a) _____; cues  for depth that are dependent on only a single eye are called (b) _____. The binocular cue for depth that arises when muscles turn your eyes inward is called (c) _____. The binocular cue for depth that arises because the two eyes send slightly different images to the brain is called (d) _____.

**8.** There are a number of monocular cues for depth. When an object appears closer because it overlaps another, the cue is called (a) _____. When parallel lines seem to stretch to a point at the horizon and create a sense of distance, the cue is called (b) _____. When two figures are expected to be the same size but one is larger and thus appears closer, the cue is called (c) _____. If dust or smog makes objects appear hazy and thus farther away, the cue is called (d) _____. As texture changes from sharp and detailed to dull and monotonous, it creates the impression of distance; this cue is called (e) _____. The play of light and shadow gives objects a three-dimensional look, a cue that is called (f) _____. As you ride in a car, the impression that near objects are speeding by and far objects are barely moving is called (g) _____.

## F. ILLUSIONS

**9.** For much of the time, our perceptions are relatively accurate reflections of the world (except for anything added by our attentional, motivational, or emotional filters). However, if perceptual cues that we have learned to use and rely on are greatly changed, the result is a distorted image, called an _____. Although illusions are extreme examples, they illustrate that perception is an active, ongoing process in which we use past experiences to interpret current sensory experiences.

## G. RESEARCH FOCUS: SUBLIMINAL PERCEPTION

**10.** Brief auditory or visual messages that are presented below the absolute threshold, which means that their chance of being heard or seen is less than 50%, are called (a) _____. Researchers have concluded that any behavioral changes attributed to subliminal messages actually result because listeners' strong belief that a behavior will change leads them to act, unknowingly, to change that behavior; this is called a (b) _____.

## H. CULTURAL DIVERSITY: INFLUENCE ON PERCEPTIONS

**11.** Experiences that are typical of a society and shared by its members are called _____ influences. These influences have significant effects on the perception of images, constancy, depth, and motion.

**12.** Because of cultural influences, Americans tend to engage more in (a) _____ thinking, while Easterners (Japanese) engage more in (b) _____ thinking.

## I. ESP: EXTRASENSORY PERCEPTION

**13.** The perception and transmission of thoughts or images by other than normal sensory channels are referred to as psychic experiences or (a) _____ phenomena. ESP, which stands for (b) _____, includes four psychic abilities. The ability to transfer one's thoughts to another or read another's thoughts is called (c) _____. The ability to foretell events is called (d) _____. The ability to perceive events or objects that are out of sight is called (e) _____. The ability to move objects without touching them is called (f) _____. Two reasons many researchers are skeptical of psychic abilities is that some supposedly psychic phenomena were actually accomplished with (g) _____ and some previous studies that supported ESP had questionable (h) _____. Although a recent study supported the occurrence of psi phenomena, many researchers are waiting for these positive results to be (i) _____.

## J. APPLICATION: CREATING PERCEPTIONS

**14.** When you view objects moving in space, it is called (a) _____ motion. When you view images of stationary objects that are presented in a rapid sequence, it is called (b) _____ motion, which is the basic principle used to create movies. The illusion that stationary lights are moving can be traced to the work of Max Wertheimer, who called this phenomenon (c) _____ movement. A perceptual experience that is created by allowing the viewer to enter and participate in computer-generated images is called (d) _____; it breaks down some of the traditional boundaries between reality and fantasy.

*Answers:* 1. absolute threshold; 2. (a) just noticeable difference, (b) Weber's; 3. (a) sensation, (b) perception, (c) experiences; 4. (a) structuralists, (b) Gestalt, (c) perceptual organization; 5. (a) figure, (b) ground, (c) simplicity, (d) similarity, (e) proximity, (f) continuity, (g) closure; 6. (a) perceptual constancy, (b) size, (c) shape, (d) color, brightness; 7. (a) binocular, (b) monocular, (c) convergence, (d) retinal disparity; 8. (a) interposition, (b) linear perspective, (c) relative size, (d) atmospheric perspective, (e) texture gradient, (f) light and shadow, (g) motion parallax; 9. illusion; 10. (a) subliminal messages, (b) self-fulfilling prophecy; 11. cultural; 12. (a) analytical, (b) holistic; 13. (a) psi, (b) extrasensory perception, (c) telepathy, (d) precognition, (e) clairvoyance, (f) psychokinesis, (g) trickery, (h) methodology, (i) replicated; 14. (a) real, (b) apparent, (c) phi, (d) virtual reality

# Critical Thinking

## Talk to a Clairvoyant?

*by Larry Lee*
SCRIPPS HOWARD NEWS SERVICE

The 800 number on TV that you scrawl onto the closest piece of scrap paper gets you a 900 number when you call—and an explanation of what they mean by 12 free minutes. It's four minutes a call for your first three calls. A bit peeved that I'd been tricked into thinking I could talk for 12 non-stop, nonpay minutes, I called anyway.

So I was put through to Victoria—a clairvoyant, she explained. It soon became apparent that she was no novice. And that it wasn't going to be easy to shake her.

Victoria: "I'm a clairvoyant. I don't use tarot cards. I use my mind."

LL (Larry Lee, the caller): OK.

Victoria: "I'm going to give you some financial information."

LL: All right.

Victoria: "I don't sense you're financially independent."

LL: You got that right.

Victoria: "There's a lot on your mind. You're all over the place—and I'm going to be, too."

LL: Shoot.

Victoria: "You don't eat or sleep well."

LL: Well, I don't sleep enough, but I eat well.

Victoria: "I see some recent sadness, depression in your life. Am I right?"

LL: No. Nothing like that. I'm happy.

Victoria: "There's a job change—a new position—in your future."

LL: I just changed jobs.

Victoria: "Relationship—you're in one now?"

LL: Strike three. I'm single. But tell me more.

To make a long psychic reading short, Victoria told me I would be meeting someone soon, someone I already know or who already knows me. She was specific down to height, eye and hair color and hair length, and she said the meeting would take place within four to six weeks.

Victoria: "Do you ever think about being self-employed? I see that in the next six to eight months."

LL: Really? (Source: *San Diego Union-Tribune*, December 2, 1997, p. E-3)

### Call the Psychics HOT LINE

### Questions

**1.** Victoria claims to be a clairvoyant. How would you determine that she really was a clairvoyant (able to see and reveal the future)?

**2.** Victoria says, "I don't sense you're financially independent." Is this a good guess or does it show that Victoria is clairvoyant?

**3.** Do these statements about LL (Larry Lee) indicate that Victoria is a clairvoyant?

**4.** What happens when Victoria makes an incorrect "clairvoyant" statement?

**5.** Because Victoria tells LL that he will meet a very specific person, does this indicate she is clairvoyant?

*Use this InfoTrac search term:* **clairvoyance.**

---

### Suggested answers to Newspaper Article questions

1. Anyone may claim to be a clairvoyant (see and reveal the future), but carefully designed tests by prominent scientists have failed to back such claims. For example, psychic forecasts that appear in many tabloids are no more accurate than chance, which means anyone's predictions would be just as accurate.

2. How many people you know are "financially independent," meaning they don't need to work for a living? Because almost everyone is not financially independent, Victoria's statement is a very accurate "guess" and may indicate that she's clever but certainly doesn't indicate that she is clairvoyant.

3. Notice that these statements—"don't eat or sleep well," "had a recent sadness," "in a relationship"—are extremely general and would apply to almost everyone.

4. Victoria's approach is the same used by many hotline psychics: they make a lot of very general statements, some of which will be true for everyone ("don't eat or sleep well," "in a relationship"). However, when Victoria is wrong, she just keeps going, hoping to guess the right thing.

5. Of all the many people LL will meet in the next six months—one of them is sure to match Victoria's description. People mistakenly think that if something a psychic or astrologist says does apply to them, then it's evidence of special powers. The psychic is saying such general things that some will be true for everyone ("don't sleep well," "recent sadness").

# Links to Learning

**Web Sites**

- WADSWORTH ONLINE STUDY CENTER
  http://psychology.wadsworth.com
  Quizzes, learning activities and exercises, a discussion forum, and hot links to Internet sites related to sensation, including:

- SENSATION AND PERCEPTION TUTORIALS
  http://psych.hanover.edu/Krantz/sen_tut.html
  Tutorials include receptive fields, Fourier analysis, and visual information in art.

- SAN FRANCISCO DIGITAL LIBRARY
  http://www.exploratorium.edu/digit/index.html
  Many of these digital exhibits from the San Francisco Exploratorium involve auditory and visual perception and show the tricks our senses sometimes play on us.

- PERCEPTION ONLINE
  http://www.pion.co.uk/perception
  This journal publishes experimental results and theories about human, animal, and machine perception.

---

**Learning Activities**

- *POWERSTUDY™ CD BY ROD PLOTNIK & TOM DOYLE*
  Check out the following sections on your CD and in the book:

| **Power Study™** |
|---|
| **Check out CD: Module 4** |
| B. Studying the Living Brain (book page 70) |
| D. Control Centers: Four Lobes (book page 74) |

- *STUDY GUIDE TO ACCOMPANY INTRODUCTION TO PSYCHOLOGY, 6TH EDITION*, by Matthew Enos
  The theme of Module 6 is that understanding how we perceive things helps us be more realistic about ourselves. Review the three basic questions about perception that psychology can answer. Consider how your personal background affects how you see things.

- *WEBTUTOR*
  http://webtutor.thomsonlearning.com
  WebTUTOR Visit this site for interactive versions of Study Guide features. Take a quiz, get your score—should you study a topic some more, or can you move on? For example, the existence of ESP is strongly supported by scientific evidence: true or false?

- *INFOTRAC Online Library*
  http://www.infotrac-college.com
   Use your password and then key in search terms such as those below to find popular and scientific articles on subjects covered in Module 6. Make the library work for you!

  Color vision          Subliminal messages
  Gestalt psychology    Virtual reality

- *PSYCHNOW!*
  CD for Macintosh and Windows includes a study guide, glossary, Web sites, and animations. For Module 6, see:

  - Perception

---

**Study Questions**

*Use InfoTrac to search for topics mentioned in the main heads below (e.g., depth perception, visual illusions, extrasensory perception).*

*A. **Perceptual Thresholds**—How does Weber's law apply to how old you perceive someone to be? (**Suggested answer page 622**)

*B. **Sensation versus Perception**—What would your life be like if your brain could receive sensations but could not assemble them into perceptions? (**Suggested answer page 622**)

C. **Rules of Organization**—Why can you still read the message on a faded and torn billboard sign?

D. **Perceptual Constancy**—If you suddenly lost all perceptual constancy, what specific problems would you have?

E. **Depth Perception**—Would a one-eyed pitcher have any particular problems playing baseball?

F. **Illusions**—What has to happen to our perceptual processes before we see an illusion?

G. **Research Focus: Subliminal Perception**—Could advertisers make any honest claims for subliminal tapes?

*H. **Cultural Diversity: Influence on Perceptions**—When foreigners visit the United States, what do you think they perceive differently? (**Suggested answer page 622**)

I. **ESP: Extrasensory Perception**—How could you test your friend's claim of having had a psychic experience?

J. **Application: Creating Perceptions**—What do illusions add to our perceptions of the world?

*These questions are answered in Appendix B.

# Module 7: Consciousness, Sleep, & Dreams

**A. Continuum of Consciousness**     **148**
* DIFFERENT STATES
* SEVERAL KINDS

**B. Rhythms of Sleeping & Waking**     **150**
* BIOLOGICAL CLOCKS
* LOCATION OF BIOLOGICAL CLOCKS
* CIRCADIAN PROBLEMS AND TREATMENTS

**C. World of Sleep**     **152**
* STAGES OF SLEEP
* NON-REM SLEEP
* REM SLEEP
* AWAKE AND ALERT
* SEQUENCE OF STAGES

**D. Research Focus: Circadian Preference**     **155**
* ARE YOU A MORNING OR NIGHT PERSON?
* BODY TEMPERATURE
* BEHAVIORAL DIFFERENCES

**E. Questions about Sleep**     **156**
* HOW MUCH SLEEP DO I NEED?
* WHY DO I SLEEP?
* WHAT IF I MISS SLEEP?
* WHAT CAUSES SLEEP?

**Concept Review**     **158**

**F. Cultural Diversity: Incidence of SAD**     **159**
* PROBLEM AND TREATMENT
* OCCURRENCE OF SAD
* CULTURAL DIFFERENCES

**G. World of Dreams**     **160**
* THEORIES OF DREAM INTERPRETATION
* TYPICAL DREAMS

**H. Application: Sleep Problems & Treatments**     **162**
* OCCURRENCE
* INSOMNIA
* NONDRUG TREATMENT
* DRUG TREATMENT
* SLEEP APNEA
* NARCOLEPSY
* SLEEP DISTURBANCES

**Summary Test**     **164**

**Critical Thinking**     **166**
* HOW GOOD IS A SLEEP-DEPRIVED DOCTOR?

**Links to Learning**     **167**

### Living in a Cave

**Would you answer this ad?**

The advertisement read: "We are looking for a hardy subject to live alone in an underground cave for four months. We'll provide board, room, and a monthly allowance. It will be necessary to take daily physiological measurements, measure brain waves, and collect blood samples."

Twenty people answered this ad, but researchers selected Stefania because she seemed to have the inner strength, motivation, and stamina to complete the entire four months. On the chosen day, Stefania crawled 30 feet underground with her favorite books into a 20-by-12-foot Plexiglas module, which had been sealed off from sunlight, radio, television, and other time cues.

During her first month underground, Stefania's concentration seemed to come and go. She appeared depressed, and she snapped at researchers when they asked her to do routine measurements. She had strange dreams—for example, that her computer monitor had turned into a TV that was talking to her. After several months, however, she became more comfortable with her underground isolation. She followed a regular routine of taking her body temperature, heart rate, and blood pressure and typing the results into a computer monitor, her only link with the outside world.

Without clocks, radio, television, or the sun, Stefania found it difficult to keep track of time, which seemed to have slowed down. When told she could leave her underground cave (photo below) because her 130 days were up, she felt certain she had been underground only about 60 days. Her time underground, which was a women's record (the men's record is 210 days), allowed researchers to closely monitor her sleeping and waking behaviors in the absence of all light and time cues (adapted from *Newsweek*, June 5, 1989).

Stefania leaves an undergound cave in which she had lived for 130 days without any time cues (clocks, sunshine, radio, TV).

Asking Stefania to live in a cave for many months was not a publicity stunt but a way to answer questions about how long a day is and how much one sleeps when there are no light cues. To answer these questions, researchers used a case study approach, which meant studying Stefania's behaviors and physiological responses in great detail and depth and doing so in a reasonably naturalistic setting. Researchers discovered that the preferred length of a day is not 24 hours and that during a particular kind of sleep Stefania's eyes moved back and forth as if she were watching a ping-pong game. The significance of these eye movements emphasizes the fact that some major discoveries in science occur quite by accident.

### Chance Discovery

**Why are your eyes moving?**

In the early days of sleep research, psychologists were observing changes in sleeping subjects and noticed that during a certain stage of sleep a person's eyes suddenly began to move rapidly back and forth. This back-and-forth eye movement can actually be seen under the eyelids in the photo below. Even more interesting, when subjects were awakened during rapid

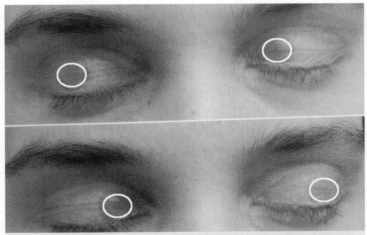

During one kind of sleep (REM—rapid eye movement sleep), the eyes dart back and forth beneath the eye lids.

eye movement they usually reported that they had been dreaming. This chance observation of rapid eye movement and its high association, or correlation, with dreaming gave researchers a reliable method to identify and study dreaming in the laboratory (Dement & Kleitman, 1957).

These examples show how researchers study waking, sleeping, and dreaming in different settings, including underground caves and sleep laboratories, and also how they were helped along by a chance discovery.

### What's Coming

We'll discuss the preferred length of a day, how you know when to sleep and wake up, what happens to your body and brain during sleep, how much sleep you need, why you sleep, and common sleep problems and their treatment. We'll also discuss the one question students always ask: "What do dreams mean?" All these areas fit neatly under a much broader phenomenon that we call awareness, or consciousness, and that is where we'll begin.

# A. Continuum of Consciousness

## Different States

**Are you conscious now?**

One curious and amazing feature of consciousness is that, at some point, the person is actually observing himself or herself (Damasio, 1999). For example, how do you know that at this very moment you are conscious?

*Consciousness* refers to different levels of awareness of one's thoughts and feelings. It may include creating images in one's mind, following one's thought processes, or having unique emotional experiences.

One way you know that you are conscious is that you are aware of your own thoughts and existence (Pinker, 2000). You may think that when awake you are conscious and when asleep you are unconscious, but there is actually a continuum of consciousness.

The *continuum of consciousness* refers to a wide range of experiences, from being acutely aware and alert to being totally unaware and unresponsive.

We'll summarize some of the experiences that make up the continuum of consciousness.

---

### Controlled Processes

A big problem with people driving while using car phones is that we have the ability to focus all of our attention on only one thing, which is an example of controlled processes.

*Controlled processes* are activities that require full awareness, alertness, and concentration to reach some goal. The focused attention required in carrying out controlled processes usually interferes with the execution of other ongoing activities.

Talking on a car phone while driving is a controlled process.

A controlled process, such as conversing on a car phone or taking an exam, represents our most alert state of consciousness. However, talking on a car phone, which is a controlled process, disrupts or distracts us from concentrating on driving. For example, people who use car phones (whether handheld or no hands) have four times the risk of having an accident. Because of increased accidents, several countries (Israel, Spain, Brazil) ban car phones, and in the United States, several states are planning to do so (Wade, 2000).

### Automatic Processes

Eating while reading is an automatic process.

Since this woman's attention is focused primarily on reading an important report, she is almost automatically eating the donut; this is an example of automatic processes.

*Automatic processes* are activities that require little awareness, take minimal attention, and do not interfere with other ongoing activities.

Examples of automatic processes include eating while reading or watching television and driving a car along a familiar route while listening to the radio or thinking of something else.

Although we seem to concentrate less during automatic processes, at some level we are conscious of what is occurring. For instance, as we drive on automatic pilot, we avoid neighboring cars and can usually take quick evasive action during emergencies.

### Daydreaming

Many of us engage in a pleasurable form of consciousness that is called daydreaming.

*Daydreaming* is an activity that requires a low level of awareness, often occurs during automatic processes, and involves fantasizing or dreaming while awake.

We may begin daydreaming in a relatively conscious state and then drift into a state between sleep and wakefulness. Usually we daydream in situations that require little attention or during repetitive or boring activities.

Most daydreams are rather ordinary, such as thinking about getting one's hair cut, planning where to eat, pondering some problem, or fantasizing a date. These kinds of

Men's and women's daydreams are similar.

daydreams serve to remind us of important things in our future. Although you might guess otherwise, men's and women's daydreams are remarkably similar in frequency, vividness, and realism (Klinger, 1987).

### Altered States

Over 3,000 years ago, Egyptians brewed alcohol to reach altered states of consciousness (Samuel, 1996).

*Altered states of consciousness* result from using any number of procedures—such as meditation, psychoactive drugs, hypnosis, or sleep deprivation—to produce an awareness that differs from normal consciousness.

For example, this woman is using a form of meditation to focus all her attention on a single image or thought, free her mind from all external restraints, and enter an altered state of consciousness.

Meditation is an altered state.

In an interesting series of studies on himself, neuropsychologist John Lilly (1972) repeatedly took LSD (when it was legal) and reported that it caused unusual, bizarre, and sometimes frightening altered states of consciousness. For example, he described leaving his body, seeing it from above, and being afraid that he would not be able to return safely to it.

The chief characteristic of altered states, whichever way they are produced, is that we perceive our internal and external environments or worlds in ways very different from normal perception.

---

### Sleep and Dreams

We enter an altered state of consciousness every night when we go to sleep.

*Sleep* consists of five different stages that involve different levels of awareness, consciousness, and responsiveness, as well as different levels of physiological arousal. The deepest state of sleep borders on unconsciousness.

Because of decreased awareness, 8 hours of sleep may seem like one continuous state. However, it is actually composed of different states of body arousal and consciousness (Kohyama et al., 1997). One interesting sleep state involves dreaming.

*Dreaming* is a unique state of consciousness in which we are asleep but experience a variety of astonishing visual, auditory, and tactile images, often connected in strange ways and often in color. People blind from birth have only auditory or tactile dreams.

Newborns sleep about 17 hours a day.

During the initial stage of sleep, we are often aware of stimuli in our environment. However, as we pass into the deepest stage of sleep, we may sleeptalk or sleepwalk and children may experience frightening night terrors but have no awareness or memory of them.

Most of this module focuses on waking, sleeping, and dreaming.

### Unconscious and Implicit Memory

Earlier we told you that one of Sigmund Freud's revolutionary ideas was his concept of the unconscious.

According to Freud's theory, when we are faced with very threatening wishes or desires, especially if they are sexual or aggressive, we automatically defend our self-esteem by placing these psychologically threatening thoughts into a mental place of which we are not aware, called the *unconscious*. We cannot voluntarily recall unconscious thoughts, images, or beliefs.

Freud believed that we can become aware of our unconscious thoughts only through a process of free association or

Freud's idea of the unconscious is different from implicit memory.

dream interpretation, both of which are explained on page 435.

In contrast to Freud's theory of the unconscious, cognitive neuroscientists have developed a different concept, called implicit or nondeclarative memory (Dienes & Perner, 1999).

*Implicit or nondeclarative memory* consists of mental and emotional processes that we are unaware of but that bias and influence our conscious feelings, thoughts, and behaviors.

For example, you cannot describe the complex motor movements your feet make as they walk down stairs because such motor memories are stored in implicit memory, whose content you are unaware of and cannot voluntarily recall. Because of implicit memory, people cannot recall and are not aware of why they greatly fear a tiny spider, fall in love, faint at the sight of blood, or learn (classically conditioned) to make a happy or sad facial expression (Dimberg et al., 2000; Lieberman, 2000b). Implicit memory emphasizes the influence of many different kinds of motor and emotional memories and is very different from Freud's unconscious, which focused on the influence of threatening memories (Kihlstrom, 1993).

### Unconsciousness

Unconsciousness can be caused by a blow to the head, disease, or general anesthesia.

**PS** If you have ever fainted, gotten general anesthesia, or been knocked out from a blow to the head, you have experienced being unconscious or unconsciousness.

*Unconsciousness*, which can result from disease, trauma, a blow to the head, or general medical anesthesia, results in total lack of sensory awareness and complete loss of responsiveness to one's environment.

For example, a boxer's goal is to knock out the opponent with a quick blow to the head that produces a temporary state of unconsciousness. Being in an accident can damage the brain and cause different levels of unconsciousness and result in different kinds of comas. In some comas, a person appears to be asleep and has absolutely no awareness or responsiveness; this is called a vegetative state. People in vegetative comas are unconscious and in some cases brain-dead, which means they will never again regain consciousness.

### Several Kinds

**What is consciousness?**

We know that consciousness is not one thing but a continuum of states, which range from the terrible unconsciousness of being in a vegetative coma to the keen alertness of controlled processes during a final exam. Each of you knows what it feels like to be conscious and aware of your thoughts and surroundings. Neuroscientists are working on the difficult problem of explaining how the interaction of microscopic brain cells gives rise to being aware and producing conscious thoughts, an experience often labeled as the mind (Pinker, 2000).

Historically, Freud viewed the unconscious as an active psychological process that defended a person against threatening sexual and aggressive thoughts, of which the person was unaware. Today, cognitive neuroscientists use the concept of implicit or nondeclarative memory to explain how you can be unaware of perceiving various stimuli, such as words, objects, faces, and emotional events, and even learn simple responses (classical conditioning), but all of these unknowingly influence your thoughts, memories, feelings, and behaviors (Damasio, 1999).

One obvious sign of consciousness is being awake, which is regulated by a clock in the brain, our next topic.

## Biological Clocks

**How long is a day?**

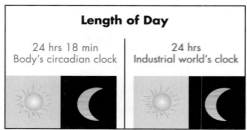

Stefania's sleep-wake cycle in the cave was regulated by a biological clock.

At the beginning of this module, we discussed how sleep researchers studied Stefania, who lived in the modernized cave shown at the left. The reason Stefania was asked to live in a cave is that researchers wanted to study her biological clocks.

*Biological clocks* are internal timing devices that are genetically set to regulate various physiological responses for different periods of time.

For example, biological clocks can be set for hours (secretion of urine), for a single day (rise and fall in internal body temperature), or for many days (sequential secretion of hormones during a woman's 28-day menstrual cycle). Here we are most interested in a biological clock that is set for about a single day and produces what is called a circadian *(sir-KAY-dee-un)* rhythm *(circa* means "about"; *diem* means "day").

A *circadian rhythm* refers to a biological clock that is genetically programmed to regulate physiological responses within a time period of 24–25 hours (about one day).

**Length of day.** The circadian rhythm you are most familiar with is the one that regulates your sleep-wake cycle. In previous studies, when researchers removed all time cues (light, clock, radio, television) from cave dwellers like Stefania, the circadian clock day was believed to lengthen from 24 hours to about 25 hours (Young, 2000). Thus, until very recently, researchers believed our sleep-wake circadian clocks were genetically set for about a 25-hour-long day. However, in a more recent and better controlled study, researchers reported that for both young (mean age 24) and older (mean age 67) adults, the sleep-wake circadian clock is genetically set for a day lasting an average of 24 hours and 18 minutes (Czeisler et al., 1999).

**Resetting the circadian clock.** Because your circadian clock is genetically set for a day that is a little longer (24 hours, 18 minutes)

### Length of Day

| 24 hrs 18 min | 24 hrs |
|---|---|
| Body's circadian clock | Industrial world's clock |

than the industrial world's agreed upon 24-hour-long day, your circadian clock must be reset by an average of 18 minutes each day. The resetting stimulus is the morning sunlight, which resets your circadian clock from a 24-hour-18-minute-long day to the industrial world's 24-hour-long day. If your circadian clock is not properly reset each day, you may have problems sleeping (see next page). Although the circadian clock was long known to exist, only recently have researchers identified its exact location.

## Location of Biological Clocks

**Where is the circadian clock?**

**PS**

It may seem strange to think of having clocks in your brain. Actually you have several clocks, including the biological circadian sleep-wake clock located in a group of cells in the brain's suprachiasmatic *(SUE-pra-kye-as-MAT-ick)* nucleus.

The *suprachiasmatic nucleus* is one of many groups of cells that make up the hypothalamus, which lies in the lower middle of the brain. The suprachiasmatic nucleus is a sophisticated biological clock that regulates a number of circadian rhythms, including the sleep-wake rhythm. Because this nucleus receives direct input from the eyes, the suprachiasmatic cells are highly responsive to changes in light.

SUPRACHIASMATIC NUCLEUS

OPTIC NERVE

The biological circadian clock is located in the suprachiasmatic nucleus.

Since light regulates sleep-wake circadian rhythms, the absence of light should disrupt circadian rhythms in blind people and cause sleep problems. Researchers found that many blind people do report sleep problems (Czeisler et al., 1995). However, a small percentage of completely blind people reported no sleep problems because the pathway for transmitting light from their eyes directly to the suprachiasmatic nucleus was intact (Moore, 1997). The pathway that transmits light from the eyes to the suprachiasmatic nucleus is not involved with seeing things but only with resetting this nucleus (Freedman et al., 1999).

Besides the 24-hour sleep-wake circadian clock, you also have other clocks in your brain, including one that measures shorter periods of time, called an interval timing clock (Gibbon, 1996).

The *interval timing clock,* which can be started and stopped like a stopwatch, gauges the passage of seconds, minutes, or hours and helps creatures time their movements, such as knowing when to start or stop doing some activity. The interval timing clock is located in a part of the brain known as the basal ganglia (see p. 541).

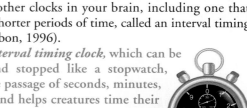

The brain has a built-in interval timing clock.

When the interval clock was destroyed in rats, they could no longer time intervals for obtaining food (Meck, 1996). Researchers believe that, like the rat's brain, the human brain has a similar interval timer that we can start and stop. In humans, the interval timing clock is used to take a one-hour nap and actually wake up about an hour later. The interval timing clock is used by both humans and animals to estimate times for starting and stopping activities.

Walking around with several fine-tuned biological clocks in your head is great for timing activities. However, if your circadian sleep-wake clock is interfered with or not properly reset, you may have various sleep-wake problems.

**What if circadian clock is upset?**

Here's the basic problem: For most of the industrial world, a day is agreed to be exactly 24 hours long, but for your genetically set sleep-wake circadian clock, a day is an average of 24 hours and 18 minutes. This difference means that your sleep-wake clock must be reset about 18 minutes each day. The resetting stimulus is bright morning sunlight, which our eyes send directly to the suprachiasmatic nucleus. This daily resetting of our sleep-wake clocks about 18 minutes usually occurs automatically. However, if our circadian clocks are not properly reset, we may experience decreased cognitive performance, work-related and traffic accidents, jet lag, and various sleep disorders (Young, 2000).

### Accidents

Staying awake when your sleep-wake clock calls for sleep results in decreased performance in cognitive and motor skills (Drummond, 2000).

| Highway Accidents | |
|---|---|
| Saturday 2–3 A.M. | 509 |
| Sunday 1–2 A.M. | 475 |
| Other hours | 203 |

Source: Data from National Highway Traffic Administration, 1992

For example, the graph above shows that highway accidents occur most often in the early morning. Although drug usage plays a significant role in traffic accidents, another factor is that the early morning hours are a time when our bodies and brains are in a sleep rhythm. Similarly, employees who work the graveyard shift (about 1–8 A.M.) also experience the highest number of accidents, reaching their lowest point, or "dead zone," about 5 A.M., when it is very difficult to stay alert (Luna et al., 1997).

The reason shift workers and late-night drivers have more accidents is that their sleep-wake clocks have prepared their bodies for sleep, which means they feel sleepy, are less attentive and alert, and are often in a lousy mood (Boivin et al., 1997).

Circadian rhythms can also create problems for cross-country travelers.

### Jet Lag

If you flew from San Diego to New York City, you would cross three time zones, experience a 3-hour difference in time, and most likely have jet lag the next day.

*Jet lag* refers to a state experienced by travelers in which their biologial circadian clock is out of step, or synchrony, with the external clock time at their new location. Jet lag results in fatigue, disorientation, lack of concentration, and reduced cognitive skills. The general rule for recovering from jet lag is that it takes about one day to reset your circadian clock for each hour of time change.

Jet lag occurs if the body's biological circadian clock does not match the new time zone.

Because genetically set circadian clocks cause problems for travelers and late-night workers, researchers have begun to find ways to more efficiently reset our biological clocks.

### Resetting Clock

Researcher Charles Czeisler (1994) spent ten years trying to convince his colleagues that

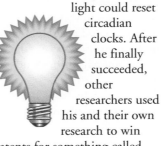

light could reset circadian clocks. After he finally succeeded, other researchers used his and their own research to win patents for something called light therapy (Nowak, 1994).

*Light therapy* is the use of bright artificial light to reset circadian clocks and so combat the insomnia and drowsiness that plague shift workers and jet-lag sufferers. It also helps people with sleeping disorders in which the body fails to stay in time with the external environment.

For example, researchers report that workers who had been exposed to bright light and then shifted to night work showed improvement in alertness, performance, and job satisfaction (Czeisler et al., 1995). Exposure to bright light (about 20 times brighter) at certain times reset the workers' suprachiasmatic nucleus and resulted in a closer match between their internal circadian clocks and their external shifted clock times. Light therapy is still a relatively new treatment but has enormous potential for resetting our sleep-wake clocks (Skerrett, 1994).

Another factor involved in setting the sleep-wake clock is a hormone from a gland that was once thought useless.

### Melatonin

One of the big scientific surprises of the mid-1990s was the discovery of a use for melatonin, which was first identified in the 1950s (Brzezinski, 1997).

*Melatonin* is a hormone that is secreted by the pineal gland, an oval-shaped group of cells that is located in the center of the human brain. Melatonin secretion increases with darkness and decreases with light. The suprachiasmatic nucleus regulates the secretion of melatonin, which plays a role in the regulation of circadian rhythms and in promoting sleep.

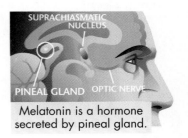

SUPRACHIASMATIC NUCLEUS

PINEAL GLAND    OPTIC NERVE

Melatonin is a hormone secreted by pineal gland.

Although early testimonials and some studies claimed that melatonin reduced jet lag, a recent double-blind study reported that melatonin was no better than a placebo (sugar pill) in reducing jet lag (Spitzer et al., 1999). However, for people with a medical problem of having chronically disrupted circadian clocks, melatonin helped them sleep better and experience less fatigue (Nagtegaal et al., 2000). Researchers identified the brain receptors for melatonin, which should further explain how it works (Reppert, 1997).

Next, we'll examine what happens inside the brain and body during sleep.

## Stages of Sleep

**Does my brain sleep?**

The first thing to know about sleep is that your brain never totally sleeps but is active throughout the night. To track your brain's activity during sleep, researchers would attach dozens of tiny wires or electrodes to your scalp and body and record electrical brain activity as you passed through the stages of sleep.

The *stages of sleep* refer to distinctive changes in the electrical activity of the brain and accompanying physiological responses of the body that occur as you pass through different phases of sleep.

As shown in the graph at the top, brain waves are described in terms of frequency

Going to sleep involves going through several different stages.

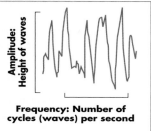

**Amplitude: Height of waves**

**Frequency: Number of cycles (waves) per second**

(speed) and amplitude (height). They are recorded by a complex machine called an EEG, or electroencephalogram. Each stage of sleep can be recognized by its distinctive pattern of EEGs, which we'll explain here.

### ALPHA STAGE

Before actually going into the first stage of sleep, you briefly pass through a relaxed and drowsy state, marked by characteristic alpha waves.

The *alpha stage* is marked by feelings of being relaxed and drowsy, usually with the eyes closed. Alpha waves have low amplitude and high frequency (8–12 cycles per second).

After spending a brief time relaxing in the alpha stage, you enter stage 1 of non-REM sleep.

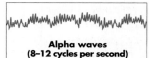

**Alpha waves (8–12 cycles per second)**

## Non-REM Sleep

**What happens during sleep?**

The second thing to know about sleep is that it is divided into two major categories, called non-REM and REM. We'll discuss non-REM first.

*Non-REM sleep* is where you spend approximately 80% of your sleep time. Non-REM is divided into sleep stages 1, 2, 3, and 4; each stage is identified by a particular pattern of brain waves and physiological responses. (REM stands for rapid eye movement.)

You begin in sleep stage 1 and gradually enter stages 2, 3, and 4 (Hirshkowitz et al., 1997).

### Stage 1

This is the lightest stage of sleep.

*Stage 1 sleep* is a transition from wakefulness to sleep and lasts 1–7 minutes. In it, you gradually lose responsiveness to stimuli and experience drifting thoughts and images. Stage 1 is marked by the presence of theta waves, which are lower in amplitude and lower in frequency (3–7 cycles per second) than alpha waves.

**Stage 1**

**Theta waves (4–7 cycles per second)**

Although stage 1 is usually labeled a sleep stage, some individuals who are aroused from it feel as if they have been awake.

Next, you enter stage 2 sleep.

### Stage 2

This is the first stage of what researchers call real sleep.

*Stage 2 sleep* marks the beginning of what we know as sleep, since subjects who are awakened in stage 2 report having been asleep. EEG tracings show high-frequency bursts of brain activity called sleep spindles.

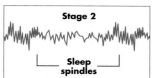

**Stage 2**

**Sleep spindles**

As you pass through stage 2, your muscle tension, heart rate, respiration, and body temperature gradually decrease, and it becomes more difficult for you to be awakened.

### Stages 3 and 4

About 30–45 minutes after drifting off into sleep, you pass through stage 3 and then enter into stage 4 sleep.

*Stage 4 sleep,* which is also called slow wave or delta sleep, is characterized by waves of very high amplitude and very low frequency (less than 4 cycles per second) called delta waves. Stage 4 is often considered the deepest stage of sleep because it is the most difficult from which to be awakened. During stage 4, heart rate, respiration, temperature, and blood flow to the brain are reduced, and there is a marked secretion of GH (growth hormone), which controls levels of metabolism, physical growth, and brain development.

As you pass through stages 3 and 4, your muscle tension, heart rate, respiration, and temperature decrease still further, and it becomes very difficult for you to be awakened.

After spending a few minutes to an hour in stage 4, you will backtrack through stages 3 and 2 and then pass into a new stage, called REM sleep, which is associated with dreaming.

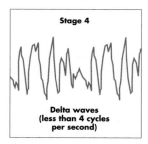

**Stage 4**

**Delta waves (less than 4 cycles per second)**

We have discussed one major category of sleep, non-REM, and now move on to the second major category of sleep, which goes by the initials REM.

*REM sleep* makes up the remaining 20% of your sleep time. It is pronounced "rem" and stands for rapid eye movement sleep because your eyes move rapidly back and forth behind closed lids. REM brain waves have high frequency and low amplitude

> **REM Sleep**
>
> ∿∿∿∿∿∿∿∿
>
> **(14–25 cycles per second)**

and look very similar to beta waves, which occur when you are wide awake and alert. During REM, your body is physiologically very aroused, but all your voluntary muscles are paralyzed. REM sleep is highly associated with dreaming.

You pass into REM sleep about five or six times throughout the night with about 30 to 90 minutes between periods. You remain in each period of REM sleep for 15 to 45 minutes and then pass back into non-REM sleep.

### Characteristics of REM Sleep

When REM sleep was first discovered in the early 1950s, researchers found it difficult to believe their unusual findings: Although you are asleep during REM, your body and brain are in a general state of

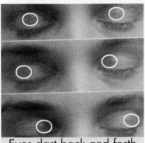

**Eyes dart back and forth as a sign of REM sleep.**

physiological arousal (Aserinsky & Kleitman, 1953). For example, during REM sleep, your heart rate and blood pressure may be twice as high as during non-REM sleep (Dement, 1999). Because of this strange combination of being asleep yet physiologically aroused REM sleep is often called *paradoxical sleep.* (A *paradox* is something with contradictory qualities.)

Another unusual feature of REM sleep is that its brain waves are very similar to those recorded when a person is wide awake and alert. By looking at brain wave recordings alone, researchers cannot tell if a person is in REM sleep or wide awake. Only the additional recording of rapid eye movements indicates the occurrence of REM sleep.

Although many physiological responses are greatly increased, you completely lose the muscle tension (tonus) in your neck and limbs so that you are essentially paralyzed. However, involuntary muscles that regulate heart, lungs, and other body organs continue to function. Researchers think that humans evolved muscle paralysis of their limbs during REM sleep so that they would not act out violent dreams by running, fighting, or jumping about and injuring themselves (Pressman & Orr, 1997). In fact, this actually happens in REM behavior disorder.

In *REM behavior disorder,* which usually occurs in older people, voluntary muscles are not paralyzed, and sleepers can and do act out their dreams. In some cases, REM behavior disorder is caused by known neurological damage, but in other cases, the causes are unknown (Plazzi et al., 1997).

So not only is REM a paradoxical sleep but it also signals dreaming.

### REM—Dreaming and Remembering

**Dreaming.** One of the biggest breakthroughs in dream research was the finding that about 80–90% of the times when subjects are awakened from a REM period, they report having vivid, complex, and relatively long dreams, such as squirrels attacking a pink house (Dement, 1999). In contrast, only about 10% of subjects awakened from non-REM sleep report similar kinds of dreams.

One of the first questions asked was what happens when people are deprived of REM sleep and dreaming by being awakened whenever their physiological signs show they are starting a REM period. Many

**Dreaming usually occurs during REM sleep.**

subjects have been deprived of REM sleep and dreaming without showing any major behavioral or physiological effects (Walsh & Lindblom, 1997). However, suppressing REM sleep does produce a curious phenomenon called REM rebound.

*REM rebound* refers to individuals spending an increased percentage of time in REM sleep if they were deprived of REM sleep on the previous nights.

**Remembering.** The occurrence of REM rebound suggests a need for REM sleep and one such need involves memory. In a recent study, subjects learned to press a button when spotting a moving target on a screen. Subjects tested on the same day as training showed a modest improvement. However, when subjects were tested the next day, those subjects allowed to get the most REM sleep (slept 8 hours) showed the greatest improvement compared to subjects who got the least REM (slept 6 hours). Researchers concluded that REM sleep helps us store or encode information in memory. Researchers advise students to get a good night's sleep so that what they studied the previous day has a chance to be stored in the brain's memory (Stickgold, 2000).

### Awake and Alert

A short time after awakening from sleep, you enter a state of being awake and alert. This state has distinctive brain activity called beta waves (right figure), which are characterized by high frequency and low amplitude and are very similar to those waves observed during REM sleep.

> **Awake and Alert**
>
> ∿∿∿∿∿∿∿∿
>
> **Beta waves**
> **(14–25 cycles per second)**

How alert you feel in the morning partly depends on whether you are a morning or night person, which we'll discuss in the upcoming Research Focus.

Although you now have an overview of the different sleep stages, you may be surprised to discover that how you go through the different stages is somewhat like riding a roller coaster.

### Sequence of Stages

**Why is sleep like a roller-coaster ride?**

When you go to sleep at night, you may think that you simply sleep for 8 hours, perhaps toss and turn a little, and even do some dreaming. But sleep is not one unbroken state but rather a series of recurring stages, similar to the ups and downs of a roller-coaster ride. We'll describe a typical night's pattern for George, a college sophomore, who goes to bed about 11 P.M. and gets up about 7 A.M. As we take you through the figure below, notice that non-REM sleep is indicated by the wide blue

A night's sleep is like a roller-coaster ride through different stages of sleep.

line and REM sleep is indicated by red inserts. The numbers 1 to 4 refer to sleep stages 1, 2, 3, and 4 of non-REM sleep, which we discussed earlier.

Researchers have studied and plotted changes in brain waves, physiological arousal, and dreaming as subjects progressed through the stages of sleep (Dement, 1999). Here's what George will experience on a typical roller-coaster-like ride through the different stages of a night's sleep.

Here's what happens during a normal night's sleep.

| 11:00 | 12:00 | 1:00 | 2:00 | 3:00 | 4:00 | 5:00 | 6:00 |

REM    REM    REM    REM    REM

1   2   3   4 ... 2 3 4 ... 2 3 ... 2 3 ... 2 3 ... 2 ... 2 ... 2   1

### STAGE 1

As George becomes drowsy, he will enter non-REM stage 1, which is the transition between being awake and asleep.

As sleep progresses, he will continue to the next stage, non-REM stage 2, which is the first stage of real sleep. During stage 2, he may experience short, fragmented thoughts, so that if he is awakened, he may think he was dreaming.

He will continue through non-REM stage 3 and finally reach non-REM stage 4. When George enters non-REM stage 4, which is slow wave, or delta, sleep, he will be very difficult to waken. After staying in stage 4 for some minutes to an hour, he will backtrack to stage 3 and then 2.

### STAGE 2

After George reaches non-REM stage 2, he does not awaken but rather enters REM sleep. He will remain in REM for 15–45 minutes and, if awakened, will likely report dreaming. When in REM, his body is in a high state of physiological arousal, but his voluntary limb muscles are essentially paralyzed. If George experiences nightmares during REM, he will not act them out or injure himself because he cannot move.

After the REM period, he goes back down through non-REM stages 2, 3, and 4.

### STAGE 4

It is during stage 4 that George may sleepwalk, sleeptalk, or perform other activities, such as partially awakening to turn off the alarm, pull up the covers, or get up and go to the bathroom. However, George will remember nothing of what happens in non-REM stage 4, such as sleeptalking with his roommate or walking to the kitchen and getting a snack. He will remain in stage 4 for a period of time before again backtracking to non-REM stages 3 and 2, and then to his second REM period of the night.

Children sometimes wake up terrified during non-REM stage 4. These experiences are called night terrors, but the children will have no memory of them the next day.

### REM

Like George, we may go in and out of REM sleep five or six times, with REM periods becoming longer toward morning. If George wants to remember his dreams, he should try when he first wakes up since his last REM period may have occurred only minutes before.

Recent findings indicate that getting as many REM periods as possible is important in helping the brain store material learned the previous day (Stickgold, 2000).

If George has a difficult time awakening from sleep, it may be because he was in stage 4, the hardest stage to awaken from.

Like George, we all go through the sleep stages in about the same sequence. However, there's a reason that some of us hate mornings more than others.

## Are You a Morning or Night Person?

**Are you an early bird or a night owl?**

Some students really hate morning classes, while others don't mind them. One reason for this difference is that some students are early birds and some are night owls. Researchers obtained a more accurate definition of these terms by developing and using a questionnaire.

A *questionnaire* is a method for obtaining information by asking subjects to read a list of written questions and check off or rate their preference for specific answers.

The morning-evening questionnaire asked subjects to rate their preferred times for going to bed, getting up, and engaging in physical and mental activities, as well as their feelings of alertness in the morning and evening. The graph here shows the results from this questionnaire.

**Score on Morning/Evening Questionnaire**

Evening person  45

Morning person  74

*Morning persons* (score above 74) prefer to get up earlier, go to bed earlier, and engage in morning activities. *Evening persons* (score below 45) prefer to get up later, go to bed later, and engage in afternoon-evening activities. Those individuals who scored between 45 and 74 did not express a strong morning or evening preference (Guthrie et al., 1995).

Individuals with strong preferences did not consciously decide to become morning or evening persons but rather are following a built-in genetic preference regulated by circadian rhythms. One reason a person may have a strong morning or evening preference is related to changes in body temperature, which rise and fall throughout the day.

Morning person

Night person

## Body Temperature

Our body has several circadian rhythms, one of them being the sleep-wake cycle, which is regulated by the suprachiasmatic nucleus in the hypothalamus. Another circadian rhythm, also thought to be regulated by the suprachiasmatic nucleus, involves body temperature, which falls as we go to sleep and rises after we get up (Boivin et al., 1997). The graph on the right shows changes in body temperature for a 24-hour period, beginning at 6 A.M.

**Getting up.** Body temperature is low in the morning and rises throughout the day, when we are most active. The temperature of a morning person rises much more quickly (so the person gets up earlier) than that of an evening person (so the person gets up later). In fact, body temperature in a morning person may rise 1–3 hours earlier than in an evening person (Tankova et al., 1994).

**Going to bed.** The body temperature of a morning person peaks earlier in the evening (so the person goes to bed earlier) than the body temperature of an evening person, which peaks 1–3 hours later (so the person goes to bed later). Researchers hypothesize that the suprachiasmatic nucleus regulates the rise and fall of body temperature, which in turn determines whether we are morning or evening people.

In addition, there are some interesting behavioral differences between morning and evening people.

**As temperature rises, you wake up; as temperature falls, you go to sleep.**

94 96 98 100 2 4 6

Body temperature (°F)

Morning person's temperature rises more quickly.

Morning person's temperature peaks earlier.

98.6°

Evening person's temperature rises 1 to 3 hours later.

Evening person's temperature peaks 1 to 3 hours later.

6 A.M.    12 noon    6 P.M.    12 midnight

## Behavioral Differences

Researchers found that students who were morning people took more classes in the morning (if they could get the classes), performed better in morning classes, and studied more in the morning than did students who were night people (Guthrie et al., 1995). This means that to get better grades, you should adjust your class schedule to best fit your particular circadian rhythm.

Researchers found that people who worked night shifts or who had to rotate through afternoon and late evening times tended to be evening persons (Adan, 1992).

Adjust class schedule to whether you're a night or day person.

When it came to eating breakfast, morning persons tend to eat a hearty, high-calorie breakfast, while evening persons tend to either skip breakfast or consume a light one.

Finally, researchers found no differences between sexes in their preferences for being a morning or night person. But, they did find that in the course of normal aging, people tend to become physiologically and behaviorally more like morning persons after the age of 50, explaining why grandparents are usually early to bed and early to rise (Tankova et al., 1994).

Although people differ in being morning or night persons, they do share similar brain structures involved in putting them to sleep or waking them up, our next topic.

Most adults need 7–8 hours of sleep.

By the time you are 25 years old, you have fallen asleep over 9,000 times and have spent about 72,000 hours asleep. There are usually four questions that students ask about sleep: How much sleep do I need? Why do I sleep? What happens if I go without sleep? What causes sleep? We'll discuss each of these questions in turn.

## How Much Sleep Do I Need?

**What's the best amount for me?**

According to a survey, 58% of adult Americans sleep 7–8 hours, 38% sleep 5–6 hours, and 4% sleep 9–10 hours (*Time,* April 19, 1993). However, if we took a survey of babies, the time spent sleeping would be dramatically different, as shown in the pie charts below.

Beginning at birth and continuing through old age, there is a gradual change in the total time we spend sleeping, the percentage of time we spend in REM sleep, and the kinds of sleep problems we experience.

**INFANCY AND CHILDHOOD**

From infancy to adolescence, the total amount of time spent in sleep and the percentage spent in REM gradually decline. For example, a newborn sleeps about 17 hours a day, and 50% of that time is spent in REM; a 4-year-old sleeps about 10 hours a day, and 25–30% of that time is spent in REM.

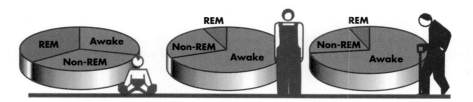

**OLD AGE**

Upon reaching our sixties, total sleep time drops to about 6.5 hours a day, but the percentage of REM sleep remains about the same (20%). In people over 60, about 30% report trouble getting to sleep, and 65% report difficulties staying asleep, which is partly due to daytime napping (Bliwise, 1997).

**ADOLESCENCE AND ADULTHOOD**   Compared to adults, researchers recently found that adolescents need more sleep (almost 10 hours) and that their circadian clocks favor going to bed later and getting up later (Carskadon, 2000). Researchers concluded that adolescents who must get up early (6 or 7 A.M.) for classes are often sleep deprived, which may interfere with performance (Hellmich, 2000). One solution is for high school classes to start an hour later so adolescents can get sufficient sleep. At about age 20, adolescents adopt the sleep pattern of adults, which is to get approximately 7-8 hours of sleep a day, with about 20% or less being REM sleep.

## Why Do I Sleep?

**Is my brain being repaired?**

One reason we know sleep is important comes from studies of animals who are deprived of sleep. Rats can live about 16 days without food (water provided) and about 17 days without sleep (Rechtschaffen, 1997). So far, the longest a human has voluntarily gone without sleep is 11 days (discussed on next page). We'll explain two currently popular theories—the repair and adaptive theories—of why we spend about one-third of each day asleep.

Repair theory says sleep restores brain and body.

The *repair theory* suggests that activities during the day deplete key factors in our brain or body that are replenished or repaired by sleep. The repair theory says that sleep is primarily a restorative process.

The repair theory is supported by several findings. First, during stage 4 sleep there is a marked secretion of growth hormone, which controls many aspects of metabolism, physical growth, and brain development (Shapiro, 1981). Second, during sleep there is increased production of immune cells to fight off infection (Born et al., 1997). Third, moderate changes in sleep schedules caused reports of decreased happiness and cheerfulness (Boivin et al., 1997). It seems the brain needs sleep to grow, repair its immune system, and maintain an optimum mood.

The *adaptive theory* suggests that sleep evolved because it prevented early humans and animals from wasting energy and exposing themselves to the dangers of nocturnal predators (Webb, 1983).

Support for the adaptive theory comes from observations that large predatory animals, such as lions, sleep a lot and wherever they wish, while smaller prey animals sleep far less and in protected areas. Also, animals (humans) that rely primarily on visual cues and have little night vision have evolved a circadian clock for sleeping at night and thus avoid becoming prey (Hirshkowitz et al., 1997).

The adaptive and repair theories are not really at odds but just focus on different reasons for our need to sleep.

Adaptive theory says sleep helps us avoid dangers.

## What If I Miss Sleep?

**Can you go without sleep?**

One method of investigating why sleep is important is to study people or animals who are sleep deprived. The record for sleep deprivation was set by a young adult who went without sleep for 11 days, or 264 hours (Johnson et al., 1965). On his 11th day without sleep, this young man beat the researcher in a pinball game, which indicates he was still awake and alert. Here's what happens when people are sleep deprived.

### EFFECTS ON THE BODY

Sleep deprivation, even for 264 hours, has minimal effect on a person's heart rate, blood pressure, and hormone secretions. It appears that many physiological functions controlled by the autonomic nervous system are not significantly disrupted by periods of sleep deprivation (Walsh & Lindblom, 1997).

However, sleep deprivation does affect our immune system, which is the body's defense against viruses, infections, and other toxic agents. In one study, men were allowed to sleep only 3–4 hours instead of their normal 8 hours. After only one night of sleep deprivation, they showed significant reductions in immune system functioning, as measured by a reduced number of killer cells (T-cells) (Irwin et al., 1994). Researchers concluded that for most people, sleep deprivation could mean increased vulnerability to some viral or bacterial infections (Dement, 1999).

### EFFECTS ON THE BRAIN

Sleep deprivation has consistently been shown to cause irritability and unhappiness and interfere with tasks that require vigilance and concentration, such as recalling and recognizing words and doing math tests (Drummond, 2000). People who are greatly sleep deprived, such as sled-dog racers who averaged 2 hours of sleep a night during the 12-day Iditarod race, reported having very vivid hallucinations, such as seeing and going to sleep in rooms with blazing fireplaces, beds, and hot showers. When they awoke some time later, they were lying in the cold snow (Balzar, 1997). Depending on its extent, sleep deprivation can cause moodiness and hallucinations as well as interfere with cognitive performance.

## What Causes Sleep?

**How do you go to sleep?**

After getting into bed, most of us fall asleep within 5–30 minutes and sleep an average of 8 hours (range about 6 to 10). Going to sleep involves a very complicated process during which different areas of the brain are activated or deactivated. The whole sleep process beings with something flipping the master switch for sleep.

### MASTER SLEEP SWITCH

VPN is the master sleep switch.

Researchers found the master switch for sleep in a nucleus of the brain called the VPN (Sherin et al., 1996).

The *VPN—ventrolateral preoptic nucleus*—is a group of cells in the hypothalamus that act like a master switch for sleep. When turned on, the VPN secretes a neurotransmitter (GABA) that turns off areas that keep the brain awake. When the VPN is turned off, certain brain areas become active and you wake up.

Although researchers have located the master switch for sleep, they haven't yet determined what turns it on and off.

One brain area that the VPN turns off is the reticular formation.

### RETICULAR FORMATION

In order for the forebrain to receive and process information from the senses, it must be aroused and alerted by the reticular formation.

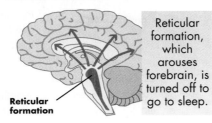

Reticular formation, which arouses forebrain, is turned off to go to sleep.

Reticular formation

The *reticular formation,* a column of cells that stretches the length of the brain stem, arouses and alerts the forebrain and prepares it to receive information from all the senses.

The reticular formation is important in keeping the forebrain alert and in producing a state of wakefulness (Munk et al., 1996). If the reticular formation is stimulated in sleeping animals, they awaken; if it is seriously damaged in animals or humans, they lapse into permanent unconsciousness or coma.

### GOING TO SLEEP

The master sleep switch and the reticular formation are but two of the factors regulating sleep. Here is the probable sequence for going to sleep (Pressman & Orr, 1997).

**First,** the time of day you go to sleep is regulated by the circadian clock, which is influenced by the suprachiasmatic nucleus of the hypothalamus.

**Second,** something turns on your master sleep switch, which is located in the VPN (ventrolateral preoptic nucleus) of the hypothalamus. In turn, the VPN turns off areas that arouse your brain, such as the reticular formation.

**Third,** a number of different chemicals and neurotransmitters, some of which are manufactured in the pons, regulate when

Going to sleep involves four factors.

you go into and out of non-REM and REM sleep and when you awaken (Gallopin, 2000).

**Fourth,** the circadian rhythm that regulates your body temperature is tied in with sleep since you go to sleep when your temperature falls and wake up when your temperature rises.

Thus, the reasons you go to sleep and wake up involve a complex interaction between the circadian clock, brain areas, sleep-inducing chemicals, and body temperature.

After the Concept Review, we'll describe a psychological problem whose cause seems related to decreased sunlight.

# Concept Review

**1.** The various levels of awareness of one's thoughts and feelings, as well as of other internal and external stimuli, are referred to as (a)_____. This experience varies on a continuum from very aware and alert to totally unaware and unresponsive. Activities that require full awareness and alertness and may interfere with other ongoing endeavors are called (b)_____. In comparison, activities that require little awareness and minimal attention and that do not interfere with other ongoing endeavors are called (c)_____.

**2.** The biological clock that is set for a day of 24–25 hours is called a (a)_____. This rhythm regulates our sleep-wake cycle, which is set to an average day of 24 hours and 18 minutes. Our circadian clock is reset by 18 minutes each day to match the industrial world's 24-hour day. The circadian clock is located in the brain's hypothalamus, in a small part called the (b)_____.

**3.** If your circadian rhythm is out of step with local time, you may feel fatigued and disoriented, a traveler's complaint called (a)_____. Workers and drivers have more accidents from 2 A.M. to 4 A.M. because their sleep-wake clock is telling them it's time to (b)_____. Researchers have reset circadian rhythms by exposing subjects and night workers to periods of bright light; this is called (c)_____ therapy.

**4.** Near the center of the human brain is an oval group of cells, collectively called the pineal gland, which secrete a hormone called (a)_____. The gland secretes the hormone during dark periods and stops when it gets light. In many animals, this hormone plays a major role in the regulation of (b)_____ rhythms.

SUPRACHIASMATIC NUCLEUS
PINEAL GLAND    OPTIC NERVE

**5.** During a night's sleep, we gradually pass through five stages. Stage 1, which is a transition between waking and sleeping, has brain waves known as (a)_____. Stage 2 has brain waves with bursts of activity that are called (b)_____. Stage 3 and especially stage 4 are marked by high-amplitude, low-frequency (c)_____. Stage 4 is often considered the deepest stage of sleep because it is the most difficult from which to be awakened. During stage 4, heart rate, respiration, temperature, and blood flow to the brain are (d)_____. Together, stages 1, 2, 3, and 4 are referred to as (e)_____, in which we spend about 80% of our sleep time. About five or six times throughout the night, we enter a paradoxical state called (f)_____, which accounts for the remaining 20% of our sleep time. This stage is characterized by increased physiological arousal, "alert and awake" brain waves, and vivid dreaming.

**6.** From birth through old age, there is a decrease in total sleep time, from about 17 hours in newborns to 6.5 hours after age 60. In addition, one stage of sleep, called _____, decreases from 50% of sleep time in infancy to 20% in adulthood.

REM    Awake
Non-REM

**7.** There are two different but not incompatible theories of why we sleep. The theory that says the purpose of sleep is to restore factors depleted throughout the day is the (a)_____. The theory that says sleep is based on an evolutionary need to conserve energy and escape nocturnal harm is the (b)_____.

**8.** Going to sleep is regulated by the following factors. An area in the hypothalamus that is the master sleep switch is called the (a)_____. An area in the hypothalamus that regulates circadian rhythms is called the (b)_____ nucleus. A brain area that contributes to our staying awake by sending neural signals that alert and arouse the forebrain is called the (c)_____. Several different sleep chemicals and (d)_____, some of which are made in the pons, regulate going into and out of the stages of sleep. In addition, we go to sleep several hours after a fall in body (e)_____ and get up when it starts to rise.

***Answers:*** *1. (a) consciousness, (b) controlled processes, (c) automatic processes; 2. (a) circadian rhythm, (b) suprachiasmatic nucleus; 3. (a) jet lag, (b) sleep, (c) light; 4. (a) melatonin, (b) circadian; 5. (a) theta waves, (b) sleep spindles, (c) delta waves, (d) reduced, (e) non-REM sleep, (f) REM sleep; 6. REM sleep; 7. (a) repair theory, (b) adaptive theory; 8. (a) VPN, or ventrolateral preoptic nucleus, (b) suprachiasmatic, (c) reticular formation, (d) neurotransmitters, (e) temperature*

## Problem and Treatment

**Does light affect your mood?**

**Problem.** For many animals, including humans, sunlight has a direct influence on resetting the circadian clock and affecting circadian rhythms. However, it was only recently that researchers found a direct nerve connection from receptors in the retina, which is located in the back of the eye, to a nucleus in the brain (the suprachiasmatic nucleus in the hypothalamus—p. 150). What is interesting about this particular nerve pathway is that it is not involved with vision or seeing things but only with sensing the presence and amount of light, either sunlight or artificial light (Young, 2000). This means that humans have a neural pathway that is very responsive to the presence of light and may also be involved in the onset of a mental health problem called seasonal affective disorder, or SAD.

*Seasonal affective disorder, or SAD,* is a pattern of depressive symptoms, such as loss of interest or pleasure in nearly all activities. Depressed feelings cycle with the seasons, typically beginning in fall or winter and going away in spring, when days are longer and sunnier. Along with depression are lethargy, excessive sleepiness, overeating, weight gain, and craving for carbohydrates (American Psychiatric Association, 1994).

Seasonal affective disorder (SAD) is worse in fall/winter.

**Treatment.** A popular nondrug treatment for SAD involves exposing a person to bright light for between 30 minutes and 1 hour, usually in the morning. Researchers reported that 69% of subjects diagnosed with SAD reported less depression after daily exposure to light, while 31% experienced little or no decrease (Terman et al., 1996). Generally, exposure to artificial light helps about 50–70% of individuals diagnosed with SAD (Lam et al., 2000).

Because decreased sunlight appears to trigger SAD, we would expect the fewest cases of SAD in southern Florida, which is almost always sunny; more cases in northern New Hampshire, which has gloomy winters; and many, many more cases in far northern Iceland (see map), which has winters with little or no sun. Let's see if this prediction holds.

## Occurrence of SAD

**Where is the highest rate of SAD?**

As predicted, the graph shows that the incidence of SAD is very low (1.4%) among residents who live in sunny Florida but about five times higher (7.3%) among residents who live under the gray winter skies of northern New Hampshire (Magnusson, 2000). However, far north of New Hampshire is Iceland (see map), which has far less sun in fall and winter than New Hampshire. In spite of having less sun, Icelanders have only about half the incidence of SAD (3.9%) compared to residents of New Hampshire.

1.4 | % SAD in Florida
3.9 | % SAD in Iceland
7.3 | % SAD in New Hampshire

When researchers try to explain any unusual or unpredicted findings, they first check the methods and procedures used to measure the dependent variable, which in this case, is the occurrence of SAD. However, researchers in Iceland used the same methods (questionnaires) and procedures that were used by researchers in the United States (Magnusson, 2000). If research methods and procedures were similar, what else would explain why the highest rates of SAD were reported in New Hampshire and not in Iceland?

## Cultural Differences

**What's different about Icelanders?**

Why did Icelanders report less than half the incidence of SAD, even though they have far less daylight in fall and winter than residents in New Hampshire (see map)?

Researchers concluded that differences in methods, questionnaires, and residents' lifestyles or occupations could not explain this discrepancy. Rather, there may be two other explanations that involve cultural and genetic differences.

For 1,000 years, Icelanders have lived rather isolated in a very demanding, low-daylight environment. Because of very harsh and unyielding environmental demands, Icelanders may have developed an emotional hardiness to deal with

Iceland

Atlantic Mid Ocean

Nova Scotia

New Hampshire

Cultural differences explain why Iceland (far north) has less SAD than New Hampshire.

especially gloomy winters that trigger almost twice as many cases of SAD among residents in the northeastern United States.

Another explanation for Icelanders' low incidence of SAD may involve genetic factors. For example, researchers studied a population of immigrants in Canada who were wholly of Icelandic decent. The incidence of SAD in the Icelandic immigrants was unexpectedly much lower than found in other residents in the same general area. Researchers concluded that the lower frequency of SAD in Icelanders is puzzling and may reflect both genetic and cultural differences, such as learning to deal with isolation and harsh environments (Magnusson et al., 2000).

Next, we'll discuss four explanations for something most of us experience every night—dreaming.

# G. World of Dreams

## Theories of Dream Interpretation

**What do my dreams mean?**

Although some people insist that they never dream, research suggests that everyone dreams during the night, even though many have forgotten their dreams by morning. In sleep laboratories, people awakened from REM periods report 80–100% of the time that they were having dreams with vivid, colorful, even bizarre images. Less frequently, people awakened from non-REM sleep or right after going to sleep may also report dreams, which may contain dull, repetitive thoughts or the colorful images reported after REM sleep (Domhoff, 1999).

For example, let's take a dream and see how others might interpret it.

I am in an elevator sitting by myself against the wall. A girl comes in, and I say, "Come sit by me," and she sits by me. (I don't even know her.) I lean over and try to kiss her, and she says, "No, don't do that." I say, "How come?" and she says something about her acne, and I say it doesn't matter and she laughs and we end up kissing and stuff on the elevator. Then these parents get on, and the elevator is real shaky, and I

There are several different interpretations of dreams.

think that the elevator will crash or get stuck (adapted from Cohen, 1979).

Figuring out what dreams mean is a popular and scholarly activity for the more than 400 psychologists, physiologists, anthropologists, artists, "dream workers," and swamis who meet for the annual Association for the Study of Dreams. The focus of this group is to discover meaning in dreams—no easy task, since there are numerous theories. For example, some say that the young man's dream is expressing his fears of having a sexual relationship; others say that his dream is expressing his fear of being in small enclosures; while still others say that his dream is a meaningless jumble of images. We'll discuss three currently popular psychological theories of dream interpretation as well as a thousand-year-old theory of dreams from the Inuit or Eskimo people.

We'll begin our discussion of dreams with the most famous and controversial theory, Freud's theory of dream interpretation.

## 1 Freud's Theory of Dream Interpretation

In the preface to his famous book, *The Interpretation of Dreams,* Freud (1900) wrote, "This book contains, even according to my present-day judgment, the most valuable of all the discoveries it has been my good fortune to make. Insight such as this falls to one's lot but once in a lifetime." Before 1900, psychologists believed that dreams were meaningless and bizarre images. However, Freud's theory changed all that when he said that dreams were a way ("the royal road") to reach our unconscious thoughts and desires.

Freud said dreams reveal repressed desires.

*Freud's theory of dreams* says that we have a "censor" that protects us from realizing threatening and unconscious desires or wishes, especially those involving sex or aggression. To protect us from having threatening thoughts, the "censor" transforms our secret, guilt-ridden, and anxiety-provoking desires into harmless symbols that appear in our dreams and do not disturb our sleep or conscious thoughts.

Freud made two main points that no one had made before: dreams had meaning and they could be understood. For example, Freud (1900) discussed the meaning of symbols: male sex symbols are long objects, such as sticks, umbrellas, and pencils; female sex symbols are hollow things, such as caves, jars, and keyholes. Freud believed a psychoanalyst's (Freudian therapist) task was to interpret or decode these disguised thoughts or symbols and help the client discover his or her internal world, which includes unconscious desires, needs, defenses, fears, and emotions (Mancia, 1999).

Current psychoanalysts agree with Freud that dreams have meaning and can represent past, present, or future concerns, fears, or worries (Greenberg & Perlman, 1999). However, as you'll see next, many non-Freudian therapists disagree with Freud's idea that a dream's contents are necessarily symbols or disguised thoughts for threatening, unconscious wishes and desires (Gardner, 1996).

## 2 Extensions of Waking Life

Many therapists and some current psychoanalysts believe that dreams are extensions of waking life (Greenberg & Perlman, 1999).

The theory that *dreams are extensions of waking life* means that our dreams reflect the same thoughts, fears, concerns, problems, and emotions that we have when awake.

Therapists believe dreams reflect waking concerns.

Therapist and researcher Rosalind Cartwright (1988), director of Rush Sleep Disorder Service, says, "The problem most therapists face is that patients' dream material is sparse and incomplete. People simply don't remember their dreams very well. The therapist's task is often like trying to reconstruct a 500-page novel from just the last page. But dreams collected from a single night in the sleep lab read like chapters in a book. They illuminate current concerns and the feelings attached to them" (p. 36).

For example, Cartwright found that people who suffered severe traumatic emotional situations have stark nightmares that re-create the traumatic situation; people who are depressed often wake each morning feeling worse than when they went to bed and have disturbed dreams (Cartwright, 1993). Cartwright believes that patients suffering from depression or marital problems cope with their problems by repeating their fears and concerns in their dreams. For this reason, therapists find dream interpretation a useful tool in helping clients reach a better understanding of themselves (Hill et al., 2000).

Rosalind Cartwright (1993) concludes that dreams are important because they represent another source of information, have a regular occurrence, and cannot be easily suppressed. But she adds that this still leaves open the question of meaning and recognizes that therapists cannot always understand the dreams that patients report.

The next theory looks at dreams as reflecting neural activity.

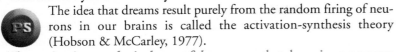
## 3 Activation-Synthesis Theory

The idea that dreams result purely from the random firing of neurons in our brains is called the activation-synthesis theory (Hobson & McCarley, 1977).

The *activation-synthesis theory of dreams* says that dreaming represents the random and meaningless activity of nerve cells in the brain. According to this theory, an area in the brain, called the pons, sends millions of random nerve impulses to the cortex. In turn, the cortex tries to make sense of these random signals by creating the feelings, imagined movements, perceptions, changing scenes, and meaningless images that we define as dreams.

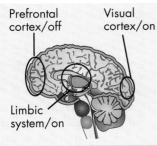

During REM sleep, prefrontal cortex turned off; visual cortex and limbic system turned on.

Hobson (1988) later revised the original activation-synthesis dream theory to acknowledge that dreams do reflect our past memories, strong hopes and fears, and personal view of the world.

**Brain scans.** Recently, researchers took pictures or PET scans of neural activity while subjects were in REM sleep. They report that during REM sleep, the area responsible for executive functions (prefrontal cortex), such as thinking, planning, and reasoning, had reduced activity, while areas involved in emotions (limbic system) and visual experiences (visual cortex) had increased activity (Braun et al., 1998). These differences in brain activity seem to explain why our dreams are often emotional (limbic system/on) and visual (visual cortex/on) but are strange, bizarre, and poorly planned out (prefrontal cortex/off) (Schwartz, 2000).

How do dream theories from European-Western cultures compare with those from native cultures, such as the Inuit (formerly called Eskimo)?

## 4 Entering the Spiritual World

The Inuit or Eskimo people have lived for thousands of years in quiet isolation along the arctic coasts of North America. The Inuit, along with other native people, believe that dreams are ways to enter the spiritual world (Foulks, 1992).

The *Inuit believes* that in dreaming, one enters the spiritual world, where the souls of animals, supernaturals, and departed relatives are made known. Through dreams, forces in the spiritual world help a living person reflect on some present or future event.

Inuits believe you enter the spiritual world through dreams.

Although the Inuit live in a far different time, place, and culture than did Sigmund Freud or Western therapists, there are numerous parallels between their theories of dreams. For example, the Inuit, Freud, and Western therapists all believed that past forces, wishes, or concerns could be revealed to the dreamer; that these wishes, concerns, or desires could take symbolic forms; and that Inuit shamans, who were thought to possess spiritual powers, function like Freudian-trained psychoanalysts or Western-trained therapists, who are sometimes needed to interpret dream symbols or unravel the meaning of dreams. Notice, however, that each dream theory has a unique focus: Freud says that dreams are ways to reach the unconscious; modern therapists hold that dreams represent waking problems; and the Inuit believe that dreams are ways to enter the spiritual world.

Next, we'll examine what people dream about.

---

## Typical Dreams

**What do people dream about?**

Although many animals, including bats, whales, monkeys, moles, dogs, and cats (but not snakes), have REM sleep, we do not know if they dream. We know that humans dream because they tell us. Thousands of descriptions of dreams have been obtained from people who had just been aroused from REM sleep and others who were asked to record their dreams at home. One researcher (Van de Castle, 1994) has catalogued these descriptions and found that typical dreams have the following characteristics:

- dreams have several characters;
- they involve motion such as running or walking;
- they are more likely to take place indoors than out;
- they are filled with visual sensations but rarely include sensations of taste, smell, or pain;
- they seem bizarre because we disregard physical laws by flying or falling without injury;
- they may be recurrent—for example, dreams of being threatened, being pursued, or trying to hide;
- they more frequently involve emotions of anxiety or fear than joy or happiness;
- they rarely involve sexual encounters and are almost never about sexual intercourse;
- rarely can we control or dream about something we intend to;

Many people dream about flying, running, falling, or hiding.

- dreams usually have visual imagery and are in color in sighted people, but in people blind from birth, dreams are never visual but only tactile, olfactory (smell), or gustatory (taste).

Researchers conclude that although individual dreams represent unique experiences, the format in which we dream, such as flying, falling, running, or hiding, is shared by others (Domhoff, 1999; Hurovitz et al., 1999). In one study, students who volunteered for dream interpretation sessions were mostly women (77%). However, not all the subjects were equally good at seeing how dreams related to and were extensions of their waking lives (Hill et al., 1997). Some of these students reported having nightmares, which we'll discuss next in considering sleep problems and treatments.

## Occurrence

**How big is the problem?**

In the United States, about 80 million people experience some kind of sleep problem. For example, some adults stop breathing in their sleep (sleep apnea); some have trouble going to or staying asleep (insomnia); a small percentage go from being wide awake to a very deep sleep quickly and without warning (narcolepsy); and about 25% of children under age 5 have a sleep disturbance (Carskadon & Taylor, 1997). We'll discuss a number of these sleep problems as well as possible treatments, beginning with one of the more common problems, insomnia.

### Insomnia

In the United States, a recent poll found that about 58% of adults report some type of insomnia (Hellmich, 2000).

*Insomnia* refers to difficulties in either going to sleep or staying asleep through the night. Insomnia is associated with a number of daytime complaints, including fatigue, impairment of concentration, memory difficulty, and lack of well-being.

**Psychological causes.** Common psychological causes of insomnia include experiencing an overload of stressful events, worrying about personal or job-related

difficulties, grieving over a loss or death, and coping with mental health problems. For many middle-aged working people, job stress is a major cause of insomnia and other sleep problems (Kalimo et al., 2000). For students, common causes of insomnia are worrying about exams, personal problems, and changes in sleep schedule, such as staying up late Saturday night and sleeping late on Sunday morning. Then Sunday night they are not tired at the usual time and may experience insomnia.

**Physiological causes.** Common physiological causes of insomnia include changing to night-shift work which upsets circadian rhythms, having medical problems or chronic pain, and abusing alcohol or other substances (sedatives). All can disrupt going to and staying asleep.

There are effective nondrug (psychological) and drug treatments for bouts of insomnia.

### Nondrug Treatment

Nondrug treatments for insomnia may differ in method, but all have the same goal: to stop the person from excessive worrying and reduce tension, which are major psychological causes of insomnia. One proven cognitive-behavioral method of reducing insomnia is to establish an optimal sleep pattern (Bootzin & Rider, 1997).

**Establishing an Optimal Sleep Pattern**

Follow these eight steps so that sleeping becomes more regular and efficient.

**1.** Go to bed only when you are sleepy, not by convention or habit.

**2.** Put the light out immediately when you get into bed.

**3.** Do not read or watch television in bed, since these are activities that you do when awake.

**4.** If you are not asleep within 20 minutes, get out of bed and sit and relax in another room until you are tired again. Relaxation can include tensing and relaxing your muscles or using visual imagery, which involves closing your eyes and concentrating on some calm scene or image for several minutes.

**5.** Repeat step 4 as often as required, and also if you wake up for any long periods of time.

**6.** Set the alarm to the same time each morning, so that your time of waking is always the same. This step is very important because oversleeping or sleeping in is one of the primary causes of insomnia the next night.

**7.** Do not nap during the day because it will throw off your sleep schedule that night.

**8.** Follow this program rigidly for several weeks to establish an efficient and regular pattern of sleep.

**Results.** People who used this or similar nondrug treatments reduced their time for going to sleep from 64 to 36 minutes. Nondrug treatment programs similar to the above were among the most effective for significantly decreasing insomnia (Bootzin & Rider, 1997; Perlis et al., 2000). More serious problems with insomnia may be treated with drugs.

### Drug Treatment

Many stressful situations, such as losing a loved one, going through a divorce, or dealing with a physical injury, may result in chronic insomnia, which is defined as lasting longer than three weeks. In these cases, doctors most often prescribe one of the benzodiazepines.

*Benzodiazepines (ben-zo-die-AS-ah-peens),* which reduce anxiety, worry, and stress, are commonly prescribed for and effective in the short-term (3–4 weeks) treatment of insomnia. However, with increasing dosage and prolonged usage, benzodiazepines (Dalmane, Xanax, Halcion, Restoril) may produce side effects that can include daytime drowsiness, loss of memory, tolerance, and dependency.

Because benzodiazepines reduce anxiety, a chief cause of insomnia, they are an effective treatment and are relatively safe when taken in moderate dosages for short periods of time (3–4 weeks) (Roan, 1999).

However, the continual use of benzodiazepines, especially at higher dosages, may lead to dependence on the drug and serious side effects, such as memory loss and excessive sleepiness. Recently, several nonbenzodiazepines have been introduced (Ambien, Sonata) which proved effective in treating insomnia with fewer side effects (Roan, 1999). For the management of long-term insomnia, clinicians often recommend a program that combines nondrug (psychological) and drug treatment.

## Sleep Apnea

In the United States, about 20 million adults have insomnia because they stop breathing, a problem called sleep apnea.

*Sleep apnea* refers to repeated periods during sleep when a person stops breathing for 10 seconds or longer. The person may repeatedly stop breathing, momentarily wake up, resume breathing, and return to sleep. Repeated awakenings during the night result in insomnia and leave the person exhausted during the day but not knowing the cause of their tiredness.

Chances of developing sleep apnea increase if a person is an intense and frequent snorer, is overweight, uses alcohol, or takes sedatives (benzodiazepines) (Chokroverty, 2000). Some individuals with sleep apnea may wake up an astonishing 400 times a night, which also results in insomnia (Dajer, 2000).

The treatment for sleep apnea partly depends on its severity. The simplest treatment is to sew tennis balls in the back of a pajama top so the person cannot lie on his or her back, which increases the chances of sleep apnea. The most popular therapy is a device that blows air into a sealed mask that the person wears over the nose. In severe cases, people with sleep apnea may have to wear a mouth device similar to a retainer or undergo surgery to remove tonsils or alter the position of the jaw (Saskin, 1997).

## Narcolepsy

"I have lived with narcolepsy for 45 years. . . . I was directly responsible for several near-fatal automobile accidents. The simple joys everyone takes for granted are, for the most part, denied me. I would literally sleep the rest of my life away" (NCSDR, 1993, p. 16).

*Narcolepsy (NAR-ko-lep-see)* is a chronic disorder that is marked by excessive sleepiness, usually in the form of sleep attacks or short periods of sleep throughout the day. The sleep attacks are accompanied by brief periods of REM sleep and by muscle paralysis (cataplexy), which may range from tilting head to buckling knees and falling to the ground.

Narcoleptics describe their sleep attacks as irresistible. They report falling asleep in very inappropriate places, such as while carrying on a conversation or driving a car. In many cases, these sleep attacks make it difficult for narcoleptics to lead normal lives.

Only recently have researchers discovered that narcolepsy results when certain brain cells, called hypocretin neurons, do not develop normally (Mignot, 2000). Researchers found that, like humans, some dogs also get narcolepsy, such as the one held here by famous sleep researcher Dr. William Dement. When these dogs were given the missing chemical, hypocretin, the narcoleptic symptoms were reversed. With the discovery that a lack of hypocretin results in narcolepsy and replacement of hypocretin can reverse the symptoms, researchers for the first time have a way to successfully treat narcolepsy, which affects about 135,000 Americans.

## Sleep Disturbances

### NIGHT TERRORS

A 4-year-old boy sits up in the night and begins screaming. This is an example of a night terror.

*Night terrors,* which occur during stage 3 or 4 (delta sleep), are frightening experiences that often start with a piercing scream, followed by sudden waking in a fearful state with rapid breathing and increased heart rate. However, the next morning the child has no memory of the frightening experience. About 3–7% of children have night terrors.

A child in the grip of night terrors is difficult to calm and, even if severely shaken, may need several minutes to regain full awareness. Night terrors are most common in children aged 4–12 and disappear by adolescence (Chokroverty, 2000). Caregivers should take enough time to comfort and soothe the frightened child, who usually will go back to sleep.

### NIGHTMARES

Besides night terrors, about 25–70% of all children aged 3–6 have nightmares; about 10% of college students report having them once a month (Siegel, 1998).

*Nightmares,* which occur during REM sleep, are very frightening and anxiety-producing images that occur during dreaming. Nightmares usually involve great danger—being attacked, injured, or pursued. Upon awakening, the person can usually describe the nightmare in great detail.

Nightmares usually stop when the person wakes, but feelings of anxiety or fear may persist for some time; it may be difficult to go back to sleep. One effective treatment for nightmares involves regular use of anxiety-reduction techniques (described in Module 21).

### SLEEPWALKING

One of the more unusual sleep disturbances is sleepwalking.

*Sleepwalking* usually occurs in stage 3 or 4 (delta sleep) and consists of getting up and walking while literally sound asleep. Sleepwalkers generally have poor coordination, are clumsy but can avoid objects, can engage in very limited conversation, and have no memory of sleepwalking.

Occasional sleepwalking is considered normal in children; frequent sleepwalking in adults may be caused by increased stress, sleep deprivation, or mental problems (Dement, 1999). Sleepwalking can be a serious problem because of the potential for injury and harm to oneself and others (imagine sleepwalking out of the house onto the highway).

Sleep researchers are alerting Americans to the growing number of people with sleep problems, especially insomnia, which leads to sleep deprivation, which in turn interferes with well-being and cognitive performance (Leehotz, 2000).

# Summary Test

## A. CONTINUUM OF CONSCIOUSNESS

**1.** The awareness of our own thoughts and feelings, as well as of other internal and external stimuli, is called (a)_____, which occurs on a continuum from being very alert to being very unresponsive.

Those activities that require our full awareness and concentration to reach some goal are called (b)_____. Those activities that require little awareness and minimal attention and that do not interfere with other ongoing activities are called (c)_____.

**2.** Fantasizing or dreaming while awake, which often occurs during automatic processes, is called (a)_____. If, under the influence of drugs, meditation, or hypnosis, we perceive our internal and external environments in ways that differ from normal, we may be said to have entered (b)_____ of consciousness. Sigmund Freud suggested that we push unacceptable wishes or desires into our (c)_____. A blow to the head or general anesthesia can produce complete loss of awareness, which is called (d)_____. Mental and emotional processes that, although we are unaware of them, influence our conscious thoughts and behaviors form a kind of memory called (e)_____.

## B. RHYTHMS OF SLEEPING & WAKING

**3.** A biological clock that is set to run on a time cycle of 24–25 hours is called a (a)_____. In animals (and probably humans) the biological clock for the sleep-wake cycle is located in a part of the hypothalamus called the (b)_____.

**4.** If we travel across time zones and our circadian rhythm gets out of phase with the local clock time, we experience difficulty in going to sleep and getting up at normal times, a condition known as (a)_____. Researchers have been able to reset circadian rhythms in workers by exposing them to bright light during certain times; this is called (b)_____ therapy.

**5.** In the center of the animal and human brain is the pineal gland, a small group of cells that secrete the hormone _____. This hormone has a major role in regulating the sleep-wake cycle in animals; its role in humans is less clear.

## C. WORLD OF SLEEP

**6.** Researchers study sleep and wakefulness by recording the activity of brain cells and muscles. Electrical brain activity is recorded in trac-

ings called an (a)_____. The height of a wave is called its (b)_____, and the number of wave cycles that occur in one second is called the (c)_____.

**7.** If you are awake and alert, your brain waves have a very high frequency and low amplitude and are called (a)_____ waves. If you close your eyes and become relaxed and drowsy, your brain waves remain low in amplitude but decrease slightly in frequency; these are called (b)_____ waves.

**8.** Researchers divide sleep into five stages. Stage 1, the transition from wakefulness to sleep, is marked by (a)_____ waves and a feeling of gradually losing responsiveness to the outside world. Stage 2 represents the first real phase of sleep and is marked by high-frequency bursts of brain activity called (b)_____. In stage 3 and especially stage 4, there are high-amplitude, low-frequency brain waves called (c)_____. Stage 4 may be considered the deepest stage of sleep, since it is the most difficult from which to wake someone. Together, stages 1, 2, 3, and 4 are referred to as (d)_____ sleep, which makes up about 80% of sleep time.

**9.** About every 30–90 minutes throughout sleep, you leave stage 4 (delta sleep) and progress backward to stage 2. From stage 2, you enter a new stage of sleep marked by high-frequency, low-amplitude brain waves that look identical to (a)_____ waves. This stage is called (b)_____ sleep because your eyes move rapidly back and forth underneath closed eyelids. During this stage, you are asleep and lose muscle tension in the neck and limbs. However, your brain waves are like those when you are awake and alert, and there is increased arousal of many physiological responses. When awakened from this stage, people usually (80–100% of the time) report that they have been (c)_____.

## D. RESEARCH FOCUS: CIRCADIAN PREFERENCE

**10.** People who prefer to get up earlier, go to bed earlier, and engage in morning activities and whose body temperature rises more quickly in the morning and peaks earlier at night are called (a)_____. People who prefer to get up later, go to bed later, and engage in afternoon-evening activities and whose body temperature rises more slowly in the morning and peaks later at night are called (b)_____.

## E. QUESTIONS ABOUT SLEEP

**11.** Going to sleep is regulated by the following factors. An area in the hypothalamus that is the master sleep switch is called the (a)_____. An area in the hypothalamus that regulates circadian rhythms is called the (b)_____. A brain area that contributes to our staying awake by sending neural signals that alert and arouse the forebrain is called the (c)_____. Several different sleep chemicals and (d)_____, some of which are made in the pons, regulate going into and out of the stages of sleep. In addition, we go to sleep several hours after a fall in body (e)_____ and get up when it starts to rise.

REM
Non-REM
Awake

**12.** From infancy through old age, there is a gradual reduction in total (a)_____ time, from about 17 to 6.5 hours, and a reduction in the percentage of (b)_____ sleep, from about 50% to 20%.

**13.** The theory that says we sleep because we use up vital factors during the day that must be replaced at night is called the (a)_____ theory. The theory that says we sleep to conserve energy and avoid potential harm and injury from nocturnal predators is called the (b)_____ theory.

**14.** When we are sleep deprived, the next day we have difficulty performing tasks that require (a)_____. Sleep deprivation also affects the body, as measured by a decrease in killer cells, which are important in the functioning of our (b)_____ system, which fights off infections and toxic agents.

## F. CULTURAL DIVERSITY: INCIDENCE OF SAD

**15.** The occurrence of a pattern of depressive symptoms that generally begin in the fall and winter and disappear in the spring is called (a)_____. Although the incidence of this disorder is lower in Florida and higher in the northeastern United States, it is not higher in Iceland, which is much farther north than New Hampshire. One reason Icelanders report a lower incidence of SAD is because of their (b)_____ values.

Iceland

## G. WORLD OF DREAMS

**16.** According to Freud's theory, we have a "censor" that protects us from (a)_____. This involves transforming threatening, unconscious desires into harmless symbols. According to Hobson and McCarley's original theory, called the (b)_____, dreams are meaningless because they result from the random and meaningless activity of neurons. During REM sleep, some parts of the brain are turned on, (c)_____, and some are turned off, (d)_____. According to many therapists and sleep-dream researchers, such as Cartwright, dreams are (e)_____ of waking thoughts and concerns, especially emotional ones, and provide clues to a person's problems. According to the Inuit culture, dreams are a way to enter the (f)_____ world.

## H. APPLICATION: SLEEP PROBLEMS & TREATMENTS

**17.** A common sleep problem that includes difficulty in going to sleep or remaining asleep throughout the night is called (a)_____. A nondrug treatment is to use a proven (b)_____ method. Drug treatment for insomnia usually involves prescribing (c)_____. Insomnia caused when the sleeper stops breathing and wakes up is called (d)_____.

**18.** If children wake up screaming and in a great fright, they have experienced (a)_____ but will remember nothing the next morning. When adults experience emotionally charged, frightening images during their dreams, they are having (b)_____. If a person walks or carries out other behaviors during sleep, it is called (c)_____, which may be caused by increased stress. A relatively rare condition that involves irresistible attacks of sleepiness, brief periods of REM, and often muscle paralysis is called (d)_____.

***Answers:*** *1. (a) consciousness, (b) controlled processes, (c) automatic processes; 2. (a) daydreaming, (b) altered states, (c) unconscious, (d) unconsciousness, (e) implicit or nondeclarative memory; 3. (a) circadian rhythm, (b) suprachiasmatic nucleus; 4. (a) jet lag, (b) light; 5. melatonin; 6. (a) electroencephalogram, or EEG, (b) amplitude, (c) frequency; 7. (a) beta, (b) alpha; 8. (a) theta, (b) sleep spindles, (c) delta waves, (d) non-REM; 9. (a) beta, (b) REM, (c) dreaming; 10. (a) morning people, (b) evening people; 11. (a) ventrolateral preoptic nucleus, (b) suprachiasmatic nucleus, (c) reticular formation, (d) neurotransmitters, (e) temperature; 12. (a) sleep, (b) REM; 13. (a) repair, (b) adaptive; 14. (a) concentration, (b) immune; 15. (a) SAD, or seasonal affective disorder, (b) cultural; 16. (a) threatening desires/wishes, (b) activation-synthesis theory, (c) limbic system and visual cortex, (d) prefrontal cortex, (e) extensions, (f) spiritual; 17. (a) insomnia, (b) cognitive- behavioral, (c) benzodiazepines or nonbenzodiazepines, (d) sleep apnea; 18. (a) night terrors, (b) nightmares, (c) sleepwalking, (d) narcolepsy*

# Critical Thinking

## Newspaper Article

### How Good Is a Sleep-Deprived Doctor?

**Questions**

**1.** When are work and traffic accidents most likely to occur?

**2.** Why do most work and traffic accidents occur early in the morning?

**3.** Why do you think the medical establishment opposed the formation of a labor union for doctors in training?

**4.** How does sleep deprivation affect the body and the brain?

**5.** Based on Dr. Dement's observations and research, why don't teaching hospitals put a stop to overworking doctors in training?

**6.** Is this doctor right or just making excuses?

It may come as a surprise to learn that some of the worst work conditions occur in some of the major hospitals in the United States. For example, the Accreditation Council for Graduate Medical Education, the official group that sets standards for medical training, reports that doctors in training often work 36-hour shifts and 100-hour weeks, which can go on for a whole year. As a result, doctors in training may spend practically all of their waking hours in the hospital, with little time to be concerned about their own physical and mental health.

The primary reason that doctors in training are usually required to work long hours, such as New York State's law that allows 24-hour shifts and 80-hour work weeks, is that teaching hospitals keep costs down by relying on young doctors to provide low-cost labor. But for the first time, doctors in training are allowed to join a labor union called the Committee of Interns and Residents, which has been working to reduce the excessive hours that doctors in training have been required to work.

A 32-year-old Stanford University doctor remembers her years in training at a major teaching hospital in Boston: "I was chronically fatigued, so tired I felt as if I was operating in a daze sometimes. You go into medicine for idealistic reasons, but by the end of a grueling internship, you see each patient you admit to the hospital as a barrier to getting sleep. That's a horrible way to interact with people. . . . I remember one night in the hospital when I told a nurse something that was wrong, the exact opposite of what I should have said about giving antibiotics to a patient. Seconds later, when I was more awake, I realized my error, but I still wonder what might have happened if I'd gone back to sleep" (Pear, p. 2D).

Dr. William Dement of Stanford University, a well-known researcher in the field of sleep, strongly believes that, based on his observations and years of research, "sleep deprivation contributes to medical errors" and that "with more hours of sleep, doctors make fewer errors" (Pear, p. 2D).

However, other doctors point out the importance of having the same doctor treat the same patient and that errors can be made when patients are handed over from the care of one physician to another. (Adapted from R. Pear, Interns' long workdays prompt first crackdown, *New York Times*, June 11, 2000, p. 2D; S. L. Cohen, Hi, I'm your doctor. I haven't slept in 36 hours, *USA Today*, March 22, 2000, p. 29A)

*Use InfoTrac to search for terms:* **sleep deprivation; medical residents; fatigue.**

---

### Suggested answers to Newspaper Article questions

1. Most highway accidents occur in the early morning hours (2 to 3 A.M.) Similarly, most work accidents occur in early morning when workers are said to reach their "dead zone," about 5 A.M., when it's hardest to stay awake.

2. Most highway and work accidents occur in the early morning because that is when our genetically set circadian rhythms say that our bodies should be asleep. For this reason, it's difficult to stay awake and alert in the early morning hours.

3. Because medical treatment and costs keep rising, training hospitals try to hold costs down by giving doctors in training long, hard hours, a potentially dangerous work practice that is permitted in no other work place where people's lives are at stake.

4. Researchers report that sleep deprivation has little effect on heart rate or blood pressure but decreases the immune system's ability to fight off infections. However, researchers found that sleep deprivation does interfere with concentration and performing cognitive tasks, such as would be required when doctors prescribe or perform medical treatment for patients.

5. Although Dr. Dement concluded that sleep deprivation contributes to medical errors, many teaching hospitals continue to overwork doctors in training primarily for economic reasons—to have a source of low-cost labor and help keep costs down.

6. While it's certainly important to have the same doctor continue to treat the same patient, would you want to be treated by the same doctor if that doctor also happened to be 36-hours sleep deprived?

# Links to Learning

## Web Sites

- WADSWORTH ONLINE STUDY CENTER
  http://psychology.wadsworth.com
  Quizzes, learning activities and exercises, a discussion forum, and hot links to Internet sites related to sensation, including:

- ASSOCIATION FOR THE SCIENTIFIC STUDY OF CONSCIOUSNESS
  http://assc.caltech.edu
  Historical and current issues in consciousness are covered in seminar transcripts, journal articles, bibliographies, and web links.

- NATIONAL SLEEP FOUNDATION
  http://www.sleepfoundation.org/
  Here you'll find the latest information on sleep-related issues, pulications, and links.

- SLEEPNET
  http://www.sleepnet.com
  Everything you wanted to know about sleep but were too tired to ask: Disorders, research, labs, and support groups.

- THE ASSOCIATION FOR THE STUDY OF DREAMS
  http://www.ASDreams.org/
  This interesting site includes a bulletin board for discussion, articles, and information on graduate study in dream-related areas.

- SLEEP AND CONSCIOUSNESS
  http://www.sawka.com/spiritwatch/whyis.htm
  This is an invited address given by sleep researcher Jayne Gackenbach, Ph.D., at the Smithsonian Institute, Washington, D.C. Topics include "Why Is Dream Forgetting Common?", "How to Have a Lucid Dream," and "Development of Pure Consciousness from Lucidity." (Warning: Whoever transcibed this speech from audiotape must have been wearing mittens! You have to put up with the strange grammar and punctuation, but it's worth it.)

## Learning Activities

- *POWERSTUDY*™ CD BY ROD PLOTNIK & TOM DOYLE
  Check out the following sections on your CD and in the book:

  > **Power Study**™
  > **Check out CD: Module 4**
  > B. Studying the Living Brain; book page 161
  > C. Organization of the Brain; book pages 149, 157, 161
  > E. Limbic Systems, Old Brain; book pages 150, 157

- *STUDY GUIDE TO ACCOMPANY INTRODUCTION TO PSYCHOLOGY, 6TH EDITION,* by Matthew Enos
  Why not turn your bed into a research laboratory? In Module 7 you're shown how to do it. Does everyone dream? Why do we often wake up just before the alarm goes off?

- *WEBTUTOR*
  http://webtutor.thomsonlearning.com
  **WebTUTOR** Visit this site for interactive versions of the Study Guide features. Take a quiz, get your score—should you study a topic some more, or can you move on? For example, is it true that humans are always either awake and conscious or asleep and unconsious?

- *INFOTRAC ONLINE LIBRARY*
  http://www.infotrac-college.com
   Use your password and then key in search terms such as those below to find popular and scientific articles on subjects covered in Module 7. Make the library work for you!

  | | | |
  |---|---|---|
  | Dreams | Night terrors | Jet lag |
  | Insomnia | REM sleep | Seasonal affective disorder (SAD) |

- *PSYCHNOW!*
  CD for Macintosh and Windows includes a study guide, glossary, Web sites, and animations. For Module 7, see:
  - Sleep and Dreaming

## Study Questions

*Use InfoTrac to search for topics mentioned in the main heads below (e.g., states of consciousness, circadian rhythms, dream analysis).*

*A. **Continuum of Consciousness**—How many different states of consciousness have you been in today? (**Suggested answer page 622**)

B. **Rhythms of Sleeping & Waking**—If an ad promised a device to cure jet lag, what would the device do?

C. **World of Sleep**—How would we know whether astronauts in space were awake, asleep, or dreaming?

*D. **Research Focus: Circadian Preference**—What kind of problems might arise if a morning person married an evening person? (**Suggested answer page 623**)

E. **Questions about Sleep**—If researchers discovered the perfect sleeping pill, how might it work?

*F. **Cultural Diversity: Incidence of SAD**—What cultural values might New Hampshire residents have that contribute to their incidence of SAD? (**Suggested answer page 623**)

G. **World of Dreams**—Which of the four theories most closely matches your personal beliefs about what dreams mean?

H. **Application: Sleep Problems & Treatments**—If you worked in a clinic that treated sleep problems, what kinds of symptoms would your patients have?

*These questions are answered in Appendix B.

# Module 8: Hypnosis & Drugs

**A. Hypnosis**                                       170
  * DEFINITION
  * THEORIES OF HYPNOSIS
  * BEHAVIORS
  * APPLICATIONS

**B. Drugs: Overview**                                174
  * REASONS FOR USE
  * DEFINITION OF TERMS
  * USE OF DRUGS
  * EFFECTS ON NERVOUS SYSTEM

**C. Stimulants**                                     176
  * DEFINITION
  * AMPHETAMINES
  * COCAINE
  * CAFFEINE
  * NICOTINE

**D. Opiates**                                        179
  * OPIUM, MORPHINE, HEROIN
  * TREATMENT

**E. Hallucinogens**                                  180
  * DEFINITION
  * LSD
  * PSILOCYBIN
  * MESCALINE
  * DESIGNER DRUGS

**F. Alcohol**                                        182
  * HISTORY AND USE
  * DEFINITION AND EFFECTS
  * RISK FACTORS
  * PROBLEMS WITH ALCOHOL

**Concept Review**                                    184

**G. Cultural Diversity: Alcoholism Rates**           185
  * DEFINITION AND DIFFERENCES IN RATES

**H. Marijuana**                                      186
  * USE AND EFFECTS

**I. Research Focus: Drug Prevention**                187
  * HOW EFFECTIVE IS THE DARE PROGRAM?

**J. Application: Treatment for Drug Abuse**          188
  * DEVELOPING A PROBLEM
  * SUBSTANCE ABUSE AND TREATMENT

**Summary Test**                                      190

**Critical Thinking**                                 192
  * CAN ALCOHOLICS STOP AFTER TWO DRINKS?

**Links to Learning**                                 193

## Hypnosis

**Why do people do stupid things?**

One night a friend and I were sitting in the front row of one of the longest-running nightclub acts in San Diego. We were going to watch a psychologist-turned-performer who entertained locals and tourists by hypnotizing volunteers from the audience and asking them to perform funny, strange, and somewhat embarrassing acts on a stage. Before the hypnotist appeared, my friend Paul repeated for the tenth time that nothing would get him up on that stage.

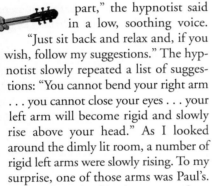

Finally the lights dimmed, and the hypnotist appeared. He was a very good performer and soon had the audience laughing at his jokes and believing that he was a wonderful, trustworthy human being.

"Now we come to the interesting part," the hypnotist said in a low, soothing voice. "Just sit back and relax and, if you wish, follow my suggestions." The hypnotist slowly repeated a list of suggestions: "You cannot bend your right arm . . . you cannot close your eyes . . . your left arm will become rigid and slowly rise above your head." As I looked around the dimly lit room, a number of rigid left arms were slowly rising. To my surprise, one of those arms was Paul's.

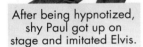

After being hypnotized, shy Paul got up on stage and imitated Elvis.

(I could not or would not raise my arm, for fear that some of my students were in the audience and would never let me forget whatever foolish behavior I might have performed.)

At the end of the show, we all filed out. Paul said nothing until we were in the car. Then he turned and asked, "Why did you let me get on that stage and be hypnotized? You better not tell anyone."

I smiled and replied, "You were terrific. That was the best imitation of Elvis Presley ever done by a reluctant friend." Then I added, "I might have been tempted to try Mick Jagger."

Although I have changed Paul's name and minor details to protect his pride and reputation, his story is essentially true and illustrates some of the strange behaviors that occur under hypnosis.

For over 200 years, psychologists have puzzled over what hypnosis really is and what it does. For example, some believe that hypnosis is a trancelike state in which people will do almost anything that is suggested by a trustworthy hypnotist. Others believe that hypnosis is just another method to induce people to comply with the demands of the situation. We'll discuss whether hypnosis is truly a trancelike state.

Many are interested in how effective hypnosis is in changing attitudes and behaviors, since our local paper carries ads claiming that hypnosis can help you stop smoking, lose weight, get rid of phobias, induce immediate relaxation, reduce pain, or increase motivation to tackle difficult projects. We'll discuss whether these claims for hypnosis are true.

## Drugs

**What was the first bicycle trip?**

While only some psychologists believe that hypnosis may change a person's state of consciousness, most agree that there are a number of drugs, legal and illegal, that can alter consciousness. One example of how a drug greatly altered consciousness happened quite by chance and began with a bike ride.

On April 19, 1943, Albert Hofmann left his laboratory, got on his bike, and began pedaling his regular route home. As Albert pedaled, the world around him began to change into threatening, wavering forms that appeared distorted, as if he was looking into a curved mirror. Once he reached home and entered his house, the familiar objects and pieces of furniture assumed grotesque and threatening forms that were in continual motion. After a while, the threatening forms disappeared, and he began to enjoy an incredible display of visual sensations and illusions. Albert saw fantastic images that opened and closed in circles and spirals that seemed to explode into colored fountains. Even stranger, sounds such as the passing of a car or opening of a door were transformed into visual images with changing forms and colors (adapted from Hofmann, 1983).

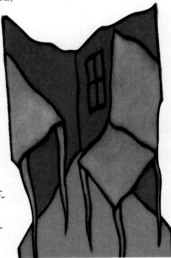

Albert Hofmann tried out his newly discovered drug (LSD) and watched his furniture change into strange shapes.

The cause of Albert Hofmann's startling visual experiences was a drug that Hofmann had previously discovered in his laboratory and had taken before his bike ride. The drug was LSD (*d*-lysergic acid diethylamide) and is now well known to cause strange and bizarre visual experiences, called hallucinations. Because Hofmann had not known about LSD's great potency (compared to other drugs, a very small dose of LSD has a very large effect), he had actually taken a dosage that was four times the usual amount. We will discuss LSD as well as other illegal and legal drugs that can alter consciousness.

## What's Coming

We'll discuss what hypnosis is, how a person is hypnotized, what a person does and does not do under hypnosis, and the uses of hypnosis. We'll examine the use and abuse of both legal and illegal drugs, such as stimulants, hallucinogens, opiates, marijuana, and alcohol. We'll discuss how drugs affect the nervous system, their dangers, and the treatments for drug abuse.

Let's begin with an interesting and supposedly mind-altering force called animal magnetism.

### Definition

#### What is hypnosis?

In the late 1700s, Anton Mesmer was the hit of Paris, France, as he claimed to cure a variety of symptoms by passing a force into a patient's body; he called this force animal magnetism. So many patients testified to the success of animal magnetism as a treatment that a committee of the French Academy of Science was appointed to investigate. The committee concluded that many of Mesmer's patients were indeed cured of various psychosomatic problems. However, the committee thought it safer to ban the future use of animal magnetism because they could neither identify what it was nor verify Mesmer's claims that such a force existed. Mesmer's name lives on in our vocabulary: We use the term *mesmerized* to describe someone who is acting strangely because he or she has been spellbound or hypnotized.

Today we know that Mesmer was not creating animal magnetism but rather was inducing hypnosis. Here's the definition agreed to by the American Psychological Association's Division of Psychological Hypnosis (1993):

*Hypnosis* is a procedure in which a researcher, clinician, or hypnotist suggests that a person will experience changes in sensations, perceptions, thoughts, feelings, or behaviors.

We'll begin by answering three questions that are often asked about hypnosis.

### Who Can Be Hypnotized?

Despite what you may have seen on television or at a stage show, not everyone can be easily hypnotized.

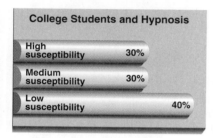

**College Students and Hypnosis**

| | |
|---|---|
| High susceptibility | 30% |
| Medium susceptibility | 30% |
| Low susceptibility | 40% |

As shown in the graph above, about 40% of college students have low susceptibility to hypnosis, which means that they cannot be easily hypnotized. About 30% of college students have medium susceptibility, and the remaining 30% have high susceptibility to being hypnotized (Bates, 1994).

Hypnotic susceptibility is not correlated with introversion, extraversion, social position, intelligence, willpower, sex, compliance, or gullibility (Kirsch & Lynn, 1995). Researchers found that people more responsive to being hypnotized fully expect to cooperate and imagine what is suggested or have a long history of engaging in vivid fantasies (Barber, 2000). Being hypnotized is something subjects do to themselves, as in responding to suggestions, rather than being under the power of a hypnotist. There are several ways to test for susceptibility to hypnosis.

### Who Is Susceptible?

The standard test for susceptibility is to hypnotize a person and then give a fixed set of suggestions (Barber, 2000). The best-known test is the Stanford Hypnotic Susceptibility Scale, which asks the individual to carry out both simple suggestions—for example, "Your arm is moving up"—and complex suggestions—for example, "Your body is heavy and you cannot stand up."

For instance, the person in the photo below is carrying out the hypnotic suggestion, "Your right arm is weightless and moving up."

Test how hypnotizable a person is by suggesting that the person's arm is rising.

Individuals who score high on the Stanford scale are usually easily hypnotized and tend to remain so across time. Compared to adults, young children, especially ages 8–12, are more susceptible to hypnosis (Bates, 1994).

Next let's see how a person is actually hypnotized.

### How Is Someone Hypnotized?

Although a number of different procedures are used, most use some of the following suggestions to induce hypnosis.

*Hypnotic induction* refers to various methods to induce hypnosis, including asking subjects to close their eyes and go to sleep, having them fix their attention on an object (such as a watch), and instructing them to go into deep relaxation.

For example, here is a commonly used method to induce hypnosis:

1. The hypnotist establishes a sense of trust, so that the subject feels comfortable in the situation.

2. The hypnotist suggests that the subject concentrate on something, such as the sound of the hypnotist's voice, an object, or an image.

Inducing hypnosis involves 3 steps.

3. The hypnotist suggests what the subject will experience during hypnosis—for example, becoming relaxed, feeling sleepy, or having a floating feeling. The hypnotist may say, "I am going to count from one to ten, and with each count you will drift more and more deeply into hypnosis" (Bates, 1994).

This procedure works on both individuals and groups, provided the individuals are all susceptible to hypnosis.

During hypnosis, subjects are affected by several powerful forces, such as the subject's desire to cooperate and respond to the hypnotist's suggestions and the hypnotist's personal skills in communicating, establishing trust, and guiding subjects to follow suggestions (Barber, 2000). During hypnosis, subjects are not asleep, retain their ability to control their behaviors, and are aware of their surroundings. Hypnosis is not a dangerous procedure when used by an experienced researcher or clinician, and hypnosis has useful medical and therapeutic benefits (Kirsch, 2000). What happens when a person is under hypnosis and why hypnosis works are our next questions.

**Why does hypnosis work?**

Explanations of hypnosis have changed significantly over the past 30 years. In the 1960s and 1970s, there were primarily two views. One view held that hypnosis was a trancelike state during which a person was more likely to carry out suggestions. The other view disagreed and held that hypnosis was not a trancelike state. After years of debate, the two views have edged more close together and dropped the idea of a trancelike state. Currently, the explanation for hypnosis can best be thought of as on a continuum, which ranges from those who hold that hypnosis is an altered state (but not a trancelike state) to those who believe that hypnosis is not an altered state but results from a combination of social pressures and personal abilities (Kirsch & Lynn, 1995). We'll discuss both ends of the continuum and their explanations for why my shy friend got the nerve to get up on stage and imitate Elvis Presley.

## *Altered State Theory of Hypnosis*

On one side of the hypnosis continuum are researchers and clinicians who view hypnosis as an altered state (Kirsch & Lynn, 1998).

The *altered state theory of hypnosis* holds that hypnosis is not a trancelike state but rather an altered state of consciousness, during which a person experiences different sensations and feelings.

Although this is currently a popular view, followers of Milton Erickson (1980/1941), who was generally recognized to be the world's leading practitioner of medical hypnosis, hold to the belief that hypnosis puts clients into a trancelike state in which their conscious limitations are partially suspended, so that they can be receptive to alternative ways of thinking and behaving. Thus, at this end of the hypnosis continuum, the most extreme view, which is held by followers of Erickson, is that hypnosis is an altered state that is also a trancelike state; the more popular, moderate view is that hypnosis is an altered state in the same way that daydreaming is an altered state, but it is not a trancelike state (Kirsch & Lynn, 1995).

**Altered state.** To explain how hypnosis might produce an altered state, psychologist Ernest Hilgard (1977) has developed the hidden observer concept. So that you can experience the hidden observer phenomenon, we'll place you in a hypnotic experiment.

Imagine being hypnotized and told that your consciousness is divided into two parts. Your hypnotized part will feel little or no pain and can answer questions orally. Your unhypnotized part will feel normal pain sensations; it cannot answer questions orally but can answer by tapping your finger—once for yes and twice for no. Now the hypnotist asks you to plunge one hand into ice water, which is painful but not injurious, with the suggestion that you will not feel pain. When asked, "Do you feel pain?" the voice controlled by your hypnotized part answers "No." But the finger controlled by your unhypnotized, hidden part taps once, indicating "Yes" (Hilgard, 1979). Findings from such experiments support the idea that hypnosis produces an altered state in which consciousness is divided into two parts. One part of the altered state is the conscious self, which can answer questions verbally and seems to be in control. Another part of the altered state, of which the conscious self is totally unaware, is the hidden observer, which can also respond to questions in nonverbal ways, such as by finger tapping.

However, the idea of hypnosis producing an altered state has been challenged by the sociocognitive theory of hypnosis.

The altered state theory says that Paul is imitating Elvis because he's in an altered state. The sociocognitive theory says Paul is responding to social influences and pressures.

## *Sociocognitive Theory of Hypnosis*

On the other side of the hypnosis continuum are researchers who currently reject the idea that hypnosis is an altered or trancelike state and propose instead the sociocognitive theory of hypnosis (Kirsch, 2000).

The *sociocognitive theory of hypnosis* says that the impressive effects of hypnosis are due to social influences and pressures as well as the subject's personal abilities.

One strong proponent of this theory is psychologist Irving Kirsch, who has published more than 75 articles on hypnosis. Kirsch and other researchers have rejected the trance or altered state theory of hypnosis for three reasons. First, in spite of 30 years of research, no behavioral, physiological, or neurological measures have been found that distinguish hypnosis from other states of consciousness (Ray, 1997). Second, all the phenomena produced by suggestions during hypnosis, such as going back to an early age or imagining and behaving in strange ways, have also been produced by subjects who are not hypnotized. Third, the markedly increased suggestibility observed during hypnosis has been duplicated and even surpassed through other procedures, such as placebo pills and imagination training (Kirsch, 2000).

For these reasons, Kirsch (2000) rejects the idea that hypnosis produces an out-of-the-ordinary, trancelike, "altered state" of consciousness. Instead, Kirsch concludes that what happens during hypnosis is NOT because the hypnotist has some power or force to put the subject into an altered state of consciousness or bring out a hidden observer. Rather, what happens during hypnosis is because of what the SUBJECT is doing to him- or herself, such as believing, imagining, trusting, expecting, and being willing to carry out suggestions made by the hypnotist. Thus, at one end of the hypnosis continuum is the altered state idea of Hilgard and at the other is the sociocognitive theory of Kirsch and others (Kirsch, 2000; Kirsch & Lynn, 1998).

**Explaining Paul's behaviors.** We can now return to our earlier question of why shy Paul got up on a public stage and imitated Elvis Presley. According to the altered state end of the hypnosis continuum, Paul got on stage and imitated Elvis Presley's gyrations and guitar-playing because he was in an altered state of consciousness (Erickson's followers would say that he was in a trancelike state), during which he was especially likely to carry out the hypnotist's suggestions. At the other end of the hypnosis continuum, sociocognitive researchers would say that Paul was motivated to get up on stage and act like Elvis because Paul felt social pressures from the audience and also because Paul wanted to please the hypnotist by following the suggestions. Although why hypnosis works has different explanations, many clinicians agree that hypnosis has proved useful in a number of treatments and therapeutic settings.

### Behaviors

**How do people behave under hypnosis?**

You have perhaps seen movies of people doing strange things, such as pretending they are chickens, after being hypnotized. However, as we describe the behaviors of people under hypnosis, keep in mind that these very same behaviors have also been performed by people who were asked to perform them without being hypnotized (Kirsch, 2000; Spanos, 1996). Thus, people who have the abilities may perform strange or unusual behaviors whether or not they are hypnotized.

#### Hypnotic Analgesia

Hypnosis has long been known to reduce pain; this is called hypnotic analgesia.

*Hypnotic analgesia (an-nall-GEEZ-ee-ah)* refers to a reduction in pain reported by clients after they had undergone hypnosis and received suggestions that reduced their anxiety and promoted relaxation.

Researchers used PET scans to show that hypnosis reduced the subjects' unpleasant feelings of pain though not the sensations of pain (Rainville et al., 1997). This means that when subjects put their hands into hot water they felt pain as usual but, depending on the hypnotic suggestions, reported it as either more or less unpleasant. Hypnotic analgesia proved useful in helping patients cope with painful medical or dental treatments (Montgomery et al., 2000).

#### Posthypnotic Suggestion

If subjects perform some behavior on cue after hypnosis, it's called a posthypnotic suggestion.

A *posthypnotic suggestion* is given to the subject during hypnosis about performing a particular behavior to a specific cue when the subject comes out of hypnosis.

Some believe that subjects who follow posthypnotic suggestions are acting automatically in response to some predetermined cue, such as smiling when they hear the word *student*. However, researchers have shown that subjects perform posthypnotic suggestions if they believe it is expected of them but stop performing if they believe the experiment is over or they are no longer being observed (Spanos, 1996).

#### Posthypnotic Amnesia

"When you wake up, you will not remember what happened." This suggestion is used to produce posthypnotic amnesia.

*Posthypnotic amnesia* is not remembering what happened during hypnosis if the hypnotist suggested that, upon awakening, the person would forget what took place during hypnosis.

One explanation is that the person forgets because the experiences have been repressed and made unavailable to normal consciousness. However, there is good evidence that, after they come out of hypnosis, what people remember or forget depends on what they think or believe the hypnotist wants them to remember or forget (Spanos, 1996).

#### Age Regression

Could the 31-year-old woman shown at the left be hypnotized and sent back to being the 3-year-old child shown below? This phenomenon is called age regression.

*Age regression* refers to subjects under hypnosis being asked to regress, or return in time, to an earlier age, such as early childhood.

Researchers have found that during age regression, hypnotized subjects do not relive their earlier experiences as some believe but rather play the role of being a child. After an exhaustive review of more than 100 years of hypnosis research on age regression, one researcher concluded that there was no evidence that adults actually went back or regressed in time (Kirsch et al., 1993). Thus, researchers believe that, during age regression, hypnotized adults are not reliving childhood experiences but merely acting as they expect children to behave (Spanos, 1996).

#### Imagined Perception

When a hypnotized subject responds to a suggestion such as "Try to swat that fly," it is called an imagined perception.

An *imagined perception* refers to experiencing sensations, perceiving stimuli, or performing behaviors that come from one's imagination.

Hypnotherapists use many forms of imagined perceptions in treating clients' problems. For example, one client imagined he was an armored knight on a great horse. After several therapy sessions, the therapist asked the client to remove the armor and discover his true self, which turned out to be a person afraid of his flaws (Eisen, 1994).

#### Conclusions

Researchers agree that most hypnotized subjects are not merely faking their responses to the hypnotist's suggestions. For example, in response to a hypnotist's suggestions, people really report being in a special state of consciousness, experience decreases in perceived pain, lose selective memory, and perform or inhibit a variety of movements (Kirsch, 2000). What researchers disagree on is whether behaviors performed and experienced under hypnosis occur because subjects are in an altered state or instead are responding to the requests of a legitimate and trusted authority figure (the hypnotist) in the same way that most of us would respond to the requests of authority figures in everyday life (Kirsch, 2000; Spanos, 1996).

Next, we'll examine some of the uses of hypnosis.

## Medical and Therapeutic Applications

You have probably seen hypnosis used in entertainment, such as when people in the audience volunteer to come up on stage and be hypnotized and then perform unusual and often funny behaviors, such as Paul's wild imitation of Elvis.

However, there are also serious and legitimate uses of hypnosis in medical, dental, therapeutic, and behavioral settings. For example, the woman in the photo below is undergoing hypnosis before a potentially painful dental treatment. Here are some of the medical, dental, therapeutic and behavioral uses of hypnosis.

### Medical and Dental Uses

In both medical and dental settings, hypnosis can be used to reduce pain through hypnotic analgesia, to reduce fear and anxiety by helping individuals relax, or to help patients deal with a terminal disease by motivating them to make the best of a difficult situation (Pinnell & Covino, 2000). However, there is considerable evidence that clients who are highly susceptible to hypnosis are better able to respond to suggestions for pain reduction and body relaxation than are low-susceptibility clients (Bates, 1994).

For example, the graph below shows that subjects who were highly susceptible to hypnosis reported significantly lower levels of pain during hypnosis than did poorly susceptible subjects (Crawford et al., 1993). Pain was produced by putting a

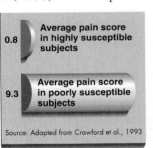

tourniquet, or binding, around the arm, which temporarily cuts off the blood supply and results in considerable pain. Researchers have only recently discovered what happens in the brains of subjects during hypnotic analgesia.

**0.8** — Average pain score in highly susceptible subjects

**9.3** — Average pain score in poorly susceptible subjects

Source: Adapted from Crawford et al., 1993

**Brain scans.** Researchers used PET scans (p. 71) to measure activity in different parts of the brain after subjects were hypnotized and told to place their hands in lukewarm (95°F) or "painfully hot" (115°F) water. Hypnotic suggestions to think of pain as *more unpleasant* (more painful) resulted in *decreased* brain activity in the frontal lobe (anterior cingulate cortex), while hypnotic suggestions to think of pain as *less unpleasant* (less painful) resulted in *increased* brain activity in the same area. In comparison, hypnotic instructions that pain was more or less unpleasant did not increase or decrease brain activity in the parietal lobe (somatosensory cortex), which indicates the reception of pain sensations (Rainville et al., 1997). Researchers concluded that hypnotic suggestions can change a person's *perception* of pain as more or less unpleasant, but hypnotic suggestions do not affect *receiving* pain sensations. This means that during hypnotic analgesia, subjects feel pain, but how much it bothers them depends on whether hypnotic suggestions are to think of pain as being more or less unpleasant. That is, the hypnotized subjects' thoughts or expectations actually change their perceptions of pain.

Client is hypnotized before painful dental work.

### Therapeutic and Behavioral Uses

Hypnosis has been used in therapy for the past 100 years. In the early 1900s, Sigmund Freud (1905) used hypnosis with his patients. More recently, Milton Erickson (1980/1941), who is generally acknowledged to be the world's leading practitioner of therapeutic hypnosis, said that hypnosis made clients more open and receptive to alternative ways of problem solving. However, hypnosis is not for all clients; some people find hypnosis frightening because they fear losing control or because they believe it indicates a lack of willpower (Kirsch, 1994).

Therapists who often use hypnosis along with other techniques generally report that it is very useful in helping clients reveal their personalities, gain insights into their lives, and arrive at solutions to their problems. Research on hypnotherapy indicates that hypnosis can be a powerful tool that leads to successful outcomes when used in therapeutic settings (Schoenberger, 2000).

Clients who are highly susceptible to hypnosis generally respond better to suggestions aimed at treating a wide range of psychosomatic problems, which involve mind-body interactions. For example, hypnosis has been successfully used to reduce pain, decrease asthma attacks, remove warts, and relieve tension. But hypnosis is not as successful with problems of self-control, such as helping clients quit smoking, stop overeating, stop excessive drinking, or overcome other habits that interfere with optimal functioning (Bates, 1994).

The graph below shows the percentage of subjects who continued to smoke after receiving three different treatment programs. Notice that after

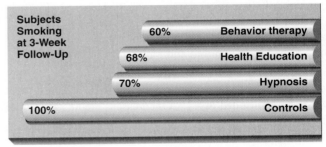

| Subjects Smoking at 3-Week Follow-Up | | |
|---|---|---|
| 60% | Behavior therapy |
| 68% | Health Education |
| 70% | Hypnosis |
| 100% | Controls |

three weeks of treatment, hypnosis was not statistically more significant in motivating people to stop smoking than was health education or behavior modification. From these results, we can conclude that all three programs were about equally effective and significantly better than controls (no treatment program) (Rabkin et al., 1984). Clinicians generally conclude that hypnosis by itself is not a miracle treatment but can be a useful technique when combined with other procedures (Lynn et al., 2000).

Although helpful in a therapeutic setting, evidence obtained under hypnosis is not allowed in most United States courts. That's because an examiner's questions or suggestions may bias or mislead a hypnotized witness into agreeing to something that was suggested but did not happen. Generally, hypnotized witnesses give unreliable testimony (Perry, 1997).

Next, we'll discuss the use, abuse, and effects of drugs.

### Reasons for Use

**Why do people use drugs?**

For the past 6,000 years, humans have used legal and illegal drugs, and current usage continues to increase as do drug-related problems (Glantz & Hartel, 1999). For example, Americans spend about $140 billion a year on legal and illegal drugs, and the resulting problems—personal, medical, legal, and job related—cost society about $71 billion a year (Schuckit, 2000).

The reasons people use drugs include obtaining pleasure, joy, and euphoria; meeting social expectations; giving in to peer pressure; dealing with or escaping stress, anxiety, and tension; avoiding pain; and achieving altered states of consciousness (Glantz & Hartel, 1999).

One researcher, reviewing 200 years of drug use in the United States, concluded that we have gone through regular cycles of tolerant and intolerant attitudes toward drug usage. Because history

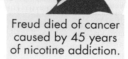

Americans spend $140 billion annually on drugs.

tends to repeat itself, the researcher warns that our society will continue to face various physical and psychological problems related to drugs (Musto, 1999).

In what follows, we'll discuss stimulants, hallucinogens, opiates, alcohol, marijuana, and other commonly used psychoactive drugs.

*Psychoactive drugs* are chemicals that affect our nervous systems and, as a result, may alter consciousness and awareness, influence how we sense and perceive things, and modify our moods, feelings, emotions, and thoughts. Psychoactive drugs are both licit (legal)—coffee, alcohol, and tobacco—and illicit (illegal)—marijuana, heroin, cocaine, and LSD.

Although all psychoactive drugs affect our nervous systems, how they affect our behaviors depends on our psychological state and other social factors, such as peer pressure and society's values. To illustrate how drug usage involves both pharmacological and psychological factors, we describe a famous person who had a serious drug problem.

### Definition of Terms

**What famous therapist had a drug problem?**

When this famous person was 38, his doctor told him to stop smoking because it was causing irregular heart beats. Although he tried to cut down, he was soon back to smoking his usual 20 cigars a day. When his heart problems grew worse, he stopped again. However, he experienced such terrible depression and mood swings that he started smoking to escape the psychological torture. When he was 67, small sores were discovered in his mouth and diagnosed as cancer. During the next 16 years, he had 33 operations on his mouth and jaw for cancer but continued smoking. By age 79, most of his jaw had been removed and replaced by an artificial one.

Freud died of cancer caused by 45 years of nicotine addiction.

He was in continual pain and was barely able to swallow or talk. However, he continued to smoke an endless series of cigars. In 1939, at age 83, he died of cancer caused by 45 years of heavy smoking (Brecher, 1972; Jones, 1953).

Our famous person is none other than Sigmund Freud, the father of psychoanalysis. Freud had a serious drug problem most of his professional life—he was addicted to tobacco (nicotine). In spite of his great insights into the problems of others, he tried but could not treat his own drug addiction. Freud's struggle with smoking illustrates four important terms related to drug use and abuse—addicton, tolerance, dependency, and withdrawal symptoms (American Psychiatric Association, 1994).

#### Addiction

One reason Freud continued to smoke despite a heart condition was that he had an addiction.

*Addiction* means a person has developed a behavioral pattern of drug abuse that is marked by an overwhelming and compulsive desire to obtain and use the drug; even after stopping, the person has a strong tendency to relapse and begin using the drug again.

The reason Freud relapsed each time he tried to give up smoking was that he was addicted to nicotine.

#### Tolerance

One reason Freud smoked as many as 20 cigars daily was that he had developed a tolerance to nicotine.

*Tolerance* means that after a person uses a drug repeatedly over a period of time, the original dose of the drug no longer produces the desired effect so that a person must take increasingly larger doses of the drug to achieve the same behavioral effect.

Becoming tolerant was a sign that Freud had become dependent on nicotine.

#### Dependency

Another reason Freud found it difficult to quit smoking was that he had developed a dependency on nicotine.

*Dependency* refers to a change in the nervous system so that a person now needs to take the drug to prevent the occurrence of painful withdrawal symptoms.

Addiction and dependency combine to make stopping doubly difficult.

#### Withdrawal Symptoms

Being dependent on nicotine, Freud had withdrawal symptoms when he stopped smoking.

*Withdrawal symptoms* are painful physical and psychological symptoms that occur after a drug-dependent person stops using the drug.

Freud described his withdrawal symptoms as being depressed, having images of dying, and feeling so tortured that it was beyond his human power to bear (Jones, 1953).

Next we'll examine a number of specific drugs that people use.

## Use of Drugs

### Which drugs do people use?

The graph on the right shows that legal and illegal drugs are widely used in the United States. People spend about $91 billion yearly on legal drugs and about $50 billion on illegal drugs (Hanson & Venturelli, 1998). About 14 million people in the United States use illegal drugs monthly.

For the past 25 years, the United States has waged a "drug war" to control the widespread use of illegal drugs. Costs of fighting the drug war were about $19 billion in 2000, with 65% spent on law enforcement and 35% on treatment. About every 20 seconds, someone in the United States is arrested for a drug violation (Egan, 1999b). Although the bulk of drug war money goes for law enforcement, a General Accounting Office study concluded that even though drug agents seized 100 tons of cocaine in 1996, such efforts ". . . have not materially reduced the availability of drugs" (Darling, 1997). For this reason, many health professionals recommend that a better way to reduce illegal drug use is to spend more money on drug

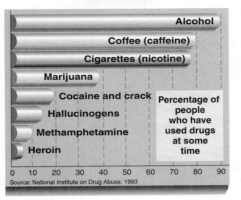

Percentage of people who have used drugs at some time

Source: National Institute on Drug Abuse, 1993

education, counseling, and treatment (Glantz & Hartel, 1999). In support of this recommendation, researchers found that drug treatment programs are more cost-effective than imprisonment (Egan, 1999a).

The cost of the war on illegal drugs and its relative ineffectiveness (illegal drugs continue to be widely available in most major cities) have prompted doctors, federal judges, and political writers to propose controlling illegal drugs either by legalization, which means illegal drugs can be used but with age restrictions, or by decriminalization, which means drugs remain illegal but removing criminal penalties and substituting fines (Nadelmann, 2000). However, no one can predict what effect drug legalization or decriminalization would have on the usage or related personal and social problems in a country as large as the United States (Schuckit, 2000).

Legal and illegal psychoactive drugs alter one's consciousness, emotional state, and thought processes by changing or interfering with the nervous system's chemical keys and locks.

## Effects on Nervous System

### How do drugs work?

You may remember from Module 3 that the nervous system communicates by using chemical messengers called neurotransmitters. You can think of neurotransmitters as acting like chemical keys that open or close chemical locks on neighboring neurons (right figure). Many drugs act by opening or closing chemical locks, which in turn results in increased or decreased neural activity. However, how drugs affect each person's nervous system partly involves genetic fac-

Neurotransmitters act like specific chemical keys.

Neurotransmitters' keys open or close chemical locks that increase or decrease neural activity.

tors. For example, researchers found that identical twins, who share 100% of their genes, were much more similar in their use and abuse of drugs than fraternal twins, who share only 50% of their genes (Kendler et al., 2000). This means that genetic factors influence the development and functioning of the nervous system, which in turn can increase or decrease the risk of a person using and abusing drugs. We'll discuss two ways that drugs affect the nervous system and change a person's psychological and physiological responses.

### 1 Drugs Mimic Neurotransmitters

Morphine and heroin are so similar to other neurotransmitters (endorphins) that they mimic or open the same chemical locks.

Your nervous system makes several dozen neurotransmitters as well as other chemicals (neuromodulators) that act like chemical messengers. After neurons release neurotransmitters, they act like chemical keys that search for and then either open or close chemical locks to either excite or inhibit neighboring neurons, organs, or muscles (right figure).

However, some drugs act like chemical keys that are so similar to neurotransmitters that these drugs can affect the same chemical locks. For example, morphine's chemical structure closely resembles that of the neurotransmitter endorphin. As a result of this similarity, morphine acts like, or mimics, the action of endorphin by affecting the same chemical locks, which decreases pain. Thus, some drugs produce their effects by mimicking the actions of neurotransmitters (Stahl, 2000).

### 2 Drugs Block Removal of Neurotransmitters

When excited, neurons secrete neurotransmitters, which move across a tiny space (synapse) and affect neighboring neurons' receptors (bottom figure). However, after a brief period, the neurotransmitters are reabsorbed back into the neuron. The action by which neurotransmitters are removed from the synapse through reabsorption is called **reuptake.** If reuptake did not occur, neurotransmitters would remain in the synapse, and neurons would be continually stimulated.

Drug blocks reuptake

Neurotransmitters

Some drugs, such as cocaine, block reuptake, which leads to increased neural stimulation that, in turn, causes increased physiological and psychological arousal (Stahl, 2000).

Next we'll look more closely at some of the more frequently used drugs.

# C. Stimulants

## Definition

### What are stimulants?

"Two pills beat a month's vacation." This marketing slogan was used to sell amphetamines in Sweden in the 1940s. It resulted in epidemic usage that peaked in the mid-1960s.

In the 1940s, American doctors prescribed amphetamines as safe energizers, mood enhancers, and appetite suppressors. By the 1960s, billions of doses of amphetamines were being used in the United States and their usage had become a serious problem.

In the 1940s, Japanese workers used amphetamines to keep factory production high during World War II. After the war, many students, night workers, and people displaced by the war began to use "wake-amines." Amphetamine use spread until, in 1954, 2 million Japanese had become abusers and addicts.

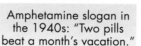

Amphetamine slogan in the 1940s: "Two pills beat a month's vacation."

By the early 1970s, most countries had brought amphetamine usage under control through a combination of measures, including regulation of prescriptions, decrease in supply, and stiffer penalties. However, at present, amphetamine-like stimulants, such as methamphetamine (crystal) and cocaine, are widely available on the black market.

All *stimulants,* including cocaine, amphetamines, caffeine, and nicotine, increase activity of the central nervous system and result in heightened alertness, arousal, euphoria, and decreased appetite and fatigue.

Dose for dose, cocaine and amphetamines are considered powerful stimulants because they produce a strong effect with a small dose; caffeine and nicotine are considered mild stimulants.

We'll discuss the more widely used stimulants—amphetamines, cocaine, caffeine, and nicotine.

## Amphetamines

### Is it still a problem?

During the 1960s, amphetamine pills were heavily prescribed to treat a wide range of problems, including fatigue, depression, and being overweight. This was also the time that young adults, called "flower children," took heavy doses of amphetamines that resulted in their having true paranoid psychotic symptoms, which resulted in their being called "speed freaks." Amphetamine usage peaked in the mid-1960s, when over 31 million prescriptions were written for dieting and about 25 tons of legitimately manufactured amphetamines were diverted to illegal sales (Hanson & Venturelli, 1998). Finally, in 1971, the Food and Drug Administration (FDA) outlawed the prescription of amphetamines for everything except attention-deficit/hyperactivity disorder (ADHD) (p. 39) and narcolepsy (p. 163).

Following a "drug war" on cocaine in the late 1980s, there was a dramatic increase in using a form of amphetamine called methamphetamine, which is manufactured in illegal home laboratories. The use of methamphetamine is spreading in the United States and worldwide. For example, methamphetamine has now become the most popular illegal drug in Japan (Magnier, 2000). In many countries, the possession or use of methamphetamine is illegal.

### Drug

In 1996, authorities raided over 800 illegal methamphetamine laboratories in California and 450 in the Midwest, where the drug has increased in popularity (Howlett, 1997).

*Methamphetamine* (D-methamphetamine) is close to amphetamine in both its chemical makeup and its physical and psychological effects. Unlike amphetamine, which is taken in pill form, methamphetamine (speed, crank, crystal, ice) can be smoked or snorted and produces an almost instantaneous high. Both amphetamine and methamphetamine cause marked increases in blood pressure and heart rate and feelings of enhanced mood, alertness, and energy.

"It's the ultimate high. . . . It makes you feel so powerful. You have tons of energy. . . . I loved it. I craved it" (Witkin, 1995, p. 50). So said 23-year-old Tara, who developed a $200-a-day habit and lost her apartment, job, and infant daughter. Her euphoria from methamphetamine soon turned into a terrible nightmare.

### Nervous System

The primary effect of amphetamines and related drugs (methamphetamine) is to increase the release of the neurotransmitter dopamine and also to block its reuptake (Stahl, 2000). Researchers are learning that the release of dopamine occurs during a wide range of pleasurable activities, such as sex (Schuster, 1997). Thus, drugs like methamphetamine are both desirable and dangerous because they increase the release of dopamine, which causes very pleasurable feelings.

### Dangers

"I couldn't get high. No matter how much I did, no matter who I was with, nothing made me happy. I was so depressed. I wanted to die," said 23-year-old Tara, who was a heavy methamphetamine user (Witkin, 1995, p. 50). At first, users of methamphetamine or ice (a concentrated form) have periods of restless activity and perform repetitive behaviors. Later, the initial euphoria is replaced with depression, agitation, insomnia, and development of true paranoid feelings. Because of its risk for addiction and dependency, as well as physical and psychological problems, methamphetamine/ice is a very dangerous drug.

Because of a crackdown on amphetamines in the 1970s, there was an enormous increase in cocaine usage, which we'll discuss next.

## Cocaine

**Why has it been
used for
3,000 years?**

A drug's increase in popularity is partly due to the particular drug that enforcement agencies target for a crackdown. For example, the U.S. government's crackdown on amphetamine usage in the 1970s was largely responsible for the increased popularity of cocaine, whose usage reached epidemic proportions in the 1980s. In turn, the 1980s were marked by the government's "war" on cocaine, which was partly responsible for an upsurge in methamphetamine usage in the 1990s.

However, despite federal efforts, government studies indicate that cocaine is still widely available (right figure) and officials estimate that the market for illegal cocaine is currently about $38 billion a year (Darling, 1997). About 80% of the cocaine smuggled into the United States comes from Colombia, whose exports of cocaine total about $16 billion, compared to the total for all of its other imports of $11 billion (McGirk, 1999). Cocaine has such a long history of usage that continues into the present because it's a very powerful stimulant that produces euphoria (happiness) and increased energy.

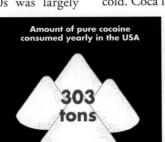

Amount of pure cocaine consumed yearly in the USA

**303 tons**

Americans spend about $38 BILLION annually on cocaine.

For 3,000 years, the ancient Incas and their descendants, the indigenous Andean people of Peru, have chewed coca leaves as they made demanding journeys through the high mountains. Some minutes after chewing the leaves, which contain cocaine, they reported feeling more vigor and strength and less fatigue, hunger, thirst, and cold. Coca leaves contain very little cocaine and produce stimulation equivalent to that experienced by coffee (caffeine) drinkers (McCarry, 1996). Few psychological or physical problems are observed in those who chew coca leaves, partly because they consume very little cocaine and because this activity is part of their culture. However, many problems have been observed among natives who have switched from coca leaves to more concentrated cocaine powder (Siegel, 1989).

In the United States, about 1.5 million people use powder cocaine monthly, 600,000 use a more concentrated version called crack, and 640,000 experience problems with cocaine usage (Egan, 1999b). Supporting a cocaine habit is estimated to cost between $500 and $1,800 per month. Since the cocaine epidemic of the late 1980s, usage of cocaine is reportedly down by 10–35%. However, cocaine remains the nonalcoholic drug of abuse in ten major cities (Sanchez-Ramos, 1993). The possession or use of cocaine is illegal.

| *Drug* | *Nervous System* | *Dangers* |
|---|---|---|

**Drug**

Cocaine can be sniffed or snorted, since it is absorbed by many of the body's membranes. If cocaine is changed into a highly concentrated form, which is called *crack,* it can be smoked or injected and produces an instantaneous but short-lived high.

*Cocaine,* which comes from the leaves of the coca plant, has physiological and behavioral effects very similar to amphetamine. Like amphetamine, cocaine produces increased heart rate and blood pressure, enhanced mood, alertness, increased activity, decreased appetite, and diminished fatigue. With higher doses, cocaine can produce anxiety, emotional instability, and suspiciousness.

When humans or monkeys have unlimited access to pure cocaine, they will use it continually, to the point of starvation and death. Only extreme shock will reduce an addicted monkey's use of cocaine, and only extreme problems involving health, legal, or personal difficulties will reduce an addicted human's intake.

**Nervous System**

Researchers have recently found that the primary effect of cocaine is to block reuptake of the neurotransmitter dopamine, which means that dopamine stays around longer to excite neighboring neurons (Stahl, 2000).

Researchers also found that cocaine excites one kind of neural receptor (dopamine) to produce pleasure/euphoria and another kind of receptor (glutamate) to produce a craving for more of the drug (Karler, 1998). Like amphetamine, cocaine results in increased physiological and psychological arousal.

When applied to an external area of the body, cocaine can block the conduction of nerve impulses. For this reason, cocaine is classified as a local anesthetic and that is its only legal usage.

**Dangers**

In *moderate doses,* cocaine produces a short-acting high (10–30 minutes) that includes bursts of energy, arousal, and alertness. Users tend to believe that they are thinking more clearly and performing better, but, in fact, they overestimate the quality of their work. In *heavy doses,* cocaine can result in serious physical and psychological problems, which may include hallucinations and feelings of bugs crawling under the skin.

Physical problems associated with cocaine abuse can include lack of appetite, insomnia, irritation, and damage to cartilage of the nose (if snorted). Sudden death, which may result from relatively low dosages, is due to respiratory failure. Heavy usage is now known to cause physical addiction (Hammer et al., 1997). Recently, cocaine was found to be one of the strongest triggers for having a heart attack (Mittleman, 1999).

Cocaine users often go through a vicious circle. As cocaine's effects wear off, the user experiences depression, fatigue, and an intense craving for more cocaine, which causes the user to seek another dose. Taking another dose is followed by depression and craving for more, which continues the vicious circle. Heavy users often require professional help to break out of this destructive pattern (Leshner, 1997).

Next we turn to two legal drugs that are the most widely used stimulants—caffeine and nicotine.

# C. Stimulants

## Caffeine

**What's the most widely used drug in the world?**

Caffeine, which has been used for the past 2,000 years, is the most widely used psychoactive drug in the world (Nehlig, 1999). One 8-ounce cup of regular coffee, two cups of regular tea, one No-Doz tablet, two diet colas, or four regular-sized chocolate bars all contain about 100 milligrams of caffeine. In the United States, the average amount of caffeine consumed is 280 milligrams per person per day, compared to 400 milligrams in Sweden and England.

### Drug

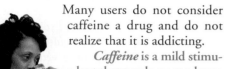

Many users do not consider caffeine a drug and do not realize that it is addicting.

*Caffeine* is a mild stimulant that produces moderate physiological arousal. The psychological effects include a feeling of alertness, decreased fatigue and drowsiness, and improved reaction times.

Both moderate doses (200–400 milligrams or 2–4 cups of coffee per day) and especially heavy doses (500–800 milligrams or five or more cups of coffee per day) result in addiction (Nehlig, 1999).

### Nervous System

Caffeine belongs to a group of chemicals called xanthines *(ZAN-thenes),* which have a number of effects. One effect is to block certain receptors (adenosine receptors) in the brain, which results in stimulation and mild physiological and psychological arousal (Stahl, 2000).

### Dangers

Researchers found that mild to heavy doses of caffeine (125–800 milligrams) can result in addiction and dependency similar to that produced by alcohol, nicotine, and cocaine (Strain et al., 1994). Higher doses of caffeine (300–1,000 milligrams) can result in feelings of depression, tension, and anxiety (DeAngelis, 1994).

Abruptly stopping the consumption of caffeine, especially medium to heavy doses, usually results in a significant number of uncomfortable withdrawal symptoms, such as increased headaches, irritability, fatigue, intense craving for caffeine, and decreased energy (Schuh & Griffiths, 1997). These symptoms usually disappear within 5–7 days. Obviously, caffeine is a real drug.

## Nicotine

**What causes the most deaths?**

After caffeine, nicotine is the world's most widely used psychoactive drug. In the United States, adult smoking declined from 42% in 1965 to 25% in 1997, but teenage smoking increased from 27% in 1991 to 36% in 1999. Most habitual smokers begin in their teens (about 3,000 teens start smoking each day) and 75% become adult daily smokers (Skaar et al., 1997). The graph at the right shows that, in the United States, the highest number of deaths (400,000) results from using tobacco (McGinnis & Foege, 1993). For this reason the United States Surgeon General concluded that cigarette smoking is the single largest avoidable cause of death in our society and the most important public health issue of our time.

| Causes of Death in the United States | |
| --- | --- |
| 400,000 Tobacco | |
| 300,000 Diet and activity patterns | |
| 100,000 Alcohol | |
| 35,000 Guns | |

### Drug

Nicotine has long been classified a stimulant drug but not until 1997 was it officially classified an addictive drug (Koch, 2000).

*Nicotine* is a stimulant because it first produces arousal but then produces calming. In low doses, nicotine improves attention, concentration, and short-term memory (Waters & Sutton, 2000). Regular use of nicotine causes addiction and dependency, and stopping leads to withdrawal symptoms.

Thus, one reason smokers find it so difficult to quit is that they are addicted to nicotine.

### Nervous System

Initially, nicotine stimulates certain receptors in the brain (cholinergic receptors) that cause arousal, but after a period of time, nicotine blocks these same receptors and produces calming. Researchers found that nicotine activates the same brain areas (nucleus accumbens) as cocaine, which means these drugs share a common neural basis for producing arousal, pleasure, and addiction (Pich et al., 1997).

### Dangers

In the United States, about 400,000 smokers die each year from lung and heart problems. Recently, researchers also found a link between smoking and sexual problems, including impotency (Hwang, 1998). Because researchers have long known that nicotine is addictive, a habitual smoker will experience withdrawal symptoms if he or she quits. These symptoms range in severity and include nervousness, irritability, difficulty in concentrating, sleep disturbances, and a strong craving for the drug—to light up again.

Professional stop-smoking programs, including those using the nicotine patch, were all about equally effective—10 to 25% remained smoke free one year later (Skaar et al., 1997). This means about 75% of smokers who stopped could not stay stopped. Nicotine is a very addicting drug that is difficult to stop using; it is even more difficult to stay stopped.

Unlike stimulants, which produce arousal, the next group of drugs, called opiates, produce the opposite effect.

## Opium, Morphine, Heroin

**How popular is heroin?**

From 6000 B.C. to the present, opiates have been used around the world. Opiates were legal in the early 1800s, when the active ingredient in the juice of the opium poppy (photo below) was found to be morphine. In the late 1800s, morphine

was chemically altered to make heroin, initially believed to be nonaddictive but later proved to be addictive. Law enforcement agencies usually refer to opiates as *narcotics*.

Opium poppy contains morphine.

In the early 1900s, the sale and use of narcotics (opium, morphine, and heroin) were made illegal, which gave rise to a lucrative worldwide opium black market. In spite of restrictive laws and billions spent on enforcement, the United States and other countries have been unable to stop the importation and use of opiates, which are readily available in most major cities (Schuckit, 2000).

The use of heroin peaked in the mid-1970s, dropped in the early 1980s as cocaine gained in popularity, but rose again in the early 1990s (Friend, 1997). This increase was partly due to a crackdown on cocaine usage as well as heroin's increased availability, decreased cost, and increased purity. In 1980, heroin was about 7% pure, while current heroin is about 50% pure; this means that now, instead of being injected, it can be smoked, which appeals to new users (beginning age has dropped to 18 years) (Leinwand, 2000).

The number of Americans who use heroin regularly is estimated to be about 350,000. On the basis of visits to emergency rooms, the primary users of heroin are men over the age of 26, both

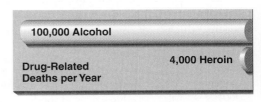

100,000 Alcohol

Drug-Related Deaths per Year

4,000 Heroin

Black (37%) and White (37%) (Stolberg, 1993). The graph above shows that, compared to 100,000 drug-related deaths a year from alcohol, there were about 4,000 heroin-related deaths (Baum, 1996; Schoemer, 1996). The possession or use of opiates—opium, morphine, and heroin—is illegal.

### Drug

Although all the opiates produce similar effects, users generally prefer to inject heroin because it reaches the brain more quickly and produces the biggest "rush," which is described as a whole-body pleasurable experience.

*Opiates,* such as opium, morphine, and heroin, produce three primary effects: analgesia (pain reduction); opiate euphoria, which is often described as a pleasurable state between waking and sleeping; and constipation. Continued use of opiates results in tolerance, addiction, and dependency.

One rock star (Steven Tyler of "Aerosmith") described using heroin as ". . . life without anxiety. It's a real floaty, godlike trip. . . . It makes you feel good" (Colapinto, 1996, p. 16). However, this rock star eventually discovered the darker side of heroin. With constant usage, his brain developed a tolerance to heroin, which means that he had to take larger and larger doses to achieve a high. Finally, he was using such large doses that getting high was almost impossible, functioning normally was out of the question, and he ended up with many personal and professional problems (Colapinto, 1996).

### Nervous System

In the 1970s, researchers discovered that the brain has naturally occurring receptors for opiates (Pert et al., 1974). When morphine reaches the brain's receptors, it produces feelings of euphoria and analgesia. In addition, the gastrointestinal tract has opiate receptors, whose stimulation results in constipation.

Researchers discovered that the brain not only has its own opiate receptors but also produces its own morphinelike chemicals. These chemicals, which function as neurotransmitters, are called *endorphins* and are found to have the same analgesic properties as morphine (Hughes et al., 1975).

### Dangers

One user (Steven Tyler) said, "But all those things it [heroin] gives you it starts to take away. Soon all you care about is the drug. You'll drag yourself through hell to get it. . . . It's killing you and you don't even care" (Colapinto, 1996, p. 16).

After several weeks of regular use, a person's brain produces less of its own endorphins and relies more on the outside supply of opiates. As a result, a person becomes addicted to taking opiates and must administer one or more doses daily to prevent withdrawal symptoms. Withdrawal symptoms, which include hot and cold flashes, sweating, muscle tremors, and stomach cramps, are not life-threatening and last 4–7 days. An overdose of opiates depresses the neural control of breathing, and a person dies from respiratory failure (Schuckit, 2000).

## Treatment

In a 24-year study of over 500 heroin addicts, researchers found that 28% died from drug overdose, 22% were abstinent, 11% were in prison, 10% were frequent users, 7% were daily users, and 6% were in methadone treatment programs; the remaining 16% could not be located (Hsea et al., 1993). Researchers concluded that, if heroin users do not quit by age 30, they are unlikely ever to stop. The most common treatment for heroin addiction is to maintain addicts on methadone, which is an addictive, synthetic drug similar to opium. Methadone maintenance is relatively effective in preventing heroin use and reducing criminal activities (Sees et al., 2000).

Next we consider the hallucinogens, which can produce strange perceptions.

## Definition

**What is a hallucinogen?**

In many parts of the world and in many different cultures, plants and fungi (mushrooms) have long been used to produce visions or hallucinations as part of cultural or religious experiences. However, Caucasians in the United States rarely used hallucinogens until the 1950s and 1960s, when these drugs gained popularity as part of the hippie subculture. Researchers have once again begun to study the potential therapeutic uses of hallucinogens, which have also gained back some of their former

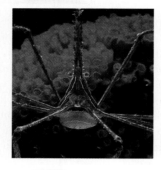

popularity (Strassman, 1995).

*Hallucinogens* are psychoactive drugs that can produce strange and unusual perceptual, sensory, and cognitive experiences, which the person sees or hears but knows that they are not occurring in reality. Such nonreality-based experiences are called *hallucinations.*

We'll focus on four of the more commonly used hallucinogens: LSD, psilocybin, mescaline, and a designer drug called ecstasy.

## LSD

**What does LSD do?**

At the beginning of this module, we told you of the strange bike ride of Albert Hofmann, who in 1943 discovered LSD (*d*-lysergic acid diethylamide). However, LSD did not become popular in America until the mid-1960s. Since then, LSD has gradually fallen in popularity, but there are reports of a slight increase in usage in the 1990s (Schuckit, 2000). Possession or use of LSD is illegal.

### Drug

LSD is a very potent drug because it produces hallucinogenic experiences at very low doses.

*LSD* produces strange experiences, which include visual hallucinations, perceptual distortions, increased sensory awareness, and intense psychological feelings.

An LSD experience, or "trip," may last 8–10 hours.

### Nervous System

LSD resembles the naturally occurring neurotransmitter serotonin. LSD binds to receptors that normally respond to serotonin, and the net effect is increased stimulation of these neurons (Schuckit, 2000). The majority of serotonin receptors are located on neurons in the brain's outermost layer, the cerebral cortex, which is involved in receiving sensations, creating perceptions, thinking, and imagining.

### Dangers

LSD's psychological effects partially depend on the setting and the person's state of mind. If a person is tense or anxious or in an unfamiliar setting, he or she may experience a bad trip. If severe, a bad trip may lead to psychotic reactions (especially paranoid feelings) that require hospitalization. Sometime after the hallucinogenic experience, users may experience frightening flashbacks that occur for no apparent reason. There have been no reports of physical addiction to LSD or death from overdose, but users do quickly develop a tolerance to LSD (Lerner et al., 2000).

## Psilocybin

**What are "magic mushrooms"?**

The existence of "magic mushrooms" was suggested by carvings of the ancient Aztec Indians, who lived around 500 B.C. In 1957, archeologists sent samples of the supposedly magic mushrooms (*Psilocybe mexicana*) to none

other than Albert Hofmann, who identified the active ingredient as psilocybin. Hofmann also tried magic mushrooms (left photo) and reported that they produced an "awake dream" that included a whirlpool of pictures rapidly changing shape and color (Hofmann, 1983). Possession or use of psilocybin is illegal.

### Drug

The active ingredient in magic mushrooms is psilocybin.

*Psilocybin* in low doses produces pleasant and relaxed feelings; medium doses produce perceptual distortions in time and space; high doses produce distortions in perceptions and body image and sometimes hallucinations.

### Nervous System

Psilocybin is chemically related to LSD and, like LSD, inhibits serotonin receptors. The hallucinatory effects produced by psilocybin are comparable to those from LSD but last half as long (Stahl, 2000).

### Dangers

The dangers of psilocybin come not from physical harm to the brain or body but rather from its potential for inducing psychotic states that may persist long after the experience is expected to end (Liska, 1994). In addition, accidental poisonings are common among those who eat poisonous mushrooms, mistaking them for magic mushrooms.

## Mescaline

**What is peyote?**

In the 1500s, Spanish soldiers noted that the Aztec Indians of South America ate peyote cactus as part of their religious ceremonies. Peyote cactus contains about 30 psychoactive chemicals; one of the more potent is the drug mescaline.

In 1965, the Native American Church of North America won a battle in the U.S. Supreme Court for the legal right to use peyote as a sacrament in their Christian ritual. Participants in this ritual usually sit around a fire and eat peyote buttons. This is followed by meditation, during which the participants feel removed from earthly cares and experience unusual visual perceptions, such as seeing a vast field of golden jewels that move and change (Liska, 1994). More recently, Native American Indians in the U.S. armed forces were allowed to use peyote in religious rituals (Richter, 1997). The possession or use of mescaline is illegal for all except those who belong to the Native American Church.

### Drug

Mescaline is about 2,000 times less potent than LSD.

*Mescaline* is the active ingredient in the peyote cactus. At high doses, mescaline produces very clear and vivid visual hallucinations, such as latticework, cobweb figures, tunnels, and spirals, which appear in various colors and intense brightness. Mescaline does not impair the intellect or cloud consciousness.

As with most hallucinogens, the setting and user's psychological state influence the experience.

### Nervous System

Mescaline reaches maximum concentration in the brain about 30–120 minutes after someone eats buttons of peyote cactus. Mescaline primarily increases the activity of the neurotransmitters norepinephrine and dopamine (Stahl, 2000). In addition, mescaline activates the sympathetic nervous system to produce physiological arousal, such as increased heart rate and temperature and sometimes vomiting.

### Dangers

During a mescaline experience, which can last 6–8 hours, users may experience headaches and vomiting. When street samples of mescaline were analyzed in a number of cities, researchers found that the chemical was rarely mescaline. Instead "street mescaline" was usually other hallucinogens, such as LSD or PCP (Hanson & Venturelli, 1998).

## Designer Drugs

**Can hallucinogens be made?**

The mid-1980s marked the appearance of so-called designer drugs.

*Designer drugs* refer to manufactured or synthetic drugs that are designed to resemble already existing illegal psychoactive drugs and to produce or mimic their psychoactive effects.

For example, a drug designer can start with an amphetamine molecule and alter it in hundreds of ways. Because designer drugs are manufactured in home laboratories, users have no guarantees that these drugs are safe to use. Of the dozen or so designer drugs available, we'll focus on one, MDMA, which was first used in the 1970s and whose street name is "ecstasy." In the late 1990s, ecstasy increased in popularity across the United States, with between 10 and 40% of teenagers and young adults having tried it (Schuckit, 2000). Ecstasy has become the drug of choice at rave parties (left photo), which feature all-night music and dancing. Since the government has not allowed research on MDMA since 1985, there are few reliable data on its effects and dangers. Possession or use of MDMA is illegal.

### Drug

The street name of MDMA is "ecstasy," which became popular in the late 1990s and early 2000s.

*MDMA,* or *ecstasy,* resembles both mescaline (hallucinogen) and amphetamine (stimulant). In anecdotal reports, users claim that MDMA causes changes in visual perceptions and increases their awareness of emotions, feelings of intimacy (hug drug), and ability to interact with others. Because it lowers inhibitions, some consider it an aphrodisiac.

### Nervous System

MDMA's primary action is to both release and block receptors that normally respond to the neurotransmitter serotonin. Of more serious concern are reports that, in animals, high doses of MDMA produced a 30% drop in stores of serotonin and may damage serotonin neurons. Researchers concluded that using MDMA is inadvisable until its potentially toxic effects on neurons can be studied (Cloud, 2000).

### Dangers

In recreational doses, MDMA trips can last 6 hours and include euphoria, jaw clenching, teeth grinding, insomnia, and high energy (Farley, 2000). In addition, at higher doses, users may experience panic, with rapid heart beat, paranoia, and psychotic-like symptoms. Prolonged use of MDMA—for a week or more—results in confusion, fatigue, depression, and nausea (Cloud, 2000). Studies of MDMA in animals indicate damage to serotonin neurons, but researchers are not yet sure if these findings apply to humans (Schuckit, 2000).

The psychoactive drug we'll examine next is widely used, potentially very dangerous, and legal.

**Power Study™**

**Check out CD: Module 3**
E. Transmitters

## History and Use

**What if alcohol was banned?**

The first brewery appeared in Egypt in about 3700 B.C., making alcohol the oldest drug to be made by humans (Samuel, 1996). Alcohol has grown in popularity worldwide, and its usage has been associated with a wide range of problems, such as motor coordination (right figure). If alcohol causes so many problems, why not just ban it?

In 1919, the U.S. Congress passed the Eighteenth Amendment, which prohibited the sale and manufacture of alcohol. However, Americans did not want to give up alcohol, so a lucrative black market developed and supplied illegal alcohol. After 14 years of black-market alcohol and failed prohibition, the U.S. Congress repealed prohibition in 1933. The lesson learned from prohibition was that it's impossible to pass a law

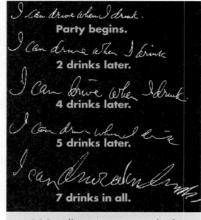

*I can drive when I drink.*
**Party begins.**

*I can drive when I drink*
**2 drinks later.**

*I Can drive when I drink.*
**4 drinks later.**

*I can draw when I drink*
**5 drinks later.**

*I can drink*
**7 drinks in all.**

110 million Americans drink alcohol and 10 to 15 million have problems.

to ban a drug that is so popular and widely used (Musto, 1996).

The U.S. government faces a similar problem today as it spends over $17 billion annually to ban illegal drugs (heroin, marijuana, cocaine, methamphetamine), which are still readily available on the black market in most cities (Schuckit, 2000).

About 110 million Americans drink alcohol and the majority do not experience problems. However, between 10 and 15 million drinkers are heavy drinkers with significant behavioral, neurological, social, legal, or medical problems. We'll discuss heavy drinkers in the Cultural Diversity section after we explain alcohol's effects on the user's brain, body, and behaviors.

## Definition and Effects

**PS** Although we'll use the term *alcohol,* we actually mean *ethyl alcohol,* which is safe to drink. The level of alcohol is measured in percentage in the blood, which is called blood alcohol content, or BAC. For example, after 3–4 drinks in an hour, the average person's BAC will range from 0.08 to 0.1. The national legal definition of being drunk is now

0.08. A drink is defined as one cocktail, one 5-ounce glass of wine, or one 12-ounce bottle of beer. It makes no difference whether you drink hard liquor, wine, or beer, since they all contain ethyl alcohol, which affects the nervous system and results in behavioral and emotional changes.

### Drug

Alcohol is not a stimulant but a depressant.

*Alcohol* (ethyl alcohol) is a psychoactive drug that is classified as a depressant, which means that it depresses activity of the central nervous system. Initially, alcohol seems like a stimulant because it reduces inhibitions, but later it depresses many physiological and psychological responses.

The effects of alcohol depend greatly on how much a person drinks. After a few drinks (0.01–0.03 BAC), alcohol causes friendliness and loss of inhibitions. After several more drinks (0.03–0.06 BAC), alcohol interferes with drinkers' ability to understand the important events going on around them. After many drinks (0.06–0.10 BAC), alcohol seriously impairs motor coordination (driving), cognitive abilities, decision making, and speech. After very many drinks (0.5 BAC and higher), alcohol may cause coma and death. For example, a fraternity pledge died after a 7-hour drinking binge that led to a BAC of 0.58—about 24 drinks (Cohen, 1997).

### Nervous System

The effects of alcohol are very complex because alcohol blocks some neural receptors and stimulates others. For example, alcohol stimulates the brain's GABA *(GAH-bah)* neural receptors, which leads to a reduction in anxiety and loss of inhibitions (Stahl, 2000). Alcohol also interferes with NMDA neural receptors, which may result in cognitive difficulties (Tsai et al., 1995). In extremely high doses (0.5 BAC), alcohol depresses vital breathing, or respiratory, reflexes in the brain stem (medulla). This can slow or stop breathing and explains why the fraternity pledge died after reaching a BAC of 0.58.

### Dangers

The morning after a bout of heavy drinking (3–7 drinks), a person usually experiences a *hangover,* which may include upset stomach, dizziness, fatigue, headache, and depression. There is presently no cure for hangovers, which are troublesome and painful but not life-threatening.

Repeated and heavy drinking can result in tolerance, addiction, and dependency. *Tolerance* means that a person must drink more to experience the same behavioral effects. *Addiction* means an intense craving for alcohol, and *dependency* means if the person stops drinking, he or she will experience serious *withdrawal symptoms,* including shaking, nausea, anxiety, diarrhea, hallucinations, and disorientation.

Another serious problem is *blackouts,* which occur after heavy and repeated drinking. During a blackout, a person seems to behave normally but when sober cannot recall what happened. If the blackout lasts for hours or days, it is probable that the person is an alcoholic.

Repeated and heavy drinking can also result in liver damage, alcoholism, and brain damage.

**Who's at risk for becoming an alcoholic?**

Of the 110 million people who drink alcohol, 10 to 12 million develop alcoholism. Researchers believe that certain individuals who drink alcohol become alcoholics because they have psychological and genetic *risk factors* that make them more likely to abuse alcohol. For example,

10 to 12 million become alcoholics.

one's risk of becoming an alcoholic is 3–4 times higher if one comes from a family whose parents are alcoholic. It is important to remember that risk factors increase the chances but do not guarantee that someone who drinks will become an alcoholic. Risk factors for abusing alcohol include both environmental/psychological and genetic factors.

### Environmental/Psychological Risk Factors

Researchers found that children whose parents (either or both) are alcoholics develop a number of unusual, abnormal, or maladaptive psychological and emotional traits that are called *environmental/psychological risk factors* (Schuckit, 2000). For example, these risk factors, which have been identified in children of alcoholic parents, include having difficulty showing trust, being overdependent in close personal relationships, and acting impulsive or overemotional when faced with stressful situations (Pandina & Johnson, 1999).

When children with these environmental/psychological risk factors become adults, they may have a tendency to imitate the behavior of their alcoholic parent and abuse alcohol when faced with personal, social, stressful, or work-related difficulties. However, besides environmental/psychological risk factors for abusing alcohol and developing alcoholism, there are also a number of genetic risk factors (Li, 2000).

### Genetic Risk Factors

Besides environmental/psychological risk factors, there are also *genetic risk factors,* which refer to inherited biases or predispositions that increase the potential for alcoholism. For example, if one identical twin was an alcoholic, there was a 39% chance that the other twin was also. In comparison, if one fraternal twin was an alcoholic, there was a 16% chance that the other twin was also. Researchers report that of those sons of alcoholic fathers who were less sensitive to alcohol, 56% became alcoholics as compared to 14% of those sons who were more sensitive to alcohol. These results indicate that a genetically set lower sensitivity to alcohol, which means that a person must drink more to feel its effects, is a risk factor for future alcoholism (Schuckit, 2000).

Findings from animals and humans indicate that genes affect a number of different neurotransmitter systems (GABA, NMDA, dopamine, and serotonin) that influence each person's susceptibility to alcohol and each person's risk for developing alcoholism (Li, 2000). Researchers caution that it's not one "alcoholic" gene that puts one at risk for alcoholism but perhaps as many as six genes, which in turn interact with the environment to increase the risk for alcoholism (Begleiter, 1997).

However, because neither every child of an alcoholic parent nor both members of a pair of identical twins became an alcoholic, genetic risk factors alone do not lead to alcoholism. Rather, researchers believe that alcoholism results from the interaction between genetic and environmental/psychological risk factors (Mann et al., 2000).

The use and abuse of alcohol are associated with a wide range of problems.

## Problems with Alcohol

**Why is alcohol so dangerous?**

The reason alcohol is considered such a dangerous drug is that its use and abuse are linked to many problems in the United States:

✔ 90% of all campus rapes involve drinking on the part of the assailant, victim, or both;

✔ 68% of manslaughter convictions and 63% of assaults involve alcohol;

✔ 63% of episodes in which husbands batter their wives involve alcohol;

✔ 41% of highway deaths involve alcohol;

✔ 43% of college men and 40% of college women said they had binged (consumed 4–5 successive drinks) at least once in the last two weeks;

Now, 52% of college students drink to get drunk—15 years ago, it was 10%.

✔ 52% of college students today drink to get drunk, whereas 15 years ago the figure was 10%;

✔ 11% of workplace accidents involve alcohol;

✔ 8–21% of suicides involve alcohol;

✔ 7% of college freshmen who drop out do so because of alcohol;

✔ alcoholism is the third leading health problem, after cancer and heart disease;

✔ alcohol is the leading cause of mental retardation due to fetal alcohol syndrome (FAS);

✔ alcohol is the most serious problem facing U.S. high schools, surpassing apathy and poor discipline by a wide margin;

✔ alcoholism and alcohol abuse cost an estimated $150 billion per year to lost production, health and welfare services, property damage, and medical expenses (Mehren, 1998; Schuckit, 2000; Ullman et al., 1999).

Because alcohol is significantly involved in so many medical, social, emotional, legal, job-related, and personal problems, many consider it to be one of the most dangerous of all the legal and illegal drugs (Mehren, 1998).

After you have had a chance to test your knowledge with the Concept Review, we'll discuss the worldwide problem of alcoholism.

# Concept Review

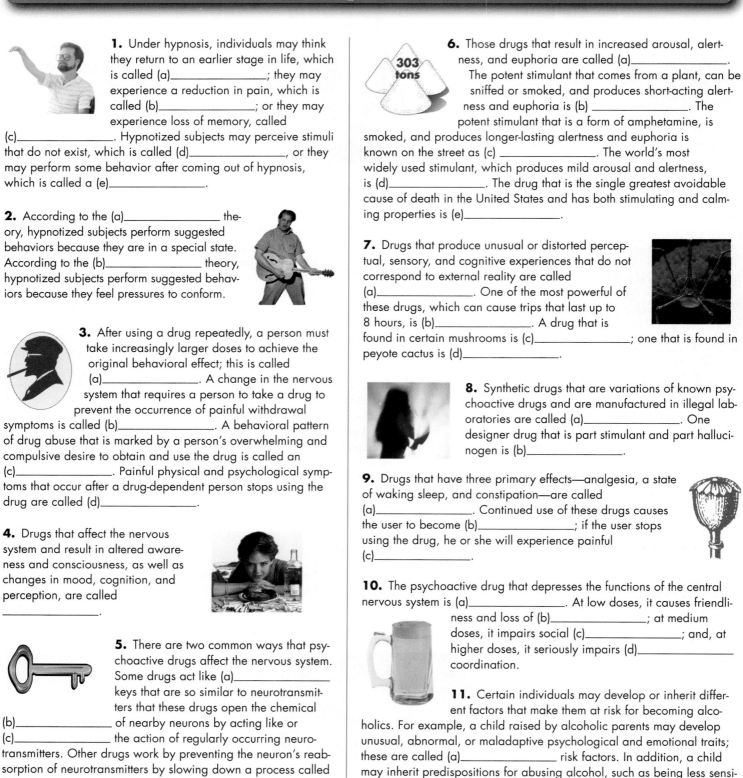

1. Under hypnosis, individuals may think they return to an earlier stage in life, which is called (a)_____; they may experience a reduction in pain, which is called (b)_____; or they may experience loss of memory, called (c)_____. Hypnotized subjects may perceive stimuli that do not exist, which is called (d)_____, or they may perform some behavior after coming out of hypnosis, which is called a (e)_____.

2. According to the (a)_____ theory, hypnotized subjects perform suggested behaviors because they are in a special state. According to the (b)_____ theory, hypnotized subjects perform suggested behaviors because they feel pressures to conform.

3. After using a drug repeatedly, a person must take increasingly larger doses to achieve the original behavioral effect; this is called (a)_____. A change in the nervous system that requires a person to take a drug to prevent the occurrence of painful withdrawal symptoms is called (b)_____. A behavioral pattern of drug abuse that is marked by a person's overwhelming and compulsive desire to obtain and use the drug is called an (c)_____. Painful physical and psychological symptoms that occur after a drug-dependent person stops using the drug are called (d)_____.

4. Drugs that affect the nervous system and result in altered awareness and consciousness, as well as changes in mood, cognition, and perception, are called _____.

5. There are two common ways that psychoactive drugs affect the nervous system. Some drugs act like (a)_____ keys that are so similar to neurotransmitters that these drugs open the chemical (b)_____ of nearby neurons by acting like or (c)_____ the action of regularly occurring neurotransmitters. Other drugs work by preventing the neuron's reabsorption of neurotransmitters by slowing down a process called (d)_____.

6. Those drugs that result in increased arousal, alertness, and euphoria are called (a)_____. The potent stimulant that comes from a plant, can be sniffed or smoked, and produces short-acting alertness and euphoria is (b)_____. The potent stimulant that is a form of amphetamine, is smoked, and produces longer-lasting alertness and euphoria is known on the street as (c)_____. The world's most widely used stimulant, which produces mild arousal and alertness, is (d)_____. The drug that is the single greatest avoidable cause of death in the United States and has both stimulating and calming properties is (e)_____.

7. Drugs that produce unusual or distorted perceptual, sensory, and cognitive experiences that do not correspond to external reality are called (a)_____. One of the most powerful of these drugs, which can cause trips that last up to 8 hours, is (b)_____. A drug that is found in certain mushrooms is (c)_____; one that is found in peyote cactus is (d)_____.

8. Synthetic drugs that are variations of known psychoactive drugs and are manufactured in illegal laboratories are called (a)_____. One designer drug that is part stimulant and part hallucinogen is (b)_____.

9. Drugs that have three primary effects—analgesia, a state of waking sleep, and constipation—are called (a)_____. Continued use of these drugs causes the user to become (b)_____; if the user stops using the drug, he or she will experience painful (c)_____.

10. The psychoactive drug that depresses the functions of the central nervous system is (a)_____. At low doses, it causes friendliness and loss of (b)_____; at medium doses, it impairs social (c)_____; and, at higher doses, it seriously impairs (d)_____ coordination.

11. Certain individuals may develop or inherit different factors that make them at risk for becoming alcoholics. For example, a child raised by alcoholic parents may develop unusual, abnormal, or maladaptive psychological and emotional traits; these are called (a)_____ risk factors. In addition, a child may inherit predispositions for abusing alcohol, such as being less sensitive to alcohol; these are called (b)_____ risk factors.

**Answers:** 1. (a) age regression, (b) hypnotic analgesia, (c) posthypnotic amnesia, (d) imagined perception, (e) posthypnotic suggestion; 2. (a) altered state, (b) sociocognitive; 3. (a) tolerance, (b) dependence, (c) addiction, (d) withdrawal symptoms; 4. psychoactive drugs; 5. (a) chemical, (b) locks, (c) mimicking, (d) reuptake; 6. (a) stimulants, (b) cocaine, (c) methamphetamine (crack, crystal, or ice), (d) caffeine, (e) nicotine; 7. (a) hallucinogens, (b) LSD, (c) psilocybin, (d) mescaline; 8. (a) designer drugs, (b) MDMA or ecstasy; 9. (a) opiates, (b) addicted, (c) withdrawal symptoms; 10. (a) alcohol (ethyl alcohol), (b) inhibitions, (c) judgment, (d) motor; 11. (a) environmental/psychological, (b) genetic

**Power Study™**

**Check out CD: Module 3**
E. Transmitters

## Definition and Differences in Rates

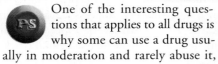

**What is alcoholism?**

One of the interesting questions that applies to all drugs is why some can use a drug usually in moderation and rarely abuse it, while others use the same drug but often abuse it and usually develop serious problems. For example, of the approximately 110 million U.S. citizens who drink alcohol, about 10 to 12 million abuse it, drink to excess, and develop alcoholism.

*Alcoholism* involves heavy drinking (sometimes a quart a day) for a long period of time, usually many years. Alcoholics are addicted (have intense craving) and are dependent on

First signs of alcoholism appear in the early 20s.

alcohol (must drink to avoid withdrawal symptoms). They continue to use alcohol despite developing major substance-related life problems, such as neglecting family, work, or school duties, having repeated legal or criminal incidents, and experiencing difficulties in personal or social relationships (American Psychiatric Association, 1994).

One answer to why only certain drinkers abuse the drug and become alcoholics comes from studying various risk factors, such as environmental/psychological and genetic influences, which we discussed earlier. Now, we'll examine another risk factor—cultural influences.

### Genetic Risk Factors

After the very first drink of alcohol, some individuals respond with a sudden reddening of the face. This reaction is called *facial flushing* and is caused by the absence of a liver enzyme involved in metabolizing alcohol.

Facial flushing from alcohol is a genetic trait and rarely occurs in Caucasians (Whites) but does occur in about 30–50% of Asians (photo below) (Schuckit, 2000). Asians who show significant facial flushing, such as Taiwanese, Chinese, and Japanese, tend to drink less and have lower rates of alcoholism than Asians who

Asians with most facial flushing have lower rates of drinking and alcoholism.

show less facial flushing, such as the Koreans (Helzer & Canino, 1992). These findings show that facial flushing, which occurs in some cultures more than others, is a *genetic risk factor* that influences the chances of becoming an alcoholic.

### Cultural Risk Factors

Different cultures have different values and pressures that may encourage or discourage alcohol abuse. For instance, researchers studied 48,000 adults (18 and older) in six different cultures to answer two questions: Do rates of alcoholism differ across cultures? What cultural values influence the rate of alcoholism?

The answer to the first question is shown in the graph below. Rates of alcoholism did differ across cultures, from a low of 0.5% among Taiwanese to a high of 22% among Koreans (Helzer & Canino, 1992).

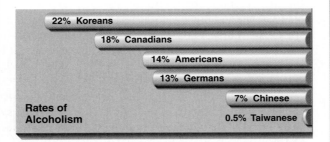

22% Koreans
18% Canadians
14% Americans
13% Germans
7% Chinese
0.5% Taiwanese
Rates of Alcoholism

The answer to the second question—What cultural values influence the rate of alcoholism?—was also partly answered. For example, the high rate of alcoholism in Korea is almost entirely in males, who are encouraged by cultural pressures to drink heavily in certain social situations, such as at the end of the workday, when coworkers are encouraged to have drinking contests. The medium rate of alcoholism found in Germany, the United States, and Canada was related to the stresses of living in heavily industrialized societies. The below average rate of alcoholism found in China and especially Taiwan was influenced by the Confucian moral code, which has strong cultural-religious taboos against drinking or showing drunken behavior in public. These findings indicate that *cultural risk factors* can either encourage or discourage the development of alcoholism.

However, despite the different rates of alcoholism across cultures, there are some striking similarities.

### Across Cultures

Although rates of alcoholism differed widely across cultures, from 0.5% to 22%, researchers found many similarities in how people developed alcoholism and the problems they had (Helzer & Canino, 1992; Peele, 1997). Here are some similarities that occurred across cultures:

■ the average age when the first symptoms of alcoholism appear was in the early twenties or midtwenties;

■ the average number of major life problems among alcoholics was 4–6;

■ the average duration of alcoholism was 8–10 years;

■ the average pattern of drinking involved daily heavy drinking, often a quart a day;

■ men were five times more likely to develop alcoholism than were women;

■ depression was about twice as likely to be diagnosed in alcoholics as in nonalcoholics;

■ the overall mortality rate from alcoholism did not differ among cultures.

Researchers concluded that although cultural—genetic and environmental—risk factors had a significant influence on the rate of alcoholism, cultural factors had little effect on the development, symptoms, sex differences, and mental disorders associated with alcoholism.

Next, we'll focus on the most widely used illegal drug in the United States.

### Use and Effects

*What's the most widely used illegal drug?*

The most widely used illegal drug in the United States is marijuana, with about 11 million who use it monthly, compared to 2.1 million cocaine users, 200,000 heroin users, and 100,000 who use ecstasy (SAMHSA, 2000). Despite the wide use, the graph on the right shows that compared to other illegal drugs, few if any deaths result from marijuana usage (Nadelmann, 1997).

Marijuana is one of the leading U.S. cash crops; growers make an estimated $24 billion yearly (top marijuana-growing states are Tennessee, Kentucky, Hawaii, California, and New York), compared to corn growers who make about $16 billion. Despite billions of dollars and years of preventive efforts, marijuana is readily available to teenagers and adults.

**Medical uses.** In 1997, the Federal Institute of Medicine issued a report on the medical uses of marijuana, which include easing

| | |
|---|---|
| 4,000 | Heroin |
| 3,618 | Cocaine |
| 0 | Marijuana |

**Drug-Related Deaths per Year**

pain and reducing nausea (Scheer, 1999). Also in 1997, the National Institutes on Drug Abuse concluded that marijuana showed promise in treating nausea and vomiting associated with chemotherapy; treatment of appetite loss in AIDS patients; and treatment of an eye disease (glaucoma) (Fackelmann, 1997a). Partly based on these reports, a number of states, including Alaska, Arizona, California, Colorado, Hawaii, Maine, Nevada, Oregon, and Washington, passed laws that allowed marijuana to be prescribed by doctors and used legally for medical problems. However, current federal law outlaws all uses of marijuana and overrides state laws. This federal-state conflict over the medical use of marijuana has not been settled. Current federal law makes it illegal to use or possess marijuana.

---

### Drug

As is true of many psychoactive drugs, some of marijuana's effects depend on the user's initial mood and state of mental health. For example, patients in their sixties who were using marijuana to treat glaucoma complained about and did not like its "strange side effects," which most young adult users desire and label as "getting high."

*Marijuana* is a psychoactive drug whose primary active ingredient is THC (tetrahydrocannabinol), which is found in the leaves of the cannabis plant. The average marijuana cigarette ("joint") contains 2.5–11.0 mg of THC, which is a tenfold increase over the amount of THC found in marijuana in the 1970s. THC is rapidly absorbed by the lungs and in 5–10 minutes produces a high that lasts for several hours. The type of high is closely related to the dose: low doses produce mild euphoria; moderate doses produce perceptual and time distortions; and high doses may produce hallucinations, delusions, and distortions of body image (Hanson & Venturelli, 1998).

Depending on the user's state of mind, marijuana can either heighten or distort pleasant or unpleasant experiences, moods, or feelings.

### Nervous System

In 1964, researchers identified and synthesized THC, the main mind-altering substance in marijuana.

In 1990, researchers discovered a specific receptor for THC in the brains of rats and humans (Matsuda et al., 1990). These THC receptors are located throughout the brain, including the hippocampus, which is involved in short-term memory; the cerebral cortex, which is involved in higher cognitive functions; the limbic system, which is involved in emotions; and the cerebellum and basal ganglia, which are involved in motor control, timing, and coordination (Iversen, 2000). Mammalian brains (such as humans) contain extremely high levels of THC receptors, which suggests they may be involved in important brain functions (Iversen, 2000).

In 1993, researchers found that the brain itself makes a chemical, called anandamide, that stimulates THC receptors. Anandamide, a naturally occurring brain chemical, has been shown to be one of the brain's neurotransmitters, whose actions are currently under study (Piomelli, 1999).

Thus, the brain not only has receptors for THC but also makes a THC-like chemical, called anandamide.

### Dangers

Marijuana can cause temporary changes in cognitive functioning, such as interfering with short-term memory and ability to drive a car, boat, or plane, because it impairs reaction time, judgment, and use of peripheral vision (Schuckit, 2000). However, there is no conclusive evidence that prolonged marijuana use causes permanent damage to brain or nervous system makeup (Block et al., 2000). Marijuana can also temporarily decrease secretion of various hormones and effectiveness of the immune system.

Marijuana causes many of the same kinds of respiratory problems as smoking tobacco, including bronchitis and asthma attacks. Because marijuana smoke contains 50% more cancer-causing substances and users hold smoke in their lungs longer, the effects of smoking 3–4 joints of marijuana are similar to those of 20 cigarettes (Tashkin, 1996).

At high doses, marijuana may cause toxic psychoses, including delusions, paranoia, and feelings of terror. However, there is no evidence that marijuana use causes long-term psychosis or schizophrenia (Schuckit, 2000).

Researchers believe that regular use of marijuana results in addiction and dependency, and if usage is stopped, there may be withdrawal symptoms (Schuckit, 2000).

We have discussed the use and potential dangers of common legal and illegal drugs. Now we'll examine a popular program to prevent drug usage in teenagers.

## How Effective Is the DARE Program?

If individuals start using illegal drugs at an early age, they are at greater risk for abusing drugs, developing future drug-related problems, or finding it more difficult to stop (Tschann et al., 1994). The graph below shows that there is reason to be concerned because the use of illegal drugs by eighth-graders more than doubled from 1991 to 1999 (11% to 28%) (Wren, 1999). A popular program developed to help teenagers say "No" to using drugs is called DARE.

*DARE* (Drug Abuse Resistance Program) is based on the idea of using social influence and role playing to discourage adolescents from starting drug use and to encourage them to refuse drugs in the future. This program is taught in grade school classrooms by trained, uniformed police officers.

Begun in 1983, DARE has become the most popular drug education school program,

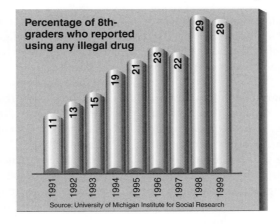

**Percentage of 8th-graders who reported using any illegal drug**

1991: 11
1992: 13
1993: 15
1994: 19
1995: 21
1996: 23
1997: 22
1998: 29
1999: 28

Source: University of Michigan Institute for Social Research

with an annual budget of about $700 million. Currently, thousands of DARE officers speak to 5 million grade school children in 70% of the school districts in the United States (Murphy, 1996).

But, here's the real question: If DARE is so popular and supposedly so effective, why has the use of illegal drugs by teenagers more than doubled during the period when millions of teenagers went through the DARE program? If DARE was so effective, you would expect the use of drugs by teenagers to drop or at least stay the same. One of the major uses of research is to evaluate the effectiveness of intervention programs that claim to change behavior, such as preventing drug use. Here's what researchers discovered about the effectiveness of the DARE program.

### *Method and Procedure*

Researchers selected 36 elementary schools in urban, suburban, and rural areas in Illinois. Schools were paired to control for ethnic differences and income levels of parents. Students in one school of a pair were the experimental group and received DARE training, while students in the other school of the pair were the control group and did not receive DARE training. A total of 1,803 students took part in the study.

Before DARE began, students were pretested to determine their attitudes toward drugs and their use of drugs. Then students in the experimental schools began the DARE program, which consisted of educational sessions lasting 45–60 minutes that are taught in the classroom by uniformed police officers.

Immediately after the DARE program and also one, two, and three years later, students were retested on their attitudes toward drugs and their actual use of drugs.

Researchers found the DARE antidrug program, which has an annual budget of $700 million, to be ineffective.

### *Results and Discussion*

Researchers found that going through project DARE had no statistically significant effect on whether students did or did not start smoking, drinking alcohol, or drinking to get drunk. These disappointing results were found immediately after the DARE program ended, as well as 1, 2, and 3 years later. There was a significant increase in self-esteem but this gain was short-lived and was apparently not strong enough to help students resist using drugs in the future.

Researchers concluded that, although the police officers were well trained and popular among students, there was little evidence that being in project DARE had any direct influence on adolescents' use of drugs or on attitudes and skills related to preventing drug use (Ennett et al., 1994).

Other researchers who analyzed dozens of similar studies involving thousands of teenagers also concluded that DARE had "a limited to essentially nonexistent effect" on drug use in teenagers (Glass, 1998; Research Triangle Institute, 1994). A recent 10-year follow-up of the DARE program also found what other studies had reported: DARE had no effect on preventing the future use of illegal drugs (Janofsky, 2000; Lynam et al., 1999).

### *Conclusion*

Despite DARE's large federal financial support and widespread popularity among police, politicians, school administrators, and parents, researchers have repeatedly found that the DARE program was ineffective in preventing future drug use in teenagers.

You may wonder how DARE became so popular. The main reason was that police officers, school administrators, and politicians gave glowing testimonials about how effective DARE was in preventing drug use.

However, as discussed in Module 2, evidence from testimonials is questionable because they are based on personal experiences, which have great potential for error and bias. The best way to evaluate the effectiveness of any program designed to change behavior, such as DARE, is to use the scientific method, which limits error and bias. This Research Focus shows the importance of basing evaluations on hard, scientific evidence rather than on glowing testimonials, which may be distorted by error and bias.

If a teenager or adult abuses drugs and develops a serious drug problem, what kind of help does he or she receive in a drug treatment program?

### Developing a Problem

**What are the risks for drug abuse?** Earlier, we discussed the genetic and environmental risks that turn a drug user into a drug abuser. In the following case study, notice the environmental risks that pushed Martin into becoming an alcoholic.

In high school, Martin got good grades but still felt insecure, especially about his sexual abilities. His solution was to act like a "rugged, hard-drinking person." Instead of helping, drinking made him feel more insecure in relationships and made it more difficult for him to perform sexually.

When Martin entered college, he continued to have low self-esteem and feared that someone would discover that his sexual performance did not match his bragging. As he had done in high school, he buried his fears in drink, often putting down 5–10 drinks on a weekend night.

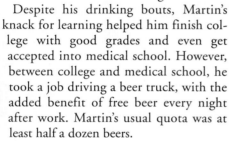

Despite his drinking bouts, Martin's knack for learning helped him finish college with good grades and even get accepted into medical school. However, between college and medical school, he took a job driving a beer truck, with the added benefit of free beer every night after work. Martin's usual quota was at least half a dozen beers.

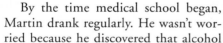

Many start out believing that alcohol is the solution.

By the time medical school began, Martin drank regularly. He wasn't worried because he discovered that alcohol made him feel "more content" and "it made it easier to live with himself." Best of all, alcohol reduced his feelings of "self-loathing" and gave him an "instant" sense of self-worth. Despite his heavy drinking, Martin's talents for mastering academic subjects helped him finish medical school.

After medical school, Martin settled in the Midwest, developed a successful medical clinic, got married, and had a family. However, throughout this period, he continued to drink heavily and was soon unable to function without alcohol. About the same time he began having blackouts, his wife refused to put up with his heavy drinking; she took the children and left. At this point, Martin began taking painkillers, for which he wrote his own prescriptions. After 10 years of abusing drugs, Martin could not escape the vicious circle of needing more and more drugs to feed his addiction.

Finally, one cold afternoon as Martin sat home with his booze and painkillers, the police arrested him for writing illegal prescriptions. Martin was saved from himself by being forced to enter a psychiatric hospital for drug treatment (adapted from Khantzian & Mack, 1994).

Some of the environmental risks that pushed Martin to become a drug abuser are clear: for most of his life, he suffered from feelings of low self-esteem and worthlessness and fears of not performing sexually. Hoping to solve his problems with drugs, Martin instead made them worse with substance abuse, the most common mental health problem among males (Kessler et al., 1994).

### Substance Abuse and Treatment

**What is a drug problem?** Like Martin, about 5–15% of those who use legal or illegal drugs develop a serious drug problem called substance abuse.

*Substance abuse* refers to a maladaptive behavioral pattern of using a drug or medicine so frequently that significant problems develop: failing to meet major obligations and having multiple legal, social, family, health, work, or interpersonal problems. These problems must occur repeatedly during the same 12-month period (American Psychiatric Association, 1994).

Individuals with substance abuse usually need professional help.

Most substance abusers need professional help and treatment to get straightened out. Martin entered a treatment program that is based on the Minnesota model, which is used in about 95% of inpatient drug treatment centers in the United States. The *Minnesota model* recognizes that the drug user has lost control when it comes to drugs, may be vulnerable to using other mood-altering substances, cannot solve the drug problem alone, must rebuild his or her life without drugs, and must strive for total abstinence (McElrath, 1997; Shorkey, 1994).

We'll follow Martin's progress as he goes through a typical drug treatment program based on the Minnesota model.

### Step 1. Admit the Problem

**Why don't people seek treatment?** The fact that Martin did not seek help for his drug problem until he was arrested points out an important difference between most individuals treated for drug problems and those treated for mental health problems.

Generally, individuals with mental health problems seek help voluntarily because they want to stop their suffering or unhappiness. In contrast, many individuals with drug problems do not recognize that they have a problem and do not seek help voluntarily. Thus, the first step in getting treatment is admitting that one has a drug problem. Although this step appears obvious, in reality it represents a hurdle that many drug abusers have a difficult time getting over. What happens is that drug users believe that drugs are the solution to their problems, fears, insecurities, and worries.

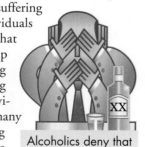

Alcoholics deny that they have a problem.

For almost 10 years, Martin believed that alcohol was the solution to his sexual and social fears. In fact, the opposite was true. Heavy drug use became the problem, even though Martin and most users refuse to admit it. Convincing heavy drug users to seek treatment often requires the efforts of their family, loved ones, and employer, as well as a judge or doctor (Schuckit, 2000).

Every day in the United States, about 700,000 people receive treatment for alcoholism in either an inpatient (hospital) or outpatient (clinic) setting (Fuller & Hiller-Sturmhofel, 1999). In Martin's case, he was required to enter an inpatient (hospital) drug treatment program because he was both addicted and depressed, would not admit to having a problem, and would not seek help on his own. In comparison, most alcoholics (85%) are treated in clinics as outpatients.

Most in- or outpatient drug treatment programs involve the following steps and goals: Martin receives a complete medical checkup and a two-week period of detoxification (getting drug free), and then a team consisting of a physician, psychologist, counselor, and nurse discusses the treatment's four goals with Martin (Winters et al., 2000).

**First goal.** Help Martin face up to his drinking problem. It is not uncommon for a drug abuser to deny that he or she has a problem with drugs, even though it is obvious to everyone else.

**Second goal.** Have Martin begin a program of stress management, so that he could reduce his anxiety and tension without drinking. Stress management involves the substitution of relaxation exercises and other enjoyable activities (sports, hobbies) for the escape and enjoyment that alcohol has provided.

**Third goal.** Give Martin an opportunity to share his experiences in group therapy. Group sessions helped Martin realize that he was not suffering alone, that it was important for him to make plans for the future, and that he might have to make new, nondrinking friends once he left the program.

**Fourth goal.** This is perhaps the most important goal and goes to the heart of the problem: Help Martin face and overcome his environmental risk factors, which include personal and social problems such as the feelings of low self-esteem and depression that had contributed to his drug abuse.

Three different therapies, including AA, were equally effective.

Regarding the fourth goal, you may wonder which kind of therapy is most effective in helping drug abusers. One answer comes from a $27-million study that took 8 years and compared three different programs. There were over 1,700 people and all were diagnosed as alcohol-dependent, which means they either drank heavily every day or went on alcohol binges that disrupted their home or work activities.

**Three therapies.** After volunteering for this study, individuals were randomly assigned to a 12-week treatment program that involved one of the following three therapies. *Cognitive-behavioral therapy* focuses on helping patients develop skills to control their thoughts about alcohol and learn to control their urges to drink. *Motivational therapy* helps clients recognize and utilize their personal resources and encourages them to take personal responsibility to abstain from drinking. The *12-step approach* is used in traditional Alcoholics Anonymous (AA) programs. This therapy or program is one of spiritual awakening that serves as a guide for recovery and abstinence. Here are two examples of the 12 steps: "Step 1: We admitted we were powerless over alcohol—that our lives had become unmanageable. Step 2: We came to believe that a Power greater than ourselves could restore us to sanity." AA believes that drug abuse is a disease, that a person must surrender to and ask God for help, and that total abstinence is the only solution.

Because these three therapies represent three different philosophies or approaches, many professionals believed that one therapy might be more effective than another.

**Effectiveness.** Researchers found that, before therapy, all individuals drank heavily on about 25 out of 30 days per month. In comparison, a year after finishing therapy, 35% reported not drinking at all, while 65% had slipped, or relapsed, into drinking again. Of the 65% who had relapsed, 40% reported periods of at least 3 consecutive days of heavy drinking.

An unexpected finding was that all three therapies were equally effective in reducing drinking (Project Match Research Group, 1997). Even though the three therapies seem to have somewhat different approaches, there was little or no difference in their effectiveness. It appears that the specific kind of therapy used is not as important as finding better ways of encouraging drug abusers to recognize and seek help for their drug problems.

**Rate of success.** The effectiveness of a drug treatment program is usually measured by how many clients remain abstinent (do not use drugs) for a period of one year. Success rates range from 30 to 45%, which means that 55 to 70% relapse or return to drinking during the year following treatment (Fuller & Hiller-Sturmhofel, 1999). For almost all drug treatment programs, such as AA, the goal is total abstinence. However, there is an ongoing debate over whether alcoholics can learn to use drugs in moderate amounts. So far, there is very little research to show that long-term alcoholics can learn to drink moderately and responsibly (Rivera, 2000).

After leaving an inpatient (hospital) or outpatient (clinic) drug treatment program, patients are strongly encouraged to join an aftercare support group in their community.

After treatment, recovering alcoholics as well as other drug addicts are encouraged to join an aftercare community support group to help fight off the temptation of returning to drugs. The most popular and successful aftercare program for alcoholics is Alcoholics Anonymous (AA); a similar program for other drug users is Narcotics Anonymous (NA). After drug treatment, AA and NA provide programs to help prevent relapse (drinking again), which occurs in 55 to 70% of former drug users.

Relapse programs teach former drug users how to avoid situations that trigger drinking (going out with drinking buddies), cope with stressors that lead to drinking, and build self-esteem to increase confidence (Larimer et al., 1999).

About 55–70% of recovering alcoholics suffer relapse.

Thus, a person with a serious drug problem initially needs treatment to get off the drug and then an aftercare support program to help prevent or deal with relapse and remain drug free.

## A. HYPNOSIS

**1.** Hypnosis is defined as an altered state of awareness, attention, and alertness, during which a person is usually much more open to the (a)_____ of a hypnotist or therapist. About 30% of college students are easily hypnotized, while 40% are difficult to hypnotize. The procedure used to hypnotize someone is called (b)_____.

**2.** Under hypnosis, subjects will experience or perform the following _____: age regression, imagined perception, posthypnotic amnesia, posthypnotic suggestions, and hypnotic analgesia.

**3.** According to the (a)_____ state theory, a hypnotized individual is in an altered state and experiences unusual sensations and feelings. According to the (b)_____ theory, the effects produced by hypnosis are due to powerful personal pressures and social influences as well as the abilities of the subject rather than to the process of being hypnotized.

**4.** In dental and medical settings, hypnosis is used to help patients deal with painful procedures by producing (a)_____. In therapeutic settings, hypnosis is used in combination with other behavioral and cognitive treatments to help clients reveal their personalities and gain insights. However, hypnosis is not very successful in dealing with problems that involve (b)_____.

## B. DRUGS: OVERVIEW

**5.** Regular use of a drug usually results in one or more of the following. A behavioral pattern of drug abuse that is marked by an overwhelming and compulsive desire to obtain and use the drug is called an (a)_____. If the nervous system becomes accustomed to having the drug and needs the drug for normal functioning, the user is said to have developed a (b)_____. If a habitual user suddenly stops taking the drug, he or she will experience unpleasant or painful (c)_____. After using a drug over a period of time, a person must take a larger dose to achieve the original behavioral effect because this person has developed a (d)_____ for the drug.

**6.** Drugs that affect the nervous system by altering consciousness, awareness, sensations, perceptions, mood, and cognitive processes are called _____ drugs.

**7.** Some drugs act like chemical keys that are so similar to the brain's own (a)_____ that drugs can open the same chemical locks. Some drugs interfere with the reabsorption, or (b)_____, of neurotransmitters back into the neuron.

## C. STIMULANTS

**8.** Drugs that increase activity of the nervous system and result in heightened alertness, arousal, and euphoria and decreased appetite and fatigue are called _____.

**303 tons**

**9.** In moderate doses, cocaine produces short-lived enhancement of _____. In heavy doses, it can produce addiction; serious psychological effects, such as frightening hallucinations; and serious physical problems, such as heart irregularity, convulsions, and death.

**10.** A form of amphetamine called _____ produces a quick high, is very addictive, and has become a major drug problem.

**11.** The most widely used legal psychoactive drug in the world is _____, which affects brain receptors and, depending on the dose, produces physiological arousal, a mild feeling of alertness, increased reaction time, and decreased fatigue and drowsiness.

**12.** The legal drug that is second to caffeine in worldwide usage is _____, which has both stimulating and calming properties.

## D. OPIATES

**13.** All opiates produce three primary effects: a reduction in pain, which is called (a)_____; a twilight state between waking and sleeping, which is called (b)_____; and (c)_____, which permits their use as a treatment for diarrhea. With continued use of opiates, users develop tolerance, addiction, and an intense craving for the drug. The brain also produces its own morphinelike chemicals, called (d)_____.

## E. HALLUCINOGENS

**14.** Drugs that act on the brain (and body) to produce perceptual, sensory, and cognitive experiences that do not match the external reality are called (a)_____. Sometime after using LSD, a user may suddenly have a frightening, drug-related experience called a (b)_____. Examples of hallucinogenic drugs are LSD, psilocybin, and mescaline. Drugs that are manufactured or altered to produce psychoactive effects are called (c)_____; an example is (d)_____.

## F. ALCOHOL

**15.** Alcohol is classified as a (a)_____ because it decreases the activity of the central nervous system by stimulating neural receptors called (b)_____ receptors. Heavy and repeated drinking can result in periods of seemingly normal behavior that the drinker, when sober, cannot recall at all; these periods are called (c)_____. Alcohol abuse is a major contributor to personal problems, fatal traffic accidents, birth defects, homicides, assaults, date rape, and suicide.

**16.** A drinker's risk of becoming an alcoholic increases 3–4 times if members of his or her family are alcoholics. The risk of developing alcoholism is increased by having difficulties in showing trust and being overdependent in relationships, which are called (a)_____ factors, and also by the inheritance of predispositions for alcoholism, which are called (b)_____ factors.

## G. CULTURAL DIVERSITY: ALCOHOLISM RATES

**17.** About 10–12% of American drinkers become _____, defined as people who have drunk heavily for a long period of time, are addicted to and have an intense craving for alcohol, and have problems in two or three major life areas caused by drinking.

| Rates of Alcoholism | |
|---|---|
| 22% | Koreans |
| 18% | Canadians |
| 14% | Americans |
| 13% | Germans |
| 7% | Chinese |
| 0.5% | Taiwanese |

**18.** One reason the Chinese and Taiwanese have low rates of alcoholism is that these societies are heavily influenced by the Confucian moral code, which discourages _____ in public.

## H. MARIJUANA

**19.** The most widely used illegal drug in the United States is (a)_____. In low doses it produces mild euphoria, in moderate doses it produces distortions in perception and time, and in high doses it may produce hallucinations and delusions. Researchers discovered that the brain has neural locks, or THC (b)_____, that are highly concentrated in the brain and respond to the THC in marijuana. The brain makes its own chemical, called (c)_____, which is one of the brain's own (d)_____ and closely resembles THC. Throughout the brain are many THC receptors that are involved in a number of behaviors, including (e)_____.

## I. RESEARCH FOCUS: DRUG PREVENTION

**20.** The most popular program to prevent drug use in teenagers is called (a)_____, which uses social influence and role playing to discourage adolescents from starting drug use and to encourage them to refuse drugs in the future. However, researchers found that this very popular and expensive program was not effective in preventing future drug use. One reason DARE grew in popularity was that early evidence for its effectiveness came primarily from (b)_____, which have a relatively high potential for error and bias.

## J. APPLICATION: TREATMENT FOR DRUG ABUSE

**21.** A maladaptive pattern of continued usage of a substance—drug or medicine—that results in significant legal, personal, or other problems over a 12-month period is called _____.

**22.** Programs that treat drug abusers have four steps: The first step is admitting that one has a (a)_____. The second step is entering a (b)_____, which has four goals. The third step is to get (c)_____ to help overcome drug abuse. The fourth step is to remain (d)_____.

**23.** Researchers found that three different kinds of therapy—cognitive-behavioral, motivational, and AA's 12-step approach—were about (a)_____ in helping alcoholics stop drinking. Although 35% of individuals stopped drinking, 65% started drinking again, which is called (b)_____. This is a big problem among recovering drug users, since about 55 to 70% will relapse at some time and may need some kind of (c)_____ to once again become drug free.

***Answers:*** *1. (a) suggestions, (b) hypnotic induction; 2. behaviors; 3. (a) altered, (b) sociocognitive; 4. (a) analgesia, (b) self-control; 5. (a) addiction, (b) dependence, (c) withdrawal symptoms, (d) tolerance; 6. psychoactive; 7. (a) neurotransmitters, (b) reuptake; 8. stimulants; 9. activity, mood, or energy; 10. methamphetamine; 11. caffeine; 12. nicotine; 13. (a) analgesia, (b) opiate euphoria, (c) constipation, (d) endorphins; 14. (a) hallucinogens, (b) flashback, (c) designer drugs, (d) MDMA, or ecstasy; 15. (a) depressant, (b) GABA, (c) blackouts; 16. (a) environmental/psychological risk, (b) genetic risk; 17. alcoholics; 18. drunkenness; 19. (a) marijuana, (b) receptors, (c) anandamide, (d) neurotransmitters, (e) memory, emotions, motor control, higher cognitive functions; 20. (a) DARE, (b) testimonials; 21. substance abuse; 22. (a) drug problem, (b) treatment program, (c) therapy, (d) drug free; 23. (a) equally effective, (b) relapse, (c) relapse program*

# Critical Thinking

Newspaper Article

## Can Alcoholics Stop After Two Drinks?

### Questions

**1.** What kind and how good is the evidence used by Kishline to back up the claims made in her book and self-help program?

**2.** How does Kishline's self-help program of learning to drink in moderation compare to AA's program?

**3.** Why do alcoholics and people who abuse drugs make rules to control their drinking?

Audrey Kishline, a housewife and a mother, was a problem drinker who believed that she could learn to stop drinking after two drinks. In fact, she wrote a book called *Moderate Drinking: The New Option for Problem Drinkers* and also started Moderation Management, a self-help treatment program which claimed to help problem drinkers learn to drink responsibly rather than have to be totally abstinent. The book and her self-help program were based on her own personal experiences of apparently learning to drink responsibly after years of problem drinking.

One reason Audrey's book and self-help program made the news was that her ideas challenged one of the basic beliefs of AA (Alcoholics Anonymous), which is that alcoholics' only hope of recovery is absolutely no drinking—total abstinence—because alcoholics cannot learn to stop after taking only two drinks.

However, most problem drinkers and alcoholics (the distinction is sometimes blurry) want more than anything to believe that they can learn to drink in moderation. The idea of facing a life without alcohol, of total abstinence, is terrifying for alcoholics who firmly believe their solution to life's problems comes in a liquor bottle. There probably isn't one recovering alcoholic who didn't struggle to drink in moderation but making rule after rule—"I won't drink until 8 P.M." or "I'll stop after two drinks"—only to find him- or herself bending the rule just this one time, which turned into two times, which turned into drinking until drunk. For many recovering alcoholics, learning to live without alcohol seemed such a terrible future that Kishline's idea of learning to drink moderately seemed the answer to their prayers.

Kishline's claim of learning to drink in moderation after years of problem drinking was tragically challenged by her own failure. After a session of binge drinking, she got into her pickup truck, drove the wrong way on an interstate freeway, smashed head-on into a car, killing a father and his daughter. She was arrested for and pleaded guilty to two counts of vehicular homicide.

Apparently, before the accident, she had given up her own program of learning to drink moderately and tried to stay sober through AA. Following her arrest, she said that her Moderation Management program was a way for "alcoholics covering up their problem." As predicted by AA and many drug treatment programs, Kishline had not learned to drink in moderation and had relapsed in a most tragic way. (Adapted from C. Knapp, An alcoholic's private anguish, *Los Angeles Times*, July 17, 2000, p. E2)

**4.** Does Kishline's personal failure to learn to drink in moderation mean that this goal is out of the question for all alcoholics?

**5.** Why is the goal of many drug treatment programs total abstinence?

*Use InfoTrac to search for topics:* alcoholism; **Alcoholics Anonymous;** moderate drinking.

---

*Suggested answers to Newspaper Article questions*

1. The kind of evidence Kishline uses to back up her claims comes from a combination of case study and testimonials (p. 30). The problem with using evidence from a case study is that it's based on personal experiences, which may be unique to the person and may not generalize to others. The problem with testimonials is that they are also based on personal experiences, which may contain errors in judgment due to personal beliefs and biases.

2. Kishline's self-help program for problem drinkers/alcoholics to learn to drink in moderation is exactly the opposite of AA's belief that alcoholics cannot learn to drink moderately and that they must give up alcohol completely and remain abstinent.

3. Alcoholics and people who abuse drugs have made drugs the focus of their lives and a major way of dealing with problems. So, the very thought of totally giving up drugs is the last thing they want. Instead, they compromise by making rules/promises about how they will control drug use, but the problem is that these rules/promises are more often broken than kept.

4. Kishline's relapse and her return to abusing alcohol are evidence that alcoholics cannot learn to drink in moderation. However, this evidence of failure in learning to drink responsibly comes from a single case study and doesn't necessarily apply to all alcoholics. It is possible that some other alcoholic or drug abuser might learn to control his or her drug use.

5. The main reason AA and other drug treatment programs insist on total abstinence from drinking or abusing other drugs (heroin, cocaine, methamphetamine) is that, like Kishline's experience, there is a very high potential for relapse (55–70%), even after successfully completing a treatment program. Because of such high relapse rates and such little evidence that most alcoholics can learn moderate drinking, the safest goal is "No more drugs."

# Links to Learning

## Web Sites

- **WADSWORTH ONLINE STUDY CENTER**
  **http://psychology.wadsworth.com**
  Quizzes, learning activities and exercises, a discussion forum, and hot links to Internet sites related to sensation, including:

- **DRUG ENFORCEMENT ADMINISTRATION (DEA)**
  **http://www.usdoj.gov/dea/index.htm**
  This government site supplies information, statistics, photos of psychoactive drugs, and information on federal drug enforcement activities.

- **NATIONAL CLEARINGHOUSE FOR ALCOHOL AND DRUG INFORMATION**
  **http://www.health.org/**
  This site provides information for those who want to overcome a drug problem—their own or someone else's.

- **MOTHERS AGAINST DRUNK DRIVING (MADD)**
  **http://www.madd.org**
  MADD promotes efforts to solve the problems of drunk driving and underage drinking. The site includes information on many alcohol-related topics, and a guide to giving a safe party.

- **HIGHER EDUCATION CENTER FOR ALCOHOL AND OTHER DRUG PREVENTION**
  **http://www.edc.org/hec/**
  Sponsored by an organization that provides support for campus alcohol and drug prevention efforts nationwide, this site covers campus drug use and features a special area for students.

## Learning Activities

- ***POWERSTUDY™ CD BY ROD PLOTNIK & TOM DOYLE***

> **Power Study™**
> **Check out CD: Module 3**
> E. Transmitters; book pages 175, 182, 185, 186
> H. Cultural Diversity: Plants and Drugs; book pages 177, 181

- ***STUDY GUIDE TO ACCOMPANY INTRODUCTION TO PSYCHOLOGY, 6TH EDITION,*** by Matthew Enos
  How do we "self-medicate" in an attempt to control and manage our thoughts, feelings, and behavior? Pay close attention to Module 8 for the answers to this and other questions, including how hypnosis and drug use are somewhat alike and whether the national DARE program is effective.

- ***WEBTUTOR***
  **http://webtutor.thomsonlearning.com**
  **WebTUTOR** Visit this site for interactive versions of the Study Guide features. Take a quiz, get your score—should you study a topic some more, or can you move on? For example, what is the number one cash crop in the United States? Is hypnosis the most effective method for quitting smoking? What substance is responsible for the most drug deaths?

- ***INFOTRAC ONLINE LIBRARY***
  **http://www.infotrac-college.com**
   Use your password and then key in search terms such as those below to find popular and scientific articles on subjects covered in Module 8. Make the library work for you!
  Addiction     Alcoholism
  Psychoactive drugs     DARE

- ***PSYCHNOW!***
  CD for Macintosh and Windows includes a study guide, glossary, Web sites, and animations. For Module 8, see:
  - Psychoactive Drugs

## Study Questions

*Use InfoTrac to search for topics mentioned in the main heads below (e.g., hypnotism, stimulants, opiates, hallucinogens, alcohol, marijuana, drug abuse).*

*A. **Hypnosis**—A student has great test anxiety, which is interfering with his success in college. Would hypnosis help? (**Suggested answer page 623**)

B. **Drugs: Overview**—Keeping in mind that Americans spend about $50 billion annually on illegal drugs, what is your position on their legalization?

C. **Stimulants**—Why don't most Americans think that caffeine and nicotine are drugs that can be addictive?

D. **Opiates**—Why do you think that our brains manufacture their own morphinelike chemicals, called endorphins?

E. **Hallucinogens**—Why is there a long history of people's use of hallucinogens in religious ceremonies?

*F. **Alcohol**—If researchers know who has an increased risk for alcoholism, at what age should such a person be told? (**Suggested answer page 623**)

G. **Cultural Diversity: Alcoholism Rates**—Why are there such striking similarities in the development of alcoholism across different cultures?

*H. **Marijuana**—A regular user of marijuana says that he can drive just fine after smoking. Would you ride with him? (**Suggested answer page 624**)

I. **Research Focus: Drug Prevention**—Can you think of reasons a 17-week course in drug abuse prevention might not be effective for adolescents?

J. **Application: Treatment for Drug Abuse**—Why are individuals who have been successfully treated for drug abuse so often tempted to relapse and use drugs again?

*These questions are answered in Appendix B.

# Module 9: Classical Conditioning

**A. Three Kinds of Learning**    **196**
* CLASSICAL CONDITIONING
* OPERANT CONDITIONING
* COGNITIVE LEARNING

**B. Procedure: Classical Conditioning**    **197**
* PAVLOV'S EXPERIMENT
* TERMS IN CLASSICAL CONDITIONING

**C. Other Conditioning Concepts**    **199**
* GENERALIZATION
* DISCRIMINATION
* EXTINCTION
* SPONTANEOUS RECOVERY

**D. Adaptive Value & Uses**    **200**
* TASTE-AVERSION LEARNING
* EXPLANATION
* EXAMPLES OF CLASSICAL CONDITIONING
* CONDITIONED EMOTIONAL RESPONSE
* CLASSICAL CONDITIONING AND DYSLEXIA

**E. Three Explanations**    **202**
* THEORIES OF CLASSICAL CONDITIONING
* STIMULUS SUBSTITUTION AND CONTIGUITY THEORY
* COGNITIVE PERSPECTIVE

**Concept Review**    **203**

**F. Research Focus: Conditioning Little Albert**    **204**
* CAN EMOTIONAL RESPONSES BE CONDITIONED?

**G. Cultural Diversity: Conditioning Dental Fears**    **205**
* IN THE DENTIST'S CHAIR
* CULTURAL PRACTICES
* ORIGINS
* EFFECTS OF FEAR

**H. Application: Conditioned Fear & Nausea**    **206**
* EXAMPLES OF CLASSICAL CONDITIONING
* SYSTEMATIC DESENSITIZATION

**Summary Test**    **208**

**Critical Thinking**    **210**
* CAN YOUR BELIEFS MAKE YOU SICK?

**Links to Learning**    **211**

PowerStudy™

## It's Only Aftershave

**What happened to Carla?**

"I've got an unusual problem and I thought you might be able to explain what happened." Carla, one of my students, looked troubled.

"I'll help if I can," I replied, and asked her to sit down.

"It all started when my dentist told me that I needed a lot of work on my teeth and gums. I spent many mornings in the dentist's chair, and even though he gave me Novocain, it was painful and very uncomfortable. But here's the strange part that I wish you would explain. I had recently bought my boyfriend a new aftershave, and as the dentist worked on my teeth, I noticed that he was using the same one. You'll think this is silly, but now when I smell my boyfriend's aftershave, I start to feel tense and anxious."

Carla stopped and waited to see if I would tell her that she was just being silly. I didn't, and she continued.

"Finally, I told my boyfriend that he would have to stop using the aftershave I had bought him because it was the same as my dentist's and the smell made me anxious. Well, we got into a big argument because he said that he was nothing like my dentist and I was just being silly. So now my teeth are great, but I feel myself getting anxious each time we get close and I smell his aftershave."

How can smelling aftershave cause anxiety?

I assured Carla that she was not being silly and that many people get conditioned in the dentist's chair. In fact, patients have reported feeling anxious when they enter the dentist's office, smell the antiseptic odor, or hear the sound of the drill (Milgrom et al., 1994). I explained that, without her knowing, she had been conditioned to feel fear each time she smelled her dentist's aftershave and how that conditioning had transferred to her boyfriend. Before I explained how to get "unconditioned," I told her how after only one terrifying experience, I too had been conditioned.

## It's Only a Needle

**What happened to Rod?**

I was about 8 years old when I had to get an injection from my local doctor, whom I really liked. He warned me in a kindly way that the injection might hurt a little. I was feeling OK until I saw the long needle on the syringe. I tried to be brave and think of my fuzzy dog, but as soon as I felt that long needle enter my little butt, everything started to spin. I remember sinking slowly to the floor, and then everything went dark. When I came to, the doctor told me that I had fainted.

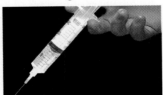

How can the sight of a syringe and needle cause terror?

Even after all these years, the sight of a needle can still strike terror into me. To prevent fainting, I always lie down when getting an injection or giving blood. But I'm not alone in my fear of needles and injections; about 10 to 20% of the general population report a similar fear (Page et al., 1997).

Besides learning to fear needles and blood, people can unknowingly learn to feel sick and nauseated, just as Michelle did.

## It's Only Dish Soap

**What happened to Michelle?**

Michelle was nervous and afraid as the nurse put a needle into the vein in her left arm and then opened a valve that allowed chemicals to drip into her bloodstream. Michelle was in the process of receiving chemotherapy to treat her cancer. One serious side effect of chemotherapy is severe nausea, which Michelle experienced after each treatment.

What Michelle wasn't prepared for was how other things could trigger her nausea. In one case, the odor of her dishwashing liquid, which smelled similar to the chemotherapy room, made her feel nauseated. She had to change her brand of detergent because its odor made her salivate, which was the first sign of oncoming nausea (Wittman, 1994). Without her awareness, Michelle had been conditioned to feel nauseated by numerous stimuli involved in her chemotherapy (Montgomery & Bovbjerg, 1997).

The cases of Michelle, Carla, and myself show how we had been conditioned to fear relatively ordinary things, such as aftershave lotion, needles, and the smell of detergent. This conditioning illustrates one kind of learning.

How can smelling dish soap cause nausea?

*Learning* is a relatively enduring or permanent change in behavior that results from previous experience with certain stimuli and responses. The term *behavior* includes both unobservable mental events (thoughts, images) and observable responses (fainting, salivating, vomiting).

In all three cases, conditioning resulted in a relatively enduring change in behavior. In fact, mine has lasted almost 50 years. What happened to each of us involved a particular kind of learning, called classical conditioning, which we'll discuss in this module.

## What's Coming

*We'll first discuss three different kinds of learning and then focus on one, classical conditioning.* We'll examine how classical conditioning is established and tested, how we respond after being classically conditioned, what we learn during classical conditioning, and how classical conditioning is used in therapy. Let's begin with a look at three different kinds of learning.

# A. Three Kinds of Learning

**Why is some learning easier?**

Some things are difficult to learn, such as all the terms in this module. Other things are easy to learn, such as fear of an injection. To understand why some learning is easy and some hard, we'll visit three different laboratories. You'll see how psychologists identified three different principles that underlie three different kinds of learning: classical conditioning, operant conditioning, and cognitive learning.

## Classical Conditioning

**Why does the dog salivate?**

It is the early 1900s, and you are working as a technician in Russia in the laboratory of Ivan Pavlov. He has already won a Nobel Prize for his studies on the reflexes involved in digestion. For example, he found that when food is placed in a dog's mouth, the food triggers the reflex of salivation (Evans, 1999).

As a lab technician, your task is to place various kinds of food in a dog's mouth and measure the amount of salivation. But soon you encounter a problem. After you have placed food in a dog's mouth on a number of occasions, the dog begins to salivate merely at the sight of the food.

At first, Pavlov considered this sort of anticipatory salivation to be a bothersome problem. Later, he reasoned that the dog's salivation at the sight of food was also a reflex, but one that the dog had somehow *learned*.

In a well-known experiment, Pavlov rang a bell before putting food in the dog's mouth.

As shown in this graph, after a number of trials of hearing a bell paired with food, the dog salivated at the sound of the bell alone, a phenomenon that Pavlov called a *conditioned reflex* and today is called classical conditioning. Classical conditioning was an important discovery because it allowed researchers to study learning in an observable, or objective, way.

*Classical conditioning* is a kind of learning in which a neutral stimulus acquires the ability to produce a response that was originally produced by a different stimulus.

Next, we'll visit a lab in the United States and observe a different kind of learning.

*[Graph: Drops of Saliva (0–60) vs. Trials (1, 10, 20, 30, 40). Source: Adapted from Anrep, 1920]*

## Operant Conditioning

**Why does the cat escape?**

It is the late 1800s, and you are now working in the laboratory of the American psychologist E. L. Thorndike. Your task is to place a cat in a box with a door that can be opened from the inside by hitting a simple latch. Outside the box is a fish on a dish. You are to record the length of time it takes the cat to hit the latch, open the door, and get the fish.

Thorndike studied how a cat learned to open a cage to get food nearby.

On the first trial, the cat sniffs around the box, sticks its paw in various places, accidentally hits the latch, opens the door, and gets the fish. You place the cat back into the box for another trial. Again the cat moves around, accidentally strikes the latch, and gets the fish. After many such trials, the cat learns to spend its time around the latch and eventually to hit the latch and get the fish in a very short time.

To explain the cat's goal-directed behavior, Thorndike formulated the law of effect.

The *law of effect* says that if some random actions are followed by a pleasurable consequence or reward, such actions are strengthened and will likely occur in the future.

Thorndike's law of effect was important because it identified a learning process different from Pavlov's conditioned reflex. Today, the law of effect has become part of operant conditioning (Evans, 1999).

*Operant conditioning* refers to a kind of learning in which the consequences that follow some behavior increase or decrease the likelihood of that behavior's occurrence in the future.

**We will discuss operant conditioning in Module 10.** Our next lab has a big plastic doll and a bunch of kids.

## Cognitive Learning

**Why do they punch the doll?**

It is the 1960s, and you are in Albert Bandura's laboratory, where children are watching a film of an adult who is repeatedly hitting and kicking a big, plastic doll. Following this film, the children are observed during play.

Bandura found that children who had watched the film of an adult modeling aggressive behavior played more aggressively than children who had not seen the film (Bandura et al., 1963). The children's change in behavior, which was increased aggressive responses, did not seem to be based on Pavlov's conditioned reflexes or Thorndike's law of effect. Instead, the entire learning process appeared to take place in the children's minds, without their performing any observable responses or receiving any noticeable rewards. These mental learning processes are part of cognitive learning, which is a relatively new approach that began in the 1960s (Lieberman, 2000b).

*Cognitive learning* is a kind of learning that involves mental processes, such as attention and memory; may be learned through observation or imitation; and may not involve any external rewards or require the person to perform any observable behaviors.

Bandura's study demonstrated a third principle of learning, which essentially says that we can learn through observation or imitation. **We will discuss cognitive learning in Modules 10, 11, and 12.**

Now, let's return to Pavlov's laboratory and examine his famous discovery in greater detail.

## Pavlov's Experiment

**What's the procedure?**

Imagine that you are an assistant in Pavlov's laboratory and your subject is a dog named Sam. You are using a procedure that will result in Sam's salivating when he hears a bell, a response that Pavlov called a *conditioned reflex*. Today, we call Pavlov's procedure *classical conditioning*, which involves the following three steps.

### Step 1. Selecting Stimulus and Response

**Terms.** Before you begin the procedure to establish classical conditioning in Sam, you need to identify three critical terms: *neutral stimulus, unconditioned stimulus,* and *unconditioned response.*

**Neutral stimulus.** You need to choose a neutral stimulus.
A *neutral stimulus* is some stimulus that causes a sensory response, such as being seen, heard, or smelled, but does not produce the reflex being tested.
Your neutral stimulus will be a tone (bell), which Sam the dog hears but which does not normally produce the reflex of salivation.

**Unconditioned stimulus.** You need to choose an unconditioned stimulus, or UCS.
An *unconditioned stimulus,* or *UCS,* is some stimulus that triggers or elicits a physiological reflex, such as salivation or eye blink.
Your unconditioned stimulus will be food, which when presented to Sam will elicit the salivation reflex, that is, will make Sam salivate.

**Unconditioned response.** Finally, you need to select and measure an unconditioned response, or UCR.
The *unconditioned response,* or *UCR,* is an unlearned, innate, involuntary physiological reflex that is elicited by the unconditioned stimulus.
For instance, salivation is an unconditioned response that is elicited by food. In this case, the sight of food, which is the unconditioned stimulus, will elicit salivation in Sam, which is the unconditioned response.

### Step 2. Establishing Classical Conditioning

**Trial.** A common procedure to establish classical conditioning is for you first to present the neutral stimulus and then, a short time later, to present the unconditioned stimulus. The presentation of both stimuli is called a *trial.*

**Neutral stimulus.** In a typical trial, you will pair the neutral stimulus, the tone, with the unconditioned stimulus, the food. Generally, you will first present the neutral stimulus (tone) and then, a short time later, present the unconditioned stimulus (food).

**+**

**Unconditioned stimulus (UCS).** Some seconds (but less than a minute) after the tone begins, you present the unconditioned stimulus, a piece of food, which elicits salivation. This trial procedure is the one most frequently used in classical conditioning.

**→**

**Unconditioned response (UCR).** The unconditioned stimulus, food, elicits the unconditioned response, salivation, in Sam. Food and salivation are said to be unconditioned because the effect on Sam is inborn and not dependent on some prior training or learning.

### Step 3. Testing for Conditioning

**Only CS.** After you have given Sam 10 to 100 trials, you will test for the occurrence of classical conditioning. You test by presenting the tone (conditioned stimulus) without showing Sam the food (unconditioned stimulus).

**Conditioned stimulus.** If Sam salivates when you present the tone alone, it means that the tone has become a conditioned stimulus. A *conditioned stimulus,* or *CS,* is a formerly neutral stimulus that has acquired the ability to elicit a response that was previously elicited by the unconditioned stimulus.
In this example, the tone, an originally neutral stimulus, became the CS.

**→**

**Conditioned response.** When Sam salivates to the tone alone, this response is called the conditioned response.
The *conditioned response,* or *CR,* which is elicited by the conditioned stimulus, is similar to, but not identical in size or amount to, the unconditioned response.
One thing to remember is that the conditioned response is usually similar in appearance but smaller in amount or magnitude than the unconditioned response. This means that Sam's conditioned response will involve less salivation to the tone (conditioned stimulus) than to the food (unconditioned stimulus).

**Predict.** One question you may ask about classical conditioning is: What exactly did Sam learn during this procedure? One thing Sam learned was that the sound of a bell predicted the very likely occurrence of food (Rescorla, 1988). Classical conditioning helps animals and humans predict what's going to happen and thus provides information that may be useful for their survival (Lieberman, 2000b).

Next we'll use the concepts of classical conditioning to explain how Carla was conditioned to her dentist's aftershave.

## Terms in Classical Conditioning

**What happened to Carla?** After many trips to her dentist, Carla unknowingly experienced classical conditioning, which explains why she now feels anxious and tense when she smells a certain aftershave lotion. As we review the steps involved in classical conditioning, you will see how they apply to Carla's situation.

### Step 1. Selecting Stimulus and Response

**Terms.** To explain how classical conditioning occurs, it's best to start by identifying three terms: *neutral stimulus, unconditioned stimulus,* and *unconditioned response.*

 The *neutral stimulus* in Carla's situation was the odor of the dentist's aftershave lotion, which she smelled while experiencing pain in the dentist's chair. The aftershave is a neutral stimulus because although it affected Carla (she smelled it), it did not initially produce feelings of anxiety. In fact, initially Carla liked the smell.

 The *unconditioned stimulus* for Carla was one or more of several dental procedures, including injections, drillings, and fillings. These dental procedures are unconditioned stimuli (UCS) because they elicited the unconditioned response (UCR), which was feeling anxious and tense.

 The *unconditioned response* was Carla's feeling of anxiety, which is a combination of physiological reflexes, such as increased heart rate and blood pressure and rapid breathing, as well as negative emotional reactions. Carla's unconditioned response (anxiety) was elicited by the unconditioned stimulus (painful dental procedure).

### Step 2. Establishing Classical Conditioning

**Trial.** One procedure to establish classical conditioning is for the neutral stimulus to occur first and be followed by the unconditioned stimulus. Each presentation of both stimuli is called a *trial.*

In Carla's case, the *neutral stimulus* was smelling the dentist's aftershave while she was experiencing a number of painful dental procedures.

**+**

Carla's many trips to the dentist resulted in her having repeated trials that involved occurrence of the *neutral stimulus,* smelling the dentist's aftershave, and occurrence of the *unconditioned stimulus,* having painful dental procedures.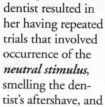

**→**

 The painful dental procedures elicited the *unconditioned response* (feelings of anxiety) as well as other physiological responses, such as increases in heart rate, blood pressure, and breathing rate.

### Step 3. Testing for Conditioning

**Only CS.** A test for classical conditioning is to observe whether the neutral stimulus, when presented alone, elicits the conditioned response.

**Conditioned stimulus.** When Carla smelled her boyfriend's aftershave, which was the same as the dentist's, she felt anxious. The aftershave's smell, formerly a neutral stimulus, had become a *conditioned stimulus* because it elicited anxiety, the conditioned response.

**→**

**Conditioned response.** Whenever Carla smelled the aftershave (conditioned stimulus) used by both her dentist and her boyfriend, it elicited the *conditioned response,* feeling anxious. However, remember that the conditioned response is similar to, but of lesser intensity than, the unconditioned response. Thus, the anxiety elicited by smelling the aftershave was similar to, but not as great as, the anxiety Carla felt during painful dental procedures.

**Dental fears.** Through classical conditioning, Carla learned that the smell of a certain aftershave predicted the likely occurrence of pain and made her feel anxious. Researchers suggest that children and adults who developed an extreme fear or phobia of dental procedures learned such fears through classical conditioning (Townsend et al., 2000). However, just as classical conditioning can elicit fears, it can also be used to treat them through an "unconditioning" procedure that we'll discuss in the Application section.

Next, we'll describe several other behaviors that are associated with classical conditioning.

**What else happened to Carla?**

Carla's experience in the dentist's office of being classically conditioned to feel anxious when she smelled a particular aftershave has several other interesting features. Carla found that similar odors also elicited anxious feelings but that other odors did not; her anxiety when smelling her boyfriend's aftershave gradually decreased, but accidentally meeting the dentist and smelling his aftershave triggered some anxiety. Pavlov found that these phenomena were associated with classical conditioning, and he named them generalization, discrimination, extinction, and spontaneous recovery.

### 1. Generalization

**Why her shampoo?**

During Carla's conditioning trials, the neutral stimulus, which was the odor of the dentist's aftershave, became the conditioned stimulus that elicited the conditioned response, anxiety. However, Carla may also feel anxiety when smelling other similar odors, such as her own hair shampoo; this phenomenon is called generalization.

*Generalization* is the tendency for a stimulus that is similar to the original conditioned stimulus to elicit a response that is similar to the conditioned response. Usually, the more similar the new stimulus is to the original conditioned stimulus, the larger will be the conditioned response.

Pavlov suggested that generalization had an adaptive value because it allowed us to make an appropriate response to stimuli that are similar to the original one. For example, although you may never see your friend's smiling face in exactly the same situation, generalization ensures that the smiling face will usually elicit positive feelings.

Reacting to similar odors is generalization.

### 2. Discrimination

**Why not her nail polish?**

Carla discovered that smells very different from that of the aftershave did not elicit anxiety; this phenomenon is called discrimination.

*Discrimination* occurs during classical conditioning when an organism learns to make a particular response to some stimuli but not to others.

For example, Carla had learned that a particular aftershave's smell predicted the likelihood of a painful dental procedure. In contrast, the smell of her nail polish, which was very different from that of the aftershave, predicted not painful dental procedures but nice-looking fingernails.

Discrimination also has an adaptive value because there are times when it is important to respond differently to related stimuli. For example, you would respond differently to the auditory stimulus of a police siren than to the auditory stimulus of a baby's cries.

Not reacting to a new odor is discrimination.

### 3. Extinction

**What about her boyfriend?**

If Carla's boyfriend did not change his aftershave and she repeatedly smelled it, she would learn that it was never followed by painful dental procedures, and its smell would gradually stop making her feel anxious; this phenomenon is called extinction.

*Extinction* refers to a procedure in which a conditioned stimulus is repeatedly presented without the unconditioned stimulus and, as a result, the conditioned stimulus tends to no longer elicit the conditioned response.

The procedure for extinguishing a conditioned response is used in therapeutic settings to reduce fears or phobias. For example, clients who had a conditioned fear of needles and receiving injections were repeatedly shown needles and given injections by qualified nurses. After exposure to the conditioned stimuli during a 3-hour period, 81% of the clients reported a significant reduction in fear of needles and receiving injections (Ost et al., 1992). This kind of exposure therapy is a practical application of Pavlov's work and will be discussed more fully in Module 22.

Not reacting to a previously powerful stimulus is extinction.

### 4. Spontaneous Recovery

**Would the anxiety come back?**

Suppose Carla's conditioned anxiety to the smell of the aftershave had been extinguished by having her repeatedly smell her boyfriend's lotion without experiencing any painful consequences. Some time later, when Carla happened to accidentally meet her dentist in the local supermarket, she might spontaneously show the conditioned response and feel anxiety when smelling his aftershave; this is called spontaneous recovery.

*Spontaneous recovery* is the tendency for the conditioned response to reappear after being extinguished even though there have been no further conditioning trials.

Spontaneous recovery of the conditioned response will not persist for long and will be of lesser magnitude than the original conditioned response. If the conditioned stimulus (smell of aftershave) is not presented again with the unconditioned stimulus (painful dental procedure), the spontaneously recovered conditioned response will again undergo extinction and cease to occur. Thus, once Carla had been classically conditioned, she would have experienced one or more of these four phenomena.

Having a reaction come back is spontaneous recovery.

Now that you are familiar with the procedure and concepts of classical conditioning, we'll explore its widespread occurrence in the real world.

Pavlov believed that animals and people evolved the capacity for classical conditioning because it had an adaptive value (Hollis, 1997).

*Adaptive value* refers to the usefulness of certain abilities or traits that have evolved in animals and humans that tend to increase their chances of survival, such as finding food, acquiring mates, and avoiding pain and injury.

We'll discuss several examples, such as learning to avoid certain tastes, salivating at the sight of food, and avoiding pain, which support Pavlov's view that classical conditioning is useful because it has an adaptive value.

## Taste-Aversion Learning

**What do you learn from getting sick?**

Rat exterminators have firsthand knowledge of classical conditioning's adaptive value. Exterminators find that while some rats eat enough bait poison to die, others eat only enough to get sick. Once rats get sick on a particular bait poison, they quickly learn to avoid its smell or taste, called *bait shyness*, and never again eat that bait poison. This kind of learning is a form of classical conditioning called taste-aversion learning (Schneider & Pinnow, 1994).

Taste-aversion learning is how rats avoid poison.

*Taste-aversion learning* refers to associating a particular sensory cue (smell, taste, sound, or sight) with getting sick and thereafter avoiding that particular sensory cue in the future.

The adaptive value of taste-aversion learning for rats is obvious: By quickly learning to avoid the smells or taste associated with getting sick, such as eating poison bait, they are more likely to survive.

**Humans.** It is likely that in your lifetime, you too will experience taste-aversion learning. For example, if you have eaten something and gotten sick after taking a thrill ride, you may avoid the smell or taste of that particular food. Similarly, people who get sick from drinking too much of a particular alcoholic drink (often a sweet or distinctive-tasting drink) avoid that drink for a long period of time (Lieberman, 2000b). Taste-aversion learning may also warn us away from eating poisonous plants that cause illness or even death, such as eating certain varieties of mushrooms. All these examples of taste-aversion learning show the adaptive value of classical conditioning, which is to keep us away from potentially unpleasant or dangerous situations, such as taking thrill rides, overdrinking, or eating poisonous plants.

I'm starting to get a sick feeling!!!

As many people have learned, taste-aversion learning can develop after a single experience and may last weeks, months, or even as long as 4 to 5 years (Logue et al., 1981; Rozin, 1986).

The study of taste-aversion learning changed two long-held beliefs about classical conditioning.

## Explanation

**Is only one trial enough?**

For a long time, psychologists believed that bait shyness was not due to classical conditioning. That's because most experimental psychologists believed that classical conditioning occurred only after many trials, and not after a single experience of getting sick. They also believed that for classical conditioning to occur, the neutral stimulus (smell or taste) must be followed closely in time (after seconds or a minute) by the unconditioned response (nausea), rather than hours later (getting sick). These findings were challenged by the work of psychologist John Garcia.

Taste-aversion learning occurs in one trial.

**One-trial learning.** Garcia showed that taste-aversion learning could occur in one trial and, more surprising, even after long intervals (minutes to hours) between the occurrence of the neutral stimulus (smell or taste) and the unconditioned response (sickness or vomiting). Although Garcia's findings first met with disbelief, there is now no question that taste-aversion learning is a unique form of classical conditioning (Lieberman, 2000b).

**Preparedness.** Another interesting finding was that rats, which have poor vision but great senses of taste and olfaction (smell), acquired taste aversion more easily to stimuli involving smell and taste cues and were rarely conditioned to stimuli involving light cues (Garcia et al., 1966). Similarly, quails, which have poor olfaction but great vision, acquired taste aversion more easily to stimuli involving visual cues (Wilcoxon et al., 1971). Garcia concluded that all stimuli do not have the same potential for becoming conditioned stimuli. These findings challenged another long-standing belief in classical conditioning: All stimuli (smell, taste, visual, auditory) have an equal chance of becoming conditioned stimuli. Garcia's finding that some stimuli were more easily conditioned than others was called preparedness (Seligman, 1970).

*Preparedness* refers to the phenomenon that animals and humans are biologically prepared to associate some combinations of conditioned and unconditioned stimuli more easily than others.

The idea of preparedness means that different animals are genetically prepared to use different senses to detect stimuli that are important to their survival and adaptation. For example, John Garcia and his colleagues (1974) applied their knowledge of preparedness and taste aversion to the problem of sheep-killing by coyotes. They baited grazing

Taste-aversion learning is used to stop coyotes from eating sheep.

areas with pieces of sheep flesh laced with a chemical that caused coyotes to become nauseated and ill. As a result, coyotes that had acquired a taste aversion showed an estimated 30–60% reduction in sheep-killing (Bower, 1997a; Gustavson et al., 1976). These findings showed that taste-aversion learning could be put to good use by sheep ranchers.

**Do bluejays avoid butterflies?**

Some animals have evolved their own taste-aversion systems that help them survive by warning off dangerous predators.

For example, bluejays feast on butterflies, but they generally learn to avoid monarch butterflies, which have a distinctive coloring pattern. Unknown to a naive bluejay is the sad fact that monarch butterflies contain a chemical that, when eaten, will make birds sick. Through taste aversion, bluejays learn that the distinctive color pattern of monarch butterflies predicts getting sick, and so smart bluejays avoid eating monarch butterflies.

Taste-aversion learning is how bluejays learn to avoid butterflies.

Like monarch butterflies, many animals have evolved with distinctive markings or colors that, through taste-aversion learning, have become conditioned stimuli that serve as warnings to predators. Thus, classically conditioned taste aversion has survival value for animals. In contrast, things that taste good can produce a classically conditioned response in humans that is also adaptive.

**Hot fudge sundaes.** The next time you enter a restaurant, read the menu, think about food, and see people eating, notice that you are salivating even though you have no food in your own mouth. Just as Pavlov's dog was conditioned to salivate at the sound of a bell, we often salivate when only thinking of, imagining, smelling, or seeing food.

This is a clear example of how many different kinds of neutral stimuli (holding a menu, reading a menu, seeing people eat, looking at food, imagining food) become conditioned stimuli that elicit a conditioned response—salivation.

Salivation is a reflex response that is normally elicited when you place food in your mouth. One purpose of salivation is to lubricate your mouth and throat to make chewing and swallowing food easier. Thus, being classically conditioned to salivate when reading a menu prepares your mouth for the soon-to-arrive food. This is an example of how classical conditioning serves an adaptive value, in this case, aiding the digestive process in humans and animals (Hollis, 1997).

Next, we'll examine how emotional responses can be classically conditioned.

## Conditioned Emotional Response

**Why do people fear needles?**

At the beginning of this module, I told a sad but true childhood story of getting an injection that elicited such pain and fear that I fainted. Even 50 years later, I still fear injections and needles and always lie down to avoid fainting. In my case, you can easily identify each element of classical conditioning: The neutral stimulus is the sight of the syringe; the unconditioned stimulus is injection; and the unconditioned response is pain and fear. After a painful injection, the formerly neutral stimulus, the syringe, becomes a conditioned stimulus and elicits the conditioned response, which is fear and even fainting. Because this situation involved the conditioning of an emotional response, my fear of injections and needles is called a conditioned emotional response.

A conditioned emotional response causes anxiety at the sight of a needle.

A *conditioned emotional response* refers to feeling some positive or negative emotion, such as happiness, fear, or anxiety, when experiencing a stimulus that initially accompanied a pleasant or painful event.

Conditioned emotional responses can have survival value, such as learning to fear and avoid stimuli that signal dangerous situations, such as the sound of a rattlesnake or wail of a siren (Forsyth et al., 2000). Conditioned emotional responses can also signal pleasant situations. For example, many couples have a special song that becomes emotionally associated with their relationship. When this song is heard by one in the absence of the other, it can elicit strong emotional and romantic feelings. Thus, different kinds of stimuli can be classically conditioned to elicit strong conditioned emotional responses.

## Classical Conditioning and Dyslexia

**Why use an eye blink?**

Problems with reading and writing, such as reversing or skipping letters and numbers, affect about 1–2% of school-age children; this is called dyslexia (see p. 320). Dyslexia is difficult to diagnose in young children who have not yet begun to read, so there is need for a nonreading test. Such a test may involve classical conditioning.

**Test.** Kevin, the young man in the photo, is dyslexic and is undergoing classical conditioning of his eye blink reflex. He is wearing a head gear that delivers a tone (conditioned stimulus) followed by a puff of air (unconditioned stimulus) that elicits his eye blink reflex (unconditioned response). Using this classical conditioning procedure, individuals who are not dyslexic learn to blink about 90% of the time

Classical conditioning is used to diagnose dyslexia.

to the tone alone (conditioned response), before the air puff occurs. However, after this same classical conditioning procedure, Kevin never learned to blink to the tone alone (conditioned response), which means his eye blink reflex could not be classically conditioned (Coffin, 2000). If these results can be repeated, classical conditioning of the eye blink reflex could diagnose dyslexia in very young children so that help in dealing with dyslexia could also begin very early.

From these examples, you can see how classical conditioning helps animals and humans survive and adapt to their environments, elicits emotional responses, and may be a test to diagnose dyslexia. Next, we'll go to the heart of classical conditioning and examine how and why classical conditioning works.

### Theories of Classical Conditioning

**Do you salivate when thinking of pizza?**

Although most of us have had the experience of salivating when thinking about or seeing a favorite food, such as a pizza, researchers have given different explanations of what happens or what is learned during conditioning. We'll discuss three theories—stimulus substitution, contiguity theory, and cognitive perspective—that offer different explanations of why nearly all of us salivate when only thinking about or seeing a delicious pizza.

### Stimulus Substitution & Contiguity Theory

**Does the bell substitute for food?**

The first explanation of classical conditioning came from Pavlov, who said the reason a dog salivated to a tone was that the tone became a substitute for the food, a theory he called stimulus substitution.

*Stimulus substitution* means that a neural bond or association forms between the neutral stimulus (tone) and unconditioned stimulus (food). After repeated trials, the neutral stimulus becomes the conditioned stimulus (tone) and acts like a substitute for the unconditioned stimulus (food). Thereafter, the conditioned stimulus (tone) elicits a conditioned response (salivation) that is similar to that of the unconditioned stimulus.

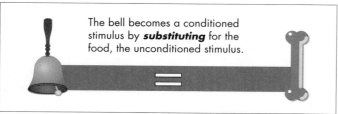

The bell becomes a conditioned stimulus by **substituting** for the food, the unconditioned stimulus.

According to stimulus substitution theory, you salivate when you see a pizza because the act of seeing a pizza (conditioned stimulus) becomes bonded in your nervous system to the pizza itself (unconditioned stimulus). Because of this neural bond or association, the sight of pizza substitutes for the pizza, so that just the sight of a pizza can elicit salivation (conditioned response).

However, researchers discovered that the responses elicited by the unconditioned stimulus were often slightly different from those elicited by the conditioned stimulus. For example, following the unconditioned stimulus, a dog salivated and always chewed, but, following the conditioned stimulus, it salivated but rarely chewed (Zener, 1937).

As a result of this and other criticisms of Pavlov's stimulus substitution theory, researchers suggested a different explanation, the contiguity theory.

The *contiguity theory* says that classical conditioning occurs because two stimuli (neutral stimulus and unconditioned stimulus) are paired close together in time (are contiguous). As a result of this contiguous pairing, the neutral stimulus becomes the conditioned stimulus, which elicits the conditioned response.

The contiguity theory says that because seeing a pizza is paired closely in time with eating it, the sight alone begins to elicit salivation. Contiguity theory was the most popular explanation of classical conditioning until the 1960s, when it was challenged by the creative research of psychologist Robert Rescorla (1966).

### Cognitive Perspective

**Does the bell predict food is coming?**

To the surprise of many researchers, Robert Rescorla (1966, 1987, 1988) showed that an association between a neutral and unconditioned stimulus did not necessarily occur when the two stimuli were closely paired in time. Instead, he found that classical conditioning occurred when a neutral stimulus contained information about what was coming next; this explanation is called the cognitive perspective.

The *cognitive perspective* says that an organism learns a predictable relationship between two stimuli such that the occurrence of one stimulus (neutral stimulus) predicts the occurrence of another (unconditioned stimulus). In other words, classical conditioning occurs because the organism learns what to expect.

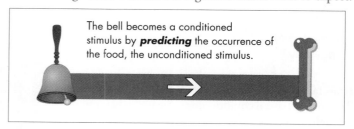

The bell becomes a conditioned stimulus by **predicting** the occurrence of the food, the unconditioned stimulus.

For example, the cognitive perspective theory would explain that you salivate to the sight of pizza because you have learned a predictable relationship: Seeing a pizza (conditioned stimulus) often leads to eating one (unconditioned stimulus), and your expectation causes salivation (conditioned response).

Support for the cognitive perspective comes from a number of findings. For example, classical conditioning occurs best if the neutral stimulus (tone) occurs slightly before the unconditioned stimulus (food). In this sequence, the organism learns a relationship between two stimuli: tone predicts food. However, if the sequence is reversed and the unconditioned stimulus appears before the neutral stimulus, this is called *backward conditioning* and does not usually result in classical conditioning.

The cognitive perspective would explain that backward conditioning makes it impossible to predict a relationship between the neutral and unconditioned stimuli and thus does not usually result in classical conditioning. Currently, there is widespread support for the cognitive perspective, which says that classical conditioning involves learning about predictable relationships, or learning about cause and effect (Hollis, 1997; Lieberman, 2000b).

After the Concept Review, we'll discuss a well-known study of classical conditioning that involves the famous "little Albert."

# Concept Review

 **1.** In classical conditioning, one of the stimuli that is chosen has two characteristics: the stimulus, such as a tone, must cause some reaction, such as being heard, seen, tasted, or smelled, but it must not elicit the unconditioned response. A stimulus with these two characteristics is called a _____.

 **2.** In classical conditioning, a second stimulus is chosen that can elicit an unlearned, involuntary physiological reflex, such as salivation. This stimulus is called an _____.

 **3.** In classical conditioning, the unconditioned stimulus elicits an unlearned, involuntary physiological reflex, such as salivation, which is called the _____.

 **4.** A typical trial in classical conditioning involves first presenting the (a)_____ and then, a short time later, presenting the (b)_____.

 **5.** On the very first conditioning trial, the neutral stimulus (tone) did not itself elicit the unconditioned response (salivation). However, on the first trial, the presentation of food, which is called the (a)_____, did elicit salivation, called the (b)_____.

**6.** After a dozen trials that paired the tone with the food, you noticed that as soon as the tone was presented, the dog salivated. Because the tone itself elicited a response similar to that elicited by the unconditioned stimulus (food), the tone is called the (a)_____. The salivation elicited by the tone itself is called the (b)_____.

 **7.** During classical conditioning there is a tendency for a stimulus similar to the original conditioned stimulus to elicit a response similar to the conditioned response. This tendency is called _____.

 **8.** During classical conditioning, an organism learns to make a particular response to some stimuli but not to others; this phenomenon is called _____.

**9.** If a conditioned stimulus is repeatedly presented *without* the unconditioned stimulus, there is a tendency for the conditioned stimulus to no longer elicit the conditioned response. This phenomenon is called _____.

 **10.** The tendency for the conditioned response to reappear some time later, even though there are no further conditioning trials, is called _____.

**11.** The kind of learning in which the cues (smell, taste, auditory, or visual) of a particular stimulus are associated with an unpleasant response, such as nausea or vomiting, is called (a)_____. This kind of learning can even occur after only a single (b)_____.

**12.** According to Pavlov's original explanation, classical conditioning occurs because of (a)_____,  which means that the conditioned stimulus (tone) bonds to the unconditioned stimulus (food). Through this bond, or association, the conditioned stimulus (tone) elicits the conditioned response (salivation) by substituting for the (b)_____ (food). Pavlov's explanation of classical conditioning was criticized, and researchers suggested instead that conditioning occurs because two stimuli are paired close together in time. This explanation, which is called (c)_____ theory, has been challenged, in turn, by more recent explanations.

**13.** The current and widely accepted explanation of classical conditioning, which is called the (a)_____ perspective, states that animals and humans learn a predictable relationship between stimuli. According to this explanation, a dog learns predictable relationships, such as a tone predicting the occurrence of (b)_____.

**Answers:** *1. neutral stimulus; 2. unconditioned stimulus (UCS); 3. unconditioned response (UCR); 4. (a) neutral stimulus, (b) unconditioned stimulus (UCS); 5. (a) unconditioned stimulus (UCS), (b) unconditioned response (UCR); 6. (a) conditioned stimulus (CS), (b) conditioned response (CR); 7. generalization; 8. discrimination; 9. extinction; 10. spontaneous recovery; 11. (a) taste-aversion learning, (b) trial; 12. (a) stimulus substitution, (b) unconditioned stimulus, (c) contiguity; 13. (a) cognitive, (b) food*

## Can Emotional Responses Be Conditioned?

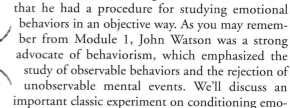

**Why do people fear spiders?**

Why does seeing a tiny, usually harmless, many-legged spider cause many people to show great fear? One reason may be that a person has developed a conditioned emotional response to spiders. Earlier we explained that conditioned emotional responses can occur through classical conditioning and may be very strong, last a long time, and even result in an intense and irrational fear.

However, in the 1920s, psychologists did not know if emotional responses could be conditioned. But with Pavlov's discovery of the conditioned reflex (classical conditioning), John Watson realized that he had a procedure for studying emotional behaviors in an objective way. As you may remember from Module 1, John Watson was a strong advocate of behaviorism, which emphasized the study of observable behaviors and the rejection of unobservable mental events. We'll discuss an important classic experiment on conditioning emotions that John Watson and his student assistant, Rosalie Rayner, published in 1920.

### Method: Identify Terms

Watson questioned the role that conditioning played in the development of emotional responses in children. To answer his question, Watson (photo) tried to classically condition an emotional response in a child.

**Subject: Nine-month-old infant.**
The subject, known later as little Albert, was described as healthy, stolid, and unemotional, since "no one had ever seen him in a state of rage and fear. The infant practically never cried" (Watson & Rayner, 1920, p. 3).

**Neutral stimulus: White rat.**
Watson briefly confronted 9-month-old Albert with a succession of objects, including a white rat, a rabbit, and a dog. "At no time did this infant ever show fear in any situation" (Watson & Rayner, 1920, p. 2).

Rat is CS.

**Unconditioned stimulus: Noise.**
Standing behind Albert, the researchers hit a hammer on a metal bar, which made a loud noise and elicited startle and crying. "This is the first time an emotional situation in the laboratory has produced any fear or crying in Albert" (Watson & Rayner, 1920, p. 3).

Bang is UCS.

**Unconditioned response: Startle/cry.**
Startle and crying were observable and measurable emotional responses that indicated the baby was feeling and expressing fear.

After Watson identified the three elements of classical conditioning, he and his assistant, Rayner, began the procedure for classical conditioning.

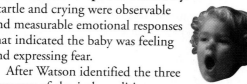

Startle is UCR.

### Procedure: Establish and Test for Classical Conditioning

**Establish.** At the age of 11 months, Albert was given repeated trials consisting of a neutral stimulus, a white rat, followed by an unconditioned stimulus, a loud noise. During early trials, he startled at the sight of the rat and on later trials he also cried.

Rat (CS) plus loud bang (UCS) elicits startle response (UCR).

**Test.** When first presented with the rat alone (no noise), Albert startled. Then he was given additional conditioning trials and retested with the rat alone (no noise). "The instant the rat was shown the baby began to cry" (Watson & Rayner, 1920, p. 5). Thus, Watson had succeeded in classically conditioning Albert's emotional response (fear).

Classical conditioning: rat (CS) alone elicits startle response (CR).

### Results and Conclusions

Watson and Rayner had shown that Albert developed a conditioned emotional response of startle and crying to the sight of a rat, which lasted about a week and then diminished, or underwent *extinction.*

After Albert was conditioned to fear a white rat, he was shown other objects to test for *generalization.* For example, he crawled away and cried at the sight of a rabbit, and he turned away and cried at the sight of a fur coat. But he showed no fear of blocks, paper, or Watson's hairy head, which indicates *discrimination.*

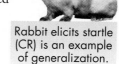

Rabbit elicits startle (CR) is an example of generalization.

Watson's conditioning of Albert was more of a demonstration than a rigorously controlled experiment. For example, Watson and Rayner did not use a standardized procedure for presenting stimuli and sometimes removed Albert's thumb from his mouth, which may have made him cry. Watson was also criticized for not unconditioning Albert's fears before he left the hospital.

Although other researchers failed to replicate Watson and Rayner's results, this was the first demonstration that emotional responses could be classically conditioned in humans (Samelson, 1980). Watson's demonstration laid the groundwork for explaining how people can learn such fear of spiders.

We've discussed how emotional responses can be conditioned; next, we'll show how conditioned emotional responses can influence a person's behavior.

## In the Dentist's Chair

**What goes on at the dentist's?**

As you sit in the dentist's chair, two interesting psychological factors are at work: the possibility of being classically conditioned and the possibility of perceiving more or less pain.

Earlier, we discussed the likely possibility of being classically conditioned during dental treatment. For example, in the dentist's chair you'll receive unconditioned stimuli (injection, drilling), which elicit unconditioned responses (pain, fear, and anxiety), which, in turn, can be conditioned to a variety of neutral stimuli

Classical conditioning: smell (CS) plus drilling (UCS) elicits pain (UCR).

(smells, sights, sounds, or images). At the beginning of this module we discussed how Carla's anxiety was conditioned to the smell of the dentist's aftershave lotion (p. 198).

As we also discussed earlier, pain is somewhat unlike other senses in that the intensity of pain can be increased or decreased by a number of psychological factors, such as your ability to relax or refocus your attention on something else (p. 112). Now we'll discuss how cultural factors can influence the conditioning of dental fears, which in turn can increase or decrease the visits to dentists in different countries (Milgrom et al., 1994).

## Cultural Practices

**Which citizens have most dental fears?**

As the graph below indicates, the percentage of children reporting high levels of dental fear is considerably greater in the United States and Asia (Singapore and Japan) than in Scandinavia (Norway and Sweden) (Chellappah et al., 1990; Klingberg & Hwang, 1994; Milgrom et al., 1994; Neverlien & Johnsen, 1991).

| | |
|---|---|
| 20% | United States |
| 17% | Singapore |
| 14% | Japan |
| Norway/Sweden | 3.5% |

**Rates of Dental Fears in Children**

One reason behind cultural differences in rates of dental fear is that the countries have different systems of dental care. In Scandinavian countries, dental care is part of a free, universal health care program available to all citizens. Because it is free and easily available, Scandinavian children tend to receive regular dental care rather than be treated only for dental emergencies. These children view dental treatment as unpleasant but necessary.

In contrast, neither America nor Japan provides free, universal dental coverage. Consequently, some children receive treatment only when there is a serious and painful dental problem. As a result, a child's first dental experience is more painful and something to be avoided. This is an example of how cultural practices influence the "painfulness" of dental treatments.

## Origins

**When did dental fears develop?**

American and Asian adults who reported high rates of dental fears were asked when their fears began. About 66% replied that they acquired their dental fears in childhood or adolescence, often after a painful treatment that was necessitated by a dental emergency (Milgrom et al., 1995; Poulton et al., 1997). These fearful adults reported that the more painful their childhood dental experiences had been, the greater was their fear (Milgrom et al., 1992).

Researchers concluded that the majority of dental fears are acquired in childhood or adolescence, often through classical conditioning. In addition, these fears can keep individuals from asking for or receiving dental treatment for future but necessary dental problems (Clay, 2000).

## Effects of Fear

**Which citizens most avoid dentists?**

Once dental fears are established, about 20–40% of these individuals report avoiding regular checkups or routine dental treatment (graph below). Usually, these individuals seek dental treatment only when they have emergency problems,

| | |
|---|---|
| 40% | England/Wales |
| 32% | Japan |
| 21% | U.S.A. |

**People Avoiding Dental Treatment**

which tend to involve very painful procedures. As a result, painful emergency dental procedures strengthen their already high level of fears and start a new vicious circle of avoiding dental treatment until the next emergency. From our knowledge of classical conditioning, we know that one way to reduce high levels of dental fear is to receive regular, nonpainful dental checkups and treatment, which will extinguish some of the conditioned emotional responses (Litt et al., 1999).

Based on these data, researchers concluded that cultural differences, such as kind and frequency of dental treatment in childhood and adolescence, affect both a child's perception of pain and the occurrence of conditioned emotional responses—in this case, fear of dentists (Milgrom et al., 1994).

Next, we'll examine another kind of treatment—chemotherapy for cancer—that also involves classical conditioning and results in a terrible problem—conditioned nausea.

## Examples of Classical Conditioning

**Why do people faint from fear?**

At the beginning of this module, I related my childhood experience of receiving an injection and then fainting. This one trial of classical conditioning resulted in my fear of needles, which remains with me to this present day. My

Conditioned emotional response

experience illustrates the powerful effect that conditioned emotional responses can have on our behavior. If you still doubt that relatively nonthreatening stimuli (needle, blood) can be conditioned to elicit such a powerful physiological response as fainting, you'll be convinced by the next study.

### Conditioned Emotional Response

Just as about 10–20% of adults report a fear of needles and injections, about the same percentage report a fear of seeing blood (Locker et al., 1997). Wondering why some people feel faint at the sight of blood, researchers asked 30 such subjects to watch a movie on open-heart surgery as their heart rates were monitored. During the movie, 4 of the 30 subjects unexpectedly fainted.

For example, the graph shows that after 4 minutes of watching the open-heart surgery movie, one subject

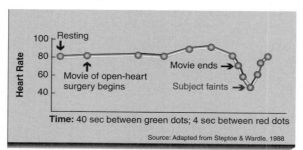

**Time:** 40 sec between green dots; 4 sec between red dots

Source: Adapted from Steptoe & Wardle, 1988

became so fearful and anxious that his body went into mild shock and he fainted. The reason this subject fainted from simply watching a movie on open-heart surgery was that he had developed a conditioned emotional response, intense fear, to the sight of blood (Steptoe & Wardle, 1988). Intense fear triggers tremendous changes in heart rate and blood pressure that can cause many physiological changes, including fainting.

Classical conditioning can also trigger nausea to a particular odor.

### Anticipatory Nausea

At the beginning of this module, we told you about Michelle, who was receiving chemotherapy treatment for breast cancer. One side effect of the powerful anticancer drugs used in chemotherapy is nausea, which may be accompanied by severe vomiting that lasts 6–12 hours.

As Michelle received additional chemotherapy injections, she experienced nausea when she smelled the treatment room or smelled her dish soap, which smelled like the treatment room. Michelle's problem is called anticipatory nausea.

*Anticipatory nausea* refers to feelings of nausea that are elicited by stimuli associated with nausea-inducing chemotherapy treatments.

Anticipatory nausea is an example of classical conditioning.

Patients experience nausea after treatment but also before or in anticipation of their treatment. Researchers believe that conditioned nausea occurs through classical conditioning.

For example, by their fourth injection, 60–70% of the patients who receive chemotherapy experience anticipatory nausea when they encounter smells, sounds, sights, or images related to treatment (Montgomery & Bovbjerg, 1997). Even 1–2 years after treatment ends, patients may continue to experience anticipatory nausea if they encounter cues associated with chemotherapy (Fredrickson et al., 1993). What makes conditioned nausea especially troublesome is that current medication does not always control it.

First we'll discuss how conditioned nausea occurs and then how it can be controlled with a nonmedical treatment.

### Conditioning Anticipatory Nausea

A few weeks after beginning her chemotherapy, Michelle began to experience anticipatory nausea that was triggered by a number of different stimuli, including the smell of her dish detergent, which smelled similar to the treatment room. Now that you know her situation, perhaps you can identify the terms and explain how classical conditioning occurred.

- **Neutral stimulus** is the smell of the treatment room and her dish detergent, which initially did not cause any nausea.
- **Unconditioned stimulus** is the chemotherapy, which elicits nausea and vomiting.
- **Unconditioned responses** are the nausea and vomiting, which were elicited by chemotherapy, the unconditioned stimulus.

- **Conditioning trials** involve presenting the neutral stimulus, smell of the treatment room (same as her detergent), with the unconditioned stimulus, the chemotherapy.
- **Conditioned stimulus** (smell of the treatment room or detergent), when presented by itself, now elicits the conditioned response (nausea).

Once established, anticipatory nausea can be very difficult to treat and control with drugs (Montgomery & Bovbjerg, 1997). Even after chemotherapy ends, anticipatory nausea may reappear for a while, which is an example of spontaneous recovery.

However, there is a nonmedical treatment for anticipatory nausea, which is also based on classical conditioning. This treatment is called systematic desensitization, which we'll discuss next.

Dish soap is CS.

## Systematic Desensitization

**Can you "uncondition" fearful things?**

Because of repeated chemotherapy sessions, Michelle developed anticipatory nausea (right photo), which was not relieved by medication. She is now going to try a nonmedical treatment called systematic desensitization.

*Systematic desensitization* is a procedure based on classical conditioning, in which a person imagines or visualizes fearful or anxiety-evoking stimuli and then immediately uses deep relaxation to overcome the anxiety. Systematic desensitization is a form of counterconditioning because it replaces, or counters, fear and anxiety with relaxation.

Learning to decrease anxiety through systematic desensitization

Essentially, systematic desensitization is a procedure to "uncondition," or overcome, fearful stimuli by pairing anxiety-provoking thoughts or images with feelings of relaxation. Systematic desensitization was developed by Joseph Wolpe in the early 1950s and has become one of the most frequently used nonmedical therapies for relief of anxiety and fears in both children and adults (Williams & Gross, 1994). Just as anticipatory nausea is based on Pavlov's classical conditioning, so too is systematic desensitization (Wolpe & Plaud, 1997).

In Michelle's case, she will try to "uncondition," or override, the anxiety-producing cues of chemotherapy, such as smells and sights, with feelings of relaxation. The procedure for systematic desensitization involves the three steps described below (Wolpe & Lazarus, 1966).

### Systematic Desensitization Procedure: Three Steps

**Step 1. Learning to relax**
Michelle is taught to relax by tensing and relaxing sets of muscles, beginning with the muscles in her toes and continuing up

1st step is learning to relax on cue.

to the muscles in her calves, thighs, back, arms, shoulders, neck, and finally face and forehead. She practices doing this intentional relaxation for about 15 to 20 minutes every day for several weeks.

After learning how to relax her body at will, she goes on to Step 2.

**Step 2. Making an anxiety hierarchy**

**MOST STRESSFUL**

8. Vomiting
7. Feeling nausea
6. Receiving injection
5. In treatment room
4. Smelling chemicals
3. In waiting room
2. Entering clinic
1. Driving to clinic

2nd step is making a list of items that elicit anxiety.

Michelle makes up a list of 7–12 stressful situations associated with chemotherapy treatment. As shown above, she arranges her list of situations in a hierarchy that goes from least to most stressful. For example, the least stressful situations are driving to and entering the clinic, and the most stressful are nausea and vomiting. Now she's ready for Step 3.

**Step 3. Imagining and relaxing**
Michelle first puts herself into a deeply relaxed state and then vividly imagines the least stressful situation, driving to the clinic. She is told to remain in a relaxed state while imagining this situation. If she becomes anxious or stressed, she is told to stop imagining this situation and return instead to a relaxed state. Once she is sufficiently relaxed, she again imagines driving to the clinic. If she can imagine driving to the clinic while remaining in a relaxed state, she goes to the next stressful situation.

She then imagines entering the clinic, while remaining in a relaxed state. She continues up the anxiety hier-

**MOST STRESSFUL**

8. Vomiting
7. Feeling nausea
6. Receiving injection
5. In treatment room
4. Smelling chemicals
3. In waiting room
2. Entering clinic
1. Driving to clinic

3rd step is combining relaxation with items in anxiety hierarchy.

archy, imagining in turn each of the eight stressful stimuli while keeping herself in a relaxed state. At the first sign of feeling anxious, she stops and returns to a relaxed state. After returning to a relaxed state, she continues with this procedure until she reaches the most stressful situation in her anxiety hierarchy.

### Effectiveness of Systematic Desensitization

As Michelle associates relaxation with each stressful situation in the hierarchy, she overcomes, or counterconditions, each stimulus in her hierarchy. In other words, systematic desensitization can be thought of as using relaxation to get rid of the stressful and anxious feelings that have become associated with a variety of stimuli that are listed in the hierarchy.

Systematic desensitization has been found to be very effective in treating a wide variety of fearful and anxiety-producing behaviors,

including conditioned nausea and fear of blood, injections, snakes, and speaking in public (Hasselt & Hersen, 1994).

We have discussed the many sides of classical conditioning, from salivation to fainting, from taste aversion to little Albert's conditioned emotional responses, from bait shyness in rats to dental fears in humans, from anticipatory nausea to systematic desensitization. It's evident that classical conditioning has a considerable influence on many of our thoughts, emotions, and behaviors.

## A. THREE KINDS OF LEARNING

**1.** A relatively permanent change in behavior that involves specific stimuli and/or responses that change as a result of experience is a definition of _____. The change in behavior includes both unobservable mental events and observable behavioral responses.

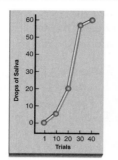

**2.** Psychologists have identified three different principles that are the basis for three different kinds of learning. One kind of learning can be traced to Pavlov's well-known experiment in which a bell was sounded and then food was placed in a dog's mouth. After a number of trials in which the bell and food were presented, the dog began to salivate to the bell alone. Pavlov called this kind of learning a conditioned reflex, which today is called _____.

**3.** A second kind of learning grew out of Thorndike's observations of cats learning to escape from a box. To explain a cat's goal-directed behavior of hitting a latch to get food, Thorndike formulated a principle of learning called the (a)_____. This law states that if certain random actions are followed by a pleasurable consequence or reward, such actions are strengthened and will likely occur in the future. Today, the law of effect has become part of the second kind of learning that is called (b)_____.

**4.** A third kind of learning involves mental processes, such as attention and memory; may be learned through observation or imitation; and may not involve any external rewards or require the person to perform any observable behaviors. This kind of learning is called _____.

## B. PROCEDURE: CLASSICAL CONDITIONING

**5.** Suppose you wanted to classically condition your roommate to salivate at the sight of a psychology textbook. One procedure for establishing classical conditioning would be to present two stimuli close together in time. The presentation of the two stimuli is called a trial. In our example, a typical trial would involve first presenting a psychology textbook, initially called the (a)_____, which does not elicit salivation. A short time later, you would present a piece of brownie, called the (b)_____ stimulus, which elicits salivation. Salivation, an innate, automatic, and involuntary physiological reflex, is called the (c)_____.

**6.** After giving your roommate about a dozen trials, you observe that, as soon as you show him the psychology text, he begins to salivate. Because the sight of the psychology textbook itself elicits salivation, the psychology text has become a (a)_____. The roommate's salivation at the sight of the psychology book, presented alone, is called the (b)_____. You know that classical conditioning is established when the neutral stimulus becomes the (c)_____ and elicits the (d)_____. Compared to the unconditioned response, the conditioned response is usually similar in appearance but smaller in amount or magnitude.

## C. OTHER CONDITIONING CONCEPTS

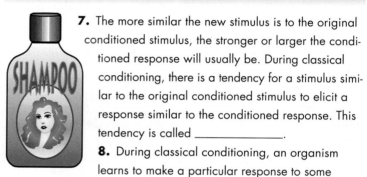

**7.** The more similar the new stimulus is to the original conditioned stimulus, the stronger or larger the conditioned response will usually be. During classical conditioning, there is a tendency for a stimulus similar to the original conditioned stimulus to elicit a response similar to the conditioned response. This tendency is called _____.

**8.** During classical conditioning, an organism learns to make a particular response to some stimuli but not to others; this phenomenon is called _____.

**9.** If a conditioned stimulus is repeatedly presented without the unconditioned stimulus, there is a tendency for the conditioned stimulus to no longer elicit the conditioned response; this phenomenon is called (a)_____. However, if some time later you again presented the psychology text to your roommate without giving him a brownie, he would show salivation, the conditioned response. This recurrence of the conditioned response after it has been extinguished is called (b)_____.

## D. ADAPTIVE VALUE & USES

**10.** After receiving an injection, people may develop fear or anxiety in the presence of stimuli associated with the treatment. If we feel fear or anxiety in the presence of some stimulus that precedes a painful or aversive event, we are experiencing a _____.

**11.** A powerful form of classical conditioning occurs in real life when a neutral stimulus is paired with an unpleasant response, such as nausea or vomiting. The result of this conditioning is called _____. This form of classical conditioning is unusual in two ways: it may be acquired in a single trial and may last a relatively long period of time; and there may be a considerable lapse of time between the presentations of the two stimuli.

**12.** We now know that animals and humans are biologically prepared to associate certain combinations of conditioned and unconditioned stimuli more easily than others. This phenomenon is called

_____.

**13.** The eye blink reflex can be classically conditioned, which means that after a number of trials, the eye blink occurs after hearing a tone and before the (a)_____ occurs. But in individuals with a reading and writing problem, called (b)_____, the eye blink reflex could not be classically conditioned.

**14.** The occurrence of salivation in response to the thought, sight, or smell of food is helpful to digestion and shows that classical conditioning has an _____ role or value.

## E. THREE EXPLANATIONS

**15.** According to Pavlov's explanation, classical conditioning occurs because a neural bond or association forms between the conditioned stimulus and unconditioned stimulus so that the conditioned stimulus eventually substitutes for the unconditioned stimulus. Pavlov's explanation is called _____.

**16.** The explanation that says that classical conditioning occurs because two stimuli (the neutral and unconditioned stimuli) are paired close together in time is called the _____ theory. However, researchers have shown that contiguity or simply pairing stimuli close together does not necessarily produce classical conditioning.

**17.** The explanation of classical conditioning that says that an organism learns a relationship between two stimuli such that the occurrence of one stimulus predicts the occurrence of the other is called the (a)_____. This theory is supported by the idea that classical conditioning is not usually learned if the unconditioned stimulus appears before the neutral stimulus, a procedure that is called (b)_____.

## F. RESEARCH FOCUS: CONDITIONING LITTLE ALBERT

**18.** An emotional response, fear, was classically conditioned in little Albert by presenting a white rat, which was the (a)_____, and then making a loud noise, which was the (b)_____; in turn, the loud noise elicited crying, which was the (c)_____. Albert's conditioned emotional response, crying, also occurred in the presence of stimuli

similar to the white rat, such as a rabbit; this phenomenon is called (d)_____. Albert did not cry at the sight of blocks or papers; this phenomenon is called (e)_____. Watson and Rayner were the first to demonstrate that (f)_____ responses could be classically conditioned in humans.

## G. CULTURAL DIVERSITY: CONDITIONING DENTAL FEARS

**19.** In the United States and Asia, the percentage of children reporting (a)_____ is considerably greater than in Scandinavia. A likely reason for this difference in dental fears is different (b)_____ practices. The majority of people with high levels of dental fears report that these fears originated in childhood, probably through the occurrence of (c)_____.

## H. APPLICATION: CONDITIONED FEAR & NAUSEA

**20.** During chemotherapy, about 60% of the patients develop nausea in anticipation of, or when encountering stimuli associated with, the actual treatment. This type of nausea, which is called _____, cannot always be treated with drugs and may persist long after the chemotherapy ends. Researchers believe that conditioned nausea is learned through classical conditioning.

| MOST STRESSFUL |
| --- |
| 8. **Vomiting** |
| 7. **Feeling nausea** |
| 6. **Receiving injection** |
| 5. **In treatment room** |
| 4. **Smelling chemicals** |
| 3. **In waiting room** |
| 2. **Entering clinic** |
| 1. **Driving to clinic** |

**21.** A nondrug treatment for conditioned nausea involves a procedure based on classical conditioning in which a person imagines or visualizes fearful or anxiety-evoking stimuli and then immediately uses deep (a)_____ to decrease the anxiety associated with these stimuli. This procedure, which is called (b)_____, is a form of counterconditioning because it uses deep relaxation to replace or decrease the fear or anxiety with particular (c)_____ that are arranged in a hierarchy.

*Answers:* 1. learning; 2. classical conditioning; 3. (a) law of effect, (b) operant conditioning; 4. cognitive learning; 5. (a) neutral stimulus, (b) unconditioned stimulus, (c) unconditioned response; 6. (a) conditioned stimulus, (b) conditioned response, (c) conditioned stimulus, (d) unconditioned response; 7. generalization; 8. discrimination; 9. (a) extinction, (b) spontaneous recovery; 10. conditioned emotional response; 11. taste-aversion learning; 12. preparedness; 13. (a) air puff, (b) dyslexia; 14. adaptive, or survival; 15. stimulus substitution; 16. contiguity; 17. (a) cognitive perspective, (b) backward conditioning; 18. (a) neutral stimulus, (b) unconditioned stimulus, (c) unconditioned response, (d) generalization, (e) discrimination (f) conditioned emotional; 19. (a) dental fears, (b) cultural, (c) classical conditioning; 20. anticipatory nausea; 21. (a) relaxation, (b) systematic desensitization, (c) stimuli or situations

# Critical Thinking

## Can Your Beliefs Make You Sick?

The dream of many snackers is to find potato chips that taste really great but are also low in calories, which means low in fat. The potato chip eater's dream came true in the late 1990s, when the U.S. Food and Drug Administration (FDA) approved a fat substitute called olestra.

Olestra is not absorbed by the body so it is calorie free and meant that potato chips suddenly lost half their calories. However, one concern with olestra are possible side effects of nausea, stomach cramps, gas, and loose stools (diarrhea), which had been reported in subjects who had eaten foods containing olestra at every meal for two months. Because of possible side effects, there's a warning label printed on bags containing olestra potato chips: "Olestra may cause abdominal cramping and loose stools." As potato chips and other foods containing olestra became widely available and very popular, there were reports of stomach problems, and critics demanded that olestra be taken off the market.

Researchers studied the side effects of eating potato chips containing olestra by giving each of 1,123 volunteers, ages 13–88, a large bag of potato chips to eat during a movie. Before the movie, volunteers were told that they were taking part in a potato chip test, that they could eat as many chips as they wished, and that there was the possibility of experiencing certain side effects, such as stomach cramps, gas, nausea, or loose stools. But they were not told that half of them randomly got bags of olestra potato chips while the other half got regular chips. To be extra careful, the researchers who analyzed the data did not know which volunteers got which bags.

When the volunteers were interviewed four days later, 15.8% who had eaten olestra potato chips (ate average of 2.1 ounces) reported having one or more side effects, such as gas, cramping, nausea, or diarrhea. However, 17.6% of those who had eaten regular potato chips (ate average of 2.7 ounces) also reported one or more of these stomach problems. There was no statistical difference between groups, which means that both groups experienced about the same number of stomach-related side effects.

Of those who ate regular potato chips, 17.6% may have reported unpleasant side effects because they were initially told that they might experience stomach problems and their expectations or beliefs somehow produced these side effects. (Adapted from N. Hellmich, Study: Olestra chips score well in digestive test, *USA Today*, January 14, 1998, p. 1D)

**Olestra may cause abdominal cramping and loose stools.**

### Questions

**1.** Why might people who ate foods containing olestra at every meal for two months be more likely to experience side effects than someone who has a bag of chips once a day?

**2.** Why wasn't olestra taken off the market when some users reported getting stomach pains or loose stools?

**3.** What is the name of this research approach in which neither the volunteers nor the researchers knew who received which kinds of potato chips?

**4.** Don't the numbers prove that those who ate regular chips reported more side effects than those who ate olestra chips?

**5.** How is it possible for a person's beliefs or expectations to produce physical side effects?

*Try InfoTrac to search for terms:* **olestra, fat substitutes.**

---

### Suggested answers to Newspaper Article questions

1. Those who ate food with olestra 3 times a day for 2 months received a larger dose of olestra than someone who eats only a bag of chips a day. Generally, the higher the dose, the greater the chances of experiencing unwanted side effects.
2. As discussed on pages 30–31, evidence based on personal experiences, which are called testimonials, has a high potential for error and bias and thus is not very reliable. In addition, we know that people's beliefs can greatly influence their responses to placebos and result in real physical benefits or problems (p. 111).
3. In studying effects of chemicals or drugs, researchers use a double-blind procedure (pp. 37, 111), in which neither the subjects nor researchers know who got which treatment. The double-blind procedure greatly reduces error and bias that can come from beliefs or expectations of either subjects or researchers.

4. The raw numbers (17.6% versus 15.8%) seem to indicate that the group that ate regular potato chips had more side effects. However, researchers used statistical tests (p. 37) and found that this difference (17.6% versus 15.8%) was not due to treatment (eating olestra) but rather to chance (other factors).
5. Most people have experienced stomach problems after eating a variety of foods, and this may result in a kind of classical conditioning called taste-aversion learning (p. 200). Similarly, if people are told and then expect or believe that they may experience stomach problems after eating potato chips (olestra or regular), their beliefs or expectations may somehow trigger or produce these stomach-related side effects (p. 111).

# Links to Learning

- WADSWORTH ONLINE STUDY CENTER
  http://psychology.wadsworth.com
  Quizzes, learning activities and exercises, a discussion forum, and hot links to Internet sites related to sensation, including:

- "CONDITIONAL"
  http://www.science.wayne.edu/
  ~wpoff/cor/mem/conditnl.html
  Look here for explanations of classical conditioning, including the generalization and extinction process.
- NOBEL BIOGRAPHY OF IVAN PAVLOV
  http://www.nobel.se/medicine/laureates/1904/pavlov-bio.html
  The Nobel e-Museum offers a detailed biography of the father of conditioning research, as well as the full text of the presentation speech given for his Nobel Prize in Physiology of Medicine in 1904.
- BEYOND FEAR—THE DENTAL PHOBIA VIRTUAL SELF-HELP GROUP
  http://www.beyondfear.org/
  This site is dedicated to helping people with dental phobia. It features online chat and discussion groups and Usenet forum.
- SPECIFIC PHOBIAS
  http://www.psyweb.com/mdisord/anxietydis/specphobia.html
  This site offers lots of information about phobias, including diagnostic criteria and therapeutic and medical treatments.
- ANXIETY DISORDERS ASSOCIATION OF AMERICA (ADAA)
  http://www.adaa.org/
  This site states, "ADAA promotes the prevention and cure of anxiety disorders and works to improve the lives of all people who suffer from them." Click on "About Anxiety Disorders" for links related to phobias.

## Learning Activities

- *POWERSTUDY*™ CD BY ROD PLOTNIK & TOM DOYLE
  A 40-minute, fully narrated, self-paced, multimedia presentation includes animations, interactive activities, videos, quizzes, pronunciation of terms, personal note-taking, and direct-to-Web connections.
- *STUDY GUIDE TO ACCOMPANY INTRODUCTION TO PSYCHOLOGY, 6TH EDITION,* by **Matthew Enos**
  In Module 9, learn why psychological terminology is so intimidating (why not just say "learning" instead of "conditioning"?), consider adopting an effectiveness strategy, and try using Pavlov's logic yourself.
- WEBTUTOR
  http://webtutor.thomsonlearning.com
  Visit this site for interactive versions of the Study Guide features. Take a quiz, get your score—should you study a topic some more, or can you move on? Can you explain why bluejays don't eat monarch butterflies? Can you retell the story of little Albert?
- *INFOTRAC ONLINE LIBRARY*
  http://www.infotrac-college.com

  Use your password and then key in search terms such as those below to find popular and scientific articles on subjects covered in Module 9. Make the library work for you!

  | | |
  |---|---|
  | Classical conditioning | Operant conditioning |
  | Emotional conditioning | Phobias |

- *PSYCHNOW!*
  CD for Macintosh and Windows includes a study guide, glossary, Web sites, and animations. For Module 9, see:
  - Classical Conditioning
  - Operant Conditioning

## Study Questions

*Use InfoTrac to search for topics mentioned in the main heads below (e.g., classical conditioning, conditioned fear).*

*A. **Three Kinds of Learning**—Can you recall situations in which you have experienced each of the three kinds of learning? (**Suggested answer page 624**)

*B. **Procedure: Classical Conditioning**—How do you explain why your heart pounds when you hear the words "There will be a test next class"? (**Suggested answer page 624**)

C. **Other Conditioning Concepts**—If a child were bitten by a small brown dog, can you predict what other animals the child would fear?

D. **Adaptive Value & Uses**—Using the terms and procedures of classical conditioning, can you explain how a person might develop a fear of flying?

E. **Three Explanations**—How would you explain why your cat runs into the kitchen and salivates each time you open the refrigerator door?

F. **Research Focus: Conditioning Little Albert**—What happens when you look into your rear-view mirror and see a police car's flashing lights?

G. **Cultural Diversity: Conditioning Dental Fears**—As a parent, how can you decrease the chances that your child will become fearful of dental treatment?

*H. **Application: Conditioned Fear & Nausea**—How would systematic desensitization be used to help reduce a student's test anxiety? (**Suggested answer page 624**)

*These questions are answered in Appendix B.

# Module 10: Operant & Cognitive Approaches

A. Operant Conditioning    214
* BACKGROUND: THORNDIKE AND SKINNER
* PRINCIPLES AND PROCEDURES
* EXAMPLES OF OPERANT CONDITIONING
* OPERANT VERSUS CLASSICAL CONDITIONING

B. Reinforcers    218
* CONSEQUENCES
* REINFORCEMENT
* REINFORCERS
* PUNISHMENT

C. Schedules of Reinforcement    220
* SKINNER'S CONTRIBUTIONS
* MEASURING ONGOING BEHAVIOR
* SCHEDULES OF REINFORCEMENT
* PARTIAL REINFORCEMENT SCHEDULES

D. Other Conditioning Concepts    222
* GENERALIZATION
* DISCRIMINATION
* EXTINCTION AND SPONTANEOUS RECOVERY

E. Cognitive Learning    223
* THREE VIEWPOINTS OF COGNITIVE LEARNING
* OBSERVATIONAL LEARNING
* BANDURA'S SOCIAL COGNITIVE THEORY
* INSIGHT LEARNING

Concept Review    227

F. Biological Factors    228
* DEFINITION
* IMPRINTING
* PREPARED LEARNING

G. Research Focus: Noncompliance    230
* HOW CAN PARENTS DEAL WITH "NO"?

H. Cultural Diversity: East Meets West    231
* DIFFERENT CULTURES BUT SIMILAR
  LEARNING PRINCIPLES

I. Application: Behavior Modification    232
* DEFINITIONS
* BEHAVIOR MODIFICATION AND AUTISM
* BIOFEEDBACK
* PROS AND CONS OF PUNISHMENT

Summary Test    234

Critical Thinking    236
* IS IT OK FOR PARENTS TO SPANK THEIR KIDS?

Links to Learning    237

PowerStudy™

## Learning 45 Commands

**How did Bart become a movie star?**

It was an unusual movie for two reasons. First, there was almost no dialogue: human actors spoke only 657 words. Second, the star of the movie was a nonspeaking, nonhuman, 12-year-old, 10-foot-tall, 1,800-pound, enormous brown Kodiak bear named Bart (shown on the left). Bart is one of the world's largest land-dwelling carnivores and can, with one swipe of his massive 12-inch paw, demolish anything in his path. Yet, in the movie, there was big bad Bart, sitting peacefully on his haunches, cradling a small bear cub in his arms. "So what?" you might say, but what you don't know is that, in the wild, a Kodiak bear normally kills and eats any cub it encounters.

Bart the bear learned to perform 45 behaviors on cue through operant conditioning.

Because Bart was found as a cub and raised by a human trainer, Bart grew to act more like an overgrown teddy bear than a natural-born killer. For his role in the movie *The Bear*, Bart learned to perform 45 behaviors on cue, such as sitting, running, standing up, roaring, and, most difficult of all, cradling a teddy bear, which is not what an adult bear does in the wild.

The training procedure seems deceptively simple: Each time Bart performed a behavior on cue, the trainer, Doug Seus, gave Bart an affectionate back scratch, an ear rub, or a juicy apple or pear. For example, when the trainer raised his arms high in the air, it was the signal for Bart to sit and hold the teddy bear. After Bart correctly performed this behavior, Doug would give him a reward. After Bart learned to perform all these behaviors with a stuffed teddy bear, a live bear cub was substituted and the scene was filmed for the movie (Cerone, 1989).

Bart learned to perform 45 behaviors on cue through a kind of learning called operant conditioning.

*Operant conditioning*, also called instrumental conditioning, is a kind of learning in which an animal or human performs some behavior, and the following consequence (reward or punishment) increases or decreases the chance that an animal or human will again perform that same behavior.

For example, if Bart performed a particular behavior, such as picking up a teddy bear, the consequence that followed—getting a rewarding apple—increased the chance that Bart would again pick up the teddy bear. Because of what Bart learned through operant conditioning, he has starred in 20 movies and is currently the highest paid animal actor, making about $10,000 a day (Brennan, 1997). That's a salary that most of us would be very happy to bear!

Operant conditioning seems rather straightforward. You perform an action or operate on your environment, such as studying hard. The consequence of your studying, such as how well you do on exams, increases or decreases the likelihood that you will perform the same behavior—studying hard—in the future.

Besides learning by having your behaviors rewarded or punished, you can also learn in a very different way.

## Learning to Golf

**What did Jack learn from just watching?**

In operant conditioning, the learning process is out in the open: Bart performs an observable response (holds a teddy bear), which is followed by an observable consequence (gets an apple). But there is another kind of learning that involves unobservable mental processes and unobservable rewards that you may give yourself. This kind of learning, called cognitive learning, is partly how Jack learned to golf.

According to his parents, Jack began watching the Golf Channel as a toddler. When he was only 13 months old, Jack was imitating the golfers he had been watching on television. He would take his tiny plastic golf club and hit Wiffle® balls (hollow plastic balls with holes) in the living room, sometimes beaning his dad on the head. Although Jack, now age 3, is much too young to play on a real golf course, he loves to practice on a range and often cries when he has to leave. Three-year-old Jack stands 3 feet 1 inch tall and can drive balls 70 yards and putt from 15 feet (right photo). His father, a casual golfer, was surprised when Jack began taking such a keen interest in golf, something he had only seen on the Golf Channel. On his own initiative and without any special encouragement or guidance from his parents, little Jack had begun imitating what he had seen on television.

The process Jack used to learn golfing is very different from the operant conditioning procedure used to teach Bart new behaviors. During operant conditioning, Bart performed observable behaviors (hold a teddy bear), which were influenced by observable consequences (getting an apple). In comparison, Jack learned how to swing a golf club through observation and imitation, which

Jack learned to play golf partly from watching the Golf Channel on TV.

involved unobservable mental processes and is called cognitive learning. We'll discuss cognitive learning later in this module.

## What's Coming

In the first half of this module, we'll discuss the history and procedure of operant conditioning, how operant conditioning differs from classical conditioning, how consequences or reinforcers work, and other examples of operant conditioning. In the second half of this module, we'll explain the history of cognitive learning, the theory behind observational learning, and the role of insight learning.

We'll begin with an important study that involved a cat, a puzzle box, and a smelly fish.

# A. Operant Conditioning

### Background: Thorndike and Skinner

**How did Bart become a movie star?**

We told you how a trainer used operant conditioning to teach Bart to perform 45 different behaviors on cue. Operant conditioning has now been applied to many different settings, such as training animals to perform, training children to use the potty, stopping retarded children from injuring themselves, and helping autistic children learn social behaviors. However, the discovery of operant behavior involved two different researchers who worked in two different laboratories on two different kinds of problems. So that you can appreciate the thinking that led to operant conditioning, we'll visit the laboratories of the two important researchers—E. L. Thorndike and B. F. Skinner.

## Thorndike's Law of Effect

**E. L. THORNDIKE (1874–1949)**

It's the late 1800s, and we're in the laboratory of E. L. Thorndike, who is interested in animal intelligence—specifically, in measuring their capacity for reasoning.

Unlike pet owners who assume from anecdotal observations that their animals are intelligent, Thorndike devised a simple but clever way to measure reasoning in a more objective way. He built a series of puzzle boxes from which a cat could escape by learning to make a specific response, such as pulling a string or pressing a bar. Outside the puzzle box was a reward for escaping—a piece of fish.

We watch Thorndike place a cat in the puzzle box and record its escape time. After Thorndike graphs the data (graph below), we see a gradual lessening in the time needed to escape. Notice that on the first trial the cat needed over 240 seconds to hit the escape latch, but by the last trial, the cat hits the escape latch in less than 60 seconds.

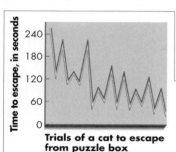

**Trials of a cat to escape from puzzle box**

Thorndike explains that, with repeated trials, the cat spends more time around the latch, which increases the chances of finding and

Law of effect: In escaping puzzle box, cat's successful responses are strengthened and this results in quicker escape times.

hitting the latch and more quickly escaping to get the fish. To explain why a cat's random trial-and-error behaviors gradually turned into efficient, goal-directed behaviors, Thorndike formulated the law of effect.

The *law of effect* states that behaviors followed by positive consequences are strengthened, while behaviors followed by negative consequences are weakened.

Thorndike's (1898) findings were significant because they suggested that the law of effect was a basic law of learning and provided an objective procedure to study it. Thorndike's emphasis on studying the consequences of goal-directed behavior was further developed and expanded by B. F. Skinner.

## Skinner's Operant Conditioning

**B. F. SKINNER (1904–1990)**

It's the 1930s, and we're in the laboratory of B. F. Skinner, who is interested in analyzing ongoing behaviors of animals. Skinner explains that Thorndike's law of effect is useful since it describes how animals are rewarded for making particular responses. However, in order to analyze ongoing behaviors, you must have an objective way to measure them. Skinner's clever solution is a unit of behavior he calls an operant response (Skinner, 1938).

An *operant response* is a response that can be modified by its consequences and is a meaningful unit of ongoing behavior that can be easily measured.

For example, suppose that out of curiosity Bart picks up a teddy bear. His picking up the teddy bear is an example of an operant response because Bart is acting or operating on the environment. The consequence of his picking up the teddy bear is that he receives an apple, which is a desirable effect. This desirable effect modifies his response by increasing the chances that Bart will repeat the same response.

By measuring or recording operant responses, Skinner can analyze animals' ongoing behaviors during learning. He calls this kind of learning *operant conditioning,* which focuses on how consequences (rewards or punishments) affect behaviors.

A simple example of operant conditioning occurs when a rat in an experimental box accidentally presses a bar. If the bar press is followed by food, this consequence increases the chance that the rat will press the bar again. As the rat presses the bar more times, more food follows, which in turn increases the chances that the rat will continue to press the bar (indicated by the rise of the blue line in the figure below).

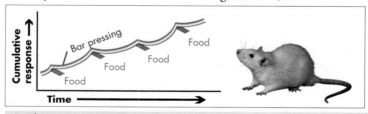

Rat learns to press a bar, which increases the chances of getting food.

Using his newly developed procedure of operant conditioning, B. F. Skinner spent the next 50 years exploring and analyzing learning in rats, pigeons, schoolchildren, and adults.

The 1920s and 1930s gave learning a mighty jolt with the discovery of two general principles—Pavlov's classical conditioning and Skinner's operant conditioning. For the first time, psychologists had two methods to analyze learning processes in an objective way.

Now we'll examine Skinner's ingenious procedure for operant conditioning in more detail.

**Why does a rat press a bar?**

A rat may initially press a bar out of curiosity, and whether it presses the bar again depends on the consequences. To show how consequences can affect behavior, imagine that you are looking over Skinner's shoulder as he places a rat into a box.

The box is empty except for a bar jutting out from one side and an empty food cup below and to the side of the bar (right figure). This box, called a **Skinner box,** is automated to record the animal's bar presses and deliver food pellets. The Skinner box is an efficient way to study how an animal's ongoing behaviors may be modified by changing the consequences of what happens after a bar press.

As you watch, Skinner explains that the rat is a good subject for operant conditioning because it can use its front paws to manipulate objects, such as a bar, and it has a tendency to explore its environment, which means that it will eventually find the bar, touch it, or even press it.

Skinner goes on to explain the following three factors that are involved in operantly conditioning a rat to press a bar in the Skinner box.

Skinner box contains bar and food cup.

**1** The rat has not been fed for some hours so that it will be active and more likely to eat the food reward. A hungry rat tends to roam restlessly about, sniffing at whatever it finds.

**2** The goal is to condition the rat to press the bar. By pressing the bar, the rat operates on its environment; thus, this response is called an *operant response.*

**3** Skinner explains that a naive rat does not usually waltz over and press the bar. In conditioning a rat to press a bar, Skinner will use a procedure called shaping.

*Shaping* is a procedure in which an experimenter successively reinforces behaviors that lead up to or approximate the desired behavior.

For example, if the desired behavior is pressing the bar, here's how shaping works.

### Shaping: Facing the Bar

Skinner places a white rat into the (Skinner) box, closes the door, and watches the rat through a one-way mirror. At first, the rat wanders around the back of the box, but when it turns and faces the bar, Skinner releases a food pellet that makes a noise as it drops into the food cup. The rat hears the pellet drop, approaches the food cup, sees, sniffs, and eats the pellet. After eating, the rat moves away to explore the box. But, as soon as the rat turns and faces the bar, Skinner releases another pellet. The rat hears the noise, goes to the food cup, sniffs, and eats the pellet. Shaping is going well.

### Shaping: Touching the Bar

As shaping continues, Skinner decides to reinforce the rat only when it actually moves toward the bar. Skinner waits and as soon as the rat faces and then moves toward the bar, Skinner releases another pellet. After eating the pellet, the rat wanders a bit but soon returns to the bar  and actually sniffs it. A fourth pellet immediately drops into the cup, and the rat eats it. When the rat places one paw on the bar, a fifth pellet drops into the cup. Notice how Skinner has shaped the rat to spend all its time near the bar.

### Shaping: Pressing the Bar

As soon as the rat actually puts its paws on the bar, Skinner releases a pellet. After eating, the rat puts its paws back on the bar and gets a pellet. Now Skinner waits until the rat puts its paws on the bar and actually happens to press down, which releases another pellet. Soon, the rat is pressing the bar over and over to get pellets. Notice how Skinner reinforced the rat's behaviors that led up to or approximated the desired behavior of bar pressing.

### Importance of Immediate Reinforcement

Depending on the rat and the trainer's experience, it may take from minutes to an hour to shape a rat to press a bar. Skinner explains that in shaping behavior, the food pellet, or *reinforcer,* should follow *immediately* after the desired behavior. By following immediately, the reinforcer is associated with the desired behavior and not with some other behavior that just happens to occur. If the reinforcer is delayed, the animal may be reinforced for some undesired or superstitious behavior.

*Superstitious behavior* is any behavior that increases in frequency because its occurrence is accidentally paired with the delivery of a reinforcer.

When I was a graduate student, I conditioned my share of superstitious rat behaviors, such as making them turn in circles or stand up instead of pressing the bar. That's because I accidentally but immediately reinforced a rat after it performed the wrong behavior.

Humans, especially professional baseball players, report a variety of superstitious behaviors that were accidentally reinforced after getting a hit. For example, a five-time batting champion (Wade Boggs) eats chicken every day he plays, allows no one else to touch his bats, and believes each bat has a certain number of hits. Once reinforced, especially after a powerful reinforcer (major league hit), superstitious behaviors can be very difficult to eliminate. You probably have some of your own! Next, we'll discuss examples of operant conditioning in humans.

### Examples of Operant Conditioning

**Have you been operantly conditioned?**

Without realizing it, you may be performing a wide range of behaviors learned through operant conditioning. For example, operant conditioning was involved if you learned to put money into a jukebox to hear music, drive through a yellow traffic light to avoid stopping, study for hours to get good grades, or give flowers to your honey to see him or her smile. And you may continually perform these behaviors be-

cause they are followed by reinforcers that increase the chances that you will perform these same behaviors again. To help you better understand how operant conditioning works, we'll discuss how its procedures and principles have been used by parents to solve two relatively common problems: getting young children to use the toilet and to stop refusing to eat a wide variety of healthy foods.

#### Toilet Training

In the 1960s, 90% of children were toilet trained by age $2^{1}/_{2}$, but in the 1990s, the number dropped to 30%. One reason is that many parents report not knowing how to go about training their child (Lemonick, 1999).

Imagine that you are a parent of 3-year-old Sheryl, who is physically mature enough to begin toilet training. Here's how operant conditioning techniques can be applied to teach toilet training.

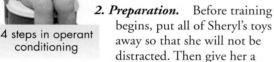

*4 steps in operant conditioning*

**1. Target behavior.** The target behavior or goal is for Sheryl to urinate in the toilet.

**2. Preparation.** Before training begins, put all of Sheryl's toys away so that she will not be distracted. Then give her a large glass of apple juice, so that she will have to urinate soon.

**3. Reinforcers.** Select reinforcers, which can be candy, verbal praise, or a hug. Each time Sheryl performs or emits a desired behavior, you immediately reinforce it. The reinforcer increases the likelihood that the behavior will be repeated.

**4. Shaping.** Just as Skinner used the shaping procedure in conditioning a rat to press a bar, you can use a similar shaping procedure in conditioning Sheryl to use the toilet. Each time Sheryl performs a behavior that leads to the target behavior (using the toilet), give her a treat, verbal praise, or a hug. For instance, when Sheryl says that she has to go potty, say, "That's great." When Sheryl enters the bathroom, say, "What a good girl." When she lowers her pants by herself, say, "You're doing really good." After Sheryl urinates into the toilet, give her a big hug and perhaps a treat.

Mothers who were supervised as they used this training procedure needed 4–18 hours to toilet train their 2- to 3-year-olds (Berk & Patrick, 1990; Matson & Ollendick, 1977).

Another difficulty parents face is when children eat only one or two favorite foods and refuse all others.

#### Food Refusal

Some young children with no medical problems may develop a habit of eating only certain foods and refusing all others, which may result in having an unhealthy diet or low weight (Timimi et al., 1997). Researchers taught parents how to use the principles of operant conditioning to overcome food refusal in their young children.

**1. Target behavior.** The target behavior or goal was for the child to taste, chew, and eat a food (usually fruits or vegetables) that she or he has persistently refused to eat.

**2. Preparation.** Researchers first showed mothers how to shape and reinforce target behaviors. Next, each mother shaped the target behavior in her child in the home setting.

**3. Reinforcers.** Each time the child performed or emitted a target behavior, the mother immediately reinforced the child with a positive reinforcer, such as praise, attention, or a smile.

**4. Shaping.** The shaping procedure consisted of having the child notice the food and let it be placed in his or her mouth, letting the child taste the food, and, finally, having the child chew and swallow the food.

The graph below explains and shows the success of using operant conditioning to overcome food refusal in young children (Werle et al., 1993).

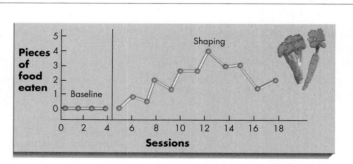

**Baseline:** During these four sessions, the mother offered nonpreferred food to her child, who refused the food each time.

**Shaping:** During these sessions, the mother shaped the child to accept nonpreferred food by giving praise, attention, and smiles each time her child made a response that was similar to or approximated the target behavior (chewing and swallowing food). Shaping proved effective in overcoming the child's habit of food refusal. Compare the child's food refusal during baseline to that during shaping sessions.

Notice that the same principles of operant conditioning apply whether the goal is to condition a child to use the potty, to overcome food refusal, or to train Bart the bear to pick up and hold a teddy bear.

Next, we'll compare the principles of operant and classical conditioning.

## Operant versus Classical Conditioning

**How are they different?**

Earlier in this module, we discussed how Bart the bear was operantly conditioned to hold a teddy bear—something he would never do in the wild. As you may remember from Module 9, we discussed how Sam the dog was classically conditioned to salivate to the sound of a bell—something he would not

Bart can be both classically and operantly conditioned.

usually do. Although both operant and classical conditioning lead to learning, they have very different procedures and principles, which may be a little confusing. We'll try to clear up any confusion by doing a side-by-side comparison of the principles and procedures of operant and classical conditioning by using the same subject, Bart, one of the world's largest subjects.

### Operant Conditioning

**1 Goal.** The goal of operant conditioning is to *increase or decrease the rate* of some response, which usually involves shaping. In Bart's case, the goal was to increase his rate of holding a teddy bear.

**2 Voluntary response.** Bart's behavior of holding a teddy bear is a voluntary response because he can perform it at will. Bart must first perform a voluntary response before getting a reward.

**3 Emitted response.** Bart voluntarily performs or emits some response, which Skinner called the operant response (holding teddy bear). Skinner used the term *emit* to indicate that the organism acts or operates on the environment. In most cases, animals and humans are shaped to emit the desired responses.

**4 Contingent on behavior.** Bart's performance of the desired response depends on, or is *contingent* on, the consequences, or what happens next. For example, each time Bart holds the teddy bear, the consequence is that he receives an apple. The apple, which is a reward (reinforcer), increases the chances that Bart will perform the desired response in the future.

The reinforcer must occur *immediately after* the desired response. In Bart's case, the reinforcer (apple) would be given immediately after Bart holds the teddy bear. If the reinforcer occurs too late, the result may be the conditioning of unwanted or superstitious responses.

**5 Consequences.** An animal or human's performance of some behavior is dependent or contingent on its *consequences*—that is, on what happens next. For example, the consequence of Bart's picking up and holding a teddy bear was to get an apple.

Thus, in operant conditioning, an animal or human learns that performing or *emitting* some behavior is followed by a *consequence* (reward or punishment), which, in turn, increases or decreases the chances of performing that behavior again.

### Classical Conditioning

**1 Goal.** The goal of classical conditioning is to create a new response to a *neutral stimulus*. In Bart's case, he will make a new response, salivation, to the sound of a horn, which is the neutral stimulus because it does not usually cause Bart to salivate.

**2 Involuntary response.** Salivation is an example of a *physiological reflex*. Physiological reflexes (salivation, eye blink) are triggered or elicited by some stimulus and therefore called involuntary responses.

**3 Elicited response.** As Bart eats an apple, it will trigger the involuntary physiological reflex of salivation. Thus, eating the apple, which is called the

*unconditioned stimulus*, triggers or elicits an involuntary reflex response, salivation, which is called the *unconditioned response*.

**4 Conditioned response.** Bart was given repeated trials during which the neutral stimulus (horn's sound) was

presented and followed by the unconditioned stimulus (apple). After repeated trials, Bart learned a relationship between the two stimuli: The horn's sound is followed by an apple. The horn's sound, or neutral stimulus, becomes the *conditioned stimulus* when its sound alone, before the occurrence of the apple, elicits salivation, which is the *conditioned response*.

For best results, the neutral stimulus is presented slightly before the unconditioned stimulus. If the unconditioned stimulus is presented before the neutral stimulus, this is called *backward conditioning* and produces little if any conditioning.

**5 Expectancy.** According to the *cognitive perspective* of classical conditioning, an animal or human learns a predictable relationship between, or develops an expectancy about, the neutral and unconditioned stimuli. This means Bart learned to *expect* that the neutral stimulus (horn's sound) is always followed by the unconditioned stimulus (apple). Thus, in classical conditioning, the animal or human learns a *predictable relationship* between stimuli.

One major difference between operant and classical conditioning is that in operant conditioning, the performance of some response depends on its consequence (rewards or punishment). We'll discuss the effects of different kinds of consequences next.

## Consequences

**Why are consequences important?**

Notice where the man is sitting as he saws off a tree limb. His behavior illustrates a key principle of operant conditioning, which is that *consequences are contingent on behavior*. In this case, the man will fall on his head (consequence) if he cuts off the tree limb (behavior). Furthermore, this consequence will make the tree trimmer think twice before repeating this stupid behavior. Thus, consequences affect behavior, and in operant conditioning, there are two kinds of consequences—reinforcement and punishment.

There are serious consequences to this man's behavior!

*Reinforcement* is a consequence that occurs after a behavior and increases the chance that the behavior will occur again.

For example, one of the main reasons you study hard for exams is to get good grades (reinforcement). The consequence of getting a good grade increases the chances that you'll study hard for future exams.

*Punishment* is a consequence that occurs after a behavior and decreases the chance that the behavior will occur again.

For example, one high school used punishment to reduce students' absentee rates. Students who got more than eight unexcused absences lost very desirable privileges (no football games, no prom). In this case, punishing consequences decreased from 15% to 4% the chance of students playing hookey from school (Chavez, 1994).

Sometimes reinforcement and punishment are used together to control some behavior, as was done in treating a serious behavioral disorder called pica.

*Pica* is a behavioral disorder, more often seen in individuals with mental retardation, which involves eating inedible objects or unhealthy substances. This can result in serious physical problems, including lead poisoning, intestinal blockage, and parasites.

Here's an example of how both reinforcement and punishment were used to treat an adolescent who suffered from pica.

### CHANGING THE CONSEQUENCES

Walt was 15 years old and suffered from profound retardation. One of Walt's problems was pica, which included eating bits of paper and clothing, metal and plastic objects, and especially paint chips, from which he had gotten lead poisoning.

To control his pica, Walt was given a tray containing nonfood items (fake paint chips made from flour) and food items (crackers). Each time Walt chose a food item, he received a reinforcement—verbal praise. Each time Walt chose a paint chip, he received a mild punishment—having his face washed for 20 seconds. The graph below shows how the consequences (reinforcement or punishment) greatly modified Walt's pica behavior (Johnson et al., 1994).

**Baseline:**
During these sessions, Walt chose the non-food items 10–80% of the time. Compare the baseline with training sessions.

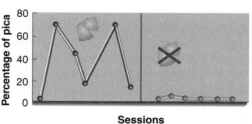

**Training:**
During these sessions, Walt was reinforced with praise for choosing food items and punished with face washing for choosing nonfood items. These consequences greatly modified his behaviors so that he chose primarily food items.

In this study, reinforcement and punishment proved an effective combination to treat a potentially dangerous problem. Next, we'll discuss two kinds of reinforcements.

## Reinforcement

**How are an apple and an "F" alike?**

Although getting an apple and getting a grade of "F" seem very different, they are both consequences that can increase the occurrence of certain behaviors. There are two kinds of reinforcements, or consequences—positive and negative—that increase the occurrence of behaviors.

### POSITIVE REINFORCEMENT

Immediately after Bart the bear emitted or performed a behavior (holding a teddy bear), the trainer gave him an apple to increase the likelihood of his repeating that behavior. This situation is an example of positive reinforcement.

*Positive reinforcement* refers to the presentation of a stimulus that increases the probability that a behavior will occur again.

A *positive reinforcer* is a stimulus that increases the likelihood that a response will occur again.

For example, if you ask a friend for money and get it, the money is a positive reinforcer that will increase the chances of your asking again. There's a second kind of reinforcement, called negative reinforcement.

### NEGATIVE REINFORCEMENT

If you have a headache and take an aspirin to get rid of it, your response of taking an aspirin is an example of negative reinforcement.

*Negative reinforcement* refers to an aversive (unpleasant) stimulus whose removal increases the likelihood that the preceding response will occur again.

If taking an aspirin removes your headache (aversive or unpleasant stimulus), then your response of taking an aspirin is negatively reinforced because it removes the headache and thus increases the chances of your taking an aspirin in the future. Don't be confused by the fact that both positive and negative reinforcers *increase* the frequency of the responses they follow.

Besides positive and negative reinforcers, there are also primary reinforcers, such as food, and secondary reinforcers, such as money and coupons.

### How are a hamburger and a coupon alike?

Sometimes we repeat a behavior because the consequence is food, a primary reinforcer, or because the consequence is a coupon, a secondary reinforcer. Let's see how primary and secondary reinforcers could be used to increase study time and maintain quiet on a school bus.

### PRIMARY REINFORCERS

If you made yourself study for 2 hours before rewarding yourself with a hamburger, you would be using a primary reinforcer.

A *primary reinforcer* is a stimulus, such as food, water, or sex, that is innately satisfying and requires no learning on the part of the subject to become pleasurable.

Food: primary reinforcer

Primary reinforcers are present from birth and require no training. In our example, a hamburger would be a primary reinforcer for studying. However, we are very often reinforced by things other than food, water, or sex.

### SECONDARY REINFORCERS

A school bus driver gave each child a coupon good for a pizza if he or she was quiet on the bus. A coupon is an example of a secondary reinforcer.

A *secondary reinforcer* is any stimulus that has acquired its reinforcing power through experience; secondary reinforcers are learned, such as by being paired with primary reinforcers or other secondary reinforcers.

Coupons, money, grades, and praise are examples of secondary reinforcers because their value is learned or acquired through experience (LeBlanc et

Bus driver uses tokens—secondary reinforcers—to encourage children's good behaviors.

al., 2000). For example, children learned that coupons were valuable since they could be redeemed for pizza. The coupons became secondary reinforcers that encouraged children to choose a seat quickly and sit quietly so that the driver could get rolling in 5 minutes (George, 1995). Many of our behaviors are increased or maintained by secondary reinforcers.

Unlike primary and secondary reinforcers, which are consequences that increase behaviors, punishment has a very different effect.

### What does punishment do?

It is helpful to distinguish between positive and negative punishment.

*Positive punishment* refers to presenting an aversive (unpleasant) stimulus (such as spanking) after a response. The aversive stimulus decreases the chances that the response will recur.

*Negative punishment* refers to removing a reinforcing stimulus (a child's allowance) after a response. This removal decreases the chances that the response will recur.

Both positive and negative punishment function as "stop signs"; they stop or decrease the occurrence of a behavior. We'll discuss negative punishment in the Application section. Here, we'll explain how positive punishment was used to treat a serious disorder called self-injurious behavior.

*Self-injurious behavior* refers to serious and sometimes life-threatening physical damage that a person inflicts on his or her own body; this may include body or head banging, biting, kicking, poking ears or eyes, pulling hair, or intense scratching.

About 8–14% of mentally retarded individuals who live in large residential treatment facilities engage in self-injurious behavior (Williams et al., 1993). Here's an example of a treatment program that used positive punishment.

### POSITIVE PUNISHMENT

Because of concerns about possible negative effects of using punishment, a special Task Force on Self-Injurious Behavior concluded that positive punishment proved effective in decreasing self-injurious behavior but should be used only when all other treatments had failed (Iwata et al., 1994).

She had to wear special gloves so she wouldn't injure herself.

Since all other treatments had failed, the State Committee for Behavior Therapy approved a program of using positive punishment to treat Suzanne's problem. Suzanne was 24 years old and profoundly mentally retarded. For many years, she engaged in such severe self-biting and eye and ear gouging that she had to continually wear a fencing mask and special gloves to prevent self-injury. Essentially, the program involved giving Suzanne an electric shock each time she bit or harmed herself. As the graph below shows, after a dozen sessions, the use of positive punishment decreased Suzanne's self-injurious behaviors by 99%, to almost zero. After 69 treatment sessions, Suzanne's protective face mask and gloves were removed, and for the first time in 15 years, Suzanne began to feed herself, perform personal care, and refrain from self-injury (Williams et al., 1993).

However, before punishment is used, other nonpunishment treatments based on operant conditioning are always tried. For example, some self-injurious behaviors decreased if the therapist gave attention (reinforcement) only when the patient stopped engaging in noninjurious behaviors or if the therapist reinforced the patient for performing particular noninjurious behaviors, such as playing games or eating candy (Olson & Houlihan, 2000).

We'll discuss the pros and cons of using punishment in the Application section on page 233.

Although somewhat confusing, remember that positive and negative punishment *decrease* the likelihood of a behavior occurring again, while positive and negative reinforcement *increase* the likelihood of a behavior occurring again.

| Self-Injurious Behaviors per Minute | |
| --- | --- |
| Before treatment | 9.3 |
| After punishment | 0.07 |

## Skinner's Contributions

**Why are consequences important?**

On September 20, 1971, *Time* magazine recognized B. F. Skinner's influence and accomplishments in psychology and education by putting him on its cover (right photo). Just a year earlier, the *American Psychologist,* which is the official publication of the American Psychological Association, rated B. F. Skinner second, after Freud, in influence on 20th-century psychology.

Skinner is perhaps best known for his discovery of operant conditioning and how consequences or reinforcers affect behavior. He also developed a powerful method for analyzing the individual behaviors of animals and humans. Part of his method was to study how different kinds of consequences or reinforcements affected behavior, and this led to his study of different schedules of reinforcement.

*TIME*

B. F. Skinner Says:
We Can't Afford Freedom

B. F. Skinner (1904–1990)

A *schedule of reinforcement* refers to a program or rule that determines how and when the occurrence of a response will be followed by a reinforcer.

Skinner pointed out many examples of how schedules of reinforcement both maintained and controlled behaviors. For example, slot machine players don't realize that they are paid off according to a schedule of reinforcement that encourages rapid responding. Similarly, some factories pay their workers by the piece, which is a schedule of reinforcement that results in steady and rapid work.

Skinner was able to study how different schedules of reinforcement affected behavior because he developed a clever method to record ongoing, individual behaviors. His method included the use of the now-famous "Skinner box" and something called the cumulative record.

## Measuring Ongoing Behavior

Skinner showed how different schedules of reinforcement affected an animal's or a human's ongoing behavior with something called a cumulative record.

A *cumulative record* is a continuous written record that shows an animal's or a human's individual responses and reinforcements.

A rat in a Skinner box is shown on the left and a cumulative record is shown below. When the rat is not pressing the bar, a pen draws a straight line on a long roll of paper that unwinds slowly and continuously to the left. When the rat presses the bar, the pen moves up a notch. When the rat makes numerous responses, the pen moves up many notches to draw a line that resembles a stairway going up. If the rat presses the bar slowly, the pen notches up gradually, resulting in a gentler slope. If the rat responds quickly, the pen notches up more quickly, resulting in a steeper slope. A downward blip indicates that the rat received a food pellet, or reinforcement (only two are shown). You'll

Rat in a Skinner box

Pen

Sloped line: series of rapid responses

Blip: reinforcement

Upward notch: one response

Blip: reinforcement

Flat line: no responses

see actual cumulative records on the next page. The cumulative record shows you an animal's ongoing responses and reinforcements across time.

We'll first look at how two general schedules of reinforcement—continuous and partial reinforcement—can greatly affect ongoing behavior.

## Schedules of Reinforcement

Each time I open my front door, my dog gives me the loudest, friendliest greeting "humanly" possible. However, when I walk into my local coffee shop, I find they have my favorite coffee only about twice a week. These situations illustrate two general schedules of reinforcement—continuous and partial.

### CONTINUOUS REINFORCEMENT

Getting a friendly greeting from my dog each and every time I walk through my front door means that my dog has me on a schedule of continuous reinforcement.

*Continuous reinforcement* means that every occurrence of the operant response results in delivery of the reinforcer.

In the real world, relatively few of our behaviors are on a continuous reinforcement schedule because very few things or people are as reliable as my dog. Continuous reinforcement is often used in the initial stages of operant conditioning because it results in rapid learning of some behavior.

Every response is reinforced.

### PARTIAL REINFORCEMENT

Finding that my favorite coffee is available only twice a week, even though I look hopefully for it almost every day, means that my coffee shop has me on a schedule of partial reinforcement.

*Partial reinforcement* refers to a situation in which responding is reinforced only some of the time.

In the real world, many of our behaviors are on a partial reinforcement schedule, which is very effective in maintaining behavior over the long run. That's why I keep walking to the coffee shop and hoping that today is the day they'll have my favorite coffee.

We'll discuss the four common schedules of partial reinforcement and show how differently they affect behavior.

Only some responses are reinforced.

# Partial Reinforcement Schedules

**Which schedule are you on?**

Skinner's analysis of the schedules of reinforcement has many practical applications. For example, one schedule of pay increases the speed of factory workers, while a different schedule of payoff increases the speed and persistence of slot machine players. There's even a schedule that explains why you keep putting money into vending machines even though the machines sometimes eat your money and why people regularly play the lottery knowing the odds of winning can be 18 million to 1. We'll discuss four different schedules of partial reinforcement, each of which has a different effect on controlling and maintaining animal and human behaviors.

## Fixed-Ratio Schedule

Suppose a pigeon is reinforced after it pecks six times. Or a factory worker is paid after packing six boxes of carrots. These are examples of a fixed-ratio schedule.

*Fixed-ratio schedule* means that a reinforcer occurs only after a fixed number of responses are made by the subject.

**Effect.** A fixed-ratio schedule is often used to pay assembly line workers because it results in fast rates of work: the more pieces of work completed, the more the worker is paid (reinforcement).

Steep slope indicates rapid response rate (reinforcers indicated by blips).

## Variable-Ratio Schedule

Suppose a pigeon gets a reinforcer after 12, 6, 8, and 2 pecks, with an average of 7 pecks. Or a slot machine pays off after an average of 25 pulls, which is called a variable-ratio schedule—in this case, VR 25.

*Variable-ratio schedule* means that a reinforcer is delivered after an average number of correct responses has occurred.

**Effect.** The variable-ratio schedule produces a high rate of responding because the subject (pigeon or slot machine player) doesn't know which response will finally produce the payoff.

Steep slope indicates rapid, steady response rate (reinforcers indicated by blips).

## Fixed-Interval Schedule

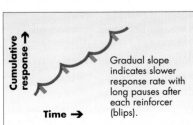

Suppose a pigeon gets a reinforcer for the first peck that occurs after 2 minutes. Or a surfer gets a big wave to ride (the reinforcer) every 30 seconds (waves come in regular sets). These are examples of a fixed-interval schedule.

*Fixed-interval schedule* means that a reinforcer occurs following the first response that occurs after a fixed interval of time.

**Effect.** A fixed-interval schedule results in slow responding at first, but as the time for the reinforcer draws near, the response rate greatly accelerates.

Gradual slope indicates slower response rate with long pauses after each reinforcer (blips).

## Variable-Interval Schedule

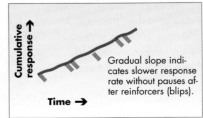

Suppose a pigeon gets a reinforcer for the first response that occurs after intervals of 12, 6, 8, and 2 minutes, with an average interval of 7 minutes. Or a bus arrives (the reinforcer) at your stop an average of 7 minutes late but at variable intervals, which is called a variable-interval schedule—in this case, VI 7. This reinforces your arriving just a few minutes late for your bus.

*Variable-interval schedule* means that a reinforcer occurs following the first correct response after an average amount of time has passed.

**Effect.** A variable-interval schedule results in a more regular rate of responding than does a fixed-interval schedule.

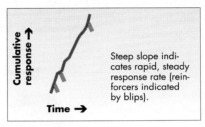

Gradual slope indicates slower response rate without pauses after reinforcers (blips).

---

In the laboratory, Skinner demonstrated that partial reinforcement, even at a rate as low as one reinforcer for an average of 200 responses, would maintain a pigeon pecking at a key. In the real world, many of our own behaviors, such as studying for exams, working at a job, or being affectionate in a relationship, are maintained on one or more of these four schedules of partial reinforcement.

During operant conditioning, a number of other things are happening, which we'll look at next.

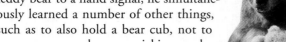

**What else did Bart learn?**

During the time that Bart was being operantly conditioned to pick up and hold a teddy bear to a hand signal, he simultaneously learned a number of other things, such as to also hold a bear cub, not to obey commands from a stranger, and to stop picking up the teddy bear if he was no longer given apples (reinforcers). You may remember these phenomena—generalization, discrimination, extinction, and spontaneous recovery—from our discussion of classical conditioning in Module 9 (p. 199). We'll explain how the same terms also apply to operant conditioning.

---

## Generalization

In the movie, Bart was supposed to pick up and hold a bear cub on command. However, in the wild, adult male Kodiak bears don't pick up and hold cubs; instead, they usually kill them.

Although Bart was relatively tame, his trainer took no chances of Bart's wilder nature coming out and killing the bear cub. For this reason, the trainer started by conducting the initial conditioning with a stuffed teddy bear. Only after Bart had learned to pick up and hold the teddy bear on cue did the trainer substitute a live bear cub. As the trainer had predicted, Bart transferred his holding the teddy bear to holding the live bear cub, a phenomenon called generalization.

Generalization: Bart's response of holding a teddy bear is transferred to holding a live cub.

In operant conditioning, *generalization* means that an animal or person emits the same response to similar stimuli.

In classical conditioning, *generalization* is the tendency for a stimulus similar to the original conditioned stimulus to elicit a response similar to the conditioned response.

A common and sometimes embarrassing example of generalization occurs when a young child generalizes the word "Daddy" to other males who appear similar to the child's real father. As quickly as possible, embarrassed parents teach their child to discriminate between the real father and other adult males.

---

## Discrimination

Since Bart had been raised and trained by a particular adult male, he had learned to obey and take cues only from his trainer and not from other males. This is an example of discrimination.

In operant conditioning, *discrimination* means that a response is emitted in the presence of a stimulus that is reinforced and not in the presence of unreinforced stimuli.

In classical conditioning, *discrimination* is the tendency for some stimuli but not others to elicit a conditioned response.

One problem with Bart was that he would repeatedly pick up and hold the teddy bear to receive an apple. To control this problem, the

Discrimination: Bart obeys hand signals from his trainer (source of reinforcers) but not signals from a stranger.

trainer used a cue—raising his arms in the air—to signal that only then would Bart receive an apple for his behavior. This is an example of a discriminative stimulus.

A *discriminative stimulus* is a cue that a behavior will be reinforced.

If you pay close attention to an animal trainer, you'll notice that discriminative stimuli, such as a hand signal or whistle, are used to signal the animal that the next behavior will be reinforced.

Young children learn to discriminate between stimuli when their parents reinforce their saying "Daddy" in the presence of their real fathers but do not reinforce their children when they call strangers "Daddy."

---

## Extinction and Spontaneous Recovery

Even after filming ended, Bart continued to perform his trained behaviors for a while. However, after a period of time when these behaviors were no longer reinforced, they gradually diminished and ceased. This is an example of extinction.

In operant conditioning, *extinction* refers to the reduction in an operant response when it is no longer followed by the reinforcer.

In classical conditioning, *extinction* refers to the reduction in a response when the conditioned stimulus is no longer followed by the unconditioned stimulus.

After undergoing extinction, Bart may show spontaneous recovery.

Extinction: Bart stops picking up a teddy bear if reinforcers (apples) stop. Spontaneous recovery: After extinction, Bart may suddenly pick up a teddy bear again.

In operant conditioning, *spontaneous recovery* refers to a temporary recovery in the rate of responding.

In classical conditioning, *spontaneous recovery* refers to the temporary occurrence of the conditioned response to the presence of the conditioned stimulus.

Remember that all four phenomena—generalization, discrimination, extinction, and spontaneous recovery—occur in both operant and classical conditioning.

One distinctive characteristic of operant conditioning is that it usually has an observable response and an observable reinforcer. Next, we turn to cognitive learning, which may have neither observable response nor observable reinforcer.

## Three Viewpoints of Cognitive Learning

**How did Jack learn?**

At the beginning of this module, we told you about Jack, who as a toddler loved to watch the Golf Channel. At 13 months, he was imitating what he saw and used a small plastic club to hit Wiffle balls in his family's living room. Jack had learned how to use a golf club not from classical or operant conditioning but from another kind of learning process called cognitive learning.

*Cognitive learning* involves mental processes, such as attention and memory; it may be learned through observation or imitation; and it may not involve any external rewards or require a person to perform any observable behaviors.

Cognitive learning involves observation and imitation.

Although interest in cognitive learning was reborn in the 1960s and became very popular in the 1990s, its roots extend back to the work of Wundt in the late 1800s (p. 12) and that of psychologist Edward Tolman in the 1930s. Today the concepts of cognitive learning have become popular in explaining both animal and human behavior as well as the development of a new area called cognitive neuroscience (p. 71) (Bandura, 1999; Higgins, 2000). We'll begin by discussing what three famous psychologists—B. F. Skinner, Edward Tolman, and Albert Bandura—had to say about cognitive learning.

### Against: B. F. Skinner

Eight days before his death, B. F. Skinner was honored by the American Psychological Association (APA) with the first APA Citation for Outstanding Lifetime Contribution to Psychology. In his acceptance speech to over 1,000 friends and colleagues, Skinner spoke of how psychology was splitting between those who were studying feelings and cognitive processes and those who were studying observable behaviors, such as animals under controlled conditions (figure below). In a sharp criticism of cognitive learning, Skinner said, "As far as I'm concerned, cognitive science is the creationism [downfall] of psychology" (Vargas, 1991, p. 1).

Skinner's severe criticism of studying cognitive processes, thoughts, and mental events caused many in the audience to gasp and only a few to applaud (Vargas, 1991).

In the 1950s and 1960s, Skinner had the major role in focusing psychology's goal on studying primarily observable behaviors rather than cognitive processes. However, beginning in the 1980s, psychologists found that human activities could not be understood or explained from observable behaviors alone. Hence, the study of cognitive processes and emotional feelings has now become a major goal of psychology (Bandura, 1999; DeGrandpre, 2000; Dougher & Hackbert, 2000).

### In Favor: Edward Tolman

In the 1930s, about the same time that Skinner was emphasizing observable behaviors, Tolman was exploring hidden mental processes. For example, he would place rats individually in a maze, such as the one shown below, and allow each rat time to explore the maze with no food present. Then, with food present in the maze's food box, he would test the rat to see which path it took. The rat learned very quickly to take the shortest path. Next, Tolman blocked the shortest path to the food box. The first time the rat encountered the blocked shortest path, it selected the next shortest path to the food box. According to Tolman (1948), the rat selected the next shortest path because it had developed a cognitive map of the maze.

A *cognitive map* is a mental representation in the brain of the layout of an environment and its features.

Tolman showed that rats, in addition to forming a cognitive map, learned the layout of a maze without being reinforced, a position very different from Skinner's. Tolman's position is making a comeback as psychologists currently study a variety of cognitive processes in animals (Lieberman, 2000b). Tolman's study of cognitive processes in animals laid the groundwork for the study of cognitive processes in humans, which is best shown by the current theory of Albert Bandura (1999).

### In Favor: Albert Bandura

Bandura began as a behaviorist in the Skinnerian tradition, which means focusing on observable behaviors and avoiding study of mental events. Since then he has almost entirely shifted to a cognitive approach. In many of his studies, Bandura (1986) has focused on how humans learn through observing things. For example, Bandura says that a child can learn to hate spiders simply by observing the behaviors of someone who shows a great fear of spiders. This is an example of social cognitive learning.

*Social cognitive learning* results from watching, imitating, and modeling and does not require the observer to perform any observable behavior or receive any observable reward.

Just as Tolman found that learning occurred while rats were exploring, Bandura found that humans learned while observing and that much (most) of human learning takes place through observation. Observational learning, which emphasizes cognitive processes, is 180 degrees from Skinner's position, which emphasizes observable, noncognitive behaviors.

Following the death of Skinner, the study of cognitive processes, including learning, continues to increase in popularity. We'll introduce you to cognitive learning by describing one of Bandura's best-known studies, which involved a doll and a considerable amount of kicking and screaming.

# E. Cognitive Learning

## Observational Learning

**Do children learn by watching?**

Perhaps a dozen experiments in psychology have become classics because they were the first to demonstrate some very important principles. One such classic experiment demonstrated the conditioning of emotional responses in "little Albert" (p. 204). Another classic is Albert Bandura (1965) and his colleagues' demonstration that children learned aggressive behaviors by watching an adult's aggressive behaviors. Learning through watching is called observational learning, which is a form of cognitive learning.

### Bobo Doll Experiment

**Why did children kick the Bobo doll?**

One reason this Bobo doll study is a classic experiment is that it challenged the earlier idea that learning occurred either through classical or operant conditioning. You'll see that children learned to perform aggressive responses simply from watching.

**Procedure.** In one part of the room, preschool children were involved in their own art projects. In another part of the room, an adult got up and, for the next 10 minutes, kicked, hit, and yelled ("Hit him! Kick him!") at a large, inflated Bobo doll. Some children watched the model's aggressive behaviors, while other children did not.

Children watched and imitated an adult's behavior of kicking doll.

Sometime later, each child was subjected to a mildly frustrating situation and then placed in a room with toys, including the Bobo doll. Without the child's knowledge, researchers observed the child's behaviors.

**Results.** Children who had observed the model's aggressive attacks on the Bobo doll also kicked, hit, and yelled ("Hit him! Kick him!") at the doll. Through observational learning alone, these children had learned the model's aggressive behaviors and were now performing them. In comparison, the children who had not observed the model's behaviors did not hit or kick the Bobo doll after they had been mildly frustrated.

**Conclusion.** Bandura's point is that these children learned to perform specific aggressive behaviors not by practicing or being reinforced but simply by watching a live model perform these behaviors. Observational learning is sometimes called modeling because it involves watching a model and later imitating the behavior.

Another interesting finding of the Bobo doll studies was that children may learn by observing but then not perform the observed behavior. This is an example of the learning-performance distinction.

### Learning versus Performance

**Do you learn but not show it?**

Is it possible that people can learn by observing but not necessarily perform what they have learned? To answer this question, Bandura and colleagues asked a group of children to watch a movie in which someone hit and kicked a Bobo doll. However, after hitting and kicking the doll, the person in the film was punished by being soundly criticized and spanked. Next, each child was left alone in a room filled with toys, including a Bobo doll.

As the experimenters watched each child through a one-way mirror, they found that more boys than girls imitated the model and performed aggressive behaviors on Bobo. But not all the children imitated the model's aggressive behaviors. Next, each child who had not imitated the model's aggressive behaviors on Bobo was offered a reward (a sticker or some fruit juice) to imitate the model's behavior. With the promise of a reward, all of the children imitated the model's aggressive behaviors. We'll examine in more detail the girls' imitated aggressive behaviors, which were similar to the boys' but more dramatic.

As the graph below shows, girls imitated an average of 0.5 aggressive behaviors after watching a film of a model who performed aggressive behaviors on Bobo and then was punished for being aggressive.

In other words, after observing a model being punished for aggressive behaviors, girls imitated almost none of the model's aggressive behaviors. However, when the same girls were promised a reward for imitating the model's aggressive behaviors, these girls imitated an average of 3.0 aggressive behaviors (Bandura, 1965).

| Average Number of Aggressive Responses | | |
| --- | --- | --- |
| 0.5 | Watched punished model | |
| 3.0 | | Reward for imitating |

So what does this experiment show? It shows that the girls had actually *learned* the model's aggressive behaviors through observation but that some did not *perform* these behaviors until they were rewarded for doing so (Bandura, 1965). This is an example of the learning-performance distinction.

The *learning-performance distinction* means that learning may occur but may not always be measured by, or immediately evident in, performance.

The learning-performance distinction may be demonstrated by young children, often to the embarrassment of their parents. For instance, a young child may overhear a "dirty" word but not repeat the word until out in public. Repeating a "dirty" word shows that the child had learned the word through observation but waited until later to imitate the parent and actually say (perform) the "dirty" word.

Child imitates adult's speech.

Based on the Bobo doll study and others, Bandura developed a theory of cognitive learning that we'll examine next.

**Would you hold this spider?**

Just as Tolman believed that rats gather information and form cognitive maps about their environments through exploring, Bandura believes that humans gather information about their environments and the behaviors of others through observation, which is part of Bandura's (1999) social cognitive theory of learning.

*Social cognitive theory* emphasizes the importance of observation, imitation, and self-reward in the development and learning of social skills, personal interactions, and many other behaviors. Unlike operant and classical conditioning, this theory says that it is not necessary to perform any observable behaviors or receive any external rewards to learn.

Bandura believes that four processes—attention, memory, imitation, and motivation—operate during social cognitive learning. We'll explain how these processes operate in decreasing fear of spiders and snakes.

### Social Cognitive Learning: Four Processes

#### 1 Attention

The observer must pay attention to what the model says or does. In the photo below, a nonfrightened woman (model) holds a huge spider while another woman (observer) looks on in amazement.

#### 2 Memory

The observer must store or remember the information so that it can be retrieved and used later. The observer in the photo will store the image of seeing a nonfrightened woman (model) holding a spider.

> The woman (above right) observes another woman who shows no fear while holding a potentially terrifying spider. Later, the observer may imitate being fearless when seeing a spider.

#### 3 Imitation

The observer must be able to use the remembered information to guide his or her own actions and thus imitate the model's behavior. The observer in the photo will later try to imitate the model's nonfrightened facial expression and manner when holding a spider.

#### 4 Motivation

The observer must have some reason or incentive to imitate the model's behavior. The observer in the photo is motivated to overcome her fear of spiders because she wants to go on camping trips.

If this observer can successfully imitate the model's calm behavior, then she will overcome her fear of spiders and be able to go camping with her friends. This example shows how Bandura's four mental processes operate during social cognitive learning.

The next study by Bandura shows how social cognitive learning, which usually takes some time and effort, decreased fear of snakes.

### Social Cognitive Learning Decreases the Fear of Snakes

**Background.** Although most people are wary of snakes, some develop an intense fear of them. Bandura and colleagues recruited subjects who had developed such an intense fear of snakes that they avoided many normal outdoor activities, such as hiking or gardening (Bandura et al., 1969). The subjects' fear of snakes was objectively measured by noting how many of 29 steps of increasingly frightening actions they would perform. For example, step 1 was approaching a glass cage containing a snake; step 29 was putting the snake in their laps and letting it crawl around while holding their hands at their sides.

*Social cognitive learning is used to decrease fear of snakes.*

**Treatment.** One group of subjects watched as a model handled a live, 4-foot, harmless king snake. After watching for 15 minutes, subjects were invited to gradually move closer to the snake. Then the model demonstrated touching the snake and asked the subjects to imitate her actions. As the model held the snake, subjects were encouraged to touch the snake with a gloved hand. Another group of subjects, who also reported an intense fear of snakes, received no treatment (control group).

**Results and conclusion.** As the graph below shows, subjects who watched a live model handle a snake and who imitated some of the model's behaviors scored an average of 27 on the 29-step approach scale.

| Average Number of Approach Responses | | |
|---|---|---|
| 10 | Control group | |
| 27 | Watched live model | |

In contrast, control subjects scored an average of only 10 approach behaviors on the 29-step scale. This study clearly showed that behavior can be greatly changed through social cognitive learning, which emphasized observation and imitation.

Bandura believes that humans acquire a great amount of information about fears, social roles, discrimination, and personal interactions through social cognitive learning. We'll discuss other aspects of cognitive learning and memory in Modules 11 and 12.

Next, we'll describe another kind of cognitive learning that involves what is often described as the "ah-ha!" feeling.

# E. Cognitive Learning

**What's the "ah-ha!" feeling?**

Earlier we told you that Thorndike studied how cats learned to escape from a puzzle box to get a piece of fish. Thorndike concluded that learning occurred through a process of trial and error as cats gradually formed associations between moving the latch and opening the door. None of the cats showed any evidence of suddenly discovering the solution of how to escape the box.

About the same time that Thorndike in America was studying the trial-and-error learning of cats escaping from a puzzle box, Wolfgang Köhler in Germany was studying how chimpanzees

**AH-HA!**

Flash of insight

learned to obtain bananas that were out of reach. Köhler challenged Thorndike's conclusion that animals learned only through trial and error. Köhler suggested instead that cats and other animals that were observed under the proper circumstances could solve a problem in a sudden flash, known as insight.

*Insight* is a mental process marked by the sudden and expected solution to a problem: a phenomenon often called the "ah-ha!" experience.

Here's an example of Köhler's chimp, Sultan, who showed insight in getting a banana that was hanging out of reach.

## *Insight in Animals*

**How did the chimp get the banana?**

This classic experiment in psychology suggested a new kind of learning.

What Köhler (1925) did was to hang a banana from the ceiling in a room that had a box placed off to one side. The banana was too high for Sultan the chimp to grab by reaching or jumping. When Sultan first entered the room, he paced restlessly for about 5 minutes. Then he seized the box, moved it toward the banana, climbed onto the box, jumped up, and seized the banana. On his second try, Sultan quickly moved the box directly beneath the banana and jumped up to get it.

What intrigued Köhler about Sultan's problem-solving behavior was that it seemed to differ greatly from the random trial-and-error behavior of Thorndike's cats. Before Sultan arrived at a solution, he might pace about, sit quietly, or vainly grasp at the out-of-reach banana. Then, all of a sudden, he seemed to hit on the solution and immediately executed a complicated set of behaviors, such as standing on a box, to get the banana. Köhler believed that Sultan's sudden solution to a problem was an example of *insight,* a mental process quite different from what Thorndike had observed in the random trial-and-error learning of cats.

However, critics of Köhler's insight studies pointed out that he did not explain how chimps solved problems; rather, he simply described the process. Critics also noted that chimpanzees that were best at solving Köhler's problems were those that had had the most experience getting or retrieving objects. Thus, the development of insight seems to depend, to a large extent, on previous experience.

Köhler replied that his studies on insight were more a way to study problem solving than an explanation of what was happening in the chimp's head. The significance of Köhler's work was that it represented a method for studying learning that was different from either classical conditioning or random trial-and-error learning (Pierce, 1999). Since the early 1990s, there has been a renewed interest in studying the workings of the animal mind, which is currently called animal cognition (Lieberman, 2000b).

Let's look at an example of insight learning in humans.

Chimp stood on a box to be able to reach the banana.

## *Insight in Humans*

**Can you solve this puzzle?**

Just as Sultan the chimp seemed to suddenly arrive at a solution to a problem, humans also report the experience of suddenly and unexpectedly solving a challenging or difficult problem. We call this phenomenon the "ah-ha!" experience or a flash of insight. You may have an "ah-ha!" experience if you can figure out what critical piece of information is needed to make the following story make sense.

*A man walks into a bar and asks for a glass of water. The bartender points a gun at the man. The man says, "Thank you," and walks out.*

If you solved this puzzle, you had an insight!

Obviously, something critical happened between two events: ". . . asks for a glass of water" and "The bartender points a gun at the man." Some subjects solved this problem in a relatively short time, while others could not solve this problem in the 2-hour time limit.

I'll admit that I never solved the problem until I read the hint: The man has hiccups. Think about cures for hiccups, and, like me, you may have an "ah-ha!" experience. The man drank the water, but it didn't cure his hiccups. The bartender thought a big surprise might do the trick, so he points a gun at the man, who is frightened, and so his hiccups stop. The man says, "Thank you," and walks out.

There was a difference between nonsolvers and solvers in the cognitive strategy that they used. The nonsolvers focused mostly on the obvious elements, such as man, bartender, gun, and glass of water, and not on new concepts (hiccups, cure) that would lead to a solution. In comparison, the solvers spent more time on bringing in new information. When the solvers finally found the missing piece of information (cure for hiccups), the solution arrived suddenly, like the "ah-ha!" experience that Köhler defined as insight (Durso et al., 1994).

We have discussed three examples of cognitive learning: Tolman's idea of cognitive maps, Bandura's theory of social cognitive learning, and Köhler's study of insightful problem solving. In addition, we'll discuss cognitive learning in Modules 11 and 12.

After the Concept Review, we'll explain why biological factors make some things easier and some things harder to learn.

# Concept Review

**1.** The kind of learning in which the consequences that follow some behavior increase or decrease the likelihood that the behavior will occur in the future is called _____.

**2.** In operant conditioning, the organism voluntarily performs or (a)_____ a behavior. Immediately following an emitted behavior, the occurrence of a (b)_____ increases the likelihood that the behavior will occur again.

**3.** Because an organism may not immediately emit the desired behavior, a procedure is used to reinforce behaviors that lead to or approximate the final target behavior. This procedure is called _____.

**4.** In operant conditioning, the term *consequences* refers to either (a)_____, which increases the likelihood that a behavior will occur again, or (b)_____, which decreases the likelihood that a behavior will occur again.

**5.** If the occurrence of some response is increased because it is followed by a pleasant stimulus, the stimulus is called a (a)_____. An increase in the occurrence of some response because it is followed either by the removal of an unpleasant stimulus or by avoiding the stimulus is called (b)_____.

**6.** A stimulus, such as food, water, or sex, that is innately satisfying and requires no learning to become pleasurable is a (a)_____. A stimulus, such as grades or praise, that has acquired its reinforcing power through experience and learning is a (b)_____.

**7.** The various ways that reinforcers occur after a behavior has been emitted are referred to as (a)_____ of reinforcement. For example, if each and every target behavior is reinforced, it is called a (b)_____ schedule of reinforcement. If behaviors are not reinforced each time they occur, it is called a (c)_____ schedule of reinforcement.

**8.** When an organism emits the same response to similar stimuli, it is called (a)_____. When a response is emitted in the presence of a stimulus that is reinforced and not in the presence of unreinforced stimuli, it is called (b)_____. A decrease in emitting a behavior because it is no longer reinforced is called (c)_____. If an organism performs a behavior without its being reinforced, it is called (d)_____.

**9.** A kind of learning that involves mental processes, that may be learned through observation and imitation, and that may not require any external rewards or the performance of any observable behaviors is referred to as _____.

**10.** Tolman studied the behavior of rats that were allowed to explore a maze without any reward given. When food was present, rats quickly learned to select the next shortest path if a previously taken path was blocked. Tolman said that rats had developed a mental representation of the layout, which he called a _____.

**11.** Although an organism may learn a behavior through observation or exploration, the organism may not immediately demonstrate or perform the newly learned behavior. This phenomenon is known as the _____ distinction.

**12.** According to Bandura, one form of learning that develops through watching and imitation and that does not require the observer to perform any observable behavior or receive a reinforcer is called (a)_____ learning. Bandura believes that humans gather much information from their (b)_____ through social cognitive learning.

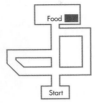

**13.** Bandura's theory of social cognitive learning involves four mental processes. The observer must pay (a)_____ to what the model says or does. The observer must then code the information and be able to retrieve it from (b)_____ for use at a later time. The observer must be able to use the coded information to guide his or her (c)_____ in performing and imitating the model's behavior. Finally, the observer must be (d)_____ to perform the behavior, which involves some reason, reinforcement, or incentive.

**14.** In Köhler's study of problem solving in chimps, he identified a mental process marked by the sudden occurrence of a solution, which he termed (a)_____. This phenomenon is another example of (b)_____ learning.

***Answers:*** *1. operant conditioning; 2. (a) emits, (b) reinforcement or reinforcer; 3. shaping; 4. (a) reinforcement, (b) punishment; 5. (a) positive reinforcer, (b) negative reinforcement; 6. (a) primary reinforcer, (b) secondary reinforcer; 7. (a) schedules, (b) continuous, (c) partial; 8. (a) generalization, (b) discrimination, (c) extinction, (d) spontaneous recovery; 9. cognitive learning; 10. cognitive map; 11. learning-performance; 12. (a) social cognitive, (b) environments; 13. (a) attention, (b) memory, (c) motor control, (d) motivated; 14. (a) insight, (b) cognitive*

# F. Biological Factors

## Definition

**Why would a monkey make a snowball?**

You may remember having difficulty learning to read, write, ride a bike, drive a car, put on makeup, or shave. But do you remember having problems learning to play? For a young child, playing just seemed to come naturally. Just as children engage in play behavior with little or no encouragement, reward, or learning, so too do monkeys. Young monkeys learn to roll snowballs and carry them around for apparently no other reason than for play (photo on right). In fact, most young mammals engage in various play behaviors, which are not easily explained by the three traditional learning procedures—classical conditioning, operant conditioning, or cognitive learning (Brownlee, 1997). Observations of animals and humans indicate that some behaviors,

Animals have innate tendencies for learning, such as playing with objects.

such as play, are easily and effortlessly learned partly because of innate biological factors.

*Biological factors* refer to innate tendencies or predispositions that may either facilitate or inhibit certain kinds of learning.

Researchers suggest that animals and humans may have evolved biological predispositions to learn play behaviors because they have adaptive functions—for example, developing social relationships among peers and learning behaviors useful for adult roles (Brown, 1994). This means that animals and humans have innate biological factors or predispositions that make certain kinds of learning, such as play behavior, very easy and effortless.

Besides play behavior, we'll discuss two other examples of learning—imprinting and preparedness—that are learned early and easily because of biological factors.

## Imprinting

**Why do young chicks follow their mother?**

Soon after they hatch and without any apparent learning, baby chicks follow their mother hen. This following behavior was not explained by any of the principles of learning identified by Pavlov (classical conditioning), Thorndike (trial-and-error learning), or Skinner (operant conditioning). The baby chick's seemingly unlearned behavior of following its mother was a different kind of learning that was first identified by ethologists.

*Ethologists* are behavioral biologists who observe and study animal behavior in the animal's natural environment or under relatively naturalistic conditions.

For example, an Austrian ethologist, Konrad Lorenz (1952), studied chicks, goslings, and ducks, which can all move around minutes after hatching. He discovered that these baby animals followed the first moving object they saw, which was usually their mother. This following behavior is an example of imprinting.

Baby ducks automatically follow first moving object.

*Imprinting* refers to inherited tendencies or responses that are displayed by newborn animals when they encounter certain stimuli in their environment.

Imprinting is an unlearned behavior that is based on biological factors and that has great survival value: It increases the chances that newly hatched birds will remain with and follow their parent instead of wandering off into the waiting jaws of predators. Besides being unlearned, Lorenz noted two other major differences between imprinting and other kinds of learning.

**Sensitive period.** Unlike classical conditioning, operant conditioning, and cognitive learning, which occur throughout an animal's life, imprinting occurs best during the first few hours after hatching. This brief time period is called the critical, or sensitive, period.

The *critical*, or *sensitive, period* refers to a relatively brief time during which learning is most likely to occur.

Normally, the first object that newly hatched ducks see is their parent, upon whom they imprint. Thus, imprinting is a way for newly hatched animals to establish social attachments to members of their species. Although newly hatched birds will imprint on almost any moving object that they first see, including a human, a colored ball, or a glove, they imprint more strongly on moving objects that look or sound like their parent. Only those birds that can walk about immediately after hatching show imprinting, which promotes their survival (Bateson, 1991).

**Irreversible.** Unlike classical conditioning, operant conditioning, and cognitive learning, whose effects are usually reversible, imprinting is essentially irreversible. Most likely, imprinting evolved to be irreversible so that a young duck would not imprint on its mother one week and then imprint on a sly fox the next week.

In a program to prevent the California condor from becoming extinct, condor chicks are hatched at the San Diego Zoo and raised by humans. Because imprinting occurs very early and is quite irreversible, special precautions are taken so that the condor will not imprint on humans.

For example, the young condor chick shown on the right is being fed by a puppet that resembles an adult condor's head rather than a human's hand. With this method of feeding, the young condor will imprint on the condor characteristics of the puppet. When this condor grows up and is reintroduced into the wild, it will establish social relationships with, and attempt to mate with, its own species.

Baby condor is fed by "mother," a puppet.

Another example of how biological factors increase the ease and speed of learning is evident in something called prepared learning.

## Prepared Learning

**Why is it so easy to speak but not read?**

I remember my mother telling me that, as a very young child, I seemed to be talking all the time. But I do remember not wanting to go to grade school because I didn't yet know how to read like my older brother. Why I very early and very easily learned to talk the same language as my parents but took many years to become a good reader illustrates the influence of biological factors. We'll discuss how biological factors help humans learn to speak thousands of different languages and birds learn to remember thousands of places where they hid food.

### Incredible Memory

**How do birds remember?**

There are small birds, called Clark's nutcrackers, that live in an area where almost no food is available in the winter. During autumn, nutcrackers gather and hide stores of food in underground places, or caches, in perhaps as many as 2,500 to 6,000 different locations. During winter, nutcrackers survive by finding and digging up their hidden stores of food. How does the nutcracker locate the thousands of stores, which were hidden weeks and months earlier? One reason is preparedness, which we also discussed earlier (p. 200).

*Remembers thousands of hidden food places*

*Preparedness,* or *prepared learning,* refers to the innate or biological tendency of animals to recognize, attend to, and store certain cues over others, as well as to associate some combinations of conditioned and unconditioned stimuli more easily than others.

Under seminatural conditions, researchers observed the amazing ability of Clark's nutcrackers to hide and find hundreds of hidden stores of food. Researchers found that nutcrackers use natural landmarks (trees, stones, bushes) to form cognitive maps that help them remember the locations of their hidden stores (Bednekoff et al., 1997; Vander Wall, 1982).

One reason nutcrackers have such phenomenal memories is that the areas of their brains involved in memory are larger than the same areas in birds that do not store food. Specifically, the hippocampus, which is involved in transferring short-term memories into long-term memories, is larger in nutcrackers than in nonstoring birds (Shettleworth, 1993). Thus, the nutcracker appears to be biologically prepared for surviving barren winters by having a larger hippocampus (green area in the figure) so that it can better remember the locations of thousands of food stores.

**Hippocampus**

Just as some birds are biologically prepared to remember the locations of critical hidden stores, humans are biologically prepared to make sounds and speak at least one of 6,000 different languages.

### Incredible Sounds

**How do infants make "word" sounds?**

In the late 1940s, two psychologists wondered if a chimp could learn to speak if it were surrounded with speaking adults and a child as a speaking companion. To answer this question, two psychologists (husband and wife) raised a chimp in their home along with their own child. However, after 6 years of trying, the chimp had learned to say a grand total of three words, "mama," "papa," and "cup" (Hayes & Hayes, 1951). At that time, these two psychologists did not know that the chimp's vocal apparatus and brain were not biologically prepared to produce sounds and words necessary for human speech (see the discussion of animal language on pp. 322–323).

*Chimp does not have vocal structures to speak.*

The reason humans but not chimps or other animals learn to speak so easily is that humans' vocal apparatus and brains are biologically prepared, or innately wired, for speaking (Pinker, 1994).

For example, the brain of a newborn infant is biologically prepared to recognize the difference between human speech sounds. Researchers discovered this ability by playing speech sounds to infants whose rate of sucking on a nipple was being recorded. After newborns heard the sound "ba" over and over, their rate of sucking slowed, indicating that they were paying little attention to the sound. But, as soon as researchers played the sound "pa," the infants' rate of sucking increased, indicating that they had noticed the relatively small change between the sounds "ba" and "pa." This study showed that infants' brains are prewired or biologically prepared (see right figure) to recognize and discriminate among sounds that are essential for learning speech (Buonomano & Merzenich, 1995). In fact, infants all around the world make similar babbling sounds, which indicates the influence and importance of biological factors in learning to speak.

*Infant's brain is prewired for speaking.*

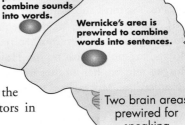

*Broca's area is prewired to combine sounds into words.*

*Wernicke's area is prewired to combine words into sentences.*

*Two brain areas prewired for speaking*

**Conclusion.** The learning principles of Pavlov, Thorndike, and Skinner do not explain how rats form cognitive maps, how infants easily produce and discriminate among human speech sounds, why monkeys roll snowballs, why chicks follow the first moving object, or how nutcrackers remember thousands of hiding places for stored food. These examples indicate that innate biological factors prepare animals and humans to learn certain kinds of behaviors useful for survival.

Next, we'll return to operant conditioning and discuss how its learning principles helped parents manage childhood problems.

## How Can Parents Deal with "NO"?

**Why study a single subject?**

When researchers study a group of subjects, information on any single subject may be lost in the group's combined scores. One advantage of operant conditioning is that a researcher can observe, study, and modify the ongoing behavior of a single subject. The ability to focus on a single subject's behavior makes operant conditioning a powerful procedure for changing undesirable behaviors. One kind of undesirable behavior in young children can be the persistent refusal of parental requests. We'll look at 4-year-old Morgan, who is becoming unmanageable because of a problem called noncompliance.

*Noncompliance* refers to a child refusing to follow directions, carry out a request, or obey a command given by a parent or caregiver.

Child constantly refusing or saying "NO" is a common complaint of many parents.

Noncompliance is a common complaint of parents in general and the most frequent problem of parents who bring their children to clinics for treatment of behavioral problems (Wierson & Forehand, 1994).

When saying "NO!" becomes a big problem, parents can be trained to use operant conditioning to decrease their child's persistent refusal. Parental training may involve different kinds of operant conditioning procedures, such as using verbal praise or giving attention to increase the occurrence of positive behaviors or using negative punishment to decrease undesirable behaviors. We'll focus on one form of negative punishment—time-out.

*Time-out* is a form of negative punishment in which reinforcing stimuli are removed after an undesirable response. This removal decreases the chances that the undesired response will recur.

Because Morgan persistently said "NO!" to her mother's requests, researchers showed Morgan's mother how to use time-out periods.

### *Study: Using Time-Out to Reduce Noncompliance*

Researchers began by explaining to parents how to use the principles of operant conditioning to overcome a child's persistent "NO!"

**Subjects.** They were 4-year-old girls who were normal in every way but had a long history of saying "NO!" to parental requests. Their mothers had volunteered for this study because they wanted help with this problem.

**Procedure.** Researchers first observed mothers making typical requests and noted the children's rate of refusal, which is called the baseline. Then, mothers were shown how to use several procedures, but we'll focus on the most successful, time-outs.

If Morgan's mother made a request and Morgan complied, her mother reinforced Morgan's response with praise. However, if Morgan refused, her mother used the time-out procedure. Morgan was led to the corner of another room and told to do nothing (no TV, books, or toys) but to sit quietly and silently in a chair facing the wall for 1 minute. After 1 minute, Morgan was allowed to leave the corner and rejoin her mother. At that point, the mother made another request of Morgan. If Morgan complied, praise was given; if she showed noncompliance ("NO!"), the time-out procedure was used. All procedures were conducted in the home by the mother.

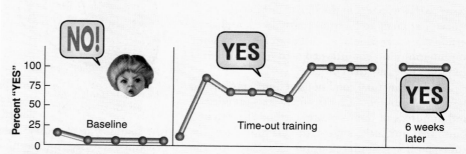

**Results.** The changes in Morgan's behavior after her mother began using time-out periods are shown in the graph below (Rortvedt & Miltenberger, 1994).

**Baseline:** Remember that during baseline, the researcher observed only the number of times that Morgan refused or agreed with her mother's request. During baseline, Morgan's mother made 5–8 requests during each session. Notice that during the last five sessions, Morgan showed mostly 0% compliance, despite her mother's scolding, pleading, or reprimanding.

**Time-out:** During time-out training, each time Morgan refused her mother's request, she was given a time-out period. Notice that Morgan's percentage of compliance started out at 12%, reached 60% on sessions 8–11, and then reached 100%.

Six weeks later, in a follow-up session using time-out, Morgan again showed 100% compliance with her mother's requests.

**Conclusion.** Studies like this show that the time-out procedure is effective in reducing undesirable behaviors, including noncompliance, temper tantrums, and disruptive activities (Taylor & Miller, 1997). The time-out procedure is an example of negative punishment, in which removing some stimuli, freedom to play, decreases the undesirable response, noncompliance. Negative punishment (time-out) is generally preferable to positive punishment (spanking) because positive punishment may cause negative emotional reactions as well as negative feelings toward the punisher (parents). The time-out procedure is an example of how operant conditioning principles may be applied to modify human behavior. We'll discuss the pros and cons of punishment more fully in the Application section.

Dealing with noncompliance is one example of how learning principles can be applied to human behavior. Another example involves learning how to play the violin.

**What's the Suzuki method?**

In the 1940s, a violin player and teacher from Japan, Shinichi Suzuki, developed a remarkably successful method for teaching violin playing to very young children (Suzuki, 1998). His method, called the *Suzuki method*, was brought to the United States in the mid-1960s and has generated incredible enthusiasm among children, parents, and music teachers ever since (Lamb, 1990).

It's interesting to learn that the basic principles of the Suzuki method for teaching young children to play the violin

Suzuki's method of teaching young children to play musical instruments has many similarities with Bandura's principles of social cognitive learning

are very similar to Bandura's four mental processes for social cognitive learning. What's different is that Suzuki developed his learning principles after years of actually teaching young children to play the violin, while Bandura developed his four mental processes of observational learning after years of research with young children. We'll discuss how even though Suzuki the teacher and Bandura the researcher lived in very different cultures thousands of miles apart, their experiences led them to very similar conclusions about how children learn.

## Different Cultures but Similar Learning Principles

### 1 Attention

*Bandura states that the observer must pay attention to what the model says and does.*

Similarly, Suzuki advises parents to teach violin information only when the child is actually looking at and watching the parent. Parents are told to stop teaching and wait if the child rolls on the floor, jumps up and down, walks backward, or talks about unrelated things.

The recommended age for starting a child with the Suzuki method is 3 for girls and 4 for boys. Parents are cautioned, however, that the attention span of the 3- to 4-year-old child is extremely limited, usually from 30 seconds to at most several minutes at a time.

### 2 Memory

*Bandura says that the observer must code the information in such a way that it can be retrieved and used later.*

Similarly, Suzuki tells parents that they should present information in ways that a young child can understand (Bandura would say code). Because a 3- to 4-year-old child does not have fully developed verbal skills or memory, little time is spent giving verbal instructions. Instead, the young child is given violin information through games and exercises. For example, children are taught how to hold the violin, use the bow, and press the strings by first playing games with their hands. Children are taught how to read music (notes) only when they are older and have gained some technical skill at playing the violin.

### 3 Imitation

*Bandura says the observer must be able to use the information to guide his or her own actions and thus imitate the model's behavior.*

Similarly, Suzuki suggests that children start at about 3 or 4 years old, the earliest age when they can physically perform the required movements and imitate their parents and teachers. Girls can start earlier than boys because girls physically mature earlier. For other instruments, the starting times are different—piano, 4–5 years; cello, 5 years; flute, 9 years—because these instruments require more physical dexterity. As you have probably guessed, 3- and 4-year-olds start with miniature violins and move up to bigger ones as they develop.

### 4 Motivation

*Bandura says that the observer must have some reason, reinforcement, or incentive to perform the model's behaviors.*

Similarly, Suzuki emphasizes that the most important role of the parent is to constantly reward and reinforce the child for observing and "doing what Mommy or Daddy is doing." Suzuki recommends several ways to keep motivation high in young children: Be an active and interested model for the child, play violin games that are fun for the child, avoid games or lessons that involve competition, and *never* push the child beyond the level that he or she is capable of reaching (Slone, 1985).

Social cognitive learning involves attention, memory, imitation, and motivation.

**Conclusion.** Parents and teachers who have used the Suzuki method report great success (Lamb, 1990). As you can judge, the basic principles of the Suzuki method for teaching violin are quite similar to Bandura's four mental processes for social cognitive learning. Both Suzuki and Bandura recognized the importance of observational learning and how much information children can learn from watching and imitating models. Suzuki's successful method of teaching violin to young children provides support for Bandura's four mental processes that he believes are involved in social cognitive learning.

Next, we'll discuss how operant learning principles were used to develop a method for teaching autistic children.

## Definitions

### What is behavior modification?

Throughout this module, we have discussed many examples of behavior modification, such as: toilet training 3-year-old Sheryl and decreasing food refusal in young children (p. 216), stopping Walt from eating paint chips (p. 218), stopping Suzanne from injuring herself (p. 219), and decreasing noncompliance (refusal) in Morgan (p. 230).

*Behavior modification* is a treatment or therapy that changes or modifies problems or undesirable behaviors by using principles of learning based on operant conditioning, classical conditioning, and social cognitive learning.

For over 35 years, psychologist and researcher Ivar Lovaas of the University of California at Los Angeles has used behavior modification or, more colloquially, behavior mod to treat autistic children (Lovaas & Buch, 1997). Lovaas's work is especially impressive because he was one of the first to adapt behavior mod procedures to treat serious problems of autistic children. We discussed autism throughout Module 1 and here we'll only summarize the kinds of problems that individuals with autism usually have.

**Behavior modification is used to treat autism.**

*Autism* is marked by especially abnormal or impaired development in social interactions, such as hiding to avoid people (see drawing), not making eye contact, not wanting to be touched. Autism is marked by difficulties in communicating, such as grave problems in developing spoken language or in initiating conversations. Autistics are characterized by having very few activities and interests, spending long periods repeating the same behaviors, or following rituals that interfere with more normal functioning. Signs of autism usually appear when a child is about 2 to 3 years old (American Psychiatric Association, 1994).

Although the social and communication deficits in autistic individuals range from moderate to severe, many autistics will remain socially unresponsive (see drawing) and lacking in communication skills unless they receive some treatment (Cowley, 2000c; McIntosh, 1999). One kind of treatment for autism comes from the work of Dr. Ivar Lovaas, who uses behavior modification techniques, which are based on the principles of operant conditioning and social cognitive learning.

## Behavior Modification and Autism

### What is the program?

Dr. Lovaas's program at UCLA is called the Young Autism Project, which treats 2- to 3-year-old autistic children with a 40-hour-per-week program that runs for 2 to 3 years. We'll describe part of the program.

**Program.** Dr. Lovaas's training program actually consists of hundreds of separate teaching programs, many of them using principles of operant conditioning: Select a specific *target behavior*, *shape the behavior*, and use *positive reinforcers* of praise and food that are given immediately after the child emits the desired behavior. For example, here's a program to help autistic children make eye contact.

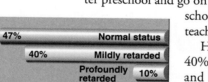

| | |
|---|---|
| 47% | Normal status |
| 40% | Mildly retarded |
| Profoundly retarded | 10% |

**Target behavior** is getting the child to make eye contact following the command "Look at me."

**Shaping the behavior** involves two steps.

Step 1. Have the child sit in a chair facing you. Give the command "Look at me" every 5–10 seconds. When the child makes a correct response of looking at you, say "Good looking" and simultaneously reward the child with food.

**47% improved**

Step 2. Continue until the child repeatedly follows the command "Look at me." Then gradually increase the duration of the child's eye contact from 1 second to periods of 2 to 3 seconds.

Using this behavior modification program, therapists and parents have had success in teaching autistic children to make eye contact, to stop constant rocking, to respond to verbal requests such as "Wash your hands," to interact with peers, to speak, and to engage in school tasks such as reading and writing (Lovaas, 1993).

**Results.** Lovaas and his colleagues did a long-term study of 19 children diagnosed as autistic. Behavior modification training went on for

at least 40 hours per week, for 2 years or more. The graph below shows that, at the end of training, 47% (9/19) of the autistic children reached normal status (Lovaas, 1987). These children acquired sufficient language, social, play, and self-help behaviors that they could enter preschool and go on to successfully complete first grade in public school. Many of the children did so well that the teachers did not know they were autistic.

However, even with such intensive training, 40% of autistic children remained mildly retarded, and 10% remained profoundly retarded and were assigned to classes for children with mental retardation. In comparison, in a control group of autistic children who received only minimal treatment, only 2% achieved normal intellectual and educational functioning, while 45% remained mildly retarded and 53% remained severely retarded (Lovaas, 1987; Lovaas & Buch, 1997; McEachin et al., 1993). Lovaas concluded that without intensive behavior modification treatment, autistic children will continue to show severe behavioral deficits.

**Follow-up.** A six-year follow-up study of the nine children who had reached normal status found that they had kept their gains and were still functioning normally (Lovaas, 1999). A recent follow-up study of the same nine children, now 20 to 30 years old, showed that eight appeared normal, that is, did not score differently from other normal adults on a variety of tests, while one had personality problems but would not be classified autistic (Lovaas, 1999). However, critics question whether the promising results from these nine individuals can be applied to all autistic children since these nine may have had less severe symptoms to begin with (Gresham et al., 1999). Dr. Lovaas is currently trying to resolve this controversy by coordinating another larger study that uses behavior modification techniques to treat autistic children (McIntosh, 1999).

## Biofeedback

*How can we reduce tension?*

Many people develop a variety of psychosomatic problems, which result from stressful or disturbing thoughts that lead to real aches and pains in the body. For example, psychosomatic problems include back pain, muscle tension, high blood pressure, stomach distress, and headaches. One procedure to reduce psychosomatic problems is based on operant conditioning and is called biofeedback.

*Biofeedback* is a training procedure through which a person is made aware of his or her physiological responses, such as muscle activity, heart rate, blood pressure, or temperature. After becoming aware of these physiological responses, a person tries to control them to decrease psychosomatic problems.

Stress may cause a buildup of muscle tension.

For example, headaches may be caused or worsened by muscle tension, of which the sufferer may be totally unaware. The left figure shows that the forehead and neck have wide bands of muscles where tension can lead to pain and discomfort. Through video or audio (bio)feedback, a person can be made aware of muscle tension and learn how to reduce the tension.

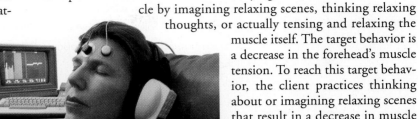

Biofeedback helps a person control his or her physiological responses.

As shown in the photo below, small sensors attached to the client's forehead detect activity in the large muscle that stretches across the top front part of the head. The woman is trying to relax her forehead muscle by imagining relaxing scenes, thinking relaxing thoughts, or actually tensing and relaxing the muscle itself. The target behavior is a decrease in the forehead's muscle tension. To reach this target behavior, the client practices thinking about or imagining relaxing scenes that result in a decrease in muscle tension. A decrease in muscle tension is signaled by a decrease in an audio signal, which acts as a reinforcer. After a number of these sessions, the client learns to decrease muscle tension with the goal of staying relaxed the next time she gets upset.

Biofeedback is often used in conjunction with other forms of medical treatment or psychotherapy and can help a person reduce blood pressure, decrease headaches, and reduce anxiety (Goldberger & Breznitz, 1993; Lehrer et al., 1994). We'll discuss other methods of reducing stress and associated psychosomatic problems in Module 21.

Our last example deals with concerns about using punishment to decrease undesirable behaviors.

## Pros and Cons of Punishment

*What are the side effects?*

In recent surveys, 42% of mothers in New York reported spanking their young children during the previous week and 64% of adults in the United States approved of spanking (Rosellini, 1998; Socolar & Stein, 1995). Although spanking remains a relatively popular form of discipline, it can have a number of negative side effects and may be a less desirable form of punishment than the time-out procedure (Geiger, 1994). We'll discuss the pros and cons of each.

### SPANKING: POSITIVE PUNISHMENT

Since spanking involves the presentation of an aversive stimulus (pain), it is an example of positive punishment. In some cases, positive punishment can decrease the occurrence of undesirable behaviors. However, a poorly chosen positive punishment, such as using harsh spanking to punish aggressive behavior, was found to have the opposite effect, increasing antisocial behavioral problems (Deater-Deckard & Dodge, 1997). In addition to increasing aggressive behaviors, studies also reported that spanking or other forms of physical punishment reduced self-esteem, made children depressed, and provided a model of aggressive behavior that the child may later imitate (Socolar & Stein, 1995).

Effects of punishment depend on its usage.

Some of the undesirable effects of positive punishment can be reduced if it is given immediately after the behavior, if it is just severe enough to be effective, if it is delivered consistently, if the child is told the reason for the punishment, and, perhaps most important, if

punishment is used in combination with positively reinforcing a desirable behavior (Lieberman, 1993). One disadvantage of positive punishment is that it points out only what the child should not do, while positive reinforcers have the advantage of encouraging the child to engage in desirable behaviors.

### TIME-OUT: NEGATIVE PUNISHMENT

Another form of discipline is time-out, which was discussed earlier (p. 230). Time-out is an example of negative punishment because it involves the removal of a reinforcing stimulus (desirable reward) so that some undesirable response will not recur. For example, after misbehaving, a child is given a time-out period (stays in a corner without any games, books, or toys). Time-out is most effective when used consistently and combined with teaching the child alternative desired behaviors using positive reinforcers (Taylor & Miller, 1997).

Time-out has fewer undesirable side effects than spanking.

Compared to punishment, time-out has fewer undesirable side effects; it does not provide a model of aggression and does not elicit severe negative emotional reactions. Thus, when it is necessary to discipline a child, care should be taken in choosing between positive punishment (spanking) and negative punishment (time-out). Although both kinds of punishment stop or suppress undesirable behaviors, spanking has more negative side effects than time-out, and time-out has been shown to be effective in eliminating undesirable behaviors. Both kinds of punishment are best used in combination with positive reinforcers so the child also learns to perform desirable behaviors (Rosellini, 1998).

# Summary Test

## A. OPERANT CONDITIONING

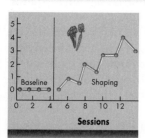

**1.** A kind of learning in which the consequences that follow some behavior increase or decrease the likelihood that the behavior will occur again is called _____.

**2.** To explain how random trial-and-error behaviors of cats became goal-directed behaviors, Thorndike formulated the _____, which says that behaviors are strengthened by positive consequences and weakened by negative consequences.

**3.** Skinner used the term *operant* (a)_____ to describe something that can be modified by its consequences. Operant responses provide one way to separate ongoing behaviors into units that can be observed and measured. Skinner believed that Pavlov's conditioning, which involves physiological (b)_____, was not very useful in understanding other forms of ongoing behaviors.

**4.** Suppose you wished to operantly condition your dog, Bingo, to sit up. The procedure would be as follows. You would give Bingo a treat, which is called a (a)_____, after he emits a desired behavior. Because it is unlikely that Bingo will initially sit up, you will use a procedure called (b)_____, which is a process of reinforcing those behaviors that lead up to or approximate the final desired behavior—sitting up. Immediately after Bingo emitted a desired behavior, you would give him a (c)_____.

**5.** Any behavior that increases in frequency because of an accidental pairing of a reinforcer and that behavior is called a _____ behavior.

**6.** The essence of operant conditioning can be summed up as follows: Consequences or reinforcers are contingent on _____.

**7.** If you compare classical and operant conditioning, you will find the following differences. In classical conditioning, the response is an involuntary (a)_____ that is elicited by the (b)_____. In operant conditioning, the response is a voluntary (c)_____ that is performed or (d)_____ by the organism. In classical conditioning, the unconditioned stimulus is presented at the beginning of a trial and elicits the (e)_____. In operant conditioning, the organism emits a behavior that is immediately followed by a (f)_____.

## B. REINFORCERS

**8.** In operant conditioning, the term *consequences* refers to what happens after the occurrence of a behavior. If a consequence increases the likelihood that a behavior will occur again, it is called a (a)_____. If a consequence decreases the likelihood that a behavior will occur again, it is called a (b)_____.

**9.** If a stimulus increases the chances that a response will occur again, that stimulus is called a (a)_____. If the removal of an aversive stimulus increases the chances that a response will occur again, that aversive stimulus is called a (b)_____. Both positive and negative reinforcements (c)_____ the frequency of the response they follow. In contrast, punishment is a consequence that (d)_____ the likelihood that a behavior will occur again.

**10.** The stimuli of food, water, and sex, which are innately satisfying and require no learning to become pleasurable, are called (a)_____. The stimuli of praise, money, and good grades have acquired their reinforcing properties through experience; these stimuli are called (b)_____.

## C. SCHEDULES OF REINFORCEMENT

**11.** A program or rule that determines how and when the occurrence of a response will be followed by a reinforcer is called a _____.

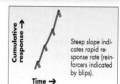

Steep slope indicates rapid response rate (reinforcers indicated by blips).

**12.** If you received reinforcement every time you performed a good deed, you would be on a (a)_____ schedule. This schedule is often used at the beginning of operant conditioning because it results in a rapid rate of learning. If your good deeds were not reinforced every time, you would be on a (b)_____ schedule. This schedule is more effective in maintaining the target behavior in the long run. There are four kinds of partial reinforcement schedules.

## D. OTHER CONDITIONING CONCEPTS

**13.** The phenomenon in which an organism emits the same response to similar stimuli is called (a)_____. If a response is emitted in the presence of a reinforced stimulus but not in the presence of unreinforced stimuli, the organism is exhibiting (b)_____. If an organism's response is no longer reinforced, it will stop emitting this behavior, which is an example of (c)_____. However, even without reinforcement, an organism may perform the behavior, which is an example of (d)_____.

## E. COGNITIVE LEARNING

**14.** The kind of learning that involves mental processes such as attention and memory, that may be learned through observation and imitation, and that may not involve any external rewards or require the person to perform any observable behaviors is called (a) _____. According to Tolman, rats developed a mental representation of the layout of their environment, which he called a (b)_____.

**15.** If an observer learns a behavior through observation but does not immediately perform the behavior, this is an example of the _____ distinction.

**16.** During his studies of problem solving in chimpanzees, Köhler used the term _____ to describe a mental process marked by the sudden occurrence of a solution.

**17.** Köhler's study of insightful problem solving, Bandura's theory of observational learning, and Tolman's idea of cognitive maps represent three kinds of _____ learning.

## F. BIOLOGICAL FACTORS

**18.** Innate tendencies or predispositions that may either facilitate or inhibit learning are referred to as _____.

**19.** The innate tendency of newborn birds to follow the first moving object that they encounter soon after birth is called (a)_____. This kind of learning occurs best during a critical or sensitive period and is essentially (b)_____. One function of imprinting is to form social attachments between members of a species.

**20.** The innate tendency of animals to recognize, attend to, and store certain cues over others and associate some combinations of conditioned and unconditioned stimuli is referred to as _____. An example of this tendency is observed in Clark's nutcrackers, which are preprogrammed to bury and remember thousands of hidden stores of food.

## G. RESEARCH FOCUS: NONCOMPLIANCE

**21.** One of the most common problems faced by parents is dealing with a child who refuses to follow directions or carry out a request or command. This refusal behavior is called _____.

**22.** An effective way to deal with a child's noncompliance is to use a procedure that involves placing a child in a situation where there is no chance of reinforcers. This mild form of nonphysical punishment is called _____.

## H. CULTURAL DIVERSITY: EAST MEETS WEST

**23.** Suzuki's method and Bandura's theory both emphasize observation, modeling, and imitation. Specifically, both Suzuki and Bandura focus on four concepts: paying (a)_____ to the model, placing the information in (b)_____, using the information to (c)_____ the model's actions, and (d)_____ to perform the behavior.

## I. APPLICATION: BEHAVIOR MODIFICATION

**24.** Using principles of operant conditioning to change human behavior is referred to as (a)_____. Using these same principles to help individuals learn to control (increase or decrease) some physiological response, such as muscle activity or temperature, is called (b)_____.

**25.** If an aversive stimulus is presented immediately after a particular response, the response will be suppressed; this procedure is called (a)_____. If a reinforcing stimulus is removed immediately after a particular response, the response will be suppressed; this procedure is called (b)_____. A poorly chosen form of punishment, such as spanking, may have undesirable side effects, such as reducing a child's (c)_____ and serving as a model for future (d)_____ behaviors.

***Answers:*** *1. operant conditioning; 2. law of effect; 3. (a) response, (b) reflexes; 4. (a) reinforcer, (b) shaping, (c) reinforcer; 5. superstitious; 6. behavior; 7. (a) reflex, (b) unconditioned stimulus, (c) behavior, (d) emitted, (e) unconditioned response, (f) reinforcer; 8. (a) reinforcer, (b) punishment; 9. (a) positive reinforcer, (b) negative reinforcer, (c) increase, (d) decreases; 10. (a) primary reinforcers, (b) secondary reinforcers; 11. schedule of reinforcement; 12. (a) continuous reinforcement, (b) partial reinforcement; 13. (a) generalization, (b) discrimination, (c) extinction, (d) spontaneous recovery; 14. (a) social cognitive learning, (b) cognitive map; 15. (a) learning-performance; 16. insight; 17. cognitive; 18. biological factors; 19. (a) imprinting, (b) irreversible; 20. preparedness, or prepared learning; 21. noncompliance; 22. time-out; 23. (a) attention, (b) memory, (c) imitate, (d) motivation; 24. (a) behavior modification, (b) biofeedback; 25. (a) positive punishment, (b) negative punishment, (c) self-esteem, (d) aggressive*

# Critical Thinking

## IS IT OK FOR PARENTS TO SPANK THEIR KIDS?

### Questions

**1.** What is your own attitude toward spanking and how much, if at all, do these findings influence your attitude?

**2.** Which approach to answering questions did this study use and what are some of the problems with this study?

**3.** How do Dr. Trumbull's beliefs about spanking differ from those of Straus's study, which shows spanking has damaging effects?

**4.** What does Dr. Larzelere conclude is important about using spanking?

**5.** How do spanking and time-out differ?

**6.** Do you agree with Dr. Hyman that spanking should be banned?

*Try InfoTrac to search for terms:* spanking; disciplining children.

Today, about 64% of American adults approve of spanking. The do-or-don't spanking controversy was sparked by a recent study.

Sociologist Murray Straus reported that the more a parent spanks a child for misbehaving, the worse—over time—that child behaves (*Archives of Pediatrics & Adolescent Medicine*, 1997). Straus says, "We are now able to show that when parents attempt to correct their child's behavior by spanking, it backfires . . . the more they spanked (3 or more times a week), the worse a child behaved two years and four years later" (Schulte, 1997, p. A1).

However, Straus's study has several problems. First, the mothers ranged in age from 14 to 21, not a representative sample of mothers in the United States. Second, the study looked at children ages 6 to 9 but not younger children. Third, the mothers were interviewed twice, two years apart, so there is a question about the reliability and truthfulness of their answers.

Dr. Den Trumbull, a pediatrician and critic of Straus's conclusions, says that spanking is effective and not harmful to development if limited to children between 18 months and 6 years. On the other hand, spanking may be humiliating and traumatic to children in the 6 to 9 years age group and lead to problems down the line. Dr. Trumbull says that he favors spanking (one or two slaps to the buttocks) only as a last resort.

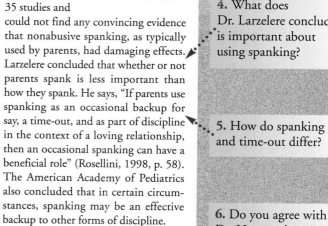

Psychologist Robert Larzelere, director of residential research at Boys Town in Nebraska, which does not allow spanking, reviewed 35 studies and could not find any convincing evidence that nonabusive spanking, as typically used by parents, had damaging effects. Larzelere concluded that whether or not parents spank is less important than how they spank. He says, "If parents use spanking as an occasional backup for say, a time-out, and as part of discipline in the context of a loving relationship, then an occasional spanking can have a beneficial role" (Rosellini, 1998, p. 58). The American Academy of Pediatrics also concluded that in certain circumstances, spanking may be an effective backup to other forms of discipline.

However, psychologist Irwin Hyman concludes, "There's enough evidence to decide we don't need spanking, even if the evidence isn't that strong." (Adapted from M. D. Lemonick, Spare the rod? Maybe, *Time*, August 25, 1997, p. 65; L. Rosellini, When to spank, *U.S. News & World Report*, April 15, 1998, pp. 52–58; B. Schulte, Spanking backfires, the latest study says, Knight-Ridder, appeared in *San Diego Union-Tribune*, August 15, 1997, p. A1)

---

### Suggested answers to Newspaper Article questions

1. Your attitude toward spanking will be influenced by how you or your brothers and sisters were disciplined by your parents, such as how much they used spanking and any negative effects. If you disapprove of spanking, this study will confirm your belief; if you approve of spanking, this study may cause you to rethink.
2. This study used the survey approach, which is an efficient method to gather data from a large number of people, but they may misremember, forget, or give answers they think the interviewers want to hear. Problems with this study include choosing a very small sample of mothers (ages 14–21) and not including younger children (below the age of 6).
3. Dr. Trumbull believes that spanking is not harmful to younger children—18 months to 6 years—who are the group of children that Straus did not study.

4. Dr. Larzelere believes that how parents spank (doing it in the context of a loving relationship and as a backup to time-out) is MORE important than if they spank.
5. Spanking is an example of positive punishment—presenting an aversive stimulus (pain); time-out is an example of negative punishment—removing a reinforcer (attention, toys, television).
6. It is almost impossible not to have an emotional reaction when discussing spanking—I feel spanking may be OK as a last resort; I feel it's never all right to hurt a child. This means that your emotional feelings will influence how you respond to research findings. Research findings rarely answer any question absolutely but rather give you some data or facts to think about. For example, if you're against spanking, you'll agree with Dr. Hyman to ban spanking, even if the research doesn't totally support such a ban.

# Links to Learning

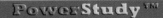

## Web Sites

● WADSWORTH ONLINE STUDY CENTER
**http://psychology.wadsworth.com**
Quizzes, learning activities and exercises, a discussion forum, and hot links to Internet sites related to sensation, including:

● OPERANT CONDITIONING AND BEHAVIORISM—A HISTORICAL OUTLINE
**http://www.biozentrum.uni-wuerzburg.de/genetics/ behavior/learning/behaviorism.html**
Here is a nice history of research on operant conditioning and behaviorism, including work by Thorndike, Watson, and Skinner.

● POSITIVE REINFORCEMENT: A SELF-INSTRUCTIONAL EXERCISE
**http://server.bmod.athabascau.ca/html/prtut/ reinpair.htm**
This site offers a tutorial in positive reinforcement, and includes examples, activities, and practice exercises.

● PARENT SOUP
**http://www.parentsoup.com/**
This site is dedicated to that ongoing experiment in operant conditioning known as parenthood. There are areas for parents of children of various ages, and special features such as how to raise moral children.

## Learning Activities

● *POWERSTUDY*™ CD, BY ROD PLOTNIK & TOM DOYLE
A 40-minute, fully narrated, self-paced, multimedia presentation that includes animations, interactive activities, videos, quizzes, pronunciation of terms, personal note-taking, and direct-to-Web connections.

● *STUDY GUIDE TO ACCOMPANY INTRODUCTION TO PSYCHOLOGY, 6TH EDITION,* **by Matthew Enos**
In Module 10, read a tribute to B. F. Skinner, decide whether Bandura's classic Bobo doll experiment disproves Skinner, and come up with everyday examples of reinforcement.

● *WEBTUTOR*
**http://webtutor.thomsonlearning.com**
Visit this site for interactive versions of the Study Guide features. Take a quiz, get your score—should you study a topic some more, or can you move on? For example, is there a difference between learning a behavior and performing it? What do you call the spanking a child gets for running into the street?

● *INFOTRAC ONLINE LIBRARY*
**http://www.infotrac-college.com**

Use your password and then key in search terms such as those below to find popular and scientific articles on subjects covered in Module 10. Make the library work for you!

Behavior modification          Biofeedback
Imprinting                     Ethologists

● *PSYCHNOW!*
CD for Macintosh and Windows includes a study guide, glossary, Web sites, and animations. For Module 10, see:
  • Classical Conditioning
  • Operant Conditioning

## Study Questions

*Use InfoTrac to search for topics mentioned in the main heads below (e.g., operant conditioning, cognitive learning, behavior modification).*

*A. **Operant Conditioning**—How do you explain why your significant other sulks every time something is wrong even though you've told him or her that it bugs you? (**Suggested answer page 625**)

*B. **Reinforcers**—How would you use operant conditioning to change a rude friend into a more likable and friendly person? (**Suggested answer page 625**)

C. **Schedules of Reinforcement**—Which schedules of partial reinforcement best apply to the following behaviors: eating, studying, going to the movies, dating?

D. **Other Conditioning Concepts**—The first time you visit your 2-year-old niece, she takes one look at you and starts to cry. What happened?

E. **Cognitive Learning**—Why should parents be especially concerned about what they say and do in the presence of their children?

F. **Biological Factors**—A 14-year-old boy graduated from college with outstanding grades. How could he learn so much so early?

G. **Research Focus: Noncompliance**—Why might parents yell, threaten, or spank rather than use a time-out to deal with a child's constant refusals?

*H. **Cultural Diversity: East Meets West**—Why do the same principles of learning work in very different cultures? (**Suggested answer page 625**)

I. **Application: Behavior Modification**—How could techniques of behavior modification be used in a computer program to teach children how to do math problems?

*These questions are answered in Appendix B.

# Module 11: Types of Memory

**A. Three Types of Memory**   240
* SENSORY MEMORY
* SHORT-TERM MEMORY
* LONG-TERM MEMORY
* MEMORY PROCESSES

**B. Sensory Memory: Recording**   241
* ICONIC MEMORY
* ECHOIC MEMORY
* FUNCTIONS OF SENSORY MEMORY

**C. Short-Term Memory: Working**   242
* DEFINITION
* TWO FEATURES
* CHUNKING
* FUNCTIONS OF SHORT-TERM MEMORY

**D. Long-Term Memory: Storing**   244
* STEPS IN THE MEMORY PROCESS
* FEATURES OF LONG-TERM MEMORY
* SEPARATE MEMORY SYSTEMS
* DECLARATIVE VERSUS PROCEDURAL

**E. Research Focus: Do Emotions Affect Memories?**   247
* HORMONES AND MEMORIES
* MEMORIES OF EMOTIONAL EVENTS

**F. Encoding: Transferring**   248
* TWO KINDS OF ENCODING
* REHEARSING AND ENCODING
* LEVELS OF PROCESSING

**G. Repressed Memories**   250
* RECOVERED MEMORIES
* DEFINITION OF REPRESSED MEMORIES
* THERAPIST'S ROLE IN RECOVERED MEMORIES
* IMPLANTING FALSE MEMORIES
* ACCURACY OF RECOVERED MEMORIES

**Concept Review**   252

**H. Cultural Diversity: Oral versus Written**   253
* UNITED STATES VERSUS AFRICA
* REMEMBERING SPOKEN INFORMATION

**I. Application: Unusual Memories**   254
* PHOTOGRAPHIC MEMORY
* EIDETIC IMAGERY
* FLASHBULB MEMORY

**Summary Test**   256

**Critical Thinking**   258
* WERE PRESCHOOL CHILDREN IMPLANTED WITH FALSE MEMORIES?

**Links to Learning**   259

PowerStudy™

## Incredible Memory

**What's a super memory?**

Rajan Mahadevan stood before the packed house of the International Congress on Yoga and Meditation. He recited, from memory, the first 31,811 digits of pi, which is often rounded off to two decimal places, or 3.14. He did not err until the 31,812th digit. This feat took 3 hours and 44 minutes and earned him a place in the *Guinness Book of World Records.*

Rajan memorized 31,811 numbers of pi in exact order.

After his record-setting memory performance, Rajan left his native India and, at age 23, entered Kansas State University. There he met Professor Charles Thompson, who made the study of memory his specialty.

Thompson discovered that Rajan can quickly recall the digit at any location within the first 10,000 digits of pi. This would be equivalent to memorizing the names of 10,000 people seated in numbered seats and then recalling the name of any single person, such as the one sitting in seat 2,141. Rajan can repeat a string of 60 numbers after a single hearing, while most of us can repeat an average of 10 random numbers. Rajan is one of only a half-dozen people in the world known to have such gargantuan memory powers.

Despite Rajan's unbelievable ability to memorize numbers, he seems to be worse than average at recalling faces, and he constantly forgets where he put his keys (Thompson et al., 1993).

No one questions the accuracy of Rajan's memories because they can be verified. However, some memories are not so easily verified, as in the case of Holly and her accused father.

## Repressed Memory

**How true are memories?**

The man in the photo at right was accused by his daughter, Holly (photo below), for allegedly molesting her as a child. When Holly was 19, she had gone into therapy for bulimia, which is an eating disorder that involves eating a large amount of food and then often inducing vomiting.

"Holly's supposed memories are the results of drugs and quackery, not anything I did."

Holly's mother had asked a therapist about the causes of bulimia, and the therapist said that one of many causes was sexual molestation. Later, the mother asked Holly if she had ever been sexually molested. "Holly became very red in the face, pushed the chair out, and was crying. She said, 'I don't know. I think so. Maybe,' and then 'Yes'" (Butler, 1994, p. 12). During therapy sessions, Holly reportedly told her therapist about other memories and images of her father molesting her.

Finally, about a year after first entering therapy, Holly accused her father of sexually molesting her. Holly's experience is an example of repressed memories, whose truthfulness and accuracy we'll discuss later in this module.

"I wouldn't be here if there was a question in my mind. I know my father molested me."

## Definitions

**What are the three processes?**

Rajan's amazing ability to recall thousands of digits and Holly's delayed remembering of terrible but difficult-to-verify childhood experiences involve three different memory processes.

*Memory* is the ability to retain information over time through three processes: encoding (forming), storing, and retrieving. Memories are not copies but representations of the world that vary in accuracy and are subject to error and bias.

We'll briefly define each of the three memory processes because they are the keys to understanding the interesting and complex process of how we remember and thus create the world we live in.

### 1 Encoding

Rajan developed a method or code to form memories for digits, a process called encoding.

*Encoding* refers to making mental representations of information so that it can be placed into our memories.

For example, Rajan encoded the number 111 by associating it with Admiral Nelson, who happened to have one eye, one arm, and one leg.

### 2 Storing

Rajan used associations to encode information because associations are also useful for storing information.

*Storing* is the process of placing encoded information into relatively permanent mental storage for later recall.

New information that is stored by making associations with old or familiar information is much easier to remember, or retrieve.

### 3 Retrieving

Rajan was able to recall, or retrieve, 31,811 digits in order.

*Retrieving* is the process of getting or recalling information that has been placed into short-term or long-term storage.

Only a half-dozen people in the entire world can match Rajan's feat of encoding, storing, and retrieving thousands of digits in order. Students are familiar with the problems of retrieving information during an exam when they try but fail to retrieve information they have studied.

We'll discuss three kinds of memory, how memories are encoded, why emotional memories are long-lasting, the issue of repressed memories, and some unusual memory abilities. We'll start with an overview of the three kinds of memory.

# A. Three Types of Memory

We often talk about memory as though it were a single process. In fact, a popular model of memory divides it into three different processes: sensory, short-term, and long-term memory (G. H. Bower, 2000). To illustrate each of these processes, we'll examine what happens as you walk through a big-city mall.

## Sensory Memory

As you walk through a busy mall, you are bombarded by hundreds of sights, smells, and sounds, including the music of a lone guitarist playing for spare change. Many of these stimuli reach your sensory memory.

*Sensory memory* refers to an initial process that receives and holds environmental information in its raw form for a brief period of time, from an instant to several seconds.

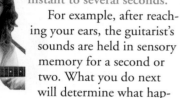

For example, after reaching your ears, the guitarist's sounds are held in sensory memory for a second or two. What you do next will determine what happens to the guitarist's sounds that are in your sensory memory.

If you pay no more attention to these sounds in sensory memory, they automatically *disappear* without a trace.

However, if you pay attention to the guitarist's music, the auditory information in sensory memory is transferred into another memory process called short-term memory (Baddeley, 2000).

## Short-Term Memory

Because a few notes of the guitarist's song sounded interesting, you shifted your attention to that particular information in sensory memory.

Paying attention to information in sensory memory causes it to be automatically transferred into short-term memory.

*Short-term memory,* also called *working memory,* refers to another process that can hold only a limited amount of information—an average of seven items—for only a short period of time—2 to 30 seconds.

Once a limited amount of information is transferred into short-term, or working, memory, it will remain there for up to 30 seconds. If during this time you become more involved in the information, such as humming to the music, the information will remain in short-term memory for a longer period of time.

However, the music will *disappear* after a short time unless it is transferred into permanent storage, called long-term memory (Brown & Craik, 2000).

## Long-Term Memory

If you become mentally engaged in humming along or wondering why the guitarist's music sounds familiar, there is a good chance that this mental activity will transfer the music from short-term into long-term memory.

*Long-term memory* refers to the process of storing almost unlimited amounts of information over long periods of time.

For example, you have stored hundreds of songs, terms, faces, and conversations in your long-term memory—information that is potentially available for retrieval. However, from personal experience, you know that you cannot always retrieve things you learned and know you know. In Module 12, we'll discuss reasons for forgetting information stored in long-term memory.

Now that you know what the three memory processes are, we'll explain how they work together.

## Memory Processes

**1** **Sensory memory.** We'll explain how the three types of memory described above work and how paying or not paying attention to something determines what is remembered and what is forgotten.

Imagine listening to a lecture. All the information that enters your sensory memory remains for seconds or less. If you *do not pay attention* to information in sensory memory, it is forgotten. If you *do pay attention* to particular information, such as the instructor's words, this information is automatically transferred into short-term memory.

**2** **Short-term memory.** If you *do not pay attention* to information in short-term memory, it is not encoded and is forgotten. If you *do pay attention* by rehearsing the information, such as taking notes, the information will be encoded for storage in long-term memory. That's why it helps to take lecture notes.

**3** **Long-term memory.** Information that is encoded for storage in long-term memory will remain there on a *relatively permanent basis.* Whether or not you can recall the instructor's words from long-term memory depends partly on how it is encoded, which we'll discuss later. This means that poor class notes may result in poor encoding and poor recall on exams. The secret to great encoding and great recall is to associate new information with old, which we'll also discuss later.

| Incoming information | → | Sensory memory | → | Selective attention | → | Short-term memory | *Rehearsing* → | Encoded for storage | → | Long-term memory |

Three types of memory, each with a different function

Sensory memory → **NO attention** → **Forgotten**

Short-term memory → **NOT encoded** → **Forgotten**

Now that we have given you an overview of memory, we'll discuss each of the three types of memory in more detail.

**Do you have a mental video recorder?**

Your brain has a mental video-audio recorder that automatically receives and holds incoming sensory information for only seconds or less. This brief period provides just enough time for you to decide whether some particular incoming sensory information is important or interesting and therefore demands your further attention. We'll examine two different kinds of sensory memory: visual sensory memory, called iconic memory, and auditory sensory memory, called echoic memory.

---

## Iconic Memory

**What happens when you blink?**

You blink about 14,000 times a day, which means your eyes are completely closed and you are totally blind for a total of about 23 minutes each waking day (LaFee, 1999). Yet the world doesn't disappear when you blink because of a special sensory memory, called iconic *(eye-CON-ick)* memory.

*Iconic memory* is a form of sensory memory that automatically holds visual information for about a quarter of a second or more; as soon as you shift your attention, the information disappears. (The word *icon* means "image.")

Because of iconic memory, you don't "go blind" when both eyes close completely during a blink (about one-third of a second) because the visual scene is briefly held in iconic memory (O'Regan et al., 2000). When your eyes reopen, you don't notice that your eyes were completely closed during the blink because "you kept seeing" the visual information that was briefly stored in iconic memory. If you did not have iconic memory, your world would disappear into darkness during each of your 14,000 blinks that occur during a waking day.

To find a memory that lasts less than a second required a clever study.

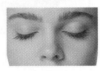

Iconic memory briefly holds visual information while eyes are shut during blinking.

### IDENTIFYING ICONIC MEMORY

Here's the first study that showed the existence and length of iconic memory.

**Procedure.** Individual subjects sat in front of a screen upon which 12 letters (three rows of four letters) appeared for a very brief period of time (50 milliseconds, or 50/1,000 of a second). After each presentation, subjects were asked to recall a particular row of letters.

**Results and conclusion.** As shown in the left graph, if subjects responded immediately (0.0-second delay) after seeing the letters, they remembered an average of nine letters. However, a delay of merely 0.5 second reduced memory to an average of six letters, and a delay of 1.0 second reduced memory to an average of only four letters (Sperling, 1960). Notice that an increased delay in responding resulted in subjects' remembering fewer letters, which indicated the brief duration of iconic memory—seconds or less.

**Number of Letters Remembered**

| Delay in Seconds | |
|---|---|
| 0.0 | 9 letters |
| 0.5 | 6 letters |
| 1.0 | 4 letters |

This study demonstrated a sensory memory for visual information, which was called iconic memory. The sensory memory for auditory information is called echoic memory.

---

## Echoic Memory

**What did you hear?**

Without realizing, you have probably already experienced auditory sensory memory, which is called echoic *(eh-KO-ick)* memory.

*Echoic memory* is a form of sensory memory that holds auditory information for 1 or 2 seconds.

For instance, suppose you are absorbed in reading a novel and a friend asks you a question. You stop reading and ask, "What did you say?" As soon as those words are out of your mouth, you realize that you can recall, or play back, your friend's exact words. You can play

Echoic memory briefly holds sounds.

back these words because they are still in echoic memory, which may last as long as 2 seconds. In addition to letting you play back things you thought you did not hear, echoic memory also lets you hold speech sounds long enough to know that a sequence of certain sounds forms words (Norman, 1982).

Because of the importance of sensory memory, both iconic and echoic, we'll review its functions.

---

## Functions of Sensory Memory

**1 Prevents being overwhelmed.** Sensory memory keeps you from being overwhelmed by too many incoming stimuli because any sensory informaton you do not attend to will vanish in seconds.

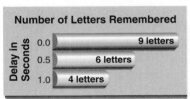

**2 Gives decision time.** Sensory memory gives you a few seconds to decide whether some incoming sensory information is interesting or important. Information you pay attention to will automatically be transferred to short-term memory.

**3 Provides stability, playback, and recognition.** Iconic memory makes things in your visual world appear smooth and continuous, such as "seeing" even during blinking. Echoic memory lets you play back auditory information, such as holding separate sounds so that you can recognize them as words.

If you attend to information in sensory memory, it goes into short-term memory, the next topic.

## Definition

**What was that phone number?**

You have just looked up a telephone number, which you keep repeating as you dial to order a pizza. After giving your order and hanging up, you can't remember the number. This example shows two characteristics of short-term memory.

*Short-term memory,* more recently called *working memory,* refers to a process that can hold a limited amount of information—an average of seven items—for a limited period of time—2 to 30 seconds. However, the relatively short duration can be lengthened by repeating or rehearsing the information.

Search for this face in a crowd.

Prefrontal cortex

For good reason, telephone numbers and postal ZIP codes are seven numbers or fewer because that is about the limit of short-term memory.

Another example of using working memory is when you keep a particular face in mind while searching for that person's face in a crowd (left figure). Brain scans taken during a similar task show that maximum neural activity occurred in an area in the front of the brain called the prefrontal cortex (left figure) (Jiang et al., 2000). Recent studies using brain scans found that when you use working memory to perform a variety of cognitive tasks, maximum neural activity occurs in various areas of the prefrontal cortex (Nyberg & Cabeza, 2000).

Although extremely useful, working or short-term memory has two features—limited duration and limited capacity—that result in several memory problems.

## Two Features

### LIMITED DURATION

The new telephone number that you looked up will remain in short-term memory for a brief time, usually from 2 to 30 seconds, and then disappear. However, you can keep information longer in short-term memory by using maintenance rehearsal.

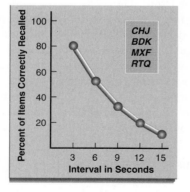

Short-term memory holds items for 2–30 seconds.

*Maintenance rehearsal* refers to the practice of intentionally repeating or rehearsing information so that it remains longer in short-term memory.

Researchers studied how long information is remembered without practice or rehearsal by asking subjects to remember a series of consonants composed of three meaningless letters, such as CHJ. Subjects were prevented from rehearsing, or repeating, these consonants by having them count backward immediately after seeing the groups of three letters.

As the graph (below right) shows, 80% of the subjects recalled the groups of three letters after 3 seconds. However, only 10% of subjects recalled the groups of three letters after 15 seconds (Peterson & Peterson, 1950).

Although this task—remembering groups of three letters—seemed easy, almost all the subjects had forgotten the groups of three letters after 15 seconds if they were prevented from rehearsing. This study clearly showed that information disappears from your short-term memory within seconds unless you continually repeat or rehearse the information.

CHJ
BDK
MXF
RTQ

*Percent of Items Correctly Recalled* — 100, 80, 60, 40, 20
Interval in Seconds — 3, 6, 9, 12, 15

You can increase the time that information remains in short-term memory by using maintenance rehearsal. However, during maintenance rehearsal, which involves repeating the same thing over and over, new information cannot enter short-term memory.

Not only does short-term or working memory have a limited duration, it also has a limited capacity.

### LIMITED CAPACITY

In previous modules, we pointed out several studies that are considered classic because they challenged old concepts or identified significant new information. One such classic study is that of George Miller (1956), who was the first to discover that short-term memory can hold only about seven items or bits, plus or minus two. Although this seems like too small a number, researchers have repeatedly confirmed Miller's original finding (Baddeley, 2000). Thus, one reason telephone numbers worldwide are generally limited to seven digits is that seven matches the capacity of short-term memory.

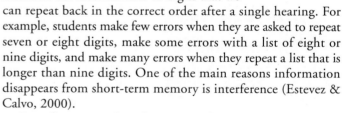

Short-term memory holds about 7 items.

It is easy to confirm Miller's finding with a *memory span test,* which measures the total number of digits that we can repeat back in the correct order after a single hearing. For example, students make few errors when they are asked to repeat seven or eight digits, make some errors with a list of eight or nine digits, and make many errors when they repeat a list that is longer than nine digits. One of the main reasons information disappears from short-term memory is interference (Estevez & Calvo, 2000).

*Interference* results when new information enters short-term memory and overwrites or pushes out information that is already there.

For example, if you are trying to remember a phone number and someone asks you a question, the question interferes with or wipes away the phone number. One way to prevent interference is through rehearsal. However, once we stop rehearsing, the information in short-term memory may disappear.

Although short-term memory has limited capacity and duration, it is possible to increase both. For example, I use a classroom demonstration in which I guarantee that any student can learn to memorize a list of 23 digits, in exact order, in just 25 seconds. This impressive memory demonstration, which always works, is accomplished by knowing how to use something called chunking.

## Chunking

**How does Rajan remember 1113121735 1802?**

Although short-term memory briefly holds an average of about seven items, it is possible to increase the length of each item by using a process called chunking (Kimball & Holyoak, 2000).

*Chunking* is combining separate items of information into a larger unit, or chunk, and then remembering chunks of information rather than individual items.

One of the interesting things about Rajan's prodigious memory for numbers is his ability to chunk. For instance, in about 2 minutes Rajan (right photo) memorized 36 random numbers (in a block of 6 × 6) written on a blackboard. He was able to repeat the numbers forward and backward and to state the numbers in any individual row, column, or diagonal.

When asked about his method for memorizing numbers, he replied that he automatically arranged the numbers into chunks and gave the chunks a name.

> I have a system for memorizing these 36 numbers in two minutes.

111312
173518
028537
873625
419803
291728

For example, here's how he chunked the first 14 numbers: 11131217351802. He chunked 111 and named it "Nelson" because Admiral Nelson had one eye, one arm, and one leg; he chunked 312 and named it the "area code of Chicago"; he chunked 1735 and named it "29" because Ben Franklin was 29 in 1735; and he chunked 1802 as "plus 2" because John Adams occupied the White House in 1800. When Rajan wants to recall the numbers, he does so by remembering a string of associations: Nelson, area code of Chicago, Ben Franklin, and John Adams. As Rajan explains, he doesn't know why he makes particular associations; they just come to him.

Sometimes we use chunking without thinking about it. For example, to remember the 11-digit phone number 16228759211, we break it into four chunks: 1-622-875-9211.

As first suggested by George Miller (1956), chunking is a powerful memory tool that greatly increases the amount of information that you can hold in short-term memory.

Next, we'll review three important functions of short-term memory.

## Functions of Short-Term Memory

**Why is it also called working memory?**

Short-term memory is like having a mental computer screen that stores a limited amount of information, but this information is automatically erased after a brief period of time and replaced by new information, and so the cycle continues. *Short-term memory* is also called *working memory* to indicate that it's an active process. Using brain scans, researchers found that short-term memory involves the front part of the brain, especially the prefrontal area (p. 242) (Markowitsch, 2000).

There are three important things regarding short-term memory: Paying attention transfers information into short-term memory, rehearsing keeps the information there, and some information is eventually transferred from short-term into permanent storage.

### 1 Attending

Imagine driving along with your radio on while a friend in the passenger seat is talking about the weekend. A tremendous amount of information is entering your sensory memory, but you avoid stimulus overload because incoming information automatically vanishes in seconds unless you pay attention to it.

The moment you pay attention to information in sensory memory, that information enters short-term memory for further processing. For example, while your friend is talking, you don't pay attention to the radio until your favorite song comes on and enters sensory memory. As you pay attention, you hear the radio, even though it has been playing the whole time. One function of short-term memory is that it allows us *to selectively attend to information that is relevant and disregard everything else.*

Once information enters short-term, or working, memory, several things may happen.

### 2 Rehearsing

Once information enters short-term memory, it usually remains for only seconds unless you rehearse it. For example, the announcer on the car radio gives a phone number to call for free movie tickets. But unless

*Rehearsing*

| Selective attention | → | Short-term memory | → | Encoded for storage |

NOT encoded

Forgotten

you rehearse or repeat the number over and over, it will probably disappear from your short-term memory because of interference from newly arriving information. Another function of short-term memory is that it allows you *to hold information for a short period of time until you decide what to do with it.*

If you rehearse the information in short-term memory, you increase the chances of storing it.

### 3 Storing

Rehearsing information not only holds that information in short-term memory but also helps *to store or encode information in long-term memory.* Later, we'll discuss two different kinds of rehearsing (p. 249) and explain why one kind of rehearsing is better than the other for storing or encoding information in long-term memory.

Next, we'll describe the steps in the memory process and why some things are stored in long-term memory.

### Steps in the Memory Process

Don't think of sensory memory, short-term memory, and long-term memory as *things* or *places* but rather as ongoing and interacting *processes*. To show how these different memory processes interact, we describe what happens as you hear a new song on the car radio and you want very much to remember the song title.

**1 Sensory memory.** As you listen to the radio, the incoming information is held for seconds or less in sensory memory. Some of the auditory information includes the announcer's words: "Remember this song title, 'Your Love Is Like Chocolate,' and win two movie tickets."

**2 Attention.** If you pay no attention to this title, it will disappear from sensory memory. If you pay attention because you want to win the tickets, the song title, "Your Love Is Like Chocolate," is automatically transferred into short-term memory.

**3 Short-term memory.** Once the song title is in short-term memory, you have a short time (2–30 seconds)  for further processing. If you lose interest or are distracted by traffic, the title will likely disappear and be forgotten. However, if you rehearse the song title, it will likely be transferred to, and encoded in, your long-term memory.

**4 Encoding.** You place information in long-term memory through a process called encoding. *Encoding* refers to the process of transferring information from short-term to long-term memory by paying attention to it, repeating or rehearsing it, or forming new associations.

For example, if a song title is catchy, unusual, or reminds you of something, such as a heart and a chocolate cake, you may easily form new associations and encode the title almost automatically and with little effort. However, if you think the title is dumb or always have trouble remembering titles, then you will have to make a deliberate effort to encode the title in long-term memory. You can improve encoding information in long-term memory (and improve future recall) by making associations between new and old information (Brown & Craik, 2000).

**5 Long-term memory.** Once the song title is encoded in long-term memory, it has the potential to remain there for your lifetime.

*Long-term memory* refers to the process of storing almost unlimited amounts of information over long periods of time with the potential of retrieving, or remembering, such information in the future.

For example, next week, month, or year, you may try to recall the song title from long-term memory by placing it back into short-term memory. How easily and accurately you can remember, recall, or retrieve information depends on many factors (Brown & Craik, 2000).

**6 Retrieving.** When people talk about remembering something, they usually mean retrieving information from long-term memory.

*Retrieving* is the process of selecting information from long-term memory and transferring it back into short-term memory.

There are several reasons you can't remember or retrieve a song's title. You simply repeated the title so it was never properly encoded in long-term memory. You heard another song that interfered with encoding the title in long-term memory. You didn't make any associations, such as imagining a heart and a chocolate cake, so the title was poorly encoded and difficult to retrieve. The key to retrieving information from long-term memory involves encoding by making associations between new and old information, which we'll soon discuss.

### Features of Long-Term Memory

**Capacity and permanency.** Researchers estimate that long-term memory has an almost unlimited capacity to store information. Anything stored has the potential to last a lifetime, provided drugs or disease do not damage the brain's memory circuits (Bahrick, 2000).

**Retrieval and accuracy.** Although all information in long-term memory has the potential to be retrieved, how much we can actually retrieve depends on a number of factors, including how it was encoded and the amount of interference from related information. In addition, researchers found that the content and accuracy of long-term memories may undergo change and distortion across time, as occurred in the following study.

**Study of long-term memory.** College freshmen were asked to recall grades from all four years of high school. As the graph below shows, students accurately recalled 89% of grades of A but only 29% of grades of D. Thus, students were much more accurate recalling positive events, grades of A, than they were for recalling negative events, grades of D (Bahrick et al., 1996). This study shows that we do not recall all events with the same accuracy, often inflating positive events and eliminating negative ones. The reasons we may change, distort, or forget information are discussed in Module 12.

Next, we'll explain how psychologists demonstrated the existence of two separate memory processes: a short-term and a long-term memory process.

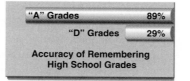

| "A" Grades | 89% |
| "D" Grades | 29% |

**Accuracy of Remembering High School Grades**

## Separate Memory Systems

**What is the evidence?** Most researchers agree that there are two memory systems (Green et al., 2000). One system involves short-term memory, which stores limited information for a brief period of time and then the information disappears. For example, a stranger tells you his or her name but a few minutes later you have totally forgotten the name because it disappeared from short-term memory. A second system involves long-term memory, which stores large amounts of information for very

long periods of time. For example, you can recall in great detail many childhood memories that years ago were stored in long-term memory. Other evidence for two memory systems comes from findings that brain damage can wipe out long-term memory while completely sparing short-term memory. Still other evidence for two memory systems comes from research on how you remember items in a relatively long list. We'll give you a chance to memorize a list of items, which will show that you have two separate memory systems—short- and long-term memory.

### Primacy versus Recency

**Can you remember this list?** Please read the following list only once and try to remember the animals' names:

> bear, giraffe, wolf, fly, deer,
> elk, gorilla, elephant, frog, snail,
> turtle, shark, ant, owl

Immediately after reading this list, write down (in any order) as many of the animals' names as you can remember.

If you examine the list of names that you wrote down, you'll discover a definite pattern to the order of the names that you remembered. For example, here's the order in which names in the above list would most likely be remembered.

**First items: Primacy effect.** In studies using similar lists, subjects more easily recalled the *first* four or five items (bear, giraffe, wolf, fly) because subjects had more time to rehearse the first words presented. As a result of rehearsing, these first names were transferred to and stored in long-term memory, from which they were recalled. This phenomenon is called the primacy effect.

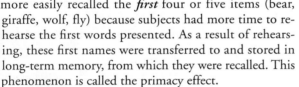

The *primacy effect* refers to better recall, or improvement in retention, of information presented at the beginning of a task.

**Middle items.** Subjects did not recall many items from the *middle* of the list (gorilla, elephant, frog) because they did not have much time to rehearse them. When they tried to remember items from the middle of the list, their attention and time were split between trying to remember the previous terms and trying to rehearse new ones. Less rehearsal meant that fewer middle names were stored in long-term memory; more interference meant that fewer names remained in short-term memory.

**Last items: Recency effect.** Subjects more easily recalled the *last* four or five items (turtle, shark, ant, owl) because they were still available in short-term memory and could be read off a mental list. This phenomenon is called the recency effect.

The *recency effect* refers to better recall, or improvement in retention, of information presented at the end of a task.

Together, these two effects are called the primacy-recency effect.

The *primacy-recency effect* refers to better recall of information presented at the beginning and end of a task.

As we'll explain next, the primacy-recency effect is evidence that short- and long-term memory are two separate processes.

### Short-Term versus Long-Term Memory

**Why didn't you remember "elephant"?** One reason you probably didn't remember the name "elephant" is that it came from the middle of the list. The middle section of a list is usually least remembered because that information may no longer be retained in short-term memory and may not have been encoded in long-term memory. Evidence for the primacy-recency effect is shown in the graph below (Glanzer & Cunitz, 1966).

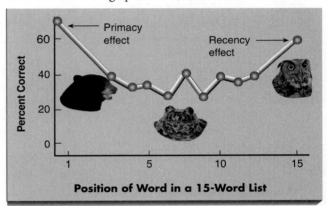

**Position of Word in a 15-Word List**

For example, subjects showed better recall (70%) for the first items presented, which is the primacy effect. The primacy effect occurs because subjects have more time to rehearse the first items, which increases the chances of transferring these items into long-term memory. Remember that rehearsal has two functions: keeping information longer in short-term memory and promoting encoding—the transfer of information into long-term memory.

In addition, subjects showed better recall (60%) for the last items presented, which is the recency effect. Sometimes subjects say that they can still "hear these words" and usually report these items first. The recency effect occurs because the last items are still in short-term memory, from which they are recalled (Glanzer & Cunitz, 1966).

The occurrence of the primacy-recency effect suggested the existence of two separate kinds of memory processes, which we now call short-term and long-term memory (Atkinson & Shiffrin, 1968; Neath, 1998).

Next, you'll discover that instead of one, there are several different kinds of long-term memory.

# D. Long-Term Memory: Storing

## Declarative versus Procedural or Nondeclarative

**Where do I store reading and skiing?**

When I ski down a hill, I can't tell you how I am able to control my muscles to keep my balance and make my turns. However, after I read a scientific article, I can tell you much of what I have read. These two activities, skiing and reading, use two different kinds of long-term memory. The discovery that there are two kinds of long-term memory is a relative new finding, and like many discoveries in science, it was found quite by accident.

Researchers were testing a patient, well known in memory circles as H. M., who suffered severe memory loss because of an earlier brain operation to reduce his seizures. H. M.'s task seemed simple: draw a star by guiding your hand while looking into a mirror. However, this mirror-drawing test is relatively difficult because looking into a mirror reverses all

hand movements: up is down and down is up. As H. M. did this task each day, his drawing improved, indicating that he was learning and remembering the necessary motor skills. But here's the strange part. Each and every day, H. M. would insist that he had never seen or done mirror-drawing before (Cohen, 1984).

How could H. M. have no memory of mirror-drawing, yet show a steady improvement in his performance as he practiced it each day? Based on H. M.'s mirror-drawing as well as data from other patients and numerous animal studies, researchers discovered that there are two different kinds of long-term memory, each involving different areas of the brain (Nyberg & Cabeza, 2000; Squire, 1994).

You'll understand why H. M. could improve at doing mirror-drawing but not remember doing it because there are two kinds of long-term memory, declarative and procedural.

### Declarative Memory

*Which bird cannot fly?*
*What did you eat for breakfast?*

You would recall or retrieve answers to these questions from one particular kind of long-term memory called declarative memory.

*Declarative memory* involves memories for facts or events, such as scenes, stories, words, conversations, faces, or daily events. We are aware of and can recall, or retrieve, these kinds of memories.

There are two kinds of declarative memory—semantic and episodic (Eichenbaum, 1997a).

**Semantic memory.**
"Which bird cannot fly?" asks you to remember a fact, which involves semantic *(sah-MANT-ic)* memory.

*Semantic memory* is a type of declarative memory and involves knowledge of facts, concepts, words, definitions, and language rules.

Most of what you *learn* in classes (facts, terms, definitions) goes into semantic memory (Schacter et al., 2000).

**Episodic memory.**
"What did you eat for breakfast?" asks you to remember an event, which involves episodic *(ep-ih-SAW-dik)* memory.

*Episodic memory* is a type of declarative memory and involves knowledge of specific events, personal experiences (episodes), or activities, such as naming or describing favorite restaurants, movies, songs, habits, or hobbies.

Most of what you *do* (activities) in college goes into episodic memory (Wheeler, 2000).

Since his brain operation, H. M. cannot remember new facts (semantic memory) or events (episodic memory). Thus, H. M. has lost declarative memory, which explains why he does not remember events, such as mirror-drawing (Cohen, 1984).

However, H. M.'s motor skills improved during mirror-drawing, which indicates another kind of long-term memory.

### Procedural or Nondeclarative Memory

*How did you learn to play tennis?*
*Why are you afraid of spiders?*

Even though you can play tennis and are afraid of spiders, you can't explain how you control your muscles to play tennis or why you're so terrified of such a tiny (usually harmless) bug. That's because motor skills and emotional feelings are stored in procedural memory.

*Procedural memory,* also called *nondeclarative memory,* involves memories for motor skills (playing tennis), some cognitive skills (learning to read), and emotional behaviors learned through classical conditioning (fear of spiders). We cannot recall or retrieve procedural memories.

Even if you have not played tennis for years, you can pick up a racket and still remember how to serve because that information is stored in procedural memory. But you cannot describe the sequence of movements needed to serve a ball because these skills are stored in procedural memory. Similarly, if you learned to fear spiders through classical conditioning, you cannot explain why you're afraid because the reasons are stored in procedural memory. Although procedural memories greatly influence our behavior, we have neither awareness of nor ability to recall these memories (Mayes, 2000).

Now we can explain H. M.'s strange behavior. He was able to improve at mirror-drawing because it involved learning a motor skill that was stored in procedural memory. But he could not talk about the skill because no one is aware of or can recall procedural memories. Although H. M. gradually improved at mirror-drawing, he could not remember the event of sitting down and drawing because that involves declarative (episodic) memories, which were damaged in his brain surgery (Hilts, 1995). The study of H. M. is a classic study because it first demonstrated the existence of two kinds of long-term memory: declarative memory and procedural memory. We'll discuss the brain systems underlying these types of long-term memory in Module 12.

## Hormones and Memories

**Do hormones affect memories?**

Many of us have vivid memories that involve highly charged emotional situations (Stein et al., 1997). For example, imagine the emotional excitement Venus Williams (right photo) felt after winning the 2000 Wimbledon tennis championship. Her winning point was followed by giant leaps around the court. Venus said, "I've been working so hard all of my life to be here. This is unbelievable" (Peyser, 2000, p. 46). She will remember this event the rest of her life because something happens during strong emotions that increases the chances of remembering the particular situation, person, or event.

What actually happens to improve memory during an emotional event involves a long-term research program that began in animals. In Module 2 we explained that researchers may use an animal model (p. 34) to answer questions that for safety, moral, or ethical reasons cannot involve human subjects. Because of safety concerns, neuropsy-

Excitatory hormones can "stamp in" memories.

chologist James McGaugh (1999) began using an animal model to study how hormones produced during emotional states affect memory. He found that certain drugs or hormones associated with emotional experiences could either increase or decrease the recall of long-term memories. For example, if rats were given an injection of a hormone (epinephrine) that is normally produced by the body during emotional or stressful states, rats remembered better what they had just learned (McGaugh, 1990). This was a new and interesting finding and made him wonder why emotional experiences should improve long-term memories for related events.

After McGaugh found that the "emotional" hormones and drugs could be safely used in animals, he began his work with human subjects. His study on animals and humans of why emotional events seemed to "stamp in" memories lasted 40 years. Here's one of his interesting studies.

## Memories of Emotional Events

**Can drugs block emotional memories?**

After almost 20 years of research using an animal model, McGaugh found a way to safely study this phenomenon in humans.

**Subjects.** Those in the experimental group received a drug (propranolol) that decreases or blocks the effects of hormones (epinephrine and norepinephrine) that are normally produced during emotional states. After taking this drug, experimental subjects would still feel emotions, but the drug would block the secretion of those emotionally produced hormones that had been shown to increase memory in animals. Subjects in the control group received a placebo, but because of the double-blind procedure, no subjects knew whether they were given a drug or a placebo.

**Procedure.** So that the drugs would have time to act, subjects were given either a placebo or the drug 1 hour before seeing a series of slides. To prevent their expectations from biasing the results, subjects did not know whether they got a drug or a placebo.

Each subject watched a series of 12 slides and heard an accompanying story. The beginning of the slide story was emotionally neutral and simply described a mother leaving home with her son to visit her husband's workplace. The middle of the slide story was emotionally charged and described the son having a terrible accident in which his feet were severed and his skull was damaged. The end of the slide story was emotionally neutral and described the mother leaving the hospital to pick up her other child from preschool. Subjects were tested for retention of the slide story a week later.

**Hypothesis.** Based on their results from the animal model, McGaugh and his colleagues guessed that if a drug blocked the effects of memory-enhancing hormones normally produced during

emotional situations, subjects who took the drug should show poor retention for emotional events.

**Results and conclusion.** Researchers found that both drug and placebo subjects remembered about the same number of neutral events. However, the graph below shows that, compared to subjects in the placebo group, subjects given a drug that blocked "emotional" hormones remembered significantly fewer emotionally charged events (Cahill et al., 1994). Other studies on humans found that, just as in rats, intense feelings triggered by emotional or stressful situations are encoded, or "carved in stone," by hormones released during emotionally charged situations and that these memories are better

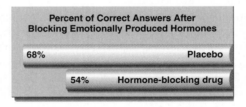

**Percent of Correct Answers After Blocking Emotionally Produced Hormones**

| | |
|---|---|
| 68% | Placebo |
| 54% | Hormone-blocking drug |

remembered (Hamann et al., 1999; McGaugh, 1999). McGaugh's research is a good example of using an animal model to lay the basis for similar studies in humans. But of what use is it to animals or humans for emotional memories to be better remembered?

Based on 40 years of research, McGaugh believed that one reason emotions seem to "stamp in" memories is to help a species survive. For instance, if emotions stamped in memories of emotional or life-threatening situations, our early ancestors would better remember to avoid these dangers and thus increase their chances of survival.

An important clinical application of McGaugh's research is that it explains why bad emotional memories, such as those formed after witnessing or being in a terrible accident or suffering physical or sexual abuse, are "stamped in" and thus become so powerful and so difficult to treat and overcome. McGaugh is now working on this problem.

While McGaugh's research shows that emotional feelings are easily encoded, you'll see next that nonemotional information, such as learning terms and definitions, can be encoded only with hard work.

## Two Kinds of Encoding

**How do we store memories?**

It's very common for someone to say, "Let me tell you about my day," and then describe in great detail a long list of mostly bad things that happened. What is amazing about our being able to repeat the bad-day list in such detail is that we initially made no effort to remember these events. We didn't have to review any notes because we didn't take any notes. We can so easily remember and recall all of these bad-day events because these events were automatically, and with no effort on our part, encoded in our long-term memories.

*Let me tell you about my awful day. First ...*

*Encoding* refers to acquiring information or storing information in memory by changing this information into neural or memory codes.

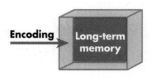

Encoding → Long-term memory

Some information, such as bad-day events or conversations with friends, seem to be encoded effortlessly and automatically and easily recalled. Other information, such as memorizing terms or definitions, usually requires deliberate effort and considerable time and may still not be easily recalled when taking exams. The difference between how you encode bad-day events versus terms in a textbook points to two different kinds of encoding: automatic and effortful encoding.

### Automatic Encoding

**Why are some things easy to encode?**

Just as most of us can easily and in great detail recall all the annoying things that happened today, the person below is recalling a long list of very detailed personal activities that were automatically encoded into his long-term memory. In fact, many personal events (often unpleasant ones), as well as things we're interested in (movies, music, sports) and a wide range of skills (riding a bike) and habits, are automatically encoded (Murnane et al., 1999).

*Automatic encoding* is the transfer of information from short-term into long-term memory without any effort and usually without any awareness.

*I bought this hat at a second-hand store for a quarter, and then I bought these shoes from a guy who said that he makes them from old tires ...*

**Personal events.** One reason many of your personal experiences and conversations are automatically encoded is that they hold your interest and attention and easily fit together with hundreds of previous associations. Because personal experiences, which are examples of *episodic information,* are encoded automatically into long-term memory, you can easily recall lengthy conversations, facts about movies and sports figures, television shows, clothes you bought, or food you ate.

**Interesting facts.** You may know avid sports fans or watchers of daily TV soap operas who remember an amazing number of facts and details, seemingly without effort. If these kinds of facts, which are examples of *semantic information,* are personally interesting and fit with previous associations, then they are automatically encoded into declarative long-term memory.

**Skills and habits.** Learning how to perform various motor skills, such as playing tennis or riding a bike, and developing habits, such as brushing your teeth, are examples of *procedural information,* which is also encoded automatically. For example, H. M. learned and remembered how to mirror-draw because mirror-drawing is a motor skill that is automatically encoded into procedural long-term memory.

On the other hand, factual or technical information from textbooks is usually not encoded automatically but rather requires deliberate, or effortful, encoding, which we'll discuss next.

### Effortful Encoding

**Why are some things hard to encode?**

The person below is pulling his hair because learning unfamiliar or complicated material almost always involves *semantic information,* such as complex terms, which is difficult to encode because such information is often uninteresting, complicated, or requires making new or difficult associations. For all these reasons, semantic information, such as terms, can be encoded only with considerable concentration and effort.

*Effortful encoding* involves the transfer of information from short-term into long-term memory either by working hard to repeat or rehearse the information or, especially, by making associations between new and old information.

You already know that some information, such as learning a skill, habit, or interesting personal event, is often encoded effortlessly and automatically. In contrast, semantic information, such as learning hundreds of new or difficult

*I've been studying these terms for hours and I still can't remember their definitions.*

terms, facts, concepts, or equations, usually requires effortful encoding because you must form hundreds of new associations. Forming new associations is often just plain hard work and is made even more difficult if you are simultaneously taking two or three difficult classes or have limited time because of other responsibilities, such as a part-time job.

Although there are two methods of effortful encoding—rehearsing and forming associations—the most effective method involves forming associations between the new information that you are trying to learn and the old information that you have already stored in long-term memory. The better the effortful encoding, the better the recall on exams. We'll explain the two methods of effortful encoding, rehearsing and forming associations, and why the second method is more effective and results in better recall.

## Rehearsing and Encoding

**How much do you remember?**

Think of encoding information in your brain as similar to saving information on a gigantic computer hard drive. Unless you have a very good system for labeling and filing the hundreds of computer files, you will have great difficulty finding or retrieving a particular file from the hard drive. Similarly, how easily you can remember or retrieve a particular memory from your brain depends on how much effort you used to encode the information. There are two kinds of effortful encoding: maintenance rehearsal and elaborative rehearsal (Brown & Craik, 2000).

### MAINTENANCE REHEARSAL

The easiest way to remember information for only a short period of time, such as a new phone number, for example, 926-4029, is to simply repeat or rehearse it. This kind of effortful encoding is called maintenance rehearsal.

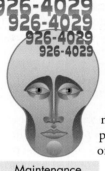

Maintenance rehearsal is not a very effective encoding process.

*Maintenance rehearsal* refers to simply repeating or rehearsing the information rather than forming any new associations.

Maintenance rehearsal works best for maintaining or keeping information longer in **short-term memory**, such as remembering a phone number for a few seconds while dialing it. However, if you want to remember the phone number later, maintenance rehearsal is not a good encoding process because it does not include a system for keeping track of how and where that particular phone number will be stored. If you need to remember a phone number for a long period of time and avoid having to keep looking it up, you'll need to use another form of effortful encoding called elaborative rehearsal.

### ELABORATIVE REHEARSAL

There are some phone numbers and much information from lectures and textbooks that you want to encode so that you remember the information for long periods of time. To have the greatest chance for remembering something, it's best to encode information using elaborative rehearsal.

*Elaborative rehearsal* involves using effort to actively make meaningful associations between new information that you wish to remember and old or familiar information that is already stored in long-term memory.

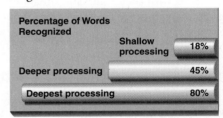


For example, using elaborative rehearsal, you could associate this phone number, 926-4029, with age: an old person is "926," I'm not "40," but I wish I were "29." To recall this number, you think of the different age associations and those associations lead to the phone number.

To test the usefulness of elaborative rehearsal, students were asked to remember many groups of three words each, such as *dog, bike,* and *street*. Students who encoded the words with maintenance rehearsal (repeating words) did poorly on recall. In comparison, students who encoded the words using elaborative rehearsal, that is, taking the effort to make associations among the three words (dog rides a bike down the street), had significantly better recall (McDaniel & Einstein, 1986).

Elaborative rehearsal is a very effective encoding process.

**Effectiveness.** Elaborative rehearsal is such an effective system of encoding because by making associations between new and old information you create cues for locating or retrieving the new information from long-term memory. For example, thinking of the association (dog rides a bike down the street) helps you remember the three words (dog, bike, street).

## Levels of Processing

**How important are associations?**

The poorest system for encoding information is to simply repeat the information, which is maintenance rehearsal. The best encoding system is to make associations, which is elaborative rehearsal. How much effort and time you put into encoding information is the basis for the levels-of-processing theory (Craik & Lockhart, 1972).

The *levels-of-processing theory* says that remembering depends on how information is encoded. If you encode by paying attention only to basic features (length of phone number), information is encoded at a shallow level and results in poor recall. If you encode by making new associations, this information will be encoded at a deeper level, which results in better recall.

For example, students were shown a series of words and asked a question after each one. The questions were of three types, designed to trigger three different levels of processing.

**1. Shallow processing question:**
"Is the word printed in capital letters?" Asks about one physical feature of the word.

**2. Deeper processing question:**
"Does the word rhyme with *rain?*" Asks about sound properties of the word.

**3. Deepest processing question:**
"Does the word fit into the sentence 'She was late for the _____'?" Asks about the meaning of the word.

After students answered these questions, they were tested to see how many of the original words they recognized.

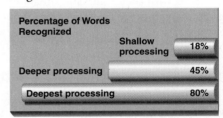

**Percentage of Words Recognized**

| | |
|---|---|
| Shallow processing | 18% |
| Deeper processing | 45% |
| Deepest processing | 80% |

As shown in the graph above, students recognized the smallest percentage of words after shallow processing and the most after the deepest processing (Craik & Tulving, 1975).

This study clearly demonstrates that the system you use to process or encode information has a great effect on how easily you can remember or retrieve the information. As we'll discuss in Module 12, a major reason for forgetting is poor encoding (Brown & Craik, 2000).

Next, we'll discuss a kind of memory that has resulted in great controversy because of the difficulties in determining whether the event ever happened.

# G. Repressed Memories

## Recovered Memories

**Who's to blame?**

At the beginning of this module, we discussed the case of Holly (left photo), who had accused her father (right photo) of sexual molestation beginning when she was 6 years old. Holly's memories of sexual abuse first surfaced during therapy sessions 13 years later, when she was 19. The father sued Holly's therapist for implanting false memories. The jury partly agreed with the father in deciding that Holly's memories were probably false and that the therapist had not implanted the memories but had carelessly reinforced them (Butler, 1994). A state appeals court dismissed Holly's case against her father because some of her testimony about sexual abuse was obtained under sodium amytal, the so-called truth serum, which was administered by her

"He abused me."   "I did not."

therapist. Because testimony taken under sodium amytal is often unreliable, it has been barred in California's courts since 1959 (*Los Angeles Times*, August 21, 1997).

Holly's case illustrates perhaps the most explosive psychological issue of the early 1990s, the problem of repressed and recovered memories. Psychiatrist Harold Lief, one of the first to question the accuracy of repressed memories, said, "We don't know what percent of these recovered memories are real and what percent are pseudomemories (false). . . . But we do know there are hundreds, maybe thousands of cases of pseudomemories and that many families have been destroyed by them" (J. E. Brody, 2000, p. D8). We'll discuss four issues related to repressed and recovered memories.

## Definition of Repressed Memories

**What's different about a repressed memory?**

The idea of repressed memories is based on Sigmund Freud's theory of repression, which underlies much of his psychoanalytic theory of personality (discussed in Module 21).

*Repression* is the process by which the mind pushes a memory of some threatening or traumatic event deep into the unconscious. Once in the unconscious, the repressed memory cannot be retrieved at will and may remain there until something releases it and the person remembers it.

Some therapists believe that children who are sexually abused cope with such traumatic situations and their feelings of guilt by repressing the memories. For example, a client may enter therapy with sexual problems or a mood disorder and later in therapy

Repressed memories are difficult to recover.

uncover repressed memories, such as being sexually abused as a child, as the cause of her current problems. Clients usually have total amnesia (loss of memory) for the traumatic experience, their recovery of repressed memories usually occurs in the first 12 months of therapy, and recovered memories usually involve specific incidents (Andrews et al., 2000).

Based on clients' experiences, therapists believe that repressed memories of sexual abuse do occur. However, a prominent memory researcher disagrees: "The idea that forgetting in abuse survivors is caused by a special repression mechanism—something more powerful than conscious suppression—is still without a scientific basis" (Schacter, 1996, p. 264). Thus, the controversy over repressed memories continues.

In the 1990s, increased reports of recovered memories were blamed partly on some therapeutic practices (Loftus, 1997b).

## Therapist's Role in Recovered Memories

**How does a therapist know?**

Therapists who treat survivors of incest and other traumatic situations maintain that repressed memories are so completely blocked that it may take deliberate suggestion and effort to release them, sometimes using images, hypnosis, or so-called truth serum, sodium amytal.

For example, in one case a client recalls that her therapist insisted that she showed signs of having been sexually abused during childhood and probably had terrible memories buried in her unconscious. The client was dubious at first but, wanting to please her therapist, finally admitted to being raped at the age of 4. However, after leaving the hospital and enlisting help from new therapists, she concluded that the sexual assaults had never happened (Bower, 1993a). Whatever the therapists' good intentions, Loftus (1993b; 1997b) wonders

The therapist may have suggested traumatic memories.

if some therapists are suggesting or implanting traumatic memories in their clients rather than releasing repressed ones. Most often, repressed memories and resulting accusations of sexual abuse were reported by women (87%) who were in therapy for depression or eating disorders (Gudjonsson, 1997).

There are also many examples of therapists who have helped clients recover and deal with terrible repressed memories (Gold et al., 1994). Thus, therapists are in the difficult position of trying to distinguish accurate accounts of repressed memories from those that may have been shaped or reinforced by the suggestions or expectations of the therapist (Byrd, 1994).

Questions about whether repressed memories can be influenced by a therapist's suggestions raised the question of whether false memories can be implanted.

## Implanting False Memories

**Do people believe "fake" memories?**

Because, in some cases, it appears that therapists' suggestions may have contributed to implanting false memories, researchers studied whether fake memories could in fact be implanted and later recalled as being "true."

Researchers gave 24 adults a booklet that contained descriptions of three events that occurred when each adult was 5 years old (Loftus, 1997a). Two of the childhood events had *really happened* because they were obtained from parents or relatives. One childhood event of being lost in a shopping mall, crying, being comforted by an elderly woman, and finally getting reunited with the family had *not happened,* according to parents and relatives. After reading the three events described in the booklet, the adults (aged 18–53) were asked to write what they remembered of the event or, if they did not remember, to write "I do not remember this."

The graph above shows that 68% of subjects remembered some or most of the two *true events* from their childhood. However, about 29% also said that they remembered having experienced the one *false event,* which was being lost in

| Percentage of Subjects Who Remembered True and False Memories | | |
|---|---|---|
| Recalled events after reading booklet | False | 29% |
| | True | 68% |
| Recalled events after 1st follow-up interview | False | 25% |
| | True | 68% |

About 25% of subjects said that they remembered a childhood event that never happened (false) and 68% remembered childhood events that did happen (true).

the mall at age 5. Even on follow-up interviews, 25% of the adult subjects continued to claim that they remembered experiencing the suggested but false event of being lost in the mall (Loftus, 1997a).

Researchers concluded that although the memory of being lost in a mall is neither as terrible nor as terrifying as the memory of being abused, this study does show that false memories can be implanted through suggestion alone. Even on follow-up, subjects continued to insist that they remembered the false event.

There are now many similar studies reporting that false memories can be implanted in both children and adults (Clancy et al., 2000; Gobbo, 2000). However, the fact that false memories can be implanted and later recalled as true does in no way disprove the occurrence of repressed memories. Rather, studies on implanting false memories simply show that a false suggestion can grow into a vivid, detailed, and believable personal memory (Ceci, 2000; Loftus, 2000).

The repeated finding that false memories can be implanted in children and adults and later remembered as "true" raises the question about the accuracy of repressed memories that are later recovered and believed to be true.

## Accuracy of Recovered Memories

**How accurate are repressed memories?**

Some individuals may initially enter therapy for help with mood disorders or eating problems but during the course of therapy, they recovered memories, apparently repressed, of childhood sexual abuse. Since researchers have shown that "false" memories can be implanted through suggestion and believed to be "true" memories, there is a question whether a client's recovered memories are accurate or were implanted by the therapist's suggestions.

In a few cases, the accuracy of recovered memories can be established. For example, a client who suffered from obesity entered a hospital weight-reduction program that also included psychotherapy. During therapy, she experienced flashbacks of being sexually abused from about age 5 by her older brother, who had since been killed in the war. When she searched through his things, she found a diary in which he had described sexual experiments with his little sister (Bower, 1993a). In this case, the woman's repressed memories of sexual abuse were proved accurate by confirming evidence, her brother's diary.

In many cases, the accuracy of recovered memories cannot be clearly established because there is no collaborating evidence of the client's report that the traumatic event really did occur 20–30 years earlier. Therapists tend to believe their client's report of recovered memories partly because there is little reason for their client to lie and partly because childhood sexual abuse may explain their client's current problems (Loftus, 1993b).

Some question the accuracy of repressed memories.

There is reason to question the accuracy of recovered memories if they were obtained under hypnosis or "truth serum" (sodium amytal). Under hypnosis or truth serum, people often become more open to suggestion and may later recall events suggested during hypnosis as being true (J. E. Brody, 2000).

Another reason to question the accuracy of recovered memories is reports of more than 300 clients who later retracted charges of childhood sexual abuse based on memories that were recovered in therapy (de Rivera, 1997). In about a dozen other cases, clients have successfully sued and won large monetary awards from their therapists for implanting false memories of child abuse (Loftus, 1999). All these examples question the accuracy of some recovered memories.

**Conclusions.** Memory researcher Elizabeth Loftus (1997a; 1999) states that there are examples of recovered memories that are accurate. However, based on her own and others' research on the possibility of implanting very detailed and later believed "false" memories, as well as on clients' later retractions of recovered memories, she questions whether all recovered memories are accurate. Loftus suggests that some recovered memories may be false because such memories might have been implanted by therapists' suggestions and/or clients needed and used these memories to explain their current psychological problems. For these reasons, recent guidelines for therapists caution against using forceful or persuasive suggestions to elicit memories from their clients (J. E. Brody, 2000). On the one hand are questions and controversies about the accuracy of repressed and recovered memories. On the other hand are cases in which recovered memories were accurate and helped clients trace the cause of their current mental difficulties (Gold et al., 1994).

# Concept Review

**1.** Three processes are involved in memory: the process in which information is placed or stored in memory by making mental representations is called (a)_____; the process of placing encoded information into a permanent mental state is called (b)_____; the process of getting information out of short-term or permanent storage is called (c)_____.

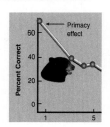

**2.** The initial step in memory is a process that holds visual and auditory information in its raw form for a very brief period of time, from an instant to several seconds; this process is called _____.

**3.** Memory that holds raw visual information for up to a quarter of a second is called (a)_____. Memory that holds raw auditory information for up to several seconds is called (b)_____. The process for controlling the transfer of information from sensory memory to the next memory process is (c)_____.

**4.** The kind of memory that has a limited capacity of about seven items (plus or minus two) and a short duration (2–30 seconds) for unrehearsed information is called either (a)_____ or _____. One way to increase this memory capacity is by combining separate pieces of information into larger units, which is called (b)_____. One way to increase the duration of this memory is by repeating the information, which is called (c)_____.

**5.** The kind of memory that can store almost unlimited amounts of information over a long period of time is _____, whose accuracy may undergo change and distortion across time.

**6.** The process for controlling the transfer of information from short-term memory into long-term memory is called _____, which may be automatic or may involve deliberate effort.

**7.** The process for selecting information from long-term memory and transferring it back into short-term memory is _____.

**8.** The better recall of items at the beginning of a list is called the (a)_____ effect. The better recall of items at the end of a list is called the (b)_____ effect. Evidence that there are two kinds of memory, short- and long-term, comes from the (c)_____ effect.

**9.** There are two kinds of encoding. Simply repeating or rehearsing the information is called (a)_____. Actively making associations between new and old information already stored is called (b)_____.

**10.** One kind of long-term memory that involves memories for facts or events, such as scenes, stories, words, conversations, faces, or daily events, is called (a)_____ memory. We can retrieve these memories and are conscious of them. One kind of declarative memory that involves events or personal experiences is called (b)_____ memory. A second kind of declarative memory that involves general knowledge, facts, or definitions of words is called (c)_____ memory.

**11.** A second kind of long-term memory that involves performing motor or perceptual tasks, carrying out habits, and responding to stimuli because of classical conditioning is called _____ memory. We cannot retrieve these memories and are not conscious of them.

**12.** Something happens that is so threatening, shocking, or traumatic that our mind pushes that memory into the unconscious, from which it cannot be retrieved at will: this phenomenon is called _____.

**13.** During very emotional or stressful situations, the body secretes chemicals called (a)_____ that act to make encoding very effective, and this results in vivid, long-term memories. Researchers believe that this hormonal encoding system for stressful or emotional events has helped our species (b)_____.

***Answers:*** *1. (a) encoding, (b) storage, (c) retrieval; 2. sensory memory; 3. (a) iconic memory, (b) echoic memory, (c) attention; 4. (a) short-term, or working, memory, (b) chunking, (c) rehearsal, or maintenance rehearsal; 5. long-term memory; 6. encoding; 7. retrieval; 8. (a) primacy, (b) recency, (c) primacy-recency; 9. (a) maintenance rehearsal, (b) elaborative rehearsal; 10. (a) declarative, (b) episodic, (c) semantic; 11. procedural or nondeclarative; 12. repression, or repressed memory; 13. (a) hormones, (b) survive*

## United States versus Africa

**What do you remember best?**

If you went to grade school in the United States, you spent considerable time in your first 8 years learning to read and write. In the U.S. culture, reading and writing skills are viewed as being not only very important for personal growth and development but also necessary for achieving success in one's career. For similar reasons, the schools of many industrialized cultures place heavy emphasis on teaching reading and writing, which allow individuals to encode great amounts of information in long-term memory. In addition, reading and writing skills are necessary for being admitted to and doing well in college.

In contrast, if you went to grade school in the more rural countries of Africa, you would have spent your first 8 or so years learning primarily through the spoken word rather than the written word. In the less industrialized countries of Africa, such as Ghana, there are fewer public

In more rural parts of Africa (Ghana) children must rely more on oral than written information.

or private schools, fewer textbooks and libraries. As a result, these cultures are said to have a strong *oral tradition*, which means that these people have considerable practice in passing on information through speaking and retelling. The Ghana culture emphasizes the oral tradition, which means encoding information after hearing it rather than after reading it.

With Ghana's emphasis on oral tradition, we would expect that African people would better encode and remember information that was spoken. In comparison, with the United States' emphasis on *written tradition*, we would expect that American people would better encode and remember information that was read rather than spoken. Let's see if this hypothesis has been supported.

## Remembering Spoken Information

**Who best remembers what they heard?**

On the left is part of a story called "War of the Ghosts," which was read aloud in English to college students at Winneba Training College in Ghana and at New York University. Each group of students heard the story twice and were told to just listen to the story so that they would not take notes on their own. They were not told that they would be tested on its content.

Although English was not the native language of the Ghanaian students, they had learned English in previous schooling, and English was used exclusively in their Training College. Sixteen days after hearing "War of the Ghosts," students were asked to write down as much of the text as they could remember. Researchers scored the amount and accuracy of recalled information by counting the number of ideas or themes and the total number of words (330). The "War of the Ghosts" story has been used frequently in memory research because it can be broken down into 21 themes, or ideas, and easily scored. For example, two of the 21 themes or ideas are (1) two young men went to hunt seals and (2) they heard war cries.

### WAR OF THE GHOSTS

One night, two young men from Egulac went down to the river to hunt seals, and while they were there it became foggy and calm. Then they heard war cries, and they thought: "Maybe this is a war party." They escaped to the shore and hid behind a log. Now canoes came up, and they heard the noise of paddles and saw one canoe coming up to them. There were five men in the canoe, and they said:

"What do you think? We wish to take you along. We are going up the river to make war on the people."

One of the young men said: "I have no arrows."

"Arrows are in the canoe," they said.

"I will not go along. I might be killed. My relatives do not know where I have gone. But you," he said, turning to the other, "may go with them."

So one of the young men went, but the other returned home.

And the warriors went up the river to a town on the other side of Kalama. The people came down to the water, and they began to fight, and many were killed. . . .

As the graph on the right shows, Ghanaian students remembered a significantly higher percentage of themes and a larger number of words than did American students. The Ghanaian students' superior performance was even more remarkable since they were tested by having to write the themes or ideas in English, which was their second language.

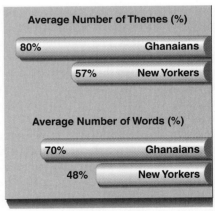

**Average Number of Themes (%)**

| 80% | Ghanaians |
| 57% | New Yorkers |

**Average Number of Words (%)**

| 70% | Ghanaians |
| 48% | New Yorkers |

These results support the idea that the Ghanaian students showed superior recall of spoken information because of their long oral tradition, which involves practicing encoding information through hearing rather than reading (Ross & Millsom, 1970). This study indicates that a culture's emphasis on how information is presented or taught can influence how information or events are encoded and how easily they can be recalled.

## Photographic Memory

She could perfectly visualize her class notes so didn't have to study for exams.

**Can you recall everything?**

One kind of unusual memory that many of us wish we had is the ability to remember everything with little or no difficulty. Such an amazing memory is commonly called a photographic memory.

*Photographic memory,* which occurs in adults, is the ability to form sharp, detailed visual images after examining a picture or page for a short period of time and to recall the entire image at a later date.

There are no reports of someone developing a photographic memory and only one or two reports of adults who had a truly photographic memory (Stromeyer, 1970). Sometimes people with exceptional memories are mislabeled as having photographic memories. For example, Rajan, who we described earlier as memorizing 31,811 numbers, denies that

he has a photographic memory.

At a recent national memory contest (U.S. Memoriad), Tatiana Cooley (left photo) came in first by doing incredible memory feats, such as pairing 70 names and faces after studying a stack of 100 faces for just 20 minutes. As a child, Tatiana's mother would read to her, and when Tatiana was $2^1/_2$ years old, she read one of the books back to her mother. In college, Tatiana says, "I remember visualizing the notes that I had taken in class and being able to recall them verbatim for tests so I didn't have to study" (Rogers & Morehouse, 1999, p. 90). To keep her memory sharp, she spends 45 minutes each day memorizing the order in which cards appear in a freshly shuffled deck. Wow! Tatiana's ability to visually remember her notes during exams comes close to satisfying the definition for having a photographic memory.

Although there are few examples of adults with photographic memories, there is a very small percentage of children who do have photographic mem-

## Eidetic Imagery

**Can you memorize this picture?**

A small number of children have the ability to look at a picture for a few seconds and then describe it in great detail. This kind of remarkable memory is called eidetic *(eye-DET-ick)* imagery.

*Eidetic imagery,* which is a form of photographic memory that occurs in children, is the ability to examine a picture or page for 10–30 seconds and then for several minutes hold in one's mind a detailed visual image of the material.

For example, an 11-year-old girl was given the following instructions: "Look at this picture from Rudyard Kipling's *The Jungle Book* for a few minutes. Hold the details of this picture in your mind's eye for several minutes. Now, close your eyes and describe what you see."

After the picture (at right) was removed, the young girl closed her eyes and, without hesitation, she described the picture in great detail, as follows: "Ground is dark greenish brown, then there's a mama and a little leopard and there's a native sitting against him. Then there's a pool with a crab coming out . . . with a fish in it, and I think there are turtles walking in front and a porcupine down near the right. There's a tree that separates a cow in half. The cow's brown and white, and there's something up in the tree—I can't see the bottom right-hand corner. There's a sun with a lot of rays on it near the top on the right . . . eight rays . . . the porcupine has a lot of bristles on it . . . the right is disappearing. I can still see that cow that's divided by the tree . . . Oh, there's a crocodile or alligator in the right-hand corner . . . It's very faint . . . It's gone" (Haber, 1980, p. 72).

What is unusual about her description is not only the amount of detail but also the fact that she seems

to be examining a vivid visual image of the actual drawing that seems to be held for a time in her mind's eye.

This girl's description is an example of eidetic imagery, which has been shown to be a real phenomenon that occurs in only about 5–8% of preadolescent children. The small percentage of children with eidetic imagery almost always lose the ability around adolescence (Neath, 1998). Why eidetic imagery drops out in adults is not known, but some suggest it may be because adults learn to use and rely more on words than on pictures (Crowder, 1992). The one or two times eidetic imagery did occur in adults it was usually called photographic memory.

Many of us have experienced a very vivid and detailed memory that is called a "flashbulb memory."

Eidetic imagery: The young girl closed her eyes and, without hesitation, she described the picture in great detail, as follows: "Ground is dark greenish brown, there's a little leopard, and there's a native sitting against him. There's a pool with a crab coming out and fish in it, and a turtle walking, and at the top a sun with lots of rays. . . ."

**What makes a memory so vivid?**

It was a crystal clear spring day with a deep blue San Diego sky and bright orange sun. I had driven the same route to my university so many times that I was doing it almost automatically, all the time thinking about something else. Suddenly brake lights began to flash in front of me. As I slowed down, I became alert and saw a black Toyota pickup truck about five cars in front of me swerve quickly to the outside to avoid hitting a stopping car. But the pickup driver had cut the turn too sharply. As if it happened in slow motion, I watched the pickup turn over and bounce as it hit the side of the freeway and then roll over again to land on its side. To this day, I can play back this terrible scene in great detail and vivid color as if I were watching a crash scene in a movie. Many individuals have had a similar experience, and this kind of memory event is called a flashbulb memory (Brown & Kulik, 1977).

*Flashbulb memories* are vivid recollections, usually in great detail, of dramatic or emotionally charged incidents that are of interest to the person. This information is encoded effortlessly and may last for long periods of time.

### EMOTIONAL EVENTS

Flashbulb memories usually deal with events that are extremely surprising, emotionally arousing, or have very important meaning or consequences for the person. For example, when people were questioned about what they were doing when they heard that President Kennedy or Reagan had been shot, or when the space shuttle *Challenger* exploded, about 80–90% could recall the exact details even seven months later (Pillemer, 1984). Apparently, only those individuals for whom these events were personally significant developed flashbulb memories, so the personal involvement in the event is one condition for the formation of these memories (Wright & Gaskell, 1995). For example, whether or not you experienced a flashbulb memory when first hearing of Princess Diana's tragic car crash and death in the fall of 1997 will depend on how much she meant to you.

### MOST-REMEMBERED EVENTS

As you can see in the center table, the top five flashbulb memories of college students involved a car accident, a college roommate, high school graduation and prom, and a romantic experience, all of which are emotionally charged events for the subjects (Rubin & Kozin, 1984).

Initially, flashbulb memories were claimed to represent a special kind of memory that was complete, accurate, vivid, and immune to forgetting (Brown & Kulik, 1977). Since then, several studies have investigated these claims and reported that flashbulb memories do not seem to be a separate, special kind of memory because flashbulb memories are subject to inaccuracies, change with retelling, and are even forgotten over time (Schooler & Eich, 2000).

### Examples of Flashbulb Memories

| Cues | Percent* |
|---|---|
| A car accident you were in or witnessed | 85 |
| When you first met your college roommate | 82 |
| Night of your high school graduation | 81 |
| Night of your senior prom (if you went or not) | 78 |
| An early romantic experience | 77 |
| A time you had to speak in front of an audience | 72 |
| When you got your college admissions letter | 65 |
| Your first date—the moment you met him/her | 57 |
| Day President Reagan was shot in Washington | 52 |
| Night President Nixon resigned | 41 |
| First time you flew in an airplane | 40 |
| Moment you opened your SAT scores | 33 |
| Your 17th birthday | 30 |
| Day of the first space shuttle flight | 24 |
| The last time you ate a holiday dinner at home | 23 |
| Your first college class | 21 |
| The first time your parents left you alone for some time | 19 |
| Your 13th birthday | 12 |

*Percentage of students in the memory experiment who reported that events on the experimenter's list were of flashbulb quality (Rubin & Kozin, 1984)

Flashbulb memories are usually vivid, detailed, emotional events of great interest to the person.

### MULTINATIONAL STUDY

In a multinational study of flashbulb memory, British and non-British people were asked what they were doing when they heard that the former Prime Minister Margaret Thatcher had resigned. Of the 215 British residents surveyed one year later, 86% reported having flashbulb memories, which occurred spontaneously and proved to be vivid, accurate, and full of detail. In comparison, less than 29% of 154 non-British subjects from North America and Denmark reported flashbulb memories of this event (Conway et al., 1994). These researchers concluded that flashbulb memories represent a special kind of automatic encoding that occurs when events are emotionally and personally very interesting.

### FLASHBULB MEMORIES AND HORMONES

Earlier, in the Research Focus (p. 247), we discussed how emotionally triggered hormones encoded long-term memories as if "in stone" (McGaugh, 1999). The presence of these hormones may help explain why emotionally charged personal experiences may be easily and automatically encoded into vivid, detailed, and long-lasting memories (Schooler & Eich, 2000).

### MEMORY: PICTURES VERSUS IMPRESSIONS

Each of us has a remarkable memory system that can encode, store, and retrieve unlimited amounts of information over long periods of time. But it's important to remember that memories are not perfect pictures of objects, people, and events but rather our personal impressions of these things. For example, the things that you remember when you're in a good mood and having a "good day" are very different from the things that you remember when you're in a bad mood and having a "bad day." This means that what you remember and recall may be changed, biased, or distorted by a wide range of emotional feelings, personal experiences, stressful situations, or social influences (Roediger & McDermott, 2000).

# Summary Test

## A. THREE TYPES OF MEMORY

**1.** The study of memory, which is the ability to retain information over time, includes three separate processes. The first process—placing information in memory—is called (a)_____. The second process, which is filing information in memory, is called (b)_____. The third process—commonly referred to as remembering—is called (c)_____.

**2.** Although we think of memory as a single event, it is really a complex sequence that may be separated into three different kinds of memory. The initial memory process that holds raw information for up to several seconds is called _____. During this time, you have the chance to identify or pay attention to new information.

**3.** If you pay attention to information in sensory memory, this information is automatically transferred into a second kind of memory process, called _____ memory.

**4.** If you rehearse or think about information in short-term memory, that information will usually be transferred or encoded into the third, more permanent kind of memory process, called _____.

## B. SENSORY MEMORY: RECORDING

**5.** Visual sensory memory, known as (a)_____ memory, lasts about a quarter of a second. Auditory memory, known as (b)_____ memory, may last as long as two seconds. Sensory memory has many functions; for example, it prevents you from being overwhelmed by too much incoming information and gives you time to identify the incoming data and pay attention to them.

## C. SHORT-TERM MEMORY: WORKING

**6.** If you pay attention to information in sensory memory, it is automatically transferred to short-term memory, which has two main characteristics. The first is that unrehearsed information will disappear after 2–30 seconds, indicating that short-term memory has a limited (a)_____. The second characteristic is that short-term memory can hold only about seven items (plus or minus two), indicating that short-term memory has a limited (b)_____. You can increase the

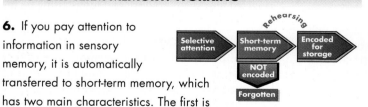

length of time that information remains in short-term memory by intentionally repeating the information, which is called (c)_____. You can considerably increase the capacity of short-term memory by combining separate items of information into larger units, which is called (d)_____.

## D. LONG-TERM MEMORY: STORING

**7.** Let's follow the progress of information from the time it enters sensory memory to its storage in long-term memory. For an instant to several seconds, incoming raw information is held in (a)_____. If you do not pay attention to this information, it disappears forever; if you pay attention, that information is automatically transferred to short-term memory. The transfer of information from sensory memory to short-term memory is controlled by the process of (b)_____.

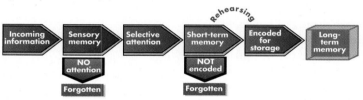

**8.** If information in short-term memory is not (a)_____, it will disappear in 2–30 seconds. If you rehearse or think about information in short-term memory, it may be transferred into long-term memory. The transfer of information from short-term into long-term memory is controlled by a process called (b)_____. In some cases, information is transferred automatically; in other cases, this transfer process may require deliberate effort.

**9.** The process of selecting information from long-term memory and transferring it back into short-term memory is called _____. Because information has been encoded into long-term memory does not guarantee that such information can always or easily be remembered or retrieved.

**10.** One demonstration of the existence of, and difference between, short-term and long-term memory is observed in the order that subjects remember items from a multiple-item list. Subjects tend to have better recall of items at the beginning of a list; this tendency is called the (a)_____ effect and involves long-term memory. Subjects tend to have better recall of items at the end of the list; this tendency is called the (b)_____ effect and involves short-term memory. The order in which subjects recall items from a long list is called the (c)_____ effect.

**11.** There are two different kinds of long-term memory. One kind involves memories of facts or events, such as scenes, stories, words, conversations, faces, or daily events. We can retrieve these memories and are conscious of them; they constitute (a)_____ memory. There are two kinds of declarative memory. One kind consists of factual knowledge of the world, concepts, word definitions, and language rules; this is called (b)_____ memory. The second kind of declarative memory consists of knowledge about personal experiences (episodes) or activities; this is called (c)_____ memory.

**12.** A second kind of long-term memory involves memories for performing motor or perceptual tasks, carrying out habits, and responding to stimuli because of classical conditioning; this is called _____ memory. We cannot retrieve these memories and are not conscious of them.

### E. RESEARCH FOCUS: DO EMOTIONS AFFECT MEMORIES?

**13.** There are times when for safety, moral, or ethical reasons researchers cannot use human subjects but instead use an (a)_____ model. Using this model, researchers found that during emotional or stressful situations, the body secretes chemicals called (b)_____, which make encoding so effective that these situations become very vivid long-term memories. One reason for the evolution of this carved-in-stone memory system is to help the species survive by remembering dangerous situations.

### F. ENCODING: TRANSFERRING

**14.** The process of storing information in memory by making mental representations is called (a)_____. There are two processes for encoding information. Most procedural and episodic information is transferred from short-term into long-term memory without any effort, and usually without any awareness, through a process called (b)_____ encoding. Much semantic information is transferred from short-term into long-term memory by deliberate attempts to repeat, rehearse, or make associations. Together, these deliberate attempts are referred to as (c)_____ encoding.

926-4029
926-4029
926-4029
926-4029

**15.** There are two kinds of effortful encoding, which differ in their effectiveness. Encoding by simply repeating or rehearsing the information is called (a)_____. This method is not very effective because it involves little thinking about the information or making new associations. Encoding that involves thinking about the information and making new associations is called (b)_____.

**16.** One theory says that memory depends on how information is encoded in the mind. If we pay attention only to basic features of the information, it is encoded at a shallow level, and poor memory results. If we form new associations, the information is encoded at a deeper level, and good memory results. This theory is called _____.

### G. REPRESSED MEMORIES

**17.** If something happens that is threatening, shocking, or traumatic, our minds may push that information deep into the unconscious, from which it may one day be released and enter consciousness. This phenomenon is called (a)_____ and is the theory behind the formation of (b)_____ memories. Unless there is corroborating evidence, the accuracy of repressed memories is difficult to establish.

### H. CULTURAL DIVERSITY: ORAL VERSUS WRITTEN

**18.** Students from Ghana, Africa, remembered more information when it was read to them than did American students who heard the same information. These results show how Ghana's tradition of passing on information orally, which is an example of _____ influences, improves both encoding and recalling or retrieving information.

### I. APPLICATION: UNUSUAL MEMORIES

**19.** The ability of certain children to examine a picture or page for 10–30 seconds and then retain a detailed visual image of the material for several minutes is called (a)_____ imagery. In adults, the ability to form sharp, detailed visual images after a short period and recall the entire image at a later date is called (b)_____ memory. Memories that are vivid recollections, usually in great detail, of dramatic or emotionally charged incidents are called (c) _____.

***Answers:*** *1. (a) encoding, (b) storing, (c) retrieving; 2. sensory memory; 3. short-term, or working; 4. long-term memory; 5. (a) iconic, (b) echoic; 6. (a) duration, (b) capacity, (c) maintenance rehearsal, (d) chunking; 7. (a) sensory memory, (b) attention; 8. (a) rehearsed, (b) encoding; 9. retrieval, or retrieving; 10. (a) primacy, (b) recency, (c) primacy-recency; 11. (a) declarative, (b) semantic, (c) episodic; 12. procedural or nondeclarative; 13. (a) animal, (b) hormones; 14. (a) encoding, (b) automatic, (c) effortful; 15. (a) maintenance rehearsal, (b) elaborative rehearsal; 16. levels of processing; 17. (a) repression, (b) repressed; 18. cultural; 19. (a) eidetic, (b) photographic, (c) flashbulb memories*

# Critical Thinking

---
### Newspaper Article
---

## Were Preschool Children Implanted with False Memories?

**Questions**

1. What major problems arise when young children are aked about being sexually abused?

2. What is unusual about this mother's accusations, and why were her accusations taken seriously?

3. Is this an example of repressed and recovered memories in children?

In Manhattan Beach, California, a grand jury accused preschool teachers of committing 115 instances of child abuse. Those accused included Ray Buckey; his mother, Peggy Buckey; his elderly grandmother and founder of the preschool, Virginia McMartin; his sister, Peggy Ann Buckey; and three other teachers. The abusive acts that the teachers allegedly committed against the preschool children (ages 2 to 5) included rape, sodomy, oral copulation, animal sacrifice, and satanic rituals. These accusations resulted in the longest (7 years) and costliest ($16 million) trial in American history.

The mother of one child, who had been at the preschool a total of only 14 times and never been in Ray Buckey's classes, accused Ray Buckey of making her boy ride naked on a horse, of molesting him while Ray was dressed as a fireman, cop, clown, and Santa Claus. The same mother also claimed that other preschool teachers had jabbed scissors into her son's eyes and staples into his ears, nipples, and tongue and that Peggy Buckey had killed a baby and made her son drink the blood.

Nearly 400 children were interviewed by social workers from the Children's Institute, who concluded that 369 of the 400 preschool children had been molested. However, before the children were interviewed, none had hinted or made any claims of being sexually abused.

During the interviews, social workers told the children about how other children had already agreed to being sexu-

ally abused. The social workers praised and told the children that they were "smart" if they agreed that sexual abuses had occurred and told them that they were "dumb" if they denied that abuse had occurred.

When the interviews, which were videotaped, were carefully reviewed, it became clear that the children soon learned what to say to please the social workers. Not only did children agree to being abused but added more instances, such as tales of horses being killed with baseball bats, of children digging up bodies at a cemetery, and of children being abused at car washes.

After a 7-year-long trial, the jury found the teachers not guilty of child abuse. The jurors agreed with the defense attorneys, who argued that during the interviews the social workers had used suggestions and persuasions to get the preschool children to agree to being abused.

After the not guilty verdict, one of the mothers said, "There is absolutely no shred of doubt in my mind that my three children were abused. I will always believe that all those teachers had abused all of those kids" (Sauer, p. D2). (Adapted from M. Sauer, Decade of accusations, *San Diego Union-Tribune*, August 29, 1993, p. D1)

4. What kind of effects might the interview techniques used by the social workers have on the young children?

5. Is there any evidence that false memories can be implanted in children?

6. After the not guilty verdict, why do you think this mother still believed that her children were molested?

*Try InfoTrac to search for terms:* false memories; interviewing children.

---

### Suggested answers to Newspaper Article questions

1. Some of the problems are that very young children do not understand what sexual abuse is or may not want to talk about such experiences, or they look to their parents or trustworthy adults for advice and answers.

2. This mother's accusations against Ray Buckey seem well beyond what could have happened in a preschool, which is a fairly public place. One reason this mother's accusations were taken seriously was that she was apparently relating what her young child had told her and her child had no reason to lie.

3. Because there is considerable controversy about the occurrence and accuracy of repressed and recovered memories in adults, there would be even more controversy about these phenomena occurring in very young children.

4. By suggesting that "smart" children would agree that the abuse had occurred while "dumb" children would deny such abuse, the interviewers were pressuring the children into giving answers that the interviewers were looking for and not trying to find out what, if anything, happened to the children.

5. There is considerable research showing that false memories can be implanted and become real in the minds of young children. Even after being told that the implanted memories were false, some children continued to believe that the "false" implanted memories were "true" and that the events "really happened."

6. This mother, through repeated questions and suggestions, may have unknowingly implanted false memories in her children. Once implanted, false memories may become real, detailed, and vivid. As a result, the children believe the "false" events happened and the mother has no reason to doubt her children.

# Links to Learning

## Web Sites

- WADSWORTH ONLINE STUDY CENTER
  http://psychology.wadsworth.com
  Quizzes, learning activities and exercises, a discussion forum, and hot links to Internet sites related to sensation, including:

- HORMONE'S AND THE MIND
  http://my.webmd.com/content/article/1700.50772
  A fascinating interview with psychologist Claire Warga, author of *Menopause and the Mind: The Complete Guide to Coping with Memory Loss, Foggy Thinking, Verbal Confusion, and other Cognitive Effects of Perimenopause and Menopause*. Includes links to related documents.

- AMERICAN PSYCHOLOGICAL ASSOCIATION: MEMORY
  http://www.apa.org/
  Type "memory" into the APA search engine to find fascinating articles on recent research, including recovered memories, false memories, memory storage, hormones and memory, and memory and aging, among others.

- RECOVERED MEMORIES OF SEXUAL ABUSE: SCIENTIFIC RESEARCH AND SCHOLARLY RESOURCES
  http://www.jimhopper.com/memory
  This thoughtful page contains links to many sites relevant to the recovered memory debate, including articles on "Verified Memory," "What the Popular Media Haven't Recorded," and "Betrayal of Children and Memory Loss."

## Learning Activities

- *POWERSTUDY*™ CD, BY ROD PLOTNIK & TOM DOYLE
  This 40-minute, fully narrated, self-paced, multimedia presentation includes animations, interactive activities, videos, quizzes, pronunciation of terms, personal note-taking, and direct-to-Web connections.

- *STUDY GUIDE TO ACCOMPANY INTRODUCTION TO PSYCHOLOGY, 6TH EDITION*, by Matthew Enos
  In Module 11, consider the statement "nothing in this module is true," and review such terms as "eidetic," "echoic," and "elaborative rehearsal."

- *WEBTUTOR*
  http://webtutor.thomsonlearning.com
  Visit this site for interactive versions of the Study Guide features. Take a quiz, get your score—should you study a topic some more, or can you move on? For example, is it true that there are four basic kinds of memory? What do we call the process of pushing bad memories into the unconscious?

- *INFOTRAC ONLINE LIBRARY*
  http://www.infotrac-college.com

  Use your password and then key in search terms such as those below to find popular and scientific articles on subjects covered in Module 10. Make the library work for you!

  | | |
  |---|---|
  | Declarative memory | Eidetic imagery |
  | Encoding | Episodic memory |

- *PSYCHNOW!*
  CD for Macintosh and Windows includes a study guide, glossary, Web sites, and animations. For Module 10, see:
  - Memory Systems

## Study Questions

*Use InfoTrac to search for topics mentioned in the main heads below
(e.g., short-term memory, long-term memory, animal research: memory, repressed memories).*

*A. **Three Types of Memory**—Why does seeing an ambulance speed by remind you of your father's heart attack and his trip to the hospital? (**Suggested answer page 625**)

B. **Sensory Memory: Recording**—Why doesn't the world disappear for the short period of time when your eyes are completely closed during blinking?

C. **Short-Term Memory: Working**—If you took a drug that blocked short-term memory, what would be different about your life?

D. **Long-Term Memory: Storing**—What would your life be like if you had declarative memory but no procedural memory?

E. **Research Focus: Do Emotions Affect Memories?**—Why do people who suffer traumatic situations, such as sexual abuse or job layoffs, have difficulty getting on with their lives?

*F. **Encoding: Transferring**—Why is it important that teachers make learning interesting and meaningful? (**Suggested answer page 626**)

G. **Repressed Memories**—What are some of the ways that therapists can guard against clients reporting repressed memories that are false?

*H. **Cultural Diversity: Oral versus Written**—How might playing video games affect a child's encoding process? (**Suggested answer page 626**)

I. **Application: Unusual Memories**—If you could have one unusual memory ability, which would you choose, and how would it make your life different?

*These questions are answered in Appendix B.

# Module 12: Remembering & Forgetting

**A. Organization of Memories**    262
* FILING AND ORGANIZING 87,967 MEMORIES
* NETWORK THEORY OF MEMORY ORGANIZATION
* ORGANIZATION OF NETWORK HIERARCHY
* CATEGORIES IN THE BRAIN

**B. Forgetting Curves**    264
* EARLY MEMORIES
* UNFAMILIAR AND UNINTERESTING
* FAMILIAR AND INTERESTING

**C. Reasons for Forgetting**    265
* OVERVIEW: FOUR REASONS FOR FORGETTING
* INTERFERENCE
* RETRIEVAL CUES
* STATE-DEPENDENT LEARNING

**D. Biological Bases of Memory**    268
* LOCATION OF MEMORIES IN THE BRAIN
* MAKING A SHORT-TERM MEMORY
* GENETICALLY ALTERING MEMORY
* MAKING A LONG-TERM MEMORY

**Concept Review**    270

**E. Mnemonics: Memorization Methods**    271
* IMPROVING YOUR MEMORY

**F. Cultural Diversity: Aborigines versus White Australians**    272
* RETRIEVAL CUES
* VISUAL VERSUS VERBAL MEMORY

**G. Research Focus: False Memories**    273
* CAN FALSE MEMORIES BE IMPLANTED?
* RESEARCH METHOD TO CREATE FALSE MEMORIES

**H. Application: Eyewitness Testimony**    274
* HOW ACCURATE IS AN EYEWITNESS?
* CAN AN EYEWITNESS BE MISLED?
* CAN QUESTIONS CHANGE THE ANSWERS?
* IS WHAT YOU SAY, WHAT YOU BELIEVE?
* WHICH INTERVIEW TECHNIQUE WORKS BEST?

**Summary Test**    276

**Critical Thinking**    278
* WHY DOES WIFE FORGET, DATE, AND REMARRY HUSBAND?

**Links to Learning**    279

PowerStudy ™

## Watching a Crime

**How much can you remember?** It was about nine at night when you entered the campus building, climbed one flight of stairs, and began walking down the long hallway. You had just finished your psychology paper and were going to slip it under the instructor's door.

Everything happened very quickly.

From about the middle of the dimly lit hallway, a man with reddish hair and wearing a brown leather jacket jumped out from behind a half-open door and ran at you. Instinctively, you threw out your hands and tried to ward off the oncoming threat. With a quick motion, the man grabbed your blue shoulder bag and pushed you down. At that instant, your eyes met. He pointed at you with a menacing gesture and said, "Don't move or make a sound." Then he checked the hallway, stepped around you, and was gone (adapted from Buckout, 1980).

A 12-second filmed sequence with a storyline similar to this one was shown on television. In the TV film, the assailant's face was on the screen for several seconds. Next, the viewers were asked to watch a lineup of six men and then to call the TV station and identify which was the assailant. Of the more than 2,000 viewers who called in, only 200 identified the correct man; 1,800 selected the wrong one (Buckout, 1980).

Without looking back, try to answer the following questions (answers at bottom):

 **A.**  **B.**  **C.**

1. What color was the mugger's jacket? _____

2. What color and type was the student's bag? _____

3. Besides the bag, what else was the student carrying? _____

4. The mugger's exact words were "Don't make a sound." True or false?

5. When thrown down, the student yelled out "Stop!" True or false?

6. Of the 2,000 viewers who called in, 1,800 identified the correct assailant. True or false?

***Answers:*** *1. brown; 2. blue, shoulder bag; 3. psychology paper; 4. false; 5. false; 6. false*

2,000 watched a televised mugging and 1,800 identified the wrong man.

## Recall versus Recognition

**Which is easier?** You probably found the first three questions harder because they involve recall.

*Recall* involves retrieving previously learned information without the aid of or with very few external cues.

For example, in questions 1–3, you were asked to recall colors or objects without having any choices. Students must use recall to answer fill-in-the-blank or essay questions.

You probably thought the last three questions were easier because they involve recognition.

*Recognition* involves identifying previously learned information with the help of more external cues.

In questions 4–6, you have only to recognize whether the information provided is correct. Students use recognition to decide which of the choices is correct on multiple-choice tests. Since multiple-choice tests involve recognition, they are generally considered easier than fill-in-the-blank and essay questions, which involve recall. Later in this module, we'll discuss why recall is more difficult than recognition.

## Eyewitness Testimony

**Which face did you see?** Question 6 asks about a very curious result. Although the assailant's face was on the television screen for several seconds, 90% of the viewers identified the *wrong* person in a six-man lineup. (For example, from the six faces below, can you identify the correct mugger? Answer below.) How can you clearly see someone's face and not remember it? The answer to this question comes from studies on how eyewitness memories can be affected by suggestions, misleading questions, and false information. Although we gen-

 **D.**  **E.**  **F.**

erally assume that eyewitness testimony is the most accurate kind of evidence, you'll see that this is not always true. We'll discuss accuracy and problems of eyewitness testimony at the end of this module. (Mugger had reddish hair.)

## What's Coming

We'll discuss how you organize thousands of events, faces, and facts and file this information in long-term memory. We'll explain the most common reasons for forgetting, the biological bases for memory, methods to improve memory, the creation of false memories, and the accuracy of eyewitness testimony.

I'll begin with my favorite theory of how information is organized and why I forget so many things—the trash can theory of memory.

## Filing and Organizing 87,967 Memories

**How do you store memories?**

One of the great puzzles of memory is how you file and store zillions of things over your lifetime. Suppose this past month you stored 91 faces, 6,340 concepts, 258 songs, 192 names, 97 definitions, 80,987 personal events, 1 dog, and 1 cat. How did you store these 87,967 memories so that you can search and retrieve one particular item from long-term memory?

There are several theories for how we file and organize memories; we'll discuss one of the more popular theories, which is called network (or connectionist) theory (McClelland, 2000).

*Network theory* says that we store related ideas in separate categories, or files, called nodes. As we make associations

Network theory: We save memories by storing them in categories (files or nodes).

among information, we create links among thousands of nodes, which make up a gigantic interconnected network of files for storing and retrieving information.

Network theory may become clearer if you imagine that the mental files, or nodes, are like thousands of cities on a map and the connections or associations between them are like roads. Just as you follow different roads to go from city to city, you follow different associative pathways to go from idea to idea. Storing new events, faces, and thousands of other things would be similar to erecting new buildings in the cities and also building new roads between the cities (Schwartz & Reisberg, 1991). Here's how one cognitive psychologist, Donald Norman, used network theory to explain how he retrieved a particular memory.

## Network Theory of Memory Organization

**Where do the roads lead?**

Just as you might follow a road map (right figure) to reach a particular city, cognitive psychologist Norman followed a cognitive map to remember the name of a particular store in San Diego. Although the mental roads that Norman takes may seem strange, these roads

represent personal associations that he created when he filed, or stored, information in long-term memory. As he follows his associations, or mental roads, he travels the cognitive network from node to node or memory to memory in search of a particular name (Norman, 1982). Please begin reading at node 1 and continue to node 6.

Norman mentally followed a cognitive map, going from file or node 1 to nodes 2, 3, 4, 5, and 6 before finding the name of a certain store.

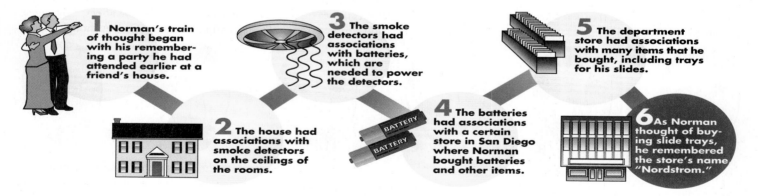

**1** Norman's train of thought began with his remembering a party he had attended earlier at a friend's house.

**2** The house had associations with smoke detectors on the ceilings of the rooms.

**3** The smoke detectors had associations with batteries, which are needed to power the detectors.

**4** The batteries had associations with a certain store in San Diego where Norman bought batteries and other items.

**5** The department store had associations with many items that he bought, including trays for his slides.

**6** As Norman thought of buying slide trays, he remembered the store's name "Nordstrom."

### *Searching for a Memory*

We've all shared Norman's problem of knowing we know something but having difficulty recalling it. This problem relates to how we store memories in long-term memory. According to the network theory of memory, we store memories in nodes that are interconnected after we make new associations. Because the network theory is somewhat complicated, we'll review how it applied to Norman's problem of trying to recall a particular memory.

**Nodes.** Norman organizes or stores related ideas in separate files, or categories, called nodes. We simplified this process by showing only six nodes, but there may be dozens. Nodes are categories for storing related ideas, such as birds, faces, friends, and store names.

**Associations.** Norman links the nodes, or categories of ideas, together by making associations or mental roads between new information and old information that was previously stored.

**Network.** Norman has thousands of interconnected nodes, which form an enormous cognitive network for arranging and storing files. Norman must search through this cognitive network to find a particular node or file, where a specific memory is stored.

Researchers have developed a theory of how we search through thousands of nodes to find a particular one (McClelland, 2000).

## Organization of Network Hierarchy

### How do you find a specific memory?

How do you find a specific memory to answer these questions: How big is a guppy? Does a rooster have feathers? Does a blue jay have skin? According to network theory, you will search for answers to these questions by using different nodes or memory files.

*Nodes* are memory files that contain related information organized around a specific topic or category.

According to network theory, the many thousands of nodes or memory files are arranged in a certain kind of order, which is called a network hierarchy (McClelland, 2000).

A *network hierarchy* refers to the arrangement of nodes or memory files in a certain order or hierarchy. At the bottom of the hierarchy are nodes with very concrete information, which are connected to nodes with somewhat more specific information, which in turn are connected to nodes with general or abstract information.

For example, a partial network hierarchy for nodes or memory files containing information about animals is shown on the right. Depending on whether you're looking for a specific memory (How big is a guppy?) or a more abstract memory (Does a blue jay have skin?), you will search different nodes, as explained next.

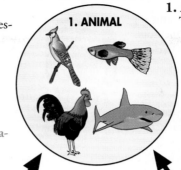

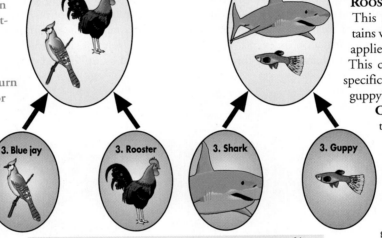

Network hierarchy: Arranging nodes or memory files with general information in top file (node #1) and specific information in bottom files (nodes #3)

### 1. ABSTRACT: ANIMAL

This node, or memory file, contains information that is very abstract and applies to all animals, such as has skin, can move around, eats, and breathes. This category has answers to very general questions about animals—"Does a blue jay have skin?"

### 2. MORE SPECIFIC: BIRD OR FISH

This node, or memory file, contains information that is somewhat more specific because it applies to many fish or birds, such as has wings, can fly, and has feathers. This category has answers to somewhat specific questions about fish or birds—"Does a rooster have feathers?"

### 3. CONCRETE: BLUE JAY, ROOSTER, SHARK, OR GUPPY

This node, or memory file, contains very concrete information that applies only to a specific animal. This category has answers to very specific questions—"How big is a guppy?" "What color is a shark?"

**Conclusion.** Because network theory doesn't have all the answers to how you file and store information, researchers are developing more complex models, such as neural networks, that try to imitate how the brain organizes and files millions of bits of information (Ratcliff & McKoon, 2000).

## Categories in the Brain

### Does the brain come with a built-in filing system?

The network theory's idea that information is filed in interconnected nodes or categories is partly supported by recent findings showing that the brain seems to have its own built-in filing system. For example, researchers found that, depending on which area of the brain is damaged, patients lose the ability to identify or process information dealing with a specific category. In some cases, patients could no longer identify faces but had no problems identifying information in other categories, such as those involving tools, animals, furniture, or plants. In other cases, patients could no longer identify plants but could identify information in other categories (tools, animals, etc.) (Schacter et al., 2000). These findings indicate that the brain has built-in categories for sorting and filing different kinds of information.

The brain seems to have built-in files or categories.

By using another research approach that involved taking pictures of neural activity in the living brain (p. 70), researchers found further evidence of the brain having different areas for different categories. When subjects were asked to think of objects in a specific category, such as faces, tools, or furniture, researchers found that maximum neural activity occurred in different areas of the brain. Researchers assume that brain areas that show maximum neural activity are where maximum thinking is occurring. For example, the left figure shows that thinking of animals produced maximum neural activity in the back of the brain, while thinking of tools produced maximum neural activity in the front of the brain (Martin et al., 1996). These kinds of findings led researchers to believe that the brain comes with prewired categories for processing information (Ishai, 1999).

The finding that the brain comes with prewired or built-in categories explains how you can so easily sort through a tremendous amount of information and so quickly find the answer to a specific question, such as "Does a camel have a hump?"

# B. Forgetting Curves

## Early Memories

**What's your earliest memory?**

Close your eyes for a moment and try to recall your earliest childhood memory. Researchers found that our earliest memories are usually sketchy, are often of personal experiences, and almost never occur before age 2 (Newcombe et al., 2000). Recently, researchers found that children as young as 13 months can recall visual events 8 months later, such as a sequence of moving toys in a certain order (Rovee-Collier & Hayne, 2000). However, these kinds of memories involving motor

Earliest memories at about age 3½

movements are not usually remembered after the age of 3½. There are two reasons we rarely remember things before age 2. First, very young children have little or no language skills so they cannot verbally encode early memories or recall them after they develop language skills. Second, very young children do not yet have a completely developed frontal cortex, which is important in encoding and retrieving memories (Newcombe et al., 2000). But even though you're now an adult and encode many things verbally, why do you still forget many of these things, especially on exams?

## Unfamiliar and Uninteresting

**Could you remember LUD, ZIB?**

From your experience studying for exams, you know that just because you verbally encode information by listening, reading, or writing doesn't mean that you'll automatically recall this information on exams. The kinds of events that you are more likely to remember or forget can be demonstrated with forgetting curves.

A *forgetting curve* measures the amount of previously learned information that subjects can recall or recognize across time.

We'll examine how two different kinds of information—unfamiliar and familiar—are remembered by using forgetting curves.

One of the earliest psychologists to study memory and forgetting was Hermann Ebbinghaus, who used himself as his only subject. He got around the fact that people have better memo-

ries for more familiar events by memorizing only three-letter nonsense syllables, such as **LUD, ZIB, MUC.** He made up and wrote down hundreds of three-letter nonsense syllables on separate cards and arranged these cards into sets of varying length. To the ticking of a metronome, he turned over each card and read aloud each of the syllables until he had read all the cards in the set. He used only rote memory (made no associations) and needed only one or two readings to memorize a set of seven cards (containing seven nonsense syllables). He needed about 45 readings to memorize a set of 24 cards (Ebbinghaus, 1885/1913).

The forgetting curve on the left shows that Ebbinghaus forgot about half the unfamiliar and uninteresting nonsense syllables within the first hour.

How long do we remember familiar information?

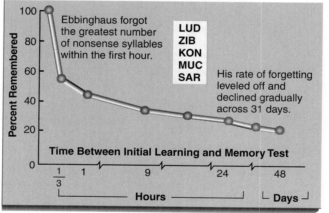

Ebbinghaus forgot the greatest number of nonsense syllables within the first hour.

LUD ZIB KON MUC SAR

His rate of forgetting leveled off and declined gradually across 31 days.

**Time Between Initial Learning and Memory Test**

## Familiar and Interesting

**Can you remember the names of your high school classmates?**

Ebbinghaus's nonsense syllables are certainly uninteresting, so it may not be surprising that he forgot half of them within the first hour. But what about the names and faces of the members of your high school graduating class? This information is both familiar and interesting and something you were exposed to for several years.

The graph on the right shows that even after 47 years, subjects correctly matched about 80% of their high school classmates' names with faces; they correctly recalled about 25% after 47 years (Bahrick et al., 1975). Subjects did better on recognition tests (matching names to faces) because they were given clues (names). They did poorer on recall tests

(seeing faces and asked to recall the names) because they were not given any clues. Similarly, students also show better memory on recognition tests (multiple-choice) than on recall tests (essay or fill-in-the-blank).

Notice that even though both kinds of information (names and nonsense syllables) were encoded verbally, subjects differed greatly in their ability to remember information. Subjects correctly recalled about 60% of familiar and interesting information (names and faces) after 7 years, while Ebbinghaus forgot about 80% of the unfamiliar and uninteresting nonsense syllables after about a week.

These two studies show that remembering is partly related to how familiar or interesting the information is. Next, we'll examine four other reasons for forgetting.

### Overview: Four Reasons for Forgetting

**What happened on her 9th birthday?**

For some reason, my sister can't remember what she did on her 9th birthday even though my brother and I can. Although researchers say that we can store enormous amounts of information for a very long time, why is it that memories of her 9th birthday seem to be missing? She says that she is forgetting, but what exactly does forgetting mean?

Forgetting has four possible reasons.

*Forgetting* refers to the inability to retrieve, recall, or recognize information that was stored or is still stored in long-term memory.

Although she says that she has forgotten her 9th birthday, it is possible that those memories were stored and are still in her long-term memory, but for some reason she cannot recall, or retrieve, them. As it turns out, there are at least four good explanations for why she may have forgotten her 9th birthday.

### 1. Repression

Perhaps my sister can't remember what happened on her 9th birthday because she repressed those memories.

*Repression,* according to Sigmund Freud, is a mental process that automatically hides emotionally threatening or anxiety-producing information in the unconscious. Once in the unconscious, repressed memories cannot be recalled voluntarily, but something may cause them to enter consciousness at a later time.

We discussed repression, repressed memories, and implanted memories in Module 11 (pp. 250–251) and will give only a brief review here. There are clinical reports of clients who, during therapy, recovered repressed memories of very emotional or traumatic events, such as sexual abuse (Andrews et al., 2000).

Repression

However, since the early 1990s, there has been a great debate over whether some of the increasing reports of recovered repressed memories involving sexual abuse were actually false memories that were unknowingly suggested or implanted by therapists (Loftus, 1999). For example, 300 women have later retracted (repressed) memories and accusations of childhood sexual abuse, and about a dozen clients have successfully sued therapists for implanting or contributing to false memories (de Rivera, 1997; Loftus, 1999).

On the one hand, there are clinical reports of clients who recalled repressed memories of traumatic events during the therapeutic process and such memories were verified by other sources (Briere & Conte, 1993). On the other hand, prominent memory researchers, such as Elizabeth Loftus (1999; 2000), have questioned the validity of repressed memories, pointing to the possibility that such memories had been suggested or implanted during the therapeutic process. For a further discussion, please see pages 250–251.

As you'll soon see, my sister's forgetting her 9th birthday was not due to repressed memories but to something more concrete.

### 2. Poor Retrieval Cues

Perhaps my sister can't remember what occurred on her 9th birthday because she was ill or had received few presents, which resulted in poor retrieval cues.

*Retrieval cues* are mental reminders that we create by forming vivid mental images or creating associations between new information and information we already know.

Many students don't realize that retrieval cues greatly influence the remembering or forgetting of new or difficult terms. For instance, if you study primarily by cramming or rote memory, you'll form poor retrieval cues. You'll make the best retrieval cues by making associations between new information and information already learned. We'll discuss how to form good retrieval cues on page 267.

Poor retrieval cues

### 3. Amnesia

What really happened to my sister on her 9th birthday was that she tried out her new ice skates. Wanting to show off, she tried a difficult spin, caught an edge, and fell hard on her head. She was knocked unconscious and, later, remembered nothing because the fall had caused amnesia (Mayes & Downes, 1997).

*Amnesia* is loss of memory that may occur after a blow or damage to the brain (temporary or permanent), after drug use, or after severe psychological stress.

Amnesia

Similar to my sister, people who strike their heads during car accidents usually have no memories of the events that occurred immediately before and during the accident.

### 4. Interference

If you try to recall your childhood birthdays, you may find that they begin to run together and get mixed up. This mix-up leads to forgetting and is called interference.

*Interference,* one of the common reasons for forgetting, means that the recall of some particular memory is blocked or prevented by other related memories.

For example, the presents, parties, or people from earlier birthdays may block out or interfere with remembering what happened on a later birthday.

Interference

Of the several reasons for forgetting, cognitive psychologists have focused primarily on interference and retrieval cues. We'll discuss these next and explain why having two exams on the same day greatly increases your chances of forgetting.

# C. Reasons for Forgetting

## Interference

**What if you study for three exams?**

Sooner or later, every student faces the problem of having to take exams in several different courses on the same day. This situation can increase the chances of forgetting material because of something called interference.

The theory of *interference* says that we may forget information not because it is no longer in storage or memory but rather because old or newer related information produces confusion and thus blocks retrieval from memory.

Students who take multiple tests on the same day often complain of studying long and hard but forgetting information that they knew they knew. In this case the culprit may be interference. Similarly, if you take two or more classes in succession, you may find that information from one class interferes with learning or remembering information from the others. We'll explain the two kinds of interference—proactive and retroactive—and how each can lead to forgetting.

### Proactive Interference

The first thing to remember about interference is that it can act forward, which is called proactive, or act backward, which is called retroactive. The prefix *pro* means "forward," so *proactive* interference "acts forward" to interfere with recalling newly learned information.

*Proactive interference* occurs when old information (learned earlier) blocks or disrupts the remembering of related new information (learned later).

Here's how proactive interference can work.

**1. Psychology information.**
From 1:00 to 3:00, you study for a test in psychology. The more psychology terms you store in memory, the more potential this psychology information has to "act forward" and disrupt whatever new and related information you study next.

**2. Psychology information acts forward.**
From 3:00 to 6:00, you study for a test in sociology. You may experience difficulty in learning and remembering this new sociology information because the previously learned psychology terms can "act forward" and interfere with remembering new and related terms from sociology.

**3. Proactive interference.**
When you take your sociology exam, you may forget some of the sociology terms you studied because of proactive interference: Previously learned psychology terms "act forward" to interfere with or block the recall of the more recently learned and related sociology terms.

Proactive interference: Material learned EARLIER (psychology) interferes with learning new information (sociology).

### Retroactive Interference

Note that the prefix *retro* means "backward," so *retroactive* interference means "acting backward" to interfere with recalling previously learned information.

*Retroactive interference* occurs when new information (learned later) blocks or disrupts the retrieval of related old information (learned earlier).

Here's how retroactive interference works.

**1. Psychology information.**
From 1:00 to 3:00, you study for a test in psychology. Then from 3:00 to 6:00, you study for a test in sociology.

**2. Sociology information acts backward.**
You may experience difficulty in remembering the psychology terms you learned earlier because the sociology terms recently learned may "act backward" and disrupt earlier learned and related psychology terms.

**3. Retroactive interference.**
When you take the psychology exam, you may forget some of the psychology terms you studied earlier because of retroactive interference: Recently learned sociology terms "act backward" to interfere with or block the recall of earlier learned and related psychology terms.

Interference, both proactive and retroactive, is one of the two common reasons for forgetting (Roediger & McDermott, 2000). Interference may also cause serious mistakes if eyewitnesses identify the wrong person, as happened in the study we discussed at the beginning of this module.

Retroactive interference: Material learned LATER (sociology) disrupts learning new information (psychology).

## Why Did Viewers Forget the Mugger's Face?

We began this module by asking why only 200 out of 2,000 viewers correctly identified a mugger's face that was shown for several seconds on television. One reason viewers forgot the mugger's face is that one or both kinds of interference were operating.

If *proactive interference* was operating, it means that previously learned faces acted forward to block or disrupt remembering of the newly observed mugger's face.

If *retroactive interference* was operating, it means that new faces learned since seeing the mugger's face acted backward to block or disrupt remembering of the mugger's face.

Thus, we may forget information that we did indeed store in long-term memory because of one or both kinds of interference.

Besides interference, the other most common reason for forgetting involves inadequate retrieval cues, our next topic.

## Retrieval Cues

**Where did I park it?**

Have you ever parked your car in a mall and later roamed around the huge lot trying to find it? In that case, the reason for your forgetting probably involved poor retrieval cues (Brown & Craik, 2000).

*Retrieval cues* are mental reminders that you create by forming vivid mental images of information or associating new information with information that you already know.

Without good retrieval cues, you cannot remember things.

Retrieval cues are also important in hiding things. Researchers asked students to hide things either in common places, such as drawers or closets, or in unusual places, such as old shoes or cereal boxes. Later, when asked to locate the hidden objects, students remembered objects hidden in common places and forgot those hidden in unusual places (Winograd & Soloway, 1986). Forgetting hiding places (which I have done) and forgetting parking places (which I have done) point to the need for creating good retrieval cues.

### Forming Effective Retrieval Cues

One reason we forget things (definitions, names, phone numbers) is that we did not take the time to create effective retrieval cues (discussed on pp. 248–249). For example, you can form effective retrieval cues by creating vivid mental images of the information, making associations between new and old information, or making somewhat bizarre but memorable associations.

For example, researchers wondered which types of sentences students would remember better: common sentences, such as "The sleek new train passes a field of fresh, juicy strawberries," or bizarre sentences, such as "The sleek new train is derailed by the fresh, juicy strawberries." As a computer randomly presented 12 common and 12 bizarre sentences, students were told to form vivid mental images of the scenes. When retested later, subjects recalled significantly more bizarre than common sentences. Researchers concluded that subjects remembered better the bizarre sentences because they formed better mental images or associations, which produced better retrieval cues (Robinson-Riegler & McDaniel, 1994). Poor retrieval cues may also be a problem in eyewitness testimony.

Vivid mental images make great retrieval cues.

**Retrieval cues and interference.** There have been cases in which eyewitnesses identified assailants who were later proven innocent based on DNA evidence. Even when told that their assailants, who had spent many years in prison, were innocent, the eyewitnesses insisted they had made the correct identifications (Dowling, 2000). One reason eyewitnesses were mistaken is that the emotional and traumatic events prevented them from forming effective *retrieval cues*. Another reason the eyewitnesses made mistakes is *interference*; that is, the faces of the accused assailants somewhat resembled and interfered with their recognizing the real assailants. These examples show that forgetting can result from poor retrieval cues, no associations, or interference (Brown & Craik, 2000).

Another example of forgetting, which involves retrieval cues and interference, usually begins with someone saying, "It's on the tip of my tongue."

### Tip-of-the-Tongue Phenomenon

Most of us have had the frustrating experience of feeling we really do know the name of a movie, person, or song but cannot recall it at this moment. This kind of forgetting is called the tip-of-the-tongue phenomenon.

The *tip-of-the-tongue phenomenon* refers to having a strong feeling that a particular word can be recalled, but despite making a great effort, we are temporarily unable to recall this particular information. Later, in a different situation, we may recall the information.

Researchers have found that the tip-of-the-tongue phenomenon is nearly universal, occurs about once a week, and most often involves names of people and objects. Its frequency increases with age, and about half of the time the thing is remembered some minutes later (Schwartz, 1999).

There are two explanations for the tip-of-the-tongue phenomenon. In some cases, information was encoded with inadequate retrieval cues, and so we must think up other associations (first letter of name, where last seen) for recall. In other cases, information is being blocked by interference from similar-sounding names or objects. Once we think of something else, the interference stops and the information pops into our memory (Schacter, 1996).

An interesting feature of retrieval cues is that such cues can also come from our states of mind.

## State-Dependent Learning

**What happens when you get angry?**

When you yell at someone for doing the same annoying thing again, why is it that a long list of related past annoyances quickly comes to mind? One answer involves state-dependent learning.

*State-dependent learning* means that it is easier to recall information when you are in the same physiological or emotional state or setting as when you originally encoded the information.

For example, getting angry at someone creates an emotional and physiological state that triggers the recall of related past annoyances. Evidence for state-dependent learning

Being in the same state (emotional) improves recall.

comes from a wide range of studies in which subjects (humans, dogs, rats) learned something while they used a certain drug, were in a certain mood, or were in a particular setting and later showed better recall of this information when tested under the original learning conditions (Brown & Craik, 2000). These state-dependent studies indicate that retrieval cues are created by being in certain physiological or emotional states or in particular settings and that returning to these original states helps recall information that was learned under the same conditions.

Next, we'll look inside the brain to see what happens during remembering and forgetting.

## Location of Memories in the Brain

**Where are memories stored?**

If you learned only 500 new things every day, that adds up to storing 180,000 new memories every year and 3,600,000 memories after twenty years. How can 3,600,000 memories (a very conservative estimate) be stored in a living container (brain) no larger than a small melon? In answering this question, researchers have studied short-term and long-term memories in normal people, brain-damaged patients, monkeys, rats, rabbits, mice, and even sea slugs to discover how and where memories are stored in the brain (Markowitsch, 2000).

Some answers came from in-depth studies of brain-damaged individuals who show deficits in some kinds of memory but not others (Zola & Squire, 2000). Some answers came from recently developed methods that take pictures of the neural activity inside the living brain while subjects are engaged in different kinds of memory (Nyberg & Cabeza, 2000). Based on these studies, researchers have identified the following areas of the brain that are involved in many different kinds of thoughts and memories.

### 1 Cortex: Short-Term Memories

When you look up a new phone number, you can hold it in short-term memory long enough to dial the number. Your ability to hold words, facts, and events in short-term memory depends on activity in the *cortex*, which is a thin layer of brain cells that covers the surface of the forebrain (indicated by thin red line around outside of brain).

People may have brain damage that prevents them from storing long-term memories, but if their cortex is intact, they may have short-term memory and be able to carry on relatively normal conversations. However, if they cannot store long-term memories, they would not later remember having those conversations.

### 2 Cortex: Long-Term Memories

If you learn the words to a song, these words are stored in long-term memory. Your ability to remember or recall songs, words, facts, and events for days, months, or years depends on areas widely spread throughout the *cortex*.

People may have brain damage that prevents them from learning or remembering any new songs. However, if they have an intact cortex, they may remember the words from songs they learned before their brain damage because such information would have already been safely stored throughout their cerebral cortex (indicated by thin red line around outside of the brain).

### 3 Amygdala: Emotional Memories

Suppose each time you hear a particular song that was associated with your first love, you have a romantic feeling. The emotional feeling associated with this memory is provided by the *amygdala*, which is an almond-shaped structure lying below the surface of the cortex in the tip of the temporal lobe. Humans with damage to the amygdala may no longer have emotions associated with memories, such as hearing a loud, unpleasant horn but no longer finding it "unpleasant" (Hamann et al., 1999). Researchers conclude that the amygdala plays a critical role in adding a wide range of emotions (pleasant and aversive) to our memories (Schooler & Eich, 2000).

### 4 Hippocampus: Transferring Memories

Just as the "Save" command on your computer transfers a file into permanent storage on your hard drive, the *hippocampus* transfers words, facts, and personal events from short-term into permanent long-term memory. The hippocampus (orange area) is a curved, fingerlike structure that lies beneath the cortex in the temporal lobe.

Four different areas of the brain are involved in memory.

People with damage to the hippocampus (and surrounding cortex) cannot save any *declarative memories*, such as new words, facts, or personal events, because the hippocampus is needed to transfer this information from short-term into long-term memory (Zola & Squire, 2000). However, people with hippocampal damage can learn and remember *nondeclarative or procedural information*, such as motor skills, but cannot remember actually doing motor skills (playing tennis) because that is a personal event (declarative memory). Thus, the hippocampus is necessary for transferring declarative information (words, facts, and events) from short-term into long-term memory but not for transferring nondeclarative or procedural information (motor skills, habits) (Zola & Squire, 2000).

### 5 Brain: Memory Model

Recent findings indicate that your *cortex* stores short-term memories as well as long-term memories; your *hippocampus* transfers or saves declarative information in long-term memory but does not transfer nondeclarative or procedural information into long-term memory; and your *amygdala* adds emotional associations to memories (Tulving & Craik, 2000). Now that you know which areas of the brain store, transfer, or add emotions to memories, we can examine how individual memories are actually formed.

## Making a Short-Term Memory

**What is a short-term memory?**

Suppose you just looked up the phone number 555-9013 and repeat it as you dial. Researchers believe that your brain may store that number in short-term memory by using interconnected groups of neurons that are called neural assemblies.

*Neural assemblies* are groups of interconnected neurons whose activation allows information or stimuli to be recognized and held briefly and temporarily in short-term memory.

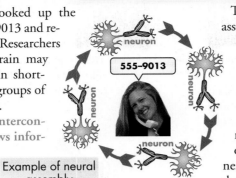

Example of neural assembly

The figure on the left shows how a very simplified neural assembly might work. Some information, such as repeating a phone number, activates a neural assembly that holds the phone number in short-term memory. However, if you switch your attention to something else before encoding the number in long-term memory, this neural assembly stops and the phone number is gone and forgotten. Researchers believe that neural assemblies are one mechanism for holding information in short-term memory (Smith, 2000). However, as you'll see next, permanently storing information in long-term memory involves chemical or structural changes in the neurons themselves.

## Genetically Altering Memory

**How is a memory made?**

How a memory is actually made in the brain has baffled researchers for 60 years. Researchers have tried to understand how a memory is made by genetically changing a mouse's brain. For example, researcher Joe Tsien (2000) inserted a special gene into a fertilized mouse egg that eventually developed into a healthy mouse. The special gene caused changes in a part of the mouse's brain (hippocampus) so that certain brain cells—neurons—could now communicate better by making stronger (synaptic) connections (see

Genes make a mouse smarter.

pp. 52–53). Researchers found that genetically altered mice, whose brain cells could better communicate, could remember which objects they had explored and which objects were new about four to five times longer than mice with unchanged or normal mice brains (see photo). Depending on the genetic changes, mice brains could be made "smarter" or "dumber." These results demonstrate that certain genes can change the *structure* of neurons so that they are either better or worse at communicating and better or worse at making memories (Tsien, 2000).

## Making a Long-Term Memory

**What is a long-term memory?**

Besides studying memory by genetically altering mice brains, researchers also study memory in sea slugs because their nervous system contains about 20,000 neurons versus billions in the human brain. After the sea slug has learned a simple task, such as tensing its muscular foot in response to a bright light, researchers can dissect the sea slug's nervous system and look for chemical or physical changes associated with learning (Kandel & Abel, 1995). We'll focus on one mechanism—long-term potentiation, or LTP—that researchers believe is involved in forming long-term memories.

### LONG-TERM POTENTIATION (LTP)

**1** You learn the name of the large-beaked bird on the left by repeating its name, "toucan," several times. Even though you learn its odd name, you are not aware of how learning changed your brain. After years of research, many neuroscientists now believe that learning changes the structure and function of the neuron itself (Izquierdo & Medina, 1997; Johnston, 1997). And one way this neural change occurs is through a very complicated process called LTP.

*Long-term potentiation,* or *LTP,* refers to the increased sensitivity of a neuron to stimulation after it has been repeatedly stimulated.

For example, by repeating the name "toucan," you are repeatedly stimulating neurons. This repeated stimulation produces LTP, which involves complex chemical and structural changes in neurons. We'll discuss a very simple version of LTP so you can understand its importance in learning and memory.

**2** Repeating the name "toucan" repeatedly stimulates neuron "A" and produces LTP in neuron "A." LTP changes the structure and functioning of neuron "A" so that it becomes more sensitive to future stimulation.

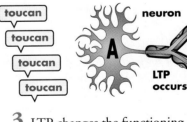

**3** LTP changes the functioning of neuron "A" so that it is associated with the name "toucan." To recall the name of this bird, you activate neuron "A," which also affects other neurons (neuron "B") that form the basis for your long-term memory of the name "toucan."

**4** In some studies, researchers found that when they chemically or genetically blocked the occurrence of LTP in sea snails or mice, these animals could not learn a classically conditioned response or learn a water maze (Tonegawa & Wilson, 1997). Thus, blocking the occurrence of LTP also blocked the formation of long-term memories. For this reason, many neuroscientists believe that the LTP process, which changes the *structure* of the neuron, is the most likely basis for learning and memory in animals and humans (Tsien, 2000).

# Concept Review

**1.** If you retrieve previously learned information without the aid of any external cues, you are using a process of remembering called (a)_____. If you identify or match information that you have previously learned, you are using a process of remembering called (b)_____.

**2.** Memory files or categories that contain related information organized around a specific topic, are called (a)_____. One theory of memory organization says that the separate memory files, or nodes, in which we file related ideas are interconnected in a gigantic system. This idea is called the (b)_____.

**3.** According to network theory, some nodes are arranged so that more concrete information is at the bottom and more abstract information is at the top; this order is called a _____.

**4.** A diagram of the amount of previously learned information that subjects can recall or recognize across time is called a _____. We tend to remember information that is familiar and interesting and forget information that is unfamiliar and uninteresting.

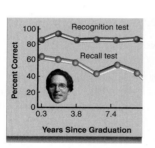

**5.** Psychologists have proposed at least four reasons for forgetting. According to Sigmund Freud, information that is threatening to our self-concept is automatically driven into our unconscious, from which we cannot retrieve it at will. This process is called _____.

**6.** One common reason for forgetting is that other related memories already stored in long-term memory may interfere with or block recall of some particular memory; this idea is called _____.

**7.** Another reason for forgetting comes from a lack of associations between new information and information we already know; this reason has to do with the quality of the _____.

**8.** A blow to the head may cause a form of forgetting called (a)_____, in which one loses all memories of events that occurred just before or just after being hit or after severe psychological (b)_____.

**9.** If we forget information not because it is lost from storage but rather because other information gets in the way and blocks its retrieval, this process is called (a)_____. If information learned earlier blocks, interferes with, or disrupts the retrieval of information that was learned later, it is called (b)_____. If information learned later blocks, interferes with, or disrupts the retrieval of information learned earlier, it is called (c)_____.

**10.** Mental reminders that we create by making images or associating new information with information that we already know are called _____.

**11.** Sometimes, despite making a great effort, we are temporarily unable to recall information that we absolutely know is in our memory. This is called the _____ phenomenon.

**12.** According to one memory model of the brain, short-term memories are formed and stored in different parts of the (a)_____. Long-term memories are also stored in different parts of the (b)_____, although these kinds of memories are not formed there. Declarative information is transferred by the (c)_____ into long-term memory, which is stored in different parts of the cortex. However, the hippocampus is not involved in transferring motor skills or habits, which are part of (d)_____ information, into long-term memory. Emotional associations are added to memories by an area in the temporal lobe called the (e)_____.

**Answers:** *1. (a) recall, (b) recognition; 2. (a) nodes, (b) network theory; 3. hierarchy; 4. forgetting curve; 5. repression; 6. interference; 7. retrieval cues; 8. (a) amnesia, (b) stress; 9. (a) interference, (b) proactive interference, (c) retroactive interference; 10. retrieval cues; 11. tip-of-the-tongue; 12. (a) cortex, (b) cortex, (c) hippocampus, (d) procedural, (e) amygdala*

## Improving Your Memory

**Do you complain about forgetting things?**

At one time or another, almost everyone complains about forgetting something. Many of my students complain about forgetting information that they really knew but couldn't recall during exams. This kind of forgetting has several causes: there may be *interference (proactive and retroactive)* from information studied for related classes; there may be *poor retrieval cues* that result from trying to learn information by using rote or straight memorization; or students may not use elaborative rehearsal (p. 249), which involves making associations between new and old information.

After about age 40, adults begin to complain about forgetting things that they never forgot before. For example, memory researcher Daniel Schacter, now 50, complains, "Reading a journal article 15 years ago, I would have it at my fingertips. Now, if I don't deliberately try to relate it to what I already know, or repeat it a few times, I'm less likely to remember it" (Schacter, 1997, p. 56). This kind of forgetting is commonly caused by poor retrieval cues, which result from being busy or distracted and not having or taking the time to create meaningful associations.

*How can I improve my memory?*

If you hear about memory courses that claim to greatly improve your memory, what these courses usually teach are how to use mnemonic methods. *Mnemonic (new-MON-ick) methods* are ways to improve encoding and create better retrieval cues by forming vivid associations or images, which improve recall.

We'll discuss two common mnemonic methods—method of loci and peg method—that improve memory (Floyd & Scogin, 1997).

### Method of Loci

If you need to memorize a list of terms, concepts, or names in a particular order, an efficient way is to use the method of loci.

The *method of loci (LOW-sigh)* is an encoding technique that creates visual associations between already memorized places and new items to be memorized.

We'll use the following three steps of the method of loci to memorize names of early psychologists: Wundt, James, and Watson.

**Step 1.** Memorize a visual sequence of places (*loci* in Latin means "places"), such as places in your apartment where you can store things. Select easily remembered places such as in your kitchen: sink, cabinet, refrigerator, stove, and closet.

**Step 2.** Create a vivid association for each item to be memorized. For example, picture Wundt hanging from a bridge and saying, "I wundt jump."

**Step 3.** Once you have created a list of vivid associations, mentally put each psychologist in one of the selected places: Wundt goes in the sink, James in the cabinet, Watson in the refrigerator.

To recall this list of early psychologists, you take an imaginary stroll through your kitchen and mentally note the image stored in each of your memorized places.

### Peg Method

Another useful mnemonic device for memorizing a long list, especially in the exact order, is the peg method.

The *peg method* is an encoding technique that creates associations between number-word rhymes and items to be memorized.

The rhymes act like pegs on which you hang items to be memorized. Let's use the two steps of the peg method to memorize our three early psychologists: Wundt, James, Watson.

**Step 1.** Memorize a list of peg-words shown on the left, which consists of a number and its rhyming word.

**one is a bun
two is a shoe
three is a tree
four is a door
five is a hive**

**Step 2.** Next, associate each of the items you wish to memorize with one of the peg-words. For instance, imagine Wundt on a bun, James with two left shoes, and Watson stuck in a tree.

To remember this list of early psychologists, you recall each peg along with its image of an early psychologist that you placed there.

### Effectiveness of Methods

A national magazine writer, who was 41 years old and complained about forgetfulness, decided to improve her memory by trying three different methods (Yoffe, 1997).

First, she took a 3-hour memory-enhancement class ($49). The teacher focused on the peg method and used it to memorize the names of the 11 students in the class. The magazine writer concluded that the peg method was impressive and if she were back in college, she would use it to memorize the endless number of facts.

Second, she listened to an audiocassette program ($79) that promised to release the "perfect photographic memory" that everyone already had. However, memory researchers report that photographic memories are as rare as duck's teeth (Schacter, 1996). The audio program focused on using the peg method without describing how it could be applied to things other than remembering grocery lists, biology terms, or names.

Third, she read a memory-improvement book ($10) that described the peg method, how to pay attention, and the importance of creating associations and images.

As this writer's experience illustrates, improving one's memory requires making the effort to use good encoding, such as elaborative rehearsal, which means creating good associations that, in turn, produce good retrieval cues and improve memory.

As the percentage of people over 50 increases, so does interest in memory-enhancing drugs. Researchers have found ways to improve memory in fruit flies and mice but say that memory-enhancing drugs in humans are years away (Weed, 2000).

Next, we'll discuss how cultural influences can affect what you remember.

## Retrieval Cues

**How do you survive in a desert versus an office meeting?**

Suppose you lived in the harsh, endless, barren desert world of western Australia, where many of the native Aborigines live (top photo). For about 30,000 years, the Aborigines have survived by using visual landmarks to remember the exact locations of water, food, and game in vast stretches of unmapped country (Gould, 1969). Because the Aborigines use few, if any, written records, their survival in this barren desert largely depends on their ability to store, or encode, enormous amounts of visual information, such as landmarks for food, water, and game. Lacking reading and writing skills, Aborigines primarily encode information about the desert by using *visual retrieval cues*, which are later used to recall information.

Survival depends on VISUAL cues.

Survival depends on VERBAL cues.

In contrast, most of us live in an industrial urban culture, in which survival largely depends on the ability to read and write and store an enormous amount of verbal, written, and computer-related information (bottom photo). Successfully surviving in an industrial culture is greatly dependent on the ability to store, or encode, enormous amounts of written and verbal information by using *verbal retrieval cues.*

These two examples show that survival in the aboriginal culture depends on encoding and remembering visual information, while surviving in an industrial culture depends on encoding and remembering verbal (written) information. This cultural difference predicts that people would perform differently on tests, depending on whether the tests emphasized visual or verbal retrieval cues.

## Visual versus Verbal Memory

Psychologist Judith Kearins was not surprised to find that Aborigines scored low on Western-style intelligence tests because these tests emphasize verbal retrieval cues and put Aborigines at a disadvantage. Considering their desert culture, she suspected that Aborigines would perform better on tests that took advantage of their ability to encode with visual retrieval cues.

### USING VISUAL CUES

To see if Aborigines were better at visual encoding, Kearins developed a test that emphasized visual retrieval cues. This test consisted of looking at 20 objects that were placed on a board divided into 20 squares. Some objects were natural—stone, feather, leaf; others were manufactured—eraser, thimble, ring. Aborigines and white Australian adolescents were told to study the board for 30 seconds (sample section on right). Then all the objects were heaped into a pile in the center of the board and the children were asked to replace the items in their original locations. The 44 Aborigine adolescents had been reared for the most part in desert tribal ways, had learned a nontraditional form of English as a second language, and were now attending school. The 44 white Australian adolescents lived and attended high school in a relatively large urban area (Perth).

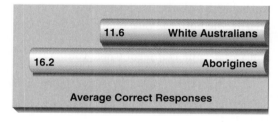

Aborigine students are better at using VISUAL cues than white Australian students.

### PERFORMANCE

Kearins tested the adolescents using four different sets of objects—all natural, all manufactured, some combined. The graph below shows that the Aborigine adolescents performed significantly better in placing objects back in their original locations than did the white Australian adolescents (Kearins, 1981). Another group of researchers essentially replicated Kearins's results using a younger population (average age of 9) of Aborigines and white Australians (Klich & Davidson, 1983).

| 11.6 | White Australians |
| 16.2 | Aborigines |

**Average Correct Responses**

### CULTURE AND RETRIEVAL CUES

Kearins concluded that the Aborigines' survival in the harsh desert landscape encouraged and rewarded their abilities to encode information using visual retrieval cues. In comparison, the urban school setting of the white Australians encouraged and rewarded their ability to encode information using verbal retrieval cues. For example, when questioned about their strategies, many of the Aborigines said that they only remembered the look of the objects on the board. In comparison, white Australians described their strategies in great detail: "I looked at the bottom row and remembered onion, banksia nut, rock, bone, and apple core." These descriptions support the idea that the Aborigines used visual retrieval cues, while the white Australians used verbal retrieval cues. These interesting results suggest that survival needs do shape and reward a particular way of encoding information in memory.

The better performance of Aborigines on visual tasks indicates that culture does influence the encoding and recall of information. Besides culture, other things, such as the age of a child, may also influence encoding and recall, as shown next in studies on implanting false memories in young children.

## Can False Memories Be Implanted?

**Is the child telling the truth?**

Each year in the United States, over 10,000 children are asked to testify about sexual abuse. In some cases, the children's testimony appears truthful and believable, and the cases are settled. In other cases, especially those involving day-care centers, children may testify about unusual or bizarre sexual practices that raise questions about the reliability of their testimony. For example, in one publicized case, Margaret Kelly Michael, a 26-year-old nursery school teacher, was said to have played the piano

Researchers implanted false memories in children.

while nude, made children drink her urine, raped and assaulted children, and licked peanut butter off children's genitals. Kelly was convicted of 115 counts of sexual abuse committed against 20 children from 3 to 5 years old. After she spent 5 years in prison, her conviction was overturned by a higher court because of concerns that the testimony of 19 child witnesses may have been unreliable due to improper interviewing by therapists (Ceci & Bruck, 1995). Improper interviewing refers to the possibility that the therapists, through repeated suggestions and specific questions, may have implanted false memories in the children. This very serious concern led researchers to study whether false memories could be implanted in young children.

## Research Method to Create False Memories

**What happens during questioning?**

Subjects: Children 3–6 years old

When questioning young children about sexual abuse charges, therapists or officials may repeatedly suggest that certain events happened. Can these repeated suggestions eventually create false memories in young children? To answer this question, psychologist Stephen Ceci and his colleagues (1994) studied 96 children from 3 to 6 years old who came from a wide range of social classes.

**Procedure.** To obtain a list of true and false events, researchers interviewed the children's parents about events that had occurred within the past 12 months of the children's lives, such as a surprise birthday party, a trip to Disney World, injury, or death of a pet. Each child was then read a list of these events, some of which were fictitious. The children were asked "to think real hard" and identify events that had actually happened to them.

Researchers emphasized that some events on the list had not happened to the children. For example, one fictitious event was "getting one's hand caught in a mousetrap and having to go to the hospital to have it removed." This testing procedure was repeated for each child in seven to ten different interviews, which were spaced about a week apart. In the last session, children were videotaped as they described the events, some true or false.

**Results.** As shown in the graph below, 91% of the time children correctly identified events that had happened to them, indicating that they had accurate recall. However, 34% of the time children said that they had experienced fictitious events that had only been suggested to them (Ceci et al., 1994). Surprisingly, children remembered fictitious events in great detail.

Here's how one 4-year-old described the fictitious event of getting his hand caught in a mousetrap: "My brother Colin was trying to get Blowtorch [an action toy] away from me, and I wouldn't let him take it from me, so he pushed me into the woodpile where the mousetrap was. And then my finger got caught in it. And then we went to the hospital, and my mommy, daddy, and Colin drove me there, to the hospital in our van, because it was far away. And the doctor put a bandage on this finger."

| | |
|---|---|
| Agreeing to false events | 34% |
| Agreeing to true events | 91% |

Some believe that children's lies or made-up stories can be detected through facial features (unsure or guilty looks) and speech patterns (stammering, correcting details). To test this belief, the same researchers asked 109 professionals (clinical and developmental psychologists, law enforcement officials, social and psychiatric workers) to judge whether events described by the children were true or fictitious. Professionals who watched videotapes of the children scored no better than chance in distinguishing true from fictitious events. Thus, children were very convincing in describing fictitious events.

**Conclusion.** When young children were asked repeatedly "to think hard" about true and fictitious events, some children became convinced that some of the fictitious events had actually happened. In addition, children gave such detailed and convincing stories of fictitious events that their stories fooled professional judges. Although this study showed that 91% of the time young children accurately recalled information about past events, it also showed that 34% of the time they turned false memories into true and believable ones.

Because very young children (aged 3 and 4 years) were more open to suggestions than older children (aged 5 and 6 years), researchers emphasize that great care must be taken when questioning young children so that repeated suggestions and interviews do not create and implant false memories (Ceci, 2000; Gobbo, 2000).

FALSE ▶ true

Children became convinced that false memories were true.

Just as some young children may respond to suggestions and misremember events, some adults may also misremember when giving eyewitness testimony, our next topic.

## How Accurate Is an Eyewitness?

The woman on the witness stand was very emotional as she recalled in vivid detail the hour of terror during which two men had forced her into her car, drove away, and later raped her in the front seat. When she was asked if one of the rapists was present in the courtroom, she pointed directly at the defendant sitting at the table and said, "There is no doubt in my mind."

*Eyewitness testimony* refers to recalling or recognizing a suspect observed during a potentially very disrupting and distracting emotional situation that may have interfered with accurate remembering.

For example, the woman's eyewitness testimony was the major piece of evidence that sent the defendant (an accused rapist) to prison. After the man spent 10 years in prison, a new defense lawyer was appointed, and he asked that the victim's clothes undergo a DNA test, which had not yet been developed at the time of the initial trial. The DNA test proved that the sperm stains on the victim's jeans did not come from the man who was in prison. The man who had been sent to prison largely on the basis of the victim's eyewitness testimony was found innocent and set free (Dolan, 1995a). This example raises at least three problems with eyewitness testimony.

First, many juries assume that eyewitness testimony is the best kind of evidence because it is so accurate and reliable. However, a study of people who were wrongfully convicted of crimes in the United States and England revealed that eyewitness testimony was the single most important source of evidence used to falsely convict people of crimes (Wells et al., 1994). Researchers estimate that

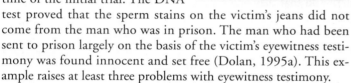

I have no doubt that he's the one who raped me!

DNA evidence proved he was not the rapist.

in the United States several thousand defendants are wrongly convicted each year of a serious crime (rape, murder) (Huff, 1995).

For example, the white woman (left figure) in this rape case may have made a mistaken identification of her alleged attacker (right figure) because she was distracted by her severe emotional state and did not get a good look. Or, she may have made the wrong identification because of interference. As it turned out, the African American man whom she confidently accused did slightly resemble the real rapist.

**Own-race bias.** The fact that the eyewitness was white and the accused rapist was black brings up another source of error. Researchers found that an eyewitness of one race will be less accurate when identifying an accused person of another race. For example, eyewitnesses are more likely to say they had previously seen an other-race face when they had not. The finding that people better recognize faces of their own race than faces of other races is called *own-race bias,* which can bias and lessen the accuracy of eyewitness testimony (Slone et al., 2000).

Second, we generally assume that the more confident an eyewitness is, the more accurate is the testimony. For example, the witness in this rape case was very confident when she said, "There is no doubt in my mind." However, six reviews of eyewitness studies concluded that there was only a weak relationship between a correct identification and how much confidence the eyewitness felt (Granhag, 1997).

Third, eyewitnesses may make errors if law enforcement officials ask misleading or biased questions. In these cases, eyewitnesses may unknowingly accept the misinformation as fact and give unreliable testimony. For example, consider the following case of mistaken identity.

## Can an Eyewitness Be Misled?

Some years ago a series of armed robberies occurred in the Wilmington, Delaware, area. The police had few leads in the case until a local citizen said that a Roman Catholic priest, Father Bernard Pagano, looked like the sketch of the robber.

At his trial, seven eyewitnesses positively identified Father Pagano (left photo) as the robber. But at the last minute, another man, Ronald Clouser (right photo), stepped forward and confessed to the robberies and Father Pagano was released (Rodgers, 1982).

As you look at these two photos, you will wonder how this case of mistaken identity could possibly have happened. Ronald Clouser is shorter, 14 years younger, and not nearly as bald as Father Pagano; besides, he has different facial features. Why, then, did seven eyewitnesses say with certainty that Father Pagano was the robber they had seen? One reason involves how the witnesses were questioned. Apparently, before the witnesses

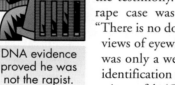

Seven people identified Father Pagano . . .

. . . but Ronald Clouser confessed to being the robber.

were questioned and shown photos of the suspects, the police had suggested the possibility that the robber was a priest. After being prompted to look for a priest, the witnesses focused on the few similarities Father Pagano had to the real robber. Because Father Pagano was the only suspect wearing a clerical collar, the witnesses concluded that he must be the robber. This example is but one of many that show how eyewitness testimony may be distorted or biased.

Because of potential problems with eyewitness testimony, the U.S. Department of Justice recently released a guide for collecting and preserving eyewitness evidence (Wells et al., 2000). This guide, based on research findings discussed in this Application section, warns law enforcement agencies about the kinds of errors that eyewitnesses may make. We'll next discuss more of the research findings that show how eyewitness testimony may be changed or biased.

## Can Questions Change the Answers?

Because of concern about the reliability of eyewitness testimony, Elizabeth Loftus (1979, 1993a) studied whether people can be misled and do misremember, especially if they are given false information. We'll describe several of Loftus's experiments that demonstrate how subjects misremembered what they saw or heard.

### DID THE CAR PASS THE BARN?

In one experiment, subjects watched a film of an automobile accident and then were questioned about what they saw. One of the questions contained a false piece of information: "How fast was the red sports car going when it passed the barn while traveling along the country road?" Although there was no barn in the film, 17% of the subjects said they had seen a barn, indicating that people may believe misinformation if it fits the overall scene or pattern (Loftus, 1975).

### WAS THERE A STOP SIGN?

In a well-known study by Loftus and colleagues, subjects were first shown slides of a traffic accident involving a stop sign and then asked a series of questions about the accident. Some of the questions were not misleading and asked about the presence of a stop sign. Other questions were deliberately misleading and did not mention the stop sign but asked about the presence of a yield sign. Later, when subjects were asked whether they had seen a stop sign or  a yield sign, those subjects who had been misled by earlier questions about a yield sign were more likely to report seeing a yield sign than subjects who were not misled (Loftus et al., 1978). These results, which show that subjects can be misled by being given false but related information, have been replicated by many other researchers (Neisser & Libby, 2000).

### HOW DOES FALSE INFORMATION ALTER MEMORY?

Based on many such studies, Loftus and Hoffman (1989) concluded that if misleading information is introduced during questioning after an event, people may believe this misinformation and report events that they did not see.

According to Loftus, eyewitnesses believed the false information they were told, rather than what they saw, because the false information altered or overwrote their original, true memory (Loftus & Loftus, 1980). This explanation, which has generated much research and  debate, says that people misremember because of a memory impairment: the true memory was erased or overwritten (Payne et al., 1994). However, other researchers argue that the original, true memory is still there but is difficult to retrieve (Zaragoza & Lane, 1994). Whatever the cause, these many studies indicate that people (witnesses) do misremember when given misleading information.

## Is What You Say, What You Believe?

The debate over whether false information overwrites the original memory has not been settled. However, what has been settled is that sometimes people do come to believe that they actually remember seeing things that were merely suggested to them; this phenomenon is called source misattribution.

*Source misattribution* is a memory error that results when a person has difficulty in deciding which of two or more sources a memory came from: Was the source something the person saw or imagined, or was it a suggestion?

For example, suppose you saw a hit-and-run accident involving a dark red car. During questioning, you are asked the color of the car that drove off. As you're thinking that the car was dark red, you remember hearing another bystander say, "The car was dark blue." Source misattribution would occur if you said that the car was dark blue (suggestion you heard) rather than dark red (something you saw). Researchers have found that false suggestions, misleading questions, and misinformation can result in source misattribution and create false memories (Roediger & McDermott, 2000). False memories that can result from source misattribution, such as suggestions or misleading questions, are one reason that court officials may question the accuracy of eyewitness testimony.

## Which Interview Technique Works Best?

Suppose you had witnessed a robbery but had trouble picking the suspect out of a police lineup. To help you provide reliable information about the suspect, you might be questioned using a procedure called the cognitive interview.

The *cognitive interview* is a technique for questioning people, such as eyewitnesses, by having them imagine and reconstruct the details of an event, report everything they remember without holding anything back, and narrate the event from different viewpoints.

The cognitive interview has proved very useful in police interrogation: Detectives trained in cognitive interview techniques obtained 47–60% more information from victims and suspects than detectives using the standard police interrogation method (Gwyer &

A cognitive interview is a more effective method for questioning eyewitnesses.

Clifford, 1997). Researchers concluded that once police officers are trained in cognitive interview procedures, it is a very effective way to increase correct recall and avoid making suggestions or giving misleading information that might create false memories and increase errors of source misattribution (Kebbell et al., 1999).

Psychologists have answered many questions about how eyewitnesses can be misled as well as how to improve the reliability of their testimony, which may result in life or death decisions. Based on this work, England has barred cases when the only evidence is an eyewitness. In the United States, many courts allow experts to testify about the reliability of eyewitnesses so that juries are made aware of the same studies and findings that you have just read (Pezdek, 1995).

# Summary Test

## A. ORGANIZATION OF MEMORIES

**1.** If you are asked to retrieve previously learned information without the aid of external cues, you are using a process of remembering called (a)_____, which is generally more difficult. If you are asked to answer multiple-choice questions, you can identify or match information and use a process of remembering called (b)_____, which is generally less difficult.

**2.** According to one theory of memory organization, we encode or file related ideas in separate categories called _____.

**3.** We form links between nodes by forming associations. The idea that the interconnected nodes form a gigantic system is called the _____ theory.

**4.** An arrangement in which nodes are organized in a logical manner, with more concrete information at the bottom and more abstract information at the top, is called a _____.

## B. FORGETTING CURVES

**5.** If the amount of previously learned information that subjects can recall or recognize across time is plotted, the resulting graph is called a _____. For example, Ebbinghaus demonstrated that the majority of nonsense syllables are forgotten relatively quickly—within hours. However, other studies showed that more relevant and interesting information may be remembered for many years.

## C. REASONS FOR FORGETTING

**6.** There are at least four reasons for forgetting. One of the most common is that other memories may interfere with or prevent retrieval of some particular memory; this is called (a)_____. One kind of interference occurs when information learned earlier interferes with information learned later; this is called (b)_____. A second kind of interference occurs when information learned later interferes with information learned earlier; this is called (c)_____.

**7.** A second reason for forgetting is that information is poorly encoded, which means that a lack of associations or reminders makes it difficult to retrieve a memory; this is called _____.

**8.** A third reason, put forth by Sigmund Freud, is that information that is threatening to our self-concept is automatically driven into our unconscious, from which we cannot retrieve it at will; this is called _____.

**9.** A fourth reason for forgetting is the effect of a blow to the head, psychological trauma, or drugs; this is called _____.

**10.** To increase the chances of remembering items from long-term memory, we can create reminders that associate new information with information that we already know; these reminders are called _____.

**11.** There are times when you are absolutely sure that certain information is stored in memory but you are unable to retrieve it. This experience is called the _____ phenomenon.

**12.** Besides creating retrieval cues, it may also be easier to recall information when you are in the same physiological or emotional state as when you originally learned it; this phenomenon is called _____.

## D. BIOLOGICAL BASES OF MEMORY

**13.** Different areas of the brain are involved in different memory processes. For example, the ability to hold words, facts, or events (declarative information) in short-term memory depends on activity in the (a)_____. The ability to transfer information about words, facts, and events (declarative information) from short-term into long-term memory depends on activity in the (b)_____. If this structure were damaged, a person could carry on a conversation but would not (c)_____ the conversation the next day.

**14.** The ability to recall words, facts, and events (declarative information) from the past involves activity in the outer covering of the brain, which is called the (a)_____. For example, if patients have an intact cortex, they can remember past events because these events are already stored in the cortex. However, they may have difficulty remembering any new words, facts, or events (declarative information) because of damage to their (b)_____.

**15.** The ability to transfer motor skills and habits, which is part of _____ memory, does not involve the hippocampus. Even though a person with damage to the hippocampus can store procedural information, that person would have no memory of having engaged in that event (declarative information).

**16.** The area of the brain that adds emotional feelings to memories is called the _____. This area is involved in forming a wide range of happy, sad, or fearful memories.

**17.** Researchers believe that the brain forms and briefly stores short-term memories by using a circuit of interconnected neurons called _____. When these interconnected neurons stop being activated, the short-term memory vanishes unless it has been encoded in long-term memory.

**18.** Researchers have evidence that the formation and storage of long-term memories involve the repeated stimulation of neurons, which in turn results in their becoming more sensitive to future stimulation; this phenomenon is called (a)_____. When this process was chemically or genetically blocked, animals were unable to form (b)_____.

### E. MNEMONICS: MEMORIZATION METHODS

**19.** Although we have the capacity to store great amounts of information, we may not be able to recall some of this information because of forgetting. Techniques that use efficient methods of encoding to improve remembering and prevent forgetting are called (a)_____. The major function of these techniques is to create strong (b)_____ that will serve as effective (c)_____.

**20.** A method that creates visual associations between memorized places and items to be memorized is called the (a)_____. With another method, one creates associations between number-word rhymes and items to be memorized; this method is called the (b)_____.

### F. CULTURAL DIVERSITY: ABORIGINES VERSUS WHITE AUSTRALIANS

**21.** Data from Aborigine and white Australian children suggest that survival needs may shape and reward a particular way of (a)_____ information in memory. For example, in the industrialized world, people (white Australians) are required to store large amounts of (b)_____. However, Aborigines in the wilds of Australia need to be able to store environmental, or (c)_____, to find their way, locate watering places, and thus increase their chances of survival. Researchers found that Aborigines performed better on tests that required (d)_____ retrieval cues and performed less well on tests that required (e)_____ cues.

### G. RESEARCH FOCUS: FALSE MEMORIES

**22.** During the past 10 years, young children have been called upon to testify in court, particularly in cases of sexual abuse. Because there are records of officials suggesting to young children that certain events have occurred, there is concern that children may come to believe these suggestions. Researchers found that, although young children can accurately recall past events, repeated suggestions may create _____ in young children.

### H. APPLICATION: EYEWITNESS TESTIMONY

**23.** One reason eyewitnesses may identify the wrong suspect is that criminal situations may be very emotionally disruptive or distracting, which may cause interference that leads to (a)_____. Another reason eyewitness testimony may not be reliable is that witnesses may be influenced by officials who ask (b)_____ questions.

**24.** When a person has difficulty deciding which of two or more sources is responsible for a memory, it is called (a)_____. Researchers found that misleading questions and false information can cause subjects to (b)_____ events.

**25.** The recall of eyewitnesses may be improved by having them imagine and reconstruct the details of an event, report everything that they remember, and report things from different viewpoints. This method is called the (a)_____. With this method, eyewitnesses remember much more information about the event than they do when asked standard questions. This questioning procedure also helps to eliminate suggestions or source misattributions, which can result in implanting (b)_____ in witnesses.

*Answers:* 1. (a) recall, (b) recognition; 2. nodes; 3. network; 4. hierarchy; 5. forgetting curve; 6. (a) interference, (b) proactive interference, (c) retroactive interference; 7. inadequate retrieval cues; 8. repression; 9. amnesia; 10. retrieval cues; 11. tip-of-the-tongue; 12. state-dependent learning; 13. (a) cortex, (b) hippocampus, (c) remember; 14. (a) cortex, (b) hippocampus; 15. procedural; 16. amygdala; 17. neural assemblies; 18. (a) long-term potentiation, or LTP, (b) long-term memories; 19. (a) mnemonics, (b) associations, (c) retrieval cues; 20. (a) method of loci, (b) peg method; 21. (a) encoding, (b) verbal information, (c) visual information, (d) visual, (e) verbal; 22. false memories; 23. (a) forgetting, (b) misleading; 24. (a) source misattribution, (b) misremember; 25. (a) cognitive interview, (b) false memories

# Critical Thinking

Newspaper Article

## Why Does Wife Forget, Date, and Remarry Husband?

*by Michael Haederle*

LAS VEGAS, N.M.—Shortly after their wedding in 1993, Krickitt suffered a severe head injury in a car crash. When she emerged from a month-long coma, she no longer knew Kim (her husband), having lost all memory of the previous 18 months—including meeting and marrying her husband.

Kim stuck by her as she struggled to heal, and against all odds, they courted and fell in love again . . .

Emerging from her coma around Christmas, Krickitt was as helpless as a newborn. She needed to be fed, diapered and bathed. The 5-foot-2 former college gymnast, who'd once performed back flips on a balance beam, had to learn to walk again.

"It was sad to see her in this condition," Kim says. But there was worse news . . .

When quizzed by a nurse, Krickitt knew she was in Phoenix—although she thought it was 1969 (it was really 1993) and Nixon was the president. She also knew who her parents were. . . . Then the nurse asked "Who's your husband?" Krickitt said, "I'm not married." Kim said, "I was devastated—I was crushed, I was hurt so bad. I hit my hand on the wall." . . .

Krickitt visited their Las Vegas home, hoping the familiar surroundings might jog her memory. She wandered through the apartment she'd shared with Kim, gazing at their wedding photos and fingering her china. Nothing clicked.

"I remember asking, 'How did I do the wife thing? Did I cook for you? Did I bring you lunch?'" she says. Krickitt was unable to drive and couldn't remember directions. Kim worried she'd get lost walking the 100 yards to the grocery store. . . . It was the therapist who suggested that Kim and Krickitt start dating as a way of rebuilding their relationship. On their "date nights," they sampled everything their small town had to offer. "We'd go to Pizza Hut," Kim says. "We'd go to Wal-Mart or go bowling." Sometimes he'd bring her roses. . . . With continued therapy and the passage of time, Krickitt has accepted her new life. . . . It was Krickitt who suggested getting married again.

On Valentine's Day he went to her office with a bunch of red roses and proposed on bended knee. . . . They married (above photo) Sept. 18, 1993, and honeymooned in Maui before settling into their new life together in this small northern New Mexico city. (Source: *Los Angeles Times*, May 23, 1996)

### Questions

**1.** Of the four reasons for forgetting, which one applies to Krickitt?

**2.** Krickitt's loss of many long-term memories means that which part of her brain was damaged?

**3.** How was Krickitt able to remember her parents but not her husband, not their apartment, and not their wedding photos?

**4.** Of the two kinds of long-term memory, which involves Krickitt's having to relearn to drive a car?

**5.** Which part of Krickitt's brain was undamaged and allowed her to store new long-term memories of Kim?

*Try InfoTrac to search for terms:* amnesia; **long-term memory; short-term memory.**

---

### Suggested answers to Newspaper Article questions

1. Because of a car accident, Krickitt suffered a severe blow to her head that caused her to go into a coma. In addition, when she came out of her coma, the severe blow to her head caused widespread amnesia, which is forgetting caused by loss of memory.

2. Since long-term memories are stored primarily in the cortex (surface of the brain), this means that areas of Krickitt's cortex were damaged in the accident.

3. Researchers have discovered that different kinds of long-term memories are stored in different parts of the cortex. Krickitt could remember her parents because those memories were stored in a part of her cortex that was undamaged. However, she lost all memory of her husband and being married because those memories were stored in a part of her cortex that was damaged.

4. There are two kinds of long-term memories: declarative and nondeclarative or procedural (p. 246). Learning motor skills and habits involves storing nondeclarative or procedural memories and does not involve the hippocampus.

5. Krickett was able to relearn who Kim was by dating him. Krickett's ability to remember that she was dating and going out with Kim means that she was able to store personal or episodic memories, which are one kind of declarative memories (p. 246). Declarative memories are transferred and stored as long-term memories by the hippocampus, which means that Krickett's hippocampus was undamaged and functioning.

# Links to Learning

## Web Sites

- **WADSWORTH ONLINE STUDY CENTER**
  **http://psychology.wadsworth.com**
  Quizzes, learning activities and e... ercises, discussion forum, and ... links to Internet sites rela... sensation, including:

- **BRAIN INJURY CEN...** support to people
  **http://www.braincen...** ...fect memory.
  This site offers in... with brain injuri...

...ETTING, MEMORY ...NEMONIC DEVICES

- **CONCENTR...**
  **IMPROVE...** ...n State University Academic
  **http://w...** ...re designed to help students
  These i... ...d test-taking abilities.
  Reso... ...UEST OF
  im... MEMORY
  ...emo.com/articles/horod.htm
  - ...n of the first ever wide-circulation ...out the SuperMemo set of learning ...oftware) by Andrej Horodenski.

...F CONSCIOUS CONTENTS
...ED FORGETTING AND
...T SUPPRESSION
...che.cs.monash.edu.au/v4/
...-16-whetstone.html

...teresting report on research into how we can ...ontrol our thoughts and suppress those we don't wish to remember. "Directed forgetting" turns out to be successful; "thought suppression" does not.

## Learning Activities

- **POWERSTUDY™ BY ROD PLOTNIK & TOM DOYLE**
  This 40-minute, fully narrated, self-paced, multimedia presentation includes animations, interactive activities, videos, quizzes, pronunciation of terms, personal note-taking, and direct-to-Web connections.

- **STUDY GUIDE TO ACCOMPANY INTRODUCTION TO PSYCHOLOGY, 6TH EDITION, by Matthew Enos**
  In Module 12, consider the implications of false memory research on psychologists and legal professionals; decide which is easier, recall or recognition; and try to remember what it's called when you can't remember someone's name.

- **WEBTUTOR**
  **http://webtutor.thomsonlearning.com**
  **WebTUTOR** Visit this site for interactive versions of the Study Guide features. Take a quiz, get your score—should you study a topic some more, or can you move on? For example, is eyewitness memory trustworthy? The spinal cord stores our memories, not the brain: true or false?

- **INFOTRAC ONLINE LIBRARY**
  **http://www.infotrac-college.com**
  Use your password and then key in search terms such as those below to find popular and scientific articles on subjects covered in Module 12. Make the library work for you!

  | | |
  |---|---|
  | Amnesia | Retroactive interference |
  | Repression | Retrieval cues |

- **PSYCHNOW!**
  CD for Macintosh and Windows includes a study guide, glossary, Web sites, and animations. For Module 12, see:
  - Forgetting

## Study Questions

*Use InfoTrac to search for topics mentioned in the main heads below (e.g., forgetting, mnemonics, false memories).*

**\*A. Organization of Memories**—How would your memory be affected if you accidentally took a drug that prevented the formation of any new nodes? (**Suggested answer page 626**)

**B. Forgetting Curves**—Why are you more likely to remember students' names than concepts from high school?

**C. Reasons for Forgetting**—If you wanted to change your study habits, how would you use information about why we forget?

**\*D. Biological Bases of Memory**—If a virus suddenly destroyed your hippocampus, what effect would it have on your performance in college? (**Suggested answer page 626**)

**E. Mnemonics: Memorization Methods**—Can you describe a mnemonic method to remember the four reasons for forgetting?

**F. Cultural Diversity: Aborigines versus White Australians**—What might be one difference between the ways in which art and English majors encode information?

**G. Research Focus: False Memories**—When young children are questioned, what precautions should be taken to minimize the creation of false memories?

**\*H. Application: Eyewitness Testimony**—If you were on a jury, what concerns would you have when listening to eyewitness testimony? (**Suggested answer page 626**)

*These questions are answered in Appendix B.

# Module 13: Intelligence

**A. Defining Intelligence**      282
* PROBLEM: DEFINITION
* TWO-FACTOR THEORY
* MULTIPLE-INTELLIGENCE THEORY
* TRIARCHIC THEORY
* CURRENT STATUS

**B. Measuring Intelligence**      284
* EARLIER ATTEMPTS TO MEASURE INTELLIGENCE
* BINET'S BREAKTHROUGH
* FORMULA FOR IQ
* EXAMPLES OF IQ TESTS
* TWO CHARACTERISTICS OF TESTS

**C. Distribution & Use of IQ Scores**      288
* NORMAL DISTRIBUTION OF IQ SCORES
* MENTAL RETARDATION: IQ SCORES
* VAST MAJORITY: IQ SCORES
* GIFTED: IQ SCORES

**D. Potential Problems of IQ Testing**      290
* BINET'S TWO WARNINGS
* RACIAL DISCRIMINATION
* CULTURAL BIAS
* CULTURE-FREE TESTS
* NONINTELLECTUAL FACTORS

**E. Nature-Nurture Question**      292
* DEFINITIONS
* TWIN STUDIES
* ADOPTION STUDIES
* INTERACTION: NATURE AND NURTURE
* RACIAL CONTROVERSY

**Concept Review**      295

**F. Cultural Diversity: Races, IQs, & Immigration**      296
* MISUSE OF IQ TESTS?

**G. Research Focus: New Approaches**      297
* CAN GENIUS BE FOUND IN THE BRAIN?
* CAN SPEARMAN'S g BE FOUND IN THE BRAIN?

**H. Application: Intervention Programs**      298
* DEFINITION OF INTERVENTION PROGRAMS
* RAISING IQ SCORES
* NEED FOR INTERVENTION PROGRAMS

**Summary Test**      300

**Critical Thinking**      302
* CAN A SUCCESSFUL BOOKIE HAVE AN IQ OF 55?

**Links to Learning**      303

© Art Wolfe (3)

## Mirror, Mirror, on the Wall, Who Is the Most Intelligent of Them All?

**How would you rank these five on intelligence?**

For the past 200 years, psychologists have been concerned with defining and measuring intelligence. However, before we discuss their findings and theories about intelligence, we would like to find out what you think intelligence is. We're going to describe five individuals and ask you to rank them in order of intelligence. We would like you to rank the five individuals now, before you read this module. After you have read the module, come back to your ranking and see if you would make any changes.

Based on my idea of intelligence, here is how I have ranked the five individuals: #1____, #2____, #3____, #4____, #5____.

**A. Gregg Cox**
At age 34, he can speak 64 languages fluently, making him, says the *Guinness Book of World Records,* the planet's greatest linguist. He broke the old record of 58 languages. He began learning languages at age 5, starting with Spanish, Portuguese, Italian, German, and Chinese. Since then, he has been learning about 5 languages a year. He's writing a book—a dictionary.

**B. Venus Williams**
At age 20, she became the first black woman to win the prestigious Wimbledon tennis tournament since 1958. Then she beat the number one ranked woman tennis player in the world to win the U.S. Open. Then she won a gold medal at the 2000 Olympics. Her winnings are in the millions, and she has a chance to become the greatest woman tennis player of all time.

**C. Bill Gates**
At age 45, he has become the richest man in the U.S.— worth around $61 billion. He began writing computer programs in the eighth grade. As a college sophomore, he dropped out of Harvard and wrote one of the first operating systems to run a computer. In his twenties, he founded Microsoft, whose software operates 90% of the computers in the world.

**D. Steve Lu**
At age 5, he scored 194 on an IQ test (average is 100). At age 9, he scored 710 on the math part of the SAT (perfect score is 800). He completed 12 years of precollege courses in just 5 years. At age 10, he was a freshman in college. At age 15, he was one of the youngest students ever to be accepted in the graduate computer science program at prestigious Stanford University.

**E. Midori**
At age 3, she began playing violin. By age 10, she was considered a musical prodigy, another name for a child genius. Also at age 10, she made a big stir in classical music circles by performing professionally with the New York Philharmonic Orchestra. From an early age she was able to memorize and flawlessly perform long and complicated pieces of classical music.

## Psychometrics

The problem you faced in trying to rank the intelligence of the above five individuals—Cox, Williams, Gates, Lu, and Midori—is similar to what psychologists faced in having to define and measure intelligence. Since the late 1800s, psychologists have debated the question, What is intelligence? and have developed a number of tests to measure intelligence. Measuring intelligence is part of an area of psychology that is called psychometrics.

*Psychometrics,* which is a subarea of psychology, is concerned with developing psychological tests that assess an individual's abilities, skills, beliefs, and personality traits in a wide range of settings—school, industry, or clinic.

As you'll discover in this module, the measurement of intelligence and the development of intelligence tests, which is one area of psychometrics, are still being debated.

## What's Coming

We'll discuss the different theories of intelligence, how intelligence is measured, the meaning of IQ scores, the problems with intelligence tests, how genetics and environment influence intelligence, and ways to improve environmental opportunities.

We'll begin with the hundred-year-old question: How do we define intelligence?

# A. Defining Intelligence

## Problem: Definition

**What is intelligence?**

Gregg Cox: speaks 64 languages

Venus Williams: world tennis champion

Bill Gates: head of Microsoft; $61 billion

Steve Lu: 194 IQ; grad school at age15

Midori: child prodigy; violin genius

I clearly remember bringing home a grade school report card and being asked by my parents why I didn't get all A's like my older brother. I thought about it and replied, "He must be smarter than me." From that time on I wondered just how smart (intelligent) I really was. When I did take a group IQ test in high school, the counselor said it was the school's policy not to tell students their exact scores. But trying to be helpful, the counselor added that I might have trouble getting through college. The point of my story is that most of us would like to find out just how intelligent we are.

But defining someone's level of intelligence is not always clear cut (Sternberg, 2000a). For example, what definition of intelligence did you use to rank the five individuals shown on the left?

Don't be surprised if you had difficulty ranking the intelligence of these five individuals. The official journal of the American Psychological Association devoted an entire issue to discussing how to define and measure intelligence as well as the value and usefulness of IQ scores (*American Psychologist,* October 1997).

For example, many psychologists believe that intelligence is best defined by measuring a variety of cognitive abilities, which in Lu's case results in determining a high IQ score. Others argue that a definition of intelligence based entirely on cognitive abilities is much too narrow. Instead, they believe that there are many kinds of intelligence, such as creative, practical or motor (movement), and musical intelligence, as in the cases of Williams and Midori. Still others argue that a definition of intelligence should include studying how people solve problems, such as how Cox learned 64 languages and Gates designed a computer operating system.

We'll discuss three popular definitions of intelligence—the two-factor, multiple-factor, and triarchic theories of intelligence. We'll begin with the oldest and most widely accepted definition of intelligence, the two-factor theory.

## Two-Factor Theory

**What is "g"?**

In 1904, Charles Spearman reported that he had measured intelligence in an objective way. Spearman was one of the first to use the psychometric approach.

The *psychometric approach* measures or quantifies cognitive abilities or factors that are thought to be involved in intellectual performance.

Spearman (1904) reasoned that by measuring related cognitive factors he would have an objective measure of intelligence. This idea led to his two-factor theory of intelligence.

Spearman's *two-factor theory* says that intelligence has two factors: a general mental ability factor, *g*, which represents what different cognitive tasks have in common, plus many specific factors, *s*, which include specific mental abilities (mathematical, mechanical, or verbal skills).

Spearman believed that factor *g*, or general mental ability, represented a person's mental energy. Today, factor *g* is defined and measured by a person's performance on various and related cognitive abilities. In other words, modern intelligence tests have essentially changed or transformed Spearman's *g* into an objective score, which is commonly known as the IQ score. Today, many psychologists believe that *g*, as represented by IQ scores, is a good measure of a person's general intelligence.

### On the basis of Spearman's two-factor theory, which of the five individuals (left photos) is most intelligent?

Many psychologists believe that *g* is the definition of general intelligence, which can be measured by an IQ test and represented by an IQ score. Thus, one way to compare people on intelligence is by using scores from IQ tests. Ranking intelligence by using IQ scores would favor Lu (IQ 194), Bill Gates (one colleague said Gates was "the smartest person he ever knew"), and probably Cox (speaks 64 languages). However, although Williams (world tennis champ) and Midori (violin genius) might score high on IQ tests, they would get little or no credit for having exceptional motor, music, and perceptual skills.

Steve Lu: 194 IQ; grad school at age15

### ADVANTAGES AND DISADVANTAGES

One advantage of *g* is that it can be objectively defined and measured by an IQ test, which gives an IQ score that is presumed to reflect a person's general intelligence. Another advantage is that *g* is a good predictor of performance in academic settings and has some success in predicting performance in certain careers (discussed later) (N. Brody, 2000).

The major disadvantage of Spearman's *g* is the continuing debate over whether it really does define and measure general intelligence. For example, one prominent researcher states, "We know how to measure something called intelligence, but we do not know what has been measured" (N. Brody, 2000, p. 30). Another disadvantage of *g* is that it focuses on cognitive abilities as the measure of general intelligence but neglects other kinds of abilities, such as motor, perceptual, musical, practical, or creative abilities, which some psychologists consider to represent other kinds of intelligence (Davidson & Downing, 2000). For this reason, psychologists critical of *g*'s narrow approach to measuring general intelligence have proposed other definitions and ways to measure intelligence. We'll discuss those next.

## Multiple-Intelligence Theory

**Multiple kinds of intelligence?**

Some psychologists reject the idea that intelligence can be reduced to *g* and expressed by a single number, an IQ score. Howard Gardner (1999) argues for broadening the definition of intelligence to include different kinds of abilities, an idea he calls the multiple-intelligence theory.

*Gardner's multiple-intelligence theory* says that instead of one kind of general intelligence, there are at least seven different kinds, which include verbal intelligence, musical intelligence, logical-mathematical intelligence, spatial intelligence, body movement intelligence, intelligence to understand oneself, and intelligence to understand others.

Gardner states that standard IQ tests measure primarily verbal and logical-mathematical intelligence and neglect other but equally important kinds of intelligence, such as the ones listed above. Gardner (1999) arrived at his theory of multiple kinds of intelligence after studying which abilities remain following brain damage, how savants and prodigies develop their specialized kinds of intelligence, and how people in different environments develop different abilities in order to adapt and be successful.

*On the basis of Gardner's multiple-intelligence theory, which of the five individuals (previous page) is most intelligent?*

According to Gardner's multiple-intelligence theory, there isn't one kind of general intelligence for ranking all individuals. Rather, Gardner views the special abilities of Williams in tennis and Midori in music as representing other kinds of intelligence.

Venus Williams: world tennis champion

Gardner argues that none of the five is more intelligent but rather that each of the five individuals shows a different kind of ability or intelligence that was developed and adapted to his or her environment.

### ADVANTAGES AND DISADVANTAGES

One advantage of Gardner's multiple-intelligence approach is that it does not reduce intelligence to a single IQ score but rather credits people with different kinds of intelligence.

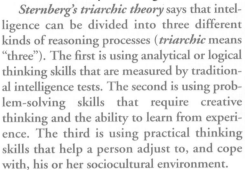

Midori: child prodigy; violin genius

Two disadvantages of this approach are not knowing how many kinds of intelligence there are and not having standard measuring techniques to assess different kinds of intelligence (Callahan, 2000).

Agreeing with Gardner that *g* is too narrow a measure of intelligence, Sternberg proposed a triarchic theory.

## Triarchic Theory

**Three kinds of intelligence?**

Criticizing Spearman's *g* as too narrow and current IQ tests as limited to measuring only problem-solving skills and cognitive abilities, psychologist Robert Sternberg defined intelligence by *analyzing* three kinds of reasoning processes that people use in solving problems. Sternberg (1985, 1997a) calls his approach the triarchic theory of intelligence.

*Sternberg's triarchic theory* says that intelligence can be divided into three different kinds of reasoning processes (*triarchic* means "three"). The first is using analytical or logical thinking skills that are measured by traditional intelligence tests. The second is using problem-solving skills that require creative thinking and the ability to learn from experience. The third is using practical thinking skills that help a person adjust to, and cope with, his or her sociocultural environment.

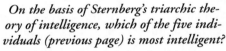

Analytical

Unlike Spearman's *g*, which measures general intelligence by measuring cognitive abilities, Sternberg's theory breaks intelligence down into three reasoning processes: analytical, problem-solving, and practical skills.

Problem solving

*On the basis of Sternberg's triarchic theory of intelligence, which of the five individuals (previous page) is most intelligent?*

According to Sternberg's triarchic theory, there isn't one kind of general intelligence for evaluating all individuals. Instead of trying to measure general intelligence, he would evaluate how much and how many of three different reasoning processes (analytical, problem solving, practical) each of the five used.

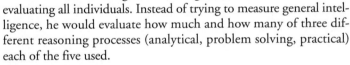

Practical

### ADVANTAGES AND DISADVANTAGES

One advantage of Sternberg's triarchic theory of intelligence is that it doesn't limit the definition of intelligence to cognitive abilities. Instead, Sternberg's theory evaluates a person's intelligence by measuring three different kinds of reasoning processes. For example, a person may be "street smart" or have exceptional practical reasoning skills but may not necessarily score high on traditional intelligence tests.

One disadvantage of the triarchic theory is that Sternberg has so far developed only a few tests to measure his proposed three kinds of reasoning processes (Lohman, 2000).

## Current Status

Currently, the majority of psychologists assume that *g* is a measure of general intelligence and that *g* is measured by current intelligence tests and represented by an IQ score (N. Brody, 2000). One reason the concept of *g* remains so popular is that most of the research on intelligence is based on the psychometric approach, from which the factor *g* was originally developed. In addition, standard intelligence tests have proved useful in predicting performance in academic settings but less so in career settings. Gardner's multiple-intelligence approach and Sternberg's triarchic approach attempt to replace *g*'s single measure of general intelligence (IQ score). These newer approaches suggest measuring additional abilities and reasoning that represent different kinds of intelligence (Sternberg, 2000a).

To see how far intelligence testing has come, we'll go back in time and discuss early attempts to define and measure intelligence.

# B. Measuring Intelligence

**Power Study™**

**Check out CD: Module 4**
B. Studying the Living Brain
H. Cultural Diversity: Brain
   Size & Racial Myths

## Earlier Attempts to Measure Intelligence

### HEAD SIZE AND INTELLIGENCE

**Are bigger brains better?**

Efforts to measure intelligence began in earnest in the late 1800s. That's when Francis Galton noticed that intelligent people often had intelligent relatives and concluded that intelligence was, to a large extent, biological or inherited. In trying to assess inherited intelligence, Galton measured people's heads and recorded the speed of their reactions to various sensory stimuli. However, his measures proved to be poorly related to intelligence or academic achievement (Gould, 1996).

Galton switched gears and tried to correlate head size with students' grade point average. For example, he reported that the average head size of Cambridge students who received A's was about 3.3% larger than that of students who received C's (Galton, 1888). However, a review of later studies showed a very low correlation of 0.19 between head size and intelligence (IQ scores) (Brody, 1992). Such a low correlation has little practical use in measuring or predicting intelligence. For this reason, using head size as a measure of intelligence was abandoned in favor of using skull or brain size.

### BRAIN SIZE AND INTELLIGENCE

Efforts to measure intelligence continued with the work of Paul Broca, a famous neurologist in the late 1800s. Broca claimed that there was a relationship between size of brain and intelligence, with larger brains indicating more intelligence. However, a later reanalysis of Broca's data indicated that measures of brain size proved to be unreliable and poorly correlated with intelligence (Gould, 1996).

More recently, MRI brain scans (p. 70) permit precise measurement of living brains and created new interest in correlating brain size and intelligence. Studies that used MRI scans reported a positive correlation of 0.32 and 0.39 between brain size and intelligence (IQ scores) (Egan et al., 1994; Wickett et al., 1994). However, such correlations indicate only that a relationship exists; they cannot tell us whether bigger brains lead to increased intelligence or whether more cognitive activity leads to bigger brains. Medium-sized correlations indicate a positive relationship between brain size and intelligence (IQ scores) but are too low to have practical value in actually predicting a person's intelligence.

### BRAIN SIZE AND ACHIEVEMENT

Early researchers were reluctant to give up the idea that bigger brains were better. They looked for a relationship between brain size and personal achievement, another measure of intelligence. However, as shown in the center illustration, there is enormous variation in brain size and achievement (Gould, 1996). Notice that Nobel Prize–winner Einstein's brain (1,230 grams) was slightly below average weight and that two famous authors, poet Walt Whitman (1,200 grams) and novelist Anatole France (1,000 grams), achieved literary fame with brains about half the weight of Jonathan Swift's (2,000 grams), one of the heaviest on record. For comparison, we have included a gorilla brain (500 grams), which is actually quite small considering the size of a gorilla head. It is difficult to test a gorilla's intelligence, but at least one is reported to have learned a vocabulary of 800 hand signs (Ross, 1991).

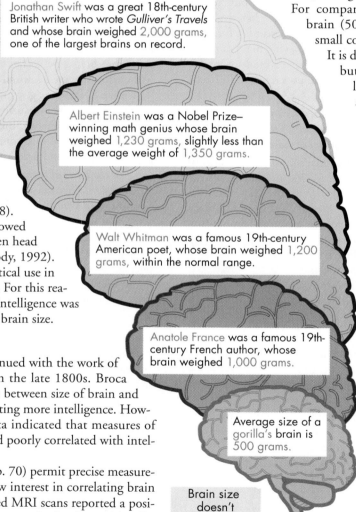

**Jonathan Swift** was a great 18th-century British writer who wrote *Gulliver's Travels* and whose brain weighed 2,000 grams, one of the largest brains on record.

**Albert Einstein** was a Nobel Prize–winning math genius whose brain weighed 1,230 grams, slightly less than the average weight of 1,350 grams.

**Walt Whitman** was a famous 19th-century American poet, whose brain weighed 1,200 grams, within the normal range.

**Anatole France** was a famous 19th-century French author, whose brain weighed 1,000 grams.

**Average size of a gorilla's brain is 500 grams.**

Brain size doesn't necessarily match performance.

### BRAIN SIZE, SEX DIFFERENCES, AND INTELLIGENCE

Still believing that bigger brains are better, some researchers claimed that women had lower IQ scores than men because women's brains weigh about 10% less than men's (Holden, 1995). However, a recent study of over 4,000 women and 6,000 men reported that there was little or no difference in intelligence (IQ scores) between men and women. Researchers concluded that the larger size of men's brains does not result in higher IQs (Colom et al., 2000).

### MEASURING INTELLIGENCE

As you have seen, there is a long history of scientists trying to measure intelligence. However, all the early attempts to use head, skull, body, or brain size to measure intelligence failed. In fact, a paper presented in 1904 to a German psychological society concluded that there was little hope of developing psychological tests to measure intelligence in an objective way (Wolf, 1973). What's interesting about this paper is that one of the authors was Alfred Binet, who went on to develop the first intelligence test.

We'll explain how Binet succeeded in developing an intelligence test when so many others had failed.

**Why did Binet develop an intelligence test?**

In the late 1800s, a gifted French psychologist named Alfred Binet realized that Broca and Galton had failed to assess intelligence by measuring brain size. Binet strongly believed that intelligence was a collection of mental abilities and that the best way to assess intelligence was to measure a person's ability to perform cognitive tasks, such as understanding the meanings of words or being able to follow directions.

Binet was very pessimistic about developing an intelligence test. By a strange twist of fate, he was appointed to a commission that was instructed to develop tests capable of differentiating children of normal intelligence from those who needed special help. Binet accepted this challenge with two goals in mind: The test must be easy to administer without requiring any special laboratory equipment, and the test must clearly distinguish between normal and abnormal mental ability (Brody, 1992). In 1905, Binet and psychiatrist Theodore Simon succeeded in developing the world's first standardized intelligence test, the Binet-Simon Intelligence Scale (Binet & Simon, 1905).

The ***Binet-Simon Intelligence Scale*** contained items arranged in order of increasing difficulty. The items measured vocabulary, memory, common knowledge, and other cognitive abilities.

Alfred Binet (1857–1911)

The purpose of this first Binet-Simon Intelligence Scale was to distinguish among mentally defective children in the Paris school system. In Binet's time, intellectually deficient children were divided into three groups: idiots (most severely deficient), imbeciles (moderate), and morons (mildest). These terms are no longer used today because they have taken on very negative meanings. The problems with this first test were that it classified children into only three categories (idiots, imbeciles, and morons) and that it did not have a way to express the results in a single score. However, several years later, Binet corrected both of these problems when he introduced the concept of mental level, or mental age.

## MENTAL AGE: MEASURE OF INTELLIGENCE

Binet and Simon revised their intelligence scale to solve several problems in their original scale. In this revised test, they arranged the test items in order of increasing difficulty and designed different items to measure different cognitive abilities. For each test item, Binet determined whether an average child of a certain age could answer the question correctly. For example, a child at age level 3 should be able to point to various parts of the face. A child at age level 9 should be able to recite the days of the week. Because the test items were arranged for each age level (age levels 3 to 13), this new test could identify which average age level the child performed at. If a particular child passed all the items that could be answered by an average 3-year-old but none of the items appropriate for older children, that child would be said to have a mental age of 3. Thus, if a 6-year-old child could answer only questions appropriate for a 3-year-old child, that child would be given a mental age of 3 and would be considered retarded in intellectual development. Binet's intelligence test became popular because a single score represented mental age.

Which items could an average 3-year-old answer?

Which items could an average 9-year-old answer?

***Mental age*** is a method of estimating a child's intellectual progress by comparing the child's score on an intelligence test to the scores of average children of the same age.

At this point, the Binet-Simon scale gave its results in terms of a mental age but not an IQ score. The idea for computing an IQ score did not occur until some years later, when it was revised by L. M. Terman.

**What was the big change?**

The first big change was when Binet and Simon introduced the concept of mental age. The second big change occurred in 1916, when Lewis Terman and his colleagues at Stanford University in California came up with a new and better method to compute the final score. Improving on the concept of expressing the test results in terms of mental age, Terman devised a formula to calculate an intelligence quotient (IQ) score (Terman, 1916).

***Intelligence quotient*** is computed by dividing a child's mental age (MA), as measured in an intelligence test, by the child's chronological age (CA) and multiplying the result by 100.

Remember that in Binet's test, mental age was calculated by noting how many items a child answered that were appropriate to a certain age. For example, if a 4-year-old girl passed the test items appropriate for a 5-year-old, she was said to have a mental age of 5. A child's chronological (physical) age is his or her age in months and years. To compute her IQ score, we use Terman's formula, shown below.

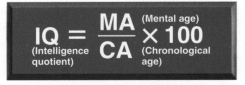
$$IQ_{\text{(Intelligence quotient)}} = \frac{MA_{\text{(Mental age)}}}{CA_{\text{(Chronological age)}}} \times 100$$

Formula for calculating IQ score

Thus, for the child in our example, we substitute 5 for MA, 4 for CA, and multiply by 100. We get: $5/4 = 1.25 \times 100 = 125$. So the child's IQ is 125. An IQ score computed in this traditional way is called a ***ratio IQ*** because the score represents a ratio of mental to chronological age. Today the ratio IQ has been replaced by the ***deviation IQ,*** whose computation is too complex to explain here. The reason for the switch from ratio IQ to deviation IQ is that deviation IQ scores more accurately reflect test performance as children get older.

Since the original Binet-Simon scale in 1905, IQ tests have become very popular and have grown into a large business. We'll look more closely at one of the most widely used IQ tests.

### Examples of IQ Tests

| **Is IQ the same as intelligence?** |
|---|

We are all curious to learn someone's IQ because we believe that this single score reveals a person's real intelligence. For example, try to match these IQ scores—104, 114, 228—with three famous people—John F. Kennedy, 35th president of the United States; J. D. Salinger, famous novelist *(Catcher in the Rye);* and Marilyn vos Savant, columnist for *Parade* magazine (answers on right). Knowing the IQ scores of these individuals tells us something of their cognitive abilities, but some psychologists believe that cognitive abilities represent only one kind of intelligence. For example, would you expect Salinger, with his average IQ, to write a very creative novel or Kennedy, with a slightly above average IQ, to become such a well-remembered president? The achievements of individuals with average or slightly above average IQs suggest that there are other kinds of intelligence, such as practical, emotional, social, and creative, which may be equally important to one's goals and success in life and career (Gardner, 1999; Sternberg, 2000a). Now, let's see how IQ scores are measured.

John F. Kennedy: 35th U.S. president

Marilyn vos Savant: columnist for *Parade* magazine

J. D. Salinger: author of *Catcher in the Rye*

**Answers:** *Salinger, 104; Kennedy, 114; and vos Savant, 228, the highest IQ on record (Cowley, 1994)*

---

### Wechsler Intelligence Scales

The most widely used IQ tests are the Wechsler Adult Intelligence Scale (WAIS-III), for ages 16 and older, and the Wechsler Intelligence Scale for Children (WISC-III), for children of ages 3–16. A trained examiner administers the Wechsler scales on a one-to-one basis.

The *Wechsler Adult Intelligence Scale (WAIS-III)* and *Wechsler Intelligence Scale for Children (WISC-III)* have items that are organized into various subtests. For example, the verbal section contains a subtest of general information, a subtest of vocabulary, and so forth. The performance section contains a subtest that involves arranging pictures in a meaningful order, one that requires assembling objects, and one that involves using codes. The verbal and performance scores are combined to give a single IQ score.

Examples of the subtests for WAIS-III are shown on the right. The Verbal Scale (top right) emphasizes language and verbal skills. Because of this emphasis, a person from a deprived environment or for whom English is a second language might have difficulty on this scale because of lack of verbal knowledge rather than lack of cognitive ability.

In an attempt to measure nonverbal skills and rule out other cultural or educational problems, Wechsler added the Performance Scale (lower right). These performance subtests, which measure problem-solving abilities, require considerable concentration and focused effort, which may be difficult for individuals who are very nervous, are poor test takers, or have emotional problems. Although these IQ tests carefully try to measure verbal and nonverbal abilities, you can see that part of one's success on IQ tests depends on nonintellectual factors, such as cultural, educational, or emotional factors (Kaplan & Saccuzzo, 2001). We'll discuss other problems with IQ tests later in this module.

One reason these IQ tests are widely used is that they have two characteristics of good tests: validity and reliability.

#### WAIS-III Verbal Scale: Subtests

**Subtests for the verbal scale include information, comprehension, arithmetic, similarities, digit span, and vocabulary. These examples resemble the WAIS-III items.**

*Information*
On what continent is France?

*Comprehension*
Why are children required to go to school?

*Arithmetic*
How many hours will it take to drive 150 miles at 50 miles per hour?

*Similarities*
How are a calculator and a typewriter alike?

*Digit span*
Repeat the following numbers backward: 2, 4, 3, 5, 8, 9, 6.

*Vocabulary*
What does *audacity* mean?

#### WAIS-III Performance Scale: Subtests

**Subtests for the performance scale include digit symbol, block design, picture completion, picture arrangement, and object assembly. These sample items shown on the right resemble those given for each WAIS-III subtest.**

*Digit symbol*

Shown:
1 2 3 4
○ □ △ ⊙

Fill in:
1 4 3 2
_ _ _ _

*Block design*
Assemble blocks to match this design.

*Picture completion*
Tell me what is missing.

*Picture arrangement*
Put the pictures in the right order.

*Object assembly*
Assemble the pieces into a complete object.

### Can you analyze handwriting?

How truthful are the claims that intelligence and other personality traits can be identified through analyzing handwriting (Searles, 1998)? For example, which one of the four handwriting samples on the right indicates the highest IQ? (Answer at bottom of page.)

Although handwriting analysis may claim to measure intelligence, research shows that its accuracy is usually no better than a good guess (Tripician, 2000).

1. So intelligent
2. so intelligent
3. so intelligent
4. so intelligent

Which handwriting sample, 1, 2, 3, or 4, is from the person with the highest IQ?

The reason handwriting analysis or so-called IQ tests in popular magazines are poor measures of intelligence (IQ) is that they lack at least one of the two important characteristics of a good test. These two characteristics are validity and reliability, which mark the difference between an accurate IQ test (WAIS-III) and an inaccurate test (handwriting analysis).

---

### Validity

Handwriting analysis is fun, but it is a very poor intelligence test because it lacks validity, which is one of the two characteristics of a good test.

*Validity* means that the test measures what it is supposed to measure.

Although the definition of validity seems simple and short, this characteristic makes or breaks a test. For example, numerous studies have shown that handwriting analysis has little or no validity as an intelligence or personality test (Basil, 1989; Feder, 1987). Because handwriting analysis lacks the characteristic of validity, it means that this test does not accurately measure what it is supposed to measure. Thus, a test with little or no validity produces results that could be produced by guessing or by chance.

The reason handwriting analysis or tests in popular magazines are not checked for validity is that checking validity is a long, expensive, and complicated process. One way to show a test's validity is to give the new test to hundreds of subjects along with other tests whose validity has already been established. Then the subjects' scores on the new test are correlated with their scores on the tests with proven validity. Another way that the validity of intelligence tests, such as the WAIS-III, was established was to show that IQ scores correlated with another measure of intelligence, such as academic performance (A. S. Kaufman, 2000).

However, if IQ scores are valid measures of cognitive abilities and correlate with academic performance, why do some individuals with high IQs do poorly in college? The developer of the Head Start program, Ed Zigler, believes that academic performance depends on three factors: cognitive abilities; achievement, or the amount of knowledge that a person has accumulated; and motivation (Zigler, 1995). This means that a person may have outstanding cognitive abilities but may lack either the achievement or the motivation to succeed in college.

Besides validity, a good intelligence test should also have reliability.

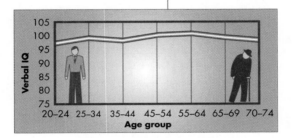

No change in VERBAL IQ scores in seven different age groups indicates that test is reliable.

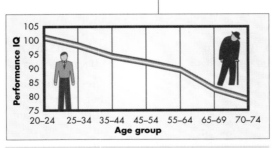

Decrease in OVERALL IQ scores across ages is due to psychological and physiological changes and not reliability problems with IQ test.

---

### Reliability

If your style of handwriting remained constant over time, such as always boldly crossing your *t*'s, then this trait would be reliable.

*Reliability* refers to consistency: A person's score on a test at one point in time should be similar to the score obtained by the same person on a similar test at a later point in time.

For example, if boldly crossed *t*'s indicated that a person is intelligent, then this measure of intelligence would be reliable. However, there is no evidence that boldly crossed *t*'s indicate that a person is intelligent. So, in this case, handwriting analysis would be a reliable test of intelligence, but since it lacks validity (doesn't measure intelligence) it is a worthless test of intelligence.

Now, suppose you took the WAIS-III as a senior in high school and then retook the test as a junior in college. You would find that your IQ scores would be much the same because each time you would be compared with others of your same age. Because your IQ scores remain similar across time, it would mean that the Wechsler scales, like other standardized IQ tests, have reliability (Berg, 2000).

For example, the top graph shows the results of verbal IQ scores when seven different age groups of subjects were given the WAIS-III. Notice that verbal IQ scores are quite stable from ages 20 to 74, indicating that the Wechsler scales score high in reliability (Kaufman et al., 1989).

But notice that the lower graph shows that there is an overall decrease in performance IQ scores from ages 20 to 74 (Kaufman et al., 1989). However, this general decrease in performance scores across one's lifetime reflects changes in psychological and physiological functioning rather than a decrease in the test's reliability.

Researchers have shown that current intelligence tests, which measure primarily cognitive abilities, have relatively good validity and reliability (Kaplan & Saccuzzo, 2001). Even though IQ scores can be measured with good reliability and validity, our next question to answer is: What good or use are IQ scores?

(Handwriting answer: I wrote all four samples so that no matter which one you picked, I would come out a winner.)

## Normal Distribution of IQ Scores

IQ 50–85

The photo on the left is of Chris Burke, who starred in the television series "Life Goes On." Burke has Down syndrome, a genetic defect that results in varying degrees of mental retardation and physical symptoms (slanting eyes, flattened nose, visual problems). Although Burke has mild or borderline mental retardation, he was able to act in the series and functions very well outside an institution. We are guessing that Burke's IQ is between 50 and 85.

In comparison, the photo on the right is of Marilyn vos Savant, who writes a column for *Parade* magazine and has a reported IQ of 228, the highest on record. To compare the IQs of Burke and vos Savant with those of other people, we need to look at the distribution of IQ scores. IQ scores from established intelligence tests, such as the WAIS-III, are said to have a normal distribution.

A *normal distribution* refers to a statistical arrangement of scores so that they resemble the shape of a bell and, thus, is said to be a bell-shaped curve. A bell-shaped curve means the vast majority of scores fall in the middle range, with fewer scores falling near the two extreme ends of the curve.

IQ 228

For example, a normal distribution of IQ scores is shown at the left and is bell-shaped. The average IQ score is 100, and 95% of IQ scores fall between 70 and 130. An IQ of 70 and below is one sign of mild retardation. An IQ of 145 or higher is one indication of a gifted individual. Thus, one widespread use of IQ tests is to provide general *categories* regarding mental abilities.

Next, we'll examine these guidelines in more detail, beginning with mental retardation.

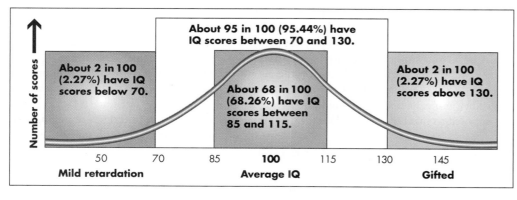

**About 95 in 100 (95.44%) have IQ scores between 70 and 130.**

**About 2 in 100 (2.27%) have IQ scores below 70.**

**About 68 in 100 (68.26%) have IQ scores between 85 and 115.**

**About 2 in 100 (2.27%) have IQ scores above 130.**

Number of scores

50    70    85    **100**    115    130    145

**Mild retardation**        **Average IQ**        **Gifted**

## Mental Retardation: IQ Scores

**What is mental retardation?**

One use of IQ scores has been to help identify individuals with mental retardation, which was Binet's original goal.

*Mental retardation* refers to a substantial limitation in present functioning that is characterized by significantly subaverage intellectual functioning, along with related limitations in two of ten areas, including communication, self-care, home living, social skills, and safety (American Association on Mental Retardation, 1993).

Psychologists caution against using IQ scores as the sole test for mental retardation. IQ tests are usually used in combination with observations of adaptive skills, which include social, home living, and communication skills. On the basis of IQ scores and adaptive skills, three levels of retardation have been identified.

**1 BORDERLINE MENTALLY RETARDED**

These individuals have IQs that range from 50 to 75. With special training and educational opportunities, they can learn to read and write, gain social competency, master simple occupational skills, and become self-supporting members of society. About 70% of individuals with retardation are in this category.

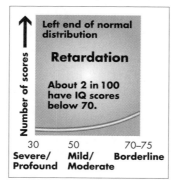

Left end of normal distribution

**Retardation**

About 2 in 100 have IQ scores below 70.

Number of scores

30    50    70–75
**Severe/**  **Mild/**  **Borderline**
**Profound**  **Moderate**

**2 MILDLY/MODERATELY MENTALLY RETARDED**

These individuals have IQs that range from 35 to 50. With special training and educational opportunities, they can learn to become partially independent in their everyday lives, provided they are in a family or self-help setting.

**3 SEVERELY/PROFOUNDLY MENTALLY RETARDED**

These individuals have IQs that range from 20 to 40. With special training and educational opportunities, they can acquire limited skills in taking care of their personal needs. However, because of retarded motor and verbal abilities, they require considerable supervision their entire lives.

**4 CAUSES**

There are two general types of mental retardation—organic and cultural-familial.

*Organic retardation* results from genetic problems or brain damage. Chris Burke is an example of someone with organic retardation.

*Cultural-familial retardation* results from a greatly impoverished environment. There is no evidence of genetic or brain damage.

Approximately 5 million Americans have various degrees of mental retardation.

Next, we move to the middle of IQ's normal distribution.

Since the vast majority of people, about 95%, have IQ scores that fall between 70 and 130, it is interesting to see what IQ scores can tell us.

### DO IQ SCORES PREDICT ACADEMIC ACHIEVEMENT?

Because IQ tests measure cognitive abilities that are similar to those used in academic settings, it is no surprise that there is a medium-strength association, or correlation, between IQ scores and grades (0.50), between IQ scores and reading scores for grade school children (0.38 to 0.46), and between IQ scores and total years of education that people complete (0.50) (Brody, 1997). These medium-strength correlations mean that IQ scores are moderately good at predicting academic performance. However, based on medium-strength correlations alone, it would be difficult to predict a *specific person's academic performance* because performance in academic settings also depends on personal characteristics, such as one's interest in school and willingness to study (Neisser et al., 1996).

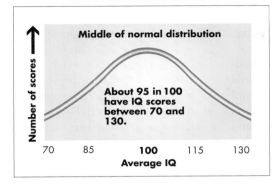

Middle of normal distribution

Number of scores

About 95 in 100 have IQ scores between 70 and 130.

70  85  **100**  115  130
**Average IQ**

IQ scores are useful for predicting academic success.

### DO IQ SCORES PREDICT JOB PERFORMANCE?

The correlation between IQ scores and job performance is about 0.30 to 0.50. This low- to medium-strength correlation means that IQ scores are weakly related to job performance (Neisser et al., 1996). Because the correlation between IQ scores and job performance is of low to medium strength, it would be very difficult to predict a *specific person's job performance* solely on the basis of his or her IQ score. In fact, researchers argue that job performance requires not only cognitive abilities, which are measured by traditional intelligence tests, but also practical intelligence, such as how to solve problems and get the job done, which is not measured by traditional intelligence tests (Sternberg & Wagner, 1993). Thus, IQ scores alone are relatively good at predicting academic performance but less successful at predicting job performance.

Now, we'll examine the right end of the normal distribution—high IQ scores.

IQ scores are somewhat useful at predicting job performance.

**What if you had a very high IQ score?**

Sometimes impressive cognitive abilities appear at a relatively early age. For instance, at 8 months Masoud Karkehadadi began talking; at 18 months he had memorized the top tunes on MTV; at 7 he took the high school equivalency exam and scored 100%; and at age 12 he graduated from the University of California at Irvine. Masoud's IQ, which is 200-plus, places him in the genius range and at the gifted end of the normal curve (*Los Angeles Times*, May 23, 1994). Although researchers and educators differ in how they define *gifted*, here is one definition that refers to academically gifted children.

A moderately *gifted* child is usually defined by an IQ score between 130 and 150; a profoundly gifted child has an IQ score about 180 or above.

When placed in *regular classrooms*, gifted children face a number of problems: They may be viewed as different—labeled as nerds or geeks—and are not challenged by the material. For these reasons, one researcher recommends that gifted children be placed in special academic programs that challenge and help gifted children develop their potentials (Winner, 2000).

### HOW DO GIFTED INDIVIDUALS TURN OUT?

In the early 1920s, Lewis Terman selected a sample of over 1,500 gifted children with IQs ranging from 130 to 200 (the average

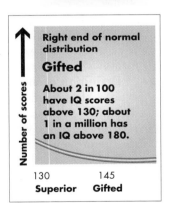

Right end of normal distribution

**Gifted**

Number of scores

About 2 in 100 have IQ scores above 130; about 1 in a million has an IQ above 180.

130  145
**Superior  Gifted**

was 151). Over the next 65 years, researchers repeatedly tested these individuals to determine what they had achieved and how they had adjusted. Although 10–30% of the more gifted males obtained advanced degrees compared with men in the general population, 30% never finished college, and 2% actually flunked out. Although gifted individuals generally showed health, adjustment, and achievement better than those of people with average IQs, about 9% had serious emotional problems, and 7% committed suicide (Holahan & Sears, 1995; Terman & Oden, 1959). As a group, these gifted individuals were generally very successful in life but not at the extraordinary level that might have been expected or predicted from their very high IQ scores (Colangelo, 1997). For example, do you think Marilyn vos Savant's (right photo) career as a magazine writer who solves difficult puzzles matches her extraordinary high IQ score?

**Conclusion.** IQ scores have proven moderately useful in predicting academic performance, in helping to define mental retardation, and in identifying the gifted, but they have low to moderate

IQ 228

success in predicting job performance. One reason IQ scores are not more predictive is that they do not measure numerous emotional, motivational, and personality factors that also influence behavior.

While IQ tests have proved useful, we'll next examine potential problems in taking and interpreting IQ tests.

# D. Potential Problems of IQ Testing

## Binet's Two Warnings

**What problems did Binet foresee?**

You may remember that Binet's original goal was to develop a test that would distinguish between normal and abnormal mental abilities and thus identify children who were mentally retarded and needed special help and education. Although previous attempts to measure intelligence had failed, Binet and Simon succeeded in developing the first scale that identified children with varying degrees of mental retardation. Binet and Simon's scale was the beginning of the modern-day IQ test. However, even in the early 1900s, Binet realized that intelligence tests could be used in two potentially dangerous ways, so he issued the following two warnings:

### BINET'S WARNINGS

**1** Binet warned that *intelligence tests do not measure innate abilities or natural intelligence;* rather, they measure an individual's cognitive abilities, which result from both heredity and environment.

**2** Binet warned that *intelligence tests, by themselves, should not be used to label people* (for example, "moron," "average," "genius"); rather, intelligence tests should be used to assess an individual's abilities and used in combination with other information to make academic or placement decisions about people.

History shows that neither of Binet's warnings were heeded. In the early 1900s it became common practice to treat IQ scores as measures of innate intelligence and to use IQ scores to label people from "moron" to "genius." The U.S. Congress went so far as to pass laws that restricted immigrants based on assumed levels of innate intelligence (Gould, 1996), an issue we'll discuss in Cultural Diversity.

Along with using IQ scores to label individuals came racial and cultural discrimination, some of which continue to the present. For example, a controversial book, *The Bell Curve* (Herrnstein & Murray, 1994), suggests that racial differences in IQ scores are due primarily to genetic factors, something we'll discuss later in this module. For now, we'll examine four issues surrounding IQ tests: racial discrimination, cultural bias, culture-free IQ tests, and nonintellectual factors.

IQ tests have a history of being used to discriminate.

## Racial Discrimination

**Are IQ tests racially biased?**

There have been a number of court cases regarding the appropriate use of IQ tests. Here is one important case and the judge's ruling.

Larry was an African American child who was assigned to special classes for the educable mentally retarded because he scored below 85 on an IQ test. However, several years later an African American psychologist retested Larry and found that his IQ score was higher than originally thought. Larry was taken out of the special classes, which were considered a dead end, and placed in regular classes that allowed for more advancement. On the basis of Larry's experience, a class action suit was brought against the San Francisco school system on behalf of all African American schoolchildren in the district. The suit was based on the finding that, although African American youngsters made up 27% of all the students enrolled in classes for the mentally retarded, they composed only 4% of the entire school population (Kaplan & Saccuzzo, 2001). African American parents wanted to know why their children were so much more numerous than White children in these special classes. They felt there must be a bias against African American children in the selection process.

IQ tests alone should not be used to define mental retardation.

Although Larry's case came to trial in the early 1970s, the final decision was given in 1979 by a judge of the federal court of appeals. The judge agreed with the African American parents and found that IQ tests being used in schools (kindergarten through grade 12) to determine mental retardation were biased against people of color. The court ruled that California schools could not place children of color in classes for children with mental retardation on the basis of the IQ test alone. The schools were instructed to come up with an intelligence test that does not favor Whites or else refrain from using a standardized test to identify slow learners.

**Definition of mental retardation.** In other states, IQ tests are used to define mental retardation, even though these states do not always agree on the definition. For example, in Ohio, a child with an IQ below 80 is considered mentally retarded, while across the border in Kentucky, the same child is placed in a regular classroom and taught along with all the other students. In 39 states, African American students are overrepresented in spe-

$$IQ = \frac{MA}{CA} \times 100$$

(Intelligence quotient) (Mental age) (Chronological age)

cial education classes, especially when they are students in predominately White school districts. Critics of the special education system argue that African American students are overrepresented not because of their especially high level of disability but because of discriminatory placement procedures, such as the culturally biased IQ tests (Shapiro et al., 1993).

**Educational decisions.** Based on the concerns discussed above, psychologists and educators recommend that IQ tests alone not be used as the primary basis for making decisions about a child's educational future. Instead, they suggest that educational decisions, especially about placing a child in a special education class, be made only after considering a wide range of information, which may include IQ scores but also samples of the child's behavior from other situations (Detterman & Thompson, 1997).

## Cultural Bias

**Can the same questions be used?**

One criticism of IQ tests is that they are culturally biased, especially in favor of industrialized communities, such as the White middle class in the United States (Serpell, 2000).

*Cultural bias* means that the wording of the questions and the experiences on which they are based are more familiar to members of some social groups than to others.

For example, consider this question from an older version of the Wechsler Intelligence Scale for Children: "What would you do if you were sent to buy a loaf of bread and the grocer said he did not have anymore?"

If you think the answer is "Go to another store," you are correct according to the developers of the Wechsler scale. However, when 200 minority children were asked this same question, 61 said they would go home. Asked to explain their answers, they gave reasonable

IQ tests are accused of being culturally biased.

explanations. Some children answered "Go home" because there were no other stores in their neighborhood. Yet the answer "Go home" would be scored "incorrect," despite its correctness in the child's experience (Hardy et al., 1976). This example shows that children of color may have different cultural influences, experiences, and standards that may penalize them on standardized tests of intelligence (Boykin, 1996).

Researchers suggest that IQ tests are culturally biased because they measure accumulated knowledge and problem-solving strategies that depend on environmental opportunities available in a particular culture or group (Suzuki & Valencia, 1997). In addition, because IQ tests involve being asked and answering questions, children who have had such experience in their homes or schools would be better able to take these tests. However, in some cultures, parents do not engage in question-and-answer sessions with their children as parents commonly do in many Western cultures (Greenfield, 1997). This is another example of how cultural influences can affect a child's performance on standard IQ tests.

## Culture-Free Tests

**Is such a test possible?**

Psychologists have attempted to develop culture-free tests.

A *culture-free test* does not contain vocabulary, experiences, or social situations that are very different from the cultural experiences of the individual taking the test.

However, the construction of culture-free tests has not been entirely successful, and some suggest that cultural bias in IQ tests cannot be avoided (Greenfield, 1997). One approach to developing culture-free tests is proposed by ecological psychology.

*Ecological psychology* says that we should measure intelligence by observing how people solve problems in their usual settings and environments.

Ecological psychology suggests measuring how people solve real problems rather than answer questions on tests.

For instance, researchers found that dairy workers, bartenders, salespeople, and waiters regularly solved complex problems in more efficient ways than standard IQ tests predict (Scribner et al., 1986).

In another setting, people from Micronesia demonstrate remarkable navigational skills as they sail long distances, using only information from stars and sea currents. These navigational abilities indicate a high degree of intelligence that might not show up on traditional IQ tests.

Ecological psychologists stress that intelligence should be measured by how well people adapt to and solve problems in their environments rather than answer questions on IQ tests (Ceci et al., 1997). Besides potential biases from cultural differences, another problem in taking IQ tests comes from nonintellectual factors.

## Nonintellectual Factors

**What if a person is nervous?**

Maria is 11 years old and has been in the United States for two years. She had a hard time learning English, is not doing well in school, and is terrified about taking tests. Maria comes to take an IQ test, and the psychologist tries to put her at ease. However, Maria is so afraid of failing the IQ test that she just sits and stares at the floor. The psychologist says, "I'm going to give you a word and you tell me what it means. What is a bed?" Maria is now so anxious that she can't concentrate or think of what to say, so she remains silent.

Maria will probably do poorly on this IQ test because of nonintellectual factors.

IQ scores are influenced by nonintellectual factors (shyness).

*Nonintellectual factors* refer to noncognitive factors, such as attitude, experience, and emotional functioning, that may help or hinder performance on tests.

For example, nonintellectual factors such as Maria's shyness, fear of strange situations, and anxiety about failing would certainly hinder her test performance. In comparison, a child who is more outgoing and used to taking tests has the kind of nonintellectual factors that would aid performance. It is well established that numerous nonintellectual factors can have a great influence on how a person performs on IQ tests (Kaplan & Saccuzzo, 2001).

Next, we'll discuss one of the oldest questions about intelligence, the nature-nurture question.

# E. Nature-Nurture Question

## Definitions

### What is the nature-nurture question?

*Midori, child prodigy: "If I went back, I would probably do everything differently."*

At the beginning of this module, we told you about Midori (right photo), who began playing violin at age 3 and made her professional debut at age 10. Because Midori was a musical genius at such an early age, her exceptional skill was due to nature or heredity, that is, something she was born with. She played professionally until age 23, when she suddenly withdrew for four months. The official reason for her sudden withdrawal was a "digestive disorder," but some reports said that she was actually suffering from an eating disorder. Midori's problem raises questions about how best to nurture or help and care for a child genius who must learn to adjust to difficult personal and professional pressures in his or her environment (Cariaga, 1995). The difficulty Midori faced in balancing nature or heredity factors (being a child genius) with nurture or environmental factors (having personal and professional pressures) raises the nature-nurture question.

The *nature-nurture question* asks how much nature—hereditary or genetic factors—and how much nurture—environmental factors—contributes to the development of intellectual, emotional, personal, and social abilities.

In the early 1900s, the answer to the nature-nurture question was nature because intelligence was believed to be inherited (Terman, 1916). In the 1950s, the answer changed because psychology was heavily influenced by behaviorism, which emphasized nurture and environmental factors affecting intelligence (Skinner, 1953). We'll discuss newer research which shows that nature and nurture contribute about equally to the development of intelligence (Grigorenko, 2000).

## Twin Studies

### How much do genes contribute?

In answering the nature-nurture question regarding intelligence, researchers compared IQ scores in siblings (brothers and sisters) and in fraternal and identical twins.

*Fraternal twins,* like siblings (brothers and sisters), develop from separate eggs and have 50% of their genes in common.

*Identical twins* develop from a single egg and thus have identical genes, which means that they have 100% of their genes in common.

If genetic factors make a significant contribution to intelligence, then IQ scores of identical twins (100% of genes in common) should be more similar than those of fraternal twins (50% of genes in common). However, in answering the nature-nurture question about the hereditary or genetic influences on intelligence, you must keep two things in mind: how intelligence is defined and what genetic influence means.

**How intelligence is defined.** Most researchers define intelligence as relating to Spearman's *g* factor (see p. 282), which is measured by performance on cognitive tests and indicated by IQ scores. However, some researchers argue that there are other, equally important kinds of intelligence, such as practical (adjusting to one's environment), social (interacting with others), emotional (perceiving and understanding emotions), as well as creative, musical, and insightful intelligence (Gardner, 1999; Sternberg, 1997a). As discussed earlier, these kinds of intelligence are not measured by standard IQ tests.

**What genetic influence means.** When researchers report that genetic factors influence intelligence (IQ scores), they mean only that genetic factors influence cognitive abilities to varying degrees (Grigorenko, 2000). It does not mean that intelligence is fixed, written in stone, or predetermined solely by genetic factors.

**Results.** There are now over 100 separate studies on over 10,000 pairs of twins and siblings. The consistent finding from all these studies is that identical twins, whether reared apart or together, were more similar in IQ scores than were fraternal twins. In turn, fraternal twins were more similar in IQ scores than siblings.

For example, the center graph shows that the correlation between IQ scores was 0.85 for identical twins reared together, 0.60 for fraternal twins reared together, and 0.45 for siblings reared together (Plomin & Petrill, 1997).

**Conclusions.** Based on these kinds of studies, researchers have concluded that genetic factors (nature) contribute about 50% to intelligence (IQ scores) and environmental factors (nurture) contribute about 50% (Grigorenko, 2000). Researchers believed that genetic influence on intelligence would be greatest in childhood but would decrease with increasing experience. However, a study of 240 twins, who were 80 years or older, found that genetic influence on intelligence remained relatively constant throughout life and did not change with increasing experience (McClearn et al., 1997).

The reason genetic factors influence but do not fix or predetermine intelligence is that genetic factors contribute 50% to intelligence (IQ scores). The other 50% comes from environmental factors, which we'll examine next.

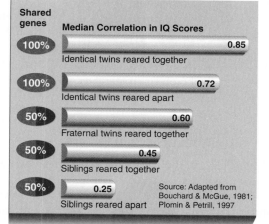

| Shared genes | Median Correlation in IQ Scores |
|---|---|
| 100% | Identical twins reared together — 0.85 |
| 100% | Identical twins reared apart — 0.72 |
| 50% | Fraternal twins reared together — 0.60 |
| 50% | Siblings reared together — 0.45 |
| 50% | Siblings reared apart — 0.25 |

Source: Adapted from Bouchard & McGue, 1981; Plomin & Petrill, 1997

**How much does environment contribute?**

What would happen if children with limited social-educational opportunities and low IQs were adopted by parents who could provide increased social-educational opportunities? Researchers reasoned that if environmental factors influence the development of intelligence, then providing increased environmental opportunities should increase IQ scores.

A group of French researchers studied children who had been abandoned as babies by their lower-class parents and adopted during the first six months of life into upper-middle-class families. The researchers found that the mean IQ of the adopted children was 14 points higher than that of similar children born and raised in lower-class settings by their natural parents. In addition, the adopted children were four times less likely to fail in school. This study suggests that by improving environmental factors—for example, increasing social-educational opportunities—intellectual development (as measured by IQ scores) and performance in the classroom can be improved (Schiff et al., 1982).

Children adopted into advantaged homes had higher IQ scores.

In a similar study, African American children from impoverished environments were adopted into middle-class families, some White and some African American; all of the families provided many social-educational opportunities for the adopted children. Researchers found that the IQs of the adopted children were as much as 10 points higher than those of African American children who were raised in disadvantaged homes (Scarr & Weinberg, 1976). In a follow-up study, researchers reported that the adopted children, now adolescents, had higher IQ scores than African American children raised in their own community (Weinberg et al., 1992).

These kinds of studies show that children with poor educational opportunities and low IQ scores can show an increase in IQ scores when they are adopted into families that provide increased educational opportunities. Based on data from adoption studies, researchers concluded that nurture or environmental factors contribute to intellectual development (Duyme, 1999).

---

**Interaction: Nature and Nurture**

**What is heritability?**

In the last 10 years, researchers have made significant progress in answering the nature-nurture question, and one tool they have used is a number called heritability.

*Heritability* is a number that indicates the amount or proportion of some ability, characteristic, or trait that can be attributed to genetic factors (nature).

For example, the figure below shows that heritability (nature) for overall intelligence (measured by IQ tests) was about 50%, which means that 50% of general cognitive ability comes from genetic factors. Researchers were also able to calculate the heritability scores for specific cognitive abilities, such as spatial ability (32%), verbal ability (55%), and memory (55%) (McClearn et al., 1997). These studies on heritability show that genetic factors (nature) contribute about half to intelligence.

The next big step in genetic research is the identification of specific genes or groups of genes that contribute to specific cognitive traits used to measure intelligence (Grigorenko, 2000).

Notice that the heritability numbers in the graph on the left are in the 50% range, which means that genes do not determine or fix these abilities, because the other 50% is coming from environmental fac-

**Estimates of Heritability**

Nature — genetic factors

Nurture — environmental factors

| Intelligence (general abilities) | |
|---|---|
| 50% | 50% |

| Spatial ability | |
|---|---|
| 32% | 68% |

| Verbal ability | |
|---|---|
| 55% | 45% |

| Memory | |
|---|---|
| 55% | 45% |

tors. You can think of genetic factors as establishing a range of potential abilities or behaviors, which are shaped and molded through interaction with one's environment. This idea of how genetic factors operate is called the reaction range (Bouchard, 1997).

*Reaction range* indicates the extent to which traits, abilities, or IQ scores may increase or decrease as a result of interaction with environmental factors.

Researchers estimate that the reaction range may vary up or down by as much as 10–15 points in one's IQ score. For example, the figure on the right shows that a person's IQ may vary from 85 to 110, depending on whether he or she has an impoverished or enriched environment (Zigler & Seitz, 1982).

**Conclusion.** The studies on heritability, twins, and adopted children provide an answer to the nature-nurture question: Nature or heredity contributes about 50% to intelligence (IQ) and environment or nurture contributes about 50%. However, a person's IQ can vary by 10–15 points (IQ reaction range), depending on how heredity interacts with different kinds of environments.

Next, we'll examine the debate over racial differences in IQ scores.

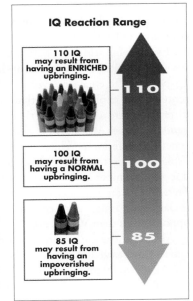

**IQ Reaction Range**

110 IQ may result from having an ENRICHED upbringing.

110

100 IQ may result from having a NORMAL upbringing.

100

85 IQ may result from having an impoverished upbringing.

85

# E. Nature-Nurture Question

## Racial Controversy

**What is the latest controversy?**

In the early 1900s, psychologists believed that intelligence was primarily inherited. This idea reappeared in a relatively recent book, *The Bell Curve,* by psychologist Richard Herrnstein and political scientist Charles Murray (1994). But what brought these authors the greatest publicity was their statement that racial differences in IQ scores were caused primarily by genetic or inherited factors. This and other statements from Herrnstein and Murray's book set off such a heated and often misguided public debate that the American Psychological Association (APA) formed a special task force of prominent researchers. The goal of the APA task force was to summarize what is currently known about intelligence (Neisser et al., 1996). We have already discussed many of the issues raised in the APA report and will now focus on the difficult and complex question of racial differences in IQ scores.

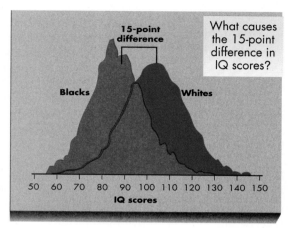

*15-point difference*

Blacks

Whites

What causes the 15-point difference in IQ scores?

50  60  70  80  90  100  110  120  130  140  150
**IQ scores**

### Difference between IQ Scores

**Findings.** To help you understand the controversy surrounding racial differences in IQ scores, please look at the figure in the upper right. Notice that there are two distributions of IQ scores: the red bell-shaped curve shows the distribution of IQ scores for African Americans (Blacks), and the blue bell-shaped curve shows the distribution of scores for Caucasians (Whites). Although there is much overlap in IQ scores (indicated by overlapping of red and blue areas), researchers generally agree that the average or mean IQ score for African Americans is about 15 points lower than the average IQ score for Caucasians (Bouchard, 1995). This 15-point average difference in IQ scores means that although there are many African Americans with high IQ scores, they are proportionally fewer in number compared to Caucasians.

**Two explanations.** There are at least two possible explanations for this 15-point difference in average IQ scores. One explanation is that the differences are due to inherited or *genetic factors:* African Americans are genetically inferior to Whites. Another explanation is that the difference is due to a number of **environmental factors:** African Americans have fewer social, economic, and educational opportunities than Whites do.

Although the authors of *The Bell Curve* emphasized the first explanation (genetic factors), you'll see that the APA task force and many other psychologists disagreed.

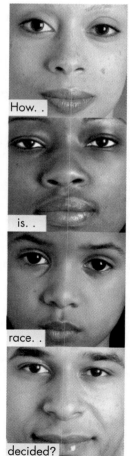

How. .

is. .

race. .

decided?

### Cause of IQ Differences

**Group differences.** In a careful review of *The Bell Curve,* one of the leading researchers in the area of intelligence concluded that the book offered no convincing evidence that genetic factors were primarily responsible for the 15-point IQ difference between African Americans and Caucasians (Sternberg, 1995). This conclusion is based largely on the distinction between whether genetic factors can influence the development of intelligence in an individual and whether they can influence different development of intelligence among races. The APA task force said that there is good evidence that genetic factors play a significant role in the development of an **individual's intelligence.** However, there is no convincing evidence that genetic factors play a primary role in the development of differences in intelligence **among races.** Thus, the APA task forced challenged Herrnstein and Murray's statement that IQ **differences among races** are caused primarily by genetic factors (Neisser et al., 1996).

Although no one knows exactly what causes the differences in IQ scores shown in the above graph, the APA task force as well as many other psychologists suggest a number of environmental factors, such as differences in social-economic classes, educational opportunities, family structure, and career possibilities (Loehlin, 2000). Thus, one of *The Bell Curve*'s major conclusions—that racial differences in IQ scores are based primarily on genetic factors—is not supported by the evidence (Neisser et al., 1996). Two prominent researchers concluded that *The Bell Curve*'s argument for racial inferiority appeared to be based on scientific evidence, but closer examination shows that it was not (Gould, 1996; Sternberg, 1995).

**Differences in skin color.** Another problem with *The Bell Curve* is its assumption that skin color is a meaningful way to separate races. For example, based on skin color, to which race would you assign the individuals in the four photos on the left? Researchers report that skin color is meaningless in identifying racial makeup because recent studies on DNA (genetic instructions) estimate that people around the world are more alike than different and that 99.9% of genetic instructions are the same in everyone (Freeman, 2000). This means that, no matter the color of one's skin, genetic instructions in people around the world vary by about 0.01%. Therefore, differences in skin color among races are essentially only "skin deep" and cannot be used to scientifically assign people to different races (Venter, 2000).

After the Concept Review, we'll discuss how early racial discrimination was based on IQ scores.

# Concept Review

**1.** One approach to measuring intelligence focuses on quantifying cognitive factors or abilities that are involved in intellectual performance; this is called the (a)_____ approach. Charles Spearman used this approach to develop a two-factor theory of intelligence: one factor is **g**, or (b)_____; the second factor is **s**, or (c)_____.

**2.** In comparison to Spearman's two-factor approach, Howard Gardner's theory says that there are seven kinds of _____, such as verbal skills, math skills, spatial skills, and movement skills.

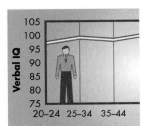

**3.** Another approach to measuring intelligence studies how people gather information to solve problems or acquire information; this is called the (a)_____ approach. An example of this approach is Robert Sternberg's (b)_____ theory of intelligence.

**4.** Alfred Binet developed an intelligence test that estimated intellectual progress by comparing a child's score on an intelligence test to the scores of average children of the same age. Binet called this concept _____.

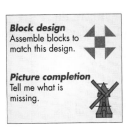

**5.** Lewis Terman revised Binet's intelligence test, and the most significant change he made was to develop a formula to compute a single score that represents a person's (a)_____. This formula is IQ = (b)_____ age divided by (c)_____ age, times (d)_____.

**6.** The most widely used series of IQ tests are the (a)_____ Intelligence Scales. These tests organize items into two subtests, which are called (b)_____ and (c)_____ scales. In an attempt to measure nonverbal skills and rule out cultural problems, Wechsler added the (d)_____ scale.

**Block design**
Assemble blocks to match this design.

**Picture completion**
Tell me what is missing.

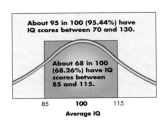

**7.** A good psychological test has two characteristics. It should give about the same score over time, which is called (a)_____, and it should measure what it is supposed to measure, which is called (b)_____.

**8.** If IQ scores can be represented by a bell-shaped curve, the pattern is called a _____. The scores have a symmetrical arrangement, so that the vast majority fall in the middle range and fewer fall near the extreme ends of the range.

About 95 in 100 (95.44%) have IQ scores between 70 and 130.

About 68 in 100 (68.26%) have IQ scores between 85 and 115.

85   100   115
**Average IQ**

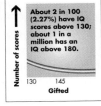

About 2 in 100 (2.27%) have IQ scores below 70.

30   50   70–75
**Mild/Moderate**

**9.** An individual who has a combination of limited mental ability (usually an IQ below 70) and difficulty functioning in everyday life is said to have some degree of (a)_____. If this condition results from genetic problems or brain damage, it is called (b)_____. If this condition results from a greatly impoverished environment, it is called (c)_____. Individuals who have above-average intelligence (usually IQ scores above 130) as well as some superior talent or skill are said to be (d)_____.

About 2 in 100 (2.27%) have IQ scores above 130; about 1 in a million has an IQ above 180.

130   145
**Gifted**

**10.** If the wording of test questions and the experiences on which they are based are more familiar to members of some social groups than to others, the test is said to have a (a)_____. The approach that measures intelligence by observing how people solve problems in their usual settings is called (b)_____ psychology.

**11.** When we ask how much genetic factors and how much environmental factors contribute to intelligence, we are asking the (a)_____ question. There is good evidence that genetic factors contribute about (b)_____ and environmental factors contribute about (c)_____ to the development of one's intelligence. The extent to which IQ scores may increase or decrease depending on environmental effects is called the (d)_____.

Intelligence (general abilities)
Spatial ability
Verbal ability
Memory

**Answers:** 1. (a) psychometric, (b) general intelligence, (c) specific abilities; 2. intelligence; 3. (a) information-processing, (b) triarchic; 4. mental age; 5. (a) intelligence quotient or IQ, (b) mental, (c) chronological, (d) 100; 6. (a) Wechsler, (b) verbal, (c) performance, (d) performance; 7. (a) reliability, (b) validity; 8. normal distribution; 9. (a) mental retardation, (b) organic retardation, (c) cultural-familial retardation, (d) gifted; 10. (a) cultural bias, (b) ecological; 11. (a) nature-nurture, (b) 50%, (c) 50%, (d) reaction range

## Misuse of IQ Tests?

**What were Binet's warnings about using IQ tests?**

After Alfred Binet developed the first intelligence tests, he gave two warnings about the potential misuse of IQ tests. He warned that IQ tests do not and should not be used to measure innate intelligence and that IQ tests should not be used to label individuals. However, in the early 1900s the area we know as psychology was just beginning, and American psychologists were very proud of how much they had improved IQ tests. With their improved IQ tests, American psychologists not only used IQ tests to measure what they thought was innate, or inherited, intelligence but also used IQ tests to label people (as morons or imbeciles). As if that weren't bad enough, early psychologists persuaded the United States Congress to pass discriminatory immigration laws based on IQ tests. As we look back now, we must conclude that the use and abuse of IQ tests in the early 1900s created one of psychology's sorriest moments. Here's what happened.

In 1924, Congress passed an immigration law to keep out those believed to have low IQs.

### Innate Intelligence

One name that we have already mentioned is that of Lewis Terman, who was the guiding force behind revising Binet's intelligence test (which became the Stanford-Binet test) and also developing the formula for computing a single IQ score. Terman, who became head of the Department of Psychology at Stanford University, firmly believed that intelligence was primarily inherited, that intelligence tests measured innate abilities, and that environmental influences were far less important.

One of Terman's goals was to test all children and, on the basis of their IQ scores, to label and sort them into categories of innate abilities. Terman argued that society could use IQ scores (usually of 70 or below) to restrain or eliminate those whose intelligence was too low for an effective moral life (Terman, 1916).

Terman hoped to establish minimum intelligence scores necessary for all leading occupations. For example, he believed that people with IQs below 100 should not be given employment that involves prestige or monetary reward. Those with IQs of 75 or below should be unskilled labor, and those with 75–85 IQs should be semiskilled labor. In Terman's world, class boundaries were to be set by innate intelligence, as measured by his Stanford-Binet IQ test (Gould, 1996; Hunt, 1993).

Terman's belief that IQ tests measured innate intelligence was adopted by another well-known American psychologist, Robert Yerkes.

### Classifying Races

Robert Yerkes was a Harvard professor who was asked to develop a test that could be used to classify applicants for the army. Under Yerkes's direction, over 1.75 million World War I army recruits were given IQ tests. From this enormous amount of data, Yerkes (1921) and his colleagues reached three conclusions:

**1.** They concluded that the average mental age of White American adults was a meager 13 years, slightly above the classification of a moron (a term psychologists used in the early 1900s). The reasons they gave for this low mental age were (using the terminology then current) the unconstrained breeding of the poor and feebleminded and the spread of Negro blood through interracial breeding.

**2.** They concluded that European immigrants could be ranked on intelligence by their country of origin. The fair peoples of western and northern Europe (Nordics) were most intelligent, while the darker peoples of southern Europe (Mediterraneans) and the Slavs of eastern Europe were less intelligent.

**3.** They concluded that Negroes were at the bottom of the racial scale in intelligence.

Many of Yerkes's outrageous and discriminatory views resurfaced in the book, *The Bell Curve* (Herrnstein & Murray, 1994), which we discussed earlier. Following Yerkes's lead, IQ scores were next used for racial discrimination.

### Immigration Laws

The fact that Yerkes ranked European races by intelligence eventually reached members of the United States Congress. Outraged by the "fact" that Europeans of "low intelligence" were being allowed into America, congressmen sought a way to severely limit the immigration of people from southern and eastern Europe. In writing the Immigration Law of 1924, Congress relied, in part, on Yerkes's racial rankings and imposed harsh quotas on those nations they believed to have inferior stock (people from southern and eastern Europe, Alpine and Mediterranean nations).

Stephen Jay Gould (1996), a well-known evolutionary biologist, reviewed Yerkes's data and pointed out a number of problems: poorly administered tests, terrible testing conditions, inconsistent standards for retaking tests, written tests given to illiterate recruits (guaranteeing a low score), and no control for educational level or familiarity with the English language. As a result of these problems, Gould concluded that Yerkes's data were so riddled with errors as to render useless any conclusions about racial differences in intelligence.

Looking back, we see clearly that early psychologists badly misused IQ tests. They forgot that IQ tests are merely one of many tools to assess cognitive abilities, which many consider to be one of many kinds of intelligence (Gardner, 1995).

We've discussed how past IQ tests have been misused and how current IQ tests may be biased. Is there a new generation of intelligence tests on the horizon?

**Power Study™**

Check out CD: Module 4
B. Studying the Living Brain

## Can Genius Be Found in the Brain?

There is one question about intelligence that has especially interested researchers: How is the brain of a genius different? For example, how was Albert Einstein able to think of riding through space on a beam of light or create his famous formula ($E = mc^2$), which led to building the atomic bomb?

When Einstein died of heart failure in 1955 at age 76, Dr. Thomas Harvey, who performed the autopsy, removed Einstein's brain and kept it at Princeton University. In 1996, Harvey contacted Dr. Sandra Witelson, a neuroscientist at McMaster University, and asked if she wished to examine Einstein's brain. McMaster University in Ontario, Canada, has a bank of over 100 brains that people have donated for research. Dr. Witelson was able to compare Einstein's 76-year-old brain with brains of similar ages from 35 men and 56 women who were known to have normal intelligence when they died. The results of Dr. Witelson's examination of Einstein's brains are discussed in the above figure.

Although the physical differences in Einstein's brain are obvious in the figure, Dr. Witelson cautions that they don't know if every

**Normal brain** weighs about 1,350 grams. This side view shows the wrinkled cortex, which contains separate areas for different functions (feeling, moving, reading, writing, seeing). Notice the yellow and red areas, which are part of the parietal lobe. The **red area, the inferior parietal lobe,** is especially used for thinking in visual-spatial terms, for mathematical thought, and for imaging how things move in space.

**Einstein's brain** weighed 1,230 grams, slightly less than normal. Einstein's brain was different in that it lacked the yellow area, which allowed his **red area, the inferior parietal lobe,** to be 15% wider than in normal brains. Researchers believe that Einstein's larger inferior parietal lobe increased his ability to think and imagine such things as space being curved and that time could slow down (Witelson et al., 1999).

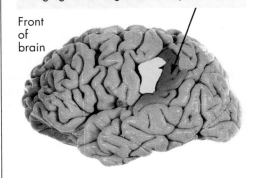

Front of brain

Front of brain

brilliant mathematician also has a larger inferior parietal lobe, which is something only further research can answer. Other researchers wonder if genius can ever be measured or located in the brain, since genius involves a mixture of creative insights, culture, and life experiences that may be unique to that person (Wang, 2000).

## Can Spearman's *g* Be Found in the Brain?

**What do brain scans show?**

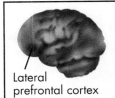

Lateral prefrontal cortex

**Hypothesis.** As you may remember, many psychologists believe that Spearman's *g* is a measure of a person's general level of intelligence or of a general mental factor shared by everyone and expressed by an IQ score. Researchers guessed that if Spearman's idea of a general mental factor of *g* was accurate, then a single brain area should be activated when solving different kinds of cognitive problems, similar to those used in IQ tests. On the other hand, if there was no general factor, but rather multiple kinds of intelligence, then many different parts of the brain should be activated when solving different kinds of cognitive problems.

**Method.** To look inside the living brain, researchers took PET scans of the brains of 13 men and women as they solved a series of difficult cognitive tasks (verbal and spatial), similar to those used in IQ tests. PET scans work by measuring the flow of blood to neurons so that a larger blood flow indicates more neural activity and a smaller blood flow indicates less neural activity (p. 71). PET scans give researchers a picture of neural activity inside the living brain.

**Results.** Researchers found that whether subjects were solving verbal or spatial problems, the same general area in the brain, the lateral prefrontal cortex, was activated (Duncan et al., 2000). Researchers concluded that because one brain area (rather than many) was activated during both spatial and verbal cognitive tasks, this single brain area (lateral prefrontal cortex) may be the neural basis for general intelligence, or Spearman's *g* (left figure).

However, researcher Robert Sternberg (2000b) points out that these results show only a correlation or association between activity in a brain area (lateral prefrontal cortex) and performance on cognitive tasks, but correlations cannot point to what causes what. In addition, the prefrontal cortex may not be the neural site for Spearman's *g* because this area also becomes active when we pay attention or use working memory. Finally, Sternberg points out that the researchers did not show whether the lateral prefrontal cortex was activated during creative or practical thought, or during thought required for people to be intelligent in their everyday lives. Thus, there is still some question about whether the lateral prefrontal cortex is the real neural basis for general intelligence or simply associated with paying attention and doing different tasks.

**Power Study™**

Check out CD: Module 10
E. Cognitive Learning

## Definition of Intervention Programs

**Why might a child need a head start?**

For a moment, imagine what will happen to Nancy's child. Nancy, who is in her mid-twenties, is a single mother with a 3-year-old child. Nancy lives in a lower-class neighborhood and earns less than $5,000 a year doing part-time work. She has completed only two years of high school, has no family and few friends. What effects do you think Nancy's background, educational level, and current impoverished environment will have on her child? Psychologists would predict that Nancy's 3-year-old child will not likely acquire the social, emotional, and cognitive skills and abilities needed to do well in school or society. Her child may need outside help, which may come from an intervention program (Ramey et al., 1982).

An *intervention program* creates an environment that offers increased opportunities for intellectual, social, and personality-emotional development while ensuring good physical health.

Intervention programs create a stimulating environment.

There are different kinds of intervention programs that could give Nancy training in how to be a good parent and provide her child with educational and social opportunities.

Perhaps the best-known intervention program in the United States is Head Start, which began in 1965 as a six-to-eight-week program with a budget of $96 million and a goal of combating poverty. Researchers soon discovered that a longer intervention program was needed, so Head Start was lengthened to two years. Head Start enrolls almost 830,000 3- to 5-year-olds in 16,000 centers and has a budget of about $4.5 billion and six different goals (Cooper, 1999).

We'll discuss Head Start's program and goals as well as another intense intervention program for disadvantaged children.

### Abecedarian Project

This project's goal was to teach youngsters from disadvantaged environments the cognitive and social skills needed for future success in school. Psychologists identified babies who were at high risk of failing in school because they lived in disadvantaged settings. Most of the mothers had low IQs, were African American, young, without a high school education, and single. With the mothers' permission, 2- to 3-month-old infants were assigned either to a control group that did not receive any special treatment or to an experimental group. Children in the experimental group spent 6 or more hours daily, five days a week, in a carefully supervised day-care center that continued for four years until the children entered public school at the age of 5.

After four years of this intense intervention program, children in the Abecedarian Project had IQ scores 12 points higher than control children from disadvantaged environments. Once children left the program, their advantage in IQ gains gradually lessened. When these children were retested at age 12 and age 15, they retained a small gain in IQ scores (Campbell & Ramey, 1990; Ramey et al., 1982).

These data indicate several things: First, the relatively large gains in IQ scores resulting from early intervention were not maintained in later years. However, at ages 12 and 15, these children did retain small gains in IQ scores, indicating the positive influence of the intervention program. Second, once children leave the intervention program and return to their disadvantaged environments, they no longer have the personal, social, or motivational support needed to maintain all their newly acquired cognitive skills (Brody, 1997).

### Head Start

Head Start, which is a day-care program for disadvantaged children, usually lasts for two years, from ages 3 to 5, and has six goals: preschool education, health screening, mental health services, hot meals, social services for the child and family, and involvement and participation of parents in the program (Zigler & Styfco, 1994). Recently, Head Start has emphasized basic academic skills, such as reading, in order to prepare disadvantaged children to do well in kindergarten (Cooper, 1999).

Head Start was initially viewed as something of a failure because two to three years after children left Head Start, few if any differences in IQ or other academic scores were found between those children and control groups (Clarke & Clarke, 1989). However, Head Start showed other important long-term beneficial effects (Zigler & Styfco, 1994):

■ Adolescents who had been in the Head Start program were more likely to be in classes appropriate for their ages rather than to have had to repeat a class, were less likely to show antisocial or delinquent behavior, and were more likely to hold jobs.

■ Mothers whose children had been in the Head Start program reported fewer psychological symptoms, greater feelings of mastery, and greater current life satisfaction.

■ Children who had two years of Head Start and an additional two to seven years of educational help were much more successful in graduating from high school (69%) than a control group (49%).

From these data we can draw two conclusions. First, early and often rather large increases (up to 10 points) in IQ scores do not last after the child leaves the intervention program. Second, Head Start programs resulted in a number of long-term benefits, such as increased social and personal well-being, to both the participating children and mothers (Zigler, 1995; Zigler & Styfco, 1994). These encouraging long-term effects indicate that Head Start should not be evaluated solely on IQ scores but also on other personality, motivational, and psychological benefits.

Head Start results in long-term personal and social gains.

## Raising IQ Scores

In the early days of Head Start, psychologists were very encouraged to find that the program initially increased disadvantaged children's IQ scores by about 10 points, a very significant amount. One reason IQ scores can be raised in young children from disadvantaged homes is that these children have not been exposed to and have not acquired the kinds of skills and cultural experiences assessed by IQ tests. However, when disadvantaged children are exposed to the enriched environment of Head Start, these children quickly acquire all kinds of new skills and abilities that help them score higher on IQ tests (Spitz, 1997).

For example, researchers compared two groups of disadvantaged children, all of whom had IQ scores below 80 (100 is considered the average IQ). Some of these children, called the experimental group, were placed in a special educational intervention program from ages 3 to 5. Other children, called the control group, were given no additional training and remained in their home environments.

The figure below shows that, after only one year, children in the experimental group (intervention program) showed a significant increase in IQ scores (about 10 points) compared to the children in the control group who remained in disadvantaged home environments (Schweinhart & Weikart, 1980). However, after the children left the intervention program at the age of 5 and entered public school, their IQ scores began a slow but consistent decline. At the same time, the IQ scores of control children began a gradual increase as they benefited from attending public school. By the age of 11, when children were in the fourth grade of public school, there was no longer any difference in IQ scores.

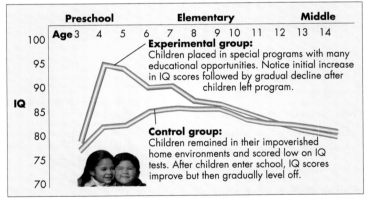

Initial increase in IQ scores (age 4) gradually disappears after children leave Head Start program and return to less stimulating environments.

One reason for this decline in IQ scores has to do with what happens to children after they leave an interventional program, such as Head Start, which usually lasts only two to three years. Once children leave the support of an intervention program and return to less stimulating environments, children receive less educational, social, and motivational support, which leads to a gradual decline in their IQ scores (Brody, 1997). For this reason, researchers recommend that programs like Head Start should be lengthened from three to at least five years so that the children have additional time to practice their newly acquired social, emotional, and academic skills (Zigler & Styfco, 1994).

Finally, as we discussed earlier, intervention programs should not be evaluated solely on IQ scores but rather on other social, emotional, and psychological gains that are found to be long-lasting.

## Need for Intervention Programs

The most successful intervention programs have a strong educational emphasis, well-trained teachers, and a low ratio of children to trained teachers.

Researchers make four important points about the need for intervention programs such as Head Start:

**1** Nearly 25% of children in the United States are growing up below the poverty line (Kassebaum, 1994). The effects of poverty include delays in young children's developmental progress, lowered aspirations and increased apathy among older children, and school failure or withdrawal (Zigler, 1994). Intervention programs help reduce the devastating effects that continuing poverty across several generations can have on families and children (Ramey & Ramey, 1998).

**2** About 25 to 30% of children live in single-parent families that are below the poverty line (Kassebaum, 1994). In some cases, impoverished family environments lead to neglect or abuse, which has very negative effects on a child's social, emotional, and intellectual development. Intensive intervention programs during the first years of life are effective in reducing and preventing the significant intellectual dysfunction that may result from continuing poverty and lack of environmental support (Ramey & Ramey, 1998).

**3** After studying intervention programs for 30 years, psychologists have learned that short periods of intervention, such as one or two years, are not as effective in promoting social, emotional, and cognitive growth as programs that last six or seven years (Reynolds, 1994; Zigler, 1994).

**4** Successful intervention programs are those that have a strong educational emphasis, which means that they have specially trained teachers, and have a low ratio of children to teachers. Good Head Start programs have these characteristics, but not all Head Start programs can meet these standards (Zigler & Styfco, 1994).

Psychologists concluded that Head Start and other intervention programs give children from impoverished environments a better opportunity for cognitive, social, and emotional development (Barnett, 1999).

# Summary Test

## A. DEFINING INTELLIGENCE

**1.** A subarea of psychology that is concerned with developing psychological tests to assess an individual's abilities, skills, beliefs, and personality traits in a wide range of settings—school, industry, or clinic—is called _____.

**2.** Spearman's two-factor theory of intelligence says there is a general factor, called (a)_____, that represents a person's ability to perform complex mental work, such as abstract reasoning and problem solving. The general factor underlies a person's performance across tests. In addition, there is a second factor, called (b)_____, that represents a person's specific mental abilities, such as mathematical or verbal skills. These specific mental abilities may differ across tests.

**3.** Gardner says that there are seven kinds of intelligence: verbal intelligence, musical intelligence, logical-mathematical intelligence, spatial intelligence, body movement intelligence, intelligence to understand oneself, and intelligence to understand others. This is called the _____ theory.

**4.** Sternberg's triarchic theory says that intelligence can be divided into three ways of gathering and processing information (*triarchic* means "three"). The first is using (a)_____ skills, which are measured by traditional intelligence tests. The second is using (b)_____ skills that require creative thinking, the ability to deal with novel situations, and the ability to learn from experience. The third is using (c)_____ skills that help a person adjust to, and cope with, his or her sociocultural environment.

## B. MEASURING INTELLIGENCE

**Block design**
Assemble blocks to match this design.

**Picture completion**
Tell me what is missing.

**5.** In trying to measure intelligence, researchers through the years have learned that neither skull size nor brain weight is an accurate predictor of _____.

**6.** The first intelligence test, which was developed by (a)_____, measured vocabulary, memory, common knowledge, and other cognitive abilities. By comparing a child's score with the scores of average children at the same age, Binet was able to estimate a child's (b)_____. Thus, the Binet-Simon Intelligence Scale gave its results in terms of mental age, while the IQ score was later developed by (c)_____,

who devised a formula to calculate an individual's intelligence quotient. The formula can be written as IQ = (d)_____.

**7.** The Wechsler Adult Intelligence Scale (WAIS-III) and Wechsler Intelligence Scale for Children (WISC-III) have items that are organized into various subtests. Subtests for general information, vocabulary, and verbal comprehension are some of those in the (a)_____ section. Subtests that involve arranging pictures in a meaningful order, assembling objects, and using codes are examples of subtests in the (b)_____ section. An individual receives a separate score for each of the subtests; these scores are then combined to yield overall scores for verbal and performance abilities, which, in turn, are combined into a single score, called an (c)_____ score.

**8.** A good psychological test must have two qualities. One quality ensures that a person's score on a test at one point in time is similar to a score by the same person on a similar test at a later date; this is called (a)_____. The other quality ensures that a test measures what it is supposed to measure; this is called (b)_____. Although the results from analyzing handwriting may be consistent from time to time, this is a poor test of personality or intelligence because handwriting analysis lacks the quality of (c)_____.

## C. DISTRIBUTION & USE OF IQ SCORES

**9.** Suppose IQ scores are in a statistical arrangement that resembles the shape of a bell, with the vast majority of scores falling in the middle range and fewer scores falling near the two extreme ends of the curve. This arrangement is called a _____.

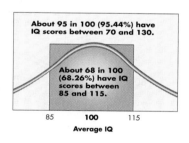

About 95 in 100 (95.44%) have IQ scores between 70 and 130.

About 68 in 100 (68.26%) have IQ scores between 85 and 115.

85    100    115
Average IQ

**10.** Substantial limitation in present functioning that is characterized by significantly below average intellectual functioning, along with related limitations in two of ten areas, including communication, self-care, home living, social skills, and safety, is called _____.

**11.** There are two general causes of mental retardation: genetic problems or brain damage give rise to (a)_____ retardation; in the absence of apparent genetic or brain damage, greatly impoverished environments can give rise to (b)_____ retardation. Mental retardation is reflected in IQ scores at one end of the normal distribution. At the other end of the normal distribution of

IQ scores are those who are considered (c)_____; such people have above average intelligence (usually IQs above 130) as well as some superior talent or skill.

## D. POTENTIAL PROBLEMS OF IQ TESTING

**12.** Binet warned that intelligence tests should not be used to measure (a)_____ mental abilities because intelligence tests measure cognitive abilities, which are influenced by both heredity and environment. Binet also warned that intelligence tests, by themselves, should not be used to (b)_____ people—for example, a moron or a genius. Current IQ tests have been criticized for including wording or experiences that are more familiar to a particular culture, which is called (c)_____. One way to avoid bias is to measure intelligence by observing people as they solve problems in natural settings; this is called (d)_____. One reason individuals may do poorly on IQ tests is noncognitive factors, such as attitude, experience, and emotional functioning, which are called (e)_____.

## E. NATURE-NURTURE QUESTION

**13.** The (a)_____ question refers to the relative contributions that genetic and environmental factors make to the development of intelligence. On the basis of twin studies, researchers generally conclude that about (b)_____ of the contribution to intelligence (IQ scores) comes from genetic factors and about (c)_____ comes from environmental factors. Adoption studies support the idea that environmental factors contribute to intellectual development (as measured by IQ scores). The idea that about half of one's intellectual development is dependent on environmental factors has resulted in (d)_____ programs that give impoverished children increased social-educational opportunities. There is little or no cause-and-effect evidence that the average difference in IQ scores between African Americans and Whites is caused primarily by (e)_____ factors.

| Intelligence (general abilities) |
| Spatial ability |
| Verbal ability |
| Memory |

## F. CULTURAL DIVERSITY: RACES, IQ, & IMMIGRATION

**14.** Early psychologists ignored Binet's warning about misusing IQ tests. For example, in the early 1900s, Terman believed that IQ tests did measure (a)_____ intelligence, and he wanted to use

IQ tests to sort people into categories. Terman's view was adopted by Robert Yerkes, who wanted to use IQ tests to rank the intelligence of (b)_____ entering the United States. In the 1920s, (c)_____ were written to exclude citizens from certain countries because Yerkes had ranked these individuals low in intelligence.

## G. RESEARCH FOCUS: NEW APPROACHES

**15.** In looking for physical differences in Einstein's brain, researchers found that he had a 15% wider (a)_____, which is involved in visual-spatial and mathematical thinking. In using PET scans to identify neural activity in the living brain, researchers found that when subjects solved verbal and spatial problems, the greatest neural activity occurred in the (b)_____. Researchers suggested that this brain area is the neural basis for (c)_____. However, the finding of a relationship between neural activity and solving cognitive problems is a (d)_____, which cannot show what causes what.

## H. APPLICATION: INTERVENTION PROGRAMS

**16.** A program that creates an environment with increased opportunities for intellectual, social, and personality-emotional development is called an (a)_____ program. Although data indicate that IQ increases resulting from intervention programs may be short-lived, there are other long-term positive benefits; for example, adolescents who have passed through such programs are more likely to complete school and hold jobs and less likely to show (b)_____ behavior. In addition, mothers involved in the Head Start program reported fewer psychological (c)_____ and had greater feelings of mastery and life satisfaction.

***Answers:*** *1. psychometrics; 2. (a)* ***g,*** *(b)* ***s;*** *3. multiple-intelligence; 4. (a) analytical, cognitive, or logical, (b) problem-solving, (c) practical; 5. intelligence; 6. (a) Binet and Simon, (b) mental age, (c) Terman, (d) MA/CA × 100; 7. (a) verbal, (b) performance, (c) IQ; 8. (a) reliability, (b) validity, (c) validity; 9. normal distribution; 10. mental retardation; 11. (a) organic, (b) cultural-familial, (c) gifted; 12. (a) innate, (b) label or classify, (c) cultural bias, (d) ecological psychology, (e) nonintellectual factors; 13. (a) nature-nurture, (b) 50%, (c) 50%, (d) intervention, (e) inherited, or genetic; 14. (a) innate, (b) immigrants, (c) immigration laws, or quotas; 15. (a) inferior parietal lobe, (b) lateral prefrontal cortex, (c) general intelligence or Spearman's* ***g,*** *(d) correlation; 16. (a) intervention, (b) antisocial or delinquent, (c) symptoms or problems*

# Critical Thinking

**Newspaper Article**

## Can a Successful Bookie Have an IQ of 55?

### Questions

**1.** How smart is Max Weisberg, who as a bookie made $700,000 but doesn't hide his illegal activities and keeps being arrested by police?

**2.** What is different about the terms used in the past to describe individuals with IQ scores at the lower end?

**3.** What are three theories of intelligence and what would each say about Max's intelligence?

Max Weisberg, who is now in his 70s, has been a very successful bookie (person who takes illegal gambling bets). But what's unusual about Max is that even after police in repeated raids have seized nearly $700,000 in cash from his rundown house, even after he's been arrested more times than he can remember, he still takes no precautions to hide his bookmaking activities. He leaves gambling slips all over his house, never hides his cash earnings, and openly takes bets on the telephone even though he's had hours of conversations recorded by the FBI. So, how smart is Max, who as a bookie made $700,000 but takes no precautions to hide his illegal activities?

Determining how smart Max is is not that easy. In 1939, when Max was 15 years old, he was committed to a state school because of "mental deficiency." Later, he was judged to be "feebleminded," and still later a probation report on Max read: "mentally deficiency: moron, causes undiagnosed." Later on, when Max scored about 55 on an IQ test, he was judged to be in the mentally retarded category.

A psychologist tested Max to find out how someone who was mentally retarded could be a successful bookie. For example, Max has no idea which direction the sun set (west), who wrote "Hamlet" (Shakespeare), who Louis Armstrong was (jazz singer and trumpet player), or why being a bookie was bad

(it's against the law in most states). However, when Max was asked to repeat 8 numbers in correct sequence, his face lit up and he repeated the numbers without an error. When something involves using numbers, Max is as good as a calculator.

Although an IQ of 55 puts Max in the range of borderline mentally retarded, Max has no trouble remembering and calculating hundreds of complex and difficult numbers related to gambling. For example, if you wanted to make an illegal bet on a professional football team, Max could give you the odds, such as Vikings to win by $10\frac{1}{2}$ points. This means that you win your bet only if the Vikings win by 11 points. If you decided to bet on two or more teams, called "parleys," or bet "over/under," which uses the total scores of games instead of a single game, Max calculates these very complicated odds without using anything more than the head on his shoulders. A person having this unusual combination of a low IQ score but excelling at some skill, such as numbers, is called a savant, which occurs in about 1 in 2,000 of mentally retarded individuals.

After every arrest, Max tells the police that he needs to get out as soon as possible so he can get to a phone and start taking bets. (Adapted from S. Braun, Max the bookie won't stop and that's a sure thing, *Los Angeles Times*, August 7, 1999, p. A1)

**4.** Based on the normal distribution, where would Max rank in intelligence and what would he be capable of doing?

**5.** Why doesn't Max understand that bookmaking is illegal and that he must stop or he will keep being arrested?

*Try InfoTrac to search for terms:* **mental retardation; multiple intelligence.**

---

### Suggested answers to Newspaper Article questions

1. As a bookie, Max has to be pretty smart to have made $700,000, but he has to be pretty dumb to leave all his gambling slips and cash lying around the house so the police have an easy time finding evidence to arrest him over and over.
2. Notice that the terms used in the past to describe individuals with lower IQs, such as "mentally deficient," "feebleminded," and "moron," were very unfavorable or derogatory and put the individual in a bad light.
3. According to Spearman's *g*, Max would be rated low in intelligence because his IQ is 55 (normal is 100) and Max is given no credit for his practical abilities (being a very successful bookie). According to Gardner's idea of multiple intelligence, Max certainly has exceptional skills in calculating numbers and is intelligent in that sense. According to Sternberg's triarchic theory, Max

certainly shows considerable practical intelligence in his ability to adapt to his environment (being a very successful bookie).
4. Based on the normal distribution of IQ scores, Max's IQ score of 55 falls in the range for borderline mentally retarded (50–75). In this range, Max should be able to read and write, master a simple occupational skill, and be self-supporting. As it turns out, Max is a very successful, self-supporting bookie.
5. Being mentally retarded means that Max has some limited cognitive capacities (not knowing which direction the sun sets). The reason Max believes that being a bookie is OK is that he says that's what he does and has been doing for 40 years. The idea that being a bookie is illegal or immoral is a concept too complex or abstract for Max to understand, no matter how many times it is explained or he is arrested.

# Links to Learning

## Web Sites

● WADSWORTH ONLINE STUDY CENTER
**http://psychology.wadsworth.com**
Quizzes, learning activities and exercises, a discussion forum, and hot links to Internet sites related to sensation, including:

● THE INTELLIGENCE PAGE
**http://www.euthanasia.org/mensal.html**
The high-IQ society, Mensa, maintains a page that includes links to related sites and a variety of mind-boggling puzzles.

● EMOTIONS AND EMOTIONAL INTELLIGENCE
**http://trochim.human.cornell.edu/gallery/young/emotion.htm**
This page is an online bibliography in the area of emotions and emotional intelligence, describing current research findings and notes of interest and including numerous Web links.

● TRADITIONAL AND MULTIPLE INTELLI-GENCE THEORIES
**http://edweb.gsn.org/edref.mi.hist.html**
On this site are summaries of intelligence theories, with an emphasis on the work of Harvard professor Howard Gardner, who for many years has put forth his theory of multiple intelligence and its potential effect on education.

● THE ARC OF THE UNITED STATES
**http://www.thearc.org/**
The national organization of people with mental retardation and related developmental disabilities and for their families.

## Learning Activities

● *POWERSTUDY™ BY ROD PLOTNIK & TOM DOYLE*

### PowerStudy™

**Check out CD: Modules 4 and 10**
CD section 4.A: Genes & Evolution; book page 292
CD section 4.B: Studying the Living Brain; book pages 284, 297
CD section 4.H: Cultural Diversity: Brain Size & Racial Myths; book pages 284, 294
CD section 10.E: Cognitive Learning; book page 298

● *STUDY GUIDE TO ACCOMPANY INTRODUCTION TO PSYCHOLOGY, 6TH EDITION,* **by Matthew Enos**
In Module 13 you have another opportunity to compare the influence of nature and nurture on intelligence and to master the differences in the intelligence theories of Spearman (*g*), Gardner (multiple), and Sternberg (triarchic).

● *WEBTUTOR*
**WebTUTOR**   **http://webtutor.thomsonlearning.com**
Visit this site for interactive versions of the Study Guide features. Take a quiz, get your score—should you study a topic some more, or can you move on? For example, what are some negative and positive uses of IQ scores? How is the measurement of intelligence affected by cultural differences? True or false: Only a small portion of intelligence is inherited.

● *INFOTRAC ONLINE LIBRARY*
**http://www.infotrac-college.com**
Use your password and then key in search terms such as those below to find popular and scientific articles on subjects covered in Module 13. Make the library work for you!

Mental retardation      Gardner's multiple intelligence theory
Wechsler's Adult Intelligence Scale      Psychometrics

● *PSYCHNOW!*
CD for Macintosh and Windows includes a study guide, glossary, Web sites, and animations. For Module 13, see:
• Infant Development      • Child Development

## Study Questions

*Use InfoTrac to search for topics mentioned in the main heads below (e.g., intelligence tests, nature-nurture).*

**\*A. Defining Intelligence**—How intelligent was Ray Kroc, who never finished high school but started the world-famous McDonald's hamburger chain? (**Suggested answer page 627**)

**B. Measuring Intelligence**—Would a new test based on a very accurate count of all the cells in your brain be a good test of intelligence?

**C. Distribution & Use of IQ Scores**—If you were hiring for a large department store, would it help to know the applicants' IQ scores?

**\*D. Potential Problems of IQ Testing**—Should we use IQ scores to assign the growing number of students from different cultures to grade levels? (**Suggested answer page 627**)

**E. Nature-Nurture Question**—If parents wanted to adopt a child, how important would it be to know the child's genetic makeup?

**F. Cultural Diversity: Races, IQs, & Immigration**—What convinced members of the United States Congress to use IQ scores as the basis for immigration laws?

**G. Research Focus: New Approaches**—Would brain scans provide a less biased, more culture-free measure of intelligence than standard IQ tests?

**\*H. Application: Intervention Programs**—Since Head Start fails to raise IQ scores over the long run, should its financial support be reduced? (**Suggested answer page 627**)

*These questions are answered in Appendix B.

# Module 14: Thought & Language

**A. Forming Concepts**     **306**
* DEFINITION THEORY
* PROTOTYPE THEORY
* EARLY FORMATION OF CONCEPTS
* CONCEPTS IN THE BRAIN
* TWO FUNCTIONS OF CONCEPTS

**B. Solving Problems**     **308**
* DIFFERENT WAYS OF THINKING
* THREE STRATEGIES FOR SOLVING PROBLEMS

**C. Thinking Creatively**     **310**
* HOW IS CREATIVITY DEFINED?
* IS IQ RELATED TO CREATIVITY?
* HOW DO CREATIVE PEOPLE THINK AND BEHAVE?
* IS CREATIVITY RELATED TO MENTAL DISORDERS?

**D. Language: Basic Rules**     **312**
* FOUR RULES OF LANGUAGE
* UNDERSTANDING LANGUAGE
* DIFFERENT STRUCTURE, SAME MEANING

**E. Acquiring Language**     **314**
* FOUR STAGES IN ACQUIRING LANGUAGE
* GOING THROUGH THE STAGES
* WHAT ARE INNATE FACTORS?
* WHAT ARE ENVIRONMENTAL FACTORS?

**Concept Review**     **317**

**F. Reason, Thought, & Language**     **318**
* TWO KINDS OF REASONING
* WHY REASONING FAILS
* WORDS AND THOUGHTS

**G. Research Focus: Dyslexia**     **320**
* WHAT KIND OF PROBLEM IS DYSLEXIA?

**H. Cultural Diversity: Influences on Thinking**     **321**
* DIFFERENCES IN THINKING
* MALE–FEMALE DIFFERENCES

**I. Application: Do Animals Have Language?**     **322**
* CRITERIA FOR LANGUAGE
* DOLPHINS
* GORILLA AND CHIMPANZEE
* BONOBO CHIMP: STAR PUPIL

**Summary Test**     **324**

**Critical Thinking**     **326**
* WHY DO PARENTS SPEAK LOUDLY AND SLOWLY?

**Links to Learning**     **327**

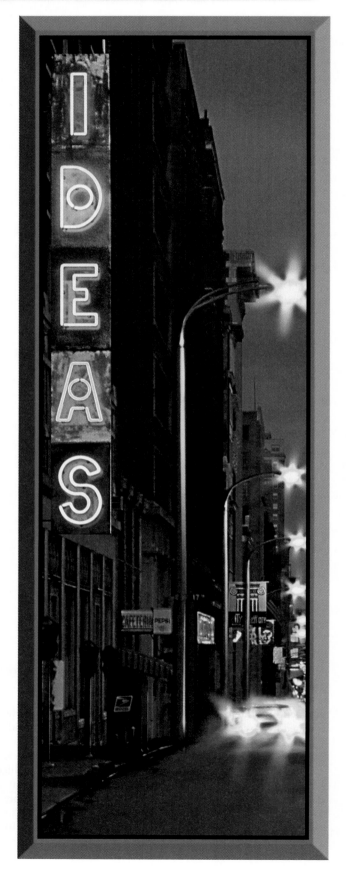

## Concepts

**What is that four-legged thing?**

Jeff, who is only 14 months old, walks up to his mother and says, in a somewhat demanding voice, "Juice." Jeff's one-word sentence, "Juice," is shorthand for "Can I please have a glass of orange juice?" Even as a toddler, Jeff already knows a considerable number of words that represent a whole range of objects, such as cookie, car, bottle, bunny, baby, juice, ball, apple, and the most hated words of all for a young child, "wash up." So when Jeff points at an object and says, "ball," his one-word sentence is short for "That is my ball." Jeff's use of these single-word "sentences" indicates that he is on his way to learning a very complex system of communicating by using language.

Jeff learned that this four-legged animal is a rabbit and not a cat or dog.

Jeff also uses one-word "sentences" to ask questions. For instance, he'll point to a picture in his animal book and ask, "Name?" This means "What is the name of that animal?" Jeff has already learned that a four-legged, fuzzy-tailed, large-eared animal is a bunny; a four-legged, long-nosed animal that barks is a dog; and a four-legged, short-eared animal with a long tail that says "meow" is a cat. Perhaps when Jeff sees an animal, such as a dog, cat, or rabbit, he takes a "mental photo" that he uses for future identifications. But that would mean storing an overwhelming number of "mental photos" of all the animals, objects, and people in his environment. We'll explain a more efficient system that Jeff probably uses to identify animals, objects, and people.

## Creativity

**How does one become creative?**

One of Jeff's most favorite things to do is to paint the animals in his picture books. Although Jeff makes a terribly wonderful mess, his parents encourage him because they hope that Jeff's early interest in painting may indicate a creative talent for painting or art. How one becomes a creative person is quite a mystery; take the case of Gordon Parks, for example.

No one thought Gordon Parks would amount to much. He was out on the streets at age 15 and never had time to finish high school, where he and his classmates were told, "Don't worry about graduating—it doesn't matter because you're gonna be porters and maids." Parks is African American and grew up in the 1920s, surrounded by segregation, discrimination, and worst of all, lynchings.

Parks was a teenager when his mother died. He was sent to live with his brother-in-law, but, Parks remembers, "That man didn't like children and didn't want to take me on, and I sensed that the minute I walked into his house." He was soon out on the street. He drifted from city to city, lived in flophouses, and worked at odd jobs. What would become of Parks (McKenna, 1994)?

With little formal schooling, Parks became a very creative person.

Parks (right photo) is now in his eighties and looks back on what he has accomplished. With little formal schooling and little professional help, he has written five volumes of poetry and a best-selling autobiography, *The Learning Tree*. He worked as a professional photographer for *Vogue* and *Life* magazines and directed several films (*Shaft* and *The Learning Tree*). He completed another novel, attended an exhibition of his photographs, and published a book of his incredible photos (Parks, 1997). Parks's early years showed no signs of his creativity. We'll discuss what creativity is and what makes creative people different.

## Cognitive Approach

**How does your mind work?**

How do toddlers like Jeff learn to speak a complex language and to recognize hundreds of objects? How did Gordon Parks, with little formal schooling, develop the ability to write and express his creativity in so many ways? The answers to these kinds of questions involve figuring out how our minds work. One way to study mental processes is to use the cognitive approach.

The **cognitive approach** is one method of studying how we process, store, and use information and how this information, in turn, influences what we notice, perceive, learn, remember, believe, and feel.

 *(decorative head graphic)*

Of all animals, humans have the greatest language ability.

We have already discussed several aspects of the cognitive approach: learning in Modules 9 and 10, and memory and forgetting in Modules 11 and 12. Here we'll explore two other cognitive processes, thinking and language.

*Thinking,* which is sometimes referred to as reasoning, involves mental processes that are used to form concepts, solve problems, and engage in creative activities.

*Language* is a special form of communication in which we learn and use complex rules to form and manipulate symbols (words or gestures) that are used to generate an endless number of meaningful sentences.

In fact, thinking and using language are two things we do much better than animals (Kosslyn, 1995).

## What's Coming

We'll discuss how we form concepts, solve problems, think creatively, acquire language, and reason. We'll also examine why people have difficulty recognizing words (dyslexia) and how language used by animals is different from the language used by humans.

We'll begin with the interesting question of how Jeff learned to distinguish a rabbit from a dog, and a dog from a cat.

# A. Forming Concepts

**Is it a dog, cat, or rabbit?**

Most of us have forgotten a problem that we faced as children: how to tell the difference among animals, such as knowing a dog is not a cat or a rabbit. One way we solved this problem was to form concepts.

A *concept* is a way to group or classify objects, events, animals, or people based on some features, traits, or characteristics that they all share in common.

How you formed the concept of a dog or cat or rabbit has two different explanations: the definition theory and the prototype theory (Medin et al., 2000).

**#1**

---

## Definition Theory

You easily recognize the animals on the left, but the question is how did you know which animal was which? Is it because your mind contains definitions of hundreds of animals?

*Definition theory* says that you form a concept of an object, event, animal, or person by making a mental list of the actual or essential characteristics of that particular thing.

According to definition theory, you formed a concept of a dog, cat, or rabbit by learning its essential characteristics. The essential characteristics of a dog might include that it barks and has a long nose, two ears, two eyes, four legs, some hair, and usually a tail. Similarly, you made mental definitions or concepts for all animals. Then, when you looked at the three animals on the left, you automatically sorted through hundreds of animal definitions until you found one that included the essential properties of a dog, cat, or rabbit. Once you found the definition, you knew what the animal was. Although the definition theory seems like a reasonable method of forming concepts, it has two serious problems.

One way to form concepts is to make definitions.

### PROBLEMS WITH DEFINITION THEORY

**Too many features.** In real life, it is very difficult to list all the features that define any object (Rey, 1983). For example, if your list of features to define a dog wasn't complete, the list might also apply to wolves, jackals, coyotes, and skunks. If your list of features to define a dog included every possible feature, such a mental list would be complete but take so long to go through that it would be very slow to use. And worse, you would need a long list of defining features for each and every animal, person, and object. Dealing with such a great number of mental lists, each one defining a separate concept, would tax the best of memories.

**Too many exceptions.** After making a list of defining features, you would also need to list all the exceptions that do not fit into the dictionary definition of dog. For example, some dogs rarely bark, some are very tiny, some are very large, some are hairless, and some are very fuzzy.

> **dog (dog, dag)** *n.; pl.* **dogs, dog.**
> 1. any of a large and varied group of domesticated animals (*Canis familiaris*) that have four legs, a tail, two ears, prominent nose, a hairy coat, and a bark.

Because of these two problems, you would need to check two mental lists—a long list that contained all the defining features and another that contained all the exceptions—before finding the concept that correctly identified the animal, person, or object.

For these reasons, the definition theory has been replaced by a different theory of how we form concepts: the prototype theory.

---

## Prototype Theory

Please look at the three animals on the right, #1, #2, and #3. Despite the great differences in size, color, and facial features of these animals, prototype theory explains why you can easily and quickly recognize each one as a dog.

*Prototype theory* says that you form a concept by creating a mental image that is based on the average characteristics of an object. This "average" looking object is called a prototype. To identify a new object, you match it to one of your already formed prototypes of objects, people, or animals.

Based on many experiences, you develop prototypes of many different objects, persons, and animals (Rosch, 1978). For example, your prototype of a dog would be a mental image of any particular animal that has *average features* (nose, tail, ears, height, weight). By using your prototype of a dog, you can easily and quickly identify all three animals on the right—the large brown mutt (#1), the tiny Chihuahua (#2) and the colorful Dalmatian (#3)—as being dogs.

**#2**

**#3**

Another way to form concepts is to form prototypes.

### ADVANTAGES OF PROTOTYPE THEORY

**Average features.** One advantage of prototype theory over definition theory is that you do not have to make a mental list of all the defining features of an object, which is often impossible. Instead, you form a prototype by creating a mental picture or image of the object, animal, or person that has only average features.

**Quick recognition.** Another advantage of prototype theory is that it can result in quick recognition, as happened when you identified these different-looking animals (#1, #2, and #3) as dogs. The more a new object resembles a prototype, the more quickly you can identify it; the less it matches your prototype, the longer it takes to identify it.

For example, what is the strange animal on the right, #4, and where is its head? Because this animal's features are not close to your dog prototype, it will take you some time to figure out that it has hair like "dreadlocks," its head is on the right, and it's an unusual dog (called a Puli).

**#4**

Prototype theory, which explains that you form concepts by creating and using prototypes, is widely accepted and has replaced the older, more traditional definition theory (Medin et al., 2000).

Next, we'll discuss when children begin forming concepts.

---

**Power Study™**

**Check out CD: Module 4**
B. Studying the Living Brain
**Check out CD: Module 10**
D. Long-Term Memory: Storing

## Early Formation of Concepts

At the beginning of this module, we described how 14-month-old Jeff had already learned a number of concepts, such as juice, cookie, car, ball, apple, and bunny. Like all children 10 to 16 months old, Jeff has formed many concepts, including correctly identifying animals that live on land or in the water (Oakes et al., 1997). Researchers found that children form concepts and place things into categories as a result of experience with objects and development of the ability to use language to name things (Gentner & Namy, 1999). For example, the child in the right photo is learning the concept *block* as she plays with them. Initially a child's categories may be very broad, such as objects, people, animals, and events. However, with more experience

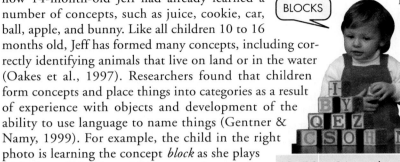

By 10 to 16 months, infants learn a number of concepts, such as block, juice, cookie.

come more concepts. Once children form one concept—for example, place the block *up*—they easily form the concept for its opposite—place the block *down;* once they form the concept for *high,* they easily form the concept for *low.*

As children gain even more experience and better use of language (as 5-year-olds), they can form more complex concepts that deal with the qualities of objects, such as *heavy, shiny, colorful,* or *sweet.* Because experience stimulates the formation of concepts, children benefit from being in stimulating environments that provide increased opportunities to encounter and interact with a wide variety of objects, animals, and people (Kagan, 1994).

Children can form a variety of concepts with relative ease and at an early age in part because of the way the brain processes information about categories.

## Concepts in the Brain

**How does the brain form concepts?**

You can quickly and easily recognize the three objects on the right as turtle, apple, and clown, And you could easily place them into three different categories: animal, fruit, and person. Researchers explain that you were able to recognize these three things by matching each to your already formed prototype of a turtle, apple, and clown (Squire & Knowlton, 1995). The reason you are not aware of forming prototypes or of matching things to prototypes is that these cognitive processes go on at an unconscious level, which means that you are unaware of and cannot recall what is happening (p. 246). Evidence that forming prototypes and matching things to prototypes occur at an unconscious (implicit) level comes from studies on patients who had suffered various forms of amnesia or memory loss due to brain damage. Although amnesic patients were able to form

The brain seems to be prewired to help us learn concepts.

prototypes and correctly match things to prototypes, they could not explain how they did it. Researchers concluded that using prototypes involves implicit processes, which we are not aware of and cannot voluntarily recall (Squire & Knowlton, 1995).

One reason children can form concepts or categories so easily and so early is that the brain is innately wired or already set up to process different concepts in different places. Based on PET scans of normal subjects and tests on brain-damaged individuals, researchers found that different concepts, such as animals, vegetables/fruits, and faces, were processed in different parts of the brain (Medin et al., 2000). These studies suggest that at birth the brain is already wired to place different concepts in different categories, which explains why children can easily and early on perform these complex cognitive tasks (Squire & Knowlton, 1995). Being able to form and use concepts has two real advantages.

## Two Functions of Concepts

**What if you lost your concepts?**

If you woke up one day to find that you had lost all your concepts, you would indeed have a very bad day. That's because concepts perform two important functions: they organize information and help us avoid relearning.

**1 Organize information.** Concepts allow you to group things into categories and thus better organize and store information in memory. For example, instead of having to store hundreds of mental images of many different kinds of dogs, you can store a single prototype of the average dog.

Concepts help us organize and classify objects.

**2 Avoid relearning.** By having concepts that can be used to classify and categorize things, you can easily classify new things without having to relearn what that thing is. For example, once you have a concept for a dog, rabbit, cat, or cookie, you do not have to relearn what that thing is on each new encounter.

Without concepts, our cognitive worlds would consist of unconnected pieces of information. In fact, some forms of brain damage destroy a person's ability to form concepts, so that the person is unable to name or categorize what he or she sees (visual agnosia; see page 79). By using concepts, you can identify, categorize, and store information very efficiently.

There is no doubt that concepts are useful for identifying objects and helping us make sense of our world. Next, you'll see that concepts are valuable for solving problems and thinking creatively.

**How do experts solve problems?**

In the photo at right, world chess champion Gary Kasparov looks very glum because for the first time he lost a chess match to a computer named Deep Blue, which had the power of 32 personal computers. This 1997 match between the world's best chess players—one human and one computer—was all about thinking and problem solving.

*Problem solving* involves searching for some rule, plan, or strategy that results in our reaching a certain goal that is currently out of reach.

In previous matches, Kasparov had always beat the computer because he was the better thinker and problem solver. For Kasparov, as well as for most of us, problem solving involves three

> A computer that was unemotional, unconcerned, and uncaring beat me at chess!

Clever computer beats human champion.

states: (1) the *initial state,* which is thinking about the unsolved problem; (2) the *operations state,* which involves trying various rules or strategies to solve the problem; and (3) the *goal state,* which is reaching the solution. One plan used by expert problem solvers, such as Kasparov, is to think in broader terms of how to solve the problem, while less successful novices become too focused on specifics (Abernethy et al., 1994). For example, expert computer programmers start with the final goal (to write a new chess program) and work their way down to specific solutions. In comparison, novices become bogged down in working on specific steps of the program and never reach the final goal of writing a complete program. Being a successful problem solver involves using different kinds of thinking.

---
### Different Ways of Thinking
---

**Can a computer think?**

In this man-machine chess match, Kasparov's thinking involved a combination of intuition (clever guesses based on years of experience) and creative mental shortcuts, called heuristics. The computer's "thinking" was more fixed because it has been programmed to use a set of rules that lead to specific outcomes, called algorithms. Solving problems by using algorithms or heuristics illustrates two very different ways of thinking (Lohman, 2000).

### Algorithms

If you wanted to win at a variety of games, such as chess, checkers, or bridge, you would follow a fixed set of rules that are called algorithms *(AL-go-rhythms).*

*Algorithms* are a fixed set of rules that, if followed correctly, will eventually lead to a solution.

For example, learning to play chess involves following algorithms that define how pieces move and the results of those moves. The reason relatively few chess players become grand masters like Kasparov is that people vary in their ability to learn and use algorithms.

Initially, Deep Blue was given little chance to beat world chess champion Kasparov because playing chess by using algorithms is a slow process. Instead of using algorithms, chess champion Kasparov was playing with a potentially more powerful set of rules called heuristics.

### Heuristics

Kasparov's unique brain, together with his years of experience, allowed him to play chess using heuristics *(hyur-RIS-ticks).*

*Heuristics* are rules of thumb, or clever and creative mental shortcuts, that reduce the number of operations and allow one to solve problems more easily and quickly.

Prior to 1997, Kasparov's clever and creative shortcuts, or heuristics, had given him the advantage over the fixed and not so creative algorithms of computer programs. In 1997, Deep Blue was programmed with new algorithms that raised its speed of "thinking" from analyzing 100,000 chess moves per second to 200,000. As a result of this increased speed, Kasparov's thinking, which focused on using clever heuristics, no longer had a clear advantage over the computer's "thinking," which involved using algorithms for analyzing 200,000 chess moves and countermoves per second (Peters, 1997).

Besides being used to solve chess problems, heuristics are often used in daily life to make decisions or draw conclusions (Bailenson et al., 2000). A commonly used heuristic is called the availability heuristic.

The *availability heuristic* says that we rely on information that is more prominent or easily recalled and overlook other information that is available but less prominent or notable.

For example, if you think the murder rate is increasing, it may be because newscasts emphasize these events and thus make murders more available (availability heuristic) in your memory. In fact, the murder rate has been going down in most major cities.

Using the availability heuristic to make a decision means taking a mental shortcut. Although heuristics allow us to make quick decisions, they may result in bad decisions since we make them using shortcuts, which limits the amount of information we use (Bower, 1997).

New computer programs, such as used in Deep Blue, are blurring some of the distinctions between how humans and machines think.

### Artificial Intelligence

It took 50 years of effort before scientists learned how to program a computer that could beat Kasparov at chess. One goal of computer science is to develop *artificial intelligence,* which means programming machines (computers, robots) to imitate human thinking and problem-solving abilities.

For example, scientists recently developed a "thinking" program modeled on how the brain thinks (neural network). Scientists programmed a computer with this "thinking" program and the basic rules of checkers. In no time, the computer taught itself to play checkers at the expert level (Fogel, 2000). Can you imagine a computer teaching itself to play expert checkers? This represents a major breakthrough in artificial intelligence—teaching machines to think like humans.

# Three Strategies for Solving Problems

**What if you get stuck?**

Most of us have had the experience of getting stuck while trying to solve a problem and wondering what to do next. By studying people who are good at problem solving, such as chess players, engineers, and computer programmers, psychologists have identified a number of useful strategies for solving problems. We'll discuss three problem-solving strategies—changing a mental set, using analogies, and forming subgoals. (Solutions to the first two problems appear on page 317.)

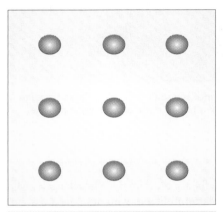

It takes new thinking to connect all dots with 4 straight lines without lifting pencil.

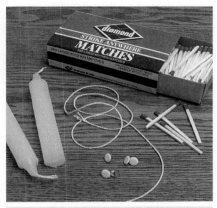

How would you mount a candle on the wall using what you see here?

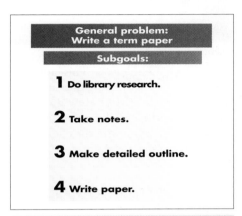

The best strategy for writing a term paper is to break the task into subgoals.

## Changing One's Mental Set

**Problem.** Connect all nine dots shown above by drawing four straight lines without lifting your pencil from the paper or retracing any lines. Try to solve it before reading any further.

If, like most people, you failed to solve this problem, it may be because of functional fixedness.

*Functional fixedness* refers to a mental set that is characterized by the inability to see an object as having a function different from its usual one.

For instance, you probably have a mental set that a straight line must begin and end on a dot. To solve the nine-dot problem, you need to break out of functional fixedness and think of a line as continuing past a dot.

As discussed in an earlier module (p. 226), some people solve this problem in a sudden flash known as insight.

*Insight* is the sudden grasp of a solution after many incorrect attempts.

You can increase your chances of solving a problem by insight if you consider the problem from many different viewpoints and unusual angles and if you decrease your anxiety and concern, which will in turn help you to overcome functional fixedness.

## Using Analogies

**Problem.** Imagine that you have a box of matches, two candles, a piece of string, and several tacks, as shown in the photo above. How would you mount a candle on the wall so that it could be used as a light?

You may solve the candle problem in a flash of insight. However, most of us have to develop a strategy to solve the problem, and a good strategy may involve using an analogy.

An *analogy* is a strategy for finding a similarity between the new situation and an old, familiar situation.

If you adopt an analogy to solve the candle problem, here's how your thinking might proceed: "I'm familiar with using a shelf to hold a candle on the wall. Which of the objects—candle, string, or box—could serve as a shelf? If I remove the matches, I can tack the box to the wall."

As you gain more experience and knowledge, you become better at using analogies to solve problems. This is one reason that businesses prefer employees with experience: these employees are more likely to use analogies to solve problems.

What about the problem every student must face—writing a paper?

## Forming Subgoals

**Problem.** Your assignment is to write a term paper titled "Creativity and Madness."

A useful strategy for writing the paper would be to divide the assignment or general problem into a number of subgoals.

Using *subgoals* is a strategy that involves breaking down the overall problem into separate parts that, when completed in order, will result in a solution.

As shown in the figure above, the first subgoal is doing library research and finding a number of articles on creativity and madness. The second subgoal is reading the articles and taking notes. The third subgoal is making a detailed outline of the whole paper. A fourth subgoal is using your outline to write the paper. By completing all four subgoals, you will have completed your paper.

The strategy of dividing a general problem into subgoals makes the overall problem seem more manageable because, at any one time, you are working on a single subgoal rather than worrying about completing the entire project.

To solve some problems, you may need to combine several of the strategies above. Another problem-solving strategy is to use creative thinking, our next topic.

At the beginning of this module, we told you about Gordon Parks (left photo). Parks grew up in the 1920s, a time of segregation, discrimination, and lynchings. As a result of the way Blacks were treated in the 1920s, Parks received little formal schooling or professional help and was told that he should be happy just to look forward to a job as a porter. Despite overwhelming odds, Parks succeeded in writing two novels and five volumes of poetry, directing two movies, and, now in his eighties, having an exhibition of his photographs (right photo) and publishing some in a book (Parks, 1997).

Gordon Parks had an HBO TV special on his 88th birthday.

This intriguing story of Gordon Parks raises four interesting questions about creativity: How is creativity defined? Is IQ related to creativity? How do creative people think and behave? Is creativity related to psychological problems? Although there are more than 60 definitions of creativity, we'll begin with the one most commonly used (Boden, 1994).

With little formal schooling, Gordon Parks became a very creative movie director and photographer.

### How Is Creativity Defined?

The definition of creative thinking is somewhat different from that of a creative individual.

*Creative thinking* is a combination of flexibility in thinking and reorganization of understanding to produce innovative ideas and new or novel solutions (Greeno, 1989).

A *creative individual* is someone who regularly solves problems, fashions products, or defines new questions that make an impact on his or her society (Gardner, 1993).

People can show evidence of creative thinking in many different ways. For example, recognized creative individuals include Albert Einstein, who formulated the theory of relativity; Michelangelo, who painted the Sistine Chapel; Sigmund Freud, who developed psychoanalysis; Dr. Seuss, who wrote rhyming books for children (and adults); the Rolling Stones, a well-known, 40-year-old rock-and-roll band; Ray Kroc, who founded McDonald's worldwide hamburger chain; and Gordon Parks, who is a writer, director, and photographer.

Because there are so many different examples (and kinds) of creativity, psychologists have used three different approaches to measure creativity: the psychometric, case study, and cognitive approaches (Sternberg & O'Hara, 2000).

#### Psychometric Approach

This approach, which uses objective problem-solving tasks to measure creativity, focuses on the distinction between two kinds of thinking—convergent and divergent (Guilford, 1967; Kitto et al., 1994).

*Convergent thinking* means beginning with a problem and coming up with a single correct solution.

Examples of convergent thinking include answering multiple-choice questions and solving math problems. The opposite of convergent thinking is divergent thinking.

*Divergent thinking* means beginning with a problem and coming up with many different solutions.

For example, the two problem-solving tasks on page 309 (nine-dot and candle-match puzzles) are used to assess divergent thinking, which is a popular psychometric measure for creativity (Amabile, 1985; Camp, 1994).

Tests of divergent thinking have good reliability, which means that people achieve the same scores across time (Domino, 1994). However, tests of divergent thinking have low validity, which means that creative persons, such as Gordon Parks, may not necessarily score high on psychometric tests of creativity (Gardner, 1993).

#### Case Study Approach

Because the psychometric approach is limited to using objective tests, it provides little insight into creative minds. In comparison, the case study approach analyzes creative persons in great depth and thus provides insight into their development, personality, motivation, and problems.

For example, Howard Gardner (1993) used the case study approach to analyze seven creative people, including Sigmund Freud. Gardner found that creative people are creative in certain areas but poor in others: Freud was very creative in linguistic and personal areas but very poor in spatial and musical areas. Although case studies provide rich insight into creative minds, their findings may be difficult to generalize: Freud's kind of creativity may or may not apply to Gordon Parks's remarkable achievements (Freyd, 1994).

#### Cognitive Approach

Although case studies provide detailed portraits of creative people, the findings are very personal or subjective and not easily applied to others. In comparison, the cognitive approach tries to build a bridge between the objective measures of the psychometric approach and the subjective descriptions provided by case studies. The cognitive approach, which is also the newest, identifies and measures cognitive mechanisms that are used during creative thinking (Freyd, 1994).

For example, many individuals have reported that one cognitive mechanism vital to creative thinking is the use of mental imagery, which involves thinking in images, without words or mathematical symbols (Finke, 1993). Thus, the cognitive approach involves analyzing the workings of mental imagery and its relationship to creative thinking.

Now, let's see what these three approaches say about creativity.

## Is IQ Related to Creativity?

In some cases, such as Michelangelo, Sigmund Freud, and Albert Einstein, creativity seems to be linked to genius. However, creativity is not the same as intelligence, as best illustrated by savants.

*Savants* refer to about 10% of autistic individuals who show some incredible memory, music, or drawing talent.

Despite their creativity, many savants score below 70 on IQ tests (the average score is 100). For instance, the detailed drawing shown on the right was done by Chris, a 16-year-old savant who has little knowledge or use of language and whose IQ is 52. After finishing a painting, Chris shows no further interest in it (Sacks, 1995).

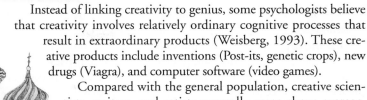

Drawn by a 16-year-old, very creative savant with an IQ of 52.

Instead of linking creativity to genius, some psychologists believe that creativity involves relatively ordinary cognitive processes that result in extraordinary products (Weisberg, 1993). These creative products include inventions (Post-its, genetic crops), new drugs (Viagra), and computer software (video games).

Compared with the general population, creative scientists, writers, and artists generally score above average, with IQs of 120 and higher. However, when the IQs of creative individuals are compared among themselves, there is little correlation between creativity and IQ. In other words, those who are generally recognized as creative do tend to have above-average IQ scores, but those with the highest IQs are not necessarily those who are the most creative (Sternberg & O'Hara, 2000).

## How Do Creative People Think and Behave?

Researchers have studied creative individuals to identify what is unusual about their work habits and psychological traits (Helson, 1996; Simonton, 2000). Here are some of their findings.

**Focus.** Creative people tend to be superior in one particular area, such as dance, music, art, science, or writing, rather than many areas. For example, Einstein (drawing at right) was superior in the logical-spatial area—the theory of relativity ($E = mc^2$)—but poor in the personal area—developing close relationships.

**Cognition.** Creative individuals have the ability to change mental directions, consider problems from many angles, and make use of mental images. They are also interested in solving unusual problems.

$$E = mc^2$$

Creative people can consider problems from different viewpoints and are driven by strong internal goals.

**Personality.** On the positive side, creative people tend to be independent, self-confident, unconventional, risk-taking, hard-working, and obsessively committed to their work. On the negative side, they tend to have large egos that make them insensitive to the needs of others. They may pursue their goals at the expense of others, and they may be so absorbed in their work that they exclude others.

**Motivation.** They are driven by internal values or personal goals; this is called intrinsic motivation. They are less concerned about external rewards such as money or recognition, which is called extrinsic motivation. They are motivated by the challenge of solving problems; their reward is the satisfaction of accomplishment. On average, creative people work on a project for about ten years before reaching their creative peaks.

One question often asked about creative people is whether their creative fires are fueled by psychological or mental problems, such as mood disorders.

## Is Creativity Related to Mental Disorders?

There are numerous historical reports of a link between creativity and madness or insanity, more correctly called mental disorders. For example, Mark Twain (Samuel Clemens), Tennessee Williams, Ernest Hemingway, Charles Mingus, Cole Porter, Edgar Allan Poe, and Herman Hesse were all reported to suffer from either depression or manic-depression (swings between euphoria and depression) (Jamison, 1995).

A more formal study of 291 creative writers, artists, composers, thinkers, and scientists indicated that 17–46% suffered from severe mental disorders, especially mood disorders. As the graph on the right shows, writers had the highest percentage of mental disorders, especially alcoholism and depression (Post, 1994).

A number of studies indicate that highly creative people experience major

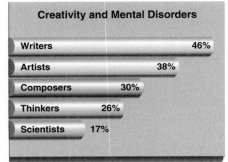

**Creativity and Mental Disorders**

| | |
|---|---|
| Writers | 46% |
| Artists | 38% |
| Composers | 30% |
| Thinkers | 26% |
| Scientists | 17% |

mood disorders more often than other groups in the general population (Jamison, 1995). But does the mood disorder contribute to creativity? One researcher suggested that severe mood change could contribute to creativity by sharpening thoughts and broadening the person's emotional, intellectual, and perceptual views of the world (Jamison, 1995). One interesting finding is that those creative individuals who reported emotional problems said that such problems often began when they were teenagers (Ludwig, 1995).

Although mental disorders may provide a sense of discomfort that may motivate creative activity, there are creative individuals, such as many scientists, who have achieved creative breakthroughs without having severe emotional problems (Waddell, 1998).

Next, we turn to an important component of creative activities, the development of language.

# D. Language: Basic Rules

**How many languages are there?**

Of all the things that humans do, none is more impressive and distinctively human than using language. Although language requires learning a very complex set of symbols and rules, most young children have little difficulty learning to speak their parents' or caretaker's language. Currently, people of planet Earth speak some 6,000 different languages (Raloff, 1995).

*Language* is a special form of communication that involves learning complex rules to make and combine symbols (words or gestures) into an endless number of meaningful sentences.

The reason language is such a successful form of communication arises from two amazingly simple principles—words and grammar.

A *word* is an arbitrary pairing between a sound or symbol and a meaning.

For example, the word *parrot* does not look like, sound like, or fly like a parrot, but it refers to a parrot because all of us memorized this pairing as children. Young adults are estimated to have about 60,000 such pairings or words in their mental dictionaries (Pinker, 1995). However, these 60,000 symbols or words would be rather useless unless the users followed similar rules of grammar.

*Grammar* refers to a set of rules for combining words into phrases and sentences to express an infinite number of thoughts that can be understood by others.

For instance, our mental rules of grammar immediately tell us that the headline "Parrot Bites Man's Nose" means something very different from "Man Bites Parrot's Nose." It may seem surprising, but speakers of all 6,000 languages learned the same four rules.

---

## Four Rules of Language

As children, each of us learned, without much trouble, the four rules of language. Now as adults, we use these rules without being aware of how or when we use them. To illustrate the four rules of language that we all learned, take the word *caterpillar*. Perhaps as a child, you put a caterpillar on your hand and watched it slowly crawl around.

Learning and using a word, such as caterpillar, involve four basic rules of language.

**1** The first language rule governs phonology.

*Phonology (FOE-nawl-uh-gee)* specifies how we make the meaningful sounds that are used by a particular language.

Any English word can be broken down into phonemes.

*Phonemes (FOE-neems)* are the basic sounds of consonants and vowels.

For example, the various sounds of *c* and *p* represent different phonemes, which are some of the sounds in the word *caterpillar*. At about 6 months, babies begin to babble and make basic sounds, or phonemes. We combine phonemes to form words by learning the second rule.

**2** The second language rule governs morphology.

*Morphology (MOR-fawl-uh-gee)* is the system that we use to group phonemes into meaningful combinations of sounds and words.

A *morpheme (MOR-feem)* is the smallest meaningful combination of sounds in a language.

For example, a morpheme may be
- a word, such as cat,
- a letter, such as the s in cats,
- a prefix, such as the un- in unbreakable,
- or a suffix, such as the -ed in walked.

The word caterpillar is actually one morpheme, and the word caterpillars is two (caterpillar-s). After we learn to combine morphemes to form words, we learn to combine words into meaningful sentences by using the third rule.

**3** The third language rule governs syntax, or grammar.

*Syntax,* or *grammar,* is a set of rules that specifies how we combine words to form meaningful phrases and sentences.

For example, why doesn't the following sentence make sense?

**Caterpillars green long and are.**

You instantly realize that this sentence is nonsensical or ungrammatical because it doesn't follow the English grammar rules regarding where we place verbs and conjunctions. If you apply the rules of English grammar, you would rearrange the combination of words to read: "Caterpillars are long and green." Although you may not be able to list all the rules of grammar, you automatically follow them when you speak. One way you know whether the word *bear* is a noun or a verb is by using the fourth rule.

**4** The fourth language rule governs semantics.

*Semantics (si-MANT-iks)* specifies the meaning of words or phrases when they appear in various sentences or contexts.

For instance, as you read "Did Pat pat a caterpillar's back?" how do you know what the word **pat** means, since it appears twice in succession. From your knowledge of semantics, you know that the first **Pat** is a noun and the name of a person, while the second **pat** is a verb, which signals some action.

Somehow you knew that the same word, **pat**, had very different meanings depending on the context. How you know what words mean in different contexts is a very intriguing question.

**Power Study™**

**Check out CD: Module 4**
D. Control Centers: Four Lobes
**Check out CD: Module 10**
F. Biological Factors

## Understanding Language

One of the great mysteries of using and understanding language can be demonstrated by the following two simple but very different sentences.

**You picked up a caterpillar.**    A caterpillar was picked up by you.

Despite a different word order, you know that these two sentences mean exactly the same thing. How you know that these different sentences mean exactly the same thing was explained by linguist Noam Chomsky (1957). His revolutionary theory involved two fundamental principles—mental grammar and innate brain program—that allow us to use and understand language (Pinker, 1994). What made Chomsky's two principles so important?

A 4-year-old unschooled child learns to speak and understand words and sentences because the brain comes with a built-in, or innate, language program.

*Broca's area is prewired to combine sounds into words.*

*Wernicke's area is prewired to combine words into sentences.*

**Mental grammar.** Almost every sentence we speak or understand is formed from a brand-new combination of words. Chomsky pointed out that the brain does not have the capacity to contain a list of all the sentences we will ever use. Instead, Chomsky argued that the brain contains a program or **mental grammar** that allows us to combine nouns, verbs, and objects in an endless variety of meaningful sentences. Chomsky's principle of mental grammar answers the question of how we can so easily create so many different sentences. The second question that Chomsky answered was: How do we acquire this mental grammar?

**Innate brain program.** How is it possible that 4-year-old children, with no formal schooling and relatively limited instruction from their parents, can speak and understand an endless variety of sentences? For example, the average 4-year-old child can already determine that the sentence "The caterpillar crept slowly across the leaf" is correct but that the sentence "The crept leaf caterpillar slowly the across" is meaningless. Chomsky's answer is that young children can learn these complex and difficult rules of grammar because our brains come with a built-in, or **innate, program** that makes learning the general rules of grammar relatively easy (p. 229). The brain's innate program for learning rules of grammar explains how a child learns most of the complex and difficult rules of grammar by the age of 4 or 5. However, it is the interaction between the innate program and a child's range of experience and kind of environment that results in learning the complicated rules of grammar (Albert et al., 2000).

But how would an innate grammar program, which could be used by any child in any culture, specify the rules for forming and understanding an endless number of meaningful sentences? The answer to this question is perhaps Chomsky's cleverest contribution.

## Different Structure, Same Meaning

One of the most difficult questions that Chomsky had to answer was how an idea can be expressed in several different ways, with different grammatical structures, yet mean the same thing.

He answered this question by making a distinction between two different structures of a sentence: surface structure and deep structure.

*Surface structure* refers to the actual wording of a sentence, as it is spoken.

*Deep structure* refers to an underlying meaning that is not spoken but is present in the mind of the listener.

We can illustrate the difference between surface and deep structures with our same two sentences.

**You picked up a caterpillar.**

A caterpillar was picked up by you.

Notice that these two sentences have different *surface structures,* which means they are worded differently. However, according to Chomsky, you are able to look underneath the different surface structures of the two sentences and recognize that they have the same *deep structure,* which is why you know they have the same meaning.

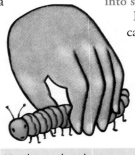

You know that the sentence "You picked up a caterpillar" means the same as "A caterpillar was picked up by you" because you recognize that both have the same deep structure.

Chomsky argues that we learn to shift back and forth between surface and deep structure by applying transformational rules.

*Transformational rules* are procedures by which we convert our ideas from surface structures into deep structures and from deep structures back into surface ones.

For example, when you hear the two sentences about picking up the caterpillar, you transform the words into their deep structure, which you store in memory. Later, when someone asks what the person did, you use transformational rules to convert the deep structure in your memory back into a surface structure, which can be expressed in differently worded sentences. The distinction between surface and deep structure is part of Chomsky's theory of language.

*Chomsky's theory of language* says that all languages share a common universal grammar and that children inherit a mental program to learn this universal grammar.

Chomsky's theory of language, which is widely accepted today, is considered a major breakthrough in explaining how we acquire and understand language (Ullman, 2000). However, one criticism of Chomsky's theory is that he downplays the importance of environmental influences (hearing and practicing sounds), which have been shown to affect language development (Albert et al., 2000).

Chomsky's idea of an innate mental grammar would predict that children around the world should go through the same stages of language development. Can this be true for all 6,000 languages?

# E. Acquiring Language

Power Study™

**Check out CD: Module 3**
B. Neurons: Structure & Function
**Check out CD: Module 4**
D. Control Centers: Four Lobes

**What do children's brains do?**

If Chomsky is correct that all children inherit the same innate program for learning grammar, then we would expect children from around the world to go through similar stages in developing language and acquiring the rules for using language. And in fact, all children, no matter the culture or the language, do go through the same stages (Pinker, 1994).

*Language stages* refer to all infants going through four different periods or stages—babbling, single words, two-word combinations, and sentences. All children go through these four stages in the same order, and in each stage, children show new and more complex language skills.

The occurrence of each of the four stages is associated with further development of the brain. At birth, an infant's brain has almost all of its neurons but they have not yet made all their connections (adult brains can grow some new neurons; p. 49).

6-month brain has few connections.

For example, a 6-month-old infant's brain (left figure) has few neural interconnections, which are associated with performing relatively simple behaviors, such as babbling. In comparison, a 24-month-old infant's brain (right figure) has hundreds of neural interconnections, which are associated with more complex behaviors, such as using two-word combinations (Bruer, 1999).

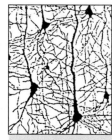

24-month brain has more connections.

Here are the four stages that each of us went through in learning to speak and understand the language of our parents or caregivers.

---

## Four Stages in Acquiring Language

### 1 Babbling

One of the key features in human development is that infants begin to make sounds long before they can say real words. Infants repeat the same sounds over and over, and these sounds are commonly called babbling.

*Babbling,* which begins at about 6 months, is the first stage in acquiring language. Babbling refers to making one-syllable sounds, such as "deedeedee" or "babababa," which are most common across all languages.

Bababa

A 6-month-old brain has limited capacity for language.

Babbling is an example of an innate "sound" program in the brain that is involved in making and processing sounds that will eventually be used to form words. Researchers have discovered that by 6 months of age, infants have already learned to discriminate between sounds, such as *ba* from *pa,* and to distinguish sounds in their native language from those used in a foreign language (Bower, 2000). These findings indicate that, at an early age, infants have already become accustomed to making and hearing sounds that make up their native languages. At about 9 months, babbling sounds begin to resemble more the vowels and consonants that children will actually use in speaking their native languages.

In children who can hear, babbling is oral. In deaf children who have been exposed only to the sign language of their deaf parents, babbling is manual and not oral. That is, these babies babble by repeating the same hand sign over and over (Petitto & Marentette, 1991). This means that the brain has an innate program for acquiring language, whether spoken or sign language.

Through endless babbling, infants learn to control their vocal apparatus so that they can make, change, and repeat sounds and imitate the sounds of their parents or caregivers (Bower, 2000). After babbling, infants begin to say their first words.

### 2 Single Word

Shortly before 1 year of age, an infant usually performs a behavior that every parent has been eagerly waiting for: to hear the child's first word. At about 1 year of age, infants not only begin to understand words but also to say single words.

*Single words* mark the second stage in acquiring language, which occurs at about 1 year of age. Infants say single words that usually refer to what they can see, hear, or feel.

An infant's ability to form sounds into words begins at about 8 months and results from an interaction between the brain's innate language program and the infant's experience with hearing sounds (Jusczyk & Hohne, 1997). About half the infant's single words refer to objects (juice, cookie, doll, dada), and the other half refer to actions, routines, or motions (up, eat, hot, more) (Pinker, 1994). The infant's single words, such as "Milk" or "Go," often stand for longer thoughts such as "I want milk" or "I want to go out."

As the infant learns to say words, parents usually respond by speaking in a specific way called parentese (motherese).

*Parentese (motherese)* is a way of speaking to young children in which the adult speaks in a slower and higher than normal voice, emphasizes and stretches out each word, uses very simple sentences, and repeats words and phrases.

In a study of mothers in the United States, Russia, and Sweden, researchers found that when talking to their infants, these mothers exaggerated certain sounds (vowel sounds), which they did not do when speaking to their husbands (Kuhl et al., 1997). Another researcher, who spent ten years traveling around the world to record child–parent interactions, concludes that parentese has several functions: getting an infant's attention and stimulating infants to make sounds they will need to speak themselves (Fernald, 1992).

Next, the young child begins to combine words.

Milk. Go.

1-year-old brain has more connections and more capacity for language.

## 3 Two-Word Combinations

Starting around age 2, children begin using single words that they have learned to form two-word combinations.

*Two-word combinations,* which represent the third stage in acquiring language, occur at about 2 years of age. Two-word combinations are strings of two words that express various actions ("Me play," "See boy") or relationships ("Hit ball," "Milk gone").

Hit ball. Me play.

A 2-year-old brain has many connections and more capacity for language.

Each of the two words provides a hint about what the child is saying. In addition, the relationship between the two words gives hints about what the child is communicating. For example, "See boy" tells us to look at a specific object; "Daddy shirt" tells us that something belongs to Daddy. The child's new ability to communicate by combining two words and changing their order marks the beginning of learning the rules of grammar. From about 2 years of age through adolescence, a child learns an average of a new word every 2 hours (Pinker, 1994).

A child's language development is partly dependent on how responsive the parent or caretaker is. A more responsive parent is one who shows more contact, awareness, and warmth during the child's verbal interactions. For example, infants whose mothers were more responsive to their speech at 13 months had significantly larger vocabularies at 21 months compared to less responsive mothers (Tamis-LeMonda et al., 1996).

By the age of 2, a child may have a vocabulary of more than 50 words, many of which will be used in two-word combinations. Although children usually go through a stage of forming single words and then two-word combinations, there is no three-word stage. Instead, at a certain point the child will begin to form sentences, which gradually increase in length through the fourth year.

## 4 Sentences

Children make a rather large language leap when they progress from relatively simple two-word combinations to using longer and more complex sentences.

*Sentences,* which represent the fourth stage of acquiring language, occur at about 4 years of age. Sentences range from three to eight words in length and indicate a growing knowledge of the rules of grammar.

However, a child's first sentences differ from adults' in that the child may omit the "small words" and speak in a pattern that is called telegraphic speech.

*Telegraphic speech* is a distinctive pattern of speaking in which the child omits articles (the), prepositions (in, out), and parts of verbs.

For example, an adult may say, "I'm going to the store." A 3- to 4-year-old child may use telegraphic speech (omit article) and say, "I go to store." However, by the time children are 4 or 5 years old, the structure of their sentences improves and indicates that they have learned the basic rules of grammar.

*Basic rules of grammar* are the rules for combining nouns, verbs, and adjectives to form meaningful sentences.

However, as children learn the rules of grammar, they often make errors of overgeneralization.

*Overgeneralization* means applying a grammatical rule to cases where it should not be used.

I goed to store. I want blue toy.

For example, after a child learns the rule of forming the past tense of many verbs by adding a *d* sound to the end, he or she may overgeneralize this rule and add a *d* to the past tense of irregular verbs (and say, for instance, "I goed to store"). By the time children enter school, they usually have a good grasp of the general rules of their language.

4- to 5-year-old brain has significantly more connections so that a child can learn the basic rules of complex grammar.

---

## Going Through the Stages

**How fast does a child go through the stages?**

Going through the four stages of language—babbling, single word, two-word combinations, and sentences—is a process that allows a child to learn a complex word code that he or she will use to communicate with and understand others.

Parents or caregivers sometimes worry about whether their child is late in developing language. In the real world, normal children pass through the four stages of language at a pace that can differ by a year or more. However, as Chomsky's theory predicts and research has shown, all normal children pass through the four stages, even though some of the stages may begin later or last for shorter or longer periods of time (Pinker, 1994).

1. Babbling    2. Single word    3. Two words    4. Sentences

Even though all children initially make the same sounds and inherit the same program for learning grammar, they must still learn the sounds, words, and word order for their particular language. For instance, the English language has the sounds "r" and "l," and phrases have nouns coming first. In the Japanese language, there are no sounds "r" or "l," and phrases have nouns coming last. In the first stage, babbling, all children make the same sounds. By the last stage, sentences, children have learned only the sounds and grammar of whatever their parents or caregivers speak.

Actually, learning language skills depends on the interaction between genetic and environmental factors, our next topic.

# E. Acquiring Language

**How does a child learn a particular language?**

It is quite amazing how children from different countries around the world, such as Africa, Bali, China, Sweden, Japan, United States, Mexico, France, Spain, Russia, and Thailand (right photo),

He learned to speak his native language, Thai.

can acquire the sounds, words, and rules of their particular native language. Each child learns his or her particular native language because of an interaction between innate (heredity) and environmental (learning) factors.

## What Are Innate Factors?

All children go through the same four language stages because of innate language factors (Albert et al., 2000).

*Innate language factors* are genetically programmed physiological and neurological features that facilitate our making speech sounds and acquiring language skills.

We'll examine three innate language features that work together so that we can learn to speak and use language.

**Innate physiological features.** We have a specially adapted vocal apparatus (larynx and pharynx) that allows us to make sounds and form words. In comparison, the structures of gorillas' and chimpanzees' vocal apparatus prevent them from making the wide variety of sounds necessary to form words (Pinker, 1994). Without our specialized vocal apparatus, we humans would be limited to making "animal" sounds.

**Innate neurological features.** When people speak or use sign language, certain brain areas are activated. The PET scan above shows a side view of the brain: red and yellow indicate most neural activity (Petitto, 1997). These findings indicate that the left hemisphere of the

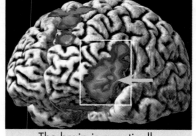

The brain is genetically programmed to speak and understand.

brain is prewired to acquire and use language, whether spoken or signed. In Module 4, we explained how damage to these same language areas (Broca's and Wernicke's areas) disrupts the use and understanding of language (p. 78). Although your brain is prewired for language, there is a best, or critical, time for learning a language.

**Innate developmental factors.** Researchers have discovered that there is a critical period when acquiring language is the easiest (Stromswold, 1995).

The *critical language period* is the time from infancy to adolescence when language is easiest to learn. Language is usually more difficult to learn anytime after adolescence.

For example, immigrant children do very well learning English as a second language, while immigrant adults, who are past the critical period, have more difficulty and do less well (Jackendoff, 1994). The critical period for learning language also explains why learning your native language was very easy as a child but, as an adult, learning a foreign language is many times more difficult.

Innate biological factors provide the programming so a child can acquire any one of 6,000 languages. Which particular language the child learns depends on his or her environment (parents).

## What Are Environmental Factors?

**Social interactions.** How each child learns a particular language depends on social interactions, one of the environmental factors.

*Environmental language factors* refer to interactions children have with parents, peers, teachers, and others who provide feedback that rewards and encourages language development, as well as providing opportunities for children to observe, imitate, and practice language skills.

What would happen if a child was deprived of almost all social interactions from ages 1 to 13? Such was the case with Genie, whose mentally disturbed father strapped her to a potty chair in a back room, punished her for making any sounds, and forbid the mother or brother to talk to her. When discovered by a social worker at age 13, Genie could not speak a single word (Curtiss, 1977). Genie's case illustrates that even though children are prewired by heredity to speak a language, they need certain environmental stimuli, such as listening, speaking, and interacting with others, in order to learn to speak and use language. Genie's case also illustrates the importance of social cognitive learning.

Parentese provides needed stimulation and feedback.

*Social cognitive learning* emphasizes the acquisition of language skills through social interactions, which give children a chance to observe, imitate, and practice the sounds, words, and sentences they hear from their parents or caregivers.

For example, within eight months of training, Genie had acquired a vocabulary of about 200 words. However, Genie's long period of social deprivation left its mark, and even after years of continued social interactions, her language ability did not develop much beyond that of a 2- or 3-year-old child (Harris, 1995).

**Parentese.** Researchers found that 2- and 3-year-old children who had the biggest vocabularies and performed best on developmental language tests were those whose parents were the most talkative during the child's first two years (Hart & Risley, 1996). These studies show the importance of environmental factors, such as parents and caregivers stimulating and encouraging language development by speaking in parentese and by being very responsive to what their child says (Monnot, 1999). All these studies show how environmental and innate factors interact and influence a child's ability to acquire the language skills of a particular culture.

When children master language, they have a powerful tool for thinking, as we'll discuss after the Concept Review.

# Concept Review

**dog** (dog, dag) n.; pl. **dogs,
dog.**
1. any of a large and varied
group of domesticated animals
(*Canis familiaris*) that have
four legs, a tail, two ears,
prominent nose, a hairy coat,
and a bark.

**1.** If you form a concept of an
object, event, or characteristic
by making a list of the properties that define it, you are forming a concept according to
_____ theory.

**2.** If you form a concept by putting together
the average characteristics of an object and
then seeing whether a new object matches
your average object, you are forming a
concept according to (a)_____
theory. If you develop an idea of a dog of
average age, height, weight, and color, you have formed a
(b)_____ of a dog.

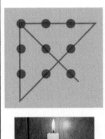

**Answers to
problems on
page 309**

**3.** If you search for some rule, plan, or
strategy that results in your reaching a
certain goal that is currently out of reach,
you are engaging in an activity called
(a)_____. During this activity,
you go through three states: contemplating
the unsolved problem, which is the
(b)_____ state; trying out
various operations, rules, or strategies
to solve the problem, which is the
(c)_____ state; and
reaching the solution, which is the
(d)_____ state.

**4.** Some problems can be solved by following certain rules. If you correctly follow
rules that lead to a certain solution, you
are using (a)_____. If you fol-
low rules that reduce the number of operations or allow you to
take shortcuts in solving problems, you are using (b)_____.

**5.** When you use a combination of flexibility in thinking and reorganization of understanding to produce innovative ideas and solutions, you are engaging in (a)_____.
If you begin with a problem and come up
with many different solutions, you are using
(b)_____ thinking, which is one
definition of creative thinking. The opposite of
this type of thinking is beginning with a problem
and coming up with the one correct solution; this
is called (c)_____ thinking.

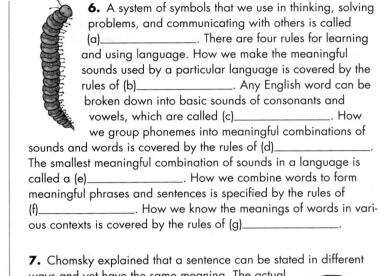

**6.** A system of symbols that we use in thinking, solving
problems, and communicating with others is called
(a)_____. There are four rules for learning
and using language. How we make the meaningful
sounds used by a particular language is covered by the
rules of (b)_____. Any English word can be
broken down into basic sounds of consonants and
vowels, which are called (c)_____. How
we group phonemes into meaningful combinations of
sounds and words is covered by the rules of (d)_____.
The smallest meaningful combination of sounds in a language is
called a (e)_____. How we combine words to form
meaningful phrases and sentences is specified by the rules of
(f)_____. How we know the meanings of words in various contexts is covered by the rules of (g)_____.

**7.** Chomsky explained that a sentence can be stated in different
ways and yet have the same meaning. The actual
wording of a sentence is called its
(a)_____ structure. The underlying
meaning of the sentence that is not spoken but is
present in the mind of the listener is called the
(b)_____ structure. To convert our
ideas from surface structures into deep structures
and from deep structures back into surface ones, we use
(c)_____ rules.

**8.** In acquiring language, all children go
through the same four stages but at different
rates. Beginning at about the age of 6
months, a baby begins making one-syllable
sounds, such as "bababa," which is called
(a)_____. By about 1 year of age, a child forms
(b)_____ words, which usually refer to what the child
can see, hear, or feel. At about 2 years of age, a child makes
(c)_____, which are strings of two words that express
various actions ("Me play") or relationships ("Hit ball," "Milk
gone"). At about 4 years of age, a child begins forming sentences,
which range from three to eight words in length and indicate a
growing knowledge of the rules of (d)_____.

**9.** One reason all children acquire a language in much
the same order is because of genetically programmed
physiological and neurological features in the brain
and vocal apparatus. These are known as
(a)_____ factors. Social interactions
between the child and others, which offer opportunities
for observation, imitation, and practice, are called
(b)_____ factors.

***Answers:*** *1. definition; 2. (a) prototype, (b) prototype; 3. (a) problem solving, (b) initial, (c) operations, (d) goal; 4. (a) algorithms,
(b) heuristics; 5. (a) creative thinking, (b) divergent, (c) convergent; 6. (a) language, (b) phonology, (c) phonemes, (d) morphology,
(e) morpheme, (f) syntax or grammar, (g) semantics; 7. (a) surface, (b) deep, (c) transformational; 8. (a) babbling, (b) single, (c) two-word
combinations, (d) grammar or syntax; 9. (a) innate, (b) environmental*

## Two Kinds of Reasoning

**Why is this fully dressed man standing in the ocean?**

If you saw a nicely dressed older man standing in the ocean, you would naturally wonder what he was doing. To figure out this man's unusual behavior, you could use the personal computer inside your brain, which has a very powerful software program called reasoning (Sloman, 1996).

*Reasoning,* which often means thinking, is a mental process that involves using and applying knowledge to solve problems, make plans or decisions, and achieve goals.

To figure out why this normal-looking, fully dressed but shoeless man is standing in the ocean, you could use two different kinds of reasoning—deductive or inductive.

### Deductive Reasoning

Since you rarely see a nicely dressed older man standing in the ocean, you might assume that he is drunk. The kind of reasoning that begins with a big assumption is called deductive reasoning.

*Deductive reasoning* begins with making a general assumption that you know or believe to be true and then drawing specific conclusions based on this assumption; in other words, reasoning from a general assumption to particulars.

Your general assumption is that only a drunk person would gleefully walk into the ocean dressed in a suit. This man is doing so. Therefore, he must be drunk. In its simplest form, deductive reasoning follows this formula: If you are given an assumption or statement as true, then there is only one correct conclusion to draw. This formula is often referred to as "If *p* (given statements), then *q* (conclusion)." For example:

Statements ("If *p*"): Only people who are over 21 years of age drink alcohol. That man is drinking alcohol. Conclusion ("Then *q*"): That man must be over 21 years of age.

One mistake people make in deductive reasoning is that they assume but do not always know if the basic statement or assumption (*p*) is true. If the basic statement is false—that is, drunkenness is not the only explanation for the man's behavior—then so are the conclusions. Another way to figure out why the man is standing in the ocean is to use inductive reasoning.

You can use either deductive or inductive reasoning to explain what this man is doing.

### Inductive Reasoning

Instead of just assuming that this man is standing in the ocean because he's drunk, you walk over and ask some specific questions. After listening to this man's answers, you reach a different explanation for why he's standing in the ocean. The kind of reasoning that starts with specific facts or observations is called inductive reasoning.

*Inductive reasoning* begins with making particular observations that you then use to draw a broader conclusion; in other words, reasoning from particulars to a general conclusion.

For example, when questioned, the man answers "No" to all the following questions: Did you drink alcohol today? Do you have a job? Are you married? Do you do this often? Have you eaten today? Are you ill? Would you like me to take you home? After considering all these particulars, you reach a general conclusion: Either this man is suffering from Alzheimer's disease or he is lying.

Researchers use inductive reasoning when they use past experiences or observations to form a general hypothesis (Evans, 1993). For instance, researchers observed that when some students take exams they have rapid heart rate, sweaty palms, muscle tension, and increased blood pressure. Based on these particulars, researchers reached the general conclusion that these students have test anxiety.

One big mistake people make in inductive reasoning is jumping to a conclusion before knowing all the facts (Levy, 1997).

Depending on the situation, deductive and inductive reasoning are powerful mental tools provided you're aware of their pitfalls.

## Why Reasoning Fails

Many students found it very difficult to solve the problem given below.

| Problem | Reasoning | Solution |
|---|---|---|
| If you drop one bullet off a table 3 feet high and fire another one straight across an empty football field, which hits the ground first? | Based on experience, it seems the dropped bullet will land first because it has only 3 feet to travel. | Based on physics, both bullets hit at the same time because downward velocity is independent of horizontal velocity. |

On the basis of their experiences, students believed that a dropped bullet would surely hit the ground before one fired parallel to the ground. However, physics principles say that both bullets would hit the ground at the same time, which is completely opposite of students' experiences.

According to Alan Cromer (1993), who taught introductory science classes for 32 years, the formal reasoning needed to solve science problems is very difficult to teach because it often runs counter to our experiences or intuitions. Researchers suggest that our brains are equipped or prewired for reasoning to meet real-world challenges, such as surviving, finding food, and finding mates, rather than solving physics problems, which requires a special kind of abstract reasoning (Cosmides & Tooby, 1994). One reason students may have difficulty in science classes is that their personal experiences interfere with using abstract reasoning.

Because words are so much a part of our reasoning process, we need to know if and how much words can influence or bias our thinking.

**Does language influence thinking?**

Almost everyone has heard it said that the Inuit (Eskimos) are supposed to have dozens of words for snow because their survival depends on knowing how to travel and hunt in different kinds of snow. This particular observation was first made by amateur linguist Benjamin Whorf (1956), who noticed that languages differed in their vocabularies depending on how much emphasis they gave to different objects and events in their environment. For example, Whorf reasoned that because the Inuit (Eskimos) have many names for snow, they must be able to perceive many more kinds of snow than Americans, for whom snow conditions are less important. On the basis of these kinds of observations, Whorf formulated the theory of linguistic relativity.

The *theory of linguistic relativity* states that the differences among languages result in similar differences in how people think and perceive the world.

Linguistic relativity theory says differences among languages lead to differences in thinking.

For example, according to the theory of linguistic relativity, people whose language divides colors into only two categories (dark or black and bright or white) should perceive fewer colors. In comparison, people whose language divides colors into eleven categories (black, white, red, yellow, green, blue, brown, purple, pink, orange, gray) should perceive many more colors in their environment. However, researchers discovered that although languages differ in their number of color categories, all languages divide colors into the same basic categories. According to Whorf's theory of linguistic relativity, we would have expected people to perceive colors differently, depending on whether their culture has two or eleven names, but this is not what researchers found (Davies & Corbett, 1997). Thus, people in different cultures seem to perceive colors in similar ways even if they do not have names for different colors (Pinker, 1994).

Now, let's examine Whorf's famous claim that Inuits have more words for snow than do Americans.

### *Inuit versus American Words for Snow*

In his original article, Whorf (1940) estimated that Inuit (Eskimos) have about seven words for snow: *falling snow, snow on the ground, snow packed hard like ice, slushy snow, drifting snow, snow drift,* and *wind-driven flying snow,* while most Americans use a single word, *snow.* Whorf reasoned that the Inuit's larger vocabulary of snow-related words should make them think and perceive snow very differently than most Americans. Since Whorf's time, the number of snow words attributed to Inuit has ranged from two dozen to about 400 (Pullum, 1991).

Another linguist did a closer examination and found that Inuit and Americans each have about eight words for snow (English words for snow include *blizzard, sleet, hail, hardpack, powder, avalanche, flurry,* and *dusting*) (Martin, 1986). So, as it turns out, Whorf was wrong about how many words Inuit and Americans have for snow. One reason Whorf's story about differences in snow words lives on is that it's a great (but untrue) story (Pullum, 1991).

We have about the same number of words for snow as you do!

Although Whorf's story about snow words was untrue, the basic question still remains: Do differences in language mean that people think and perceive the world in different ways? One way to answer this question is to examine how individuals who are bilingual—that is, fluent in two languages—think about and perceive their world.

### *Thinking in Two Languages*

Suppose your native language is Chinese but you are also fluent in English. You are asked to read descriptions of two different people in either Chinese or English and then to write impressions of these individuals. You read a Chinese and an English description of a type of person easily labeled in Chinese—*shi gu,* a person with strong family ties and much worldly experience—but not easily labeled in English. You read an English and a Chinese description of a type of person easily labeled in English—an *artistic* character, a person with artistic abilities who is very temperamental—but not easily labeled in Chinese. Researchers found that when subjects were reading and thinking in Chinese, they formed a clearer impression of the *shi gu* person; when reading and thinking in English, they formed a clearer impression of the artistic character (Hoffman et al., 1986). This is one of the few studies that supports the linguistic relativity theory and the idea that language influences thinking (Hardin & Banaji, 1993).

My native language is Chinese but I also speak English, so which do I think in?

Other prominent linguists argue that thoughts or ideas are not the same thing as words (Pinker, 1994, 1995). For example, sometimes we find it difficult to put a thought or idea into words, which would not be the case if every thought had a matching word. Also, how would new words be formed if thoughts depended on words that did not yet exist? For all these reasons, psychologists have generally found little or only weak support for Whorf's theory of linguistic relativity (Davies & Corbett, 1997; Pinker, 1994).

We know that words are important tools for reasoning, so what happens to an individual's thinking if he or she has great difficulty recognizing printed words? Our next topic is dyslexia.

# G. Research Focus: Dyslexia

## What Kind of Problem Is Dyslexia?

**Power Study™**

**Check out CD: Module 9**
D. Adaptive Value & Uses

**Was that word "bark" or "dark"?**

In the right photo, 16-year-old Steve Goldberg is wearing a number of medals that he won for projects he submitted to science fairs. Steve does very well in engineering and mechanics classes, such as designing a wind tunnel and making windmills more efficient. However, Steve cannot spell the name of his high school, read a phone number, or distinguish between the words *pine* and *fine* or *dark* and *bark*. Steve has difficulty reading and spelling because of dyslexia.

*Why can't I spell the name of my high school?*

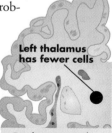

*Dyslexia* refers to reading, spelling, and writing difficulties that may include reversing or skipping letters and numbers. Dyslexia affects 1–2% of children, about an equal number of boys and girls, and is now regarded as a neurological problem rather than a reading problem.

There are about 2.5 million American schoolchildren with learning disabilities and, of these, about 80% have dyslexia (Roush, 1995). Individuals with dyslexia can have a wide range of long-lasting reading or writing difficulties, but they may have normal or above average IQ scores (Shaywitz, 1999b).

In studying dyslexia, psychologists combined the cognitive and biological approaches. We'll discuss new and important research findings on the causes and treatments for dyslexia.

## Why Can't Dyslexics Read?

For most children, learning to speak comes easily because their brains have prewired areas for learning how to speak, which means the instructions for speaking are in their genes (p. 316). However, for some children, learning to read is a struggle because, unlike speaking, instructions for reading are not in their genes, and that means they have to spend many years working to acquire reading skills (Shaywitz, 1999a).

You may not realize that in learning to read, the first step involves learning to change letters on a page into sounds and then distinguishing between sounds so that you can arrange sounds into correct words. As it turns out, to read normally, you must recognize the differences between sounds, such as differences between *ba, pa,* and *la*, very quickly (40 milliseconds). Researchers found that unlike normal readers, dyslexic children take much longer (500 milliseconds) to recognize differences between sounds (Tallal, 1995). Because dyslexics cannot distinguish between sounds (*ba, pa, la*), they cannot see differences between words (*bark, park, lark*). Researchers concluded that the dyslexics' inability to recognize differences between sounds results in various reading difficulties (Shaywitz, 1999a).

Looking for a neurological basis for dyslexia, researchers autopsied brains from five dyslexics and five controls who had no reading problems. Researchers focused on a part of the brain called the thalamus, which receives and processes auditory signals from the ears and transfers these signals to higher brain centers for further analysis important in reading. As shown in the right figure, researchers found fewer neural cells in the left thalamus of dyslexic brains (the left hemisphere is involved primarily with speech and language) (Galaburda et al., 1994). Problems in the thalamus would cause initial problems in processing and recognizing differences between sounds.

More recently, researchers used brain scans to take pictures of neural activity while children were reading. Researchers reported that compared to brains of normal readers, the brains of dyslexics showed less neural activity in the thalamus as well as faulty neural connections between temporal and parietal areas, which are involved in processing visual and auditory information (Klingberg et al., 2000; Talcott et al., 2000). These neural deficits are believed to be largely inherited and involve at least four different genes (Shaywitz, 1999a). Researchers believe that these neural deficits cause a slowdown in processing visual and auditory information, which, in turn, prevents dyslexics from recognizing differences between sounds and words and thus causes difficulties in reading.

Based on the above neurological findings, researchers are developing programs to help dyslexics train their brains to better process visual and auditory information and improve their reading skills. And these programs seem to be working.

**Left thalamus has fewer cells**

Dyslexia may be related to damage to the left thalamus.

## Can Training Help?

One of the first steps in helping dyslexics is to diagnose the problem early, ideally between the ages of 5 and 7, when underlying reading skills are most easily learned (Lyon, 1999). There are now a number of screening tests that identify children with potential reading problems. The key is early intervention, which may involve different kinds of training, such as reading aloud to them and using rhyme games.

More recently, researchers have developed a computer program based on the finding that learning to read requires our brains to quickly distinguish between sounds (40 milliseconds). Because dyslexic children need much longer (500 milliseconds) to distinguish between sounds, they find reading difficult. If dyslexics' brains could be trained to process auditory sounds more quickly, would it also improve their reading skills?

Researchers programmed a computer to play games that increased auditory processing, improved working memory, and gradually helped dyslexic children to distinguish sounds more quickly. After 4 to 8 weeks of repeating thousands of these "reading" games, dyslexics gained one to two years' worth of language ability compared to no change in dyslexics who played the computer games but did not practice identifying and distinguishing between very short sounds (Merzenich et al., 1996). These results appear very promising because they point to a new kind of therapy that helps dyslexics learn to process brief sounds and thus gain the skills needed for reading (Tallal, 1998).

## Differences in Thinking

**Can culture influence thinking?**

You probably don't realize how much your culture influences your thinking because you may not know how people in other cultures think (Hong et al., 2000). For example, look at the underwater scene (top right) and then look away and describe what you saw.

**Differences.** When American students looked at this underwater scene (top right) and then thought about what they saw, they usually began by describing the biggest, brightest, or most outstanding feature—in this case, focusing on the large fish and what it was doing (swimming to the right). In contrast, when Japanese students looked at the same underwater scene and then thought about what they saw, they usually began by describing the background and saying that the bottom was rocky (Had you noticed?) and the water was green (Had you noticed?). They usually discussed how the fish interact with the background, such as the big fish was swimming toward the seaweed. On average, Japanese subjects made 70% more statements about how the background looked than Americans and 100% more statements about the way the objects (fish) interact with the background.

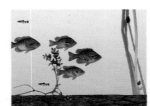

American students' descriptions of these drawings differed from Japanese students'.

Based on these kinds of findings, researchers concluded that Americans usually analyze each object separately, which is called analytical thinking, such as seeing a forest and focusing on the biggest or strangest trees. In comparison, Asian people (Japanese, Chinese, and Koreans) think more about the relationship between objects and backgrounds, which is called holistic thinking, such as seeing a forest and thinking about how the many different trees make up a beautiful forest (Norenzayan & Nisbett, 2000). Researchers suggest that differences in thinking between Americans and Asians—analytical versus holistic—come from differences in social and religious practices and languages (Nisbett, 2000).

Other cultural differences in thinking were revealed when American and Asian (Japanese, Chinese, and Koreans) students were asked to watch an animated film that showed one fish swimming in front of other fish (bottom left). As you look at this figure, what do you think is happening? American students more often thought that the fish in front was a leader for the other fish. In comparison, Asian students more often thought that the fish in front was being chased by the other fish (Hong et al., 2000). Researchers concluded that cultural factors influence how you think much more than you realize.

## Male–Female Differences

**Do men and women think differently?**

Just as culture influences how we think, so do gender differences. For about 20 years, linguist Deborah Tannen (1990, 1994) has been recording and analyzing the conversations of men and women. She found that men and women think and use language differently.

### MALES AND FEMALES USE LANGUAGE DIFFERENTLY

■ Men more frequently use language to express ideas and solve problems. Women more frequently use language to share concerns, daily experiences, and ordinary thoughts.

■ Men use language to maintain their independence and position in their group. Women use language to create connections and develop feelings of intimacy.

■ Men prefer to attack problems, while women prefer to listen, give support, or be sympathetic.

Tannen concluded that neither the female nor the male use of language, which strongly reflects how they think, is necessarily better; the two styles are just different. She added, however, that men and women need to be aware of basic differences in thinking and using language so they can reduce hurt feelings, avoid misunderstandings, and work to improve communication between the sexes.

### BRAINS PROCESS WORDS DIFFERENTLY

One reason for the difference in how males and females use language may be found in a report that male and female brains process language differently.

For the first time, researchers reported clear evidence that the brains of men and women process words differently. Researchers took MRI scans that showed which areas of the brain were most active while men and women performed different language tasks. The left MRI scan shows that, in women, activity during certain word processing tasks occurred almost equally in both the right and left hemispheres (red and yellow areas indicate maximum activity). In contrast, the right MRI scan shows that, in men, activity during the same word processing tasks occurred only in the left hemisphere (Shaywitz et al., 1995).

Researchers concluded that there were many similarities in how male and female brains functioned. However, the significant neurological differences shown in the MRIs may be the basis for behavioral differences between how males and females process words, which reflects their thinking (Rugg, 1995).

Next, we'll discuss the interesting question of whether animals have language.

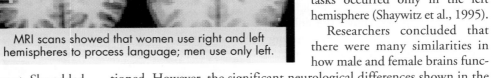

MRI scans showed that women use right and left hemispheres to process language; men use only left.

## Criteria for Language

**What does my dog understand?**

Like most pet owners, I talk to my dog and he usually behaves as if he understands what I say. For example, my dog Bear (photo below) behaves as if he understands "get your toy," "go for walk," "time to eat," and "watch television." The obvious question is: Has Bear learned a language? The answer to this question hinges on the difference between communication and language. As do many animals, Bear has the ability to communicate.

*Communication* is the ability to use sounds, smells, or gestures to exchange information.

But language is much more than just communication.

*Language* is a special form of communication in which an individual learns complex rules for using words or gestures to generate and understand an endless number of meaningful sentences.

Although Bear can communicate, that is, understand my commands and act accordingly, he, like most animals, shows no evidence of meeting the four criteria for having real language.

Dogs communicate but don't have a language.

**1** Language, which is a special form of communication, involves *learning a set of abstract symbols* (whether words for spoken language or hand signs for sign language).

**2** Language involves *using abstract symbols* (words or signs) to express thoughts or indicate objects and events that may or may not be present.

**3** Language involves *learning complex rules of grammar* for forming words into meaningful phrases and sentences.

**4** Language involves using the rules of grammar to *generate an endless number of meaningful sentences.*

Because some animals, such as dolphins and pygmy chimps, show an amazing ability to communicate, researchers are debating whether animals can satisfy all four criteria for language (Begley, 1998a; Savage-Rumbaugh & Lewin, 1994). We'll examine how close several animals come to satisfying the four criteria for language.

## Dolphins

**Do dolphins use language?**

Dolphins are considered very intelligent, not only because of their ability to learn but also because in proportion to the size of their bodies, dolphins' brains are the largest of nonhuman mammals (smaller than human brains but larger than that of great apes) (Tyack, 2000). Because dolphins have relatively large brains, researchers are interested in how well they communicate.

In the wild, dolphins use two kinds of sounds for communication: clicks, which they use to probe the sea and "see" their environment, and whistles, which they use in dolphin-to-dolphin communication, probably to express emotional states and identify the animal to the group (Herman, 1999).

In testing the ability of dolphins to communicate, psychologist Louis Herman (1999) has been training dolphins to respond to hand signals or whistles. He has taught two dolphins to respond to approximately 50 such signals.

For example, in the top right photo, Herman is raising his hands, which is part of a signal for "person over," which means "jump over the person in the pool." The bottom right photo shows the dolphin carrying out the command by jumping over the person and not the surfboard.

Herman found that dolphins can understand a variety of hand signals and perform behaviors in sequence. For example, the hand signal combination "basket, right, Frisbee, fetch" means "Go to the Frisbee on the right and take it to the basket."

Hand signals in top photo tell dolphin to "jump over person," which it does in bottom photo.

More recently, Herman combined "words" by using gestures or whistles in basic "sentences," such as "ball fetch surface hoop." The two dolphins responded correctly to both familiar and novel "sentences" about 85% of the time. Herman concluded that the ability of these two dolphins to pass tests of language comprehension (understanding "sentences"), which indicates an understanding of grammar or syntax, means that dolphins have a relatively sophisticated ability to use language (Herman, 1999). Herman's next step is to determine if dolphins use sounds to communicate information to each other.

However, despite Herman's impressive findings, some scientists remain skeptical. For example, David Kastak, a researcher of animal cognition, said, "What dolphins do may turn out to be a lot more complex than what we thought originally, but do they have what we would call language? No. They are not animals using nouns and verbs" (Mastro, 1999, p. E4).

Although dolphins understand a variety of signals, perform behaviors in sequence, form concepts, and even understand "sentences," they show little evidence of using abstract symbols and applying rules of grammar to generate meaningful sentences to communicate information to other dolphins. It is these criteria that distinguish the ability to use language from the ability to communicate with signs, sounds, or gestures.

Next, let's turn to the greater apes, which in terms of evolution are the animals closest to humans.

## Gorilla and Chimpanzee

**What does a gorilla know?**

Gorillas and chimpanzees have relatively large and well-developed brains. A gorilla's brain weighs about 500 grams, a chimpanzee's about 400 grams, and a human's about 1,350 grams. However, because gorillas and chimpanzees lack the vocal apparatus necessary for making speech sounds, researchers have taught them other forms of language, such as American Sign Language (Ross, 1991).

Shown on the right is researcher Francine Patterson using sign language to communicate with Koko the gorilla, who has a vocabulary of about 800 signs. Similarly, Beatrice and Allen Gardner (1975) taught sign language to a chimpanzee named Washoe, who after four years of training had learned about 160 signs. The finding that gorillas and chimps can learn sign language raised the question of whether they use language in the same way as humans.

*Francine Patterson taught Koko the gorilla a vocabulary of about 800 hand signs.*

Psychologist Herbert Terrace (1981) analyzed videotapes of chimps using sign language with their trainers. He was particularly interested in the videotapes of a chimp named Nim, who has learned more than 125 signs, such as "give orange me." After observing over 20,000 of Nim's signs on videotape, Terrace concluded that Nim was using signs more as tools to obtain things than as abstract symbols or words and that Nim never learned to form combinations of more than a few words. Perhaps the most devastating criticism was that Nim had primarily learned to imitate or respond to cues from human teachers rather than learning and using rules of grammar to initiate or produce new sentences.

As a result of criticisms by Terrace and others, research monies to study language in animals mostly disappeared in the 1980s (Savage-Rumbaugh & Lewin, 1994). However, in the late 1980s, new findings on bonobos again raised the question of language in animals.

## Bonobo Chimp: Star Pupil

**Is this the first real sign of language?**

The best evidence for language in animals comes from the work of psychologist Sue Savage-Rumbaugh. She reported that Kanzi, a bonobo (commonly called a pygmy chimp), has remarkable language skills that surpass previous accomplishments of common chimps (Savage-Rumbaugh, 1991; Savage-Rumbaugh & Lewin, 1994).

Instead of using sign language, Kanzi "speaks" by touching one of 256 symbols on a board (top right photo), each of which stands for a word. For example, Kanzi (bottom right photo) might signal "Want a drink" by touching the symbol for "drink" or signal "Want to play" by touching in sequence two symbols for "hiding" and "play biting."

By the time Kanzi was 6 years old, he had a vocabulary of 90 symbols; at age 12, he knew about 190 symbols but used about 128 regularly. Even more surprising, Kanzi understands about 200 spoken English words, something that common chimps have failed to master.

Perhaps Kanzi's greatest accomplishment is his knowledge of word order. Psychologists tested the ability of Kanzi to respond to 600 spoken English commands that he had not previously encountered, such as "Put the melon in the potty." Savage-Rumbaugh suggests that Kanzi, now 17 years old, has an ability to use abstract symbols (keyboard) and a kind of primitive grammar (word order) for combining symbols that equals the language ability of a 2-year-old child (Savage-Rumbaugh, 1998).

| BLACKBERRIES | BUTTER | VELVET PLANT |
|---|---|---|
| SHOT | STRING | PINE CONE |

*Examples of symbols and their meanings*

*Kanzi has an amazing ability to use and respond to either symbols or English words.*

One reason the findings on Kanzi's language abilities are receiving new attention is that Savage-Rumbaugh used strict control procedures. Savage-Rumbaugh used one-way mirrors to eliminate the possibility that Kanzi was simply imitating or responding to human cues, which had been the major criticism of previous research with chimps.

Doubts about the chimpanzees' ability to learn and use language were based partly on the belief that they lacked a brain area similar to the one that humans use for language. The considerable language ability of humans comes from a specific brain area (Wernicke's area) that is larger in the left than right hemisphere. However, researchers recently reported that chimpanzees do have a similar brain area and that, as in humans, this area is larger in the left hemisphere (Gannon et al., 1998). Researchers suggest that human language originated from this brain structure in the left hemisphere and that language began more than 8 million years ago in the common ancestor of chimpanzees and humans.

Researchers who study evolution speculate that as early humans began to form social groups, the great pressure to keep track of their physical needs and enormously complex personal and social interactions led to the development of language abilities (Linden, 1993).

## A. FORMING CONCEPTS

**1.** There are two theories of how you might have formed your concept of a dog and how you form concepts generally. If you form a concept of an object, event, or characteristic by making a list of the properties that define it, you are using (a)_____ theory. If you form a concept by constructing an idea of the ideal object and then seeing whether a new object matches that idea, you are using (b)_____ theory.

**2.** A concept is a way to group objects, events, or characteristics on the basis of some common property they all share. Concepts perform two important functions: They allow us to (a)_____ objects and thus better organize and store information in memory, and to identify things without (b) _____.

## B. SOLVING PROBLEMS

**3.** The process of searching for some rule, plan, or strategy that results in reaching a certain goal that is currently out of reach is called (a)_____. We usually go through three states in solving problems: (b)_____, _____, and _____.

**4.** We win at games by following rules. If we correctly follow a set of rules that lead to a solution, these rules are called (a)_____. As you gain experience with solving problems, you may use rules of thumb that reduce the number of operations or allow you to take shortcuts in solving problems; these shortcuts are called (b)_____. In making everyday decisions, you rely on information that is more prominent or easily recalled and overlook other information that is available but less prominent or notable; this is an example of using the (c)_____ heuristic.

**5.** By studying how people eventually solve problems, psychologists have discovered a number of useful strategies, including changing our (a)_____. This often involves breaking out of a pattern called (b)_____, in which we cannot see an object as having a function different from its usual one.

**6.** The sudden grasp of a solution after many incorrect attempts is called (a)_____. Another kind of thinking that is useful in solving problems is to find (b)_____, which are similarities between new situations and familiar situations. Still another useful strategy for solving problems is to break the problem down into a number of (c)_____, which, when completed in order, will result in a solution.

## C. THINKING CREATIVELY

**7.** A combination of flexibility in thinking and reorganization of understanding to produce innovative ideas and solutions is referred to as (a)_____. Psychologists distinguish between two different kinds of thinking. If you begin with a problem and come up with the one correct solution, it is called (b)_____. If you begin with a problem and come up with many different solutions, it is called (c)_____, which is another definition of creative thinking.

## D. LANGUAGE: BASIC RULES

**8.** Our most impressive skill is thought to be a special form of communication in which an individual learns complex rules to manipulate symbols (words or gestures) and so generates an endless number of meaningful sentences; this form of communication is called _____.

**9.** All of the 6,000 known languages share four basic language rules, which are normally learned during childhood. The first language rule governs (a)_____, which specifies how we make meaningful sounds that are used by a particular language. The second language rule governs (b)_____, which specifies how we group phonemes into meaningful combinations of sounds and words. The third language rule governs (c)_____, which specifies how we combine words to form meaningful phrases and sentences. The fourth language rule governs (d)_____, which specifies the meanings of words in various contexts.

**10.** The linguist Noam Chomsky distinguished between how a sentence is worded, which he called the (a)_____ structure, and the meaning of the sentence, which he called the (b)_____ structure. Procedures for converting our ideas from surface structures into deep structures and from deep structures back into surface ones are called (c)_____.

## E. ACQUIRING LANGUAGE

**11.** Children around the world acquire language in the same four stages that are associated with growth and development of the (a)_____. In the first stage, generally at about the age of 6 months, the infant makes one-syllable sounds; this is called (b)_____. By about 1 year of age, a child forms (c)_____, which usually refer to what the child can see,

hear, or feel. At about 2 years of age, a child makes (d)_____ to express various actions or relationships. At about 4 years of age, a child is forming sentences, which range from three to eight words in length and indicate a growing knowledge of the (e)_____.

**12.** A child's beginning sentences differ from adult sentences. A child's speech is called (a)_____ because it omits articles, prepositions, and parts of verbs. In learning the rules for combining nouns, verbs, and adjectives into meaningful sentences, children often apply a grammatical rule to cases where it should not be used. This type of error is called (b)_____. Although all children pass through these stages in the same order, they may go through them at different ages and speeds.

**13.** Children are able to acquire a language with so little formal training because of genetically programmed physiological and neurological features in the brain and vocal apparatus; these features are called (a)_____ factors. One innate factor is the period of time from infancy to adolescence when language is easier to learn, called the (b)_____. Children acquire the sounds and rules of a particular language because of their interactions with their surroundings; these interactions are called (c)_____ factors. The approach that emphasizes observation, exploration, and imitation in language acquisition is (d)_____.

### F. REASON, THOUGHT, & LANGUAGE

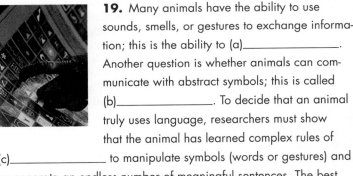

**14.** The process by which we use and apply knowledge to achieve certain goals that involve solving problems or making decisions is called (a)_____. This process has two different forms: If you begin with a general assumption and draw specific conclusions, you are using (b)_____ reasoning; if you begin with specific observations and then draw a general conclusion, you are using (c)_____ reasoning.

**15.** Whorf has suggested that language determines or influences the way people think and that people with different languages think and perceive their world differently. This is called the theory of _____. There is only weak support for Whorf's theory.

### G. RESEARCH FOCUS: DYSLEXIA

**16.** A neurological disorder whose symptoms include reversing or skipping letters and numbers, with accompanying difficulties in reading, spelling, and writing, is called (a)_____. These

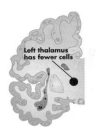

Left thalamus has fewer cells

symptoms are believed to be caused by maldevelopment in a particular part of the brain, called the (b)_____, which processes auditory information necessary for hearing differences in sounds that are used to make words. Dyslexia is not an all-or-nothing condition but rather is on a continuum that includes a wide range of reading difficulties, which may be accompanied by normal IQ scores.

### H. CULTURAL DIVERSITY: INFLUENCES ON THINKING

**17.** Men tend to use language to express ideas, maintain their position in the group, and solve (a)_____, while women use language more to share concerns, daily experiences, and develop feelings of (b)_____.

**18.** MRI scans of the brain have shown that women process some words equally in both (a)_____, while men process words only in the (b)_____ hemisphere.

### I. APPLICATION: DO ANIMALS HAVE LANGUAGE?

**19.** Many animals have the ability to use sounds, smells, or gestures to exchange information; this is the ability to (a)_____. Another question is whether animals can communicate with abstract symbols; this is called (b)_____. To decide that an animal truly uses language, researchers must show that the animal has learned complex rules of (c)_____ to manipulate symbols (words or gestures) and so generate an endless number of meaningful sentences. The best evidence for language in animals is the (d)_____, who has matched the language ability of a 2-year-old child.

***Answers:*** *1. (a) definition, (b) prototype; 2. (a) categorize, (b) relearning; 3. (a) problem solving, (b) initial state, operations state, goal state; 4. (a) algorithms, (b) heuristics, (c) availability; 5. (a) mental set, (b) functional fixedness; 6. (a) insight, (b) analogies, (c) subgoals; 7. (a) creative thinking, (b) convergent thinking, (c) divergent thinking; 8. language; 9. (a) phonology, (b) morphology, (c) syntax or grammar, (d) semantics; 10. (a) surface, (b) deep, (c) transformational rules; 11. (a) brain, (b) babbling, (c) single words, (d) two-word combinations, (e) rules of grammar; 12. (a) telegraphic, (b) overgeneralization; 13. (a) innate, (b) critical language period, (c) environmental, (d) social cognitive learning; 14. (a) reasoning, (b) deductive, (c) inductive; 15. linguistic relativity; 16. (a) dyslexia, (b) thalamus; 17. (a) problems, (b) intimacy; 18. (a) hemispheres, (b) left; 19. (a) communicate, (b) language, (c) grammar, (d) bonobo (pygmy chimp)*

# Critical Thinking

## WHY DO PARENTS SPEAK LOUDLY AND SLOWLY?

*by Robert Lee Hotz*

The singsong crooning that every adult instinctively adopts for conversation with a newborn baby is more than patronizing gibberish passing between the generations. It is a universal teaching mechanism rooted in the biology of language and the developing human brain, say neuroscientists Patricia Kuhl and her colleagues at the University of Washington in Seattle, who studied how native speakers of English, Swedish, and Russian talk to infants.

Linguists call the special tone adults reserve for speech with infants "parentese," and the new research indicates it is the same in every culture around the world.

To examine the role of parentese, Kuhl and her colleagues in Russia and Sweden investigated differences in how American, Swedish, and Russian mothers speak to their infants and to other adults. The three languages were chosen because each has a significantly different number of vowel sounds. Russian has five vowel sounds, English nine, and Swedish 16.

The researchers recorded 10 women from each of the three countries talking for 20 minutes to their babies, who ranged in age from 2 to 5 months. Then they recorded the same women talking to other adults. The mothers were told to talk naturally, but were given a list of words containing three common vowel sounds and instructed to work them into their conversations.

For those speaking English, the target words were "bead" for its "ee" vowel sound, "pot" for its "ah" sound, and "boot" for its "oo" sound. Similar words were chosen from Russian and Swedish.

The researchers then used a spectrograph to analyze more than 2,300 instances of how the target words were used in the conversations and discovered that, in all three language groups, the speech directed at infants was stretched out to emphasize the vowel sounds, in contrast to the more normal tone used with adults.

The researchers concluded that the exaggerated speech allowed the mothers to expand the sounds of the vowels so they would be more distinct from each other. It also appears to allow the mothers to produce a greater variety of vowel pronunciations without overlapping other vowel sounds. (Source: *Los Angeles Times*, September 18, 1997)

### Questions

**1.** What is the term for and what is the purpose of the "baby talk" that parents or caregivers use with their infants?

**2.** What would happen if parents or caregivers never spoke to their children?

**3.** Why did the researchers study English, Russian, and Swedish?

**4.** Why did researchers compare how mothers talked to infants and other adults?

**5.** What might happen if mothers or caregivers spoke to infants the same way they spoke to adults?

**6.** How do the mothers' speaking parentese fit in with the critical period for language?

*Try InfoTrac to search for terms:* baby talk; language acquisition.

---

### Suggested answers for Newspaper Article questions

1. "Baby talk" is called parentese (motherese). The purpose of parentese is to teach infants the particular sounds or phonetic building blocks that will be used to form and speak words.
2. For her first 13 years, Genie was punished for making sounds and was never spoken to by her parents. As a result, Genie could not speak a single word and, even with training, developed language skills of only a 2- to 3-year-old child. (Discussion is on page 316.)
3. Researchers chose three different languages because each of these languages had a different number of vowel sounds and researchers wanted to know if mothers would exaggerate the vowel sounds particular to their different languages.
4. Researchers compared how mothers spoke to infants versus adults to see if they used parentese only with infants. It turned out that mothers exaggerated vowel sounds when speaking to their babies but did not when speaking to other adults.
5. If mothers spoke the same to infants and adults, then infants would not hear the slow, exaggerated vowel sounds (parentese) and would have difficulty learning the particular sounds that make up the particular language of their parents.
6. The critical period says that language is easiest to learn between infancy and adolescence. The use of parentese at the beginning of the critical period gives the infant a great start in developing language and successfully going through the four stages of language (babbling, one word, two-word combinations, sentences).

# Links to Learning

## Web Sites

- **WADSWORTH ONLINE STUDY CENTER**
  http://psychology.wadsworth.com
  Quizzes, learning activities and exercises, a discussion forum, and hot links to Internet sites related to sensation, including:

- **THE HUMAN LANGUAGES PAGE**
  http://www.ilovelanguages.com
  Interested in linguistics? Here is a comprehensive index to 2,000 relevant Internet sites.

- **DYSLEXIA: THE GIFT**
  http://www.dyslexia.com/
  This site offers support for people with dyslexia, including a newsletter, library, games, and links.

- **NATIONAL APHASIA ASSOCIATION**
  http://www.aphasia.org/
  Aphasia is a common cause of language problems, especially among older people. This site offers news, research, and readings to anyone interested in aphasia.

- **FUN WITH LANGUAGES**
  http://www.ncbe.gwu.edu/classroom/fun.htm
  Have fun with word play, pick up useful foreign phrases, compare how animal sounds are expressed in different languages, and learn how to draw your name in Egyptian hieroglyphs!

## Learning Activities

- **POWERSTUDY™ BY ROD PLOTNIK & TOM DOYLE**

  **PowerStudy™**

  **Check out CD: Module 14**

  | | |
  |---|---|
  | CD section 3.B: | Neurons: Structure and Function; book page 314 |
  | CD section 4.B: | Studying the Living Brain; book page 307 |
  | CD section 4.D: | Control Centers: Four Lobes; book pages 313, 314, 316 |
  | CD section 9.D: | Adaptive Values and Uses; book page 320 |
  | CD section 10.D: | Long-Term Memory; Storing; book page 307 |
  | CD section 10.F: | Biological Factors; book page 313 |

- **STUDY GUIDE TO ACCOMPANY INTRODUCTION TO PSYCHOLOGY, 6TH EDITION, by Matthew Enos**
  In Module 14, there's a thoughtful discussion about what makes us human, and advice for applying things you know outside of school to what you learn in class.

- **WEBTUTOR**
  http://webtutor.thomsonlearning.com
  **Web**TUTOR  Visit this site for interactive versions of the Study Guide features. Take a quiz, get your score—should you study a topic some more, or can you move on? For example, who are Koko and Washoe? What might keep you from solving the nine-dot problem?

- **INFOTRAC ONLINE LIBRARY**
  http://www.infotrac-college.com
   Use your password and then key in search terms such as those below to find popular and scientific articles on subjects covered in Module 14. Make the library work for you!

  | | | |
  |---|---|---|
  | Noam Chomsky | Dyslexia | Inductive reasoning |
  | Morphology | Phonology | Savants |

- **PSYCHNOW!**
  CD for Macintosh and Windows includes a study guide, glossary, Web sites, and animations. For Module 14, see:
  - Cognition and Language
  - Problem Solving and Creativity

## Study Questions

*Use InfoTrac to search for topics mentioned in the main heads below (e.g., problem solving, creative thinking, language acquisition).*

*A. **Forming Concepts**—Why is it difficult to explain to your younger sister or brother that a whale is a mammal and not a fish? (**Suggested answer page 628**)

B. **Solving Problems**—Why is it easier to win at checkers the longer you have been playing?

C. **Thinking Creatively**—How would you teach people to think more creatively?

D. **Language: Basic Rules**—To develop a secret code for sending computer messages across a network, which language rule should you break?

E. **Acquiring Language**—Why might students in college have more difficulty learning a foreign language than students in grade school?

*F. **Reason, Thought, & Language**—What problems might result when heads of government speak through translators? (**Suggested answer page 628**)

G. **Research Focus: Dyslexia**—Why does dyslexia cause difficulties with reading but not with engineering and inventive abilities?

*H. **Cultural Diversity: Influences on Thinking**—What kinds of social problems can arise from finding differences between male and female brains? (**Suggested answer page 628**)

I. **Application: Do Animals Have Language?**—When a parrot speaks perfect English and understands dozens of commands, can we conclude it is using language?

*These questions are answered in Appendix B.

# Module 15: Motivation

**A. Theories of Motivation**　　330
* INSTINCT THEORY
* DRIVE-REDUCTION THEORY
* INCENTIVE THEORY
* COGNITIVE THEORY
* EXPLAINING HUMAN MOTIVATION

**B. Biological & Social Needs**　　332
* BIOLOGICAL NEEDS
* SOCIAL NEEDS
* SATISFYING NEEDS
* MASLOW'S HIERARCHY OF NEEDS

**C. Hunger**　　334
* OPTIMAL WEIGHT
* OVERWEIGHT
* THREE HUNGER FACTORS
* BIOLOGICAL HUNGER FACTORS
* GENETIC HUNGER FACTORS
* PSYCHOSOCIAL HUNGER FACTORS

**D. Sexual Behavior**　　338
* GENETIC INFLUENCES ON SEXUAL BEHAVIOR
* BIOLOGICAL INFLUENCES
* PSYCHOLOGICAL INFLUENCES ON SEXUAL BEHAVIOR
* MALE–FEMALE SEX DIFFERENCES
* HOMOSEXUALITY
* SEXUAL RESPONSE, PROBLEMS, AND TREATMENTS
* AIDS

**E. Cultural Diversity: Female Circumcision**　　346
* GOOD TRADITION OR CRUEL MUTILATION?

**Concept Review**　　347

**F. Achievement**　　348
* KINDS OF ACHIEVEMENT
* FEAR OF FAILURE
* UNDERACHIEVEMENT
* THREE COMPONENTS OF SUCCESS
* COGNITIVE INFLUENCES
* INTRINSIC MOTIVATION

**G. Research Focus: Immigrant Students**　　351
* WHY DID IMMIGRANT CHILDREN DO WELL?

**H. Application: Eating Problems & Treatments**　　352
* DIETING: PROBLEMS, CONCERNS, AND BENEFITS
* SERIOUS EATING DISORDERS

**Summary Test**　　354

**Critical Thinking**　　356
* HOW EFFECTIVE IS VIAGRA?

**Links to Learning**　　357

## Motivation

**Why would a paraplegic climb a mountain?**

On a cool September morning, two men began to climb a nearly vertical slope rising over 2,200 feet from the floor of Yosemite National Park. Because of the slope's crumbly granite, fewer than 30 people had completed this particular route up Half Dome, Yosemite's well-known landmark. What made this particular climb very difficult and dangerous was that one of the men, Mark Wellman, is a paraplegic.

Some years ago, on a different climb, Mark fell 50 feet into a crevice, hurt his back, and was paralyzed from the waist down. Mark now climbs with his friend Mike Corbett, who takes the lead and sets the supports. Because Mark's legs are paralyzed, he climbs by using the supports to pull himself up inch by inch.

Mark figured that by doing the equivalent of 5,000 pull-ups, each of which would raise him about 6 inches, he could climb the 2,200 feet in seven days. By the end of day seven, however, Mark and Mike were only a little more than halfway up the slope and had to sleep by hanging in sleeping bags anchored to the sheer granite wall.

By day ten, Mark was becoming exhausted as his arms strained to raise his body's weight up the vertical face (left photo). By day 12, the men were almost out of food and water. Finally, on day 13, six days later than planned, Mark pulled himself up the last 6 inches and over the top of Half Dome. When Mark was asked later why he still climbed and risked further injury, he said, "Everyone has their own goals. . . . Never underestimate a person with a disability" (adapted from the *Los Angeles Times,* September 19, 1991, p. A-3).

Reporters who questioned Mark about why he risked his life to climb were really asking about his motivation.

Mark Wellman, a paraplegic, was motivated to do the equivalent of 5,000 pull-ups to climb the almost vertical face of Half Dome.

*Motivation* refers to the various physiological and psychological factors that cause us to act in a specific way at a particular time.

When you are motivated, you usually show three characteristics:

1. You are *energized* to do or engage in some activity.
2. You *direct* your energies toward reaching a specific goal.
3. You have differing *intensities* of feelings about reaching that goal.

We can observe these three characteristics in Mark's behavior:

1. He was energized to perform the equivalent of 5,000 pull-ups during his 13-day climb.
2. He directed his energy toward climbing a particular slope that fewer than 30 other climbers had completed.
3. He felt so intensely about reaching that goal that even when totally exhausted he still persisted in reaching his goal, the top of Half Dome.

We'll discuss several kinds of motivating forces, including those involved in eating and drinking, sexual behavior, achievement, underachievement, failure, and of course, climbing mountains.

## Achievement

**Why did friends call him a "White boy"?**

Victor remembers being in the seventh grade when some of his Black buddies called him a "White boy" because they thought he was studying too hard. "You can't be cool if you're smart," says Victor, who was Mission Bay High's student body president, had a 3.7 (A–) grade point average, and planned to attend the University of Southern California in the fall (adapted from the *San Diego Union-Tribune,* June 17, 1994).

Victor (photo below) grew up with an obstacle that goes largely unnoticed and is rarely discussed in public: pressure from students in the same racial or ethnic group not to succeed in the classroom. Faced with this negative peer pressure, some minority students (principally Latino, African American, and Native American teenage boys) stop studying, don't do homework, avoid answering questions in class, join gangs, and even drop out of school.

Educators believe that the high dropout rates for some minorities along with peer pressure not to succeed in school result, in part, from a cultural bias against appearing to be too smart or intellectual (McWhorter, 2000). How Victor overcame this negative peer pressure and did succeed will be discussed later in this module.

Victor was proud of his A– average even though some of his peers believed "you can't be cool if you're too smart."

## What's Coming

We'll look at four general theories that psychologists use to explain motivation, discuss the differences between social and biological needs, and then focus on specific examples, such as hunger, sexual behavior, and achievement. We'll examine why some people are achievers and others are underachievers. We'll discuss why people become overweight and why dieting is so difficult. We'll look at two serious eating disorders that result more from psychological than from biological factors.

We'll begin with four general theories that psychologists use to explain motivation.

**Why does Mark climb?**

For 13 days, sightseers on the Yosemite valley floor watched Mark pull himself up the granite face of Half Dome. Many asked, "Why is he doing that?" The inquisitive onlookers were asking about Mark's motivation: Why was he pulling himself up this impossibly steep mountain? To understand what motivates Mark's behavior, we'll discuss four general theories—the instinct, drive-reduction, incentive, and cognitive theories.

### Instinct Theory

**Is he driven by instincts?**

If you could travel back to the early 1900s, you would hear William McDougall (1908) claim that humans were motivated by a number of different instincts.

*Instincts* are innate tendencies or biological forces that determine behavior.

Initially, McDougall listed about a half-dozen instincts, such as flight, repulsion, curiosity, pugnacity, and self-abasement. By the 1920s, psychologists had proposed over 6,000 instincts to explain every kind of human motivation.

#### DOES MARK HAVE AN INSTINCT FOR CLIMBING?

In the 1920s, Mark's desire to climb mountains would probably have been explained in terms of an instinct for seeking excitement or novelty. But just labeling climbing or some other behavior as an instinct does nothing more than name or describe the behavior; it does not explain why a person engages in that behavior. Because instincts became labels rather than explanations, psychologists abandoned the use of instincts to explain human motivation. However, psychologists and ethologists—biologists who study animal behavior—have now redefined instinct as being a fixed action pattern (FitzGerald, 1993).

A *fixed action pattern* is an innate biological force that predisposes an organism to behave in a fixed way in the presence of a specific environmental condition.

Animals have innate biological tendencies to behave in certain ways.

For example, in the above photo, the baboon is innately predisposed to behave in a fixed way (opens mouth, stares, rises on hind feet) in the presence of a specific environmental condition (a cheetah, a threatening stimulus).

**PS** Ethologists observe how animals use fixed action patterns in adapting to their natural environments. Earlier (p. 228), we discussed ethologist Konrad Lorenz (1952) and his well-known work on imprinting in birds. Lorenz found that soon after birth a bird usually becomes attached to, or imprinted on, the first moving object (animal, human, or basketball) it encounters, and it continues to interact with that object as if it were its parent. This is an example of a fixed action pattern.

The second theory of motivation focuses on biological factors.

### Drive-Reduction Theory

**Does he have a need to climb?**

By the 1930s, so many human instincts had been proposed that instinct was no longer a useful concept to explain motivation. In the 1940s and 1950s, psychologists developed two new concepts to explain human motivation—needs and drives (Hull, 1952).

A *need* is a biological state in which the organism lacks something essential for survival, such as food, water, or oxygen. The need produces a *drive,* which is a state of tension that motivates the organism to act to reduce that tension.

Once the need is satisfied, the body returns to a more balanced state.

*Homeostasis* is the tendency of the body to return to, and remain in, a more balanced state.

By combining these three concepts—need, drive, and homeostasis—we have the key components of the drive-reduction theory.

The *drive-reduction theory* says that a need results in a drive, which is a state of tension that motivates the organism to act to reduce the tension and return the body to homeostasis.

As an example, not eating for a period of time causes a need for food, which produces a *drive,* or state of tension. In

We all have a biological need for food, which is essential for our survival.

turn, the drive, or tension, energizes the person to *act,* perhaps by raiding the refrigerator, thereby reducing the tension and returning the body to *homeostasis.*

According to drive-reduction theory, drives motivate us to engage in a wide variety of behaviors to satisfy biological needs. For example, psychologists might refer to an organism as having a hunger drive or a thirst drive. However, drive-reduction theory has difficulty explaining why, after we satisfy our hunger need with a complete meal and say we are full, we then eat a dessert.

#### DOES MARK HAVE A NEED TO CLIMB?

Mark probably does not have a biological need for climbing, which in most cases results in fear and excitement that increase rather than decrease body arousal or tension. Drive-reduction theory cannot explain why we sometimes act to increase needs and drives (Locke & Latham, 1994). It is more likely that Mark climbs to satisfy a variety of psychological needs, including the need for excitement, novelty, or challenge.

Needs and drives are processes that we assume are going on inside Mark's body. Researchers have also identified motivational forces that occur in our environments or in our minds.

## Incentive Theory

**Why do you study?**

The issue of motivation becomes very personal when we ask you to explain why you sacrificed so much and worked so hard to get into college. Now that you're in college, what is motivating you to study for all those exams and write all those papers? One answer is that you want to get a college degree, which is considered a very big incentive (Atkinson & Birch, 1978; Skinner, 1953).

*Incentives* are environmental factors, such as external stimuli, reinforcers, or rewards, that motivate our behaviors.

The degree was worth the hard work!

Your behaviors can be motivated by a variety of incentives, including grades, praise, money, and a high school or college degree. Because incentives are external—in the environment—they are thought of as *pulling* us to obtain them. In comparison, because drives are internal, they are thought of as *pushing* us to reduce needs. This push-pull difference between drives and incentives explains some otherwise perplexing behaviors.

For instance, what motivates us to continue performing the same behavior after our need is already met? Why do we eat a dessert after complaining of being stuffed, or buy more clothes when our closet is already full? Incentive theory explains that, even though our immediate needs are met, incentives such as stylish clothes or highly desired foods continue to pull us toward them.

Why do we engage in risky behaviors that increase arousal, such as mountain climbing, or behaviors that deliberately tax or damage our bodies, such as vigorous sports? Incentive theory explains that when we perform arousing or life-threatening behaviors, we are motivated by positive incentives, such as praise, recognition, or excitement.

### DOES MARK CLIMB TO OBTAIN INCENTIVES?

One reason Mark may climb is to obtain incentives, such as recognition in the form of national press coverage, invitations for speaking, and monies ($100,000) from corporate sponsors that he donates to help others with disabilities. However, other equally powerful reasons for Mark's climbing probably involve cognitive factors (Little, 1999).

## Cognitive Theory

**Why do people run marathons?**

Thousands of people train for months to run grueling 26-mile-long marathons, in which only the top two or three receive any prize money. What motivates people to endure such agony? Beginning in the 1960s, psychologists such as Albert Bandura (1986), Richard deCharms (1980), Edward Deci (Deci & Ryan, 1985), and Bernard Weiner (1991) began applying cognitive concepts to explain human motivation. These cognitive researchers said that one reason people run marathons, usually for no reward other than a T-shirt, has to do with the difference between extrinsic and intrinsic motivation.

*Extrinsic motivation* involves engaging in certain activities or behaviors that either reduce biological needs or help us obtain incentives or external rewards.

*Intrinsic motivation* involves engaging in certain activities or behaviors because the behaviors themselves are personally rewarding or because engaging in these activities fulfills our beliefs or expectations.

Intrinsic motivation explains that people volunteer their services, spend hours on hobbies, run marathons, or work on personal projects because these activities are personally rewarding, fulfilling, or challenging. Intrinsic motivation emphasizes that we do many things because of personal beliefs, expectations, or goals, rather than external incentives. The concept of intrinsic motivation provides quite a different way of explaining human motivation.

I need to prove to myself that I can do it!

### DOES MARK CLIMB BECAUSE OF INTRINSIC MOTIVATION?

Besides the explanations offered by the drive-reduction and incentive theories, cognitive theory's concept of intrinsic motivation suggests another reason for Mark's dangerous behavior: Climbing itself was rewarding; climbing allowed him to meet his own personal goals, beliefs, and expectations. As Mark said, "Everyone has their own goals." And so does Mark.

## Explaining Human Motivation

**Which theory is correct?**

We have discussed four theories of motivation that try to explain what *energizes* people and what *directs* their behavior into specific actions. The theory of *fixed action patterns* explains the behaviors of animals. The *drive-reduction theory*, a pushing force, explains our actions to meet biological or physiological needs. The *incentive theory*, a pulling force, explains that we may do things to obtain external rewards. The *cognitive theory* explains that we may do things to satisfy personal beliefs or meet personal goals. For example, you may work years to obtain a degree, or Mark may have undertaken his life-threatening climb because of strong personal beliefs (Deci et al., 1999).

One reason the cognitive theory of human motivation has grown in popularity is that it focuses on the importance of personal beliefs and expectations, which are primary forces in many human behaviors (Little, 1999).

Two interesting questions about human motivation are: How many needs do we have? and In which order will we satisfy them? Next, we'll answer these questions.

## B. Biological & Social Needs

| **How do you spend your day?** | Recent television programs ("Survivor") let you watch what happened when a group of strangers were isolated in very deserted places. What you saw was how individuals in each group spent considerable time and effort trying to satisfy numerous biological and social needs. Here's how biological and social needs differ. |

---

### Biological Needs

| **What are this man and his pet pig doing?** | One of our most popular activities is eating, which fulfills a basic biological need. |

*Biological needs* are physiological requirements that are critical to our survival and physical well-being.

Researchers have identified 10–15 biological needs, six of which are listed on the right (Madsen, 1973). We all share the same biological needs, many of which we must satisfy daily to survive and to keep our bodies functioning at their best.

These two are satisfying biological needs.

In extreme cases, people may seriously interfere with meeting their biological needs. Such is the case with the eating disorder anorexia nervosa, in which individuals may starve themselves to death. We'll discuss this disorder in the Application section. In other cases, people may choose to suffer considerable pain and injury, as happens in football, boxing, and climbing. These examples demonstrate how psychological factors can override basic biological needs.

Although there are a limited number of biological needs, there are many social needs.

Biological Needs
Food
Water
Sex
Oxygen
Sleep
Avoid pain

---

### Social Needs

| **Why did they get married?** | One reason that about 90% of adults in the United States get married is that being married satisfies a number of social needs. |

*Social needs* are needs that are acquired through learning and experience.

Depending on one's learning and experiences, there are dozens of social needs, some of which are listed on the right (Murray, 1938). Notice that being married can satisfy a number of these social needs, such as affiliation, nurturance, play, dominance, and achievement. The need for affiliation, or forming lasting and positive interpersonal attachments, is one of our stronger social needs and is important to maintaining physical health and psychological well-being (Baumeister & Leary, 1995).

Getting married satisfies a number of social needs.

In some cases, the distinction between biological and social needs is blurred. For example, we may eat or drink not only to satisfy biological needs but to make social contact as well. Similarly, we may engage in sex for reproduction, which is a biological need, or to express love and affection, which are social needs. Even if needs overlap, we have only so much time and energy to satisfy a relatively large number of biological and social needs. This condition leaves us with a problem: How do we decide which needs to satisfy first?

Social Needs
Achieve
Form social bonds
Nourish & protect
Be independent
Influence others
Have fun, relax

---

### Satisfying Needs

| **Which need gets satisfied?** | As you may remember from Module 1, Abraham Maslow was one of the founders of the humanistic approach in psychology. Maslow was particularly interested in human motivation, |

especially in how we choose which biological or social need to satisfy. For example, should you study late for an exam and satisfy your social need to achieve, or go to bed at your regular time and satisfy your biological need for sleep? Maslow (1970) proposed that we satisfy our needs in a certain order or according to a set hierarchy.

Are you most likely to satisfy biological needs before social needs?

*Maslow's hierarchy of needs* is an ascending order, or hierarchy, in which biological needs are placed at the bottom and social needs at the top. This hierarchy indicates that we satisfy our biological needs before we satisfy our social needs.

Maslow hypothesized that, after we satisfy needs at the bottom level of the hierarchy, we advance up the hierarchy to satisfy the needs at the next level. However, if we are at a higher level and basic needs are not satisfied, we may come back down the hierarchy. Let's examine Maslow's hierarchy of needs in more detail.

**Which needs do you satisfy first?**

If you were very hungry and very lonely at the same time, which need would you satisfy first, your biological need (hunger) or your social need (affiliation)? One answer to this question can be found in Maslow's hierarchy of needs, which says that you satisfy your biological needs before you can turn your attention and energy to fulfilling your personal and social needs. According to Maslow, when it comes to satisfying your needs, you begin at the bottom of the needs hierarchy, with physiological needs, and then work your way toward the top. As you meet the needs at one level, you

advance to the next level. For example, if your physiological needs at Level 1 are satisfied, you advance to Level 2 and work on satisfying your safety needs. Once your safety needs are satisfied, you advance to Level 3, and so forth, up the needs hierarchy.

Maslow's hierarchy of needs is represented by a pyramid and shows the order in which you satisfy your biological and social needs. The first needs you satisfy are physiological or biological ones, so please go to the bottom of the pyramid and begin reading Level 1. Then continue reading Levels 2, 3, 4, and 5, which takes you up the pyramid.

**Level 5  Self-actualization: Fulfillment of one's unique potential.** If we face roadblocks in reaching our true potential, we will feel frustrated. For example, if you are majoring in business and your real interest and talent is music, your need for self-actualization may be unsatisfied. According to Maslow, the highest need is self-actualization, which involves developing and reaching our full potential as unique human beings. However, Maslow cautioned that very few individuals reach the level of self-actualization because it is so difficult and challenging. Examples of individuals who might be said to have reached the level of self-actualization would include Abraham Lincoln, Albert Einstein, Eleanor Roosevelt, and Martin Luther King, Jr.

**Level 4  Esteem needs: Achievement, competency, gaining approval and recognition.** During early and middle adulthood, people are especially concerned with achieving their goals and establishing their careers. As we develop skills to gain personal achievement and social recognition, we turn our energies to Level 5.

**Level 3  Love and belonging needs: Affiliation with others and acceptance by others.** Adolescents and young adults, who are beginning to form serious relationships, would be especially interested in fulfilling their needs for love and belonging. After we find love and affection, we advance to Level 4.

**Level 2  Safety needs: Protection from harm.** People who live in high-crime or dangerous areas of the city would be very concerned about satisfying their safety needs. After we find a way to live in a safe and secure environment, we advance to Level 3.

**Level 1  Physiological needs: Food, water, sex, and sleep.** People who are homeless or jobless would be especially concerned with satisfying their physiological needs above all other needs. We must satisfy these basic needs before we advance to Level 2.

Maslow's hierarchy of needs suggests order in which we satisfy our needs.

**Conclusion.**   One advantage of Maslow's hierarchy is that it integrates biological and social needs into a single framework and proposes a list of priorities for the order in which we satisfy various biological and social needs (Frick, 2000).

One problem with Maslow's hierarchy is that researchers have found it difficult to verify whether his particular order of needs is accurate or to know how to assess some of his needs, especially self-actualization, which very few individuals are able to reach (Geller, 1982). Another problem is that people give different priorities to needs: some may value love over self-esteem

or vice versa (Neher, 1991). We'll discuss Maslow's hierarchy of needs later on when we explain humanistic theories of personality (p. 443). Despite criticisms of Maslow's hierarchy, it remains a useful reminder of the number and complexity of human needs.

To give you a sample of how psychologists study human motivation, we have selected two biological needs—hunger and sex—from Maslow's Level 1 and one social need—achievement—from Maslow's Level 4. We consider these needs in the following sections.

# C. Hunger

## Optimal Weight

**Why don't you see fat wolves?**

The reason you never see fat wolves is that they, like all animals, have an inherited biological system that carefully regulates their eating so that they maintain their optimal, or ideal, weights (Kolata, 2000b).

*Optimal* or *ideal weight* results from an almost perfect balance between how much food an organism eats and how much it needs to meet its body's energy needs.

In the wild, animals usually eat only to replace fuel used by their bodies, and thus they rarely get fat. In addition, most wild animals use up a tremendous amount of energy in finding food. In comparison, home pets may become fat because

Animals rely on a biological system to regulate weight.

their owners, having the best of intentions, give the pets too much food or food so tasty that their pets eat too much. And unlike wild animals, home-bound pets may have few opportunities to run around and burn off the extra food or surplus calories.

A *calorie* is simply a measure of how much energy food contains. For example, food high in fats (pizza, cheeseburger, french fries, donuts) usually have twice the calories of foods high in protein (fish, chicken, eggs) or high in carbohydrates (vegetables, fruits, grains). The same factors that make pets overweight also make humans overweight.

## Overweight

**Why do people become overweight?**

Like animals, we humans also have an inherited biological system that regulates hunger to keep us at our ideal weights. However, if just like pets we eat more food than is required to fuel the body's energy needs or we don't get enough exercise to burn off extra food (surplus calories), we become overweight (Rosenblatt, 2000).

*Overweight* means that a person is 20% over the ideal body weight.

*Obesity* means that a person is 30% or more above the ideal body weight.

The numbers on the right show that during the last 25 years, the percentage of adult Americans who are overweight has increased dramatically, from 26% in 1976 to 55% in 2000 (Mestel, 2000). Researchers found that a person's body fat typically doubles

| 1976 | 26% |
| 2000 | 55% |

Increase in percent of Americans (ages 20–74) who are overweight

between ages 20 and 50 unless there is a program to get more exercise (Roberts, 1997).

Being overweight has become a major health problem in the United States because it significantly increases the risk for heart disease, stroke, high blood pressure, clogged arteries, adult-onset diabetes, and early death (Manson, 1999). For example, during the 1990s, the diabetes rate among U.S. adults increased at an alarming 33%, which experts say was caused primarily by being overweight and not exercising (being a couch potato) (Vinicor, 2000). In 1994, almost 6% of all health problems were weight related, for a total annual bill of $39 billion (Azar, 1994b).

However, you'll see that solving the problem of being overweight is complicated by the fact that eating is influenced by three different hunger factors.

## Three Hunger Factors

**So, what controls your eating?**

Hunger is considered a biological drive because eating is essential to our survival. However, the way in which you satisfy your hunger drive—when, where, and how much you eat—is influenced by three different factors: biological, psychosocial, and genetic.

*Biological hunger factors* come from physiological changes in blood chemistry and signals from digestive organs that provide feedback to the brain, which, in turn, triggers us to eat or stop eating.

If your eating was regulated primarily by biological factors, as in most animals, you would keep your weight at optimal levels. The fact that 50% of adults are overweight and some individuals suffer from serious eating problems indicates the influence of both psychosocial and genetic factors.

*Psychosocial hunger factors* come from learned associations between food and other stimuli, such as

In humans, psychosocial hunger factors can override biological and genetic hunger factors.

snacking while watching television; sociocultural influences, such as pressures to be thin; and various personality problems, such as depression, dislike of body image, or low self-esteem.

*Genetic hunger factors* come from inherited instructions found in our genes. These instructions determine the number of fat cells or metabolic rates of burning off the body's fuel, which push us toward being normal, overweight, or underweight.

These three hunger factors interact to influence your weight. For example, because of psychosocial factors, some of us eat when we should not, such as during stress. Because of biological factors, some of us may respond too much or too little to feedback from our digestive organs. Because of genetic factors, some of us can eat more calories and still maintain optimal weight. We'll discuss these three hunger factors, beginning with biological factors.

| **Why do you start or stop eating?** |
|---|

The Japanese sumo wrestler on the right is Konishiki, nicknamed Meat Bomb. He is 6 feet 1 inch tall and weighs 580 pounds, which is considered normal by sumo standards but obese by Western medical charts. He maintains his huge body by consuming about 10,000 calories daily, which is 3–5 times the amount required by an average-sized male. Konishiki starts or stops eating partly because of biological hunger factors that come from two different sources—peripheral and central cues (Woods et al., 2000).

*Peripheral cues* come from changes in blood chemistry or signals from digestive organs.

*Central cues* come from the activity of chemicals and neurotransmitters in different areas of the brain.

Peripheral and central cues are part of an elaborate biological system that evolved over millions of years to help humans and animals maintain their optimal weights.

## Peripheral Cues

Signals for feeling hungry or full come from a number of body organs that are involved in digestion and regulation of blood sugar (glucose) levels, which is the primary source of fuel for the body and brain.

**1** The *stomach* monitors the amount and kinds of nutrients our body needs to restore our depleted stores of fuel. In addition, after we eat a meal, the stomach's walls are distended and their stretch receptors signal fullness or time to stop eating.

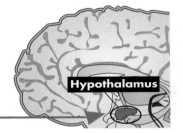

The stomach's signals about fullness are monitored by a particular area of the brain, the hypothalamus, which is the master control center for hunger and eating behaviors (Gershon, 2000).

**2** The *liver* monitors nutrients, especially the level of glucose (sugar) in the blood. When the level of glucose falls, the liver signals hunger; when the level of glucose rises, the liver signals fullness.

The liver's signals about being hungry or full are monitored by a certain part of the hypothalamus (Woods et al., 2000).

**3** The *intestines* respond to the presence of food, especially fats, by secreting a hormone called CCK (cholecystokinin), which inhibits eating.

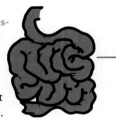

The intestine's signals about fullness are monitored by a certain part of the hypothalamus (Carlson, 1998).

**4** *Fat cells* secrete a hormone (leptin) that is monitored by the brain. In turn, the brain signals a person to eat or stop eating so that a certain level of body fat remains constant over a person's lifetime.

As fat cells secrete the hunger-related hormone (leptin), it is monitored by a certain part of the hypothalamus (Woods et al., 2000).

There are also central cues for hunger.

## Central Cues

Located in the lower middle of the brain are groups of cells that are collectively called the hypothalamus. We have greatly simplified the hypothalamus's role in motivation by focusing only on its role in hunger.

**Hypothalamus**

**1** The *hypothalamus* has many different groups of cells that are involved in a number of different behaviors having to do with motivation, such as thirst, sexual behavior, and regulation of hunger.

Two particular groups of cells, the lateral and ventromedial hypothalamus, affect eating in opposite ways.

**2** The *lateral hypothalamus* is a group of cells that regulates hunger by creating feelings of being hungry (Woods et al., 2000).

For example, rats begin eating when the lateral hypothalamus is electrically stimulated. They stop eating, and may starve, if the lateral hypothalamus is destroyed. In addition, the lateral hypothalamus has cells that increase or decrease activity depending on the blood level of glucose.

**3** The *ventromedial hypothalamus* is a group of cells that regulates hunger by creating feelings of satiety *(say-TIE-ah-tea)* or fullness.

For example, in humans, the brain signals fullness about 10 minutes after we start eating (Liu et al., 2000). In rats, electrical stimulation of the ventromedial hypothalamus causes rats to stop eating, while destruction of the ventromedial hypothalamus causes rats to overeat and become obese. In addition, various chemicals affect other cells of the hypothalamus and regulate our appetites for specific foods.

**4** *Galanin,* which is a chemical produced by the brain, acts on the hypothalamus and stimulates eating fat. Norepinephrine, which is a neurotransmitter produced by the brain, acts on the hypothalamus and stimulates eating carbohydrates (Woods et al., 2000).

Thus, the hypothalamus has several centers involved in eating: one to start eating (lateral hypothalamus), another to stop eating (ventromedial hypothalamus), and others for eating specific foods (fats or carbohydrates).

Although each of us has a sophisticated biological system to keep us at our ideal weight, you'll see that various genetic and psychological factors can change or interfere with this system.

# C. Hunger

## Genetic Hunger Factors

**Are identical twins always the same weight?**

Last semester I had a set of identical twins in my class. They looked similar except that one twin weighed about 10 pounds more than the other. Researchers generally find that identical twins (photo on right), even when separated soon after birth and reared in adopted families, were much more alike in weight than fraternal twins reared apart (Bouchard et al., 1990). This similarity in weight is due to genetic hunger factors.

*Genetic hunger factors* come from inherited instructions found in our genes. These instructions determine the number of fat cells or metabolic rates of burning off the body's

Identical twins share the same genes and thus are similar in weight.

fuel, which push us toward being normal, overweight, or underweight.

On the basis of twin studies, researchers concluded that inherited factors contribute about 70% to the maintenance of a particular body size and weight, while environmental factors contribute the other 30% (Hewitt, 1997).

The finding that genetic hunger factors contribute about 70% to having a certain body size and weight explains why identical twins have similar body types. The finding that environmental factors contribute about 30% to body size explains why one twin may weigh a little more or less than the other. So far, psychologists have identified four genetic hunger factors: fat cells, metabolic rate, set point, and weight-regulating genes.

**1** We inherit different numbers of fat cells.

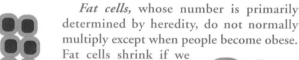

*Fat cells,* whose number is primarily determined by heredity, do not normally multiply except when people become obese. Fat cells shrink if we are giving up fat and losing weight (left) and greatly enlarge if we are storing fat and gaining weight (right) (Carlson, 1998).

People who inherit a larger number of fat cells have the ability to store more fat and are more likely to be fatter than average.

**2** We inherit different rates of metabolism.

*Metabolic rate* refers to how efficiently our bodies break food down into energy and how quickly our bodies burn off that fuel.

For example, if you had a low metabolic rate, you would burn less fuel, be more likely to store excess fuel as fat, and thus may have a fatter body. In comparison, if you had a high metabolic rate, you would burn off more fuel, be less likely to store fat, and thus may have a thinner body (left figure). This means that people can consume the same number of calories but, because of different metabolic rates, may maintain, lose, or gain weight. There are only two known activities that can raise metabolic rate: exercise and smoking cigarettes. Researchers found that exercise raises metabolic rate 10–20% and that nicotine raises it 4–10%. That's the reason exercise helps dieters lose weight and smokers generally gain weight when they stop smoking (Audrain et al., 1995).

**3** We inherit a set point to maintain a certain amount of body fat.

The *set point* refers to a certain level of body fat (adipose tissue) that our bodies strive to maintain constant throughout our lives.

For example, a person whose body (right figure) has a higher set point will try to maintain a higher level of fat stores and thus have a fatter body. In comparison, a person whose body has a lower set point will maintain a lower level of fat stores and thus have a thinner body (Woods et al., 2000). If a person diets to reduce the level of fat stores, the body compensates to maintain and build back fat stores by automatically lowering metabolic rate and thus consuming less fuel. That's the reason dieters may lose weight for the first two or three weeks and then stop losing because the body has lowered its metabolic rate. Researchers concluded that because the body protects its fat stores, long-term dieting will be unsuccessful in treating overweight people unless they also exercise (Leibel et al., 1995).

**4** The most recent findings indicate that we inherit weight-regulating genes.

*Weight-regulating genes* play a role in influencing appetite, body metabolism, and secretion of hormones (leptin) that regulate fat stores.

For example, the mouse on the left has a gene that increases a brain chemical (neuropeptide Y) that increased eating so that it weighs three times as much as the normal-weight mouse on the right (Gura, 1997). Researchers have also found a gene that can jack up metabolism so that calories are burnt off as heat rather than stored as fat (Warden, 1997). This latter finding may explain why about 10% of the population can stay trim on a diet that would make others fat.

You have seen how genetic hunger factors are involved in the regulation of body fat and weight.

Next, we'll explore several psychological factors involved in the regulation of eating and weight.

**Why is there always room for dessert?**

Many of us have a weakness for certain foods, and mine is for desserts. No matter how full, I can always fit a dessert along the sides of my stomach. Even though my biological and genetic hunger factors may tell me (my brain) when to start and stop eating, I can use my large forebrain to override my innately programmed biological and genetic factors. My forebrain allows me to rationalize that one dessert can do no harm. This kind of rationalizing comes under the heading of psychosocial factors.

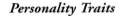

*Psychosocial hunger factors* come from learned associations between food and other stimuli, such as snacking while watching television; sociocultural influences, such as pressures to be thin; and various personality traits, such as depression, dislike of body image, or low self-esteem.

Psychosocial hunger factors can have an enormous effect on our eating habits and weight and contribute to many problems associated with eating, such as becoming overweight, eating when stressed or depressed, and bingeing (Ward et al., 2000). We'll discuss three psychosocial hunger factors—learned associations, social-cultural influences, and personality traits.

## *Learned Associations*

The best examples of how *learned associations* influence eating are that we often eat not because we're hungry but because it's "lunchtime," because foods smell good, or because our friends are eating.

More evidence that learned associations influence eating comes from marketing and advertising pressures to sell foods by offering huge servings. For example, movie theaters offer an extra large box of popcorn, which, at almost 900 calories, is equivalent to a major meal. Health professionals warn that as children, adolescents, and adults learn to prefer large portions and tasty foods high in fat,

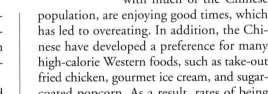

Extra large box of popcorn has same calories as a meal!

sugar, and calories, there has been a corresponding increase in rates of being overweight (from 26% in 1976 to 55% in 2000) (National Center for Health Statistics, 1997).

Researchers are especially concerned about the continued rise in rates of overweight and obesity in children since childhood obesity is very difficult to treat and an obese child has a high probability of becoming an obese adult with the associated health risks we discussed earlier (Manning, 2000).

Health professionals suggest that to avoid future increases in rates of overweight and obesity, we need to unlearn many of our learned food associations, which primarily involves decreasing the size of food portions, decreasing the amount of high-fat foods, and increasing levels of activity to burn off excess calories (Watson & Wu, 1996).

## *Social-Cultural Influences*

Examples of how *social-cultural influences* affect food preferences and body weight may be cited from around the world.

In the Czech Republic, the government subsidized cheap fatty sausage and dairy products in the 1970s, with the result that 45% of Czech women and a smaller percent of men are obese. The Czech Republic has the world's highest death rates from heart disease and has begun programs to teach the difficult lesson of adopting better nutrition (Elliott, 1995).

In China, many current parents grew up in the 1950s, when poverty was common and there was never enough food. Today, these same parents, along with much of the Chinese population, are enjoying good times, which has led to overeating. In addition, the Chinese have developed a preference for many high-calorie Western foods, such as take-out fried chicken, gourmet ice cream, and sugar-coated popcorn. As a result, rates of being overweight, strokes, and heart attacks have greatly increased (Wong, 1994).

In the United States, there are many cultural pressures on women to be thin. As a result, American women are more likely to be unhappy with and *overestimate* their weights (right figure), which contributes to developing eating disorders. In comparison, American men are less concerned with and usually *underestimate* their weights and develop fewer eating problems (Heatherton et al., 1997).

## *Personality Traits*

If a person has certain *personality traits,* he or she may be at greater risk for overeating as well as developing serious eating disorders, such as overeating when stressed or depressed, going on food binges (bulimia nervosa), or starving oneself (anorexia nervosa). We'll discuss serious eating problems in the Application section.

The particular personality traits that have been associated with eating problems include being overly sensitive to rejection; being excessively concerned about approval from others; having high personal standards for achievement; having suffered physical or sexual abuse; and experiencing bouts of depression, anxiety, or mood swings (Fairburn et al., 1997; Tanofsky et al., 1997). An individual who has these kinds of personality traits, which are often accompanied by stress, anxiety, and emotional upset, may find it very difficult and sometimes almost impossible to control his or her eating. As we'll discuss in the Application section, individuals with serious eating problems may find it necessary to seek professional help and counseling.

Although hunger is considered a biological need, you have seen how numerous psychosocial hunger factors can greatly influence where, when, and how the hunger drive is satisfied. And, as we'll discuss in the Application section, there are extreme cases in which psychosocial factors can completely override the hunger drive.

Next, we'll discuss another very important biological need, sexual behavior.

I look too fat!

Certain personality traits influence eating patterns.

# D. Sexual Behavior

**Why do lions know how to do it?**

Although we don't look, sound, or behave the same as lions do, we share similar biological and genetic factors that regulate sexual behavior. The sexual behavior of lions and most animals is controlled chiefly by genetic and biological factors, which means that most animals engage in sex primarily for reproduction.

*Genetic sex factors* include inherited instructions for the development of sexual organs, the secretion of sex hormones, and the wiring of the neural circuits that control sexual reflexes.

*Biological sex factors* include the action of sex hormones, which are involved in secondary sexual characteristics (facial hair, breasts), sexual motivation (more so in animals than in humans), and the development of ova and sperm.

Lions, like most animals, generally avoid sexual interactions unless the female is in heat, which means she is ovulating and can be

In most animals, sexual behavior is regulated by genetic and biological factors.

impregnated. In comparison, humans engage in sexual behavior for many reasons, which point to psychological sex factors.

*Psychological sex factors* play a role in developing a sexual or gender identity, gender role, and sexual orientation. In addition, psychological factors can result in difficulties in the performance or enjoyment of sexual activities.

For example, otherwise healthy men and women may report difficulties in sexual activities arising from stress, anxiety, or guilt, which can interfere with the functioning of genetic and biological sex factors. One reason psychological factors play such an important role in human sexual behavior is that our large forebrains have the capacity to think, reason, and change our minds and thus increase, interfere with, or completely block sexual motivation, performance, or enjoyment.

As we did for the hunger drive, we'll discuss, in order, the influences of genetic, biological, and psychological factors on sexual behavior.

---

## Genetic Influences on Sexual Behavior

**Which sex organ?**

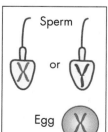

How we develop a particular sex organ, male or female, is determined primarily by a genetic program that is contained in a single human cell about the size of a grain of sand.

### SEX CHROMOSOME

Unlike the other cells of our body, which contain 46 chromosomes (23 pairs), the sperm and egg each contain half that number and are called sex chromosomes (figure below).

The *sex chromosome,* which is in the sperm or the egg, contains 23 chromosomes, which in turn have genes that contain instructions for determining the sex of the child.

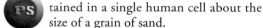

As we discussed earlier (p. 68), each chromosome is made up of a long strand of DNA (deoxyribonucleic acid). On this long strand of DNA are hundreds of genes, which contain the chemically coded instructions for the development and maintenance of our bodies. In the figure above, notice that some sperm have an **X** chromosome and some have a **Y,** which contain different genetic instructions and, as you'll see, result in the development of different sex organs (penis or vagina).

**1** The human egg contains one of the sex chromosomes, which is always an **X** chromosome. Thus, each human egg has a single **X** chromosome.

Egg with **X** chromosome

**2** A human sperm also contains one of the sex chromosomes. However, the sperm's chromosome can be either an **X** chromosome, which has instructions for development of *female sex organs* and body, or a **Y** chromosome, which has instructions for *male sex organs* and body. Thus, the sperm (**X** or **Y**) determines the sex of the infant.

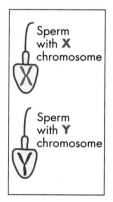

Sperm with **X** chromosome

Sperm with **Y** chromosome

**3** During fertilization, a single sperm penetrates an egg and results in a fertilized egg with 23 pairs of chromosomes. If the last pair has the combination **XY,** it means the egg contains the genetic instructions for developing a male's sex organs (top right figure). If the last pair has the combination **XX,** it means the egg contains the genetic instructions for developing a female's sex organs (bottom right figure).

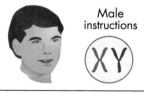

Male instructions

Female instructions

Following fertilization, the human cell, which is called a *zygote,* will divide over and over many thousands of times during the following weeks and months and eventually develop into a female body with female sex organs or a male body with male sex organs.

How an unborn infant actually develops male or female sex organs is an interesting story, especially since everyone begins as a female.

## ——— Genetic Influences (continued) ———

### DIFFERENTIATION

Although it would seem that at fertilization you are destined to be either a male or a female, there is actually no physical difference between a male and a female embryo for the first four weeks of development in the womb. During this time period, the embryos are identical and have the potential to develop into either a male or a female (Federman, 1994). At about the fifth week, the embryo begins to differentiate into either a male or a female because of the presence or absence of certain sex hormones.

### MALE SEX ORGAN AND MALE BRAIN

In an embryo that began from an **XY** fertilized egg, the **Y** sex chromosome has instructions for the development of male testes. At about the fifth week, the testes begin to grow and produce tiny amounts of male hormones or *androgens*, one of which most people know as *testosterone*.

The presence of testosterone does two things: it triggers the development of the male sexual organ (penis), and it programs a particular area of the brain, called the hypothalamus, so that at puberty it triggers the pituitary gland to secrete hormones on a continuous basis, which results in the continuous production of sperm.

**Presence** of testosterone results in a male brain.

### FEMALE SEX ORGANS AND FEMALE BRAIN

In an embryo that began from an **XX** fertilized egg, the second **X** sex chromosome contains instructions for the development of ovaries, which do not secrete testosterone.

The absence of testosterone in the developing embryo means two things: the automatic development of female sexual organs (clitoris and vagina), and the hypothalamus, which is normally programmed for female hormonal functions, keeps its female program. Thus, at puberty, this female-programmed hypothalamus triggers the pituitary gland to secrete hormones on a cyclic basis, which results in the menstrual cycle.

**Absence** of testosterone results in a female brain.

### IMPORTANCE OF TESTOSTERONE

The *presence* of testosterone, which is secreted by fetal testes, results in male sexual organs and a male hypothalamus; the *absence* of testosterone results in female sexual organs and a female hypothalamus (Carlson, 1998).

When the infant is born, the doctor identifies the infant's sex organs and says those famous words, "It's a boy" or "It's a girl." At that point a hormonal clock begins ticking and its alarm will set off biological factors at puberty.

## ——— Biological Influences ———

You have seen how genetic sex factors influence the development and growth of the body's sex organs. The next big event to affect a person's sex organs and sexual motivation occurs at puberty as a result of biological sex factors.

The sex hormones secreted during puberty either directly or indirectly affect our bodies, brains, minds, personalities, self-concepts, and mental health. Here, we'll focus on how sex hormones affect our bodies.

**Sex hormones.** At puberty, some yet unknown signal activates cells in the hypothalamus, which triggers a 10- to 20-fold increase in the secretion of sex hormones.

*Sex hormones*, which are chemicals secreted by glands, circulate in the bloodstream to influence the brain, body organs, and behaviors. The major male sex hormones secreted by the testes are *androgens*, such as testosterone; the major female sex hormones secreted by the ovaries are *estrogens*.

**Male–female differences.** Because of neural programming in the womb resulting from the presence or absence of testosterone, the male hypothalamus functions differently from the female hypothalamus.

The *male hypothalamus* triggers a continuous release of androgens, such as testosterone, from the testes. The increased level of androgens causes the development of male secondary sexual characteristics, such as facial and pubic hair, muscle growth, and lowered voice.

**Male hypothalamus** triggers release of testosterone.

The *female hypothalamus* triggers a cyclical release of estrogens from the ovaries. The increased level of estrogens causes the development of female secondary sexual characteristics, such as pubic hair, breast development, and widening of the hips. The cyclical release of hormones (estrogen and progesterone) also regulates the menstrual cycle.

**Female hypothalamus** triggers release of estrogen.

### SEXUAL MOTIVATION

In animals, sexual motivation is primarily regulated by the rise and fall in levels of sex hormones.

In contrast, human sexual motivation shows little correlation with levels of sex hormones, provided they are within the normal range. For example, the normal rise and fall in levels of androgens or estrogens have no clear-cut effect on sexual motivation (Schiavi & Segraves, 1995). Provided a person has a normal level of sex hormones, increases or decreases in sexual motivation are more dependent on psychological factors, such as feelings, desires, and expectations (Tiefer & Kring, 1995).

At the same time that genetic and biological factors are guiding our bodies toward physical sexual maturity, numerous psychological factors are preparing our minds for psychological sexual maturity. Next, we'll examine these psychological sex factors.

## Psychological Influences on Sexual Behavior

**How do boys and girls become men and women?**

As boys and girls develop and go through puberty, their genetic and biological factors prepare their bodies for sexual maturity. At the same time that their bodies are developing, boys and girls are observing, imitating, and learning the behaviors of their mothers and fathers, older brothers and sisters, and other adults in their environments. This is when psychological sex factors come into play.

**XY =**
Testosterone

**XX =**
Estrogen

**Sex hormones** activate many physical and psychological changes.

*Psychological sex factors* play a role in developing a sexual or gender identity, gender role, and sexual orientation. In addition, psychological factors can result in difficulties in the performance or enjoyment of sexual activities.

It's through psychological sex factors that boys and girls develop into men and women and achieve psychological sexual maturity.

Three psychological sex factors are especially important—gender identity, gender role, and sexual orientation. One factor leads to the next, so we'll discuss each in turn, beginning with gender identity.

### 1st Step: Gender Identity

One question that children learn to answer correctly between the ages of 2 and 3 is "Are you a little girl or a little boy?" The young child proudly answers, "I'm a girl" or "I'm a boy," indicating that he or she has already acquired the beginnings of a gender identity (Fagot et al., 2000).

*Gender identity,* which was formerly called sexual identity, refers to the individual's subjective experience and feelings of being either a male or a female.

When a doctor proclaims "It's a girl" or "It's a boy," these well-known words set in motion the process for acquiring a gender identity. From that point on, parents, siblings, grandparents, and others behave toward male and female infants differently, so that they learn and acquire their proper gender identity (Fagot et al., 2000). For example, the little girl in the right photo is checking out her pretty dress in the mirror, a behavior that she has observed her mother doing many times.

Gender identity is a psychological sex factor that exerts a powerful influence on future sexual thoughts and behavior, as clearly illustrated in the case of someone with a gender identity disorder, who is commonly referred to as a transsexual.

By age 3, children know if they **are** boys or girls.

*Gender identity disorder* is commonly referred to as transsexualism. A transsexual is a person who has a strong desire or feeling of wanting to be the other sex, is uncomfortable about being one's assigned sex, and may wish to live as a member of the other sex (American Psychiatric Association, 1994).

Transsexuals usually have normal genetic instructions and biological (hormonal) factors, but for some reason, they feel and insist that they are trapped in the body of the wrong sex and may adopt the behaviors, dress, and mannerisms of the other sex. There is no clear understanding of why transsexuals reject their biological sex. Current data indicate that the incidence of transsexualism is about the same for males and females (Bradley & Zucker, 1997). Infrequently, adults with gender identity disorder may seek surgery to change the sex organs that they were born with to the other sex. Because transsexuals acquire gender identities that do not match their external sex organs, they experience problems in thinking and acting and may not easily fit into or be accepted by society (Bradley & Zucker, 1997). However, the vast majority of people do acquire gender identities that match their external sex organs.

As you acquire a male or female gender identity, you are also acquiring a matching gender role.

### 2nd Step: Gender Roles

The first step in becoming psychologically sexually mature is acquiring a male or female gender identity, which results in your knowing that you are a boy or a girl. The second step in becoming psychologically sexually mature involves acquiring a gender role.

*Gender roles,* which were formerly called sex roles, refer to traditional or stereotypic behaviors, attitudes, and personality traits that society designates as masculine or feminine. Gender roles greatly influence how we think and behave.

Between the ages of 3 and 4, American children learn the stereotypic or traditional expectations

By age 5, children know how a boy or girl **behaves.**

regarding the kinds of toys, clothes, and occupations for men and women. By the age of 5, children have acquired many of the complex thoughts, expectations, and behaviors that accompany their particular gender role of male or female (Eckes & Trautner, 2000).

For example, young boys learn stereotypic male behaviors, such as playing sports, competing in games, engaging in rough and tumble play, and acquiring status in his group. In comparison, girls learn stereotypic female behaviors, such as providing and seeking emotional support, emphasizing physical appearance, clothes, and fashion, and learning to cooperate and share personal experiences (Eagly et al., 2000).

As children, we all learned and adopted a male or female gender role, often without being aware or realizing how subtly we were rewarded for imitating and performing appropriate behaviors. Learning and adopting a gender role continue through adolescence and into adulthood and result in very different gender roles. For instance, adult American women tend to show stereotypic gender roles that can be described as socially sensitive, nurturing, and concerned with others' welfare. In comparison, adult American men tend to show gender roles that can be described as dominant, controlling, and independent (Eagly et al., 2000).

**Dominant Controlling Independent**

**Sensitive Nurturing Concerned**

**Function.** A major function of gender roles is that they influence how we think and behave. Notice that male gender roles—dominant, controlling, and independent—can lead to different kinds of sexual thoughts and behaviors than female gender roles—socially sensitive, nurturing, and concerned. Thus, some of the confusion, conflict, and misunderstanding over sexual behavior come from underlying differences in gender roles. A major task a couple will have in establishing a healthy, loving relationship is to work out the many differences in thoughts, beliefs, and expectations that come from combining two different gender roles.

After we acquire a gender role, the next step involves knowing one's sexual orientation.

### 3rd Step: Sexual Orientation

In answering the question "Do you find males or females sexually arousing?" you are expressing your sexual orientation, which is the third step in reaching psychological sexual maturity.

*Sexual orientation,* also called sexual preference, refers to whether a person is sexually aroused primarily by members of his or her own sex, the opposite sex, or both sexes.

*Homosexual orientation* refers to a pattern of sexual arousal by persons of the same sex.

*Bisexual orientation* refers to a pattern of sexual arousal by persons of both sexes.

*Heterosexual orientation* refers to a pattern of sexual arousal by persons of the opposite sex.

The vast majority of the American population, about 96–97%, have a heterosexual orientation. The remaining 3–4% have a homosexual orientation, and a very small percentage of these individuals have a bisexual orientation (Laumann et al., 1994).

Of several models that explain how we develop a particular sexual orientation, the interactive model is perhaps the most popular (Money, 1987; Zucker, 1990).

The *interactive model of sexual orientation* says that genetic and biological factors, such as genetic instructions and prenatal hormones, interact with psychological factors, such as the individual's attitudes, personality traits, and behaviors, to influence the development of sexual orientation.

1. Gender identity

2. Gender role

3. Sexual orientation

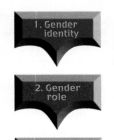

Developing a sexual orientation depends on several factors.

**Genetic and biological factors.** There is considerable debate over how much genetic and biological factors influence sexual orientation. Some researchers prefer the term *sexual preference* because it suggests that we have considerable freedom in choosing a particular sexual orientation and that genetic and biological factors do not play a major role (Baumrind, 1995; Byne, 1997). Other researchers prefer the term *sexual orientation* because they believe that genetic and biological factors play a major role in sexual orientation (Diamond & Sigmundson, 1997). This debate was intensified by a case that involved changing a person's gender identity.

**Changing gender identity.** In the 1960s, genetic and biological factors were thought to play minor roles in developing gender identity. That's because some babies who were born with inconclusive sex organs (tiny penis, no testicles) were said to be girls and were raised as girls; others were said to be boys and were raised as boys. Later, when these children reached puberty, doctors discovered that some of these "girls" actually had the chromosomes of males and some of the "boys" had the chromosomes of females. However, some of those raised as "girls" decided to remain female and received corrective surgery (a vagina) and hormones (developed breasts). Others raised as "boys" decided to remain male and also received corrective surgery and hormones. In these cases, children chose the gender identity and orientation that matched their upbringing, not their genetic makeup. Based on such cases, researchers believed that gender identity and gender orientation could be changed if, before the age of 2, infants were assigned a gender identity and raised accordingly (Money, 1987). However, another case has questioned this belief.

**Tragic case.** While doctors were doing a routine medical procedure to repair an 8-month-old male's foreskin, they accidentally destroyed the infant's penis. As a result, doctors advised the parents to raise the boy (John) as a girl (Joan). However, since about the age of 8, Joan had been unhappy being and acting like a female and began to suspect that she was really a boy. By the time Joan was 14, she had received corrective surgery (a vagina) and hormonal treatment to physically look like a girl (developed breasts) but was so unhappy she threatened suicide and told doctors she thought she was a boy. After much discussion, doctors agreed to help Joan change back to John. Now in his 30s, John is married and reports that he never liked being a female and is very happy being a male. Based on Joan-John's experience, researchers believe that individuals are genetically and biologically predisposed for having a male or female gender identity, which is not easily changed by being raised a certain way (boy or girl) (Diamond & Sigmundson, 1997). This case suggests that, unlike previously believed, humans may have a genetic predisposition to develop a male or female gender identity and gender orientation.

### Male–Female Sex Differences

**How are males different from females?**

After we have acquired a gender identity, gender role, and sexual orientation, there remain sometimes difficult decisions about when, where, and with whom sexual behavior is appropriate. Virtually every sex survey during the past 30 years reports similar differences in sexual behavior between males and females. For example, a national survey of 3,500 Americans, ages 18–29, reported that males engage in more sexual behaviors and with greater frequency and have more sexual partners than do females (Baldwin & Baldwin, 1997; Laumann et al., 1994). Why males consistently report more sexual desire, motivation, and activity than females is explained by two different theories—social role theory and evolutionary theory.

The *social role theory*, which emphasizes social and cultural forces, states that sexual differences between males and females arise from different divisions of labor, which lead to developing different social roles.

According to social role theory, men and women developed different social roles: men were traditionally providers and protectors, while women were homemakers and caregivers (Eagly et al., 2000). These different social roles for males and females resulted in society developing a different set of norms for male–female sexual behaviors, which is commonly known as the double standard.

The *double standard for sexual behavior* refers to a set of beliefs, values, and expectations that subtly encourages sexual activity in males but discourages the same behavior in females.

According to social role theory, one reason males are more interested in and engage in more sexual activities is that our cultural and social standards permit greater sexual freedom for males than for females. A different explanation for male–female sexual differences comes from evolutionary theory.

The *evolutionary theory,* which emphasizes genetic and biological forces, says that current sexual differences are a continuation of the behaviors that evolved from early men and women who developed these different behaviors as they tried to survive the problems of their time (Archer, 1997; Buss, 1995).

We'll discuss how each theory explains some of the major male–female sexual differences.

**Male–Female Sex Differences**

**11 to 30 sexual partners since the age of 18**
Men 33%
Women 9%

**Think about sex daily**
Men 54%
Women 19%

**Reached orgasm during sex**
Men 75%
Women 29%

**Masturbated during past year**
Men 85%
Women 45%

Source: Laumann et al., 1994

### Social Role Theory

Researchers consistently find at least two male–female differences in sexual behavior. First, men consistently report greater interest in sex as shown by increased frequency of sexual activities, greater percentage of extramarital affairs, and desire for more sex partners (about 18 partners) than women (about 4–5 partners) (Buss & Schmitt, 1993). Second, in an international study of 37 cultures, 10,000 individuals were asked to state their top priorities in choosing a mate. Across all cultures and all racial, political, and religious groups, men generally valued physical attractiveness more than women, while women valued the financial resources of prospective mates twice as much as men (Buss et al., 1990).

According to social role theory, these differences in sexual activities and priorities in mate selection developed from traditional cultural divisions of labor, in which women were childbearers and homemakers, while men were providers and protectors (right photo) (Eagly et al., 2000). These different social roles (men—providers and protectors; women—childbearers and homemakers) resulted in men and women performing different duties and developing different sex roles and sexual behaviors. Social role theory points to different social and cultural pressures as being the basis for males and females developing different sexual roles and behaviors.

**Provider Protector**

**Childbearer Homemaker**

### Evolutionary Theory

A different explanation for the differences in sexual behavior between men and women comes from evolutionary theory. According to evolutionary theory, men developed a greater interest in sex and desire for many attractive sex partners because it maximized their chances for reproduction. In comparison, women would not benefit from indiscriminate and frequent mating because it would place them at risk for having offspring of low quality and create an unstable environment for raising their children. Instead, women placed a high priority on finding a man who was a good protector and provider, which means that she and her children would have a better chance for survival, especially during her childbearing years (Buss et al., 1998). According to evolutionary theory, our current male–female differences in sexual behavior arise from genetic and biological forces that evolved from an ancient set of mating patterns, which helped the species survive (Ketelaar & Ellis, 2000).

We have discussed how two different theories explain differences in male–female sexual behaviors. However, some researchers suggest that the best explanation of male–female sex differences comes from combining social role theory, which emphasizes cultural forces, with evolutionary theory, which emphasizes genetic and biological forces (Baldwin & Baldwin, 1997).

Next, we'll return to a controversial question in sexual behavior: Why does an individual develop a homosexual orientation?

**Were the brothers born gay?**

Although four major professional health organizations—American Psychological Association, American Psychiatric Association, American Medical Association, American Psychoanalytic Association—have concluded that homosexuality is a normal form of sexual expression, national surveys usually find that only a slight majority (56%) of adult Americans approve of homosexuality, while about half disapprove for a variety of reasons (Goldberg, 1998). According to current national surveys, about 1–3% of the American male population are homosexual (gay) and about 1.4% of the female population are homosexual (lesbian). These recent surveys are considered more accurate than earlier estimates of 10% of the population being homosexual (Kinsey et al., 1948).

Both brothers are gay and share similar genetic factors.

Many people say that they would be more accepting of homosexuality if it were shown to be a genetic predisposition, since it would be similar to inheriting other preferences, such as being left-handed (Leland, 1994). We'll discuss recent genetic/biological and psychological factors that bear on the question of whether brothers Rick and Randy (left photo) were genetically predisposed to be gay or chose to be gay.

## *Genetic/Biological Factors*

During the past 10 years, there has been an increasing search for genetic and hormonal influences that contribute to the development of homosexuality (Lalumiere et al., 2000). Some of this evidence comes from the study of sexual orientation in twins. For example, a number of studies on identical male and female twins have found that, if one male or female twin of an identical pair was gay, about 48–65% of the time so was the second twin; this compared to 26–30% for fraternal twins and 6–11% for adopted brothers or sisters (Bailey & Zucker, 1995). However, one criticism of these studies is that some of the twins were not reared separately so it is impossible to determine the effects of similar environments on sexual orientation. Another kind of evidence comes from studies on genetic similarities among brothers.

Researchers studied 40 families, each of which had two gay brothers (including Rick and Randy in the photo above). Researchers identified an area at the end of the

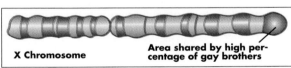

**X Chromosome**    Area shared by high percentage of gay brothers

**X** chromosome that was shared by 33 out of 40 pairs of gay brothers (left figure).

Thus, although they are not twins, Rick and Randy, who are gay, share the same section of genetic material (Hammer, 1995). Researchers cautioned that they have not found a "homosexual gene" but only identified shared genetic material that may contribute to sexual orientation. This study is the best evidence to date that homosexual orientation is strongly influenced by genetic factors. There is some question about the results, though, since not all researchers have been able to replicate these findings (Rice et al., 1999).

If there were a genetic/biological predisposition to homosexuality, we might expect that a person would become aware of his or her homosexual orientation before learning about or actually engaging in homosexual behavior and despite considerable pressure from parents, siblings, or peers to develop a heterosexual orientation. Researchers report that most gays report becoming aware of their orientation around puberty, usually before actually knowing much about or engaging in homosexual behavior and despite being almost totally surrounded by heterosexual role models (Pillard & Bailey, 1995).

All the above findings suggest that, to a certain extent, Rick and Randy were born with genetic or biological predispositions or tendencies that played a role in the development of a homosexual orientation (Bailey et al., 2000). However, if genetic predisposition was decisive, then we would expect 100% of the pairs of identical twins to have exactly the same sexual orientation, but only about 50% do (Lalumiere et al., 2000). This means that besides genetic/biological factors influencing the development of a homosexual orientation, there may also be psychological factors.

## *Psychological Factors*

In studying psychological factors, researchers ask whether young children who later develop a heterosexual orientation differ from children who develop a homosexual orientation. In answering this question, researchers observed the behaviors of young children and consistently found that young boys who preferred girl playmates and girls' toys, avoided rough-and-tumble play, and engaged in wearing girls' clothing had a tendency to develop a homosexual orientation (Dawood et al., 2000). In addition, adult gay men and lesbian women recalled engaging in more behaviors of the opposite sex as children than did heterosexual adults (Bailey & Zucker, 1995). Although these studies are correlational and cannot show cause and effect, they do suggest that certain psychological factors (kinds of play behaviors and preferences) are associated with developing a homosexual orientation (Dawood et al., 2000).

I knew I was gay before I did anything.

One psychological factor that influenced attitudes on homosexuality was that, until the 1970s, virtually all professional health organizations considered homosexuality to be an abnormal condition that often required psychotherapy to change. However, over the past 30 years, countless studies found that homosexuals scored about the same as heterosexuals on a wide variety of mental health tests, meaning that homosexuals are as mentally healthy as heterosexuals (Rosenberg, 1994). For these reasons, most professional health organizations now consider homosexuality a normal form or expression of sexual behavior and discourage all discriminatory practices toward homosexuals.

Next, we'll discuss several of the more common sexual problems and their treatments.

## Sexual Response, Problems, and Treatments

**What is the sexual response?**

A recent survey reported that up to 30% of men and women, aged 18 to 59, married and unmarried, experienced a variety of sexual problems (Leland, 1999). Some seek help for their problem, while others are ashamed or embarrassed and suffer in silence. There are two categories of sexual problems—paraphilias and sexual dysfunctions.

*Paraphilias,* commonly called sexual deviations, are characterized by repetitive or preferred sexual fantasies involving nonhuman objects, such as sexual attractions to particular articles of clothing (shoes, underclothes).

*Sexual dysfunctions* refer to problems of sexual arousal or orgasm that interfere with adequate functioning during sexual behavior.

When a person seeks help for a sexual problem, the clinician will check whether the causes are organic or psychological.

*Organic factors* refer to medical conditions or drug or medication problems that lead to sexual difficulties.

For example, certain medical conditions (such as diabetes mellitus), medications (such as antidepressants), and drugs (such as alcohol abuse) can interfere with sexual functioning.

*Psychological factors* refer to performance anxiety, sexual trauma, guilt, or failure to communicate, all of which may lead to sexual problems.

**Four-stage model.** To understand how psychological factors cause sexual problems, it helps to know Masters and Johnson's (1966) four-stage model of the sexual response.

Masters and Johnson proposed four stages of the human sexual response.

**1st stage: Excitement.** The body becomes physiologically and sexually aroused, resulting in erection in the male and vaginal lubrication in the female.

**2nd stage: Plateau.** Sexual and physiological arousal continues in males and females.

**3rd stage: Orgasm.** Men have rhythmic muscle contractions that cause ejaculation of sperm. Women experience similar rhythmic muscle contractions of pelvic area. During orgasm, women and men report very pleasurable feelings.

**4th stage: Resolution.** Physiological responses return to normal.

**Problems.** Sexual problems can occur at different stages. For example, some individuals cannot reach stage 1, excitement, while others can reach stages 1 and 2 but not stage 3, orgasm.

There were few successful treatments for sexual problems until Masters and Johnson (1970) published their treatment program, which has several stages. First, the therapist provides basic information about the sexual response and helps the couple communicate their feelings. Then the therapist gives the couple "homework," which is designed to reduce performance anxiety. Homework involves learning to pleasure one's partner without genital touching or making sexual demands. This nongenital pleasuring is called *sensate focus.* After using sensate focus, the couple moves on to genital touching and intercourse. Sex therapists have expanded and modified Masters and Johnson's program and report considerable success with treating many sexual problems (Wincze & Carey, 1991).

We'll discuss two common sexual problems and their treatments.

### Premature Ejaculation

John and Susan had been married for three years and were both 28 years old. When the clinician asked about their problem, Susan said that sex was over in about 30 seconds because that's how long it took for John to have an orgasm. John replied that he had always reached orgasm very quickly and didn't realize it was a problem. Susan said that it was a problem for her (Althof, 1995). John's problem is called premature ejaculation.

*Premature* or *rapid ejaculation* refers to persistent or recurrent absence of voluntary control over ejaculation, in which the male ejaculates with minimal sexual stimulation before, upon, or shortly after penetration and before he wishes to.

Premature ejaculation is the most common male sexual problem, which is reported by about 30% of adult men (Leland, 1999). A common treatment for it is called the squeeze technique. First, the partner stimulates the man's penis to nearly full erection. Then, the partner squeezes the head of the penis, which reduces arousal and erection. This squeeze procedure is repeated until the male develops a sense of control over arousal and ejaculation (Metz & Pryor, 2000). This procedure has proved successful in treating premature ejaculation.

### Inhibited Female Orgasm

Greta and Bill had been married for five years and were in their late twenties. When asked about their problem, Greta said that she didn't think she had ever had an orgasm. She added that she loved Bill very much but that she was becoming less interested in sex (Barlow & Durand, 1995). Greta's problem is called inhibited female orgasm.

*Inhibited female orgasm* refers to a persistent delay or absence of orgasm after becoming aroused and excited.

About 5–10% of females never or almost never reach orgasm, and about 30% do not have orgasms during intercourse. Difficulty in reaching orgasm is the most common complaint of women seeking help for sexual problems (Sarwer & Durlak, 1997).

Psychological treatment begins with sensate focus, during which the couple learns to pleasure each other and the woman learns to relax and enjoy her body's sensations. The man is told how to help a woman reach orgasm, for example, by using his hand or, in Greta's case, using a vibrator (Barlow & Durand, 1995). This program has proved successful in treating inhibited female orgasm.

Next, we'll discuss a sexual problem that involves a potentially deadly transmitted disease—AIDS.

## AIDS: Acquired Immune Deficiency Syndrome

On June 5, 1981, the United States Centers for Disease Control issued a brief report describing five gay men in Los Angeles who had a rare form of pneumonia; eventually this pneumonia was determined to be one symptom of the HIV virus that is believed to cause AIDS.

*HIV positive* refers to the presence of HIV antibodies, which means that the individual has been infected by the human immunodeficiency virus (HIV).

*AIDS (Acquired Immune Deficiency Syndrome)* is a life-threatening condition that, by the latest definition, is present when the individual is HIV positive and has a level of T-cells (CD4 immune cells) of no more than 200 per cubic milliliter of blood (one-fifth of the level of a healthy person) or has developed one or more of 26 specified illnesses (including recurrent pneumonia and skin cancer).

The criterion of T-cell levels below 200 became a part of the definition of AIDS in 1993. T-cells are a critical part of the body's immune system, which fights against toxic agents (viruses and bacteria). Because of this change, some people who were previously defined as being HIV positive are now defined as having AIDS, even if no obvious symptoms have developed.

In 1999, there were about 34 million people worldwide infected with the human immunodeficiency virus (HIV), which is believed to cause AIDS (Cohen, 2000). As shown in the map on the left, the AIDS virus is widely spread and has reached dangerous and epidemic levels in Sub-Saharan Africa (24.5 million cases). AIDS kills 11 people worldwide every minute, and since 1981 it has killed a total of about 14 million (Forsyth, 2000). Researchers now have evidence that, in the 1950s, the HIV virus jumped from chimpanzees to humans who lived in the Congo (Africa) (Cohen, 1999). We'll discuss three major issues involving AIDS.

**HIV Infections Worldwide**

North America 900,000
Caribbean 360,000
Latin America 1.3 million
Eastern Europe & Central Asia 420,000
Southeast Asia 5.6 million
North Africa & Middle East 220,000
East Asia 530,000
Sub-Saharan Africa 24.5 million

### Risk for AIDS

The HIV virus cannot survive in air, in water, or on things that people touch. There are no reports of getting AIDS through casual contact, such as through touch. The HIV virus survives best in blood tissues and some bodily fluids (semen and vaginal fluids). Thus people who come in physical contact with blood or bodily fluids (semen or vaginal fluids) from someone who has the HIV virus are at risk for getting AIDS.

The graph on the right shows that in the United States, those at greatest risk for AIDS are gay men and heterosexual intravenous drug users. However, the risk of AIDS among women in the United States increased from 7% in the early 1980s to 23% in 1998. In the rest of the world, about 75% of AIDS is spread through heterosexual intercourse (Piot, 2000).

**How people get AIDS**

| | |
|---|---|
| 7% | Gay intravenous drug users |
| 11% | Heterosexual contact |
| 12% | Other |
| 25% | Heterosexual intravenous drug users |
| 45% | Homosexual contact |

Source: Centers for Disease Control and Prevention, 1999

### Progression of Disease

After infection, the AIDS virus replicates rapidly and intensively. As a result, newly infected individuals are 100–1,000 times more infectious than they are throughout the remainder of the disease (Koopman, 1995). In addition, newly infected individuals have no symptoms and the presence of antibodies to the HIV virus cannot be confirmed biochemically for at least 60 days. Thus, the newly infected person is regarded as a walking time bomb.

HIV destroys T-cells (CD4 cells), which are immune cells that fight off toxic agents (viruses and bacteria). It takes an average of 7 years for a person infected with HIV to develop AIDS (T count below 200) and another 2–3 years after that to develop diseases that result in death. The reason a person with AIDS is especially susceptible to infections and diseases is that the HIV virus slowly destroys a person's immune system's defenses, which means the body loses its ability to fight off toxic agents (infections or diseases).

Because of yet unknown qualities of their immune systems, about 10 to 17% of HIV-infected individuals will be AIDS-free 20 years after infection. Researchers are studying these AIDS-free individuals to find out how their immune systems can fight off AIDS (Kolata, 2000a).

### Treatment

In 1996 the number of AIDS-related deaths in the United States fell 23%; in 1997 it fell 45%; and in 1998 it fell 11%. This decrease in AIDS-related deaths was primarily due to several new breakthroughs in drugs that were introduced in 1995. The new drug treatment program has patients taking a drug "cocktail" of many pills daily, which include several new drugs (protease inhibitors and HIV-inhibiting drugs) (Steinhauer, 2000). In many  cases, these new drugs reduce the levels of the HIV virus so that they are undetectable. However, the new drugs do not totally wipe out the virus. Instead, the HIV virus somehow "hides out" in the body and returns if patients stop taking the drug cocktail (Fauci, 2000). The new drug cocktails to treat the HIV virus have reduced life-threatening symptoms and given AIDS patients a longer and better life (Maugh, 2000).

However, besides the new drug's troublesome side effects (nausea, kidney stones), if patients stop taking these drugs, the HIV virus returns (Roberts, 2000). More troubling, the HIV virus is becoming immune to some of the current drugs, which means that new drugs or vaccines must be found to treat the HIV virus or the death rate from AIDS will start to increase again (Koplan, 1999).

Now, we'll discuss a cruel cultural influence on female sexual behavior.

## Good Tradition or Cruel Mutilation?

**What is female circumcision?**

Males have a long history of trying to control the sexual motivation of females. In many countries, men want to marry virgins and insist that women remain so until marriage, although the men do not hold themselves to the same standards. One extreme example of men controlling the sexual motivation and behavior of women is found in parts of Africa and the Arabian Peninsula, where young girls are circumcised before they become sexually mature (Caldwell et al., 1997).

*Female circumcision* involves cutting away the female's external genitalia, usually including her clitoris and surrounding skin (labia minora). The remaining edges are sewn together, which leaves only a small opening for urination and menstruation.

Soraya Mire (above photo) remembers the day that her mother said, "I'm going to buy you some gifts." Soraya, who was

At age 13, Soraya Mire underwent female circumcision.

13, obediently got into the car with her mother and driver. They didn't go shopping but stopped at a doctor's house. Once inside, they went into an operating room where a doctor asked Soraya to lie on the operating table. He tied her feet down with a rope so she could not move. Her mother said that it was time for Soraya to become a woman and undergo female circumcision.

Like her mother and her mother's mother, Soraya underwent this ancient rite of passage. But unlike them, Soraya has decided to break the silence and fight this cruel mutilation. Now 36, Soraya has made a documentary film called *Fire Eyes* to protest the current practice of female circumcision (Tawa, 1995).

Researchers estimate that about 2 million women a year and a total of about 100 million women have undergone circumcision. Female circumcision is currently practiced in about 28 African countries by peoples of different socioeconomic classes and ethnic and cultural groups (Caldwell et al., 1997; Nour, 2000).

### What Is Its Purpose?

In many of the poorer societies of Africa and Ethiopia, female circumcision is a common ritual to physically mark young girls and increase their chances for future marriage. Recently, conservative Muslim clerics in Egypt overturned a government ban on female circumcision, which serves no hygienic or medically useful purpose (Daniszewski, 1997).

Girls are commonly circumcised before they reach puberty, usually between the ages of 4 and 10. The primary reason for female circumcision is the male's belief that if females are surgically deprived of receiving sexual pleasure, they will remain clean and virginal until marriage. Men in these societies often refuse to marry a woman who has not been circumcised because they believe that she is unclean and not a virgin (Walker & Parmar, 1993).

The male equivalent of female circumcision would be amputation of the male's penis.

Young girl is being held while undergoing female circumcision.

### Are There Complications?

Because of the high social status of Soraya's father, who was a general, her circumcision was performed by a doctor. However, in the majority of cases, it is done by someone with no medical training who uses a razor blade and less than sterile procedures.

Because the genital area has a high percentage of nerves and blood vessels, female circumcision results in severe pain, bleeding, and even hemorrhaging, which can lead to shock and death. Because of poor surgical procedures, girls endure a number of medical complications, including infections, cysts, and permanent scarring. This procedure also makes menstruation and intercourse painful and childbirth dangerous (Nour, 2000).

Girls submit to the fear, pain, and trauma of circumcision for varied and complex reasons. Female circumcision is done in the belief that it is for the good of their daughters; that their religion requires it; that it will make their daughters marriageable; and that it is necessary to maintain female chastity (Nour, 2000). However, many circumcised women suffer chronic anxiety and depression from worry about their disfigured genitals, difficulties with menstruation, and fear of infertility (Caldwell et al., 1997).

### Is There a Solution?

The United Nations health organizations have endorsed anticircumcision laws, but such laws would not eliminate the strong sociocultural traditions that exist in many of the villages that currently practice this procedure. As one supporter of circumcision said, "This procedure helps to keep women's sexual drives at acceptable and reasonable levels" (Daniszewski, 1997). Although Westerners are horrified by this barbaric practice, many African societies consider this practice part of their culture and do it out of love for their daughters. For example, when a newspaper in Ghana, Africa, published articles in favor of banning female circumcision, local women had great success in drumming up support for keeping this ancient practice and rejecting values from the outside world.

A number of feminists in Africa and Egypt have formed a society to fight the sexual mutilation of females, but they have encountered considerable resistance from both men and women who wish to maintain the practice (Caldwell et al., 1997). Female circumcision is an extreme example of how far human societies (men) have gone to control the sexual behavior of females.

We have discussed two biological drives, hunger and sex. After the Concept Review, we'll examine an important social need—achievement.

# Concept Review

**1.** Physiological or psychological factors that cause us to act in a specific way at a particular time are included in the definition of _____.

**2.** Innate biological forces predispose an animal to behave in a particular way in the presence of a specific environmental condition. These ways of behaving are called _____.

**3.** A biological need produces a state of arousal during which the organism engages in behaviors to reduce the need. This state of arousal is called a (a)_____. Once a need is satisfied, the body returns to a more balanced state, called (b)_____. This need-drive-homeostasis sequence is described by the (c)_____ theory.

**4.** External stimuli, reinforcers, goals, or rewards that may be positive or negative and that motivate one's behavior are called _____.

**5.** When we perform behaviors to reduce biological needs or obtain various incentives, we are acting under the influence of (a)_____ motivation. When we perform behaviors because they are personally rewarding or because we are following our personal goals, beliefs, or expectations, we are acting under the influence of (b)_____ motivation.

**6.** Needs that are not critical to your survival but that are acquired through learning and socialization, such as the needs for achievement and affiliation, are called (a)_____ needs. Needs that are critical to your survival and physical well-being, such as food, water, and sex, are called (b)_____ needs.

**7.** The ascending order or hierarchy with biological needs at the bottom and social needs at the top is _____. This idea assumes that we satisfy our biological needs before satisfying our social needs.

**8.** There are three major factors that influence eating. Cues that come from physiological changes are called (a)_____ factors. Cues that come from inherited instructions are called (b)_____ factors. Cues that come from learning and personality traits are called (c)_____ factors.

**9.** Biological cues for hunger that come from the stomach, liver, intestines, and fat cells are called (a)_____ cues. Biological cues that come from the brain are called (b)_____ cues.

**10.** The part of the hypothalamus that is involved in feelings of being hungry is called the (a)_____; the part that is involved in feelings of being full is called the (b)_____.

**11.** We inherit the following genetic factors involved in weight regulation: a certain number of (a)_____ cells that store fat; a certain (b)_____ rate that regulates how fast we burn off fuel; a certain (c)_____ point that maintains a stable amount of body fat; and weight-regulating (d)_____ that influence appetite, metabolism, and hormone secretion.

**12.** Psychological factors that influence eating include (a)_____ associations, (b)_____ influences, and (c)_____ variables.

**13.** Genetic sex factors involve the 23rd chromosome, called the (a)_____, which determines the sex of the child. Biological sex factors include sex hormones, which for the male are called (b)_____ and for the female are called (c)_____. Psychological sex factors include the subjective feeling of being male or female, which is called (d)_____; adopting behaviors and traits that society identifies as male or female, which is called (e)_____; and being more sexually aroused by members of the same or opposite sex, which is called (f)_____.

**14.** Evidence from the sexual orientation of identical twins and the shared genetic material from gay brothers are examples of (a)_____ factors in the development of a homosexual orientation. Young boys who prefer girls' toys and girl playmates and engage in opposite-sex behaviors show a tendency to develop a homosexual orientation, which shows the effects of (b)_____ factors on sexual orientation.

**15.** A person who has been infected by the human immuno-deficiency virus but has not yet developed any illnesses is said to be (a)_____. A person whose level of T-cells has dropped to 200 per cubic milliliter of blood but who may or may not have developed an illness is defined as having (b)_____.

**Answers:** *1. motivation; 2. fixed action patterns; 3. (a) drive, (b) homeostasis, (c) drive-reduction; 4. incentives; 5. (a) extrinsic, (b) intrinsic; 6. (a) social, (b) biological; 7. Maslow's hierarchy of needs; 8. (a) biological, (b) genetic, (c) psychosocial; 9. (a) peripheral, (b) central; 10. (a) lateral hypothalamus, (b) ventromedial hypothalamus; 11. (a) fat, (b) metabolic, (c) set, (d) genes; 12. (a) learned, (b) social-cultural, (c) personality; 13. (a) sex chromosome, (b) androgens, (c) estrogens, (d) gender identity, (e) gender role, (f) sexual orientation; 14. (a) genetic, (b) psychological; 15. (a) HIV positive, (b) AIDS*

### Kinds of Achievement

**Why did Victor succeed when his friends didn't?**

At the beginning of the module, we told you about Victor, an African American high school student whose buddies called him a "White boy" because they thought he was studying too hard. "You can't be cool if you're smart," says Victor, who was Mission Bay High's student body president, had a 3.7 (A–) grade point average, and planned to attend the University of Southern California in the fall (adapted from the *San Diego Union-Tribune,* June 17, 1994).

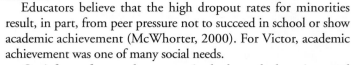

It doesn't look cool if you work hard for grades.

Victor (right photo) grew up with an obstacle that goes largely unnoticed and is rarely discussed in public: pressure from students in the same racial or ethnic group not to succeed in the classroom (Steele, 1995). Faced with this negative peer pressure, principally from Latino, African American, and Native American teenage boys, some minority students stop studying, don't do homework, avoid answering questions in class, join gangs, or even drop out of school.

Educators believe that the high dropout rates for minorities result, in part, from peer pressure not to succeed in school or show academic achievement (McWhorter, 2000). For Victor, academic achievement was one of many social needs.

*Social needs* are those acquired through learning and experience.

Social needs include desire for affiliation or close social bonds; nurturance or need to help and protect others; dominance or need to influence or control others; and achievement or need to excel (Murray, 1938). The fact that you are in college suggests that you are showing your social need for achievement.

The *achievement need* refers to the desire to set challenging goals and to persist in pursuing those goals in the face of obstacles, frustrations, and setbacks.

The achievement need not only is a major concern of college students but also ranks high (Level 4 out of 5) in Maslow's hierarchy of needs. We'll discuss four questions related to the achievement need: How is the need for achievement measured? What is high need for achievement? What is fear of failure? What is underachievement?

### *How Is the Need for Achievement Measured?*

You could simply ask people if they had a great need to achieve, but, depending on social pressures, their answers might be biased, untrue, or otherwise unreliable. To obtain a more reliable measure of a person's need for achievement, psychologists David McClelland and John Atkinson used the Thematic Apperception Test (TAT).

What do you think is going on in this TAT card?

The *Thematic Apperception Test,* commonly called the *TAT,* is a personality test in which subjects are asked to look at pictures of people in ambiguous situations and to make up stories about what the characters are thinking and feeling and what the outcome will be.

For example, the sample TAT card on the left shows a young man with a sad expression and a bright sun and fruit tree in the background. If you were taking the TAT, you would be asked to describe what is happening in this card. To measure the level of achievement, your stories would be scored in terms of achievement themes such as setting goals, competing, or overcoming obstacles (Atkinson, 1958; McClelland et al., 1953). The TAT assumes that the strength of your need to achieve will be reflected in the kinds of thoughts and feelings that you use to describe the TAT cards. However, TAT stories are difficult to score reliably because there is no objective way to identify which thoughts and feelings indicate level of achievement (Keiser & Prather, 1990). For that reason, achievement is often measured with more objective paper-and-pencil tests because they are easier to administer and score and have better reliability and validity than does the TAT (Kaplan & Saccuzzo, 2001).

### *What Is High Need for Achievement?*

There is perhaps no better example of individuals with high need for achievement than Olympic athletes. One example is Shannon Miller (photo below), who from a very early age trained for hours each day, gave up the fun and games that most children take for granted, and endured the stress and frustration of competition for a dozen years to achieve her final goal, winning four medals in gymnastics at the summer Olympics. Shannon is a perfect example of someone with a high need for achievement (Atkinson & Raynor, 1974; McClelland, 1985).

*High need for achievement* is shown by those who persist longer at tasks; perform better on tasks, activities, or exams; set challenging but realistic goals; compete with others to win; and are attracted to careers that require initiative.

Although the vast majority of us will not make the Olympics or achieve an A average, most of us exhibit varying degrees of need to achieve, by doing our best, striving for social recognition, and working to achieve material rewards (Snow & Jackson, 1994). The need for achievement influences and motivates many of your behaviors.

If we consider one side of a coin to be a need for achievement, the other side is fear of failure, which also involves making excuses for failing.

Shannon Miller showed her high need for achievement by winning an Olympic medal.

## Fear of Failure

**Why do some fail?**

Just as some individuals may be motivated by a need for achievement, others may be motivated by a fear of failure. Atkinson (1964) believed that, in order to understand fully why a person succeeds or fails in reaching a goal, we must examine not only that person's need for achievement but also his or her fear of failure.

*Fear of failure* is shown by people who are motivated to avoid failure by choosing easy, nonchallenging tasks where failure is more unlikely to occur.

For example, fear of failure may motivate a student to study just enough to avoid failing an exam but not enough to get a good grade or set higher academic goals. In fact, the fear of failure is a good predictor of poor grades: the greater a student's fear of failure, the poorer his or her grades (Herman, 1990). Atkinson believed that, just as people vary in their need for achievement, they also vary in their motivation to avoid failure. Atkinson said that individuals who are motivated primarily by a fear of failure would never do as well, work as hard, or set goals as high as those who were motivated by a need for achievement.

**Self-handicapping.** If a person is motivated primarily by the fear of failure, how does this individual explain his or her poor performances yet keep a good self-image? One solution to this problem is to make up excuses, which is called self-handicapping (Jones & Berglas, 1978).

*Self-handicapping* refers to doing things that contribute to failure and then using these things, knowingly or unknowingly, as excuses for failing to achieve some goal.

Researchers found that individuals with low self-esteem are most likely to engage in self-handicapping, apparently to protect their already low self-esteem when they fail (Spalding & Hardin, 1999). Some of the more popular self-handicapping excuses involve health (missed sleep, have a cold), drug usage (have a hangover), chance/fate (it was bad luck, could only happen to me), unrealistically high goals (how could I possibly do that), or procrastination (I didn't have enough time). Although self-handicapping excuses that explain why we failed do help preserve our positive self-image and self-esteem, such excuses interfere with taking personal responsibility to achieve our goals (Covington, 2000).

One example of how fear of failure affects motivation is seen in individuals who are underachievers.

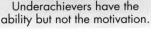

Underachievers have the ability but not the motivation.

## Underachievement

**Why do some underachieve?**

One of my friends described his 14-year-old son, Rich, as having all the brains in the world but doing nothing with them. Although Rich is a computer wizard, he gets terrible grades in school, never does his homework, and doesn't seem to have any ambition. Rich might be called an underachiever.

*Underachievers* are individuals who score relatively high on tests of ability or intelligence but perform more poorly than their scores would predict.

The most common examples of underachievers are students who score relatively high on ability or intelligence tests but perform poorly in school or academic settings (Lupart & Pyryt, 1996). Researchers found that underachievement is not related to socioeconomic class, that there are two or three male underachievers for every female, and that about 15% of students are underachievers (McCall, 1994).

**Characteristics.** The psychological characteristics of underachievers include having a poor self-concept, low self-esteem, and poor peer relations and being shy or depressed. The cognitive characteristics of underachievers include fear of failure, poor perceptions of their abilities, and lack of persistence. This means that underachievers are less likely to persist in getting their college degrees, holding on to jobs, or maintaining their marriages (McCall, 1994). Thus, underachievement reduces performance in academic, job, and marital settings, and its effects may last through adulthood.

The paradox of underachievement is that underachievers have the abilities but are not motivated to use them. Clinicians, counselors, and researchers are developing treatment programs to help underachievers change their psychological traits and cognitive perceptions so they will have the motivation to use their considerable abilities (McCall, 1994).

## Three Components of Success

**Why is a person successful?**

Explaining why some students are more successful than others involves the interaction of three components that we have just discussed: need for achievement, fear of failure, and psychological factors (self-concept, self-esteem, and confidence in one's abilities). For example, researchers wondered why some minority children from low-income homes were successful in school while others were not. Those minority students who succeeded had higher self-esteem, greater confidence in their abilities, and received more support and encourage-

ment from a parent or caregiver (Finn & Rock, 1997). Researchers also found that students who were more successful in school had come from more stimulating home environments (parents spoke more to children, children had more books and watched less television) (Cleveland et al., 2000). Thus, having a stimulating home environment leads to a higher need for achievement, which in turn leads to more success in life. Finally, successful students not only worked harder but also liked what they were doing. This "enjoyment of work" is an important cognitive factor that greatly influences motivation and is our next topic.

Need for achievement | Fear of failure | Psychological factors

**Being successful**

## Cognitive Influences

Intrinsic
Motivation

Competence
Determination
Curiosity
Enjoyment

Extrinsic
Motivation

Competition
Recognition
Incentive
Money

**Do you work for love or money?**

Each year, over 1,600 seniors compete in the Westinghouse Science Talent Search to win the most prestigious high school science award in the United States. One winner was Ann Chen (photo at right), a high school senior from California. Chen's project involved studying how genes function in the spread of cancer. When interviewed after receiving her award, Chen said that science has been a lifelong love and interest for her (Balint, 1995). Chen's love of science translates into a motivating force that comes from cognitive factors.

*Cognitive factors in motivation* refer to how people evaluate or perceive a situation and how these evaluations and perceptions influence their willingness to work.

Ann Chen perceives science projects as interesting and enjoyable and works hard to complete them. She plans to go to Harvard and get a doctorate in chemistry. Compared to Chen's love of science, other students find science projects hard and boring and take science courses only because they are

required. The difference between taking science courses because of a love of science or because of course requirements illustrates the difference between two kinds of motivation—intrinsic motivation and extrinsic motivation.

*Intrinsic motivation* involves engaging in certain activities or behaviors without receiving any external rewards because the behaviors themselves are personally rewarding or because engaging in these activities fulfills our beliefs or expectations.

*Extrinsic motivation* involves engaging in certain activities or behaviors that either reduce biological needs or help us obtain incentives and external rewards.

Being motivated because you love the work (Chen's love of science) indicates *intrinsic motivation,* which is related to competence, self-determination, curiosity, enjoyment, and interest. Being motivated because the work is required indicates *extrinsic motivation,* which is related to competition, evaluation, recognition, money, and incentives, such as a nice house. The major advantage of working because of intrinsic motivation (loving what you're doing) is that you will feel powerfully motivated. Without intrinsic motivation, there would be very little charitable work or donations; very few people would volunteer their time or donate their blood (Deci et al., 1999).

## Intrinsic Motivation

**What happens if volunteers get paid?**

What would happen if people who were intrinsically motivated to give blood (wanting to do their duty, wanting to help others) were now given an external reward (money) for giving blood? Would receiving money "turn them off" or decrease their intrinsic motivation to the point that they might give less blood or none at all?

Researchers generally thought that if people were given external rewards (money, awards, prizes, or tokens) for doing tasks (donating blood) that they formerly did from intrinsic motivation, their performance of and interest in these tasks would decrease (Deci et al., 1999). Because the finding that external rewards decreased intrinsic motivation was widely accepted, many books advised that rewards should not be used in educational settings, hospitals, or volunteer organizations because such rewards would do more harm than good. Recent reviews of this question indicate that the effects of external rewards on intrinsic motivation are more complex than originally thought.

There are three general conclusions from the recent reviews (Deci et al., 1999; Eisenberger et al., 1999; Lepper et al., 1999). First, giving unexpected

People who donate blood are usually intrinsically motivated.

external rewards does not decrease intrinsic motivation, but people may come to expect such rewards. Second, giving positive verbal feedback for doing work that was better than others may actually increase intrinsic motivation. Third, giving external rewards for doing minimal work or completing a specific project may decrease intrinsic motivation. These studies show that, unlike previously thought, external rewards that are unexpected or involve positive verbal feedback may increase intrinsic motivation. External rewards that are tied to doing minimal work or completing a specific project may decrease intrinsic motivation.

For a long time it was also thought that external rewards automatically decreased creative work and interest. But researchers have found that the effects of giving children a reward for completing a creative task depend on how they perceive the reward. If they perceive the reward as a treat, it will increase their intrinsic interest, but if they see the reward as an external pressure to be creative, it will decrease their intrinsic interest (Eisenberger & Armeli, 1997). All of these studies show that external rewards influence cognitive factors, which in turn may increase or decrease intrinsic motivation.

Next, we'll examine how cognitive factors influenced children's motivation and achievement in school.

## Why Did Immigrant Children Do Well?

**Why were researchers surprised?**

One goal of research is to solve puzzles about human behavior. We're about to describe a situation that was very puzzling because what psychologists guessed should happen, did not and what should not happen, did. Here's the situation.

Psychologists visited a junior high school and the teacher explained that some of the students only recently immigrated to the United States and had to learn English and adjust to all the cultural differences. All the other students were born in the United States. The psychologists were asked to guess which students—those born

Why did immigrant children who first had to learn English do well in school?

in the United States or those who had recently immigrated—were doing better in school and getting better grades.

The psychologists guessed that children who had been born in the United States would be doing better and getting higher grades because they knew the language and the customs. They guessed that the newly arrived immigrant children would not be doing as well because the immigrant students would be seriously handicapped by not knowing the language or the customs. To answer this question, researchers began a large study which ended in a puzzle.

### Procedure and Results

To find out which students were doing better in school, researchers analyzed data from a representative sample of 24,599 eighth-grade students who came from 1,052 randomly selected schools in the United States. Researchers focused on two groups of students, who were Latino, Asian, Black (mostly from the Caribbean) and White (Kao & Tienda, 1995). One group of students was called first generation because both the student and his or her mother were foreign born and had difficulties with the language and customs. The other group was called third generation because both the student and his or her mother were native born (born in the United States) and knew the language and were familiar with the customs.

Researchers compared how first- and third-generation students performed on well-known tests for math and reading. At the end of the test, students were asked about their future academic plans, such as whether they planned to go to college.

In the graph on the right, notice that there are three pairs of bars, and each pair compares the math scores of first- and third-generation Asian, Latino, and Black *immigrant* students. Notice that in each case, the first-generation immigrant students, who faced the most difficulties in language and social adjustment, performed better on math tests (and other tests not shown) than did the third-generation students who were born in the United States.

There were two puzzling findings: Why did first-generation students perform better, and why did more first-generation students plan to go to college?

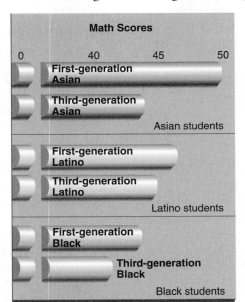

**Math Scores**

| 0 | 40 | 45 | 50 |

First-generation Asian

Third-generation Asian

Asian students

First-generation Latino

Third-generation Latino

Latino students

First-generation Black

Third-generation Black

Black students

### Conclusions

The puzzle is why and how immigrant students, who are handicapped by language problems, consistently score higher on tests than native-born students. Perhaps this difference in scores between first- and third-generation students was due to different socioeconomic conditions. However, after controlling (by using statistics) for socioeconomic class differences, researchers found that the major reason for the better performance of first-generation minority students was that they had adopted their parents' *hopeful values* about education.

**Parental values.** The first-generation immigrant mothers and fathers believed that their children would achieve social and economic advantages by obtaining a good education. The parents' hopeful values about educational opportunities translated into encouraging their children to work together, help one another, and spend a significant amount of time doing homework (three hours nightly).

In comparison, third-generation parents who have lived for some years in the United States have become less hopeful about making advances through education. Because they are less hopeful about educational opportunities, they pass along a negative attitude about doing well in school. In turn, negative parental attitudes translate into their children having less motivation, spending less time doing homework, performing poorer on tests, and having less desire to go on to college (Kao & Tienda, 1995).

**Implications.** There is much discussion of how to improve public schools, such as by decreasing class size or making teachers more accountable for their students. This study points to another factor in improving schools, which is to encourage parents to become more involved in their children's education. As this study found, parents' positive or negative attitudes toward education translate into encouraging or discouraging their children, which in turn increases or decreases their children's motivation, performance, and academic achievement.

We have discussed how cognitive factors can influence social needs, such as achievement. Next, we'll discuss how cognitive factors can also influence a biological need, hunger, and result in serious eating disorders.

## Dieting: Problems, Concerns, and Benefits

**Why is dieting so difficult?** Some of us have learned to eat at certain times (learned associations) or eat when stressed (personality variables), or we come from families that encourage eating to show appreciation (cultural influences). Any of these psychosocial factors—learned associations, personality variables, or cultural influences—can override our genetic and biological factors and result in becoming overweight. Currently, about 55% of adults in the United States are overweight and they spend about $40 billion annually trying to lose weight (Grady, 2000).

Losing weight is very difficult because the body is genetically designed to store extra calories as fat and because our large forebrains are very good at rationalizing why we need to eat another piece of pizza and at making excuses for not exercising. We'll use the dieting experiences of television talk-show host Oprah Winfrey to illustrate the difficulties of dieting and maintaining an optimal weight.

### Before

In the 1970s, when Oprah Winfrey was in her twenties, she weighed about 140 pounds. By the mid-1980s, Oprah weighed about 190 pounds (right photo), which is considered overweight for her height and frame. Oprah admitted to loving foods high in fat content (caramels, cheese popcorn) and had no time for exercise. She described getting home from work and being overwhelmed by a compulsion to eat. Her weight reached 200 pounds, and she felt depressed. When her weight reached 211, she decided it was time for a diet program (Greene & Winfrey, 1996).

*190 pounds*

### 1 Year Later

In 1988, Oprah went on a well-publicized diet in which she lost 67 pounds and weighed 142 pounds. She showed off her slim figure on television (right photo) and said she was finally cured of overeating.

**Physiological factors.** However, Oprah was probably not aware of two physiological factors that make it difficult to keep off lost weight and explain why about 90% of dieters regain their lost weight in the first year. The first physiological factor is that her body automatically adjusts to any decrease in fat stores by lowering its rate of *metabolism* from 10% to 28% (Leibel et al., 1995). As a result, her body becomes more efficient at burning fuel so she must eat even less to avoid regaining lost weight.

The second physiological factor is that Oprah's body has a genetically fixed *set point*, which maintains her fat stores at a stable level. If the level of fat stores drops below her set point, her body will compensate by reducing the metabolic rate to return fat stores to their former level (Vogel, 1999). To raise her metabolic rate, she would need a regular exercise program. Could Oprah make major changes in her lifestyle, such as more exercise, or would she regain her lost weight?

*142 pounds*

### 2 Years Later

Oprah did not make the necessary changes in her lifestyle; she regained all her lost weight and then some, reaching about 237 pounds (left photo). After she gained back all her weight, Oprah admitted, "I didn't do whatever the maintenance program was. I thought I was cured. And that's just not true. You have to find a way to live in the world with food" (*People,* January 14, 1991, p. 84). Researchers find that 90–95% of people who diet and lose weight gradually gain back their lost weight, usually within 1–2 years and almost certainly after 5 years (Vogel, 1999). The reason people regain the lost weight is that they don't have a *maintenance program* that involves eating less and exercising more. Oprah finally found the motivation to exercise.

*237 pounds*

### 8 Years Later

One day while writing in her journal, Oprah decided that the reason she had regained her weight was that she had lost it primarily to please others. Now she would try again but this time do it to please herself. She also realized that food had become more than nutrition. "For me, food was comfort, pleasure, love, a friend, everything. Now I consciously work every day at not letting food be a substitute for emotions" (Tresniowski & Bell, 1996, p. 81). Oprah changed her attitude toward eating, hired a personal trainer, lost 67 pounds, and maintained her weight at a comfortable 170 pounds (left photo) (Greene & Oprah, 1996).

**Best weight-control program.** Oprah's continuing difficulties in controlling her weight confirm the experiences of many dieters who found it not only difficult to lose weight but even more difficult to keep the weight off. Most researchers agree that the best way to reduce and keep weight off is not by going on a one-time, six-month diet or the latest fad diet but rather by committing to a long-term program of exercise and careful diet (Evans, 2000). Researchers found that a program of exercise and diet involves four factors: (1) changing one's attitudes toward food (making it less important); (2) changing one's eating patterns (consuming fewer calories); (3) developing a regular exercise program (a critical part of a weight program); and (4) perhaps the most important, sticking to this weight program over the long term, often for a lifetime (Brody, 2000).

Next, we'll discuss the causes and treatments of two eating disorders.

*170 pounds*

## Serious Eating Disorders

**Why does a person starve?**

For six seasons (1985–1992), Tracey Gold starred on the highly rated ABC sitcom "Growing Pains." However, in 1992, she was forced to leave the show as her weight plummeted and finally hit 80 pounds, which made her body look almost like skin and bones. She said, "All life meant was losing weight and counting calories." One night Tracey caught sight of herself in the mirror. "I saw somebody who would die of anorexia, and I had a panic attack." That marked a turning point, and Tracey began her fight to live (Levitt & Wagner, 1994). Tracey's progress in overcoming her eating disorder is seen in the photo at the right. She is back to her normal weight (108 pounds), happily married, and the proud mother of a daughter. How could someone like Tracey, a young TV star who seemed to have it all, develop anorexia nervosa?

Actress Tracey Gold recovered from anorexia.

### Anorexia Nervosa

Tracey's eating disorder, anorexia nervosa *(an-uh-REX-see-ah ner-VOH-sah)*, almost exclusively affects individuals who are female (90%), White (99%), 15–24 years old (60%), and from the two highest socioeconomic classes (75%) (Garner & Garfinkel, 1997). Contrary to reports in the popular press, anorexia nervosa, as defined by the symptoms below, is a relatively rare disorder, occurring in only about 0.10–1.0% of the population (Walters & Kendler, 1995).

*Anorexia nervosa* is a serious eating disorder characterized by refusing to eat and not maintaining weight at 85% of what is expected, having an intense fear of gaining weight or becoming fat, and missing at least three consecutive menstrual cycles. Anorexics also have a disturbed body image: They see themselves as fat even though they are very thin (American Psychiatric Association, 1994).

The very skinny legs in the right photo belong to a White female, age 20, who once weighed a normal 140 pounds but now weighs a mere 90 pounds and is being treated for anorexia nervosa (Fox, 1997).

**Personality and genes.** Many clinicians search for causes of anorexia nervosa in personality development. Studies of anorexics indicate that as children they were conforming, compulsive, tense, sensitive, and ambitious, with difficult temperaments (too restrained or too emotional). When they faced the pressures of adolescence, their personality difficulties came out in abnormal eating patterns (self-starvation) because they believed that the love and support they needed so badly were given only if they controlled their impulses (Crisp, 1997). One very dramatic way to control one's impulses is to starve oneself to the point of death.

**Treatment.** Treatment for anorexics initially involves in-hospital programs that focus on encouraging weight gain, usually through behavior modification (Module 10), and then dealing with psychological problems through psychotherapy. Drugs have been of limited use in treating this disorder (Garfinkel & Walsh, 1997). Outcome after 12 years showed that 12% of anorexics had died and 14% had poor, 27% intermediate, and 47% good outcomes (Herzog et al., 2000).

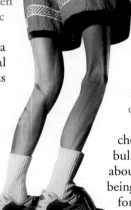

Anorexics do not see themselves as skinny.

### Bulimia Nervosa

Another kind of eating disorder is illustrated by Carol, a college sophomore. Her life seemed perfect when she was growing up, but all the time something was terribly wrong. "It was like I had to live in this fantasy world where everything was sweet and good and I got straight A's," Carol explains. "I started work when I was really young and I would do anything for anyone there and everyone thought I was so nice and so sweet. And I was just dying inside, literally." At 5 feet 7 inches tall and 127 pounds, she shows no external sign of an eating disorder, but Carol began binge eating at the age of 15. She would eat large numbers of calories in one brief period and then force herself to vomit as a way of avoiding weight gain (adapted from the *Daily Aztec,* March 22, 1984).

Carol's disorder is called bulimia nervosa *(boo-LEE-me-ah ner-VOH-sah)*, which affects about 1–3% of women (primarily adolescent and young White women) and only 0.3% of males (American Psychiatric Association, 1994).

*Bulimia nervosa* is characterized by a minimum of two binge-eating episodes per week for at least three months; fear of not being able to stop eating; regularly engaging in vomiting, use of laxatives, or rigorous dieting and fasting; and excessive concern about body shape and weight (American Psychiatric Association, 1994).

**Risk factors.** Researchers have identified a number of psychological factors that make a young woman like Carol at risk for bulimia nervosa. Risk factors include being excessively concerned about approval from others in order to feel good about themselves, being too sensitive to rejection, and having high personal standards for achievement. Some bulimics experience bouts of depression, anxiety, mood swings, and problems with social relationships that may persist for years after treatment (Keel et al., 2000).

**Treatment.** Two kinds of treatment, which may be combined, are used to treat bulimia nervosa. One treatment involves psychotherapy (cognitive-behavior therapy or interpersonal therapy), which may focus on substituting positive thoughts for negative ones or improving a person's social functioning. A second method, generally less preferred because of unwanted side effects, is the use of antidepressant drugs. Researchers reported success with both kinds of treatments, whether used singly or in combination (Bacaltchuk et al., 2000). A ten-year follow-up of bulimics showed that 52% were fully recovered, 39% had some symptoms, and 9% had serious symptoms (Collings & King, 1994).

The eating disorders of anorexia and bulimia nervosa clearly illustrate how various personality and psychosocial factors not only can influence but even override the normal functioning of one of our basic biological needs, hunger.

## A. THEORIES OF MOTIVATION

**1.** The combined physiological and psychological factors that cause you to act in specific ways at particular times are referred to as (a)_____. When motivated, you usually exhibit three characteristics: you are (b)_____ to do something; you (c)_____ your energies toward a specific goal; and you have different (d)_____ of feelings about reaching that goal.

**2.** There are four general theories to explain human motivation. One theory, which applies primarily to animal motivation, involves innate biological forces that determine behavior. This is called the (a)_____ theory. Another theory explains human motivation in terms of a need that results in a drive, by which we are motivated to engage in activities to return to a more balanced state. This is called the (b)_____ theory. Because this theory does not explain why we continue to perform after our needs are met or why we perform risky behaviors, other theories were developed. The theory that says that we are motivated by external rewards is called the (c)_____ theory. The theory that distinguishes between extrinsic and intrinsic motivations is called the (d)_____ theory. If we are motivated because we find the activities personally rewarding or because they fulfill our beliefs or expectations, our motivation is said to be (e)_____.

## B. BIOLOGICAL & SOCIAL NEEDS

**3.** Food, water, and sleep are examples of (a)_____ needs. In comparison, needs that are acquired through learning and socialization are called (b)_____ needs. The theory that we satisfy our needs in ascending order, with physiological needs first and social needs later, is called (c)_____. According to this theory, needs are divided into five levels: biological, safety, love and belongingness, esteem, and self-actualization.

## C. HUNGER

**4.** If there is an almost perfect balance between how much food an organism needs to maintain the body's energy needs and how much the organism actually eats, the organism's weight is said to be (a)_____. Three different factors influence the hunger drive. Factors that come from physiological changes in blood chemistry and signals from digestive organs that provide feedback to the brain, which, in turn, triggers us to eat or stop eating, are called (b)_____ factors. Factors that come from learned associations between food and other stimuli, sociocultural influences, and various personality problems are called (c)_____ factors. Factors that come from inherited instructions contained in our genes are called (d)_____ factors.

**5.** Biological factors that influence eating come from two different sources. Cues arising from physiological changes in your blood chemistry and signals from your body organs are called (a)_____; cues from your brain are called (b)_____.

**6.** Genetic factors that influence hunger come from four different sources: the number of cells that store fat, which are called (a)_____; your rate of burning the body's fuel, which is called your (b)_____; the body's tendency to keep a stable amount of fat deposits, which is called the (c)_____; and a number of (d)_____ genes that influence appetite, metabolism, and secretion of hormones regulating fat stores.

## D. SEXUAL BEHAVIOR

**7.** Human sexual behavior is influenced by three different factors. Inherited instructions for the development of sexual organs, hormonal changes at puberty, and neural circuits that control sexual reflexes are called (a)_____ factors. The fact that humans engage in sexual behavior for many reasons besides reproduction and the fact that humans experience sexual difficulties that have no physical or medical basis indicate the influence of (b)_____ factors on sexual behavior. Factors that regulate the secretion of sex hormones, which play a role in the development of secondary sexual characteristics, influence sexual motivation (more so in animals than in humans), regulate the development of ova and sperm, and control the female menstrual cycle, are called (c)_____ factors.

**8.** Biological sex factors include the secretion of sex hormones, which is controlled by an area of the brain called the (a)_____. The major male sex hormones secreted by the testes are called (b)_____, and the major female sex hormones secreted by the ovaries are (c)_____. When hormone levels are within the normal range, there is little (d)_____ between levels of sex hormones and sexual motivation in humans.

**9.** Three psychological sex factors include the individual's subjective experience and feelings of being a male or a female, which is called (a)_____; traditional or stereotypic behaviors, attitudes, and personality traits that society designates as masculine or feminine, which are called (b)_____; and whether a person is sexually aroused primarily by members of his or her own sex, the opposite sex, or both sexes, which is called (c)_____.

**10.** The findings that identical twins are often alike in their sexual orientation and that homosexual brothers shared similar inherited material indicate the influence of (a)_____ factors on homosexual orientation. The finding that genetic factors do not necessarily determine sexual orientation indicates the influence of (b)_____ factors on sexual orientation.

**11.** There are two kinds of sexual problems. Problems that are characterized by repetitive or preferred sexual fantasies involving nonhuman objects (articles of clothing) are called (a)_____. Problems of sexual arousal or orgasm that interfere with adequate functioning during sexual behavior are called (b)_____. When a person seeks help for a sexual problem, the clinician will check whether the causes are (c)_____ or _____.

**12.** If a person has been infected by the human immunodeficiency virus (HIV) but has not yet developed one or more of 26 illnesses, that person is said to be (a)_____. A person whose level of T-cells (CD4 immune cells) has dropped to below 200 per cubic milliliter of blood (one-fifth the level of a healthy person) and who may or may not have any other symptoms is said to have (b)_____.

## E. CULTURAL DIVERSITY: FEMALE CIRCUMCISION

**13.** In some cultures the female's external genitalia, usually including her clitoris and surrounding skin (labia minora), are cut away; this practice is called _____. Girls often submit to the fear, pain, and trauma of this procedure so as to gain social status, please their parents, and comply with peer pressure. A number of feminists in Africa have formed a society to fight the sexual mutilation of females.

## F. ACHIEVEMENT

**14.** High in Maslow's needs hierarchy is a desire to set challenging goals and persist in pursuing those goals in the face of obstacles, frustrations, and setbacks. This social need is called the (a)_____. Someone who persists longer at tasks, shows better performance on tasks, activities, or exams, sets challenging but realistic goals, competes with others to win, and is attracted to careers that require initiative is said to have a high (b)_____. Individuals who score relatively high on tests

of ability or intelligence but perform more poorly than their scores would predict are called (c)_____. Individuals who either choose easy, nonchallenging tasks or challenging tasks where failure is probable and expected are said to be motivated by (d)_____.

**15.** If you engage in behaviors without receiving any external reward but because the behaviors themselves are personally rewarding, you are said to be (a)_____ motivated. If you engage in behaviors to reduce biological needs or obtain external rewards, you are said to be (b)_____ motivated.

## G. RESEARCH FOCUS: IMMIGRANT STUDENTS

**16.** Researchers found that the major reason for the greater success of first-generation immigrant students was that they had taken on their (a)_____ hopeful outlook toward advancement through education. This study shows that parents' optimistic or pessimistic attitudes toward education, which are examples of (b)_____ factors, influence their children's academic achievement.

## H. APPLICATION: EATING PROBLEMS & TREATMENTS

**17.** A healthy weight-maintenance program, which can reduce the risk of serious medical problems of (a)_____ people, involves changing (b)_____ toward food, changing (c)_____ patterns, developing an (d)_____ program, and sticking to a long-term (e)_____ program. Two serious eating disorders include a pattern characterized by bingeing, fear of not being able to stop eating, and regularly purging the body, which is called (f)_____; and another pattern in which a person starves to remain thin, has a fear of being fat, and has a disturbed body image, which is called (g)_____.

***Answers:*** *1. (a) motivation, (b) energized, (c) direct, (d) intensities; 2. (a) instinct, (b) drive-reduction, (c) incentive, (d) cognitive, (e) intrinsic; 3. (a) biological, (b) social, (c) Maslow's hierarchy of needs; 4. (a) ideal or optimal, (b) biological, (c) psychosocial, (d) genetic; 5. (a) peripheral cues, (b) central cues; 6. (a) fat cells, (b) metabolic rate, (c) set point, (d) weight-regulating; 7. (a) genetic, (b) psychological, (c) biological; 8. (a) hypothalamus, (b) androgens, (c) estrogens, (d) correlation or association; 9. (a) gender identity, (b) gender roles, (c) sexual orientation; 10. (a) genetic, (b) psychological; 11. (a) paraphilias, (b) sexual dysfunctions, (c) psychological, physiological; 12. (a) HIV positive, (b) AIDS; 13. female circumcision; 14. (a) achievement motive, (b) need for achievement, (c) underachievers, (d) fear of failure; 15. (a) intrinsically, (b) extrinsically; 16. (a) parents', (b) cognitive or psychological; 17. (a) overweight, (b) attitudes, (c) eating, (d) exercise, (e) maintenance, (f) bulimia nervosa, (g) anorexia nervosa*

# Critical Thinking

## How Effective Is Viagra?

### Questions

**1.** What are the two different causes of sexual problems (dysfunctions) and which one applies to Eric?

**2.** Why do you think that Viagra was discovered by accident?

**3.** How is the transmitter involved in producing an erection (a gas called nitric oxide) different from most other transmitters discussed earlier (p. 54)?

Eric (not his real name), who was 64 and happily married, was diagnosed with prostate cancer. He chose to have his prostate gland removed, knowing there was a 50–50 chance of becoming impotent, which is the inability to have an erection (also called erectile dysfunction). After surgery, Eric did become impotent and developed a terrible fear that his wife would leave him. Eric volunteered for a study on a brand new drug to treat impotence. For Eric, the new drug worked so well that he called it a "wonder drug" because it gave him back a normal married life. This drug later became known as Viagra (sildenafil).

What's unusual about Viagra is that it was discovered by accident. Scientists were looking for drugs to treat heart disease and found that, while one drug didn't work on heart disease, it did cause erections. Scientists changed goals and began testing the particular drug on men who were impotent.

It was not until the early 1980s that scientists figured out the plumbing behind erections. They discovered that when a man feels aroused, his penis releases a gas, nitric oxide, which activates an enzyme (cyclic GMP), which triggers the blood vessels in the penis to relax, which allows blood to rush in and cause stiffness (erection). Scientists found that Viagra worked by keeping the enzyme around longer so that blood vessels stayed relaxed longer, which allowed blood to flow in and cause an erection.

Estimates are that between 10 and 20 million American men suffer some degree of impotence. For many of these men, the idea of having an erection 20 to 40 minutes after taking Viagra was very appealing. In the first 3 months, sales of Viagra hit $411 million, making it the most successful prescription drug ever. However, after 7 months, sales had fallen 66% to $141 million for a number of reasons.

One reason was that Viagra did not work in 30–40% of men who tried it. Some men experienced unwanted side effects, such as one man who stopped taking Viagra because "your face gets very hot, you feel like your heart is beating faster than it should, there's anxiety" (Leland, 1998, p. 68). Also, although Viagra can cause erections, it may not resolve the underlying sexual difficulties in unhappy relationships. Finally, 61 deaths have been associated with Viagra, which resulted in a new warning label about not prescribing Viagra for men with certain heart problems.

In women with decreased sexual desire, Viagra has not proved effective, since the percentage of women (21%) who reported improved sexual functioning after Viagra was about the same as for those who took placebos.

For about 70% of men who suffer some degree of impotency, especially after prostate surgery, Viagra appears to be a very good deal. (Adapted from Horowitz, 1999; Leland, 1998; Roan, 1998; Mestel, 1999)

**4.** Why might men who were not impotent want to try Viagra?

**5.** What is one reason that Viagra did not work in 30–40% of those who tried it?

**6.** What is one reason that Viagra did not improve sexual functioning in women?

*Try InfoTrac to search for terms:* prostate cancer; impotence; Viagra.

---

*Suggested answers to Newspaper Article questions*

1. There are two general causes of sexual dysfunctions. One cause involves organic factors, such as medical problems or problems caused by drugs. The other cause involves psychological factors, such as anxiety, sexual trauma, guilt, or communication difficulties, all of which lead to sexual problems. In Eric's case, the cause was organic, since he had no problems with having an erection until his prostate gland was removed.

2. Although finding a pill to treat impotence was a high priority, scientists did not yet understand how erections occurred and so did not know where to look for a drug to treat impotence. It was by accident that scientists, who were initially studying a drug to treat heart disease, found a drug that produced erections.

3. All the transmitters discovered earlier were chemicals (pp. 54–55). That's why finding that the transmitter involved in erections was a gas (nitric oxide) was completely unexpected.

4. Men with no erectile problems may want to try Viagra because they incorrectly believed that Viagra would increase not only erections but also sexual desire and motivation, which it doesn't.

5. The reasons Viagra did not work in 30–40% of men with erectile problems may be serious organic (medical) problems or psychological problems (low sexual motivation, fear or anxiety about performing), which Viagra doesn't necessarily help.

6. One reason Viagra was no more effective than a placebo in improving female sexual functioning was that Viagra essentially deals with the flow of blood into and out of sexual organs and doesn't seem to improve sexual desire. Thus, women's low sexual desire or motivation, which may be a psychological problem, is a difficulty that Viagra doesn't seem to help.

# Links to Learning

## Web Sites

- WADSWORTH ONLINE STUDY CENTER
  **http://psychology.wadsworth.com**
  Quizzes, learning activities and exercises, a discussion forum, and hot links to Internet sites related to sensation, including:

- THE PROCRASTINATOR'S AID
  **http://www.geocities.com/SouthBeach/1915/**
  Warning: This page is completely and intentionally silly. If you are lacking in motivation and want a variety of jokes, book lists, and suggestions on how to waste time, this is your site.

- THE CENTER FOR EATING DISORDERS
  **http://www.eating-disorders.com**
  This comprehensive site offers hope, support, and advice for people with eating disorders, including a discussion group and mailing list.

- OVEREATERS ANONYMOUS
  **http://www.overeaters.com**
  OA is a 12-Step group dedicated to helping people who compulsively overeat. The site contains information on the organization, a quiz to help determine whether overeating is a problem for you, advice to professionals, and meeting locations.

- SEXUAL ORIENTATION: SCIENCE, EDUCATION, AND POLICY
  **http://pychology-ucdavis.edu/rainbow/index.html**
  This site features work by Gregory Herek, a noted authority on sexual prejudice, hate crimes, and AIDS stigma. Many links under main topics provide "factual information about sexual orientation, to promote the use of scientific knowledge for education and enlightened public policy."

## Learning Activities

- *POWERSTUDY™* BY ROD PLOTNIK & TOM DOYLE

  **PowerStudy™**

  **Check out CD: Module 15**
  CD section 4.A:  Genes & Evolution; book page 338
  CD section 4.E:  Limbic System: Old Brain; book page 335
  CD section 4.F:  Endocrine System; book page 339
  CD section 10.B:  Biological Factors; book page 15

- *STUDY GUIDE TO ACCOMPANY INTRODUCTION TO PSYCHOLOGY, 6TH EDITION,* by Matthew Enos
  In Module 15, you can clarify the distinction between extrinsic reinforcement and intrinsic motivation, learn which day of school you absolutely must not miss, and decide what of everything you've done was the hardest and what that says about your motivation.

- *WEBTUTOR*
  **http://webtutor.thomsonlearning.com**
  **WebTUTOR** Visit this site for interactive versions of the Study Guide features. Take a quiz, get your score—should you study a topic some more, or can you move on? For example, define "paraphilia" and "set point," and explain social role theory.

- *INFOTRAC ONLINE LIBRARY*
  **http://www.infotrac-college.com**
  Use your password and then key in search terms such as those below to find popular and scientific articles on subjects covered in Module 15. Make the library work for you!

  Motivation          Homeostasis      Gender identity disorder
  Female circumcision  Anorexia         Bulimia

- PSYCHNOW!
  CD for Macintosh and Windows includes a study guide, glossary, Web sites, and animations. For Module 15, see:
  • Motivation

## Study Questions

*Use InfoTrac to search for topics mentioned in the main heads below (e.g., motivation, female circumcision, achievement).*

*A. **Theories of Motivation**—Which theory best explains why students work hard to get good grades? (**Suggested answer page 628**)

*B. **Biological & Social Needs**—How would your needs change if you won a $20-million lottery? (**Suggested answer page 629**)

C. **Hunger**—As a parent, what would you do to keep you and your children from becoming overweight?

D. **Sexual Behavior**—What would happen to someone's sexual behavior if, at puberty, no sex hormones were secreted?

E. **Cultural Diversity: Female Circumcision**—Are there any American cultural traditions that are detrimental to the sexual behavior of men or women?

F. **Achievement**—Why might some students get the "sophomore blues" and feel less motivated about doing well in college?

G. **Research Focus: Immigrant Students**—What is one key to unlocking the potential of students from different cultures?

*H. **Application: Eating Problems & Treatments**—Would you believe an ad that promised you could "lose weight easily and quickly without dieting or exercise by practicing self-hypnosis"? (**Suggested answer page 629**)

*These questions are answered in Appendix B.

# Module 16: Emotion

**A. Peripheral Theories**    360
* SEQUENCE FOR EMOTIONS
* JAMES-LANGE THEORY
* FACIAL FEEDBACK THEORY

**B. Cognitive Appraisal Theory**    362
* SCHACHTER-SINGER EXPERIMENT
* WHICH COMES FIRST: FEELING OR THINKING?
* COGNITIVE APPRAISAL THEORY
* AFFECTIVE-PRIMACY THEORY

**C. Universal Facial Expressions**    364
* DEFINITION OF UNIVERSAL
* CROSS-CULTURAL EVIDENCE
* GENETIC EVIDENCE

**D. Functions of Emotions**    365
* SEND SOCIAL SIGNALS
* ADAPT AND SURVIVE
* AROUSE AND MOTIVATE

**E. Happiness**    366
* KINDS OF HAPPINESS
* ADAPTATION LEVEL THEORY
* LONG-TERM HAPPINESS

**F. Cultural Diversity: Emotions Across Cultures**    367
* SHOWING EMOTIONS
* PERCEIVING EMOTIONS

**Concept Review**    368

**G. Research Focus: Emotional Intelligence**    369
* WHAT IS EMOTIONAL INTELLIGENCE?

**H. Application: Lie Detection**    370
* WHAT IS THE THEORY?
* WHAT IS A LIE DETECTOR TEST?
* HOW ACCURATE ARE LIE DETECTOR TESTS?

**Summary Test**    372

**Critical Thinking**    374

* WHY DO THEY HAVE TO LEARN TO SMILE?

**Links to Learning**    375

## Emotional Experience

**What did Rick feel during a shark attack?**

What happened to Rick at 7:30 in the morning on a warm Thursday was something he would never forget. He had paddled his surfboard about 150 feet from shore to catch the best waves. As he waited, he saw a large green sea turtle swim by and disappear under the deep blue surface. Moments later he felt the water under him start to move and saw some colors and swirls but thought it must be the turtle swimming around. It wasn't a turtle but a 14-foot tiger shark, a very dangerous killing machine. With one quick motion of its head, the shark tossed Rick and his surfboard out of the water. When the board landed, Rick was hanging onto the back of the board while the shark was sinking its rows of jagged teeth into the front of the board.

As Rick hung on, he heard his heart pounding like a hammer and then a loud snapping sound as the shark broke off a piece of Rick's surfboard. Looking down into the water, Rick saw one of the shark's big eyes staring right at him, and he felt his adrenaline pumping. After what seemed like forever, the shark swam away with a big piece of Rick's surfboard stuck in its mouth.

Rick pulled himself onto what was left of his surfboard and paddled toward shore. When he reached the shallows, he stood up on still-shaking knees and walked to the beach, where a crowd had gathered. Rick showed them his board with the big piece missing (left photo) and was thankful he wasn't missing a leg or an arm.

Rick was attacked by a shark, which bit off a large piece of his surfboard!

It was almost a month before Rick was able to go surfing again. As he paddled out, this time with about 20 others, he began to have a weird, terrible feeling that something bad was going to happen again (adapted from the *Los Angeles Times,* February 8, 1993).

Rick experienced a variety of different emotions during and after his shark attack. During the attack, he felt intense anxiety and fear for his life. When he reached shore safely, he felt relief and happiness for having survived with all his limbs intact. Sometime later, he felt some fright and apprehension about surfing again. Although Rick experienced a half-dozen different emotions, they all shared the same four components (Frijda, 2000).

An *emotion* is defined in terms of four components. First, you interpret or appraise some stimulus (event, object, or thought) in terms of your well-being. Second, you have a subjective feeling, such as fear or happiness. Third, you experience physiological responses, such as changes in heart rate or breathing. Fourth, you may show observable behaviors, such as smiling or crying.

By analyzing Rick's experience with the shark, you can identify the four components of an emotion:

First, he *interpreted* or *appraised* the stimulus, a shark attack, as being a threat to his well-being and survival.

Second, he had the *subjective experience* or *feeling* of fear and terror.

Third, he experienced a variety of *physiological responses,* such as heart pounding and adrenaline pumping.

Fourth, he showed *overt* or *observable behaviors,* such as fearful facial expressions and frantic swimming to escape the shark. In some cases, such as playing poker, a person may experience a wide range of emotions but try to hide his or her overt behaviors by showing no facial expression, commonly known as a "poker face."

Although there is general agreement that emotions have four components, there is a debate over the order in which these four components occur (Frijda, 2000). For instance, did Rick have to think about the shark before he felt fear, or did he feel fear immediately and then think how terrified he was? We'll discuss this as well as many other questions about emotions.

## Staying Happy

**How long do emotions last?**

Being attacked by a shark results in a very different emotional experience than winning big bucks in a lottery. Since lotteries began in the late 1970s, about 4,000 people have become instant millionaires. Immediately after winning, the new millionaires reported feeling intense pleasure, being ecstatic, being unbelievably happy, and living in a dream world (Angelo, 1991). But what happens when a winner finally realizes that for the next 20 years he or she will receive a large monthly check? Will the emotional high continue, or will being a millionaire become a taken-for-granted experience?

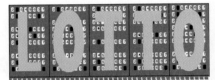

Ten years after winning a $20-million lottery, would you still be very happy?

Researchers have studied lottery winners to find out what effect such an enormous windfall has had on their lives (Gould, 1995). Later in this module, we'll tell you what the researchers discovered about happiness and how it applies to lottery winners.

## What's Coming

To realize the importance of emotions, just imagine going through one day without them. We'll discuss how emotions occur; how much our physiological responses, facial expressions, and interpretations contribute to emotions; whether feeling or thinking comes first in experiencing an emotion; if there is a set of basic or universal facial expressions that occur across all cultures; what the functions of emotions are; how specific emotions work; and how emotions are used in lie detection.

We'll begin our discussion of emotions with how a swimmer's sight of a shark causes him or her to feel fear.

### Sequence for Emotions

**Why do you feel fear?**

Imagine swimming in the ocean and suddenly seeing a large shark fin coming right at you. This situation has the four components of an emotion that we discussed earlier. First, you interpret a stimulus—shark fin—as dangerous. Second, you have an emotional feeling—fear. Third, you have physiological changes—increased heart rate. Fourth, you show observable behaviors—screaming and making a fearful facial expression. Psychologists agree that these four components usually occur,

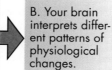

Why does a shark cause fear?

but they have not always agreed on what the correct sequence is. We'll describe several theories of emotions, each of which proposes a different sequence of the four components. These theories generally fit into two categories: peripheral and cognitive appraisal theories.

*Peripheral theories of emotions* emphasize that physiological changes in the body give rise to your emotional feelings.

*Cognitive appraisal theories of emotions* emphasize that your interpretations or appraisals of situations give rise to your emotional feelings.

We'll begin with the historic James-Lange theory.

### James-Lange Theory

This theory, proposed independently in the late 1800s by two psychologists, William James and Carl Lange, emphasizes physiological patterns as causing emotional feelings.

The *James-Lange theory* says that our brains interpret specific physiological changes as feelings or emotions and that

there is a different physiological pattern underlying each emotion.

Here's how the James-Lange theory would explain why seeing a skark fin coming at you makes you feel fear.

#### 1 PHYSIOLOGICAL CHANGES

The awful sight of an approaching shark fin affects an area of the brain called the hypothalamus, which controls the autonomic nervous system. One division of the autonomic nervous system, called the sympathetic division, activates various physiological responses, such as increases in heart rate, blood pressure, breathing, and secretion of various hormones.

#### 2 INTERPRETATION OF CHANGES

The James-Lange theory assumes that there is a different pattern of physiological responses for each different emotion. Your brain analyzes each different pattern of physiological responses and interprets each pattern as a different emotion.

Interpret

#### 3 EMOTIONAL FEELING

According to the James-Lange theory, the reason

SHARK!

you feel fear at seeing a shark fin is because you experienced a specific pattern of physiological responses that your brain interpreted as a specific emotion, in this case, fear. You may also show observable behaviors, such as a fearful facial expression. Notice that the James-Lange theory points to a specific pattern of physiological responses as giving rise to a particular emotion.

#### 4 JAMES-LANGE THEORY: SEQUENCE FOR EMOTIONAL COMPONENTS

Before the James-Lange theory, people thought that the sequence for feeling an emotion was that you see a shark, feel fear, and perhaps scream. James-Lange reversed the sequence: You see a shark and experience certain physiological changes, which result in feeling fear and perhaps screaming. The James-Lange theory is summarized below:

| | | | |
|---|---|---|---|
| A. Stimulus (shark) triggers different physiological changes in your body. | B. Your brain interprets different patterns of physiological changes. | C. Different physiological changes produce different emotions (fear). | D. You may or may not show observable responses (scream). |

Instead of a shark, James (1884/1969) used the now-famous example of seeing a bear in the forest. James said that, if you see a bear, "you are frightened because you run" rather than run because you are frightened.

#### 5 CRITICISMS

There are three major criticisms of the James-Lange theory.

First, different emotions are not necessarily associated with different patterns of physiological responses. For instance, anger, fear, and sadness share similar physiological patterns of arousal (Cacioppo et al., 2000). Thus, James's bear example was backward: Instead of the act of running making you feel fear, you feel fear and then run.

Second, people whose spinal cords have been severed at the neck are deprived of most of the feedback from their physiological responses (autonomic nervous system), yet they experience emotions with little or no change in intensity. These data are the opposite of what the James-Lange theory would predict, which is that these people should experience little or no emotion (Bermond et al., 1991; Chwalisz et al., 1988).

Third, some emotions, such as feeling guilty or jealous, may require a considerable amount of interpretation or appraisal of the situation. The sequence involved in feeling a complex emotion like guilt or jealousy points to the influence of cognitive factors on emotional feelings (Johnson-Laird & Oatley, 2000).

**Intensity.** Although researchers showed that physiological changes are not the primary cause of emotions, physiological changes may increase the intensity of emotional experiences (Cacioppo et al., 2000).

Next we turn to a different peripheral theory, the facial feedback theory, which offers a different sequence for the four components of emotions.

The James-Lange theory said that different patterns of physiological responses give rise to different emotions. A very different explanation for what causes emotions involves the activation of facial muscles that are used in smiling, frowning, or raising your eyebrows in fear. The idea that feedback from facial muscles causes emotional feelings originated with the work of Charles Darwin (1872/1965). Today, Darwin's theory is called the facial feedback theory (Keltner & Ekman, 2000).

The *facial feedback theory* says that the sensations or feedback from the movement of your facial muscles and skin are interpreted by your brain as different emotions.

Here's how the facial feedback theory explains why you feel fear when you see a rapidly approaching shark fin.

## 1 PHYSIOLOGICAL CHANGES

The sight of a rapidly approaching shark fin results in a number of physiological responses. These responses include the movement of your facial muscles and skin, such as raising your eyebrows, opening your mouth, and widening your eyes to show fear.

## 2 INTERPRETATION OF CHANGES

As you perceive different situations, you automatically make different facial expressions (Keltner & Ekman, 2000). Different movements of muscles and skin cause different facial expressions whose feedback is sent to your brain. In turn, your brain interprets the feedback from different facial muscles and skin patterns as different emotions. For example, when you see an approaching shark fin, you automatically raise your eyebrows, open your mouth, and widen your eyes. This "fearful" facial expression gives rise to your feeling the emotion of fear.

## 3 EMOTIONAL FEELING

According to the facial feedback theory, when you see a shark fin, the muscles in your face automatically move in a distinct pattern, such as raising your eyebrows, opening your mouth, and widening your eyes, and this feedback is interpreted by your brain as the emotion of fear. Note that the facial feedback theory says that feedback from your various facial skin and muscles results in your feeling different emotions.

## 4 SEQUENCE FOR EMOTIONS

Similar to the James-Lange theory, the facial feedback theory assumes that physiological changes—in this case, feedback from facial muscles and skin—are the primary causes of emotions. Here's the facial feedback theory's explanation of how we feel an emotion.

| A. Stimulus (shark) triggers changes in facial muscles and skin. | B. Your brain interprets feedback from facial muscles and skin. | C. Different facial feedback results in feeling different emotions (fear). | D. You may or may not show various observable reponses (scream). |

## 5 CRITICISMS

Facial feedback has been widely studied, and here are the conclusions.

**Different patterns.** Current supporters of the facial feedback theory of emotions report that the facial feedback involved in expressions of anger, fear, happiness, sadness, and disgust produces different muscle-skin patterns that may influence the occurrence of different emotions (Keltner & Ekman, 2000). However, individuals whose facial muscles are completely paralyzed can also experience emotions without any facial feedback (McIntosh, 1996). Thus, facial feedback may influence the occurrence of specific emotions, but emotions can also be felt without any facial feedback.

**Mood and intensity.** Researchers have reported that facial feedback may contribute to your mood, or overall emotional feeling. For example, subjects asked to hold a smile later reported being in a better mood than those asked to hold a frown. And compared with control subjects, people holding a smile reported that cartoons were funnier, that pleasant scenes produced more positive feelings, and that electric shocks were less painful (Laird, 1974; Lanzetta et al., 1976; Zuckerman et al., 1981). Researchers generally report that facial feedback also contributes to the intensity of your subjective emotional experience (Adelmann & Zajonc, 1989; Izard, 1990). For example, if you smile when you are happy or cry when you are sad, the feedback from facial muscles involved in smiling and crying may *intensify* your emotional feeling.

**Darwin's original theory.** Current researchers have not confirmed Darwin's original theory that feedback from facial muscles *alone* is sufficient to produce emotions. That's because individuals whose facial muscles are paralyzed can still feel emotions. However, researchers have found that facial feedback can influence the occurrence of emotions as well as influence general mood and emotional intensity (Dimberg & Ohman, 1996).

**Conclusion.** We have discussed two peripheral theories of emotions, the James-Lange and facial feedback theories. Both theories were found to influence the intensity of emotions and general mood, and one (facial feedback theory) was reported to influence the occurrence of emotions. However, neither peripheral theory *alone* was shown to be sufficient to cause different emotional feelings.

Our search for the cause or sequence of the four components of emotions now moves from the peripheral responses (specific changes in the body's organs or facial skin and muscles) that occur outside the brain to the central or cognitive processes that go on inside the brain or mind.

**Can thoughts cause emotions?**

You have arranged to meet your girlfriend at 7 P.M. at the movie theater. You arrive a few minutes early and are shocked to see her in the arms of a stranger. Feeling very angry and jealous, you rush over to confront them. Just as you arrive, she turns and says, "I want you to meet my brother, whom I haven't seen in years." Her explanation immediately changes your anger and jealousy into relief and happiness. Your girlfriend's explanation flip-flopped your emotional state and illustrates the cognitive appraisal theory of emotions.

The *cognitive appraisal theory* says that your interpretation or appraisal of a situation, object, or event can contribute to, or result in, your experiencing different emotional states.

For example, believing that your girlfriend is being hugged by an attractive stranger triggers jealousy, but hearing that the stranger is her brother changes your jealousy to relief and happiness.

Current cognitive appraisal theories can be traced back to the original work of Stanley Schachter and Jerome Singer (1962). We'll focus on one part of their now-classical experiment that shows the importance of cognitive interpretation, or appraisal, in emotions.

## Schachter-Singer Experiment

Throughout this text, we have pointed out classic experiments, so called because these studies challenged and dramatically changed how we think about something. The Schachter-Singer study was the first to show that thoughts are important in generating and identifying emotional feelings. Here's what they did in their groundbreaking experiment.

### 1 PHYSIOLOGICAL AROUSAL

First, Schachter and Singer injected some of their subjects with a hormone, epinephrine (adrenaline), that caused physiological arousal, such as increased heart rate and blood pressure.

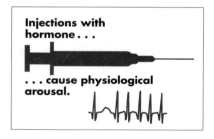

Injections with hormone . . .

. . . cause physiological arousal.

However, subjects were told that the injections were vitamins and were not told that they would experience physiological arousal.

### 2 INTERPRETATION OF CUES

Second, after the injections, subjects were placed in different situations—a happy one or an angry one.

In the **happy situation,** a confederate of the researchers created a happy atmosphere by laughing and throwing paper airplanes around.

In the **angry situation,** another confederate created an angry atmosphere by complaining about filling out a long questionnaire.

### 3 EMOTIONAL FEELING

Those subjects in the happy situation often reported feeling happy, and their observable behaviors were smiles. However, those in the angry situation often reported feeling angry, and their observable behaviors were angry facial expressions. Schachter and Singer explained that subjects did not know that their physiological arousal was caused by hormone injections and looked for other causes in their environment. Subjects interpreted environmental cues, such as being in a happy or angry situation, as the cause of their arousal and thus reported feeling happy or angry.

### 4 SEQUENCE FOR EMOTIONS

The Schachter-Singer explanation assumes that our interpretation or appraisal of a situation is the primary cause of emotions. This sequence is shown below:

| A. Injection of hormone causes physiological arousal (rise in heart rate, etc.). | B. Explain physiological arousal by using situational cues. | C. Depending on situation, feel different emotions (happy or angry). | D. Subjects show observable behaviors that matched emotions. |

### 5 CRITICISMS

The Schachter-Singer cognitive theory led to a classic study that was the first to show that cognitive factors, such as one's interpretation of events, could trigger and give rise to emotional feelings. However, their explanation has undergone two general revisions.

First, researchers recognize that emotions may occur without earlier experiences of physiological arousal (Cacioppo et al., 1993). For example, suppose a friend walked up to you and said, "I just saw somebody back into your car and drive away." Your appraisal of that situation would trigger feelings of anger before your physiological arousal kicked in.

Second, researchers argue that emotions may result not only from situational or environmental cues but also from your own cognitive processes, such as thoughts, interpretations, and appraisals (Johnson-Laird & Oatley, 2000). For example, your friend's explanation of who the stranger was changed your jealous anger into feelings of happy relief.

Schachter and Singer's cognitive theory triggered a number of other cognitive appraisal theories that were developed independently in the 1980s (Frijda, 1986; Ortony et al., 1988; Smith & Ellsworth, 1985; Weiner, 1986). The cognitive appraisal theory of emotions points to thoughts, interpretations, and appraisals as being some of the primary ways that emotions are triggered and develop (Johnson-Laird & Oatley, 2000).

Next, we'll explain the current form of the cognitive appraisal theory.

## Which Comes First: Feeling or Thinking?

There's no question that thinking can trigger emotions, but the question is whether you think before you feel emotions. For example, suppose you picked the winning lottery numbers and won $55 million. At that moment, you felt incredibly happy. Did that emotional feeling occur before or after you thought about winning the lottery? This example raises the primacy question (Scherer, 1999).

Would you feel happy immediately after hearing you won $55 million or would you need to think about it first?

The *primacy question* asks whether we can experience an emotion immediately, without any thinking, or whether we must engage in some kind of thinking or appraisal before feeling an emotion.

We'll examine two different theories that propose two different but somewhat complementary answers to the primacy question.

---

### Cognitive Appraisal Theory

One theory says that you usually think before you feel.

The *cognitive appraisal theory* assumes that your interpretation or appraisal of a situation is often the primary cause of emotions.

According to the cognitive appraisal theory, here's the sequence for feeling happy if you win a lottery.

**1** The stimulus could be an event, object, or thought. In this example, the stimulus is holding a winning lottery ticket for $55 million.

**2** You appraise or interpret how the stimulus affects your well-being; in this case, your appraisal is extremely positive since you have won $55 million.

**3** Your appraisal of having won $55 million gives rise to your emotional feelings of happiness and joy. In this example, you think or appraise before you feel an emotion.

**4** Along with feeling comes a variety of bodily responses, including physiological arousal and overt (observable) behaviors, such as smiling.

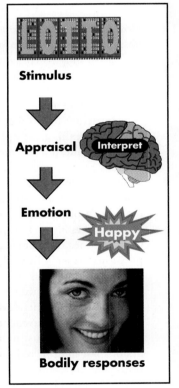
Stimulus
Appraisal — Interpret
Emotion — Happy
Bodily responses

**5** THINKING BEFORE FEELING

The spokesperson for this position is Richard Lazarus (1999), who argues that, for an emotion to occur, it is necessary, at some level, to first think about or appraise the situation. There are many cases where thinking obviously precedes feelings, as in the example of jealousy changing to relief after hearing your girlfriend's explanation of the event. In other cases, such as winning a lottery, the emotion (happiness) seems to occur very quickly. However, even in these situations, researchers explain that the thinking or appraising occurs at an automatic, unconscious level, without our awareness (Ohman, 2000).

---

### Affective-Primacy Theory

Another theory says that you often feel before you think.

The *affective-primacy theory* says that, in some situations, you feel an emotion before you have time to interpret or appraise the situation.

According to the affective-primacy theory, here's the sequence for feeling happy if you win a lottery.

**1** The stimulus could be an event, object, or thought. In this example, the stimulus is holding a winning lottery ticket for $55 million.

**2** Holding and seeing the winning lottery ticket trigger an emotional experience, feeling happy, so quickly that there seems to be little or no thinking or appraisal preceding your feeling.

**3** You already feel happy, but as you appraise or think about how you will spend the $55 million, you may feel even happier. In this example, you feel an emotion before you think.

**4** Along with feeling comes a variety of bodily responses, including physiological arousal and overt (observable) behaviors, such as smiling.

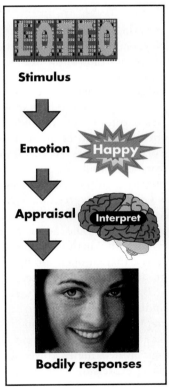
Stimulus
Emotion — Happy
Appraisal — Interpret
Bodily responses

**5** FEELING BEFORE THINKING

The spokesperson for this position is Robert Zajonc (1984), who believes that feelings or emotions may occur before thinking. Although Zajonc does not deny that cognition may sometimes precede emotions, he gives examples, such as reactions to winning a lottery or seeing a snake, in which emotions occur so rapidly there seems to be little time for thinking. Other researchers point out that thinking or appraising can occur quickly, automatically, and without our awareness and that some kind of appraisal precedes feelings or emotions (Ohman, 2000).

Now that you know the general theories for how we feel emotions, we'll discuss how people across cultures feel and express emotions.

### Definition of Universal

Suppose you survived a plane crash in the jungles of Borneo. After crawling out of the plane and finding cuts and bruises but no broken bones, you look up and see two native people with blow-dart guns aimed at you. Not knowing their language, how would you communicate that you were friendly? Your best bet is to break into a big smile because the native people will most likely recognize that a smile means you're friendly. In fact, smiling is a sign of being happy (friendly) and is one of the universal emotional expressions (Keltner & Ekman, 2000).

*Universal emotional expressions* refer to a number of specific inherited facial patterns or expressions that

Why do people from different cultures smile the same way?

signal specific feelings or emotional states, such as a smile signaling a happy state.

For example, notice that although the four individuals in the photos come from four different countries, they display similar facial expressions—smiles—which you would interpret as showing happiness. Universal emotional expressions are thought to have evolved because they served adaptive and survival functions for our ancestors.

The existence of universal emotions was scientifically formulated by Charles Darwin (1872/1965), and his ideas have inspired modern-day researchers to study universal emotional expressions (Keltner & Ekman, 2000). We'll review two kinds of evidence—cross-cultural and genetic—that support the idea of universal emotional expressions.

### Cross-Cultural Evidence

How do individuals from relatively isolated cultures in New Guinea, Burma, Thailand, and Borneo (photos top to bottom) know how to smile or what a smile means? One answer is that a smile is one of the unlearned, inherited universal emotional expressions. For example, researchers showed photos of different facial expressions to individuals in 20 different Western cultures and 11 different primitive (illiterate and isolated) cultures. As the graph below indicates, researchers found that individuals in both Western and primitive cultures showed significant agreement on which facial expressions signaled which emotions. Most individuals in Western and primitive cultures agreed that a smile indicated happiness. However, the fewest individuals in Western and primitive cultures agreed that an open-mouth and raised-eyebrows expression indicated surprise.

Based on the cross-cultural findings shown in the right graph, researchers concluded that there are innately or biologically determined universal facial expressions for emotions. Universal emotional signals most likely include facial expressions for happiness, surprise, fear, anger, contempt, disgust, and sadness (Ekman, 1994; Keltner & Ekman, 2000).

Besides cross-cultural evidence, support for universal emotional expressions comes from observing the emotional development of infants.

**Recognition of Facial Expressions**

| | |
|---|---|
| Happiness Western | 96% |
| Happiness Primitive | 92% |
| Surprise Western | 88% |
| Surprise Primitive | 36% |
| Anger Western | 81% |
| Anger Primitive | 46% |
| Sadness Western | 80% |
| Sadness Primitive | 52% |

### Genetic Evidence

How does an infant who is born blind learn to smile? Is it possible that the programming of specific facial expressions, such as smiling, is contained in our DNA, or chemically coded genetic instructions? The answer to this question comes from observing the development of emotional expressions in infants.

Researchers found that at 4–6 weeks of age, infants begin to smile; this greatly pleases parents, who usually smile back. The question is whether an infant's smiling is biologically programmed or whether the infant has learned to smile by observing and imitating the parents' facial expressions. An ethologist studied the facial expressions of infants born blind and found that, at around 4–6 weeks, blind infants also begin to smile. This observation supports the idea of biologically programmed emotional expressions, since blind children have never seen their parents' smiling faces (Eibl-Eibesfeldt, 1973).

Additional evidence for universal emotions comes from reports that all infants develop facial expressions in a predictable order. For instance, newborns show facial expressions signaling disgust in response to foul tastes or odors; infants 3–4 months old show angry and sad facial expressions; infants 4–6 weeks old begin to smile; and infants 5–7 months old show fear. Since infants in all cultures develop these emotional expressions at about the same age, we have further evidence for the existence of universal emotions (Izard, 1993).

Researchers conclude that evidence from cross-cultural studies on facial expressions and on the development of emotional expressions in infants indicates strong biological (genetic) influences on the development of emotional expressions (Frijda, 2000). But why should humans have an innate, genetic program for the development of facial emotional expressions? There are several interesting answers to this question.

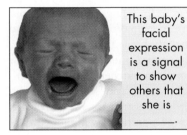

**What good are emotions?**

To appreciate the value and worth of emotions, try living a single day without feeling or expressing any emotions. It would be one of the worst days of your life because emotions have three important functions. Emotions send powerful *social signals* about how you feel; emotions help you *adapt and survive* in your world; and emotions *arouse and motivate* many of your behaviors. We'll examine each emotional function in turn.

### — Send Social Signals —

As you look at the photo below, guess the baby's emotional state.

This baby's facial expression is a signal to show others that she is _____.

You immediately recognize this baby's emotional facial expression because it is a powerful social signal that the child is feeling unhappy, distressed, or is in pain.

In turn, this particular social signal usually elicits help, sympathy, or compassion from the parents or caregiver. This example illustrates how we send social signals through a variety of facial expressions.

*Facial expressions* that go with emotions communicate personal feelings and provide social signals, which may elicit a variety of responses from those around you (Frijda & Mesquita, 1994).

We often make facial expressions so that others respond to us in certain ways. For example, smiling elicits friendly feelings, while crying elicits sympathy and aid.

In some cases, facial expressions are a more accurate signal of a person's emotional state than the person's denial, "There's nothing wrong," when his or her face says there is something wrong.

In other cases, a lack of facial expressions may be a symptom of serious emotional problems or mental disorders, such as anxiety, depression, and schizophrenia, which we'll discuss in Modules 22 and 23 (MacLeod, 1999; Power, 1999).

### — Adapt and Survive —

According to Charles Darwin (1872/1965), our early ancestors evolved the ability to smile, cry, laugh, and display other emotional expressions because such facial expressions helped the species adapt and survive. Building on Darwin's idea, current researchers have proposed the psychoevolutionary theory of emotions (Ekman, 1994; Izard, 1994).

The *psychoevolutionary theory of emotions* says that we inherit the neural structure and physiology to express and experience emotions and that we evolved emotional patterns to adapt to our environment and solve problems important for our survival.

This man's facial expression is a signal to show that he is _____, which may help him survive _____ situations.

There are many examples of emotion having survival value: expressing anger (above photo) may help you escape or survive a dangerous situation; showing disgust may signal the presence of poisonous or rotten food; and crying may indicate the need for help. The fact that all animals have basic emotional expressions supports the idea that emotions have evolved because of their survival value (Plutchik, 1993).

Emotions also have adaptive value in dealing with basic social problems because they signal how you intend to act (McIntosh, 1996). You may smile to show you are being friendly and sociable; you may look angry to threaten or settle some conflict; or you may look hurt or jealous when competing for some goal. Besides being adaptive and helping us survive, emotions can also provide energy and motivation.

### — Arouse and Motivate —

You may spend hours playing a challenging computer or video game because this activity arouses and motivates you to work harder. In contrast, you may have difficulty spending time studying a foreign language because this difficult activity reduces your arousal and motivation. These examples show that emotions function to arouse or depress many of our behaviors (Lang, 1995). In fact, there is a relationship between emotional arousal and your performance on a task. That relationship is called the Yerkes-Dodson law.

The *Yerkes-Dodson law* says that performance on a task is an interaction between the level of physiological arousal and the difficulty of the task. For difficult tasks, low arousal results in better performance; for most tasks, moderate arousal helps performance; and for easy tasks, high arousal may facilitate performance.

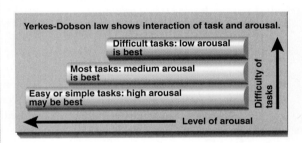

Yerkes-Dobson law shows interaction of task and arousal.
Difficult tasks: low arousal is best
Most tasks: medium arousal is best
Easy or simple tasks: high arousal may be best
Difficulty of tasks
Level of arousal

For example, suppose we apply the Yerkes-Dodson law to taking difficult exams (figure above). We would predict that a person with high test anxiety (high arousal) would do more poorly than someone with comparable ability but low test anxiety. Researchers tested this idea by comparing students who were highly aroused because of either high test anxiety or drinking much coffee (caffeine) with students who had low test anxiety or were given little coffee. Highly aroused students scored more poorly on difficult tasks than less aroused students (Anderson, 1994; Endler et al., 1994). The well-established fact that emotions increase physiological arousal is the basis for the so-called lie detector test, which we'll discuss in the Application section (pp. 370–371).

Another interesting fact about emotions is that negative emotions (fear, anger, hate) seem to last longer than positive ones (happiness, joy). Why doesn't happiness last longer?

## Kinds of Happiness

**What is happiness?**

Pam was unmarried, eight months pregnant, and holding down two jobs when she stopped in at Jackson's Food Store for her morning orange juice, doughnut, and one lottery ticket.

She remembers praying, "Please, God, let something happen so I can afford a small studio apartment" (Reed & Free, 1995, p. 63). The next day she pulled out her lottery ticket and discovered that she had won $87 million. She felt very, very, very happy.

*Happiness* includes smiling and laughing resulting from momentary pleasures, such as seeing a funny commercial; short-term joys, such as seeing an enjoyable movie or having a great time; and long-term satisfaction, such as having an enjoyable relationship, career, or life (Averill & Moore, 2000).

For example, Pam's happiness included the momentary pleasure of laughing and smiling when she received the check (photo above) and the short-term joy of going on a buying spree that included new cars for herself and her family, a new home, and several trips. However, whether Pam experienced long-term happiness from winning the lottery is questionable. Some months later she said, "I thought I'd drop everything and travel the world. But my idea of a good time is still to hang out at my brother's house, have dinner, or have a friend over for videos" (Reed & Free, 1995, p. 64). Like other lottery winners, Pam discovered that money helps and makes life easier but it doesn't buy long-term happiness. Why not?

## Adaptation Level Theory

**How much happiness can money buy?**

Researchers have interviewed hundreds of lottery winners and found that after winning, they initially experience a short period of great happiness and wild euphoria, just as Pam did when she went on a spending spree. But this is often followed by a long period of mixed emotions because of indecision about what to do with one's life, job, or career, as well as potential problems with friends, relatives, or in-laws who are envious and insist on sharing the riches (Gould, 1995).

When researchers interviewed lottery winners 1 to 12 months after they had won large sums of money, the majority reported positive changes, such as financial security, more leisure time, and earlier retirement. However, when asked to rate their happiness one year after winning, lottery winners were no happier than before (Diener & Diener, 1996). This curious finding that the happiness of being a millionaire lasts a relatively short time (less than a year) is explained by the adaptation level theory.

The *adaptation level theory* says that we quickly become accustomed to receiving some good fortune (money, job, car, degree); we take the good fortune for granted within a short period of time; and as a result, the initial impact of our good fortune fades and contributes less to our long-term level of happiness.

According to the adaptation level theory, the immediate emotional high of obtaining good fortune—such as graduating from college, getting married, buying a new car, getting a much-wanted job, or winning a lottery—will fade with time and contributes less and less to our long-term happiness (Brickman et al., 1978). For example, three weeks after winning $87 million, Pam gave birth to Nicholas, and she said, "Winning the lottery was pretty exciting, but it can't compare to Nicholas. I want him to grow up caring about people and knowing the value of work" (Reed & Free, 1995, p. 64).

Pam said, "Winning the lottery was great but it can't compare to my baby."

Researchers find that setting and achieving long-term goals, such as Pam's goals for her son, will contribute more to Pam's long-term feeling of happiness than winning the lottery (Averill & Moore, 2000). Thus, according to adaptation theory, money cannot buy happiness because we adapt to the continuous satisfaction of having plenty of money.

## Long-Term Happiness

**How long will you be happy?**

Although worldwide surveys indicate that the vast majority (84%) of people report being happy, some people report being happier on average than others (Diener & Diener, 1996). Reasons for being happy come from both personal/environmental and genetic/inherited factors.

**Genetic/inherited factors.** For example, researchers found that identical twins (share 100% of genes), who were reared together or apart, showed significantly higher correlations in their happiness ratings (0.44 to 0.52) than did fraternal twins (share 50% of their genes), who were raised together or apart (0.08 to −0.02). Based on these data, researchers estimated that about half of your level of happiness comes from inherited or genetic influences, which affect the development of cognitive and personality traits (Lykken & Tellegen, 1996).

**Personal/environmental factors.** A long-term level of happiness is associated with making an effort to enjoy simple, daily pleasurable events, people, or situations, which provide a daily

Happiness from winning a lottery fades away.

diet of little highs. In comparison, the level of happiness resulting from big pleasurable events (college degree, exam grade, lottery, new car) disappears in a relatively short time (several months to a year) (Goleman, 1996). In addition, a long-term level of happiness is associated with setting and achieving personal goals that include having a close relationship, a network of friends, a purpose in life, and a good dose of hope and optimism (Buss, 2000; Myers, 2000).

Next we'll examine how cultural influences affect emotions.

## Showing Emotions

**Why don't grown men cry?**

Although many emotional expressions are shared and recognized across cultures, it is also true that each culture has unique gestures and differs in its display of emotions. For example, in the United States, it is very rare and considered a character weakness for a grown man to cry in public, while it is relatively common and considered part of a grown woman's character to cry in public. One explanation for this American male–female cultural difference involves display rules (Ekman, 1993; Ekman & Friesen, 1969).

*Display rules* refer to specific cultural norms that regulate how, when, and where we should express emotion and how much emotion is appropriate.

There are many examples of how display rules differ across and within different cultures. For instance, in some European cultures it is acceptable and expected that males greet each other with a kiss to the cheek or lips, while such a male gesture of greeting is not observed or acceptable in most Western cultures. Among the Inuit (Eskimos), feelings of anger are strongly condemned, but among certain Arab groups, a man's failure to respond with anger is seen as dishonorable (Abu-Lughod, 1986; Briggs, 1970).

Although there is cross-cultural evidence for the universal facial expression and recognition of emotions, this does not mean that all individuals use exactly the same facial expressions. For example:

1. Japanese and Chinese have more difficulty identifying facial expressions of fear and anger than do North Americans (Biehl et al., 1997; Tang, 1998).
2. North Americans were worse at identifying contempt than Japanese, Poles, or Hungarians (Biehl et al., 1997).
3. Vietnamese were worse at identifying disgust than Japanese, Poles, or North Americans (Biehl et al., 1997).

These examples illustrate how cultural influences create display rules, which in turn affect how frequently facial expressions occur and how easily specific facial expressions are identified (Ekman, 1993; Tang, 1998).

Not only do different cultures have different display rules but they also have different interpretations of what causes emotions. For example, in the United States, people interpret negative events initiated by other people (insult, automobile accident, rudeness) as evoking anger. In comparison, negative events caused by fate, chance, or circumstances beyond anyone's control (earthquake, flood, or tornado) are interpreted as evoking sorrow (Ellsworth, 1994a). Thus, each culture has different ways of interpreting events, which in turn affect the kind of emotion we feel.

Cultures also influence how much emotion their citizens are "permitted" to display.

**Surprise**

**Sadness**

**Anger**

## Perceiving Emotions

**Why do Japanese and Americans disagree?**

When I visited Japan, I noticed that the Japanese tended not to display emotions in public and often covered their mouths when they laughed. In comparison, I have never seen any of my fellow citizens use their hands to cover or hide their mouths when they laugh. These kinds of obvious cultural differences in displaying emotions led researchers to wonder if citizens would also differ in how they perceived or judged the intensity of emotions.

Researchers showed photos of five emotional expressions—surprise, anger, happiness, disgust, and sadness (similar to the photos on this page)—to a group of Japanese and a group of Americans (Matsumoto & Ekman, 1989). Each group looked at two sets of photos: one depicted a Japanese showing five facial emotional expressions, and the other depicted a Caucasian showing the same five expressions.

The Japanese and Americans were asked to rate the intensity of each emotional expression in each set. The Japanese gave significantly lower ratings of *emotional intensity* to all five emotional expressions than did the Americans. These results indicate differences in cultural display rules: Japan has a long history of discouraging any show of emotional intensity in public, while America encourages the show of emotional intensity in public (Reitman, 1999).

When asked to rate which of the five emotions is most intense—surprise, anger, happiness, disgust, or sadness—the Japanese rated disgust as the most intense emotion, while the Americans rated happiness as the most intense.

This and other studies illustrate how cultural influences affect not only the display of emotions in public but also the perception of an emotion's intensity (Tang, 1998).

After the Concept Review, we'll discuss the exciting new area of emotional intelligence.

**Japanese** rated *disgust* as the most intense of five emotions.

**Disgust**

**Americans** rated *happiness* as the most intense of five emotions.

**Happiness**

# Concept Review

**1.** An emotion is defined in terms of four components: you interpret or (a)_____ some stimulus, thought, or event in terms of your well-being; you have a subjective (b)_____, such as being happy or fearful; you experience bodily responses, such as increased heart rate and breathing, which are called (c)_____ responses; and you often show (d)_____ behaviors, such as crying or smiling.

**2.** One theory says that emotions result from specific physiological changes in our bodies and that each emotion has a different physiological pattern. This theory, which says that we feel fear because we run, is called the (a)_____ theory. Two major criticisms of this theory are that researchers have not identified a different (b)_____ response pattern to match each emotion and that individuals with severed spinal cords, which prevents feedback from the body's physiological responses, still experience (c)_____.

**3.** A second theory says that feedback from the movement of facial muscles and skin is interpreted by your brain as an emotion; this theory is called the (a)_____ theory. Researchers found that emotions do occur without feedback from facial muscles and skin. However, facial feedback may initiate the occurrence of emotions and contribute to the (b)_____ of an emotion, as well as to our mood.

**4.** A third theory of emotions, which grew out of the work of Schachter and Singer, says that you interpret or appraise a situation as having a positive or negative impact on your life and this results in a subjective feeling that you call an emotion; this is called the _____ theory.

**5.** The fourth theory of emotions, which says that in some situations you feel an emotion before you have time to interpret or appraise the situation, is called the (a)_____. This theory says that, for some emotions, you (b)_____ before you think. In comparison, the cognitive appraisal theory says that you (c)_____ before you feel. This question about which comes first, feeling or thinking, is called the (d)_____.

**6.** Specific inherited facial patterns or expressions that signal specific feelings or emotional states across cultures, such as a smile signaling a happy state, are called _____. These emotions are thought to have evolved because they had important adaptive and survival functions for our ancestors.

**7.** According to one theory, we inherit the neural structure and physiology to express and experience emotions and we evolved basic emotional patterns to adapt to and solve problems important for our survival; this is called the (a)_____ theory. Facial expressions that accompany emotions communicate the state of our personal or subjective (b)_____ and provide (c)_____ signals that communicate with, and elicit responses from, those around us.

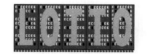

**8.** Your performance on a task depends on the amount of physiological arousal and the difficulty of the task. For many tasks, moderate arousal helps performance; for new or difficult tasks, low arousal is better; and for easy or well-learned tasks, high arousal may facilitate performance. This relationship between arousal and performance is known as the _____.

**9.** According to one theory, big events in your life, such as doing well on final exams, getting a car, obtaining a degree, or winning the lottery, do not produce long-lasting increases in happiness because in a relatively short period of time you become accustomed to your good fortune and it contributes less to your level of happiness; this theory is called the (a)_____. Long-term happiness is less dependent upon wealth and more dependent upon developing and achieving long-term (b)_____.

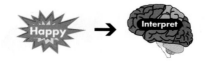

**10.** Specific cultural norms that regulate when, where, and how much emotion we should or should not express in different situations are called _____. These rules explain why the expression and intensity of emotions differ across cultures.

***Answers:*** *1. (a) appraise, (b) feeling, (c) physiological, (d) observable; 2. (a) James-Lange, (b) physiological, (c) emotions; 3. (a) facial feedback, (b) intensity; 4. cognitive appraisal; 5. (a) affective-primacy theory, (b) feel, (c) think, (d) primacy question; 6. universal emotions; 7. (a) psychoevolutionary, (b) feelings, (c) social; 8. Yerkes-Dodson law; 9. (a) adaptation level theory, (b) goals; 10. display rules*

# G. Research Focus: Emotional Intelligence

## What Is Emotional Intelligence?

**What is it and who has it?**

One of the exciting things about being a researcher is the chance to come up with new ideas. Beginning in the early 1990s, researchers came up with the idea of emotional intelligence, which they suggested made people more effective in social situations (Salovey & Mayer, 1990). By the mid-1990s, popular magazines, such as *Time,* declared that emotional intelligence may redefine what it means to be smart and may be the best predictor of success in life (Gibbs, 1995). In the 2000 presidential campaign, emotional intelligence took a practical turn. Most reporters agreed that George W. Bush's approach (above left photo) made him seem like an old friend—someone you might want to sit down and talk to. In comparison, most reporters agreed that Al Gore's approach (right photo) made him seem like a college professor—someone who could give an intelligent lecture on almost any topic (Miller, 2000). These different

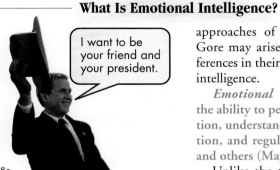

approaches of Bush and Gore may arise from differences in their emotional intelligence.

*Emotional intelligence* is the ability to perceive and express emotion, understand and reason with emotion, and regulate emotion in oneself and others (Mayer et al., 2000b).

Unlike the traditional idea of intelligence involving performance on cognitive tests (IQ scores; p. 282), emotional intelligence involves how well people perceive, express, and regulate emotions in themselves and others. For example, Al Gore was judged to be very knowledgeable in many areas and thus more intelligent in the traditional sense of having better cognitive skills. In comparison, George W. Bush was judged to be better at connecting with people by making them feel as if he was one of them. How would we measure the difference in emotional intelligence between Al Gore and our 46th president, George W. Bush?

## How Do We Measure Emotional Intelligence?

In the mid-1990s there was a best-selling book titled *Emotional Intelligence: Why It Can Matter More Than IQ* (Goleman, 1995). The author, a Harvard-educated psychologist, claimed that emotional intelligence was involved in some of the most important things in our lives, such as managing bad moods, maintaining hope after setbacks, getting along with people, and making critical decisions. This book sparked tremendous interest in educators, businesspeople, parents, and many others, who asked, "Could I teach others how to acquire emotional intelligence as well as improve my own?" However, it would be difficult if not impossible to teach or increase emotional intelligence unless there were some way to accurately measure it. What was needed was a valid and reliable way to measure emotional intelligence (validity and reliability are discussed on page 287).

We have already discussed problems in measuring complex behaviors, such as autism (p. 3), ADHD (p. 39), Alzheimer's disease (p. 47), alcoholism (p. 185), and intelligence (p. 282). In some cases, researchers use a set of behavioral symptoms to measure behaviors, such as autism, ADHD, Alzheimer's disease, and alcoholism. In other cases, researchers use paper-and-pencil tests to measure behavior, such as intelligence. Similarly, psychologists are currently developing paper-and-pencil tests to measure the many complex abilities believed to underlie emotional intelligence, such as the ability to express, label, regulate, and understand emotions (Mayer et al., 2000a).

However, researchers are just in the early stages of trying to define and measure emotional intelligence, and even though early results seem promising, it's too early to tell if someday emotional intelligence will be as important as IQ (Ciarrochi et al., 2000). In any case, no one denies that emotions can have powerful influences on many of our behaviors.

Emotional intelligence has been difficult to measure.

## Is Emotional Intelligence Important?

Here are some common remarks that show how emotions can influence our behaviors.

- "I was so angry, I couldn't think straight."
- "I get worse when people tell me to calm down."
- "When we argue, I often get mad and say the wrong thing and make it worse."
- "You never try to understand how I feel."
- "Sometimes I act on my feelings, right or wrong."

These kinds of statements point to the influence that emotions can have on what we say and do and on our success in life. According to supporters of emotional intelligence, the better our understanding of how emotions work, the more likely we are to find a compromise between our often strong emotional feelings ("I felt like doing that") and our equally strong rational thoughts ("I knew I should not have done that") (Mayer et al., 2000b).

Emotional intelligence plays an important role in our lives.

Supporters of emotional intelligence also point out that IQ scores are relatively poor at predicting success in life because they don't account for a variety of emotional factors. Knowing more about emotional intelligence will help us better understand and predict who will likely succeed in life and help those who are more likely to fail (Gibbs, 1995).

Although emotional intelligence seems important, its future depends entirely on whether researchers can develop a reliable and valid test to measure it.

**How did a spy pass a lie detector test twice?**

From 1985 to 1994, the Russians paid or promised $4.6 million to Aldrich Ames (photo on right), who was a high-level Central Intelligence Agency official. Later, Ames pleaded guilty to espionage, which involved selling secrets to the Russians. Ames is currently serving a life sentence in prison. The Ames case brings up the issue of lie detection because he reportedly

*I lied, but I passed two lie detector tests.*

passed at least two lie detector (polygraph) tests during the time that he was selling U.S. secrets to Russia (Jackson, 1994). The publicity surrounding this case made people ask, "How could Ames be selling secrets and pass two lie detector tests?" The Ames case raises three questions: What is the theory behind lie detection? How is a lie detector test given? How accurate are lie detector tests?

---

## What Is the Theory?

**Does the test measure lying?**

The lie detector test is based on the four components of an emotion that we discussed earlier. The first component of an emotion is interpreting or appraising a stimulus. In this case, Ames will need to interpret questions such as "Have you ever sold secrets to Russia?" The second component of an emotion is a subjective feeling, such as whether Ames will feel any guilt or fear when he answers "Yes" or "No" to the question "Have you ever sold secrets to Russia?" The third component of an emotion is the occurrence of various physiological responses (figure below). If Mr. Ames feels guilty about selling secrets, then his guilt feeling will be accompanied by physiological arousal, which includes increases in heart rate, blood pressure, breathing, and sweating of the hands. These physiological responses occur automatically and are usually involuntary because they are controlled by the autonomic nervous system (discussed in Module 4). The fourth component of an emotion is the occurrence of some overt behavior, such as a facial expression. Mr. Ames may be able to control his facial expressions and put on a nonemotional poker face. However, neither the presence nor the absence of expressions is critical to the theory behind lie detector tests.

*Lie detector (polygraph) tests* are based on the theory that, if a person tells a lie, he or she will feel some emotion, such as guilt or fear. Feeling guilty or fearful will be accompanied by involuntary physiological responses, which are difficult to suppress or control and can be measured with a machine called a polygraph.

A polygraph (lie detector) is about the size of a laptop computer (right figure) and measures chest and abdominal muscle movement during respiration, heart rate, blood pressure, and skin conductance or galvanic skin response.

The *galvanic skin response* refers to changes in sweating of the fingers (or palms) that accompany emotional experiences and are independent of perspiration under normal temperatures (Cacioppo et al., 1993).

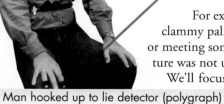

Chest movement during respiration
Abdominal movement during respiration
Heart rate and blood pressure
Skin conductance

Man hooked up to lie detector (polygraph)

For example, you may remember having sweaty or clammy palms when taking exams, giving a public talk, or meeting someone important, even though the temperature was not unduly hot.

We'll focus on the galvanic skin response because its changes are often the most obvious.

---

## What Is a Lie Detector Test?

**Is the suspect lying?**

Very few details have been released about how Mr. Ames, who apparently lied, passed two lie detector tests. Instead, we'll use a more detailed report of a man named Floyd, who told the truth but failed two lie detector tests.

Floyd was very surprised when two police officers came to his home. They had a warrant and arrested him for the armed robbery of a liquor store. However, the case against Floyd was weak, since none of the witnesses could positively identify him as the robber. Soon after his arrest, the prosecutor offered to drop all charges if Floyd agreed to take, and pass, a lie detector test. Floyd jumped at the chance to prove his innocence and took the test. He failed the lie detector test but insisted that he had not lied and that he be allowed to take a second one, which he also failed. Eventually Floyd was tried, found guilty, and sent to prison. He served several years behind bars before his lawyer tracked down the real robbers, which proved Floyd's innocence (*Los Angeles Times,* December 22, 1980).

Floyd was given the most commonly used procedure for lie detection in criminal investigations, which is called the Control Question Technique (Bashore & Rapp, 1993; Saxe, 1994).

The *Control Question Technique* refers to a lie detection procedure in which the examiner asks two kinds of questions: neutral questions that elicit little emotional response, and critical questions that are designed to elicit large emotional responses. The person answers only "Yes" or "No" to the questions and, if guilty, is expected to show a greater emotional response to the critical questions than to the neutral questions.

| NEUTRAL QUESTIONS | CRITICAL QUESTIONS |
|---|---|
| These are general questions, such as "Is your name Floyd?" or "Do you live at a particular place?" These questions are designed to elicit few if any emotional responses and are used to establish a baseline for normal physiological responding. | These are specific questions about some particular crime or misconduct that only a person who committed the crime would know, such as "Did you rob the liquor store on 5th and Vine?" Critical questions are designed to elicit emotional responses, such as guilt or fear, if the person tells a lie. |

As shown in the figure below, Floyd showed very little physiological arousal—as measured by the galvanic skin response—when asked a neutral question, "Is your name Floyd?" However, he showed great physiological arousal when asked a critical question, "Did you rob the liquor store?"

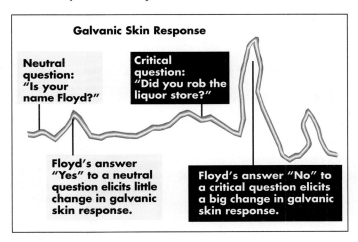

**Galvanic Skin Response**

Neutral question: "Is your name Floyd?"

Critical question: "Did you rob the liquor store?"

Floyd's answer "Yes" to a neutral question elicits little change in galvanic skin response.

Floyd's answer "No" to a critical question elicits a big change in galvanic skin response.

The examiner decides whether the client is lying or telling the truth by comparing differences in physiological responses between neutral and critical questions. In Floyd's case, he answered "No" to a number of critical questions, such as "Did you rob the liquor store?" But his "No" answers were accompanied by large increases in galvanic skin response (as well as other responses). For those reasons, the examiner decided that Floyd had lied and thus failed the polygraph test. However, when the real robbers were eventually caught, tried, and sentenced, it proved that Floyd had not lied even though he failed the lie detector test twice. Floyd's case, as well as the Ames case, questions the accuracy of lie detector tests.

**Why aren't tests allowed in most courts?**

If Floyd was innocent, why did he fail two lie detector exams? If Ames was lying, why did he pass two lie detector tests?

The basic problem with lie detector tests is that researchers have been unable to identify a pattern of physiological responses specific to lying. This means that a number of different emotions—such as guilt, fear, nervousness, or worry—can trigger physiological responses that make a person appear to be lying when he or she may be telling the truth (Iacono & Lykken, 1997; Johnson, 1999). Because of this serious problem, researchers estimate that lie detector tests are wrong about 25–75% of the time (graph below) (Saxe, 1994).

**Percentage of Errors in Polygraph (Lie Detector) Tests**

75% — High estimate

25% — Low estimate

Although very low error scores (5–10%) for lie detector tests have been reported, these data come from less realistic laboratory settings that use simple tasks, such as identifying some object about which the subject—often a college student—has been told to lie. The much higher error scores reported in the graph come from field studies that simulate more realistic conditions, in which subjects actually steal objects that they are told will be replaced after the test (Bashore & Rapp, 1993; Honts, 1994).

Besides high error scores, lie detector tests have two other problems: in one field study, about 40% of subjects were judged to be lying or maybe lying when they were telling the truth (Honts, 1994); and in another field study, about 50% of guilty people who were told to both press their toes to the ground and bite their tongues during control questions passed lie detector tests (Honts et al., 1994).

Because of these problems, federal law now prohibits most employers from using polygraph tests to screen employees and most state and federal courts prohibit the use of polygraph evidence (Saxe, 1994). In 1998, the United States Supreme Court ruled that polygraph evidence cannot be used in most courts. However, 62% of local law enforcement agencies use lie detectors to screen new employees, and 75% of police believe that polygraph tests are between 86 and 100% effective (Johnson, 1999).

For about the last ten years, researchers have studied the possibility of using brain waves to detect deception. One particular brain wave, called the P300, is associated with processing oddball stimuli, such as "Do you take your coffee black or with ketchup?" The oddball pairing of coffee with ketchup would generate a P300 brain wave. Although researchers have reported that the P300 brain wave has shown promise in detecting deception, more work needs to be done to prove its validity (Rosenfeld, 1995).

One curious and little-known fact about lie detector tests is that they are used primarily in the United States. Lie detector (polygraph) tests are almost unknown and are not used in the rest of the industrialized world (Shenour, 1990).

## A. PERIPHERAL THEORIES

**1.** We can define an emotion in terms of four components: we interpret or appraise a (a)_____ in terms of our well-being; we have a subjective (b)_____; we experience various (c)_____ responses, such as changes in heart rate and respiration; and we often show (d)_____ behaviors, such as crying or smiling.

**2.** Several theories explain what causes emotions. Theories that emphasize changes in the body are called (a)_____ theories. One such theory states that emotions result from specific physiological changes in your body and that each emotion has a different physiological basis; this is called the (b)_____ theory. The major criticism of this theory is that different emotions do not always cause different patterns of physiological arousal. However, feedback from physiological changes may increase the (c)_____ of emotional feelings.

**3.** According to another peripheral theory, sensations or feedback from the movement of facial muscles and skin are interpreted by your brain and result in an emotion; this is called the (a)_____ theory. One criticism of this theory is that facial skin and muscles do not initiate emotions. However, they may contribute to the (b)_____ of emotional feelings and also contribute to our mood.

## B. COGNITIVE APPRAISAL THEORY

**4.** Theories about emotions that emphasize the importance of how you interpret a stimulus are called (a)_____ theories. One such theory is Schachter and Singer's cognitive theory of emotions. According to their theory, a stimulus causes physiological arousal, which creates a need for an explanation. To find the explanation, the person checks out the environment and (b)_____ the situational cues in order to label his or her emotional feeling. This theory has been revised to recognize that emotions may occur without prior physiological arousal and that emotions may result from our (c)_____ processes.

**5.** According to the current cognitive appraisal theory of emotions, here is the sequence for how you have an emotional experience: first, some stimulus (thought, event, or object) occurs; second, you (a)_____ this stimulus as to how it will affect your well-being; third, your appraisal results in an (b)_____; fourth, the emotional feeling includes (c)_____, such as changes in heart rate and blood pressure, and may include overt behaviors.

**6.** Some researchers believe that certain emotions, such as feeling afraid when you see a snake, involve feeling before thinking; however, other emotions, such as feeling jealous when seeing your partner with someone else, involve complex thought processes where thinking precedes feeling. The interesting question regarding the order of feeling and thinking is called the (a)_____ question. The most likely answer to this question is that some thinking or appraisal always precedes an emotional feeling but that this appraisal may occur quickly, automatically, and without our (b)_____.

## C. UNIVERSAL FACIAL EXPRESSIONS

**7.** Specific inherited facial patterns or expressions that signal specific feelings or emotional states, such as a smile signaling a happy state, are called (a)_____. These emotions, which are said to include happiness, surprise, fear, anger, contempt, disgust, and sadness, are thought to have evolved because they had important adaptive and survival functions for our ancestors. There are two kinds of evidence for the existence of universal emotions: people in different cultures from around the world recognize the same (b)_____ expressions; across cultures, infants show a predictable (c)_____ in developing facial expressions, and even blind children, who cannot observe their parents' faces, develop smiling at the same time as sighted children.

## D. FUNCTIONS OF EMOTIONS

**8.** We communicate the state of our personal feelings and provide social signals that communicate with, and elicit responses from, those around us with (a)_____ expressions. In some cases, the lack of facial expressions is one of the symptoms of certain mental (b)_____.

| Difficult tasks: low arousal is optimal |
| Most tasks: medium arousal is optimal |
| Easy or simple tasks: high arousal may be optimal |

Difficulty of tasks

Level of arousal

**9.** According to one theory of emotions, we have inherited the neural structure and physiology to express and experience emotions and we evolved basic emotional patterns to adapt to and solve problems important for our survival; this is called the _____ theory.

**10.** There is a relationship between emotional arousal and your performance on a task; this relationship is called the (a)_____ law. According to this law, low arousal results in better performance on (b)_____ tasks; for most tasks, (c)_____ arousal helps performance; and for easy tasks, (d)_____ arousal may facilitate performance.

## E. HAPPINESS

**11.** Being happy involves three components: you feel a (a)_____ emotion, you are very satisfied with your (b)_____, and you are not experiencing any (c)_____ emotions. Reasons for being happy come from factors that involve both (d)_____ and _____ influences. The finding that identical twins (share 100% of genes) are significantly more similar in happiness ratings than fraternal twins (share 50% of genes) supports the influence of (e)_____ factors.

**12.** One theory explains that we quickly become accustomed to receiving some good fortune (money, job, car, degree) and, within a short period of time, take the good fortune for granted; as a result, it contributes little to our long-term level of happiness; this is called the (a)_____ theory. According to this theory, very positive significant events—such as graduating from college, getting married, winning the lottery, or buying a new car—have huge initial emotional impacts, but these emotional highs fade with time. Instead of wealth, factors that are most associated with long-term happiness involve developing and achieving long-term (b)_____ and developing and maintaining close (c)_____.

## F. CULTURAL DIVERSITY: EMOTIONS ACROSS CULTURES

**13.** Although many emotional expressions are shared and recognized across cultures, it is also true that cultures have unique rules that regulate how, when, and where we should express emotion and how much emotion is appropriate; these rules are called _____. For example, among the Inuit (Eskimos), feelings of anger are strongly condemned, but among certain Arab groups, a man's failure to respond with anger is seen as dishonorable.

**14.** Another example of display rules is from a study in which Americans and Japanese rated the intensity of five emotions—surprise, anger, happiness, disgust, and sadness—on a scale from 1 to 10. The emotion rated most intense by the Japanese was (a)_____, while the Americans rated (b)_____ as the most intense of the five emotions. This study illustrates how cultural display rules

may differently influence how people perceive the (c)_____ of emotions.

## G. RESEARCH FOCUS: EMOTIONAL INTELLIGENCE

**15.** The ability to perceive and express emotion, understand and reason with emotion, and regulate emotion in oneself and others is called (a)_____. The major problem in studying emotional intelligence is that researchers have not yet developed a reliable and valid method or test to (b)_____ it. One reason researchers believe that emotional intelligence is important is that the better we understand how emotions operate, the better are our chances of finding a way to work out compromises between our strong (c)_____ feelings and our equally strong rational (d)_____. However, research on emotional intelligence is slowed until a better way is found to (e)_____ it.

## H. APPLICATION: LIE DETECTION

**16.** The instrument mistakenly referred to as a lie detector is correctly called a (a)_____; it measures a person's heart rate, blood pressure, respiration, and emotionally induced hand sweating, which is called the (b)_____ response.

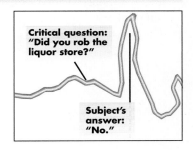
Critical question: "Did you rob the liquor store?"
Subject's answer: "No."

To determine whether a person is telling the truth or a lie, the examiner compares the person's physiological responses to (c)_____ and _____ questions. The basic problem with lie detector tests is that no pattern of physiological responses has been specifically associated with lying. This means that many emotions can cause increased physiological responses that make the person appear to be lying. Because of the relatively high (d)_____ rate, evidence from lie detector tests is not admitted in most courts of law.

***Answers:*** *1. (a) stimulus, (b) feeling, (c) physiological, (d) overt; 2. (a) peripheral, (b) James-Lange, (c) intensity; 3. (a) facial feedback, (b) intensity; 4. (a) cognitive appraisal, (b) interprets or appraises, (c) cognitive; 5. (a) interpret or appraise, (b) emotion, (c) physiological arousal; 6. (a) primacy, (b) awareness or conscious awareness; 7. (a) universal emotions, (b) facial, (c) order; 8. (a) facial, (b) disorders; 9. psychoevolutionary; 10. (a) Yerkes-Dodson, (b) difficult, (c) medium, (d) high; 11. (a) positive, (b) life, (c) negative, (d) personal/environmental, genetic/inherited, (e) genetic; 12. (a) adaptation level, (b) goals, (c) relationships or friends; 13. display rules; 14. (a) disgust, (b) happiness, (c) intensity; 15. (a) emotional intelligence, (b) measure, (c) emotional, (d) thoughts, (e) measure; 16. (a) polygraph, (b) galvanic skin, (c) neutral, critical, (d) error*

# Critical Thinking

## Why Do They Have to Learn to Smile?

### Questions

**1.** In the United States, why is smiling in social situations considered an acceptable and even desirable way to behave in public?

**2.** When having to make money is bucking cultural traditions, what do you think will happen?

**3.** Even though emotional expressions, such as smiling, are considered universal facial expressions, why don't the Japanese smile more?

In the United States it's very common to see people smiling in public because it's a friendly way to interact socially. In fact, many businesses insist that their salespeople smile at customers because smiling makes the customers feel more comfortable and more likely to buy something. But in Japan, people are very reluctant to show emotions in public and that's become a problem.

Japan is currently going through a recession or downturn in business, so there is increased competition to get new customers and keep current customers happy. Said one gas station attendant, who is trying to learn to smile more, "In this recession, customers are getting choosy about their gas stations, so you have to think positively. Laughter and a smile are representative of this positive thinking" (Reitman, 1999, p. A1).

But getting salespeople to smile is a radical change in Japan, whose cultural tradition has long emphasized suppressing any public display of emotions, be it happy, sad, or angry. For example, women never smile at their husbands and members of families rarely touch in public and never hug, even when greeting after a long separation. It's still common for women to place a hand over their mouths when they laugh, and men believe that the correct and proper behavior is to show no emotions in public. Unlike American salespeople who

often smile and make eye contact with their customers, Japanese salespeople are very reserved and greet customers with a simple "welcome"; smiling, up until now, was totally frowned upon.

Because getting salespeople to smile is going against a strong tradition, learning how to smile has grown into a big business in Japan. Employees are now being sent to "smile school," which uses various techniques to teach reluctant and bashful students to smile. For example, one technique in learning how to smile is biting on a chop stick (left photo) and then lifting the edges of the mouth higher than the chopstick. Another technique is to follow "smile" instructions: "Relax the muscle under your nose, loosen up your tongue. Put your hands on your stomach and laugh out loud, feeling the 'poisons' escape" (Reitman, 1999, p. A1).

What is driving all this smiling in Japan is sales and morale. As is well known by American businesses, happy, friendly salespeople are usually the most successful and are great at building company morale. The same is holding true in Japan, where smiley clerks are racking up the most sales and creating a friendly morale. In fact, some foreign firms in Japan, such as McDonald's, put such a high premium on smiling that they turn down applicants with poker faces. (Adapted from Reitman, 1999)

**4.** Why is it so difficult for many highly motivated Japanese to learn to smile?

**5.** Why do you think that smiley, friendly salespeople are more successful and better at building morale?

*Try InfoTrac to search for terms:* smile; Japanese and smiling.

---

### Suggested answers to Newspaper Article questions

1. Smiling is one of the universal facial expressions, which means it occurs and is recognized as a friendly social signal worldwide. However, different countries have different display rules, which regulate how, when, and where its citizens can express emotions. The display rules for the United States encourage the public display of emotional expressions, such as smiling.

2. Cultural display rules have a strong influence on people's behavior (in the United States, women can cry but men should not). It takes a strong motivating force, such as money, to change the cultural display rules, such as making it OK to smile in Japan.

3. Unlike the United States, whose cultural display rules encourage public display of smiling, Japan has had a long tradition of cultural display rules that ban most public display of emotions.

4. Even though many businesses in Japan are now sending their employees to "smile school," employees are finding it difficult to learn to smile because they must first overcome a lifetime habit of being told not to show emotions. Imagine how men in the United States would feel if they were now encouraged to cry in public and were sent to "cry school" to learn how!

5. One reason smiley salespersons are usually more successful is that all their customers come with a built-in or inherited detector for facial expressions, such as smiling. When seeing a salesperson smile (universal facial expression), customers immediately detect that it's a friendly social signal and that the salesperson is acting friendly. As a result, customers feel more friendly and more motivated to agree with the salesperson's suggestions and buy.

# Links to Learning

## Web Sites

● WADSWORTH ONLINE STUDY CENTER
http://psychology.wadsworth.com
Quizzes, learning activities and exercises, a discussion forum, and hot links to Internet sites related to sensation, including:

● HOW DO WE STUDY EMOTION?
http://www.psy.ulaval.ca/~arvid/R2e.html
At this well-organized and very interesting site you can learn about the scientific study of emotions (not the same as feelings) through psychophysiology, facial expressions, and the encoding and decoding of voice signals.

● WALKERS IN DARKNESS
http://www.walkers.org/
This long-established and award-winning site is dedicated to helping people with schizophrenia, bipolar illness, and related mood disorders. Included are descriptions of each disorder, information on medication and therapy, links to a variety of resources, forums, chat rooms, and mailing lists.

● CONTROLLING ANGER BEFORE IT CONTROLS YOU
http://www.apa.org/pubinfo/anger.html
The topics in this succinct APA brochure are "What Is Anger?," "Anger Management," "Strategies to Keep Anger at Bay," and "Do You Need Counseling?."

## Learning Activities

● *POWERSTUDY™ BY ROD PLOTNIK & TOM DOYLE*

**PowerStudy™**

**Check out Module 16**
CD section 4.E:  Limbic System: Old Brain; book page 360
CD section 11.F: Encoding: Transferring; book page 363

● *STUDY GUIDE TO ACCOMPANY INTRODUCTION TO PSYCHOLOGY, 6TH EDITION,* **by Matthew Enos**
In Module 16, consider which comes first, a thought or an emotion? And while you're on the subject, take some good advice on how to beat test anxiety.

● *WEBTUTOR*
http://webtutor.thomsonlearning.com

Visit this site for interactive versions of the Study Guide features. Take a quiz, get your score—should you study a topic some more, or can you move on? For example, are some emotions universal, or are they all defined by culture? Is it necessary to express our emotions? Is it possible to conceal them?

● *INFOTRAC ONLINE LIBRARY*
http://www.infotrac-college.com
Use your password and then key in search terms such as those below to find popular and scientific articles on subjects covered in Module 16. Make the library work for you!

Galvanic skin response          Happiness
Anger                           Polygraph

● **PSYCHNOW!**
CD for Macintosh and Windows includes a study guide, glossary, Web sites, and animations. For Module 16, see:
• Emotion

## Study Questions

*Use InfoTrac to search for topics mentioned in the main heads below (e.g., emotions, facial expressions, brain and emotions).*

*A. **Peripheral Theories**—Does someone with many facial expressions experience more emotions than someone with few facial expressions? (**Suggested answer page 630**)

B. **Cognitive Appraisal Theory**—Why would you get very angry if someone backed into your car but calm down as soon as you discovered your mother had done it?

C. **Universal Facial Expressions**—Do animals express emotions with facial expressions that are similar to humans'?

*D. **Function of Emotions**—Why might people who are madly in love have difficulty making the right decisions? (**Suggested answer page 630**)

*These questions are answered in Appendix B.

E. **Happiness**—How might your level of happiness change after you reach a big goal in your life, such as getting a college degree, new job, or relationship?

F. **Cultural Diversity: Emotions Across Cultures**—Is there any truth to the stereotypes that Italians are emotional, British hide their feelings, Germans are serious, and Americans are impulsive?

G. **Research Focus: Emotional Intelligence**—If PET scans could identify emotions, would our criminal justice system benefit from knowing whether violent criminals felt guilt for their crimes?

*H. **Application: Lie Detection**—Would it be fair to use lie detector tests to identify students who are suspected of cheating on exams? (**Suggested answer page 630**)

# Module 17: Infancy & Childhood

**A. Prenatal Influences**     **378**
* NATURE AND NURTURE
* GENETIC AND ENVIRONMENTAL FACTORS
* PRENATAL PERIOD: THREE STAGES
* DRUGS AND PRENATAL DEVELOPMENT

**B. Newborns' Abilities**     **382**
* GENETIC DEVELOPMENTAL PROGRAM
* SENSORY DEVELOPMENT
* MOTOR DEVELOPMENT

**C. Emotional Development**     **384**
* DEFINITION AND KINDS OF TEMPERAMENT
* TEMPERAMENT AND EMOTIONS
* ATTACHMENT

**D. Research Focus: Temperament**     **386**
* ARE SOME INFANTS BORN FEARFUL?

**E. Cognitive Development**     **388**
* PIAGET'S THEORY
* PIAGET'S STAGES OF COGNITIVE DEVELOPMENT
* EVALUATION OF PIAGET'S THEORY

**F. Social Development**     **392**
* FREUD'S PSYCHOSEXUAL STAGES
* ERIKSON'S PSYCHOSOCIAL STAGES
* BANDURA'S SOCIAL COGNITIVE THEORY
* RESILIENCY
* GENDER DIFFERENCES
* DIFFERENCES IN GENDER TRAITS
* QUESTIONS ABOUT GENDER DIFFERENCES
* REVIEW: THE BIG PICTURE

**Concept Review**     **398**

**G. Cultural Diversity: Gender Roles**     **399**
* IDENTIFYING GENDER ROLES
* GENDER ROLES ACROSS CULTURES
* TWO ANSWERS

**H. Application: Child Abuse**     **400**
* KINDS OF ABUSE
* WHO ABUSES CHILDREN?
* WHAT PROBLEMS DO ABUSED CHILDREN HAVE?
* HOW ARE ABUSIVE PARENTS HELPED?

**Summary Test**     **402**

**Critical Thinking**     **404**
* CAN AN ANGRY CHILD BE CHANGED?

**Links to Learning**     **405**

### Nature-Nurture Question

**Who should be Jessica's parents?**

For the first $2\frac{1}{2}$ years of her life, Jessica's parents were Roberta and Jan DeBoer, who had raised her and tried hard to adopt her. However, the Iowa court ruled that they could not adopt Jessica and that she must be returned to her biological parents. At Jessica's birth, her mother, Clara Clausen, was single and had put Jessica up for adoption. Later, Clara changed her mind and married Jessica's biological father, and now the biological parents wanted Jessica back.

Roberta and Jan had viewed Jessica as their daughter and had legally fought for over two years to adopt her. But the court decided that Jessica must be returned to her biological parents, even though Jessica had never known them and only recently met them. On the court-appointed day, a lawyer took Jessica away from the DeBoers' home, placed her in a car seat (left photo), and drove Jessica to where Dan and Clara waited. On the way, Jessica cried and said, "I want my daddy. Where's my daddy?" (Moss, 1993, p. 3A).

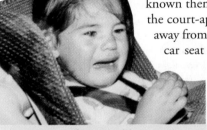

Jessica, $2\frac{1}{2}$ years old, is crying because she is being taken away from her adoptive parents.

The Baby Jessica case triggered a national debate: Why was Jessica taken from the parents who had raised and loved her and wanted to adopt her, and returned to her biological parents, whom Jessica had never known? This debate brings up an interesting question that in developmental psychology is referred to as the nature-nurture question.

The *nature-nurture question* asks how much nature (genetic factors) and how much nurture (environmental factors) contribute to a person's biological, emotional, cognitive, personal, and social development.

Although the nature-nurture question seems like an abstract intellectual issue, it has very practical consequences. For example, in the United States, most courts have traditionally sided with biological parents (nature) over adoptive parents (nurture) when awarding custody of an adopted child. Likewise, in Jessica's case, the Iowa court declared that the rights of her biological parents were primary and came before the rights of her adoptive parents. A number of child development experts criticized the Iowa court for basing its decision solely on nature. Professor Solnit, senior research scientist at Yale Child Study Center, argued that removing a child as young as Jessica from a loving home and placing her with strangers could have serious consequences. Solnit says, "One of the basic capacities that children develop in that period is the ability to trust an adult so that they can look ahead to a world that seems to them safe and reasonable, rather than a world that is unpredictable and unstable" (Gibbs, 1993a, p. 49).

More recently, however, some courts have begun to favor adoptive parents (nurture) over biological parents (nature). Denver juvenile court judge Dana Wakefield says that he invariably considers the child's needs over the parents' demands. "In my courtroom, they stay where they've been nurtured," he says flatly. "You have to consider who the child feels is the psychological parents. If they have a good bond in that home, I'm not about to break it" (Gibbs, 1993a, p. 49).

### Developmental Psychologists

In another court case, state supreme court justices refused to take an adopted 4-year-old boy named Michael away from his adoptive parents and return him to his biological father. In their ruling, the justices sided with nurture when they explained that Michael, who had lived for all his four years with adoptive parents, might suffer psychological harm if taken from the only parents he had known since birth (Dolan, 1995b).

These kinds of real-life decisions, which involve the psychological well-being of adopted children such as Michael and Baby Jessica, illustrate the kinds of issues and questions studied by developmental psychologists.

*Developmental psychologists* study a person's biological, emotional, cognitive, personal, and social development across the life span, from infancy through late adulthood.

For example, developmental psychologists are interested in how young children such as Jessica adjust to adoption or divorce and whether such changes result in any long-term psychological problems.

Later in this module, we'll explain how Jessica was doing at age 3 (she has a new name) and why she is smiling again (photo below). From the work of developmental psychologists, we have learned that the age-old question of whether nature or nurture is more important has been answered. The answer is that nature and nurture are both important and that their interaction is the key to understanding how an infant develops into a very complex adult man or woman with his or her own personality, behaviors, and goals (Collins et al., 2000).

Eight months after Jessica was returned to her biological parents, she seems adjusted.

### What's Coming

We'll discuss how development is affected by various prenatal factors, such as alcohol, which is the leading known cause of mental retardation. We'll explain the amazing abilities of newborns, the early appearance of a basic emotional makeup, the surprising growth of mental abilities, the different factors influencing social development, and the terrible occurrence of child abuse, which affects over a million children a year.

We'll begin with a family whose infant son's unusual musical abilities showed how nature and nurture interact.

# A. Prenatal Influences

## Nature and Nurture

**Was he born a violin player?**

The reviewer for the *San Francisco Examiner* had listened to an inspired performance and wrote that the violinist "would one day be a master among masters" (Magidoff, 1973, p. 35).

At that point, the "master" was all of 5 years old and had been taking lessons for only six months. His name was Yehudi Menuhin. When Yehudi was 8 years old, he made his first professional appearance. The reviewer wrote, "This is not talent; it is genius!" (Magidoff, 1973, p. 46). Yehudi made his debut in New York at the age of 10, and the reviewer wrote, "What built the world in six days is what contrived the genius of Yehudi. He walks on the waves" (Magidoff, 1973, p. 52).

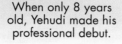

When only 8 years old, Yehudi made his professional debut.

The amazing musical abilities of young Yehudi certainly classify him as a prodigy.

A *prodigy* is a child who shows a highly unusual talent, ability, or genius at a very early age and does not have mental retardation. A small percentage of autistic children, who have some degree of mental retardation, may also show unusual artistic or mathematical abilities; they are called savants.

Because prodigies demonstrate such unusual abilities so early, they are excellent examples of the interaction between nature (genetic influences) and nurture (learned influences).

## Genetic and Environmental Factors

One reason Yehudi Menuhin was a prodigy and could give an inspiring violin performance at the age of 5 was the prenatal (before birth) effects of genetic influences. Prenatal influences, in the form of genetic instructions, regulated the development of Yehudi's brain and body.

**Parents.** The father contributed half of Yehudi's genetic instructions (23 chromosomes) and the mother contributed half of the genetic instructions (23 chromosomes).

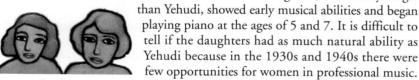

The father and mother were teachers, and both had musical interests. The father had taken six violin lessons when he was a boy, but his grandfather had forbidden him to play any further. The mother had musical ability and took regular cello lessons. Through their chromosomes, the parents passed some of their musical talents on to their three children, Yehudi and his two younger sisters.

**Daughters.** The two daughters each received half of their genetic instructions from their mother and half from their father. Both daughters, who were younger than Yehudi, showed early musical abilities and began playing piano at the ages of 5 and 7. It is difficult to tell if the daughters had as much natural ability as Yehudi because in the 1930s and 1940s there were few opportunities for women in professional music. As a result, these negative environmental influences actively discouraged the two daughters from developing their potential musical abilities.

**Son.** Yehudi received half of his genetic instructions from his mother and half from his father. The unique pairing of chromosomes from the mother and father results in different physical and mental traits for each of the three children. Because Yehudi and his two younger sisters showed great musical ability by age 5, we can assume that their early musical ability was primarily due to genetic or inherited instructions that came from their parents' chromosomes. However, certain environmental factors, such as few opportunities for women musicians, discouraged the sisters from developing their talents. Different environmental factors, such as many opportunities for male musicians, encouraged Yehudi to develop his musical talents.

**Interaction.** Yehudi Menuhin, who was universally hailed as the greatest child prodigy since Mozart, developed into a legendary violin performer (Magidoff, 1973). The development of Yehudi's musical talents is a perfect example of how nature and nurture interact. You can see that genetic influences (nature) played a major role in wiring his brain so that his incredible musical abilities appeared at a very early age, before he had a chance to learn them. You can also see that environmental influences (nurture), such as being taken to concerts from age 2 on and being encouraged to practice and take lessons, encouraged Yehudi to develop the musical talents that he had inherited from his parents.

Psychologists have long recognized the importance of learning influences, but it is only for about the past ten years that psychologists have also recognized the importance of genetic influences on almost every aspect of behavior, including cognitive, social, emotional, and personality development (Plomin & Caspi, 1999). Today, researchers no longer focus on which is more important, nature or nurture, but rather on how nature and nurture interact to influence and regulate our behaviors (Reiss, 2000).

Genetic instructions from our parents can result in our having a wide range of abilities. Next, we'll explain what happens when genetic instructions are damaged—for example, if the mother uses drugs during the prenatal period.

You began as a single cell about the size of a grain of sand. In this tiny cell was the equivalent of about 300,000 pages of instructions for the development of your brain and body. This single cell marks the beginning of the prenatal period.

The *prenatal period* extends from conception to birth and lasts about 266 days (around nine months). It consists of three successive phases: the germinal, embryonic, and fetal stages. During the prenatal period, a single cell will divide and grow to form 200 billion cells.

As we examine the prenatal period, we'll unravel one of the great puzzles of science—how a human being begins, develops, and is born. We'll start with the germinal stage.

**Prenatal Period: Three Stages**

1. Germinal stage
2. Embryonic stage
3. Fetal stage

## 1 *Germinal Stage*

The germinal stage marks the beginning of our development into a human being.

The *germinal stage* is the first stage of prenatal development and refers to the two-week period following conception.

To understand how conception occurs, we need to back up a little and explain ovulation.

*Ovulation* refers to the release of an ovum or egg cell from a woman's ovaries.

In most cases, only a single ovum is released during ovulation, but sometimes two ova are released. If two separate ova are released and fertilized, the result is fraternal twins, who can be two brothers, two sisters, or a brother and sister. Because fraternal twins come from two separate eggs, they are no more genetically alike than any other two children of the same parents. In contrast, if a single ovum splits into two parts after fertilization, the result is identical twins, who share the same genes and thus are genetically alike.

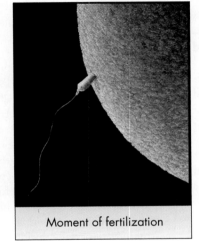
Moment of fertilization

### How does conception take place?

If no sperm are present, there can be no fertilization, and the ovum, together with the lining of the uterus, is sloughed off in the process called *menstruation.* If, however, sperm have been deposited in the vagina (100–500 million sperm may be deposited with each act of intercourse), they make their way to the uterus and into the fallopian tubes in search of an ovum to be fertilized.

*Conception,* or *fertilization,* occurs if one of the millions of sperm penetrates the ovum's outer membrane. After the ovum has been penetrated by a single sperm (above photo), its outer membrane changes and becomes impenetrable to the millions of remaining sperm.

Once the ovum has been fertilized, it is called a *zygote,* which is a single cell that is smaller than the dot in the letter *i.* The zygote begins a process of repeated division and, after about a week, consists of about 150 cells. After two weeks, it has become a mass of cells and attaches itself to the wall of the uterus. Once the zygote is implanted, or attached to the wall of the uterus, the embryonic stage begins.

## 2 *Embryonic Stage*

During this next stage, the organism begins to develop body organs.

The *embryonic stage* is the second stage of the prenatal period and spans the 2–8 weeks that follow conception; during this stage, cells divide and begin to differentiate into bone, muscle, and body organs.

At about 21 days after conception, the beginnings of the spinal cord and eyes appear; at about 24 days, cells differentiate to form what will become part of the heart; at about 28 days, tiny buds appear that will develop into arms and legs; and at about 42 days, features of the face take shape.

During this stage, the embryo is very fragile, since all of its basic organs are being formed. This is the time when most miscarriages occur and when most major birth defects occur (Mortensen et al., 1991).

Toward the end of the embryonic stage, the organism has developed a number of body organs, such as the heart. The embryo is only about an inch long but already has the beginnings of major body organs and limbs and begins to look somewhat human.

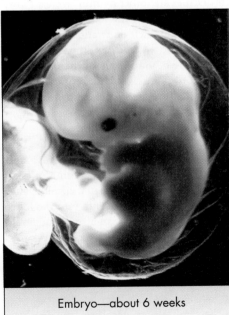
Embryo—about 6 weeks

In the left photo, you can see the head as the large rounded structure at the top, and the black dot on the side of the head is the developing eye. After this second stage of development, which is called the embryonic stage and lasts from 2–8 weeks, comes the last stage, which is called the fetal stage.

*3* *Fetal Stage*

**What is the fetal stage?**

The embryonic stage is followed by the fetal stage.

The *fetal stage,* which is the third stage in prenatal development, begins two months after conception and lasts until birth.

At the end of the fetal stage, usually 38–42 weeks after conception (or roughly nine months), birth occurs and the fetus becomes a newborn.

During this stage, the fetus develops vital organs, such as lungs, and physical characteristics that are distinctively human. For example, at about six months a fetus has eyes and eyelids that are completely formed (right photo), a fine coating of hair, relatively well-developed external sex organs, and lungs that are beginning to function.

Infants born very prematurely (under six months) will have difficulty surviving because their lungs are not completely formed and they have difficulty breathing. However, a six-month-old fetus usually has lungs well enough developed to begin to show irregular breathing and, for this reason, can survive if born prematurely.

During stage 2, embryonic stage, and stage 3, fetal stage, the developing organism is especially vulnerable to toxic agents and chemicals. To help keep out these potentially harmful agents, the developing organism is protected by the placenta.

**Placenta and teratogens.** Because the fetus experiences rapid body growth and development of the nervous system, it is highly vulnerable to the effects of drugs and other harmful agents. However, the blood supply of the fetus is partly protected by the placenta (left illustration).

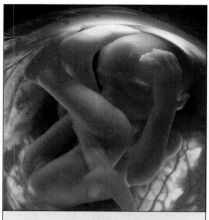
Fetus in womb at 6 months

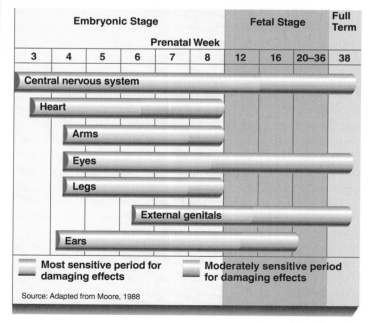

**Placenta**

**Umbilical cord**

The *placenta* is an organ that connects the blood supply of the mother to that of the fetus. The placenta acts like a filter, allowing oxygen and nutrients to pass through while keeping out some toxic or harmful substances.

However, certain viruses, such as the HIV virus, and many drugs, including nicotine, caffeine, marijuana, cocaine, and heroin, pass from the placenta into the fetus's blood vessels and thus can affect fetal development. These potentially dangerous agents are called teratogens.

A *teratogen* is any agent that can harm a developing fetus (causing deformities or brain damage). It might be a disease (such as genital herpes), a drug (such as alcohol), or another environmental agent (such as chemicals).

Besides harmful chemicals, drugs, or viruses, the developing fetus can also be affected by genetic problems, especially if the parents are carriers of potentially harmful genes (Tay-Sachs) or if the mother is in her forties, which increases the risk for certain fetal genetic problems

(Down syndrome). In these cases where there is greater potential for fetal genetic problems, the mother may wish to have her fetus tested by a relatively safe process called amniocentesis (Marcus, 2000).

**Birth defects and amniocentesis.** During the fetal stage, it is possible to test for a number of genetic errors by amniocentesis *(AM-nee-oh-sen-TEE-sis).*

*Amniocentesis,* which is a medical test done between weeks 14 and 20 of pregnancy, involves inserting a long needle through the mother's abdominal muscles into the amniotic fluid surrounding the fetus. By withdrawing and analyzing fetal cells in the fluid, doctors can identify a number of genetic problems.

One example of a genetic problem identified by amniocentesis is Down syndrome, whose likelihood is greater in mothers who are in their forties (Marcus, 2000).

*Down syndrome* results from an extra 21st chromosome and causes abnormal physical traits (a fold of skin at the corner of each eye, a wide tongue, heart defects) and abnormal brain development, resulting in degrees of mental retardation.

Besides Down syndrome (p. 288), more than 450 other genetic disorders can now be tested for and identified (Painter, 1997). As shown in the figure below, birth defects can occur if something (toxin, drug, genetic malfunction) interferes with developing structures, especially during the embryonic stage (Lie et al., 1994).

| | Embryonic Stage | | | | | | Fetal Stage | | | Full Term |
|---|---|---|---|---|---|---|---|---|---|---|
| Prenatal Week | | | | | | | | | | |
| 3 | 4 | 5 | 6 | 7 | 8 | 12 | 16 | 20–36 | 38 |
| Central nervous system | | | | | | | | | | |
| Heart | | | | | | | | | | |
| Arms | | | | | | | | | | |
| Eyes | | | | | | | | | | |
| Legs | | | | | | | | | | |
| External genitals | | | | | | | | | | |
| Ears | | | | | | | | | | |

Most sensitive period for damaging effects

Moderately sensitive period for damaging effects

Source: Adapted from Moore, 1988

Next, we'll discuss several teratogens (from the Greek word *tera,* meaning "monster") that can pass through the placenta and interfere with fetal growth and development.

**How well is the fetus protected?** In the womb, the fetus is protected from physical bumps by a wraparound cushion of warm fluid. The fetus is also protected from various teratogens (certain chemicals and drugs) by the filtering system of the placenta (described on p. 380). However, we'll discuss several drugs, both legal and illegal, that can pass through the placenta, reach the fetus, and cause potential neurological, physiological, and psychological problems.

### Multiple Drug/Cocaine Usage

In the 1980s and early 1990s, the media reported that mothers who had used "crack" cocaine during pregnancy had "crack babies," who suffered serious brain damage and would likely be mentally retarded. Many of these early reports on crack babies were based on cases that researchers were not able to confirm. What researchers did confirm were somewhat less drastic but still potentially harmful short- and long-term effects resulting from the use of cocaine (usually combined with other drugs) during pregnancy.

**Short-term effects.** Researchers report that pregnant women who reported using crack cocaine usually used a combination of other drugs as well, such as alcohol, tobacco, marijuana, or opiates. Infants who had been exposed in the womb to cocaine and other drugs had lower birth weight, were more irritable, and had poor feeding habits (Richardson & Day, 1994). However, because women who had used cocaine had simultaneously used other drugs, the short-term problems shown by their newborns may have resulted from the combination of drugs, rather than from cocaine alone. In any case, pregnant women who use cocaine, usually with other drugs, have infants with low birth weight, which may place the newborn at risk for developing other medical problems (Bendersky & Lewis, 1999).

**Long-term effects.** Besides the short-term problem of low birth weight, researchers wondered whether exposure in the womb to crack cocaine would result in long-term behavioral problems. Several follow-up studies found that children from 4 to 7 years old who had been exposed in the womb to cocaine (usually combined with other drugs) were more impulsive, were less able to adapt to stressful situations, and had more behavioral problems later in life than did a control group of children whose mothers had not used drugs (Chasnoff, 1997).

In addition, 4- to 7-year-old children exposed in the womb to cocaine (usually combined with other drugs) were found to have significantly lower IQ scores and significantly lower scores in using and understanding language. Researchers concluded that, although children exposed in the womb to cocaine (usually combined with other drugs) are not hopelessly damaged, they do show reliable deficits in cognitive development (Lester et al., 1998).

Researchers strongly recommend that pregnant women not use cocaine or other drugs because children exposed to such drugs may show behavioral (acting impulsively) and cognitive (lower IQ scores and poorer language abilities) problems later in life.

**Tobacco Cocaine Alcohol Opiates Marijuana**

These drugs can affect the developing fetus.

### Alcohol

**Heavy drinking.** In the United States, alcohol is the leading known cause of mental retardation. Alcohol (ethanol) is a teratogen that crosses the placenta, affects the developing fetus, and can result in fetal alcohol syndrome (Young, 1997).

*Fetal alcohol syndrome (FAS)* results from a mother drinking heavily during pregnancy, especially in the first 12 weeks. FAS results in a combination of physical changes, such as short stature, flattened nose, and short eye openings (right photo), and psychological deficits, such as degrees of mental retardation and hyperactivity (Jones & Smith, 1973).

Notice the facial features.

Children with fetal alcohol syndrome continue to have problems into adolescence and adulthood. In two follow-up studies conducted 5–14 years after the original diagnosis, researchers retested adolescents and adults (age range 12–40 years). Subjects tended to remain short, their average IQ was 68 (normal is 100), and they tended to be easily distracted and to misperceive social cues (Spohr et al., 1993; Streissguth et al., 1999). Thus, various physical, behavioral, and cognitive problems associated with fetal alcohol syndrome are long-lasting.

**Moderate drinking.** Recently, researchers found that moderate drinking (7–14 drinks per week) by pregnant women does not usually result in fetal alcohol syndrome (FAS). However, moderate drinking may result in prenatal exposure to alcohol (PEA), which is less severe than fetal alcohol syndrome but three times more prevalent (Jacobson & Jacobson, 1999). Researchers reported that children with prenatal exposure to alcohol showed deficits in a number of cognitive tasks (work comprehension), academic skills, and fine motor speed and coordination (Mattson et al., 1998). Because even moderate drinking (1–2 drinks a day) during pregnancy may result in serious problems, researchers recommend that women who are pregnant or are planning a pregnancy should not drink any alcohol (Christensen, 2000).

Although the fetus is vulnerable to various drugs (teratogens), over 90% of babies are normal, and many of those born with birth defects have mild, temporary, or reversible problems (Sigelman & Shaffer, 1995).

We have discussed the three stages of prenatal development, which end with the baby's birth. After the baby gets a pat on the backside and lets out a cry, he or she is ready to take on the world.

# B. Newborns' Abilities

**Power Study™**

Check out CD: Module 3
A. Overview: Human Brain
B. Neurons: Structure & Function

**Why can't a newborn walk?**

Some animals, such as baby elephants (150 pounds), can walk immediately after birth. In comparison, baby humans (7 pounds) cannot walk because neither their leg muscles nor brain areas are well enough developed. However, human infants are born with a surprising number of sensory and motor abilities, such as hearing, grasping, and sucking. How these abilities develop is explained by an inherited genetic program.

## Genetic Developmental Program

Conception results in a fertilized egg, which has a genetic program that is equivalent to 300,000 pages of typed instructions for developing the body and brain. The mother contributes 23 chromosomes and the father contributes 23, so that each child receives a unique genetic program.

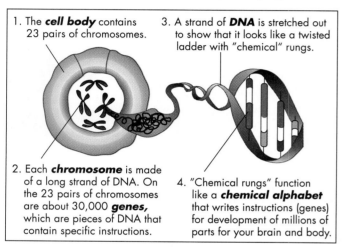

1. The **cell body** contains 23 pairs of chromosomes.

2. Each **chromosome** is made of a long strand of DNA. On the 23 pairs of chromosomes are about 30,000 **genes,** which are pieces of DNA that contain specific instructions.

3. A strand of **DNA** is stretched out to show that it looks like a twisted ladder with "chemical" rungs.

4. "Chemical rungs" function like a **chemical alphabet** that writes instructions (genes) for development of millions of parts for your brain and body.

**Brain growth.** After birth, the genetic program regulates how the brain develops, such as making thousands of connections between neurons. For example, during the first three months of life, the most active areas of the newborn's brain are involved in processing sights, sounds, and touches, preparing the infant for dealing with sensory information from the surrounding environment.

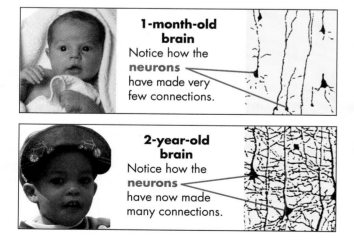

**1-month-old brain**
Notice how the **neurons** have made very few connections.

**2-year-old brain**
Notice how the **neurons** have now made many connections.

In the figures above, notice that a 1-month-old brain has very few neural connections, while a 2-year-old brain has many thousands (Wiznitzer, 2000). This enormous increase in neural connections partly explains why the baby's brain increases from 340 grams at birth to about 900 grams at 2 years old.

## Sensory Development

During the nine months of development in the womb, the genetic program is guiding the development of a number of motor and sensory functions that are important for the newborn's survival. For example, each newborn is equipped with a sucking reflex to ensure getting food and a very loud cry to demand attention. Here's a summary of a newborn's sensory and perceptual abilities.

**Faces.** At 1 month of age, an infant can distinguish his or her mother's face from that of a stranger, provided the infant also hears the mother's voice. By 3 months of age, an infant can visually distinguish his or her mother's face from a stranger's (Burnham, 1993). By 3 to 4 years of age, an infant's visual abilities are equal to those of an adult.

**Hearing.** One-month-old infants have very keen hearing and can discriminate small sound variations, such as the difference between *bah* and *pah*. By 6 months, infants have developed the ability to make all the sounds that are necessary to learn the language in which they are raised (Bower, 1994).

**Touch.** Newborns also have a well-developed sense of touch and will turn their head when lightly touched on the cheek. Touch will also elicit a number of reflexes, such as grasping and sucking.

**Smell and taste.** Researchers found that 1-day-old infants could discriminate between a citrus odor

The senses develop relatively fast.

and a floral odor (Sullivan et al., 1991). Six-week-old infants can smell the difference between their mother and a stranger (Macfarlane, 1975). Newborns have an inborn preference for both sweet and salt and an inborn dislike of bitter-tasting things.

**Depth perception.** By the age of 6 months, infants have developed depth perception, which was tested by observing whether they would crawl off a visual "cliff" (Gibson & Walk, 1960).

A *visual cliff* is a glass tabletop with a checkerboard pattern over part of its surface; the remaining surface consists of clear glass with a checkerboard pattern several feet below, creating the illusion of a clifflike drop to the floor.

An infant is placed on the area with the checkerboard pattern and is encouraged to creep off the cliff. Six-month-old infants hesitate when they reach the clear glass "dropoff," indicating that they have developed depth perception.

Although the genetic program is largely responsible for the early appearance of these sensory abilities, *environmental stimulation,* such as parental touch and play, encourages the infant to further develop these sensory abilities (Collins et al., 2000).

**Why do infants crawl before they walk?**

"Gloria just took her first step." Mothers and fathers proudly relate their children's motor accomplishments, which are primarily due to the child's genetic program. As infants learn to crawl and walk, they change from passive observers into very active participants in the family's social life. The first area studied by early developmental psychologists was motor skill development (Thelen, 1995).

*Motor development* refers to the stages of motor skills that all infants pass through as they acquire the muscular control necessary for making coordinated movements.

Because each child has a unique genetic program, he or she will acquire motor skills at different times. The development of early motor skills, such as sitting, crawling, and walking, follows two general rules, called the proximodistal and cephalocaudal principles.

**1** The *proximodistal principle* states that parts closer to the center of the infant's body (*proximo* in Latin means "near") develop before parts farther away (*distal* in Latin means "far").

For example, activities involving the trunk are mastered before activities involving the arms and legs. For that reason, infants can roll over before they can walk or bring their arms together to grasp a bottle.

**2** The *cephalocaudal principle* states that parts of the body closer to the head (*cephalo* in Greek means "head") develop before parts closer to the feet (*caudal* in Greek means "tail").

For example, infants can lift their heads before they can control their trunks enough to sit up, and they can sit up before they can control their legs to crawl. In the figure below, notice the head area (larger) developing before the feet area (smaller).

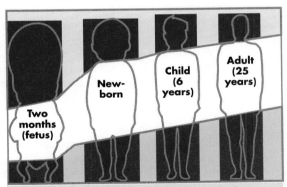

Two months (fetus) · Newborn · Child (6 years) · Adult (25 years)

Head size decreases in proportion to body size.

**3** The cephalocaudal and proximodistal principles, which regulate the sequence for developing early motor skills, are part of a process known as maturation.

*Maturation* refers to developmental changes that are genetically or biologically programmed rather than acquired through learning or life experiences.

In developing motor skills (three right photos), such as sitting up alone, crawling, and walking, all infants in all parts of the world go through the same developmental stages at about the same times. However, if children are given more opportunities to practice their stepping reflex earlier in life, they will begin to walk at an earlier age than children who lack such opportunities (Thelen, 1995). Thus, the development of early motor development is heavily influenced by maturation (genetic program) but the timing can be partly slowed or speeded up by experience/learning (nurture).

**4** Parents often note the major milestones in their infants' motor development, such as their first time crawling or walking, because they want to know if their children are within the developmental norms.

*Developmental norms* refer to the average age at which children perform various kinds of skills or exhibit abilities or behaviors.

Sitting up alone— average 5.5 months (range 4.5–8.0 months)

Some examples of developmental norms for stages in walking accompany the three photos. Because norms for motor development represent average ages rather than absolute ages, parents should not be disturbed if their infant's motor progress does not match the norms.

By the age of 2, infants have grown into toddlers who can walk up and down stairs and use their hands to hold glasses of juice, operate toys, and, of course, get into a lot of trouble.

**5** The reason infants develop skills and abilities at different times is that neural connections develop at different rates. This means that infants cannot perform complex cognitive, sensory, or motor tasks, such as walking, talking, and reading, until appropriate areas of their brains develop neural connections.

Crawling—average 10 months (range 7.0–12.0 months)

Although we have focused on the role of the genetic developmental program (nature), it's important to remember that nature interacts with the environment (nurture) to encourage or discourage the development of various motor, sensory, and cognitive abilities (Shatz, 1997). For example, infants need appropriate *environmental stimulation* for development of their visual systems (see things), for learning to speak (hear parents speaking), for emotional development (get loving care), and for motor development (explore objects). These examples show how the genetic program needs and interacts with environmental stimulation for the proper development of most of a child's sensory, motor, and cognitive abilities (Lach, 1997; Nash, 1997).

Walking alone— average 12.1 months (range 11.5–14.5 months)

Next, we'll discuss emotional development.

# C. Emotional Development

## Definition and Kinds of Temperament

**Why are babies so different?**

A colleague who had just had her second baby was explaining how different the new baby is. "My first baby was very fussy and required constant attention. But my new baby is a dream. He's such a good, happy baby and totally unlike how his older sister was." My colleague is actually discussing how each of her two babies has a very different temperament.

*Temperament* refers to individual differences in attention, arousal, and reactivity to new or novel situations. These differences appear early, are relatively stable and long-lasting, and are influenced in large part by genetic factors.

Most parents with two or more children have noticed differences in their babies' temperaments. Using a more scientific approach, researchers studied differences in infants' temperaments by interviewing mothers with 2- to 3-month-old infants and then observing these same infants repeatedly over the next seven years. Researchers rated each infant on nine components of temperament, including activity level, attention span, fussiness, and mood. On the basis of these ratings, they were able to divide the infants into four categories (Thomas & Chess, 1977).

**1 Easy babies,** who made up 40% of the sample, were happy and cheerful, had regular sleeping and eating habits, and adapted quickly to new situations.

**2 Slow-to-warm-up babies,** who made up 15% of the sample, were more withdrawn, were moody, and tended to take longer to adapt to new situations.

**3 Difficult babies,** who made up 10% of the sample, were fussy, fearful of new situations, and more intense in their reactions. During the course of the seven-year study, difficult babies developed more serious emotional problems than the easy or slow-to-warm-up babies.

**4 No-single-category babies,** who made up 35% of the sample, had a variety of traits and could not be classified into one of the other three categories.

**Genetic influence.** From this and other studies, researchers concluded that the majority of infants develop distinct temperaments very early, usually in the first 2–3 months of life, and that these distinct temperaments occur largely because of genetic factors rather than learning experiences (Bates, 2000). Additional evidence that differences in temperament result primarily from a genetic developmental program comes from the finding that about 10–15% of Caucasian babies inherit an inhibited or fearful temperament, such as showing great physiological arousal and distress in new or novel situations. In comparison, about 40% of Caucasian babies inherit a fearless temperament, such as remaining relaxed and calm in novel or strange situations (Kagan, 1998).

15% fearful

**Long-lasting.** Although some fearful infants became less so as they grew up, most individuals retained their generally fearful or fearless traits into adolescence and adulthood (Kagan, 1998).

Other studies also report that a distinct temperament developed in infancy can have long-lasting effects. For example, babies who developed a difficult temperament (negative mood, intense crying) were found to have a negative attitude and mood and significantly more behavioral problems at age 12 (Guerin et al., 1997). Thus, temperament is a genetic influence that affects a child's level of arousal and reactivity to new situations, which, in turn, affects whether a child develops healthy or unhealthy personality traits and social relationships (Caspi, 2000).

40% fearless

## Temperament and Emotions

**What are sextuplets like?**

Becki is describing the personalities of her sextuplets (photo below). "Brenna, the oldest by 30 seconds, is the affectionate one. Julinan, the second child delivered, is 'Mr. Smiley.' Quinn, the third, is sweet and generous and most adventurous. Claire,

Each sextuplet has a different temperament.

fourth oldest, is the boss, as charming as she is tough. Ian, the fifth, is the smallest and loves music, drawing, and sleep. Adrian, the youngest, is the biggest and most gentle" (Reed & Breu, 1995, p. 127). Each of these 2-year-old sextuplets is already showing a distinct personality, partly a result of his or her unique emotional development (Bates, 2000).

*Emotional development* is an interaction between temperament (nature) and positive or negative environmental feedback (nurture), which children receive as they explore their worlds.

**Interaction.** Similar to all infants, the sextuplets initially expressed their temperaments through a limited number of inherited emotional expressions, including showing interest, startle, distress, disgust, and a neonatal smile (a sort of half-smile that appears spontaneously for no apparent reason). Also, similar to all infants, during the first two years the sextuplets developed a wide range of emotional expressions and feelings, including *social smiling* (age 4–6 weeks); *anger, surprise,* and *sadness* (age 3–4 months); *fear* (age 5–7 months); *shame* and *shyness* (age 6–8 months); and *contempt* and *guilt* (age 24 months) (Lewis, 2000). Thus, during the first two years, the different and mostly inherited temperaments of each of the sextuplets interacted with different environmental feedback (especially parental) to result in developing very different emotional traits, ranging from being sweet and gentle to being charming, adventurous, and tough.

Think of an infant's temperament as setting a range for later emotional development, which in turn has an influence on the bond or attachment between parent and child, our next topic.

## Attachment

**Do infants and parents form a special bond?**

For the first $2\frac{1}{2}$ years of her life, Jessica was lovingly cared for by the only parents she ever knew, her adoptive parents, Roberta and Jan DeBoer. When the court decided that Jessica must be returned to her biological parents, whom Jessica did not know, she cried as she was taken away (right photo). Taking Jessica away from her adoptive parents broke a special bond that she had developed with Roberta and Jan. This emotional bond is called attachment.

Jessica, $2\frac{1}{2}$ years old, is being taken away from her adoptive parents.

*Attachment* refers to a close, fundamental emotional bond that develops between the infant and his or her parents or caregiver.

The interesting theory behind attachment comes from psychologist John Bowlby (1969), who believed that attachment behavior evolved through a process of natural selection. According to his idea, attachment evolved because of its adaptive value. Attachment gave the infant a better chance of surviving because the parent was close by to provide care and protection. Much of the research on attachment was initiated by Mary Ainsworth (1989), who asked three general questions: How does attachment occur? Are there different kinds of attachment? What are the long-term effects of attachment?

### How Does Attachment Occur?

According to attachment theory, Jessica, like most babies, would have formed an attachment to her parents through a gradual process that begins shortly after birth and continues through infancy. As a newborn, Jessica has a powerful social signal, crying, which elicits care and sympathy. As a 4- to 6-week-old infant, she will begin social smiling (smiling at others), which will elicit joy and pleasure in her parents. At about 6 months, Jessica begins to give her parents a happy greeting (smiling, holding out her arms) when they reappear after a short absence. All of these behaviors contribute to building a good parent–child attachment (Thompson, 1998).

As the infant develops a closer attachment to her parents, she also shows more distress when her parents leave; this is called separation anxiety.

*Separation anxiety* is an infant's distress—as indicated by loud protests, crying, and agitation—whenever the infant's parents temporarily leave.

According to Ainsworth, separation anxiety is a clear sign that the infant has become attached to one or both parents. By the end of the first year, an infant usually shows a close attachment to her parents as well as to one or more other family members.

However, depending on the infant's temperament (easy or difficult) and the mother's attitude (caring or not responsive), different kinds of attachment occur.

### Are There Different Kinds of Attachment?

Ainsworth (1979) is best known for developing a method for studying infants' reactions to being separated from, and then reunited with, their mothers. She used these reactions to indicate the kind or quality of the infants' attachment. There are now four different kinds of attachment, but we'll focus on two, which are called secure (65% of infants) and insecure attachment (20% of infants).

*Secure attachment* is characteristic of infants who use their parent as a safe home base from which they can wander off and explore their environments.

For example, when infants are placed in an unfamiliar room containing many interesting toys, securely attached infants tend to explore freely as long as their parent looks on. If the parent leaves, most of the infants cry. On the parent's return, securely attached infants happily greet the caregiver and are easily soothed. By contrast, some infants show insecure attachment.

*Insecure attachment* is characteristic of infants who avoid or show ambivalence or resistance toward their parent or caregiver.

For example, insecurely attached infants may cling and want to be held one minute but squirm and push away the next minute, apparently displaying a lack of trust in the parent or caregiver.

Researchers found that an infant's sense of trust or attachment was not affected by whether or how long a child was in day care. Instead, what most affected the infant's attachment was a mother's sensitivity, caring, and responsiveness to the infant's needs (NICHD, 1997). As you'll see, attachments may affect later behaviors and relationships.

### What Are Effects of Attachment?

After spending $2\frac{1}{2}$ years with her adoptive parents, Jessica was taken from them. Psychologists worried that breaking this original attachment might have long-term effects on Jessica's sense of security and trust. However, after being with her biological parents for eight months, Jessica (now called Anna) seemed to have formed a healthy attachment to them (photo below left) and, as yet, shows no obvious symptoms of being insecure or untrusting.

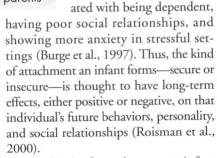

Eight months after Jessica was returned to her biological parents

The kind of attachment an infant forms during the first five years is thought to be associated with future behaviors. For example, a secure attachment is associated with being better at resolving conflicts, being more trusting, enjoying relationships, and dealing better with stress and anxiety; an insecure attachment is associated with being dependent, having poor social relationships, and showing more anxiety in stressful settings (Burge et al., 1997). Thus, the kind of attachment an infant forms—secure or insecure—is thought to have long-term effects, either positive or negative, on that individual's future behaviors, personality, and social relationships (Roisman et al., 2000).

The kind of attachment an infant forms is also partly dependent on the infant's temperament. We'll next discuss a classic study on kinds of temperaments.

## Are Some Infants Born Fearful?

We're going to discuss a series of classic studies by Jerome Kagan (1998), which changed the way we think about children's temperaments. Kagan wanted to answer a question asked by many parents: Why do children raised by the same parents in the same family grow up with such different emotional makeups? For instance, Eric's parents wondered why he (similar to circled child in right photo) was more shy and fearful than his two brothers. Eric would never leave his mother's side to play with other children, was afraid to tell a story to his grade school class, and feared going into the swimming pool with other children (Elias, 1989). Kagan wondered if fearful children like Eric were born that way and if they changed as they grew up.

Why is only one child shy?

The first problem Kagan faced was to select between two different research methods—longitudinal and cross-sectional methods—to study developmental changes. As we discuss the advantages and disadvantages of each method, you'll understand why Kagan selected the longitudinal method to study temperament.

### Longitudinal Method

One method researchers use to study developmental changes, such as a child's temperament, is the longitudinal method.

A *longitudinal method* means that the same group of individuals is studied repeatedly at many different points in time.

For example, as shown in the figure below, researchers first measure temperaments in a group of 2-year-old children, retest this same group again at age 7, then test them again at age 12, and so on.

**Advantages and disadvantages.** A major advantage of the longitudinal method is that it allows researchers to study the developmental patterns or changes of the

| Age | **2** | **7** | **12** |
|-----|-------|-------|--------|
| Year | **1989** | **1994** | **1999** |

same subjects across time. One disadvantage is that researchers must wait many years for their subjects to grow older and must deal with the problem of subjects dropping out of the study (due to relocation, illness, or death). However, researchers generally prefer using the longitudinal method to study developmental changes because they can track the behaviors of the same subjects across time.

### Cross-Sectional Method

A *cross-sectional method* means that several groups of different-aged individuals are studied at the same time.

For example, in the figure below, researchers are using the cross-sectional method because they selected a group of 2-year-olds, a group of 7-year-olds, and a group of 12-year-olds and measured their temperaments at the same time.

**Advantages and disadvantages.** One advantage of the cross-sectional method is that researchers can immediately compare any

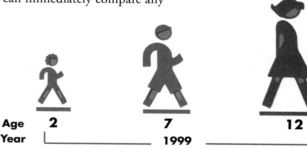

| Age | **2** | **7** | **12** |
|-----|-------|-------|--------|
| Year | | **1999** | |

developmental differences, such as in temperaments, across many different age groups. A major disadvantage of the cross-sectional approach is that it cannot tell us if the same individuals remain the same or change across time. For this reason, the longitudinal method is preferable to the cross-sectional method for studying developmental differences.

### Procedure

Using the longitudinal method, Jerome Kagan and his colleagues (Kagan, 1998; Kagan & Snidman, 1991) began by studying the temperaments of 4-month-old infants. The same infants would be retested several times, at different ages, until they turned 12. Kagan found that some 4-month-olds were shy and fearful; he called them inhibited children.

*Inhibited children* show avoidance, anxiety, or fear (measured by avoiding, fretting, or crying) when in a strange or novel environment; these children also show increased physiological arousal (increased heart rate) to novel or strange situations.

After identifying a group of inhibited—shy or fearful—infants, Kagan next asked if these inhibited infants would grow into inhibited children. We'll discuss some of Kagan's interesting findings.

## Results

### First question: How many infants are classified as fearful?

As shown in the graph below, Kagan and his colleagues observed several hundred 4-month-old infants and reported that about one-fourth were classified as inhibited, or highly fearful. An inhibited, or highly fearful, infant showed a high degree of avoidance, fretting, and crying in novel or strange situations. About one-third of the infants were classified as uninhibited, or low-fear, individuals, and the remaining infants were classified in between.

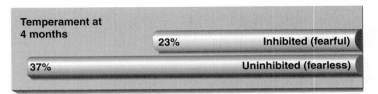

Temperament at 4 months

23% — Inhibited (fearful)

37% — Uninhibited (fearless)

The vast majority of infants who showed high fear at 4 months continued to show high fear at 21 months (Kagan et al., 1988; Kagan & Snidman, 1991). Thus, the answer to our first question is that some infants are born with a tendency to develop either an inhibited (fearful) or uninhibited (fearless) temperament. Data from twin studies indicate that the influence of genetic factors on temperament ranges from 50 to 60% (Kagan, 1998). An infant's temperament may influence the kind of attachment formed with its mother. Infants who have a fearful or distressed temperament may develop an insecure attachment if raised by a rigid or less affectionate mother, but the same infant may develop a secure attachment if raised by a more flexible, affectionate mother (Kagan, 1998). This means an infant's temperament interacts with a mother's traits to result in the development of a secure or insecure attachment.

### Second question: Do infants change their temperaments?

To answer this question, researchers repeatedly tested the same group of infants until they were 7 years old. As the graph below shows, between the ages of 21 months and 7 years, about 70% of the children showed moderate changes in their temperaments, becoming less inhibited or uninhibited, while about 30% retained their original temperaments. How do these inhibited and uninhibited children differ in behavior?

Temperament Changes Between 21 Months and 7 Years

30% — Retained temperament

70% — Moderate changes in temperament

**Profile of inhibited child.**   A typical inhibited child stayed at the periphery of a large group of peers, reading a book, painting at an easel, or standing in a corner quietly watching another child. One of the best indicators of an inhibited child was that he or she spoke very little or initiated very little spontaneous conversation with unfamiliar peers or adults.

**Profile of uninhibited child.**   A typical uninhibited child was involved in group activities, was very talkative, initiated spontaneous interactions, engaged in conversations, often with smiling and laughter, and showed enthusiasm for social interactions not observed in inhibited children.

This brings up another question: What should parents do to help an inhibited child overcome his or her fear and shyness?

## Conclusions

One reason children raised by the same parents in the same family can be so different is that they inherit different temperaments. Kagan's (1994, 1998) series of longitudinal studies showed that there are at least two distinct temperaments, which he called inhibited (shy or fearful) and uninhibited (outgoing or fearless). These two temperaments are relatively stable across time, involve both observable behaviors and physiological arousal, and probably involve the excitability of different brain areas.

The appearance of these temperaments in very young infants indicates the influence of genetic factors (nature). However, the finding that about 70% of the children's temperaments changed moderately indicates the influence of environmental or learning experiences (nurture). Kagan estimates that about 10–15% of the general population have an inhibited (fearful) temperament, while about 20–40% have an uninhibited (fearless) temperament.

Being shy is one kind of temperament.

Another interesting finding was that although children differed in temperament—inhibited or uninhibited—they did not differ in IQ scores, intellectual abilities, language, memory, or reasoning abilities (Kagan, 1998).

### What should parents do if their child is inhibited?

Researchers advise parents with inhibited children to be very caring and supportive and to consistently help their inhibited child deal with minor stressors. With such support, inhibited children learned to control their initial urges to withdraw from strange people or situations. Additionally, researchers suggest that if parents avoid becoming too anxious, overprotective, or angry at their children's extreme fearfulness and timidity, there will be a better chance that the inhibited child will become less anxious in adolescence (Kagan, 1994).

Eric's parents followed this advice. As an infant and child, Eric (similar to right photo) showed signs of being fearful or inhibited. For example, Eric spent two weeks worrying about having to give a book report, which meant standing in front of, and speaking to, the whole class. Eric was sure he couldn't do it. His parents encouraged Eric to role-play giving his book report. Eric performed his speech over and over at home until he felt comfortable. When Eric gave his book report to the class, he did very well and felt great afterward (Elias, 1989). With support and understanding, parents can help a shy or fearful child become more expressive and outgoing.

At the same time that an infant is developing emotional behaviors, he or she is also acquiring numerous cognitive skills and abilities, which we'll discuss next.

# E. Cognitive Development

**What are blocks for?**

We have explained how a newborn's brain and senses develop relatively quickly so that an infant is soon ready to creep and walk and explore and learn about a wondrous world through a process called cognitive development.

*Cognitive development* refers to how a person perceives, thinks, and gains an understanding of his or her world through the interaction and influence of genetic and learned factors.

For example, if you gave blocks to Sam, who is 5 months old (top right photo), he would surely put one into his mouth. If you gave the same blocks to Sam when he was 2 years old, he might stack them (bottom right photo). If you gave the same blocks to Sam when he was an adolescent, he might play a game of throwing them into a can. What Sam does with blocks depends on his experience and level of cognitive development.

**Jean Piaget.** In the history of developmental psychology, the person who had the greatest impact on the study of cognitive development was Jean Piaget, who was both a biologist and a psychologist. From the 1920s to his death in 1980, Piaget (1929) studied how children solved problems in their natural settings, such as cribs, sandboxes, and playgrounds. Piaget developed one of the most influential theories of cognitive development (Roth et al., 2000).

Piaget believed that from early on, a child acts like a tiny scientist who is actively involved in making guesses or hypotheses about how the world works. For example, when given blocks, 5-month-old Sam puts them into his mouth, while 2-year-old Sam tries to stack them, and adolescent Sam laughs and plays a game of tossing blocks into a can. Piaget believed that children learned to understand things, such as what to do with blocks, through two active processes that he called assimilation and accommodation.

## ASSIMILATION

If you gave 5-month-old Sam a block, he would first try to put it into his mouth because at that age, infants "think" that objects are for sucking on. This mouthing behavior is an example of assimilation.

Blocks are for putting in mouth.

*Assimilation* is the process by which a child uses old methods or experiences to deal with new situations.

At 5 months, Sam will first put a new object into his mouth because his knowledge of objects is that they are for eating or sucking. Thus, Sam will assimilate the new object as something too hard to eat but all right for sucking.

Depending on their age and knowledge, children assimilate blocks in different ways: infants assimilate blocks as something to suck; toddlers assimilate blocks as something to stack or throw; adolescents assimilate blocks as something used to play games; and adults assimilate blocks as something to give to children. The assimilation of new information leads to Piaget's next process—accommodation.

## ACCOMMODATION

If you gave 2-year-old Sam the same blocks, he would not try to eat them, but he might try to stack them, which is an example of accommodation.

Blocks are for stacking.

*Accommodation* is the process by which a child changes old methods to deal with or adjust to new situations.

For example, because of Sam's experience with different kinds of objects, he has learned that square, hard objects are not food but things that can be handled and stacked. Sam's learning to change existing knowledge because of new information (blocks are for stacking, not eating) is an example of accommodation, which is one way that mental growth occurs.

As an infant or child is actively involved in exploring his or her environment, there are many opportunities for assimilation and accommodation, which result in different kinds of cognitive growth and development.

According to Piaget, children make big gains in reasoning, thinking, and understanding through active involvement and the processes of assimilation and accommodation. Using these two processes, children go through a series of cognitive stages.

---

## Piaget's Stages of Cognitive Development

**What is Sam thinking?**

Piaget is best known for describing the changes or different stages in cognitive development that occur between infancy and adulthood (Roth et al., 2000).

*Piaget's cognitive stages* refer to four different stages—sensorimotor, preoperational, concrete operations, and formal operations—each of which is more advanced than the preceding stage because it involves new reasoning and thinking abilities.

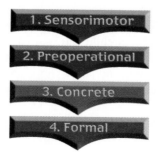

1. Sensorimotor
2. Preoperational
3. Concrete
4. Formal

Although Piaget believed that all people go through the same four cognitive stages, he acknowledged that they may go through the stages at different rates.

Piaget's hypothesis that cognitive development occurs in stages and that each stage involves different kinds of thinking was one of his unique contributions to developmental psychology. We'll explain Piaget's four stages by following Sam through his cognitive development.

## 1. Sensorimotor

Imagine Sam as a newborn infant. His primary way of interacting with the world is through reflexive responses, such as sucking and grasping. By 5 months, Sam has developed enough voluntary muscle control so that he can reach out, grasp things, and put them into his mouth to discover if the things are good to suck on. Sam is in the sensorimotor stage.

The *sensorimotor stage* (from birth to about age 2) is the first of Piaget's cognitive stages. During this stage, infants interact with and learn about their environments by relating their sensory experiences (such as hearing and seeing) to their motor actions (mouthing and grasping).

**Hidden objects.** At the beginning of sensorimotor stage, Sam has one thinking problem: remembering that hidden objects still exist. For example, notice in the top left photo that 5-month-old Sam is shown a toy dog. Sam immediately tries to

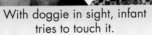

grab it and put part of it in his mouth. This is another example of assimilation; Sam believes that objects are mostly for mouthing.

However, notice in the bottom left photo that when a screen is placed in front of the dog, Sam looks away. He doesn't push the screen away to get at the toy because, at this point, Sam behaves as if things that are out of sight are out of mind and simply no longer exist. Sam has not learned object permanence.

With doggie in sight, infant tries to touch it.

With doggie hidden, infant acts as if there is no doggie.

**Object permanence.** Beginning at around 9 months, if Sam is shown a toy dog that is then covered by a screen, he will try to push the screen away and look for the dog. Sam has learned that a toy dog that is out of sight still exists behind the screen. This new concept is called object permanence.

*Object permanence* refers to the understanding that objects or events continue to exist even if they can no longer be heard, touched, or seen.

The concept of object permanence develops slowly over a period of about nine months. By the end of the sensorimotor period (about age 2), an infant will search long and hard for lost or disappeared objects, indicating a fully developed concept of object permanence.

At the end of the sensorimotor stage, 2-year-old Sam can think about things that are not present and can form simple plans for solving problems, such as searching for things.

According to Piaget, after the sensorimotor stage, Sam enters the next stage, called the preoperational stage.

## 2. Preoperational

As a 4-year-old, Sam is busy pushing a block around the floor and making noises as he pretends the block is a car. The cognitive ability to pretend is a sign that Sam is going through the preoperational stage.

The *preoperational stage* (from about 2 to 7 years old) is the second of Piaget's cognitive stages. During this stage, children learn to use symbols, such as words or mental images, to solve simple problems and to think or talk about things that are not present.

At this stage, Sam is acquiring the cognitive ability to pretend things and to talk about or draw things that are not physically present. Although Sam is learning to use words and images in speech and play, his thinking has a number of interesting limitations that make his thinking different from an adult's. During the preoperational stage, two of his cognitive limitations involve problems with conservation and engaging in egocentric thinking.

**Conservation.** As 4-year-old Sam watches you pour milk from a tall, thin glass into a short, wide glass, will he know that the amount of milk remains the same even though its shape changes? This is called the problem of conservation.

*Conservation* refers to the fact that even though the shape of some object or substance is changed, the total amount remains the same.

Here's what happens when 4-year-old Sam is faced with a conservation problem.

**In photo #1,** 4-year-old Sam watches as his mother fills two short, wide glasses with equal amounts of milk.

**In photo #2,** Sam sees his mother pour the milk from one short, wide glass into a tall, thin glass. Mother asks, "Does one glass have more milk?"

**In photo #3,** Sam points to the tall, thin glass as having more milk because the tall glass looks larger. He makes this mistake even though he just saw his mother pour the milk from a short, wide glass.

Sam, like other children at the preoperational stage, will not be able to solve conservation problems until the next stage.

**Egocentric thinking.** A second problem that Sam has during the preoperational stage is that he makes mistakes or misbehaves because of egocentric thinking.

*Egocentric (ee-goh-SEN-trick) thinking* refers to seeing and thinking of the world only from your own viewpoint and having difficulty appreciating someone else's viewpoint.

Piaget used the term *egocentric thinking* to mean that preoperational children cannot see situations from another person's, such as a parent's, point of view. When they don't get their way, children may get angry or pout because their view of the world is so self-centered.

# E. Cognitive Development

## 3. Concrete
### Stage 3

Between the ages of 7 and 11, Sam learns that even if things change their shape, they don't lose any quantity or mass, a new concept that occurs during the concrete operations stage.

The *concrete operations stage* (from about 7 to 11 years) is the third of Piaget's cognitive stages. During this stage, children can perform a number of logical mental operations on concrete objects (ones that are physically present).

**Conservation.** As you may remember, when Sam was 4 years old and in the preoperational stage, he had not mastered the concept of conservation. In the preoperational stage, Sam thought a tall, thin glass held more milk than a short, wide glass. And if 4-year-old Sam watched as a ball of clay (top left photo) was flattened into a long piece (bottom left photo), he would say the long piece was larger.

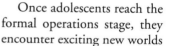

Can these two pieces of clay be the same size?

However, Sam is now 10 years old and has just watched you flatten a ball of clay into a long piece. Sam now says that the long, flattened piece contains the same amount of clay as the ball, even if the shape changed. Similarly, if 10-year-old Sam watched you pour cola from a short glass into a tall glass, he would correctly answer that the amount of cola remained the same. Children gradually master the concept of conservation during the concrete operations stage, and they also get better at classification.

**Classification.** If you gave 4-year-old, preoperational Sam some trail mix (photo below), he would be able to classify the pieces according to a single category, such as size. However, during the concrete operations stage, 10-year-old Sam has acquired the ability to classify trail mix according to two categories, such as color and size, indicating that he has learned a new cognitive skill.

During the concrete stage, children learn to sort objects by both size and color.

**New abilities.** During the concrete operations stage, children learn to classify or sort objects according to more than one category and learn to solve a variety of conservation problems. The reason Piaget called this the *concrete* operations stage is that children can easily classify or figure out relationships between objects provided the objects are actually physically present or "concrete."

However, children at the concrete operations stage still have difficulty figuring out relationships among objects that are not present or situations that are imaginary. Thinking about imaginary or hypothetical situations occurs in Piaget's fourth stage.

## 4. Formal
### Stage 4

Sam is now 17 years old and is surfing the Web for a paper he's writing on what killed the dinosaurs. This kind of abstract thinking indicates that Sam is in the formal operations stage.

The *formal operations stage* (from about 12 years old through adulthood) is Piaget's fourth cognitive stage. During this stage, adolescents and adults develop the ability to think about and solve abstract problems in a logical manner.

Piaget believed that it is during the formal operations stage that adolescents develop thinking and reasoning typical of adults. For example, 17-year-old Sam can compare several theories about why the dinosaurs died, including being destroyed by a giant asteroid, radical temperature change, or some terrible virus. In the formal operations stage, Sam will learn to solve abstract problems in a systematic, logical manner. In comparison, seven years ago when Sam was in the concrete operations stage, he lacked the ability to solve abstract problems. Now that Sam is 17 and in the formal operations stage, Sam is learning to use a computer graphics program as well as solving the latest video game that involves careful planning to outthink seven layers of evil creatures.

Once adolescents reach the formal operations stage, they encounter exciting new worlds

How much does the thinking of a 17-year-old differ from that of a 15-year-old?

of abstract ideas and hypothetical concepts. For example, Sam can discuss abstract ideas, such as whether computer hackers should go to jail, if going steady is a good idea, and how strict parents should be. Acquiring the ability to think in a logical, systematic, and abstract way is one of the major characteristics of the formal operations stage and opens up a whole new world of ideas. The cognitive skills associated with the formal operations stage are the very ones that you will need to do well in college.

### PIAGET'S KEY IDEAS
We have discussed Piaget's cognitive stages in some detail, but there are three ideas that stand out (Larivee et al., 2000):

**1** Children gradually and in a step-by-step fashion develop reasoning abilities through the active processes of assimilation and accommodation.

**2** Children are naturally curious and intrinsically or self-motivated to explore their worlds and, in the process, develop numerous cognitive skills.

**3** Children acquire different kinds of thinking and reasoning abilities as they go through different stages of cognitive development.

Over the past 45 years, researchers have tested Piaget's theories and ideas and made some revisions and modifications.

**How does Piaget stand today?**

Piaget's theory, especially his descriptions of how thinking differs at each of the four cognitive stages, had a tremendous influence on the area of cognitive development (Roth et al., 2000). However, beginning in the late 1960s and continuing to the present, there have been numerous criticisms of Piaget's theory (Piaget died in 1980). We'll discuss these criticisms along with the current direction of cognitive development.

### Criticisms

**Four stages.** A major part of Piaget's theory involves his four cognitive stages with their differences in thinking and reasoning that all children go through. However, one criticism of Piaget's four stages is that they are not as rigid as he originally proposed. Researchers have found that children can solve certain kinds of problems at stages earlier than Piaget proposed. For example, preoperational children can solve some abstract problems, such as who is taller or shorter than someone else, provided the problems are presented simply and are repeated many times. According to Piaget (far right illustration), preoperational children should not be able to solve these simple abstract problems. However, researchers have found that children do show certain thinking skills earlier than would be predicted from Piaget's cognitive stages. For this reason, Piaget's stages are now viewed as being neither as rigid nor as complete as he originally proposed (Haith & Benson, 1998).

**Description versus explanation.** One advantage of Piaget's stages is that each stage described what a child could and could not do, such as an infant learns object permanence but not conservation during the sensorimotor stage. Although Piaget's theory describes the kind of thinking a child can and cannot do at different ages and at different stages, his theory does not explain how this change occurs. Thus, another criticism of Piaget's cognitive stages is that they describe rather than explain what causes children's thinking to change from one stage to another (Bruner, 1997).

**Current status.** Essentially, Piaget began an area that we now know as cognitive development (Flavell, 1996). Many of his contributions, such as using observational research to study children and viewing children as active explorers who gradually discover their worlds, are still considered important ideas today. However, because of more recent criticism discussed above, Piaget's theory is now viewed as having great historical importance but no longer being the major force in guiding research in childhood cognitive development (Roth et al., 2000). Today, there are several guiding forces.

### Current Directions

Since Piaget developed his theory, there have been at least three major changes or advances in the study of cognitive development.

**1 Genetic factors.** One of the biggest changes has been in the identification of genetic factors that influence memory, learning, and cognitive skills. For example, research on identical and fraternal twins has shown that genetic factors account for between 20 and 60% of the influence on verbal, spatial, and perceptual abilities as well as on memory (Petrill, 1998). In Piaget's time, the influence of genetic factors on cognitive abilities had not been as clearly established. In the last 10 years there has been an increasing number of studies showing how genetic cognitive factors (nature) influence and interact with a child's environment (nurture). Researchers conclude that genetic factors set a range for many cognitive abilities, whose growth can be either facilitated by a stimulating environment or depressed by an impoverished environment (Plomin & Caspi, 1999).

**2 Basic abilities.** A second major change is the discovery that infants and young children have many more basic cognitive skills and abilities than Piaget believed. For example, researchers report that infants are aware that objects continue to exist even when screened from view; that infants have a basic concept of how objects move; that infants understand the concept of addition; and that they have remarkable abilities to recognize speech sounds (Haith & Benson, 1998). The fact that infants and young children possess a relatively large number of cognitive skills means that they are even more actively involved in learning about and discovering their environments than Piaget or anyone previously believed (Haith & Benson, 1998).

Jean Piaget (1896–1980)

**3 New theories.** A third major change in the field of cognitive development is that there is no longer a single grand theory, such as Piaget's theory of four cognitive stages. Although Piaget's original theory had and still has some influence on cognitive development studies, the findings described above point out the weaknesses in his theory. For this reason, psychologists are constructing new theories; one has the unusual name of theory theory.

*Theory theory* says that children have innate abilities to make guesses about how things are, test their guesses through interactions with the environment, and change their guesses as they gather new or conflicting information.

According to theory theory, a child develops cognitively by acting like an everyday scientist who makes guesses about how the world works, tests these guesses by gathering new information, and changes these guesses in the face of conflicting information (Gopnik & Meltzoff, 1997). Theory theory is one example of the new theories being developed to replace Piaget's theory.

We have discussed cognitive development by itself, but cognitive development is closely intertwined with social development, which we'll examine next.

# F. Social Development

**What will happen to Baby Jessica?**

At the beginning of this module we described how Baby Jessica at age $2\frac{1}{2}$ was taken away from the adoptive parents who had raised her from birth and returned to her biological parents, whom she had never met. Some psychologists wonder how Jessica's early emotional difficulties will affect her future social development.

*Social development* refers to how a person develops a sense of self or a self-identity, develops relationships with others, and develops the kinds of social skills important in personal interactions.

In Baby Jessica's case, we know that after eight months with her new, biological parents, she seemed to have made a very good adjustment. However, some psychologists believe that Jessica's first five years are the most important and that her early emotional troubles may lead to social problems as an adult.

Jessica's social development is a long and complicated process, which is influenced by many of the emotional and cognitive factors that we have just discussed. We'll describe three different theories of social development, each of which emphasizes a different aspect of behavior.

## Freud's Psychosexual Stages

One of the best-known theories is that of Sigmund Freud (1940/1961), who said that each of us goes through five successive psychosexual stages.

The *psychosexual stages* are five different developmental periods—oral, anal, phallic, latency, and genital stages—during which the individual seeks pleasure from different areas of the body that are associated with sexual feelings. Freud emphasized that a child's first five years were most important to social and personality development.

In Freud's theory, there is often conflict between the child and parent. The conflict arises because the child wants immediate satisfaction or gratification of its needs, while the parents often place restrictions on when, where, and how the child's needs should be satisfied. For example, a child may wish

Does an infant's experience during breast feeding have lasting effects?

to be fed immediately, while the parent may want to delay the feeding to a more convenient time. Freud believed that interactions between parent and child in satisfying these psychosexual needs—for example, during breast feeding or toilet training—greatly influence the child's social development and future social interactions. In addition, Freud emphasized the importance of a child's first five years in influencing future social development or future personality problems.

According to Freud, Jessica will go through five developmental stages, some of which contain potential conflicts between her desires and her parents' wishes. If her desires are over- or undersatisfied, she may become fixated at one of the first three stages. As you'll see, becoming fixated at one of these stages will hinder her normal social development.

**1 Oral Stage**

**Period:** Early infancy—first 18 months of life.

**Potential conflict:** The *oral stage* lasts for the first 18 months of life and is a time when the infant's pleasure seeking is centered on the mouth.

Pleasure-seeking activities include sucking, chewing, and biting. If Jessica were locked into or fixated at this stage because her oral wishes were gratified too much or too little, she would continue to seek oral gratification as an adult.

**2 Anal Stage**

**Period:** Late infancy—$1\frac{1}{2}$ to 3 years.

**Potential conflict:** The *anal stage* lasts from the age of about $1\frac{1}{2}$ to 3 and is a time when the infant's pleasure seeking is centered on the anus and its functions of elimination.

If Jessica were locked into or fixated at this stage, she would continue to engage in behavioral activities related to retention or elimination. Retention may take the form of being very neat, stingy, or behaviorally rigid. Elimination may take the form of being generous or messy.

**3 Phallic Stage**

**Period:** Early childhood—3 to 6 years.

**Potential conflict:** The *phallic (FAL-ik) stage* lasts from about age 3 to 6 and is a time when the infant's pleasure seeking is centered on the genitals.

During this stage, Jessica will compete with the parent of the same sex (her mother) for the affections and pleasures of the parent of the opposite sex (her father). Problems in resolving this competition (called the Electra complex and discussed in Module 19) may result in feelings of inferiority for women and of having something to prove for men.

**4 Latency Stage**

**Period:** Middle and late childhood—from 6 to puberty.

**Potential conflict:** The *latency stage*, which lasts from about age 6 to puberty, is a time when the child represses sexual thoughts and engages in nonsexual activities, such as developing social and intellectual skills.

At puberty, sexuality reappears and marks the beginning of a new stage.

**5 Genital Stage**

**Period:** Puberty through adulthood.

**Potential conflict:** The *genital stage* lasts from puberty through adulthood and is a time when the individual has renewed sexual desires that he or she seeks to fulfill through relationships with members of the opposite sex.

If Jessica successfully resolved conflicts in the first three stages, she will have the energy to develop loving relationships and a healthy and mature personality.

According to Freud, Jessica's future personality and social development will depend, to a large extent, on what she experiences during the first three psychosexual stages, which occur during her first five years. Freud's psychosexual stages are part of his larger psychoanalytic theory of personality, which we'll discuss more fully in Module 19.

# Erikson's Psychosocial Stages

**How important is trust?**

According to well-known psychologist Erik Erikson, Jessica will encounter kinds of problems very different from the psychosexual ones proposed by Freud. Unlike Freud's emphasis on psychosexual issues, Erikson (1963, 1982) focused on psychosocial issues and said that each of us goes through eight psychosocial stages.

The *psychosocial stages* are eight developmental periods during which an individual's primary goal is to satisfy desires associated with social needs: the eight periods are associated, respectively, with issues of trust, autonomy, initiative, industry, identity, intimacy, generativity, and ego integrity.

Erikson hypothesized that from infancy through adulthood we proceed through these stages, each of

Are the effects of psychosocial problems long-lasting?

which is related to a different problem that needs to be resolved. If we successfully deal with the potential problem of each psychosocial stage, we develop positive personality traits and are better able to solve the problem at the next stage. However, if we do not successfully handle the psychosocial problems, we may become anxious, worried, or troubled and develop social or personality problems.

Unlike Freud, Erikson believed that psychosocial needs deserve the greatest emphasis and that social development continues throughout one's lifetime. Thus, Erikson would emphasize Jessica's psychosocial needs and downplay the importance of sexuality in the first five years.

*We'll explain Erikson's first five stages here and discuss the remaining three stages in Module 18, which deals with social development in adolescents and adults.*

| Stage **1** Trust versus Mistrust | Stage **2** Autonomy versus Shame and Doubt | Stage **3** Initiative versus Guilt | Stage **4** Industry versus Inferiority | Stage **5** Identity versus Role Confusion |
|---|---|---|---|---|
| **Period:** Early infancy—birth through first year. **Potential problem:** Jessica comes into the world as a helpless infant who needs much care and attention. If her parents are responsive and sensitive to her needs, Jessica will develop what Erikson calls basic trust, which makes it easier for her to trust people later in life. If Jessica's parents neglect her needs, she may view her world as uncaring, learn to become mistrustful, and have difficulty dealing with the second stage. It appears that both sets of parents gave Jessica care and attention. | **Period:** Late infancy—1 to 3 years. **Potential problem:** As Jessica begins walking, talking, and exploring, she is bound to get into conflict with the wishes of her parents. Thus, this second stage is a battle of wills between her parents' wishes and Jessica's desires to do as she pleases. If her parents encourage Jessica to explore, she will develop a sense of independence, or autonomy. If her parents disapprove of or punish Jessica's explorations, she may develop a feeling that independence is bad and feel shame and doubt. | **Period:** Early childhood—3 to 5 years. **Potential problem:** As a preschooler, Jessica has developed a number of cognitive and social skills that she is expected to use to meet the challenges in her small world. Some of these challenges involve assuming responsibility and making plans. If her parents encourage initiative, Jessica will develop the ability to plan and initiate new things. However, if they discourage initiative, she may feel uncomfortable or guilty and may develop a feeling of being unable to plan her future. | **Period:** Middle and late childhood—5 to 12 years. **Potential problem:** Jessica's grade school years are an exciting time, filled with participating in school, playing games with other children, and working to complete projects. If Jessica can direct her energy into working at and completing tasks, she will develop a feeling of industry. If she has difficulty applying herself and completing homework, she may develop a feeling of inferiority and incompetence. | **Period:** Adolescence. **Potential problem:** Adolescents need to leave behind the carefree, irresponsible, and impulsive behaviors of childhood and develop the more purposeful, responsible, planned behaviors of adults. If Jessica is successful in making this change, she will develop a sense of confidence and a positive identity. If she is unsuccessful, she will experience role confusion, which will result in having low self-esteem and becoming socially withdrawn. |

According to Erikson, Jessica will encounter a particular psychosocial problem at each stage. If she successfully solves the problem, she will develop positive social traits that will help her solve the next problem. If she does not solve the problem, she will develop negative social traits that will hinder her solving a new problem at the next stage.

**Evaluation of Erikson's and Freud's theories.** Many psychologists agree with Erikson that psychosocial conflicts, which are based on interpersonal and environmental interactions, do contribute to social-emotional development (Bugental & Goodnow, 1998). Erikson said that the first five years were not necessarily the most important and that social development continues throughout one's life. In fact, longitudinal studies show that personality change and development continue well into middle adulthood (McCrae & Costa, 1990).

Many psychologists also agree with Freud that childhood events are important to social development. However, they criticize Freud for emphasizing childhood sexuality while neglecting the influences

of social and cognitive factors on social development (Bugental & Goodnow, 1998). In addition, longitudinal studies show that children may overcome a variety of problems during the first five years and still have a well-adjusted personality, contrary to Freud's predictions (Werner, 1995).

The strength of Erikson's and Freud's theories is that they explain the whole of social development, from infancy through adulthood. Their weakness, however, is that many of their concepts (trust, autonomy, oral stage, fixation) are more descriptive than explanatory and are very difficult to verify or test experimentally. Next, we'll examine the social cognitive theory of social development.

## F. Social Development

### Bandura's Social Cognitive Theory

**What is the 3-year-old doing?**

After watching his daddy bowl, this 3-year-old boy walked up to his daddy, pointed at the ball, and said, "Me too ball." Neither Freud's nor Erikson's theory explains why this 3-year-old child wanted to learn to bowl, what motivated him to ask his daddy, or why he clapped his hands just like his daddy when the ball hit the pins. Albert Bandura (1989a, 1999) says that this little boy, like all of us, develops many of his behaviors and social skills through a variety of social cognitive processes.

The *social cognitive theory* emphasizes the importance of learning through observation, imitation, and self-reward in the development of social skills, interactions, and behaviors. According to this theory, it is not necessary that you perform any observable behaviors or receive any external rewards in order to learn new social skills because many of your behaviors are self-motivated, or intrinsic.

He watched his daddy bowl and then he wanted to.

Social cognitive theory stresses how you learn by modeling and imitating behaviors that you observe in social interactions and situations. For example, after watching his daddy, this 3-year-old is intrinsically motivated to imitate many of his daddy's social behaviors. Social cognitive theory emphasizes that children develop social behaviors and skills by watching and imitating the social behaviors of their parents, grandparents, teachers, and peers.

In comparing Bandura's, Freud's, and Erikson's theories, notice that although the three theories are very different, they are complementary because they each emphasize a different process. Social cognitive theory emphasizes learning through modeling; Freud's theory focuses on parent–child interactions that occur in satisfying innate biological needs; and Erikson's theory points to the importance of dealing with social needs.

We'll use these theories to explain how some children overcame terrible childhood experiences to develop normal social behaviors.

### Resiliency

**How do children survive early problems?**

Based on observations of his patients, Freud concluded that social and personality development is essentially completed in the first five years. That is, even though an individual might undergo later social changes, his or her basic social and personality traits are primarily established during the first five years. One way to test Freud's hypothesis is to do a long-term study of children who are faced with major problems. One such child was Delia.

During her first year, Delia's unwed mother was withdrawn and showed little interest in Delia; her father was rarely around. But, during her second year, she was sent to live with her grandparents, who raised Delia in a warm, loving, and caring home environment and later adopted her.

Delia was part of a study of 600 children from a small rural community on the Hawaiian island of Kauai. In this study, conducted by psychologist Emmy Werner (1989), the children (right photo) were followed from birth to almost 20. Like Delia, all the children were exposed to numerous life stresses, including problems during mother's pregnancy, family instability, parents' mental and financial difficulties, and a lower social class environment with limited environmental stimulation. How these life stressors affect children depends on their vulnerability and resiliency.

*Vulnerability* refers to psychological or environmental difficulties that make children more at risk for developing later personality, behavioral, or social problems.

*Resiliency* refers to various personality, family, or environmental factors that compensate for increased life stresses so that expected problems do not develop.

Some children suffered childhood traumas but developed normal personalities.

In Delia's group of 600 children, about 200 showed increased vulnerability and later developed serious behavioral or learning problems. However, the most remarkable finding is that over 400 of the children showed resiliency and developed into competent and autonomous young adults (Werner, 1989; Werner & Smith, 1982).

Children like Delia are called resilient, or stress-resistant. These children defy expectations because they develop into well-adapted individuals in spite of serious life stressors (Masten & Coatsworth, 1998). For example, despite having an insensitive, unresponsive young mother and an absent father, Delia at age 20 had developed adequate self-esteem, high achievement motivation, a fair degree of insight into her life, and realistic plans for the future.

Researchers identified several factors that contribute to resiliency. One factor was genetic: Children born with *positive temperaments,* meaning they are more smiley and socially responsive, elicited more attention and care. Another factor was related to social cognitive processes: Resilient children had a *substitute caregiver* whose caring behaviors and social skills could be observed and imitated; as a result, resilient children were socially popular. Another factor involved Erikson's psychosocial stages: Resilient children received *social support, care,* and *trust* from their peers and caregivers and developed well-adjusted social behaviors (Werner, 1989).

Studies on resilient children show three things. First, early traumatic emotional events do not necessarily lead to later social-emotional problems, as Freud predicted. Second, a loving, supportive caregiver can substitute for a disinterested parent. Third, children observe and imitate normal social behaviors modeled by caregivers (Masten & Coatsworth, 1998; Werner, 1995).

**What three words change your life forever?**

A very important part of our social development begins with three little words. If the doctor says, "It's a girl," one kind of social development is started. If the doctor says, "It's a boy," a different kind of social development is begun. In fact, when you look at the photo on the right, you can't help asking, "Is it a girl or a boy?" This question has to do with gender identity.

**Gender identity.** Between the ages of 2 and 3, most children learn to label themselves as boys or girls and can classify others as being the same sex or the other sex.

*Gender identity* refers to the individual's subjective experience and feelings of being a female or male.

Once they know their correct sex, they begin to learn sex-appropriate behaviors, which are called gender roles.

**Gender roles.** By the time they are 3 years old, American children know the traditional expectations of how

By age 2–3, this male infant will know he's a boy.

gender roles relate to toys, clothes, games, and tools. From ages 4 to 5, children develop a clear idea of which occupations are stereotypically for men and for women. And by the relatively early age of 5, children have already learned the thoughts, expectations, and behaviors that accompany their particular gender roles (Eckes & Trautner, 2000).

*Gender roles* are the traditional or stereotypic behaviors, attitudes, and personality traits that parents, peers, and society expect us to have because we are male or female.

Gender roles have a relatively powerful effect on how we behave, think, and act.

How children acquire gender roles is explained by two somewhat different but related theories: social role theory and cognitive developmental theory.

## Social Role Theory

In many families, the parents expect a son to behave and act differently than a daughter. How parental expectations influence a child's gender identity is explained by the social role theory (Eagly et al., 2000).

The *social role theory* emphasizes the influence of social and cognitive processes on how we interpret, organize, and use information. Applied to gender roles, it says that mothers, fathers, teachers, grandparents, friends, and peers expect, respond to, and reward different behaviors in boys than in girls. Under the influence of this differential treatment, boys learn a gender role that is different from girls'.

For example, the stereotypic gender roles for males include being controlling, dominant, and independent, while gender roles for females include being sensitive, nurturing, and concerned (Wood et al., 1997). According to social role theory, these gender differences originate, to a large extent, because mothers and fathers respond to and reward different behaviors in girls than in boys.

Why does she want to be a model?

For instance, parents buy more sports equipment, tools, and toy cars for boys and more dolls and child's furniture for girls (Pomerleau et al., 1990). In playing with boys, fathers were observed to model being assertive and dominant, while in playing with girls, mothers were observed to model being concerned and nurturing (Leaper, 2000). Parents are more likely to encourage dependence in girls, generally reward boys for conforming to traditional play activities, and generally reward girls for doing traditional household chores (Keenan & Shaw, 1997). These differences in parents' behaviors support the social role theory idea that parents encourage or discourage behaviors depending on whether these behaviors match traditional boy–girl gender roles.

One criticism of social role theory is that it focuses too much on rewarding and discouraging behaviors and too little on cognitive influences, which are emphasized in the cognitive developmental theory.

## Cognitive Developmental Theory

When you were a child, you probably learned that there were ways or rules about what boys and girls could and could not do. This childhood experience supports the cognitive developmental theory (Martin, 2000).

The *cognitive developmental theory* says that, as children develop mental skills and interact with their environments, they learn one set of rules for male behaviors and another set of rules for female behaviors.

In this view, children actively process information that results in their learning gender rules regarding which behaviors are correct for girls and wrong for boys and vice versa. On the basis of these rules, children form mental images of how they should act; these images are called gender schemas.

*Gender schemas* are sets of information and rules organized around how either a male or a female should think and behave (Bem, 1985).

Why does he want to be baseball player?

For instance, the traditional gender schema for being a boy includes engaging in rough-and-tumble play and sports, initiating conversations, and exploring; the traditional gender schema for being a girl includes playing with dolls, expressing emotions, listening, and being dependent.

Cognitive developmental theory emphasizes that a child is an active participant in learning a male or female set of rules and schemas, which result in different gender roles (Bem, 1981).

Both social role theory and cognitive developmental theory predict that the sexes will develop different gender roles.

### Differences in Gender Traits

Some of the reliable differences in gender roles are that girls develop traits of being concerned, sensitive, and nurturing (left figure), while boys develop traits of being independent, controlling, and dominant (right figure) (Eckes & Trautner, 2000). These differences in gender traits are explained by two different theories.

concerned
sensitive
nurturing

According to *social role theory*, the expectations of parents, peers, and others *reward* or *discourage* different gender roles and behaviors for boys and girls. According to *cognitive developmental theory*, children acquire gender schemas or *cognitive rules* that indicate which gender roles and behaviors are right or wrong for boys and girls. Notice that each of these theories focuses on different factors in developing gender-role differences. The social role theory focuses on boys and girls learning different gender roles and behaviors because of outside pressures from society. In comparison, cognitive developmental theory focuses on boys and girls developing different gender roles and behaviors because of inside pressures from acquiring personal rules. Thus, these two theories are not mutually exclusive but rather emphasize different factors in the development of gender-role differences and behaviors (Eckes & Trautner, 2000).

independent
controlling
dominant

We'll discuss how differences in gender traits have important influences on personal, social, and career choices.

### Questions about Gender Differences

*Are There Gender Differences in Career Choices?*

As boys and girls grow into men and women, gender roles are further strengthened by pressures from parents, peers, and society and result in stereotypic ways for men and women to think about appropriate behaviors, social interactions, and career choices (Eckes & Trautner, 2000). For example, until the early 1990s, gender roles for women did not include careers in law enforcement, armed forces, or management of large corporations, while gender roles for men did not include careers as nurses, secretaries, or elementary school teachers. However, beginning in the early 1990s, gender roles began to change so that men and especially women were given more flexibility and freedom in making job and career choices. As a result of changes in gender roles, men and especially women have more career opportunities open to them than ever before. (But, is the United States ready for a female president?)

*Are There Gender Differences in Aggression?*

Is there any truth to the common belief that males are more aggressive than females? Researchers find that, from the age of 2 through college age, males tend to show more rough-and-tumble play, to display more aggressive physical and verbal behavior, and to commit about four times more delinquent or antisocial acts than girls. Reasons for gender differences in aggression include both biological and psychological influences. Studies on identical twins indicate that genetic factors account for about 50% of aggressive behavior, which suggests a biological basis for boys being more aggressive than girls (Cadoret et al., 1997). Although biological factors are estimated to account for 50% of aggressive behavior, the remaining 50% is due to psychosocial influences. For example, researchers found that parents, peers, and society reward boys for acting out, being competitive, and settling their conflicts with fighting. In comparison, "nice girls" don't fight and tend to settle conflicts through talking (Coie & Dodge, 1998). As a result of these biological and psychosocial influences, the gender role for males encourages aggressive behavior and helps explain why the majority of aggressive acts, both social and criminal, are committed by males (Halpern, 2000).

*Are There Gender Differences in Cognitive Abilities?*

There is a long history of viewing women as less intellectually bright, which was an argument men used to deny women the right to vote. No differences between men and women have been found on tests of general intelligence; however, there are sex differences in tests of specific cognitive abilities. For example, women generally score higher on tests of word fluency (p. 84), word memory, and reading and writing comprehension. In comparison, men generally score higher on tests of mathematical problem solving, mental rotation of objects (p. 84), and mechanical reasoning (Halpern, 2000).

In studying why women are generally better at processing words, scientists found that women process language by using both sides of their brains, while men use only the left side (right figure) (Shaywitz et al., 1995). This study suggests that sex differences in some cognitive abilities, such as processing language, come from biological differences in how male and female brains function.

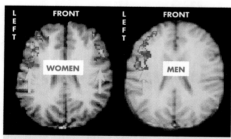

MRI scans show women process language using both sides of the brain.

*Conclusion*

Some researchers argue that most gender differences are relatively small and have little practical significance (Hyde, 1994). Others argue that there are some medium to large gender differences (aggression) that suggest real male and female differences (Eagly, 1995a). However, all researchers warn that gender differences, no matter how large they may be, do not indicate that one gender is better or smarter than the other. Gender-role differences indicate only that sexes are different and that any difference should not be used as the basis for discrimination (Halpern, 2000).

**What's going on?**

We have discussed how during infancy and childhood there are amazing increases in sensory abilities and motor skills and wondrous development of emotions, cognitive skills, social interactions, and gender roles. We'll briefly review and summmarize these changes so that you can see the big picture of infant and child development.

6 months old          10 months old          1 year old          3 years old

## 1  NEWBORNS' ABILITIES

Newborns come with more sensory and perceptual abilities than previously thought. They have a well-developed sense of touch, show an innate preference for sweet and salt, and recognize (smell) their mothers' odors. In a few more months, infants can recognize their mothers' faces, produce speech sounds, perceive depth, and have a basic concept of addition. This new and improved version of infants' abilities better explains how they discover the world.

## 2  MOTOR DEVELOPMENT

Infants gradually acquire the **coordinated movements** that they need to crawl, sit, stand, and walk. Many motor skills occur in a set sequence called **maturation** that is regulated by genetic programming. Two principles for motor development are that parts closest to the center of the body develop first—the **proximodistal** principle—and parts closer to the head develop first—the **cephalocaudal** principle. With motor development comes the ability to get up and explore.

## 3  EMOTIONAL DEVELOPMENT

"Good" babies and "difficult" babies show signs of differences in temperament, which is largely influenced by genetic factors. **Temperament** refers to stable differences in attention, arousal, and reaction to new situations; it also affects level of arousal and the development of emotional behaviors. Infants develop many **emotions,** which allow a wide range of wordless communication with the parent and the world. Infants form a close emotional bond with parents (caregiver). This emotional bond, which is called **attachment,** is thought to influence the development of future emotional and social behaviors.

## 4  COGNITIVE DEVELOPMENT

One theory of cognitive development is **Piaget's theory,** which says that children play an active role in cognitive development by incorporating new information into existing knowledge **(assimilation)** or changing existing knowledge through experience **(accommodation).** Children pass through four different cognitive stages—**(1) sensorimotor, (2) preoperational, (3) concrete operations,** and **(4) formal operations**—in that order but at different rates. With each stage, the child adds a new and qualitatively different kind of thinking or reasoning skill that helps the child make better sense of the world.

## 5  SOCIAL DEVELOPMENT

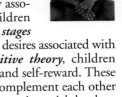

At the same time that children are developing emotionally and cognitively, they are also developing socially. **Freud** said that children develop socially by going through five **psychosexual stages** and that during the first three stages, the individual seeks pleasure from different areas of the body associated with sexual feelings. **Erikson** said that children develop socially by going through eight **psychosocial stages** during which an individual's primary goal is to satisfy desires associated with social needs. According to **Bandura's social cognitive theory,** children develop social skills through imitation, observation, and self-reward. These three theories are not mutually exclusive but rather complement each other by focusing on different factors believed to be important in social development. Freud's is the only theory that says the first five years are critical.

## 6  IMPORTANCE OF CHILDHOOD

How important are events that occur during childhood? In some cases, traumatic events (poverty, parental disinterest) result in later behavioral and social problems, but in other cases, a loving, supportive parent or caregiver compensates for early problems, which results in a resilient child. Although childhood may be an important time for emotional, social, and personality development, both positive and negative personality and social changes continue into middle adulthood.

After the Concept Review we'll examine an interesting and related question: Do children from very different cultures acquire similar or different gender roles and behaviors?

# Concept Review

**1.** The question that asks how much genetic factors and how much environmental factors contribute to a person's biological, emotional, cognitive, personal, and social development is called the _____ question.

**2.** The prenatal period, which begins at conception and ends at birth, is composed of three different stages. The first stage of prenatal development refers to the two-week period following conception; this is called the (a)_____ stage. The second stage of the prenatal period spans the 2–8 weeks that follow conception; this is called the (b)_____ stage. The third stage of the prenatal period begins two months after conception and lasts until birth; this is called the (c)_____ stage.

**3.** The organ that connects the blood supply of the mother to that of the fetus is called the (a)_____, which acts as a filter. However, some agents, such as drugs, viruses, and chemicals, pass into the fetal blood supply and harm the developing fetus; these agents are called (b)_____. One example of these agents is alcohol, which if drunk heavily during pregnancy can result in a combination of physical changes and mental retardation called (c)_____.

**4.** Newborns have some visual acuity, respond to touch, and are able to hear, smell, and taste. This indicates that they have relatively well-developed _____.

**5.** The acquisition of the muscular control necessary for coordinated physical activity, which is called (a)_____ development, follows two general principles. The principle that parts of the body closer to the head develop before parts closer to the feet is the (b)_____ principle. The principle that parts closer to the center of the infant's body develop before parts farther away is the (c)_____ principle. Development of motor skills occurs in a sequential and orderly fashion because of a genetic plan; this process is called (d)_____.

**6.** An individual's stable pattern of behavioral and emotional reactions that appear early and are influenced in large part by genetic factors is called his or her _____.

**7.** The close fundamental emotional bond that develops between the infant and his or her parent or caregiver is called (a)_____. Infants who use their parent as a safe home base from which they can wander off and explore their environments are said to have formed a (b)_____ attachment. Infants who avoid or show ambivalence toward their parents are said to have formed an (c)_____ attachment.

**8.** Piaget believed that children are actively involved in understanding their world through two basic processes: incorporating new information or experience into existing knowledge is called (a)_____; changing existing knowledge or experience as a result of assimilating some new information is called (b)_____.

**9.** Piaget's theory of cognitive development includes four stages, each of which is characterized by the development of particular kinds of reasoning. The first stage, during which infants learn about their environments by relating their sensory experiences (such as hearing and seeing) to their motor actions, is called the (a)_____ stage. The second stage, during which infants learn to use symbols to think about things that are not present and to help them solve simple problems, is called the (b)_____ stage. The third stage, during which children learn to perform a number of logical mental operations on objects that are physically present, is called the (c)_____ stage. The fourth stage, during which adolescents and adults develop the ability to think about and solve abstract problems in a logical manner, is called the (d)_____ stage.

**10.** According to Freud's theory of social development, children go through five developmental periods, which he called _____ stages. During these stages, a child's primary goal is to satisfy desires associated with innate biological needs.

**11.** According to Albert Bandura's social cognitive theory, we learn social skills through _____, _____, and self–reward.

**12.** According to Erik Erikson, a person goes through eight developmental periods during which the primary goal is to satisfy desires associated with social needs. Each of these eight periods is called a _____ stage, during which the person works to resolve a potential problem.

***Answers:*** *1. nature-nurture; 2. (a) germinal, (b) embryonic, (c) fetal; 3. (a) placenta, (b) teratogens, (c) fetal alcohol syndrome; 4. senses; 5. (a) motor, (b) cephalocaudal, (c) proximodistal, (d) maturation; 6. temperament; 7. (a) attachment, (b) secure, (c) insecure; 8. (a) assimilation, (b) accommodation; 9. (a) sensorimotor, (b) preoperational, (c) concrete operations, (d) formal operations; 10. psychosexual; 11. observation, imitation; 12. psychosocial*

## Identifying Gender Roles

**Do cultures have different gender roles?**

Although we know that young boys and girls acquire different gender roles, the intriguing question is, Why do little boys generally grow up to be more aggressive and independent, while little girls grow up to be less aggressive and more nurturing? To answer this question, researchers tested hundreds of 5-, 8-, and 11-year-old children in 24 countries to find out if young children from so many different cultures developed similar or different male–female gender roles and behaviors (Williams & Best, 1990).

> **1.** One of these people is a very affectionate person. When they like someone, they hug and kiss them a lot. Which person likes to hug and kiss a lot?

For younger children (5- and 8-year-olds), researchers told 32 brief stories and then asked whether the person in the story was more like a man or a woman; an example is given on the left. For older children (11-year-olds), researchers gave a list of 300 adjectives, such as aggressive, affectionate, calm, bossy, sensitive, loud, and helpful, and asked which adjectives were more likely to be associated with males and which with females. Unlike 5- and 8-year-old children, 11-year-olds were able to understand the meanings of the adjectives and indicate their preferences by checking off adjectives that they thought best suited males or females.

## Gender Roles across Cultures

**Similarities.** Researchers found that across the 24 countries, relatively young children showed remarkable similarities in the characteristics that they associated with gender roles.

About 57% of 5-year-old children made stereotyped responses about gender roles by associating people in the stories with a particular sex, either male or female. For example, 5-year-old children associated being strong, aggressive, and dominant with males, while they associated being gentle and affectionate with females. Eight-year-old children had learned even more stereotypic behaviors. They associated being weak, emotional, appreciative, excitable, gentle, softhearted, meek, and submissive with females, while they associated being disorderly, cruel, coarse, adventurous, independent, ambitious, loud, and boastful with males (see photos). By the age of 11, the percentage of children who made stereotyped responses about gender roles jumped to 90%.

Strong, aggressive, dominant, independent, coarse, loud, boastful

Emotional, appreciative, excitable, gentle, submissive

**Differences.** Researchers also found that across countries and cultures, interesting differences occurred in children's perceptions of gender roles. For example, in Germany, children associated being adventurous, confident, jolly, and steady with females, while in most other countries, these characteristics were typically associated with males.

In Japan, children associated being dominant and steady with females, while in other countries, these characteristics were typically associated with males.

**Conclusions.** Researchers concluded that children in 24 different countries and cultures developed knowledge of gender roles relatively early and showed remarkable similarities in choosing different gender roles and behaviors for males and females. Although there were some differences due to cultural values, there were generally more similarities in male–female gender roles across the 24 countries (Williams & Best, 1990).

## Two Answers

We began with the question, Why do little boys generally grow up to be more aggressive and independent, while little girls grow up to be less aggressive and more nuturing? To this we add another question, Why do little boys and little girls from 24 different countries and cultures develop such similar male–female gender roles? There are two different but somewhat complementary answers.

The **social role theory (discussed earlier, p. 396)**, which emphasizes social and cultural influences, states that gender differences between males and females arise from different divisions of labor.

According to social role theory, male–female gender differences developed from traditional cultural divisions of labor, in which women were childbearers and homemakers, while men were providers and protectors (Eagly et al., 2000). Because men and women performed different duties, men and women were under different social-cultural pressures to develop different gender roles. Another answer comes from a relatively new theory.

The **evolutionary theory**, which emphasizes genetic and biological forces, says that current gender differences are a continuation of the behaviors that evolved from early men and women who adapted these different behaviors in their attempts to survive the problems of their time.

According to evolutionary theory, men increased their chances for reproduction by being dominant, controlling, and aggressive. In comparison, women increased their chances of raising their children by being concerned, sensitive, and nurturing. According to evolutionary theory, the current male–female gender differences arise from genetic and biological forces that evolved from an ancient set of mating patterns that had initially helped the species survive (Buss, 1999).

Because social role theory emphasizes cultural influences and evolutionary theory emphasizes genetic and biological forces, researchers suggest that by combining the two theories we can better explain the development of our current male–female gender differences (Baldwin & Baldwin, 1997).

**What was her terrible secret?**

The family had all the trappings of being perfect, including wealth, status, and prestige.

**Father.** The father was a handsome, intelligent man who served as president of the Denver Area Boy Scout Council and helped establish Denver's Cleo Wallace Village for Handicapped Children. He was a millionaire socialite and a pillar of the Denver community.

**Mother.** The mother was a good homemaker, who spent all of her time caring for her four children, all girls.

**Marilyn.** Marilyn was the youngest daughter and described as a golden-haired beauty. In college she was a straight-A student and a swimming champion. At the age of 20, she was crowned Miss America (left photo).

**The secret.** Marilyn had been sexually abused by her father from the time she was 5 until she was 18, when she moved away to college. However, Marilyn had completely repressed any knowledge of sexual abuse by her father until she was 24 (repressed memories are discussed on pages 250–251). She was having a conversation with a former youth minister at her church when she broke down and told her painful secret. She made the minister promise not to tell anyone except her fiancé, who was very sympathetic and understanding, and her oldest sister, who said, "Oh, no! I thought I was the only one" (van Derbur Atler, 1991, p. 91).

At 20, she was crowned Miss America.

**Dealing with abuse.** Marilyn says that she didn't tell anyone because she didn't want to destroy her family and was afraid her father would go to jail. Thus, she kept her secret and survived by splitting into a day child who seemed normal and happy and a night child who feared her father and suffered his abuse.

**Facing the abuser.** When Marilyn was 40 years old, the sight of her own 5-year-old daughter triggered terrible memories of her father's abuse and gave her frightening physical symptoms. She knew that her misery would remain until she confronted her father. She met and talked to him for 20 minutes. He did not deny anything and said, "If I had known what this would do to you, I never would have done it" (van Derbur Atler, 1991, p. 94).

**Aftermath.** At 47, Marilyn van Derbur was named the Outstanding Woman Speaker in America. But she was having terrible bouts of anxiety and couldn't continue her career. Finally, she told her mother about being abused and spent the next seven years in therapy. At 54, Marilyn (right photo) stood before the Adult Incest Survivors Group and publicly revealed her secret: She had been abused for 13 years by her father. Her goal now is to help others who have been abused.

At 24, she remembered being sexually abused by her father.

Marilyn was a victim of one kind of child abuse, sexual abuse. There are several kinds of child abuse.

---

### Kinds of Abuse

**How many children suffer abuse?**

In the Unites States, about 1.4 million children a year suffer some form of child abuse (Pizarro & Billick, 1999). In 1997, there were 1,300 deaths confirmed to have resulted from abuse, and of these, 85% were children under the age of 5.

*Child abuse and neglect* (physical and emotional) result from inadequate care or acts of the parent that put the child in danger, cause physical harm or injury, or involve sexual molestation.

As the graph below shows, the most common abuse is neglect (60%), followed in order by physical abuse and sexual abuse. The "other" category includes emotional neglect and other kinds of abuse that do not easily fit into any category.

The second most frequently confirmed kind of child abuse (23%) is *physical abuse.* For example, Karen, who was 10 years old, vividly remembered how much and how often her mother beat her. Her

Every year in the USA, about 1.4 million children suffer abuse.

mother would get angry over the tiniest things, grab something handy (shoes, father's belt, potato masher), and start hitting her. One time her mother beat her so hard that Karen's legs turned black and blue. When Karen threatened to tell the police, her mother replied in an angry voice, "Go ahead. They won't believe you and they'll put you in the darkest prison" (*Time,* September 5, 1983).

The third most frequently confirmed kind of child abuse (9%) is *sexual abuse.* For example, Marilyn's case shows that very often the abuser is the father or stepfather and that many children are too fearful of the abuser to report their maltreatment. Surveys of sexual abuse in 21 different countries indicate that 7–36% of women and 3–29% of men have been sexually abused; females are 2–3 times more likely to suffer abuse than males (Emery & Laumann-Billings, 1998). This indicates that sexual abuse, which may result in serious long-term behavioral, social, and personality problems, is an international problem.

We'll focus on three questions related to abuse and neglect: Who abuses children? What problems do abused children suffer? How are abusive parents helped?

**Kinds of Child Abuse**

| | |
|---|---|
| Neglect | 60% |
| Physical abuse | 23% |
| Sexual abuse | 9% |
| Other | 8% |

Source: National Committee to Prevent Child Abuse

**What are the parents' problems?**

Parents who abuse their children are likely to have low self-esteem and a wide range of personal problems. They are apt to be impulsive, anxious, defensive, aggressive, and socially isolated. Often, serious marital problems add to their numerous life stresses (Emery & Laumann-Billings, 1998). Studies show that about 60% of *physical* abuse is committed by mothers and about 90% of *sexual* abuse is committed by fathers or stepfathers (Miller, 1995). In addition, about 30% of abused children become parents who abuse their own children (Kaufman & Zigler, 1989).

Although an abused child is at risk for becoming an abusive parent, a number of *compensatory factors* can prevent this from happening. These compensatory factors include having a positive attachment to a caregiver, resolving not to repeat the abuse, having an awareness of one's early abusive experiences, experiencing fewer stressful life events than the abusive parents did, and having a supportive spouse or good social support. The path from being abused to becoming an abusive parent is neither direct nor fixed and can be reversed by these compensatory factors (Belsky, 1993).

A child's characteristics can also increase or decrease the chances of being abused. For example, a fussy, irritable, dependent, sickly, or physically handicapped child is more difficult to care for if the parents have personal problems of their own (Knutson, 1995). The interaction between a difficult child and troubled parents illustrates the principle of bidirectionality (Maccoby, 1984).

The *principle of bidirectionality* says that a child's behaviors influence how his or her parents respond, and in turn the parents' behaviors influence how the child responds.

According to this principle, child abuse results from an interaction between a child's difficult traits, which tend to elicit maltreatment or abuse from the parents, and the parents' social-emotional and caregiving problems, which make it difficult for them to recognize and meet the needs of their child (Miller, 1995). Thus, the combination of a difficult child and parents who have their own personal or drug-related problems results in a potentially explosive parent–child interaction that increases the risk for child abuse. Abused children can develop a variety of problems.

Children who suffer sexual abuse have physical and psychological problems.

## What Problems Do Abused Children Have?

**Are there long-term problems?**

Children who suffer abuse may experience a number of physical and psychological problems. The *physical problems* include stomachaches, headaches, bedwetting, and abnormal hormonal changes that indicate their systems are trying to deal with large doses of stress (Yehuda, 2000). Abused children also suffer a number of *psychological problems,* which include increased anxiety, social withdrawal, delays in social, cognitive, and emotional development, poor school performance, attention problems, and fearful nightmares.

When abused children become teenagers, they may experience continuing problems, such as having poor self-esteem, more depression, loneliness, and suicidal impulses, more conflicts with friends, and more delinquent behaviors. Thus, child abuse may result in many psychological and physiological problems, some of which may persist for some time (Davis & Petretic-Jackson, 2000).

Long-term or longitudinal studies on sexually abused children report that within 12–18 months after sexual abuse stopped, 55–65% of children showed a substantial decrease in symptoms, but 10–24% appeared to get worse. Those children who showed the best recovery were those who received strong support and care from their mothers (Saywitz et al., 2000).

## How Are Abusive Parents Helped?

**How can abusive parents be changed?**

Treatment for abusive parents focuses on solving their personal and marital problems and improving their child-rearing skills. A number of therapy programs that use some combination of cognitive-behavior therapy (Module 25) and parent-training programs (Module 10) have proven relatively successful in decreasing child abuse. In general, these programs have at least two goals (Peterson & Brown, 1994).

**1. Overcoming the parent's personal problems.** Abusive parents need help in learning about and developing social relationships, which are needed for positive bonding and attachment between parent and child. Abusive parents also need training in basic caregiving skills, which involves learning how to meet the physical, social, and emotional needs of their children. Dealing with abusive parents' personal or drug problems usually requires long-term professional therapy. As parents get their personal or marital problems under control, they can concentrate on improving their interactions with their child.

**2. Changing parent–child interactions.** Researchers have found that abusive parents are less likely to use positive behaviors such as smiling, praising, and touching and are more likely to use negative behaviors such as threatening, disapproving, and showing anger when dealing with their child (Reid et al., 1981). This means that abusive parents need to learn more positive ways of interacting with their children. Parent-training programs, which use behavior modification techniques (discussed in Module 10), are effective in helping parents learn to reduce negative interactions with their children (Kolko, 1995).

Clinicians and researchers recognize that, in many countries, neglect, physical abuse, and sexual abuse are serious social problems that deserve more attention and treatment than they currently receive (Emery & Laumann-Billings, 1998).

# Summary Test

## A. PRENATAL INFLUENCES

**1.** The time from conception to birth is called the (a)_____ period, which is divided into three parts. The two-week period that immediately follows conception is called the (b)_____ period; it is marked by the zygote dividing into many cells. The period that includes the 2–8 weeks after conception, during which cells continue to divide and begin to differentiate into bone, muscle, and body organs, is called the (c)_____ period. The period of development that begins two months after conception and lasts for about seven months is called the (d)_____ period. At the end of this period, birth occurs and the fetus becomes a newborn.

Placenta

Umbilical cord

**2.** The development of the fetus can be interrupted or damaged by a variety of toxic agents, called (a)_____, which cause malformation of the brain or body and result in birth defects. For example, heavy drinking during pregnancy can cause a combination of physical and psychological deficits called (b)_____, which is the leading known cause of mental retardation in the United States.

## B. NEWBORNS' ABILITIES

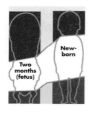

Two months (fetus)

New-born

**3.** The newborn comes into the world with relatively well-developed sensory and perceptual responses. For example, the newborn can see, but his or her ability to see details, which is called (a)_____, is poor. Six-month-old infants will not crawl off the visual cliff, indicating that they have developed (b)_____ perception. Newborns have good hearing, touch, and smell and an inherited preference for sweet and salt tastes.

**4.** Motor development, which is the acquisition of the muscle control required for coordinated physical activity, follows two general principles. The principle that parts of the body closer to the head develop before those closer to the feet is called the (a)_____ principle. The principle that parts closer to the center of the body develop before those farther away is called the (b)_____ principle.

**5.** Development that occurs in a sequential and orderly fashion because of a genetic plan is called (a)_____. The average age at which individuals perform various kinds of motor skills or exhibit abilities or behaviors is reflected in (b)_____.

## C. EMOTIONAL DEVELOPMENT

**6.** Early and stable individual differences in attention, arousal, and reaction to new things refer to an infant's _____, which is greatly influenced by genetic, or inherited, factors.

**7.** Newborns have a limited range of emotional expressions that include interest, startle, distress, disgust, and neonatal smile. During the first two years, infants develop a wide range of _____ expressions and feelings that signal the infant's physiological needs and psychological moods.

**8.** The close emotional bond that develops between infant and parent (caregiver) is called (a)_____. As the infant develops a closer attachment to her parents, she also shows more distress when her parents leave; this distress is called (b)_____.

**9.** There are two kinds of attachment. Infants who use their caregiver as a safe home base from which they can wander off and explore their environments are said to be (a)_____ attached. This kind of attachment may contribute to better emotional bonds later in life. Infants who avoid or show ambivalence toward their caregivers are said to be (b)_____ attached. For example, these infants may cling and want to be held one minute but squirm and push away the next minute.

## D. RESEARCH FOCUS: TEMPERAMENT

Age   2        7

**10.** Researchers use two different methods to study developmental processes. Repeatedly studying the same group of individuals at different ages is using the (a)_____ method. Studying different groups of individuals who are of different ages is using the (b)_____ method.

**11.** Researchers estimate that about 10–15% of the general population show reluctance, anxiety, or fear and increased physiological arousal when in a strange or novel situation. These individuals are called shy or _____. This finding supports the idea that temperaments appear early, are stable across time, and are partially under genetic control (nature).

## E. COGNITIVE DEVELOPMENT

**12.** Piaget believed that children participate in their own cognitive development by active involvement through two different processes: incorporating new information or experiences into existing knowledge is called (a)_____; and changing one's knowledge or experiences as a result of assimilating some new information is called (b)_____.

**13.** Piaget divided cognitive development into four stages. In the first, lasting from birth to about age 2, infants interact with and learn about their environments by relating their sensory experiences to their motor actions; this is called the (a)_____ stage. A significant development of this stage is the concept that objects or events continue to exist even if they cannot be heard, touched, or seen; this is called (b)_____.

**14.** In the second stage, lasting from the age of about 2 to 7, children learn to use symbols to think about things that are not present and to help solve simple problems; this is the (a)_____ stage. A limitation in this stage is the tendency to think of the world only from one's own viewpoint, called (b)_____ thinking.

**15.** The third stage, which lasts from the age of about 7 to 11, is called the (a)_____ stage. During this stage, children can perform a number of logical mental operations on concrete objects (ones that are physically present). The idea that the amount of a substance remains the same even in different shapes, known as (b)_____, is mastered during the third stage.

**16.** During the fourth and last stage, which lasts from about age 12 through adulthood, the individual develops the ability to think about and solve abstract problems logically; this is called the (a)_____ stage. Each of Piaget's cognitive stages is thought to be qualitatively different from the previous one because each new stage represents the development of some new (b)_____ ability.

## F. SOCIAL DEVELOPMENT

**17.** How a person develops social relationships, develops a sense of self, and becomes a social being is called (a)_____ development. Three theories of such development each emphasize a different aspect. According to Freud, a person goes through five developmental periods, called (b)_____ stages, during which the primary goal is to satisfy innate biological needs. In contrast, Erikson divided development into eight developmental periods, in which the primary goal is to satisfy social needs; he called these (c)_____ stages. Bandura emphasizes the importance of learning through imitation, observation, and reinforcement; this is called (d)_____ theory.

**18.** Freud's five psychosexual stages are called the (a)_____, (b)_____, (c)_____, (d)_____, and (e)_____ stages. Freud believed that the first five years leave a lasting impression on the individual's personality and social development.

**19.** The first five of Erikson's eight stages involve the resolution of a potential social problem between the child and his or her environment. In stage 1, the infant deals with resolving issues surrounding trust versus (a)_____. In stage 2, the toddler must resolve issues surrounding autonomy versus shame and (b)_____. In

stage 3, the younger child deals with issues of initiative versus (c)_____. In stage 4, the older child deals with issues that involve industry versus (d)_____. In stage 5, the adolescent deals with issues that involve identity versus (e)_____.

**20.** Early psychological difficulties increase a child's (a)_____, which in turn increases the risk for developing later social or personality problems. However, certain emotional traits, family factors, and outside emotional support help a child overcome early problems and are said to help make the child (b)_____ and thus develop normal social behaviors.

**21.** Expectations of how we should think or behave because we are male or female are called (a)_____. One theory says that these roles develop because parents or caregivers expect, treat, and reward different kinds of behaviors depending on the child's sex; this is the (b)_____ theory. Another theory says that children learn rules for male or female behavior through active involvement with their environments; this is the (c)_____ theory.

## G. CULTURAL DIVERSITY: GENDER ROLES

**22.** Although children's perceptions of gender roles show some variation across countries and cultures, it appears that their _____ of gender roles develops in a generally similar way at similar times.

## H. APPLICATION: CHILD ABUSE

**23.** Inadequate care, neglect, or acts of the parent that put the child in danger or that cause physical harm or injury or involve sexual molestation compose the definition of (a)_____. According to the principle of (b)_____, the child's behaviors influence how the parents respond and the parents' behaviors influence how the child responds. Two goals of treatment to stop or prevent child abuse are to help parents overcome their (c)_____ problems and to change parent–child interactions from negative to positive.

*Answers:* 1. (a) prenatal, (b) germinal, (c) embryonic, (d) fetal; 2. (a) teratogens, (b) fetal alcohol syndrome (FAS); 3. (a) visual acuity, (b) depth; 4. (a) cephalocaudal, (b) proximodistal; 5. (a) maturation, (b) developmental norms; 6. temperament; 7. emotional; 8. attachment, (b) separation anxiety; 9. (a) securely, (b) insecurely; 10. (a) longitudinal, (b) cross-sectional; 11. inhibited; 12. (a) assimilation, (b) accommodation; 13. (a) sensorimotor, (b) object permanence; 14. (a) preoperational, (b) egocentric; 15. (a) concrete operations, (b) conservation; 16. (a) formal operations, (b) reasoning or thinking; 17. (a) social, (b) psychosexual, (c) psychosocial, (d) social cognitive; 18. (a) oral, (b) anal, (c) phallic, (d) latent, (e) genital; 19. (a) mistrust, (b) doubt, (c) guilt, (d) inferiority, (e) role confusion; 20. (a) vulnerability, (b) resilient; 21. (a) gender roles, (b) social role, (c) cognitive developmental; 22. knowledge; 23. (a) child abuse, (b) bidirectionality, (c) personal

# Critical Thinking

## Can an Angry Child Be Changed?

*by Michael Ryan*

### Questions

**1.** What are some of the reasons these children developed into emotionally troubled individuals?

**2.** Why don't teachers just punish a bad or disruptive child every time he or she behaves badly in school?

**3.** What can happen if an angry parent uses harsh spanking to control a misbehaving child?

"There are some children you become familiar with before you ever teach them," Janet Johnson told me. After nearly 20 years as a first-grade teacher at Chadwell Elementary School in Nashville, Johnson knows when trouble is coming. "You hear their names repeatedly," she said. "These are the children that other teachers have given up on. They're angry, they're self-centered. They do poor in school."

Chadwell Elementary School is participating in a research project to see if children at risk for developing chronic aggressive problems—such as bullying, truancy, or other angry, disruptive behavior——can be identified and changed before their lives go irretrievably wrong.

The project, called Fast Track, is an intervention program that first identifies children at failing in school and at risk for becoming aggressive and disruptive because of parental violence in the home. Then, teachers intervene to change the child's poor social and academic behaviors.

Special training sessions were set up for all teachers so they could learn how to help their students deal with anger, aggression, sharing, and getting along with each other. "We start very basically," explained Taylor Martin, a specially trained teacher who has worked with

children at risk. "The rules are: No fighting, no hitting, no putdowns, and listen to the teachers." Students soon learn that their disruptive behaviors result in lack of attention, while their good behaviors are rewarded.

The program also involved parental training. "I had one parent who had absolutely no communication with her child," Davis recalled. "The best she could do was say, 'Get over here and sit down'—that sort of thing. We do a lot of role-playing and talking about how the parent should relate to the child."

The program, now in its sixth year, has some promising results. When Fast Track began in Nashville, all the at-risk children were in regular kindergarten classes. By the fourth grade, 40% of the at-risk children who had received no special help were doing poorly and had been placed into special education classes. However, only 23% of the at-risk children given the intervention program were in special education classes. These results suggest that the Fast Track program helps at-risk kids to a better future. (Adapted from "An Angry Child Can Change" by Michael Ryan, *Parade,* April 14, 1996, pp. 20–21. Copyright © 1996 by *Parade.* Reprinted by permission of Parade and Scovil, Chichak & Galen Literary Agency on behalf of the author.)

**4.** Is the intervention program the teachers are using an example of classical conditioning (p. 198) or operant conditioning using behavior modification (p. 232)?

**5.** Which theory says that what parents expect and how they reward different behaviors of boys and girls lead to the development of the "right" gender roles?

**6.** Is this intervention program an example of doing an experiment (p. 36) or looking for a correlation (p. 32)?

*Try InfoTrac to search for terms:* anger in children; agression in children.

---

### Suggested answers to Newspaper Article questions

1. These emotionally troubled children may have started life as difficult babies, who are more likely to develop serious emotional problems. Freud might say they were fixated at the oral stage and Erikson might say they may not have solved the problem of trust versus mistrust.
2. Although the use of punishment (p. 233) can decrease undesired behaviors, it can also produce undesirable effects, such as increasing antisocial behaviors in other settings.
3. A parent who uses harsh punishment to control an aggressive child may actually increase aggression because the child may imitate the aggressive acts of the parent in other settings (school).
4. This intervention program is primarily an example of operant conditioning—when used to change human behavior, it's called

behavior modification. Behavior modification teaches the child that his or her behaviors are followed by rewards or punishments, such as time-outs (p. 233).
5. The social role theory emphasizes how the parents' expectations and rewarding of certain behaviors lead to boys and girls developing different gender roles.
6. This intervention program is an example of doing an experiment in the field. Researchers evaluated the effects of a treatment or intervention program (independent variable) on behaviors of at-risk children (dependent variable).

# Links to Learning

### Web Sites

● WADSWORTH ONLINE
STUDY CENTER
**http://psychology.wadsworth.com**
Quizzes, learning activities and exercises, a discussion forum, and hot links to Internet sites related to sensation, including:

● OBSTETRICS ULTRASOUND
**http://www.ob-ultrasound.net**
At this site you can survey fetal development in ultrasound images of each stage. Also included are text, sound, graphics, and links to related sites.

● CLASSIC THEORIES OF CHILD
DEVELOPMENT
**http://idealist.com/children/cdw.html**
This site is a great place to review the theoris of Margaret Mahler, Sigmund Freud, and Erik Erikson. Click on a child's age in months from birth to 3 years to call up each theorist's analysis of the specific developmental stage.

● CHILD ABUSE YELLOW PAGES
**http://www.idealist.com/cayp**
Here are more than 300 current (1996–2000) annotated links to child abuse resources on the Web.

● BOOKS ILLUSTRATING NONTRADITIONAL
GENDER ROLES
**http://fuji.acpl.lib.in.us/Childrens_Services/
gender.html**
This list, prepared at an Indiana library, is a great source of books for liberated kids. Print it and use it as a guide when you're looking for something special to share with a child.

### Learning Activities

● *POWERSTUDY™ BY ROD PLOTNIK & TOM DOYLE*

**PowerStudy™**

**Check out CD: Module 17**
CD section 3.A: Overview: Human Brain; book
page 382
CD section 3.B: Neuron: Structure and Function;
book page 382
CD section 4.A: Genes and Evolution; book
page 380
CD section 4.G: Research Focus: Sex Differences
in the Brain?; book page 397

● *STUDY GUIDE TO ACCOMPANY INTRODUCTION TO
PSYCHOLOGY, 6TH EDITION,* **by Matthew Enos**
In Module 17, try to decide whether infants are helpless or competent, ponder the insoluble nature-nurture question, and re-examine the popular belief that childhood is a happy time.

● *WEBTUTOR*
**http://webtutor.thomsonlearning.com**
**WebTUTOR** Visit this site for interactive versions of the Study Guide feature. Take a quiz, get your score—should you study a topic some more, or can you move on? For example, what is the visual cliff? Does Piaget mean surgery when he talks about "operation"?

● *INFOTRAC ONLINE LIBRARY*
**http://www.infotrac-college.com**

Use your password and then key in search terms such as those below to find poular and scientific articles on subjects covered in Module 17. Make the library work for you!

Developmental psychology    Fetal alcohol syndrome (FAS)
Gender roles                Maturation
Resilience                  Temperament

● *PSYCHNOW!*
CD for Macintosh and Windows includes a study guide, glossary, Web sites, and animations. For Module 17, see:
   • Infant Development          • Child Development

## Study Questions

*Use InfoTrac to search for topics mentioned in the main heads below (e.g., prenatal influences, cognitive development, child abuse).*

*A. **Prenatal Influences**—A pregnant woman asks, "Why do I have to worry about ingesting chemicals, since my unborn child has a separate blood supply?" What is your response? (**Suggested answer p. 630**)

B. **Newborns' Abilities**—A father gives his infant son practice in walking so that the boy will develop early and grow up to be a professional track star. Will this early practice help?

C. **Emotional Development**—"Parents, stop worrying—emotions depend on genes, not discipline." Is this headline statement correct?

*D. **Research Focus: Temperament**—Marcie and Jeff love their 6-month-old son but find that he is easily irritated and frightened. What should they do? (**Suggested answer p. 630**)

E. **Cognitive Development**—Why is it that a 1-year-old child likes to play the game of peek-a-boo but a 7-year-old thinks it is silly?

*F. **Social Development**—How would Freud's and Erikson's theories apply to a 3-year-old child whose parents are getting divorced? (**Suggested answer p. 631**)

G. **Cultural Diversity: Gender Roles**—Why do you think that young boys and girls around the world develop relatively similar gender roles?

H. **Application: Child Abuse**—If one were abused as a child, what kinds of problems might one face as a parent?

*These questions are answered in Appendix B.

# Module 18: Adolescence & Adulthood

**A. Puberty & Sexual Behavior**  408
* GIRLS DURING PUBERTY
* BOYS DURING PUBERTY
* ADOLESCENTS: SEXUALLY MATURE

**B. Cognitive & Emotional Changes**  410
* DEFINITION
* PIAGET'S COGNITIVE STAGES: CONTINUED
* BRAIN DEVELOPMENT: REASON AND EMOTION
* KOHLBERG'S THEORY OF MORAL REASONING
* PARENTING STYLES AND EFFECTS
* ADOLESCENCE: BIG PICTURE
* BEYOND ADOLESCENCE

**C. Personality & Social Changes**  416
* DEFINITION
* DEVELOPMENT OF SELF-ESTEEM
* ADULTHOOD: ERIKSON'S PSYCHOSOCIAL STAGES
* PERSONALITY CHANGE

**D. Gender Roles, Love, & Relationships**  418
* DEFINITION: GENDER ROLES
* EXPECTATIONS
* KINDS OF LOVE
* CHOOSING A PARTNER
* LONG-TERM RELATIONSHIP: SUCCESS OR FAILURE?

**Concept Review**  421

**E. Research Focus: Happy Marriages**  422
* WHY DO MARRIAGES SUCCEED OR FAIL?

**F. Cultural Diversity: Preferences for Partners**  423
* MEASURING CULTURAL INFLUENCES
* DESIRABLE TRAITS
* REASONS FOR MARRYING

**G. Physical Changes: Aging**  424
* KINDS OF AGING
* REASONS FOR AGING
* SEXUAL CHANGES WITH AGING

**H. Application: Suicide**  426
* TEENAGE SUICIDE
* PROBLEMS RELATED TO TEENAGE SUICIDE
* PREVENTING TEENAGE SUICIDE
* SUICIDE IN THE ELDERLY

**Summary Test**  428

**Critical Thinking**  430
* AM I LOSING MY MEMORY?

**Links to Learning**  431

## Adolescence

**Will Branndi become president?**

"Do not label me as anything. I'm an individual."

"I will eventually become president. In 2017. I think. I've figured it out. I don't want people to think, 'She's just a kid. She doesn't know what's ahead of her.' I know the presidency will not come easy to me. I'm black, first of all, and I'm a woman. I want to be a lawyer, then work my way up in politics, become like mayor, then senator, then governor . . .

"I know people will look into my past and say, 'Years ago, she did this, she did that, blah, blah, blah.' The worst thing I've ever done is to steal two little five-cent Bazooka gums from a 7-Eleven when I was nine. I don't think they'll count that against me . . .

"Sometimes people just expect me to make trouble because I'm 'one of the black kids.' Do not label me as anything. Label me as individual . . .

"I want everyone to know that some 12-year-olds really do think seriously about the future. I want to be a role model. I'm glad I was born black. I want to tell others, 'Stay in there because you can do just as much good as any other person.'"

Besides talking like a philosopher, Branndi is a fun-loving adolescent who likes rap music, hanging out at the mall with her friends, and "dumb" movies. She is an above-average student, likes to write fairy tales for children, and sings in the youth choir at the neighborhood church (*Los Angeles Times*, December 22, 1991, pp. E-1, E-12).

At age 12, Branndi is just beginning adolescence.

*Adolescence* is a developmental period, lasting from about ages 12 to 18, during which many biological, cognitive, social, and personality traits change from childlike to adultlike.

While it is true that adolescents, like Branndi, go through dramatic changes, experts now believe that adolescence is not necessarily marked by great psychological turmoil. Psychologists have learned that the majority of teenagers, unlike the terrible adolescents portrayed in the media, do develop a healthy sense of identity, maintain close relationships with their families, and avoid major emotional disorders (Compas et al., 1995; Lerner & Galambos, 1998). After making it through adolescence, most teenagers are ready and eager to enter the adult world.

## Adulthood

**Did the prom queen live happily ever after?**

"I remember standing on stage in front of all the students. I was thinking, 'Can this really happen to me?' It was my junior year of high school, and I had been elected prom queen. It was like being in a fairy tale.

"I cried at my high school graduation, but I was excited about going away to college and being on my own. I considered myself a very sensible, logical, and levelheaded person. So what did I do? I began seriously dating a guy who was my opposite. He was a fun-loving, kidding-around, cocky-type person. I met him in January, got engaged in February, and was married in September. What had love done to my sensible head?

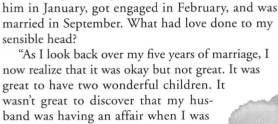

"Only some of the things turned out the way I hoped."

"As I look back over my five years of marriage, I now realize that it was okay but not great. It was great to have two wonderful children. It wasn't great to discover that my husband was having an affair when I was pregnant the second time. We got divorced soon after my daughter was born. It was hard being single again, with two children and no job. Later, my 12-year-old son developed a brain tumor and after two years of suffering, he died. How does one prepare for the death of one's child? Without help from my parents and friends, I would never have survived.

"I'm almost 40 now. My daughter and I are doing pretty well. I think about getting married again. I don't know if I will. You see, I also like my independence. Come back and see me when I'm 70 and I'll tell you what happened" (Wallechinsky, 1986).

Susan had dreamed of finishing college, getting married, and having a family, all of which she did. However, she did not figure on a divorce, having to support herself and her children, and her son's dying of a brain tumor, all before she reached 40. These are some of the joys and pains of adulthood.

### MAJOR PERIODS OF CHANGE

Both Susan and Branndi went through periods of great change. Each of us goes through three major developmental periods marked by significant physical, cognitive, personality, and social changes. We discussed childhood in Module 17. Now we'll turn to the other two periods: adolescence and adulthood. Generally, adolescents are more concerned about their physical appearance and finding their identities, while adults are more concerned with establishing a long-term relationship and finding a good job. Thus, the individual's concerns and goals undergo major changes between adolescence and adulthood.

## What's Coming

We'll explain the personality, social, cognitive, and physical changes that individuals undergo from adolescence through adulthood and discuss some of the challenges and problems that adolescents and adults face during each of these periods.

We'll begin with perhaps the biggest change in adolescence—puberty.

**Why is puberty such a big deal?**

A teenager leaves behind the mind and body of a child and begins to take on the mind and body of an adult. This great change from child to adult is full of challenge, excitement, and anxiety for both the adolescent and the parents. Perhaps the biggest event in changing from a child to an adult is the onset of puberty, which is altogether interesting, wondrous, and potentially very stressful.

*Puberty* refers to a developmental period, between the ages of 9 and 17, when the individual experiences significant biological changes that result in developing secondary sexual characteristics and reaching sexual maturity.

As puberty triggers dramatic changes in the structure and function of our bodies, we simultaneously experience dramatic changes in our thoughts, personalities, and social behaviors. To understand why puberty changed our minds, we first need to know how puberty changed our bodies.

## Girls During Puberty

Every girl wants to grow up so she can finally be a woman. Becoming a woman means going through puberty and experiencing three major biological changes that occur between ages 9 and 13. The onset of puberty usually occurs about two years earlier in girls (average of 10.5 years) than in boys (average of 12.5 years).

**1** Puberty sets off a surge in *physical growth,* which is marked by an increase in height that starts on average at 9.6 years. This growth spurt begins about 6–12 months before the onset of breast development.

**2** Puberty triggers a physiological process that results in a girl's reaching *female sexual maturity,* which primarily involves the onset of menarche.

*Menarche* is the first menstrual period; it is a signal that ovulation may have occurred and that the girl may have the potential to conceive and bear a child.

In the United States, menarche occurs on average at 12.5 years, about 2.5 years after the beginning of breast development. For reasons of diet, exercise, family stress, and genes, age of menarche varies with society and country (Lemonick, 2000).

The onset of menarche is triggered by an area of the brain called the *hypothalamus,* which stimulates the pituitary to produce hormones that travel throughout the bloodstream. These hormones stimulate the ovaries to greatly increase production of female hormones.

*Estrogen* is one of the major female hormones. At puberty, estrogen levels increase eightfold, which stimulates the development of both primary and secondary sexual characteristics.

**3** Puberty marks a major change in the girl's body as she develops female secondary sexual characteristics.

*Female secondary sexual characteristics,* whose development is triggered by the increased secretion of estrogen, include growth of pubic hair, development of breasts, and widening of hips.

In girls, the onset of secondary sexual characteristics begins at 10.5 years (the range is from age 9 to age 18) and continues for about 4.5 years.

**Early versus late maturing.** Girls who are early maturing— that is, who go through puberty early—may be more shy and introverted, rate lower on social skills, and try cigarettes and alcohol ahead of their later-maturing classmates (Wilson et al., 1994). One reason girls who mature early physically may encounter psychological problems is that they have not yet acquired the adult personality traits and social skills that are needed for normal and healthy functioning in their newly developed adult bodies (Lerner & Galambos, 1998).

## Boys During Puberty

Every boy wants to grow up so he can finally be a man. Becoming a man means going through puberty and experiencing three major biological changes that occur between ages 10 and 14. The onset of puberty in a boy usually occurs about two years later than in a girl.

**1** Puberty triggers an increase in *physical growth,* especially height, generally at 13–14 years of age. The increase in height may be dramatic, and a boy may feel strange as he discovers that he is taller than his mother and as tall as or taller than his father.

**2** Puberty starts a physiological process that results in a boy's reaching *male sexual maturity,* which includes growth of the genital organs—testes and penis—and production of sperm. The onset of genital growth begins at around 11.5 years (the range is from age 9 to age 16) and continues for approximately three years. The production and release of sperm begin at 12–14 years of age.

The increase in genital growth and the production of sperm are triggered by the *hypothalamus,* which stimulates the male pituitary gland. The pituitary in turn triggers the testes to increase production of testosterone by as much as 18 times more than before puberty.

*Testosterone,* which is the major male hormone, stimulates the growth of genital organs and the development of secondary sexual characteristics.

**3** The increased production of testosterone triggers the development of male secondary sexual characteristics.

*Male secondary sexual characteristics,* which are triggered by the increased secretion of testosterone, include the growth of pubic and facial hair, development of muscles, and a change (deepening) in voice.

These changes usually occur between 12 and 16 years of age, but there is a wide range in their development.

**Early versus late maturing.** Generally, boys who are early maturing, which means they go through puberty earlier, are found to be more confident, relaxed, socially responsible, popular, and highly regarded by their peers. In comparison, boys who go through puberty later (are late maturing) are found lacking in self-confidence and self-esteem, more dependent on their parents, and less highly regarded by peers.

However, many of the psychological differences between early- and late-maturing girls and boys decrease and disappear with age (Sigelman & Shaffer, 1995). One interesting difference between boys and girls during puberty is that generally boys see themselves as being physically attractive, while many girls doubt their attractiveness and are constantly comparing themselves with other girls (Rodriguez-Tome et al., 1993).

During puberty, boys and girls become physically sexually mature, a brand-new body state that raises many difficult questions for adolescents.

**Now what do I do?**

In the United States, about 30 million youths between the ages of 10 and 17 are looking for answers to a very important and burning question, "Now that I am sexually mature, what do I do?" For example, a survey of teenage girls reported that the number one problem they faced revolved around issues of sex and pregnancy (Henry, 1999). Part of the difficulty that adolescents have in making decisions about how to behave sexually is that they receive conflicting answers.

## Conflicting Answers

On the one hand, the media (movies, television, magazines), as well as peers, friends, and classmates, often discuss or portray sex in exciting ways that stimulate and encourage adolescents to try sex, often before they are emotionally ready (Lammers et al., 2000). For example, in a study of 174 girls, most said that they had been too young (average age was 13) at the time of their first intercourse. The reasons (in order of frequency) that they gave for engaging in sex were that they were physically attracted or curious, were alone with their partner, or knew that all their friends were having sex. Looking back, most of these girls wished they had waited longer before having sexual intercourse because they had not been ready and had not appreciated the risks of pregnancy and disease (Rosenthal et al., 1997).

On the other hand, most parents, mental health organizations, and religious groups advise adolescents not to engage in sex too early and to wait until they are more emotionally mature and involved in an intimate relationship (Rabasca, 1999).

Faced with conflicting pressures, many adolescents don't know what to do about becoming sexually active. For example, here's what one young female said: "My school taught us what our sexual anatomy did. But when the time came, what I really needed to know was all the dimensions of having a sexual relationship with my boyfriend. . . . Was I ready to make love with a man who I perceived I loved deeply?" (Minton, 1995, p. 8).

These thoughts reflect adolescents' concerns about the relationship between sex and love and introduce a new model of adolescent sexual development, called the BioPsychoSocial model (Compas et al., 1995).

Generally, teenage boys are more sexually active than girls.

The *BioPsychoSocial model* views adolescent development as a process that occurs simultaneously on many levels and includes sexual, cognitive, social, and personality changes that interact and influence each other.

According to the BioPsychoSocial approach, sexual behavior cannot be discussed independently of other cognitive, personality, or emotional behaviors. For example, sex hormones not only trigger important physical changes but also influence mood changes (Buchanan et al., 1992). Adolescents may experience wide mood swings and desires that lead them to seek answers in intimate relationships, which may involve sexual activity.

## Decisions about Becoming Sexually Active

In the United States, the waiting time between becoming sexually mature and committing to a permanent relationship has increased. The average age for marriage increased from 22 in 1970 to 26 in 1997. Similarly, the number of adolescents becoming sexually active has increased, from 29% in 1970 to about 50% today (Haney, 2000). For example, one survey (graph below) found that by age 17, about 60% of adolescents had engaged in sex, and boys were more sexually active than girls (Leigh et al., 1994).

**Girls.** A recent survey reported that 56% of girls had had sexual intercourse by age 17, compared to 42% in 1980. Although the median age for first intercourse was 17.4 years for girls, about half the girls (48%) said that the best age for first intercourse is

| Teenagers and Intercourse (percentage) | | |
|---|---|---|
| | Have NOT | Have |
| Age 12 | 95 | 5 |
| Age 14 | 73 | 27 |
| Age 16 | 52 | 48 |
| Age 17 | 39 | 61 |

between 18 and 20 years old. Almost half of girls who were sexually active reported not using contraceptives.

**Boys.** The survey reported that 67% of boys had had sexual intercourse by age 17. The median age for first intercourse was 16.6 years for boys, but almost half the boys (47%) said that the best age for first intercourse is between 18 and 20 years old. About 43% of boys who were sexually active reported not using contraceptives.

**Conclusions.** Based on recent surveys, we can draw several conclusions (Haney, 2000; Healy, 1999).

**First,** most surveys report that the age at which teenagers actually engage in sexual activity is earlier than what they think is the best age. Teenage girls report that sex and pregnancy are the number one issues they face today. However, curiosity, media coverage, and peer pressure play a large role in motivating sexual activity (Henry, 1999).

**Second,** a relatively large percentage of adolescents (39%) had *not* engaged in sex by age 17. There are a number of programs to reduce sexual activity in teenagers, ranging from abstinence-only to providing information about safer sex. Researchers report that some of these programs do reduce teens' risky sexual behaviors (Rabasca, 1999).

**Third,** about half the boys and girls did not use contraceptives, which contributes to two major problems: the spread of sexually transmitted diseases, including AIDS, and births among unwed teenage girls (Leigh et al., 1994).

Although puberty prepares teenage bodies for engaging in sexual behavior, the majority of teenagers (especially girls) report not being emotionally, psychologically, or mentally prepared to deal with strong sexual desires and feelings. We'll next examine a number of mental and psychological changes that accompany the teenage years.

---------------------------------------- **Definition** ----------------------------------------

**Why is Branndi's head spinning?**

When most adults and especially current parents of teenagers hear the word *adolescence,* they often get a pained look as they remember a time full of problems. Until the early 1990s, researchers believed that adolescence was primarily a time of storm and stress, of intense feelings, huge mood swings, and irritating parental conflicts. However, current research paints a different picture of adolescence. Yes, storm and stress and intense mood swings and parental conflicts are more likely to occur during adolescence, but they come and go and not all adolescents have a terrible time (Arnett, 2000a). Current research also finds that among the storm and stress, adolescence is a time for tremendous growth in emotional, social, and cognitive development as teenagers go from childhood to adulthood (Lerner & Galambos, 1998).

We have already discussed the dramatic physical changes and sexual feelings that occur during puberty and the problems adolescents have in deciding what to do with their newly developed sexual maturity. Along with sexual maturity, adolescents develop new ways of thinking and reasoning, which represents a major change in cognitive development.

*Cognitive development* refers to how a person perceives, thinks, and gains an understanding of his or her world through the interaction and influence of genetic and learned factors.

"I believe God lets awful things happen to teach us a lesson."

For example, at the beginning of this module we told you that, during adolescence, Branndi (left photo) would undergo major changes in reasoning and thinking. For example, here are some of her thoughts about the condition of the world: "I don't believe in the Pledge of Allegiance. I don't say it, because they're telling a lie—'liberty and justice for all.'. . . My first step into politics will be mayor. I write lots of letters to Tom Bradley [former mayor of Los Angeles] about things like animal rights. But he just sent me, you know, one of those typed things. I don't think it's right . . . I'm very outspoken. I worry about things—sex, rape, and stuff like that . . . I believe in God. I believe God lets awful things happen to teach us a lesson . . ." (*Los Angeles Times,* December 22, 1991, p. E-13).

There's no question that 12-year-old Branndi is full of abstract thinking, is very outspoken, and holds absolute opinions on a variety of concrete and abstract issues. Her views illustrate one of the most significant changes in cognitive development during adolescence, which is the ability to think about abstract issues, such as the meaning of liberty, justice, and God. This kind of abstract thinking indicates that Branndi is entering Piaget's fourth cognitive stage, called formal operations, which marks the beginning of thinking and reasoning like an adult.

---------------------------------------- **Piaget's Cognitive Stages: Continued** ----------------------------------------

**What's new about a teenager's thinking?**

As you may remember from Module 17, Piaget's theory of cognitive development is that we all go through four distinct cognitive stages (left figure). As we go through each *cognitive stage,* we acquire a new and distinct kind of reasoning and thinking that is different from and more advanced than the reasoning abilities we possessed at our previous stage. We discussed Piaget's four cognitive stages in Module 17, but we'll review stage 4, the formal operations stage, because it begins in adolescence.

### STAGE 4: FORMAL OPERATIONS

The fact that 12-year-old Branndi is using abstract concepts, such as liberty, justice, animal rights, and God, is good evidence that she is entering the formal operations stage.

The *formal operations stage,* the last of Piaget's four cognitive stages, extends from about age 12 through adulthood. During this stage, adolescents and adults develop the abilities to think about abstract or hypothetical concepts, to consider an issue from another's viewpoint, and to solve cognitive problems in a logical way.

Having the ability to think about and discuss abstract concepts means that adolescents can critically consider their beliefs, attitudes, values, and goals as well as discuss a wide range of topics important to their becoming adults. For instance, when adolescents were asked about their major concerns, tops on their lists were getting married, having friends, getting a good job, and doing well in school. Each of these concerns involves the ability to discuss abstract concepts, which is a cognitive skill that they are learning at the formal operations stage.

1. Sensorimotor Birth to age 2

2. Preoperational Ages 2 to 7

3. Concrete Ages 7 to 11

4. Formal Ages 12 thru adulthood

"My major concerns are doing well in school and having friends."

One of the interesting questions about adolescents is why some seem so slow to develop thinking and reasoning skills that prepare them to deal with typical problems and stressful situations that occur during adolescence. For example, many adolescents report that they were not prepared to have sex but it just happened, or they fight continually with their parents, or they do stupid things like drink and then drive. Researchers have only recently discovered that the answer involves the developing adolescent's brain.

## Brain Development: Reason and Emotion

One of my colleagues has a teenage son whose most recent irritating behavior was to throw a party for his friends when his parents were gone for the day. The son raided his father's wine cellar and proceeded to drink or break many of his father's most prized bottles. When asked by his parents why he didn't think before destroying his father's prized wines, the teenage son replied, "It just seemed like the thing to do." This seemingly irresponsible teenage behavior, not thinking before acting, drives many parents crazy because they believe their teens should and do know better. Until recently, and in agreement with parents, researchers thought that teenage brains were fully developed by puberty. However, new findings indicate that teenagers' brains are still in the developmental process, especially areas related to clear thinking and reasoning (Spear, 2000).

### 1 Prefrontal cortex: executive functions

Every company has an executive officer who is responsible for making decisions, day-to-day planning, organizing, and thinking about the future. Similarly, our brains have an executive area, called the *prefrontal cortex*, which is involved in similar functions and is located near the front of the brain (right figure).

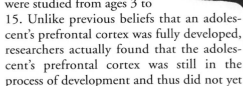

Researchers used MRI scans (p. 70) to take pictures of neural growth and development inside the brains of children who were studied from ages 3 to 15. Unlike previous beliefs that an adolescent's prefrontal cortex was fully developed, researchers actually found that the adolescent's prefrontal cortex was still in the process of development and thus did not yet have the ability to think, reason, decide, or plan like an adult (Gieddes, 1999, 2000). One researcher summed up the findings by saying that the teenage brain is developing in fits and starts, is far from mature, and is a work in progress that will not be completed until about the early twenties (Witelson, 1999).

**Risk-taking behavior.** The finding that executive functions in the adolescent's brain are not yet fully developed helps explain many of the adolescent's seemingly irresponsible behaviors, such as engaging in risky behaviors. For example, adolescents have about twice the rates of adults in transmitting venereal diseases because only 50% of adolescents think to use condoms; they have 20 times the rate of automobile accidents as adults because adolescents don't worry about drinking, driving, and speeding; and they have the lowest rate for using seat belts (50% do not) of any age group (Adler, 1993; Jelalian et al., 2000). The previous explanation for why adolescents engaged in risk-taking behavior was that they felt invulnerable and had no fear of accident or injury. A more basic reason adolescents have a tendency to engage in risk-taking behaviors is that the executive manager of their behaviors, their prefrontal cortex, is underdeveloped, which means they simply don't have the neural bases to think very far ahead or make intelligent decisions (Spear, 2000).

Another reason adolescents have a tendency to engage in risk-taking behaviors involves a different part of their brain that's involved in emotional behaviors.

"As executive, officer, I'm responsible for thinking, planning, and making good decisions."

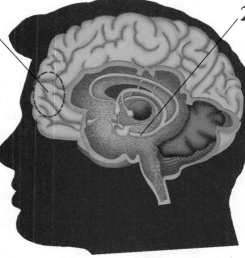

### 2 Limbic system: emotional behaviors

Teenagers are known to act impulsively, such as getting a tongue pierced on a dare, and experience wide mood swings. As one parent said, "It's hot and cold, nasty and nice. One minute loving me, one minute hating me." What parents don't realize is that a teenager's prefrontal cortex, which acts like an executive officer, is not fully developed, so an adolescent has less control over his or her emotional and impulsive behaviors, which involve other brain structures.

**Moody and impulsive behaviors.** As shown in the above figure, in the center of the brain is a circle of structures (shown in yellow) that make up our emotional brain, called the limbic system. The *limbic system* is involved in a wide range of emotional behaviors, such being ecstatic over getting a date, feeling depressed when failing a test, or getting angry when insulted. Researchers found that sex hormones (testosterone in males and estrogen in females), which are secreted in abundance during puberty, increase the growth of limbic system structures (amygdala, hippocampus). Researchers believe that this increased structure and function of the limbic system account for a teenager's irritability as well as the increase in aggressiveness in adolescent males (Gieddes, 1999).

"I was dared to get my lip and nose pierced."

**Conclusion.** Researchers are finding that the adolescent's brain has an underdeveloped prefrontal cortex, or executive officer, but a well-developed limbic system or emotional center (Spear, 2000). This combination of a weak executive officer and a strong emotional center results in many of the unthinking and irritating behaviors of adolescents, such as taking risks, switching moods, and acting impulsively. As one researcher summarized, "Good judgment is learned but you can't learn it if you don't have the necessary hardware (neural development)" (Yurgelun-Todd, 1999, p. 48).

"One minute I'm laughing and the next I'm crying."

An adolescent's lack of a strong executive officer (prefrontal cortex) will also affect moral judgment, our next topic.

# B. Cognitive & Emotional Changes

## Kohlberg's Theory of Moral Reasoning

**Would you steal to save a friend?**

Suppose your best friend is dying of cancer. You hear of a chemist who has just discovered a new wonder drug that could save her life. The chemist is selling the drug for $5,000, many times more than it cost him to make. You try to borrow the full amount but can get only $2,500. You ask the chemist to sell you the drug for $2,500 and he refuses. Later that night, you break into the chemist's laboratory and steal the drug. Should you have done that? Did you decide that it would be all right to steal the drug to save the life of your dying friend? If you did, how did you justify your moral decision? Lawrence Kohlberg (1984) and associates presented similar dilemmas to individuals who were asked to explain their moral decisions. On the basis of such studies, Kohlberg explained the development of moral reasoning in terms of three levels.

### Three Levels of Moral Reasoning

#### Level 1 Self-Interest

The *preconventional level,* which represents Kohlberg's lowest level of moral reasoning, has two stages. At stage 1, moral decisions are based primarily on fear of punishment or the need to be obedient; at stage 2, moral reasoning is guided most by satisfying one's self-interest, which may involve making bargains.

For example, individuals at stage 1 might say that you should not steal the drug because you'll be caught and go to jail. Individuals at stage 2 might say that you can steal the drug and save your best friend, but in return you'll have to give up some freedom by going to jail. Most children are at the preconventional level.

#### Level 2 Social Approval

The *conventional level,* which represents an intermediate level of moral reasoning, also has two stages. At stage 3, moral decisions are guided most by conforming to the standards of others we value; at stage 4, moral reasoning is determined most by conforming to laws of society.

Individuals at stage 3 might say that you should steal the drug since that is what your family would expect you to do. Individuals at stage 4 might say that you should not steal the drug because of what would happen to society if everybody took what they needed. Many adolescents and adults are at this level.

#### Level 3 Abstract Ideas

The *postconventional level,* which represents the highest level of moral reasoning, has one stage. At stage 5, moral decisions are made after carefully thinking about all the alternatives and striking a balance between human rights and laws of society.

Individuals at stage 5 might say that one should steal the drug because life is more important than money. (Stage 6, which appeared in earlier versions of Kohlberg's theory, has been omitted in later versions because too few people had reached it.) Some, but not all, adults reach the postconventional level.

Kohlberg's theory has two distinct features. First, he classifies moral reasoning into three distinct levels—preconventional, conventional, and postconventional. Second, he suggests that everyone progresses through the levels in order, from lowest to highest. However, not everyone reaches the higher levels of moral development.

Next, we'll evaluate Kohlberg's theory and its present status.

### Evaluating Kohlberg's Theory

**Stages.** Kohlberg hypothesized that everyone goes through the five stages in sequence. That is, you begin at stage 1 and cannot reach stage 4 without going through stages 2 and 3. Researchers reviewed 45 Kohlberg-type studies conducted in 27 cultures. The vast majority of these studies supported Kohlberg's assumption that individuals progress through the stages in order but that not everyone reaches the higher stages (Damon, 1999; Helwig, 1997).

**Criticisms.** There are three criticisms of Kohlberg's stages. The first is that Kohlberg's moral stages indicate different kinds of moral thinking that may or may not predict how an individual actually behaves. Thus, Kohlberg focused on development of moral thinking rather than on development of moral behavior (Damon, 1999).

The second criticism, made by Carol Gilligan (1982), is that men and women may differ in their moral thinking: Men use a justice orientation and women use a care orientation.

A *care orientation* is making moral decisions based on issues of caring, on avoiding hurt, on how things affect interpersonal relationships, and on concerns for others.

A *justice orientation* is making moral decisions based more on issues of law and equality and individual rights.

However, after 15 years of studies, there is only weak support for Gilligan's idea that women use predominately a care orientation and men use a justice orientation. Recent reviewers concluded that what is more likely is that men and women use a mixture of care and justice orientations, depending on the particular moral situation (Jaffee & Hyde, 2000).

The third criticism is that when Kohlberg constructed his theory, he did not know about recent advances in studying the neural structure and function of the living brain. We have already discussed how the teenage brain has an underdeveloped prefrontal cortex, which results in an underdeveloped executive area, which in turn restricts a teenager's ability to think, reason, and make intelligent decisions needed for moral reasoning (Gieddes, 2000). Also supporting the role of the prefrontal cortex in moral reasoning are findings that individuals who had their prefrontal cortex damaged in infancy had difficulty learning the normal social and moral rules in childhood and adolescence. As adults, these individuals showed no guilt or remorse for their extremely bad behaviors and could not get along in social situations (Damasio, 1999). Thus, there is growing evidence that moral reasoning is, to a large extent, dependent on an intact and well-functioning prefrontal cortex.

Finally, moral reasoning and cognitive development are also influenced by the kinds of rules that parents use, which is our next topic.

## Parenting Styles and Effects

**Were your parents easy or strict?**

During adolescence, teenagers experience several major changes in cognitive and emotional development. These changes are influenced by both biological factors, such as brain development, and environmental factors, such as the influence of peers and parents. For instance, if someone asked how your parents raised you, would you answer that they were strict, supportive, easy, or hard? It turns out that parents' rules, standards, and codes of conduct influence how a teenager develops a sense of independence and achievement (Baumrind, 1991). We'll discuss how parental rules can affect the cognitive and emotional development of teenagers.

### Personal Experiences

When teenagers were asked how they responded to their parents' rules, here's what Ida and Chris replied (photos below).

**Ida, age 17.** "I live in a strict Italian home. Sometimes my parents are really, really great, but their rules for me are absolutely ridiculous. So I get around them. My friends will tell you I'm a good kid. I don't drink. I don't do drugs. I don't smoke. But my parents think that, if I've gone out on a Friday night and I ask to go out Saturday, too, I'm asking for the world . . . So I lie a lot . . . A lot of people know I do this, but nobody yells at me for it, because I'm a good kid, and my parents' rules are so ridiculous."

**Chris, age 18.** "My parents never make their punishments stick. Like, I'll get my Jeep taken away for a week, and I'll get it back within six hours. Why? Because my parents hate to see their kids unhappy, and I know it, so I play right into it. They'll punish me by not letting me go out, so I'll walk around the house, slam the door occasionally, this, that . . . and after awhile this just plays on them, and they feel bad, and they let me out" (*Parade* magazine, July 14, 1991, pp. 6–7. Reprinted with permission from Parade. Copyright © 1991).

Ida says, "I had to get around my parents' strict rules."

Chris says, "I acted unhappy so my parents gave in."

After reading these two descriptions, you can see that Ida's parents are the opposite of Chris's. How do such different styles of parenting affect adolescents' development? To answer this question, psychologist Diana Baumrind (1991, 1993) has been carrying out a series of longitudinal studies on parent–child and parent–adolescent interactions. She has identified a number of parenting styles that are associated with different kinds of adolescent development.

### Different Styles of Parenting

We'll focus on three of Baumrind's parenting styles: authoritarian parents, authoritative parents, and permissive parents.

*Authoritarian parents* attempt to shape, control, and evaluate the behavior and attitudes of their children in accordance with a set standard of conduct, usually an absolute standard that comes from religious or respected authorities.

For these parents, obedience is a virtue, and they punish and use harsh discipline to keep the adolescent in line with their rules. This parenting style seems to describe Ida's parents. Boys from authoritarian families are found to be relatively hostile, while girls are found to be relatively dependent and submissive. This description fits Ida, who admits to problems with being independent.

*Authoritative parents* attempt to direct their children's activities in a rational and intelligent way. They are supportive, loving, and committed, encourage verbal give-and-take, and discuss their rules and policies with their children.

Authoritative parents value being expressive and independent but are also demanding. The children of such parents tend to be competent. In addition, girls are achievement-oriented and boys are friendly and cooperative.

*Permissive parents* are less controlling and behave with a nonpunishing and accepting attitude toward their children's impulses, desires, and actions; they consult with their children about policy decisions, make few demands, and tend to use reason rather than direct power.

This parenting style seems to describe Chris's parents. Girls with such parents are less socially assertive, and both boys and girls are less achievement-oriented.

### Effects of Parenting Styles

It is clear that each of the three parenting styles has different costs and benefits. Authoritarian parents, who are very demanding, benefit by preventing adolescent behavioral problems but at some cost to adolescents, who tend to be more conforming and have lower self-esteem. Authoritative parents, who state their values clearly, benefit by having loving and supportive parent–teenager interactions, which further benefit their teenagers, who tend to be more friendly, cooperative, achievement-oriented, and better adjusted to college (Hickman et al., 2000). Permissive parents benefit by having to make fewer demands and enforcing fewer rules but at some cost to adolescents, who may be less socially assertive and less achievement-oriented than adolescents with authoritative parents (Baumrind, 1991, 1993).

Which is better, being too easy or too strict?

The style of parenting also influences whether and how often adolescents engage in risky behaviors (drugs, early sex). Researchers report that the better the communication is between the adolescent and parent, the less likely the adolescent will engage in risky behaviors. This is true as long as adolescents can openly communicate with at least one of the parents (Marta, 1997; Resnick et al., 1997). Thus, different parenting styles can have significantly different effects on the cognitive, social, and personality development of adolescents.

### Adolescence: Big Picture

There are 30 million of us.

**What are the major changes?** In the United States, there are about 30 million youths (ages 10 to 17) who are currently going through adolescence, a period of considerable physical, neurological (brain), cognitive, and emotional change. Although adolescence is a time of some storm and stress, it is also a time for tremendous personal growth. We'll review some of the major changes that occur during adolescence.

**1 GIRLS DURING PUBERTY**

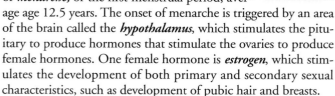

Puberty sets off a surge in physical growth, which is marked by an increase in height that starts on average at 9.6 years. Puberty triggers a physiological process that results in a girl's reaching *female sexual maturity,* which involves primarily the onset of *menarche,* or the first menstrual period, average age 12.5 years. The onset of menarche is triggered by an area of the brain called the *hypothalamus,* which stimulates the pituitary to produce hormones that stimulate the ovaries to produce female hormones. One female hormone is *estrogen,* which stimulates the development of both primary and secondary sexual characteristics, such as development of pubic hair and breasts.

**2 BOYS DURING PUBERTY**

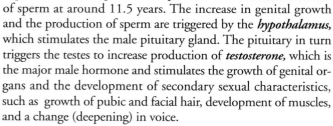

Puberty triggers an increase in physical growth, especially height, generally at 13 or 14 years of age. Puberty starts a physiological process that results in a boy's reaching *male sexual maturity,* which includes growth of the genital organs—testes and penis—and production of sperm at around 11.5 years. The increase in genital growth and the production of sperm are triggered by the *hypothalamus,* which stimulates the male pituitary gland. The pituitary in turn triggers the testes to increase production of *testosterone,* which is the major male hormone and stimulates the growth of genital organs and the development of secondary sexual characteristics, such as growth of pubic and facial hair, development of muscles, and a change (deepening) in voice.

**3 SEXUAL MATURITY**

The waiting time between becoming sexually mature and committing to a more permanent relationship (marriage) continues to increase. As a result, the number of adolescents becoming sexually active has generally been increasing, from 29% in 1970 to about 50% today (Haney, 2000). For example, a survey of thousands of adolescents found that by age 17, about 60% of adolescents had engaged in sex, with boys being more sexually active than girls (Leigh et al., 1994).Teenage girls report that sex and pregnancy are the number one issues they face today. However, curiosity, media coverage, and peer pressure play a large role in motivating early participation in sexual activity (Henry, 1999).

**4 PIAGET'S STAGES: CONTINUED**

According to Piaget's theory, children pass through four different cognitive stages—(1) sensorimotor, (2) preoperational, (3) concrete operations, and (4) formal operations—in that order but at different rates. With each stage, the child adds a new and qualitatively different kind of thinking or reasoning skill that helps the child make better sense of the world. Adolescents are entering Piaget's fourth stage, called the formal operations stage, which begins at about age 12 and extends through adulthood. During this stage, adolescents develop the abilities to think about abstract or hypothetical concepts, to consider an issue from another's viewpoint, and to solve cognitive problems in a logical way. These cognitive abilities are very useful during adulthood.

**5 BRAIN DEVELOPMENT: REASON & EMOTION**

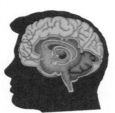

Researchers are finding that the adolescent's brain has an underdeveloped prefrontal cortex or executive officer but a well-developed limbic system or emotional center (Spear, 2000). This combination of a weak executive officer and a strong emotional center results in many of the unthinking, irresponsible, and irritating behaviors of adolescents. For example, the lack of a strong executive officer (prefrontal cortex) explains why adolescents engage in risky behaviors, switch moods suddenly, and act impulsively. As one researcher summarized, "Good judgment is learned but you can't learn it if you don't have the necessary hardware (neural development)" (Yurgelun-Todd, 1999, p. 48).

**6 KOHLBERG'S THEORY OF MORAL REASONING**

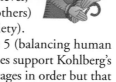

Kohlberg hypothesized that everyone goes through three levels of moral reasoning. Level 1, the preconventional level, involves stage 1 (fear of punishment) and stage 2 (self-interest). Level 2, the conventional level, involves stage 3 (conforming to the standards of others) and stage 4 (conforming to the standards of society). Level 3, the postconventional level, has only stage 5 (balancing human rights and society's laws). The vast majority of studies support Kohlberg's assumption that individuals progress through the stages in order but that not everyone reaches the higher stages (Damon, 1999; Helwig, 1997).

As adolescents grow up and become adults, they will experience a number of cognitive changes that become noticeable in their forties and fifties and continue on through later life. We'll discuss some of the cognitive changes that make people realize that they're not kids anymore.

**Power Study™**

**Check out CD: Module 12**
B. Forgetting Curves
D. Reasons for Forgetting
E. Mnemonics

## Beyond Adolescence

As teenagers enter their 20s, they face a number of major changes, such as deciding about going to college, leaving home for perhaps the first time, choosing a career or major, entering the job market, and searching for a serious relationship (Arnett, 2000b). The 20s are a time when executive abilities (thinking, planning, deciding, remembering) are sharp, partly because the brain's prefrontal cortex is now fully developed. Cognitive or executive abilities usually remain sharp through the 30s. But beginning in the 40s and continuing through the 50s and 60s, there is a gradual decline in some cognitive abilities, especially in the ability to remember things. We'll discuss some of the slowing in cognitive abilities.

In the 20s and 30s, cognitive abilities are usually at their peak.

In the 40s and 50s, memory problems usually begin and continue.

In the 60s, 70s, and 80s, there's slowing in cognitive processes.

### Changes in Cognitive Speed

From about ages 20 to 40, cognitive skills remain relatively stable. However, between 40 and 80, there is a general slowing of some cognitive processes (Verhaeghen & Salthouse, 1997).

Beginning in the late fifties, there is a slowing in *processing speed*, which is the rate at which we encode information into long-term memory or recall or retrieve information from long-term memory.

For example, 20-year-olds can memorize and recall significantly more words than 60-year-olds can. Older adults appear to have more problems in encoding and storing lists of information as well as greater difficulty in reliably retrieving and recalling specific information (Salthouse, 1994).

Beginning in the late fifties, there is a slowing in *perceptual speed*, which is the rate at which we can identify a particular sensory stimulus.

For instance, in a set period of time, subjects were given a list of words and were instructed to find and draw a line through all words that contained the letter *a*. On this task, 25-year-old subjects canceled significantly more words than 67-year-old subjects did (52 versus 48 words). Researchers believe that slower perceptual speed in older adults results from slower encoding of information (Salthouse et al., 1990).

Beginning in the late fifties, there is a slowing in *reaction time,* which is the rate at which we respond (see, hear, move) to some stimulus.

For instance, 20- to 29-year-old subjects were fastest in pressing a button when a light appeared, while older subjects were slowest (Tranel et al., 1997).

This slowing in processing, perceiving, and reacting partly explains why older people react more slowly when driving a car or playing golf and are slower to make decisions or understand and follow instructions. For example, partly because of the slowdown in these processes, there is a professional golf tour for seniors only (over 50); they can no longer keep up with younger golfers.

"Why is my golf game slowing down?"

Besides a slowing in processing, perceiving, and reacting, older adults also experience a problem in remembering things.

### Changes in Memory

Beginning in the 40s and continuing into old age, most people complain about not remembering things. Researchers concluded that older adults have no trouble remembering the big picture (name of a movie) but do forget many of the small details (who played the starring role). In comparison, young adults easily remember the big picture plus all the details (Schacter, 1996). So as people move into their 50s, 60s, and 70s, their complaints are true: they do forget details (names, places, groceries) that may be bothersome but are usually unimportant.

**Memory differences.** Differences between 20-year-olds and 50-year-olds are that young adults excel at encoding (storing) and recalling vast amounts of detail but are not as good at making sense of what all the details mean. In comparison, mature adults excel at making sense of information but at the cost of forgetting much of the detail.

Am I losing my memory?

**Normal forgetting.** After the age of 60, people often worry about what their memory problems mean. For example, a 69-year-old professor wanted to know if she was "losing it" because she had difficulty recalling the names of new faculty members, the number of her classroom when ordering audiovisual equipment, and one morning could not think of the name for the thing you turn over eggs with. However, after a physical examination, the doctor told her that she was just experiencing memory problems that often occur in people 60 and over (Powell & Whitla, 1994).

Researchers report that decreases in memory skills, such as this professor shows, result from the slowing down of processing speed and are signs of normal aging (Lindenberger & Baltes, 1997).

**Memory advice.** Because aging, especially entering the 40s and 50s, is associated with memory problems, Americans are spending billions on memory improvement products, ranging from memory courses to food supplements. For example, Americans spend $350 million annually on a supplement called ginkgo biloba, whose claims of improving memory have not been rigorously tested and, at this writing, remain largely unproven (Herbert, 1999).

Memory experts advise that the best way to deal with age-related memory difficulties is to maintain physical fitness (having a regular exercise program) and mental fitness (engaging in cognitive activities—reading, taking courses, doing crosswords) (Herbert, 1999).

Next, we turn to changes in personality and social development.

# C. Personality & Social Changes

## Definition

**Who am I?**

So far we have discussed many of the major changes that occur during adolescence. One more change during adolescence is their developing a sense of who they are, which involves personality and social development.

*Personality* and *social development* refers to how a person develops a sense of self or self-identity, develops relationships with others, and develops the skills useful in social interactions.

Like it or not, this is the real me!

For example, the teenager in the left photo shows her independence and what she believes is her real identity by having a very noticeable hairstyle and piercings.

*Personal identity* or *self-identity* refers to how we describe ourselves and includes our values, goals, traits, perceptions, interests, and motivations.

Personal identity grows and changes as adolescents acquire many new values, goals, beliefs, and interests (Bandura, 1999). A major influence on the kind of identity teenagers develop is how they feel about themselves, which is called self-esteem.

## Development of Self-Esteem

**What influences self-esteem?**

Throughout this module, we have discussed 12-year-old Branndi, who, like other teenagers, has many beliefs and goals, such as being proud to be Black and female, having high hopes for her future, and wanting to be a role model. How Branndi perceives herself, which is called self-esteem, has a significant influence on her developing personality.

*I'm proud to be Black and female.*

*Self-esteem* is how much one likes oneself and includes feelings of self-worth, attractiveness, and social competence.

For example, in adolescents, self-esteem is influenced by a number of factors, including how *physically attractive* and how *socially competent* they appear to their peers (DuBois et al., 2000). As teenagers develop sexually mature bodies, they wonder how physically attractive they are; as teenagers begin dating, they wonder how socially skilled they are. Researchers measure changes in adolescents' self-esteem by using longitudinal studies that begin in adolescence and continue through adulthood, such as measuring self-esteem at ages 14, 18, and 23. We'll discuss three different patterns of self-esteem development in adolescents (Zimmerman et al., 1997).

*High Self-Esteem—develop and maintain high levels.* A large percentage of adolescents (about 60%) develop and maintain a strong sense of self-esteem through junior high school. These individuals do well in school, develop rewarding friendships, participate in social activities, and are described as cheerful, assertive, emotionally warm, and unwilling to give up if frustrated.

*Low Self-Esteem—develop and maintain low levels.* A small percentage of adolescents (about 15%) develop and maintain a chronically low sense of self-esteem that continues through junior high school. These adolescents usually have continuing personal and social problems (shy, lonely, depressed), which have been present for some time and contribute to this low self-esteem.

*Reversals—reverse levels.* A moderate percentage of adolescents (about 25%) show dramatic reversals in self-esteem, either from high to low or from low to high. For example, some boys change from being stern, unemotional, and lacking social skills into being open and expressive. Researchers think that reversals in self-esteem may result from changes in peer groups, personal attractiveness, or parental relationships.

Next, we'll describe some influences on the development of self-esteem.

**Forces shaping self-esteem.** The development of self-esteem in adolescents involves many factors, such as physical attractiveness, acceptance by peers, parental support, and performance in social and academic settings. However, boys and girls respond to different forces.

In girls, self-esteem is especially dependent upon the ability to relate well to others. Probably the most disturbing finding is that, compared to boys, girls are more likely to be the ones showing declining or low self-esteem. In boys, self-esteem is especially dependent upon looking cool in public, which means not letting stress or anxiety make them look bad (Block & Robins, 1993). Compared to girls, who are more likely to develop lower levels of self-esteem, boys are more likely to show increasing or high levels (Zimmerman et al., 1997).

Perhaps the most encouraging finding is that many adolescent boys and girls who show lowered self-esteem during adolescence were able to recover and reach a higher level of self-esteem during their early adult years (Block & Robins, 1993).

**Importance of self-esteem.** Self-esteem is important because developing a high level is associated with positive outcomes, such as being cheerful and happy and promoting personal adjustment, while developing a low level is associated with negative outcomes, such as depression, anxiety, and poor personal adjustment (Leary et al., 1995). Also, concern over levels of self-esteem in adolescence is important because many personality traits, once

There's nothing wrong with us!

clearly established, are difficult to change and often last a lifetime (Caspi & Roberts, 1999). We'll discuss all aspects and theories of personality in Modules 19 and 20.

One theory of how self-esteem and personal identity develop is found in Erikson's psychosocial stages.

**What will I have to deal with?**

*What happened to all my dreams?*

At the beginning of this module, we described how Susan went from teenage prom queen to middle-aged adult. Along the way, she dealt with dating, going to college, getting married, having children, getting divorced, finding a job, and losing her son. How dealing with these life events might affect Susan's social and personality development was something that Erik Erikson (1982) tried to explain. As you may remember from Module 17, Erikson divided life into eight *psychosocial stages,* each of which contained a unique psychosocial conflict, such as intimacy versus isolation. If Susan successfully solved each psychosocial conflict, she would develop a healthy personality; if unsuccessful in solving these conflicts, she might develop an unhealthy personality and future psychological problems. In Module 17, we discussed Erikson's stages related to childhood; now, we'll discuss stages related to adolescence and adulthood.

## Stage 5   Identity versus Role Confusion

**Period.** Adolescence (12–20)

**Potential conflict.** Adolescents need to leave behind the carefree, irresponsible, and impulsive behaviors of childhood and develop the more purposeful, planned, and responsible behaviors of adulthood. If adolescents successfully resolve this problem, they will develop a healthy and confident sense of *identity.* If they are unsuccessful in resolving the problem, they will experience *role confusion,* which results in their having low self-esteem and becoming unstable or socially withdrawn.

## Stage 6   Intimacy versus Isolation

**Period.** Young adulthood (20–40)

**Potential conflict.** Young adulthood is a time for finding intimacy by developing loving and meaningful relationships. On the positive side, we can find *intimacy* in caring relationships. On the negative side, without intimacy we will have a painful feeling of *isolation,* and our relationships will be impersonal.

## Stage 7   Generativity versus Stagnation

**Period.** Middle adulthood (40–65)

**Potential conflict.** Middle adulthood is a time for helping the younger generation develop worthwhile lives. On the positive side, we can achieve *generativity* through raising our own children. If we do not have children of our own, we can achieve generativity through close relationships with children of friends or relatives. Generativity can also be achieved through mentoring at work and helping others. On the negative side, a lack of involvement leads to a feeling of *stagnation,* of having done nothing for the younger generation.

## Stage 8   Integrity versus Despair

**Period.** Late adulthood (65 and older)

**Potential conflict.** Late adulthood is a time for reflecting on and reviewing how we met previous challenges and lived our lives. On the positive side, if we can look back and feel content about how we lived and what we accomplished, we will have a feeling of satisfaction or *integrity.* On the negative side, if we reflect and see a series of crises, problems, and bad experiences, we will have a feeling of regret and *despair.*

**Conclusions.** Erikson believed that achieving a personally satisfying identity was the very heart and soul of an adolescent's development (Hirsch, 1997). As adolescents developed into adults and reached middle adulthood (stage 7), Erikson described a shift from concerns about identity to concerns about being productive, creative, and nurturing (Bradley, 1997).

Researchers have found evidence that we do go through a sequence of psychosocial stages and that how we handle conflicts at earlier stages affects our personality and social development at later stages (Van Manen & Whitbourne, 1997).

## Personality Change

**How much will I change?**

When Mick Jagger, lead singer of the Rolling Stones, was in his early 20s (below), he boasted, "I'd rather be dead than sing 'Satisfaction' when I'm 45." Now in his 50s, Jagger (right) has changed his tune; he and the Stones recently completed a world tour and sang "Satisfaction" dozens of times. As Jagger found out, some of the things that we say and do at 20 may seem stupid at 50. The differences in Jagger at 20 and 50 raise an interesting question: How much do our personalities change and how much do they remain the same?

In his 20s, he said he'd rather be dead than singing at 45.

Now in his 50s, Jagger is still touring and singing.

Researchers answer such questions with longitudinal studies, which measure personality development across time in the same group of individuals. One study found that from adolescence to middle adulthood, individuals became more trusting and intimate and developed a better sense of control and identity. Researchers also found that possessing certain personality traits as a young adult (early 20s) led to developing related traits in middle adulthood (middle 40s). For example, individuals with a high level of identity in their early 20s showed more independence, warmth, and compassion later on in their mid-40s (Vandewater et al., 1997).

From these kinds of longitudinal studies researchers draw these conclusions: First, from the end of adolescence through middle adulthood, there are less dramatic but still continuing changes in personality traits, such as becoming more trusting and intimate. Second, possessing certain personality traits in early adulthood is the foundation for developing related traits later on (Caspi & Roberts, 1999). Third, adults appear to pass through psychosocial stages and face conflicts in personality development similar to those proposed by Erikson (Van Manen & Whitbourne, 1997).

One of the major social and personality changes that women and men go through involves gender roles.

# D. Gender Roles, Love, & Relationships

## Definition: Gender Roles

**Why couldn't women be firefighters?**

As boys and girls grow to become men and women, they acquire a set of behavioral and cognitive rules, called gender roles.

*Gender roles* are traditional or stereotypic behaviors, attitudes, values, and personality traits that society says are how males and females are to think and behave.

You can become aware of gender roles by noticing how differently males and females dress, behave, think, and express emotions. For example, gender roles played a major role in whether firefighters could be women. For as long as people could remember, firefighters had always been men because they were considered strong and cool in the face of danger, while women were considered weak and nervous. In the

Women fought for 20 years to become firefighters.

1970s, when women applied to become firefighters, a local paper warned against the city's "futile exercise in trying to fit women into jobs which common sense tells us are best filled by men." Only after 20 years of heated political and legal battles were gender roles changed and women, found to be strong and cool under pressure, were allowed to become firefighters.

During the past 20 years, there have been some changes in gender roles in the United States. As a result, women can now enter careers traditionally reserved for men, such as firefighters, doctors, police officers, senators, astronauts, and soldiers. Similarly, men can now enter careers traditionally reserved for women, such as nurses, single parents, and grade school teachers. We'll discuss some of the issues surrounding current gender roles and their functions.

## Current Gender Roles: U.S. and Worldwide

Because each of us acquired a male or female gender role with little conscious effort or awareness, we often do not notice the effect of gender roles on the development of our personality and social behaviors.

**U.S. gender roles.** The influence of gender roles on personality became clear when researchers asked U.S. college students to describe the traits of a typical female and a typical male. Students generally agreed that the female gender role included being caring, insecure, helpful, emotional, social, and shy. In comparison, students said that the male gender role included being arrogant, self-confident, aggressive, ambitious, not emotional, and dominant (Helgeson, 1994). These results matched previous descriptions of traditional, stereotypic gender roles that other researchers had found—females were generally concerned, sensitive, and nurturing, while males were considered independent, controlling, and dominant (Eckes & Trautner, 2000).

**Worldwide gender roles.** Not only in the U.S. but college students from around the world agreed remarkably well that the male gender role included being ambitious, dominant, and independent, while the female gender role included being submissive, affectionate, and emotional (Williams & Best, 1990). Researchers concluded that differences in male and female gender roles are clearly defined because society (family, peers, bosses, and colleagues) encourages and rewards behaviors and thoughts that match expected gender roles and discriminates against those that don't fit in (Eckes & Trautner, 2000).

**Changes.** During the past 20 years in the United States, women have struggled to broaden their gender role by assuming traits, behaviors, and occupations traditionally associated with the male gender role. Although women are trying to assume some of the traits traditionally associated with the male gender role (ambitious, dominant, assertive, confident), males have been less eager to take on traits traditionally associated with the female gender role (caring, emotional, helpful, nurturing) (Twenge, 1997).

Why do gender roles develop worldwide and what are their functions?

caring
insecure
helpful
emotional
social
shy

## Gender Roles: Development and Function

The question of why gender roles develop in every culture has two different but related answers.

**Evolutionary psychology theory.** One answer comes from *evolutionary psychology theory*, which says that differences in gender roles arose because there were different evolutionary demands placed on the survival of each sex; for example, men needed to be aggressive and dominant to protect their families, while women needed to be caring and helpful to raise their children (Buss, 1996).

**Social role theory.** A different but related answer comes from *social role theory*, which says that gender differences arose because men traditionally had occupational roles and society encouraged them to be assertive, while women traditionally had family roles and society encouraged them to be caring (Eagly et al., 2000). These two theories do not disagree but rather emphasize different factors, either biological or psychological. Researchers caution that differences in gender roles do not mean that one role is better or worse and that any differences should not be used for discriminatory practices (Zemore et al., 2000).

Next, you'll see that gender roles affect not only our cognitive, social, and personality development but also our expectations about relationships.

arrogant
confident
aggressive
ambitious
unemotional
dominant

## Expectations

**Did Susan recognize Mr. Right?**

As we acquire a male or female gender role, we also develop expectations about who we would like for an intimate relationship (Fletcher & Simpson, 2000). For example, here are the expectations of Susan, the high school prom queen.

"When I went away to college, I was a very sensible, logical, and levelheaded person. That's probably why the first person I dated was very much like me. We had wonderful serious talks, read poetry, discussed philosophy, but never had much passion. After we broke up, a friend of mine fixed me up

*Susan's expectations changed.*

with Charlie, who was a fun-loving, arrogant, cocky, abrasive basketball player and my complete opposite. We dated, got engaged, and about a year later were married. Oh, yes, I knew we were complete opposites, but I passionately loved Charlie and knew he was the one" (Wallechinsky, 1986).

Susan's first choice for someone to love was someone like her, but it didn't last. Then she chose someone very different from her and decided he was the right one to marry. After five years of marriage, she got divorced.

Susan's experience brings up three issues: kinds of love, choosing a partner, and what makes a relationship a success or failure.

## Kinds of Love

**Which kind of love are you in?**

Previous researchers had thought love too mysterious for scientific study, but current researchers have begun to analyze love into various components. As a starting point, researchers distinguish between passionate and companionate love (Hatfield & Rapson, 1995).

*Passionate love* involves continuously thinking about the loved one and is accompanied by warm sexual feelings and powerful emotional reactions.

*Companionate love* involves having trusting and tender feelings for someone whose life is closely bound up with one's own.

For example, when people fall madly in love, it's usually passionate love. When mature couples talk about enjoying each other's company, it's usually companionate love, which may or may not involve sexual behaviors. Thus, love is more complex than many think. One of the better known theories of love is Robert Sternberg's (1999) triangular theory of love.

Commitment | Intimacy
Love Triangle
Passion

Three components of love

The *triangular theory of love* has three components: passion, intimacy, and commitment. *Passion* is feeling physically aroused and attracted to someone. *Intimacy* is feeling close and connected to someone; it develops through sharing and communicating. *Commitment* is making a pledge to nourish the feelings of love and to actively maintain the relationship.

What makes you feel in love is the component of passion, which rises quickly and strongly influences and biases your judgment. What makes you want to share and offer emotional and material support is the component of intimacy. What makes you want to form a serious relationship, such as getting married, and to promise support through difficult times is the component of commitment. Sternberg believes that the kind of love most of us strive for is complete or consummate love, which is a balanced combination of all three components—passion, intimacy, and commitment.

Sternberg (1999) uses his triangular theory to answer some of the most commonly asked questions about love.

---

**Is there love at first sight?**

Love at first sight occurs when we are overwhelmed by passion, without any intimacy or commitment. Sternberg calls this *infatuated love,* which can arise in an instant, involves a great deal of physiological arousal, and lasts varying lengths of time. Because there is no intimacy or commitment, infatuated love is destined to fade away.

**Why do some people get married after being in love for a very short time?**

Sternberg calls this *Hollywood love,* which is a combination of passion and commitment but without any intimacy. In Hollywood love, two people make a commitment based on their passion for each other. Unless they develop intimacy over time, the relationship is likely to fail.

**Can there be love without sex?**

Sternberg calls love without sex *companionate love,* which is a combination of intimacy and commitment without any sexual passion. An example of companionate love is a married couple who are committed to each other and share their lives but whose physical attraction has waned.

**Why doesn't romantic love last?**

*Romantic love,* which is a combination of intimacy and passion, usually doesn't last because there is no commitment. As soon as the passion dies and the intimacy fades, the individuals no longer feel in love and go their separate ways.

---

About 90% of adults report having fallen in love, 10% report never being in love, and some individuals report finding love so painful that they will never love again (Thompson & Borrello, 1992). Researchers believe that when we first fall in love, the excitement and happiness we feel are fueled by passion, but we need to gradually develop commitment and intimacy if the relationship is to last (Sternberg, 1999). Most often we use the term *in love* to mean

emotional feelings plus sexual attraction. However, as couples age and reach their senior years, sexual attraction may lessen and give way to a different kind of love that includes feelings of tenderness, support, and commitment (Meyers & Berscheid, 1997).

Falling in love is but the first step in developing an intimate relationship and making a more permanent commitment, such as marriage. Developing a long-term relationship is our next topic.

## Choosing a Partner

**What am I looking for?**

The fact that about 90% of adults in the United States marry means that most of us will eventually select a partner for a long-term relationship. However, the fact that 40 to 60% of new marriages and an even higher percentage of second marriages end in divorce means that selecting the right partner can be a very difficult, demanding, and somewhat mysterious process (Gottman, 1999).

Researchers suggest that one way we choose a partner for a long-term relationship is by finding someone who most closely matches our ideal-partner schema (Fletcher & Simpson, 2000).

A *schema* refers to an organized mental or cognitive list that includes characteristics, facts, values, or beliefs about people, events, or objects.

An ideal-partner schema is a mental list of the most desirable characteristics that we are seeking. For instance, an ideal-partner schema in order of preference for unmarried college students (averaged for men and women) is shown above (Buss, 1994b). Researchers con-

**IDEAL PARTNER**
1. Kind and understanding
2. Exciting personality
3. Intelligent
4. Physically attractive (men)
5. Healthy
6. Easygoing
7. Creative
8. Wants children
9. Educated
10. Good earning potential (women)

cluded that men and women form ideal-partner schemas with two major differences: men rank physical attractiveness as more important, and women rank good earning capacity higher (Buss, 1994a, 1995).

One reason we date different people is to find the ideal partner who best matches the traits on our ideal-partner schema list. However, when we become passionately attracted to a person, we lose the ability to rationally decide whether a person really has the traits on our list (Rossi, 1994). Even though our parents or best friends may warn us that our ideal partner has some negative traits, we usually turn a deaf ear because in our love-blinded state the person looks ideal.

After selecting Mr. or Ms. Right, the couple is ready to make a commitment, such as getting married (92%) or living together (8%). What happens during the next 7–10 years usually determines the success or failure of a long-term relationship (Kurdek, 1999).

Looking for partner with good earning potential

Looking for partner who is physically attractive

## Long-Term Relationship: Success or Failure?

**How do I make my marriage last?**

The graph below shows that a couple's rating of marital satisfaction falls during the next 7–10 years (Benin & Robinson, 1997). To find out why some of these marriages succeed but about 40 to 60% fail, researcher John Gottman analyzed videotapes of many couples' social interactions and physiological responses (heart rates) across a period of 14 years. From these data, Gottman was able to predict with an amazing 91% accuracy which couples would stay together and which would divorce (Gottman, 2000).

**Unhappy relationships.** As Gottman analyzed couples' social interactions, he found that couples who later divorced had four major problems: One or both partners spent too much time criticizing the other; one or both partners became too defensive when one of their faults was criticized; one or both partners showed contempt for the other, especially during disagreements; and one or both partners, usually the male, engaged in stonewalling or being unwilling to talk about some problem (Gottman, 2000). The continual stress arising from these four problems—criticism, defensiveness, contempt, and stonewalling—resulted in couples becoming more unhappy and distressed through the years. For example, couples who were happily married had at least five times as many positive as negative experiences. In comparison, couples who grew more unhappy and later divorced had about the same number of positive and negative experiences (Gottman, 1995a).

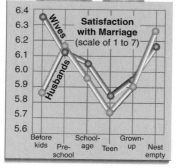

**Satisfaction with Marriage** (scale of 1 to 7)

Wives

Husbands

6.4
6.3
6.2
6.1
6.0
5.9
5.8
5.7
5.6

Before kids | Pre-school | School-age | Teen | Grown-up | Nest empty

In some cases, couples in unhappy relationships may not know what's wrong or may not have the necessary social or communication skills. Couples who participated in programs on how to manage conflicts and learn effective communication skills showed lower rates of both divorce and domestic violence (Prince & Jacobson, 1997).

**Happy relationships.** Couples in happy and successful marriages find a way to deal with the four major problems—criticism, defensiveness, contempt, and stonewalling. For example, successful couples learn to confront and deal with stonewalling by settling disagreements in an open, straightforward way; try to be less defensive about negative feedback; criticize their partners less and try to be more supportive; and agree to overlook small problems they are unlikely to change (one partner is messy and one is neat) (Gottman, 1999). Gottman's research shows that falling in love is grand but it takes work to achieve long-term success.

**Happiness graph.** Every couple knows there are ups and downs in marital happiness (left graph). The lowest point in happiness is when adolescent children are learning to be independent and disagree with their parents' rules (Benin & Robinson, 1997). One of the high points is when the children leave home and parents are given peace and quiet so they can again share some good times together.

# Concept Review

**1.** Puberty is accompanied by a number of biological and physical changes, which are triggered by male or female (a)_____. These chemicals result in the development of male and female secondary (b)_____ characteristics and, for females, their first menstrual cycle, which is called (c)_____.

**2.** The idea that adolescent development consists of a number of cognitive, sexual, social, and personality changes that occur simultaneously is called the _____ model.

**3.** Piaget hypothesized that cognitive development is made up of four distinct stages of reasoning, each of which is qualitatively different from and more advanced than the previous one. According to Piaget, from adolescence through adulthood, we are at the _____ stage, which involves the ability to think about hypothetical concepts, consider an issue from another's viewpoint, and solve abstract problems in a logical manner.

**4.** New findings indicate that teenagers do not yet have a fully developed part of their brains, called the (a)_____, which has (b)_____ functions, such as thinking, planning, and making decisions.

**5.** One reason adolescents engage in more risky behaviors is that they have an underdeveloped (a)_____ but a fully functioning emotional center, called the (b)_____.

**6.** The idea that moral reasoning can be classified into three distinct levels and that everyone goes through these levels in order is a theory of moral development proposed by (a)_____. The level of moral reasoning based primarily on punishment is called (b)_____; the one based on conforming to laws and society is called (c)_____; and the one based on balancing rights and laws is called (d)_____. Most research supports Kohlberg's idea that people do go through (e)_____ of moral development but that not everyone reaches the higher stages.

**7.** Carol Gilligan has proposed two basic approaches to moral decisions. Basing moral decisions on avoiding hurt and on concerns about interpersonal relationships is called the (a)_____ orientation. Making moral decisions based more on issues of law and equality is called the (b)_____ orientation.

**8.** The development of independence and achievement during adolescence is shaped by a number of different kinds of parenting styles—in particular, (a)_____, (b)_____, and (c)_____—each of which has different costs and benefits to parents and adolescents.

**9.** In late adulthood, individuals experience a decline in three cognitive processes: an increase in the time required to respond to some sensory stimulus, which is called the (a)_____; a decrease in the rate at which we identify some sensory stimulus as different from other stimuli, which is called the (b)_____; and a decrease in the rate at which we encode information into long-term memory or retrieve it, which is called the (c)_____ speed.

*Am I losing my memory?*

**10.** According to Erik Erikson, across our lifetimes we proceed through eight (a)_____, each of which presents a particular kind of personality or social problem. For adolescents, stage 5 is most relevant and involves (b)_____ versus role confusion. Finding one's identity has many aspects; the aspect that involves how much we like ourselves and our feelings of worth, attractiveness, and social competence is called (c)_____. Erikson believed that the most important part of personality development for an adolescent was to achieve a satisfying sense of (d)_____, while adults are more concerned about being (e)_____.

*What happened to all my dreams?*

**11.** Males and females think, act, and behave in different ways, and these are called _____, which are enforced by expectations of parents and peers and by society rewarding traditional roles and punishing roles that are different.

**12.** One way we select a partner for a long-term relationship is by first forming a mental list of characteristics and then looking for someone who matches our mental list, which is called a _____.

**13.** The theory of love that has three components—passion, intimacy, and commitment—is called the _____.

**14.** Couples are more likely to have successful long-term relationships if they learn to deal with (a)_____ in a straightforward way and have at least five times more positive (b)_____ than negative ones.

**Answers:** *1. (a) hormones, (b) sexual, (c) menarche; 2. BioPsychoSocial; 3. formal operations; 4. (a) prefrontal cortex, (b) executive; 5. (a) prefrontal cortex, (b) limbic system; 6. (a) Kohlberg, (b) preconventional, (c) conventional, (d) postconventional, (e) stages; 7. (a) care, (b) justice; 8. (a) authoritarian, (b) authoritative, (c) permissive; 9. (a) reaction time, (b) perceptual speed, (c) processing; 10. (a) psychosocial stages, (b) identity, (c) self-esteem, (d) identity, (e) productive, creative, nurturing; 11. gender roles; 12. schema; 13. triangular theory; 14. (a) conflicts, (b) experiences*

---

## Why Do Marriages Succeed or Fail?

**Power Study™**

Check out CD: Module 4
E. Limbic System: Old Brain

**What's the key to a successful relationship?**

Imagine being a researcher who wants to predict one of the most complex human behaviors: Which couples will succeed and which will fail in long-term relationships? The fact that 40 to 60% of marriages fail indicates that something is leading to success or failure. How would you design a research program to figure out what that "something" is?

Every research program aims for the same four goals, which are to describe, explain, predict, and control behavior. The first two goals—describe and explain—are relatively easy. However, the last two goals—predict and control—are very difficult because many human behaviors are so complex that they cannot be completely explained, much less predicted or controlled. Now,

along comes psychologist and researcher John Gottman, who claims that not only can he explain the "something" but he can also predict with 91% accuracy which marriages will succeed or fail. Since very few human behaviors can be predicted with 91% accuracy, his claim is nothing but amazing.

In the past, researchers used primarily self-reports or questionnaires to study the success or failure of long-term relationships. However, self-reports and questionnaires are not totally reliable since marriage partners could knowingly (out of embarrassment) or unknowingly (out of defensiveness) bias their answers. Gottman's breakthrough in studying and predicting the success or failure of long-term relationships was to develop a better research method that goes by the zany name of "Love Lab."

### Method

**PS** In the Love Lab, one partner sits facing the other (photos below). For 15 minutes they discuss a topic that is a known sore point while their facial and physiological responses are recorded.

**Facial responses.** The advantage of recording each of the partners' nonverbal facial responses is that facial responses reflect a wide range of emotional expressions (surprise, interest, anger, disgust, contempt) that one or both partners may be unaware of or try to deny. Nonverbal behaviors are very important ways of communicating in real life. For example, it's not uncommon for one partner to notice the other partner's facial expression and ask, "What's bothering you?" By recording nonverbal facial cues, which are difficult to hide or fake by normal (untrained) individuals, Gottman can reliably identify if certain kinds of social interactions cause problems for the partners.

**Physiological responses.** Gottman also wants to know how long the emotional feelings last. He measures the duration of emotional feeings by recording physiological responses (heart and breathing rate, sweating). These responses reflect the start and duration of increased physiological or emotional arousal, which one or both partners may be unaware of or try to deny. For example, if one or both part-

In the Love Lab, a video camera (in circle) records facial expressions, and white bands (visible on her fingers and his wrist) record various physiological responses.

ners experience frequent and long-lasting bad feelings, it often signals the marriage is in trouble (Gottman, 1999).

**Longitudinal method.** So far, you can see that Gottman's Love Lab solved the problem of how to reliably measure a couple's emotional responses and feeings. But how would he know if these measures predicted a marriage's success or failure? To answer this question, Gottman used the longitudinal research method, which means he retested the same couples regularly during 14 years. By retesting the same couples over time, he could determine if a couple's social interactions and emotional responses recorded during early sessions could be used to predict whether this particular marriage would succeed or fail.

### Results and Conclusions

After retesting the same 79 couples for 14 years, Gottman (1999) reported that he could predict, based on previous observations in the Love Lab, which of the marriages would succeed or fail. Here are some of the findings that allowed him to predict with such accuracy.

**Unsuccessful relationships.** We have already discussed the four major problems that couples experience early on and that, if not dealt with successfully, predict failure in long-term relationships. These four problems are giving too many *criticisms*, becoming too *defensive*, showing *contempt* of a partner, and *stonewalling* or refusing to settle disagreements in an open, straightforward discussion.

**Successful relationships.** There are several things that predict successful relationships. First, happy marriages had *husbands* who were good at not immediately rejecting their wives' advice but either accepted it or found something reasonable in it. In contrast, unhappy marriages had husbands who were autocratic, failed to listen, and dismissed their wives' advice, often with contempt.

Second, happy marriages had *wives* who were careful to express their complaints and advice in gentle, soothing ways, which were easier for their husbands to accept. In contrast, unhappy marriages had wives who phrased their complaints and advice in angry, fighting words that, in turn, triggered equally angry replies from their husbands.

**Advice.** Gottman's advice is for a couple to work at managing conflict, which means men have to be more accepting of a woman's position, and women have to be more gentle in starting up discussions.

Although in the United States most people marry for love, that's not true in other cultures.

## Measuring Cultural Influences

**Can 9,000 people agree?**

Imagine being born and raised in a country different from your own, such as Nigeria, Germany, China, Iran, Brazil, Japan, France, or India. Now imagine being asked to list, in order, those traits that you consider most desirable in a potential partner. How much would your culture influence the order of desirable traits? To answer this

What if you were born in Egypt?

question, researchers surveyed over 9,000 young adults (males and females), all in their 20s, who lived in 37 different countries (Buss, 1994b; Buss et al., 1990). Subjects were given a list of 32 traits and asked to rank the traits from most to least desirable in a potential partner. The results indicate that 9,000 individuals from many different cultures seemed to agree reasonably well in ranking traits.

## Desirable Traits

**What is considered desirable in a potential partner?** The list on the near right shows the most desirable traits for potential partners averaged across cultures. Men and women have similar lists of desirable traits, as indicated by a high correlation of +0.87 between lists. The numerous similarities between males' and females' lists indicate similar cultural influences.

The list on the far right shows that there were also some interesting differences between males and females. Males almost always ranked physical appearance in a partner higher, while females almost always ranked earning potential in a partner higher.

| Average ranking of desirable traits |
|---|
| 1 Kind and understanding |
| 2 Intelligent |
| 3 Exciting personality |
| 4 Healthy |
| 5 Emotionally stable and mature |
| 6 Dependable character |
| 7 Pleasing disposition |

| Differences in desirable traits |
|---|
| 8 Good looks (ranked higher by males) |
| 9 Good financial prospect (ranked higher by females) |
| 10 Virginity (ranked higher by males) |

**How much is virginity valued around the world?** In two-thirds of all the cultures measured, men desired virginity or chastity (the lack of previous sexual intercourse) in marriage partners more than women did; there were no cultures where women valued virginity in a prospective partner more than men did (Buss, 1994b). For example, in China, virginity is indispensable in a partner; marrying a nonvirgin is simply out of the question (Buss, 1994b). In addition, people in India, Taiwan, and Iran placed great value on virginity, while people in the Netherlands, Sweden, and Norway placed little value on virginity in a prospective partner. These differences in the value placed on the virginity of females indicate how cultural influences can raise or lower the desirability of certain traits in potential marriage partners.

## Reasons for Marrying

**How much is love valued?** As the figure on the right shows, cultures in different countries place different values on marrying for love. In the United States and other Western countries, marrying for love is highly valued, but it is valued less in some Middle East, Asian, and African nations.

**How do women decide?** Some anthropologists have argued that women, who invest more time in caring for offspring, would adopt more discriminating standards for potential mates than would men, who invest less time in rearing children. Thus, women would be more careful in deciding whom to marry. This proved true: In nearly every culture, women expressed more stringent standards across a wide range of characteristics (Buss, 1994b).

**How Citizens in Different Nations Rank the Importance of Love in Choosing a Spouse**

**United States: First**
These citizens ranked love first or most important in choosing a spouse.

**Iran: Third**
Citizens ranked higher: education, ambition, chastity

**Nigeria: Fourth**
Citizens ranked higher: good health, refinement/neatness, desire for home and children

**China: Sixth**
Citizens ranked higher: health, chastity, homemaker

**South Africa-Zulu: Seventh**
Citizens ranked higher: emotionally stable, mature, dependable

**How do men decide?** Across cultures, men generally decide to marry younger women who are physically attractive. In those societies where men purchase their wives, younger women command a higher bride price. Also, across cultures, the most common reason that men use to dissolve marriages is infertility, or the inability to have children (Buss, 1994b).

From surveys of desirable traits in marriage partners, researchers found many similarities across cultures but found considerable differences among cultures in reasons for getting married.

We have primarily discussed development in adolescents and young to middle-aged adults. Next, we'll examine the physical changes that come with aging.

# G. Physical Changes: Aging

**Power Study™**

**Check out CD: Module 3**
B. Neurons: Structure & Function

## Kinds of Aging

**Why do we grow old?**

**PS**

As you look at the photo on the right, the difference you see between grandmother and granddaughter is an example of normal aging, which is very different from pathological aging.

*Normal aging* is a gradual and natural slowing of our physical and psychological processes from middle through late adulthood.

*Pathological aging* may be caused by genetic defects, physiological problems, or diseases, such as Alzheimer's (p. 47), all of which accelerate the aging process.

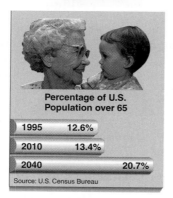

**Percentage of U.S. Population over 65**

| | |
|---|---|
| 1995 | 12.6% |
| 2010 | 13.4% |
| 2040 | 20.7% |

Source: U.S. Census Bureau

One goal of the study of aging, which is called *gerontology*, is to separate the causes of normal aging from those of pathological aging. The study of aging will grow in importance because the percentage of people in the United States over 65 is expected to almost double by the year 2040 (left graph). Life expectancy in the United States was 45 years in 1945 but is now a record 76.7 years. In the 1920s, there were only 3,700 people over 100, but currently there are about 61,000 over that age (women outnumber men 4 to 1) (Sharp, 1999).

We'll examine two related questions about aging: Why do our bodies age? How do our bodies and behaviors change with age?

## Reasons for Aging

How long you will live and how fast your body will age depend about 50% on heredity (genes) and 50% on other factors (diet, exercise, lifestyle, diseases) (Finch & Tanzi, 1997). Researchers have two general theories to explain the aging process.

### AGING BY CHANCE

The *aging by chance theory* says that our bodies age because of naturally occurring problems or breakdowns in the body's cells, which become less able to repair themselves.

These cellular changes, which occur as a result of normal wear and tear, may include a buildup of waste products that interferes with the cells' functioning; a breakdown in the immune system, which destroys the body's defenses against toxic agents; and an increased number of errors in the genetic mechanism (DNA code), which interferes with cell structure and function (Wallace, 1997).

### AGING BY DESIGN

The *aging by design theory* says that our bodies age because there are preset biological clocks that determine the number of times cells can divide and multiply; after that limit is reached, cells begin to die and aging occurs.

Evidence suggests that our bodies age from a combination of biological clocks, which are set by genetic mechanisms, wear and tear, and environmental factors, such as diet, disease, exercise, and lifestyle. Currently, all of these factors (genes, wear and tear, and environment) limit the human life span to a maximum of about 120 years (Marx, 2000).

As we age, our bodies undergo many physiological changes.

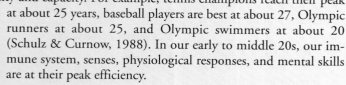

### Early Adulthood

The finding that most athletes peak in their 20s indicates that this is a period of maximum physical ability and capacity. For example, tennis champions reach their peak at about 25 years, baseball players are best at about 27, Olympic runners at about 25, and Olympic swimmers at about 20 (Schulz & Curnow, 1988). In our early to middle 20s, our immune system, senses, physiological responses, and mental skills are at their peak efficiency.

### Middle Adulthood

In our 30s and 40s, we usually gain weight, primarily because we are less active. By the late 40s, there is a slight decrease in a number of physiological responses, including heart rate, lung capacity, muscle strength, kidney function, and eyesight.

### Late Adulthood

In our 50s and 60s, we may experience a gradual decline in height because of loss of bone, a further decrease in output of lungs and kidneys, an increase in skin wrinkles, and a deterioration in joints. Sensory organs become less sensitive, resulting in less acute vision, hearing, and taste. The heart, which is a muscle, becomes less effective at pumping blood, which may result in as much as a 35% decrease in blood flow through the coronary arteries. A general decrease occurs in both the number and diameter of muscle fibers, which may explain some of the slowing in motor functions that usually accompanies old age.

### Very Late Adulthood

In our 70s and 80s, we undergo further decreases in muscle strength, bone density, speed of nerve conduction, and output of lungs, heart, and kidneys. More than 10% have Parkinson's or Alzheimer's disease. In 1997, the oldest living person in the world died at age 117; in 1999, the oldest living person died at 119. At current rates, life expectancy is projected to reach about 100 toward the end of this century.

As many of the body's physical responses slow down with aging, there are corresponding decreases in related behaviors. Earlier in this module we discussed decreases in memory with aging (p. 415), and now we'll discuss decreases in sexual behavior.

**How does sex change with aging?**

Surveys of sexual behavior, which usually sample people between ages 17 and 59, generally report that single men have more sex partners, experience orgasm more frequently, and masturbate more frequently than single women and that about one-third of married couples have sex 2–3 times a week (Laumann et al., 1994). However, people in late adulthood (60–80) are often not included in these surveys because of the common stereotype that they no

longer have any interest in sexual activity or that it is inappropriate for them to engage in sex (Masters & Johnson, 1981). However, other surveys reported that about 30% of healthy men and women over 65 (average age was 77) were sexually active, primarily those who were married (Matthias et al., 1997). This survey indicates that adults can enjoy sexual activity well into their later years, especially if they know how sexual responses change and learn ways to deal with these changes.

## Sexual Changes in Women

The single most significant effect on women's sexual behavior in later adulthood is menopause.

*Menopause* occurs in women at about age 50 (range 35–60) and involves a gradual stoppage in secretion of the major female hormone (estrogen), which, in turn, results in cessation of both ovulation and the menstrual cycle.

Menopause is not the end of sexual behavior.

Over the next 20 years, approximately 40 million baby boomers will enter menopause, and most can expect to live nearly one-third of their lives after menopause (Fackelmann, 1995b). During and immediately after menopause, about 15% of women experience physical symptoms that are severe enough to require medical help; 65% of women experience mild symptoms that do not require medical help; and 20% of women have few if any of the physical symptoms described below (Hooyman & Niyak, 1999).

### PHYSICAL SYMPTOMS
Most women experience hot flashes, some sleep disturbance, and dryness of the vagina, which results from a decrease and eventual stoppage in the secretion of the female hormone estrogen. A lack of estrogen results in thinning of the vaginal wall and reduction of lubrication during arousal. However, there is little or no change in the ability to become sexually aroused or to reach orgasm. Potential problems with lack of lubrication or painful intercourse may be compensated for by hormone replacement therapy or the use of vaginal creams. Because researchers find no correlation between decrease in hormones and sexual activity, it means that women's continued sexual activity after menopause is due primarily to psychological rather than physiological factors (Dennerstein et al., 1997; Hooyman & Niyak, 1999).

### PSYCHOLOGICAL SYMPTOMS
Researchers followed more than 400 healthy women through menopause and observed many psychological changes. They found that women did report psychological symptoms, such as moodiness, depression, anxiety, and anger. However, these symptoms were more related to other stressful issues—for example, growing older in a society that glorifies being young—rather than the physical symptoms of menopause. In addition, women's expectations greatly influence the psychological outlook during menopause. Women with positive expectations about what they hope to accomplish have few psychological symptoms, compared to women who expect their lives to be over and thus feel depressed and angry during menopause (Dennerstein et al., 1997; Neugarten, 1994).

### SEXUAL ACTIVITIES
Researchers report that those women who experienced sexual activity as fulfilling and enriching before menopause will likely continue to enjoy sexual activity after menopause and into late adulthood. On the other hand, women who experienced sexual activity as just tolerable or worse before menopause may gradually discontinue sexual activity after menopause (Hooyman & Niyak, 1999).

Interestingly enough, women in cultures where menopause results in increased social status look forward to menopause and have fewer symptoms than women in the United States (Richters, 1997).

## Sexual Changes in Men

As men reach late adulthood (60s, 70s, and 80s) they may experience some physiological changes that decrease sexual responsiveness.

### SEXUAL RESPONDING
Because many of the body's physiological responses slow down, older men may require more time and stimulation to have an erection and to reach orgasm. Upon ejaculation, there may be a reduction in the force and amount of fluid. However, in healthy men, there is usually no difficulty in becoming sexually aroused or reaching orgasm. Some men worry that their decreased ability to have an erection or reach orgasm means an end to their sexuality (Masters & Johnson, 1981). In 1998, a new drug (Viagra) was approved for the treatment of impotency, which is the inability to have an erection. Early reports are that about 80% of men with impotency can be helped by the drug (Mann, 1998).

### PSYCHOLOGICAL PROBLEMS
Although older men are generally more sexually active than older women, some men see their decreased sexual abilities as a threat to their self-esteem (Matthias et al., 1997). However, any increased time and stimulation required for erection and orgasm can usually be compensated for by longer periods of stimulation and more imaginative sexual activity by the couple.

Some things may take longer but that's OK.

According to one researcher, as we grow older we also learn more skills—for example, being more understanding and sensitive to our partner's needs—and these skills help maintain sexual enjoyment and activity (Rossi, 1994).

Next, we'll discuss a serious problem that is shared by both adolescents and seniors, a high rate of suicide.

### Teenage Suicide

**What is the third leading cause of death?**

Suicides for teenagers aged 15–19 almost quadrupled from about 3.5 per 100,000 in 1960 to 11.1 per 100,000 in 1994 (Nazario, 1997). In this age group, suicide is now the third leading cause of death. White boys have the highest suicide rate among teens (18 per 100,000). A recent survey of high school students reported that about 22% had considered suicide during the past year (Moran, 2000).

We'll focus on the two most-asked questions: What are the problems related to teenage suicide? How can teenage suicide be prevented? We'll use four real-life examples to illustrate how complex the issues and causes are. In a span of five weeks, four teenage boys—one a straight-A student, one the class clown, one deeply religious person, and one very troubled boy—committed suicide in the small southern town of Sheridan, Arkansas (adapted from *People*, May 21, 1990, pp. 56–59). Here are their sad and tragic stories.

**1  March 28, 1990: Raymond, 17 Years Old**

According to the police chief, Ray had threatened to kill himself in the past, but the threats were considered teenage histrionics. He had a drinking problem, had been arrested for drunken driving, and had been sent to a rehabilitation center for several weeks. Before Ray shot himself, however, his life seemed to be improving, and he had made plans to go to college. A suicide note to his girlfriend said, "Don't blame yourself. It's nobody's fault."

**3  April 30, 1990: Thomas, 19 Years Old**

Thomas was a straight-A student who liked to read, listen to oldies, and hunt and fish. He did not drink, smoke, or swear. He lived too far out of town to have many buddies. His father had died when he was 9. Two years earlier, his grandfather, who had terminal cancer, committed suicide with a pistol to his head. Tommy had shot himself in the afternoon, and that very night Thomas did the same. In his suicide note he said, "Where shall I begin? I really don't know. It's hard to say what's going on anymore. A long time now I have felt like I am on the edge and slipping fast. I guess I've finally slipped over the edge."

**2  April 30, 1990: Tommy, 16 Years Old**

His teenage peers considered Tommy a clown, but his best friend, Rhonda, didn't believe that. She thought Tommy's clever wit and clowning were a mask for his insecurity. On April 29, Tommy called Rhonda, which he did regularly, and told her that he was going to kill himself. Certain he would not carry out his threat, she made him promise to come to school the next day. Tommy came to school, and in one of his classes he got up and stated that he had two things to say. He said that he loved Rhonda, although they had never dated. "The other thing," he said, "is this." He pulled out a pistol and shot himself.

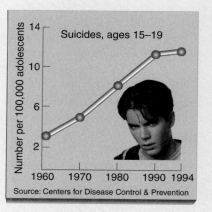

Suicides, ages 15–19

14

10

6

2

Number per 100,000 adolescents

1960  1970  1980  1990  1994

Source: Centers for Disease Control & Prevention

**4  May 2, 1990: Jerry, 17 Years Old**

Jerry's suicide was the last of the four and the most troubling. He was popular, gregarious, good-looking, and so deeply religious that he was nicknamed "preacher boy." The night after Tommy's suicide he told his mother, "I can't understand how anyone would commit suicide—that was the coward's way." That same night he called his girlfriend and said, "I love you. I'll talk to you tomorrow." The next day he stayed home from school, and around noon he shot himself in the head. The family insists that Jerry's death was accidental.

### Problems Related to Teenage Suicide

**Why do teens take their own lives?**

Notice that in the above examples, family and friends could not believe that two of the four adolescents would ever even think of committing suicide. That's because one was a straight-A student and the other was very popular and deeply religious. In the other two cases, one adolescent had said he was thinking about suicide and one had made a previous attempt. Thus, if and when adolescents talk about committing suicide, parents and friends need to take such talk seriously. In other cases, the problems, symptoms, or events leading up to or triggering suicide may be difficult to recognize. However, clinicians find that the following problems may lead to or trigger suicide attempts.

**Problems and symptoms.**  The most common *psychological problems* include depression, feelings of helplessness, and drug-related problems, such as Raymond's alcohol problem. Usually these problems have persisted for some time (Haliburn, 2000). The most common *behavioral symptoms* include decline in school performance; social isolation and withdrawal; intense difficulties with parents, siblings, and peers; and antisocial behavior (Patton et al., 1997). For example, Thomas's suicide note says, "A long time now I have felt like I am on the edge and slipping fast."

**Precipitators.**  In most cases, there are *precipitators* of suicide, which may be certain events, feelings, or situations. For example, common precipitators include problems with relationships, bouts of depression, drinking problems, or relatively ordinary stressors, such as difficulties with dating, parents, or school. A high percentage of victims had either expressed the wish to die or threatened suicide, as was true for both Raymond and Tommy.

One reason parents and friends are shocked by an adolescent's suicide is that the problems or precipitators may be hard to spot.

## Preventing Teenage Suicide

**What can be done to help teens?**

A survey by the Centers for Disease Control and Prevention found that 1 in 12 high school students have attempted suicide and about 24 out of 100 students have seriously thought about committing suicide (Nazario, 1997). Because suicide is the third leading cause of death in adolescents, therapists have proposed a three-step program to help identify the risk factors and ultimately prevent suicide.

### Identify Risk Factors

The first step is to identify risk factors, including depression, drug abuse, previous suicide attempt, recent suicide of a friend, and major life stressors, such as family turmoil or parental separation (Lewinsohn et al., 1994). A youth with one or more of these risk factors is in imminent danger of committing suicide (Berman & Jobes, 1994). Methods for identifying risk factors include special programs on suicide prevention in schools and support groups among families to deal with life and environmental stressors (Garland & Zigler, 1993).

### Crisis Management

The Centers for Disease Control and Prevention (1988) recommend that, following a suicide in a school or local community, a team of mental health professionals be sent to the location to screen for students who may be at risk for suicide. For example, in a questionnaire screening of 2,000 students, about 3% requested help from a counselor (Berman & Jobes, 1994).

### Hot-Line Services

The rationale for 24-hour hot-line services is that suicidal behavior is often associated with a crisis situation during which the person may have a strong need or desire to talk to someone in a last cry for help (Garland & Zigler, 1993). Hot-line services may reach adolescents, such as those in poverty or without health coverage, who would not otherwise be served by mental health facilities.

The combination of these programs in schools and communities can aid in identifying and preventing potential suicides in adolescents (Berman & Jobes, 1995). In one case, suicides decreased by 50% after an antisuicide program in schools (Kalafat, 1997).

Although adolescents have a high rate of suicide, the highest rate of any group is one you rarely hear about.

## Suicide in the Elderly

**Why are rates so high?**

Although suicides are the third leading cause of death among adolescents, the highest suicide rate for any group is among the elderly. For individuals 65 and older, the suicide rate in the United States is almost double (20 per 100,000) that of the national average (12 per 100,000). A number of risk factors contribute to the high rate of suicide in the elderly.

**Risk factors.** The common risk factors for suicide among the elderly are depression and loneliness, but the major contributing cause in 69–85% of the cases was a serious health problem (Cattell & Jolley, 1995). Thus, the major factor leading to suicide in the elderly, which is physical illness, is very different from the major factors in adolescent suicide, which involve psychological problems. How the elderly deal with serious physical problems brings up the question of physician-assisted suicide.

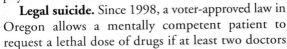

"I have six months to live and I'm in constant pain."

**Assisted suicide.** During the 1990s, Dr. Jack Kevorkian assisted in the suicides of 130 adults who were terminally ill, were in great pain or fear of pain, and had made known their wishes to die. After five trials, Kevorkian was convicted of one murder and, in 1999, was sentenced to 10–25 years in prison (Slater, 1999). At least 28 states have laws banning assisted suicide by anyone. However, the state of Oregon has recently legalized physician-assisted suicide.

**Legal suicide.** Since 1998, a voter-approved law in Oregon allows a mentally competent patient to request a lethal dose of drugs if at least two doctors determine that the person has less than six months to live. In 1999, 27 terminally ill residents of Oregon decided on doctor-assisted suicide. Legalization is now being considered in a number of states.

### Opponents of Doctor-Assisted Suicide

Opponents say that allowing people to take their own lives opens the door to many potential abuses. For example, making assisted suicide easier may increase the chances that people who are suffering from mental problems or temporary emotional difficulties will take their own lives without exploring other possibilities for living. Some fear that the profit motive may make assisted suicide or euthanasia a lucrative business (Hendin, 1994). Others argue that when people are distressed they are unlikely or unable to think clearly or make a rational decision about committing suicide (Clay, 1997a).

### Proponents of Doctor-Assisted Suicide

Proponents explain that each of us has the moral right to end our lives if we find that life has become unbearable for health reasons. In 1990, public opinion polls found that 66% believed that someone in great pain and with no hope of improvement has the moral right to commit suicide (euthanasia) (Blendon et al., 1992). The *New England Journal of Medicine* published an article by a group of doctors who proposed a policy of legalized physician-assisted death with safeguards to protect patients, preserve the integrity of physicians, and ensure that voluntary physician-assisted death occurs only as a last resort (F. G. Miller et al., 1994). For example, in Oregon, most of the 27 individuals who chose doctor-assisted suicide were well-educated, elderly cancer patients who had health insurance and were concerned about loss of bodily functions and increasing pain (McMahon & Koch, 2000).

The pros and cons of doctor-assisted suicide will continue to be debated, especially since the population of the elderly will almost double in the next 35 years.

# Summary Test

## A. PUBERTY & SEXUAL BEHAVIOR

**1.** Girls and boys experience three major biological changes as they go through a period called (a)_____. For both girls and boys, one of these changes is the development of (b)_____ maturity, which for girls includes the first menstrual cycle, called (c)_____, and for boys includes the production of sperm. These physical changes in girls and boys are triggered by a portion of the brain called the (d)_____. A second change is the development of (e)_____ sexual characteristics, such as pubic hair and gender-specific physical changes. A third change is a surge in (f)_____ growth, especially height. The changes for girls tend to start about a year earlier than those for boys.

## B. COGNITIVE & EMOTIONAL CHANGES

**2.** Piaget's fourth cognitive stage, which begins in adolescence and continues into adulthood, is called the (a)_____ stage. During this stage, adolescents and adults develop the ability to think about (b)_____ concepts, plan for the future, and solve abstract problems. One reason adolescents engage in more risky behaviors is that they have an underdeveloped (c)_____ but a fully functioning emotional center, called the (d)_____.

**3.** According to Kohlberg's theory, moral reasoning can be classified into three distinct levels, and everyone progresses through the levels in the same order. However, not all adults reach the higher levels. The first level, the (a)_____ level, has two stages. In stage 1, moral decisions are determined primarily through fear of punishment, while at stage 2 they are guided by satisfying one's self-interest. The second level, the (b)_____ level, also has two stages. In the first of these, stage 3, people conform to the standards of others they value; in stage 4, they conform to the laws of society. In the third level, the (c)_____ level, moral decisions are made after thinking about all the alternatives and striking a balance between human rights and the laws of society.

**4.** There is only limited support for Gilligan's proposal that women may tend to make moral decisions based on a (a)_____ orientation, while men tend to make moral decisions based on a (b)_____ orientation.

## 5.

**5.** Parenting styles affect many aspects of adolescents' development. Parents who attempt to shape and control their children in accordance with a set standard of conduct are termed (a)_____. Parents who attempt to direct their children's activities in a rational and intelligent way and are supportive, loving, and committed are called (b)_____. Parents who are less controlling and behave with a nonpunishing and accepting attitude toward their children's impulses are called (c)_____.

## C. PERSONALITY & SOCIAL CHANGES

**6.** How you describe yourself, including your values, goals, traits, interests, and motivations, is a function of your sense of (a)_____, which is part of the problem to be faced in stage 5 of Erikson's eight (b)_____ stages. Those who are unsuccessful in resolving the problems of this stage will experience (c)_____, which results in low self-esteem, and may become socially withdrawn.

**7.** An adolescent's feeling of worth, attractiveness, and social competence is called _____, which is influenced particularly by physical appearance, social acceptability, and management of public behaviors (anxiety and stress).

**8.** The challenges of adulthood are covered in the last three of Erikson's eight (a)_____ stages. According to his theory, in stage 6, young adults face the problems of intimacy versus (b)_____. In stage 7, middle adults face problems of generativity versus (c)_____. In stage 8, older adults reflect on their lives; if they feel positive and content about how they lived and what they accomplished, they will have a feeling of satisfaction or (d)_____; if not, they will have a feeling of regret and (e)_____.

## D. GENDER ROLES, LOVE, & RELATIONSHIPS

**9.** During childhood and adolescence, males and females experience pressures and expectations from parents, peers, and society to behave in different ways. These expected patterns of behavior and thought, called _____, influence cognitive, personality, and social development.

**10.** The kind of love that involves continually thinking about the loved one and is accompanied by sexual feelings and powerful emotional reactions is called (a)_____ love. The kind of love that involves trusting and tender feelings for someone whose life is closely bound up with one's own is called (b)_____ love. Sternberg has developed a triangular theory of love, dividing it into three components. Feeling physically aroused and attracted to someone is called (c)_____; feeling close and connected to someone, which develops through sharing and communicating, is called (d)_____; making a pledge to nourish the feelings of love and to maintain the relationship is called (e)_____. Sternberg believes that most of us strive for (f)_____, which is a balanced combination of these three components.

**11.** One way that we select a mate is by developing an organized mental list of desirable characteristics and then looking for someone who matches this mental list, which is called a _____.

### E. RESEARCH FOCUS: HAPPY MARRIAGES

**12.** Gottman identified four problems that can result in the failure of a long-term relationship: these problems involve (a)_____, _____, _____, and _____. In successful marriages, wives learn to express their (b)_____ in gentle ways so their husbands are more likely to listen and accept, and husbands learn not to reject their wives' (c)_____ without listening and finding something reasonable in it.

### F. CULTURAL DIVERSITY: PREFERENCES FOR PARTNERS

**13.** People's lists of desirable traits for a mate show remarkable similarity across cultures. However, there are some differences in ranking between the genders; for example, men rank (a)_____ higher than women do, and women rank (b)_____ higher than men do. Also, different cultures place different values on the desirability of marrying someone who is a (c)_____ and marrying someone primarily because of being in (d)_____.

United States: **First**
Ranked love first

Iran: **Third**
Ranked higher: education/ intelligence, ambition, chastity

### G. PHYSICAL CHANGES: AGING

**14.** The gradual and natural slowing of physical and psychological processes from middle through late adulthood is called (a)_____ aging and is explained by two theories, each of which emphasizes a different mechanism. According to one theory, our bodies age because of naturally occurring problems or breakdowns in the cells. This theory is called aging by (b)_____. According to another theory, our bodies age because of a biological limit on the number of times that cells can divide and multiply; after

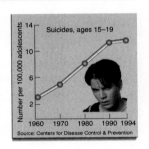

that limit is reached, cells begin to die and aging occurs. This is called aging by (c)_____.

**15.** The aging that may be caused by genetic defects, physiological problems, or diseases is called _____ aging, an example of which is Alzheimer's disease.

**16.** In later adulthood (about age 50), women experience a gradual reduction in the secretion of estrogen, which results in cessation of ovulation and the menstrual cycle; this is called (a)_____. In late adulthood (60–80), men do not stop producing testosterone, but they may experience a decrease in sexual responsiveness due to (b)_____ changes.

### H. APPLICATION: SUICIDE

**17.** A number of factors have been found to be related to teenage suicide. Before committing suicide, adolescents usually have a number of (a)_____ problems, such as depression, feelings of helplessness, or drug-related problems; adolescents also show a number of (b)_____ symptoms, such as falling grades, social isolation and withdrawal, difficulties with family and peers, and antisocial behavior. Usually, suicide is preceded by events or feelings called (c)_____; these may include problems with relationships or bouts of depression or drinking.

**18.** Among the risk factors for suicide in the elderly are depression and loneliness, but the major contributing cause is (a)_____ problems. Currently, there is considerable discussion in the United States over the right of a person with a terminal disease to end his or her life through (b)_____ suicide.

**Answers:** *1. (a) puberty, (b) sexual, (c) menarche, (d) hypothalamus, (e) secondary, (f) physical; 2. (a) formal operations, (b) abstract or hypothetical, (c) prefrontal cortex, (d) limbic system; 3. (a) preconventional, (b) conventional, (c) postconventional; 4. (a) care, (b) justice; 5. (a) authoritarian, (b) authoritative, (c) permissive; 6. (a) identity or self, (b) psychosocial, (c) identity confusion; 7. self-esteem; 8. (a) psychosocial, (b) isolation, (c) stagnation, (d) integrity, (e) despair; 9. gender roles; 10. (a) passionate, (b) companionate, (c) passion, (d) intimacy, (e) commitment, (f) complete or consummate love; 11. schema; 12. (a) criticism, defensiveness, contempt, stonewalling, (b) complaints, (c) advice; 13. (a) good looks, virginity, (b) financial prospects, (c) virgin, (d) love; 14. (a) natural, (b) chance, (c) design; 15. pathological; 16. (a) menopause, (b) physiological; 17. (a) psychological, (b) behavioral, (c) precipitators; 18. (a) health or medical, (b) assisted*

# Critical Thinking

## Newspaper Article

## Am I Losing My Memory?

### Questions

**1.** Why is Polly shocked at her memory problems since she had observed similar memory problems in her own parents?

**2.** When you are in your 40s and 50s, what kind of memory problems will you experience?

**3.** Besides a loss in speed of processing, what other cognitive changes occur with normal aging?

**4.** What is the difference between normal aging and pathological aging?

**5.** Why do some individuals who take ginkgo biloba claim that it has greatly improved their memory?

**6.** Why might boomers prefer taking herbal supplements rather than going on a proven program for a healthy memory?

*Try InfoTrac to search for terms:* **adulthood; adolescence; sociology; life expectancy.**

Polly van Benthusen worked in a Social Security office for 28 years. Whenever someone wanted to know details about any of the hundreds of cases, everyone said, "Ask Polly. She will remember that."

So it was a real shock for Polly to discover that about the time she turned 42, her famous memory was slipping: she could no longer remember details or give even a simple presentation without having detailed notes. With her memory going, Polly worried, "Well, I really am losing my mind. This is how it happens, in little bits and states" (Herbert, 1999, p. 45). She remembered laughing at her parents' forgetting things; was that now happening to her?

Like Polly, about 10,000 baby boomers turn 50 every day and find that they cannot remember where the keys are, forget names of new friends, and walk from one room to another only to forget what they're looking for. Aging boomers find they can't remember the name of an old song, movie actor, or book title that's on the "tip of their tongue," and they hate having to search for a word or term that they know they know but has momentarily "slipped their minds."

Some of these memory problems are simply due to a loss of processing speed that increases with age. This means that trying to remember previously learned things or learn new things simply takes longer and requires more effort.

Although boomers in their 40s and 50s are bothered by memory problems, what they really fear is that these beginning memory problems may be the first signs of something much worse, such as Alzheimer's disease. Alzheimer's disease is caused by progressive damage to brain cells, which results in progressive loss of cognitive abilities, including greater and greater memory loss. The only good news for aging boomers is that their small but bothersome memory losses are so common that they're considered normal and are not usually a sign of Alzheimer's, a disease affecting about 5% of the population over 65.

Aging boomers' memory problems have driven them to spend millions of dollars annually on "memory boosters," which include various drugs or herbal supplements that claim to boost brain power. For example, last year Americans spent $350 million on ginkgo biloba, an herbal supplement (ginkgo tree) that claims to improve brain power and memory. To date, there is no reliable scientific evidence that ginkgo biloba improves memory.

The only known ways for an aging boomer to maintain a healthy memory are to keep physically fit (exercising), increase mental stimulation (reading more or taking a memory course), and have control of one's life (being optimistic). (Adapted from Herbert, 1999; Kluger, 2000)

---

### *Suggested answers for Newspaper Article questions*

1. Children rarely believe that the failings or problems they observe in their "older" parents will ever happen to them. I for one never believed I would forget things like my parents did.

2. No matter how firmly you believe it won't happen, you will experience exactly the same kind of memory problems as described here: a gradual increase in forgetting things (keys, names, words) that you have known all your life.

3. Besides changes in memory, aging also results in several other cognitive problems, such as a slowing of perceptual speed and a slowing of reaction time, which partly accounts for more driving accidents in older persons (p. 415).

4. Normal aging is a gradual and naturally occurring slowing of physiological and psychological (cognitive) processes. In contrast,

pathological aging (Alzheimer's) is caused by some abnormal genetic or physiological condition (p. 424).

5. To date, there is no reliable scientific evidence that ginkgo biloba improves memory. People who claim that ginkgo really improved their memories are most likely experiencing the placebo effect, which is known to produce powerful psychological effects (p. 31).

6. One reason aging boomers are spending millions on unproven supplements to boost memory is because that's the easiest way—even if it doesn't work. The other alternatives for keeping a healthy memory (increase mental stimulation) require much more time and effort.

# Links to Learning

## Web Sites

- **WADSWORTH ONLINE STUDY CENTER**
  **http://psychology.wadsworth.com**
  Quizzes, learning activities and exercises, a discussion forum, and hot links to Internet sites related to adolescence and adulthood, including:

- **AMERICAN ACADEMY OF CHILD AND ADOLESCENT PSYCHIATRY**
  **http://www.aacap.org/**
  What special psychiatric risks do adolescents face? Look here for information on mental disorders, including research findings and breaking news.

- **COLLEGE VIEW**
  **http://www.collegeview.com/index.html**
  College often links adolescence and adulthood. This site provides virtual college tours, a survival guide, financial information, and more.

- **SUICIDE: READ THIS FIRST**
  **http://www.metanoia.org/suicide/**
  A compassionate address to people who are considering suicide. Valuable links point to ways of reducing pain and increasing coping resources.

- **CAREGIVER SURVIVAL RESOURCES**
  **http://www.caregiver911.com/**
  Caring for an ill or aging person can be one of life's biggest challenges. This site offers resources for support, a reading list, and an advice section.

## Learning Activities

- ***POWERSTUDY*™ BY ROD PLOTNIK & TOM DOYLE**

**PowerStudy™**

**Check out CD: Module 18**
CD 3.B:  Neurons: Structure & Function; book page 424
CD 4.B:  Studying the Living Brain; book page 411
CD 4.D:  Control Centers: Four Lobes; book page 411
CD 4.E:  Limbic System: Old Brain; book pages 411, 422
CD 12.B:  Forgetting Curves; book page 415
CD 12.D:  Reasons for Forgetting; book page 415
CD 12.E:  Mnemonics; book page 415

- ***STUDY GUIDE TO ACCOMPANY INTRODUCTION TO PSYCHOLOGY, 6TH EDITION,* by Matthew Enos**
  In Module 18 you can dig deep into your teenage years, enjoy the author's tribute to his 93-year-old mother, and take a special rock and roll quiz on adolescence!

- ***WEBTUTOR***
  **http://webtutor.thomsonlearning.com**
  **WebTUTOR** Visit this site for interactive versions of the Study Guide features. Take a quiz, get your score—should you study a topic some more, or can you move on? For example, how do authoritative parents differ from authoritarian ones? All cognitive abilities decline with age: true or false? Who finds it easier to adjust, the early maturing girl or boy or the late maturing boy or girl?

- ***INFOTRAC ONLINE LIBRARY***
  **http://www.infotrac-college.com**

  Use your password and then key in search terms such as those below to find popular and scientific articles on subjects covered in Module 18. Make the library work for you!

  Estrogen     Perceptual speed     Sexual maturity
  Suicide     Schema     Testosterone

## Study Questions

*Use InfoTrac to search for topics mentioned in the main heads below (e.g., teenage sexuality, parenting, love relationships, aging).*

**\*A. Puberty & Sexual Behavior**—How are the sexual concerns of adolescents and senior adults similar but also different? (**Suggested answer page 631**)

**B. Cognitive & Emotional Changes**—If you heard an adolescent discussing politics with her grandfather, what cognitive differences between them would you notice?

**\*C. Personality & Social Changes**—If you became a parent, what special concerns might you have when your own children go through adolescence? (**Suggested answer page 631**)

**D. Gender Roles, Love, & Relationships**—If you are beginning a long-term relationship, what two things should you and your partner do to ensure success?

**E. Research Focus: Happy Marriages**—What is different about the interactions of couples who are happy from those of couples who are unhappy?

**F. Cultural Diversity: Preferences for Partners**—What are the advantages and disadvantages of having parents arrange marriages for their children?

**G. Physical Changes: Aging**—Of two people who are both 65, why might one seem much older and the other much younger?

**\*H. Application: Suicide**—If your grandmother had incurable cancer and unbearable pain and asked you to help her commit suicide, would you do it? (**Suggested answer page 631**)

*These questions are answered in Appendix B.

# Module 19: Freudian & Humanistic Theories

### A. Freud's Psychodynamic Theory    434
* **DEFINITION**
* **CONSCIOUS VERSUS UNCONSCIOUS FORCES**
* **TECHNIQUES TO DISCOVER THE UNCONSCIOUS**

### B. Divisions of the Mind    436
* **ID, EGO, AND SUPEREGO**
* **ANXIETY**
* **DEFENSE MECHANISMS**

### C. Developmental Stages    438
* **DEVELOPMENT: DEALING WITH CONFLICTS**
* **FIXATION: POTENTIAL PERSONALITY PROBLEMS**
* **FIVE PSYCHOSEXUAL STAGES**

### D. Freud's Followers & Critics    440
* **DISAGREEMENTS**
* **NEO-FREUDIANS**
* **FREUDIAN THEORY TODAY**

### E. Humanistic Theories    442
* **THREE CHARACTERISTICS OF HUMANISTIC THEORIES**
* **MASLOW: NEED HIERARCHY AND SELF-ACTUALIZATION**
* **ROGERS: SELF THEORY**
* **APPLYING HUMANISTIC IDEAS**
* **EVALUATION OF HUMANISTIC THEORIES**

### Concept Review    447

### F. Cultural Diversity: Unexpected High Achievement    448
* **BOAT PEOPLE: REMARKABLE ACHIEVEMENT**
* **VALUES AND MOTIVATION**
* **PARENTAL ATTITUDES**

### G. Research Focus: Shyness    449
* **WHAT IS SHYNESS AND WHAT CAUSES IT?**
* **PSYCHODYNAMIC APPROACH**
* **SOCIAL COGNITIVE THEORY**

### H. Application: Assessment—Projective Tests    450
* **DEFINITION OF PROJECTIVE TESTS**
* **EXAMPLES OF PROJECTIVE TESTS**
* **TWO CHARACTERISTICS**
* **USEFULNESS OF PROJECTIVE TESTS**

### Summary Test    452

### Critical Thinking    454
* **FRIENDS, OTHERS OFFER COMPLEX VIEW OF RATHBUN**

### Links to Learning    455

## Personality

**When he had it all, why did he end it all?**

In the early 1990s, the top punk rock band was Nirvana, and their hit song "Smells Like Teen Spirit" was number one in the charts and in the hearts of millions of fans. Nirvana's founder, song writer, and lead guitar player was Kurt Cobain, whose troubled life was beginning to unravel. Just as his band and career had finally reached the top in the United States and his music was getting international acclaim, he wrote a very revealing one-page note, part of which reads as follows:

At the height of his popularity, Kurt Cobain, founder of punk band Nirvana, killed himself.

"I haven't felt the excitement of listening to as well as creating music, along with really writing for too many years now. I feel guilty beyond words about these things. For example, when we're backstage and the lights go out and manic roar of the crowd goes up, it doesn't affect me the way in which it did for Freddie Mercury, who seemed to love and relish in the love and admiration from the crowd, which is something I totally admire and envy. The fact is, I can't fool you, any one of you. It simply isn't fair to you or to me. The worst crime I can think of would be pull people off by faking it and pretending as if I'm having a hundred percent fun. . . . I've tried everything that's in my power to appreciate it, and I do. God, believe me, I do. But it's not enough . . ."(N. Strauss, 1994, p. 40).

After writing this note, Kurt Cobain, 27 years old and at the height of his popularity, opened his wallet to his Washington driver's license and tossed it on the floor. He apparently drew up a chair to the window, sat down, took some drugs, pressed the barrel of a 20-gauge shotgun to his head, and—eventually using his thumb—pulled the trigger (N. Strauss, 1994).

How could someone with so much going for him—youth, a family (wife and baby daughter), the number-one band in the United States, hit records, fame, and money—turn away from all that and commit suicide? Cobain's tragic story introduces some of the most puzzling and fascinating issues about our innermost selves, our personalities.

*Personality* refers to a combination of long-lasting and distinctive behaviors, thoughts, motives, and emotions that typify how we react and adapt to other people and situations.

Cobain's rocket to stardom and tragic ending raise a number of questions about personality: How does personality develop? Why do personalities differ? How well do we know ourselves? These kinds of questions are answered by theories of personality.

A *theory of personality* is an organized attempt to describe and explain how personalities develop and why personalities differ.

On the one hand, personality theories try to explain why Cobain's personality put him at risk for suicide. On the other hand, personality theories also try to explain why some individuals have personalities that help them overcome horrendous problems and achieve personal success. One such individual is Charles Dutton.

## Changing Personality

**How did he change from a criminal to an actor?**

Charles Dutton had been in and out of reform schools since he was 12 years old and was finally sent to prison for manslaughter and illegal possession of a firearm. While in prison, he got into trouble for being a ringleader of a riot and was punished with solitary confinement. To pass his time, he took along a friend's book of plays by black authors. Dutton was so moved by the plays' messages that for the first time he thought about channeling his rage and anger into acting.

At one point he spent more than 60 painful days in the prison hospital after a fellow inmate had plunged an ice pick through his neck. During those long days in the hospital, he decided that it was time to put his life in order and accomplish something worthwhile during his remaining time in prison. He obtained a high school equivalency certificate and then a two-year college degree, read dozens of plays, and even started a prison theater. After his parole, he attended college and got his B.A. in drama. His high point came when he was accepted into Yale drama school.

By 1992, ex-problem boy, ex-con, ex-prison terrorist Charles Dutton (right photo) had turned into a very successful actor and was starring in "Roc," his own television series (*Los Angeles Times,* August 25, 1991). Dutton's story is an emotionally painful search for identity, culminating in the discovery and development of his acting potential. We'll discuss a theory of personality that emphasizes the development of our full potential.

Charles Dutton, formerly a convict and prison terrorist, becomes a respected actor and director.

## What's Coming

We'll discuss two very different theories of personality: Sigmund Freud's psychodynamic theory emphasizes unconscious forces, irrational thoughts, and the lasting impressions of childhood experiences, whereas humanistic theories emphasize our rational processes and our natural striving to reach our true potentials.

We'll begin with a look at Kurt Cobain's problems and where his inner demons came from.

# A. Freud's Psychodynamic Theory

## Definition

**Why suicide at age 27?**

Freud's theory of personality begins with a controversial assumption that is an important key to unlocking the secrets of personality. To understand how Freud found this key idea, we'll journey back in time to the late 1800s.

At that time, Freud was wondering why several of his women patients had developed very noticeable physical symptoms, such as losing all sensation in their hands or being unable to control the movements of their legs. What most puzzled Freud, who was a medical doctor, was that despite these obvious physical complaints, he could not identify a single physical cause for these symptoms. Somehow, Freud's brilliant mind solved this problem and, in so doing, found an important key to unlocking the secrets of personality. Freud reasoned that since there were no observable physical or neurological causes of the women's physical symptoms, the causes must come from unconscious psychological forces (Westen & Gabbard, 1999).

In the 1800s, Freud's belief that human behavior was influenced by unconscious psychological forces was revolutionary, and it led to his equally revolutionary theory of personality.

*Freud's psychodynamic theory of personality* emphasizes the importance of early childhood experiences, unconscious or repressed thoughts that we cannot voluntarily access, and the conflicts between conscious and unconscious forces that influence our feelings, thoughts, and behaviors.

Freud believed not only that unconscious psychological forces had a powerful influence on personality but that these forces originated in early childhood. This means that if Freud were alive today, he would look for reasons behind Kurt Cobain's suicide at age 27 by searching through Kurt's childhood. Here's what Freud would find.

**Childhood.** When Kurt was 8 years old, his mother filed for divorce, and his parents began their endless fighting. Now Kurt, who had been an outgoing, happy child, became sullen and withdrawn. Because he was skinny and frail, the local town bullies gave him a bad time. Kurt lived sporadically with his father, grandparents, and three sets of aunts and uncles, never finding a real home or anyone to give him love and support. Kurt developed some behavioral problems, such as trouble paying attention, and was given Ritalin (a drug similar in effect to amphetamine) because he was thought to be hyperactive. As if his own problems weren't difficult enough for him to deal with, two of his uncles committed suicide. Friends had only to look into Kurt's eyes to see his sadness and loneliness (Mundy, 1994).

Freud would say that childhood experiences and unconscious forces played a role in Kurt's suicide.

According to Freud, Kurt's childhood, which was full of hurt, pain, and rejection, greatly affected his personality development and caused problems that eventually overwhelmed him. To explain the complex development of someone's personality, such as Kurt Cobain's, is such a difficult task that only a dozen or so psychologists have tried. One of the best-known attempts to explain personality is included in Sigmund Freud's (1901/1960, 1924, 1940) overall theory of psychoanalysis, which includes two related theories: a method of psychotherapy, which we'll discuss in Module 24, and a theory of personality development, which we'll focus on here.

We'll begin with Freud's controversial and revolutionary assumption that unconscious psychological forces influence behavior.

## Conscious versus Unconscious Forces

**Was Kurt Cobain aware of all his feelings?**

Cobain's life was full of inconsistencies. The closer he got to the top, the less happy he became. "Sometime during the months leading up to the recording sessions for Nirvana's last album, Kurt Cobain wrote a song called 'I Hate Myself and Want To Die.' It was a phrase he used a lot at the time—ever since the band's Australian tour—as a backhanded response to people who kept asking him how he was doing. Cobain thought it was so funny he wanted it to be the title of the album" (Fricke, 1994, p. 63).

Kurt indicated that the title of his song was a joke. In doing so, he was expressing a conscious thought.

*Conscious thoughts* are wishes, desires, or thoughts that we are aware of, or can recall, at any given moment.

However, Freud theorized that our conscious thoughts are only a small part of our total mental activity, much of which involves unconscious thoughts or forces (Westen & Gabbard, 1999).

*Unconscious forces* represent wishes, desires, or thoughts that, because of their disturbing or threatening content, we automatically repress and cannot voluntarily access.

Did Cobain write the song "I Hate Myself and Want To Die" because of some unconscious forces that he was unaware of and had repressed? According to Freud, although repressed thoughts are unconscious, they may influence our behaviors through unconscious motivation.

*Unconscious motivation* is a Freudian concept that refers to the influence of repressed thoughts, desires, or impulses on our conscious thoughts and behaviors.

Freud used the concept of unconscious forces and motivation to explain why we say or do things that we cannot explain or understand. Once he assumed that there were unconscious forces and motivations, Freud needed to find ways to explore the unconscious.

Freud would say that unconscious or repressed thoughts, desires, and feelings influence many of our behaviors.

## Techniques to Discover the Unconscious

**What was in Kurt's unconscious?**

It was one thing for Freud to propose the existence of powerful unconscious psychological forces and motivations but it was quite another thing for him to show that such unconscious forces actually existed. For example, were there any signs that unconscious psychological forces were making Cobain more and more unhappy as he became more and more successful and popular?

Looking back at Kurt Cobain's suicide, we see there was more truth than jest to the title of his song, "I Hate Myself and Want To Die." One music critic wrote that Cobain was very clever at hiding the true meanings of his lyrics under a layer of the funny or bizarre (Fricke, 1994). The fact that he committed suicide at the height of his career puts a different and tragic light on many of his verses. For example, did Cobain hide some of his unconscious feelings in the following lyrics?

*"Everything is my fault / I'll take all the blame"* ("All Apologies")
*"Monkey see monkey do / I don't know why I'd rather be dead than cool"* ("Stay Away")

Freud proposed ways to unlock and examine unconscious wishes and feelings.

*"One more special message to go / And then I'm done, then I can go home"* ("On a Plain")

**Unconscious.** If Freud were to examine these lyrics, he might say that they reflected some of Cobain's repressed and unconscious thoughts, desires, and wishes about death and dying. Because neither Cobain nor any of us can easily or voluntarily reveal or talk about our unconscious thoughts and desires, Freud needed to find ways for his patients to reveal their unconscious thoughts and desires, some of which may be psychologically threatening or disturbing. From observing his patients during therapy, Freud believed that he had found three techniques that uncovered, revealed, or hinted at a person's unconscious wishes and desires.

**Three techniques.** Freud's three techniques to uncover the unconscious were free association, dream interpretation, and analysis of slips of the tongue (commonly known as Freudian slips) (Macmillan, 1997).

### Free Association

One technique for revealing the unconscious was to encourage his patients to relax and to sit back or lie down on his now-famous couch and talk freely about anything. He called this process free association.

*Free association* is a Freudian technique in which clients are encouraged to talk about any thoughts or images that enter their head; the assumption is that this kind of free-flowing, uncensored talking will provide clues to unconscious material.

Free association, which is one of Freud's important discoveries, continues to be used today by some therapists (Macmillan, 1997). However, not all therapists agree that free associations actually reveal a client's unconscious thoughts, desires, and wishes (Grunbaum, 1993).

### Dream Interpretation

Freud listened to and interpreted his patients' dreams because he believed that dreams represent the purest form of free association and a path to the unconscious.

Freud's three ways to explore the unconscious: free association, dreams, and slips

*Dream interpretation,* a Freudian technique of analyzing dreams, is based on the assumption that dreams contain underlying, hidden meanings and symbols that provide clues to unconscious thoughts and desires. Freud distinguished between the dream's obvious story or plot, called manifest content, and the dream's hidden or disguised meanings or symbols, called latent content.

For example, Freud interpreted the hidden meaning of dreams' objects, such as sticks and knives, as being symbols for male sexual organs and interpreted other objects (such as boxes and ovens) as symbols for female sexual organs. The therapist's task is to look behind the dream's manifest content (bizarre stories and symbols) and interpret the symbols' hidden or latent content, which provides clues to a person's unconscious wishes, feelings, and thoughts (Greenberg & Pearlman, 1999).

### Freudian Slips

At one time or another, most of us, according to Freud, unintentionally reveal some unconscious thought or desire by making what is now called a Freudian slip (Macmillan, 1997).

*Freudian slips* are mistakes or slips of the tongue that we make in everyday speech; such mistakes, which are often embarrassing, are thought to reflect unconscious thoughts or wishes.

For example, one of my colleagues was lecturing on the importance of regular health care. She said, "It is important to visit a veterinarian for regular checkups." According to Freud, mistakes like substituting *veterinarian* for *physician* are not accidental but rather "intentional" ways of expressing unconscious desires. As it turns out, my colleague, who is in very good health, was having serious doubts about her relationship with a person who happened to be a veterinarian.

Freud assumed that free association, dream interpretation, and slips of the tongue share one thing in common: They are all mental processes that are the least controlled by our conscious, rational, and logical minds. As a result, he believed that these three techniques allowed uncensored clues to slip out and reveal our deeper unconscious wishes and desires (Macmillan, 1997).

According to Freud's theory, there is a continuing battle going on in our minds between conscious thoughts and unconscious forces. How our minds fight these battles is perhaps one of Freud's best-known theories, and you'll easily recognize many of the terms, including id, ego, and superego.

# B. Divisions of the Mind

## Id, Ego, and Superego

**What was in his suicide note?** Kurt Cobain's suicide note revealed some of his problems and internal struggle. Here are some excerpts from his suicide note (N. Strauss, 1994, p. 40):

"I'm too sensitive. I must be one of those narcissists who only appreciate things when they're alone. Thank you all from the pit of my burning nauseous stomach. It's better to burn out than to fade away."

 Freud might say that Cobain's aggressive acts result from inner conflicts between his id and superego.

Cobain's final thoughts suggest that he was fighting a number of psychological and emotional battles. Sometimes his problems became public when, for no apparent reason, he would violently throw or smash his guitar during concerts. According to Freud's theory, some of Cobain's driving forces were arising from unconscious battles among three separate mental processes, which you know as the id, ego, and superego.

## Three Mental Processes

**Iceberg example.** To understand how the id, ego, and superego interact, imagine an iceberg floating in the sea. The part of the iceberg that is above water represents conscious forces of which we are aware, while parts below the water indicate unconscious forces of which we are not aware.

Freud divided the mind into three separate processes, each with a different function. Because of their different functions, Freud believed that interactions among the id, ego, and superego would result in conflicts (O'Shaughnessy, 1999).

Please begin at top left with number 1, the id.

## 1 Id: Pleasure Seeker

Freud believed that mental processes must have a source of energy, which he called the id.

The *id,* which is Freud's first division of the mind to develop, contains two biological drives—sex and aggression—that are the source of all psychic or mental energy; the id's goal is to pursue pleasure and satisfy the biological drives.

Freud assumed that the id operated at a totally unconscious level, which is analogous to an iceberg's massive underwater bulk. The id operates according to the pleasure principle.

The *pleasure principle* operates to satisfy drives and avoid pain, without concern for moral restrictions or society's regulations.

You can think of the id as a spoiled child who operates in a totally selfish, pleasure-seeking way without regard for reason, logic, or morality. Simply following the pleasure principle leads to conflict with others (parents), and this conflict results in the development of the ego.

**2. Ego:** Reality principle. Tip of iceberg represents the conscious part of the ego.

The lower, hidden part of the iceberg represents a part of the ego that is unconscious.

**3. Superego:** Moral standards. Tip represents conscious part of superego.

**1. ID: Pleasure principle.** The iceberg's huge, hidden, underwater bulk represents the id, which Freud assumed was totally unconscious.

Huge, hidden, underwater bulk represents a part of the superego that is unconscious.

## 2 Ego: Executive Negotiator Between Id and Superego

As infants discover that parents put restrictions on satisfying their wishes, infants learn to control their wishes through the development of an ego.

The *ego,* which is Freud's second division of the mind, develops from the id during infancy; the ego's goal is to find safe and socially acceptable ways of satisfying the id's desires and to negotiate between the id's wants and the superego's prohibitions.

Freud said that a relatively large part of the ego's material is conscious (iceberg above water), such as information that we have gathered in adapting to our environments. Smaller parts of the ego's material are unconscious (below water), such as threatening wishes that have been repressed. In contrast to the id's pleasure principle, the ego follows the reality principle.

The *reality principle* has a policy of satisfying a wish or desire only if there is a socially acceptable outlet available.

You can think of the ego as an executive negotiator that operates in a reasonable, logical, and socially acceptable way in finding outlets for satisfaction. The ego works to resolve conflicts that may arise because of different goals of the id and superego.

## 3 Superego: Regulator

As children learn that they must follow rules and regulations in satisfying their wishes, they develop a superego.

The *superego,* which is Freud's third division of the mind, develops from the ego during early childhood; the superego's goal is to apply the moral values and standards of one's parents or caregivers and society in satisfying one's wishes.

Think of the iceberg's visible tip as representing that part of the superego's moral standards of which we are conscious or aware and the huge underwater bulk as representing the part of the superego's moral standards that are unconscious or outside our awareness.

A child develops a superego through interactions with the parents or caregivers and by taking on or incorporating the parents' or caregivers' standards, values, and rules. The superego's power is in making the person feel guilty if the rules are disobeyed. Because the pleasure-seeking id wants to avoid feeling guilty, it is motivated to listen to the superego. You can think of a superego as a moral guardian or conscience that is trying to regulate or control the id's wishes and impulses.

**Disagreements.** Freud believed that in some situations there is little or no disagreement between the goals of the id and superego, which means a person experiences little if any conflict. However, in other situations, there could be disagreements between the goals of the id and superego, which result in the ego (executive negotiator) trying to mediate this conflict. Freud describes a number of mental processes that the ego uses to mediate conflicts between the id and superego. We'll next discuss these mental processes, called defense mechanisms.

## Anxiety

**Why do you feel anxious?**

Suppose you know that you should study for tomorrow's exam but at the same time you want to go to a friend's party. Freud explained that in this kind of situation there is a conflict between the desires of the pleasure-seeking id and the goals of the conscience-regulating superego and this conflict causes anxiety.

*Anxiety,* in Freudian theory, is an uncomfortable feeling that results from inner conflicts between the primitive desires of the id and the moral goals of the superego.

What happens if you want to go to a party but know you should stay home and study?

For example, the study-or-party situation sets up a conflict between the pleasure-seeking goal of the id, which is to go to the party, and the conscience-keeping goal of the superego, which is to stay home and study. Caught in the middle of this id-superego conflict is the ego, which like any good executive, tries to negotiate an acceptable solution. However, this id-superego conflict along with the ego's continuing negotiations to resolve this conflict causes anxious feelings. Freud suggested that the ego, as executive negotiator, tries to reduce the anxious feelings by using a number of mental processes, which he called defense mechanisms (Barlow & Durand, 2001).

## Defense Mechanisms

**Have you ever rationalized?**

In trying to decide whether to go to a friend's party or stay home and study for an important exam, a student would experience increasing levels of anxiety. Freud reasoned that anxiety is a sure sign of the id-superego inner conflict and that in order to reduce levels of anxiety, the ego may use defense mechanisms (Cramer, 2000).

*Defense mechanisms* are Freudian processes that operate at unconscious levels and that use self-deception or untrue explanations to protect the ego from being overwhelmed by anxiety.

According to Freud, a student's ego has two ways to reduce anxiety over deciding to party or study. The student's ego can take realistic steps to reduce anxiety, such as motivating or convincing the student to stay home and study. Or the student's ego can use a number of defense mechanisms, which reduce anxiety by deceiving the student to think it's OK to party and study tomorrow. Here is a brief summary of some of Freud's more popular defense mechanisms (Barlow & Durand, 2001).

*Rationalization* involves covering up the true reasons for actions, thoughts, or feelings by making up excuses and incorrect explanations.

A student may rationalize that by going to a party tonight he or she will feel more motivated to study for the exam tomorrow, even if he or she will be very tired and in no mood or condition to study tomorrow.

*Denial* is refusing to recognize some anxiety-provoking event or piece of information that is clear to others.

Defense mechanisms function like a mental traffic cop trying to reduce conflict and anxiety.

Heavy smokers would be using denial if they disregarded the scientific evidence that smoking increases the risk of lung cancer and cardiovascular disease and in addition would be using rationalization if they say they can quit any time they want.

*Repression* involves blocking and pushing unacceptable or threatening feelings, wishes, or experiences into the unconscious.

Having feelings of jealousy about your best friend's academic success might be threatening to your self-concept, so you unknowingly block these unwanted feelings by also unknowingly pushing them into your unconscious.

*Projection* falsely and unconsciously attributes your own unacceptable feelings, traits, or thoughts to individuals or objects.

A student who refuses to accept responsibility for cheating during exams may look at other students and decide that they are cheating.

*Reaction formation* involves substituting behaviors, thoughts, or feelings that are the direct opposite of unacceptable ones.

A person who feels guilty about engaging in sexual activity may use reaction formation by joining a religious group that bans sex.

*Displacement* involves transferring feelings about, or response to, an object that causes anxiety to another person or object that is less threatening.

If you were anxious about getting angry at your best friend, you might unknowingly displace your anger by picking an argument with a safer individual, such as a salesclerk, waiter, or stranger.

*Sublimation,* which is a type of displacement, involves redirecting a threatening or forbidden desire, usually sexual, into a socially acceptable one.

For instance, a person might sublimate strong sexual desires by channeling that energy into physical activities.

**Conclusions.** Freud believed that defense mechanisms are totally unconscious, which means that, if a best friend or spouse points out that you are being defensive, you will absolutely deny it. We all use defense mechanisms at some time and they can be helpful or harmful. For example, the occasional use of defense mechanisms is normal and helps reduce conflict and anxiety so that we can continue to function as we work on the real cause of our anxiety. However, the overuse of defense mechanisms may prevent us from recognizing or working on the real causes of our anxiety. There is growing scientific evidence that we do indeed use unconscious defense mechanisms much as Freud theorized, which is to reduce anxiety and conflict. In fact, many of us have a dominant or most-often-used defense mechanism, which may be effective in reducing short-term but not necessarily long-term anxiety (Cramer, 2000).

We have discussed the three divisions of the mind—id, ego, and superego—and how the ego may use defense mechanisms to reduce anxiety. Now we'll turn to how one's ego and personality develop.

### Development: Dealing with Conflicts

**What shaped Kurt's personality?**

Imagine a theory so broad that it is able to describe almost exactly how and why your personality developed the way it did and why you did or did not develop certain personality problems along the way. Such is Sigmund Freud's personality theory, which can give a complex description of how each of us develops a different personality.

**Case study.** For example, let's return to the case of Kurt Cobain, especially his childhood. When Kurt was 5 years old, he was described as an artistic, inquisitive, and energetic child, who was the center of attention, especially at family gatherings. To the delight of all the relatives, Kurt sang, drew pictures, and acted out imaginative skits. Just three years later, when he was 8, Kurt's mother filed for divorce, which triggered years of parental fighting with Kurt caught in the middle. During this time, Kurt changed from being happy, outgoing, and energetic to becoming sullen, shy, and withdrawn (Mundy, 1994).

**Psychosexual stages.** According to Freud, the development of

According to Freud, Kurt Cobain's personality developed as he passed through five psychosexual stages.

Kurt's personality, such as becoming outgoing and energetic and then changing to shy and withdrawn, was primarily influenced by how he dealt with the five different kinds of conflicts that occurred at five different times or stages. According to Freud (1940), our personality develops as we pass through and deal with potential conflicts at five psychosexual stages.

*Psychosexual stages* are five developmental periods—oral, anal, phallic, latency, and genital stages—each marked by potential conflict between parent and child. The conflicts arise as a child seeks pleasure from different body areas that are associated with sexual feelings (different *erogenous zones*). Freud emphasized that the child's first five years were most important in personality development.

You can think of each psychosexual stage as being a source of potential *conflict* between the child's id, which seeks immediate gratification, and the parents, who place restrictions on when, where, and how the gratification can take place. For example, the child may want to be fed immediately, while the parent may wish to delay the feeding to a more convenient time. The kind of interactions that occur between parent and child in satisfying these psychosexual needs and the way a child learns to deal with psychosexual conflicts, especially during breast feeding or toilet training, will greatly influence the personality development as well as future problems and social interactions.

One of Freud's controversial ideas is the relationship between early psychosexual stages and development of later personality, social, and emotional problems. Here is Freud's explanation of how different problems may arise.

### Fixation: Potential Personality Problems

**Why did Kurt develop problems?**

Freud explained that the way a person deals with early psychosexual conflicts lays the groundwork for personality growth and future problems. This means that, to a large extent, Kurt's later personality problems grew out of early childhood experiences. Freud would say that Kurt's problems in finding his identity and dealing with fame and fortune began in childhood, which included being caught in the middle of parents fighting over a divorce, becoming shy and withdrawn, being sent to live with various relatives, and finally hearing about the suicides of two uncles (DeCurtis, 1994).

**Fixation.** As an adult, there were times when Kurt was happy and smiley (right photo), but at other times he was eerily moody and withdrawn (drawing below). The problem for any theory of personality is to explain how problems and contradictions in personal-

Healthy personality involves resolving potential conflicts during psychosexual stages.

ity occur. For example, why did Kurt continue to play on center stage and go on world tours yet complain of not enjoying it and having to pretend to be happy? Freud would explain that the development of Kurt's personality depended, to a large extent, on the way he dealt with early psychosexual conflicts. One way a child can deal with or resolve these conflicts—wanting to satisfy all desires but not being allowed to by the parents—is to become fixated at a certain stage.

*Fixation,* which can occur during any of the first three stages—oral, anal, or phallic—refers to a Freudian process through which an individual may be locked into a particular psychosexual stage because his or her wishes were either overgratified or undergratified.

For example, if a person were fixated at the oral stage because of *too little* gratification, he might go through life trying to obtain oral satisfaction through eating too much, boasting too much, or focusing on other oral behaviors. If fixation had occurred at the oral stage because of *too much* gratification, he might focus on seeking oral gratification while neglecting to develop other aspects of his personality.

Next, we'll briefly summarize each of Freud's psychosexual stages, pointing out the possible parent–child conflicts, problems developing from fixation, and implications for future personality and social development.

Fixation at one of the psychosexual stages could cause problems, such as intense moodiness.

**What happens during the stages?**

According to Freud, every child goes through certain situations, such as nursing, bottle feeding, and toilet training, that contain potential conflicts between the child's desire for instant satisfaction or gratification and the parents' wishes, which may involve delaying the child's satisfaction. How these conflicts are resolved and whether a child becomes fixated at one stage because of too much or too little satisfaction greatly influence development of personality and onset of future problems.

## 1 Oral Stage

**Time.** Early infancy: first 18 months of life.
**Potential conflict.** The *oral stage* lasts for the first 18 months of life and is a time when the infant's pleasure seeking is centered on the mouth.

Pleasure-seeking activities include sucking, chewing, and biting. If we were locked into or fixated at this stage because our oral wishes were gratified too much or too little, we would continue to seek oral gratification as adults. *Fixation* at this stage results in adults who continue to engage in oral activities, such as overeating, gum chewing, or smoking; oral activities can be symbolic as well, such as being overly demanding or "mouthing off."

## 2 Anal Stage

**Time.** Late infancy: $1\frac{1}{2}$ to 3 years.
**Potential conflict.** The *anal stage* lasts from the age of about $1\frac{1}{2}$ to 3 and is a time when the infant's pleasure seeking is centered on the anus and its functions of elimination.

*Fixation* at this stage results in adults who continue to engage in activities of retention or elimination. Retention may take the form of being very neat, stingy, or behaviorally rigid (thus the term *anal retentive*). Elimination may take the form of being generous, messy, or behaving very loose or carefree.

## 3 Phallic Stage

**Time.** Early childhood: 3 to 6 years.
**Potential conflict.** The *phallic* (*FAL-ik*) *stage* lasts from the age of about 3 to 6 and is a time when the infant's pleasure seeking is centered on the genitals.

Freud theorized that the phallic stage is particularly important for personality development because of the occurrence of the Oedipus complex (named for Oedipus, the character in Greek mythology who unknowingly killed his father and married his mother).

The *Oedipus* (*ED-ah-pus*) *complex* is a process in which a child competes with the parent of the same sex for the affections and pleasures of the parent of the opposite sex.

According to Freud, the Oedipus complex causes different problems for boys and girls.

**Boys.** When a boy discovers that his penis is a source of pleasure, he develops a sexual attraction to his mother. As a result, the boy feels hatred, jealousy, and competition toward his father and has fears of castration. The boy resolves his Oedipus complex by identifying with his father. If he does not resolve the complex, fixation occurs and he may go through life trying to prove his toughness.

**Girls.** When a girl discovers that she does not have a penis, she feels a loss that Freud called *penis envy.* Her loss makes her turn against her mother and develop sexual desires for her father. A girl resolves her Oedipus complex, sometimes called the Electra complex (for Electra, a woman in Greek mythology who killed her mother), by identifying with her mother. If this complex is not resolved, fixation occurs and the woman may go through life feeling inferior to men.

Over the years, the idea of the Oedipus complex has waned in popularity and credibility, both within psychoanalysis and within the culture at large. That's because there's almost no way to scientifically test this idea and also Freud's assertion that the Oedipus complex occurs universally is not supported by data from other cultures (Crews, 1996).

Freud would say that Kurt's personality depended to a large extent on what happened during five psychosexual stages.

## 4 Latency Stage

**Time.** Middle and late childhood: 6 to puberty.
**Potential conflict.** The *latency stage,* which lasts from about age 6 to puberty, is a time when the child represses sexual thoughts and engages in nonsexual activities, such as developing social and intellectual skills.

At puberty, sexuality reappears and marks the beginning of a new stage, called the genital stage.

## 5 Genital Stage

**Time.** Puberty through adulthood.
**Potential conflict.** The *genital stage* lasts from puberty through adulthood and is a time when the individual has renewed sexual desires that he or she seeks to fulfill through relationships with other people.

How a person meets the conflicts of the genital stage depends on how conflicts in the first three stages were resolved. If the individual is fixated at an earlier stage, less energy will be available to resolve conflicts at the genital stage. If the individual successfully resolved conflicts in the first three stages, he or she will have the energy to develop loving relationships and a healthy and mature personality.

**Summary.** Freud's psychodynamic theory of personality development made a number of assumptions that, at the time, were revolutionary. His assumptions included the influence of unconscious forces; the division of the mind into the id, ego, and superego; the importance of resolving conflicts at five psychosexual stages; the importance of fixation; and the importance of the first five years to personality development.

Next, we'll discuss what Freud's critics have had to say about his theory and assumptions.

# D. Freud's Followers & Critics

## Disagreements

**What did they argue about?**

Because Freud's theory was so creative and revolutionary for its time, it attracted many followers, who formed a famous group called the Vienna Psychoanalytic Society. However, it was not long before members of the society began to disagree over some of Freud's theories and assumptions, such as whether Freud placed too much emphasis on biological urges (sex and aggression), psychosexual stages, and importance of early childhood experience in personality development (Horgan, 1996). We'll focus on three influential followers who eventually broke with Freud's theory.

### Carl Jung

Jung disagreed on the importance of the sex drive.

**Why did Freud's "crown prince" stop talking to him?**

In 1910 Carl Jung, with the whole-hearted support of Sigmund Freud, became the first president of the Vienna Psychoanalytic Society. Freud said that Jung was to be his "crown prince" and personal successor. However, just four years later, Jung and Freud ended their personal and professional relationship and never again spoke to each other.

The main reason for the split was that Jung disagreed with Freud's emphasis on the sex drive. Jung believed the collective unconscious—and not sex—to be the basic force in the development of personality.

The *collective unconscious,* according to Jung, consists of ancient memory traces and symbols that are passed on by birth and are shared by all peoples in all cultures.

Jung's theory of collective unconscious and his elaborate theory of personality, called *analytical psychology,* had more influence on the areas of art, literature, philosophy, and counseling/therapy than on current areas of psychology.

### Alfred Adler

Adler disagreed on the importance of biological urges.

**Why did one of the society's presidents resign?**

Alfred Adler was another contemporary of Freud's who later became president of the Vienna Psychoanalytic Society. However, after Adler voiced his disagreement with Freud at one of the society's meetings, he was so badly criticized by the other members that he resigned as president.

Like Jung, Adler disagreed with Freud's theory that humans are governed by biological and sexual urges. Adler believed that the main factors influencing a child's development were sibling influences and child-rearing practices.

In contrast to Freud's biological drives, Adler proposed that humans are motivated by *social urges* and that each person is a social being with a unique personality. Adler formed his own group, whose philosophy became known as *individual psychology.* In contrast to Freud's emphasis on unconscious forces that influence our behaviors, Adler suggested that we are aware of our motives and goals and have the capacity to guide and plan our futures.

### Karen Horney

Horney disagreed on the importance of penis envy.

**What would a woman say about penis envy?**

Karen Horney was trained as a psychoanalyst; her career reached its peak shortly after Freud's death in 1939. For many years, Horney was dean of the American Institute of Psychoanalysis in New York.

Horney strongly objected to Freud's view that women were dependent, vain, and submissive because of biological forces and childhood sexual experiences. She especially took issue with Freud's idea that penis envy affects girls' development.

In contrast to Freud's psychosexual conflicts, Horney insisted that the major influence on personality development, whether in women or men, can be found in child–parent *social interactions.* Unlike Freud, who believed that every child must experience child–parent conflicts, Horney theorized that such conflicts are avoidable if the child is raised in a loving, trusting, and secure environment. Karen Horney would now be called a feminist and is credited with founding the psychology of women.

## Neo-Freudians

Karen Horney is sometimes referred to as a *neo-Freudian* because she changed and renovated Freud's original theory. One of the best-known neo-Freudians was Erik Erikson, who formulated his own theory of personality development, which we discussed in Modules 17 and 18. Erikson proposed that everyone goes through a series of *psychosocial* stages, rather than the *psychosexual* stages proposed by Freud.

Neo-Freudians generally agreed with Freud's basic ideas, such as the importance of the unconscious; the

Neo-Freudians focused on social and cultural factors.

division of the mind into the id, ego, and superego; and the use of defense mechanisms to protect the ego. However, they mostly disagreed with Freud's placing so much emphasis on biological forces, sexual drives, and psychosexual stages. The neo-Freudians turned the emphasis of Freud's psychodynamic theory away from biological drives toward psychosocial and cultural influences (Westen & Gabbard, 1999).

From early on, followers of Freud criticized his theory and, as you'll see, criticisms continue to the present day.

## Freudian Theory Today

**What is the current status of Freud's theory?**

In 1993, *Time* magazine's cover featured a picture of Sigmund Freud with the question "Is Freud Dead?" Answering this question with a loud "Yes" are four scholarly books that seriously question Freud's theory and all its assumptions (Crews, 1996). Answering this question with a loud "No" are 400 members of the American Psychological Association's psychoanalysis division, who meet the attacks on Freud with equally strong defenses (Horgan, 1996). To give you an idea of where Freud's theory stands today, we'll focus on four questions: How valid is Freud's theory? How important are the first five years? Are there unconscious forces? What was the impact of Freud's theory?

## 1 HOW VALID IS FREUD'S THEORY?

**Too comprehensive.** Freud's psychodynamic theory, which includes how the mind develops (id, ego, and superego), how personality develops (psychosexual stages), and how to do therapy (psychoanalysis), is so comprehensive that it can explain almost any behavior. For example, Freud's theory predicts that fixation at the anal stage may result in a person being at one extreme very messy and at the other extreme very neat. Critics argue that Freud's theory is too comprehensive to be useful in explaining or predicting behaviors of specific individuals (Horgan, 1996).

**Difficult to test.** Current followers agree that some of Freud's concepts, such as the id being the source of energy, the importance of the Oedipus complex in personality development, and basic drives limited to sex and aggression, have proved difficult to test or verify and are now out of date. The same followers add that other Freudian concepts, such as the influence of unconscious forces, long-term effects of early childhood patterns, and existence of defense mechanisms and conflicting cognitive processes, have been experimentally tested and received support (Westen & Gabbard, 1999).

**Must be updated.** However, even supporters suggest that if psychoanalysis or psychodynamic theory is to survive in the 2000s, Freud's theory must continue to be tested experimentally as well as updated with findings from other areas of psychology. For example, psychodynamic theory needs to include how *genetic factors* account for 20 to 50% of a wide range of behaviors and take into account how *brain development,* which is not complete until early adulthood, is associated with and necessary for the development of related behaviors, thoughts, and feelings (Westen, 1998).

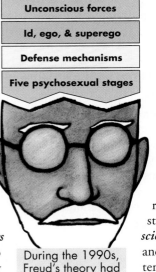

Theory of Personality

Unconscious forces

Id, ego, & superego

Defense mechanisms

Five psychosexual stages

During the 1990s, Freud's theory had several major revisions.

## 3 ARE THERE UNCONSCIOUS FORCES?

One of Freud's major assumptions was that unconscious forces influence our conscious thoughts and behaviors. There is good evidence that unconscious influences do affect our conscious behaviors, but these influences are not the repressed, threatening desires proposed by Freud. In contrast to Freud's theory of the unconscious, cognitive neuroscientists have developed a different concept, called implicit or nondeclarative memory (Dienes & Perner, 1999).

*Implicit* or *nondeclarative memory* consists of mental and emotional processes that we are unaware of but that bias and influence our conscious feelings, thoughts, and behaviors.

Examples of what's in implicit memory include procedural memories (p. 246), such as motor skills and habits (typing), and classical or conditioned emotional responses (fears or phobias). Thus, there is strong evidence for the *influence of unconscious forces* on conscious thoughts, feelings, and behaviors, but it is part of a cognitive system rather than a battleground for conflicts among the id, ego, and superego (Westen & Gabbard, 1999).

## 2 HOW IMPORTANT ARE THE FIRST FIVE YEARS?

Based on observations of his patients, Freud concluded that personality development is essentially complete after the first five years. However, Freud never did systematic research or collected longitudinal observations to support his hypothesis that personality development is fixed during a child's first five years (Bruer, 1999). In fact, there are two lines of research showing the opposite. First, our earlier discussion of *resilient children* (p. 394) indicated that the occurrence of serious psychological and physical problems during the first five years does not necessarily stunt or inhibit personality development, as Freud predicted. Many children who had experienced poverty, the death of or separation from their parents, or a poor home life developed into healthy, mature adults provided the children had a loving caregiver (Werner, 1995).

Second, a number of *longitudinal studies* that followed children into adulthood indicate that personality development is not complete in the first five years but rather continues well into middle adulthood (Caspi & Roberts, 1999). For these reasons, current psychologists question Freud's idea that personality development is complete in the first five years.

## 4 WHAT WAS FREUD'S IMPACT?

Freud's theory has had an enormous impact on society, as can be seen in the widespread use of Freudian terms (ego, id, rationalization) in literature, art, and our everyday conversations. Freud's theory also had a great impact on psychology: Many of his concepts have been incorporated into the fields of personality, development, abnormal psychology, and psychotherapy. However, as we have discussed, some of Freud's terms are out of date (Oedipus complex) and Freud's psychoanalytic or psychodynamic theory was modified in the 1990s (Westen & Gabbard, 1999).

Unlike Freud's psychodynamic theory, which paints a picture of humans filled with irrational and unconscious forces with little free choice, we next discuss a family of theories—humanistic theory—that is almost the direct opposite of Freud's theory.

# E. Humanistic Theories

**How did he develop his real potential?**

At the beginning of this module, we told you about two very different people. One was rock musician Kurt Cobain, who struggled with numerous personal and drug-related problems. At age 27, when his band, Nirvana, had reached the peak of its fame and popularity, he committed suicide.

The other person was Charles Dutton, who had been in and out of reform schools since he was 12 years old, was sent to prison on charges of manslaughter, and spent time in solitary confinement for his ringleader role in a prison riot. Just when most people would have given up on reforming Dutton, he began to reform himself. Inspired by reading a book of plays, he began to channel his rage against society into becoming a student and then an actor. After leaving prison, Charles Dutton (right photo) worked hard to become a very successful actor and starred in "Roc," his own television series, and a number of movies.

When most would have given up, Charles Dutton turned his life completely around.

What Dutton and Cobain shared in common as young men was that neither showed particular evidence of having special talents or great potentials. Few people would have predicted that skinny, frail Cobain would discover the raw power of punk rock and take it further than anyone had before with his band, Nirvana. No one would have predicted that angry, tough, mean Charles Dutton would discover, of all things, acting and would channel his anger into becoming a very successful professional actor. The lives of these two men demonstrate the difficulty in predicting someone's potential and whether he or she will develop it. Developing our potential is at the heart of humanistic theory.

*Humanistic theories* emphasize our capacity for personal growth, development of our potential, and freedom to choose our destiny.

Humanistic theories reject the biological determinism and the irrational, unconscious forces of Freud's psychodynamic theory. Humanistic theories emphasize freely choosing to go after one's dream and change one's destiny, as Kristi Yamaguchi did.

## Three Characteristics of Humanistic Theories

**What did she do to reach her goal?**

For Kristi Yamaguchi, reaching her goal of winning a gold medal meant giving her whole life to ice skating. From early childhood on, she spent thousands of hours practicing, entering grueling competitions, struggling with disappointments, and sacrificing her life to reach the final contest—the winter Olympics. After so many years of preparation, Kristi's grace, skill, and artistry (photo below) dazzled the audience and impressed the judges. She reached her lifelong dream: a gold medal in figure skating at the winter Olympics.

Kristi Yamaguchi's life illustrates the three characteristics that distinguish humanistic theory from other theories of personality. We'll describe each of the three characteristics unique to humanistic theory: having a phenomenological perspective, a holistic view, and a goal of self-actualization (Wertz, 1998).

**1** Humanistic theories stress learning about the world through personal experiences, which illustrates the phenomenological *(feh-nom-in-no-LODGE-uh-cal)* perspective.

The *phenomenological perspective* means that your perception or view of the world, whether or not it is accurate, becomes your reality.

For instance, Kristi's phenomenological perspective of how she perceived her skating abilities may or may not have been accurate. However, because she believed so strongly that she had the abilities, this perception became her reality. Other examples of phenomenological perspectives are long-held beliefs that women could not perform certain jobs—for example, police officer, doctor, plumber, truck driver, or lawyer. Since women have demonstrated that they can perform these jobs, this particular perception has been proven false. As a result, people (especially men) have developed a new perspective and accepted the reality of what women can accomplish.

Kristi worked hard to develop her skating potential and win an Olympic gold medal.

**2** Humanistic theories emphasize looking at the whole situation or person, which illustrates the holistic *(hole-LIS-tick)* view.

The *holistic view* means that a person's personality is more than the sum of its individual parts; instead, the individual parts form a unique and total entity that functions as a unit.

For example, the holistic view would explain that Kristi outperformed her competitors because of her unique combination of many traits—discipline, ability, motivation, persistence, desire—rather than any single trait.

**3** Humanistic theories highlight the idea of developing one's true potential, which is called self-actualization.

*Self-actualization* refers to our inherent tendency to develop and reach our true potentials.

By winning an Olympic gold medal, Kristi is a wonderful example of someone who has developed and reached her true potential and thus achieved a high level of self-actualization. According to humanistic theories, no matter what our skills or abilities, each of us has the capacity for self-actualization and can reach our potentials as whoever we are.

The beginning of humanistic theory can be traced to two psychologists—Abraham Maslow and Carl Rogers. They had surprisingly different backgrounds, but they arrived at the same uplifting ideas.

**Why did a behaviorist become a humanist?**

We can trace the official beginning of the humanistic movement to the early 1960s and the publication of the *Journal of Humanistic Psychology*. One of the major figures behind establishing this journal was Abraham Maslow. Interestingly enough, Maslow was trained as a behaviorist, but along the way he felt there was too much emphasis on rewards and punishments and observable behaviors and too little emphasis on other important

aspects of human nature, such as feelings, emotions, and beliefs. For these reasons, Maslow (1968) broke away from the reward/punishment/observable behavior mentality of behaviorism and developed his humanistic theory, which emphasized two things: our capacity for growth, or self-actualization, and our desire to satisfy a variety of needs, which he arranged in a hierarchy.

## Maslow's Hierarchy of Needs

**Maslow's Hierarchy of Needs**

**Level 5**
Self-actualization: fulfillment of one's unique potential

**Level 4**
Esteem needs: achievement, competency, gaining approval and recognition

**Level 3**
Love and belonging needs: affiliation with others and acceptance by others

**Level 2**
Safety needs: protection from harm and concern about safety and survival

**Level 1**
Physiological needs: hunger, thirst, sex, and sleep

For just a moment, think of all the needs that you try to meet each day: eating, having a safe place to live, talking to your friends, perhaps working at a part-time job, caring for loved ones, and studying for exams. Maslow believed that you satisfy these needs in a certain order. As you may remember from Module 15 (p. 333), Maslow arranged all human needs into a hierarchy of five major needs.

*Maslow's hierarchy of needs* arranges needs in ascending order (figure on left), with biological needs at the bottom and social and personal needs at the top. Only when needs at a lower level are met can we advance to the next level.

According to Maslow's hierarchy, you must satisfy your biological and safety needs before using energy to fulfill your personal and social needs. Finally, you can devote time and energy to reaching your true potential, which is called self-actualization, your highest need.

Maslow divided our needs into two general categories: deficiency and growth needs.

*Deficiency needs* are physiological needs (food, sleep) and psychological needs (safety, love, esteem) that we try to fulfill if they are not met.

*Growth needs* are those at the higher levels and include the desire for truth, goodness, beauty, and justice.

According to Maslow, we must satisfy our deficiency needs before having the time and energy to satisfy our growth needs and move toward self-actualization.

## Self-Actualization

One of the major characteristics of the humanistic movement is the emphasis on a process called self-actualization.

*Self-actualization* refers to the development and fulfillment of one's unique human potential.

Maslow (1971) developed the concept of self-actualization after studying the lives of highly productive and exceptional people, such as Abraham Lincoln, Albert Einstein, and Eleanor Roosevelt. Maslow believed that these individuals had been able to reach the goal of self-actualization because they had developed the following personality characteristics.

**Characteristics of Self-Actualized Individuals**

- They perceive reality accurately.
- They are independent and autonomous.
- They prefer to have a deep, loving relationship with only a few people.
- They focus on accomplishing their goals.
- They report peak experiences, which are moments of great joy and satisfaction.

Maslow believed that, although very few individuals reach the level of self-actualization, everyone has a self-actualizing tendency. This tendency motivates us to become the best kind of person we are capable of becoming.

Civil rights leader, Martin Luther King, Jr., is an example of a self-actualized person.

There is no doubt that Maslow would also have considered Martin Luther King, Jr., an example of a self-actualized person. Martin Luther King, Jr., devoted his life to achieving civil rights for all people. Here he delivers his famous "I Have a Dream" speech at a civil rights rally in Washington, D.C. He was awarded the Nobel Prize for peace at age 35. He was gunned down by an assassin's bullet at age 39. King's achievements exemplify the humanistic idea of self-actualization.

About the same time that Maslow was making this journey from behaviorism to humanism and developing the concept of self-actualization, another psychologist by the name of Carl Rogers was developing a different but related humanistic theory.

## Rogers: Self Theory

**What are the two most important concepts?**

Carl Rogers was initially trained in the psychodynamic approach, which he used in his practice as a clinical psychologist. However, Rogers began to feel that Freud placed too much emphasis on unconscious, irrational forces and on biological urges, and too little emphasis on human potential for psychological growth. As a result, Rogers gradually abandoned the psychodynamic approach in favor of a new theory of personality that he developed in the 1960s. Rogers's new humanistic theory is often called self theory because of his emphasis on the self or self-concept.

*Self theory,* also called *self-actualization theory,* is based on two major assumptions: that personality development is guided by each person's unique self-actualization tendency, and that each of us has a personal need for positive regard.

Rogers's first major assumption about self-actualization is similar but slightly different from Maslow's use of the term.

*Rogers's self-actualizing tendency* refers to an inborn tendency for us to develop all of our capacities in ways that best maintain and benefit our lives.

The self-actualizing tendency refers to **biological functions,** such as meeting our basic need for food, water, and oxygen, as well as **psychological functions,** such as expanding our experiences, encouraging personal growth, and becoming self-sufficient. The self-

Because of different experiences, the girl in the wheelchair will likely develop a different concept of self than the other girl.

actualizing tendency guides us toward positive or healthful behaviors rather than negative or harmful ones. For example, one of the two girls in the photo below has lost the use of her legs and must use a wheelchair. Part of her self-actualizing process will include learning to deal with her disability, engaging in positive healthful behaviors, and getting to know herself.

*Self* or *self-concept* refers to how we see or describe ourselves. The self is made up of many self-perceptions, abilities, personality characteristics, and behaviors that are organized and consistent with one another.

Because of very different experiences, the girl in the wheelchair will develop a self-concept different from that of her friend who has normal use of her legs. According to Rogers (1980), self-concept plays an important role in personality because it influences our behaviors, feelings, and thoughts. For example, if you have a **positive self-concept,** you will tend to act, feel, and think optimistically and constructively; if you have a **negative self-concept,** you will tend to act, feel, and think pessimistically and destructively.

Sometimes a person may be undecided about his or her real self. As we discover our real self, we may undergo a number of changes in personality.

### *Real Self versus Ideal Self*

**Who is the real David Bowie?**

We all change how we see ourselves but probably not as much as rock star David Bowie, who, through the years, has radically changed his looks, clothes, and personal values. For example, Bowie's earlier looks (top photo) and behaviors might be described as having pushed society's limits. Now, however, Bowie is in his 50s and appears quite conventional in hairstyle and clothes (bottom photo), and he has adopted many of society's values, such as getting married. The question is, Which is Bowie's real self?

Carl Rogers said that his clients often asked questions related to their selves: "How do I find myself?" "Why do I sometimes feel that I don't know myself?" "Why do I say or do things that aren't really me?" Rogers developed a clever answer to these relatively common and perplexing questions. He said that there are two kinds of selves: a real self and an ideal self.

The *real self,* according to Rogers, is based on our actual experiences and represents how we really see ourselves.

The *ideal self,* according to Rogers, is based on our hopes and wishes and reflects how we would like to see ourselves.

*My ideal self is based on my hopes and wishes.*

*My real self is based on my actual experience.*

In some cases, the hopes and wishes of one's ideal self may contradict the abilities and experiences of the real self. For example, a student's ideal self may be someone who is very responsible and studies hard, but the real self may be someone who puts things off and studies less than is required.

**Contradiction between ideal and real self.** According to Rogers, a glaring contradiction between the ideal and real self can result in personality problems. Rogers suggested that we can resolve contradictions between the ideal and real self by paying more attention to our actual experiences, working to have more positive experiences, and paying less attention to the expectations of others. In working out discrepancies between our ideal and real selves, we may undergo changes in looks, clothes, and behavior.

Now that you know what the self is, here's how it develops.

**Why are there millions of dog owners?**

One reason I am one of the millions of dog owners is that my dog Bear, like most dogs, is especially good at showing real appreciation, no matter how angry, grouchy, depressed, or sad I may feel or act. In fact, researchers found that residents in nursing homes were more alert and sociable when allowed to have a pet to play with and care for (Hendy, 1984).

The need to feel appreciated is so important that in the United States we have a number of days throughout the year that are officially designated for appreciation, such as Mother's, Father's, Grandparent's, and Secretary's days, as well as birthdays and Valentine's Day.

*It's so nice you're always glad to see me.*

The creation of national appreciation days and the popularity of pets illustrate the second assumption of Carl Rogers's self theory, which is that all humans have a need for positive regard.

*Positive regard* includes love, sympathy, warmth, acceptance, and respect, which we crave from family, friends, and people important to us.

Rogers believed that positive regard was essential for the healthy development of one's self as well as for successful interpersonal relations (Liebert & Spiegler, 1994). When we are children, positive regard comes mainly from our parents, siblings, or grandparents. But as we become adults, we learn to provide some of our own positive regard.

## Conditional and Unconditional Positive Regard

**What's a big problem for teenagers?**

Unlike friends and family, pets never pass judgment; they provide endless amounts of positive regard no matter how their owners look, feel, dress, or talk. In contrast, friends and family can be very judgmental and may give only conditional positive regard.

*Conditional positive regard* refers to the positive regard we receive if we behave in certain acceptable ways, such as living up to or meeting the standards of others.

For instance, one way teenagers display their newly developed independence is by choosing different (radical, awful, outrageous) hairstyles and fashions. In this case, if the teenagers receive conditional positive regard based on conforming to the more traditional fashion standards of their parents, they may develop a negative self-concept or feel bad or worthless because they displeased or disappointed their parents.

No matter how she dresses, she hopes to get unconditional positive regard.

Rogers believed that the development of a healthy and positive self-concept depends on receiving as much unconditional positive regard as possible.

*Unconditional positive regard* refers to the warmth, acceptance, and love that others show you because you are valued as a human being even though you may disappoint people by behaving in ways that are different from their standards or values or the way they think.

Parents who provide love and respect, even if a teenager does not always abide by their fashion standards, are showing unconditional positive regard, which will foster the development of a healthy self-concept. Nevertheless, however much we need, want, and enjoy unconditional positive regard, it appears to be more the exception; conditional positive regard appears to be more the rule (Culp et al., 1991).

## Importance of Self-Actualization

**What would you do to reach your potential?**

In 1945, Russian leader Stalin exiled writer Aleksandr Solzhenitsyn (right photo) to Siberia for publishing essays critical of Stalin's abuse of power. In 1976, Solzhenitsyn received the Nobel Prize for his novels, such as *One Day in the Life of Ivan Denisovich,* and was allowed to come to the United States, where he said, "you can be free."

The life of Solzhenitsyn is a case study in self-actualization. He persisted in developing his potential as a thinker and writer, despite being persecuted for years, exiled to the terrible living conditions of Siberia, and forbidden to publish his works. Rogers would

*I survived Siberia and prison so I could keep writing.*

explain that Solzhenitsyn persisted in writing because of the tendency for self-actualization, which provides direction and motivation to develop one's potential. Rogers recognized that our tendency for self-actualization may be hindered or blocked by situational hurdles or personal difficulties. But Rogers believed that we will experience the greatest self-actualization if we work to remove situational problems, resolve our personal problems, and receive unconditional positive regard.

Humanistic theories contain powerful positive messages, but do these messages work?

# E. Humanistic Theories

## Applying Humanistic Ideas

**What problems do young African Americans face?**

Unlike almost every other theory of personality, humanism holds that people are basically good and can achieve their true potentials if the roadblocks placed by society, poverty, drugs, or other evil influences are removed (Megargee, 1997). Based on this belief, one of the primary goals of the humanistic approach is to find ways of removing blocking influences so that people can grow and self-actualize. In the United States, psychologists have identified African American boys as one group of individuals whose paths are often filled with roadblocks. Some of the roadblocks that prevent African American boys from reaching their potentials include peer pressure to act out, to "take nothing from nobody," to turn down educational opportunities and to not "act White" by excelling in school, to hang out on the streets, to join gangs, and to take part in a variety of antisocial and illicit activities (Franklin, 1995; McWhorter, 2000).

To help remove these roadblocks to healthy personality development in African American boys, counselors are using humanistic ideas, such as providing positive regard and role models for self-actualization. For example, for the past dozen years, counselor Roland Gilbert in San Francisco has been conducting a mentoring program for African American boys who are at high risk for developing

I try to show these young boys that someone really cares.

personality problems. These boys live in neighborhoods with daily occurrences of violence and drugs; their fathers are often absent; and they have few adult male role models to help them through adolescence's difficult times. At the heart of Gilbert's program are twice-weekly meetings between young African American boys and adult men from the community. During these meetings, the African American men discuss the importance of getting regular jobs, demonstrate how to deal with anger by talking rather than hitting, and provide positive regard by showing that someone really cares (Smith, 1993).

In the United States, there are now numerous mentoring programs, such as Big Brothers/Big Sisters of America, which instill a sense of pride and self-worth and give children the motivation to achieve success (Hill, 1995). For example, children who participated in mentoring programs reported significantly higher self-concepts than children without mentors (Turner & Scherman, 1996). Thus, applying humanistic principles helped improve the self-concept of children who came from problem families or neighborhoods.

Next, we'll summarize the important humanistic concepts and discuss what critics have to say about humanistic theories.

## Evaluation of Humanistic Theories

**How popular is humanism?**

Perhaps the main reason humanistic theories, such as those of Maslow and Rogers, continue to be popular is that they view people as basically good and believe that people can develop their true potentials (Elkins, 2000). However, these optimistic views of human nature have triggered a number of criticisms.

### Impact

In the African American mentoring programs described above, the self-worth of boys at risk is increased when mentors are successful role models who also provide positive regard. These programs illustrate the humanistic theories' emphasis on building self-worth through positive regard. In a real sense, the mentors are removing roadblocks so that each boy can find a path to his true potential through a process called self-actualization (Sapienza & Bugental, 2000).

Humanistic theories have had their greatest impact in counseling, clinical settings, and personal growth programs, where ideas like self-concept, self-actualization, and self-fulfillment have proven useful in the development of healthy personalities and interpersonal relationships (Ford, 1991). Compared to Freud's idea that we are driven by unconscious irrational forces, humanism says that we are driven by positive forces that point us toward realizing our good and true selves.

### Criticisms

Humanistic theories have come under considerable criticism because Rogers and Maslow provide little or no scientific evidence that an inherent (biological) tendency to self-actualization really exists. Because the major assumption of self-actualization and other humanistic concepts, such as positive regard and self-worth, are difficult to demonstrate experimentally, critics argue that humanistic theories primarily describe how people behave rather than explain the causes of their behaviors. For these reasons, critics regard humanistic theories more as a wonderfully positive view of human nature or a very hopeful philosophy of life rather than as a scientific explanation of personality development (Liebert & Spiegler, 1994). Critics note that because humanistic concepts are too descriptive and limited in scope, humanistic theories have had less impact on mainstream psychology and more on humanities. Another major problem is that humanistic theories generally ignore research showing that 20 to 60% of the development of intellectual, emotional, social, and personality traits comes from genetic factors (McClearn et al., 1997). This means that genetic factors must be considered when discussing a person's true potential or a person's ability to achieve self-actualization.

Maslow hoped that humanistic theories would become a third major force in psychology, along with behavioral and psychoanalytic theories. Although it appears that the humanistic approach has not achieved Maslow's goal, many of humanism's ideas gave birth to the human potential movements in the 1960s and 1970s and have been incorporated into approaches for counseling and psychotherapy (Wertz, 1998).

# Concept Review

**1.** The combination of long-lasting and distinctive behaviors, thoughts, and emotions that are typical of how we react and adapt to other people and situations forms our _____.

**2.** Freud's theory of personality, which emphasizes the importance of early childhood experiences and of conflicts between conscious thoughts and unconscious forces, is called a _____ theory.

**3.** Freud developed three techniques for probing the unconscious. A technique that encourages clients to talk about any thoughts or images that enter their head is called (a)_____. A technique to interpret the hidden meanings and symbols in dreams is called (b)_____. With a third technique, the therapist analyzes the mistakes or (c)_____ that the client makes in everyday speech.

**4.** Freud considered the mind to have three major divisions. The division that contains the biological drives and is the source of all psychic or mental energy is called the (a)_____. This division operates according to the (b)_____ principle, which demands immediate satisfaction. The division that develops from the id during infancy and whose goal is finding safe and socially acceptable ways of satisfying the id's desires is called the (c)_____. This division operates according to the (d)_____ principle, which involves satisfying a wish only if there is a socially acceptable outlet. The division that develops from the id during early childhood and whose goal is applying the moral values and standards of one's parents and society is called the (e)_____.

**5.** Conflicts between the id and the superego over satisfaction of desires may cause the ego to feel threatened. When threatened, the ego generates an unpleasant state that is associated with feelings of uneasiness, apprehension, and heightened physiological arousal; this unpleasant state is called (a)_____. Freud suggested that the ego may reduce anxiety by using unconscious mechanisms that produce self-deception; these are called (b)_____.

**6.** Freud proposed that the major influence on personality development occurs as we pass through five developmental periods that he called the (a)_____ stages, each of which results in conflicts between the child's wishes and parents' restrictions. The result of a person's wishes being overgratified or undergratified at any one of the first three stages is called (b)_____.

**7.** Personality theories that emphasize our capacity for personal growth, the development of our potential, and freedom to choose our destinies are referred to as _____ theories.

**8.** Humanistic theories have three characteristics in common. They take the perspective that our perception of the world, whether or not it is accurate, becomes our reality; this is called the (a)_____ perspective. Humanistic theories see personality as more than the sum of individual parts and consider personality as a unique and total entity that functions as a unit; this is the (b)_____ view of personality. Humanistic theories point to an inherent tendency that each of us has to reach our true potential; this tendency is called (c)_____.

**9.** The idea that our needs occur in ascending order, with biological needs at the bottom and social and personal needs toward the top, and that we must meet our lower-level needs before we can satisfy higher ones is called (a)_____. Our physiological needs (food, sleep) and psychological needs (safety, belongingness, esteem) are called (b)_____ needs because we try to fulfill them if they are not met. The highest need of self-actualization, which includes the desire for truth, goodness, beauty, and justice, is called a (c)_____ need.

**10.** Carl Rogers's self theory of personality makes two basic assumptions. The first is that personality development is guided by an inborn tendency to develop our potential; this idea is called (a)_____. The second assumption is that each of us has a personal need for acceptance and love, which Rogers called (b)_____. According to Rogers, it is important that we receive love and acceptance despite the fact that we sometimes behave in ways that are different from what others think or value; this type of acceptance is called (c)_____.

**11.** Rogers proposes that we have two kinds of selves: the self that is based on real-life experiences is called the (a)_____ self; the self that is based on how we would like to see ourselves is called the (b)_____ self.

***Answers:*** *1. personality; 2. psychodynamic; 3. (a) free association, (b) dream interpretation, (c) Freudian slips or slips of the tongue; 4. (a) id, (b) pleasure, (c) ego, (d) reality, (e) superego; 5. (a) anxiety, (b) defense mechanisms; 6. (a) psychosexual, (b) fixation; 7. humanistic; 8. (a) phenomenological, (b) holistic, (c) self-actualization; 9. (a) Maslow's hierarchy of needs, (b) deficiency, (c) growth; 10. (a) self-actualization, (b) positive regard, (c) unconditional positive regard; 11. (a) real, (b) ideal*

## Boat People: Remarkable Achievement

**What was different about these children?**

I have always been puzzled by why students with similar academic skills perform so differently: some do well on my exams, while others do poorly. A humanist would look at the same differences and ask, "Why are some students developing their potential, while others are not?" One answer comes from studying thousands of Indo-Chinese refugees, known as the boat people, who were allowed to resettle in the United States in the 1970s and 1980s.

On their arrival in America, the boat people's only possessions were the clothes they wore. They knew virtually no English, had almost no knowledge of Western culture, and had no one to turn to for social or financial support. In spite of horrendous difficulties, refugee children achieved such remarkable academic success that American educators were scratching their heads and asking why.

**Background.** Researchers set out to discover why these refugee children had achieved astonishing scholastic success against overwhelming odds (Caplan et al., 1992). The researchers selected a random sample of 200 Indo-Chinese refugee families with a total of 536 school-age children. The children had been in the United States for

Refugee boat people's children, who first had to learn English, went on to achieve remarkable academic success.

an average of $3\frac{1}{2}$ years. They had generally lived in low-income metropolitan areas with troublesome neighborhoods and run-down schools that were plagued with problems and not known for their high academic standards. Despite all these problems, children of the boat people performed remarkably well in school. Here's what researchers found.

**Amazing success.** The researchers computed the mean grade point average for the 536 children, who were fairly evenly distributed among grades 1 to 12. They found that 27% of the children had a grade point average (GPA) in the A range, 52% had a GPA in the B range, 17% in the C range, and only 4% had a GPA below C. Equally noteworthy was the children's overall performance in math: almost 50% of the children earned A's, while another 33% earned B's. On national math tests, the Indo-Chinese children's average scores were almost three times higher than the national norm.

After analyzing all these data, researchers were able to identify several reasons why immigrant Indo-Chinese students achieved such high grades.

## Values and Motivation

**What were their values?**

Although Indo-Chinese refugee children had been in the United States for an average of only $3\frac{1}{2}$ years, they were doing better in math than 90% of their peers. It could not be the quality of their schools, which were average, undistinguished low-income schools in metropolitan areas. But clearly there were powerful factors helping these children overcome the problems of learning a second language and adapting to a new culture. Researchers located these powerful factors in the values of the Asian family.

The *primary values* held by the Indo-Chinese families were that parents and children have mutual respect, cooperate freely, and are committed to accomplishment and achievement. A clear example of commitment to accomplishment is the amount of time Indo-Chinese children spend doing homework: They average about 3 hours a day, while American students average about $1\frac{1}{2}$ hours. Thus, among refugee families, doing homework, not watching television, is the main activity; the older children help the younger children.

Another primary value is that parents were very involved in their children's education: Over 50% of parents read aloud and helped with homework. When children were asked, "What accounts for your academic success?" the children most often checked the category, "having a love of learning." Love of learning was one of the values nourished and passed on from parent to child. When children were asked, "How much do you choose your own destiny?" the children answered that they did not trust luck or fate but were the masters of their own destinies.

**Parental Values**

**Children**

Parental values on the importance of education motivated the children.

## Parental Attitudes

**How did parents help?**

One reason Indo-Chinese children earned great academic success was the personal and cultural values transmitted by their parents, who were committed to help their children succeed through educational performance. After studying the immigrant parents' values and how they instilled these values in their children, researchers concluded that for American schools to succeed, parents must become more committed to the education of their children. In this case, Americans can truly learn from the values of these refugees.

In explaining the immigrant children's wonderful academic achievement, humanists would emphasize how parental values served to remove mental roadblocks that otherwise might have hindered their children from developing their true potentials and reaching self-fulfillment.

Next, we turn to a relatively common personality problem, shyness, and discuss how different theories of personality explain its causes.

## What Is Shyness and What Causes It?

**What's it like to be shy?**

It's one thing to discuss Freud's psychodynamic theory of personality but it's another to see it in action, in this case, to treat shyness.

At some time and in some situations, we have all felt a little shy. However, there are degrees of shyness, and a high degree of shyness can interfere with enjoying personal and social interactions. For example, when Alan was a child, he would walk home from school through alleys to avoid meeting any of his classmates. Although he received a perfect math score on his SAT, he dropped out of the University of Texas because he always felt like a stranger and was continually frustrated by not being able to reach out and make contact with people. He was so shy that he could not even use the Internet. Finally, feeling so lonely, Alan

20–40% are shy.

sought help at the Shyness Clinic, which was founded in the 1970s by well-known shyness researcher, Philip Zimbardo of Stanford University (Noriyuki, 1996).

*Shyness* is a feeling of distress that comes from being tense, stressed, or awkward in social situations and from worrying about and fearing rejection.

Surveys indicate that about 40% of adults report mild but chronic shyness and although they are good at hiding their shyness, internally they feel distress. About 20% report more severe shyness and are unable to hide their pain and distress (Carducci & Zimbardo, 1995). The cause and treatment for shyness depend partly on which theory of personality guides our thinking. We'll contrast answers from two different theories: Freud's psychodynamic theory and social cognitive theory.

## Psychodynamic Approach

**Is shyness due to unresolved conflicts?**

As a practicing psychoanalyst, Donald Kaplan (1972) uses his clinical experience and psychodynamic concepts to answer the question, What causes shyness? Kaplan traces the causes of shyness back to *unresolved conflicts* at one or more of Freud's psychosexual stages. For example, one very shy client reported that his mother constantly fed him so that he would never cry or whimper. As a result, Kaplan suggests that this client's unresolved conflict during the oral stage resulted in his feelings of inadequacy and shyness in later social interactions.

According to Kaplan, the symptoms of shyness include both conscious fears, such as having nothing to say, and unconscious fears of being rejected. Shy people may deal with these anxieties by using *defense mechanisms;* for example, one client reduced his anxiety through displacement, by changing his fears of being rejected into opposite feelings of self-righteousness and contempt.

One *advantage* of the psychodynamic approach is that it suggests that a number of causes, such as conscious and unconscious fears, as well as unresolved psychosexual conflicts are involved in shyness.

One *disadvantage* of the psychodynamic approach is that Freudian concepts (unconscious fears, unresolved psychosexual stages) are difficult to verify by experimental methods (Macmillan, 1997). For example, saying that being fixated at the oral stage may result in a person becoming a shy adult is mostly a descriptive guess rather than a testable hypothesis.

A very different account of what causes shyness comes from the social cognitive theory of personality.

The cause and treatment for shyness depend partly on which theory of personality the therapist follows.

## Social Cognitive Theory

**What are the three factors?**

Unlike the Freudian approach, which relies primarily on therapists' personal observations, social cognitive theory uses primarily experimental studies to answer questions about personality. Social cognitive theory breaks shyness down into three measurable or observable components—cognitive, behavioral, and environmental—which can be studied using the experimental method described in Module 2 (Carducci & Zimbardo, 1995). For example, in a series of longitudinal studies, researchers found that about 10–15% of the population have a shy personality that, to a large extent, comes from genetic factors—for example, inheriting a nervous system that is easily aroused by novel stimuli (Kagan, 1998). By observing the social interactions (the behavioral component) of shy people, researchers found that shy people have too few social and communication skills and, as a consequence, they are continually punished during social interactions (Jackson et al., 1997). By giving personality tests (the cognitive component), researchers found that shy people are overly self-conscious, which leads to worrisome thoughts and irrational beliefs that interfere with social functioning (Romney & Bynner, 1997). According to social cognitive theory, which we'll discuss more fully in Module 20, shyness can be understood by analyzing the interaction among cognitive, behavioral, and environmental components (Carducci & Zimbardo, 1995).

One *advantage* of social cognitive theory is that it breaks shyness down into three measurable or observable components, each of which can be studied using the experimental method.

One *disadvantage* of this approach is that researchers may overlook certain influences that we are neither conscious nor aware of, such as conditioned emotional responses, that can also trigger shy behaviors (Westen, 1998).

Our discussion of shyness raises the interesting question of how psychologists measure or assess personality traits, such as shyness.

## Definition of Projective Tests

**How did friends describe Kurt's personality?**

At the beginning of this module, we discussed Kurt Cobain, the 27-year-old singer and songwriter, who committed suicide at the height of his fame and fortune. When friends, schoolteachers, and writers described Cobain's personality, some said that he was a nice young man, very quiet, a kind, sweet man, and a sincere listener (top photo). Other friends said that he was very moody, extremely intimidating, unhappy, filled with anger, and never close to anyone (bottom drawing) (DeCurtis, 1994). When friends were describing Kurt's personality, they were making a kind of psychological assessment.

*Psychological assessment* refers to the use of various tools, such as psychological tests and/or interviews, to measure various characteristics, traits, or abilities in order to understand behaviors and predict future performances or behaviors.

Psychological tests are usually divided into ability tests and personality tests, which differ considerably. For

Was Kurt Cobain generally a kind, sweet man or an angry, moody one?

example, when Kurt entered a drug treatment program, he was most likely given personality tests to identify his personal problems.

*Personality tests* are used to measure observable or overt traits and behaviors as well as unobservable or covert characteristics. Personality tests are used to identify personality problems and psychological disorders as well as to predict how a person might behave in the future.

Although you may not have taken a personality test, you certainly have taken many ability tests, such as exams.

*Ability tests* include achievement tests, which measure what we have learned; aptitude tests, which measure our potential for learning or acquiring a specific skill; and intelligence tests, which measure our general potential to solve problems, think abstractly, and profit from experience (Kaplan & Saccuzzo, 2001).

The primary tools of assessment are tests of ability and personality. There are two kinds of personality tests. Here we'll focus on one kind, projective personality tests, and we'll discuss the second kind, objective personality tests, in Module 20.

## Examples of Projective Tests

In describing Cobain's personality, some listed observable behaviors, such as quiet, kind, and nice, while others hinted at unobservable behaviors, such as filled with anger, not close to anybody. In Freud's psychodynamic theory, observable behaviors reflect conscious wishes, desires, and thoughts, while unobservable behaviors may reflect unconscious forces. Freud developed three techniques for revealing unconscious forces—free association, dream interpretation, and interpretation of slips of the tongue. We now add a fourth technique to reveal hidden or unconscious forces: projective tests.

*Projective tests* require individuals to look at some meaningless object or ambiguous photo and describe what they see. In describing or making up a story about the ambiguous object, individuals are assumed to project both their conscious and unconscious feelings, needs, and motives.

Although projective tests were not developed by Freud, they are assumed to reveal unconscious thoughts (Masling, 1997). We'll examine the two most widely used projective tests—Rorschach (*ROAR-shock*) inkblot test and Thematic Apperception Test (TAT).

### RORSCHACH INKBLOT TEST

#### What do you see in this inkblot?

The Rorschach inkblot test, which was published in the early 1920s by a Swiss psychiatrist, Hermann Rorschach (1921/1942), contains five inkblots printed in black and white and five that have color (the inkblot shown on the left is similar to but is not an actual Rorschach inkblot).

What might this be?

The *Rorschach inkblot test* is used to assess personality by showing a person a series of ten inkblots and then asking the person to describe what he or she thinks an image is.

This test is used primarily in the therapeutic setting to assess personality traits and identify potential problems of adolescents and adult clients (Weiner, 2000).

### THEMATIC APPERCEPTION TEST (TAT)

#### What's happening in this picture?

A person would be shown a picture like the one on the right and asked to make up a plot or story about what the young man is thinking, feeling, or doing. This is an example but not a real TAT card.

What's happening?

The *Thematic Apperception Test,* or *TAT,* involves showing a person a series of 20 pictures of people in ambiguous situations and asking the person to make up a story about what the people are doing or thinking in each situation.

The TAT, which was developed by Henry Murray (1943), is used to assess the motivation and personality characteristics of normal individuals as well as clients with personality problems (Kaplan & Saccuzzo, 2001).

Before we discuss how well the Rorschach inkblot test and the TAT assess personality traits and identify potential problems, we'll look at another personality test that you have probably heard of: handwriting analysis. How much can someone learn from just your handwriting?

Which handwriting reveals an honest and sincere person?

**What does handwriting show?**

Handwriting analysts (graphologists) charge about $75 an hour to do personality assessments that they claim reveal a person's strengths and weaknesses, which are important in selecting job applicants and identifying people who may not be trusted (Scanlon & Mauro, 1992).

However, researchers report that handwriting analysis is no better than chance at assessing personality characteristics, rating the success of job applicants, or identifying one's profession (Basil, 1989; Tripician, 2000). In order for handwriting analysis or any personality assessment test to be an effective personality assessment tool, it must have two characteristics, validity and reliability. Handwriting analysis is no better than chance in assessing personality because it lacks validity.

### VALIDITY

Handwriting analysis is fun but no better than chance as a personality test because it lacks validity.

*Validity* means that the test measures what it says it measures or what it is supposed to measure.

For example, for a personality test to be valid, it must measure personality traits specific to the person rather than general traits that apply to almost everyone. Handwriting analysis does not measure, identify, or predict traits specific to an individual, so it has no validity as a personality test (Basil, 1989; Tripician, 2000).

In addition to validity, a good personality test must also have a second characteristic, reliability.

### RELIABILITY

In judging the usefulness of any personality test, the major question is always the same: How good are the test's validity and reliability?

*Reliability* refers to having a consistent score at different times. A person who takes a test at one point in time should receive the same score on a similar test taken at a later time.

For example, handwriting analysis may have good reliability provided your handwriting remains about the same across time. But, even if handwriting analysis has good reliability, it is still no better than chance at assessing or predicting an individual's personality traits because graphology lacks the important characteristic of validity.

This means that the usefulness of projective personality tests, such as the Rorschach test and TAT, depends on their validity and reliability.

## Usefulness of Projective Tests

**Are they valid and reliable?**

Projective tests, such as the Rorschach inkblot test, have been used for over 75 years. However, there is still a debate between therapists, who report that projective tests are useful in assessing personality traits and problems, and researchers, who continue to question the reliability and validity of projective tests (Weiner, 2000). This debate involves the advantages and disadvantages of projective tests.

### ADVANTAGES

Individuals who take projective tests do not know which are the best, correct, or socially desirable answers to give because the stimuli—the inkblot or the TAT picture—are ambiguous and have no right or wrong answers. Thus, one advantage of projective tests such as the Rorschach and the TAT is that they are difficult to fake or bias since there are no correct or socially desirable answers.

When clients respond to Rorschach's meaningless inkblots or make up stories about what is happening in TAT's ambiguous pictures, clinicians assume that clients will project their hidden feelings, thoughts, or emotions onto these ambiguous stimuli. Based on this assumption, some clinicians believe that a second advantage of projective tests is that they are another method for assessing a client's hidden and unconscious thoughts and desires of which he or she is normally unaware (Weiner, 2000). Other researchers suggest that the Rorschach test is useful as an interview technique in eliciting unique information about the person (Aronow et al., 1995). Thus, the Rorschach test's advantage is obtaining information about the person in a setting where there are no right or wrong answers.

Clinician's experience affects reliability and validity of projective tests.

### DISADVANTAGES

One disadvantage of projective tests comes from the use of ambiguous stimuli to which there are no right or wrong answers. This means clinicians are responsible for learning and using a complex scoring procedure that includes many different variables, such as content, theme, and popularity (commonly given responses) (Weiner, 2000). The problem is that because of differences in experience or training, different clinicians may not always agree on the scoring of responses and thus their interpretations and scoring may differ. For this reason, it is difficult to know if the interpretation and scoring of the client's responses accurately assess the client's personality traits and problems or rather reflect the biases or lack of experience of the interpreting clinician (Acklin et al., 2000). Because of potential problems in scoring and interpreting, projective tests tend to have relatively low reliability and validity, their major disadvantages (Kaplan & Saccuzzo, 2001).

However, well-trained and experienced clinicians who regularly use projective tests, often combined with other assessment techniques, report that projective tests can provide reliable and valid information about a client's personality and problems (Weiner, 2000). Thus, a clinician's training and experience play a major role in the accuracy of assessing a client's personality and problems using projective tests (Kaplan & Saccuzzo, 2001).

# Summary Test

## A. FREUD'S PSYCHODYNAMIC THEORY

**1.** The lasting behaviors, thoughts, and emotions that typify how we react and adapt to other people and situations make up our (a)_____. An organized attempt to explain how personalities develop and why they differ is called a (b)_____ of personality.

**2.** Freud's approach, which emphasizes the importance of early childhood experiences and conflicts between conscious and unconscious forces, is called a (a)_____ theory of personality. According to Freud, those wishes, desires, or thoughts of which we are aware or that we can readily recall are (b)_____; those that we automatically repress because of their disturbing or threatening content are (c)_____.

**3.** Freud's technique of encouraging clients to talk about any thoughts or images that enter their heads is called (a)_____. His assumption that dreams provide clues to unconscious thoughts and desires gave rise to his technique of (b)_____. Mistakes that we make in everyday speech that are thought to reflect unconscious thoughts or wishes are called (c)_____.

## B. DIVISIONS OF THE MIND

**4.** According to Freud, the biological drives of sex and aggression are the source of all psychic or mental energy and give rise to the development of the (a)_____. Because this division of the mind strives to satisfy drives and avoid pain without concern for moral or social restrictions, it is said to be operating according to the (b)_____. During infancy, the second division of the mind develops from the id; it is called the (c)_____. The goal of this second division is to find safe and socially acceptable ways of satisfying the id's desires. The ego follows a policy of satisfying a wish or desire only if a socially acceptable outlet is available; thus it is said to operate according to the (d)_____. During early childhood, the third division of the mind develops from the id; it is called the (e)_____. The goal of this division is to apply the moral values and standards of one's parents and society in satisfying one's wishes.

**5.** When the id, ego, and superego are in conflict, an unpleasant state of uneasiness, apprehension, and heightened physiological arousal may occur; this is known as (a)_____. The Freudian processes that operate at unconscious levels to help the ego reduce anxiety through self-deception are called (b)_____; they can be helpful or harmful, depending on how much we rely on them.

## C. DEVELOPMENTAL STAGES

**6.** The essence of Freud's theory of personality development is a series of five developmental stages, called (a)_____, during which the individual seeks pleasure from different parts of the body. The stage that lasts for the first 18 months of life is called the (b)_____ stage. It is followed by the (c)_____ stage, which lasts until about the age of 3. The next stage, until about the age of 6, is called the (d)_____ stage. The stage that lasts from about 6 to puberty is called the (e)_____ stage; it is followed by the (f)_____ stage, which lasts through adulthood.

**7.** The resolution of the potential conflict at each stage has important implications for personality. A Freudian process through which individuals may be locked into earlier psychosexual stages because their wishes were overgratified or undergratified is called _____; it can occur at any of the first three stages.

## D. FREUD'S FOLLOWERS & CRITICS

**8.** Jung believed that the basic force is not the sex drive, as Freud believed, but ancient memory traces and symbols shared by all peoples in all cultures, called the (a)_____. According to Adler's philosophy, each person is a social being with a unique personality and is motivated by (b)_____. Karen Horney disagreed with Freud's emphasis on biological urges and insisted that the major influence on personality development was (c)_____ between parents and child.

**9.** Those who generally agreed with Freud's basic ideas but disagreed with his emphasis on biological forces, sexual drives, and psychosexual stages are referred to as _____; they turned the emphasis of psychodynamic theory to psychosocial and cultural influences.

**10.** Criticisms of Freud's psychodynamic theory include that it is so comprehensive that it is not very useful for explaining or predicting behaviors of a specific (a)_____; that some Freudian terms (Oedipal complex) are out of date because they could not be (b)_____; that psychodynamic theory must be updated with findings about (c)_____ factors and the association between (d)_____ development and related behaviors.

## E. HUMANISTIC THEORIES

**11.** Humanistic theories emphasize our capacity for personal growth, development of our potential, and freedom to choose our (a)_____. They stress that our perception of the world becomes our reality; this is called the (b)_____ perspective. These theories emphasize that one's personality is unique, functions as a unit, and is more than the sum of individual parts; together these ideas make up the (c)_____ view. These theories also highlight the idea of an inherent tendency to reach our true potentials, which is called (d)_____.

**12.** According to Maslow, our needs are arranged in a hierarchy with (a)_____ at the bottom and (b)_____ toward the top.

**13.** How we see or describe ourselves, including how we perceive our abilities, personality characteristics, and behaviors, is referred to as our (a)_____. According to Carl Rogers, the development of self-concept depends on our interactions with others. If we receive (b)_____ positive regard even when our behavior is disappointing, we will develop a positive self-concept and tend to act, feel, and think optimistically and constructively.

## F. CULTURAL DIVERSITY: ACHIEVEMENT

**14.** Indo-Chinese children overcame problems of language and culture and excelled in American schools in part because of the _____ held by their families, including mutual respect, cooperation, parental involvement, and the belief that they, not fate, controlled their destinies.

© Jason Goltz

## G. RESEARCH FOCUS: SHYNESS

**15.** As a practicing psychoanalyst, Donald Kaplan traces the causes of shyness back to unresolved conflicts at one or more of Freud's

(a)_____. The Freudian approach primarily uses therapists' (b)_____ to answer questions about personality. In comparison, social cognitive theory breaks shyness down into three measurable or observable components that can be investigated using (c)_____.

## H. APPLICATION: ASSESSMENT—PROJECTIVE TESTS

**16.** Tests that are used to measure observable traits and behaviors as well as unobservable characteristics of a person and to identify personality problems and psychological disorders are called _____ tests.

**17.** Achievement tests measure what we have learned; aptitude tests measure our potential for learning or acquiring a specific skill; and intelligence tests measure our general potential to solve problems, think abstractly, and profit from experience. Collectively, these are called _____ tests.

**18.** For a test to be useful, it must have two characteristics. First, a test must measure what it is supposed to measure; this is called (a)_____. Second, a person's score on a test at one point in time should be similar to the score obtained by the same person on a similar test at a later point in time; this is called (b)_____.

**19.** Typically, a combination of tests is used to assess personality. Tests that involve presenting an ambiguous stimulus and asking the person to describe it are called (a)_____ tests. A test used to assess personality in terms of how the subject interprets a series of inkblots is called the (b)_____ test. A test in which the subject is to make up a story about people shown in ambiguous situations is called the (c)_____.

*Answers:* 1. (a) personalities, (b) theory; 2. (a) psychodynamic, (b) conscious thoughts, (c) unconscious forces or thoughts; 3. (a) free association, (b) dream interpretation, (c) slips of the tongue or Freudian slips; 4. (a) id, (b) pleasure principle, (c) ego, (d) reality principle, (e) superego; 5. (a) anxiety, (b) defense mechanisms; 6. (a) psychosexual stages, (b) oral, (c) anal, (d) phallic, (e) latency, (f) genital; 7. fixation; 8. (a) collective unconscious, (b) social urges, (c) social interactions; 9. neo-Freudians; 10. (a) individual or person, (b) tested or verified, (c) genetic, (d) brain; 11. (a) destinies, (b) phenomenological, (c) holistic, (d) self-actualization; 12. (a) biological needs, (b) social and personal needs; 13. (a) self or self-concept, (b) unconditional; 14. primary values; 15. (a) psychosexual stages, (b) personal observations, (c) experimental studies; 16. personality; 17. ability; 18. (a) validity, (b) reliability; 19. (a) projective, (b) Rorschach inkblot, (c) Thematic Apperception Test (TAT)

# Critical Thinking

**Newspaper Article**

## Friends, Others Offer Complex View of Rathbun

*by Robert J. Lopez and Eric Slater*

### Questions

**1.** Which part of Freud's psychodynamic theory might explain why Charles Rathbun murdered a woman?

**2.** What roles might the Freudian concepts of the id, ego, and superego have had in Rathbun's earlier charge of raping a woman?

**3.** Following Freud's psychodynamic theory, what kinds of questions might you ask or techniques might you use to understand Rathbun's behavior?

Charles E. Rathbun is a skilled automobile photographer who was on his way to the top in his highly specialized field.

Yet, as Rathbun sits in Men's Central Jail downtown—charged with murdering model Linda Sobek—a more complex portrait of the 38-year-old is beginning to emerge, one of a man who seemed to have different facets of his personality that he showed to different people— friendly and easygoing to some, a loner who had difficulties with women to others, and an aggressive hothead in some eyes. Problems with women are not new since as a young college student in Ohio, court records show, he was charged and then acquitted of raping a female friend in 1979.

Moving to California eight years ago, Rathbun had no run-ins with the law until he was arrested in Sobek's death and led investigators to her shallow grave. "There is nothing about this guy that would ever suggest that he is in any way capable of this," said Steve Spence, managing editor of *Car and Driver* magazine.

The son of a management consultant, Rathbun was born on Oct. 2, 1957, and was raised in a quiet, middle-class neighborhood in Worthington, a suburb of Columbus. He was the youngest of four children, and has two sisters and a brother. At Worthington High School in the early 1970s, Rathbun developed an interest in photography, taking photos for the school's biweekly newspaper, the *Chronicle.*

After several years of college in Ohio, Rathbun made his way to the car-manufacturing center of Detroit, an ideal place for an ambitious automobile photographer to leave his mark. Jim Haefner hired Rathbun as an assistant in 1985. "He was a nice enough guy— there was just something a little bit different about him," Haefner recalled. "It was just an anger that would come out from time to time. If something frustrated him, he might pick up [a piece of photo equipment] and throw it across the studio. I don't know what was bothering him."

But others in Michigan did not see Rathbun that way. Pamela Powell, who has been a friend of Rathbun's for 10 years, said he was a well-adjusted man who liked old rock 'n' roll and adventure movies. Contrary to some reports, Powell insisted that Rathbun was comfortable around men and women alike, and dated frequently. (Source: *Los Angeles Times,* December 11, 1995)

**4.** Can you explain why different people offer such different descriptions of Rathbun?

**5.** How might humanistic theories explain Rathbun's actions?

*Try InfoTrac to search for terms:* personality development; self-actualization; rape.

---

### Suggested answers to Newspaper Article questions

1. The part of Freud's psychodynamic theory that focuses on the development of personality involves how a person goes through the five psychosexual stages and whether fixation occurs. For example, Rathbun may have become fixated at the phallic stage and found it necessary to prove his toughness with women.

2. Rathbun's id, which follows the pleasure principle, wanted to have sex with women. Rathbun's superego, which contains moral standards, would argue against forcing women to have sex. Rathbun's ego, which follows the reality principle, tried to find a socially acceptable outlet for the id's desires. In Rathbun's case, the id's desires apparently won out.

3. Since Freud believed that most personality development and seeds of problems occurred during the first five years, you would ask questions about his early childhood, especially his relationship with his parents. To reveal Rathbun's unconscious forces, you might use free association and dream interpretation.

4. People might have very different impressions of Rathbun because he might have behaved very differently depending on how much he was influenced by different unconscious feelings and thoughts, repressed wishes or desires, or defense mechanisms.

5. Humanistic theories are better at describing positive human growth than criminal behavior. However, a humanist might say that because Rathbun had not received enough love or unconditional positive regard, he developed a poor or negative self-concept, which interfered with his self-actualization and instead led to committing destructive actions.

# Links to Learning

## Web Sites

- **WADSWORTH ONLINE STUDY CENTER**
  **http://psychology.wadsworth.com**
  Quizzes, learning activities and exercises, a discussion forum, and hot links to internet sites related to Freudian and humanistic theories and other subjects in this module, including:

- **SIGMUND FREUD MUSEUM**
  **http://freud.t0.or.at/freud/index-e.htm**
  The online service of the Sigmund Freud Society provides a detailed time line of Freud's life, links to Freud sites on the Internet, discussions of major themes in Freud's professional work, audio and video clips, and, under "Topography," photographs of many of the homes and other buildings that have historical significance.

- **ASSOCIATION FOR HUMANISTIC PSYCHOLOGY**
  **http://ahpweb.org/index.html**
  This site includes *The Journal of Humanistic Psychology* and *AHP Perspective* magazine (also available in Spanish), news, articles, and extensive annotated bibliography of resources for humanistic psychology, and information about degree programs.

- **RESOURCES FOR SHY PEOPLE**
  **http://www.base.com/shy/**
  Created by and for shy people, this extensive site offers links to articles on shyness in general and to articles that give advice, a bibliography, news groups, chat rooms (open only to shy people), information on shyness clinics, classes, and counseling, email lists, links to other relevant sites, and the *Shy Digest*, in which several mail messages are collected every day and sent to subscribers every 1 to 3 days.

## Learning Activities

- **POWERSTUDY™ BY ROD PLOTNIK & TOM DOYLE**

  **PowerStudy™**
  **Check out CD: Module 19**
  CD 11.D: Long-Term Memory: Storing

- **STUDY GUIDE TO ACCOMPANY INTRODUCTION TO PSYCHOLOGY, 6TH EDITION, by Matthew Enos**
  In Module 19 you're faced with various theories of personality and reminded to evaluate each one on your own terms. You are also let in on "Three Secrets of Effective Writing" and encouraged to track and analyze your Freudian slips.

- **WEBTUTOR**
  **http://webtutor.thomsonlearning.com**
  Visit this site for interactive versions of the Study Guide features. Take a quiz, get your score— should you study a topic some more, or can you move on? For example, What are defense mechanisms and how do they work? Carl Rogers says happiness is an illusion: true or false?

- **INFOTRAC ONLINE LIBRARY**
  **http://www.infotrac-college.com**

  Use your password and then key in search terms such as those below to find popular and scientific articles on subjects covered in Module 19. Make the library work for you!

  Psychological tests    Abraham Maslow    Boat people

- **PSYCHNOW!**
  CD for Macintosh and Windows includes a study guide, glossary, Web sites, and animations. For Module 19, see:
  - Theories of Personality

## Study Questions

*Use InfoTrac to search for topics mentioned in the main heads below (e.g., shyness, projective tests).*

*A. **Freud's Psychodynamic Theory**—According to Freud, why do some students plan to study on the weekend but end up partying? (**Suggested answer p. 632**)

B. **Divisions of the Mind**—Sheryl wears sexy clothes but claims to be a feminist. How would Freud explain that?

C. **Developmental Stages**—How would Freud's theory explain why you are neat and outspoken while your sister is messy and demanding and feels inferior?

D. **Freud's Followers & Critics**—Which factors in the development of your personality support Freud's theory and which do not?

E. **Humanistic Theories**—How would humanistic theories explain why many students change their majors three to five times during their college careers?

*F. **Cultural Diversity: Unexpected High Achievement**—If you were the principal of a grade school, what might you do to improve overall student performance? (**Suggested answer p. 632**)

G. **Research Focus: Shyness**—Carl says that he's always been shy and it can't be helped. Would a Freudian respond to Carl's problem in the same way as a cognitive behaviorist?

*H. **Application: Assessment**—Projective Tests—How useful would projective tests be for identifying students who are most likely to cheat on exams? (**Suggested answer p. 632**)

*These questions are answered in Appendix B.

# Module 20: Social Cognitive & Trait Theories

**A. Social Cognitive Theory**     **458**
* REVIEW AND DEFINITION
* INTERACTION OF THREE FACTORS
* BANDURA'S SOCIAL COGNITIVE THEORY
* EVALUATION OF SOCIAL COGNITIVE THEORY

**B. Trait Theory**     **462**
* DEFINITION
* IDENTIFYING TRAITS
* FINDING TRAITS: BIG FIVE
* PERSON VERSUS SITUATION
* STABILITY VERSUS CHANGE

**C. Genetic Influences on Traits**     **466**
* BEHAVIORAL GENETICS
* STUDYING GENETIC INFLUENCES
* DATA FROM TWIN STUDIES
* INFLUENCES ON PERSONALITY

**D. Evaluation of Trait Theory**     **468**
* HOW GOOD IS THE LIST?
* CAN TRAITS PREDICT?
* WHAT INFLUENCES TRAITS?

**Concept Review**     **469**

**E. Research Focus: 180-Degree Change**     **470**
* HOW MUCH CAN PEOPLE CHANGE IN A DAY?

**F. Cultural Diversity: Resolving Conflicts**     **471**
* INTERPERSONAL CONFLICTS
* CULTURAL DIFFERENCES
* USING DIFFERENT STRATEGIES

**G. Four Theories of Personality**     **472**
* PSYCHODYNAMIC THEORY
* HUMANISTIC THEORIES
* SOCIAL COGNITIVE THEORY
* TRAIT THEORY

**H. Application: Assessment—Objective Tests**     **474**
* DEFINITION
* EXAMPLES OF OBJECTIVE TESTS
* RELIABILITY AND VALIDITY
* USEFULNESS

**Summary Test**     **476**

**Critical Thinking**     **478**
* COMPANIES USING PERSONALITY TESTS FOR MAKING HIRES THAT FIT

**Links to Learning**     **479**

Courtesy of Sony Electronics, Inc.

## Power of Beliefs

**Why did he suffer in prison for 27 years?**

He chose to remain in prison rather than change his major beliefs.

Nelson Mandela had been born into a royal tribal African family, but he lost his father at an early age and was raised by a guardian in the tribe. According to tradition, Mandela became a man at 16, when he went through an elaborate public circumcision ceremony. When he was 21, he ran away to the big city. In Johannesburg, he entered college, received his law degree, and began his lifetime struggle to free the black people of South Africa (Ransdell & Eddings, 1994).

In 1964, Nelson Mandela (left photo) was found guilty of plotting against the all-white South African government and sentenced to prison for life. In his defense he said: "During my lifetime I have dedicated myself to this struggle of the African people. I have fought against white domination, and I have fought about black domination. I have cherished the ideal of a democratic and free society in which all persons live together in harmony and with equal opportunities. It is an ideal which I hope to live for and to achieve. But, if need be, it is an ideal for which I am prepared to die" (Bernstein, 1994, p. 11).

While in prison, he slept on a narrow bed in a barren cubicle, 7 feet wide and 9 feet long. He ate corn porridge, with a piece of meat every other day. He was allowed to write one letter and have one visitor every six months. Mandela endured these long, terrible years because he believed that one day he would be free to continue his fight against oppression. Many times he was offered his release from prison provided that he make no public speeches and cease his freedom-fighting activities. Mandela refused these conditional releases and remained in prison.

Finally, in 1990, at the age of 71, he was released from prison. His time had indeed come, and he repeated the moving speech that he had spoken 27 years earlier (quoted above). Mandela lost no time in resuming his fight against White domination and for equal opportunities for Blacks. For these efforts, Mandela was awarded the Nobel Peace Prize in 1993.

The fulfillment of his life's dream finally came in 1994. At the age of 76, Mandela was elected the first Black president of South Africa. His election marked the end to the horrible and discriminatory practice of apartheid, which had been in effect for almost 300 years and had permitted the White minority to dominate and suppress the Black majority.

What were the forces that shaped Mandela's personality and gave him the strength and motivation to persist in the face of overwhelming adversity? In this module, we'll discuss three forces that shape and mold our personalities.

In a different nation, an ocean away, Beverly Harvard was waging her own personal struggle against forces that said no African American woman should be doing what she wanted to do.

## Determination

**What's unusual about this woman?**

In the 1970s, Beverly Harvard, an African American woman in a southern city (Atlanta, Georgia), was trying to become a police officer. In those days, female police recruits, Black or White, faced rejection, discrimination, and harassment by their male peers, who believed strongly that women had neither the physical strength nor the mental toughness to be police officers (Fletcher, 1995). From the 1970s through the 1980s, there were intense legal and political battles in the United States, in which women had to prove that they have what it takes to be good cops. Their struggle is slowly paying off: By the early 1990s, about 10% of this country's police officers were women.

With incredible determination, Beverly Harvard (photo below) worked her way up through the Atlanta police ranks. She put up with the male officers' sarcastic, hurtful, and discriminatory comments and concentrated on doing the best possible job. Finally, after struggling for almost 20 years, she was appointed head of the Atlanta police department. Her appointment in 1994 marks the first time an African American woman has headed a police department in a major city. She has 1,700 police officers under her command, and her motto is "You can talk about what's wrong with the world or help fix it" (Eddings, 1994, p. 87).

For her beliefs, Beverly Harvard fought against sex discrimination for 20 years.

Beverly Harvard, like thousands of female police officers around the country, has shown that women make good cops, partly because of their particular personality traits: women are less authoritarian, more open, better listeners, and less likely to trigger showdowns than are their male counterparts (Fletcher, 1995; Nazario, 1993). Apparently, what women may lack in sheer muscle power, they make up for in a winning combination of personality traits.

In this module, we'll discuss personality traits, which are powerful motivating forces that we all have, cannot live without, like to talk about, may be critical of, and are often asked to change but find it difficult to do so.

## What's Coming

We'll discuss two theories of personality, each with a different emphasis. The first is social cognitive theory (previously called social learning theory), which stresses the influences of cognitive, learning, and social processes on personality development. The second is trait theory, which focuses on measuring traits and describing how traits make up our different personalities and influence our behaviors.

We'll begin with three social cognitive forces that helped shape Nelson Mandela's personality.

457

# A. Social Cognitive Theory

**What shaped his personality?**

How many of us would have stayed in prison for 27 years, as Mandela did, if the only condition for our release was that we not speak in public against the government? What were the forces that shaped Mandela's personality and gave him such courage, self-confidence, and perseverance? In Module 19, we discussed two answers to this question, Freud's psychodynamic theory and humanistic theories.

Freud's psychodynamic theory said that our personality is shaped primarily by our inborn biological urges, especially sex and aggression, and by how we resolve conflicts during the psychosexual stages, especially during the first five years.

Humanistic theories, such as those of Abraham Maslow and Carl Rogers, assume that we are basically good and that our personality is shaped

*What gave him the courage to fight for the presidency?*

primarily by our inborn tendency for self-actualization, or self-fulfillment, which includes both biological and psychological factors.

Now we discuss two more answers: first, social cognitive theory and, later, trait theory.

*Social cognitive theory* says that personality development is shaped primarily by three forces: environmental conditions (learning), cognitive-personal factors, and behavior, which all interact to influence how we evaluate, interpret, organize, and apply information.

Social cognitive theory grew out of the research of a number of psychologists, including Julian Rotter (1966), Albert Bandura (1986), and Walter Mischel (1990). According to social cognitive theory, we are neither good nor bad but shaped primarily by three influential factors.

## Interaction of Three Factors

For almost his entire life, Nelson Mandela has been fighting the White domination of Blacks in South Africa. During this time, he suffered tremendous personal hardships, including 27 years in prison. You can't help wondering what shaped his personality and gave him the strength,

1. Cognitive factors
2. Behaviors
3. Environmental factors

YOU

determination, and character to sacrifice so much to reach his goal of freedom for his people. According to social cognitive theory, Mandela's personality was influenced and shaped by the interactions among three significant forces—namely, cognitive-personal, behavioral, and environmental factors.

### Cognitive-Personal Factors

Mandela was born to an African tribal royal family, and he was expected and trained to be a leader someday (photo below). Mandela's family encouraged him to be self-confident, have dignity, and, if needed, be ruthless and determined to achieve his goal (Mathews et al., 1990). Being born into a royal family and being taught to view himself as a leader are examples of cognitive-personal factors that helped shape Mandela's personality.

*Cognitive factors* include our beliefs, expectations, values, intentions, and social roles. *Personal factors* include our emotional makeup and our biological and genetic influences.

Cognitive factors guide personality development by influencing the way we view and interpret information. For example, Mandela viewed the world from the standpoint of someone trained to lead and help his people. These kinds of beliefs (cognitions) gave Mandela the strength and determination to fight for freedom. Thus, cognitive-personal factors influence our personalities by affecting what we think, believe, and feel, which in turn affect how we act and behave.

*Born to a royal family but . . .*

### Behaviors

All his life Mandela spoke forcefully against oppression (photo top of page), organized political groups, and led marches against unfair domination of his people. These are examples of the kinds of behaviors that also shaped his personality.

*Behaviors* include a variety of personal actions, such as the things we do and say.

In Mandela's case, the political and social behaviors that he engaged in to help his people achieve freedom in turn strengthened his belief that apartheid (discriminatory practices against Blacks) was morally and politically wrong.

Just as behavior influences our beliefs, so too does our environment influence both.

*. . . Mandela grew up amid racial hatred.*

### Environmental Factors

Mandela lived in a society based on apartheid, which meant strict separation of the races, limited opportunities for non-Whites, and the fostering of intense racial hatred (bottom photo). These environmental factors certainly affected Mandela's personality development.

*Environmental factors* include our social, political, and cultural influences, as well as our particular learning experiences.

Just as our cognitive factors influence how we perceive and interpret our environment, our environment in turn affects our beliefs, values, and social roles.

We can assume that living in such an oppressive environment strengthened Mandela's determination to get a law degree and to devote his life to obtaining freedom for all.

According to Bandura (1999), personality development is influenced by the interactions among these three factors. He especially focused on cognitive-personal factors.

**Why are beliefs important?**

Albert Bandura (1986, 1999) originally called his theory of personality development the social learning theory. However, to emphasize the importance of cognitive factors in personality development, he has recently changed the name to the social cognitive theory.

*Bandura's social cognitive theory* assumes that personality development, growth, and change are influenced by four distinctively human cognitive processes: highly developed language ability, observational learning, purposeful behavior, and self-analysis.

Bandura believes that these four cognitive processes reach their highest level of functioning in humans and that much of human

Cognitive factors—beliefs, values, and goals—influence their personalities.

personality and behavior is shaped by our own thoughts and beliefs.

For example, the young Black men in the photo on the left are wearing T-shirts that say "ANC LIVES." Nelson Mandela helped found a social-political organization whose initials, ANC, stand for African National Congress. For many years Mandela was the head of ANC, whose goal is freedom and equal opportunities for Black Africans. According to Bandura's social cognitive theory, these young men's personalities will, to a large extent, be molded by cognitive factors such as the beliefs, values, and goals of the African National Congress. We'll briefly explain each of Bandura's cognitive factors.

## Four Cognitive Factors

At the heart of Bandura's social cognitive theory is the idea that much of personality development is shaped and molded by cognitive processes that influence how we view and interpret the world. And, in turn, how we view and interpret the world influences how we behave. Here's how Bandura's cognitive processes apply to the young Black men who have joined the ANC.

**1 Language ability.** This is a powerful tool for processing and understanding information that influences personality development. We turn this information into ideas, beliefs, values, and goals, which shape, guide, and motivate our behaviors. For example, the ANC talks about, teaches, and values fighting for freedom. This information motivates its members to become assertive, self-confident, and determined.

**2 Observational learning.** Almost all of us "people watch"; we observe parents, brothers, sisters, peers, friends, and teachers; by doing so, we learn a great deal. Observational learning involves watching, imitating, and modeling. Most of the time, the observer provides his or her own reward for developing some belief or performing some behavior. For example, observational learning allows the young Black men to imitate and model the personality characteristics of adult role models in the ANC.

**3 Purposeful behavior.** Our capacity to anticipate events, plan ahead, and set goals influences our personality development, growth, and change. For instance, in fighting for freedom, the young Black men will organize, plan marches, and develop political strategies, which will encourage them to become responsible, confident, and energetic.

**4 Self-analysis.** This is a powerful internal process that allows us to monitor our own thoughts and actions. By deciding to change our goals or values, we can significantly affect our personality development. For instance, the young Black men use self-analysis to check their personality progress as well as to reward themselves for meeting goals of the ANC.

According to Bandura's social cognitive theory, these four cognitive processes influence our personality development, growth, and change.

To make the relationship between cognitive factors and personality more concrete, we'll focus on three specific beliefs: locus of control (this page), delay of gratification, and self-efficacy (next page).

## Locus of Control

### Can you control when you'll graduate?

This is the kind of question that intrigued Julian Rotter (1990), who was interested in how social cognitive theory applied to human behavior. Rotter developed a well-known scale to measure a person's expectancies about how much control he or she has over situations, which Rotter called the locus of control.

Can you control when you will graduate?

*Locus of control* refers to our beliefs about how much control we have over situations or rewards. We are said to have an *internal locus of control* if we believe that we have control over situations and rewards. We are said to have an *external locus of control* if we believe that we do not have control over situations and rewards and that events outside ourselves (fate) determine what happens.

For example, if you believe that when you graduate depends primarily on your motivation and determination, then you have more of an internal locus of control. If you believe that when you graduate depends mostly on chance or things outside your control, then you have more of an external locus of control. Having more of an internal locus of control is an advantage because hundreds of studies report a positive correlation (0.20 to 0.30) between internal locus of control and mental health and psychological functioning (Janssen & Carton, 1999; Smith et al., 1997). For example, people with an internal locus of control were generally higher achievers and were likely to take preventive health measures, to report less stress, and to be less depressed than were those with an external locus of control (Carducci, 1998).

These findings indicate that a specific belief, such as how much control you believe you have, influences how you perceive your world; and this, in turn, affects how you behave. Next, we'll examine two other beliefs that influence behavior.

## Delay of Gratification

**Have it now or wait?**

When I was a young child, I hated vegetables but loved candy. I remember that one night at the dinner table, my father showed me a handful of candy that made me so excited I clapped my hands and reached to grab as much as I could. My father stopped me and said, "Rod, you can have one piece now, but if you finish your corn, you can have four pieces." I remember this event as clearly as the day it happened because it was the biggest and hardest decision of my young life. You can imagine my surprise when I read later that researchers were studying what my father had asked me to do: wait for a reward, or delay my gratification.

*Delay of gratification* refers to voluntarily postponing an immediate reward and continuing to complete some task with the promise of a future reward.

My father had said I needed to develop my willpower. Walter Mischel and his colleagues have recast this old concept into the idea of delay of gratification (Mischel et al., 1989).

A technique that Mischel used to measure delay of gratification was to show children two objects, one less preferred (a single marshmallow) and one more preferred (two marshmallows). The children were told that to obtain the more preferred reward they had to wait until the experimenter, who had to leave the room, returned after some delay (about 15 minutes). Children were free to end the waiting period by ringing a bell, but then they would get only the less preferred reward. Thus, the child had a real conflict: accept immediate gratification and take the less preferred reward, or delay gratification and obtain the more preferred reward.

Should I take one marshmallow now or wait and get two later?

Researchers found that 4-year-old children differed greatly in the length of time they could delay gratification. This time was, in turn, significantly associated with a number of psychological variables. For example, when children were told to picture the marshmallows in their minds, they waited an average of over 15 minutes; however, when they could see the real marshmallows, they could wait an average of only 6 minutes (Mischel et al., 1989).

**Conclusion.** The ability to delay gratification was related to a number of personality variables. For example, 4-year-old children good at delaying gratification tended to be more intelligent, to have greater social responsibility, and to strive for higher achievement. When these same 4-year-old children were later retested at age 14, they were rated by parents as more competent, more intelligent, and better able to concentrate than those who did not delay gratification. Taken together, these studies make an important point: The beliefs and cognitive processes involved in the ability to delay gratification also affect personality development and influence a number of personal and social behaviors (Green et al., 1994; Mischel, 1990).

Another cognitive process that affects personality and behavior is how much we believe in our own capabilities.

## Self-Efficacy

**Can I get better grades?**

Students often ask about how to improve their grades. According to Albert Bandura (1999), one reason students differ in whether they receive high or low grades is related to self-efficacy.

*Self-efficacy* refers to our personal beliefs regarding how capable we are in controlling events and situations in our lives, such as performing or completing specific tasks and behaviors.

For example, saying "I think that I am capable of getting a high grade in this course" is a sign of strong self-efficacy. You judge your self-efficacy by combining four sources of information (Bandura, 1999; Zimmerman, 2000):

1. You *use previous experiences* of success or failure on similar tasks to estimate how you will do on a new, related task.
2. You *compare* your capabilities with those of others.
3. You *listen* to what others say about your capabilities.
4. You *use feedback* from your body to assess your strength, vulnerability, and capability.

Why do my friends say that I should be getting better grades?

You would have strong self-efficacy for getting good grades if you have had previous success with getting high grades, if you believe you are as academically capable as others, if your friends say you are smart, and if you do not become too stressed during exams.

**Influence of self-efficacy.** According to Bandura's self-efficacy theory, your motivation to achieve, perform, and do well on a variety of tasks and situations is largely mediated or influenced by how strongly you believe in your own capabilities. For example, people with higher self-efficacy were better at succeeding on a number of different tasks: stopping smoking, losing weight, overcoming a phobia, performing well in school, adjusting to new situations, coping with job stress, playing video games, or tolerating pain (Bandura, 1999; Laganer et al., 2000). These findings indicate that having either high or low self-efficacy can increase or decrease your performance on a variety of tasks. Twenty years of research show that students' levels of self-efficacy are good predictors of their motivation and learning during college (Zimmerman, 2000).

**Conclusion.** So far we have discussed three important beliefs: whether you have an internal or external locus of control, how much you can delay gratification, and whether you have high or low self-efficacy. Research on these three beliefs supports the basic assumption of social cognitive theory: Cognitive factors influence personality development, which in turn affects performance of a variety of behaviors.

**Where does he get the courage to keep trying?**

Sometimes a person's experience better illustrates the power and importance of beliefs than all the research in the world. Such an experience is that of Christopher Reeve, who once played the role of Superman in movies. Since his spinal cord was severed in a tragic riding accident, Christopher Reeve has not been able to move or feel any part of his body below his neck. This means that when Reeve wakes up in the morning, he can move only the muscles of his face and eyes. Although he knows his head is attached to his body, he cannot so much as raise his head to look down at his body. Someone else must move, clothe, and feed him and take care of all his bodily needs.

When Reeve recently fell and broke his arm, he felt no pain because nothing that happens to

his body is able to reach his perfectly functioning brain. When he goes to sleep, he experiences being whole again through his vivid dreams of riding, acting, or being with his family. Strapped to his electric wheelchair, which he controls by breathing, Reeve is able to move about and appear on numerous news and talk shows. He says, "I'm not trying to be a hero. I'm just trying to cope the best I can" (*People*, May 5, 1998, p. 216).

One reason Reeve is coping so well is his belief that researchers will find a way to regrow spinal nerves so that he'll be able to walk by his 50th birthday (Reeve, 1998). This single belief gives Reeve the courage to live inside his head while someone else takes care of his body. Reeve's story illustrates a major assumption of social cognitive theory: Beliefs have a great influence on personality and behavior.

We'll evaluate social cognitive theory's approach to personality development and compare it with other theories.

*What keeps me going is my belief that I'll walk on my 50th birthday.*

### 1 Comprehensive Approach

Social cognitive theory focuses on the interaction of three primary forces in the development of personality: cognitive-personal factors, which include beliefs, expectations, social roles, and genetic influences; behaviors, which include actions, conversations, and emotional expressions; and environmental influences, such as social, political, and cultural forces.

Bandura (1999) points out that other theories of personality tend to focus on one or two of these factors but neglect the interaction among all three factors. For example, Freudian and humanistic theories emphasize the effects of personal and cognitive forces on personality development but neglect the significant behavioral, learning, and environmental influences. Thus, one advantage of social cognitive theory is that its approach to personality development is more comprehensive and includes more influential factors than other theories.

### 2 Experimentally Based

Many of the concepts used in social cognitive theory have been developed from, and based on, objective measurement, laboratory research, and experimental studies. Because social cognitive theory's concepts—such as locus of control, delay of gratification, and self-efficacy—are experimentally based, they can be manipulated, controlled, and tested and are less subject to error and bias.

In comparison, many concepts from Freudian and humanistic theories of personality were developed from clinical interviews and practice and, for that reason, these concepts (oral stage, Oedipal complex, self-actualization, positive regard) are more difficult to test and validate and more open to error and bias.

### 3 Programs for Change

Because many of the concepts of social cognitive theory are experimentally based and objectively defined (observational learning, self-reward, modeling behavior, self-analysis, and planning), these concepts have been used to develop very successful programs for changing behavior and personality. For example, in Module 10, we discussed an observational and modeling program based on social cognitive theory that decreased intense fear, such as fear of snakes.

Also in Module 10, we explained how children may learn to be aggressive by watching a model behave in an aggressive manner. These are just two of many examples of applied programs for behavioral changes based on the concepts of social cognitive theory (Bandura, 1999, 2000).

### 4 Criticisms and Conclusions

Critics say that because social cognitive concepts focus on narrowly defined behaviors, such as self-efficacy, locus of control, and delay of gratification, social cognitive theory is a somewhat piecemeal explanation of personality development. They add that social cognitive theory needs to combine these objectively but narrowly defined concepts into a more integrated theory of personality. Finally, critics contend that social cognitive theory pays too little attention to the influence of genetic factors, emotional influences, and childhood experiences on personality development (Liebert & Spiegler, 1994; Plomin & Crabbe, 2000).

Despite these criticisms, social cognitive theory has made a profound impact on personality theory by emphasizing the objective measurement of concepts, the influence of cognitive processes, and the application of concepts to programs for behavioral change.

Next, we'll discuss an interesting theory of personality that emphasizes describing and assessing differences between individuals and explaining why we do not always act in a consistent way.

## B. Trait Theory

— Definition —

**Do women make better cops?**

At the beginning of this module, we told you about Beverly Harvard (photo below), who in 1994 became the first African American woman appointed to head a police department in a major city (Atlanta, Georgia). In 1992, Elizabeth Watson was the first Caucasian woman to head a major metropolitan police force (Houston, Texas).

Throughout the 1970s, 1980s, and 1990s women have had to fight discrimination and harassment from male police officers who believed that women did not have the physical or mental stuff to be police officers (Copeland, 1999). However, a number of studies have shown that women do make good police officers and, in situations involving domestic abuse, they are more successful than policemen because policewomen have better interpersonal skills than men (Johnson, 1998).

Which traits of policewomen make them better at keeping the peace?

**Peacekeeper.** For example, police officer Kelly, who is female, patrols an area known for problems with street thugs. Although we may think that the best way to control thugs is with threat or force, Kelly rarely uses either. Kelly readily admits that her physical strength cannot always match that of some of the macho males she encounters. "Coming across aggressively doesn't work with gang members," Kelly explains. "If that first encounter is direct, knowledgeable, and made with authority, they respond. It takes a few more words but it works" (McDowell, 1992, p. 70). This example suggests that, in some ways, women make better cops than men because they have different personality traits (figure below).

**Women.** Some traits of female police officers include being compassionate, sympathetic, and diplomatic, which help them act as peacekeepers.

**Men.** Some traits of male police officers include being assertive, aggressive, and direct, which help them act as enforcers and crime fighters.

The reason female police officers act more as peacekeepers and male police officers act more as enforcers may be explained by trait theory (Johnson, 1997).

*Trait theory* is an approach for analyzing the structure of personality by measuring, identifying, and classifying similarities and differences in personality characteristics or traits.

The basic unit for measuring personality characteristics is the trait.

A *trait* is a relatively stable and enduring tendency to behave in a particular way.

For example, traits of female police officers include being compassionate and diplomatic, while those of male police officers include being assertive and direct. Determining exactly how many traits are needed to describe someone's personality took psychologists almost 60 years.

— Identifying Traits —

**How to describe these five persons?**

How would you describe the personalities of a criminal, clown, graduate, nun, and beauty queen? This seemingly impossible task was the major goal of personality researchers. They were determined to find a list of traits whose two characteristics seemed mutually exclusive: The list had to contain very few traits but at the same time be able to describe differences among anyone's and everyone's personality, from avocado grower to zookeeper. The search for this elusive list began in the 1930s with, of all things, a dictionary.

### How many traits can there be?

In the 1930s, Gordon Allport and an associate went through the dictionary and selected every term that could distinguish differences among personalities (Allport & Odbert, 1936). They found about 18,000 terms that dealt with all kinds of personality differences; of these, about 4,500 were considered to fit their definition of personality traits. Allport defined *traits* as stable and consistent tendencies in how an individual adjusts to his or her environment. The advantage of Allport's list was that it was comprehensive enough to describe anyone's and everyone's personality. The disadvantage was that it was incredibly long and thus impractical to use in research.

Allport's search for a list of defining traits set the stage for future research. However, his list of thousands of traits needed to be organized into far fewer basic traits. This task fell to Raymond Cattell.

### Aren't some traits related?

In the 1940s, Raymond Cattell (1943) took Allport's list of 4,500 traits and used factor analysis to reduce the list to the most basic traits.

*Factor analysis* is a complicated statistical method that finds relationships among many different or diverse items and allows them to be grouped together.

Cattell used factor analysis to search for *relationships* among hundreds of traits on Allport's list so that the original list could be reduced to 35 basic traits, which Cattell called *source traits*. He claimed that these 35 basic traits could describe all differences among personalities. Although Cattell's achievement was remarkable, his list of 35 traits—and even his further reduction of the list to 16 traits—still proved too long to be practical for research and only moderately useful in assessing personality differences. Obviously, Cattell's list needed more reducing, but that was to take another 30 years.

Which . . .

. . . five . . .

. . . traits . . .

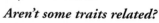

. . . describe . . .

. . . each of these five different personalities?

## Finding Traits: Big Five

From the 1960s to the early 1990s, about a dozen researchers in several countries were using factor analysis to find relationships among lists of adjectives that described personality differences. Doing the impossible, researchers reduced the list of 35 traits to only 5, which make up the five-factor model of personality (John & Srivastava, 1999).

The *five-factor model* organizes personality traits and describes differences in personality using five categories, which are *openness, conscientiousness, extraversion, agreeableness,* and *neuroticism.*

These five factors became known as the *Big Five* and are easy to remember if you note that their first letters make the acronym OCEAN. Each of the five factors actually represents a continuum of behavior, as briefly described in the figure below.

**Openness**

Is open to novel experiences. | Has narrow interests.

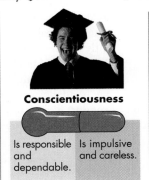

**Conscientiousness**

Is responsible and dependable. | Is impulsive and careless.

**Extraversion**

Is outgoing and decisive. | Is retiring and withdrawn.

**Agreeableness**

Is warm and good-natured. | Is unfriendly and cold.

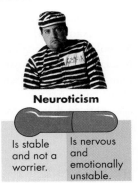

**Neuroticism**

Is stable and not a worrier. | Is nervous and emotionally unstable.

**Hot and cold.** You can think of each Big Five factor as a *supertrait* because each factor's thermometer includes dozens of related traits at the hot and cold ends. For example, conscientiousness, at the hot end, includes the traits of being dependable, responsible, deliberate, hardworking, and precise; at the cold end are the traits of being impulsive, careless, late, lazy, and aimless. Although it took 30 years of research, coming up with the Big Five means that trait theory finally achieved its major goal, which was to describe and organize personality characteristics using the fewest number of traits (John & Srivastava, 1999).

### Importance of the Big Five

Unlike earlier attempts to identify traits, there is now convincing evidence that the Big Five or five-factor theory can indeed describe personality differences among many thousands of individuals by using only five categories or traits. For example, the personalities of children and adults in the United States as well as in six other very different cultures or countries (Germany, Portugal, Israel, Hong Kong, South Korea, and Japan) were described by using the Big Five traits (John & Srivastava, 1999).

**Big question.** Since the five-factor model has been replicated in seven different countries, researchers asked if the structure of personality was shaped primarily by different *cultural factors* (child-rearing practices, religious and moral values, language similarities) or primarily by differences in the *basic human ways* of acting and experiencing that are universal, or similar across all peoples and countries.

Because support for the five-factor model was found in seven very different countries or cultures, researchers concluded that the basic structure of human personality arises from some universal living experience or biological basis rather than being shaped by individual countries or cultures (McCrae & Costa, 1999). If basic human personality structure is universal, it means that the personalities of individuals in different countries can be described by using the Big Five traits.

Each letter in the word OCEAN is the first letter of one of the Big Five traits.

### Big Five in the Real World

When you describe a friend's personality, what you are doing (usually without knowing) is using the five supertraits described in the Big Five or five-factor theory. Because personality similarities and differences can be described by five categories, questionnaires based on the five-factor theory can more accurately assess personality and personality problems, which is one of the major tasks of therapists, clinicians, and psychologists.

Although the five-factor theory has proven very useful in describing and organizing personality traits, this theory does not explain how these traits develop across one's lifetime or account for people's behavior in unusual situations, such as risking one's life to climb Mount Everest (McCrae & Costa, 1999).

For instance, the Big Five traits can be used to describe differences between male and female police officers. Compared with policemen, policewomen are generally more agreeable (sympathetic, friendly, helpful), more open (insightful, intelligent), and more extraverted (sociable, talkative). These kinds of traits result in policewomen being less authoritarian, more diplomatic, and better at defusing potentially dangerous situations (Spillar & Harrington, 2000).

Researchers generally agree that the five-factor theory is a giant leap forward in trait theory and is a useful tool for defining personality structures and differences, predicting behaviors, and identifying personality problems (McCrae & Costa, 1999).

Although each of us possesses at least five relatively enduring supertraits that push us to behave in a stable way, why do we sometimes contradict ourselves and behave differently in different situations?

### Person versus Situation

**How should a dean behave?**

Suppose that being honest was one of your traits, which are defined as relatively stable and enduring tendencies to behave in particular ways. How would you explain making up an excuse (lying) to postpone an exam? This example of a person having a trait (being honest) but in some situations behaving inconsistently (lying) caused a problem for trait theory.

For example, the Dean of Harvard Divinity School was very religious and moral, an eminent scholar, Lutheran minister, and happily married man with two children. However, when the dean's computer was being upgraded, a technician noticed that the computer contained an extensive collection of hard-core pornography. After the technician reported finding the

**HARVARD UNIVERSITY**
**THE DIVINITY SCHOOL**
**ANDOVER HALL**
**ROCKEFELLER HALL →**

Do you think a Dean of Divinity would have a pornography collection?

dean's pornography collection, a Harvard spokesperson said that the dean's conduct was not only inappropriate but also contrary to the faculty handbook, which specifically banned obscene material on school computers (Gegax, 1999). Of course, the dean resigned.

The Dean of Divinity having a pornography collection is certainly an example of inconsistent behavior and illustrates that our behaviors depend not only on traits but also on particular situations. This observation, that individuals do not necessarily behave consistently across different situations, led psychologist Walter Mischel (1968) to question the basic assumption of trait theory, which is that traits create tendencies to behave in particular ways. Mischel went on to conduct a series of now well-known experiments on the interaction between a person's traits and different situations.

### *Experiment: Person-Situation*

To test trait theory's basic assumption of behavioral consistency across situations, Walter Mischel and Philip Peake (1982) asked college students, "How conscientious are you?" If students answer that they are "very conscientious," trait theory predicts that they would behave conscientiously in many different situations. Mischel then observed how conscientious college students behaved in 19 different situations, such as attending classes, going to study sessions, getting homework in on time, and keeping their rooms neat.

Students who rated themselves as very conscientious behaved that way day after day in similar situations. However these same students did not behave conscientiously across all 19 conditions.

For example, very conscientious students might clean their rooms daily but not get their homework in on time, or they might attend all their classes but not clean their rooms. Researchers concluded that, as trait theory would predict, students behaved with great consistency in the *same* situation. But trait theory did not predict that students behaved *differently* or with low consistency across different situations. This finding led to what is now called the person-situation interaction (Mischel & Shoda, 1995).

The *person-situation interaction* means that a person's behavior results from an interaction between his or her traits and the effects of being in or responding to cues from a particular situation.

The person-situation interaction explains that even if you were an extravert, you would behave differently at a wedding than at a funeral because each of these situations creates different cues to which you respond. Similarly, the person-situation interaction describes how Harvard's Dean of Divinity could behave in a very moral and religious way in public situations but, in private situations, act in a completely contradictory way by collecting hard-core pornography.

The person-situation interaction says that to understand or predict a person's behavior, we must consider both the person's traits and the cues that come from being in different situations (Malle et al., 2000).

If you consider yourself open to new experiences, would you engage in this new experience?

### *Conclusions*

There is no question that humans have stable and consistent parts of their personalities, which are called traits. There is no question that personality differences can be accurately described by using the Big Five traits. However, people may act or behave inconsistently or contradictorily because traits interact with and are partly dependent upon situational cues. This means that even though you consider yourself open to new experiences and often try new things, you might very well draw the line and say "NO!" to rock climbing (left photo). Although researchers have found that traits are not consistent across all situations, the concept of traits is still very useful for two reasons (Wiggins, 1997).

**Descriptions.** First, traits are useful because they provide a kind of shorthand method for describing someone's personality. In fact, if I asked you to describe your best friend, you would essentially list this person's traits.

**Predictions.** Second, traits are useful because they help predict someone's behavior in future situations. However, you must keep in mind the person-situation interaction, which means you must take into account how the person's traits will interact with the situation's cues. For example, my friends would predict that I generally watch my weight but they also know that when placed in front of a dessert counter, I can easily consume my weight in chocolate. Researchers found that accuracy in predicting behaviors across situations can be significantly increased if an individual is observed under a number of different conditions (Wiggins, 1997).

Most personality researchers agree that traits, such as the Big Five, are useful in describing our stable and consistent behavioral tendencies, yet they warn that traits may not predict behaviors across different situations (Malle et al., 2000).

Does saying that traits are stable and consistent mean that one's personality gradually becomes fixed?

| **How changeable are your traits?** | If you are now 16, 18, 20, 25, or 30, what will your personality be like when you're 40, 50, 60, 70, or 80? The question of how much your personality traits remain the same and how much they change is answered by using a research approach called the longitudinal method. | *Longitudinal method* means that the same group of individuals is studied repeatedly at many different points in time.

For example, if you asked your parents to list your personality traits at age 3, would these traits match your traits at age 21? In other words, how changeable or fixed are your personality traits? |

### 3 to 18 Years Old

To answer the question of how much personality traits change or remain the same, researchers did a longitudinal study on 1,000 children, whose traits were assessed at age 3 and then reassessed when the same children were 21 years old. Based on their assessment, the personality traits of 3-year-old children were divided into five different personality groups that were labeled undercontrolled, inhibited, confident, reserved, and well-adjusted (Caspi, 2000).

Will this 3-year-old child's personality traits . . .

. . . be similar to those he has at 18 years old?

**Consistency.** Researchers found significant consistencies between traits assessed at 3 years and at 21 years old. For example, traits of 3-year-old children in the *undercontrolled group* included being impulsive, restless, and distractible. When these 3-year-old children were retested at age 21, their traits were similar and included being reckless, careless, and favoring dangerous and exciting activities. In comparison, traits of 3-year-old children in the *well-adjusted group* included being confident, having self-control, and easily adjusting to new or stressful situations. When these 3-year-old children were retested at age 18, their traits were similar and included being in control, self-confident, and all-around well-adjusted and normal adults. Researchers concluded that the origin or development of a person's more stable personality traits begins around age 3. This means that traits observed at age 3 predict personality traits observed later in the same young adults (Caspi, 2000).

**Change.** Although there were remarkable consistencies in personality traits between age 3 and age 18, researchers point out that there are often major changes in emotional traits during adolescence. During adolescence individuals may become less responsible, less cautious, and more moody or impulsive (Caspi & Roberts, 1999).

What happens to personality development after age 18, and does personality ever stop changing?

### 20 to 80 Years Old

If you are 18, 20, 25, or 30 now, what will your personality be like at 50, 60, 70, 80? Answers come from a series of longitudinal studies by psychologists Robert McCrae and Paul Costa, Jr. (1994, 1997, 1999), who reached the following conclusions.

**1** Major changes in personality occur during childhood, adolescence, and young adulthood. Between 20 and 30, both men and women become less emotional, less likely to be thrill seekers, and somewhat more likely to be cooperative and self-disciplined. These personality changes are often associated with becoming more mature.

**2** In fact, longitudinal studies find that most changes in personality occur before the age of 30 because adolescents and young adults are more willing to adopt new values and attitudes or revise old ones.

**3** Personality traits are relatively fixed by age 30, after which changes in personality are few and small. However, after 30, adults continue to grow in their ideas, beliefs, and attitudes as they respond to changing situations and environments. For example, an eager tennis player may, with age, become an eager gardener, but an eager liberal is unlikely to become an eager conservative.

**4** Men and women, healthy and sick people, and Blacks and Whites all show the same stable personality pattern after age 30. Because personality is stable, it is somewhat predictable. However, individuals may struggle to overcome or change certain traits (become less shy, more confident), which brings up the question of how much personality changes during adulthood.

**5** When middle-aged and older adults were asked to describe the course of their personality development, they all described increases in desirable traits (energetic, realistic, intelligent) as they grew older. But on objective tests, these same individuals showed little or no change in these same traits (Krueger & Heckhausen, 1993). Researchers believe these findings show that as people grow older, they tend to report more socially desirable or stereotypic responses rather than what actually has occurred (McCrae & Costa, 1999).

**Conclusions.** Your personality is more likely to change the younger you are, but after age 30, personality traits are fairly stable and fixed. Thus, personality has the interesting distinction of being both stable and changeable (up to a point). One reason personality traits remain relatively stable across time is that they are influenced by genetic factors, which we'll discuss next.

Before age 30, personality may go through major changes, but . . .

. . . after age 30, personality is relatively fixed and difficult to change.

## Behavioral Genetics

**Why are twins so similar?**

Jim Lewis (top photo) and Jim Springer (bottom photo) drove the same model blue Chevrolet, chain-smoked the same brand of cigarettes, owned dogs named Toy, held jobs as deputy sheriff, enjoyed the same woodworking hobby, and had vacationed on the same beach in Florida. When they were given personality tests, they scored almost alike on traits of flexibility, self-control, and sociability. The two Jims are identical twins who were separated four weeks after birth and reared separately. When reunited at age 39, they were flabbergasted at how many things they had in common (Leo, 1987).

These surprising coincidences come from an ongoing University of Minnesota project on genetic factors (Bouchard, 1994; Bouchard et al., 1990). One of the project's major questions is whether the similarities between the two Jims are simply coincidence or reflect the influence of genetic factors on personality traits.

Most of us grew up hearing one or both of these phrases: "You're acting just like your father" or "You're behaving just like your mother." What these phrases suggest is that genetic factors that we inherited from our parents are influencing our behaviors. Psychologists have only recently recognized the importance and influence of genetic factors, which have resulted in a new area called behavioral genetics.

*Behavioral genetics* is the study of how inherited or genetic factors influence and interact with psychological factors to shape our personality, intelligence, emotions, and motivation and also how we behave, adapt, and adjust to our environments.

Many of us have a difficult time accepting the idea of genetic influences because we equate genetic with *fixed*. However, genetic factors do not fix behaviors but establish a range for a behavior, which environmental factors foster or impede. For example, genetic factors set a range for our height and weight. But our actual height and weight will also depend on how genetic factors interact with environmental influences, such as whether we have a good diet and exercise program.

We'll examine studies showing that genetic factors also set a range for personality traits. As we discuss the influence of genetic factors on personality traits, please remember that our actual traits result from the interaction between genetic factors and environmental influences.

*Why did they drive the same kind of car, smoke the same cigarettes, . . .*

*. . . hold the same kind of job, and both name their dogs Toy?*

## Studying Genetic Influences

**What's in the genes?**

Few studies have made such an impact on beliefs about what shapes personality and behavior as the ongoing twin study at the University of Minnesota. Until the early 1990s, most psychologists recognized the existence of genetic factors in shaping personality but believed that genetic factors had much less impact than environmental factors. While psychologists knew that human genes contained chemical instructions (middle figure) for development of the brain and body parts, they were less sure of how much genes shaped development of psychological traits. Then in 1990, Thomas Bouchard and his colleagues (1990) published the first study to simultaneously compare four different groups of twins: identical twins reared together, identical twins reared apart, fraternal twins reared together, and fraternal twins reared apart. Remember that identical twins share 100% of their genes, while fraternal twins share only 50% of their genes and thus are no more genetically alike than ordinary brothers and sisters. This study allowed researchers to separate genetic factors (identical versus fraternal twins) and environmental factors (reared together versus reared apart).

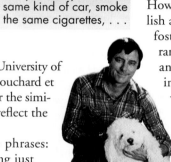

This is a piece of the genetic code, which uses a chemical alphabet (A, C, G, T) to write instructions that influence the development of personality traits.

*We're identical twins, and we share 100% of our genes.*

More than 100 sets of twins in the United States, Great Britain, and many other countries participated in this initial study. Each participant was given over 50 hours of medical and psychological assessment, including four different tests to measure personality traits. Those identical and fraternal twins who were reared apart were adopted shortly after birth and had not met their twin until this study brought them together for testing. The measure that researchers use to estimate genetic influences is called heritability.

*Heritability* is a statistical measure that estimates how much of some cognitive, personality, or behavioral trait is influenced by genetic factors.

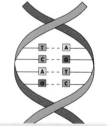

*We're fraternal twins, and we share only 50% of our genes.*

Heritability is expressed on an increasing scale of influence from 0.0 to 1.0. For example, if genetic factors have no influence, the heritability would be 0.0; having half the influence is indicated by 0.5; and having total control over behavior is indicated by 1.0. For example, in Module 13, you learned that the heritability of IQ is in the range of 50–70%, which means that about 50–70% of an individual's IQ score is explained by genetic factors (Gottesman, 1997). We're now interested in a different question: What are the heritability estimates for personality traits?

**Do genes influence the Big Five?**

Identical twins Jim Lewis and Jim Springer (photos opposite page) were subjects in the now famous Minnesota twin study. Their scores were similar on personality tests that measured the Big Five traits—openness, conscientiousness, extraversion, agreeableness, and neuroticism. (Note that by taking the first letter of each Big Five trait, you make the word OCEAN.) One reason the two Jims' scores on personality tests were so similar was that their genetic factors were identical.

There are now many studies on thousands of twins, both identical and fraternal, who were reared together and apart, and whose data were analyzed by different groups of researchers

### Heritability of Big Five Personality Traits

| | |
|---|---|
| Earlier twin studies | 0.51 |
| Loehlin twin studies | 0.42 |
| Minnesota twin studies | 0.41 |

(Bouchard et al., 1990; Plomin & Caspi, 1999). Results from earlier studies and two large and recent studies are shown in the graph below (Bouchard, 1994). Researchers estimate that the heritability of personality traits ranges from 0.41 to about 0.51, which means that genetic factors contribute about 40 to 50% to the development of an individual's personality traits.

Even though genetic factors are responsible for about half of each of the Big Five personality traits we develop, that still leaves about half coming from environmental factors. We'll describe two kinds of environmental factors—shared and nonshared—that influence personality development.

## Influences on Personality

**What shapes personality?**

As I was growing up, I remember hearing my parents talking (when they thought I wasn't listening) about how different I was from my older brother and sister. My parents questioned how my brother and sister and I could be so (very) different even though we had the same parents, lived in the same house, in the same town, and even went to the same school and church. One reason that brothers and sisters develop such different personalities is that 50% of their genes are different (and 50% are shared). And another important reason that brothers and sisters develop different personalities is that each brother's or sister's unique set of genetic factors interacts differently with his or her environment. Researchers have broken down the contributions to personality development into the following four factors.

### 40% Genetic Factors

The fingerprints of the two Jims were almost identical because they shared 100% of their genes, and genetic factors contribute 97% to the

development of ridges on finger tips (Bouchard et al., 1990). In comparison, the two Jims' scores were similar but not identical on personality traits of self-control, flexibility, and sociability because, although they share 100% of their genes, genetic factors contribute about 40 to 50% to the kind of personality traits they developed. Thus, while genetic factors contribute about half to the development of certain personality traits, the next biggest factor is something of a surprise.

### 27% Nonshared Environmental Factors

Although we know that the two Jims show remarkable similarities in personality, they also display unique differences. Jim Lewis (left photo)

says that he is more easygoing and less of a worrier than his identical twin, Jim Springer (right photo). When the twins get on a plane, Jim Springer worries about the plane being late, while Jim Lewis says that there is no use worrying (*San Diego Tribune*, November 12, 1987). One of the reasons that the two Jims developed different personality traits is that about 27% of the influence on personality development comes from how each individual's genetic factors react and adjust to his or her own environment. These factors are called *nonshared environmental factors* because they involve how each individual's genetic factors react and adjust to his or her particular environment.

### 26% Error

About 26% of the influence on personality development cannot as yet be identified and is attributed to errors in testing and measurement procedures. As methodology improves, this error percentage will decrease and other factors will increase.

### 7% Shared Environmental Factors

About 7% of the influence on personality development comes from environmental factors that involve parental patterns and shared family experiences. These factors are called *shared environmental factors* because they involve how family members interact and share experiences. One of the major surprises to come out of the twin studies was how little impact parental practices and shared family experiences have on personality development. Researchers concluded that being raised in the same family contributes little (about 7%) to personality development. Far

more important for personality development are nonshared environmental factors (27%), which refer to how each child's unique genetic factors react and adjust to being in that family (Bouchard, 1994; Plomin & Caspi, 1999). You can think of genetic factors as pushing and pulling personality development in certain directions, while environmental factors join in to push and pull it in the same or different directions.

Next, we'll take a last look at the impact of trait theory.

# D. Evaluation of Trait Theory

**Could we live without traits?**

It would be very difficult to live without traits because you use them constantly, usually without knowing it. For example, whenever you describe someone, or predict how he or she will behave, your descriptions of personality and predictions of behaviors are based almost entirely on knowing the person's

**Personal Want Ad**

Personal ads are based on traits.

traits. Newspapers are full of personal ads, which are essentially a list of most-desired traits.

Although traits are very useful as a shorthand to describe a person's personality and predict a person's behaviors, critics raise three major questions about traits: How good is the list? Can traits predict? What influences traits? We'll discuss each issue in turn.

---

### How Good Is the List?

The Big Five or five-factor trait theory assumes that all similarities and differences among personalities can be described by an amazingly short but comprehensive list of five traits—openness, conscientiousness, extraversion, agreeableness, and neuroticism (OCEAN). Each of the *Big Five traits* has two poles or two dimensions, which include dozens of related traits. The Big Five traits' ability to describe personality has now been verified in many different countries, with different populations and age groups (John, 1990; McCrae & Costa, 1997).

The Big Five traits have the ability to describe personalities of children and adults in many different countries.

Critics of the five-factor model point out that the data for the model came from questionnaires that may be too structured to give real and complete portraits of personalities. As a result, data from questionnaires may paint too simplistic a picture of human personality and may not reflect its depth and complexity (Block, 1995b). Critics also point out that traits primarily describe a person's personality rather than explain or point out its causes (Digman, 1997).

In defense of the five-factor theory, researchers have shown that the Big Five traits provide a valid and reliable way to describe personality differences and consistencies in our own lives and in our social interactions with others (McCrae & Costa, 1999).

---

### Can Traits Predict?

One of the more serious problems faced by early trait theory involved the assumption that, since traits are consistent and stable influences on our behaviors, traits should be very useful in predicting behaviors.

Dean of Divinity behaved morally in public situations but in private situations had a pornography collection.

But how does trait theory explain why the Dean of the Harvard Divinity School was so moral and religious in public behaviors but a little shady and immoral in having a private pornography collection?

One explanation is that the dean generally behaved consistently in the same situation (public behaviors) but did not necessarily behave the same across many different situations (private behaviors). This problem in predicting behavior across situations became known as the *person-situation interaction*. Researchers found that situations may have as much influence on behavior as traits do, so situational influences must be taken into account when predicting someone's behavior (Wiggins, 1997). Researchers found that traits could better predict behaviors if traits were measured under different conditions and situations.

Currently, the Big Five traits are considered useful concepts for describing consistent and stable behavioral tendencies in similar situations, but traits do not necessarily predict behaviors across different situations.

---

### What Influences Traits?

One major surprise coming from twin studies was how relatively little effect parental practices or shared family experiences have on personality development (graph below). Researchers concluded that parental practices or *shared factors* contributed only about 7% to personality development. In contrast, how each child personally reacts or adjusts to parental or family practices, called *nonshared factors*, contributed about 27% to personality development (Bouchard, 1994; Plomin & Crabbe, 2000). This finding questioned a major belief of developmental psychologists, who hold that sharing parental or family environment greatly influenced personality development among the siblings (brothers and sisters). Instead, twin research suggests that psychologists need to look more closely at each child's reactions to his or her family environment as a major influence on personality development.

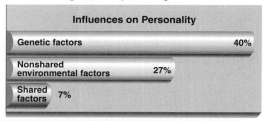

**Influences on Personality**

| | |
|---|---|
| Genetic factors | 40% |
| Nonshared environmental factors | 27% |
| Shared factors | 7% |

Personality development depends more on genetic and nonshared factors (child's individual reactions) than on shared parental influences.

According to behavioral geneticists, the idea of genes influencing complex human behaviors was unthinkable as recently as 15 years ago. Today, however, there is convincing evidence that genetic factors exert a considerable influence on many complex human behaviors, including intelligence, mental health, and personality traits (Plomin & Crabbe, 2000). Yet these same researchers warn that *genetic influences* on human behavior should not be blown out of proportion. Because heritability scores generally do not exceed 50%, this means the remaining 50% or more involves *environmental influences,* especially nonshared environmental influences.

# Concept Review

**1.** Social cognitive theory says that personality development is primarily shaped by three interacting forces: _____, _____, and _____.

**2.** The above three forces all interact to influence how we evaluate, interpret, and organize _____ and apply such knowledge to ourselves and others.

**3.** An example of the social cognitive approach is Bandura's social cognitive theory, which says that personality development, growth, and change are influenced by four distinctively human cognitive processes: highly developed (a)_____ ability, (b)_____ learning, (c)_____ behavior, and (d)_____.

**4.** Three different beliefs based on social cognitive theory have been shown to influence personality development and behavior. Rotter referred to beliefs concerning how much control we have over situations or rewards. If we believe that we have control over situations and rewards, we are said to have an (a)_____. If we believe that we do not have control over situations and rewards and that events outside ourselves (fate) determine what happens, we are said to have an (b)_____.

Should I take one marshmallow now or wait and get two?

**5.** According to Bandura, our personal beliefs regarding how capable we are of exercising control over events in our lives—for example, carrying out certain tasks and behaviors—is called (a)_____, which, in turn, affects our performance on a wide variety of behaviors. Mischel devised ways of measuring our ability to voluntarily postpone an immediate reward and persist in completing a task for the promise of a future reward, which is called (b)_____.

**6.** The approach to describe the structure of personality that is based on identifying and analyzing ways in which personalities differ is known as _____ theory.

**7.** A relatively stable and enduring tendency to behave in a particular way is called a (a)_____. A statistical procedure that may be used to find relationships among many different or diverse items, such as traits, and form them into selected groups is called (b)_____.

## OCEAN

**8.** The model that organizes all personality traits into five categories that can be used to describe differences in personality is called the (a)_____ model. This model uses the Big Five traits, which are (b)_____, _____, _____, _____, and _____.

**9.** Research supports the five-factor model and the Big Five traits. Each of the Big Five traits has two poles or dimensions and represents a wide range of _____.

**10.** Walter Mischel said that to predict a person's behavior we must take into account not only the person's traits but also the effects of the situation; this became known as the (a)_____. According to this idea, a person's behavior results from an (b)_____ between his or her traits and the effects of being in a particular situation.

**11.** To investigate whether personality changes as people grow older, psychologists study the same individuals at different times; this is called a (a)_____ study. In general, studies have shown that personality is more likely to change if a person is under (b)_____ years old. After that, changes usually involve variations on the same behavioral theme or accompany changes in social roles.

**12.** The field that focuses on how inherited or genetic factors influence and interact with psychological factors is called (a)_____. A statistical measure that estimates how much of some behavior is due to genetic influences is called (b)_____.

**13.** Studies have found that about 40% of the influence on personality development comes from (a)_____; about 27% comes from how each person adjusts to his or her own environment, which is called (b)_____; and about 7% comes from parental patterns and family experiences, which are called (c)_____.

**Answers:** *1. cognitive-personal factors, behavior, environmental influences; 2. information; 3. (a) language, (b) observational, (c) purposeful, (d) self-analysis; 4. (a) internal locus of control, (b) external locus of control; 5. (a) self-efficacy, (b) delay of gratification; 6. trait; 7. (a) trait, (b) factor analysis; 8. (a) five-factor, (b) openness, conscientiousness, extraversion, agreeableness, neuroticism; 9. behaviors; 10. (a) person-situation interaction, (b) interaction; 11. (a) longitudinal, (b) 30; 12. (a) behavioral genetics, (b) heritability; 13. (a) genetic factors, (b) nonshared environmental factors, (c) shared environmental factors*

469

## How Much Can People Change in a Day?

**What triggers a major change?**

Sometimes researchers study unusual behaviors that seem to contradict what is known. For example, anyone who has ever tried to change some behavior finds it difficult because traits are relatively stable and enduring. For this reason, it's difficult to believe people who claim to have totally changed their personalities in minutes, hours, or a single day. Researchers call these sudden and dramatic changes quantum personality changes (Miller & C'deBaca, 1994).

A *quantum personality change* refers to making a very radical or dramatic shift in one's personality, beliefs, or values in minutes, hours, or a day.

For example, here's the quantum personality change of Bill Wilson, who cofounded Alcoholics Anonymous (AA). He was in the depths of alcoholic despair and depression when he suddenly saw his room lit with a bright light. In his mind's eye, he

What causes a person to have a major personality change in a day?

saw himself on a mountaintop and felt that spirit winds were blowing through him. Then, suddenly, a simple but powerful thought burst upon him: he was a free man (Kurtz, 1979). This dramatic experience changed Wilson's personality 180 degrees as he went from being a desperate and hopeless drunk to being a sober and dedicated worker who devoted his life to helping others overcome alcoholism.

Reports of sudden and major changes in personality challenge two well-established findings: first, personality traits are stable and enduring tendencies that may change gradually but rarely undergo sudden and dramatic changes; and second, even when people want to change their personalities, as in therapy, it doesn't happen overnight but takes considerable time and effort. Then how can quantum personality changes occur, often in a single day? To answer this question, researchers first had to develop a method to study quantum changes.

### Method

Researchers found people who had experienced a quantum personality change through a feature story in the local paper (Albuquerque, New Mexico). Researchers asked for volunteers who, in a relatively short period of time, had experienced a transformation in their basic values, feelings, attitudes, or actions. Out of a total of 89 people who responded, 55 were found acceptable. These 55 subjects were given a series of personality tests and structured interviews (average length 107 minutes).

*Structured interviews* involve asking each individual the same set of relatively narrow and focused questions so that the same information is obtained from everyone.

During structured interviews, all subjects were asked the same detailed questions about the what, when, and where of the unusual experiences that had apparently transformed their personalities so completely.

Structured interviews use the subjects' self-reports to provide information about subjective thoughts, feelings, and experiences, which are most often unobservable cognitive and emotional processes.

### Results

Researchers used a variety of personality tests to make sure the subjects (31 females and 24 males) performed within the normal range on personality tests, had no strange problems, and showed no striking or unusual things in common. In fact, based on the battery of personality tests and interviews, all subjects seemed to be largely normal, ordinary individuals who had had extraordinary experiences (Miller & C'deBaca, 1994). Here are some of the study's major findings:

■ A majority of subjects (58%) could specify the date and time of day when the quantum experience occurred even though the experience had occurred, on average, 11 years earlier.

■ A majority of subjects (75%) reported that the quantum experience began suddenly and took

Quantum personality change

Began suddenly: As if struck by light or hearing a voice

them by surprise. For some the experience lasted only minutes (13%), and for most it was over within 24 hours (64%). The actual experiences included being struck by an intense thought, making a total commitment, hearing a voice, and hearing God's voice.

■ A majority of subjects (56%) reported a high level of emotional distress and a relatively high level of negative life experiences in the year before the quantum experience.

■ Most (96%) reported that the quantum experience had made their lives better, and most (80%) stated that the changes had lasted.

■ Most (87%) said that, during the quantum experience, an important truth was revealed to them; 78% said that they were relieved of a mental burden; and 60% said that they felt completely loved.

All of these 55 individuals reported that they had, in a single day or less, experienced a 180-degree change in personality. For the vast majority, the quantum change in personality seems to have resulted from or been triggered by a period of bad times. After the quantum change, subjects reported that their lives had improved.

### Conclusions

Researchers concluded that the quantum personality changes reported by the subjects were dramatically larger than are ordinarily observed, occurred in a quicker period of time than is normally reported, and lasted for years (Miller & C'deBaca, 1994).

For most of the subjects, the changes represented an increased sense of meaning, happiness, and satisfaction; some reported a sense of closeness to God. This study suggests that quantum changes in personality do occur and may be one way a person solves some long-standing and stressful personal problem.

In many cases, people who experienced quantum personality changes also reported subsequent changes in behavior.

As you'll see next, how much personality influences behavior is partly dependent on one's culture.

## Interpersonal Conflicts

**How do you settle conflicts?**

One reason psychologists have been studying personality traits for over 60 years is that traits are stable and enduring tendencies to behave in certain ways. Knowing if a friend is usually on time or late will help predict your friend's behavior. Similarly, knowing a person's level of assertiveness will partly predict how he or she will handle an interpersonal conflict.

*Interpersonal conflict* refers to your disagreeing with another person who opposes your getting some wish, goal, or expectation.

For example, imagine that your best friend suddenly decides to get married and insists that you be at the wedding the same week you have a major paper due. You explain the problem to your professor and ask for a week's extension of the deadline. Your professor replies that if you turn your paper in late, you will receive a grade of D. How would you handle this interpersonal conflict? People generally use one of two different strategies for resolving interpersonal conflicts—a passive or an active strategy (Hocker & Wilmot, 1991).

In a *passive strategy,* you resolve the conflict by avoiding further discussion or restating your request or opinion.

In an *active strategy,* you resolve the conflict by making compromises or persuading the other person to adopt your position.

Which strategy you choose depends partly on cultural values, which reinforce your being assertive or passive. We'll examine how two different cultures—the United States and Japan—influence personality traits that, in turn, influence how their citizens solve interpersonal conflicts.

## Cultural Differences

One of the major cultural differences between Western and Eastern countries is how citizens rate their priorities and goals. Generally, citizens in Western countries place individual goals over group goals, while citizens in Eastern countries place group or collective goals over individual ones.

As a Western nation, the United States is considered an individualistic culture (Triandis, 1989).

An *individualistic culture* places a high priority on attaining personal goals and striving for personal satisfaction, often by being competitive and assertive.

Since the focus in many Western cultures is on individual goals, citizens are generally encouraged to be independent, competitive, and assertive (Ohbuchi & Takahashi, 1994). In contrast, many Eastern nations, such as Japan, have a collectivistic culture.

The United States is an individualistic culture, which OKs being assertive to reach personal goals.

A *collectivistic culture* places a high priority on group goals and norms over personal goals and values. Individuals in these cultures work to control their behaviors and maintain harmonious relationships with others.

Since the focus in many Asian cultures is on collective or group goals, citizens are generally encouraged to be dependent on and submissive to group values (Ohbuchi & Takahashi, 1994). Will these cultural differences result in different strategies for solving interpersonal conflicts?

Japan is a collectivistic culture, which places reaching group goals over personal goals.

## Using Different Strategies

Researchers predicted that because of these cultural differences, students in the United States would use different strategies to resolve interpersonal conflicts compared to students in Japan. In this study, college students in the United States and Japan were asked to recall their interpersonal conflicts during the past several weeks and describe what they had actually done to resolve these conflicts. Two trained raters divided students' responses into two different strategies for resolving interpersonal conflicts: passive strategy, which is to avoid further discussion, and active strategy, which is to engage in persuasion or compromise.

**Different strategies.** As shown in the graph at right, Japanese students usually used the passive strategy, which means they were more likely to solve interpersonal conflicts by avoiding any further discussion of the conflict. Japanese students were less likely to use the active strategy, which means that they did not try to resolve problems through persuasion, bargaining, or compromise (Ohbuchi & Takahashi, 1994).

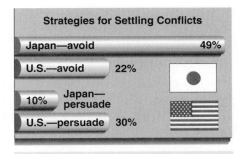

**Strategies for Settling Conflicts**

| | |
|---|---|
| Japan—avoid | 49% |
| U.S.—avoid | 22% |
| Japan—persuade | 10% |
| U.S.—persuade | 30% |

Japanese use passive strategy (avoid—49%), while Americans use active strategy (persuade—30%) to settle conflicts.

In comparison, American students used the opposite strategies: they were significantly more likely to use the active strategy and to resolve the problem through persuasion, bargaining, or compromise. American students were significantly less likely to use the passive strategy—to settle the interpersonal conflict by avoiding further discussion.

Researchers concluded that the collectivistic culture of Japan rewards personality traits that lead to avoiding the public discussion of conflicts. In comparison, the individualistic culture of the United States rewards personality traits that lead individuals to settle conflicts through public persuasion or compromise (Ohbuchi & Takahashi, 1994). This study is a good example of how culture influences the development of different personality traits, which, in turn, lead to different behaviors.

Next, we'll briefly review the four major theories of personality to give you a better overview of their similarities and differences.

## Psychodynamic Theory

Freud's psychodynamic theory, which was developed in the early 1900s, grew out of his work with patients.

Freud's ***psychodynamic theory of personality*** emphasizes the importance of early childhood experiences, the importance of repressed thoughts that we cannot voluntarily access, and the conflicts between conscious and unconscious forces that influence our thoughts and behaviors. (Freud used the term *dynamic* to refer to mental energy force.)

***Conscious thoughts*** are wishes, desires, or thoughts that we are aware of or can recall at any given moment.

***Unconscious forces*** represent wishes, desires, or thoughts that, because of their disturbing or threatening content, we automatically repress and cannot voluntarily access.

Freud believed that a large part of our behavior was guided or motivated by unconscious forces.

***Unconscious motivation*** is a Freudian concept that refers to the influence of repressed thoughts, desires, or impulses on our conscious thoughts and behaviors.

Freud developed three methods to uncover unconscious processes: ***free association, dream interpretation***, and ***slips of the tongue*** (Freudian slips).

### Divisions of the Mind

Freud divided the mind into three divisions: id, ego, and superego.

The first division is the ***id***, which contains two biological drives—sex and aggression—that are the source of all mental energy. The id follows the pleasure principle, which is to satisfy the biological drives.

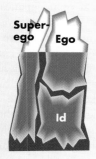

The second division is the ***ego***, whose goal is to find socially acceptable ways of satisfying the id's desires within the range of the superego's prohibitions. The ego follows the reality principle, which is to satisfy a wish or desire only if there is a socially acceptable outlet available.

The third division is the ***superego***, whose goal is to apply the moral values and standards of one's parents or caregivers and society in satisfying one's wishes.

### Psychosexual Stages

Freud assumed that our personality develops as we pass through a series of ***five psychosexual stages.***

During these developmental periods—the ***oral, anal, phallic, latency***, and ***genital stages***—the individual seeks pleasure from different areas of the body associated with sexual feelings. Freud emphasized that the child's first five years were the most important in personality development.

## Humanistic Theories

Humanistic theories emphasize our capacity for personal growth, development of our potential, and freedom to choose our destiny. ***Humanistic theories*** stress three major points—phenomenological perspective, holistic view, and self-actualization.

The ***phenomenological perspective*** means that our perception of the world, whether or not it is accurate, becomes our reality.

The ***holistic view*** means that a person's personality is more than the sum of its individual parts; instead, the individual parts form a unique and total entity that functions as a unit.

***Self-actualization*** refers to our inherent tendency to reach our true potentials.

Humanistic theories reject the biological determinism and the irrational, unconscious forces of Freud's psychodynamic theory. Humanistic theories emphasize freely choosing to go after one's dream and change one's destiny.

The beginning of humanistic theory can be traced to two psychologists: Abraham Maslow, who rejected behaviorism's system of rewards and punishment, and Carl Rogers, who rejected Freud's psychodynamic theory with its emphasis on unconscious forces.

### Abraham Maslow

Maslow (1968) broke away from the reward/punishment/observable behavior mentality of behaviorism and developed his humanistic theory. ***Maslow's humanistic theory*** emphasized two things: our capacity for growth or self-actualization and our desire to satisfy a variety of needs.

***Maslow's hierarchy of needs*** arranges needs in ascending order, with biological needs at the bottom and social and personal needs toward the top; as needs at one level are met, we advance to the next level.

### Carl Rogers's Self Theory

Carl Rogers rejected the psychodynamic approach because it placed too much emphasis on unconscious, irrational forces. Instead, Rogers developed a new humanistic theory, which is called self theory. ***Rogers's self theory***, also called self-actualization theory, has two primary assumptions: Personality development is guided by each person's unique self-actualization tendency, and each of us has a personal need for positive regard.

Rogers said that the ***self*** is made up of many self-perceptions, abilities, personality characteristics, and behaviors that are organized and consistent with one another.

## Social Cognitive Theory

Freud's *psychodynamic theory*, developed in the early 1900s, grew out of his work with patients. Humanistic theories were developed in the 1960s by an ex-Freudian (Rogers) and ex-behaviorist (Maslow), who believed that previous theories had neglected the positive side of human potential and fulfillment.

In comparison, *social cognitive theory*, developed in the 1960s and 1970s, grew out of a strong research background that emphasized a more experimental approach to developing and testing concepts that could be used to understand and explain personality development.

*Social cognitive theory* says that personality development is primarily shaped by three factors: environmental conditions (learning), cognitive-personal factors, and behavior. *Behavior* includes a variety of actions, such as what we do and say. *Environmental influences* include our social, political, and cultural influences, as well as our particular learning experiences. Just as our cognitive factors influence how we perceive and interpret our environment, our environment in turn affects our beliefs, values, and social roles. *Cognitive-personal factors* include our beliefs, expectations, values, intentions, and social roles as well as our biological and genetic influences. Thus, what we think, believe, and feel affects how we act and behave.

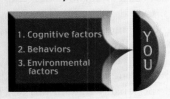

1. Cognitive factors
2. Behaviors
3. Environmental factors

YOU

### *Bandura's Social Cognitive Theory*

Perhaps the best example of the social cognitive approach is Bandura's social cognitive theory, which he developed in the 1970s. *Bandura's social cognitive theory* says that personality development, growth, and change are influenced by four distinctively human cognitive processes: highly developed language ability, observational learning, purposeful behavior, and self-analysis.

Bandura's theory emphasizes *cognitive factors*, such as personal values, goals, and beliefs. Three particular beliefs have been shown to influence personality development: *locus of control*, which refers to how much control we think we have over our environment; *delay of gratification*, which involves our voluntarily postponing an immediate reward for the promise of a future reward; and *self-efficacy*, which refers to our personal beliefs of how capable we are in performing specific tasks and behaviors.

Should I take one marshmallow now or wait and get two?

One of the *basic assumptions* of social cognitive theory is that our beliefs, values, and goals influence the development of our personalities, which, in turn, affects how we behave.

## Trait Theory

For over 50 years, a *major goal* of personality researchers was to find a way to define the structure of personality with the fewest possible traits. The search for a list of traits that could describe personality differences among everyone, including criminals and nuns, began in the 1930s with a list of about 4,500 traits and ended in the 1990s with a list of only 5 traits.

In the 1990s, trait theory developed the five-factor model, which is based on laboratory research, especially questionnaires and statistical procedures. *Trait theory* refers to an approach for analyzing the structure of personality by measuring, identifying, and classifying similarities and differences in personality characteristics or traits. The basic unit for measuring personality characteristics is the trait. *Traits* are relatively stable and enduring tendencies to behave in particular ways, but behavior is not always the same across different situations.

Trait theory says relatively little about the development or growth of personality but instead emphasizes measuring and identifying differences among personalities.

### *Five-Factor Model*

The *five-factor model* organizes all personality traits into five categories—openness, conscientiousness, extraversion, agreeableness, and neuroticism (OCEAN). These traits, which are referred to as the *Big Five traits*, raise three major issues.

First, although traits are stable tendencies to behave in certain ways, this stability does not necessarily apply across situations. According to the *person-situation interaction*, you may behave differently in different situations because of the effects of a particular situation.

O
C
E
A
N

Second, personality traits are both *changeable and stable:* most change occurs before age 30 because adolescents and young adults are more willing to adopt new values and attitudes or revise old ones; most stability occurs after age 30, but adults do continue to grow in their ideas, beliefs, and attitudes.

Third, *genetic factors* have a considerable influence on personality traits and behaviors. Genetic factors push and pull the development of certain traits, whose development may be helped or hindered by environmental factors.

*Traits* are useful in that they provide shorthand descriptions of people and predict certain behaviors.

## Definition

**Why are traits big business?**

The study of traits has become big business because traits are used in many kinds of personality tests. For instance, suppose you're applying for a fast-food job and your employer asks you to fill out a written questionnaire, which is really a honesty test. The employer knows that about 62% of fast-food workers steal money or give away food to friends and hopes this honesty test will help select a honest employee (Murphy, 1993). To help employers make hiring decisions, about 5,000 companies administer honesty tests to almost 5 million people each year (Lilienfeld, 1993). Honesty tests, which are the most frequently administered psychological tests in the United States, are examples of objective personality tests.

*I've heard others do, but I would never steal from my employer.*

*Objective personality tests,* also called *self-report questionnaires,* consist of specific written statements that require individuals to indicate, for example, by checking "true" or "false," whether the statements do or do not apply to them.

Because objective personality tests or self-report questionnaires use very specific questions and require very specific answers, they are considered to be highly *structured,* or *objective.* In comparison, projective tests (pp. 450–451) use ambiguous stimuli (inkblots, photos), have no right or wrong answers, and are considered to be *unstructured,* or *projective,* personality tests.

It is most likely that, as part of a job interview, you will be asked to take a variety of self-report questionnaires. That's because employers, clinicians, researchers, and government and law enforcement agencies use self-report questionnaires to identify and differentiate personality traits.

The basic assumption behind self-report questionnaires brings us back to the definition of traits. We defined traits as stable and enduring tendencies to behave in certain ways. Self-report questionnaires identify traits, which employers use to predict how prospective employees will behave in their particular jobs or situations (Ozer, 1999).

Before we discuss how valid and reliable self-report questionnaires are in predicting behavior, we'll examine two of the more popular self-report questionnaires.

## Examples of Objective Tests

**How honest are most employees?**

Objective personality tests are used in both business and clinical settings. In business settings, self-report questionnaires are often used in selecting employees for certain traits, such as being honest and trustworthy, which is why integrity tests are often used (Alliger & Title, 2000).

### INTEGRITY TESTS

Integrity or honesty tests are supposed to assess whether individuals have high levels of the trait of honesty. Questions asked on honesty tests are similar to those below (Lilienfeld, 1993).

1. Have you ever stolen merchandise from your place of work?

2. Have you ever been tempted to steal a piece of jewelry from a store?

3. Do you think most people steal money from their workplace every now and then?

4. A person has been a loyal and honest employee at a firm for 20 years. One day, after realizing that she has neglected to bring lunch money, she takes $10 from her workplace but returns it the next day. Should she be fired?

Would you buy a gold watch from this man?

People strong in the trait of honesty answer: (1) no, (2) no, (3) no, (4) yes.

Notice that some self-report questionnaires, such as the integrity test, focus on measuring a single personality trait, in this case honesty. The next self-report questionnaire, called the MMPI-2, is used primarily in clinical settings and measures a number of traits and personality problems.

### MINNESOTA MULTIPHASIC PERSONALITY INVENTORY-2

Suppose a parole board needed to decide if a convicted murderer had changed enough in prison to be let out on parole. To help make this decision, they might use a test that identifies the range of normal and abnormal personality traits, such as the well-known Minnesota Multiphasic Personality Inventory-2 (MMPI-2).

The *Minnesota Multiphasic Personality Inventory (MMPI-2)* is a true-false self-report questionnaire that consists of 567 statements describing a wide range of normal and abnormal behaviors. The purpose of the MMPI-2 is to measure the personality style and emotional adjustment in individuals with mental illness.

The MMPI-2 asks about and identifies a variety of specific personality traits, including depression, hostility, high energy, and shyness, and plots whether these traits are in the normal or abnormal range. A few of the 567 statements used in the MMPI are given below:

- I do not tire quickly.
- I am worried about sex.
- When I get bored, I like to stir up some excitement.
- I believe I am being plotted against.

One advantage of this test is that it contains three kinds of scales: *validity scales,* which assess whether the client was faking good or bad answers; *clinical scales,* which identify psychological disorders, such as depression, paranoia, or schizophrenia; and *content scales,* which identify specific areas, such as the anger scale, whose content includes references to being irritable and hotheaded and to difficulties controlling anger (Kaplan & Saccuzzo, 2001).

Could a test show if a person were ready for parole?

The MMPI-2 is commonly used to assess a wide range of personality traits, numerous behaviors, health and psychosomatic symptoms, and many well-known psychotic symptoms (Greene & Clopton, 1994). The MMPI-2 and the integrity questionnaire are examples of objective tests used to identify personality traits.

Another method that claims to identify your particular traits involves astrology.

## Reliability and Validity

About 78% of women and 70% of men read horoscopes, and many believe that they are so correct that they were written especially for them (Halpern, 1998). As you read the horoscope on the right, note how many traits apply to you. Because horoscopes contain general traits, people believe horoscopes were written especially for them, a phenomenon called the Barnum principle (Snyder et al., 1977).

The *Barnum principle* (named after the famous circus owner P. T. Barnum) refers to the method of listing many general traits so that almost everyone who reads the horoscope thinks that these traits apply specifically to him or her. But, in fact, these traits are so general that they apply to almost everyone.

Astrologers claim they can identify your personality traits by knowing the sign under which you were born. However, researchers found that horoscopes do not assess personality traits for a particular individual, which means horoscopes lack one of the two characteristics of a good test—validity.

You are bright, sincere, and likable. At times you can be too independent and too critical of yourself.

### VALIDITY

Students claim that the Scorpio horoscope, which I wrote, is accurate for them. The reason I can write "accurate" horoscopes is that I use the *Barnum principle*, which means that I state personality traits in a general way so that they apply to everyone.

I read my horoscope every day, and it's always right on the mark.

*Validity* means that the test measures what it claims or is supposed to measure.

A personality test that has no validity is no better than chance at describing or predicting a particular individual's traits. For example, researchers found that the 12 zodiac signs were no better than chance at identifying traits for a particular individual (Svensen & White, 1994). Because horoscopes cannot identify or predict traits for a particular person, horoscopes lack validity. The reason horoscopes remain popular and seem to be "accurate" is that astrologers essentially use the Barnum principle, which means their horoscopes are "accurate" for almost everyone. In comparison, integrity tests generally have low validity, while the MMPI-2 has good validity, which means it can describe and predict behaviors for particular individuals (Kaplan & Saccuzzo, 2001). In addition to validity, a good personality test must also have reliability.

### RELIABILITY

Even though horoscopes lack validity, they may actually have the second characteristic of a good personality test, reliability.

*Reliability* refers to consistency: A person's score on a test at one point in time should be similar to the score obtained by the same person on a similar test at a later point in time.

Horoscopes may be reliable if the astrologer remains the same. In comparison, integrity tests and the MMPI-2 have good reliability. However, the MMPI-2 is better than integrity tests because the MMPI-2 has both good validity and reliability, while the integrity test has good reliability but low validity (Kaplan & Saccuzzo, 2001).

## Usefulness

Self-report questionnaires or objective personality tests are popular and widely used because they assess information about traits in a structured way so that such information can be compared with others who have taken the same tests. For example, employers and government and law enforcement agencies use objective personality tests, such as integrity tests, to compare and select certain traits in job applicants. Researchers use objective personality tests to differentiate between people's traits. Counselors and clinicians use objective personality tests, such as the MMPI-2, to identify personality traits and potential psychological problems (Ozer, 1999). We'll discuss the disadvantages and advantages of objective personality tests.

### DISADVANTAGES

One disadvantage of objective personality tests is that their questions and answers are very structured and critics from the psychodynamic approach point out that such structured tests may not assess deeper or unconscious personality factors. A second disadvantage comes from the straightforward questions, which often allow people to figure out what answers are most socially desirable or acceptable and thus bias the tests' results. For example, one problem with integrity tests is that the answers can be faked so the person appears more trustworthy (compare the devil's and monk's responses on the right) (Wanek, 1999). Third, many self-report questionnaires measure specific traits, which we know may predict behavior in the same situations but not across situations. This means a person may behave honestly with his or her family but not necessarily with his or her employer.

Of course I'm a very, very honest person.

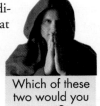

I'm not as honest as I should be.

### ADVANTAGES

One advantage of objective personality tests is that they are easily administered and can be taken individually or in groups. A second advantage is that since the questions are structured and require either a true-false or yes-no answer, the scoring is relatively straightforward. Third, many of the self-report questionnaires have good reliability. For example, the reliability of the MMPI-2 ranges from 0.68 to 0.92 (1.0 is perfect reliability) (Kaplan & Saccuzzo, 2001). Fourth, the validity of self-report questionnaires varies with the test; it ranges from poor to good. For example, the validity of integrity tests appears to be poor: In one study, a group of monks and nuns scored "more dishonest" than a group of prisoners in jail (Rieke & Guastello, 1995). In comparison, many studies on the MMPI-2 indicate its validity to be good (Kaplan & Saccuzzo, 2001).

Which of these two would you trust?

Because objective personality tests and projective personality tests (pp. 450-451) have different advantages and disadvantages, counselors and clinical psychologists may use a combination of both to assess a client's personality traits and problems.

## A. SOCIAL COGNITIVE THEORY

**1.** One theory says that personality development is shaped primarily by environmental conditions (learning), cognitive-personal factors, and behavior, which all interact to influence how we evaluate, interpret, and organize information and apply that information to ourselves and others; this is called the _____ theory.

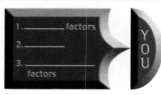

**2.** Albert Bandura called the version of his original social learning theory the (a)_____ theory. Bandura's theory assumes that four distinctively human cognitive processes—highly developed language ability, observational learning, purposeful behavior, and self-analysis—influence the growth, development, and change in (b)_____.

**3.** Our highly developed (a)_____ ability provides us with a tool for processing and understanding information, which is critical to personality development. Our capacity for (b)_____ learning allows us to learn through watching, without observable behavior or a reinforcer. Our capacity for forethought enables us to plan ahead and set goals—to perform (c)_____ behavior. Finally, the fact that we can monitor our thoughts and actions as well as set and change goals and values gives us the capacity for (d)_____.

**4.** The power of beliefs and ideas to change the way that we interpret situations and events is one of the basic assumptions of social cognitive theories. Rotter developed a scale to measure our belief about how much control we have over situations or rewards; he called this belief (a)_____. If we believe that we have control over situations and rewards, we are said to have an (b)_____ locus of control. In contrast, if we believe that we do not have control over situations and rewards and that events outside ourselves determine what happens, we are said to have an (c)_____ locus of control.

**5.** According to Bandura, our personal belief regarding how capable we are of exercising control over events in our lives is called (a)_____. According to Mischel, our voluntary postponement of an immediate reward and persistence in completing a task for the promise of a future reward is called delay of (b)_____.

## B. TRAIT THEORY

**6.** A relatively stable and enduring tendency to behave in a particular way is called a (a)_____. An approach to understanding the structure of personality by measuring, identifying, and analyzing differences in personality is called (b)_____ theory. In attempting to pare down a list of traits by finding relationships among them, researchers have used a statistical method called (c)_____.

**7.** The model that organizes all personality traits into five categories is called the (a)_____. These five categories, known as the Big Five, are (b)_____, _____, _____, _____, and _____; their initial letters spell out the word OCEAN.

**8.** Mischel questioned the basic assumption of trait theory, saying that, if traits represent consistent behavioral tendencies, they should predict behaviors across many different (a)_____. Instead, he found that people behaved with great consistency in the same situation but behaved with low consistency across different situations. Mischel pointed out that predicting a person's behavior must take into account not only the person's traits but also the effects of the situation; this idea became known as the (b)_____ interaction.

## C. GENETIC INFLUENCES ON TRAITS

**9.** How inherited or genetic factors influence and interact with psychological factors—for example, the ways we behave, adapt, and adjust to our environments—is the focus of the field of behavioral (a)_____. Current thinking about genetic factors is that they do not fix behaviors but rather set a range for behaviors. Researchers estimate genetic influences with a measure that estimates how much of some behavior is due to genetic influences; this measure is referred to as (b)_____.

**10.** Considering the various influences on personality development, researchers estimated that about 40% of the influence comes from (a)_____, which are inherited. About 27% of the influence on personality development comes from environmental factors that involve how each individual reacts and adjusts to his or her own environment; these are called (b)_____ factors. About 7% of the influence on personality development comes from environmental factors that involve parental patterns and shared family experiences; these are called (c)_____ factors. The remaining 26% of the influence on personality development cannot as yet be identified and is attributed to errors in testing and measurement procedures.

## D. EVALUATION OF TRAIT THEORY

**11.** Trait theory assumes that differences among personalities can be described by a short but comprehensive list of traits. Critics of the current list, known as the

(a)_____, point out that the data for the model may paint too simplistic a picture of human personality and may not reflect its depth and complexity. Trait theory assumes that traits are consistent and stable influences on our (b)_____, but critics argue that when traits are measured in one situation, they do not necessarily predict behaviors in other situations.

**12.** The biggest changes in personality occur during childhood, adolescence, and young adulthood because young men and women are somewhat more likely to be open to new ideas. Personality is less likely to change after age (a)_____. Observations from over 10,000 pairs of twins indicate that (b)_____ factors significantly influence personality traits. Critics warn that inherited factors should not be exaggerated because 50% or more of the influence on traits comes from (c)_____ influences.

## E. RESEARCH FOCUS: 180-DEGREE CHANGE

**13.** If you were to experience a sudden and radical or dramatic

shift in personality, beliefs, or values, you would be said to have experienced a (a)_____ in personality. One way researchers studied these changes in personality was to ask each individual the same set of relatively narrow and focused questions so that the same information was obtained from everyone; this method is called the (b)_____.

## F. CULTURAL DIVERSITY: RESOLVING CONFLICTS

**14.** A culture that places a high priority on attaining personal goals and striving for personal satisfaction is called an (a)_____ culture. A culture that places a high priority on group goals and norms over personal goals and values is called a (b)_____ culture.

**15.** The strategy that Japanese students used most frequently to resolve interpersonal conflicts was to (a)_____ discussion of the conflict; the strategy favored by American students was to resolve the problem through (b)_____. In addition, Japanese students reported that the vast majority of their interpersonal conflicts were (c)_____, while American students reported that the vast majority of their conflicts were (d)_____.

## G. FOUR THEORIES OF PERSONALITY

**16.** How does personality grow and develop? We discussed four different answers. The theory that emphasizes the importance of early childhood, unconscious factors, the three divisions of the mind, and psychosexual stages is called

(a)_____. The theories that focus on the phenomenological perspective, a holistic view, and self-actualization are called (b)_____ theories. The theory that says that personality development is shaped by the interaction among three factors—environmental conditions, cognitive-personal factors, and behavior—is called (c)_____ theory. The theory that emphasizes measuring and identifying differences among personalities is called (d)_____ theory.

## H. APPLICATION: ASSESSMENT—OBJECTIVE TESTS

**17.** Self-report questionnaires, which consist of specific written statements that require structured responses—for example, checking "true" or "false"—are examples of _____ personality tests.

**18.** A true-false self-report questionnaire containing hundreds of statements that describe a wide range of normal and abnormal behaviors is called the (a)_____. The purpose of this test is to distinguish normal from (b)_____ groups.

**19.** The method of listing a number of traits in such a general way that almost everyone who reads a horoscope thinks that many of the traits apply specifically to him or her is called the _____ principle.

***Answers:*** *1. social cognitive; 2. (a) social cognitive, (b) personality; 3. (a) language, (b) observational, (c) purposeful, (d) self-analysis; 4. (a) locus of control, (b) internal, (c) external; 5. (a) self-efficacy, (b) gratification; 6. (a) trait, (b) trait, (c) factor analysis; 7. (a) five-factor model, Big Five, (b) openness, conscientiousness, extraversion, agreeableness, neuroticism; 8. (a) situations, (b) person-situation; 9. (a) genetics, (b) heritability; 10. (a) genetic factors, (b) nonshared environmental, (c) shared environmental; 11. (a) Big Five, (b) behaviors; 12. (a) 30, (b) genetic, (c) environmental; 13. (a) quantum change, (b) structured interview; 14. (a) individualistic, (b) collectivistic; 15. (a) avoid, (b) persuasion, bargaining, or compromise, (c) covert, (d) overt; 16. (a) Freud's psychodynamic theory, (b) humanistic, (c) social learning, (d) trait; 17. objective; 18. (a) Minnesota Multiphasic Personality Inventory-2, or MMPI-2, (b) abnormal; 19. Barnum*

# Critical Thinking

Newspaper Article

## Companies Using Personality Tests for Making Hires That Fit

*by Carol Smith*

Like a growing number of white-collar workers, Stacy McCollough discovered that an interview and a resume review are no longer the only hurdles to landing a job in today's competitive marketplace. Today, workers going for mid- and upper-level management or sales positions are increasingly likely to have to take hard-to-fool psychological exams as well.

When McCollough applied to work at a medical malpractice insurance brokerage firm, she took a 2-hour test to determine how psychologically fit she was for the job. The test revealed she didn't have the aggressive traits needed to excel as a broker, but it helped the company steer her into a job that made the most of her skills.

Increasingly, companies are finding that an individual's past performance may not be the best predictor of success, because work requirements are changing so rapidly. Instead, companies are looking for new ways to assess intangible skills, such as how people work on teams, how organized they are, or how strategic they are in their thinking.

Although many employers like the tests, applicants aren't always as comfortable. "Some people say they think it's kind of weird—they've already made it to upper management and suddenly they're being given a test," said Barry Lawrence of the Society for

Human Resource Management. "Their attitude is, 'My experience should speak for itself.'"

Most candidates, however, accept testing as part of the hiring process. And test advocates point out that sometimes testing can help a candidate overcome a lack of experience by showing he or she has the right potential for the job.

The tests range from standard psychological profiles, or "personality tests," such as the 60-year-old Minnesota Multiphasic Personality Inventory, to specialized tests such as the Caliper Profile, which has been developed specifically for use in hiring.

While people can sometimes act their way through an interview, it's hard to fool the tests, which have built-in safeguards against cheating.

They are a good reality check on how someone appears in the interview, said human resources specialist Philip Barquer. "You can't fake your character." (Source: *Los Angeles Times*, February 9, 1997)

### Questions

**1.** Why do some employers use both interviews and objective personality tests in deciding whom to hire?

**2.** Why do companies look for certain traits in selecting employees and why would Freud question the importance of selecting for traits?

**3.** If you were using the Big Five traits to design a test for salespeople who work as a team, which traits would you look for?

**4.** What are some objections to or disadvantages of objective personality tests?

**5.** When might the MMPI-2 be used in assessing job applicants?

**6.** Which objective personality test has a scale to detect lying? Can objective personality tests prevent a person from "faking his or her character"?

*Try InfoTrac to search for terms:* **personality tests; Big Five personality traits.**

---

### Suggested answers to Newspaper Article questions

1. Some employers believe that applicants may not always be truthful in interviews and that objective personality tests may be more difficult to fool.

2. Employers are looking for certain traits because, according to trait theory, traits are relatively stable and enduring tendencies to behave in certain ways and traits predict how people will behave in similar situations. Freud would point out that traits are important but that behaviors and feelings may be influenced by unconscious forces, of which applicants would not be aware and which are not easily measured by objective personality tests.

3. Salespeople who work as a team might be selected for being high in openness (open to new experiences), extraversion (outgoing and decisive), agreeableness (warm and good-natured), and con-

   scientiousness (responsible and dependable) but low in neuroticism (stable and not a worrier).

4. Since objective personality tests use very structured questions, simplified yes-no answers, and objective scoring, an applicant can sometimes figure out and give socially acceptable answers and thus bias the test in his or her favor.

5. The MMPI-2 was designed to distinguish normal people from abnormal groups, so it is sometimes used to check for potential personality problems in applicants for sensitive or stressful jobs, such as law enforcement or air-traffic controllers.

6. The MMPI-2 has a scale to detect lying. To some degree, people can "fake their character" on objective personality tests provided they can figure out the socially acceptable or desirable answers.

# Links to Learning

## Web Sites

- **WADSWORTH ONLINE STUDY CENTER**
  http://psychology.wadsworth.com
  Quizzes, learning activities and exercises, a discussion forum, and hot links to Internet sites related to personality, including:

- **GREAT IDEAS IN PERSONALITY**
  http://personalityresearch.org/
  This Web site deals with scientific research programs in personality psychology. They are offered as candidates for the title "great ideas"; the site authors add, "whether they are indeed great remains an open question." Help decide! A section especially for students includes a glosary, self-test, and tips for becoming a better speaker and writer.

- **PERSONALITY AND CONSCIOUSNESS**
  http://www.wynja.com/personality/theorists.html
  This well-organized site has drop menus where you can link to book lists and other information about each of 14 personality psychologists, plus Buddhist psychology. Magazine subscriptions are offered at discount prices. If you write a good paper, send it in and you may well find it posted online.

- **RESOURCES FOR SHY PEOPLE**
  http://www.base.com/shy/
  Created by and for shy people, this extensive site offers links to articles on shyness in general and to articles that give advice; a bibliography, news groups, chat rooms (open only to shy peole), information on shyness clinics, classes, and counseling; email lists, links to other relevant sites, and the *Shy Digest,* in which several mail messages are collected every day and sent to subscribers every 1 to 3 days.

## Learning Activities

- ***POWERSTUDY*™ BY ROD PLOTNIK & TOM DOYLE**

  **PowerStudy™**

  **Check out CD: Module 20**
  CD 4.A: Genes & Evolution; book page 466

- ***STUDY GUIDE TO ACCOMPANY INTRODUCTION TO PSYCHOLOGY, 6TH EDITION,* by Matthew Enos**
  In Module 20, test your own personality by listing, honestly, all the reasons you're enrolled in college. What is your age in relation to "the Big Three-Oh," and what does that indicate about your personality? Have you ever had a quantum personality change?

- ***WEBTUTOR***
  http://webtutor.thomsonlearning.com
  **WebTUTOR** Visit this site for interactive versions of the Study Guide features. Take a quiz, get your score—should you study a topic some more, or can you move on? For example, What are the five factors summed up by the acronym OCEAN? What is the MMPI? What is the Barnum principle?

- ***INFOTRAC ONLINE LIBRARY***
  http://www.infotrac-college.com
   Use your password and then key in search terms such as those below to find popular and scientific articles on subjects covered in Module 20. Make the library work for you!

  | | | |
  |---|---|---|
  | Behavioral genetics | Trait theory | Albert Bandura |
  | Minnesota Multiphasic Personality Inventory | Nelson Mandela | |

- ***PSYCHNOW!***
  CD for Macintosh and Windows includes a study guide, glossary, Web sites, and animations. For Module 20, see:
  - Theories of Personality

## Study Questions

*Use InfoTrac to search for topics mentioned in the main heads below (e.g., social cognitive theory, conflict resolution).*

*A. **Social Cognitive Theory**—Why do students invest thousands of dollars and 4–6 years of hard work to obtain a college degree? (**Suggested answer p. 632**)

*B. **Trait Theory**—Would knowing about the Big Five traits help you write an ad to find the perfect roommate or life mate? (**Suggested answer p. 633**)

C. **Genetic Influences on Traits**—How is it possible that, in the same family, one child may be lively and outgoing and another may be shy and withdrawn?

D. **Evaluation of Trait Theory**—Why might newlyweds discover that the person they married is not the person they thought they knew?

E. **Research Focus: 180-Degree Change**—What are some of the reasons that we should be cautious in believing self-reports of dramatic behavioral changes?

*F. **Cultural Diversity: Resolving Conflicts**—What could happen when U.S. officials negotiate public trade agreements with Japanese officials? (**Suggested answer p. 633**)

G. **Four Theories of Personality**—Do you think that all four theories of personality could be or should be reduced to just one?

H. **Application: Assessment—Objective Tests**—A psychological test in a magazine promises to tell you what kind of mate is perfect for you. Can you believe it?

*These questions are answered in Appendix B.

# Module 21: Health, Stress, & Coping

**A. Appraisal**  **482**
* PRIMARY APPRAISALS
* SITUATIONS AND PRIMARY APPRAISALS
* APPRAISAL AND STRESS LEVEL
* SAME SITUATION, DIFFERENT APPRAISALS
* SEQUENCE: APPRAISAL TO AROUSAL

**B. Physiological Responses**  **484**
* FIGHT-FLIGHT RESPONSE
* PSYCHOSOMATIC SYMPTOMS
* KINDS OF SYMPTOMS
* GENERAL ADAPTATION SYNDROME
* MIND-BODY CONNECTION
* IMMUNE SYSTEM

**C. Stressful Experiences**  **490**
* KINDS OF STRESSORS
* SITUATIONAL STRESSORS
* CONFLICT
* ANXIETY

**D. Personality & Social Factors**  **494**
* HARDINESS
* LOCUS OF CONTROL
* OPTIMISM VERSUS PESSIMISM
* TYPE A BEHAVIOR
* SOCIAL SUPPORT

**Concept Review**  **498**

**E. Kinds of Coping**  **499**
* APPRAISAL
* KINDS OF COPING
* CHOOSING A COPING STRATEGY

**F. Research Focus:
Coping with Trauma**  **500**
* HOW DO PEOPLE COPE
  WITH SEVERE BURNS?

**G. Cultural Diversity: Tibetan Monks**  **501**
* MONKS' AMAZING CLAIMS
* MIND-BODY INTERACTION

**H. Application:
Stress Management Programs**  **502**
* DEFINITION
* CHANGING THOUGHTS
* CHANGING BEHAVIORS
* CHANGING PHYSIOLOGICAL RESPONSES

**Summary Test**  **504**

**Critical Thinking**  **506**
* THE DIAGNOSIS

**Links to Learning**  **507**

## Stress

### Why do I faint when giving blood?

The doctor explains that, as part of my physical exam, the nurse will take a couple of samples of my blood. The nurse enters the room, smiles, and says, "This will only take a minute." She asks me to sit on the edge of the examining table and to roll up my sleeve. I slowly roll up my sleeve and look at my bare arm as if it were about to be cut off.

After the nurse tightens a rubber tourniquet around my upper arm, she says in a gentle voice, "Please make a fist and hold it." As the nurse brings the needle to my vein, she says, "You'll feel a tiny prick but it won't hurt." With a swift and practiced movement, she sticks the thin needle into my vein.

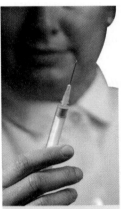

How can seeing a needle cause me to pass out?

She pulls the plunger back and I see my blood, which is a deep red color, flow rapidly into the syringe.

I say to myself, "It's almost over."

She removes the first syringe and starts to fill a second.

By now my heart is beating crazily and I have broken out in a fine, cold sweat. I try to distract myself by looking away and thinking about my wonderful fuzzy dog that has the head of a lion and the heart of a true friend.

Now I am floating in space, and all is white and so peaceful. In the distance I hear someone calling my name, "Rod, Rod," but I'm frozen in a deep dream and cannot move a single muscle.

As I come to with the odor of smelling salts, the nurse tells me that I fainted and should just lie still for several minutes. I raise my arm and see a small Band-Aid, which covers the tiny hole made by the needle. The nurse looks down and asks, "What's the big deal about giving a little blood?"

The big deal concerns what is going on in my head. I have developed an overwhelming fear of seeing blood or seeing an injury, and this fear causes me to faint, as it does in about 15% of the population (equally in males and females) (Page, 1994). Compared with other strong fears, such as fear of snakes, heights, or small spaces, the fear of blood or needles is one of the few fears that cause people to actually faint (Page, 1994). This means that for about 15% of the population (including me), seeing blood is a very stressful experience.

*Stress* is the anxious or threatening feeling that comes when we interpret or appraise a situation as being more than our psychological resources can adequately handle (Lazarus, 1999).

The study of stress is very much the study of how the mind and body interact. For instance, the fear generated by my mind alone is so intense that it causes my body's physiological responses to overreact, and the result is fainting. In this module, you'll find out what happens to your body during stressful situations.

Just as we can use our mind to overreact to stress, we can also use it to cope with stress, which is something Sandra must do almost every minute of her life.

## Coping

### What's a day like for Sandra?

It's 6:30 A.M. With a groan Sandra slaps at the alarm, rolls out of bed, and stands grimacing at herself in the bathroom mirror. She ducks into the shower. A few minutes later she wakes Jesse, 5, and Caiti, 3, and the morning rush is on. She sits the kids down at the dinette for breakfast, packs their lunches, and reminds them Auntie Erika is picking them up after school today. She scoops up a stack of books, almost forgetting the 15-page religion paper she slaved over all weekend. She turns off the TV, bundles up the kids, and is out the door.

This is a normal day for Sandra Sullivan, a 27-year-old single mother of two wonderful kids. Sandra is a recovering drug addict and former homeless person. She is surviving without child support, needs food stamps to make ends meet, and is trying against all odds to go to college. And not just any college, but Wellesley, one of the most prestigious women's colleges in the nation.

The turning point for Sandra was the day she got the disappointing news that her husband had forged a check. She felt that she had come to the very end of her rope. She got down on her knees and prayed, and in a flash, it seemed that her old self had died and she was ready to make a new beginning. She swallowed her pride and made some very tough decisions. She left her husband, who had been

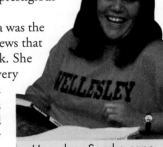

How does Sandra cope with being the single mother of two children and a college student?

in and out of jobs for five years, quit drugs, and moved with her babies into a homeless shelter. She decided to do something about her life and enrolled in a community college. She worked hard enough and did well enough to be accepted into Wellesley College (adapted from *Life,* April 1992, pp. 62–65).

For Sandra, every day is a series of nonstop potential stressors. To keep these stressors from growing out of control, she uses a variety of coping techniques. Some days she copes better than others, and she must continually guard against being overwhelmed by college, by kids, by duties, and by life. One of the interesting topics we'll discuss in this module is the different ways to cope with stressors.

## What's Coming

We'll discuss how you decide something is stressful, your physiological and psychological responses to stress, how your immune system works, how you develop psychosomatic symptoms, which situational, personality, and social factors help or hinder your coping processes, and how you can develop your own stress management program.

We'll begin with how my mind can overpower my body and make me faint for no good reason.

### Primary Appraisals

**What makes giving blood so stressful?**

If there is no real threat to my physical survival in giving a sample of blood, why do I and millions of others overreact to the point of fainting? One answer may be obtained by questioning people about the origin of their fear of blood . As was true for me, 76% reported that it began with a traumatic event (Kleinknecht, 1994). Through conditioning, this traumatic event makes the blood a powerful emotional stimulus that automatically triggers a chain of intense mental events (feelings of fear) and overactive physiological responses (changes in blood pressure to produce fainting). In my case, I was about 8 years old when I saw my father almost cut off his thumb. As I saw his hand covered with blood, I thought he was going to die. Thereafter, each time I saw blood, I automatically interpreted this situation as a severe emotional threat. The initial interpretation of a potentially stressful situation is called a primary appraisal (Lazarus, 1999, 2000).

*My mind creates my fear.*

*Primary appraisal* refers to our initial, subjective evaluation of a situation, in which we balance the demands of a potentially stressful situation against our ability to meet these demands.

For example, there can be three different primary appraisals of giving blood. If giving blood doesn't matter one way or another to your well-being, your primary appraisal is that the situation is *irrelevant* and therefore mostly nonstressful. If you're giving blood to help a friend, your primary appraisal is that the situation is *positive* and mostly nonstressful because it makes you feel good. If giving blood triggers uncontrollable fear, your primary appraisal is that the situation is *stressful,* meaning that it overtaxes your emotional and psychological recourses. Your primary appraisal that a situation is stressful involves three different interpretations: harm/loss, threat, or challenge.

---

#### Harm/Loss

If you broke your arm in a bike accident, you would know that you have suffered harm or loss.

*Harm/loss appraisal*

A *harm/loss appraisal* of a situation means that you have already sustained some damage or injury.

Because the harm/loss appraisal *elicits negative emotions,* such as fear, depression, fright, and anxiety, you will feel stressed; and the more intense your negative emotions are, the more stressful and overwhelming the situation will seem.

#### Threat

If you have a terrible fear of giving blood and are asked to do so, you would automatically interpret giving blood as a threat to your well-being.

*Threat appraisal*

A *threat appraisal* of a situation means that the harm/loss has not yet taken place but you know it will happen in the near future.

Because a threat appraisal also **elicits negative emotions,** such as fear, anxiety, and anger, the situation or event may seem especially stressful. In fact, just imagining or anticipating a threatening situation, such as giving blood or taking a final exam, can be as stressful as the actual event itself.

#### Challenge

If you are working hard in college but find that you have to take two more classes, you might interpret taking these classes as a way to achieve a major goal—that is, you use a challenge appraisal.

*Challenge appraisal*

A *challenge appraisal* of a situation means that you have the potential for gain or personal growth but also need to mobilize your physical energy and psychological resources to meet the challenging situation.

Because a challenge appraisal *elicits positive emotions,* such as eagerness or excitement, it is usually less stressful than a harm/loss or a threat appraisal.

---

### Situations and Primary Appraisals

**First reaction.** Your first reaction to potentially stressful situations, such as waiting in line, dealing with a sloppy roommate, giving blood, making a public speech, dealing with a rude salesperson, taking an exam, seeing a vicious dog, or being in a car accident, is to appraise the situation in terms of whether it harms, threatens, or challenges your physical or psychological well-being.

Making primary appraisals about complex situations, such as whether to take a certain job, get married, or go on to graduate school, may require considerable time as you think over the different ways a situation will affect you. In comparison, making primary appraisals about very emotional situations, such as taking a surprise quiz, presenting a report in class,

This person made a primary appraisal that giving a speech was a threat to her self-esteem.

or, in my case, giving blood, may occur quickly, even automatically (Lazarus, 2000). However, not all appraisals neatly divide into harm/loss, threat, or challenge. Some primary appraisals are a combination of threat and challenge. For instance, if you are about to ask someone for a first date, you may feel threatened by the possibility of being rejected yet challenged by the chance to prove yourself.

Later in this module, we'll discuss how you can change a threat appraisal into more of a challenge appraisal and thus reduce your stressful feelings. At this point, just keep in mind that making a primary appraisal is the first step in experiencing stress. Depending on the kind of primary appraisal, your level of stress may either increase or decrease.

## Appraisal and Stress Level

**Would it stress you to watch a bloody accident?**

If you were asked to watch a film of bloody accidents caused by power saws, how much would your primary appraisal affect your level of stress? This is exactly what researchers asked subjects to do while recording a major sign of physiological arousal, called the galvanic skin response.

The *galvanic skin response* is a measure of how much a person's hand sweats due to physiological arousal and not to normal temperature changes.

As subjects watched the accident film, they were given instructions that would result in making a primary appraisal of challenge or threat. To encourage challenge appraisals, subjects were told to watch the film objectively, to consider how these accidents might be prevented, but not to identify with the injured. To encourage threat appraisals, subjects were told to put themselves in the place of men who accidentally cut off their fingers with power saws and imagine how they would feel in these situations.

Level of stress from watching a bloody accident depended on threat or challenge appraisal.

As the graph below shows, subjects using threat appraisals showed significantly more physiological arousal—that is, high levels of galvanic skin responses—than subjects using challenge appraisals (Dandoy & Goldstein, 1990). Researchers concluded that in threatening or disturbing situations, your feelings of stress increase with the kind of appraisal: Threat appraisals raise levels of stress more than challenge appraisals do. However, when people are asked to identify the cause of their stressful feelings, they usually—and often incorrectly—point to a particular situation rather than to their primary appraisals. But as you'll see next, people often appraise the same situation in different ways.

**Average Physiological Arousal Scores**

| | |
|---|---|
| Threat appraisal | 64 |
| Challenge appraisal | 24 |

## Same Situation, Different Appraisals

**How stressful is waiting in line?**

When I ask my students, "What stresses you?" they always list a variety of situations, including many of those situations listed in the table below right. Notice especially how the same situation was stressful for some but not for others. For example, 65% said waiting for a late person was stressful, but 35% reported it wasn't. Similarly, 61% said waiting in line was stressful, but 39% said that it wasn't. Because people don't agree on which situations are stressful, researchers concluded that level of stress depends not only on the kind of situation but also on the kind of *primary appraisal* one makes (Rasmussen et al., 2000). For example, you could appraise waiting in line to get your favorite beverage as a challenge, which elicits positive emotions and little stress. In contrast, you could appraise waiting in line as a threat or real test of your patience, which elicits negative emotions (growing impatient) and considerable stress. Thus, similar situations (waiting in line) can result in different levels of stress depending on your primary appraisals.

Why are 61% stressed by waiting in line while 39% are not?

| | Percentage rating it | |
|---|---|---|
| **Situation** | **stressful** | **not stressful** |
| Waiting for someone who is late | 65 | 35 |
| Being caught in traffic | 63 | 37 |
| Waiting in line | 61 | 39 |
| Waiting in a doctor's office | 59 | 41 |
| Waiting for the government to act | 51 | 49 |
| Waiting for a repair person | 46 | 54 |
| Looking for a parking space | 42 | 58 |
| Waiting for an airplane to take off | 26 | 74 |

## Sequence: Appraisal to Arousal

**How does stress start?**

The first step in feeling stress depends on your primary appraisal, which can be one of harm/loss, threat, or challenge. In turn, harm/loss and threat appraisals elicit negative emotions, which, in turn, increase levels of stress. In comparison, challenge appraisals elicit positive emotions, which, in turn, decrease levels of stress. Thus, when you say that a situation is causing you stress, such as giving blood, taking an exam, making a public speech, changing your job, asking for a date, arguing with your boss, having to move, getting married, or arguing with your roommate, you are forgetting that part of the stress is coming from whether you make a harm/loss or threat appraisal versus a challenge appraisal (Lazarus, 2000).

The moment after you make an appraisal, especially a harm/loss or threat appraisal, your body changes from a generally calm state into one of heightened physiological arousal as it prepares to deal with the stressor, whether it involves a car accident, a mugger, a public speech, or giving blood. We'll look inside the body and see what happens when you are stressed.

Making a threat or harm/loss appraisal results in increased physiological arousal.

# B. Physiological Responses

**Power Study™**

**Check out CD: Module 4**
C. Organization of the Brain
E. Limbic System: Old Brain

## Fight-Flight Response

**What happens when you're frightened?**

Imagine walking to the front of the class-room, turning around, and facing 35 other students. As you look at their faces, you feel your heart pounding, mouth becoming dry, hands sweating, stomach knotting, and muscles tensing; you take in short, rapid breaths. Your body is fully aroused before you have spoken a single word (Tanouye, 1997).

Since speaking in public is no threat to your physical survival and you can neither fight nor flee, why is your body in this state of heightened physiological arousal? The answer is that once you make a primary appraisal that something is a threat—whether it's giving a speech or facing a mugger—these threatening and fearful thoughts automatically trigger one of the body's oldest physiological response systems, the fight-flight response (White & Porth, 2000).

The *fight-flight response* (a) directs great resources of energy to the muscles and the brain, (b) can be triggered by either physical stimuli that threaten our survival or psychological situations that are novel, threatening, or challenging, and (c) involves numerous physiological responses that arouse and prepare the body for action—fight or flight.

The fight-flight response helps us survive by preparing the body for action—fleeing or fighting.

We know that the fight-flight response is evolutionarily very old because it can be found in animals such as the alligator, which has been around for millions of years. We presume that our early ancestors evolved a similar fight-flight response to help them survive attacks by wild animals and enemies.

**Physical stimuli.** Today you have almost no need to fight wild animals or flee attacking enemies, so you rarely activate your fight-flight response for the reasons important to our early ancestors. However, you would activate the fight-flight response when faced with a potentially dangerous physical stimulus, such as a mugger, accident, police siren, snake, tornado, or other situation that threatened your physical survival.

**Psychological stimuli.** Today the most common reason you activate the fight-flight response is exposure to potentially bothersome or stressful psychological stimuli, such as worrying about exams, being impatient in traffic, having to wait in lines, getting angry over a putdown, or arguing with someone (Lazarus, 1999, 2000). We'll trace the sequence of how psychological or physical stimuli can trigger the fight-flight response and transform your body into a state of heightened physiological arousal (White & Porth, 2000).

### Sequence for Activation of the Fight-Flight Response

**1 Appraisal**
A number of potentially dangerous physical stimuli, such as seeing a snake or being in an accident, can automatically trigger the fight-flight response. But much more common triggers of the fight-flight response are hundreds of psychological stimuli that you appraise as threatening, such as making a public speech or taking an exam. Thus, either *physically or psychologically threatening stimuli* can trigger the fight-flight response and negative emotional feelings (fear, rage).

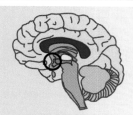

**2 Hypothalamus**
If you appraise making a public speech as psychologically threatening, these thoughts activate a part of your brain called the *hypothalamus.* In turn, the hypothalamus simultaneously activates two stress-related responses: it triggers the pituitary gland to release a stress-fighting hormone called *ACTH* (adrenocorticotropic hormone); it also activates the sympathetic division of the autonomic nervous system.

**3 Sympathetic Division**
As we discussed in Module 4, the autonomic nervous system has two divisions. The *sympathetic division,* which is activated by the hypothalamus, triggers a number of physiological responses that make up the fight-flight response, which prepares the body to deal with potentially threatening physical or psychological stimuli. In contrast, the *parasympathetic division,* also activated by the hypothalamus, returns the body to a more calm, relaxed state.

**4 Fight-Flight Response**
The sympathetic division triggers the very primitive *fight-flight response*, which causes great *physiological arousal*, by increasing heart rate, blood pressure, respiration, secretion of excitatory hormones, and many other responses that prepare the body to deal with the impending threat, whether it is public speaking or facing a mugger.

Next, we'll describe the many interesting physiological responses that literally transform the body into a powerful fighting or fleeing machine.

*Fight-Flight: Physiological and Hormonal Responses*

Students often have trouble remembering that their fight-flight response can just as easily be triggered by potentially threatening psychological stimuli, such as speaking in public or taking exams, as by potentially threatening physical stimuli, such as seeing a rattlesnake. In fact, in the course of a week, you experience relatively few potentially threatening physical stimuli, such as seeing a snake, but many psychological situations occur that you appraise as threatening ("Boy, did I have a bad day"). As soon as you appraise a situation as threatening, your hypothalamus starts the fight-flight response, which in turn prepares your body for action (White & Porth, 2000). We'll describe some of those physiological changes.

Which physical or psychological stimuli can trigger the fight-flight response?

**1 Stress appraisal** activates the *hypothalamus* (yellow in figure at right), which simultaneously triggers the pituitary gland (green) and sympathetic division of the autonomic nervous system. The *pituitary gland* releases ACTH (adrenocorticotropic hormone), which acts on part of the adrenal gland (adrenal cortex). The *sympathetic division* causes physiological arousal by automatically increasing heart rate, blood pressure, and many other responses (Rosch, 1994).

**2 Respiration,** which is increased by the sympathetic division, is more rapid and shallow so that there is a greater flow of oxygen into the body. However, if breathing is too rapid and shallow, we can feel light-headed or "spacey" from lack of oxygen.

**3 Heart rate,** which is increased by the sympathetic division, can rocket from a normal 70–90 beats per minute to an incredible 200–220 beats per minute (Sloan et al., 1994). Rapid heart rate increases blood flow to muscles and vital organs (lungs, kidneys). Rapid heart rate during stressful experiences can lead to a "pounding heart" and, in extreme cases, result in heart attack and death.

**4 Liver** releases its stores of blood sugar (glycogen) to provide a ready source of energy during stress. After a stressful experience, we may feel fatigued because our supply of blood sugar is low.

   **Stomach** and **intestinal activity** is reduced by the sympathetic division. During stressful experiences, the blood that is normally used by digestive organs is rerouted to muscles and vital organs. Because the sympathetic division shuts down the digestive system, people may experience problems with digestion, such as stomach pain, constipation, and diarrhea during stressful times.

**Liver**

**Stomach**

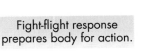

Fight-flight response prepares body for action.

**5 Pupils** are dilated by the sympathetic division. As a result, more light enters our eyes so we can see better if we have to fight or flee in dim light. One way to check for physiological arousal is to see how much a person's pupils are dilated: more dilation usually indicates more arousal (except in the case of drug use).

**6 Hair** stands up; this is called piloerection (goose bumps) and is more noticeable in dogs and cats. Piloerection, which occurs when we are stressed (frightened or angry) or cold (fluffy fur or hair conserves heat), is triggered by the sympathetic division, which also regulates sweating. The next time you are feeling stressed, look for piloerection and sweaty hands.

**7 Adrenal glands** (tan) have an outside—adrenal cortex—and an inside—adrenal medulla. The *adrenal medulla,* which is activated by the sympathetic division, secretes two powerful activating hormones, epinephrine (adrenaline) and norepinephrine. These hormones increase heart rate, blood pressure, blood flow to muscles, and release of blood sugar (glucose) as a source of energy. Epinephrine and norepinephrine may be regarded as the body's own stimulants; they can result in euphoria, loss of appetite, and sleeplessness.

   The *adrenal cortex,* which is activated by the pituitary gland's release of ACTH, secretes a group of hormones called corticoids, which regulate levels of minerals and glucose in the body.

**Kidney** **Kidney**

**8 Muscle tension** is increased during stressful experiences, so that we are better able to coordinate and move quickly if needed. However, if you are feeling stressed for long periods of time, you may end up with muscle aches and pains because of increased muscle tension throughout your body.

   **Male–female difference.** The fight-flight response is automatically triggered to increase physiological arousal and prepare our bodies for action. However, researchers recently found that while men are more likely to fight or flee when stressed, women show a different response to stress, called tend and befriend, which involves nurturing (children) and seeking social support (Taylor et al., 2000b). Researchers suggest that this male–female difference in responding to stress may have developed from evolutionary pressures on primitive men to fight and protect their families and on primitive women to nurture their children and seek help and social support for themselves and their families.

   Although the fight-flight response is designed to aid survival in stressful situations, if the fight-flight response is continuously triggered over a period of time (days, weeks), you may develop painful physical problems, which we'll describe next.

## Psychosomatic Symptoms

**What causes stomach pains?**

Today it's rather common for students to be faced with many difficult personal, academic, or financial problems. For example, Joan, a college freshman, was stressed out from taking 3 classes, spending 28 hours a week on homework, working another 10 hours a week at a part-time job, not getting enough sleep, and always being behind in the rent. She's one of the 30% of college freshmen in the United States who reported feeling "frequently overwhelmed" by all they have to do. In comparison, only 16% of college freshmen reported feeling stressed in 1985 (Carpenter, 2000). Not only does stress make one feel overwhelmed but it also triggers the fight-flight response, which greatly increases physiological arousal.

*But how can worrying cause my awful stomach pains?*

One of the first researchers to recognize that stressful experiences trigger the fight-flight response was Hans Selye (1956, 1993). His pioneering work showed that prolonged or continuing stress caused continued physiological arousal, which in turn may cause psychosomatic (also called psychophysiological) symptoms.

*Psychosomatic (SIGH-ko-so-MAH-tik) symptoms* refer to real and often painful physical symptoms, such as headaches, muscle pains, and stomach problems, that are caused by psychological factors, such as worry, stress, and anxiety. (The word *psychosomatic* is derived from *psyche* meaning "mind" and *soma* meaning "body.")

College freshmen, as well as anyone who feels "frequently overwhelmed," are at great risk for developing psychosomatic symptoms. That's because *threat appraisals* result in *stress*, which triggers the *fight-flight response.* Triggering the flight-fight response infrequently is not usually damaging. But if the fight-flight response is triggered frequently across days, weeks, and months, this increased and prolonged arousal can result in a variety of *psychosomatic symptoms,* such as stomach pains, intestinal problems, and heart attacks (Wimbush & Nelson, 2000). We'll discuss the kinds and the development of common psychosomatic symptoms.

## Kinds of Symptoms

**Do you have any of these symptoms?**

Doctors estimate that 50–80% of patients seen in general medical practice have stress-related problems (Wimbush & Nelson, 2000). For example, 56% of patients complaining of stomach pain were diagnosed as having psychosomatic or stress-related symptoms since no organic causes could be identified. Of interest is that all the patients whose problems were stress-related reported that they had experienced a serious stressor (breakup of a relationship, family member leaving home) during the previous six months (Creed, 1993). Some of the more common stress-related or psychosomatic symptoms are listed below (Smith & Seidel, 1982). My students (and I) usually report having at least one of these psychosomatic symptoms.

### Common Psychosomatic Symptoms

- **Stomach symptoms:** feelings of discomfort, pain, pressure, or acidity
- **Muscle pain and tension:** occurring in neck, shoulders, and back
- **Fatigue:** feeling tired or exhausted without doing physical activity
- **Headaches:** having either tension or migraine headaches
- **Intestinal difficulties:** having either constipation or diarrhea
- **Skin disorders:** exaggerated skin blemishes, pimples, oiliness
- **Eating problems:** either feeling a compulsion to eat or losing one's appetite
- **Insomnia:** having recurring bouts of being unable to get to sleep or stay asleep
- **Asthmatic** or **allergic problems:** worsening of problems
- **High blood pressure** or **heart pounding**
- **Colds or flus:** recurring problems

### DEVELOPMENT OF PSYCHOSOMATIC SYMPTOMS

Researchers believe that developing a psychosomatic symptom is a three-step process.

Step **1: Genetic predisposition and lifestyle.** We may have a genetic predisposition for the breakdown of certain organs, such as heart, blood vessels, or stomach lining, or our lifestyle may promote poor health practices, such as smoking, being overweight, or not exercising. This means that the development of psychosomatic problems involves not only stressful feelings but also inherited predispositions or poor lifestyle practices that target certain body organs for future problems (Plomin & Crabbe, 2000).

Stress can cause a variety of stomach and intestinal problems.

Step **2: Prolonged stress.** Some of us may be more likely than others to appraise situations as threatening, thus eliciting negative emotions and automatically triggering the fight-flight response. The continual activation of the fight-flight response produces a state of heightened physiological arousal (increased heart rate, blood pressure, and secretion of arousing hormones) that will put a strain on our body organs and immune system (Cohen, 1996).

Step **3: Psychosomatic symptoms.** The interaction of body organs that are already targeted or weakened from genetic predispositions or poor lifestyle practices and prolonged physiological arousal from stressful experiences can result in a variety of psychosomatic problems (Wimbush & Nelson, 2000).

Next, we'll examine how prolonged stressful experiences affect the body.

## General Adaptation Syndrome

**What does stress do?**

One thing continued stress does is activate the fight-flight response. The continual activation of fight-flight responses results in what Hans Selye (1993) has described as the general adaptation syndrome.

The *general adaptation syndrome* (GAS) refers to the body's reaction to stressful situations during which it goes through a series of three stages—alarm, resistance, and exhaustion—that gradually increase the chances of developing psychosomatic symptoms.

Selye's general adaptation syndrome explains how coed Joan, who felt continually overwhelmed, developed a psychosomatic symptom, stomach pain.

### 1 Alarm Stage

Alarm: initial reaction

As sleep-deprived Joan worries about having too little time for all she has to do, she appraises that situation as a terrible threat to her well-being, which causes her body to be in the alarm stage.

The *alarm stage* is the initial reaction to stress and is marked by activation of the fight-flight response; in turn, the fight-flight response causes physiological arousal.

During stress, the body goes through 3 stages.

Your body may go into and out of the alarm stage (fight-flight response) many times during the day as stressful experiences come and go. Normally, you do not develop psychosomatic problems during the alarm stage because the fight-flight responses come and go. However, if stress continues for a longer period of time, your body goes into the resistance stage.

### 2 Resistance Stage

Resistance: fighting back

As the semester comes to an end, Joan's continual feelings of being overwhelmed cause almost continual fight-flight responses, which in turn cause her body to go into the resistance stage.

The *resistance stage* is the body's reaction to continued stress during which most of the physiological responses return to normal levels but the body uses up great stores of energy.

During the resistance stage, Joan's body will use up vital reserves of hormones, minerals, and glucose (blood sugar) because her body is almost continually in the fight-flight state. Joan doesn't realize that the resistance stage is taking a toll on her stomach by interfering with digestion and causing stomach pain, a psychosomatic symptom. If her stress continues, her body will go into the exhaustion stage and her psychosomatic symptom will worsen.

### 3 Exhaustion Stage

Exhaustion: breakdown in organs

As Joan's feeling of being overwhelmed continues over many weeks, her body may enter the exhaustion stage.

The *exhaustion stage* is the body's reaction to long-term, continuous stress and is marked by actual breakdown in internal organs or weakening of the infection-fighting immune system.

During the exhaustion stage, Joan's stomach problems may become more serious. Like Joan, extended periods of stress, such as during final exams, may cause your body to go into the stage of resistance or exhaustion. During this time you may develop a variety of psychosomatic symptoms, such as a cold, flu, cold sore, sore throat, allergy attack, aching muscles, or stomach problem. For example, researchers found that individuals who had prolonged and high levels of anger, signaling stages of resistance and exhaustion, were more likely to develop high blood pressure than those with normal levels (Jorgensen et al., 1996). As you'll see, psychosomatic symptoms develop because of a mind-body interaction.

## Mind-Body Connection

**Why do I faint?**

At the beginning of this module, I told you that my fear of human blood is so intense that just seeing or giving blood can make me faint. This is a perfect example of the mind-body connection (Benson, 1997).

The *mind-body connection* refers to how your thoughts, beliefs, and emotions can produce physiological changes that may be either beneficial or detrimental to your health and well-being.

For example, the mind-body connection explains why fearful or threatening thoughts cause about 15% of the adult population to faint at the sight of blood, needles, or injections (Kleinknecht, 1994). For these individuals (including me), fearful thoughts or appraisals trigger the fight-flight response, which greatly increases blood pressure. This is shortly followed by a rebound drop in blood pressure, which lowers blood flow to the brain and results in fainting (Roan, 1997a). The mind-body connection also explains why, after a prolonged period of fearful or anxious thoughts that continually trigger fight-flight responses, there may be a breakdown in body organs and development of psychosomatic symptoms (Wimbush & Nelson, 2000).

Continuing research on the importance and implications of the mind-body connection has given rise to an area called mind-body therapy (Goleman & Gurin, 1993).

*Mind-body therapy* is based on the finding that thoughts and emotions can change physiological and immune responses. Mind-body therapy uses mental strategies, such as relaxation, meditation, and biofeedback, as well as social support groups to help individuals change negative beliefs, thoughts, and emotions into more positive ones.

Mind and body interact during times of stress.

At the end of this module, we'll discuss specific mind-body therapies, called stress management programs, which help people recognize and deal with stress overload and thus prevent or reduce painful psychosomatic symptoms.

The mind-body connection is involved in the prevention as well as the development and maintenance of psychosomatic symptoms. More unexpectedly, the mind-body connection was found to be involved in the strengthening or weakening of our immune systems, which is the next topic.

### Immune System

Getting a cold is partly due to the effects of too much stress in your life.

**Why did you get a cold?**

How often have you gotten a cold, strep throat, or some other bacterial or viral infection when final exams were over? This rather common experience of "coming down with something" when exams are over indicates how prolonged stressful experiences can decrease the effectiveness of your immune system.

The *immune system* is the body's defense and surveillance network of cells and chemicals that fight off bacteria, viruses, and other foreign or toxic substances.

For many years, researchers had firmly believed that the immune system was a totally independent system without any input from the brain and certainly not influenced by your thoughts. In the mid-1970s, quite by chance, a psychologist and an immunologist found the first good evidence that there was a mind-body connection—that psychological factors influenced the immune system (Ader & Cohen, 1975). Their results and subsequent studies by other researchers led to the development of an entirely new area of medical science that is called psychoneuroimmunology *(SIGH-ko-new-row-im-you-NAWL-ah-gee)*.

### *Psychoneuroimmunology*

Researchers Ader and Cohen (1975) were trying to figure out why some of their rats were dying so young when they chanced upon one of the important scientific discoveries of the 1970s. For the previous 50 years, immunologists had believed that the immune system operated independently of psychological influences. To the surprise of all and disbelief of many, Ader and Cohen reported that psychological factors influenced the immune system's functioning, a finding that challenged 50 years of thinking. Today, no one doubts their findings, which single-handedly launched the field of psychoneuroimmunology.

*Psychoneuroimmunology* is the study of the relationship among three factors: the central nervous system (brain and spinal cord), the endocrine system (network of glands that secrete hormones), and psychosocial factors (stressful thoughts, personality traits, and social influences).

Coming down with something (cold, flu) after a stressful period results from the interaction among these three factors—central nervous system, immune system, and psychosocial factors—that can suppress or strengthen the immune system and in turn make the body more or less susceptible to disease and infection (Witek-Janusek & Mathews, 2000). For example, researchers reported that taking exams suppressed the immune systems of students with high but not low anxiety. These results explain why some students, those highly anxious, are more likely to come down with something after exams or stressful events (Borella et al., 1999).

The immune system has several ways to kill foreign invaders. In the left photo, an immune system cell actually sends out a footlike extension to engulf and destroy the small green bacterial cell (inside white oval).

However, as you'll see next, the immune system's defenses can be decreased by psychosocial factors (Ader, 1999).

An immune system cell sends out a footlike extension to destroy a bacterial cell (in white oval).

### *Evidence for Psychoneuroimmunology*

Researchers were faced with a difficult question: Why doesn't everyone who is exposed to a disease virus or bacteria actually get the disease? They tackled this question head-on by giving the same amount of cold virus to 394 subjects, all of whom were quarantined for a week. During this period, the researchers checked for symptoms of colds and related the percentage of colds to the levels of stress that subjects had reported before they received the virus. As shown in the graph below, researchers found that those individuals who reported high levels of psychological stress were significantly more likely to develop colds than were those who reported low stress levels (Cohen et al., 1997).

**Subjects with Colds (%)**

| | |
|---|---|
| Subjects reporting HIGH psychological stress | 48% |
| Subjects reporting LOW psychological stress | 38% |

Individuals who reported high levels of stress described their lives as somewhat unpredictable, uncontrollable, and overwhelming. Researchers concluded that, with every increase in psychological stress, there's an increased likelihood of developing a cold—provided we are exposed to the cold virus. (There is no truth to the folk wisdom that people get colds simply by being cold or damp.)

**Fight-flight response.** Another reason stressed individuals are more likely to get colds is that they are continually activating their fight-flight responses, which depresses the effectiveness of the immune system. When the fight-flight response is activated, your body produces two groups of hormones (corticoids and catecholamines), which suppress the immune system, and this suppression makes the body more susceptible to diseases, viruses, and other infections (Cohen & Williamson, 1991).

**Conclusion.** Ader and Cohen's (1975) basic research on animals' immune systems resulted in the unexpected discovery that the immune system was influenced by psychosocial factors, such as the amount of stress in one's life (Witek-Janusek & Mathews, 2000).

How psychological factors affect the immune system will become clearer as we describe a really clever experiment.

**Power Study™**

**Check out CD: Module 9**
B. Procedure: Classical
   Conditioning
H. Application: Conditioned
   Fear

## Conditioning the Immune System

**Could artificial flowers make you sneeze?**

There is an interesting story of a woman who was in therapy for having severe allergic reactions to flowers. The therapist was curious about what caused her allergic reaction. It could be caused either by organic factors, which refer to the physical properties of flowers, or by psychosomatic factors, which refer to thoughts, beliefs, or conditioned responses to flowers. To determine whether the cause was organic or psychosomatic, one day the therapist took a dozen red roses from under her desk, gave them to the woman, and asked her what the flowers reminded her of. The woman held them for a short time and then began to have allergic responses, including nasal congestion and tears. What the woman did not know was the flowers were artificial.

Why do artificial flowers make my nose run?

The woman's allergic reaction to artificial flowers clearly demonstrated that the cause of her allergy was not physical but psychosomatic (caused by the woman's own thoughts). As the woman later explained, her husband had regularly given her flowers as a sign of affection, but now that he was seeking a divorce, the flowers had become a depressing or aversive stimulus. This means that, through classical conditioning, flowers had become conditioned stimuli capable of eliciting a conditioned response, in this case an allergic reaction (classical conditioning is discussed on pages 197–199). Just to be sure, researchers designed the following experiment that left no doubt that the immune system could be classically conditioned (Maier et al., 1994).

---

### CLASSICAL CONDITIONING EXPERIMENT

If the immune system could be classically conditioned, it would clearly show the influence of psychological factors. As explained in Module 9, classical conditioning involves changing a neutral stimulus, such as a flashing light or a humming fan, into a conditioned stimulus so that it alone can elicit a conditioned response, in this case an allergic reaction in a rat. Here's how an immune response (allergic reaction) was classically conditioned in rats (MacQueen et al., 1989).

**Conditioned stimuli:** flashing light and humming fan.

**Unconditioned stimulus:** injection of a substance that produces allergy.

**Unconditioned response:** allergic reaction elicited by injected substance.

**1** For the first three trials, each rat was first presented with two conditioned (neutral) stimuli, a light flashing and a fan humming. A short time later, each rat was given an injection of an allergy-producing substance, which was the unconditioned stimulus. In turn, the unconditioned stimulus elicited an allergic reaction, which was the unconditioned response.

**2** On the fourth trial the animals were divided into two groups: control and experimental groups.
*Control group* received a trial with the regular sequence: flashing light and fan humming, then the injection of the substance, which elicited the allergic reaction.
*Experimental group* of rats received a different trial: Rats were exposed only to the conditioned stimuli of flashing light and fan humming, with no injection.

**3** The *experimental group* of animals showed a conditioned response, which means that just being given or exposed to the conditioned stimuli (flashing light and humming fan) caused the allergic reaction, which is the *conditioned response.*

**4** **Discussion.** During classical conditioning, animals or people learn that the neutral or conditioned stimulus signals or predicts what will happen next. In this study, rats learned that the flashing light and humming fan predicted an allergic reaction. And in fact, by the fourth trial, the conditioned stimuli (light and fan) alone elicited the allergic reaction—the conditioned response. Researchers concluded that the psychological factors can trigger an allergic reaction in animals (MacQueen et al., 1989).

**5** **Conclusion.** The amazing fact that immune responses can be conditioned demonstrates a method through which purely psychological or cognitive factors can affect immune function. Although the immune system was originally thought to act independently, it is now known that psychological factors influence the immune system in both animals and humans (Ader, 1999).
These findings in rats explain why the woman had an allergic reaction to artificial flowers: The artificial flowers had become conditioned stimuli that, by themselves, could elicit conditioned responses—in this case, allergic reactions of congestion and running eyes.

---

The history of psychoneuroimmunology reads like a mystery story. For 50 years, researchers had written in stone that the immune system was totally independent and only a fool would believe otherwise. In the early 1970s, Ader the psychologist and Cohen the immunologist were studying something entirely different (why animals were dying prematurely) when they discovered the reason was that the animals' immune systems had been weakened through clas-

sical conditioning (Ader & Cohen, 1975). This revolutionary finding meant the immune system could be influenced by psychological factors, and this led to the birth of a whole new field, called psychoneuroimmunology (Ader, 1999).

We have discussed how stressful experiences trigger the fight-flight response and affect the immune system. Next, we'll examine which situations are the most likely to become stressful.

### Kinds of Stressors

**What are Sandra's stressors?**
We began this module with a description of Sandra's busy day as a single mother and college student: She gets up at 6:30 A.M., wakes her two children, yells for them to get dressed, rushes to get her kids on the school bus, panics when she can't find her paper that's due today, and speeds out the door to make her first class. Every day of Sandra's life is filled with small annoyances that are called hassles, which can add up to make what she would probably call "a very bad day."

Sandra has dozens of hassles and experienced several major life changes.

Besides dealing with daily hassles, Sandra has also gone through a number of major life changes: She left her husband; quit using drugs; began group therapy; did well in a community college; and went on to Wellesley College. Unlike hassles, which seem relatively small, major life events have had a significant impact on Sandra's life and can be very big stressors.

Both hassles and major life events have the potential to become stressful experiences that influence mood and development of psychosomatic problems.

### Hassles

When someone asks, "And how was your day?" you usually reply with a list of hassles.

*Hassles* are those small, irritating, frustrating events that we face daily and that we usually appraise or interpret as stressful experiences.

Hassles are usually measured with questionnaires that ask about work, time pressures, health, friends, interpersonal relationships, and financial status (Setterlind & Larsson, 1995). Hassles are important because the score on a hassle scale is a reasonably good predictor of a person's daily mood, perceived level of stress, depression, and development of future psychosomatic symptoms (Macnee & McCabe, 2000). The opposite of a hassle is a wonderful experience called an uplift.

This man is experiencing a hassle (must work late), which puts him in a bad mood.

*Uplifts* are those small, pleasurable, happy, and satisfying experiences that we have in our daily lives.

If you were to keep a record of your daily hassles and uplifts, you would probably discover that hassles, which put you in a bad mood, may far outnumber uplifts, which put you in a good mood. One way to decrease your daily stress is to pay more attention to and enjoy the uplifts while trying to reduce hassles. In contrast to hassles, researchers have found that more daily uplifts are associated with less depression and better functioning (Macnee & McCabe, 2000).

Another source of stress is major life events.

### Major Life Events

Experiencing a major life event (getting married) can be stressful.

Not only do hassles increase stress levels and predict daily mood and health, but so too do major life events.

*Major life events* are potentially disturbing, troubling, or disruptive situations, both positive and negative, that we appraise as having a significant impact on our lives.

Researchers measure life events using the recently updated Social Readjustment Rating Scale (below), which is a shortened version of the original 44-item list (Miller & Rahe, 1997). The number after each event rates the impact that the event would have on one's life; death of one's spouse has the maximum rating (119). To obtain your score, add the numbers associated with each event you experienced in the last year. The total reflects how much life change you have experienced. Researchers predicted that experiencing an increased number of life changes would increase levels of stress and, in turn, increase chances of developing psychosomatic problems.

In the updated scale at the right, events in a six-month period that total over 300 and events in a one-year period that total over 500 indicate high recent life stress and a greatly increased risk of developing psychosomatic problems (Miller & Rahe, 1997). Researchers do report a modest correlation (+0.20 to +0.30) between number of major life events experienced and development of psychosomatic symptoms (Werner & Frost, 2000).

One problem with the Social Readjustment Rating Scale is that it makes no distinction between appraisal of positive events (getting married) and negative events (getting divorced). More recent scales found that the appraisal of negative life events was more important in predicting illnesses or depression than were positive events (Dixon & Reid, 2000). Both major life events and daily hassles are ways of assessing current level of stress, which contributes to our daily moods and chances of developing psychosomatic symptoms.

**Female–male difference.** Researchers found that females reported significantly more and intense stressful events and more symptoms of depression, anxiety, and psychosomatic problems than did males. Researchers suggest that this female–male difference may result from females being socialized to be more sensitive and responsive to stressful and emotional events, while males are socialized to just "grin and bear it" (Davis et al., 1999).

One characteristic of stressful events, such as major life events and hassles, is that they are generally frustrating experiences. We'll discuss frustration and its long-term effects.

| SOCIAL READJUSTMENT RATING SCALE | |
|---|---|
| Life event | Mean value |
| Death of spouse | 119 |
| Divorce | 98 |
| Death of close family member | 92 |
| Fired at work | 79 |
| Personal injury or illness | 77 |
| Death of a close friend | 70 |
| Pregnancy | 66 |
| Change in financial state | 56 |
| Change in work conditions | 51 |
| Marriage | 50 |
| Sex difficulties | 45 |
| Change in living conditions | 42 |
| Change in residence | 41 |
| Beginning or ending school | 38 |
| Great personal achievement | 37 |
| Change in school | 35 |
| Trouble with boss | 29 |
| Revision of personal habits | 27 |
| Change in sleeping habits | 26 |
| Vacation | 25 |
| Minor violations of the law | 22 |

## Situational Stressors

**What makes situations stressful?** We're going to examine three situations—being frustrated, feeling burned out, and experiencing interpersonal violence—that have the potential to be highly stressful. What can make these situations especially stressful is they can all elicit very negative emotions, which can greatly increase levels of stress.

### Frustration

Don Nelson (right photo), former coach of a professional basketball team, checked into a hospital complaining of exhaustion. To reduce his stress, he was forced to take a month-long vacation.

This coach shows his frustration by shouting at a player.

A Los Angeles district attorney was forced to take a break from the famous O. J. Simpson murder trial when he experienced chest pains after working many "eighteen-hour days" (Hancock et al., 1995). These examples illustrate the difficulties of having a job where success is judged by whether you win or lose, and losing can be very frustrating.

*Frustration* is the awful feeling that results when your attempts to reach some goal are blocked.

You may be blocked from reaching a goal because of *personal limitations,* such as losing your temper, making dumb mistakes on an exam, or not having the skills to pass a course. Or you may be blocked from reaching a goal because of *social* or *environmental limitations,* such as having to work eighteen-hour days. One reason frustrating situations are especially stressful is because they seem to be out of your control and they usually elicit *strong negative emotions,* such as anger or rage (Goldberger & Breznitz, 1993).

**Monday versus Friday.** One survey found that compared to Fridays, Mondays were more stressful and frustrating because of having to return to work, having too many things to do, not having enough time, and expecting but not getting as much done. The stress and frustration experienced on Mondays resulted in 33% more heart attacks than occurred on Fridays (Friend, 1994). This is a graphic example of how stress and frustration can contribute to dangerous psychosomatic problems.

If frustration lasts for a long period of time, the result can be burnout.

### Burnout

About 5 to 20% of nurses, lawyers, police officers, social workers, managers, counselors, teachers, and others whose jobs demand intense involvement with people suffer from burnout (Farber, 2000a, 2000b).

*Burnout* refers to feelings of physically wearing out and becoming emotionally exhausted due to the constant stress of working too hard or working at a monotonous job that demands too much of one's time and energy and provides too little reward or satisfaction.

Burnout is accompanied by intense feelings and negative emotions that trigger the fight-flight response, keep the body in a continual stage of heightened physiological arousal, and cause most of the psychosomatic symptoms that we have discussed: stomach disorders, frequent and prolonged colds, headaches, sleep problems, muscular pain (especially lower back and neck), and chronic fatigue (Schaufeli & Peeters, 2000).

This man feels burned out after years of working as a correctional officer.

Idealistic people, such as new teachers, who work very hard with little reward are the most susceptible to burnout, while cynical people who want to succeed at whatever cost are least likely to burn out (Farber, 2000a).

**Student burnout.** College counselors report that burnout often causes students to drop out of college before they obtain their degrees. Counselors suggest that before students decide to drop out they should consider ways to reduce their work and class load so that life and school seem less overwhelming and more manageable (Leafgren, 1989).

The next situation is so stressful that it leaves a terrible, lasting mark that may trigger years of problems.

### Interpersonal Violence

The one situation that can produce horrible psychological aftereffects and nightmares involves experiencing interpersonal violence and can result in posttraumatic stress disorder.

*Posttraumatic stress disorder,* or *PTSD,* is a disabling condition that results from personally experiencing an event that involves actual or threatened death or serious injury or from witnessing such an event or hearing of such an event happening to a family member or close friend. People suffering from PTSD experience a number of psychological symptoms, including recurring and disturbing memories, terrible nightmares, and intense fear and anxiety (American Psychiatric Association, 2000).

For example, about 32% of women report having PTSD after being raped; about 15% of soldiers report having PTSD after serving in war; and about 15% of people report having PTSD after being in a natural disaster or serious car accident (Hidalgo & Davidson, 2000). These horrible memories and feelings of fear keep stress levels high and result in a wide range of psychosomatic symptoms, including sleep problems, pounding heart, high blood pressure, and stomach problems (Murberg, 1994).

**Treatment.** The treatment of posttraumatic stress disorder usually involves a form of cognitive-behavior therapy (p. 568), which provides emotional support so victims can begin the healing process, helps to slowly eliminate the horrible memories by bringing out the

About 15% of soldiers returning from wars report having PTSD.

details of the experience, and gradually replaces the feeling of fear with a sense of courage to go on with one's life (Foa, 2000).

We'll examine two more situations with high potential for stress because they involve conflict or anxiety.

## Conflict

**Why are decisions so hard to make?**

Sometimes situations can be stressful because they involve making difficult decisions. For example, what decisions would you make in the following situations?

- You can either go to a great party or see a good friend who is visiting town for just one day.
- You can study for a psychology exam or write a paper for a history class.
- You can ask a new acquaintance to have lunch, but then you risk being rejected.

In making these kinds of decisions you are most likely to feel stressed because they each involve facing a different kind of conflict.

*Conflict* is the feeling you experience when you must choose between two or more incompatible possibilities or options.

The reason the situations above put you in conflict is that, no matter which option you choose, you must give up something you want to get or want to avoid. We'll describe three common kinds of conflicts: approach-approach, avoidance-avoidance, and approach-avoidance.

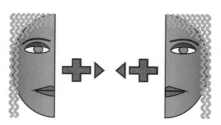

**Approach-approach.** Deciding between going to a party or seeing a friend involves choosing between two pleasurable options.

*Approach-approach conflict* involves choosing between two situations that both have pleasurable consequences.

At first it seems that approach-approach conflicts are the least stressful of the three kinds because, whichever option you choose, you will experience a pleasurable consequence. But on second thought, approach-approach conflicts can be the most stressful because you must give up one of the very pleasurable consequences. The result is that you will feel considerably stressed as you agonize over which one of the two great possibilities to give up.

**Avoidance-avoidance.** Deciding between studying for a psychology exam or writing a paper for a history class involves choosing between two undesirable options.

*Avoidance-avoidance conflict* involves choosing between two situations that both have disagreeable consequences.

In an avoidance-avoidance conflict, you may change your mind many times and wait until the last possible minute before making the final decision. You delay choosing as long as possible in trying to avoid the disagreeable or unpleasant outcome.

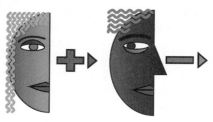

**Approach-avoidance.** Deciding between asking a new acquaintance to lunch and being afraid of being rejected involves a single situation that has both desirable and undesirable possibilities.

*Approach-avoidance conflict* involves a single situation that has both pleasurable and disagreeable aspects.

In this example, asking the person to lunch would make you feel good, but at the same time, being rejected is something you want to avoid because it makes you feel bad. Our lives are full of approach-avoidance conflicts, and trying to decide what to do about them can turn into very stressful experiences.

### Five Styles of Dealing with Conflict

Researchers have identified five different styles of dealing with conflict, one of which may be similar to yours and one of which is better than the rest (Sternberg & Soriano, 1984).

**1. Avoidance.** These individuals find dealing with conflicts unpleasant. They hope that by avoiding or ignoring the conflict it will disappear or magically go away. Sadly, the conflict usually gets worse and will have to be dealt with eventually.

**2. Accommodation.** These individuals also hate conflicts and just give in to make the disagreement go away. They tend to please people and worry about approval. Unfortunately, giving in does not solve the problem, which in the long term will need to be solved.

**3. Domination.** In conflicts, these individuals go to any lengths to win, even if it means being aggressive and manipulative. However, aggressively solving conflicts results in hostility rather than intimate human relationships.

What is the best way to settle conflicts?

**4. Compromise.** These individuals recognize that others have different needs and try to solve conflicts through compromise. Unfortunately, they may use manipulation and misrepresentation to further their own goals, so compromise isn't always the best solution.

**5. Integration.** These individuals try to resolve conflicts by finding solutions to please both partners. They don't criticize the other person, they try to be open, and they emphasize similarities rather than differences.

Perhaps the best way to resolve relationship conflicts is to try to be as much of an integrator as possible because this style avoids criticism and has the best chance of pleasing both individuals (Williams & Knight, 1994).

Situations involving conflict can be very stressful because you must often make undesirable choices. The next situations are stressful because they involve anxiety.

**Power Study™**

**Check out CD: Module 9**
B. Procedure: Classical Conditioning
H. Application: Conditioned Fear

**Check out CD: Module 10**
E. Cognitive Learning
I. Application: Behavior Modification

# Anxiety

This module began with two stories that involved anxiety. One story was about my intense personal fear and anxiety over giving blood. The other was about Sandra's fear and anxiety over whether she had the brains and motivation to compete with all the excellent students who attend Wellesley College. Like my and Sandra's experiences, everyone at some time will feel the terrible grip of anxiety.

*Anxiety* is an unpleasant state characterized by feelings of uneasiness and apprehension as well as increased physiological arousal, such as increased heart rate and blood pressure.

There are three ways of developing anxiety: classical conditioning, observational learning, and unconscious conflict.

## Classical Conditioning

My fear of blood comes from a traumatic childhood incident: I had seen my father almost cut off his thumb. For me and about 76% of people surveyed, fear of blood began with a traumatic event that involved classical conditioning (Kleinknecht, 1994). In my case, the neutral stimulus was the sight of blood. It was paired with an unconditioned stimulus—seeing my father almost cut off his thumb—which caused an unconditioned response—anxiety, fear, and the fight-flight response. After this single pairing, the sight of blood became the conditioned stimulus, which now elicits the unconditioned response—great anxiety. My fear of blood is an example of a conditioned emotional response.

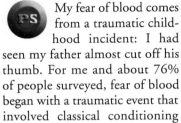

I developed anxiety through classical conditioning.

A *conditioned emotional response* results when an emotional response, such as fear or anxiety, is classically conditioned to a previously neutral stimulus.

A conditioned emotional response is not only highly resistant to extinction but can also cause very stressful feelings (p. 201).

## Observational Learning

One way that Sandra developed anxiety about being at Wellesley College was through observational learning on campus and in the classroom.

*Observational learning,* which is a form of cognitive learning, results from watching and modeling and does not require the observer to perform any observable behavior or receive a reinforcer.

In Sandra's case, her observations of younger and seemingly better prepared students made her feel anxious about being able to compete academically and socially. Her initial anxiety decreased somewhat as she earned good grades and made friends. Albert Bandura (1999) believes that the majority of human learning, including feeling anxious in the classroom, occurs through observational learning (p. 225). However, having to compete will no doubt continue to make Sandra feel anxious, which in turn will keep her stress level high.

Sandra developed anxiety from observing competing students.

## Unconscious Conflict

Sigmund Freud suggested a cause of anxiety that is very different from classical conditioning or observational learning. Freud hypothesized that there are three divisions of the mind—id, ego, and superego—that at times may be in conflict over how a need should be satisfied (p. 436). This internal, unconscious conflict may result in feeling anxiety.

*Anxiety,* according to Freud, arises when there is an unconscious conflict between the id's and superego's desires regarding how to satisfy a need, with the ego caught in the middle. The ego's solution to this conflict is to create a feeling of anxiety.

According to Freud, we may try to decrease our anxiety by using a number of *defense mechanisms*, which are discussed below.

Depending on whether anxiety occurs because of classical conditioning (conditioned emotional responses), through observational learning, or from unconscious conflicts between the id and superego, there are several different ways to cope with anxiety.

## Coping with Anxiety

We would use different methods to cope with anxiety, depending on whether it developed through classical conditioning, observational learning, or unconscious conflicts.

**Extinction.** If our anxious feelings were learned through classical conditioning or observational learning, we could use a number of extinction techniques discussed earlier (pp. 207, 233). As a quick review, these extinction methods include systematic desensitization and behavior modification, which are ways to unlearn responses. All extinction procedures involve actively working to change certain thoughts, behaviors, or physiological responses associated with our anxious feelings. These procedures might be characterized as *problem-focused, conscious coping techniques,* since they represent active attempts by us to deal with the problem itself.

**Freudian defense mechanisms.** In comparison to extinction procedures, which constitute conscious, problem-focused coping, Freud's defense mechanisms represent *emotion-focused, unconscious coping techniques.* Defense mechanisms are unconscious, emotion-focused coping techniques because they try to manage a person's emotions rather than resolving the problem that is causing the anxiety. As you may remember, defense mechanisms are processes that operate at unconscious levels to help the ego reduce anxiety through various forms of self-deception, such as denial, repression, projection, and rationalization (p. 437).

According to Freud, the occasional use of defense mechanisms is normal and helps reduce anxiety so that we can continue to function as we work on the real causes of our problems. However, the overuse of defense mechanisms may prevent us from recognizing or working on the real causes of our anxiety (Cramer, 2000).

Next, we'll examine how different kinds of personality variables can help or hinder our coping with anxiety and stress.

## Hardiness

**How can he work 12 hours a day, every day?**

The door opens. Dr. Michael DeBakey enters and walks quickly to the operating table. His assistants have already opened the patient's chest and removed the diseased heart. With the skill and precision of a master, DeBakey (right photo) transplants a healthy donor heart into the patient's chest. It takes about an hour. When DeBakey finishes, he leaves the operating suite and goes to the scrub room. He takes off his operating clothes, scrubs down, and puts on clean, sterilized clothes. In a matter of minutes, he enters another operating suite, and the whole process starts over. In a normal working day, DeBakey operates on five to nine patients. He normally spends 12–15 hours a day, seven days a week, in the hospital and performs as many heart operations in one month as most surgeons do in a year. There is one more thing you should know about DeBakey. He is over 90 years old (Sternberg, 1998).

How can Dr. DeBakey, at age 90, work 12-hour days in extremely stressful conditions?

**Appraisal.** There are two primary reasons Dr. Michael DeBakey functions so successfully in such a potentially stressful environment. The first is that he appraises these situations—doing complicated heart transplants—as challenges rather than as threats. The advantage of *challenge appraisals* is that they help a person focus on making particular decisions or solving particular problems. In turn, problem-focused coping brings out positive feelings and emotions, such as excitement and eagerness, which help reduce stress levels. In contrast, *threat appraisals* elicit negative emotional feelings, such as fear or anxiety, which raise levels of stress. Because emotion-focused coping is directed at managing negative emotional feelings, the person isn't motivated to solve his or her problem.

**Personality.** A second reason DeBakey functions so well is that he has a winning combination of personality factors that help him perform under great stress. He has what is known as a hardy personality.

### Definition

Why is it that certain people, like Dr. DeBakey, seem to handle stressful situations better than others? This was exactly the question researchers asked as they studied the personality characteristics of middle- and upper-level executives and lawyers who had experienced considerable stress in the previous three years (Kobasa, 1982; Kobasa et al., 1982a, 1982b). Researchers discovered that those executives and lawyers who stayed healthy in spite of stressful life situations had three personality traits, which, taken together, were labeled hardiness.

*Hardiness* is a combination of three personality traits—control, commitment, and challenge—that protect or buffer us from the potentially harmful effects of stressful situations and reduce our chances of developing psychosomatic illnesses.

From what we know of Dr. DeBakey, he appears to be the perfect example of a hardy person who has the three Cs—control, commitment, and challenge. For example, his worldwide medical reputation shows he has *commitment,* which means he knows and pursues his goals and values. His desire to do open-heart surgery shows he likes a *challenge,* which means he actively confronts and solves problem situations. His role as head of surgery indicates his desire to be in *control,* which means he believes that his actions directly affect how situations turn out.

Being hardy gives people a real edge in dealing with potentially stressful situations.

### Function

What would happen to your heart rate if you were told that you had to listen to a 4-minute lecture and then repeat the lecture as best you could to two professors, who would grade the accuracy of your performance?

This is exactly what male college students were told while their heart rates were being recorded. Researchers predicted that hardy students (those who scored higher in control, commitment, and challenge) would appraise this situation as more challenging and less threatening than would students who were less hardy.

In the graph on the right, notice that both low and high hardy subjects had similar heart rates during rest. (Heart rate changes are good indicators of physiological arousal and stress levels.) However, as soon as students were put into a potentially stressful situation (told about repeating a lecture), low hardy subjects' heart rates shot up significantly higher than did those of high hardy subjects. And low hardy subjects' heart rates remained higher after the stressor, while high hardy subjects calmed down more. These data indicate that high hardy subjects had the cognitive and personality traits that allowed them to appraise the potentially stressful task as more challenging and less threatening (Wiebe, 1991).

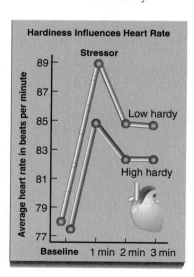

**Hardiness Influences Heart Rate**

*Average heart rate in beats per minute*

- Stressor
- 89
- 87
- 85 — Low hardy
- 83 — High hardy
- 81
- 79
- 77
- Baseline  1 min  2 min  3 min

Generally, hardiness is a personality factor that functions to decrease the chances of developing psychosomatic symptoms and to increase protection against the harmful and physiologically arousing effects of stress (Ford-Gilboe & Cohen, 2000).

Researchers have especially studied control, one of the three traits composing hardiness, because feelings of being in control reduce stressful feelings.

## Locus of Control

**Why can waiting be such a hassle?**

A daily hassle that most of us hate is being made to wait for something or somebody, such as a doctor's appointment, red light, friend, or bus. One reason we find waiting so stressful is that we have little or no control in this situation. How much control you feel you have over a situation is a personal belief that is called locus of control.

*Locus of control* represents a continuum: At one end is the belief that you are basically in control of life's events and that what you do influences the situation; this belief is called an internal locus of control. At the other end is the belief that chance and luck mostly determine what happens and that you do not have much influence; this belief is called an external locus of control.

Most of us lie somewhere along the locus of control continuum, rather than being at one end or the other (Carducci, 1998). For example, when students discuss how much their studying affects their grades, they are, to a large extent, talking about their locus of control, which in turn affects their stress level.

> What's the use of studying when I do poorly on exams?

**External locus of control.** "No matter how much I study, it never seems to help," says a student with an external locus of control. This student will likely appraise exams and papers as less of a challenge and more of a threat, which in turn will generate negative emotions (fear, anxiety, anger) and increase stress levels.

**Internal locus of control.** "If I study hard and apply myself, I can get good grades," says a student with an internal locus of control. This student will likely appraise exams and papers less as threats and more as challenges, which in turn will generate positive emotions (excitement, enthusiasm) and decrease stress levels. This means that students with internal locus of control have lower levels of stress and, as a result, report fewer psychosomatic symptoms than those with external locus of control (Ruiz-Bueno, 2000).

An example of how locus of control relates to psychosomatic symptoms is shown on the right. In this study, subjects with an external locus of control perceived situations as uncontrollable, which

| Illness Score | |
|---|---|
| 1,100 | High controllability |
| Low controllability | 1,850 |

led to increased levels of stress that were associated with significantly more psychosomatic symptoms (they developed more physical illnesses). In comparison, subjects with an internal locus of control appraised situations as less stressful and developed fewer psychosomatic symptoms (Stern et al., 1982).

From many studies on locus of control, we learn that our personality traits influence our appraisal (more or less challenging or threatening), which, in turn, increases or decreases our feelings of stress and our chances of developing psychosomatic symptoms.

Another personality trait that can influence stress levels is how pessimistic or optimistic we generally are.

## Optimism versus Pessimism

**Why is it better to be an optimist?**

If you want to experience more positive than negative emotions and reduce your levels of stress, try being more optimistic.

*Optimism* is a relatively stable personality trait that leads to believing and expecting that good things will happen. *Pessimism* is a relatively stable personality trait that leads to believing and expecting that bad things will happen.

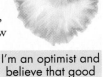

**Optimists.** One way optimists reduce their levels of stress is by focusing on the good things that are happening or have happen, a process called *positive reappraisal.* Forms of positive reappraisal include discovering new opportunities for personal growth, noticing actual personal growth, or seeing how your actions can benefit others. By using positive reappraisal, you can change the meaning or appraisal of situations into seeming more positive and thus feel positive emotions (Folkman & Moskowitz, 2000). Researchers have

I'm an optimist and believe that good things will happen.

generally found that optimists experienced more positive emotions and reported lower stress levels and decreased psychosomatic symptoms (Taylor et al., 2000a).

**Pessimists.** Because pessimists expect bad things to happen, they are likely to change the meaning or appraisal of situations into seeming more negative and thus experience more negative emotions, such as anger, hostility, rage, fear, or anxiety, and are less able to ask for or receive social support.

For example, researchers found that men with high levels of negative emotions, such as anger, were four times more likely to suffer sudden heart death. Patients were more likely to die during the next eight months if they had a pessimistic attitude toward treatment and recovery from cancer (Kawachi et al., 1994; Schulz, 1994). In comparison, optimistic patients who received heart transplants reported more positive emotions and dealt better with setbacks than patients with a pessimistic outlook (Leedham et al., 1995).

I'm a pessimist and believe that bad things will happen.

Numerous studies associate pessimism and negative emotions with increasing stress levels, decreasing functioning of the immune system, and experiencing a wide range of psychosomatic symptoms such as high blood pressure, heart problems, headaches, allergies, and stomach problems (Vahtera et al., 2000).

**Personality factors.** During the past 10 years, a number of personality factors, such as optimism/pessimism, locus of control, and hardiness, have been associated with feeling more or less positive or negative emotions, which in turn are involved in increasing or decreasing stress levels and increasing or decreasing chances of developing psychosomatic symptoms (Salovey et al., 2000).

Next, we'll examine one particular combination of personality traits that has been labeled Type A behavior, which has been associated with increasing the chances of having a heart attack.

### Type A Behavior

In the mid-1970s, a new expression—"You're a Type A person"—was coined when two doctors published the book *Type A Behavior and Your Heart* (Friedman & Rosenman, 1974). At that time, the best-known risk factors associated with developing heart disease were diet, exercise, and smoking. This book startled the medical world by describing a combination of personality traits that made up a psychological risk factor, which was called Type A behavior. No one had ever before suggested that any psychological factor could possibly influence getting heart disease. However, after 30 years of study, you'll see that researchers have been changing their definition of what makes up a Type A behavior.

## *1970s:* *Type A Behavior—Impatient, Hostile, Workaholic*

Impatient, hostile, and workaholic

We'll begin with the original 1970s definition of Type A behavior (Friedman & Rosenman, 1974).

*Type A behavior* referred to a combination of personality traits that included an overly competitive and aggressive drive to achieve, a hostile attitude when frustrated, a habitual sense of time urgency, a rapid and explosive pattern of speaking, and being a workaholic. *Type B behavior* was characterized by being easygoing, calm, relaxed, and patient.

The reason Type A behavior made such a big scientific splash was that compared to Type B's, Type A's were found to have experienced two to three times as many heart attacks. By 1978, Type A behavior was officially recognized as an independent risk factor for heart disease by a National Institutes of Health panel.

However, at about the same time that Type A behavior was declared a risk factor, researchers began having trouble replicating earlier findings and began to seriously question the definition of Type A behavior.

## *1980s:* *Type A Behavior—Depressed, Angry, Competitive*

Depressed, angry, and competitive

In the late 1970s and throughout most of the 1980s, researchers ran into a number of problems with the original description of Type A behavior. In particular, a number of large-scale studies failed to replicate the earlier and revolutionary finding that Type A behavior was a risk factor for the onset of heart disease. Researchers thought the reason for this failure was that the original definition of Type A behavior wasn't quite accurate.

The 1970s definition of Type A behavior included being hurried, impatient, and a workaholic, but researchers found that coronary disease was not associated with being impatient or a workaholic, so both traits were dropped from the new definition (Booth-Kewley & Friedman, 1987; Matthews & Haynes, 1986).

*Type A behavior* was defined in the 1980s as being depressed, aggressively competitive, easily frustrated, anxious, and angry, or some combination of these traits.

Despite using this new and improved definition, researchers analyzed 83 relevant studies but reported only a modest association between Type A behavior and heart disease (Booth-Kewley & Friedman, 1987). These data again raised the question of whether Type A behavior is a risk factor for coronary heart disease (Miller et al., 1991). And that brings us to the 1990s.

## *1990s:* *Type A Behavior—Hostile, Angry*

Prolonged hostility

A review of about 100 relevant Type A behavior studies between 1983 and 1992 led one researcher to conclude that the relationship between Type A behavior and cardiac disease is so low as to have no practical meaning and that Type A behavior is no longer a valid or useful concept (Myrtek, 1995). Because of the continuing failure to replicate the original relationship, researchers have again redefined Type A behavior.

The 1990s definition of *Type A behavior* specifies an individual who feels angry and hostile much of the time but may or may not express these emotions publicly.

This definition made prolonged hostility (felt or expressed) the major component of Type A behavior (Leventhal & Patrick-Miller, 2000). In support of this definition, researchers found that behavioral ratings for hostility were reasonably good predictors of heart disease (Friedman et al., 1994).

## *2000s:* *Type A Behavior—Hostile, Depressed*

Hostile plus depressed?

Although some researchers have found a relationship between Type A behavior—defined as hostility/anger—and heart disease, others have not (Friedman et al., 1994). For example, recent research reported that hostility alone did not predict heart disease but that hostility plus a tendency to depression was predictive (Ravaja et al., 2000). At this point, researchers are working on solving two problems. The first is developing a more reliable method to define and measure hostility, which seems to combine a number of different emotions (anger, rage). The second is explaining why high levels of hostility predict heart disease in men but do not predict heart disease in women (Ravaja et al., 2000). Researchers hope that a better definition of hostility will result in a better definition of Type A behavior (Donker et al., 2000).

Research on Type A behavior was the first to recognize personality factors as risk factors for diseases. Now researchers are also looking at how various social factors increase or decrease the effects of stressful experiences.

**Do friends help you deal with stress?**

We have told you how important findings are often discovered by chance. Here's a "chance" finding that began a new area of research.

In the small town of Roseto, Pennsylvania, people were relatively obese and ate a lot of animal fat. They smoked as much and exercised as little as residents of other neighboring towns. Despite the citizens' awful diet and lifestyle—obvious risk factors for developing heart disease—only one man in 1,000 died of a heart attack, compared with a national rate of 3.5 per 1,000, and the rates for women were even lower. Citizens of Roseto also had lower rates for ulcers and emotional problems compared with rates in the rest of the United States and their neighboring towns.

This puzzling question—why the citizens of Roseto should enjoy such good physical and mental health in the face of obvious risk factors—was answered by a study of the town's social order. "One striking feature did set Roseto apart from its neighbors," says Stewart Wolf, vice president for medical affairs at St. Luke's Hospital in Bethlehem, Pennsylvania, and a principal investigator of the Roseto phenomenon. "We found that family relationships were extremely close and mutually supportive, and this wonderful social support system extended to neighbors and to the community as a whole" (Greenberg, 1978, p. 378). But the story of Roseto does not have a happy ending.

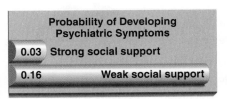

We're always helping one another.

Social support reduces stress.

As families of Roseto prospered, they moved into larger and finer homes in the countryside, and their social support system began to break down. Families no longer had helpful friends for neighbors, which meant fewer family and friendly get-togethers and far less social support. One of the most interesting and deadly findings was that with the breakdown in social support came an increase in heart attacks, especially in younger men. This study on families in Roseto was one of the first to suggest that dealing with stress and overcoming health risks were in large part aided by one's social support.

*Social support* refers to three factors: having a group or network of family or friends who provide strong social attachments; being able to exchange helpful resources among family or friends; and feeling, or making appraisals, that we have supportive relationships and behaviors.

Thirty years ago, no one would have thought that loneliness and lack of social support were major factors that contributed to becoming ill and developing psychosomatic symptoms. Today, social support is reported to be one of the most important coping methods that individuals use to decrease the effects of stressful situations and cope with psychosomatic problems (Underwood, 2000). We'll discuss several studies that illustrate how social support buffers us from stress and helps maintain our mental health.

## *Buffer Against Stress*

Many of us have asked for help in solving a variety of problems, which range from feeling lonely to needing to borrow money. In these troublesome situations, social support helps us cope with stress by giving us confidence, raising our self-esteem, and increasing our feelings of self-worth, which in turn promote and maintain psychological adjustment.

For example, many of you have experienced the common psychosomatic symptom of a pounding heart while having to speak in public. Researchers wondered if the presence of a supportive person would buffer or decrease the stressful experience of college students who were asked to do public speaking. Changes in stress levels were assessed by measuring changes in blood pressure, which increases dramatically during the fight-flight response that is triggered by stressful situations.

The graph below shows that students speaking in public

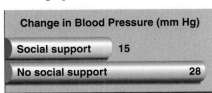

**Change in Blood Pressure (mm Hg)**

| Social support | 15 |
| No social support | 28 |

with no supportive person present had almost double the increase in blood pressure compared to that of students who spoke in public with a supportive person present (Lepore et al., 1993). From this and similar studies, researchers concluded that social support, such as the help, advice, sympathy, and reassurance from family or friends, can decrease effects of stressful experiences (Underwood, 2000).

## *Maintaining Mental Health*

One reason we tell a friend or family member about how our day went and the problems we had is that the telling elicits support and sympathy, which make us feel better (Kowalski, 1996). Besides making us feel better, researchers wondered if social support would also help prevent individuals who already had mild psychiatric symptoms, such as anxiety or depression, from getting worse. In a 10-year study, researchers interviewed the same individuals several times to see how social support affected levels of anxiety or depression.

The graph below shows that individuals with strong social support had a low chance of worsening psychiatric symptoms even if they had faced

**Probability of Developing Psychiatric Symptoms**

| 0.03 | Strong social support |
| 0.16 | Weak social support |

two to six stressful life events in the previous year. In comparison, individuals with a weak social support system had a significantly greater chance of worsening anxiety or depression.

Researchers concluded that a good social support system, such as having one or more close friends or neighbors, decreases the effects of stressful life events, prevents the worsening of anxiety and depression, and thus helps maintain a person's mental health (Dalgard et al., 1995).

These kinds of studies indicate that, in a very real sense, a good social support system facilitates our maintaining good mental health and protects us from developing illnesses and psychosomatic symptoms (Underwood, 2000). One of the important functions of a good social support system is to help us develop ways of coping with stress, which we'll discuss after the Concept Review.

# Concept Review

**1.** The cognitive and behavioral efforts that we use to manage a situation that we have appraised as exceeding, straining, or taxing our personal resources are referred to as _____.

**2.** Our initial, subjective evaluation of a situation, in which we balance environmental demands against our ability to meet them, is referred to as _____. We may appraise the situation in three ways: as irrelevant, positive, or stressful.

**3.** If we appraise a situation as stressful, we go on to determine whether it represents (a)_____, _____, or _____. If our primary appraisal is one of harm/loss or threat, we will experience more (b)_____ than if our appraisal is one of challenge, because harm/loss or threat appraisals elicit (c)_____ emotions.

**4.** A combination of physiological responses that arouse and prepare the body for action is referred to as the (a)_____ response. This response begins in a part of the brain called the (b)_____, which triggers the (c)_____ division of the autonomic nervous system. This response is especially triggered by threat appraisals.

**5.** Real and painful physical symptoms that are caused by psychological factors, such as our reactions to stress, are called _____ symptoms.

**6.** A series of three stages—alarm, resistance, and exhaustion—that the body goes through in dealing with stress is referred to as the (a)_____. The alarm stage is our initial reaction to stress and is marked by activation of the (b)_____. The resistance stage is the body's reaction to continued stress and is marked by most physiological responses returning to (c)_____ levels. The exhaustion stage is the body's reaction to long-term, continuous stress and is marked by the actual breakdown or weakening of (d)_____.

**7.** The body's defense and surveillance network of cells and chemicals that fight off bacteria, viruses, and other foreign matter is called the _____ system.

**8.** The study of how three factors—the central nervous system, the endocrine system, and psychosocial factors—interact to affect the immune system is called _____.

**9.** Potentially disturbing, troubling, or disruptive situations—both positive and negative—that we appraise as having considerable impact on our lives are called (a)_____ events. In comparison, those small, irritating, frustrating events that we face in our daily lives are called (b)_____ and those small, pleasurable, daily experiences that make us feel happy are called (c)_____.

**10.** When our attempts to reach some goal are blocked, the feeling we have is called (a)_____. The feeling of doing poorly at one's job, physically wearing out, and becoming emotionally exhausted due to intense involvement with people is called (b)_____. The problem arising from direct personal experience of an event that involves actual or threatened death or serious injury or from witnessing such an event or hearing of such an event happening to a family member or close friend is called (c)_____.

**11.** There are three general kinds of conflict. A single situation that has both pleasurable and disagreeable aspects is called (a)_____ conflict; choosing between two options that both have pleasurable consequences is called (b)_____ conflict; choosing between two options that both have disagreeable consequences is called (c)_____ conflict.

**12.** We can become anxious in at least three different ways. If an emotional response is classically conditioned to a previously neutral stimulus, this procedure results in a (a)_____ response. If we become anxious through watching and do not perform any observable behavior or receive a reinforcer, this is called (b)_____ learning. If we become anxious because of unconscious conflicts between the id and the superego, this is (c)_____ explanation of anxiety.

**13.** A combination of three personality traits—control, commitment, and challenge—that protect or buffer us from the potentially harmful effects of stressful situations and reduce our chances of developing psychosomatic illness is referred to as (a)_____. The belief that you are basically in control of life's events and that what you do influences the situation is called an (b)_____ locus of control. The belief that chance and luck mostly determine what happens is called an (c)_____ locus of control.

**14.** If we have family or friends who provide strong social attachments, if we can exchange helpful resources among friends, and if we appraise our relationships as supportive, we would be said to have strong _____.

*Answers:* 1. stress or stressful; 2. primary appraisal; 3. (a) harm/loss, threat, challenge, (b) stress, (c) negative; 4. (a) fight-flight, (b) hypothalamus, (c) sympathetic; 5. psychosomatic; 6. (a) general adaptation syndrome, (b) fight-flight response, (c) normal, (d) internal organs or the immune system; 7. immune; 8. psychoneuroimmunology; 9. (a) major life, (b) hassles, (c) uplifts; 10. (a) frustration, (b) burnout, (c) posttraumatic stress disorder; 11. (a) approach-avoidance, (b) approach-approach, (c) avoidance-avoidance; 12. (a) conditioned emotional, (b) observational, (c) Freud's; 13. (a) hardiness, (b) internal, (c) external; 14. social support

## Appraisal

**Why is arguing stressful?**

Sooner or later, every couple gets into an argument. For example, Susan complained about Bill always getting home late, but Bill was angry from having a bad day and said that he didn't want to talk about it (photo at left). Bill's reply made Susan angrier, and she made a few more complaints that made Bill mad.

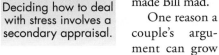

Deciding how to deal with stress involves a secondary appraisal.

One reason a couple's argument can grow into a very stressful situation is that arguing causes feelings of conflict and frustration, elicits negative emotional feelings (anger, fear, rage, hurt, depression), and activates the fight-flight response, which increases physiological arousal and intensifies negative feelings. One reason Bill and Susan's argument quickly grew in intensity was that Bill's *primary appraisal* of Susan's complaints was that of threat. Bill's primary appraisal that Susan's complaints were threatening triggered negative emotions, increased his stress, and left him deciding what to do next, which is called secondary appraisal (Lazarus, 2000).

*Secondary appraisal* involves deciding to deal with a potentially stressful situation by using one or both of two different coping patterns: problem-focused coping means doing something about the problem, while emotion-focused coping means dealing with our emotions.

Which coping strategy Bill and Susan adopt during their argument—that is, whether they use problem-focused or emotion-focused coping—will affect how their argument gets resolved and what happens to their levels of stress.

We'll discuss how each coping strategy—problem-focused or emotion-focused coping—has both short- and long-term disadvantages and advantages.

## Kinds of Coping

**How to cope with arguing?**

During their argument, Susan and Bill each make a secondary appraisal, sometimes out of habit and without thinking, about dealing with this potentially stressful situation by choosing one of two coping strategies, either problem-focused or emotion-focused coping. If Bill or Susan focused on trying to change the situation and stop arguing, he or she would be using problem-focused coping.

*Problem-focused coping* means we solve the problem by seeking information, changing our own behavior, or taking whatever action is necessary.

For example, if Bill agreed to find ways to avoid being late, he would be using problem-focused coping. If Susan agreed to interpret Bill's being late as something he cannot always control and something she should not get angry about, she would be using problem-focused coping.

However, if they don't use problem-focused coping, whose goal is to solve the problem and reduce stress, they are likely to continue arguing and to get angrier and to use emotion-focused coping.

*Emotion-focused coping* means that we do things primarily to deal with our emotional distress, such as seeking support and sympathy or avoiding or denying the situation.

For example, Bill may use emotion-focused coping to deal with his anger by going to a sports bar to drink and watch television. Susan may use emotion-focused coping to deal with her hurt feelings by calling her friends to get sympathy and support. Emotion-focused coping is a short-term coping strategy to help Bill and Susan deal with negative emotions but does not solve the basic problems that are causing their stressful feelings (Lazarus, 2000). In contrast, problem-focused coping is a long-term coping strategy to identify and solve whatever problems are causing stressful situations and negative emotional feelings.

**Emotion-focused**

**Stress**

**Problem-focused**

These are two kinds of coping strategies.

## Choosing a Coping Strategy

**Which coping is best?**

Suppose you're in a relationship and your partner complains about something you do. Which coping strategy you choose depends partly on the situation and on your personality (Lazarus, 2000).

One *personality factor* that influences whether you use primarily problem-focused or emotion-focused coping is how much *control* you believe you have over the situation. For example, if you appraise a situation such as being late as something under your control, you can use primarily problem-focused coping to deal with the situation. On the other hand, if you appraise a situation such as dealing with your partner's complaints as being out of your control, you may first need to use primarily emotion-focused coping to manage your negative emotional state. Once you calm down, you can use problem-focused coping to take some direct action to solve the basic problem, which often involves changing some undesirable behavior.

The more frustrating a situation is, the more likely you will need to use both emotion-focused and problem-focused coping (Lazarus, 2000). For example, in dealing with the breakup of a relationship, you may need to use emotion-focused coping to deal with your hurt feelings and problem-focused coping to keep your life going and decide on how to meet someone new. Similarly, in dealing with finals, you may need to use emotion-focused coping to deal with test anxiety and problem-focused coping to arrange time for studying.

One of the biggest mistakes we often make when coping with a stressful situation is that we use primarily emotion-focused coping, which is usually a *short-term solution*, to cope with our negative emotional feelings. However, to identify the cause of a stressful problem, we need to use problem-focused coping, which is a long-term solution that involves changing our behaviors (Lazarus, 2000).

A common mistake is to use only emotion-focused coping.

## How Do People Cope with Severe Burns?

We have discussed stress and coping in general, and now we turn to the specific case of Harold Dennis. It was late at night, and Harold had fallen asleep in the school bus, which was returning from a trip to an amusement park. Out of nowhere came a pickup truck, traveling the wrong way on the freeway, and it drove head-on into the bus. Later, it was found that the truck driver was drunk. The bus burst into flames, and before Harold could be pulled out the back, he suffered severe burns to his face. At the young age of 13, Harold would need to cope with terrible pain, multiple surgeries, and, worst of all, the sight of his disfigured face in a mirror (photo below) (Fisher, 1995). One reason psychologists study burn victims such as Harold is to discover how they cope with traumatic and chronic stress.

## 1 Research Methods

In Module 2, we discussed several ways psychologists answer questions, including experiments and case studies, each of which has advantages and disadvantages.

An *experiment* is a method for identifying cause-and-effect relationships by following a set of guidelines that describe how to control, manipulate, and measure variables, while at the same time minimizing the possibility of error and bias.

Although experiments permit great control over manipulating treatments and measuring subjects' responses, it would be unethical to inflict burns on individuals to study how they cope. This brings us to situations that result from accidents, natural disasters, or cruel fate, and involve the use of a case study.

How did Harold cope with a face so badly burned that he could not speak?

A *case study* is more of an in-depth analysis of the thoughts, feelings, beliefs, or behaviors of individuals without much ability to control or manipulate situations or variables.

For example, much of the initial information on how the brain functions came from case studies on individuals who had tumors, gunshot wounds, or accidental damage. Similarly, psychologists learn much about how people cope with traumatic events by observing the recovery and adjustment of burn victims. A case study approach would involve observing, questioning, and perhaps administering various personality tests to burn victims, such as Harold, to identify how they cope and adjust to their condition.

## 2 Coping with Initial Stressful Effects

Harold's face was so badly burned that he could not speak and had to communicate by writing notes. Harold kept asking for a mirror to see how he looked, but doctors had told the nurses not to give him one. A new nurse, who had not heard the doctors' orders, gave Harold a mirror, and when he looked at his terribly disfigured face, he began to scream. When his mother explained to Harold that 27 children had died in the bus crash and how lucky Harold was just to be alive, he got the courage to go on. Over the weeks and months following injury, burn patients undergo painful changes of their dressings, plastic surgery, skin grafting, and rehabilitation. Each of these procedures is stressful and elicits a variety of emotional reactions, the most common of which are confusion, anxiety, and depression. In dealing with these emotional reactions, burn victims use a number of emotion-focused coping strategies, which include complaining ("Why me?"), denying the severity of the problem (being too cheerful), rationalizing ("I'm being punished"), and trying to have a positive outlook (looking on the bright side) (Patterson et al., 1993). One emotion-focused coping strategy that Harold used to deal with his disfigured face was "I'm just lucky to be alive."

## 3 Coping with Long-Term Stressful Effects

About five months after his face was severely burned, Harold started high school. He constantly worried how fellow students, especially girls, would react when seeing his disfigured face (left photo). It was Harold's quiet courage, charm, and smile that won students over and helped him find a girlfriend (Fisher, 1995).

Researchers found that both personality traits and social factors helped burn victims cope with long-term stressful effects, such as the anxiety and depression that come from being disfigured by burns. For example, burn victims with high self-esteem and strong social support are better able to cope with long-term stressful aftereffects of their burn injuries (Patterson et al., 1993). Harold kept his self-esteem high by finding a girlfriend and going out for football his sophomore year. In addition, he received strong social support from his mother and girlfriend.

## 4 Conclusions

Based on case studies, researchers found that the majority of people (50–80%) hospitalized for severe burns did not develop major psychological problems and showed good psychological adjustment to their physical problems. Burn victims coped better when they had high self-esteem and a good social support system. When it came to coping strategies, burn victims used problem-focused coping to deal with social, family, and job situations and used emotion-focused coping to deal with anxiety and depression that result from being disfigured (Patterson et al., 1993). By using in-depth case studies, researchers learned how burn victims cope and adjust to severe physical, personal, and emotional trauma.

Next, we'll look at how some monks develop mind-over-body control.

**Power Study™**

**Check out CD: Module 4**
E. Limbic System: Old Brain

## Monks' Amazing Claims

Tibetan monks claim that by meditating they can voluntarily control their autonomic nervous systems to perform a number of responses, such as warming their hands (photo below). Since many Western researchers believe that voluntary control of the autonomic nervous system is very, very difficult, Western researcher Herbert Benson and his colleagues from Harvard Medical School have traveled to India to test the monks' amazing claims (Benson et al., 1982, 1990).

Western researchers studied Eastern monks who claimed to use meditation to control the responses of the very difficult-to-control autonomic nervous system.

The *autonomic nervous system* has two divisions that are not usually under voluntary control: the sympathetic division causes physiological arousal by increasing heart rate, breathing, blood pressure, and secretion of hormones; the parasympathetic division calms and relaxes the body by decreasing physiological responses and stimulating digestion.

The only two responses of the autonomic nervous system that you can control *easily, voluntarily,* and *without practice* are breathing and eye blinking. All other responses of the autonomic nervous system, such as increasing or decreasing blood pressure, temperature, or heart rate, dilating or constricting blood vessels, are controlled automatically and, without considerable practice, are not under voluntary control. For example, your hands automatically warm up when blood vessels in the fingers are automatically and involuntarily dilated and cool down when blood vessels are constricted. Because dilating blood vessels is not usually under voluntary control, it takes considerable practice to learn how to warm your hands. Compared to Westerners, some Tibetan monks are very good at warming their hands.

## Mind-Body Interaction

If you wish to voluntarily control one of your autonomic nervous system's responses, such as dilating blood vessels to warm your hands, sit quietly in a chair, close your eyes, and think relaxing thoughts. If your thoughts are truly relaxing, they will activate your parasympathetic division, which will dilate blood vessels and result in warm hands. However, the first time you try this your hands will probably become colder because by trying so hard to relax you may be doing the reverse, which is to activate your sympathetic system, which causes arousal and constricts the blood vessels in your fingers.

The reason Westerners find it takes considerable practice to learn to warm our hands is that we usually spend little time practicing relaxation exercises and thus are unfamiliar with how to concentrate on thoughts or images that will result in hand warming. Those Western individuals who have used biofeedback training have managed to raise their finger temperatures by only about 0.25–2°F, on average (Freedman, 1991). In comparison, certain Tibetan monks, through various forms of meditation, claim that they can warm their hands and bodies 9–12°F, which is sufficient to dry wet towels placed on their shoulders. This was exactly the kind of claim that excited and puzzled Benson's group of researchers.

**Voluntary control.** Benson's group obtained permission from three monks at a monastery in Upper Dharamsala, India, to measure skin temperature during heat meditation, or g Tum-mo yoga. The monks sat in the lotus position, closed their eyes, and began meditating. As shown in the graph below, within a short period of time, one monk had raised his finger temperature as much as 7–9°C or 9–12°F with no change in heart rate (Benson et al., 1982). The monks' success at warming their hands was about five times as great as Westerners had managed (0.25–2°F). One reason monks can learn to voluntarily control their autonomic nervous systems (dilating blood vessels to warm their hands) is that they practice this task daily for many years.

**Explanation.** Westerner Benson explains that monks are able to raise hand temperature by activating the parasympathetic division, which dilates tiny blood vessels that lie near the surface of

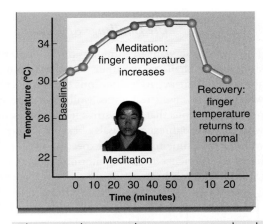

Tibetan monks use meditation to increase hand temperature, a response very difficult to control.

the skin. The monks' explanation is much more interesting: During meditation, they gather winds scattered in consciousness and focus the winds into a "central channel" that generates internal heat (Benson et al., 1982).

**Application.** The monks' ability to voluntarily control their physiological responses clearly shows the mind-body interaction. In this case, the monks' minds (thoughts) control hand warming, which is a physiological response (blood vessel dilatation) of the normally automatic and involuntary autonomic nervous system. Similarly, without being aware of doing so and usually without voluntary control, you also experience daily mind-body interactions when your thoughts, beliefs, and emotional feelings automatically activate physiological responses, such as triggering the fight-flight response or weakening the immune responses. As we explained earlier, overactivation of the fight-flight response can result in continuous physiological arousal and put you at risk for developing a variety of psychosomatic symptoms.

One way to turn down activation of the fight-flight response and decrease the risk of developing psychosomatic symptoms is to have a stress management program.

## Definition

**How can I reduce my stress levels?**

One reason 30% of college freshmen feel continuously overwhelmed is that their classes, exams, papers, personal problems, and part-time jobs combine to take more time and energy than they have (Carpenter, 2000). Being overwhelmed means increased levels of stress and increased risk of developing psychosomatic symptoms. One way to reduce levels of stress is with a stress management program.

A **stress management program** uses a variety of strategies to reduce anxiety, fear, and stressful experiences by changing three different aspects of our lives: thoughts (appraisals), behaviors, and physiological responses.

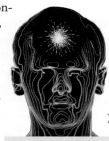

By controlling your thoughts you can control your body.

Psychologists have developed a number of very effective stress management programs that reduce stress levels, which in turn decrease the occurrence of psychosomatic symptoms. Although stress management programs have different names, they all focus on ways to change three major contributors to stressful experiences: your thoughts and beliefs (appraisals), your behaviors, and your emotional and physiological responses (Granvold, 1994).

We'll describe several methods that psychologists have developed for effectively changing each of these three factors, beginning with changing your thoughts.

## Changing Thoughts

**Can you learn to think more positively?**

Many daily hassles—dealing with long lines, slow traffic, rude people, loud neighbors, and sloppy roommates—can be made more or less stressful depending on how you appraise these situations. Since your appraisal of a situation as threatening or challenging is related to increasing or decreasing your stress levels, it follows that an effective way to decrease stressful experiences is to work at changing how you initially appraise a situation (Lazarus, 2000). We'll explain two effective strategies for changing your appraisals: thinking of potentially stressful situations as challenging rather than threatening, and changing negative self-statements into positive ones.

### Use Challenge Appraisals

The reason you want to think or appraise potentially stressful situations as challenging rather than threatening is that threat appraisals elicit negative emotions (fear, anxiety, depression), which in turn raise stress levels, while challenge appraisals elicit positive emotions that lower stress levels. For example, students who emphasize threat appraisals of exams, such as thinking they will not have time to study or expecting to do poorly, are more likely to experience negative emotions such as anxiety and fear (Shannon, 1994). In turn, anxiety and fear trigger the fight-flight response, which raises the level of stress and often leads to emotion-focused coping, such as complaining, seeking sympathy, or avoiding studying. However, emotion-focused coping does not usually motivate actions, such as studying, that are needed to prepare students for exams.

I see life as one big challenge!

In comparison, students who emphasize challenge appraisals of exams, such as wanting to do their best or to prove themselves, are more likely to experience positive emotions, such as excitement or eagerness, which decrease levels of stress. In turn, challenge appraisals are more likely to result in problem-focused coping, which means taking direct action to deal with the situation itself, such as developing a study program.

Thus, a good way to deal with potentially stressful situations is to focus on challenging rather than threatening appraisals (Lazarus, 1999, 2000).

### Substitute Positive Self-Statements

Another way to prevent a situation, such as taking an exam, from becoming more stressful is to work at removing negative self-statements by substituting positive ones. Specifically, on one side of a sheet of paper write your negative self-statements; then next to them on the other side write the positive ones that you can substitute. The example below shows negative self-statements changed into positive ones.

| Negative self-statements | Positive self-statements |
|---|---|
| "I know I'll do badly." | "I know I can do OK." |
| "I always get so anxious." | "I'm going to stay calm." |
| "I'm not smart enough." | "I've got plenty of ability." |
| "I'm never going to learn it." | "I can learn the material." |

The reason you want to avoid making negative self-statements is that they elicit negative emotions (fear, anger, anxiety) that increase stress levels. By substituting positive self-statements, which elicit positive emotions, you can decrease stress levels. For example, each time you begin to think of a negative self-statement, stop yourself and substitute a positive one. For regularly occurring stressors, such as taking exams, waiting in lines, fighting with traffic, and dealing with rude people, it is best to have prepared a different list of self-statements to go with each different situation. Researchers found that a program of substituting self-statements proved very effective in helping people change their thought patterns and reduce their stress levels (Meichenbaum & Fitzpatrick, 1993).

You better be good, better not pout, and better think positively.

## Changing Behaviors

**How do you get ready for an exam?**

There are generally two different ways that students get ready for exams. Some students get ready for an exam by complaining about how much work there is, making excuses about not studying, or blaming the instructor for too much material. All these behaviors involve *emotion-focused coping,* which in the short term serves to reduce stress by reducing negative emotional feelings. However, in the long run, students may need to change these behaviors and engage in *problem-focused coping,* which means developing a study plan (Lazarus, 1999).

Because some students are not aware of whether they use emotion-focused or problem-focused coping, stress

I'd rather complain than change.

management programs include an observation period of 1–2 weeks. During this time, a student observes or monitors his or her own behaviors to identify emotion-focused versus problem-focused behaviors. If a student is using primarily *emotion-focused coping* (making excuses, procrastinating, or blaming others), he or she will likely do poorly on exams. Instead, a student would need to start a program of *problem-focused coping* (making a study program, rewriting class notes) by using some of the self-reward and behavior modification techniques that we discussed in Module 10 (Granvold, 1994; Meichenbaum & Fitzpatrick, 1993). Thus, one way to reduce stress is to change your behaviors—that is, to emphasize problem-focused over emotion-focused activities.

## Changing Physiological Responses

**How do you learn to relax?**

There are two good reasons it is difficult for you to relax at will. First, the autonomic nervous system, which controls relaxing responses, is not normally under voluntary control (except by Tibetan monks). Second, learning to have some voluntary control over the autonomic nervous system involves learning a mind-over-body program that takes considerable effort and practice. However, learning to relax at will is an important part of a stress management program. We'll describe three techniques that have proved almost equally effective in learning to relax (Shapiro et al., 2000).

### Biofeedback

You could learn a relaxing response, such as decreasing muscle tension, by having small sensors placed on your forehead. The sensors are attached to a machine that records, amplifies, and displays changes in muscle tension. Each time you think thoughts or images that increase tension, you hear a high tone; if you decrease tension, you hear a low tone. This procedure is called biofeedback.

*Biofeedback* refers to voluntarily learning to control physiological responses, such as muscle activity, blood pressure, or temperature, by recording and displaying these responses.

After 12–30 biofeedback training sessions (about 20 minutes per session), most individuals have some success in turning on relaxing responses. You could also learn to relax with progressive relaxation.

### Progressive Relaxation

You could learn to relax your body's muscles by first tensing and relaxing your toes and then continuing up the body, tensing and relaxing the muscles of your calves, thighs, pelvis, stomach, shoulders, arms, hands, neck, face, and forehead. This procedure is called progressive relaxation.

*Progressive relaxation* involves practicing tensing and relaxing the major muscle groups of the body until you are able to relax any groups of muscles at will.

After several weeks of daily practice, about 20 minutes per session, you would be able to use this exercise to relax your body. You could also relax by meditating.

### Meditation

There are many kinds of meditation exercises. We'll describe two of the more popular ones.

*Transcendental meditation* (TM) involves assuming a comfortable position, closing one's eyes, and repeating and concentrating on a sound to clear one's head of all thoughts (worrisome and otherwise).

TM is an Eastern form of meditation. A Western counterpart is the relaxation response (Benson, 1975).

The *relaxation response* involves sitting or lying in a comfortable position while silently repeating a sound over and over to rid oneself of anxious thoughts.

Meditation involves removing all stressful thoughts and replacing them with peaceful ones. Becoming competent at using meditation to relax usually requires practicing about 20 minutes a day for about six weeks.

You may hear claims that a particular form of meditation, such as Zen or yoga, is effective in reducing stress. However, researchers report that most relaxation techniques, whether biofeedback, progressive relaxation, or various forms of meditation, are about equally effective in producing relaxation and reducing stress (Shapiro et al., 2000). For example, different relaxation techniques were about equally effective in reducing anxiety and decreasing a variety of psychosomatic complaints, such as headaches, high blood pressure, insomnia, stomach pain, and intestinal problems (irritable bowel syndrome) (Cruess et al., 2000; Sandlund & Norlander, 2000; Speca et al., 2000). Since methods of relaxation are about equally effective, the one you choose comes down to personal preference. More important than which relaxation technique you choose is the need for daily practice so that you will be able to relax at will. All researchers agree that continued use of relaxation techniques is a critical part of any effective stress management program (Clay, 1997b).

# Summary Test

## A. APPRAISAL

**1.** The uncomfortable feeling we have when we appraise a situation as something that overloads or strains our psychological resources is called _____.

**2.** Our initial, subjective evaluation of a situation in which we balance various environmental demands against our ability to meet them is called _____.

**3.** There are three outcomes of primary appraisal. Those situations that do not matter to our well-being are called (a)_____; those that will enhance or preserve our well-being are called (b)_____; and those that overtax our resources are called (c)_____.

**4.** A stressful situation has the potential for three different kinds of personal experiences. If you have already sustained some damage or injury, this is referred to as (a)_____. If the injury has not yet taken place but you anticipate it in the near future, this is referred to as (b)_____. If you have the potential for gain or personal growth but need to use physical energy and psychological resources, this is referred to as (c)_____. Not all appraisals are clear-cut; some may represent a combination of threat and challenge.

## B. PHYSIOLOGICAL RESPONSES

**5.** A combination of physiological responses that arouse and prepare the body for action is called the (a)_____ response. Although this response originally evolved to help our ancestors survive dangerous and life-threatening situations, it can also be triggered by psychological stimuli, such as our primary (b)_____ of a situation as harm/loss, threatening, or challenging.

**6.** Threat appraisals activate a part of the brain called the (a)_____, which triggers two responses simultaneously. It causes the (b)_____ gland to release ACTH (adreno-corticotropic hormone), which acts on the adrenal cortex to secrete hormones that regulate levels of minerals and glucose in the body. The hypothalamus also triggers the (c)_____ division of the autonomic nervous system, which causes physiological arousal.

**7.** Our psychological reactions to stressful situations can result in real, painful, physical symptoms called (a)_____ symptoms. According to Selye, we develop psychosomatic symptoms because the body's response to stress involves going through three stages that he called the (b)_____ syndrome. The first is called the (c)_____ stage, which is our initial reaction to stress and is marked by physiological arousal. The second is called

the (d)_____ stage, in which most physiological responses return to normal levels as the body uses up great stores of energy. The third is called the (e)_____ stage, which is marked by the actual breakdown in body organs or weakening of the infection-fighting immune system.

**8.** The body's network of cells and chemicals that automatically fight off bacteria, viruses, and other foreign matter is known as the (a)_____. The study of the relationship between the central nervous system, the endocrine system, and psychosocial factors is called (b)_____. The interaction among these factors affects the immune system and, in turn, makes the body more or less susceptible to disease and infection.

## C. STRESSFUL EXPERIENCES

**9.** Situations that are potentially disturbing or disruptive and that we appraise as having an impact on our lives are called (a)_____ events. Small, irritating daily events are called (b)_____, and small, pleasant daily experiences are called (c)_____. How we cope with hassles predicts our daily mood and the occurrence of psychosomatic symptoms.

**10.** The feeling that results when our attempts to reach some goal are blocked is called (a)_____. Feelings of wearing out or becoming exhausted because of too many demands on our time and energy are referred to as (b)_____. A direct personal experience of actual or threatened death or serious injury or witnessing such an event could result in terrible stress symptoms called (c)_____.

**11.** When we must decide between two or more incompatible choices, we are in (a)_____, which can include at least three possibilities. If we must choose between two options with pleasurable consequences, we experience (b)_____ conflict. If we must choose between two options that both have disagreeable consequences, we are in (c)_____ conflict. If a single situation has both pleasurable and disagreeable aspects, we are in (d)_____ conflict.

**12.** An unpleasant state in which we have feelings of uneasiness and apprehension as well as increased physiological arousal is called (a)_____. This feeling has at least three causes. One is classical conditioning of an emotional response to a previously neutral stimulus; the result is called a (b)_____ response. A second cause is a form of learning that develops through watching and does not require any observable behavior or reinforcer; this is called (c)_____ learning. According to Freud, anxiety arises when the id and superego disagree, resulting in an (d)_____ conflict, which results in the ego producing a feeling of anxiety.

## D. PERSONALITY & SOCIAL FACTORS

**13.** Three personality traits that decrease the potentially harmful effects of stressful situations are control, commitment, and challenge, which together are called _____.

**14.** If you believe that what you do influences what happens, you are said to have an (a)_____ of control. In contrast, if you believe that chance and luck mostly determine what happens and that you do not have much influence, you are said to have an (b)_____ of control. People with an external locus of control experience more negative emotions, higher levels of stress, and more psychosomatic symptoms than do those whose locus of control is internal.

**15.** Because the original association between Type A behavior and the occurrence of cardiovascular disease was not replicated, researchers redefined Type A behavior as having two primary traits, _____ and _____. Even with the new definition, researchers have questioned an association between Type A behavior and cardiovascular disease.

**16.** One factor that buffers us from stressful experiences is having a group or network of family or friends who provide strong support and this is called _____.

## E. KINDS OF COPING

**17.** After we make a primary appraisal, we then must decide what action to take, which is called a (a)_____ appraisal. This involves two different kinds of coping. If we seek information about what needs to be done, change our own behavior, or take whatever action will solve the problem, we use (b)_____ coping. If we use our energies to deal with emotional distress caused by a harm or threat appraisal, we are using (c)_____ coping. Compared to emotion-focused coping, problem-focused coping is better at reducing long-term effects of stress because it solves the problem.

## F. RESEARCH FOCUS: COPING WITH TRAUMA

**18.** Psychologists use a number of different research methods. One method identifies cause-and-effect relationships by following a set of guidelines that describe how to control and manipulate variables; this is called the (a)_____ method. Another method is a more in-depth analysis of the thoughts,

feelings, beliefs, or behaviors of individuals; this is called the (b)_____. Researchers found that burn victims use (c)_____-focused coping to adjust to social, family, and job situations, and (d)_____-focused coping to deal with anxiety and depression that may result from disfigurement.

## G. CULTURAL DIVERSITY: TIBETAN MONKS

**19.** Many of our physiological responses involved in relaxation (heart rate, blood pressure, temperature, and secretion of hormones) are not under voluntary control because they are regulated by the (a)_____ system. Researchers discovered that some monks have learned a method to voluntarily control temperature, which involves relaxation. This demonstrates that the (b)_____ can be used to control the (c)_____ physiological responses.

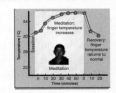

## H. APPLICATION: STRESS MANAGEMENT PROGRAMS

**20.** A program for reducing anxiety, fear, and stressful experiences by using a variety of strategies to change three different aspects of our lives— thoughts, behaviors, and physiological responses—is called a _____.

**21.** One component of a stress management program is learning to relax at will, which can be accomplished with three different methods. Recording and amplifying physiological signals from the body and displaying these signals so that we can learn to increase or decrease them is known as (a)_____. An exercise of tensing and relaxing the major muscle groups is called (b)_____. Meditation can take many forms. Sitting or lying in a comfortable position while repeating a meaningless sound over and over to rid oneself of anxious thoughts is called (c)_____ or the _____ response. Researchers found that all three techniques are about equally effective in learning to relax.

***Answers:*** *1. stress; 2. primary appraisal; 3. (a) irrelevant, (b) positive, (c) stressful; 4. (a) harm/loss, (b) threat, (c) challenge; 5. (a) fight-flight, (b) appraisal; 6. (a) hypothalamus, (b) pituitary, (c) sympathetic; 7. (a) psychosomatic, (b) general adaptation, (c) alarm, (d) resistance, (e) exhaustion; 8. (a) immune system, (b) psychoneuroimmunology; 9. (a) major life, (b) hassles, (c) uplifts; 10. (a) frustration, (b) burnout, (c) posttraumatic stress disorder; 11. (a) conflict, (b) approach-approach, (c) avoidance-avoidance, (d) approach-avoidance; 12. (a) anxiety, (b) conditioned emotional, (c) observational, (d) unconscious; 13. hardiness; 14. (a) internal locus, (b) external locus; 15. hostility, anger; 16. social support; 17. (a) secondary, (b) problem-focused, (c) emotion-focused; 18. (a) experimental or scientific, (b) case study, (c) problem, (d) emotion; 19. (a) autonomic nervous or parasympathetic, (b) mind, (c) body's; 20. stress management program; 21. (a) biofeedback, (b) progressive relaxation, (c) transcendental meditation (TM), relaxation*

# Critical Thinking

## The Diagnosis

*by Mary Herczog*

**Questions**

**1.** After Mary found a lump in her breast, which Freudian defense mechanism does she use to deal with this potentially damaging news and what is her primary appraisal of the situation?

**2.** After she has a biopsy to see if the lump is cancerous, which two Freudian defense mechanisms does she use to cope with the stress?

**3.** Which kinds of personality traits would help this person cope with the stress of knowing that she has breast cancer?

Early last year, a mammogram and an ultrasound diagnosed some lumps in my breasts as cysts. One month later, when I found another lump, I dismissed it as a cyst the doctor had certainly noticed. And continued to dismiss it for a few weeks until it grew to more than the size of a peach pit and turned very hard. When a lump turned up in my armpit, I knew.

A biopsy was taken on a Thursday and I was told to call on Monday for news that I was still almost certain would be that this lump was a fibroadenoma—totally benign. My husband, Steve, and I spent a weekend telling ourselves this would turn out to be nothing.

After all, I'm 33, way too young to have breast cancer. There is no history in my family. I never drank, smoked, did drugs, or drank coffee, tea, or soda. So how could I have breast cancer?

But on Monday I was told that the biopsy result was "suspicious for cancer." So I wasn't exactly surprised when the doctor told me the pathologist would "bet his children's lives" that this was cancer. In both lump and lymph node, the latter being the bad news as this meant the cancer had spread.

The plan was to hit me with four months of chemotherapy, remove both the lump and the lymph node,

and follow up with six weeks of radiation, then four more weeks of chemo.

You can spend a week thinking, "What if I have cancer. OK, so I'm going to lose my hair, which is bad, but I love hats, and I can explore my inner drag queen by wearing wigs" and other Pollyanna things. But, actually hearing someone tell you that removing your breast is a possibility in your future—well, pass the Kleenex.

Damn, damn, damn.

The next few days passed in a haze of more biopsies and tests. In between them were phone calls. Many, many phone calls. Soon the phone lines were buzzing. The reactions poured in, and while one does not enjoy creating anguish for one's friends, the love and concern that result are as good as any medicine—in some ways better than a medicine that makes you vomit, lose your hair, and gain weight. (Over the course of several years, the cancer spread to her brain and caused her death.) Source: *Los Angeles Times,* December 8, 1997)

**4.** Should this person use problem-focused or emotion-focused coping to deal with having breast cancer?

**5.** Why is it good news that her phone lines were buzzing with calls from her friends?

*Try InfoTrac to search for terms:* mammogram;  ultrasound; breast cancer; chemotherapy; radiation.

---

*Suggested answers to Newspaper Article questions*

1. After finding a new lump in her breast, she initially dismissed the problem, which is using the Freudian defense mechanism of denial to cope with the problem. However, after the lump grew and hardened, her primary appraisal changed to one of threat (will the lump be cancer), which increased her level of stress.
2. While waiting to find out the biopsy results, she again uses the Freudian mechanism of denial ("It will turn out to be nothing") and also rationalization ("I'm too young to have breast cancer").
3. She will be better able to cope with the news of having breast cancer if she has the personality traits of hardiness (control, commitment, challenge), if she has an internal rather than an external locus of control, and if she is has a more optimistic than pessimistic attitude toward life.

4. In dealing with the frightening news of having breast cancer, she would have to use both problem-focused and emotion-focused coping. Problem-focused coping is a long-term strategy to deal with the stressful problem itself, in this case getting information on and then getting the best kind of treatment for breast cancer. Emotion-focused coping is a strategy of dealing with negative emotional feelings that are triggered by a stressful situation (having breast cancer), such as fear, depression, and sadness.
5. This person is using emotion-focused coping to deal with her fear and depression by seeking support and encouragement from her many friends (phone lines were buzzing). Social support is a very powerful way to reduce levels of stress as well as help prepare and be a buffer for future stressful situations.

# Links to Learning

## Web Sites

- **WADSWORTH ONLINE STUDY CENTER**
  http://psychology.wadsworth.com
  Quizzes, learning activities and exercises, a discussion forum, and hot links to Internet sites related to health, stress, and coping, including:

- **THE AMERICAN INSTITUTE OF STRESS**
  http://www.stress.org/
  "Dedicated to increasing our knowledge of the role of stress in health and disease," this site offers a monthly newsletter, informational packets, expert consultations, and links to other sites.

- **THE MEDICAL BASIS OF STRESS, DEPRESSION, ANXIETY, SLEEP PROBLEMS, AND DRUG USE**
  http://www.teachhealth.com/
  This informative site includes information on the biological bases of stress, how to recognize stress, a self-test for stress levels, stress management techniques, and more, all in clear straightforward language. A Spanish version is also available.

- **TRAUMA INFORMATION PAGES**
  http://www.trauma-pages.com/
  This excellent site by psychologist David Baldwin contains detailed information about trauma and its aftermath, and includes articles and relevant Web links, disaster handouts, support resources, and a bookstore. Translations are available into and from French, German, Italian, Portuguese, and Spanish.

## Learning Activities

- *POWERSTUDY*™ **BY ROD PLOTNIK & TOM DOYLE**

  ### PowerStudy™

  **Check out CD: Module 21**
  CD 4.C: Organization of the Brain; book page 484
  CD 4.E: Limbic System: Old Brain; book pages 484, 485, 501
  CD 4.F: Endocrine System; book page 485
  CD 9.B: Procedure: Classical Conditioning; book pages 489, 493
  CD 9.H: Application: Conditioned Fear; book pages 489, 493
  CD 10.E: Cognitive Learning; book page 493
  CD 10.I: Application: Behavior Modification; book page 493

- *STUDY GUIDE TO ACCOMPANY INTRODUCTION TO PSYCHOLOGY, 6TH EDITION,* **by Matthew Enos**
  In Module 21—This module could save your life!—you'll be convinced that stress is a serious health hazard. Would you change your life to reduce stress?

- *WEBTUTOR*
  http://webtutor.thomsonlearning.com

  Visit this site for interactive versions of Study Guide features. Take a quiz, get your score—should you study a topic some more, or can you move on? For example, why doesn't the fight-flight response work as well today as it did early in human evolution? What is the relationship between frustration and stress? Can you define psychoneuroimmunology?

- *INFOTRAC Online Library*
  http://www.infotrac-college.com
  Use your password and then key in search terms such as those below to find popular and scientific articles on subjects covered in Module 21. Make the library work for you!

  | Biofeedback | Immune system | Meditation |
  | Burnout | Type A behavior | Posttraumatic stress disorder |

- *PSYCHNOW!*
  CD for Macintosh and Windows includes a study guide, glossary, Web sites, and animations. For Module 21, see: • Coping with Emotions • Stress and Health

## Study Questions

*Use InfoTrac to search for topics mentioned in the main heads below (e.g., personality and social factors, coping, stress management).*

**\*A. Appraisal**—Sue says that some situations always cause her stress, but John says it's how she thinks about them. Who's right? (**Suggested answer p. 633**)

**B. Physiological Responses**—Why are people so very reluctant to admit that some painful physical symptoms can be caused by their thoughts?

**C. Stressful Experiences**—Why does Sally always feel a little anxious when she goes to parties where she doesn't know anyone?

**D. Personality & Social Factors**—Greg did great in high school, so why is he doing poorly in his first year of college, away from home?

**E. Kinds of Coping**—How would you cope with finding out that, because of major differences, you must break off your current relationship?

**\*F. Research Focus: Coping with Trauma**—What can you learn from how burn victims cope with stress that would apply to dealing with stress in your own life? (**Suggested answer p. 634**)

**G. Cultural Diversity: Tibetan Monks**—Why is it so much easier for most of us to use our minds to trigger the fight-flight response than to calm or relax our body?

**\*H. Application: Stress Management Programs**—Why is it better to cope with stress by changing three things—thoughts, behaviors, and physiological responses—rather than just one? (**Suggested answer p. 634**)

*\*These questions are answered in Appendix B.*

# Module 22: Assessment & Anxiety Disorders

A. Three Approaches     510
* CAUSES OF ABNORMAL BEHAVIOR
* DEFINITIONS OF ABNORMAL BEHAVIOR

B. Assessing Mental Disorders     512
* DEFINITION OF ASSESSMENT
* THREE METHODS OF ASSESSMENT

C. Diagnosing Mental Disorders     513
* REAL-LIFE ASSESSMENT
* DSM-IV-TR
* NINE MAJOR PROBLEMS: AXIS I
* OTHER PROBLEMS AND DISORDERS: AXES II, III, IV, V
* POTENTIAL PROBLEMS WITH USING DSM-IV-TR
* FREQUENCY OF MENTAL DISORDERS

D. Anxiety Disorders     517
* GENERALIZED ANXIETY DISORDER
* PANIC DISORDER
* PHOBIAS
* OBSESSIVE-COMPULSIVE DISORDERS

E. Somatoform Disorders     520
* DEFINITION AND EXAMPLES
* MASS HYSTERIA

Concept Review     521

F. Cultural Diversity:
An Asian Disorder     522
* TAIJIN KYOFUSHO, OR TKS
* SOCIAL CUSTOMS

G. Research Focus: School Shootings     523
* WHAT DROVE TEENS
TO KILL FELLOW STUDENTS AND TEACHERS?

H. Application: Treating Phobias     524
* SPECIFIC PHOBIA: FLYING
* COGNITIVE-BEHAVIORAL THERAPY
* EXPOSURE THERAPY
* SOCIAL PHOBIA: PUBLIC SPEAKING
* DRUG TREATMENT OF PHOBIAS

Summary Test     526

Critical Thinking     528
* PRISONERS OF LOVE

Links to Learning     529

## Mental Disorder

**How did a serial killer go unnoticed?**

His eyes are hazel, placid, almost vacant, and his appearance is neither sinister nor scary. Until the day he was caught, his neighbors considered him an "average Joe." But over a period of three years, Jeffrey Dahmer planned and carried out the murders of 15 young men, while 5 more potential victims managed to escape.

In a very real sense, Dahmer led two different lives. In public, Dahmer seemed like a harmless, quiet guy who held down a job in a chocolate factory. However, in private, Dahmer would con potential victims into coming to his apartment, where he would drug them, commit sexual acts, and then kill, mutilate, and sometimes eat parts of them.

Although no two serial killers are alike, Dahmer fits the typical pattern. Serial killers are almost always young, White males who are quite intelligent and often come from broken homes; they may have been physically or sexually abused during childhood; and they have serious personality defects, such as low self-esteem and a lifelong sense of loneliness. Over half of all serial killers have mutilated their victims (Hickey, 1991). John Douglas, investigative chief at the FBI's National Center for Analysis of Violent Crime, adds that serial killers are obsessed with control, manipulation, and dominance and often con their victims into agreeing to their requests.

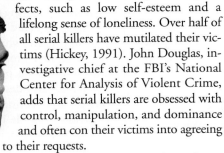

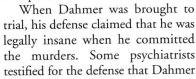
Jeffrey Dahmer, who murdered 15 people, fits the pattern of serial killers.

When Dahmer was brought to trial, his defense claimed that he was legally insane when he committed the murders. Some psychiatrists testified for the defense that Dahmer was insane; others testified for the prosecution that he was sane.

*Insanity,* according to its legal definition, means not knowing the difference between right and wrong.

The jury rejected Dahmer's plea of insanity and agreed with the prosecution that Dahmer was legally sane. The jury found Dahmer guilty on 15 counts of murder and characterized him as a con man who killed for his own selfish interests. On February 17, 1992, a Milwaukee County judge sentenced 31-year-old Dahmer to 15 consecutive life terms (*Newsweek,* August 5, 1992). In 1994, Dahmer was beaten to death in prison.

When mental health professionals examine Dahmer's behaviors, they are trying to identify his particular mental disorder.

A *mental disorder* is generally defined as a prolonged or recurring problem that seriously interferes with an individual's ability to live a satisfying personal life and function adequately in society.

Deciding whether a person has a mental disorder can be difficult because so many factors are involved in defining what is abnormal. As you'll learn in this module, someone's behavior may be described as abnormal but the person may or may not have a mental disorder.

## Phobia

**What's so scary about flying?**

There is no doubt that Jeffrey Dahmer's murder and mutilation of 15 young men indicate a severe mental disorder and extremely abnormal behavior. In other cases, mental disorders may involve a relatively common behavior or event that, through some learning, observation, or other process, has the power to elicit tremendous anxiety and becomes a phobia (Hackmann et al., 2000).

A *phobia (FOE-bee-ah)* is an anxiety disorder characterized by an intense, excessive, and irrational fear that is out of all proportion to the danger elicited by the object or situation.

Kate Premo's phobia of flying began in her childhood, when she experienced a turbulent flight that left her scared and anxious. Later, as a young adult, her fear of flying was worsened by memories of the 1988 terrorist bombing of Pan Am flight 103, which killed several of her fellow students from Syracuse University. After that incident, her phobia of flying kept her from visiting friends and family. She would try to fly and even make reservations but always cancel them at the last minute.

Kate Premo is trying to overcome her phobia of flying.

An estimated 25 million Americans have a similar irrational and intense fear of flying, which is called *aerophobia;* they refuse to get on a plane. Another 30 million Americans report moderate to high degrees of anxiety when they fly (Wilhelm & Roth, 1997). To treat her phobia, Kate Premo (photo above) took part in a weekend seminar that included actually flying in a plane. We'll tell you about Kate's phobia and treatment later in this module.

These two examples of Jeffrey Dahmer and Kate Premo raise a number of questions about mental disorders: How do they develop? How are they diagnosed? How are they treated? We'll answer these three questions as we discuss mental disorders.

## What's Coming

In this module, we'll discuss three approaches to understanding mental disorders. We'll explain how mental disorders are assessed and diagnosed and go into some specific examples of mental disorders, such as generalized anxiety, phobias, obsessive-compulsive behaviors, and somatoform disorders. Finally, we'll discuss how common phobias, such as fear of flying, are treated.

We'll begin with the three approaches that are used to define, explain, and treat abnormal behaviors, such as that of Jeffrey Dahmer.

# A. Three Approaches

## Causes of Abnormal Behavior

The view of mental disorders has changed greatly through the centuries. In the Middle Ages, mental disorders were thought to be the result of demons or devils who inhabited individuals and made them do strange and horrible things. In the 1600s, mental disorders were thought to involve witches, who were believed to speak to the devil. This was the case in Salem, Massachusetts, in 1692, where, in a short span of four months, 14 women and 5 men were hanged as witches on the testimony of young girls and God-fearing adults (Shapiro, 1992).

Three approaches to understanding mental disorders

We'll discuss three popular approaches to understanding and treating mental disorders: medical, cognitive-behavioral, and psychodynamic or psychoanalytic approaches. In the discussion of serial killer Jeffrey Dahmer, you'll see that each approach emphasizes different factors.

### Medical Model Approach

Researchers looking for biochemical or neurological causes of Jeffrey Dahmer's mental disorder are using the medical model approach.

According to the *medical model approach,* mental disorders involve genetic, physiological, or neurological factors that cause symptoms that can be diagnosed and treated.

Mental disorders may involve biochemical or neurological problems.

Similar to doctors using drugs to treat physical diseases, psychiatrists use psychoactive drugs to treat mental disorders.

**Advantage.** One advantage of the medical model is that it emphasizes the role of the nervous system, genetic makeup, and chemical factors in mental disorders. For example, researchers have found that mental disorders run in families, which points to genetic factors (Sullivan et al., 2000). In addition, researchers have reported both anatomical and chemical differences in the brains of individuals with mental disorders, which points to the importance of neurological factors (Selemon, 2000).

**Disadvantage.** One difficulty with the current medical model is that genetic or neurological factors underlying mental disorders cannot always be identified. In addition, treatment with psychoactive drugs is not always effective, and in some disorders, psychotherapy without drugs has proven equally effective (Barlow & Durand, 2001).

Beginning in the early 1990s, the medical model approach benefited from using newer genetic and brain-imaging techniques that allow researchers to analyze anatomical and chemical differences in living brains (Kendler et al., 2000; Wright et al., 2000).

### Cognitive-Behavioral Approach

Psychologists looking for strange beliefs, thoughts, or behaviors underlying Jeffrey Dahmer's disorder are using the cognitive-behavioral approach.

The *cognitive-behavioral approach* emphasizes that mental disorders result from deficits in cognitive processes, such as thoughts and beliefs, and from behavioral problems, such as deficits in skills and abilities.

Mental disorders may involve unusual thoughts.

The *cognitive* part of this approach grew out of research on how faulty beliefs, attitudes, and thoughts can result in serious mental and behavioral problems, such as depression and anxiety. The *behavioral* part of this approach grew out of research on how inappropriate behavior or behavioral deficits may lead to cognitive and behavioral problems such as shyness, loneliness, or helplessness. The cognitive-behavioral approach is supported by data showing that cognitive-behavior therapy can be as effective in treating depression as various antidepressant drugs (Barlow & Durand, 2001).

The cognitive-behavioral approach views mental disorders as resulting from maladaptive ways of thinking and behaving. Accordingly, treatment for mental disorders focuses on changing a person's maladaptive thoughts and behaviors.

### Psychoanalytic Approach

Psychotherapists looking for unconscious psychological conflicts underlying Jeffrey Dahmer's disorder are using the psychodynamic (psychoanalytic) approach.

The *psychodynamic* or *psychoanalytic approach* focuses on unconscious or repressed conflicts underlying mental disorders.

Sigmund Freud developed the psychoanalytic approach, which today is often called the psychodynamic approach. Freud's major contribution was pointing out that some of our beliefs and desires may be unconscious but yet have considerable influence on our behaviors (Module 19).

The psychodynamic approach recognizes the importance of thoughts and beliefs, especially ones that have been repressed and are therefore unconscious. According to the psychodynamic approach, treatment of mental disorders centers on the therapist's helping the patient identify and resolve his or her unconscious conflicts.

Mental disorders may involve unconscious forces.

**Today's approach.** Many psychologists recognize that mental disorders result from the interaction of physiological/neurological factors, cognitive processes, and unconscious thoughts or desires of which we may be totally or somewhat unaware. For example, the development of antisocial behaviors may involve a neurological problem with the prefrontal cortex (involved in planning and making decisions) combined with poor upbringing (lack of moral training) to result in antisocial personality (psychopath) (Damasio, 1999).

One problem with abnormal behaviors is that there are several ways to define them.

## Definitions of Abnormal Behavior

**Is Mr. Thompson abnormal?**

In some cases, such as Jeffrey Dahmer's murder and mutilation of 15 young men, we have no doubt that he demonstrated an extremely abnormal behavior pattern. In other cases, such as Kate Premo's phobia of flying, we would probably say that most of her life appears to be normal except for a small piece—flying in airplanes—that is abnormal. In still other cases, such as that of 54-year-old Richard Thompson (right photo), it is less clear what is abnormal behavior.

The City of San Diego evicted Thompson and all his belongings from his home. His belongings included shirts, pants, dozens of shoes, several Bibles, a cooler, a tool chest, lawn chairs, a barbecue grill, tin plates, bird cages, two pet rats, and his self-fashioned bed. For the previous nine months, Thompson had lived happily and without any problems in a downtown storm drain (sewer). Because the city does not allow people to live in storm drains, Thompson was evicted from his underground storm-drain home and forbidden to return. Although Thompson later lived in several care centers and mental hospitals, he much preferred the privacy and comfort of the sewer (Grimaldi, 1986).

There are three different ways to decide whether Richard Thompson's behavior—living in the sewer—was abnormal.

Is it abnormal to live in a storm drain if you don't bother anyone?

### Statistical Frequency

Although Thompson caused no problems to others except to violate a city law against living in a storm drain, his preferred living style could be considered abnormal according to statistical frequency.

The *statistical frequency approach* says that a behavior may be considered abnormal if it occurs rarely or infrequently in relation to the behaviors of the general population.

According to statistical frequency, living in a monastery is abnormal.

By this definition, Thompson's living in a storm drain would be considered very abnormal since, out of over 280 million people in the United States, a very few prefer his kind of home. This illustrates that even though statistical frequency is a relatively precise measure, it is not a very useful measure of abnormality. By this criterion, getting a Ph.D., being president, living in a monastery, and selling a million records are abnormal, although some of these behaviors would be considered very desirable by most people. In fact, the *Guinness Book of Records* (1995) lists thousands of people who have performed some statistically abnormal behaviors and are very proud of them. We would not consider any of these individuals to necessarily have mental disorders.

As all these examples demonstrate, the statistical frequency definition of abnormality has very limited usefulness.

### Deviation from Social Norms

Thompson's behavior—preferring to live in a sewer—could also be considered abnormal based on social norms.

The *social norms approach* says that a behavior is considered abnormal if it deviates greatly from accepted social standards, values, or norms.

Thompson's decision to live by himself in a storm drain greatly deviates from society's norms about where people should live. However, a definition of abnormality based solely on deviations from social norms runs into problems when social norms change with time. For example, 25 years ago, very few males wore earrings, while today many males consider earrings very fashionable. Similarly, 40 years ago, a woman who preferred to be very thin was considered to be ill and in need of medical help. Today, our society pressures women to be thin like the fashion models in the media.

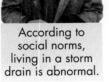

According to social norms, living in a storm drain is abnormal.

Thus, defining abnormality on the basis of social norms can be risky, as social norms may, and do, change over time. The definition of abnormality most used by mental health professionals is the next one.

### Maladaptive Behavior

The major problem with the first two definitions of abnormal behavior—statistical frequency and deviation from social norms—is that they don't say if a particular behavior is psychologically damaging or maladaptive.

The *maladaptive behavior approach* defines a behavior as psychologically damaging or abnormal if it interferes with the individual's ability to function in one's personal life or in society.

For example, being terrified of flying, hearing voices that dictate dangerous acts, feeling compelled to wash one's hands for hours on end, starving oneself to the point of death (anorexia nervosa), and Jeffrey Dahmer's committing serial murders and eating parts of the victims would all be considered maladaptive and, in that sense, abnormal.

However, Thompson's seemingly successful adaptation to living in a sewer may not be maladaptive for him and certainly has no adverse consequences to society.

**Most useful.** Of the three definitions discussed here, mental health professionals find the most useful definition of abnormal behaviors is the one based on the maladaptive definition—that is, whether a particular behavior or behavior pattern interferes with a person's ability to function normally (Barlow & Durand, 2001).

According to the maladaptive definition, some behavior is abnormal if it interferes with a person's ability to function.

However, you'll see that deciding if behavior is truly maladaptive is not always so easy.

## Definition of Assessment

**How do you find out what's wrong?**

In some cases, it's relatively easy to identify what's wrong with a person. For example, it's clear that Jeffrey Dahmer was a serial killer and that Kate Premo has an intense and irrational fear of flying. But in other cases, it's more difficult to identify exactly what the person's motivation and mental problem are. Take the tragic case of Susan Smith.

Susan Smith appeared on the "Today" show, crying for the return of her two little boys (right photo), Michael, 3 years old, and Alex, 14 months old, who, she said, had been kidnapped. She begged the kidnapper to feed them, care for them, and please, please, return them. And then, nine days later, after a rigorous investigation turned up doubts about the kidnapping story, the police questioned Susan again. Not only did she change her story, but she made the teary confession that she had killed her two children. She said that she had parked her car by the edge of the lake,

Susan first said her sons were kidnapped but later confessed that she had drowned them.

strapped her two children into their car seats, shut the windows and doors, got out of the car, walked to the rear, and pushed the car into the lake. She covered her ears so she couldn't hear the splash. The car disappeared under the water. The two little boys, strapped into their seats, drowned.

Susan's confession stunned the nation as everyone asked, "How could she have killed her own children?" "What's wrong with Susan?" To answer these questions, mental health professionals evaluated Susan's mental health with a procedure called the clinical assessment.

A *clinical assessment* involves a systematic evaluation of an individual's various psychological, biological, and social factors, as well as identifying past and present problems, stressors, and other cognitive or behavioral symptoms.

A clinical assessment is the first step in figuring out which past or current problems may have contributed to Susan killing her own children (Begley, 1998). We'll discuss how a clinical assessment is done.

## Three Methods of Assessment

**How was Susan evaluated?**

After Susan's arrest, mental health professionals did clinical assessments to try to discover what terrible forces pushed her over the edge. Depending on their training, mental health professionals use one or more of three major techniques—clinical interviews, psychological tests, and neurological exams—to do clinical assessments.

### Neurological Tests

We can assume that Susan was given a number of *neurological tests* to check for possible brain damage or malfunction. These tests might include evaluating reflexes, brain structures (MRI scans), and brain functions (fMRI scans, p. 70).

Neurological exams are part of a clinical assessment because a variety of abnormal psychological symptoms may be caused by tumors, diseases, or infections of the brain.

Did Susan have neurological problems?

Neurological tests are used to distinguish physical or organic causes (tumors) from psychological ones (strange beliefs) (Howieson & Lezak, 1997). Susan was not reported to have neurological problems.

### Clinical Interview

As part of her clinical assessment, several psychiatrists spent many hours interviewing Susan. This method is called a clinical interview.

The *clinical interview* is one method of gathering information about a person's past and current behaviors, beliefs, attitudes, emotions, and problems. Some clinical interviews are unstructured, which means they have no set questions; others are structured, which means they follow a standard format of asking a similar set of questions.

During the clinical interview, Susan would have been asked about the history of her current problems, such as when they started and what other events accompanied them. The focus of the interview would have been on Susan's current problem, killing her children, especially on the

What are Susan's past and current psychological problems?

details of the symptoms that led up to the killing. The clinical interview is perhaps the primary technique used to assess abnormal behavior (Barlow & Durand, 1995).

Based on 15 hours of interviews, Dr. Seymour Halleck testified that Susan was scarred by her father's suicide and her stepfather sexually abusing her, which led to periods of depression, her current problem (Towle, 1995).

### Psychological Tests

As part of her assessment, psychologists may have given Susan a number of personality tests (pp. 450, 474).

*Personality tests* include two different kinds of tests: objective tests (self-report questionnaires), such as the MMPI, which consist of specific statements or questions to which the person responds with specific answers, and projective tests, such as the Rorschach inkblot test, which have no set answers but consist of ambiguous stimuli that a person interprets or makes up a story about.

As we also discussed in Modules 19 and 20, personality tests help clinicians evaluate a person's traits, attitudes, emotions, and beliefs.

**Purpose.** A major goal of doing a clinical assessment is to decide which mental health disorder best accounts for a client's symptoms. For example, based on her symptoms, Susan was described as having a mood disorder, which you'll see next is one of many possible mental health problems.

### Real-Life Assessment

**How many mental disorders?**

In criminal trials that involve questions of mental health, the defense and prosecution usually hire their own psychiatrists or psychologists because they are looking for different problems or symptoms. In Susan's case, at least two psychiatrists did clinical assessments to answer a number of questions: What are her current symptoms? What past events and situations caused these symptoms? What role did her symptoms play in the killing of her children?

#### Her Past

During clinical interviews, the psychiatrist found that when Susan was 8 years old, her father shot himself. When she was 13, psychologists wanted to admit her to a hospital to treat her depression, but her mother and stepfather refused to cooperate. Later, when Susan was 15, her stepfather sexually molested her, but her mother refused to press charges. When she was in high school, she had periods of depression and attempted suicide. However, she did well academically, was an honor student and a member of the math club, and was voted the "friendliest female" in the class of 1989. She married David in 1991, but one year after the birth of their second son, their marriage fell apart and they filed for divorce (Bragg, 1995).

Dr. Seymour Halleck testified that Susan was scarred by her father's suicide, her stepfather's sexual abuse, and her periods of depression, which contributed to her current difficulties (Towle, 1995).

Susan's clinical assessment revealed a disturbed person. She is being led away to serve a life sentence.

#### Her Present

The psychiatrist found that Susan's present problems included becoming depressed after being rejected by her current boyfriend. She confessed to being so lonely in the months before the killings that she had multiple sexual encounters: with her stepfather, who had molested her as a teenager; with her estranged husband, whom she was divorcing; with her current boyfriend, who later wrote the good-bye letter; and with her boyfriend's father. In addition, Susan was drinking heavily during this period.

Dr. Halleck testified that Susan suffered from severe depression, drinking, and an adjustment disorder that caused her to have a heightened emotional reaction to stress (Morgan, 1995).

In just $2\frac{1}{2}$ hours, the jury decided that Susan Smith was guilty of murder. She was led from the courthouse (upper left photo) to serve a life sentence.

As a result of her clinical assessment, Susan was diagnosed as having a mood disorder and was treated in prison with antidepressants.

A clinical assessment is a method of identifying a client's symptoms, which are used to make a diagnosis. Making a diagnosis requires matching the symptoms to a particular disorder, which involves using the DSM-IV-TR.

### DSM-IV-TR

**How many mental disorders?**

Those who knew Susan tried to diagnose the problem that led to her tragic crime.

"Maybe Susan was just plain crazy." "Maybe she was too depressed to know what she was doing." "Maybe she had bad genes." "Maybe something bad happened to her as a child."

Using a more rigorous method, mental health professionals conduct clinical assessments to identify symptoms, which are then used to make a clinical diagnosis.

A *clinical diagnosis* is a process of matching an individual's specific symptoms to those that define a particular mental disorder.

Making a clinical diagnosis was very difficult prior to the 1950s because there was no uniform code or diagnostic system. However, since 1952, the American Psychiatric Association (APA) has been developing a uniform diagnostic system, whose most recent version is known as the *Diagnostic and Statistical Manual of Mental Disorders*-IV-Text Revision, abbreviated as DSM-IV-TR (American Psychiatric Association, 2000).

The *Diagnostic and Statistical Manual of Mental Disorders*-IV-Test Revision, or DSM-IV-TR, describes a uniform system for assessing specific symptoms and matching them to almost 300 different mental disorders.

The first *Diagnostic and Statistical Manual of Mental Disorders* (1952) described about 100 mental disorders, as compared to the almost 300 in DSM-IV-TR (right figure).

A major improvement in DSM-II (1968) was to give general descriptions of mental problems based on Sigmund Freud's concepts of *psychoses* (severe mental disorders, such as schizophrenia) and *neuroses* (less severe forms of psychological conflict, such as anxiety). Because these Freudian-based descriptions were rather general and based more on expert opinion than on research findings, there were considerable disagreements in making clinical diagnoses.

To decrease such disagreements, the DSM-III (1980) dropped Freudian terminology and instead listed specific symptoms and criteria for mental disorders. However, since criteria for mental disorders were still based primarily on clinical opinion, disagreements continued over making uniform diagnoses.

A major improvement in the current DSM-IV-TR is that it establishes criteria and symptoms for mental disorders based more on research findings than on expert clinical opinion (Clark et al., 1995).

We'll use the cases of Jeffrey Dahmer (serial killer), Susan Smith (murderer), and Kate Premo (phobia of flying) to show how mental health professionals use the DSM-IV-TR to make a diagnosis.

| Number of Disorders | |
| --- | --- |
| DSM-I | 106 |
| DSM-II | 182 |
| DSM-III | 265 |
| DSM-IV-TR | 297 |

# C. Diagnosing Mental Disorders

**Power Study™**

**Check out CD: Module 3**
B. Neurons: Structure &
Function
**Check out CD: Module 12**
C. Reasons for Forgetting

--- **Nine Major Problems: Axis I** ---

**How do we make a diagnosis?**

In making a clinical diagnosis, a mental health professional first assesses the client's specific symptoms and then matches these symptoms to those described in the DSM-IV-TR. The DSM-IV-TR has five major dimensions, called *axes,* which serve as guidelines for making decisions about symptoms. We'll first describe Axis I and show how it can be used to diagnose the very different problems of Susan Smith and Kate Premo. (The numbered items below and on the opposite page are based on the *Diagnostic and Statistical Manual of Mental Disorders*-Text Revision [2000], American Psychiatric Association.)

## Axis I: Nine Major Clinical Syndromes

Axis I contains lists of symptoms and criteria about the onset, severity, and duration of these symptoms. In turn these lists of symptoms are used to make a clinical diagnosis of the following nine major clinical syndromes.

**1. Disorders usually first diagnosed in infancy, childhood, or adolescence.**

This category includes disorders that arise before adolescence, such as attention deficit disorders, autism, mental retardation, enuresis, and stuttering (discussed in Modules 1, 2, and 13).

**2. Organic mental disorders.**

PS These disorders are temporary or permanent dysfunctions of brain tissue caused by diseases or chemicals, such as delirium, dementia (Alzheimer's; p. 50), and amnesia (p. 265).

**3. Substance-related disorders.**

This category refers to the maladaptive use of drugs and alcohol. Mere consumption and recreational use of such substances are not disorders. This category requires an abnormal pattern of use, as with alcohol abuse and cocaine dependence (pp. 188–189).

**4. Schizophrenia and other psychotic disorders.**

The schizophrenias are characterized by psychotic symptoms (for example, grossly disorganized behavior, delusions, and hallucinations) and by over six months of behavioral deterioration. This category, which also includes delusional disorder and schizoaffective disorder, will be discussed in Module 23.

**5. Mood disorders.**

The cardinal feature is emotional disturbance. Patients may or may not have psychotic symptoms. These disorders, including major depression, bipolar disorder, dysthymic disorder, and cyclothymic disorder, are discussed in Module 23. Susan Smith is an example of a person with a mood disorder.

**Susan Smith: Diagnosis—Mood Disorder**

From childhood on, Susan's symptoms include being depressed, attempting suicide, seeking sexual alliances to escape loneliness, drinking heavily, and having feelings of low self-esteem and

Diagnosis:
Mood disorder

hopelessness, all of which match the DSM-IV-TR's list of symptoms for a mood disorder. In Susan's case, the specific mood disorder most closely matches major depressive disorder but without serious thought disorders and delusions.

In diagnosing major depression, the DSM-IV-TR distinguishes between early (before age 21) and late onset depression—Susan would be early; and between mild and severe depression, as judged by how many episodes of depression she had and whether she showed a decreased capacity to function normally, such as the inability to work or care for children. Susan's ability to hold a job and care for her children suggest mild depression. This example shows how the guidelines of Axis I are used to arrive at one of nine major clinical syndromes—in this case, major depression.

**6. Anxiety disorders.**

These disorders are characterized by physiological signs of anxiety (for example, palpitations) and subjective feelings of tension, apprehension, or fear. Anxiety may be acute and focused (phobias) or continual and diffuse (generalized anxiety disorder). An example of an anxiety disorder is that of Kate Premo.

**Kate Premo: Diagnosis—Specific Phobia**

Kate Premo's symptoms include having an intense fear of flying, knowing that her fear is irrational and that she can't control it, going out of her way to avoid flying, and making reservations that she later cancels. Kate's symptoms most closely match the DSM-IV-TR's list of symptoms for an anxiety disorder called a specific phobia. The DSM-IV-TR's symptoms for a specific phobia match those of Premo—experiencing intense and irrational fear when exposed to a feared situation (flying) and

Diagnosis:
Specific phobia
(aerophobia)

having to avoid that situation at all costs, which interferes with part of her normal activities (going to meetings).

**7. Somatoform disorders.**

These disorders are dominated by somatic symptoms that resemble physical illnesses. These symptoms cannot be accounted for by organic damage. There must also be strong evidence that these symptoms are produced by psychological factors or conflicts. This category, which includes somatization and conversion disorders and hypochondriasis, will be discussed in this module.

**8. Dissociative disorders.**

These disorders all feature a sudden, temporary alteration or dysfunction of memory, consciousness, identity, and behavior, as in dissociative amnesia and multiple personality (discussed in Module 23).

**9. Sexual and gender-identity disorders.**

There are three types of disorders in this category: gender-identity disorders (discomfort with identity as male or female), paraphilias (preference for unusual acts to achieve sexual arousal), and sexual dysfunctions (impairments in sexual functioning) (discussed in Module 15).

## Other Problems and Disorders: Axes II, III, IV, V

We have explained how Axis I is used to make clinical diagnoses of such mental disorders as major depression (mood disorder) and specific phobias (fear of flying). Now, we'll briefly describe how the other four axes are used in diagnosing problems.

### Axis II: Personality Disorders

This axis refers to disorders that involve patterns of personality traits that are long-standing, maladaptive, and inflexible and involve impaired functioning or subjective distress. Examples include borderline, schizoid, and antisocial personality disorders. Personality disorders will be discussed in Module 23. An example of a personality disorder is that of Dahmer.

Diagnosis:
Antisocial
personality disorder

#### Jeffrey Dahmer: Diagnosis—Antisocial Personality Disorder

Jeffrey Dahmer's symptoms include sexually assaulting and killing 15 young men, in some cases eating parts of them, feeling no guilt or remorse, and exhibiting this behavior over a considerable period of time. Dahmer's symptoms may indicate a combination of mental disorders, but here we'll focus on only one from the DSM-IV-TR, a personality disorder. According to DSM-IV-TR, the essential features of an antisocial personality disorder are the existence of strange inner experiences that differ greatly from the expectations of one's culture, that lead to significant impairment in personal, occupational, or social functioning, and that form a pattern of disregard for, and violation of, the rights of others. This list of symptoms from DSM-IV-TR matches those of Dahmer.

### Axis III: General Medical Conditions

This axis refers to physical disorders or conditions, such as diabetes, arthritis, and hemophilia, that have an influence on someone's mental disorder.

### Axis IV: Psychosocial and Environmental Problems

This axis refers to psychosocial and environmental problems that may affect the diagnosis, treatment, and prognosis of mental disorders in Axes I and II. A psychosocial or environmental problem may be a negative life event (experiencing a traumatic event), an environmental difficulty or deficiency, a familial or other interpersonal stress, an inadequacy of social support or personal resources, or another problem that describes the context in which a person's difficulties have developed (PTSD was discussed on p. 491).

### Axis V: Global Assessment of Functioning Scale

This axis is used to rate the overall psychological, social, and occupational functioning of the individual on a scale from 10 (severe danger of hurting self) to 100 (superior functioning in all activities).

**Using All Five Axes.** Mental health professionals use all five axes to make a clinical diagnosis. For example, in making a clinical diagnosis of Jeffrey Dahmer, his unusual sexual symptoms may match those of a sexual disorder in *Axis I*. His other maladaptive symptoms match those of an antisocial personality disorder in *Axis II*. Dahmer apparently had no related medical conditions listed in *Axis III*. Dahmer was a loner with poor self-esteem and poor social skills, which match some of the psychological, social, and environmental factors listed in *Axis IV*. Amazingly, Dahmer functioned well enough to hold a job and go unnoticed in his neighborhood, which would be used to rate his general functioning listed in *Axis V.* As you can see, each of the five axes in DSM-IV-TR focuses on a different factor that contributes to making an overall clinical diagnosis of a person's mental health.

### USEFULNESS OF DSM-IV-TR

The figure below shows the steps in making a clinical diagnosis. Mental health professionals begin by using three different methods to identify a client's symptoms, a process called clinical assessment. Next, the client's symptoms are matched to the five axes in the DSM-IV-TR to arrive at a diagnosis of each client's particular mental disorder.

> 1. Clinical interview
> 2. Personality tests
> 3. Neurological tests
>
> Clinical assessment:
> identify symptoms
>
> DSM-IV-TR:
> Use symptoms
> to diagnose
> mental disorder

For mental health professionals, there are three advantages of using DSM-IV-TR's uniform system to diagnose and classify mental disorders (Widiger & Clark, 2000).

First, mental health professionals use the classification system to communicate with one another and discuss their clients' problems.

Second, researchers use the classification system to study and explain mental disorders.

Third, therapists use the classification system to design their treatment program so as to best fit a particular client's problem.

Although using the DSM-IV-TR system to diagnose mental problems has advantages, it also has a number of potential problems. For example, mental health professionals do not always agree on whether a client fits a particular diagnosis. In addition, there are a number of social, political, and labeling problems, which we'll discuss next.

### Potential Problems with Using DSM-IV-TR

**Is labeling a problem?** It's not uncommon to hear people use labels, such as "Jim's really anxious," "Mary Ann is compulsive," or "Vicki is schizophrenic." Although the goal of the DSM-IV-TR is to give mental disorders particular diagnostic labels, once a person is labeled, the label itself may generate a negative stereotype. In turn, the negative stereotype results in negative social and political effects, such as biasing how others perceive and respond to the labeled person (Corrigan, 2000).

#### Labeling Mental Disorders

David Oaks, a sophomore at Harvard University, was having such fearful emotional experiences that he was examined by a psychiatrist. Although David believed that he was having a mystical experience, the psychiatrist interpreted and labeled David's fearful experiences as indicating a kind of short-term schizophrenic disorder (Japenga, 1994). As in David's case, when a mental health professional makes a clinical diagnosis the result is to give the client's problem a label.

*Labeling* refers to identifying and naming differences among individuals. The label, which places individuals into specific categories, may have either positive or negative associations.

At first David felt relieved to know that his problem had a diagnosis or label. Later he realized that his new label was changing his life for the worse. People no longer responded to him as David-the-college-sophomore but as David-with-schizophrenic-disorder.

As David's case shows, the advantage of diagnostic labels is their ability to summarize and communicate a whole lot of information in a single word or phrase. But, the disadvantage is that if the label has negative associations—for example, mentally ill, retarded, schizo—the very label may elicit negative or undesirable responses. For this reason, mental health professionals advise that we avoid responding to people with mental disorders by their labels and instead respond to the person behind the label (Foxhall, 2000).

Some labels (anxious, depressed) generate negative stereotypes.

#### Social and Political Implications

A dramatic example of the power of labels was the public announcement by television actress Ellen DeGeneres that she was a lesbian. As a result, millions of viewers who had never tuned in to watch Ellen-the-sitcom-star now tuned in to watch Ellen-the-lesbian (Marin & Miller, 1997). Similarly, diagnostic labels, such as anxious, compulsive, or mentally ill, can change how an individual is perceived and thus have important political and social implications.

For instance, in the early 1970s, gays protested that homosexuality should not be included in DSM-I and II as a mental disorder. When studies found that homosexuals were no more or less mentally healthy than heterosexuals, homosexuality as a mental disorder was eliminated from DSM-III. Dropping this label had a powerful social and political effect because no longer would being homosexual be considered a mental disorder.

In the 1980s, women protested the DSM label of self-defeating personality disorder because this disorder applied primarily to women who were said to make destructive life choices, such as to stay in abusive relationships (Japenga, 1994). This label was dropped from DSM-IV because it suggested that women were deliberately choosing bad relationships, which wasn't true (Caplan, 1994).

These two examples illustrate the social and political implications of labeling individuals with mental disorders. One advantage of the current DSM-IV-TR is that labels or diagnostic categories are based more on empirical findings, which reduces the potential for bias (Widiger & Clark, 2000). For this reason, the DSM-IV-TR is considered a great improvement over previous manuals.

### Frequency of Mental Disorders

Although labels are a fact of life, researchers and clinicians try to apply the DSM labels as fairly as possible. For example, researchers interviewed a national sample of over 8,000 noninstitutionalized civilians between 15 and 54 years old and diagnosed their problems using the DSM's diagnostic system. As the graph shows, almost 50% of those surveyed reported at least one lifetime disorder (Kessler et al., 1994). The most common mental disorder was substance abuse, especially problems with alcohol. What was surprising was that about 60% of

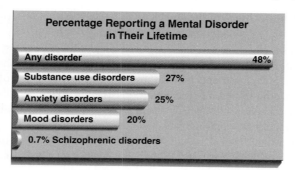

**Percentage Reporting a Mental Disorder in Their Lifetime**

| | |
|---|---|
| Any disorder | 48% |
| Substance use disorders | 27% |
| Anxiety disorders | 25% |
| Mood disorders | 20% |
| 0.7% Schizophrenic disorders | |

those with a lifetime mental disorder had neither asked for nor received any professional treatment. This study also replicated findings that a larger proportion of women (24%) than of men (15%) report mood disorders, while a larger proportion of men (35%) than of women (18%) report substance use disorder.

Researchers concluded that the accuracy of their interview method revealed a greater prevalence of mental disorders than had previously been recorded and that most individuals with a mental disorder do not seek treatment.

Next, we'll examine the symptoms and treatment of specific disorders, beginning with anxiety.

**How common is anxiety?**

The second most common mental disorder reported by adults in the United States is any kind of anxiety disorder (right graph) (Emmelkamp & van Oppen, 1994; Kessler et al., 1994). In addition, anxiety is either the first or second most commonly reported mental disorder in children and adolescents (Strauss, 1994). We have already discussed one serious anxiety problem, posttraumatic stress disorder (PTSD), in Module 21. Here we'll discuss six of the more common forms of anxiety, including generalized anxiety disorder, panic disorder, three kinds of phobias, and obsessive-compulsive disorders.

**Anxiety Disorders**

| | |
|---|---|
| 25% | Any anxiety disorder |
| 13% | Social phobia |
| 11% | Specific phobia |
| 5% | Generalized anxiety |
| 5% | Agoraphobia |
| 4% | Panic disorder |
| 3% | Obsessive-compulsive |

## Generalized Anxiety Disorder

During his initial therapy interview, Fred was sweating, fidgeting in his chair, and repeatedly asking for water to quench a never-ending thirst. From all indications, Fred was visibly distressed and extremely nervous. At first, Fred spoke only of his dizziness and problems with sleeping. However, it soon became clear that he had nearly always felt tense. He admitted to a long history of difficulties in interacting with others, difficulties that led to his being fired from two jobs. He constantly worried about all kinds of possible disasters that might happen to him (Davison & Neale, 1990). Fred's symptoms showed that he was suffering from generalized anxiety disorder.

*Generalized anxiety disorder* is characterized by excessive or unrealistic worry about almost everything or feeling that something bad is about to happen. These anxious feelings occur on a majority of days for a period of at least six months (American Psychiatric Association, 2000).

### SYMPTOMS

Generalized anxiety disorder includes both psychological and physical symptoms. Psychological symptoms include being irritable, having difficulty concentrating, and being unable to control one's worry, which is out of proportion to the actual event. Constant worrying causes significant distress or impaired functioning in social, occupational, or other areas (American Psychiatric Association, 2000). Physical symptoms include restlessness, being easily fatigued, sweating, flushing, pounding heart, insomnia, clammy hands, headaches, and muscle tension or aches. Along with Fred, about 5% of adults in the United States report suffering from generalized anxiety disorder (Hunt, 2000).

Anxiety can be treated with drugs and psychotherapy.

### TREATMENT

Generalized anxiety disorder is commonly treated with psychotherapy (Module 24), with or without drugs. The drugs most frequently prescribed are tranquilizers such as alprazolam and diazepam, which belong to a group known as the *benzodiazepines (ben-zoh-die-AS-ah-peens)*. In moderate doses, the benzodiazepines are not usually physically addicting. In higher doses, however, these drugs are addicting and interfere with the ability to remember newly learned information (Stahl, 2000).

Researchers found that about 40 to 50% of clients treated for generalized anxiety disorder with either psychotherapy (cognitive-behavioral) or drugs (tranquilizers) were free of symptoms one year later (Gould et al., 1997).

## Panic Disorder

Karen went down the street to Antoine's Beauty Shop to have her hair set. As she was sitting under the dryer, a sudden feeling swept over her. She thought she was losing her mind. Her heart started beating fast, her legs felt weak, and her body trembled. As a wave of fear spread over her, she wanted to scream. Suddenly Karen jumped up with all the pins still in her hair, slapped a $5 bill on the counter, and ran all the way home (*Los Angeles Times,* December 13, 1981). Karen's symptoms indicate that she had a panic disorder.

*Panic disorder* is characterized by recurrent and unexpected panic attacks. Plus, the person is so worried about having another panic attack that this intense worrying interferes with normal psychological functioning (American Psychiatric Association, 2000).

Like Karen, about 4% of adults in the United States suffer from panic disorder, and women are 2–3 times more likely to report it than are men (Kessler et al., 1994). People who suffer from panic disorder have an increased risk of alcohol and other drug abuse, an increased incidence of suicide, decreased social functioning, and decreased marital happiness; about a third suffer from depression (Emmelkamp & van Oppen, 1994).

### SYMPTOMS

Karen's symptoms in the beauty shop indicate that she was having a panic attack, which may occur in several different anxiety disorders but is the essential feature of panic disorder.

A *panic attack* is a period of intense fear or discomfort in which four or more of the following symptoms are present: pounding heart, sweating, trembling, shortness of breath, feelings of choking, chest pain, nausea, feeling dizzy, and fear of losing control or dying (American Psychiatric Association, 2000).

### TREATMENT

Panic disorders are usually treated with a combination of benzodiazepines or antidepressants and/or psychotherapy. Successful treatment may require 3–8 months of drug therapy and psychotherapy (Bakker et al., 1999). However, some clients relapsed once drug treatment was stopped. Researchers found that, one year after treatment with a combination of psychotherapy and drugs, about 30 to 50% of clients were symptom-free (Pollack & Otto, 1997).

Another kind of anxiety disorder that is relatively common involves a number of phobias.

## Phobias

**Can fear go wild?**

We all have fears of various things, such as exams, seeing blood, spiders, injections, mice, meeting new people, speaking in public, flying, or being in small places. But sometimes these common fears turn into very intense fears, called phobias.

A *phobia (FOE-bee-ah)* is an anxiety disorder characterized by an intense and irrational fear that is out of all proportion to the possible danger of the object or situation. Because of this intense fear, which is accompanied by increased physiological arousal, a person goes to great lengths to avoid the feared event. If the feared event cannot be avoided, the person feels intense anxiety.

Reseachers believe that, because 75% of individuals with phobias could trace their onset to specific traumatic events, the majority of phobias are learned through conditioning or observation (Menzies & Clarke, 1995). However, since 25% of those with phobias could not recall their onset, there may also be other causes of phobias.

We discussed blood injection phobias earlier (pp. 201, 487). Here we'll discuss three more common phobias—social phobias, specific phobias, and agoraphobia (graph above) (Kessler et al., 1994).

| Common Phobias | |
| --- | --- |
| Social phobia | 13% |
| Specific phobia | 11% |
| Agoraphobia | 5% |

### Social Phobia

**Why didn't Billy talk up in class?**

In junior high school, Billy never, never spoke up in class or answered any questions. The school counselor said that Billy would be sick to his stomach the whole day if he knew that he was going to be called on. Billy began to hide out in the restrooms to avoid going to class. Billy's fear of speaking up in class is an example of a social phobia (Barlow & Durand, 1995).

*Social phobias* are characterized by irrational, marked, and continuous fear of performing in social situations. The individuals fear that they will humiliate or embarrass themselves (American Psychiatric Association, 2000).

| Social Phobias | |
| --- | --- |
| 8% | Speaking in public |
| 5% | Speaking to strangers |
| 4% | Eating in public |

Source: Eaton et al., 1991

As a fearful social situation approaches (graph above), anxiety builds up and may result in considerable bodily distress, such as nausea, sweating, and other signs of heightened physiological arousal. Although a person with a social phobia realizes that the fear is excessive or irrational, he or she may not know how to deal with it, other than by avoiding the situation.

### Specific Phobias

**Why couldn't Kate get on a plane?**

In the beginning of this module, we told you about Kate Premo (left photo), whose  traumatic childhood and adult experiences with flying turned into a phobia of flying, which is called a specific phobia.

*Specific phobias,* formerly called simple phobias, are characterized by marked and persistent fears that are unreasonable and triggered by anticipation of, or exposure to, a specific object or situation (flying, heights, spiders, seeing blood) (American Psychiatric Association, 2000).

| Specific Phobias | |
| --- | --- |
| Bugs, snakes, etc. | 23% |
| Heights | 22% |
| Water | 13% |
| Closed places | 10% |

Source: Eaton et al., 1991

Among the more common specific phobias seen in clinical practice (graph above) are fear of animals (zoophobia), fear of heights (acrophobia), fear of confinement (claustrophobia), fear of injury or blood, and fear of flying (Emmelkamp & van Oppen, 1994).

The content and occurrence of specific phobias vary with culture. For example, fears of spirits or ghosts are present in many cultures but become specific phobias only if the fear turns excessive and irrational (American Psychiatric Association, 2000).

### Agoraphobia

**Why couldn't Rose leave her house?**

Fear trapped Rose in her house for years. If she thought about going outside to do her shopping, pain raced through her arms and chest. She grew hot and perspired. Her heart beat rapidly and her legs felt like rubber. She said that thinking about leaving her house caused stark terror, sometimes lasting for days. This 39-year-old mother of two is one of millions of Americans suffering from an intense fear of being in public places, which is called agoraphobia (*Los Angeles Times,* October 19, 1980).

*Agoraphobia* is characterized by anxiety about being in places or situations from which escape might be difficult or embarrassing (graph below) if a panic attack or paniclike symptoms (sudden dizziness or onset of diarrhea) were to occur (American Psychiatric Association, 2000).

Agoraphobia arises out of an underlying fear of either having a full-blown panic attack (discussed on the previous page) or having a sudden and unexpected onset of paniclike symptoms.

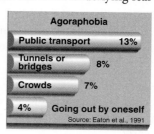

| Agoraphobia | |
| --- | --- |
| Public transport | 13% |
| Tunnels or bridges | 8% |
| Crowds | 7% |
| Going out by oneself | 4% |

Source: Eaton et al., 1991

After any of these phobias are established, they are extremely persistent and may continue for years if not treated (Leahy & Holland, 2000). We'll discuss drug and psychological treatments for phobias later in this module—in the Application section.

Next, we'll look at another form of anxiety that can be very difficult to deal with—obsessive-compulsive disorders.

**Why was Shirley always late?**

Shirley was an outgoing, popular high school student with average grades. Her one problem was that she was late for school almost every day. Before she could leave the house in the morning, she had to be very sure that she was clean, so she needed to take a shower that lasted a full 2 hours. After her 2-hour shower, she spent a long time dressing, because for each thing she did, such as putting on her stockings, underclothes, skirt, and blouse, she had to repeat each act precisely 17 times. When asked about her washing and counting, she said she knew that it was crazy but that she just had to do it and couldn't explain why. She said that she had struggled against this problem for three years without success (Rapoport,

**Anxiety Disorders**

| | |
|---|---|
| Social phobia | 13% |
| 5% Agoraphobia | |
| 3% Obsessive-compulsive | |

1988). Shirley's symptoms would be diagnosed as indicative of an anxiety problem called an obsessive-compulsive disorder.

An *obsessive-compulsive disorder* consists of obsessions, which are persistent, recurring irrational thoughts, impulses, or images that a person is unable to control and that interfere with normal functioning, and compulsions, which are irresistible impulses to perform over and over some senseless behavior or ritual (hand washing, checking things, counting, putting things in order) (American Psychiatric Association, 2000).

Only five years ago, obsessive-compulsive disorder (OCD) was considered relatively rare, but now it is known to affect about 3% of adults in the United States (left graph) (Stanley & Turner, 1995). Worldwide, about 2 to 3% of the general population suffer from OCD (Horwath & Weissman, 2000).

## *Symptoms*

Shirley's symptoms included both obsession— her need to be very clean and careful about dressing—and compulsions—her need to take 2-hour showers and to perform each act of dressing precisely 17

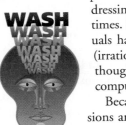

times. Some individuals have obsessions (irrational, recurring thoughts) without compulsions.

Because compulsions are usually very time-consuming, they often take an hour or more to complete each day. Although doing the compulsive behaviors may help individuals reduce their anxiety in the short term, in the long term the compulsive behaviors interfere with normal daily functioning.

The most common compulsions involve cleaning, checking, and counting; the less common include buying, hoarding, and putting things in order. For example, individuals obsessed with being dirty or contaminated reduce their anxiety by washing their hands until their skin is raw, while those obsessed with leaving a door unlocked may be driven to check the lock every few minutes (American Psychiatric Association, 2000). These kinds of obsessive-compulsive behaviors interfere with normal functioning and make holding a job or engaging in social interactions difficult.

## *Treatment*

In the late 1980s, obsessive-compulsive disorder was thought to be an incurable disorder. Currently, however, about half the patients report improvement after being treated with some combination of exposure psychotherapy and several drugs (Hollander et al., 2000; Neziroglu et al., 2000).

**Exposure therapy.** Shirley's compulsive behaviors are thought to be one way that she reduces or avoids anxiety—in her case, anxiety associated with feeling dirty. The most successful treatment programs involve exposure therapy.

*Exposure therapy* consists of gradually exposing the person to the real anxiety-producing situations or objects that he or she is attempting to avoid and continuing exposure treatments until the anxiety decreases.

For example, Shirley would be exposed to dirt or dirty things over and over until such exposure elicited little or no anxiety. After *exposure therapy*, about 85% of patients reported being improved and 55% of them reported being much improved (Neziroglu et al., 2000).

**Antidepressant drugs.** Clients who cannot tolerate exposure therapy or are not motivated to undergo exposure therapy may be given drugs. For example, Shirley refused to try exposure therapy and insisted that she had to continue her washing and counting rituals. But after taking an antidepressant drug (clomipramine) for about three weeks, her urges to wash and count faded sufficiently that she could try exposure therapy (Rapoport, 1988). However, about 50% of clients with obsessive-compulsive disorder (OCD) are not helped by antidepressants or even a newer class of drugs called selective serotonin reuptake inhibitors (sertraline) (Hollander et al., 2000).

For those 50% of individuals with OCD for whom drug treatment is not effective, exposure or cognitive-behavioral therapy may be helpful, especially since these psychotherapies have no unwanted physical side effects. Researchers found that both exposure and cognitive-behavioral therapy were either equal to or more effective than antidepressant drugs or the newer selective serotonin reuptake inhibitors. In some cases, a combination of exposure therapy and drug treatments proved best (Hollander et al., 2000).

Researchers have found that OCD has both genetic (runs in families) and neurological (malfunctioning basal ganglia) factors (Baxter, 2000; Wolff et al., 2000). Because of these underlying genetic and neurological factors, OCD tends to be a chronic problem that requires treatment with drugs, psychotherapy, or some combination (Neziroglu et al., 2000).

Next, we'll discuss how people create real physical symptoms that also interfere with normal functioning.

Treatment for obsessive-compulsive behavior is psychotherapy and/or several drugs.

# E. Somatoform Disorders

Imagine someone whose whole life centers around physical symptoms, some of which are imagined and others that appear real, such as developing paralysis in one's legs. This intense focus on imagined, painful, or uncomfortable physical symptoms is characteristic of individuals with somatoform disorders.

*Somatoform (so-MA-toe-form) disorders* are marked by a pattern of recurring, multiple, and significant bodily (somatic) symptoms that extend over several years. The bodily symptoms (pain, vomiting, paralysis, blindness) are not under voluntary control, have no known physical causes, and are believed to be caused by psychological factors (American Psychiatric Association, 2000).

Although the term *somatoform disorders* is not well known, these disorders are among the most common health problems seen in general medical practice (Kirmayer et al., 1994). The DSM-IV-TR lists seven kinds of somatoform disorders. We'll discuss two of the more common forms—somatization and conversion disorders.

### SOMATIZATION DISORDER

One kind of somatoform disorder, which was historically called hysteria, is now called somatization disorder and is relatively rare (2.7% of population).

*Somatization disorder* begins before age 30, lasts over several years, and is characterized by multiple symptoms—including pain, gastrointestinal, sexual, and neurological symptoms—that have no physical causes but are triggered by psychological problems or distress (American Psychiatric Association, 2000).

A psychologically distressed individual may have painful physical symptoms that have no physical causes.

This disorder is reported in most cultures, and women are five times more likely to report it than men (Gureje et al., 1997). Those having this disorder use health services frequently and tend to have many hospitalizations and surgeries (Wool & Barsky, 1994). Researchers found that this disorder is frequently associated with a variety of personality problems, such as paranoia (Kirmayer et al., 1994). Somatization disorders are apparently a means of coping with a stressful situation, indicating distress, or obtaining wanted attention (Barlow & Durand, 2001).

### CONVERSION DISORDER

Sometimes individuals report serious physical problems, such as blindness, which have no physical causes and are examples of a somatoform disorder called conversion disorder.

A *conversion disorder* refers to changing anxiety or emotional distress into real physical, motor, sensory, or neurological symptoms (headaches, nausea, dizziness, loss of sensation, paralysis) for which no physical or organic cause can be identified (American Psychiatric Association, 2000).

For example, individuals have reported paralysis of a limb, lack of balance, blindness, or seizures, when in fact no physical, organic, or neurological damage could be identified. Usually the symptoms of a conversion disorder are associated with psychological factors, such as depression, concerns about health, or the occurrence of a stressful situation. The development of physical symptoms gets the person attention, effectively removes the person from threatening or anxiety-producing situations, and thus reinforces the occurrence and maintenance of the symptoms involved in the conversion disorder (Barlow & Durand, 2001). Researchers found that in some cultures, bodily complaints (somatoform disorders) are used instead of emotional complaints to express psychological problems (Gureje et al., 1997).

The same kind of painful or uncomfortable physical symptoms observed in

As more than 500 students from various schools began to give a choir and orchestra concert, they suddenly began to complain of headaches, dizziness, weakness, abdominal pain, and nausea. These symptoms spread rapidly until about half the students developed one or more of the symptoms. Students who became ill were most often those who saw someone near them take ill. Students from one school, particularly girls in the soprano section, experienced the highest rate of symptoms. Younger members reported more symptoms than older ones, and girls (51%) reported more symptoms than boys (41%). At first, someone thought that a gas line had broken, but no one in the audience developed any symptoms. There was no ruptured gas line. The students' symptoms resulted from mass hysteria (Small et al., 1991).

*Mass hysteria* refers to a condition experienced by a group of people who, through suggestion, observation, or other psychological processes, develop similar fears, delusions, abnormal behaviors, or physical symptoms.

In this case, several of the most popular and visible girls complained of feeling dizzy and nauseous (they had been standing for hours). Soon, other students were complaining about having similar physical symptoms until over 200 students eventually developed these physical symptoms. A similar case of mass hysteria was recently reported in a group of high school students, 80 of whom were hospitalized with headache, nausea, shortness of breath, and dizziness (Jones, 2000).

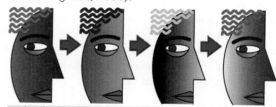

Individuals who are emotionally aroused in a group may experience similar physical symptoms.

In the Middle Ages, hysteria was attributed to possession by evil spirits or the Devil. Today, mass hysteria is known to involve members of a group who experience and share emotional arousal or excitement, which spreads through the group and results in its members developing *real physical symptoms* with no known physical causes (Barlow & Durand, 2001). Mass hysteria is another example of somatoform disorders.

After the Concept Review, we'll discuss how symptoms of mental disorders can vary between cultures, as we examine a disorder that seems to be unique to Asian cultures, especially Japan.

# Concept Review

**1.** A prolonged or recurring problem that seriously interferes with the ability of an individual to live a satisfying personal life and function in society is called a _____.

**2.** There are three approaches to studying mental disorders. Viewing mental disorders as diseases is using the (a)_____ approach. Looking for the causes of mental disorders in unconscious conflicts or problems with unresolved conflicts is using the (b)_____ approach. Combining information from cognitive processes and learning-conditioning factors to understand mental disorders is using the (c)_____ approach.

**3.** There are three definitions of abnormality. A behavior that occurs infrequently in the general population is abnormal, according to the (a)_____ definition. A behavior that deviates greatly from accepted social norms is abnormal, according to the (b)_____ definition. Behavior that interferes with the individual's ability to function as a person or in society is abnormal, according to the (c)_____ definition, which is used by most mental health professionals.

**4.** When performed by a mental health professional, a systematic evaluation of an individual's various psychological, biological, and social factors that may be contributing to his or her problem is called a clinical (a)_____. A mental health professional who determines whether an individual's specific problem meets or matches the standard symptoms that define a particular mental disorder is doing a clinical (b)_____. One of the primary techniques used to gather an enormous amount of information about a person's past behavior, attitudes, and emotions and details of current problems is the clinical (c)_____.

**5.** The manual that describes the symptoms for almost 300 different mental disorders is called the (a)_____. The manual's primary goal is to provide mental health professionals with a means of (b)_____ mental disorders and (c)_____ that information in a systematic and uniform way. The DSM-IV-TR has five major dimensions, called (d)_____, which serve as guidelines for making decisions about symptoms.

| Number of Disorders | |
| --- | --- |
| DSM-I | 106 |
| DSM-II | 182 |
| DSM-III | 265 |
| DSM-IV-TR | 297 |

**6.** There are several kinds of anxiety disorders. An anxiety disorder that is characterized by excessive and/or unrealistic worry or feelings of general apprehension about events or activities, when those feelings occur on a majority of days for a period of at least six months, is called (a)_____ disorder. An anxiety disorder marked by the presence of recurrent and unexpected panic attacks, plus continued worry about having another panic attack, when such worry interferes with psychological functioning, is called a (b)_____ disorder. Suppose a person has a period of intense fear or discomfort during which four or more of the following symptoms are present: pounding heart, sweating, trembling, shortness of breath, feelings of choking, chest pain, nausea, feeling dizzy, and fear of losing control or dying. That person is experiencing a (c)_____.

**7.** An anxiety disorder characterized by an intense and irrational fear and heightened physiological arousal that is out of all proportion to the danger elicited by the object or situation is called a (a)_____, of which there are several kinds. Unreasonable, marked, and persistent fears that are triggered by anticipation of, or exposure to, a specific object or situation are called a (b)_____. An anxiety that comes from being in places or situations from which escape might be difficult or embarrassing if a panic attack or paniclike symptoms were to occur is called (c)_____. Irrational, marked, and continuous fear of performing in social situations and feeling humiliated or embarrassed is called a (d)_____.

**8.** A disorder that consists of persistent, recurring irrational thoughts, impulses, or images that a person is unable to control and irresistible impulses to perform over and over some senseless behavior or ritual is called (a)_____ disorder. A nondrug treatment for this disorder, which consists of gradually exposing the person to the real anxiety-producing situations or objects that he or she is attempting to avoid, is called (b)_____ therapy.

**9.** When something happens to a group of people so that all share the same fears or delusions, or develop similar physical symptoms, it is called (a)_____. There is a disorder that involves a pattern of recurring, multiple, and significant bodily complaints that have no known physical causes. This is called (b)_____ disorder, and one of its more common forms is somatization disorder.

***Answers:*** *1. mental disorder; 2. (a) medical, (b) psychoanalytic, (c) cognitive-behavioral; 3. (a) statistical, (b) social norms, (c) maladaptive; 4. (a) assessment, (b) diagnosis, (c) interview; 5. (a) Diagnostic and Statistical Manual—IV-TR, (b) diagnosing, (c) communicating, (d) axes; 6. (a) generalized anxiety, (b) panic, (c) panic attack; 7. (a) phobia, (b) specific phobia, (c) agoraphobia, (d) social phobia; 8. (a) obsessive-compulsive, (b) exposure; 9. (a) mass hysteria, (b) somatoform*

## Taijin Kyofusho, or TKS

**Can a culture create a disorder?**

Anxiety is a worldwide concern and is the second most common mental disorder in the United States and several Asian nations, notably Japan. We have described how the symptoms of one kind of anxiety disorder, somatoform disorder, occur in very similar form in many cultures around the world (Gureje et al., 1997). However, it's also true that the unique cultural values of some countries, such as Japan, can result in the development of a unique anxiety order not found in Western cultures, such as the United States.

If you had a *social phobia* in the United States, it would usually mean that you had a great fear or were greatly embarrassed about behaving or performing in social situations, such as making a public speech. But if you had a social phobia in several Asian cultures, especially Japan, it might mean that you had a very different kind of fear or embarrassment, called taijin kyofusho, or TKS.

In Japan, the fear of offending others, such as by staring, is considered a kind of social phobia.

*Taijin kyofusho (tie-GIN quo-FOO-show)*, or TKS, is a kind of social phobia characterized by a terrible fear of offending others through awkward social or physical behavior, such as staring, blushing, giving off an offensive odor, having an unpleasant facial expression, or having trembling hands (Kirmayer, 1991).

Although many Westerners are also concerned or embarrassed about offending others through staring, having offensive body odors, or blushing, TKS is different in that it is an intense, irrational, morbid fear—in other words, a true phobia. In desperately trying to avoid TKS symptoms, Asians may try to avoid social interactions altogether. The Japanese word *taijin-kyofu* literally means "fear of interpersonal relations."

**Occurrence.** The graph below shows that TKS is the third most common psychiatric disorder treated in Japanese college students (Kirmayer, 1991). TKS is more common in males than in females, with a ratio of about 5:4. Most patients have a primary symptom, which has changed during the past 40 years. Initially, fear of blushing was the primary symptom, but it has currently been replaced by fear of making eye contact or staring (Yamashita, 1993). In comparison, making eye contact is very common in Western cultures; if you did not make eye contact in social interactions, you would be judged as shy or lacking in social skills.

| Percentage of Students | |
|---|---|
| Psychosomatic disorders | 24% |
| Depressive reactions | 20% |
| TKS | 19% |

TKS begins around adolescence, when interpersonal interactions play a big role in one's life. TKS is rarely seen after the late 20s because, by then, individuals have learned the proper social behaviors. TKS seems to develop from certain cultural influences that are unique to Japan.

**Cultural values.** The Japanese culture places great emphasis on the appropriate way to conduct oneself in public, which means a person should avoid making direct eye contact, staring, blushing, having trembling hands, or giving off offensive odors. To emphasize the importance of avoiding these improper behaviors, mothers often use threats of abandonment, ridicule, and embarrassment as punishment. Through this process of *socialization*, the child is made aware of the importance of avoiding improper public behaviors, which result in a loss of face and reflect badly on the person's family and social group. Thus, from early on, Japanese children are strongly encouraged to live up to certain cultural expectations about avoiding improper public behaviors, especially staring and blushing, which are considered to be rude and disgraceful.

## Social Customs

In Japan, individuals are expected to know the needs and thoughts of others by reading the emotional expressions of faces rather than asking direct questions, which is considered rude social behavior. In contrast, Westerners may ask direct questions to clarify some point and often use direct eye contact to show interest. Individuals in Japan who make too much eye contact or ask too direct questions are likely to be viewed as insensitive to others, unpleasantly bold, or aggressive. In fact, Japanese children are taught to fix their gaze at the level of the neck of people they are talking to. This Japanese social custom that emphasizes not making eye contact, blushing, or having trembling hands or offensive body odors during social interactions results in about 20% of Japanese teenagers and young adults developing the intense, irrational fear called TKS. This social phobia is so common in Japan that there are special clinics devoted only to treating TKS. The Japanese TKS clinics are comparable in popularity to the numerous weight-loss clinics found in the United States. Interestingly, TKS is a kind of social phobia that doesn't occur in Western cultures (Kleinknecht et al., 1997; Yamashita, 1993).

**Cultural differences.** Although people in many cultures report anxiety about behaving or performing in public, the particular fears that they report may depend on their own culture's values. For example, TKS—the fear and embarrassment of making eye contact, blushing, or having trembling hands during social interactions—is a social phobia unique to Asian cultures and unknown in Western cultures. Because of cultural differences, clinicians emphasize the importance of taking cultural values, influences, and differences into account when diagnosing behaviors across cultures (Kleinman & Cohen, 1997).

In Japan, it is very important to know and show the proper public behaviors.

Next, we'll discuss a very serious problem in the United States culture: school shootings.

## What Drove Teens to Kill Fellow Students and Teachers?

**What is their problem?**

Sometimes researchers are faced with answering tragic questions, such as why teenage boys had taken guns to schools and shot and killed at least 32 and wounded another 79, including students and teachers. Everyone wondered what had turned these adolescents into killers. In some cases, but not all, these adolescents might be clinically diagnosed with conduct disorder.

*Conduct disorder* refers to a repetitive and persistent pattern of behaving that has been going on for at least a year and that violates the established social rules or the rights of others. Problems may include aggressive behaviors such as threatening to harm people, abusing or killing animals, destroying property, being deceitful, or stealing.

The diagnosis of conduct disorder seems to apply to Kipland Kinkel, age 15, who was charged with firing 50 rounds from a semiautomatic rifle into the school cafeteria, killing 2 students and injuring 22.

There have been 9 incidents of boys involved in school shootings—32 killed.

Those who knew him said that Kinkel had a violent temper and a history of behavioral problems, which included killing his cat by putting a firecracker in its mouth, blowing up a dead cow, stoning cars from a highway overpass, and making bombs (Witkin et al., 1998). In trying to answer the question, Why did these adolescents shoot their fellow students and teachers, mental health professionals have primarily used the case study approach.

A *case study* is an in-depth analysis of the thoughts, feelings, beliefs, experiences, behaviors, or problems of a single individual.

Researchers used the case study approach to do an in-depth analysis of the behaviors of shooters 1 to 8, listed below left (Verlinden et al., 2000). As you'll see, case studies revealed several social-emotional problems that put these boys at risk for committing antisocial acts of violence.

### Adolescents Involved in School Shootings

**1 Moses Lake, Washington: February 2, 1996**
Barry Loukaitis, 14, confessed to firing on his algebra class, killing three and wounding one. He said that he wanted to get back at a popular boy who had teased him. Loukaitis shot the boy dead.

**2 Bethel, Alaska: February 19, 1997**
Evan Ramsey, 16, was convicted of killing a student and principal. Ramsey thought it was "cool" to shoot up the school.

**3 Pearl, Mississippi: October 1, 1997**
Luke Woodham, 16, was found guilty of stabbing his mother, shooting and killing his ex-girlfriend and another student, and wounding seven other students.

**4 West Paducah, Kentucky: December 1, 1997**
Michael Caneal, 14, allegedly killed three students and wounded five more when he fired on a prayer circle outside the high school. Caneal said, "It was kind of like I was in a dream."

**5 Jonesboro, Arkansas: March 24, 1998**
Andrew Golden, 11, and Mitchell Johnson, 13, were charged with killing five and wounding 10 when they fired on students and teachers leaving school after a fire alarm was pulled.

**6 Springfield, Oregon: May 21, 1998**
Kipland Kinkel, 15, was sentenced to 111 years for killing his parents, two students, and wounding 22 students at Thurston High School.

**7 Littleton, Colorado: April 20, 1999**
In 16 minutes, Eric Harris, 18, and Dylan Klebold, 17, killed 12 students and 1 teacher, wounded 22 at Columbine High School, and then allegedly shot and killed themselves.

**8 Conyers, Georgia: May 20, 1999**
T.J. Solomon, 15, was charged with firing on and injuring six students at Heritage High. School officials said he wasn't a discipline problem.

**9 Fort Gibson, Oklahoma: December 6, 1999**
Seth Trickey, 13, was charged with shooting and wounding 6 students at Fort Gibson Middle School. School officials said he was a good student and had no behavioral problems.

### Risks Shared by Adolescent School Shooters

Although there are differences among the shooters (#1–8) listed on the left, researchers identified a number of risk factors that the boys shared (Verlinden et al., 2000).

■ Most of the boys (shooters) showed uncontrolled anger and depression, blaming others for problems and threatening violence. Most had a history of aggression, either physical or verbal or both, and discipline problems at school or home.

■ Half of the boys had been given little parental supervision, had troubled family relationships, and perceived themselves as receiving little support from their families. Most of the boys had recently experienced the breakup of a relationship, a stressful event, or loss of status.

■ Most of the boys were generally isolated and rejected by their peers in school. Most had poor social skills and felt picked on and persecuted and had friends who were also antisocial. The most commonly stated motives for shootings were to obtain justice against peers or adults who the teenage shooters believed had wronged them and/or to obtain status or importance among their peers.

■ In all cases, the boys had easy access to firearms, which were in their homes and were used in the school shootings.

■ Most teenage shooters gave warning signs of their violent intentions, which were not taken seriously. For example, Kinkel (#6) read a graphic journal entry to his class about killing fellow students. Loukaitis (#1) wrote a poem: "I look at his body on the floor / Killing a bastard that deserves to die / Ain't nothing like it in the world." Woodham (#3) wrote, "I do this to show society . . . No one truly loves me" (Egan, 1998).

The National Association of School Psychologists has made a list of 17 risks (uncontrolled anger, suicidal threats, social isolation, history of aggression, etc.) that increase the chances of violent acts. Most of the teenage shooters (#1–8) had 13 or more of these 17 risks. Researchers recommend that when a child is reported or known to have a number of these 17 risk factors, the child should be given a complete assessment with a focus on intervention or helping the child decrease these risks (Verlinden et al., 2000).

This module has focused on describing various mental disorders. Next we turn to explaining several ways of treating two relatively common anxiety disorders—social and specific phobias.

## Specific Phobia: Flying

At the beginning of this module, we told you about Kate Premo (right photo), who developed a phobia of flying. In some cases, people don't remember what caused their phobias, but Premo remembers exactly when her phobia began. Her fear began as a child when she was on a very turbulent and stressful flight. Her fear was further intensified by her memories of the terrorist bombing of Pan Am flight 103, which killed several of her fellow students. After that incident, her fear of flying turned into a real phobia that kept her from flying to visit friends and family. An estimated 25 million Americans have a phobia of flying called aerophobia,

Kate is undergoing exposure therapy for fear of flying.

which may include fear of flying, crashing, heights, being in small enclosed spaces, or not having control of the situation (Van Gerwen et al., 1997).

Most phobias do not disappear without some treatment, and on the few occasions that Premo was forced to fly, she dosed herself so much with alcohol and tranquilizers that she was groggy for days. Finally, she joined a weekend seminar that helps people overcome their fears of flying (Sleek, 1994). Treatment for phobias can involve psychotherapy or drugs, or some combination of them. We'll discuss psychotherapy and drug treatment, beginning with cognitive-behavioral and exposure therapy.

## Cognitive-Behavioral Therapy

Kate's phobia of flying involves fearful and irrational thoughts, which in turn cause increased physiological arousal. She can learn to reduce her irrational and fearful thoughts and reduce her arousal through cognitive-behavioral therapy (Cottraux et al., 2000).

*Cognitive-behavioral therapy* involves using a combination of two methods: changing negative, unhealthy, or distorted thoughts and beliefs by substituting positive, healthy, and realistic ones; and changing limiting or disruptive behaviors by learning and practicing new skills to improve functioning.

**Thoughts.** Cognitive-behavioral therapy is useful in helping Kate control her fearful thoughts and eliminate dangerous beliefs about flying. For example, Kate had learned to fear various noises during flight, which she believed indicated trouble. To change these fearful thoughts, an airplane pilot explained the various noises, such as the thumps meant the landing gear was retracting after takeoff or being put down for landing. Thus, when Kate has a fearful thought, for example, "That noise must mean trouble," she immediately stops herself and substitutes a realistic thought, "That's just the landing gear."

**Behaviors.** Because Kate automatically gets nervous and fearful when just thinking about flying, she is instructed to do breathing, relaxation, and imagery exercises that will help her calm down. Deep and rhythmic breathing is an effective calming exercise because it distracts Kate from her fears and focuses her attention on a pleasant activity. Relaxing and tensing groups of muscles are also calming and help to decrease physiological arousal. Finally, imagery exercises are calming because focusing on pleasant images is a very powerful way of using her mind to control (relax) her body's fight-flight response.

Cognitive-behavioral methods have proved effective in treating a variety of phobias (Cottraux et al., 2000). Sometimes cognitive-behavioral therapy is combined with another kind of therapy, called exposure therapy.

## Exposure Therapy

In treating phobias, cognitive-behavior therapy is often combined with exposure therapy. The most difficult part of Kate's phobia treatment involves exposure therapy, when she must actually confront her most feared situation.

*Exposure therapy* consists of gradually exposing the person to the real anxiety-producing situations or objects that he or she is attempting to avoid and continuing exposure treatments until the anxiety decreases.

The first part of Kate's treatment involved cognitive-behavioral therapy, in which she learned how to control her irrational thoughts and acquire some basic relaxation techniques. The second part of her treatment involves exposure therapy, in which she is required to fly on a regularly scheduled airline, meaning that she would be exposed to her most feared situation. To help Kate deal with her fear of flying, Captain Michael Freebairn (photo below) sat next to Kate. Each time Kate tensed or looked fearful, the captain reassured Kate that all was normal and then reminded her to begin relaxation exercises (breathing and relaxing muscles), to use pleasant images, and to substitute positive, healthy thoughts for negative, fearful ones. When the plane landed, Kate was all smiles (left photo) after realizing that exposure therapy had significantly reduced her fear or phobia of flying.

Kate smiles after successfully flying without feeling intense fear.

Programs that treat specific phobias, such as fear of flying, often use some combination of cognitive-behavioral and exposure therapy, which significantly reduces fear in the majority of clients (Lang & Craske, 2000).

Clients not helped by cognitive-behavioral or exposure therapy may be given drug therapy (see next page) or may try virtual reality therapy.

**Virtual reality therapy.** Although clients never leave the ground, they sit in real airplane seats that vibrate to the sound of airplane engines. Clients wear head-mounted displays that surround them with 3-D experiences of "taking off" and "flying." Everything appears so real that clients who have a fear of flying begin to sweat and their hearts pound just as on real flights. This is the virtual reality version of exposure therapy, which, combined with relaxation exercises and thought substitution, has proved successful in treating a variety of specific phobias, including fear of flying (Wiederhold, 2000).

## Social Phobia: Public Speaking

**When does a fear become a phobia?**

Just as specific phobias can be successfully treated with psychotherapy, so too can social phobias, such as public speaking. Almost everyone is somewhat anxious about getting up and speaking in public. For a fear to become a full-blown phobia, however, the fear must be intense, irrational, and out of all proportion to the object or situation. For example, individuals with social phobias have such intense, excessive, and irrational fears of doing something humiliating or embarrassing that they will go to almost any lengths to avoid speaking in public. There are a number of very effective, nondrug programs for treating social phobias (fear of speaking, performing, or acting in public). These programs combine cognitive-behavioral and exposure therapies and usually include the following four components (Leahy & Holland, 2000).

**1 Explain.** Clinicians *explain* to the person that, since the fears involved in social phobias are usually learned, there are also methods to unlearn or extinguish such fears. The person is told how both thoughts and physiological arousal can exaggerate the phobic feelings and make the person go to any lengths to avoid the feared situation.

Treating social phobias involves four components.

**2 Learn and substitute.** Clinicians found that some individuals needed to *learn* new social skills (initiating a conversation, writing a speech) so that they would function better in social situations. In addition, individuals were told to record their thoughts immediately after thinking about being in a feared situation. Then they were shown how to *substitute* positive and healthy thoughts for negative and fearful ones.

**3 Expose.** Clinicians first used *imaginary exposure,* during which a person imagines being in the situation that elicits the fears. For example, some individuals imagined presenting material to their coworkers, making a classroom presentation, or initiating a conversation with the opposite sex. After imaginary exposure, clinicians used *real (in vivo) exposure,* in which the person gives his or her speech in front of a group of people or initiates conversations with strangers.

**4 Practice.** Clinicians asked subjects to *practice* homework assignments. For instance, individuals were asked to imagine themselves in feared situations and then to eliminate negative thoughts by substituting positive ones. In addition, individuals were instructed to gradually expose themselves to making longer and longer public presentations or having conversations with the opposite sex.

Researchers report that programs similar to the one above resulted in reduced social fears in about 30–80% of those who completed the program (Cottraux et al., 2000).

## Drug Treatment of Phobias

**How effective are drugs?**

Imagine being told to walk into a room and meet a group of strangers while you are stark naked. For most of us, this idea would cause such embarrassment, fear, and anxiety that we would absolutely refuse. This imagined situation is similar to the terrible kind of negative emotions that individuals with social phobia feel when they must initiate a conversation, meet strangers, or give a public presentation. As we have discussed, social phobias can be treated with cognitive-behavioral/exposure therapy (Cottraux, 2000). However, some individuals with social phobia do not choose to or are too fearful to complete a therapy program that includes exposure to the feared situation. Instead, these individuals may choose drug therapy, which may involve either tranquilizers (benzodiazepines) or several kinds of antidepressants (Stahl, 2000).

Drug therapy for anxiety involves tranquilizers or antidepressants.

The graphs below show the results of a double-blind study in which individuals with social phobia were given either a placebo or a tranquilizer, in this case one of the benzodiazepines (clonazepam). After ten weeks of treatment, individuals given benzodiazepines showed a significant clinical reduction in scores on both anxiety and avoidance tests, which means they were able to function relatively well in social situations (Davidson, 1994). Although 73% of those on benzodiazepines showed a significant decrease in fear and anxiety, a remarkable 22% of those given placebos (sugar pills) showed a similar decrease. This means that the significant decrease in the social fears of almost one out of four individuals resulted from purely psychological factors, such as a client's expectations and beliefs ("The pill is powerful medicine and will reduce my fear").

**Average Score on Fear Scale: Drug reduced fear more than placebo**

| Placebo | 32 |
|---------|----|
| Drug | 21 |

**Average Score on Fear Scale: Drug reduced avoidance more than placebo**

| Placebo | 30 |
|---------|----|
| Drug | 21 |

Although drug treatments are effective in reducing social phobias, there are two potential problems. First, about 50–75% of individuals relapse when drugs are discontinued, which means that their original intense social phobic symptoms return. Second, long-term maintenance on drugs can result in tolerance and increases in dosage, which, in turn, can result in serious side effects, such as loss of memory (Stahl, 2000). Compared to drug treatment of phobias, psychotherapy programs have the advantages of having no problems with tolerance or unwanted physical side effects.

**Which treatment to choose?** Whether a client chooses psychotherapy or drug treatment for phobias depends to a large extent on the client's preference. That's because the treatment of different phobias, including specific phobias, social phobias, and agoraphobia, is about equally effective following either drug therapy (tranquilizers or antidepressants) or cognitive-behavioral/exposure therapy (Liebowitz et al., 1999).

## A. THREE APPROACHES

**1.** A prolonged or recurring problem that seriously interferes with an individual's ability to live a satisfying personal life and function in society is a _____. This definition takes into account genetic, behavioral, cognitive, and environmental factors, all of which may contribute to a mental disorder.

**2.** One approach to understanding and treating mental disorders views psychological problems as similar to diseases, and a major part of the treatment involves the use of psychoactive drugs. This approach is called the (a) _____ model. An approach that looks for the causes of mental disorders in unconscious or unresolved conflicts is the (b)_____ approach. An approach that uses a combination of information from cognitive processes and learning-conditioning factors to understand and treat mental disorders is the (c)_____ approach. According to this approach, people have learned maladaptive ways of responding to or thinking about themselves and their environments.

**3.** If a behavior is considered abnormal because it occurs infrequently in the general population, we are using a definition based on (a)_____ frequency. If a behavior is considered abnormal because it deviates greatly from what's acceptable, we are using a definition based on (b)_____. If a behavior is considered abnormal because it interferes with an individual's ability to function as a person or in society, we are using a definition based on (c)_____ behavior.

## B. ASSESSING MENTAL DISORDERS

**4.** A systematic evaluation of an individual's various psychological, biological, and social factors that may be contributing to his or her problem is called a (a)_____. The primary method used in clinical assessments is to get information about a person's background, current behavior, attitudes, and emotions and also details of present problems through a (b)_____. A complete clinical assessment usually includes three major methods: (c)_____, _____, and _____.

**5.** Assessing mental disorders may be difficult because (a)_____ vary in intensity and complexity. The assessment must take into account past and present problems and current stressors. The accurate assessment of symptoms is important because it has significant implications for the kind of (b)_____ that the client will be given.

## C. DIAGNOSING MENTAL DISORDERS

**6.** When mental health professionals determine whether an individual's specific problem meets or matches the standard symptoms that define a particular mental disorder, they are making a (a)_____. In trying to reach an agreement on the clinical diagnosis, mental health professionals use a set of guidelines developed by the American Psychiatric Association, which are called the (b)_____, abbreviated as DSM-IV-TR.

**7.** The DSM-IV-TR is a set of guidelines that uses five different dimensions or (a)_____ to diagnose mental disorders. The advantage of the DSM-IV-TR is that it helps mental health professionals communicate their findings, conduct research, and plan for treatment. One disadvantage of using the DSM-IV-TR to make a diagnosis is that it places people into specific categories that may have bad associations; this problem is called (b)_____.

## D. ANXIETY DISORDERS

**8.** A mental disorder that is marked by excessive and/or unrealistic worry or feelings of general apprehension about events or activities, when those feelings occur on a majority of days for a period of at least six months, is called _____. This anxiety disorder is treated with some form of psychotherapy and/or drugs known as benzodiazepines.

**9.** One mental disorder is characterized by recurring and unexpected panic attacks and continued worry about having another panic attack; such worry interferes with psychological functioning. This problem is called a _____ disorder.

**10.** Suppose you experience a period of intense fear or discomfort in which four or more of the following symptoms are present: pounding heart, sweating, trembling, shortness of breath, feelings of choking, chest pain, nausea, feeling dizzy, and fear of losing control or dying. You are having a (a) _____. Panic disorders are treated with a combination of benzodiazepines or antidepressants and (b)_____.

**11.** Another anxiety disorder characterized by increased physiological arousal and an intense, excessive, and irrational fear that is out of all proportion to the danger elicited by the object or situation is called a _____.

**12.** DSM-IV-TR divides phobias into three categories. Those that are triggered by common objects, situations, or animals (such as snakes or heights) are called (a)_____ phobias. Those that are brought on by having to perform in social situations and expecting to be humiliated and embarrassed are called (b)_____ phobias. Those that are characterized by fear of being in public places from which it may be difficult or embarrassing to escape if panic symptoms occur are called (c)_____. Once established, phobias are extremely persistent, continue for years, and may require professional treatment.

**13.** Persistent, recurring irrational thoughts that a person is unable to control and that interfere with normal functioning are called (a)_____. Irresistible impulses to perform some ritual over and over, even though the ritual serves no rational purpose, are called (b)_____. A disorder that consists of both of these behaviors and that interferes with normal functioning is called (c)_____. The most effective nondrug treatment for obsessive-compulsive disorder is (d)_____ therapy.

### E. SOMATOFORM DISORDERS

**14.** The appearance of real physical symptoms and bodily complaints that are not under voluntary control, have no known physical causes, extend over several years, and are believed to be caused by psychological factors is characteristic of (a)_____ disorders. DSM-IV-TR lists seven kinds of somatoform disorders. The occurrence of multiple symptoms—including pain, gastrointestinal, sexual, and neurological symptoms—that have no physical causes but are triggered by psychological problems or distress is referred to as (b)_____ disorder; a disorder characterized by unexplained and significant physical symptoms or deficits that affect voluntary motor or sensory functions and that suggest a real neurological or medical problem is called a (c)_____ disorder. A recent survey reported that somatoform disorders occur worldwide, although their symptoms may differ across cultures.

### F. CULTURAL DIVERSITY: AN ASIAN DISORDER

**15.** A social phobia found in Asia, especially Japan, that is characterized by morbid fear of making eye-to-eye contact, blushing, giving off an offensive odor, having an unpleasant or tense facial expression, or having trembling hands is called

| Percentage of Students | |
| --- | --- |
| Psychosomatic disorders | 24% |
| Depressive reactions | 20% |
| TKS | 19% |

_____. This phobia appears to result from Asian cultural and social influences that stress the importance of showing proper behavior in public.

### G. RESEARCH FOCUS: SCHOOL SHOOTINGS

**16.** A method of investigation that involves an in-depth analysis of the thoughts, feelings, beliefs, experiences, behaviors, or problems of a single individual is called a (a)_____. This method was used to decide if teenage school shooters had repetitive and persistent patterns of behavior that had been going on for at least a year and involved threats or physical harm to people or animals, destruction of property, being deceitful, or stealing. These symptoms define a mental disorder that is called (b)_____.

### H. APPLICATION: TREATING PHOBIAS

**17.** There are several different treatments for phobias. A nondrug treatment combines changing negative, unhealthy, or distorted thoughts and beliefs by substituting positive, healthy, and realistic ones and learning new skills to improve functioning; this treatment is called (a)_____ therapy. Another therapy that gradually exposes the person to the real anxiety-producing situations or objects that he or she has been avoiding is called (b)_____ therapy. Individuals who are unwilling or too fearful to be exposed to fearful situations or objects may choose drug therapy.

**18.** Social and specific phobias have been successfully treated with tranquilizers called (a)_____. Although these drugs are effective, they have two problems: when individuals stop taking these drugs, the original fearful symptoms may return, which is called (b)_____; and, if individuals are maintained on drugs for some length of time, they may develop tolerance, which means they will have to take larger doses, which in turn may cause side effects such as loss of (c)_____. Researchers found that drug therapy was about equally effective as cognitive-behavioral or exposure therapy in reducing both social and specific phobias, including agoraphobia.

***Answers:*** *1. mental disorder; 2. (a) medical, (b) psychoanalytic, (c) cognitive-behavioral; 3. (a) statistical, (b) social norms, (c) maladaptive; 4. (a) clinical assessment, (b) clinical interview, (c) clinical interview, psychological tests, neurological tests; 5. (a) symptoms, (b) treatment; 6. (a) clinical diagnosis, (b) Diagnostic and Statistical Manual of Mental Disorders—IV-TR; 7. (a) axes, (b) labeling; 8. generalized anxiety; 9. panic; 10. (a) panic attack, (b) psychotherapy; 11. phobia; 12. (a) specific, (b) social, (c) agoraphobia; 13. (a) obsessions, (b) compulsions, (c) obsessive-compulsive disorder, (d) exposure; 14. (a) somatoform, (b) somatization, (c) conversion; 15. taijin kyofusho, or TKS; 16. (a) case study, (b) conduct disorder; 17. (a) cognitive-behavioral, (b) exposure; 18. (a) benzodiazepines, (b) relapse, (c) memory*

# Critical Thinking

## Prisoners of Love

*by Pamela Varrick*

### Questions

**1.** According to the three definitions of abnormal behavior, is this girlfriend abnormal?

**2.** According to the three definitions of abnormal behavior, is this lawyer abnormal?

**3.** According to Freud's psychodynamic theory of personality, why is it difficult to explain why women fall in love with killers?

**4.** How would clinicians decide if women who fall in love with killers have a mental disorder?

O h, what they do for love. The girlfriend of the "Hillside Strangler" tries to strangle a woman herself to throw police off her sweetheart's trail. Her murder attempt fails and she goes to jail for life.

A promising young female lawyer assigned to defend a murder suspect finds her client so appealing, she helps him escape. She is disbarred and goes to prison.

What is there about a murderer that can make him so irresistible? What is it about some women that makes them find killers so lovable?

Although there is little formal research on the psychology of prison romance, those who observe the dynamics of such couplings say the relationships aren't as bizarre as they seem. The relationships often feel especially exciting, passionate, and dangerous.

According to Sheila Isenberg, who interviewed dozens of women for her 1990 book *Women Who Love Men Who Kill* (Dell), those who fall for men convicted of serious crimes are themselves often surprisingly accomplished.

"They are very likely to be attractive and intelligent, often successful in their profession, and almost always unacquainted with the world of crime and criminals," Isenberg says. "In the eyes of these women, these men are a magnetic mix of evil and vulnerability, danger and safety."

Although such women refuse to be categorized as naïve, needy, or lonely, Isenberg and others who have inter-

Woman fell in love with a convicted and jailed killer.

viewed prisoners' wives find that most such women do at the very least share one important trait: they come from loveless homes or suffered unhealthy, even abusive, marriages in the past.

Here's the scenario: You're madly in love with someone who you're forbidden to love. You are separated by forces greater than yourselves, so you see each other very infrequently. You dream of a happy life together but know in your hearts that it may never happen—It's Romeo and Juliet. It's the definition of the perfect prison marriage.

Most of those who study prisons and prisoners agree that women who fall in love with killers often share an idealized version of romantic love. They believe that love is based upon "constant passion, unsatisfied yearnings, and ungratified desires," as author Isenberg puts it.

Because passion is never reduced to the daily tedium and predictability of many marriages outside prison, it burns all the hotter. (Source: *Los Angeles Times*, January 23, 1997.)

**5.** Which of the five axes in DSM-IV-TR best describes the problems these women share?

**6.** What are the advantages and disadvantages of labeling these women's problems?

*Try InfoTrac to search for terms:* **murderers; DSM-IV; romantic love.**

---

### *Suggested answers to Newspaper Article questions*

1. A woman who tries to help her jailed sweetheart killer by repeating the killer's crime of strangling women is certainly abnormal in terms of statistical frequency, in terms of deviation from social norms, and in terms of engaging in maladaptive behavior.

2. A female lawyer who falls in love with a suspected killer she represents and then helps the killer escape from jail is certainly abnormal in terms of statistical frequency, in terms of deviation from social norms, and in terms of engaging in maladaptive behavior (helping the suspect results in her going to prison).

3. According to Freud's psychodynamic theory of personality, women who fall in love with killers are influenced by unconscious forces, wishes, and repressed desires, which are difficult to examine

and understand because they are unconscious and not easily revealed or brought to the surface.

4. Clinicians would use a clinical assessment (neurological and psychological/personality tests and interviews) to identify symptoms and then match symptoms to the mental disorders listed in the DSM-IV-TR.

5. To identify potential problems of women who fall in love with killers, clinicians might use axis II, which focuses on long-standing personality traits that are maladaptive or impair functioning.

6. One advantage in labeling these women's problem is that it may help decide on which therapy is best. One disadvantage is that giving women a label may bias how others perceive and respond.

# Links to Learning

## Web Sites

- **WADSWORTH ONLINE STUDY CENTER**
  **http://psychology.wadsworth.com**
  Quizzes, learning activities and exercises, a discussion forum, and hot links to Internet sites related to mental assessment and anxiety disorders, including:

- **INTERNET MENTAL HEALTH**
  **http://www.mentalhealth.com**
  This many-layered, award-winning site, which originates in Canada, has American and European descriptions of 54 mental disorders, including diagnosis, treatment, and research findings for each disorder and for 72 medications.
  There are also interactive message boards for bipolar disorder, depression, and schizophrenia; an online magazine that includes recovery stories; and links to other sites.

- **ANXIETY DISORDERS EDUCATION PROGRAM**
  **http://www.nimh.nih.gov/anxiety/**
  The National Institute of Mental Health maintains this site to educate the public about anxiety disorders. Sections include news, a library, and links to educational resources and mental health organizations.

- **THE ANXIETY-PANIC INTERNET RESOURCE (tAPir)**
  **http://www.algy.com/anxiety**
  "tAPir is a true grassroots project, unaffiliated with any business organization and created and sustained by its users. Because of this, you won't find professional counseling here, nor will you find guaranteed resolution to your personal situation. What you will find is a nonprogrammatic, unbiased self-help resource where you can interact with tens of thousands of others who share an interest in anxiety and its treatment, and where you will find open and friendly information from people who actually live with these disorders." Includes a newsletter, bulletin board, and store.

## Learning Activities

- **POWERSTUDY™ BY ROD PLOTNIK & TOM DOYLE**

  ### PowerStudy™
  **Check out CD: Module 22**
  CD 3.B: Neurons: Structure and Function; book page 514
  CD 4.B: Studying the Living Brain; book page 512
  CD 12.C: Reasons for Forgetting; book page 514

- **STUDY GUIDE TO ACCOMPANY INTRODUCTION TO PSYCHOLOGY, 6TH EDITION, by Matthew Enos**
  In Module 22, examine your assumptions about being bored, face your obsessive-compulsive tendencies, and decide whether psychology is based more in art or in science.

- **WEBTUTOR**
  **http://webtutor.thomsonlearning.com**
  **WebTUTOR** Visit this site for interactive versions of the Study Guide features. Take a quiz, get your score—should you study a topic some more, or can you move on? For example, can you define *taijin kyofusho?* Agoraphobia is characterized by recurrent panic attacks: true or false?

- **INFOTRAC Online Library**
  **http://www.infotrac-college.com**

  Use your password and key in search terms such as those below to find popular and scientific articles on subjects covered in Module 22. Make the library work for you!

  | | | |
  |---|---|---|
  | Serial killers | Phobias | Deviant behavior |
  | Mass hysteria | Personality tests | Psychosomatic disorders |

- **PSYCHNOW!**
  CD for Macintosh and Windows includes a study guide, glossary, Web sites, and animations. For Module 23, see:
  - Assessment
  - Abnormality and Psychopathology
  - Nonpsychotic, Psychotic, and Affective Disorders

## Study Questions

*Use InfoTrac to search for topics mentioned in the main heads below (e.g., anxiety disorders, somatoform disorders, school shootings).*

**\*A. Three Approaches**—The night before a big exam, John gets drunk to relax. However, the next day he has a terrible hangover and does poorly on the exam. Is his behavior abnormal? (**Suggested answer p. 634**)

**\*B. Assessing Mental Disorders**—Why must mental health professionals spend so much time and effort in assessing their clients' symptoms? (**Suggested answer p. 634**)

**C. Diagnosing Mental Disorders**—Why are negative attitudes or stereotypes associated with mental illness but not with physical illness?

**D. Anxiety Disorders**—Some of the things that make you anxious have no effect on other people. How do you explain this?

**E. Somatoform Disorders**—Why do you think some people express their psychological distress or emotional problems by exhibiting bodily symptoms?

**F. Cultural Diversity: An Asian Disorder**—What kind of cultural influences and pressures make the vast majority of us afraid to speak in public?

**G. Research Focus: School Shootings**—What are some characteristics that teenage school shooters have in common?

**\*H. Application: Treating Phobias**—If you were very shy and uncomfortable about meeting strangers and talking to groups, what could you do about this problem? (**Suggested answer p. 635**)

*These questions are answered in Appendix B.

### A. Mood Disorders     532
* KINDS OF MOOD DISORDERS
* CAUSES OF MOOD DISORDERS
* TREATMENT OF MOOD DISORDERS

### B. Electroconvulsive Therapy     535
* DEFINITION AND USAGE
* EFFECTIVENESS OF ECT

### C. Personality Disorders     536
* DEFINITION
* ANTISOCIAL PERSONALITY DISORDER
* PSYCHOPATHS: CAUSES AND TREATMENT

### D. Schizophrenia     538
* DEFINITION AND TYPES
* SYMPTOMS
* BIOLOGICAL CAUSES
* NEUROLOGICAL CAUSES
* ENVIRONMENTAL CAUSES
* TREATMENT
* EVALUATION OF NEUROLEPTIC DRUGS

### Concept Review     543

### E. Dissociative Disorders     544
* DEFINITION
* DISSOCIATIVE AMNESIA
* DISSOCIATIVE FUGUE
* DISSOCIATIVE IDENTITY DISORDER

### F. Cultural Diversity: Interpreting Symptoms     546
* SPIRIT POSSESSION
* CULTURAL DIFFERENCES IN OCCURRENCE
* CULTURAL DIFFERENCES IN GENDER ROLES

### G. Research Focus: Exercise versus Drugs     547
* CHOICES OF THERAPY FOR DEPRESSION
* EXERCISE EXPERIMENT: SEVEN RULES

### H. Application: Dealing with Mild Depression     548
* MILD VERSUS MAJOR DEPRESSION
* BECK'S THEORY OF DEPRESSION
* OVERCOMING MILD DEPRESSION

### Summary Test     550

### Critical Thinking     552
* LIVES REDISCOVERED

### Links to Learning     553

## Mood Disorder

**Why do his thoughts speed up?**

Chuck Elliot (photo below) was checking out the exhibits at an electronics convention in Las Vegas when suddenly his mind seemed to go wild and spin at twice its regular speed. His words could not keep up with his thoughts, and he was talking in what sounded like some strange code, almost like rapid fire "dot, dot, dot." Then he stripped off all his clothes and ran stark naked through the gambling casino of the Hilton Hotel. The police were called and Chuck was taken to a mental hospital. After his symptoms were reviewed, Chuck was diagnosed with what was then called manic depression.

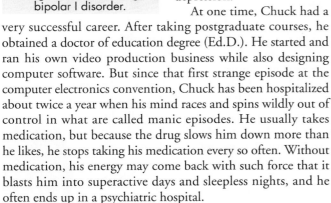

Chuck Elliot's mind spins and whirls out of contol. He was diagnosed with having bipolar I disorder.

At one time, Chuck had a very successful career. After taking postgraduate courses, he obtained a doctor of education degree (Ed.D.). He started and ran his own video production business while also designing computer software. But since that first strange episode at the computer electronics convention, Chuck has been hospitalized about twice a year when his mind races and spins wildly out of control in what are called manic episodes. He usually takes medication, but because the drug slows him down more than he likes, he stops taking his medication every so often. Without medication, his energy may come back with such force that it blasts him into superactive days and sleepless nights, and he often ends up in a psychiatric hospital.

His last regular job ended when he was in the middle of another manic attack. He was going on 100 hours without sleep when he went out to his car, grabbed a bunch of magazines, books, fruits, and vegetables, and piled them all on the desk in his office. When his boss came by and found a desk piled high with junk and Chuck sitting there with his mind spinning, the boss fired him on the spot (Brooks, 1994). Since that time, despite his very good academic, computer, and business qualifications, he has not been able to hold a steady job.

More recently, Chuck married a woman he had been dating for only ten days. She understands Chuck very well because she too is a manic-depressive and has similar mental health problems. She hopes that they can care for each other. She says, "Chuck is the most brilliant man I have ever met. I am so lucky" (Brooks, 1994, p. 4).

In this module, we'll explain Chuck's illness, his treatment, and how he is dealing with his problem.

## Schizophrenia

**Why was he hearing voices?**

When Michael McCabe was 18 years old, Marsha, his mother, thought that he was just about over his rebellious phase. She was looking forward to relaxing and enjoying herself. But then Michael said that he was hearing voices. At first Marsha thought that Michael's voices came from his smoking marijuana. But the voices persisted for two weeks, and Marsha checked Michael into a private drug treatment center. He left the center after 30 days and seemed no better off than he had been before. Several days later, Marsha found Michael in her parents' home, a couple of miles down the road from her own house. Michael was sitting on the floor, his head back, holding his throat and making grunting sounds like an animal. Marsha got really scared and called the police, but before they arrived, Michael ran off.

Michael spent time with his grandparents, who finally called Marsha and said that they couldn't take his strange behavior anymore. Once again Marsha called the police. Just as Michael (photo below) tried to run away, the police caught him and took him to the community psychiatric hospital.

Marsha received a call from a psychiatrist at the hospital, who explained that Michael had been diagnosed as having schizophrenia, a serious mental disorder that includes hearing voices and having disoriented thinking. A few days later, Michael escaped from the hospital. He was later returned by police, put into leather restraints, and given antipsychotic drugs that would also calm him down. Michael remained in the hospital and was treated with drugs for about a month, with little success.

Michael McCabe, 18 years old, began hearing voices and was diagnosed with having schizophrenia.

Just about the time Marsha was at her wits' end about what to do next, Michael was put on a new antipsychotic drug, clozapine. After about a month on the new drug, Michael improved enough to be discharged back into Marsha's care (Brooks, 1994, 1995a).

In this module, we'll explain what schizophrenia is, describe the drugs Michael was given, and report how his treatment is working.

## What's Coming

We'll discuss several different mental disorders and their treatments. We'll explain mood disorders and their treatments, including the treatment of last resort for depression, electroconvulsive shock therapy. We'll also examine several personality disorders and different kinds of schizophrenia, along with old and new antipsychotic drugs. We'll end with a group of strange and unusual disorders, one of which is multiple personality.

We'll begin with Chuck Elliot's problem, which is an example of one kind of mood disorder.

## Kinds of Mood Disorders

**How bad is it?**

You'll probably recognize some of these well-known names: Mike Wallace, television reporter for "60 Minutes"; Joan Rivers, comedian; William Styron, Pulitzer Prize–winning author; Jules Feiffer, cartoonist; Dick Cavett, television and radio talk show host; and Rod Steiger, Academy Award–winning actor. Each of them suffers from major depression, a mood disorder (Brody, 1998).

A *mood disorder* is a prolonged and disturbed emotional state that affects almost all of a person's thoughts, feelings, and behaviors.

Most of us have experienced a continuum of moods, with depression on one end and elation on the other. However, the depression or blues that most of us feel is like having a paper cut on our finger, while major depression is more like undergoing open-heart surgery.

Actor Rod Steiger says that he spent most of the 1980s in major depression. When he tried to work, it was a disaster; even after a lifetime of making movies, he couldn't remember his lines (Brooks, 1995b). The DSM-IV-TR lists ten different mood disorders, but we'll focus on the symptoms of three of the more common forms: major depressive disorder, bipolar I disorder, and dysthymic disorder.

### Major Depression

Actor Rod Steiger (photo below) says that during his depression, his self-esteem hit bottom; he was consumed with self-pity; he felt worthless and guilty. Many days he couldn't get

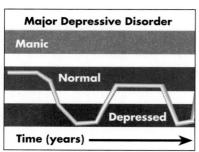

out of bed; often he didn't wash or do anything. He remembers thinking about putting a quick end to his pain and misery through suicide (Brooks, 1995a). Steiger's symptoms match those of a major depressive disorder.

*Major depressive disorder* is marked by at least two weeks of continually being in a bad mood, having no interest in anything, and getting no pleasure from activities. In addition, a person must have at least four of the following symptoms: problems with eating, sleeping, thinking, concentrating, or making decisions, lacking energy, thinking about suicide, and feeling worthless or guilty (American Psychiatric Association, 2000).

Steiger says that the misery he felt during depression was more severe and long-lasting than the pain he felt after a death or divorce. About 17% of the adults surveyed in the United States reported a lifetime episode of major depression; women (21%) reported significantly more episodes than did men (13%) (Kessler et al., 1994).

**Major Depressive Disorder**

Manic

Normal

Depressed

Time (years) ➡

To help understand mood disorders, look at the left graph, which shows three general mood states. At the top are manic episodes or periods of incredible energy and euphoria. In the middle are normal periods—times when mood and emotions are not interfering with normal psychological functioning. At the bottom are major depressive disorders, during which a person fluctuates between normal behavior and bouts of severe depression. Mike Wallace, well-known television reporter on the news program "60 Minutes," calls his three terrible bouts with depression a crushing and paralyzing time of endless darkness (Brody, 1998).

### Bipolar I Disorder

Unlike Rod Steiger, who has a major depressive disorder, Chuck Elliot (photo below) fluctuates between

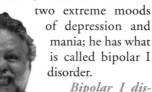

two extreme moods of depression and mania; he has what is called bipolar I disorder.

*Bipolar I disorder* is marked by fluctuations between episodes of depression and mania. A manic episode goes on for at least a week, during which a person is unusually euphoric, cheerful, and high and has at least three of the following symptoms: has great self-esteem, has little need for sleep, speaks rapidly and frequently, has racing thoughts, is easily distracted, and pursues pleasurable activities (American Psychiatric Association, 2000).

**Bipolar I Disorder**

Manic

Normal

Depressed

Time (years) ➡

As the graph above shows, a person with bipolar I disorder fluctuates between two extreme moods. For example, Chuck Elliot fluctuates among periods of being normal, manic, or depressed. Less than 1% of the population suffers from bipolar I disorder.

### Dysthymic Disorder

Another mood disorder that is less serious than major depression is called dysthymic *(dis-THY-mick)* disorder.

*Dysthymic disorder* is characterized by being chronically but not continuously depressed for a period of two years. While depressed, a person experiences at least two of the following symptoms: poor appetite, insomnia, fatigue, low self-esteem, poor concentration, and feelings of hopelessness (American Psychiatric Association, 2000).

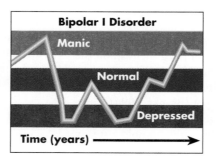

Individuals with dysthymic disorder, which affects about 6% of the population, are often described as "down in the dumps." Some of these individuals become accustomed to such feelings and describe themselves as "always being this way."

Besides these three mood disorders, we have also discussed another mood disorder, seasonal affective disorder, or SAD (p. 159). People with SAD become depressed as a result of a decrease in the number of sunny days, such as occurs in fall and winter months.

Next, we'll examine two common and related causes of depression.

# Causes of Mood Disorders

Chuck Elliot (right photo) had his first manic episode in his early thirties when his mind began to spin and he ran naked out of a convention. Because his mood swings fluctuated between manic and depressed, he was diagnosed as having bipolar I disorder.

What caused Chuck's bipolar I disorder?

The reason Chuck and about 15 million other Americans each year develop a mood disorder involves the interaction of biological and psychosocial factors.

## Biological Factors

The past ten years have seen a very active search for genetic, chemical (neurotransmitters), and neurological factors involved in mood disorders. These three factors are part of the biological theory of depression.

The *biological theory of depression* emphasizes underlying genetic, neurological, or physiological factors that may predispose a person to developing a mood disorder.

For example, how much are Elliot's mood swings affected by genes, neurotransmitters, or abnormal brain structures?

**Genetic factors.** Evidence that genetic factors contribute to mood disorders is clearly found from studies on twins (McGue & Christensen, 1997). For example, as the graph on the left shows, if one identical twin has a bipolar disorder, the risk that the other twin will develop the disorder is about 80%. In comparison, the chance of both fraternal twins developing this disorder is only about 16% (Moldin et al., 1991). Currently, researchers believe that there is no single gene but rather a combination of genes that produce a risk, or predisposition, for developing a mood disorder such as depression (Serretti et al., 2000). Since genes are involved in the regulation of neurotransmitters, researchers are searching for the neurotransmitters that control mood disorders.

**Risk of Developing Bipolar Disorder**

| | |
|---|---|
| Identical twins | 80% |
| 16% | Fraternal twins |

**Neurological factors.** Researchers know that abnormal levels of certain neurotransmitters can cause disturbances in brain circuits and, in turn, predispose or put individuals at risk for developing mood disorders (Nemeroff, 1998). One group of neurotransmitters, called the *monoamines* (especially serotonin and norepinephrine), are known to be involved in mood problems. On the next page, we'll discuss several drugs that change the levels of certain monoamines; the result is a decrease in the symptoms of depression (Mayberg et al., 1997).

**Brain scans.** Researchers took computerized photos of the structure and function of living brains and compared brains of depressed patients with those of individuals with normal moods. Researchers reported that a brain area called the prefrontal cortex (left figure) was about 40% smaller in depressed patients (Drevets et al., 1997). The prefrontal cortex, which has executive functions (planning and deciding; p. 75), was also found to be less active in depressed patients (Videbech, 2000). These studies on the living brains of depressed patients suggest that faulty brain structure or function, especially in the prefrontal cortex, contributes to the onset and/or maintenance of mood disorders (Robbins, 2000).

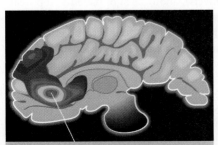

The red circle marks an area in the prefrontal cortex that was about 40% smaller in patients who had depression caused by hereditary (genetic) factors (Drevets et al., 1997).

## Psychosocial Factors

We've just explained how biological factors make some individuals more vulnerable to depression. Another reason individuals may be more at risk for depression involves a number of psychosocial factors.

*Psychosocial factors,* such as underlying personality traits, amount of social support, and the ability to deal with stressors, are believed to interact with predisposing biological factors that combine to put one at risk of developing a mood disorder.

Researchers believe that psychosocial factors may combine to increase stress and thus increase a person's risk of developing a mood disorder.

**Personality factors.** One important psychosocial factor is the kind of personality a person has developed. For example, some individuals have the kind of personality that makes their self-esteem primarily dependent on what others say or think and how much they are liked and accepted. Individuals with this kind of *socially dependent personality* are more vulnerable to becoming seriously depressed when faced with a particular kind of life stressor, namely, the failure of a close personal relationship or friendship.

Certain personality factors increase risk for mood disorders.

Other individuals, however, may not become depressed by the failure of a relationship because they have a different kind of personality. Some have the kind of personality that makes their self-esteem primarily dependent on reaching certain personal standards or achieving certain career goals. Individuals with this kind of *achievement personality* are more vulnerable to becoming seriously depressed when faced with a different kind of life stressor, namely, the failure to meet or reach one of their cherished goals (Coyne & Whiffen, 1995). These examples show how psychosocial factors—having a dependent or achievement-oriented personality—interact with major stressors to increase one's risk of developing a mood disorder, such as depression (Kessler, 1997).

The answer to the question Why do some people get depressed while others do not? is complex because it depends on the interaction between biological and psychosocial factors. For this reason, you'll see that there is both a psychosocial and a biological treatment of depression.

### Treatment of Mood Disorders

**What's the treatment?** We have discussed Rod Steiger, who was diagnosed with a major depressive disorder, and Chuck Elliot, who was diagnosed with bipolar I disorder (manic-depressive disorder). Because of their different diagnoses, they would be treated with different drugs, psychotherapy, or some combination. We'll discuss the effectiveness of drugs and psychotherapy.

#### Major Depression and Dysthymic Disorder

Rod Steiger decided to fight the stigma of having a mental disorder by making his fight with depression public and seeking treatment. He was given an antidepressant drug.

*Antidepressant drugs* act by increasing levels of a specific group of neurotransmitters (monoamines, such as serotonin) that is believed to be involved in the regulation of emotions and moods.

Major depression: treated with antidepressants

**Selective serotonin reuptake inhibitors—SSRIs.**
About 80% of prescribed antidepressant drugs, such as Prozac (fluoxetine), belong to a group of drugs called *SSRIs* (selective serotonin reuptake inhibitors) (Sussman & Ginsberg, 1998). The SSRIs are relatively new and work primarily by raising the level of a single neurotransmitter, serotonin. When the effectiveness of older antidepressant drugs (tricyclics) was compared with SSRIs (Prozac), both groups of drugs proved effective, but the older drugs (tricyclics) had more undesirable side effects than SSRIs (Hirschfeld, 2000). Because SSRIs are better tolerated, clinicians recommend that SSRIs be tried first in treating depression (Mendlewicz & Lecrubier, 2000).

**Effectiveness of antidepressants.** Although antidepressants may take 4 to 6 weeks before they begin to work, about 70% of patients show improvement, while the remaining 30% receive little or no benefit from antidepressant drugs (Rivas-Vazquez & Blais, 1997). Although antidepressant drugs initially help about 70% of patients, how do antidepressants compare with nondrug treatments, such as psychotherapy?

**Psychotherapy.** Researchers have compared patients who received antidepressant drugs, psychotherapy, or a combination of drugs and psychotherapy to treat major depression. For patients with less severe depression, psychotherapy was as effective as antidepressant drugs (Elkin et al., 1989; Thase et al., 1997). For patients with more severe or chronic depression, a combination of antidepressant drugs (SSRIs) and psychotherapy was more effective than either one alone (Keller et al., 2000).

Antidepressants and psychotherapy are about equally effective for many patients.

**Relapse.** However, when patients who had recovered were followed for 18 months, the results were discouraging because within that time, 70% of the patients had relapsed, that is, had become depressed again and required additional treatment. Of those who maintained their recovery and were doing well, 30% had been treated with psychotherapy, 20% with antidepressant drugs, and 20% with placebos. Thus, patients treated with psychotherapy were somewhat less likely to relapse than those treated with drugs or given placebos (Shea et al., 1992).

The big problem is that 70% of patients treated for depression relapse within 18 months and 82% relapse during the first five years. For this reason, clinicians concluded that major depression is a long-term or chronic disorder that may require further treatments during the patient's lifetime (Hirschfeld, 2000).

#### Bipolar I Disorder

Unlike Rod Steiger's problem, which was major depressive disorder, Chuck Elliot has bipolar I disorder, which means that he cycles between episodes of depression and mania. For example, one of Elliot's manic episodes lasted four days, during which he was in almost constant motion and did not sleep. Several times, when he lost control, he screamed at his wife (right photo) and ripped the blinds from the windows. When his wife called the police, whom Elliot wanted to avoid meeting at all costs, he immediately left the house. The police caught and handcuffed him and drove him to a psychiatric hospital for drug treatment. The medication that Elliot takes for his bipolar I disorder is called lithium.

Bipolar I disorder: treated with lithium

*Lithium (LITH-ee-um)*, which is a naturally occurring mineral salt, is the most effective treatment for bipolar I disorder because it reduces or prevents manic episodes.

Lithium is thought to prevent manic episodes by preventing neurons from being overstimulated (Lenox & Hahn, 2000). When Elliot takes his medication, he functions well enough that he has enrolled in law school and is currently working toward his degree. The problem arises when Elliot doesn't take his lithium. Within four weeks of stopping lithium, about 50% of patients experience a manic episode (Moncrieff, 1997).

In terms of effectiveness, about 50% of bipolar patients are greatly helped with lithium; 30% are partially helped; and 20% get little or no help (Baldessarini & Tondo, 2000). Because of lithium's serious side effects (weight gain and toxic effects), about 28% of patients stop treatment on their own and may relapse (Maj et al., 1997).

**Mania.** Lithium has been found to be effective in treating individuals with *mania*—that is, manic episodes without the depression (Bowden, 2000). Because lithium prevents mania, patients may stop taking it to experience the euphoria they miss, as Elliot did several times.

**Relapse.** For both major depression and bipolar I disorder, 10–30% of patients receive no help from current drugs and 30–70% initially improve but later relapse. Researchers are constantly searching for new ways to treat mood disorders and prevent relapse.

For individuals with major depression who are not helped by drugs, there is a treatment of last resort.

## Definition and Usage

**What's it like to get ECT?**

Because the use of shock as therapy has often been wrongly portrayed in the media, it helps to see the treatment from the eyes of an actual patient.

". . . As far as manic-depressive tales go, my stories are typical. My illness went undiagnosed for a decade, a period of euphoric highs and desperate lows highlighted by $25,000 shopping sprees, impetuous trips to Tokyo, Paris, and Milan, drug and alcohol binges . . . After seeing eight psychiatrists, I finally received a diagnosis of bipolar disorder on my 32nd birthday. Over the next year and a half, I was treated unsuccessfully with more than 30 medications. My suburban New Jersey upbringing, my achievements as a film major at Wesleyan, and a thriving career in public relations couldn't help me . . . As a last resort, I'm admitted to the hospital for ECT, electroconvulsive therapy, more commonly known as electroshock. . . . The doctor presses a button. Electric current shoots through my brain for an instant, causing a grand-mal seizure for 20 seconds . . . I wake up 30 minutes later and think I'm in a hotel room in Acapulco. My head feels as if I've just downed a frozen margarita too quickly . . . After four treatments, there is marked improvement. No more egregious highs or lows. But there are huge gaps in my memory. I avoid friends and neighbors because I don't know their names anymore. I can't remember the books I've read or the movies I've seen. I have trouble recalling simple vocabulary. I forget phone numbers . . . But I continue treatment because I'm getting better . . . On the one-year anniversary of my first electroshock treatment, I'm clearheaded and even-keeled. I call my doctor to announce my 'new and improved' status . . . Two and a half years later, I still miss ECT. But medication keeps my illness in check, and I'm more sane than I've ever been" (Behrman, 1999, p. 67).

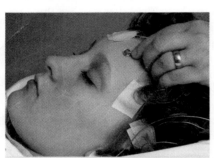

ECT: Electrodes placed on this patient's forehead will carry electricity through the brain and cause a major seizure.

This patient received electroconvulsive therapy (ECT).

*Electroconvulsive therapy,* or *ECT,* involves placing electrodes on the skull and administering a mild electric current that passes through the brain and causes a seizure. Usual treatment consists of a series of 10–12 ECT sessions, at the rate of about three per week.

**Usage.** Because antidepressants fail to decrease depression in up to 30% of patients in the United States, the only other available treatment is ECT—the last resort. As shown in the right graph, ECT's use has been increasing since 1980 and is currently estimated at 100,000 patients per year (Fischer, 2000). ECT is used primarily to treat mood disorders (84%), especially depression.

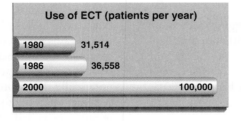

**Use of ECT (patients per year)**

| | |
|---|---|
| 1980 | 31,514 |
| 1986 | 36,558 |
| 2000 | 100,000 |

We'll discuss the pros and cons of electroconvulsive therapy.

## Effectiveness of ECT

**Why is ECT considered the last resort?**

Because antidepressants had not worked, the patient we just described agreed to ECT. The reason ECT is the last resort for treating depression is that ECT produces major brain seizures and may cause varying degrees of memory loss. However, even as a treatment of last resort, ECT is effective in reducing depressive symptoms in about 60–80% of patients (Sackeim et al., 2000). For example, the graph below shows the results for eight out of nine seriously depressed patients who had received no help from antidepressants. After a series of ECT treatments, they showed a rather dramatic reduction in depressive symptoms and remained symptom-free after one year (Paul et al., 1981). However, the relapse rate after ECT treatment is about 50%, which means that patients may need additional ECT treatments for depression (Bourgon & Kellner, 2000). Researchers are not sure how ECT works but suggest that it may temporarily reduce blood flow to certain brain areas or change the levels of neurotransmitters (Nobler & Sackeim, 1998).

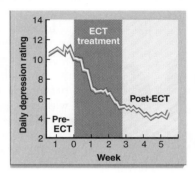

**Modern ECT.** Unlike patients who received ECT in the movie *One Flew Over the Cuckoo's Nest,* there is no evidence that modern ECT procedures cause brain damage or turn people into "vegetables" (Ende et al., 2000). Modern ECT procedures include the proper placement of electrodes on the scalp and reduced levels of electric current (Sackeim et al., 2000).

**Memory loss.** A serious side effect of ECT is memory loss, which, similar to the patient we described on the left, may range from a persistent loss of memory for events experienced during the weeks of treatment to include events before and after treatment. Following ECT treatment, there is a gradual improvement in memory functions, and researchers have reported that long-term impairment of memory following ECT was minimal and returned to pretreatment levels within six months (Sackeim & Stern, 1997). In spite of the finding that some memories return, about 50% of patients given ECT reported considerable memory loss, more so for information about the world than about themselves (personal memories), as long as three years after treatment (Lisanby et al., 2000).

A National Institute of Mental Health panel of experts gave a cautious endorsement of the use of ECT as a treatment of last resort for some types of severe depression. The panel added that every patient should be informed as fully as possible of the potential risks, such as memory loss (Holden, 1985).

Next, we'll discuss a disorder shared by many serial killers.

# C. Personality Disorders

## Definition

### What are serial killers like?

We have all heard the expression "Don't judge a book by its cover." That advice proved absolutely true when we heard what their friends and neighbors said about the following individuals.

A high school classmate of Joel Rifkin said that he was "quiet, shy, not the kind of guy who would do something like this." Rifkin confessed to killing 17 prostitutes.

His boss said David Berkowitz was "quiet and reserved and kept pretty much to himself. That's the way he was here, nice—a quiet, shy fellow." Berkowitz, known as "Son of Sam," was convicted of killing 6 people.

A neighbor of Westley Allan Dodd said that he "seemed so harmless, such an all-around, basic good citizen." Dodd was executed for kidnapping, raping, and murdering 3 small boys.

A neighbor said John Esposito "was such a quiet, caring person. He was a very nice person." Esposito was charged with kidnapping a young girl and keeping her in an underground bunker for 16 days.

A friend said Jeffrey Dahmer "didn't have much to say, was quiet, like the average Joe." Dahmer confessed to killing and dismembering 15 people (*Time*, July 12, 1993, p. 18).

### Why do friends describe serial killers as quiet, nice, and caring?

Notice how friends and neighbors judged all these cold-blooded killers to be "quiet" and "nice" and even "caring" individuals. However, while these individuals appeared very ordinary in public appearance and behavior, each was hiding a deep-seated, serious, and dangerous personality disorder (Hickey, 1991).

A *personality disorder* consists of inflexible, long-standing, maladaptive traits that cause significantly impaired functioning or great distress in one's personal and social life (American Psychiatric Association, 2000).

Personality disorders are found in about 12% of the adult population in the United States (Weissman, 1993). Of the ten different personality disorders described in DSM-IV-TR, here are six of the more common types.

■ *Paranoid personality disorder* is a pattern of distrust and suspiciousness and perceiving others as having evil motives (0.5–2.5% of population).

■ *Schizotypal personality disorder* is characterized by an acute discomfort in close relationships, distortions in thinking, and eccentric behavior (3–5% of population).

■ *Histrionic personality disorder* is characterized by excessive emotionality and attention seeking (2% of population).

■ *Obsessive-compulsive personality disorder* is an intense interest in being orderly, achieving perfection, and having control (4% of population).

■ *Dependent personality disorder* refers to a pattern of being submissive and clingy because of an excessive need to be taken care of (2% of population).

■ *Antisocial personality disorder* refers to a pattern of disregarding or violating the rights of others without feeling guilt or remorse (3% of population, predominantly males) (American Psychiatric Association, 2000).

Individuals with personality disorders often have the following characteristics: troubled childhoods, childhood problems that continue into adulthood, maladaptive or poor personal relationships, and abnormal behaviors that are at the extreme end of the behavioral continuum. Their difficulties arise from a combination of genetic, psychological, social, and environmental factors (Vargha-Khadem, 2000).

We'll focus on one particular personality disorder, the antisocial personality, because it is the one most mentioned by the media.

## Antisocial Personality Disorder

The five "nice," "quiet" killers we described would probably be diagnosed as having antisocial personality disorder or some combination of personality disorders. These individuals are more commonly called psychopaths or sociopaths, whose symptoms are on a continuum. At one end of the continuum are chronic delinquents, bullies, and lawbreakers; at the other end are the serial killers (Widiger & Costa, 1994).

**Delinquent.** An example of someone on the delinquent end of the continuum is Tom, who always seemed to be in trouble. As a child he would steal items (silverware) from home and sell or swap them for things he wanted. As a teenager, he skipped classes in school, set deserted buildings on fire, forged his father's name on checks, stole cars, and was finally sent to a federal institution. After Tom served his time, he continued to break the law, and by the age of 21, he had been arrested and imprisoned 50–60 times (Spitzer et al., 1994).

**Serial killer.** At the other end of the psychopathic continuum is serial killer Jeffrey Dahmer, whom we also discussed in Module 22. Dahmer would pick up young gay men, bring them home, drug them, strangle them, have sex with their corpses, and then, in some cases, eat their flesh. As Dahmer said in an interview, "I could completely control a person—a person that I found physically attractive, and keep them with me as long as possible, even if it meant just keep a part of them" (Gleick et al., 1994, p. 129).

Jeffrey Dahmer was diagnosed as having an antisocial personality disorder (being a psychopath).

**Two characteristics.** One characteristic of psychopaths is their consistent pattern of disregard for or violation of the rights or properties of others; they may steal, harass, or beat people, destroy property, kidnap, or kill. Another characteristic of psychopaths is their dishonesty, lying, or deceitful manipulation of others. The combination of these two groups of characteristics makes psychopaths potentially dangerous to deal with and, as you'll see, very difficult to treat or change into more responsible individuals.

**Power Study™**

**Check out CD: Module 4**
A. Genes & Evolution
B. Studying the Living Brain

## Psychopaths: Causes and Treatment

**How does one become a psychopath?**
Researchers have found genetic and neurological factors that may predispose individuals for developing an antisocial personality, which involves behaving irresponsibly, being a habitual and convincing liar, having no guilt or remorse, being impulsive and reckless, and failing to learn from experience (Lewis, 1991). Psychopaths are more likely to be men (2–4.5%) than women (0.5–1%), and they usually have a number of other related problems, such as alcoholism and depression (Black et al., 1995). We'll discuss the causes and treatment of antisocial personality disorder.

### Causes

What makes psychopaths such puzzling and potentially dangerous individuals is a disorder that involves complex psychosocial and biological factors (Brennan & Raine, 1997).

**Psychosocial factors.** To identify psychosocial factors, researchers followed more than 500 cases of children who had been referred for behavioral problems (Robins et al., 1991). Many of these problem children, who later developed into full-blown psychopaths, had originally been brought

Developing into a psychopath involves psychosocial and biological factors.

to the clinic because of aggressive and antisocial behaviors, such as truancy, theft, disobeying their parents, and frequent lying with no signs of remorse. Thus, an aggressive and antisocial child whom parents find almost impossible to control is at risk for developing an antisocial personality (Morey, 1997).

Another psychosocial factor that may contribute to developing an antisocial personality is physical or sexual abuse in childhood, which is reported by 59–70% of psychopaths (Ruegg & Frances, 1995). However, since many abused children do not become psychopaths, it is difficult to determine how much childhood abuse contributes to the development of antisocial personality disorders.

**PS** **Biological factors.** Many parents reported that, from infancy on, their children had temper tantrums, became furious when frustrated, bullied other children, did not respond to punishment, and were generally unmanageable. Researchers suggest that the early appearance of serious behavioral problems suggests that underlying biological factors, both genetic and neurological, may predispose or place a child at risk for developing antisocial personality disorders.

Evidence for *genetic factors* comes from twin and adoption studies that show that genetic factors contribute 30–50% to the development of antisocial personality disorders (Thapar & McGuffin, 1993). Evidence for *neurological factors* comes from individuals with brain damage and from MRI studies on the brains of individuals with antisocial personality disorder.

For example, researchers found that early brain damage to the *prefrontal cortex* resulted in two children who did not learn normal social and moral behaviors and showed no empathy, remorse, or guilt as adults. In addition, MRI scans (p. 70) indicated that individuals diagnosed with antisocial personality disorder had 11% fewer brain cells in their prefrontal cortex (Raine et al., 2000). Since the prefrontal cortex is known to be involved in important executive functions, such as making decisions and planning, researchers suggest that damage to or maldevelopment of the prefrontal cortex predisposes or increases the risk of an individual developing an antisocial personality disorder. Researchers believe that biological factors can predispose individuals to act in certain ways but that the interaction between biological and psychosocial factors results in the development and onset of personality disorders (Morgan & Lilienfeld, 2000).

### Treatment

Psychotherapy has not proved very effective in treating psychopaths because psychopaths are guiltless, mistrusting, irresponsible, and practiced liars, who fail to see that many of their behaviors are antisocial and maladaptive. As a result, psychotherapists have a very difficult time modifying or changing the behavior of psychopaths (Bateman & Fonagy, 2000).

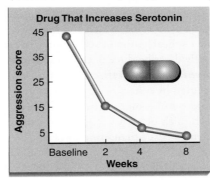

Psychopaths do not recognize their problems or want to change.

Because of the relative ineffectiveness of psychotherapy, clinicians have tried various drugs, including antidepressants, that act to raise levels of serotonin in the brain. Currently, researchers believe that some abnormality in the brain's serotonin system may underlie the impulsive, aggressive, and self-destructive behaviors observed in personality disorders (Coccaro & Kavoussi, 1997). Following this line of reasoning,

**Drug That Increases Serotonin**

researchers have used several relatively new drugs (sertraline, fluoxetine, Prozac) whose primary action is to raise levels of serotonin. As shown in the left graph, patients who took a serotonin-increasing drug (sertraline) reported significant decreases in their aggressive behaviors across eight weeks of treatment. However, researchers caution that aggressive behaviors may return once patients stop taking these serotonin-increasing drugs (Coccaro & Kavoussi, 1997).

A major question is whether psychopaths improve over time. Researchers did a 29-year follow-up of 71 men who had been treated for antisocial personality disorder. They found that only 31% continued to show improvement; the remaining 69% either showed no improvement or relapsed (Black et al., 1995). Researchers concluded that, for more than two-thirds of the patients, antisocial personality disorders are an ongoing, relatively stable, long-term problem that may need continual treatment (Parker, 2000).

Next, we'll examine one of the most tragic mental disorders—schizophrenia.

### Definition and Types

**What if you lose touch with reality?**

At the beginning of this module, we described 18-year-old Michael McCabe (photo below), who said that his mind began to weaken during the summer of 1992. "I totally hit this point in my life where I was so high on life, it was amazing. I had this sense of independence. I was 18 and turning into an adult. Next thing I knew I got this feeling that people were trying to take things from me. Not my soul, but physical things from me. I couldn't sleep because they [his mother and sister] were planning to do something to me. I think there was a higher power inside the 7-Eleven that was helping me out the whole time, just bringing me back to a strong mental state" (Brooks, 1994, p. 9). Michael was diagnosed as having schizophrenia *(skit-suh-FREE-nee-ah)*.

Michael McCabe had many of the symptoms described on the right.

*Schizophrenia* is a serious mental disorder that lasts for at least six months and includes at least two of the following symptoms: delusions, hallucinations, disorganized speech, disorganized behavior, and decreased emotional expression. These symptoms interfere with personal or social functioning (American Psychiatric Association, 2000).

Michael has a number of these symptoms, including delusions (higher power inside the 7-Eleven), hallucinations (hearing voices), and disorganized behavior. Schizophrenia affects about 0.2–2% of the adult population or about 4.5 million people (equal numbers of men and women) in the United States (American Psychiatric Association, 2000). Of the inpatients in mental hospitals, about 30% are there because of schizophrenia, and this percentage is the highest of any mental disorder (Robins & Regier, 1991).

#### SUBCATEGORIES OF SCHIZOPHRENIA

Michael's case illustrates some of the symptoms that occur in schizophrenia. In fact, no two patients have exactly the same set of symptoms, which are described in the list on the right. The DSM-IV-TR describes five different subcategories of schizophrenia, each of which is characterized by different symptoms. We'll briefly describe three of the more common schizophrenic subcategories.

*Paranoid schizophrenia* is characterized by auditory hallucinations or delusions, such as thoughts of being persecuted by others or thoughts of grandeur.

*Disorganized schizophrenia* is marked by bizarre ideas, often about one's body (bones melting), confused speech, childish behavior (giggling for no apparent reason, making faces at people), great emotional swings (fits of laughing or crying), and often extreme neglect of personal appearance and hygiene.

*Catatonic schizophrenia* is characterized by periods of wild excitement or periods of rigid, prolonged immobility; sometimes the person assumes the same frozen posture for hours on end.

Differentiating between types of schizophrenia can be difficult because some symptoms, such as disordered thought processes and delusions, are shared by all types.

#### CHANCE OF RECOVERY

Chances of recovery are dependent upon a number of factors, which have been grouped under two major types of schizophrenia (Crow, 1985).

*Type I schizophrenia* includes having positive symptoms, such as hallucinations and delusions, which are a distortion of normal functions. In addition, this group has no intellectual impairment, good reaction to medication, and thus a good chance of recovery.

*Type II schizophrenia* includes having negative symptoms, such as dulled emotions and little inclination to speak, which are a loss of normal functions. In addition, this group has intellectual impairment, poor reaction to medication, and thus a poor chance of recovery.

According to this classification system, the best predictor of a schizophrenic's recovery is his or her symptoms: those with positive symptoms have a good chance of recovery, while those with negative symptoms have a poor chance (Andreasen et al., 1994).

Next, we'll describe the major symptoms of schizophrenia.

### Symptoms

Schizophrenia is a serious mental disorder that lasts for at least six months and includes at least two of the following symptoms:

**1 Disorders of thought.** These are characterized by incoherent thought patterns, formation of new words (called *neologisms*), inability to stick to one topic, and irrational beliefs or delusions. For example, Michael believed that his mother and sister were plotting against him.

**2 Disorders of attention.** These include difficulties in concentration and in focusing on a single chain of events. For instance, one patient said that he could not concentrate on television because he couldn't watch and listen at the same time.

**3 Disorders of perception.** These include strange bodily sensations and hallucinations.

*Hallucinations* are sensory experiences without any stimulation from the environment.

The most common hallucinations are auditory, such as hearing voices. Other distorted perceptions include feeling that parts of the body are too small or too large.

**4 Motor disorders.** These include making strange facial expressions, being extremely active, or (the opposite) remaining immobile for long periods of time.

**5 Emotional (affective) disorders.** These may include having little or no emotional responsiveness or having emotional responses that are inappropriate to the situation—for example, laughing when told of the death of a close friend.

The cause of these schizophrenic symptoms involves the interaction among biological, neurological, and environmental factors.

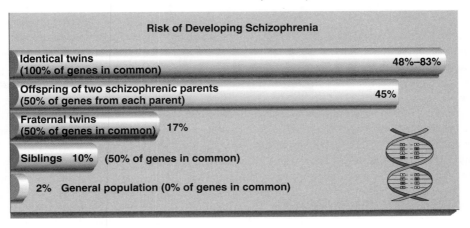

Marsha tries to help her son, Michael, who has schizophrenia.

When Michael was in the hospital, his mother, Marsha (photo below ), began going to a support group to get help and find out about schizophrenia. At one meeting Marsha said, "I haven't been doing very well with this, to be perfectly honest. How in the hell were we dealt this hand?" (Brooks, 1994, p. 8).

The psychiatrist who led Marsha's group answered that about 1 in 100 people get schizophrenia but the odds increase to 1 in 10 if it's already in the family. If a person inherits a predisposition for schizophrenia, any number of things—such as drugs, a death in the family, growing-up problems—can trigger its onset (Brooks, 1994). The psychiatrist was pointing out three major factors—biological, neurological, and environmental—that interact in the development of schizophrenia. We'll begin with biological factors, specifically genetic causes.

## GENETIC PREDISPOSITION

In 1930, the birth of four identical baby girls (quadruplets) was a rare occurrence (1 in 16 million) and received great publicity. By the time the girls had reached high school, all four were labeled "different." They sometimes broke light bulbs, tore buttons off their clothes, complained of bones slipping out of place, and had periods of great confusion. By young adulthood, all four girls, who are called the Genain quadruplets and share 100% of their genes, were diagnosed with schizophrenia (Mirsky & Quinn, 1988). The finding that all four Genain quadruplets (above photo) developed schizophrenia indicates that increased genetic similarity is associated with increased risk for developing schizophrenia and suggests that a person inherits a *predisposition* for developing the disorder. Support for a genetic predisposition also comes from twin studies.

All four of these identical quadruplets developed schizophrenia, pointing to genetic causes.

## GENETIC MARKERS

Because researchers knew that schizophrenia might have a genetic factor, they compared rates of schizophrenia in identical twins, who share 100% of their genes, with rates in fraternal twins and siblings (brothers and sisters), who share only 50% of their genes. The right graph shows the risk of developing schizophrenia for individuals

who share different percentages of genes and thus have different degrees of genetic similarity. Notice that if one identical twin is schizophrenic, there is a 48–83% chance that the other twin will also develop the disorder. In comparison, if one brother or sister (sibling or fraternal twin) is schizophrenic, there is only about a 10–17% chance that the other will develop the disorder (Gottesmann, 1991). In a recent study, researchers reported that if one identical twin was schizophrenic, there was an 83% chance that the other twin was also (Cannon et al., 1998). These twin data show that genetic factors are involved in developing schizophrenia and that the range is from 48 to 83%.

With this finding in mind, researchers have been searching for the location of specific genes involved in schizophrenia; such genes are called a genetic marker (Byerley & Coon, 1995).

A **genetic marker** refers to an identifiable gene or number of genes or a specific segment of a chromosome that is directly linked to some behavioral, physiological, or neurological trait or disease.

During the past ten years, researchers have reported about half a dozen genetic markers for schizophrenia, but none proved valid because none could be repeated or replicated by other laboratories (Marshall, 1995). However, a major breakthrough in identifying genetic markers for schizophrenia has been recently reported.

**Breakthrough.** Researchers studied 22 families and their relatives because many had been diagnosed as schizophrenic. These families and relatives were found to share a certain part of chromosome 1, which means these individuals shared many genes in common (Brzustowicz et al., 2000). The next step will be to identify the specific genes that researchers believe are involved in the development of schizophrenia. Researchers believe that they will find not a single gene but a combination of genes that interact to produce a predisposition (a greater risk) for developing schizophrenia (Brzustowicz et al., 2000). Genetic factors are most likely to act during the 9th to 15th week of the fetal stage, when brain cells (neurons) show a fantastic rate of development and growth (Waddington et al., 2000).

One way that genes could produce a predisposition for schizophrenia would be to cause faulty development of certain structures or functions in the brain. We'll examine what might go wrong in the brain to predispose one to develop schizophrenia.

**Risk of Developing Schizophrenia**

Identical twins
(100% of genes in common) — 48%–83%

Offspring of two schizophrenic parents
(50% of genes from each parent) — 45%

Fraternal twins
(50% of genes in common) — 17%

Siblings — 10% (50% of genes in common)

2% General population (0% of genes in common)

## D. Schizophrenia

**Power Study™**

**Check out CD: Module 3**
B. Neurons: Structure &
Function
**Check out CD: Module 4**
B. Studying the Living Brain
D. Control Centers: Four Lobes

### Neurological Causes

**Is the brain different?**

During the past ten years, advances in studying the living brain, such as by using PET and MRI scans (p. 70), have revealed several major differences between brains of schizophrenics and brains of mentally healthy individuals. Researchers found that the brains of schizophenics, partly as a result of faulty genetic instructions, have larger ventricles and decreased activity in the prefrontal cortex (Selemon, 2000).

#### VENTRICLE SIZE

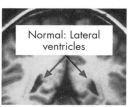

Normal: Lateral ventricles

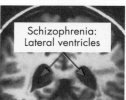

Schizophrenia: Lateral ventricles

Fluid-filled ventricles are enlarged in brains of schizophrenic patients.

Most us of don't realize that our brains have four fluid-filled cavities called ventricles (left figure). The fluid in these cavities helps to cushion the brain against blows and also serves as a reservoir of nutrients and hormones for the brain. One early finding was that ventricles in the brains of schizophrenics were larger. Using MRI scans, researchers studied 15 pairs of identical twins, one of whom was diagnosed as schizophrenic while the other was mentally healthy (normal). Researchers found that the brains of schizophrenic twins had *larger ventricles* compared to the brains of the mentally healthy twins (left figures) (Suddath et al., 1990). However, not all brains of schizophrenics have larger ventricles or an overall decrease in brain size. Researchers conclude that some schizophrenics have abnormally large ventricles, which results in a reduction in the overall size of the brain, which in turn may contribute to the development of schizophrenia (Wright et al., 2000).

#### FRONTAL LOBE: PREFRONTAL CORTEX

Another brain structure involved in many executive functions, such as reasoning, planning, remembering, paying attention, and making decisions, is the the prefrontal cortex (figure below). Researchers report that in pairs of identical twins where one twin was schizophrenic and the other was not, the brain of the schizophrenic twin was characterized by significantly *less activation of the prefrontal cortex* (Torrey et al., 1994). This decreased prefrontal lobe activity is consistent with the deficits in many executive functions observed in schizophrenics, such as disorganized thinking, irrational beliefs, and lack of concentration (Rajkowska et al., 1997).

After finding less activation in the prefrontal cortex of schizophrenics, researchers searched for the causes. In a breakthrough finding, researchers found that, in the brains of schizophrenics, neurons in the prefrontal cortex are packed so close together that there is less room for the needed lines of communication (dendrites and axons; p. 50) between neurons (Sanfilipo et al., 2000). As a result, the reduced lines of communication cause deficits in transmitting information and thus cause deficits in executive functions (disorganized thinking and reasoning) that are observed in patients diagnosed with schizophrenia (Selemon, 2000).

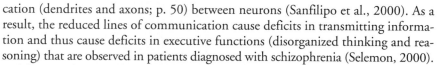

Frontal lobe

Prefrontal cortex

These studies point to neurological causes—abnormal brain structure and function—that may underlie and contribute to the development of schizophrenia. Next, we'll turn to environmental factors involved in developing schizophrenia.

### Environmental Causes

**Can stress act as a trigger?**

If biological factors alone explained why people develop schizophrenia, then the risk for developing schizophrenia in identical twins would be 100% rather than, from what is reported, from 48 to 83%. Because biological factors alone cannot explain the development of schizophrenia, researchers look at the influence of environmental factors, such as the incidence of stressful events and how individuals cope. For example, when Michael McCabe (right photo) was 18, he began to develop schizophrenic symptoms. The onset of these symptoms occurred after the death of his father and during the well-known potentially stressful period of going through adolescence and becoming an adult.

Stressful events may have led to his onset of schizophrenia.

Researchers believe that stressful events, such as having hostile parents, poor social relations, the death of a parent or loved one, and career or personal problems, can contribute to the development and onset of schizophrenia (Walker & Diforio, 1997). This relationship between stress and onset of schizophrenia is called the diathesis stress theory.

The *diathesis (die-ATH-uh-sis) stress theory* of schizophrenia says that some people have a genetic predisposition (a diathesis) that interacts with life stressors to result in the onset and development of schizophrenia.

The diathesis stress theory assumes that biological or neurological factors have initially produced a *predisposition for schizophrenia*. If a person already has a predisposition for schizophrenia, then being faced with stressful environmental factors can increase the risk and vulnerability for developing schizophrenia as well as trigger the onset of schizophrenic symptoms (Benes, 1997). Thus, the diathesis stress theory says that biological/neurological factors first create a predisposition that may lead to schizophrenia in dealing with stressful factors.

Now we'll examine the drugs used to treat schizophrenia.

**How is Michael treated?**

After Michael (right photo) was taken to the psychiatric hospital, his symptoms were assessed and he was diagnosed as schizophrenic. Schizophrenic symptoms are commonly divided into positive and negative symptoms.

*Positive symptoms of schizophrenia* reflect a distortion of normal functions: distorted thinking results in delusions; distorted perceptions result in hallucinations; distorted language results in disorganized speech.

*Negative symptoms of schizophrenia* reflect a decrease in or loss of normal functions: decreased range and intensity of emotions,

Michael was given a neuroleptic drug to treat his schizophrenia.

decreased ability to express thoughts, and decreased initiative to engage in goal-directed behaviors (American Psychiatric Association, 2000).

Like most individuals diagnosed with schizophrenia, Michael had both positive symptoms, such as delusions that people were going to steal from him, and negative symptoms, such as loss of emotional expression. To reduce these symptoms, he was given haloperidol, which is an example of an antipsychotic or neuroleptic (meaning "taking hold of the nerves") drug.

*Neuroleptic drugs,* also called *antipsychotic drugs,* are used to treat serious mental disorders, such as schizophrenia, by changing levels of neurotransmitters in the brain.

There are two kinds of neuroleptic drugs, typical and atypical.

## Typical Neuroleptics

**Typical neuroleptics: decrease dopamine**

Typical neuroleptics were discovered in the 1950s and were the first effective medical treatment for schizophrenia.

*Typical neuroleptic drugs* primarily reduce levels of the neurotransmitter dopamine. Two of the more common are phenothiazines (Thorazine) and butrophenones (haloperidol). These drugs primarily reduce positive symptoms and have little effect on negative symptoms (Casey, 2000).

Because typical neuroleptics primarily reduce levels of dopamine, their method of action supports the dopamine theory of schizophrenia (Kapur et al., 2000).

The *dopamine theory* says that in schizophrenia the dopamine neurotransmitter system is somehow overactive and gives rise to a wide range of symptoms.

The dopamine theory involves neurons in one particular brain structure, the *basal ganglia* (right figure), which use dopamine in communicating; these communications are significantly blocked by typical neuroleptics. Problems with typical neuroleptics include causing unwanted motor movements and not helping about 20% of schizophrenics. For this reason, clinicians are using new drugs, called atypical neuroleptics, whose effectiveness casts some doubt on the dopamine theory (Schulz, 2000).

Basal ganglia

## Atypical Neuroleptics

In Michael's case and for about 20% of all schizophrenics, typical neuroleptic drugs (haloperidol or Thorazine) have little or no effect on their symptoms. Many of these patients are now being helped by atypical neuroleptic drugs (Casey, 2000).

**Atypical neuroleptics: decrease dopamine & serotonin**

*Atypical neuroleptic drugs* lower levels of dopamine but, more important, reduce levels of other neurotransmitters, especially serotonin. One group of these drugs is the benzamides (such as clozapine). These drugs primarily reduce positive symptoms and may also improve negative symptoms (Schulz, 2000).

The first atypical neuroleptic, clozapine, was approved for use in schizophrenia in 1990. Since then, a number of atypical neuroleptics have proven effective in decreasing schizophrenic symptoms, especially in patients who were not helped by typical neuroleptics (Purdon et al., 2000).

Michael, for example, showed little improvement with typical neuroleptics (haloperidol). However, the atypical neuroleptic clozapine reduced his positive symptoms to the point that he was allowed to leave the psychiatric hospital and return home. A year later, Michael is still taking clozapine and is making slow progress in overcoming his symptoms, such as paranoia.

On most days, Michael comes home from group therapy and job-training classes, puts on a Bob Marley record, and sits and listens, afraid to do much else. As Michael explains, "I can't go out and skate or do anything because I'm afraid I'm going to have a paranoia attack" (Brooks, 1995b, p. D-3). His mother

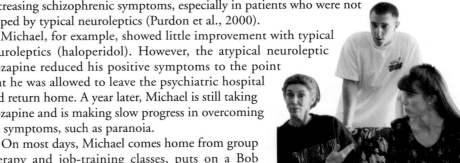

Michael (with mother and sister) was switched to atypical neuroleptics, which reduced his symptoms.

and sister (right photo) provide Michael (standing in back) with financial and social support but wish Michael would take greater initiative to improve his own life. Michael and many other patients with schizophrenia face a daily struggle to overcome their symptoms, which may last for months, years, or in some cases, a lifetime (Kane, 1997).

**Atypical neuroleptics.** Many studies have found that about 50% of patients who did poorly on typical neuroleptics showed significant improvement on atypical neuroleptics (Purdon et al., 2000). For this reason, typical neuroleptics (phenothiazines) have lost their standing as the first choice in treating schizophrenia. The first choice in the drug treatment of schizophrenia is now one of the new atypical neuroleptics.

Although typical neuroleptics and the newer atypical neuroleptics represent major advances in the treatment of schizophrenia, both can produce significant and undesirable side effects, which we'll discuss next.

---

### Evaluation of Neuroleptic Drugs

---

**What are the side effects?**

The major advantage of neuroleptic drugs is that they effectively reduce positive symptoms so that many patients can regain some degree of normal functioning. However, neuroleptics also have two potentially serious disadvantages: they may produce undesirable side effects, and they may not prevent relapse or return of the original schizophrenic symptoms. We'll first explain the side effects.

**NEUROLEPTICS**

| Typical: decrease dopamine | Atypical: decrease dopamine & serotonin |

---

#### *Typical Neuroleptics*

**Side effects.** One group of typical neuroleptics, called the phenothiazines *(pheen–no–THIGH–ah–zines),* is widely prescribed to treat schizophrenia. Phenothiazines can produce unwanted motor movements, which is a side effect called tardive dyskinesia.

*Tardive dyskinesia (TARD-if dis-cah-KNEE-zee-ah)* involves the appearance of slow, involuntary, and uncontrollable rhythmic movements and rapid twitching of the mouth and lips, as well as unusual movements of the limbs. This condition is associated with the continued use of typical neuroleptics.

As shown in the graph below, the risk for developing tardive dyskinesia increases with use: after three months, 16% developed

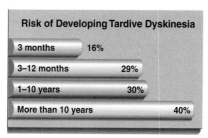

**Risk of Developing Tardive Dyskinesia**

| | |
|---|---|
| 3 months | 16% |
| 3–12 months | 29% |
| 1–10 years | 30% |
| More than 10 years | 40% |

this side effect; after ten years, 40% developed it (Sweet et al., 1995). About 30% of patients with tardive dyskinesia will experience a reduction in symptoms if they are taken off typical neuroleptics, but the remaining 70% may continue to have the problem when the drug therapy is stopped (Roy-Byrne & Fann, 1997).

**Relapse.** The basic problem with taking patients off typical neuroleptics is that they may relapse. For example, after an average of 19 months, 53% of patients taken off typical neuroleptics experienced a relapse as compared to a relapse rate of 16% for those who were maintained on atypical neuroleptics (Gilbert et al., 1995). In treating patients with phenothiazines, clinicians must balance the dangers of a patient relapsing against those of developing tardive dyskinesia.

**Effectiveness.** Researchers have completed several long-term follow-up studies on patients who were treated for schizophrenia with typical neuroleptics. They found that, 2–12 years after treatment, about 20–30% of patients showed a good outcome, which means they needed no further treatment and had no relapse; about 40–60% continued to suffer some behavior impairment and relapse, although their symptoms reached a plateau in about 5 years and did not worsen after that; and about 20% were not helped by these drugs and remained schizophrenic.

Researchers concluded that, for the majority of patients, schizophrenia can be a chronic problem with a high risk for relapse and the need for additional drug treatment during the person's lifetime (Harding & Hall, 1997).

---

#### *Atypical Neuroleptics*

**Side effects.** One advantage of atypical neuroleptics, such as clozapine, is that these drugs produce tardive dyskinesia in only about 5% of patients. However, about 15–35% of patients taking clozapine reported side effects of feeling fatigued and emotionally indifferent to what was happening around them (Gerlach & Peacock, 1994). The most serious side effect of clozapine is sudden loss of infection-fighting white blood cells, which occurs in only 1–2% of patients but can result in death if not detected early. Besides clozapine, there are almost a half dozen new atypical neuroleptics that have fewer side effects than clozapine (Casey, 2000).

Unwanted motor movements (lip smacking) are a side effect of typical neuroleptics but less so with atypical neuroleptics.

**Effectiveness.** From the 1950s through the middle of the 1990s, the drug of choice for treating schizophrenia was typical neuroleptics, especially the phenothiazines. Beginning in the late 1990s and continuing to the present, the drug of choice for treating schizophrenia has made a dramatic switch to atypical neuroleptics.

There are two reasons atypical neuroleptics are now the drug of choice in treating schizophrenia: First, atypical neuroleptics have proved as effective and often more effective in reducing positive and negative symptoms compared to typical neuroleptics; and second, compared to typical neuroleptics (phenothiazines), atypical neuroleptics are less likely to cause tardive dyskinesia (Casey, 2000).

Studies on the effectiveness of atypical neuroleptics indicate that, after a year, 31–60% of patients who were initially treated with atypical neuroleptics or who did poorly on typical neuroleptics and were switched to atypical neuroleptics showed significant improvement (Schulz, 2000). The most surprising finding was that of the 50% who improved on clozapine, about 10% showed very dramatic improvement, almost as if they were suddenly "awakened" from a long and silent sleep (Weiden et al., 1996).

**Second revolution.** The new atypical neuroleptics (olanzapine, risperidone, quetiapine), which appeared in the late 1990s, now account for the majority of antipsychotic prescriptions (Schulz, 2000). Clozapine, which was the first atypical neuroleptic, is no longer the first choice because of its unwanted side effects (life-threatening loss of white blood cells).

The discovery of phenothiazines was considered the first revolution in treating schizophrenia, while the discovery of atypical neuroleptics is now considered the second revolution (Casey, 2000).

After the Concept Review, we'll discuss a disorder that has a very strange symptom—the person does not know who he or she is.

# Concept Review

**1.** A prolonged emotional state that affects almost all of a person's thoughts and behaviors is called a _____ disorder.

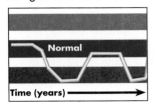

**2.** The most common form of mood disorder is marked by at least two weeks of daily being in a bad mood, having no interest in anything, or getting no pleasure from activities and having at least four of these additional symptoms: problems with weight or appetite, insomnia, fatigue, difficulty thinking, and feeling worthless and guilty. This problem is called _____ disorder.

**3.** Another depressive disorder is characterized by being chronically depressed for many but not all days over a period of two years and having two of the following symptoms: poor appetite, insomnia, fatigue, low self-esteem, and feelings of hopelessness. This problem is called _____ disorder.

**4.** Another mood disorder is characterized by a fluctuation between a depressive episode and a manic episode that lasts about a week, during which a person is unusually euphoric, cheerful, or high, speaks rapidly, feels great self-esteem, and needs little sleep. This problem is called _____ disorder.

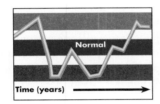

**5.** The theory that underlying genetic, neurological, or physiological factors may predispose a person to developing a mood disorder is called the _____ of depression.

| Risk of Developing Bipolar Disorder | |
|---|---|
| Identical twins | 80% |
| Fraternal twins | 16% |

**6.** Factors such as dealing with stressors and stressful life events are believed to interact with predisposing biological factors and contribute to the development, onset, or maintenance of mood disorders. These are called _____ factors.

**7.** One treatment for major depression involves placing electrodes on the skull and administering a mild electric current that passes through the brain and causes a seizure. Usual treatment consists of a series of 10–12 such sessions, at the rate of about three per week. This treatment is called _____.

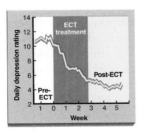

**8.** Certain psychoactive drugs act by increasing levels of a specific group of neurotransmitters (monoamines, such as serotonin) that

is believed to be involved in the regulation of emotions and moods. These are called (a)_____ drugs. A naturally occurring mineral salt that is an effective treatment for bipolar I disorder because it reduces or prevents manic episodes is called (b)_____.

**9.** A person who has inflexible, long-standing, maladaptive traits that cause significantly impaired functioning or great distress in his or her personal and social life is said to have a (a)_____ disorder. Examples of this disorder include a pattern of distrust and suspiciousness and perceiving others as having evil motives, which is called a (b)_____ personality disorder; a pattern of being submissive and clingy because of an excessive need to be taken care of, which is called a (c)_____ personality disorder; and a pattern of disregarding or violating the rights of others without feeling guilt or remorse, which is called an (d)_____ personality disorder.

**10.** A serious mental disturbance that lasts for at least six months and that includes at least two of the following persistent symptoms—delusions, hallucinations, disorganized speech, grossly disorganized behavior, and decreased emotional expression—is called (a)_____. There are subcategories of this disorder: the one characterized by auditory hallucinations or delusions, such as thoughts of being persecuted by others or thoughts of grandeur, is called (b)_____ schizophrenia.

**11.** Drugs that are used to treat schizophrenia and that act primarily to reduce levels of dopamine are called (a)_____ drugs and include phenothiazines. Drugs that are used to treat schizophrenia and that reduce levels of dopamine and levels of serotonin are called (b)_____ drugs and include clozapine. The theory that, in schizophrenia, the dopamine neurotransmitter system is somehow overactive and gives rise to many of the symptoms observed in schizophrenics is called the (c)_____ theory, which is supported by the actions of (d)_____ drugs but not by the action of (e)_____ drugs.

***Answers:*** *1. mood; 2. major depressive or unipolar depression; 3. dysthymic; 4. bipolar I; 5. biological theory; 6. psychosocial; 7. electroconvulsive therapy, or ECT; 8. (a) antidepressant, (b) lithium; 9. (a) personality, (b) paranoid, (c) dependent, (d) antisocial; 10. (a) schizophrenia, (b) paranoid; 11. (a) typical neuroleptic, (b) atypical neuroleptic, (c) dopamine, (d) typical neuroleptic, (e) atypical neuroleptic*

# E. Dissociative Disorders

## Definition

You have probably had the experience of being so absorbed in a fantasy, thought, or memory that, for a short period of time, you cut yourself off from the real world. However, if someone calls your name, you quickly return and explain, "I'm sorry, I wasn't paying attention. I was off in my own world." This is an example of a normal "break from reality," or dissociative experience, which may occur when you are self-absorbed, hypnotized, or fantasizing (Kihlstrom et al., 1994). Now imagine a

*What if you had a split or breakdown in your self?*

dissociative experience so extreme that your own self splits, breaks down, or disappears.

A *dissociative disorder* is characterized by a person having a disruption, split, or breakdown in his or her normal integrated self, consciousness, memory, or sense of identity. This disorder is relatively rare and unusual (American Psychiatric Association, 2000).

We'll discuss three of the five more common dissociative disorders listed in the DSM-IV-TR. These are dissociative amnesia (Who am I?), dissociative fugue (Where am I?), and dissociative identity disorder (formerly called multiple personality disorder).

## Dissociative Amnesia

Mark is brought into the hospital emergency room by police. He looks exhausted and is badly sunburned. When questioned, he gives the wrong date, answering September 27th instead of October 1st. He has trouble answering specific questions about what happened to him. With much probing, he gradually remembers going sailing with friends on about September 25th and hitting bad weather. He cannot recall anything else; he doesn't know what happened to his friends or the sailboat, how he got to shore, where he has been, or where he is now. Each time he is told that it is really October 1st and he is in a hospital, he looks very surprised (Spitzer et al., 1994). Mark is suffering from dissociative amnesia.

*Dissociative amnesia* is characterized by the inability to recall important personal information or events and is usually associated with stressful or traumatic events. The importance or extent of the information forgotten is too great to be explained by normal forgetfulness (American Psychiatric Association, 2000).

In Mark's case, you might think his forgetfulness was due to a blow to the head suffered on the sailboat in rough seas. However, doctors found no evidence of head injury or neural problems. To help Mark recall the events between September 25th and October 1st, he was given a drug (sodium amytal) that helps people relax and recall events that may be blocked by stressful experiences. While under the drug, Mark recalled a big storm that washed his companions overboard but spared him because he had tied himself to the boat. Thus, Mark did suffer from dissociative amnesia, which was triggered by the stressful event of seeing his friends washed overboard (Spitzer et al., 1994). In dissociative amnesia, the length of memory loss varies from days to weeks to years and is often associated with a series of stressful events (Eich et al., 1997).

As we'll see next, a person may forget who he or she is.

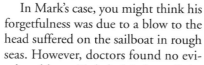

*What if you forgot a month in your life?*

## Dissociative Fugue

He got into a fight with a customer at the diner where he worked. When the police arrived, he gave his name as Burt Tate but had no identification. He said he had drifted into town a couple of weeks ago and taken a job as a cook at the diner. Burt could not recall where he had come from, where he had worked before, whether he was married or had children, or anything from his past. When the police ran a missing persons' check on Burt, they discovered that he matched a person, Gene Saunders, who had disappeared a month before from a city 200 miles away. When Mrs. Saunders arrived, she identified Burt Tate as her husband, Gene Saunders (Spitzer et al., 1994). Gene Saunders had experienced dissociative fugue.

*Dissociative fugue* is a disturbance marked by suddenly and unexpectedly traveling away from home or place of work and being unable to recall one's past. The person may not remember his or her identity or may be confused about his or her new, assumed identity (American Psychiatric Association, 2000).

Before clinicians diagnosed Gene-alias-Burt as suffering from dissociative fugue, they ruled out drugs, medications, and head injuries.

*What if you found yourself in another city with no clue as to who you were?*

Mrs. Saunders explained that, for about 18 months before Gene disappeared, he had been having great trouble at work; he had been criticized for his poor performance and passed over for promotion. The stress at work had made him difficult to live with at home. Formerly easygoing and sociable, he had become sullen and withdrawn.

As Gene's case illustrates, the onset of dissociative fugue is related to stressful or traumatic life events. Usually, fugue states end quite suddenly, and the individual recalls most or all of his or her identity and past.

In other cases, a person's self seems to split into two or more "true" selves or identities. This condition is called dissociative identity disorder.

The idea that one individual could possess two or more "different persons" who may or may not know one another and who may appear at different times to say and do different things describes one of the more remarkable and controversial mental disorders (Eich et al., 1997). Previously, this disorder was called multiple personality but now it's called dissociative identity disorder. We'll discuss a real case of dissociative identity disorder and its possible causes.

### Definition

Mary noticed something very peculiar about her car's gas gauge. Each night when she returned home from work, the gauge registered a nearly full tank of gas. However, when she got in to drive to work the next morning, the gauge registered about half full. Thinking that something suspicious was going on, she noted the mileage on the odometer each evening and compared it with the morning's. Someone was driving her car between 50 to 100 miles each night, and she had no idea who it was.

During a hypnotic treatment for pain, the physician asked Mary about the mileage someone was putting on her car. Suddenly a different voice answered, "It's about time you knew about me." This new voice said that her name was Marian and that she drove the car around at night to work out difficulties. Marian was as hostile and unfriendly as Mary was pleasing and sociable. During the course of therapy, six other personal-

Formerly called multiple personality, dissociative identity disorder is said to have two very different causes.

ities came out, some of whom were independent and aggressive, while others were dependent and submissive. At times, the different personalities fought for control; each reported different memories. As a child, Mary had been physically and sexually abused by her father (Spitzer et al., 1994). The physician diagnosed Mary as suffering from dissociative identity disorder.

*Dissociative identity disorder* (formerly called multiple personality disorder) is the presence of two or more distinct identities or personality states, each with its own pattern of perceiving, thinking about, and relating to the world. Different personality states may take control of the individual's thoughts and behaviors at different times (American Psychiatric Association, 2000).

As in Mary's case, the personalities are usually quite different and complex, and the original personality is seldom aware of the others. After four years of psychotherapy, Mary managed to integrate the personalities into just two, which continued to fight with each other (Spitzer et al., 1994).

How common is dissociative identity disorder, and what causes it?

### Occurrence and Causes

As shown in the right graph, the worldwide occurrence of dissociative identity disorder was very rare before 1970, with only 36 cases reported. However, an "epidemic" occurred in the 1970s and 1980s, with estimates ranging from 300 to 2,000 cases (Spanos, 1994). Reasons for the upsurge include incorrect diagnosis, renewed professional interest, the trendiness of the disorder, and therapists' (unknowing) encouragement of patients to play the roles. Whatever the reasons, the vast majority (70–80%) of mental health professionals are skeptical about the upsurge in occurrence of dissociative identity disorder (Lilienfeld et al., 1999). The patients most often diagnosed with dissociative identity disorder (DID) are females, who outnumber males by 8:1. In addition, patients with DID usually have a history of other mental disorders.

**Explanations.** There are two opposing explanations for DID. One is that DID results from the severe trauma of childhood abuse, which causes a mental splitting or dissociation of identities as one way to defend against or cope with the terrible trauma. In one study, 89% of patients diagnosed with DID were women, and of these, 98% reported having been physically or sexually abused during childhood (Ellason & Ross, 1997). A second explanation is that DID has become commonplace because of cultural factors, such as DID becoming a legitimate way for people to express their frustrations or to use DID as a way to manipulate or gain personal rewards (Lilienfeld et al., 1999). These opposing explanations reflect the current controversy in why so many patients have been diagnosed with DID.

**Treatment.** Patients diagnosed with DID may also have problems with depression, anxiety, interpersonal relations, and substance abuse. As a result, treatment for DID involves helping patients with these related problems as well as helping them integrate their various personalities into one unified self, which may take years. For example, after two years of treatment, patients diagnosed with DID who showed the greatest improvement were those who showed the greatest ability to integrate or bring together and resolve the differences of their separate selves and see themselves as a person with a single self. Clinicians concluded that treatment for DID is a long-term process that usually involves some form of psychotherapy (Kluft & Foote, 1999).

**Worldwide Cases of Dissociative Identity Disorder**

1971–1988

1874–1920

1921–1970

28

8

300

## Spirit Possession

**How does the world view mental disorders?**

Imagine being a clinician and interviewing a 26-year-old female client who reports the following symptoms: "Sometimes a spirit takes complete control of my body and mind and makes me do things and say things that I don't always remember. The spirit is very powerful and I never know when it will take control. The spirit first appeared when I was 16 and has been with me ever since."

As a clinician, you would of course conduct a much more in-depth clinical interview and administer a number of psychological tests. But on the basis of these symptoms alone, would you say that she has delusions and hallucinations and possibly schizophrenia or that she has multiple identities and possibly dissociative identity disorder? In this case, both diagnoses would be incorrect. This female client comes from a small village in Northern

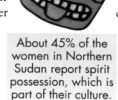

About 45% of the women in Northern Sudan report spirit possession, which is part of their culture.

Sudan, where spirit possession is part of their culture and about 45% of married women over 15 years of age report spirit possession (Boddy, 1988). While in the United States symptoms of spirit possession would probably be interpreted as delusional and abnormal, in Northern Sudan spirit possession is interpreted as a normal behavior and an expression of the women's culture. To deal with possible cultural differences, the DSM-IV-TR now includes an appendix that describes how to diagnose symptoms within the context of a person's culture (American Psychiatric Association, 2000).

Spirit possession is an example of how cultural factors determine whether symptoms are interpreted as normal or abnormal. Researchers are also finding that cultural factors influence the occurrence of certain other kinds of mental disorders (Lopez & Guarnaccia, 2000). We'll examine how cultural factors influence their occurrence.

## Cultural Differences in Occurrence

Just as there is a manual to guide the diagnosis of mental disorders in the United States, the *Diagnostic and Statistical Manual,* 4th edition Text Revision (DSM-IV-TR), there is also a worldwide classification system, called the *International Classification of Disease and Related Health Problems,* 10th revision (ICD-10) (World Health Organization, 1993). Since 1970, the ICD-10 has been used to make uniform, worldwide diagnoses of mental disorders. Using this worldwide diagnostic system, clinicians report remarkable differences in the frequencies of certain mental disorders.

■ Since 1970, the United States recorded the greatest increase in dissociative identity disorders (DIDs), while DIDs were rarely diagnosed in France, Great Britain, Russia, Japan, or Switzerland (Spanos, 1994).

■ Paranoid schizophrenia is 50% more common in developed countries. Catatonic schizophrenia, which has almost disappeared in developed nations, is 60% more common in developing countries (Kleinman & Cohen, 1997).

■ The suicide rate in China is about twice that of the United States and is highest among rural women. In the United States, the suicide rate is highest among White males (Kleinman & Cohen, 1997).

Although we know that biological factors play a role in the development of mental disorders, the examples above show the importance of cultural factors in the development of mental disorders.

Cultural factors influence not only the occurrence of disorders but also the rates of occurrence in males and females.

## Cultural Differences in Gender Roles

Many mental disorders in the United States, such as bipolar I disorder and schizophrenia, are reported about equally by women and men. However, several disorders, such as major depression and dysthymic disorders, are reported significantly more frequently by women than by men (graph below) in the United States as well as in other countries, such as Chile, China, Taiwan, and Uganda (Kleinman & Cohen, 1997).

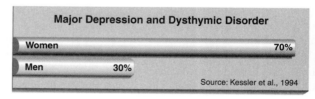

**Major Depression and Dysthymic Disorder**

| Women | 70% |
| Men | 30% |

Source: Kessler et al., 1994

Some clinicians attribute the higher percentage of women reporting depression to cultural differences in gender roles. Although gender roles have been gradually changing, the stereotypic gender role for men is to be independent and assertive and to take control, which tends to reduce levels of stress. In comparison, the stereotypic gender role for women is to be dependent, passive, and emotionally sensitive to the needs of others. This stereotypic role for women serves to reinforce women's feelings of being dependent, not having control, and being helpless, which in turn are known to increase levels of stress and thus place women at greater risk for developing emotional disorders such as depression (Barlow & Durand, 2001).

Compared with men, over twice as many women report problems with depression.

These differences in reported depression between men and women point to cultural differences that influence gender roles, which in turn have the potential to increase women's risk of developing mood disorders, such as major depression (Kleinman & Cohen, 1997).

Just as cultural factors affect mental disorders, so too do neurological factors, which show what happens inside the brains of patients with mental disorders.

# G. Research Focus: Exercise versus Drugs

## Choices of Therapy for Depression

**Can exercise help?**

What would you think if you were in the middle of feeling very depressed and someone recommended running three times a week as a good treatment? It seems hard to believe that something as simple as exercising could be as effective as antidepressants. Remember that major depression is not how you feel from having a bad day or doing poorly on an exam. Major depression must include a number of the following symptoms.

*Major depressive disorder* is marked by at least two weeks of continually being in a bad mood, having no interest in anything, and getting no pleasure from activ-

Can depressed people get help from walking?

ities. In addition, a person must have at least four of the following symptoms: problems with eating, sleeping, thinking, concentrating, or making decisions, lacking energy, thinking about suicide, and feeling worthless or guilty (American Psychiatric Association, 2000).

We have already discussed how psychotherapy, antidepressants, or a combination of the two have proven effective in treating major depression (Elkin et al., 1989; Keller et al., 2000). Now researchers are asking if regular exercise can also be effective in treating major depression.

This Research Focus shows how scientists often try to answer questions that potentially have very practical or applied benefits.

## Exercise Experiment: Seven Rules

### METHOD AND RESULTS

You may remember that there are seven rules for doing an experiment (pp. 36–37). We'll review these seven rules by showing how researchers followed them in their study (Babyak et al., 2000).

**Rule 1: Ask.** Every experiment asks a specific question that is changed into a hypothesis or educated guess. In this study, the *hypothesis* is that exercise will be as effective a treatment for major depression as are antidepressants.

**Rule 2: Identify.** Researchers *identify* the treatment, which is called the *independent variable* because researchers are able to control or administer it to the subjects. Here, the independent variable has three levels of treatments: first level is 30 minutes of exercise (stationary bike or walking/jogging) 3 times a week; second level is taking antidepressants (Zoloft); and third level is a combination of exercising and taking antidepressants.

**Zoloft**

Antidepressants: independent variable

Exercise: independent variable

Next, researchers *identify* the behavior(s), called the *dependent variable,* which depends on the treatment, and measure its effectiveness. In this study, the dependent variable is a scale (Hamilton rating scale for depression) that measures increases or decreases in subjects' depression.

Scale to measure depression: dependent variable

**Rule 3: Choose.** Researchers *choose* subjects, who in this study are 156 adult volunteers (50 years or older) who have been diagnosed with major depression (according to the above definition).

**Rule 4: Assign.** The chosen patients are *randomly assigned* to groups, which means that each of the 156 patients has an equal chance of being assigned to one of the three treatment groups.

**Rule 5: Manipulate.** Researchers administer or *manipulate* the three levels of the treatment by giving one level of treatment to each of the three groups of patients.

**Rule 6: Measure.** After 4 months of treatments, researchers use the depression scale to *measure* how effective each one of the three levels of treatment was in decreasing the patients' depression.

**Rule 7: Analyze.** Researchers found that about 60% of patients in the exercise group had greatly improved, compared with 66% of subjects taking antidepressants and 69% of those who combined exercise and antidepressants. Although these percentages look different, *statistical analysis* indicated that the three treatments were equally effective. This means that exercise alone was as effective in reducing depression as were antidepressants or the combination, which supports the researchers' original hypothesis.

### RELAPSE

We discussed how, after treatment for a mental disorder, a certain percentage of patients relapse or again return to having serious symptoms. Of the 60 to 69% of patients in each of the three treatment groups who showed significant improvement (few if any depressive symptoms), some patients had relapsed during the 6-month period following treatment. Researchers reported (above graph) that 38% of patients who had received antidepressants had relapsed and 31% of patients who had received both exercise and antidepressants had relapsed. However, a major finding was that only 8% of patients relapsed who were in the exercise-only treatment.

**Relapse Rate after Treatment**

| 38% | Antidepressants |
| 31% | Combination |
| 8% | Exercise |

### CONCLUSIONS

Researchers found that after 4 months of treatment for major depression, patients in all three treatment groups showed significant improvement. However, when patients were retested 6 months later, those who had received exercise only showed significantly less relapse. Researchers suggest that exercise helps patients develop a sense of personal mastery and positive self-regard, which helps patients get over being depressed and also decreases the risk of future relapse (Babyak et al., 2000). Researchers found that as a treatment for major depression, exercise is very effective, inexpensive, and without unwanted physical side effects. Researchers suggest that a regular exercise program will help patients avoid relapse.

Next, we'll discuss several ways to overcome mild depression.

# H. Application: Dealing with Mild Depression

### Mild versus Major Depression

**How does depression differ?**

There is a big difference between mild and major depression. Earlier, we discussed actor Rod Steiger, who experienced a major depressive disorder. Symptoms of major depressive disorder include being in a bad mood for at least two weeks, having no interest in anything, and getting no pleasure from activities. Additionally, to be diagnosed with major depression, a person must have at least two of the following problems: difficulty in sleeping, eating, thinking, and making decisions or having no energy and feeling continually fatigued. Compared with the symptoms of major depressive disorder, the symptoms of mild depression are milder and generally have less impact on a person's functioning. For example, take the case of Janice, who has what is often called the sophomore blues.

There is a big difference between the symptoms of major and mild depression.

"At first I was excited about going off to college and being on my own," explains Janice. "But now I feel worn out from the constant pressure to study, get good grades, and scrape up enough bucks to pay my rent. I've lost interest in classes, I have trouble concentrating, I'm doing poorly on exams, and I'm thinking about changing my major—again. And to make everything even more depressing, my boyfriend just broke up with me. I sit around wondering what went wrong or what I did or why he broke it off. What did I do that was so bad? My friends are tired of my moping around and complaining, and I know they are starting to avoid me. Yeah, everyone says that I should just get over him and get on with my life. But exactly what do I do to get out of my funk?"

**Continuum.** Some researchers have argued that the kind of depression reported by college students is related more to general distress and does not represent any of the particular symptoms and feelings found in major depression (Coyne, 1994). However, other researchers find that depression is best thought of as on a continuum. At one end of the continuum is mild depression, such as that experienced by college students, which is basically similar in quality but just a milder form of major depression, which is at the other end of the continuum (Flett et al., 1997).

**Similarities.** There are a number of similarities between the symptoms of mild and major depression that support the idea of depression being on a continuum. For example, about 40–60% of individuals with major depression report thinking about suicide; similarly, about 50% of depressed college students also report thinking about suicide (Hill et al., 1987). In fact, thinking about suicide is 50% more common among college students than among nonstudents of the same age, and suicides are estimated to be the second leading cause of death among college students (Vredenburg et al., 1994). College students also experience almost all the major stressors of adulthood, including coping with a new environment, dealing with academic pressures, trying to establish intimate personal relationships, experiencing financial difficulties, and trying to achieve some independence from parents and family (Pennebaker et al., 1990).

**Vulnerability.** There are three major factors that increase an individual's vulnerability or risk for developing mild depression. The first factor is being a young adult who is facing new, challenging, and threatening situations, events, and feelings. The second factor is having a high and chronic level of troubling or negative life events. Since college students experience both of these factors, they are at high risk for developing mild depression in college, which may lead to a more serious or a major depressive disorder later in life. The third factor involves an individual's pattern of thinking, which is the basis for Beck's theory of depression.

### Beck's Theory of Depression

**How much do thoughts matter?**

Janice thinks that her depression is caused by outside forces, such as academic pressures, financial concerns, personal difficulties, and family pressures. There is no question that stressful events or negative situations can depress Janice's mood. However, another factor that Janice may not be aware of and that may contribute to her depression is a particular pattern of thinking, which is described by Aaron Beck's (1991) cognitive theory of depression.

*Beck's cognitive theory of depression* says that when we are feeling down, automatic, negative thoughts that we rarely notice occur continually throughout the day. These negative thoughts distort how we perceive and interpret the world and thus influence our behaviors and feelings, which in turn contribute to our feeling depressed.

Often these automatic, negative thoughts are centered on personal inadequacies, such as thinking one is a failure, is not liked, or never gets anything done. Beck has identified a number of *specific negative, maladaptive thoughts* that he believes contribute to developing anxiety and depression. For example, thinking "I'm a failure" after doing poorly on one test is an example of *overgeneralization*—that is, making a blanket judgment about yourself based on a single incident. Thinking "People always criticize me" is an example of *selective attention*—that is, focusing on one detail so much that you do not notice other positive events, such as being complimented.

Beck believes that maladaptive thought patterns cause a distorted view of oneself and one's world, which in turn may lead to various emotional problems, such as depression. Thus, one of the things that Janice must work on to get out of her depressed state is to identify and change her negative, maladaptive thoughts.

We'll discuss how negative thoughts and two other factors maintain depression, as well as ways to change them.

1. Academic pressures
2. Financial concerns
3. Family pressures
4. Negative thought patterns

Increased risk for depression

**What can one do?** Once we get "down in the dumps," we are likely to stay there for some time unless we work at changing certain thoughts and behaviors, such as improving social skills, increasing social support, and eliminating negative thoughts. We'll describe several ways to "get out of the dumps" and overcome mild depression.

## Improving Social Skills

**Problem.** In some cases, a person may feel mildly depressed because he or she has poor social skills, which lead to problems in having good social interactions.

For example, researchers found that depressed teenagers and college students may be overly dependent, competitive, aggressive, or mistrustful, which in turn caused problems in developing and maintaining close social relationships (Reed, 1994). If part of being depressed involves poor social skills, a person can learn new ways of interacting with friends.

**Program.** Psychologists have developed a number of programs for improving social skills, which include developing better verbal skills, learning to initiate conversations, expressing positive feelings, eliminating complaining, and learning to listen (Granvold, 1994).

Individuals with poor social skills have poor social relationships, which increases their chances of feeling depressed.

As with every behavioral change program, the first step is to monitor our social interactions to notice what we are doing wrong, such as complaining too much to our friends. Once we become aware of our bad habits, such as complaining too much, not asking questions or showing interest, or not being sympathetic, we can begin to take positive steps. That means making a real effort to stop complaining and to show more interest in our friends' activities and to be more sensitive to their feelings. By proceeding in gradual steps, we can learn to improve our social skills and get more rewards from social interactions, which in turn will make us feel better and help us get over our mild depression.

**Problem.** In other cases, our negative attitudes and behaviors begin to irritate our friends, who tire of interacting with someone who is continually down and complaining. In this situation, even the best of friends may withdraw, or avoid us, and give less social support when we need it most to help overcome mild depression. This situation usually results in a vicious cycle: A depressed person's negative behaviors turn off friends, who respond by avoiding and providing less support, thus making the person feel even more depressed (Hokanson & Butler, 1992).

Researchers find that individuals often become and remain mildly depressed because they do not give themselves credit for any success (however small), make every situation (however small) into a bad or unpleasant experience, and constantly blame themselves for every failure. In addition, individuals who are depressed are more likely to attribute their failures to faults within themselves, which lowers their self-esteem and contributes to negative attitudes (Nurius & Berlin, 1994). Because of this, depressed individuals may be caught in another vicious cycle: Self-blame lowers individuals' self-esteem, which makes them more depressed, which elicits more negative reactions from friends.

**Program.** A behavior change program can increase our self-esteem. The first step is to become aware of self-blame by monitoring our thoughts and noticing all the times we blame ourselves for things, no matter how small. Once we become aware of self-blame, we can substitute thoughts of our past or recent accomplishments, no matter how small. By substituting thoughts of accomplishment and focusing on recent successes, we will gradually improve our self-esteem. As our self-esteem improves, we slowly get a more positive attitude, which in turn increases the social support of our friends (Granvold, 1994).

By learning to take credit for our actions we can increase our self-esteem and get over feelings of mild depression.

## Eliminating Negative Thoughts

**Problem.** According to Beck's theory of depression, a depressed person thinks negative, maladaptive thoughts, which, in turn, cause the person to pay attention to, perceive, and remember primarily negative and depressing situations, events, and conversations (Beck, 1991; Hartlage et al., 1993). Thus, besides improving social skills and increasing social support, depressed individuals also need to stop the automatic, negative thought pattern that maintains depression.

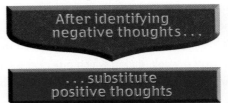

After identifying negative thoughts...
...substitute positive thoughts

Researchers found that depressed individuals have a tendency to select and remember unhappy, critical, or depressing thoughts, events, or remarks. In addition, depressed individuals remember fewer good things than bad things and take a more pessimistic view of life (Dykman et al., 1989; Ingram et al., 1994). One solution to this problem is to change a negative thought pattern (Beck, 1991).

**Program.** The first step in every behavior change program is to monitor our thoughts and behaviors—in this case, to monitor negative and depressive thoughts. The second step is to eliminate the depressive thoughts by substituting positive ones. This second step is difficult because it requires considerable effort to stop thinking negative thoughts ("I really am a failure") and substitute positive ones ("I've got a lot going for me"). With practice, we can break the negative thought pattern by stopping negative thoughts and substituting positive ones, which in turn will help us overcome mild depression (Reed, 1994).

Psychologists find that by doing all three things—improving social skills, increasing social support, and eliminating negative thoughts—individuals can break out of the vicious cycle of mild depression, get out of the dumps, and enjoy life more.

# Summary Test

## A. MOOD DISORDERS

**1.** A prolonged emotional state that affects almost all of a person's thoughts and behaviors is called a _____ disorder.

**Risk of Developing Bipolar Disorder**

| | |
|---|---|
| Identical twins | 80% |
| 16% | Fraternal twins |

**2.** One mood disorder is marked by being in a daily bad mood, having no interest in anything, or getting no pleasure from activities and having at least four of the following symptoms: problems with weight, appetite, sleep, fatigue, thinking, or making decisions and having suicidal thoughts. This is called (a)_____ disorder, which is the most common form of mood disorder. Another mood disorder is characterized by being chronically depressed for many but not all days over a long period of time and having two of the following symptoms: problems with appetite and sleep, fatigue, low self-esteem, and feelings of hopelessness. This is called (b)_____ disorder.

**3.** A mood episode that is characterized by a distinct period, lasting at least a week, during which a person is unusually euphoric, cheerful, or high and has at least three of the following symptoms—has great self-esteem, needs little sleep, speaks rapidly and frequently, experiences racing thoughts, is easily distracted—is called a (a)_____ episode. A disorder characterized by periods of fluctuation between episodes of depression and mania is called (b)_____ disorder.

**4.** The theory that underlying genetic, neurological, or physiological factors may predispose a person to developing a mood disorder is called the (a)_____ theory of depression. Factors such as dealing with stressors and stressful life events are believed to interact with predisposing biological influences and contribute to the development, onset, or maintenance of mood disorders. These are called (b)_____ factors.

**5.** Psychoactive drugs that act by increasing levels of a specific group of neurotransmitters (monoamines, such as serotonin) believed to be involved in the regulation of emotions and moods, such as major depression, are called (a)_____. These drugs may take 4–6 weeks before they begin working, during which time up to 50% of patients drop out because of undesirable (b)_____. Currently the most popular antidepressant drug is (c)_____, which is no more effective but has fewer side effects than do previous antidepressants.

**6.** The most effective treatment for bipolar I depression is a natural mineral salt called (a)_____, which reduces manic episodes in about half the patients. Lithium is also used to treat euphoric episodes without depression; this disorder is called (b)_____.

## B. ELECTROCONVULSIVE THERAPY

**7.** If antidepressant drugs fail to treat major depression, the treatment of last resort involves placing electrodes on the skull and administering a mild electric current that passes through the brain and causes a seizure. This treatment is called (a)_____ therapy. A potentially serious side effect of this treatment is impairment or deficits in (b)_____, which usually affects events experienced during the weeks of treatment, as well as events before and after treatment. However, following ECT treatment, there is a gradual improvement in memory functions.

## C. PERSONALITY DISORDERS

**8.** A disorder that involves inflexible, long-standing, maladaptive traits that cause significantly impaired functioning or great distress in one's personal and social life is called a (a)_____ disorder. Ten of these disorders are listed in the DSM-IV-TR, including: a pattern of being submissive and clingy because of an excessive need to be taken care of, which is called a (b)_____ disorder; and a pattern of disregarding or violating the rights of others without feeling guilt or remorse, which is called an (c)_____ disorder. There is evidence that personality disorders develop from an interaction of (d)_____ and _____ factors.

**9.** Evidence that genetic factors influence personality disorders comes from studies on (a)_____, which show that genetic factors contribute 30–50% to the development of these personality disorders. Evidence for neurological factors comes from studies on (b)_____, which indicate that individuals with antisocial personality disorders may have up to a 25% reduction in serotonin.

## D. SCHIZOPHRENIA

**10.** Schizophrenia is a serious mental disturbance that lasts for at least six months and includes at least two of the following

**NEUROLEPTICS**

| Typical: decrease dopamine | Atypical: decrease dopamine & serotonin |
|---|---|

persistent symptoms: delusions, hallucinations, disorganized speech, grossly disorganized behavior, and decreased emotional expression. These symptoms interfere with personal or social _____.

**11.** DSM-IV-TR lists five categories of schizophrenia, which include the following three. A category characterized by bizarre ideas, confused speech, childish behavior, great emotional swings, and often extreme neglect of personal appearance and hygiene is called (a)_____ schizophrenia. Another form marked by periods of wild excitement or periods of rigid, prolonged immobility is called (b)_____ schizophrenia. A third form characterized by thoughts of being persecuted or thoughts of grandeur is called (c)_____ schizophrenia.

**12.** Researchers have searched for an identifiable gene or a specific segment of a chromosome that is directly linked to developing schizophrenia. This genetic link is called a _____.

**13.** Two kinds of neuroleptic drugs are used to treat schizophrenic symptoms by changing levels of neurotransmitters in the brain. Drugs that act primarily to reduce levels of the neurotransmitter dopamine are called (a)_____ neuroleptics. An example is the phenothiazines. Drugs that lower levels of dopamine but, more important, also reduce levels of other neurotransmitters, especially serotonin, are called (b)_____ neuroleptics. The current drug of choice for treating schizophrenia is one of the new (c)_____ neuroleptics.

**14.** One side effect of continued use of phenothiazines is the appearance of slow, involuntary, and uncontrollable rhythmic movements and rapid twitching of the mouth and lips, as well as unusual movements of the limbs. This side effect is called _____.

**15.** One theory of schizophrenia says that it develops when the (a)_____ neurotransmitter is overactive. Another related theory says that some people have a genetic predisposition, called a (b)_____, that interacts with life stressors to result in the onset and development of schizophrenia.

## E. DISSOCIATIVE DISORDERS

**16.** A dissociative disorder is characterized by a (a)_____ in a person's normally integrated functions of memory, identity, or perception of the environment. The DSM-IV lists five types of dissociative disorder, which include the following three. If a person is unable to recall important personal information or events, usually in connection with a stressful or traumatic event, and the information forgotten is too important or lengthy to be explained by normal forgetfulness, it is called (b)_____. If a person suddenly and unexpectedly travels away from home or place of work and is unable to recall the past and may assume a new identity, it is called (c)_____. If a person experiences the presence of two or more distinct identities or personality states, each with its own pattern of perceiving, thinking about, and relating to the world, it is called (d)_____ disorder.

**17.** One theory says that dissociative identity disorder (DID) develops as a way to cope with the severe trauma of childhood (a)_____. A second explanation is that DID has become

a culturally approved way for people to express their (b)_____ or to control others or gain personal rewards.

## F. CULTURAL DIVERSITY: INTERPRETING SYMPTOMS

**18.** Spirit possession is one example of how cultural factors determine whether symptoms are interpreted as (a)_____ or _____. An example of how cultural factors may increase the risk for development of mood disorders can be traced to the differences in assigned (b)_____ roles: males are expected to be independent and in control, and females are expected to be dependent and not have control.

## G. RESEARCH FOCUS: EXERCISE VERSUS DRUGS

**19.** After three different treatments, including exercise only, researchers found that at least 60% of patients diagnosed with (a)_____ showed significant improvement. Another finding was that when patients were retested 6 months later, those who had received exercise only showed significantly less (b)_____. Researchers suggest that (c)_____ helps patients develop a sense of personal mastery and positive self-regard, which helps prevent relapse.

## H. APPLICATION: DEALING WITH MILD DEPRESSION

**20.** Beck's cognitive theory of depression says that when we are depressed, we have automatically occurring (a)_____, which center around being personally inadequate. In turn, these negative thoughts (b)_____ how we perceive and interpret the world and thus influence our behaviors and feelings. Three factors that maintain mild depression are having poor social skills, lacking social support, and thinking negative thoughts or paying attention to negative events. Psychologists have developed effective programs to change these three behaviors.

*Answers:* 1. mood; 2. (a) major depressive, (b) dysthymic; 3. (a) manic, (b) bipolar I; 4. (a) biological, (b) psychosocial; 5. (a) antidepressants, (b) side effects, (c) Prozac; 6. (a) lithium, (b) mania; 7. (a) electroconvulsive, (b) memory; 8. (a) personality, (b) dependent, (c) antisocial, (d) biological, psychological; 9. (a) twins, (b) neurotransmitters; 10. functioning; 11. (a) disorganized, (b) catatonic, (c) paranoid; 12. genetic marker; 13. (a) typical, (b) atypical, (c) atypical; 14. tardive dyskinesia; 15. (a) dopamine, (b) diathesis; 16. (a) disruption, split, breakdown, (b) dissociative amnesia, (c) dissociative fugue, (d) dissociative identity; 17. (a) physical or sexual abuse, (b) frustrations, fears; 18. (a) normal, abnormal, (b) gender; 19. (a) major depression, (b) relapse, (c) exercise; 20. (a) negative thoughts, (b) bias or distort

# Critical Thinking

## Lives Rediscovered

*by Shari Roan*

### Questions

**1.** What is one reason that the onset of schizophrenia often occurs in the late teens and early twenties?

**2.** What is the difference between positive and negative symptoms? Are these symptoms reduced by neuroleptic drugs?

**3.** How do neuroleptic drugs that made up the first revolution in treating schizophrenia differ from neuroleptics making up the second revolution?

For the 100,000 people each year who are found to have schizophrenia—the onset usually in the late teens for men and early 20s for women—the disease begins to warp reality at a time when most young adults are drawing up ambitious plans for the future.

Despite what is shaping up to be a decade of startling progress in the development of new drugs to treat the disease, the road back from the horrors of schizophrenia remains tough indeed.

The fact that thousands of people with schizophrenia are making steady, if not spectacular, recoveries, say mental health experts, is due not only to sophisticated new medications but to the very commitment of helping patients "start over."

This vigorous rehabilitation concept—called reintegration—is altering the view of schizophrenia from a hopeless disease to one that can be lived with and successfully managed.

"Patients are getting better at rates we never dreamed were possible 10 years ago," says Kim Littrell, founder of the Schizophrenia Treatment and Rehabilitation centers. "There are five drugs we expect to be approved between now and the turn of the century. That's seven new antipsychotics in the '90s, whereas we hadn't had any new antipsychotics in 20 years. . . . But part of the problem is we need to make sure we have the ancillary

services. Dishing out meds is the easy part."

As thousands of people with schizophrenia rekindle their ability to return to jobs, school, or independent living, mental health experts across the nation bemoan the dearth of reintegration services to help these now cogent-thinking patients reassemble their shattered lives.

The barriers include the cost of rehabilitative services—vocational as well as social skills training; the lack of supportive people in their lives; and a society that still wrongheadedly regards mental illness as a personal weakness.

"It's like a schizophrenic being locked in the house and medication unlocks the door. But you need someone to take you outside and show you around," says Littrell. "I don't ever remember a patient taking an [antipsychotic] medication and saying, 'Good God, I'm a mess. Get me to Supercuts. And I need a job application.'" (Source: *Los Angeles Times,* January 30, 1996)

**4.** After individuals recover from schizophrenia, what potentially dangerous problem may occur in the next 2 to 5 years?

**5.** Would you respond differently if you were told that a person was a schizophrenic?

**6.** Why does someone need to take a schizophrenic out in the real world and show him or her how to get around and behave?

*Try InfoTrac to search for terms:* **schizophrenia; schizophrenia rehabilitation; neuroleptic drugs.**

## Suggested answers to Newspaper Article questions

1. The years between adolescence and adulthood can be especially stressful. According to the diathesis theory, increased stress can be a factor in the onset and development of schizophrenia.
2. Positive symptoms involve a *distortion* of normal functioning, such as distorted thinking (delusions). Negative symptoms involve a *decrease* in normal functions, such as decreased emotions. Typical neuroleptics decrease positive but not negative symptoms, while atypical neuroleptics decrease positive symptoms and somewhat improve negative symptoms.
3. The first revolution in treating schizophrenia occurred in the 1950s with the discovery of the *typical* neuroleptics, which decrease levels of dopamine. The second revolution in drug treatment occurred in the 1990s with the discovery of *atypical* neuroleptics, which decrease levels of dopamine and serotonin.
4. Following successful treatment of a mental disorder, such as depression or schizophrenia, about 30 to 70% of patients may relapse and need further treatment involving drugs, psychotherapy, or both.
5. Because some people have a negative attitude toward people with mental problems, hearing a person labeled as a schizophrenic may bias our perception and response to that person. Clinicians suggest we make a special effort not to stereotype or discriminate against a person with a mental disorder.
6. In the text we discussed how Michael, who was treated for schizophrenia, was afraid to do things on his own. This is an example of how people recovering from mental disorders often need help and social support in learning how to behave and deal with problems and daily hassles in the real world.

# Links to Learning

## Web Sites

- **WADSWORTH ONLINE STUDY CENTER**
  http://psychology.wadsworth.com
  Quizzes, learning activities and exercises, a discussion forum, and hot links to Internet sites related to mood disorders and schizophrenia, including:

- **SCREENING TEST FOR DEPRESSION**
  http://www.med.nyu.edu/Psych/screens/depres.html
  The New York University Department of Psychiatry offers this simple test, with results and referrals.

- **HARBOR OF REFUGE**
  http://www.Harbor-of-Refuge.org/
  This site was created to serve people who are receiving appropriate medical treatment for their bipolar illness, including appropriate medications, as well as their friends and relatives. "Our greatest strength is the peer to peer support we offer one another, but we are not licensed mental health professionals." Includes a newsletter, self-care strategies, discussion forums, FAQs, and many Web links.

- **THE EXPERIENCE OF SCHIZOPHRENIA**
  http://www.chovil.com
  This is the personal site of Ian Chovil, who began struggling with schizophrenia in late adolescence and suffered greatly until he began taking medication in 1990. He tells his own story in unsparing detail, describes the biology of schizophrenia, recommends books and movies on the subject, and provides many links.

## Learning Activities

- **POWERSTUDY™ BY ROD PLOTNIK & TOM DOYLE**

  **PowerStudy™**

  **Check out CD: Module 23**
  CD 3.B: Neurons: Structure and Function; book page 540
  CD 4.A: Genes and Evolution; book page 537
  CD 4.B: Studying the Living Brain; book pages 533, 537
  CD 4.D: Control Centers: Four Lobes; book pages 533, 540

- **STUDY GUIDE TO ACCOMPANY INTRODUCTION TO PSYCHOLOGY, 6TH EDITION,** by Matthew Enos
  In Module 23, try completing "an exercise in understanding"; without actually having a disorder, decide which one is closest to your own personality; and get busy learning a challenging list of new terms.

- **WEBTUTOR**
  http://webtutor.thomsonlearning.com
  **WebTUTOR** Visit this site for interactive versions of the Study Guide features. Take a quiz, get your score—should you study a topic some more, or can you move on? For example, what do the Genain quadruplets represent? What do all the dissociative disorders have in common? Tardive dyskinesia is used to treat bipolar disorder: true or false?

- **INFOTRAC ONLINE LIBRARY**
  http://www.infotrac-college.com
   Use your password and then key in search terms such as those below to find popular and scientific articles on subjects covered in Module 23. Make the library work for you!
  Neuroleptic drugs     Dissociation     Electroconvulsive therapy
  Lithium     Hallucinations     Antisocial personality disorder

- **PSYCHNOW!**
  CD for Macintosh and Windows includes a study guide, glossary, Web sites, and animations. For Module 23, see:
  - Abnormality and Psychopathology
  - Non-Psychotic, Psychotic, and Affective Disorders

## Study Questions

*Use InfoTrac to search for topics mentioned in the main heads below (e.g., mood disorders, personality disorders, brain imaging).*

**\*A. Mood Disorders**—A student is brought into the health clinic for being depressed and having attempted suicide. What will be her treatment program? (**Suggested answer p. 635**)

**\*B. Electroconvulsive Therapy**—How would you compare the effectiveness and side effects of electroconvulsive shock therapy with those of antidepressant drugs? (**Suggested answer p. 635**)

**C. Personality Disorders**—A teenager is arrested by police for maliciously breaking car windows. How would you determine if this teenager is a potential psychopath?

**D. Schizophrenia**—Why do you think that drugs are more effective than psychotherapy in treating schizophrenia?

**E. Dissociative Disorders**—How would you decide whether someone really has dissociative fugue or is just faking it to avoid dealing with stressful life events?

**F. Cultural Diversity: Interpreting Symptoms**—What differences in our cultural gender roles contribute to men's reporting significantly more alcohol abuse than women do?

**G. Research Focus: Exercise versus Drugs**—How might a brain image of a person with a mental disorder differ from an image of a person without a mental disorder?

**\*H. Application: Dealing with Mild Depression**—When some people get depressed, why do they prefer to spread their gloom rather than do something to get over it? (**Suggested answer p. 635**)

*These questions are answered in Appendix B.

# Module 24: Therapies

### A. Historical Background     556
* ❊ DEFINITION
* ❊ EARLY TREATMENTS
* ❊ REFORM MOVEMENT
* ❊ PHENOTHIAZINES AND DEINSTITUTIONALIZATION
* ❊ COMMUNITY MENTAL HEALTH CENTERS

### B. Questions about Psychotherapy     558
* ❊ DO I NEED PROFESSIONAL HELP?
* ❊ ARE THERE DIFFERENT KINDS OF THERAPISTS?
* ❊ ARE THERE DIFFERENT APPROACHES?
* ❊ HOW EFFECTIVE IS PSYCHOTHERAPY?

### C. Insight Therapies     560
* ❊ PSYCHOANALYSIS
* ❊ TECHNIQUES TO REVEAL THE UNCONSCIOUS
* ❊ PROBLEMS DURING THERAPY
* ❊ PSYCHOANALYSIS: EVALUATION
* ❊ CLIENT-CENTERED THERAPY
* ❊ COGNITIVE THERAPY

### D. Behavior Therapy     566
* ❊ DEFINITION
* ❊ SYSTEMATIC DESENSITIZATION
* ❊ COGNITIVE-BEHAVIOR THERAPY
* ❊ KINDS OF PROBLEMS

### Concept Review     569

### E. Review: Evaluation of Approaches     570
* ❊ ASSUMPTIONS, METHODS, AND TECHNIQUES
* ❊ EFFECTIVENESS OF PSYCHOTHERAPY
* ❊ COMMON FACTORS

### F. Cultural Diversity: Different Healer     572
* ❊ CASE STUDY: YOUNG WOMAN
* ❊ HEALER'S DIAGNOSIS AND TREATMENT
* ❊ HEALERS VERSUS WESTERN THERAPISTS

### G. Research Focus: EMDR—New Therapy     573
* ❊ DOES NEW THERAPY METHOD ELIMINATE TRAUMATIC MEMORIES?

### H. Application: Cognitive-Behavior Techniques     574
* ❊ THOUGHT PROBLEMS
* ❊ THOUGHT-STOPPING PROGRAM
* ❊ THOUGHT SUBSTITUTION
* ❊ TREATMENT FOR INSOMNIA

### Summary Test     576

### Critical Thinking     578
* ❊ WHAT IS EXORCISM?

### Links to Learning     579

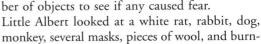

## Beginning of Psychoanalysis

***Why couldn't she drink a glass of water?***

It is the late 1800s, and we are listening to a young, intelligent woman named Anna O. She explains that she was perfectly healthy until she was 21 years old, when she began to experience strange physical symptoms. She developed a terrible squint that blurred her vision, a gagging feeling when she tried to drink a glass of water, and a paralysis in her right arm that would spread down her body. These symptoms occurred at about the time her father developed a serious illness and she felt the need to care for him by spending endless hours at his bedside. When her symptoms persisted, she consulted her doctor, Joseph Breuer.

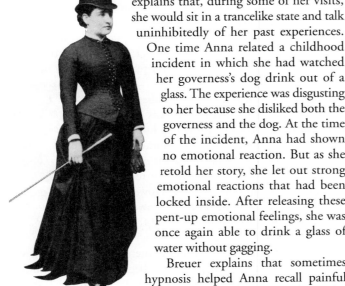

Dr. Breuer takes up Anna's story and explains that, during some of her visits, she would sit in a trancelike state and talk uninhibitedly of her past experiences. One time Anna related a childhood incident in which she had watched her governess's dog drink out of a glass. The experience was disgusting to her because she disliked both the governess and the dog. At the time of the incident, Anna had shown no emotional reaction. But as she retold her story, she let out strong emotional reactions that had been locked inside. After releasing these pent-up emotional feelings, she was once again able to drink a glass of water without gagging.

Breuer explains that sometimes hypnosis helped Anna recall painful past experiences. She told of sitting by her father's sickbed, falling asleep, and having a horrifying dream in which a snake attacked him. She could not reach out and stop the snake because her arm had fallen asleep from hanging over the chair. As Anna relived her powerful guilt feelings of not being able to protect her father, the paralysis of her right arm disappeared. Breuer describes how, each time Anna recalled a past, traumatic experience, a physical symptom associated with that trauma would vanish. Breuer would often discuss Anna's case with his friend and colleague, Sigmund Freud.

Her right arm became paralyzed with no physical or neurological cause.

Dr. Freud interpreted Anna's symptoms as being caused by strong, primitive forces, probably related to unconscious sexual desires (Breuer & Freud, 1895/1955). The case of Anna O. is important because it played a role in the development of Freud's system of psychoanalysis, which was the start of what we currently call psychotherapy.

Just as psychoanalysis had its beginning with Anna O., another very different kind of therapy had its beginning with Little Albert.

## Beginning of Behavior Therapy

***Why was Albert afraid of a white rat?***

It was the early 1900s when John Watson, an up-and-coming behaviorist, showed 9-month-old Albert a number of objects to see if any caused fear. Little Albert looked at a white rat, rabbit, dog, monkey, several masks, pieces of wool, and burning newspapers without showing the slightest sign of fear.

Later, when Albert was about 11 months old, Watson retested Albert. This time, as Albert sat on a mattress, Watson suddenly took a white rat out of a basket and showed it to Albert. At the very moment Albert touched the animal, another experimenter standing behind Albert struck a steel bar with a hammer. The sudden loud noise made Albert jump violently and fall forward into the mattress. Five more times Watson showed Albert the white rat and each time a loud sound rang out from behind. Finally, Watson showed Albert the rat but there was no loud sound. The instant the rat appeared, Albert began to cry and turn away from the rat. From this demonstration, Watson concluded that he had shown, for the first time, that an emotional reaction—in this case, fear—could be conditioned to any stimulus (Watson & Rayner, 1920).

This white rat caused no fear until . . .

The case of Little Albert could be considered the starting point for a very different kind of psychotherapy, known as behavior therapy. Behavior therapists believe that emotional problems may arise through conditioning and thus may be treated—or unconditioned—by using other principles of learning.

The cases of Little Albert and Anna O. illustrate two very different assumptions about how psychotherapy works. According to behavior therapy, emotional problems are learned and thus can be unlearned through conditioning techniques. According to psychoanalysis, emotional problems arise from unconscious fears, which can be uncovered and revealed only with special techniques. We'll discuss these two assumptions along with those of several other therapies as well as whether different therapies produce different results.

. . . Little Albert was classically conditioned.

## What's Coming

In this module we'll discuss the history of psychotherapy and how current therapists are trained. We'll explain Freud's psychoanalysis, and how those who disagreed with Freud developed their own kinds of therapies. We'll examine three of the more popular forms of psychotherapy: behavior therapy, cognitive therapy, and humanistic therapy. Finally, we'll answer one of the most interesting questions: Do therapies differ in their effectiveness?

Let's begin with how psychotherapy came about and how it has developed into a multibillion-dollar business.

# A. Historical Background

## Definition

Today, there are over 400 different forms of psychotherapy, some of them tested and some based purely on personal beliefs. For example, 22 states do not require the licensing of therapists; almost anyone can hang out a sign and go into practice (Singer & Lalich, 1997). The remaining states require licensing and training of therapists. There are about a dozen tested psychotherapies that may differ in assumptions and methods but generally share the following three characteristics.

*Psychotherapy* has three basic characteristics: verbal interaction between therapist and client(s); the development of a supportive relationship in which a client can bring up and discuss traumatic or bothersome experiences that may have led to current problems; and analysis of the client's experiences and/or suggested ways for the client to deal with or overcome his or her problems.

Over the past 60 years, clinicians have developed different forms of psychotherapy to treat a variety of mental disorders. We'll review the major changes in the treatment of mental disorders, beginning with early barbaric treatments and ending with the establishment of modern-day community mental health centers.

## Early Treatments

**Why did hospitals sell tickets?**

From the 15th to the 17th centuries, people who today would be diagnosed as schizophrenics were considered insane and called lunatics. They were primarily confined to asylums or hospitals for the mentally ill, where the treatment was often inhumane and cruel. For example, patients were placed in a hood and straitjacket, padlocked to a cell wall, swung back and forth until they were quieted, strapped into a chair (right drawing), locked in handcuffs, hosed down with water until they were exhausted, or twirled until they passed out.

Some doctors developed their own peculiar methods of treating mental patients. In the late 1700s, Dr. Benjamin Rush, who is considered the father of American psychiatry, developed the "tranquilizing chair" (bottom drawing), into which a patient was strapped and remained until the patient seemed calmed down. Dr. Rush believed that mental disorders were caused by too much blood in the brain. He tried to cure patients by withdrawing huge amounts of blood, as much as six quarts over a period of

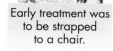

Early treatment was to be strapped to a chair.

months. Another strange treatment that Dr. Rush developed was to frighten patients—for example, to convince them that they were about to die by placing them in coffins. Despite his unusual and sometimes inhumane treatments, Dr. Rush encouraged his staff to treat patients with kindness and understanding (Davison & Neale, 1994).

In the 1700s, some hospitals even sold tickets so that the public could walk through and view the mentally disordered and make fun of their troubling and pathetic behaviors. However, by the early 1800s, the first reforms in treating the mentally ill emerged.

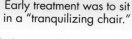

Early treatment was to sit in a "tranquilizing chair."

## Reform Movement

**What did she change?**

In the 1800s, a Boston schoolteacher named Dorothea Dix (right photo below) began to visit the jails and poorhouses where most of the mental patients in the United States were kept. Dix publicized the terrible living conditions and the lack of reasonable treatment of mental patients. Her work was part of the reform movement that emphasized moral therapy.

*Moral therapy,* which was popular in the early 1800s, was the belief that mental patients could be helped to function better by providing humane treatment in a relaxed and decent environment.

During the reform movement, pleasant mental hospitals were built in rural settings so that moral therapy could be used to treat patients. However, these mental hospitals soon became overcrowded, the public lost interest, funds became tight, and treatment became scarce.

Dorothea Dix began a humane treatment of the mentally ill.

By the late 1800s, the belief that moral therapy would cure mental disorders was abandoned. Mental hospitals began to resemble human snake pits, in which hundreds of mental patients, in various states of dress or undress, milled about in a large room while acting out their symptoms with little or no supervision. Treatment went backward, and once again patients were put into straitjackets, handcuffs, and various restraining devices (Routh, 1994).

By the early 1930s, Sigmund Freud had developed psychoanalysis, the first psychotherapy. Psychoanalysis eventually spread from Europe to the United States and reached its peak of popularity in the 1950s. However, psychoanalysis was more effective in treating less serious mental disorders (neuroses) than in treating the serious mental disorders (psychoses) that kept people in mental hospitals.

Thus, the wretched conditions and inhumane treatment of patients with serious mental disorders persisted until the early 1950s. By then, more than half a million patients were locked away. But in the mid-1950s, two events dramatically changed the treatment of mental patients: one was the discovery of antipsychotic drugs, and the other was the development of community mental health centers.

Freud developed first psychotherapy.

## Phenothiazines and Deinstitutionalization

**What was the first break-through?**
The discovery of drugs for treating mental disorders often occurs by chance. Such was the case in the 1950s as a French surgeon, Henri Laborit, searched for a drug that would calm down patients before surgery without causing unconsciousness. He happened to try a new drug on a woman about to have surgery and who was also schizophrenic. To the doctor's great surprise, the drug not only calmed the woman down but also decreased her schizophrenic symptoms. This is how the drug, chlorpromazine, was discovered to be a treatment for schizophrenia. Chlorpromazine (*klor-PRO-ma-zeen*) belongs to a group of drugs called phenothiazines.

*Phenothiazines (fee-no-THIGH-ah-zeens),* which were discovered in the early 1950s, block or reduce the effects of the neurotransmitter dopamine and reduce schizophrenic symptoms, such as delusions and hallucinations.

**Discovery.** After 200 years of often cruel and inhumane treatments for mental disorders, chlorpromazine was the first drug shown to be effective in reducing severe mental symptoms such as delusions and hallucinations. For this reason, the discovery of chlorpromazine is considered the first revolution in the drug treatment of mental disorders. Earlier we discussed the phenothiazines, now called typical neuroleptics, as well as the newer discovery of atypical neuroleptics (p. 541), which are used in the treatment of schizophrenia.

In 1954, one of the phenothiazines, chlorpromazine (trade name: Thorazine), reached the United States and had two huge effects. First, it stimulated research on neurotransmitters and on the development of new drugs to treat mental disorders. Second, chlorpromazine reduced severe mental symptoms such as delusions and hallucinations to the point that patients could function well enough to be released from mental hospitals, a policy called deinstitutionalization.

*Deinstitutionalization* refers to the release of mental patients from mental hospitals and their return to the community to develop more independent and fulfilling lives.

In 1950, before the discovery of phenothiazines, there were 550,000 patients in mental hospitals in the United States. After the use of phenothiazines and deinstitutionalization, the number of patients in mental hospitals had dropped to about 150,000 in 1970 and to about 80,000 in 2000 (Manderscheid & Sonnenschein, 1992). However, deinstitutionalization has created a related problem.

**Homeless.** The goal of deinstitutionalization, which is to get patients back into the community, has been only partly realized. Some former mental patients do live in halfway houses that provide help and support in making the transition from mental hospitals to the community. However, there are not enough halfway houses to accommodate all the patients who have been deinstitutionalized. As a result, mental patients with serious disorders make up about 25–50% of today's homeless and receive little or no treatment (Morrissey et al., 1997). In addition, up to 25% of prisoners in county jails are homeless and show some form of mental disorder but are receiving little or no treatment (Rivera, 2000). To provide mental health treatment for the homeless as well as those released from hospitals, there is a new place to receive help, called community mental health centers.

About 25–50% of the homeless have some degree of mental problems.

## Community Mental Health Centers

**Where can they go for treatment?**
There is a need for treatment of mental disorders in the homeless, county prisoners, those released from mental hospitals, as well as about 20% of Americans who experience a mental disorder in the course of a year (Satcher, 2000). Some of these individuals may have less serious mental disorders that may require professional help but not hospitalization. One way to provide professional help to individuals with less serious mental disorders is through community mental health centers.

*Community mental health centers* offer low-cost or free mental health care to members of the surrounding community, especially the under-privileged. The services may include psychotherapy, support groups, or telephone crisis counseling.

This therapist is treating a client in a community mental health center, which helps those who need it but can't afford it.

Just as the 1950s saw the introduction of a new drug treatment for mental disorders, the phenothiazines, the 1960s saw the growing availability of new treatment facilities, the community mental health centers. The goal of these centers is to provide treatment for the poor and those who have no other means of treatment for their mental health problems. These centers provide briefer forms of therapy that are needed in emergencies, and they focus on the early detection and prevention of psychological problems (Barlow & Durand, 2001). To meet these ambitious goals required an enormous change in mental health personnel.

Previously, *psychiatrists* provided the majority of psychological services, which consisted of mainly psychoanalysis and served individuals in the middle and upper social classes who were not very seriously disturbed. Because of the limited number of psychiatrists, community mental health centers turned to *clinical psychologists* and *social workers* to provide the new mental health services. This demand increased the number of clinical and counseling psychologists and social workers and stimulated the development of new therapy approaches (Garfield & Bergin, 1994).

Before we discuss specific psychotherapies, we'll answer four basic questions about psychotherapy in general.

**What do I need to know?**

If you or a family member, friend, relative, or acquaintance has a mental health problem, there are at least four questions that you might ask about seeking professional help or psychotherapy: Do I need professional help? Are there different kinds of therapists? Are there different approaches? How effective is psychotherapy? We'll answer each question in turn.

## Do I Need Professional Help?

Each year, more than 30 million Americans need help in dealing with a variety of mental disorders, which range from those that cause some problems in daily activities to those that interfere with a person's normal functioning (American Psychological Association, 1995). For example, a person may feel overwhelmed by a sense of sadness, depression, or helplessness so that he or she cannot form a meaningful relationship. A person may worry or expect such terrible things to happen that he or she cannot concentrate or carry out everyday activities. A person may become so dependent on drugs that he or she has difficulty functioning in personal, social, or professional situations. If these problems begin to interfere with daily functioning in social, personal, business, academic, or professional interactions and activities, then a person may need help from a mental health professional (Satcher, 2000).

*Each year, about 30 million Americans need help in dealing with mental disorders.*

In Module 23, we discussed how a well-known actor, Rod Steiger, suffered from major depression for several years before he sought professional help (p. 532). He delayed seeking professional help because of the public stigma attached to having a mental disorder. This is also one of the reasons that about 40% of individuals with psychological problems do not seek professional help (Kessler et al., 1994). However, the stigma of having a mental disorder has decreased in recent years as people have become aware of the need for professional treatment (Swindle, 2000).

In Module 23, we also discussed the treatment of individuals with more serious mental symptoms (p. 531). In one case, Michael McCabe heard voices and believed people were going to steal things from him (schizophrenia); and in another case, Chuck Elliot went sleepless for four nights and had trouble controlling his behavior (bipolar I disorder). Although both of these individuals needed professional treatment, neither wanted nor asked for it. Thus, individuals with serious mental disorders may not be able to decide what is best, and their friends or family may need to help them get professional help.

Currently, there are a number of different kinds of mental health professionals who may provide a drug or nondrug treatment program or some combination.

## Are There Different Kinds of Therapists?

We'll discuss three of the more common kinds of therapists: psychiatrists, clinical psychologists, and counseling psychologists, each of whom receives a different kind of training in psychotherapy techniques.

*Psychiatrists* go to medical school, receive an M.D. degree, and then take a psychiatric residency, which involves additional training in pharmacology, neurology, psychopathology, and psychotherapeutic techniques.

Psychiatrists focus on biological factors and usually prescribe drugs to treat mental health disorders. Psychiatrists who receive additional training in psychoanalytic institutes are called *psychoanalysts*.

*Clinical psychologists* go to graduate school in clinical psychology and earn a doctorate degree (Ph.D., Psy.D., or Ed.D.). This training, which includes one year of work in an applied clinical setting, usually requires five to six years of work after obtaining a college degree.

Clinical psychologists who receive additional training in psychoanalytic institutes can also use psychoanalysis. Clinical psychologists focus on psychosocial and environmental factors and use psychotherapy to treat mental health disorders because, as of yet, they cannot generally prescribe drugs. Recently however, in a trial program, clinical psychologists were trained in prescribing drugs for a variety of mental disorders. Evaluators of this program concluded that, with proper training, clinical psychologists can provide safe and high-quality drug treatment for their patients (Smith, 2000). However, despite this very positive recommendation, clinical psychologists have not yet been given the general authority to prescribe drugs to treat mental disorders, primarily because of political opposition from psychiatrists.

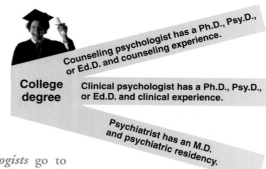

Counseling psychologist has a Ph.D., Psy.D., or Ed.D. and counseling experience.

**College degree**

Clinical psychologist has a Ph.D., Psy.D., or Ed.D. and clinical experience.

Psychiatrist has an M.D. and psychiatric residency.

*Counseling psychologists* go to graduate school in psychology or education and earn a doctorate degree (Ph.D., Psy.D., or Ed.D). This training, which includes work in a counseling setting, usually requires about four to six years after obtaining a bachelor's degree.

Counseling psychologists receive training similar to that of clinical psychologists but with less emphasis on research and more emphasis on counseling in real-world settings. Counseling psychologists, who function in settings such as schools, colleges, industry, and private practice, generally deal more with problems of living than with the mental disorders that are treated by clinical psychologists.

In addition, other mental health professionals, such as *clinical social workers* and *psychiatric nurses,* also provide mental health services.

Just as there are different kinds of therapists, there are also different kinds of therapeutic approaches from which to choose.

## Are There Different Approaches?

If you were to seek professional help for a mental problem, you could choose from a number of different therapeutic approaches: some use primarily psychotherapy, some use primarily drugs, and others use a combination of psychotherapy and drugs. These different therapies can be divided into three groups: insight therapy, cognitive-behavior therapy, and medical therapy.

With *insight therapy,* the therapist and client talk about the client's symptoms and problems with the goal of reaching or identifying the cause of the problem. Once the client has an insight into the cause of the problem, possible solutions can be discussed with the therapist.

The classic example of insight therapy is psychoanalysis, whose goal is to help clients get insights into their problems. But because psychoanalysis requires hundreds of sessions, it is very costly; and since it is no more effective than other, briefer therapies, its popularity has significantly decreased since the 1950s. The next kind of therapy, called cognitive-behavior therapy, combines some features of insight therapy with a much more directive approach.

*Cognitive-behavior therapy* involves the application of principles of learning that were discussed in Modules 9 and 10. The therapist focuses on the client's problem, identifies specific thoughts and behaviors that need to be changed, and provides techniques based on learning principles to make desired changes.

Here's my problem . . .

There are several kinds of drug and non-drug therapies for mental disorders.

Unlike psychoanalysis, which focuses on insight and gives little direction for change, cognitive-behavior therapy focuses on changing specific undesirable or problematic thoughts and behaviors. This approach, which is sometimes called behavior therapy, has become very popular today.

Currently, the most popular approach, used by about 68% of therapists, is the eclectic approach (Lambert & Bergin, 1994).

The *eclectic (ee-KLEK-tik) approach* involves combining and using techniques and ideas from many different therapeutic approaches.

For example, a therapist using an eclectic approach might combine some of the nondirective techniques from psychoanalysis with more directive techniques from cognitive-behavior therapy. Unlike insight and cognitive-behavioral approaches, which focus on psychosocial factors, the next kind of therapy focuses on changing biological factors.

*Medical therapy* involves the use of various psychoactive drugs to treat mental disorders by changing biological factors, such as the levels of neurotransmitters in the brain.

In Modules 22 and 23, we discussed medical therapies and how various psychoactive drugs are used to treat a wide variety of mental disorders, including anxiety, mood disorders, and schizophrenia. Unlike medical therapies, in which drugs may have undesirable physical side

A number of different drugs (neuroleptics, antidepressants) may be used to treat more serious mental disorders.

effects, no undesirable side effects are associated with psychotherapy. In this module, we'll focus on several psychotherapies, specifically insight and cognitive-behavioral approaches.

With so many different therapeutic approaches, is one kind of psychotherapy more effective than another?

## How Effective Is Psychotherapy?

When we have problems, we sometimes say, "I'll just wait and maybe the problem will go away by itself." This kind of remark raises a major question: Is psychotherapy more effective than just waiting for problems to go away?

To answer this question and determine the effectiveness of psychotherapy, researchers have used a complex statistical procedure called meta-analysis.

*Meta-analysis* is a powerful statistical procedure that compares the results of dozens or hundreds of studies to determine the effectiveness of some variable or treatment examined in these studies.

Researchers have done meta-analysis on over 1,500 studies that examined the effects of psychotherapy on a variety of problems, such as depression, anxiety disorders, family problems, eating disorders, and headaches (Nathan et al., 2000; Shadish et al., 2000). We'll discuss three of the major findings:

■ Psychotherapy was effective in relieving a wide variety of psychological and behavioral symptoms in comparison with control groups who were on a waiting list to receive therapy or who received no systematic treatment.

■ There was little or no significant difference in effectiveness between the approaches used by different therapies. In other words, the same psychological or behavioral symptoms were, in most cases, treated effectively with different approaches.

■ The vast majority of patients (75%) showed measurable improvement by the end of six months of once-a-week psychotherapy sessions (24 sessions).

Psychotherapy has proved effective for a wide variety of mental disorders.

Thus, on the basis of data on thousands of patients, psychotherapy proved effective in treating numerous mental and behavioral problems, and the greatest improvement occurred in a relatively brief period of time (Lambert & Bergin, 1994). Generally, about 10–20% of clients who seek psychotherapy experience great improvement, 30–50% receive some improvement, and about 10–30% show little or no improvement (Bergin & Garfield, 1994; Mohr, 1995). Thus, although psychotherapy has proved to be an effective treatment, the amount of improvement varies across patients (VandenBos, 1996).

Although many different therapies seem to be about equally effective overall, we'll discuss how some approaches are preferred for certain problems and that clients may prefer a certain approach.

We'll begin with one of the oldest and best-known therapy approaches—Freud's system of psychoanalysis.

---

**Psychoanalysis**

---

**What happens in psycho-analysis?** One reason almost everyone knows the name Freud is that he constructed one of the first amazingly complete and interesting descriptions of personality development, mental disorder, and treatment, which was a monumental and revolutionary accomplishment at the time. In fact, Sigmund Freud's theory of psychoanalysis includes two related theories. The first is his comprehensive theory of personality development (id, ego, superego, and psychosexual stages), which we discussed in Module 19. His second theory involves the development and treatment of various mental disorders, which we'll examine here.

In the late 1800s, Freud developed the first psychotherapy, called psychoanalysis.

*Psychoanalysis* focuses on the idea that each of us has an unconscious part that contains ideas, memories, desires, or thoughts, which have been hidden or repressed because they are psychologically dangerous or threatening to our self-concept. To protect our self-concept from these threatening thoughts and desires, we automatically build a mental barrier that we cannot voluntarily remove. However, the presence of these threatening thoughts and desires gives rise to unconscious conflicts, which, in turn, can result in psychological and physical symptoms and mental disorders.

Freud began developing the theory of psychoanalysis in the late 1800s. From 1902 onward, a number of young doctors and interested laypersons gathered around Freud to learn the principles and practice of psychoanalysis. In 1908, Freud was invited to America to discuss his approach, which reached the height of its popularity in the 1950s. Psychoanalysis makes three major assumptions (Wolitzky & Eagle, 1997).

**1** Freud believed that *unconscious conflicts* were the chief reason for the development of psychological problems (paranoia) and physical symptoms (loss of feeling in a hand). To treat psychological and physical problems, patients needed to become aware of, and gain insight into, their unconscious conflicts and repressed thoughts.

**2** Freud developed *three techniques*—free association, dream interpretation, and analysis of slips of the tongue—that he believed provide clues to unconscious conflicts and repressed thoughts.

**3** Freud found that at some point during therapy the patient would react to the therapist as a substitute parent, lover, sibling, or friend and, in the process, project or *transfer* strong emotions onto the therapist.

Freud developed these three assumptions gradually, over a period of about ten years, when he was treating patients for a variety of psychological problems and physical symptoms.

We'll explain how Freud used these three assumptions to develop the therapy he called psychoanalysis.

**Therapy session.** To give you an appreciation of what happens during psychoanalysis, we'll begin with an excerpt from a therapy session and then explain what goes on between client and psychoanalyst.

Henry is in his mid-forties and is well advanced in treatment. As he arrives, he casually mentions his somewhat late arrival at the analyst's office, which might otherwise have gone unnoticed.

"You will think it is a resistance," Henry remarked sarcastically, "but it was nothing of the kind. I had hailed a taxi that would have gotten me to the office on time. However, the traffic light changed just before the cab reached me, and someone else got in instead. I was so annoyed that I yelled 'F___ you!' after the cab driver."

A brief pause ensued, followed by laughter as Henry repeated "F___ you!"—this time clearly directed to the analyst.

The analyst interpreted this interaction to mean that the cabbie had represented the analyst in the first place. Henry's anger at the analyst was relieved by the opportunity to curse out the analyst (cabbie).

After another brief pause, it was the analyst who broke the silence and injected his first and only interpretation of the 50-minute session. He asserted that Henry seemed to be angry about a previously canceled therapy session.

Henry was furious over the interpretation. "Who are you that I should care about missing that session?" he stormed.

Henry paused again, and then reflected more tranquilly, "My father, I suppose."

This time it was the word *father* that served as the switch word to a new line of thought.

"My father was distant, like you," he began. "We never really had a conversation" (adapted from Lipton, 1983).

### ROLE OF ANALYST

This brief excerpt from a psychoanalytic session illustrates the basic assumptions of psychoanalysis.

> I was thinking how my mother didn't make me feel appreciated and how I felt bad but I still loved her but it still hurt and . . .

■ **Free association.** Notice that the patient is encouraged to free-associate or say anything that comes into his mind, while the analyst makes few comments.

■ **Interpretation.** When the analyst does comment, he or she interprets or analyzes something the patient says, such as the meaning of the anger at the cab driver.

■ **Unconscious conflicts.** By analyzing the client's free associations, the analyst hopes to reveal the client's unconscious and threatening desires, which are causing unconscious conflicts that, in turn, cause psychological problems.

One of Freud's techniques was the use of free association.

We'll examine three of Freud's therapy techniques in more detail.

## Techniques to Reveal the Unconscious

One of Freud's major challenges was to find ways to uncover unconscious conflicts, which, he believed, led to psychological problems that he labeled neuroses.

*Neuroses,* according to Freud, are maladaptive thoughts and actions that arise from some unconscious thought or conflict and indicate feelings of anxiety.

In order to treat neuroses or neurotic symptoms, such as phobias, anxieties, and obsessions, Freud wanted to discover what was in the patient's unconscious. To do this, he developed two major techniques: free association and dream interpretation. To show how these techniques work, we'll describe two of Freud's most famous cases, Rat Man and Wolf-Man.

### Rat Man: Free Association

Freud encouraged patients to relax, sit back, or lie down on his now-famous couch and engage in something called free association.

*Free association* is a technique that encourages clients to talk about any thoughts or images that enter their heads; the assumption is that this kind of free-flowing, uncensored talking will provide clues to unconscious material.

Rat Man believed that rats would destroy his father and lover.

For example, here is how Freud described a session with one of his most famous patients, a 29-year-old lawyer later named the Rat Man because of his obsession that rats would destroy his father and lover.

Freud writes, "The next day I made him [Rat Man] pledge himself to submit to the one and only condition of the treatment—namely, to say everything that came into his head even if it was *unpleasant* to him, or seemed *unimportant* or *irrelevant* or *senseless.* I then gave him leave to start his communications with any subject he pleased" (Freud, 1909/1949, p. 297; italics in the original).

Freud is actually telling Rat Man to free-associate. By this means, Freud uncovered a number of Rat Man's repressed memories, such as how Rat Man, as a child, would get into rages and bite people, just like a rat.

Free association was one of Freud's important methodological discoveries. Psychoanalysts still use this technique today to probe a client's unconscious thoughts, desires, and conflicts (Kernberg, 1999).

### Wolf-Man: Dream Interpretation

Freud listened to and interpreted his patients' dreams because he believed that dreams represent the purest form of free association.

*Dream interpretation* is a psychoanalytic technique based on the assumption that dreams contain underlying, hidden meanings and symbols that provide clues to unconscious thoughts and desires.

For example, here is one of the best-known dreams in psychoanalytic literature. This dream was told to Freud by a 23-year-old patient who was later named Wolf-Man because he had a phobia of wolves and other animals (Buckley, 1989).

Wolf-Man dreamt there were wolves sitting in the tree outside his room.

"I dreamt that it was night and that I was lying in my bed. Suddenly the window opened of its own accord, and I was terrified to see that some white wolves were sitting on the big walnut tree in front of the window. There were six or seven of them. The wolves were quite white, and looked more like foxes or sheep-dogs, for they had big tails like foxes and they had their ears pricked like dogs when they are attending to something. In great terror, evidently of being eaten up by the wolves, I screamed and woke up . . . I was 3, 4, or at most 5 years old at the time. From then until my 11th or 12th year I was always afraid of seeing something terrible in my dreams" (Freud, 1909/1949, p. 498).

Freud's interpretation of this dream was that, as a young boy, Wolf-Man was "transformed" into a wolf and had witnessed his parents' sexual intercourse (looking through the bedroom window). Later, sexual fears created unconscious conflicts and resulted in a phobia of wolves and other animals.

As Freud demonstrates, the psychoanalyst's task is to look behind the dream's often bizarre disguises and symbols and decipher clues to unconscious, repressed memories, thoughts, feelings, and conflicts (Greenberg & Pearlman, 1999).

### Case Studies: Anna O., Rat Man, and Wolf-Man

Case studies, such as those of Rat Man, Wolf-Man, and Anna O., whom we discussed at the beginning of the module, were very important because from these Freud developed the major concepts of psychoanalysis. For example, from cases like that of Anna O., who had physical symptoms (paralyzed arm, blurred vision) but no apparent physical causes, Freud developed the idea that repressed feelings and unconscious conflicts could affect behavior but that the person would have no awareness of this happening. In support of Freud's belief that unconscious forces were causing Anna O.'s physical problems, each

Were Anna O.'s physical symptoms caused by unconscious forces?

time she let out some apparently repressed emotional experience, one of her physical symptoms disappeared.

Freud's case studies read like mystery stories with Freud being the master detective who searches for psychological clues that will reveal the person's repressed feelings and unconscious conflicts. At the time, Freud's assumptions and theories, such as repressed feelings and unconscious motivation, were revolutionary. However, as we'll discuss later, Freud's theories and assumptions have been very difficult to verify or prove with experimental methods (Grunbaum, 1993).

Besides developing methods to reveal unconscious thoughts and conflicts, Freud discovered two other concepts that are central to psychoanalysis.

### Problems During Therapy

**Why did clients get angry?** Freud was the first to notice that, during therapy, his clients became somewhat hostile toward him, a problem he called transference. He also found that patients became very resistant about dealing with their feelings. Freud believed that how these two problems, called transference and resistance, were handled determined how successful therapy would be. We'll explain these two concepts by using the cases of Rat Man and Wolf-Man.

### Rat Man: Transference

Freud describes a patient, later labeled Rat Man, as expressing powerful, aggressive feelings toward him. For example, Rat Man refused to shake hands with Freud, accused Freud of picking his nose, called Freud a "filthy swine," and said that Freud needed to be taught some manners (Freud, 1909/1949).

During therapy, Rat Man called Freud a "filthy swine," which Freud believed resulted from transference.

According to Freud, Rat Man was projecting negative traits of his own very controlling mother onto Freud, who became a "substitute mother." This process of transferring feelings to the therapist is called transference.

*Transference* is the process by which a client expresses strong emotions toward the therapist because the therapist substitutes for someone important in the client's life, such as the client's mother or father.

Freud believed that the main part of therapy involved working through the transference—that is, resolving the emotional feelings that the client has transferred to the therapist. Freud said that if the feelings involved in transference are not worked out, therapy would stall and treatment would not occur. For this reason, Freud believed that one of the major roles of the analyst was to help the client deal with, work through, and resolve the transferred feelings. Identifying the process of transference, which occurs in many therapeutic relationships, is considered one of Freud's greatest insights (Eagle, 2000).

### Wolf-Man: Resistance

For most patients, working out transference and achieving insight into their problems are long and difficult processes. One reason for the difficulty is that the client has so many defenses against admitting repressed thoughts and feelings into consciousness. These defenses lead to resistance.

*Resistance* is characterized by the client's reluctance to work through or deal with feelings or to recognize unconscious conflicts and repressed thoughts.

Resistance may show up in many ways: clients may cancel sessions or come late, argue continually, criticize the analyst, or develop physical problems. For example, the patient named Wolf-Man constantly complained of severe constipation. Freud said that Wolf-Man used constipation as an obvious sign that he was resisting having to deal with his feelings (Freud, 1909/1949).

During therapy, Wolf-Man complained of constipation, which Freud believed indicated resistance.

Freud overcame Wolf-Man's resistance by promising that his constipation would disappear with continued therapy, and it did (Buckley, 1989). Freud cautioned that the analyst must use tact and patience to break down the client's resistance so that the client faces his feelings.

A necessary role of the analyst is to overcome the client's resistance so that the therapy can proceed and stay on course (Kernberg, 1999).

### Short-Term Dynamic Psychotherapy

The cases of Rat Man and Wolf-Man illustrate two difficulties that psychoanalysts face in helping clients achieve insight into the causes of their problems. One difficulty is helping clients work out their strong emotional feelings involved in transference or else therapy will not succeed. Another difficulty is helping clients overcome their resistance and begin dealing with threatening or undesirable feelings. However, resolving these problems of transference and resistance may take years. One reason psychoanalysis has greatly decreased in popularity is that it often requires several years of 2–4 weekly sessions, while other current forms of psychotherapy are relatively short term. For this reason, a briefer version of psychoanalysis has been developed; it is called short-term dynamic psychotherapy (Della Selva, 1996).

*Short-term dynamic psychotherapy,* which is a shortened version of psychoanalysis, assumes that symptoms are signs of more basic underlying problems, that transference needs to be worked out, and that the client's behaviors need to be interpreted. The main goal is to bring the client's underlying feelings to the surface. To do this, therapists take a more active and directive role in identifying and discussing the client's problems and suggesting solutions.

Unlike traditional psychoanalysis, which requires an average of 200–600 sessions over several years, short-term dynamic psychotherapy occurs in a maximum of 25–30 sessions. In addition, short-term dynamic psychotherapy has proven effective for the treatment of stress and eating disorders, depression, and several personality disorders (Blagys & Hilsenroth, 2000; Della Selva, 1996). Several kinds of short-term dynamic psychotherapy have now become more popular than long-term psychoanalysis (Blagys & Hilsenroth, 2000).

How long will it take for me to get over my fears?

Short-term versions of traditional psychoanalysis have been developed and proved effective.

Next, we'll evaluate the current importance of psychoanalysis.

## Psychoanalysis: Evaluation

The 50th anniversary of Sigmund Freud's death (1939) was marked by a series of articles in the *Psychoanalytic Quarterly* titled, "Is There a Future for American Psychoanalysis?" One author said that such a question was unheard of in the 1950s, when psychoanalysis was at the height of its popularity (Kirsner, 1990). However, following the 1950s, there has been a gradual decline in the popularity of psychoanalysis (Henry et al., 1994). At the start of the new millennium, the *Journal of the American Psychoanalytic Association* devoted its issue to examining where psychoanalysis is and where it's going (Gabbard, 2000). We'll discuss the decline in popularity of psychoanalysis, as well as its future.

### 1 Decline in Popularity

How did it happen that psychoanalysis, the number one therapy in the 1950s, lost its popularity and is now struggling to compete with other therapies? Here are some of the reasons according to its own members (Wallerstein & Fonagy, 1999; Westen & Gabbard, 1999).

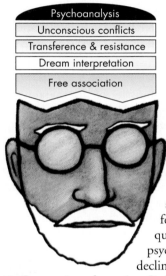

■ **Lack of research.** In the 1970s, critics pointed out that almost no research had been done on whether the psychoanalytic process was an effective form of therapy. For example, psychoanalysts have been very slow to analyze their own profession in terms of education—how best to train analysts—and to conduct research into what goes on during analysis and how to make it more effective. This criticism, which questioned the effectiveness of psychoanalysis, contributed to its decline in popularity.

■ **Competing therapies.** Perhaps the major reason for the decrease in popularity of psychoanalysis was that, beginning in the 1970s, a number of competing psychotherapies (discussed later in this module) were developed that were proven equally effective but had a great advantage in that they are much quicker and far less costly. For example, psychoanalysis may require 200–600 sessions (2–4 per week for several years) versus 25 for other therapies. This last point is particularly important since most major health insurance plans limit either the amount of money or the number of sessions (usually 23–25) for treatment of psychological problems. Because of this policy, health plans would not pay the costs of therapy for patients choosing psychoanalysis.

■ **Psychoactive drugs.** Another reason for the decline of psychoanalysis was the discovery of many new psychoactive drugs that proved effective in treating many of the problems formerly dealt with in psychoanalysis, such as anxiety and mood disorders. Some patients preferred drugs to psychoanalysis.

All of the above factors—lack of research on its effectiveness, development of new and less costly therapies, and discovery of psychoactive drugs—resulted in psychoanalysis experiencing a great decline from its popularity in the 1950s.

### 2 Current Status

Beginning in the 1980s and continuing to the present, there has been a major effort by psychoanalytic societies and their members to encourage research on the methods, concepts, and outcomes of therapy. This shift toward research indicates a major turning point in psychoanalysis. Previously, psychoanalysts almost exclusively reported and discussed individual case studies but rarely studied the psychoanalytic process or its effectiveness using the experimental approach that had been adopted by newly developed and competing therapies.

**Freudian concepts.** Current followers agree that some of Freud's concepts, such as the id being the source of energy, the importance of the Oedipus complex in personality development, and basic drives limited to sex and aggression, have proved difficult to test or verify and are now out of date. The same followers add that other Freudian concepts, such as the influence of unconscious forces, long-term effects of early childhood patterns, and existence of defense mechanisms and conflicting cognitive processes, have been experimentally tested and supported (Westen & Gabbard, 1999). For example, researchers discovered that we do have memories, called procedural or nondeclarative (p. 246), that are outside our awareness (unconscious) but affect a variety of behaviors, including performing motor skills and acquiring strong emotional responses (fears and phobias) through classical conditioning (Dienes & Perner, 1999). Thus, two basic concepts behind psychoanalysis—influence of unconscious forces and use of defense mechanisms—have received support.

### 3 Conclusion

The right graph shows that the most popular therapy today is not psychoanalysis but the eclectic approach, which combines techniques and methods from many different therapies. The second most popular therapy, the psychodynamic approach, is different from traditional psychoanalysis. Although the psychodynamic approach shares some of its concepts with classical psychoanalysis (transference, resistance, unconscious forces), this newer approach has the therapist taking a more directive role that significantly reduces the number of sessions but seems equally effective (Henry et al., 1994).

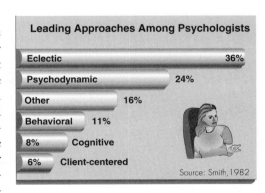

**Leading Approaches Among Psychologists**

| | |
|---|---|
| Eclectic | 36% |
| Psychodynamic | 24% |
| Other | 16% |
| Behavioral | 11% |
| Cognitive | 8% |
| Client-centered | 6% |

Source: Smith, 1982

Next, we'll discuss an approach that had an interesting beginning. This therapy approach was developed by a clinician who had been using Freud's psychoanalytic approach but became very displeased with it.

**Client-Centered Therapy**

**What is a therapist's role?**

As a therapist, Carl Rogers used the most popular therapy in his time, which was Freud's psychoanalytic approach. However, before long Rogers became dissatisfied with Freud's view that human nature was dependent on biological urges and instincts—sex and aggression—and that psychological problems arose from unconscious thoughts and desires that threatened one's self-concept. Rogers also disagreed with Freud's belief that the analyst—and not the client—was responsible for the client's progress. Instead, Rogers said that clients themselves have the capacity and are responsible for change. Using these ideas, Rogers developed client-centered therapy (Rogers, 1951, 1986).

*Client-centered therapy* (also called person-centered therapy) assumes that each person has an actualizing tendency, which is a tendency to develop one's full potential. The therapist's task is to be nondirective and show compassion and positive regard in helping the client reach his or her potential.

Rogers believed that each person has a tendency to develop his or her potential.

In client-centered therapy, Rogers changed the therapist's role from that of an all-knowing expert to a helper or facilitator, whose personal characteristics would foster growth and change (Rogers, 1986).

**Therapy session.** To illustrate some of the differences between psychoanalysis and client-centered therapy, here is a brief excerpt of a client-centered therapy session where a mother is talking about her problems with letting her daughter be more independent.

**Client:** I'm having a lot of problems dealing with my daughter. She's 20 years old; she's in college; I'm having a lot of trouble letting her go . . . And I have a lot of guilt feelings about her; I have a real need to hang on to her. And it's very hard with a lot of empty places now that she's not with me.

**Rogers:** The old vacuum, sort of, when she's not there.

**Client:** Yes, yes. I also would like to be the kind of mother that could be strong and say, you know, "go and have a good life," and it's really hard for me to do that.

**Rogers:** It's very hard to give up something that's been so precious in your life, but also something that I guess has caused you pain when you mentioned guilt.

**Client:** Yeah, and I'm aware that I have some anger toward her that I don't always get what I want. I have needs that are not met. And, uh, I don't feel I have a right to those needs. You know . . . she's a daughter; she's not my mother—though sometimes I feel as if I'd like her to mother me . . . It's very difficult for me to ask for that and have a right to it.

**Rogers:** So it may be unreasonable, but still, when she doesn't meet your needs, it makes you mad.

**Client:** Yeah. I get very angry, very angry with her. (*pause*)

**Rogers:** You're also feeling a little tension at this point, I guess.

**Client:** Yeah, yeah. A lot of conflict . . .

**Rogers:** A lot of pain.

**Client:** A lot of pain.

**Rogers:** A lot of pain. Can you say anything more what that's about? (adapted from Rogers, 1989).

**Client-centered approach.** In this brief except, you can see two of the hallmarks of client-centered therapy. First, Rogers avoids giving any suggestions, advice, or disapproval and primarily shows the client that he understands what the client is feeling. Second, one technique Rogers uses for showing understanding is *reflecting* or restating the client's concerns. Reflecting the client's feelings is one of the basic techniques of the person-centered approach. In addition, humanistic therapists believe that clients have the capacity to discover and reach their true potential and it is the therapist's role to help and remove any roadblocks in their paths (Greenberg & Rice, 1997).

### THERAPIST'S TRAITS

Rogers believed that personal characteristics of the therapist—empathy, positive regard, genuineness—would bring about the client's change. *Empathy* is the ability to understand what the client is saying and feeling. *Positive regard* is the ability to communicate caring, respect, and regard for the client. *Genuineness* is the ability to be real and nondefensive in interactions with the client. Rogers and his followers assumed that a therapist with these three characteristics would be able to help a client change and grow.

However, numerous studies have shown that these three characteristics are not always related to successful outcomes (Hill & Nakayama, 2000). The success of client-centered therapy appears to be due more to developing a good working client–therapist partnership and to the client's attitudes of wanting to and working hard to change (Greenberg & Rice, 1997).

What's blocking my path to developing my true potential?

### EFFECTIVENESS

A recent review of client-centered therapy reported that it was effective in producing significant changes in clients in comparison with no-treatment control groups, but it was no more or less effective than were other forms of therapy (Hill & Nakayama, 2000). Although client-centered therapy has emphasized the importance of empathy in producing change, studies have generally failed to find such an association. In addition, client-centered therapists who were very reflective and gave very little direction were less effective than therapists who made more suggestions and gave more direction (Greenberg & Rice, 1997).

Although client-centered therapy is currently used by only 6% of psychologists, it has greatly contributed to making therapists aware of the importance and need to develop a positive working relationship with their clients (Hill & Nakayama, 2000).

The therapist takes a much more directive role in the next kind of insight therapy, called cognitive therapy.

Similar to Carl Rogers's experience, Aaron Beck was also trained in psychoanalytic techniques and used them to treat patients, many of whom were suffering from depression. When he asked them to free-associate, he noticed that depressed patients often expressed negative or distorted thoughts about themselves—"I'm a failure, no one likes me, nothing turns out right." What really caught his attention was how patients would express a string of negative thoughts almost automatically, without paying much attention. Beck reasoned that these automatically occurring negative thoughts had a great impact on the patients' lives, such as by lowering their self-esteem and encouraging self-blame and self-criticism. Beck developed his form of cognitive therapy to stop these thoughts and so treat depression and other problems (Beck, 1976, 1991).

*Cognitive therapy,* as developed by Aaron Beck, assumes that we have automatic negative thoughts that we typically say to ourselves without much notice. By continually repeating these automatic negative thoughts, we color and distort how we perceive and interpret our world and influence how we behave and feel.

Negative things we say to ourselves—for example, "Nothing ever goes right," "I'm a failure," or "Everybody criticizes me"—can bias and distort our thoughts and feelings. Cognitive therapy was developed to make a person aware of, and stop, negative self-statements.

**Therapy session.** To give you an idea of how negative thoughts occur, here is a brief excerpt from one of Dr. Beck's sessions.

The client is a 26-year-old graduate student who has bouts of depression.

**Client:** I get depressed when things go wrong. Like when I fail a test.

**Therapist:** How can failing a test make you depressed?

**Client:** Well, if I fail, I'll never get into law school.

**Therapist:** Do you agree that the way you interpret the results of the test will affect you? You might feel depressed, you might have trouble sleeping, not feel like eating, and you might even wonder if you should drop out of the course.

*Why do I keep thinking all those negative thoughts?*

**Client:** I have been thinking that I wasn't going to make it. Yes, I agree.

**Therapist:** Now what did failing mean?

**Client:** (*tearful*) That I couldn't get into law school.

**Therapist:** And what does that mean to you?

**Client:** That I'm just not smart enough.

**Therapist:** Anything else?

**Client:** That I can never be happy.

**Therapist:** And how do these thoughts make you feel?

**Client:** Very unhappy.

**Therapist:** So it is the meaning of failing a test that makes you very unhappy. In fact, believing that you can never be happy is a powerful factor in producing unhappiness. So,

you get yourself into a trap—by definition, failure to get into law school equals "I can never be happy" (Beck et al., 1979, pp. 145–146).

**Cognitive approach.** Notice how the client tries to avoid admitting that her thoughts influence her feelings. Also notice her negative self-statements, such as "I'm just not smart enough" and "I can never be happy." Beck believes that these kinds of negative self-statements will influence this client's thoughts and feelings and contribute to her major symptom, depression.

**IMPORTANT FACTORS**

Beck has identified a number of specific maladaptive thoughts that contribute to various symptoms, such as anxiety and depression. Thus, thinking "I'm a failure" after doing poorly on one test is an example of *overgeneralization,* which is making blanket judgments about yourself on the basis of a single incident. Thinking "Most people don't like me" is an example of *polarized thinking,* which is sorting information into one of two categories, good or bad. Thinking "People always criticize me" is an example of *selective attention,* which is focusing on one detail so much that you do not notice other events, such as being complimented. Beck believes that maladaptive thought patterns cause a distorted view of oneself and one's world, which in turn may lead to various emotional problems. Thus, the primary goals of cognitive therapy are to identify and change maladaptive thoughts.

**Cognitive techniques.** Beck's approach, which is an example of cognitive therapy, works to change thought patterns, which, in turn, play a critical role in influencing behavior and emotions. In cognitive therapy, clients are told how their maladaptive thoughts and irrational beliefs can result in feelings of depression, anxiety, or other symptoms. Clients are shown how to monitor their thoughts and beliefs, how to recognize maladaptive thought patterns, such as overgeneralization and polarized thinking, and how to substitute rational thought patterns. In the Application section, we'll give several examples of specific techniques for stopping negative thoughts and substituting positive ones.

**EFFECTIVENESS**

Cognitive therapy, which is used by about 8% of therapists, has proved effective in treating a variety of symptoms. For example, it was as effective as various drugs in treating depression, general anxiety, agoraphobia, panic attacks, stopping smoking, and eating disorders, and reducing anger (Beck & Fernandez, 1998; Deffenbacher et al., 2000; Dobson & Khatri, 2000). In some cases, the benefits of cognitive therapy were longer lasting than those of other forms of therapy (Hollon & Beck, 1994).

Increasingly, methods of cognitive therapy are combined with those of the next approach, behavior therapy. The result is a very popular approach called cognitive-behavior therapy. However, before explaining cognitive-behavior therapy, we'll need to discuss behavior therapy, which is our next topic.

Overgeneralization

Polarized thinking

Selective attention

EMOTIONAL PROBLEMS

**Power Study™**

**Check out CD: Module 9**
F. Research Focus: Little Albert
**Check out CD: Module 10**
I. Application: Behavior Modification

## Definition

### What's so important about Little Albert?

The 1950s was the time Carl Rogers developed client-centered therapy and Aaron Beck developed cognitive therapy. Both were motivated to develop new approaches because they had become disillusioned with the techniques and results of the psychoanalytic approach, which they had used in clinical practice.

This was also the time Joseph Wolpe (1958, 1990), a physician in South Africa, became disillusioned with psychoanalysis and developed a new, quicker, and more effective procedure to reduce fear and anxiety.

At the beginning of this module, we told you about Little Albert, who initially wanted to touch and play with a white rat but, after being conditioned, came to fear it (Watson & Rayner, 1920). This demonstration, which occurred in the 1920s, showed that emotional responses could be conditioned. But it was not until the 1950s that a clinician developed a procedure to unlearn emotional responses.

*Through classical conditioning, this pet rat . . .*

In a real sense, Wolpe finished what John Watson had started: Watson had conditioned Little Albert to fear an object, while Wolpe conditioned patients to be less fearful. Wolpe's procedure was the first experimental demonstration of reducing fear through conditioning and gave a real jump-start to the development of behavior therapy (Persons, 1997).

*. . . came to be feared by Little Albert.*

*Behavior therapy,* also called behavior modification, uses the principles of classical and operant conditioning to change disruptive behaviors and improve human functioning. It focuses on changing particular behaviors rather than the underlying mental events or possible unconscious factors.

We'll first give you an example of a behavior therapy session and then describe Wolpe's conditioning procedure to reduce fear.

**Therapy session.** In this session, the therapist is talking to a woman who feels bad because she has great difficulty being assertive.

**Client:** The basic problem is that I have the tendency to let people step all over me. I don't know why, but I just have difficulty in speaking my mind.

**Therapist:** So you find yourself in a number of different situations where you don't respond the way you would really like to and you would like to learn how to behave differently.

**Client:** Yes. But you know, I have tried to handle certain situations differently, but I just don't seem to be able to do so.

**Therapist:** Well, maybe you tried to do too much or didn't quite know the right technique. For example, imagine yourself at the bottom of a staircase, wanting to get to the top. It's too much to ask to get there in one gigantic leap. Perhaps a better way to go about changing your reaction in these situations is to take it one step at a time.

**Client:** That would seem to make sense, but I'm not sure if I see how it could be done.

**Therapist:** Well, there are probably certain situations in which it would be less difficult for you to assert yourself, such as telling your boss that he forgot to pay you for the past four weeks.

**Client:** (*laughing*) I guess in that situation, I would say something. Although I must admit, I would feel uneasy about it.

**Therapist:** But not as uneasy as if you went in and asked him for a raise.

**Client:** No. Certainly not.

**Therapist:** So, the first situation would be low on the staircase, whereas the second would be higher up. If you can learn to handle easier situations, then the more difficult ones would present less of a problem. And the only way you can really learn to change your reactions is through practice.

**Client:** In other words, I really have to go out and actually force myself to speak up more, but taking it a little bit at a time?

**Therapist:** Exactly. And it's easier and safer to run through some of these situations here because you can't really get into trouble if you make a mistake. Once you learn different ways to speak your mind, you can try them out in the real world (adapted from Goldfried & Davison, 1976).

**Behavioral approach.** Notice that the behavior therapist does not encourage the client to free-associate, which is a major technique of psychoanalysis. The behavior therapist does not repeat or reflect what the client says, which is a major technique of client-centered therapy. The behavior therapist does not discuss the client's tendency to automatically think negative thoughts, which is a major technique of cognitive therapy.

Instead, the behavior therapist quickly identifies the specific problem, which is the woman's tendency to be unassertive when she really wants to speak her mind. Next, the behavior therapist will discuss a program for behavioral change that will help this woman learn to behave more assertively.

**Two goals.** Behavior therapy has two goals. The first is to modify undesirable behaviors, using many of the principles of operant conditioning, and teach the client how to perform new behaviors, which for this woman involves learning ways to be more assertive. The second goal of behavior therapy is to help the client meet specific behavioral goals through constant practice and reward. For example, this woman would be asked to practice initiating conversations and stating her opinions, perhaps beginning in the safety of the therapist's office and gradually practicing these new assertive behaviors in the more threatening situations of the real world (Fishman & Franks, 1997).

*Why do I let people walk all over me?*

The next example of behavior therapy illustrates a specific technique that is used to help clients overcome phobias.

## Systematic Desensitization

### CASE STUDY

Jack had developed a phobia of blood that interfered with his plans. He was a high school senior who wanted to be an ambulance driver. But the problem was that he passed out at the sight or discussion of blood. He had been afraid of blood for years and had fainted about 20 times in science and biology classes. He even felt queasy when bloody accidents or operating-room scenes were shown on television. If his supervisor found out about his phobia, Jack might lose his chance to be an ambulance driver. Except for his phobia, Jack was happy at school, rarely became depressed, and was generally easygoing. (Yule & Fernando, 1980).

*Jack's fear of blood interfered with his being an ambulance driver.*

Some therapies for phobias might require years of treatment; for instance, a psychoanalyst would search for unconscious conflicts causing the phobia. In contrast, behavior therapists would take a direct approach to the treatment, requiring 5–30 sessions. The technique used today by behavior therapists is based on the one that Wolpe (1958) developed in the 1950s and is called systematic desensitization.

*Systematic desensitization* is a technique of behavior therapy in which the client is gradually exposed to the feared object while simultaneously practicing relaxation. Desensitization involves three steps: learning to relax; constructing a hierarchy with the least feared situation on the bottom and the most feared situation at the top; and being progressively exposed to the feared situation.

Behavior therapists assume that since Jack's phobia was acquired through a conditioning process, his phobia can be unconditioned by gradually exposing him to the feared object through a process called systematic desensitization.

### 1 Relaxation

Jack, whose phobia was a fear of blood, underwent systematic desensitization, a very effective treatment for phobias (Wolpe & Plaud, 1997). In the first step, Jack learned to relax by practicing progressive relaxation. This method involves tensing and relaxing various muscle groups, beginning with the toes and working up to the head. With this procedure, Jack learned how to put himself into a relaxed state. For most individuals, learning progressive relaxation requires several weeks with at least one 15-minute session every day.

### 2 Stimulus Hierarchy

The second step was for Jack to make a *stimulus hierarchy,* which is a list of feared stimuli, arranged in order from least to most feared. With the help of his therapist, Jack made the stimulus hierarchy shown on the right, which lists various situations associated with blood. A rating of 1 indicates little fear if confronted by this stimulus, while a rating of 7 indicates that he would probably pass out from this stimulus.

**MOST STRESSFUL**
7. Needle drawing blood
6. Finger dripping blood
5. Seeing someone cut
4. Needle entering arm
3. Watching blood on TV
2. Cutting own finger
1. Seeing word "blood"

*Stimulus hierarchy ranks fearful situation from least (1) to most (7).*

### 3 Exposure

Systematic desensitization training means that, after successfully completing steps 1 and 2, Jack was ready for step 3, which was to systematically desensitize himself by exposing himself to the fear stimuli. Desensitization occurs through relaxing while simultaneously imagining the feared stimuli.

Jack put himself into a relaxed state and then imagined the first or least feared item in his hierarchy, seeing the word *blood.* He tried to remain in a relaxed state while vividly imagining the word *blood.* He repeated this procedure until he felt no tension or anxiety in this situation. At this point, he went on to the next item in his hierarchy. Jack repeated the procedure of pairing relaxation with images of each feared item until he reached the last and most feared item.

*A necessary part of therapy is exposure to the feared situation.*

Through the desensitization program described here, Jack's blood phobia was treated in five one-hour sessions. A follow-up five years later indicated that Jack was still free of his blood phobia, had not developed any substitute symptoms, and was training to be an ambulance driver (Yule & Fernando, 1980).

### 4 Exposure: Imagined or In Vivo

Systematic desensitization appears to be most effective if, instead of just imagining the items on the list, which is called *imagined exposure,* clients gradually expose themselves to the actual situation, which is called *in vivo exposure* (the phrase *in vivo* is Latin for "in real life") (Emmelkamp & van Oppen, 1994). For example, in Module 22 we described the case of Kate Premo (right photo), who signed up for a treatment course that used in vivo exposure to treat her lifetime phobia of flying. In her case, a modified systematic desensitization program included in vivo exposure, which meant taking an actual flight while doing the breathing and relaxation exercises that she had learned. The in vivo exposure worked for Premo, who was able to overcome her phobia of flying.

*Kate is being exposed to the actual situation (in vivo) that causes her fear, flying in an airplane.*

Clinicians also found that in vivo exposure was a very effective treatment for about 55% of obsessive-compulsives, who were once viewed as having chronic, incurable problems (Abramowitz, 1997). Thus, systematic desensitization has proved to be a very effective treatment for a variety of anxiety disorders, especially when combined with in vivo exposure (Gould et al., 1997).

The next therapy is actually a combination of behavior and cognitive therapies.

## Cognitive-Behavior Therapy

**Why combine two different therapies?** As psychoanalysis reached its peak of popularity in the 1950s, a number of clinicians and researchers were becoming dissatisfied with its procedures, which were too time-consuming, too costly, and too ineffective, except in treating a very small number of people who had relatively minor psychological problems (Franks, 1994).

At this same time, there was a great increase in the popularity of learning principles that came from Pavlov's work on classical conditioning and Skinner's work on operant conditioning. Researchers and clinicians began to apply these learning principles to change human behavior with methods based on a strong experimental foundation rather than Freud's unverified beliefs about unconscious conflicts. Both behavior and cognitive therapies developed out of dissatisfaction with psychoanalysis and the belief that learning principles would provide more effective methods of changing human behavior than would the concepts of psychoanalysis.

**Combining therapies.** One of the interesting developments in therapy has been occurring since the late 1970s as both behavior and cognitive therapies have become increasingly popular. The major difference between them is that *behavior therapy* focuses on identifying and changing specific behaviors, while *cognitive therapy* focuses on identifying and changing specific maladaptive thought patterns. Beginning in the early 1990s, researchers and clinicians have been combining methods of behavior and cognitive therapies into what is now called cognitive-behavior therapy (K. G. Wilson et al., 1997).

*Cognitive-behavior therapy* combines the cognitive therapy technique of changing negative, unhealthy, or distorted thought patterns with the behavior therapy technique of changing maladaptive or disruptive behaviors by learning and practicing new skills to improve functioning.

I need to stop thinking all those negative thoughts.

Currently, the difference between cognitive therapy and behavior therapy has become blurred as techniques from these two approaches are combined into what is commonly called cognitive-behavior therapy (Dobson & Khatri, 2000).

**Cognitive-behavior approach.** Cognitive-behavior therapists use a number of techniques to change thoughts and behaviors and thus improve functioning. These techniques include monitoring one's own thoughts and behaviors; identifying thoughts and behaviors that need to be changed; setting specific goals that increase in difficulty; learning to reinforce oneself for reaching a goal; imitating or modeling new behaviors; substituting positive for negative thoughts; and doing homework, which involves practicing new behaviors in a safe setting before performing them in the real world (Larkin & Edens, 1994). These cognitive-behavior techniques are the basis for almost all *self-help programs,* which may be completed without the assistance of a therapist. For more serious problems or additional support, the aid and help of a therapist may be needed (Gambrill, 1994; Marks, 1994).

## Kinds of Problems

**Who can be helped?** Throughout this text, we have discussed how behavior therapy, cognitive therapy, and the popular cognitive-behavior therapy have been used to treat the following problems:

■ **Insomnia:** cognitive-behavior program was as effective as drugs in helping people get to sleep (p. 162).

■ **Conditioned nausea:** individuals undergoing chemotherapy developed conditioned nausea and were treated with behavior therapy (p. 207).

■ **Noncompliance in children:** behavior therapy, also called behavior modification, was used to treat young children who refused to eat healthy foods (p. 230).

■ **Autistic children:** behavior modification helped some autistic children develop sufficient academic and social skills to enter public schools and function very well (p. 232).

■ **Psychosomatic problems:** behavior therapy (biofeedback) helped people decrease stress-related symptoms by reducing headaches and physiological arousal (p. 233).

I need to learn assertive behaviors.

■ **Abusive parents:** cognitive-behavior therapy that involved training in social skills helped parents deal with their own personal problems as well as daily difficulties related to caring for demanding children (p. 401).

■ **Stress management:** cognitive-behavior techniques are basic to all programs for reducing stress (p. 502).

■ **Phobias:** various phobias, such as fear of specific situations (flying, public speaking) or objects (snakes, bugs, blood), have been treated with cognitive-behavior techniques (pp. 225, 524, 525).

We'll also discuss several other examples of cognitive-behavior techniques in the upcoming Application section.

**Effectiveness.** Cognitive-behavior therapy is currently being used to treat a wide variety of problems, including eating disorders, marital problems, anxiety and phobias, depression, and sexual dysfunction. Programs based on cognitive-behavior therapy are widely used to help people stop smoking, become more assertive, improve communication and interpersonal skills, manage stress, and learn to control anger. Researchers report that cognitive-behavior therapy was significantly more effective in treating this wide variety of problems than were control procedures (Beck & Fernandez, 1998; Dobson & Khatri, 2000). And in some cases, cognitive-behavior therapy was as effective as drugs in treating some forms of anxiety, phobia, depression, and compulsive behavior (Abramowitz, 1997; Basco et al., 2000; Garety et al., 2000).

After the Concept Review, we'll review and compare the development, techniques, and effectiveness of all the major therapies that we have discussed.

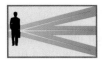

**1.** If you first trained as a physician and then went into a psychiatric residency, which involves additional training in pharmacology, neurology, and psychotherapeutic techniques, you would be a (a)_____. If you completed a Ph.D. program in psychology, including one year of work in a clinical setting, you would be a (b)_____. If you completed a Ph.D. program in psychology or education, including work in a counseling setting, you would be a (c)_____.

**2.** A process characterized by verbal interaction between therapist and client and the development of a supportive relationship, during which a therapist may analyze or suggest ways for the client to deal with and overcome his or her problems, is called _____.

**3.** One approach to therapy is characterized by the idea that we have an unconscious part whose activities and thoughts are hidden behind a mental barrier that we cannot voluntarily remove. Behind this barrier are repressed and psychologically dangerous thoughts that give rise to unconscious conflicts, which, in turn, can result in psychological and physical symptoms. This approach is called _____.

**4.** Freud developed two techniques to uncover unconscious thoughts. One was to encourage clients to talk about any thoughts or images that entered their heads, which is called (a)_____. The second technique was based on the assumption that dreams contain hidden meanings and symbols and the therapist's role was to (b)_____ these dream symbols.

**5.** Freud said that, during therapy, a patient may respond as if the therapist were a father or mother and project strong feelings toward the therapist. This process is called (a)_____. Also during therapy, a patient may be reluctant to work through feelings or to recognize unconscious conflicts and repressed thoughts; this is called (b)_____.

**6.** The second most popular approach to therapy shares many of the features of psychoanalysis—for example, discussing the client's feelings; breaking down the client's defenses and resistances; and interpreting the client's behaviors—but may not necessarily use free association or agree that many problems result from unconscious sexual conflicts. This approach, which takes less time than psychoanalysis, is called _____ psychotherapy.

**7.** One approach to therapy assumes that each person has an actualizing tendency—that is, a tendency to develop his or her full potential. In this approach, the therapist's task is to show compassion and positive regard in helping the client reach his or her potential. This approach was developed by (a)_____ and is called (b)_____ therapy.

**8.** Another approach to therapy assumes that we have automatic negative thoughts that we usually say to ourselves without much notice. By continually repeating these automatic negative thoughts, we color and distort how we perceive and interpret our world and influence how we behave and feel. This approach to therapy was developed by (a)_____ and is called (b)_____ therapy.

**9.** One approach to therapy primarily uses the principles of classical and operant conditioning to change disruptive behaviors and improve human functioning. This approach, which focuses on changing particular behaviors rather than on the underlying mental events or possible unconscious factors, is called _____ therapy.

**10.** One approach combines changing negative, unhealthy, or distorted thoughts and beliefs by substituting positive, healthy, and realistic ones and changing one's undesirable or disruptive behaviors by learning and practicing new skills to improve functioning. This approach, which combines two therapies, is called _____ therapy.

**11.** There is a technique of behavior therapy in which the client is gradually exposed to the feared object while simultaneously practicing relaxation. This technique, which involves three steps—learning to relax; constructing a hierarchy with the least feared situation on the bottom and the most feared situation at the top; and being progressively exposed to the feared situation—is called _____.

**12.** Because of its effectiveness, cognitive-behavior therapy has become the basis for many self-help programs to stop smoking, reduce insomnia, decrease conditioned nausea, help autistic children develop academic and social skills, and reduce intense and irrational fears called _____.

***Answers:*** *1. (a) psychiatrist, (b) clinical psychologist, (c) counseling psychologist; 2. psychotherapy; 3. psychoanalysis; 4. (a) free association, (b) interpret; 5. (a) transference, (b) resistance; 6. psychodynamic; 7. (a) Carl Rogers, (b) client-centered; 8. (a) Aaron Beck, (b) cognitive; 9. behavior; 10. cognitive-behavior; 11. systematic desensitization; 12. phobias*

# E. Review: Evaluation of Approaches

## Assumptions, Methods, and Techniques

**How do they differ?**

We have discussed five different approaches to psychotherapy, including psychoanalysis, client-centered therapy, cognitive therapy, behavior therapy, and the increasingly popular cognitive-behavior therapy. We'll briefly review the different backgrounds, assumptions, and techniques for four of these approaches, and then discuss their effectiveness.

### PSYCHOANALYSIS

**Background.** Psychoanalysis, which was developed by Sigmund Freud in the late 1800s and early 1900s, marked the beginning of psychotherapy. Freud gradually developed his major assumptions from treating patients for a variety of symptoms and problems. Thus, Freud's assumptions are based on case studies rather than on experimental data.

**Basic assumption.** Freud believed that unacceptable or threatening thoughts were repressed and unavailable to conscious recall. Repressed thoughts could produce unconscious conflicts that, in turn, could result in feelings of anxiety and a variety of psychological and emotional problems.

**Techniques.** Freud developed two techniques for uncovering and revealing unconscious thoughts: free association and dream interpretation. Freud was also the first to identify and recognize the importance of transference and resistance during therapy. He believed that patients overcame their problems by bringing up and dealing with underlying unconscious conflicts.

### CLIENT-CENTERED THERAPY

**Background.** In the late 1940s and early 1950s, Carl Rogers became disillusioned with the psychoanalytic role of the therapist as expert and in charge of changing the client. To give the client a greater role in making decisions and changes, he developed his client-centered approach.

**Basic assumption.** Rogers assumed that the client has the capacity to actualize and reach his or her full potential and the client, not the therapist, is responsible for change. He believed that, although the client had the major role in making changes, there were certain characteristics of the therapist that helped the client change.

**Techniques.** The client-centered therapist uses the technique of repeating or reflecting what the client says and thereby showing interest and understanding. Rogers believed that therapists would be effective if they had three characteristics: empathy, positive regard, and genuineness. These characteristics produced a warm and supportive atmosphere in which the client felt comfortable and could better deal with solving his or her problems.

### COGNITIVE THERAPY

**Background.** In the late 1960s and early 1970s, Aaron Beck became dissatisfied with the psychoanalytic assumption that unconscious conflicts were the chief cause of psychological problems. As Beck treated patients, he noticed that they would often repeat a string of negative statements, almost without notice. Beck believed that these automatic, negative self-statements played a major role in emotional problems.

**Basic assumption.** Beck pointed out that our automatic, irrational thoughts and beliefs can color our feelings and actions, distort our perceptions, and result in various psychological and emotional problems. He assumed that these irrational self-statements, such as polarized thinking, needed to be changed.

**Techniques.** The techniques of cognitive therapy include having the client monitor and identify his or her automatic, negative, irrational thoughts and replace them with positive ones. Thus, clients deal with and solve their problems by gradually substituting positive thoughts for distorted self-statements.

### BEHAVIOR THERAPY

**Background.** Developed in the 1950s, behavior therapy was based on principles of learning from classical and operant conditioning. Behavior therapy was a reaction against psychoanalysis, whose emphasis was on unconscious and unobservable conflicts and whose concepts lacked a scientific foundation.

**Basic assumption.** Behavior therapy assumes that just as emotional reactions can be learned or conditioned, so too can they be unlearned using the same principles of learning. Behavior therapy focuses on observable behaviors, while cognitive-behavior therapy also emphasizes changing thought patterns.

**Techniques.** The behavior therapist identifies specific behaviors that need to be changed and provides the client with particular methods for carrying out the changes. Specific behavioral techniques include self-observation, self-reward, modeling, and role playing. For treatment of anxiety, fears, and phobias, systematic desensitization combined with in vivo exposure has proved effective.

Currently, techniques of cognitive and behavior therapies are combined into cognitive-behavior therapy, which has proved effective for a variety of psychological problems and self-help programs.

These four approaches differ in their assumptions and techniques. The interesting question is whether one approach is more effective than another.

## Effectiveness of Psychotherapy

**How helpful is psycho-therapy?**

About 10–15% of the adult population in the United States do seek help and treatment for mental illness from various mental services, such as community mental health centers (Satcher, 2000). However, about half of all individuals who have a serious mental problem do not seek treatment because they want to avoid the stigma that many in our society attach to mental illness (Satcher, 2000). Mental health professionals have tried to erase this stigma by explaining that mental illness is not a character flaw but a real health problem that can often be successfully treated with therapy programs that may involve drug, nondrug, or a combination of therapies (right graph).

For only a small percentage (10–20%) of individuals with psychological problems, simply waiting for the problem to go away will work. However, clinicians do not know how to identify these individuals beforehand and give them the option of waiting. For a very large percentage (80–90%) of individuals with psychological problems, simply waiting is not effective and their problems may either continue or worsen (Eysenck, 1994). For these individuals with psychological problems, professional help is the better choice.

Researchers have analyzed over 1,500 studies that examined the effects of psychotherapy on a variety of problems, such as depression, various kinds of anxieties, family problems, interpersonal difficulties, and eating disorders. Researarchers found that psychotherapy was more effective in relieving a wide variety of psychological and behavioral symptoms than were control procedures such as being on a waiting list to receive therapy or just being in a group that received no systematic treatment. In addition, most improvement occurs in a relatively short period of time, about 25 to 40 sessions (Shadish et al., 2000).

Knowing that psychotherapy is an effective treatment brings us to the second question: Is one kind of psychotherapy more effective than another?

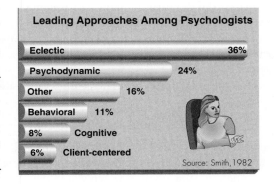

**Leading Approaches Among Psychologists**

| Approach | Percentage |
|---|---|
| Eclectic | 36% |
| Psychodynamic | 24% |
| Other | 16% |
| Behavioral | 11% |
| Cognitive | 8% |
| Client-centered | 6% |

Source: Smith, 1982

## Common Factors

**Is one approach more effective?**

If you lived fifty years ago and needed professional help for a mental illness, your only choice was psychoanalysis, which was very time-consuming and expensive. In contrast, if you need professional help today, you can choose from a number of different therapies (graph above), which are available at a variety of mental health facilities. However, because the current therapy approaches begin with different assumptions and use different methods, you might wonder if one therapy is more effective than another. In answer to this question, researchers have consistently found that there is very little, if any, difference in effectiveness among various therapies (Nathan et al., 2000). However, for a small number of specific disorders, including *panic attacks, phobias, compulsions,* and *depression,* behavior, cognitive, and cognitive-behavior therapies have generally been shown to be more effective than traditional talk therapies, such as the psychodynamic approaches (Dobson & Khatri, 2000).

It may seem surprising that therapies with such different assumptions and techniques have been found to be equally effective. One reason different therapies using different techniques can achieve the same results is that they all share common factors (Arkowitz, 1997).

*Common factors* refer to a basic set of procedures and experiences that different therapies share and that explain why different approaches are equally effective. Common factors include the growth of a supportive and trusting relationship between therapist and client and the development of an accepting atmosphere, in which the client feels willing to admit problems and is motivated to work on changing.

The fact that certain common factors are basic to all approaches explains why different therapies are equally effective and why different techniques can be effectively combined into the most popular form of therapy, the eclectic approach (graph above) (Messer & Wachtel, 1997).

For example, one common factor—development of a warm, trusting, and accepting relationship between client and therapist—has been shown to play a major role in helping clients work out their problems and change their behaviors (Lambert & Bergin, 1994). Since the client–therapist relationship is important in influencing the effectiveness of treatment, researchers suggest that a client select a therapist to whom he or she can relate (Dawes, 1994).

The client-consumer should know that psychotherapy is generally effective and that (except for depression and anxiety disorders, such as phobias and obsessive-compulsive behavior) the particular therapy approach does not matter as much as do common factors.

Common factors may also explain why the next treatment, which seems very strange to Westerners, proved effective.

> I need professional help but I don't know which therapy to choose.

> I found out that many of the therapies are about equally effective.

## Case Study: Young Woman

**What was Putu's problem?**

In Bali, which is a province of Indonesia, as well as in parts of Africa and China, many psychological problems that Western clinicians would diagnose as anxiety, mood disorders, or schizophrenia are believed to be caused by possession by evil spirits (Kua et al., 1993; Straker, 1994). For example, take the case of Putu, a young unmarried woman, who was about 20 years old.

Putu lived with her family in a small village on the beautiful island of Bali. Putu's family had made her break off her loving relationship with one man and become engaged to another, whom she did not want to marry. Since her new engagement, Putu had lost all interest in things around her, ate very little, and did not take part in normal activities or conversation. Putu was taken to the local nurse,

who gave an injection of multivitamins to treat her low energy level and general apathy. The injection did not help and the nurse recommended that the family take Putu to a local witch doctor or healer, who could use special rituals to cure Putu (Connor, 1982).

In Western terminology, clinicians would say that Putu was suffering from depression, which was most certainly brought on by having to break off her loving relationship and being forced by her family to become engaged to someone she did not like. Western therapists would have treated her depression with some form of psychotherapy and, if possible, would have brought the whole family in for therapy. However, in Bali, Putu was believed to be the victim of witchcraft, which could be cured by taking her to a traditional healer, who is called a *balian*.

## Healer's Diagnosis and Treatment

**What is healing smoke?**

The family took the depressed Putu to a well-respected healer or balian, a woman named Jero. Balians, such as Jero, believe their powers come from supernatural forces. The balians often undergo periods of fasting and isolation that induce trances through which the spirits speak to them. Balians are considered special healers who are asked to help individuals with a variety of personal and mental problems (Stephen & Suryani, 2000).

In Putu's case, Jero located a small pulsation beneath Putu's jawbone that indicated the presence of an evil wind spirit. The rejected lover had placed the evil spirit into Putu's body, and there was now a great danger that this evil spirit might travel throughout her body: if it reached Putu's ears, she would go deaf; if it reached her brain, she would become violent and insane. Jero (right photo) said that she would mix special medicine and that the family should return in two days for an exorcism of the evil wind spirit.

As part of the exorcism rites, two small human effigies, a male and a female, were made out of cooked rice and were set on the ground to

You are possessed of an evil wind spirit.

Indonesian healers, called balians, function like Western therapists.

the south of the girl. When the evil spirit was driven out of Putu's body by smoke, the evil spirit would be attracted to the effigies, which would then be broken to destroy the spirit.

In the morning, Jero asked Putu to stand in the middle of healing smoke. After about 40 minutes, the evil wind spirit left Putu's body and entered the small male and female rice figures, which were broken and thrown away. Then Putu's body was purified with holy water. During the course of the afternoon, Putu began to talk, show interest in food and things around her, and generally get over her former apathy.

For two more weeks, Putu stayed with Jero, who continued to perform purification ceremonies and drive away any lingering evil wind spirits. As part of the purification ceremonies, Putu was asked to take part in everyday activities, such as gathering and making food, engaging in normal conversations, washing clothes, and doing other chores. Through this process, Putu was helped and encouraged to resume her normal duties and take part in social activities.

## Healers versus Western Therapists

**Is a balian a therapist?**

The case of Putu shows that the beliefs and treatments used in the traditional healing practices of African and Asian balians or healers are very different from those used by Western therapists to treat psychological problems. But notice that the balian's exorcism rites, purification rituals, and herbal medicines did reduce Putu's depression. In many parts of Asia, China, Africa, and Indonesia, healers use herbal medicines, exorcism, and purification rituals to successfully treat a variety of psychological problems (Kua et al., 1993; Stephen & Suryani, 2000).

There are several explanations of why a balian's potions and rituals are effective treatments for various mental and physical problems. First, studies on Western patients find that about 10–30% of

patients suffering from a variety of psychological and physical problems show remarkable improvement after receiving placebo treatments (Talbot, 2000). The balian's rituals and herbs may function like Western placebos (p. 111), which create positive beliefs and expectations to help individuals recover from a variety of physical and psychological problems. Second, the balian's purification ceremonies involve the development of a close relationship with the sufferer, and this relationship may involve common factors similar to those found effective in Western therapy. Thus, placebos and psychotherapy's common factors may explain the success of balians in treating a variety of mental problems in different cultures.

Next, we'll discuss treatment of one of the more difficult psychological problems, getting over a terrible and traumatic situation.

## Does New Therapy Method Eliminate Traumatic Memories?

**What is EMDR?**

During the past 50 years, there have been literally hundreds of therapies that were claimed to be uniquely effective, were popular for a time, and then disappeared because their claims were not supported (Pitman, 1994). Strong claims have been made for another new therapy, called Eye Movement Desensitization and Reprocessing, or EMDR (Shapiro, 1989, 1991).

*Eye Movement Desensitization and Reprocessing (EMDR) involves focusing on a traumatic memory while visually following the back-and-forth movement*

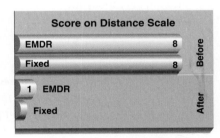

Can watching a hand moving back and forth erase terrible memories?

of a therapist's hand or pen. One memory may trigger another, which the client focuses on while again visually following the back-and-forth movement. This process usually continues for a 90-minute session, during which the traumatic memories are said to be reprocessed by eye movements that help replace traumatic memories with pleasant ones (Shapiro, 1991).

Francine Shapiro discovered EMDR after noticing that her own troubling thoughts had disappeared after being associated with her back-and-forth eye movements. However, for the past 10 years, researchers have hotly debated the claims and effectiveness of EMDR therapy (McNally, 1999).

### Evidence from Case Studies

All of the early support for the effectiveness of EMDR came from testimonials and case studies, many of them as dramatic as the following:

After one individual lost both arms and hearing in a tragic fire and explosion, he experienced terrible flashbacks and nightmares for the next six years. When he finally consulted a psychiatrist, he was desperate and agreed to try the then-new EMDR procedure. During the EMDR procedure, he vividly recalled the fire, the shouts of the employees, and other terrible images, while visually following the back-and-forth movement of the therapist's hand. However, as he continued imagining terrible images and following the therapist's hand movements, he began to feel a flowing sensation of peace. Following a number of sessions, he was reported to be free of flashbacks and nightmares, had taught himself to drive a car, and had joined a group that helps children who need artificial limbs (Wartik, 1994).

Dramatic case studies supported claims that EMDR could erase traumatic flashbacks.

Dramatic cases like this suggested that EMDR was a simple but effective treatment for traumatic memories, one of the most difficult problems therapists face. Shapiro (1991) explained that EMDR somehow functions like the eye movements during rapid eye movement (REM) sleep and may help to unlock and reprocess traumatic memories. However, Shapiro provides no evidence for her neurological interpretation.

Although the effectiveness of EMDR was supported by case studies and testimonials, we must remember that such methods have great potential for error and bias and cannot demonstrate cause and effect. Thus, to evaluate the effectiveness of EMDR, researchers turned to the experimental method.

### Evidence from Experiments

**Method.** The major question is whether eye movements are uniquely effective for the treatment of traumatic memories. To answer this question, researchers who had been trained by Shapiro recruited subjects who satisfied the DSM-IV criteria for experiencing traumatic events. The subjects were randomly divided into three groups, two of which we'll describe here. One group received EMDR treatment, in which subjects recalled traumatic events while their eyes moved back and forth as they tracked the end of a moving pen; another group recalled traumatic events while staring straight ahead at a fixed light. All subjects filled out questionnaires that evaluated their level of distress before and after treatment.

**Results.** As shown in the right graph, subjects who received EMDR treatment showed a significant reduction in distress. However, the treatment that involved fixed staring produced a similar significant reduction in distress. Researchers concluded that the back-and-forth eye movements used in EMDR were not necessary for effective treatment, since fixed staring produced equally good results (Renfrey & Spates, 1994).

**Score on Distance Scale**

| | | Before |
|---|---|---|
| EMDR | 8 | |
| Fixed | 8 | |

| | | After |
|---|---|---|
| 1 | EMDR | |
| | Fixed | |

**Conclusions.** Because the treatments with fixed staring and watching hand movements were equally effective in reducing distress from traumatic memories, researchers suggest that hand movements are not the critical feature in reducing stressful thoughts. Rather, the critical feature in EMDR is what goes along with watching the hand movements: The individual recalls and confronts his or her most feared feelings, images, or situations. Researchers suggest that EMDR is a form of exposure therapy (p. 567), which has been proven very effective for treating fearful thoughts, images, and situations (McNally, 1999).

This Research Focus shows that it usually takes years to verify the claims of case studies and testimonials. For example, it took about 10 years for researchers to show that EMDR is no more effective than cognitive-behavior therapy, that EMDR's hand movements are not critical, that what is critical is having individuals confront their fears (exposure therapy), and that in a 5-year follow-up study, the beneficial effects of EMDR had disappeared, which suggests the need for additional therapy sessions (Macklin et al., 2000).

Next, we'll review several cognitive-behavior techniques that have proven effective in treating a number of relatively common psychological problems.

# H. Application: Cognitive-Behavior Techniques

## Thought Problems

**What's a common problem?**

We have discussed different kinds of therapy approaches for a number of mental disorders. However, there are a variety of psychological or behavioral problems that are not usually considered serious mental disorders but that can be very bothersome and interfere with our functioning normally.

For example, if you happened to do poorly on an exam, were criticized by someone important to you, broke up with someone, got rejected, or had an accident, you often cannot stop replaying and reliving that troublesome scene. At some point a friend may advise, "It's time

*How do I battle crazy thoughts?*

to just stop thinking about that!" Although this is good advice, many of us have discovered that it is very difficult to stop thinking about a troubling event. In fact, trying very hard to not think of something often makes us think about that particular event even more. As it turns out, clinicians have developed a number of very useful cognitive-behavior techniques that can be used to solve a variety of psychological or behavior problems. We'll discuss techniques that can be used to stop recurring and troubling thoughts, to change negative thoughts into positive ones, and to deal with mild insomnia.

## Thought-Stopping Program

**Could you not think about a white bear?**

Researchers asked college students to try very hard to suppress or stop any thoughts having to do with a large white bear. But researchers found that no matter how hard students tried to suppress such thoughts, they had thoughts about a white bear on average once a minute during a 5-minute period (Wenzlaff & Wegner, 2000). These kinds of recurring and unwanted thoughts are called intrusive thoughts.

*Intrusive thoughts* are thoughts that we repeatedly experience, are usually unwanted or disruptive, and are very difficult to stop or eliminate.

Researchers found that just trying to stop thinking about something, called *thought suppression*, is not very effective, especially when the thoughts involve emotional situations. Instead of using thought suppression (trying not to think that thought), which is not effective, researchers suggest using a mental program that either distracts us or helps us change our goals (Wenzlaff & Wegner, 2000). For example, we'll describe a cognitive behavior program to identify and change intrusive thoughts. This program can be carried out on one's own or with the help and support of a therapist.

Here's a real-life example of Carol, who couldn't stop thinking about her former boyfriend, Fred, with whom she had just broken up. No matter how much she tried, she thought about Fred almost every day, and her thinking triggered a chain of other negative thoughts about herself: "I feel that I am a failure. I feel ugly and useless. I keep thinking about not being able to have a relationship. I feel really depressed and I don't want to do anything" (Martin, 1982).

Carol's problem is that she has been unable to stop the intrusive thoughts about Fred, which results in her feeling depressed. An effective cognitive-behavior technique for stopping intrusive thoughts has three steps.

### 1 Self-Monitoring

In all behavior-changing procedures, the first step is *self-monitoring,* which is observing one's own behavior without making any changes. In Carol's case, it meant that for one week she wrote down all depressing thoughts about Fred that lasted for more than a couple of minutes. In addition, the therapist asked Carol to bring in pictures of herself that showed her in pleasurable activities. These pictures would provide cues for thinking rational thoughts.

### 2 Thought Stopping

Each time Carol began to experience a disturbing thought, she would stop what she was doing, clasp her hands, close her eyes, silently yell "Stop!" to herself, and silently count to ten. This was the *thought-stopping procedure.*

### 3 Thought Substitution

After counting silently to ten, she would open her eyes and take five photographs out of her purse. She would look at each photograph and read what she had written on the back. For example, one photograph showed her about to board an airplane for a trip. On the back she had written, "I'm my own boss. My life is ahead of me. I can do what I want to do." Carol would then think about the trip and how much she liked to travel. She would do the same for all five photographs.

*How do I stop thinking of my former boyfriend?*

This *thought-substituting procedure* took 1–2 minutes. After that, she would return to whatever she had been doing.

During Carol's first week of self-monitoring, she thought about Fred constantly and spent from 15 minutes to an hour each day crying. However, after using the thought-stopping and thought-substituting procedures for eight weeks, Carol had reduced the time thinking about Fred to the point that she rarely cried or was depressed. A follow-up interview four months after therapy revealed that Carol was no longer having intrusive thoughts about Fred, was no longer depressed, had developed no new symptoms, and had a new boyfriend (Martin, 1982).

In Carol's case, thought suppression alone (trying not to think that thought) did not stop intrusive thoughts about Fred but a thought-substitution program proved very effective. As you'll see next, thought substitution is a very useful technique for a number of problems, including fear and anxiety.

## Thought Substitution

*How can I change fearful thoughts?*

For many years Rose was trapped in her house by intrusive thoughts that resulted in an intense fear of going out into public places, which is called **agoraphobia**. If she even thought about going outside to do her shopping, she felt pain in her arms and chest, she began to perspire, her heart beat rapidly, and her feet felt like rubber. However, after cognitive-behavior therapy, she overcame her agoraphobia.

As part of the overall therapy program, a cognitive therapist asked Rose a number of questions to identify her irrational thoughts. For example, she may have overgeneralized, thinking, "The last time I went out I was terrified; it's sure to happen again." Or Rose may have engaged in polarized thinking: "All my happiness is right here in this house; nothing outside could give me any pleasure." Her thinking might have been distorted by selective attention, such as remembering all those activities outside the house that terrified her and forgetting all those activities that she had once found pleasurable, such as shopping and going to movies.

Rose was asked to make a list of all her irrational thoughts on one side of a sheet of paper. Then, next to each irrational thought, she was asked to write down a rational response that could be substituted for the irrational one. Here are some examples:

| IRRATIONAL THOUGHTS | RATIONAL THOUGHTS |
|---|---|
| ■ I am much safer if I stay at home. | ■ Rarely has anything bad happened when I have gone out. |
| ■ I feel more protected if I do not have to walk through crowds. | ■ I have never been harmed by a crowd of people. |
| ■ I think something awful will occur if I go to a supermarket. | ■ Thousands of people go to supermarkets and do their shopping unharmed. |
| ■ I can't bear the thought of going to a movie theater. | ■ Many people enjoy going to movies. |

Thought substitute

Like Rose, you can follow the same three steps of the thought-substitution program, which is a very effective technique for changing feelings and behaviors.

**1** Through self-monitoring, write down as many irrational thoughts as possible. If you are in a habit of thinking irrational thoughts, it may require special attention to identify them.

*How do I change my fearful thoughts so I can go out in public?*

**2** Next to the column of irrational thoughts, compose a matching list of rational thoughts. The rational thoughts should be as detailed or specific as possible.

**3** Begin to practice substituting rational thoughts for irrational ones. Each time you make a substitution, give yourself a mental reward for your effort.

One reason therapists give clients homework, such as using thought substitution in daily life, is to encourage clients to practice thinking rationally (Kazantzis et al., 2000). Cognitive-behavior therapists see irrational thoughts and beliefs as the primary causes of emotional and behavioral problems (Stanley & Novy, 2000).

Worrisome, annoying, and irrational thoughts are one of the major causes of insomnia, which can also be treated with a cognitive-behavior program.

## Treatment for Insomnia

*How can I get to sleep?*

Two of the major causes of insomnia are excessive worry and tension. There are several nondrug treatments for insomnia that differ in method, but all have the same goal: to stop the person from excessive worrying and reduce tension. One proven cognitive-behavioral method to reduce insomnia is to establish an optimal sleep pattern (Bootzin & Rider, 1997).

### Establishing an Optimal Sleep Pattern

Cognitive-behavior program for insomnia.

By following the eight steps below, your sleep pattern will become more regular and efficient and help reduce insomnia.

**1.** Go to bed only when you are **sleepy**, not by convention (it's time for bed) or habit.

**2.** Put the **light out** immediately when getting into bed.

**3.** **Do not read or watch television** in bed since these are activities that you do when awake.

**4.** If you are not asleep within **20 minutes,** get out of bed and sit and relax in another room until you are **sleep tired** again. Relaxation can include tensing and relaxing one's muscles or using **visual imagery**, which involves closing one's eyes and concentrating on some calm scene or image for several minutes.

**5.** **Repeat step 4** as often as required, and also if you wake up for any long periods of time.

**6.** **Set the alarm to the same time each morning** so that your time of waking is always the same. This step is very important because oversleeping or sleeping in is one of the primary causes of insomnia the next night.

**7.** **Do not nap during the day** because it will throw off your sleep schedule that night.

**8.** **Follow this program** rigidly for several weeks to establish an efficient and regular pattern of sleep.

**Results.** Nondrug treatment programs, such as the eight-step program described here, were among the most effective programs for significantly decreasing insomnia (Perlis et al., 2000).

We have discussed several cognitive-behavior techniques that can be used on one's own or with the aid of a therapist. These techniques are effective for treating a wide range of mild to severe mental problems (Dobson & Khatri, 2000).

## A. HISTORICAL BACKGROUND

**1.** In the early 1800s, the popular belief that mental patients could be helped to function better by providing humane treatment in a relaxed and decent environment was called (a)_____. In the early 1950s, the first drugs to reduce schizophrenic symptoms were discovered. These drugs, called (b)_____, reduced the effects of the neurotransmitter (c)_____.

**2.** Following the use of phenothiazines, many mental patients were released from mental hospitals and returned to the community to develop more independent and fulfilling lives; this process was called (a)_____. People with mental disorders that do not require hospitalization often seek treatment in (b)_____ centers.

## B. QUESTIONS ABOUT PSYCHOTHERAPY

**3.** If you go to medical school, receive an M.D. degree, and then take a psychiatric residency, you can become a (a)_____. If you go to graduate school in clinical psychology and complete a Ph.D. program, including at least one year of work in a clinical setting, you can become a (b)_____. If you go to graduate school in psychology or education and complete a Ph.D. program, including work in a counseling setting, you can become a (c)_____.

**4.** Therapy in which the therapist and client talk about the client's symptoms and problems with the goal of reaching or identifying the cause of the problem is called (a)_____ therapy. Therapy that involves the application of learning principles and focuses on identifying and changing specific behaviors is called (b)_____ therapy. Therapy that involves the use of various psychoactive drugs, such as tranquilizers and neuroleptics, to treat mental disorders is called (c)_____ therapy.

## C. INSIGHT THERAPIES

**5.** Freud developed one of the first forms of insight therapy, which he called (a)_____. At the core of psychoanalysis is the idea that psychological and physical symptoms arise from (b)_____ that a person cannot voluntarily uncover or recall.

**6.** Freud developed two techniques that he believed provide clues to unconscious thoughts and conflicts: when clients are encouraged to talk about any thoughts or images that enter their heads, this is called (a)_____; when a therapist looks for hidden meanings and symbols in dreams, this is called (b)_____.

**7.** During the course of therapy, a patient will project conflict-ridden emotions onto the therapist; this process is called (a)_____. Working through transference is one of the two essential requirements for improvement in psychoanalysis; the other is that the patient achieves (b)_____ into the causes of his or her problem. A patient's reluctance to work through feelings or recognize unconscious conflicts and repressed thoughts is called (c)_____.

**8.** The second most popular approach to therapy shares many of the features of psychoanalysis—such as discussing the client's feelings and breaking down the client's defenses and resistances—but does not necessarily use free association. This approach, which greatly shortens the therapy time, is called _____ psychotherapy.

**9.** A form of insight therapy developed by Carl Rogers emphasizes our creative and constructive tendencies and the importance of building caring relationships. This is called (a)_____ therapy. One of its basic techniques is to restate or (b)_____ the client's concerns and feelings.

**10.** Rogers believed that the therapist's characteristics foster growth and change. The therapist needs to have the ability to understand what the client is saying and feeling, a trait called (a)_____; the ability to communicate caring, respect, and regard for the client, called (b)_____; and the ability to be real and nondefensive in interactions with the client, called (c)_____.

**11.** Another form of insight therapy is the cognitive therapy developed by Aaron Beck. The basic assumption of Beck's cognitive theory is that our (a)_____ negative thoughts distort how we perceive and interpret things, thus influencing our behaviors and feelings. For example, making blanket judgments about yourself on the basis of a single incident is called (b)_____. Sorting information into one of two categories is (c)_____. Focusing on one detail so much that you do not notice other events is using (d)_____. Beck believes that maladaptive thought patterns cause a distorted view of one's world, which in turn may lead to various emotional problems.

**12.** Cognitive therapy has been shown to have approximately the same effectiveness as do drugs in treating major _____ and has been used effectively to treat other psychological problems.

## D. BEHAVIOR THERAPY

**13.** Therapy that emphasizes treatment of specific behaviors and working toward specific goals without focusing on mental events or underlying unconscious factors is known as _____ therapy. This form of therapy is based on classical and operant conditioning principles.

**14.** A technique of behavior therapy in which the client is gradually exposed to the feared object while simultaneously practicing relaxation is called (a)_____. As part of this technique, the client must prepare a list of feared stimuli, arranged in order from least to most feared; this is called a (b)_____ hierarchy. Another technique is for the client to be gradually exposed to the actual feared or anxiety-producing situation; this is called (c)_____ exposure.

**15.** One form of therapy combines two methods: changing negative thoughts by substituting positive ones; and changing unwanted or disruptive behaviors by learning and practicing new skills to improve functioning. This approach is called _____ therapy.

## E. REVIEW: EVALUATION OF APPROACHES

**16.** Sigmund Freud developed psychoanalysis, whose basic assumption is that emotional problems are caused by underlying (a)_____. Techniques used to uncover unconscious conflicts include (b)_____ and _____.

**17.** Carl Rogers developed (a)_____ therapy, whose basic assumption is that the client is responsible for change and has the capacity to grow and reach his or her full potential. Techniques include (b)_____ the client's concerns; therapists must also show the characteristics of empathy, positive regard, and genuineness.

**18.** Aaron Beck's cognitive theory assumes that automatic, negative, and irrational (a)_____ can color our feelings and actions, distort our perceptions, and result in various problems. Its techniques include recognizing negative thoughts and (b)_____ positive ones.

**19.** An approach to therapy based on learning principles is called (a)_____ therapy, whose basic assumption is that emotional problems are (b)_____ and thus can be unlearned by using learning principles. Its techniques include systematic desensitization, role playing, imitation, and modeling.

**20.** Despite differences in approaches and techniques, the six most popular forms of psychotherapy differ little in (a)_____, except for a small number of disorders, such as phobias, panic attacks, and depression, in which (b)_____ therapy is found more effective. Most improvement in therapy occurs in a relatively short period of (c)_____.

**21.** One reason therapies tend to be equally effective is that they all share _____. For example, the development of a supportive and trusting relationship between therapist and client results in an accepting atmosphere, in which the client feels willing to admit problems and is motivated to work on changing.

## F. CULTURAL DIVERSITY: DIFFERENT HEALER

**22.** In many cases, the healers in Asia and Africa are as effective as Western therapists. One explanation is that these healers may rely on the (a)_____ effect, which is found to produce significant improvement in 10–30% of Western patients. Another is that the healers' ceremonies may involve some of the (b)_____ that underlie the effectiveness of Western therapy.

## G. RESEARCH FOCUS: EMDR—NEW THERAPY

**23.** A number of studies report that Eye Movement Desensitization Reprocessing (EMDR) therapy is an effective method to reduce distress, anxiety, and depression following a (a)_____ experience. However, studies have not shown that (b)_____ movements are necessary or that EMDR is more effective than cognitive-behavior therapies.

## H. APPLICATION: COGNITIVE-BEHAVIOR TECHNIQUES

**24.** Behavior or cognitive-behavior therapy usually involves three steps in changing thought patterns. The first step is observing one's own behavior without making any changes; this is called (a)_____. The second step is to identify those (b)_____ thoughts that need to be changed. The third step is to (c)_____ a positive thought for a negative one. Another step that is sometimes included is to actively stop (d)_____ thoughts.

> Thought substitute

**Answers:** 1. (a) moral therapy, (b) phenothiazines, (c) dopamine; 2. (a) deinstitutionalization, (b) community mental health; 3. (a) psychiatrist, (b) clinical psychologist, (c) counseling psychologist; 4. (a) insight, (b) behavior, (c) medical; 5. (a) psychoanalysis, (b) unconscious conflicts; 6. (a) free association, (b) dream interpretation; 7. (a) transference, (b) insight, (c) resistance; 8. psychodynamic; 9. (a) client-centered, (b) reflect; 10. (a) empathy, (b) positive regard, (c) genuineness; 11. (a) automatic, (b) overgeneralization, (c) polarized thinking, (d) selective attention; 12. depression; 13. behavior; 14. (a) systematic desensitization, (b) stimulus, (c) in vivo; 15. cognitive-behavior; 16. (a) unconscious conflicts, (b) free association, dream interpretation; 17. (a) client-centered, (b) reflecting or restating; 18. (a) thoughts, (b) substituting; 19. (a) behavior, (b) learned; 20. (a) effectiveness, (b) behavior or cognitive-behavior, (c) time; 21. common factors; 22. (a) placebo, (b) common factors; 23. (a) traumatic, (b) eye; 24. (a) self-monitoring, (b) negative or automatic, (c) substitute, (d) intrusive or annoying

# Critical Thinking

## Newspaper Article

## What Is Exorcism?

### Questions

**1.** Besides the United States, what other country did we discuss in which people believe that they can be possessed by evil spirits?

**2.** Do you think exorcism and its related problems are listed in the American Psychiatric Association's official guide to mental disorders, called the DSM-IV-TR?

**3.** Can exorcism be considered a kind of psychotherapy?

A deep growling sound came from Karen, a 42-year-old medical student. The terrible voice said it was a demon who had entered Karen and forced her to have evil sex and would continue to use her as it wanted. An evangelical minister, holding a Bible in one hand, shouted, "Witchcraft, face me! We break every curse! I now call down to you the wrath of God. Go now to the pit!" (Watanabe, 2000, p. A1). Immediately Karen's contorted face relaxed and she called out thanks to Jesus. Later, Karen said her demons were "completely gone." What Karen experienced is called exorcism, which is a ritual for banishing evil demons or devils that are believed to have entered and caused a person to experience or perform terrible or sinful behaviors.

Fordham University Associate Professor Michael W. Cuneo, author of a book on exorcism, believes that recent interest in exorcism can be traced partly to the very popular movie *The Exorcist*, which first appeared in 1973 and was re-released in 2000, and to the appearance of exorcists on many popular TV talk shows and the Internet. Currently, there are about 600 charismatic and evangelical Protestant ministries devoted to exorcism. The Roman Catholic Church has increased the number of exorcists in the United States from one in 1990 to about 15–20 today.

Along with exorcism's rise in popularity has come a heated debate over whether a person's problems come from possession by devils and whether these problems can be erased through exorcism. The Catholic Church allows exorcism only after all physical and psychological causes for the person's problems have been ruled out. In other ministries, a variety of personal and social behaviors may be taken as evidence of possession by devils. For example, Karen (described above) underwent exorcism because she had apparently been forced (by the demon) to engage in evil sex.

Albert Landry, a lay pastor at the Harvest Rock Church (Pasadena, CA), looks at whether the possessed person had traumatic childhood experiences, which he believes can create Satan's strongholds and cause anger, bitterness, and lack of forgiveness. Landry explains that initially when devils were cast out, they returned and caused more problems. Now, he combines exorcism with counseling to get at the root of the person's problems.

In some cases, exorcisms are performed out of spiritual compassion to help troubled individuals, while in other cases, there have been reports of beatings and in one case death. "And experts say the psychological dangers of what some see as playing with people's minds and telling them they are possessed can be great" (Watanabe, 2000, p. A16). (Adapted from Watanabe, 2000)

**4.** In what ways do Landry and Freud give similar explanations of what causes mental illness?

**5.** What big problem can result from telling people that their mental problems are caused by demons?

*Try InfoTrac to search for terms:* **demonic possession; exorcism.**

---

### Suggested answers to Newspaper Article questions

1. Earlier (p. 546) we explained that about 45% of the married women in Northern Sudan complain of being possessed by spirits that can make the women do and think strange things.
2. The American Psychiatric Association's official guide to mental disorders (DSM-IV-TR) (p. 514) does not list exorcism as a mental disorder. However, the DSM-IV-TR has an appendix that discusses a variety of mental illnesses that are found in particular cultures. For example, members of some American Indian tribes report ghost sickness, which includes various psychological problems such as hallucinations, fear, anxiety, and confusion.
3. Besides the three or four major therapy approaches discussed in this module, there are hundreds of other kinds of psychotherapy. Almost any approach, even exorcism, could be called a therapy, since exorcism is a ritual that is reported to treat mental illnesses.

However, unlike many exorcists, mental health professionals first do a careful evaluation of the client's problems and only then develop a program for therapy. In addition, mental health professionals use therapy approaches whose effectiveness has been investigated and evaluated through systematic research.

4. Both Landry and Freud suggest that early traumatic childhood experiences can make a lasting impact and contribute to the future development of mental health problems. However, the similarity ends when Landry talks of "Satan's strongholds."
5. Telling people that their mental problems are caused by devil possession may create a self-fulfilling prophecy (p. 30) in which the person not only believes the prophecy ("I'm possessed by devils") but then acts to fulfill the prophecy by developing a variety of undesirable symptoms for which they take no responsibility.

# Links to Learning

## Web Sites

● WADSWORTH ONLINE
STUDY CENTER
**http://psychology.wadsworth.com**
Quizzes, learning activities and exercises, a discussion forum, and hot links to Internet sites related to therapies, including:

● THE CBT WEB SITE
**http://www.cognitivetherapy.com/index.html**
Cognitive-behavior therapy for emotional and behavioral problems is well represented at this site, which includes detailed explanations of the approach, including its historic origins (the Greek philosopher Epictitus and Siddhartha Guatama—Buddha—are viewed as original practitioners), length of treatment and medication issues, how to find a therapist, and links to numerous resources.

● JOURNAL OF PSYCHOTHERAPY PRACTICE
AND RESEARCH
**http://jppr.psychiatryonline.org/**
The online journal of the "American Psychiatric Association "presents original research and clinical reports related to psychotherapy research and education, cognitive and behavioral treatment of selected disorders, integration of multiple treatment modalities, and descriptions of new techniques and educational methodologies."

● ORGANIZATION OF AFRICAN TRADITIONAL
HEALERS (OATH)
**http://www.mamiwata.com/OATH.html**
"OATH is . . . committed to the positive promotion of African Traditional Religions, and the legitimization of practitioners of ATRs." A fascinating site.

## Learning Activities

● *POWERSTUDY*™ BY ROD PLOTNIK & TOM DOYLE

**PowerStudy™**

**Check out CD: Module 24**
CD 1.I: Application: Behavior Modification; book page 566
CD 9.F: Research Focus: Little Albert; book pages 555, 566
CD 9.H: Application: Conditioned Fear and Nausea; book page 567
CD 11.D: Long-Term Memory: Storing; book page 563

● *STUDY GUIDE TO ACCOMPANY INTRODUCTION TO PSYCHOLOGY, 6TH EDITION,* **by Matthew Enos**
In Module 24, consider advice to take courses outside your major; learn how modern psychotherapy originated from Freud's interpretation of dreams; and sort out the three main versions of insight therapy.

● *WEBTUTOR*
**http://webtutor.thomsonlearning.com**
WebTUTOR Visit this site for interactive versions of the Study Guide features. Take a quiz, get your score—should you study a topic some more, or can you move on? For example, can you explain eye movement desensitization and reprocessing? Can you defend the statement that psychotherapy is the witchcraft of the modern world?

● *INFOTRAC ONLINE LIBRARY*
**http://www.infotrac-college.com**

Use your password and then key in search terms such as those below to find popular and scientific articles on subjects covered in Module 24. Make the library work for you!

Meta-analysis        Clinical psychology        Moral therapy
Behavior therapy     Community mental health centers

● *PSYCHNOW!*
CD for Macintosh and Windows includes a study guide, glossary, Web sites, and animations. For Module 24, see:  • Major Psychological Therapies

## Study Questions

*Use InfoTrac to search for topics mentioned in the main heads below (e.g., psychotherapy, behavior therapy, EMDR).*

*A. **Historical Background**—Should our major cities spend more money to develop care and treatment programs for the homeless? (**Suggested answer p. 635**)
B. **Questions about Psychotherapy**—Suppose your friend or loved one has a relatively serious psychological problem. Should you suggest that he or she get professional help?
C. **Insight Therapies**—Several computer programs have been written to "do psychotherapy." Could a computer program be written to "do psychoanalysis"?
*D. **Behavior Therapy**—Susan complains of having terrible test anxiety. What would a behavior therapist do to help her? (**Suggested answer p. 636**)

E. **Review: Evaluation of Approaches**—Janice has a phobia of going out in public. Which approach would be most effective for treating her problem?
F. **Cultural Diversity: Different Healer**—If a Westerner believed that he or she was possessed by the devil, would therapy or an exorcism ritual be the more effective treatment?
G. **Research Focus: EMDR—New Therapy**—Why do you think that people are often more convinced by dramatic case studies than by sound experimental evidence?
*H. **Application: Cognitive-Behavior Techniques**—Frank has very little self-confidence and self-esteem. What is one way that he could work on raising them? (**Suggested answer p. 636**)

*These questions are answered in Appendix B.

# Module 25: Social Psychology

**A. Perceiving Others**      **582**
* PERSON PERCEPTION
* PHYSICAL APPEARANCE
* STEREOTYPES
* SCHEMAS

**B. Attributions**      **585**
* DEFINITION
* INTERNAL VERSUS EXTERNAL
* KELLEY'S MODEL OF COVARIATION
* BIASES AND ERRORS

**C. Research Focus:
Attributions & Grades**      **587**
* CAN CHANGING ATTRIBUTIONS CHANGE GRADES?

**D. Attitudes**      **588**
* DEFINITION
* COMPONENTS OF ATTITUDES
* FUNCTIONS OF ATTITUDES
* ATTITUDE CHANGE
* PERSUASION

**E. Social & Group Influences**      **592**
* CONFORMITY
* COMPLIANCE
* OBEDIENCE
* HELPING: PROSOCIAL BEHAVIOR
* WHY PEOPLE HELP
* GROUP DYNAMICS
* BEHAVIOR IN CROWDS
* GROUP DECISIONS

**Concept Review**      **599**

**F. Aggression**      **600**
* DEFINITION
* BIOLOGICAL FACTORS
* SOCIAL COGNITIVE AND PERSONALITY FACTORS
* ENVIRONMENTAL FACTORS
* SEXUAL HARASSMENT AND AGGRESSION

**G. Cultural Diversity: National
Attitudes & Behaviors**      **603**
* NIGER: BEAUTY IDEAL
* JAPAN: ORGAN TRANSPLANTS
* EGYPT: WOMEN'S RIGHTS

**H. Application:
Controlling Aggression**      **604**
* CASE STUDY
* CONTROLLING AGGRESSION IN CHILDREN
* CONTROLLING ANGER IN ADULTS
* CONTROLLING SEXUAL AGGRESSION

**Summary Test**      **606**

**Critical Thinking**      **608**
* TEEN PREGNANCIES FORCE TOWN TO GROW UP

**Links to Learning**      **609**

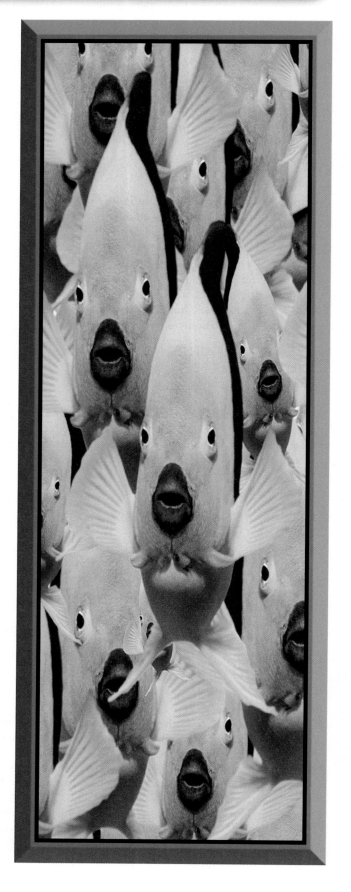

## Stereotypes

**Why did he take a $90,000 pay cut?**

Lawrence Graham wanted to get a job at a country club and had phoned numerous clubs to set up personal interviews. Here's what happened when he arrived for one of his interviews.

"We don't have any job openings—and if you don't leave the building, I will have to call security," the receptionist said at the first club Graham visited.

"But I just spoke to Donna, your dining manager, and she said to come by and discuss the waiter job."

"Sorry, but there are no jobs and no one here named Donna" (Graham, 1995, p. 4).

Graham finally got two job offers and decided on the exclusive Greenwich Country Club. This club had been in existence for 100 years and was *the* country club in the very affluent, prestigious, and White town of Greenwich, Connecticut. The club's members included a former president, a number of high-ranking government officials, and dozens of *Fortune* 500 executives, bankers, and Wall Street lawyers.

A posh country club would offer Graham only the job of a busboy.

Although Graham wanted a job as a waiter, he was hired to be a busboy. Except when one of the members wanted something and deliberately looked for him, Graham's job as a busboy made him quite invisible and able to overhear members' conversations.

"Here, busboy. Here, busboy," a woman called out. "Busboy, my coffee is cold. Give me a refill."

"Certainly, I would be happy to," said Graham.

Before he returned to the kitchen, Graham heard the woman say to her companion, "My goodness. Did you hear that? That busboy has diction like an educated White person" (Graham, 1995, p. 12).

In real life, Lawrence Graham is a Harvard Law School graduate, has a job as an associate in a New York law firm, and makes $105,000 a year. Although he is ready to move up the social ladder, Graham, who is African American, received no invitations to join a country club, as his White associates did. So to find out what goes on in country clubs that do not admit African Americans, he got in the only way he could, as a busboy making $7 an hour.

Graham's example points out how people often make judgments about others on the basis of physical appearance and accompanying stereotypes, which are both major topics of social psychology.

*Social psychology* is a broad field whose goals are to understand and explain how our thoughts, feelings, perceptions, and behaviors are influenced by the presence of, or interactions with, others.

One relatively new, rapidly growing, and important subarea of social psychology is social cognition.

*Social cognition* is a subarea of social psychology that focuses on cognitive processes—for example, how we perceive, store, and retrieve information about social interactions and events. It rose to prominence in the 1980s (Hamilton et al., 1994).

Social psychologists study how we form impressions and perceive others, how we form attitudes and stereotypes, how we evaluate social interactions, and why racism exists—all of which are involved in Lawrence Graham's story.

Another major topic of social psychology is how people behave in groups.

## Behavior in Groups

**Why did they follow him to their deaths?**

David Koresh, a 34-year-old high school dropout, rock musician, polygamist, and preacher, built his church on a simple message: "If the Bible is true, then I'm Christ." This message drew more than a hundred people to join him at an armed fortress near Waco, Texas, where they waited for the end of the world.

Koresh's followers would do anything for him. For example, he taught that all the women in the world belonged to him. At one point, Koresh had 18 "wives"; some were only 12 years old. One of the young girls said, "You're going to marry this guy and he's God, and someday he will be resurrected as a perfect human being." Koresh fathered numerous children.

Koresh laid down strict rules for his followers. They were not allowed beer, meat, air conditioning, or MTV, had to turn over all their money and possessions to him, and were not allowed to marry. Sometimes Koresh enforced his rules with beatings and other punishment.

Agents of the Bureau of Alcohol, Tobacco, and Firearms became concerned about Koresh's

As group leader, Koresh had 18 "wives" but forbade his followers to marry.

increasing stash of weapons. After negotiations failed, they fired tear gas into the Koresh compound. A fire started. Fueled by kerosene in the compound and 30-mile-an-hour winds, the fire swept through the buildings. After the fire was put out, agents sifted through the burned rubble and found the bodies of Koresh and 85 other adults and children (Gibbs, 1993b; Kantrowitz et al., 1993). Why 85 adults and children stayed with Koresh and burned to death is one of the topics we'll discuss when we examine behavior in groups.

## What's Coming

We'll discuss how we perceive people, how we explain the causes of our behaviors, why we develop attitudes, and how we respond to persuasion. We'll also explore a variety of social influences and group behaviors, such as how we respond to group pressures, what motivates us to help others, and why we are aggressive.

We'll begin with Graham's story, which raises the question of how we form impressions of others.

### Person Perception

**How do you form first impressions?**

As you compare the photo of Lawrence Graham on the left with that on the right, notice that your first impressions automatically change. In the left photo, your first impression is that Graham is a busboy or waiter. In the right photo, your first impression is that Graham is a confident businessman or professional. Your first impressions were formed in seconds, required little conscious deliberation, and were biased or distorted by your past experiences. For instance, if you were once a busperson, you might feel sympathetic toward Graham. This example illustrates some of the different factors that go into person perception.

When interviewing for jobs at posh country clubs, Graham was offered only a job as busperson.

Graham did not reveal that he was actually a graduate of Harvard Law School.

*Person perception* refers to the process by which we form impressions of, and make judgments about, the traits and characteristics of others.

As you looked at each photo of Graham and formed a first impression, four things were simultaneously influencing your judgment (Wyer & Lambert, 1994).

**1 Physical appearance.** Your initial impressions and judgments of Graham are heavily influenced and biased by physical appearance. When Graham is dressed as a busboy he makes a very different impression than when he is dressed as a professional.

**2 Need to explain.** You don't just look at or observe Graham, but rather you try to explain why he looks, dresses, or behaves in a certain way. You might explain that Graham-as-busboy is working his way through college, while Graham-as-professional is starting his career.

**3 Influence on behavior.** Your first impressions of Graham will influence how you would interact with him. For example, if your first impression of Graham is as a $7-an-hour busboy, you would interact very differently than if your impression of him was as a $100,000-a-year professional working for a large corporation.

**4 Effects of race.** Researchers have found that members of one race generally recognize faces of their own race more accurately than faces of other races (Ng & Lindsay, 1994). This means that we may perceive faces that are racially different from our own in a biased or distorted way because they do not appear as distinctly as faces from our own race. For this reason, your first impressions of Graham will depend on your race and racial attitudes.

Researchers report that first impressions, which usually occur automatically, function to influence or bias future social interactions in a positive or negative direction (Hassin & Trope, 2000). One factor that plays a major role in person perception, especially forming first impressions, is physical attractiveness.

### Physical Appearance

**What makes a face attractive?**

When looking at a someone's face, you automatically and usually without thinking rate its attractiveness. For example, rate the attractiveness of pop singer Britney Spears (left photo) and the mystery face (right photo). To determine what makes a face attractive, researchers created faces by combining and averaging physical features (mouth, eyes, nose, etc.) taken from different faces. They found that a face created by averaging features from 32 faces was judged as more attractive than a face created by averaging features from 16 or fewer faces (Langlois et al., 1994). In support of the idea that a beautiful face results from averaging facial features, look at the face on the far right. This very attractive face is not a real person but was actually created by averaging thousands of faces (Johnston, 2000).

Is Britney more or less attractive . . .

. . . than this person (identified in text)?

Unlike what many believe, researchers found that both within and across cultures there is a strong agreement (correlation about 0.90) among Whites, African Americans, Asians, and Hispanics about which faces of adults and children are and are not attractive (Langlois et al., 2000). Evolutionary psychologists suggest that the seemingly "built-in" ability of people across cultures to agree on attrac-

tiveness is due to signs of being fit, healthy, and a potentially good mate (Langlois et al., 2000). Social psychologists have studied the effects of facial attractiveness on how we feel, think, and behave in social interactions. For example, a widely cited early conclusion from research on physical attractiveness is the phrase "What is beautiful is good" (Dion et al., 1972). This phrase means that physically attractive people were found to create more favorable impressions than did less attractive people. That is, physically attractive people are considered to be more responsive, interesting, sociable, intelligent, kind, outgoing, and likely to be recommended for job promotions (Kalick et al., 1998).

Besides an attractive face, certain *psychological characteristics* make a person more or less attractive. For instance, women rated men as more physically and sexually attractive if they were also willing to be helpful and considerate of others (Jensen-Campbell et al., 1995). Thus, physical appearance plays an important role in creating positive first impressions but whether those first impressions are confirmed depends on psychological factors that come to light in longer relationships.

One reason first impressions occur quickly and automatically is that we often form them based on already formed stereotypes.

# Stereotypes

**What could bias medical treatment?**

On the right are photos of actors who played the roles of patients complaining of chest pains. While describing their symptoms, the actor-patients were videotaped. These videotapes were shown to over 700 physicians who were asked to recommend appropriate treatments. Because the actor-patients all described the same physical symptoms, all the physicians should have generally recommended the same treatments. However, researchers found that physicians recommended different treatments that depended on the physicians' particular sexual and racial stereotypes (Schulman et al., 1999).

*Stereotypes* are widely held beliefs that people have certain traits because they belong to a particular group. Stereotypes are often inaccurate and frequently portray the members

Which of these individuals received the best treatment for heart problems?

of less powerful, less controlling groups more negatively than members of more powerful or controlling groups.

Stereotypes played an important role in the study we just described. Researchers found that, although all the actor-patients reported the same physical symptoms and should have received about the same kinds of treatment, physicians were 40% less likely to recommend sophisticated medical tests for women and African Americans compared to White men (Schulman et al., 1999).

This study clearly demonstrates that racial and sexual stereotypes (with or without awareness) biased the physicians' perceptions and in turn their professional medical judgments. As you'll see next, one of the problems with negative stereotypes is that once formed, they are difficult to change.

## Development of Stereotypes

Psychologists believe that we develop stereotypes when parents, peers, coworkers, teachers, and others reward us with social approval for holding certain attitudes and beliefs. There are also cultural pressures to adopt certain values and beliefs about members of different groups. For example, in the weight-conscious culture of the United States, there is an emphasis on being thin (Module 15), so we might expect a negative stereotype to apply to women who are overweight (Sands et al., 1997).

To test this idea, researchers asked subjects to watch videotapes of job applicants and decide if they would hire them. The applicants were professional male and female actors made up to appear normal weight or overweight (about 28–35 pounds heavier). When asked to make hiring decisions, subjects showed a significant bias against hiring overweight applicants, especially overweight women (Pingitore et al., 1994). This bias against hiring overweight women is an example of a negative stereotype, which is often accompanied by prejudice and discrimination.

*Prejudice* refers to an unfair, biased, or intolerant attitude toward another group of people.

An example of prejudice is believing that overweight women are not as intelligent, competent, or capable as women of normal weight.

*Discrimination* refers to specific unfair behaviors exhibited toward members of a group.

An employer's bias against hiring overweight applicants would be an example of discrimination.

The history of the United States provides many examples of racist and sexist cultural stereotypes, such as beliefs that women are not smart enough to vote and that African Americans are inferior to Whites (Swim et al., 1995). When we apply stereotypes to all members of a different group from our own, we usually use extreme stereotypes (they're all smart, dumb, lazy, hardworking), which can be either positive or negative. One reason we frequently use stereotypes to make judgments about people is that stereotypes save us thinking time.

*Why do you think I wasn't hired?*

## Functions of Stereotypes

Social cognitive psychologists suggest that, just as we have developed physical tools, such as hammers and saws, to help us build things more efficiently, we have also developed cognitive tools, such as stereotypes, to help us think and make decisions more efficiently. For example, instead of having to analyze in detail the person in the right photo, you can simply assign the person to a social group, such as teenage-punker, and use the information that you have stored in that stereotype. A stereotype for teenage-punker might include: disregards standard social customs and fashions, is independent, dislikes authority, goes to rave parties, experiments with drugs, and so on. From this example, you can see that stereotypes are used frequently because they serve at least two major functions (Macrae et al., 1994).

*Why don't adults like me?*

**Source of information.** A stereotype is like an information file stored in your brain. As soon as you assign someone to a stereotype, you mentally open that file and use the stored information to make judgments.

**Thought-saving device.** Stereotypes are ways to conserve time and energy when making decisions in social situations. By using stereotypes, you make quick (and sometimes inaccurate) decisions and thus save time and energy by not having to analyze an overwhelming amount of personal and social information.

However, a major problem with stereotypes is that they are, once formed, very difficult to change (Hewstone & Hamberger, 2000). One reason we don't easily change stereotypes is that we are often unaware of using them. Another reason we hold on to stereotypes is that we usually dismiss information that does not fit our stereotypes (Greenwald & Banaji, 1995). This means that biased stereotypes live on and on and lead to inaccurate judgments and decisions.

Some social psychologists describe stereotypes as representing hundreds of information files or categories, called schemas, that influence what we see and think.

**A.** *PERCEIVING OTHERS*    583

## Schemas

**How are schemas like social filters?**

In 1975, Fran Conley reached her goal of becoming a board-certified neuro-surgeon. At the time, she was one of only two female board-certified neuro-surgeons in the United States. Yet despite her exceptional accomplishments, Dr. Conley has had to put up with sexist attitudes from male colleagues. For example, as a young neurosurgeon, she was repeatedly propositioned by fellow doctors in front of others, primar-ily for effect. Dr. Conley admits that she tolerated this kind of behavior because she wanted to advance in her profession and be accepted by her colleagues. However, even after Dr. Conley had achieved the status of a full professor at Stanford Medical Center (right photo), the sex-ism continued. For instance, whenever Dr. Conley disagreed with male colleagues, they would jokingly attribute her lack of agreement to a difficult menstrual period. But disagreements between male colleagues were viewed as honest differences of opinion (Manning, 1998). One reason male colleagues

**Why did fellow neurosurgeons show her less respect?**

responded to Dr. Conley in sexist ways is that they had developed mental categories, called schemas, about women that were biased.

*Schemas* are mental categories that, like computer files, contain knowledge about people, events, and concepts. Because schemas affect what we attend to and how we interpret things, schemas can influence, bias, and distort our thoughts, perceptions, and social behaviors.

The social relationships between Dr. Conley and her male colleagues show how schemas, in this case sexist, served at least three functions (Higgins, 2000).

**Functions.** Schemas provided male colleagues with *information* about social stimuli, such as because Dr. Conley was a woman, she was inferior and less intelligent than men. Schemas influenced what male colleagues would pay *attention* to, such as noticing when Dr. Conley disagreed with a male colleague. Schemas influenced how some male colleagues *responded* to women, such as making sexual advances to Dr. Conley. Thus, schemas are important in social relationships because schemas contain files of information that influ-ence our thoughts, behaviors, and feelings toward others (Higgins, 2000).

### Kinds of Schemas

Schemas are part of *social cognition*, which studies how and what people learn about social relationships. Schemas, which are like hundreds of different infor-mation files in your brain, are generally divided into four types: person, role, event, and self schemas.

*Person schemas* include our judgments about the traits that we and others possess.

For example, when meeting someone new, we may rely on person schemas to provide general informa-tion about that person. Person schemas that contain general information about people who have member-ship in groups are *stereotypes*.

*Role schemas* are based on the jobs people perform or the social positions they hold.

The reason you often ask "What do you do?" is so you can use your role schemas to provide any missing information about the person and provide men-tal shortcuts about what you might say or how you might act in social situations.

*Event schemas,* also called scripts, contain behaviors that we associate with familiar activities, events, or procedures.

The event schema for graduation is to celebrate getting your degree. In contrast, the event schema for a college class is to be silent, pay attention, and take notes. Event schemas help us know what to expect and provide guide-lines on how to behave in different kinds of situations.

*Self schemas* contain personal information about ourselves, and this information influences, modifies, and distorts what we perceive and remember and how we behave.

What's interesting about our self schemas is that they overemphasize our good points, which explains why being criticized in public easily hurts our feelings.

We especially look for information or feedback to support our schemas and tend to disregard information that doesn't. For this reason, once schemas are formed, they are difficult to change (Macrae & Bodenhausen, 2000).

Person schema has information on how to act with a new date.

Event schema has information on how to act at graduation.

### Advantages and Disadvantages

There are two *disadvantages* of schemas. The first is that schemas may *restrict, bias,* or *distort* what we attend to and remember and thus cause us to over-look important information (Devine et al., 1994). For example, if your self schema is that of being a good student, you may not pay atten-tion to suggestions from parents, teachers, or friends that may make you a better student.

The second disadvantage of schemas is that they are highly *resistant to change* because we gen-erally select and attend to informa-tion that supports our schemas and deny any information that is in-consistent with them (Macrae & Bodenhausen, 2000). For example, you might pay attention to positive written comments on a class paper and reject any constructive suggestions about ways to improve your writing skills.

Your person schema may cause you to reject valid criticisms of your work.

Schemas have several *advantages.* For example, if someone says "I'm a freshman," you use your "fresh-man schema," which contains *information* about how freshmen think and behave, to help you analyze and respond appropriately in this particular social sit-uation. Schemas also provide *guidelines* for how to behave in various social events (event schemas) and help us explain the social behavior of others (role schemas) (Higgins, 2000). Explaining social behav-ior is one of the most intriguing areas of social cogni-tion, and it's our next topic.

### Definition

**What is unusual about this umpire?**

After 13 seasons and 2,000 games in the minor leagues, this umpire was passed over for promotion to the major leagues and released. An evaluation report by the Office for Umpire Development claimed that this umpire's work had "deteriorated in areas of enthusiasm and execution," even though earlier in the season the rating had been "better than average." What is unusual about this umpire is that she is a woman. Pam Postema (right photo) claims the reason she was passed over for promotion and released was that she was a woman and there are no female

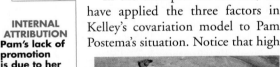

Because I'm a woman, I wasn't promoted.

umpires in major league baseball. She filed a sex discrimination suit because, as Pam says, "Baseball wasn't ready for a woman umpire no matter how good she was" (Reed & Stambler, 1992).

Most sports fans would have an explanation as to why Pam Postema was not promoted to be an umpire in major league baseball. These kinds of explanations are called attributions.

*Attributions* are things we point to as the causes of events, other people's behaviors, and our own behaviors.

If you had to explain why there are no female umpires in major league baseball, you would choose between internal and external attributions.

### Internal versus External

A famous social psychologist, Fritz Heider (1958), believed that we all function to some extent like social psychologists as we try to explain everyday behaviors. Heider was the first to distinguish between internal and external causes or attributions for behaviors.

*Internal attributions* are explanations of behavior based on the internal characteristics or dispositions of the person performing the behavior. They are sometimes referred to as dispositional attributions.

For example, if you used internal attributions to explain why Postema was not made a major league umpire, you would point to her personal characteristics or dispositions, such as saying that she was not a good judge of balls and strikes.

*External attributions* are explanations of behavior based on the external circumstances or situations. They are sometimes called situational attributions.

If you used external attributions to explain why Postema was not promoted, you would point to external circumstances, such as saying that major league baseball is run by men, and they do not want to have a woman umpire.

Thus, making internal or external attributions has important implications for personal and social behaviors (Weiner & Graham, 1999). For example, if you use internal attributions, you would say that Postema does not have the skill or talent to be a major league umpire. If you use external attributions, you would say that, although she has the skills, the league discriminated against her because she is a woman. How people make the distinction between internal and external attributions is a rather complicated process.

### Kelley's Model of Covariation

How do we decide whether Pam was passed over for promotion because of dispositional or situational factors? To answer this question, social psychologist Harold Kelley (1967) developed the covariation model.

The *covariation model,* developed by Harold Kelley, says that, in making attributions, we should look for factors that are present when the behavior occurs and factors that are absent when the behavior does not occur.

Kelley proposed that, in explaining someone's behavior, we should look for information about three factors: consensus, consistency, and distinctiveness.

*Consensus* means determining whether other people engage in the same behavior in the same situation.

*Consistency* means determining whether the person engages in this behavior every time he or she is in a particular situation.

*Distinctiveness* means determining how differently the person behaves in one situation when compared to other situations.

In the examples on the left, we have applied the three factors in Kelley's covariation model to Pam Postema's situation. Notice that high

**1. HIGH CONSISTENCY**
Pam performs about the same every time.

**2. LOW DISTINCTIVENESS**
Pam makes good decisions in calling strikes but not in calling base runners out.

**3. LOW CONSENSUS**
Pam does not show the same skills as other umpires.

**INTERNAL ATTRIBUTION**
Pam's lack of promotion is due to her poor umpiring skills.

**1. HIGH CONSISTENCY**
Pam performs about the same every time.

**2. HIGH DISTINCTIVENESS**
Pam makes good decisions in all aspects of the game.

**3. HIGH CONSENSUS**
Pam shows the same skills as other umpires.

**EXTERNAL ATTRIBUTION**
Pam's lack of promotion is due to discrimination by the league.

How do you decide if internal or external attributions apply to Pam?

consistency, low distinctiveness, and low consensus result in an internal, or dispositional, attribution (fired because she's a poor umpire). But high consistency, high distinctiveness, and high consensus result in an external or situational attribution (fired because of sexual discrimination). Thus, Kelley's covariation model helps us determine if Postema's firing was due to internal or external attributions (Smith, 1994). However, if we don't follow Kelley's model, which demands considerable time and effort, we make errors in attributing causes. We'll discuss three major errors in making attributions, that is, in deciding what caused what.

### Biases and Errors

**Can we make the wrong attributions?**

Most people have heard the phrase *glass ceiling*, which refers to a real but invisible barrier that keeps women and people of color from reaching the top positions in a business or organization. Evidence that there is a very thick glass ceiling came from a survey of *Fortune* magazine's top 1,000 companies. In these companies, 97% of the senior managers were White and 95% were male (Michaelson, 1995). One person who is trying to break the glass ceiling is Mary Contreras-Sweet (right photo), who was born in Guadalajara, Mexico, and now lives in Los Angeles. Through perseverance, hard work, and a winning personality, she broke through the glass ceiling at age 30 by becoming vice-president for public affairs at 7-Up/RC Bottling Company of Southern California. She is working to find ways of helping others break through the ceiling.

Breaking through the glass ceiling involves decisions about attributions. Do women and people of color fail to be appointed to senior-level positions because they lack skills and intelligence, which is an internal or dispositional attribution, or because they face discrimination from senior-level White males, which is an external or situational attribution? Although Kelley's covariation model would help decide this issue, many want a quicker way and use the cognitive miser model (Taylor, 1981).

The ***cognitive miser model*** says that, in making attributions, people feel they must conserve time and effort by taking cognitive shortcuts.

We have already discussed several cognitive shortcuts that we use in selecting, gathering, remembering, and using information—for example, relying on stereotypes and schemas. Besides these, researchers have identified a number of other cognitive shortcuts that we frequently use in making attributions (Weiner & Graham, 1999). Although these cognitive shortcuts save mental time and effort, they may result in biased or incorrect attributions. We'll discuss three of the most common biases in making attributions: the fundamental attribution error, the actor-observer effect, and self-serving bias.

*Let me tell you how I broke through the glass ceiling.*

---

#### Fundamental Attribution Error

If you believe that women and people of color cannot break through the glass ceiling because they lack the skills and intelligence to do so, you may be making the fundamental attribution error.

The ***fundamental attribution error*** refers to our tendency, when we look for causes of a person's behavior, to focus on the person's disposition or personality traits and overlook how the situation influenced the person's behavior.

*When you explain someone's behavior, you may be wrong.*

An example of the ***fundamental attribution error*** would be to conclude that women and people of color cannot break through the glass ceiling because of personal or dispositional factors, such as a lack of assertiveness or intelligence. This may not be the real reason, however. Because it was found that 97% of senior management in *Fortune*'s 1,000 top companies were White and 95% were male, another possible reason that women and people of color have difficulty breaking through the glass ceiling may be biased or discriminatory hiring practices.

#### Actor-Observer Effect

John angrily explains that he got to his car to put more money in the meter just as the police officer was driving away. John adds that he's very responsible and the ticket was bad luck because he was only 45 seconds late. John says the reason he got the ticket was that the police officer was just being mean. John's explanation is a good example of the actor-observer effect.

The ***actor-observer effect*** refers to the tendency, when you are behaving (or acting), to attribute your own behavior to situational factors. However, when you are observing others, you attribute another's behavior to his or her personality traits or disposition.

In the parking ticket example, John, the ***actor***, attributes his getting the ticket to situational factors, just having bad luck, rather than to his own behavior, being late. In addition, John, the ***observer***, explains that the police officer ticketed him because of a dispositional or personality factor—the officer was mean. The actor-observer error is very common. You can tell if you're making it by putting yourself in the position of the one you are observing (S. R. Wilson et al., 1997).

#### Self-Serving Bias

When we look for the causes of our own behaviors, such as why we received a good or bad grade on a test, we may make errors because of the self-serving bias (Sedikides et al., 1998).

The ***self-serving bias*** refers to explaining our successes by attributing them to our dispositions or personality traits and explaining our failures by attributing them to the situations.

The self-serving bias can be considered another part of the actor-observer effect. According to the self-serving bias, if you get an A on an exam, you tend to attribute your success to your personality traits or disposition, such as intelligence and perseverance. However, if you get a D on an exam, you tend to attribute your failure to the situation, such as a difficult test or unfair questions. Thus, according to the ***self-serving bias***, we try to keep ourselves in the best possible light by making different and even opposite attributions, depending on whether we have performed well or poorly.

*I didn't do well on this exam because the text was confusing.*

The three errors in attributions that we just discussed show the need to be on guard so that these errors don't bias or distort our attributions.

Although biased attributions can create problems, they can also be an advantage when they help us change our behaviors, as we'll discuss next.

## Can Changing Attributions Change Grades?

***What problems do freshmen face?***

Perhaps 20% of the students I counsel tell me about getting poor grades in their freshman year, and their reasons are very similar. Either they didn't develop good study habits in high school so they weren't academically prepared for college or they spent too much time partying or dealing with stressful personal, social, or financial difficulties. What is interesting is that some of the freshmen who got poor grades their first year were

I'm having problems with my grades and wonder if I should drop out.

able to bounce back academically their second year, while others became discouraged and dropped out of college. Researchers discovered many differences in students' attributions—that is, how students explained why they bounced back or dropped out. Because one goal of psychology is to apply scientific findings to real-world problems, researchers used findings on attributions to develop a program for improving grades and lowering the dropout rate (Wilson & Linville, 1982). Here's what actually happened.

### Kinds of Attributions

In explaining why a freshman is having academic problems, researchers may point to personal or dispositional attributions, such as the lack of necessary academic skills. Or researchers may point to external or situational attributions, such as pressures to party rather than study. Once a freshman has developed a pattern of getting poor grades, another question is whether the causes are permanent or temporary. For example, if freshmen attributed their academic problems to relatively permanent conditions, such as poor abilities, they would have little motivation and would expect little improvement. In addition, poor academic performance would make new students worried and anxious, which in turn would interfere with their ability to study.

However, if freshmen attributed their academic problems to temporary conditions, such as poor study habits, they could expect to improve if they developed better study skills. Researchers thought that if they could change students' attributions about poor academic performance and help them realize that it was a temporary rather than a permanent state, students could improve their grades.

### Method: Changing Attributions

I did terribly my freshman year but I got my act together and didn't drop out.

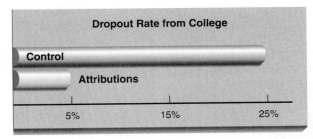

Researchers recruited freshmen who were having academic problems, such as scoring poorly on exams, not keeping up with assignments, and considering dropping out of college. These students were randomly divided into two different groups.

Students in the *experimental group* (attributions group) were given a number of procedures that changed their attributions about poor academic performance from a permanent cause to only a temporary condition. For example, students in the experimental group read a booklet about previous freshmen who had similar academic problems but showed improvement later in college. These subjects watched videotapes of previous students who described very convincingly how their grade point averages had risen after their freshman year. Next, these subjects were asked to write down all the reasons they could think of why grade point averages might increase after the freshman year.

The other group of freshmen with academic problems did not receive any of this information and served as a ***control group.***

### Results and Conclusions

Researchers found that changing students' attributions for poor academic performance from permanent to temporary had two significant positive effects.

**Change in Grade Point Average after Program**

| | | |
|---|---|---|
| Control | | |
| Attributions | | |

−0.50          0.00          +0.50

First, in the graph above, notice that freshmen who were told how to attribute their academic problems to temporary conditions (attributions group) had a significant improvement in grade point averages one year after the completion of this program.

Second, as shown in the graph below, only 5% of freshmen who changed their attributions for poor academic performance from permanent to temporary dropped out of college, while 25% of those in the control group dropped out.

**Dropout Rate from College**

| | | |
|---|---|---|
| Control | | |
| Attributions | | |

5%          15%          25%

On the basis of these data, researchers reached two important conclusions. First, it is possible to change students' attributions and expectations about academic performance. Second, changing students' attributions and expectations actually improved academic performance and reduced the dropout rate. This study illustrates how social psychologists used the concept of attribution to solve a real-world problem (Wilson & Linville, 1982).

Next, we'll discuss one of the most active areas of social cognition—forming and changing attitudes.

## D. Attitudes

---
### Definition
---

**Can your attitudes get you fired?**

We often remark that a certain person has a great attitude or a bad attitude or should change his or her attitude. The media regularly report on people's attitudes toward a wide range of topics, such as illegal drug usage, assisted suicide, sexual harassment, skinheads, or fat-free potato chips. All this talk about attitude demonstrates that it is not only a very popular term but also one of the most important terms in social psychology (Petty et al., 1997).

An example of how important an attitude can be comes from a letter received by an airport sales agent named Terri. The letter was brief and to the point: "Terri . . . it is our decision to terminate your employment as an airport sales agent . . . for insubordination." Terri's insubordination was that she had refused to wear makeup (lipstick, eyeliner) as specified in Continental Airlines' new 45-page appearance code manual. Terri had never worn makeup in her 11 years in the airline industry, and no one had ever complained before. Her attitude was that she was doing a good job without wearing makeup, so why should she start now? Terri (right photo) stuck to her attitude and was fired. However, several weeks later, Continental announced that it had changed its mind, apologized to Terri, and allowed her to keep her job without having to wear makeup (Mehren, 1991).

Terri's story introduces the concept of *attitude,* which in the 1930s was called the single most indispensable term in social psychology (Allport, 1935).

> Can they fire me because of my attitude toward wearing makeup?

An *attitude* is any belief or opinion that includes an evaluation of some object, person, or event along a continuum from negative to positive and that predisposes us to act in a certain way toward that object, person, or event.

In a very real sense, as demonstrated by Terri's experience, our attitudes can have a significant impact on our behaviors. Because attitudes are so important in influencing behaviors, attitude research has become very big business. For example, billions of dollars are spent each year in measuring or trying to change buyers' attitudes toward consumer products and in measuring and trying to change attitudes of voters toward candidates (Bassili, 1995; Dinh et al., 1995).

Although there are many definitions of attitude, they all share the following features (Ostrom et al., 1994):

■ An attitude is *evaluative:* it involves likes and dislikes. An attitude is like a point on a thermometer that ranges from very negative to very positive. For example, Terri makes a negative evaluation of using makeup, which means she has developed a negative attitude toward cosmetics.

■ The evaluation is always *targeted* toward some object, person, or event. Terri's negative attitude is targeted against a specific event, wearing makeup.

■ An attitude *predisposes* us to behave in a certain way. This means that we approach some objects, people, and events and avoid others because of corresponding positive or negative attitudes. Terri's attitude toward wearing makeup predisposed her to fight against wearing it, even to the point of losing her job.

Just as attitudes have the three general features discussed above, they also have the following three components.

---
### Components of Attitudes
---

If you closely examine how Terri's attitude toward wearing makeup affects her thoughts, feelings, and behaviors, you will discover that an attitude has three components: cognitive, affective, and behavioral (Eagly et al., 1994).

### 1 Cognitive Component

One reason Terri doesn't approve of wearing makeup is that some cosmetics are tested on animals, which she believes is a cruel practice.

Terri's belief that animals should not be used for cosmetic testing is an example of the cognitive component of attitudes. Thus, the *cognitive component* of our attitudes involves both thoughts and beliefs, which can strongly influence how we behave. For example, one reason vegetarians do not eat meat is based on the cognitive component of their attitude, namely, their firm belief that eating meat is immoral (Rozin et al., 1997).

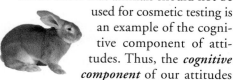

### 2 Affective Component

Another reason Terri doesn't approve of using makeup is that when she does, she feels uncomfortable because she does not like what she sees in the mirror. Terri's strong negative feeling about how she looks in makeup is an example of the *affective component* of attitudes. Thus, the affective component of attitudes involves emotional feelings, which also influence our behaviors. For example, we in the United States do not eat dogs because we are emotionally attached to our pets. But in some parts of Asia, dog meat is considered a delicacy.

### 3 Behavioral Component

Terri's negative attitude toward cosmetics predisposed or influenced her behavior; although she refused to wear makeup, she also fought to save her job. Terri's strong actions—refusing to wear makeup and fighting to save her job—are examples of the *behavioral component* of attitudes. Thus, attitudes influence how we behave, and how we behave can also influence the development of attitudes.

Attitudes not only influence our behavior but also have other important functions, which we'll discuss next.

**What if attitudes collide?**

Shannon Faulkner (right photo, front) had an attitude about going to college that set off an enormous personal and legal struggle. In the early 1990s, she applied to and was accepted at the Citadel, a military college in Charleston, South Carolina. But almost immediately, she was rejected because officials discovered that Shannon was a woman (she had eliminated all references to gender on her application). During the next two years, there was a battle of attitudes between the Citadel, which wanted to continue its 150-year-old tradition as a male-only college, and Shannon, who wanted to be given the same opportunities as males. She challenged the Citadel's all-male attitude and policy on legal grounds: Since the Citadel received 28% of its financial support from the state's tax dollars, it should be open to all the state's residents, male or female.

Why are they harassing me?

Shannon's attitude—that she be allowed to attend the Citadel—elicited death threats, hate mail, harassing phone calls, and hissing in restaurants. However, after two years of legal battles, the court ruled that the Citadel had to admit Shannon, and she was escorted into the Citadel by her parents and federal marshals.

But her first week at the Citadel, which is called hell week because of the terrible harassment new cadets must endure, was triple hell for Shannon. Not a single male cadet, new or old, would speak to her or offer any support (Reed & Esselman, 1995).

Shannon's struggle to become the first female cadet at the all-male Citadel resulted in a fierce battle between opposing attitudes. We'll use Shannon's experience to illustrate three general functions of attitudes: how they affect our predispositions, interpretations, and evaluations (Ostrom et al., 1994).

## 1 Predispose

Shannon had heard about the Citadel in her senior year of high school and said, "There was just something inside of me that wanted to do this" (Baum, 1994, p. 4). As Shannon's battle dragged on for two years, she explained, "It really has been a long struggle. When I started this lawsuit, I was told I would *never* enter the Citadel" (Reed & Esselman, 1995, p. 44). However, Shannon's attitude that women must be given the same opportunities as men predisposed her to behave in a certain way.

The *predisposing function* of attitudes means that they guide or influence us to behave in specific ways.

Shannon's attitude predisposed her to apply to the Citadel, so that she could obtain the same education and profit from the same network as males.

Because attitudes predispose us to behave in specific ways, attitudes are often used to predict behavior. A meta-analysis of 88 studies on how attitudes predispose behavior reported that attitudes significantly and substantially predicted future behaviors (Kraus, 1995). The fact that attitudes can and do predispose us to behave in certain ways is the primary reason that politicians survey voters' attitudes and manufacturers measure consumers' attitudes.

Although attitudes predispose us to behave in specific ways, they do not force us to do so, which explains why voters don't always vote as they say and consumers don't always buy what they say they like (Petty et al., 1997).

## 2 Interpret

New cadets' first week at the Citadel is called hell week because they endure constant harassment—for example, being yelled at for almost everything or being punished by having to take scalding showers until they throw up (Peyser et al., 1995). One reason cadets endure such harassment is that their attitudes influence how they interpret this cruel treatment.

The *interpreting function* of attitudes means that they provide convenient guidelines for interpreting and categorizing objects and events and deciding whether to approach or avoid them.

Cadets with very positive attitudes toward the Citadel's proud traditions will interpret hell week's harassment as one way to prove themselves. In contrast, cadets with less positive attitudes may question and rebel against such cruel harassment. Although Shannon had fought hard to enter the Citadel, she decided to drop out during hell week, as did 24 male cadets.

## 3 Evaluate

During the two years Shannon fought for admission to the Citadel, garbage was heaped on her car, hate mail called her every ugly name, and she was jeered and hissed at in restaurants. One reason Shannon put up with this harassment was that attitudes help us evaluate situations and stand up for our beliefs.

The *evaluative function* of attitudes means that they help us stand up for those beliefs and values that we consider very important to ourselves.

For example, Shannon's strong attitude that women should have equal opportunities for education, especially in publicly supported institutions, helped her endure two years of harassment and struggle.

The evaluative function of attitudes explains why people with strong attitudes about equal rights, the homeless, religion, freedom, abortion, gays, and politics often endure great personal hardships in standing up and fighting for their beliefs.

Although Shannon dropped out of the Citadel in 1995, four more women entered the Citadel in 1996. Although the Citadel promised to halt harassment, two of the four women dropped out because of excessive harassment (having their clothes set on fire, made to drink iced tea until they vomited). The Citadel officially punished 10 cadets for excessive hazing (Gleick, 1997). One reason male cadets continue to excessively harass female cadets is that the Citadel knowingly or unknowingly has fostered negative attitudes toward women cadets. However, despite negative attitudes, 41 women have enrolled at the Citadel, which saw the first woman graduate magna cum laude in 1999.

Researchers have found that strong negative attitudes are very difficult to change (Petty et al., 1997). Changing attitudes is our next topic.

## Attitude Change

**What made a skinhead reform?**

At one time, Gregory Withrow (right photo) was an out-and-out hatemonger who belonged to the White Aryan Resistance, the Ku Klux Klan, the skinheads, and the American Nazi Party. His goal was "the complete and total extermination of all nonwhites from the face of the American continent." He preached hatred and bashed and robbed Japanese tourists in San Francisco. Then he met Sylvia, who completely rejected Gregory's white supremacist notions. As Gregory grew to love Sylvia, he found himself caught between her disapproval of his Nazi values and his years of preaching hate. Gregory finally resolved his personal dilemma by

*I was a racist and a skinhead until I met Sylvia.*

renouncing his previous white supremacist values and abandoning the hate organizations. He now speaks against hate and racism (Wride, 1989).

Social psychologists are interested in the process of changing attitudes, such as Gregory's radical change from preaching hate and racism to denouncing these beliefs. We'll discuss two popular theories that explain why people change their attitudes: the theory of cognitive dissonance and self-perception theory (Petty et al., 1997).

### Cognitive Dissonance

After meeting Sylvia, Gregory's life became one big conflict. He had spent most of his adult life practicing racism and hate, but now he was in love with Sylvia, who was tolerant and peace-loving. Because Gregory's hateful beliefs clashed with Sylvia's nonhateful attitudes, he found himself in the middle of a very troubling inconsistency, which Leon Festinger (1957) called cognitive dissonance.

*Cognitive dissonance refers to a state of unpleasant psychological tension that motivates us to reduce our cognitive inconsistencies by making our beliefs more consistent with each other.*

There are two main ways to reduce cognitive dissonance—that is, to make our beliefs and attitudes consistent with our behavior (Aronson, 1997).

**Adding or changing beliefs.** We can reduce cognitive dissonance by adding new beliefs or changing old beliefs and making them consistent with our behavior. In Gregory's case, cognitive dissonance was created by the conflict between Sylvia's nonviolent values and his own racist and hate-filled beliefs. To decrease his cognitive dissonance, Gregory renounced his hateful beliefs so that his attitudes became consistent with his behavior, which was loving Sylvia and her nonviolent ways (Gibbons et al., 1997).

**Counterattitudinal behavior.** Another way we can reduce cognitive dissonance is by engaging in opposite or counterattitudinal behavior (Leippe & Eisenstadt, 1994).

*Counterattitudinal behavior involves taking a public position that runs counter to your private attitude.*

*Did he change his racist attitudes to resolve his cognitive dissonance?*

A classic study by Festinger and Carlsmith (1959) illustrates how counterattitudinal behavior works. In this study, subjects were asked to do an extremely boring task, such as turning pegs in a board. At the end of the task, the experimenter asked the subjects to help out by telling the next group of subjects how interesting the task was. Subjects were asked to lie about the task and say it was interesting, which is engaging in counterattitudinal behavior. For saying the task was interesting, some subjects received $1 and some received $20. Sometime later, the original subjects were asked how much they had liked the boring task. A curious finding emerged. Subjects paid just $1 had a more favorable attitude to the boring task than those who were paid $20. That's because subjects paid $20 felt they were paid well for lying. Subjects paid $1 had no good reason for lying, and so, to resolve the cognitive dissonance between what they'd said (it was interesting) and what they felt (it was boring), they convinced themselves that the task was somewhat interesting. This shows that engaging in opposite or counterattitudinal behaviors can change attitudes. However, there's a different explanation for this experiment's results.

### Self-Perception Theory

Perhaps subjects in the previous experiment came to believe their own lies (task was interesting) after engaging in counterattitudinal behavior not to reduce cognitive dissonance but because of changing their own self-perceptions.

*Self-perception theory says that we first observe or perceive our own behavior and then, as a result, we change our attitudes.*

Daryl Bem (1967), who developed self-perception theory, would explain that subjects paid only $1 for lying would recall their behavior and conclude that they would never have lied for only $1, so the task must have actually been interesting.

At first glance, cognitive dissonance theory and self-perception theory seem to be similar, since they both indicate that if we say something, it must be true. However, each theory points to different reasons. According to *cognitive dissonance theory*, the belief "if I said it, it must be true" occurs because we are trying to reduce the inconsistency in our beliefs and behaviors. In comparison, according to *self-perception theory*, concluding that "if I said it, it must be true" simply reflects another way of explaining our own behaviors.

Self-perception theory also challenges the traditional assumption that attitudes give rise to behavior. According to self-perception theory, behaviors give rise to attitudes. For example, after Gregory began speaking out against racism, his attitudes changed radically. Researchers have shown that behavior can influence attitudes (Leippe & Eisenstadt, 1994).

*Did he change his racist attitudes because he spoke against racism?*

We may change our own attitudes in response to cognitive dissonance or self-perception. However, others are continually trying to change our attitudes through various forms of persuasion, our next topic.

Political candidates spend much of their time, energy, and money trying to persuade people to vote for them. What politicians have to decide is whether to use an intellectual or emotional appeal, how to appear honest, and what arguments to use. We'll begin with choosing between two different routes—central or peripheral (Dalto et al., 1994; Petty & Cacioppo, 1986).

## Central Route

If the audience is interested in and will think about the real issues, a politician should seek votes using the central route.

The *central route for persuasion* presents information with strong arguments, analyses, facts, and logic.

> I think logical arguments and hard facts work best.

A political candidate using the central route for persuasion must present clear and detailed information about his or her views and accomplishments and about opponents' records. The candidate should appear *credible* by demonstrating knowledge and commitment to the issues and be perceived as *honest* (Priester & Petty, 1995).

Politicians should choose the central route when they are trying to persuade voters who have a high need for cognition—that is, a high need to know the facts and issues (Cacioppo & Petty, 1982). The central route for persuasion works with people who think about and analyze the issues. However, not all voters can be persuaded by the central route. For some, a peripheral route for persuasion proves the better method.

## Peripheral Route

If the audience is interested in the candidate's personality or image, a politician should seek votes using the peripheral route.

> I think emotional and personal appeals work best.

The *peripheral route for persuasion* emphasizes emotional appeal, focuses on personal traits, and generates positive feelings.

The peripheral route assumes that not all voters will spend the time and energy to digest or discuss the issues. Instead, some audiences are more interested in the excitement a candidate can generate by an *energetic* and *enthusiastic delivery*. For this audience, politicians should choose the peripheral route for seeking votes (Priester & Petty, 1995). This route includes bands, banners, parties, and personal appearances, which build an inviting and exciting image and create a positive attitude toward the candidate. If audiences like the candidate's image, they will more likely agree with the candidate's views (Carlson, 1990).

The peripheral route is more concerned with style and image, and the central route is more concerned with substance and ideas. Researchers generally find that the central route produces more enduring results, while the peripheral route produces more transient results (Mackie & Skelly, 1994). Whether the central or peripheral route is used, a number of specific elements are important in persuasion.

## Elements of Persuasion

Figuring out which elements are important in persuading people was begun in the 1950s by the Yale Communication Program, which is still considered one of the best models. This communication program identified a number of important elements in persuasion, including the source, message, and audience (Mackie & Skelly, 1994; Petty et al., 1997).

**Source.** One element in persuading someone to adopt your point of view involves the *source of the message:* We are more likely to believe sources who appear honest and trustworthy, have expertise and credibility, are attractive, or appear similar to us (Priester & Petty, 1995). For example, national newscasters, such as ABC's Peter Jennings, receive multi-million-dollar contracts because they appear attractive, honest, and credible. Can you name one national newscaster who is not physically attractive?

**Message.** Another element of persuasion involves the *content of the message.* If the persuader is using the *central route,* the messages will contain convincing and understandable facts. If the facts are complicated, a written message is better than a spoken one (Chaiken & Eagly, 1976).

If the persuader is using the *peripheral route,* the messages will be designed to arouse emotion, sentiment, and loyalty. One type of message that uses the peripheral route is the *fear appeal.* Could we, for example, change people's attitudes toward smoking by showing them blackened lungs? Researchers find that fearful messages are more effective if the audience is already fearful and the message is relevant to their lives (Baron et al., 1994).

Some messages are better presented as *one-sided,* that is, you present only the message that you want accepted. Other messages are better presented as *two-sided,* that is, you include both the message and arguments against any potential disagreements. Thus, a good persuader will select not only the best route (central or peripheral) but also the kind of message (one- or two-sided) (Jacks & Devine, 2000).

Why is ABC's newscaster Peter Jennings paid millions for reading the evening news?

**Audience.** Another element of being an effective persuader involves knowing the *characteristics of the audience.* For example, audiences who are interested in facts are best persuaded using the central route, while audiences interested in personal traits are best persuaded using the peripheral route. If the audience is leaning toward the persuader, a one-sided message is best; if an audience is leaning away from the persuader, a two-sided message is best.

Thus persuasion is a complicated process that involves the persuader's traits, the central or peripheral route, and the audience's characteristics (Wood, 2000).

Besides being influenced by the source's traits and the message's route, we are also influenced by social forces, which we'll discuss next.

**Why did they die with him?**

At the beginning of this module, we told you about David Koresh. He was a 34-year-old high school dropout, rock musician, polygamist, and preacher, whose teaching attracted more than a hundred people to join him at an armed fortress near Waco, Texas. Koresh's followers would do anything for him. He taught that all the women in the world belonged to him, and at one point, Koresh had 18 "wives," some as young as 12 years old. Koresh (left photo) laid down strict rules for his followers. They were not allowed beer or meat; they had to turn over all their money and possessions to him; and they were not allowed to marry. Koresh enforced his rules with beatings and other punishment.

Why did Koresh's 85 followers remain with him . . .

Concerned about Koresh's stash of weapons, federal agents assaulted the Koresh compound but were held off by returning gunfire. However, after 51 days of unsuccessful negotiations, the agents moved up armored vehicles and fired tear gas. Somehow, a fire started and, driven by strong winds, grew into a blazing inferno (photo below). Later, agents found the bodies of Koresh and 85 other adults and children (Gibbs, 1993b; Kantrowitz et al., 1993).

What happened to Koresh and his followers is an extreme example of social and group influences. However, some of the reasons these people followed Koresh even to their deaths are similar to the reasons we obey people in authority and conform to group and social pressures. We'll examine why people conform and obey.

. . . as a deadly fire destroyed them?

## Conformity

The followers of David Koresh worked in the commune, recognized his leadership, and followed his teaching, all examples of conformity.

*Conformity* refers to any behavior you perform because of group pressure, even though that pressure might not involve direct requests.

For example, you may conform by wearing clothes that are in style, using common slang phrases, and buying the latest and most popular products. A recent example of conformity in the United States began in the late 1990s, when increasing numbers of people began carrying small plastic bottles of drinking water wherever they went. This increased need to carry plastic bottles of water wasn't because of water shortages or warmer climates but most likely because of conforming to the social pressures of seeing others carrying similar bottles of water (Cialdini, 2001). We'll begin our discussion of conformity with a classic study in social psychology.

### ASCH'S EXPERIMENT

A classic experiment is one that causes us to change the way we think about something—in this case, how social pressures can influence conformity (Conner, 2000). Solomon Asch's (1958) classic experiment showed very clearly how an individual can be pressured to conform to a group's standards. As we describe Asch's experiment, imagine that you are a subject and guess how you might have behaved.

### *Procedure*

You are seated at a round table with five others and have been told that you are taking part in a visual perception experiment. Your group is shown a straight line and then is instructed to look at three more lines of different lengths and pick out the line equal in length to the original one. The three choices are different enough that it is not hard to pick out the correct one. Each person at the round table identifies his or her choice out loud, with you answering next to last. When you are ready to answer, you will have heard four others state their opinions. What you do not know is that these four other people are the experimenter's accomplices. On certain trials, they will answer correctly, making you feel your choice is right. On other trials, they will deliberately answer incorrectly, much to your surprise. In these cases you will have heard four identical incorrect answers before it is your turn to answer. You will almost certainly feel some group pressure to conform to the others' opinion. Will you give in?

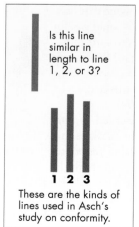

Is this line similar in length to line 1, 2, or 3?

**1 2 3**

These are the kinds of lines used in Asch's study on conformity.

### *Results*

Out of 50 subjects in Asch's experiment, 75% conformed on some of the trials, but no one conformed on all the trials; 25% never conformed. These data indicate that the desire to have your attitudes and behaviors match those of others in a group can be a powerful force.

Although Asch's original results are rather dramatic, they have not always been replicated. Researchers have concluded that group conformity is dependent upon the makeup and culture of the group (Mackie & Skelly, 1994). Regarding group makeup, conformity in Asch-type studies increases as the size of the majority increases and as the proportion of females increases. Regarding culture, conformity in Asch-type studies decreases in cultures that value the role of the individual over the group (individualism), such as the United States, and increases in cultures that value the good of the group over the individual's needs (collectivism), such as some Arab countries (Bond & Smith, 1996).

Asch's study is considered a classic because it was the first to clearly show that group pressures can influence conformity. However, we may conform publicly but disagree privately and this is an example of compliance.

## Compliance

**Were the subjects just pretending?**

One interpretation of Asch's data is that subjects were not really changing their beliefs but rather just pretending to go along with the group. For example, when subjects in Asch's experiment privately recorded their answers, conforming drastically declined. This decline indicated that subjects were conforming but not really changing their beliefs, which is one kind of compliance.

*Compliance* is a kind of conformity in which we give in to social pressure in our public responses but do not change our private beliefs.

For example, you may conform to your instructor's suggestions on rewriting a paper although you do not agree with the suggestions. In this case, you would be complying with someone in authority.

One particular technique of compliance is used by many sales-

Salespeople use the foot-in-the-door technique to obtain customer compliance.

people. Those in sales soon learn that if they can get the customer to comply with a small request (get a foot in the door), the customer is more likely to comply with a later request to buy the product.

The *foot-in-the-door technique* refers to the technique of starting with a little request to gain eventual compliance with a later request.

A common example of the foot-in-the-door technique is that used by telemarketers who first get you to answer a simple question, "How are you today?" so that you'll stay on the phone and answer their other questions. The foot-in-the-door technique is one relatively successful way to obtain compliance (Cialdini, 2001).

If you are officially or formally asked to comply with a request, such as "Take a test on Friday," your compliance is called obedience.

## Obedience

**Do you run red lights?**

When it comes to signs, laws, rules, and regulations, such as speed limits, traffic lights, smoking restrictions, parental requests, instructors' assignments, and doctors' orders, people differ in what they choose to obey.

*Obedience* refers to performing some behavior in response to an order given by someone in a position of power or authority.

A serious problem in California is drivers who run red lights and cause accidents. To increase obedience, cameras automatically take photos of drivers who run red lights and these drivers are mailed tickets with expensive fines ($270). Here's a case of using punishment to decrease accidents by increasing obedience (42% reduction in running red lights) (Halladay, 2001).

Most of us obey orders, rules, and regulations that are for the general good. But what if the orders or rules are cruel or immoral?

### MILGRAM'S EXPERIMENT

Stanley Milgram's (1963) experiment on obedience is a classic experiment in social psychology because it was the first to study whether people would obey commands that were clearly inhumane and immoral (Conner, 2000). As we describe this famous experiment, imagine being the "teacher" and consider whether you would have obeyed the experimenter's commands.

### *The Setup*

Imagine that you have volunteered for a study on the effects of punishment on learning. After arriving in the laboratory at Yale University, you are selected to be the "teacher" and another volunteer is to be the "learner." What you don't know is that the *learner* is actually an accomplice of the experimenter. As the *teacher*, you watch the learner being strapped into a chair and having electrodes placed on his wrists. The electrodes are attached to a shock generator in the next room. You and the researcher then leave the learner's room, close the door, and go into an adjoining room.

The researcher gives you a list of questions to ask the learner over an intercom, and the learner is to signal his answer on a panel of lights in front of you. For each wrong answer, you, the teacher, are to *shock the learner* and to increase the intensity of the shock by 15 volts for each succeeding wrong answer. In front of you is the shock machine, with 30 separate switches that indicate increasing intensities. The first switch is marked "15 volts. Slight shock," and the last switch is marked "XXX 450 volts. Danger: Severe shock." You begin to ask the learner questions, and as he misses them, you administer stronger and stronger shocks.

> Whenever you make a mistake, you'll receive an electric shock.

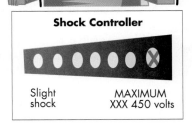

**Shock Controller**

Slight shock — MAXIMUM XXX 450 volts

### *The Conflict*

As the teacher, you give the learner shocks that increase in intensity up to 300 volts, when the learner pounds on the wall. You continue and after the next miss, you give the learner a 315-volt shock, after which the learner pounds on the wall and stops answering any more questions. Although you plead with the researcher to stop the experiment, the researcher explains that, as the teacher, you are to continue asking questions and shocking the learner for incorrect answers. Even though the learner has pounded the wall and stopped answering any questions after a 315-volt shock, would you continue the procedure until you deliver the XXX 450 volts?

What you, the teacher, didn't know is that the learner is part of the experiment and acts like being shocked but never received a single one. The teacher was misled into believing that he or she was really shocking the learner. The question was whether a teacher would continue and deliver the maximum shock.

## Milgram's Results

**How many obeyed?**

The scary question was how many "teachers" (subjects) would deliver the maximum intensity shock to the "learner."

**0.12%** When psychiatrists were asked to predict how many subjects would deliver the full range of shocks, including the last 450 volts, they estimated that only 0.12% of the subjects would do so.

**2%** When members of the general public were asked the same question, they predicted that only 2% of the subjects would deliver the maximum 450 volts.

**65%** To the surprise and dismay of many, including Milgram, 65% of the subjects (no difference between males and females) delivered the full range of shocks, including the final XXX 450 volts.

When Stanley Milgram conducted these studies on obedience in the early 1960s, they demonstrated that people will obey inhumane orders simply because they are told to do so. This kind of unthinking obedience to immoral commands was something that psychiatrists, members of the general population, and Milgram had not predicted. Milgram (1974) repeated variations of this experiment many times and obtained similar results. Additionally, Milgram's experiment was repeated in various parts of the world with similar results (Blass, 2000).

The results of these experiments helped answer a question people had asked since World War II: Why had Germans obeyed Hitler's commands? And why did the followers of Koresh obey his rigid rules and even commit mass suicide by being burned alive? According to Milgram's experiments, social situations that involve power and authority greatly increase obedience to the point that a large percentage of people will obey orders even if they are clearly unreasonable and inhumane.

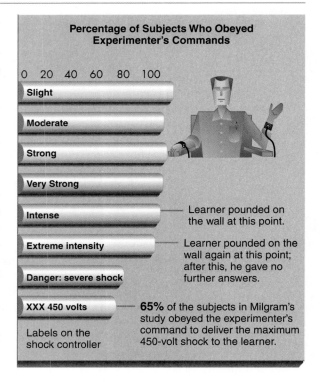

**Percentage of Subjects Who Obeyed Experimenter's Commands**

0   20   40   60   80   100

Slight

Moderate

Strong

Very Strong

Intense — Learner pounded on the wall at this point.

Extreme intensity — Learner pounded on the wall again at this point; after this, he gave no further answers.

Danger: severe shock

XXX 450 volts — **65%** of the subjects in Milgram's study obeyed the experimenter's command to deliver the maximum 450-volt shock to the learner.

Labels on the shock controller

## Why Do People Obey?

Psychologists have suggested several reasons why about 65% of the subjects in Milgram's experiment agreed to deliver the maximum shock to learners. Perhaps the major reason is that people have learned to follow the orders of *authority figures,* whether they are religious leaders, army commanders, doctors, scientists, or parents. However, people are more likely to obey authority figures when they are present. In one of his follow-up studies, Milgram (1974) found that when subjects received their instructions over the telephone, they were more likely to defy authority than when they received their instructions in person. This also explains why patients don't follow doctors' orders once they leave their offices.

People also obey because they have *learned to follow orders* in their daily lives, whether in traffic, on the job, or in personal interactions. However, people are more likely to obey if an authority figure is present (police officer, boss, or parent). What Milgram's study showed was that blind obedience to unreasonable authority or inhumane orders is more likely than we think.

Why do some show blind obedience to immoral orders?

## Were Milgram's Experiments Ethical?

Although the Milgram experiments provided important information about obedience, it is unlikely that they could be conducted under today's research guidelines. As we discussed (p. 40), all experiments today, especially those with the potential for causing psychological or physical harm, are carefully screened by research committees, a practice that did not exist at the time of Milgram's research. Currently, committees must determine whether proposed experiments on animals or humans have the potential for psychological or physical harm and whether these potentially damaging effects can be eliminated or counteracted. When there is a possibility of an experiment causing *psychological harm,* the researchers must propose ways to eliminate or counteract the potential harmful effects. This is usually done by thoroughly debriefing the subjects.

*Debriefing* occurs after an experimental procedure and involves explaining the purpose and method of the experiment, asking the subjects about their feelings about being in the experiment, and helping the subjects deal with possible doubts or guilt arising from their behaviors in the experiment.

After the Milgram experiments, the subjects were debriefed. For example, subjects were told that, contrary to what they believed, no shock was actually delivered to the learner. The subjects were also given the opportunity to discuss their feelings about the experiment and their own actions during it. In addition, some of the subjects were sent questionnaires or were interviewed a year later by a psychiatrist to determine whether there were any long-lasting harmful effects of having been a teacher. Although Milgram's subjects were debriefed, critics doubted that the question of whether any psychological harm had been done to the subjects was successfully resolved. Because the potential for psychological harm to the subjects was so great in Milgram's studies, researchers seriously doubt if such studies could be approved under current ethical standards for conducting safe research.

Next, we'll turn to another interesting question: Why do people help?

## Helping: Prosocial Behavior

**Would you help an accident victim?**

About 60 people had gathered around a serious car crash in a downtown area. They were talking about the accident and pointing at the victims, but no one was helping. One of the victims was a woman, obviously pregnant and unconscious. One person in the crowd, Ken Von, came forward and tried to save the woman with cardiopulmonary and mouth-to-mouth resuscitation that he had learned by watching television. He kept her alive until paramedics arrived (*San Diego Tribune,* September 9, 1983).

Ken's quick action is an example of helping, or prosocial behavior.

*Prosocial behavior,* which is also called *helping,* is any behavior that benefits others or has positive social consequences.

In our society, professionals, such as paramedics, are trained and paid to provide help. However, in Ken's case, he was the only one of 60 onlookers

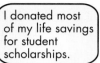

I donated most of my life savings for student scholarships.

who came forward to help the unconscious traffic victim. Ken's helping may be described as altruistic, since he expected no external reward.

*Altruism* is one form of helping or doing something, often at a cost or risk, for reasons other than the expectation of a material or social reward.

Altruistic people often do things that touch our hearts. Consider 87-year-old Osceola McCarty, who handwashed clothes most of her life for grateful clients. When she finally retired at age 86, she donated most of her life savings, an amazing $150,000, to the University of Southern Mississippi to finance scholarships for the area's African American students. "I want them to have an education," said McCarty, who never married and has no children of her own. "I had to work hard all my life. They can have the chance that I didn't have" (Plummer & Ridenhour, 1995, p. 40). As these examples show, some people help in emergencies, and others help by donating time or money.

## Why People Help

**Would you help?**

Why did Osceola McCarty, who spent her life washing clothes, donate most of her hard-earned life savings to finance scholarships instead of using her savings to make her retirement more comfortable? Researchers suggest at least three different motivations—empathy, personal distress, and norms and values—to explain why people, like McCarty, are altruistic and help others without thought of rewards (Batson, 1998; Schroeder et al., 1995):

■ We may help because we feel *empathy*—that is, we identify with what the victim must be going through. Osceola McCarty may have donated her life savings for scholarships because she felt empathy for other African American students.

■ We may help because we feel *personal distress*—that is, we have feelings of fear, alarm, or disgust from seeing a victim in need. Osceola said that she didn't want other young African American people to have to go through the hard times that she had faced.

■ We may help because of our *norms* and *values*—that is, we may feel morally bound or socially responsible to help those in need.

Researchers have combined these three motivations along with several other ideas to construct two different theories of why people come out of a crowd and help perfect strangers. We can use these two theories to explain why Ken Von was the only person in a crowd of 60 spectators to help a pregnant woman who was seriously injured in a car accident.

### DECISION-STAGE MODEL

Ken may have decided to help after going through five stages, which involved making five different decisions.

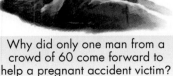

Why did only one man from a crowd of 60 come forward to help a pregnant accident victim?

The *decision-stage model of helping* says that you go through five stages in deciding to help: (1) you notice the situation; (2) you interpret it as one in which help is needed; (3) you assume personal responsibility; (4) you choose a form of assistance; and (5) you carry out that assistance.

According to the decision-stage model, Ken helped because he went through all five stages. Most onlookers stopped at stage 3 and decided it was not their responsibility; so they did not help. This model explains that people may recognize a situation as an emergency (stages 1 and 2) yet fail to help because they do not take personal responsibility for the situation (Latané & Darley, 1970).

### AROUSAL-COST-REWARD MODEL

Ken also may have helped the pregnant woman because he thought about the costs and rewards.

The *arousal-cost-reward model of helping* says that we make decisions to help by calculating the costs and rewards of helping.

For example, seeing an accident may cause you to be unpleasantly and emotionally *aroused,* which you wish to reduce. In deciding how to reduce these unpleasant feelings, you calculate the *costs* and *rewards* of helping. For example, those who decided not to help may have felt that the costs of helping, such as getting involved in a potentially dangerous situation, outweighed the rewards (Piliavin et al., 1982).

According to these two models, Ken experienced five stages (five decisions) and then decided to help, or Ken possibly considered the costs and rewards of reducing his unpleasant emotional feelings and then decided to help. Although the arousal-cost-reward model and the decision-stage model focus on different factors, they are not mutually exclusive.

Next, we'll explain how social forces influence people in groups.

---

## Group Dynamics

---

**What happens in groups?**

When you're with family, friends, or coworkers, you may or may not be aware of the numerous group influences that can greatly change how you think, feel, and behave.

*Groups* are collections of two or more people who interact, share some common idea, goal, or purpose, and influence how their members think and behave.

To illustrate the powerful influences of groups, we'll describe the case of Dennis Jay, who almost died in a drunken coma and later heard that his fraternity brothers had lied about the initiation that had almost killed him.

### *Group Cohesion and Norms*

As a pledge at a fraternity initiation party, Dennis Jay and 19 others were forced to drink from a "beer bong," a funnel into which beer was poured; the beer ran down a plastic hose placed in the mouth (left photo). The rule was that once you threw up you could stop drinking from the beer bong. Because he did not throw up, Jay was given straight shots of whiskey until he fell on his face. By the time his frat brothers got Jay to the hospital 30 minutes later, he was in a coma and barely breathing. His blood alcohol content was 0.48, and a level of 0.50 is usually fatal (legally drunk in many states is 0.08).

> My fraternity brothers lied about why I was in a coma.

At first, Jay refused to describe what happened because he wanted to be loyal to his fraternity. Then he heard that the fraternity brothers had lied and said that he had stumbled drunk into their frat house and that they had brought him to the emergency ward just to help out. The fraternity brothers' lies made Jay angry and he told the truth (Grogan et al., 1993).

Why would a group of fraternity members make up a story about what happened to Jay, who was one of their pledges? Social psychologists would point to the powerful influence of two group forces: group cohesion and group norms.

*Group cohesion* is group togetherness, which is determined by how much group members perceive that they share common attributes.

One reason many groups have some form of initiation rites and rituals is to have all members share a common experience and thus increase group cohesion.

*Group norms* are the formal or informal rules about how group members should behave.

Group norms, written or unwritten, can exert powerful influences, both good and bad, on group members' behaviors (Abrams et al., 2000). For example, fraternity members apparently lied about what happened to Jay to protect their group. But this leaves the question of why Jay and others like him endure potentially harmful hazing to join a group.

### *Why Do We Form Groups?*

In his hierarchy of human motivation (p. 333), humanistic psychologist Abraham Maslow identified *the need for love and belonging* as fundamental to human happiness (Maslow, 1970). One way to satisfy this social need is by joining a group, which helps individuals feel a sense of belonging. For instance, in high school and college, students often join various groups to feel they belong, form friendships, and receive social support. The need for belonging carries into adulthood as individuals join various community and business organizations. According to Maslow's theory, the social need to belong points to a ***motivational reason*** for joining groups.

At about the same time Maslow published his work on the hierarchy of motivation, Leon Festinger (1954) offered another reason for joining groups, based on the social comparison theory.

*Social comparison theory* says that we are driven to compare ourselves to others who are similar to us, so that we can measure the correctness of our attitudes and beliefs. According to Festinger, this drive motivates us to join groups.

According to Festinger's theory, the drive to compare and judge our attitudes and beliefs against those of others who are similar to us points to a ***cognitive reason*** for joining groups.

An additional reason for forming groups is that we can accomplish things in groups that we simply cannot do alone. For example, students form study groups because they want academic help, social support, and motivation. However, there are two kinds of study groups, each with different goals: task-oriented and socially oriented groups.

In a ***task-oriented group,*** members have specific duties to complete.

In task-oriented groups, especially if there is high cohesiveness (togetherness), students will perform much better than those in groups that have less cohesiveness or are more socially oriented (Mullen & Cooper, 1994).

In a ***socially oriented group,*** the members are primarily concerned about fostering and maintaining social relationships among the members of the group.

This group of young Mormon adults are being trained in bringing their religion to others.

Compared to a task-oriented group, which helps members achieve certain academic, business, political, or career goals, a socially oriented group primarily provides a source of friends, fun activities, and social support.

The fact that members may invest considerable time, effort, and money indicates how important groups can become in satisfying a variety of needs.

Next, we'll discuss how groups and crowds can influence our behaviors.

## Behavior in Crowds

**How do you behave in a crowd?**

When a person is in a crowd, he or she may think and behave very differently than when alone.

A *crowd* is a large group of persons, most of whom are strangers and unacquainted.

Being in a crowd can facilitate or inhibit certain behaviors, can lead to antisocial behaviors, such as riots, or may result in refusals to help someone in need. We'll discuss how crowds influence these kinds of behaviors.

### Facilitation and Inhibition

Performing before a large crowd can facilitate or inhibit certain behaviors.

If a runner has a history of successful competition, he may turn in a better performance in front of a large crowd as a result of social facilitation.

*Social facilitation* is an increase in performance in the presence of a crowd.

In contrast, if a runner has a spotty history in competition, he may turn in a worse performance in front of a large crowd because of social inhibition.

*Social inhibition* is a decrease in performance in the presence of a crowd.

Whether we show facilitation or inhibition depends partly on our previous experience. Generally, the presence of others will facilitate well-learned, simple, or reflexive responses but will inhibit new, unusual, or complex responses. An example of social facilitation occurs during championship games when a player is awarded the title of "most valuable player." An example of social inhibition also occurs during championship games when a star player, who is expected to do great, instead feels anxiety about performing and plays poorly or "chokes" (Baumeister, 1995; Schlenker et al., 1995). Thus, the presence of a crowd can either facilitate or inhibit behaviors, depending on the situation.

### Deindividuation in Crowds

During the Los Angeles riots in the early 1990s, people were arrested for looting, setting fires, and beating others. Individuals in a crowd are more likely to commit such antisocial acts because being in a crowd conceals the person's identity, a process called deindividuation.

*Deindividuation* refers to the increased tendency for subjects to behave irrationally or perform antisocial behaviors when there is less chance of being personally identified.

Looting is more likely to occur in a crowd because of deindividuation.

For example, researchers found that drivers are more likely to honk their horns long and hard if they have little chance of being identified (Ellison et al., 1995).

One researcher thinks that deindividuation occurs because being in a crowd reduces guilt and self-awareness so that people are less controlled by internal standards and more willing to engage in deviant or antisocial roles (Zimbardo, 1970). Researchers report some support for deindividuation but emphasize that just being in a rowdy crowd, such as at a competitive sporting event, can turn individuals into potential mobsters (Postmes & Spears, 1998).

### The Bystander Effect

As a person lies unconscious on a city sidewalk, dozens or hundreds of people may walk by without helping. There are several reasons no one stops to help, including fear of the person's reactions, inexperience with providing help, and the bystander effect.

The *bystander effect* says that an individual may feel inhibited from taking some action because of the presence of others.

Data from over 50 studies indicate that 75% of people offer assistance when alone, but fewer than 53% do so when in a group (Latané & Nida, 1981). There are two explanations for the bystander effect.

The *informational influence theory* says that we use the reactions of others to judge the seriousness of the situation.

If other bystanders are taking no action, we conclude that no emergency exists and do nothing to offer help or aid (Cialdini, 2001).

The *diffusion of responsibility theory* says that, in the presence of others, individuals feel less personal responsibility and are less likely to take action in a situation where help is required (Latané, 1981).

Researchers report a significant negative correlation between helping and increased population density in small, medium, and large cities in the United States (Levine et al., 1994). Thus, an individual may feel less responsibility to offer help or aid the more crowded a city becomes.

Just being in the presence of other strangers can inhibit an individual from helping somone in need.

The presence of others also influences how we make decisions, which we'll examine next.

## Group Decisions

**Does being in a group affect thinking?**

All of us have been in groups—families, fraternities, sororities, various social or business clubs. What you may not realize is that being in a group creates social pressures that influence how you think and make decisions. We'll discuss two interesting factors in making decisions: group polarization and groupthink.

### Group Polarization

Imagine that a young lawyer is trying to decide between two job offers. The first offer is from a large, well-established firm that promises more security, financial opportunities, and prestige. However, it has a poor record as an equal opportunity employer of women and currently has no women partners. The second offer is from a small, recently established firm that can promise little security or prestige. However, this firm is doing well and has an excellent record in promoting women as partners. Which offer should she accept? Using dilemmas such as this, a researcher compared the recommendations from individuals in a group with those made by the group after it had engaged in discussion (Gigone & Hastie, 1997; Pruitt, 1971). Group discussions change individuals' judgments, such as when a group urges a more risky recommendation than do individuals. This phenomenon became known as the *risky shift.*

Researchers later discovered that the direction of a group's risky shift depends on how conservative or liberal the group was to begin with. If a group's members are initially more conservative, group discussion will shift its recommendation to an even more conservative one. If a group's members are initially more liberal, group discussion will shift its recommendation to an even more liberal one.

The group's shift to a more extreme position is called polarization. *Group polarization* is a phenomenon in which group discussion reinforces the majority's point of view and shifts that view to a more extreme position.

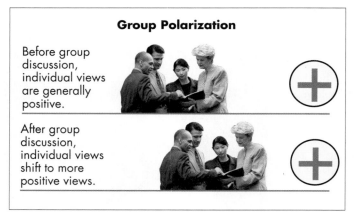

**Group Polarization**

Before group discussion, individual views are generally positive.

After group discussion, individual views shift to more positive views.

Whether this group polarization (figure above) is in a liberal or conservative direction depends on the initial leanings of the group's members. Researchers also found that the more the group repeated each other's arguments, the more polarized the group became (Brauer et al., 1995). Thus, repetition of the same arguments resulted in stronger formation of attitudes and more group polarization.

### Groupthink

In the early 1960s, President John F. Kennedy took the world to the brink of nuclear war when he ordered the invasion of Cuba. This invasion, which occurred at the Bay of Pigs, was a terrible decision and a well-remembered failure. Researchers have analyzed group decision-making processes involved in bad decisions, such as the Bay of Pigs, the escalation of war in Vietnam, the Watergate cover-up, and the *Challenger* disaster, as well as flawed group decisions in business and other organizations. One reason that groups made bad decisions in the above examples is a phenomenon called groupthink (Granstrom & Stiwne, 1998; Janis, 1982, 1989).

*Groupthink* occurs when group discussions emphasize sticking together and agreement over the use of critical thinking to make the best decisions (right figure).

According to psychologist Irving Janis (1982, 1989), groupthink has a number of clearly defined characteristics: discussions are limited, few alternatives are presented, and there is increased pressure to conform. For example, the group usually has

**Groupthink**

What's most important is that we stick together.

a member that Janis calls a *mindguard,* whose job is to discourage ideas that might be a threat to the group's unity. In addition, groupthink results in viewing the world in very simple terms: there is the *ingroup,* which includes only the immediate members of the group, versus the *outgroup,* which includes everyone who is not a part of the group. When a group adopts the ingroup–outgroup attitude and mentality, the result is that it strengthens groupthink by emphasizing the protection of the group's members over making the best decisions.

Psychologists suggest several ways to avoid groupthink. The first is to allow the group's members the freedom to express differing opinions without being criticized or being considered a threat to the group. A second is to make sure that communication and gathering of information are kept open and unbiased within the group.

When studying group decisions, researchers also found that the more socially focused a group becomes, the poorer the decisions it makes; the more task oriented a group becomes, the better its decisions (Mullen et al., 1994). Additionally, if being in a group makes its members anxious, their performance and decisions will worsen (Camacho & Paulus, 1995). Thus, the best decisions would come from groups whose members feel free to express opinions, value gathering information, are task oriented, and are not made anxious by being in groups (Kramer et al., 1997; Rowatt et al., 1997).

After the Concept Review, we'll discuss a potentially very disruptive social behavior—aggression.

# Concept Review

**1.** A broad field that studies how our thoughts, feelings, perceptions, and behaviors are influenced by interactions with others is called (a)_____. A major branch of this field that studies how people perceive, store, and retrieve information about social interactions is called (b)_____.

**2.** Making judgments about the traits of others through social interactions and gaining knowledge from our social perceptions are called _____.

**3.** Widely held beliefs that people have certain traits because they belong to a particular group are known as (a)_____. An unfair, biased, or intolerant attitude toward another group of people is called (b)_____. Specific unfair behaviors exhibited toward members of a group are known as (c)_____.

**4.** Cognitive structures that represent an organized collection of knowledge about people, events, and concepts are called _____. They influence what we perceive and remember and how we behave.

**5.** The process by which we look for causes to explain a person's behavior is known as (a)_____. If we attribute behavior to the internal characteristics of a person, we are attributing the behavior to the person's (b)_____. If we attribute behavior to the external circumstances or context of that behavior, we are attributing the behavior to the (c)_____.

**6.** If we attribute the cause of a behavior to a person's disposition and overlook the demands of the environment or situation, we are committing the (a)_____ error. If we attribute our own behavior to situational factors but the behaviors of others to their disposition, we are committing the (b)_____ error. If we attribute success to our disposition and failure to the situation, we are using the (c)_____ bias.

**7.** Beliefs or opinions that include a positive or negative evaluation of some target (object, person, or event) and that predispose us to act in a certain way toward the target are called _____.

**8.** There are two different theories about why we change our attitudes. One theory says that experiencing cognitive inconsistencies produces psychological tension that we try to reduce by making our beliefs more consistent. This is called (a)_____ theory. If we take a public position that is counter to our private attitude, we are engaging in (b)_____ behavior.

**9.** Another theory of attitude change says that we first observe our own behaviors, which in turn causes us to change our attitudes. This is called _____ theory.

**10.** If a politician tries to get votes by presenting information with strong arguments, analyses, facts, and logic, he or she is using the (a)_____ route of persuasion. If a politician seeks votes by emphasizing emotional appeals, focusing on personal accomplishments, and generating positive feelings, he or she is using the (b)_____ route of persuasion.

**11.** Persuasion involves at least three elements: we are likely to believe a (a)_____ who appears honest and trustworthy; if we disagree with the message, it is better if the persuader presents a (b)_____ message; if the (c)_____ is less interested in issues, the peripheral route is more effective.

**12.** Any behavior we perform because of social influences or group pressure, even if that pressure involves no direct requests, is called (a)_____. A kind of conformity in which we give in to social pressure in our public responses but do not change our private beliefs is called (b)_____. Any behavior performed in response to an order given by someone in a position of authority is called (c)_____.

**13.** An increase in performance in the presence of a crowd is called social (a)_____; a decrease in performance in the presence of a crowd is called social (b)_____. An increased tendency for individuals to behave irrationally or perform antisocial behaviors if there is less chance of being personally identified is called (c)_____. Being socially inhibited to take some action, such as helping, because of the presence of others is called the (d)_____ effect.

**14.** A collection of two or more people who interact and share some common attribute or attributes is called a (a)_____. Togetherness, which is determined by how much group members perceive that they share common attributes, is called group (b)_____.

**15.** The phenomenon by which group discussion reinforces the majority's point of view and shifts that view to a more extreme position is called group (a)_____. Emphasizing group cohesion and agreement over critical thinking and making the best decisions is called (b)_____.

**Answers:** 1. (a) social psychology, (b) social cognition; 2. person perception; 3. (a) stereotypes, (b) prejudice, (c) discrimination; 4. schemas; 5. (a) attribution, (b) disposition, (c) situation; 6. (a) fundamental attribution, (b) actor-observer, (c) self-serving; 7. attitudes; 8. (a) cognitive dissonance, (b) counterattitudinal; 9. self-perception; 10. (a) central, (b) peripheral; 11. (a) source, (b) two-sided, (c) audience; 12. (a) conformity, (b) compliance, (c) obedience; 13. (a) facilitation, (b) inhibition, (c) deindividuation, (d) bystander; 14. (a) group, (b) cohesion; 15. (a) polarization, (b) groupthink

Shock Controller

Slight shock — MAXIMUM XXX 450 volts

# F. Aggression

## Definition

**Why so much violence?**

With frightening regularity, we hear reports of drive-by killings, spouse and child abuse, violent behaviors in schools, revenge-shooting by angry workers, and other forms of violence and aggression (Stanton et al., 1997a).

*Aggressive behavior* is any act that is intended to do physical or psychological harm.

As the right graph shows, in 1996 about 48% of homes in the United States have guns compared to about 1% of the homes in Japan. In 1994, there were 32 gun murders in Japan compared to 15,456 in the United States (Kristof, 1996). Experts predict that by the year 2003, guns will surpass traffic accidents as the leading cause of injuries and death in the United States (Squitieri, 1994). Although gun restrictions do not keep guns out of the hands of criminals, gun control does cut down on murders within families and gun crimes by teenagers, which account for a high percentage of violent deaths (Kristof, 1996).

**Percentage of Homes with Guns**

Japan 1.0
England & Wales 4.4
Germany 8.9
Australia 15.1
Canada 24.2
Switzerland 27.2
United States 48.0

Source: United Nations Interregional Crime and Justice Research Institute, 1996

Expert psychologists discuss a number of factors that contribute to aggression, including genetic factors, neurotransmitters in the brain, personality characteristics, social feedback, exposure to violence in neighborhoods and in the media, and family environment (Azar, 1994a). Based on their findings, psychologists developed the following model of aggression.

**Model of aggressive behavior.** One model of why we act aggressively assumes that we go through the following series of steps: (1) A person encounters a provoking or dangerous situation. (2) The person's initial emotional response is to feel threatened or bad. (3) The person's initial behavioral response is either to fight or to flee. (4) The person chooses between fighting and fleeing on the basis of the interaction among three major factors that differ for each person: predisposing biological factors (genetic predispositions or brain neurotransmitters), social learning factors, and environmental or situational factors (Berkowitz, 1994).

According to this model, one person may flee the provoking situation while another may stay and fight, depending on the interaction of biological, social, and situational factors. To help you understand these factors, we'll discuss each one in more detail.

## Biological Factors

**What are some biological factors?**

You can clearly see how biological factors regulate aggression by watching the behavior of animals. Ethologists, who study animal behavior in natural settings, have identified numerous social signals that animals have evolved to stop fights and avoid injury. For example, the photo below shows an interaction between two wolves: One wolf makes a submissive gesture, rolling on its back, which stops the dominant wolf from attacking. Many dominant and submissive gestures observed in animals are programmed innate biological responses that regulate and control aggression.

**Aggression and neurotransmitters.** There is growing evidence that biological factors also influence aggression in humans. For example, from twin and adoption studies, researchers estimate that from 20 to 70% of human aggression is regulated by genetic factors (Manuck et al., 2000). One way that genetic factors can influence aggression is through the regulation of neurotransmitters, especially serotonin, in the brain.

Unlike humans, aggression in animals is largely controlled by biological factors.

For example, researchers studied psychiatric patients who scored high on aggression and impulsive behaviors, such as engaging in physical fights, assaults on people, and antisocial behavior involving police. Compared to patients who scored low, patients who scored high in aggression were found to have significantly lower levels of the neurotransmitter serotonin (Stanley et al., 2000).

Other researchers found a relationship between genes involved in manufacturing serotonin and levels of aggression. Specifically, those individuals who had higher levels of aggression and impulsive behavior shared genetic factors that resulted in lower levels of serotonin (Manuck et al., 2000). These lines of research point to an association among genetic factors, lower levels of serotonin, and higher levels of aggression and impulsive behaviors.

**Piece of Genetic Code**

Genetic factors control levels of serotonin, which are associated with aggression.

**Mutant mice.** Evidence supporting the involvement of serotonin in aggression comes from studies on mice whose genes have been altered so that they lack serotonin receptors in their brains. These mutant mice attack intruder mice faster and with more intensity, indicating that serotonin is involved in aggression (Shih, 1996).

Thus, both human and mice studies suggest that biological factors, such as genetic influences on levels of serotonin, are involved in levels of aggressive behavior (Manuck et al., 2000). However, researchers caution against using biological factors alone to label, prosecute, or imprison individuals for aggressive acts, since the influence of environmental factors on aggression accounts for at least 50% (Berman et al., 1997).

Besides biological factors, human aggression is also influenced by social and environmental factors.

## Social Cognitive and Personality Factors

**PS** Although biological factors may predispose a person to be aggressive, whether a person actually becomes aggressive also depends on his or her learning experiences and personality traits. One theory that explains how people learn to be aggressive is Bandura's (1965, 1999) social cognitive theory.

*Social cognitive theory* says that much of human behavior, including aggressive behavior, may be learned through watching, imitating, and modeling and does not require the observer to perform any observable behavior or receive any observable reward.

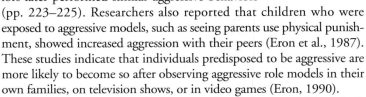

I like to bully kids and make them do things.

Support for social cognitive theory comes from both laboratory and naturalistic studies. A classic laboratory study by Bandura (1965) found that children who observed a model's aggressive behaviors later performed similar aggressive behaviors (pp. 223–225). Researchers also reported that children who were exposed to aggressive models, such as seeing parents use physical punishment, showed increased aggression with their peers (Eron et al., 1987). These studies indicate that individuals predisposed to be aggressive are more likely to become so after observing aggressive role models in their own families, on television shows, or in video games (Eron, 1990).

**Three factors.** Researchers suggest that aggressive children (bullies) develop into aggressive adults from an interaction of three factors: *genetic factors* that affect neurotransmitters and predispose individuals to develop an irritable or angry temperament; *social cognitive factors* that involve the imitation and modeling of aggressive behaviors observed in adults; and *personality factors*, such as being impulsive, having little empathy, and wanting to dominate others, which contribute to developing aggressive behaviors. The interaction of these three factors increases the chances of a child developing into an aggressive adolescent and adult (Elkins et al., 1997).

**Television/video games.** Current concern about the availability of violent television shows and video games is that children and adolescents, especially those with a predisposition to be aggressive, will imitate and model what they see. For example, after watching about 2,500 hours of television (no sports or newscasts), researchers concluded that the majority of programs on cable and network television contain violence, that 73% of aggressive actions go unpunished, and that 53%

Concern is that adolescents will imitate aggressive behaviors on television and in video games.

of all violent portrayals show no painful or negative consequences (Wilson, 1996). Mental health professionals analyzed over 1,000 studies and concluded that violence portrayed on television and in video games is associated with increased aggression in some children (American Academy of Pediatrics, 2000).

We have discussed how biological and social cognitive factors influence aggression. There are also environmental factors that can increase or trigger aggressive behavior.

## Environmental Factors

**How do you deal with frustration?**

In 1998, a new kind of violence was identified: road rage. This is the angry response of a driver frustrated by another's annoying driving habits to the point of aggressively pursuing, ramming, fighting, and even shooting the other driver. Road rage is an extreme example of a common environmental situation in which our goals are blocked and we feel frustrated. Another cause of frustration is hot weather (above 90° F), when incidences of violence significantly increase (Anderson et al., 1997). The idea that frustration plays a major role in aggression was proposed more than 60 years ago by a group of researchers at Yale University (Dollard et al., 1939).

The *frustration-aggression hypothesis* says that when our goals are blocked, we become frustrated and respond with anger and aggression.

However, researchers soon discovered that although frustration may lead to aggression, the link between the two is not absolute. Leonard Berkowitz (1989) reviewed the research on the frustration-aggression hypothesis and concluded the following:

- Frustration doesn't always lead to aggression.
- Social rules may inhibit aggression.
- Frustration may result in behaviors other than aggression.
- Cognitive factors can override aggression.

Thus, Berkowitz (1993) modified the original hypothesis.

The *modified frustration-aggression hypothesis* says that although frustration may lead to aggression, a number of situational and cognitive factors may override the aggressive response.

I'll get you for cutting me off, you dumb . . . !

Although our daily lives are often filled with frustrations, we usually find ways to control our frustrations and don't express them in anger, violence, or road rage. However, a child is more likely to react to frustration with violence if he or she has observed and imitated the aggressive behaviors of adults (Osofsky, 1995). Similarly, adults with a trait or tendency to be aggressive are more likely to react to frustration with aggression (Lindsay & Anderson, 2000).

**Three factors.** We have discussed three factors—biological, social cognitive, and environmental—that combine and interact to influence levels of aggressive behavior. Formerly, psychologists focused primarily on social cognitive and environmental factors in aggression. However, recent studies indicate that biological factors, which may account for 20 to 50% of aggressive behavior, need to be given equal consideration (Manuck et al., 2000).

One terrifying and degrading form of aggression is sexual aggression, which we'll examine next.

## Sexual Harassment and Aggression

**Why do men rape?**

According to a very reliable 1995 National Crime Victimization Survey, which pooled 100,000 U.S. citizens aged 12 and older, the annual number of rapes and sexual assaults was 354,670. About 51% of rape victims were under 18 years old, and of those, 85% were raped by either a relative or an acquaintance. However, only about a third of rape victims report their attacks to the police.

> In the United States, a woman is raped about every 3 minutes.

National surveys of female college students report that about 27% of college females had experienced either rape or attempted rape, and about 42% had experienced forced sexual encounters, some of which led to nonconsensual sexual intercourse (Flores, 1999).

Most researchers agree that the primary motivation for rape is not sexual but rather a combination of aggression, power, and control (Polaschek et al., 1997). For example, in interviews with ten convicted rapists, nine stated that sex was of secondary importance in motivating their assaults. Rather, these rapists stressed that either anger or the need to dominate was the most important factor to them (Levine & Koenig, 1980).

Another form of aggression occurs during sexual harassment. Researchers found that sexual harassment is widespread and was reported by 42% of women and 15% of men in occupational settings and by 73% of women and 22% of men during medical training. Although sexual harassment produces psychological and physical effects in 90% of the victims, only about 1 to 7% of victims file formal complaints (Charney & Russell, 1994).

Here, we'll focus on rape and sexual assault and begin by describing the more common types of rapists.

### *Characteristics and Kinds of Rapists*

Psychologists have identified several developmental factors that are associated with men who rape: they often come from broken homes, did not have a loving caregiver, were sexually or physically abused, were neglected, and spent time in penal institutions (Polaschek et al., 1997). However, these factors alone do not produce rapists; other men who have suffered similar development problems do not become rapists. At present, there is no generally accepted theory of what turns men into rapists.

Researchers have interviewed rapists to understand the motivation behind their sexual aggression. Rapists reported different degrees and combinations of anger, sexual violence, power, and control. Here are descriptions of four types of rapists (Knight, 1992).

> The most common rapist is a man who wants to possess his victim.

■ The *power rapist*, who commits 70% of all rapes, is not out to hurt physically but to possess. His acts are premeditated and are often preceded by rape fantasies. He may carry a weapon, not to hurt but to intimidate the victim.

■ The *sadistic rapist* accounts for fewer than 5% of rapes, but he is the most dangerous because for him sexuality and aggression have become fused, and using physical force is arousing and exciting.

■ For the *anger rapist*, rape is an impulsive, savage attack of uncontrolled physical violence. The act is of short duration, accompanied by abusive language, and the victim usually suffers extensive physical trauma, such as broken bones and bruises.

■ The *acquaintance* or *date rapist* knows his victim and uses varying amounts of verbal or physical coercion to force his partner to engage in sexual activities.

These examples indicate that men rape for a number of or combination of reasons, such as to exercise power and control, express anger, and become sexually aroused.

Other factors that contribute to rape are the false beliefs, called rape myths, that some men hold about women.

### *Rape Myths*

One consistent finding about rapists is that they hold negative and demeaning attitudes toward women. For example, here are some of their negative attitudes:

■ Healthy women cannot be raped against their will.

■ Women often falsely accuse men of rape.

■ Rape is primarily a sex crime committed by sex-crazed maniacs.

■ Only bad girls get raped.

■ If a girl engages in necking or petting and lets things get out of hand, it is her own fault if her partner forces sex on her.

> Some men mistakenly believe that only bad women get raped.

These kinds of statements are called rape myths (Foubert & Marriott, 1997).

*Rape myths* are misinformed, false beliefs about women, and these myths are frequently held by rapists.

Men who believe in rape myths tend to have a more traditional view of sex roles and hold more negative attitudes toward women. Although researchers have found that acceptance of rape myths is more common among men who have raped, rape myths are also held by men in general. For example, one survey of male college students reported that from 17 to 75% of the students agreed with one or more of nine rape myths (Giacopassi & Dull, 1986). This association between rape myths and rapists illustrates how negative beliefs and attitudes can contribute to sexual aggression (Johnson et al., 1997).

In the United States, it is estimated that during their lifetime 20–30% of women will be victims of some type of sexual aggression. Researchers are currently starting a number of rape prevention programs to both prevent rape and stop the perpetuation of rape myths (Ullman, 1997). We'll discuss ways to prevent rape in the upcoming Application section.

Next, we'll discuss how cultures differ in their attitudes toward beauty, heart transplants, and women's rights.

## Niger: Beauty Ideal

**How do African women judge beauty?**

One reason that the concept of attitude has been so dominant in social psychology is that our attitudes push or predispose us to think and behave in certain ways. What we often don't realize is how much our culture shapes our attitudes. For example, in the United States, the current attitude, especially among the middle and upper classes, is that for a woman to be attractive, she should be slender. This thin-is-beautiful attitude can pressure women to behave in certain ways, such as to constantly worry about their weight and go on strict diets, which in some cases may result in eating disorders (Heatherton et al., 1997).

But thin is not always beautiful. For example, in Niger, Africa, a small group of young women were discussing who had the most beautiful body. They all agreed on Monique, age 15, because she was already heavy for her age and on her way to being

The beauty ideal in Niger is to be heavy.

very rotund. As one woman said, "I want to gain weight like Monique. I don't want to be thin" (Onishi, 2001, p. A4).

In Niger, as well as in many parts of Africa, being fat is the beauty ideal for women and beauty contests are won by the heaviest women. Before getting married, young brides-to-be are sent to so-called fattening rooms, where the goal is to eat to get fat and round so that the bride will be admired for her fullness. If a married woman is not round and fleshy, the villagers will accuse the husband of not taking care of her.

As one African doctor said, "In America, you are rich and have everything and the women want to be thin as if they had nothing. Here in Africa, we have nothing but women buy products to become fat and show they had everything" (Onishi, 2001, p. A4). This comparison of beauty attitudes between America and Africa clearly shows how cultural values not only shape attitudes but also predispose us to behave in certain ways.

A different debate over attitudes is going on in Japan.

## Japan: Organ Transplants

**How do Japanese view heart transplants?**

Miss Wakana Kume, who lives in Japan, was going to die unless she received a liver transplant. However, since 1968, it has been illegal in Japan to transplant organs from donors who are brain-dead. Like all Japanese, Miss Kume grew up with the attitude that brain-dead was not really dead, so she was very reluctant to get a transplant from a brain-dead donor. But because of the seriousness of her condition, Miss Kume flew to Australia, where she underwent a liver transplant. In a very real sense, Miss Kume engaged in counterattitudinal behavior by doing a behavior opposite of what she believed—getting a transplanted organ. Since her life-saving transplant, Miss Kume has changed her attitude toward transplant organs and now approves of them. This is a real example of changing attitudes by engaging in counterattitudinal behavior.

There are almost no organ transplants in Japan.

The reason there were about 24,000 organ transplants in the United States in 1997 but none in Japan is that cultures have different definitions of death. In the United States, death is defined as brain death—when a person's brain no longer shows electrical activity, even though the heart is still beating. In Japan, however, death is defined only as the moment when a person's heart stops beating, and donor organs can be removed only after the heart stops. But to be useful, donor organs must be removed when a person's heart is still beating. Currently, the Japanese are debating changing their definition of death to include brain death, which goes against a long cultural tradition. If brain death is legalized in Japan, organ transplants will be possible, provided that the Japanese change their attitudes toward death and accept organ transplants (WuDunn, 1997).

A debate over attitudes and behaviors is also going on in Egypt.

## Egypt: Women's Rights

**How do Egyptians view women?**

Since the early 1900s, Egyptian women have been fighting for their sexual, political, and legal rights in a society that is dominated by Muslim religious principles, which grant women few rights. For example, while women are supposed to wear veils to preserve their dignity, a husband may strike his wife as long as he doesn't hit her in the face and hits lightly. Many women are not given birth certificates, which means that they cannot vote, get a passport, or go to court. Although female circumcision is illegal in Egypt, virtually all women in certain areas have been circumcised (p. 346). There are no public hotlines to help battered women and no statistics on rape,

Egyptian women are fighting for equal rights.

although both are common in certain areas. Although Egyptian women are currently fighting for equal rights, such as not wearing veils in public (photo below), they are having limited success because these traditional attitudes are backed by powerful social forces, including political, cultural, and religious institutions (Daniszewski, 1999; Lief, 1994). In getting Egyptians to change their attitudes toward women, the persuaders will need to use some of the methods that we have discussed, such as using trustworthy and honest sources, presenting one- or two-sided arguments, and, depending on the audience, using either the central or peripheral approach.

Next, we'll examine programs psychologists have developed to change attitudes toward aggression.

# H. Application: Controlling Aggression

Why did only one of six children develop into a violent teen and adult?

The finding that about half the contribution to aggressiveness comes from genetic factors and about half from environmental ones explains what happened in this family of six children. One, called Monster Kody Scott, became a gang member and shot his first victim at age 11. He continued to engage in violent behavior until he was arrested, convicted, and sentenced to jail for robbery. When he wrote his autobiography from his prison cell, he blamed his prob-

lems and violent behavior on his parents' poverty and destitution and on his belonging to a violent gang. But as it turned out, Monster Kody Scott had three brothers and two sisters who grew up in the same poverty and destitution but developed into law-abiding citizens who are leading very productive lives (Azar & Sleek, 1994).

The fact that only one of the six children became an aggressive adult illustrates how the development of aggressive behavior depends on the interaction of biological, social cognitive, and environmental factors. Because biological and environmental factors are sometimes difficult to change, recent programs focus on social cognitive factors to reduce and control aggression.

## Controlling Aggression in Children

Most children show occasional outbursts of anger and aggression, but if these outbursts become frequent, young children may develop a pattern of using aggressive behaviors to deal with problems (Lemerise & Dodge, 2000). If this aggressive behavioral pattern is not treated early, it may persist and increase the risk of aggressive children developing later problems, such as substance abuse, criminality, and various mental health disorders (Herrenkohl et al., 2000). Researchers have discovered that aggressive children have a number of cognitive-behavioral deficits that make them perceive, remember, and react to a world that appears more hostile than it really is. We'll first discuss these cognitive-behavioral deficits and then a treatment program.

Treatment programs can prevent aggressive children from becoming violent adults.

### COGNITIVE-BEHAVIORAL DEFICITS

Parents and teachers need to realize that an aggressive child or teenager does not perceive the world, take feedback, or act as regular nonaggressive children do. Here are some of the ways that aggressive children differ (Spielman & Staub, 2000).

■ An aggressive child *does not accurately perceive or recall social cues.* For example, the aggressive child selectively attends to aggressive or hostile actions and overlooks positive social cues. When an aggressive child is asked to recall what happened that day, the child tends to remember all the hostile actions rather than any friendly cues.

■ An aggressive child *does not make accurate explanations* or attributions of the situation. For instance, aggressive children tend to attribute hostile actions to other children when, in fact, other children are not behaving in an aggressive or hostile way.

■ An aggressive child *does not have many adaptive solutions* to problems. This means that aggressive children tend to use hostile and aggressive actions to solve many of their problems rather than using nonhostile or verbal solutions.

■ An aggressive child *is reinforced for aggressive behaviors* rather than for positive social behaviors. That's because aggressive children get their way by using hostile actions, which in turn are reinforced. Aggressive children *have poor social skills,* which means they rarely solve problems in nonaggressive ways, such as by discussion.

Because of these cognitive-behavioral deficits, aggressive children perceive a more hostile world and respond with more aggressive behaviors (Spielman & Staub, 2000). There are successful programs that teach children how to control their aggression.

### PROGRAMS TO CONTROL AGGRESSION

Children who engage in a variety of antisocial and aggressive behaviors are usually described by the term *conduct disorder,* which is one of the most frequent reasons for referral to treatment programs (Kazdin, 2000). We'll discuss two successful programs for treating conduct disorder.

**Cognitive problem-solving skills training.** A well-researched treatment program involves helping aggressive children overcome the deficits in cognitive-behavioral skills that we just discussed. For example, because

You know I've got a quick temper so don't make me angry!

an aggressive child does not know how to stop thinking and acting in aggressive ways, therapists teach the child specific rules, such as no matter how angry the child gets, he or she must not hit, yell, or kick. The child receives special reinforcement for obeying these rules. The child learns to use self-statements to inhibit impulsive behavior, including "I can stop myself." The child learns to use alternative, nonaggressive solutions when frustrated. These might be hand clapping, scribbling on a sheet of paper, or tensing and relaxing muscles. Cognitive programs have reduced the aggression of children in home and school (Kazdin, 2000).

**Parent Management Training (PMT).** One of the best researched treatment programs for conduct disorder is called Parent Management Training or PMT. In this program, a therapist teaches the parents how to use specific procedures in the home to alter angry interactions with their child, to decrease deviant behaviors, and, very important, to promote positive or prosocial behaviors. For example, parents learn to not reinforce aggressive behaviors that a child uses to get his or her way, to establish and enforce reasonable rules, and to reinforce appropriate behaviors. PMT has proven very effective in decreasing aggressive behaviors in the home and school (Kazdin, 2000).

Now, we'll examine methods of controlling aggression in adults.

## Controlling Anger in Adults

**What should I do?**

You've probably known people who get mad, rant and rave, and then take their anger out on whoever happens to be near. Then, after their violent outbursts, they may apologize, say they're sorry, or explain that they have to let out their angry feelings or they'll explode. Is it true that "letting it all out" is a good way to deal with anger?

### CATHARSIS

A popular idea for reducing and controlling aggression involves the idea of cartharsis.

*Catharsis* refers to a psychological process through which anger or aggressive energy is released by expressing or letting out powerful negative emotions.

According to the concept of catharsis, a good way to deal with anger or aggression is to "let off steam," which means expressing strong negative emotions by yelling, arguing, hitting, or kicking something.

Sigmund Freud used the term *catharsis* to mean that engaging in aggressive behavior can get rid of pent-up emotions and thus be helpful for reducing aggression. However, most research does not support Freud's conclusion about the usefulness of catharsis. For example, researchers measured the levels of aggression in fans before and after a football game. On the basis of catharsis, we would predict that the losing fans who showed the most aggression during the game should have the lowest levels after the game. Instead, researchers found that both losing and winning fans showed increased levels of aggression at the end of the game (Goldstein, 1989).

Researchers report that it is difficult to find appropriate people on whom to vent cathartic aggression, since these people feel obliged to respond with aggression (Tavris, 1982). Thus, venting aggression may actually trigger aggression (Lippa, 1994). Generally, the notion that catharsis is a method for reducing aggression by letting out strong aggressive emotions has received little scientific support (Deaux et al., 1993).

*When I get angry, I like to let it all out!*

### COGNITIVE-BEHAVIORAL PROGRAM

A more successful method than catharsis for dealing with anger involves a program that combines cognitive-behavioral methods and learning new social skills.

Researchers selected college students who reported a personal problem with getting angry and were interested in learning how to better manage their anger. The students were randomly assigned to either a control group, which was promised future treatment, or an experimental group, which received eight weekly 1-hour sessions in using a cognitive-behavioral program for controlling anger.

For example, many students said that they got angry while driving. For their first three sessions, students were asked to observe themselves (called self-monitoring), write down those situations in which they got angry, and describe their negative thoughts and behaviors. They were also asked to write down positive thoughts and behaviors that they could use to stop getting angry. In sessions 4–8, students reviewed their self-monitoring experiences and role-played using anger-lowering thoughts and behaviors in the sessions and then practiced them while driving.

Four weeks after treatment, subjects were asked to rate their level of anger in situations that had been previously identified as causing anger. Compared to control subjects, those in the cognitive-behavioral program reported a large and significant reduction in both experiencing and expressing anger in situations that previously caused anger. Researchers concluded that cognitive-behavioral programs proved effective in reducing anger and that reductions were maintained in a 15-month follow-up (Deffenbacher et al., 2000).

## Controlling Sexual Aggression

**What are the risks?**

According to feminist writers, sexually aggressive male behavior is the result of normal male socialization in the American culture (Rozee, 1993). This idea is supported by data suggesting that when sexual aggression is broadly defined, the majority of men admit to being sexually aggressive (Hall & Barongan, 1997). Part of socialization involves exposure to situations that may reinforce and increase the risk of males being sexually aggressive. For example, the media (movies, videos, songs) portray situations in which men believe that being sexually aggressive does no harm and may even be arousing to their partners, or may be necessary to achieve their goals (Lonsway & Fitzgerald, 1994). These media portrayals reinforce the idea that sexual aggression is acceptable and even arousing to women and increase the risk that men will be sexually aggressive and not be perceptive and responsive to a woman's wishes or refusals.

Somehow the socialization creates a difference between men who are sexually aggressive and those who are not. For

One of the risks in sexual aggression is that males do not take "NO!" for an answer.

instance, men who report higher levels of sexual aggression also perceived women as showing higher levels of sexual interest in nonsexual, mundane situations (having a conversation). Researchers concluded that, in these cases, it is not the women's behaviors that put them at risk for sexual aggression but rather it is that sexually aggressive males misperceive women as showing sexual interest when they are not (Bondurant & Donat, 1999). These researchers suggest that prevention programs need to educate sexually aggressive men about how they overperceive sexual interest of women, even in mundane situations.

According to researchers, one way to avoid sexual aggression on a date is for men and women to know the risk factors. For women, these include the heavy use of alcohol or other drugs that dull reason and perception. For men, these include overuse of drugs, thinking that paying the expenses entitles him to sex, misperceiving his date's sexual interest, and not recognizing that "NO" means "NO!" (Shotland & Hunter, 1995; Ullman, 1997).

# Summary Test

## A. PERCEIVING OTHERS

**1.** How our thoughts, feelings, perceptions, and behaviors are influenced by interactions with others is studied in the field of (a)_____ psychology. A branch of this field studies how people perceive, store, and retrieve information about social interactions; this branch is called social (b)_____.

**2.** Making judgments about the traits of others through social interactions and gaining knowledge from our social perceptions are part of person (a)_____. This process is aided by a wealth of social information that is stored in our memories. However, some memories can bias our perceptions. Widely held beliefs that people have certain traits because they belong to a particular group are called (b)_____. Negative beliefs that are often accompanied by an unfair, biased, or intolerant attitude toward another group of people are called (c)_____. Specific unfair behaviors exhibited toward members of a group are called (d)_____.

**3.** Cognitive structures that represent an organized collection of knowledge about people, events, and concepts are called _____. They help us select and interpret relevant information from a tremendous amount of incoming social information and provide guidelines for how we should behave in different situations.

**4.** There are different kinds of schemas: those that include our judgments about the traits that we and others possess are called (a)_____ schemas; those that are based on the jobs people perform or the social positions they hold are called (b)_____ schemas; those that contain behaviors that we associate with familiar activities, events, or procedures are called (c)_____ schemas, or scripts.

## B. ATTRIBUTIONS

**5.** The factors or events that we point to as causes or explanations for people's behavior are called (a)_____. If we attribute behavior to the internal characteristics of the person performing the behavior, we are using (b)_____ explanations; if we attribute behavior to the circumstances or context of that behavior, we are using (c)_____ explanations.

**6.** Harold Kelley proposed that in deciding between dispositional and situational explanations, we should look for factors that change along with the behavior we are trying to explain; this is called the _____ model. To decide between dispositional and situational explanations, we should look for consensus, consistency, and distinctiveness.

**7.** An error that we make by attributing the cause of a behavior to a person's disposition and overlooking the demands of the environment or situation is the (a)_____ attribution error. If we attribute our own behavior to situational factors but others' behaviors to their dispositions, we fall prey to the (b)_____ effect. If we attribute success to our disposition and failure to the situation, we use the (c)_____ bias.

## C. RESEARCH FOCUS: ATTRIBUTIONS & GRADES

**Dropout Rate from College**

Percent leaving school — 25, 15, 5 — Control, Change

**8.** Researchers found that freshmen who were encouraged to attribute their academic problems to _____ conditions, such as poor study habits, showed a significant improvement in grade point average and were less likely to drop out than were students who continued to attribute their poor performance to permanent factors.

## D. ATTITUDES

**9.** Beliefs or opinions that include a positive or negative evaluation of an object, person, or event and that predispose us to act in a certain way are called (a)_____. General attitudes are convenient guidelines for interpreting and categorizing objects and events and deciding whether to approach or avoid them. Attitudes have three components: beliefs and ideas make up the (b)_____ component; emotions and feelings make up the (c)_____ component; and predispositions make up the (d)_____ component.

**10.** A state of unpleasant psychological tension that motivates us to reduce our inconsistencies and return to a more consistent state is called (a)_____. To reduce this tension and return to a more consistent state, we may add or change (b)_____ or take a public position that is counter to our private attitude, which is called engaging in (c)_____ behavior. According to Daryl Bem's theory, we first observe or perceive our own behavior and then infer attitudes from that behavior; this is called (d)_____ theory.

**11.** One method of persuasion presents information with strong arguments, analyses, facts, and logic; this is the (a)_____ route, which works primarily on the cognitive component of our attitudes. Another route emphasizes emotional appeal, focuses on personal traits, and generates positive feelings; this is called the (b)_____ route and works primarily on the affective or feeling component. Three factors to consider in persuasion are the source, (c)_____, and (d)_____.

## E. SOCIAL & GROUP INFLUENCES

**12.** If you perform a behavior because of group pressure, you are exhibiting (a)_____. Giving in to social pressure in your public responses but not changing your private beliefs is called (b)_____. A sales technique that relies on the increased probability of getting a second request if you obtain compliance with a small, first request is called the (c)_____ technique. Performing a behavior in response to an order given by someone in authority is called (d)_____.

**13.** Any behavior that benefits others or has positive social consequences is called (a)_____ behavior. A form of helping that involves doing something, often at a cost or risk, for reasons other than the expectation of a material or social reward is called (b)_____. Two different models explain how we make our decisions to help. The model that frames our decision as a five-stage process is called the (c)_____ model. According to another model, we make decisions to help by calculating the costs and rewards of helping; this is called the (d)_____ model.

**14.** A collection of two or more people who interact and share some common attribute or attributes is called a (a)_____. How much group members perceive that they share common attributes determines group (b)_____. The formal or informal rules about how group members should behave are called group (c)_____. According to Leon Festinger's (d)_____ theory, we compare ourselves to others who are similar to us so that we can measure the correctness of our attitudes and beliefs.

**15.** If the presence of a crowd increases performance, it is called social (a)_____; if it decreases performance, it is called social (b)_____. If people in a crowd take on antisocial roles because they cannot be identified easily, it is called (c)_____. If an individual in a crowd is inhibited from helping someone in need, it is called the (d)_____ effect.

**16.** The effect in which a group discussion reinforces the majority's point of view and shifts that view to a more extreme position is called (a)_____. The phenomenon in which group discussions tend to emphasize cohesion and agreement over critical thinking and making the best decisions is called (b)_____.

## F. AGGRESSION

**17.** Three major factors influence aggression. The finding that aggressive male relatives all shared the same gene supports the influence of (a)_____ factors. The finding that people can learn aggressive behavior through observation, imitation, and self-reinforcement supports the influence of (b)_____ factors. The finding that frustration may lead to or trigger aggression supports the influence of (c)_____ factors.

**18.** The primary motivation for rape is not sexual but a combination of (a)_____, _____, and _____. Men who rape have been classified into four types: power, sadistic, anger, and acquaintance/date rapists. The misinformed beliefs that are frequently held by rapists and that are contributing factors to rape are called (b)_____.

## G. CULTURAL DIVERSITY: NATIONAL ATTITUDES & BEHAVIORS

**19.** National attitudes are important because they push or predispose citizens to (a)_____ in certain ways. For example, Niger women's attitude toward beauty motivates them to (b)_____ to become heavy. Because of Japan's attitude toward brain death, they do not approve of (c)_____. One reason Egyptian women are having such difficulty changing (d)_____ toward them is that these discriminatory policies are backed by social, political, and religious forces.

## H. APPLICATION: CONTROLLING AGGRESSION

**20.** An aggressive child perceives and reacts to a world that appears more hostile than normal because this child has a number of (a)_____ deficits. One program to decrease aggressive behavior teaches children how to control their (b)_____. Freud theorized that one way to control aggression in adults was to release emotional tension. This process, known as (c)_____, is supposed to get rid of pent-up anger, but there is little experimental support for this idea. A proven method to decrease anger involves a combination of cognitive, relaxation, and social skills training.

**Answers:** 1. (a) social, (b) cognition; 2. (a) perception, (b) stereotypes, (c) prejudice, (d) discrimination; 3. schemas; 4. (a) person, (b) role, (c) event; 5. (a) attributions, (b) internal (dispositional), (c) external (situational); 6. covariation model; 7. (a) fundamental, (b) actor-observer, (c) self-serving; 8. temporary; 9. (a) attitudes, (b) cognitive, (c) affective, (d) behavioral; 10. (a) cognitive dissonance, (b) beliefs, (c) counterattitudinal, (d) self-perception; 11. (a) central, (b) peripheral, (c) message, (d) audience; 12. (a) conformity, (b) compliance, (c) foot-in-the-door, (d) obedience; 13. (a) prosocial or helping, (b) altruism, (c) decision stage, (d) arousal-cost-reward model; 14. (a) group, (b) cohesion, (c) norms, (d) social comparison; 15. (a) facilitation, (b) inhibition, (c) deindividuation, (d) bystander; 16. (a) group polarization, (b) groupthink; 17. (a) biological, (b) social learning, (c) environmental; 18. (a) power, aggression, control, (b) rape myths; 19. (a) behave, (b) eat, (c) organ transplants, (d) attitudes; 20. (a) cognitive-behavioral, (b) anger, (c) catharsis

# Critical Thinking

Newspaper Article

## Teen Pregnancies Force Town to Grow Up

*by Sheryl Stolberg*

### Questions

**1.** Why is the new doctor surprised that, in this small community, about 12% of the births were to teenage mothers?

**2.** How could the residents of this small town, where everyone usually knows everything, not know that teenage pregnancy was a problem?

**3.** Which group attitudes or norms do the citizens of this small town share? How does a group benefit by sharing norms?

After 20 years of practicing obstetrics and gynecology in Indianapolis, 52-year-old physician William Stone was eager to set up shop in a community where he might make a difference. He chose Tipton, a small town in Indiana, and what a difference the doctor has made.

The first thing he noticed were the teenagers. Girls, some as young as 14, growing babies in their bellies. And not the stereotypical troubled teens, but girls from good families, girls in the National Honor Society at school.

In his first year of practice, Stone delivered infants to 16 teenagers. He did a little checking and discovered that unwed teens accounted for 12% of births in Tipton County—a rate slightly higher than both Indiana's and the nation's.

So it was that in August 1994, the doctor boldly informed his new hometown that it had a teen pregnancy problem. It was a declaration that opened a Pandora's box of questions about teenage sexuality, unwed motherhood, and, most important, the values that parents impart to children.

Listen to the troubled voices of Tipton and one can hear the voices of a troubled America. Adults preach abstinence but secretly expect their kids to have sex—and then worry that they are creating a self-fulfilling prophecy. A local minister wonders aloud whatever happened to shame.

In a community that prides itself on neighbor helping neighbor, people are now chiding themselves for coddling teen mothers. Educators fret over whether they have made it too easy for pregnant girls to get a diploma. Some are suggesting that teen fathers be banned from school sports.

At Tipton High School, the administration has cracked down on necking in the hallways. The quarterback got his girlfriend pregnant—and married her. His teammates think that's cool.

"I don't know of a society in the history of the world that has simultaneously stretched out marriage so long and has successfully preached abstinence before marriage," said William Galston, who heads the "religious and public values" task force of the National Campaign to Prevent Teen Pregnancy.

"My guess," he said, "is that most people in their heart of hearts, wish that teens would abstain. But they are not sure that they will and are not sure what the best response is to the fact that many of them won't." (Source: *Los Angeles Times,* November 29, 1996)

**4.** Why might parents experience cognitive dissonance after their good and loving daughter became pregnant?

**5.** Why has preaching abstinency not been more successful in preventing teenage pregnancy?

*Try InfoTrac to search for terms:* teenage pregnancy; norms; sexual abstinence.

---

### Suggested answers to Newspaper Article questions

1. The stereotype of a small community is usually close-knit families who raise their children with high standards and moral values that would completely discourage teenage sex and certainly teenage pregnancy.
2. Small towns often function like an ingroup whose members think alike and work together to protect the group's reputation. As an ingroup, the citizens would take measures, such as denying or hiding knowledge of teenage pregnancies, to protect itself against the opinions of outsiders (outgroups).
3. One of the main attitudes or norms that the community shares is that abstinence, especially for teenagers, is the best policy before marriage. The group comes together and develops group cohesion by sharing common attitudes or norms.
4. The parents expected their good and loving teenage daughter to follow their advice and abstain from premarital sex. But their good and loving daughter did not follow their advice and got pregnant. The parent's conflicting beliefs that their daughter was good but had gotten pregnant would cause cognitive dissonance. They might resolve this dissonance by believing that, although their daughter had become pregnant, she was now doing the good and right thing by getting married.
5. The problem is that changing attitudes and beliefs is difficult, especially in this case, when national surveys report that about 50% of teenagers have sex by age 17. In attempts to change attitudes through persuasion, many factors are involved: whether to use facts and logic, the central route, or use emotional appeals, the peripheral route; whether a one-sided or a two-sided message will be more effective; and who will be the most believable and trusted source of the message, the parents, teachers, minister, peers, or boyfriends.

# Links to Learning

## Web Sites

- **WADSWORTH ONLINE STUDY CENTER**
  **http://psychology.wadsworth.com**
  Quizzes, learning activities and exercises, a discussion forum, and hot links to Internet sites related to social psychology, including:

- **SOCIAL PSYCHOLOGY NETWORK**
  **http://www.socialpsychology.org/**
  This is the largest social psychology database on the Internet and is supported by the National Science Foundation. It features more than 5,000 links to related resources. May be read in English, French, Spanish, Italian, Dutch, and Portuguese.

- **CROSS-CULTURAL PSYCHOLOGY**
  **http://www.vanguard.edu/psychology/ webculture.html**
  This home page consists of links to a great variety of cross-cultural resources, including, for example, "Connectedness vs. Separateness: Applicability of Family Therapy to Japanese Families"; "American Indian Learning Styles"; "Refugee Health and Immigration Problems"; and "The Universal Black Pages."

- **CULTS**
  **http://www.kassiber.de/cults.htm**
  This page, devoted to secret societies and religious cults, consists of an extensive list of links, such as "Aum Supreme Truth," "Branch Davidians," "Killer Cults," and many more, including some you might not have thought of in cult terms.

## Learning Activities

- **POWERSTUDY™ BY ROD PLOTNIK & TOM DOYLE**

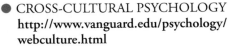

  **Check out CD: Module 25**
  CD 10.E: Cognitive Learning; book page 566

- **STUDY GUIDE TO ACCOMPANY INTRODUCTION TO PSYCHOLOGY, 6TH EDITION, by Matthew Enos**
  In Module 25, you're advised to honor your need to be effective in the world and congratulated for working your way through the course, the textbook, and the Study Guide. Reward yourself!

- **WEBTUTOR**
  **http://webtutor.thomsonlearning.com**
  Visit this site for interactive versions of the Study Guide features. Take a quiz, get your score—should you study a topic some more, or can you move on? For example, try defending and opposing the statement that humans are naturally aggressive. Define counterattitudinal behavior. "Prejudice" and "discrimination" mean the same thing: true or false?

- **INFOTRAC ONLINE LIBRARY**
  **http://www.infotrac-college.com**
  Use your password and then key in search terms such as those below to find popular and scientific articles on subjects covered in Module 25. Make the library work for you!

  Altruism     Prejudice     Social cognition     Stereotypes

- **PSYCHNOW!**
  CD for Macintosh and Windows includes a study guide, glossary, Web sites, and animations. For Module 25, see:
  - Helping Others
  - Attribution
  - Social Influence: Obedience and Conformity
  - Attitudes and Prejudice
  - Aggression
  - Environmental; Psychology
  - Gender and Stereotyping

## Study Questions

*Use InfoTrac to search for topics mentioned in the main heads below (e.g., attitudes, aggression, domestic violence).*

*A. **Perceiving Others**—Mark says that he doesn't make snap judgments but waits until he knows people. Do you think Mark does what he claims? (**Suggested answer p. 636**)

*B. **Attributions**—What should you be aware of when you try to explain the behaviors of your friend or mate? (**Suggested answer p. 637**)

C. **Research Focus: Attributions & Grades**—As a senior in college, what advice would you give to your younger brother or sister who is an incoming freshman?

D. **Attitudes**—You are trying to persuade your loved one to be more neat and tidy around the house. How would you do this?

E. **Social & Group Influences**—A family of five is trying to decide where to go on vacation. What problems might arise?

*F. **Aggression**—One of your friends says, "Getting angry and being aggressive are just part of human nature." What would you reply? (**Suggested answer p. 637**)

G. **Cultural Diversity: National Attitudes & Behaviors**—In changing national attitudes, do you think the central or peripheral route for persuasion is more effective?

H. **Application: Controlling Aggression**—Why do you think that about 4 million women each year are victims of domestic violence initiated by their spouses?

*These questions are answered in Appendix B.

# STATISTICS IN PSYCHOLOGY

## Descriptive Statistics

***Frequency Distributions***
***Measures of Central Tendency***
***Measures of Variability***

## Inferential Statistics

***Chance and Reliability***
***Tests of Statistical Significance***
***Analysis of Variance***
***Chi-Square***

## Descriptive Statistics

### Do numbers speak for themselves?

Suppose you are curious about how many people are capable of being hypnotized. You read up on how to induce hypnosis and put together a list of five things that people under hypnosis have been known to do, such as feeling no pain when a finger is pricked, being unable to bend an arm when told that the arm will remain stiff, and acting like a young child when told to regress to infancy.

You next persuade 20 people to participate in a little test. You attempt to hypnotize them and then ask them to do each of the things on your list. Of your 20 subjects, 2 follow none of your suggestions, 4 follow only one, 7 go along with two suggestions, 4 go along with three, 2 go along with as many as four, and only 1 follows all five.

The next day, a friend asks you how your study worked out. How would you make generalizations about your findings?

To answer this type of question, psychologists rely on *statistics*. Although you often hear that numbers "speak for themselves," this is not really true. Numbers must be sorted, organized, and presented in a meaningful fashion before they tell us much.

*Statistics* are the tools researchers use to analyze and summarize large amounts of data.

If the very word *statistics* brings to mind complex formulas you think you could never master, you may be surprised to realize how much you already use statistics in your everyday life. When you hear that a ball player has a batting average of .250 and you know this means he has gotten one hit in every four times at the plate, you are using statistics. When you understand that a rise in the median income means that people, on average, are earning more money, you are understanding statistics. When you know that scoring in the 90th percentile on a final exam means you did better than nine out of ten of your classmates, you are showing a grasp of statistics—specifically, descriptive statistics.

*Descriptive statistics* are numbers used to present a collection of data in a brief yet meaningful form.

One important part of descriptive statistics is presenting distributions of measurements and scores.

### FREQUENCY DISTRIBUTIONS

Individual differences show up in everything that can be measured. There are no measurements—whether of height, heart rate, memory capability, shyness, or political opinion—that do not show individual variation.

The *frequency distribution* is the range of scores we get and the frequency of each one when we measure a sample of people regarding some trait.

Frequency distributions are often presented in graphic form so their patterns can be seen at a glance. We'll discuss two of these distributions, normal and skewed.

### What is a normal distribution?

For many traits in a large population, the frequency distribution has a characteristic pattern. For instance, if you measured the height of 500 students chosen at random from your school, you would find a few very short people and a few very tall people, while the height of the majority of students would be somewhere in the middle. Height, like weight, IQ, years of education, and many other characteristics, has what is known as a ***normal distribution.*** When graphed, a normal distribution produces a normal curve.

A ***normal curve*** is a graph of a frequency distribution in which the curve tapers off equally on either side of a central high point.

This characteristic bell shape (Figure A.1) shows that most of the measurements fall near the center, with as many falling to one side as to the other. When you measure a trait that is distributed normally throughout a population, your measurements should produce an approximately normal curve, provided that your sample is large enough.

### What is a skewed distribution?

Not all traits are distributed normally.

*Skewed distributions* are distributions in which more data fall toward one side of the scale than toward the other.

When plotted on a graph, skewed distributions do not have a symmetrical shape. Instead, they have a "tail" on one end, which shows that relatively fewer frequencies occur on that side of the horizontal scale. When the

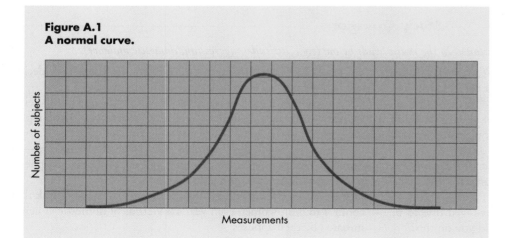

**Figure A.1
A normal curve.**

Number of subjects

Measurements

tail is on the right, as in Figure A.2, we say the distribution is skewed to the right, or has a *positive skew* (there are fewer frequencies at the higher end of the horizontal scale). When the tail is on the left, as in Figure A.3, we say the distribution is skewed to the left, or has a *negative skew* (there are fewer frequencies at the lower end of the horizontal scale).

The data you collected about susceptibility to hypnosis present a skewed distribution. If you plotted them on a graph, with score along the horizontal axis and number of people along the vertical one, the curve would be skewed to the right. This would show at a glance that more people in the sample fell at the low end of your hypnotic susceptibility scale than fell at the high end.

In fact, your sample is fairly representative of the general population. About twice as many people are poor hypnotic subjects as are excellent ones. But note that to be assured of obtaining the true distribution in a large population, you would usually have to test quite a large representative sample.

## MEASURES OF CENTRAL TENDENCY

Suppose you want to summarize in a few words the average height of people, the typical susceptibility to hypnosis, or the most common performance on an IQ test. For this you would need another kind of descriptive statistic, called a ***measure of central tendency.*** There are three measures of central tendency: the mean, the median, and the mode. Each is a slightly different way of describing what is "typical" within a given distribution.

The ***mean*** is the arithmetic average of all the individual measurements in a distribution.

Suppose that ten students in a seminar took an exam. Their scores were 98, 96, 92, 88, 88, 86, 82, 80, 78, and 72. You would find the mean by adding all the scores and dividing the sum by the total number of scores. In this case, the sum of all the scores is 860; dividing this by 10 gives a mean of 86.

The ***median*** is the score above and below which half the scores in the distribution fall.

If you took our ten test results and arranged them in order from highest to lowest, the median would be the point right in the middle, between the fifth and sixth scores on the list. That would be 87.

The ***mode*** is the most frequent measurement in a distribution.

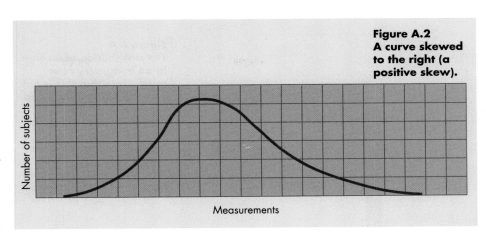

**Figure A.2**
**A curve skewed to the right (a positive skew).**

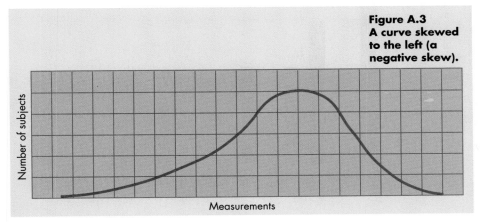

**Figure A.3**
**A curve skewed to the left (a negative skew).**

In this group of scores, the mode, the score that occurs most often, is 88.

In the example just given, the mean, median, and mode are very close together, but this is not always true. In some distributions, particularly those that are strongly skewed, these three measures of central tendency may be quite far apart. In such cases, all three of the measures may be needed to give a complete understanding of what is typical.

For instance, look at the graph in Figure A.4, which shows the distribution of income in an imaginary company. The mean income of its 50 employees is $30,600 a year. But look at the distribution. The president of the company earns $140,000, three other executives earn $80,000, and another four earn $60,000 a year. There are also six lower-level managers at $40,000, six salespeople at $30,000, and ten foremen at $25,000. The rest of the employees, the 20 people who keep the company records and run the machines, earn only $12,000 each. Thus, the mean of $30,600 does not really give an accurate indication of a typical income of an employee at this firm.

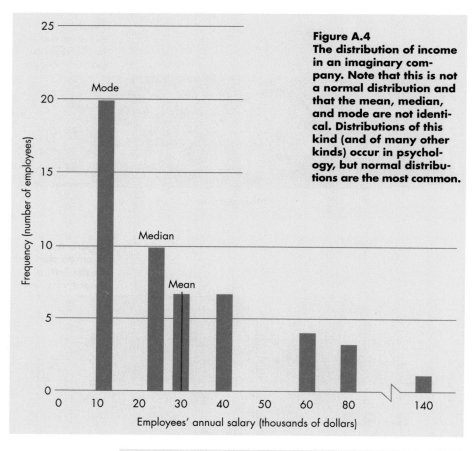

**Figure A.4**
**The distribution of income in an imaginary company. Note that this is not a normal distribution and that the mean, median, and mode are not identical. Distributions of this kind (and of many other kinds) occur in psychology, but normal distributions are the most common.**

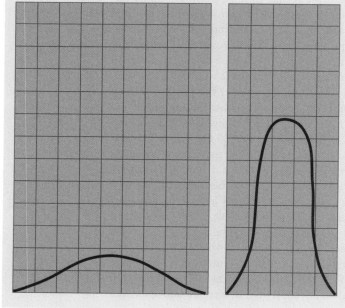

**Figure A.5**
**At left, a distribution with a great deal of variability. At right, a distribution with little variability.**

A better measure of central tendency in this instance is probably the median, or $25,000. It tells us that half the people at the company earn no more than this amount. Also revealing is the mode, or most common salary; it is only $12,000 a year. As you can see, the mean, median, and mode can provide us with very different figures.

## MEASURES OF VARIABILITY

If you get an A in a course and are told that the grades ranged from A to F, you will feel a greater sense of accomplishment than if the grades ranged only from A to B. Why this difference in how you perceive a grade? The answer is that it is often important to take into account the extent to which scores in a distribution are spread out. In other words, it is often informative to have a measure of variability.

A *measure of variability* is an indication of how much scores vary from one another.

On a graph, scores that vary greatly produce a wide, flat curve; scores that vary little produce a curve that is narrow and steep. Figure A.5 illustrates these two patterns.

One measure of variability is the range.

The *range* consists of the two most extreme scores at either end of a distribution.

Another measure is the standard deviation.

The *standard deviation* shows how widely all the scores in a distribution are scattered above and below the mean.

If scores cluster closely around the mean, the standard deviation will be small; if scores are dispersed widely from the mean, the standard deviation will be large. Thus, the standard deviation is an indication of how representative the mean is. If the standard deviation is small, we know that the mean is representative of most scores in the distribution. Conversely, if the standard deviation is large, we know that many scores are quite far from the mean.

Figure A.6 shows that the standard deviation divides a normal curve into several portions, each of which has a certain percentage of the total distribution. As you can see, 68.2% of all scores fall somewhere between the mean and one standard deviation to either side of it. If you move two standard deviations to either side of the mean, you will take in 95.4% of all the scores in the distribution. Finally, 99.8% of all the scores will fall between the mean and three standard

## How to Find the Standard Deviation

Finding the standard deviation of a distribution is not difficult, although it is tedious without the aid of a calculator. To compute the standard deviation, follow these five steps:

**1.** Determine the mean of all the measurements in the distribution.
**2.** Subtract the mean from each measurement and square the difference. (Squaring the difference eliminates the negative signs that result when dealing with measurements that fall below the mean.)
**3.** Add the squares together.
**4.** Divide the sum of the squares by the number of measurements.
**5.** Take the square root of the value you obtained in step 4. This figure is the standard deviation.

deviations from it. Only a scant 0.2% fall beyond three standard deviations.

Knowing the mean and the standard deviation of any normal distribution allows you to determine just how "average" any given score is.

For instance, suppose you take a difficult test consisting of 100 questions and receive a score of 80. How well did you perform? If you learn that the mean is 60 and the standard deviation is 8, you know that your score of 80 is very good indeed. The overwhelming majority of people—95.4%—scored no better than 76, or two standard deviations above the mean. Thus, relative to what most others have done, an 80 is excellent. By the same token, a 40 is not very good at all; 95.4% of people scored 44 or higher on this test. Thus, if you received a 40 you are near the bottom of the distribution and had better start studying much harder.

## Inferential Statistics

### Can scientists be 100% certain?

In the mid-1970s, many Americans were puzzled to learn that a distinguished panel of scientists could not determine with absolute certainty whether the artificial sweetener called cyclamate posed a risk of cancer. The scientists announced that, after months of research, costing millions of dollars, they could be only 95% sure that cyclamate was safe. Why this remaining margin of doubt? Why can't a team of

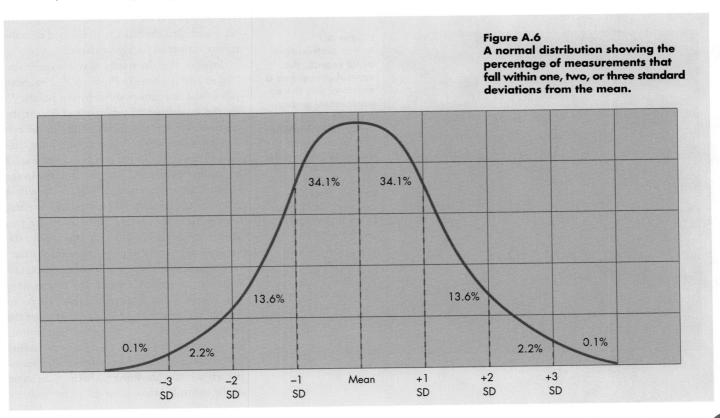

**Figure A.6**
**A normal distribution showing the percentage of measurements that fall within one, two, or three standard deviations from the mean.**

highly skilled researchers, backed by government funds, manage to tell us absolutely if a substance is hazardous to our health?

## CHANCE AND RELIABILITY

No one can totally eliminate the influence of chance on scientific findings. Even when you randomly select groups of subjects, there is always the possibility that, just by chance, those groups will differ slightly in ways that affect your experiment. This is why scientists must rely on statistics to tell them the likelihood that a certain set of results could have happened purely by chance. If this likelihood is small—5% or less—the researchers are justified in rejecting the chance explanation and in concluding instead that their findings are probably reliable. *Reliable* means that the investigators would probably obtain similar results if they repeated their study over and over with different groups of subjects.

Determining the reliability of experimental findings is a major way in which psychologists use inferential statistics.

*Inferential statistics* are a set of procedures for determining what conclusions can be legitimately inferred from a set of data.

These procedures include what are called *tests of statistical significance.* Tests of statistical significance were used to determine the 95% certainty of the finding that cyclamate is safe to eat. Different tests of statistical significance are needed for different kinds of data.

## TESTS OF STATISTICAL SIGNIFICANCE

Suppose you are an educational psychologist who has put together a special program to raise the IQ levels of children with learning disabilities. You expose one group of children with learning deficits to the special program and another group, with equal learning deficits, to the standard curriculum. At the end of a year, you give all the subjects an IQ test. Those in the special program score an average of ten points higher than those in the standard curriculum. Is this enough of a difference to reject the chance explanation and conclude that the program was a success? The procedure most frequently used to answer questions like this is a test of statistical significance called the *t* test.

### What is a t test?

The *t* test is an estimate of reliability that takes into account both the size of the mean difference and the variability in distributions. The *greater* the mean difference and the *less* the variability, the less the likelihood that the results happened purely by chance.

Imagine that the results of your experiment looked like the ones in Figure A.7. The mean IQs of the two groups differ by ten points: 75 for the experimental subjects and 65 for the controls. But look at the variability in the two distributions: there is almost none. All the children in the experimental group received a score within five points of 75; all the children in the control group received a score within five points of 65. It seems that some genuine effect is at work here. The IQ patterns in the two groups are distinctly different and are not the kinds of differences usually caused by chance.

Unfortunately, the results of most experiments are not this clear-cut. Far more often, the distributions look more like those in Figure A.8. In this figure, you can see that the mean difference in scores is still ten points, but now there is a sizable amount of variability in the two groups. In fact, some of the experimental subjects are doing no better than some of the controls, while some of the controls are

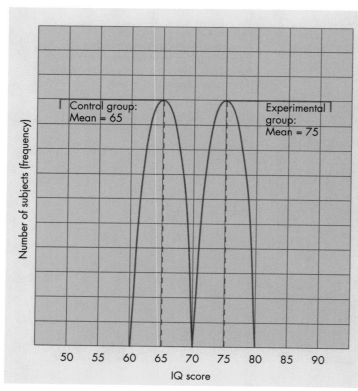

**Figure A.7**
**In this distribution of IQ scores, the control group has a mean of 65; the experimental group, a mean of 75. When distributions in a study show this little variability and no overlap between the two curves, they are not very likely to have happened purely by chance.**

Control group: Mean = 65

Experimental group: Mean = 75

Number of subjects (frequency)

50  55  60  65  70  75  80  85  90

IQ score

scoring higher than some of those in the experimental program. Is a mean difference of ten points in this case large enough to be considered reliable?

### When should you use a t test?

The *t* test also considers how many subjects are included in the study. You should not put much faith in a comparison of educational programs that tries out each approach on only two or three children. There is too great a likelihood that such samples are not representative of the larger population from which they are drawn. Let's say that, in the hypothetical experiment we have been describing, you included 100 randomly selected children in each of the two groups. It is much less likely that samples of this size would be biased enough to distort the research's findings.

To learn the steps involved in actually performing the *t* test, please read the accompanying box.

### ANALYSIS OF VARIANCE

Not all data lend themselves to a *t* test, however. Often researchers want to compare the mean scores of more than two groups, or they want to make comparisons among groups that are classified in more than one way. (For instance, does age or sex have an effect on how much children benefit from our special education program?) In such cases another test of statistical significance is needed. This test is

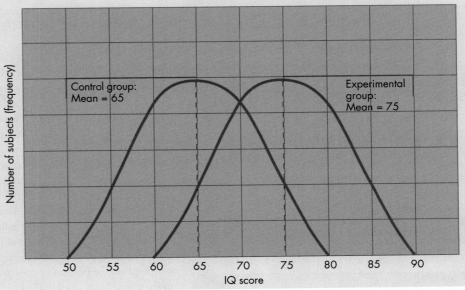

**Figure A.8**
**This set of distributions is much more likely than the one in Figure A.7. The mean is still 65 for the control group and 75 for the experimental group. But now the variability of the distributions is substantially greater. There is also substantial overlap between the two curves. Is the mean difference in this case statistically significant? A *t* test can provide the answer.**

called an ***analysis of variance,*** or ***ANOVA*** for short. An analysis of variance is rather like a more complex *t* test. To learn more about the ANOVA technique, consult any introductory statistics text.

---

### How to Perform the t Test

The *t* test is an estimate of how reliable the difference between two means is. To determine the likelihood that the outcome occurred by chance, you first need to know the size of the mean difference (mean 1 minus mean 2). In general, the larger the mean difference, the less likely that it happened by chance alone. You also need to know the variance within each group.

The *variance* is a measure of the variability within the two distributions.

In general, the lower the variance, the less likely that chance alone caused the results. Finally, you need to know how many subjects are in the random samples. In general, the larger the samples, the less the likelihood of a purely chance explanation.

To calculate the *t* test just follow these steps:

**1.** Determine the mean of the scores for each group and subtract one from the other.
**2.** Go back to the box on standard deviation and work through that calculation for each of your distributions, stopping at step 4. This gives you the variance of each distribution.
**3.** Add the two variances.
**4.** Add the total number of subjects minus 2 (in our example 200 – 2 = 198).
**5.** Divide the summed variances by the number obtained in step 4 and take the square root.
**6.** Divide the mean difference between the two groups by the square root from step 5.

If the samples add up to more than 50 individuals, any value of *t* over 2 is statistically reliable more than 95% of the time.

## CHI-SQUARE

Sometimes the data psychologists collect do not consist of sets of scores with means or averages. Instead, the researchers have recorded who does what, or who falls into which of several categories. For instance, psychologists have found that chess players are more apt to be introverts than they are to be extroverts. Is this just a chance association? To answer such questions, statisticians often use the *chi (ky) square,* a test of statistical significance.

Suppose you are a psychologist and you want to study the usefulness of fear tactics in changing people's behavior. You randomly select 200 habitual smokers who are willing to participate in an experiment. You expose half to a 20-minute talk on the known health hazards of smoking, complete with graphic illustrations of diseased lungs and hearts. You expose the rest to a 20-minute talk on the history of tobacco. After the talks, the members of each group are given the opportunity to sign up for a free "quit smoking" clinic. Some people from each group sign up for the clinic; some do not. The easiest way to present their choices is with a 2 × 2 table, like the one set up in Table A.1.

Table A.2 shows how the distribution worked out in your study. Of the 100 subjects in your experimental group (the ones exposed to the fear tactics), 60 signed up for the quit-smoking clinic and 40 did not. Of the 100 subjects in the control group, 40 signed up for the free clinic and 60 did not. Is this difference in the distribution of choices statistically significant? The chi-square can be used to estimate the reliability of this difference.

The *chi-square* is a test of statistical significance that compares the actual observed distribution of people (or events) among various categories with the distribution expected purely on the basis of chance.

If people had made their decisions purely by chance—for instance, by the toss of a coin—the same number of people would be expected to sign up for the clinic in each of the two groups. The accompanying box gives a step-by-step description of how to do the chi-square calculation.

**Table A.1: The Format of a 2 × 2 Table**

| Talk heard | Signed up for clinic | Didn't sign up | Row total |
|---|---|---|---|
| Fear tactics | | | 100 |
| No fear tactics | | | 100 |
| Column totals | | | 200 (grand total) |

**Table A.2: Study Results in Our Example**

| Talk heard | Signed up for clinic | Didn't sign up | Row total |
|---|---|---|---|
| Fear tactics | 60 | 40 | 100 |
| No fear tactics | 40 | 60 | 100 |
| Column totals | 100 | 100 | 200 (grand total) |

### How to Calculate Chi-Square

Chi-square ($\chi^2$) is an estimate of how sure we can be that a distribution of events or of people did not happen just by chance. In our example, chi-square calculates the *expected* number of people that a chance distribution would place in each of the categories represented by the four cells in the table. This expected number is then compared with the actual *observed* number of people in each of these categories, shown by cells (the data presented in Table A.2). If the difference between the expected and observed numbers is large enough, the distribution is not likely to have happened by chance alone.

Here are the steps in making the chi-square calculation:

**1.** Figure out how many people, by chance alone, would be likely to fall into the upper-left cell. To do this, multiply the first row total by the first column total (100 × 100) and divide by the grand total (200). The expected number is 50.

**2.** Subtract the expected number (50) from the observed number in the upper-left cell (60). The difference is 10 (60 − 50 = 10). Square the difference to eliminate negative signs (10 × 10 = 100) and divide the result by the expected number: 100 ÷ 50 = 2.

**3.** Repeat steps 1 and 2 for each of the four cells. In this example, the expected values are the same for each cell, but that won't always be true.

**4.** Add the four values you get from calculating the difference between the expected and observed number for each cell. This is the chi-square.

The reliability of the chi-square value must be looked up in a table. In this example, the fear-tactic subjects signed up for the clinic so much more often than the control subjects did that this distribution could have occurred by chance only two times in a hundred.

## DESCRIPTIVE STATISTICS

**1.** The tools that researchers use to analyze and summarize large amounts of data are called (a)_____. Numbers that are used to present a collection of data in a brief yet meaningful form are (b)_____ statistics, which are often used to present distributions of measurements and scores. The range of scores and the frequency of each one are called the (c)_____; this is often presented in graphic form so the patterns can be seen at a glance.

**2.** When graphed, a normal distribution produces a curve that tapers off equally on either side from a central high point; this is called a (a)_____ curve. This curve has the characteristic shape of a (b)_____ and shows that most of the measurements fall near the center, with as many falling to one side as to the other. However, not all traits are distributed normally. If more data fall toward one side of the scale than toward the other, it is called a (c)_____ distribution. Such distributions do not have symmetrical shapes when plotted; instead, they have a "tail" on one end. When there are fewer frequencies at the higher end of the horizontal scale (the tail is on the right), we say the distribution is skewed to the right or has a

(d)_____ skew. When there are fewer frequencies at the lower end of the horizontal scale (the tail is on the left), we say the distribution is skewed to the left or has a (e)_____ skew.

**3.** Ways of describing what is "typical" within a given distribution are called measures of (a)_____. The arithmetic average of all the individual measurements in a distribution is the (b)_____. The score above and below which half the scores in the distribution fall is the (c)_____. The measurement that occurs most often in a distribution is the (d)_____.

**4.** The extent to which scores in a distribution are spread out—in other words, how much scores vary from one another—is the measure of (a)_____. The two most extreme scores at either end of a distribution indicate the range. The measure of variability that shows how widely all the scores in a distribution are scattered above and below the mean is called the (b)_____.

## INFERENTIAL STATISTICS

**5.** Because the influence of chance on scientific findings cannot be completely avoided, procedures are necessary to determine what conclusions can be properly inferred from a set of data; these procedures are called

(a)_____ statistics. If the likelihood that the results could have occurred purely by chance is small, researchers can reject the chance explanation and conclude that their findings are probably (b)_____; that is, they would probably obtain similar results if they repeated the study over and over with different groups.

**6.** Different kinds of data require different tests of statistical significance. An estimate of reliability that takes the size of the mean difference and the variability in distributions into account is called the (a)_____; it estimates how reliable the difference between two means is. In general, the larger the difference between (b)_____, the less likely that it happened by chance alone.

**7.** A measure of the variability within two distributions is called the (a)_____. In general, the lower the variance, the less likely that chance alone caused the results. An analysis of variance, or (b)_____ test, is similar to, but more complex than, the *t* test.

**8.** How sure we can be that a distribution of events or of people did not happen just by chance is measured by another test of statistical significance, called the _____.

**Answers:** 1. (a) statistics, (b) descriptive, (c) frequency distribution; 2. (a) normal, (b) bell, (c) skewed, (d) positive, (e) negative; 3. (a) central tendency, (b) mean, (c) median, (d) mode; 4. (a) variability, (b) standard deviation; 5. (a) inferential, (b) reliable; 6. (a) t test, (b) mean difference; 7. (a) variance, (b) ANOVA; 8. chi-square

# CRITICAL THINKING STUDY QUESTIONS WITH ANSWERS

## *Why Answer the Critical Thinking Study Questions?*

As you read and study a module, you will learn new concepts, terms, and theories. We hope you will think about how you can apply these concepts to your own lives and to the problems and events in your own environment. To give you some practice, we have included answers to some of the Critical Thinking study questions that appear at the end of each module. Other kinds of questions may have a single correct answer, but study questions are open to a variety of interpretations. Answering them will help you learn to think about and discuss issues in greater depth.

Just as you must put extra effort into acquiring any complex skill, from tennis to algebra, you will have to exert yourself mentally to answer the study questions. To make the task easier, we have provided possible answers for selected questions. The first study question in each module is discussed in considerable detail to give you a strategy for answering other questions. Remember that our answers are only suggestions; you may think of other, equally good responses. If you use our answers as examples when you answer study questions on your own, you will acquire the very important skill of knowing how to apply concepts, terms, and theories to significant questions that often have no single correct answer. In fact, you will discover that many of the issues you face in the real world are very similar to the ones included here. When you have practiced answering our study questions, you will be better equipped to respond to related questions in your own life.

In this appendix we answer three to four study questions from each module. We always include a detailed response to the first question in each module and then suggest briefer answers to the following questions. As a result, you have an opportunity both to study a model for answering questions and to practice answering them more fully on your own.

At first you may find it difficult to answer study questions by yourself, but with practice you'll get the knack and actually find it fun to apply the concepts that you have learned. Remember, the more you stretch your mind by answering study questions, the bigger and stronger your mind will become. Unlike a balloon that bursts when expanded too far, your mind loves to be stretched and will never explode.

*Rod Plotnik*
*Katie Townsend-Merino*

# Module 1
## DISCOVERING PSYCHOLOGY

### A. Definition & Goals

STUDY QUESTION: How would you rank the four goals of psychology in terms of importance?

**1. Need to Know:** What specific information do I need to answer this question?

I need to know the four goals of psychology: **describe, explain, predict,** and **control.**

**2. Defining Terms:** Do I need to use my own words to define or review any terms?

I need to define each of the four goals.

**Describe:** Psychologists want to describe in detail the particular behavior. What is the organism doing?

**Explain:** Psychologists want to explain why organisms behave in a particular way. What causes this behavior to occur?

**Predict:** Psychologists want to make predictions about how organisms will behave in the future. If I know something about the causes of a particular behavior, I can predict who will demonstrate that behavior.

**Control:** Psychologists want to control the behavior of an organism. This may allow for positive change in an individual's behavior.

**3. Identify Key Words:** Which words in the question hold the key to the best answer?

The key words are "rank" and "importance." Both are dependent on the nature of a *particular* question. For example, if you are trying to understand what *causes* schizophrenia, the goals **describe** and **explain** would be ranked 1 and 2. However, if you want to *treat* or *prevent* schizophrenia, the goals **predict** and **control** would be ranked 1 and 2. Keep in mind, though, that it is impossible to predict and control without first describing and explaining!

### D. Cultural Diversity: Early Discrimination

STUDY QUESTION: Why would discriminatory practices exist in psychology, an area devoted to studying human behavior?

**Possible Answer:** In our culture people can be privileged in a number of ways. Privilege by race (White), gender (male), and class (upper) are among the most common types of special status. Historically, advantaged groups have had a difficult time seeing that status differences are real, or they have attributed them to differences in abilities. The founders of psychology were themselves privileged and saw no harm in their beliefs regarding women and minorities. For example, being Black and female in the early days of psychology meant that you were doubly disadvantaged. Disadvantages took a number of forms: difficulties for a minority member in obtaining an education, problems finding work in academia, and discrimination in employment as a clinical psychologist.

### H. Application: Study Skills

STUDY QUESTION: What changes would you make to study most efficiently?

**Possible Answer:** There is no simple relationship between the amount of time spent studying and the grades one receives. Study time is judged by its *quality* rather than its *quantity.*

In-class time must not be wasted. To make the most of it, I must keep my attention focused. I will ask myself questions during class, or I will participate in discussion when the opportunity arises. Note-taking in my own words demands more attention than direct dictation.

Good planning is the key to using study time efficiently. My plan will include specific goal setting, a realistic time schedule, and self-reinforcement. Such planning is *present-oriented* because it emphasizes getting down to work right away on tasks that will result in my meeting short-term goals. When I think, "How will I ever graduate?!" I'm looking beyond the here and now to do some rather destructive "global worrying."

When learning, I will focus on specific material and concepts, dividing the course into manageable chunks. I will do the self-tests that are contained in the text.

# Module 2
## PSYCHOLOGY & SCIENCE

### A. Methods for Answering Questions

STUDY QUESTION: Which method would you use to find out if caffeine improves memory?

**1. Need to Know:** What specific information do I need to answer this question?

I need to know the methods for answering questions: **survey, case study,** and **experiment.**

I need to know the **advantages** and **disadvantages** of each method.

**2. Defining Terms:** Do I need to use my own words to define or review any terms? Do I know the advantages and disadvantages of each?

I need to define each of the methods and list the advantages and disadvantages.

**Survey:** This is a way to get information by asking people directly to respond to a set of questions. This can be done in person, over the phone, or through the mail. An advantage is that you can easily get a lot of information relatively quickly, but it may be biased in accord with the beliefs and truthfulness of the respondents.

**Case study:** This is a way to get information by studying a particular individual in depth. You get a lot of information about one person, but this information may not apply to anyone else.

**Experiment:** This is a way to get information in a controlled environment so you can systematically manipulate treatments and measure their effects on behavior. You can identify cause-and-effect relationships, but information gained in a controlled environment may not apply in the real world.

**3. Identify Key Words:** Which words in the question hold the key to the best answer?

The key terms are "caffeine" and "improves memory." Although you might get interesting stories using the survey approach, your data would not be particularly valuable: it would be distorted by error and bias. That is, the placebo effect might be strong in this case. If you used the case-study method, you would learn a lot about the relationship between one individual's memory response and caffeine. But you would not know whether that information applied to anyone else. The best method of assessing cause-and-effect relationships ("Does caffeine cause memory improvement?") is to do an experiment. You could have two groups of students tested on the same material. Before the test, one group would drink a cup of caffeinated coffee and the other would drink one cup of decaffeinated coffee. You would then compare their test performances. This method would provide the most accurate answer to this question.

## D. Cultural Diversity: Use of Placebos

STUDY QUESTION: Why do Americans think it strange that Asians use rhino horn as medicine?

**Possible Answer:** Belief is the most important factor in generating the placebo effect. In some Asian cultures there is a strong belief that rhino horn is an aphrodisiac and a potent medicine. Therefore, there is a high incidence of rhino horn treatments available in those countries. In the United States, we hold no beliefs about the medicinal value of rhino horn and recognize it as a placebo. Therefore, we regard those who use rhino horn as strange! But Americans do not regard taking vitamin C as unusual because we believe it has medicinal value.

## F. Decisions about Doing Research

STUDY QUESTION: Which research techniques and settings would you use to study mental problems in the homeless?

**Possible Answer:** To decide on the best way of answering this question, let's look at each of the methods at our disposal and assess their utility.

*Questionnaires and interviews.* We could interview people who live in homeless shelters or on the street about their mental conditions. We could also talk to people who work with the homeless, asking their opinions about mental illness and the homeless.

*Standardized tests.* We could administer tests designed to detect different kinds of mental illness to homeless individuals. This might give us information about the prevalence and type of mental illness in that population.

*Laboratory experiment: behaviors.* It would be impossible to do a true experiment on this question. You cannot randomly assign someone to homelessness or mental illness. It would be difficult to get homeless people to a laboratory setting. You could possibly assess the effects of treatments for mental illness on the homeless.

*Laboratory experiment: physiological and genetic techniques.* Again, it may be difficult to get homeless individuals to a laboratory. If you could, you might be able to compare brain structure and function in the mentally ill and the non-mentally ill homeless.

## Module 3
## BRAIN'S BUILDING BLOCKS

### A. Overview: Human Brain

STUDY QUESTION: Why is it really smart to drive a car only if it is equipped with driver- and passenger-side airbags?

**1. Need to Know:** What specific information do I need to answer this question?

I need to know the advantages of airbags and to relate them to the information regarding the brain provided in this module.

**2. Defining Terms:** Do I need to use my own words to define or review any terms?

I need to know that airbags reduce the incidence of head injury in auto accidents.

**3. Identify Key Words:** Which words in the question hold the key to the best answer?

The key words are "really smart to drive . . . only." In the context of the current module, we should focus on the fact that airbags can help prevent head injuries during auto accidents. Severe blows to the head during a traffic accident can damage neurons in the brain and spine. Because mature primate brains are capable of very little growth of new neurons, such damage is usually permanent.

This is very serious because the brain controls almost all of our most important functions. So airbags are advantageous because they might help prevent irreversible damage to the brain.

### D. Sending Information

STUDY QUESTION: How are the structure and function of the axon like those of a battery?

**Possible Answer:** Both batteries and neurons must generate electrical impulses. They both achieve this by transforming chemical energy into electrical energy. Like batteries, neurons get their potential to generate electrical impulses from an imbalance between positive and negative charges. When the barrier between these charges is removed, positive and negative charges are attracted to each other like opposite poles of magnets. In a battery, a built-up charge is released when a connection is made between the negative and positive terminals. In the axon, the barrier between positive and negative ions is broken when the axon membrane becomes permeable.

Once the charge has been spent, both batteries and neurons must be recharged. For the neuron, this involves pumping the positively charged sodium ions back outside the axon membrane, which returns to its semipermeable state.

### H. Cultural Diversity: Plants, Drugs, & Transmitters

STUDY QUESTION: What are the different ways that drugs can affect neurotransmitters?

**Possible Answer:** Some of the ways drugs can affect neurotransmitters are by blocking reuptake, blocking receptors, and mimicking neurotransmitters. A drug like cocaine blocks the process of reuptake, so that the neurotransmitter stays in the synapse and continues to activate the receiving neuron. Other drugs block the receptors on the receiving neuron by occupying the receptor sites, which prevents the neurotransmitter from relaying its message. Finally, some drugs, such as mescaline, actually mimic one of the brain's natural neurotransmitters. These drugs bind to receptor sites, thereby activating neurons.

## Module 4
## INCREDIBLE NERVOUS SYSTEM

### A. Genes & Evolution

STUDY QUESTION:  If a species of humans with 5-pound brains was discovered, would their behavior differ from ours?

**1. Need to Know:** What specific information do I need to answer this question?

I need to know how much an average human brain weighs. Furthermore, I must know how much our ancestors' brains weighed on average.

**2. Identify Key Words:** Which words in the question hold the key to the best answer?

The key words are "would their behavior differ from ours?" In the context of the current module, we see that our brain has already tripled in size since the time of our earliest known ancestors. It is believed that these early humans did not make tools, make fire, or use language. Later, humans with a brain twice as large as our earliest ancestors' walked upright and made precise tools. By the time the human brain was as large as ours today, our ancestors were growing crops, living in communities, developing language, and painting representations of animals and humans. It seems that large changes in brain size are associated with large changes in human capabilities and behaviors. If we had 5-pound brains, our behavior would probably be very different. *How* different is impossible to predict. Much science fiction has been written on this topic.

### B. Studying the Living Brain

STUDY QUESTION:  How would you know if a professional boxer had brain damage?

**Possible Answer:** If the behavior or capabilities of this boxer have changed in ways that make us suspect brain damage, we could examine the brain using one or more imaging techniques.

*Computerized axial tomography—CAT scan.* We could take a sophisticated x-ray of the patient's brain to check for possible abnormalities. This would give us video images that represented slices of the brain. In this way, we could penetrate brain tissue to search for possible causes of the changes in the boxer's behavior.

*Magnetic resonance imaging—MRI.* We could penetrate farther into the boxer's brain with a device that sends nonharmful magnetic fields and radio frequencies through it. This gives us more detailed and clearer pictures and, unlike the CAT scan, does not expose the patient to radiation.

*Positron emission tomography—PET scan.* PET scans allow us to analyze brain function by providing a video image whose colors correspond to various levels of brain activity and abnormality. In our diagnosis of the boxer, we could compare these images to PET scans of age- and gender-matched controls to see if there are any *functional* differences.

### H. Cultural Diversity: Brain Size & Racial Myths

STUDY QUESTION:  Why is there a continuing interest in whether a bigger brain is more intelligent?

**Possible Answer:** Scientists might hope for a relationship between brain size and intelligence for a number of reasons. First of all, brain size is measurable, and thus we would have another quantifiable indicator of intelligence, of which there are precious few. Second, individuals' brain sizes can be quite easily compared. Group comparisons of intelligence have always intrigued science, though their usefulness to society has been questioned.

Other reasons have more to do with historical sociology than psychology. For example, Marx might have said that finding consistent differences in brain size that correlate with intelligence would be of interest to the ruling class, as a means of maintaining the status quo. An individual's ticket to aristocracy would be an MRI.

Finally, racism and sexism may play a part in the continuing interest in establishing differences. If such a measure were found to be reliably true, some would argue that, because their brains are somewhat smaller, women cannot be regarded as men's equal in intelligence.

## Module 5
## SENSATION

### A. Eye: Vision

STUDY QUESTION:  What kinds of problems in the visual system could result in some forms of blindness?

**1. Need to Know:** What specific information do I need to answer this question?

I need to know: the structure and function of the parts of the eye; how light gets to the retina; how the light is transformed into a neural message; and the pathway that the neural message takes to the brain.

**2. Identify Key Words:** Which words in the question hold the key to the best answer?

The key words are "problems in the visual system" and "result in . . . blindness." In order to effectively answer this question, we need to examine the entire process of normal vision and to imagine all the possible ways that this process could be interrupted.

Let's examine the structure and function of the eye. First, we see that if the cornea or lens is damaged or occluded, the light waves cannot reach the retina, and vision cannot occur. If the retina or any of its cells are damaged, the light waves cannot be transformed into neural messages that are sent to the brain; in other words, there can be no vision.

Second, if any part of the optic nerve is damaged, the neural messages cannot be sent to the brain. Damage to the part of the thalamus responsible for sending messages about vision to the occipital lobe would also cause blindness.

Finally, if an individual sustains damage to the primary visual cortex or the association cortex, either total or partial blindness would occur.

## B. Ear: Audition

STUDY QUESTION: What kinds of problems in the auditory system could result in some form of deafness?

**Possible Answer:** If we examine the structure of the auditory system, we can see where problems could occur that would result in some form of deafness. First, if the tympanic membrane lost flexibility (as sometimes occurs in children with frequent ear infections), the vibrations could lose strength and fail to be transmitted to the ossicles, which would prevent those sound vibrations from reaching the cochlea. Second, if any of the ossicles became calcified or fused together, sound vibrations would again be stopped before reaching the cochlea. These types of damage result in conduction deafness.

In the event of damage to any part of the cochlea, particularly the hair cells, the vibrations would not be changed into nerve impulses that are sent to the brain. Consequently, no sound would be heard. If there is any damage to the auditory nerve, the primary auditory cortex, or the auditory association areas, various types of nerve deafness will occur.

## D. Chemical Senses

STUDY QUESTION: How might a master chef's chemical senses differ from yours?

**Possible Answer:** It makes sense that a master chef would have a particularly acute sense of taste. The number of taste buds on the human tongue varies widely from individual to individual. Very likely, the tongue of a master chef would have more taste buds than the average person's. Also, because flavor is actually the combination of taste and smell, a master chef might have a very sensitive sense of smell (olfaction). It's reasonable to guess that a master chef could distinguish very subtle differences in flavor that the average person could not.

## Module 6
## PERCEPTION

### A. Perceptual Thresholds

STUDY QUESTION: How does Weber's law apply to how old you perceive someone to be?

**1.** *Need to Know:* What specific information do I need to answer this question?

I need to know what Weber's law states and what a "just noticeable difference" is.

**2.** *Defining Terms:* Do I need to use my own words to define or review any terms?

I need to define *just noticeable difference* and Weber's law.

**Just noticeable difference (JND):** The smallest increase or decrease in the intensity of a stimulus that a person can manage to detect.

**Weber's law:** This law states that the amount of increase in a stimulus needed to provide a just noticeable difference grows with the intensity of the stimulus.

**3.** *Identify Key Words:* Which words in the question hold the key to the best answer?

The key words are "how old you perceive someone to be." When people are babies, just a few months make a huge difference in how old we perceive them to be. As humans age, the increase in time before someone looks older becomes longer; it may even be many years. For example, it might take five or more years before someone of 60 looks older to us, while if we saw a child at 3 it might take only six months before the child looks different. This follows directly from Weber's law. If the person's age is the stimulus, Weber's law says that the change in the person's age that we are able to notice increases with increase in intensity of the stimulus—that is, as the person gets older.

### B. Sensation versus Perception

STUDY QUESTION: What would your life be like if your brain could receive sensations but could not assemble them into perceptions?

**Possible Answer:** Sensations are just the bits of information that we first become aware of from an outside stimulus. The receptors have transformed the stimulus into a neural impulse that the brain can understand. However, without perception, those neural impulses have *no meaning*. For example, if you had no ability to form visual perceptions, you would be aware that something was out there in the environment, but you would not be able to know or to tell anyone what it was.

If you lost *all* your perceptual abilities, you would be extremely disadvantaged; in fact, the world would cease to have meaning. You would be unable to form a relationship with the world.

### H. Cultural Diversity: Influence on Perceptions

STUDY QUESTION: When foreigners visit the United States, what do you think they perceive differently?

**Possible Answer:** It is very difficult to answer this question because the way we perceive our own world is invisible to us. However what is normal in one culture may be abnormal in another. For example, it may seem weird to us that women in India cover their heads. But, to Indians, it is the custom. So to answer this question, we have to step outside ourselves and our culture.

The new visitor might notice that American teenagers are more heavily monitored by their parents than are teenagers in Europe. It is normal in many European countries for adolescents of 16 to smoke, drink, and dance the night away (with no curfew) at the local discos.

## Module 7
## CONSCIOUSNESS, SLEEP, & DREAMS

### A. Continuum of Consciousness

STUDY QUESTION: How many different states of consciousness have you been in today?

**1.** *Need to Know:* What specific information do I need to answer this question?

I need to know what the different states of consciousness are.

The states of consciousness include controlled processes, automatic processes, daydreaming, altered states of consciousness, sleep and dreams, the unconscious, and unconsciousness.

**2.** *Defining Terms:* Do I need to use my own words to define or review any terms?

I need to define each of the states of consciousness.

**Controlled processes:** These activities require our full awareness and concentration to complete. Usually we cannot perform other tasks at the same time.

**Automatic processes:** These tasks (eating, driving, listening to the radio) are performed on autopilot and can be done in conjunction with other activities.

**Daydreaming:** This occurs with very low levels of awareness and often *during* automatic processes. In this state, we are fantasizing or imagining while we are awake.

**Altered states of consciousness:** We experience these states under the influence of an external source or technique, such as meditation, psychoactive drugs, sleep deprivation, or hypnosis.

**Sleep and dreams:** During **sleep,** we go through five different stages of awareness and consciousness. When we **dream,** we experience visual and auditory images, both in black and white and in color.

**The unconscious: Freud's theory of the unconscious** says that when we experience something threatening (sexual or aggressive events or thoughts), we put these in a place in our mind that cannot be accessed during ordinary recall. The updated theory of the **cognitive unconscious** says that a mental structure of which we are unaware influences our conscious behaviors and thoughts.

**Unconsciousness:** This refers to a state in which we are completely unaware and unresponsive, most often as a result of a head injury, disease, or surgical anesthesia.

**3.** *Identify Key Words:* Which words in the question hold the key to the best answer?

The key words are "How many . . . states . . . have you been in today?" Simply review what you have learned about the different states and apply it to what you have experienced so far today.

### D. Research Focus: Circadian Preference

STUDY QUESTION: What kind of problems might arise if a morning person married an evening person?

**Possible Answer:** The lifestyles of these two people are likely to be quite different. The morning person would wake up early and get a number of things accomplished in the morning. She or he would eat a large breakfast before beginning the day. The evening partner would probably be annoyed by all this early activity. She or he would wake up later, skip breakfast (or eat lightly), and not feel like beginning the day's activities until the afternoon or evening. During the evening, when the night owl still had energy to spare, the early bird would be wound down and ready for bed. This couple would need to understand that their differences in this regard are innate and that

one style is not superior to the other. They would need to compromise and have realistic expectations (which is difficult for any of us!).

### F. Cultural Diversity: Incidence of SAD

STUDY QUESTION: What cultural values might New Hampshire residents have that contribute to their incidence of SAD?

**Possible Answer:** This question is difficult to answer for those of us who have never been to New Hampshire. The answer given here is based purely on film and TV portrayals of New Hampshirites, which are probably full of stereotypes.

Icelanders appear to have lower expectations of the good life than do New Hampshirites. When New Hampshirites' expectations are not met, depression may be one outcome. Also, the text reports that Icelanders tend not to complain. In New Hampshire, complaining is more socially acceptable and, in fact, may be a lifestyle itself. Complaining may cause New Hampshirites to dwell on problems that might trigger SAD. Further, if New Hampshirites have fewer support systems than do Icelanders, that would also contribute to the higher incidence of SAD. (It also seems possible that there could be fewer people who are susceptible to SAD in Iceland—from an evolutionary perspective.)

## Module 8
## HYPNOSIS & DRUGS

### A. Hypnosis

STUDY QUESTION: A student has great test anxiety, which is interfering with his success in college. Would hypnosis help?

**1.** *Need to Know:* What specific information do I need to answer this question?

I need to know what type of hypnotic tool I could use and whether hypnosis helps with relaxation.

I could give the student a posthypnotic suggestion to be relaxed during test taking.

**2.** *Identify Key Words:* Which words in the question hold the key to the best answer?

The key words are "would hypnosis help [with test anxiety]?" I know from the text that I can give a posthypnotic suggestion, and the text further reports that hypnosis appears to relieve tension. So, in this case hypnosis might be worth a try—if my student is susceptible.

### F. Alcohol

STUDY QUESTION: If researchers know who has an increased risk for alcoholism, at what age should such a person be told?

**Possible Answer:** Before we tell people that they are at increased risk for any condition, we must have clear evidence that a risk exists. What is the evidence that we can confidently predict increased risk for alcoholism when someone is still in childhood?

**Environmental and genetic risk factors** can be reliably identified in childhood. For example, an adoption study has shown that babies born to alcoholic parents are three or four times more likely to become alcoholics than are babies born to nonalcoholics. There are also some environmental risk factors associated with growing up in a home in which the parents are alcoholic: specifically, children can learn to turn to alcohol as a way of coping with problems. In addition, they may learn different norms regarding how much alcohol consumption is appropriate, or where and when it is appropriate to consume alcohol.

What are the possible benefits of telling children that they are at risk? It might act as an early warning, alerting children that they should exercise extreme caution when consuming alcohol. This might reduce the likelihood that they will become alcoholics.

Are there any reasons why we shouldn't tell children that they are at risk? We should bear in mind that children of different ages have different levels of comprehension. Our warning would be lost on young children, who could not understand the notion of a risk much later in their lives. Adolescents might benefit from the warning, but we would have to be careful not to make the risk seem thrilling. Telling some people that they are at risk for something actually increases the likelihood that they will bring it on; the warning becomes a self-fulfilling prophecy. We would also have to be careful to accompany our warning with clear advice on how the risk can be lowered.

Given all this, we can state the following guidelines about informing children of their risk for alcoholism. Don't bring up the idea before the child is old enough to understand the notion of long-term risk. If talking with adolescents, don't make the notion of risk sound attractive to thrill seekers. Finally, be sure to accompany the warning with clear advice regarding how the risk can be reduced.

## H. Marijuana

STUDY QUESTION:   A regular user of marijuana says that he can drive just fine after smoking. Would you ride with him?

**Possible Answer:** Only if I was driving. Otherwise, *no way!*

This person is overlooking a number of factors. The most obvious is that marijuana acts as a depressant: it decreases reaction time, judgment, and the use of peripheral vision. In addition, larger dosages can produce time and perceptual distortions and hallucinations, none of which are conducive to the safe operation of heavy machinery, such as a car.

## Module 9
## CLASSICAL CONDITIONING

### A. Three Kinds of Learning

STUDY QUESTION:   Can you recall situations in which you have experienced each of the three kinds of learning?

**1. Need to Know:** What specific information do I need to answer this question?

I need to know what the three types of learning are.

They are classical conditioning, operant conditioning, and cognitive learning.

**2. Defining Terms:** Do I need to use my own words to define or review any terms?

**Classical conditioning:** This kind of learning involves *involuntary* responses. A neutral stimulus is paired with an unconditioned stimulus, so that the response that occurred to the unconditioned stimulus now occurs to what was the neutral stimulus (which is now called the conditioned stimulus).

**Operant conditioning:** This kind of learning involves *voluntary* behavior. The responses that follow a behavior will either increase or decrease the likelihood of that behavior's recurrence.

**Cognitive learning:** This kind of learning involves our mental processes. A behavior can be learned through observation or imitation.

**3. Identify Key Words:** Which words in the question hold the key to the best answer?

The key words are "you have experienced." Since we all have learned something in these three ways, you just need to come up with a personal example for each learning method.

### B. Procedure: Classical Conditioning

STUDY QUESTION:   How do you explain why your heart pounds when you hear the words "There will be a test next class"?

**Possible Answer:** In this example, the pounding heart would be considered a *conditioned response.* (In fact, it's a *conditioned emotional response.*) The heart is stimulated to beat faster by the sympathetic nervous system when danger is perceived. In this case, the teacher's words are perceived to be anxiety provoking (or "dangerous") because of learning that has taken place via classical conditioning.

The words "There will be a test next time" constitute the conditioned stimulus. We know this is a conditioned stimulus because words are not inherently dangerous. Also, someone who has never taken a test and, therefore, has had no opportunity to be conditioned would not experience the same change in heart rate.

### H. Application: Conditioned Fear & Nausea

STUDY QUESTION:   How would systematic desensitization be used to help reduce a student's test anxiety?

**Possible Answer:** I would use the three steps of the systematic desensitization procedure to help reduce the test anxiety in a student. (To avoid the complication of saying "he or she," I'll assume, arbitrarily, that the student is female.) First, she must learn how to relax intentionally. I would teach her to tense and relax all the muscles in her body from her toes to her head. The student must practice this for 15–20 minutes every day for several weeks before we could proceed. The second step would be for this student to make up a list of 7–12 stressful situations associated with test taking and to rank them from least to most stressful. Finally, my student friend would put herself in a deeply relaxed state and vividly imagine the least stressful situation. At the first sign of stress, I would stop her and have her put herself in a deeply relaxed state again. She would then begin imagining the situation again until she could continue without becoming stressed. When she had mastered that stressful situation, we would move up the hierarchy to the next stressful scenario. In this way, she would move all the way up her hierarchy until she could actually take a test with reduced anxiety.

## Module 10
### OPERANT & COGNITIVE APPROACHES

### A. Operant Conditioning

STUDY QUESTION: How do you explain why your significant other sulks every time something is wrong even though you've told him or her that it bugs you?

**1. Need to Know:** What specific information do I need to answer this question?

I need to know why people persist in a particular behavior.

BICOC: behavior is contingent on consequences. This is the essence of operant conditioning.

**2. Defining Terms:** Do I need to use my own words to define or review any terms?

**BICOC:** This means that someone performs or does not perform a specific behavior because of the consequences that will follow. If the consequence is a reinforcer, the person will likely repeat the behavior. If the consequence is a punisher, the person will not repeat that behavior.

**Operant conditioning:** This kind of learning involves voluntary behavior. The responses that follow a behavior will either increase or decrease the likelihood of that behavior's recurrence.

**3. Identify Key Words:** Which words in the question hold the key to the best answer?

The key words are "explain why [the person] sulks." From an understanding of the concepts involved, it is clear that whatever I am doing when my partner sulks is reinforcing that behavior. I need to change my behavior before my partner's behavior will change.

### B. Reinforcers

STUDY QUESTION: How would you use operant conditioning to change a rude friend into a more likable and friendly person?

**Possible Answer:** This question asks me to design a program that **shapes** my friend toward a desired **goal**, that of polite behavior. In order to do this operantly, I must find a relevant reinforcer for my friend. If my friend does not like people very much, that might be difficult. However, I'll assume that anyone likes the company of another as long as it is pleasant and the attention the person receives is positive.

This means that the reinforcer in this case will be that positive attention my friend receives from others. One way to accomplish this is to enlist the help of my other friends. I'll tell them to give this positive attention in the form of smiles, compliments, and general concerned attention whenever my friend exhibits the desired behaviors.

If I'm going to shape my friend, then I will have to move him or her gradually away from rude behavior toward more polite, likable behavior. I cannot simply wait for the desired final behavior before giving any reinforcement. In the beginning of the program, my other friends must be instructed to provide reinforcement whenever my problematic friend is in their company and not being rude. This might mean reinforcing him or her for just standing quietly.

From there, my friends must become more particular in the criteria they use for giving reinforcement. They will wait until the friend does or says something that is polite or pleasant. For example, if the friend asks someone how she is today, the person must respond very positively and ask after his or her welfare as well. If the friend offers to get someone a cup of coffee or help carry something, that must be reinforced strongly as well.

If this program works, my friend will learn that rude behavior gets him or her ignored, whereas polite, considerate behavior leads to social rewards in the form of pleasant attention from others. This program won't be easy to put into practice, because rude behavior is hard to ignore, and it makes people less interested in persevering to find polite behavior in the person. Still, people can be shaped by the social reinforcement they receive.

### H. Cultural Diversity: East Meets West

STUDY QUESTION: Why do the same principles of learning work in very different cultures?

**Possible Answer:** Actually, this shows that learning principles come close to being laws of human nature, just like the laws of physics or chemistry. There is no reason why these principles *should* be different in other cultures. What is learned varies—for example, using a fork and knife or using chopsticks. It is also true that what an individual perceives as a reinforcer or punisher varies between cultures. However, once we know what is reinforcing to an individual, we can use that reinforcer to increase the likelihood that a response will occur again. Social mores are culturally dependent; the principles of learning are not.

## Module 11
### TYPES OF MEMORY

### A. Three Types of Memory

STUDY QUESTION: Why does seeing an ambulance speed by remind you of your father's heart attack and his trip to the hospital?

**1. Need to Know:** What specific information do I need to answer this question?

I need to know what processes are involved in memory formation and retrieval.

The basic process is sensory memory to short-term memory to long-term memory.

**2. Defining Terms:** Do I need to use my own words to define or review any terms?

**Sensory memory:** Visual images are stored here for a quarter of a second or more, and auditory images last for about 2 seconds.

**Short-term memory:** If we attend to information, we can hold it for about 30 seconds in the working memory.

**Long-term memory:** Unlimited amounts of information can be held here for an unlimited amount of time. This information can go back and forth between long-term memory and short-term memory.

**3. Identify Key Words:** Which words in the question hold the key to the best answer?

The key words are "why does seeing an ambulance . . . remind you?" The visual and probably also auditory image of the ambulance was put into my short-term memory and, while exploring ambulance-related thoughts from my long-term memory, I stumbled upon an emotional memory related to my father's heart attack.

### F. Encoding: Transferring

STUDY QUESTION: Why is it important that teachers make learning interesting and meaningful?

**Possible Answer:** Most of what you learn and need to remember from teachers requires that you use **effortful encoding.** You have to work hard to transfer information from short-term to long-term memory either by using **maintenance rehearsal** or by making new associations. We know from research that simple maintenance rehearsal results in reduced retention and retrieval. When teachers make material *interesting* to you, you pay attention, which in itself makes it more likely you will remember—because the information got through the first process in memory. When teachers make the material *meaningful,* it means something to you individually, and you can connect this information to other information in your memory. By **making associations** between this new learning and previous learning, you will process this meaningful information at the deepest **level of processing.** Thus, you will have the best retention and recall for information learned in this manner.

### H. Cultural Diversity: Oral versus Written

STUDY QUESTION: How might playing video games affect a child's encoding process?

**Possible Answer:** The text points out that we in the United States spend most of our time encoding information with words—by reading and writing—and that we excel at retrieving information in that form. But individuals in cultures with a strong oral tradition excel at retrieval of information that they have heard. This suggests that using a particular form of encoding over a period of time may improve your recall for information encoded in that way. Video games are organized around visual images. Children who play them get a lot of practice at encoding visual-spatial images. It seems likely that children who play video games would have better recall for visual-spatial information than do children (or adults) who do not play video games.

## Module 12
## REMEMBERING & FORGETTING

### A. Organization of Memories

STUDY QUESTION: How would your memory be affected if you accidentally took a drug that prevented the formation of any new nodes?

*1. Need to Know:* What specific information do I need to answer this question?

I need to know what a node is and how it relates to memory formation.

*2. Defining Terms:* Do I need to use my own words to define or review any terms?

**Node:** A node is a memory file in which information is organized around a specific topic.

**Memory process and nodes:** Nodes are linked to one another in a hierarchy.

*3. Identify Key Words:* Which words in the question hold the key to the best answer?

The key words are "memory be affected" and "prevented the formation of any new nodes." Probably the nature of the memory damage would be related to the age at which I took this drug. Presuming I'm an adult when this happens, I would appear normal much of the time because I would already have had time to form many hundreds (thousands) of nodes. But I would be unable to learn any new concepts. I would have to try and fit any new information into an already existing node. This would greatly impair the sophistication of my network hierarchy.

### D. Biological Bases of Memory

STUDY QUESTION: If a virus suddenly destroyed your hippocampus, what effect would it have on your performance in college?

**Possible Answer:** The hippocampus is crucial for transferring semantic information and episodic information from short-term to long-term memory. However, it is not involved in the processing of procedural information—for example, motor skills.

Therefore, my performance in English would be impaired because I would not be able to encode details from what I read into long-term memory. Thus, it would be impossible for me to discuss a novel I read because I could not remember its plot. I would also have great difficulty in mathematics. The rules for solving quadratic equations or finding the area under a curve wouldn't be in long-term memory when I needed them.

My physical education class would be a slightly different story. I would not lose my motor skills, so if I had been a talented athlete before losing my hippocampus, I would still be one after losing it. My coordination would not be affected. However, if I had played a sport in which there were any rule changes after my hippocampus had been destroyed, I would have to be reminded of them all the time because I would not be able to encode them.

### H. Application: Eyewitness Testimony

STUDY QUESTION: If you were on a jury, what concerns would you have when listening to eyewitness testimony?

**Possible Answer:** Most jurors regard eyewitness testimony as a very important form of evidence, yet it is prone to biases and errors. If I were on a jury, I would listen carefully to the way the lawyers phrased their questions to the witnesses because, as the textbook points out, this phrasing can influence the witnesses' testimony.

I would remember that witnesses are often not completely sure of the accuracy of their accounts. This makes them susceptible to influence. So if the lawyer used an especially strong verb, such as "smashed," to describe a collision, the witness might tend to give a higher estimate of the vehicle's speed. The lawyer can also introduce potentially false information as background to a question, so that the witness will verify that information at a later time.

Witnesses are often trying to recall events they experienced under considerable emotional duress. Thus, encoding the information must have been difficult in the first place. Now, under more duress on the witness stand, the person is expected to recall with accuracy something that occurred as an emotional blur perhaps six months or a year ago.

Finally, I would try hard to remember that there is no correlation between the accuracy of an eyewitness's testimony and the person's confidence in that accuracy. So when a lawyer asks a witness if she is sure she is right, the fact that the witness answers yes does not verify the accuracy of the testimony.

## Module 13
### INTELLIGENCE

### A. Defining Intelligence

STUDY QUESTION: How intelligent was Ray Kroc, who never finished high school but started the world-famous McDonald's hamburger chain?

**1. Need to Know:** What specific information do I need to answer this question?

I need to know the different ways intelligence is defined.

Intelligence has been defined in three ways: using a two-factor approach; using Gardner's theory of multiple intelligences; and using Sternberg's triarchic theory.

**2. Defining Terms:** Do I need to use my own words to define or review any terms?

**Two-factor theory:** This theory of intelligence says that there is a general factor, *g,* that represents a person's ability to perform complex mental functions. Standard IQ tests are presumed to measure *g.*

A second factor, *s,* measures specific mental skills such as mathematical skills and verbal skills.

**Theory of multiple intelligences:** This theory concludes that there are seven kinds of intelligence: verbal, musical, logical-mathematical, spatial, body movement, understanding oneself, and understanding others.

**Triarchic Theory:** This theory concludes that there are three kinds of intelligence: analytical and logical thinking; the ability to deal creatively with new situations and learn from experience; and the ability to use practical skills to adjust to one's sociocultural environment.

**3. Identify Key Words:** Which words in the question hold the key to the best answer?

The key words are "how intelligent was Ray Kroc?" The answer to this question lies in the way we define intelligence. We could try comparing Ray Kroc to Albert Einstein using each approach.

**Two-factor approach:** There are two basic tenets to this approach. First, intelligence can be quantified in the form of tests, most notably the IQ test. Second, there is a general trait called intelligence, *g,* that is supplemented by a few specific abilities, *s.* In this approach, if Albert Einstein scored higher on an IQ test than Ray Kroc, he would be considered more intelligent.

**Multiple-intelligence approach:** Gardner also considers intelligence to be quantifiable, but not into one composite score. Instead, he considers intelligence to be multidimensional: there are many different kinds of intelligence. It may be that Ray Kroc would have scored very high on measures of insight about others and verbal skills, whereas Einstein would have scored higher on math skills. Using this approach, we would not talk about one person being more intelligent than another; rather (provided some skills were demonstrated), we'd say the individuals had different kinds of intelligence.

**Triarchic approach:** According to this approach, intelligence should not be defined by how much you know, but by how you came to know it. In other words, *thinking skills*—logic, problem-solving, and practicality—are the hallmark of intelligence. It could be assumed that both Kroc and Einstein had impressive problem-solving skills, though some might want to debate which man was working on the more complex problems. Certainly, it is hard to build a business empire without some ability to think practically. Einstein's thinking could stay at a very abstract level, which does not necessitate practicality. Again, this approach does not make comparisons between people in terms of a global trait called intelligence. Rather, the emphasis is on the way the person thinks.

### D. Potential Problems of IQ Testing

STUDY QUESTION: Should we use IQ scores to assign the growing number of students from different cultures to grade levels?

**Possible Answer:** First of all, unless IQ tests were also being used to assess nonminority students' grade levels (which they are not), the possibility should not even be considered. However, for the sake of discussion, let's assume that IQ tests are used to place children into grade levels. Given that, the question is whether IQ tests are a good means of deciding at which grade level a child should be placed.

Experience (for example, the story of Larry described in the text) leads us to predict that if IQ tests were used as the sole criterion for placement, minority students would be overrepresented at the lower levels and underrepresented at the upper levels. This would mean that, at each grade level, the average age of minority children would be higher than that of nonminority children. This is due, in no small part, to the **cultural bias** in most IQ tests.

The problem, then, is that IQ tests are not valid criteria for placement; rather, they are *discriminatory*. The conclusion would be to avoid the use of IQ tests as the sole criterion for placement. Perhaps the best strategy is to use a number of criteria, including past academic performance and the child's behaviors both in and out of the classroom.

### H. Application: Intervention Programs

STUDY QUESTION: Since the Head Start program fails to raise IQ scores over the long run, should its financial support be reduced?

**Possible Answer:** This is another question that probes the value of IQ scores in decision-making—in this case, in evaluating the efficacy of the intervention program Head Start.

It is true that Head Start has not yielded long-term changes in children's IQs. However, research quite clearly indicates other very tangible benefits of the program. The text cites research demonstrating that the Head Start children were less likely to repeat classes and less likely to show antisocial or delinquent behavior. People who had been in the Head Start program were more likely to be holding jobs.

Research has also shown that the program has benefited other family members. Mothers of children who had been in the program reported fewer psychological symptoms, greater feelings of mastery, and greater current life satisfaction.

Given all the problems in assessing what an IQ score really means, it should not be used as the sole measure of a program's success. The Head Start program should not be dropped.

## Module 14
## THOUGHT & LANGUAGE

### A. Forming Concepts

STUDY QUESTION: Why is it difficult to explain to your younger sister or brother that a whale is a mammal and not a fish?

**1. Need to Know:** What specific information do I need to answer this question?

I need to know how people form concepts like "fish" and "mammal."

The two theories of concept formation are **definition theory** and **prototype theory.**

**2. Defining Terms:** Do I need to use my own words to define or review any terms?

**Definition theory:** This theory suggests that we make a concept by listing all the properties that define it.

**Prototype theory:** This theory says we form a concept by forming a prototype, which is a mental picture of an average example of the thing we are defining.

**3. Identify Key Words:** Which words in the question hold the key to the best answer?

The key words are "difficult to explain . . . that a whale is a mammal and not a fish." The answer to this question lies in the way we form concepts. Let's look at the two different approaches in terms of whales.

**Definition theory** helps us understand why your younger sister (provided she is quite young) might have difficulty understanding that a whale is not a fish. The problem is that a whale and a fish share many common **defining properties**: they both swim in water; they both have similar shapes; they have similar tails; and so on. In fact, the property that defines a whale as a mammal—the fact that it gives birth to its young—is not readily apparent to a young child.

You might have more success taking a **prototype** approach. With this approach, you would show the child a picture of a typical whale—one that was an average of most whale types. Perhaps a killer whale would be a good prototype. This would lead the child to the rather straightforward and often-correct conclusion that whales are larger than fish. The disadvantage, of course, is that you haven't really taught the child what a mammal is.

### F. Reason, Thought, & Language

STUDY QUESTION: What problems might result when heads of governments speak through translators?

**Possible Answer:** The text explores the different ways a person can think depending on which language the person is using. This reminds us that there is more to language than mere words; language is inextricably tied to culture. Not only are there words that exist in one language but not in another; there are also *ideas* that are not shared across cultures. This means that *literal translations* often lack clarity and, in fact, can be misunderstood.

To be a translator is difficult, therefore, when words and concepts encountered in one language do not have equivalents in another. For example, to call someone "a character" in English does not translate well into French. The French might use a word like "type" (pronounced "teep") to describe an unusual or eccentric person. In English we would use "type" to describe certain personalities, like "the nervous type" or "the outgoing type."

We can see how potentially dangerous translation can become when applied to something as important as diplomatic relations and communication. Translators must have a very good working knowledge of the nuances of both languages and the way words are used in each cultural context.

### H. Cultural Diversity: Influences on Thinking

STUDY QUESTION: What kinds of social problems can arise from finding differences between male and female brains?

**Possible Answer:** In an ideal world, the fact that there are gender differences in the brain should not cause any social dissension. Historically, though, we have seen that differences (for example, in skin color, genitalia, presumed brain size, IQ) have been used to imply that one is better than another. So, instead of a "different but equal" philosophy, we see attitudes that "mine is better than yours" or "you can't play with me."

One problem is that when most people hear about gender differences, they assume that all males are different from all females, when, in fact, there is a huge overlap. For example, there is a gender difference in height, but this *doesn't* mean that all males are taller than all females. These false beliefs may translate into social policy that would unfairly discriminate against people because of their gender and not because of their individual abilities. A woman who is applying to be an air traffic controller might be told, "Well, women have a smaller amount of brain area devoted to visual-spatial skills than men do, so we don't want to hire you."

These findings may be used to enforce a difference in status between men and women in our social structure.

## Module 15
## MOTIVATION

### A. Theories of Motivation

STUDY QUESTION: Which theory best explains why students work hard to get good grades?

**1.** *Need to Know:* What specific information do I need to answer this question?

I need to know the various theories regarding human motivation.

The four theories of motivation are **instinct theory, drive-reduction theory, incentive theory,** and **cognitive theory.**

**2.** *Defining Terms:* Do I need to use my own words to define or review any terms?

**Instinct theory:** This theory suggests that there are innate, inborn forces that cause us to behave in certain ways or inborn forces that cause a particular behavior when we are faced with a specific environmental condition.

**Drive-reduction theory:** This theory states that a biological need produces a drive to fill that need. To bring our body back to homeostasis, we are motivated to produce a particular need-reducing behavior.

**Incentive theory:** This theory suggests that we are motivated to behave in certain ways by external and environmental factors (rewards, money, and other reinforcers).

**Cognitive theory:** This theory proposes that our beliefs can influence our behavior and that our motivation is intrinsic: we engage in particular behaviors because we find them personally rewarding or because they fulfill our beliefs and expectations.

**3.** *Identify Key Words:* Which words in the question hold the key to the best answer?

The key words are "which theory *best explains?*" I need to evaluate each of the theories in terms of its account of why students work hard to get good grades. Then I can decide which is the best explanation.

**Instinct theory:** It is unlikely that a student's hard work is purely instinctual: we are not born with the biological determination to study and attain good grades. You might want to say that a desire for survival motivates students, but it would be much easier to argue that notion from a cognitive, rather than instinctual, point of view.

**Drive-reduction theory:** This approach is also too biological to explain something as cognitively based as studying in college. Some students might tell you that if they don't get good grades, their parents will stop sending them money and so they will go hungry! Nevertheless, the brain does not monitor *homeostasis* in terms of grade maintenance, and so if students are driven, it is not likely to be because of biological necessity.

**Incentive theory:** Now we come to a perspective that will help us explain the hard work of college students. People with college degrees tend to have higher salaries than those without such degrees, and money can be translated into other material incentives, such as clothes, a nice apartment, and a Ford Explorer. Beyond material incentives, there are also social incentives, such as praise and status. Just having a college degree confers status in our culture.

**Cognitive theory:** The focus here is on intrinsic motivators. In a humanistic sense, students might think that they have the potential to excel academically, and they believe that the best way to reach that potential is by getting good grades. In those terms, they get considerable satisfaction from their success. This means that some students do not need praise or encouragement from others, nor do they need the promise of a big salary at the end of their studies. Their motivation is self-determined and independent of these external factors. If these students decide to go into academic life, they are well advised to be motivated by cognitive, rather than external, factors.

## B. Biological & Social Needs

STUDY QUESTION: How would your needs change if you won a $20-million lottery?

**Possible Answer:** We have all heard the cliché "Money can't buy happiness." Money can help us satisfy some, but not all, of our needs. After winning a lottery, I should be able to look after most *biological needs,* unless I become ill or am physically threatened (for instance, kidnapped for ransom). Money can also help with the attainment of *social needs,* to the extent that it allows the person to meet others, be generous, and just plain have fun.

However, money might be less helpful in my attempt to satisfy my need to achieve. Getting $1 million per year would eliminate the need to work for a living, but many people satisfy most of their achievement needs at work. I could travel the world; I could have servants, expensive cars, and wild parties; but boredom might set in anyway because I would not be *achieving* anything through all this. Such lack of self-actualization might explain why people's lives don't change as much as they expect when they win large sums of money.

Another problem in terms of social needs is that an abrupt change in financial status might bring about an unwelcome change in my friendship network. I might like to continue as always with my friends, but they now perceive me to be rich and, therefore, different from them.

## H. Application: Eating Problems & Treatments

STUDY QUESTION: Would you believe an ad that promised you could "lose weight easily and quickly without dieting or exercise by practicing self-hypnosis"?

**Possible Answer:** A good starting question would be, "What is the physiological basis for weight loss via hypnosis?" Since the only known means of losing weight are reducing consumption of certain foods and increasing metabolism, usually by exercise, it is hard to imagine that a hypnosis program could work without at least one of those components.

Another question, therefore, would be, "What is the content of the hypnotic suggestion?" A strong hunch would be that it would involve repressing urges to eat by desensitizing us to external food cues. That might be all right, depending on the answers to the next questions.

"How quickly will I lose weight with this program, and what long-term coping strategies does it include?" If the hypnosis provides little more than the means to survive a crash diet, it isn't a good idea. Staying within healthy weight limits involves controlling aspects of one's *lifestyle.* Self-hypnosis can play a part in this, especially with confidence building and relaxation (since some people eat more when anxious), but people should probably be skeptical of "lose-weight-quick" schemes that rely on self-hypnosis. In fact, any plan to lose weight quickly should be given careful scrutiny.

## Module *16*
### EMOTION

### A. Peripheral Theories

STUDY QUESTION: Does someone with many facial expressions experience more emotions than someone with few facial expressions?

**1. Need to Know:** What specific information do I need to answer this question?

I need to know what facial expressions have to do with emotions. Specifically, what is facial feedback theory?

**2. Defining Terms:** Do I need to use my own words to define or review any terms?

**Facial feedback theory:** This theory suggests that sensations or feedback from the movement of the facial muscles are interpreted as emotions.

**3. Identify Key Words:** Which words in the question hold the key to the best answer?

The key words are "experience more emotions." The answer to this question lies in the validity of facial feedback theory.

At first glance, the answer would seem to be yes. If facial feedback theory is correct, the individual with few expressions is having fewer emotions than is the individual with a lot of facial expressions. But the text reports that facial feedback theory has not been demonstrated to be correct. A relationship has, however, been found between facial expression and the *intensity* of our subjective emotional experience. So, the person with a lot of facial expressions would be having more *intense* experiences than would someone with fewer expressions, but not *more* emotions.

### D. Function of Emotions

STUDY QUESTION: Why might people who are madly in love have difficulty making the right decisions?

**Possible Answer:** When individuals are madly in love, they are in a state of high physiological arousal. According to the Yerkes-Dodson law, high levels of arousal improve our performance on easy tasks but impair performance on difficult tasks. When we are making an important decision (which is certainly a difficult task), it's best to be in a relaxed state of low arousal. If we are in a heightened state of arousal, the decision that we make at this time—for example, "Should I marry this person?"—might not be the best one for us.

### H. Application: Lie Detection

STUDY QUESTION: Would it be fair to use lie detector tests to identify students who are suspected of cheating on exams?

**Possible Answer:** Let's start with the assumption that your students did not, in fact, cheat on the exams. Can you prove their innocence via the polygraph? Putting the question another way, could an innocent person fail a lie detector test?

The answer to this question appears to be yes. The text points out that such tests lead to false conclusions from 5 to 75% of the time. There are many reasons for this. The most important follows from the fundamental assumptions of the lie detector test—that lying is accompanied by guilt, and guilt yields arousal.

No one has doubted that a polygraph can detect physiological arousal. The problem is in the interpretation of that arousal. Your students might respond with arousal to a critical question about the exam because they know that they are under suspicion and the exam is very relevant to that suspicion. Perhaps they saw someone who seemed to be cheating during the exam, and the mention of that makes them anxious. In short, there are many reasons why the students might show a positive response to the critical question.

It would be extremely unfair to use the lie detector to assess guilt (or innocence) of cheating.

## Module *17*
### INFANCY & CHILDHOOD

### A. Prenatal Influences

STUDY QUESTION: A pregnant woman asks, "Why do I have to worry about ingesting chemicals, since my unborn child has a separate blood supply?"

**1. Need to Know:** What specific information do I need to answer this question?

I need to know whether fetuses in fact have their own blood supply.

**2. Identify Key Words:** Which words in the question hold the key to the best answer?

The key words are "separate blood supply." To answer this question, I must establish whether the blood supplies of mother and fetus are shared.

This pregnant woman is wrong. The blood supplies of mother and fetus are connected via the **placenta,** which is the life-support system for the fetus. In fact, the chemicals that this woman injects might very well be **teratogens**—agents that can cause birth defects. Here is some evidence that the mother's bloodstream can supply teratogens to the fetus.

Heavy maternal drinking during pregnancy results in **fetal alcohol syndrome,** which is characterized by a number of physical and psychological defects. Mothers who smoke heavily during pregnancy have a higher rate of stillbirths and premature births and have babies with significantly lower birth weight. Finally, pregnant women who are cocaine and heroine addicts experience problems such as the premature birth, lower birth weight, and smaller head circumference of babies. These babies are also born with dependencies on the drugs and must go through drug withdrawal after birth.

### D. Research Focus: Temperament

STUDY QUESTION: Marcie and Jeff love their 6-month-old son but find that he is easily irritated and frightened. What should they do?

**Possible Answer:** Marcie and Jeff should be told that, for reasons that have nothing to do with parenting, children differ in the early emotional patterns they display. Their son would fit into a category called **inhibited children.** Inhibited children show reluctance, anxiety, and fear when approaching a strange child, exploring new objects, playing with peers, or speaking to adults.

Once they know they have not done anything wrong, Marcie and Jeff can be told that there are things they can do that might reduce their son's relatively high fear response. They need to be caring and supportive and to consistently help their child with minor stressors. Marcie and Jeff should also avoid becoming too anxious, overprotective, or angry at their child's fearfulness. If they can provide their infant son with the love and support he needs, this inhibited baby will have a better chance of becoming less and less fearful as he approaches adolescence. Parents can help their shy or fearful child become more expressive and outgoing.

### F. Social Development

STUDY QUESTION: How would Freud's and Erikson's theories apply to a 3-year-old child whose parents are getting divorced?

Possible Answer: Let's consider Freud's and Erikson's approaches in turn.

*Freud.* Freud would probably say that the parents' separation will cause more problems when the child approaches puberty than at age 3. The child had both parents around when he or she was going through some of the early stages that Freud considered vital—breast feeding and toilet training. The next critical stage will be near puberty, when the child begins to develop subconscious sexual urges. Freud believed that, for a boy, these subconscious urges are directed at the mother, and that the father is then seen as a rival. (For a girl, the parents' roles are reversed.) All of this arouses subconscious guilt in the child. With one of the parents missing, this process will be disrupted. (This Oedipal analysis is presented later in the text.)

*Erikson.* In Erikson's view, this 3-year-old is making a transition between stages 2 and 3 in terms of psychosocial development. This means that the child might be working to establish autonomy over shame and initiative over guilt. The parents can play an important role in the resolution of both these conflicts. If they encourage the child to try things on his or her own—for example, getting dressed in the morning—the child is more likely to develop autonomy. If they also encourage the child to take on appropriate challenges—for example, building things or cleaning up his or her room—the child will develop initiative.

The problem is that both these processes require parental presence. The parents must take the time to encourage and praise the child when he or she shows autonomy and initiative. Unfortunately, divorce often becomes the focus of the parents' attention. In addition, the child might feel partly to blame for the parents' difficulties, which makes shame and guilt more likely.

## Module 18
## ADOLESCENCE & ADULTHOOD

### A. Puberty & Sexual Behavior

STUDY QUESTION: How are the sexual concerns of adolescents and senior adults similar but also different?

**1.** *Need to Know:* What specific information do I need to answer this question?

I need to know what the sexual concerns of adolescents and senior adults are.

**2.** *Identify Key Words:* Which words in the question hold the key to the best answer?

The key words are "similar but also different." To answer this question, I need to examine the sexual concerns of people in these age groups.

One of the biggest concerns for teenagers is whether to become sexually active. And there is considerable peer pressure for them to do so. Once they have decided to be sexually active, avoiding pregnancy and sexually transmitted diseases is of great concern. Many teens are not viewed as sexually active by adults, in the same way that senior adults are not viewed as sexually active. Senior adults are often confused by the physical changes in their bodies (just like teens!) that make sex different than it once was. Seniors have to fight the stereotype that they are asexual: research indicates that many senior couples are happier with their sex lives now than when they were individuals in the singles scene.

### C. Personality & Social Changes

STUDY QUESTION: If you become a parent, what special concerns might you have when your own children go through adolescence?

**Possible Answer:** According to the text, one of the primary tasks an adolescent has is to develop a **self-identity** and **self-esteem.** This also corresponds to Erikson's **stage 5: identity versus role confusion.** Erikson suggests that if teens do not develop a purposeful life, they will experience **identity confusion** and they will be unstable or socially withdrawn. So I would be concerned about their successful development of self-identity.

A parent might not only want teenagers to be happy with their self-identity but also hope that they will find productive work that they love and form deep and lasting relationships with their family and friends. Safety is another concern: can the teenagers explore their developing selves without getting AIDS, having bad experiences with drugs, or becoming enmeshed in unhealthy relationships with other people?

### H. Application: Suicide

STUDY QUESTION: If your grandmother had incurable cancer and unbearable pain and asked you to help her commit suicide, would you help her?

**Possible Answer:** Here is what I would do for my grandmother. Other people might have different responses.

I would not get angry with her or say that her desire to end her life was silly or selfish. Instead, I would say that her wishes were perfectly understandable. Then I would suggest that we find a hospice facility willing to do its utmost to reduce her pain and allow her to retain her dignity.

If, in the hospice, she found that the pain was still intolerable, I would have to face the moral dilemma of whether to help her commit suicide. Probably, I would first try to convince her caregivers to let her end her life peacefully and with dignity. I could not actively kill my grandma but, if it came to it, I would help her to do what it takes to commit suicide—to gather pills, and so on.

# Appendix B

## Module 19
### FREUDIAN & HUMANISTIC THEORIES

#### A. Freud's Psychodynamic Theory

STUDY QUESTION: According to Freud, why do some students plan to study on the weekend but end up partying?

**1. Need to Know:** What specific information do I need to answer this question?

I need to know what Freud's psychodynamic theory of personality is.

It is a theory about our personality development that emphasizes early childhood experiences, the importance of repressed thoughts that we can't access, and conflicts between our conscious and our unconscious desires. These conflicts are used to explain why we do things that we don't intend.

**2. Defining Terms:** Do I need to use my own words to define or review any terms?

**Conscious thoughts:** These are wishes and desires that we can express at any time.

**Unconscious thoughts:** These are our wishes and desires that are repressed because of their disturbing content. We cannot access them.

**3. Identify Key Words:** Which words in the question hold the key to the best answer?

The key words are "plan to study . . . but end up partying." This question asks us to explain why we do things we don't intend to do.

Our conscious desire is to study. But every weekend we end up partying and don't understand why. Freud would say that we had an unconscious desire to seek pleasure (remember Module 17?) in the form of partying. We aren't aware that we desire to party every weekend (this wish is repressed), because to recognize that we'd rather party than graduate from college threatens our sense of who we are. The unconscious desire is winning over our conscious desire.

#### F. Cultural Diversity: Unexpected High Achievement

STUDY QUESTION: If you were the principal of a grade school, what might you do to improve overall student performance?

**Possible Answer:** The experiences of Indochinese immigrants outlined in the text suggest that you must pay attention to particular **primary values** in order to improve overall student performance at your school. These primary values include mutual respect, cooperation, a love of learning, a commitment to accomplishment and achievement, and the belief that you cannot let fate or luck control your life. Instead, students must believe that they are the masters of their own destiny.

Parental involvement appears to be vital. Over half the Indochinese parents read aloud to their children. Parents at your school should be encouraged to make homework a family activity. This doesn't mean that parents do their children's homework. Instead, it means that, each night, every family member has something to do that enhances his or her learning. This makes it clear that all family members are committed to accomplishment and achievement. Students should be expected to do more homework than the national average, perhaps as much as three hours per night, to the

exclusion of television. You should also encourage strong family ties, so that parents and children feel mutual respect and obligation, and family members strive to maintain cooperation and harmony.

All of this would be very difficult to achieve because, as principal, you are going beyond the principles of pedagogy; you are attempting to make changes to our culture by borrowing from the strengths of another.

#### H. Application: Assessment—Projective Tests

STUDY QUESTION: How useful would projective tests be in identifying students who are most likely to cheat on exams?

**Possible Answer:** Strong proponents of projective tests might claim that they have this type of predictive power. Others would suggest that projective tests can provide insights into general personality traits or more global behavioral tendencies but that they could not be used to predict a behavior as specific as cheating on exams. Still others would argue that projective tests are too open to interpretation by the clinician to be predictive of anything.

If projective tests were to be used in this way, many different testings would have to be conducted with a variety of projective tests. If a student showed consistent trends indicative of extreme mark anxiety, external pressure, poor moral development, or perhaps an animosity toward the instructor or toward authority in general, we could perhaps infer that this student would be more likely to cheat than would students who do not show these tendencies. Of course, the problem comes in ascertaining these tendencies from the open-ended responses of the student.

## Module 20
### SOCIAL LEARNING & TRAITS

#### A. Social Cognitive Theory

STUDY QUESTION: Why do some students invest thousands of dollars and 4–6 years of hard work to obtain a college degree?

**1. Need to Know:** What specific information do I need to answer this question?

I need to know what social cognitive theory says about our behaviors—in this case, going to college.

Social cognitive theory suggests that our beliefs and feelings influence our behavior. What beliefs (cognitive factors) might be related to our behavior of going to college?

**2. Defining Terms:** Do I need to use my own words to define or review any terms?

**Cognitive factors:** Four cognitive factors are important, according to social cognitive theory. Specifically, there are three important beliefs: locus of control, self-efficacy, and delay of gratification.

**3. Identify Key Words:** Which words in the question hold the key to the best answer?

The key word is "why?" We are asked to examine what motivates a person to go to college, from a social cognitive perspective. Let's look at the relevant cognitive factors.

One important belief that would help explain students' desire to attain a university degree is their **locus of control.** Most people who put out considerable effort and resources to attain a goal believe that its attainment is within their control. In other words, they have an *internal locus of control.*

Students' sense of **self-efficacy** refers to their beliefs regarding how capable they are of achieving their goals. Individuals who have a history of success in similar tasks, who feel they are as good as or better than others, and who have received positive feedback about their capabilities will have a high sense of self-efficacy. Students generally come to university with a fairly high sense of self-efficacy, since they were successful in high school. However, university presents new challenges that might make immediate success difficult. The danger, therefore, is that students' self-efficacy will drop dramatically in their first year. This can start a damaging cycle for them, in which they do not succeed because they feel they can't. In turn, their lack of success reinforces their low self-efficacy.

Students who invest all this money and effort must be willing to **delay gratification** for long periods of time. While some of their friends have full-time jobs that allow them to buy new cars and stereos, students live in residence halls or noisy apartments and drive beaters. To be successful students, they must persist at a number of difficult tasks for the promise of future reward.

### B. Trait Theory

STUDY QUESTION: Would knowing about the Big Five traits help you write an ad to find the perfect roommate or life mate?

**Possible Answer:** This question is as concerned with attraction and compatibility as it is with trait theory. The literature on attraction makes it quite clear that similarity is a stronger unifying force than is dissimilarity, or complementary differences. Given that, it would be reasonable to assume that you are better advised to look for a roommate or a life partner who is similar to you.

Remember also that the definition of personality includes behavioral tendencies. Indeed, personality theorists assume that it is our personalities that predispose us to act in certain ways. This means that compatible personalities will engage in similar behaviors, such as keeping the apartment tidy, going to bed at similar times, and respecting other people's privacy. Similarity in these behaviors reduces the likelihood of conflict.

Knowing how you measure in the Big Five traits—openness, conscientiousness, extraversion, agreeableness, and neuroticism—might help you in finding someone who is more similar than different to share your apartment. Of course, this assumes that you can measure these traits in ways that will predict behavior in this particular situation (living together). To do this with some reliability, you must have made observations in related contexts.

It seems unlikely that you could find a life partner from a simple ad in the paper using the Big Five traits. You could find someone who appears to be very similar to you on a paper-and-pencil test but have no interpersonal or sexual attraction to that person.

### F. Cultural Diversity: Resolving Conflicts

STUDY QUESTION: What could happen when United States officials negotiate public trade agreements with Japanese officials?

**Possible Answer:** Interpersonal conflict is associated with opposing interests or disagreements in which one person's goal interferes with that of another person. Trade conflicts between countries are very similar to interpersonal conflicts. The research has indicated that, in general, citizens of the United States tend to resolve conflicts by being independent, assertive, and competitive in achieving their personal goals. Citizens of Japan, in general, place a higher priority on group goals than on personal goals and often avoid discussion of the conflict. This contrast between the **collectivist culture** of Japan and the **individualistic culture** of the United States can make negotiating trade agreements very difficult.

It is possible that, because of this difference, the U.S. could appear to bully Japan into agreement by engaging in public discussion of the conflict and using persuasive, assertive negotiating techniques. The research with students suggests that the Japanese might back away from, or cut off, discussion of topics that cause serious conflict. Presumably, women and men who are trained in cross-cultural differences are advising politicians on matters such as these.

## Module 21
## HEALTH, STRESS, & COPING

### A. Appraisal

STUDY QUESTION: Sue says that some situations always cause her stress, but John says it is how she thinks about them. Who's right?

**1.** *Need to Know:* What specific information do I need to answer this question?

I need to know what the research indicates about how situations cause stress.

**2.** *Identify Key Words:* Which words in the question hold the key to the best answer?

The key words are "some situations always cause her stress" and "how she thinks about them." The question is asking if the way we think about situations can change the amount of stress we feel in reaction to the situation.

According to the text, any situation (even a nonthreatening one) can cause stress through a process called **primary appraisal.** This is our first evaluation of the situation and how it relates to us. We may appraise the situation in one of three ways: as *irrelevant,* which means that the situation doesn't affect us at all; as *positive,* meaning that the situation will benefit us in some way; or as *stressful,* meaning that it overtaxes our resources. This would indicate that John is right and that how we appraise, or think about, the situation greatly affects whether or not we feel stressed.

The text also reports that in an experimental setting, the type of appraisal that individuals gave a stressful situation (whether they were told to view an industrial accident film objectively or to think about how they would feel) changed the physiological reaction to the stress. Subjects who were told to think about how they would feel in an industrial accident demonstrated higher physiological stress responses. This also supports John's position that how Sue thinks about a situation causes (or increases) her stress.

### F. Research Focus: Coping with Trauma

STUDY QUESTION: What can you learn from how burn victims cope with stress that would apply to dealing with stress in your own life?

**Possible Answer:** Research on burn victims helps us understand what factors contribute to successfully coping with major trauma in life. High self-esteem was the most important personality trait in long-term coping with burn aftereffects. Also, patients with a strong social support network of family and friends were better able to adjust to their burn injuries than those lacking social support.

In terms of our own lives, this research indicates that we should cultivate warm and lasting friendships and that family members should support one another. Additionally, if we do not have high self-esteem, it would be wise to find and become involved in activities that increase our esteem levels. If these factors can help victims of burn trauma cope, they must also be powerful enough to help the rest of us.

### H. Application: Stress Management Program

STUDY QUESTION: Why is it better to cope with stress by changing three things—thoughts, behaviors, and physiological responses—rather than just one?

**Possible Answer:** Our thoughts, behaviors, and physiological reactions all contribute to our feelings of stress. So it makes sense that the *best* way to reduce or manage stress is by changing all three factors. We can make our acid stomach better by popping antacids, thereby reducing the physiological reaction, but this is only temporary and doesn't change our reactions to stress.

Changing our thoughts means, for example, appraising events as a challenge rather than a threat and substituting positive self-statements when we notice ourselves making negative self-statements. Changing our behaviors means taking a problem-solving approach (taking action) rather than using emotion-focused temporary solutions to our stressors. Finally, changing our physiological reaction to stress means learning how to relax. Relaxation methods can include biofeedback, progressive relaxation, or meditation. Successful long-term stress management involves changing all three of the factors affecting our stress levels.

## Module 22
## ASSESSMENT & ANXIETY DISORDERS

### A. Three Approaches

STUDY QUESTION: The night before a big exam, John gets drunk to relax. However, the next day he has a terrible hangover and does poorly on the exam. Is his behavior abnormal?

**1. Need to Know:** What specific information do I need to answer this question?

I need to know how *abnormal* is defined.

Abnormality can be defined by three different methods: statistical frequency, deviation from the social norm, and maladaptive behavior.

**2. Defining Terms:** Do I need to use my own words to define or review any terms?

**Statistical frequency:** This method defines behavior as abnormal if it occurs rarely in the population as a whole.

**Deviation from social norm:** Behavior is considered abnormal if it differs greatly from the prevailing social standards.

**Maladaptive behavior:** Behavior is regarded as abnormal if it interferes with an individual's ability to function in society and as a person.

**3. Identify Key Words:** Which words in the question hold the key to the best answer?

The key words are "is his behavior abnormal?" If we look at John's behavior in the context of each method of defining what is abnormal, we will be able to answer the question.

If we use the statistical frequency approach and compare John's behavior to the general population of college students, his behavior would probably be considered abnormal. Most college students do not get so drunk before an exam that they are hung over.

On the basis of deviation from social norms, we would call John's behavior abnormal. It is not socially acceptable to drink so much that it interferes with your ability to take a test. However, it is probably more acceptable among young college students than in the population at large.

On the basis of the maladaptive behavior approach, we would say that if this is an isolated incident, John's behavior is not abnormal and will not greatly interfere with his responsibilities. However, if this behavior were to increase in frequency, it would interfere with his ability to function as a person and in society and would thus be considered abnormal.

### B. Assessing Mental Disorders

STUDY QUESTION: Why must mental health professionals spend so much time and effort in assessing their clients' symptoms?

**Possible Answer:** There are a number of reasons why a detailed and usable diagnosis of mental disorders is essential to the understanding of mental health and the treatment of those disorders. Here are some of them.

*Human behavior covers an extremely broad range.* Because people are capable of so many different behaviors, it can be difficult to determine which are normal and which are abnormal. It might be that a behavior is infrequent and unusual but not maladaptive. Also, the possible range of abnormal behaviors is very broad, and it takes a great deal of time and experience to put names to each type.

*The consequences of diagnosis are considerable.* Passing diagnosis on a person carries considerable implications for that person. It could mean the difference between a prison term and psychiatric treatment, for example, or the difference between getting a job and being passed over. For this reason, the classification system must be detailed enough to gain diagnosticians' confidence. Also, diagnoses of mental disorders often carry a social stigma. This stigma can be reduced if the language is carefully chosen; for example, "antisocial personality disorder" sounds less condemning than "psychopath."

*Treatment depends on classification.* As with any intervention, the type of treatment is determined by the diagnosis.

## H. Application: Treating Phobias

STUDY QUESTION:   If you were very shy and uncomfortable about meeting strangers and talking to groups, what could you do about this problem?

**Possible Answer:** A number of cognitive-behavioral programs could help me. These programs use four components that I can try on my own. First, I would try to understand and believe that, since social fears are learned, they can be unlearned; after reading all the modules so far, this is easy to believe. I need to understand that I avoid meeting people and talking to groups of people in order to avoid the thoughts and physiological arousal that I experience in these situations.

Second, I would learn and substitute new social skills. I would carefully watch individuals who successfully meet others, so as to learn what the appropriate behaviors are. I would begin to write down my thoughts when I think about a group social situation or when I am in one. Then I would write a list of positive and healthy thoughts that I can use instead.

Third, I would begin to imagine myself successfully meeting others and talking to groups of strangers, until I am comfortable with these thoughts. Then I would begin actually to participate in these social situations.

Finally, I would continue doing homework by imagining these situations and also actually participate in group situations. If I was unable to treat myself to my satisfaction, I would get a referral to a therapist.

## Module 23
## MOOD DISORDER & SCHIZOPHRENIA

### A. Mood Disorders

STUDY QUESTION:   A student is brought into the health clinic for being depressed and having attempted suicide. What will be her treatment program?

**1. Need to Know:** What specific information do I need to answer this question?

I need to know what treatments are usually given for severe depression.

According to the text, the usual treatment consists of antidepressant drug therapy and/or psychotherapy.

**2. Identify Key Words:** Which words in the question hold the key to the best answer?

The key words are "what will be her treatment program?" The treatment options for major depression that are discussed in this section are antidepressant drug therapy and psychotherapy.

Generally, someone who has just attempted suicide is hospitalized for two reasons. First, constant monitoring will ensure the safety of the individual while he or she is deeply depressed. Second, this student will immediately begin a regimen of antidepressant drugs, as well as intensive psychotherapy. After the individual is no longer a suicide risk and if the depression has remitted somewhat, he or she will be released. It is important to continue the drug treatment and/or psychotherapy in order to prevent relapse.

### B. Electroconvulsive Therapy

STUDY QUESTION:   How would you compare the effectiveness and side effects of electroconvulsive shock therapy with those of antidepressant drugs?

**Possible Answer:** The text notes that about half of those patients for whom antidepressant drugs were initially prescribed quit because of the negative side effects. So there are obviously some significant side effects. Of those who remain on the drugs, about 30% show no benefit from the treatment; they still have major depression.

The question for those with unremitting depression is Are the side effects and risks of ECT worth the benefits? One of the side effects of ECT is significant memory impairment. Consequently, ECT should not be undertaken without first attempting to treat the depression with several different antidepressants under the direction of qualified therapists. However, the effectiveness rate of ECT is 60–80%. This is very high, considering that only the most depressed people ever get ECT. It may be that ECT is worth the risks when all else fails.

### H. Application: Dealing with Mild Depression

STUDY QUESTION:   When some people get depressed, why do they prefer to spread their gloom, rather than do something to get over it?

**Possible Answer:** The essential problem is that those who are mildly depressed are used to this condition and often do not know that help is available. What's more, the state of depression leaves a person without the motivation or energy to do anything. Taken together, these problems mean that depressed people are unlikely to get unsolicited help or to help themselves. So where does the impetus to get help come from?

People with mild depression get caught in a cycle that cuts off social contact. It usually begins with deficiencies in social behavior, such as overdependence or general mistrust of others. Not surprisingly, people react negatively to depressed individuals, who interpret this to mean that they are right about themselves: they are worthless. In addition, friends tend to withdraw social support. This deepens the person's depressed state, which makes it less likely that the person will try to do anything to remedy the situation. Often, it takes a persistent, true friend to start the change, by getting the depressed person to seek professional help.

## Module 24
## THERAPIES

### A. Historical Background

STUDY QUESTION:   Should our major cities spend more money to develop care and treatment programs for the homeless?

**1. Need to Know:** What specific information do I need to answer this question?

I need to know why the homeless would need care and treatment programs.

According to the text, one of the results of deinstitutionalization has been that many former mental patients are no longer able to get the care and medication that they need. It is estimated that 25–50% of the current homeless population have serious mental disorders.

**2.** *Identify Key Words:* Which words in the question hold the key to the best answer?

The key words are "should our major cities spend more money?" This is a question of personal values. What do I think government should do?

Many homeless individuals are actually very ill and are untreated. In some cases, good treatment might be able to rehabilitate an individual as a functioning member of society. In other cases, even though treatment would improve the quality of an individual's life, he or she would never become an independent, functioning member of society. I think that it is important to deliver humane psychological and medical care and housing to individuals in *both* cases. How we choose to spend our money reflects what we value.

### D. Behavior Therapy

STUDY QUESTION: Susan complains of having terrible test anxiety. What would a behavior therapist do to help her?

**Possible Answer:** A behavior therapist would look at **behaviors** that are causing Susan's problems, with the hope of replacing these with new **target behaviors.** The therapist would also look at **stimuli** that might be eliciting these unwanted responses, with the hope of desensitizing Susan so that the stimuli no longer bring on the unwanted response. For example, Susan might feel her heart pound before an exam. She might shake and feel nauseated. She might avoid studying because it is associated with the test; she goes jogging or hits the fridge instead. The therapist would like Susan to remain relaxed when she thinks about her exam and when she approaches the exam room. This will allow her to concentrate when she studies and when she takes the exam. After identifying which behaviors to change and which new ones to replace them with, the therapist could use **desensitization** to help Susan overcome her test anxiety. The steps of systematic desensitization include relaxation, stimulus hierarchy, and desensitization training. Susan and the therapist together would design a stimulus hierarchy. The therapist would slowly take Susan through each step, making sure that she is fully relaxed and comfortable before proceeding to the next level of the hierarchy. This might take weeks, but the end result would be a reduction in Susan's test anxiety.

### H. Application: Cognitive-Behavior Techniques

STUDY QUESTION: Frank has very little self-confidence and self-esteem. What is one way that he could work on raising them?

**Possible Answer:** There are a few cognitive-behavior techniques that can be practiced without the assistance of a therapist. Two very good strategies are called **thought stopping** and **thought substitution.**

Thought stopping has two basic components. In the first step, Frank must close his eyes each time he has a thought that is self-deprecating, silently yell "Stop!" and then silently count to ten. In the second step, Frank uses a collection of five photographs that he has pulled from albums. These photos show Frank having a good time with friends. On the back of each photo, he has written positive self-statements—for example, "I am a good person with good friends" or "My life is under my control. " He thinks about each picture for a moment, then turns over the photo, and repeats the sentence to himself. The entire process takes from one to two minutes.

Frank can follow up on this by making plans to improve his self-confidence. He can engage in activities for which he has some ability. Also, he can make a list of the irrational thoughts that have accompanied these activities—for example, "I can never do well" or "People will hate me if I don't do well. " These can be replaced with positive statements like those on the back of his photos. He must also be willing to reinforce himself when he succeeds. This can take the form of self-praise or tangible reinforcers—things he likes to eat and do.

## Module 25
## SOCIAL PSYCHOLOGY

### A. Perceiving Others

STUDY QUESTION: Mark says that he doesn't make snap judgments but waits until he knows people. Do you think Mark does what he claims?

**1.** *Need to Know:* What specific information do I need to answer this question?

I need to know how we normally form first impressions.

Normally, our first impression of an individual is shaped by the person's physical appearance; our need to explain why the individual looks, dresses, or behaves as he or she does, and the person's race. Our first impression is formed in seconds, and it influences how we interact with that person.

**2.** *Identify Key Words:* Which words in the question hold the key to the best answer?

The key words are "do you think Mark does what he claims?" The question is asking whether or not anyone can stop making first impressions.

Mark might reserve judgment about people until he gets to know them better. If so, he's in a very small minority. Most of us do form judgments about others on meeting them. Let's look at some of the reasons why we form these first impressions.

As the text points out, making judgments about others has *social consequences:* the behavior we exhibit toward another person is guided by our impressions of that person. It is very difficult to treat someone in an entirely neutral way; our behavior can be placed on a continuum of friendliness, or of patience, tolerance, and so on. In order for Mark to reserve judgment, he must treat everyone *the same way* until he makes a judgment that helps dictate how he will treat the person. While this is possible, it is not the way most people operate.

Another factor is that, in order to avoid forming first impressions, Mark will have to either ignore some very salient social data or store it in memory without acting upon it. He must remain totally uninfluenced by appearance, accent, nonverbal behavior, and the first things a person says to him. Again, if Mark can do this, he has set himself apart from most of us, who pay quite close attention to these things.

In summary, Mark will have to control powerful motivational and cognitive factors in order to avoid these snap judgments. It's unlikely that he does so. Perhaps a more realistic goal is to admit to making first impressions but to allow for changes in them as you get to know a person better.

## B. Attributions

STUDY QUESTION: What should you be aware of when you try to explain the behaviors of your friend or your mate?

**Possible Answer:** This question requires a knowledge of biases and errors in attribution. Let's look at each of the three discussed in the text and see how they can be avoided.

*Fundamental attribution error.* According to fundamental attribution error, we place inordinate weight on dispositional factors when making attributions. This means that we fail to appreciate the power that a situation can exert on behavior. For example, when someone does poorly on a test, we think the person isn't very smart, rather than thinking that the person might have been prevented from studying by a family crisis. To avoid this error, we must force ourselves to look at the situations in which people find themselves and acknowledge that they can have a strong influence on behavior.

*Actor-observer effect.* The actor-observer effect describes our tendency to attribute our own behavior to the situation and other people's behavior to their dispositions. We have eliminated some fundamental attribution error by gaining an appreciation of how the situation can influence our own behavior, but we still are insensitive to the effect the situation can have on the behavior of others. To avoid this effect requires that we show *empathy* for other people when they are in situations that bring out behavior that is less than their best. It also requires that we realize how favorable situations can sometimes make other people look better than they really are.

*Self-serving bias.* As its name implies, self-serving bias applies to our explanations of our own behavior. This isn't directly relevant to explanations of your friend's behavior, but it is worth reviewing as an addendum to the question.

We attribute our successes to our dispositions and our failures to the situation. In so doing, we protect our self-esteem. Though this protection has benefits as a short-term strategy, it does little to help us reduce the likelihood of failure in the future. If we were to be truly honest with ourselves, we would admit that some of our success is due to good fortune and the hard work of others, both of which are situational factors. Also, we would acknowledge that some of our failures could have been avoided if we had worked harder or if we had the talent to do better.

On the other hand, this honesty is not necessarily the best way to improve ourselves. A large body of research indicates that attributing all our outcomes to our own effort is most likely to result in self-improvement and high motivation.

## F. Aggression

STUDY QUESTION: One of your friends says, "Getting angry and being aggressive are just part of human nature." What would you reply?

**Possible Answer:** The key phrase in my friend's sentence is "human nature." This term implies that being aggressive is inborn and that nothing can be done to change aggressive behavior. Although there is research suggesting that some aggressive behavior is related to neurotransmitter levels and thus is inborn, much more evidence points to external contributors to aggressive behavior, such as social learning and environmental factors. If all anger (an emotion that probably is inborn) were expressed aggressively, there would be even more worldwide cross-cultural aggression than we see now.

I would further suggest to my friend that his belief is more likely to cause his own anger to be expressed as aggression. Research has shown that cognitive factors can override aggression and also indicates that social rules can inhibit aggression. If we have rules that say aggressive behavior is unacceptable, we are less likely to experience aggression.

**ability tests** Achievement tests, which measure what we have learned; aptitude tests, which measure our potential for learning or acquiring a specific skill; and intelligence tests, which measure our general potential to solve problems, think abstractly, and profit from experience.

**absolute threshold** The intensity level of a stimulus such that a person has a 50% chance of detecting it.

**accommodation** The process by which a person changes old methods to deal with or adjust to new situations.

**achievement need** The desire to set challenging goals and to persist in pursuing those goals in the face of obstacles, frustrations, and setbacks.

**Acquired Immune Deficiency Syndrome** *See* AIDS.

**action potential** A tiny electric current that is generated when the positive sodium ions rush inside the axon. The enormous increase of sodium ions inside the axon causes the inside of the axon to reverse its charge: the inside becomes positive, while the outside becomes negative.

**activation-synthesis theory of dreams** The idea that dreaming represents the random and meaningless activity of nerve cells in the brain. According to this theory, the pons, an area in the brain, sends millions of random nerve impulses to the cortex; in turn, the cortex tries to make sense of these signals by creating the feelings, imagined movements, perceptions, changing scenes, and meaningless images that we define as dreams.

**actor-observer effect** Our tendency, when we are behaving (or acting), to attribute our own behavior to situational factors but, when we are observing, to attribute another person's behavior to his or her personality traits or disposition.

**acupuncture** An ancient Chinese procedure for relief of pain, in which a trained practitioner inserts thin needles into various points on the body's surface, often far from the site of the pain, and then manually twirls or electrically stimulates the needles.

**adaptation** The decreasing response of the sensory organs as they are exposed to a continuous level of stimulation.

**adaptation level theory** The idea that we quickly become accustomed to receiving some good fortune (money, job, car, degree); we take the good fortune for granted within a short period of time; and, as a result, the initial impact of our good fortune fades and contributes less to our long-term level of happiness.

**adaptive theory** A theory suggesting that sleep evolved as a survival mechanism, since it prevented early humans and animals from wasting energy and exposing themselves to the dangers of nocturnal predators.

**adaptive value** The usefulness of certain abilities or traits that have evolved in animals or humans that tend to increase their chances of survival, such as the ability to find food, acquire mates, and avoid illness and injury.

**addiction** A behavioral pattern of drug abuse that is marked by an overwhelming and compulsive desire to obtain and use the drug. Even after stopping, the addict has a tendency to relapse and begin using the drug again.

**adolescence** A developmental period, lasting from about the ages of 12 to 18, that marks the end of childhood and the beginning of adulthood; it is a transitional period of considerable biological, cognitive, social, and personality changes.

**adrenal glands** Structures in the endocrine system. The adrenal cortex (outer part) secretes hormones that regulate sugar and salt balances and help the body resist stress; they are also responsible for the growth of pubic hair, a secondary sexual characteristic. The adrenal medulla (inner part) secretes two hormones that arouse the body to deal with stress and emergencies: epinephrine (adrenaline) and norepinephrine (noradrenaline).

**affective-primacy theory** The idea that, in some situations, we feel an emotion before we have time to interpret or appraise the situation.

**afferent neurons** Neurons that carry information from the senses to the spinal cord; also called sensory neurons.

**afterimage** A visual image that continues after the original stimulus is removed.

**age regression** In hypnosis, the suggestion that subjects regress, or return, to an earlier time in their lives—for example, to early childhood.

**aggressive behavior** Any act intended to do physical or psychological harm.

**aging by chance theory** The idea that our bodies age because of naturally occurring problems or breakdowns in the body's cells, which become less able to repair themselves.

**aging by design theory** The idea that our bodies age because preset biological clocks determine the number of times cells can divide and multiply; after that limit is reached, cells begin to die and aging occurs.

**agoraphobia** An anxiety about being in places or situations from which escape might be difficult or embarrassing if a panic attack or paniclike symptoms (sudden dizziness or onset of diarrhea) were to occur.

**AIDS (Acquired Immune Deficiency Syndrome)** A life-threatening condition that, by the latest definition, is present when the individual is HIV positive and has a level of T-cells (CD4 immune cells) of no more than 200 per cubic milliliter of blood (one-fifth of the level of a healthy person) or has developed one or more of 26 specified illnesses (including recurrent pneumonia and skin cancer).

**alarm stage** In the general adaptation syndrome, our initial reaction to stress, marked by activation of the fight-flight response, which causes physiological arousal.

**alcohol (ethyl alcohol)** A psychoactive drug classified as a depressant; it depresses activity of the central nervous system. Alcohol causes friendliness and loss of inhibitions at low doses; impairs drinkers' social judgment and understanding at medium doses; and seriously impairs motor coordination, cognitive abilities, decision making, and speech at higher doses. Very high doses may result in coma and death.

**alcoholism** A problem involving addiction to alcohol. An alcoholic is a person who has drunk heavily for a long period of time, is addicted to and has an intense craving for alcohol, and, as a result, has problems in two or three major life areas (social, personal, and financial areas, for example).

**algorithms** Rules that, if followed correctly, will eventually lead to the solution of a problem.

**all-or-none law** The fact that, once a nerve impulse starts in a small segment at the very beginning of the axon, it will continue at the same speed, segment by segment, to the very end of the axon.

**alpha stage** In sleep, a stage marked by feelings of being relaxed and drowsy, usually with the eyes closed. Alpha waves have low amplitude and high frequency (8–12 cycles per second).

**altered state of consciousness** An awareness differing from normal consciousness; such awareness may be produced by using any number of procedures, such as meditation, psychoactive drugs, hypnosis, or sleep deprivation.

**altered state theory of hypnosis** The idea that hypnosis is not a trancelike state but rather an altered state of consciousness, during which a person experiences different sensations and feelings. No physiological measures have been found to indicate that a person is in a trance. For another view of hypnosis, see the sociocognitive theory of hypnosis.

**altruism** Helping or doing something, often at a cost or risk, for reasons other than the expectation of a material or social reward.

**Alzheimer's disease** A disorder that usually begins after people reach age 50 and is always fatal; it results from widespread damage to the brain, including the hippocampus, and produces deterioration in personality, emotions, cognitive processes, and memory.

**Ames room** A viewing environment, designed by Albert Ames, that demonstrates how our perception of size may be distorted by manipulating our depth cues.

**amnesia** Memory loss that may occur after damage to the brain (temporary or permanent), following drug use, or after severe psychological stress.

**amniocentesis** A medical test performed between weeks 14 and 20 of pregnancy. A long needle is inserted through the mother's abdominal muscles into the amniotic fluid surrounding the fetus. By withdrawing and analyzing fetal cells in the fluid, doctors can identify a number of genetic problems.

**amygdala** A structure in the limbic system that is located in the tip of the temporal lobe and is involved in forming, recognizing, and remembering emotional experiences and facial expressions.

**anal stage** Freud's second psychosexual stage, lasting from the age of about $1\frac{1}{2}$ to 3. In this stage, the infant's pleasure seeking is centered on the anus and its functions of elimination.

**analogy** A strategy for finding a similarity between a new situation and an old, familiar situation.

**androgens** Male sex hormones.

**anencephaly** The condition of being born with little or no brain. If some brain or nervous tissue is present, it is totally exposed and often damaged because the top of the skull is missing. Survival is usually limited to days; the longest has been 2 months.

**animal model** An approach to studying some human problem, situation, or disease by observing, testing, and measuring animals' behavioral, physiological, or neurological changes under conditions that closely approximate it.

**anorexia nervosa** A serious eating disorder characterized by refusing to eat and not maintaining weight at 85% of what is expected, having an intense fear of gaining weight or becoming fat, and missing at least three consecutive menstrual cycles. Anorexics also have a disturbed body image: they see themselves as fat even though they are very thin.

**anterior pituitary** The front part of the pituitary gland, a key component of the endocrine system. It regulates growth through the secretion of growth hormone and produces hormones that control the adrenal cortex, pancreas, thyroid, and gonads.

**anticipatory nausea** Feelings of nausea that are elicited by stimuli associated with nausea-inducing chemotherapy treatments. Patients experience nausea after treatment but also in anticipation of their treatment. Researchers believe that anticipatory nausea occurs through classical conditioning.

**antidepressant drugs** Drugs used to combat depression. They act by increasing levels of a specific group of neurotransmitters (monoamines, such as serotonin) that is believed to be involved in the regulation of emotions and moods.

**antipsychotic drugs** See neuroleptic drugs.

**antisocial personality disorder** A pattern of disregarding or violating the rights of others without feeling guilt or remorse. It is found in 3% of the population, predominantly in males.

**anxiety** An unpleasant state that is associated with feelings of uneasiness, apprehension, and heightened physiological arousal, such as increased heart rate and blood pressure. According to Freud, it arises when there is an unconscious conflict between the id's and superego's desires regarding how to satisfy a need; the ego, caught in the middle, reacts by creating a feeling of anxiety. More modern theories of anxiety are based on conditioned emotional responses and observational learning.

**apparent motion** An illusion that a stimulus or object is moving in space when, in fact, it is stationary. This illusion is created by rapidly showing a series of stationary images, each of which has a slightly different position or posture than the one before.

**approach-approach conflict** Having to choose between two situations that both have pleasurable consequences.

**approach-avoidance conflict** The conflict that arises in a single situation that has both pleasurable and disagreeable aspects.

**approaches to understanding behavior** Distinctive psychological viewpoints that may involve different methods or techniques—for example, the psychobiological, cognitive, behavioral, psychoanalytic, humanistic, and cross-cultural approaches.

**arousal-cost-reward model of helping** The idea that we make decisions to help by calculating the costs and rewards of helping.

**assimilation** The process by which a child uses old methods or experiences to deal with new situations and then incorporates the new information into his or her existing knowledge.

**atmospheric perspective** In three-dimensional vision, a monocular depth cue that comes into play in the presence of dust, smog, or water vapor. Hazy objects are interpreted as being farther away.

**attachment** A close fundamental emotional bond that develops between the infant and his or her parent or caregiver.

**attention-deficit/hyperactivity disorder (ADHD)** A condition diagnosed on the basis of the occurrence of certain behavioral problems, rather than medical tests. A child must have six or more symptoms of inattention (such as making careless mistakes in schoolwork) and six or more symptoms of hyperactivity (such as fidgeting or talking excessively). These symptoms should have been present from an early age, persisted for at least six months, and contributed to maladaptive development.

**attitude** Any belief or opinion that includes a positive or negative evaluation of some object, person, or event and that predisposes us to act in a certain way toward that object, person, or event.

**attributions** Our explanations of the causes of events, other people's behaviors, and our own behaviors.

**atypical neuroleptic drugs** Neuroleptics that somewhat lower levels of dopamine but, more importantly, reduce levels of other neurotransmitters, especially serotonin. One group of these drugs is the benzamides, such as clozapine. These drugs primarily reduce positive symptoms and may slightly improve negative symptoms.

**auditory association area** An area directly below the primary auditory cortex that receives and transforms meaningless auditory sensations into perceptions or meaningful sounds, such as melodies or words.

**auditory canal** A long tube in the ear that funnels sound waves down its length so that the waves strike a thin, taut membrane—the eardrum, or tympanic membrane.

**auditory nerve** A band of fibers that carries impulses (electrical signals) from the cochlea to the brain, resulting in the perception of sounds.

**authoritarian parents** Parents who attempt to shape, control, and evaluate the behavior and attitudes of their children in accordance with a set standard of conduct, usually an absolute standard that comes from religious or respected authorities.

**authoritative parents** Parents who attempt to direct their children's activities in a rational and intelligent way. They are supporting, loving, and committed, encourage verbal give-and-take, and discuss their rules and policies with their children.

**autism** A condition marked by especially abnormal or impaired development in social interactions, spoken language, and sensory-motor systems. Autistics characteristically have few activities or interests and spend long periods repeating the same ritualistic physical behaviors. Signs of autism begin in a child's first three years.

**automatic encoding** The transfer of information from short-term into long-term memory without any effort and usually without any awareness.

**automatic processes** Activities that require little awareness, take minimal attention, and do not interfere with other ongoing activities.

**autonomic nervous system** That portion of the peripheral nervous system that regulates heart rate, breathing, blood pressure, digestion, hormone secretion, and other functions, as well as maintaining the body in a state of optimal balance, or homeostasis. It usually functions without conscious effort, which means that only a few of its responses, such as breathing, can also be controlled voluntarily. Its two subdivisions are the sympathetic division and the parasympathetic division.

**availability heuristic** A rule of thumb by which we rely on information that is more prominent or easily recalled and overlook other information that is available but less prominent or notable.

**avoidance-avoidance conflict** Having to choose between two situations that both have disagreeable consequences.

**axon** A single threadlike structure within the neuron. It extends from, and carries signals away from, the cell body to neighboring neurons, organs, or muscles.

**axon membrane** The axon wall, which contains chemical gates that may be opened or closed to control the inward and outward flow of electrically charged particles called ions.

**babbling** The first stage in acquiring language, in which infants, at an age of about 6 months, begin to make one-syllable sounds such as "deedeedee" or "bababa." Many of these sounds are common across languages.

**Bandura's social cognitive theory** A personality theory that assumes that personality development, growth, and change are influenced by four distinctively human cognitive processes: highly developed language ability, observational learning, purposeful behavior, and self-analysis. Bandura emphasizes the importance of learning through observation, imitation, and self-reward in the development of social skills, interactions, and behaviors. He contends that we can learn new social skills without performing any observable behaviors or receiving any external rewards. See also social cognitive theory.

**Barnum principle** A technique used in horoscopes and elsewhere, in which a number of traits are listed in such a general way that almost everyone who reads them thinks that these traits apply specifically to him or her. This technique was named after circus owner P. T. Barnum.

**basal ganglia** A group of structures in the center of the brain that are involved in regulating movements. To function properly, neurons in the basal ganglia must have a sufficient supply of the neurotransmitter dopamine.

**basic rules of grammar** Rules for combining nouns, verbs, and adjectives into meaningful sentences.

**basilar membrane** A membrane within the cochlea that contains the auditory receptors, or hair cells.

**Beck's cognitive theory of depression** The idea that when we are depressed, automatic, negative thoughts that we rarely notice occur continually throughout the day. These negative thoughts distort how we perceive and interpret the world and thus influence our behaviors and feelings, which in turn contribute to our feeling depressed.

**Beck's cognitive therapy** *See* cognitive therapy.

**behavior modification** A treatment or therapy that changes or modifies problems or undesirable behaviors by using learning principles based on operant conditioning, classical conditioning, and social cognitive learning.

**behavior therapy** A form of psychotherapy in which disruptive behaviors are changed and human functioning is improved on the basis of principles of classical and operant conditioning. It focuses on changing particular behaviors rather than on the underlying mental events or possible unconscious factors. Sometimes called behavior modification or cognitive-behavior therapy.

**behavioral approach** A psychological viewpoint that analyzes how organisms learn new behaviors or modify existing ones, depending on whether events in their environments reward or punish these behaviors. Historically, as founded by John B. Watson, the behavioral approach emphasized the objective, scientific analysis of observable behaviors.

**behavioral genetics** The study of how inherited or genetic factors influence and interact with psychological factors to shape our personality, intelligence, emotions, and motivation and also how we behave, adapt, and adjust to our environment.

**benzodiazepines** Minor tranquilizers (Librium, Valium, Xanax, Dalmane, Halcion) that reduce anxiety and stress. They are frequently prescribed for short-term (3–4 weeks) treatment of insomnia. Side effects associated with high doses or prolonged usage include daytime drowsiness, loss of memory, tolerance, and dependency.

**Binet-Simon Intelligence Scale** The world's first standardized intelligence test, containing items arranged in order of increasing difficulty. The items measured vocabulary, memory, common knowledge, and other cognitive abilities.

**binocular depth cues** In three-dimensional vision, depth cues that depend on the movement of both eyes (*bi* means "two"; *ocular* means "eye").

**biofeedback** A training procedure through which a person is made aware of his or her physiological responses, such as muscle activity, heart rate, blood pressure, or temperature, and then tries to increase or decrease these physiological responses.

**biological approach** A psychological viewpoint that examines how our genes, hormones, and nervous systems interact with our environments to influence learning, personality, memory, motivation, emotions, coping techniques, and other traits and abilities.

**biological clocks** The body's internal timing devices that are genetically set to regulate various physiological responses for certain periods of time.

**biological factors** Innate tendencies or predispositions that may either facilitate or inhibit certain kinds of learning.

**biological hunger factors** Physiological changes in blood chemistry and signals from digestive organs that provide feedback to the brain, which, in turn, triggers us to eat or stop eating.

**biological needs** Physiological requirements that are critical to our survival and physical well-being.

**biological psychology** *See* psychobiology.

**biological sex factors** The action of sex hormones, which are involved in secondary sexual characteristics (facial hair, breasts), sexual motivation (more so in animals than in humans), and the development of ova and sperm.

**biological theory of depression** The idea that underlying genetic, neurological, or physiological factors may predispose a person to developing a mood disorder.

**BioPsychoSocial model** The representation of adolescent development as a process that occurs simultaneously on many levels and includes sexual, cognitive, social, and personality changes that interact and influence each other.

**bipolar I disorder** A mood disorder characterized by fluctuations between episodes of depression and mania. A manic episode goes on for at least a week, during which a person is unusually euphoric, cheerful, and high and has at least three of the following symptoms: has great self-esteem, has little need of sleep, speaks rapidly and frequently, has racing thoughts, is easily distracted, and pursues pleasurable activities. Formerly called manic-depressive illness.

**bisexual orientation** A pattern of sexual arousal by persons of either sex.

**brightness constancy** Our tendency to perceive brightness as remaining the same in changing illumination.

**Broca's aphasia** An inability to speak in fluent sentences while retaining the ability to understand written or spoken words. It is caused by damage to Broca's area.

**Broca's area** An area usually located in the left frontal lobe that is necessary for combining sounds into words and arranging words into meaningful sentences. *See* Broca's aphasia.

**bulimia nervosa** An eating disorder characterized by a minimum of two binge-eating episodes per week for at least three months; fear of not being able to stop eating; regularly engaging in vomiting, use of laxatives, or rigorous dieting and fasting; and excessive concern about body shape and weight.

**burnout** Feelings of doing poorly at one's job, physically wearing out, and becoming emotionally exhausted due to intense involvement with people who demand too much of one's time and energy and provide too little reward or satisfaction.

**bystander effect** The phenomenon in which an individual feels inhibited from taking some action because of the presence of others.

**caffeine** A mild stimulant that produces dilation of blood vessels, increased secretion of stomach acid, and moderate physiological arousal. Psychological effects include a feeling of alertness, decreased fatigue and drowsiness, and improved reaction times. Caffeine, which is present in coffee, tea, chocolate, and other foods, can be addictive, especially in higher doses.

**care orientation** Making moral decisions based on issues of caring, on avoiding hurt, on how things affect interpersonal relationships, and on concern for others.

**case study** An in-depth analysis of the thoughts, feelings, beliefs, experiences, behaviors, or problems of an individual. This research method offers little opportunity to control or manipulate situations or variables.

**CAT scan** *See* computerized axial tomography.

**catatonic schizophrenia** A subcategory of schizophrenia characterized by periods of wild excitement or periods of rigid, prolonged immobility; sometimes the person assumes the same frozen posture for hours on end.

**catharsis** A psychological process through which anger or aggressive energy is released by expressing or letting out powerful negative emotions. Freud's view that catharsis can be helpful in reducing aggression is not supported by most research.

**cell body** For neurons, a relatively large, egg-shaped structure that provides fuel, manufactures chemicals, and maintains the entire neuron in working order; also called the soma.

**central cues** Hunger cues associated with the activity of chemicals and neurotransmitters in different areas of the brain.

**central nervous system** Neurons located in the brain and spinal cord. From the bottom of the brain emerges the spinal cord, which is made up of neurons and bundles of axons and dendrites that carry information back and forth between the brain and the body. Neurons in the central nervous system normally have almost no capacity to regrow or regenerate if damaged or diseased.

**central route for persuasion** Presenting information with strong arguments, analyses, facts, and logic.

**cephalocaudal principle** The rule that parts of the body closer to the infant's head develop before parts closer to the feet.

**cerebellum** A region of the hindbrain that is involved in coordinating movements but not in initiating voluntary movements. It is also involved in cognitive functions, such as short-term memory, following rules, and carrying out plans. Surprising new evidence suggests the cerebellum is also involved in learning to perform timed motor responses, such as those required in playing games or sports.

**challenge appraisal** Our conclusion that we have the potential for gain or personal growth in a particular situation but that we also need to mobilize our physical energy and psychological resources to meet the challenging situation.

**chi-square** A test of statistical significance that compares the actual observed distribution of people (or events) among various categories with the distribution expected purely on the basis of chance.

**child abuse and neglect** Inadequate care or acts by the parent(s) (physical or emotional abuse) that put a child in danger, cause physical harm or injury, or involve sexual molestation.

**Chomsky's theory of language** The idea that all languages share a common universal grammar and that children inherit a mental program to learn this universal grammar. This theory includes the concepts of deep structure and surface structure and of transformational rules to convert from one to the other.

**chromosome** A hairlike structure that contains tightly coiled strands of deoxyribonucleic acid (DNA). Each cell of the human body (except for the sperm and egg) contains 46 chromosomes, arranged in 23 pairs.

**chunking** Combining separate items of information into a larger unit, or chunk, and then remembering chunks of information rather than individual items. A technique of memory enhancement.

**circadian rhythm** A biological clock that is genetically programmed to regulate physiological responses within a time period of 24 or 25 hours (about a day); one example is the sleep-wake cycle.

**clairvoyance** The ability to perceive events or objects that are out of sight.

**classical conditioning** A kind of learning in which a neutral stimulus acquires the ability to produce a response that was originally produced by a different stimulus.

**client-centered therapy** An approach developed by Carl Rogers that assumes that each person has an actualizing tendency—that is, a tendency to develop his or her own potential; the therapist's task is to show compassion and positive regard in helping the client reach his or her potential. Also called person-centered therapy.

**clinical assessment** A systematic evaluation of an individual's various psychological, biological, and social factors, as well as the identification of past and present problems, stressors, and other cognitive and behavioral symptoms.

**clinical diagnosis** A process of determining how closely an individual's specific symptoms match those that define a particular mental disorder.

**clinical interview** In assessment, a method of gathering information about relevant aspects of a person's past as well as current behaviors, attitudes, emotions, and details of present difficulties or problems. Some clinical interviews are unstructured, which means that they have no set questions; others are structured, which means that they follow a standard format of asking the same questions.

**clinical psychologist** An individual who has a Ph.D., has specialized in the clinical subarea, and has spent an additional year in a supervised therapy setting to gain experience in diagnosing and treating a wide range of abnormal behaviors. To train as a clinical psychologist usually requires 4–6 years of work after obtaining a college degree.

**closure rule** A perceptual rule stating that, in organizing stimuli, we tend to fill in any missing parts of a figure and see the figure as complete.

**cocaine** A stimulant produced from the leaves of the coca plant. Its physiological and behavioral effects are very similar to those of amphetamine: it produces increased heart rate and blood pressure, enhanced mood, alertness, increased activity, decreased appetite, and diminished fatigue. At higher doses, it can produce anxiety, emotional instability, and suspiciousness.

**cochlea** A coiled, fluid-filled structure in the inner ear that contains the receptors for hearing. Its function is transduction—transforming vibrations into nerve impulses that are sent to the brain for processing into auditory information.

**cochlear implant** A miniature electronic device that is surgically implanted into the cochlea to restore hearing in those with neural deafness. It converts sound waves to electrical signals, which are fed into the auditory nerve and hence reach the brain for processing.

**cognitive appraisal theory** The idea that our interpretation or appraisal of a situation is often the primary cause of emotions.

**cognitive approach** *See* cognitive psychology.

**cognitive-behavior therapy** A treatment for phobias and other mental disorders based on a combination of two methods: changing negative, unhealthy, or distorted thoughts and beliefs by substituting positive, healthy, and realistic ones; and changing limiting or disruptive behaviors by learning and practicing new skills to improve functioning. Sometimes called behavior therapy.

**cognitive-behavioral approach** The view that mental disorders result from deficits in cognitive processes, such as thoughts and beliefs, and from behavioral problems, such as deficits in skills and abilities. In this approach, mental disorders are treated by changing the person's maladaptive thoughts and behaviors.

**cognitive development** How a person perceives, thinks, and gains an understanding of his or her world through the interaction and influence of genetic and learned factors.

**cognitive developmental theory** The idea that, as they develop mental skills and interact with their environments, children learn one set of

rules for male behavior and another set of rules for female behavior.

**cognitive dissonance** A state of unpleasant psychological tension that motivates us to reduce our cognitive inconsistencies by making our beliefs more consistent with one another.

**cognitive factors** According to social cognitive theory, factors that include our beliefs, expectations, values, intentions, and social roles—all of which help to shape our personalities.

**cognitive factors in motivation** The influence of individuals' evaluations or perceptions of a situation on their willingness to work.

**cognitive interview** A technique for questioning eyewitnesses and others by having them imagine and reconstruct the details of an event, report everything they remember without holding anything back, and narrate the event from different viewpoints.

**cognitive learning** A kind of learning that involves mental processes, such as attention and memory; may proceed through observation or imitation; and may not involve any external rewards or require the person to perform any observable behaviors.

**cognitive map** A mental representation of the layout of an environment and its features.

**cognitive miser model** The idea that, in making attributions, people feel they must conserve time and effort by taking cognitive shortcuts.

**cognitive neuroscience** An approach to studying cognitive processes that involves taking pictures of the structures and functions of the living brain during performance of a wide variety of mental or cognitive processes, such as thinking, planning, naming, and recognizing objects.

**cognitive perspective** The theory that an organism learns a predictable relationship between two stimuli such that the occurrence of one stimulus (neutral stimulus) predicts the occurrence of another (unconditioned stimulus). In other words, classical conditioning occurs because the organism learns what to expect. Formerly called information theory.

**cognitive psychology** The study of how we process, store, retrieve, and use information and how cognitive processes influence what we attend to, perceive, learn, remember, believe, feel, and do.

**cognitive therapy** An approach to therapy that focuses on the role of thoughts in our emotions and actions. The widely used version developed by Aaron Beck assumes that we have automatic negative thoughts that we typically say to ourselves without much notice. By continuously repeating these automatic negative thoughts, we color and distort how we perceive and interpret the world and influence how we behave and feel. The goal of the therapy is to change these automatic negative thoughts.

**cognitive unconscious** Mental structures and processes that, although we are unaware of them, automatically and effortlessly influence our conscious thoughts and behaviors.

**collective unconscious** According to Jung, ancient memory traces and symbols that are passed on by birth and are shared by all people in all cultures.

**collectivistic culture** A culture that places a high priority on group goals and norms over personal goals and values. Individuals in these cultures work to control their behaviors and maintain harmonious relationships with others.

**color blindness** Inability to distinguish between two or more shades in the color spectrum. There are several kinds of color blindness. *See* monochromats and dichromats.

**color constancy** Our tendency to perceive colors as remaining stable despite differences in lighting.

**commitment** In Sternberg's triangular theory of love, the component of love associated with making a pledge to nourish the feelings of love and to actively maintain the relationship.

**common factors** A basic set of procedures and experiences shared by different therapies that account for those therapies' comparable effectiveness despite their different fundamental principles and techniques. Common factors include the growth of a supportive and trusting relationship between therapist and client and the accompanying development of an accepting atmosphere in which the client feels willing to admit problems and is motivated to work on changing.

**communication** The ability to use sounds, smells, or gestures to exchange information.

**community mental health centers** Government-sponsored centers that offer low-cost or free mental health care to members of the surrounding community, especially the underprivileged. The services may include psychotherapy, support groups, or telephone crisis counseling.

**companionate love** A condition associated with trusting and tender feelings for someone whose life is closely bound up with one's own.

**compliance** A kind of conformity in which we give in to social pressure in our public responses but do not change our private beliefs.

**computerized axial tomography (CAT scan)** A technique used to study the structure of the living brain. Low levels of X rays are passed through the brain. A computer measures the amount of radiation absorbed by the brain cells, which depends on their density, and produces a relatively good image of the brain.

**concept** A way to group objects, events, or characteristics on the basis of some common property they all share.

**conception** The process in which one of the millions of sperm penetrates the ovum's outside membrane; also called fertilization. After penetration, the outside membrane changes and becomes impenetrable to the millions of remaining sperm.

**concrete operations stage** The third of Piaget's cognitive stages, lasting from about the age of 7 to 11 years. During this stage, children can perform a number of logical mental operations on concrete objects that are physically present.

**conditional positive regard** Positive regard that depends on our behaving in certain ways—

for example, living up to or meeting others' standards.

**conditioned emotional response** The feeling of some positive or negative emotion, such as happiness, fear, or anxiety, when experiencing a stimulus that previously accompanied a pleasant or painful event. This is an example of classical conditioning.

**conditioned response (CR)** A response elicited by the conditioned stimulus; it is similar to the unconditioned response but not identical in magnitude or amount.

**conditioned stimulus (CS)** A formerly neutral stimulus that has acquired the ability to elicit a response previously elicited by the unconditioned stimulus.

**conduct disorder** A repetitive and persistent pattern of aggressive behavior that has been going on for at least a year and that violates the established social rules or the rights of others. Problems may include threatening to harm people, abusing or killing animals, destroying property, being deceitful, or stealing.

**conduction deafness** Deafness caused by wax in the auditory canal, injury to the tympanic membrane, or malfunction of the ossicles.

**cones** Photoreceptors that contain three chemicals called opsins, which are activated in bright light and allow us to see color. Unlike rods, cones are wired individually to neighboring cells; this one-on-one system of relaying information allows us to see fine details.

**conflict** The feeling we experience when we must decide between two or more incompatible choices.

**conformity** Any behavior you perform because of group pressure, even though that pressure might not involve direct requests.

**conscious thoughts** Wishes, desires, or thoughts that we are aware of, or can recall, at any given moment.

**consciousness** An individual's different levels of awareness of his or her thoughts and feelings. Creating images in the mind, following thought processes, and having unique emotional experiences are all part of consciousness.

**consensus** In making attributions, determining whether other people engage in the same behavior in the same situation.

**conservation** The idea that even though the shape of some object or substance is changed, the total amount remains the same.

**consistency** In making attributions, determining whether an individual engages in a certain behavior every time he or she is in a particular situation.

**contiguity theory** The view that classical conditioning occurs because two stimuli (the neutral stimulus and the unconditioned stimulus) are paired close together in time (are contiguous). Eventually, as a result of this contiguous pairing, the neutral stimulus becomes the conditioned stimulus, which elicits the conditioned response.

**continuity rule** A perceptual rule stating that, in organizing stimuli, we tend to favor smooth or

continuous paths when interpreting a series of points or lines.

**continuous reinforcement** The simplest reinforcement schedule, in which every occurrence of the operant response results in delivery of the reinforcer.

**continuum of consciousness** The wide range of human experiences, from being acutely aware and alert to being totally unaware and unresponsive.

**control group** In an experiment, subjects who undergo all the same procedures as the experimental subjects do, except that the control subjects do not receive the treatment.

**Control Question Technique** A lie detection procedure in which the examiner asks two kinds of questions: neutral questions that elicit little emotional response; and critical questions that are designed to elicit greater emotional responses. The person answers only "Yes" or "No" to the questions and, if guilty, is expected to show a greater emotional response to the critical questions than to the neutral questions.

**controlled processes** Activities that require full awareness, alertness, and concentration to reach some goal. Because of the strongly focused attention they require, controlled processes often interfere with other ongoing activities.

**conventional level** Kohlberg's intermediate level of moral reasoning. It consists of two stages: At stage 3, moral decisions are guided most by conforming to the standards of others we value; at stage 4, moral reasoning is determined most by conforming to the laws of society.

**convergence** In three-dimensional vision, a binocular cue for depth perception based on signals sent from the muscles that turn the eyes. To focus on near or approaching objects, these muscles turn the eyes inward, toward the nose. The brain uses the signals sent by these muscles to determine the distance of the object.

**convergent thinking** Beginning with a problem and coming up with a single correct solution.

**conversion disorder** A type of somatoform disorder characterized by unexplained and significant physical symptoms—headaches, nausea, dizziness, loss of sensation, paralysis—that suggest a real neurological or medical problem but for which no physical or organic cause can be identified. Anxiety or emotional distress is apparently converted to symptoms that disrupt physical functioning.

**cornea** The rounded, transparent covering over the front of the eye. As the light waves pass through the cornea, its curved surface bends, or focuses, the waves into a narrower beam.

**corpus callosum** A wide band of fibers that connects the left and right hemispheres of the brain. It has 200 million nerve fibers that allow information to pass back and forth between the hemispheres.

**correlation** An association or relationship between the occurrence of two or more events.

**correlation coefficient** A number that indicates the strength of a relationship between two or more events: the closer the number is to −1.00

or +1.00, the greater is the strength of the relationship.

**cortex** A thin layer of cells that essentially covers the entire surface of the forebrain. The cortex consists of the frontal, parietal, occipital, and temporal lobes, whose control centers allow us to carry out hundreds of cognitive, emotional, sensory, and motor functions.

**counseling psychologist** An individual who has a Ph.D. in psychology or education and whose training included work in a counseling setting. Counseling psychologists generally have a less extensive research background than clinical psychologists and work in real-world settings, such as schools, industry, and private practice. Whereas clinical psychologists treat mental disorders, counseling psychologists deal largely with problems of living. To train as a counseling psychologist generally takes 4–6 years after obtaining a bachelor's degree.

**counterattitudinal behavior** Taking a public position that runs counter to your private attitude.

**covariation model** A model developed by Harold Kelley that may be used in deciding between internal and external attributions. The model says that, in determining attributions, we should look for factors that are present when the behavior occurs and factors that are absent when the behavior does not occur.

**creative individual** Someone who regularly solves problems, fashions products, or defines new questions that make an impact on his or her society.

**creative thinking** A combination of flexibility in thinking and reorganization of understanding to produce innovative ideas and solutions.

**critical language period** A period of time from infancy to adolescence when language is easiest to learn; in the period after adolescence through adulthood, language is more difficult to learn.

**critical period** In imprinting, a relatively brief time during which learning is most likely to occur. Also called the sensitive period.

**cross-cultural approach** A psychological viewpoint that studies the influence of cultural and ethnic similarities and differences on psychological and social functioning.

**cross-sectional method** A research design in which several groups of different-aged individuals are studied at the same time.

**crowd** A large group of persons, most of whom are unacquainted.

**cultural bias** In testing, the situation in which the wording of the questions and the experiences on which they are based are more familiar to members of some social groups than to others.

**cultural-familial retardation** Mental retardation that results from greatly impoverished environments, with no evidence of genetic or brain damage.

**cultural influences** Pervasive pressures that encourage members of a particular society or ethnic group to conform to shared behaviors, values, and beliefs.

**culture-free test** Test that does not contain vocabulary, experiences, or social situations greatly different from the cultural experiences of the individual taking the test.

**cumulative record** A continuous written record that shows an organism's responses and reinforcements.

**curare** A drug that enters the bloodstream, reaches the muscles, and blocks receptors on the muscles. As a result, acetylcholine, the neurotransmitter that normally activates muscles, is blocked, and the muscles are paralyzed.

**DARE (Drug Abuse Resistance Program, sometimes referred to as DARE)** A program taught in the classroom by trained, uniformed police officers. It is based on the idea of using social influence and role playing to discourage adolescents from starting drug use and to encourage them to refuse drugs in the future.

**daydreaming** An activity that requires a low level of awareness, often occurs during automatic processes, and involves fantasizing or dreaming while awake.

**debriefing** A procedure administered to subjects after an experiment to minimize any potential negative effects. It includes explaining the purpose and method of the experiment, asking the subjects their feelings about having been in the experiment, and helping the subjects deal with possible doubts or guilt arising from their behaviors in the experiments.

**decibel** A unit to measure loudness. Our threshold for hearing ranges from 0 decibels, which is absolutely no sound, to 140 decibels, which can produce pain and permanent hearing loss.

**decision-stage model of helping** The idea that we go through five stages in deciding to help: (1) we notice the situation; (2) we interpret it as one in which help is needed; (3) we assume personal responsibility; (4) we choose a form of assistance; and (5) we carry out that assistance.

**declarative memory** Memories of facts or events, such as scenes, stories, words, conversations, faces, or daily events. We are aware of these kinds of memories and can retrieve them.

**deductive reasoning** Reasoning from the general to the particular: deriving a conclusion about particulars that is based on a general assumption that one knows or believes to be true.

**deep structure** According to Chomsky, a sentence's underlying meaning that is not spoken but is present in the mind of the listener.

**defense mechanisms** Freudian processes that operate at unconscious levels to help the ego reduce anxiety through self-deception.

**deficiency needs** Physiological needs (food, sleep) and psychological needs (safety, belongingness, and esteem) that we try to fulfill if they are not met.

**definition theory** The idea that we form a concept of an object, event, animal, person, or characteristic by making a mental list of the actual or essential properties that define it.

**deindividuation** The increased tendency for subjects to behave irrationally or perform antisocial behaviors when there is less chance of being personally identified.

**deinstitutionalization** The release of mental patients from mental hospitals and their return to the community to develop more independent and fulfilling lives.

**delay of gratification** Voluntarily postponing an immediate reward to persist in completing a task for the promise of a future reward.

**dendrites** Branchlike extensions that arise from the cell body; they receive signals from other neurons, muscles, or sense organs and pass them to the cell body.

**denial** Refusal to recognize some anxiety-provoking event or piece of information.

**dependency** A change in the nervous system such that a person addicted to a drug now needs to take it to prevent the occurrence of painful symptoms.

**dependent personality disorder** A pattern of being submissive and clingy because of an excessive need to be taken care of. It is found in 2% of the population.

**dependent variable** In an experiment, one or more of the subjects' behaviors that are used to measure the potential effects of the treatment or independent variable.

**depth perception** In visual perception, the ability of the eye and brain to add a third dimension, depth, to visual perceptions, even though the images projected on our retina have only two dimensions, height and width.

**descriptive statistics** Numbers used to present a collection of data in brief yet meaningful form.

**designer drugs** Manufactured or synthetic drugs designed to resemble already existing illegal psychoactive drugs and to produce or mimic their psychoactive effects.

**developmental norms** The average ages at which children perform various skills or exhibit particular abilities or behaviors.

**developmental psychologists** Psychologists who study a person's biological, emotional, cognitive, personal, and social development across the life span, from infancy through late adulthood.

**developmental psychology** The study of moral, social, emotional, and cognitive development throughout a person's entire life.

***Diagnostic and Statistical Manual of Mental Disorders-IV-TR* (DSM-IV-TR)** The 2000 edition of the American Psychiatric Association's uniform diagnostic system for assessing specific symptoms and matching them to almost 300 different mental disorders. The DSM-IV-TR has five major dimensions, or axes.

**diathesis stress theory of schizophrenia** The idea that some people have a genetic predisposition (a diathesis) that interacts with life stressors to result in the onset and development of schizophrenia.

**dichromats** People who have trouble distinguishing red from green because their eyes have just two kinds of cones. This is an inherited condition, found mostly in males, that results in seeing mostly shades of green, but it differs in severity.

**diffusion of responsibility theory** The idea that, in the presence of others, individuals feel less personal responsibility and are less likely to take action in a situation where help is required.

**direction of a sound** The brain determines the direction of a sound by calculating the slight difference in time that it takes sound waves to reach the two ears, which are about 6 inches apart.

**discrimination** In classical conditioning, the tendency for some stimuli but not others to elicit a conditioned response. In operant conditioning, the tendency for a response to be emitted in the presence of a stimulus that is reinforced but not in the presence of unreinforced stimuli. In social psychology, specific unfair behaviors exhibited toward members of a group.

**discriminative stimulus** In conditioning, a cue that behavior will be enforced.

**disgust** A universal facial expression—closing the eyes, narrowing the nostrils, curling the lips downward, and sometimes sticking out the tongue—that indicates the rejection of an item of food.

**disorganized schizophrenia** A subcategory of schizophrenia marked by bizarre ideas, often about one's body (bones melting), confused speech, childish behavior (giggling for no apparent reason, making faces at people), great emotional swings (fits of laughing or crying), and often extreme neglect of personal appearance and hygiene.

**displacement** Transferring feelings from their true source to another source that is safer and more socially acceptable.

**display rules** Specific cultural norms that regulate when, where, and how much emotion we should or should not express in different situations.

**dispositional attributions** *See* internal attributions.

**dissociative amnesia** A dissociative disorder characterized by inability to recall important personal information or events and usually associated with stressful or traumatic events. The importance of the information forgotten or the duration of the memory lapse is too great to be explained by normal forgetfulness.

**dissociative disorder** A disorder characterized by a disruption, split, or breakdown in a person's normally integrated and functioning consciousness, memory, sense of identity, or perception.

**dissociative fugue** A disturbance in which an individual suddenly and unexpectedly travels away from home or place of work and is unable to recall his or her past. The person may not remember his or her identity or may be confused about his or her new, assumed identity.

**dissociative identity disorder** The presence in a single individual of two or more distinct identities or personality states, each with its own pattern of perceiving, thinking about, and relating to the world. Different personality states may take control of the individual's thoughts and behaviors at different times. Formerly called multiple personality disorder.

**distinctiveness** In making attributions, determining how differently the person behaves in one situation in comparison with other situations.

**divergent thinking** Beginning with a problem and coming up with many different solutions.

**dopamine theory** The idea that, in schizophrenia, the dopamine neurotransmitter system is somehow overactive and gives rise to a wide range of symptoms.

**double-blind procedure** An experimental design in which neither the researchers nor the subjects know which group is receiving which treatment. This design makes it possible to separate the effects of medical treatment from the participants' beliefs or expectations about the treatment.

**double standard for sexual behavior** A set of beliefs, values, and expectations that subtly encourages sexual activity in males but discourages the same behavior in females.

**Down syndrome** A genetic disorder that results from an extra 21st chromosome and causes abnormal physical traits (a fold of skin at the corner of each eye, a wide tongue, heart defects) and abnormal brain development, resulting in degrees of mental retardation.

**dream interpretation** A Freudian technique of dream analysis, based on the assumption that dreams contain underlying, hidden meanings and symbols that provide clues to unconscious thoughts and desires. Freud distinguished between a dream's manifest content—the plot of the dream at the surface level—and its latent content—the hidden or disguised meaning of the plot's events.

**dreaming** A unique state of consciousness in which we are asleep but we experience a variety of images, often in color. People blind from birth have only auditory or tactile dreams, while sighted people have dreams with astonishing visual, auditory, and tactile images.

**drive** A state of tension, produced by a need, that motivates the organism to act to reduce that tension.

**drive-reduction theory** The idea that a need results in a drive, which is a state of tension that motivates the organism to act to reduce the tension and return the body to homeostasis.

**Drug Abuse Resistance Program** *See* DARE.

**DSM-IV-TR** *See Diagnostic and Statistical Manual of Mental Disorders-IV-TR.*

**dyslexia** Reading, spelling, and writing difficulties that may include reversing or skipping letters and numbers. This condition affects 1–2% of children and is now regarded as a neurological disorder rather than a reading problem.

**dysthymic disorder** A mood disorder characterized by feeling chronically but not continuously depressed for a period of two years. While depressed, a person experiences at least two of the following symptoms: poor appetite, insomnia, fatigue, low self-esteem, poor concentration, and feelings of hopelessness.

**eardrum** *See* tympanic membrane.

**echoic memory** A form of sensory memory that holds auditory information for one or two seconds.

**eclectic approach** An approach to therapy in which the psychotherapist combines techniques and ideas from many different schools of thought.

**ecological psychology** An approach to measuring intelligence by observing how people solve problems in their usual settings.

**ECT** *See* electroconvulsive therapy.

**efferent neurons** Neurons that carry information away from the spinal cord to produce responses in various muscles and organs throughout the body. Also called motor neurons.

**effortful encoding** The transfer of information from short-term into long-term memory either by working hard to repeat or rehearse the information or by making associations between new and old information.

**ego** Freud's second division of the mind, which develops from the id during infancy; its goal is to find safe and socially acceptable ways of satisfying the id's desires and to negotiate between the id's wants and the superego's prohibitions.

**egocentric thinking** Seeing and thinking of the world only from your own viewpoint and having difficulty appreciating someone else's viewpoint. *See also* adolescent egocentric thinking.

**eidetic imagery** The ability to examine a picture or page for 10–30 seconds and then retain a detailed visual image of the material for several minutes. Eidetic memory is found in a small percentage of children and almost always disappears around adolescence.

**elaborative rehearsal** Making meaningful associations between information to be learned and information already learned. An effective strategy for encoding information into long-term memory.

**Electra complex** *See* Oedipus complex.

**electroconvulsive therapy (ECT)** A treatment for depression in which electrodes are placed on the skull and a mild electric current is administered. As it passes through the brain, the current causes a seizure. Usual treatment consists of 10–12 ECT sessions, at the rate of about three per week.

**embryonic stage** The second stage of the prenatal period, spanning the 2–8 weeks that follow conception; during this stage, cells divide and begin to differentiate into bone, muscle, and body organs.

**EMDR** *See* Eye Movement Desensitization and Reprocessing.

**emotion** A response consisting of four components: interpreting or appraising a stimulus (event, object, or thought) in terms of one's well-being; having a subjective feeling, such as happiness or sadness; experiencing physiological responses, such as changes in heart rate or breathing; and possibly showing overt behaviors, such as smiling or crying.

**emotion-focused coping** Making some effort to deal with the emotional distress caused by a harm/loss or threat appraisal. These efforts include seeking support and sympathy, avoiding or denying the situation, or redirecting our attention.

**emotional development** The process in which we learn to produce facial expressions and experience associated emotional feelings, as a result of the interaction between our biological capacity to produce emotional expressions (nature) and the positive or negative feedback we receive from our environment (nurture).

**emotional intelligence** The ability to perceive and express emotion, understand and reason with emotion, and regulate emotion in oneself and others.

**encoding** Placing or storing information—such as images, events, or sounds (music, noise, speech)—in memory by making mental representations.

**end bulbs** Bulblike swellings at the extreme ends of axons' branches that store chemicals called neurotransmitters, which are used to communicate with neighboring cells.

**endocrine system** Numerous glands, located throughout the body, that secrete various chemicals called hormones, which affect organs, muscles, and other glands in the body.

**endorphins** Chemicals produced by the brain and secreted in response to injury or severe physical or psychological stress. Their powerful pain-reducing properties are similar to those of morphine.

**environmental factors** Our social, political, and cultural influences, as well as our particular learning experiences.

**environmental language factors** Interactions that children have with parents, peers, teachers, and others whose feedback rewards and encourages language development; these interactions also provide opportunities for children to observe, imitate, and practice language skills.

**episodic memory** A type of declarative memory, consisting of knowledge about one's personal experiences (episodes) or activities, such as naming or describing favorite restaurants, movies, songs, habits, or hobbies.

**ESP** *See* extrasensory perception.

**estrogen** One of the major female hormones. At puberty, estrogen levels increase eightfold and stimulate the development of both primary and secondary sexual characteristics.

**ethologists** Behavioral biologists who observe and study animal behavior in the animal's natural environment or under relatively naturalistic conditions.

**evaluative function** The role of our attitudes in helping us to stand up for those beliefs and values that we consider very important to ourselves.

**evening persons** People who prefer to get up late, go to bed late, and engage in afternoon or evening activities. *See* morning persons.

**event schemas** Social schemas containing behaviors that we associate with familiar activities, events, or procedures. Also called scripts.

**evolution** *See* theory of evolution.

**evolutionary theory (of gender differences)** The idea in sociobiology, which emphasizes genetic and biological forces, that current behavioral and cognitive differences between men and women can be traced back to different survival problems faced by early women and men and the different behaviors they adapted to survive.

**exhaustion stage** The third stage in the general adaptation syndrome. In reaction to long-term, continuous stress, there is actual breakdown in internal organs or weakening of the infection-fighting immune system.

**experiment** A method for identifying cause-and-effect relationships by following a set of rules and guidelines that minimize the possibility of error, bias, and chance occurrences. *See also* laboratory experiment.

**experimental group** In an experiment, the subjects who receive the treatment.

**experimental psychology** The study of sensation, perception, learning, human performance, motivation, and emotion in carefully controlled laboratory conditions, with both animal and human subjects.

**exposure therapy** A treatment for anxiety in which the person is gradually exposed to the real anxiety-producing situations or objects that he or she is attempting to avoid; exposure treatment is continued until the anxiety decreases.

**external attributions** Explanations of behavior based on the external circumstances or situations. Also called situational attributions.

**external ear** An oval-shaped structure that protrudes from the side of the head. Its function is to pick up sound waves and send them along the auditory canal.

**extinction** In classical conditioning, the reduction in a response when the conditioned stimulus is no longer followed by the unconditioned stimulus. As a result, the conditioned stimulus tends to no longer elicit the conditioned response. In operant conditioning, reduction in the operant response when it is no longer followed by the reinforcer.

**extrasensory perception (ESP)** A group of psychic experiences that involve perceiving or sending information (images) outside normal sensory processes or channels. ESP includes four general abilities—telepathy, precognition, clairvoyance, and psychokinesis.

**extrinsic motivation** Engaging in certain activities or behaviors that either reduce biological needs or help us to obtain incentives or external rewards.

**Eye Movement Desensitization and Reprocessing (EMDR)** A new technique in which the client focuses on a traumatic memory while visually following the back-and-forth movement of a therapist's hand or pen. One memory may trigger another, which the client focuses on while again visually following the back-and-forth movement. The process usually continues throughout a 90-minute session, during which the traumatic memories are said to be reprocessed by eye movements that help replace traumatic memories with pleasant ones.

**eyewitness testimony** Recollection or recognition of a suspect observed during a possibly disruptive emotional situation that may have interfered with accurate remembering.

**facial expressions** Social signals that accompany emotions and express the state of our personal feelings; they provide social signals that elicit a variety of responses from those around us.

**facial feedback theory** The idea that sensations or feedback from the movement of facial muscles and skin are interpreted by your brain as emotional feelings.

**factor analysis** A complicated statistical method that finds relationships among different or diverse items and allows them to be grouped together.

**farsightedness** A visual acuity problem that may result when the eyeball is too short, so that objects are focused at a point slightly behind the retina. The result is that distant objects are clear, but near objects are blurry.

**FAS** *See* fetal alcohol syndrome.

**fat cells** Cells that store body fat. The number of fat cells in the body is primarily determined by heredity. They do not normally multiply except when we become obese. Fat cells shrink as we give up fat and lose weight and greatly enlarge as we store fat and gain weight.

**fear** A realistic response to a threatening situation.

**fear of failure** A tendency to avoid failure by choosing easy, nonchallenging tasks where failure is unlikely or difficult.

**female circumcision** The practice of cutting away the female's external genitalia, usually including her clitoris and surrounding skin (labia minora). The remaining edges are sewn together, which leaves only a small opening for urination and menstruation.

**female hypothalamus** Because of neural programming in the womb, the hypothalamus, a structure in the brain that controls the endocrine system, functions differently in the male and female. The female hypothalamus triggers a cyclical release of estrogens from the ovaries. The increased estrogen level is responsible for female secondary sexual characteristics, such as pubic hair, breast development, and widening of the hips. The cyclic release of hormones (estrogen and progesterone) also regulates the menstrual cycle.

**female secondary sexual characteristics** Sexual characteristics whose development in the female is triggered by the increased secretion of estrogen during puberty; they include the growth of pubic hair, development of breasts, and widening of hips.

**fertilization** *See* conception.

**fetal alcohol syndrome (FAS)** A condition caused by heavy maternal drinking during pregnancy. It results in a combination of physical changes, such as short stature, flattened nose, and short eye openings, and psychological defects, such as degrees of mental retardation and hyperactivity.

**fetal stage** The third stage in prenatal development, beginning two months after conception and lasting until birth.

**fight-flight response** A state of increased physiological arousal that (a) directs great resources of energy to the muscles and brain, (b) can be triggered by either physical stimuli that threaten our survival or psychological situations that are novel, threatening, or challenging, and (c) involves numerous physiological responses that arouse and prepare the body for action—fight or flight. Caused by the activation of the sympathetic nervous system, it helps us to cope with, and survive, threatening situations.

**figure-ground rule** A perceptual rule stating that, in organizing stimuli, we tend to automatically distinguish between a figure and a ground: the figure, with more detail, stands out against the background, which has less detail.

**five-factor model** An approach to personality in which all traits are organized under five categories—openness, conscientiousness, extraversion, agreeableness, and neuroticism—that are used to describe differences in personality.

**fixation** A Freudian process through which an individual may be locked into any one of the three psychosexual stages—oral, anal, or phallic—because his or her wishes were either overgratified or undergratified in that stage.

**fixed action pattern** An innate biological force that predisposes an organism to behave in a fixed way in the presence of a specific environmental condition. Previously called instinct.

**fixed-interval schedule** In conditioning, a schedule in which a reinforcer occurs following a subject's first response after a fixed interval of time.

**fixed-ratio schedule** In conditioning, a schedule in which a reinforcer occurs only after a fixed number of responses by the subject.

**flashbulb memories** Vivid recollections, usually in great detail, of dramatic or emotionally charged incidents, which are encoded effortlessly and may last for long periods of time.

**flavor** What we experience when we combine the sensations of taste and smell.

**fMRI** *See* functional magnetic resonance imaging.

**foot-in-the-door technique** A method of persuasion that relies on the increased probability of compliance to a second request if a person complies with a small, first request.

**forebrain** The largest part of the brain, consisting of left and right hemispheres, which are connected by a wide band of fibers, the corpus callosum. The hemispheres are responsible for a vast array of responses, including learning and memory, speaking and language, emotional responses, experiencing sensations, initiating voluntary movements, planning, and making decisions.

**forgetting** Inability to retrieve, recall, or recognize information that was stored or is still stored in long-term memory.

**forgetting curve** A graph measuring the amount of previously learned information that subjects can recall or recognize across time.

**formal operations stage** Piaget's fourth cognitive stage, lasting from about 12 years of age through adulthood. During this stage, adolescents and adults develop the ability to think about abstract or hypothetical concepts, to consider an issue from another person's viewpoint, and to solve cognitive problems in a logical manner.

**fragile X syndrome** A defect in the X chromosome that can result in physical changes such as a relatively large head with protruding ears, as well as mild to profound levels of mental retardation.

**fraternal twins** Twins who develop from separate eggs and share 50% of their genes.

**free association** A Freudian technique in which clients are encouraged to talk about any thoughts or images that enter their heads; the assumption is that this kind of free-flowing, uncensored talking will provide clues to unconscious material.

**frequency distribution** The range of scores we get and the frequency of each one, when we measure a sample of people (or objects) regarding some trait.

**frequency theory** In explaining pitch perception, the idea that, for low-frequency sound waves (1,000 cycles or less), the rate at which nerve impulses reach the brain determines how low a sound is. A rate of 50 impulses per second would be interpreted as a lower sound than a rate of 200 impulses per second.

**Freud's psychodynamic theory of personality** A personality theory that emphasizes the importance of early childhood experiences; repressed thoughts that we cannot voluntarily access; and the conflicts between conscious and unconscious forces that influence our thoughts and behaviors. *See also* psychoanalytic approach.

**Freud's theory of dreams** A theory that says we have a "censor" that protects us from realizing threatening and unconscious desires or wishes, especially those involving sex or aggression, by transforming them into harmless symbols that appear in our dreams and do not disturb our sleep or conscious thoughts.

**Freud's theory of the unconscious** The idea that, when faced with very threatening—especially sexual or aggressive—wishes or desires, we automatically defend our self-esteem by placing these psychologically dangerous thoughts into a mental place, the unconscious, that is sealed off from voluntary recall.

**Freudian slips** Mistakes or slips of the tongue that we make in everyday speech; such mistakes are thought to reflect unconscious thoughts or wishes.

**frontal lobe** An area in the front part of the brain that includes a huge area of cortex. The frontal lobe is involved in many functions: performing voluntary motor movements, interpreting and performing emotional behaviors, behaving normally in social situations, maintaining a healthy personality, paying attention to things in the environment, making decisions, and carrying out plans.

**frontal lobotomy** A surgical procedure in which about one-third of the front part of the frontal lobe is separated from the rest of the brain.

**frustration** The feeling that results when our attempts to reach some goal are blocked.

**frustration-aggression hypothesis** The idea that, when our goals are blocked, we become frustrated and respond with anger and aggression. *See also* modified frustration-aggression hypothesis.

**functional fixedness** A mental set characterized by the inability to see an object as having a function different from its usual one.

**functional magnetic resonance imaging (fMRI)** A brain scan that measures the activity of specific neurons that are functioning during cognitive tasks, such as thinking, listening, or reading.

**functionalism** An early school of psychological thought that emphasized the function rather than the structure of consciousness and was interested in how our minds adapt to our changing environment.

**fundamental attribution error** Our tendency, when we look for causes of a person's behavior, to focus on the person's disposition or personality traits and overlook how the situation influenced the person's behavior.

**galvanic skin response** Changes in sweating of the fingers (or palms) that accompany emotional experiences and are independent of perspiration under normal temperatures.

**Ganzfeld procedure** A controlled method for eliminating trickery, error, and bias while testing telepathic communication between two people.

**Gardner's multiple-intelligence theory** The idea that, instead of one kind of general intelligence, there are at least seven different kinds: verbal intelligence, musical intelligence, logical-mathematical intelligence, spatial intelligence, body movement intelligence, intelligence to understand oneself, and intelligence to understand others.

**GAS** *See* general adaptation syndrome.

**gate control theory** The idea that nonpainful nerve impulses compete with pain impulses as they enter the spinal cord, creating a neural gate through which only the nonpainful impulses pass; the pain impulses do not reach the brain. Thus, feelings of pain may be reduced by rubbing an injured area or becoming absorbed in other activities.

**gender identity** The individual's subjective experience and feelings of being either a male or a female; formerly called sexual identity.

**gender identity disorder** Commonly referred to as transsexualism, it is an individual's strong desire or feeling of wanting to be the opposite sex, discomfort with being one's assigned sex, and the wish to live as a member of the other sex.

**gender roles** Traditional or stereotypic behaviors, attitudes, and personality traits that parents, peers, and society designate as masculine or feminine. Gender roles affect how we think and behave; formerly called sex roles.

**gender schemas** Sets of information and rules organized around how either a male or a female should think and behave.

**gene** A specific segment on the strand of DNA (the chromosome) that contains instructions for making proteins, the chemical building blocks from which all the parts of the brain and body are constructed.

**general adaptation syndrome (GAS)** According to Selye, a series of three stages—alarm, resistance, and exhaustion—that correspond to the three different reactions of the body to stressful situations and that gradually increase the chances of developing psychosomatic symptoms.

**generalization** In classical conditioning, the tendency for a stimulus that is similar to the original conditioned stimulus to elicit a response that is similar to the conditioned response. Usually, the more similar the new stimulus is to the original conditioned stimulus, the larger will be the conditioned response. In operant conditioning, the situation in which an animal or a person emits the same response to similar stimuli.

**generalized anxiety disorder** A psychological disorder primarily characterized by excessive and/or unrealistic worry or feelings of general apprehension about events or activities. These anxious feelings occur on a majority of days for a period of at least six months.

**genetic hunger factors** Inherited instructions found in our genes that influence our hunger; these instructions may determine our number of fat cells or our metabolic rate of burning off the body's fuel, for example, and push us toward being normal, overweight, or underweight.

**genetic marker** An identifiable gene or number of genes or a specific segment of a chromosome that is directly linked to some behavioral, physiological, or neurological trait or disease.

**genetic sex factors** Inherited instructions for the development of sexual organs, the secretion of sex hormones, and the wiring of the neural circuits that control sexual reflexes.

**genital stage** Freud's fifth, and final, psychosexual stage, lasting from puberty through adulthood. In this stage, the individual has renewed sexual desires that he or she seeks to fulfill through relationships with other people.

**germinal stage** The first stage of prenatal development, lasting two weeks from the moment of conception.

**Gestalt approach** An older theoretical approach that emphasized the idea that perception is more than the sum of its parts. In contrast to the structuralists, the Gestalt psychologists believed that perceptions are formed by the brain on the basis of a set of rules specifying how individual elements may be organized to form a meaningful pattern—that is, a perception.

**gifted** A term applied to an individual (usually to a child) who has above-average intelligence as well as some superior talent or skill. A moderately gifted child is usually defined by an IQ score between 130 and 150; a profoundly gifted child has an IQ score of 180 or above.

**glial cells** Cells in the nervous system that have at least three functions: they provide scaffolding to guide the growth of developing neurons and support mature neurons; they wrap themselves around neurons and form a kind of insulation to prevent interference from other electrical sig-

nals; and they release chemicals that influence a neuron's growth and function.

**gonads** Glands—the ovaries in females and the testes in males—that produce hormones to regulate sexual development, ovulation or sperm production, and the growth of sex organs. They are part of the endocrine system.

**grammar** A set of rules for combining words into phrases and sentences to express an infinite number of thoughts that can be understood by others.

**group** A collection of two or more people who interact and share some common attribute or purpose. A group also influences how its members think and behave.

**group cohesion** Group togetherness, which is determined by how much group members perceive that they share common attributes.

**group norms** Formal or informal rules about how group members should behave.

**group polarization** The phenomenon in which group discussion reinforces the majority's point of view and shifts that view to a more extreme position.

**groupthink** Poor group decision making that occurs when group discussions emphasize cohesion and agreement rather than critical thinking and the best possible outcome.

**growth needs** According to Maslow, higher-level needs that are not essential to existence, such as the desire for truth, goodness, beauty, and justice.

**hair cells** The auditory receptors. These miniature hair-shaped cells rise from the basilar membrane in the cochlea.

**hallucinations** Sensory experiences without any stimulation from the environment. Common symptoms of schizophrenia, hallucinations may be auditory, such as hearing voices; or they may include distorted perceptions, such as feeling that parts of one's body are too small or too large.

**hallucinogens** Psychoactive drugs that can produce hallucinations—strange perceptual, sensory, and cognitive experiences that the person sees or hears but knows are not occurring in reality. Such unreal experiences are called hallucinations.

**happiness** A mental state that includes three components: feeling positive emotions, being satisfied with one's life, and not experiencing negative emotions.

**hardiness** A combination of three personality traits—control, commitment, and challenge—that protect or buffer us from the potentially harmful effects of stressful situations and reduce our chances of developing psychosomatic illness.

**harm/loss appraisal** Our conclusion that we have already sustained some damage or injury in a particular situation.

**hassles** Small, irritating, frustrating events that we face daily and that we usually appraise as stressful experiences.

**helping** *See* prosocial behavior.

**heritability** A statistical measure that estimates the amount or proportion of some ability, characteristic, or trait that can be attributed to genetic factors.

**heterosexual orientation** A pattern of sexual arousal by persons of the opposite sex.

**heuristics** Rules of thumb that reduce the number of operations or allow us to take shortcuts in solving problems.

**hierarchy of needs** *See* Maslow's hierarchy of needs.

**high need for achievement** A tendency to persist longer at tasks; show better performance on tasks, activities, or exams; set challenging but realistic goals; compete with others to win; and be attracted to careers that require initiative.

**hindbrain** An area at the base of the brain that is involved in sleeping, waking, coordinating body movements, and regulating vital reflexes (heart rate, blood pressure, and respiration).

**hippocampus** A curved structure within the temporal lobe that is involved in transforming many kinds of fleeting memories into permanent storage. It forms part of the limbic system.

**histrionic personality disorder** A disorder characterized by excessive emotionality and attention seeking. It is found in 2% of the population.

**HIV positive** Having HIV antibodies, which implies infection by the human immunodeficiency virus (HIV).

**holistic view** The idea, emphasized in humanistic theories, that a person's personality is more than the sum of its individual parts; instead, the individual parts form a unique and total entity that functions as a unit.

**homeostasis** The tendency of the sympathetic and parasympathetic divisions of the autonomic nervous system to work together to maintain the body's level of arousal in balance for optimal functioning.

**homosexual orientation** A pattern of sexual arousal by persons of the same sex.

**humanistic approach** A psychological viewpoint emphasizing that each individual has great freedom in directing his or her future, considerable capacity for achieving personal growth, intrinsic worth, and enormous potential for self-fulfillment.

**humanistic theories** *See* humanistic approach.

**hypnosis** A situation or set of procedures in which a researcher, clinician, or hypnotist suggests to another person that he or she will experience various changes in sensation, perception, cognition, or control over motor behaviors.

**hypnotic analgesia** Reduction in pain reported by clients after undergoing hypnosis and receiving suggestions that reduced anxiety and promoted relaxation.

**hypnotic induction** Various methods of inducing hypnosis, such as asking subjects to close their eyes and go to sleep, having them fix their attention on an object (for example, a watch), and instructing them to go into deep relaxation.

**hypothalamus** A structure of the limbic system that is located near the bottom middle of the brain and regulates many motivational and emotional behaviors. It controls much of the endocrine system by regulating the pituitary gland.

**hypothesis** An educated guess about some phenomenon, stated in precise, concrete language so as to rule out any confusion or error in the meaning of its terms.

**iconic memory** A form of sensory memory that holds visual information for about a quarter of a second or more. (The word *icon* means "image.")

**id** Freud's first division of the mind, which contains two biological drives—sex and aggression—that are the source of all psychic or mental energy; the id's goal is to pursue pleasure and satisfy the biological drives.

**ideal self** According to Rogers, the self that is based on our hopes and wishes and reflects how we would like to see ourselves; its complement is the real self.

**ideal weight** *See* optimal weight.

**identical twins** Twins who develop from a single egg and thus have exactly the same genes.

**identity** How we describe ourselves, including our values, goals, traits, interests, and motivations.

**illusion** Perception of an image so distorted that, in reality, it cannot and does not exist. An illusion is created when space, size, and depth cues are manipulated so that our brains can no longer correctly interpret them.

**imagined perception** In hypnosis, the subject's willingness, at the hypnotist's suggestion, to respond to nonexistent stimuli and imaginary perceptions. It can also include bizarre behaviors, such as imitating Elvis Presley in public.

**immune system** The body's defense and surveillance network of cells and chemicals that fight off bacteria, viruses, and other foreign or toxic substances.

**implicit or nondeclarative memory** Mental and emotional processes that we are unaware of but that bias and influence our conscious feelings, thoughts, and behaviors. *See* procedural memory.

**impossible figure** A perceptual experience in which a drawing seems to defy basic geometric laws.

**imprinting** Inherited tendencies or responses that are displayed by newborn animals when they encounter certain stimuli in their environment.

**incentives** Environmental factors, such as external stimuli, reinforcers, or rewards, that motivate our behavior.

**independent variable** In an experiment, a treatment or something else that the researcher controls or manipulates.

**individualistic culture** A culture that places a high priority on attaining personal goals and striving for personal satisfaction, often by being competitive and assertive.

**inductive reasoning** Reasoning from particulars to the general: using particular experiences or observations to draw a broader conclusion.

**inferential statistics** A set of procedures for determining what conclusions can be legitimately inferred from a set of data.

**informational influence theory** The theory that we use the reactions of others to judge the seriousness of the situation.

**inhibited children** Kagan's term for children who show reluctance, anxiety, or fear (measured by motor activity, fretting, or crying) when approaching a strange child, exploring novel objects, playing with a peer, or talking to an unfamiliar adult. In addition, inhibited children show increased physiological arousal to novel or strange situations.

**inhibited female orgasm** A persistent delay or absence of orgasm after becoming aroused and excited.

**innate language factors** Genetically programmed physiological and neurological features of the brain and vocal apparatus that facilitate our making speech sounds and learning language skills.

**insanity** According to the legal definition, not knowing the difference between right and wrong.

**insecure attachment** An emotional bond characteristic of infants who avoid, or show ambivalence toward, their parents.

**insight** A mental process marked by the sudden and unexpected solution to a problem: a phenomenon often called the "ah-ha!" experience.

**insight therapy** An approach in which the therapist and client talk about the client's symptoms and problems, with the goal of identifying the cause of the problem. Once the client has an insight into the cause of the problem, possible solutions can be discussed with the therapist.

**insomnia** Difficulties in going to sleep or in staying asleep through the night. Associated daytime complaints include fatigue, impairment of concentration, memory difficulty, and lack of well-being. About 20–40% of adult Americans report bouts of insomnia.

**instincts** According to McDougal (1908), innate tendencies or biological forces that determine behavior; now used as a synonym for fixed action pattern.

**intelligence quotient (IQ)** A measure of intelligence computed by dividing a child's mental age, as measured in an intelligence test, by the child's chronological age and multiplying the result by 100.

**interactive model of sexual orientation** The theory that genetic and biological factors, such as genetic instructions and prenatal hormones, interact with psychological factors, such as the individual's attitudes, personality traits, and behaviors, to influence the development of sexual orientation.

**interference** The forgetting process in which the recall of some particular memory is blocked or prevented by new information that overwrites or interferes with it. *See also* proactive interference and retroactive interference.

**internal attributions** Explanations of behavior on the basis of the internal characteristics (or dispositions) of the person performing the behavior. Also referred to as dispositional attributions.

**interneuron** A relatively short neuron whose primary task is to make connections between other neurons.

**interpersonal conflict** A situation characterized by opposing interests or disagreements, in which one person interferes with a goal, a wish, or an expectation of another.

**interposition** In three-dimensional vision, a monocular depth cue that comes into play when objects overlap. The overlapping object appears closer, and the object that is overlapped appears to be farther away.

**interpreting function** The role played by our attitudes in providing convenient guidelines by means of which we can interpret and categorize objects and events and decide whether to approach or avoid them.

**interval timing clock** A sort of timing device, located in the basal ganglia of the brain, that gauges the passage of seconds, minutes, or hours and helps creatures know when to start or stop doing some activity.

**intervention program** A program for disadvantaged children that creates an environment offering increased opportunities for intellectual, social, and personality-emotional development while ensuring good physical health.

**interview** A technique for obtaining information by asking questions, ranging from open-ended to highly structured, about a subject's behaviors and attitudes, usually in a one-on-one situation.

**intestines** The body organ that responds to the presence of food, especially fats, by secreting a hormone called CCK (cholecystokinin), which inhibits eating.

**intimacy** In Sternberg's triangular theory of love, the component of love associated with feeling close and connected to someone; it develops through sharing and communicating.

**intrinsic motivation** Engaging in certain activities or behaviors because they are personally rewarding or because we are fulfilling our beliefs or expectations.

**introspection** A method of exploring conscious mental processes adopted by the structuralists: subjects were asked to look inward and report their sensations and perceptions.

**intrusive thoughts** Thoughts that we repeatedly experience, that are usually unwanted or disruptive, and that are very difficult to stop or eliminate.

**Inuit beliefs about dreams** The Inuit, or Eskimo, people, like other isolated indigenous people, believe that dreams are ways to enter the spiritual world, where the souls of departed animals, supernaturals, and relatives are made known.

**ions** Electrically charged chemical particles, which obey the rule that opposite charges attract and like charges repel.

**IQ** *See* intelligence quotient.

**iris** A circular muscle that surrounds the pupil and controls the amount of light that enters the eye. In dim light, the iris relaxes, allowing more light to enter—the pupil dilates; in bright light, the iris constricts, allowing less light to enter—the pupil constricts. The iris muscle contains the pigment that gives the eye its characteristic color.

**James-Lange theory** The idea that our brains interpret specific physiological changes as feelings or emotions and that there is a different physiological pattern underlying each emotion.

**jet lag** A condition in which travelers' internal circadian rhythm is out of step, or synchrony, with the external clock time at their new location. They experience fatigue, disorientation, lack of concentration, and reduced cognitive skills. It takes about one day to reset the circadian clock for each hour of time change.

**just noticeable difference (JND)** The smallest increase or decrease in the intensity of a stimulus that a person can manage to detect.

**justice orientation** Making moral decisions based more on issues of law and equality and individual rights.

**labeling** A process of identifying differences among individuals and placing them into specific categories, which may have either positive or negative associations.

**laboratory experiment** A technique to gather information by studying behavior in a controlled environment that permits the careful manipulation of some treatment and the measurement of the treatment's effects on behavior.

**laboratory setting** An environment in which individuals may be studied under systematic and controlled conditions, thus eliminating many of the real-world influences.

**language** A form of communication in which we learn and use complex rules to form and manipulate symbols (words or gestures) that are used to generate an endless number of meaningful sentences.

**language stages** Four different periods in a child's acquisition of language and grammar—babbling, single words, two-word combinations, and sentences; in each subsequent stage, a child displays new and more complex language skills.

**latency stage** The fourth of Freud's psychosexual stages, lasting from the age of about 6 to puberty. In this stage, the child represses sexual thoughts and engages in nonsexual activities, such as developing social and intellectual skills.

**lateral hypothalamus** A group of brain cells that regulates hunger by creating feelings of being hungry.

**law of effect** The principle that behaviors followed by positive (pleasurable) consequences are strengthened (and thus will likely occur in the future), while behaviors followed by negative consequences are weakened.

**learning** A relatively permanent change in behavior (both unobservable mental events and observable responses) associated with specific stimuli and/or responses that change as a result of experience.

**learning-performance distinction** The idea that learning may occur but may not always be measured by, or immediately evident in, performance.

**lens** A transparent, oval structure in the eye whose curved surface functions to bend and focus light waves into an even narrower beam. The lens is attached to muscles that adjust the curve of the lens, which, in turn, adjusts the focusing.

**levels-of-processing theory** The theory that memory depends on how well information is encoded in the mind. Information is encoded at a shallow level if we simply pay attention to its basic features but is encoded at a deep level if we form new associations with existing information. According to the theory, poor memory corresponds to information encoded at a shallow level, and good memory to information encoded at deep levels.

**lie detector tests** *See* polygraph tests.

**light and shadow** A monocular depth cue: brightly lit objects appear closer, while objects in shadows appear farther away.

**light therapy** The use of bright, artificial light to reset circadian rhythms and so combat the insomnia and drowsiness that plague shift workers and jet-lag sufferers; it is also used to help people with sleeping disorders in which the body fails to stay in time with the external environment.

**limbic system** A group of about half a dozen interconnected structures in the core of the forebrain that are involved in many motivational behaviors, such as obtaining food, drink, and sex; organizing emotional behaviors such as fear, anger, and aggression; and storing memories. It is sometimes referred to as our primitive, or animal, brain because the same structures are found in the brains of animals that are evolutionarily very old.

**linear perspective** In three-dimensional vision, a monocular depth cue associated with the convergence of parallel lines in the far distance.

**linguistic relativity** *See* theory of linguistic relativity.

**lithium** A naturally occurring mineral salt that is the most effective treatment for bipolar I disorder. It reduces or prevents manic episodes.

**liver** The body organ that monitors nutrients, especially the level of glucose (sugar) in the blood. When the level of glucose falls, the liver signals hunger; when the level of glucose rises, the liver signals fullness.

**lobes** The four areas into which the brain's cortex is divided.

**locus of control** Our beliefs concerning how much control we have over situations or rewards. For each of us, these beliefs lie somewhere on a continuum between internal and external locus of control. We have an internal locus of control if we believe that we have control over situations and rewards and an external locus of control if we believe that we do not have control over situations and rewards and that events outside ourselves (fate) determine what happens.

**long-term memory** The process that can store almost unlimited amounts of information over long periods of time.

**long-term potentiation (LTP)** The increased sensitivity of a neuron to stimulation after it has been repeatedly stimulated. Neuroscientists believe that the LTP process may be the basis for learning and memory in animals and humans.

**longitudinal method** A research design in which the same group of individuals is studied repeatedly at many different points in time.

**loudness** Our subjective experience of a sound's intensity, which is determined by the height (amplitude) of the sound wave. The brain calculates loudness from the rate of nerve impulses that arrive in the auditory nerve.

**LSD (*d*-lysergic acid diethylamide)** A very potent hallucinogen. Very small doses can produce experiences such as visual hallucinations, perceptual distortions, increased sensory awareness, and emotional responses that may last 8–10 hours.

**LTP** *See* long-term potentiation.

**magnetic resonance imaging (MRI scan)** A technique for studying the structure of the living brain. Nonharmful radio frequencies are passed through the brain, and a computer measures their interaction with brain cells and transforms this interaction into an incredibly detailed image of the brain (or body).

**maintenance rehearsal** The practice of intentionally repeating or rehearsing information (rather than forming any new associations) so that it remains longer in short-term memory.

**major depressive disorder** A mood disorder marked by at least two weeks of continually being in a bad mood, having no interest in anything, and getting no pleasure from activities. In addition, a person must have at least four of the following symptoms: problems with eating, sleeping, thinking, concentrating, or making decisions; lacking energy, thinking about suicide, and feeling worthless or guilty. Also called unipolar depression.

**major life events** Potentially disturbing, troubling, or disruptive situations, both positive and negative, that we appraise as having a significant impact on our lives.

**maladaptive behavior approach** In defining abnormality, the idea that a behavior is psychologically damaging or abnormal if it interferes with the individual's ability to function in one's personal life or in society.

**male hypothalamus** Because of neural programming in the womb, the hypothalamus, a structure in the brain that controls the endocrine system, functions differently in the male and female. The male hypothalamus triggers a continuous release of androgens, such as testosterone, from the testes. The increased androgen level is responsible for male secondary sexual characteristics, such as facial and pubic hair, muscle growth, and lowered voice.

**male secondary sexual characteristics** Sexual characteristics whose development in the male is triggered by the increased secretion of testosterone during puberty; they include the growth of pubic hair, muscle development, and a change (deepening) of the voice.

**marijuana** A psychoactive drug whose primary active ingredient is THC (tetrahydrocannabinol), which is found in the leaves of the cannabis plant. Low doses produce mild euphoria; moderate doses produce perceptual and time distortions; and high doses may produce hallucinations, delusions, and distortions of body image.

**Maslow's hierarchy of needs** An ascending order, or hierarchy, in which biological needs are placed at the bottom and social needs at the top. As needs at lower levels are met, we advance to the next higher level. This hierarchy indicates that we satisfy our biological needs before we satisfy our social needs.

**mass hysteria** A condition experienced by a group of people who, through suggestion, observation, or other psychological processes, develop similar fears, delusions, abnormal behaviors, and in some cases, similar physical symptoms.

**maturation** The succession of developmental changes that are genetically or biologically programmed rather than acquired through learning or life experiences.

**MDMA** A stimulant and hallucinogen that appeared in the early 1980s. Users claim that this designer drug, whose street name is ecstasy, causes changes in visual perceptions, increased emotional awareness, feelings of intimacy, and ability to interact with others. Because it lowers inhibitions, some consider it an aphrodisiac.

**mean** The arithmetic average of all the individual measurements in a distribution.

**measure of variability** An indication of how much scores in a distribution vary from one another.

**median** The score above and below which half the scores in the distribution fall.

**medical model approach** The view that mental disorders are similar to physical diseases and that both have symptoms that can be diagnosed and treated. Just as doctors use drugs to treat physical diseases, psychiatrists use psychoactive drugs to treat mental disorders.

**medical therapy** Any approach that uses psychoactive drugs, such as tranquilizers and neuroleptics, to treat mental disorders by changing biological factors, such as the levels of neurotransmitters in the brain.

**medulla** An area in the hindbrain, located at the top of the spinal cord, that includes a group of cells that control vital reflexes, such as respiration, heart rate, and blood pressure.

**melatonin** A hormone secreted by the pineal gland, an oval group of cells in the center of the human brain. Melatonin secretion, controlled by the suprachiasmatic nucleus, increases with darkness and decreases with light; thus, it plays a role in the regulation of circadian rhythms and in promoting sleep.

**memory** The ability to retain information over time through the processes of encoding, storing, and retrieving. Memories are not copies but representations of the world that vary in accuracy and are subject to error and bias.

**menarche** The first menstrual period; it is a signal that ovulation may have occurred and that the girl may have the potential to conceive and bear a child.

**Meniere's disease** Sudden attacks of dizziness, nausea, vomiting, and head-splitting buzzing sounds that result from a malfunction of the semicircular canals in the vestibular system.

**menopause** A gradual stoppage in the secretion of the major female hormone (estrogen). This process, which occurs in women at about age 50 (range 35–60), results in the cessation of ovulation and the menstrual cycle.

**mental age** The estimation of a child's intellectual progress, which is calculated by comparing the child's score on an intelligence test to the scores of average children of the same age.

**mental disorder** A prolonged or recurring problem that seriously interferes with an individual's ability to live a satisfying personal life and function adequately in society.

**mental retardation** Substantial limitation in present functioning, characterized by significantly subaverage intellectual functioning along with related limitations in two of ten areas, including communication, self-care, home living, social skills, and safety.

**mescaline** The active ingredient in the peyote cactus. At high doses, mescaline produces physiological arousal and very clear, colorful, and vivid visual hallucinations. It primarily increases the activity of the neurotransmitters norepinephrine and dopamine. Mescaline does not impair the intellect or cloud consciousness.

**meta-analysis** A powerful statistical procedure that compares the results of dozens or hundreds of studies to determine the effectiveness of some variable or treatment examined in those studies (for example, a type of therapy).

**metabolic rate** The efficiency with which the body breaks food down into energy and the speed with which the body burns off that fuel. An inherited trait, it can be raised by exercise or smoking.

**methamphetamine (D-methamphetamine)** A stimulant similar to amphetamine in both its chemical makeup and its physical and psychological effects. It causes marked increases in blood pressure and heart rate and feelings of enhanced mood, alertness, and energy. Methamphetamine, whose street names are crystal and ice, produces an almost instantaneous high when smoked and is highly addictive.

**method of loci** A mnemonic device, or encoding technique, that improves encoding by creating visual associations between memorized places and new items to be memorized.

**midbrain** The smallest division of the brain; it makes connections with the hindbrain and forebrain and alerts the forebrain to incoming sensations.

**middle ear** A bony cavity that is sealed at each end by a membrane. The two membranes are connected by three small bones, collectively called ossicles. Because of their shapes, these bones are referred to as the hammer, anvil, and stirrup. The ossicles act like levers that greatly amplify vibrations from the eardrum and transmit them to the oval window and inner ear.

**mind-body connection** The ability of our thoughts, beliefs, and emotions to produce physiological changes that may be either beneficial or detrimental to our health and well-being.

**mind-body question** The debate about how complex mental activities, such as feeling, thinking, learning, imagining, and dreaming, can be generated by the brain's physical membranes, fluids, and chemicals.

**mind-body therapy** An approach to healing based on the finding that thoughts and emotions can change physiological and immune responses. It attempts to increase physical and mental well-being by means of mental strategies such as relaxation, meditation, and biofeedback, as well as social support groups.

**Minnesota Multiphasic Personality Inventory-2 (MMPI-2)** A true-false self-report questionnaire that consists of 567 statements describing a wide range of normal and abnormal behaviors. The purpose of MMPI-2 is to help distinguish normal from abnormal groups.

**mnemonic methods** Very effective ways to improve encoding and create better retrieval cues by forming vivid associations or images, which facilitate recall and decrease forgetting.

**mode** The most frequent measurement in a distribution.

**modified frustration-aggression hypothesis** The idea that although frustration may lead to aggression, a number of situational and cognitive factors may override the aggressive response.

**monochromats** Individuals who have total color blindness; their world looks like a black-and-white movie. This kind of color blindness is rare and results from individuals having only rods or only one kind of functioning cone instead of three.

**monocular depth cues** In three-dimensional vision, depth cues produced by signals from a single eye. They are most commonly determined by the way objects are arranged in the environment.

**mood disorder** A prolonged and disturbed emotional state that affects almost all of a person's thoughts and behaviors.

**moral therapy** The belief that mental patients could be helped to function better by providing humane treatment in a relaxed and decent environment; this approach was fundamental to the reform movement of the early 1800s.

**morning persons** People who prefer to get up early, go to bed early, and engage in morning activities. *See* evening persons.

**morphemes** The smallest meaningful combination of sounds in a language.

**morphology** A system that we use to group phonemes—consonants and vowels—into meaningful combinations of sounds and words.

**motion parallax** In three-dimensional vision, a monocular depth cue based on the speed of moving objects: objects that appear to be moving at high speed are interpreted as closer to us than those moving more slowly.

**motion sickness** Feelings of nausea and dizziness experienced in a moving vehicle when information from the vestibular system (that your head is bouncing around) conflicts with that reported by your eyes (that objects in the distance look fairly steady).

**motivation** Various physiological and psychological factors that cause us to act in a specific way at a particular time.

**motor cortex** A narrow strip of cortex that is located on the back edge of the frontal lobe and extends down its side. It is involved in the initiation of all voluntary movements. The right motor cortex controls muscles on the left side of the body and vice versa.

**motor development** The stages of motor skills that all infants pass through as they acquire the muscular control necessary for making coordinated movements.

**motor neurons** *See* efferent neurons.

**MRI scan** *See* magnetic resonance imaging.

**multiple-intelligence theory** *See* Gardner's multiple-intelligence theory.

**myelin sheath** A tubelike structure of fatty material that wraps around and insulates an axon, preventing interference from electrical signals generated in adjacent axons.

**narcolepsy** A relatively rare, chronic disorder in which the individual abruptly falls asleep at intervals throughout the day. Brief periods of REM sleep are accompanied by muscle paralysis (cataplexy), which may range from tilting of the head to buckling of the knees and falling. Narcolepsy has a genetic component that interferes with the neural mechanisms that control the sleep-wake cycle.

**naturalistic setting** A relatively normal environment in which researchers gather information by observing individuals' behaviors without attempting to change or control the situation.

**nature-nurture question** The debate concerning the relative contribution of genetic factors (nature) and environmental factors (nurture) to a person's intelligence, as well as to his or her biological, emotional, cognitive, personal, and social development.

**nearsightedness** A visual acuity problem that may result when the eyeball is too long, so that objects are focused at a point slightly in front of the retina. The result is that near objects are clear, but distant objects appear blurry.

**need** A biological state in which the organism lacks something essential for survival, such as food, water, or oxygen. The need produces a drive, which is a state of tension that motivates the organism to act to reduce that tension.

**negative punishment** Removal of a reinforcing stimulus (for example, taking away a child's allowance) after a response. This removal decreases the chances that the response will recur.

**negative reinforcement** The occurrence of an operant response that either stops or removes an aversive stimulus. Removal of the aversive stimulus increases the likelihood that the response will occur again.

**negative symptoms of schizophrenia** Symptoms that reflect a decrease in or loss of normal functions: decreased range and intensity of emotions, decreased ability to express thoughts, and decreased initiative to engage in goal-directed behaviors.

**neglect syndrome** The failure of a patient to see objects or parts of the body on the side opposite the brain damage when the damage is to an association area, usually in occipital and parietal lobes, and usually in the right hemisphere.

**nerve impulse** A series of separate action potentials that take place, segment by segment, as they move down the length of an axon.

**nerves** Stringlike bundles of axons and dendrites that are held together by connective tissue. Nerves in the peripheral nervous system have the ability to regrow, regenerate, or reattach if severed or damaged. They carry information from the senses, skin, muscles, and the body's organs to and from the spinal cord.

**network hierarchy** In the network theory of memory, the arrangement of nodes or categories so that concrete ideas are at the bottom of the hierarchy and are connected to more abstract ideas located above them. The most abstract ideas are at the top of the hierarchy.

**network theory** The theory that we store related ideas in separate memory categories, or files, called nodes. As we make associations between information, we create links among thousands of nodes, which make up a gigantic interconnected network for storing and retrieving information.

**neural assemblies** Groups of interconnected neurons whose activation allows information or stimuli to be recognized and held briefly and temporarily in short-term memory.

**neural deafness** Deafness caused by damage to the auditory receptors (hair cells), which prevents the triggering of impulses, or by damage to the auditory nerve, which prevents impulses from reaching the brain. *See also* cochlear implant.

**neuroleptic drugs** Drugs that change levels of neurotransmitters in the brain. They are used to treat serious mental disorders, such as schizophrenia. Also called antipsychotic drugs.

**neurons** Cells that have specialized extensions for the reception and transmission of electrical signals.

**neuroses** According to Freud, maladaptive thoughts and actions that arise from some unconscious thought or conflict and indicate feelings of anxiety.

**neurotransmitters** About a dozen different chemicals that are made by neurons and then used for communication between neurons during the performance of mental or physical activities.

**neutral stimulus** A stimulus that causes a sensory response, such as being seen, heard, or smelled, but does not produce the reflex being tested.

**nicotine** A stimulant; it first produces arousal but then produces calming. Present in cigarettes, nicotine increases both heart rate and blood pressure. It improves attention and concentration, may improve short-term memory, but may interfere with complex processing. Regular use of nicotine causes addiction, and stopping leads to withdrawal symptoms.

**night terrors** Sleep disruptions in children that occur during stage 3 or stage 4 (delta) sleep. They usually start with a piercing scream, after which the child wakes suddenly in a fearful state, with rapid breathing and increased heart rate. The next morning, the child has no memory of the frightening experience.

**nightmares** Dreams that contain frightening and anxiety-producing images. They usually involve great danger—being attacked, injured, or pursued. Upon awakening, the dreamer can usually describe the nightmare in considerable detail. Nightmares occur during REM sleep.

**nodes** Memory files that contain related information organized around a specific topic or category.

**noncompliance** In children, refusal to follow directions, carry out a request, or obey a command given by a parent or caregiver. Noncompliance is one of the most common complaints of parents in general and the most frequent problem of parents who bring their children to clinics for treatment of behavioral problems.

**nonintellectual factors** Factors such as attitude, experience, and emotional functions that may help or hinder an individual's performance on intelligence tests.

**non-REM sleep** Stages 1–4 of sleep, in which rapid eye movement does not occur; it makes up about 80% of sleep time.

**normal aging** A gradual and natural slowing of our physical and psychological processes from middle through late adulthood.

**normal curve** A graph of a frequency distribution in which the curve tapers off equally on either side of a central high point—in other words, a graph of a normal distribution.

**normal distribution** A bell-shaped frequency distribution curve: the scores are arranged symmetrically so that the vast majority fall in the middle range, with fewer scores near the two extreme ends of the curve.

**obedience** Behavior performed in response to an order given by someone in a position of authority.

**obesity** A body weight 30% or more above the ideal value.

**object permanence** The understanding that objects or events continue to exist even if they can no longer be heard, touched, or seen.

**objective personality tests** Tests consisting of specific written statements that require individuals to indicate—for example, by checking "true" or "false"—whether the statements do or do not apply to them; also called self-report questionnaires.

**observational learning** *See* social cognitive learning.

**obsessive-compulsive disorder** An anxiety disorder consisting of obsessions, which are persistent, recurring, irrational thoughts, impulses, or images that a person is unable to control and that interfere with normal functioning; and compulsions, which are irresistible impulses to perform over and over some senseless behavior or ritual (hand washing, checking things, counting, putting things in order).

**obsessive-compulsive personality disorder** A personality disorder characterized by an intense interest in being orderly, achieving perfection, and having control. It is found in 4% of the population.

**occipital lobe** A region at the very back of the brain that is involved in processing visual information, which includes seeing colors and perceiving and recognizing objects, animals, and people.

**Oedipus complex** According to Freud, a process in which a child competes with the parent of the same sex for the affections and pleasures of the parent of the opposite sex; called the Electra complex in girls.

**olfaction** The sense of smell. Its stimuli are various chemicals that are carried by the air.

**olfactory cells** The receptors for smell, located in the uppermost part of the nasal passages. As volatile molecules dissolve in the mucus covering the cells, they stimulate the receptors, which send nerve impulses to the brain.

**operant conditioning** A kind of learning in which the consequences—reward or punishment—that follow some behavior increase or decrease the likelihood of that behavior's occurrence in the future. Also called instrumental conditioning.

**operant response** A response that can be modified by its consequences. Operant responses offer a way of dividing ongoing behavior into meaningful and measurable units.

**opiates** Drugs derived from the opium poppy, including opium and morphine, which is chemically altered to make heroin. All opiates have three primary effects: analgesia (pain reduction); opiate euphoria, which is often described as a pleasurable state between waking and sleeping; and constipation. Continued usage of opiates results in tolerance, physical addiction, and an intense craving for the drug.

**opponent-process theory** A theory of color vision suggesting that ganglion cells in the retina and cells in the thalamus respond to two pairs of colors: red-green and blue-yellow. When these cells are excited, they respond to one color of the pair; when inhibited, they respond to the complementary pair.

**optimal weight** The body weight resulting from an almost perfect balance between how much food an organism eats and how much it needs to meet its body's energy needs; also called ideal weight.

**optimism** A relatively stable personality trait that leads one to believe and expect that good things will happen. It is one of the personality factors associated with lower stress levels and fewer chances of developing psychosomatic symptoms. *See* pessimism.

**oral stage** Freud's first psychosexual stage, which lasts for the first 18 months of life. In this stage, the infant's pleasure seeking is centered on the mouth.

**organic causes** Medical conditions or drug or medication problems that lead to sexual difficulties.

**organic retardation** Mental retardation that results from genetic problems or brain damage.

**ossicles** *See* middle ear.

**outer ear** Three structures important to the hearing process: the external ear, auditory canal, and tympanic membrane (eardrum).

**overgeneralization** A common error during language acquisition, in which children apply a grammatical rule to cases where it should not be used.

**overweight** A body weight 20–30% over the ideal value.

**ovulation** The release of an ovum or egg cell from a woman's ovaries.

**pain** Sensations caused by various stimuli that activate the pain receptors, free nerve endings. Nerve impulses from these pain receptors travel to the somatosensory and limbic areas of the brain, where they are transformed into pain sensations. Pain is essential for survival: it warns us to avoid or escape dangerous situations or stimuli and makes us take time to recover from injury.

**pancreas** An organ that regulates the level of sugar in the bloodstream by secreting insulin. It forms part of the endocrine system.

**panic attack** A period of intense fear or discomfort in which four or more of the following symptoms are present: pounding heart, sweating, trembling, shortness of breath, feelings of choking, chest pain, nausea, feeling dizzy, and fear of losing control or dying.

**panic disorder** A mental disorder characterized primarily by recurrent and unexpected panic attacks, plus continued worry about having another attack; such worry interferes with psychological functioning.

**paranoid personality disorder** A pattern of distrust and suspiciousness and perceiving others as having evil motives. It is found in 0.5–2.5% of the population.

**paranoid schizophrenia** A subcategory of schizophrenia characterized by auditory hallucinations or delusions, such as thoughts of being persecuted by others or delusions of grandeur.

**paraphilias** Repetitive or preferred sexual fantasies involving nonhuman objects, such as sexual attractions to particular articles of clothing (shoes, underwear); commonly called sexual deviations.

**parasympathetic division** The subdivision of the autonomic nervous system that decreases physiological arousal and helps return the body to a calmer, more relaxed state. It also stimulates digestion during eating.

**parentese** A way of speaking to young children in which the adult speaks in a voice that is slower and higher than normal, emphasizes and stretches out each word, uses very simple sentences, and repeats words and phrases. Formerly known as motherese.

**parietal lobe** An area of the cortex located directly behind the frontal lobe. Its functions include: processing sensory information from body parts, which includes touching, locating positions of limbs, and feeling temperature and pain; and carrying out several cognitive functions, such as attending to and perceiving objects.

**Parkinson's disease** A condition caused by the destruction of neurons that produce the neurotransmitter dopamine. Symptoms include tremors and shakes in the limbs, a slowing of voluntary movements, and feelings of depression. As the disease progresses, patients develop a peculiar shuffling walk and may suddenly freeze in space for minutes or hours at a time.

**partial reinforcement** A schedule of reinforcement in which the response is reinforced only some of the time.

**passion** In Sternberg's triangular theory of love, the component of love associated with feeling physically aroused and attracted to someone.

**passionate love** A condition that is associated with continuously thinking about the loved one and is accompanied by warm sexual feelings and powerful emotional reactions.

**pathological aging** Acceleration of the aging process, which may be caused by genetic defects, physiological problems, or diseases.

**peg method** A mnemonic device, or encoding technique, that creates associations between number-word rhymes and items to be memorized.

**perception** The experience of a meaningful pattern or image that the brain assembles from thousands of individual, meaningless sensations; a perception is normally changed, biased, colored, or distorted by a person's unique set of experiences.

**perceptual constancy** Our tendency to perceive sizes, colors, brightness, and shapes as remaining the same even though their physical characteristics are constantly changing.

**perceptual sets** Learned expectations that are based on our personal, social, or cultural experiences. These expectations automatically add information, meaning, or feelings to our perceptions and thus change or bias our perceptions.

**perceptual speed** The rate at which we can identify a particular sensory stimulus; this rate slows down noticeably after age 60.

**peripheral cues** Hunger cues associated with changes in blood chemistry or signals from digestive organs.

**peripheral nervous system** All the nerves that extend from the spinal cord and carry messages to and from various muscles, glands, and sense organs located throughout the body. It has two divisions: the somatic nervous system and the autonomic nervous system.

**peripheral route for persuasion** Approaches to persuasion that emphasize emotional appeal, focus on personal traits, and generate positive feelings.

**peripheral theories of emotions** Theories attributing our subjective feelings primarily to our body's physiological changes.

**permissive parents** Parents who are less controlling and behave with a nonpunishing and accepting attitude toward their children's impulses, desires, and actions. They consult with their children about policy decisions, make few demands, and tend to use reason rather than direct power.

**person perception** The process by which we form impressions of, and make judgments about, the traits and characteristics of others.

**person schemas** Social schemas including our judgments about the traits that we and others possess.

**person-situation interaction** The interaction between a person's traits and the effects of being in a particular situation, which, according to Mischel, determines the person's behavior.

**personal factors** According to social cognitive theory, factors that include our emotional makeup and our biological and genetic influences and that help to shape our personalities.

**personality** A combination of long-lasting and distinctive behaviors, thoughts, motives, and emotions that typify how we react and adapt to other people and situations. *See also* theory of personality.

**personality development** *See* social development.

**personality disorder** Any psychological disorder characterized by inflexible, long-standing, maladaptive traits that cause significantly impaired functioning or great distress in one's personal and social life.

**personality psychology** The study of personality development, personality change, assessment, and abnormal behaviors.

**personality tests** Tests used to measure a person's observable traits and behaviors and unobservable characteristics. In addition, some are used to identify personality problems and psychological disorders, as well as to predict how a person might behave in the future. Objective personality tests (self-report questionnaires), such as the MMPI, consist of specific statements or questions to which the person responds with specific answers; projective tests, such as the Rorschach inkblot test, have no set answers but consist of ambiguous stimuli that a person interprets or makes up stories about.

**pessimism** A relatively stable personality trait that leads one to believe and expect that bad things will happen. It is one of the personality factors associated with increased stress levels and chances of developing psychosomatic symptoms. *See* optimism.

**PET scan** *See* positron emission tomography.

**phallic stage** Freud's third psychosexual stage, lasting from the ages of about 3 to 6. In this stage, the infant's pleasure seeking is centered on the genitals.

**phantom limb** The experience of sensations and feelings coming from a limb that has been amputated. The sensations and feelings are extremely vivid, as if the amputated limb were still present.

**phenomenological perspective** The idea that our perspective of the world, whether or not it is accurate, becomes our reality. This idea is stressed in humanistic theories.

**phenothiazines** The first group of drugs to reduce schizophrenic symptoms, such as delusions and hallucinations. Discovered in the early 1950s, the phenothiazines operate by blocking or reducing the effects of the neurotransmitter dopamine.

**phi movement** The illusion that stationary lights are moving. The illusion of movement—today called apparent motion—is created by flashing closely positioned stationary lights at regular intervals.

**phobia** An anxiety disorder characterized by an intense and irrational fear that is out of all proportion to the danger elicited by the object or situation. In comparison, fear is a realistic response to a threatening situation.

**phonemes** The basic sounds of consonants and vowels.

**phonology** Rules specifying how we make the meaningful sounds used by a particular language.

**photographic memory** The ability to form sharp, detailed visual images after examining a picture or page for a short period of time and to recall the entire image at a later date. Photographic memory is similar to eidetic imagery but occurs in adults.

**physiological psychology** *See* psychobiology.

**Piaget's cognitive stages** Four different stages—the sensorimotor, preoperational, concrete operations, and formal operations stages—each of which is more advanced than the preceding stage because it involves new reasoning and thinking abilities.

**pica** A behavioral disorder in which individuals eat inedible objects or nonnutritive substances. Pica can lead to serious physical problems, including lead poisoning, intestinal blockage, and parasites, and is more often seen in individuals with mental retardation.

**pitch** Our subjective experience of how low or high a sound is. The brain calculates pitch from the speed (frequency) of the sound waves. The frequency of sound waves is measured in cycles, which refers to how many sound waves occur in one second.

**pituitary gland** A key component of the endocrine system, which hangs directly below the hypothalamus, to which it is connected by a narrow stalk. Its anterior section regulates growth and controls much of the endocrine system, while its posterior section regulates water and salt balance.

**place theory** The theory that the brain perceives the pitch of a sound by receiving information about where on the basilar membrane a given sound vibrates the most; it applies to medium and higher pitches.

**placebo** An intervention—taking a pill, receiving an injection, or undergoing an operation—that resembles medical therapy but that, in fact, has no medical effects.

**placebo effect** A change in the patient's illness that is attributable to an imagined treatment rather than to a medical treatment.

**placenta** An organ that connects the blood supply of the mother to that of the fetus. The placenta acts like a filter, allowing oxygen and nutrients to pass through while keeping out certain toxic or harmful substances.

**pleasure principle** The satisfaction of drives and avoidance of pain, without concern for moral restrictions or society's regulations; according to Freud, this is the id's operating principle.

**polygraph tests** Tests based on the theory that, if a person tells a lie, he or she will feel some emotion, such as guilt or fear. Feeling guilty or fearful will usually be accompanied by involuntary physiological responses, which are difficult to suppress or control and can be measured with a machine called a polygraph.

**pons** A bridge that connects the spinal cord with the brain and parts of the brain with one another. Cells in the pons manufacture chemicals involved in sleep.

**positive punishment** The presentation of an aversive stimulus (for example, spanking) after a response. The aversive stimulus decreases the chances that the response will recur.

**positive regard** Love, sympathy, warmth, acceptance, and respect, which we crave from family, friends, and people important to us.

**positive reinforcement** The presentation of a stimulus that increases the probability of a behavior's recurrence.

**positive reinforcer** A stimulus that increases the likelihood that a response will occur again.

**positive symptoms of schizophrenia** Symptoms that reflect a distortion of normal functions: distorted thinking results in delusions; distorted perceptions result in hallucinations; distorted language results in disorganized speech.

**positron emission tomography (PET scan)** A technique to measure the function of the living brain. A slightly radioactive solution is injected into the blood and the amount of radiation absorbed by the brain cells is measured. Very active brain cells—neurons—absorb more radioactive solution than less active ones. A computer transforms the different levels of absorption into colors that indicate activity of neurons. The colors red and yellow indicate maximum activity of neurons, while blue and green indicate minimal activity.

**postconventional level** Kohlberg's highest level of moral reasoning, at which moral decisions are made after carefully thinking about all the alternatives and striking a balance between human rights and laws of society.

**posterior pituitary** The rear part of the pituitary gland, a key component of the endocrine system. It regulates water and salt balance.

**posthypnotic amnesia** Inability to remember what happened during hypnosis, prompted by a specific suggestion from the hypnotist.

**posthypnotic suggestion** A suggestion given to the subject during hypnosis about performing a particular behavior, in response to a predetermined cue, when the subject comes out of hypnosis.

**posttraumatic stress disorder** A disabling condition that results from direct personal experience of an event that involves actual or threatened death or serious injury or from witnessing such an event or hearing that such an event has happened to a family member or close friend.

**precognition** The ability to foretell events.

**preconventional level** Kohlberg's lowest level of moral reasoning. It consists of two stages: At stage 1, moral decisions are based primarily on fear of punishment or the need to be obedient; at stage 2, moral reasoning is guided most by satisfaction of one's self-interest, which may involve making bargains.

**predisposing function** The role of our attitudes in guiding or influencing us to behave in specific ways.

**prejudice** An unfair, biased, or intolerant attitude toward another group of people.

**premature ejaculation** Persistent or recurrent absence of voluntary control over ejaculation, in that the male ejaculates with minimal sexual stimulation before, upon, or shortly after penetration and before he wishes to; also called rapid ejaculation.

**prenatal period** The period from conception to birth, which lasts about 266 days (about nine months). It is divided into three phases: the germinal, embryonic, and fetal periods. During the prenatal period, a single cell will divide and grow to form 200 billion cells.

**preoperational stage** The second of Piaget's cognitive stages, lasting from the ages of about 2 to 7. During this stage, children learn to use symbols (such as words or mental images) to think about things that are not present and to help them solve simple problems.

**preparedness** The innate or biological tendency of animals and humans to recognize, attend to, and store certain cues over others, as well as to associate some combinations of conditioned and unconditioned stimuli more easily than others. Also called prepared learning.

**primacy effect** Better recall, or improvement in retention, of information presented at the beginning of a task.

**primacy question** The question of whether we can experience an emotion immediately, without any thinking, or whether we must engage in some kind of thinking before feeling.

**primacy-recency effect** Better recall of information presented at the beginning and end of a task.

**primary appraisal** Our initial, subjective evaluation of a situation, in which we balance the demands of a potentially stressful situation against our ability to meet them.

**primary auditory cortex** An area at the top edge of the temporal lobe that transforms nerve impulses (electrical signals) into basic auditory sensations, such as meaningless sounds and tones of varying pitch and loudness. Next, it sends impulses (sensations) to the auditory association areas.

**primary reinforcer** A stimulus, such as food, water, or sex, that is innately satisfying and requires no learning on the part of the subject to become pleasurable.

**primary visual cortex** A small area, located at the back of each occipital lobe, that receives electrical signals from receptors in the eyes and transforms these signals into meaningless, basic visual sensations, such as lights, lines, shadows, colors, and textures.

**principle of bidirectionality** The idea that a child's behaviors influence how his or her parents respond and, in turn, the parents' behaviors influence how the child responds.

**proactive interference** A forgetting process in which information that we learned earlier blocks or disrupts the retrieval of related information that was learned later.

**problem-focused coping** Solving a problem by seeking information, changing our own behavior, or taking whatever action is necessary.

**problem solving** Searching for some rule, plan, or strategy in order to reach a certain goal that is currently out of reach.

**procedural memory** Memories of performing motor or perceptual tasks (playing sports), carrying out habitual behaviors (brushing teeth), and responding to stimuli because of classical conditioning (fearing spiders). We cannot retrieve these memories and are not conscious of them.

**processing speed** The rate at which we encode information into long-term memory or recall or retrieve information from long-term memory; this rate slows down after age 60.

**procrastination** The tendency to always put off completing a task to the point of feeling anxious or uncomfortable about one's delay.

**prodigy** A child who shows unusual talent, ability, or genius at a very early age and does not have mental retardation. A small percentage of autistic children, who have some degree of mental retardation, may also show unusual artistic or mathematical abilities; they are called savants.

**progressive relaxation** An exercise in which the major muscle groups of the body are tensed and relaxed repeatedly until the individual can relax any group of muscles at will.

**projection** Unconsciously transferring unacceptable traits to others.

**projective tests** Tests in which the subject is presented with some type of ambiguous stimulus—such as a meaningless object or ambiguous photo—and then asked to make up a story about the stimulus. The assumption is that the person will project conscious or unconscious feelings, needs, and motives in his or her responses.

**prosocial behavior** Any behavior that benefits others or has positive social consequences. Also called helping.

**prototype theory** The idea that we form a concept by first constructing a prototype of an object—that is, a mental image based on its average characteristics. Once we have formed a set of prototypes, we identify new objects by matching them against our prototypes.

**proximity rule** A perceptual rule stating that, in organizing stimuli, objects that are physically close to one another will be grouped together.

**proximodistal principle** The rule that parts closer to the center of the infant's body develop before parts that are farther away.

**psi** The processing of information or transfer of energy by methods that have no known physical or biological mechanisms and that seem to stretch the laws of physics.

**psilocybin** A hallucinogen, the active ingredient in magic mushrooms. Low doses produce pleasant and relaxed feelings; medium doses produce distortions in the perception of time and space; and high doses produce distortions in perceptions and body image and sometimes hallucinations.

**psychiatrist** A medical doctor (M.D.) who has taken a psychiatric residency, which involves additional training in pharmacology, neurology, psychopathology, and therapeutic techniques. In diagnosing the possible causes of abnormal behaviors, psychiatrists focus on biological factors; they tend to view mental disorders as diseases and to treat them with drugs. Psychiatrists who receive additional training in psychoanalytic institutes are called psychoanalysts.

**psychoactive drugs** Chemicals that affect the nervous system and, as a result, may alter consciousness and awareness, influence sensations and perceptions, and modify moods and cognitive processes. Some are legal (coffee, alcohol, and tobacco) and some are illegal (marijuana, heroin, cocaine, and LSD).

**psychoanalysis** A form of psychotherapy based on the idea that each of us has an unconscious part that contains ideas, memories, desires, or thoughts, which have been hidden or repressed because they are psychologically dangerous or threatening to our self-concept. To protect our self-concept, we automatically build a mental barrier that we cannot voluntarily remove. But the presence of these thoughts and desires gives rise to unconscious conflicts, which, in turn, can result in psychological and physical symptoms and mental disorders.

**psychoanalyst** *See* psychiatrist.

**psychoanalytic approach** A psychological viewpoint that stresses the influence of unconscious fears, desires, and motivations on thoughts and behaviors and also the impact of childhood experiences on the development of later personality traits and psychological problems. As applied to mental disorders, this approach traces their origin to unconscious conflicts or problems with unresolved conflicts at one or more of Freud's psychosexual stages. Treatment of mental disorders, in this approach, centers on the therapist's helping the patient to identify and resolve his or her unconscious conflicts.

**psychobiological approach** *See* biological approach.

**psychobiology** The scientific study of the physical and chemical changes that occur during stress, learning, and emotions, as well as how our genetic makeup and nervous system interact with our environments and influence our behaviors.

**psychodynamic psychotherapy** An approach that shares many of the features of psychoanalysis—for example, discussing the client's feelings; breaking down the client's defenses and resistances; interpreting the client's behaviors; and working through transference problems. However, these therapies take a more directive role than do classical psychoanalysts and thus shorten the total time in therapy. *See also* short-term dynamic psychotherapy.

**psychodynamic theory of personality** *See* Freud's psychodynamic theory of personality.

**psychoevolutionary theory of emotions** The idea that we inherit the neural structure and physiology to express and experience emotions and that we evolved basic emotional patterns to adapt to our environment and solve patterns important for our survival.

**psychokinesis** The ability to exert mind over matter—for example, by moving objects without touching them.

**psychological assessment** The use of various tools—including psychological tests and interviews—to measure characteristics, traits, or abilities in order to understand behavior and predict future performance or behavior.

**psychological causes** Performance anxiety, sexual trauma, guilt, or failure to communicate, all of which may lead to sexual problems.

**psychological sex factors** Factors involved in the development of a gender identity, gender role, and sexual orientation, as well as in difficulties in sexual performance or enjoyment.

**psychologist** An individual who has completed four to five years of postgraduate education and has obtained a Ph.D. in psychology; in some states, an individual with a master's degree.

**psychology** The systematic, scientific study of behaviors and mental processes.

**psychometric approach** An approach to the assessment of intelligence that measures or quantifies cognitive abilities or factors that are thought to be involved in intellectual performance.

**psychometrics** A subarea of psychology concerned with the development of tests to assess an individual's abilities, skills, intelligence, personality

traits, and abnormal behaviors in a wide range of settings—school, the workplace, or a clinic.

**psychoneuroimmunology** The study of the relationship among the central nervous system, the endocrine system, and psychosocial factors such as cognitive reactions to stressful events, the individual's personality traits, and social influences.

**psychosexual stages** According to Freud, five developmental periods—the oral, anal, phallic, latency, and genital stages—each marked by potential conflict between parent and child. The conflicts arise as the child seeks pleasure from different bodily areas associated with sexual feelings (different erogenous zones). Freud emphasized that the child's first five years were most important in social and personality development.

**psychosocial factors** Underlying personality traits, amount of social support, and ability to deal with stressful life events—these factors are believed to combine and interact with predisposing biological factors to either increase or decrease a person's vulnerability to the development and maintenance of a mood disorder.

**psychosocial hunger factors** Learned associations between food and other stimuli, such as snacking while watching television; sociocultural influences, such as pressures to be thin; and various personality problems, such as depression, dislike of body image, or low self-esteem.

**psychosocial stages** According to Erikson, eight developmental periods during which an individual's primary goal is to satisfy desires associated with social needs: the eight periods are associated, respectively, with issues of trust, autonomy, initiative, industry, identity, intimacy, generativity, and ego integrity.

**psychosomatic symptoms** Real, physical, and often painful symptoms, such as headaches, muscle pain, and stomach problems, that are caused by psychosomatic factors, such as worry, tension, and anxiety.

**psychotherapy** Approaches to treating psychological problems that share three characteristics: verbal interaction between therapist and client(s); the development of a supportive relationship during which a client can bring up and discuss traumatic or bothersome experiences that may have led to current problems; and analysis of the client's experiences and/or suggested ways for the client to deal with or overcome his or her problems.

**puberty** A developmental period, corresponding to the ages of 9–17, when the individual experiences significant biological changes and, as a result, develops secondary sexual characteristics and reaches sexual maturity.

**punishment** A consequence that occurs after behavior and decreases the likelihood that that behavior will recur.

**pupil** The round opening at the front of the eye that allows light waves to pass through into the eye's interior.

**quantum personality change** A sudden and radical or dramatic shift in personality, belief, or values.

**questionnaire** A method for obtaining information by asking subjects to read a list of written questions and to check off, or rate their preference for, specific answers.

**random selection** A research design such that each subject in a sample population has an equal chance of being selected to participate in the experiment.

**range** The two most extreme scores at either end of a distribution.

**rape myths** Misinformed false beliefs about women that are frequently held by rapists, as well as by other men.

**rationalizations** Inventing acceptable excuses for behaviors that make us feel anxious.

**reaction formation** Turning unacceptable wishes into acceptable behaviors.

**reaction range** The extent to which traits, abilities, or IQ scores may increase or decrease as a result of interaction with environmental factors.

**reaction time** The rate at which we respond (see, hear, move) to some stimulus; this rate slows down noticeably after age 60.

**real motion** Our perception of any stimulus or object that actually moves in space; the opposite of apparent motion.

**real self** According to Rogers, the self that is based on our actual experiences and represents how we really see ourselves; its complement is the ideal self.

**reality principle** A policy of satisfying a wish or desire only if a socially acceptable outlet is available; according to Freud, this is the ego's operating principle.

**reasoning** A mental process by which we apply knowledge to achieve goals that involve solving problems or making plans and decisions.

**recall** Retrieval of previously learned information without the aid of or with very few external cues.

**recency effect** Better recall, or improvement in retention, of information presented at the end of a task.

**recognition** The identification of previously learned information with the help of external cues.

**reflex** An unlearned, involuntary reaction to some stimulus. The neural connections of the network underlying a reflex are prewired by genetic instructions.

**reinforcement** A consequence that occurs after behavior and increases the likelihood that that behavior will recur.

**relative size** In three-dimensional vision, a monocular depth cue that results when we expect two objects to be the same size, and they are not. In that case, the larger of the objects will appear closer, and the smaller will be farther away.

**relaxation response** A physiological response induced by sitting or lying in a comfortable position while repeating a meaningless sound over and over to drive out anxious thoughts.

**reliability** The extent to which a test is consistent: a person's score on a test at one point in time should be similar to the score obtained by the same person on a similar test at a later point in time.

**REM (rapid eye movement) sleep** The stage of sleep in which our eyes move rapidly back and forth behind closed eyelids. This stage makes up 20% of our sleep time; in a normal night, we experience 5–6 periods of REM sleep, each one lasting 15–45 minutes. REM brain waves, which have a high frequency and a low amplitude, look very similar to the beta waves that are recorded when we are wide awake and alert; the body's voluntary muscles, however, are paralyzed. Dreams usually occur during REM sleep.

**REM behavior disorder** A disorder, usually found in older people, in which the voluntary muscles are not paralyzed during REM sleep; sleepers can and do act out their dreams.

**REM rebound** The tendency of individuals to spend proportionally longer in the REM stage after they have been deprived of REM sleep on previous nights.

**repair theory** A theory of sleep suggesting that activities during the day deplete key factors in the brain or body that are replenished or repaired by sleep.

**repression** According to Freud, a mental process that automatically hides emotionally threatening or anxiety-producing information in the unconscious. Repressed information cannot be retrieved voluntarily, but something may cause it to be released and to reenter the person's consciousness at a later time.

**resiliency** Various personal, family, or environmental factors that compensate for increased life stresses so that expected problems do not develop.

**resistance** In psychotherapy, especially psychoanalysis, the client's reluctance to work through or deal with feelings or to recognize unconscious conflicts and repressed thoughts.

**resistance stage** The second stage in the general adaptation syndrome. In reaction to continued stress, most physiological responses return to normal levels, but the body uses up great stores of energy.

**resting state** A condition in which the axon, like a battery, has a charge, or potential, because the axon membrane separates positive ions on the outside from negative ions on the inside.

**reticular formation** A column of brain cells that arouses and alerts the forebrain and prepares it to receive information from all the senses. It plays an important role in keeping the forebrain alert and producing a state of wakefulness. Animals or humans whose reticular formation is seriously damaged lapse into permanent unconsciousness or coma.

**retina** A thin film, located at the very back of the eyeball, that contains cells, called photoreceptors, that are extremely sensitive to light. The retina consists of three layers, the third and deepest of which contains two kinds of photore-

ceptors, rods and cones, that perform transduction—that is, they change light waves into nerve impulses.

**retinal disparity** A binocular depth cue that depends on the distance between the two eyes. Because of their different positions, the two eyes receive slightly different images. The difference between these images is the retinal disparity. The brain interprets large retinal disparity to mean a close object, and small retinal disparity to mean a distant object.

**retrieval cues** Mental reminders that we create by forming vivid mental images of information or associating new information with information that we already know. Forgetting can result from not taking the time to create effective retrieval cues.

**retrieving** The process of getting or recalling information that has been placed into short-term or long-term storage.

**retroactive interference** A forgetting process in which information that we learned later blocks or disrupts the retrieval of related information that was learned earlier.

**reuptake** The process by which some neurotransmitters, such as dopamine, are removed from the synapse by being transported back into the end bulbs.

**rods** Photoreceptors containing the chemical rhodopsin, which is activated by small amounts of light. Because rods are extremely light sensitive, they allow us to see in dim light but to see only black, white, and shades of gray.

**Rogers' self-actualizing tendency** An inborn tendency for us to develop all of our capacities in ways that best maintain and benefit our lives.

**role schemas** Social schemas based on the jobs people perform or the social positions they hold.

**Rorschach inkblot test** A projective test used to assess personality in which a person is shown a series of ten inkblots and then asked to describe what he or she sees in each.

**rules of organization** Rules identified by Gestalt psychologists that specify how our brains combine and organize individual pieces or elements into a meaningful whole—that is, a perception.

**SAD** *See* seasonal affective disorder.

**savants** Autistic individuals who show some incredible memory, music, or drawing talent. They represent about 10% of the total number of autistics.

**schedule of reinforcement** In conditioning, a program or rule that determines how and when a response will be followed by a reinforcer.

**schemas** Mental categories that, like computer files, contain knowledge about people, events, and concepts. Because schemas influence which stimuli we attend to, how we interpret stimuli, and how we respond to stimuli, they can bias and distort our thoughts, perceptions, and behaviors. *See also:* event schemas; gender schemas; person schemas; role schemas; and self schemas.

**schizophrenia** A serious mental disturbance that lasts at least six months and includes at least two

of the following symptoms: delusions, hallucinations, disorganized speech, grossly disorganized behavior, and decreased emotional expression. These symptoms interfere with personal or social functioning. *See also* Type I and Type II schizophrenia.

**schizotypical personality disorder** A disorder characterized by acute discomfort in close relationships, distortions in thinking, and eccentric behavior. It is found in 3–5% of the population.

**scientific method** A general approach to gathering information and answering questions so that errors and biases are minimized.

**scripts** *See* event schemas.

**seasonal affective disorder (SAD)** A pattern of depressive symptoms that cycle with the seasons, typically beginning in fall or winter. The depression is accompanied by feelings of lethargy, excessive sleepiness, overeating, weight gain, and craving for carbohydrates.

**secondary appraisal** Deciding what we can do to deal with a potentially stressful situation. We can choose some combination of problem-focused coping, which means doing something about the problem, and emotion-focused coping, which means dealing with our emotions.

**secondary reinforcer** Any stimulus that has acquired its reinforcing power through experience; secondary reinforcers are learned, for example, by being paired with primary reinforcers or other secondary reinforcers.

**secure attachment** An emotional bond characteristic of infants who use their parent as a safe home base from which they can wander off and explore their environments.

**self** How we see or describe ourselves; also called self-concept. The self is made up of many self-perceptions, abilities, personality characteristics, and behaviors that are organized so as to be consistent with one another.

**self-actualization** Our inherent tendency to reach our true potentials. The concept of self-actualization, developed by Maslow, is central to humanistic theories. *See also* Rogers's self-actualizing tendency.

**self-actualization theory** *See* self theory.

**self-concept** *See* self.

**self-efficacy** Our personal beliefs regarding how capable we are of exercising control over events in our lives, such as completing specific tasks and behaviors.

**self-esteem** How much an individual likes himself or herself; it includes feelings of self-worth, attractiveness, and social competence.

**self-fulfilling prophecy** A situation in which a person has a strong belief or makes a statement (prophecy) about a future behavior and then acts, usually unknowingly, to fulfill or carry out that behavior.

**self-handicapping** A tendency to adopt tactics that are prone to failure and then to use those tactics as excuses for failures in performance, activities, or achieving goals.

**self-identity** *See* identity.

**self-injurious behavior** A behavior pattern in which an individual inflicts serious and sometimes life-threatening physical damage on his or her own body; this may take the form of body or head banging, biting, kicking, poking ears or eyes, pulling hair, or intense scratching.

**self-perception theory** The idea, developed by Daryl Bem, that we first observe or perceive our own behavior and then, as a result, change our attitudes.

**self-report questionnaires** *See* objective personality tests.

**self schemas** Social schemas containing personal information about ourselves. They can influence how we behave, as well as what we perceive and remember.

**self-serving bias** Attributing our successes to our dispositions or personality traits and our failures to the situations.

**self theory** Rogers's humanistic theory, based on two major assumptions: that personality development is guided by each person's unique self-actualization tendency; and that each of us has a personal need for positive regard.

**semantic memory** A type of declarative memory consisting of factual knowledge about the world, concepts, word definitions, and language rules.

**semantics** A set of rules specifying the meaning of words or phrases when they appear in various sentences or contexts.

**sensation** Our first awareness of some outside stimulus. The stimulus activates sensory receptors, which in turn produce electrical signals that are transformed by the brain into meaningless bits of information.

**sensitive period** *See* critical period.

**sensorimotor stage** The first of Piaget's cognitive stages, lasting from birth to about age 2. During this stage, infants interact with and learn about their environments by relating their sensory experiences (such as hearing and seeing) to their motor actions (mouthing and grasping).

**sensory homunculus** A drawing of the somatosensory cortex that shows the relationship between the size of each body part and the degree of its sensitivity to external stimulation. *Homunculus* means "little man."

**sensory memory** An initial memory process that receives and holds environmental information in its raw form for a brief period of time, from an instant to several seconds.

**sensory neurons** *See* afferent neurons.

**sentence stage** The fourth stage in acquiring language, which begins at about 4 years of age. Sentences range from three to eight words in length and indicate a growing knowledge of the rules of grammar.

**separation anxiety** An infant's distress—as indicated by loud protests, crying, and agitation—whenever his or her parents temporarily leave.

**set point** A certain level of body fat (adipose tissue) that our body strives to maintain constant throughout our lives; the set point is an inherited characteristic.

**sex chromosome** The sperm or the egg. Each contains only 23 chromosomes, on which are the genes bearing the instructions that determine the sex of the child.

**sex (gender) differences in the brain** Structural or functional differences in cognitive, behavioral, or brain processes that arise from being male or female.

**sex hormones** Chemicals, secreted by glands, that circulate in the bloodstream and influence the brain, other body organs, and behaviors. The major male sex hormones secreted by the testes are androgens, such as testosterone; the major female sex hormones secreted by the ovaries are estrogens.

**sexual dysfunctions** Problems of sexual arousal or orgasm that interfere with adequate functioning during sexual behavior.

**sexual orientation** A person's pattern of primary sexual arousal: by members of his or her own sex, the opposite sex, or both sexes; also called sexual preference.

**shape constancy** Our tendency to see an object as remaining the same shape when viewed at different angles—that is, despite considerable change in the shape of its image on the retina.

**shaping** In operant conditioning, a procedure in which an experimenter successively reinforces behaviors that lead up to or approximate the desired behavior.

**short-term dynamic psychotherapy** A shortened version of psychoanalysis. It retains the principles that symptoms are signs of more basic underlying problems, that transference needs to be worked out, and that clients' behaviors need to be interpreted. In contrast to traditional psychoanalysis, however, therapists take a more active and directive role in identifying and discussing the client's problems and suggesting solutions. *See also* psychodynamic psychotherapy.

**short-term memory** A process that can hold a limited amount of information—an average of seven items—for a short time (2–30 seconds), which can be lengthened if you rehearse the information. Sometimes called working memory.

**shyness** The tendency to feel tense, worried, or awkward in social situations.

**similarity rule** A perceptual rule stating that, in organizing stimuli, elements that appear similar are grouped together.

**simplicity rule** A perceptual rule stating that stimuli are organized in the simplest way possible.

**single-word stage** The second stage in acquiring language, which begins when the child is about 1 year old. Infants say single words that usually refer to what they can see, hear, or feel.

**situational attributions** *See* external attributions.

**size constancy** Our tendency to perceive objects as remaining the same size even when their images on the retina are continually growing or shrinking.

**skewed distributions** Distributions in which more data fall toward one side of the scale than toward the other.

**sleep** A condition in which we pass through five different stages, each with its own level of consciousness, awareness, responsiveness, and physiological arousal. In the deepest stage of sleep, we enter a state that borders on unconsciousness.

**sleep apnea** A condition characterized by a cycle in which a sleeper stops breathing for intervals of 10 seconds or longer, wakes up briefly, resumes breathing, and returns to sleep. This cycle can leave apnea sufferers exhausted during the day but oblivious to the cause of their tiredness. It is more common among habitual snorers.

**sleepwalking** Walking or carrying out behaviors while still asleep. Sleepwalkers generally are clumsy and have poor coordination but can avoid objects; they can engage in very limited conversations. Sleepwalking behaviors can include dressing, eating, performing bathroom functions, and even driving a car. Sleepwalking usually occurs in stage 3 or stage 4 (delta) sleep.

**social cognition** A subarea of social psychology that focuses on cognitive processes—for example, how we perceive, store, and retrieve information about social interactions and events. It rose to prominence in the 1980s.

**social cognitive learning** A form of learning that results from watching, imitating, and modeling and does not require the observer to perform any observable behavior or receive any observable reward. Formerly called observational learning.

**social cognitive theory** The theory that grew out of the research of a number of psychologists—Rotter, Bandura, and Mischel—that says that personality development is primarily shaped by three forces: environmental conditions, cognitive-personal factors, and behavior, which all interact to influence how we evaluate, interpret, organize, and apply information. *See also* Bandura's social cognitive theory; social learning theory.

**social comparison theory** The idea that we are driven to compare ourselves to others who are similar to us, so that we can measure the correctness of our attitudes and beliefs. According to Festinger, this drive motivates us to join groups.

**social development** How a person develops a sense of self or self-identity, develops relationships with others, and develops the skills useful in social interactions.

**social facilitation** An increase in performance in the presence of a crowd.

**social inhibition** A decrease in performance in the presence of a crowd.

**social learning approach** A theory that emphasizes the role of observation, exploration, and imitation in acquiring language skills.

**social learning theory** The idea that personality development is primarily shaped by environmental conditions (learning), cognitive-personal factors, and behavior, which all interact to influence how we evaluate, interpret, and organize information and apply that information to ourselves and others. As applied to gender roles, it says that mothers, fathers, teachers, grandparents, friends, and peers expect, respond to, and reward different behaviors in boys than in girls. In response to this differential treatment, boys learn a gender role that is different from girls'. As applied to aggression, it says that such behavior may be learned and maintained through observation, imitation, and self-reinforcement. *See also* social cognitive theory.

**social needs** Needs that are acquired through learning and experience.

**social norms approach** In defining abnormality, the idea that a behavior is considered abnormal if it deviates greatly from accepted social standards, values, or norms.

**social phobias** Irrational, marked, and continuous fear of performing in social situations. The individuals fear that they will humiliate or embarrass themselves.

**social psychology** A broad field whose goals are to understand and explain how our thoughts, feelings, perceptions, and behaviors are influenced by interactions with others. It includes the study of stereotypes, prejudices, attitudes, conformity, group behaviors, and aggression.

**social role theory** The theory that emphasizes the importance of social and cultural influences on gender roles and states that gender differences between males and females arise from different divisions of labor.

**social support** A stress-reducing factor that includes three components: having a group or network of family or friends who provide strong social attachments; being able to exchange helpful resources among family or friends; and feeling, or making appraisals, that we have supportive relationships or behaviors.

**socially oriented group** A group in which members are primarily concerned about fostering and maintaining social relationships among the members of the group.

**sociobiology theory** *See* evolutionary theory.

**sociocognitive theory of hypnosis** The idea that the impressive effects of hypnosis are due to social influences and pressures as well as the subject's personal abilities. For another view, see the altered state theory of hypnosis.

**sodium pump** A chemical transport process that picks up any sodium ions that enter the axon's chemical gates and returns them back outside. In this way, the sodium pump is responsible for keeping the axon charged by returning and keeping sodium ions outside the axon membrane.

**somatic nervous system** A network of nerves that are connected either to sensory receptors or to muscles that you can move voluntarily, such as muscles in your limbs, back, neck, and chest. Nerves in the somatic nervous system usually contain two kinds of fibers: afferent, or sensory, fibers that carry information from sensory receptors in the skin, muscles, and other organs to the spinal cord and brain; and efferent, or motor, fibers that carry information from the brain and spinal cord to the muscles.

**somatization disorder** A somatoform disorder that begins before age 30, lasts several years, and is characterized by multiple symptoms—including pain, gastrointestinal, sexual, and neurological symptoms—that have no physical causes

but are triggered by psychological problems or distress.

**somatoform disorder** A pattern of recurring, multiple, and significant bodily (somatic) complaints that extend over several years. The physical symptoms (pain, vomiting, paralysis, blindness) are not under voluntary control, have no known physical causes, and are believed to be caused by psychological factors.

**somatosensory cortex** A narrow strip of the cortex that is located at the front edge of the parietal lobe and extends down its side. It processes sensory information about touch, location of limbs, pain, and temperature. The right somatosensory cortex receives information from the left side of the body and vice versa.

**sound waves** The stimuli for hearing, or audition. Similar to ripples on a pond, sound waves travel through space with varying heights and speeds. Height, or amplitude, is the distance from the bottom to the top of a sound wave; speed, or frequency, is the number of sound waves that occur within one second.

**source misattribution** A memory error that results when a person has difficulty in deciding which of two or more sources a memory came from: Was the source something the person saw or imagined, or was it a suggestion?

**Spearman's *g*** *See* two-factor theory.

**specific phobias** Unreasonable, marked, and persistent fears triggered by anticipation of, or exposure to, a specific object or situation (flying, heights, spiders, seeing blood); formerly called simple phobias.

**split-brain operation** A procedure for moderating severe, uncontrollable seizures by cutting the corpus callosum, a wide band of nerve fibers that connects the right and left hemispheres.

**spontaneous recovery** In classical conditioning, the temporary occurrence of the conditioned response to the presence of the conditioned stimulus. In operant conditioning, a temporary recovery in the rate of responding.

**stage 1** In sleep, a stage lasting 1–7 minutes in which the individual gradually loses responsiveness to stimuli and experiences drifting thoughts and images. This stage marks the transition from wakefulness to sleep and is characterized by the presence of theta waves, which are lower in amplitude and lower in frequency (3–7 cycles per second) than alpha waves.

**stage 2** In sleep, the stage that marks the beginning of what we know as sleep; subjects awakened in stage 2 report having been asleep. EEG tracings show high-frequency bursts of brain activity called sleep spindles.

**stages 3 and 4** About 30–45 minutes after drifting off to sleep, we pass rapidly through stage 3 and enter stage 4 sleep, a stage characterized by delta waves, which are of very high amplitude and very low frequency (less than 4 cycles per second). Stage 4 is often considered the deepest stage of sleep, because it is the most difficult from which to be awakened. During stage 4, heart rate, respiration, temperature, and blood flow to the brain are reduced, and there is a

marked secretion of growth hormone, which controls many aspects of metabolism, physical growth, and brain development. This stage is also called slow-wave or delta sleep.

**stages of sleep** Distinctive changes in the electrical activity of the brain and accompanying physiological responses of the body that occur as we pass through different stages of sleep. *See also* stage 1, stage 2, stages 3 and 4.

**standard deviation** A statistic indicating how widely all the scores in a distribution are scattered above and below the mean.

**standardized test** A technique to obtain information by administering a psychological test that has been standardized, which means that the test has been given to hundreds of people and shown to reliably measure thought patterns, personality traits, emotions, or behaviors.

**state-dependent learning** The idea that we recall information more easily when we are in the same physiological or emotional state or setting as when we originally encoded the information.

**statistical frequency approach** In defining abnormality, the idea that a behavior may be considered abnormal if it occurs rarely or infrequently in relation to the behaviors of the general population.

**statistical procedures** In experiments, procedures to determine whether differences observed in dependent variables (behaviors) are due to independent variables (treatment) or to error or chance occurrence.

**statistics** Tools researchers use to analyze and summarize large amounts of data.

**stereotaxic procedure** A method used for the introduction of material at a precise location within the brain. The patient's head is fixed in a holder, and a small hole is drilled through the skull. The holder has a syringe that can be precisely guided to a predetermined location in the brain.

**stereotypes** Widely held beliefs that people have certain traits because they belong to a particular group. Stereotypes are often inaccurate and frequently portray the members of less powerful, less controlling groups more negatively than members of more powerful or more controlling groups.

**Sternberg's triangular theory of love** The idea that love has three components: passion, intimacy, and commitment. *Passion* is feeling physically aroused and attracted to someone; *intimacy* is feeling close and connected to someone, through sharing and communicating; and *commitment* is pledging to nourish the feelings of love and actively maintain the relationship.

**Sternberg's triarchic theory** The idea that intelligence can be divided into three ways of gathering and processing information (*triarchic* means "three"): using analytical or logical thinking skills that are measured by traditional intelligence tests; using problem-solving skills that require creative thinking, the ability to deal with novel situations, and the ability to learn from experience; and using practical thinking skills that help a person adjust to, and cope with, his or her sociocultural environment.

**stimulants** Drugs, such as cocaine, amphetamines, caffeine, and nicotine, that increase activity in the nervous system and result in heightened alertness, arousal, and euphoria and decreased appetite and fatigue.

**stimulus substitution** The theory that, in classical conditioning, a neural bond or association is formed between the neutral stimulus and unconditioned stimulus. After repeated trials, the neutral stimulus becomes the conditioned stimulus, which, in turn, substitutes for the unconditioned stimulus. Thereafter, the conditioned stimulus elicits a response similar to that of the unconditioned stimulus.

**stomach** The body organ that monitors the amount and kinds of nutrients our body needs to restore our depleted stores of fuel. In addition, after we eat a meal, the stomach's walls are distended and their stretch receptors signal fullness or time to stop eating.

**storing** The process of placing encoded information into relatively permanent mental storage for later recall.

**stress** The anxious or threatening feeling that comes when we interpret or appraise a situation as being more than our psychological resources can adequately handle.

**stress management program** A program to reduce anxiety, fear, and stressful experiences by using a variety of strategies to change three different aspects of our lives: thoughts (appraisals), behaviors, and physiological responses.

**structuralism** An early school of psychological thought that emphasized the study of the basic elements—primarily sensations and perceptions—that make up conscious mental experiences. Structuralists argued that we can understand how perceptions are formed by breaking them down into smaller and smaller elements. Then we can analyze how these basic elements are recombined to form a perception. They believed that a perception is simply the sum of its parts.

**structured interviews** A research technique in which each individual is asked the same set of relatively narrow and focused questions, so that the same information is obtained from everyone.

**subgoals** In problem solving, a strategy by which the overall problem is broken into separate parts that, when completed in order, will result in a solution.

**sublimation** A type of displacement in which threatening or forbidden desire, usually sexual, is redirected into socially acceptable forms.

**subliminal messages** Brief auditory or visual messages that are presented below the absolute threshold, so that their chance of perception is less than 50%.

**subliminal stimulus** A stimulus whose intensity is such that a person has a less than 50% chance of detecting it.

**substance abuse** A maladaptive pattern of frequent and continued usage of a substance—a drug or medicine—that results in significant problems, such as failing to meet major obligations and having multiple legal, social, family, health, work, or interpersonal difficulties. These problems must occur repeatedly during a single 12-month period to be classified as substance abuse.

**superego** Freud's third division of the mind, which develops from the ego during early childhood; its goal is to apply the moral values and standards of one's parents or caregivers and society in satisfying one's wishes.

**superstitious behavior** In operant conditioning, any behavior that increases in frequency because its occurrence is accidentally paired with the delivery of a reinforcer.

**suprachiasmatic nucleus** A sophisticated biological clock, located in the hypothalamus, that regulates a number of circadian rhythms, including the sleep-wake cycle. Suprachiasmatic cells are highly responsive to changes in light.

**surface structure** According to Chomsky, the actual wording of a sentence, as it is spoken.

**survey** A way to obtain information by asking many individuals—person to person, by telephone, or by mail—to answer a fixed set of questions about particular subjects.

**sympathetic division** The subdivision of the autonomic nervous system that is triggered by threatening or challenging physical or psychological stimuli, increasing the body's physiological arousal and preparing the body for action.

**synapse** An infinitely small space (20–30 billionths of a meter) between an end bulb and its adjacent body organ, muscle, or cell body; it is a space over which chemical messages are transmitted.

**syntax** *See* grammar.

**systematic desensitization** A technique of behavior therapy, based on classical conditioning, in which a person is gradually and progressively exposed to fearful or anxiety-evoking stimuli while practicing deep relaxation. Systematic desensitization is a form of counterconditioning because it replaces, or counters, fear and anxiety with relaxation.

***t* test** An estimate of reliability that takes into account both the size of the mean difference and the variability in distributions.

**taijin kyofusho (TKS)** A mental disorder found only in Asian cultures, particularly Japan. This social phobia is characterized by a morbid fear of offending others through awkward social or physical behavior, such as making eye-to-eye contact, blushing, giving off an offensive odor, having an unpleasant or tense facial expression, or having trembling hands.

**tardive dyskinesia** A condition characterized by the appearance of slow, involuntary, and uncontrollable rhythmic movements and rapid twitching of the mouth and lips, as well as unusual movements of the limbs. This condition is a side effect of the continued use of typical neuroleptics.

**task-oriented group** A group in which members have specific duties to complete.

**taste** A chemical sense that makes use of various chemicals as stimuli.

**taste-aversion learning** The association of a particular sensory cue (smell, taste, sound, or sight) with an unpleasant response, such as nausea or vomiting, resulting in future avoidance of that particular sensory cue.

**taste buds** Onion-shaped structures on the tongue that contain the receptors for taste.

**TAT** *See* Thematic Apperception Test.

**telegraphic speech** A distinctive speech pattern observed during language acquisition in which the child omits articles, prepositions, and parts of verbs.

**telepathy** The ability to transfer thoughts to another person or to read the thoughts of others.

**temperament** An individual's distinctive pattern of attention, arousal, and reactivity to new or novel situations. This pattern appears early, is relatively stable and long-lasting, and is influenced in large part by genetic factors.

**temporal lobe** A segment of the brain located directly below the parietal lobe that is involved in hearing, speaking coherently, and understanding verbal and written material.

**teratogen** Any agent that can harm a developing fetus (causing deformities or brain damage). It might be a disease (such as genital herpes), a drug (such as alcohol), or another environmental agent (such as chemicals).

**test anxiety** A combination of physiological, emotional, and cognitive components that are caused by the stress of taking exams and that may interfere with a student's ability to think, reason, and plan.

**testimonial** A statement in support of a particular viewpoint based on personal experience.

**testosterone** The major male hormone, which stimulates the growth of genital organs and the development of secondary sexual characteristics.

**texture gradient** In three-dimensional vision, a monocular depth cue: areas with sharp, detailed texture are interpreted as being closer, and those with less sharpness and detail as more distant.

**thalamus** A structure of the limbic system that is located in the middle of the forebrain and is involved in receiving sensory information, doing some initial processing, and then relaying the sensory information to appropriate areas of the cortex, including the somatosensory cortex, primary auditory cortex, and primary visual cortex.

**Thematic Apperception Test (TAT)** A personality test in which subjects are asked to look at pictures of people in ambiguous situations and to make up stories about what the characters are thinking and feeling and what the outcome will be.

**theory of evolution** Darwin's theory that different species arose from a common ancestor and that those species survived that were best adapted to meet the demands of their environments.

**theory of linguistic relativity** Whorf's theory that the differences among languages result in differences in the ways people think and perceive the world.

# Glossary

**theory of personality** An organized attempt to describe and explain how personalities develop and why personalities differ.

**theory theory** The idea that children have innate abilities to make guesses about how things are, test their guesses through interactions with the environment, and change their guesses as they gather new or conflicting information.

**thinking** Mental processes by which we form concepts, solve problems, and engage in creative activities. Sometimes referred to as reasoning.

**threat appraisal** Our conclusion that harm or loss has not yet taken place in a particular situation but we anticipate it in the near future.

**threshold** A point above which a stimulus is perceived and below which it is not perceived. *See also* absolute threshold.

**thyroid** A gland located in the neck that regulates metabolism through secretion of hormones. It forms part of the endocrine system.

**time-out** In training children, a form of negative punishment in which reinforcing stimuli are removed after an undesirable response. This removal decreases the chances that the response will recur. In time-out, the child is told to sit quietly in the corner of a room or put in some other situation where there is no chance to obtain reinforcers or engage in pleasurable behaviors.

**tip-of-the-tongue phenomenon** The situation in which, despite making a great effort, we are temporarily unable to recall information that we absolutely know is in our memory.

**TKS** *See* taijin kyofusho.

**tolerance** The reaction of the body and brain to regular drug use, whereby the person has to take larger doses of the drug to achieve the same behavioral effect.

**touch** The skin senses, which include temperature, pressure, and pain. Touch sensors change mechanical pressure or changes in temperature into nerve impulses that are sent to the brain for processing.

**trait** A relatively stable and enduring tendency to behave in a particular way.

**trait theory** An approach for analyzing the structure of personality by measuring, identifying, and classifying similarities and differences in personality characteristics or traits.

**transcendental meditation (TM)** A meditation exercise in which individuals assume a comfortable position, close their eyes, and repeat and concentrate on a sound to clear their head of all thoughts (worrisome and otherwise).

**transduction** The process by which a sense organ changes, or transforms, physical energy into electrical signals that become neural impulses, which may be sent to the brain for processing.

**transference** In psychotherapy, the process by which a client expresses strong emotions toward the therapist because the therapist substitutes for someone important in the client's life, such as the client's mother or father. Freud first developed this concept.

**transformational rules** According to Chomsky, procedures by which we convert our ideas from surface structures into deep structures and from deep structures back into surface structures.

**transmitter** A chemical messenger that transmits information between nerves and body organs, such as muscles and heart. *See also* neurotransmitters.

**transsexualism** *See* gender identity disorder.

**triangular theory of love** *See* Sternberg's triangular theory of love.

**triarchic theory** *See* Sternberg's triarchic theory.

**trichromatic theory** The idea that there are three different kinds of cones in the retina, and each cone contains one of three different light-sensitive chemicals, called opsins. Each opsin is most responsive to wavelengths that correspond to each of the three primary colors—blue, green, and red—from which all other colors can be mixed.

**two-factor theory** A theory of intelligence proposed by Spearman, according to which a general mental ability factor, *g*, represents a person's ability to perform complex mental work, such as abstract reasoning and problem solving, while many specific factors, *s*, represent a person's specific mental abilities, such as mathematical, mechanical, or verbal skills. Thus, *g* is constant across tests, while *s* may vary across tests.

**two-word combinations** The third stage in acquiring language, which begins at about 2 years of age. The infant says strings of two words that express various actions ("Me play," "See boy") or relationships ("Hit ball," "Milk gone").

**tympanic membrane** The thin, taut membrane, commonly called the eardrum, that is the boundary between the outer ear and middle ear. Struck by sound waves, it vibrates and passes the vibrations to the ossicles.

**Type A behavior** A combination of personality traits that may be a risk factor for coronary heart disease. According to the original (1970s) definition, these traits included an overly competitive and aggressive drive to achieve, a hostile attitude when frustrated, a habitual sense of time urgency, a rapid and explosive pattern of speaking, and workaholic tendencies; in contrast, type B behavior was easygoing, calm, relaxed, and patient. In the 1980s, the list of traits was reduced to being depressed, aggressively competitive, easily frustrated, anxious, and angry. In the 1990s, the list was reduced again, to frequent feelings of anger and hostility, which may or may not be publicly expressed. At this point, the association between Type A behavior and risk of coronary disease is much in doubt.

**Type I schizophrenia** A type of schizophrenia characterized by positive symptoms, such as hallucinations and delusions, which are distortions of normal functions. Individuals diagnosed with Type I schizophrenia have no intellectual impairment, good reaction to medication, and thus a good chance of recovery.

**Type II schizophrenia** A type of schizophrenia characterized by negative symptoms, such as dulled emotions and little inclination to speak, which are a loss of normal functions. Individuals diagnosed with Type II schizophrenia have intellectual impairment, poor reaction to medication, and thus a poor chance of recovery.

**typical neuroleptic drugs** Neuroleptics that primarily reduce the levels of the neurotransmitter dopamine. Two of the more common are phenothiazines (for example, Thorazine) and butrophenones (for example, haloperidol). These drugs primarily reduce positive symptoms but have little or no effects on negative symptoms.

**unconditional positive regard** The warmth, acceptance, and love that others show us because we are valued human beings even though we may behave in ways that disappoint them by behaving in ways that differ from their standards and values or the way they think.

**unconditioned response (UCR)** An unlearned, innate, involuntary physiological reflex that is elicited by the unconditioned stimulus.

**unconditioned stimulus (UCS)** A stimulus that triggers or elicits some physiological response, such as salivation or eye blink.

**unconscious** *See* Freud's theory of the unconscious; cognitive unconscious.

**unconscious forces** Wishes, desires, or thoughts that, because of their disturbing or threatening content, we automatically repress and cannot voluntarily access.

**unconscious motivation** A Freudian concept that refers to the influence of repressed thoughts, desires, or impulses on our conscious thoughts and behaviors.

**unconsciousness** Total loss of awareness and responsiveness to the environment. It may be due to disease, trauma, a blow to the head, or general medical anesthesia.

**underachievers** Individuals who score relatively high on tests of ability or intelligence but perform more poorly than their scores would predict.

**unipolar depression** *See* major depressive disorder.

**universal emotional expressions** A number of specific inherited facial patterns or expressions that signal specific feelings or emotional states, such as a smile signaling a happy state.

**uplifts** Small, pleasurable, happy, and satisfying experiences that we have in our daily lives.

**validity** The extent to which a test measures what it is supposed to measure.

**variable-interval schedule** A conditioning schedule such that the time between the response and the subsequent reinforcer is variable.

**variable-ratio schedule** A conditioning schedule in which the subject must make a different number of responses for the delivery of each reinforcer.

**variance** A measure of the variability within two distributions.

**ventrolateral preoptic nucleus (VPN)** A group of cells in the hypothalamus that acts like a master switch for sleep. Turned on, the VPN secretes a neurotransmitter (GABA) that turns off areas that keep the brain awake; turned off, certain brain areas become active and we wake up.

**ventromedial hypothalamus** A group of brain cells that regulates hunger by creating feelings of satiety *(say-TIE-ah-tea)* or fullness.

**vertigo** Feelings of dizziness and nausea resulting from malfunction of the semicircular canals in the vestibular system.

**vestibular system** Three semicircular canals in the inner ear that sense the position of the head, keep the head upright, and maintain balance. Fluid in the semicircular canals moves in response to movements of the head, and sensors (hair cells) in the canals respond to the movement of the fluid.

**virtual reality** A perceptual experience—of being inside an object, moving through an environment, or carrying out some action—that is, in fact, entirely simulated by a computer.

**visible spectrum** The one particular segment of electromagnetic energy that we can see because these waves are the right length to stimulate receptors in the eye.

**visual acuity** The ability to see fine details.

**visual agnosia** A condition caused by damage to the visual association area. An individual with visual agnosia is unable to recognize some object, person, or color and yet is able to see and even describe parts of some visual stimulus.

**visual association area** An area of the brain, located next to the primary visual cortex, that transforms basic sensations, such as lights, lines, colors, and textures, into complete, meaningful visual perceptions, such as persons, objects, or animals.

**visual cliff** A glass tabletop with a checkerboard pattern over part of its surface; the remaining surface consists of clear glass with a checkerboard pattern several feet below, creating the illusion of a clifflike drop to the floor.

**VPN** *See* ventrolateral preoptic nucleus.

**vulnerability** Psychological or environmental difficulties that make children more at risk for developing later personality, behavioral, or social problems.

**Weber's law** A psychophysics law stating that the increase in intensity of a stimulus needed to produce a just noticeable difference grows in proportion to the intensity of the initial stimulus.

**Wechsler Adult Intelligence Scale (WAIS-III)** and **Wechsler Intelligence Scale for Children (WISC-III)** Intelligence tests that are divided into various subtests. The verbal section contains a subtest of general information, a vocabulary subtest, and so forth. The performance section contains a subtest that involves arranging pictures in a meaningful order, one that requires assembling objects, and one that involves using codes. The verbal and performance scores are combined to give a single IQ score.

**weight-regulating genes** Genes that play a role in influencing appetite, body metabolism, and secretion of hormones (such as leptin) that regulate fat stores.

**Wernicke's aphasia** Difficulty in understanding spoken or written words and in putting words into meaningful sentences, as a result of injury to Wernicke's area in the brain.

**Wernicke's area** An area usually located in the left temporal lobe that plays a role in understanding speech and speaking in coherent sentences. *See* Wernicke's aphasia.

**withdrawal symptoms** Painful physical and psychological symptoms that occur when a drug-dependent person stops using a drug.

**word** An arbitrary pairing between a sound or symbol and a meaning.

**working memory** *See* short-term memory.

**Yerkes-Dodson law** The principle that performance on a task is an interaction between the level of physiological arousal and the difficulty of the task. For difficult tasks, low arousal results in better performance; for most tasks, moderate arousal helps performance; and for easy tasks, high arousal may facilitate performance.

**zygote** The cell that results when an egg is fertilized. It contains 46 chromosomes, arranged in 23 pairs.

**Abernethy, B., Neal, R. J., & Koning, P.** (1994). Visual-perceptual and cognitive differences between expert, intermediate, and novice snooker players. *Applied Cognitive Psychology, 8,* 185–211.

**Abramov, I., & Gordon, J.** (1994). Color appearance: On seeing red—or yellow, or green, or blue. *Annual Review of Psychology, 45,* 451–485.

**Abramowitz, J. S.** (1997). Effectiveness of psychological and pharmacological treatments for obsessive-compulsive disorder: A quantitative review. *Journal of Consulting and Clinical Psychology, 65,* 44–52.

**Abrams, D., Marques, J. M., Bown, N., & Henson, M.** (2000). Pro-norm and anti-norm deviance within and between groups. *Journal of Personality and Social Psychology, 78,* 906–912.

**Abrams, R. L., & Greenwald, A. G.** (2000). Parts outweigh the whole (word) in unconscious analysis of meaning. *Psychological Science, 11,* 118–124.

**Abu-Lughod, L.** (1986). *Veiled sentiments.* Berkeley: University of California Press.

**Acklin, M. W., McDowell, C. J., II., Verschell, M. S., & Chan, D.** (2000). Interobserver agreement, intraobserver reliability, and the Rorschach comprehensive system. *Journal of Personality Assessment, 74,* 15–47.

**Adams, C.** (1991). Qualitative age differences in memory for text: A life-span developmental perspective. *Psychology and Aging, 6,* 323–336.

**Adan, A.** (1992). The influence of age, work schedule and personality on morningness dimensions. *International Journal of Psychophysiology, 12,* 95–99.

**Adelmann, P. K., & Zajonc, R. B.** (1989). Facial efference and the experience of emotion. *Annual Review of Psychology, 40,* 249–280.

**Ader, F.** (1999, June). Cited in B. Azar, Father of PNI reflects on the field growth. *Monitor: American Psychological Association,* 18.

**Ader, R., & Cohen, N.** (1975). Behaviorally conditioned immunosuppression. *Psychosomatic Medicine, 37,* 333–340.

**Adler, J., & Rosenberg, D.** (1994, December 19). The endless binge. *Newsweek.*

**Adler, L. L., & Denmark, F. L.** (1995). *Violence and the prevention of violence.* Westport, CT: Praeger.

**Adler, T.** (1993, April). Sense of invulnerability doesn't drive teen risks. *APA Monitor.*

**Adler, T.** (1994). Comprehending those who can't relate. *Science News, 145,* 248–249.

**Aghajanian, G. K.** (1994). Serotonin and the action of LSD in the brain. *Psychiatric Annals, 24,* 137–141.

**Ainsworth, M. D. S.** (1979). Infant-mother attachment. *American Psychologist, 34,* 932–937.

**Ainsworth, M. D. S.** (1989). Attachments beyond infancy. *American Psychologist, 44,* 709–716.

**Aitchison, K., & Kerwin, R. W.** (1997). Cost-effectiveness of clozapine. *British Journal of Psychiatry, 171,* 125–130.

**Alanen, P. P.** (1997). A critical review of genetic studies of schizophrenia: I. Epidemiological and brain studies. *Acta Psychiatrica Scandinavica, 95,* 1–5.

**Albert, M. L., Connor, L. T., & Obler, L. K.** (2000). Brain, language, and environment. *Brain and Language, 71,* 4–6.

**Alcock, J.** (1995, May/June). Why faith in anecdotal reports? *Skeptical Inquirer.*

**Alexander, G. E., Furey, M. L., Grady, C. L., Pietrini, P., Brady, D. R., Mentis, M. J., & Schapiro, M. B.** (1997). Association of premorbid intellectual function with cerebral metabolism in Alzheimer's Disease: Implications for the cognitive reserve hypothesis. *American Journal of Psychiatry, 154,* 165–172.

**Ali, S. I., & Begum, S.** (1994). Fabric softeners and softness perception. *Ergonomics, 37,* 801–806.

**Alivisatos, B., & Petrides, M.** (1997). Functional activation of the human brain during mental rotation. *Neuropsychologia, 35,* 111–118.

**Allen, G., Buxton, R. B., Wong, E. C., & Courchesne, E.** (1997). Attentional activation of the cerebellum independent of motor involvement. *Science, 275,* 1940–1943.

**Allen, J. E.** (2000, May 8). How do you know if it's attention deficit/hyperactivity disorder? *Los Angeles Times,* S3.

**Allen, R. P., & Mirabile, J.** (1997, June 18). Cited in E. Woo, How to get A's, not Zzzz. *Los Angeles Times.*

**Allgood, W. P., Risko, V. J., Alvarez, M. C., & Fairbanks, M. M.** (2000). Factors that influence study. In R. F. Flippo & D. C. Caverly (Eds.), *Handbook of college reading and study strategy research.* Mahwah, NJ: Lawrence Erlbaum.

**Alliger, G. M., & Title, S. A.** (2000). A meta-analytic investigation of the susceptibility of integrity tests to faking and coaching. *Educational & Psychological Measurement, 60,* 59–72.

**Allport, G. W.** (1935). Attitudes. In C. Murchison (Ed.), *Handbook of social psychology* (Vol. 2). Worcester, MA: Clark University Press.

**Allport, G. W., & Odbert, H. S.** (1936). Trait-names: A psycho-lexical study. *Psychological Monographs, 47* (Whole No. 211).

**Althof, S. E.** (1995). Pharmacologic treatment of rapid ejaculation. *The Psychiatric Clinics of North America, 18,* 85–94.

**Altman, L. K.** (1997, January 19). With AIDS advance, more disappointment. *New York Times.*

**Amabile, T. M.** (1985). Motivation and creativity: Effects of motivational orientation on creative writers. *Journal of Personality and Social Psychology, 48,* 393–399.

**American Academy of Pediatrics.** (2000, July 26). Joint statement on the impact of entertainment violence on children. Congressional public health summit. *http://www.aap.org*

**American Association on Mental Retardation.** (1993). *Mental retardation* (9th ed.). Annapolis Junction, MD: AAMR Publications.

**American Psychiatric Association.** (1952). *Diagnostic and statistical manual of mental disorders.* Washington, DC: Author.

**American Psychiatric Association.** (1968). *Diagnostic and statistical manual of mental disorders* (2nd ed.). Washington, DC: Author.

**American Psychiatric Association.** (1980). *Diagnostic and statistical manual of mental disorders* (3rd ed.). Washington, DC: Author.

**American Psychiatric Association.** (1994). *Diagnostic and statistical manual of mental disorders* (4th ed.). Washington, DC: Author.

**American Psychiatric Association.** (2000). *Diagnostic and statistical manual of mental disorders* (4th ed., Text revision). Washington, DC: Author.

**American Psychological Association.** (1992). Ethical principles of psychologists and code of conduct. *American Psychologist, 47,* 1597–1611.

**American Psychological Association.** (1995). *How to choose a psychologist.* Washington, DC: Author.

**American Psychological Association, Division of Psychological Hypnosis.** (1993). Hypnosis. *Psychologial Hypnosis, 2*(3).

**Anastasi, A., & Urbina, S.** (1997). *Psychological testing.* Upper Saddle River, NJ: Prentice-Hall.

**Anderson, A. K., & Phelps, E. A.** (2000). Expression without recognition: Contributions of the human amygdala to emotional communication. *Psychological Science, 11,* 106–111.

**Anderson, C. A., Bushman, B. J., & Groom, R. W.** (1997). Hot years and serious and deadly assault: Empirical tests of the heat hypothesis. *Journal of Personality and Social Psychology, 73,* 1213–1223.

**Anderson, K. J.** (1994). Impulsivity, caffeine, and task difficulty: A within-subjects test of the Yerkes-Dodson law. *Personality and Individual Differences, 16,* 813–819.

**Andreasen, N. C.** (1997a). The role of the thalamus in schizophrenia. *Canadian Journal of Psychiatry, 42,* 27–33.

**Andreasen, N. C.** (1997b). Linking mind and brain in the study of mental illnesses: A project for a scientific psychopathology. *Science, 275,* 1586–1593.

**Andreasen, N. C., Nopoulos, P., Schultz, S., Miller, D., Gupta, S., Swayze, V., & Flaum, M.** (1994). Positive and negative symptoms of schizophrenia: Past, present, and future. *Acta Psychiatrica Scandinavica, 90,* 510–519.

**Andrews, B., Brewin, C. R., Ochera, J., Morton, J., Bekerian, D. A., Davies, G. M., & Mollon, P.** (2000). The timing, triggers and qualities of recovered memories in therapy. *British Journal of Clinical Psychology, 39,* 11–26.

**Angelo, B.** (1991, November 4). Life at the end of the rainbow. *Time.*

**Antonuccio, D. O., Thomas, M., & Danton, W. G.** (1997). A cost-effective analysis of cognitive behavior therapy and fluoxetine (Prozac) in the treatment of depression. *Behavior Therapy, 28,* 187–210.

**Archer, J.** (1996). Sex differences in social behavior. *American Psychologist, 51,* 909–917.

**Archer, J.** (1997). On the origins of sex differences in social behavior: Darwinian and non-Darwinian accounts. *American Psychologist, 52,* 1383–1384.

**Arena, J. G., Bruno, G. M., & Rozantine, G. S.** (1997). A comparison of tension headache sufferers and non-pain controls on the state-trait anger expression inventory: An exploratory study with implications for applied psychophysiologists. *Applied Psychophysiology and Biofeedback, 22,* 209–214.

**Arendt, J., & Deacon, S.** (1997). Treatment of circadian rhythm disorders—melatonin. *Chronobiology International, 14,* 185–204.

**Arkowitz, H.** (1997). Integrative theories of therapy. In P. L. Wachtel & S. B. Messer (Eds.), *Theories of psychotherapy: Origins and evolution.* Washington, DC: American Psychological Association.

**Armbruster, B. B.** (2000). Taking notes from lectures. In R. F. Flippo & D. C. Caverly (Eds.), *Handbook of college reading and study strategy research.* Mahwah, NJ: Lawrence Erlbaum.

**Arnett, J. J.** (2000a). Adolescent storm and stress, reconsidered. *American Psychologist, 54,* 317–326.

**Arnett, J. J.** (2000b). Emerging adulthood. *American Psychologist, 55,* 469–480.

**Aronow, E., Reznikoff, M., & Moreland, K. L.** (1995). The Rorschach: Projective technique or psychometric test? *Journal of Personality Assessment, 64,* 213–218.

**Aronson, E.** (1997). Back to future: Retrospective review of Leon Festinger's *A theory of cognitive dissonance. American Journal of Psychology, 110,* 127–157.

**Asch, S. E.** (1958). Effects of group pressure upon modification and distortion of judgments. In E. E. Maccoby, T. M. Newcomb, & E. L. Hartley (Eds.), *Readings in social psychology* (3rd ed.). New York: Holt, Rinehart & Winston.

**Aserinsky, E., & Kleitman, N.** (1953). Regularly occurring periods of eye motility, and concomitant phenomena during sleep. *Science, 118,* 273–274.

**Ashton, H.** (1994). The treatment of benzodiazepine dependence. *Addiction, 89,* 1535–1541.

**Atkinson, J. W.** (1964). *An introduction to motivation.* Princeton, NJ: Van Nostrand Reinhold.

**Atkinson, J. W.** (Ed.). (1958). *Motives in fantasy, action and society.* Princeton, NJ: Van Nostrand Reinhold.

Atkinson, J. W., & Birch, D. (1978). *Introduction to motivation.* New York: Van Nostrand.

Atkinson, J. W., & Raynor, J. O. (Eds.). (1974). *Motivation and achievement.* Washington, DC: V. H. Winston.

Atkinson, R. C., & Shiffrin, R. M. (1968). Human memory: A proposed system and its control processes. In K. W. Spence & J. T. Spence (Eds.), *The psychology of learning and motivation: Advances in research and theory* (Vol. 2). New York: Academic Press.

Atkinson, R. C., & Shiffrin, R. M. (1971). The control of short-term memory. *Scientific American, 225,* 82–90.

Attias, J., Gordon, C., Ribak, J., Binah, O., & Arnon, R. (1987). Efficacy of transdermal scopolamine against seasickness: A 3-day study at sea. *Aviation, Space and Environmental Medicine, 58,* 60–62.

Audrain, J. E., Klesges, R. C., & Klesges, L. M. (1995). Relationship between obesity and the metabolic effects of smoking in women. *Health Psychology, 14,* 116–123.

Averill, J. R., & Moore, T. A. (2000). Happiness. In M. Lewis & J. M. Haviland-Jones (Eds.), *Handbook of emotions* (2nd ed.). New York: Guilford.

Azar, B. (1994a, October). Scientists eye complexities of aggression. *APA Monitor.*

Azar, B. (1994b, November). Mixed messages fuel dieting dilemmas. *APA Monitor.*

Azar, B. (1997, August). When research is swept under the rug. *APA Monitor.*

Azar, B., & Sleek, S. (1994, October). Do roots of violence grow from nature or nurture? *APA Monitor.*

Babyak, M., Blumenthal, J. A., Herman, S., Khatri, P., Doraiswamy, M., Moore, K., Craighead, W. E., Baldewizc, T. T., & Krishnan, K. R. (2000). Exercise treatment for major depression: Maintenance of therapeutic benefit at 10 months. *Psychosomatic Medicine, 62,* 633–638.

Bacaltchuk, J., Trefiglio, R. P., Oliveira, I. R., Hay, P., Lima, M. S., & Mari, J. J. (2000). Combination of antidepressants and psychological treatments for bulimia nervosa: A systematic review. *Acta Psychiatrica Scandinavica, 101,* 256–264.

Baddeley, A. (1994). The magical number seven: Still magic after all these years? *Psychological Review, 101,* 353–356.

Baddeley, A. (2000). Short-term and working memory. In E. Tulving & F. M. Craik (Eds.), *The Oxford handbook of memory.* New York: Oxford University Press.

Bahrick, H. P. (2000). Long-term maintenance of knowledge. In E. Tulving & F. M. Craik (Eds.), *The Oxford handbook of memory.* New York: Oxford University Press.

Bahrick, H. P., Bahrick, P. O., & Wittlinger, R. P. (1975). Fifty years of memory for names and faces. *Journal of Experimental Psychology: General, 104,* 54–75.

Bahrick, H. P., Hall, L. K., & Berger, S. A. (1996). Accuracy and distortion in memory for high school girls. *Psychological Science, 7,* 265–271.

Bailenson, J. N., Shum, M. S., & Uttal, D. H. (2000). The initial segment strategy: A heuristic for route selection. *Memory & Cognition, 28,* 306–318.

Bailey, J. M., Dunne, M. P., & Martin, N. G. (2000). Genetic and environmental influences on sexual orientation and its correlates in an Australian twin sample. *Journal of Personality and Social Psychology, 78,* 524–536.

Bailey, J. M., & Zucker, H. J. (1995). Childhood sextyped behavior and sexual orientation: A conceptual analysis and quantitative review. *Developmental Psychology, 31,* 43–55.

Bakker, A., van Dyck, R., Spinhoven, P., & van Balkom, A. J. L. M. (1999). Paroxetine, clomipramine, and cognitive therapy in the treatment of panic disorder. *Journal of Clinical Psychiatry, 60,* 831–838.

Baldessarini, R. J., & Tondo, L. (2000). Does lithium treatment still work? *Archives of General Psychiatry, 57,* 187–190.

Baldwin, J. D., & Baldwin, J. I. (1997). Gender differences in sexual interest. *Archives of Sexual Behavior, 26,* 181–210.

Balint, K. (1995, March 4). La Jolla senior, 17, wins top U.S. science prize. *San Diego Union-Tribune.*

Ball, E. M. (1997). Sleep disorders in primary care. *Comprehensive Therapy, 23,* 25–30.

Ball, G. F., & Hulse, S. H. (1998). Birdsong. *American Psychologist, 53,* 37–58.

Balter, M. (1996). New clues to brain dopamine control, cocaine addiction. *Science, 271,* 909.

Balzar, J. (1997, March 8). A passion for canines, cold winds. *Los Angeles Times.*

Banati, R. B., Goerres, B. W., Tjoa, C., Aggleton, J. P., & Grasby, P. (2000). The functional anatomy of visual-tactile integration in man: A study using positron emission tomography. *Neuropsychologia, 38,* 115–124.

Bandura, A. (1965). Influence of models' reinforcement contingencies on the acquisition of imitative responses. *Journal of Personality and Social Psychology, 1,* 589–596.

Bandura, A. (1986). *Social foundations of thought and action: A social cognitive theory.* Englewood Cliffs, NJ: Prentice-Hall.

Bandura, A. (1989a). Human agency in social cognitive theory. *American Psychologist, 44,* 1175–1184.

Bandura, A. (1989b). Social cognitive theory. In R. Vasta (Ed.), *Annals of child development* (Vol. 6). Greenwich, CT: JAI Press.

Bandura, A. (1989c). Regulation of cognitive processes through perceived self-efficacy. *Developmental Psychology, 25,* 729–735.

Bandura, A. (Ed.). (1995). *Self-efficacy in changing societies.* New York: Cambridge University Press.

Bandura, A. (1999). Social cognitive theory of personality. In L. A. Pervin & O. P. John (Eds.), *Handbook of personality: Theory and research* (2nd ed.). New York: Guilford.

Bandura, A. (2000). Exercise of human agency through collective efficacy. *Current Directions in Psychological Science, 9,* 75–78.

Bandura, A., Blanchard, E. B., & Ritter, B. (1969). Relative efficacy of desensitization and modeling approaches for inducing behavioral, affective and attitudinal changes. *Journal of Personality and Social Psychology, 13,* 173–179.

Bandura, A., Ross, D., & Ross, S. A. (1963). Imitation of film-mediated aggressive models. *Journal of Abnormal and Social Psychology, 66,* 3–11.

Barber, T. X. (2000). A deeper understanding of hypnosis: Its secrets, its nature, its essence. *American Journal of Clinical Hypnosis, 42,* 208–272.

Barinaga, M. (1992). The brain remaps its own contours. *Science, 258,* 216–218.

Barinaga, M. (1996). Backlash strikes at affirmative action programs. *Science, 271,* 1908–1910.

Barinaga, M. (1997a). A mitochondrial Alzheimer's gene? *Science, 276,* 682.

Barinaga, M. (1997b). Ban has mixed impact on Texas, California grad schools. *Science, 277,* 633–634.

Barinaga, M. (2000a). Family of bitter taste receptors found. *Science, 287,* 2133–2135.

Barinaga, M. (2000b). Fetal neuron grafts pave the way for stem cell therapies. *Science, 287,* 1421–1422.

Barkley, R. (1994, July 18). Cited in C. Wallis, Life in overdrive. *Time.*

Barkley, R. A. (1997). Behavioral inhibition, sustained attention, and executive functions: Constructing a unifying theory of ADHD. *Psychological Bulletin, 121,* 65–94.

Barkley, R. A. (1998, September). Attention-deficit hyperactivity disorder. *Scientific American,* 66–71.

Barling, J., Kelloway, E. K., & Cheung, D. (1996). Time management and achievement striving to predict car sales performance. *Journal of Applied Psychology, 81,* 821–826.

Barlow, D. H., & Durand, V. M. (1995). *Abnormal psychology: An integrative approach.* Pacific Grove, CA: Brooks/Cole.

Barlow, D. H., & Durand, V. M. (2001). *Abnormal psychology* (2nd ed.). Belmont, CA: Wadsworth/Thomson.

Barnard, N. D., & Kaufman, S. R. (1997, February). Animal research is wasteful and misleading. *Scientific American,* 80–82.

Barnett, S. (1999, October 22). Cited in T. H. Maugh II, Study finds major benefits from quality day care. *Los Angeles Times,* A3.

Baron, R., Logan, H., Lilly, J., Inman, M., & Brennan, M. (1994). Negative emotion and message processing. *Journal of Experimental Social Psychology, 30,* 181–201.

Barrett, S. (1995, January–February). The dark side of Linus Pauling's legacy. *Skeptical Inquirer.*

Bartol, C. R., Bergen, G. T., Volckens, J. S., & Knoras, K. M. (1992). Women in small-town policing. *Criminal Justice and Behavior, 19,* 240–259.

Bartoshuk, L. M. (1997). Cited in K. Fackelmann, The bitter truth. *Science News, 152,* 24–25.

Bartoshuk, L. M., & Beauchamp, G. K. (1994). Chemical senses. *Annual Review of Psychology, 45,* 419–449.

Basco, M. R., Blickman, M., Wetherford, P., & Ryser, N. (2000). Cognitive-behavioral therapy for anxiety disorders: Why and how it works. *Bulletin of the Menninger Clinic, 64* (Suppl. A), A52–A70.

Bashore, T. R., Osman, A., & Heffley, E. F., III. (1989). Mental slowing in elderly persons: A cognitive psychophysiological analysis. *Psychology and Aging, 4,* 235–244.

Bashore, T. R., & Rapp, P. E. (1993). Are there alternatives to traditional polygraph procedures? *Psychological Bulletin, 113,* 3–22.

Basil, R. (1989). Graphology and personality: Let the buyer beware. *Skeptical Inquirer, 13,* 241–248.

Bassili, J. N. (1995). Response latency and the accessibility of voting intentions: What contributes to accessibility and how it affects vote choice. *Personality and Social Psychology Bulletin, 21,* 686–695.

Basso, A. (2000). The aphasias: Fall and renaissance of the neurological model. *Brain and Language, 71,* 15–17.

Bateman, A. W., & Fonagy, P. (2000). Effectiveness of psychotherapeutic treatment of personality disorder. *British Journal of Psychiatry, 177,* 138–143.

Bates, B. L. (1994). Individual differences in response to hypnosis. In J. W. Rhue, S. J. Lynn, & I. Kirsch (Eds.), *Handbook of clinical hypnosis.* Washington, DC: American Psychological Association.

Bates, J. (2000). Temperament as an emotion construct: Theoretical and practical issues. In M. Lewis & J. M. Haviland-Jones (Eds.), *Handbook of emotions* (2nd ed.). New York: Guilford.

Bateson, P. (1991). Is imprinting such a special case? In J. R. Krebs & G. Horn (Eds.), *Behavioural and neural aspects of learning and memory.* Oxford: Oxford University Press.

Batson, C. D. (1998). Who cares? When? Where? Why? How? *Contemporary Psychology, 43,* 108–109.

Bauer, P. J. (1996). What do infants recall of their lives? *American Psychologist, 51,* 29–41.

Baum, D. (1996). *Smoke and mirrors: The war on drugs and the politics of failure.* New York: Little, Brown.

Baum, G. (1994, February 13). Storming the Citadel. *Los Angeles Times.*

Baumeister, R. F. (1995). Disputing the effects of championship pressures and home audiences. *Journal of Personality and Social Psychology, 68,* 644–648.

Baumeister, R. F., & Leary, M. R. (1995). The need to belong: Desire for interpersonal attachments as a fundamental human motivation. *Psychological Bulletin, 117,* 497–529.

Baumrind, D. (1991). Effective parenting during the early adolescent transition. In P. A. Cowan & E. M. Hetherington (Eds.), *Advances in family research.* Hillsdale, NJ: Erlbaum.

Baumrind, D. (1993). The average expectable environment is not good enough: A response to Scarr. *Child Development, 64,* 1299–1317.

Baumrind, D. (1995). Commentary on sexual orientation: Research and social policy implications. *Developmental Psychology, 31,* 130–136.

Baxter, L. R. (2000, March 21). Cited in A. Fuentes, Finding hope amid despair in treating compulsive disorders. *New York Times,* D7.

Beaman, A. L., Cole, C. M., Preston, M., Lentz, B., & Steblay, N. M. (1983). Fifteen years of foot-in-the-door research. *Personality and Social Psychology Bulletin, 9,* 181–196.

Bear, M. F., Connors, B. W., & Paradiso, M. A. (1996). *Neuroscience: Exploring the brain.* Baltimore: Williams & Wilkins.

Beardsley, T. (1997, August). The machinery of thought. *Scientific American,* 78–83.

Bechara, A., Damasio, H., Tranel, D., & Damasio, A. R. (1997). Deciding advantageously before knowing the advantageous strategy. *Science, 275,* 1293–1295.

Bechara, A., Tranel, D., Damasio, H., Adolphs, R., Rockland, C., & Damasio, A. R. (1995). Double dissociation of conditioning and declarative knowledge relative to the amygdala and hippocampus in humans. *Science, 269,* 1115–1120.

Beck, A. T. (1976). *Cognitive therapy and the emotional disorders.* New York: International Universities Press.

Beck, A. T. (1991). Cognitive therapy: A 30-year retrospective. *American Psychologist, 46,* 368–375.

Beck, A. T., Rush, A. J., Shaw, B. F., & Emery, G. (1979). *Cognitive therapy of depression.* New York: Guilford Press.

Beck, R., & Fernandez, E. (1998). Cognitive-behavioral therapy in the treatment of anger: A meta-analysis. *Cognitive Therapy and Research, 22,* 63–74.

Becker, J. V., & Kaplan, M. S. (1994). Sexual disorders. In V. B. Van Hasselt & M. Mersen (Eds.), *Advanced abnormal psychology.* New York: Plenum Press.

Bednekoff, P. A., Kamil, A. C., & Balda, R. P. (1997). Clark's nutcracker (Aves: Corvidae) spatial memory; Interference effects on cache recovery performance? *Ethology, 103,* 554–565.

Begleiter, H. (1997). Cited in Children of alcoholics show brain deficits identical to fathers. *American Psychological Society Observer,* 15.

Begley, S. (1994, August 29). Why Johnny and Joanie can't read. *Newsweek.*

Begley, S. (1997, February 24). Mammogram war. *Newsweek.*

Begley, S. (1998a, January 19). Aping language. *Newsweek.*

Begley, S. (1998b, January 26). Is everybody crazy? *Newsweek,* 51–55.

Begley, S. (2000, April 10). Decoding the human body. *Newsweek,* 50–57.

Behrman, A. (1999, January 27). Electroboy. *New York Times Magazine,* 67.

Bell, A. P., Weinberg, M. S., & Hammersmith, S. K. (1981). *Sexual preference: Its development in men and women.* Bloomington: Indiana University Press.

Bell, S. M., McCallum, R. S., Bryles, J., Driesler, K., McDonald, J., Park, S. H., & Williams, A. (1994). Attributions for academic success and failure: An individual difference investigation of academic achievement and gender. *Journal of Psychoeducational Assessment, 13,* 4–13.

Belsky, J. (1993). Etiology of child maltreatment: A developmental-ecological analysis. *Psychological Bulletin, 114,* 413–434.

Bem, D. (1967). Self-perception: An alternative interpretation of cognitive dissonance phenomena. *Psychological Review, 74,* 183–200.

Bem, D. J., & Honorton, C. (1994). Does psi exist? Replicable evidence for an anomalous process of information transfer. *Psychological Bulletin, 115,* 4–18.

Bem, S. L. (1981). Gender schema theory: A cognitive account of sex-typing. *Psychological Review, 88,* 354–364.

Bem, S. L. (1985). Androgyny and gender schema theory: Conceptual and empirical integration. In T. B. Sonderegger (Ed.), *Nebraska symposium on motivation.* Lincoln: University of Nebraska Press.

Bendersky, M., & Lewis, M. (1999). Prenatal cocaine exposure and neonatal condition. *Infant Behavior & Development, 22,* 353–366.

Benes, F. M. (1997). The role of stress and dopamine—GABA interactions in the vulnerability for schizophrenia. *Journal of Psychiatric Research, 31,* 57–275.

Benin, M. H., & Robinson, L. B. (1997, August 25). Marital happiness across the family life cycle: A longitudinal analysis. Cited in *Time,* 24.

Benjamin, L. T., Jr. (2000). The psychology laboratory at the turn of the 20th century. *American Psychologist, 55,* 318–321.

Ben-Shakhar, G., Bar-Hillel, M., Bilu, Y., Ben-Abba, E., & Flug, A. (1986). Can graphology predict occupational success? Two empirical studies and some methodological ruminations. *Journal of Applied Psychology, 71,* 645–653.

Benson, H. (1975). *The relaxation response.* New York: Morrow.

Benson, H. (1997). Cited in W. Roush & Herbert Benson, Mind-body maverick pushes the envelope. *Science, 276,* 357–359.

Benson, H., Lehmann, J. W., Malhotra, M. S., Goldman, R. F., Hopkins, P. J., & Epstein, M. D. (1982). Body temperature changes during the practice of g Tum-mo yoga. *Nature, 295,* 234–235.

Benson, H., Malhotra, M. S., Goldman, R. F., Jacobs, G. D., & Hopkins, P. J. (1990). Three case reports of the metabolic and electroencephalographic changes during advanced Buddhist meditation techniques. *Behavioral Medicine, 16,* 90–95.

Berg, C. A. (2000). Intellectual development in adulthood. In R. J. Sternberg, *Handbook of intelligence.* New York: Cambridge University Press.

Berger, J., & Cunningham, C. (1994). Active intervention and conservation: Africa's pachyderm problem. *Science, 263,* 1241–1242.

Bergin, A. E., & Garfield, S. L. (1994). Overview, trends, and future issues. In A. E. Bergin & S. L. Garfield (Eds.), *Handbook of psychotherapy and behavior change* (4th ed.). New York: Wiley.

Berglas, S. (1989). Self-handicapping behavior and the self-defeating personality disorder. In R. C. Curtis (Ed.), *Self-defeating behaviors: Experimental research, clinical impressions, and practical implications.* New York: Plenum Press.

Berk, L. B., & Patrick, C. F. (1990). Epidemiologic aspects of toilet training. *Clinical Pediatrics, 29,* 278–282.

Berkowitz, L. (1989). Frustration-aggression hypothesis: Examination and reformulation. *Psychological Bulletin, 106,* 59–73.

Berkowitz, L. (1993). *Aggression: Its causes, consequences, and control.* New York: McGraw-Hill.

Berkowitz, L. (1994, October). Cited in B. Azar, Scientists eye complexities of aggression. *APA Monitor.*

Berman, A. L., & Jobes, D. A. (1994). Treatment of the suicidal adolescent. *Death Studies, 18,* 375–389.

Berman, A. L., & Jobes, D. A. (1995). Suicide prevention in adolescents (age 12–18). *Suicide and Life-Threatening Behavior, 25,* 143–154.

Berman, M. E., Tracy, J. I., & Coccaro, E. R. (1997). The serotonin hypothesis of aggression revisited. *Clinical Psychology Review, 17,* 651–665.

Bermond, B., Nieuwenhuyse, B., Fasotti, L., & Schuerman, J. (1991). Spinal cord lesions, peripheral feedback, and intensities of emotional feelings. *Cognition and Emotion, 5,* 201–220.

Berney, T. P. (2000). Autism—an evolving concept. *British Journal of Psychiatry, 176,* 20–25.

Bernstein, D. A. (1993, March). Excuses, excuses. *APS Observer.*

Bernstein, P. W. (1994, May 9). The words Nelson Mandela lives by. *U.S. News & World Report.*

Betancourt, H., & Lopez, S. R. (1993). The study of culture, ethnicity, and race in American psychology. *American Psychologist, 48,* 629–637.

Biederman, J., Faraone, S., Milberger, S., Guite, J., Mick, E., Chen, L., Mennin, D., Marrs, A., Ouellette, C., Moore, P., Spencer, T., Norman, D., Wilens, T., Kraus, I., & Perrin, J. (1996). A prospective 4-year follow-up study of attention-deficit hyperactivity and related disorders. *Archives of General Psychiatry, 53,* 437–446.

Biehl, M., Matsumoto, D., Ekman, P., Hearn, V., Heider, K., Kudoh, T., & Ton, V. (1997). Matsumoto and Ekman's Japanese and Caucasian facial expressions of emotion (JACFEE): Reliability data and cross-national differences. *Journal of Nonverbal Behavior, 21,* 3–21.

Billy, J. O. G., Tanfer, K., Grady, W. R., & Klepinger, D. H. (1993). The sexual behavior of females in the United States. *Family Planning Perspectives, 25,* 52–60.

Binet, A., & Simon, T. (1905). Methodes nouvelles pour le diagnostic du niveau intellectual des anormaux. *L'Annee Psychologique, 11,* 191–244.

Bisserbe, J. C., Lane, R. M., Flament, M. R., & Franco-Belgian OCD Study Group. (1997). A double-blind comparison of sertraline and clomipramine in outpatients with obsessive-compulsive disorder. *European Psychiatry, 12,* 82–93.

Bjorklund, A. (2000). Cited in M. Barinaga, Fetal neuron grafts pave the way for stem cell therapies. *Science, 287,* 1421–1422.

Black, D. W., Baumgard, C. H., & Bell, S. E. (1995). A 16- to 45-year follow-up of 71 men with antisocial personality disorder. *Comprehensive Psychiatry, 36,* 130–140.

Blackmore, S. (1994). Psi in psychology. *Skeptical Inquirer, 18,* 351–356.

Blagys, M. D., & Hilsenroth, M. J. (2000). Distinctive features of short-term psychodynamic-interpersonal psychotherapy: A review of the comparative psychotherapy process literature. *Clinical Psychology: Science and Practice, 7,* 167–188.

Blakely, M. R. (1994, May 15). A place of belonging. *Los Angeles Times Magazine.*

Blakeslee, S. (2000a, January 12). Researchers developing bold new theories to explain autism. *San Diego Union-Tribune.*

Blakeslee, S. (2000b, March 14). Just what's going on inside that head of yours? *New York Times,* D6.

Blakeslee, S. (2000c, April 25). "Rewired" ferrets overturn theories of brain growth. *New York Times,* D1.

Blanchard, E. B., Andrasik, F., Guarnieri, P., Neff, D. F., & Rodichok, L. D. (1987). Two-, three-, and four-year follow-up on the self-regulatory treatment of chronic headache. *Journal of Consulting and Clinical Psychology, 55,* 257–259.

Blass, T. (Ed.). (2000). *Obedience to authority.* Mahwah, NJ: Lawrence Erlbaum.

Blendon, R. J., Szalay, U. S., & Knox, R. A. (1992). Should physicians aid their patients in dying? The public perspective. *New England Journal of Medicine, 267,* 2658–2662.

Bliwise, D. L. (1997). Sleep and aging. In M. R. Pressman & W. C. Orr (Eds.), *Understanding sleep: The evaluation and treatment of sleep disorders.* Washington, DC: American Psychological Association.

Block, J. (1995a). A contrarian view of the five-factor approach to personality description. *Psychological Bulletin, 117,* 187–215.

Block, J. (1995b). Going beyond the five factors given: Rejoinder to Costa & McCrae (1995) and Goldberg & Saucier (1995). *Psychological Bulletin, 117,* 226–229.

Block, J., & Robins, R. W. (1993). Longitudinal study of consistency and change in self-esteem from early adolescence to early adulthood. *Child Development, 64,* 909–923.

Block, R. I. (1996). Does heavy marijuana use impair human cognition and brain functioning? *Journal of the American Medical Association, 275,* 560–561.

Block, R. I., O'Leary, D. S., Ehrhardt, J. C., Augustinack, J. C., Ghoneim, M. M., Arndt, S., & Hall, J. A. (2000). Effects of frequent marijuana use on brain tissue volume and composition. *Brain Imaging, 11,* 491–496.

Blunt, A. K., & Pychyl, T. A. (2000). Task aversiveness and procrastination: A multi-dimensional approach to task aversiveness across stages of personal projects. *Personality and Individual Differences, 28,* 153–167.

Boddy, J. (1988). Spirits and selves in northern Sudan: The cultural therapeutics of possession and trance. *American Ethnologist, 15,* 4–27.

Boden, M. A. (1994). Précis of the creative mind: Myths and mechanisms. *Behavioral and Brain Sciences, 17,* 519–570.

Boivin, D. B., Czeisler, C. A., Kijk, D. J., Duffy, J. F., Folkard, S., Minors, D. S., Totterdell, P., & Waterhouse, J. M. (1997). Complex interaction of sleep-wake cycle and circadian phase modulates mood in healthy subjects. *Archives of General Psychiatry, 54,* 145–152.

Bond, R., & Smith, P. B. (1996). Culture and conformity: A meta-analysis of studies using Asch's (1952b, 1956) line judgment task. *Psychological Bulletin, 119,* 11–13.

Bondolfi, G., Dufour, H., Patris, M., May, J. P., Billeter, U., Eap, C. B., & Baumann, P. (1998). Risperidone versus clozapine in treatment-resistant chronic schizophrenia: A randomized double-blind study. *American Journal of Psychiatry, 155,* 499–504.

Bondurant, B., & Donat, P. L. N. (1999). Perceptions of women's sexual interest and acquaintance rape. *Psychology of Women Quarterly, 23,* 691–705.

Bonebakker, A. E., Jelicic, M., Passchier, J., & Bonke, B. (1996). Memory during general anesthesia: Practical and methodological aspects. *Consciousness and Cognition, 5,* 542–561.

Booth-Kewley, S., & Friedman, H. S. (1987). Psychological predictions of heart disease: A quantitative review. *Psychological Bulletin, 101,* 343–362.

Bootzin, R. R., & Rider, S. P. (1997). Behavioral techniques and biofeedback for insomnia. In M. R. Pressman & W. C. Roo (Eds.), *Understanding sleep: The evaluation and treatment of sleep disorders.* Washington, DC: American Psychological Association.

Borella, P., Bargellini, A., Rovesti, S., Pinelli, M., Vivoli, R., Solfrini, V., & Vivoli, G. (1999). Emotional stability, anxiety, and natural killer activity under examination stress. *Psychoneuroendocrinology, 224,* 613–627.

Born, J., Lange, T., Hansen, K., Molle, M., & Fehm, H. L. (1997). Effects of sleep and circadian rhythm on human circulating immune cells. *Journal of Immunology, 158,* 4454–4464.

Botting, J. H., & Morrison, A. R. (1997, February). Animal research vital to medicine. *Scientific American,* 83–85.

Bouchard, T. J., Jr. (1994). Genes, environment, and personality. *Science, 264,* 1700–1701.

Bouchard, T. J., Jr. (1995). Breaking the last taboo. *Contemporary Psychology, 40,* 415–418.

Bouchard, T. J., Jr. (1997). IQ similarity in twins reared apart: Findings and responses to critics. In R. J. Sternberg & E. Grigorenko (Eds.), *Intelligence, heredity, and environment.* New York: Cambridge University Press.

Bouchard, T. J., Jr., Lykken, D. T., McGue, M., Segal, N. L., & Tellegen, A. (1990). Sources of human psychological differences: The Minnesota study of twins reared apart. *Science, 250,* 223–228.

Bouchard, T. J., & McGue, M. (1981). Familial studies of intelligence: A review. *Science, 212,* 1055–1059.

Bourgon, L. N., & Kellner, C. H. (2000). Relapse of depression after ECT: A review. *Journal of ECT, 16,* 19–31.

Bowden, C. L. (2000). Efficacy of lithium in mania and maintenance therapy of bipolar disorder. *Journal of Clinical Psychiatry, 61*(Suppl. 9), 35–40.

Bower, B. (1991). Oedipus wrecked. *Science News, 140,* 248–250.

Bower, B. (1993a). Sudden recall. *Science News, 144,* 184–186.

Bower, B. (1993b). Flashbulb memories: Confident blunders. *Science News, 143,* 166–167.

Bower, B. (1994). Babies' brains charge up to speech sounds. *Science News, 146,* 71.

Bower, B. (1996). Creatures in the brain. *Science News, 149,* 234–235.

Bower, B. (1997a). Forbidden flavors. *Science News, 151,* 198–199.

Bower, B. (1997b). Thanks for the memories: Scientists evaluate interviewing tactics for boosting eyewitness recall. *Science News, 151,* 246–247.

Bower, F. (1997). The power of limited thinking. *Science News, 152,* 334–335.

Bower, F. (2000). Building blocks of talk. *Science News, 157,* 344–346.

Bower, G. H. (2000). A brief history of memory research. In E. Tulving & F. M. Craik (Eds.), *The Oxford handbook of memory.* New York: Oxford University Press.

Bowers, K., & Farvolden, P. (1996). Revisiting a century-old Freudian slip—From suggestion disavowed to the truth repressed. *Psychological Bulletin, 119,* 335–380.

Bowlby, J. (1969). *Attachment and loss: Vol. 1. Attachment.* New York: Basic Books.

Boykin, A. W. (1996, August). The case of African-American inner-city schools. In R. Serpell & B. Nsamenang (Convenors), *Basic education for the modern world: Alternatives to Western cultural hegemony.* Quebec City, Quebec, Canada: International Society for the Study of Behavioral Development.

Bradley, C. L. (1997). Generativity-stagnation: Development of a status model. *Developmental Review, 17,* 262–290.

Bradley, S. J., & Zucker, K. J. (1997). Gender identity disorder: A review of the past 10 years. *Journal of the American Academy of Child Adolescence Psychiatry, 36,* 87–88.

Bragg, R. (1995, July 16). In South Carolina, a mother's defense, and life, could hinge on 2 choices. *New York Times.*

Brainerd, C. J., & Poole, D. A. (1997). Long-term survival of children's false memories: A review. *Learning and Individual Differences, 9,* 125–151.

Brannon, L., & Feist, J. (1997). *Health psychology* (3rd ed.). Pacific Grove, CA: Brooks/Cole.

Brauer, M., Judd, C. M., & Gliner, M. D. (1995). The effects of repeated expressions on attitude polarization during group discussions. *Journal of Personality and Social Psychology, 68,* 1014–1029.

Braun, A. R., Balkin, T. J., Wesensten, N. J., Gwadry, F., Carson, R. E., Varga, M., Baldwin, P., Belenky, G., & Herscovitch, P. (1998). Dissociated pattern of activity in visual cortices and their projections during human rapid eye movement sleep. *Science, 279,* 91–95.

Brecher, E. M. (1972). *Licit and illicit drugs.* Boston: Little, Brown.

Brennan, J. (1997, September 28). This 1,800-pound bear is no 800-pound gorilla. *Los Angeles Times/ Calendar.*

Brennan, P. A., & Raine, A. (1997). Biosocial bases of antisocial behavior: Psychophysiological, neurological, and cognitive factors. *Clinical Psychology Review, 17,* 589–604.

Breuer, J., & Freud, S. (1955). Studies on hysteria. In J. Strachey (Ed. and Trans.), *The standard edition of the complete psychological works of Sigmund Freud.* London: Hogarth. (Original work published 1895)

Brewer, J. D. (1991). Hercules, Hippolyte, and the Amazons—or policewomen in the RUC. *British Journal of Sociology, 42,* 231–247.

Brickman, P., Coates, D., & Janoff-Bulman, R. (1978). Lottery winners and accident victims: Is happiness relative? *Journal of Personality and Social Psychology, 36,* 917–927.

Briere, J., & Conte, J. (1993). Self-reported amnesia for abuse in adults molested as children. *Journal of Traumatic Stress, 6,* 21–31.

Briggs, J. L. (1970). *Never in anger: Portrait of an Eskimo family.* Cambridge, MA: Harvard University Press.

Bristol, M. M., Cohen, D. J., Costello, E. J., Denckla, M., Eckberg, T. H., Kallen, R., Kraemer, H. C., Lord, C., Maurer, R., McIlvane, W. J., Minskew, N., Sigman, M., & Spence, M. A. (1996). State of the science in autism: Report to the National Institute of Health. *Journal of Autism and Developmental Disorders, 26,* 121–154.

Brody, H. (2000, August 14). Tapping the power of the placebo. *Newsweek,* 66.

Brody, J. E. (1996, April 16). Vitamin C by the numbers: 200 milligrams gets the nod. *San Diego Union-Tribune.*

Brody, J. E. (1998, January 6). Depression: 2 famous men tell their stories. *San Diego Union-Tribune.*

Brody, J. E. (2000a, April 25). Memories of things that never were. *New York Times,* D8.

Brody, J. E. (2000b, October 17). One-two punch for losing pounds: Exercise and careful diet. *New York Times,* D6.

Brody, N. (1992). *Intelligence.* New York: Academic Press.

Brody, N. (1997). Intelligence, schooling, and society. *American Psychologist, 52,* 1046–1050.

Brody, N. (2000). Theories and measurements of intelligence. In R. J. Sternberg, *Handbook of intelligence.* New York: Cambridge University Press.

Brooks, C. (1994, February 27). Breakdown into the shadows of mental illness. [Special report]. *San Diego Union-Tribune.*

Brooks, C. (1995a, February 27). Shadowlands: Three profiled in mental illness series are striving to improve their conditions. *San Diego Union-Tribune.*

Brooks, C. (1995b, June 5). Rod Steiger is powerful voice for mentally ill. *San Diego Union-Tribune.*

Brown, A. S. (1991). A review of the tip-of-the-tongue experience. *Psychological Bulletin, 109,* 204–223.

Brown, R., & Kulik, J. (1977). Flashbulb memories. *Cognition, 5,* 73–99.

Brown, S. C., & Craik, F. I. M. (2000). Encoding and retrieval of information. In E. Tulving & F. M. Craik (Eds.), *The Oxford handbook of memory.* New York: Oxford University Press.

Brown, S. L. (1994, December). Animals at play. *National Geographic.*

Brown, T. A., Barlow, D. H., & Liebowitz, M. R. (1994). The empirical basis of generalized anxiety disorder. *American Journal of Psychiatry, 151,* 1271–1280.

Brown, W. A. (1997, January). The placebo effect. *Scientific American,* 90–95.

Brownell, K. D., & Rodin, J. (1994). The dieting maelstrom. *American Psychologist, 49,* 781–791.

Brownlee, S. (1997, February 3). The case for frivolity. *U.S. News & World Report.*

Brownlee, S., & Schrof, J. M. (1997, March). The quality of mercy. *U.S. News & World Report.*

Bruer, J. T. (1999). *The myth of the first three years.* New York: Free Press.

Bruner, J. (1997). Celebrating divergence: Piaget and Vygotsky. *Human Development, 40,* 63–73.

Brunner, H. G., Nelen, M., Breakefield, X. O., Ropers, H. H., & van Oost, B. A. (1993). Abnormal behavior associated with a point mutation in the structural gene for monoamine oxidase A. *Science, 262,* 578–580.

Brzezinski, A. (1997). Melatonin in humans. *New England Journal of Medicine, 336,* 186–195.

Brzustowicz, L. M., Hodgkinson, E. A., Chow, E. W. C., Honer, W. G., & Bassett, A. S. (2000). Location of a major susceptibility locus for familial schizophrenia on chromosome 1q21–q22. *Science, 288,* 678–681.

Buchanan, C., Eccles, J., & Becker, J. (1992). Are adolescents the victims of raging hormones? Evidence for activational effects of hormones on moods and behavior at adolescence. *Psychological Bulletin, 111,* 62–107.

Buck, K. J., Metten, P., Belknap, J. K., & Crabbe, J. C. (1997). Quantitative trait loci involved in genetic predisposition to acute alcohol withdrawal in mice. *Journal of Neuroscience, 17,* 3946–3955.

Buck, L. (1999). Cited in J. Travis, Making sense of scents. *Science News, 155,* 236–238.

Buckley, P. (1989). Fifty years after Freud: Dora, the Rat Man, and the Wolf-Man. *American Journal of Psychiatry, 146,* 1394–1403.

Buckout, R. (1980). Nearly 2,000 witnesses can be wrong. *Bulletin of the Psychonomic Society, 16,* 307–310.

Buehler, R., Griffin, D., & Ross, M. (1994). Exploring the "planning fallacy": Why people underestimate their task completion times. *Journal of Personality and Social Psychology, 67,* 366–381.

Bugental, B. B., & Goodnow, J. J. (1998). Socialization processes. In W. Damon & N. Eisenberg (Eds.), *Handbook of child psychology* (5th ed.). New York: John Wiley & Sons.

Buitelaar, J. K., Jan van der Gaag, R., Swaab-Barneveld, H., & Kuiper, M. (1996). Pindolol and methlphenidate in children with attention-deficit hyperactivity disorder. Clinical efficacy and side effects. *Journal of Child Psychology and Psychiatry, 37,* 587–595.

Bunce, S. C., Bernat, E., Wong, P. S., & Shevrin, H. (1999). Further evidence for unconscious learning: Preliminary support for the conditioning of facial EMG to subliminal stimuli. *Journal of Psychiatric Research, 33,* 341–347.

Buonomano, D. V., & Merzenich, M. M. (1995). Temporal information transformed into a spatial code by a neural network with realistic properties. *Science, 267,* 1028–1030.

Burcham, B., Carlson, L., & Milich, R. (1993). Promising school-based practices for students with attention deficit disorder. *Exceptional Children, 60,* 174–180.

Burge, D., Hammen, C., Davila, J., Daley, S. E., Paley, B., Herzberg, D., & Lindberg, N. (1997). Attachment cognitions and college and work functioning two years later in late adolescent women. *Journal of Youth and Adolescence, 26,* 285–301.

Burnette, E. (1994, November). Psychology makes top 10% of country's hottest careers. *Monitor American Psychological Association.*

Burnham, D. (1993). Visual recognition of mother by young infants: Facilitation by speech. *Perception, 22,* 1133–1153.

Buss, D. (1996, August). Cited in B. Azar, Modern mating: Attraction or survival? *APA Monitor,* 31–32.

Buss, D. M. (1994a). *The evolution of desire.* New York: Basic Books.

Buss, D. M. (1994b). Mate preferences in 37 cultures. In W. J. Lonner & R. Malpass (Eds.), *Psychology and culture.* Boston: Allyn & Bacon.

Buss, D. M. (1995). Psychological sex differences. *American Psychologist, 50,* 164–168.

Buss, D. M. (1999). Human nature and individual differences: The evolution of human personality. In L. A. Pervin & O. P. John (Eds.), *Handbook of personality* (2nd ed.). New York: Guilford.

Buss, D. M. (2000). The evolution of happiness. *American Psychologist, 55,* 15–23.

Buss, D. M., Abbott, M., Angleitner, A., Asherian, A., Biaggio, A., Blanco-VillaSenor, A., Bruchon-Schweitzer, M., Ch'u, H. Y., Czapinski, J., DeRaad, B., Ekehammar, B., Fioravanti, M., Georgas, J., Gjerde, P., Guttman, R., Hazan, F., Iwawaki, S., Janakiramaiah, H., Khosroshani, F., Kreitler, S., Lachenicht, L., Lee, M., Liik, K., Little, B., Lohamy, N., Makun, S., Mika, S., Moadel-Shahid, M., Moane, G., Montero, M., Mundy-Casde, A. C., Niit, T., Nsenduluka, E., Peltzer, K., Pienkowski, R., Pirttila-Backman, A., Ponce De Leon, J., Rousseau, J., Runco, M. A., Safir, M. P., Samuels, C., Sanitioso, R., Schweitzer, B., Serpell, R., Smid, N., Spencer, C., Tadinac, M., Todorova, E. N., Troland, K., Van den Brande, L., Van Heck, G., Van Langenhove, L., & Yang, K. S. (1990). International preferences in selecting mates. *Journal of Cross-Cultural Psychology, 21,* 5–47.

Buss, D. M., Haselton, M. G., Shackelford, T. K., Bleske, A. L., & Wakefield, J. C. (1998). Adaptations, explanations, and spandrels. *American Psychologist, 53,* 533–548.

Buss, D. M., & Schmitt, D. P. (1993). Sexual strategies theory: An evolutionary perspective on human mating. *Psychological Review, 100,* 204–232.

Butcher, J. N., Dalhstrom, W. G., Graham, J. R., Tellegen, A. M., & Kaemmer, B. (1989). *MMPI-2: Manual for administration and scoring.* Minneapolis: University of Minnesota Press.

Butler, K. (1994, June 26). A house divided. *Los Angeles Times Magazine.*

Butterworth, B. (1999). A head for figures. *Science, 284,* 928–929.

Byerley, W., & Coon, H. (1995). Strategies to identify genes for schizophrenia. *American Psychiatric Press Review of Psychiatry* (Vol. 14). Washington, DC: American Psychiatric Press.

Byne, W. (1994). The biological evidence challenged. *Scientific American, 270,* 50–55.

Byne, W. (1997). Why we cannot conclude that sexual orientation is primarily a biological phenomenon. *Journal of Homosexuality, 34,* 73–80.

Byrd, K. R. (1994). The narrative reconstructions of incest survivors. *American Psychologist, 49,* 439–440.

Cabeza, R., & Nyberg, L. (1997). Imaging cognition: An empirical review of PET studies with normal subjects. *Journal of Cognitive Neuroscience, 9,* 1–26.

Cacioppo, J. T., Berntson, G. G., Larsen, J. R., Poehlmann, K. M., & Ito, T. A. (2000). The psychophysiology of emotion. In M. Lewis & J. M. Haviland-Jones (Eds.), *Handbook of emotions* (2nd ed., pp. 173–191). New York: Guilford.

Cacioppo, J. T., Klein, D. J., Berntson, G. G., & Hatfield, E. (1993). The psychophysiology of emotion. In M. Lewis & J. M. Haviland (Eds.), *Handbook of emotions.* New York: Guilford Press.

Cacioppo, J. T., & Petty, R. E. (1982). The need for cognition. *Journal of Personality and Social Psychology, 42,* 116–131.

Cacioppo, J. T., Petty, R. E., Feinstein, J. A., & Jarvis, W. B. G. (1996). Dispositional differences in cognitive motivation: The life and times of individuals varying in need for cognition. *Psychological Bulletin, 119,* 197–253.

Cadoret, R. J., Leve, L. D., & Devor, E. (1997). Genetics of aggressive and violent behavior. *Psychiatric Clinics of North America, 20,* 301–322.

Cahill, L., Prins, B., Weber, M., & McGaugh, J. L. (1994). B-adrenergic activation and memory for emotional events. *Nature, 371,* 702–704.

Caldwell, J. C., Orubuloye, I. O., & Caldwell, P. (1997). Male and female circumcision in Africa from a regional to a specific Nigerian examination. *Social Science & Medicine, 44,* 1181–1193.

Callahan, C. M. (2000). Intelligence and giftedness. In R. J. Sternberg, *Handbook of intelligence.* New York: Cambridge University Press.

Calvo, M. G., & Carreiras, M. (1993). Selective influence of test anxiety on reading processes. *British Journal of Psychology, 84,* 375–388.

Camacho, L. M., & Paulus, P. B. (1995). The role of social anxiousness in group brainstorming. *Journal of Personality and Social Psychology, 68,* 1071–1080.

Cameron, J., & Pierce, D. (1994). Reinforcement, reward, and intrinsic motivation: A meta-analysis. *Review of Educational Research, 64,* 363–423.

Camp, G. C. (1994). A longitudinal study of correlates of creativity. *Creativity Research Journal, 7,* 125–144.

Campbell, R. A., & Ramey, C. T. (1990). The relationship between cognitive development, mental test performance, and academic achievement in high-risk students with and without early educational experience. *Intelligence, 14,* 293–308.

Cannon, T. D., Kaprio, J., Lonnqvist, J., Huttunen, M., & Koskenvuo, M. (1998). The genetic epidemiology of schizophrenia in a Finnish twin cohort. *Archives of General Psychiatry, 55,* 67–74.

Caplan, N., Choy, M. H., & Whitmore, J. K. (1992). Indochinese refugee families and academic achievement. *Scientific American, 266,* 36–42.

Caplan, P. (1994, June 5). Cited in A. Japenga, DMS. *Los Angeles Times Magazine.*

Cardon, L. R., Smith, S. D., Fulker, D. W., Kimberling, W. J., Pennington, B. F., & DeFries, J. C. (1994). Quantitative trait locus for reading disability on chromosome 6. *Science, 266,* 276–279.

Carducci, B. J. (1998). *The psychology of personality.* Pacific Grove, CA: Brooks/Cole.

Carducci, B. J., & Zimbardo, P. G. (1995, November/December). Are you shy? *Psychology Today,* 34–40.

Carey, K. B., & Correia, C. J. (1997). Drinking motives predict alcohol-related problems in college students. *Journal of Studies on Alcohol, 58,* 100–185.

**Cariaga, D.** (1995, April 9). The return of the prodigy. *Los Angeles Times/Calendar,* 54–55.

**Carlin, A.** (2000, July 4). Cited in J. Robbins, Virtual reality finds a real place as a medical aid. *New York Times,* D6.

**Carlin, A. S., Hofman, H. G., & Weghorst, S.** (1997). Virtual reality and tactile augmentation in the treatment of spider phobia: A case report. *Behavior Research and Therapy, 35,* 153–158.

**Carlson, J. G., Chemtob, C. M., Rusnak, K., Hedlund, N. L., & Muraoka, M. Y.** (1998). Eye movement desensitization and reprocessing (EDMR) treatment for combat-related posttraumatic stress disorder. *Journal of Traumatic Stress, 11,* 3–24.

**Carlson, J. M.** (1990). Subjective ideological similarity between candidates and supporters: A study of party elites. *Political Psychology, 11,* 485–492.

**Carlson, N. R.** (1998). *Physiology of behavior* (6th ed.). Boston: Allyn & Bacon.

**Carpenter, S.** (2000, February 1). Girl, stressed out. *Los Angeles Times,* E1.

**Carskadon, M.** (2000, March 28). Cited in N. Hellmich, Teen's thing: Losing sleep. *USA Today,* 1A.

**Carskadon, M. A., & Taylor, J. F.** (1997). Public policy and sleep disorders. In M. R. Pressman & W. C. Orr (Eds.), *Understanding sleep: The evaluation and treatment of sleep disorders.* Washington, DC: American Psychological Association.

**Carton, J. S.** (1996). The differential effects of tangible rewards and praise on intrinsic motivation: A comparison of cognitive evaluation theory and operant theory. *Behavior Analyst, 19,* 237–255.

**Cartwright, R.** (1988, July–August). Cited in *Psychology Today.*

**Cartwright, R. D.** (1993). Who needs their dreams? The usefulness of dreams in psychotherapy. *Journal of the American Academy of Psychoanalysis, 21,* 539–547.

**Casey, D. E.** (2000). Antipsychotic standard of care: Redefining the definition of atypical antipsychotics. *Journal of Clinical Psychiatry, 61*(Suppl. 3), 3.

**Caspi, A.** (2000). The child is father of the man: Personality continuities from childhood to adulthood. *Journal of Personality and Social Psychology, 78,* 158–172.

**Caspi, A., & Roberts, B. W.** (1999). Personality continuity and change across the life course. In L. A. Pervin & O. P. John (Eds.), *Handbook of personality* (2nd ed.). New York: Guilford.

**Cattell, H., & Jolley, D. J.** (1995). One hundred cases of suicide in elderly people. *British Journal of Psychiatry, 166,* 451–457.

**Cattell, R. B.** (1943). The description of personality: Basic traits resolved into clusters. *Journal of Abnormal and Social Psychology, 38,* 476–506.

**Cauchon, D.** (1995, December 6). Shock therapy. *USA Today.*

**Cavett, D.** (1992, August 3). Goodbye, darkness. *People.*

**Ceci, S. J.** (2000, April 25). Cited in J. E. Brody, Memories of things that never were. *New York Times,* D8.

**Ceci, S. J., & Bruck, M.** (1995). *Jeopardy in the courtroom: A scientific analysis of children's testimony.* Washington, DC: American Psychological Association.

**Ceci, S. J., & Huffman, M. L. C.** (1997). How suggestible are preschool children? Cognitive and social factors. *Journal of the American Academy of Child and Adolescence Psychiatry, 36,* 948–958.

**Ceci, S. J., Huffman, M. L. C., Smith, E., & Loftus, E.** (1994). Repeatedly thinking about a non-event: Source misattributions among preschoolers. *Consciousness and Cognition, 3,* 388–407.

**Ceci, S. J., Rosenblum, T., de Bruyn, E., & Lee, D. Y.** (1997). A bio-ecological model of intellectual development: Moving beyond h². In R. J. Sternberg & E. Grigorenko (Eds.), *Intelligence, heredity, and environment.* New York: Cambridge University Press.

**Ceniceros, S., & Brown, G. R.** (1998). Acupuncture: A review of its history, theories, and indications. *Southern Medical Journal, 91,* 1121–1125.

**Centers for Disease Control and Prevention.** (1988). CDC recommendations for a plan for the prevention and containment of community clusters. *Monthly Morbidity and Mortality Weekly Reports,* (Suppl. 37), 1–12.

**Centers for Disease Control and Prevention.** (1992, December 18). 1993 revised classification system for HIV infection and expanded surveillance case definition for AIDS among adolescents and adults. *Morbidity and Mortality Weekly Report.*

**Centers for Disease Control and Prevention.** (1997). Update: Trends in AIDS incidence, deaths, and prevalence—United States, 1996. *Journal of the American Medical Association, 277,* 874–875.

**Cerone, D.** (1989, October 22). How to train an 1,800-pound star. *Los Angeles Times/Calendar.*

**Cervone, D.** (1997). Social-cognitive mechanisms and personality coherence: Self-knowledge, situational beliefs, and cross-situational coherence in perceived self-efficacy. *Psychological Science, 8,* 43–50.

**Chaiken, S., & Eagly, A. H.** (1976). Communication modality as a determinant of message persuasiveness and message comprehensibility. *Journal of Personality and Social Psychology, 34,* 605–614.

**Chalmers, D. J.** (1995, December). The puzzle of conscious experience. *Scientific American,* 80–86.

**Chamberlin, J.** (2000, February). Where are all these students coming from? *Monitor on Psychology.*

**Chang, K.** (2000, August 1). Laser eye surgery's turf war. *New York Times,* D1.

**Channouf, A., Canac, D., & Gosset, O.** (2000). Nonspecific effects of subliminal advertising. *European Review of Applied Psychology, 49,* 20–21.

**Chapman, C. R., & Nakamura, Y.** (1999). A passion of the soul: An introduction to pain for consciousness researchers. *Consciousness and Cognition, 8,* 391–422.

**Charney, D. A., & Russell, R. C.** (1994). An overview of sexual harassment. *American Journal of Psychiatry, 151,* 10–17.

**Chasnoff, I.** (1997, December). Cited in B. Azar, Researchers debunk myth of the "crack baby." *APA Monitor.*

**Chaves, J. F.** (1994). Hypnosis in pain management. In J. W. Rhue, S. J. Lynn, & I. Kirsch (Eds.), *Handbook of clinical hypnosis.* Washington, DC: American Psychological Association.

**Chavez, S.** (1994, January 3). Tough stand on attendance pays off at South Gate High. *Los Angeles Times.*

**Chellappah, N. K., Viegnehas, H., Milgrom, P., & Lo, B. L.** (1990). Prevalence of dental anxiety and fear in children in Singapore. *Community Dentistry Oral Epidemiology, 18,* 269–271.

**Chen, G., Li, S., & Jiang, C.** (1986). Clinical studies on neurophysiological and biochemical basis of acupuncture analgesia. *American Journal of Chinese Medicine, 14,* 86–95.

**Chen, J., Chang, S., Duncan, S. A., Okano, H. J., Fishell, G., & Aderem, A.** (1996). Disruption of the MacMARCKS gene prevents cranial neural tube closure and results in anencephaly. *Proceedings of the National Academy of Sciences, 93,* 6275–6279.

**Chen, Y., Mestek, A., Liu, J., Hurley, J. A., & Yu, L.** (1993). Molecular cloning and functional expression of a u-opioid receptor from rat brain. *Molecular Pharmacology, 44,* 8–12.

**Chisholm, A. H.** (1996). Fetal tisssue transplantation for the treatment of Parkinson's disease: A review of the literature. *Journal of Neuroscience Nursing, 28,* 329–338.

**Chokroverty, S.** (2000). *Sleep disorders medicine* (2nd ed.). Boston: Butterworth-Heinemann.

**Chomsky, N.** (1957). *Syntactic structures.* The Hague: Mouton.

**Christensen, D.** (2000). Sobering work: Unraveling alcohol's effects on the developing brain. *Science News, 138,* 28–29.

**Christopher, K.** (2000, September/October). Magnet therapy update: Support for your feet, but little support from science. *Skeptical Inquirer,* 7.

**Chuang, D.** (1998). Cited in J. Travis, Stimulating clue hints how lithium works. *Science News, 153,* 165.

**Chwalisz, K., Diener, E., & Gallagher, D.** (1988). Autonomic arousal feedback and emotional experience: Evidence from the spinal cord injury. *Journal of Personality and Social Psychology, 54,* 820–828.

**Cialdini, R. B.** (2001). *Influence: Science and practice* (4th ed.). New York: Allyn & Bacon.

**Ciarrochi, J. V., Chan, A. Y. C., & Caputi, P.** (2000). A critical evaluation of the emotional intelligence construct. *Personality and Individual Differences, 28,* 539–561.

**Cimons, M.** (1997, September 19). New AIDS cases show decline in U.S. *Los Angeles Times,* A12.

**Cirelli, C., Pompeiano, M., & Tononi, G.** (1996). Neuronal gene expression in the waking state: A role for locus coeruleus. *Science, 274,* 1211–1215.

**Clancy, S. A., Schacter, D. L., McNally, R. J., & Pitman, R. K.** (2000). False recognition in women reporting recovered memories of sexual abuse. *Psychological Science, 11,* 26–31.

**Clark, L. A., Watson, D., & Reynolds, S.** (1995). Diagnosis and classification of psychopathology: Challenges to the current system and future directions. *Annual Review of Psychology, 46,* 121–153.

**Clarke, A. M., & Clarke, A. D. B.** (1989). The later cognitive effects on early intervention. *Intelligence, 13,* 289–297.

**Clay, R. A.** (1997a, April). Is assisted suicide ever a rational choice? *APA Monitor.*

**Clay, R. A.** (1997b, September). Meditation is becoming more mainstream. *APA Monitor.*

**Clay, R. A.** (2000, July/August). The mental/dental connection. *Monitor on Psychology,* 52–53.

**Cleveland, H. H., Jacobson, K. C., Lipinski, J. J., & Rose, D. C.** (2000). Genetic and shared environmental contributions to the relationship between the home environment and child and adolescent achievement. *Intelligence, 28,* 69–86.

**Cloud, J.** (2000, June 5). The lure of ecstary. *Time,* 66.

**Coccaro, E. F., & Kavoussi, R. J.** (1997). Fluoxetine and impulsive aggressive behavior in personality-disordered subjects. *Archives of General Psychiatry, 54,* 1081–1088.

**Coe, W. C.** (1994). Expectations and hypnotherapy. In J. W. Rhue, S. J. Lynn, & I. Kirsch (Eds.), *Handbook of clinical hypnosis.* Washington, DC: American Psychological Association.

**Coffin, J.** (2000, April 6). Cited in K. Thomas, Better reading in the blink of the eye. *USA Today,* 9D.

**Cohen, A.** (1997, September 8). Battle of the binge. *Time.*

**Cohen, B., & Murphy, G. L.** (1984). Models of concepts. *Cognitive Science, 8,* 27–58.

**Cohen, D. B.** (1979). *Sleep and dreaming: Origins, nature and functions.* New York: Pergamon Press.

**Cohen, D. J., & Volkmar, F. R.** (Eds.). (1997). *Handbook of autism and pervasive developmental disorders* (2nd ed.). New York: John Wiley & Sons.

**Cohen, J.** (1994). New fight over fetal tissue grafts. *Science, 263,* 600–601.

**Cohen, J.** (1999). AIDS virus traced to chimp subspecies. *Science, 283,* 772–773.

Cohen, J. (2000). Ground zero: AIDS research in Africa. *Science, 288*, 2150–2153.

Cohen, N. J. (1984). Preserved learning capacity in amnesia: Evidence for multiple memory systems. In L. R. Squire & N. Butters (Eds.), *Neuropsychology of memory.* New York: Guilford Press.

Cohen, S. (1996). Psychological stress, immunity, and upper respiratory infections. *Current Directions in Psychological Science, 5,* 86–89.

Cohen, S., Tyrrell, D. A. J., & Smith, A. P. (1997). Psychological stress in humans and susceptibility to the common cold. In T. W. Miller (Ed.), *Clinical disorders and stressful life events.* Madison, CT: International Universities Press.

Cohen, S., & Williamson, G. M. (1991). Stress and infectious disease in humans. *Psychological Bulletin, 109,* 5–24.

Coie, J. D., & Dodge, K. A. (1998). Aggression and antisocial behavior. In W. Damon & R. M. Lerner (Eds.), *Handbook of child psychology* (Vol. 1). New York: John Wiley & Sons.

Coie, J. D., Lochman, J. E., Terry, R., & Hyman, C. (1992). Predicting early adolescent disorder from childhood aggression and peer rejection. *Journal of Consulting and Clinical Psychology, 60,* 783–792.

Colangelo, N. (1997). The "termites" grow up and grow old. *Contemporary Psychology, 42,* 208–209.

Colapinto, J. (1996, May 30). Rock & roll heroin. *Rolling Stone.*

Cole, K. C. (1997, April 28). Upsetting our sense of self. *Los Angeles Times.*

Collacott, E. A., Zimmerman, J. T., White, D. W., & Rindone, J. P. (2000). Bipolar permanent magnets for the treatment of chronic low back pain. *Journal of the American Medical Association, 283,* 1322–1325.

Collings, S., & King, M. (1994). Ten-year follow-up of 50 patients with bulimia nervosa. *British Journal of Psychiatry, 164,* 80–87.

Collins, A. M., & Quillian, M. R. (1969). Retrieval time from semantic memory. *Journal of Verbal Learning and Verbal Behavior, 8,* 240–247.

Collins, W. A., Maccoby, E. E., Steinberg, L., Hetherington, E. M., & Bornstein, M. H. (2000). Contemporary research on parenting. *American Psychologist, 55,* 218–232.

Colom, R., Juan-Espinosa, M., Abad, F., & Garcia, L. F. (2000). Negligible sex differences in general intelligence. *Intelligence, 28,* 57–68.

Compas, B. E., Hinden, B. R., & Gerhardt, C. A. (1995). Adolescent development: Pathways and processes of risk and resilience. *Annual Review of Psychology, 46,* 265–293.

Conner, A. (2000, March). Classic experiments in social psychology. *APS Observer, 9.*

Connor, L. (1982). In A. J. Marsella & G. M. White (Eds.), *Cultural conceptions of mental health and therapy.* Boston: D. Reidel.

Conway, M. A., Anderson, S. J., Larsen, S. F., Donnelly, C. M., McDaniel, M. A., McClelland, A. G. R., Rawles, R. E., & Logie, R. H. (1994). The formation of flashbulb memories. *Memory and Cognition, 22,* 326–343.

Cook, E., Courchesne, R., Lord, C., Cox, N. J., Lincoln, A., Haas, R., Courchesne, E., & Leventhal, B. L. (1997). Evidence of linkage between the serotonin transporter and autistic disorder. *Molecular Psychiatry, 2,* 247–250.

Cookson, J. (1997). Lithium: Balancing risks and benefits. *British Journal of Psychiatry, 171,* 113–119.

Cooper, R. T. (1999, April 14). Head Start's fresh start. *Los Angeles Times,* B2.

Copeland, L. (1999, December 16). Meet South's new sheriffs. *USA Today,* A1.

Coren, S., & Ward, L. M. (1993). *Sensation and perception* (4th ed.). San Diego: Harcourt Brace Jovanovich.

Cork, L. C., Clarkson, T. B., Jacoby, R. O., Gaertner, D. J., Leary, S. L., Linn, J. M., Pakes, S. P., Ringler, D. H., Strandberg, J. D., & Swindle, D. (1997). The costs of animal research: Origins and options. *Science, 276,* 758–759.

Corrigan, P. W. (2000). Mental health stigma as social attribution: Implications for research methods and attitude change. *Clinical Psychology: Science and Practice, 7,* 48–67.

Cosmides, L., & Tooby, J. (1994). Cited in B. Bower, Roots of reason. *Science News, 145,* 72–75.

Costa, P. T., Jr., & McCrae, R. R. (1995). Solid ground in the wetlands of personality: A reply to Block. *Psychological Bulletin, 117,* 216–220.

Costa, P. T., Jr., & McCrae, R. R. (1997). Longitudinal stability of adult personality. In R. Hogan, J. Johnson, & S. Briggs (Eds.), *Handbook of personality psychology.* New York: Academic Press.

Cottraux, J., Note, I., Albuisson, E., Yao, S. N., Note, B., Mollard, E., Bonasse, F., Jalenaques, I., Guerin, J., & Coudert, A. J. (2000). Cognitive behavior therapy versus supportive therapy in social phobia: A randomized controlled trial. *Psychotherapy and Psychosomatics, 69,* 137–146.

Courchesne, E., Townsend, J., Akshoomoff, N. A., Saiton, O., Yeung-Courchesne, R., Lincoln, A. J., James, H. E., Haas, R. I. T., Schreibman, L., & Lau, L. (1994). Impairment in shifting attention in autistic and cerebellar patients. *Behavioral Neuroscience, 108,* 848–865.

Covington, M. V. (2000). Goal theory, motivation, and school achievement: An integrative review. *Annual Review of Psychology, 51,* 171–200.

Cowley, G. (1994, October 24). Testing the science of intelligence. *Newsweek.*

Cowley, G. (1997, June 30). How to live to 100. *Newsweek.*

Cowley, G. (2000a, January 31). Alzheimer's: Unlocking the mystery. *Newsweek,* 46–51.

Cowley, G. (2000b, April 24). Looking beyond Viagra. *Newsweek,* 77–78.

Cowley, G. (2000c, July 31). Understanding autism. *Newsweek,* 46–55.

Cowley, G., Miller, S., Crandall, R., & Hager, M. (1995, February). RoboDocs and mousecalls. *Newsweek.*

Cowley, G., & Underwood, A. (2000, April 10). A revolution in medicine. *Newsweek,* 58–62.

Coyle, J. T., & Schwarcz, R. (2000). Mind glue: Implications of glial cell biology for psychiatry. *Archives of General Psychiatry, 57,* 90–93.

Coyne, J. C. (1994). Self-reported distress: Analog or ersatz depression? *Psychological Bulletin, 116,* 29–45.

Coyne, J. C., & Whiffen, V. E. (1995). Issues in personality as diathesis for depression: The case of sociotropy—dependency and autonomy—self-criticism. *Psychological Bulletin, 118,* 358–378.

Craik, F. I. M., & Lockhart, R. S. (1972). Levels of processing: A framework for memory research. *Journal of Verbal Learning and Verbal Behavior, 11,* 671–684.

Craik, F. I. M., & Tulving, E. (1975). Depth of processing and the retention of words in episodic memory. *Journal of Experimental Psychology: General, 104,* 268–294.

Cramer, P. (2000). Defense mechanisms in psychology today. *American Psychologist, 55,* 637–646.

Cravatt, B. F., Prospero-Garcia, O., Siuzdak, G., Gilula, N. B., Henriksen, S. J., Boger, D. L., & Lerner, R. A. (1995). Chemical characterization of a family of brain lipids that induce sleep. *Science, 268,* 1506–1509.

Crawford, H. J., Gur, R. C., Skolnick, B., Gur, R. E., & Benson, D. M. (1993). Effects of hypnosis on regional cerebral blood flow during ischemic pain with and without suggested hypnotic analgesia. *International Journal of Psychophysiology, 15,* 181–195.

Cray, D. (2000, July). Incredible shrinking doctors. *Popular Science,* 63–65.

Creed, F. (1993). Stress and psychosomatic disorders. In L. Goldberger & S. Breznitz (Eds.), *Handbook of stress: Theoretical and clinical aspects* (2nd ed.). New York: Free Press.

Crews, F. (1996). The verdict on Freud. *Psychological Science, 7,* 63–68.

Crichton, S. (1995, February). Caught between east and west, Rushdie keeps on. *Newsweek.*

Crick, F. (1994). *The astonishing hypothesis.* New York: Scribner's.

Crick, F., & Koch, C. (1997). The problem of consciousness [Special issue]. *Scientific American,* 19–26.

Crisp, A. H. (1997). Anorexia nervosa as flight from growth: Assessment and treatment based on the model. In D. M. Garner & P. E. Garfinkel (Eds.), *Handbook of treatment for eating disorders* (2nd ed.). New York: Guilford Press.

Croce, C. M. (1996, April 5). Cited in F. Flam, Scientists identify gene that triggers smokers' lung cancer. *San Diego Union-Tribune.*

Cromer, A. (1993). *Uncommon sense: The heretical nature of science.* New York: Oxford University Press.

Cross, S. E., & Madson, L. (1997). Models of the self: Self-construals and gender. *Psychological Bulletin, 122,* 5–37.

Crow, T. J. (1985). The two syndrome concept: Origins and current status. *Schizophrenia Bulletin, 11,* 471–486.

Crowder, R. G. (1992). Eidetic imagery. In L. R. Squire (Ed.), *Encyclopedia of learning and memory.* New York: Macmillan.

Crowe, R. A. (1990). Astrology and the scientific method. *Psychological Reports, 67,* 163–191.

Cruess, D. G., Antoni, M. H., McGregor, B. A., Kilbourn, K. M., Boyers, A. E., Alferi, S. M., Carver, C. S., & Kumar, M. (2000). Cognitive-behavioral stress management reduces serum cortisol by enhancing benefit finding among women being treated for early stage breast cancer. *Psychosomatic Medicine, 62,* 304–308.

Cull, W. L., & Zechmeister, E. B. (1994). The learning ability paradox in adult metamemory research: Where are the metamemory differences between good and poor learners? *Memory & Cognition, 22,* 249–257.

Culp, R. E., Culp, A. M., Osofsky, J. D., & Osofsky, H. J. (1991). Adolescent and older mothers' interaction patterns with their six-month-old infants. *Journal of Adolescence, 14,* 195–200.

Cunningham, M. R., Roberts, A. R., Barbee, A. P., Druen, P. B., & Wu, C. (1995). "Their ideas on beauty are, on the whole, the same as ours": Consistency and variability in the cross-cultural perception of female physical attractiveness. *Journal of Personality and Social Psychology, 68,* 261–279.

Curtiss, S. (1977). *Genie: A psycholinguistic study of a modern-day "wild child."* New York: Academic Press.

Czeisler, C. A. (1994). Cited in R. Nowak, Chronobiologists out of sync over light therapy patents. *Science, 263,* 1217–1218.

Czeisler, C. A., Duffy, J. F., Shanahan, T. L., Brown, E. N., Mitchell, J. F., Rimmer, D. W., Ronda, J. M., Siva, E. J., Allan, J. S., Emens, J. S., Dijk, K., & Kronauer, R. E. (2000). Stability, precision, and near-24-hour period of the human circadian pacemaker. *Science, 284,* 2177–2181.

Czeisler, C. A., Shanahan, T. L., Klerman, E. B., Martens, H., Brotman, D. J., Emens, J. S., Klein, T., & Rizzo, J. F. (1995). Suppression of melatonin secretion in some blind patients by exposure to bright light. *New England Journal of Medicine, 332,* 6–11.

**Dadds, M. R., Bovbjerg, D. H., Redd, W. H., & Cutmore, T. R. H.** (1997). Imagery in human classical conditioning. *Psychological Bulletin, 122,* 80–103.

**Dahmer, L.** (1994). *A father's story.* New York: Morrow.

**Dajer, T.** (2000, May). Breathless. *Discover,* 34–35

**Dalgard, O. S., Bjork, S., & Tambs, K.** (1995). Social support, negative life events and mental health. *British Journal of Psychiatry, 166,* 29–34.

**Dallos, P., & Evans, B. N.** (1995). High-frequency motility of outer hair cells and the cochlear amplifier. *Science, 267,* 2006–2010.

**Dalto, C. A., Ossoff, E. P., & Pollack, R. B.** (1994). Processes underlying reactions to a campaign speech: Cognition, affect, and voter concern. *Journal of Social Behavior and Personality, 9,* 701–713.

**Damasio, A.** (1999, October 19). Cited in S. Blakeslee, Brain damage during infancy stunts moral learning, study finds. *Los Angeles Times,* A1.

**Damasio, A.** (2000, May 7). Cited in A. Star, What feelings feel like. *New York Times Magazine,* 50.

**Damasio, A. R.** (1999, December). How the brain creates the mind. *Scientific American,* 112–117.

**Damasio, H., Brabowski, T., Frank, R., Galaburda, A. M., & Damasio, A. R.** (1994). The return of Phineas Gage: Clues about the brain from the skull of a famous patient. *Science, 264,* 1102–1105.

**Damon, W.** (1999, August). The moral development of children. *Scientific American,* 73–78.

**Dandoy, A. C., & Goldstein, A. G.** (1990). The use of cognitive appraisal to reduce stress reactions: A replication. *Journal of Social Behavior and Personality, 5,* 275–285.

**Daniel, M. H.** (1997). Intelligence testing. *American Psychologist, 52,* 1038–1045.

**Daniszewski, J.** (1997, June 25). Female circumcision ban nullified. *Los Angeles Times,* A4.

**Daniszewski, J.** (1999, January 5). Egypt bets on school for girls. *Los Angeles Times,* A1.

**Darling, J.** (1997, March 29). Drug war appears to make little dent in supply. *Los Angeles Times.*

**Darwin, C.** (1859). *The origin of species by means of natural selection or the preservation of favored races in the struggle for life.* London: John Murray.

**Darwin, C.** (1965). *The expression of the emotions in man and animals.* Chicago: University of Chicago Press. (Original work published 1872)

**Davidson, J. E., & Downing, C. L.** (2000) Contemporary models of intelligence. In R. J. Sternberg, *Handbook of intelligence.* New York: Cambridge University Press.

**Davidson, J. R. T.** (1994). International advances in the treatment of social phobia. *Journal of Clinical Psychiatry, 55,* 123–129.

**Davidson, J. R. T., Tupler, L. A., & Potts, N. L. S.** (1994). Treatment of social phobia with clonazepam and placebo. *Journal of Clinical Psychopharmacology, 13,* 423–428.

**Davidson, L., & McGlashan, T. H.** (1997). The varied outcomes of schizophrenia. *Canadian Journal of Psychiatry, 42,* 34–43.

**Davies, I. R. L., & Corbett, G. G.** (1997). A cross-cultural study of colour grouping: Evidence for weak linguistic relativity. *British Journal of Psychology, 88,* 493–517.

**Davis, J. L., & Petretic-Jackson, P. A.** (2000). The impact of child sexual abuse on adult interpersonal functioning: A review and synthesis of the empirical literature. *Aggression and Violent Behavior, 5,* 291–328.

**Davis, M. C., Matthews, K. A., & Twamley, E. W.** (1999). Is life more difficult on Mars or Venus? A meta-analytic review of sex differences in major and minor life events. *Annals of Behavioral Medicine, 21,* 83–97.

**Davison, G. C., & Neale, J. M.** (1990). *Abnormal psychology* (3rd ed.). New York: Wiley.

**Davison, G. C., & Neale, J. M.** (1994). *Abnormal psychology* (6th ed.). New York: Wiley.

**Dawes, R. M.** (1994). *House of cards.* New York: Free Press.

**Dawood, K., Pillard, R. C., Horvath, C., Revelle, W., & Bailey, J. M.** (2000). Familial aspects of male homosexuality. *Archives of Sexual Behavior, 29,* 155–163.

**Dawson, D. D.** (1996). Cited in B. Bower, Alcoholics synonymous. *Science News, 151,* 62–63.

**Deaconson, R. F., O'Hair, D. P., Levy, M. R., Lee, M. B. F., Schuenerman, A. L., & Condon, R. E.** (1988). Sleep deprivation and resident performance. *Journal of the American Medical Association, 260,* 1721–1727.

**DeAngelis, T.** (1966, March). Women's contributions large; recognition isn't. *Monitor American Psychological Association.*

**DeAngelis, T.** (1994, February). People's drug of choice offers potent side effects. *APA Monitor.*

**Deater-Deckard, K., & Dodge, K. A.** (1997). Externalizing behavior problems and discipline revisited: Nonlinear effects and variation by culture, context, and gender. *Psychological Inquiry, 8,* 161–175.

**Deaux, K., Dane, F. C., Wrightsman, L. S., & Sigelman, C. K.** (1993). *Social psychology* (6th ed.). Pacific Grove, CA: Brooks/Cole.

**DeCarvalho, R. J.** (1990). A history of the "Third Force" in psychology. *Journal of Humanistic Psychology, 30,* 22–44.

**deCharms, R.** (1980). The origins of competence and achievement motivation in personal causation. In L. J. Fyans, Jr. (Ed.), *Achievement motivation.* New York: Plenum Press.

**Deci, E. L., Koestner, R., & Ryan, R. M.** (1999). A meta-analytic review of experiments examining the effects of extrinsic rewards on intrinsic motivation. *Psychological Bulletin, 125,* 627–668.

**Deci, E. L., & Ryan, R. M.** (1985). *Intrinsic motivation and self-determination in human behavior.* New York: Plenum Press.

**DeCurtis, A.** (1994, June 2). Kurt Cobain, 1967–1994. *Rolling Stone.*

**Deffenbacher, J. L., Dahlen, E. R., Lynch, R. S., Morris, C. D., & Gowensmith, W. N.** (2000). An application of Beck's cognitive therapy to general anger reduction. *Cognitive Therapy and Research, 24,* 689–697.

**DeGrandpre, R. J.** (2000). A science of meaning. *American Psychologist, 55,* 721–739.

**Dehaene-Lambertz, G., & Dehaene, S.** (1994). Cited in B. Bower, Babies' brains charge up to speech sounds. *Science News, 146,* 71.

**Della Selva, P. C.** (1996). *Intensive short-term dynamic psychotherapy: Theory and technique.* New York: Wiley.

**Dement, W. C.** (1999). *The promise of sleep.* New York: Random House.

**Dement, W. C., & Kleitman, N.** (1957). The relation of eye movements during sleep to dream activity: An objective method for the study of dreaming. *Journal of Experimental Psychology, 53,* 339–346.

**Dennerstein, L., Dudley, E., & Burger, H.** (1997). Well-being and the menopausal transition. *Journal of Psychosomatic Obstetrics and Gynecology, 18,* 95–101.

**Deregowski, J. B.** (1980). *Illusions, patterns and pictures: A cross-cultural perspective.* Orlando, FL: Academic Press.

**de Rivera, J.** (1997). The construction of false memory syndrome: The experience of retractors. *Psychological Inquiry, 8,* 271–292.

**DeRubeis, R. J., & Crits-Christoph, P.** (1998). Empirically supported individual and group psychological treatments for adult mental disorders. *Journal of Consulting and Clinical Psychology, 66,* 37–52.

**Detterman, D. K., & Thompson, L. A.** (1997). What is so special about special education? *American Psychologist, 52,* 1082–1090.

**Deutsch, G., & Halsey, J. H., Jr.** (1991). Cortical blood flow indicates frontal asymmetries dominate in males but not in females during task performance. *Journal of Cerebral Blood Flow and Metabolism, 11,* S787.

**Devine, P. G., Hamilton, D. L., & Ostrom, T. M.** (Eds.). (1994). *Social cognition: Impact on social psychology.* New York: Academic Press.

**Diamond, J.** (1994, November). Race without color. *Discover.*

**Diamond, M., & Sigmundson, H. K.** (1997). Sex reassignment at birth. *Archives of Pediatric Adolescent Medicine, 151,* 298–304.

**Diener, E., & Diener, C.** (1996). Most people are happy. *Psychological Science, 7,* 181–185.

**Dienes, Z., & Perner, J.** (1999). A theory of implicit and explicit knowledge. *Behavioral and Brain Science, 22,* 735–808.

**Digman, J. M.** (1997). Higher-order factors of the Big Five. *Journal of Personality and Social Psychology, 73,* 1246–1256.

**Dimberg, U., & Ohman, A.** (1996). Behold the wrath: Psychophysiological responses to facial stimuli. *Motivation and Emotion, 20,* 149–182.

**Dimberg, U., Thunberg, M., & Elmehed, K.** (2000). Unconscious facial reactions to emotional facial expressions. *Psychological Science, 11,* 86–89.

**Dinh, K. T., Sarason, I. G., Peterson, A. V., & Onstad, L. E.** (1995). Children's perceptions of smokers and nonsmokers: A longitudinal study. *Health Psychology, 14,* 32–40.

**Dinsmore, J. H.** (2000). Cited in N. Seppa, Pig-cell grafts ease symptoms of Parkinson's. *Science News, 157,* 197.

**Dion, K. K., Berscheid, E., & Walster, E.** (1972). What is beautiful is good. *Journal of Personality and Social Psychology, 24,* 285–290.

**Dixon, W. A., & Reid, J. K.** (2000). Positive life events as a moderator of stress-related depressive symptoms. *Journal of Counseling & Development, 78,* 343–347.

**Dobelle, W.** (2000, January 17). Cited in M. Ritter, Camera wired to brain provides some useful vision for blind man. *San Diego Union-Tribune,* A-6.

**Dobson, K. S., & Khatri, N.** (2000). Cognitive therapy: Looking backward, looking forward. *Journal of Clinical Psychology, 56,* 907–923.

**Docherty, J. P., & Streeter, M. J.** (1995). Advances in psychotherapy research. *Current Opinion in Psychiatry, 8,* 145–149.

**Dodes, J. E.** (1997, January–February). The mysterious placebo. *Skeptical Inquirer.*

**Dolan, M.** (1995a, February 11). When the mind's eye blinks. *Los Angeles Times.*

**Dolan, M.** (1995b, August 1). Justices rule for adoptive parents of San Diego boy. *Los Angeles Times.*

**Dollard, J., Doob, L. W., Miller, N. E., Mower, O. H., & Sears, R. R.** (1939). *Frustration and aggression.* New Haven, CT: Yale University Press.

**Domhoff, G. W.** (1999). Drawing theoretical implications from descriptive empirical findings on dream content. *Dreaming, 9,* 201–210.

**Domino, G.** (1994). Assessment of creativity with the ACL: An empirical comparison of four scales. *Creativity Research Journal, 7,* 21–33.

**Domjan, M.** (1998). *The principles of learning and behavior* (4th ed.). Pacific Grove, CA: Brooks/Cole.

Domjan, M., & Purdy, J. E. (1995). Animal research in psychology. *American Psychologist, 50,* 496–503.

Donker, F. J. S., Breteler, M. H. M., & van der Staak, C. P. F. (2000). Assessment of hostility in patients with coronary heart disease. *Journal of Personality Assessment, 75,* 158–177.

Dougher, M. J., & Hackbert, L. (2000). Establishing operations, cognitions, and emotion. *Behavior Analyst, 23,* 11–24.

Doupe, A. J. (1996). Plasticity of a different feather. *Science, 274,* 1851–1853.

Dowd, E. T. (1994). Cognitive-developmental hypnotherapy. In J. W. Rhue, S. J. Lynn, & I. Kirsch (Eds.), *Handbook of clinical hypnosis.* Washington, DC: American Psychological Association.

Dowling, C. G. (2000, August, 14). Mistaken identity. *People,* 50–55.

Downey, K. K., Stelson, F. W., Pomerleau, O. F., & Giordani, B. (1997). Adult attention deficit hyperactivity disorder: Psychological test profiles in a clinical population. *Journal of Nervous and Mental Disease, 185,* 32–38.

Doyle, R. P. (1994). *Books challenged or banned in 1993–1994.* Chicago: American Library Association.

Drevets, W. C., Price, J. L., Simpson, J. R., Jr., Todd, R. D., Reich, T., Vannier, M., & Raiche, M. E. (1997). Subgenual prefrontal cortex abnormalities in mood disorders. *Nature, 386,* 824–827.

Drewnowski, A. (1997). Cited in K. Fackelmann, The bitter truth. *Science News, 152,* 24–25.

Driver, J., & Baylis, G. C. (1996). Edge-assignment and figure-ground segmentation in short-term visual matching. *Cognitive Psychology, 31,* 248–306.

Drummond, S. P. A. (2000). Cited in B. Bower, Sleepyheads' brains veer from restful path. *Science News, 157,* 103.

DuBois, D. L., Tevendale, H. D., Burk-Braxton, C., Swenson, L. P., & Hardesty, J. L. (2000). Self-system influences during early adolescence: Investigation of an integrative model. *Journal of Early Adolescence, 20,* 12–43.

Duncan, J., Seitz, R. J., Kolodny, J., Bor, D., Herzog, H., Ahmed, A., Newell, F. N., & Emslie, H. (2000). A neural basis for general intelligence. *Science, 289,* 457–460.

Dunnerstein, L., Dudley, E., & Burger, H. Well-being and the menopausal transition. *Journal of Psychosomatic Obstetrics and Gynecology, 18,* 95–101.

DuPaul, G. J., & Eckert, T. L. (1997). The effects of school-based interventions for attention deficit hyperactivity disorder: A meta-analysis. *School Psychology Review, 26,* 5–27.

Durso, F. T., Rea, C. B., & Dayton, T. (1994). Graph-theoretic confirmation of restructuring during insight. *Psychological Science, 5,* 94–98.

Duyme, M. (1999). Cited in B. Bower, Kids adopted late reap IQ increases. *Science News, 156,* 54–55.

Dykman, B. M., Abramson, L. Y., Alloy, L. B., & Hartlage, S. (1989). Processing of ambiguous and unambiguous feedback by depressed and nondepressed college students: Schematic biases and their implications for depressive realism. *Journal of Personality and Social Psychology, 56,* 431–445.

Eagle, M. N. (2000). A critical evaluation of current conceptions of transference and countertransference. *Psychoanalytic Psychology, 17,* 24–37.

Eagly, A. H. (1995a). The science and politics of comparing women and men. *American Psychologist, 50,* 145–158.

Eagly, A. H. (1995b). Reflections on the commenters' views. *American Psychologist, 50,* 169–171.

Eagly, A. H. (1997). Sex differences in social behavior: Comparing social role theory and evolutionary psychology. *American Psychologist, 52,* 1303–1382.

Eagly, A. H., Ashmore, R. D., Makhijani, M. G., & Longo, C. C. (1991). What is beautiful is good, but . . . : A meta-analytic review of research on the physical attractiveness stereotype. *Psychological Bulletin, 110,* 109–128.

Eagly, A. H., Mladinic, A., & Otto, S. (1994). Cognitive and affective bases of attitudes toward social groups and social policies. *Journal of Experimental Social Psychology, 30,* 113–137.

Eagly, A. H., Wood, W., & Diekman, A. B. (2000). Social role theory of sex differences and similarities: A current appraisal. In T. Eckes & H. M. Trautner, (Eds.), *The developmental social psychology of gender.* Mahwah, NJ: Lawrence Erlbaum.

Eaton, M. J., & Dembo, M. H. (1997). Differences in the motivational beliefs of Asian American and non-Asian students. *Journal of Educational Psychology, 89,* 433–440.

Eaves, L., Silberg, J., Hewitt, J. K., Meyer, J., Rutter, M., Simonoff, E., Neale, M., & Pickles, A. (1993). Genes, personality, and psychopathology: A latent class analysis of liability to symptoms of attention-deficit hyperactivity disorder in twins. In R. Plomin & G. E. McClearn (Eds.), *Nature, nurture and psychology.* Washington, DC: American Psychological Association.

Ebbinghaus, H. (1913). *Memory: A contribution to experimental psychology* (H. A. Ruger C. & E. Bussenius, Trans.). New York: Teachers College Press. (Original work published 1885)

Eberhardt, J. L., & Randall, J. L. (1997). The essential notion of race. *Psychological Science, 8,* 198–203.

Eckensberger, L. H. (1994). Moral development and its measurement across cultures. In W. J. Lonner & R. Malpass (Eds.), *Psychology and culture.* Boston: Allyn & Bacon.

Eckes, T., & Trautner, H. M. (2000). *The developmental social psychology of gender.* Mahwah, NJ: Lawrence Erlbaum.

Eddings, J. (1994, December 26). Atlanta's new top cop makes her mark. *U.S. News & World Report.*

Edwards, R. (1995, January). Is hyperactivity label applied too frequently? *APA Monitor.*

Egan, T. (1998, June 14). From adolescent angst to shooting up schools. *New York Times.*

Egan, T. (1999a, February 28). The war on crack retreats, still taking prisoners. *New York Times,* 1.

Egan, T. (1999b, June 25). In the war against drugs, treatment is proving a winner. *San Diego Union-Tribune,* E14.

Egan, V., Chiswick, A., Santosh, C., Naidu, K., Rimmington, J. E., & Best, J. K. (1994). Size isn't everything: A study of brain volume, intelligence and auditory evoked potentials. *Personality and Individual Differences, 17,* 357–367.

Eibl-Eibesfeldt, I. (1973). The expressive behavior of the deaf-and-blind-born. In M. von Cranach & I. Vine (Eds.), *Social communication and movement.* San Diego, CA: Academic Press.

Eich, E. (1995). Searching for mood-dependent memory. *Psychological Science, 6,* 67–75.

Eich, E., Macaulay, D., Loewenstein, R. J., & Dihle, P. H. (1997). Memory, amnesia, and dissociative identity disorder. *Psychological Science, 8,* 417–422.

Eichenbaum, H. (1993). Thinking about brain cell assemblies? *Science, 261,* 993–994.

Eichenbaum, H. (1997a). Declarative memory: Insights from cognitive neurobiology. *Annual Review of Psychology, 48,* 547–572.

Eichenbaum, H. (1997b). How does the brain organize memories? *Science, 277,* 330–332.

Eisen, M. R. (1994). Psychoanalytic and psychodynamic models of hypnoanalysis. In J. W. Rhue, S. J. Lynn, & I. Kirsch (Eds.), *Handbook of clinical hypnosis.* Washington, DC: American Psychological Association.

Eisenberger, R., & Armeli, S. (1997). Can salient reward increase creative performance without reducing intrinsic creative interest? *Journal of Personality and Social Psychology, 72,* 652–663.

Eisenberger, R., & Cameron, J. (1996). Detrimental effects of reward: Reality or myth? *American Psychologist, 51,* 1153–1166.

Eisenberger, R., Pierce, W. D., & Cameron, J. (1999). Effects of reward on intrinsic motivation—negative, neutral, and positive: Comment on Deci, Koestner, and Ryan (1999). *Psychological Bulletin, 125,* 677–691.

Ekman, P. (1993). Facial expression and emotion. *American Psychologist, 48,* 384–392.

Ekman, P. (1994). Strong evidence for universals in facial expressions: A reply to Russell's mistaken critique. *Psychological Bulletin, 115,* 268–287.

Ekman, P., & Davidson, R. J. (1993). Voluntary smiling changes regional brain activity. *Psychological Science, 4,* 342–345.

Ekman, P., & Friesen, W. V. (1969). The repertoire of nonverbal behavior: Categories, origins, usage, and coding. *Semiotica, 1,* 49–98.

Elias, M. (1989, August 9). With guidance, a child can control negative traits. *USA Today.*

Elkin, I., Shea, M. T., Watkins, J. T., Imber, S. D., Sotsky, S. M., Collins, J. F., Glass, D. R., Pilkonis, P. A., Leber, W. R., Docherty, J. P., Fiester, S. J., & Parloff, M. B. (1989). NIMH treatment of depression collaborative research program: 1. General effectiveness of treatments. *Archives of General Psychiatry, 46,* 971–982.

Elkind, D. (1978). Understanding the young adolescent. *Adolescence, 13,* 127–134.

Elkins, D. N. (2000). Old Saybrook I and II: The visioning and re-visioning of humanistic psychology. *Journal of Humanistic Psychology, 40,* 119–127.

Elkins, I. J., Iacono, W. G., Doyle, A. E., & McGue, M. (1997). Characteristics associated with the persistence of antisocial behavior: Results from recent longitudinal research. *Aggression and Violent Behavior, 2,* 101–124.

Ellason, J. W., & Ross, C. A. (1997). Two-year follow-up of inpatients with dissociative identity disorder. *American Journal of Psychiatry, 154,* 832–839.

Elliott, D. (1995, March 20). The fat of the land. *Newsweek.*

Ellis, A. (1997). Extending the goals of behavior therapy and of cognitive behavior therapy. *Behavior Therapy, 28,* 333–339.

Ellison, P. A., Govern, J. M., Petri, H. L., & Figler, M. H. (1995). Anonymity and aggressive driving behavior. *Journal of Social Behavior and Personality, 10,* 265–272.

Ellsworth, P. C. (1994a). William James and emotion: Is a century of fame worth a century of misunderstanding? *Psychological Review, 101,* 222–229.

Ellsworth, P. C. (1994b). Sense, culture, and sensibility. In S. Kitayama & H. R. Markus (Eds.), *Emotion and culture.* Washington, DC: American Psychological Association.

Elmer-Dewitt, P. (1997, January 6). Turning the tide. *Time.*

Emery, R. E., & Laumann-Billings, L. (1998). An overview of the nature, causes, and consequences of abusive family relationships. *American Psychologist, 53,* 121–135.

Emmelkamp, P. M. G., & van Oppen, P. (1994). Anxiety disorders. In V. B. Van Hasselt & M. Hersen (Eds.), *Advanced abnormal psychology.* New York: Plenum Press.

Ende, G., Braus, D. F., Walter, S., Weber-Fahr, W., & Henn, R. A. (2000). The hippocampus in patients treated with electroconvulsive therapy. *Archives of General Psychiatry, 57,* 937–943.

**Endler, N. S., Kantor, L., & Parker, J. D. A.** (1994). State-trait coping, state-trait anxiety and academic performance. *Personality and Individual Differences, 16,* 663–670.

**Ennett, S. T., Rosenbaum, D. P., Flewelling, R. L., Bieler, G. S., Ringwalt, C. L., & Bailey, S. L.** (1994). Long-term evaluation of drug abuse resistance education. *Addictive Behaviors, 19,* 113–125.

**Epley, N., Savitsky, K., & Kachelski, R. A.** (1999, September/October). What every skeptic should know about subliminal persuasion. *Skeptical Inquirer,* 40–45.

**Epstein, L. H., Valoski, A. M., Vara, L. S., McCurley, J., Wisniewski, L., Kalarchian, M. A., Klein, K. R., & Shrager, L. R.** (1995). Effects of decreasing sedentary behavior and increasing activity on weight change in obese children. *Health Psychology, 14,* 109–115.

**Erickson, J. S.** (1994). The use of hypnosis in anesthesia: A master class commentary. *International Journal of Clinical and Experimental Hypnosis, 42,* 8–12.

**Erickson, M. H.** (1980). Hypnosis: A general review. In E. L. Rossie (Ed.), *The collected papers of Milton H. Erickson on hypnosis* (Vol. 30). New York: Irvington. (Original work published 1941)

**Erikson, E. H.** (1963). *Childhood and society.* New York: Norton.

**Erikson, E. H.** (1982). *The life cycle completed: Review.* New York: Norton.

**Eron, L. D.** (1990). Understanding aggression. *Bulletin of the International Society for Research on Aggression, 12,* 5–9.

**Eron, L. D., Huesmann, L. R., Dubow, E., Romanoff, R., & Yarmel, P. W.** (1987). Aggression and its correlates over 22 years. In D. H. Crowell, I. M. Evans, & C. R. O'Donnell (Eds.), *Childhood aggression and violence: Sources of influence, prevention, and control.* New York: Plenum Press.

**Espy, K. A., Riese, M. L., & Francis, D. J.** (1997). Neurobehavior in preterm neonates exposed to cocaine, alcohol, and tobacco. *Infant Behavior and Development, 20,* 297–309.

**Estevez, A., & Calvo, M. G.** (2000). Working memory capacity and time course of predictive inferences. *Memory, 8,* 51–61.

**Estrich, S.** (1998, June 25). Staring up close at eyeball surgery. *USA Today,* 15A.

**Evans, J.** (1993). The cognitive psychology of reasoning: An introduction. *Quarterly Journal of Experimental Psychology, 46A,* 561–567.

**Evans, R. B.** (1999, December). A century of psychology. *Monitor on Psychology.*

**Evans, W.** (2000, October 17). Cited in J. E. Brody, One-two punch for losing pounds: Exercise and careful diet. *New York Times,* D6.

**Everson, C. A.** (1997). Sleep deprivation and the immune system. In M. R. Pressman & W. C. Orr (Eds.), *Understanding sleep: The evaluation and treatment of sleep disorders.* Washington, DC: American Psychological Association.

**Everson, H. T., Smodlaka, I., & Tobias, S.** (1994). Exploring the relationship of test anxiety and meta-cognition on reading test performance: A cognitive analysis. *Anxiety, Stress, and Coping, 7,* 85–96.

**Eysenck, H. J.** (1994). The outcome problem in psychotherapy: What have we learned? *Behaviour Research and Therapy, 32,* 477–495.

**Fackelmann, K. A.** (1993). Marijuana and the brain. *Science News, 143,* 88–94.

**Fackelmann, K. A.** (1995a). Forever smart: Does estrogen enhance memory? *Science News, 147,* 74–75.

**Fackelmann, K. A.** (1995b). Staying alive: Scientists study people who outwit the AIDS virus. *Science News, 147,* 172–174.

**Fackelmann, K. A.** (1997a). Marijuana on trial. *Science News, 151,* 178–179.

**Fackelmann, K. A.** (1997b). The bitter truth. *Science News, 152,* 24–25.

**Fagot, B. I., Rodgers, C. S., & Leinbach, M. D.** (2000). Theories of gender socialization. In T. Eckes & H. M. Trautner (Eds.), *The developmental social psychology of gender.* Mahwah, NJ: Lawrence Erlbaum.

**Fahy, T. A.** (1988). The diagnosis of multiple personality disorder: A critical review. *British Journal of Psychiatry, 153,* 597–606.

**Fairburn, C. G., Welch, S. L., Doll, H. A., Davies, B. A., & O'Connor, M. E.** (1997). Risk factors for bulimia nervosa. *Archives of General Psychiatry, 54,* 509–517.

**Farb, P., & Armelagos, G.** (1980). *Consuming passions.* Boston: Houghton Mifflin.

**Farber, B. A.** (2000a). Introduction: Understanding and treating burnout in a changing culture. *Journal of Clinical Psychology/In Session, 56,* 589–594.

**Farber, B. A.** (2000b). Treatment strategies for different types of teacher burnout. *Journal of Clinical Psychology/In Session, 56,* 675–689.

**Farley, C. J.** (2000, June 5). Rave new world. *Time.*

**Fauci, A.** (2000, July 12). Cited in S. Sternberg, Break from HIV drugs strengthens immune system. *USA Today,* 10D.

**Fava, M., & Kaji, J.** (1994). Continuation and maintenance treatments of major depressive disorder. *Psychiatric Annals, 24,* 281–290.

**Favell, J. E., Azrin, N. H., Baumeister, A. A., Carr, E. G., Dorsey, M. F., Forehand, R., Foxx, R. M., Lovaas, O. I., Rincover, A., Risley, T. R., Romanczyk, R. G., Russo, D. C., Schroeder, S. R., & Solnick, J. V.** (1982). The treatment of self-injurious behavior. *Behavior Therapy, 13,* 529–554.

**Fechner, G. T.** (1860). *Elemente der psychophysik* (Vol. 1). Leipzig: Brietkopf & Marterl. (H. E. Alder, D. H. Howes, & E. G. Boring, Trans.). New York: Holt, Rinehart & Winston.

**Feder, L.** (1987). The cold reading of writing. *Skeptical Inquirer, 11,* 346–348.

**Federman, D. D.** (1994). Life without estrogen. *New England Journal of Medicine, 331,* 1088–1089.

**Feingold, B. R.** (1975). Hyperkinesis and learning disabilities linked to artificial food flavors and colors. *American Journal of Nursing, 75,* 797–803.

**Feng, A. S., & Ratnam, R.** (2000). Neural basis of hearing in real-world situations. *Annual Review of Psychology, 51,* 699–725.

**Fenly, L.** (1996, August 4). Computer technology can virtually wipe out phobias. *San Diego Union-Tribune,* E-1.

**Fernald, A.** (1992). Human maternal vocalizations to infants as biologically relevant signals: An evolutionary perspective. In J. H. Barkow, L. Cosmides, & J. Tooby (Eds.), *The adapted mind: Evolutionary psychology and the generation of culture.* New York: Oxford University Press.

**Ferrari, J. R.** (1994). Dysfunctional procrastination and its relationship with self-esteem, interpersonal dependency, and self-defeating behaviors. *Personality and Individual Differences, 17,* 673–679.

**Ferrari, J. R., McCown, W., & Johnson, J.** (1997). *Procrastination and task avoidance: Theory, research, and treatment.* New York: Plenum Press.

**Ferrari, J. R., & Tice, D. M.** (2000). Procrastination as a self-handicap for men and women: A task-avoidance strategy in a laboratory setting. *Journal of Research in Personality, 34,* 73–83.

**Ferster, D., & Spruston, N.** (1995). Cracking the neuronal code. *Science, 270,* 756–757.

**Feske, U., & Goldstein, A. J.** (1997). Eye movement desensitization and reprocessing treatment for panic disorder: A controlled outcome and partial dismantling study. *Journal of Consulting and Clinical Psychology, 65,* 1026–1035.

**Festinger, L.** (1954). A theory of social comparison processes. *Human Relations, 7,* 117–140.

**Festinger, L.** (1957). *A theory of cognitive dissonance.* Palo Alto, CA: Stanford University Press.

**Festinger, L., & Carlsmith, J. M.** (1959). Cognitive consequences of forced compliance. *Journal of Abnormal and Social Psychology, 58,* 203–210.

**Fiez, J. A., & Petersen, S. E.** (1993). PET as part of an interdisciplinary approach to understanding processes involved in reading. *Psychological Science, 4,* 287–293.

**Finch, C. E., & Tanzi, R. E.** (1997). Genetics of aging. *Science, 278,* 407–411.

**Fineman, M., & Pyes, C.** (1996, June 6). Cocaine traffic to U.S. finds holes in high-tech "fence." *Los Angeles Times.*

**Finke, R. A.** (1993). Mental imagery and creative discovery. In B. Roskos-Ewoldsen, M. J. Intons-Peterson, & R. E. Anderson (Eds.), *Imagery, creativity, and discovery: A cognitive perspective.* Amsterdam: North Holland.

**Finn, J. D., & Rock, D. A.** (1997). Academic success among students at risk for school failure. *Journal of Applied Psychology, 82,* 221–234.

**Firestein, S., Breer, H., & Greer, C. A.** (1996). Olfaction: What's new in the nose. *Journal of Neurobiology, 30,* 1–2.

**Fisch, G. S., Simensen, R., Tarleton, J., Chalifoux, M., Holden, J. J. A., Carpenter, N., Howard-Peebles, P. N., & Maddalena, A.** (1996). Longitudinal study of cognitive abilities and adaptive behavior levels in fragile X males: A prospective multicenter analysis. *American Journal of Medical Genetics, 64,* 356–361.

**Fischbach, G. D.** (1992). Mind and brain. *Scientific American, 267,* 48–57.

**Fischer, J. S.,** (2000, January 24). Taking the shock out of electroshock. *U.S. News & World Report,* 46.

**Fisher, C. B., & Fryberg, D.** (1994). Participant partners. *American Psychologist, 49,* 417–427.

**Fisher, L.** (1995, October 16). Tested by fire. *People.*

**Fisher, R. P., & Geiselman, R. E.** (1992). *Memory-enhancing techniques for investigative interviewing.* Springfield, IL: Charles C Thomas.

**Fisher, R. P., & McCauley, M. R.** (1994). Improving eyewitness memory with the cognitive interview. In D. Ross, J. Read, & M. Toglia (Eds.), *Eyewitness memory: Current trends and developments.* New York: Springer-Verlag.

**Fishman, D. B., & Franks, C. M.** (1997). The conceptual evolution of behavior therapy. In P. L. Wachtel & S. B. Messer (Eds.), *Theories of psychotherapy: Origins and evolution.* Washington, DC: American Psychological Association.

**Fishman, S.** (1988). *A bomb in the brain.* New York: Scribner's.

**Fisk, J. E., & Pidgeon, N.** (1997). The conjunction fallacy: The case for the existence of competing heuristic strategies. *British Journal of Psychology, 88,* 1–27.

**FitzGerald, G. J.** (1993). The reproductive behavior of the stickleback. *Scientific American, 268,* 80–85.

**Flavell, J. H.** (1996). Piaget's legacy. *Psychological Science, 7,* 200–203.

**Fleischhacker, W. W., Hummer, M., Kurz, M., Kurzthaler, I., Lieberman, J. A., Pollack, S., Safferman, A. Z., & Kane, J. J.** (1994). Clozapine dose in the United States and Europe: Implications for therapeutic and adverse effects. *Journal of Clinical Psychiatry, 55,* 78–80.

Fletcher, C. (1995). *Breaking and entering: Women cops talk about life in the ultimate men's club.* New York: HarperCollins.

Fletcher, G. J. O., & Simpson, J. A. (2000). Ideal standards in close relationships: Their structure and functions. *Directions in Psychological Science, 9,* 102--105.

Flett, G. L., Vredenburg, K., & Krames, L. (1997). The continuity of depression in clinical and nonclinical samples. *Psychological Bulletin, 121,* 395–416.

Flippo, R. F., Becker, M. J., & Wark, D. M. (2000). Preparing for and taking tests. In R. F. Flippo & D. C. Caverly (Eds.), *Handbook of college reading and study strategy research.* Mahwah, NJ: Lawrence Erlbaum.

Flippo, R. F., & Caverly, D. C. (Eds.). (2000). *Handbook of college reading and study strategy research.* Mahwah, NJ: Lawrence Erlbaum.

Flor, H., Elbert, T., Knecht, S., Wienbruch, C., Pantev, C., Birbaumer, N., Larbig, W., & Taub, E. (1995). Phantom-limb pain as a perceptual correlate of cortical reorganization following arm amputation. *Nature, 375,* 482–483.

Flores, S. A. (1999). Attributional biases in sexually coercive males. *Journal of Applied Social Psychology, 29,* 2425–2442.

Floyd, M., & Scogin, F. (1997). Effects of memory training on the subjective memory functioning and mental health of older adults: A meta-analysis. *Psychology and Aging, 12,* 150–161.

Foa, E. B. (2000). Psychosocial treatment of posttraumatic stress disorder. *Journal of Clinical Psychology, 61*(Supplement 5), 43–48.

Foa, E. B., & Meadows, E. A. (1997). Psychosocial treatments for posttraumatic stress disorder: A critical review. *Annual Review of Psychology, 48,* 449–480.

Fogel, D. B. (2000, July 25). Cited in J. Glanz, It's only checkers, but the computer taught itself. *New York Times,* D1.

Folkman, S., & Moskowitz, J. T. (2000). Stress, positive emotion, and coping. *Current Directions in Psychological Science, 9,* 115–118.

Ford, J. G. (1991). Rogers's theory of personality: Review and perspectives. *Journal of Social Behavior and Personality, 6,* 19–44.

Ford-Gilboe, M., & Cohen, J. A. (2000). Hardiness: A model of commitment, challenge, and control. In V. R. Rice (Ed.), *Handbook of stress, coping and health.* Thousand Oaks, CA: Sage.

Forsyth, B. W. C. (2000). The AIDS epidemic: Past and future. *Child and Adolescent Psychiatric Clinics of North America, 9,* 267–277.

Forsyth, J. P., Daleiden, E. L., & Chorpita, B. F. (2000). *Psychological Record, 50,* 17–33.

Foster, G. D., Wadden, T. A., Vogt, R. A., & Brewer, G. (1997). What is reasonable weight loss? Patients' expectations and evaluations of obesity treatment outcomes. *Journal of Consulting and Clinical Psychology, 65,* 79–85.

Foubert, J. D., & Marriott, K. A. (1997). Effects of a sexual assault peer education program on men's belief in rape myths. *Sex Roles, 36,* 259–268.

Foulks, E. G. (1992). Reflections on dream material from arctic native people. *Journal of the American Academy of Psychoanalysis, 20,* 193–203.

Fowers, B. J., & Richardson, F. C. (1996). Why is multiculturalism good? *American Psychologist, 51,* 609–621.

Fox, C. (1997, December). Starved out. *Life.*

Foxhall, K. (2000, July/August). APA is key to antistigma campaign. *APA Monitor on Psychology,* 48–49.

Foxx, R. M. (1996). Twenty years of applied behavior analysis in treating the most severe problem behavior: Lessons learned. *Behavior Analyst, 19,* 225–235.

Franklin, A. (1995, June). Cited in E. Burnette, Black males retrieve a noble heritage. *APA Monitor.*

Franks, C. M. (1994). Behavioral model. In V. B. Van Hasselt & M. Hersen (Eds.), *Advanced abnormal psychology.* New York: Plenum Press.

Franz, V. H., Gegenfurtner, K. R., Bulthoff, H. H., & Fahle, M. (2000). Grasping visual illusions: No evidence for a dissociation between perception and action. *Psychological Science, 11,* 20–25.

Fredrickson, M., Hursti, T., Salmi, P., Borjeson, S., Furst, C. J., Peterson, C., & Steineck, G. (1993). Conditioned nausea after cancer chemotherapy and autonomic nervous system conditionability. *Scandinavian Journal of Psychology, 34,* 318–317.

Freed, C. (1999). Cited in L. Helmuth, Fetal cells help Parkinson's patients. *Science, 286,* 886–887.

Freed, C. R., Breeze, R. E., Rosenberg, N. L., Schneck, S. A., Kriek, E., Qi, J., Lone, T., Zhang, Y., Snyder, J. A., Wells, T. H., Ramig, L. O., Thompson, L., Mazziotta, J. C., Huang, S. C., Grafton, S. T., Brooks, D., Sawle, G., Schroter, G., & Ansari, A. A. (1992). Survival of implanted fetal dopamine cells and neurologic improvement 12 to 46 months after transplantation for Parkinson disease. *New England Journal of Medicine, 327,* 1549–1555.

Freedman, M. S., Lucas, R. J., Soni, B., von Schantz, M., Munoz, M., David-Gray, A., & Foster, R. (1999). Regulation of mammalian circadian behavior by non-rod, non-cone, ocular photoreceptors. *Science, 284,* 502–504.

Freedman, R. R. (1991). Physiological mechanisms of temperature biofeedback. *Biofeedback and Self-Regulation, 16,* 95–115.

Freeman, H. (2000, August 22). Cited in N. Angier, Do races differ: Not really, genes show. *New York Times,* D1.

Freiberg, P. (1998, February). We know how to stop the spread of AIDS: So why can't we? *APA Monitor, 32.*

Freud, S. (1891; reprinted 1966). Hypnosis. In J. Strachey (Ed. and Trans.), *The standard edition of the complete psychological works of Sigmund Freud* (Vol. 1). London: Hogarth.

Freud, S. (1900; reprinted 1980). *The interpretation of dreams* (J. Strachey, Ed. and Trans.). New York: Avon.

Freud, S. (1901; reprinted 1960). The psychopathology of everyday life. In J. Strachey (Ed. and Trans.), *The standard edition of the complete psychological works of Sigmund Freud* (Vol. 6). London: Hogarth.

Freud, S. (1905; reprinted 1953). Three essays on the theory of sexuality. In J. Strachey (Ed. and Trans.), *The standard edition of the complete psychological works of Sigmund Freud* (Vol. 7). London: Hogarth.

Freud, S. (1909; reprinted 1949). Notes upon a case of obsessional neurosis. In *Collected papers* (Vol. 3), (Alix and James Strachey, Trans.). London: Hogarth.

Freud, S. (1924). *A general introduction to psychoanalysis.* New York: Boni & Liveright.

Freud, S. (1940; reprinted 1961). An outline of psychoanalysis. In J. Strachey (Ed. and Trans.), *The standard edition of the complete psychological works of Sigmund Freud* (Vol. 23). London: Hogarth.

Freyd, J. J. (1991, August). *Memory repression, dissociative states, and other cognitive control processes involved in adult sequelae of childhood trauma.* Paper presented at the Second Annual Conference of Psychodynamics–Cognitive Science Interface, University of California, San Francisco.

Freyd, J. J. (1994). Circling creativity. *Psychological Science, 5,* 122–126.

Frick, W. B. (2000). Remembering Maslow: Reflections on a 1968 interview. *Journal of Humanistic Psychology, 40,* 128–147.

Fricke, D. (1994, June 2). Heart-shaped noise: The music and the legacy. *Rolling Stone.*

Friedman, H. S., Hawley, P. H., & Tucker, J. S. (1994). Personality, health and longevity. *Current Directions in Psychological Science, 3,* 37–41.

Friedman, M., & Rosenman, R. (1974). *Type A behavior and your heart.* New York: Knopf.

Friedman, S., & Stevenson, M. (1980). Perception of movements in pictures. In M. Hagen (Ed.), *Perception of pictures: Vol. 1. Alberti's window: The projective model of pictorial information.* Orlando, FL: Academic Press.

Friend, T. (1994, July 19). Monday just got worse: It's a coronary day. *USA Today,* D1.

Friend, T. (1996, August 21). Teens and drugs. *USA Today.*

Friend, T. (1997a, February 5). Heroin spreads across the USA. *USA Today.*

Friend, T. (1997b, December 9). The race to save the wild tiger from extinction. *USA Today.*

Frijda, N. H. (1986). *The emotions.* Cambridge, England: Cambridge University Press.

Frijda, N. H., & Mesquita, B. (1994). The social roles and functions of emotions. In S. Kitayama & H. R. Markus (Eds.), *Emotion and culture.* Washington, DC: American Psychological Association.

Frijda, N. S. (2000). The psychologists' point of view. In M. Lewis & J. M. Haviland-Jones (Eds.), *Handbook of emotions* (2nd ed.). New York: Guilford.

Friman, P. C., Allen, K. D., Kerwin, L. E., & Larzelere, R. (1993). Changes in modern psychology. *American Psychologist, 48,* 658–644.

Fritz, S. (1995, June). Found: Wonders in a secret cave. *Popular Science.*

Fucci, D., Harris, D., Petrosino, L., & Banks, M. (1993). Effects of preference for rock music on magnitude-production scaling behavior in young adults: A validation. *Perceptual and Motor Skills, 77,* 811–815.

Fuller, R. K., & Hiller-Sturmhofel, S. (1999). Alcoholism treatment in the United States. *Alcohol Research and Health, 23,* 69–77.

Furumoto, L. (1989). The new history of psychology. In I. S. Cohen (Ed.), *The G. Stanley Hall lecture series* (Vol. 9). Washington, DC: American Psychological Association.

Furumoto, L., & Scarborough, E. (1986). Placing women in the history of psychology. *American Psychologist, 41,* 35–42.

Gabbard, G. O. (2000). American psychoanalysis in the new millennium. *Journal of the American Psychoanalytic Association, 48,* 293–295.

Gabrieli, J. (1998, December 7). Cited in A. Rogers, Thinking differently. *Newsweek,* 60.

Gabrieli, J. D. E., Brewer, J. B., Desmond, J. E., & Glover, G. H. (1997). Separate neural bases of two fundamental memory processes in the human medial temporal lobe. *Science, 276,* 264–266.

Gabrieli, J. D. E., Fleischman, D. A., Keane, M. M., Reminger, S. L., & Morrell, F. (1995). Double dissociation between memory systems underlying explicit and implicit memory in the human brain. *Psychological Science, 6,* 76–82.

Gage, F. (1997). Cited in B. Bower, Enriched mice show adult neuron boost. *Science News, 151,* 206.

Gage, F. (1999, September 29). Cited in S. LaFee, The living brain. *San Diego Union-Tribune,* E-1.

Gajilan, A. T., & Leland, J. (1999, February 8). To have and hold. *Newsweek,* 50–53.

Galaburda, A. M., Menard, M. T., & Rosen, G. D. (1994). Evidence for aberrant auditory anatomy in developmental dyslexia. *Proceedings of the National Academy of Science, 91,* 8010–8013.

Gallopin, T. (2000, May 2). Cited in J. O'Neil, The brain cells that make you sleepy. *New York Times*, D7.

Gallup, G. H., Jr., & Newport, F. (1991). Belief in paranormal phenomena among adult Americans. *Skeptical Inquirer, 15,* 137–146.

Galton, F. (1888). Head growth in students at the University of Cambridge. *Nature, 38,* 14–15.

Gambrill, E. D. (1994). Concepts and methods of behavioral treatment. In D. K. Granvold (Ed.), *Concepts and methods of cognitive treatment.* Pacific Grove, CA: Brooks/Cole.

Gannon, P. J., Holloway, R. L., Broadfield, D. C., & Braun, A. R. (1998). Asymmetry of chimpanzee planum temporale: Humanlike pattern of Wernicke's brain language area homolog. *Science, 279,* 220–222.

Gannon, R. (1995, March). Why we throw up. *Popular Science,* 97–101.

Garcia, J., Ervin, F. R., & Koelling, R. A. (1966). Learning with prolonged delay of reinforcement. *Psychonomic Science, 5,* 121–122.

Garcia, J., Hankins, W. G., & Rusinak, K. W. (1974). Behavioral regulation of the milieu interne in man and rat. *Science, 185,* 824–831.

Gardner, B. T., & Gardner, R. A. (1975). Evidence for sentence constituents in the early utterances of child and chimpanzee. *Journal of Experimental Psychology: General, 104,* 244–267.

Gardner, H. (1976). *The shattered mind.* New York: Vintage Books.

Gardner, H. (1993). *Creating minds.* New York: Basic Books.

Gardner, H. (1995, November). Reflections on multiple intelligences. *Phi Delta Kappan.*

Gardner, H. (1997). Six afterthoughts: Comments on "Varieties of intellectual talent." *Journal of Creative Behavior, 31,* 120–124.

Gardner, H. (1999). *Intelligence reframed.* New York: Basic Books.

Gardner, H., Hatch, T., & Torff, B. (1997). A third perspective: The symbol systems approach. In R. J. Sternberg & E. Grigorenko (Eds.), *Intelligence, heredity, and environment.* New York: Cambridge University Press.

Gardner, M. (1995, November/December). Waking up from Freud's theory of dreams. *Skeptical Inquirer,* 10–12.

Gardner, M. (1996, January/February). Post-Freudian dream theory. *Skeptical Inquirer,* 7–9.

Garety, P. A., Fowler, D., & Kuipers, E. (2000). Cognitive-behavioral therapy for medication-resistant symptoms. *Schizophrenia Bulletin, 26,* 73–86.

Garfield, S. L., & Bergin, A. E. (1994). Introduction and historical overview. In A. E. Bergin & S. L. Garfield (Eds.), *Handbook of psychotherapy and behavior change* (4th ed.). New York: Wiley.

Garfinkel, P. E., & Walsh, B. T. (1997). Drug therapies. In D. M. Garner & P. E. Garfinkel (Eds.), *Handbook of treatment for eating disorders* (2nd ed.). New York: Guilford Press.

Garland, A. R., & Zigler, E. (1993). Adolescent suicide prevention. *American Psychologist, 48,* 169–182.

Garner, D. M., & Garfinkel, P. E. (Eds.). (1997). *Handbook of treatment for eating disorders* (2nd ed.). New York: Guilford Press.

Gazzaniga, M. S. (1983). Right hemisphere language following brain bisection. *American Psychologist, 39,* 525–537.

Gazzaniga, M. S. (1994). *Nature's mind.* New York: Basic Books.

Gazzaniga, M. S. (1996). Cited in B. Bower, Whole-brain interpreter. *Science News, 149,* 124–125.

Gazzaniga, M. S. (1997). Brain, drugs, and society. *Science, 275,* 459.

Gazzaniga, M. S. (1998, July). The split brain revisited. *Scientific American,* 50–55.

Gazzaniga, M. S., Bogen, J. E., & Sperry, R. W. (1962). Some functional effects of sectioning the cerebral commissures in man. *Proceedings of the National Academy of Science, 48,* 1765–1769.

Gegax, T. T. (1999, May 31). An odd fall from grace. *Newsweek,* 70.

Geiger, R. (1994, October). What the experts say. *Parenting.*

Geller, L. (1982). The failure of self-actualization theory: A critique of Carl Rogers and Abraham Maslow. *Journal of Humanistic Psychology, 22,* 56–73.

Gentner, D., & Namy, L. L. (1999). Comparison in the development of categories. *Cognitive Development, 14,* 487–513.

George, K. I. (1995, December 6). Driver gets children to mind pizzas and Qs. *USA Today.*

George, M. S., Ketter, T. A., Parekh, P. T., Herscovitch, P., & Post, R. M. (1996). Gender differences in regional cerebral bloodflow during transient self-induced sadness or happiness. *Biological Psychiatry, 40,* 859–871.

Georgopoulos, A. (1999). Cited in I. Wickelgren, Memory for order found in the motor cortex, *Science, 283,* 1617–1618.

Gerber, L. (1996, June 22). After 16 years, he's cleared. *San Diego Union-Tribune.*

Gergen, K. J., Gulerce, A., Lock, A., & Girishwar, M. (1996). Psychological science in cultural context. *American Psychologist, 51,* 496–503.

Gerlach, J., & Peacock, L. (1994). Motor and mental side effects of clozapine. *Journal of Clinical Psychiatry, 55,* 107–109.

Gershoff-Stowe, L., Thal, J. J., Smith, L. B., & Namy, L. L. (1997). Categorization and its developmental relation to early language. *Child Development, 68,* 843–859.

Gershon, M. (2000, April 3). The wisdom of the gut. *U.S. News & World Report,* 50–51.

Giacopassi, D. J., & Dull, R. T. (1986). Gender and racial differences in the acceptance of rape myths within a college population. *Sex Roles, 15,* 63–75.

Gibbon, J. (1996). Cited in V. Morell, Setting a biological stopwatch. *Science, 271,* 905–906.

Gibbons, A. (1991). Deja vu all over again: Chimp-language wars. *Science, 251,* 1561–1562.

Gibbons, A. (1998). Which of our genes make us human? *Science, 281,* 1432–1434.

Gibbons, F. X., Eggleston, T. J., & Benthin, A. C. (1997). Cognitive reactions to smoking relapse: The reciprocal relation between dissonance and self-esteem. *Journal of Personality and Social Psychology, 72,* 184–195.

Gibbs, N. (1993a, July 19). In whose best interest? *Time.*

Gibbs, N. (1993b, May 3). Tragedy in Waco. *Time.*

Gibbs, N. (1995, October 2). The EQ factor. *Time,* 60–68.

Gibbs, W. W. (1996, August). Gaining on fat. *Scientific American,* 88–94.

Gibson, E. J., & Walk, R. (1960). The visual "cliff." *Scientific American, 202,* 64–71.

Giedd, J. N., Castellanos, F. X., Casey, B. J., Kozuch, P., King, A. C., Hamburger, S. D., & Rapoport, J. L. (1994). Quantitative morphology of the corpus callosum in attention deficit hyperactivity disorder. *American Journal of Psychiatry, 151,* 665–669.

Giedd, J. N., Castellanos, F. X., & Rapoport, J. L. (1995). Corpus callosum morphology in ADHD: Dr. Giedd and colleagues reply. *American Journal of Psychiatry, 152,* 1105–1106.

Gieddes, J. (1999, August 9). Cited in S. Brownlee, Inside the teen brain. *U.S. News & World Report,* 45–54.

Gieddes, J. (2000, March 9). Cited in R. L. Hotz, Scientists map pattern of growth in young brains. *Los Angeles Times,* A1.

Gigone, D., & Hastie, R. (1997). Proper analysis of the accuracy of group judgments. *Psychological Bulletin, 121,* 149–167.

Gilbert, P. L., Harris, J. H., McAdams, L. A., & Jeste, D. V. (1995). Neuroleptic withdrawal in schizophrenic patients. *Archives of General Psychiatry, 52,* 173–188.

Gilligan, C. (1982). *In a different voice: Psychological theory and women's development.* Cambridge, MA: Harvard University Press.

Gladue, B. A. (1994). The biopsychology of sexual orientation. *Current Directions in Psychological Science, 3,* 150–154.

Glantz, M. D., & Hartel, C. R. (1999). *Drug abuse: Origins & interventions.* Washington, DC: American Psychological Association.

Glanzer, M., & Cunitz, A. R. (1966). Two storage mechanisms in free recall. *Journal of Verbal Learning and Verbal Behavior, 5,* 351–360.

Glass, S. (1998, March 5). Truth & D.A.R.E. *Rolling Stone,* 42–43.

Gleick, E. (1997, January 27). And then there were two. . . . *Time,* 38–39.

Gleick, E., Alexander, B., Eskin, L., Pick, G., Skolnik, S., Dodd, J., & Sugden, J. (1994, December 12). The final victim. *People.*

Glenberg, A. M., Sanocki, T., Epstein, W., & Morris, C. (1987). Enhancing calibration of comprehension. *Journal of Experimental Psychology: General, 116,* 119–136.

Gobbo, C. (2000). Assessing the effects of misinformation on children's recall: How and when makes a difference. *Applied Cognitive Psychology, 14,* 163–182.

Gold, I., & Stoljar, D. (1999). A neuron doctrine in the philosophy of neuroscience. *Behavioral and Brain Sciences, 22,* 809–869.

Gold, P. E., & McGaugh, J. L. (1975). A single-trace, two-process view of memory storage processes. In D. Deutsch & J. A. Deutsch (Eds.), *Short-term memory.* New York: Academic Press.

Gold, S. N., Hughes, D., & Hohnecker, L. (1994). Degrees of repression of sexual abuse memories. *American Psychologist, 49,* 441–442.

Goldberg, C. (1998, May 31). Acceptance of gay men and lesbians is growing, study says. *New York Times,* 15.

Goldberger, L., & Breznitz, S. (Eds.). (1993) *Handbook of stress: Theoretical and clinical aspects.* New York: Free Press.

Goldfried, M. R., & Davison, G. C. (1976). *Clinical behavior therapy.* New York: Holt, Rinehart & Winston.

Goldman, D. (1996). High anxiety. *Science, 274,* 1483.

Goldsborough, J. O. (1997, July 3). Harvesting the (sour) fruits of the U.C. regents' labors. *San Diego Union-Tribune.*

Goldsmith, H. H., Buss, K. A., & Lemery, K. S. (1997). Toddler and childhood temperament: Expanded content, stronger genetic evidence, new evidence for the importance of environment. *Developmental Psychology, 33,* 891–905.

Goldstein, A. P. (1989). Aggression reduction: Some vital steps. In J. Groebel & R. A. Hinde (Eds.), *Aggression and war: Their biological and social bases.* Cambridge, England: Cambridge University Press.

Goldstein, E. B. (1999). *Sensation and perception* (5th ed.). Pacific Grove, CA: Brooks/Cole.

Goleman, D. (1995). *Emotional intelligence: Why it can matter more than IQ.* New York: Bantam Books.

Goleman, D. (1996, July 16). Forget money; Nothing can buy happiness, some researchers say. *New York Times.*

Goleman, D., & Gurin, J. (1993). *Mind/body medicine: How to use your mind for better health.* New York: Consumer Reports.

Goode, E. (2000, August 8). How culture molds habits of thought. *New York Times,* D1.

Goodman, G. S., & Quas, J. A. (1997). Trauma and memory: Individual differences in children's recounting of a stressful experience. In N. L. Stein, P. A. Ornstein, B. Tversky, & C. Brainerd (Eds.), *Memory for everyday and emotional events.* Mahwah, NJ: Lawrence Erlbaum.

Goodwin, F. K., & Jamison, K. R. (1990). *Manic-depressive illness.* New York: Oxford University Press.

Gopnik, A., & Meltzoff, A. N. (1997). *Words, thoughts, and theories.* Cambridge: The MIT Press.

Gordon, C. M., Dougherty, D. D., Rauch, S. L., Emans, S. J., Grace, E., Lamm, R., Alpert, N. M., Majzoub, J. A., & Fischman, A. J. (2000). Neuroanatomy of human appetitive function: A positron emission tomography investigation. *International Journal of Eating Disorders, 27,* 163–171.

Gore, R. (1997, February). The first steps. *National Geographic,* 72–99.

Gottesman, I. I. (1997). Twins: En route to QTLs for cognition. *Science, 276,* 1522–1523.

Gottesmann, I. I. (1991). *Schizophrenia genesis: The origins of madness.* New York: W. H. Freeman.

Gottlieb, G., Wahlsten, D., & Lickliter, R. (1998). The significance of biology for human development: A developmental psychobiological systems view. In W. Damon & R. M. Lerner (Eds.), *Handbook of child psychology* (Vol. 1). New York: John Wiley & Sons.

Gottman, J. (1995a, February). Cited in R. Edwards, New tools help gauge marital success. *APA Monitor.*

Gottman, J. (1995b). *Why marriages succeed or fail.* New York: Simon & Schuster.

Gottman, J. M. (1998). Psychology and the study of marital processes. *Annual Review of Psychology, 49,* 169–197.

Gottman, J. M. (1999). *Seven principles for making marriage work.* New York: Three Rivers Press.

Gottman, J. M. (2000, September 14). Cited in K. S. Peterson, "Hot" and "cool" phases could predict divorce. *USA Today,* 9D.

Gottman, J. M., Coan, J., Carrere, S., & Swanson, C. (1998). Predicting marital happiness and stability from newlywed interactions. *Journal of Marriage and the Family, 60,* 5–22.

Gould, E. (1999). Cited in B. Bower, Learning to make, keep adult neurons. *Science News, 155,* 170.

Gould, E., Reeves, A. J., Graziano, S. A., & Gross, C. G. (1999). Neurogenesis in the neocortex of adult primates. *Science, 286,* 548–551.

Gould, L. (1995, April 23). Ticket to trouble. *New York Times Magazine.*

Gould, R. A. (1969). Subsistence behaviour among the Western Desert Aborigines of Australia. *Oceania, 39,* 253–274.

Gould, R. A., Otto, M. W., Pollack, M. H., & Yap, L. (1997). Cognitive behavioral and pharmacological treatment of generalized anxiety disorder: A preliminary meta-analysis. *Behavior Therapy, 28,* 285–305.

Gould, S. J. (1981). *The mismeasure of man.* New York: Norton.

Gould, S. J. (1994, November). The geometer of race. *Discover.*

Gould, S. J. (1996). *The mismeasure of man* (revised and expanded). New York: W. W. Norton.

Graber, J. A., Brooks-Gunn, J., & Warren, M. P. (1995). The antecedents of menarcheal age: Heredity, family environment, and stressful life events. *Child Development, 66,* 346–359.

Grabowska, A., & Nowicka, A. (1996). Visual-spatial frequency model of cerebral asymmetry: A critical survey of behavioral and electrophysiological studies. *Psychological Bulletin, 120,* 434–449.

Grady, D. (2000, October 12). Exchanging obesity's risks for surgery's. *New York Times,* A1.

Graham, L. O. (1995). *Member of the club.* New York: HarperCollins.

Granhag, P. A. (1997). Realism is eyewitness confidence as a function of type of event witnessed and repeated recall. *Journal of Applied Psychology, 82,* 599–613.

Granstrom, K., & Stiwne, D. (1998). A bipolar model of groupthink: An expansion of Janis's concept. *Small Group Research, 29,* 32–56.

Granvold, D. K. (Ed.). (1994). *Cognitive and behavioral treatment.* Pacific Grove, CA: Brooks/Cole.

Gray, R. (1996). Cited in B. Bower, Clues to nicotine's memory, plaque impact. *Science News, 150,* 263.

Graziano, W. B., & Eisenberg, N. H. (1997). Agreeableness: A dimension of personality. In R. Hogan, J. Johnson, & S. Briggs (Eds.), *Handbook of personality psychology.* New York: Academic Press.

Green, A. J., Prepscius, C., & Levy, W. B. (2000). *Learning & Memory, 7,* 48–57.

Green, J. T., & Woodruff-Pak, D. S. (2000). Eyeblink classical conditioning: Hippocampus formation is for neutral stimulus associations as cerebellum is for association-response. *Psychological Bulletin, 126,* 1138–1158.

Green, L., Fry, A. R., & Myerson, J. (1994). Discounting of delayed rewards: A life-span comparison. *Psychological Science, 5,* 33–36.

Greenberg, J. (1978). The Americanization of Roseto. *Science News, 113,* 378–382.

Greenberg, L., Elliott, R., & Lietaer, G. (1994). Research on experiential psychotherapies. In A. E. Bergin & S. L. Garfield (Eds.), *Handbook of psychotherapy and behavior change* (4th ed.). New York: Wiley.

Greenberg, L. S., & Rice, L. N. (1997). Humanistic approaches to psychotherapy. In P. L. Wachtel & S. B. Messer (Eds.), *Theories of psychotherapy: Origins and evolution.* Washington, DC: American Psychological Association.

Greenberg, R., & Perlman, C. A. (1999). The interpretation of dreams: A classic revisited. *Psychoanalytic Dialogues, 9,* 749–765.

Greene, B., & Winfrey, O. (1996). *Make the connection.* New York: Hyperion.

Greene, R. L., & Clopton, J. R. (1994). Minnesota Multiphasic Personality Inventory–2. In M. E. Maruish (Ed.), *The use of psychological testing for treatment planning and outcome assessment: Introduction.* Hillsdale, NJ: Lawrence Erlbaum.

Greenfield, P. M. (1997). You can't take it with you. *American Psychologist, 52,* 1115–1124.

Greengard, P. (2000, January 31). Cited in G. Cowley, Alzheimer's: Unlocking the mystery. *Newsweek,* 46–51.

Greeno, J. G. (1989). A perspective on thinking. *American Psychologist, 44,* 134–141.

Greenwald, A. G., & Banaji, M. R. (1995). Implicit social cognition: Attitudes, self-esteem, and stereotypes. *Psychological Review, 102,* 4–27.

Greenwald, A. G., Draine, S. C., & Abrams, R. L. (1996). Three cognitive markers of unconscious semantic activation. *Science, 273,* 1699–1702.

Greenwald, A. G., Spangenberg, E. R., Pratkanis, A. R., & Eskenazi, J. (1991). Double-blind tests of subliminal self-help audiotapes. *Psychological Science, 2,* 119–122.

Gregory, R. L. (1974). Recovery from blindness: A case study. In R. L. Gregory (Ed.), *Concepts and mechanisms of perception.* London: Gerald Duckworth.

Gresham, F. M., Beebe-Frankenberger, M. E., & MacMillan, D. L. (1999). A selective review of treatments for children with autism: Description and methodological considerations. *School Psychology Review, 28,* 559–575.

Grether, J. K. (2000, May 4). Cited in T. H. Maugh, II, Test identifies newborns likely to develop autism. *Los Angeles Times,* A1.

Grigorenko, E. L. (2000). Heritability and intelligence. In R. J. Sternberg, *Handbook of intelligence.* New York: Cambridge University Press.

Grimaldi, J. V. (1986, April 16). "The mole" evicted from sewer. *San Diego Tribune.*

Grinspoon, L., Bakalar, J. B., Zimmer, L., & Morgan, J. P. (1997). Marijuana addiction. *Science, 277,* 751–752.

Grogan, B., Shaw, B., Ridenhour, R., Fine, A., & Eftimiades, M. (1993, May). Their brothers' keepers? *People.*

Gron, G., Wunderlich, A. P., Spitzer, M., Tomczak, R., & Riepe, M. W. (2000). Brain activation during human navigation: Gender-different neural networks as substrate of performance. *Nature Neuroscience, 3,* 404–408.

Grunbaum, A. (1993). *Validation in the clinical theory of psychoanalysis.* Madison, CT: International Universities Press.

Guastello, S. J., Guastello, D. D., & Craft, L. L. (1989). Assessment of the Barnum effect in computer based test interpretations. *Journal of Psychology, 12,* 477–484.

Gudjonsson, G. H. (1997). Accusations by adults of childhood sexual abuse: A survey of the members of the British False Memory Society (BFMS). *Applied Cognitive Psychology, 11,* 3–18.

Guerin, D. W., Gottfried, A. W., & Thomas, C. W. (1997). Difficult temperament and behaviour problems: A longitudinal study from 1.5 to 12 years. *International Journal of Behavioral Development, 21,* 71–90.

Guida, F. V., & Ludlow, L. H. (1989). A cross-cultural study of test anxiety. *Journal of Cross-Cultural Psychology, 20,* 178–190.

Guilford, J. P. (1967). *The nature of human intelligence.* New York: McGraw-Hill.

*Guinness book of records, The.* (1995). New York: Bantam.

Gullette, E. C. D., Blumenthal, J. A., Babyak, M., Jiang, W., Waugh, R. B., Frid, D. J., O'Connor, C. M., Morris, J. J., & Krantz, D. S. (1997). Effects of mental stress on myocardial ischemia during daily life. *Journal of American Medical Association, 277,* 1521–1526.

Gur, R. C., Mozley, L. H., Mozley, P. D., Risnick, S. M., Karp, J. S., Alavi, A., Arnold, S. E., & Gur, R. E. (1995). Sex differences in regional cerebral glucose metabolism during a resting state. *Science, 267,* 528–531.

Gur, R. E., Cowell, P., Turetsky, B. I., Gallacher, F., Cannon, T., Bilker, W., & Gur, R. C. (1997). A follow-up magnetic resonance imaging study of schizophrenia. *Archives of General Psychiatry, 55,* 145–152.

Gura, T. (1997). Obesity sheds its secrets. *Science, 275,* 751–753.

Gureje, O., Simon, G. E., Ustun, T. B., & Goldberg, D. P. (1997). Somatization in cross-cultural perspective: A World Health Organization study in primary care. *American Journal of Psychiatry, 154,* 989–995.

Gurman, E. B. (1994). Debriefing for all concerned: Ethical treatment of human subjects. *Psychological Science, 5,* 139.

Gustavson, C. R., Kelly, D. J., Sweeney, M., & Garcia, J. (1976). Prey-lithium aversion I: Coyotes and wolves. *Behavioral Biology, 17,* 61–72.

Guthrie, J. P., Ash, R. A., & Bendapudi, V. (1995). Additional validity evidence for a measure of morningness. *Journal of Applied Psychology, 80,* 186–190.

Guthrie, R. V. (1976). *Even the rat was white.* New York: Harper & Row.

Gutkin, A. J., Holborn, S. W., Walker, J. R., & Anderson, B. A. (1994). Cost-effectiveness of home relaxation training for tension headaches. *Journal of Behavior Therapy and Experimental Psychiatry, 25,* 69–74.

Gwyer, P., & Clifford, B. R. (1997). The effects of the cognitive interview on recall, identification, confidence, and the confidence/accuracy relationship. *Applied Cognitive Psychology, 11,* 121–145.

Haber, N. R. (1980, November). Eidetic images are not just imaginary. *Psychology Today.*

Hackmann, A., Clark, D. M., & McManus, F. (2000). Recurrent images and early memories in social phobia. *Behaviour Research and Therapy, 38,* 601–610.

Hager, M. (1997, February 24). Beyond the mammogram. *Newsweek.*

Haidt, J., Koller, S. H., & Dias, M. G. (1993). Affect, culture, and morality, or is it wrong to eat your dog? *Journal of Personality and Social Psychology, 65,* 613–628.

Haidt, J., McCauley, C., & Rozin, P. (1994). Individual differences in sensitivity to disgust: A scale sampling seven domains of disgust elicitors. *Personality and Individual Differences, 16,* 701–713.

Haier, R. (1996, October 17). Cited in J. Marquis, A real brain teaser. *Los Angeles Times.*

Haier, R. J., Chueh, D., Touchette, P., Lott, I., Buchsbaum, M. S., MacMillan, D., Sandman, C., LaCasse, L., & Sosa, E. (1995). Brain size and glucose metabolic rate in mental retardation and Down syndrome. *Intelligence, 20,* 199–210.

Haith, M. M., & Benson, J. B. (1998). Infant cognition. In W. Damon & R. M. Lerner (Eds.), *Handbook of child psychology* (Vol. 1). New York: John Wiley & Sons.

Haliburn, J. (2000). Reasons for adolescent suicide attempts. *Journal of the American Academy of Child Adolescent Psychiatry, 29,* 13.

Hall, C. I. (1997). Cultural malpractice. *American Psychologist, 52,* 642–651.

Hall, G. C. N., & Barongan C. (1997). Prevention of sexual aggression. *American Psychologist, 52,* 5–14.

Halliday, J. (2001, February 28). Red-light scofflaws run but can't hide. *USA Today,* 13A.

Halpern, D. F. (1992). *Sex differences in cognitive abilities* (2nd ed.). Hillsdale, NJ: Lawrence Erlbaum.

Halpern, D. F. (1998). Teaching critical thinking for transfer across domains. *American Psychologist, 53,* 449–455.

Halpern, D. F. (2000). *Sex differences in cognitive abilities* (3rd ed.). Hillsdale, NJ: Lawrence Erlbaum.

Hamann, S. B., Ely, T. D., Grafton, S. T., & Kilts, C. D. (1999). Amygdala activity related to enhanced memory for pleasant and aversive stimuli. *Nature Neuroscience, 2,* 289–294.

Hamer, D. H., Hu, S., Maagnuson, V. L., Hu, H., & Pattatucci, A. M. L. (1993). Male sexual orientation and genetic evidence: Response. *Science, 262,* 265.

Hamilton, D. L., Devine, P. G., & Ostrom, T. M. (1994). Social cognition and classic issues in social psychology. In P. G. Devine, D. L. Hamilton, & T. M. Ostrom (Eds.), *Social cognition: Impact on psychology.* New York: Academic Press.

Hammer, D. (1995). Cited in C. Holden, More on genes and homosexuality. *Science, 268,* 1571.

Hammer, R. P., Egilmez, Y., & Emmett-Oglesby, M. W. (1997). Neural mechanisms of tolerance to the effects of cocaine. *Behavioural Brain Research, 84,* 225–239.

Han, S., & Humphreys, G. W. (1999). Interactions between perceptual organization based on Gestalt laws and those based on hierarchical processing. *Perception & Psychophysics, 61,* 1287–1298.

Hancock, L. (1996, March 18). Mother's little helper. *Newsweek.*

Hancock, L., Rosenberg, D., Springen, K., King, P., Rogers, P., Brant, M., Kalb, C., & Gegax, T. T. (1995, March 6). Breaking point. *Newsweek.*

Haney, D. Q. (2000, July 11). Teens' sexual activity in USA on decline during past decade. *USA Today,* 9D.

Hansen, J. T. (2000). Psychoanalysis and humanism: A review and critical examination of integrationist efforts with some proposed resolutions. *Journal of Counseling and Development, 78,* 21–28.

Hanson, G., & Venturelli, P. J. (1998). *Drugs and society* (5th ed.). Boston: Jones and Bartlett.

Happé, F., & Frith, U. (1996). The neuropsychology of autism. *Brain, 119,* 1377–1400.

Hardin, C., & Banaji, M. R. (1993). The influence of language on thought. *Social Cognition, 11,* 277–308.

Harding, C. M., & Hall, G. M. (1997). Long-term outcome studies of schizophrenia: Do females continue to display better outcome as expected? *International Review of Psychiatry, 9,* 409–418.

Hardy, J. B., Welcher, D. W., Mellits, E. D., & Kagan, J. (1976). Pitfalls in the measurement of intelligence: Are standardized intelligence tests valid for measuring the intellectual potential of urban children? *Journal of Psychology, 94,* 43–51.

Harmon, A. (1995, October 1). High-tech hidden persuaders. *Los Angeles Times.*

Harriott, J., & Ferrari, J. R. (1996). Prevalence of procrastination among samples of adults. *Psychological Reports, 78,* 611–616.

Harris, B. (1979). Whatever happened to little Albert? *American Psychologist, 34,* 151–160.

Harris, G., Thomas, A., & Booth, D. A. (1990). Development of salt taste in infancy. *Developmental Psychology, 26,* 534–538.

Harris, J. C. (1995). *Developmental neuropsychiatry* (Vol. 1). New York: Oxford Press.

Harris, J. L., Salus, D., Rerecich, R., & Larsen, D. (1996). Distinguishing detection from identification in subliminal auditory perception: A review and critique of Merikle's study. *Journal of General Psychology, 123,* 41–50.

Hart, F., & Risley, T. (1996). Cited in B. Bower, Talkative parents make kids smarter. *Science News, 150,* 100.

Harter, S. (1990). Self and identity development. In S. S. Feldman & G. R. Elliott (Eds.), *At the threshold: The developing adolescent.* Cambridge, MA: Harvard University Press.

Hartlage, S., Alloy, B., Vazquez, C., & Dykman, B. (1993). Automatic and effortful processing in depression. *Psychological Bulletin, 113,* 247–278.

Harvey, J. (1997, December). Cited in B. Azar, Researchers debunk myth of the "crack baby." *APA Monitor.*

Hasselt, V. B., & Hersen, M. (Eds.). (1994). *Advanced abnormal psychology.* New York: Plenum Press.

Hassin, R., & Trope, Y. (2000). Facing faces: Studies on the cognitive aspects of physiognomy. *Journal of Personality and Social Psychology, 78,* 837–852.

Hatfield, E., & Rapson, R. L. (1995). *A world of passion: Cross-cultural perspective on love and sex.* New York: Allyn & Bacon.

Hausmann, M., & Gunturkun, O. (1999). Sex differences in functional cerebral asymmetries in a repeated measures design. *Brain and Cognition, 41,* 263–275.

Hayamizu, T. (1997). Between intrinsic and extrinsic motivation: Examination of reasons for academic study based on the theory of internalization. *Japanese Psychological Research, 39,* 98–108.

Hayes, B. K., & Delamothe, K. (1997). Cognitive interviewing procedures and suggestibility in children's recall. *Journal of Applied Psychology, 82,* 562–577.

Hayes, J. A., & Mitchell, J. C. (1994). Mental health professionals' skepticism about multiple personality disorder. *Professional Psychology: Research and Practice, 25,* 410–425.

Hayes, K. J., & Hayes, C. H. (1951). The intellectual development of a home-raised chimpanzee. *Proceedings of the American Philosophical Society, 95,* 105–109.

Hayes, S. C., Munt, E. D., Korn, Z., Wulfert, E., Rosenfarb, I., & Zettle, R. D. (1986). The effect of feedback and self-reinforcement instructions on studying performance. *Psychological Record, 36,* 27–37.

Healy, M. (1999, December 28). Sex and the teenage girl: Curiosity wins out over love. *USA Today,* 6D.

Healy, M. (2000, November 29). Computer improves mammogram results. *USA Today,* 9D.

Heatherton, T. F., Mahamedi, F., Striepe, M., Gield, A. E., & Keel, P. (1997). A 10-year longitudinal study of body weight, dieting, and eating disorder symptoms. *Journal of Abnormal Psychology, 106,* 117–125.

Heatherton, T. F., & Weinberger, J. L. (Eds.). (1994). *Can personality change?* Washington, DC: American Psychological Association.

Heider, F. (1958). *The psychology of interpersonal relations.* New York: Wiley.

Helgeson, V. S. (1994). Prototypes and dimensions of masculinity and feminity. *Sex Roles, 31,* 653–682.

Hellige, J. B. (1993). Unity of thought and action: Varieties of interaction between the left and right cerebral hemispheres. *Current Directions in Psychological Science, 2,* 21–30.

Hellmich, N. (2000, March 29). One way to get to sleep: Get up. *USA Today,* 1A.

Hellstrom, A. (2000). Sensation weighting in comparison and discrimination of heaviness. *Journal of Experimental Psychology, 26,* 6–17.

Helmers, K. H., Krantz, D. S., Merz, C. N. B., Klein, J., Kop, W. J., Gottdiener, J. S., & Rozanski, A. (1995). Defensive hostility: Relationship to multiple markers of cardiac ischemia in patients with coronary disease. *Health Psychology, 14,* 202–209.

Helson, R. (1993). Comparing longitudinal studies of adult development: Toward a paradigm of tension between stability and change. In D. C. Funder, R. D. Parke, C. Tomlinson-Keasey, & K. Widaman (Eds.), *Studying lives through time.* Washington, DC: American Psychological Association.

Helson, R. (1996). In search of the creative personality. *Creativity Research Journal, 9,* 295–306.

Helwig, C. C. (1997). Making moral cognition respectable (again): A retrospective review of Lawrence Kohlberg. *Contemporary Psychology, 42,* 191–195.

Helzer, J. E., & Canino, G. J. (Eds.). (1992). *Alcoholism in North America, Europe, and Asia.* New York: Oxford University Press.

Hendin, H. (1994). *Suicide in America.* New York: Norton.

Hendy, H. (1984). Effects of pets on the sociability and health activities of nursing home residents. In R. K. Anderson, B. J. Hart, & L. A. Hart (Eds.), *The pet connection.* Minneapolis: Center to Study Human-Animal Relationships and Environments, University of Minnesota.

Henker, B., & Whalen, C. K. (1989). Hyperactivity and attention deficits. *American Psychologist, 44,* 216–233.

Henry, T. (1999, September 15). Sex is No. 1 struggle, teen girls say. *USA Today*, 9D.

Henry, W. A., III. (1994, June 27). Pride and prejudice. *Time*.

Henry, W. P., Strupp, H. H., Schacht, T. E., & Gaston, L. (1994). Psychodynamic approaches. In A. E. Bergin & S. L. Garfield (Eds.), *Handbook of psychotherapy and behavior change* (4th ed.). New York: Wiley.

Herbert, W. (1999, July 26). Losing your mind. *U.S. News & World Report*, 45–51.

Herkenham, M. (1996, December 16). Cited in D. Ferrell, Scientists unlocking secrets of marijuana's effects. *Los Angeles Times*.

Herman, L. (1989, April). Cited in S. Chollar, Conversations with the dolphins. *Psychology Today*.

Herman, L. (1993, March 22). Cited in S. Linden, Can animals think? *Time*.

Herman, L. (1999, July 21). Cited in J. Mastro, Dialogue with a dolphin. *San Diego Union-Tribune*, E1.

Herman, W. E. (1990). Fear of failure as a distinctive personality trait measure of test anxiety. *Journal of Research and Development in Education, 23,* 180–185.

Herrenkohl, T. I., Maguin, E., Hill, K. G., Hawkins, J. D., Abbott, R. D., & Catalano, R. F. (2000). Developmental risk factors for youth violence. *Journal of Adolescent Health, 26,* 176–186.

Herrnstein, R. J., & Murray, C. (1994). *The bell curve.* New York: Free Press.

Herzog, H. (1993). Animal rights and wrongs. *Science, 262,* 1906–1908.

Herzog, W., Deter, H. C., Fiehn, W., & Petzold, E. (2000). Medical findings and predictors of long-term physical outcome in anorexia nervosa: A prospective, 12-year follow-up study. *Psychological Medicine, 27,* 269–279.

Hewitt, J. K. (1997). The genetics of obesity: What have genetic studies told us about the environment? *Behavior Genetics, 27,* 353–358.

Hewstone, H., & Hamberger, J. (2000). Perceived variability and stereotype change. *Journal of Experimental Social Psychology, 36,* 103–124.

Hickey, E. W. (1991). *Serial murderers and their victims.* Pacific Grove, CA: Brooks/Cole.

Hickman, G., Bartholomae, S., & McKenry, P. C. (2000). Influence of parenting styles on the adjustment and academic achievement of traditional college freshmen. *Journal of College Student Development, 41,* 41–54.

Hidalgo, R. B., & Davidson, J. R. T. (2000). Posttraumatic stress disorder: Epidemiology and health-related considerations. *Journal of Clinical Psychiatry, 61*(Supplement 7), 5–13.

Higgins, E. T. (1997). Beyond pleasure and pain. *American Psychologist, 52,* 1280–1300.

Higgins, E. T. (2000). Social cognition: Learning about what matters in the social world. *European Journal of Social Psychology, 30,* 3–39.

Hilgard, E. R. (1977). *Divided consciousness: Multiple controls in human thought and action.* New York: Wiley.

Hilgard, E. R. (1979). Divided consciousness in hypnosis: The implications of the hidden observer. In E. Fromm & R. E. Shor (Eds.), *Hypnosis: Developments in research and new perspectives* (2nd ed.). New York: Aldine.

Hill, A., Niven, C. A., & Knussen, C. (1996). Pain memories in phantom limbs: A case study. *Pain, 66,* 381–384.

Hill, A. B., Kemp-Wheeler, S. M., & Jones, S. A. (1987). Subclinical and clinical depression: Are analogue studies justifiable? *Personality and Individual Differences, 8,* 113–120.

Hill, C. E., Diemer, R. A., & Heaton, K. J. (1997). Dream interpretation sessions: Who volunteers, who benefits, and what volunteer clients view as most and least helpful. *Journal of Counseling Psychology, 44,* 53–62.

Hill, C. E., & Nakayama, E. Y. (2000). Client-centered therapy: Where has it been and where is it going? A comment on Hathaway (1948). *Journal of Clinical Psychology, 56,* 861–875.

Hill, C. E., Zack, J. S., Wonnell, T. L., Hofffman, M. A., Rochlen, A. B., Goldberg, J. K., Nakayama, E. Y., Heaton, K. R., Kelley, F. A., Eiche, K., Tomlinson, M. J., & Hess, S. (2000). Structured brief therapy with a focus on dreams or loss for clients with troubling dreams and recent loss. *Journal of Counseling Psychology, 47,* 90–101.

Hill, P. (1995, June). Cited in E. Burnette, Black males retrieve a noble heritage. *APA Monitor.*

Hilts, P. H. (1995). *Memory's ghost: The strange tale of Mr. M and the nature of memory.* New York: Simon & Schuster.

Hirsch, B. J. (1997). Where are the interventions? *Contemporary Psychology, 42,* 1113–1114.

Hirschfeld, R. M. A. (2000). Antidepressants in long-term therapy: A review of tricyclic antidepressants and selective serotonin reuptake inhibitors. *Acta Psychiatrica Scandinavica, 101*(Supplement 403), 35–38.

Hirshkowitz, M., Moore, C. A., & Minhoto, G. (1997). The basics of sleep. In M. R. Pressman & W. C. Orr (Eds.), *Understanding sleep: The evaluation and treatment of sleep disorders.* Washington, DC: American Psychological Association.

Hobson, J. A. (1988). *The dreaming brain.* New York: Basic Books.

Hobson, J. A., & McCarley, R. W. (1977). The brain as a dream state generator: An activation-synthesis hypothesis of the dream process. *American Journal of Psychiatry, 134,* 1335–1348.

Hoch, T. A., Babbitt, R. L., Coe, D. A., Krell, D. M., & Hackbert, L. (1994). Contingency contacting. *Behavior Modification, 18,* 106–128.

Hocker, J. L., & Wilmot, W. W. (1991). *Interpersonal conflict.* Dubuque, IA: William C Brown.

Hodgson, R. (1994). Treatment of alcohol problems. *Addiction, 89,* 1529–1534.

Hoffman, C., Lau, I., & Johnson, D. R. (1986). The linguistic relativity of person cognition: An English-Chinese comparison. *Journal of Personality and Social Psychology, 51,* 1097–1105.

Hoffman, H. (2000, July 4). Cited in J. Robbins, Virtual reality finds a real place as a medical aid. *New York Times,* D6.

Hoffman, P. (1999, November 8). Can I grow a new brain? *Time,* 94–96.

Hofmann, A. (1983). *LSD: My problem child.* Los Angeles: J. P. Tarcher.

Hogan, J., & Ones, D. S. (1997). Conscientiousness and integrity at work. In R. Hogan, J. Johnson, & S. Briggs (Eds.), *Handbook of personality psychology.* New York: Academic Press.

Hokanson, J. E., & Butler, A. C. (1992). Cluster analysis of depressed college students' social behaviors. *Journal of Personality and Social Psychology, 62,* 273–280.

Holahan, C. K., & Sears, R. R. (1995). *The gifted group in later maturity.* Stanford, CA: Stanford University Press.

Holden, C. (1985). A guarded endorsement for shock therapy. *Science, 228,* 1510–1511.

Holden, C. (1995). Sex and the granular layer. *Science, 268,* 807.

Holden, C. (1996). Researchers find feminization a two-edged sword. *Science, 271,* 1919–1920.

Holden, C. (1997). Thumbs up for acupuncture. *Science, 278,* 1231.

Hollander, E., Kaplan, A., Allen, A., & Cartwright, C. (2000). Pharmacotherapy for obsessive-compulsive disorder. *The Psychiatric Clinics of North America, 23,* 643–656.

Hollis, K. L. (1997). Contemporary research on Pavlovian conditioning. *American Psychologist, 52,* 956–965.

Hollon, S. D., & Beck, A. T. (1994). Cognitive and cognitive behavioral therapies. In A. E. Bergin & S. L. Garfield (Eds.), *Handbook of psychotherapy and behavior change* (4th ed.). New York: Wiley.

Holmes, C., & Lovestone, S. (1997). The molecular genetics on mood disorders. *Current Opinion in Psychiatry, 10,* 79–83.

Holmes, T. H., & Rahe, R. H. (1967). The social readjustment rating scale. *Journal of Psychosomatic Research, 11,* 203–218.

Holt, R. R. (1993). Occupational stress. In L. Goldberger & S. Breznitz (Eds.), *Handbook of stress: Theoretical and clinical aspects* (2nd ed.). New York: Free Press.

Hong, Y., Morris, M. W., Chiu, C., & Benet-Martinez, V. (2000). Multicultural minds. *American Psychologist, 55,* 709–720.

Honts, C. R. (1994). Psychophysiological detection of deception. *Current Directions in Psychological Science, 3,* 77–82.

Honts, C. R., Raskin, D. C., & Kircher, J. C. (1994). Mental and physical countermeasures reduce the accuracy of polygraph tests. *Journal of Applied Psychology, 79,* 252–259.

Hooyman, N., & Kiyak, H. (1999). *Social gerontology* (5th ed.). New York: Allyn & Bacon.

Hoptman, M. J., & Davidson, R. J. (1994). How and why do the two cerebral hemispheres interact? *Psychological Bulletin, 116,* 195–219.

Horgan, J. (1996, December). Why Freud isn't dead. *Scientific American,* 106–111.

Horowitz, J. M. (1999, March 22). Libido letdown. *Time,* 115.

Horowitz, J. M. (2000, August 28). High five for a new hand. *Time,* 44.

Horwath, E., & Weissman, M. M. (2000). The epidemiology and cross-national presentation of obsessive-compulsive disorder. *The Psychiatric Clinics of North America, 23,* 493–507.

Hotz, R. (1997, October 27). Chemical in pot cuts severe pain, study says. *Los Angeles Times.*

Hotz, R. L. (2000, January 24). A scalpel, a life and language. *Los Angeles Times,* A1.

Howard, K. I., Krause, M. S., Saunders, S. M., & Kopta, S. M. (1997). Trials and tribulations in the meta-analysis of treatment differences: Comment on Wampold et al. (1997). *Psychological Bulletin, 122,* 221–225.

Howard, K. I., Moras, K., Brill, P. L., Martinovich, Z., & Lutz, W. (1996). Evaluation of psychotherapy: Efficacy, effectiveness, and patient progress. *American Psychologist, 51,* 1059–1064.

Howe, M. L., & Courage, M. L. (1997). The emergence and early development of autobiographical memory. *Psychological Review, 104,* 499–525.

Howe, T. (1997, June). Cited in T. DeAngelis, Abused children have more conflicts with friends. *APA Monitor.*

Howieson, D. B., & Lezak, M. D. (1997). The neuropsychological evaluation. In S. C. Yodofsky & R. E. Hales (Eds.), *The American Psychiatric Press textbook of neuropsychiatry* (3rd ed.). Washington, DC: American Psychiatric Press.

Howlett, D. (1997, September 10). Easy-to-concoct drug often makes users turn violent. *USA Today.*

**Howlin, P.** (1997). Prognosis in autism: Do specialist treatments affect long-term outcome? *European Child & Adolescent Psychiatry, 6,* 55–72.

**Hsea, Y., Anglin, D., & Powers, K.** (1993). A 24-year follow-up of California narcotics addicts. *Archives of General Psychiatry, 50,* 577–584.

**Hsu, D. T.** (1996). Acupuncture: A review. *Regional Anesthesia, 21,* 361–370.

**Hubel, D. H., & Wiesel, T. N.** (1979). Brain mechanisms of vision. *Scientific American, 241,* 150–162.

**Huff, R.** (1995, February 11). Cited in M. Dolan, When the mind's eye blinks. *Los Angeles Times.*

**Hughes, J., Smith, T. W., Kosterlitz, H. W., Fothergill, L. A., Morgan, B. A., & Morris, H. R.** (1975). Identification of two related pentapeptides from the brain with potent opiate agonist activity. *Nature, 258,* 577–579.

**Hughes, R. J., & Badia, P.** (1997). Sleep-promoting and hypothermic effects of daytime melatonin administration in humans. *Sleep, 20,* 124–131.

**Hui, K. K. S., Liu, J., Makris, N., Gollub, R. L., Chen, An J. W., Moore, C. I., Kennedy, D. N., Rosen, B. R., & Kwong, K. K.** (2000). Acupuncture modulates the limbic system and subcortical gray structures of the human brain: Evidence from fMRI studies in normal subjects. *Human Brain Mapping, 9,* 13–25.

**Hull, C. L.** (1952). *A behavior system: An introduction to behavior theory concerning the individual organism.* New Haven, CT: Yale University Press.

**Hultquist, C. M., Meyers, A. W., Whelan, J. P., Klesges, R. C., Preacher-Ryan, H., & DeBon, M. W.** (1995). The effect of smoking and light activity on metabolism in men. *Health Psychology, 14,* 124–131.

**Humphreys, G. W., & Muller, H.** (2000). A search asymmetry reversed by figure-ground assignment. *Psychological Science, 11,* 196–210.

**Hunt, C.** (2000). The diagnosis and nature of generalized anxiety disorder. *Current Opinions in Psychiatry, 13,* 157–161.

**Hunt, M.** (1993). *The story of psychology.* New York: Doubleday.

**Hwang, S. L.** (1998, November 13). Threat of impotence aids war on smoking. *San Diego Union-Tribune,* A29.

**Hyde, J. A.** (1994). Can meta-analysis make feminist transformations in psychology? *Psychology of Women Quarterly, 18,* 451–462.

**Hyde, J. S., Fennema, E., & Lamon, S. J.** (1990). Gender differences in mathematics performance: A meta-analysis. *Psychological Bulletin, 107,* 139–155.

**Hyde, J. S., & Linn, M. C.** (1988). Are there sex differences in verbal abilities: A meta-analysis. *Psychological Bulletin, 104,* 53–69.

**Hyde, J. S., & Plant, E. A.** (1995). The magnitude of psychological gender differences: Another side to the story. *American Psychologist, 50,* 159–161.

**Hyman, R.** (1994). Anomaly or artifact? Comments on Bem and Honorton. *Psychological Bulletin, 115,* 19–24.

**Hyman, R.** (1996a, March/April). Evaluation of the military's twenty-year program on psychic spying. *Skeptical Inquirer.*

**Hyman, R.** (1996b, March/April). The evidence for psychic functioning: Claims vs. reality. *Skeptical Inquirer.*

**Iacono, W. G., & Lykken, D. T.** (1997). The validity of the lie detector: Two surveys of scientific opinion. *Journal of Applied Psychology, 82,* 426–433.

**Ingram, R. E., Partridge, S., Scott, W., & Bernet, C. Z.** (1994). Schema specificity in subclinical syndrome depression: Distinctions between automatically versus effortfully encoded state and traits depressive information. *Cognitive Therapy and Research, 18,* 195–209.

**Irwin, M., Mascovich, A., Gillin, J. C., Willoughby, R., Pike, J., & Smith, T. L.** (1994). Partial sleep deprivation reduces natural killer cell activity in humans. *Psychosomatic Medicine, 56,* 493–498.

**Ishai, A.** (1999). Cited in S. Carpenter, A new look at recognizing what people see. *Science News, 156,* 102.

**Ito, T. A., Miller, N., & Pollock, V. E.** (1996). Alcohol and aggression: A meta-analysis on the moderating effects of inhibitory cues, triggering events, and self-focused attention. *Psychological Bulletin, 120,* 60–82.

**Iversen, L. L.** (2000). *The science of marijuana.* New York: Oxford University Press.

**Iwata, B. A., Pace, G. M., Dorsey, M. F., Zarcone, J. R., Vollmer, T. R., Smith, R. G., Rodgers, T. A., Lerman, D. C., Shore, B. A., Mazaleski, J. L., Goh, H. L., Cowdery, G. E., Kalsher, M. J., McCosh, K. C., & Kimberly, D. W.** (1994). The functions of self-injurious behavior: An experimental-epidemiological analysis. *Journal of Applied Behavior Analysis, 27,* 215–240.

**Izard, C. E.** (1990). Facial expressions and the regulation of emotions. *Journal of Personality and Social Psychology, 58,* 487–498.

**Izard, C. E.** (1993). Four systems for emotion activation: Cognitive and noncognitive processes. *Psychological Review, 100,* 68–90.

**Izard, C. E.** (1994). Innate and universal facial expressions: Evidence from developmental and cross-cultural research. *Psychological Bulletin, 115,* 288–299.

**Izquierdo, I., & Medina, J. H.** (1997). The biochemistry of memory formation and its regulation by hormones and neuromodulators. *Psychobiology, 25,* 1–9.

**Jackendoff, R.** (1994). *Patterns in the mind: Language and human nature.* New York: Basic Books.

**Jacklin, C. N.** (1989). Female or male: Issues of gender. *American Psychologist, 44,* 127–133.

**Jacks, J. Z., & Devine, P. G.** (2000). Attitude importance, forewarning of message content, and resistance to persuasion. *Basic and Applied Social Psychology, 22,* 19–29.

**Jackson, R. L.** (1994, May 4). A false sense of sincerity: Some cases belie polygraph results. *Los Angeles Times.*

**Jackson, T., Towson, S., & Narduzzi, K.** (1997). Predictors of shyness: A test of variables associated with self-presentational models. *Social Behavior and Personality, 25,* 149–154.

**Jacobs, B.** (1993, January 19). In M. Elias, Brain power a case of "use it or lose it." *USA Today.*

**Jacobson, J. L., & Jacobson, S. W.** (1999). Drinking moderately and pregnancy. *Alcohol Research and Health, 23,* 25–30.

**Jacobson, N. S., & Christensen, A.** (1996). Studying the effectiveness of psychotherapy: How well can clinical trials do the job? *American Psychologist, 51,* 1031–1039.

**Jaffee, S., & Hyde, J. S.** (2000). Gender differences in moral orientation: A meta-analysis. *Psychological Bulletin, 126,* 703–726.

**James, W.** (1969). What is an emotion? In *William James: Collected essays and reviews.* New York: Russell & Russell. (Original work published 1884)

**James, W.** (1890). *The principles of psychology.* New York: Dover.

**Jamison, K. R.** (1995). Manic-depressive illness and creativity. *Scientific American, 272,* 62–67.

**Jan, J. E., Espezel, H., & Appelton, R. E.** (1994). The treatment of sleep disorders with melatonin. *Developmental Medicine and Child Neurology, 36,* 97–107.

**Janca, A., Isaac, M., Bennett, L. A., & Tacchini, G.** (1995). Somatoform disorders in different cultures: A mail questionnaire survey. *Social Psychiatry and Psychiatric Epidemiology, 30,* 44–48.

**Janis, I. L.** (1982). *Groupthink* (2nd ed.). Boston: Houghton Mifflin.

**Janis, I. L.** (1989). *Crucial decisions: Leadership in policy-making and crisis management.* New York: Free Press.

**Janofsky, M.** (2000, September 16). Antidrug program's end stirs up Salt Lake City. *New York Times,* A8.

**Jansen, A. S. P., Nguyen, X. V., Karpitskiy, V., Mettenleiter, T. C., & Loewy, A. D.** (1995). Central command neurons of the sympathetic nervous system: Basis of the fight-or-flight response. *Science, 270,* 644–646.

**Janssen, T., & Carton, J. S.** (1999). The effects of locus of control and task difficulty on procrastination. *The Journal of Genetic Psychology, 160,* 436–442.

**Janus, S. S., & Janus, C. L.** (1993). *The Janus report on sexual behavior.* New York: John Wiley & Sons.

**Japenga, A.** (1994, June 5). Rewriting the dictionary of madness. *Los Angeles Times Magazine.*

**Jelalian, E., Alday, S., Spirito, A., Rasile, D., & Nobile, C.** (2000). Adolescent motor vehicle crashes: The relationship between behavioral factors and self-reported injury. *Journal of Adolescent Health, 27,* 84–93.

**Jensen, P.** (1999). A 14-month randomized clinical trial of treatment strategies for attention-deficit/hyperactivity disorder. *Archives of General Psychiatry, 56,* 1073–1086.

**Jensen, P. S., & Hoagwood, K.** (1997). The book of names: DSM-IV in context. *Development and Psychopathology, 9,* 231–249.

**Jensen-Campbell, L. A., Graziano, W. G., & West, S. G.** (1995). Dominance, prosocial orientation, and female preferences: Do nice guys really finish last? *Journal of Personality and Social Psychology, 68,* 427–440.

**Jiang, Y., Haxby, J. V., Martin, A., Ungerleider, L. G., & Parasuraman, R.** (2000). Complementary neural mechanisms for tracking items in human working memory. *Science, 287,* 643–646.

**Johanson, D. C.** (1996, March). Face-to-face with Lucy's family. *National Geographic,* 96–117.

**John, O. P.** (1990). The "big five" factor taxonomy: Dimensions of personality in the natural language and in questionnaires. In L. A. Previn (Ed.), *Handbook of personality.* New York: Guilford Press.

**John, O. P., & Srivastava, S.** (1999). The big five trait taxonomy: History, measurement and theoretical perspectives. In L. A. Pervin & O. P. John (Eds.), *Handbook of personality* (2nd ed.). New York: Guilford.

**Johnson, B. E., Kuck, D. L., & Schander, P. R.** (1997). Rape myth acceptance and sociodemographic characteristics: A multidimensional analysis. *Sex Roles, 36,* 693–707.

**Johnson, C. R., Hunt, F. M., & Siebert, J. J.** (1994). Discrimination training in the treatment of pica and food scavenging. *Behavior Modification, 18,* 214–229.

**Johnson, J. A.** (1997). Units of analysis for the description and explanation of personality. In R. Hogan, J. Johnson, & S. Briggs (Eds.), *Handbook of personality psychology.* New York: Academic Press.

**Johnson, K.** (1998, November 28). Survey: Women muscled out by bias, harassment. *USA Today,* A1.

**Johnson, K.** (1999, April 5). Government agencies see truth in polygraphs. *USA Today,* 11A.

**Johnson, L. C., Slye, E. S., & Dement, W.** (1965). Electroencephalographic and autonomic during and after prolonged sleep deprivation. *Psychosomatic Medicine, 27,* 415–423.

**Johnson, S. L., & Roberts, J. E.** (1995). Life events and bipolar disorder: Implications from biological theories. *Psychological Bulletin, 117,* 434–449.

**Johnson-Laird, P. N., & Oatley, K.** (2000). Cognitive and social construction in emotions. In M. Lewis & J. M. Haviland-Jones (Eds.), *Handbook of emotions* (2nd ed.). New York: Guilford.

Johnston, D. (1997). A missing link? LTP and learning. *Science, 278,* 401–403.

Johnston, V. (2000, February). Cited in B. Lemley, Isn't she lovely. *Discover,* 43–49.

Jones, D. R., Levy, R. A., Gardner, L., Marsh, R. W., & Patterson, J. C. (1985). Self-control of psychophysiologic response to motion stress: Using biofeedback to treat airsickness. *Aviation, Space and Environmental Medicine, 56,* 1152–1157.

Jones, E. (1953). *The life and work of Sigmund Freud* (3 vols.). New York: Basic Books.

Jones, E., & Berglas, S. (1978). Control of attributions about the self through self-handicapping strategies: The appeal of alcohol and the role of underachievement. *Personality and Social Psychology Bulletin, 4,* 200–206.

Jones, K. L., & Smith, D. W. (1973). Recognition of the fetal alcohol syndrome in early infancy. *Lancet, 2,* 999–1001.

Jones, T. F. (2000). Cited in B. Bower, Mass illness tied to contagious fear. *Science News, 157,* 37.

Jorgensen, R. S., Johnson, B. T., Kolodziej, M. E., & Schreer, G. D. (1996). Elevated blood pressure and personality: A meta-analytic review. *Psychological Bulletin, 120,* 293–320.

Jusczyk, P. W., & Hohne, E. A. (1997). Infants' memory for spoken words. *Science, 277,* 1984–1986.

Just, M. A., Carpenter, P. A., Keller, T. A., Eddy, W. F., & Thulborn, K. R. (1996). Brain activation modulated by sentence comprehension. *Science, 274,* 114–116.

Kagan, J. (1994). *The nature of the child* (10th anniversary edition). New York: Basic Books.

Kagan, J. (1998). Biology and the child. In W. Damon & R. M. Lerner (Eds.), *Handbook of child psychology* (Vol. 1). New York: John Wiley & Sons.

Kagan, J., Reznick, J. S., & Snidman, N. (1988). Biological bases of childhood shyness. *Science, 240,* 167–171.

Kagan, J., & Snidman, N. (1991). Temperamental factors in human development. *American Psychologist, 46,* 856–862.

Kagitcibasi, C., & Poortinga, Y. H. (2000). Cross-cultural psychology. *Journal of Cross-Cultural Psychology, 31,* 129–147.

Kaiser, A. P., & Hester, P. P. (1997). Prevention of conduct disorder through early intervention: A social-communicative perspective. *Behavioral Disorders, 22,* 117–130.

Kaiser, J. (1997). A new way to resist AIDS? *Science, 275,* 1258.

Kalafat, J. (1997, March 10). Cited in S. Nazario, Schools struggle to teach lessons in life and death. *Los Angeles Times.*

Kalick, S. M., Zebrowitz, L. A., Langlois, J. H., & Johnson, R. M. (1998). Does human facial attractiveness honestly advertise health? *Psychological Science, 9,* 8–13.

Kalimo, R., Tenkanen, L., Harma, M., Poppius, E., & Heinsalmi, P. (2000). Job stress and sleep disorders: Findings from the Helsinki heart study. *Stress Medicine, 16,* 65–75.

Kalof, L. (1993). Rape-supportive attitudes and sexual victimization experiences of sorority and nonsorority women. *Sex Roles, 29,* 767–780.

Kandel, E., & Abel, T. (1995). Neuropeptides, adenylyl cyclase, and memory storage. *Science, 268,* 825–826.

Kane, J. M. (1997). Update of treatment strategies. *International Review of Psychiatry, 9,* 419–427.

Kanner, A. D., & Feldman, S. S. (1991). Control over uplifts and hassles and its relationship to adaptational outcomes. *Journal of Behavioral Medicine, 14,* 187–201.

Kanner, L. (1943). Autistic disturbances in affective contact. *Nervous Child, 2,* 217–250.

Kantrowitz, B., Carroll, G., Annin, P., Barrett, T., Cohn, B., & Liu, M. (1993, May 3). The killing ground. *Newsweek.*

Kao, G., & Tienda, M. (1995). Optimism and achievement: The educational performance of immigrant youth. *Social Science Quarterly, 76,* 1–19.

Kaplan, D. M. (1972). On shyness. *International Journal of Psycho-Analysis, 53,* 439–453.

Kaplan, H. B., & Damphousse, K. R. (1997). Reciprocal relationships between life events and psychological distress. *Stress Medicine, 13,* 75–90.

Kaplan, P. S. (1998). *The human odyssey: Life-span development* (3rd ed.). Pacific Grove, CA: Brooks/Cole.

Kaplan, R. M., & Saccuzzo, D. P. (1997). *Psychological testing: Principles, applications, and issues* (4th ed.). Pacific Grove, CA: Brooks/Cole.

Kaplan, R. M., & Saccuzzo, D. P. (2001). *Psychological testing: Principles, applications, and issues* (5th ed.). Belmont, CA: Wadsworth.

Kapur, S., Zipursky, R., Jones, C., Remington, G., & Houle, S. (2000). Relationship between dopamine D2 occupancy, clinical response, and side effects: A double-blind PET study of first-episode schizophrenia. *American Journal of Psychiatry, 157,* 514–520.

Kareken, D. A., Gur, R. C., Mozley, D., Mozley, L. H., Saykin, A. J., Shtasel, D. L., & Gur, R. E. (1995). Cognitive functioning and neuroanatomic volume measures in schizophrenia. *Neuropsychology, 9,* 211–219.

Karler, R. (1998). Cited in I. Wickelgren, Teaching the brain to take drugs. *Science, 280,* 2045–2047.

Karney, B. R., & Bradbury, T. N. (1995). The longitudinal course of marital quality and stability: A review of theory, method, and research. *Psychological Bulletin, 118,* 3–34.

Kassebaum, N. L. (1994). Head Start: Only the best for America's children. *American Psychologist, 49,* 123–126.

Katz, J. (1992). Psychophysiological contributions to phantom limbs. *Canadian Journal of Psychiatry, 37,* 282–298.

Kaufman, A. S. (2000). Tests of intelligence. In R. J. Sternberg, *Handbook of intelligence.* New York: Cambridge University Press.

Kaufman, A. S., Reynolds, C. R., & McLean, J. E. (1989). Age and WAIS-R intelligence in a national sample of adults in the 20 to 74 age range: A cross-sectional analysis with educational level controlled. *Intelligence, 13,* 235–253.

Kaufman, J., & Zigler, E. (1989). The intergenerational transmission of child abuse. In C. Cicchetti & V. Carlson (Eds.), *Child maltreatment: Theory and research on the causes and consequences of child abuse and neglect.* Cambridge, England: Cambridge University Press.

Kaufman, L. (2000). Cited in B. Bower, The moon also rises—and assumes new sizes. *Science News, 157,* 22.

Kavoussi, R. J., Liu, J., & Coccaro, E. F. (1994). An open trial of sertraline in personality disordered patients with impulsive aggression. *Journal of Clinical Psychiatry, 55,* 137–141.

Kawachi, I., Sparrow, D., Vokonas, P. S., & Weiss, S. T. (1994). Symptoms of anxiety and risk of coronary heart disease. *Circulation, 90,* 2225–2229.

Kawakami, K., Dion, K. L., & Dovidio, J. F. (1998). Racial prejudice and stereotype activation. *Personality and Social Psychology Bulletin, 24,* 407–416.

Kay, S. A. (1997). PAS, present, and future: Clues to the origins of circadian clocks. *Science, 276,* 753–754.

Kazantzis, N., Deane, F. P., & Ronan, K. R. (2000). Homework assignments in cognitive and behavioral

therapy: A meta-analysis. *Clinical Psychology: Science and Practice, 7,* 189–202

Kazdin, A. E. (2000). Treatments for aggressive and anti-social children. *Juvenile Violence, 9,* 841–857.

Kearins, J. M. (1981). Visual spatial memory in Australian Aboriginal children of desert regions. *Cognitive Psychology, 13,* 434–460.

Kebbell, M. R., Milne, R., & Wagstaff, G. F. (1999). The cognitive interview: A survey of its forensic effectiveness. *Psychology, Crime & Law, 5,* 101–115.

Keefe, F. J., & France, C. R. (1999). Pain: Biopsychosocial mechanisms and management. *Current Directions in Psychological Science, 8,* 137–141.

Keefe, F. J., & Lefebure, J. C. (1997). Introduction to the featured section: Pain—From mechanisms to management. *Health Psychology, 16,* 307–309.

Keel, P. K., Mitchell, J. E., Miller, K. B., Davis, T. L., & Crow, S. J. (2000). Social adjustment over 10 years following diagnosis with bulimia nervosa. *International Journal of Eating Disorders, 27,* 21–28.

Keenan, K., & Shaw, D. (1997). Developmental and social influences on young girl's early problem behavior. *Psychological Bulletin, 121,* 95–113.

Keiser, R. E., & Prather, E. N. (1990). What is the TAT? A review of ten years of research. *Journal of Personality Assessment, 55,* 800–803.

Keller, H., & Greenfield, P. M. (2000). History and future of development in cross-cultural psychology. *Journal of Cross-Cultural Psychology, 31,* 52–62

Keller, M. B., McCullough, J. P., Klein, D. N., Arnow, B., Dunner, D. L., Gelenberg, A. J., Markowitz, J. C., Nemeroff, C. B., Russell, J. M., Thase, M., Trivedi, M. H., & Zajecka, J. (2000). A comparison of nefazodone, the cognitive-behavioral analysis system of psychotherapy, and their combination for the treatment of chronic depression. *New England Journal of Medicine, 342,* 1462–1470.

Kelley, H. H. (1967). Attribution theory in social psychology. In D. Levine (Ed.), *Nebraska symposium on motivation* (Vol. 15). Lincoln: University of Nebraska Press.

Kelly, A. E., & Kahn, J. H. (1994). Effects of suppression of personal intrusive thoughts. *Journal of Personality and Social Psychology, 66,* 998–1006.

Keltner, D., & Ekman, P. (2000). Facial expression of emotion. Cognitive and social construction in emotions. In M. Lewis & J. M. Haviland-Jones (Eds.), *Handbook of emotions* (2nd ed.). New York: Guilford.

Kempermann, G., & Gage, F. H. (1999, May). New nerve cells for the adult brain. *Scientific American,* 48–53.

Kendall-Tackett, K., Williams, M., & Finkelhor, D. (1993). Impact of sexual abuse on children: A review and synthesis of recent empirical studies. *Psychological Bulletin, 113,* 164–180.

Kendler, K. S., Karkowski, L. M., Neale, M. C., & Prescott, C. A. (2000). Illicit psychoactive substance use, heavy use, abuse, and dependence in a U.S. population-based sample of male twins. *Archives of General Psychiatry, 57,* 261–269.

Kennedy, D. V., & Doepke, K. J. (1999). Multicomponent treatment of a test anxious college student. *Education and Treatment of Children, 22,* 203–217.

Kennedy, S. H., Javanmard, M., & Vaccarino, F. J. (1997). A review of functional neuroimaging in mood disorders: Positron emission tomography and depression. *Canadian Journal of Psychiatry, 42,* 467–475.

Kenrick, D. T., & Funder, D. C. (1988). Profiting from controversy. *American Psychologist, 43,* 23–34.

Kernberg, O. F. (1999). Psychoanalysis, psychoanalytic psychotherapy and supportive psychotherapy: Contemporary controversies. *International Journal of Psychoanalysis, 80,* 1076–1091.

Kernis, M. H., Cornell, D. P., Sun, C., Berry, A., & Harlow, T. (1993). There's more to self-esteem than whether it is high or low: The importance of stability of self-esteem. *Journal of Personality and Social Psychology, 65,* 1190–1204.

Kessler, R. C. (1997). The effects of stressful life events on depression. *Annual Review of Psychology, 48,* 191–214.

Kessler, R. C., McGonagle, K. A., Zhao, S., Nelson, C. B., Higher, M., Eshleman, S., Wittchen, H., & Kendler, K. S. (1994). Lifetime and 12-month prevalence of DSM-III-R psychiatric disorders in the United States. *Archives of General Psychiatry, 51,* 8–19.

Ketelaar, T., & Ellis, B. J. (2000). Are evolutionary explanations unfalsifiable? Evolutionary psychology and the Lakatosian philosophy of science. *Psychological Inquiry, 11,* 1–21.

Khantzian, E. J., & Mack, J. E. (1994). How AA works and why it's important for clinicians to understand. *Journal of Substance Abuse Treatment, 11,* 77–92.

Kiecolt-Glaser, J. K., & Glaser, R. (1989). Psychoneuroimmunology: Past, present, and future. *Health Psychology, 8,* 677–682.

Kihlstrom, J. F. (1993). The continuum of consciousness. *Consciousness and Cognition, 2,* 334–354.

Kihlstrom, J. F., Glisky, M. L., & Angiulo, M. J. (1994). Dissociative tendencies and dissociative disorders. *Journal of Abnormal Psychology, 103,* 117–124.

Kihlstrom, J. R. (1996). Perception without awareness of what is perceived, learning without awareness of what is learned. In M. Velmans (Ed.), *The science of consciousness.* New York: Routledge.

Kilbride, H., Castor, C., Hoffman, E., & Fuger, K. (2000). Thirty-six month outcome of prenatal cocaine exposure for term or near-term infants: Impact of early case management. *Developmental and Behavioral Pediatrics, 21,* 19–26.

Kimball, D. R., & Holyoak, K. J. (2000). Transfer and expertise. In E. Tulving & F. M. Craik (Eds.), *The Oxford handbook of memory.* New York: Oxford University Press.

Kimura, D. (1992). Sex differences in the brain. *Scientific American, 267,* 119–125.

King, A. (1992). Comparison of self-questioning, summarizing, and notetaking-review as strategies for learning from lectures. *American Educational Research Journal, 29,* 303–323.

King, D. P., Zhao, Y., Sangoram, A. M., Wilsbacher, L. D., Tanaka, M., Antoch, M. P., Steeves, T. D. L., Vitaterna, M. H., Kornhauser, J. M., Lowrey, P. L., Turek, F. W., & Takahashi, J. S. (1997). Positional cloning of the mouse circadian clock gene. *Cell, 89,* 641–653.

King, F. A., Yarbrough, C. J., Anderson, D. C., Gordon, T. P., & Gould, K. G. (1988). Primates. *Science, 240,* 1475–1482.

Kinsbourne, M. (1994). Sugar and the hyperactive child. *New England Journal of Medicine, 330,* 355–356.

Kinsey, A. C., Pomeroy, W. B., & Martin, C. E. (1948). *Sexual behavior in the human male.* Philadelphia: Saunders.

Kirk, M. S. (1972, March). Head-hunters in today's world. *National Geographic.*

Kirmayer, L. J. (1991). The place of culture in psychiatric nosology: Taijin kyofusho and DSM-III-R. *Journal of Nervous and Mental Disease, 179,* 19–28.

Kirmayer, L. J., Robbins, J. M., & Paris, J. (1994). Somatoform disorders: Personality and social matrix of somatic distress. *Journal of Abnormal Psychology, 103,* 125–136.

Kirsch, I. (1994). Cognitive-behavioral hypnotherapy. In J. W. Rhue, S. J. Lynn, & I. Kirsch (Eds.), *Handbook of clinical hypnosis.* Washington, DC: American Psychological Association.

Kirsch, I. (1997). Suggestibility or hypnosis: What do our scales really measure? *International Journal of Clinical and Experimental Hypnosis, 45,* 212–225.

Kirsch, I. (2000). The response set theory of hypnosis. *American Journal of Clinical Hypnosis, 42,* 274–292.

Kirsch, I., & Lynn, S. J. (1995). The altered state of hypnosis. *American Psychologist, 50,* 846–858.

Kirsch, I., & Lynn, S. J. (1998). Dissociation theories of hypnosis. *Psychological Bulletin, 123,* 100–115.

Kirsch, I., Lynn, S. J., & Rhue, J. W. (1993). Introduction to clinical hypnosis. In J. W. Rhue, S. J. Lynn, & I. Kirsch (Eds.), *Handbook of clinical hypnosis* (pp. 3–23). Washington, DC: American Psychological Association.

Kirsner, D. (1990). Is there a future for American psychoanalysis? *Psychoanalytic Review, 77,* 175–200.

Kitayama, S., & Markus, H. R. (Eds.). (1994). *Emotion and culture.* Washington, DC: American Psychological Association.

Kitto, J., Lok, D., & Rudowicz, E. (1994). Measuring creative thinking: An activity-based approach. *Creativity Research Journal, 7,* 59–69.

Kleijn, W. C., van der Ploeg, H. M., & Topman, R. M. (1994). Cognition, study habits, test anxiety, and academic performance. *Psychological Reports, 75,* 1219–1226.

Klein, S. B. (2000). *Biological psychology.* Upper Saddle River, NJ: Prentice-Hall.

Kleinhenz, J., Streitberger, K., Windeler, J., Gubbacher, A., Mavridis, G., & Eiki, M. (1999). Randomized clinical trial comparing the effects of acupuncture and a newly designed placebo needle in rotator cuff tendinitis. *Pain, 83,* 235–241

Kleinknecht, R. A. (1994). Acquisition of blood, injury, and needle fears and phobias. *Behavior Research and Therapy, 32,* 817–823.

Kleinknecht, R. A., Dinnel, D. L., & Kleinknecht, E. E. (1997). Cultural factors in social anxiety: A comparison of social phobia symptoms and *taijin kyofusho. Journal of Anxiety Disorders, 11,* 157–177.

Kleinman, A., & Cohen, A. (1997, March). Psychiatry's global challenge. *Scientific American,* 86–89.

Klich, L. Z., & Davidson, G. R. (1983). A cultural difference in visual memory: On le voit, on ne le voit plus. *International Journal of Psychology, 18,* 189–201.

Klingberg, G., & Hwang, C. P. (1994). Children's dental fear picture test (CDFP): A projective test for the assessment of child dental fear. *Journal of Dentistry for Children, 62,* 89–96.

Klingberg, T., Hedehus, M., Temple, E., Salz, T., Gabrielli, J. D. E., Moseley, M. E., & Poldrack, R. A. (2000). Microstructure of temporo-parietal white matter as a basis for reading ability: Evidence from diffusion tensor magnetic resonance imaging. *Neuron, 25,* 493–500.

Klinger, E. (1987, October). The power of daydreams. *Psychology Today.*

Kluft, R. P., & Foote, B. (2000). Dissociate identity disorder: Recent developments. *American Journal of Psychotherapy, 53,* 283–319.

Kluger, J. (1999, November 8). Will Christopher Reeve walk again? *Time,* 85.

Kluger, J. (2000, June 12). The battle to save your memory. *Time,* 46–57.

Knapp, C. (2000, July 12). An alcoholic's private anguish. *Los Angeles Times,* E2.

Knight, R. A. (1992, July). Cited in N. Youngstrom, Rapist studies reveal complex mental map. *APA Monitor.*

Knowlton, B. J., Mangels, J. A., & Squire, L. R. (1996). A neostriatal habit learning system in humans. *Science, 273,* 1399–1402.

Knutson, J. R. (1995). Psychological characteristics of maltreated children: Putative risk factors and consequences. *Annual Review of Psychology, 46,* 401–431.

Kobasa, S. C. (1982). Commitment and coping in stress resistance among lawyers. *Journal of Personality and Social Psychology, 42,* 707–717.

Kobasa, S. C., Maddi, S. R., & Kahn, S. (1982a). Hardiness and health: A prospective study. *Journal of Personality and Social Psychology, 42,* 168–177.

Kobasa, S. C., Maddi, S. R., & Puccetti, M. C. (1982b). Personality and exercise as buffers in the stress-illness relationship. *Journal of Behavioral Medicine, 5,* 391–404.

Koch, P. B. (1993). Promoting healthy sexual development during early adolescence. In R. M. Lerner (Ed.), *Early adolescence: Perspectives on research, policy, and intervention.* Hillsdale, NJ: Lawrence Erlbaum.

Koch, W. (2000, June 16). Big tobacco tells Florida jury it has reformed. *USA Today,* 13A.

Kockro, R. A., Serra, L., Tseng-Tsai, Y., Chan, C., Yih-Yian, S., Gim-Guan, C., Lee, E., Hoe, L. Y., Hern, N. G., & Nowinski, W. L. (2000). Planning and simulation of neurosurgery in a virtual reality environment. *Neurosurgery, 46,* 118–137.

Koegel, L. K., Valdez-Menchacha, M. C., & Koegel, R. L. (1994). Autism: Social communication difficulties and related behaviors. In V. B. Van Hasselt & M. Hersen (Eds.), *Advanced abnormal psychology.* New York: Plenum Press.

Kohlberg, L. (1984). *The psychology of moral development: Essays on moral development* (Vol. 11). San Francisco: Harper & Row.

Kohler, T., & Troester, U. (1991). Changes in the palmar sweat index during mental arithmetic. *Biological Psychology, 32,* 143–154.

Köhler, W. (1917; reprinted 1925). *The mentality of apes* (E. Winter, Trans.). New York: Harcourt Brace & World.

Kohyama, J., Shimohira, M., & Iwakawa, Y. (1997). Maturation of motility and motor inhibition in rapid-eye-movement sleep. *Journal of Pediatrics, 130,* 117–122.

Kolata, G. (2000a, May 15). Sharing of profits is debated as the value of tissue rises. *New York Times,* A1.

Kolata, G. (2000b, October 17). How the body knows when to gain or lose. *New York Times,* D1.

Kolko, D. (1995, April). Cited in T. DeAngelis, Research documents trauma of abuse. *APA Monitor.*

Kondo, D. S. (1997). Strategies for coping with test anxiety. *Anxiety, Stress, and Coping, 10,* 203–215.

Koopman, J. M. (1995, February 20). Cited in M. Cimons & T. H. Maugh, II, New strategies fuel optimism in AIDS fight. *Los Angeles Times.*

Koplan, J. P. (1999, August 31). Cited in M. Cimons, New data suggest limits to AIDS drugs. *Los Angeles Times,* A1.

Kordower, J. H., Rosenstein, J. M., Collier T. J., Burke, M. A., Chen, E., Li, J. M., Martel, L., Levey, A. E., Mufson, E. J., Freeman, T. B., & Olanow, W. (1996). Functional fetal nigral grafts in a patient with Parkinson's disease: Chemoanatomic, ultrastructural, and metabolic studies. *Journal of Comparative Neurology, 370,* 203–230.

Koss, M. P., Gidycz, C. A., & Wisniewski, N. (1987). The scope of rape: Incidence and prevalence of sexual aggression and victimization in a national sample of higher education students. *Journal of Consulting and Clinical Psychology, 55,* 162–170.

Kosslyn, S. M. (1995). Introduction. In M. S. Gazzaniga (Ed.), *The cognitive neurosciences.* Cambridge, MA: MIT Press.

Kowalski, R. M. (1996). Complaints and complaining: Functions, antecedents, and consequences. *Psychological Bulletin, 119,* 179–196.

Kramer, M. W., Kuo, C. L., & Dailey, J. C. (1997). The impact of brainstorming techniques on subsequent group processes: Beyond generating ideas. *Small Group Research, 28,* 218–242.

Kraus, S. J. (1995). Attitudes and the prediction of behavior: A meta-analysis of the empirical literature. *Personality and Social Psychology Bulletin, 21,* 58–75.

Kristof, N. D. (1996, March 10). Guns: One nation bars, the other requires. *New York Times,* E-3.

Krueger, J., & Heckhausen, J. (1993). Personality development across the adult life span: Subjective conceptions vs. cross-sectional contrasts. *Journal of Gerontology: Psychological Sciences, 48,* P100–P108.

Kua, E. H., Chew, P. H., & Ko, S. M. (1993). Spirit possession and healing among Chinese psychiatric patients. *Acta Psychiatrica Scandinavica, 88,* 447–450.

Kubovy, M., & Wagemans, J. (1995). Grouping by proximity and multistability in dot lattices: A quantitative Gestalt theory. *Psychological Science, 6,* 225–234.

Kuch, K., Cox, B. J., Evans, R., & Shulman, I. (1994). Phobias, panic, and pain in 55 survivors of road vehicle accidents. *Journal of Anxiety Disorders, 8,* 181–187.

Kuffer, D. J., & Reynolds, C. R. (1997). Management of insomnia. *New England Journal of Medicine, 336,* 341–346.

Kugelmann, R. (1998). The psychology and management of pain: Gate control as theory and symbol. In S. J. Henderikus (Ed.), *The body and psychology.* London, England: Academy of Hebrew Language.

Kuhl, P. K., Andruski, J. E., Christovich, I. A., Christovich, L. A., Kolzhevnikova, E. V., Ryskina, V. L., Stolyarova, E. I., Sundberg, U., & Lacerda, F. (1997). Cross-language analysis of phonetic units in language addressed to infants. *Science, 277,* 684–687.

Kulman, L. (1999, April 26). What'd you say? *U.S. News & World Report,* 66–74.

Kurahashi, T., & Menini, A. (1997). Mechanism of odorant adaptation in the olfactory receptor cell. *Nature, 385,* 725–729.

Kurdek, L. A. (1999). The nature and predictors of the trajectory of change in marital quality for husbands and wives over the first 10 years of marriage. *Developmental Psychology, 35,* 1283–1296.

Kurten, B. (1993). *Our earliest ancestors.* New York: Columbia University Press.

Kurtz, E. (1979). *Not-God: A history of Alcoholics Anonymous.* Center City, MN: Hazelden.

Kurtz, P. (1995, May/June). Is John Beloff an absolute paranormalist? *Skeptical Inquirer.*

Laan, E., & van Lunsen, R. H. W. (1997). Hormones and sexuality in postmenopausal women: A psychophysiological study. *Journal of Psychosomatic Obstetrics and Gynecology, 18,* 126–133.

LaBar, K. S., & LeDoux, J. E. (1996). Partial disruption of fear conditioning in rats with unilateral amygdala damage: Correspondence with unilateral temporal lobectomy in humans. *Behavioral Neuroscience, 110,* 991–997.

Labouvie-Vief, G. (1996). Emotion, thought, and gender. In C. Magai & S. H. McFadden (Eds.), *Handbook of emotion, adult development, and aging.* San Diego: Academic Press.

Lach, J. (1997, Spring/Summer). Cultivating the mind (Special issue). *Newsweek.*

LaFee, S. (1996, September 11). Fragile lives. *San Diego Union-Tribune.*

LaFee, S. (1999, October 13). Face value. *San Diego Union-Tribune,* E1.

LaFee, S. (2000, March 29). Sight to behold. *San Diego Union-Tribune,* E-12.

Laganer, A., Kraft, P., & Roysamb, E. (2000). Perceived self-efficacy in health behaviour research: Conceptual-

izations, measurement and correlated. *Psychology and Health, 15,* 51–69.

Laird, J. D. (1974). Self-attribution of emotion: The effects of expressive behavior on the quality of emotional experience. *Journal of Personality and Social Psychology, 29,* 475–486.

Lalumiere, M. L., Blanchard, R., & Zucker, K. J. (2000). Sexual orientation and handedness in men and women: A meta-analysis. *Psychological Bulletin, 126,* 575–592.

Lam, R. W., Tam, E. M., Shiah, I., Yatham, L. N., & Zis, A. P. (2000). Effects of light therapy on suicidal ideation in patients with winter depression. *Journal of Clinical Psychiatry, 61,* 30–32.

Lamb, N. (1990). *Guide to teaching string* (5th ed.). Dubuque, IA: William C Brown.

Lambert, M. J., & Bergin, A. E. (1994). The effectiveness of psychotherapy. In A. E. Bergin & S. L. Garfield (Eds.), *Handbook of psychotherapy and behavior change* (4th ed.). New York: Wiley.

Lammers, C., Ireland, M., Resnick, M., & Blum, R. (2000). Influences on adolescents' decision to postpone onset of sexual intercourse: A survival analysis of virginity among youths aged 13–18 years. *Journal of Adolescent Health, 26,* 42–48.

Lane, H. (1997, July). Cited in R. A. Clay, Do hearing devices impair deaf children? *APA Monitor.*

Lane, R. D., Reiman, E. M., Ahern, G. L., Schwartz, G. E., & Davidson, R. J. (1997). Neuroanatomical correlates of happiness, sadness, and disgust. *American Journal of Psychiatry, 154,* 926–933.

Lang, A. J., & Craske, M. G. (2000). Manipulations of exposure-based therapy to reduce return of fear: A replication. *Behaviour Research and Therapy, 38,* 1–12.

Lang, P. J. (1995). The emotion probe. *American Psychologist, 50,* 372–385.

Langlois J. H., Kalakanis, L., Rubenstein, A. J., Larson, A., Hallam, M., & Smoot, M. (2000). Maxims or myths of beauty? A meta-analysis and theoretical review. *Psychological Bulletin, 136,* 390–423.

Langlois, J. H., Roggman, L. A., & Musselman, L. (1994). What is average and what is not average about attractive faces? *Psychological Science, 5,* 214–220.

Lanyado, M., & Horne, A. (Eds.). (1999). *The handbook of child and adolescent psychotherapy.* New York: Routledge.

Lanzetta, J. T., Cartwright-Smith, J., & Kleck, R. E. (1976). Effects of nonverbal discrimination on emotional experience and autonomic arousal. *Journal of Personality and Social Psychology, 33,* 354–370.

Larimer, M. E., Palmer, R. S., & Marlatt, G. A. (1999). Relapse prevention. *Alcohol Research and Health, 23,* 151–160.

Larivee, S., Normandeau, S., & Parent, S. (2000). The French connection: Some contributions of French-language research in the post-Piagetian era. *Child Development, 71,* 823–839.

Larkin, K. T., & Edens, J. L. (1994). Behavior therapy. In V. B. Van Hasselt & M. Hersen (Eds.), *Advanced abnormal psychology.* New York: Plenum Press.

Latané, B. (1981). The psychology of social impact. *American Psychologist, 36,* 343–356.

Latané, B., & Darley, J. M. (1970). *The unresponsive bystander: Why doesn't he help?* New York: Appleton-Century-Crofts.

Latané, B., & Nida, S. (1981). Ten years of research on group size and helping. *Psychological Bulletin, 89,* 308–324.

Laumann, E., Michael, R. T., Gagnon, J. H., & Kolata, G. (1994). *The social organization of sexuality.* Chicago: University of Chicago Press.

Lawrie, S. M., & Abukmeil, S. S. (1998). Brain abnormality in schizophrenia. *British Journal of Psychiatry, 172,* 110–120.

Lazarus, R. S. (1990). Psychological stress in the workplace. *Journal of Social Behavior and Personality, 6,* 1–13.

Lazarus, R. S. (1991). Cognition and motivation in emotion. *American Psychologist, 46,* 352–367.

Lazarus, R. S. (1993). Why we should think of stress as a subset of emotion. In L. Goldberger & S. Breznitz (Eds.), *Handbook of stress: Theoretical and clinical aspects* (2nd ed.). New York: Free Press.

Lazarus, R. S. (1999a). *Stress and emotion.* New York: Springer Publishing.

Lazarus, R. S. (1999b). The cognition-emotion debate: A bit of history. In T. Dalgleish & M. Power (Eds.), *Handbook of cognition and emotion.* New York: Wiley.

Lazarus, R. S. (2000). Evolution of a model of stress, coping and discrete emotions. In V. R. Rice (Ed.), *Handbook of stress, coping and health.* Thousand Oaks, CA: Sage.

Leafgren, A. (1989). Health and wellness programs. In M. L. Upcraft & J. N. Gardner (Eds.), *The freshman year experience.* San Francisco: Jossey-Bass.

Leahy, R. L., & Holland, S. J. (2000). *Treatment plans and interventions for depression and anxiety disorders.* New York: Guilford.

Leaper, C. (2000). Gender, affiliation, assertion, and the interactive context of parent-child play. *Developmental Psychology, 36,* 381–393.

Leary, M. R., Tambor, E. S., Terdal, S. K., & Downs, D. L. (1995). Self-esteem as an interpersonal monitor: The sociometer hypothesis. *Journal of Personality and Social Psychology, 68,* 518–530.

Leavy, J. (1996, March 18). With Ritalin, the son also rises. *Newsweek.*

LeBlanc, L. A., Hagopian, L. P., & Maglieri, K. A. (2000). Use of a token economy to eliminate excessive inappropriate social behavior in an adult with developmental disabilities. *Behavioral Interventions, 15,* 135–143.

LeDoux, J. (1996). *The emotional brain: The mysterious underpinnings of emotional life.* New York: Simon & Schuster.

LeDoux, J., & Phelps, E. A. (2000). In M. Lewis & J. M. Haviland-Jones (Eds.), *Handbook of emotions* (2nd ed., pp. 157–172). New York: Guilford.

Lee, C., & Bobko, P. (1994). Self-efficacy beliefs: Comparison of five measures. *Journal of Applied Psychology, 79,* 364–369.

Leedham, B., Meyerowitz, B. E., Muirhead, J., & Frist, W. H. (1995). Positive expectations predict health after heart transplantation. *Health Psychology, 14,* 74–79.

Leehotz, R. (2000, March 16). Losing sleep over fatigue. *Los Angeles Times,* B2.

Lehrer, P. M., Carr, R., Sargunaraj, D., & Woolfolk, R. L. (1994). Stress management techniques: Are they all equivalent, or do they have specific effects? *Biofeedback and Self-Regulation, 19,* 353–401.

Leibel, R. L., Rosenbaum, M., & Hirsch, J. (1995). Changes in energy expenditure resulting from altered body weight. *New England Journal of Medicine, 332,* 621–628.

Leiblum, S. R. (1990). Sexuality and the midlife woman. *Psychology of Women Quarterly, 14,* 495–508.

Leigh, B. C., Morrison, D. M., Trocki, K., & Temple, M. T. (1994). Sexual behavior of American adolescents: Results from a U.S. National Survey. *Journal of Adolescent Health, 15,* 117–125.

Leinwand, D. (2000, May 9). Heroin's resurgence closes drug's traditional gender gap. *USA Today,* 1A.

**Leippe, M. R., & Eisenstadt, D.** (1994). Generalization of dissonance reduction: Decreasing prejudice through induced compliance. *Journal of Personality and Social Psychology, 67,* 395–413.

**Leland, J.** (1994, February 14). Homophobia, *Newsweek.*

**Leland, J.** (1998, October 26). Not quite Viagra nation. *Newsweek,* 68.

**Leland, J.** (1999, February 22). Bad news in the bedroom. *Newsweek,* 47.

**Lemerise, E. A., & Dodge, K. A.** (2000). The development of anger and hostile interactions. In M. Lewis & J. M. Haviland-Jones (Eds.), *Handbook of emotions* (2nd ed.). New York: Guilford.

**Lemley, B.** (2000, February). Isn't she lovely? *Discover,* 42–49.

**Lemonick, M. D.** (1999, January 25). War of the diapers. *Time,* 64.

**Lemonick, M. D.** (2000, October 30). Teens before their time. *Time,* 66–74.

**Lemonick, M. D., & Dorfman, A.** (1999, August 23). Up from the apes. *Time,* 50–58.

**Lendon, C. L., Ashall, F., & Goate, A. M.** (1997). Exploring the etiology of Alzheimer disease using molecular genetics. *Journal of the American Medical Association, 277,* 825–831.

**Lenox, R. H., & Hahn, C.** (2000). Overview of the mechanism of action of lithium in the brain: Fifty-year update. *Journal of Clinical Psychiatry, 2000*(Supplement 9), 5–15.

**Leo, J.** (1987, January 12). Exploring the traits of twins. *Time.*

**Lepore, S. J., Mata Allen, K. A., & Evans, G. W.** (1993). Social support lowers cardiovascular reactivity to an acute stressor. *Psychosomatic Medicine, 55,* 518–524.

**Lepper, M. R., Henderlong, J., & Gingras, I.** (1999). Understanding the effects of extrinsic rewards on intrinsic motivation—Uses and abuses of meta-analysis: Comment on Deci, Koestner, and Ryan (1999). *Psychological Bulletin, 125,* 669–676.

**Lerner, A. G., Gelkopf, M., Oyfee, I., Finkel, B., Katz, S., Sigal, M., & Weizman, A.** (2000). LSD-induced hallucinogen persisting perception disorder treatment with clonidine: An open pilot study. *International Clinical Psychopharmacology, 115,* 35–37.

**Lerner, R. M., & Galambos, N. L.** (1998). Adolescent development: Challenges and opportunities for research, programs, and policies. *Annual Review of Psychology, 49,* 413–446.

**Leshner, A. I.** (1997). Drug abuse and addiction treatment research. *Archives General Psychiatry, 54,* 691–693.

**Lester, B.** (1997, December). Cited in B. Azar, Researchers debunk myth of the "crack baby." *APA Monitor.*

**Lester, B. M., LaGasse, L. L., & Seifer, R.** (1998). Cocaine exposure and children: The meaning of subtle effects. *Science, 282,* 633–634.

**Leung, P. W. L., Luk, S. L., Ho, T. P., Taylor, E., Mak, R. L., & Bacon-Shone, J.** (1996). The diagnosis and prevalence of hyperactivity in Chinese schoolboys. *British Journal of Psychiatry, 168,* 486–496.

**LeVay, S., & Hamer, D. H.** (1994). Evidence for a biological influence in male homosexuality. *Scientific American, 270,* 44–49.

**Levenson, R. W., Carstensen, L. L., & Gottman, J. M.** (1994). The influence of age and gender on affect, physiology, and their interrelations: A study of long-term marriages. *Journal of Personality and Social Psychology, 67,* 56–68.

**Leventhal, H., & Patrick-Miller, L.** (2000). Emotions and physical illness: Causes and indicators of vulnerability. In M. Lewis & J. M. Haviland-Jones (Eds.), *Handbook of emotions* (2nd ed.). New York: Guilford.

**Levin, R.** (1994). Sleep and dreaming characteristics of frequent nightmare subjects in a university population. *Dreaming, 4,* 127–137.

**Levine, R. V., Martinez, T. S., Brase, G., & Sorenson, K.** (1994). Helping in 36 U.S. cities. *Journal of Personality and Social Psychology, 67,* 69–82.

**Levine, S., & Koenig, J.** (Eds.). (1980). *Why men rape: Interviews with convicted rapists.* Toronto: Macmillan.

**Levitt, S., & Wagner, J.** (1994, January 21). Weight and see. *People.*

**Levy, D.** (1997). *Tools of critical thinking.* New York: Allyn & Bacon.

**Levy, J.** (1985, May). Right brain, left brain: Fact and fiction. *Psychology Today.*

**Levy, J., & Trevarthen, C.** (1976). Metacontrol of hemispheric function in human split-brain patients. *Journal of Experimental Psychology: Human Perception and Performance, 2,* 299–312.

**Levy, J., Trevarthen, C., & Sperry, R. W.** (1972). Perception of bilateral chimeric figures following hemispheric deconnection. *Brain, 95,* 61–68.

**Lewin, R.** (1993). *The origin of modern humans.* New York: Scientific American Library.

**Lewinsohn, P. M., Rohde, P., & Seeley, J. R.** (1994). Psychosocial risk factors for future adolescent suicide attempts. *Journal of Consulting and Clinical Psychology, 62,* 297–305.

**Lewis, C. E.** (1991). Neurochemical mechanisms of chronic antisocial behavior (psychopathy). *Journal of Nervous and Mental Disease, 179,* 720–727.

**Leyens, J. P., & Fiske, S. T.** (1994). Impression formation: From recitals to Symphonie Fantastique. In P. G. Devine, D. L. Hamilton, & T. M. Ostrom (Eds.), *Social cognition: Impact on social psychology.* New York: Academic Press.

**Li, T. K.** (2000). Pharmacogenetics of responses to alcohol and genes that influence alcohol drinking. *Journal of Studies on Alcohol, 61,* 5–12.

**Libman, J.** (1991, June 7). Sudden end to a trailblazing career. *Los Angeles Times,* E-1.

**Liddle, P. F.** (1997). Dynamic neuroimaging with PET, SPET, or fMRI. *International Review of Psychiatry, 9,* 331–337.

**Lie, R. T., Wilcox, A. J., & Skjaerven, R.** (1994). A population-based study of the risk of recurrence of birth defects. *New England Journal of Medicine, 331,* 1–4.

**Lieberman, D. A.** (1993). *Learning* (2nd ed.). Pacific Grove, CA: Brooks/Cole.

**Lieberman, D. A.** (2000). *Learning: Behavior and cognition* (3rd ed.). Belmont, CA: Wadsworth.

**Lieberman, M. D.** (2000). Intuition: A social cognitive neuroscience approach. *Psychological Bulletin, 126,* 109–137.

**Liebert, R. M., & Spiegler, M. D.** (1994). *Personality: Strategies and issues* (7th ed.). Pacific Grove, CA: Brooks/Cole.

**Liebowitz, M. R., Heimberg, R. G., Schneier, F. R., Hope, D. A., Davies, S., Holt, C. S., Goetz, D., Juster, H. R., Lin, S. H., Bruch, M. A., Marshall, R. D., & Klein, D. F.** (1999). Cognitive-behavioral group therapy versus phenelzine in social phobia: Long-term outcome. *Depression and Anxiety, 10,* 89–98.

**Lief, H. I., & Fetkewicz, J.** (1995). Retractors of false memories: The evolution of pseudo-memories. *Journal of Psychiatry & Law, 23,* 411–436.

**Lief, L.** (1994, August 29/September 5). An old oasis of tolerance runs dry. *U.S. News & World Report.*

**Lilienfeld, S. O.** (1993). Do "honesty" tests really measure honesty? *Skeptical Inquirer, 18,* 32–41.

**Lilienfeld, S. O., Kirsch, I., Sarbin, T. R., Lynn, S. J., Chaves, J. F., Ganaway, G. K., & Powell, R. A.** (1999). Dissociative identity disorder and the sociocognitive model: Realing the lessons of the past. *Psychological Bulletin, 125,* 507–523.

**Lilly, J. C.** (1972). *The center of the cyclone.* New York: Bantam.

**Lin, J. G.** (1996). A concept in analgesic mechanisms of acupuncture. *Chinese Medical Journal, 109,* 179–192.

**Linden, E.** (1993, March 22). Can animals think? *Time.*

**Lindenberger, U., & Baltes, P. B.** (1997). Intellectual functioning in old and very old age: Cross-sectional results from the Berlin aging study. *Psychology and Aging, 12,* 410–432.

**Lindsay, J. J., & Anderson, C. A.** (2000). From antecedent conditions to violent actions: A general affective aggression model. *Personality and Social Psychological Bulletin, 26,* 533–547.

**Lipkin, R.** (1995). Additional genes may affect color vision. *Science News, 147,* 100.

**Lippa, R. A.** (1994). *Introduction to social psychology* (2nd ed.). Pacific Grove, CA: Brooks/Cole.

**Lipton, S. D.** (1983). A critique of so-called standard psychoanalytic technique. *Contemporary Psychoanalysis, 19,* 35–52.

**Lisanby, S. H., Maddox, J. H., Prudic, J., Devanand, D. P., & Sackeim, H. A.** (2000). The effects of electroconvulsive therapy of memory of autobiographical and public events. *Archives of General Psychiatry, 57,* 581–590.

**Liska, K.** (1994). *Drugs & the human body* (4th ed.). New York: Macmillan.

**Litt, M. D., Kalinowski, L., & Shafer, D.** (1999). A dental fears typology of oral surgery patients: Matching patients to anxiety interventions. *Health Psychology, 18,* 614–624.

**Little, B. R.** (1999). Personality and motivation: Personal action and the conative evolution. In L. A. Pervin & O. P. John (Eds.), *Handbook of personality* (2nd ed.). New York: Guilford.

**Liu, W., & McGucken, E.** (1997a, March). Cited in D. Stover, *Popular Science.*

**Liu, W., & McGucken, E.** (1997b, August). Cited in M. Shaffer, Restoring sight. *Popular Science.*

**Liu, Y., Gao, J., Liu, H., & Fox, P. T.** (2000). The temporal response of the brain after eating revealed by functional MRI. *Nature, 405,* 1058–1062.

**Lochman, J. E., & Lenhart, L. A.** (1993). Anger coping intervention for aggressive children: Conceptual models and outcomes effects. *Clinical Psychology Review, 13,* 785–805.

**Locke, E. A., & Latham, G. P.** (1994). Goal setting theory. In H. F. O'Neil, Jr., & M. Drillings (Eds.), *Motivation: Theory and research.* Hillsdale, NJ: Lawrence Erlbaum.

**Locker, D., Shapiro, D., & Liddell, A.** (1997). Overlap between dental anxiety and blood-injury fears: Psychological characteristics and response to dental treatment. *Behaviour Research and Therapy, 35,* 583–590.

**Loeber, R., & Hay, D.** (1997). Key issues in the development of aggression and violence from childhood to early adulthood. *Annual Review of Psychology, 48,* 371–410.

**Loehlin, J. C.** (1992). *Genes and environment in personality.* Newbury Park, CA: Sage.

**Loehlin, J. C.** (2000). Group differences in intelligence. In R. J. Sternberg, *Handbook of intelligence.* New York: Cambridge University Press.

**Loftus, E.** (1999). Repressed memories. *Forensic Psychiatry, 22,* 61–69.

**Loftus, E.** (2000, April 25). Cited in J. E. Brody, Memories of things that never were. *New York Times,* D8.

Loftus, E. F. (1975). Leading questions and the eyewitness report. *Cognitive Psychology, 7,* 560–572.

Loftus, E. F. (1979). The malleability of memory. *American Scientist, 67,* 312–320.

Loftus, E. F. (1993a). Psychologists in the eyewitness world. *American Psychologist, 48,* 518–537.

Loftus, E. F. (1993b). The reality of repressed memories. *American Psychologist, 48,* 518–537.

Loftus, E. F. (1994). The repressed memory controversy. *American Psychologist, 49,* 443–445.

Loftus, E. F. (1997a, September). Creating false memories. *Scientific American,* 70–75.

Loftus, E. F. (1997b). Repressed memory accusations: Devastated families and devastated patients. *Applied Cognitive Psychology, 11,* 25–30.

Loftus, E. F., & Hoffman, H. G. (1989). Misinformation and memory: The creation of new memories. *Journal of Experimental Psychology: General, 118,* 409–420.

Loftus, E. F., & Loftus, G. R. (1980). On the performance of stored information in the human brain. *American Psychologist, 35,* 409–420.

Loftus, E. F., Miller, D. G., & Burns, H. J. (1978). Semantic integration of verbal information into a visual memory. *Journal of Experimental Psychology: Human Learning and Memory, 4,* 19–31.

Loftus, E. F., Polonsky, S., & Fullilove, M. T. (1994). Memories of childhood sexual abuse. *Psychology of Women Quarterly, 18,* 67–84.

Logothetis, N. K. (1999, November). Vision: A window on consciousness. *Scientific American,* 69–75.

Logue, A. W., Ophir, I., & Strauss, K. E. (1981). The acquisition of taste aversions in humans. *Behavior Research and Therapy, 19,* 319–335.

Lohman, D. F. (2000). Complex information processing and intelligence. In R. J. Sternberg, *Handbook of intelligence.* New York: Cambridge University Press.

Long, J. D., Gaynor, P., Erwin, A., & Williams, R. L. (1994). The relationship of self-management to academic motivation, study efficiency, academic satisfaction, and grade point average among prospective education majors. *Psychology, A Journal of Human Behavior, 31,* 22–30.

Longo, L. C., & Ashmore, R. D. (1995). The looks-personality relationship: Global self-orientations as shared precursors of subjective physical attractiveness and self-ascribed traits. *Journal of Applied Social Psychology, 25,* 371–398.

Lonsway, K. A., & Fitzgerald, L. F. (1994). Rape myths: In review. *Psychology of Women Quarterly, 18,* 133–164.

Lopez, S. R., & Guarnaccia, P. J. (2000). Cultural psychopathology: Uncovering the social worlds of mental illness. *Annual Review of Psychology, 51,* 571–598.

Lore, R. K., & Schultz, L. A. (1993). Control of human aggression. *American Psychologist, 48,* 16–25.

Lorenz, K. (1952). *King Solomon's ring.* New York: Crowell.

Lovaas, I. (1999, September). Cited in H. McIntosh, Two autism studies fuel hope—and skepticism. *Monitor: American Psychological Association, 28.*

Lovaas, O. I. (1987). Behavioral treatment and normal educational and intellectual functioning in young autistic children. *Journal of Consulting and Clinical Psychology, 55,* 3–9.

Lovaas, O. I. (1993). The development of a treatment-research project for developmentally disabled autistic children. *Journal of Applied Behavior Analysis, 26,* 617–630.

Lovaas, O. I., & Buch, G. (1997). Intensive behavioral intervention with young children. In N. N. Singh (Ed.), *Prevention and treatment of severe behavior problems.* Pacific Grove, CA: Brooks/Cole.

Lowry, J. L., & Ross, M. J. (1997). Expectations of psychotherapy duration: How long should psychotherapy last? *Psychotherapy, 34,* 272–277.

Lubart, T. I. (1994). Creativity. In R. J. Sternberg (Ed.), *Thinking and problem solving.* San Diego, CA: Academic Press.

Lucking, C. B., Durr, A., Bonifati, V., Vaughan, J., De Michele, G., Gasser, T., Harhangi, B. S., Pollak, P., Bonnet, A., Nichol, D., De Mari, M., Marconi, R., Broussolle, E., Rascol, O., Rosier, M., Arnould, I., Oostra, B. A., Breteler, M. M. B., Filla, A., Meco, G., Denefle, P., Wood, N. W., Agid, Y., & Brice, A. (2000). Association between early-onset Parkinson's disease and mutations in the parkin gene. *New England Journal of Medicine, 342,* 1560–1567.

Ludwig, A. M. (1995). *The price of greatness: Resolving the creative and madness controversy.* New York: Guilford Press.

Luna, T. D., French, J., & Mitcha, J. I. (1997). A study of USAF air traffic controller shiftwork: Sleep, fatigue, activity, and mood analyses. *Aviation, Space, and Environmental Medicine, 68,* 18–23.

Luo, L., & Shih, J. B. (1997). Sources of happiness: A qualitative approach. *Journal of Social Psychology, 137,* 181–187.

Lupart, J. L., & Pyryt, M. C. (1996). "Hidden gifted" students: Underachiever prevalence and profile. *Journal for the Education of the Gifted, 20,* 36–53.

Lutz, J., Means, L. W., & Long, T. E. (1994). Where did I park? A naturalistic study of spatial memory. *Applied Cognitive Psychology, 8,* 439–451.

Lykken, D., & Tellegen, A. (1996). Happiness is a stochastic phenomenon. *Psychological Science, 7,* 186–189.

Lynam, D. R., Milich, R., Zimmerman, R., Novak, S. P., Logan, T. K., Martin, C., Leukefeld, C., & Clayton, R. (1999). Project DARE: No effects at 10-year follow-up. *Journal of Counsulting and Clinical Psychology, 67,* 590–593.

Lynn, S. J. (1997). Automaticity and hypnosis: A sociocognitive account. *International Journal of Clinical and Experimental Hypnosis, 45,* 239–250.

Lynn, S. J., Kirsch, I., Barabasz, A., Cardena, E., & Patterson, D. (2000). Hypnosis as an empirically supported clinical intervention: The state of the evidence and a look to the future. *International Journal of Clinical and Experimental Hypnosis, 48,* 239–259.

Lyon, R. (1999, November 22). Cited in B. Kantrowitz & A. Underwood, Dyslexia and the new science of reading. *Newsweek,* 72–78.

Maccoby, E. E. (1984). Socialization and developmental change. *Child Development, 55,* 317–328.

MacCoun, R. J. (1993). Drugs and the law: A psychological analysis of drug prohibition. *Psychological Bulletin, 113,* 497–512.

Macfarlane, A. J. (1975). Olfaction in the development of social preferences in the human neonate. *CIBA Foundation Symposium, 33,* 103–117.

Mackenzie, D. (2000, July). Remote heart surgery. *Popular Science,* 65.

Mackie, D. M., & Skelly, J. J. (1994). The social cognition analysis of social influence: Contributions to the understanding of persuasion and conformity. In P. G. Devine, D. L. Hamilton, & T. M. Ostrom (Eds.), *Social cognition: Impact on social psychology.* New York: Academic Press.

Macklin, M. L., Metzger, L. J., Lasko, N. B., Berry, N. J., Orr, S. P., & Pitman, R. K. (2000). Five-year follow-up study of eye movement desensitization and reprocessing therapy for combat-related posttraumatic stress disorder. *Comprehensive Psychiatry, 41,* 24–27.

MacLeod, C. (1999). Anxiety and anxiety disorders. In T. Dalgleish & M. Power (Eds.), *Handbook of cognition and emotion.* New York: Wiley.

Macmillan, M. (1997). *Freud evaluated.* Cambridge, MA: MIT Press.

Macnee, C. L., & McCabe, S. (2000). Microstressors and health. In V. R. Rice (Ed.), *Handbook of stress, coping and health.* Thousand Oaks, CA: Sage.

MacQueen, G., Marshall, J., Perdue, M., Siegel, S., & Biennenstock, J. (1989). Pavlovian conditioning of rat mucosal mast cells to secrete rat mast cell protease II. *Science, 243,* 83–85.

Macrae, C. N., & Bodenhausen, G. V. (2000). Social cognition: Thinking categorically about others. *Annual Review of Psychology, 51,* 93–120.

Macrae, C. N., Bodenhausen, G. V., & Milne, A. B. (1998). Saying no to unwanted thoughts: Self-focus and the regulation of mental life. *Journal of Personality and Social Psychology, 74,* 578–589.

Macrae, C. N., Milne, A. B., & Bodenhausen, G. V. (1994). Stereotypes as energy-saving devices: A peek inside the cognitive toolbox. *Journal of Personality and Social Psychology, 66,* 37–47.

Madon, S., Jussim, L., & Eccles, J. (1997). In search of the powerful self-fulfilling prophecy. *Journal of Personality and Social Psychology, 72,* 791–809.

Madsen, K. B. (1973). Theories of motivation. In B. B. Wollman (Ed.), *Handbook of general psychology.* Englewood Cliffs, NJ: Prentice-Hall.

Magidoff, R. (1973). *Yehudi Menuhin.* London: Robert Hale.

Magnier, M. (2000, March 25). Japanese on a fast track to addiction. *Los Angeles Times,* A2.

Magnusson, A., & Stefansson, J. G. (1993). Prevalence of seasonal affective disorder in Iceland. *Archives of General Psychiatry, 50,* 941–946.

Magnusson, A. (2000). An overview of epidemiological studies on seasonal affective disorder. *Acta Psychiatria Scandinavica, 101,* 176–184.

Magnusson, A., Axelsson, J., Karlsson, M. M., & Oskarsson, H. (2000). Lack of seasonal mood change in the Icelandic population: Results of a cross-sectional study. *American Journal of Psychiatry, 157,* 234–238.

Mah, Z., & Bryant, H. E. (1997). The role of past mammography and future intentions in screening mammography usage. *International Society for Preventive Oncology, 21,* 213–220.

Maier, S. R., Watkins, L. R., & Fleshner, M. (1994). Psychoneuroimmunology. *American Psychologist, 49,* 1004–1007.

Maj, M., Pirozzi, R., Magliano, L., & Bartoli, L. (1997). Long-term outcome of lithium prophylaxis in bipolar disorder: A 5-year prospective study of 402 patients at a lithium clinic. *American Journal of Psychiatry, 155,* 30–55.

Maldonado, P. E., Godecke, I., Gray, C. M., & Bonhoffer, T. (1997). Orientation selectivity in pinwheel centers in cat straite cortex. *Science, 276,* 1551–1555.

Malle, B. F., Knobe, J., O'Lauglin, M. J., Pearce, G. E., & Nelson, S. E. (2000). Conceptual structure and social functions of behavior explanations: Beyond person-situation attributions. *Journal of Personality and Social Psychology, 79,* 309–326.

Mancia, M. (1999). Psychoanalysis and the neurosciences: A topical debate on dreams. *International Journal of Psychoanalysis, 80,* 1205–1213.

Manderscheid, R. W., & Sonnenschein, M. A. (1992). *Mental health, United States, 1992.* Washington, DC: U.S. Department of Health and Human Services.

Mann, A. (1998, April 6). Cross-gender sex pill. *Time.*

Mann, K., Hermann, D., & Heinz, A. (2000). One hundred years of alcoholism: The twentieth century. *Alcohol & Alcoholism, 35,* 10–15.

**Manning, A.** (1996, September 17). Caught dirty-handed: Many fail to wash when they should. *USA Today*.

**Manning, A.** (1998, February 23). Operating with sexism. *USA Today*, D-1.

**Manning, A.** (2000a, May 2). The changing deaf culture. *USA Today*, 1D.

**Manning, A.** (2000b, June 13). Kid obesity tips scales towards diabetes epidemic. *USA Today*, 8D.

**Mannuzza, S., Klein, R. G., Bessler, A., Malloy, P., & LaPadula, M.** (1993). Adult outcome of hyperactive boys. *Archives of General Psychiatry, 50,* 565–576.

**Manson, J.** (1999, October 8). Overweight people risk early death. *San Diego Union-Tribune*, A16.

**Manuck, S. B., Flory, J. D., Ferrell, R. E., Mann, J. J., & Muldoon, M. F.** (2000). A regulatory polymorphism of the monoamine oxidase-A gene may be associated with variability in aggression, impulsivity, and central nervous system serotonergic reponsivity. *Psychiatry Research, 95,* 9–23.

**Manuel, L. L., Retzlaff, P., & Sheehan, E.** (1993). Policewomen personality. *Journal of Social Behavior and Personality, 8,* 149–153.

**Maquet, P.** (1997). Positron emission tomography studies of sleep and sleep disorders. *Journal of Neurology, 244*(Supplement 1), S23–S28.

**Maratsos, M., & Matheny, L.** (1994). Language specificity and elasticity: Brain and clinical syndrome studies. *Annual Review of Psychology, 45,* 487–516.

**Marcus, M. B.** (2000, October 2). Don't let false alarms scare you off prenatal tests, but do get the facts first. *U.S. News & World Report,* 69–70.

**Marecek, J.** (1995). Gender, politics, and psychology's ways of knowing. *American Psychologist, 50,* 162–163.

**Marin, R., & Miller, S.** (1997, April 14). Ellen steps out. *Newsweek*.

**Markman, H. J.** (1995, February). Quoted in R. Edwards, New tools help gauge marital success. *APA Monitor*.

**Markowitsch, H. J.** (2000). Neuroanatomy of memory. In E. Tulving & F. M. Craik (Eds.), *The Oxford handbook of memory*. New York: Oxford University Press.

**Marks, I.** (1994). Behavior therapy as an aid to self-care. *Current Directions in Psychological Science, 3,* 19–22.

**Marshall, E.** (1995). Dispute splits schizophrenia study. *Science, 268,* 792–794.

**Marta, E.** (1997). Parent-adolescent interactions and psychosocial risk in adolescents: An analysis of communication, support, and gender. *Journal of Adolescence, 20,* 471–487.

**Martin, A., Wiggs, C. L., Ungerfelder, L. G., & Haxby, J. V.** (1996). Neural correlates of category-specific knowledge. *Nature, 379,* 649–652.

**Martin, C. L.** (2000). Cognitive theories of gender development. In T. Eckes & H. M. Trautner (Eds.), *The developmental social psychology of gender*. Mahwah, NJ: Lawrence Erlbaum.

**Martin, G. L.** (1982). Thought-stopping and stimulus control to decrease persistent disturbing thoughts. *Journal of Behavior Therapy and Experimental Psychiatry, 13,* 215–220.

**Martin, L.** (1986). Eskimo words for snow: A case study in the genesis and decay of an anthropological example. *American Anthropologist, 88,* 418–423.

**Martin, R. P., Wisenbaker, J., & Baker, J.** (1997). Gender differences in temperament at six months and five years. *Infant Behavior and Development, 20,* 339–347.

**Martin, S.** (1995, January). Field's status unaltered by the influx of women. *APA Monitor*.

**Maruish, M. E.** (Ed.). (1994). *The use of psychological testing for treatment planning and outcome assessment: Introduction*. Hillsdale, NJ: Lawrence Erlbaum.

**Marx, J.** (2000). Chipping away at the causes of aging. *Science, 287,* 2390.

**Masling, J. M.** (1997). On the nature and utility of projective tests and objective tests. *Journal of Personality Assessment, 69,* 357–370.

**Maslow, A. H.** (1968). *Toward a psychology of being* (2nd ed.). New York: Van Nostrand.

**Maslow, A. H.** (1970). *Motivation and personality*. New York: Harper & Row.

**Maslow, A. H.** (1971). *The farther reaches of human nature*. New York: Viking Press.

**Massimini, R., & Fave, A. D.** (2000). Individual development in a bio-cultural perspective. *American Psychologist, 55,* 24–33.

**Masten, A. S., & Coatsworth, J. D.** (1998). The development of competence in favorable and unfavorable environments. *American Psychologist, 53,* 205–220.

**Masters, W. H., & Johnson, V. E.** (1966). *Human sexual response*. Boston: Little, Brown.

**Masters, W. H., & Johnson, V. E.** (1970). *Human sexual inadequacy*. Boston: Little, Brown.

**Masters, W. H., & Johnson, V. E.** (1981). Sex and the aging process. *Journal of the American Geriatrics Society, 19,* 385–389.

**Mastro, J.** (2000, July 21). Dialogue with a dolphin. *San Diego Union-Tribune*, E1.

**Mathews, R. C.** (1997). Commentaries. *Psychonomic Bulletin & Review, 4,* 38–42.

**Mathews, T., Reiss, S., & Artholet, J.** (1990, February 19). The threat of a white backlash. *Newsweek*.

**Matson, J. L., & Ollendick, T. H.** (1977). Issues in toilet training normal children. *Behavior Therapy, 8,* 549–553.

**Matsuda, L. A., Lolait, S. J., Brownstein, M. J., Young, A. C., & Bonner, T. I.** (1990). Structure of a cannabinoid receptor and functional expression of the cloned cDNA. *Nature, 346,* 561–564.

**Matsumoto, D., & Ekman, P.** (1989). American-Japanese cultural differences in intensity ratings of facial expressions of emotion. *Motivation and Emotion, 13,* 143–157.

**Matt, G. E., & Navarro, A. M.** (1997). What meta-analyses have and have not taught us about psychotherapy effects: A review of future directions. *Clinical Psychology Review, 17,* 1–32.

**Matthews, K. A., & Haynes, S. G.** (1986). Type A behavior pattern and coronary disease risk. *American Journal of Epidemiology, 123,* 923–960.

**Matthias, R. E., Lubben, J. E., Atchison, K. A., & Schweitzer, S. T.** (1997). Sexual activity and satisfaction among very old adults: Results from a community-dwelling Medicare population survey. *Gerontologist, 37,* 6–14.

**Mattson, S., Riley, E. P., Gramling, L., Delis, D. C., & Jones, K. L.** (1998). Neuropsychological comparison of alcohol-exposed children with or without physical features of fetal alcohol syndrome. *Neuropsychology, 12,* 146–153.

**Maugh, T. H.** (1997, July 11). Heroin use soars in state, study says. *Los Angeles Times*.

**Maugh, T. H., II.** (1998, February 21). Study's advice to husbands: Accept wife's influence. *Los Angeles Times*.

**Maugh, T. H., II.** (2000, July 8). Experts fear resurgence of HIV infection. *Los Angeles Times*, A1.

**Mayberg, H. S., Mahurin, R. K., & Brannan, S. K.** (1997). Neuropsychiatric aspects of mood and affective disorders. In S. C. Yudofsky & R. E. Hales (Eds.), *American Psychiatric Press textbook of neuropsychiatry* (3rd ed.). Washington, DC: American Psychiatric Press.

**Mayer, J. D., Caruso, D., & Salovey, P.** (2000). Emotional intelligence meets traditional standards for an intelligence. *Intelligence, 27,* 267–298.

**Mayer, J. D., & Salovey, P.** (1997). What is emotional intelligence? In P. Salovey & D. Sluyter (Eds.), *Emotional development and emotional intelligence: Implications for educators*. New York: Basic Books.

**Mayer, J. D., Salovey, P., & Caruso, D.** (2000). Models of emotional intelligence. In R. J. Sternberg (Ed.), *Handbook of intelligence*. New York: Cambridge University Press.

**Mayes, A. R.** (2000). Selective memory disorders. In E. Tulving & F. M. Craik (Eds.), *The Oxford handbook of memory*. New York: Oxford University Press.

**Mayes, A. R., & Downes, J. J.** (1997). What do theories of the functional deficit(s) underlying amnesia have to explain? *Memory, 5,* 3–36.

**Mays, V. M., Rubin, J., Sabourin, M., & Walker, L.** (1996). Moving toward a global psychology. *American Psychologist, 51,* 485–487.

**Mazzoni, G., & Cornoldi, C.** (1993). Strategies in study time allocation: Why is study time sometimes not effective? *Journal of Experimental Psychology: General, 122,* 47–60.

**McAninch, W.** (1995, July 16). Cited in R. Bragg, In South Carolina, a mother's defense, and life, could hinge on 2 choices. *New York Times*.

**McCall, R. B.** (1994). Academic underachievers. *Current Directions in Psychological Science, 3,* 15–19.

**McCarry, J.** (1996, May). Peru begins again. *National Geographic*.

**McClearn, G. E., Johansson, B., Berg, S., Pedersen, N. L., Ahern, F., Petrill, S. A., & Plomin, R.** (1997). Substantial genetic influence on cognitive abilities in twins 80 or more years old. *Science, 276,* 1560–1563.

**McClelland, D. C.** (1985). *Human motivation*. Glenview, IL: Scott, Foresman.

**McClelland, D. C., Atkinson, J. W., Clark, R. W., & Lowell, E. L.** (1953). *The achievement motive*. New York: Appleton-Century-Crofts.

**McClelland, J. L.** (2000). Connectionist models of memory. In E. Tulving & F. M. Craik (Eds.), *The Oxford handbook of memory*. New York: Oxford University Press.

**McConnell, J. V., Cutler, R. L., & McNeil, E. B.** (1958). Subliminal stimulation: An overview. *American Psychologist, 13,* 229–242.

**McCrae, R. R., & Costa, P. T., Jr.** (1990). *Personality in adulthood*. New York: Guilford Press.

**McCrae, R. R., & Costa, P. T., Jr.** (1994). The stability of personality: Observations and evaluations. *Current Directions in Psychological Science, 3,* 173–175.

**McCrae, R. R., & Costa, P. T., Jr.** (1997). Personality trait structure as a human universal. *American Psychologist, 52,* 509–516.

**McCrae, R. R., & Costa, P. T., Jr.** (1999). A five-factor theory of personality. In L. A. Pervin & O. P. John (Eds.), *Handbook of personality* (2nd ed.). New York: Guilford.

**McDaniel, M. A., & Einstein, G. O.** (1986). Bizarre imagery as an effective memory aid: The importance of distinctiveness. *Journal of Experimental Psychology: Learning, Memory and Cognition, 12,* 54–65.

**McDonald, H. E., & Hirt, E. R.** (1997). When expectancy meets desire: Motivational effects in reconstructive memory. *Journal of Personality and Social Psychology, 72,* 5–23.

**McDougall, W.** (1908). *Social psychology*. New York: Putnam.

**McDougle, C. J.** (1997). Update on pharmacologic management of OCD: Agents and augmentation. *Journal of Clinical Psychiatry, 58*(Supplement 12), 11–17.

**McDowell, D. M., & Kleber, H. D.** (1994). MDMA: Its history and pharmacology. *Psychiatric Annals, 24,* 127–130.

**McDowell, J.** (1992, February 17). Are women better cops? *Time*.

McEachin, J. J., Smith, T., & Lovaas, O. I. (1993). Long-term outcome for children with autism who received early intensive behavioral interventions. *American Journal on Mental Retardation, 97,* 359–372.

McElrath, D. (1997). The Minnesota model. *Journal of Psychoactive Drugs, 29,* 141–144.

McGaugh, J. L. (1990). Significance and remembrance: The role of neuromodulatory systems. *Psychological Science, 1,* 15–25.

McGaugh, J. L. (1999, February). Cited in B. Azar, McGaugh blazes on down his own path to keys of memory. *APA Monitor,* 18.

McGinnis, J. M., & Foege, W. H. (1993). Actual causes of death in the United States. *Journal of the American Medical Association, 270,* 2207–2212.

McGirk, T. (1999, August 9). A carpet of cocaine. *Time,* 51.

McGrady, A. V., Bush, E. G., & Grubb, B. P. (1997). Outcome of biofeedback-assisted relaxation for neurocardiogenic syncope and headache: A clinical replication series. *Applied Psychophysiology and Biofeedback, 22,* 63–72.

McGue, M., Bouchard, T. J., Jr., Iacono, W. G., & Lykken, D. T. (1993). Behavioral genetics of cognitive ability: A life-span perspective. In R. Plomin & G. E. McClearn (Eds.), *Nature, nurture, and psychology.* Washington, DC: American Psychological Association.

McGue, M., & Christensen, K. (1997). Genetic and environmental contributions to depression symptomatology: Evidence from Danish twins 75 years of age and older. *Journal of Abnormal Psychology, 106,* 439–448.

McGuire, P. K. (1993, September 29). Cited in D. Goleman, Thinking, not hearing voices. *San Diego Union-Tribune.*

McIntosh, D. N. (1996). Facial feedback hypothesis: Evidence, implications, and directions. *Motivation and Emotion, 20,* 121–147.

McIntosh, H. (1999, September). Research unearths new treatments for autism. *Monitor: American Psychological Association, 29.*

McKenna, K. (1994, November 13). He just did it. *Los Angeles Times Calendar.*

McLellan, A. T., Grossman, D. S., Blaine, J. D., & Haverkos, H. W. (1993). Acupuncture treatment for drug abuse: A technical review. *Journal of Substance Abuse Treatment, 10,* 569–576.

McMahon, P. (1998, July 14). Law has changed how Oregonians die. *USA Today,* 3A.

McMahon, P., & Koch, W. (2000, February 24). Oregon assisted-suicide law is not abused, study finds. *USA Today,* 6A.

McNally, R. J. (1999). On eye movements and animal magnetism: A reply to Greenwald's defense of EMDR. *Journal of Anxiety Disorders, 13,* 617-620.

McWhorter, J. H. (2000). *Losing the race.* New York: Free Press.

Meck, W. (1996). Cited in V. Morell, Setting a biological stopwatch. *Science, 271,* 905–906.

Medin, D. L., Lynch, E. B., & Solomon, K. O. (2000). Are there kinds of concepts? *Annual Review of Psychology, 51,* 121–147.

Meeus, W., & Raaijmakers, Q. (1989). Obedience to authority in Milgram-type studies: A research review. *Zeitschrift für Sozialpsychologie, 20,* 70–85.

Megargee (1997). Internal inhibitions and controls. In R. Hogan, J. Johnson, & S. Briggs (Eds.), *Handbook of personality psychology.* New York: Academic Press.

Mehren, E. (1991, May 27). Grounded for cosmetic reasons. *Los Angeles Times,* E-1.

Mehren, E. (1998, September 16). It's still the old college cry: Drink! *Los Angeles Times,* B2.

Meichenbaum, D., & Fitzpatrick, D. (1993). A constructivist narrative perspective on stress and coping: Stress inoculation applications. In L. Goldberger & S. Breznitz (Eds.), *Handbook of stress: Theoretical and clinical aspects* (2nd ed.). New York: Free Press.

Meissner, J. S., Blanchard, E. B., & Malamood, H. S. (1997). Comparison of treatment outcome measures for irritable bowel syndrome. *Applied Psychophysiology and Biofeedback, 22,* 55–62.

Melzack, R. (1989). Phantom limbs, the self and the brain. *Canadian Psychology, 30,* 1–16.

Melzack, R. (1997). Phantom limbs (Special issue). *Scientific American,* 84–91.

Melzack, R., & Wall, P. D. (1983). *The challenge of pain.* New York: Basic Books.

Mendlewicz, J., & Lecrubier, Y. (2000). Antidepressants selection: Proceedings from a TA–SSRI consensus conference. *Acta Psychiatrica Scandinavica, 101*(Supplement 403*),* 5–8.

Menzies, R. G., & Clarke, J. C. (1995). The etiology of phobias: A nonassociative account. *Clinical Psychology Review, 15,* 23–48.

Merzenich, M. M., Jenkins, W. M., Johnston, P., Schreiner, C., Miller, S. L., & Tallal, P. (1996). Temporal processing deficits of language-learning impaired children ameliorated by training. *Science, 271,* 77–81.

Mesirow, K. H. (1984). *Report on animal research survey.* Paper presented at the American Psychological Association, Toronto.

Messer, S. B., & Wachtel, P. L. (1997). The contemporary psychotherapeutic landscape: Issues and prospects. In P. L. Wachtel & S. B. Messer (Eds.), *Theories of psychotherapy: Origins and evolution.* Washington, DC: American Psychological Association.

Mestel, R. (1993, July 31). Cannibis: The brain's other supplier. *New Scientist.*

Mestel, R. (1999, January). Sexual chemistry. *Discover,* 32.

Mestel, R. (2000, February 7). Wired for hunger. *Los Angeles Times,* S1.

Metz, M. E., & Pryor, J. L. (2000). Premature ejaculation: A psychophysiological approach for assessment and management. *Journal of Sex & Marital Therapy, 26,* 293–320.

Meyers, S. A., & Berscheid, E. (1997). The language of love: The difference a preposition makes. *Personality and Social Psychology Bulletin, 23,* 347–362.

Michaelson, J. (1995, July 16). Front and center. *Los Angeles Times.*

Middlebrooks, J. C., Clock, A. E., Xu, L., & Green, D. M. (1994). A panoramic code for sound location by cortical neurons. *Science, 264,* 842–884.

Mignot, E. (1997). Behavioral genetics '97: Genetics of narcolepsy and other sleep disorders. *American Journal of Human Genetics, 60,* 1289–1302.

Mignot, E. (2000, August 30). Cited in A. Manning, Narcolepsy is caused by loss of particular brain cells. *USA Today,* 10D.

Miles, D. R., & Carey, G. (1997). Genetic and environmental architecture of human aggression. *Journal of Personality and Social Psychology, 72,* 207–217.

Milgram, N. A., Dangour, W., & Raviv, A. (1992). Situational and personal determinants of academic procrastination. *Journal of General Psychology, 119,* 123–133.

Milgram, S. (1963). Behavioral study of obedience. *Journal of Abnormal and Social Psychology, 67,* 371–378.

Milgram, S. (1974). *Obedience to authority.* New York: Harper & Row.

Milgrom, P., Mancl, L., Kng, B., & Weinstein, P. (1995). Origins of childhood dental fear. *Behaviour Research and Therapy, 33,* 313–319.

Milgrom, P., Quang, J. Z., & Tay, K. M. (1994). Cross-cultural validity of a parent's version of the Dental Fear Survey Schedule for children in Chinese. *Behavior Research and Therapy, 32,* 131–135.

Milgrom, P., Vigehesa, H., & Weinstein, P. (1992). Adolescent dental fear and control: Prevalence and theoretical implications. *Behavior Research and Therapy, 30,* 367–373.

Millan, M. J. (1986). Multiple opioid systems and pain. *Pain, 27,* 303–347.

Miller, A. (2000, October 27). Why Bush will win this election. *San Diego Union-Tribune,* B9.

Miller, D. D., Perry, P. J., Cadoret, R. J., & Andreasen, N. C. (1994). Clozapine's effect on negative symptoms in treatment-refractory schizophrenics. *Comprehensive Psychiatry, 35,* 8–15.

Miller, F. G., Quill, T. E., Brody, H., Fletcher, J. C., Gostin, L. O., & Meier, D. E. (1994). Regulating physician-assisted death. *New England Journal of Medicine, 331,* 119–122.

Miller, G. (1956). The magical number seven, plus or minus two: Some limits on our capacity for information processing. *Psychological Review, 48,* 337–442.

Miller, I. J., Jr. (1993, February 10). Cited in J. Williams, Survival of the sweetest. *San Diego Union-Tribune.*

Miller, J. (1995, April). Cited in T. DeAngelis, Research documents trauma of abuse. *APA Monitor.*

Miller, L. K. (1999). The savant syndrome: Intellectual impairment and exceptional skill. *Psychological Bulletin, 125,* 31–46.

Miller, M. A., & Rahe, R. H. (1997). Life changes scaling for the 1990s. *Journal of Psychosomatic Research, 43,* 279–292.

Miller, N. S., & Gold, M. S. (1994). LSD and ecstasy: Pharmacology, phenomenology, and treatment. *Psychiatric Annals, 24,* 131–133.

Miller, P. H. (1993). *Theories of developmental psychology* (3rd ed.). New York: Freeman.

Miller, R. W., & C'deBaca, J. (1994). Quantum change: Toward a psychology of transformation. In T. F. Heatherton & J. L. Weinberger (Eds.), *Can personality change?* Washington, DC: American Psychological Association.

Miller, T. Q., Turner, C. W., Tindale, R. S., Posavac, E. J., & Dugoni, B. L. (1991). Reasons for the trend toward null findings in research on Type A behavior. *Psychological Bulletin, 110,* 469–485.

Miller, W. R., & Brown, S. A. (1997). Why psychologists should treat alcohol and drug problems. *American Psychologist, 52,* 1269–1279.

Millon, T. (1981). *Disorders of personality.* New York: Wiley.

Milstein, M. (1993, October 27). A dizzying dilemma. *San Diego Union-Tribune.*

Miltner, W., Matjek, M., Braun, C., Diekmann, H., & Brody, S. (1994). Emotional qualities of odors and their influence on the startle reflex in humans. *Psychophysiology, 31,* 107–110.

Milton, J., & Wiseman, R. (1999). Does Psi exist? Lack of replication of an anomalous process of information transfer. *Psychological Bulletin, 125,* 387–391.

Mindell, J. A. (1997). Children and sleep. In M. R. Pressman & W. C. Orr (Eds.), *Understanding sleep: The evaluation and treatment of sleep disorders.* Washington, DC: American Psychological Association.

Minshew, N. J., Goldstein, G., & Siegel, D. J. (1995). Speech and language in high-functioning autistic individuals. *Neuropsychology, 9,* 255–261.

Minton, L. (1995, May 8). Fresh voices. *Parade.*

Miranda, A., & Presentacion, M. J. (2000). Efficacy of cognitive-behavioral therapy in the treatment of children with ADHD with and without aggressiveness. *Psychology in the School, 37*, 169–182.

Mirsky, A. F., & Quinn, O. W. (1988). The Genain quadruplets. *Schizophrenia Bulletin, 14*, 595–612.

Mischel, W. (1968). *Personality and assessment.* New York: Wiley.

Mischel, W. (1990). Personality dispositions revisited and revised: A view after three decades. In L. A. Previn (Ed.), *Handbook of Personality.* New York: Guilford Press.

Mischel, W., & Peake, P. K. (1982). Beyond deja vu in the search for cross-situational consistency. *Psychological Review, 89*, 730–755.

Mischel, W., & Shoda, Y. (1995). A cognitive-affective system theory of personality: Reconceptualizing situations, dispositions, dynamics, and invariance of personality structure. *Psychological Review, 102*, 246–268.

Mischel, W., Shoda, Y., & Rodriguez, M. L. (1989). Delay of gratification in children. *Science, 244*, 933–937.

Mitchell, S. (1996, September). Cited in T. DeAngelis, Psychoanalysis adapts to the 1990s. *APA Monitor.*

Mittleman, M. A. (1999). Cited in S. Carpenter, Cocaine use boosts heart-attack risk. *Science News, 155*, 358.

Miyashita, Y. (1995). How the brain creates imagery: Projection to primary visual cortex. *Science, 268*, 1719–1720.

Mizes, J. S. (1994). Eating disorders. In V. B. Van Hasselt & M. Hersen (Eds.), *Advanced abnormal psychology.* New York: Plenum Press.

Mohr, D. C. (1995). Negative outcome in psychotherapy: A critical review. *Clinical Psychology: Science and Practice, 2*, 1–27.

Moldin, S. O., Reich, T., & Rice, J. P. (1991). Current perspectives on the genetics of unipolar depression. *Behavior Genetics, 21*, 211–242.

Moncrieff, J. (1997). Lithium: Evidence reconsidered. *British Journal of Psychiatry, 171*, 113–119.

Mondain, M., Sillon, M., Vieu, A., Lanvin, M., Reuillard-Artieres, F., Tobey, E., & Uziel, A. (1997). Speech perception skills and speech production intelligibility in French children with prelingual deafness and cochlear implants. *Archives of Otolaryngology, Head and Neck Surgery, 123*, 181–184.

Money, J. (1987). Sin, sickness or status? *American Psychologist, 42*, 384–399.

Monnot, M. (1999). Function of infant-directed speech. *Human Nature, 10*, 415–443.

Montgomery, G., & Kirsch, I. (1996). Mechanisms of placebo pain reduction: An empirical investigation. *Psychological Science, 7*, 174–176.

Montgomery, G. H., & Bovbjerg, D. H. (1997). The development of anticipatory nausea in patients receiving adjuvant chemotherapy for breast cancer. *Physiology & Behavior, 61*, 737–741.

Montgomery, G. H., DuHamel, K. N., & Redd, W. H. (2000). A meta-analysis of hypnotically induced analgesia: How effective is hypnosis? *International Journal of Clinical and Experimental Hypnosis, 48*, 138–153.

Moore, R. Y. (1997). Circadian rhythms: Basic neurobiology and clinical applications. *Annual Review of Medicine, 48*, 253–266.

Moran, C. (2000, February 19). 20% of surveyed S.D. students weighed suicide. B-4.

Morash, M., & Greene, J. R. (1986). Evaluating women on patrol: A critique of contemporary wisdom. *Evaluation Review, 10*, 230–255.

Morell, V. (1996). Life at the top: Animals pay the high price for dominance. *Science, 271*, 292.

Morey, L. C. (1997). Personality diagnosis and personality disorders. In R. Hogan, J. Johnson, & S. Briggs (Eds.), *Handbook of personality psychology.* New York: Academic Press.

Morgan, A. B., & Lilienfeld, S. O. (2000). A meta-analytic review of the relation between antisocial behavior and neuropsychological measures of executive function. *Clinical Psychology Review, 20*, 113–136.

Morgan, D. (1995, July 11). Cited in C. Sullivan, Mother called fit for trial in sons' deaths. *San Diego Union-Tribune.*

Morgan, M. (1985). Self-monitoring of attained subgoals in private study. *Journal of Educational Psychology, 77*, 623–630.

Morganthau, T. (1995, February 13). What color is black? *Newsweek.*

Morrison, A. (1993). Cited in H. Herzog, Animal rights and wrongs. *Science, 262*, 1906–1908.

Morrison-Bogorad, M. (2000, January 31). Cited in G. Cowley, Alzheimer's: Unlocking the mystery. *Newsweek*, 46–51.

Morrison-Bogorad, M., Phelps, C., & Buckoltz, N. (1997). Alzheimer's disease research comes of age. *Journal of the American Medical Association, 277*, 837–840.

Morrissey, J., Calloway, M., Johnsen, M., & Ullman, M. (1997). Service System performance and integration: A baseline profile of the ACCESS demonstrations sites. *Psychiatric Services, 48*, 374–380.

Mortensen, M. E., Sever, L. E., & Oakley, G. P. (1991). Teratology and the epidemiology of birth defects. In S. G. Gabbe, J. R. Niebyl, & J. L. Simpson (Eds.), *Obstetrics: Normal and problem pregnancies.* New York: Churchill Livingstone.

Moscovitch, M. (1997). Cited in C. Holden, A special place for faces in the brain. *Science, 278*, 41.

Moss, D. (1993, August 3). A painful parting in Michigan. *USA Today.*

Muehlenhard, C. L., & Linton, M. A. (1987). Date rape and sexual aggression in dating situations: Incidence and risk factors. *Journal of Counseling Psychology, 34*, 186–196.

Mukerjee, M. (1997, February). Trends in animal research. *Scientific American*, 86–93.

Mullen, B., Anthony, T., Salas, E., & Driskell, J. E. (1994). Group cohesiveness and quality of decision making: An integration of tests of the groupthink hypothesis. *Small Group Research, 25*, 189–204.

Mullen, B., & Cooper, C. (1994). The relation between group cohesiveness and performance: An integration. *Psychological Bulletin, 115*, 210–227.

Mullen, M. K. (1994). Earliest recollections of childhood: A demographic analysis. *Cognition, 52*, 55–79.

Muller, R. A., Behen, M. E., Rothermel, R. D., Chugani, D. C., Muzik, O., Mangner, T. J., & Chugani, H. T. (1999). Brain mapping of language and auditory perception in high-functioning autistic adults: A PET study. *Journal of Autism and Developmental Disorders, 29*, 19–31.

Mumford, D., Rose, A. S., & Goslin, D. A. (1995). *An evaluation of remote viewing: Research and applications.* Washington, DC: The American Institutes for Research.

Mundy, C. (1994, June 2). The lost boy. *Rolling Stone.*

Munk, M. H. J., Roelfsema, P. R., Konig, P., Engel, A. K., & Singer, W. (1996). Role of reticular activation in the modulation of intracortical synchronization. *Science, 272*, 271–277.

Murberg, M. (Ed.). (1994). *Catecholamine function in post-traumatic stress disorder: Emerging data on child sexual abuse.* Beverly Hills, CA: Sage.

Murnane, K., Phelps, M. P., & Malmberg, K. (1999). Context-dependent recognition memory: The ICE theory. *Journal of Experimental Psychology: General, 128*, 403–415.

Murphy, G. G., & Glanzman, D. L. (1997). Mediation of classical conditioning in *Aplysia californica* by long-term potentiation of sensorimotor synapses. *Science, 278*, 467–471.

Murphy, K. (1996, November 19). Seattle dares to seek DARE alternatives. *Los Angeles Times.*

Murphy, K. R. (1993). *Honesty in the workplace.* Pacific Grove, CA: Brooks/Cole.

Murray, B. (1997, May). Is it a rise in ADHD, or in students' false claims? *APA Monitor.*

Murray, B. (2000, March). Cognitive psychology: A meeting of the mind and education? *Monitor on Psychology.*

Murray, D. J., Kilgout, A. R., & Wasykliw, L. (2000). Conflicts and missed signals in psychoanalysis, behaviorism, and Gestalt psychology. *American Psychologist, 55*, 422–426.

Murray, H. (1938). *Explorations in personality.* New York: Oxford University Press.

Murray, H. (1943). *Thematic apperception test manual.* Cambridge, MA: Harvard University Press.

Musto, D. F. (1991). Opium, cocaine and marijuana in American history. *Scientific American, 265*, 40–47.

Musto, D. F. (1996, April). Alcohol in American history. *Scientific American*, 78–83.

Musto, D. F. (1999). The impact of puboic attitudes on drug abuse research in the twentieth century. In M. D. Glantz & C. R. Hartel (Eds.), *Drug abuse: Origins & interventions.* Washington, DC: American Psychological Association, 63–78.

Mydans, S. (1997, February 2). Legal euthanasia: Australia faces a grim reality. *New York Times International.*

Myers, D. G. (2000). The funds, friends, and faith of happy people. *American Psychologist, 55*, 56–67.

Myers, D. G., & Diener, E. (1996, May). The pursuit of happiness. *Scientific American*, 70–72.

Myers, L. (1992, March 12). Nerd-for-a-day is harassed, teased, shunned. *San Diego Union-Tribune*, A-3.

Myrtek, M. (1995). Type A behavior pattern, personality factors, disease, and physiological reactivity: A meta-analytic update. *Personality and Individual Differences, 18*, 491–502.

Nadelmann, E. A. (1997, February 20). Reefer Madness 1997: The new bag of scare tactics. *Rolling Stone*, 51.

Nadelmann, E. A. (2000, January 2). Cited in C. S. Wren, Small coalition crusades against the war on drugs. *San Diego Union-Tribune*, A14.

Nagarahole, E. L. (1994, March 28). Tigers on the brink. *Time.*

Nagtegaal, J. E., Laurant, M. W., Kerkof, G. A., Smits, M. G., van der Meer, Y. G., & Coenen, A. M. L. (2000). Effects of melatonin on the quality of life in patients with delayed sleep phase syndrome. *Journal of Psychosomatic Research, 48*, 45–50.

NAMHC (National Advisory Mental Health Council). (1996). Basic behavioral science research for mental health: Perception, attention, learning, and memory. *American Psychologist, 51*, 133–142.

Nash, J. M. (1997, February 3). Fertile minds. *Time.*

Nash, M. (1987). What, if anything, is regressed about hypnotic age regression? A review of the empirical literature. *Psychological Bulletin, 102*, 42–52.

Naslund, J., Haroutunian, V., Mohs, R., Davis, K. L., Davies, P., Greengard, P., & Buxbaum, J. D. (2000). Correlation between elevated levels of amyloid B-peptide in the brain and cognitive decline. *Journal of the American Medical Association, 283*, 1571–1577.

Nathan, P. E., Stuart, S. P., & Dolan, S. L. (2000). Research of psychotherapy efficacy and effectiveness: Between Scylla and Charybdis. *Psychological Bulletin, 126*, 964–981.

Nathans, J., Piantanida, T. P., Eddy, R. L., Shows, T. B., & Hogness, D. S. (1986). Molecular genetics of inherited variation in human color vision. *Science, 232*, 203–210.

National Advisory Mental Health Council. (1996). Basic behavioral science research for mental health: A national investment. *American Psychologist, 50*, 838–845.

National Center for Health Statistics. (1997). Update: Prevalence of overweight among children, adolescents, and adults—United States, 1988–1994. *Journal of the American Medical Association, 277*, 1111.

National Task Force on the Prevention and Treatment of Obesity. (1994). Weight cycling. *Journal of the American Medical Association, 272*, 1196–1202.

Nazario, S. (1993, July 5). Force to be reckoned with. *Los Angeles Times.*

Nazario, S. (1997, March 10). Schools struggle to teach lessons in life and death. *Los Angeles Times.*

NCSDR (National Commission on Sleep Disorders Research). (1993). *Wake up America: A national sleep alert.* Washington, DC: Department of Health and Human Services.

Neath, I. (1998). *Human memory.* Pacific Grove, CA: Brooks/Cole.

Neher, A. (1991). Maslow's theory of motivation: A critique. *Journal of Humanistic Psychology, 31*, 89–112.

Nehlig, A. (1999). Are we dependent upon coffee and caffeine? A review of human and animal data. *Neuroscience and Biobehavioral Reviews, 23*, 563–576.

Neisser, U. (1997). Never a dull moment. *American Psychologist, 52*, 79–81.

Neisser, U., Boodoo, G., Bourchard, T. J., Jr., Boykin, A. W., Brody N., Ceci, S. J., Halpern, D. R., Loehlin, J. C., Perloff, R., Sternberg, R. J., & Urbina, S. (1996). Intelligence: Knowns and unknowns. *American Psychologist, 51*, 77–101.

Neisser, U., & Libby, L. K. (2000). Remembering life experiences. In E. Tulving & F. M. Craik (Eds.), *The Oxford handbook of memory.* New York: Oxford University Press.

Neitz, J., Neitz, M., & Kainz, P. M. (1996). Visual pigment gene structure and the severity of color vision defects. *Science, 274*, 801–803.

Neitz, M., & Neitz, J. (1995). Numbers and ratios of visual pigment genes for normal red-green color vision. *Science, 267*, 1013–1016.

Nelson, R. J., Demas, G. E., Huang, P. L., Fishman, M. C., Dawson, V. L., Dawson, T. M., & Snyder, S. H. (1995). Behavioural abnormalities in male mice lacking neuronal nitric oxide synthase. *Nature, 378*, 383–386.

Nelson, T. O. (1993). Judgments of learning and the allocation of study time. *Journal of Experimental Psychology: General, 122*, 269–273.

Nelson, T. O. (1996). Consciousness and metacognition. *American Psychologist, 51*, 102–116.

Nemeroff, C. B. (1998, June). The neurobiology of depression. *Scientific American*, 42–49.

Neugarten, B. (1994, May). Cited in B. Azar, Women are barraged by media on "the change." *APA Monitor.*

Neverlien, P. O., & Johnsen, T. B. (1991). Optimism-pessimism dimension and dental anxiety in children aged 10–12. *Community Dentistry Oral Epidemiology, 19*, 342–346.

Newcombe, N. S., Drummey, A. B., Fox, N. A., Lie, E., & Ottinger-Alberrts, W. (2000). Remembering early childhood: How much, how, and why (or why not). *Current Directions in Psychological Science, 9*, 55–58.

Newman, L. S., Duff, K. J., & Baumeister, R. F. (1997). A new look at defensive projection: Through suppression, accessibility, and biased person perception. *Journal of Personality and Social Psychology, 72*, 980–1001.

Neziroglu, F., Hsla, C., & Yargura-Tobias, J. A. (2000). Behavioral, cognitive, and family therapy for obsessive-compulsive and related disorders. *The Psychiatric Clinics of North America, 23*, 657–670.

Ng, W., & Lindsay, R. C. L. (1994). Cross-race facial recognition. *Journal of Cross-Cultural Psychology, 25*, 217–232.

NICHD. (1997). The effects of infant child care on infant-mother attachment security: Results of the NICHD study of early child care. *Child Development, 68*, 860–879.

Nichelli, P., Grafman, J., Pietrini, P., Alway, D., Carton, J. C., & Miletich. (1994). Brain activity in chess playing. *Nature, 369*, 191.

Niedenthal, P. M. (1992). Affect and social perception: On the psychological validity of rose-colored glasses. In R. Bornstein & T. Pittman (Eds.), *Perception without awareness.* New York: Guilford.

Niedenthal, P. M., & Setterlund, M. C. (1994). Emotion congruence in perception. *Personality and Social Psychology Bulletin, 20*, 401–411.

NIH Consensus Development Panel on cochlear implants in adults and children. (1995). Cochlear implants in adults and children. *Journal of the American Medical Association, 274*, 1955–1961.

Nisbet, M. (1998, May/June). Psychic telephone networks profit on yearning, gullibility. *Skeptical Inquirer*, 5–6.

Nisbett, R. (2000, August 8). Cited in E. Goode, How culture molds habits of thought. *New York Times*, D1.

Nishizawa, S., Benkelfat, C., Young, S. N., Leyton, M., Mezengeza, S., de Montigny, C., Plier, P., & Diksic, M. (1997). Differences between males and females in rates of serotonin synthesis in human brain. *Proceedings of the National Academy of Science, 94*, 5308–5313.

Noah, T. (1997, March 3). OK, OK, cigarettes do kill. *U.S. News & World Report.*

Nobler, M. S., & Sackeim, H. A. (1998). Mechanisms of action of electroconvulsive therapy: Functional brain imaging studies. *Psychiatric Annals, 28*, 23–29.

Nordin, V., & Gillberg, C. (1998). The long-term course of autistic disorders: Update on follow-up studies. *Acta Psychiatrica Scandinavica, 97*, 99–108.

Norenzayan, A., & Nisbett, R. E. (2000). Culture and causal cognition. *Current Directions in Psychological Science, 9*, 132–135.

Noriyuki, D. (1996, February). Breaking down the walls. *Los Angeles Times*, E-1.

Norman, D. A. (1982). *Learning and memory.* New York: Freeman.

Nottebohm, F. (1989). From bird song to neurogenesis. *Scientific American, 260*, 74–79.

Nour, N. (2000, July 11). Cited in C. Dreifus, A life devoted to stopping the suffering of mutilation. *New York Times*, D7.

Nousaine, T. (1996, July). Hear today, gone tomorrow. *Stereo Review*, 71–73.

Novy, D. M., Nelson, D. V., Francis, D. J., & Turk, D. C. (1995). Perspectives of chronic pain: An evaluative comparison of restrictive and comprehensive models. *Psychological Bulletin, 118*, 238–247.

Nowak, R. (1994). Chronobiologists out of sync over light therapy patents. *Science, 263*, 1217–1218.

Nurius, P. S., & Berlin, S. S. (1994). Treatment of negative self-concept and depression. In D. K. Granvold (Ed.), *Cognitive and behavioral treatment: Methods and applications.* Pacific Grove, CA: Brooks/Cole.

Nyberg, L., & Cabeza, R. (2000). Brain imaging of memory. In E. Tulving & F. M. Craik (Eds.), *The Oxford handbook of memory.* New York: Oxford University Press.

Oakes, L. M., Coppage, D. J., & Dingel, A. (1997). By land or by sea: The role of perceptual similarity in infant's categorization of animals. *Developmental Psychology, 33*, 396–407.

O'Brien, M., Peyton V., Mistry, R., Hruda, L., Jacobs, A., Caldera, Y., Houston, A., & Roy, C. (2000). Gender-role cognition in three-year-old boys and girls. *Sex Roles, 42*, 1007–1025.

Ohbuchi, K., & Takahashi, Y. (1994). Cultural styles of conflict management in Japanese and Americans: Passivity, covertness, and effectiveness of strategies. *Journal of Applied Social Psychology, 24*, 1345–1366.

Ohman, A. (2000). Fear and anxiety: Evolutionary, cognitive and clinical perspectives. In M. Lewis & J. M. Haviland-Jones (Eds.), *Handbook of emotions* (2nd ed.). New York: Guilford.

Ojemann, J. G., Buckner, R. L., Corbetta, M., & Raichle, M. E. (1997). Imaging studies of memory and attention. *Neurosurgery Clinics of North America, 8*, 307–319.

Olanow, C. W., Kordower, J. H., & Freeman, T. B. (1996). Fetal nigral transplantation as a therapy for Parkinson's disease. *Trends in Neurosciences, 19*, 102–109.

O'Leary, A., Brown, S., & Suarez-Al-Adam, M. (1997). Stress and immune function. In T. W. Miller (Ed.), *Clinical disorders and stressful life events.* Madison, CT: International Universities Press.

Olmos, D. R. (1997, January 7). Seeing the light. *Los Angeles Times.*

Olson, L., Cheng, H., & Cao, Y. (1997, January). Cited in J. Goldberg, Mending spinal cords. *Discover.*

Olson, L., & Houlihan, D. (2000). A review of behavioral treatments used for Lesch-Nylan syndrome. *Behavior Modification, 24*, 202–222.

Olweus, O. (1995). Bullying or peer abuse at school: Facts and intervention. *Current Directions in Psychological Science, 4*, 196–200.

O'Neil, H. R., Jr., & Drillings, M. (Eds.). (1994). *Motivation: Theory and research.* Hillsdale, NJ: Lawrence Erlbaum.

Onishi, N. (2001, February 12). On the scale of beauty, weight weighs heavily. *New York Times*, A4.

O'Regan, J. K., Deubel, H., Clark, J. J., & Rensink, R. A. (2000). Picture changes during blinks: Looking without seeing and seeing without looking. *Visual Cognition, 7*, 191–211.

Orne, M. T., & Evans, F. J. (1965). Social control in the psychological experiment: Antisocial behavior and hypnosis. *Journal of Personality and Social Psychology, 1*, 189–200.

Ornish, D. (1998). *Love & survival.* New York: Harper-Collins.

Ortony, A., Clore, G., & Collins, A. (1988). *The cognitive structure of emotions.* New York: Cambridge University Press.

O'Shaughnessy, E. (1999). Relating to the superego. *International Journal of Psychoanalysis, 80*, 861–870.

Osofsky, J. D. (1995). The effects of exposure to violence on young children. *American Psychologist, 50*, 782–788.

Ost, L., Helstrom, K., & Kaver, A. (1992). One versus five sessions of exposure in the treatment of injection phobia. *Behavior Therapy, 23*, 263–282.

Ostrom, T. M., Skowronski, J. J., & Nowak, A. (1994). The cognitive foundation of attitudes: It's a wonderful construct. In P. G. Devine, D. L. Hamilton, & T. M. Ostrom (Eds.), *Social cognition: Impact on social psychology.* New York: Academic Press.

Ozer, D. J. (1999). Four principles for personality assessment. In L. A. Pervin & O. P. John (Eds.), *Handbook of personality* (2nd ed.). New York: Guilford.

Page, A. C. (1994). Blood-injury phobia. *Clinical Psychology Review, 14,* 443–461.

Page, A. C., Bennett, K. S., Carter, O., Smith, M., & Woodmore, K. (1997). The blood-injection symptoms scale (BISS) assessing a structure of phobic symptoms elicited by blood and injections. *Behaviour Research and Therapy, 35,* 457–464.

Paikoff, R. L., & Brooks-Gunn, J. (1991). Do parent-child relationships change during puberty? *Psychological Bulletin, 110,* 47–66.

Painter, K. (1997, August 15–17). Doctors have prenatal test for 450 genetic diseases. *USA Today.*

Pandina, R. J., & Johnson, V. L. (1999). In M. D. Glantz & C. R. Hartel (Eds.), *Drug abuse: Origins & interventions.* Washington, DC: American Psychological Association, 119–147.

Pappas, G. D., Lazorthes, Y., Bes, J. C., Tafani, M., & Winnie, A. P. (1997). Relief of intractable cancer pain by human chromaffic cell transplants: Experience at two medical centers. *Neurological Research, 19,* 71–77.

Park, B., DeKay, M. L., & Kraus, S. (1994). Aggregating social behavior in person models: Perceiver-induced consistency. *Journal of Personality and Social Psychology, 66,* 437–459.

Parker, G. (2000). Personality and personality disorder: Current issues and directions. *Psychological Medicine, 30,* 1–9.

Parks, G. (1997). *Half past autumn.* New York: Bulfinch Press & Little, Brown & Company.

Patterson, D. R., Everett, J. J., Bombadier, C. H., Questad, K. A., Lee, V. K., & Marvin, J. A. (1993). Psychological effects of severe burn injuries. *Psychological Bulletin, 113,* 362–378.

Patterson, G. R. (1994, October). Cited in B. Azar & S. Sleek, Do roots of violence grow from nature or nurture? *APA Monitor.*

Patton, G. C., Harris, R., Carlin, J. B., Hibbert, M. E., Coffey, C., Schwartz, M., & Bowes, G. (1997). Adolescent suicidal behaviours: A population-based study of risk. *Psychological Medicine, 27,* 715–724.

Paul, S. M., Extein, I., Calil, H. M., Potter, W. Z., Chodoff, P., & Goodwin, F. K. (1981). Use of ECT with treatment-resistant depressed patients at the National Institute of Mental Health. *American Journal of Psychiatry, 138,* 486–489.

Paulesu, E., Frith, C. D., & Frackowiak, R. S. J. (1993). The neural correlates of the verbal component of working memory. *Nature, 362,* 342–345.

Paulhus, D. L., Fridhandler, B., & Hayes, S. (1997). Psychological defense. In R. Hogan, J. Johnson, & S. Briggs (Eds.), *Handbook of personality psychology.* New York: Academic Press.

Payne, D. G., Toglia, M. P., & Anastasi, J. S. (1994). Recognition performance level and the magnitude of the misinformation effect in eyewitness memory. *Psychonomic Bulletin and Review, 1,* 376–382.

Payte, J. T. (1997). Methadone maintenance treatment: The first thirty years. *Journal of Psychoactive Drugs, 29,* 149–153.

Peele, S. (1997). Utilizing culture and behaviour in epidemiological models of alcohol consumption and consequences of western nations. *Alcohol & Alcoholism, 32,* 51–64.

Pelham, W. E., Bender, M. E., Caddell, J., Booth, S., & Moorer, S. H. (1985). Methylphenidate and children with attention deficit disorder. *Archives of General Psychiatry, 42,* 948–952.

Pennebaker, J. W., Colder, M., & Sharp, L. (1990). Accelerating the coping process. *Journal of Personality and Social Psychology, 58,* 528–537.

Pennebaker, J. W., & Memon, A. (1996). Recovered memories in context: Thoughts and elaborations on Bowers and Farvolden (1996). *Psychological Bulletin, 119,* 381–385.

Pennisi, E. (2000). And the gene number is . . . ? *Science, 288,* 1146–1147.

Perlis, M., Aloia, M., Millikan, A., Boehmler, J., Smith, M., Greenblatt, D., & Giles, D. (2000). Behavioral treatment of insomnia: A clinical case series study. *Journal of Behavioral Medicine, 22,* 149–161.

Perry, C. (1997). Admissibility and per se exclusion of hypnotically elicited recall in American courts of law. *International Journal of Clinical and Experimental Hypnosis, 45,* 266–279.

Perry, D. (2000). Patients' voices: The powerful sound in the stem cell debate. *Science, 287,* 1423.

Perry, T. (1995, May 28). Woman's work. *Los Angeles Times.*

Persons, J. B. (1997). Dissemination of effective methods: Behavior therapy's next challenge. *Behavior Therapy, 28,* 465–471.

Pert, C. B., Snowman, A. M., & Snyder, S. H. (1974). Localization of opiate receptor binding in presynaptic membranes of rat brain. *Brain Research, 70,* 184–188.

Peters, J. (1997, May 12). After sudden defeat, it's Kasparov who's blue. *Los Angeles Times.*

Peterson, K. S. (1997, July 22). Helping procrastinators get to it. *USA Today.*

Peterson, L., & Brown, D. (1994). Integrating child injury and abuse-neglect research: Common histories, etiologies, and solutions. *Psychological Bulletin, 116,* 293–315.

Peterson, L. R., & Peterson, M. J. (1950). Short-term retention of individual verbal terms. *Journal of Experimental Psychology, 58,* 193–198.

Peterson, M. A., & Gibson, B. S. (1994). Must figure-ground organization precede object recognition? *Psychological Science, 5,* 253–259.

Petitto, L. A. (1997, December 11). Cited in R. L. Hotz, The brain: Designed to speak the mind. *Los Angeles Times.*

Petitto, L. A., & Marentette, P. F. (1991). Babbling in the manual mode: Evidence for the ontogeny of language. *Science, 251,* 1493–1496.

Petrill, S. A. (1998). Molarity versus modularity of cognitive functioning? A behavioral genetic perspective. *Current Directions in Psychological Science, 6,* 96–99.

Petty, R. E., & Cacioppo, J. T. (1986). *Attitudes and persuasion: Classic and contemporary approaches.* Dubuque, IA: William C Brown.

Petty, R. E., Wegener, D. T., & Fabrigar, L. R. (1997). Attitudes and attitude change. *Annual Review of Psychology, 46,* 609–647.

Peyser, M. (2000, July 17). Venus rising. *Newsweek, 46.*

Peyser, M., Biddle, N. A., Brant, M., Wingert, P., Hackworth, D. H., & O'Shea, M. (1995, August 28). Sounding retreat. *Newsweek.*

Pezdek, K. (1995, February 11). Cited in M. Dolan, When the mind's eye blinks. *Los Angeles Times.*

Piaget, J. (1929). *The child's conception of the world.* New York: Harcourt Brace.

Pich, E. M., Pagliusi, S. R., Tessari, M., Talabot-Ayer, D., van Huijsduijnen, R. H., & Chiamulera, C. (1997). Common neural substrates for the addictive properties of nicotine and cocaine. *Science, 275,* 83–86.

Pierce, B. H. (1999). An evolutionary perspective on insight. In D. H. Rosen & M. D. Luebbert (Eds.), *Evolution of the psyche. Human evolution, behavior, and intelligence.* Westport, CT: Praeger/Greenwood Publishing, 227–245.

Piliavin, J. A., Dovidio, J. F., Gaertner, S. L., & Clark, R. D. (1982). Responsive bystanders: The process of intervention. In V. J. Derlega & J. Grzelak (Eds.), *Cooperation and helping behavior.* Orlando, FL: Academic Press.

Pillard, R. C., & Bailey, M. J. (1995). A biologic perspective on sexual orientation. *The Psychiatric Clinics of North America, 18,* 71–84.

Pillemer, D. B. (1984). Flashbulb memories of the assassination attempt on President Reagan. *Cognition, 16,* 63–80.

Pines, A. M. (1993). Burnout. In L. Goldberger & S. Breznitz (Eds.), *Handbook of stress: Theoretical and clinical aspects* (2nd ed.). New York: Free Press.

Pingitore, R., Dugoni, B. L., Tindale, R. S., & Spring, B. (1994). Bias against overweight job applicants in a simulated employment interview. *Journal of Applied Psychology, 79,* 909–917.

Pinker, S. (1994). *The language instinct.* New York: William Morrow.

Pinker, S. (1995). Introduction. In M. S. Gazzaniga (Ed.), *The cognitive neurosciences.* Cambridge, MA: MIT Press.

Pinker, S. (2000, April 10). Will the mind figure out how the brain works? *Time,* 90–91.

Pinnell, C. M., & Covino, N. A. (2000). Empirical findings on the use of hypnosis in medicine. *International Journal of Clinical and Experimental Hypnosis, 48,* 170–194.

Piomelli, D. (1997). Cited in J. Travis, Brain doubles up on marijuana-like agents. *Science News, 152,* 118.

Piomelli, D. (1999). Cited in J. Travis, Marijuana mimic reveals brain role. *Science News, 155,* 215.

Piot, P. (2000). Global AIDS epidemic: Time to turn the tide. *Science, 288,* 2176–2178

Pitman, R. (1994, August 4). Cited in N. Wartik, The amazingly simply inexplicable therapy that just might work. *Los Angeles Times Magazine.*

Pizarro, R. A., & Billick, S. B. (1999). Current issues in child abuse. *Current Opinion in Psychiatry, 12,* 665–668.

Plazzi, B., Corsini, R., Provini, R., Pierangeli, G., Martinelli, P., Montagna, P., Lugaresi, E., & Cortelli, P. (1997). REM sleep behavior disorders in multiple system atrophy. *Neurology, 48,* 1094–1097.

Plomin, R. (1997, May). Cited in B. Azar, Nature, nurture: Not mutually exclusive. *APA Monitor.*

Plomin, R. (2000). Behavioural genetics in the 21th century. *International Journal of Behavioral Development, 24,* 30–34.

Plomin, R., & Caspi, A. (1999). Behavioral genetics and personality. In L. A. Pervin & O. P. John (Eds.). *Handbook of personality* (2nd ed.). New York: Guilford.

Plomin, R., & Crabbe, J. (2000). DNA. *Psychological Bulletin, 126,* 806–828.

Plomin, R., Owen, M. J., & McGuffin, P. (1994). The genetic basis of complex human behaviors. *Science, 264,* 1733–1739.

Plomin, R., & Petrill, S. A. (1997). Genetics and intelligence: What's new? *Intelligence, 24,* 53–77.

Plomin, R., & Rutter, M. (1998). Child development, molecular genetics and what to do with genes once they are found. *Child Development, 69,* 68–71.

Plug, C., & Ross, H. E. (1994). The natural mood illusion: A multifactor angular account. *Perception, 23,* 321–333.

Plummer, W., & Ridenhour, R. (1995, August 28). Saving grace. *People*.

Plutchik, R. (1993). Emotions and their vicissitudes: Emotions and psychopathology. In M. Lewis & J. M. Haviland (Eds.), *Handbook of emotions*. New York: Guilford Press.

Polaschek, D. L. L., Ward, T., & Hudson, S. M. (1997). Rape and rapists: Theory and treatment. *Clinical Psychology Review, 17*, 117–144.

Pollack, M. H., & Otto, M. W. (1997). Long-term course and outcome of panic disorder. *Journal of Clinical Psychiatry, 58*(Supplement 2), 57–60.

Polymeropoulos, M. H., Higgins, J. J., Golbe, L. I., Johnson, W. G., Ide, S. E., Iorio, G. D., Sanges, G., Stenroos, E. S., Pho, L. T., Schaffer, A. A., Lazzarini, A. M., Nussbaum, A. L., & Duvoisin, R. C. (1996). Mapping of a gene for Parkinson's disease to chromosome 4q21–q23. *Science, 274*, 1197–1198.

Pomerleau, A., Bolduc, D., Malcuit, G., & Cossette, L. (1990). Pink or blue: Environmental gender stereotypes in the first two years of life. *Sex Roles, 22*, 359–367.

Ponsi, M. (1997). Interaction and transference. *International Journal of Psycho-Analysis, 78*, 243–263.

Porkka-Heiskanen, T., Strecker, R. E., Thakkar, M., Bjorkum, A. A., Greene, R. W., & McCarley, R. W. (1997). Adenosine: A mediator of the sleep-inducing effects of prolonged wakefulness. *Science, 276*, 1265–1268.

Portillo, E., Jr. (1994, June 17). Minority graduates choose to succeed. *San Diego Union-Tribune*.

Portin, P., & Alanen, Y. O. (1997). A critical review of genetic studies of schizophrenia: II. Molecular genetic studies. *Acta Psychiatrica Scandinavica, 95*, 73–80.

Portman, K., & Radanov, B. P. (1997). Dental anxiety and illness behaviour. *Psychotherapy and Psychosomatics, 66*, 141–144.

Posner, M. I. (1997). Introduction: Neuroimaging of cognitive processes. *Cognitive Psychology, 33*, 2–4.

Posner, M. I. (2000). Exploiting cognitive brain maps. *Brain and Cognition, 42*, 64–67.

Posner, M. I., & Dehaene, S. (1994). Attentional networks. *Trends in Neuroscience, 17*, 75–79.

Posner, M. I., & Raichle, M. E. (1994). *Images of mind*. New York: W. H. Freeman.

Post, R. (1994). Creativity and psychopathology: A study of 291 world-famous men. *British Journal of Psychiatry, 165*, 22–34.

Postmes, T., & Spears, R. (1998). Deindividuation and antinormative behavior: A meta-analysis. *Psychological Bulletin, 13*, 238–259.

Potter, J. (2000). Post-cognitive psychology. *Theory & Psychology, 10*, 31–37.

Poulton, R., Thomson, W. M., Davies, S., Kruger E., Brown, R. H., & Silva, P. (1997). Good teeth, bad teeth, and fear of the dentist. *Behaviour Research and Therapy, 35*, 327–334.

Powell, D. H., & Whitla, D. K. (1994). Normal cognitive aging: Toward empirical perspectives. *Current Directions in Psychological Science, 3*, 27–31.

Power, M. J. (1999). Sadness and its disorders. In T. Dalgleish & M. Power (Eds.), *Handbook of cognition and emotion*. New York: Wiley.

Pratkanis, A. R. (1992). The cargo cult science of subliminal persuasion. *Skeptical Inquirer, 16*, 260–286.

Prescott, C. A., Hewitt, J. K., Truett, K. R., Heath, A. C., Neale, M. C., & Eaves, L. J. (1994). Genetic and environmental influences on alcohol-related problems in a volunteer sample of older twins. *Journal of Studies on Alcohol, 55*, 184–202.

Pressley, M., Yokoi, L., van Meter, P., Van Etten, S., & Freebern, G. (1997). Some of the reasons why preparing for exams is so hard: What can be done to make it easier? *Educational Psychology Review, 9*, 1–38.

Pressman, M. R., & Orr, W. C. (Eds.). (1997). *Understanding sleep: The evaluation and treatment of sleep disorders*. Washington, DC: American Psychological Association.

Price, D. D. (2000). Psychological and neural mechanisms of the affective dimension of pain. *Science, 288*, 1769–1772.

Priest, R. G., Terzano, M. G., & Boyer, P. (1997). Efficacy of zolpidem in insomnia. *European Psychiatry, 12*(Supplement), 5s–14s.

Priester, J. R., & Petty, R. E. (1995). Source attributions and persuasion: Perceived honesty as a determinant of message scrutiny. *Personality and Social Psychology Bulletin, 21*, 637–654.

Prince, A., & Smolensky, P. (1997). Optimality: From neural networks to universal grammar. *Science, 75*, 1604–1610.

Prince, S. E., & Jacobson, N. S. (1997). A review and evaluation of marital and family therapies for affective disorders. *Journal of Marital and Family Therapy, 21*, 377–402.

Project Match Research Group. (1997). Matching alcoholism treatments to client heterogeneity: Project MATCH posttreatment drinking outcomes. *Journal of Studies on Alcohol, 58*, 7–29.

Pruitt, D. G. (1971). Choice shifts in group discussion: An introductory review. *Journal of Personality and Social Psychology, 20*, 339–360.

Pullum, G. K. (1991). *The great Eskimo vocabulary hoax*. Chicago: University of Chicago Press.

Purdon, S. E., Jones, B. D. W., Stip, E., Labelle, A., Addington, D., David, S. R., Breier, A., & Tollefson, G. D. (2000). Neuropsychological change in early phase schizophrenia during 12 months of treatment with olanzapine, rispeidone, or haloperidol. *Archives of General Psychiatry, 57*, 249–258.

Putnam, P. (1995, April). Cited in T. DeAngelis, Research documents trauma of abuse. *APA Monitor*.

Quadrel, M. J., Fischhoff, B., & Davis, W. (1993). Adolescent (in)vulnerability. *American Psychologist, 48*, 102–116.

Rabasca, L. (1999, December). Not enough evidence to support "abstinence-only." *Monitor of American Psychological Association, 39*.

Rabasca, L. (2000, November). In search of equality. *Monitor on Psychology*, 30–31.

Rabheru, K., & Persad, E. (1997). A review of continuation and maintenance electroconvulsive therapy. *Canadian Journal of Psychiatry, 42*, 476–484.

Rabkin, J. G., & Ferrando, S. (1997). A "second life" agenda. *Archives of General Psychiatry, 54*, 1049–1053.

Rabkin, S. W., Boyko, E., Shane, F., & Kaufert, J. (1984). A randomized trial comparing smoking cessation programs utilizing behavior modification, health education or hypnosis. *Addictive Behaviors, 9*, 157–173.

Raichle, M. E. (1994). Visualizing the mind. *Scientific American, 270*, 58–64.

Raine, A., Lencz, T., Bihrle, S., LaCasse, L., & Colletti, P. (2000). Reduced prefrontal gray matter volume and reduced autonomic activity in antisocial personality disorder. *Archives of General Psychiatry, 57*, 119–127.

Rainville, P., Duncan, G. H., Price, D. D., Carrier, B., & Bushnell, M. C. (1997). Pain affect encoded in human anterior cingulate but not somatosensory cortex. *Science, 277*, 968–971.

Rajkowska, G., Selemon, L. D., & Goldman-Rakic, P. S. (1997). Neuronal and glial somal size in the prefrontal cortex. *Archives of General Psychiatry, 55*, 215–224.

Rakic, P. (1985). Limits of neurogenesis in primates. *Science, 227*, 1054–1055.

Rakoff, D. (2000, October 29). Time warp: Questions for Dick Cavett. *New York Times Magazine*, 25.

Raloff, J. (1995). Languishing languages: Cultures at risk. *Science News, 147*, 117.

Raloff, J. (1997). FDA can regulate tobacco as a device. *Science News, 151*, 268.

Ralph, M. R., Foster, R. G., Davis, F. C., & Menaker, M. (1990). Transplanted suprachiasmatic nucleus determines circadian period. *Science, 247*, 975–978.

Ralston, J. (1989, April). Cited in S. Chollar, Conversations with the dolphins. *Psychology Today*.

Ramachandran, V. S., & Anstis, S. M. (1986). The perception of apparent motion. *Scientific American, 254*, 102–109.

Ramey, C. T., MacPhee, D., & Yeates, K. O. (1982). Preventing developmental retardation: A general system model. In D. K. Detterman & R. J. Sternberg (Eds.), *How and how much can intelligence be increased?* Norwood, NJ: Ablex Publishing.

Ramey, C. T., & Ramey, S. L. (1998). Early intervention and early experience. *American Psychologist, 53*, 109–120.

Ransdell, E., & Eddings, J. (1994, May 9). The man of the moment. *U.S. News & World Report*.

Rao, S. C., Rainer, G., & Miller, E. K. (1997). Integration of what and where in the primate prefrontal cortex. *Science, 276*, 821–824.

Rapoport, J. L. (1988). The neurobiology of obsessive-compulsive disorder. *Journal of the American Medical Association, 260*, 2888– 2890.

Rapoport, J. L., Buchsbaum, M. S., Weingartner, H., Zahn, T. P., Ludlow, C., & Mikkelsen, E. J. (1980). Dextroamphetamine: Its cognitive and behavioral effects in normal and hyperactive boys and normal men. *Archives of General Psychiatry, 37*, 933–942.

Rapport, M. D. (1994). Attention-deficit hyperactivity disorder. In V. B. Van Hasselt & M. Hersen (Eds.), *Advanced abnormal psychology*. New York: Plenum Press.

Rapport, M. D., Denney, C., DuPaul, G. J., & Bardner, M. J. (1994). Attention deficit disorder and methylphenidate; Normalization rates, clinical effectiveness, and response prediction in 76 children. *Journal of the American Academy of Child and Adolescent Psychiatry, 33*, 882–893.

Rasmussen, C., Knapp, T. J., & Garner, L. (2000). Driving-induced stress in urban college students. *Perceptual and Motor Skills, 90*, 437–443.

Ratcliff, R., & McKoon, G. (2000). Memory models. In E. Tulving & F. M. Craik (Eds.), *The Oxford handbook of memory*. New York: Oxford University Press.

Rauch, S. L., & Renshaw, P. F. (1995). Clinical neuroimaging in psychiatry. *Harvard Review of Psychiatry, 2*, 297–312.

Ravaja, N., Kauppinen, T., & Keltikangas-Jarvinen, L. (2000). Relationships between hostility and physiological coronary disease risk factors in young adults: The moderating tendencies of depressive tendencies. *Psychological Medicine, 30*, 381–393.

Ray, W. J. (1997). EEG concomitants of hypnotic susceptibility. *International Journal of Clinical and Experimental Hypnosis, 45*, 301–313.

Rechtschaffen, A. (1997, August). Cited in T. Geier, What is sleep for? *U.S. News & World Report*.

Redelmeier, D. A., & Tibshirani, R. J. (1997). Association between cellular-telephone calls and motor vehicle collisions. *New England Journal of Medicine, 336*, 453–458.

Reed, C. F. (1996). The immediacy of the moon illusion. *Perception, 25,* 1295–1300.

Reed, M. K. (1994). Social skills training to reduce depression in adolescents. *Adolescence, 29,* 293–302.

Reed, S., & Breu, G. (1995, June 6). The wild ones. *People.*

Reed, S., & Cook, D. (1993, April 19). Realm of the senses. *People.*

Reed, S., & Esselman, M. (1995, August 28). Catching hell. *People.*

Reed, S., & Free, C. (1995, October 16). The big payoff. *People.*

Reed, S., & Stambler, L. (1992, May 25). The umpire strikes back. *People,* 87–88.

Reeve, C. (1998). *Still me.* New York: Random House.

Register, A. C., Beckham, J. C., May, J. G., & Gustafson, D. J. (1991). Stress inoculation bibliotherapy in the treatment of test anxiety. *Journal of Counseling Psychology, 38,* 115–119.

Reid, J. B., Taplin, P. S., & Lorber, R. (1981). A social interactional approach to the treatment of abusive families. In R. B. Stuart (Ed.), *Violent behavior: Social learning approaches to prediction, management and treatment.* New York: Brunner/Mazel.

Reiman, E. M., Lane, R. D., Ahern, G. L., Schwartz, G. E., Davidson, R. J., Friston, K. J., Yun, L. S., & Cen, K. (1997). Neuroanatomical correlates of externally and internally generated human emotion. *American Journal of Psychiatry, 154,* 918–925.

Reiss, D. (2000). *The relationship code.* Cambridge, MA: Harvard University Press.

Reitman, V. (1999, February 22). Learning to grin—and bear it. *Los Angeles Times,* A1.

Relman, A. S. (Ed.). (1982). *Marijuana and health.* Washington, DC: National Academy Press.

Renfrey, G., & Spates, C. R. (1994). Eye movement desensitization: A partial dismantling study. *Journal of Behavior Therapy and Experimental Psychiatry, 25,* 231–239.

Reppert, S. (1997). Cited in M. Barinaga, How jet-lag hormone does double duty in the brain. *Science, 277,* 480.

Rescorla, R. A. (1966). Predictability and number of pairings in Pavlovian fear conditioning. *Psychonomic Science, 4,* 383–384.

Rescorla, R. A. (1987). A Pavlovian analysis of goal-directed behavior. *American Psychologist, 42,* 119–129.

Rescorla, R. A. (1988). Pavlovian conditioning. *American Psychologist, 43,* 151–160.

Research Triangle Institute. (1994). *Past and future directions of the D.A.R.E. program: An evaluation review.* National Institute of Justice.

Resnick, M., Bearman, P. S., Blum, R. W., Bauman, K. E., Harris, K. H., Jones, J., Tabor, J., Beuhring, T., Sieving, R. E., Shew, M., Ireland, M., Bearinger, L. H., & Udry, J. R. (1997). Protecting adolescents from harm. *Journal of the American Medical Association, 278,* 823–832.

Rey, G. (1983). Concepts and stereotypes. *Cognition, 15,* 237–262.

Reyna, V. F., & Lloyd, F. (1997). Theories of false memory in children and adults. *Learning and Individual Differences, 9,* 95–123.

Reyneri, A. (1984). The nose knows, but science doesn't. *Science.*

Reynes, R. L. (1996). The dream, communication, and attunement. *Psychotherapy, 33,* 479–483.

Reynolds, A. J. (1994). Effects of a preschool plus follow-on intervention for children at risk. *Developmental Psychology, 30,* 787–804.

Rhodes, G., & Tremewan, T. (1996). Averageness, exaggeration, and facial attractiveness. *Psychological Science, 7,* 105–110.

Rhue, J. W., Lynn, S. J., & Kirsch, I. (Eds.). (1994). *Handbook of clinical hypnosis.* Washington, DC: American Psychological Association.

Rice, G., Anderson, C., Risch, N., & Ebers, G. (1999). Male homosexuality: Absence of linkage to microsatellite markers at Xq28. *Science, 284,* 665–667.

Richardson, G. (1997, December). Cited in B. Azar, Researchers debunk myth of the "crack baby." *APA Monitor.*

Richardson, G. E., & Day, N. L. (1994). Detrimental effects of prenatal cocaine exposure: Illusion or reality. *Journal of the American Academy of Child and Adolescent Psychiatry, 33,* 28–34.

Richardson, L. (1994, June 7). OK, so I'll never be a waif. *Los Angeles Times.*

Richmond, R. L., Kehoe, L., & de Almeida Neto, A. C. (1997). Effectiveness of a 24-hour transdermal nicotine patch in conjunction with a cognitive behavioural programme: One year outcome. *Addiction, 92,* 27–31.

Richter, P. (1997, April 17). Pentagon to OK peyote for religious rites. *Los Angeles Times.*

Richters, J. M. A. (1997). Menopause in different cultures. *Journal of Psychosomatic Obstetrics and Gynecology, 18,* 73–80.

Rieke, M. L., & Guastello, S. J. (1995). Unresolved issues in honesty and integrity testing. *American Psychologist, 50,* 458–459.

Rieker, P. P., & Carmen, E. H. (1986). The victim-to-patient process: The discomfirmation and transformation of abuse. *American Journal of Orthopsychiatry, 56,* 360–370.

Rilling, M. (2000). John Watson's paradoxical struggle to explain Freud. *American Psychologist, 55,* 301–312.

Rimland, B. (1964). *Infantile autism.* New York: Appleton-Century-Crofts.

Risold, P. Y., & Swanson, L. W. (1996). Structural evidence for functional domains in the rat hippocampus. *Science, 272,* 1484–1486.

Risse, G. L., Gates, J. R., & Fangman, M. C. (1997). A reconsideration of bilateral language representation based on the intracarotid amobarbital procedure. *Brain and Cognition, 33,* 118–132.

Ritter, M. (2000, January 17). Camera wired to brain provides some useful vision for blind man. *San Diego Union-Tribune,* A-6.

Riva, G. (2000). Virtual reality in rehabilitation of spinal cord injured: A case report. *Rehabilitation Psychology, 45,* 81–88.

Rivas-Vazquez, R. A., & Blais, M. A. (1997). Selective serotonin reuptake inhibitors and atypical antidepressants: A review and update for psychologists. *Professional Psychology: Research and Practice, 28,* 526–536.

Rivera, C. (2000, June 9). Helping hands for mentally ill. *Los Angeles Times,* A1.

Rivera, E. (2000, July 31). License to drink. *Time,* 47.

Rivers, P. C. (1994). *Alcohol and human behavior.* Englewood Cliffs, NJ: Wiley.

Roan, S. (1997a, March 26). Faint chances. *Los Angeles Times.*

Roan, S. (1997b, June 11). A losing gamble. *Los Angeles Times.*

Roan, S. (1998, March 16). A reason for hope. *Los Angeles Times,* S1.

Roan, S. (1999, October 25). Elusive sleep, elusive cure. *Los Angeles Times,* S1.

Robbins, J. (2000a, April). Wired for sadness. *Discover,* 77–81.

Robbins, J. (2000b, July 4). Virtual reality finds a real place as a medical aid. *New York Times,* D6.

Roberts, K, J. (2000). Barriers to and facilitators of HIV-positive patients' adherence to antiretroviral treatment regimes. *AIDS Patient Care and STDs, 14,* 155–168.

Roberts, M. J. (1993). Human reasoning: Deduction rules or mental models, or both. *Journal of Experimental Psychology, 46A,* 569–589.

Roberts, S. B. (1997). Cited in J. Raloff, Getting older—and a little rounder? *Science News, 152,* 282.

Robins, L. N., & Regier, D. A. (Eds.). (1991). *Psychiatric disorders in America.* New York: Free Press.

Robins, L. N., Tipp, J., & Przybeck, T. (1991). Antisocial personality. In L. N. Robins & D. A. Regier (Eds.), *Psychiatric disorders in America.* New York: Free Press.

Robinson, R. G. (1995). Mapping brain activity associated with emotion. *American Journal of Psychiatry, 152,* 327–329.

Robinson-Riegler, B., & McDaniel, M. A. (1994). Further constraints on the bizarreness effect: Elaboration at encoding. *Memory and Cognition, 22,* 702–712.

Rock, I., & Palmer, S. (1990). The legacy of Gestalt psychology. *Scientific American, 263,* 84–90.

Rodgers, J. E. (1982). The malleable memory of eyewitnesses. *Science.*

Rodier, P. M. (2000, February). The early origins of autism. *Scientific American,* 36–63.

Rodriguez-Tome, H., Bariaud, F., Cohen-Zardi, M. F., Delmas, C., Jeanvoine, F., & Szylagyi, P. (1993). The effects of pubertal changes on body image and relations with peers of the opposite sex in adolescence. *Journal of Adolescence, 16,* 421–438.

Roediger, H. L., & McDermott, K. B. (2000). Distortions of memory. In E. Tulving & F. M. Craik (Eds.), *The Oxford handbook of memory.* New York: Oxford University Press.

Rogers, C. R. (1951). *Client-centered therapy: Its current practice, implications, and theory.* Boston: Houghton Mifflin.

Rogers, C. R. (1980). *A way of being.* Boston: Houghton Mifflin.

Rogers, C. R. (1986). Client-centered therapy. In I. L. Kutash & A. Wolf (Eds.), *Psychotherapists' casebook.* San Francisco: Jossey-Bass.

Rogers, C. R. (1989). Cited in N. J. Raskin & C. R. Rogers, Person-centered therapy. In R. J. Corsini & D. Wedding (Eds.), *Current psychotherapies* (4th ed.). Itasca, IL: F. E. Peacock.

Rogers, P., & Morehouse, W., III. (1999, April 12). She's got it. *People,* 89.

Rogoff, B., & Chavajay, P. (1995). What's become of research on the cultural basis of cognitive development? *American Psychologist, 50,* 859–877.

Roisman, G. I., Bahadur, M. A., & Oster, H. (2000). Infant attachment security as a discriminant predictor of career development in late adolescence. *Journal of Adolescent Research, 15,* 531–545.

Rokicki, L. A., Holroyd, K. A., France, C. R., Lipchik, G. L., France, J. L., & Kvaal, S. A. (1997). Change mechanisms associated with combined relaxation/EMG biofeedback training for chronic tension headache. *Applied Psychophysiology and Biofeedback, 22,* 21–41.

Rolls, E. T. (2000). Memory systems in the brain. *Annual Review of Psychology, 51,* 599–630.

Romney, D. M., & Bynner, J. M. (1997). A re-examination of the relationship between shyness, attributional style, and depression. *Journal of Genetic Psychology, 158,* 261–270.

Rorer, L. G. (1990). Personality assessment: A conceptual survey. In L. A. Pervin (Ed.), *Handbook of personality: Theory and research.* New York: Guilford Press.

**Rorschach, R.** (Original work published 1921; reprinted 1942). *Psychodiagnostics.* Bern: Hans Huber.

**Rortvedt, A. K., & Miltenberger, R. G.** (1994). Analysis of a high-probability instructional sequence and time-out in the treatment of child noncompliance. *Journal of Applied Behavior Analysis, 27,* 327–330.

**Rosch, E.** (1978). Principles of categorization. In E. Rosch & B. B. Lloyd (Eds.), *Cognition and categorization.* Hillsdale, NJ: Lawrence Erlbaum.

**Rosch, P. J.** (1994). Does stress cause hypertension? *Stress Medicine, 10,* 141–143.

**Rose, F. D., Attree, E. A., & Johnson, D. A.** (1996). Virtual reality: An assistive technology in neurological rehabilitation. *Current Opinion in Neurology, 9,* 461–467.

**Rosellini, L.** (1998, April 13). When to spank. *U.S. News & World Report,* 52–58.

**Rosenberg, H.** (1993). Prediction of controlled drinking by alcoholics and problem drinkers. *Psychological Bulletin, 113,* 129–139.

**Rosenberg, K. P.** (1994). Notes and comments: Biology and homosexuality. *Journal of Sex and Marital Therapy, 20,* 147–150.

**Rosenblatt, R. A.** (2000, May 30). At summit, U.S. plans to weigh in on increase of diet doctors. *Los Angeles Times,* A5.

**Rosenfeld, J. P.** (1995). Alternative views of Bashore and Rapp's (1993) alternatives to traditional polygraphy: A critique. *Psychological Bulletin, 117,* 159–166.

**Rosenfeld, J. V.** (1996). Minimally invasive neurosurgery. *Australian Journal of Surgery, 66,* 553–559.

**Rosenfeld, M.** (1998, November 30). Was it depression or disease? *Los Angeles Times,* E4.

**Rosenthal, M. S.** (1994). The 1993 distinguished lecturer in substance abuse. *Journal of Substance Abuse Treatment, 11,* 3–7.

**Rosenthal, N. E.** (1993). Diagnosis and treatment of seasonal affective disorder. *Journal of the American Medical Association, 270,* 2717–2720.

**Rosenthal, R.** (1994). Science and ethics in conducting, analyzing, and reporting psychological research. *Psychological Science, 5,* 127–134.

**Rosenthal, R. H.** (1993). Relationships of the type A behavior pattern with coronary heart disease. In L. Goldberger & S. Breznitz (Eds.), *Handbook of stress: Theoretical and clinical aspects* (2nd ed.). New York: Free Press.

**Rosenthal, S. L., Burklow, K. A., Lewis, L. M., Succop, P. A., & Biro, F. M.** (1997). Heterosexual romantic relationships and sexual behaviors of young adolescent girls. *Journal of Adolescent Health, 21,* 238–243.

**Rosenzweig, M. R.** (1992). Psychological science around the world. *American Psychologist, 47,* 718–722.

**Ross, B. M., & Millsom, C.** (1970). Repeated memory of oral prose in Ghana and New York. *International Journal of Psychology, 5,* 173–181.

**Ross, P. E.** (1991). Hard words. *Scientific American, 264,* 138–147.

**Rossi, A. S.** (Ed.). (1994). *Sexuality across the life course.* Chicago: University of Chicago Press.

**Rostan, S. M.** (1994). Problem finding, problem solving, and cognitive controls: An empirical investigation of critically acclaimed productivity. *Creativity Research Journal, 7,* 79–110.

**Roth, D., Slone, M., & Dar, R.** (2000). Which way cognitive development? *Theory and Psychology, 10,* 353–373.

**Rothbart, M. K., & Bates, J. E.** (1998). Temperament. In W. Damon & R. M. Lerner (Eds.), *Handbook of child psychology* (Vol. 1). New York: John Wiley & Sons.

**Rothenberg, S. A.** (1997). Introduction to sleep disorders. In M. R. Pressman & W. C. Orr (Eds.), *Under-standing sleep: The evaluation and treatment of sleep disorders.* Washington, DC: American Psychological Association.

**Rotter, J. B.** (1966). Generalized expectancies for internal versus external locus of control of reinforcement. *Psychological Monographs: General and Applied, 80*(Whole No. 609).

**Rotter, J. B.** (1990). Internal versus external control of reinforcement: A case history of a variable. *American Psychologist, 45,* 489–493.

**Roush, W.** (1995). Arguing over why Johnny can't read. *Science, 267,* 1896–1898.

**Routh, D. K.** (1994). *The founding of clinical psychology (1896) and some important early developments: Introduction.* New York: Plenum Publishing.

**Rovee-Collier, C., & Hayne, H.** (2000). Memory in infancy and early childhood. In E. Tulving & F. M. Craik (Eds.), *The Oxford handbook of memory.* New York: Oxford University Press.

**Rowatt, W. C., Nesselroade, K. P., Jr., Beggan, J. K., & Allison, S. T.** (1997). Perceptions of brainstorming in groups: The quality-over-quantity hypothesis. *Journal of Creative Behavior, 31,* 131–151.

**Rowe, D. C.** (1997). Genetics, temperament, and personality. In R. Hogan, J. Johnson, & S. Briggs (Eds.), *Handbook of personality psychology.* New York: Academic Press.

**Roy-Byrne, P. P., & Fann, J. R.** (1997). Psychopharmacologic treatments for patients with neuropsychiatric disorders. In S. C. Yudofsky & R. E. Hales (Eds.), *American Psychiatric Press textbook of neuropsychiatry* (3rd ed.). Washington, DC: American Psychiatric Press.

**Rozee, P. D.** (1993). Forbidden or forgiven? Rape in cross-cultural perspective. *Psychology of Women Quarterly, 17,* 499–514.

**Rozin, P.** (1986). One-trial acquired likes and dislikes in humans: Disgust as a U.S. food predominance, and negative learning predominance. *Learning and Motivation, 17,* 180–189.

**Rozin, P., Haidt, J., & McCauley, C. R.** (2000). Disgust. In M. Lewis & J. M. Haviland-Jones (Eds.), *Handbook of emotions* (2nd ed., 637–653). New York: Guilford.

**Rozin, P., Markwith, M., & Stoess, C.** (1997). Moralization and becoming a vegetarian. *Psychological Science, 8,* 67–73.

**Rubin, D. C., & Kozin, M.** (1984). Vivid memories. *Cognition, 16,* 81–95.

**Rubin, R.** (1999a, December 21). Do mammograms pass the test? *USA Today,* 1A.

**Rubin, R.** (1999b, December 21). Going digital: Proponents say it's time the FDA updates mammography system. *USA Today,* 9D.

**Ruble, D. N., & Martin, C. L.** (1998). Gender development. In W. Damon & R. M. Lerner (Eds.), *Handbook of child psychology* (Vol. 1). New York: John Wiley & Sons.

**Ruegg, R., & Frances, A.** (1995). New research in personality disorders. *Journal of Personality Disorders, 9,* 1–48.

**Rugg, M.** (1995). La difference vive. *Nature, 373,* 561–562.

**Ruiz-Bueno, J. B.** (2000). Locus of control, perceived control, and learned helplessness. In V. R. Rice (Ed.), *Handbook of stress, coping and health.* Thousand Oaks, CA: Sage.

**Rushdie, S.** (1988). *The satanic verses.* New York: Viking-Penguin.

**Rutter, M.** (2000). Genetic studies of autism: From the 1970s into the millennium. *Journal of Abnormal Child Psychology, 28,* 3–14.

**Saarni, C., Mumme, D. L., & Campos, J. J.** (1998). Emotional development: Action, communication, and understanding. In W. Damon & N. Eisenberg (Eds.), *Handbook of child psychology* (5th ed.). New York: John Wiley & Sons.

**Sackeim, H. A., Prudic, J., Devanand, D. P., Nobler, M. S., Lisanby, S., Peyser, S., Fitzsimons, L., Moody, B. J., & Clark, J.** (2000). A prospective, randomized, double-blind comparison of bilateral and right unilateral electroconvulsive therapy at different stimulus intensities. *Archives of General Psychiatry, 57,* 425–434.

**Sackeim, H. A., & Stern, Y.** (1997). Neuropsychiatric aspects of memory and amnesia. In S. C. Yudofsky & R. E. Hales (Eds.), *The American Psychiatric Press textbook of neuropsychiatry* (3rd ed.). Washington, DC: American Psychiatric Press.

**Sacks, O.** (1995). *An anthropologist on Mars.* New York: Alfred A. Knopf.

**Saffran, J. R., Aslin, R. N., & Newport, E. L.** (1996). Statistical learning by 8-month-old infants. *Science, 274,* 1926–1928.

**Salgado, J. F.** (1997). The five-factor model of personality and job performance in the European Community. *Journal of Applied Psychology, 82,* 30–43.

**Salovey, P., & Mayer, J. D.** (1990). Emotional intelligence. *Imagination, Cognition, and Personality, 9,* 185–211.

**Salovey, P., Rothman, A. J., Detweiller, J. B., & Steward, W. T.** (2000). Emotional states and physical health. *American Psychologist, 55,* 110–121.

**Salthouse, T. A.** (1994). The aging of working memory. *Neuropsychology, 8,* 535–543.

**Salthouse, T. A., Legg, S., Palmon, R., & Mitchell, D.** (1990). Memory factors in age-related differences in simple reasoning. *Psychology and Aging, 5,* 9–15.

**Salzman, C.** (1998). ECT, research, and professional ambivalence. *American Journal of Psychiatry, 155,* 1–2.

**Salzman, C., Miyawaki, E. K., le Bars, P., & Kerrihard, T. N.** (1993). Neurobiologic basis of anxiety and its treatment. *Harvard Review of Psychiatry, 1,* 197–206.

**Samelson, F.** (1980). J. B. Watson's little Albert, Cyril Burt's twins, and the need for a critical science. *American Psychologist, 35,* 619–625.

**SAMHSA.** (2000). 1999 National household survey on drug abuse. *www.SAMHSA.gov*

**Sammons, M. T., & Gravitz, M. A.** (1990). Theoretical orientation of professional psychologists and their former professors. *Professional Psychology: Research and Practice, 21,* 131–134.

**Samuel, D.** (1996). Cited in N. Williams, How the ancient Egyptians brewed beer. *Science, 273,* 432.

**Sanchez-Ramos, J. R.** (1993). Psychostimulants. *Neurologic Clinics, 11,* 535–553.

**Sandlund, E. S., & Norlander, T.** (2000). The effects of Tai Chi Chuan relaxation and exercise on stress responses and well-being. An overview of research. *International Journal of Stress Management, 7,* 139–149.

**Sands, R., Tricker, J., Sherman, C., Armatas, C., & Maschette, W.** (1997). Disordered eating patterns, body image, self-esteem, and physical activity in preadolescent school children. *International Journal of Eating Disorders, 21,* 159–166.

**Sanfilipo, M., Lafargue, T., Rusinek, H., Arena, L., Loneragan, C., Lautin, A., Feiner, D., Rotrosen, J., & Wolkin, A.** (2000). Volumetric measure of the frontal and temporal lobe regions in schizophrenia. *Archives of General Psychiatry, 57,* 471–480.

**Sanyal, S., & van Tol, H. M.** (1997). Review of the role of dopamine D4 receptors in schizophrenia and antipsychotic action. *Journal of Psychiatric Research, 31,* 219–232.

Sapienza, B. G., & Bugental, J. F. T. (2000). Keeping our instruments finely tuned: An existential-humanistic perspective. *Professional Psychology: Research and Practice, 31,* 458–460.

Sapolsky, R. M. (1992). *Stress: The aging brain and the mechanism of neuron death.* Cambridge, MA: MIT Press.

Sapp, M. (1994). The effects of guided imagery on reducing the worry and emotionality components of test anxiety. *Journal of Mental Imagery, 18,* 165–180.

Sarason, I. G., Sarason, B. R., & Johnson, J. H. (1985). Stressful life events' measurement, moderators and adaptation. In S. R. Burchfield (Ed.), *Stress: Psychological and physiological interactions.* New York: Hemisphere.

Sarter, M., Berntson, G. G., & Cacioppo, J. T. (1996). Brain imaging and cognitive neuroscience. *American Psychologist, 51,* 13–21.

Sarwer, D. B., & Durlak, J. A. (1997). A field trial of the effectiveness of behavioral treatment for sexual dysfunctions. *Journal of Sex & Marital Therapy, 23,* 87–97.

Saskin, P. (1997). Obstructive sleep apnea: Treatment options, efficacy, and effects. In M. R. Pressman & W. C. Orr (Eds.), *Understanding sleep: The evaluation and treatment of sleep disorders.* Washington, DC: American Psychological Association.

Sasson, Y., Zohar, J., Chopra, M., Lustig, M., Iancu, I., & Hendler, T. (1997). Epidemiology of obsessive-compulsive disorder: A world view. *Journal of Clinical Psychiatry, 58*(Supplement 12), 7–10.

Satcher, D. (2000). Mental health: A report of the Surgeon General—executive summary. *Professional Psychology, Research and Practice, 31,* 5-13.

Saudino, K. J., & Plomin, R. (1997). Cognitive and temperamental mediators of genetic contributions to the home environment during infancy. *Merrill-Palmer Quarterly, 43,* 1–23.

Savage, D. G. (1996, September 13). Calls for legalization remain as Dole's anti-drug rhetoric rises. *Los Angeles Times.*

Savage-Rumbaugh, S. (1991). Cited in A. Gibbons, Deja vu all over again: Chimp-language wars. *Science, 251,* 1561–1562.

Savage-Rumbaugh, S. (1998, January 19). Cited in S. Begley, Aping language. *Newsweek.*

Savage-Rumbaugh, S., & Lewin, R. (1994). *Kanzi.* New York: Wiley.

Saxe, L. (1994). Detection of deception: Polygraph and integrity tests. *Current Directions in Psychological Science, 3,* 69–73.

Saywitz, K. J., Mannarino, A. P., Berliner, L., & Cohen, J. A. (2000). Treatment for sexually abused children and adolescents. *American Psychologist, 55,* 1040–1049.

Scanlon, M., & Mauro, J. (1992, November–December). The lowdown on handwriting analysis. *Psychology Today.*

Scarr, S., & Weinberg, R. A. (1976). IQ test performance of black children adopted by white families. *American Psychologist, 31,* 726–739.

Schachter, S., & Singer, J. (1962). Cognitive, social and physiological determinants of emotional state. *Psychological Review, 69,* 379–399.

Schacter, D. L. (1996). *Searching for memory.* New York: Basic Books.

Schacter, D. L. (1997, October). Cited in E. Yoffe, How quickly we forget. *U.S. News & World Report.*

Schacter, D. L., & Tulving, E. (Eds.). (1994). *Memory systems 1994.* Cambridge, MA: MIT Press.

Schacter, D. L., Wagner, A. D., & Buckner, R. L. (2000). Memory systems of 1999. In E. Tulving & F. M. Craik (Eds.), *The Oxford handbook of memory.* New York: Oxford University Press.

Schaie, K. W. (1994). The course of adult intellectual development. *American Psychologist, 49,* 304–313.

Schaller, M. (1997). Beyond "competing," beyond "compatible." *American Psychologist, 52,* 1379–1387.

Schaufeli, W. B., & Peeters, M. C. W. (2000). Job stress and burnout among correctional officers: A literature review. *International Journal of Stress Management, 7,* 19–48.

Scheck, M. M., Schaeffer, J. A., & Gillette, C. (1998). Brief psychological intervention with traumatized young women: The efficacy of eye movement desensitization and reprocessing. *Journal of Traumatic Stress, 11,* 25–44.

Scheer, R. (1999, March 23). A drug war fought on ideology alone. *Los Angeles Times,* B7.

Scheier, M. F., & Carver, C. S. (1992). Effects of optimism on psychological and physical well-being: Theoretical overview and empirical update. *Cognitive Therapy and Research, 16,* 201–228.

Schemo, D. J. (1997, March 30). Heroin is proving a growth industry for Colombia. *New York Times International.*

Scherer. K. R. (1999). Appraisal theory. In T. Dalgleish & M. Power (Eds.), *Handbook of cognition and emotion.* New York: Wiley.

Schiavi, R. C., & Segraves, R. T. (1995). The biology of sexual function. *Clinical Sexuality, 18,* 7–23.

Schiff, M., Duyme, M., Dumaret, A., & Tomkiewicz, S. (1982). How much could we boost scholastic achievement and IQ scores? A direct answer from a French adoption study. *Cognition, 12,* 165–196.

Schlenker, B. R., Phillips, S. T., Boniecki, K. A., & Schlenker, D. R. (1995). Where is the home choke? *Journal of Personality and Social Psychology, 68,* 649–652.

Schlosser, E. (1994, August). *Reefer madness.* Atlantic.

Schmidt, M. Germany. (1997). In D. J. Cohen & F. R. Volkmar (Eds.), *Handbook of autism and pervasive developmental disorders* (2nd ed.). New York: John Wiley & Sons.

Schneider, G. E. (1995). Cited in C. Holden, Why neurons won't regenerate. *Science, 269,* 925.

Schneider, K., & Pinnow, M. (1994). Olfactory and gustatory stimuli in food-aversion learning in rats. *Journal of General Psychology, 12,* 169–183.

Schoemer, K. (1996, August 26). Heroin. *Newsweek.*

Schoenberger, N. E. (2000). Research on hypnosis as an adjunct to cognitive-behavioral psychotherapy. *International Journal of Clinical and Experimental Hypnosis, 48,* 154–169.

Schooler, J. W., & Eich, E. (2000). Memory for emotional events. In E. Tulving & F. M. Craik (Eds.), *The Oxford handbook of memory.* New York: Oxford University Press.

Schroeder, D. A., Penner, L. A., Dovidio, J. F., & Piliavin, J. A. (1995). *The psychology of helping and altruism: Problems and puzzles.* New York: McGraw-Hill.

Schuckit, M. A. (1990, August). Are there dangers to marijuana? *Drug Abuse and Alcoholism Newsletter.* Vista Hill Foundation.

Schuckit, M. A. (1994a). Can marijuana cause a long-lasting psychosis? *Vista Hills Foundation Newsletter, 23,* 1–4.

Schuckit, M. A. (1994b). Low level of response to alcohol as a predictor of future alcoholism. *American Journal of Psychiatry, 151,* 184–189.

Schuckit, M. A. (2000). *Drug and alcohol abuse* (5th ed.). New York: Kluwer Academic.

Schuckit, M. A., & Smith, T. L. (1997). Assessing the risk for alcoholism among sons of alcoholics. *Journal of Studies of Alcohol, 58,* 141–145.

Schuh, K. J., & Griffiths, R. R. (1997). Caffeine reinforcement: The role of withdrawal. *Psychopharmacology, 130,* 320–326.

Schuker, E. (1979). Psychodynamics and treatment of sexual assault victims. *Journal of the American Academy of Psychoanalysis, 7,* 553–573.

Schuler, G. D., Boguski, M. S., Stewart, E. A., Stein, L. D., Gyapay, G., Rice, K., White, R. E., Rodriguez-Tome, P., Agarwal, A., Bajorek, E., Bentolila, S., Birren, B. B., Butler, A., Castle, A. B., Chiannikulchai, N., Chu, A., Clee, C., Cowles, S., Day, P. J. R., Dibling, T., Drouot, N., Dunham, I., Duprat, S., East, C., Edwards, C., Fan, J. B., Fang, N., Fizamex, C., Garrett, C., Green, L., Hadley, D., Harris, M., Harrison, P., Brady, S., Hicks, A., Holloway, E., Hui, L., Hussain, S., Couis-Dit-Sully, C., Ma, J., MacGlvery, A., Mader, C., Maratukulam, A., Matise, T. C., McKusick, K. B., Morissette, J., Mangall, A., Muselet, D., Nusbaum, H. C., Page, D. C., Peck, A., Perkins, S., Piercy, M., Quin, F., Quackenbush, J., Ranby, S., Reif, T., Rozen, S., Sanders, C., She, S., Silva, J., Slonim, D. K., Soderlund, C., Sun, W. L., Tabar, P., Thangarajah, T., Vega-Czarny, N., Vollrath, D., Voyticky, S., Wilmer, T., Wu, X., Adams, M. D., Auffray, C., Walter, N. A. R., Brandon, R., Dehejia, A., Goodfellow, P. N., Houlgatte, R., Hudson, J. R., Jr., Ide, S. E., Ioorio, K. R., Lee, W. Y., Seki, L. N., Nagase, T., Ishikawa, K., Nomura, N., Phillips, C., Polymeropoulos, M. H., Sandusky, M., Schmitt, K., Berry, R., Swanson, K., Torres, R., Venter, J. C., Sikela, J. M., Beckmann, J. S., Weissenbch, J., Myers, R. M., Cox, D. R., James, M. R., Bentley, D., Deloukas, P., Lander, E. S., & Hudson, T. J. (1996). A gene map of the human genome. *Science, 274,* 540–546.

Schultz, R. T., Gauthier, I., Klin, A., Fulbright, R. K., Anderson, A. W., Volkmar, F. R., Schudlarski, P., Lacadie, C., Cohen, D. J., & Gore, J. C. (2000). Abnormal ventral temporal cortical activity during face discrimination among individuals with autism and Asperger syndrome. *Archives of General Psychiatry, 57,* 331–340.

Schulz, R. (1994, April 18). Cited in M. Elias, Pessimism takes toll on the ill. *USA Today.*

Schulz, R., & Curnow, C. (1988). Peak performance and age among superathletes: Track and field, swimming, baseball, tennis, and golf. *Journal of Gerontology, 43,* 113–120.

Schulz, S. C. (2000). New antipsychotic medications: More than old wine in new bottles. *Bulletin of the Menninger Clinic, 64,* 60–75.

Schuster, C. (1997, May 5). Cited in J. M. Nash, Addicted. *Time.*

Schusterman, R. (1993, March 22). Cited in S. Linden, Can animals think? *Time.*

Schwartz, B., & Reisberg, D. (1991). *Learning and memory.* New York: Norton.

Schwartz, B. L. (1999). Sparkling at the end of the tongue: The etiology of tip-of-the-tongue phenomenology. *Psychonomic Bulletin & Review, 6,* 379–393.

Schwartz, G. J. (1996). Cited in J. Raloff, How the brain knows when eating must stop. *Science News, 150,* 343.

Schwartz, N. (1999). Self-reports: How the questions shape the answers. *American Psychologist, 54,* 93–105.

Schwartz, R. H. (1991). Heavy marijuana use and recent memory impairment. *Psychiatric Annals, 21,* 80–82.

Schwartz, S. (2000). A historical loop of one hundred years: Similarities between 19th century and contemporary dream research. *Dreaming, 10,* 55–66.

# References

**Schweinhart, L. J., & Weikart, D. P.** (1980). *Young children grow up: The effects of the Perry Preschool Program on youth through age 15* (Monograph No. 7). High/Scope Educational Research Foundation.

**Schweitzer, J. B., Faber, T. L., Grafton, S. T., Tune, L. E., Hoffman, J. M., & Kilts, C. D.** (2000). Alterations in the functional anatomy of working memory in adult attention deficit hyperactivity disorder. *American Journal of Psychiatry, 157,* 278–280.

**Sciutto, M. J., Terjesen, M. D., & Bender Frank, A. S.** (2000). Teacher's knowledge and misperceptions of attention-deficit/hyperactivity disorder. *Psychology in the Schools, 37,* 115–122.

**Scott, J.** (1997). Advance in cognitive therapy. *Current Opinion in Psychiatry, 10,* 256–260.

**Scott, J. D., & Pawson, T.** (2000, June). Cell communication: The inside story. *Scientific American,* 72–79.

**Scott, K. S., Young, A. W., Calder, A. J., Hellawell, D. J., Aggleton, J. P., & Johnson, M.** (1997). Impaired auditory recognition of fear and anger following bilateral amygdala lesions. *Nature, 385,* 254–257.

**Scribner, S.** (1986). Thinking in action: Some characteristics of practical thought. In R. J. Sternberg & R. K. Wagner (Eds.), *Practical intelligence: Nature and origins of competence in the everyday world.* Cambridge, England: Cambridge University Press.

**Seaman, D.** (1996, November 24). Learning to beat a fear of flying. *New York Times.*

**Searles, J.** (1998, September). Write on! Learn to read his handwriting and read his mind. *Cosmopolitan,* 310–311.

**Sedikides, C., Campbell, W. K., Reeder, G. D., & Elliot, A. J.** (1998). The self-serving bias in relational context. *Journal of Personality and Social Psychology, 74,* 378–386.

**Seeley, R. J., & Schwartz, M. W.** (1997). The regulation of energy balance: Peripheral hormonal signals and hypothalamic neuropeptides. *Current Directions in Psychological Science, 6,* 39–44.

**Seeman, M. V.** (1994). Schizophrenia: D4 receptor elevation. What does it mean? *Journal of Psychiatry and Neuroscience, 19,* 171–176.

**Sees, K. L., Delucchi, K. L., Masson, C., Rosen, A., Clark, H. W., Robillard, H., Banys, P., & Hall, S. M.** (2000). Methadone maintenance vs. 180-day psychosocially enriched detoxification for treatment of opiod dependence. *Journal of American Medical Association, 283,* 1303–1310.

**Seidenberg, M. S.** (1997). Language acquisition and use: Learning and applying probabilistic constraints. *Science, 275,* 1599–1603.

**Selemon, L. D.** (2000). A measured milestone in schizophrenia research. *Archives of General Psychiatry, 57,* 74–75.

**Self, D. W., Barnhart, W. J., Lehman D. A., & Nestler, E. J.** (1996). Opposite modulation of cocaine-seeking behavior by $D_1$- and $D_2$-like dopamine receptor agonists. *Science, 271,* 1586–1569.

**Seligman, M. E. P.** (1970). On the generality of the laws of learning. *Psychological Review, 77,* 406–418.

**Selkoe, D. J.** (1997). Alzheimer's disease: Genotypes, phenotype, and treatments. *Science, 275,* 630–631.

**Selye, H.** (1956). *The stress of life.* New York: McGraw-Hill.

**Selye, H.** (1993). History of the stress concept. In L. Goldberger & S. Breznitz (Eds.), *Handbook of stress: Theoretical and clinical aspects* (2nd ed.). New York: Free Press.

**Semin, G. R., & De Poot, C. J.** (1997). The question–answer paradigm: You might regret not noticing how a question is worded. *Journal of Personality and Social Psychology, 73,* 472–480.

**Senden, M. von.** (1960). *Space and sight: The perception of space and shape in the congenitally blind before and after operation* (P. Heath, Trans.). New York: Free Press.

**Senécal, C., Koestner, R., & Vallerand, R. J.** (1995). Self-regulation and academic procrastination. *Journal of Social Psychology, 135,* 607–619.

**Seppa, N.** (2000). Stem cells repair rat spinal cord damage. *Science News, 157,* 6.

**Serpell, R.** (2000). Intelligence and culture. In R. J. Sternberg, *Handbook of intelligence.* New York: Cambridge University Press.

**Serretti, A., Macciardi, F., Cusin, C., Lattuada, E., Souery, D., Lipp, O., Mahieu, B., Van Broeckhoven, C., Blackwood, D., Muir, W., Aschauer, H. N., Heiden, A. M., Ackenheil, M., Fuchshuber, S., Raeymaekers, P., Verheyen, G., Kaneva, R., Jabelsky, A., Papadimitrou, G. N., Dikeos, D. G., Stefanis, C. N., Smeraldi, E., & Mendlewicz, J.** (2000). Linkage of mood disorders with D2, D3, and Th genes: A multicenter study. *Journal of Affective Disorders, 58,* 51–61.

**Setterlind, S., & Larsson, G.** (1995). The stress profile: A psychological approach to measuring stress. *Stress Medicine, 11,* 85–92.

**Shadish, W. R., Navarro, A. M., Matt, G. E., & Phillips, G.** (2000). The effects of psychological therapies under clinically representative conditions: A meta-analysis. *Psychological Bulletin, 126,* 512–529.

**Shannon, C.** (1994). Stress management. In D. K. Granvold (Ed.), *Cognitive and behavioral treatment.* Pacific Grove, CA: Brooks/Cole.

**Shapiro, C. M.** (1981). Growth hormone sleep interaction: A review. *Research Communications in Psychology, Psychiatry and Behavior, 6,* 115–131.

**Shapiro, F.** (1989). Efficacy of the eye movement desensitization procedure in the treatment of traumatic memories. *Journal of Traumatic Stress, 2,* 199–223.

**Shapiro, F.** (1991). Eye movement desensitization and reprocessing: From MD to EMD/R—A new treatment model for anxiety and related trauma. *Behavior Therapist, 14,* 133–135.

**Shapiro, F.** (1995). Cited in B. Bower, EMDR: Promise and dissent. *Science News, 148,* 270–271.

**Shapiro, J. P., Loeb, P., Bowermaster, D., Wright, A., Headden, S., & Toch, T.** (1993, December 13). Special report. *U.S. News & World Report.*

**Shapiro, L.** (1992, August 31). The lesson of Salem. *Newsweek.*

**Shapiro, S. L., Shapiro, D. E., & Schwartz, G. E. R.** (2000). Stress management in medical education: A review of the literature. *Academic Medicine, 75,* 748–759.

**Sharp, D.** (1999, December 27). 100-year club grows. *USA Today,* A1.

**Sharp, D.** (2000, August 10). Family embraces ear implants. *USA Today,* 9D.

**Shatz, C.** (1997, February 3). Cited in J. Madeleine Nash, Fertile minds. *Time.*

**Shaywitz, B. A., Shaywitz, S., Pugh, K. R., Constable, R. T., Skudlarski, P., Fulbright, R. K., Bronen, R. A., Fletcher, J. M., Shankweiler, D. P., Katz, L., & Gore, J. C.** (1995). Sex differences in the functional organization of the brain for language. *Nature, 373,* 607–609.

**Shaywitz, B. A., Sullivan, C. M., Anderson, G. M., Gillespie, S. M., Sullivan, B., & Shaywitz, S. E.** (1994). Aspartame, behavior, and cognitive function in children with attention deficit disorder. *Pediatrics, 93,* 70–75.

**Shaywitz, W.** (1999a, November 22). Cited in B. Kantrowitz & A. Underwood, Dyslexia and the new science of reading. *Newsweek,* 72–78.

**Shaywitz, W.** (1999b, December 7). Cited in M. Elias, Dyslexia is a handicap throughout school years. *USA Today,* D1.

**Shea, M. T., Elkin, I., Imber, S. D., Sotsky, S. M., Watkins, J. T., Collins, J. F., Pilkonis, P. A., Beckham, E., Glass, D. R., Dolan, R. T., & Parloff, M. B.** (1992). Course of depressive symptoms over follow-up: Findings from the National Institute of Mental Health Treatment of Depression Collaborative Research Program. *Archives of General Psychiatry, 49,* 782–787.

**Sheaffer, R.** (1997, May/June). Psychic departures and a discovery institute. *Skeptical Inquirer, 21.*

**Shenour, E. A.** (1990). Lying about polygraph tests. *Skeptical Inquirer, 14,* 292–297.

**Sherin, J. E., Shiromani, P. J., McCarley, R. W., & Saper, C. B.** (1996). Activation of ventrolateral preoptic neurons during sleep. *Science, 271,* 216–219.

**Sherman, L.** (1997, April 17). Cited in F. Butterfield, Popular anti-crime programs called ineffective. *San Diego Union-Tribune.*

**Shettleworth, S. J.** (1993). Where is the comparison in comparative cognition? *Psychological Science, 4,* 179–184.

**Shetty, A. K., & Turner, D. A.** (1996). Development of fetal hippocampal grafts in intact and lesioned hippocampus. *Progress in Neurobiology, 50,* 597–653.

**Shevrin, H., Bond, J. A., Brakel, A. W., Hertel, R. K., & Williams, W. J.** (1996). *Conscious and unconscious processes.* New York: Guilford Press.

**Shiffrin, R. M., & Nosofsky, R. M.** (1994). Seven plus or minus two: A commentary on capacity limitations. *Psychological Review, 101,* 357–361.

**Shih, J. C.** (1996, June 6). Cited in T. Monmaney, Of mice and mayhem. *Los Angeles Times,* B-2.

**Shilts, R.** (1988). *And the band played on.* New York: Penguin.

**Shimaya, A.** (1997). Perception of complex line drawings. *Journal of Experimental Psychology: Human Perception and Performance, 23,* 25–50.

**Shipley, M. T., & Ennis, M.** (1996). Functional organization of olfactory system. *Journal of Neurobiology, 30,* 123–176.

**Shorkey, C. T.** (1994). Use of behavioral methods with individuals recovering from substance dependence. In D. V. Granvold (Ed.), *Concepts and methods of cognitive treatment.* Pacific Grove, CA: Brooks/Cole.

**Shotland, R. L., & Hunter, B. A.** (1995). Women's "token resistant" and compliant sexual behaviors are related to uncertain sexual intentions and rape. *Personality and Social Psychology Bulletin, 21,* 226–236.

**Shute, N., Locy, T., & Pasternak, D.** (2000, March 6). The perils of pills. *U.S. News & World Report,* 43–50.

**Shweder, R. A., & Haidt, J.** (1993). The future of moral psychology: Truth, intuition, and the pluralist way. *Psychological Science, 4,* 360–365.

**Sidtis, J. J., Volpe, B. T., Wilson, D. H., Rayport, M., & Gazzaniga, M. S.** (1981). Variability in right hemisphere language function after callosal section: Evidence for a continuum of generative capacity. *Journal of Neuroscience, 1,* 323–331.

**Siegel, A.** (1998). *Dreamcatching: Every parent's guide to exploring and understanding children's dreams and nightmares.* New York: Three Rivers Press.

**Siegel, J. M.** (2000, January). Narcolepsy. *Scientific American,* 77–81.

**Siegel, R. K.** (1989). *Intoxication.* New York: Dutton.

**Sigelman, C. K., & Shaffer, D. R.** (1995). *Life-span human development.* Pacific Grove, CA: Brooks/Cole.

**Siliciano, R.** (1997). Cited in M. Balter, HIV survives drug onslaught by hiding out in T cells. *Science, 278,* 1227.

Silver, W. (1997, July 8). Cited in S. L. Jones, High schoolers learn that smell is a matter of taste. *San Diego Union-Tribune*.

Simonton, D. K. (1994). *Greatness*. New York: Guilford Press.

Simonton, D. K. (2000). Creativity: Cognitive, personal, developmental, and social aspects. *American Psychologist, 55*, 151–158.

Sinclair, R. C., Hoffman, C., Mark, M. J., Martin, L. L., & Pickering, T. L. (1994). Construct accessibility and the misattribution of arousal: Schachter and Singer revisited. *Psychological Science, 5*, 15–25.

Singelis, T., Choo, P., & Hatfield, E. (1995). Love schemas and romantic love. *Journal of Social Behavior and Personality, 10*, 15–36.

Singer, M. T., & Lalich, J. (1997). *Crazy therapies: What are they? Do they work?* San Francisco: Jossey-Bass.

Skaar, K. L., Tsho, J. Y., McClure, J. B., Cinciripini, P. M., Friedman, K., Wetter, D. W., & Gritz, E. R. (1997). Smoking cessation: 1. An overview of research. *Behavioral Medicine, 23*, 5–13.

Skerrett, P. J. (1994, October). Turning back the clock. *Popular Science*.

Skinner, B. F. (1938). *The behavior of organisms*. New York: Appleton-Century-Crofts.

Skinner, B. F. (1953). *Science and human behavior*. New York: Macmillan.

Skinner, B. F. (1957). *Verbal behavior*. New York: Appleton-Century-Crofts.

Skinner, B. F. (1989). The origin of cognitive thought. *American Psychologist, 44*, 13–18.

Slater, E. (1999, April 14). Kevorkian is sentenced to 10 to 25 years. *Los Angeles Times*, A1.

Sleek, S. (1994, December). Psychology takes the fear out of flying. *APA Monitor*.

Sleek, S. (1995, June). Unlocking the restrictions on drinking. *APA Monitor*.

Sloan, R. P., Shapiro, P. A., Bagiella, E., Boni, S. M., Paik, M., Bigger, J. T., Jr., Steinman, R. C., & Gorman, J. M. (1994). Effect of mental stress throughout the day on cardiac autonomic control. *Biological Psychology, 37*, 89–99.

Sloman, S. A. (1996). The empirical case for two systems of reasoning. *Psychological Bulletin, 119*, 3–22.

Slone, A. E., Brigham, J. C., & Meissner, C. A. (2000). Social and cognitive factors affecting the own-race bias in white. *Basic and Applied Social Psychology, 22*, 71–84.

Slone, K. C. (1985). *They're rarely too young . . . and never too old "to twinkle"!* Ann Arbor, MI: Shar Publications.

Slutske, W. S., Heath, A. C., Dinwiddie, S. H., Madden, P. A. F., Bucholz, K. K., Dunne, M. P., Statham, D. J., & Martin, N. G. (1997). Modeling genetic and environmental influences in the etiology of conduct disorder: A study of 2,682 adult twin pairs. *Journal of Abnormal Psychology, 106*, 266–279.

Small, G. W., Propper, M. W., Randolph, E. T., & Spencer, E. (1991). Mass hysteria among student performers: Social relationship as a symptom predictor. *American Journal of Psychiatry, 148*, 1200–1205.

Smiley, J. (2000, May 7). The good life. *New York Times Magazine*, 58–59.

Smith, C. A., & Ellsworth, P. C. (1985). Patterns of cognitive appraisal in emotion. *Journal of Personality and Social Psychology, 48*, 813–838.

Smith, D. (1982). Trends in counseling and psychotherapy. *American Psychologist, 37*, 802–809.

Smith, D. (2000, December). An Rx privilege project gets another look. *Monitor on Psychology*, 34.

Smith, E. E. (2000). Neural bases of human working memory. *Current Directions in Psychological Science, 9*, 45–49

Smith, E. E., & Jonides, J. (1997). Working memory: A view from neuroimaging. *Cognitive Psychology, 33*, 5–42.

Smith, E. R. (1994). Social cognition contributions to attribution theory and research. In P. G. Devine, D. L. Hamilton, & T. M. Ostrom (Eds.), *Social cognition: Impact on social psychology*. New York: Academic Press.

Smith, J. C., & Seidel, J. M. (1982). The factor structure of self-reported physical stress reactions. *Biofeedback and Self-Regulation, 7*, 35–47.

Smith, L. (1993, July 13). Men in the making. *Los Angeles Times*.

Smith, P. B., Dugan, S., & Trompenaars, F. (1997). Locus of control and affectivity by gender and occupational status: A 14-nation study. *Sex Roles, 36*, 51–77.

Snow, R. E., & Jackson, D. N., III. (1994). Individual differences in conation: Selected constructs and measures. In H. F. O'Neil, Jr., & M. Drillings (Eds.), *Motivation: Theory and research*. Hillsdale, NJ: Lawrence Erlbaum.

Snyder, C. R., Shenkel, R. J., & Lowery, C. R. (1977). Acceptance of personality interpretations: The "Barnum effect" and beyond. *Journal of Consulting and Clinical Psychology, 45*, 104–114.

Sobin, C., Sackeim, H. A., Prudic, J., Devanant, D. P., Moody, B. J., & McElhiney, M. C. (1995). Predictors of retrograde amnesia following ECT. *American Journal of Psychiatry, 152*, 995–1001.

Socolar, R., & Stein, R. E. K. (1995). Spanking infants and toddlers: Maternal belief and practice. *Pediatrics, 95*, 105–111.

Solomon, D. A., Keller, M. B., Leon, A. C., Mueller, T. I., Shea, M. R., Warshaw, M., Maser, J. D., Coryell, W., & Endicott, J. (1997). Recovery from major depression. *Archives of General Psychiatry, 54*, 1001–1006.

Somers, V. K., Phil, D., Dyken, M. E., Mark, A. L., & Abboud, F. M. (1993). Sympathetic-nerve activity during sleep in normal subjects. *New England Journal of Medicine, 328*, 303–307.

Sorbi, M. J., Maassen, G. H., & Spierings, E. L. H. (1996). A time series analysis of daily hassles and mood changes in the 3 days before the migraine attack. *Behavioral Medicine, 22*, 103–113.

Sozzi, G., Veronese, M. L., Negrini, M. J., Baffa, R., Cohicelli, M. G., Inoue, H., Tornielli, S., Pilotti, S., DeGregorio, L., & Pastorino, U. (1996). The FHIT gene 3p14.2 is abnormal in lung cancer. *Cell*, 17–26.

Spalding, L. R., & Hardin, C. D. (1999). Unconscious unease and self-handicapping: Behavioral consequences of individual differences in implicit and explicit self-esteem. *Psychological Science, 10*, 535–539.

Spangler, D. L., Simons, A. D., Monroe, S. M., & Thase, M. E. (1997). Response to cognitive-behavioral therapy in depression: Effects on pretreatment cognitive dysfunction and life stress. *Journal of Consulting and Clinical Psychology, 65*, 568–575.

Spanos, N. P. (1994). Multiple identity enactments and multiple personality disorder: A sociocognitive perspective. *Psychological Bulletin, 116*, 143–165.

Spanos, N. P. (1996). *Multiple identities and false memories: A sociocognitive perspective*. Washington, DC: American Psychological Association.

Spear, L. P. (2000). Neurobehavioral changes in adolescence. *Current Directions in Psychological Science, 9*, 111–114.

Spearman, C. (1904). "General intelligence" objectively determined and measured. *American Journal of Psychology, 15*, 201–293.

Speca, M., Carlson, L. E., Goodey, E., & Angen, M. (2000). A randomized, wait-list controlled clinical trial: The effect of a mindfulness meditation-based stress reduction program on mood and symptoms of stress in cancer outpatients. *Psychosomatic Medicine, 62*, 613–622.

Spelke, E. S., Breinlinger, K., Jacobson, K., & Phillips, A. (1993). Gestalt relations and object perception: A developmental study. *Perception, 22*, 1483–1501.

Spencer, T., Biederman, J., & Wilens, T. (2000). Pharmacotherapy of attention deficit hyperactivity disorder. *Psychopharmacology, 9*, 77–97.

Sperling, G. A. (1960). The information available in brief visual presentations. *Psychological Monographs, 74*(Whole No. 498).

Sperry, R. W. (1974). Lateral specialization in the surgically separated hemisphere. In R. O. Schmitt & F. G. Worden (Eds.), *The neurosciences: Third study program*. Cambridge, MA: MIT Press.

Sperry, R. W. (1993, August). Cited in T. Deangelis, Sperry plumbs science for values and solutions. *APA Monitor*.

Spiegel, D. A., & Bruce, T. J. (1997). Benzodiazepines and exposure-based cognitive behavior therapies for panic disorder: Conclusions from combined treatment trials. *American Journal of Psychiatry, 154*, 773–781.

Spielman, D. A., & Staub, E. (2000). Reducing boys aggression: Learning to fulfill basic needs constructively. *Journal of Applied Developmental Psychology, 21*, 165–181.

Spillar, K., & Harrington, P. (2000, February, 18). This is what you get when men rule the roost. *Los Angeles Times*, B7.

Spitz, H. H. (1997). Some questions about the results of the Abecedarian early intervention project cited by the APA task force on intelligence. *American Psychologist, 52*, 72.

Spitzer, R. L., Gibbon, M., Skodol, A. E., Williams, J. B. W., & First, M. B. (Eds.). (1994). *DSM-IV casebook*. Washington, DC: American Psychiatric Association.

Spitzer, R. L., Terman, M., Williams, J. B., Terman, J. S., Malt, U. F., Singer, F., & Lewy, A. J. (1999). Jet lag. *American Journal of Psychiatry, 156*, 1392–1396.

Spohr, M. L., Willms, J., & Steinhausen, H. C. (1993). Prenatal alcohol exposure and long-term developmental consequences. *Lancet, 341*, 907–910.

Springer, S. P., & Deutsch, G. (1997). *Left brain, right brain* (5th ed.). New York: W. H. Freeman.

Squire, L. R. (1994). Declarative and nondeclarative memory: Multiple brain systems supporting learning and memory. In D. L. Schacter & E. Tulving (Eds.), *Memory systems 1994*. Cambridge, MA: MIT Press.

Squire, L. R., & Knowlton, B. J. (1995). Memory, hippocampus, and brain systems. In M. S. Gazzaniga (Ed.), *The cognitive neurosciences*. Cambridge, MA: MIT Press.

Squire, L. R., & Slater, P. C. (1983). Electroconvulsive therapy and complaints of memory dysfunction: A prospective three-year follow-up study. *British Journal of Psychiatry, 142*, 1–8.

Squire, L. R., & Zola-Morgan, S. (1991). The medial temporal lobe memory system. *Science, 253*, 1380–1386.

Squitieri, T. (1994, January 28–30). Guns soon to be No. 1 cause of injury deaths. *USA Today*.

Stahl, S. M. (1996). *Essential psychopharmacology*. New York: Cambridge University Press.

Stahl, S. M. (2000). *Essential psychopharmacology* (2nd ed.). New York: Cambridge University Press.

Stanley, B., Molcho, A., Stanley, M., Winchel, R., Gameroff, M. J., Parsons, B., & Mann, J. J. (2000).

Association of aggressive behavior with altered serotonergic function in patients who are not suicidal. *American Journal of Psychiatry, 157,* 609–614.

Stanley, M. A., & Novy, D. M. (2000). Cognitive-behavior therapy for generalized anxiety in late life: An evaluative overview. *Journal of Anxiety Disorders, 14,* 191–207.

Stanley, M. A., & Turner, S. M. (1995). Current status of pharmacological and behavioral treatment of obsessive-compulsive disorder. *Behavior Therapy, 26,* 163–186.

Stanton, B., Baldwin, R. M., & Rachuba, L. (1997a). A quarter century of violence in the United States. *Psychiatric Clinics of North America, 20,* 269–282.

Stanton, B., Fang, X., Li, X., Feigelman, S., Galbraith, J., & Rocardo, I. (1997b). Evolution of risk behaviors over 2 years among a cohort of urban African American adolescents. *Archives of Pediatrics and Adolescent Medicine, 151,* 398–406.

Stanton, M. D., & Shadish, W. R. (1997). Outcome, attrition, and family-couples treatment for drug abuse: A meta-analysis and review of the controlled, comparative studies. *Psychological Bulletin, 122,* 170–191.

Steele, C. (1995, December 11). Cited in E. Woo, Can racial stereotypes psych out students? *Los Angeles Times,* A1.

Stein, J. (1997, March 12). A child's heavy burden. *Los Angeles Times.*

Stein, N. L., Ornstein, P. A., Tversky, B., & Brainerd, C. (Eds.). (1997). *Memory for everyday and emotional events.* Mahwah, NJ: Lawrence Erlbaum.

Steiner, R. (1989). Live TV special explores, tests psychic powers. *Skeptical Inquirer, 14,* 2–6.

Steinhauer, J. (2000, June 25). The new landscape of AIDS. *New York Times,* 16–17.

Stephen, M., & Suryani, L. K. (2000). Shamanism, psychosis, and autonomous imagination. *Culture, Medicine and Psychiatry, 24,* 5–40.

Steptoe, A., & Wardle, J. (1988). Emotional fainting and the psychophysiologic response to blood and injury: Autonomic mechanisms and coping strategies. *Psychosomatic Medicine, 50,* 402–417.

Steriade, M. (1966). Arousal: Revisiting the reticular activating system. *Science, 72,* 225–226.

Stern, G. S., McCants, T. R., & Pettine, P. W. (1982). Stress and illness: Controllable and uncontrollable life events' relative contributions. *Personality and Social Psychology Bulletin, 8,* 140–143.

Stern, R. M., & Koch, K. L. (1996). Motion sickness and differential susceptibility. *Current Directions in Psychological Science, 5,* 115–119.

Sternberg, R. J. (1985). Human intelligence: The model is the message. *Science, 230,* 1111–1118.

Sternberg, R. J. (1986). A triangular theory of love. *Psychological Review, 93,* 119–135.

Sternberg, R. J. (1988). Triangulating love. In R. J. Sternberg & M. L. Barnes (Eds.), *The psychology of love.* New Haven, CT: Yale University Press.

Sternberg, R. J. (1995). For whom the Bell Curve tolls: A review of *The Bell Curve. Psychological Science, 6,* 257–261.

Sternberg, R. J. (1997a). The concept of intelligence and its role in lifelong learning and success. *American Psychologist, 52,* 1030–1037.

Sternberg, R. J. (1997b). Intelligence and lifelong learning. *American Psychologist, 52,* 1034–1039.

Sternberg, R. J. (1999). *Cupid's arrow: The course of love through time.* New York: Cambridge University Press.

Sternberg, R. J. (2000a). The concept of intelligence. In R. J. Sternberg, *Handbook of intelligence.* New York: Cambridge University Press.

Sternberg, R. J. (2000b). The holy grail of general intelligence. *Science, 289,* 399–401.

Sternberg, R. J., & Grigorenko, E. (Eds.). (1997). *Intelligence, heredity, and environment.* New York: Cambridge University Press.

Sternberg, R. J., & Lubart, T. I. (1996). Investing in creativity. *American Psychologist, 51,* 677–688.

Sternberg, R. J., & O'Hara, L. A. (2000). Intelligence and creativity. In R. J. Sternberg, *Handbook of intelligence.* New York: Cambridge University Press.

Sternberg, R. J., & Soriano, L. J. (1984). Styles of conflict resolution. *Journal of Personality and Social Psychology, 47,* 115–126.

Sternberg, R. J., & Wagner, R. K. (1993). The *g*-ocentric view of intelligence and job performance is wrong. *Current Directions in Psychological Science, 2,* 1–5.

Sternberg, S. (1998, November 2). Michael DeBakey's living legacy. *USA Today,* D1.

Stevens, J. E. (1994, February 27). Tribeswomen disfigure themselves in name of tourism. *San Diego Union-Tribune.*

Stickgold, R. (2000, March 7). Cited in S. Blakeslee, For better learning, researchers endorse "sleep on it" adage. *New York Times,* D2.

Stolberg, S. (1993, July 14). Long-term study gives grim picture of heroin addiction. *Los Angeles Times.*

Stolberg, S. (1994, August 29). Study shows drug abuse programs are cost-effective. *Los Angeles Times.*

Stone, B. (1997, June 2). Zapping the eye. *Newsweek,* 80–81.

Strain, E. C., Mumford, G. K., Silverman, K., & Griffiths, R. R. (1994). Caffeine dependence syndrome. *Journal of the American Medical Association, 272,* 1043–1048.

Straker, G. (1994). Integrating African and Western healing practices in South Africa. *American Journal of Psychotherapy, 48,* 455–467.

Strassman, R. J. (1995). Hallucinogenic drugs in psychiatric research and treatment: Perspectives and prospects. *Journal of Nervous and Mental Diseases, 183,* 127–138.

Strauss, C. C. (1994). Anxiety disorders. In V. B. Van Hasselt & M. Hersen (Eds.), *Advanced abnormal psychology.* New York: Plenum Press.

Strauss, N. (1994, June 2). Kurt Cobain 1967–1994. *Rolling Stone.*

Streissguth, A. P., Aase, J. M., Clarren, S. K., Randels, S. P., LaDue, R. A., & Smith, D. F. (1991). Fetal alcohol syndrome in adolescents and adults. *Journal of the American Medical Association, 265,* 1961–1967.

Streissguth, A. P., Barr, H. M., Bookstein, F. L., Sampson, P. D., & Olson, H. C. (1999). The long-term neurocognitive consequences of prenatal alcohol exposure: A 14-year study. *Psychological Science, 10,* 186–190.

Stritzke, W. G. K., Lang, A. R., & Patrick, C. J. (1996). Beyond stress and arousal: A reconceptualization of alcohol—Emotion relations with reference to psychophysiological methods. *Psychological Bulletin, 120,* 376–395.

Stromeyer, C. F., III. (1970, November). Eidetikers. *Psychology Today.*

Stromswold, K. (1995). The cognitive and neural bases of language acquisition. In M. S. Gazzaniga (Ed.), *The cognitive neurosciences.* Cambridge, MA: MIT Press.

Stumpf, D. A., Cranford, R. E., Elias, S., Fost, N. C., McQuillen, M. P., Myer, E., Poland, R., & Queenam, J. T. (1990). The infant with anencephaly. *New England Journal of Medicine, 322,* 669–674.

Suddath, R. L., Christison, G. W., Torrey, E. F., Casanova, M. R., & Weinberger, D. R. (1990). Anatomical abnormalities in the brains of monozygotic twins discordant for schizophrenia. *New England Journal of Medicine, 322,* 789–794.

Sullivan, P. F., Neale, M. C., & Kendler, K. S. (2000). Genetic epidemiology of major depression: Review and meta-analysis. *American Journal of Psychiatry, 157,* 1552–1562.

Sullivan, R. M., Taborsky-Barba, S., Mendoza, R., Itano, A., Leon, M., Cotman, C. W., Payne, T. R., & Lott, I. (1991). Olfactory classical conditioning in neonates. *Pediatrics, 87,* 511–518.

Sussman, N., & Ginsberg, D. (1998). Rethinking side effects of the selective serotonin reuptake inhibitors: Sexual dysfunction and weight gain. *Psychiatric Annals, 28,* 89–97.

Suzuki, L. A., & Valencia, R. R. (1997). Race—Ethnicity and measured intelligence: Educational implications. *American Psychologist, 5,* 1103–1114.

Suzuki, S. (1998, January 27). Cited in Shinichi Suzuki: Started music classes for toddlers. *Los Angeles Times,* B8.

Svensen, S., & White, K. (1994). A content analysis of horoscopes. *Genetic, Social and General Psychology Monographs, 12,* 5–38.

Svirsky, M. A., Robbins, A. M., Kirk, K. I., Pisoni, D. B., & Miyamoto, R. T. (2000). Language development in profoundly deaf children with cochlear implants. *Psychological Science, 11,* 153–158.

Swanson, J. M., McBurnett, K., Wigal, T., Pfiffner, L. J., Lerner, M. A., Williams, L., Christian, D. L., Tamm, L., Willcutt, E., Crowley, K., Clevenger, W., Khouzam, N., Woo, C., Crinella, F. M., & Fisher, T. D. (1993). Effect of stimulant medication on children with attention deficit disorder: A "review of reviews." *Exceptional Children, 60,* 154–162.

Swayze, V. W., II. (1995). Frontal leukotomy and related psychosurgical procedures in the era before antipsychotics (1935–1954): A historical overview. *American Journal of Psychiatry, 152,* 505–515.

Sweet, R. A., Mulsant, B. H., Gupta, B., Rifai, A. H., Pasternak, R. E., McEachran, A., & Zubenko, G. S. (1995). Duration of neuroleptic treatment and prevalence of tardive dyskinesia in late life. *Archives of General Psychiatry, 52,* 478–486.

Swets, J. A., Dawes, R. M., & Monahan, J. (2000). Psychological science can improve diagnostic decisions. *Psychological Science in the Public Interest, 1,* 1–26.

Swim, J. K., Aikin, K. J., Hall, W. S., & Hunter, B. A. (1995). Sexism and racism: Old-fashioned and modern principles. *Journal of Personality and Social Psychology, 68,* 199–214.

Swindle, R. (2000, July 3). Cited in D. Ho, Americans relaxing views on stigma of nervous breakdown. *San Diego Union-Tribune,* A9.

Szyfelbein, S. K., Osgood, P. F., & Carr, D. B. (1985). The assessment of pain and plasma B-endorphin immunoactivity in burned children. *Pain, 22,* 173–182.

Taddese, A., Nah, S. Y., & McCleskey, E. W. (1995). Selective opiod inhibition of small nociceptive neurons. *Science, 270,* 1366–1369.

Takahashi, J. S. (1999). Narcolepsy genes wake up the sleep field. *Science, 285,* 2076–2077.

Talbot, J. D., Marrett, S., Evans, A. C., Meyer, E., Bushnell, M. C., & Duncan, G. H. (1991). Multiple representations of pain in human cerebral cortex. *Science, 251,* 1355–1358.

Talbot, M. (2000, January 9). The placebo prescription. *New York Times Magazine,* 34.

Talcott, J. B., Witton, C., McLean, M. F., Hansen, P. C., Rees, A., Green, G. G. R., & Stein, J. F. (2000).

Dynamic sensory sensitivity and children's word decoding skills. *Proceedings of the National Academy of Science, USA, 97,* 2952–2957.

Tallal, P. (1995, August 29). Cited in S. Begley, Why Johnny and Joanie can't read. *Newsweek.*

Tallal, P. (1998, October 18). Cited in R. L. Hotz, In art of language, the brain matters. *Los Angeles Times,* A1.

Tallal, P., Miller, S. L., Bedi, G., Byma, G., Wang, Z., Nagarajan, S. S., Shreiner, C., Jenkins, W. M., & Merzeich, M. M. (1996). Language comprehension in language-learning impaired children impaired with acoustically modified speech. *Science, 271,* 81–84.

Tamis-LeMonda, C. S., Bornstein, M. H., Baumwell, L., & Dakmast, A. M. (1996). Responsive parenting in the second year: Specific influences on children's language and play. *Early Development and Parenting, 5,* 173–183.

Tamminga, C. A. (1997). The promise of new drugs for schizophrenia treatment. *Canadian Journal of Psychiatry, 42,* 264–273.

Tang, S. W. (1998, January 9). Cited in S. Emmons, Emotions at face value. *Los Angeles Times.*

Tankova, I., Adan, A., & Buela-Casal, G. (1994). Circadian typology and individual differences. A review. *Personality and Individual Differences, 16,* 671–684.

Tannen, D. (1990). *You just don't understand: Women and men in conversation.* New York: William Morrow.

Tannen, D. (1994). *Talking from 9 to 5.* New York: William Morrow.

Tanner, L. (2000, May). Pediatrician guidelines issued to spot disorder. *San Diego Union-Tribune,* A-1.

Tanofsky, M. B., Wilfley, D. E., Spurrell, E. B., Welch, R., & Brownell, K. D. (1997). Comparison of men and women with binge eating disorder. *International Journal of Eating Disorders, 21,* 49–54.

Tanouye, E. (1997, July 7). Got a big public speaking phobia? *San Diego Union-Tribune.*

Tanzi, R. (2000, January 31). Cited in G. Cowley, Alzheimer's: Unlocking the mystery. *Newsweek,* 46–51.

Tao, K. (1987). Infantile autism in China. *Journal of Autism and Developmental disorders, 2,* 289.

Tao, K. T., & Yang, X. L. (1997). China. In D. J. Cohen & F. R. Volkmar (Eds.), *Handbook of autism and pervasive developmental disorders* (2nd ed.). New York: John Wiley & Sons.

Tashkin, D. (1996, December 16). Cited in D. Ferrell, Scientists unlocking secrets of marijuana's effects. *Los Angeles Times.*

Taubes, G. (1994, December). Surgery in cyberspace. *Discover.*

Taubes, G. (1995). Averaged brains pinpoint a site for schizophrenia. *Science, 266,* 221.

Taubes, G. (1997). The breast-screening brawl. *Science, 275,* 1056–1059.

Taubman, B. (1997). Toilet training and toileting refusal for stool only: A prospective study. *Pediatrics, 99,* 54–58.

Tavris, C. (1982). *Anger: The misunderstood emotion.* New York: Simon & Schuster.

Tawa, R. (1995, March 12). Shattering the silence. *Los Angeles Times.*

Taylor, J., & Miller, M. (1997). When time-out works some of the time: The importance of treatment integrity and functional assessment. *School Psychology Quarterly, 12,* 4–22.

Taylor, S. E. (1981). The interface of cognitive and social psychology. In J. Harvey (Ed.), *Cognition, social behavior, and the environment.* Hillsdale, NJ: Erlbaum.

Taylor, S. E., & Armor, D. A. (1996). Positive illusions and coping with adversity. *Journal of Personality, 64,* 873–898.

Taylor, S. E., Kemeny, M. E., Reed, G. M., Bower, J. E., & Gruenewald, T. L. (2000a). Psychological resources, positive illusions, and health. *American Psychologist, 55,* 99–109.

Taylor, S. E., Klein, L. C., Lewis, B. P., Gruenwald, T. L., Gurung, R. A. R., & Updegraff, J. A. (2000b). Biobehavioral responses to stress in females: Tend and befriend, not fight-or-flight. *Psychological Review, 107,* 411–439.

Te, G. O., Hamilton, M. J., Rizer F. M., Schatz, K. A., Arkis, P. N., & Oose, H. E. (1996). Early speech changes in children with multichannel cochlear implants. *Archives of Otolaryngology, Head and Neck Surgery, 115,* 508–512.

Tebbutt, J., Swanston, H., Oates, R. K., & O'Tolle, B. I. (1997). Five years after child sexual abuse: Persisting dysfunction and problems of prediction. *Journal of American Academy of Child Adolescent Psychiatry, 36,* 330–339.

Teicher, M. (2000, April 10). Cited in J. S. Fischer, Taking a picture of a mind gone awhirl. *U.S. News & World Report,* 48.

Terman, L. M. (1916). *The measurement of intelligence.* Boston: Houghton Mifflin.

Terman, L. M., & Oden, M. H. (1959). *The gifted group at mid-life* (Vol. 5). Stanford, CA: Stanford University Press.

Terman, M., Amira, L., Terman, J. S., & Ross, D. C. (1996). Predictors or response and nonresponse to light treatment for winter depression. *American Journal of Psychiatry, 153,* 1423–1429.

Terrace, H. S. (1981). A report to an academy, 1980. *Annals of the New York Academy of Sciences, 364,* 94–114.

Thapar, A., & McGuffin, P. (1993). Is personality disorder inherited? An overview of the evidence. *Journal of Psychopathology and Behavioral Assessment, 15,* 325–345.

Thase, M. E., Greenhouse, J. B., Frank, E., Reynolds, C. F., Pilkonis, P. A., Hurley, K., Grochorinski, V., & Kupfer, D. J. (1997). Treatment of major depression with psychotherapy or psychotherapy-pharmacotherapy combinations. *Archives of General Psychiatry, 54,* 1009–1015.

Thelen, E. (1995). Motor development. *American Psychologist, 50,* 79–95.

Thomas, A., & Chess, S. (1977). *Temperament and development.* New York: Brunner/Mazel.

Thomas, K. (2000, August 15). "Let talk about what I can do." *USA Today,* 1D–2D.

Thombs, D. L. (1995). Problem behavior and academic achievement among first-semester college freshmen. *Journal of College Student Development, 36,* 280–288.

Thompson, B., & Borrello, G. M. (1992). Different views of love: Deductive and inductive lines of inquiry. *Current Directions in Psychological Science, 1,* 154–156.

Thompson, C., Cowan, T., & Frieman, J. (1993). *Memory search by a memorist.* Hillsdale, NJ: Lawrence Erlbaum.

Thompson, J. W., Weiner, R. D., & Myers, C. P. (1994). Use of ECT in the United States in 1975, 1980, and 1986. *American Journal of Psychiatry, 151,* 1657–1661.

Thompson, R. A. (1998). Early sociopersonality development. In W. Damon & R. M. Lerner (Eds.), *Handbook of child psychology* (Vol. 1). New York: John Wiley & Sons.

Thorndike, E. L. (1898). Animal intelligence: An experimental study of the associative process in animals. *Psychological Review Monograph Supplement, 2*(8).

Thurfjell, E. (1994). Mammography screening. One versus two views and independent double reading. *Acta Radiology, 35,* 345–350.

Tice, D. M., & Baumeister, R. F. (1997). Longitudinal study of procrastination, performance, stress, and health: The costs and benefits of dawdling. *Psychological Science, 8,* 454–458.

Tiefer, L., & Kring, B. (1995). Gender and the organization of sexual behavior. *Clinical Sexuality, 18,* 25–37.

Timimi, S., Douglas, J., & Taiftsopoulou, K. (1997). Selective eaters: A retrospective study. *Child: Care, Health and Development, 23,* 265–278.

Tolman, E. C. (1948). Cognitive maps in rats and men. *Psychological Review, 55,* 189–208.

Tomaka, J., Blascovich, J., Kibler, J., & Ernst, J. M. (1997). Cognitive and physiological antecedents of threat and challenge appraisal. *Journal of Personality and Social Psychology, 73,* 63–72.

Tomes, H. (2000, July/August). Why did APA take so long? *Monitor on Psychology,* 57.

Tonegawa, S., & Wilson, M. (1997). Cited in W. Roush, New knockout mice point to molecular basis of memory. *Science, 275,* 32–33.

Torrey, E. F. (1986). *Witchdoctors and psychiatrists: The common roots of psychotherapy and its future.* New York: Harper & Row.

Torrey, F. E., Bowler, A. E., Taylor, E. H., & Gottesman, I. I. (1994). *Schizophrenia and manic-depressive disorder.* New York: Basic Books.

Toshio, I., Witter, M. P., Ichikawa, M., Tominaga, T., Kajiwara, R., & Matsumoto, G. (1996). Entorhinal-hippocampal interactions revealed by real-time imaging. *Science, 272,* 1176–1179.

Towle, L. H. (1995, July 31). Elegy for lost boys. *Time.*

Townsend, E., Dimigen, G., & Fung, D. (2000). A clinical study of child dental anxiety. *Behaviour Research and Therapy, 38,* 31–46.

Tranel, D., Benton, A., & Olson, K. (1997). A 10-year longitudinal study of cognitive changes in elderly persons. *Developmental Neuropsychology, 13,* 87–96.

Travis, J. (1994). Glia: The brain's other cells. *Science, 266,* 970–972.

Tresniowski, A., & Bell, B. (1996, September 9). Oprah buff. *People,* 81.

Triandis, H. C. (1989). The self and social behavior in differing cultural contexts. *Psychological Review, 96,* 506–520.

Triandis, H. C. (1996). The psychological measurement of cultural syndromes. *American Psychologist, 51,* 407–415.

Tripathi, H. L., Olson, K. G., & Dewey, W. L. (1993). Borphin response to endurance exercise: Relationship to exercise dependence. *Perceptual and Motor Skills, 77,* 767–770.

Tripician, R. J. (2000, January/February). Confessions of a (former) graphologist. *Skeptical Inquirer,* 44–47.

Troiano, R. (1997, March 7). Cited in Associated Press and Reuters, Americans keep getting fatter; soft living is cited as reason. *San Diego Union-Tribune.*

Troster, A. I. (2000). Introduction to neurobehavioral issues in the neurosurgical treatment of movement disorders: Basic issues, thalamotomy, and nonablative treatemts. *Brain and Cognition, 42,* 173–182.

Tsai, G., Gastfriend, D. R., & Coyle, J. T. (1995). The glutamatergic basis of human alcoholism. *American Journal of Psychiatry, 152,* 332–340.

Tschann, J. M., Adler, N. E., Irwin, C. E., Jr., Millstein, S. B., Turner, R. A., & Kegeles, S. M. (1994). Initiation of substance use in early adolescence: The roles of puberty timing and emotional distress. *Health Psychology, 13,* 326–333.

Tsien, J. Z. (2000). Building a brainier mouse. *Scientific American,* 62–68.

Tucker, G. J. (1998). Putting DSM-IV in perspective. *American Journal of Psychiatry, 155,* 159–161.

Tully, T. (1997, May). Cited in B. Azar, Research in fruit flies sheds light on behavior. *APA Monitor.*

Tulving, E., & Craik, F. M. (Eds.). (2000). *The Oxford handbook of memory.* New York: Oxford University Press.

Turk, D. (1996, December). Cited in B. Azar, Psychosocial factors provide clues to pain. *APA Monitor.*

Turnbull, C. (1961). Some observations regarding the experiences and behavior of the Bambuti pygmies. *American Journal of Psychology, 74,* 304–308.

Turner, J. A., Deyo, R. A., Loeser, J. D., Von Korff, M., & Fordyce, W. E. (1994). The importance of placebo effects in pain treatment and research. *Journal of the American Medical Association, 271,* 1609–1614.

Turner, M., & Griffin, M. J. (1999). Motion sickness in public road transport: The relative importance of motion, vision and individual differences. *British Journal of Psychology, 90,* 519–530.

Turner, S. M., Beidel, D. C., Cooley, M. R., Woody, S. R., & Messer, S. C. (1994). A multicomponent behavioral treatment for social phobia: Social effectiveness therapy. *Behavior Research and Therapy, 32,* 381–390.

Turner, S., & Scherman, A. (1996). Big brothers: Impact on little brothers' self-concepts and behaviors. *Adolescence, 31,* 875–882.

Tversky, A., & Kahneman, D. (1983). Extensional versus intuitive reasoning: The conjunction fallacy in probability judgment. *Psychological Review, 90,* 293–315.

Twenge, J. M. (1997). Changes in masculine and feminine traits over time: A meta-analysis. *Sex Roles, 36,* 305–325.

Tyack, P. L. (2000). Dolphins whistle a signature tune. *Science, 289,* 1310–1313.

Tykocinski, O., Higgins, E. T., & Chaiken, S. (1994). Message framing, self-discrepancies, and yielding to persuasive messages: The motivational significance of psychological situations. *Personality and Social Psychology Bulletin, 20,* 107–115.

Ullman, M. T. (2000). How the brain made language. *Science, 289,* 251.

Ullman, S. E. (1997). Review and critique of empirical studies of rape avoidance. *Criminal Justice and Behavior, 24,* 177–204.

Ullman, S. E., Karabatsos, G., & Koss, M. P. (1999). Alcohol and sexual aggression in a national sample of college men. *Psychology Women Quarterly, 23,* 673–689.

Underwood, P. W. (2000). Social support: The promise and the reality. In V. R. Rice (Ed.), *Handbook of stress, coping and health.* Thousand Oaks, CA: Sage.

Unger, R. H. (1997). Cited in J. Travis, Hormone may directly trim fat from cells. *Science News, 151,* 271.

Ursin, H. (1997). Sensitization, somatization, and subjective health complaints. *International Journal of Behavioral Medicine, 4,* 105–116.

Vahtera, J., Kivimaki, M., Uutela, A., & Pentti. (2000). Hostility and ill health: Role of psychosocial resources in two contexts of working life. *Journal of Psychosomatic Research, 48,* 89–98.

Vaillant, G. E. (1996). A long-term follow-up of male alcohol abuse. *Archives of General Psychiatry, 53,* 243–249.

Valenstein, E. S. (1986). *Great and desperate cures.* New York: Basic Books.

Van de Castle, R. L. (1994). *Our dreaming mind.* New York: Ballantine.

VandenBos, G. R. (1996). Outcome assessment of psychotherapy. *American Psychologist, 51,* 1005–1006.

van Derbur Atler, D. (1991, June). The darkest secret. *People.*

Vander Wall, S. B. (1982). An experimental analysis of cache recovery in Clark's nutcracker. *Animal Behavior, 30,* 84–94.

Vandewater, E. A., Ostrove, J. M., & Stewart, A. J. (1997). Predicting women's well-being in midlife: The importance of personality development and social role involvements. *Journal of Personality and Social Psychology, 72,* 1147–1160.

Van Essen, D. (1997, January 13). Cited in S. Brownlee & T. Watson, The senses. *U.S. News & World Report,* 51–59.

Van Essen, D. C., Anderson, C. H., & Felleman, D. J. (1992). Information processing in the primate visual system: An integrated systems perspective. *Science, 255,* 419–423.

Van Gerwen, L. J., Spinhoven, P., Diekstra, R. F. W., & Van Dyck, F. (1997). People who seek help for fear of flying: Typology of flying phobics. *Behavior Therapy, 28,* 237–251.

Van Manen, K., & Whitbourne, S. K. (1997). Psychosocial development and life experiences in adulthood: A 22-year sequential study. *Psychology and Aging, 12,* 239–246.

van Praag, H. (1999). Cited in B. Bower, Learning to make, keep adult neurons. *Science News, 155,* 170.

Vargas, J. S. (1991). B. F. Skinner: The last few days. *Journal of the Experimental Analysis of Behavior, 55,* 1–2.

Vargha-Khadem, F. (2000, November 20). Cited in J. Fischman, Seeds of a sociopath. *U.S. News & World Report,* 82.

Vargha-Khadem, F., Gadian, D. G., Watkins, K. E., Connelly, A., Van Paesschen, W., & Mishkin, M. (1997). Differential effects of early hippocampal pathology on episodic and semantic memory. *Science, 227,* 376–380.

Venter, J. C. (2000, August 22). Cited in N. Angier, Do races differ: not really, genes show. *New York Times,* D1.

Verhaeghen, P., & Salthouse, T. A. (1997). Meta-analyses of age-cognition relations in adulthood: Estimates of linear and nonlinear age effects and structural models. *Psychological Bulletin, 122,* 231–249.

Verlinden, S., Hersen, M., & Thomas, J. (2000). Risk factors in school shootings. *Clinical Psychology Review, 29,* 3–56.

Videbech, P. (2000). PET measurements of brain glucose metabolism and blood flow in major depressive disorder: A critical review. *Acta Psychiatrica Scandinavica, 101,* 11–20.

Viglione, D. J., Jr. (1997). Problems in Rorschach research and what to do about them. *Journal of Personality Assessment, 68,* 590–599.

Vinicor, F. (2000, August 24). Obesity spurs an alarming rise in U.S. diabetes, experts say. *San Diego Union-Tribune,* A11.

Vogel, S. (1999, April). Why we get fat. *Discover,* 94–99.

Vonk, R. (1995). Effects of inconsistent behaviors on person impressions: A multidimensional study. *Personality and Social Psychology Bulletin, 21,* 674–685.

Vredenburg, K., Flett, G. L., & Krames, L. (1994). Analogue versus clinical depression: A critical reappraisal. *Psychological Bulletin, 113,* 327–344.

Waddell, C. (1998). Creativity and mental illness: Is there a link? *Canadian Journal of Psychiatry, 43,* 166–172.

Waddington, J. L., Lane, A., Scully, P., Meagher, D., Quinn, J., Larkin, C., & O'Callaghan, E. (2000). Early cerebro-craniofacial dysmorphogenesis in schizophrenia: A lifetime trajectory model from neurodevelopmental basis to "neuroprogressive" process. *Journal of Psychiatric Research, 33,* 477–489.

Wade, B. (2000, January 6). Driving while phoning has a whole lot of people groaning. *San Diego Union-Tribune,* F-8.

Wade, N. (2001, February 13). Genome's riddle: Few genes, much complexity. *New York Times,* D1.

Waldman, I. D., Weinberg, R. A., & Scarr, S. (1994). Racial-group differences in IQ in the Minnesota transracial adoption study: A reply to Levin and Lynn. *Intelligence, 19,* 29–44.

Waldron, S., Jr. (1997). How can we study the efficacy of psychoanalysis? *Psychoanalytic Quarterly, 66,* 283–321.

Walker, A., & Parmar, P. (1993). *Warrior marks: Female genital mutilation and sexual blinding of women.* New York: Harcourt Brace.

Walker, E. G., & Diforio, D. (1997). Schizophrenia: A neural diathesis-stress model. *Psychological Bulletin, 104,* 667–685.

Walker, L. J. (1991). Sex differences in moral reasoning. In W. M. Kurtines & J. L. Gerwitz (Eds.), *Handbook of moral behavior and development: Vol. 2. Research.* Hillsdale, NJ: Erlbaum.

Wallace, D. C. (1997, August). Mitochondrial DNA in aging and disease. *Scientific American,* 40–47.

Wallechinsky, D. (1986). *Midterm report.* New York: Viking.

Wallerstein, R. S., & Fonagy, P. (1999). Psychoanalytic research and the IPA: History, present status and future potential. *International Journal of Psychoanalysis, 80,* 91–109.

Walsh, J. K., & Lindblom, S. S. (1997). Psychophysiology of sleep deprivation and disruption. In M. R. Pressman & W. C. Orr (Eds.), *Understanding sleep: The evaluation and treatment of sleep disorders.* Washington, DC: American Psychological Association.

Walter, H. J., Vaughan, R. D., Armstrong, B., Krakoff, R. Y., Maldonado, L. M., Tiezzi, L., & McCarthy, J. R. (1995). Sexual, assaultive, and suicidal behaviors among urban minority junior high school students. *Journal of the American Academy of Child and Adolescent Psychiatry, 34,* 73–80.

Walters, E. E., & Kendler, K. S. (1995). Anorexia nervosa and anorexic-like syndromes in a population-based female twin sample. *American Journal of Psychiatry, 152,* 64–71.

Waltz, J. A., Knowlton, B. J., Holyoak, K. J., Boone, K. B., Mishkin, F. S., de Menezes Santos, M., Thomas, C. R., & Miller, B. L. (1999). A system for relational reasoning in human prefrontal cortex. *Psychological Science, 10,* 119–125.

Wampold, B. E., Mondin, G. W., Moody, M., Stich, F., Benson, K., & Ahn, H. (1997). A meta-analysis of outcome studies comparing bona fide psychotherapies: Empirically, "All must have prizes." *Psychological Bulletin, 122,* 203–215.

Wanek, J. E. (1999). Integrity and honesty testing: What do we know? How do we use it? *International Journal of Selection and Assessment, 7,* 183–196.

Wang, S., Sun, C., Walczak, C. A., Ziegle, J. S., Kipps, B. R., Goldin, L. R., & Diehl, S. (1995). Evidence for a susceptibility locus for schizophrenia on chromosome 6pter-p22. *Nature Genetics, 10,* 41–46.

Wang, S. C. (2000). In search of Einstein's genius. *Science, 289,* 1477.

Wann, D. L., & Dolan, T. J. (1994). Attributions of highly identified sports spectators. *Journal of Social Psychology, 134,* 783–792.

Ward, A., Tiller, J., Treasure, J., & Russell, G. (2000). Eating disorders: Psche or soma? *International Journal of Eating Disorders, 27,* 279–287.

Warden, C. H. (1997). Cited in J. Travis, Gene heats up obesity research. *Science News, 151,* 142.

Warga, C. (1987, August). Pain's gatekeeper. *Psychology Today.*

Wartik, N. (1994, August 7). The amazingly simple, inexplicable therapy that just might work. *Los Angeles Times.*

Watanabe, T. (2000, October 31). Exorcism flourishing once again. *Los Angeles Times*, A1.

Waterhouse, L., Fein, D., & Modahl, C. (1996). Neurofunctional mechanisms in autism. *Psychological Review, 103,* 457–489.

Waters, A. J., & Sutton, S. R. (2000). Direct and indirect effects of nicotine/smoking on cognition in humans. *Addictive Behaviors, 25,* 29–42.

Watson, J. B. (1924). *Behaviorism.* Chicago: University of Chicago Press.

Watson, J. B., & Rayner, R. (1920). Conditioned emotional reactions. *Journal of Experimental Psychology, 3,* 1–14.

Watson, J. B., & Watson, R. R. (1920). Studies in infant psychology, *Scientific Monthly, 13,* 492–515.

Watson, T., & Wu, C. (1996, January 8). Are you too fat? *U.S. News & World Report,* 52–61.

Weatherburn, D., & Lind, B. (1997). The impact of law enforcement activity on a heroin market. *Addiction, 92,* 557–569.

Weatherby, W. J. (1990). *Salman Rushdie: Sentenced to die.* New York: Carroll & Graf.

Webb, W. B. (1983). Theories in modern sleep research. In A. Mayes (Ed.), *Sleep mechanisms and functions.* Wokingham, England: Van Nostrand Reinhold.

Weber, E. H. (1834). *De pulsu, resorptione, auditu et tactu: Annotationes anatomical et physiological.* Liepzig: Koehler.

Weed, W. S. (2000, June). Smart pills. *Discover,* 82.

Wegner, D. M., & Gold, D. B. (1995). Fanning old flames: Emotional and cognitive effects of suppressing thoughts of a past relationship. *Journal of Personality and Social Psychology, 68,* 782–792.

Weiden, P., Aquila, R., & Standard, J. (1996). Atypical antipsychotic drugs and long-term outcome in schizophrenia. *Journal of Clinical Psychiatry, 57*(Supplement 11), 53–60.

Weinberg, R. A., Scarr, S., & Waldman, I. D. (1992). The Minnesota transracial adoption study: A follow-up of IQ test performance at adolescence. *Intelligence 16,* 117–135.

Weinberger, D. R., Goldberg, T. E., & Tamminga, C. A. (1995). Prefrontal leukotomy. *American Journal of Psychiatry, 152,* 330–331.

Weinberger, J. (1995). Common factors aren't so common: The common factors dilemma. *Clinical Psychology: Science and Practice, 2,* 45–69.

Weiner, B. (1986). *An attributional theory of motivation and emotion.* New York: Springer-Verlag.

Weiner, B. (1991). Metaphors in motivation and attribution. *American Psychologist, 46,* 921–930.

Weiner, B., & Graham, S. (1999). Attribution in personality psychology. In L. A. Pervin & O. P. John (Eds.), *Handbook of personality* (2nd ed.). New York: Guilford.

Weiner, I. B. (2000). Making Rorschach interpretations as good as it can be. *Journal of Personality Assessment, 74,* 164–174.

Weiner, I. R. (1997). Current status of the Rorschach inkblot method. *Journal of Personality Assessment, 68,* 5–19.

Weiner, M. F. (1997). Alzheimer's disease: Diagnosis and treatment. *Harvard Review of Psychiatry, 4,* 206–316.

Weisberg, R. W. (1993). *Creativity: Beyond the myth of genius.* New York: Freeman.

Weiss, G. L. (1996). Attitudes of college students about physician-assisted suicide: The influence of life experiences, religiosity, and belief in the autonomy. *Death Studies, 20,* 587–599.

Weiss, K. R. (1997, January 13). Survey finds record stress in class of 2000. *Los Angeles Times.*

Weissman, M. M. (1993, Spring). The epidemiology of personality disorders. A 1990 update. *Journal of Personality Disorders* (Supplement), 44–62.

Welling, H. (1994). Prime number identification in idiots savants: Can they calculate them? *Journal of Autism and Developmental Disorders, 24,* 199–207.

Wellman, H. M., & Gelman, S. A. (1998). Knowledge acquisition in foundational domains. In W. Damon & R. M. Lerner (Eds.), *Handbook of child psychology* (Vol. 1). New York: John Wiley & Sons.

Wells, G. L., Luus, E., & Windschitl, P. D. (1994). Maximizing the utility of eyewitness identification evidence. *Current Directions in Psychological Science, 3,* 194–197.

Wells, G. L., Malpass, R. S., Lindsay, R. C. L., Fisher, R. P., Turtle, J. W., & Fulero, S. M. (2000). From the lab to the police station. *American Psychologist, 55,* 581–598.

Wenzlaff, R. M., & Wegner, D. M. (2000). Thought suppression. *Annual Review of Psychology, 51,* 59–91.

Werle, M. A., Murphy, T. B., & Budd, K. S. (1993). Treating chronic food refusal in young children: Home-based parent training. *Journal of Applied Behavior Analysis, 26,* 421–433.

Werner, E. E. (1989). Children of the garden island. *Scientific American, 260,* 106–111.

Werner, E. E. (1995). Resilience in development. *Current Directions in Psychological Science, 4,* 81–85.

Werner, E. E., & Smith, R. S. (1982). *Vulnerable but invincible.* New York: McGraw-Hill.

Werner, J. S., & Frost, M. H. (2000). Major life stressors and health outcomes. In V. R. Rice (Ed.), *Handbook of stress, coping and health.* Thousand Oaks, CA: Sage.

Wertz, F. J. (1998). The role of the humanistic movement in the history of psychology. *Journal of Humanistic Psychology, 38,* 42–70.

West, R. L. (1996). An application of prefrontal cortex function theory to cognitive aging. *Psychological Bulletin, 120,* 272–292.

Westen, D. (1990). Psychoanalytic approaches to personality. In L. A. Previn (Ed.), *Handbook of personality.* New York: Guilford Press.

Westen, D. (1998a). Unconscious thought, feeling, and motivation: The end of a century-long debate. In R. F. Bornstein & J. M. Masling (Eds.), *Empirical perspectives on the psychoanalytic unconscious.* Washington, DC: American Psychological Association.

Westen, D. (1998b). The scientific legacy of Sigmund Freud: Toward a psychodynamically informed psychological science. *Psychology Bulletin, 124,* 333–371.

Westen, D., & Gabbard, G. O. (1999). Psychoanalytic approaches to personality. In L. A. Pervin & O. P. John (Eds.), *Handbook of personality* (2nd ed.), New York: Guilford.

Wheeler, M. A. (2000). Episodic memory and autonoetic awareness. In E. Tulving & F. M. Craik (Eds.), *The Oxford handbook of memory.* New York: Oxford University Press.

Wheeler, M. A., Stuss, D. T., & Tulving, E. (1997). Toward a theory of episodic memory: The frontal lobes and autonoetic consciousness. *Psychological Bulletin, 121,* 331–354.

Whitaker-Azmitia, P. (1997, December). Cited in B. Azar, Researchers debunk myth of the "crack baby." *APA Monitor.*

Whitbourne, S. K., Zuschlag, M. K., Elliot, L. B., & Waterman, A. S. (1992). Psychosocial development in adulthood: A 22-year sequential study. *Journal of Personality and Social Psychology, 63,* 260–271.

White, J. M., & Porth, C. M. (2000). Evolution of a model of stress, coping and discrete emotions. In V. R. Rice (Ed.), *Handbook of stress, coping and health.* Thousand Oaks, CA: Sage.

Whorf, B. L. (1940). In J. B. Carroll (Ed.), *Language, thought, and reality: Selected writing of Benjamin Lee Whorf.* Cambridge, MA: MIT Press.

Whorf, B. L. (1956). *Language, thought, and reality.* New York: Wiley.

Wickelgren, I. (1997a). Getting a grasp on working memory. *Science, 275,* 1580–1582.

Wickelgren, I. (1997b). Marijuana: Harder than thought? *Science, 276,* 1967–1968.

Wickett, J. C., Vernon, P. A., & Lee, D. H. (1994). In vivo brain size, head perimeter, and intelligence in a sample of healthy adult females. *Personality and Individual Differences, 16,* 831–838.

Widiger, T. A., & Clark, L. A. (2000). Toward DSM-V and the classification of psychopathology. *Psychological Bulletin, 126,* 946–963.

Widiger, T. A., & Costa, P. T., Jr. (1994). Personality and personality disorders. *Journal of Abnormal Psychology, 103,* 78–91.

Widman, M., Platt, J. J., Lidz, V., Mathis, D. A., & Metzger, D. S. (1997). Patterns of service use and treatment involvement. *Journal of Substance Abuse Treatment, 14,* 29–35.

Wiebe, D. J. (1991). Hardiness and stress moderation: A test of proposed mechanisms. *Journal of Personality and Social Psychology, 60,* 89–99.

Wiebe, D. J., & Smith, T. W. (1997). Personality and health: Progress and problems in psychosomatics. In R. Hogan, J. Johnson, & S. Briggs (Eds.), *Handbook of personal psychology.* New York: Academic Press.

Wiederhold, B. (2000, July 4). Cited in J. Robbins, Virtual reality finds a real place as a medical aid. *New York Times,* D6.

Wierson, M., & Forehand, R. (1994). Parent behavioral training for child noncompliance: Rationale, concepts, and effectiveness. *Current Directions in Psychological Science, 3,* 146–150.

Wiggins, J. S. (1997). In defense of traits. In R. Hogan, J. Johnson, & S. Briggs (Eds.), *Handbook of personality psychology.* New York: Academic Press.

Wilcoxon, H. C., Dragoin, W. B., & Kral, P. A. (1971). Illness-induced aversions in rat and quail: Relative salience of visual and gustatory cues. *Science, 171,* 826–828.

Wildavsky, B. (1999, March 22). Whatever happened to minority students? *U.S. News & World Report.*

Wilde, M. C., & Cinciripini, P. M. (1994). Biological model. In V. B. Van Hasselt & M. Hersen (Eds.), *Advanced abnormal psychology.* New York: Plenum Press.

Wilens, T. E., Biederman, J., Mick, E., Farone, S., & Spencer, T. (1997). Attention deficit hyperactivity disorder (ADHD) is associated with early onset substance use disorders. *Journal of Nervous and Mental Disease, 185,* 475–482.

Wilfley, D. E., & Cohen, L. R. (1997). Psychological treatment of bulimia nervosa and binge eating disorder. *Psychopharmacology Bulletin, 33,* 437–454.

Wilhelm, F. H., & Roth, W. T. (1997). Clinical characteristics of flight phobia. *Journal of Anxiety Disorders, 11,* 241–261.

Willett, W. C. (1994). Diet and health: What should we eat? *Science, 264,* 532–537.

Williams, B. K., & Knight, S. M. (1994). *Healthy for life.* Pacific Grove, CA: Brooks/Cole.

Williams, D. (1992). *Nobody nowhere.* New York: Times Books.

Williams, D. (1994). *Somebody somewhere.* New York: Times Books.

Williams, D. E., Kirkpatrick-Sanchez, S., & Iwata, B. A. (1993). A comparison of shock intensity in the treatment of longstanding and severe self-injurious behavior. *Research in Development Disabilities, 14,* 207–219.

Williams, J. (1994, February 10). Survival of the sweetest. *San Diego Union-Tribune.*

# References

Williams, J. E., & Best, D. L. (1990). *Measuring sex stereotypes* (Vol. 6, rev. ed.). Newbury Park, CA: Sage Publications.

Williams, M. A., & Gross, A. M. (1994). Behavior therapy. In V. B. Hasselt & M. Hersen (Eds.), *Advanced abnormal psychology*. New York: Plenum Press.

Williams, P. (1997, December 7). Town wants to move on, but past won't be ignored. *San Diego Union-Tribune*.

Wilson, B. (1996, February 7). Cited in G. Braxton, TV violence poses risk to viewers, study says. *Los Angeles Times*, F-1.

Wilson, D., Killen, J. D., Hayward, C., Robinson, T. N., Hammer, L. D., Kraemer, H. C., Varady, A., & Taylor, C. B. (1994). Timing and rate of sexual maturation and the onset of cigarette and alcohol use among teenage girls. *Archives of Pediatric and Adolescent Medicine, 148*, 789–795.

Wilson, G. T. (1994). Behavioral treatment of obesity: Thirty years and counting. *Advances in Behavior, Research and Therapy, 16*, 31–75.

Wilson, K. G., Hayes, S. C., & Gifford, E. V. (1997). Cognition in behavior therapy: Agreements and differences. *Journal of Behavior Therapy and Experimental Psychiatry, 28*, 53–63.

Wilson, S. A., Becker, L. A., & Tinker, R. H. (1997). Fifteen month follow-up of eye movement desensitization and reprocessing (EMDR) treatment for posttraumatic stress disorder and psychological trauma. *Journal of Consulting and Clinical Psychology, 65*, 1047–1056.

Wilson, S. R., Levine, K. J., Cruz, M. G., & Rao, N. (1997). Attribution complexity and actor-observer bias. *Journal of Social Behavior and Personality, 12*, 709–726.

Wilson, T. D., & Linville, P. W. (1982). Improving the academic performance of college freshmen: Attribution therapy revisited. *Journal of Personality and Social Psychology, 42*, 367–376.

Wimbush, F. B., & Nelson, M. L. (2000). Stress, psychosomatic illness, and health. In V. R. Rice (Ed.), *Handbook of stress, coping and health*. Thousand Oaks, CA: Sage.

Wincze, J. P., & Carey, M. P. (1991). *Sexual dysfunction: A guide for assessment and treatment*. New York: Guilford Press.

Wink, P., & Helson, R. (1996). Personality change in women and their partners. *Journal of Personality and Social Psychology*.

Winkler, J., Suhr, S. T., Gage, F. H., Thai, L. J., & Fisher, L. J. (1995). Essential role of neocortical acetylcholine in spatial memory. *Nature, 375*, 484–487.

Winn, P. (1995). The lateral hypothalamus and motivated behavior: An old syndrome reassessed and a new perspective gained. *Current Directions in Psychological Science, 4*, 182–187.

Winner, E. (1997). Exceptionally high intelligence and schooling. *American Psychologist, 52*, 1070–1081.

Winner, E. (2000). The origins and ends of giftedness. *American Psychologist, 55*, 159–169.

Winograd, E., & Neisser, U. (Eds.). (1992). *Studies of "flashbulb" memories*. New York: Cambridge University.

Winograd, E., & Soloway, R. M. (1986). On forgetting the locations of things stored in special places. *Journal of Experimental Psychology: General, 115*, 366–372.

Winter, K. A., & Kuiper, N. A. (1997). Individual differences in the experience of emotions. *Clinical Psychology Review, 17*, 791–821.

Winters, K. C., Stinchfield, R. D., Opland, E., Weller, C., & Latimer, W. W. (2000). The effectiveness of the Minnesota Model approach in the treatment of adolescent drug abusers. *Addiction, 95*, 601–612.

Witek-Janusek, L., & Mathews, H. L. (2000). Stress, immunity, and health outcomes. In V. R. Rice (Ed.), *Handbook of stress, coping and health*. Thousand Oaks, CA: Sage.

Witelson, S. (1999, August 9). Cited in S. Brownlee, Inside the teen brain. *U.S. News & World Report*, 45–54.

Witelson, S. F., Glezer, I. I., & Kigar, D. L. (1995). Women have greater density of neurons in posterior temporal cortex. *Journal of Neuroscience, 15*, 3418–3428.

Witelson, S. F., Kigar, D. L., & Harvey, T. (1999). The exceptional brain of Albert Einstein. *Lancet, 353*, 2149–2153.

Witkin, G. (1995, November 13). A new drug gallops through the West. *U.S. News & World Report*.

Witkin, G., Tharp, M., Schrof, J. M., Toch, T., & Scattarella, C. (1998, June 1). Again. *U.S. News & World Report*, 16–18.

Wittman, J. (1994, January 5). Nausea, euphoria alternate marks of chemotherapy. *San Diego Union-Tribune*.

Wiznitzer, M. (2000, Fall/Winter). Cited in J. Raymond, The world of the senses [Special edition]. *Newsweek*. 16–18.

Wolf, T. H. (1973). *Alfred Binet*. Chicago: University of Chicago Press.

Wolff, M., Alsobrook J. P., II, & Pauls, D. L. (2000). Genetic aspects of obsessive-compulsive disorder. *The Psychiatric Clinics of North America, 23*, 535–544.

Wolitzky, D. L., & Eagle, M. N. (1997). Psychoanalytic theories of psychotherapy. In P. L. Wachtel & S. B. Messer (Eds.), *Theories of psychotherapy: Origins and evolution*. Washington, DC: American Psychological Association.

Wolpe, J. (1958). *Psychotherapy by reciprocal inhibition*. Stanford, CA: Stanford University Press.

Wolpe, J. (1990). *The practice of behavior therapy* (4th ed.). London: Pergamon Press.

Wolpe, J., & Lazarus, A. A. (1966). *Behavior therapy techniques*. London: Pergamon Press.

Wolpe, J., & Plaud, J. J. (1997). Pavlov's contributions to behavior therapy. *American Psychologist, 52*, 966–972.

Wolraich, M. L., Lindgren, S. D., Stumbo, P. L., Stegink, L. D., Appelbaum, M. J., & Kiritsy, M. C. (1994). Effects of diets high in sucrose or aspartame on the behavior and cognitive performance of children. *New England Journal of Medicine, 330*, 301–308.

Wong, J. (1994, February 26). Obesity weighing in as life-style for modern Chinese. *San Diego Union-Tribune*.

Wood, W. (2000). Attitude change: Persuasion and social influence. *Annual Review of Psychology, 51*, 539–570.

Wood, W., Christensen, P. N., Hebl, M. R., & Rothgerber, H. (1997). Conformity to sex-typed norms, affect and the self-concept. *Journal of Personality and Social Psychology, 73*, 523–535.

Woods, S. C., Schwartz, M. W., Baskin, D. G., & Seeley, R. J. (2000). Food intake and the regulation of body weight. *Annual Review of Psychology, 51*, 255–277.

Woody, E. Z. (1997). Have the hypnotic susceptibility scales outlived their usefulness? *International Journal of Clinical and Experimental Hypnosis, 45*, 226–238.

Wool, C. A., & Barsky, A. J. (1994). So women somatize more than men? *Psychosomatics, 35*, 445–452.

World Health Organization. (1993). *International classification of disease and related health problems* (10th rev.). Geneva: Author.

Wren, C. S. (1999, December 19). Study sees little change in youth drug use. *New York Times*, 41.

Wride, N. (1989, June 14). Odyssey of a skinhead. *Los Angeles Times*.

Wright, D. B., & Gaskell, G. D. (1995). Flashbulb memories: Conceptual and methodological issues. *Memory, 3*, 67–80.

Wright, I. C., Rabe-Hesketh, S., Woodruff, P. W. R., David, A. S., Murray, R. M., & Bullmore, E. T. (2000). Meta-analysis of regional brain volumes in schizophrenia. *American Journal of Psychiatry, 157*, 16–25.

Wu, K. K., & Lam, D. J. (1993). The relationship between daily stress and health: Replicating and extending previous findings. *Psychology and Health, 8*, 329–344.

WuDunn, S. (1997, May 11). In Japan, use of dead has the living uneasy. *New York Times*, 1.

Wyer, R. S., Jr., & Srull, T. K. (1994). The role of trait constructs in person perception: A historical perspective. In P. G. Devine, D. L. Hamilton, & T. M. Ostrom (Eds.), *Social cognition: Impact on social psychology*. New York: Academic Press.

Yamashita, I. (1993). *Taijin-kyofu or delusional social phobia*. Sapporo, Japan: Hokkaido University Press.

Yapko, M. D. (1994). Suggestibility and repressed memories of abuse: A survey of psychotherapists' beliefs. *American Journal of Clinical Hypnosis, 36*, 163–171.

Ybarra, M. J. (1991, September 13). The psychic and the skeptic. *Los Angeles Times*.

Yehuda, R. (2000, August 2). Cited in E. Goode, Childhood abuse and adult stress. *New York Times*, A14.

Yerkes, R. M. (1921). *Psychological examining in the United States Army*. Washington, DC: (Memoir No. 15). National Academy of Sciences, No. 15.

Yoffe, E. (1997, October). How quickly we forget. *U.S. News & World Report*.

Young, M. W. (2000, March). The tick-tock of the biological clock. *Scientific American*, 64–71.

Young, N. K. (1997). Effects of alcohol and other drugs on children. *Journal of Psychoactive Drugs, 29*, 23–42.

Yule, W., & Fernando, P. (1980). Blood phobia: Beware. *Behavior Research and Therapy, 18*, 587–590.

Yurgelun-Todd, D. (1999, August 9). Cited in S. Brownlee, Inside the teen brain. *U. S. News & World Report*, 44–45.

Zajonc, R. B. (1984). On the primacy of affect. *American Psychologist, 39*, 117–123.

Zald, D. H., & Pardo, J. (1997). Emotion, olfaction, and the human amygdala: Amygdala activation during aversive olfactory stimulation. *Proceedings of the National Academy of Science, 94*, 4119–4124.

Zane, J. P. (1996, April 15). Time wasted, money lost. *San Diego Union-Tribune*.

Zaragoza, M. S., & Lane, S. M. (1994). Source misattributions and the suggestibility of eyewitness memory. *Journal of Experimental Psychology: Learning Memory, and Cognition, 20*, 934–935.

Zeidner, M. (1998). *Test anxiety: The state of the art*. New York: Plenum Press.

Zeifman, D., & Hazan, C. (1997). Cited in B. Bower, The ties that bond. *Science News, 152*, 94–95.

Zeiler, M. D. (1996). On books: Whither behaviorism? *Behavior Analyst, 19*, 301–309.

Zeki, S. (1993). *A vision of the brain*. Cambridge, MA: Blackwell Scientific.

Zemore, S. E., Fiske, S. T., & Kim, H. (2000). Gender stereotypes and the dynamics of social interaction. In T. Eckes & H. M. Trautner (Eds.), *The developmental social psychology of gender*. Mahwah, NJ: Lawrence Erlbaum.

Zener, K. (1937). The significance of behavior accompanying conditioned salivary secretion for theories of the conditioned response. *American Journal of Psychology, 50*, 384–403.

**Zeng, R. G., & Shannon, R. V.** (1994). Loudness-coding mechanisms inferred from electric stimulation of the human auditory system. *Science, 264,* 564– 566.

**Zigler, E.** (1994). Reshaping early childhood intervention to be a more effective weapon against poverty. *American Journal of Community Psychology, 22,* 37–47.

**Zigler, E.** (1995, January). Cited in B. Azar, DNA-environment mix forms intellectual fate. *APA Monitor.*

**Zigler, E., & Seitz, V.** (1982). Social policy and intelligence. In R. J. Sternberg (Ed.), *Handbook of human intelligence.* Cambridge, England: Cambridge University Press.

**Zigler, E., & Styfco, S. J.** (Eds.). (1993). *Head Start and beyond.* New Haven, CT: Yale University Press.

**Zigler, E., & Styfco, S. J.** (1994). Head Start: Criticisms in a constructive context. *American Psychologist, 49,* 127–132.

**Zimbardo, P. G.** (1970). The human choice: Individuation, reason and order versus deindividuation, impulse and chaos. In W. J. Arnold & D. Levine (Eds.), *Nebraska symposium on motivation.* Lincoln: University of Nebraska Press.

**Zimmer, C.** (1993, June). Making senses. *Discover.*

**Zimmer, L., & Morgan, J. P.** (1997). *Marijuana myths, marijuana fact: A review of scientific evidence.* New York: Lindesmith Center.

**Zimmerman, B. J.** (2000). Self-efficacy: An essential motive to learn. *Contemporary Educational Psychology, 25,* 82–91.

**Zimmerman, M. A., Copeland, L. A., Shope, J. T., & Gielman, T. E.** (1997). A longitudinal study of self-esteem: Implications for adolescent development. *Journal of Youth and Adolescence, 26,* 117–141.

**Zito, J. M., Safer, D. J., dosReis, S., Gardner, J. F., Boles, M., & Lynch, F.** (2000). Trends in prescribing of psychotropic medications to preschoolers. *Journal of American Medical Association, 283,* 1025–1030.

**Zola, S. M., & Squire, L. R.** (2000). The medial temporal lobe and the hippocampus. In E. Tulving & F. M. Craik (Eds.), *The Oxford handbook of memory.* New York: Oxford University Press.

**Zucker, K. J.** (1990). Gender identity disorders in children: Clinical descriptions and natural history. In R. Blanchard & B. W. Steiner (Eds.), *Clinical management of gender identity disorders in children and adults.* Washington, DC: American Psychiatric Press.

**Zuckerman, M., Klorman, R., Larrance, D. T., & Speigel, N. H.** (1981). Facial, autonomic, and subjective components of emotion: The facial feedback hypothesis versus the externalizer-internalizer distinction. *Journal of Personality and Social Psychology, 41,* 929–944.

# Photo Credits

This page constitutes an extension of the copyright page. We have made every effort to trace the ownership of all copyrighted material and to secure permission from copyright holders. In the event of any question arising as to the use of any material, we will be pleased to make the necessary corrections in future printings. Thanks are due to the following authors, publishers, and agents for permission to use the material indicated.

## Front Matter

**x:** (#A) Craig McClain; **xi:** (#B) © George Frey; **xiii:** (#I) © Michael Nichols/Magnum Photos; **xiv:** (#C,F,G) PhotoDisc, Inc.; **xv:** (#A) PhotoDisc, Inc.; (#G) © Werner Bokerberg/The Image Bank, altered by Doug Stern/ *U.S. News & World Report;* **xvi:** (#C,H) PhotoDisc, Inc.; **xix:** (#A) PhotoDisc, Inc.; **xxiii:** (baby's face) PhotoDisc, Inc.; (owl face) © Chase Swift-CORBIS; (panther face) © Susan Middleton & David Liitschwager-CORBIS; **xxiv:** (woman & donut) © Tony Freeman/Photo Edit, Inc.; **xxv:** (#1) STONE/© Warren Bolster; (#6) Digital Stock Corporation; (#7) © Topham/OB/ The Image Works; **xxvi:** (Egyptian woman) © Thomas Hartwell/Saba Press Photos; **xxvii:** Figures (left) adapted from "Sex Differences in the Brain," by D. Kimura, 1992, *Scientific American, 267,* 119–125; **xxviii:** (top) Agence France Presse [AFP]/ Archive Photos; (center) Redrawn from an illustration by John Tom Seetin in "Working Knowledge," *Scientific American, 277 (6),* December, 1997, p. 132. Reprinted by permission of the illustrator. All rights reserved.; (photo below left) by Joel Reicherter, reprinted by permission and courtesy of the photographer; **xxix:** (#7) *People Weekly* © 1992 Taro Yamasaki; **xxxiv** (rhino) © Joe McDonald/Animals, Animals Earth Science; (bear) © Peter Weimann/Animals, Animals Earth Science; (tiger) © Belinda Wright/DRK Photo; **xxxv:** (Module 4: alligator) STONE/Paul Berger; **xxxvi:** (MRI) Digital Stock Corporation; **xxxvii:** (female w/guitar) PhotoDisc, Inc.; **xxxviii:** (baby & toy) PhotoDisc, Inc.

## Module 1

**2:** NASA **4:** Courtesy of Doubleday/AB/Times Books/Random House, by permission of Donna Williams; **5:** (right #5) Reprinted with permission of Times Books; **5:** (far left above) Craig McClain; **6:** (center left) Craig McClain; **10:** (top) Reprinted with permission of Times Books; **12:** (bottom left) © C Squared Studios/PhotoDisc, Inc. **13:** (center below) © Tony Freeman/Photo Edit; **14:** (center above) Courtesy, Margaret Clapp Library Archives, Wellesley College, photo by Patridge; **14:** (left) Robert Guthrie Collection; **14:** (right) The Institute of Texan Cultures, University of Texas, San Antonio; **15:** (left #1) Courtesy of Doubleday/AB/Times Books/Random House, by permission of Donna Williams; **15:** (right #11) © Tony Freeman/Photo Edit; **15:** (left #7) Reprinted with permission of Times Books; **15:** (left #3) Craig McClain; **15:** (right #9) © C Squared Studios/PhotoDisc, Inc. **18:**

(left) David Young-Wolff/Photo Edit; **18:** (center) © STONE/Lori Adamski Peek; **19:** (left) © Doug Menuez/Saba Press Photos, Inc.; **19:** (right) © 1988 Joel Gordon; **20:** (bottom) © Hangarter/The Picture Cube/Index Stock; **22:** (left #1) Courtesy of Doubleday/AB/Times Books/Random House, by permission of Donna Williams; **22:** (right bottom) Courtesy, Margaret Clapp Library Archives, Wellesley College, photo by Patridge; **22:** (left #3) Craig McClain; **23:** (Left #16) © Doug Menuez/ Saba Press Photos, Inc.; **23:** (right #18) © Hangarter/ The Picture Cube/Index Stock.

## Module 2

**26:** © William James Warren/CORBIS; **27:** (top) © Jose Azel/Aurora Quanta Productions; **27:** (right) © Joe McDonald/Animals, Animals; **28:** © Jose Azel/Aurora Quanta Productions; **31:** (left) © Joe McDonald/Animals, Animals; **31:** (center) © Peter Weimann/Animals, Animals; **31:** (right) © Belinda Wright/DRK Photo; **32:** (top) © Jose Azel/Aurora Quanta Productions; **33:** (left) © Edward Thomas/ Leo DeWys; **34:** (bottom left) *People Weekly* © 1995/Alan S. Weiner; **34:** (bottom right) John Sholtis, The Rockefeller University, New York. Copyright © 1995 Amgen, Inc.; **34:** (right top) © Richard E. Schultz; **35:** (left) © Michael McLoughlin; **36:** (top & bottom) © Jose Azel/ Aurora Quanta Productions; **38:** (left #2) © Joe McDonald/Animals, Animals; **38:** (left #1) © Jose Azel/Aurora Quanta Productions; **38:** (left #4) © Richard E. Schultz; **39:** © Michael McLoughlin; **40:** (center) Craig McClain; **40:** (bottom) Craig McClain; **41:** Courtesy of the Foundation for Biomedical Research; **42:** (left #1) © Jose Azel/ Aurora Quanta Productions; **42:** (left #4) © Joe McDonald/ Animals, Animals; **43:** (right #14) Craig McClain; **44:** PhotoDisc, Inc.

## Module 3

**45:** Detail from illustration by John Karapelou in *Discover,* January 1998, p. 67. Copyright © 1998 by Discover (Disney Magazine Publishing, Inc.); **46:** Detail from illustration by John Karapelou in *Discover,* January 1998, p. 67. Copyright © 1998 by Discover (Disney Magazine Publishing, Inc.); **47:** © Melchior Digiacomo; **48:** © Melchior Digiacomo; **49:** Courtesy of Center on Aging and Department of Molecular and Medical Pharmacology, University of California, Los Angeles; **50:** Alfred Pasika-SPL/ Photo Researchers, Inc.; **51:** (top left) *People Weekly* © 1992 Taro Yamasaki; **51:** (right center) *People Weekly* © 1998 Photo by Frank Veronsky; **55:** (right below) Courtesy of Johns Hopkins University, Office of Public Affairs; **55:** (right above) Courtesy of Miles Herkenham, Ph.D., Section of Functional Neuroanatomy, NIMH; **55:** (left ) PhotoDisc, Inc.; **58:** AP/Wide World Photos; **59:** (center above) © Borys Malkin/Anthro-Photo; **59:** center below) © G.I. Bernard/Animals, Animals/Earth Sciences; **59:** (top) © Adalberto Rios Szal Sol/PhotoDisc; **61:** (center) From "Survival of Implanted Fetal Dopamine Cells and Neurologic Improvement 12

to 46 months after Transplantation for Parkinson's Disease," by C.R. Freed, et al. 1992, New England Journal of Medicine, 327: 1549-1555. Copyright © 1992 by the Massachusetts Medical Society. Courtesy of Dr. Curt R. Freed; **62:** (right #7) *People Weekly* © 1992 Taro Yamasaki; **63:** (right #13) AP/Wide World Photos.

## Module 4

**66:** © Gary Bartholomew/CORBIS; **67:** (left) Patrick Farrell/ *Miami Herald* photo; **67:** (top right) © Peter A. Simon/Phototake, NYC; **67:** (right center) By courtesy and kind permission of Cynthia de Gruchy; **68:** (bottom) By courtesy and kind permission of Cynthia de Gruchy; **69:** (top) © Kevin O'Farrell Concepts; **69:** (right center) Craig McClain; **70:** (left) Digital Stock Corporation; **70:** (top) PhotoDisc, Inc.; **70:** (right) From "A Head for Figures," by Brian Butterworth, *Science, 284,* p. 928, by permission of B. Butterworth; **71:** (top center-2) Courtesy of Dr. Marcus Raichle, University of Washington; **71:** Courtesy of Dr. Marcus Raichle, University of Washington; **71:** (bottom center, right) Digital Stock Corporation; **72:** (bottom right) STONE/David Stewart; **74:** (right) Patrick Farrell/ *Miami Herald* photo; **74:** (left) Martin Sereno/© 1996. Reprinted with permission of *Discover* Magazine; **74:** (right) Patrick Farrell/ *Miami Herald* photo; **75:** (left) Courtesy of Dr. Hanna Damasio, Human Neuroanatomy & Neuroimaging Laboratory, Dept of Neurology, University of Iowa College of Medicine. Published in 1994 in *Science, 264,* p 1104. Copyright © 1994 by the American Association for the Advancement in Science. Reprinted with permission of author and publisher; **76:** (bottom) Courtesy of J.A. Fiez, Dept of Neurology, Washington University School of Medicine; **80:** (left) STONE/ Paul Berger; **80:** (right) © Topham/OB/The Image Works; **80:** (bottom) Tomas del Amo/Aristock; **81:** (center right) STONE/David Stewart; **83:** (left #2) Digital Stock Corporation; **83:** (right #5) STONE/ David Stewart; **85:** (right) © PhotoDisc, Inc.; **88:** (left #3) Courtesy of Dr. Marcus Raichle, University of Washington; **89:** (left#16) STONE/Paul Berger.

## Module 5

**92:** (top) © PhotoDisc; **92:** (center) © Chase Swift/ CORBIS; **92:** (bottom) © Susan Middleton & David Liitschwager/CORBIS; **93:** (center #2) PhotoDisc, Inc.; **98:** (center) Digital Stock Corporation; **99:** (bottom right) Courtesy of Graham- Field, Inc.; **99:** (top & right center ) Normal and altered re-production of Vincent van Gogh self-portrait reprinted by permission of Los Angeles Times Syndicate, originally appearing in *Popular Science,* July 1995 issue, "Color for the Color Blind: Self-Portrait of Van Gogh; **100:** (left center) © Tony Freeman/Photo Edit; **101:** (man & drill) PhotoDisc, Inc.; **101:** (couple) PhotoDisc, Inc.; **101:** (sunset) PhotoDisc, Inc.; **104:** (right) © Tony Freeman/Photo Edit; **104:** (left) © M.P. Kahl/DRK Photo; **105:** PhotoDisc, Inc.; **107:** (bottom) © 1989 Jonathan

Levine; **108:** (left) © 1986 Steven Green-Armytage/ The Stock Market; **110:** (right) Danielle Pellegrini/ Photo Researchers, Inc.; **110:** (top) © Burt Glinn/ Magnum Photos; **110:** (left) © Malcolm S. Kirk; **110:** (center) © Guy Mary-Rousseliere; **110:** (bottom) © Malcolm S. Kirk; **112:** Digital Stock Corporation; **113:** (bottom) © Leonard Freed-Magnum Photos; **113:** (top) © P.R. Miller/Focus on Sports; **114:** (right) AP/Wide World Photos; **115:** (bottom) © James M. Kubus, Greensburg, PA; **117:** (left #17) © Danielle Pellegrini/Photo Researchers, Inc.

## Module 6

**120:** Robert Estall Photographs, © Angela Fisher and Carol Beckwith; **121:** © Howard Sochurek/ The Stock Market; **122:** © Howard Sochurek/ The Stock Market; **123:** (left) © Al Francekevich/ The Stock Market; **123:** (bottom) © Pat Bruno/ Positive Images; **124:** (bottom) Custom Medical Stock Photo; **126:** Painting by Richard Haas, photo © Bill Horsman; **127:** (top) Painting by Richard Haas, photo © Bill Horsman; **128:** (right 2) © Pat Bruno/ Positive Images; **129:** (center) Random House photo by Charlotte Green; **130:** (left) © Peter Turner/The Image Bank; **130:** (top) Photo Courtesy of Nikon Inc., photography © Jerry Friedman; **130:** (bottom) © Bob Daemmrich/Stock, Boston; **130:** (right) Digital Stock Corporation; **131:** (top left) © Stephen Firsch/Stock, Boston; **131:** (bottom left) © Garry Gay/The Image Bank; **131:** (top right) © Gamma Press Images/Liaison Agency; **131:** (bottom right) © Robert Holmes/ CORBIS; **132:** (left) © Robert P. Comport/ Animals, Animals/Earth Sciences; **132:** (right) © John Elk/Stock, Boston; **133:** (top left) © Baron Wolman/Woodfin Camp & Associates; **133:** (center right 2) Craig McClain; **134:** (left #4) Painting by Richard Haas, photo © Bill Horsman; **134:** (left #3) Custom Medical Stock Photo; **134:** (right #13) © Garry Gay/The Image Bank; **135:** PhotoDisc, Inc.; **136:** (center) Digital Stock Corporation; **136:** (right & left) PhotoDisc, Inc.; **136:** (top) © Ric Ergenbright/CORBIS; **136:** (bottom) By courtesy of Takahiko Masuda and Dr. Richard Nisbett, University of Michigan; **137:** (left) Digital Stock Corporation; **137:** (center) Digital Stock Corporation; **137:** (right) © 1991 Jim Amentler; **138:** © Dana Fineman/CORBIS-Sygma; **140:** (center) PhotoDisc, Inc.; **140:** (center below) © Globus Brothers/The Stock Market; **140:** (top right) © Gianni Dagli Orti/ CORBIS; **141:** (Howard Stern) © Allen Tannenbaum/ Sygma Photos illustration by Doug Stern. *U.S. News & World Report.* Reproduced by permission; **141:** (Schwarzenegger) Courtesy of Colors Magazine; **141:** (Queen Elisabeth) Courtesy of Colors Magazine; **141:** (left) 2000 Computer Motion Photograph by Bobbi Bennett; **141:** (Marilyn Monroe) © Doc Alain/ Retna, Inc., Julia Roberts © Bill Davila/ Retna, Inc., Howard Stern © Allen Tannenbaum/ Sygma. Photos illustration by Doug Stern. *U.S. News & World Report.* Reproduced by permission.

**141:** (top right) Ames Research Center/NASA, photo by Walt Sisler; **142:** (left #1) © Al Francekevich/The Stock Market; **142:** (right #7) © Peter Turner/The Image Bank; **143:** (right #14) Courtesy of Colors Magazine.

## Module 7

**146:** © Louis Psihoyos/Matrix, Inc.; **147:** (left) © Murrae Haynes/Mercury Pictures; **147:** (right) © Alan Hobson/Science Source/Photo Researchers; **148:** (near right) © STONE/David Stewart; **148:** (far left) © Michael S. Yamashita/CORBIS; **148:** (near left) © Tony Freeman/Photo Edit; **148:** (far right) Craig McClain; **149:** (left) © STONE/ Robert E. Daemmrich; **149:** (center) © Cesar Paredes/The Stock Market; **149:** (right) Neil Leifer/ *Sports Illustrated,* © Time-Pix; **150:** (top left) © Murrae Haynes/Mercury Pictures; **153:** (left) © Alan Hobson/Science Source/Photo Researchers, Inc.; **158:** (left #1) © Michael S. Yamashita/ CORBIS; **159:** (top) Digital Stock Corporation; **161:** (bottom) Craig McClain; **162:** (left) © Paul Buddle; **162:** (center) © STONE/Carol Fords; **163:** (right) © Dan McCoy/ Rainbow; **163:** (center) © Louis Psihoyos/Matrix; **164:** (left #1) © Michael S. Yamashita/CORBIS; **165:** (right #17) © Paul Buddle; **166:** © Fran Heyl & Associates.

## Module 8

**168:** © David Muench/CORBIS; **169:** (left) Craig McClain; **170:** (center) Craig McClain; **171:** Craig McClain; **172:** (top) © Michael Salas/The Image Bank; **172:** (right center) © Myrleen Ferguson/ Photo Edit; **173:** (top) Courtesy, Rainbow Babies and Children's Hospital, University Hospitals of Cleveland, Dr. Howard Hall. Photo © Joe Glick; **174:** (top) © James Porto; **178:** Craig McClain; **180:** (center below) © Joy Spurr/Bruce Coleman Inc.; **180:** (top) © Robert Pickett/CORBIS; **180:** (bottom left) © Andy Small/CORBIS; **180:** (center left) © Michael and Patricia Fogden/CORBIS; **181:** (top) © David Muench/CORBIS; **181:** (left above) © Joseph Sohm/Chromosohm, Inc./CORBIS; **181:** (center below) © Scott Houston/CORBIS-Sygma; **181:** (left below) © Scott Houston/CORBIS Sygma; **182:** (center) Craig McClain; **182:** (top) Courtesy, Joseph E. Seagram's and Sons, Inc.; **183:** © Andrew Lichtenstein/CORBIS-Sygma; **184:** (left #1) Craig McClain; **184:** (right #10) Craig McClain; **184:** (left #2) Craig McClain; **184:** (left #4) © James Porto; **184:** (right #7) © Robert Pickett/CORBIS; **184:** (right #8) © J. Cloud/ CORBIS-Sygma; **185:** (left) © Richard Kalvar/ Magnum Photos; **185:** (top) © Pat Bruno/Positive Images; **186:** (left) © Brooks Kraft/CORBIS-Sygma; **187:** Courtesy of D.A.R.E. America; **188:** (left) © Pat Bruno/Positive Images; **189:** © Pat Bruno/Positive Images; **190:** (left #1) Craig McClain; **190:** (right #14) © Robert Pickett/ CORBIS; **191:** (right #20) Courtesy of D.A.R.E. America; **191:** (left #19) © Brooks Kraft/CORBIS-Sygma; **192:** © Pat Bruno/Positive Images.

## Module 9

**194:** © Carl Vanderschuit/Index Stock Imagery; **195:** Digital Stock Corporation; **196:** Craig McClain; **200:** (right below) Courtesy of Professor Stuart Ellins, California State University, San Barnardino, CA.; **200:** (right above) PhotoDisc, Inc.; **201:** (left) © Runk/Schoenberger/Grant Heilman Photography; **201:** (right) © Michael Stuckey/Comstock; **201:** (center above) AP/ Wide World Photos; **201:** (bottom) © Christian Abraham; **202:** top, (left) PhotoDisc, Inc.; **204:** (toddler smiling & yelling) Digital Stock Corporation; **204:** (rat) PhotoDisc, Inc.; **204:** (rabbit) PhotoDisc, Inc.; **205:** (top) © Schmid-Langsfeld/The Image Bank; **206:** Digital Stock Corporation; **207:** Digital Stock Corporation; **209:** (toddler) Digital Stock Corporation; **209:** (rat) PhotoDisc, Inc.

## Module 10

**212:** © Cydney Conger/CORBIS; **213:** (left) © George Frey; **213:** (right) © Frederick Charles; **214:** (right) PhotoDisc, Inc.; **216:** (left) © Peter Southwick/Stock, Boston; **216:** (top) Courtesy of Wurlitzer Jukebox Company; **217:** (top & bottom) © George Frey; **217:** (apple) PhotoDisc, Inc.; **218:** (right) PhotoDisc, Inc.; **218:** (left) STONE/ Henley & Savage; **219:** (left) PhotoDisc, Inc.; **220:** (top) © 1971 *Time* Inc. Reprinted by permission; **221:** (top left) STONE/ Andy Sacks; **221:** (top right) © Michael P. Gadomski/Photo Researchers, Inc.; **221:** (left below) © Vince Cavataio/Allsport Photographic Ltd./USA.; **221:** (right below) STONE/Norman Mosallem; **222:** (cub) © Stephen Kraseman/DRK Photo; **222:** (Bart & Bart/trainer) © George Frey; **222:** (bottom) PhotoDisc, Inc.; **222:** (spider) PhotoDisc, Inc.; **223:** (rat) PhotoDisc, Inc.; **223:** (top) © Frederick Charles; **224:** (bobo doll) Craig McClain; **225:** (left) © Barry Lewis/ Network/Saba; **225:** (top) PhotoDisc, Inc.; **226:** (left) From *The Mentality of Apes,* by Wolfgang Koehler, Routledge & Kegan Paul. Reproduced by permission of International Thomson Publishing Services, Ltd.; **226:** (banana) Craig McClain; **226:** (right) PhotoDisc, Inc.; **226:** (gun) PhotoDisc, Inc.; **227:** (right #11) Craig McClain; **227:** (left #8) © Stephen Kraseman/DRK Photo; **227:** (left #6) PhotoDisc, Inc.; **227:** (left #4) PhotoDisc, Inc.; **227:** (right #13) PhotoDisc, Inc.; **228:** (right) Photo by Ron Garrison, © Zoological Society of San Diego; **228:** (top) Mitsuaki Iwago/National Geographic Society; **228:** (left) PhotoDisc, Inc.; **229:** (left) Arthur C. Smith, III/ Grant Heilman Photography; **229:** (right) Kennan Ward Photography/CORBIS; **231:** (top, right) © Hiroji Kubota/Magnum Photos; **233:** (top) © Dan McCoy/ Rainbow; **233:** (right) © 1998 Danny Gonzalez; **234:** (right #13) © Stephen Kraseman/ DRK Photo; **234:** (right #8) PhotoDisc, Inc.; **235:** (right #23) © Hiroji Kubota/Magnum Photos; **235:** (left #19) Photo by Ron Garrison, © Zoological Society of San Diego.

# Photo Credits

## Module 11

**238:** PhotoDisc, Inc.; **239:** (top right) AP/Wide World Photos; **239:** (right below) © John Harding; **239:** (left) Chris Assaf/ © *The Washington Post;* **240:** (left) PhotoDisc, Inc.; **241:** (eyes) PhotoDisc, Inc.; **242:** (top) PhotoDisc, Inc.; **243:** (top) Chris Assaf/© *The Washington Post;* **244:** (cake) PhotoDisc, Inc.; **244:** (right) PhotoDisc, Inc.; **244:** (left) PhotoDisc, Inc.; **245:** (frog) PhotoDisc, Inc.; **245:** (owl) PhotoDisc, Inc.; **245:** (bear) PhotoDisc, Inc.; **246:** (left) Digital Stock Corporation; **246:** (right) PhotoDisc, Inc.; **247:** (top) AP/Wide World Photos; **250:** (top right) AP/Wide World Photos; **250:** (top left) © John Harding; **252:** (left #5) Chris Assaf/ © *The Washington Post;* **252:** (left #7) PhotoDisc, Inc.; **252:** (right #13) AP/Wide World Photos; **253:** (top) Bob Carey/*Los Angeles Times* Photo; **254:** (top) © Doug Levere; **254:** (bottom) Courtesy of Prof. Ralph Norman Haber; **256:** (left #5) PhotoDisc, Inc.; **257:** (right #18) Bob Carey/*Los Angeles Times* Photo; **257:** (left #13) AP/Wide World Photos; **258:** AP/Wide World Photos.

## Module 12

**260:** © Karl Weatherly/PhotoDisc, Inc.; **263:** (bottom) Digital Stock Corporation; **264:** (top) © Laura Dwight; **264:** (faces in graph) PhotoDisc, Inc.; **265:** (cupcake) PhotoDisc, Inc.; **265:** (present) PhotoDisc, Inc.; **267:** (bottom) © Topham/OB/ The Image Works; **267:** (strawberry) PhotoDisc, Inc.; **268:** (computer) PhotoDisc, Inc.; **268:** (left) PhotoDisc, Inc.; **268:** (tennis player) PhotoDisc, Inc.; **269:** (top) PhotoDisc, Inc.; **269:** (center) © Bill Ballenberg; **270:** (right #7) PhotoDisc, Inc.; **270:** (left #6) PhotoDisc, Inc.; **272:** (meeting) PhotoDisc, Inc.; **272:** (top) © Tad Janocinski/The Image Bank; **274:** (bottom 2) UPI/CORBIS-Bettmann; **276:** (right #13) PhotoDisc, Inc.; **276:** (left #5)PhotoDisc, Inc.; **277:** (right #23) UPI/ CORBIS-Bettmann; **277:** (left #21) © Tad Janocinski/The Image Bank; **278:** *People Weekly* © 1996 Adolphe Pierre-Louis.

## Module 13

**280:** (3) © Art Wolfe; **281:** (far left) © Stephen Ellison/CORBIS-Outline; **281:** (center) AP/Wide World Photos; **281:** (far right) Bob Chamberlin/ *Los Angeles Times* Photo; **281:** (near right) Photo by Brigitte Lacombe, courtesy of Cerritos Center for the Performing Arts, California; **281:** (near left) AP/Wide World Photos; **282:** (top left) © Stephen Ellison/CORBIS-Outline; **282:** (2nd left) AP/Wide World Photos; **282:** (3rd left) AP/Wide World Photos; **282:** (4th left & right) Bob Chamberlin/ *Los Angeles Times* Photo; **282:** (bottom left) Photo by Brigitte Lacombe, courtesy of Cerritos Center for the Performing Arts, California; **282:** (right) Bob Chamberlin/*Los Angeles Times* Photo; **283:** (top right) PhotoDisc, Inc.; **283:** (right center) PhotoDisc, Inc.; **283:** (bottom right) PhotoDisc, Inc.; **283:** AP/Wide World Photos; **283:** (center) Photo by Brigitte Lacombe, courtesy of Cerritos Center for

the Performing Arts, California; **285:** (top) Corbis-Bettmann; **285:** (left) PhotoDisc, Inc.; **285:** (center) PhotoDisc, Inc.; **286:** (left) Courtesy, John Fitzgerald Kennedy Library/Museum, #C283-51-63; **286:** (center) Deborah Feingold, courtesy of *Parade Magazine* and Marilyn vos Savant; **286:** (right) Corbis-UPI/Bettmann; **288:** (left) Courtesy of Marian Burke; **288:** (right) Deborah Feingold, courtesy of *Parade Magazine* and Marilyn vos Savant; **289:** (left) PhotoDisc, Inc.; **289:** (right) PhotoDisc, Inc.; **289:** (bottom) Deborah Feingold, courtesy of *Parade Magazine* and Marilyn vos Savant; **291:** (center) © Rick Smolan/Stock, Boston; **291:** (bottom) PhotoDisc, Inc.; **292:** (top) Photo by Brigitte Lacombe, courtesy of Cerritos Center for the Performing Arts; **292:** (center) © Myrleen Ferguson/Photo Edit; **293:** (top) © Anne Rippy/The Image Bank; **293:** (left) PhotoDisc, Inc.; **293:** (right) PhotoDisc, Inc.; **294:** (center-4) © Anthony Barboza; **295:** (left #3) PhotoDisc, Inc.; **295:** (left #4) PhotoDisc, Inc.; **295:** (left #1) Bob Chamberlin/*Los Angeles Times* Photo; **295:** (left #2) Photo by Brigitte Lacombe, courtesy of Cerritos Center for the Performing Arts, California; **296:** CORBIS-UPI/Bettmann; **297:** (above) Adapted from S.F. Witelson, D. L. Kigar, & T. Harvey, Fig. 2, *The Lancet,* 353, 1999, with permission of the authors; **298:** © 1991 Ira Block/The Image Bank; **299:** (right) © Jacques Chenet/Woodfin Camp & Associates; **299:** (left) PhotoDisc, Inc.; **300:** (left #1) Bob Chamberlin/*Los Angeles Times Photo;* **301:** (left #12) © Rick Smolan/Stock, Boston; **301:** (right #14) UPI/Bettmann-CORBIS; **302:** © Judy Griesedieck.

## Module 14

**304:** © Third Eye Images/ CORBIS; **305:** (right) © 1994 Paul Morse, *Los Angeles Times.* Reprinted by permission; **305:** (left) © Charles Allen/The Image Bank; **306:** (top left) PhotoDisc, Inc.; **306:** (left center) PhotoDisc, Inc.; **306:** (left below) PhotoDisc, Inc.; **306:** (right #1) PhotoDisc, Inc.; **306:** (right #2) PhotoDisc, Inc.; **306:** (right #3) PhotoDisc, Inc.; **306:** (right #4) © Animals/ Animals; **307:** (top) PhotoDisc, Inc.; **307:** (turtle) PhotoDisc, Inc.; **307:** (apple) PhotoDisc, Inc.; **307:** (clown) PhotoDisc, Inc.; **308:** (top) © Richard Pohle/Sipa Press; **308:** (bottom) PhotoDisc, Inc.; **309:** (center) Craig McClain; **310:** (left) © 1994 Paul Morse, *Los Angeles Times.* Reprinted by permission; **310:** (right) © 1994 Gordon Parks; **311:** (top) Courtesy of and by permission of John Johnson, Ltd. on behalf of Stephen Wilshire; **314:** (left) © Romilly Lockyer/The Image Bank; **314:** (right) © Al Hamdan/The Image Bank; **315:** (left) © Laura Dwight; **315:** (right) © Frank Bates/The Image Bank; **315:** (bottom #1) © Romilly Lockyer/ The Image Bank; **315:** (bottom #2) © Al Hamdan/ The Image Bank; **315:** (bottom #3) © Laura Dwight; **315:** (bottom #4) © Frank Bates/The Image Bank; **316:** (bottom) PhotoDisc, Inc.; **316:** (center) Courtesy of Robert Zatorre, and Denise Klein, McGill University; **316:** (top) © Jeremy Horner/CORBIS; **317:** (left #4) Craig McClain;

**317:** (right #8) © Romilly Lockyer/The Image Bank; **317:** (right #9) © Jeremy Horner/CORBIS; **318:** PhotoDisc, Inc.; **319:** (left) STONE/P H Cornut; **319:** (right) PhotoDisc, Inc.; **320:** (top) © Brian Vander Brug; **321:** (bottom) Shaywitz, et al., 1995 NMR Research/Yale Medical School; **321:** (top) By courtesy of Takahiko Masuda and Dr. Richard Nisbett, University of Michigan; **322:** (bottom- 2) By Ed Kashi © 1989; **322:** (top) Author's collection; **323:** (bottom) © Michael Nichols/Magnum Photos; **323:** (top) © Ronald H. Cohn/The Gorilla Foundation, Woodside, California 94062; **323:** (center) Courtesy of Language Research Center, Georgia State University, Dr. Duane Rumbaugh, © 1991 Public Sphere; **324:** (right #7) Courtesy of and by permission of John Johnson, Ltd. on behalf of Stephen Wilshire; **324:** (left #3) Craig McClain; **325:** (right #17) Shaywitz, et al., 1995 NMR Research/Yale Medical School; **325:** (right #19) © Michael Nichols/Magnum Photos; **325:** (left #11) © Jeremy Horner/CORBIS; **326:** Digital Stock Corporation.

## Module 15

**328:** © Francisco Cruz/Superstock; **329:** (left) © Jay Mather/CORBIS-Sygma; **329:** (right) *Union-Tribune/*John McCutchen; **330:** (left) John Dominis, *LIFE* Magazine © Time, Inc.; **330:** (right) © Michael Melford/The Image Bank; **331:** (left) © Richard Sjoberg; **331:** (right) © Mike Malyszko/ Stock, Boston; **332:** (top left) WIlliam Campbell/ *Time* Magazine; **332:** (left center) PhotoDisc, Inc.; **332:** (bottom) PhotoDisc, Inc.; **334:** (center) © Les Stone/CORBIS-Sygma; **334:** (top) PhotoDisc, Inc.; **335:** (right) © Kim Newton/Woodfin Camp & Associates; **336:** (bottom) Courtesy of Jeffrey M. Friedman, Rockefeller University; **336:** (top) © Bob Sacha; **337:** (center) © FoodPix; **337:** (top) © FoodPix; **338:** © George B. Shaller/Bruce Coleman, Inc.; **340:** (center) © Tony Freeman/Photo Edit; **340:** (bottom) © George Simian-CORBIS; **341:** (top left) PhotoDisc, Inc.; **341:** (top right) PhotoDisc, Inc.; **341:** (bottom) © Left Lane Productions/ CORBIS; **342:** (center above) PhotoDisc, Inc.; **343:** Red Morgan/*Time Magazine;* **345:** © S. Wanke/PhotoLink/PhotoDisc, Inc.; **346:** (top) © 1995 Gina Ferazzi, *Los Angeles Times.* Reprinted by permission; **346:** (bottom) © Mariella Furrer/Saba Press Photos; **347:** (left #1) © Michael Melford/The Image Bank; **347:** (left #4) © Mike Malyszko/ Stock, Boston; **347:** (right #15) © S. Wanke/ PhotoLink/PhotoDisc, Inc.; **348:** (top) *Union-Tribune/*John McCutchen; **348:** (right) © Dave Black; **350:** (bottom) PhotoDisc, Inc.; **350:** (top center) Photo by Dr. Alfred McLaren. Reprinted with permission from *Science News,* the weekly newsmagazine of science, copyright 1995 by Science Service, Inc.; **350:** (top right) PhotoDisc, Inc.; **351:** © Jason Goltz; **352:** (top right) CORBIS-UPI/Bettmann; **352:** (top left) CORBIS-UPI/ Bettmann; **352:** (bottom left) AP/Wide World Photos; **352:** (bottom right) © L. Schwartzwald/ CORBIS-Sygma; **353:** (top) © Jim McHugh/ Outline Press Syndicate; **353:** (center) © Nina

Berman/Sipa Press Photos; **354:** (left #4) Courtesy of Jeffrey M. Friedman, Rockefeller University; **354:** (left #1) © Richard Sjoberg; **355:** (right #17) CORBIS UPI/Bettmann; **355:** (left #13) © Mariella Furrer/ Saba Press Photos; **355:** (left #14) PhotoDisc, Inc.

## *Module 16*

**358:** © Lisa Means, Dallas, TX; **359:** (left) STONE/ © Warren Bolster; **360:** (bottom left) PhotoDisc, Inc.; **361:** (bottom left) PhotoDisc, Inc.; **362:** (center & left above) PhotoDisc, Inc.; **362:** (right & bottom left) PhotoDisc, Inc.; **363:** (bottom-2) PhotoDisc, Inc.; **364:** (center) Digital Stock Corporation; **365:** (center) © Topham/OB/ The Image Works. **365:** (left) Digital Stock Corporation; **366:** (left) *Idaho Statesman*/© Tom Shanahan; **366:** (center below) PhotoDisc, Inc.; **366:** (right) PhotoDisc, Inc.; **367:** (left below) © Topham/OB/The Image Works; **367:** (right above) © Burt Glinn/Magnum Photos; **367:** (left above) PhotoDisc, Inc.; **367:** (left center) © Ray Ellis/Photo Researchers, Inc.; **367:** (right below) PhotoDisc, Inc.; **368:** (left #1) STONE/© Warren Bolster; **368:** (right #7) ©Topham/OB/The Image Works; **368:** (right #6) Digital Stock Corporation; **369:** (top left) © Christopher Morris/Black Star; **369:** (top right) © David Burnett/Contact Press; **370:** (top) Agence France Presse [AFP]/Archive Photos; **370:** (Photo below left) by Joel Reicherter; reprinted by permission and courtesy of the photographer; **371:** Agence France Presse [AFP]/ Archive Photos; **372:** (right #7) Digital Stock Corporation; **373:** (left #11) *Idaho Statesman*/ © Tom Shanahan; **374:** Noboru Hashimoto/*Los Angeles Times* photo.

## *Module 17*

**376:** © Terry Whitaker/Frank Lane Agency/ CORBIS; **377:** (left) AP/Wide World Photos; **377:** (right) © Melchoir Digiacomo; **378:** (top) CORBIS-Bettmann;/UPI; **379:** (left) © Francis Leroy/BioCosmos/Science Photo Library/Photo Researchers, Inc.; **379:** (right) © Petit Format/ Science Source/Photo Researchers, Inc.; **380:** (top) Lennart Nilsson, *The Incredible Machine,* National Geographic Society, by permission of Bokforlaget Bonnier Alba AB; **381:** (right) © George Steinmetz; **381:** (center) PhotoDisc, Inc., **382:** (left above) PhotoDisc, Inc.; **382:** (left below) PhotoDisc, Inc.; **382:** (right) PhotoDisc, Inc.; **383:** (right center) © Laura Dwight; **383:** (bottom) © Elyse Lewin/The Image Bank; **383:** (top) © Laura Dwight; **384:** (right) *People Weekly* © 1995 Taro Yamaski; **384:** (center above) © David M. Grossman/Photo Researchers, Inc; **384:** (center below) PhotoDisc, Inc.; **385:** (top) AP/Wide World Photos; **385:** (center) © Melchoir Digiacomo; **386:** (right) © Joseph Nettis/Stock, Boston; **386:** (bottom) © Brad Martin/The Image Bank; **387:** (right below) © Joseph Nettis/Stock, Boston; **387:** (right above) © Brad Martin/The Image Bank; **388:** (center above) PhotoDisc, Inc; **388:** (center below) PhotoDisc, Inc; **389:** (left-2) ) © Doug Goodman; **389:** (right-3) Craig McClain; **390:** (right) PhotoDisc, Inc.;

**390:** (left bottom) PhotoDisc, Inc.; **390:** (left above) Craig McClain; **390:** (left below) Craig McClain; **391:** © Yves DeBraine/ Black Star; **391:** *Jean Piaget* © Etienne Delessert; **392:** PhotoDisc, Inc.; **393:** PhotoDisc, Inc.; **394:** (below) © Mike Teruya/Free Spirit Photography; **394:** (above) PhotoDisc,Inc.; **395:** (top) © Jon Feingersh/The Stock Market; **395:** (left) © Bob Daemmrich/Stock, Boston; **395:** (right) © Charles Gupton/Stock, Boston; **396:** (top left) PhotoDisc, Inc; **396:** Shaywitz, et al., 1995 NMR Research/ Yale Medical School; **397:** Olivero Toscani for BENETTON; **397:** (right #10) PhotoDisc, Inc.; **397:** (center left) PhotoDisc, Inc.; **397:** (top right) PhotoDisc, Inc.; **398:** (right #10) PhotoDisc, Inc.; **399:** (left) © Steven Winn/AnthroPhoto; **399:** (right) © Lila Abu Lughod/AnthroPhoto; **400:** (left) UPI/CORBIS-Bettmann; **400:** (right) © Christopher Little/ Outline; **401:** Private Collection; **402:** (right #7) © Melchoir Digiacomo; **403:** (right #23) Private Collection; **403:** (right #22) © Steven Winn/AnthroPhoto; **403:** (left #17) PhotoDisc, Inc.

## *Module 18*

**406:** PhotoDisc, Inc.; **407:** (right) H. Armstrong Roberts; **407:** (left) Tammy Lechner/*Los Angeles Times* Photo; **408:** © David Michael Kennedy; **409:** (left) Lauren Greenfield; **410:** (top) Tammy Lechner/*Los Angeles Times* Photo; **410:** (right) PhotoDisc, Inc.; **411:** (left) PhotoDisc, Inc.; **411:** (right above) PhotoDisc, Inc.; **411:** (right below) PhotoDisc, Inc.; **413:** (left) © David Michael Kennedy; **413:** (right) PhotoDisc, Inc.; **414:** (top) © Lawrence Manning/CORBIS; **414:** (left above & center) © David Michael Kennedy; **414:** (left bottom) © Lauren Greenfield; **415:** (right) PhotoDisc., Inc.; **415:** (left) PhotoDisc., Inc.; **415:** (top left) PhotoDisc, Inc.; **415:** (top center) PhotoDisc, Inc.; **415:** (top right) PhotoDisc, Inc.; **416:** (center) Tammy Lechner/*Los Angeles Times* Photo; **416:** (bottom) © David Michael Kennedy; **416:** (top) PhotoDisc, Inc.; **417:** (bottom left) © Bob Grant/Archive Photos; **417:** (bottom right) © All Action/LGI Photo Agency; **417:** (left) H. Armstrong Roberts; **418:** (top) © 1995 Dave Garley, *Los Angeles Times.* Reprinted by permission; **418:** (center right) PhotoDisc., Inc.; **418:** (center left) PhotoDisc., Inc.; **419:** H. Armstrong Roberts; **420:** (left, right & center) PhotoDisc, Inc.; **421:** (right #9) PhotoDisc., Inc.; **421:** (right #11) PhotoDisc., Inc.; **421:** (right #8) © PhotoDisc, Inc.; **421:** (right #10)H. Armstrong Roberts; **422:** (top) PhotoDisc., Inc.; **422:** (center) © Andrew Brusso/CORBIS/Outline; **423:** (top) CORBIS-Bettmann; **424:** (center) © Werner Bokeberg/The Image Bank; altered by Doug Stern/ *U.S. News & World Report;* **424:** (top) © David J. Sams/Stock, Boston; **425:** (left) PhotoDisc., Inc.; **425:** (right) PhotoDisc., Inc.; **426:** PhotoDisc., Inc.; **427:** PhotoDisc,Inc.; **428:** (right #7) © David Michael Kennedy; **428:** (right #9) PhotoDisc, Inc.; **428:** (left #1) © Lawrence Manning/CORBIS; **429:** (right #14) © David J. Sams/Stock, Boston; **429:** (right #17) PhotoDisc, Inc.

## *Module 19*

**432:** © Ralph A. Clevenger/CORBIS; **433:** (right) © Fox/Shooting Star; **433:** (right) © Sin/Doralba Picerno/LGI Photo Agency; **436:** © Frank Micelotta/ Outline Press; **438:** © Mike Hashimoto/NGI/LGI Photo Agency; **439:** © Mike Hashimoto/NGI/LGI Photo Agency; **440:** (center) Courtesy, Adler School of Professional Psychology. Reproduced by permission of Kurt Adler; **440:** (left) National Library of Medicine, Bethesda, MD; **440:** (right) Courtesy, Association for the Advancement of Psychoanalysis; **442:** (top) © Fox/Shooting Star; **442:** (bottom) © Photo 3045 Pool: by J.O. Alber/Liaison Agency; **443:** (bottom) © Bob Adelman/Magnum Photos; **443:** (top) J. Howard Miller/National Archives/CORBIS-Bettmann; **444:** (center below) © Francois Lochon/Liaison Agency; **444:** (center above) © Nancy Moran/CORBIS-Sygma; **444:** (top) © Laura Dwight/CORBIS; **445:** (bottom) © Harry Benson; **445:** (center) PhotoDisc, Inc.; **445:** (top) © Jose Azel/Woodfin Camp & Associates; **446:** © Robert Durell; **447:** (right #10) © Jose Azel/Woodfin Camp & Associates; **448:** © Jason Goltz; **449:** (bottom) © Walter Wick/ Telegraph Colour Library/FPG International; **449:** (top) © Walter Wick/Telegraph Colour Library/ FPG International; **450:** (top) © Mike Hashimoto/ NGI/LGI Photo Agency; **453:** (left #14) © Jason Goltz; **453:** (left #11) © Robert Durell; **453:** (right #15) © Walter Wick/Telegraph Colour Library/ FPG International; **454:** *Los Angeles Times* Photos/ Rick Meyer.

## *Module 20*

**456:** Courtesy of Sony Electronics, Inc.; **457:** (right) © Alan Weiner/ Liaison Agency; **457:** (left) © Tomas Muscionico/Contact Press Images; **458:** (left) IDAF/Sipa Press; **458:** (top) © Nils Jorgensen/ RDR Productions/Rex Features, London; **458:** (right) © David Turnley, *Detroit Free Press*/ Black Star; **459:** (right) PhotoDisc, Inc.; **459:** (top) © Peter Turnley/Black Star; **460:** (left) PhotoDisc, Inc.; **460:** (right) PhotoDisc, Inc.; **461:** *People Weekly* © 1998 Photo by Frank Veronsky; **462:** (top left) © Alan Weiner/Liaison Agency; **462:** (criminal) PhotoDisc, Inc.; **462:** (clown) PhotoDisc, Inc.; **462:** (graduate) PhotoDisc, Inc.; **462:** (nun) PhotoDisc, Inc.; **462:** (beauty queen) © Joshua-Ets-Hokin/ PhotoDisc, Inc.; **463:** (criminal) PhotoDisc, Inc.; **463:** (clown) PhotoDisc, Inc.; **463:** (graduate) PhotoDisc, Inc.; **463:** (nun) PhotoDisc, Inc.; **463:** (beauty queen) © Joshua Ets-Hokin/PhotoDisc, Inc.; **464:** (top) © Ira Wyman-CORBIS/Sygma; **464:** (center) © Galen Rowell-CORBIS; **465:** (left above) © Barbara Penoyar/PhotoDisc, Inc.; **465:** (left below) © Barbara Penoyar/PhotoDisc, Inc.; **465:** (right) © Werner Bokeberg/The Image Bank; altered by Doug Stern/ *U.S. News & World Report;* **466:** (top) © Michael Nichols/Magnum Photos; **466:** (center) © Michael Nichols/Magnum Photos; **466:** (left) PhotoDisc, Inc.; **466:** (right) PhotoDisc, Inc.; **467:** (left) © Michael Nichols/Magnum Photos; **467:** (center) © Michael Nichols/Magnum

# Photo Credits

Photos; **467:** (right) PhotoDisc, Inc.; **468:** (center) © Ira Wyman-CORBIS/Sygma; **469:** (left #5) PhotoDisc, Inc.; **469:** (left #4) PhotoDisc, Inc.; **469:** (right #9) PhotoDisc, Inc.; **469:** (right #10) PhotoDisc, Inc.; **469:** (right #11-2) © Barbara Penoyar/PhotoDisc, Inc.; **469:** (right #11–2) © Barbara Penoyar/PhotoDisc, Inc.; **471:** (left) PhotoDisc, Inc.; **471:** (bottom) PhotoDisc, Inc.; **472:**(top right) © Photo 3045 Pool: by J.O. Alber/ Liaison Agency; **473:** (top left) © Nils Jorgensen/ RDR Productions/Rex Features, London; **473:** (center above) PhotoDisc, Inc.; **473:** (center below) PhotoDisc, Inc.; **473:** (center bottom) © Michael Nichols/Magnum Photos; **473:** (bottom left) PhotoDisc, Inc.; **474:** (left) PhotoDisc, Inc.; **474:** (right above) PhotoDisc, Inc.; **474:** (right below) PhotoDisc, Inc.; **475:** (right above) PhotoDisc, Inc.; **475:** (right below) PhotoDisc, Inc.; **475:** (left) Photodisc, Inc.; **475:** (center top) Corel Gallery; **478:** PhotoDisc, Inc.

## Module 21

**480:** © Barbara Cesery/Superstock; **481:** (right) Arlene Gottfried, *Life Magazine* © Time Inc.; **481:** (left) Craig McClain; **482:** (left) PhotoDisc, Inc.; **482:** (center) PhotoDisc, Inc.; **482:** (right) PhotoDisc, Inc.; **483:** (left) PhotoDisc, Inc.; **484:** (right) STONE/© Paul Berger; **484:** (center left) PhotoDisc, Inc.; **484:** (center right) PhotoDisc, Inc.; **486:** PhotoDisc, Inc.; **487:** (center) PhotoDisc, Inc.; **488:** © Lennart Nilsson, *The Incredible Machine,* National Geographic Society; **488:** (top) Digital Stock Corporation; **489:** (top) PhotoDisc, Inc.; **490:** (center below) © Photo Edit; **490:** (center above) Arlene Gottfried, *Life* Magazine © *Time* Inc.; **490:** (left) © L.D. Gordon/The Image Bank; **491:** (top) © David Liam Kyle/Sportslight; **491:** (right) © 1991 David Turnley, *Detroit Free Press*/Black Star; **491:** (center) PhotoDisc, Inc.; **493:** (right) Arlene Gottfried, *Life* Magazine © Time Inc.; **493:** (left) PhotoDisc, Inc. **494:** © Chuck Fishman/ Contact Press Images; **495:** (left) PhotoDisc, Inc.; **495:** (right below) PhotoDisc, Inc.; **497:** PhotoDisc, Inc.; **498:** (right #13) © Chuck Fishman/Contact Press Images; **498:** (right #12) Craig McClain; **498:** (left #9) © L.D. Gordon/The Image Bank; **498:** (right #10) PhotoDisc, Inc.; **498:** (right #14) PhotoDisc, Inc.; **499:** PhotoDisc, Inc.; **500:** © Ann States/Saba; **501:** (left and right) Photo by Dr. John W. Lehman, courtesy of Dr. Herbert Bensen, Mind/ Body Medical Institute; **502:** (top) PhotoDisc, Inc.; **502:** (left) PhotoDisc, Inc.; **502:** (right) PhotoDisc, Inc.; **503:** (top) PhotoDisc, Inc.; **503:** (bottom) PhotoDisc, Inc.; **505:** (left #17) PhotoDisc, Inc.; **505:** (left #18) © Ann States/Saba; **505:** (right #20) PhotoDisc, Inc.; **505:** (right #19) Photo by Dr. John W. Lehman, courtesy of Dr. Herbert Bensen, Mind/Body Medical Institute; **506:** *Los Angeles Times* Photo/Gina Ferazzi.

## Module 22

**508:** © Roger Ressmeyer/CORBIS; **509:** (left) Reuters/CORBIS-Bettmann; **509:** (right) © Elizabeth

Roll; **510:** top & center) © Henrik Drescher; **511:** (bottom right) © Henrik Drescher; **511:** (left) PhotoDisc, Inc.; **511:** (top right and center) *San Diego Union-Tribune*/Rick McCarthy; **512:** (top) William Cambell/*Time* Magazine; **512:** (center below) AP/Wide World Photos; **513:** AP/Wide World Photos; **514:** (right) © Elizabeth Roll; **514:** (top) AP/Wide World Photos; **515:** Reuters/ CORBIS-Bettmann; **518:** (center) © Elizabeth Roll; **520:** © Marvin Mattelson; **521:** (left #4) AP/Wide World Photos; **521:** (left #3) *San Diego Union-Tribune*/Rick McCarthy; **522:** (left) © David Young-Wolff/Photo Edit; **522:** (right) PhotoDisc, Inc.; **524:** © Elizabeth Roll; **526:** (left #4) AP/Wide World Photos; **526:** (left #1) *San Diego Union-Tribune*/Rick McCarthy; **527:** (left #14) © Marvin Mattelson; **528:** *Los Angeles Times* Photo/Perry C. Riddle.

## Module 23

**530:** © Joseph McNally; **531:** (left) *San Diego Union-Tribune*/Robert Gauthier; **531:** (right) *San Diego Union-Tribune*/Robert Gauthier; **532:** (center) *San Diego Union-Tribune*/Robert Gauthier; **532:** (left) *San Diego Union-Tribune*/John Gastaldo; **533:** (bottom left) © 1997 *Time* Inc., Reprinted by permission; **533:** (top) *San Diego Union-Tribune*/ Robert Gauthier; **533:** (right) Matthew Klein/ CORBIS; **534:** (left) *San Diego Union-Tribune*/ John Gastaldo; **534:** (right) *San Diego Union-Tribune*/Robert Gauthier; **535:** (right) © Photo Researchers, Inc.; **536:** (right) Reuters/ CORBIS-Bettmann; **538:** *San Diego Union-Tribune*/Robert Gauthier; **539:** (left) *San Diego Union-Tribune*/ Robert Gauthier; **539:** (center) Courtesy of Edna Morlok; **540:** (right) *San Diego Union-Tribune*/ Robert Gauthier; **540:** (left) Courtesy of Drs. E. Fuller Torrey & Daniel R. Weinberger, NIMH, Neuroscience Center, Washington D.C; **541:** (top) *San Diego Union-Tribune*/Robert Gauthier; **541:** (right) *San Diego Union-Tribune*/Jim Baird; **543:** (right #10) *San Diego Union-Tribune*/Robert Gauthier; **545:** Craig McClain; **547:** (top and left) © PhotoLink/PhotoDisc, Inc.; **551:** (left #16) Craig McClain; **551:** (right #19) © PhotoLink/ PhotoDisc, Inc.

## Module 24

**554:** © Michael Freeman/CORBIS; **555:** (left) Mary Evans /Sigmund Freud Copyrights/Sulloway; **555:** Digital Stock (right below) Corporation; **555:** (right above) PhotoDisc, Inc.; **556:** (left center) National Library of Medicine, #A-13394; **556:** (left below) National Library of Medicine, neg. 93072; **556:** (right) Photo by Ken Smith of painting in Harrisburg State Hospital/LLR Collection; **557:** (right) © Bernard Gotfryd/Woodfin Camp & Associates; **557:** (left) AP/Wide World Photos; **558:** (right) PhotoDisc, Inc.; **559:** (left) S. Wanke/ PhotoLink/PhotoDisc, Inc.; **561:** (bottom) Mary Evans /Sigmund Freud Copyrights/Sulloway; **566:**

(center) Digital Stock Corporation; **566:** (left) PhotoDisc, Inc.; **567:** © Elizabeth Roll; **572:** © Roger Dashow/AnthroPhoto; **574:** (top) PhotoDisc, Inc.; **574:** (bottom) PhotoDisc, Inc.; **575:** (right) © Paul Buddle; **576:** (left #1) National Library of Medicine; **577:** (right #22) © Roger Dashow/ AnthroPhoto.

## Module 25

**580:** © Ralph A Clevenger/CORBIS; **581:** (right) Channel 9 Australia/Gamma Agency; **581:** (left) © Ted Hardin; **582:** (bottom right) By permission of Dr. Victor Johnston, author of *Why We Feel;* **582:** (top) © Ted Hardin; **582:** (bottom left) AP/Wide World Photos; **583:** (below left) PhotoDisc, Inc.; **583:** (below right) PhotoDisc, Inc.; **584:** (left) PhotoDisc, Inc.; **584:** (right) PhotoDisc, Inc.; **584:** (center below) PhotoDisc, Inc.; **584:** (center above) © James Wilson/Woodfin Camp & Associates; **585:** (top) © Robert Johnson/Liaison Agency; **585:** (right) PhotoDisc, Inc.; **586:** (left) PhotoDisc, Inc.; **586:** (right) PhotoDisc, Inc.; **586:** (center above) Vince Campagnore/*Los Angeles Times* Photo; **587:** (center) PhotoDisc, Inc.; **587:** (left) PhotoDisc, Inc.; **588:** (center & right) AP/Wide World Photos; **588:** (left) PhotoDisc, Inc.; **589:** © Wade Spees; **590:** Photo by A. L. Wendrof, courtesy of the Anti Defamation League of B'nai B'rith, San Francisco and Gregory Withrow; **591:** (below) © 1997 Gregory Pace/ CORBIS-Sygma; **591:** (center above) © Reuters News Media-Jason Cohn/CORBIS; **592:** (left) Channel 9 Australia/Liaison Agency; **592:** (right) *Dallas Morning News*/Gamma Agency; **595:** Alan Weiner/*New York Times* Photo; **596:** (left) *People Weekly* © 1993 Taro Yamasaki; **596:** (right) Jim LoScalzo/*U.S. News & World Report;* **597:** (right) © Dan Miller/ Woodfin Camp & Associates; **597:** (center) Reuters/ CORBIS-Bettmann; **597:** (left) © Bill Ross/Woodfin Camp & Associates; **598:** (left) PhotoDisc, Inc.; **598:** (right) PhotoDisc, Inc.; **599:** (left #1) © Ted Hardin; **599:** (right #13) © Bill Ross/Woodfin Camp & Associates; **599:** (left #4) PhotoDisc, Inc.; **599:** (left #8) Photo by A. L. Wendrof, courtesy of the Anti Defamation League of B'nai B'rith, San Francisco and Gregory Withrow; **599:** (right #15) PhotoDisc, Inc.; **599:** (right #6) PhotoDisc, Inc.; **599:** (right #10) © Reuters News Media-Jason Cohn/CORBIS; **600:** (right) © Zig Leszcynski/Animals Animals; **601:** (left bottom) PhotoDisc, Inc.; **601:** (center above) PhotoDisc, Inc.; **602:** (center) PhotoDisc, Inc.; **602:** (left/ right) PhotoDisc, Inc.; **603:** (bottom) © Thomas Hartwell/ Saba Press Photos; **604:** (center below) PhotoDisc., Inc.; **604:** (right) ©Topham/OB/The Image Works; **604:** (left) © Arte & Imagini srt/CORBIS; **605:** (center) PhotoDisc, Inc.; **606:** (left #1) © James Wilson/Woodfin Camp & Associates; **606:** (left #5) PhotoDisc, Inc.; **606:** (right #9) © ReutersNewsMedia-Jason Cohn/ CORBIS; **607:** (right #20) PhotoDisc., Inc.; **607:** (left #13) Jim LoScalzo/*U.S. News & World Report;* **608:** PhotoDisc, Inc.

This page constitutes an extension of the copyright page. We have made every effort to trace the ownership of all copyrighted material and to secure permission from copyright holders. In the event of any question arising as to the use of any material, we will be pleased to make the necessary corrections in future printings. Thanks are due to the following authors, publishers, and agents for permission to use the material indicated.

## Module 1

**6:** Bottom graph: Graph data from "Changes in the Palmar Sweat Index During Mental Arithmetic," by T. Kohler and U. Troester, 1991, *Biological Psychology, 32,* 143–154; **7:** Graph data from "Isolating Gender Differences in Test Anxiety: A Confirmatory Factor Analysis of the Test Anxiety Inventory," by Howard T. Everson, Roger E. Millsap, & Caroline M. Rodriguez, 1991, *Educational and Psychological Measurement, 51,* p. 247; **8:** Bar graph data from "The Relationship of Self-Management to Academic Motivation, Study Efficiency, Academic Satisfaction, and Grade Point Average Among Prospective Education Majors," by J. D. Long, P. Gaynor, A. Erwin and R. L. Williams, 1994, *Psychology: A Journal of Human Behavior, 31,* 22–30; **16:** Graph data from "Comparison of Self-Questioning, Summarizing, and Notetaking-Review as Strategies for Learning from Lectures," by A. King, 1992, *American Educational Research Journal, 29,* 303–23; **17:** Pie graph data from "Psychological Science Around the World," by M. R. Rosenzweig, 1992, *American Psychologist, 47,* 718–22; **21:** Excuses list from "Excuses, Excuses," by D. A. Bernstein, 1993, *APS Observer,* March, 1993 p. 4. Copyright © 1993 by the American Psychological Society. Reprinted by permission of the author.

## Module 2

**30:** Bar graph data from "Aspartame, Behavior, and Cognitive Function in Children with Attention Deficit Disorder," by B.A Shaywitz, C. M. Sullivan, G. Anderson, S. M. Gillespie, B. Sullivan & S. E. Shaywitz, *Pediatrics, 93,* 70–5; **44:** Adapted from "Frequent Sexual Activity May Help Men Live Longer, Study Finds" by Lawrence K. Altman, 1997, New York Times News Service. Copyright © 1997 by The New York Times Company. Adapted by permission.

## Module 3

**46:** Detail from illustration by John Karapelou in Discover, January 1998, p. 67. Copyright © 1998 by Discover (Disney Magazine Publishing, Inc.); **64:** Article adapted from S. Lafee, "At Hand and Ahead." *San Diego Union-Tribune,* March 8, 2000, p. E–1.

## Module 4

**68:** Chromosome drawing (right) redrawn by permission from an illustration on page 126 by Michael Goodman in "DNA's New Twists," by

John Rennie, *Scientific American,* March, 1993. All rights reserved; **70:** (right) From "A Head for Figures," by Brian Butterworth, *Science, 284,* p. 928, by permission of B. Butterworth; **79:** From "Language Specificity and Elasticity: Brain and Clinical Syndrome Studies," by M. Maratsos and L. Matheny, 1994, *Annual Review of Psychology, 45,* 487–516; **84:** Figures (left) adapted from "Sex Differences in the Brain," by D. Kimura, 1992, *Scientific American, 267,* 119–125; **90:** Article adapted from "Brain damage during infancy stunts moral learning, study finds," by Sandra Blakesless, New York Times News Service in *The Los Angeles Times,* October 9. 1999, A–1.

## Module 5

**97:** (bottom right) Adapted from *Images of the Mind* by M. I. Posner & M. E. Raichle, 1994. W. H. Freeman and Company; **99:** (bottom right) Courtesy of Graham-Field, Inc.; **114:** John Karapelou/© 1993 The Walt Disney Co. Reprinted with permission of *Discover Magazine;* **114:** (top & left) Illustration by K. Daniel Clark from "Newsfronts-Science & Technology," by Dawn Stover, *Popular Science,* August 1997 p. 29. Reprinted by permission; **117:** (right #20) John Karapelou/© 1993 The Walt Disney Co. Reprinted with permission of *Discover Magazine;* **118:** Adapted from J. Weiss, "So-called Mozart Effect May be (yawn) Just a Dream," *San Diego Union-Tribune,* 2/12/2000, p. E–5.

## Module 6

**135:** Bar graph (right) based on data from "Emotion congruence in Perception," by P. M. Niedenthal and M. C. Sutterlund, *Personality and Social Psychology, 20,* 401–411; **139:** Corel Gallery; **144:** Excerpt from *San Diego Union-Tribune,* December 2, 1997, p. E–3. Used by permission of Scripps Howard News Service.

## Module 7

**147:** Living in a cave text adapted from an article in Newsweek, June 5, 1989; **155:** Temperature graph adapted from *Wide Awake at 3am by Choice or Chance?* by R. M. Coleman. Coyright © 1986 by Richard M. Coleman. Used with permission of W. H. Freeman and Company; **166:** Adapted from "Interns' Long Workdays Prompt First Crackdown," by Robert Pear, *The New York Times,* June 11, 2000, p. 2D; "Hi, I'm Your Doctor. I Haven't Slept in 36 Hours," by S. L. Cohen, *USA Today,* March 22, 2000, p. 29A.

## Module 8

**170:** Bar graph data from "Individual Differences in Response to Hypnosis," by B. L. Bates, 1994. In J. W. Rhue, S. J. Lynn & I. Kirsch (Eds.), *Handbook of Clinical Hypnosis.* American Psychological Association; **173:** Bar graph on left Adapted from "Effects of Hypnosis on Regional Cerebral Blood Flow During Ischemic Pain with and without

Suggested Hypnotic Analgesia," by H. J. Crawford, R. C. Gur, B. Skolnick, R. E. Gur & D. M. Benson, *International Journal of Psychophysiology, 15,* 181–195; **173:** Bar graph on right Adapted from "A Randomized Trial Comparing Smoking Cessation Programs Utilizing Behavior Modification, Health, Education or Hypnosis," by S. W. Rabkin, E. Boyko, F. Shane & J. Kaufert, 1984, *Addictive Behaviors, 9,* 157-173; **178:** Bar graph data from "Actual Causes of Death in the United States," by J. M. McGinnis and W. H. Foege, 1993, *Journal of the American Medical Association, 270,* 2207–2212; **188:** Adapted from "How AA Works and Why It's Important for Clinicians to Understand," by E. J. Khantzian and J. E. Mack, 1994, *Journal of Substance Abuse Treatment, 11,* 77–92.

## Module 9

**195:** Adapted from "Cross-Cultural Validity of a Parent's Version of the Dental Fear Survey Schedule for Children in Chinese," by P. Milgrom, J. Z Quang, K. M. Tay, 1994, *Behavior Research and Therapy, 32,* 131–135; **196:** Bar graph data from "Pitch Discrimination in the Dog," by H. M. Anrep, 1920, *Journal of Physiology, 53,* 367–385; **206:** Adapted from "Emotional Fainting and the Psychophysiologic Response to Blood and Injury: Autonomic Mechanisms and Coping Strategies," by A. Steptoe and J. Wardle, 1988, *Psychosomatic Medicine, 50,* 402–417; **210:** Adapted from "Study: Olestra Chips Score Well in Digestive Test," by Nanci Hellmich, *USA Today,* January 14, 1998. Copyright © 1998 by *USA Today.* Adapted by permission.

## Module 10

**214:** Graph on right Based on *Behavior of Organisms,* by B. F. Skinner, 1938. Appleton-Century-Crofts; **215:** Skinner box illustration from *Introduction to Psychology* by E. Bruce Goldstein, 1995. Brooks/Cole; **216:** Adapted from "Treating Chronic Food Refusal in young Children: Home-Based Parent Training," by M. A. Werle, T. B. Murphy & K. S. Budd, 1993, *Journal of Applied Behavior Analysis, 26,* 421–433; **218:** Graph adapted from "Discrimination Training in the Treatment of Pica and Food Scavenging," by C. R. Johnson, F. M. Hunt & J. J. Siebert, 1994, *Behavior Modification, 18,* 214–229; **219:** Bar graph data from "A Comparison of Shock Intensity in the Treatment of Longstanding and Severe Self-Injurious Behaviors," by D. E. Williams, S. Kirkpatrick-Sanchez & B. A. Iwata, 1993, *Research in Development Disabilities, 14,* 207–219; **220:** Reinforcement diagram from *Psychology: Themes and Variations,* by Wayne Weiten, 2nd ed., figure 6.13. Copyright © 1992 by Wadsworth, Inc. Reproduced by permission; **220:** Skinner box illustration from *Introduction to Psychology* by E. Bruce Goldstein, 1995. Brooks/Cole; **223:** (left) Skinner box illustration from *Introduction to Psychology* by E. Bruce Goldstein, 1995, Brooks/Cole; **224:** Bar graph data from "Influence of Models' Reinforcement Contingenices on the

# Figure/Text Credits

Acquisition of Imitative Responses," by A. Bandura, 1965, *Journal of Personality and Social Psychology, 1,* 589–596; **225:** Bar graph data from "Relative Efficacy of Densensitization and Modeling Approaches for Inducing Behavior, Affective and Attitudinal Changes" by A. Bandura, E. B. Blanchard & B. Ritter, 1969, *Journal of Personality and Social Psychology, 13,* 173–179; **227:** (left #1) Skinner box illustration from *Introduction to Psychology* by E. Bruce Goldstein, 1995. Brooks/Cole; **230:** Graph from "Analysis of a High-Probability Instructional Sequence and Time-Out in the Treatment of Child Noncompliance," by A. K. Rortvedt and R. G. Miltenberger, 1994, *Journal of Applied Behavior Analysis, 27,* 327–330, figure 1a. Copyright © 1993 Society for the Experimental Analysis of Behavior. Reprinted by permission of the author; **232:** Bar graph data from "Behavioral Treatment and Normal Educational and Intellectual Functioning in Young Autistic Children," by O. I. Lovaas, 1987, *Journal of Consulting and Clinical Psychology, 55,* 3–9; **236:** Adapted from M.D. Lemonick, "Spare the Rod? Maybe," *Time,* August 25, 1997, 65; L. Rosellini, "When to Spank," *U.S. News & World Report,* April 15, 1998, 52–58; B. Schulte, "Spanking Backfires, the Latest Study Says," Knight-Ridder; appeared in *San Diego Union-Tribune,* August 15, 1997, A1.

## Module 11

**241:** Bar graph data from "The Information Available in Brief Visual Presentations," by G. A. Sperling, 1960, *Psychological Monographs, 74* (Whole No. 498); **242:** Graph data from "Short-Term Retention of Individual Verbal Items," by L. R. Peterson and M. J. Peterson, 1950, *Journal of Experimental Psychology, 58,* 193–198; **244:** Bar graph data from "Accuracy and Distortion in Memory for High School Girls," by H. P. Bahrick, L. K. Hall & S. A. Berger, 1996, *Psychological Science, 7,* 265–271; **245:** Graph data from "Two Storage Mechanisms in Free Recall," by M. Glanzer and A. R. Cunitz, 1966, *Journal of Verbal Learning and Verbal Behavior, 5,* 351–360; **247:** Bar graph data from "B-Adrenergic Activation and Memory for Emotional Events," by L. Cahill, B. Prins, M. Webert & J. McGaugh, 1994, *Nature, 371,* 702–704; **249:** Bar graph data from "Depth of Processing and the Retention of Words in Episodic Memory," by E. I. M. Craik and E. Tulving, 1975, *Journal of Experimental Psychology, General, 104,* 268–294; **251:** Bar graph data from "Repressed memory Accusations: Devastated Families and Devastated Patients," by E. F. Loftus, 1997, *Applied Cognitive Psychology, 11,* 25–30; **253:** Excerpt from *Remembering: A Study in Experimental and Social Psychology,* by F. C. Bartlett, p. 65, 1932. Cambridge University Press. Copyright © 1932. Reprinted with the permission of Cambridge University Press; **253:** Bar graph data from "Repeated Memory of Oral Prose in Ghana and New York," by B. M. Ross and C. Millson, 1970, *International Journal of Psychology, 5,* 173–181; **255:** Adapted from "Vivid Memories," by D. C. Rubin and M. Kozin, 1984,

*Cognition, 16,* 81–95. Copyright © 1984 by Elsevier Science Publishers BV. Adapted by permission from Elsevier Science; **258:** (Sauer, August 29, 1993, p. D2.) (Adapted from "Decade of Accusations" by M. Sauer, *San Diego Union-Tribune,* August 29, 1993, D1.)

## Module 12

**261:** Adapted from "Nearly 2,000 Witnesses Can Be Wrong," by R. Buckout, 1980, *Bulletin of the Psychonomic Society, 16,* 307–310; **262:** Memory figure based on Learning and Memory, by D. A. Norman, 1982. W. H. Freeman & Company; **263:** Network hierarchy based on "Retrieval Time from Semantic Memory," by A. M. Collins and M. R. Quillian, 1969, *Verbal Learning and Verbal Behavior, 8,* 240–247; **264:** Graph (bottom) data from "Fifty Years of Memory for Names and Faces," by H. P. Bahrick, P. O. Bahrick & R. P. Wittlinger, 1975, *Journal of Experimental Psychology: General, 104,* 54–75; **272:** Bar graph data from "Visual Spatial Memory in Australian Aboriginal Children of Desert Regions," by J. M. Kearins, 1981, *Cognitive Psychology, 13,* 434–460; **273:** Bar graph data from "Repeatedly Thinking About a Non-Event: Source Misattributions Among Pre-Schoolers," by S. J. Ceci , M. L. C. Huffman, E. Smith & E. Loftus, 1994, *Consciousness and Cognition, 3,* 388–407; **278:** Adapted from "Second Time Around," by Michael Haederle, *Los Angeles Times,* May 23, 1996 p. E–1. Copyright © 1996 by *Los Angeles Times.* Adapted by permission of the publisher.

## Module 13

**287:** (center) Graphs: Adapted from "Age and WAIS-R A Cross-Sectional Analysis with Educational Level Controlled, " by A. S. Kaufman, C. R. Reynolds & J. E. McLean, 1989, *Intelligence, 13,* pp. 246, 247. Copyright © 1989 by Ablex Publishing Company. Adapted by permission; **292:** Bar graph data from "Familial Studies of Intelligence: A Review," by T. J. Bouchard and M. McGue, 1981, *Science, 212,* 1055–1059. American Association for the Advancement of Science; **294:** Graph adapted with the permission of The Free Press, a Division of Simon & Schuster Inc. from *The Bell Curve: Intelligence and Class Structure in American Life,* by Richard Hernstein and Charles Murray, 1994, p. 279. Copyright © 1994 Richard J. Hernstein and Charles Murray; **295:** (right #7) Graph adapted from "Age and WAIS-R A Cross-Sectional Analysis with Educational Level Controlled," by A. S. Kaufman, C. R. Reynolds & J. E. McLean, 1989, *Intelligence, 13,* pp. 246, 247. Copyright © 1989 by Ablex Publishing Company. Adapted by permission; **297:** (below) From "A Head for Figures," by Brian Butterworth, *Science, 284,* p. 928. By permission of B. Butterworth; **299:** Graph adapted from "Young Children Grow Up: The Effects of the Perry Preschool Program on Youth Through Age 15," by L. J. Schweinhart and D. P. Weikart, 1980, *Monographs of the High/Scope Educational Research Foundation,* 1980, No. 7. Courtesy of L. J.

Schweinhart; **301:** (right #15) From "A Head for Figures," by Brian Butterworth, *Science, 284,* p. 928. By permission of B. Butterworth; **302:** Adapted from S. Braun, "Max the Bookie Won't Stop and That's a Sure Thing," *Los Angeles Times,* August 7, 1999, A1.

## Module 14

**309:** Top left and p. 317: Adapted from *Conceptional Blockbusting: A Guide to Better Ideas,* by James L. Adams, pp. 17–18. Copyright © 1974 by James L. Adams. Used with permission of W. H. Freeman & Co., Publishers; **311:** Bar graph data from "Creativity and Psychopathology: A Study of 291 World-Famous Men," by F. Post, 1994, *British Journal of Psychiatry, 165,* 22–34; **314:** (top right) From Conel, J. L. 1939, 1941, 1959 *The Postnatal Development of the Human Cerebral Cortex, 6 Volumes,* Cambridge: Harvard; **321:** (center) From Corel 2, p. B138; **326:** Article adapted from "The Language of Learning," by Robert Lee Hotz, 1997, *Los Angeles Times,* Sept. 18, 1997, p. B2. Copyright © 1997 by the *Los Angeles Times.* Adapted by permission of the publisher.

## Module 15

**342:** Bar graph data from *The Social Organization of Sexuality,* by E. Laumann, R. T. Michael, J. H. Gagnon & G. Kolata, 1994. University of Chicago Press; **348:** (TAT) From *Abnormal Psychology* by Barlow/Durand, 2/E, pg 79. Copyright © 1997. Brooks/Cole Publishing; **351:** Math scores data from *National Educational Longitudinal Study of 1988,* National Opinon Research Center, University of Chicago.

## Module 16

**370:** (center) Redrawn from an illustration by John Tom Seetin in "Working Knowlege," *Scientific American, 277*(6), December, 1997, p. 132. Reprinted by permission the illustrator. All rights reserved; **371:** Bar graph data from "Detection of Deception: Polygraph and Integrity Tests," by L. Saxe, 1994, *Current Directions in Psychological Science, 3,* 69–73.

## Module 17

**380:** Bar graph adapted from a figure in *The Developing Human: Clinically Oriented Embryology, 4th ed.,* by Keith L. Moore. W. B. Saunders Co., Copyright © 1988 by Keith L. Moore. Adapted by permission of the author; **387:** Data from "Temperamental Factors in Human Development," by J. Kagan and N. Snidman, *American Psychologist, 46,* 856–862; **387:** Data from "Biology and the Child," by J. Kagan, 1998. In W. Damon and R. M. Lerner (Eds.), *Handbook of Child Psychology, Vol. 1.* John Wiley & Sons, Inc.; **391:** *Jean Piaget* © Etienne Delessert; **404:** Adapted from "An Angry Child Can Change" by Michael Ryan, Parade, April 14, 1996 pp. 20–21. Copyright © 1996 by *Parade.* Reprinted by permission of Parade and Scovil, Chichak & Galen Literary Agency on behalf of the author.

## Module 18

**407:** Adapted from the *Los Angeles Times,* December 22, 1991, p. E–1, E–12; **407:** Adapted from *Midterm Report,* by D. Wallechinsky, 1986. Viking Press; **409:** Bar graph data from "Sexual Behavior of American Adolescents: Results from a U.S. National Survey," by B. C. Leigh, D. M. Morrison, K. Trocki & M. T. Temple, 1994, *Journal of Adolescent Health, 15,* 117–125; **410:** Adapted from the *Los Angeles Times,* December 22, 1991, p. E–13; **413:** Excerpt from *Parade Magazine,* July 14, 1991, pp. 6–7 Reprinted with permission from Parade. Copyright © 1991; **420:** List adapted from "Preferences in Human Mate Selection," by D. M. Buss and M. Barnes, 1986, *Journal of Personality and Social Psychology, 7,* 3–15. American Psychological Association; **423:** List [bottom] adapted from "International Preferences in Selecting Mates," by D. M. Buss, M. Abbott, A. Angleitner, A. Asherian, A. Biaggio, A. Blanoco-Villasenor, A. Bruchon-Scwietzer, H. Y. Ch'U, J. Czapinski, B. Deraad, B. Ekehammar, N. E. Lohamy, M. Fioravanti, J. Georgas, P. Gjerde, R. Guttmann, E. Hazan, S. Iwawaki, H. Jankiramaiah, F. Khosroshani, D. Kreitler, L. Lachenicht, M. Lee, K. Kiik, B. Little, S. Mika, M., Moadel-Shahid, G. Moane, M. Montero, A. C. Mundy-Castle, T. Niit, E. Nsenduluka, R. Pienkowski, A. M. Pirttila-Backman, L. P. DeLeon, J. Rousseau, M. A. Runco, M. P. Safir, C. Samuels, R. Sanitioso, R. Serpell, N. Simid, C. Spencer, M. Tadinac, E. N. Tordorova, Z. K. Troland, L. Van Den Brande, G. Van Heck, L. Van Langenhove & K. S. Yang, 1990, *Journal of Cross-Cultural Personality, 21,* 5–47; **423:** List [center] adapted from "Mate Preferences in 37 Cultures," by D. M. Buss , 1994. In W. J. Lonner & R. Malpass (Eds.), *Psychology and Culture.* Allyn & Bacon; **426:** Center text adapted from *People Magazine,* May 21, 1990, pp. 56–59.

## Module 19

**450:** (TAT) From *Abnormal Psychology* by Barlow/Durand, 2/E, p. 79. Copyright © 1997. Brooks/Cole Publishing; **451:** (TAT) From *Abnormal Psychology* by Barlow/Durand, 2/E, pg. 79. Copyright © 1997. Brooks/Cole Publishing; **454:** Adapted from "Friends, Others Offer Complex View of Rathbun," by Robert J. Lopez and Eric Slater, Los Angeles Times, December 11, 1995, p. B–1. Copyright © 1995 by *Los Angeles Times.* Adapted by permission of the publisher.

## Module 20

**456:** Courtesy of Sony Electronics Corporation; **467:** Bar graph data from "Genes, Environment, and Personality," by T. J. Bouchard, 1994, *Science, 264,* 1700–1701. American Association for the Advancement of Science; **468:** Bar graph data from "Genes, Environment, and Personality," by T. J. Bouchard, 1994, *Science, 264,* 1700–1701. American Association for the Advancement of Science; **471:**

Bar graph data from "Cultural Styles of Conflict Management in Japanese and Americans: Passivity, Covertness and Effectiveness of Strategies," by K. Ohbushi and Y. Takahaski, 1994, *Journal of Applied Social Psychology, 24,* 1345–1366; **475:** (center top) Corel Gallery; **478:** Adapted from "Companies Using Personality Tests for Making Hire That Fit," by Carol Smith, *Los Angeles Times,* February 9, 1997 p. D5. Copyright © 1997 by Los Angeles Times. Adapted by permission of the publisher.

## Module 21

**481:** Text about Sandra Sullivan, adapted from an article by Sasha Nyary, *Life Magazine,* April, 1992 pp. 62–65; **483:** Bar graph data from "The Use of Cognitive Appraisal to Reduce Stress Reactions: A Replication," by A. C. Dandoy and A. G. Goldstein, 1990, *Journal of Social Behavior and Personality, 5,* 272–285; **483:** Situation list data from *USA Today,* August 19, 1987, p. 4D; **486:** List Adapted from "The Factor Structure of Self-Reported Physical Stress Reactions," by J. C. Smith and J. M. Seidel, 1982, *Biofeedback and Self-Regulation, 7,* 35–47; **488:** Bar graph data from "Psychological Stress and Susceptibility to the Common Cold," by S. Cohen, D. A. J. Tyrrell & A. P. Smith, 1997, *New England Journal of Medicine, 325,* 606–612; **490:** Scale: Reprinted from *Journal of Psychosomatic Research,* 11 by T. H. Holmes and R. H. Rahe in "The Social Readjustment Rating Scale," 213–218, Copyright © 1967, with permission from Elsevier Science; **490:** Text about Sandra Sullivan, adapted from an article by Sasha Nyary, *Life Magazine,* April, 1992 pp. 62–65; **494:** Graph adapted from "Hardiness and Stress Moderation: A Test of Proposed Mechanisms," by D.J. Wiebe, 1991, *Journal of Personality and Social Psychology, 60,* pp. 89–99, p. 94. American Psychological Association; **495:** Bar graph data from "Stress and Illness: Controllable and Uncontrollable Life Events' Relative Contributions," by G. S. Stern, T. R. McCants & P.W. Pettine, 1982, *Personality and Social Psychology Bulletin, 8,* 140–143; **497:** Probability graph data from "Social Support, Negative Life Events and Mental Health," by O. S. Dalgard, S. Bjork & K. Tambs, 1995, *British Journal of Psychiatry, 166,* 29–34; **497:** Change in blood pressure data from "Social Support Lowers Cardiovascular Reactivity to an Acute Stressor," by S. J. Lepore, K. A. Mata Allen & G. W. Evans, 1993, *Psychosomatic Medicine, 55,* 518–524; **501:** Graph data from "Body Temperature Changes During the Practice of g Tum-mo-Yoga," by H. Bensen, J. W. Lehmann, M. S. Malhotra, R. F. Goldman, P. J. Hopkins & M. D. Epstein, 1982, *Nature, 295,* 234–235; **505:** (right #19) Graph data from "Body Temperature Changes During the Practice of g Tum-mo-Yoga," by H. Bensen, J. W. Lehmann, M. S. Malhotra, R. F. Goldman, P. J. Hopkins & M. D. Epstein, 1982, *Nature, 295,* 234–235; **506:** Adapted from "The Diagnosis," by Mary Herczog, *Los Angeles Times,* December 8, 1997, p S-1. Copyright © 1997 by the Los Angeles Times. Adapted by permission of the publisher.

## Module 22

**514:** Pages 514–515: Syndrome titles from *Diagnostic and Statistical Manual of Mental Disorders,* Fourth Edition. Copyright © 1994 American Psychiatric Association; **514:** Pages 514–520: Disorder definitions are based on descriptions in *DSM-IV,* American Psychiatric Association, 1994; **516:** Bar graph data from "Lifetime and 12-month Prevalence of DSM-III-R Psychiatric Disorders in the United States," by R. C. Kessler, K. A. McGonagle, S. Zhao, C. B. Nelson, M. Hugher, S. Eshleman, H. Wittchen & K. S. Kendler, 1994, *Archives of General Psychiatry,* 51, 8–19; **518:** Bar graphs data from "Panic and Phobia" by W. W. Eaton, A. Dryman & M. M. Weissman, 1991. In L. N. Robins & D. A. Regier (Eds.), *Psychiatric Disorders in America: The Epidemiological Catchment Area Study.* Free Press; **519:** Bar graph data from "Current Status of Pharmacological and Behavioral Treatment of Obsessive-Compulsive Disorder," by G. B. Stanley and S. M. Turner, 1995, *Behavior Therapy, 26,* 163–186; **522:** Bar graph data from "The Place of Culture in Psychiatric Nosology: Taijin Kyofusho and DSM-III-R," by L. J. Kirmayer, 1991, *Journal of Nervous and Mental Disease, 179,* 19–28; **525:** Graphs adapted from "International Advances in the Treatment of Social Phobia," by J. R. T. Davidson, 1994, *Journal of Clinical Psychiatry, 55,* 123–129; **528:** Adapted from "Prisoners of Love" by Pamela Warrick, *Los Angeles Times,* January 23, 1997, p. E–1. Copyright © 1997 by the *Los Angeles Times.* Adapted by permission of the publisher.

## Module 23

**531:** Adapted from "Breakdown into the Shadows of Mental Illness," by C. Brooks, *San Diego Union-Tribune,* February 27, 1994, p. 4; **531:** Adapted from "Shadowland: Three Profiled in Mental Illness Series Are Strving to Improve Their Condition" by C. Brooks, *San Diego Union-Tribune,* February 27, 1995; **533:** Bar graph data from "Current Perspectives on the Genetics of Unipolar Depression," by S. O. Moldin, T. Reich & J. P. Rice, 1991, *Behavior Genetics, 21,* 211–242; **535:** Excerpt from "Electroboy," by Andy Behrman, *New York Times Magazine,* January 27, 1999, p. 67. Reprinted by permission of *The New York Times;* **535:** ECT treatment graph adapted from "Use of ECT with Treatment-Resistant Depressed Patients at the National Institute of Mental Health," by S. M. Paul, I. Extein, H. M. Calil, W. Z. Potter, P. Chodiff & F. K. Goodwin, 1981, *American Journal of Psychiatry, 13,* 486–489; **535:** Bar graph data from "Use of ECT in the United States in 1975, 1980 and 1986," by J. W. Thompson, R. D. Weiner & C. P. Myers, 1994, *American Journal of Psychiatry, 151,* 1657–1661. 1995 data from "Shock Therapy," by D. Cauchon, *USA Today,* December 6, 1995; **537:** Graph data from "An Open Trial of Sertraline in Personality Disordered Patients with Impulsive Aggression," by R. J. Kavoussi, J. Liu & E. F. Caccaro, 1994, *Journal of Clinical Psychiatry, 55,*

# Figure/Text Credits

137–141; **539:** Bar graph data from *Schizophrenia Genesis: The Origins of Madness,* by I. I. Gottesmann, 1991. W. H. Freeman & Company; with additional data from "The Epidemiology of Schizophrenia in a Finnish Twin Cohort," by T. D. Cannon, J. Kaprio, J. Lonnqvist, M. Huttunen & M. Koskenvuo, 1998, *Archives of General Psychiatry, 55,* 67–74; **542:** Data from "Duration of Neuroleptic Treatment and Prevalence of Tardive Dyskinesia in Late Life," by R. A. Sweet, B. H. Mulsant, B. Gupta, A. H. Rifai, R. E. Pasternak, A. McEachran & G. S. Zubenko, 1995, *Archives of General Psychiatry, 52,* 478–486; **543:** (left #5) Bar graph data from "Current Perspectives on the Genetics of Unipolar Depression," by S. O. Moldin, T. Reich & J. P. Rice, 1991, *Behavior Genetics, 21,* 211–242; **543:** (left #7) ECT treatment graph adapted from "Use of ECT with Treatment-Resistant Depressed Patients at the National Institute of Mental Health," by S. M. Paul, I. Extein, H. M. Calil, W. Z. Potter, P. Chodiff & F. K. Goodwin, 1981, *American Journal of Psychiatry, 138,* 486–489; **545:** Bar graph data from "The diagnosis of Multiple Personality Disorder: A Critical Review, by T. A. Fahy, 1988, *British Journal of Psychiatry, 153,* 597–606; and "Multiple Identity Enactments and Multiple Personality Disorder: A Sociocognitive Perspective," by N. P. Spanos, 1994, *Psychological Bulletin, 116,* 1434–1465; **546:** Bar graph data from "Lifetime and 12-month Prevalence of DSM-III-R Psychiatric Disorders in the United States," by R. C. Kessler, K. A. McGonagle, S. Zhao, C. B. Nelson, M. Higher, S. Eshleman, H. Wittchen, & K. S. Kendler, 1994, *Archives of General Psychiatry, 51,* 8–19; **552:** Adapted from "Recovered" by Shari Roan, *Los Angeles Times,* January 30, 1996, p. E–1. Copyright © 1996 by the Los Angeles Times: Reprinted by permission of the Los Angeles Times.

## Module 24

**560:** Therapy Session Adapted from " A Critique of So-Called Standard Psychoanalytic Technique," by S. D. Lipton, 1983, *Contemporary Psychoanalysis, 19,* 35–52; **563:** Bar graph adapted from "Trends in Counseling and Psychotherapy," by D. Smith, 1982, *American Psychologist, 37,* 802–809. American Psychological Association. Adapted by permission; **564:** Therapy Session: Adapted from "Person-Centered Therapy," by N. J. Raskin and C. R. Rogers, 1989. In R. J. Corsini and D. Wedding (Eds.), *Current Psychotherapies,* 4th ed. F. E. Peacock; **565:** Therapy Session: Adapted from *Cognitive Therapy of Depression,* by A. T. Beck, A. J. Rush, B. F. Shaw & G. Emery, 1979, pp. 145–146. Guilford Press; **566:** Therapy Session: Adapted from *Clinical Behavior Therapy,* by M. R. Goldfried and G. C. Davison, 1976. Holt, Rinehart & Winston; **571:** Bar Graph adapted from "Trends in Counseling and Psychotherapy," by D. Smith, 1982, *American Psychologist, 37,* 802–809. Copyright © 1982 by the American Psychological Association. Adapted by permission; **573:** Bar graph data from "Eye Movement Desensitation: A Partial Dismantling Study," by G. Renfrey and C. R. Spates, 1994, *Journal of Behavior Therapy and Experimental Psychiatry, 25,* 231–239.

## Module 25

**587:** Bar graphs adapted from "Improving the Academic Performance of College Freshman," by T. D. Wilson and P. W. Linville, 1982, *Journal of Personality and Social Psychology, 42,* 367–376, Copyright © 1982 by the American Psychological Association. Adapted by permission of the author; **594:** Bar graph adapted from "Behavioral Study of Obedience," by S. Milgram, 1963, *Journal of Abnormal and Social Psychology, 67,* 371–378; **606:** (right #8) Bar graph adapted from "Improving the Academic Performance of College Freshman," by T. D. Wilson and P. W. Linville, 1982, *Journal of Personality and Social Psychology, 42,* 367–376, Copyright © 1982 by the American Psychological Association. Adapted by permission of the author. **608:** Adapted from "Teen Pregnancies Force Town to Grow Up" by Sheryl Stolberg, *Los Angeles Times,* November 29, 1996. Copyright © 1996 the Los Angeles Times. Adapted by permission.

**A**

Abel, T., 269
Abernethy, B., 308
Abramov, I., 98
Abramowitz, J. S., 567, 568
Abrams, D., 596
Abrams, R. L., 121, 135
Abu-Lughod, L., 367
Acklin, M. W., 451
Adan, A., 155
Adelmann, P. K., 361
Ader, F., 489
Ader, R., 488, 489
Adler, Alfred, 440
Adler, T., 411
Ainsworth, Mary, 385
Albert, M. L., 313, 316
Ali, S. I., 123
Alivisatos, B., 84
Allen, G., 73
Allen, J. E., 29, 35, 39
Alliger, G. M., 474
Allport, G. W., 462, 588
Althof, S. E., 344
Amabile, T. M., 310
Ames, Albert, 133
Anastasi, A., 33, 34
Anderson, A. K., 80
Anderson, C. A., 601
Anderson, K. J., 365
Andreasen, N. C., 538
Andrews, B., 250, 265
Angelo, B., 359
Anstis, S. M., 140
Archer, J., 342
Arkowitz, H., 571
Armbruster, B. B., 16, 21
Armeli, S., 350
Arnett, J. J., 410, 415
Aronow, E., 451
Aronson, E., 590
Asch, Solomon, 592
Aserinsky, E., 153
Atkinson, John W., 331, 348, 349
Atkinson, R. C., 245
Attias, J., 105
Audrain, J. E., 336
Averill, J. R., 366
Azar, B., 84, 334, 600, 604

**B**

Babyak, M., 547
Bacaltchuk, J., 353
Baddeley, A., 240, 242
Bahrick, H. P., 244, 264
Bailey, J. M., 343
Bailey, M. J., 343
Bakker, A., 517
Baldessarini, R. J., 534
Baldwin, J. D., 342, 399

Baldwin, J. I., 342, 399
Balint, K., 350
Ball, G. F., 49
Baltes, P. B., 415
Balzar, J., 157
Banaji, M. R., 319, 583
Banati, R. B., 77
Bandura, Albert, 8, 196, 223, 224, 225, 231, 331, 394, 458, 459, 460, 461, 473, 493, 601
Barber, T. X., 170
Barinaga, M., 14, 49, 60, 61, 106
Barkley, R. A., 32
Barling, J., 20
Barlow, D. H., 344, 437, 510, 511, 512, 518, 520, 546, 557
Barnard, N. D., 41
Barnett, S., 299
Baron, R., 591
Barongan, C., 605
Barsky, A. J., 520
Bartoshuk, L. M., 106, 107
Basco, M. R., 568
Bashore, T. R., 370, 371
Basil, R., 287, 451
Bassili, J. N., 588
Basso, A., 78
Bateman, A. W., 537
Bates, B. L., 170, 173
Bates, J., 384
Bateson, P., 228
Batson, C. D., 595
Baum, D., 179
Baum, G., 589
Baumeister, R. F., 332, 597
Baumrind, Diana, 341, 413
Baxter, L. R., 519
Bear, M. E., 77
Beauchamp, G. K., 106, 107
Beck, Aaron T., 548, 549, 565, 568
Bednekoff, P. A., 229
Begleiter, H., 183
Begley, S., 68, 80, 322, 512
Begum, S., 123
Behrman, A., 535
Bell, B., 352
Bell, S. M., 10
Belsky, J., 401
Bem, Daryl J., 138, 139, 590
Bem, S. L., 395
Bendersky, M., 381
Benes, F. M., 540
Benin, M. H., 420
Benjamin, L. T., Jr., 12

Benson, H., 487, 501, 503
Benson, J. B., 391
Berg, C. A., 287
Berger, J., 31
Bergin, A. E., 557, 559, 571
Berk, L. B., 216
Berkowitz, Leonard, 600, 601
Berlin, S. S., 549
Berman, A. L., 427
Berman, M. E., 600
Bermond, B., 360
Berney, T. P., 3, 4, 6
Bernstein, D. A., 21
Bernstein, P. W., 457
Berscheid, E., 419
Best, D. L., 399, 418
Betancourt, H., 11
Biederman, J., 29
Biehl, M., 367
Billick, S. B., 400
Billy, J. O. G., 34
Binet, Alfred, 284, 285, 290
Birch, D., 331
Bjorklund, A., 51
Black, D. W., 537
Blagys, M. D., 562
Blais, M. A., 534
Blakely, M. R., 5, 8
Blakeslee, S., 4, 49, 70
Blass, T., 594
Blendon, R. J., 427
Bliwise, D. L., 156
Block, J., 416, 468
Block, R. I., 186
Blunt, A. K., 9, 21
Boddy, J., 546
Boden, M. A., 310
Bodenhausen, G. V., 584
Boivin, D. B., 151, 155, 156
Bond, R. R., 592
Bondurant, B., 605
Booth-Kewley, S., 496
Bootzin, R. R., 162, 575
Borella, P., 488
Born, J., 156
Borrello, G. M., 419
Botting, J. H., 41
Bouchard, T. J., Jr., 293, 294, 336, 466, 467, 468
Bourgon, L. N., 535
Bovbjerg, D. H., 195, 206
Bowden, C. L., 534
Bower, B., 79, 200, 251, 382
Bower, F., 308, 314
Bower, G. H., 240
Bowlby, John, 385

Boykin, A. W., 291
Bradley, C. J., 417
Bradley, S. J., 340
Bragg, R., 513
Brauer, M., 598
Braun, A. R., 161
Brecher, E. M., 174
Brennan, J., 213
Brennan, P. A., 537
Breu, G., 384
Breuer, J., 555
Breznitz, S., 491
Brickman, P., 366
Briere, J., 265
Briggs, J. L., 367
Broca, Paul, 284
Brody, H., 31
Brody, J. E., 250, 251, 289, 532
Brody, N., 282, 283, 284, 285, 298, 299, 352
Brooks, C., 531, 532, 538, 539, 541
Brown, D., 401
Brown, G. R., 113
Brown, R., 255
Brown, S. C., 240, 244, 245, 249, 267
Brown, S. L., 228
Brownlee, S., 228
Brown, W. A., 31, 111
Bruck, M., 273
Bruer, J. T., 314, 441
Bruner, J., 391
Brzezinski, A., 151
Brzustowicz, L. M., 539
Buch, G., 232
Buchanan, C., 409
Buck, L., 107
Buckley, P., 561, 562
Buckout, R., 261
Buehler, R., 20
Bugental, B. B., 393
Bugental, J. F. T., 446
Bunce, S. C., 135
Buonomano, D. V., 229
Burge, D., 385
Burnham, D., 382
Buss, D., 418
Buss, D. M., 342, 366, 399, 420, 423
Butler, A. C., 549
Butler, K., 239, 250
Butterworth, B., 70
Byerley, W., 539
Byne, W., 341
Bynner, J. M., 449
Byrd, K. R., 250

**C**

Cabeza, R., 242, 246, 268
Cacioppo, J. T., 81, 360, 362, 591
Cadoret, R. J., 396

Cahill, L., 247
Caldwell, J. C., 346
Calkins, Mary, 14
Callahan, C. M., 283
Calvo, M. G., 7, 242
Camacho, L. M., 598
Camp, G. C., 310
Campbell, R. A., 298
Canino, G. J., 185
Cannon, T. D., 539
Caplan, N., 448
Caplan, P., 516
Carducci, B. J., 449, 459, 495
Carey, K. B., 124
Carey, M. P., 344
Cariaga, D., 292
Carlin, Albert, 141
Carlsmith, J. M., 590
Carlson, J. M., 591
Carlson, N. R., 335, 336, 339
Carpenter, S., 486, 502
Carreiras, M., 7
Carskadon, M., 156
Carton, J. S., 459
Cartwright, Rosalind, 160
Casey, D. E., 541, 542
Caspi, A., 378, 384, 391, 416, 417, 441, 465, 467
Casrkadon, M. A., 162
Cattell, H., 427
Cattell, Raymond, 462
Caverly, D. C., 20
C'deBaca, J., 470
Ceci, Stephen J., 251, 273, 291
Ceniceros, S., 113
Cerone, D., 213
Chaiken, S., 591
Chamberlin, J., 17
Chang, K., 95
Channouf, A., 135
Chapman, C. R., 112
Charney, D. A., 602
Chasnoff, I., 381
Chavez, S., 218
Chellappah, N. K., 205
Chen, J., 74
Chen, Y., 113
Chess, S., 384
Chokroverty, S., 163
Chomsky, Noam, 311
Christensen, D., 381
Christensen, K., 533
Christopher, K., 31
Chwalisz, K., 360
Cialdini, R. B., 592, 593, 597
Ciarrochi, J. V., 369, 370
Cirelli, C., 73
Clancy, S. A., 251
Clark, L. A., 513, 515, 516

Clarke, A. D. B., 298
Clarke, A. M., 298
Clarke, J. C., 518
Clay, R. A., 205, 427, 503
Cleveland, H. H., 349
Clifford, B. R., 275
Clopton, J. R., 474
Cloud, J., 181
Coatsworth, J. D., 394
Coccaro, E. F., 537
Coffin, J., 201
Cohen, A., 182, 522, 546
Cohen, D. B., 160
Cohen, J., 345
Cohen, J. A., 494
Cohen, N., 488, 489
Cohen, N. J., 246
Cohen, S., 486, 488
Coie, J. D., 396
Colangelo, N., 289
Colapinto, J., 179
Collacott, E. A., 31
Collings, S., 353
Collins, W. A., 377, 382
Colom, R., 284
Compas, B. E., 407, 409
Conner, A., 592, 593
Connor, L., 572
Conte, J., 265
Conway, M. A., 255
Cook, D., 9
Cooley, Tatiana, 254
Coon, H., 539
Cooper, C., 596
Cooper, R. T., 298
Copeland, L., 462
Corbett, G. G., 319
Coren, S., 132, 137
Cornoldi, C., 20
Correia, C. J., 124
Corrigan, P. W., 516
Cosmides, L., 318
Costa, P. T., Jr., 393, 463, 465, 468, 536
Cottraux, J., 524, 525
Covington, M. V., 349
Covino, N. A., 173
Cowley, G., 31, 47, 48, 68, 138, 232
Coyle, J. T., 48
Coyne, J. C., 533, 548
Crabbe, J., 461, 468, 486
Craik, F. I. M., 240, 244, 245, 249, 267
Cramer, P., 437, 493
Craske, M. G., 524
Crawford, H. J., 173
Cray, D., 141
Creed, F., 486
Crews, F., 439, 441
Crick, Francis, 49
Crisp, A. H., 353
Cromer, Alan, 318

Crow, T. J., 538
Crowder, R. G., 254
Cruess, D. G., 503
Cull, W. L., 20
Culp, R. E., 445
Cunningham, C., 31
Curnow, C., 424
Curtiss, S., 316
Czeisler, Charles A., 150, 151

**D**

Dajer, T., 163
Dalgard, O. S., 497
Dalto, C. A., 591
Damasio, A. R., 49, 75, 80, 149, 412, 510
Damasio, H., 148
Damon, W., 412, 414
Dandoy, A. C., 483
Daniszewski, J., 346, 603
Darley, J. M., 595
Darling, J., 175, 177
Darwin, Charles, 69, 361, 364, 365
Davidson, G. R., 272
Davidson, J. E., 282
Davidson, J. R. T., 491, 525
Davies, I. R. L., 319
Davis, J. L., 401
Davis, M. C., 490
Davison, G. C., 517, 556, 566
Dawes, R. M., 571
Dawood, K., 343
Day, N. L., 381
DeAngelis, T., 14, 178
Deater-Deckard, K., 233
Deaux, K., 605
DeBakey, Michael, 494
deCharms, Richard, 331
Deci, Edward L., 331, 350
DeCurtis, A., 438, 450
Deffenbacher, J. L., 565, 605
DeGrandpre, R. J., 223
Dement, William C., 147, 153, 154, 157, 163
Dennerstein, L., 425
Deregowski, J. B., 136
de Rivera, J., 251
Detterman, D. K., 290
Deutsch, G., 79, 84, 87
Devine, P. G., 591
Diamond, M., 341
Diener, C., 366
Diener, E., 366
Dienes, Z., 149, 441, 563

Diforio, D., 540
Digman, J. M., 468
Dimberg, U., 149, 361
Dinsmore, J. H., 60, 61
Dion, K. K., 582
Dixon, W. A., 490
Dobelle, W., 114
Dobson, K. S., 565, 568, 571, 575
Dodge, K. A., 233, 396, 604
Doepke, K. J., 8
Dolan, M., 274, 377
Dollard, J., 601
Domhoff, G. W., 160, 161
Domino, G., 310
Donat, P. L. N., 605
Donker, F. J. S., 496
Dorfman, A., 69
Dougher, M. J., 223
Douglas, John, 509
Dowling, C. G., 267
Downes, J. J., 265
Downing, C. L., 282
Drevets, W. C., 533
Drewnowski, A., 106
Drummond, S. P. A., 151, 157
DuBois, D. L., 416
Dull, R. T., 602
Duncan, J., 297
DuPaul, G. J., 29
Durand, V. M., 344, 437, 510, 511, 512, 518, 520, 546, 557
Durlak, J. A., 344
Durso, F. T., 226
Duyme, M., 293
Dykman, B. M., 549

**E**

Eagle, M. N., 560, 562
Eagly, A. H., 340, 341, 342, 395, 396, 399, 418, 588, 591
Ebbinghaus, H., 264
Eckert, T. L., 29
Eckes, T., 340, 395, 396, 418
Eddings, J., 457
Edens, J. L., 568
Eddings, J., 457
Egan, T., 175, 177, 284, 523
Eibl-Eibesfeldt, I., 364
Eich, E., 255, 268, 544, 545
Eichenbaum, H., 246
Einstein, G. O., 249
Eisen, M. R., 172
Eisenberger, R., 350
Eisenstadt, D., 590
Ekman, P., 361, 364, 365, 367
Elias, M., 386, 387
Elkin, I., 534, 547

Elkins, D. N., 446
Elkins, I. J., 601
Ellason, J. W., 545
Elliott, D., 337
Ellis, B. J., 342
Ellison, P. A., 597
Ellsworth, P. C., 362, 367
Emery, R. E., 400, 401
Emmelkamp, P. M. G., 517, 518, 567
Ende, G., 535
Endler, N. S., 7, 365
Ennett, S. T., 187
Epley, N., 135
Erickson, Milton, 171, 173
Erikson, Erik, 393, 417
Eron, L. D., 601
Esselman, M., 589
Estevez, A., 242
Evans, J., 318
Evans, R. B., 12, 13, 14, 196
Evans, W., 352
Everson, H. T., 7
Eysenck, H. J., 571

**F**

Fackelmann, K. A., 55, 106, 186, 425
Fagot, B. I., 340
Fairburn, C. G., 337
Fann, J. R., 542
Farber, B. A., 491
Farley, C. J., 181
Fauci, A., 345
Fave, A. D., 11
Fechner, Gustav, 122
Feder, L., 287
Federman, D. D., 339
Feingold, B. R., 28, 30
Feng, A. S., 78, 103
Fernald, A., 314
Fernandez, E., 565, 568
Fernando, P., 567
Ferrari, J., 9
Ferrari, J. R., 21
Ferster, D., 108
Festinger, Leon, 590, 596
Fiez, J. A., 76
Finch, C. E., 424
Finke, R. A., 310
Finn, J. D., 349
Firestein, S., 107
Fisch, G. S., 67, 68
Fischbach, G. D., 48
Fischer, J. S., 535
Fisher, C. B., 40
Fisher, L., 500
Fishman, D. B., 566
Fishman, S., 67
FitzGerald, G. J., 330
Fitzgerald, L. F., 605

Fitzpatrick, D., 502, 503
Flavell, J. H., 391
Fletcher, C., 457
Fletcher, G. J. O., 419, 420
Flett, G. L., 548
Flippo, R. F., 20, 21
Flor, H., 58
Flores, S. A., 602
Floyd, M., 271
Foa, E. B., 491
Foege, W. S., 178
Fogel, D. B., 308
Folkman, S., 495
Fonagy, P., 537, 563
Foote, B., 545
Ford, J. G., 446
Ford-Gilboe, M., 494
Forehand, R., 230
Forsyth, B. W. C., 345
Forsyth, J. P., 201
Foster, G. D., 34
Foubert, J. D., 602
Foulks, E. G., 161
Fox, C., 353
Foxx, R. M., 219
Fragile X syndrome, 68
France, C. R., 112
Frances, A., 537
Franklin, A., 446
Franks, C. M., 566, 568
Franz, V. H., 132
Fredrickson, M., 206
Free, C., 366
Freed, C., 61
Freedman, M. S., 150
Freedman, R. R., 501
Freeman, H., 294
Freud, Sigmund, 9, 160, 173, 392, 434–441, 472, 473, 555, 556, 560, 561, 562
Freyd, J. J., 310
Frick, W. B., 333
Fricke, D., 434, 435
Friedman, H. S., 496
Friedman, M., 496
Friedman, S., 137
Friedman, S., 137
Friend, T., 31, 179, 491
Friesen, W. V., 367
Frijda, N. H., 362, 365
Frijda, N. S., 359, 364
Fritz, S., 140
Frost, M. H., 490
Fryberg, D., 40
Fucci, D., 124
Fuller, R. K., 189
Furumoto, L., 14

**G**

Gabbard, G. O., 434, 440, 441, 563
Gabrieli, J. D. E., 35
Gage, F., 87
Gage, F. H., 49

Gage, Phineas, 75
Gajilan, A. T., 51
Galaburda, A. M., 320
Galambos, N. L., 407, 408, 410
Gallopin, T., 157
Gallup, G. H., Jr., 138
Galton, Francis, 284
Gambrill, E. D., 568
Gannon, P. J., 323
Garcia, John, 200
Gardner, Allen, 323
Gardner, Beatrice, 323
Gardner, Howard, 78, 283, 286, 292, 296
Gardner, M., 160
Garety, P. A., 568
Garfield, S. L., 557, 559
Garfinkel, P. E., 353
Garland, A. R., 427
Garner, D. M., 353
Gaskell, G. D., 255
Gazzaniga, Michael S., 86
Gegax, T. T., 464
Geiger, R., 233
Geller, L., 333
Gentner, D., 307
George, K. I., 219
George, M. S., 84
Georgopoulos, A., 76
Gerlach, J., 542
Gershon, M., 335
Giacopassi, D. J., 602
Gibbon, J., 150
Gibbons, F. X., 590
Gibbs, N., 369, 377, 581, 592
Gibson, B. S., 127
Gibson, E. J., 382
Gieddes, J., 411, 412
Gigone, D., 598
Gilbert, P. L., 542
Gilbert, Roland, 446
Gillberg, C., 7
Gilligan, Carol, 412
Ginsberg, D., 534
Glantz, M. D., 174, 175
Glanzer, M., 245
Glass, S., 187
Gleick, E., 536, 589
Glenberg, A. M., 20
Gobbo, C., 251, 273
Gold, I., 49, 71
Gold, S. N., 250, 251
Goldberg, C., 343
Goldberger, L., 233, 491
Goldfried, M. R., 566
Goldstein, A. G., 483
Goldstein, A. P., 605
Goldstein, E. B., 98, 104, 125, 133
Goleman, D., 366, 369, 487

Goode, E., 136
Goodnow, J. J., 393
Gopnik, A., 391
Gordon, C. M., 70
Gordon, J., 98
Gore, R., 69
Gottesman, I. I., 466
Gottesmann, I. I., 539
Gottman, John, 420, 422
Gould, E., 49, 87
Gould, L., 359, 366
Gould, R. A., 272, 517, 567
Gould, Stephen Jay, 84, 85, 284, 290, 294, 296
Grady, D., 352
Graham, Lawrence, 581
Graham, S., 585
Granhag, P. A., 274
Granstrom, K., 598
Granvold, D. K., 502, 503, 549
Green, A. J., 245
Green, J. T., 73
Green, L., 460
Greenberg, J., 497
Greenberg, L. S., 564
Greenberg, R., 160, 435, 561
Greene, B., 352
Greene, R. L., 474
Greenfield, P. M., 11, 291
Greengard, P., 47
Greeno, J. G., 310
Greenwald, A. G., 121, 135, 583
Gregory, R. L., 128
Gresham, F. M., 4, 232
Grether, J. K., 6
Griffin, M. J., 105
Griffiths, R. R., 178
Grigorenko, E. L., 292, 293
Grimaldi, J. V., 511
Grogan, B., 596
Gron, G., 84
Gross, M. A., 207
Grunbaum, A., 435, 561
Guarnaccia, P. J., 546
Guastello, S. J., 475
Gudjonsson, G. H., 250
Guerin, D. W., 384
Guilford, J. P., 310
Gunturkun, O., 84
Gura, T., 34, 68, 336
Gureje, O., 520, 522
Gurin, J., 487
Gurman, E. B., 40
Gustavson, C. R., 200
Guthrie, J. P., 155
Guthrie, R. V., 14
Gwyer, P., 275

## H

Haber, N. R., 254
Hackbert, L., 223
Hackmann, A., 509
Hahn, C., 534
Haith, M. M., 391
Haliburn, J., 426
Hall, G. C. N., 605
Hall, G. M., 542
Halleck, Seymour, 512, 513
Halliday, J., 593
Halpern, D. F., 84, 396, 475
Hamann, S. B., 247, 268
Hamberger, J., 583
Hamilton, D. L., 581
Hammer, D., 343
Hammer, R. P., 177
Han, S., 127
Hancock, L., 35, 491
Haney, D. Q., 409, 414
Hansen, J. T., 9, 10
Hanson, G., 175, 176, 181, 186
Hardin, C., 319
Hardin, C. D., 349
Harding, C. M., 542
Hardy, J. B., 291
Harrington, P., 463
Harriott, J., 21
Harris, J. C., 316
Hart, E., 316
Hartel, C. R., 174, 175
Hartlage, S., 549
Harvey, Thomas, 297
Hasselt, V. B., 207
Hassin, R., 582
Hastie, R., 598
Hatfield, E., 419
Hausmann, M., 84
Hayes, C. H., 229
Hayes, K. J., 229
Hayne, H., 264
Haynes, S. G., 496
Healy, M., 122, 409
Heatherton, T. F., 337, 603
Heckhausen, J., 465
Heider, Fritz, 585
Helgeson, V. S., 418
Hellmich, N., 156, 162
Hellstrom, A., 123
Helson, R., 311
Helwig, C. C., 412, 414
Helzer, J. E., 185
Hendin, H., 427
Hendy, H., 445
Henker, B., 35
Henry, T., 409, 414
Henry, W. P., 563
Herbert, W., 415
Hering, Ewald, 99

Herkenham, M., 55
Herman, Louis, 322
Herman, W. E., 349
Herrenkohl, T. I., 604
Herrnstein, Richard J., 290, 294, 296
Hersen, M., 207
Herzog, W., 353
Hewitt, J. K., 336
Hewstone, H., 583
Hickey, E. W., 509, 536
Hickman, G., 413
Hidalgo, R. B., 491
Higgins, E. T., 223, 584
Hilgard, Ernest, 171
Hill, A., 58
Hill, A. B., 548
Hill, C. E., 160, 161, 564
Hill, P., 446
Hiller-Sturmhofel, S., 189
Hilsenroth, H. L., 562
Hilts, P. H., 246
Hirsch, B. J., 417
Hirschfeld, R. M. A., 534
Hirshkowitz, M., 152, 156
Hobson, J. A., 161
Hocker, J. L., 471
Hoffman, C., 319
Hoffman, H., 141
Hoffman, H. G., 275
Hoffman, P., 49
Hofmann, Albert, 169
Hohne, E. A., 314
Hokanson, J. E., 549
Holahan, C. K., 289
Holden, C., 85, 113, 284, 535
Holland, S. J., 518, 525
Hollander, E., 519
Hollis, K. L., 200, 201, 202
Hollon, S. D., 565
Holyoak, K. J., 243
Hong, Y., 321
Honorton, Charles, 138, 139
Honts, C. R., 371
Hooyman, N., 425
Horgan, J., 440, 441
Horne, A., 9
Horney, Karen, 440
Horowitz, J. M., 51
Horwath, C., 519
Hotz, R. L., 78
Houlihan, D., 219
Howard, Ruth, 14
Howieson, D. B., 512
Howlett, D., 176
Howlin, P., 4
Hsea, Y., 179
Hubel, David, 97
Huff, R., 274

Hughes, J., 55, 179
Hui, K. K. S., 113
Hull, C. L., 330
Hulse, S. H., 49
Humphreys, G. W., 127
Hunt, C., 517
Hunt, M., 12, 296
Hunter, B. A., 605
Hurovitz, 161
Hwang, C. P., 205
Hwang, S. L., 178
Hyde, J. S., 396, 412
Hyman, R., 139

## I

Iacono, W. G., 371
Irwin, M., 157
Ishai, A., 71, 263
Iversen, L. L., 186
Iwata, B. A., 219
Izard, C. E., 364, 365
Izquierdo, I., 269

## J

Jackendoff, R., 316
Jacks, J. Z., 591
Jackson, D. N., III, 348
Jackson, R. L., 370
Jackson, T., 449
Jacobson, J. L., 381
Jacobson, N. S., 420
Jacobson, S. W., 381
Jaffee, S., 412
James, William, 12, 360
Jamison, K. R., 311
Janis, Irving, 598
Janofsky, M., 187
Jansen, A. S. P., 81
Janssen, T., 459
Janus, C. L., 34
Janus, S. S., 34
Japenga, A., 516
Jelalian, E., 411
Jensen, P., 28, 35, 39
Jensen-Campbell, L. A., 582
Jiang, Y., 242
Jobes, D. A., 427
Johanson, D. C., 67
John, O. P., 463, 468
Johnsen, T. B., 205
Johnson, B. E., 602
Johnson, C. R., 218
Johnson, J. A., 462
Johnson, K., 371, 462
Johnson, L. C., 157
Johnson, V. E., 344, 425
Johnson, V. L., 183
Johnson-Laird, P. N., 360, 362
Johnston, D., 269
Johnston, V., 582
Jolley, D. J., 427

Jones, D. R., 105
Jones, E., 174, 349
Jones, K. L., 381
Jones, T. F., 520
Jorgensen, R. S., 487
Jung, Carl, 440
Jusczyk, P. W., 314

## K

Kagan, Jerome, 307, 384, 386, 387, 449
Kagitcibasi, C., 11
Kalafat, J., 427
Kalick, S. M., 582
Kalimo, R., 162
Kandel, E., 269
Kane, J. M., 541
Kanner, L., 11
Kantrowitz, B., 581, 592
Kao, G., 351
Kaplan, Donald, 449
Kaplan, R. M., 286, 287, 290, 291, 348, 450, 451, 474, 475
Kapur, S., 541
Karler, R., 177
Kassebaum, N. L., 299
Kastak, David, 322
Katz, J., 58
Kaufman, A. S., 287
Kaufman, J., 401
Kaufman, L., 132
Kaufman, S. R., 41
Kavoussi, R. J., 537
Kawachi, I., 495
Kazantzis, N., 575
Kazdin, A. E., 604
Kearns, Judith, 272
Kebbell, M. R., 275
Keefe, F. J., 112
Keel, P. K., 353
Keenan, K., 395
Keiser, R. E., 348
Keller, H., 11, 534
Keller, M. B., 547
Kelley, Harold, 585
Kellner, C. H., 535
Keltner, D., 361, 364
Kempermann, G., 49
Kendler, K. S., 175, 353, 510
Kennedy, D. V., 8
Kernberg, O. F., 561, 562
Kessler, R. C., 188, 516, 517, 518, 532, 533, 558
Ketelaar, T., 342
Khantzian, E. J., 188
Khatri, N., 565, 568, 571, 575
Kihlstrom, J. F., 149, 544
Kimball, D. R., 243
Kimura, D., 84
King, A., 16, 21

King, Frederick, 41
King, M., 353
Kinsbourne, M., 30, 36, 39
Kinsey, A. C., 34, 343
Kirk, M. S., 110
Kirmayer, L. J., 520, 522
Kirsch, Irving, 170, 171, 172, 173
Kirsner, D., 563
Kitto, J., 310
Kleijn, W. C., 10
Klein, S. B., 55
Kleinhenz, J., 113
Kleinknecht, R. Z., 482, 487, 493, 522
Kleinman, A., 522, 546
Kleitman, N., 147, 153
Klich, L. Z., 272
Klingberg, G., 205
Klingberg, T., 320
Klinger, E., 148
Kluft, R. P., 545
Kluger, J., 51
Knight, R. A., 602
Knight, S. M., 492
Knowlton, B. J., 307
Knutson, J. R., 401
Kobasa, S. C., 494
Koch, K. L., 105
Koch, W., 178, 427
Koenig, J., 602
Koffka, Kurt, 13
Köhler, Wolfgang, 13, 226
Kohyama, J., 149
Kolata, G., 334, 345
Kolko, D., 401
Koopman, J. M., 345
Koplan, J. P., 345
Kosslyn, S. M., 305
Kowalski, R. M., 497
Kozin, M., 255
Kramer, M. W., 598
Kraus, S. J., 589
Kring, B., 339
Kristof, N. D., 600
Krueger, J., 465
Kua, E. H., 572
Kubovy, M., 127
Kugelmann, R., 112
Kuhl, P. K., 314
Kulik, J., 255
Kulman, L., 101
Kurahashi, T., 107
Kurdek, L. A., 420
Kurten, B., 69
Kurtz, E., 470
Kurtz, P., 138

## L

Laborit, Henri, 557

Lach, J., 383
LaFee, S., 67, 114, 241
Laganer, A., 460
Lalich, J., 556
Lalumiere, M. L., 343
Lam, R. W., 159
Lamb, N., 231
Lambert, A. J., 582
Lambert, M. J., 559, 571
Lammers, C., 409
Lane, H., 115
Lane, S. M., 275
Lang, A. J., 524
Lang, P. J., 365
Lange, Carl, 360
Langlois, J. H., 582
Lanyado, M., 9
Lanzetta, J. T., 361
Larimer, M. E., 189
Larivee, S., 390
Larkin, K. T., 568
Larsson, G., 490
Latané, B., 595, 597
Latham, G. P., 330
Laumann, E., 341, 342, 425
Laumann-Billings, L., 400, 401
Lazarus, A. A., 207
Lazarus, Richard S., 363, 481, 482, 483, 484, 499, 502, 503
Leafgren, A., 491
Leahy, R. L., 518, 525
Leaper, C., 395
Leary, M. R., 332, 416
Leavy, J., 30
LeBlanc, L. A., 219
Lecrubier, Y., 534
LeDoux, J., 80
Leedham, B., 495
Leehotz, R., 163
Lehrer, P. M., 233
Leibel, R. L., 336, 352
Leigh, B. C., 409, 414
Leinwand, D., 179
Leippe, M. R., 590
Leland, J., 51, 343, 344
Lemerise, E. A., 604
Lemley, B., 141
Lemonick, M. D., 69, 216
Lenox, R. H., 534
Leo, J., 466
Lepore, S. J., 497
Lepper, M. K., 350
Lerner, A. G., 180
Lerner, R. M., 407, 408, 410
Leshner, A. I., 177
Lester, B. M., 381
Leung, P. W. L., 29
Leventhal, H., 496
Levine, R. V., 597
Levine, S., 602

Levitt, S., 353
Levy, D., 318
Levy, Jerre, 87
Lewin, R., 69, 322, 323
Lewinsohn, P. M., 427
Lewis, 384
Lewis, C. E., 537
Lewis, M., 381
Li, T. K., 183
Libby, L. K., 275
Lie, R. T., 380
Lieberman, M. D., 149, 196, 197, 200, 202, 223, 226
Liebert, R. M., 445, 446, 461
Liebowitz, M. R., 525
Lief, Harold, 250
Lief, L., 603
Lilienfeld, S. O., 474, 537, 545
Lilly, John, 148
Lindblom, S. S., 153, 157
Linden, E., 323
Lindenberger, U., 415
Lindsay, J. J., 601
Lindsay, R. C. L., 582
Linville, P. W., 587
Lipkin, R., 98
Lippa, R. A., 605
Lipton, S. D., 560
Lisanby, S. H., 535
Liska, K., 180, 181
Litt, M. D., 205
Little, B. R., 331
Liu, Y., 335
Locke, E. A., 330
Locker, D., 206
Lockhart, R. S., 249
Loehlin, J. C., 294
Loftus, Elizabeth F., 250, 251, 265, 275
Loftus, G. R., 275
Logothetis, N. K., 79
Logue, A. W., 200
Lohman, D. F., 283, 308
Long, J. D., 8
Lonsway, K. A., 605
Lopez, S. R., 11, 546
Lorenz, Konrad, 228, 330
Lovaas, O. Ivar, 232
Lucking, C. B., 60
Ludwig, A. M., 311
Luna, T. D., 151
Lupart, J. L., 349
Lykken, D., 366, 371
Lynam, D. R., 187
Lynn, S. J., 170, 171, 173
Lyon, R., 320

**M**
Maccoby, E. E., 401

Macfarlane, A. J., 382
Mack, J. E., 188
Mackie, D. M., 591, 592
Macklin, M. L., 573
MacLeod, C., 365
Macmillan, M., 435, 449
Macnee, C. L., 490
MacQueen, G., 489
Macrae, C. N., 583, 584
Madon, S., 30, 31
Madsen, K. B., 332
Magidoff, R., 378
Magnusson, A., 159
Mahadevan, Rajan, 239
Maier, S. R., 489
Maj, M., 534
Maldonado, P. E., 79
Malle, B. F., 464
Mancia, M., 160
Manderscheid, R. W., 557
Mann, A., 425
Manning, A., 29, 115, 337, 584
Manson, J., 334
Manuck, S. B., 600, 601
Maratsos, M., 79
Marcus, M. B., 380
Marentette, P. F., 314
Marin, R., 516
Markowitsch, H. J., 243, 268
Marks, I., 568
Marriott, K. A., 602
Marshall, E., 539
Marta, E., 413
Martin, A., 71, 263
Martin, C. L., 395
Martin, G. L., 574
Martin, L., 319
Marx, J., 424
Masling, J. M., 450
Maslow, Abraham, 10, 332, 443, 472, 596
Massimini, R., 11
Masten, A. S., 394
Masters, W. H., 344, 425
Mastro, J., 322
Matheny, L., 79
Mathews, H. L., 488
Mathews, T., 458
Matson, J. L., 216
Matsuda, L. A., 186
Matsumoto, D., 367
Matthews, K. A., 496
Matthias, R. E., 425
Mattson, S., 381
Maugh, T. H., II, 345
Mauro, J., 451
Mayberg, H. S., 533
Mayer, J. D., 369

Mayes, A. R., 246, 265
Mazzoni, G., 20
McCabe, S., 490
McCall, R. B., 349
McCarley, R. W., 161
McCarry, J., 177
McClearn, G. E., 292, 293, 446
McClelland, David, 348
McClelland, J. L., 262, 263
McConnell, J. V., 135
McCrae, R. R., 393, 463, 465, 468
McDaniel, M. A., 249, 267
McDermott, K. B., 255, 266, 275
McDougall, William, 330
McDowell, J., 462
McEachin, J. J., 232
McElrath, D., 188
McGaugh, James L., 247, 255
McGinnis, J. M., 178
McGirk, T., 177
McGue, M., 533
McGuffin, P., 537
McIntosh, D. N., 361, 365
McIntosh, H., 232
McKenna, K., 305
McKoon, G., 263
McMahon, P., 427
McNally, R. J., 573
McWhorter, J. H., 329, 348, 446
Meck, W., 150
Medin, D. L., 306, 307
Medina, J. H., 269
Megargee, 446
Mehren, E., 183, 588
Meichenbaum, D., 502, 503
Meltzoff, A. N., 391
Melzack, Ronald, 58, 112
Mendlewicz, J., 534
Menini, A., 107
Menzies, R. G., 518
Merzenich, M. M., 229, 320
Mesmer, Anton, 170
Mesquita, B., 365
Messer, S. B., 571
Mestel, R., 334
Metz, M. E., 344
Meyers, S. A., 419
Michaelson, J., 586
Mignot, E., 163
Milgram, P., 9
Milgram, Stanley, 593, 594
Milgrom, P., 195, 205
Millan, M. J., 113

Miller, A., 369
Miller, F. G., 427
Miller, George, 242, 243
Miller, J., 401
Miller, L. K., 7
Miller, M., 230, 233
Miller, M. A., 490
Miller, R. W., 470
Miller, S., 516
Miller, T. Q., 496
Millsom, C., 253
Milstein, M., 105
Miltenberger, R. G., 230
Milton, J., 139
Minshew, N. J., 7
Minton, L., 409
Miranda, A., 39
Mirksky, A. F., 539
Mischel, Walter, 458, 460, 464
Mittleman, M. A., 177
Mohr, D. C., 559
Moldin, S. O., 533
Moncrieff, J., 534
Mondain, M., 115
Money, J., 341
Moniz, Egas, 75
Monnot, M., 316
Montgomery, G. H., 172, 195, 206
Moore, R. Y., 150
Moore, T. A., 366
Moran, C., 426
Morehouse, W., III, 254
Morey, L. C., 537
Morgan, A. B., 537
Morgan, D., 513
Morgan, M., 20
Morrison, Adrian, 41
Morrison, J. R., 41
Morrison-Bogorad, M., 47
Morrissey, J., 557
Mortensen, M. E., 379
Morton, Samuel George, 85
Moscovitch, M., 71
Moskowitz, J. T., 495
Moss, D., 377
Mukerjee, M., 41
Mullen, B., 596, 598
Muller, H., 127
Muller, R. A., 7
Mundy, C., 434, 438
Munk, M. H. J., 157
Murberg, M., 491
Murnane, K., 248
Murphy, K., 187
Murphy, K. R., 474
Murray, B., 7, 39
Murray, Charles, 290, 294, 296
Murray, D. J., 13, 126
Murray, Henry, 332, 348, 450

Musto, D. F., 174, 182
Myers, D. G., 366
Myrtek, M., 496

**N**
Nadelmann, E. A., 175, 186
Nagarahole, E. L., 31
Nagtegaal, J. E., 151
Nakamura, Y., 112
Nakayama, E. Y., 564
Namy, L. L., 307
Nash, J. M., 383
Naslund, J., 47
Nathan, P. E., 559, 571
Nazario, S., 426, 427, 457
Neale, J. M., 517, 556
Neath, I., 245, 254
Neher, A., 333
Nehlig, A., 178
Neisser, U., 275, 289, 294
Neitz, J., 98, 99
Neitz, M., 98
Nelson, M. L., 486, 487
Nelson, R. J., 55
Nemeroff, C. B., 533
Neugarten, B., 425
Neverlien, P. O., 205
Newcombe, N. S., 264
Newport, F., 138
Neziroglu, F., 519
Ng, W., 582
Nichelli, P., 77
Nida, S., 597
Niedenthal, P. M., 135
Nisbet, M., 138, 139
Nisbett, R., 136, 321
Nisbett, R. E., 321
Niyak, H., 425
Nobler, M. S., 535
Nordin, V., 7
Norenzayan, A., 321
Noriyuki, D., 449
Norlander, T., 503
Norman, Donald A., 241, 262
Nour, N., 346
Novy, D. M., 575
Nowak, R., 151
Nurius, P. S., 549
Nyberg, L., 242, 246, 268

**O**
Oakes, L. M., 307
Oatley, K., 360, 362
Odbert, H. S., 462
Oden, M. H., 289
O'Hara, L. A., 310, 311
Ohbuchi, K., 471
Ohman, A., 361, 363
Ollendick, T. H., 216
Olson, L., 51, 219
Onishi, N., 603

O'Regan, J. K., 241
Orr, W. C., 153, 157
Ortony, A., 362
O'Shaughnessy, E., 436
Osofsky, J. D., 601
Ost, L., 199
Ostrom, T. M., 588, 589
Otto, M. W., 517
Ozer, D. J., 474, 475

**P**
Page, A. C., 195, 481
Painter, K., 380
Palmer, S., 126
Pandina, R. J., 183
Pappas, G. D., 113
Parker, G., 537
Parmar, P., 346
Patrick, C. F., 216
Patrick-Miller, L., 496
Patterson, D. R., 500
Patterson, Francine, 323
Patton, G. C., 426
Paul, S. M., 535
Paulesu, E., 77
Paulus, P. B., 598
Pavlov, Ivan, 196, 197, 228, 568
Pawson, T., 51
Payne, D. G., 275
Peacock, L., 542
Peake, Philip, 464
Peele, S., 185
Peeters, M. C. W., 491
Pelham, W. E., 37
Pennebaker, J. W., 548
Perlis, M., 162, 575
Perlman, C. A., 160, 435, 561
Perner, J., 149, 441, 563
Perry, C., 173
Perry, D., 60, 61
Persons, J. B., 566
Peters, J., 308
Petersen, S. E., 76
Peterson, K. S., 21
Peterson, L., 401
Peterson, L. R., 242
Peterson, M. A., 127
Peterson, M. J., 242
Petitto, L. A., 314, 316
Petretic-Jackson, P. A., 401
Petrides, M., 84
Petrill, S. A., 292, 391
Petty, R. E., 588, 589, 590, 591
Peyser, M., 247, 589
Pezdek, K., 275
Phelps, E. A., 80
Piaget, Jean, 388–391, 414
Pich, E. M., 178
Pierce, B. H., 226

Piliavin, J. A., 595
Pillard, R. C., 343
Pillemer, D. B., 255
Pingitore, R., 583
Pinker, S., 49, 148, 149, 229, 312, 313, 314, 315, 316, 319
Pinnell, C. M., 173
Pinnow, M., 200
Piomelli, D., 186
Piot, P., 345
Pitman, R., 573
Pizarro, R. A., 400
Plaud, J. J., 207, 567
Plazzi, B., 153
Plomin, R., 6, 292, 378, 391, 461, 467, 468, 486
Plummer, W., 595
Plutchik, R., 365
Polaschek, D. L. L., 602
Pollack, M. H., 517
Pomerleau, A., 395
Poortinga, Y. H., 11
Porth, C. M., 484, 485
Posner, M. I., 97
Post, R., 311
Postmes, T., 597
Potter, J., 7
Poulton, R., 205
Powell, D. H., 415
Power, M. J., 365
Prather, E. N., 348
Pratkanis, A. R., 135
Presentacion, M. J., 39
Pressman, M. R., 153, 157
Price, D. D., 112
Priester, J. R., 591
Prince, S. E., 420
Pruitt, D. G., 598
Pryor, J. L., 344
Pullum, G. K., 319
Purdon, S. E., 541
Pychyl, T. A., 9, 21
Pyryt, M. C., 349

**Q**
Quinn, O. W., 539

**R**
Rabasca, L., 14, 409
Rabkin, S. W., 173
Rahe, R. H., 490
Raichle, M. E., 71, 97
Raine, A., 537
Rainville, P., 172, 173
Rajkowska, G., 540
Rakic, P., 49
Raloff, J., 312
Ramachandran, V. S., 140
Ramey, C. T., 298, 299
Ramey, S. L., 299
Randi, James, 138

Ransdell, E., 457
Rapoport, J. L., 519
Rapp, P. E., 370, 371
Rapson, R. L., 419
Rasmussen, C., 483
Ratcliff, R., 263
Ratnam, R., 78, 103
Ravaja, N., 496
Ray, W. J., 171
Rayner, Rosalie, 204, 555, 566
Raynor, J. O., 348
Rechtschaffen, A., 156
Reed, M. K., 549
Reed, S., 9, 366, 384, 585, 589
Reeve, Christopher, 461
Regier, D. A., 538
Reid, J. B., 401
Reid, J. K., 490
Reisberg, D., 262
Reiss, D., 378
Reitman, V., 367
Renfrey, G., 573
Reppert, S., 151
Rescorla, R. A., 197, 202
Resnick, M., 413
Rey, G., 306
Reyneri, A., 107
Reynolds, A. J., 299
Rice, G., 343
Rice, L. N., 564
Richardson, G. E., 381
Richter, P., 181
Richters, J. M. A., 425
Ridenhour, R., 595
Rider, S. P., 162, 575
Rieke, M. L., 475
Rilling, M., 13
Rimland, B., 11
Risley, T., 316
Risse, G. L., 78
Ritter, M., 114
Rivas-Vazquez, R. A., 534
Rivera, C., 557
Rivera, E., 189
Roan, S., 162, 487
Robbins, J., 141, 533
Roberts, B. W., 416, 417, 441, 465
Roberts, K. J., 345
Roberts, S. B., 334
Robins, L. N., 537, 538
Robins, R. W., 416
Robinson, L. B., 420
Robinson-Riegler, B., 267
Rock, D. A., 349
Rock, I., 126
Rodgers, J. E., 274
Rodier, P. M., 4
Rodriguez-Tome, H., 408

Roediger, H. L., 255, 266, 275
Rogers, Carl, 444, 445, 472, 564
Rogers, P., 254
Roisman, G. I., 385
Rolls, E. T., 80
Romney, D. M., 449
Rorschach, Hermann, 450
Rortvedt, A. K., 230
Rosch, E., 306, 485
Rosellini, L., 233
Rosenberg, K. P., 343
Rosenblatt, R. A., 334
Rosenfeld, J. P., 371
Rosenfeld, M., 105
Rosenman, R., 496
Rosenthal, R., 40
Rosenthal, S. L., 409
Rosenzweig, M. R., 17
Ross, B. M., 253
Ross, C. A., 545
Ross, P. E., 284, 323
Rossi, A. S., 420, 425
Roth, D., 388, 391
Roth, W. T., 509
Rotter, Julian, 458
Roush, W., 320
Routh, D. K., 556
Rovee-Collier, C., 264
Rowatt, W. C., 598
Roy-Byrne, P. P., 542
Rozee, P. D., 605
Rozin, P., 110, 200, 588
Rubin, D. C., 255
Rubin, R., 122
Ruegg, R., 537
Rugg, M., 321
Ruiz-Bueno, J. B., 495
Rush, Benjamin, 556
Russell, R. C., 602
Ryan, R. M., 331

**S**
Saccuzzo, D. P., 286, 287, 290, 291, 348, 450, 451, 474, 475
Sackeim, H. A., 535
Sacks, O., 311
Salovey, P., 369, 495
Salthouse, T. A., 415
Samelson, F., 204
Samuel, D., 148, 182
Sanchez, George, 14
Sanchez-Ramos, J. R., 177
Sandlund, E. S., 503
Sands, R., 583
Sanfilipo, M., 540
Sapienza, B. G., 446
Sarwer, D. B., 344
Saskin, P., 163
Satcher, D., 557, 558, 571

Savage-Rumbaugh, S., 322, 323
Saxe, L., 370
Saywitz, K. J., 401
Scanlon, M., 451
Scarborough, E., 14
Scarr, S., 293
Schachter, Stanley, 362
Schacter, D. L., 246, 250, 263, 267, 271
Schaufeli, W. B., 491
Scheer, R., 186
Scherer, K. R., 363
Scherman, A., 446
Schiavi, R. C., 339
Schiff, M., 293
Schlenker, B. R., 597
Schmidt, M., 11
Schmitt, D. P., 342
Schneider, G. E., 49
Schneider, K., 200
Schoenberger, N. E., 173
Schooler, J. W., 255, 268
Schroeder, D. A., 595
Schuckit, M. A., 174, 175, 179, 180, 181, 182, 183, 185, 186, 188
Schuh, K. J., 178
Schulman, 583
Schultz, R. T., 6
Schulz, R., 424, 495
Schulz, S. C., 541, 542
Schuster, C., 176
Schwarcz, R., 48
Schwartz, B., 262
Schwartz, B. L., 267
Schwartz, S., 29, 161
Schweinhart, L. J., 299
Sciutto, M. J., 27
Scogin, F., 271
Scott, J. D., 51
Scribner, S., 291
Searles, J., 287
Sears, R. R., 289
Sedikides, C., 586
Sees, K. L., 179
Segraves, R. T., 339
Seidel, J. M., 486
Seitz, V., 293
Selemon, L. D., 510, 540
Seligman, M. E. P., 200
Selye, Hans, 486, 487
Selemon, L. D., 540
Senden, M. von, 127
Senécal, C., 9, 21
Seppa, N., 51
Serpell, R., 291
Serretti, A., 533
Setterlind, S., 490
Setterlund, M. C., 135
Shadish, W. R., 559, 571
Shaffer, D. R., 381, 408
Shannon, C., 502

Shannon, R. V., 100
Shapiro, C. M., 156, 510
Shapiro, Francine, 573
Shapiro, J. P., 290
Shapiro, S. L., 503
Sharp, D., 115, 424
Shatz, C., 383
Shaw, D., 395
Shaywitz, B. A., 30, 320, 321, 396
Shea, M. T., 534
Sheaffer, R., 139
Shenour, E. A., 371
Sherin, J. E., 157
Shettleworth, S. J., 229
Shetty, A. K., 60
Shiffrin, R. M., 245
Shih, J. C., 600
Shilts, R., 84
Shimaya, A., 127
Shoda, Y., 464
Shoemer, K., 179
Shorkey, C. T., 188
Shotland, R. L., 605
Shute, N., 27
Sidis, J. J., 86
Siegel, A., 163
Siegel, R. K., 177
Sigelman, C. K., 381, 408
Sigmundson, H. K., 341
Silver, W., 107
Simon, T., 285
Simonton, D. K., 311
Simpson, J. A., 419, 420
Singer, Jerome, 362
Singer, M. T., 556
Skaar, K. L., 178
Skelly, J. J., 591, 592
Skerrett, P. J., 151
Skinner, B. F., 8, 13, 214, 215, 220, 221, 223, 228, 292, 331, 568
Slater, E., 427
Sleek, S., 524, 604
Sloan, R. P., 485
Sloman, S. A., 318
Slone, A. E., 274
Slone, K. C., 231
Small, G. W., 520
Smiley, J., 29
Smith, C. A., 362
Smith, D. W., 381
Smith, E. E., 269, 558
Smith, E. R., 585
Smith, J. C., 486
Smith, L., 446
Smith, P. B., 592
Smith, R. S., 394
Snidman, N., 386, 387
Snow, R. E., 348
Snyder, C. R., 475
Socolar, R., 233

Soloway, R. M., 267
Sonnenschein, M. A., 557
Soriano, L. J., 492
Sozzi, G., 33
Spalding, L. R., 349
Spanos, N. P., 172, 545, 546
Spates, C. R., 573
Spear, L. P., 411, 414
Spearman, Charles, 282
Spears, R., 597
Speca, M., 503
Spelke, E. S., 127
Spencer, T., 27
Sperling, G. A., 241
Sperry, Roger, 49
Sperry, R. W., 87
Spiegler, M. D., 445, 446, 461
Spielman, D. A., 604
Spillar, K., 463
Spitz, H. H., 299
Spitzer, R. L., 151, 536, 544, 545
Spohr, M. L., 381
Springer, S. P., 79, 84, 87
Spruston, N., 108
Squire, L. R., 80, 246, 268, 307
Squitieri, T., 600
Srivastava, S., 463
Stahl, S. M., 59, 175, 176, 177, 178, 180, 517, 525
Stambler, L., 585
Stanley, B., 600
Stanley, M. A., 519, 575
Stanton, B., 600
Staub, E., 604
Steele, C., 348
Stein, R. E. K., 233
Steiner, R., 138
Steinhauer, J., 345
Stephen, M., 572
Steriade, M., 73
Stern, G. S., 495
Stern, R. M., 105
Stern, Y., 535
Sternberg, Robert J., 282, 283, 286, 289, 292, 294, 297, 310, 419, 492, 494
Stevens, J. E., 137
Stevenson, M., 137
Stickgold, R., 153, 154
Stiwne, D., 598
Stolberg, S., 179
Stoljar, D., 49, 71
Strain, E. C., 178
Straker, G., 572
Strassman, R. J., 180
Strauss, C. C., 517
Strauss, N., 433, 436
Streissguth, A. P., 381

# Name Index

Stritzke, W. G., 124
Stritzke, W. G. K., 55
Stromeyer, C. F., III, 254
Stromswold, K., 316
Stumpf, D. A., 74
Styfco, S. J., 298, 299
Suddath, R. L., 540
Sullivan, P. F., 510
Sullivan, R. M., 382
Suryani, L. K., 572
Sussman, N., 534
Sutton, S. R., 178
Suzuki, L. A., 291
Suzuki, Shinichi, 231
Svensen, S., 475
Svirsky, M. A., 115
Swayze, V. W., II, 75
Sweet, R. A., 542
Swets, J. A., 121
Swim, J. K., 583
Swindle, R., 558
Szyfelbein, S. K., 113

**T**

Taddese, A., 113
Takahashi, Y., 471
Talbot, J. D., 31
Talbot, M., 111, 572
Talcott, J. B., 320
Tallal, P., 320
Tamis-LeMonda, C. S., 315
Tang, S. W., 367
Tankova, I., 155
Tannen, Deborah, 321
Tanner, L., 27, 35, 39
Tanofsky, M. B., 337
Tanouye, E., 484
Tanzi, R., 47
Tanzi, R. E., 424
Tao, K., 11
Tao, K. T., 11
Tashkin, D., 186
Tavris, C., 605
Tawa, R., 346
Taylor, J., 230, 233
Taylor, J. F., 162
Taylor, S. E., 485, 495, 586
Teicher, M., 34
Tellegen, A., 366
Terman, Lewis M., 285, 289, 292, 296

Terman, M., 159
Terrace, Herbert, 323
Thapar, A., 537
Thase, M. E., 534
Thelen, E., 383
Thomas, A., 384
Thomas, K., 39
Thombs, D. L., 20
Thompson, B., 419
Thompson, Charles, 239
Thompson, L. A., 290
Thompson, R. A., 385
Thorndike, E. L., 196, 214, 226, 228
Tice, D. M., 9
Tiefer, L., 339
Tienda, M., 351
Timimi, S., 216
Title, S. A., 474
Tolman, Edward, 223
Tomes, H., 14
Tondo, L., 534
Tonegawa, S., 269
Tooby, J., 318
Torrey, F. E., 540
Towle, L. H., 512, 513
Townsend, E., 198
Tranel, D., 415
Trautner, H. M., 340, 395, 396, 418
Tresniowski, A., 352
Trevarthen, C., 87
Triandis, H. C., 471
Tripathi, H. L., 113
Tripician, R. J., 287, 451
Troester, U., 6
Trope, Y., 582
Troster, A. I., 60
Tsai, G., 55, 182
Tschann, J. M., 187
Tsien, Joe Z., 269
Tulving, E., 249, 268
Turk, D., 112
Turner, D. A., 60
Turner, M., 105
Turner, S., 446
Turner, S. M., 519
Twenge, J. M., 418
Tyack, P. L., 322

**U**

Ullman, M. T., 313, 602
Ullman, S. E., 183, 605

Underwood, A., 68
Underwood, P. W., 497
Urbina, S., 33, 34

**V**

Vahtera, J., 495
Valencia, R. R., 291
Valenstein, E. S., 75
Van de Castle, R. L., 161
VandenBos, G. R., 559
van Derbur Atler, D., 400
Vander Wall, S. B., 229
Vandewater, E. A., 417
Van Essen, D. C., 97
Van Gerwen, L. J., 524
Van Manen, K., 417
van Oppen, P., 517, 518, 567
van Praag, H., 87
Vargas, J. S., 223
Vargha-Khadem, F., 536
Venter, J. C., 294
Venturelli, P. J., 175, 176, 181, 186
Verhaeghen, P., 415
Verlinden, S., 523
Videbech, P., 533
Vinicor, F., 334
Vogel, S., 352
Vredenburg, K., 548

**W**

Wachtel, P. L., 571
Waddell, C., 311
Waddington, J. L., 539
Wade, B., 148
Wade, N., 68
Wagemans, J., 127
Wagner, J., 353
Wagner, R. K., 289
Wakefield, Dana, 377
Walk, R., 382
Walker, A., 346
Walker, E. G., 540
Wall, P. D., 112
Wallace, D. C., 424
Wallechinsky, D., 407, 419
Wallerstein, R. S., 563
Walsh, B. T., 353
Walsh, J. K., 153, 157

Walters, E. E., 353
Waltz, J. A., 76
Wanek, J. E., 475
Wang, S. C., 297
Ward, A., 337
Ward, L. M., 132, 137
Warden, C. H., 336
Warga, C., 112
Wartik, N., 573
Waters, A. J., 178
Watson, John B., 13, 204, 555, 566
Watson, R. R., 204
Watson, T., 337
Webb, W. B., 156
Weber, E. H., 123
Weed, W. S., 271
Wegner, D. M., 574
Weiden, P., 542
Weikart, D. P., 299
Weinberg, R. A., 293
Weinberger, D. R., 75
Weiner, B., 362, 585
Weiner, Bernard, 331
Weiner, I. B., 450, 451
Weisberg, R. W., 311
Weiss, K. R., 29
Weissman, M. M., 519, 536
Wells, G. L., 274
Wenzlaff, R. M., 574
Werle, M. A., 216
Werner, Emmy E., 393, 394, 441
Werner, J. S., 490
Wertheimer, Max, 13, 140
Wertz, F. J., 442, 446
Westen, D., 434, 440, 441, 449, 563
Whalen, C. K., 35
Wheeler, M. A., 76, 246
Whiffen, V. E., 533
Whitbourne, S. K., 417
White, J. M., 484, 485
White, K., 475
White, Robert J., 64
Whitla, D. K., 415
Whorf, Benjamin, 319
Wickett, J. C., 85, 284
Widiger, T. A., 515, 516, 536
Wiebe, D. J., 494

Wiederhold, B., 524
Wierson, M., 230
Wiesel, Torsten, 97
Wiggins, J. S., 464, 468
Wilcoxon, H. C., 200
Wildavsky, B., 14
Wilens, T. E., 39
Wilhelm, F. H., 509
Williams, A. M., 207
Williams, B. K., 492
Williams, D. E., 219
Williams, Donna, 3, 6, 7, 10
Williams, J., 106
Williams, J. E., 399, 418
Williamson, G. M., 488
Wilmot, W. W., 471
Wilson, B., 601
Wilson, D., 408
Wilson, K. G., 568
Wilson, M., 269
Wilson, S. R., 586
Wilson, T. D., 587
Wimbush, F. B., 486, 487
Wincze, J. P., 344
Winfrey, O., 352
Winner, E., 289
Winograd, E., 267
Winters, K. C., 189
Wiseman, R., 139
Witek-Janusek, L., 488
Witelson, Sandra F., 85, 297, 411
Witkin, G., 176, 523
Wittman, J., 195
Wiznitzer, M., 382
Wolf, T. H., 284
Wolff, M., 519
Wolitzky, D. L., 560
Wolpe, Joseph, 207, 566
Wong, J., 337
Wood, W., 395, 591
Woodruff-Pak, D. S., 73
Woods, S. C., 335, 336
Wool, C. A., 520
Wren, C. S., 187
Wride, N., 590
Wright, D. B., 255
Wright, I. C., 510, 540
Wu, C., 337

WuDunn, S., 603
Wundt, Wilhelm, 12, 223
Wyer, R. S., Jr., 582

**Y**

Yamashita, I., 522
Yang, X. L., 11
Ybarra, M. J., 138
Yehuda, R., 401
Yerkes, Robert, 296
Yoffe, E., 271
Young, John, 98
Young, M. W., 150, 151, 159
Young, N. K., 381
Yule, W., 567
Yurgelun-Todd, D., 411, 414

**Z**

Zajonc, Robert B., 361, 363
Zane, J. P., 21
Zaragoza, M. S., 275
Zechmeister, E. B., 20
Zeidner, M., 3, 6, 7, 11
Zeki, S., 97
Zemore, S. E., 418
Zener, K., 202
Zeng, R. G., 100
Zigler, Ed, 287, 293, 298, 299, 401, 427
Zimbardo, Philip G., 449, 597
Zimmerman, B. J., 460
Zimmerman, M. A., 416
Zito, J. M., 27
Zola, S. M., 268
Zola-Morgan, S., 80
Zucker, H. J., 343
Zucker, K. J., 340, 341
Zuckerman, M., 361

## A

AA (Alcoholics Anonymous), 189, 470
Abecedarian Project, 298
Ability tests, 450
Aborigines, 272
Absolute threshold, 122
Academic achievement, 288, 448, 587
Academic settings, 17
Accommodation (cognitive development), 388
Accommodation (conflict style), 492
Acetylcholine, 59
Achievement, 329, 348–351, 448, 533
Achievement personality, 533
Acquaintance (date) rapists, 602
Acquired Immune Deficiency Syndrome (AIDS), 345
Action potential, 52–53
Activation-synthesis theory of dreams, 161
Active strategies for interpersonal conflicts, 471
Actor-observer effect, 586
Acupuncture, 113
Acute pain, 112
Adaptation, sensory, 93, 108
Adaptation level theory of emotions, 366
Adaptive theory of sleep, 156
Adaptive value, 200–201, 365. See also Evolution
Addiction, 174, 182
ADHD. See Attention-deficit/hyperactivity disorder
Adolescence, 407, 408–414
   cognitive development, 390, 410–413
   personality, 416
   pregnancy, 608
   puberty, 408–409
   review and study questions, 421, 431
   school shootings, 523
   sleep, 156
   social development, 392, 393
   suicide, 426–427
   summary test, 428–429
   Web sites, 431
Adoption, 377, 385, 392
Adoption studies, 293
Adrenal cortex, 485
Adrenal glands, 82, 113, 485
Adrenaline, 362
Adrenal medulla, 485
Adulthood, 407, 415–420, 422–425
   aging, 424–425
   cognitive development, 390, 415
   gender roles, 418
   memory, 415, 430
   personality, 417
   relationships, 419–420, 422–423
   review and study questions, 421, 431

sleep, 156
social development, 392, 393
summary test, 428–429
Web sites, 431
Affective component of attitudes, 588
Affective-primacy question of emotions, 363
Afferent (sensory) neurons, 56
African Americans:
   intelligence, 290, 294
   mentoring programs, 446
   psychologists, 14
   See also Race
Afterimage, 99
Age regression, 172
Aggression, 600–602, 604–605
   and antisocial personality disorder, 536–537
   gender differences, 396
   and neurotransmitters, 55
   and observational learning, 224
   sexual, 602, 605
   See also Violence
Aging, 424–425. See also Adulthood; Old age
Aging by chance theory, 424
Aging by design theory, 424
Agoraphobia, 518, 575
AIDS (Acquired Immune Deficiency Syndrome), 345
Alarm stage of stress, 487
Alcohol, 182–184, 192
   cultural diversity, 185
   and nervous system, 55
   prenatal effects, 381
   See also Drug use
Alcoholics Anonymous (AA), 189, 470
All-or-none law, 52
Alpha stage of sleep, 152
Altered states of consciousness, 148. See also Drug use; Hypnosis
Altered state theory of hypnosis, 171
Altruism, 595
Alzheimer's disease, 47, 48, 49, 50, 61
American Academy of Pediatrics, 27
American Psychological Association (APA), 14, 40, 294
Ames, Aldrich, 370
Ames room, 133
Amnesia, 544
Amniocentesis, 380
Amphetamines, 176, 177
Amygdala, 80, 268
Analogies, 309
Anal stage of psychosexual development, 392, 439
Assimilation, 388
Analysis of variance (ANOVA), 615
Analytical psychology, 440
Anandamide, 55, 186
Androgens, 339
Anencephaly, 74
Anger, 604–605
Anger rapists, 602

Animal magnetism, 170
Animal models, 34, 247
Animals:
   brain, 49
   classical conditioning, 196–197, 200
   fetal tissue transplants, 60
   imprinting, 228
   insight learning, 226
   language, 322–323
   memory, 247
   as models, 34, 247
   preparedness, 200, 229
   research on, 41
Anmesia, 265
Anorexia nervosa, 332, 353
ANOVA (analysis of variance), 615
ANS (autonomic nervous system), 72, 81, 360, 501, 503
Anterior pituitary, 82
Anticipatory nausea, 206
Antidepressant drugs, 517, 519, 534, 547
Antisocial personality disorder, 515, 536–537
Anvil (ear), 102
Anxiety, 493
   Freudian theory, 437
   and insomnia, 162
   reduction techniques, 163, 207
   test anxiety, 3, 6–11
   See also Anxiety disorders
Anxiety disorders, 514, 517–519, 522, 524–525
Apparent motion, 140
Appraisal, 482–483, 484, 486, 494, 499, 502
Approach-approach conflict, 492
Approach-avoidance conflict, 492
Arousal:
   and autonomic nervous system, 81
   and emotions, 360, 362, 365
   and lie detector tests, 365, 370–371
   and REM sleep, 153
   and stress, 483, 484, 485
   and temperament, 384
   and test anxiety, 6
Arousal-cost-reward model of helping, 595
Artificial intelligence, 308
Artificial senses, 114
Aspartame (Nutrasweet), 30
Assessment:
   mental disorders, 512–513
   personality, 450–451, 474–475, 478, 512
   See also Diagnosis
Assisted suicide, 427
Association areas, 78, 79, 97, 103, 125
Associations, forming, 248, 249, 262
Atmospheric perspective, 131
Attachment, 385, 387
Attention, 231, 240, 243, 244

Attention-deficit/hyperactivity disorder (ADHD), 27–28, 29, 39
   experimental research, 28, 34, 35, 36–37
Attitudes, 588–591, 603
Attractiveness, 582, 603
Attributions, 10, 585–587
Atypical neuroleptic drugs, 541, 542
Audience, 591
Audition. See Hearing
Auditory association area, 78, 103
Auditory canal, 102
Auditory nerve, 103
Australopithecus afarensis, 67, 69
Authoritarian parents, 413
Authoritative parents, 413
Authority, 593–594
Autism, 3, 6–11, 24
   behavior therapy, 232, 568
   and savants, 311
Autistic savants, 7
Automatic encoding, 248
Automatic processes, 148
Autonomic nervous system (ANS), 72, 81, 360, 501, 503
Autonomy vs. shame/doubt stage of psychosocial development, 393
Availability heuristic, 308
Avoidance-avoidance conflict, 492
Awareness. See Consciousness
Axes, 514
Axon membrane, 52
Axons, 50, 51, 52, 55

## B

Babbling, 314
Backward conditioning, 202, 217
Bait shyness, 200
Balance, 105
Bali, 572
Bandura's theory. See Social cognitive theory
Barnum principle, 475
Basal ganglia, 60, 519, 541
Basilar membrane, 103
Bear gallbladders, 31
Beauty, 603
Beck's cognitive theory of depression, 548, 549
Behavioral approach, 5, 8, 13. See also Behavior therapy; Classical conditioning; Cognitive-behavioral approach; Operant conditioning; Social cognitive theory
Behavioral genetics, 466
Behavior modification. See Behavior therapy
Behaviors, 4, 458, 459, 473, 588
Behavior therapy, 236, 555, 556–557
   autism, 232
   biofeedback, 233, 501, 503
   dyslexia, 201
   and mood disorders, 549
   operant conditioning, 216
   systematic desensitization, 207, 567

time-out, 230, 233
*See also* Classical conditioning; Operant conditioning
Beliefs, 27, 30, 210
*The Bell Curve* (Herrnstein & Murray), 294
Benzodiazepines, 162, 517, 525
Bias:
  and attributions, 586
  in case studies, 30
  and double-blind procedures, 40
  and IQ tests, 290–291, 296
  and perception, 124
  and standardized tests, 34
  and surveys, 28, 29
  *See also* Discrimination
Bidirectionality principle, 401
Big Five traits, 463, 468, 473
Bilingualism, 319
Binet-Simon Intelligence Scale, 285
Binocular depth cues, 129
Biofeedback, 233, 501, 503, 568
Biological approach, 5, 6. *See also* Biological factors
Biological clocks, 150–151, 155, 156, 159
Biological factors, 6
  aggression, 600
  gender identity, 341
  hunger, 334, 335
  learning, 228–229
  memory, 263, 268–269
  mood disorders, 533
  personality disorders, 537
  schizophrenia, 539
  sexual behavior, 338, 339, 341, 343
  *See also* Brain; Nature-nurture question
Biological needs, 332. *See also* Hunger; Sexual behavior
Biological psychology, 19
BioPsychoSocial model of adolescence, 409
Bipolar I disorder, 532, 534
Birth defects, 380
Bisexual orientation, 341
Blackouts, 182
Blindness, 114, 150, 161
Blind spot, 96
Blinking, 241
Blood, as food, 110
Blood-brain barrier, 59
Boat people, 448
Bobo doll study, 224
Body temperature, 155
Bonobos, 323
Bowie, David, 444
Brain, 67–91
  adolescence, 411
  and autism, 6, 7
  and biological clocks, 150, 155
  and concept formation, 307
  control centers, 74–79
  and deception, 371
  development, 48, 382
  and dreams, 161

and dyslexia, 320
and endocrine system, 82
evolution, 69
and Freudian theory, 441
gender differences, 84, 85, 284, 321
head transplants, 64
hemispheres, 7, 73, 86–87
and hunger, 335
and intelligence, 85, 284, 297
and language, 313, 316, 323
and limbic system, 80–81
and memory, 76, 77, 80, 263, 268
and mental disorders, 519, 533, 537, 539–540
mind-body question, 49
neurons, 48–49, 50
and perception, 125
and phantom limb, 58
regrowth, 49
review and study questions, 83, 91
and senses, 78, 79, 97, 103, 108
size, 85, 284, 297
and speech, 78, 87, 229
structure, 48
study techniques, 70–71
summary test, 88–89
Web sites, 91
*See also* Nervous system
Brain scans, 61
Breast cancer, 122
Brightness constancy, 128
Broca's aphasia, 78
Broca's area, 78, 316
Bulimia nervosa, 353
Burke, Chris, 288
Burnout, 491
Bystander effect, 597

## C

Caffeine, 178
Calories, 334
Cancer, 33, 122, 195, 206–207, 506
Careers, 17–19
Care orientation, 412
Case studies, 28, 30, 35
  on consciousness, 147
  on creativity, 310
  and Freudian theory, 561
  on school shootings, 523
  on stress, 500
Catatonic schizophrenia, 538
Catharsis, 605
Causation, 33
Cell body (soma), 50, 382
Central cues, 335
Central nervous system (CNS), 51, 72
Central route for persuasion, 591
Central tendency, measures of, 611–612
Cephalocaudal principle of motor development, 383
Cerebellum, 73
Challenge, 494. *See also* Challenge appraisals

Challenge appraisals, 482, 483, 494, 502
Chemical alphabet, 68, 382
Chemical senses, 106–107
Chemotherapy, 195, 206
Child abuse, 400–401, 568
Childhood, 397, 404
  abuse during, 400–401, 568
  aggression, 604
  cognitive development, 388, 389, 390
  concept formation, 307
  and dental fears, 205
  dyslexia, 320
  language, 315
  memory, 251, 258, 264, 273
  mentoring programs, 446
  and nature-nurture question, 377
  operant conditioning, 216
  sleep, 156
  social development, 392, 393, 394, 395
  socialization, 522
Chile, 11
Chimpanzees, 323
China, 11
Chi-square, 616
Chomsky's theory of language, 313, 315
Chromosomes, 68, 382
Chronic pain, 112
Chunking, 243
Cigarettes, 178, 336
Circadian rhythms, 150–151, 155, 156, 162
Citadel, 589
Clairvoyance, 138, 144
Class. *See* Socioeconomic status
Classical conditioning, 195–211
  adaptive value, 200–201
  and brain structure, 73
  emotions, 201, 204–205
  vs. operant conditioning, 217
  procedure, 197–198
  review and study questions, 203, 211
  and stress, 489, 493
  summary test, 208–209
  theories of, 202
  Web sites, 211
Classification, 390
Class notes, 16
Client-centered therapy, 564
Clinical assessment, 512
Clinical interview, 512
Clinical psychologists, 17, 557, 558
Clinical scales, 474
Clinical social workers, 558
Closure rule of perception, 127, 140
Clozapine, 541, 542
CNS. *See* Central nervous system
Cobain, Kurt, 433–436, 438, 450
Cocaine, 59, 175, 177, 381
Cochlea, 102–103
Cochlear implants, 115
Cognitive appraisal theory of emotions, 360, 362–363

Cognitive approach, 5, 7
  attitudes, 588
  and classical conditioning, 202
  creativity, 310
  depression, 548, 549
  emotions, 360, 362–363
  gender identity, 395, 396
  mental disorders, 548
  motivation, 331, 350
  personality, 458, 459, 473
  psychotherapy, 565
  and unconscious, 441
  *See also* Cognitive-behavioral approach; Cognitive-behavioral therapy; Learning; Memory
Cognitive-behavioral approach:
  aggression, 604
  mental disorders, 510
  *See also* Cognitive-behavioral therapy
Cognitive-behavioral therapy, 559, 568, 574–575
  aggression, 604, 605
  drug use, 189
  insomnia, 162
  mood disorders, 549
  parenting, 401
  phobias, 225, 524, 525, 568, 575
  stress management programs, 6, 502–503, 568
  thought substitution, 574, 575
  trauma, 491
Cognitive development, 388–391
  adolescence, 390, 410–413
  adulthood, 390, 415
  and gender identity, 395, 396
Cognitive development theory of gender identity, 395, 396
Cognitive dissonance, 590
Cognitive factors. *See* Cognitive approach
Cognitive interviews, 275
Cognitive learning, 196, 213, 223–226. *See also* Cognitive approach
Cognitive maps, 223
Cognitive miser model of attribution, 586
Cognitive neuroscience, 7, 19, 71, 149
Cognitive processes:
  review and study questions, 317, 327
  summary test, 324–325
  *See also* Language; Thinking
Cognitive psychology, 19
Cognitive therapy, 565. *See also* Cognitive-behavioral therapy
Cohesion, 596
Collective unconscious, 440
Collectivistic cultures, 471, 592
Color, 98
Color blindness, 99
Color constancy, 128
Commitment, 419, 494
Communication, 322. *See also* Language

Community mental health centers, 557
Companionate love, 419
Compensatory factors, 401
Compliance, 593
Compromise, 492
Concept formation, 306–307
Conception (fertilization), 68, 379
Concept reviews, 15
  adolescence/adulthood, 421
  brain, 83
  cognitive processes, 317
  consciousness, 158
  developmental psychology, 398
  emotions, 368
  intelligence, 295
  learning, 203, 227
  memory, 252, 270
  mental disorders, 521, 543
  motivation, 347
  nervous system, 57
  perception, 134
  personality, 447, 469
  psychotherapy, 569
  research, 38
  senses, 109
  social psychology, 599
  stress, 498
Concrete operations stage of cognitive development, 390
Conditional positive regard, 445
Conditioned emotional response, 201, 493
Conditioned nausea, 195, 206–207
Conditioned reflexes, 196
Conditioned response, 201, 217, 489, 493
Conditioned stimulus, 217
Conduct disorder, 523
Conduction deafness, 115
Cones, 96
Conflict, 471, 492
Conformity, 592–594
Conley, Fran, 584
Consciousness, 147–167
  biological clocks, 150–151, 155, 156, 159
  continuum, 148–149
  dreams, 149, 153, 160–162, 435, 561
  review and study questions, 158, 167
  seasonal affective disorder, 159
  summary test, 164–165
  Web sites, 167
  See also Drug use; Hypnosis; Sleep
Conscious thoughts, 434, 472
Consensus, 585
Consequences, 217, 218
Conservation, 389, 390
Consistency, 585
Content scales, 474
Contiguity theory of classical conditioning, 202
Continuity rule of perception, 127
Continuous reinforcement, 220

Continuum of consciousness, 148–149
Control:
  of behavior, 4
  locus of, 459, 473, 495
  and stress, 4, 494, 495
Control group, 37, 489
Controlled processes, 148
Control Question Technique, 370–371
Conventional level of moral reasoning, 412
Convergence, 129
Convergent thinking, 310
Conversion disorder, 520
Coping, 481, 499–500. See also Stress
Cornea, 95
Correlation, 32–33, 85
Correlation coefficient, 32
Cortex, 74, 268
Counseling psychologists, 17, 558
Counterattitudinal behavior, 590
Covariation model of attribution, 585
Cox, Gregg, 281
Creativity, 305, 310–311
Critical language period, 316
Critical (sensitive) period, 228
Cross-cultural approach, 5, 11
  emotions, 364
  gender, 418
  Oedipus complex, 439
  trait theory, 463
  See also Cultural diversity
Cross-sectional method, 386
Crowds, 597
Cultural bias, 291, 329
Cultural diversity, 5, 11
  alcoholism, 185
  attitudes, 603
  autism, 11
  conformity, 592
  dental fears, 205
  discrimination, 14
  drug use, 59
  emotions, 367, 374
  gender roles, 399
  IQ test bias, 290–291
  learning, 231
  memory, 253, 272
  mental disorders, 518, 522, 546
  perception, 136–137
  personality, 448, 471
  psychotherapy, 572, 578
  relationships, 423
  seasonal affective disorder, 159
  senses, 110
  stress, 501
  test anxiety, 11
  thinking, 321
  and trait theory, 463
  See also Cross-cultural approach; Race
Cultural-familial retardation, 288
Cultural influences, 136. See also Cultural diversity

Cultural risk factors, 185
Culture-free tests, 291
Cumulative record, 220
Curare, 59

## D

Dahmer, Jeffrey, 509, 515, 536
DARE (Drug Abuse Resistance Program), 187
Date (acquaintance) rapists, 602
Daydreaming, 148
Deafness, 101, 115
Debriefing, 40, 594
Deception, 40
Decibels, 101
Decision-stage model of helping, 595
Declarative memory, 246, 268
Deductive reasoning, 318
Deep Blue, 308
Deep structure, 313
Defense mechanisms, 437, 449, 493
Deficiency needs, 443
Definition theory of concept formation, 306
Deindividuation, 597
Deinstitutionalization, 557
Delay of gratification, 460, 473
Dendrites, 50, 55
Denial, 437
Dennis, Harold, 500
Dental fears, 195, 199, 205
Dependency, 174
Dependent personality disorder, 536
Dependent variables, 36
Depression, 496, 532, 533, 534, 548–549. See also Mood disorders
Depth perception, 129–131, 382
Describing behavior, 4
Descriptive statistics, 610–613
Designer drugs, 181
Developmental norms, 383
Developmental psychology, 18, 376–405, 377, 407–431
  adolescence, 408–414
  adulthood, 415–420, 422–425
  child abuse, 400–401
  cognitive development, 388–391, 410–413, 415
  gender, 395–396, 399
  infancy, 382–388, 397
  nature-nurture question, 377
  old age, 155, 156, 415, 425, 427, 430
  prenatal period, 378–382
  review and study questions, 398, 405
  social development, 392–396
  summary test, 402–403
  Web sites, 405
  See also Adolescence; Adulthood; Childhood
Deviation IQ, 285
Diagnosis:
  ADHD, 27, 28, 39
  Alzheimer's disease, 47

dyslexia, 201
  mental disorders, 513–516
  See also Assessment
Diagnostic and Statistical Manual of Mental Disorders-IV-Test Revision (DSM-IV-TR), 513–516, 546
Diathesis stress theory of schizophrenia, 540
Dichromats, 99
Dieting, 336, 352
Diffusion of responsibility theory of the bystander effect, 597
Direction of sound, 104
Discrimination, 378, 457
  and attributions, 585, 586
  and gender differences, 84
  in psychology field, 14
  and schemas, 584
  and stereotypes, 583
  See also Bias
Discrimination (classical conditioning), 199, 204, 222
Discriminative stimulus, 222
Disgust, 110
Disorganized schizophrenia, 538
Displacement, 437
Display rules, 367
Dissociative disorders, 9, 514, 544–545
Dissociative identity disorder (DID) (multiple personality disorder), 9, 545, 546
Distinctiveness, 585
Divergent thinking, 310
Dix, Dorothea, 556
DNA, 68, 382
Dolphins, 322
Domination, 492
Dopamine, 59, 60
Dopamine theory of schizophrenia, 541
Double-blind experiments, 37, 40, 111, 135
Double standard for sexual behavior, 342
Down syndrome, 380
Dream interpretation, 435, 561
Dreams, 160–162
  and continuum of consciousness, 149
  Freudian theory, 160, 435, 561
  and sleep stages, 153
Drive-reduction theory of motivation, 330
Drives, 330
Drug effects on nervous system:
  alcohol, 182
  hallucinogens, 180, 181
  marijuana, 186
  opiates, 179
  stimulants, 59, 175, 176, 177
  traditional plants, 59
Drug treatments:
  ADHD, 27, 28, 30, 39
  AIDS, 345
  anxiety disorders, 517, 519, 525

eating disorders, 353
insomnia, 162
mood disorders, 534, 547
Parkinson's disease, 60
personality disorders, 537
and psychotherapy, 563
Ritalin, 27
schizophrenia, 541, 542
Drug use, 169, 174–193
alcohol, 55, 182–184, 185, 192, 381
cultural diversity, 59
definitions, 174
extent of use, 175
hallucinogens, 180–181
marijuana, 186
opiates, 179
prenatal effects, 381
prevention, 187
review and study questions, 184, 192
stimulants, 176–178
summary test, 190–191
treatment, 188–189
Web sites, 193
See also Drug effects on nervous system; Drug treatments
DSM-IV-TR (Diagnostic and Statistical Manual of Mental Disorders-IV-Test Revision), 513–516, 546
Dutton, Charles, 433, 442
Dyslexia, 201, 320
Dysthymic disorder, 532, 534

**E**

Ear, 102–103. See also Hearing
Early humans, 67, 69, 140
Eating. See Food
Eating disorders, 332, 337, 353
Echoic memory, 241
Eclectic approach to psychotherapy, 559
Ecological psychology, 291
Ecstasy (MDMA), 181
ECT (electroconvulsive therapy), 535
Education, 289, 290, 298
Efferent (motor) neurons, 56
Effortful encoding, 248
Ego, 436, 437, 472
Egocentric thinking, 389
Eidetic imagery, 254
Einstein, Albert, 284, 297
Elaborative rehearsal, 249
Electra complex, 439
Electroconvulsive therapy (ECT), 535
Elliot, Chuck, 531, 532, 533, 534
Embryonic stage, 379
EMDR (Eye-Movement Desensitization and Reprocessing), 573
Emotional intelligence, 369
Emotional intensity, 360, 361, 367
Emotion-focused coping, 499, 503

Emotions, 359–375
adolescence, 411
and attitudes, 588
and brain structure, 80
classical conditioning, 201, 204–205
cognitive appraisal theory, 360, 362–363
cross-cultural approach, 364
cultural diversity, 367, 374
development, 384–385
emotional intelligence, 369
functions of, 365
gender differences, 84
happiness, 366
and lie detector tests, 365, 370–371
and memory, 247, 255, 267
review and study questions, 368, 375
and schizophrenia, 538
sequence of, 360–361
and stress, 482, 499, 503
summary test, 372–373
and temperament, 384
and test anxiety, 6
universal facial expressions, 364
Web sites, 375
See also Stress
Empathy, 564
Encoding, 239, 244, 248–249
End bulbs, 50, 53, 54
Endocrine system, 82
Endorphins, 55, 113, 175
Environmental factors:
aggression, 601
emotions, 366
intelligence, 292–293, 294
language, 313, 316
mental disorders, 540
motor development, 383
personality, 458, 467, 468, 473
prodigies, 378
sensory development, 382
temperament, 387
weight, 336
See also Nature-nurture question
Environmental/psychological risk factors, 183
Environmental stimulation, 383
Epinephrine, 247, 362
Episodic memory, 246, 248
Erikson's psychosocial stages of development, 393, 394, 417, 440
Erogenous zones, 438
Error, 29, 30
ESP. See Extrasensory perception
Estrogen, 408, 425
Ethics, 40–41, 594
Ethologists, 228
European Americans, 272, 384. See also Race
Evaluative function of attitudes, 589
Evening persons, 155
Event schemas, 584
Evolution:
and brain, 69

and emotions, 361, 365
and gender, 84, 342, 399, 418, 485
and taste, 106
Excitatory transmitters, 54
Executive function of brain, 76
Exercise, 336, 352, 547
Exhaustion stage of stress, 487
Exorcism, 578
Experimental group, 37, 489
Experimental psychology, 18
Experiments, 28, 500, 547
conducting, 36–37
laboratory, 34, 35
Explaining behavior, 4
Exposure therapy, 519, 524, 567
Extensions of waking life theory of dreams, 161
External attributions, 585
External ear, 102
External locus of control, 459, 495
Extinction, 199, 204, 222, 493
Extrasensory perception (ESP), 138–139, 144
Extrinsic motivation, 331, 350
Eye, 94–95, 485. See also Vision
Eye Movement Desensitization and Reprocessing (EMDR), 573
Eyewitness testimony, 261, 274–275

**F**

Facial expressions, 361, 364, 365, 374
Facial feedback theory of emotions, 361
Facial flushing, 185
Factor analysis, 462
Failure, fear of, 349
False memories, 251, 258, 273. See also Repressed memory
Farsightedness (presbyopia), 95
FAS (fetal alcohol syndrome), 381
Fat cells, 335, 336
Faulkner, Shannon, 589
Fear of failure, 349
Female circumcision, 346
Fertilization, 68, 379
Fetal alcohol syndrome (FAS), 381
Fetal stage, 380
Fetal tissue transplants, 60–61
Fight-flight response, 81, 484–485, 486, 488, 501
Figure-ground rule of perception, 127
First impressions, 141
Fish eyes, 110
Five-factor model of trait theory, 463, 468, 473
Fixation, 438, 439
Fixed action pattern, 330
Fixed-interval reinforcement schedule, 221
Fixed-ratio reinforcement schedule, 221
Flashbulb memory, 255
Flavor, 106
fMRI (functional magnetic resonance imaging), 70

Food:
dieting, 336, 352
and disgust, 110
eating disorders, 332, 337, 353
flavor, 106
and operant conditioning, 216
See also Hunger
Foot-in-the-door technique, 593
Forebrain, 73, 74
Forgetting, 264–267, 278, 415. See also Memory
Forgetting curves, 264
Formal operations stage of cognitive development, 390, 410
Four-stage model of sexual response, 344
Fovea, 96
France, Anatole, 284
Fraternal twins, 292
Free association, 435, 560, 561
Free nerve endings, 108
Frequency, 100, 104
Frequency distributions, 610
Frequency theory of pitch, 104
Freud, Sigmund, 174, 310. See also Freudian theory
Freudian slips, 435
Freudian theory, 5, 9, 434–441, 472
criticisms of, 440
current, 441
divisions of mind, 436, 472
and dreams, 160, 435, 561
and mental disorders, 510, 513
psychoanalysis, 555, 560–563
psychosexual stages, 392, 393, 438–439, 472
and repressed memories, 250, 265
and shyness, 449
unconscious, 9, 149, 434–435, 472, 493, 560
Frontal lobe, 74, 75–76
Frontal lobotomy, 75
Frustration, 491
Frustration-aggression hypothesis, 601
Fugue, 544
Functional fixedness, 309
Functionalism, 12
Functional magnetic resonance imaging. See fMRI
Fundamental attribution error, 586

**G**

GABA neurons, 55, 157, 182
Gage, Phineas, 75
Galanin, 335
Galvanic skin response, 370–371, 483
Ganglion cells, 96
Ganzfeld procedure, 139
Gardner's theory. See Multiple-intelligence theory
GAS (general adaptation syndrome), 487
Gate control theory of pain, 112
Gates, Bill, 281

Gay men. *See* Homosexual orientation
Gender differences, 396
aggression, 396
brain, 84, 85, 284, 321
color blindness, 99
cultural diversity, 399
language, 321, 396
and mental disorders, 546
moral reasoning, 412
relationships, 423
sexual behavior, 339, 342
social development, 395
stress, 485, 490, 496
*See also* Gender identity; Gender roles
Gender identity, 340, 341, 395, 514
Gender-identity disorders, 340, 514
Gender roles, 340–341, 395
adulthood, 418
cultural diversity, 399
and sexual aggression, 602, 605
and sexual orientation, 343
General adaptation syndrome (GAS), 487
General goals, 20
Generalization, 199, 204, 222
Generalized anxiety disorder, 517
Generativity vs. stagnation stage of psychosocial development, 417
Genes, 48, 68, 382. *See also* Genetic factors
Genetic factors:
ADHD, 32
aggression, 601
alcoholism, 183, 185
Alzheimer's disease, 48
autism, 6
brain development, 68
classical conditioning, 200
cognitive development, 391
color vision, 98
drug use, 175
eating disorders, 353
emotional development, 384
emotions, 364, 366
Freudian theory, 441
gender identity, 341
and humanistic theories, 446
hunger, 334, 336
infancy, 382, 387
intelligence, 292–293, 294
mental disorders, 519, 537
mood disorders, 533
motion sickness, 105
motor development, 383
obesity, 34
personality, 466–467, 468, 473
prodigies, 378
schizophrenia, 539
seasonal affective disorder, 159
sensory development, 382
sexual behavior, 338–339, 341, 343
stress, 486
temperament, 387

*See also* Nature-nurture question
Genetic markers, 539
Genital stage of psychosexual development, 392, 439
Genuineness, 564
Germany, 11
Germinal stage, 379
Gerontology, 424
Gestalt approach, 13, 126–127
G (general intelligence) factor, 282, 283, 297
Giftedness, 289
Glass ceiling, 586
Glial cells, 48
Goal-setting, 20–21, 309
Gold, Tracey, 353
Gonads, 82
Goose bumps (piloerection), 485
Gorillas, 323
Graham, Lawrence, 581
Grammar (syntax), 312, 314, 315
Gratification, delay of, 460, 473
Grojsman, Sophia, 107
Group cohesion, 596
Group dynamics, 596–598
Group norms, 596
Group polarization, 598
Groupthink, 598
Growth needs, 443
Grubs, 110

**H**
Hair, 485
Hair cells, 103
Hair receptors, 108
Hallucinations, 538
Hallucinogens, 180–181
Haloperidol, 541
Hammer (ear), 102
Handwriting analysis, 451
Happiness, 366, 420. *See also* Emotions
Hardiness, 494
Harm/loss appraisals, 482
Harvard, Beverly, 457, 462
Hassles, 490
Head Start, 298–299
Head transplants, 64
Hearing, 100–104, 115, 382
and brain structure, 78, 103
and memory, 241
Heart rate, 485
Helping, 595
Hemispheres (brain), 7, 73, 86–87
Hereditary factors. *See* Genetic factors
Heritability, 293, 320, 466. *See also* Genetic factors
Heroin, 175, 179
Heterosexual orientation, 341
Heuristics, 308
Hidden observer, 171
Hindbrain, 73, 74
Hippocampus, 80, 84, 268
Hispanic Americans. *See* Latinos
Historical approaches, 12–13

Histrionic personality disorder, 536
HIV positive status, 345. *See also* AIDS
Hofmann, Albert, 169, 180
Holistic view, 442, 472
Hollywood love, 419
Homelessness, 557
Homeostasis, 81, 330
*Homo erectus,* 69
*Homo sapiens,* 69
Homosexual orientation, 341, 343, 516
Honesty tests, 474
Hormones, 82
and hunger, 335, 336
and memory, 247, 255
and sexual behavior, 339
Horoscopes, 475
Hostility, 496
Humanistic approach, 5, 10
Humanistic theories, 5, 10, 442–446
Maslow's hierarchy of needs, 332–333, 348, 443, 472
Human potential movement, 446
Hunger, 334–337
eating disorders, 332, 337, 353
Hypnosis, 169, 170–173
review and study questions, 184
summary test, 190–191
Hypnotic analgesia, 172, 173
Hypnotic induction, 170
Hypocretin neurons, 163
Hypothalamus, 80, 81, 82
and biological clocks, 150, 155
and hunger, 335
and puberty, 408
and sexual behavior, 339
and stress, 484, 485
Hypothesis, 36

**I**
Iconic memory, 241
Id, 436, 437, 472
Ideal (optimal) weight, 334
Ideal self, 444
Identical twins, 292
Identity, 416
Identity vs. role confusion stage of psychosocial development, 393, 417
Illusions, 132–133, 140
Imagined perception, 172
Imitation, 231
Immigrants:
achievement, 351, 448
intelligence, 296
language acquisition, 316
Immune system, 111, 488–489
Implicit (nondeclarative/procedural) memory, 149, 246, 248, 268, 441
Impossible figures, 132, 137
Imprinting, 228
Incentive theory of motivation, 331
Independent variables, 36
Individualistic cultures, 471, 592

Individual psychology, 440
Inductive reasoning, 318
Industrial settings, 17
Industry vs. inferiority stage of psychosocial development, 393
Infancy, 382–388, 397
cognitive development, 388, 389
emotional development, 384–385
facial expressions, 364
language, 314
motor development, 383
and nature-nurture question, 377
sensory development, 382
sleep, 156
social development, 392, 393
temperament, 384, 386–387
Infatuated love, 419
Inferential statistics, 613–616
Inferior parietal lobe, 297
Informational influence theory of the bystander effect, 597
Ingroup, 598
Inhibited children, 386, 387
Inhibited female orgasm, 344
Inhibitory transmitters, 54
Initiative vs. guilt stage of psychosocial development, 393
Innate language factors, 313, 316
Inner ear, 102–104
Insanity, 509
Insects, as food, 110
Insecure attachment, 385
Insight, 309
Insight learning, 226
Insight therapies, 559, 560–565
client-centered therapy, 564
cognitive therapy, 565
short-term dynamic psychotherapy, 562
Insomnia, 162, 568, 575
Instinct theory of motivation, 330
Integration, 492
Integrity vs. despair stage of psychosocial development, 417
Intelligence, 281–303
artificial, 308
and brain size, 85, 284, 297
and correlation, 33, 85
and creativity, 311
definitions, 282–283, 292
early measurement, 284–285, 296
emotional, 369
gender differences, 396
intervention programs, 298–299
IQ score distribution, 288–289
IQ test limitations, 290–291
IQ tests, 286–287
nature-nurture questions, 292–294
new approaches, 297
and race, 290, 294, 296
review and study questions, 295, 303
summary test, 300–331
Web sites, 303
Intelligence quotient (IQ), 33, 282
and emotional intelligence, 369

and g factor, 282
historical origins, 285
and intervention programs, 298–299
limitations of, 290–291, 296
score distribution, 288–289
tests, 286–287
Intensity, 123
Interactive model of sexual orientation, 341
Interference, 242, 265, 266, 267, 271
Internal attributions, 585
Internal locus of control, 459, 495
*International Classification of Disease and Related Health Problems* (ICD-10), 546
Interneurons, 56
Interpersonal conflicts, 471, 492
Interposition, 130
Interpreting function of attitudes, 589
Interval timing clock, 150
Intervention programs, 298–299
Interviews, 34
Intestines, 335, 485
Intimacy vs. isolation stage of psychosocial development, 417
Intrinsic motivation, 331, 350
Introspection, 12
Intrusive thoughts, 574, 575
Inuit, 161, 319
Ions, 52
IQ. *See* Intelligence quotient
Iris, 95

**J**
James-Lange theory of emotions, 360
Jet lag, 151
JND (just noticeable difference), 123
Job performance, 288
*Journal of Cross-Cultural Psychology,* 11
*Journal of Humanistic Psychology,* 10
Justice orientation, 412
Just noticeable difference (JND), 123

**K**
Kasparov, Gary, 308
Kennedy, John F., 286
Kevorkian, Jack, 427
King, Martin Luther, Jr., 443
Kinkel, Kipland, 523
Kohlberg's theory of moral reasoning, 412
Koresh, David, 581, 592

**L**
Labeling, 516
Laboratory experiments, 34, 35
Laboratory settings, 34, 35
Language, 305, 312–316
acquisition, 314–316
animals, 322–323
and autism, 7
dyslexia, 320
gender differences, 321, 396
oral vs. written, 253

and personality, 459
review and study questions, 317, 327
summary test, 324–325
and thinking, 319
Web sites, 327
*See also* Speech
Language stages, 314
LASIK surgery, 95
Latency stage of psychosexual development, 392, 439
Lateral hypothalamus, 335
Lateral prefrontal cortex, 297
Latinos, 14
Law of effect, 196, 214
L-dopa, 60
Learned associations, 337
Learning, 195–196
biological factors, 228–229
cognitive learning, 196, 213, 223–226
observational, 223, 224–225, 459, 493
review and study questions, 203, 211, 227, 237
summary test, 234–235
Suzuki method, 231
Web sites, 211, 237
*See also* Classical conditioning; Operant conditioning
Learning-performance distinction, 224
Lens, 95
Leptin, 335, 336
Lesbians. *See* Homosexual orientation
Levels-of-processing theory, 249
Lie detector (polygraph) tests, 365, 370–371
Light and shadow, 131
Light waves, 94, 96, 98
Limbic system, 80–81, 411
Limitations, 491
Linear perspective, 130
Linguistic relativity, theory of, 319
Lithium, 534
Liver, 335, 485
Lobotomies, 75
Locus of control, 459, 473, 495
Longitudinal method, 386, 441, 465
Long-term memory, 240, 244–246, 269
Long-term potentiation (LTP), 269
Loudness, 100, 104
Love, 419–420, 423
LSD, 169, 180
LTP (long-term potentiation), 269
Lu, Steve, 281
Lucy (*Australopithecus afarensis*), 67, 69
Lung cancer, 33

**M**
Magic, 138
Magnetic resonance imaging (MRI), 70

Magnets, 31
Maintenance rehearsal, 242, 249
Major depressive disorder, 532, 534, 547
Major life events, 490
Maladaptive behavior approach to mental disorders, 511
Male-female differences. *See* Gender differences
Mammograms, 122
Mandela, Nelson, 457–458
Mania, 534
Marijuana, 186
Marriage, 409, 420, 422–423
Maslow's hierarchy of needs, 332–333, 348, 443, 472
Maslow's theory. *See* Humanistic theories
Mass hysteria, 520
Maturation, 383
McCabe, Michael, 531, 538–541, 558
MDMA (ecstasy), 181
Mean, 611
Measurement, 37, 369. *See also* Diagnosis; Intelligence quotient; Statistics
Measures of central tendency, 611–612
Measures of variability, 612–613
Median, 611–612
Medical model approach to mental disorders, 510
Medical therapy, 559
Medications. *See* Drug treatments
Meditation, 501, 503
Medulla, 73
Melatonin, 151
Memory, 239–279, 260–279
adulthood, 415, 430
amnesia, 544
biological factors, 263, 268–269
and brain structure, 76, 77, 80, 263, 268
cultural diversity, 253, 272
definitions, 239
and emotions, 247, 255, 267
encoding, 239, 244, 248–249
and eyewitness testimony, 261, 274–275
false, 251, 258, 273
forgetting, 264–267, 278, 415
long-term, 240, 244–246, 269
mnemonics, 271
organization of, 262–263
repressed, 239, 250–251, 265
review and study questions, 252, 259, 270, 279
and senses, 107, 240, 241
short-term, 240, 242–243, 244, 245, 269
and sleep, 153
and social cognitive theory, 231
summary tests, 256–257, 276
types of, 240
unusual, 254–255
Web sites, 259, 279

Memory span test, 242
Men. *See* Gender differences; Gender roles; Sexism
Menarche, 408
Meniere's disease, 105
Menopause, 425
Mental age, 285
Mental disorders, 509–529, 531–553
anxiety disorders, 514, 517–519, 522, 524–525
assessment, 512–513
cause theories, 510
and creativity, 311
cultural diversity, 518, 522, 546
definitions, 509, 511
diagnosis, 513–516
dissociative disorders, 9, 514, 544–545
frequency of, 516
mood disorders, 514, 531, 532–535, 547–549
personality disorders, 515, 536–537
review and study questions, 521, 529, 543, 553
schizophrenia, 514, 536, 538–542, 552
and school shootings, 523
somatoform disorders, 514, 520
summary tests, 526–527, 550–551
Web sites, 529, 553
Mental grammar, 313
Mental processes, 4. *See also* Cognitive processes
Mental retardation, 288, 290, 302
Menuhin, Yehudi, 378
Mescaline, 59, 181
Message, 591
Meta-analysis, 559
Metabolic rate, 336
Metabolism, 82
Methadone, 179
Methamphetamine, 176, 177
Method of loci, 271
Midbrain, 73
Middle ear, 102
Midori, 281, 292
Mild depression, 548–549
Mind-body connection:
and autonomic nervous system, 501
and hypnosis, 173
and placebos, 111
and stress, 487
Mind-body question, 49
Mind-body therapy, 487
Mind-guard, 598
Minnesota Multiphasic Personality Inventory (MMPI-2), 474, 475
Minorities. *See* People of color
MMPI-2 (Minnesota Multiphasic Personality Inventory), 474
Mnemonics, 271
Mode, 611
Modeling. *See* Observational learning
Modified frustration-aggression hypothesis, 601

Monoamines, 533
Monochromats, 99
Monocular depth cues, 130–131
Mood disorders, 514, 531, 532–535, 547–549
Morality, 90, 412
Moral reasoning, 412
Moral therapy, 556
Morning persons, 155
Morphine, 175, 179
Morphology, 312
Motherese. See Parentese
Motion parallax, 131
Motion sickness, 105
Motivation, 329–357
   achievement, 329, 348–351, 448
   and brain structure, 80
   and creativity, 311
   and emotions, 365
   and groups, 596
   hunger, 334–337
   and needs, 330, 332–333, 348
   review and study questions, 347, 357
   and rewards, 21
   and social cognitive theory, 231
   summary test, 354–355
   theories, 330–331
   unconscious, 434
   Web sites, 357
   See also Hunger; Sexual behavior
Motivational therapy, 189
Motor cortex, 76
Motor development, 383
Motor (efferent) neurons, 56
Motor homunculus, 76
MRI (magnetic resonance imaging), 70
Müller-Lyer illusion, 133
Multiple-intelligence theory, 283
Multiple personality disorder (dissociative identity disorder) (DID), 9, 545, 546
Muscles, 361, 485
Music, 231
Myelin sheath, 50, 53
Myopia (nearsightedness), 95

N
NA (Narcotics Anonymous), 189
Narcolepsy, 163
Narcotics Anonymous (NA), 189
Naturalistic research settings, 35
Nature-nurture question, 292–294, 377, 378. See also Biological factors; Environmental factors; Genetic factors
Nausea, 195, 206–207
Nazi Germany, 594
Nearsightedness (myopia), 95
Needs, 330, 332–333, 348, 443
Negative correlation coefficient, 32
Negative punishment, 219
Negative reinforcement, 218
Neglect, 400
Neglect syndrome, 79

Neo-Freudian theory, 440
Neologisms, 538
Nerve impulse, 52–53, 96
Nerves, 51
Nervous system, 47–65
   action potential, 52–53
   and aggression, 600
   autonomic, 72, 81, 360, 501, 503
   central, 51, 72
   and emotions, 360
   fetal tissue transplants, 60–61
   head transplants, 64
   and hunger, 335
   and mental disorders, 519, 533, 534, 537
   nerve impulse, 52–53
   organization of, 72
   peripheral, 51, 72
   phantom limb, 58
   reflexes, 56, 73
   review and study questions, 57, 65
   and sleep, 157
   somatic, 72
   summary test, 62–63
   transmitters, 53, 54–55
   Web sites, 65
   See also Brain; Drug effects on nervous system
Network hierarchies, 263
Network theory of memory organization, 262–263
Neural assemblies, 269
Neural deafness, 115
Neuroleptic drugs, 541, 542
Neurological factors. See Brain; Nervous system
Neurological tests, 512
Neurons, 48–49, 50, 161. See also Nervous system
Neuroses, 513
Neurotransmitters, 54–55
   and aggression, 600
   and drug use, 59, 175
   and hunger, 335
   and mood disorders, 534
   and Parkinson's disease, 60
   and sleep, 157
   See also Nervous system
Neutral stimulus, 197, 198, 217. See also Classical conditioning
Nicotine, 178, 336
Nightmares, 163
Night terrors, 163
Nitric oxide, 55
Nodes, 263
Noncompliance, 230, 568
Nondeclarative (procedural/implicit) memory, 149, 246, 248, 268, 441
Nonintellectual factors, 291
Non-REM sleep, 152, 154
Nonshared environmental factors, 467, 468
Norepinephrine, 59, 247, 335
Normal aging, 424
Normal curve, 610

Normal distribution, 288, 610
Norms, 596
Note-taking strategies, 16, 21
Nutrasweet (aspartame), 30

O
Obedience, 593–594
Obesity, 34, 334, 337
Objective personality tests, 474, 475
Object permanence, 389
Observation, 35
Observational learning, 223, 224–225, 459, 493
Obsessive-compulsive disorder (OCD), 519
Obsessive-compulsive personality disorder, 536
Occipital lobe, 74, 79
OCD (obsessive-compulsive disorder), 519
OCEAN (Big Five traits), 463
Oedipus complex, 439
Old age. See Adulthood; Aging
Old age, 424
   memory, 415, 430
   sexual behavior, 425
   sleep, 155, 156
   suicide, 427
Olestra, 210
Olfaction. See Smell
Olfactory cells, 107
One-trial learning, 200
Operant conditioning, 196, 213–222, 230
   applications, 216
   vs. classical conditioning, 217
   origins of, 214
   procedures, 215
   reinforcement, 215, 216, 218–219
   reinforcement schedules, 220–221
Operant response, 214, 215
Opiates, 179
Opium, 179
Opponent-process theory, 99
Optic nerve, 96, 97
Optimal (ideal) weight, 334
Optimal sleep pattern, 162, 575
Optimism, 495
Oral stage of psychosexual development, 392, 439
Oral tradition, 253
Organic factors in sexual problems, 344
Organic mental disorders, 514
Organic retardation, 288
Organ transplants, 603
Orgasm, 344
Ossicles, 102
Outer ear, 102
Outgroup, 598
Ovaries, 82
Overgeneralization, 315, 548, 565
Overlapping, 130
Overweight, 334–335, 337
Ovulation, 379
Own-race bias, 274

P
Pacinian corpuscle, 108
Pain, 108, 112–113
   and adaptation, 93
   and hypnosis, 172, 173
   and placebos, 111
Palmar sweating, 6
Pancreas, 82
Panic attacks, 517
Panic disorder, 517
Paradoxical sleep, 153
Paranoid personality disorder, 536
Paranoid schizophrenia, 538, 546
Paraphilias, 344
Parasympathetic division (nervous system), 72, 81, 484, 501
Parentese, 314, 316
Parenting, 404
   and achievement, 351, 448
   and adolescence, 413
   and behavior therapy, 216, 230, 233, 236
   and child abuse, 400–401, 568
   See also Childhood; Environmental factors; Infancy
Parent Management Training (PMT), 604
Parietal lobe, 74, 77, 297, 320
Parkinson's disease, 60–61
Parks, Gordon, 305, 310
Partial reinforcement, 220–221
Passionate love, 419
Passive strategies for interpersonal conflicts, 471
Pathological aging, 424
Pavlov, Ivan. See Classical conditioning
Peg method, 271
Penis envy, 439, 440
People of color, 14, 329. See also Discrimination; Race
Perception, 121–145
   constancy, 128
   creating, 140–141
   and cultural diversity, 136–137
   depth, 129–131, 382
   extrasensory, 138–139, 144
   illusions, 132–133, 140
   imagined, 172
   organizational rules, 126–127
   person, 582–584
   review and study questions, 134, 145
   vs. sensations, 93, 103, 124–125
   subliminal, 122, 135
   summary test, 142–143
   thresholds, 122–123
   Web sites, 145
   See also Senses
Perceptual constancy, 128
Perceptual sets, 137
Perceptual speed, 415
Perfect negative correlation coefficient, 32
Perfect positive correlation coefficient, 32

Performance goals, 20
Peripheral cues, 335
Peripheral nervous system (PNS), 51, 72
Peripheral route for persuasion, 591
Peripheral theories of emotions, 360
Permissive parents, 413
Personal beliefs, 27, 30, 210
Personal factors, 458, 473
Personal identity (self-identity), 416
Personality, 433–479, 457–479
    adolescence, 416
    adulthood, 417
    and aggression, 601
    assessment, 450–451, 474–475, 478, 512
    and creativity, 311
    cultural diversity, 448, 471
    disorders, 515, 536–537
    and eating disorders, 353
    humanistic theories, 442–446, 472
    and hunger, 337
    and mood disorders, 533
    review and study questions, 447, 455, 469, 479
    shyness, 449
    social cognitive theory, 449, 458–461, 473
    stability, 465, 470, 473
    and stress, 494–496, 499
    summary tests, 452–453, 476–477
    theory overview, 472–473
    trait theory, 450–451, 462–468, 473
    Web sites, 455, 479
    See also Freudian theory
Personality disorders, 515, 536–537
Personality psychology, 18
Personality tests, 450
Person-centered therapy (client-centered therapy), 564
Person perception, 582–584
Person schemas, 584
Person-situation interaction, 464, 473
Persuasion, 591
Pessimism, 495
PET (positron emission tomography) scan, 71, 76, 77, 84
Peyote, 59
Phallic stage of psychosexual development, 392, 439
Phantom limb, 58
Phenomenological perspective, 442, 472
Phenothiazines, 542, 557
Phi movement, 140
Phobias, 195, 509, 518, 522
    treatment for, 198, 225, 524–525, 567, 568, 575
Phonemes, 312
Phonology, 312
Photographic memory, 254
Photoreceptors, 95, 96
Physical abuse, 400
Physical appearance, 582, 603
Physical growth, 408
Physiological reflexes. See Reflexes

Piaget's cognitive stages, 388–391, 410
Pica, 218
Piloerection (goose bumps), 485
Pineal gland, 151
Pitch, 100, 104
Pituitary gland, 82, 485
Placebo effects, 31, 111
Placebos, 30, 31, 111
Placenta, 380
Place theory of pitch, 104
Pleasure principle, 436
PMT (Parent Management Training), 604
PNS (peripheral nervous system), 51, 72
Polarization, 598
Polarized thinking, 565
Polygraph (lie detector) tests, 365, 370–371
Pons, 73, 161
Ponzo illusion, 133
Position, sense of, 105
Positive correlation coefficient, 32
Positive punishment, 219, 233, 236
Positive reappraisal, 495
Positive regard, 445, 564
Positive reinforcement, 218
Positron emission tomography (PET) scan, 71, 76, 77, 84
Postconventional level of moral reasoning, 412
Posterior pituitary, 82
Posthypnotic amnesia, 172
Posthypnotic suggestion, 172
Posttraumatic stress disorder (PTSD), 491
Poverty, 288, 299
Power rapists, 602
Precognition, 138
Preconventional level of moral reasoning, 412
Prediction, of behavior, 4
Predictions, 33
Predisposing function of attitudes, 589
Predispositions, 539, 540. See also Genetic factors
Prefrontal cortex, 297, 411, 537, 540
Prejudice, 583
Premature (rapid) ejaculation, 344
Premo, Kate, 514
Prenatal period, 378–382
Preoperational stage of cognitive development, 389
Prepared learning. See Preparedness
Preparedness, 200, 229
Presbyopia (farsightedness), 95
Primacy effect, 245
Primacy question of emotions, 363
Primacy-recency effect, 245
Primary appraisals, 482, 483, 499
Primary auditory cortex, 78, 103
Primary reinforcers, 219
Primary visual cortex, 79, 97
Primates, 49

Principles of Psychology (James), 12
Private practice, 17
Proactive interference, 266
Problem-focused coping, 499, 503
Problem-solving, 84, 291, 308–309. See also Learning
Procedural (nondeclarative/implicit) memory, 149, 246, 248, 268, 441
Processing speed, 415
Procrastination, 9, 21
Prodigies, 378
Progressive relaxation, 503
Project Genome, 68
Projection, 437
Projective personality tests, 450–451, 474
Propranolol, 247
Prosocial behavior, 595
Proteins, 68
Prototype theory of concept formation, 306
Proximity rule of perception, 127
Proximodistal principle of motor development, 383
Prozac, 534
Psi, 138
Psilocybin, 180
Psychiatric nurses, 558
Psychiatrists, 17, 557, 558
Psychic hotlines, 139, 144
Psychoactive drugs, 174. See also Drug use
Psychoanalysis, 555, 560–563
Psychoanalytic theory. See Freudian theory
Psychobiologists, 6. See also Biological approach
Psychodynamic theory. See Freudian theory
Psychoevolutionary theory of emotions, 361
Psychokinesis, 138
Psychological assessment, 450–451, 474–475, 478
Psychological factors:
    sexual behavior, 338, 340–341, 343
    sexual problems, 344
    See also Psychosocial factors
Psychological harm, 594
Psychologists, 17, 557, 558
Psychology:
    careers in, 17–19
    defined, 4
    goals of, 4
    historical approaches, 12–13
    modern approaches, 5, 6–11
    review and study questions, 15, 25
    summary test, 22–23
    Web sites, 25
Psychometric approach, 282, 310
Psychometrics, 19, 281. See also Intelligence
Psychoneuroimmunology, 488
Psychopaths, 536–537
Psychoses, 513

Psychosexual stages of development, 392, 393, 438, 439, 472
Psychosocial factors:
    hunger, 334, 337
    mood disorders, 533
    personality disorders, 537
    stress, 488–489, 497
    See also Psychological factors
Psychosocial stages of development, 393, 394, 417, 440
Psychosomatic symptoms, 81, 486–487, 489
    and biofeedback, 233, 568
    and hypnosis, 173
Psychotherapy, 555–579
    anxiety disorders, 524–525
    common factors, 571
    cultural diversity, 572, 578
    dissociative disorders, 545
    and dreams, 160
    and drug use, 189
    eating disorders, 353
    effectiveness, 559, 571
    historical background, 555–557
    and humanistic theories, 446
    and hypnosis, 173
    insight therapies, 555, 559, 560–565
    mind-body therapy, 487
    mood disorders, 534
    personality disorders, 537
    and psychology careers, 17
    and repressed memory, 250–251
    review and study questions, 569, 579
    sexual problems, 344
    summary test, 576–577
    trauma, 491, 573
    types of, 558–559, 570
    and virtual reality, 141, 524
    Web sites, 579
    See also Behavior therapy
Psychotic mental disorders, 514
PTSD (posttraumatic stress disorder), 491
Puberty, 408–409. See also Adolescence
Punishment, 218, 219, 233, 236
Pupil, 95, 485

Q
Quantum personality change, 470
Questionnaires, 34

R
Race:
    and brain size, 85
    and eyewitness testimony, 274
    and intelligence, 290, 294, 296
    and perception, 141
    and person perception, 582, 583
Random selection, 36
Range, 612
Rape, 602
Rape myths, 602
Rapid eye movement (REM) sleep, 147, 153, 154

Rapid (premature) ejaculation, 344
Ratio IQ, 285
Rationalization, 437
Reaction formation, 437
Reaction range, 293
Reaction time, 415
Reading, 320
Reality principle, 436
Real motion, 140
Real self, 444
Reasoning, 318–319
Recall, 261, 264
Recency effect, 245
Receptors, 54
Recognition, 261, 264
Reeve, Christopher, 51, 461
Reflecting, 564
Reflexes, 56, 73
    and classical conditioning, 196,
        197, 201, 217
Rehearsing, 240, 243, 249
Reinforcement, 215, 216, 218–219
    schedules of, 220–221
Relationships, 419–420, 422–423,
    497
Relative size, 130
Relaxation, 207, 501, 503, 567
Relaxation exercises, 6
Relaxation response, 503
Reliability, 287, 451, 475, 614
REM behavior disorder, 153
REM (rapid eye movement) sleep,
    147, 153, 154
REM rebound, 153
Repair theory of sleep, 156
Replication, 139
Repressed memory, 239, 250–251,
    265
Repression, 437. See also Repressed
    memory
Research, 27–45
    case studies, 28, 30, 35
    choosing techniques, 34
    controversies, 39
    correlation, 32–33, 85
    and discrimination, 84
    and ESP, 139
    ethics, 40–41
    experiments, 28
    longitudinal vs. cross-sectional
        methods, 386
    and placebos, 31, 111
    replication, 139
    review and study questions, 38, 45
    settings, 35
    specialization areas, 17–18
    statistics, 37, 610–617
    summary test, 42–43
    surveys, 28, 29
    Web sites, 45
Resiliency, 394, 441
Resistance, 562
Resistance stage of stress, 487
Respiration, 485
Resting state, 53
Reticular formation, 157

Retina, 95, 96
Retinal disparity, 129
Retrieval cues, 265, 267, 271
Retrieving (memory), 239, 244
Retroactive interference, 266
Reuptake, 59, 175
Rewards, 21, 331, 350. See also
    Operant conditioning
Rhino horn, 31
Rhodopsin, 96
Risk factors, 183, 427
Risk-taking behavior, 411, 413
Risky shift, 598
Ritalin, 27, 28, 30, 39
Rods, 96
Rogers's self theory, 444–445, 472
Role schemas, 584
Romantic love, 419
Rorschach inkblot test, 450, 451

S
Sadistic rapists, 602
SAD (seasonal affective disorder),
    159, 532
Salinger, J. D., 286
Salivation, 196, 197, 201, 202
Savants, 7, 302, 311
Schachter-Singer experiment, 362
Schedules of reinforcement, 220–221
Schemas, 420, 584
Schizophrenia, 514, 536, 538–542,
    546, 552
Schizophrenic personality disorder,
    536
School psychologists, 17
School shootings, 523
School uniforms, 33
Scientific method, 36
Scripts (event schemas), 584
Seasonal affective disorder (SAD),
    159, 532
Secondary appraisals, 499
Secondary reinforcers, 219
Secondary schools, 17
Secondary sexual characteristics, 408
Secure attachment, 385
Seizures, 86
Selective attention, 548, 565
Selective serotonin reuptake
    inhibitors (SSRIs), 534
Self-actualization, 333, 442, 443,
    445, 472. See also Self theory
Self-actualizing tendency, 444
Self-analysis, 459
Self-concept, 444
Self-defeating personality disorder,
    516
Self-efficacy, 460, 473
Self-esteem, 416
Self-fulfilling prophecies, 30, 31, 135
Self-handicapping, 349
Self-help programs, 568
Self-identity (personal identity), 416
Self-injurious behavior, 219
Self-management skills, 8
Self-monitoring, 574, 575

Self-perception theory, 590
Self-reinforcement, 21
Self-report questionnaires, 474, 475
Self schemas, 584
Self-serving bias, 586
Self-statements, 502
Self theory (self-actualization theory),
    444–445, 472
Semantic memory, 246, 248
Semantics, 312
Semicircular canals, 105
Sensate focus, 344
Sensations, 93, 103, 124–125.
    See also Senses
Senses, 93–119
    artificial, 114
    and classical conditioning, 200
    common characteristics, 93
    development, 382
    hearing, 78, 100–104, 115, 241,
        382
    and memory, 107, 240, 241
    pain, 111–113
    review and study questions, 109,
        119
    smell, 106–107, 382
    summary test, 116–117
    taste, 106, 382
    touch, 77, 108, 382
    vestibular system, 105
    Web sites, 119
    See also Perception; Vision
Sensitive (critical) period, 228
Sensorimotor stage of cognitive
    development, 389
Sensors, 56
Sensory homunculus, 77
Sensory memory, 240, 241
Sentence stage, 315
Separation anxiety, 385
Serial killers, 509, 515, 536–537
Serotonin, 534, 541, 600
Set point, 336
Sex chromosome, 338
Sex differences. See Gender differences
Sex hormones, 339
Sexism, 14, 378, 457
    and attitudes, 589
    and attributions, 585, 586
    and schemas, 584
    and stereotypes, 583
Sex roles. See Gender roles
Sexual abuse, 400–401
    and false memories, 251, 258, 273
    and repressed memory, 239,
        250–251, 265
Sexual aggression, 602, 605
Sexual behavior, 338–346
    adolescence, 409
    and aging, 425
    and AIDS, 345
    and autism, 10
    biological factors, 338, 339, 341,
        343
    female circumcision, 346
    and gender, 340–341

gender differences, 339, 342
genetic factors, 338–339, 341, 343
homosexual orientation, 341, 343
and longevity, 44
and marriage, 423
problems, 344
psychological factors, 338,
    340–341, 343
sexual orientation, 341
Viagra, 356
Sexual disorders, 514
Sexual dysfunctions, 344
Sexual harassment, 602
Sexual orientation, 341
Sexual preference. See Sexual
    orientation
Shape constancy, 128
Shaping, 215, 216
Shared environmental factors, 467,
    468
Shift work, 151
Shock therapy (ECT), 535
Short-term dynamic psychotherapy,
    562
Short-term memory, 240, 242–243,
    244, 245, 269
Shyness, 449
Similarity rule of perception, 127
Simplicity rule of perception, 127
Single word stage, 314
Size constancy, 128
Skewed distribution, 610–611
Skin, 108, 361, 370. See also Touch
Skinner box, 215, 220
Sleep:
    and biological clocks, 150, 151,
        155, 156, 159
    and continuum of consciousness,
        149
    deprivation, 157, 166
    need for, 156–157
    problems, 162–163, 568, 575
    rapid eye movement, 147
    review and study questions, 158
    sleep-wake cycle, 150–151, 155
    stages of, 152–154
    See also Dreams
Sleep apnea, 163
Sleep-wake cycle, 150–151, 155
Sleepwalking, 163
Smell, 106–107, 382
Smiling, 364
Smith, Susan, 512, 513, 514
Smoking, 178, 336
Social cognition, 581, 584
Social cognitive theory, 8, 223, 225,
    231, 473
    and aggression, 601
    development, 394
    and language acquisition, 316
    personality, 449, 458–461, 473
Social comparison theory, 596
Social-cultural influences, 337
Social development, 392–396
Social facilitation, 597
Social factors. See Psychosocial factors

# Subject Index

Social inhibition, 597
Socialization, 522, 605. *See also* Gender roles
Social learning approach. *See* Social cognitive theory
Socially dependent personality, 533
Socially oriented groups, 596, 598
Social needs, 332, 348
Social norms approach to mental disorders, 511
Social phobias, 518, 522, 525
Social psychology, 18, 581–609
  aggression, 600–602, 605
  attitudes, 588–591, 603
  attributions, 10, 585–587
  conformity, 592–594
  group dynamics, 596–598
  person perception, 582–584
  prosocial behavior, 595
  review and study questions, 599, 609
  summary test, 606–607
  Web sites, 609
Social role theory of gender, 342, 395, 396, 399, 418
Social skills, 549
Social support, 497
Social workers, 557
Sociocognitive theory of hypnosis, 171
Socioeconomic status, 288, 299
Sodium pump, 53
Soma (cell body), 50
Somatic nervous system, 72
Somatization disorder, 520
Somatoform disorders, 514, 520
Somatosensory cortex, 77, 108
Sound waves, 100–101
Source, 591
Source misattribution, 275
Source traits, 462
Sozhenitsyn, Aleksandr, 445
Spanking, 233, 236
Spearman's theory. *See* G (general intelligence) factor
Specialization areas, 17–18
Specific phobias, 518, 524
Speech:
  and brain structure, 78, 87, 229
  and cochlear implants, 115
  and preparedness, 229
Spinal cord, 72. *See also* Nervous system
Spinal cord injuries, 51, 360
Spirit possession, 546
Split-brain operation, 86–87
Spontaneous recovery, 199, 222
SSRIs (selective serotonin reuptake inhibitors), 534
Standard deviation, 612–613
Standardized tests, 34
Stanford Hypnotic Susceptibility Scale, 170
State-dependent learning, 267
Statistical frequency approach to mental disorders, 511

Statistics, 37, 610–617
  descriptive, 610–613
  inferential, 613–616
  summary test, 617
Steiger, Rod, 532, 534, 558
Stereotaxic procedure, 61
Stereotypes, 583, 584
Sternberg's theory. *See* Triarchic theory of intelligence
Stimulants, 176–178
  and ADHD, 27, 28, 30, 39
Stimulus hierarchy, 567
Stimulus substitution theory of classical conditioning, 202
Stirrup (ear), 102
Stomach, 335, 485
Storing, 239, 243
Stress, 481–507
  appraisals, 482–483, 484, 486, 494, 499, 502
  and autonomic nervous system, 81
  coping, 6, 481, 499–500, 502–503, 568
  cultural diversity, 501
  fight-flight response, 81, 484–485, 486, 488, 501
  and immune system, 111, 488–489
  and pain, 111
  and personality, 494–496, 499
  psychosocial factors, 488–489, 497
  and psychosomatic symptoms, 81, 233, 486–487
  review and study questions, 498, 507
  and schizophrenia, 540
  and sleep problems, 162
  stressors, 490–493
  summary test, 504–505
  and test anxiety, 6
  Web sites, 507
Stress management programs, 6, 502–503, 568
Stressors, 490–493
Strology, 475
Structuralism, 12, 126
Structured interviews, 470
Study questions, 25
  adolescence/adulthood, 431
  brain, 91
  cognitive processes, 327
  consciousness, 167
  developmental psychology, 405
  emotions, 375
  intelligence, 303
  learning, 211, 237
  memory, 259, 279
  mental disorders, 529, 553
  motivation, 357
  nervous system, 65
  perception, 145
  personality, 455, 479
  psychotherapy, 579
  research, 45
  senses, 119
  social psychology, 609
  stress, 507

Study skills, 20–21
Subgoals, 309
Subject selection, 36
Sublimation, 437
Subliminal perceptions, 122, 135
Substance abuse, 188. *See also* Drug use
Substance-related mental disorders, 514
Success, 349
Suicide, 426–427, 433–436, 546, 548
Summary tests, 22–23
  adolescence/adulthood, 428–429
  brain, 88–89
  cognitive processes, 324–325
  consciousness, 164–165
  developmental psychology, 402–403
  drugs, 190–191
  emotions, 372–373
  intelligence, 300–331
  learning, 208–209, 234–235
  memory, 256–257, 276
  mental disorders, 526–527, 550–551
  motivation, 354–355
  nervous system, 62–63
  perception, 142–143
  personality, 452–453, 476–477
  psychotherapy, 576–577
  research, 42–43
  senses, 116–117
  social psychology, 606–607
  statistics, 617
  stress, 504–505
Superego, 436, 437, 472
Superstitious behavior, 215
Supertasters, 106
Supertraits, 463
Suprachiasmatic nucleus, 150, 155
Surface structure, 313
Surveys, 28, 29
Suzuki method, 231
Swift, Jonathan, 284
Sympathetic division (nervous system), 72, 81, 484, 485, 501
Synapse, 50
Syntax (grammar), 312
Systematic desensitization, 207, 567

## T

Taijin kyofusho (TKS), 522
Tardive dyskinesia, 542
Target behavior, 216
Task-oriented groups, 596, 598
Taste, 106, 382
Taste-aversion learning, 200–201
Taste buds, 106
TAT (Thematic Apperception Test), 348, 450, 451
Telegraphic speech, 315
Telepathy, 138
Television, 601
Temperament, 384, 386–387, 394
Temperature, 108
Temporal lobe, 74, 78, 320
Teratogens, 380
Test anxiety, 3, 6–11

Test entry, 24–25
Testes, 82
Testimonials, 30, 31, 138
Testosterone, 339, 408
Tests, 34
  assessment, 450–451, 474–475, 478
  intelligence, 286–287
  neurological, 512
Tests of statistical significance, 614–616
Texture gradient, 131
Thalamus, 80, 97, 320
Thematic Apperception Test (TAT), 348, 450, 451
Theory of evolution, 69
Theory of linguistic relativity, 319
Theory theory of cognitive development, 391
Therapy. *See* Psychotherapy
Thinking, 305, 306–311
  concept formation, 306–307
  creativity, 305, 310–311
  cultural diversity, 321
  egocentric, 389
  intrusive thoughts, 574
  problem-solving, 84, 291, 308–309
  reasoning, 318–319
  review and study questions, 317, 327
  summary test, 324–325
  *See also* Cognitive approach; Cognitive-behavioral therapy
Thomas, John, 51
Thorazine, 541
Thoughts. *See* Cognitive approach; Thinking
Thought-stopping procedure, 574
Thought substitution, 574, 575
Thought suppression, 574
Threat appraisals, 482, 483, 486, 494
Thresholds, 122–123
Thyroid, 82
Tibetan monks, 501
Tiger bones, 31
Time goals, 20
Time management, 20
Time-out, 230, 233
Tip-of-the-tongue phenomenon, 267
TKS (taijin kyofusho), 522
TM (transcendental meditation), 503
Toilet training, 216
Tolerance, 174, 182
Touch, 77, 108, 382
Trait theory, 462–468, 473
  assessment, 450–451, 474–475, 478
  evaluation of, 468
  five-factor model, 463, 468, 473
  genetic factors, 466–467
  person-situation interaction, 464, 468, 473
  stability, 465
Trance, 171

Tranquilizers, 525
Transcendental meditation (TM), 503
Transduction, 93, 96, 125
Transference, 560, 562
Transformational rules, 313
Transmitters, 53, 54–55
Transsexuals, 340
Trauma, 491, 500, 506, 573
Triangular theory of love, 419
Triarchic theory of intelligence, 283
Trichromatic theory, 98
Trust vs. mistrust stage of psychosocial development, 393
*T* tests, 614–615
Twelve-step approach, 189
Twin studies, 32, 292, 336, 343, 467
Two-factor theory, 282
Two-word combination stage, 315
Tympanic membrane, 102
Type A behavior, 496
Typical neuroleptic drugs, 541, 542

**U**
Unconditional positive regard, 445
Unconditioned response (UCR), 197, 198, 217. *See also* Classical conditioning
Unconditioned stimulus (UCS), 197, 198, 217. *See also* Classical conditioning
Unconscious, 9, 149, 434–435, 472
 and cognitive approach, 441
 and psychotherapy, 560
 and stress, 493
Unconsciousness, 149
Underachievement, 349

Unresolved conflicts, 449
Uplifts, 490
Uprima, 31

**V**
Validity, 287, 451, 474, 475
Validity scales, 474
Variability, measures of, 612–613
Variable-interval reinforcement schedule, 221
Variable-ratio reinforcement schedule, 221
Variables, 36
Ventricles, 540
Ventrolateral preoptic nucleus (VPN), 157
Ventromedial hypothalamus, 335
Verbal retrieval cues, 272
Vestibular system, 105
Vetigo, 105
Viagra, 356
Violence, 183, 523. *See also* Aggression
Virginity, 423
Virtual reality, 141, 524
Visible spectrum, 94
Vision, 93, 94–99
 artificial, 114
 and brain structure, 79, 97
 and dreams, 161
 infancy, 382
 and memory, 241, 254, 272
 organizational rules, 126–127, 140
Visual agnosia, 79, 97, 307
Visual association area, 79, 97
Visual cliff, 382

Visual retrieval cues, 272
Vocal apparatus, 316
Vos Savant, Marilyn, 286, 288, 289
VPN (ventrolateral preoptic nucleus), 157
Vulnerability, 394

**W**
WAIS-III (Wechsler Adult Intelligence Scale), 286
Watson, John B., 13
Weber's law, 123
Web sites:
 adolescence/adulthood, 431
 brain, 91
 consciousness, 167
 developmental psychology, 405
 drug use, 193
 emotions, 375
 general psychology resources, 25
 intelligence, 303
 language, 327
 learning, 211, 237
 memory, 259, 279
 mental disorders, 529, 553
 motivation, 357
 nervous system, 65
 perception, 145
 personality, 455, 479
 psychotherapy, 579
 research, 45
 senses, 119
 social psychology, 609
 stress, 507
Wechsler Adult Intelligence Scale (WAIS-III), 286

Wechsler Intelligence Scale for Children (WISC-III), 286
Weight, 334–336, 352, 583
Weight-regulating genes, 336
Wellman, Mark, 329, 330, 331
Wernicke's area, 78, 316, 323
Whale fat, 110
Whitman, Walt, 284
Williams, Venus, 247, 281
Wilson, Bill, 470
WISC-III (Wechsler Intelligence Scale for Children), 286
Withdrawal symptoms, 174, 178, 179, 182
Women:
 and Freudian theory, 440
 sexual aggression against, 602, 605
 *See also* Gender differences; Gender roles; Sexism
Working memory. *See* Short-term memory
Worrying, 7
Written tradition, 253
Wyman, Donald, 58

**X**
Xanthines, 178

**Y**
Yamaguchi, Kristi, 442
Yerkes-Dodson law, 365

**Z**
Zener cards, 139
Zero correlation coefficient, 32
Zygotes, 68, 338, 379

I'd like to ask you a small favor. I have worked very hard to make this book readable and stimulating and would like to know if I have succeeded. Would you take a few minutes to fill out this form and tell me your reactions to this textbook? I will use your comments, suggestions, and criticisms to improve the next edition of *Introduction to Psychology, 6th Edition.*

School: _____

Instructor's name: _____

1. What did you like most about *Introduction to Psychology*? _____

   _____

   _____

2. What did you like least about the book? _____

   _____

3. Were all the modules assigned for you to read? Yes _____ No _____ Which ones were omitted? _____

4. Did you use the Concept Review sections? Yes _____ No _____ Did you find them useful? Yes _____ No _____

5. How interesting and informative did you find the Cultural Diversity sections, which told you about behaviors in other cultures?

   _____

   _____

6. Did you use the Summary Test sections? Yes _____ No _____ Did you find them useful? Yes _____ No _____

7. How interesting and informative did you find the Research Focus? _____

   _____

   _____

8. Did you purchase the *Study Guide*? Yes _____ No _____

   If so, in electronic _____ or print _____ format?

9. Do you own a computer? Yes _____ No _____

   If so, what type? _____

10. Do you use the Internet? Yes _____ No _____

    If so, do you use it at school _____, at home _____, or both _____?

11. Did you go to the Psychology Study Center Web site? Yes _____ No _____

    If so, did you use the quizzes or other activities? Yes _____ No _____

12. Did your text come with PowerStudy? Yes _____ No _____ Did you purchase it? Yes _____ No _____

13. How useful did you find PowerStudy? _____

14. In the space below (or in a separate letter) please make any other comments that you have about the book. (For example, did you like the way that photos and figures were integrated with the text?) I would really like to hear from you.

    _____

    _____

Many thanks for taking the time to fill out this survey.

Best wishes,
*Rod Plotnik*

Optional:

Your name: _____ Date: _____

May Wadsworth quote you, either in promotion for *Introduction to Psychology, 6th Edition* or in future publishing ventures?

Yes: _____ No: _____

Sincerely,

*Rod Plotnik*

---

FOLD HERE

FOLD HERE